U.S. INDUSTRY & TRADE OUTLOOK® '99

U.S. INDUSTRY & TRADE OUTLOOK® '99

The McGraw-Hill Companies

U.S. Department of Commerce/International Trade Administration

McGraw-Hill

A Division of The **McGraw·Hill** *Companies*

1 2 3 4 5 6 7 8 9 0   POO/POO   9 0 4 3 2 1 0 9

ISBN 0-07-018135-7

The sponsoring editor for this book was Susan Barry, the editing manager was Joe Faulk, and the production supervisor was Suzanne Rapcavage. The book was set in Times Roman with Univers by North Market Street Graphics.

At the back of the book is a list of associations, organizations, and companies that have given permission to use data and other information for this publication.

Printed and bound by The Press of Ohio.

McGraw-Hill books are available at special quantity discounts to use as premiums and sales promotions, or for use in corporate training programs. For more information please write to the Director of Special Sales, McGraw-Hill, 11 West 19th Street, New York, NY 10011. Or contact your local bookstore.

ACKNOWLEDGMENTS

The *U.S. Industry & Trade Outlook '99*® is the product of a partnership between The McGraw-Hill Companies and the U.S. Department of Commerce. Contributing McGraw-Hill companies are Standard & Poor's DRI for industry analysis and the Professional Book Group for production and distribution. Within Professional Book, special thanks go to Philip Ruppel, Publisher; Susan Barry, Editorial Director; Roger Kasunic, Production Director; Griffin Hansbury, Assistant Editor; Joe Faulk, Editing Manager; and Suzanne W. B. Rapcavage, Senior Production Supervisor. Cynthia H. Braddon is Vice President, Washington Affairs, for The McGraw-Hill Companies, and Tracey Thomson is Manager, Government Marketing & Communications.

The Office of Trade and Economic Analysis within the U.S. Department of Commerce provided concept development, authorship, interagency coordination within the government, U.S. government data, and editorial support. Those with major responsibilities for this edition include the following: Jonathan C. Menes, Project Director; Richard A. Eberhart, Project Manager; John J. Bistay, Managing Editor; Howard L. Schreier, Computer Support Coordinator; Rebecca Krafft, Francine Krasowska, Technical Editors; Jeffrey W. Lins, Senior Economist/Economic Reviewer; Kemble Stokes, Senior Economist; Michael Goodwin, Joanne Hepburn, Indumati Jasani, Marjorie Pavliscak, Allen Unsworth, Economic/Statistical Reviewers; Bruce Miller, Heather West, Policy Reviewers; John Jelacic, Sabrina Montes, Consulting Economists; David Barton, Statistical Support; Miralette Herbert, Administrative Support.

The National Technical Information Service, of which Sandy Waters is Director of Strategic Planning, is McGraw-Hill's distribution partner.

The Bureau of the Census provided most of the data on which the analyses are based. Many other federal agencies also contributed data, but special recognition goes to the Bureau of Economic Analysis, the Bureau of Labor Statistics, the Council of Economic Advisers, the Board of Governors of the Federal Reserve System, the Department of Transportation, the Department of the Interior, the Department of Health and Human Services, the Securities and Exchange Commission, and the Commodity Futures Trading Commission.

Special appreciation also goes to the Department of Energy for its coverage of crude petroleum and natural gas and petroleum refining; the U.S. Geological Survey of the Department of the Interior for the chapter on metal and industrial minerals mining; the Maritime Administration and Federal Railroad Administration of the Department of Transportation for the chapters on shipbuilding and repair and transportation; and the Federal Deposit Insurance Corporation for the chapter on financial services.

THE SECRETARY OF COMMERCE
Washington, D.C. 20230

The 1999 *U.S. Industry & Trade Outlook*®—the result of a public-private partnership between the Department of Commerce and The McGraw-Hill Companies—presents an illuminating portrait of America's industrial economy and our prospects for the future. We are making a special effort in this 37th edition to show U.S. business activity not only in the domestic marketplace, but in the world economy as well.

The health of the U.S. economy is evidenced by the first Federal Government surplus since 1969, the lowest rates of inflation and unemployment in a generation, and robust business investment. Our economic expansion set a record in 1998 as the longest peacetime expansion to date. The data and forecasts in this book reflect our country's vigorous and dynamic business activity.

While the U.S. economic expansion will likely continue in 1999, the risks to the U.S. economy from the turmoil in Asia, Russia, and other regions are very real, though the magnitude of their impact is uncertain. To help U.S. business understand global industrial trends, the more than 100 contributors have incorporated information and data on the international competitive situations of their industries. Using the *Outlook's* data and forecasts as a basis, strategies can be developed to succeed in this intense competitive environment.

As we approach the millennium, opportunities abound for business to develop new products and services to improve our country's productivity and living standards. One such development with far-reaching relevance is electronic commerce. The Clinton Administration and the Department of Commerce have been working vigorously within the United States and with our trading partners in organizations such as the Organization for Economic Cooperation and Development, World Trade Organization, United Nations Commission on International Trade Law, and Asia Pacific Economic Cooperation forum to ensure that the vast potential of electronic commerce is realized for all—large and small businesses, workers, consumers and governments. To achieve this goal, we believe the development of electronic commerce must be industry-led and, where government involvement is needed, such development should support and enforce a predictable, minimalist, and consistent legal environment. This year's *Outlook* includes a special feature article on electronic commerce and its link with information technology and our economic future. In addition, a number of industry specific chapters include discussion of electronic commerce's effect on those industries.

Coping with the challenges and opportunities posed by the world economic situation is the shared responsibility of business and government. It is our hope that the information and forecasts contained in the *U.S. Industry & Trade Outlook*® will contribute to the success of our efforts.

William M. Daley

1221 Avenue of the Americas
New York, NY 10020-1095

Harold McGraw III
President and
Chief Executive Officer

The **McGraw·Hill** *Companies*

For over three decades the *U.S. Industrial Outlook®* proved to be a critical reference tool for government, businesses, and nonprofit entities both in the United States and abroad. Under the title *U.S. Industry & Trade Outlook®*, the 1999 edition marks the second year of The McGraw-Hill Companies' collaboration with the U.S. Department of Commerce in producing this important publication. We are proud to be a part of the process and to assist in providing the public with this vital economic and trade information.

Founded in 1888, The McGraw-Hill Companies is a leading information services provider meeting worldwide needs in education, business, finance, the professions, and government. Because of our expertise in financial information and publishing, we are in a unique position to assist in creating an updated objective outlook on U.S. industry and trade.

The McGraw-Hill Companies is pleased that both Standard & Poor's DRI and our Professional Publishing group are able to make a valuable contribution to the revival of this important resource volume. *Outlook '99* encompasses deeper, richer content, is more customer friendly, provides a more global perspective, and promotes wide distribution of valuable information.

In addition, *Outlook '99* preserves underlying government information principles, strongly supported by The McGraw-Hill Companies, which assure that such information remains available to the public. The McGraw-Hill Companies provides the government with free copies for distribution to depository libraries and the Library of Congress as well as for internal government use. We strongly support products such as the *Outlook* entering into the National Depository Library program.

The *U.S. Industry & Trade Outlook®* partnership is a prime example of how the government and the private sector can successfully work together and provide valuable information that the public wants and needs.

HAROLD McGRAW III

Contents

INDUSTRIAL MATERIALS AND COMPONENTS

PRODUCTION AND MANUFACTURING EQUIPMENT

INFORMATION AND COMMUNICATIONS

THE CONSUMER ECONOMY

TRANSPORTATION

HEALTH CARE

FINANCIAL, BUSINESS, AND EDUCATION SERVICES

U.S. INDUSTRY & TRADE OUTLOOK® '99

Getting the Most Out of *Outlook '99*

Welcome to the second edition of the *U.S. Industry & Trade Outlook*®, a joint publication of the U.S. Department of Commerce and The McGraw-Hill Companies. This volume replaces the *U.S. Industrial Outlook*®, which the Department of Commerce had published annually until 1994. Like its predecessor, the *U.S. Industry & Trade Outlook*® is a single reference source that business professionals, investors, researchers, and students can use to get information on U.S. industries, how these industries affect the U.S. economy, and where they are going in an increasingly global marketplace. Most of the chapters have been written by government analysts; also participating were McGraw-Hill authors (principally from Standard & Poor's DRI and Standard & Poor's Equity Investor Services) and independent analysts and industry experts. To ensure that the articles and forecasts are objective and unbiased, government economists have reviewed all chapters.

ANALYTICAL APPROACH: SIC CODES

The *'99 Outlook* continues to be based on the Standard Industrial Classification system, which classifies industries by SIC codes and uses these codes as the basis for collecting most of the data on domestic industries. This classification system includes all sectors, from manufacturing and service industries to construction, agriculture and natural resources. The SIC system begins with nine major categories: (1) agriculture, forestry, and fishing; (2) mining; (3) construction; (4) manufacturing; (5) transportation, communications and public utilities; (6) wholesale trade; (7) retail trade; (8) finance, insurance and real estate; and (9) services. These basic categories are, in turn, divided into groups with two-digit, three-digit, and four-digit industry codes, where each additional digit indicates a greater degree of specificity.

WHAT TO LOOK FOR IN EACH CHAPTER

Economic and Trade Trends Graphs

Each chapter begins with this full-page feature. Most manufacturing industries, which make up 29 of the 50 chapters, have a standard set of these graphs. In addition to U.S. international trade, the graphs include the following:

World Export Market Share. The world export market share data have been developed from international trade information provided by the United Nations, which collects such information from various countries. These data are classified by Standard International Trade Classifications (SITC), Revision 3, which does not correspond to the 1987 SIC system used for U.S. domestic industries. To resolve this disparity, the two classification systems were matched where possible at the four-digit SIC level. Where the worldwide international trade data would not accurately reflect the SIC industries included in the chapter, no data are presented. The world export market share graph reflects available data through 1996. Such data account for about 75 percent of total world trade in 1996.

Export Dependence and Import Penetration. The export dependence ratio is derived by dividing exports by comparable domestic shipments; the import penetration ratio is derived by dividing imports by the sum of shipments and imports less exports (apparent consumption). The ratios do not necessarily use the shipments data included in the Trends and Forecasts tables (discussed below); shipments data were modified to reflect all traded commodities of a particular sector.

Output and Output Per Worker. Constant-dollar industry shipments are used as a proxy for output. Output per worker for each industry is defined as industry shipments (adjusted for price changes) divided by total employment and expressed as an index based in 1992. The raw data are presented in the trends and forecasts tables. At the national level, output is for private nonfarm business, adjusted for inflation. Private nonfarm business output is gross domestic product (GDP) minus the sum of agricultural output and the output of the government sector. The Bureau of Labor Statistics (BLS) has provided data on total employment.

Trends and Forecasts Tables

The Trends and Forecasts table is a standard feature of every chapter. Tables in manufacturing chapters follow a specific format. The industry is defined by SIC codes, and the table contains up to 8 years of statistics. Tables in this edition contain industry and product data from 1992 through 1999. Shipments data through 1996 are actual; for 1997 and 1998, estimates; and 1999, forecasts. (Trade data through 1997 are actual.) The value of shipments in the trends and forecasts tables is generally shown in both "current" and "constant" dollars. The constant dollars in the *Outlook*'s Trends and Forecasts tables are identified as "value of shipments (1992$)." This means that output is valued using 1992 prices. (See the accompanying glossary for further explanation.) Historical data are also provided for capital investment and earnings (both in current dollars) and for employment.

The difference between industry and product shipments is important for interpreting the statistics in this book. Shipments data are collected separately for individual factories or establishments rather than for entire companies. Although most factories or establishments make or sell a variety of

products, for statistical purposes individual concerns are classified under the industry of their most prominent product. For instance, if 80 percent of a plant's total output is tires and 20 percent is hose and belting, then that plant is classified as a tire industry plant. The total output of all such plants make up the industry shipments for the industry. Other measures of activity under the "industry" heading, such as employment and hourly earnings, are reported for the establishments classified in that industry.

The value of all tires shipped by all establishments is added to derive "product shipments." In other words, "industry shipments" refers to the total value of all activities conducted by establishments classified in an industry. "Product shipments" can be thought of as the total value of specific products classified within an industry shipped by all establishments, regardless of how these establishments are classified.

When a plant's products change substantially, the industry under which the plant is classified may change as well. Despite such changes, historical data are not revised, which can result in significant discontinuities. The reader should, therefore, use care in relating industry statistics (such as employment) to product statistics because an industry's product mix may change.

Trade Patterns Tables

These tables include data on exports and imports for the six major areas of the world and on the United States' top purchasers and suppliers of merchandise. The six major regions are

NAFTA (North American Free Trade Agreement countries of Canada and Mexico), Latin America (all other countries in the western hemisphere, except Canada and Mexico), Western Europe (all countries in the region, whether a European Union member or not), Japan/Chinese Economic Area (Japan, China, Hong Kong, and Taiwan), Other Asia (all countries on the Asian continent except the Japan/Chinese Economic Area and the Middle East), and Rest of world (Eastern Europe and former Soviet states, the Middle East, Africa, Australia, New Zealand, and other Pacific countries and territories).

Data Sources and Methods

Industry and Product Data. For manufacturing industries, the most reliable and consistent federal data source of historical data on such items as value of shipments, employment and wages, and capital investments is the *1992 Census of Manufactures,* revised and updated by the *Annual Survey of Manufactures.* Mining industry data are published in the *1992 Census of Minerals;* data for subsequent years are available from the U.S. Department of the Interior, Bureau of Mines. Data for many service industries are included in the Census Bureau's Service Annual Surveys, which are current through 1996.

Trade Data. Census trade data (exports and imports) are tabulated following the Bureau of the Census' trade concordance, as adjusted by the various analysts to approximate their four-

---

WHERE TO FIND MORE INFORMATION

Two federal government resources of general interest to U.S. businesses are *A Basic Guide to Exporting,* which discusses exporting strategies and related issues, and the U.S. Trade Information Center (1-800-USA-TRADE), the definitive source for information on U.S. government export programs and activities.

Free catalogs listing government publications may be ordered from the Superintendent of Documents at the Government Printing Office (GPO) by calling (202) 512-1800 or by faxing an order to (202) 512-2250. (The GPO's Internet address is www.access.gpo.gov.) Call the National Technical Information Service at (703) 487-4650 for ordering information and catalogs on thousands of government publications or visit the Web site at www.ntis.gov. In addition, the U.S. Bureau of the Census has made statistical information available on its Web site at www.census.gov.

The government documents mentioned can be found in the reference section of many libraries or on the Web sites of university and state libraries participating in the Federal Depository Library program. Useful nongovernment sources of business information include *Thomas' Register, Standard & Poor's Register, Ward's Business Directory, Dun's Industrial Guide,* and reports by Dun & Bradstreet and Standard & Poor's, among others. Directories of trade associations that can be found in reference sections of libraries include the *Encyclopedia of Associations, National Trade & Professional Associations of the U.S.,* and the *Yearbook of International Organizations.*

---

digit SIC industry grouping. Census data on U.S. merchandise trade are current through 1997. Trade data are collected using the Harmonized System (HS), a procedure the United States adopted in 1989. Most major industrial countries and many less-developed countries use the HS, making it easier to assess and compare recent (but not pre-1989) international trade by commodity for various countries.

Analysis of trade data over a longer period is more difficult, however. Since trade data used to be collected and tabulated differently, it cannot be determined if apparent changes in the value of trade by category before and after 1989 are due to actual trade developments or to changes in reporting and classifying practices.

GLOSSARY OF KEY TERMS

APEC: The Asia-Pacific Economic Cooperation group was established in 1989 in response to the growing interdependence among Asia-Pacific economies. Begun as an informal dialogue group, APEC has become the primary regional vehicle for promoting open trade and economic cooperation within the region. As of November 1998, its members are (in order of joining) Australia, Brunei Darussalam, Canada, Indonesia, Japan, South Korea, Malaysia, New Zealand, Philippines, Singapore, Thailand, the United States, China, Hong Kong, Taiwan, Mexico, Papua New Guinea, Chile, Peru, Russia, and Vietnam.

Antidumping duty: A duty imposed by the United States to offset any profits that a foreign firm attempts to make by dumping merchandise on the U.S. market. (See Dumping.)

ASEAN: Association of Southeast Asian Nations, consisting of Brunei Darussalam, Cambodia, Indonesia, Laos, Malaysia, Myanmar, Philippines, Singapore, Thailand, and Vietnam.

CAGR: Compound annual growth rate.

Caribbean Basin Initiative (CBI): An inter-American program, led by the United States, of increased economic assistance and trade preferences to Caribbean and Central American countries. CBI provides duty-free access to the U.S. market for most products from the region and promotes private sector development in the region.

c.i.f.: Cost, insurance and freight. A pricing term indicating that the cost of the goods, insurance, and freight are included in the quoted price.

Constant dollars (or "real" dollars): Output values converted to a base price level, calculated by dividing current (or actual) dollars by a deflator. Use of constant dollars eliminates the effects of price changes between the year of measurement and the base year and allows calculation of real changes in output.

Consumer Price Index (CPI): Measures a weighted average price level of a representative basket of goods and services purchased by consumers.

Countervailing duty: A retaliatory charge that a country places on imported goods to counter direct or indirect subsidies or bounties granted to the exporters of the goods by their home governments.

Current dollars: The actual dollar amount paid in sales transactions.

Dumping: A term used in international trade that refers to the sale of a product in export markets below the selling price for the same product in the exporter's domestic market, or lower than the cost of manufacturing and marketing such goods in the domestic market.

Durable goods (durables): Items with a normal life expectancy of 3 years or more, such as automobiles, furniture, and major household appliances. Sales of durable goods are generally postponable and, therefore, are the most volatile component of consumer expenditures.

Euro: The basic unit of the new common European currency, which will begin to be used on January 1, 1999. Initially, only 11 of the 15 European Union member countries will participate. Denmark, Greece, Sweden, and the United Kingdom will continue to maintain their national currencies.

Eurodollars: Deposits held in denominations of U.S. dollars in commercial banks outside the United States.

European Currency Unit (ECU): An international unit of account created for the European Monetary System (EMS), to be used as the denominator of EMS debts and credits and as a reserve credit in the European Monetary Cooperation Fund (EMCF). The ECU is an index composed of a weighted basket of currencies of EU members. The ECU will go out of existence upon the introduction of the euro on January 1, 1999.

European Union (EU): A regional economic/political organization forming the largest trading bloc in the world. Its 15 members are Austria, Belgium, Denmark, Finland, France, Germany, Greece, Ireland, Italy, Luxembourg, the Netherlands, Portugal, Spain, Sweden, and the United Kingdom.

Export-Import Bank (Eximbank): An autonomous agency of the U.S. Government created in 1934 to facilitate the export trade of the United States.

f.a.s. (free alongside ship): The transaction price of an export product, including freight, insurance, and other charges incurred in placing the merchandise alongside the carrier in the U.S. port.

f.o.b. (free on board): Without charge for delivery of export merchandise to, and placing on board, a carrier at a specified point.

Foreign trade zones (FTZs): Designated areas in the United States, usually near ports of entry, considered to be outside the customs territory of the United States. Also known as free trade zones.

G-7 (Group of Seven): Seven industrial countries: the United States, Japan, Germany, France, the United Kingdom, Italy, and Canada. G-7 heads of state and/or government have met at annual economic summits since 1975. G-7 finance ministers meet periodically to discuss economic issues of common concern.

General Agreement on Tariffs and Trade (GATT): An international organization and code of tariffs and trade rules that has evolved out of the multilateral trade treaty signed in 1947. It was replaced by the World Trade Organization (WTO) on January 1, 1995.

Generalized Agreement on Trade in Services (GATS): Expands the rules on trade in goods that were negotiated under GATT auspices to include trade in services.

Generalized System of Preference (GSP): A system approved by GATT in 1971 that authorizes developed countries to give preferential tariff treatment to developing countries.

Gross domestic product (GDP): The value of all goods and services produced in a country during a specified time period. (See Value added)

Harmonized System (HS): An international convention, implemented by the United States in 1989, for classifying imports and exports so that data from different countries are comparable.

Industry shipments: The total value of products shipped by establishments classified as being in the industry, plus miscellaneous receipts.

Intellectual property: Includes trademarks, copyrights, patents, and trade secrets.

International Monetary Fund (IMF): Established in 1945, the IMF serves as a permanent forum for its member countries to discuss and to coordinate economic and financial policies. Its capital is derived from subscriptions from member countries and is used to provide assistance to members facing relatively short-term economic difficulties.

IPR: Intellectual property rights; in general, the right to possess or control the use of intellectual property.

ISO 9000: A series of five standards (9000–9004) of the International Standards Organization (ISO), an international agency that promotes quality standards in products and systems.

Maquila (maquiladora): Mexican assembly plant generally, but not necessarily, near the U.S.-Mexican border; most of its production is exported to the United States.

Most-favored-nation (MFN) trade status: An arrangement in which GATT (now WTO) countries must extend to all other members the most favorable treatment granted to any trading partner, thus assuring that any tariff reductions or other trade concessions are automatically extended to all GATT parties.

n.e.c.: Not elsewhere classified.

NIC/NIE: Newly industrialized country/economy. A country that has experienced rapid growth in GDP, industrial production, and exports in recent years.

Nondurable goods (nondurables): Items which last for less than 3 years, such as food, beverages, and clothing. Generally, purchases of these items cannot be significantly postponed.

North American Free Trade Agreement (NAFTA): Agreement creating a free trade area among the United States, Canada, and Mexico. The agreement became effective January 1, 1994.

North American Industry Classification System (NAICS): A new system, adopted by the United States, Canada, and Mexico to replace SIC as the standard for defining industries and classifying establishments by industry.

Organization for Economic Cooperation and Development (OECD): A group of 29 industrialized, market economy countries that aims to promote its members' economic and social welfare, and to stimulate economic development efforts in developing countries. The OECD was established in 1961 and is headquartered in Paris. Member countries as of October 1998 are Austria, Australia, Belgium, Canada, Czech Republic, Denmark, Finland, France, Germany, Greece, Hungary, Iceland, Ireland, Italy, Japan, Luxembourg, Mexico, New Zealand, the Netherlands, Norway, Poland, Portugal, South Korea, Spain, Sweden, Switzerland, Turkey, the United Kingdom, and the United States.

Organization of Petroleum Exporting Countries (OPEC): An association of important oil-exporting countries that are highly dependent on oil revenues, formed in 1960. Its major purpose is to coordinate the petroleum production and pricing of its 12 members: Algeria, Gabon, Indonesia, Iran, Iraq, Kuwait, Libya, Nigeria, Qatar, Saudi Arabia, the United Arab Emirates, and Venezuela.

Pacific Rim: A term that technically means all countries bordering on the Pacific Ocean, although it often refers only to East Asian countries.

Product shipments: The total value of specific products shipped by all establishments, irrespective of these establishments' industry classification.

Standard industrial classification (SIC): U.S. government-established standard for defining industries and classifying establishments by industry.

Uruguay Round: Eighth and final round of multilateral trade negotiations held under GATT auspices. It is named for the country where initial discussions began in September 1986 and concluded in December 1993; most of the negotiations have taken place in Geneva, Switzerland.

Value added: The difference between the value of goods produced and the cost of materials and services purchased to produce them. It includes wages, interest, rent, and profits. The sum of value added of all sectors of the economy equals GDP.

Voluntary restraint agreement (VRA): An import relief device to limit foreign trade in a particular commodity to protect domestic industry from injury by foreign competition. Sometimes referred to as a "voluntary export restraint" or an "orderly marketing agreement."

World Bank: This term refers to the International Bank for Reconstruction and Development (IBRD) and the International Development Association (IDA). The World Bank is the largest provider of development assistance to developing countries and countries in transition, committing about $20 billion in new loans each year. Its main focus is to help people in developing countries raise their standards of living through finance for agriculture, schools, health programs, transportation, and other essential needs.

World Trade Organization (WTO): Created by the Uruguay Round to succeed GATT on January 1, 1995, it expands GATT's rules to apply to trade in services and intellectual property rights. A tribunal to adjudicate trade disputes was also established.

Economic Assumptions of *Outlook '99*

U.S. Industry & Trade Outlook '99 provides estimates of near-term growth for major sectors of the economy. Those estimates reflect, in part, the major economic assumptions that are described in this chapter. The estimates also reflect the knowledge of analysts from the U.S. Department of Commerce and from Data Resources Incorporated (DRI) of the specific circumstances influencing the industries that the analysts follow. That knowledge is conveyed in Chapters 1 through 50.

U.S. Economy in 1997 and 1998

A brief review of economic developments in 1997 and 1998 provides a helpful introduction to the projections for 1999 and 2000. The current expansion celebrated its seventh birthday in March 1998. In November 1998, the expansion will set an endurance record for peace-time expansions of 92 months, bettering the record posted in the 1983–1990 expansion. The longest expansion on record, in 1961–1969, lasted 106 months and coincided with the Vietnam War.

The health of the economy has been demonstrated by the first federal government surplus since 1969, the lowest rates of inflation and unemployment in a generation, and robust business investment. The momentum of these trends is being slowed by the influence from overseas economies, especially those in Asia. A strike at GM and a fall in inventory investment contributed to slower growth in real gross domestic product (GDP) in the second quarter. Deterioration in the trade deficit also subtracted from overall growth in the first half of 1998. Available data at midyear were consistent with moderate growth in the second half of the year.

As of September 1998, private analysts (*Blue Chip* consensus) anticipated that real GDP would grow 3.4 percent in 1998 (year over year), down slightly from the robust 1997 gain of 3.9 percent. Analysts also expected consumer prices to rise about 1.6 percent in 1998, down from the 1997 pace of 2.3 percent. Lower prices for energy accounted for the overall moderation.

Federal Government's Budget

The economy's strong growth in 1997 and early 1998, combined with modest growth in outlays, led to the elimination of the federal government's deficit. The administration's efforts to restore federal fiscal responsibility can be traced back to the effects of the Omnibus Budget Reconciliation Act of 1993. Data available in late September indicated a budget surplus of roughly $70 billion for the fiscal year (FY) 1998, the largest surplus as a percent of GDP since the 1950s. The budget, as a percent of GDP, shifted from a 4.7 percent deficit in FY1993 to a surplus of roughly 0.8 percent in FY1998.

The elimination of the deficit since FY1989, the fiscal year before the last recession, reflected almost equal rise in receipts relative to GDP and a drop in outlays relative to GDP (see Figure B-1).

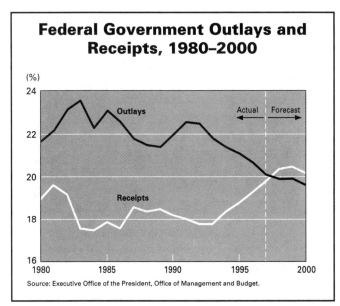

Federal Government Outlays and Receipts, 1980–2000

Source: Executive Office of the President, Office of Management and Budget.

FIGURE B-1

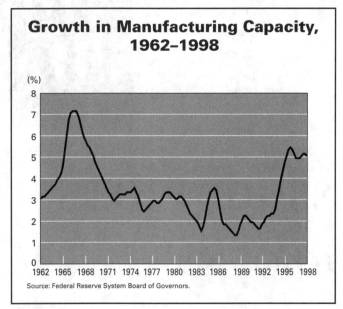

Growth in Manufacturing Capacity, 1962–1998

(%)

Source: Federal Reserve System Board of Governors.

FIGURE B-2

The dramatic swing from deficit to surplus has freed financial resources for the private market and has lowered interest rates. Between the fourth quarter of 1989 and the second quarter of 1998, federal government spending for goods and services (adjusted for inflation) fell 2.9 percent at an annual rate. Over these 33 quarters, private spending for consumption and investment rose 3.2 percent at an annual rate.

Business Investment

As new federal borrowing has been reduced, private investment has flourished. Strong growth in business investment in structures and equipment has contributed importantly to the health

of the current expansion. Its contribution has been both direct and indirect. Business investment (after adjusting for inflation) accounted directly for roughly one-third of overall GDP growth between 1993 and the first half of 1998, although it accounted for only 9 percent of the level of GDP in 1997.

The advances in investment have indirectly contributed to the expansion's health by significantly boosting the rate of capacity growth—the capacity of the overall economy to produce goods and services. Figure B-2 shows that manufacturing capacity has grown over 5 percent per year since mid-1995, the fastest pace since mid-1969 and more than twice the rate of increase posted at the end of the last expansion in 1989. Since 1990, the growth of capacity has essentially matched the gains in manufacturing production and, as a consequence, pressures on capacity have not developed in the current expansion. Capacity utilization in 1997 and so far in 1998 has remained close to its long-term average and well below rates posted toward the end of all recent expansions.

The moderate levels of capacity utilization from 1997 through mid-1998 contributed importantly to the low inflation in the U.S. economy. Moderate operating rates indicate an absence of inflationary pressures from capacity constraints. The longer-term downward trend in U.S. prices for imported goods has also contributed to the absence of inflationary pressures. Lower import prices directly affect the prices paid by consumers for imported goods at the retail level. Lower prices also indirectly affect the prices charged by domestic producers, via lower costs for materials inputs and greater competitive pressures.

Inflation

All post-World War II expansions have come to an end because serious imbalances developed which, in turn, led to inflationary

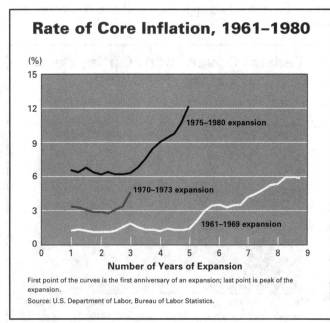

Rate of Core Inflation, 1961–1980

(%)

1975–1980 expansion

1970–1973 expansion

1961–1969 expansion

Number of Years of Expansion

First point of the curves is the first anniversary of an expansion; last point is peak of the expansion.

Source: U.S. Department of Labor, Bureau of Labor Statistics.

FIGURE B-3

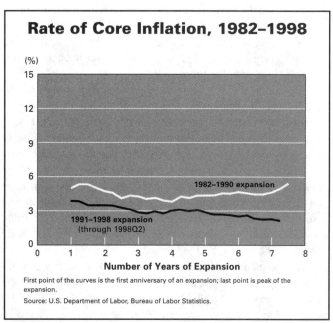

Rate of Core Inflation, 1982–1998

(%)

1982–1990 expansion

1991–1998 expansion
(through 1998Q2)

Number of Years of Expansion

First point of the curves is the first anniversary of an expansion; last point is peak of the expansion.

Source: U.S. Department of Labor, Bureau of Labor Statistics.

FIGURE B-4

TABLE B-1: Nonfinancial Corporations' Performance
(percent change, fourth quarter to fourth quarter)

	1997 Share of Total Payments	1995	1996	1997	1998Q2[1]
Compensation per hour		2.6	3.4	3.9	4.3
Productivity		2.2	2.4	2.6	3.0
Unit labor costs	65	0.4	0.9	1.2	1.3
Unit nonlabor costs	21	−0.3	−1.4	−1.8	−1.6
Unit profits	13	4.9	4.3	0.2	−5.1
Implicit price deflator		0.8	0.8	0.4	−0.2
Addendum					
Core CPI		3.1	2.6	2.2	2.2
Core Gross Domestic Purchases Index		2.2	1.3	1.4	0.8

[1] 1997Q1 to 1998Q1.
Source: U.S. Department of Commerce, Bureau of Economic Analysis.

pressures and rising interest rates. In past expansions, the rate of core inflation (as measured on consumer prices excluding food and energy) always accelerated in the latter stages of the expansion after trending down early in the expansion (see Figures B-3 and B-4). The rate of inflation was rising rapidly at the end of the 1975–1980 expansion and modestly at the end of the 1982–1990 expansion. In strong contrast, the rate of core inflation has continued to trend down in the current expansion. In the seventh year of this expansion (March 1997 to March 1998), core prices increased just 2.1 percent, less than in prior years.

The tight labor markets in 1997 and early 1998 put some upward pressure on labor costs. Hourly compensation rose 4.3 percent in the second quarter of 1998 from the year-ago level, a pickup from the 3.1 percent rise in the year 1996 (see Table B-1). Faster growth in hourly compensation, however, does not necessarily translate into a higher rate of inflation. Prices charged by nonfinancial corporations actually edged down 0.2 percent in the second quarter of 1998 from their level a year before. For these businesses, the rapid growth in compensation has been accommodated by a combination of strong productivity gains, declines in nonlabor costs per unit of output, and a drop in profit margins.

The profit margins of nonfinancial corporations (the ratio of profits to nominal GDP) have declined from the 29-year high posted in 1997 but remained at a relatively high level in mid-1998. If that decline persists, it will dampen future investment levels.

International Trade

The appreciation in the U.S. dollar's value relative to most foreign currencies in recent years, the financial and economic turmoil in the Asian developing countries in the second half of 1997, and the recession in Japan in late 1997 and early 1998 contributed to a sharply higher trade deficit in mid-1998.

The U.S. trade deficit in goods and services jumped to $176 billion at an annual rate in the second quarter, well above the $110 billion deficit for all of 1997. As a percent of GDP, the deficit rose

Exports and Imports of Goods and Services

Imports

Exports

Based on 1992 chained dollars, National Income Accounts basis.
Source: U.S. Department of Commerce, Bureau of Economic Analysis.

FIGURE B-5

to 2.1 percent from 1.4 percent for all of 1997. Although the current deficit is the largest ever in nominal dollars, the deficits in the mid-1980s were much higher as a percent of GDP.

The deterioration in the trade deficit in 1998 reflected weak exports and continued strength in imports (see Figure B-5). Exports of goods and services adjusted for inflation have dropped as a share of GDP. In contrast, real imports as a share of GDP have continued their strong upward trend.

Exchange rates have an effect on U.S. international trade. The trade-weighted value of the U.S. dollar moved sharply upward in late 1997 and early 1998 to its highest level since 1986. In contrast, during the 1987–1996 period, the value of the dollar fluctuated with no clear upward or downward trend. In early October 1998, the dollar stood about 10 percent above its 1987–1996 average. This relatively high level, if sustained, will likely dampen the growth rate of U.S. exports in 1999 and boost the growth rate of U.S. imports.

Recession and declining investment through much of east Asia have depressed U.S. exports since the high reached in October 1997. Most U.S. exports to the area are capital goods. The value of goods exports to several Asian countries dropped sharply in the first 7 months of 1998 from their year-ago level— down 52 percent to Indonesia, 46 percent to Korea, 29 percent to Thailand, and 12 percent to Japan (see Table B-2). Goods exports to other regions continued to expand in 1998 but, in many cases, at slower rates than in 1997. For example, exports to Canada rose 5 percent in the first 7 months of 1998 from their year-ago level, down from the 1997 pace of 13 percent.

Economic Outlook for 1999 and 2000

Consumer spending, which accounts for roughly two-thirds of overall spending, should remain fairly vigorous in 1999. Consumer spending, after adjusting for inflation, increased at a 4.4

TABLE B-2: U.S. Merchandise Exports

	Share of 1997 Exports	Percent Change from Year-Ago Level	
		1997	Jan.-July 1998
Total exports	100	10.3	1.8
Indonesia	1	13.7	−52.1
South Korea	4	−5.9	−46.0
Thailand	1	2.1	−29.1
Japan	10	−3.0	−11.7
Mexico	10	25.7	16.6
South and Central America	9	19.8	7.2
Canada	22	13.1	4.7
Western Europe	23	9.8	3.5

Source: U.S. Department of Commerce, Bureau of the Census.

percent annual rate in the six quarters ending in mid-1998. Healthy advances in real disposable personal income (income after taxes and adjusted for inflation) and payroll employment, combined with historically high levels of consumer confidence, have supported the sizable increase in consumer spending so far in 1998.

Growth in consumer spending may be slowed, however, by the decline in the stock market or even a plateau. In 1997, households received $60 billion in dividends from mutual funds that were derived from capital gains that represent 0.9 percent of personal income, up from an estimated 0.3 percent in 1987. The 1987 fall in stock prices had little effect on consumer spending, but the influence may be more apparent this year because of the larger impact on income.

The outlook for slower economic growth rests primarily on the prospects for a widening trade deficit. In each of the first two quarters of 1998, falling net exports pulled down the GDP growth rate by more than 2 percent. Total exports, after adjusting for

TABLE B-3: Economic Forecasts for 1999 and 2000[1]

	Actual 1997	Forecasts		
		1998	1999	2000
Real GDP (year-over-year percent change)				
Outlook '99			1.7 to 2.2	2.2 to 2.7
Blue Chip consensus	3.9	3.4	1.6 to 2.9	NA[2]
Administration			2.0	2.0
Consumer Price Index (percent change)				
Outlook '99			2.4 to 2.9	2.7 to 3.2
Blue Chip consensus	2.3	1.6	1.9 to 2.6	NA
Administration			2.1	2.2
Unemployment rate (percent)				
Outlook '99			4.5 to 5.1	5.4 to 6.2
Blue Chip consensus	5.4	4.5	4.3 to 5.1	NA
Administration			5.0	5.2

[1] The Outlook '99 forecast was prepared in late March 1998, administration forecasts were published in June, and the Blue Chip consensus in September.
[2] NA = not available.

inflation, declined in the first two quarters of 1998. Employment in capital equipment and electronic components, two manufacturing sectors most sensitive to exports, fell at a 3 percent rate from their peak in the spring of 1998 to the fall. (See "World Economic Outlook" for a discussion of the economic prospects for Asia and other regions of the global economy.)

The events in Asia appear to have accelerated a longer-term downward trend in U.S. prices for imported nonpetroleum goods. The ongoing drop in these import prices no doubt has contributed to the favorable performance in the rate of inflation of consumer goods. Lower import prices directly affect the prices paid by consumers for imported goods at the retail level. Lower prices also indirectly affect the prices charged by domestic producers via lower costs for materials inputs and greater competitive pressures. In addition, slower domestic growth will reduce price pressures caused by tight labor markets.

The Asian effect on international capital flows and the outlook for slower U.S. growth no doubt has put downward pressures on U.S. interest rates. The yield on 30-year Treasury bonds trended downward from its peak of 7.12 percent in April 1997 to less than 5 percent in October, the lowest yield for a long-term government bond since 1967. Lower long-term interest rates, combined with favorable weather patterns, boosted home-building activity to record levels in the first 8 months of 1998. Lower rates have also helped to sustain an upward trend in private nonresidential construction.

Looking ahead, the Department of Commerce and DRI expect moderate growth, moderate inflation, and somewhat higher unemployment rates in 1999 and 2000 (see Table B-3). Forecasts, however, always involve uncertainties. To signal the uncertainties, the forecasts of key indicators that underlie Outlook '99 are presented as ranges rather than point estimates.

The economy should grow between 1.7 and 2.7 percent per year in 1999 and 2000, a favorable performance but down considerably from the expected 1998 gain of 3.4 percent. It is anticipated that in 1999 the rate of inflation, as measured by changes in the consumer price index, would remain below 3 percent and the unemployment rate slightly below 5 percent. The expected pickup in the overall inflation from the anticipated 1998 pace reflects, in large part, the expected end of the price declines at the retail level that were related, in turn, to the weakness in crude oil prices during 1997 and so far in 1998.

Outlook '99 forecasts essentially match those prepared by private analysts and the administration (see Table B-3). The Blue Chip estimates shown in the table are the averages of the highest and lowest 10 forecasts that make up the Blue Chip consensus. Blue Chip forecasts of GDP growth for 1999 range from 1.9 to 2.9 percent. The difference between Outlook '99 and Blue Chip estimates for 1999 is on the upper bound and likely reflects the date the forecasts were prepared. The economy performed better than anticipated in early 1998. The Blue Chip estimates published in September 1998 reflect that performance while the Outlook '99 estimates prepared in March do not.

Lee Price, Chief Economist, U.S. Department of Commerce.

World Economic Outlook

In 1997 the world economy grew an estimated 4 percent, about the same growth that occurred in the previous year, marking 4 consecutive years of solid growth (International Monetary Fund, *World Economic Outlook,* May 1998). The expectations for economic growth in 1998 and the outlook for 1999 are far less positive than they were in late 1997, owing to the economic turmoil that began in Asia and spread to Russia, Latin America, and other emerging markets. The current forecast is that economic growth in 1998 and 1999 will average more than a percentage point less than growth in 1997 because of the downturn in Asia and because of the repercussions that are impacting other parts of the world economy. This outlook assumes that the problems in Asia will not become worse, and that no further shocks will destabilize the situation even more than has already occurred. Growth is expected to be slower in the industrial countries (as a group) as well as in the developing countries. Only the transition economies of east and central Europe are expected to grow slightly more rapidly during this period, but even in this group the outlook for growth has been pared down because of the fallout from the financial situation in Russia. World and regional growth rates are summarized in Table C-1.

Besides the outlook for world growth, other indicators of economic activity are looking less robust. World trade volume will certainly grow much less in 1998 than the 9 percent growth of 1997, but there should be a slight rebound in the rate of growth of both trade and world output in 1999. The outlook for inflation is mixed. In some industrial countries the cycle of expansion has reached a point where wage pressures are beginning to pose a threat to price stability. In Japan, however, prices have been on a downward trend and deflation is more of a problem. Among the developing countries a similar dichotomy can be found. In the Asian countries that have been most severely impacted by the crisis, rapid price inflation is a problem. The crisis, however, has resulted in a decline in demand for several industrial and food commodities that are important exports of many developing countries. In general, however, price inflation is not the problem that it was in most developing countries just a few years ago. In Latin America, for example, overall inflation is approaching single-digit levels, a rate of price increase

not seen in many years. The transition economies of Europe also have reduced price inflation significantly.

As a group, the industrial countries are expected to grow by about half a percentage point less in 1998–1999 compared to 1997 when growth was nearly 3 percent. In contrast to 1997, however, economic growth rates among the major economies are expected to converge during the 1998–1999 period, unlike 1997 when the United States, Canada, and the United Kingdom grew at paces that were above long-term potential growth rates while the major continental European countries grew at rates that were somewhat slower than potential would allow in the long term. In 1998–1999 slower growth in the United States, the United Kingdom, and Canada will be offset to some extent by faster growth in continental Europe. The exception to this scenario will be in Japan, where fiscal tightening in early 1997 slowed the economy to a crawl for the final three quarters of the year in comparison to 1996 when Japan's growth was the fastest

POSTSCRIPT ON THE ONGOING WORLD ECONOMIC CRISIS

The research and writing of this report was largely completed in mid-1998 during a period in which the worst of the financial turbulence connected with the Asian financial crisis seemed to have been realized. In the weeks that followed, however, new and increased turmoil—beginning in Russia in mid-August and quickly spreading to Latin America—unleashed a new round of financial market instability and economic uncertainty. Some editing of the paper was completed at that time to reflect what was then seen as the most probable outcome of these new events, most importantly a more severe contraction of economic growth in most regions than was foreseen earlier in the year. Nevertheless, major uncertainties remained when the draft was sent to the publisher in early autumn. The most important uncertainty is whether or not the latest spread of market instability will be contained and world financial market confidence gradually restored, or if a new round of "financial meltdown" in yet undetermined countries will occur with even more adverse consequences than were expected at this writing.

TABLE C-1: World, Regional, and Country Growth, 1987–1999

	Average 1987–1992	1993	1994	1995	1996	1997	1998 Forecast (Low/High)	1999 Forecast (Low/High)
World	3.3	2.7	3.8	3.7	4.3	3.9	1.8/2.5	2.2/3.2
Industrial countries	2.7	0.9	2.9	2.2	2.7	2.8	2.0/2.6	1.8/2.4
United States	2.2	2.3	3.5	2.3	3.4	3.9	3.1/3.5	2.0/2.4
Canada	1.8	2.5	3.9	2.2	1.2	3.6	3.0/3.6	2.2/2.8
Japan	4.2	0.3	0.6	1.5	3.9	0.5	-2.0/-1.5	0.0/1.0
European Union	2.7	-0.5	2.9	2.4	1.6	2.5	2.5/2.9	2.4/3.0
Germany[1]	3.4	-1.2	2.7	1.8	1.4	2.4	2.3/2.7	2.2/2.8
France	2.6	-1.3	2.8	2.1	1.5	2.3	2.7/3.1	2.5/3.1
Australia	2.5	3.9	5.4	4.1	3.7	2.9	2.9/3.4	2.5/3.1
Emerging market countries by region	4.2	4.9	5.0	5.3	5.9	5.2	1.6/2.2	3.0/3.8
Africa	2.5	0.8	2.5	3.0	5.5	3.2	2.0/3.0	4.2/5.0
Asia	7.5	9.4	9.7	9.1	8.3	6.6	1.5/1.9	3.8/4.6
NICs[2]	8.1	6.3	7.6	7.3	6.4	6.0	-1.6/-1.2	1.0/2.0
China	8.9	13.5	12.6	10.5	9.7	8.8	6.0/7.0	6.5/7.5
ASEAN[3]	7.8	7.0	7.5	7.8	6.9	3.1	-10.0/-8.0	-2.0/2.0
Middle East and Europe[4]	4.0	3.9	0.7	3.6	4.9	4.3	3.0/3.6	3.0/4.0
Central and South America	2.3	3.9	5.0	0.7	3.6	5.1	2.6/3.2	2.4/3.1
Mexico	3.2	2.0	4.5	-6.2	5.2	7.0	4.3/4.8	4.0/5.0
Big Emerging Markets[5]	6.4	8.3	8.4	7.1	7.2	6.2	1.5/2.5	3.5/4.5
East Europe and former Soviet Union	-3.5	-6.2	-8.1	-1.2	-0.6	0.9	1.5/2.5	2.5/3.5
Russia	NA[6]	-8.7	-12.6	-4.0	-2.8	0.4	-4.0/-1.0	-6.0/-4.0
Poland	-2.0	3.8	5.2	7.0	6.1	5.6	5.0/5.5	5.0/6.0
World trade volume	6.0	4.0	9.3	9.5	6.6	9.4	4.0/5.0	5.6/6.6

[1] Data prior to 1990 refer to West Germany only.
[2] Newly Industrialized Countries (Hong Kong, Singapore, South Korea, Taiwan).
[3] Association of Southeast Asian Nations (Indonesia, Malaysia, Philippines, Thailand, Singapore, Brunei Darrussalam, Vietnam).
[4] Developing countries in Europe are Turkey, Cyprus, and Malta.
[5] Argentina, Brazil, Mexico, Chinese Economic Area, ASEAN, India, South Korea, Poland, South Africa, and Turkey.
[6] Not available.
Sources: Historical data from the IMF, the OECD, and various country sources; forecasts by the U.S. Department of Commerce, International Trade Administration.

among the G-7 group of countries. The recession that began in the last months of 1997 continued well into 1998, and Japan's growth in 1998 is expected to be negative.

Among the seven major industrial countries, the economies of the United States and the United Kingdom have reached full capacity and must slow to avoid higher rates of inflation. Monetary policy has been tightened in the United Kingdom, while tight fiscal policy and the trade repercussions of the Asian crisis will slow growth in the United States. Most of the other countries are below capacity and can grow at their current pace in the near term. Japan, of course, must take action to reverse the course of its economy. In addition to the restraining influence of the fiscal policy tightening in early 1997, Japan's economy has been hurt by a lack of reserves in the banking system, by falling business and consumer confidence, by falling asset prices, and by the negative impact of the Asian crisis on its exports.

As a group, economic growth in the smaller industrial countries was even better than growth in the major seven during 1997, and while growth is expected to be somewhat slower for these smaller countries in 1998–1999, they are expected to outperform the industrial countries as a group. Growth rates in some of the smaller European economies were particularly impressive during 1997, especially in Ireland and Finland.

For the developing countries as a whole, the forecast is that they will grow between 2 and 3 percent in 1998 and slightly more in 1999. These expected rates of growth are 3 to 4 percent-

age points less than in the last decade. Most of this slowdown is related to the Asian crisis, of course, but growth in all regions is expected to be slower in 1998–1999 compared to 1997 with the possible exception of Africa, where growth is forecast to accelerate from around 3 percent in 1997 to 4 percent or more in 1998 and 1999.

Developing countries in Africa, Latin America, Europe, and the Middle East have been adversely impacted by the fallout of the crisis in Asia. Falling petroleum prices have dampened growth prospects in the Middle East and in the energy-exporting Latin American and African countries. Lower prices for other raw materials have slowed growth in many other countries as well. For example, in Chile falling copper prices have seriously cut export earnings, fiscal balances, and investment plans. Another element of the fallout from Asia is that there has been a flight of short-term capital as investors have pulled back from developing economies. This reduction in foreign investment has led to higher interest rates and will adversely affect growth in the 1998–1999 period.

Growth in the developing countries of the Middle East and Europe is forecast to decrease from around 4 percent in 1997 to around 2.5 to 3 percent in 1998 and slightly more in 1999, when petroleum prices are expected to recover. In Latin America, very strong growth in Mexico, Argentina, Chile, and Venezuela propelled the region's overall growth to an estimated 5 percent in 1997. Because of the fallout from Asia—less foreign investment, higher interest rates, reduced exports, and fiscal and monetary tightening—growth in 1998 will be a only about half as high, before recovering slightly in 1999.

In the transition economies of central and eastern Europe and in the countries of the former Soviet Union, 1997 marked the first year since economic transition began that, as a group, these countries recorded positive economic growth. In just a few months, however, the generally positive outlook for the region has turned sour because of the Russian economic "meltdown." In one sense the collapse of Russia's economy was a consequence of fallout from the Asian crisis as rapidly falling prices for Russia's chief exports—oil, nickel, and other primary commodities—eroded the country's current account balance. On a more fundamental level, however, the fallout from Asia served to expose the fact that Russian economic reforms were incomplete and flawed. Large fiscal debts owing to poor tax collection, a lack of bank supervision, and a failure to protect the property rights of foreign investors are among the many problems that could no longer be ignored once the country began to hemorrhage foreign exchange reserves as the ruble came under attack. The other countries in the region will suffer the fallout from the Russian crisis, and growth in these countries is expected to be much lower, if not negative, compared to expectations at the beginning of the year.

Among the 20 countries that constitute the leading export markets for U.S. manufactured goods, growth was quite robust in 1997. The trade-weighted growth rate for the 20 was an estimated 4.3 percent in 1997, nearly a percentage point higher than the 3.6 percent growth in the previous year (see Table C-2 and Figure C-1). Much of the increase was the result of very

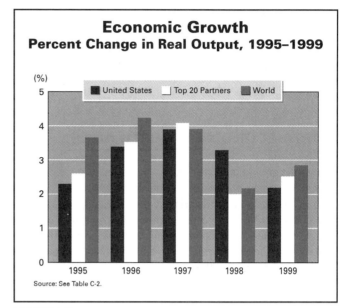

Economic Growth
Percent Change in Real Output, 1995–1999

Source: See Table C-2.

FIGURE C-1

TABLE C-2: Economic Growth in the Top 20 Markets for U.S. Manufactures

U.S. Exports of Manufactures to the Top 20 Markets in 1996[1]	U.S. Exports			Growth of Real GDP (year-over-year percent change)							
	Exports ($ billions)	Share of Total Exports (%)	Share of Top 20 Markets (%)	Average Growth 1983–1992	1993	1994	1995	1996	1997	1998 Forecast	1999 Forecast
1. Canada (1)	120.0	23.0	28.2	2.9	2.5	3.9	2.2	1.2	3.6	3.3	2.5
2. *Mexico (3)*	48.8	9.3	11.5	1.8	2.0	4.5	−6.2	5.2	7.0	4.5	4.6
3. Japan (2)	47.0	9.0	11.0	3.9	0.3	0.6	1.5	3.9	0.5	−1.8	0.5
4. United Kingdom (4)	28.7	5.5	6.7	2.4	2.1	4.3	2.7	2.2	3.4	2.2	1.5
5. Germany[2] (5)	21.2	4.1	5.0	3.1	−1.2	2.7	1.8	1.4	2.4	2.5	2.5
6. *South Korea (7)*	20.4	3.9	4.8	9.5	5.8	8.6	8.9	7.1	5.5	−5.0	−0.5
7. *Singapore (8)*	16.0	3.1	3.8	6.9	10.4	10.5	8.7	6.9	7.8	1.0	2.5
8. *Taiwan (7)*	14.4	2.8	3.4	8.5	6.3	6.5	6.0	5.7	6.9	4.5	4.5
9. Netherlands (10)	13.4	2.6	3.2	2.8	0.8	3.2	2.3	3.3	3.2	3.7	3.3
10. France (8)	13.2	2.5	3.1	2.2	−1.3	2.8	2.1	1.5	2.3	2.9	2.8
11. *Hong Kong (11)*	11.8	2.3	2.8	6.5	6.1	5.4	3.9	4.9	5.3	−2.5	1.5
12. Australia (13)	11.3	2.2	2.7	3.0	3.9	5.4	4.1	3.7	2.9	3.1	2.8
13. *Brazil (12)*	11.3	2.2	2.7	2.1	4.9	5.9	4.2	2.8	3.0	1.0	0.5
14. Belgium (13)	9.8	1.9	2.3	2.1	−1.5	2.4	2.1	1.5	2.4	2.7	2.7
15. *China (14)*	9.1	1.7	2.1	10.1	13.5	12.6	10.5	9.7	8.8	6.5	7.0
16. Switzerland (18)	8.2	1.6	1.9	2.2	−0.5	0.5	0.8	−0.2	0.5	1.9	2.2
17. *Malaysia (16)*	7.7	1.5	1.8	6.4	8.3	9.2	9.5	8.6	7.8	−4.0	0.0
18. Italy (17)	6.8	1.3	1.6	2.3	−1.2	2.2	2.9	0.7	1.3	2.3	3.2
19. Saudi Arabia (20)	6.5	1.2	1.5	1.5	−0.6	0.5	0.5	1.4	2.7	0.1	1.0
20. Thailand (19)	6.4	1.2	1.5	8.4	8.5	8.6	8.8	5.5	−4.0	−7.0	0.5
Trade Weighted Sum of Top 20	425.4	81.4	100.0	4.1	3.0	4.7	2.6	3.5	4.1	2.0	2.5
PPP GDP Weighted Sum of Top 20				4.2	3.7	5.3	4.2	4.5	4.0	2.2	3.1
United States				3.1	2.3	3.5	2.3	3.4	3.9	3.3	2.2
World	522.7			3.4	2.7	3.8	3.7	4.3	3.9	2.1	2.7

[1] Number in parentheses shows rank in 1995. Big Emerging Market economies (BEMs) are shown in bold italics.
[2] Data for years through 1990 apply to West Germany only.
Source: Historic data are from the IMF, World Bank, the United Nations, the OECD, and official country sources; forecasts by the U.S. Department of Commerce, International Trade Administration.

good growth in the economies of the United States' NAFTA partners, Mexico and Canada. Most of the European countries in the list of top markets also did better in 1997, but the crisis in Asia slowed 1997 growth in virtually all U.S. markets in this region. In 1998, for the first time since 1992, U.S. growth is expected to outpace the trade-weighted growth of the country's major export markets, and the growth rate of this group of countries may be lower than in any year since 1982. In 1999, with the expected slowdown in the U.S. economy and the hoped-for rebound in Asia, growth among the major U.S. export markets should again outpace U.S. growth, if only by a small amount.

NAFTA ECONOMIES: NORTH AMERICA

Economic growth in North America will cool during 1998-1999 compared to its blistering pace in 1997 when the U.S. and Canada led the major industrial countries, each growing by 3.8 percent, while Mexico's economy boomed with a growth rate of 7 percent. The U.S. economy is operating at or slightly above capacity, and growth rates should return to long-term trend levels of 2 to 2.5 percent. Slower growth in the United States will reduce export growth in both Mexico and Canada since both countries send roughly 80 percent of their exports to the United States (see Figure C-2). The Asian crisis is having negative impacts on all countries in NAFTA, but particularly on Canada and Mexico which are very dependent on commodity exports whose prices have fallen in the wake of the Asian slowdown.

Canada
While Canada's economic growth in 1998 will slow a few tenths of a percent below its 1997 growth, economic growth in Canada, still the largest single U.S. export market, is expected to be the fastest among the G-7 economies in 1998, the first

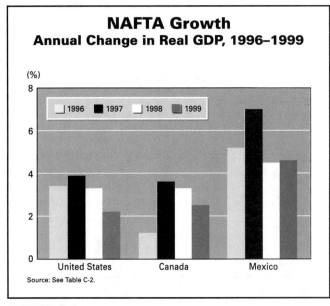

NAFTA Growth
Annual Change in Real GDP, 1996–1999

(%)

Legend: 1996, 1997, 1998, 1999

Source: See Table C-2.

FIGURE C-2

time in 30 years that Canada has led the group. But the economy slowed sharply in the second quarter, and projections for economic growth in the second half of 1998 and for 1999 have been scaled back. In 1997 business investment and consumer spending were the major driving forces behind the economy, and they were expected to play the same role in 1998–1999. However, declines in commodity prices, an increase in lending rates, lower consumer expectations, and a weaker export market in the United States have combined to produce a less optimistic outlook, although the economy remains fundamentally sound. As in the United States, the federal budget is in balance, and government fiscal policy is expected to be slightly expansionary in 1998–1999, after several years of austerity. The trade sector is the only one that will subtract from growth in 1998 as import growth again outpaces export growth. The gap between export growth and import growth is expected to be smaller in 1998 than in 1997, when imports, spurred by strong consumer spending, grew 13.4 percent while exports increased 8.6 percent.

In addition to the potential of more spillover effects from Asia, Canada's current account balance is the other area of major concern. The account deficit is expected to approach 3 percent of gross domestic product (GDP) in 1998, and it is a leading factor behind the decline in the value of the Canadian dollar, which fell to record lows against the U.S. dollar in mid-1998. The weakness of the Canadian dollar led to four hikes in short-term interest rates between late 1997 and mid-1998 by the Bank of Canada. With exports to Asia declining because of the crisis, and prices for materials exports falling for the same reason, there is concern that additional interest rate increases might be required to slow the decline in the value of the Canadian dollar if the trade balance continues to deteriorate. But higher interest rates might further dampen consumer spending and slow the economy. Any slowdown could hurt the job market. Canada's unemployment rate has fallen significantly during the current expansion, but it remains quite high (8.4 percent in mid-1998) compared with that of the United States.

The longer-term outlook for the Canadian economy is relatively positive. The tough fiscal tightening of the last several years has eliminated the federal budget deficit as well as deficits in most of the provinces. The government has discussed splitting any future surpluses between the restoration of some social spending and tax cuts.

Mexico
Mexico's economy grew a strong 7 percent in 1997, and inflation slowed to around 15 percent. The economy has completely recovered the lost ground following the 1995 peso crisis. From the depth of the depression in 1995, the recovery took roughly 2 years, a very rapid rebound compared to the 9 years required to recover from the 1982 crisis. Significantly, real wages also began to increase again. Real wages are projected to increase about 4 percent in 1998, making up part of the 25 percent decline in real monthly earnings that workers suffered following the 1994–1995 crisis. The increase in earnings is an impor-

tant factor behind strong consumption growth during the first half of 1998 as the economy grew 5.4 percent.

Most of Mexico's growth in 1997 was driven by domestic consumption spending and investment. Fiscal policy remained tight as government spending increased only slightly, while net exports detracted from growth for the second straight year. A similar pattern in spending growth is expected through 1999, although consumer spending and private investment are expected to grow less rapidly than in 1997, and net export growth is expected to remain negative through 1999. Fiscal policy was expected to be neutral to slightly positive, but lower petroleum prices have forced three rounds of cuts in planned government expenditures in 1998, equal to around 1 percent of GDP. Revenues from petroleum sales constitute more than 30 percent of government tax revenues and around 10 percent of Mexico's export earnings.

Besides the adverse impact on petroleum and other material prices, the Asian crisis has impacted Mexico in other ways. As in the case of most Latin American economies that were favored by international investors in the first half of 1997, inflows of foreign capital have stopped and have been reversed in most cases. Mexico's stock prices have suffered along with equity prices in other countries in the region despite very good growth potential and solid macroeconomic fundamentals. The loss of foreign investment is particularly troublesome for Mexico, and for the region in general, because relatively low savings rates leave the country unable to generate enough investment domestically to grow the estimated 6 percent per year required to absorb the country's burgeoning labor force. The loss of foreign investment inflows has pushed the value of the peso down, forced interest rates higher, and contributed to increasing inflationary pressure in the economy. Finally, the Asian crisis has meant that Mexico's exports have come under increasing competition from lower-priced Asian exports because of Asia's currency devaluations. The competitiveness effect on Mexico is limited, however, since only about 20 percent of Mexico's exports—primarily footwear and textile products—are in direct competition with Asian exports in the U.S. market. To date, the Asian crisis has had little impact on the booming textile and clothing export business as many firms have shifted plants from Asian countries to Mexico since tariff and quota restrictions were removed with the birth of NAFTA. Mexico has replaced China as the leading source of U.S. textile imports.

As the Asian crisis continues to unwind, the economy of Mexico may face new crises. Moreover, the country faces problems that could sidetrack the recovery. Perhaps the greatest of these is the pending issue of the government's attempt to convert billions in bad bank loans to public sector debt. The loans were acquired by the country's deposit insurance fund as the result of bank failures following the 1995 crisis, but there is a strong resistance to the debt conversion by members of the opposition party in Mexico's Congress. The bad loans total around $65 billion, and their conversion to public sector debt would increase the ratio of debt to GDP from around 30 percent to more than 40 percent.

INDUSTRIAL ECONOMIES: WESTERN EUROPE

Were it not for the Asian and Russian crises, the move to a single European currency on January 1, 1999, would undoubtedly be the biggest event in the world economy. The process that began at Maastricht in early 1992 will come to its final fruition in July 2002, when the national currencies of most of the current European Union (EU) members will cease to exist. Between January 1, 1999, and July 2002, the national currencies will circulate along with the new currency, the euro. Of the 15 EU member states, 11 countries are first-round participants in the launching of the euro, with Greece scheduled to join later. Only the United Kingdom, Denmark, and Sweden have elected not to become members for the time being.

Although there was significant doubt that the launching of the euro would get off on schedule as recently as late 1997, the current momentum toward the January 1999 launch looks unstoppable. The gains from establishing a single currency are largely in efficiency as markets will become more transparent, price competition will increase across national borders, and transactions costs will be reduced. The EU has put the value of these anticipated benefits at around 0.5 percent of GDP. Offsetting these potential benefits are some unresolved issues that may become problems in the future. The theory that posits the gains from a single currency also stipulates that the economies covered by the one currency should possess certain characteristics that would allow adjustments if and when particular regions of the single-currency area are adversely impacted by economic shocks. Among these characteristics are mobile labor forces, flexible prices, and a shared fiscal policy—the latter to allow assistance to the region or regions that may suffer adverse impacts. The problem is that the EU single-currency area possesses none of these characteristics to any meaningful degree. The true test of the system may come when the first major economic crisis hits.

Aside from these issues, the launch of the euro could hardly come at a better time as the EU region is in the process of an economic expansion better than any in the last decade. Even some adverse spillover effects from Asia will dampen the recovery only slightly. After growing only 1.7 percent in 1996, the EU economy expanded 2.5 percent in 1997 and is projected to grow at a slightly faster rate in the 1998–1999 period. Inflation is very low, long-term interest rates have dropped, and fiscal budgets are in their best condition in decades, thanks to the "convergence criteria" that were set in the original Maastricht agreement. [The Maastricht treaty stipulated five convergence criteria that potential members would have to meet before they could join the euro: (1) to have total national debt equal or less than 60 percent of GDP; (2) to have a fiscal deficit no larger than 3 percent of GDP; (3) to have inflation at an annual rate of 3.2 percent or less; (4) to have long-term interest rates at 7.7 percent or lower; (5) and to be a member of the Exchange Rate Mechanism. The ERM is a policy of maintaining the value of the country's currency within 15 percent of the central rate.] In addition, consumer confidence and business confidence are growing stronger because of improvements in the job markets, increases in real earnings and, in a few countries, some equity asset appreciation.

While the EU as a group is in a strong recovery, there are significant differences among the European economies regarding their position in the business cycle. In mid-1997 one group of countries, led by the United Kingdom, had reached or was near to reaching full economic capacity. These countries either were in the process of slowing or were in danger of overheating. A second group of countries, led by three of the four largest economies—Germany, France, and Italy—were in the recovery stage and were still well short of full capacity. Indeed, the major economic problem in these countries, as well as in most of Europe, is the high level of unemployment. The fact that strong growth is expected in Germany, France, and Italy, economies that account for well over half of total EU output, is behind the expectation that EU growth will average nearly 3 percent per year in the 1998–1999 period (see Figure C-3). These projections are made with important caveats: that the Asian crisis will not deepen; that the fallout from the collapse of the Russian economy will be minimal; that the transition to the new euro currency proceeds as smoothly and with as little trouble as is currently expected. Compared to the United States, Europe is even more isolated from the fallout from the Asian crisis. A smaller share of its output is exported to countries outside the region, and with virtually no raw material exports and few farm shipments, the region has only benefited from the decline in commodity prices, whereas both Canada and the United States have suffered because of declines in export prices of these products.

The economic recovery in France and Germany was led by export growth. Exports increased by more than 10 percent in both countries in 1997. Low price inflation, strong productivity growth, a depreciation of their currencies relative to the dollar, and strong growth in their export markets, such as the United States, were the factors behind export growth. In 1998 and beyond, growth will be less dependent on exports as domestic spending increases. All sectors of domestic spending—private consumption, investment, and fiscal policy—are expected to be stronger in the forecast period. Interest rates, particularly at the long end, have dropped significantly, spurring investment in capital goods and in housing. Consumer confidence has finally returned as the growth of the last 2 years has put a small dent in Europe's high unemployment rates and real compensation to employees has begun to grow. Finally, after several years of government austerity programs to meet the Maastricht criteria on government debt and deficits, fiscal policy will become neutral in most countries, removing the fiscal drag that had existed as deficits were brought down.

Germany

Germany remains the one major EU economy where internal demand has continued at a subdued pace. Exports, along with inventory investment, were the primary sources of growth in 1997. Exports should continue to provide an impetus to growth in 1998–1999. Investment spending is also expected to increase. Interest rates are low and capacity utilization is high. The big uncertainty, however, is consumer spending. There has been a modest improvement in consumer sentiment as well as job creation, but wages have been stagnant. Another area of weakness has been in construction, especially in the eastern sector. In the east unemployment remains very high, and productivity and incomes are far behind the west despite continued large transfer payments into the area. As in other European countries, fiscal policy will ease, providing some stimulus to the economy in 1998–1999. Growth in 1998 is forecast at around 2.5 percent, with slightly faster growth expected in 1999.

France

Consumer spending in France, in contrast to Germany, has been an important source of growth since mid-1997, supplementing export growth which led growth in the first half of the year. Import growth picked up as consumption grew, but the year ended with the current account surplus equal to 2.8 percent of GDP, a record. Despite the pickup in demand and lower interest rates, investment spending increased very little in 1997, in part because of uncertainty surrounding a controversial government proposal to reduce the work week to 35 hours in an effort to generate more jobs. As business and consumer confidence improve, business investment and residential investment are expected to increase. Average growth in the 1998–1999 period is expected to be nearly 3 percent, with the Asian situation being the biggest downside risk.

Italy

The recovery in Italy has been much slower than in either France or Germany. Although private consumption, especially for cars, expanded briskly in 1997, investment spending was tepid except for inventory spending. Fiscal policy was restrictive and net exports subtracted 1 percent from growth. The con-

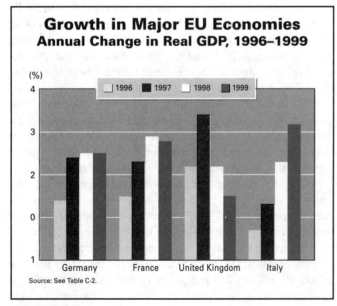

Growth in Major EU Economies
Annual Change in Real GDP, 1996–1999

Source: See Table C-2.

FIGURE C-3

traction of the Italian fiscal deficit was quite remarkable. The year ended with a deficit equal to 2.7 percent of GDP, 4 percentage points lower than the previous year. No other European country could boast of such fiscal rectitude. In the near-term outlook, fiscal policy is expected to be slightly expansionary and net exports are expected to turn positive, in contrast to net exports in 1997 when they were a drag on economic growth. In addition, private investment is expected to increase since interest rates have fallen and demand is up.

Italy, as in the case of Germany and France, has a high rate of unemployment—in the double-digit range. Recent and expected growth is projected to bring the rate down only modestly. In addition, like Germany, Italy suffers from a large regional disparity in unemployment rates, with rates in the south averaging some 16 percentage points higher than in the industrial north.

United Kingdom

The performance of the British economy in 1997 was notably good, and for many of the same reasons that the U.S. economy sparkled. Growth was strong, 3.1 percent, above estimated trend growth. Unemployment fell to 4.8 percent in early 1998, a rate not enjoyed in nearly 20 years. At the same time prices were falling, at least until mid-1997. Since then there has been an increase in the rate of inflation, and the Bank of England has tightened monetary policy through a series of interest rate hikes beginning in the spring of 1997. Fiscal policy also became restrictive. As a result of these policy moves, the British pound appreciated and export growth slowed. The manufacturing sector has taken the brunt of the impact of tighter fiscal and monetary policy. Consumption and the service industries continue at a strong pace.

The outlook is for U.K. economic growth to fall by a percentage point or slightly more in 1998, with a further half point decline in 1999. The outlook has several uncertainties, however. For one, there is a fear that the full impact of the Sterling appreciation has yet to be felt and that the drag from the trade sector will become more severe in the months ahead. Second, the advent of the euro in January 1999 may result in a weaker pound relative to the euro because of relatively lower interest rates in the United Kingdom. This development would then give U.K. exports a competitive boost. This expectation, like all projections about the impact of the euro, is very uncertain. Third, as in the United States, there is debate about the level of sustainable growth in the economy. Some believe that it is higher than current estimates because of unmeasured increases in productivity.

Other European Countries

Because of their relative size, accounting for nearly three-quarters of the EU output, developments in the four major European economies dominate statistics for average growth in the EU region. In terms of interest, however, recent trends in some of the smaller countries at the periphery of the EU have been quite notable. For one, economic growth in most of the smaller economies was faster than overall average EU growth in 1997. Growth rates in Ireland and Finland were particularly notable at 10.5 percent and 5.9 percent, respectively. Denmark, the Netherlands, Spain, and Portugal also grew at rates well above the EU average. Of these countries, all except Spain and Portugal are expected to grow somewhat slower in the 1998–1999 period, but still at rates that are above the EU average. Spain and Portugal are expected to continue growing at roughly their same rate as in 1997, about 3.5 percent. Despite their rapid growth, inflation in all of these countries was just about at the EU average of 2 percent in 1997, and inflation is expected to remain under control in the 1998–1999 period.

In addition to strong growth and low inflation, most of these smaller economies have been as successful as the big four in bringing down fiscal deficits to within the Maastricht limits. In fact, among all of the EU economies, only Greece had a 1997 fiscal deficit (4 percent of GDP) that was larger than 3 percent of GDP. The average fiscal deficit for the EU economies in 1997 was 2.4 percent, a remarkable improvement from the deficit in 1993 when it was 6.4 percent of GDP. Some of the success in reducing deficits below the Maastricht limit was the result of temporary measures to constrain spending and boost revenues. Therefore, there will be some relaxation of fiscal restraint in most of these EU countries in the 1998–1999 period, but strong growth should keep the ratio of deficit to GDP at current low levels.

While each of the smaller economies had its own unique factors behind their generally strong growth in 1997, there were a few characteristics that most of them shared. For one, their trade sectors benefited from the acceleration of growth in the major economies—France, Germany, and Italy. Spain, for example, ships around 30 percent of its exports to Italy and France. Also, consumers across most of Europe have seen their confidence boosted as a result of low inflation, wage gains, and improvements in labor markets. Finally, the tight fiscal policies in conjunction with monetary policies that generally shadow the German Bundesbank have reduced interest rates along with inflation, spurring investment in most of the economies.

INDUSTRIAL ECONOMIES IN THE EAST: JAPAN, AUSTRALIA, AND NEW ZEALAND

In mid-1998 the economy of Japan was in recession, having just recorded a third consecutive quarter of economic decline. Japan became the fifth country in Asia to change governments as a result of the Asian financial crisis, and many analysts considered Japan's response to the crisis to be the key in determining the near-term outlook for the economies of Asia and the world. Australia, feeling the effects of the Asian financial crisis, is expected to grow more slowly in 1998–1999, while New Zealand's economy, more dependent on exports to Asia, contracted in the first two quarters of 1998 (see Figure C-4).

Japan

In 1996 the Japanese economy recorded the highest growth rate among the G-7, and the rapid growth continued into the first quarter of 1997, the first real expansion of the economy in

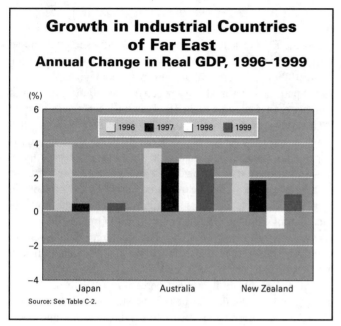

Growth in Industrial Countries of Far East
Annual Change in Real GDP, 1996–1999

Source: See Table C-2.

FIGURE C-4

nearly 5 years. Then fiscal policy was tightened through a series of tax increases and spending cuts, and the economy dropped by an unexpectedly high 10.6 percent (an annual rate) in the second quarter. (Of course, it was during this same quarter that the Thai baht was coming under increasing pressure, and was devalued on July 2.) A slight recovery during the third quarter (the "dead cat bounce") was negated by the unfolding economic calamity in Asia, the ongoing credit crunch in the banking system, and the failure of three large financial institutions late in the year. Japanese business and consumer confidence began to collapse along with Japan's Asian export markets and the yen. The recession that began in the fall of 1997 is the first since the OPEC oil price shock of 1974. Attempts to revive the economy through a series of supplemental budgets that included temporary tax cuts and new fiscal spending initiative failed to reignite the economy, and when Japanese voters went to the polls on July 11, 1998, they expressed their lack of confidence in the government's economic programs.

Most analysts agree that Japan needs further fiscal stimulus combined with a recapitalization of the banking system and structural reform of much of its economy. The government did initiate six packages of fiscal stimulus between 1992 and 1995, and these programs had moderate success in reviving the economy. However, since the banking system is burdened with an acknowledged 77 trillion yen in bad loans (equal to approximately 15% of GDP), the credit creation necessary to fuel the nascent recoveries was not forthcoming, and the expansions were short-lived. The new government announced an additional fiscal stimulus package in August and came to an agreement on a new plan to deal with the weakest of the big banks in late September. A final resolution to the shaky financial sector is nowhere in sight, however, and asset prices and confidence continue to slide.

Interest rates began falling soon after the bubble economy burst and are at record low levels. Many economists now believe that even if the banking system were free of the debt overhang, a credit expansion would not occur because with interest rates at rock-bottom levels the country is in a Keynesian "liquidity trap." No one would be willing to extend credit at such low rates.

The yen peaked in value in mid-1995 and has been on a downward trend since then. The economy did get some boost from export growth in 1997, but the economic collapse in Asia—the market for 40 percent of Japan's exports—severely restricted the trade avenue as an engine of recovery. In addition, while the yen has fallen by roughly 40 percent with respect to the dollar since 1995, it has appreciated with respect to most of the currencies in Asia, including some, like that of Korea, with which it is in direct competition.

The outlook for the Japanese economy in the 1998–1999 period is not good. The consensus seems to be that the bottom of the current recession may not be reached until late in the year and that growth in 1999 will be minimal. The picture, however, should not be painted too bleak. The Japanese economy is home to some of the world's most efficient and dynamic manufacturing corporations. Japan is a huge net creditor to the world economy. Its work force is well-educated and dedicated. The problem is mustering the political will to implement the necessary reforms that will probably lead to more economic hardship in the short run but will return faster growth in the future.

Australia and New Zealand

In Australia and New Zealand, two countries that have enjoyed six years of economic expansion, 1998–1999 promised to bring more growth in the 3.0 to 3.5 percent range. Well after the Asian crisis occurred, most analysts who follow the two economies predicted that the impact on them would be minimal. By mid-1998, however, forecasts were lowered a notch or two for Australia and drastically downgraded for New Zealand as the adverse spillover effects took hold. Agricultural products and raw materials dominate the exports of both countries, and the Asian crisis has reduced both prices and volumes of exports. (Since many of these export commodities are priced in U.S. dollars, and the depreciation of the currencies has outpaced price declines, prices received by commodity producers in the two countries have actually increased in some cases.) In Australia, commodity exports are expected to fall for the first time in 20 years. The recession in Japan, which takes around a third of Australia's exports, has hit Australia particularly hard. New Zealand, in turn, is dependent on Australia as a market for around half of its shipments and on Asia for another third. The current account balance in both countries is deteriorating, and their currencies have depreciated. Business confidence and consumer confidence have fallen. Nevertheless, in both countries inflation is low and fiscal budgets are in balance. The heavy dependence of New Zealand on commodity exports, a severe drought on its east coast, and high interest rates have pushed the New Zealand economy into recession. Output fell for the second consecutive quarter ending in June 1998. In Australia domestic demand is expected to continue at a strong pace, and the spillover effects from Asia are expected to slow the economy but not cause a recession.

EMERGING MARKETS: LATIN AMERICA

Economic growth in South America in 1997 was around 5 percent, the best showing since 1994 when the Mexican peso crisis and subsequent "tequila effect" slowed growth throughout the region. The aftermath of the Asian and Russian crises will have a similar impact on growth in the region in the 1998–1999 period, but the slowdown should not be as drastic as occurred following Mexico's problems (see Figure C-5). Governments throughout the region tightened monetary and fiscal policies when international financial markets began to apply pressure on the region as the Asian crisis spread during the fall of 1997. While these measures worked in the short term, they were derailed when the Russian financial meltdown in mid-August 1998 set off another round of capital flight from the emerging markets of South America. A good example of swift and decisive action in the spreading crisis is found in the sharp increase of interest rates and the tightening of fiscal policy by Brazil in October 1997, when the Asian crisis was rocking the economies of southeast Asia. Brazil's actions will result in slower growth for the country in 1998–1999, but the decisive action apparently stopped the Asian crisis from spreading in the region. However, as in the entire region, the fallout from the Russian crisis in August brought renewed financial pressure—increased levels of capital flight, plunging equity prices, and soaring interest rates. There is an air of uncertainty about whether the latest round of tightening will be enough to prevent a regional economic meltdown.

Maintaining the confidence of international investors is probably more important in South America than in Asia. With its relatively low savings rates, the region is much more dependent on outside financing for its growth and development. As it is, the fallout from Russia's problems has drained the region of much needed foreign investment. Growth will slow until commodity prices rebound and confidence is restored in international capital markets and investors return to the region.

Despite the best efforts of governments throughout the region to limit capital flight as a result of the Asian crisis, the spillover effects from the events in Asia created consequences in South America that neither prudent fiscal nor monetary policies could avert. Perhaps most importantly, the fall in commodity prices that resulted from falling Asian demand widened the balance of payments deficits throughout the region because of the dependence on commodity exports. Additionally, long-term foreign capital investments in these same commodity industries—copper, petroleum—have been reduced and/or postponed. As a consequence, several countries were forced either to place a greater reliance on short-term financing of payments deficits or to devalue their currencies by greater amounts than planned or desired. Large currency devaluations, in turn, have exacerbated efforts to bring down inflation.

Another feature of the falling commodity prices and exports is that they have seriously dented government revenue collections in several of the countries that depend on this source for financing government programs. This development has forced sharp contractions in government spending. Coincidently, since several countries in the region are facing elections during the period, the government spending cutbacks have fueled the prospects of populist opposition parties in a region where incomes have always been sharply unequal and are growing more unequal as a result of the spending cuts and the reform and privitization programs of recent years. The resulting political uncertainty adds to the perceived risks in the outlook of foreign investors.

Brazil

Brazil's economy, by far South America's largest, came under pressure in late 1997 as the Asian crisis began to spread to other areas. The Cardoso government responded swiftly with a series of fiscal and monetary measures to shore up international confidence which was troubled in large part by the country's large fiscal and external deficits. The moves, doubling interest rates and slashing spending, worked for a time as foreign capital returned, and interest rates began to come down in early 1998. However, the collapse of the Russian ruble in mid-August and the subsequent suspension of payments on some of Russia's foreign debt immediately led to a new round of capital flight from emerging markets, including Brazil and other South American countries. During the month following the Russian meltdown, Brazil lost around $1 billion in foreign exchange reserves per day in its efforts to support the value of its currency, the real. Interest rates were once again boosted, doubling to over 40 percent, and Brazil's credit rating was downgraded by international rating agencies. All of these measures will slow growth sharply in the 1998–1999 period.

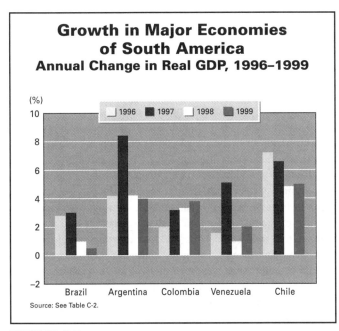

Growth in Major Economies of South America
Annual Change in Real GDP, 1996–1999

Source: See Table C-2.

FIGURE C-5

In early autumn of 1998 there remained great uncertainty as to whether or not the economy would avoid an Asian-type financial meltdown. Such a scenario will be avoided if at all possible because of the importance of the Brazilian economy to the region. To this end the International Monetary Fund (IMF) and the United States have been leading an effort to put together a rescue package of loans to stabilize the situation and ensure that the real maintains its value. Aside from the "contagion effect" from the Asian and Russian problems, several issues remain which could unsettle the economy and impede foreign investment flows in the months ahead. The increase in interest rates has added significantly to the government's debt service burden and pushed up the fiscal deficit, estimated at around 7 percent of GDP. The trade deficit also continues to be a problem despite the slowing of the economy and a lower bill for oil imports. Some have argued that the real is overvalued and should be devalued or allowed to float. But a devaluation, it is feared, would quickly lead to a domino effect throughout the region and an economic implosion of the type that has crippled Asia.

Argentina

In Argentina the economy grew 8.4 percent in 1997, but there are signs of slowing in the wake of spillover effects from Asia. Recently the government, following the "advice" of the IMF, shelved plans to spend billions on highways. Other austerity measures are in the works as the government attempts to cut the country's burgeoning foreign trade deficit, which doubled the country's current account deficit from just less than 2 percent of GDP in 1996 to nearly 4 percent of GDP in 1997. The trade gap has worsened because the Argentine peso is tied to the dollar and, as the dollar has gained in value, Argentina's exports have become less competitive, and less expensive imports from places like China have poured in. Also, Brazil is Argentina's major export market, and when Brazil's economy slowed, Argentina's exports suffered. Falling commodity prices have also hurt Argentina's exports. The government is facing elections next year, and there is growing opposition to its policies, particularly its plans to liberalize the country's labor laws in view of the high unemployment rate. Argentina's privatization programs, while they have attracted billions in foreign investment and have narrowed the government deficit, have created a large and growing number of unemployed. Income distribution is increasingly less equal and crime is worsening, as it is in Mexico and in other South American countries where the drive to efficiency has increased unemployment and poverty.

Colombia

Colombia is South America's third largest economy, and it has enjoyed largely uninterrupted growth for several decades, even during the "lost decade" of the 1980s when most countries in the region grew very little or even declined. In the past few years, however, the country has had problems with a growing fiscal deficit, and growth in 1996 was only 2 percent, well below the region's average. Growth rebounded to 3.2 percent in

1997. Spillover effects from the Asian crisis, adverse El Niño impacts, and continuing problems with leftist and rightist guerrilla and paramilitary groups will slow the economy below the goal of 4.5 percent growth, but output should expand at a slightly faster pace in the 1998–1999 period. In early September 1998, Colombia was forced to devalue its currency around 5 percent to stem further losses of foreign exchange reserves that had increased as part of the post-Russian "flight to quality." The move was seen as putting more pressure on other currencies in the region, particularly Colombia's neighbor, Venezuela, with whom the country shares close trade ties.

Venezuela

In sharp contrast to the relative stability of Colombia's economy, the Venezuelan economy has been one of the more unstable economies in Latin America over the years. The country's dependence on one commodity, oil, largely explains its economic instability. Economic growth in 1997 was a strong 5.1 percent as the economy rebounded from negative growth in the previous year. The good performance was fueled by developments in the petroleum sector which the government has opened to foreign investment. However, the recent fall in oil prices has reduced the country's balance of payments surplus and increased the government deficit. Nearly half of all government revenues come from oil sales. In response, the government has cut expenditures and raised interest rates to protect the value of the country's currency. Low oil prices and soaring interest rates will slow the economy sharply in the coming year. As in the case of the finances of other countries in the region, Venezuela's finances were rocked by the Russian situation in late summer. Capital flight increased, the stock market plunged, interest rates soared, and there was increasing speculation that the currency would have to be devalued.

Chile and Peru

Chile and Peru both enjoyed strong economic growth in 1997, but like most economies in South America with a heavy dependence on commodity exports, the price declines have hurt export earnings and government finances. Chile has been especially impacted because of its heavy dependence on copper exports which account for about 40 percent of its shipments. Also, Chile ships around 30 percent of its exports to Asia, and these sales have suffered with the economic decline in that region. In addition, these two countries, with their long Pacific coastlines, have been hurt by the El Niño damage to the fish meal industry, another source of export earnings. The softness in commodity prices has, in turn, resulted in delays or cancellations in foreign capital investments in the impacted industries, putting pressures on foreign exchange reserves and exchange rates. Chile, whose controls on short-term capital flows were touted as an example of how emerging market economies should isolate themselves from short-term, "hot money" capital flows, has had to relax those controls in order to help finance its balance of payments deficits. Both countries will grow more slowly in 1998–1999 than in 1997.

After 3 years of good economic growth, the sharp decline in oil prices in early 1998 will slow economic growth in the Middle East in the 1998–1999 period. Estimated growth in 1997 was 4.4 percent, but will be more than a percentage point lower in 1998 (see Figure C-6). Most of the countries in the region depend on oil exports for a major portion of their export earnings and for government finance. Government spending is being scaled back, particularly for capital projects, in an attempt to bring budgets into line. The decline in oil prices will also eliminate the small balance of payments surplus that the region enjoyed in 1997.

The decrease in oil prices, which fell to price-adjusted levels not seen since before the 1973 oil crisis, has been blamed on a variety of supply and demand factors. On the supply side, the Organization of Oil Producing Countries (OPEC) made a decision to increase production quotas in November 1997 when the Asian financial crisis was still unfolding. Also, Iraq, which has been under U.N. sanctions that limit the country's petroleum sales, has been permitted to bring additional supplies onto the market. On the demand side, the Asian crisis has reduced demand for oil from most Asian economies, and the warm winter in much of the Northern Hemisphere as a result of El Niño effects further reduced demand. In the first half of 1998, oil-producing countries reached new agreements to cut back on output quotas, but chronic problems in enforcing quotas and the severity of the downturn in Asia will do little more than prevent further price erosion until late 1998 or early 1999.

Four economies in this region—Egypt, Iran, Turkey, and Saudi Arabia—account for about three-quarters of the region's total output. Of the four, Egypt has made the most progress in implementing stabilization and structural reforms. From a starting point of nearly total economic collapse at the beginning of the decade, a series of reform measures combined with debt relief under the aegis of the Paris Club has resulted in several years of solid growth. In addition, inflation rates have declined, and government budget deficits have been virtually eliminated. Economic growth in 1997 was an estimated 5 percent and was expected to increase to a higher level in 1998–1999, but two crises—the Asian financial crisis and the murder of dozens of foreign tourists at the Luxor archeological site—have lowered growth expectations. The latter incident has cut deeply into Egypt's tourist revenue, costing the country an estimated 0.5 percent in GDP growth. The Asian crisis, meanwhile, has resulted in higher interest rates, reduced workers' remittances, and lower oil export revenues. Oil exports account for roughly half of the country's merchandise exports. Despite the setbacks, economic reform efforts are continuing with a focus on privatization in the capital markets, particularly insurance and banking, in an effort to increase domestic saving.

Turkey, another of the area's major economies, has also enjoyed rapid growth in recent years, but in most other respects Turkey's economy differs greatly from that of Egypt. While the economy has grown rapidly in the last 3 years, inflation is very high. It reached into the triple-digit levels in late 1997. Furthermore, efforts at deregulation, privatization, and structural reform have been limited. Government efforts to tighten fiscal and monetary policy have met with limited success, in part because of weak coalition governments in recent years. Nevertheless, the ripple effects from Asia have had little impact on the country, but the more recent turmoil in Russia, a major trading partner, will have adverse consequences. As a fuel importer, Turkey benefited from lower oil prices, and its exports of textiles, steel, and foodstuffs largely flow toward Europe, where economic growth has been on the upswing.

The remaining major economies in the region—Saudi Arabia and Iran—and most of the smaller economies depend on petroleum production and exports to propel them. With oil prices at their current low levels, growth in these economies will be reduced in the 1998–1999 period. In most of these economies, the oil industry is state-owned and state-controlled. Progress on economic reform has been slow and spotty, but even in Saudi Arabia there has been progress in economic diversification even if the economy is still heavily dependent on oil sales for export earnings. Finally, the instability created by the continued tensions in the Middle East are only increased when economic conditions are on the downswing.

EMERGING MARKETS: AFRICA

Following a good year in 1996, when the region's growth exceeded 5 percent, Africa's growth slowed to around 3 percent in 1997. The outlook for 1998–1999 is for slightly higher growth, but as in the case of other regions, most of the risks to the outlook are on the downside. The general story that explains

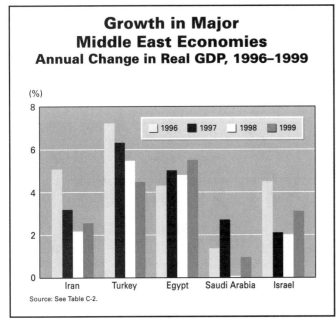

Growth in Major Middle East Economies
Annual Change in Real GDP, 1996–1999

Source: See Table C-2.

FIGURE C-6

much of the 1997 slowdown includes lower agricultural output, lower commodity prices, and continued civil unrest in several countries. Nevertheless, output per person increased for the third consecutive year after declining for most of the previous two decades (see Figure C-7).

Many countries in the region have undertaken long-needed steps to reform their economies. Trade has been liberalized, commodity boards have been eliminated, and state-owned companies have been privatized. Several countries have made significant progress toward reform, and the World Economic Forum gives a handful of Africa's countries—South Africa, Mauritius, Ghana, Côte d'Ivoire—high competitiveness rankings. Still, much needs to be done before the region can hope to begin to attract the private investment capital needed for more rapid growth. (Somewhat perversely, because the continent has been largely isolated from world financial markets, the capital flight that has impacted other regions, notably Latin America, has caused little or no impact in this region.) Sub-Sahara Africa attracts barely 5 percent of the total of foreign direct investment in emerging markets, down from more than 20 percent in 1980. Furthermore, only a handful of African countries receive the bulk of foreign investment, with South Africa getting by far the largest share. At the same time, official assistance has been on the decline as industrial countries have cut back on foreign aid. High levels of indebtedness also impede efforts to increase investment in many African countries.

The region is very dependent on commodity exports. El Niño weather effects hurt agriculture output in the last year, and Asian ripple effects have hurt prices for commodity exports. But aside from the vagaries of the weather or international markets, perhaps Africa's biggest challenge continues to be ethnic strife which in its mildest form leads to political deadlock and corruption, but all too often degenerates into armed conflict. A recent study (William Easterly and Ross Levine, "Africa's Growth Tragedy: Policies and Ethnic Divisions, *The Quarterly Journal of Economics,* Vol. 112, No. 4, 1997, pp. 1203–1250.) concluded that ethnic group polarization of the type commonly found in Africa leads to public policies that are often unfavorable for generating the country characteristics, such as high levels of education and stable financial systems, that are required for strong economic growth.

EMERGING MARKETS: ASIA

With the onset of the Asian financial crisis in mid-1997, growth throughout the region slowed dramatically, with some of the most severely impacted countries falling into sharp recessions. While only five of the nearly two dozen countries in the region suffered severe financial destabilization, the impact of the crisis has been felt throughout Asia and beyond (see Figure C-8). [These five "crisis economies" are Thailand, Indonesia, Malaysia, South Korea, and the Philippines. Collectively they account for about one-fourth of total economic output in "emerging Asia" and about one-fifth of Asian total output, which includes Japan, Australia, and New Zealand.]

Early assessments of the depth of the prospective downturn and subsequent recovery have proven to be too optimistic. A natural tendency to reference the last large financial crisis, the Mexican peso crisis of late 1994, led many analysts to conclude that Asia's economies would follow a recovery path similar to the "V-shaped" path of Mexico's economy. [There is a very extensive body of reporting and analysis of the crisis. For example, the homepage of New York University professor Nouriel Roubini provides a detailed chronology of the crisis,

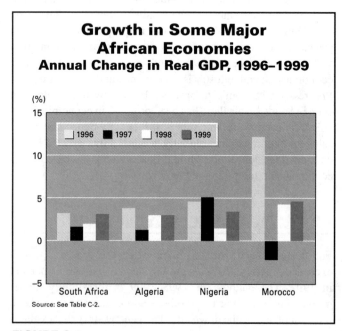

Growth in Some Major African Economies
Annual Change in Real GDP, 1996–1999

Source: See Table C-2.

FIGURE C-7

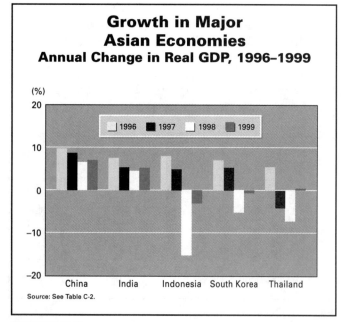

Growth in Major Asian Economies
Annual Change in Real GDP, 1996–1999

Source: See Table C-2.

FIGURE C-8

and links to much of the analysis. (http://www.stern.nyu.edu/~nroubini).] Although there were some characteristics shared by Mexico and the five Asian "crisis economies"—weak banking systems with less than perfect transparency in reporting, large and growing current account deficits, and overvalued exchange rates—there were important differences as well. Perhaps most notable were two. First, Mexico's major trading partner is the United States, and at the time of the crisis the U.S. economy was growing rapidly and was able to absorb a large and growing volume of Mexican exports, which allowed Mexico's economy to recover rather quickly. In contrast, the most important export markets of the Asian crisis economies are other countries in the region, including (most importantly) Japan. The ongoing recession in Japan did not provide the crisis economies with a strong and growing market for exports. In addition, the depreciation of the yen eliminated much of the competitive advantage of Asian country exports following their own currency devaluations.

A second important difference is that much of Mexico's external debt at the time of the crisis was government, sovereign debt while most of the debt of the crisis economies of Asia was private, borrowed by private banks and financial institutions from private investors in the international financial community. This difference in the nature of the debt had two important consequences. First, in the case of Asia it was much more difficult to organize and arrange a financial stabilization agreement between debtors and creditors because of the many parties involved. Second, the conditions imposed by the IMF as part of its financial rescue package for three of the crisis countries resulted in high interest rates and a credit crunch which starved the private sector in these countries of needed hard currency. Export trade finance was unavailable, and bankruptcies proliferated.

In mid-1998 the magnitude of the impact of the Asian financial crisis on the "real" economy began to be revealed as government data on economic growth for the first half of the year was reported. Generally speaking, the reports showed the economic decline to be more severe than was initially projected. Throughout the region, official estimates for growth in the 1998–1999 period have been downgraded. Of the major emerging economies in the region, only China, Taiwan, and India are expected to have solid growth in 1998. Even so, in each case growth will be less than projected at the beginning of 1998. These three economies, accounting for nearly two-thirds of the output in emerging Asia, will grow 5 to 7 percent in 1998 and perhaps a little faster in 1999. The remaining large, medium, and smaller economies are expected to grow very little in 1998 or to suffer outright declines in output. Thailand, Korea, Hong Kong, Malaysia, and Indonesia will certainly contract in 1998, and it seems increasingly likely that Pakistan may also record negative growth. Others in the region—the Philippines, Singapore, Bangladesh—will grow by only 1 to 3 percent, and these rates, by past Asian growth standards, are very low. Most forecasts call for slightly higher growth throughout the region in 1999, but continuing economic contraction and growing pessimism in Asia make this outlook very uncertain.

TRANSITIONAL ECONOMIES

For the first time since the transition from planned to market economy began, the countries in this group collectively recorded positive economic growth in 1997. In general, the outlook for growth in the 1998–1999 period is that the economies of many of these countries will accelerate further, but with the meltdown of the Russian economy this outlook is very uncertain. Set off by the financial collapse in Asia and the Russian crisis, the currencies in this region came under pressure as financial market speculators perceived weaknesses in the macroeconomic fundamentals of the Czech Republic, Estonia, and Ukraine (see Figure C-9).

Russia
In the case of Russia, a porous tax collection system left the country without the revenue to finance its operations. The Russian central bank raised interest rates in February 1998 to increase the attractiveness of the country's official debt. However, higher interest rates exacerbated the fiscal deficit situation since nearly half of the outlays of government went toward paying interest on the debt. The IMF announced a rescue package of $22.6 billion at midyear under conditions that Russia implement necessary fiscal reforms, including spending cuts and tax increases. But political opposition to some of the more painful measures left the economy's finances in an uncertain and perilous state. Foreign investors were also losing confidence in the Russian stock market, and prices there fell by more than half since the beginning of the year. As confidence in the economy and the government fell, Russia continued to support the ruble under growing speculation that its value would soon fall. When the government finally abandoned its attempt to support the ruble on August 17, the ruble's value slipped moderately but

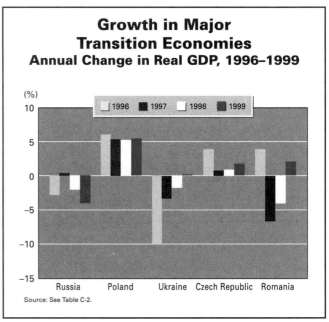

Growth in Major Transition Economies
Annual Change in Real GDP, 1996–1999

Source: See Table C-2.

FIGURE C-9

collapsed a few days later. At the same time, Russia unilaterally declared a moratorium on payments of foreign-held debt and restructured some of them under very unattractive terms in what amounted to a default according to most analysts. These actions in Russia then loosed fears in financial markets throughout the world, beginning a rush to exit virtually all emerging markets.

Russia's economy recorded positive economic growth in 1997 for the first time in many years, and data indicate that average real incomes increased and poverty fell slightly. But the fiscal reforms required to repair Russia's finances and save the ruble have yet to be implemented.

European Countries

Except for the Czech Republic, the countries of Central Europe enjoyed solid economic growth in 1997. The economies of Poland, the Slovak Republic, and Slovenia grew 6.9 percent, 5.7 percent, and 3.7 percent, respectively. These countries have enjoyed several consecutive years of good growth and are now being helped by the recovery in western Europe. Hungary's economy accelerated to a 4 percent growth rate in 1997 following 2 years of anemic growth during which painful fiscal adjustments were made to rein in fiscal and current account deficits. In the case of the Czech Republic, little progress toward needed reforms and structural adjustments resulted in a run on the koruny in the spring of 1997, and a devaluation occurred in May. Tighter monetary and fiscal policies were implemented, and the economy slowed, growing a little more than 1 percent for the year. For the 1998–1999 period these countries are expected to continue growing at about the same rate as in 1997, including the Czech Republic where a rebound to faster growth is not expected until late in the period. There should be only a limited direct impact from the Russian crisis on these economies since they have redirected much of their economic activities toward the west in recent years.

In contrast to Central Europe, the economies of the Balkans did poorly in 1997. Only Croatia and Macedonia recorded positive growth in 1997 (no data were available for Bosnia). Bulgaria and Romania were in the process of implementing stabilization and structural reforms during the year, and their economies shrank. Albania suffered a financial crisis because of the collapse of massive pyramid investment schemes early in 1997, and Yugoslavia is under U.N. economic sanctions and facing a civil war in its southern province of Kosovo. In 1998–1999 the economies of Romania and Bulgaria, the two largest in the Balkans, may begin to recover, but Romania is still lagging in the process of reform and Bulgaria maintains strong trade ties with Russia. Croatia is also expected to continue expanding at or near current rates, particularly since tourists are once again flocking to the Adriatic coast, a major source of foreign exchange for the country. The conflict in Kosovo makes the economic outlook for Yugoslavia and the two adjacent countries, Albania and Macedonia, quite uncertain.

In eastern Europe and the Baltics States, economic growth in the smaller countries was quite good in 1997, but the two largest economies, Belarus and Ukraine, suffered economic declines. The downturn in Belarus was the first after 4 years of solid growth. In Ukraine, 1997 marked yet another year of economic decline. Fiscal imbalances, underdeveloped financial markets, delays in structural reform and poor economic management continue to plague the economy of Ukraine, the second largest (after Russia) of the republics in the former Soviet Union. Ukraine's continued close ties to Russia will mean continued economic stagnation.

The remaining republics of the former Soviet Union, in central Asia and in the Transcaucases, enjoyed as a group a second consecutive year of economic growth in 1997. In this group of nine countries, only Turkmenistan suffered economic decline in 1997. The best performance was turned in by Georgia, which grew at double-digit rates for the second consecutive year. The two largest countries in the region, Uzbekistan and Kazakhstan, grew 2.4 percent and 2.1 percent, respectively. The outlook for these nine countries is uncertain, in part because of the depression in commodity prices, including oil, and in part because of the unresolved issue of how best to transport oil from the reserves in the Caspian Sea basin to markets in the west and in Asia.

SUMMARY AND CONCLUSIONS

The world economic outlook has changed remarkably compared to a year ago when most economic signals were blinking green almost everywhere in the world. In mid-1998 the outlook is far less positive. There seems to be little doubt that world economic output in 1998 will record its slowest growth since 1991, when the world economy expanded only 1.8 percent. Growth in 1999 may be slightly faster than this rate, but the risks and uncertainties were increasing as 1998 entered its last quarter and most of these were on the downside.

In North America, the United States and Canada are at or near the peaks in their current expansion, while Mexico continues to make good progress in recovering from the 1995 peso crisis. In western Europe, the macroeconomic conditions throughout the region, unemployment rates excepted, are in better condition than they have been in years. The fiscal and monetary discipline that the region has imposed on itself in preparation for the adoption of a single currency has laid an economic foundation that promises good economic performance for years to come. Furthermore, there were some signs in mid-1998 that the current expansion may reduce unemployment more than was anticipated at the beginning of the year. On the downside, in Japan the new government that assumed leadership in mid-1998 has moved slowly in its efforts to resolve that country's economic problems.

Emerging markets undoubtedly have taken the brunt of the impact of the fallout from Asia because of the impact on commodity prices and because of the financial "flight to quality." International "hot money" capital fled most emerging markets despite no appreciable changes in the stable economic policy that the governments of these countries were following. Nevertheless, most emerging markets will see slower growth in 1998 because of the adverse impacts already experienced. Emerging markets in South America, Africa, the Middle East, and Europe, as well as the transition economies, will grow somewhat slower in the 1998–1999 period because of lost export earnings and higher interest payments.

In terms of the current outlook, a great concern is growth in 1999 when an anticipated slowdown in the U.S. economy will have to be offset by a recovery in Asia to prevent world growth from sinking to an even lower rate. The worry is that most of the uncertainties with this outlook are on the downside. Few of the structural problems in the financial institutions of Asia have yet been repaired. The banking system throughout the region needs to be recapitalized before new growth can be adequately financed. In Europe, the advent of the euro promises gains in economic efficiencies and growth in the long run, but there is still apprehension that the conversion will not go smoothly. The uncertain state of the Russian financial system still looms large in the outlook for that country as well as for Russia's neighbors and for European banks that hold much of Russia's debt.

John Jelacic, U.S. Department of Commerce, Office of Trade and Economic Analysis, (202) 482-2403, October 8, 1998.

Electronic Commerce: The Key to the Evolving Digital Economy

One of the most important phenomena to cut across all industries in the 1990s is the arrival of the Internet as a mass medium and the emergence of electronic commerce over the Internet. An interconnected worldwide network of computer networks, the Internet moved from the province of academics and government researchers into the mainstream during the early 1990s due to the development of a relatively easy-to-use interface (the World Wide Web) and new access technologies (Web browsers). These factors, combined with the rapid decrease of computer prices, led to a dramatic expansion of the number of computers connected to the Internet and the number of people online. Hosts, computers with unique Internet Protocol (IP) addresses, increased from 1.3 million in January 1993 to 19.5 million in July 1997. Over the same period, the number of domains—names registered within the Internet's domain name system—increased from 21,000 to 1.3 million (Network Wizards, 1998). Estimates range from 51 million to 62 million people online in the United States, and to as many as 101 million people online worldwide in 1997 (CommerceNet/Nielsen, 1997; IntelliQuest, 1998; NUA, 1998). While absolute numbers vary by source, few analysts disagree that Internet usage is growing rapidly. As the Internet has expanded, businesses have begun to explore its commercial potential, both in terms of a new marketplace and as a medium for internal and external business communications.

Just as the concept of commerce is not defined simply as sales, electronic commerce is not simply sales over the Internet. In fact, there is no single widely accepted definition of electronic commerce. At its narrowest, electronic commerce describes transactions where both the money and the product are exchanged over the Internet. More broadly, electronic commerce may also apply to a consumer surfing the Web to learn about a product before driving to the local mall to buy it. Furthermore, electronic commerce encompasses transactions between firms, organizations, governments, and individuals at all levels of market participation:

- the enterprise level—between firms in supply and production chains
- the organization level—within and between firms and organizations
- the business to customer level—between suppliers and final customers (other businesses and/or consumers)
- the person to person level—between individuals (Hawkins, 1998)

While discussions of electronic commerce usually center on activities on the Internet, many transactions on various nonpublic networks are also typically included as electronic commerce. Many companies, for example, use Internet technologies to create private networks for company only use (intranets) or for use among their employees and their business partners (extranets).

Many of the most common examples of the electronic commerce are those of the online sale of goods that are ultimately delivered physically. Books, compact discs, computers, and electronics equipment are among items sold online, then shipped to a location provided by the consumer. The Internet, however, is also a medium for the online delivery of digital products, such as software or newspaper articles. Anything that can be digitized—text, images, sounds, video—can be delivered electronically.

While the delivery of radio, movies, and other streaming video products, such as live audio or video feeds (WebCasting), are available, their practicality is dependent on a number of factors, including the bandwidth of the user's connection to the Internet; the limitations of the provider's infrastructure (i.e., the number of people who can simultaneously log onto a site is still fairly limited); and the availability of sufficient bandwidth from the starting point to the destination of the transmission to deliver a product without noticeable breaks.

Bandwidth measures the amount of information that can flow over the communications connection. Bandwidth-intensive products, such as video, require the consumer to have a high-bandwidth Internet connection. It would, for example, take a user with a 28.8-kbps modem connection to the Internet 46 minutes to download a 10 megabyte file (the approximate size of a 3.5 minute video clip). If the user had a 10-mbps cable modem, the same file would take 8 seconds to download (FCC, 1997). Residential Internet users are typically constrained by low-bandwidth Internet connections; businesses can often afford faster connections for their employees.

Technological advances are increasing connection speeds and enabling agreements on methods of handling and reserving bandwidth. While the delivery of many bandwidth-intensive products over the Internet may be unrealistic today, their delivery may be possible in the near future.

The Internet is also being used to deliver many services. The travel industry, for instance, has seen services such as reservations and ticketing begin to shift to the Internet. Financial service industries, such as banks and brokerage houses, are also beginning to deliver services online. The emergence and development of online brokerage services, for instance, has already led to dramatic pricing changes in that industry.

INDICATORS OF THE GROWTH OF ELECTRONIC COMMERCE

Electronic commerce is young, expanding, and changing rapidly; therefore it is difficult to find direct measures of its growth, development, and impact. Because electronic commerce is closely linked to the technologies (computers and software) that make it possible and the communications infrastructure over which it takes place, many measures of electronic commerce rely on information technology industry statistics to indicate the growth and potential of electronic commerce. Generally speaking, information technologies are included in the following industries: computer equipment (SIC 35), telecommunications equipment (SIC 36), telecommunications services (SIC 48), and computer software and networking (SIC 73).

Growth in investment by businesses in information processing equipment, for example, suggests a widespread and continuing acceptance in the business community of the technologies that underlie electronic commerce. Information processing equipment's share of business producers' durable equipment investment in real dollars increased from 32 percent in 1991 to 49 percent by the second quarter of 1998 (Bureau of Economic Analysis, various years).

The amount of venture capital funds pouring into business sectors associated with electronic commerce provides additional evidence that investors anticipate continued growth in these industries. The share of venture capital going to the information technology sectors—software and information, communications, computer and peripherals, electronics and instrumentation, and semiconductors and equipment industries—has increased as a share of overall U.S. venture capital. In 1995, these categories represented $3.3 billion (44.2 percent) of a total of $7.6 billion in U.S. venture capital. In 1997, they accounted for $7.1 billion (55.8 percent) of $12.8 billion in U.S. venture capital (Price Waterhouse, various years).

Surveys also suggest an increasing willingness by Web users to make purchases online. The CommerceNet/Nielsen survey of fall 1997 revealed that 10.1 million people (16.1 percent of their estimate of recent Web users in the United States and Canada) had made purchases online. This estimate was up from 7.4 million 6 months earlier.

Work is under way in various forms, such as the Organization for Economic Cooperation and Development, to develop better indicators of the growth, development, and effects of electronic commerce.

ONLINE RETAIL TRADE

Business-to-consumer electronic commerce has received widespread attention in the media despite the fact that the dollar value of online sales is insignificant relative to total final sales in the U.S. economy. Analysts estimate Internet retail sales at between $1.3 billion and $4 billion in 1997, a small fraction of the $2.5 trillion consumer retail market.

Nonetheless, companies across the economy are exploring sales and marketing online. Books, compact discs, newspaper articles, plane tickets, concert tickets, bus passes, flowers, gardening tools, computers, electronics equipment, networking hardware, and even durable goods such as cars and refrigerators are being sold online. More than 2,700 newspapers, for example, have online businesses, and all but three of the top 50 magazines in the country (based on paid circulation) had a Web presence by January 1998 (U.S. Department of Commerce, 1998a). Approximately 12 percent of retailers and 9 percent of manufacturers currently sell on the Internet.

The Internet has also generated the development of companies that exist entirely online with no physical outlets—the "virtual firm" or "cyber-trader." In a few situations, these companies are providing competition for the dominant firms in the industry. For example, Amazon.com, one of the most frequently cited examples of the virtual firm, since its opening in July 1995 has become an important competitor to established booksellers such as Barnes and Nobel and Borders. In 1997, Amazon.com generated $148 million in online sales. Barnes and Noble opened its own online business in May 1997 and has generated $14 million in its first 9 months of business.

Electronic commerce may generate cost savings for online retailers such as reducing or eliminating the need to maintain the physical store infrastructure (rent, utilities, store personnel). Firms may be able to reduce the amount of stock they keep in inventory—leaving order fulfillment activities (warehousing and distribution) to third parties.

Electronic commerce also has the potential to reduce distribution costs. In the airline industry, for example, it costs $8 to process an airline ticket if a travel agent books the ticket using a computer reservation system. It costs $6 if the travel agent books it directly with the airline. It costs $1 for the same ticket if the customer books an "electronic ticket" directly with the airline (Air Transport Association of America, 1997).

Electronic commerce may also enable companies to provide more customized products and services. For example, by tracking a customer's purchases an online company might tailor online advertising to that customer's preferences. Companies may also be able to tailor their products and services according to a customer's preferences, allowing them to develop one-to-one marketing via customer profiling.

Bank of America's "Build Your Own Bank" is an example of electronic commerce–enabled customization. The customer provides the bank with personal information, such as occupation, age, income, gender, home ownership status, and the types of bank accounts that he or she has, as well as information on his or her financial interests and priorities—saving and investing, home buying, home improvement, etc. The bank uses this information to deliver "Money Tips," news items, and special offers geared to the customer's preferences (U.S. Department of Commerce, 1998a).

Electronic commerce enables businesses to provide more efficient and effective customer services and to reduce sales and marketing costs. Posting product information, technical information, frequently asked questions, and order status information online frees customer service staff to handle more complicated questions and to manage customer relations. Companies that use the Internet for customer service—order tracking, software downloads, technical support information, etc.—report improved customer satisfaction and costs savings. Cisco Systems, for example, reports that customer service productivity has increased 200 to 300 percent, which has resulted in savings of $125 million in customer service costs (U.S. Department of Commerce, 1998a).

Electronic commerce based on the Internet also has the capacity to give a small company an international reach. The Internet is international in scope. Almost every country has some connectivity, although the level of access varies by country—ranging from E-mail only to full Internet access. A company that opens an online business potentially has a worldwide market. There are, however, certain limiting factors. International shipping costs are an important factor for tangible goods. For intangible goods, limited bandwidth in other countries may be a constraint. In both cases, language, cultural differences, and differing commercial rules may create significant barriers to trade.

The Internet also opens up new opportunities for businesses to manage their sales and inventories. Airlines are using the Internet to fill seats on flights at the last minute. American Airlines, for example, sends weekly E-mail messages listing special discounted fares for the upcoming weekend to more than 1 million "NetSAAvers" subscribers (U.S. Department of Commerce, 1998a). Electronic commerce auctions, such as the online interactive auction for surplus electronic components created by FastParts, Inc., have also emerged in the Internet.

Electronic commerce, however, is not a positive force for all firms. An example is the case of Encyclopedia Britannica. After 1990, with the advent of CD-ROM encyclopedias such as Encarta, Britannica's sales decreased by more than 50 percent. Microsoft's Encarta, which costs about $50, was typically given free to customers with the purchase of a personal computer. The printed version of the Encyclopedia Britannica, however, cost from $1,500 to $2,200. Realizing the threat, Britannica created a CD-ROM version of its encyclopedia. To avoid undercutting its sales force, the company included the CD-ROM free with the printed version and charged $1,000 for the CD-ROM alone. Revenues continued to decline and Britannica's owner eventually sold the business. The new owners are now trying to rebuild the business around the Internet (Evans and Wurster, 1997).

While many companies are exploring electronic commerce, the factors that generate a successful online business are not yet clear. Many companies engaged in electronic commerce over the Internet are still struggling to develop profitable online business models. Even highly visible companies, such as Amazon.com, have yet to make a profit.

The Internet is an active, rather than a passive, medium. It is not enough for a company to simply develop a Web site for its online business. Since there are millions of Web sites, it is crucial also to develop a means to bring users to the company's site.

One way of doing this is for a company to link its site to a Web site that receives heavy traffic by Web users. Companies, such as Microsoft Corp., Netscape Communications Inc., America Online Inc., Yahoo Inc., and Compaq Computers Corp., have recently begun to develop their Web sites around this concept—creating "portals" or starting points for Internet users. These companies are selling premium advertising space and links from their sites to other companies in the hopes that a link from a portal will be the Internet equivalent of a main street storefront. It remains to be seen whether the portals will be a successful strategy for the companies developing them or for the companies that hope to generate traffic at their Web site by advertising on a portal (Chandrasekaran, 1998).

Another key factor appears to be the development or promotion of a recognizable brand name. Trust is an important component in any business transaction, and the use of brands appears to be one means of establishing credibility and developing trust in the online marketplace. In order to generate brand recognition, virtual firms may need to develop advertising campaigns offline—using television, radio, and print media. This factor also may create an advantage for established companies that develop online businesses over virtual firms and new entrants.

Another important factor in Internet-based electronic commerce is the development of secure online payment systems. Most Internet purchases are currently made by the consumer entering a credit card number and delivery address information onto an online form. While this practice is likely as secure as giving a credit card number over the phone, consumers' fear that credit card information will be misused or stolen is often cited as the largest barrier to growth of retail sales on the Internet (U.S. Department of Commerce, 1998a).

Technologies for making Internet transactions more secure, as well as new forms of payment such as smart cards and digital cash, are being developed to address these issues. Smart cards contain microchips that store data, such as the consumer's name, address, and credit card information. Digital cash is a card or electronic purse that stores a set amount of money but no identifying information about the consumer. Thus, the consumer can purchase goods and services electronically with the same anonymity offered by cash. Digital cash also offers a potential mechanism for micropayments, i.e., very small online cash transactions. This would enable a consumer, for example, to pay 25 cents to read a single magazine article instead of purchasing access to the full magazine.

BUSINESS-TO-BUSINESS ELECTRONIC COMMERCE

While the proliferation of business-to-consumer activity on the World Wide Web receives the lion's share of attention from the media, many analysts anticipate that business-to-business electronic commerce has a larger potential impact on economic activity.

Business-to-business electronic commerce in the form of electronic data interchange (EDI) has existed since the 1970s. EDI is the exchange of standardized data usually within or between large companies over private telecommunications networks, known as value-added networks (VANs). Businesses that have implemented EDI have typically realized considerable cost savings. For example, companies using EDI for procurement commonly save 5 to 10 percent in procurement costs (Lundstrom, 1997).

Historically, the costs involved in installing and maintaining VANs precluded all but very large companies. VANs used their own proprietary communications technologies, and a supplier firm would have to maintain a separate terminal for each VAN used by the companies with which it communicated using EDI. Small and medium-sized companies typically relied on fax and telephone communications for routine transactions. Large companies did not realize the full potential savings of EDI because a share of their business partners did not use it.

By standardizing business communications on the relatively open Transmission Control Protocol/Internet Protocol (TCP/IP) technologies, small and medium-sized companies are more able to explore the efficiencies and opportunities inherent in automating routine business transactions. However, because the public Internet is not secure enough for many sensitive business communications, businesses may use intranets and extranets, private networks using the Internet's TCP/IP protocols. The use of Internet technologies instead of proprietary technologies reduces one of the barriers to business-to-business communications.

Reducing Procurement Costs and Increasing the Supplier Base

Use of the Internet for EDI communications reduces transmission costs relative to using private networks, such as VANs. The use of Internet technologies also potentially increases the number of firms able to act as suppliers; many small and medium-sized companies, which cannot afford to install and maintain a VAN, have access to the Internet.

GE Lighting, a General Electric division, is a case of Internet-based electronic commerce reducing procurement costs while increasing the supplier base. In 1996, GE Lighting implemented the company's first online procurement system, TPN Post, over an extranet developed by GE Information Services. Using the system, the sourcing department receives requisitions for low-value machine parts from internal customers, and the system automatically attaches the necessary drawings to the requisition and sends the electronic bid package to suppliers around the world via E-mail, fax, or EDI.

TPN Post enabled GE Lighting to reduce processing time for outgoing bid packages from at best 7 days to 2 hours. It also increased the number of suppliers receiving requests for quotes; prior to the implementation of TPN Post, the process was so complex that the department normally sent bid packages to only two or three suppliers at a time. TPN Post is also more efficient than the previous process. Prior to TPN Post, one out of four invoices had to be investigated and reworked to reconcile it with purchase orders and receipts; these invoices are reconciled automatically in the course of the TPN Post process.

According to GE, the division's labor costs have decreased 30 percent, and 60 percent of the procurement staff has been redeployed. Materials costs have also declined up to 20 percent due, in part, to the wider supply base and greater competition among suppliers (U.S. Department of Commerce, 1998a).

Managing Inventory

By increasing communications, electronic commerce technologies may enable businesses to reduce the inventory they keep in stock and manage it better. Better communications among factories, purchasing departments, and marketing make it easier for businesses to keep less inventory in stock and "turn" it more frequently. This in turn lowers operating costs—e.g., storage and handling costs—as well as increasing the likelihood of stocking products that are currently in demand and of using current manufacturing capacity effectively.

IBM's Personal Systems Group, for example, uses inputs on supply and demand from across the company to determine and adjust the production schedules for each factory and to determine procurement needs for negotiations with suppliers. The group's Advanced Planning System increased inventory turns 40 percent and sales volume 30 percent during its first year (U.S. Department of Commerce, 1998a). Automotive companies are also taking advantage of these technologies by using EDI to communicate production and scheduling requirements to suppliers. By more closely coordinating production and assembly processes, North American assembly locations turn inventory 130 times per year, up from 7 to 10 times per year in the past (U.S. Department of Commerce, 1998a).

Reducing Product Cycle Time

Electronic commerce enables businesses to reduce product cycle time, thereby reducing fixed costs associated with production. These costs include depreciation of equipment, most utility and building costs, and most managerial and supervisory time. By reducing the time it takes for companies to transmit, receive, and process routine business communications, such as purchase orders, invoices, and shipping notifications, electronic commerce reduces the length of the production cycle. Businesses have also used electronic commerce technologies to increase communications in the product development stage.

For example, the Manufacturing Assembly Pilot (MAP) enabled Chrysler, Ford, GM, Johnson Controls, and 12 of their suppliers to improve material flows within a four-tier seat assembly supply chain. By electronically connecting the companies, MAP enabled them to reduce the time that information took to reach the bottom of the supply chain, from 4–6 weeks to less than 2 weeks. On-time shipments improved 6 percent. Error rates decreased 72 percent. Labor costs were reduced by up to 8 hours per week per customer (Hoy and Margolin, 1996).

ELECTRONIC COMMERCE POLICY ISSUES

The global reach of the Internet and its ability to enable instant cross-border communications and transactions raises a host of questions about how the established rules and norms of commercial activities apply to electronic commerce, both within countries and across international borders. The U.S. government took the lead in fostering discussion of these issues when, in July 1997, President Clinton issued the strategy paper *A Framework for Global Electronic Commerce*. This report, which promotes a private sector–led approach, precipitated a worldwide discussion of policy issues related to electronic commerce. These issues include, but are not limited to, privacy, security, standards, intellectual property rights, taxation, tariffs, the development of electronic payment systems, and handling laws related to content, advertising, gambling, etc., that differ across countries. The examples of security and privacy that are given below illustrate the importance and complexity of electronic commerce policy issues.

Electronic commerce technologies enable companies to collect and store information about their customers. On the positive side, these technologies enable businesses to offer features, such as customization and one-to-one marketing, that were not previously possible. The proliferation of these technologies, however, also raises numerous issues related to the collection, use, and sale of data collected over the Internet; these issues include:

- Businesses' responsibilities to report to the user what data are being collected, how the data will be used, whether data will be sold to third parties, and whether the consumer has the right to opt out of the collection and/or resale of personal data

- The consumer's right to access and, if necessary, correct personal data held in business databases

- The collection of personal data from minors

- The collection of data without the Internet user's knowledge (e.g., "cookies," programs that a Web page can cache on a user's computer, are able to track a Web user's movements around the Internet and send that information to Web sites)

Protection of privacy remains one of the critical issues associated with the development of electronic commerce. The U.S. goverment approach has been to encourage a private sector–led self-regulatory approach. Industry, however, has only recently begun to undertake serious efforts to address privacy issues. These efforts include the formation of the OnLine Privacy Alliance. This alliance of more than 50 of the largest companies doing business on the Internet and 15 business organizations that represent thousands of other companies has committed to implement policies encompassing notice, choice, access, third-party enforcement mechanisms (including complaint and redress mechanisms), and the prohibition of the collection of data from children without prior parental permission. The U.S. government has already passed into law the Online Children's Privacy Protection Act, which protects the privacy of children online.

Privacy issues are in some ways closely related to security issues—those issues associated with making sure that electronic commerce communications and transactions are not altered or tampered with and that consumers and businesses engaged in electronic commerce have the means to verify the authenticity of electronic communications. For example, a consumer making an online purchase with a credit card requires assurance that the credit card number will not be stolen as the message travels across the Internet. Similarly, companies using the Internet to communicate business plans want to make sure that their competitors cannot open Internet messages and gain access to or tamper with confidential information.

Many security issues are associated with the development and implementation of technologies, such as:

- Encryption—A technology that encodes a message before it is sent and decodes it when it is received. Encryption is used to protect a message from unauthorized viewing and alteration.

- Digital signatures—An electronic version of a signature. One of a number of signature alternative technologies, it uses cryptographic techniques to verify that the person who apparently sent the message in fact sent the message and that the contents have not been altered since the message was sent.

- Digital certificates—An electronic third-party "voucher" that a message is authentic. This is conceptually similar to paper-based certificates, such as birth certificates, passports, and drivers licences. The certificate (e.g., a driver's license) issued by a credible third party (state government) indicates that the information carried in the message (name, address, etc.) is authentic.

Equally important among security issues is the development of means to make sure that the technologies used to ensure the security, confidentiality, and authenticity of electronic communications are not used to shield illegal activities such as money laundering or terrorist activities.

While many of the electronic commerce policy issues are still under discussion within the United States, within other countries, and in multinational organizations, such as the World Trade Organization, the World Intellectual Property Organization, and the Organization for Economic Cooperation and Development, policy makers have made progress on developing a reliable legal environment for electronic commerce. Important steps in ths process include enactment into law of the Internet Tax Freedom Act, the Digital Millennium Copyright Act, the Government Paperwork Elimination Act, and the Online Children's Privacy Protection Act. These new laws and the evolution of other policy issues will play major roles in the future development of electronic commerce.

Sabrina Montes, U.S. Department of Commerce, Office of Trade and Economic Analysis, (202) 482-5242.

■ REFERENCES

Air Transport Association of America, November 20, 1997. Cited in U.S. Department of Commerce, 1998a.

Bureau of Economic Analysis, *Survey of Current Business,* Government Printing Office, Washington, DC, January/February 1996; September 1997; August 1998.

Chandrasekaran, Rajiv, "One-Stop Surfing: Today's Hot Web Concept is 'Portals.' Tomorrow, Who Knows?", *The Washington Post,* October 11, 1998, p. H1.

Chronister, Kristian, "Site Adds Parts Auction," *Electronic Buyers News,* September 1, 1997, p. 62.

CommerceNet, "Electronic Commerce on the Rise According to CommerceNet/Nielsen Media Research Survey," Press Release, December 11, 1997. http://www.commerce.net/news/press/121197.html.

CommerceNet/Nielsen, "Internet Demographic Study: Dec '96/Jan '97," 1997 [the fall 1997 statistics were provided by a CommerceNet/Nielsen representative].

Evans, Philip B., and Thomas S. Wurster, "Strategy and the New Economics of Information," *The Harvard Business Review,* September-October, 1997. Cited in OECD, 1998.

Federal Communications Commission, "Annual Assessment of the Status of Competition in the Market for the Delivery of Video Programming," CS Docket No. 96-496, January 2, 1997. http://www.fcc.gov/Bureaus/Cable/Reports/fcc97423.html.

Hawkins, Richard, "Creating a Positive Environment for Electronic Commerce in Europe," Information, Networks & Knowledge Science Policy Research Unit, Working Paper No. 36, March 1998.

Hoy, Tom, and David Margolin, "Charting the Course," *Action Line,* September 1996. Cited in U.S. Department of Commerce, 1998a.

IntelliQuest, "Latest IntelliQuest Survey Reports 62 Million American Adults Access the Internet/Online Services," IntelliQuest Press Release, February 4, 1998.

Lundstrom, Scott, "Internet Enabled Indirect Procurement: A Low Risk/High Return Project," *The Report on Supply Chain Management,* Advanced Manufacturing Research, Inc., July 1997. Cited in U.S. Department of Commerce, 1998a.

Network Wizards, Internet Domain Name Survey. http://www.nw.com.

NUA, "How Many on Line?", NUA Web site. Accessed on January 23, 1998. http://www.nua.ie/surveys/how_many_online/index.html.

Organization for Economic Cooperation and Development, "The Economic and Social Impacts of Electronic Commerce: Preliminary Findings and Research Agenda," OECD, Paris, 1998. http://www.oecd.org/subject/e_commerce/summary.html.

Price Waterhouse, "Price Waterhouse National Venture Capital Survey," 1995–1998. http://www.pw.com/vc. Cited in U.S. Department of Commerce, 1998b.

U.S. Department of Commerce, *The Emerging Digital Economy,* U.S. Department of Commerce, Washington, DC.; April 1998a. http://www.ecommerce.gov.

U.S. Department of Commerce, *The Emerging Digital Economy Appendices,* U.S. Department of Commerce, Washington, DC.; April 1998b. http://www.ecommerce.gov.

The White House, *A Framework for Global Electronic Commerce,* Washington, DC, July 1997. http://www.ecommerce.gov.

■ RELATED CHAPTERS

Highlights of *Outlook '99*

The U.S. economy has done extremely well in recent years, as robust economic growth has pushed the unemployment rate down to around 4.5 percent while inflation has remained low. In this setting, most industry sectors have done well. However, the economy is now in transition to a lower and more sustainable rate of growth of 2 to 2.5 percent (in contrast to the more than 3 percent growth of 1998). Consumer and investment spending, which have been major sources of domestic demand, are expected to slow in 1999. Weakness in international trade, especially as a result of the Asian crisis, will be an important factor in weakening demand for manufactures, which will in turn impact on other elements of the economy. Business activity in services will tend to slow as growth in incomes and employment subsides in the overall economy.

These trends are reflected in the forecasts for industry shipments and production of services. Industry shipments have generally tracked GDP closely (see Figure E-1). Shipments for the

manufacturing sectors forecast in the *Outlook* are expected to slow considerably in 1999.

TRADE EFFECTS

International trade has a great impact on the overall economy. Trade (exports plus imports) has grown relative to the domestic economy from under 10 percent of the total economy in 1960 to 25 percent in 1998. The dependence on international trade is even more apparent in goods trade (that is, excluding services and construction), where exports have risen to over 25 percent of goods GDP (see Figure E-2).

Economic growth abroad is expected to be relatively weak in 1999, as it was in 1998. Combined with the strong U.S. dollar, this will result in a weak U.S. export performance. Despite the

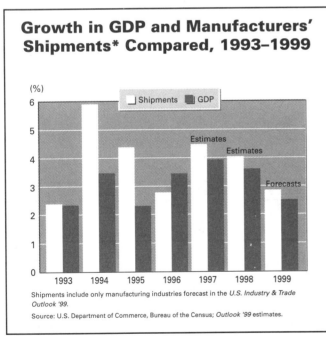

FIGURE E-1

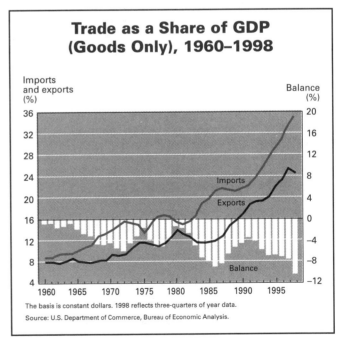

FIGURE E-2

TABLE E-1: Trends in Selected Manufacturing Sectors

(billions of 1992 dollars except where noted)

Sector	Value of Industry Shipments, 1999	Percent Change at Annual Rates		
		92–97	97–98	98–99
Aerospace	143	–3.0	20.9	4.7
Chemicals	213	1.5	0.7	1.9
Construction materials	37	4.9	3.1	2.3
Consumer durables (selected)	85	3.3	2.2	1.2
Food and kindred products	451	1.4	1.6	2.0
Industrial supplies	404	3.1	2.3	2.0
Information technology	420	11.4	7.6	8.0
Instruments, medical and dental equipment	108	5.8	5.0	5.0
Machinery and equipment	184	6.4	0.9	1.1
Motor vehicles and parts	353	5.3	3.3	0.7
Printing and publishing	173	0.4	1.0	1.0
Textiles, apparel, and leather	167	1.2	0.7	0.9

Source: *U.S. Industry & Trade Outlook '99.*

deterioration in international trade and its concomitant impact on the manufacturing sector, the economy overall is expected to grow moderately during 1998 and 1999. Nevertheless, there will be substantial variation by sector. Table E-5 provides a summary of forecasts for the manufacturing sector.

MANUFACTURING SECTORS

Information technologies will continue to be a mainstay of growth and especially of capital spending. Demand for computers, networking equipment, and telecommunications equipment are expected to continue their strong growth, though at a slower pace than in recent years. Other capital goods sectors will be slowing even more. Shipments of the aerospace industries will return to a more moderate growth rate in 1999 after surging in 1997 and 1998. Traditional capital goods industries such as machinery will slow even more, with construction equipment and oil and gas field equipment posting negative growth. Cyclical industries (those whose ups and downs closely track the economy) will reflect the slowing of the economy. This is especially true for chemicals and other

industrial supplies. Shipments of construction materials and supplies had picked up in the mid-1990s with the resurgence of construction, but with construction growth slowing, demand for materials will also fall off in 1999. Weak export markets are also an important factor in the dampened prospects for chemicals and machinery, since both are very dependent on export sales. Shipments of selected consumer durables as shown in Table E-1 will grow slowly. Consumer expenditures on consumer durables as measured in the National Accounts can be expected to grow more rapidly since the category includes expenditures on computers and related equipment. Shipments of motor vehicles and parts is expected to show only modest growth after a good 1998 performance, but deliveries will still be in the 15 million unit plus range. Other industries closely tied to consumer spending on non-durables—food processing and textiles and apparel—are expected also to show only modest growth, reflecting the overall slowing of consumer demand in 1999.

The fastest growing industries are, with one exception, high-technology industries, and all are industries in which the United States is highly competitive worldwide (see Table E-2). Three of these sectors are centered on aerospace—aircraft engines and

TABLE E-2: Ten Fastest Growing Manufacturing Industries in 1999

(based on shipments valued in 1992 dollars)

SIC	Industry	Chapter	Annual Growth Rates, %		
			92–97	97–98	98–99
3672	Printed circuit boards	16	11.1	9.0	14.0
3769	Space vehicle equipment, nec	21	–4.8	9.0	12.8
3761	Guided missiles and space vehicles	21	–2.8	16.0	11.0
3674	Semiconductors and related devices	16	24.6	8.9	10.2
3663	Radio and TV communications equipment	31	13.0	15.0	10.0
3764	Space propulsion units and parts	21	–10.1	12.6	9.9
357A	Computers and peripherals	27	11.3	8.5	8.7
367A	Passive components	16	8.2	6.3	8.0
3548	Welding apparatus	17	2.9	6.2	7.3
3661, 3663	Telecommunications equipment	31	11.5	9.8	6.9

Source: *U.S. Industry & Trade Outlook '99.*

TABLE E-3: Ten Slowest Growing Manufacturing Industries in 1999

(based on shipments valued in 1992 dollars)

SIC	Industry	Chapter	Annual Growth Rates, %		
			92–97	97–98	98–99
3171	Women's handbags and purses	34	−14.7	−13.9	−11.1
3172	Personal leather goods, nec	34	−9.8	−9.4	−9.5
3531	Construction machinery	18	11.2	−3.6	−6.4
3812	Search and navigation equipment	31	−4.5	−3.9	−3.9
3532	Mining machinery	18	4.4	−9.6	−3.5
3151	Leather gloves and mittens	34	−3.5	−17.9	−3.1
3111	Leather tanning and finishing	34	0.3	0.7	−3.0
3555	Printing trades machinery	18	6.0	2.6	−2.6
3634	Electric housewares and fans	38	0.7	−4.2	−1.9
2711	Newspapers	25	−1.5	−1.0	−1.5

Source: *U.S. Industry & Trade Outlook '99.*

TABLE E-4: Trends in Nonmanufacturing Industries

Sector	Chapter	Unit of Measure	1999 Value	Annual Growth Rates, %		
				95–97	97–98	98–99
Nonservices						
Coal mining	2	Production, millions of short tons	1,128	2.6	3.1	0.5
Natural gas production	3	Production, trillions of cubic feet	20	0.7	1.1	6.8
Crude petroleum	3	Production, thousands of barrels/day	6,280	−1.1	−0.3	−1.7
Refined petroleum	4	U.S. refinery output, millions of barrels/day	17	2.4	1.1	0.9
Electricity	5	Sales, billions of kilowatt-hours	3,258	2.0	2.7	1.5
Construction	5	Value put in place, billions of $1992	525	3.4	2.5	1.0
Titanium ingot	6	Production, thousands of metric tons	63	21.5	2.0	5.0
Lead	14	Production, thousands of metric tons	1,435	2.4	−3.8	4.7
Refined copper	14	Production, thousands of metric tons	2,610	3.4	3.7	3.2
Aluminum	14	Shipments, thousands of metric tons	10,890	3.6	3.1	3.0
Zinc	14	Production, thousands of metric tons	402	3.3	3.4	0.5
Services						
Environmental services	20	Revenues, $ billions	94	n.a.	2.2	2.0
Information retrieval services	26	Value added, $ billions	8	13.1	26.7	26.7
Data processing and network services	26	Value added, $ billions	34	13.5	15.0	15.1
Professional computer services	26	Value added, $ billions	95	13.3	14.7	15.1
CAD/CAM/CAE software	28	Revenues, $ billions	3	n.a.	13.0	14.0
Space commerce	29	Launch revenues, $ millions	992	24.6	16.0	14.0
Telecommunications services	30	Value added, $ billions	270	10.3	8.0	8.0
Cable television	32	Revenues, $ billions	32	17.0	16.1	11.1
Movies: box office	32	Revenues, $ billions	7	7.9	4.7	4.5
Home video	32	Revenues, $ billions	18	5.8	2.4	2.3
Recorded music	32	Revenues, $ billions	13	−0.4	0.8	1.6
Merchandise, wholesale	41	Sales, $ billions	2,776	5.6	5.7	4.0
Retailing	42	Sales, $ billions	2,804	5.5	4.5	3.7
Railroads	43	Billions of ton-miles	1,390	1.6	1.6	1.5
Health care	44	Expenditures, $ billions	1,200	4.5	5.0	5.6
Life and health insurance	46	Premium receipts, $ billions	395	3.9	3.8	3.9
Commercial banking	46	Business loans, $ billions	964	8.9	7.1	6.3
Mutual funds industry	47	Assets, $ billions	6,196	26.2	17.3	17.6
Securities industry	47	Revenues, $ billions	268	20.3	14.4	12.8
Commodity trading	48	Futures contracts, millions	462	1.0	5.0	5.5
Management, consulting, and public relations	48	Revenues, $ billions	147	10.6	12.1	13.1
Accounting, auditing, and bookkeeping	48	Revenues, $ billions	72	10.9	9.6	9.5
Advertising	49	Revenues, $ billions	37	9.6	6.3	7.1
Legal services	49	Revenues, $ billions	148	6.3	6.1	6.5
Public and private education	49	Receipts, $ 1994/95 billions	546	2.2	2.1	1.5

Source: *U.S. Industry & Trade Outlook '99.*

parts, guided missiles, and space vehicles. Growth in shipments in these areas was very strong in 1998 but will slow somewhat in 1999. Exports have been the most dynamic part of the current cyclical upswing in the aerospace industry. The continued strength of computers, semiconductors, and communications equipment reflects the ongoing digital revolution, which is transforming the ways in which goods and services are produced, the kinds of goods consumed, and the modes of personal communication and interaction.

The manufacturing industries with the slowest growth reflect a number of trends (see Table E-3). Footwear and leather goods reflect slow growth in demand as well as a continued shift to overseas suppliers. Other declining industries present a different picture. Shipments of oil and gas field machinery are dropping in the wake of lower oil prices and hence less drilling. Construction machinery shipments are off as a result of a slowdown in construction, while the decline in search and navigation equipment shipments reflects continued weakness in defense procurement. Though newspapers continue to contract, the aging baby boomer population is expected to give a boost to readership of print and online versions.

SERVICES

Trends in the services sector to a significant degree mirror those in manufacturing (see Table E-4). The fastest-growing services industries are dominated by information technologies, including information services, data processing, and professional computer services. Not surprisingly, the mutual fund and securities industries are expected to continue to grow apace, as the stock and bond markets continue to post record trading volumes. Strong growth is also expected in management consulting and accounting. This growth partly reflects the continued trend by many companies to contract out, or "outsource," for a host of business services. Noticeably absent from the top ten rapid growth sectors is health services. While growth in health services continues to be well above the rate of inflation, it is significantly below the double digit rates common in the 1980s and early 1990s.

(See the following table for forecasts in the manufacturing sector.)

Jonathan C. Menes, U.S. Department of Commerce, Office of Trade and Economic Analysis, December 1998.

TABLE E-5: Forecast Growth Rates for 137 Manufacturing Industries and Groups
(millions of 1992 dollars except as noted)

SIC	Industry	Chapter	Value of Industry Shipments, 1999	Annual Growth Rates, % 92–97[1]	Annual Growth Rates, % 98–99	1999 Rank	Rank Based on 92–97 Growth
2015	Poultry slaughtering and processing	35	29,710	3.1	3.3	26	65
201A	Red meat	35	74,300	0.3	1.0	89	112
206A	Snack foods	35	12,310	3.0	2.1	49	67
2082	Malt beverages	35	18,050	0.4	1.0	86	108
2084	Wines, brandy, and brandy spirits	35	5,766	4.8	3.0	35	36
2085	Distilled and blended liquors	35	3,457	−0.2	1.7	61	115
2096	Potato chips and similar snacks	35	9,030	3.5	2.0	56	55
221	Cotton broadwoven fabric mills	9	6,650	2.2	0.8	98	78
222	Man-made broadwoven fabric mills	9	10,000	2.1	1.0	85	79
223	Wool broadwoven fabric mills	9	1,800	2.0	0.6	104	83
225A	Weft, lace, and warp knit fabric mills	9	7,870	0.7	1.8	58	101
227	Carpets and rugs	9	11,150	2.0	1.6	64	84
2281	Yarn spinning mills	9	8,750	2.3	0.6	103	75
2311	Men's and boys' suits and coats	33	1,911	−4.7	0.7	99	139
2321	Men's and boys' shirts	33	5,134	−3.2	−0.4	122	134
2322	Men's and boys' underwear and nightwear	33	576	−6.8	0.5	105	142
2323	Men's and boys' neckwear	33	646	0.4	−0.8	127	106
2325	Men's and boys' trousers and slacks	33	7,167	2.3	−1.2	136	76
2326	Men's and boys' work clothing	33	1,820	4.2	−1.0	134	46
2331	Women's and misses' blouses and shirts	33	3,694	−1.7	0.0	116	131
2335	Women's, juniors', and misses' dresses	33	7,036	5.4	1.4	73	30
2337	Women's and misses' suits and coats	33	3,995	−2.3	1.1	82	132
2341	Women's and children's underwear	33	2,315	−0.8	−0.2	120	124
2342	Bras, girdles, and allied garments	33	1,794	2.9	−1.4	137	71
2361	Girls' and children's dresses, blouses	33	1,693	−0.2	1.3	77	116
2369	Girls' and children's outerwear, nec[2]	33	2,325	8.7	−0.3	121	9
2386	Leather and sheep-lined clothing	34	211	0.4	−0.9	131	109
239A	Textile house furnishings	33	7,079	0.6	−0.5	124	103
239B	Miscellaneous textile products	33	14,212	3.3	0.5	107	62

[1] Compound annual growth rate.
[2] nec = not elsewhere classified.
[3] Shipments are valued in current dollars.
Source: U.S. Department of Commerce, Bureau of the Census; *U.S. Industry & Trade Outlook '99* forecasts.

(millions of 1992 dollars except as noted)

SIC	Industry	Chapter	Value of Industry Shipments, 1999	Annual Growth Rates, % 92–97[1]	Annual Growth Rates, % 98–99	1999 Rank	Rank Based on 92–97 Growth
2421	Sawmills and planing mills, general	7	23,900	1.9	1.5	70	86
2435	Hardwood veneer and plywood	7	2,298	0.1	1.1	80	114
2436	Softwood veneer and plywood	7	5,335	−0.3	0.7	100	118
2451	Mobile homes	8	7,075	9.7	1.3	76	8
2452	Prefabricated wood buildings	8	2,275	1.2	−0.9	130	95
2493	Reconstituted wood products	7	4,755	2.7	2.1	50	72
251	Household furniture	38	25,629	3.3	2.0	54	59
2611	Pulp mills	10	5,050	−1.4	2.0	53	128
2653	Corrugated and solid fiber boxes	10	23,114	1.8	3.3	25	88
2657	Folding paperboard boxes	10	9,042	1.8	1.8	59	89
26PM	Paper and paperboard mills	10	54,390	1.4	2.5	40	93
2711	Newspapers	25	30,559	−1.5	−1.5	138	130
2721	Periodicals	25	23,538	0.8	1.0	90	99
2731	Book publishing	25	18,491	1.6	1.5	68	91
2732	Book printing	25	5,200	1.8	1.0	92	87
2741	Miscellaneous publishing	25	10,876	−0.6	1.2	78	122
275	Commercial printing	25	63,759	1.7	2.0	52	90
2761	Manifold business forms	25	5,164	−6.6	3.1	30	141
2771	Greeting cards	25	4,129	−0.5	0.6	101	121
2782	Blankbooks and looseleaf binders	25	4,665	3.0	2.3	42	68
2789	Bookbinding and related work	25	1,634	3.7	2.5	38	52
279	Printing trade services	25	4,985	−0.3	−0.5	123	117
281	Industrial inorganic chemicals	11	25,800	−0.9	1.2	79	125
2821	Plastics materials and resins	11	40,160	3.5	3.2	29	56
2822	Synthetic rubber	12	4,891	2.1	2.1	48	82
282A	Man-made fibers	9	13,845	1.1	1.1	83	98
283	Drugs	11	83,702	3.1	2.5	41	64
286	Industrial organic chemicals	11	66,550	0.6	1.6	63	104
289	Miscellaneous chemical products	11	23,600	2.4	1.9	57	73
3011	Tires and inner tubes	12	15,767	5.3	0.9	95	33
3069	Fabricated rubber products, nec[2]	12	8,038	2.9	0.3	109	70
3111	Leather tanning and finishing	34	2,881	0.3	−3.0	141	111
3142	House slippers	34	96	−16.5	3.2	28	146
3143	Men's footwear, except athletic	34	2,022	−1.4	3.0	33	129
3144	Women's footwear, except athletic	34	363	−16.5	1.1	81	147
3149	Footwear, except rubber, nec[2]	34	413	7.0	2.0	55	19
3151	Leather gloves and mittens	34	93	−3.5	−3.1	142	136
3161	Luggage	34	1,044	2.1	3.3	27	81
3171	Women's handbags and purses	34	160	−14.7	−11.1	147	145
3172	Personal leather goods, nec[2]	34	209	−9.8	−9.5	146	143
3211	Flat glass	8	2,595	3.7	2.6	37	51
3241	Cement, hydraulic	8	4,820	3.1	0.8	97	66
3251	Brick and structural clay tile	8	1,290	3.3	−1.0	132	60
3253	Ceramic wall and floor tile	8	1,115	7.3	3.8	22	17
3275	Gypsum products	8	2,525	4.0	−0.9	129	48
331A	Steel mill products	13	73,200	4.3	1.5	65	45
343A	Plumbing parts	8	8,185	6.3	4.4	18	21
3441	Fabricated structural metal	8	11,740	4.4	2.2	46	43
3448	Prefabricated metal buildings	8	4,285	7.6	2.6	36	15
3451	Screw machine products	15	6,301	7.1	2.5	39	18
3452	Bolts, nuts, rivets, and washers	15	7,050	4.7	3.0	34	37
345A	General components	15	29,335	4.3	2.2	47	44
349A	Valves and pipe fittings	15	10,696	3.3	2.0	51	58
3511	Turbines and turbine generator sets	19	6,306	1.2	−0.2	119	94
3523	Farm machinery and equipment	18	14,905	7.8	2.3	44	14
3524	Lawn and garden equipment	38	7,143	6.1	1.0	88	23
3531	Construction machinery	18	20,142	11.2	−6.4	145	5
3532	Mining machinery	18	1,678	4.4	−3.5	143	41

[1] Compound annual growth rate.
[2] nec = not elsewhere classified.
[3] Shipments are valued in current dollars.
Source: U.S. Department of Commerce, Bureau of the Census; *U.S. Industry & Trade Outlook '99* forecasts.

SIC	Industry	Chapter	Value of Industry Shipments, 1999	Annual Growth Rates, % 92–97[1]	Annual Growth Rates, % 98–99	1999 Rank	Rank Based on 92–97 Growth
3533	Oil and gas field machinery	18	4,244	3.5	0.2	111	57
3544	Special dies, tools, jigs, and fixtures	17	14,329	7.9	2.3	45	13
3545	Machine tool accessories	17	6,284	8.0	6.5	11	12
3546	Power-driven handtools	17	3,857	4.4	4.4	19	42
3548	Welding apparatus	17	3,600	2.9	7.3	9	69
354A	Machine tools	17	6,575	3.6	1.5	69	54
3554	Paper industries machinery	18	3,040	4.5	–1.1	135	40
3555	Printing trades machinery	18	3,527	6.0	–2.6	140	24
3556	Food products machinery	18	2,814	1.5	4.0	20	92
3562	Ball and roller bearings	15	5,288	3.3	1.0	91	61
3565	Packaging machinery	18	4,117	3.9	4.0	21	50
357A	Computers and peripherals[3]	27	125,000	11.3	8.7	7	4
3585	Refrigeration and heating equipment	18	26,115	5.8	2.3	43	26
3612	Transformers, except electronic	19	5,414	5.7	0.2	110	28
3613	Switchgear and switchboard apparatus	19	6,905	4.1	0.1	113	47
3621	Motors and generators	19	10,887	6.5	–1.0	133	20
3625	Relays and industrial controls	19	10,690	6.2	0.5	106	22
3631	Household cooking equipment	38	3,725	3.9	0.9	94	49
3632	Household refrigerators and freezers	38	5,815	5.5	1.5	71	29
3633	Household laundry equipment	38	4,650	5.9	1.4	75	25
3634	Electric housewares and fans	38	2,820	0.7	–1.9	139	102
3635	Household vacuum cleaners	38	2,280	3.2	1.0	84	63
3639	Household appliances, nec[2]	38	3,350	–0.6	1.5	66	123
3661	Telephone and telegraph apparatus	31	35,731	10.1	3.3	24	7
3663	Radio and TV communications equipment	31	45,397	13.0	10.0	5	2
3671	Electron tubes	16	4,294	4.5	5.2	13	38
3672	Printed circuit boards	16	15,401	11.1	14.0	1	6
3674	Semiconductors and related devices	16	115,882	24.6	10.2	4	1
367A	Passive components	16	52,871	8.2	8.0	8	11
371A	Automotive parts and accessories	37	156,677	7.5	1.4	74	16
371B	Motor vehicles and bodies	36	195,919	3.7	0.1	115	53
3721	Aircraft	21	65,760	–4.0	3.5	23	137
3724	Aircraft engines and engine parts	21	25,884	–1.4	3.1	31	127
3728	Aircraft parts and equipment, nec[2]	21	23,744	–0.3	3.0	32	119
3731	Ship building and repairing	22	11,080	–1.1	5.0	15	126
3732	Boat building and repairing	39	5,153	1.9	0.6	102	85
3761	Guided missiles and space vehicles	21	21,645	–2.8	11.0	3	133
3764	Space propulsion units and parts	21	3,713	–10.1	9.9	6	144
3769	Space vehicle equipment, nec[2]	21	1,889	–4.8	12.8	2	140
3812	Search and navigation equipment	31	25,698	–4.5	–3.9	144	138
3825	Instruments to measure electricity	23	14,712	8.5	4.9	16	10
382A	Laboratory instruments	23	14,010	5.1	4.6	17	34
382B	Measuring and controlling instruments	23	23,629	5.4	5.3	12	32
384	Medical instruments and supplies	45	56,060	5.4	5.0	14	31
3861	Photographic equipment and supplies	24	26,200	2.3	1.8	60	77
3911	Jewelry, precious metal	40	4,313	0.4	0.0	117	105
3931	Musical instruments	40	1,035	0.4	1.5	72	110
3949	Sporting and athletic goods, nec[2]	39	10,211	5.0	1.7	62	35
394A	Dolls, toys, and games	39	4,426	0.2	0.1	114	113
3961	Costume jewelry	40	1,505	0.4	1.0	87	107

[1] Compound annual growth rate.
[2] nec = not elsewhere classified.
[3] Shipments are valued in current dollars.
Source: U.S. Department of Commerce, Bureau of the Census; *U.S. Industry & Trade Outlook '99* forecasts.

METALS AND INDUSTRIAL MINERALS MINING
Economic and Trade Trends

U.S. Production of Industrial Minerals in 1997

Total: 2,720 million metric tons

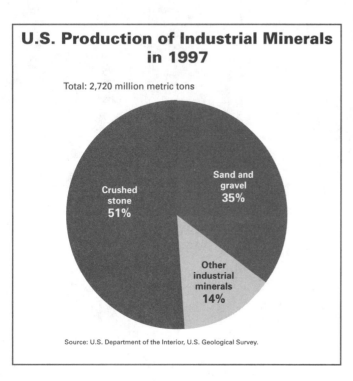

Source: U.S. Department of the Interior, U.S. Geological Survey.

U.S. Production of Major Construction Materials, 1992–1996

(millions of metric tons [log scale])

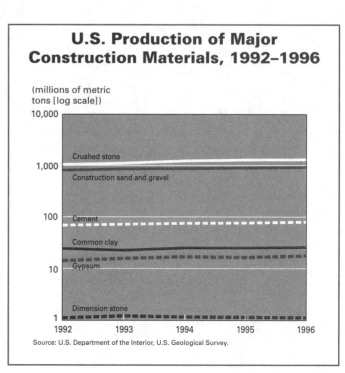

Source: U.S. Department of the Interior, U.S. Geological Survey.

U.S. Production of Major Chemical Minerals, 1992–1996

(millions of metric tons)

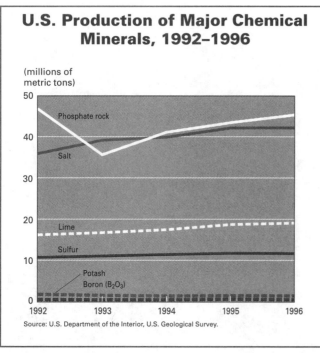

Source: U.S. Department of the Interior, U.S. Geological Survey.

U.S. Production of Other Major Industrial Minerals, 1992–1996

(millions of metric tons)

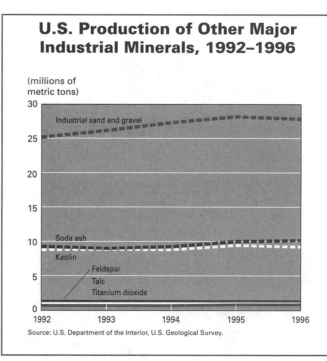

Source: U.S. Department of the Interior, U.S. Geological Survey.

Metals and Industrial Minerals Mining

INDUSTRY DEFINITION The U.S. nonfuel minerals industry, as it is described in this chapter, includes the mining of ores containing metals (SIC 10) such as copper, gold, iron, lead, lithium, molybdenum, silver, and zinc and the production of industrial minerals (SIC 14) such as boron, clays, phosphate rock, potash, salt, sand and gravel, soda ash, and stone.

FACTORS AFFECTING FUTURE U.S. INDUSTRY GROWTH

Recent Industry Trends

The nonfuel mining industries have continued to benefit from growth in the world economy between 1995 and 1997. Industrial production indexes calculated by the Federal Reserve Board show that production in U.S. metal mining and industrial mineral mining grew about 5.4 percent and 5.3 percent, respectively, in that period. This growth, however, did not keep pace with the growth of the U.S. economy as measured by the gross domestic product, which increased approximately 6.6 percent over that 2-year period when adjusted for inflation.

While physical production of both metal and industrial minerals mining increased between 1995 and 1997, the values of the production in each broad industry group moved in different directions. The current and the inflation-adjusted values of production for metal mining declined about 11.4 percent and 6.4 percent, respectively, during that period, partly because of flat or falling metal prices. In contrast, the current and inflation-adjusted values of production for industrial minerals mining grew 10.2 percent and 6.7 percent, respectively. In the 1990s so far, the inflation-adjusted value of production for metal mining is estimated to have registered a compound annual growth rate of −0.7 percent, while inflation-adjusted production of industrial minerals has been estimated at a growth rate of 1.5 percent.

The United States is dependent on foreign producers for many important metals, including cadmium, chromium, cobalt, magnesium compounds, manganese, nickel, the platinum-group metals, tin, and tungsten. For metal ores and concentrates, the value of imports has exceeded the value of exports for most of the 1990s, while the United States has exported more raw industrial minerals than it has imported.

Employment in the U.S. nonfuel minerals industry totaled about 160,000 in 1997, approximately 4.0 percent lower than the figure at the beginning of the decade. Average hourly earnings in both metal and industrial minerals mining continued to increase in 1996 and 1997, but data tabulated by the Bureau of Labor Statistics for all mining show that inflation-adjusted earnings have been falling since the late 1980s (see Table 1-1).

Southeast Asian Economic Crisis

In mid-1997 a devaluation of the Thai baht sparked a currency and economic crisis in several southeast Asian countries. Between the end of June and December 1997, the Thai baht, Malaysian ringgit, Korean won, and Japanese yen depreciated 45, 34, 40, and 12 percent, respectively, against the U.S. dollar. Before the crisis, most Asian countries had been experiencing strong economic growth, except for Japan, whose economy has been locked in a pattern of sluggish growth since 1991.

For nonfuel minerals, the most immediate effect of the crisis was on prices for nonferrous metals. As building and production in southeast Asia slowed or stopped, prices for aluminum, copper, lead, and zinc began to drop. Between the end of June and December 1997, for example, inventory levels of copper held on the London Metal Exchange almost tripled, while the closing spot price of that metal declined 32 percent.

TABLE 1-1: Metals and Industrial Minerals Mining (SIC 10, 14) Trends

(millions of dollars unless otherwise noted)

	1990	1992	1993	1994	1995	1996	1997	Percent Change 95–96	Percent Change 96–97	Compound Annual Growth Rate, % 90–97
Industry data										
Value of mine production										
SIC 10	12,442	11,547	10,800	12,100	14,000	12,900	12,400	−7.9	−3.9	0.0
SIC 14	20,992	20,574	21,200	23,100	24,600	25,800	27,100	4.9	5.0	3.7
Value of mine production (1992$)										
SIC 10	11,530	11,547	10,880	11,983	11,690	11,435	10,947	−2.2	−4.3	−0.7
SIC 14	21,460	20,574	20,714	21,816	22,365	23,092	23,855	3.3	3.3	1.5
Total employment (thousands)										
SIC 10	58	53	50	49	51	54	54	5.9	0.0	−1.0
SIC 14	110	102	102	104	105	106	107	1.0	0.9	−0.4
Production workers (thousands)										
SIC 10	46	42	40	39	41	42	42	2.4	0.0	−1.3
SIC 14	83	76	76	78	80	81	81	1.3	0.0	−0.4
Average hourly earnings ($)										
SIC 10	14.05	15.26	15.29	16.08	16.77	17.35	17.82	3.5	2.7	3.5
SIC 14	11.58	12.25	12.68	13.10	13.38	13.75	14.22	2.8	3.4	2.9
Trade data										
Value of exports										
SIC 10	1,137	1,084	799	1,018	1,562	1,091	1,251	−30.2	14.6	1.4
SIC 14	837	1,148	1,107	1,199	1,296	1,302	1,375	0.5	5.6	7.3
Value of imports										
SIC 10	1,500	1,167	1,108	1,283	1,413	1,407	1,407	−0.4	0.0	−0.9
SIC 14	882	734	767	839	894	1,035	1,619[1]	15.8	56.4	9.1

[1] The U.S. Geological Survey regards this 1997 value as overstated because it includes a large dollar value for polished diamonds. Normally, SIC 14 would include only the imported value of crude diamonds.
Source: U.S. Department of the Interior, U.S. Geological Survey (USGS); U.S. Department of Labor, Bureau of Labor Statistics (BLS); and U.S. Department of Commerce, Bureau of the Census. Value of mine production in 1992 dollars was estimated by the USGS using commodity-based producer price indexes (BLS codes 101, 102, 13).

The financial crisis in southeast Asia strongly affected the metal markets because that region is a major consumer of refined metals. In 1996 the major southeast Asian countries, including Japan and China, consumed 34 percent of the world's total refined copper, 30 percent of its aluminum, 25 percent of its lead, and 30 percent of its zinc.

In addition, southeast Asia is an important market for metal ores and concentrates. In 1995 Japan, the Philippines, and South Korea received a total of 31 percent of exports of U.S. copper ore and concentrates. In that year Japan and South Korea received 22 percent of U.S. exports of lead ore and concentrates and 21 percent of U.S. exports of zinc ores.

For the most part, southeast Asia is not a major consumer of U.S. mined industrial minerals, but there are exceptions. The United States is the world's second largest producer of boron compounds and exports about half of its production. In 1995, 17 percent of U.S. exports of sodium borates and 39 percent of U.S. exports of boric acid went to southeast Asia. The United States also exported 36 percent of its production of soda ash to that region in 1995.

Because the currencies of the southeast Asian countries have fallen dramatically against the U.S. dollar, many companies in that region cannot afford to import raw materials priced in dol-

lars which they need to stay in business. In the near term the outlook for the Pacific region is not encouraging. Economic trends calculated by several organizations, such as the Center for International Business Cycle Research in New York City, indicate that most of the Pacific region is experiencing a significant economic slowdown which could worsen in 1999.

Long-Term Issues and Regulation

The health of the U.S. mining industries is affected by long-term factors such as access to public lands, the regulatory environment, advances in mining technology, and the location, quality, and potential profitability of ore deposits. For nonfuel mining, the most important of these factors in recent years have been access to public lands for the exploration and development of mineral deposits and environmental regulation.

In the United States, access to federal lands for mining is determined by the 1872 Mining Law, which allows anyone to enter open public lands to explore for hard-rock minerals such as copper, gold, lead, silver, and zinc. That law also allows anyone filing a claim to extract minerals found on those lands. There are currently more than 330,000 active claims on federal lands operating under this law. However, legislation has been introduced in Congress over the years to change the 1872 Mining Law because of three major concerns: (1) Hard-rock mining companies pay no royalties to the federal government for mining minerals on public lands; (2) mining companies with approved claims can "patent" or buy land for $2.50 or $5.00 per acre, depending on the type of claim; and (3) mining on federal lands has caused environmental damage.

In 1997 several bills were proposed in Congress that would reform the 1872 Mining Law, but none were enacted. Among the proposed changes have been setting a royalty (e.g., 5 percent of net proceeds on the production of hard-rock minerals), establishing guidelines for mineral exploration and claim maintenance, repealing the percentage depletion for certain hard-rock mines, and charging a fee to reclaim abandoned hard-rock mines. Efforts to reform the mining law and restrict access to public lands probably will continue in the future.

Nonfuel mining and minerals processing are subject to environmental regulation at the federal and state levels. At the federal level, environmental impacts are regulated primarily by the Resource Conservation and Recovery Act (RCRA), which covers the treatment and disposal of hazardous and nonhazardous solid wastes; the Clean Water Act, which regulates discharges into surface waters; the Clean Air Act, which is designed to prevent and control air pollution; and the Comprehensive Environmental Response, Compensation, and Liability Act (CERCLA), which establishes a mechanism for cleaning up closed and abandoned hazardous waste sites.

In December 1997 at Kyoto, Japan, the United States agreed to an international treaty that would cut greenhouse emissions to a level 7 percent below the 1990 level in the period 2008–2012. At a minimum, enactment of this treaty will increase energy costs for mining and minerals processing companies, since the burning of fossil fuels is the major source of greenhouse gases. The United States is not obligated to begin reducing emissions until the protocol is approved by Congress, and this may not occur because some congressional members object to the fact that the proposed treaty does not require emissions reductions by developing nations. There is growing public support for reducing greenhouse emissions, however, and the United States probably will undertake some kind of effort to reduce them in the future.

Outlook

Nonfuel minerals are feedstock for U.S. construction and durable goods manufacturing (see Table 1-2), which are affected by the business cycle, the level of interest rates, and the health of the overall economy. The U.S. economy was in its eighty-first straight month of expansion at the end of 1997, and the consensus among most economists was that it would grow at a slower rate in 1998 than the 3.8 percent rate of 1997, with early forecasts ranging from 2.0 percent (Council of Economic Advisers) to 2.6 percent (National Association of Business Economists).

Early economic indicators did not show a significant change in growth in the first quarter of 1998, but most economists did not expect growth to slow until the middle or latter part of that year. In regard to metal mining, while physical production could increase, the value of production is likely to decline in

TABLE 1-2: U.S. Manufacturing Industries' Dependence on Minerals[1]

Industry	Percent of Inputs
Metal containers	61
Screw machine products and stampings	47
Heating, plumbing, and fabricated structural metal products	46
Other fabricated metal products	33
Miscellaneous machinery, except electrical	32
Engines and turbines	26
Electrical industrial equipment	25
Metalworking machinery and equipment	25
Electric lighting and wiring equipment	24
Materials-handling machinery and equipment	24
Truck and bus bodies, trailers, and motor vehicle parts	24
Special industry machinery and equipment	21
Farm, construction, and mining machinery	20
General industrial machinery and equipment	20
Service industry machines	20
Household appliances	19
Other transportation equipment	14
Miscellaneous manufacturing	13
Construction	13
Miscellaneous electrical machinery and supplies	13
Furniture and fixtures	10

[1] U.S. manufacturing industries for which raw and processed nonfuel minerals account for 10 percent or more of the total value of intermediate inputs. Intermediate inputs consist of the materials and services purchased by each industry from other industries to produce output.
Source: "Benchmark Input-Output Accounts for the U.S. Economy, 1992," *Survey of Current Business,* November 1997.

1998 and 1999 because of low prices caused by high levels of inventories of some metals worldwide and falling demand in southeast Asia for materials and capital goods.

Long-term U.S. interest rates were low at the end of 1997, hovering near 6.0 percent, and were expected to remain near that level through 1998. Low interest rates, moderate growth in the U.S. economy, and increased federal funding for highway construction should help increase construction activity and the demand for construction materials. That should result in increases in the physical production of industrial minerals and higher values of mine production in 1998 and 1999.

METALS MINING

Metals have faced strong competition from other materials. Their production value overall, either in constant 1992 or current dollars, decreased slightly in the United States in 1997 compared with that of 1990 (see Table 1-1). The total value of metal mine production in current dollars peaked in 1995, then declined in 1996 and 1997 because of lower prices. However, the current-dollar trend during the 1990s has been upward, indicating an average annual growth of about 1.7 percent. The value-of-output trend in constant dollars for all metals in the United States was nearly flat over this period, but is projected by Standard and Poor's DRI to grow 2 percent or less annually in the period 1996–2002. Although output growth has been weak, demand for metal commodities has kept pace with the U.S. economy. U.S. use of all metals is high compared with use in most other countries, but the total quantity of metal mine production in the United States is relatively low for many metal commodities, with some important exceptions. For example, the United States is nearly self-sufficient in the production of iron ore, with a net import reliance of only 14 percent in 1997. Other important commodities in which the United States produces the majority of its supply and has a low net import reliance are gold and molybdenum, of which it is a net exporter; zinc, 35 percent; silicon, 34 percent; lead, 14 percent; and copper, 12 percent. While the United States is completely dependent on imports of bauxite and alumina, it is the world's largest producer of aluminum metal. Total employment in U.S. metal mining was 54,000 in 1997, unchanged from the level in 1996.

In terms of the value of mine production, copper was the highest among the metals at $4.6 billion, followed by gold at $3.4 billion, iron ore at $1.7 billion, zinc at $1.1 billion, molybdenum at $0.46 billion, and lead at $0.43 billion. The value of raw steel production was about $26 billion, and primary aluminum produced at U.S. smelters was valued at $5.9 billion. Generally favorable economic conditions, particularly in automobile manufacturing and housing, created a relatively high demand for metals. The index of motor vehicle and parts manufacturing rose 4.4 percent from 1996 to 1997, and the index of industrial production for chemicals and chemical products rose 4.25 percent. Construction, another key indicator, was strong but leveling off. Housing starts rose only 0.5 percent compared with those in 1996 but were 19.6 percent above those in 1990. Demand for stainless steel strengthened in 1997 after weakening in 1996 following 2 consecutive years of growth in excess of 10 percent. Recycling of metals continued to be an important element in the domestic supply. The commodities in which recycling was most significant in terms of old or obsolete scrap metal as a percentage of apparent consumption were lead at 68 percent, steel at 49 percent, nickel at 32 percent, aluminum at 25 percent, chromium at 24 percent, copper at 15 percent, tin at 15 percent, and zinc at 11 percent; the balance consisted of primary metal. The value of metal exports ($1.25 billion) increased 14.6 percent from 1996 to 1997, while the value of imports was unchanged at $1.4 billion. Financial problems in Asia had little impact on U.S. metal markets through early 1998. However, Asian countries are significant consumers and producers of metal commodities, and the potential exists for a significant impact on metal commodity markets worldwide if Asian financial problems spread or become more severe. The early effects of the Asian financial crisis were evident in lower prices of steel scrap, of which several Asian countries are major importers.

Ferrous Metals

Besides iron, the ferrous metals include chromium, cobalt, columbium (niobium), manganese, molybdenum, nickel, silicon, tungsten, and vanadium. These metals are commonly alloyed with iron and therefore may follow trends in the steel industry or related industries and be referred to as ferroalloys. The United States is a major producer of iron ore for the steel

industry and provides 80 percent of the domestic consumption. From 1993 to 1997 the production of iron ore trended upward from 55.7 million metric tons (Mt) to an estimated 62 Mt, an annual growth rate of 2.2 percent (see Figure 1-1). The production, consumption, and trade of iron ore in 1997 were about the same as the levels in 1996. Steel shipments outpaced iron ore production in 1997, growing approximately 3.3 percent. The difference may be accounted for by a slightly increased share of the steel supply held by imports in 1997. Average annual growth of

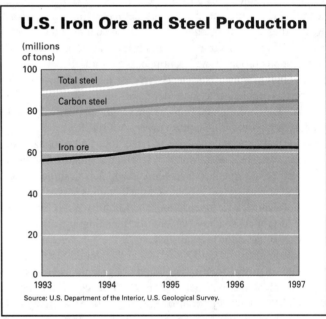

FIGURE 1-1

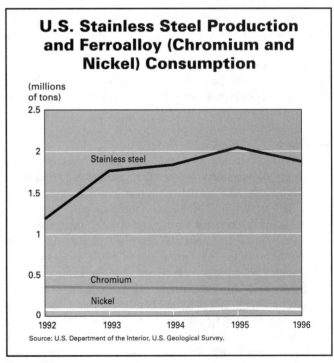

FIGURE 1-2

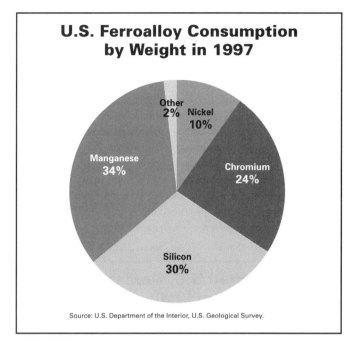

FIGURE 1-3

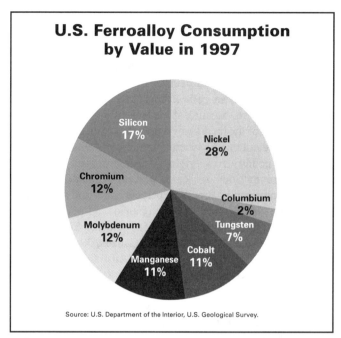

FIGURE 1-4

output in constant dollars for iron and ferroalloy ores has been projected by DRI at 2 percent over the period 1996–2002.

Because of concern about the availability of low-residue scrap, investment in alternative ironmaking technologies has become more attractive, particularly direct reduction of iron, and several projects are planned or under way. The ratio of steel production from basic oxygen furnaces, which use mostly primary ore products, to that from electric arc furnaces, using mostly scrap or direct reduced iron, was nearly unchanged over the period 1993–1996, holding at about 60:40. Strong demand and the large share of steel production continuing to be supplied by primary ore products was reflected in ore and steel product prices. Iron ore and steel prices rose about 23 and 8 percent, respectively. The iron and steel industry and ferrous foundries produced goods valued at about $35 billion. To maintain this strength, capital expenditures on blast furnaces and cold-rolling and galvanizing facilities by integrated steel makers totaled an estimated $2.1 billion in 1997, an increase of 24 percent over 1996.

Carbon steel has shown slower but steadier growth compared with specialty steel. While the trend has been upward for most ferroalloys, there have been some significant fluctuations in demand, notably in chromium, which is dependent on the specialty steel industry. This sector of the steel industry continued to account for only about 2 percent of raw steel production in 1996, the last year for which data are available. The specialty steel industry was a major consumer of chromium and nickel (see Figure 1-2). Stainless steel is subject to market conditions that may be different from those which apply to carbon steel.

The share of total ferroalloy consumption accounted for by the major types is shown in Figure 1-3. The markets for the bulk ferroalloys silicon and manganese are tied to the markets for carbon steel and show similar patterns of use. The share of U.S.

consumption held by each ferrous metal in terms of value is shown in Figure 1-4. In comparing the relative sizes of ferroalloy markets by weight and value, there is a much more even distribution of the commodities when they are compared by value.

There was a fairly high degree of net import reliance in the ferrous metals, with the exception of molybdenum and iron and steel scrap, for which the United States was a net exporter (see Figure 1-5). The United States had a 100 percent reliance on

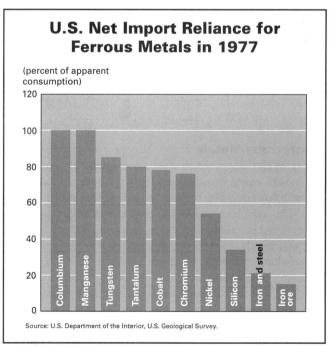

FIGURE 1-5

imports of manganese and columbium. The United States was partially dependent on imports for tungsten at 85 percent, tantalum at 80 percent, cobalt at 78 percent, chromium at 76 percent, vanadium at an estimated 60 percent, nickel at 54 percent, silicon at 34 percent, iron and steel at 21 percent, and iron ore at 15 percent. For all these commodities except silicon, iron and steel, and iron ore, because of the lack of domestic mine production, most of the balance of supply was from domestic scrap material. The commodities with high import reliance and their significant countries of origin (4-year average, 1993–1996) were chromium (South Africa, 37 percent), cobalt (Norway, 21 percent), columbium (Brazil, 66 percent), iron and steel (European Union, 30 percent), iron ore (Canada, 54 percent), manganese (Gabon, manganese ore, 58 percent; South Africa, ferromanganese, 38 percent), nickel (Canada, 39 percent), silicon (Norway, 24 percent), tantalum (Australia, 28 percent), tungsten (China, 35 percent), and vanadium (Russia, ferrovanadium, 36 percent; South Africa, vanadium pentoxide, 79 percent). Russia was determined by the International Trade Commission to have dumped ferrovanadium in the U.S. market in 1995–1996, and duties were levied. Since that time imports of ferrovanadium from Russia have virtually ceased.

Although raw steel production trended upward in the United States, prices decreased to lower levels for manganese ore and the principal manganese ferroalloys. Prices for silicon materials in the U.S. market declined through at least the first three quarters of 1997, especially for 75 percent–grade ferrosilicon. The domestic industry was operating in an environment whose uncertainties included the outcomes of lawsuits and trade actions. Chromium markets strengthened in 1997, and stainless steel production was expected to increase. This resulted in similar growth in ferrochromium demand. The world nickel supply began to exceed demand in mid-1997, causing the price on the London Metal Exchange to fall below $2.99 per pound, the lowest price since 1994. Recently discovered nickel reserves at Voisey's Bay, Canada, were scheduled to begin producing in 2002, and concentrates were to be smelted in Argentia, Newfoundland. When brought into production, the Argentia complex would be the largest nickel smelting and refining complex outside Russia. Unfortunately, low prices for nickel forced postponement of these plans in mid-1998.

Nonferrous Metals

The term nonferrous metals covers more than four dozen metals that are mined in quantities that range from several million tons to a few kilograms per year and that have extremely diverse uses. The most economically important nonferrous metals are the base metals (aluminum, copper, lead, tin, and zinc) and the precious metals (gold, silver, and the six platinum-group metals—iridium, osmium, palladium, platinum, rhodium, and ruthenium). The base metals are important because they are produced and used in large tonnages, and the precious metals because they have high unit values. The United States uses large quantities of all these economically important nonferrous metals and produces large quantities of most of them. In terms of the dollar value of production or consumption, all these metals

rank among the top 22 of the 90 or so mineral commodities used in the domestic economy (see Figure 1-6). Average annual growth of output in constant dollars for miscellaneous nonferrous ores has been projected by DRI at 1.2 percent over the period 1996–2002.

The United States is the world's largest producer and user of aluminum (see Table 1-3). In addition to the substantial imports of aluminum metal, this country is completely dependent on foreign sources for the aluminum ore (metallurgical bauxite) needed for its smelters. It also imports large quantities of the intermediate product alumina, of which more than 90 percent is smelted to the metal; the balance of this alumina, along with some of the domestically produced alumina, is used in refractories, abrasives, and several other applications. Domestic pri-

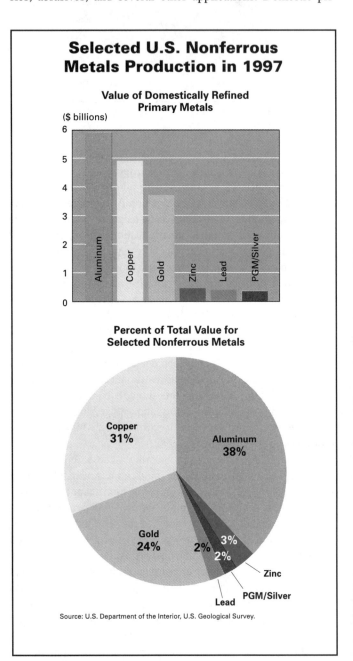

FIGURE 1-6

TABLE 1-3: Percent of Total Quantity of World Refined Consumption of Selected Nonferrous Metals in 1996

	Aluminum	Copper	Lead	Zinc Slab
Southeast Asia				
China	9.8	9.3	8.1	11.7
Hong Kong	0.7	0.3		0.1
Indonesia	0.7	0.8	1.5	1.1
Japan	11.9	11.9	5.7	8.8
Malaysia	0.7	1.2	1.3	0.4
Philippines	0.1	0.3	0.5	0.6
South Korea	3.4	4.7	4.0	4.2
Taiwan	1.6	4.4	2.2	2.3
Thailand	1.1	1.2	1.4	1.3
Total	30.0	34.2	24.7	30.4
United States	25.5	21.0	28.4	14.4
Western Europe	24.4	27.8	27.3	33.6

Source: World Bureau of Metal Statistics; U.S. Department of the Interior, U.S. Geological Survey.

mary aluminum production was 3.7 Mt in 1993, it dipped to 3.3 Mt in 1994 at the peak of imports of metal from the former Soviet Union, and then it rebuilt to 3.6 Mt in 1997. Secondary production from old scrap, which in aluminum has been important for many years, constituted a third of domestic metal production in 1997. U.S. apparent consumption of aluminum amounted to about 6.9 Mt in 1997.

The United States is the second largest mine producer and the largest consumer of copper, a metal that competes with aluminum in several electrical, thermal transfer, and structural applications. Mine production grew slowly but steadily from 1.8 Mt in 1993 to an estimated 1.94 Mt in 1997, while consumption rose more rapidly from 2.5 Mt in 1993 to more than 2.8 Mt in 1997. The output of copper mines in constant dollars has been projected by DRI to grow 1.6 percent per year between 1996 and 2002.

The United States is the second largest producer and the largest consumer of lead. Lead is the preeminent metal in batteries for automotive starting, lighting, ignition systems, and industrial backup power systems. Domestic lead mine production grew substantially from 362,000 tons in 1993 to 448,000 tons in 1997, and lead consumption kept pace, growing from 1.34 Mt in 1993 to 1.66 Mt in 1997. Lead is an extensively recycled metal. In the United States, lead from postconsumer scrap provides more than two-thirds of the metal consumed.

The United States is the fifth largest mine producer of zinc and by far the largest consumer. Because of limited refinery capacity, it imports more than two-thirds of its refined metal requirement. Conversely, the United States exports large quantities of zinc in concentrate to foreign smelters. Mine production grew substantially from 488,000 tons of recoverable zinc in 1993 to 605,000 tons in 1997. Consumption grew at a lesser pace, increasing from 1.34 Mt in 1993 to an estimated 1.5 Mt in 1997. Although zinc is an important constituent of brass, bronze, and die casting alloys and has a variety of other uses, more than half the metal consumed domestically is used as a protective coating on galvanized steel.

Since 1992 the United States has been the second largest mine producer of gold after South Africa. Mine production of gold in the United States increased dramatically in the 1970s and 1980s and in 1993 reached 331 tons per year. In 1997 gold production was an estimated 358 tons, but with the bullion price slipping dramatically late in that year, it appeared unlikely that the high level would be sustained in 1998. The United States is the third largest fabricator of gold after India and Italy; as is the case elsewhere in the world, the largest end use by far is for jewelry. Except for a 9 percent dip in 1994, annual domestic mine production of silver has remained nearly flat at about 1,600 tons, the level estimated for 1997. Domestic fabrication demand, more than half of which is attributed to photographic uses, is estimated to be in the vicinity of 4,300 tons. Like lead, silver is recycled extensively. The sole domestic mine for platinum-group metals (PGM), which yields palladium and platinum in a 3.3:1 ratio along with minor quantities of rhodium, increased its production substantially, from 8.8 tons in 1993 to 10.8 tons in 1997. The use of PGM in jewelry is almost negligible in the United States, in contrast to some other countries. The six metals in the group have many technological uses; their use as catalysts, especially automotive emissions control catalysts, is the most important quantitatively.

U.S. net import reliance (NIR), expressed as a percentage of consumption, ranges widely among the nonferrous metals (see Figure 1-7). About 75 percent of aluminum is imported, principally as bauxite, alumina, and aluminum metal and its alloys. Other NIR figures are copper, 12 percent; lead, 14 percent; pal-

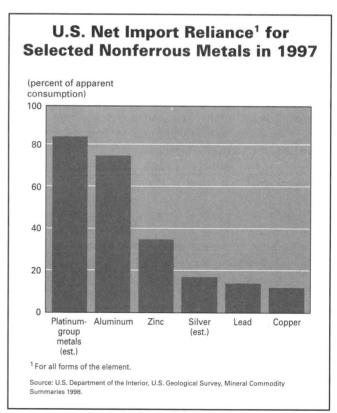

U.S. Net Import Reliance[1] for Selected Nonferrous Metals in 1997

(percent of apparent consumption)

[1] For all forms of the element.

Source: U.S. Department of the Interior, U.S. Geological Survey, Mineral Commodity Summaries 1998.

FIGURE 1-7

ladium, 78 percent (estimated); platinum, 84 percent (estimated); silver, 17 percent; and zinc, 35 percent. The United States is a net exporter of gold.

The annual average price per pound for aluminum ingot in the United States increased about 6 cents in 1997, to 77 cents. The price for copper cathode remained essentially static at $1.07, and the price of lead dropped about 2 cents to 47 cents per pound. The price of zinc, reflecting a shortfall in the world supply that began in 1996 and lasted through the first 8 months of 1997, rose almost 30 cents to 79 cents per pound in August. The average price of zinc in 1997 was 65 cents. The average price per troy ounce for gold and silver fell in 1997 by 14 percent and 6 percent, respectively. The price for platinum remained unchanged, and increasing demand for palladium for automotive emissions control catalysts drove price up 41 percent. At year end the price of gold was still falling, averaging about $290 in December, while silver was rallying strongly. The platinum price was a few percent lower, and palladium was still moving upward, reaching $203 in December.

METAL INDUSTRY SUBSECTORS

Aluminum

Domestic Production and Use. The domestic supply of aluminum includes three major components: primary ingot production, secondary (scrap) recovery, and trade. In 1997, 3.6 Mt of primary aluminum metal was produced by 13 companies operating 22 primary aluminum smelters in 13 states. Montana, Oregon, and Washington accounted for 40 percent of the production, and Kentucky, North Carolina, South Carolina, and Tennessee accounted for 20 percent; the remaining states produced 40 percent. Based on published market prices, the value of primary metal production was $6.1 billion. The secondary metal sector, which includes both postconsumer scrap and prompt industrial scrap, has maintained steady growth in its share of the domestic supply and now accounts for more than 35 percent of the domestic aluminum supply.

Imports for consumption increased in 1997, reversing a downward trend that began in 1995. Canada is the dominant U.S. trading partner for aluminum imports and exports, accounting for about 70 percent of U.S. imports of ingot and between 55 and 60 percent of both imported mill products and scrap. Although Russia remained second only to Canada as a major shipper of aluminum materials to the United States, the level of Russian shipments has declined over recent years from the record high level reached in 1994 and appears to have stabilized at about 400,000 tons per year. Canada receives about 40 percent of U.S. ingot exports, and Japan takes an additional 30 percent.

The transportation sector continued to be the dominant market for aluminum in the United States, surpassing the packaging industry, which dominated the market before 1995. Transportation uses for aluminum accounted for more than one-third of domestic consumption, with packaging accounting for approximately another 25 percent. Building and construction, electri-cal equipment, consumer durables, machinery and equipment, and other uses accounted for the remainder.

Recent Events, Trends, and Issues. The 1997 Defense Authorization Act authorized the Defense Logistics Agency to sell the entire inventory of 57,000 tons of aluminum metal from the National Defense Stockpile. Sales began on April 15, 1997, and by the end of October virtually the entire inventory had been sold.

Domestic primary aluminum production remained relatively stable in 1997. Domestic smelters continued to operate at about 85 percent of engineered or rated capacity. World production, however, increased as producers continued to bring back on-stream the primary capacity that had been temporarily idled and to start up new capacity expansions.

World demand for aluminum continued to grow, led by increases in the United States and western Europe. Demand grew despite the economic slowdown in Asia, which began during the latter months of 1997. The United States and western Europe remain the major markets for primary aluminum, with each accounting for about one-fourth of world consumption.

Copper

Domestic Production and Uses. Copper mine production has generally trended upward since 1983. Copper mine production in 1997 totaled 1.94 Mt, an increase of 20,000 tons from that in 1996. The five principal mining states in descending order—Arizona, Utah, New Mexico, Nevada, and Montana—accounted for 98 percent of domestic production; copper also was recovered at mines in six other states. Although copper was recovered at about 35 U.S. mines, 15 of those accounted for about 97 percent of the production. Mine production was processed through to refined copper at seven primary and four secondary smelters, seven electrolytic and six fire refineries, and 15 electrowinning operations. Approximately 35 brass mills, 15 wire-rod mills, and 600 foundries, chemical plants, and miscellaneous plants consumed refined copper and/or copper base scrap. Consumption of refined copper in 1997 rose about 6 percent to a record high of 2.77 Mt. The principal markets for copper and copper alloy products were building construction (43 percent), electric and electronic products (24 percent), industrial machinery and equipment (12 percent), transportation equipment (12 percent), and consumer and general products (9 percent). U.S. net imports of refined copper, principally from Canada, Chile, and Mexico, amounted to about 550,000 tons, or adjusting for stock increases, 14 percent of the domestic demand for refined copper.

Recent Events, Trends, and Issues. World mine production of copper rose significantly for the third consecutive year, increasing about 3 percent in 1997. Most of the increase in production came from Chile, where an estimated 300,000 tons of new capacity came on stream. Most U.S. mining companies continued to expand their investment in South American copper production. The United States maintained its position as the second largest mine producer of copper and the world's largest smelter, refiner, and consumer of that metal. U.S. mine production and capacity were essentially unchanged. There was increased production from a major new mine in Nevada which began production in 1996 and from a new solvent extraction–electrowinning (SX-EW) operation in Arizona. However, it was offset by the closing of two smaller mines in Arizona in 1996 and the depletion of ore at a third mine in Wisconsin in 1997. Production also declined at several SX-EW operations where mining of leach ore was curtailed and production was limited to existing heaps. Although domestic production of refined copper rose more than 4 percent in 1997, it remained well below capacity owing to a shortage of anode copper during the first half of the year. The smelter in Utah, which had been plagued by problems since its commissioning in 1995, was closed for 6 weeks in the first half of 1997 for replacement of anode casting equipment, but by year end it was operating above design capacity. The increased consumption of refined copper was driven by strong demand for wire mill products. Despite its expansion of capacity in 1996, at least one major wire rod producer reported operating above design capacity in 1997. Copper recovery from both old and new scrap rose during that year despite the indefinite closing of a secondary smelter in Pennsylvania. Copper supply remained tight in the first 6 months of the year, and prices trended upward, with the U.S. producer price averaging almost $1.16 per pound. In July 1997, domestic and global inventories began to rise and prices declined. By year end, domestic refined inventories were more than double those at the end of 1996 and the U.S. producer price had fallen to a low of $0.80 per pound. In constant dollar terms, these were the lowest prices since the depth of the depression in 1932–1933. The long-projected potential for an oversupply of copper resulting from rapid expansion of global capacity, particularly in Chile, was compounded by the economic crisis in Asia, where forecasts of demand growth did not materialize. With most analysts projecting a continued buildup of inventories and low prices, both domestic and foreign producers began to announce the curtailment of some of their higher-cost production early in 1998 and delays in start-ups of new projects. It was projected that domestic mine production in 1998 would decline by about 100,000 tons.

Gold

Domestic Production and Use. In 1997 the United States was the second largest producer of gold after South Africa with more than 358 metric tons of production. Gold is produced by more than 200 mines, mostly in the western states and Alaska. Thirty lode mines were responsible for more than 90 percent of the gold produced domestically in 1997. Mines in Nevada and California continued to dominate U.S. gold production. The value of 1997 U.S. gold production stood at about $3.9 billion. The most important use of gold in the United States is for jewelry. Canada supplies the overwhelming majority of American gold imports. Palladium, platinum, and silver are leading substitutes for gold in jewelry and a few other uses.

Recent Events, Trends, and Issues. As did many mineral commodity producers, U.S. gold-mining companies sought opportunities abroad. Much of the foreign investment took place in Latin American countries with their promising geo-

logic terranes and liberalized regulations on foreign direct investment. Additional gold-related foreign direct investment took place in Australia as well as parts of Africa, the Pacific and southeast Asia, and Canada.

Although the average price of gold has remained stable in recent years, there was a deterioration in price toward the end of 1996 that continued through 1997. Gold prices dipped in December 1997 to their lowest level in 18 years. The fear of significant central bank selling to reduce gold reserves dominated market sentiment. In early January 1997 the Dutch central bank confirmed that it sold more than 20 percent of its gold reserves in 1996. Gold-mining shares remained at approximately the same level because investors viewed this sell-off as an exercise in the recalibration of reserves. In July 1997 the Australian central bank surprised the world with an announcement that it had sold more than 60 percent of its gold reserves. Subsequently, gold-mining shares fell more than 4 percent because investors saw no specific need for Australia to sell gold. In October 1997 the Swiss central bank was considering selling off gold reserves sometime in the next century, and gold-mining shares continued to fall. This sell-off reportedly was sparked by the news of a plan proposed by a Swiss-commissioned panel of financial experts to mobilize 54 percent of Switzerland's gold resources.

Iron Ore

Domestic Production and Use. The value of usable ore shipped from mines in Minnesota, Michigan, and six other states in 1997 was estimated at $1.9 billion. Iron ore was produced by 14 mines which had 10 concentration plants and 10 pelletizing plants. These mines included 13 open pits and 1 underground operation. Virtually all the ore was concentrated before shipment. Nine mines managed by five companies accounted for 99.5 percent of production. Estimated production of iron ore in 1997 was 63.0 Mt; consumption was 79.5 Mt.

Recent Events, Trends, and Issues. Virtually all iron ore is consumed by the steel industry. The domestic iron ore industry provides about 80 percent of the ore used in the United States. Nearly all domestic iron ore reserves are low grade and require extensive processing. The U.S. iron ore industry is able to compete with foreign producers largely because of its proximity to the domestic steel industry. Nearly all domestic iron ore production capacity and most of the integrated steel industry are located near the Great Lakes, which offer low-cost transportation. Most, if not all, east and Gulf coast integrated steelmakers are supplied by foreign producers. Virtually all exports consisted of pellets shipped via the Great Lakes to Canadian steel companies that are partners in U.S. taconite projects in Michigan and Minnesota.

The U.S. steel industry is undergoing a structural change that has the potential to affect the domestic iron ore industry. It can be viewed as having two primary parts: the integrated steelmakers, which use iron ore as feedstock, and the minimills, which use iron and steel scrap as feed. The minimills' share of the steel market has increased steadily, rising from

15 percent in 1970 to more than 43 percent in 1997. This trend is expected to continue and will affect the iron ore industry negatively if the steel sector uses less iron ore. The trend will have a positive effect on any iron ore producer that also produces direct reduced iron, which is used in minimills as an alternative to scrap.

Lead

Domestic Production and Use. Based on the net quantity of lead recovered in the smelting of concentrate, mine production increased about 5.1 percent in 1997 to 448,000 tons. Lead was produced at 16 mines in Alaska, Colorado, Idaho, Missouri, Montana, New York, and Tennessee, among which 9 mines in Alaska and Missouri accounted for about 92 percent of production. The value of the recovered lead was about $460 million, calculated on the basis of an average North American producer price of $0.4654 per pound. Lead concentrate was processed at two smelter-refineries in Missouri and a smelter in Montana. Primary refinery production increased 5.1 percent in 1997 as refineries began to adjust to the permanent closing of one refinery in mid-1996.

Lead was consumed principally in the transportation industries, where about 70 percent was used in automotive-type starting-lighting-ignition (SLI) storage batteries, bearings, fuel tanks, seals, and solder. The use of lead in communications, electrical, and electronic applications, including industrial-type lead-acid storage batteries, and its use in ammunition, construction, protective coatings, radiation shielding, and television glass accounted for approximately 23 percent of consumption. The balance was consumed in ballast and weights, ceramics and crystal glass, tubes, containers, foil, and wire. The demand for lead in all forms of lead-acid storage batteries, SLI-type and industrial-type, represented about 87 percent of consumption in 1997. SLI-type batteries include those used for automobiles, buses, marine craft, motorcycles, tractors, and trucks. Industrial-type batteries include those used in telecommunications and mainframe computer networks, load-leveling equipment for commercial electrical power systems, and uninterruptible power supply equipment for hospitals. Traction batteries, such as those used in airline ground equipment, industrial forklifts, mining equipment, and personalized medical assistance vehicles, represent another type of industrial battery.

Recent Events, Trends, and Issues. Exploration and development activities were conducted in 1997 at two lead-producing mines in Alaska and one in Idaho. Efforts were continued to reopen two mines: one in Washington and one in Utah. If these activities and reopenings proceed as currently planned, it is estimated that by 2000 an additional 90,000 tons of lead could be produced each year from these operations.

In 1997 the price of lead decreased in the U.S. and world markets. The average North American Producer and London Metal Exchange prices declined about 5 percent and 19 percent, respectively, compared with the average prices in 1996. Average stock levels in the industrialized countries increased marginally in 1997, and a modest surplus of supply over

demand in the industrialized countries was anticipated for 1998. Although the growing U.S. economy provided the basis for continued strong demand for lead in 1997, that demand was tempered by the general absence of significant weather extremes nationwide. Significant temperature extremes tend to shorten the life of automotive-type batteries, increasing the demand for replacement batteries. The replacement battery end-use sector represented about 60 percent of the 1997 U.S. demand for lead.

Molybdenum

Domestic Production and Use. In 1997, 11 U.S. mines produced molybdenum with a value of approximately $406 million. Major end-use applications for molybdenum include machinery, 35 percent; electrical products, 15 percent; transportation, 15 percent; chemicals, 10 percent; and the oil and gas industry, 10 percent. The U.S. ratio of exports to imports was about 3:1. Potential substitutes for molybdenum include chromium, vanadium, columbium, and boron in alloy steels; tungsten in tool steels; and graphite, tungsten, and tantalum for refractory materials in high-temperature electric furnaces.

Recent Events, Trends, and Issues. In 1997 molybdenum mine production increased 11 percent and reported consumption was about the same as in 1996. This change contrasts with 1996, when mine production of molybdenum decreased about 10 percent while reported consumption increased about 2 percent. Exports and imports in 1997 were about the same as in 1996. The United States produces about 44 percent of the world's mined molybdenum.

Zinc

Domestic Production and Use. In 1997 the production of zinc in concentrate was about 630,000 tons, of which 95 percent came from four states: Alaska, Missouri, New York, and Tennessee. More than half the zinc in concentrate originated in Alaska. The production of zinc metal was 367,000 tons valued at about $520 million. Zinc metal was produced by 3 primary smelters and 10 secondary smelters. After a small decline in 1996, apparent consumption of zinc metal reached 1.2 Mt in 1997. About 75 percent of the zinc output was used in Illinois, Indiana, Michigan, New York, Ohio, and Pennsylvania. Of the total zinc consumed, about 54 percent was used in galvanizing, 19 percent in zinc-base alloys, 13 percent in brass and bronze, and 14 percent in other uses. Zinc compounds and dust were used mainly by the agriculture, chemical, paint, and rubber industries. Major coproducts of zinc mining and smelting, in decreasing order, were lead, sulfur, cadmium, silver, gold, and germanium. Major competitors for zinc include aluminum, cadmium, magnesium, plastics, and steel.

Recent Events, Trends, and Issues. The small decline in ore production in 1996 should be reversed in 1998 and 1999 as a result of an expected increase in production at Cominco's Red Dog Mine in Alaska. However, this increase in concentrate production will have only a negligible short-term effect on metal production because all three primary smelters are producing at or near capacity. Only Korea Zinc Co. Ltd. is planning to gradually expand production at its Sauget, IL, smelter from the current 88,000 to 120,000 tons per year. In the meantime, inadequate domestic metal production will have to be augmented with foreign imports of zinc metal. Because of their geographic proximity and low tariffs, most of the imports come from Canada and Mexico. As a result of strict environmental protection laws, a larger share of the zinc in use is being recycled. Currently, about 30 percent of consumption is met by secondary production.

INDUSTRIAL MINERALS

The production and use of industrial minerals showed important growth in the 1990s, generally following the trend of the domestic economy. In 1996 and 1997, in both current and constant dollar terms, the value of industrial minerals production grew at a slightly lower rate than did the economy as a whole. Owing to the low unit value of most industrial minerals, production for the most part comes from domestic resources. Most industrial minerals are produced for their physical or chemical properties and require little processing other than sizing or separation from other minerals before their end use. Several are produced from brines, which are concentrated by solar evaporation or chemically processed into end-use products. Many industrial minerals are building blocks for end-use manufactured products.

In terms of the value of mine production, crushed stone was the largest commodity at $7.7 billion in 1997, followed by construction sand and gravel at $4.3 billion. These two commodities were also the largest in terms of volume at 1,390 and 961 Mt, respectively. Cement at $6 billion was used to make portland cement concrete that had an ex-plant value of about $26 billion. Chemical minerals of important value to the economy were lime ($1.13 billion), phosphate rock ($1.1 billion), salt, ($0.96 billion), soda ash ($0.822 billion), boron ($0.5 billion), and sulfur ($0.45 billion). Titanium dioxide pigment was valued at about $2.76 billion. By-product production of industrial minerals from nonmining sources is significant for sulfur and sodium sulfate and has significant potential for flue-gas desulfurization gypsum. Very few industrial minerals are recycled; refractory brick, construction and demolition concrete, and road asphalt are exceptions.

The value of trade in industrial minerals has shown considerable growth in value during the 1990s. The value of exports increased about $500 million from 1990 to 1996, and the value of imports increased about $200 million. U.S. import reliance, expressed as a percentage of domestic consumption, varies widely among industrial minerals. The United States is totally dependent on foreign sources for fluorspar, graphite, sheet mica, and strontium minerals and more than 50 percent dependent for barite, dimension stone, gemstones, iodine, peat, and potash. Although the United States is among the top three producers in the world, it has some import dependence for cement, gypsum, lime, salt, and sulfur. The United States is an important exporter of soda ash, talc, and titanium dioxide. Industrial minerals have contributed positively to U.S. exports; chemicals, compounds, and finished products are based solely or partly on domestically produced materials.

INDUSTRIAL MINERALS INDUSTRY SUBSECTORS

Aggregates

Domestic Production and Use. Preliminary estimates indicate that 2.36 billion metric tons of aggregates were produced in 1997 in the United States. Of this total, nearly 1.4 billion tons consisted of crushed stone produced by 1,500 companies at 3,645 quarries, and 961 Mt consisted of construction sand and gravel produced by 3,838 companies at 5,562 operations. U.S. production of aggregates has increased steadily since 1991 in response to continued high-level activity in the commercial, public, and private sectors of the construction industry. Production for consumption of both mineral commodities in 1997 represented the highest U.S. production levels ever recorded.

Fifty-one percent of the crushed stone produced in 1997 came from 10 states, listed in descending order of volume: Pennsylvania, Texas, Florida, Missouri, Illinois, Ohio, Georgia, Virginia, Kentucky, and North Carolina. For sand and gravel, the leading states in order of volume were California, Michigan, Texas, Ohio, Minnesota, Arizona, Washington, Illinois, Wisconsin, and Colorado, which together accounted for about 52 percent of total U.S. output. Aggregates are used mainly for construction purposes in portland cement concretes, asphalt concretes, and road base materials. A small percentage of crushed stone is used for chemical and metallurgical processes, including cement and lime manufacture; in agricultural uses; and in environmental applications such as soil erosion control, water purification, and the reduction of sulfur dioxide emissions generated mostly by electric power plants. The widespread distribution of domestic deposits of aggregates and the high cost of transportation have combined to limit foreign trade to mostly local transactions across international borders. U.S. imports and exports of aggregates are small, representing less than 1 percent of domestic consumption.

Outlook. The demand for aggregates is expected to continue to grow on the basis of the volume of work on the infrastructure that will be financed by the new Surface Transportation Efficiency Act and as a result of the health of the U.S. economy in general. The projected increases will be influenced by construction activity in the public as well as the private construction sectors. The demand for crushed stone in 1998 was expected to be about 1,450 Mt, a 3.6 percent increase over 1997. The demand for construction sand and gravel in 1998 was expected to be 975 Mt, a 2 percent increase over 1997. Gradual increases in the demand for aggregates are anticipated after 1998 as well. The free on board (FOB) mine prices for aggregates are not expected to increase significantly in the near future. The delivered prices, however, are expected to increase, especially in and near metropolitan areas, mainly because more aggregates will be transported from distant sources.

Gypsum and By-product Gypsum

Domestic Production and Use. In 1997 U.S. output of mined gypsum reached a record high of 18.4 Mt valued at $130 million. The leading producer states were Oklahoma, Texas, Iowa, Michigan, Nevada, California, and Indiana, which together accounted for about 75 percent of the total output. Overall, 30 companies produced gypsum at 61 mines in 20 states and 10 companies calcined gypsum at 67 plants in 28 states. More than two-thirds of domestic consumption, which was estimated to be more than 26 Mt, was accounted for by manufacturers of wallboard and plaster products. About 5 Mt for cement production, 2 Mt for agricultural applications, and small amounts of high-purity gypsum for a wide range of industrial processes, such as smelting and glassmaking, accounted for the remaining consumption. About one-third of U.S. consumption was supplied by imports, almost all from Canada and Mexico.

By-product gypsum is generated by various industrial processes and by flue-gas desulfurization (FGD) operations at coal-burning power plants. Some by-product gypsum is used for wallboard manufacturing, agriculture, roadbase, and fill material. Industrial plants in at least 11 states sold an estimated 2.5 Mt of by-product gypsum in 1997, principally for agricultural uses. Also, approximately 60 domestic coal-fired power plants generated at least 24 Mt of FGD product in 1997. Although less than 10 percent of this material is used as a substitute for mined gypsum, primarily for wallboard manufacturing (900,000 tons in 1997), consumption has been increasing in recent years.

Recent Events, Trends, and Issues. Forecasts indicate that overall gypsum demand in North American markets will rise about 2 percent annually in the next several years. This demand will be driven primarily by the construction industry, particularly in the United States, where more than 90 percent of the gypsum consumed is used for wallboard products (whose use reached a record high in 1997), building plasters, and the manufacture of portland cement. Several large wallboard plants under construction are designed to use only FGD gypsum generated at coal-fired electric utilities by processes that reduce sulfur emissions. When operational, these plants will significantly accelerate the use of by-product gypsum from industrial processes as an alternative to mined gypsum.

Lithium

Cyprus Foote Mineral Co. and FMC Corp.'s Lithium Division have long been the principal producers of lithium compounds worldwide. In 1997 these companies maintained their dominance as leading producers, but the center of lithium carbonate production shifted from the United States to South America. The shift to South American production began in 1984, when Cyprus Foote opened the Sociedad Chilena de Litio Ltda.

(SCL) lithium carbonate plant in Antofagasta, Chile, where it recovers lithium carbonate from brines, which are concentrated at the Salar de Atacama in the Chilean Andes.

Sociedad Minera Salar de Atacama S.A. (Minsal), a subsidiary of the Chilean fertilizer producer Sociedad Quimica y Minera de Chile, began production at a second operation on the salar late in 1996 and was ramping up to full capacity throughout 1997. Combined lithium carbonate capacity at the plants in Chile is about 32,000 tons per year.

FMC was building a lithium carbonate plant in Argentina at the Salar de Hombre Muerto. Production began in late 1997, although technical problems had delayed initial production for about a year. After the completion of the Argentine project, FMC was planning to close its North Carolina spodumene mine and lithium carbonate plant, using the products from the new plant to meet its sales requirements and as the starting material for its downstream lithium products.

Lithium brines have become the primary lithium chemical resource because it is much less costly to produce lithium carbonate from brines than it is from spodumene or other lithium ores. Lithium ores must be heated to very high temperatures during lithium carbonate production, making the process energy- and capital-intensive. Lithium brines are concentrated through solar evaporation, and no cost is incurred for the energy required. Because brines are concentrated at solar ponds, these operations are established in desert areas. Lithium carbonate is produced at brine operations because it is the starting material for all other lithium compounds. Lithium has received a lot of interest in recent years because of its use in batteries. Although more lithium is consumed in other end uses, such as ceramics and glass, primary aluminum production, production of synthetic rubbers and pharmaceuticals, and multipurpose greases, batteries represent a tremendous potential for growth. Consumption of lithium in batteries has grown significantly in the past 10 years, and research continues in an attempt to develop and improve lithium batteries of many different sizes and types. The most noteworthy application for rechargeable lithium batteries is expected to be in electrical vehicles (EVs). Currently, one major automobile manufacturer is offering an EV powered by a lithium ion battery. Other automakers are using other types of batteries, but many people believe that as advances are made in EVs and their power systems, lithium ion will become the preferred battery material.

Phosphate

In 1997 phosphate rock ore was mined by 10 companies in four states and was upgraded into 45.1 Mt of marketable product, slightly below the 1996 output. Mines in Florida and North Carolina accounted for 83 percent of domestic production; the remainder was produced in Idaho and Utah. Approximately 90 percent of domestic demand was for conversion into wet-process phosphoric acid and superphosphoric acid, which were used as intermediates in the manufacture of granulated and liquid fertilizers. The remaining 10 percent was used in industrial applications. The production of phosphoric acid in 1997 was about the same as that in 1996. More than 50 percent of U.S.

phosphoric acid production was consumed in the form of fertilizer materials and merchant-grade phosphoric acid for export. The United States accounted for 43 percent of estimated concentrated phosphate production worldwide. U.S. exports of phosphate rock decreased significantly in 1997 as producers switched their emphasis to exporting higher-value phosphoric acid and fertilizer materials. Imports of marketable phosphate rock were estimated at 1.8 Mt, primarily from Morocco.

Consolidation of the domestic phosphate industry continued in 1997. IMC Global merged with Freeport McMoRan, Inc., leaving IMC Global as the surviving entity. As a result, IMC Global became the controlling partner of IMC-Agrico (IMCA), the largest domestic producer of phosphate rock and fertilizers. In 1997 IMCA temporarily closed two of its seven mines in response to market conditions. The company also exchanged reserves with another company to prolong the life of one of its mines.

Agrium Inc. acquired the Rasmussen Ridge Mine in Idaho from Rhône-Poulenc Basic Chemicals Co. Agrium had been purchasing phosphate rock ore from that mine since 1994 for use in the production of phosphoric acid and ammonium phosphate fertilizer. Monsanto Co. spun off its chemical products group to form a new company, Solutia, Inc., which operated a phosphate mine and elemental phosphorus plant in Idaho under a joint venture agreement with Monsanto. Mulberry Phosphates, Inc., received permission from Manatee County in Florida to reopen its Wingate Creek Mine and Piney Point phosphate plant, which had been idle for more than 5 years; both were expected to resume production late in 1998.

Domestic consumption of phosphate rock has been helped by the 1996 Freedom to Farm Act, which changed the method used to determine income support payments to farmers. This law allows farmers to plant unlimited acreage of any crop they prefer. Plantings of corn and soybeans, which use the most phosphate crop nutrients, have increased since the passage of this law. Attempts to increase corn yields and grain stocks were expected to increase domestic demand in 1998. International demand for crop nutrients has increased for 3 consecutive years (1995–1997), with the highest growth occurring in developing countries in Asia. U.S. producers should continue to play a major role as a supplier to that region.

Soda Ash

Soda ash is the trade name for sodium carbonate, a chemical refined from the mineral trona or naturally occurring sodium carbonate–bearing brines (natural soda ash) or manufactured from one of several chemical processes (synthetic soda ash). It is an essential raw material in glass, chemicals, detergents, and other important industrial products. In 1997 soda ash was the eleventh largest inorganic chemical in terms of the production of all domestic inorganic and organic chemicals, excluding petrochemical feedstocks. Although soda ash represented 2 percent of the total $39 billion U.S. nonfuel mineral industry, its use in many diversified products consequently contributed substantially to the gross domestic product of the United States. Because soda ash is used to make flat glass and fiberglass,

which are used by the domestic automotive and construction industries, monthly soda ash production statistics canvassed by the U.S. Geological Survey are used to develop monthly economic indicators for industrial production that measure the conditions of the U.S. economy.

Production. Total U.S. soda ash production in 1997 increased 5 percent, reaching a record high of 10.7 Mt. The domestic soda ash industry included five companies in Wyoming and one company in California. The names and annual nameplate capacities of the Wyoming producers are FMC Wyoming Corp., 3.22 Mt; General Chemical Corp., 2.18 Mt; OCI Chemical Corp., 2.09 Mt; Solvay Minerals Inc., 2.09 Mt; and Tg Soda Ash Inc., 1.18 Mt. North American Chemical Co.'s plant in California has an annual capacity of 1.31 Mt. In 1997 the industry produced 12.07 Mt, operating at 89 percent of total nameplate capacity. Each U.S. company is wholly or partially owned by foreign soda ash–producing companies or foreign soda ash consumers. These countries include Australia, Belgium, France, Japan, and the Republic of South Korea. U.S. ownership represented slightly more than half of total production capacity.

World soda ash production in 1997 was estimated at 32.1 Mt. Among the 29 countries that produce natural and synthetic soda ash, the United States is the world's largest producer, accounting for 33 percent of total output. Only the United States, Botswana, China, and Kenya produce soda ash from natural sources; other countries manufacture it through various chemical processes, primarily the Solvay process. Total world natural soda ash production represented about 35 percent of combined world soda ash production. The five leading nations that produce soda ash are the United States, China, Russia, India, and Germany, which together accounted for 69 percent of world production in 1997.

Consumption. Soda ash is a mature commodity that tends to grow in parallel with population and gross domestic product. U.S. reported consumption in 1997 was 6.48 Mt, a slight increase over 1996. The distribution of soda ash by end use was glass, 49 percent (containers 49 percent, flat 35 percent, fiber and specialty 8 percent each); chemicals (mainly sodium phosphates, sodium silicates, sodium bicarbonate, and sodium chromate), 26 percent; soaps and detergents, 12 percent; distributors, 5 percent; FGD, 3 percent; pulp and paper and miscellaneous uses, 2 percent each; and water treatment, 1 percent. Domestic soda ash consumption has been relatively flat for several years, with domestic markets growing only about 1 percent annually. The glass container sector, which is the single largest consuming market, has been declining since about 1980 because of competition from polyethylene terephthalate (PET) plastic beverage containers, which are lighter-weight and unbreakable. Glass container recycling also has adversely affected soda ash consumption in glass container manufacturing. In 1997 the domestic recycling rate for glass containers was about 36 percent. In certain uses, particularly in the pulp and paper, water treatment, and some chemical sectors, sodium hydroxide (also known as caustic soda) can be substituted for soda ash. The price and availability of both commodities usually determine which chemical is preferred by those sectors. Normally, about 300,000 tons of displacement can occur between both chemicals when the cycle shifts from one to the other. Caustic soda can be produced from soda ash and can substitute for the traditional electrolytic form of sodium hydroxide.

U.S. Trade. The export market is the major growth sector for U.S. soda ash. In 1997 exports amounted to 4.19 Mt and represented 39 percent of total U.S. soda ash production. In comparison, exports accounted for only 5 percent of U.S. production in 1970. Export sales have increased 75 percent since 1990, 322 percent since 1980, and 1,273 percent since 1970. With world soda ash demand estimated to grow about 2.5 to 3 percent annually, the United States will continue to be the main supplier to many foreign markets for the foreseeable future.

The percentage distribution of U.S. soda ash exports on a regional basis in 1997 was Asia, 47 percent; South America, 18 percent; North America, 17 percent; Europe, 7 percent; the Middle East, 4 percent; Africa and Oceania, 3 percent each; and Central America, 1 percent. The 10 leading nations for U.S. soda ash exports in 1997 were Mexico (11 percent), Japan (10 percent), Indonesia (9 percent), the Republic of Korea (7 percent), Thailand (7 percent), Canada (6 percent), Taiwan (5 percent), Brazil (5 percent), Chile (4 percent), and Malaysia (3 percent); together they accounted for 67 percent of total U.S. exports.

The economic downturn in Asia late in 1997 did not affect year-end exports to that region; however, it has been estimated that shipments to Asia in 1998 will be approximately 300,000 tons less than they were in 1997. On the positive side, the U.S. soda ash export association, the American Natural Soda Ash Corp. (ANSAC), successfully convinced Brazilian trade authorities that it did not dump soda ash in Brazil in 1997. The threat of an antidumping duty on soda ash imports would have eliminated exports to Brazil. Soda ash consumption in that country was forecast to increase in mid-1998 as new flat glass manufacturing facilities were scheduled to come on-stream to supply demand in housing and automobile construction.

The majority of U.S. soda ash imports come from Canada, where General Chemical Corp. operates a synthetic soda ash facility at Amherstburg, Ontario. That plant produces dense and light soda ash, a large quantity of which is shipped to the United States for special markets that require soda ash with a lighter bulk density, such as the market for detergents.

Outlook. World soda ash consumption will remain strong through 2000 because of growing demand for soda ash in developing nations, especially in the Far East and South America. Exports will continue to be the most important category for increased U.S. soda ash sales. Domestic soda ash consumption will remain about the same in the short term; however, the introduction of polyethylene naphthalate (PEN) plastic to the food-packaging sector may displace part of the glass container market, especially in the food container category, and this would further reduce soda ash consumption. PEN is the next generation of plastics and has better performance properties than do PET plastic products. PEN is highly suited for hot fill products such as baby foods, jams, and jellies, as well as beverage containers for enhanced oxygen and carbon dioxide resistance. It also screens ultraviolet light to extend a product's shelf life and preserve a drink's natural flavor. Amoco Corp. began PEN production at its Decatur, AL, plant in April 1997. PEN has been test-marketed in Japan and Latin America, and it is forecast that PEN plastic may be introduced to select U.S. markets within the next few years.

Sulfur

The United States has been the world's leading sulfur producer since it surpassed Italy around 1915, shortly after the Frasch method for mining sulfur was perfected in Louisiana. In this unusual mining process, native sulfur is melted underground with superheated water and brought to the surface by compressed air. More recent years have seen significant changes in the sulfur industry, although the United States has maintained its dominance and is expected to continue to do so in the foreseeable future.

In 1982 the most important change in sulfur production was the shift from Frasch sulfur to recovered sulfur as the most important source. Recovered sulfur is produced primarily to comply with environmental regulations that are applicable directly to emissions from a processing facility or indirectly by restricting the sulfur content of the fuels sold or used by a facility. Recovered sulfur is produced at oil refineries, natural gas processing plants, and coking plants in the United States. Another important source of domestic sulfur is by-product sulfuric acid from nonferrous metal smelters.

In the United States more elemental sulfur is recovered from petroleum refining than from natural gas processing and Frasch mining combined. Natural gas processing is a more important source of sulfur in the world market than is any other source. Because of its high sulfur content, pyrite is also an important source of sulfur in a few countries, although its importance is diminishing everywhere.

The general trend in sulfur production is for intentional production (in which elemental sulfur, sulfur ores, or pyrites are produced for the sole purpose of providing sulfur raw materials) to decline, and there is little likelihood of reversing that trend. Sulfur that is produced in compliance with environmental regulation is expanding globally, and as economies improve in developing countries, this expansion is likely to accelerate.

Trends in sulfur consumption are relatively stable. The production of phosphate fertilizers is by far the largest consumer of sulfur and sulfuric acid. Consumption in phosphate production and other agricultural areas varies from year to year for a variety of reasons, including weather conditions in various regions, economic circumstances in different locations, and government programs that increase or decrease agricultural support programs over time. Although difficult to predict over the short term, sulfur consumption in the phosphate industry is expected to rise moderately as new projects are completed around the world. Little growth is expected in the United States.

An agricultural use that has the potential to cause a global increase in demand is plant nutrient sulfur. Sulfur has been recognized as a requirement for the growth of healthy crops. Sulfur deficits in soil have been identified around the world and could represent a large market for additional sulfur, but the application of sulfur as a fertilizer is not expanding quickly.

Other uses for sulfur are considerably less significant than those in agriculture, and their growth is harder to predict. In general, growth in other areas will be moderate at best. In all end uses, growth in sulfur consumption is expected to lag behind increased production. Unless additional requirements for sulfur are developed, supply will continue to surpass demand.

Titanium

Production and Uses. Commercial forms of titanium concentrates used to produce titanium pigment and metal include ilmenite, leucoxene, rutile, synthetic rutile, and titaniferous slag. The leading producing countries of titanium concentrates are Australia, Canada, Norway, and South Africa. In the United States, E. I. du Pont de Nemours & Co. Inc. (DuPont) and RGC (USA) Mineral Sands, Inc. produce titanium mineral concentrates from heavy-mineral sands operations in Florida and Virginia, and P. W. Gillibrand Co. produces ilmenite in California as a by-product of sand and gravel production. Kerr McGee Chemical Corp. produces synthetic rutile from purchased ilmenite concentrate at Mobile, AL. In 1997 domestic mineral production data were withheld to avoid revealing company proprietary data.

The leading producing countries of titanium pigments include France, Germany, Japan, the United Kingdom, and the United States. Major end uses of titanium dioxide (TiO_2) are paint, paper, and plastics, while minor end uses include catalysts, ceramics, coated fabrics and textiles, floor coverings, printing ink, and roofing granules. U.S. producers of titanium pigment include DuPont, Millennium Inorganic Chemicals Inc., Kemira, Inc., Kerr-McGee, and Louisiana Pigment Co. Domestic production of titanium dioxide pigment in 1997 was 1.34 Mt, a 10 percent increase over 1996.

Producers of titanium sponge, the primary form of titanium metal, are located in China, Japan, Kazakstan, Russia, and the United States. In the United States titanium sponge is produced by Oregon Metallurgical Corp. (Oremet) in Albany, OR, and Titanium Metals Corp. (Timet) in Henderson, NV. In 1997 an estimated 65 percent of titanium metal was used in aerospace applications; the remaining 35 percent was used in the chemical process industry and for power generation, marine, ordnance, medical, and other nonaerospace applications. In 1997 domestic sponge production data were withheld to avoid revealing company proprietary data.

Events, Trends, and Issues. After a flat year of demand growth in 1996, global demand for titanium dioxide pigment rebounded in 1997, with an estimated increase of about 5 percent. On a gross weight basis, apparent consumption of titanium dioxide in the United States in 1997 increased about 7 percent from 1996. Meanwhile, owing to increased consumption of titanium metal by the commercial aerospace industry, net U.S. shipments of titanium metal mill products in 1997 were estimated to be 9 percent higher than the level in 1996.

Allegheny Teledyne Inc. (ATI) announced plans to expand its business in specialty metals through the acquisition of the titanium metal producer Oremet. Currently, Teledyne subsidiaries in the titanium industry include Wah Chang in Albany, OR, and Allvac in Monroe, NC. Before its acquisition, Oremet began the construction of a new electron-beam cold-hearth melting facility near Richland, WA. The facility, with a rated capacity of 10,000 tons per year, was expected to begin commercial production by middle to late 1998. The ATI subsidiary Allvac commissioned a new furnace for producing titanium ingot at its Monroe, NC, facility. The new furnace, 2,270 tons per year, is based on plasma-arc cold-hearth melting technology. Allvac's total melt capacity is estimated to be 10,000 to 12,000 tons per year after the addition of the new furnace.

In 1997 Anglo American Corp. was proceeding with plans to expand its Namakwa Sands operation near Saldanha, South Africa. The Namakwa expansion will add a second smelting furnace for the production of titanium slag, raising capacity from 97,000 to 235,000 tons per year. Rutile production is expected to rise to 42,000 tons per year. The expansion is expected to be completed in 1999, with full production achieved in 2001.

BHP Minerals commissioned its mining operations at Beenup, Australia. Beenup's designed production rate is 600,000 tons of ilmenite per year, of which approximately 50 percent will be processed at the BHP-Tinfos joint venture slag operation in Tyssedal, Norway. The Tyssedal joint venture is expected to produce 200,000 tons of chloride-grade slag per year and 40,000 tons of sulfate-grade slag. DuPont announced an agreement to acquire several of Imperial Chemical Industries PLC's (ICI) businesses, including ICI's white pigment business outside North America. Under the agreement, DuPont would acquire the ICI subsidiary Tioxide's titanium pigment facilities in France, Italy, Malaysia, South Africa, Spain, and the United Kingdom. However, Tioxide's 50 percent interest in Louisiana Pigment Co. in Lake Charles and its finishing operations in Quebec, Canada, will not be included in the acquisition. The acquisition includes about 535,000 tons of annual capacity. According to ICI, options are being developed for the disposal of its North American titanium dioxide businesses. At the end of 1997 the acquisition was still awaiting approval from the Federal Trade Commission. DuPont also announced plans to idle its 36,000 tons per year pigment plant at Antioch, CA. However, finishing and slurry operations at the Antioch facility are expected to remain on-stream. The Antioch pigment plant was opened in 1963, using DuPont's original chloride process technology. DuPont indefinitely delayed the development of a deposit in Georgia near the eastern edge of the Okefenokee National Wildlife Refuge while it held discussions with interested parties regarding the environmental impact of developing the 38,000 acres.

Kerr-McGee Chemical Corp. expanded chloride-route capacity at its Hamilton, MS, plant from 145,000 to 160,000 tons per year. Kerr-McGee is the only U.S. pigment maker that produces its own synthetic rutile feedstock.

In 1997 SCM Chemicals Inc. changed its name to Millennium Inorganic Chemicals Inc. Millennium agreed to acquire Rhône-Poulenc Thann et Mulhouse S.A. Rhône-Poulenc titanium dioxide operations are located in France at Le Havre and Thann. In addition to 138,000 tons of combined titanium dioxide pigment capacity per year, the plants have 100,000 tons per year capacity to produce specialty chemicals and intermediate chemicals.

Timet began the construction of a 9,000 tons per year expansion of ingot capacity through its wholly owned subsidiary Titanium Hearth Technologies in Morgantown, PA. The new furnace will employ electron-beam cold-hearth melting technology.

Outlook. On a global basis, about 95 percent of demand for titanium mineral feedstocks is used to produce titanium pigments. Flat demand for titanium pigment in 1996 caused many producers to delay expansion projects. However, growth in 1997 caused some producers to run at close to operating capacity and prompted the resumption of many expansion programs. In the next decade demand for titanium dioxide pigment is forecast to grow at an average rate of 3 percent annually. Over the long term, adequate mineral supplies of titanium dioxide exist or are being developed to meet increased demand.

Global demand for titanium metal products is driven primarily by the commercial and military aerospace industries. The recent surge in demand has been primarily a result of increased consumption from commercial aircraft. Demand in this sector is expected to remain high in the short term. However, long-term growth for titanium metal is expected to rely on growth in nonaerospace markets.

Minerals Information Team, U.S. Department of the Interior, U.S. Geological Survey, (703) 648-4919, October 1998.

■ REFERENCES

American Geological Institute, Government Affairs Program, http://www.agiweb.org.

"Benchmark Input-Output Accounts for the U.S. Economy, 1992," *Survey of Current Business,* November 1997, Bureau of Economic Analysis, U.S. Department of Commerce.

H.10 Foreign Exchange Rates, Federal Reserve Board.

Minerals Yearbook, Metals and Minerals, vol. I, 1995, U.S. Geological Survey, Department of the Interior.

Mining Engineering, January 1998, page 6.

The New York Times.

The Wall Street Journal.

World Metal Statistics, February 1998, World Bureau of Metal Statistics.

■ RELATED CHAPTERS

COAL MINING
Economic and Trade Trends

U.S. International Trade

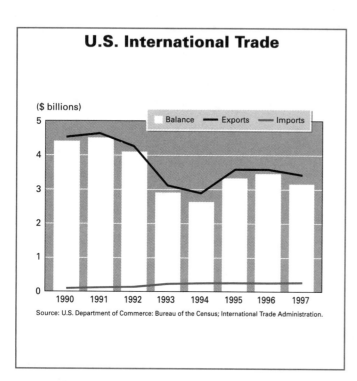

($ billions)

Legend: Balance — Exports — Imports

Source: U.S. Department of Commerce: Bureau of the Census; International Trade Administration.

World Export Market Shares

(%)

Legend: United States ■ Australia □ Canada ■ South Africa

Source: United Nations; U.S. Department of Commerce, International Trade Administration.

U.S. Coal Mining Productivity by Mine Type

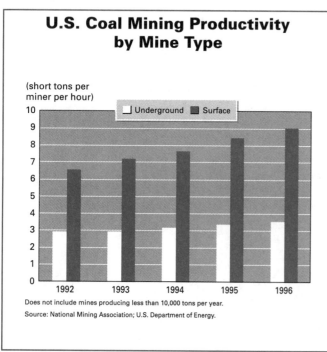

(short tons per miner per hour)

Legend: □ Underground ■ Surface

Does not include mines producing less than 10,000 tons per year.

Source: National Mining Association; U.S. Department of Energy.

Output and Output per Hour

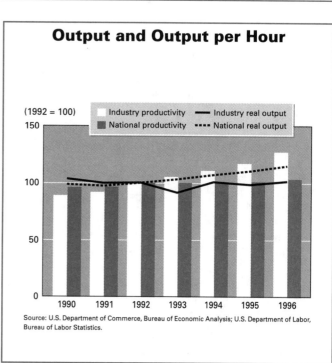

(1992 = 100)

Legend: Industry productivity — Industry real output
National productivity - - - National real output

Source: U.S. Department of Commerce, Bureau of Economic Analysis; U.S. Department of Labor, Bureau of Labor Statistics.

See "Getting the Most Out of *Outlook '99*" for definitions of terms.

Coal Mining

INDUSTRY DEFINITION The coal industry is composed of establishments primarily engaged in producing and developing bituminous coal or lignite at surface mines (SIC 1221), bituminous coal or lignite at underground mines (SIC 1222), and anthracite (SIC 1231). The industry includes underground mining, auger mining, strip mining, culm bank mining, and other surface mining, as well as coal preparation plants engaged in cleaning, crushing, screening, or sizing. It also includes establishments that perform primarily coal mining services for others on a contract or fee basis (SIC 1241).

GLOBAL INDUSTRY TRENDS

The role of coal in energy use worldwide has undergone a dramatic transformation over the last several decades. Once a fuel used extensively in all sectors of the economy, coal now is employed primarily for electricity generation and in a few key industries, including steel, cement, and chemicals. World coal reserves will last another 200 years if energy consumption remains at current levels. Of the three fossil fuels used worldwide—coal, natural gas, and oil—coal use grows at the slowest rate; the relatively high level of carbon emissions per British thermal unit (Btu) of energy from coal leads to higher levels of emissions than do oil and gas (see Figures 2-1 and 2-2). Nevertheless, the rise in overall coal use has been substantial and is expected to continue. In 1996 coal accounted for 26 percent of the world's energy consumption and 36.4 percent of energy consumption for electricity generation. By most forecasts, the use of coal should remain strong through 2015, accounting for approximately 24 percent of energy consumption in the world.

In the 1990s coal use in the United States and the generation of electricity are closely linked (see Figure 2-3). The establishment of coal as a major energy resource over the last two decades has been supported by a steadily growing commitment to its use by electric utilities. From less than 400 million tons annually during the 1970s, utility coal consumption rose to 863 million tons in 1996, an increase of 36 million tons over 1995. Coal's share of electricity generation in that period increased from 46 percent to about 55 percent. In 1996 almost 8 of every 10 tons of U.S. coal consumed was used to produce electricity.

However, coal is at a crossroads. Potential problems abound—serious, unresolved challenges to coal's future as a dominant energy source that can be summed up in two words: the environment. The acid rain rules of the 1990 Clean Air Act require utilities to cut sulfur dioxide and nitrogen oxide emissions and have led to a sharp reduction in high-sulfur coal production. The U.S. Environmental Protection Agency (EPA) has also proposed new regulations for fine particulates and ozone.

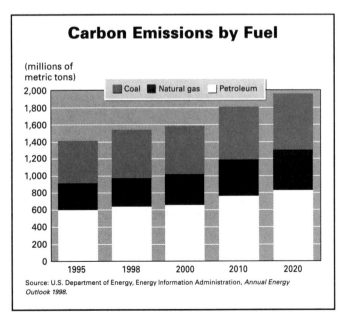

Carbon Emissions by Fuel

Source: U.S. Department of Energy, Energy Information Administration, *Annual Energy Outlook 1998*.

FIGURE 2-1

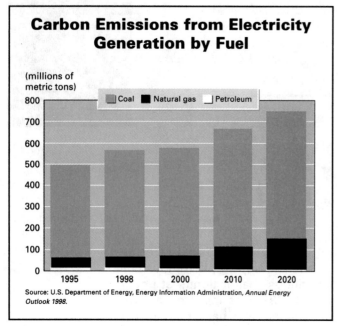

Carbon Emissions from Electricity Generation by Fuel

(millions of metric tons)

Legend: Coal, Natural gas, Petroleum

Source: U.S. Department of Energy, Energy Information Administration, *Annual Energy Outlook 1998.*

FIGURE 2-2

Air toxics such as mercury pollution are another new concern. Possibly the biggest challenge for coal consists of carbon dioxide. Coal in recent years has been criticized by those who fear that an increase in so-called greenhouse gases—atmospheric carbon dioxide from the burning of fossil fuels—is warming the earth, perhaps to dangerous levels by the middle of the twenty-first century. The global warming debate formed the backdrop for climate change treaty negotiations in Japan in December

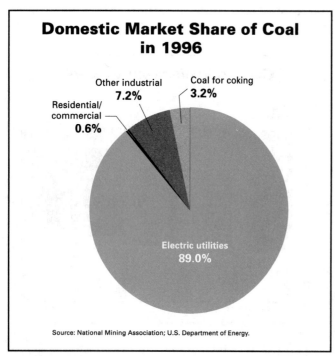

Domestic Market Share of Coal in 1996

Other industrial 7.2%

Coal for coking 3.2%

Residential/commercial 0.6%

Electric utilities 89.0%

Source: National Mining Association; U.S. Department of Energy.

FIGURE 2-3

1997. The resulting Kyoto Treaty, tentatively embraced by the representatives of 35 industrialized nations, including the United States, aims to reduce carbon dioxide emissions by 7 percent below the 1990 levels no later than 2012.

To reach that goal, the Clinton administration and environmentalists are targeting the coal industry and electric utilities because of their synergistic relationship. By 2015 the U.S. Energy Information Administration predicts that coal will account for 47 percent of total U.S. electricity generation even as more utilities switch to cleaner-burning natural gas. As the leading emitter of carbon dioxide emissions in the United States, the world leader in that category, utilities are increasingly looking for ways to meet their obligations under the treaty.

To be legally binding on the United States, the treaty must be ratified by the Senate, but there appears to be little chance of that before 1999, given the Republicans' majority status. The refusal of China and India, projected to account for 32 percent of the world's total increase in energy consumption through 2015, and of other major developing countries, such as South Korea and Mexico, to be bound by the treaty essentially means that the accord will not be passed by the Senate in 1998 and probably 1999. Indeed, the Senate voted 95–0 before U.S. negotiators left for Kyoto to reject any treaty that did not apply to developing nations as well as traditional industrial powers.

While environmental concerns cloud the long-term future of coal use, the present and the near term remain bright. In the United States coal is a $20 billion industry that had a record production year in 1996 with 1.064 billion short tons (U.S. tons, as opposed to metric tons, here referred to only as tons), an increase of 3 percent. Once again Wyoming led the way, followed by West Virginia and Kentucky. Wyoming's coal production in 1996 jumped 6 percent over its 1995 level to reach a record 278 million tons. West Virginia increased coal production 5 percent to a level of 170 million tons, only 3 percent below its record level of 176 million tons in 1947. Kentucky, though, saw coal production decline by 1 percent in 1996, falling to 152 million tons. In fact, only 11 of the 25 coal-producing states showed an increase in 1996.

Still, coal production in the United States is expected to undergo a gradual rise to 1.16 billion tons annually by 2015. Worldwide, coal use increased from 4.1 billion tons in 1980 to a peak of 5.3 billion tons in 1989. Recently, growth in coal consumption in the developing countries of Asia led a recovery in worldwide coal use from a low of 5 billion tons in 1992 to 5.1 billion tons in 1995. Coal use is projected to rise 45 percent through 2015, reaching 7.4 billion tons in that year.

With the exception of China, coal for electricity generation will account for virtually all the projected growth in coal consumption worldwide through 2015. In the nonelectricity sectors other fuels—mainly natural gas—are expected to gain market share. In China, however, coal should continue to be the fuel of choice for industrial applications because of that country's abundant reserves and limited access to alternative sources of energy. Consumption of coking coal will decline slightly in most regions as a result of technological advances in steelmaking, increasing output from electric arc furnaces, and the substitution of other materials for steel in end-use applications.

China is the world's largest consumer of coal and is projected to remain so in the foreseeable future. Chinese economic policy favors the use of its coal resources to spur development at the possible expense of environmental protection, the main reason why China has rejected the Kyoto Treaty. Pollution control technologies used in the industrialized countries to reduce the environmental impact of coal use are not widely employed in China. If that policy changed, China would be forced to make major adjustments in its energy system.

Slow growth in coal-fired generating capacity in industrialized countries is expected to be offset by rapid expansion in the rest of the world, primarily in Asia. The large increase in electricity consumption in developing countries in Asia—particularly in China and India—accounts for a major portion of the overall rise in coal-fired generation. Both countries are rich in coal reserves and have well-developed infrastructures for coal mining and distribution; also, because their oil and natural gas infrastructures are relatively less developed, coal is their most economical fuel. India has some of the largest coal reserves in the world. At India's present production rate of about 800,000 tons daily, its reserves are likely to last more than 100 years.

Although metallurgical coal, which is used to make coke for steel manufacturing, historically has dominated world coal trade, its share has declined steadily, falling from 55 percent in 1980 to about 40 percent in 1996. Projections call for its share of world coal trade to continue to dwindle, falling to 28 percent by 2015. Among the reasons for this decline are the additional penetration of steel production by electric arc furnaces, which do not use coal coke as input, and technological improvements at blast furnaces, including a greater use of pulverized coal injection (PCI) equipment as well as higher average injection rates per ton of hot metal produced. One ton of pulverized coal used in steel production displaces approximately 1.4 tons of coking coal. In 1996 an estimated 17 million tons of coal for PCI was traded worldwide, representing 8 percent of total coal imports for consumption at coke plants and blast furnaces. Partly offsetting the downward pressure on metallurgical coal trade is an expected rise in imports by South Korea, Taiwan, India, and Brazil.

Australia is expected to remain the major coal exporter to Asia, accounting for almost half of that region's total coal import demand over the next 15 years. Coal exports from China and Indonesia, Asia's internal coal suppliers, should keep pace with overall growth in Asian import demand. Together, these three countries are projected to meet 23 percent of Asia's total import needs by 2015. In the 1980s Australia became the leading coal exporter in the world, mainly by meeting increased demand for steam coal in Asia. Some of the largest coal producers in the United States, including the Peabody Group, have stepped up coal production in Australia.

European coal imports also are expected to rise over the next decade or so, though at a slower rate than in Asia. Several unknowns cloud the prospects for European imports, including the extent and pace of the decline in indigenous coal produc-

tion, especially in Germany and the United Kingdom, and the extent to which natural gas and other sources of energy will substitute for coal in electricity generation.

In the future the United States and South America are projected to take an increasing share of European coal import demand, primarily at the expense of Australia and South Africa. Coal exporters in Australia and South Africa are expected to direct most of their additional shipments of coal to the rapidly expanding Asian import markets.

U.S. coal exports grew from 88.5 million tons in 1995 to 90.4 million tons in 1996, with increased shipments to Canada, Mexico, and several African countries accounting for much of the increase. Prices also rose from a tonnage average of $40.27 in 1995 to $40.76 in 1996. Coal exports from the United States are expected to continue increasing at a modest rate to 102.2 million tons in 2000 and 120.6 million tons in 2015. Steam coal exports, particularly to Europe, should underpin much of the increase.

DOMESTIC TRENDS

More than half the 48 contiguous states plus Alaska sit atop a wealth of coal resources. Demonstrated coal reserves totaled 496 billion tons in year end 1995, more than 480 times U.S. annual coal production. But almost half those reserves are either inaccessible or likely to be lost in the mining process. Nearly half the reserves—an estimated 241 billion tons—are found in western states, mainly Wyoming, Utah, and Montana (see Figure 2-4). There the reserves are mostly low in sulfur content, making them more attractive to electric utilities in compliance with the EPA's Clean Air Act than are the higher-sulfur reserves in the midwest and the east. Western coal deposits, particularly

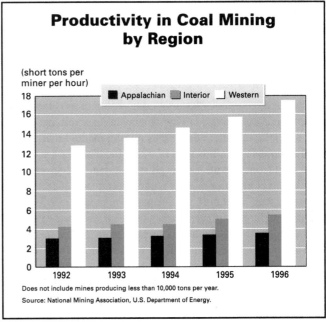

FIGURE 2-4

in the Powder River Basin of Wyoming, are found in thick, relatively shallow seams, and so they can be extracted easily by surface mining, a more efficient production method than deep mining, which generally is more labor-intensive and less productive on a per-employee basis. In recent years environmental regulations have been responsible for a shift westward in U.S. coal production. The big three of coal production—Wyoming, West Virginia, and Kentucky—accounted for more than 570 million tons of production in 1996, more than half the nation's total. While the coal industry is growing only modestly in West Virginia and is declining slightly in Kentucky, it continues to expand about 10 percent annually in Wyoming. The west also is the home of the nation's largest coal mines. Thunder Basin Coal Co.'s Black Thunder surface mine in Wyoming is approaching 50 million tons annually, nearly six times the output of the largest deep mine in the United States: CONSOL Inc.'s Enlow Fork mine in Pennsylvania.

Despite the recent trend toward the mining of the vast low-sulfur coalfields of the west, total low-sulfur, medium-sulfur, and high-sulfur coal reserves in the United States are roughly even. Nationwide, low-sulfur coal reserves are estimated to amount to 171 billion tons, or 34 percent of all reserves. Medium-sulfur coal accounts for 28 percent of reserves, and high-sulfur coal accounts for about 37 percent. In regard to estimated recoverable reserves, low-sulfur coal leads the way at 37 percent. Estimated high-sulfur and medium-sulfur recoverable reserves each make up about 31.5 percent. Among the predominant low-sulfur coal regions, eastern Wyoming is best positioned to meet increasing demand for low-sulfur coal over the next 15 years. Active surface mines in eastern Wyoming report an estimated 6 billion tons of low-sulfur recoverable reserves, representing nearly 75 percent of low-sulfur reserves at active surface mines and almost 60 percent of low-sulfur reserves at all active mines.

In the midwest and east new trends are at work. Production from longwall mines, which use equipment to cut coal from large faces of coal deposits, eclipsed production from continuous mining mines in 1996 by about 10 million tons—194 million tons compared with 184 million tons. In continuous mining, a traditional staple in the U.S. coal industry, machines cut or rip coal from the face and load it onto conveyors or shuttle cars in a continuous fashion. Longwall mining is more efficient than is continuous mining or conventional mining, an old, less efficient, and more dangerous mining method that is waning in popularity; in this type of mining explosives are used to blast coal from a seam. Longwall mining requires fewer workers, saving companies money. Largely as a result of technological advances, including the increased popularity of longwall mining and larger surface mines in the west, the number of miners has continued to dwindle, dropping from 90,252 in 1995 to 83,462 in 1996. Some traditional coal-mining states, such as Illinois, have been hit hard by this downsizing. In the early part of this century Illinois had as many as 100,000 miners; in 1997 the total was barely 5,000, and it is still dropping.

Illinois was not alone in this regard. Of the 25 coal-producing states, 18 had a decrease in employment. Although all regions of the country have experienced declines in coal-mining employment, the western region, which recorded a 13.1 percent drop, accounted for the largest proportion of the decrease. The Appalachian region in the east had a 7 percent decline, while the interior or midwestern region had a decline of 8 percent.

Productivity, however, remains on the rise. In 1996 coal miners working daily averaged 5.69 tons per miner per hour, an increase of 5.8 percent over 1995. Increases occurred in all regions, with the west showing the largest hike: 11 percent. Over the past decade productivity has risen at an average annual rate of 6.3 percent; deep mines went up 5.5 percent, and surface mines 6.9 percent.

Another trend in some areas, especially in Illinois, is micromining. Instead of the large, labor-intensive deep mines that once dotted the landscapes of Illinois and other midwestern states, tiny mines are springing up, often with no more than a dozen or two employees, to extract coal from smaller reserves either ignored or unwanted by larger producers. Micromines operate on a relatively shoestring budget, usually producing no more than 100,000 to 150,000 tons of coal annually. They generally serve niche markets or just one customer.

The biggest and most far-reaching change in the U.S. coal industry is restructuring. A volatile industry since its inception more than a century ago, the U.S. coal industry is undergoing dramatic, frequent shifts in company ownership. Consolidation is the byword, especially among coal producers that are undercapitalized. The combination of government environmental and safety regulations and, in some states, worker's compensation program costs has caused thousands of smaller producers to go out of business in the last few years. Kentucky alone has lost more than 1,000 producers—mostly small, with production of 100,000 or tons or less—in the last 5 years.

Larger companies are benefiting from consolidation. Recent developments appear to bear this out. The London-based Hanson Industries Plc announced a "demerger" in which Peabody Holding Co., the parent of Peabody Coal Co., joined with Hanson's British electric utility, the Eastern Group, to form an energy resources company called The Energy Group. Another British company, Costain Plc, sold its Kentucky properties to Rencoal, Inc. Coastal Corp. also announced plans to sell its western subsidiaries to Atlantic Richfield Co. (ARCO), while the off-again, on-again merger between Ashland Coal, Inc., and Arch Mineral Corp. finally was consummated. The new company is called Arch Coal Inc.

Those transactions only served as a prelude to the wave of mergers that occurred in late 1997 and 1998. Five of the nation's 10 largest coal producers either changed ownership or formally placed at least a portion of their properties on the block. After a protracted bidding war between PacifiCorp, a Portland, OR, investor-owned electric utility, and Texas Utilities, The Energy Group was sold to Texas Utilities for $7.3 billion. Shortly afterward the Peabody Group, which included the former Peabody Holding Co. and Peabody Coal Co., was sold by Texas Utilities to Lehman Merchant Banking Partners for $2.3 billion, including assumed debt. Peabody, the nation's largest coal producer, sold more than 165 million tons of coal worldwide in 1997. It operates 24 mines in the United States and 3 in Australia, where a fourth mine is under construction. Peabody's U.S. market share was 14.2 percent in 1997, approximately twice that of its nearest competitor. The company supplied 92 percent of its U.S. production to electric utilities, 5 percent to the export market, and 3 percent to the U.S. industrial sector. Peabody has approximately 9.4 billion tons of proven and probable reserves.

Cyprus Amax Minerals Co., the nation's number three coal producer, sold operating coal properties in Kentucky, West Virginia, Indiana, and Tennessee to AEI Holding Co. Cyprus retained two big mines in Pennsylvania and one in southern Illinois. ARCO disposed of its U.S. coal assets in Wyoming, Colorado, and Utah in a sale to Arch Coal for $1.14 billion after a tentative deal with the Beacon Group fell through.

Two other top 10 coal producers—Kerr-McGee Corp. and Zeigler Coal Holding Co.—evaluated proposals for their coal properties. Kerr-McGee offered its Jacobs Ranch surface mine in Wyoming and its Galatia deep mine in southern Illinois, while Zeigler considered the sale of properties in Illinois, West Virginia, Wyoming, and Ohio. Meanwhile, rumors abounded about other major coal producers considering divestitures, underscoring the volatility of the U.S. coal market and the uncertainty surrounding the future of coal in the face of stricter environmental regulations.

To the list of uncertainties confronting the U.S. coal industry as the millennium nears can be added deregulation of the electric utility industry. The federal Energy Policy Act of 1992 set the stage for the current deregulatory activity. At least a half dozen states have agreed to open their electric industries to retail competition or are seriously considering such a move. Legislatures in perhaps three dozen more states are pondering deregulation bills. What this means for the coal industry as a whole is open to debate, although some observers theorize that it will mean a decrease in coal prices. Stripped of their longtime monopoly status, utility executives, the argument goes, will be under intense pressure to reduce operating costs to become more competitive. Because fuel is the principal expense for a utility, accounting for as much as 50 percent of its costs, coal contracts will come under even greater scrutiny. Already there is evidence to support this theory. Long-term coal contracts, sometimes lasting for 20 or 30 years and once a staple of the utility industry, are a thing of the past. They largely have been replaced by short-term "spot" contracts or coal supply agreements of no more than 2 or 3 years. This lack of a guaranteed long-term market for coal makes it increasingly difficult for newcomers to obtain the financing needed to get into the coal business.

However, some authorities believe that deregulation can be a boon for coal use if regulators require utilities to participate in independent system operators (ISOs), in which groups of utilities turn control of their transmission systems over to an independent entity. The multistate, multisystem ISO structure erases the breakup of the transmission system according to price, system ownership, and congestion at key interfaces. Under such a scenario, coal could be burned at one end of the regional market and sold at the other without the need to pay for transporting the coal.

On the positive side, labor disruptions have subsided in U.S. coalfields. The debilitating nationwide strikes by the United Mine Workers of America (UMWA) in 1977–1978 and 1981—and to a lesser extent the union's strike against "selected" coal company targets in 1993—have been replaced by a new working relationship between the UMWA and the Bituminous Coal Operators Association (BCOA), the main industry bargaining group, based on an overriding mutual interest in survival. For this reason, the two sides put aside their historic differences in December 1997 to negotiate a new 5-year labor agreement 8 months before the old one was due to expire. Instead of the usual rancor and distrust that have marked contract bargaining in the coal industry, the UMWA and the BCOA have agreed to work together to oppose the Kyoto Treaty. For the union, whose active membership has dwindled from about 100,000 a decade ago to perhaps 30,000, vocal opposition to the Clinton administration's environmental policies represents a significant development. The union enthusiastically supported Clinton in his two successful campaigns in the 1990s. Now it views the President's strong endorsement of tougher air pollution regulations as perhaps the greatest threat the U.S. coal industry has ever faced.

OUTLOOK

In the future it remains uncertain whether the opportunities in regard to coal can be realized and the challenges can be overcome. Many answers will arrive in the next few years as electric utilities, the traditional market for steam coal in the United States, decide whether to invest in expensive and in some cases still experimental clean-coal technologies to comply with government air quality regulations. If utilities decide that it is too risky to invest the billions of dollars that will be necessary to enable coal to remain the dominant fuel in electricity generation, the continued shift to natural gas may accelerate. Many utilities soon will be faced with a still bigger decision—whether to construct new generating capacity fired by coal or by another fuel source. By 2015 fully 90 percent of existing generating capacity in the United States will need to be replaced. Aging and inefficient coal-burning plants account for most of that existing capacity. Coal also faces a small but growing challenge from renewable energy sources, including wind, solar, geothermal, hydropower, and photovoltaic. Proponents of renewables believe that these "clean," alternative sources of energy could capture 10 to 15 percent of the U.S. energy market over the next decade.

Between 1995 and 1996 hydropower generation increased 12 percent in the United States, with more than half the power derived from hydro plants in California, Oregon, and Washington. Nonhydro renewable generation, though, declined 5 percent between 1995 and 1996, largely because of a 7.2 percent drop in geothermal production. Overall, nonhydro renewable generation currently represents less than 1 percent of total electric utility generation in the United States. Nevertheless, interest among utilities in renewable energy continues to grow. Some utilities for the first time are offering customers so-called green power originating from such sources. Any green power actually incorporated into a utility's energy portfolio is likely to displace at least some existing coal supplies.

As has been the case through most of the 1990s, consolidation will remain the byword of the coal industry. Mergers, joint ventures, and buyouts will persist as price, always an important factor in the coal production and marketing mix, assumes pre-eminent proportions. Larger companies will find it easier to secure financing to develop new mines and make other acquisitions as utilities continue to turn away from long-term coal supply contracts in favor of shorter-term or spot purchases. Coal producers will continue to look for ways to trim even a penny or two off the price of a ton of coal. Even that small difference can sometimes decide who wins or loses a coal supply contract. With the advent of competition in the utility industry, price has taken on an importance not seen in the coal industry in decades. A deregulated utility industry favors electric generators that can offer the lowest-cost power. Since fuel represents up to one-third of a utility's total operational costs, utilities will feel more pressure to buy the least expensive coal on the market.

Nonutility generation (NUG) has had a definite impact on the generation of electricity from traditional utilities. NUG increased from 40,000 gigawatt-hours (GWh) in 1985 to 116,500 GWh in 1990 and more than 200,000 GWh in 1996. For coal, this is a problem because only 15 percent or so of this generation is coal-fired, while about half uses natural gas. NUG is most important in the northeast and the Pacific region. Although these are not traditional coal areas, at least in the short term, NUG is having an effect on the rate of increase in total coal burning.

Coal producers will strive to become even more efficient. They will invest in bigger, remote-controlled mining equipment that will reduce the number of miners on payrolls as well as faster longwall mining systems that extract pockets of coal that ordinarily would have to be left behind. Producers will search for ways to keep the equipment up and running, since downtime equates to higher costs and ultimately higher coal prices. On the transportation front, railroads will begin switching to aluminum rail cars, which are lighter and are considered more reliable.

Traditional energy companies will leave the industry and investment groups with new management approaches will enter as the business environment undergoes an enormous change. One of the first moves after Lehman Merchant Banking Partners, a New York City investment group, acquired the Peabody Group in 1998 was to realign Peabody's organizational structure, an action that resulted in major office closings and relocations and staff reductions. More and more coal also will be sold by traders as a commodity in many markets, and coal options will become commonplace.

U.S. coal production is expected to continue to grow about 1 percent annually to 1.24 billion tons in 2015, with most of the increase attributable to a modest though steady rise in coal consumption for the generation of electricity (see Table 2-1). Most of this continued surge in production should take place in the

west, with that region producing about 142 million tons a year more by the end of the forecast period. Production should rise in the east as well, though only 103 million tons annually. In addition to growth in coal consumption for electricity generation, eastern production benefits from a projected increase in U.S. coal exports over the next decade or so. Coal production in the midwest, meanwhile, should decline about 38 million tons annually as a consequence of that region's increasingly unpopular high-sulfur coal.

Indeed, stricter air quality standards mandated by the 1990 Clean Air Act could cause low-sulfur western and in some cases eastern coal to continue to gain market share at the expense of high-sulfur coal. Medium-sulfur coal production will decline through 2000 and then recover as Clean Air Act compliance strategies shift from fuel switching to installing flue gas desulfurization units, or scrubbers, in phase 2 of the Clean Air Act, starting January 1, 2000.

There are different versions of this scenario. Some researchers suggest that as many as 58 coal-fired power plants in the United States, representing 20,706 megawatts of generating capacity, could be forced to close as utilities are coerced to comply with the EPA's tougher new air quality standards. Just to meet pending emissions rules under the Clean Air Act, the utility industry would need to spend about $23 billion. If the Kyoto Treaty is ratified by the U.S. Senate, more coal plants will close because utilities simply do not have a sufficient revenue stream from their current rate base to cover the cost of compliance. Compliance with the Kyoto accords could result in the shutting down of 50 percent of U.S. coal-fired generation. As a result, utilities may be less likely to spend the millions of dollars needed to invest in new pollution controls because of the prevailing uncertainty that any changes they make may be followed by even stricter air quality rules and regulations.

High-sulfur coal could make a comeback of sorts as a result of deregulation in the electricity industry. With utilities competing for customers in the years ahead—the utility industry could be totally deregulated within a decade—they may turn to lower-cost, abundant supplies of fuel. Already some utilities that are facing capacity shortages during peak generation periods have taken older, coal-fired plants out of mothballs on at least a temporary basis. This trend bodes well for high-sulfur coal, as does electric industry competition. Traditional high-sulfur coal states such as Kentucky, Illinois, and Ohio hope to take advantage of competition by constructing new coal-fired generating plants that could utilize locally mined, less expensive coal to generate electricity for other, high-cost regions of the country.

Coal mine mouth prices should decline slightly through 2015 because of increasing productivity, flat real wage increases, and competitive pressures on long-term contracts. In 2010 the mine mouth price should be $17.43 per ton, compared with $23.30 in 1995. Average electricity prices are expected to remain essentially flat through the forecast period because the projected fossil fuel prices are lower. Coal will remain the primary fuel for electricity generation. Total coal consumption will grow at an average annual rate of just under 1 percent, with 90 percent of the coal used for generation. Natural gas, however, will increase

TABLE 2-1: Coal Trends and Forecasts
(million short tons per year unless otherwise noted)

	1995	1996	1997	1998	1999	2003	2005	2010	2015	2020	96–20
Production[1]											
Appalachia	435	452	458	478	480	507	506	505	505	513	0.5%
Midwest	169	173	166	177	171	172	176	177	167	166	−0.2%
West	430	439	464	467	477	504	525	583	654	697	1.9%
East of the Mississippi	544	564	560	589	585	607	608	602	609	623	0.4%
West of the Mississippi	489	500	528	532	543	576	599	663	717	754	1.7%
Total	1,033	1,064	1,088	1,122	1,128	1,183	1,207	1,265	1,326	1,376	1.1%
Imports	7	7	7	7	7	8	8	8	8	8	0.4%
Exports	88	90	87	90	92	101	104	112	119	128	1.4%
Net imports	−81	−83	−80	−83	−85	−94	−96	−104	−112	−120	1.5%
Total supply[2]	952	981	1,008	1,039	1,043	1,089	1,111	1,161	1,215	1,256	1.0%
Consumption by sector											
Residential and commercial	6	6	6	6	6	6	6	6	7	6	0.4%
Industrial[3]	72	70	69	70	71	75	77	81	81	81	0.6%
Coke plants	33	32	32	32	32	29	28	26	24	23	−1.4%
Electric generators[4]	847	896	903	943	936	979	1,000	1,049	1,103	1,147	1.0%
Total	958	1,003	1,009	1,051	1,044	1,090	1,112	1,162	1,215	1,257	0.9%
Delivery price (1996$/short ton)[5]											
Industrial	33.14	32.28	32.01	31.62	31.32	30.28	29.92	29.29	28.90	28.57	−0.5%
Coke plants	48.39	47.33	48.62	48.00	47.56	46.31	45.90	45.10	44.78	44.61	−0.2%
Electric generators	27.61	26.45	25.72	25.27	25.05	23.87	23.37	22.09	20.72	19.52	−1.3%
1996 dollars/million Btu[6]	1.35	1.29	1.25	1.23	1.22	1.16	1.14	1.09	1.03	0.97	−1.2%
Average	28.75	27.52	26.88	26.40	26.16	24.92	24.40	23.12	21.76	20.56	−1.2%
Exports[7]	41.17	40.77	40.29	39.51	38.96	37.00	36.40	35.02	33.75	32.47	−0.9%

[1] Includes anthracite, bituminous coal, and lignite.
[2] Production plus net imports and net storage withdrawals.
[3] Includes consumption by cogenerators.
[4] Includes all electric power generators except cogenerators.
[5] Sectoral prices weighted by consumption tonnage; weighted average excludes residential/commercial and export (f.a.s.) prices.
[6] Btu = British thermal unit.
[7] f.a.s. = price at U.S. port of exit.
Note: Totals may not equal the sum of components due to independent rounding.
Source: U.S. Department of Energy, Energy Information Administration, *Annual Energy Outlook 1998*.

an average of 1.6 percent annually as gas-fired generation will more than double by 2015. Petroleum consumption also will grow a bit faster than coal, with two-thirds of the petroleum used for transportation. Coal and natural gas will combine to take more market share from nuclear power. Only one new nuclear unit, Watts Bar 1, was completed in the 1990s. No other new nuclear units are projected by 2015. With about 40 percent of American nuclear capacity scheduled to be retired by 2015, nuclear generation will decline after 2000.

Recoverable coal reserves at existing active mines for some coal types and regions will be exhausted over the next decade or so, and new mine capacity will be needed in many areas of the country. Despite the opening window of opportunity for high-sulfur coal with the advent of electric industry deregulation, low-sulfur regions of the United States, particularly the Powder River Basin of Wyoming, remain best positioned to meet demand for new mine capacity. For medium-sulfur coal, substantial investments in new surface mine capacity are likely in eastern Kentucky, while somewhat smaller investments should take place in Virginia, Tennessee, and Alabama. As is the case for low-sulfur coal reserves, recoverable reserves of medium-

sulfur coal at active surface mines in these regions also are small. For high-sulfur coal, recoverable reserves at active surface mines are sufficient to meet the projected demand in all supply regions over most of the forecast period.

Robert Matyi, Henderson, KY, (502) 827-8145, October 1998.

■ REFERENCES

Coal Statistics International, The McGraw-Hill Companies, 1200 G Street, NW, Suite 900, Washington, DC 20005.
National Mining Association, 1130 17th Street, NW, Washington, DC 20036. (202) 463-9780.

The following are published by the U.S. Department of Energy, Energy Information Administration, and are available from the U.S. Government Printing Office, P.O. Box 371954, Pittsburgh, PA 15250:

Annual Energy Outlook, 1998.
Coal Industry Annual, 1996.

International Energy Annual, 1996 and 1997.
Performance Profiles of Major Energy Producers, 1994.
Quarterly Coal Report, 1998.
State Coal Profiles, January 1994.
U.S. Coal Reserves: A Review and Update, August 1996.

Information about DOE/EIA publications may be obtained from the National Energy Information Center, EI-231, Energy Information Administration, U.S. Department of Energy, Washington, DC 20585. (202) 586-8800, infoctr@eia.doe.gov.

■ **RELATED CHAPTERS**

3: Crude Petroleum and Natural Gas
4: Petroleum Refining
5: Electricity Production and Sales
13: Steel Mill Products
18: Production Machinery
20: Environmental Technologies and Services
37: Automotive Parts
43: Transportation

■ **GLOSSARY**

Bituminous coal: The most common coal, with moisture content less than 20 percent and a calorific value of 10,500 to 14,000 Btu per pound; typically found in the midwestern United States.

Coke: A hard, dry carbon substance produced by heating coal to a very high temperature in the absence of air; used in the manufacture of iron and steel.

Continuous mining: Underground mining method using a machine that rips or cuts coal from the solid seam and loads it onto conveyors or into shuttle cars for removal from the mine.

Conventional mining: A deep mining method that includes inserting explosives in a coal seam, blasting the seam, and removing the coal onto a conveyor or shuttle car.

Demonstrated reserve base: The portion of the identified resource base that is measured and indicated and published by the Department of Energy.

Identified resources: Measured, indicated, and inferred resources that are published by the Department of Energy and the U.S. Geological Survey.

Lignite coal: A brownish-black coal that contains a high moisture content and volatile matter and has a low heat content, ranging from 6,300 to 8,300 Btu per pound.

Longwall mining: An underground mining method that uses equipment that cuts coal from large faces of coal deposits. Conveyors then remove the coal, and movable hydraulic roof supports collapse the roof evenly once mining from an area is complete. More of the coal can be removed than with more traditional methods that leave pillars to support the ceilings.

Metallurgical coal: Various grades of coal suitable for carbonization to make coke for steel manufacturing.

Mine-mouth price: The price of coal that is sold from the mine and therefore does not include transportation and other consumer costs.

Pulverized coal processes: Processes that use pulverized, powderlike coal and are predominantly found in utilities that burn coal, and are increasingly used in blast furnaces.

Recoverable reserve base: The portion of the demonstrated reserve that is likely to be recovered using standard technologies, taking economics into account, as published by the Department of Energy.

Steam coal: Coal used by electric power plants and industrial steam boilers to produce electricity.

Subbituminous coal: A coal that is ranked between bituminous and lignite.

Total resources: Estimates of both identified resources and undiscovered resources, as published by the Department of Energy and the U.S. Geological Survey.

CRUDE PETROLEUM AND NATURAL GAS
Economic and Trade Trends

U.S. International Trade

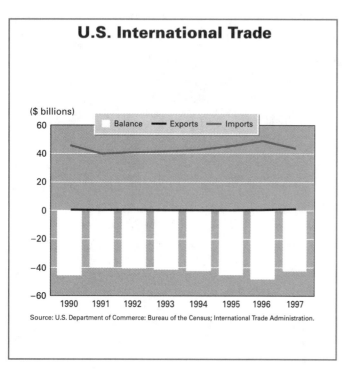

($ billions)

Legend: Balance — Exports — Imports

Source: U.S. Department of Commerce: Bureau of the Census; International Trade Administration.

U.S. Crude Oil and Gas Production, 1974–2000

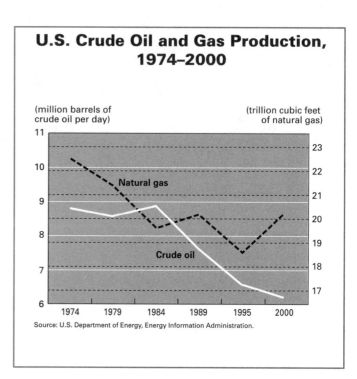

(million barrels of crude oil per day)

(trillion cubic feet of natural gas)

Natural gas

Crude oil

Source: U.S. Department of Energy, Energy Information Administration.

World Crude Oil Consumption, 1999

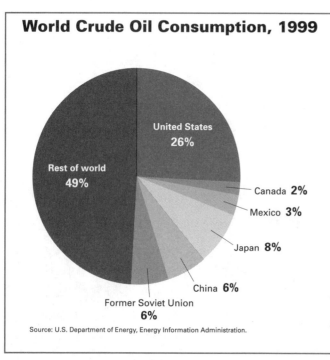

United States 26%
Canada 2%
Mexico 3%
Japan 8%
China 6%
Former Soviet Union 6%
Rest of world 49%

Source: U.S. Department of Energy, Energy Information Administration.

Output and Output per Hour

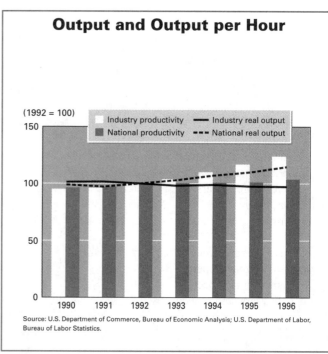

(1992 = 100)

Legend: Industry productivity — Industry real output — National productivity — National real output

Source: U.S. Department of Commerce, Bureau of Economic Analysis; U.S. Department of Labor, Bureau of Labor Statistics.

See "Getting the Most Out of *Outlook '99*" for definitions of terms.

Crude Petroleum and Natural Gas

INDUSTRY DEFINITION The crude oil and natural gas extraction industry (SIC 1311) consists of establishments engaged in operating oil and gas fields. The industry's activities include exploration for crude oil and natural gas; drilling, completing, and equipping wells; operating separators, emulsion breakers, and desilting equipment; and all other activities involved in making crude oil and natural gas marketable up to the point of shipment from the producing property. This industry also includes the mining and extraction of oil from oil shale and oil sands and the production of gas and hydrocarbon liquids through gasification, liquefaction, and pyrolysis of coal at the mine site.

OVERVIEW

The production of crude oil in the United States is projected to increase slightly in 1998 and decline 2.3 percent in 1999 (see Table 3-1). Consumption is forecast to grow 2.2 percent in 1998 and 1 percent in 1999 (see Table 3-2). As a result, a slight reduction in crude oil imports is forecast in 1998, while a 3 percent increase is forecast in 1999 (see Table 3-3). The prices of imported crude oil are expected to fluctuate over the next 2 years but should generally decline overall. A 10 percent reduction is expected in 1998, followed by an increase of almost 5 percent in 1999.

In contrast, natural gas production is expected to increase slightly over those 2 years, rising 1 percent in 1998 and slightly more than 1 percent in 1999. Meanwhile, natural gas prices paid to producers are forecast to fall more than 13 percent in 1998 and an additional 1 percent in 1999. However, residential natural gas prices are expected to fall only 4 percent in 1998 and then increase almost 1 percent in 1999. The growth in natural gas consumption is expected to exceed the increase in production in both years, and as a consequence imports of natural gas are expected to increase 9 percent in 1998 and 7 percent in 1999 (see Table 3-3). [See the boxed note: "Natural Gas Production, Consumption, and Imports Through 2005."]

WORLDWIDE INDUSTRY TRENDS

Worldwide Supply

It is expected that most oil-producing regions will increase their petroleum production between 1997 and 2005. The United States, with a forecast 5 percent reduction in crude oil output, is an exception to this worldwide trend (see Table 3-1). The Organization of Petroleum Exporting Countries (OPEC) is expected to account for about 40 percent of the projected increase in world oil supply between 1997 and 2005. Non-OPEC Latin America, Asia, and the countries of the former Soviet Union (FSU) are forecast to contribute almost 40 percent of that increase. The balance of increased crude oil production will be provided by the developed countries, chiefly from the North Sea.

OPEC. The member countries of OPEC accounted for almost 40 percent of world crude oil production in 1997. By the end of 2005 OPEC's share is expected to be essentially unchanged, creating an 11-year period of steady world dependence on OPEC crude oil. This period of little-changing world dependence follows a 6-year period (1987–1993) of increasing world dependence on OPEC crude oil production during which OPEC's share of world production rose from 31 percent to 42 percent. Although OPEC's share is forecast to remain stable

TABLE 3-1: Historical and Forecast World Crude Oil Production by Region, 1995–2005

(millions of barrels per day unless otherwise noted)

	1995	1996	1997	1998	1999	2000	2001	2002	2003	2004	2005
OECD	22.296	23.033	23.293	23.811	24.259	24.822	24.952	25.072	25.235	25.339	25.463
United States	9.399	9.445	9.429	9.439	9.220	9.110	9.060	9.000	8.980	8.960	8.960
Canada	2.448	2.474	2.560	2.643	2.741	2.840	2.910	2.980	3.050	3.121	3.191
Mexico	3.092	3.306	3.420	3.482	3.630	3.781	3.832	3.884	3.937	3.990	4.044
Japan	0.081	0.081	0.080	0.079	0.084	0.090	0.095	0.100	0.106	0.111	0.116
Australia and New Zealand	0.699	0.721	0.775	0.796	0.812	0.830	0.831	0.832	0.834	0.836	0.837
OECD Europe	6.577	7.006	7.029	7.094	6.941	6.804	8.224	8.276	8.329	8.322	8.315
Developing countries	37.066	37.854	39.419	40.470	40.468	41.219	42.378	43.599	44.722	46.022	47.404
Other South and Central America	3.006	3.257	3.393	3.687	3.867	4.050	4.133	4.216	4.301	4.385	4.471
Pacific Rim	2.087	2.091	2.163	2.263	2.345	2.428	2.529	2.631	2.732	2.835	2.937
OPEC	27.507	27.906	29.237	29.770	29.460	29.895	30.696	31.556	32.315	33.248	34.261
Other developing countries	4.466	4.600	4.625	4.750	4.795	4.845	5.020	5.196	5.375	5.554	5.735
Eurasia	10.405	10.477	10.660	10.753	10.954	11.162	11.595	12.030	12.468	12.907	13.347
Former Soviet Union	7.146	7.082	7.189	7.261	7.377	7.497	7.900	8.303	8.708	9.114	9.522
Eastern Europe	0.269	0.264	0.253	0.259	0.280	0.301	0.311	0.321	0.331	0.342	0.352
China	2.990	3.131	3.218	3.233	3.297	3.364	3.385	3.406	3.428	3.451	3.473
Total production	69.767	71.364	73.372	75.034	75.680	77.203	78.926	80.702	82.425	84.267	86.214
Presumed world oil prices (1996$ per barrel)	17.61	20.52	18.18	18.00	18.57	19.11	19.36	19.51	19.79	19.99	20.19

Source: U.S. Department of Energy, Energy Information Administration, *International Energy Outlook 1998,* April 1998.

TABLE 3-2: Historical and Forecast World Crude Oil Consumption by Region, 1995–2005

(millions of barrels per day unless otherwise noted)

	1995	1996	1997	1998	1999	2000	2001	2002	2003	2004	2005
OECD	42.409	43.328	43.869	44.435	45.123	45.623	46.186	46.745	47.201	47.714	48.267
United States (states and territories)	17.979	18.565	18.870	19.191	19.653	19.923	20.252	20.591	20.841	21.151	21.501
Canada	1.755	1.799	1.822	1.845	1.862	1.876	1.905	1.933	1.960	1.986	2.012
Mexico	1.855	1.895	1.941	2.007	2.091	2.197	2.233	2.268	2.301	2.334	2.367
Japan	5.711	5.867	5.982	6.100	6.208	6.307	6.376	6.448	6.519	6.592	6.670
Australia and New Zealand	0.988	0.935	0.963	0.992	1.020	1.047	1.058	1.068	1.078	1.088	1.098
OECD Europe	14.121	14.267	14.291	14.300	14.290	14.274	14.362	14.437	14.502	14.562	14.621
Developing countries	18.477	19.149	19.904	20.657	20.929	21.617	22.440	23.291	24.168	25.075	26.016
Other Central and South America	3.459	3.544	3.820	4.100	4.381	4.669	4.843	5.022	5.207	5.399	5.597
Pacific Rim	4.394	4.548	4.733	4.917	5.095	5.267	5.554	5.856	6.171	6.502	6.850
OPEC	5.226	5.394	5.596	5.786	5.498	5.624	5.753	5.885	6.020	6.158	6.300
Other developing countries	5.398	5.663	5.755	5.854	5.955	6.057	6.290	6.528	6.770	7.016	7.268
Eurasia	9.040	9.047	9.317	9.615	9.928	10.263	10.600	10.966	11.357	11.778	12.232
Former Soviet Union	4.617	4.379	4.328	4.309	4.319	4.361	4.464	4.585	4.725	4.885	5.067
Eastern Europe	1.092	1.120	1.220	1.316	1.408	1.497	1.514	1.533	1.554	1.577	1.601
China	3.331	3.548	3.770	3.990	4.201	4.405	4.622	4.847	5.078	5.317	5.564
Total consumption	69.926	71.524	73.090	74.707	75.980	77.503	79.226	81.002	82.726	84.567	86.515
Presumed oil prices (1996$ per barrel)	17.61	20.52	18.18	18.00	18.57	19.11	19.36	19.51	19.79	19.99	20.20

Source: U.S. Department of Energy, Energy Information Administration, *International Energy Outlook Projection Systems,* 1998.

between 1997 and 2005, OPEC could easily increase its production and world share over that period because of its low production costs. The production costs of the OPEC countries in the Persian Gulf are among the lowest in the world, varying between $1 and $1.50 per barrel.

Former Soviet Union. In 1997, the FSU was the world's third largest oil-producing region (after Saudi Arabia and the United States). However, between 1992 [when the FSU led world crude oil producers with more than 12 million barrels per day (b/d)] and 1996, FSU production steadily declined, reaching a low of 7 million b/d. Recent western investment in the FSU, particularly in Russia, implies that the perceived risk of investing in the oil and gas industry of the FSU may be diminishing. Consequently, production is forecast to increase an average of 4 percent annually between 1997 and 2005.

The growth in FSU oil production between 1997 and 2005 may be substantially higher than 4 percent annually, depending on the resolution of many unanswered questions. Nonetheless, the relatively low level of investment currently held by the major

U.S. oil companies in the FSU (see Table 3-6) indicates that caution is being exercised. Recent developments suggest that Russia still is determined to open its petroleum industry to western investment, which may stimulate additional future investment. For example, on April 1, 1998, the Russian government announced that it would abolish an excise tax on the pumping of oil. Other, so far undisclosed, tax relief measures also are planned, all of which may spur unforecast western investment in Russian oil production, depending on how significant the tax relief is. Prospects for both future crude oil production and foreign investment in the countries of the FSU were substantially enhanced when Russia and Kazakhstan agreed in April 1998 to divide the Caspian Sea into sections among the countries bordering that sea. The agreement improves the chances for substantial foreign investment in the area. (See the boxed note: "Resource Development in the Caspian Sea Region.")

Latin America. Latin America (including Mexico but excluding the OPEC member Venezuela) has had substantial growth in crude oil production in recent years, reaching 14 percent of world output in 1997. Between 1990 and 1997 production of Latin American crude oil increased 55 percent. Latin America is expected to add almost 2 million b/d of productive capacity between 1997 and 2005 (see Table 3-1).

The recent growth in Latin America's level of petroleum production is due partially to the discovery of new fields as well as privatizations of state-owned petroleum companies and the opening of petroleum resources to foreign investment. Brazil opened its upstream petroleum industry to foreign investment through a constitutional amendment in 1996 that allowed foreign investment in the exploration, production, and development of crude oil within that nation's boundaries (including offshore). This reform is expected to increase crude oil production substantially by increasing the level of investment in Brazil's upstream petroleum industry. Colombia already has substantial foreign investment in its upstream petroleum industry. Brazil and Colombia are expected to join Venezuela as 1-million-b/d producers of crude oil before 2005. (In 1996 only 14 countries worldwide produced 1 million barrels of crude oil per day, according to the Energy Information Administration.)

Asia. The oil production of non-OPEC Asian nations grew 22 percent between 1990 and 1996 and accounted for 11 percent of world production in 1997. China is the largest Asian oil producer. Although China has expanded its productive capacity greatly in recent years, it has not become a major oil-exporting

---

NATURAL GAS PRODUCTION, CONSUMPTION, AND IMPORTS THROUGH 2005

The worldwide consumption of natural gas has grown far more rapidly than has the consumption of crude oil in recent years. Natural gas consumption increased 25 percent between 1987 and 1996 and petroleum consumption increased 13 percent in that period, according to the Energy Information Administration. Strong growth in the consumption of natural gas is projected for the period 1997–2005, with consumption in Asia expected to show the greatest increases, although the recent financial crisis in that region may limit growth somewhat for a while.

Trade in natural gas grew 9 percent in 1996. Three-fourths of world gas trade is transported by pipeline. Two major pipeline projects were completed during 1997, in Latin America and in Europe. The balance of natural gas trade is in the form of liquefied natural gas (LNG) transported by LNG tankers. The majority of LNG trade occurs in Asia. For example, 62 percent of the LNG produced worldwide was imported by Japan in 1996 and 58 percent was imported in 1997.

Overall domestic natural gas production is forecast to increase 1 percent in 1998 and 7 percent in 1999 (see Table 3-4). Between 1997 and 2005, domestic production is expected to increase an average of slightly more than 2 percent annually, with onshore production increasing an average of 2 percent per year and offshore production increasing an average of almost 3 percent per year. Nevertheless, natural gas production in the United States occurs chiefly onshore. Although the onshore share declined from 80 to 85 percent between 1974 and 1989 to 70 to 72 percent between 1995 and 1997, the onshore share is forecast to remain at around 70 percent through 2005. Increases in U.S. natural gas production have

lagged behind increases in demand in recent years, and the shortfall is expected to increase in the future, leading to increased levels of imports (see Tables 3-4 and 3-5). Canada is the main source for U.S. natural gas imports, accounting for 99 percent of the 1997 imported total. Canada, which more than doubled its natural gas production between 1986 and 1996, currently accounts for 13 percent of the U.S. natural gas market. Canada is expected to continue to increase its exports of natural gas to the United States in the future. Imports of natural gas are expected to increase 9 percent in 1998 and 7 percent in 1999 and an average of 5 percent annually between 1997 and 2005 (see Table 3-3). The growing integration of the U.S. and Canadian natural gas markets bodes well for future U.S. investment in Canadian petroleum resources. In 1996 the major U.S. petroleum companies accounted for nearly 14 percent of Canadian production of natural gas.

Natural gas consumption in the United States is expected to grow steadily over the next few years (see Table 3-5), matching the forecast average expansion in the value of domestic output of 2.3 percent and exceeding the growth in overall domestic energy consumption. This substantial expansion in the consumption of natural gas results partly from its environmental advantage over crude oil. Additionally, most new electricity generation capacity planned for 1997 through 2005 will be natural gas–fired. Natural gas has become relatively less expensive as a fuel for electricity generation, an advantage that has been magnified by the impending deregulation of the domestic electricity industry. Prices of natural gas are expected to decline at an average annual rate of about 1.5 percent, with most of the reduction anticipated between 1997 and 1999.

TABLE 3-3: U.S. Net Imports[1] of Energy by Source, 1987–2005

Year	Crude Oil, millions of barrels per day	Petroleum Products, millions of barrels per day	Natural Gas,[2] (trillion cubic feet)
1987	4.52	1.39	0.94
1988	4.95	1.63	1.22
1989	5.70	1.50	1.28
1990	5.79	1.38	1.45
1991	5.67	0.96	1.64
1992	5.99	0.94	1.92
1993	6.69	0.93	2.21
1994	6.96	1.09	2.46
1995	7.14	0.75	2.69
1996	7.40	1.10	2.78
1997[3]	7.89	1.05	2.85
1998[4]	7.88	1.37	3.11
1999[4]	8.15	1.36	3.34
2000[4]	8.75	1.42	3.84
2001[4]	9.03	1.59	3.87
2002[4]	9.46	1.64	3.89
2003[4]	9.58	1.75	3.94
2004[4]	9.95	1.82	3.98
2005[4]	10.14	1.96	4.02

[1] Gross imports minus gross exports.
[2] Dry natural gas.
[3] Estimate.
[4] Forecast.
Source: U.S. Department of Energy, Energy Information Administration, *Short-Term Energy Outlook* (1987–1999), *Annual Energy Outlook* (2000–2005).

TABLE 3-4: U.S. Crude Oil and Natural Gas Production, Selected Years

	1974	1979	1984	1989	1995	1996	1997	1998	1999	2000	2001	2002	2003	2004	2005
Crude oil production (thousands of barrels per day)															
Onshore crude oil	7,285	7,485	7,596	6,486	5,035	4,931	4,931	4,931	4,931	4,931	4,931	4,931	4,931	4,931	4,931
Lower 48 crude oil	7,092	6,084	5,874	4,612	3,820	3,760	3,720	3,660	3,510	3,390	3,300	3,230	3,180	3,150	3,130
Alaska crude oil	193	1,401	1,722	1,874	1,484	1,400	1,300	1,210	1,170	1,130	1,090	1,050	1,020	980	930
Offshore crude oil	1,489	1,067	1,283	1,127	1,260	1,320	1,400	1,530	1,590	1,650	1,690	1,720	1,740	1,750	1,750
Total crude oil	8,774	8,552	8,879	7,613	6,560	6,480	6,410	6,390	6,280	6,170	6,080	6,010	5,940	5,880	5,820
Natural gas production (trillion cubic feet)															
Onshore natural gas	19.34	17.06	15.56	16.30	13.25	13.51	13.57	13.59	14.57	14.39	14.65	14.82	15.22	15.43	15.82
Offshore natural gas	3.18	4.33	4.06	3.92	5.35	5.50	5.28	5.47	5.78	5.88	5.95	6.12	6.22	6.38	6.43
Total natural gas	22.52	21.39	19.62	20.22	18.60	19.01	18.85	19.06	20.35	20.27	20.60	20.94	21.44	21.81	22.25
Crude oil production (percent of total U.S. production)															
Onshore crude oil	83.03	87.52	85.55	85.20	76.75	76.10	76.93	77.17	78.52	79.92	81.10	82.05	83.01	83.86	84.73
Lower-48 crude oil	80.83	71.14	66.16	60.58	58.23	58.02	58.03	57.28	55.89	54.94	54.28	53.74	53.54	53.57	53.78
Alaska crude oil	2.20	16.38	19.39	24.62	22.62	21.60	20.28	18.94	18.63	18.31	17.93	17.47	17.17	16.67	15.98
Offshore crude oil	16.97	12.48	14.45	14.80	19.21	20.37	21.84	23.94	25.32	26.74	27.80	28.62	29.29	29.76	30.07
Natural gas gross withdrawals (percent of total U.S. production)															
Onshore natural gas	85.9	79.8	79.3	80.6	71.2	71.1	72.0	71.3	71.6	71.0	71.1	70.8	71.0	70.7	71.1
Offshore natural gas	14.1	20.2	20.7	19.4	28.8	28.9	28.0	28.7	28.4	29.0	28.9	29.2	29.0	29.3	28.9

Source: U.S. Department of Energy, Energy Information Administration, *Annual Energy Review 1996,* and the National Energy Modeling System.

TABLE 3-5:   U.S. Consumption of Energy by Selected Sources, 1987–2005

	Petroleum Products, millions of barrels per day	Natural Gas,[1] trillion cubic feet per year	Coal, millions of short tons per year	Nuclear Power, quadrillion Btu per year
1987	16.72	17.21	837	4.91
1988	17.34	18.03	884	5.66
1989	17.37	18.80	891	5.68
1990	17.04	18.72	897	6.16
1991	16.77	19.03	894	6.58
1992	17.10	19.54	907	6.61
1993	17.24	20.28	944	6.52
1994	17.72	20.71	951	6.84
1995	17.72	21.58	962	7.19
1996	18.31	21.96	1,007	7.17
1997[2]	18.61	22.10	1,034	7.24
1998[3]	18.97	22.87	1,053	7.34
1999[3]	19.36	23.84	1,044	7.35
2000[3]	19.62	24.08	1,058	7.36
2001[3]	19.94	24.44	1,087	7.26
2002[3]	20.27	24.81	1,084	7.31
2003[3]	20.52	25.33	1,090	7.16
2004[3]	20.81	25.72	1,097	7.03
2005[3]	21.15	26.22	1,112	6.87

[1] Dry natural gas.
[2] Estimate.
[3] Forecast.
Source: U.S. Department of Energy, Energy Information Administration, *Short-Term Energy Outlook* (1987–1999), *Annual Energy Outlook* (2000–2005).

TABLE 3-6:   Petroleum Exploration and Development Expenditures of Major U.S. Petroleum Companies by Region for Selected Years
(millions of dollars)

	1986	1989	1994	1995	1996
U.S. exploration and development expenditures					
Onshore	12,496	8,973	7,815	7,695	7,913
Offshore	4,906	6,016	4,773	4,739	6,719
Total	17,402	14,989	12,588	12,434	14,632
Foreign exploration and development expenditures					
Canada	1,126	6,266	1,835	1,899	1,563
OECD Europe	3,168	3,539	4,439	5,204	5,551
FSU and eastern Europe		0	297	359	461
Africa	1,064	1,024	1,392	2,043	2,798
Middle East	340	406	445	361	463
Other Eastern Hemisphere	1,186	2,284	2,758	2,430	4,625
Other Western Hemisphere	642	609	743	875	1,638
Total	7,526	14,128	11,909	13,171	17,099

Source: U.S. Department of Energy, Energy Information Administration, *Performance Profiles of Major Energy Producers 1996,* February 1998.

nation because consumption has exceeded production since 1992. Chinese crude oil production is expected to continue to grow almost 8 percent between 1997 and 2005. However, domestic consumption is forecast to expand even faster at a rate of 48 percent over that period (see Table 3-2).

North Sea. Organization of Economic Cooperation and Development (OECD) European production, most of which comes from the North Sea, has increased substantially in recent years despite earlier predictions that North Sea crude oil production would peak in the late 1980s. For example, between 1991 and 1997 North Sea production rose at an average annual rate of 7 percent after achieving only 2 percent average annual growth between 1985 and 1990. The introduction of horizontal drilling and other technological advances have dramatically increased oil production in the North Sea over this decade. North Sea production is expected to peak around 2003 at 8.33 million b/d and to decline only slightly to 8.32 million b/d by 2005 (see Table 3-1).

Worldwide Demand

On the demand side, recent growth of world oil consumption has resulted largely from a 3-year global economic expansion.

The Caspian Sea is a landlocked body of water whose coastal states include Azerbaijan, Iran, Kazakhstan, Russia, and Turkmenistan. Over 42 billion barrels of recoverable oil reserves are believed to lie beneath it. Some experts estimate that the Caspian Sea Basin possesses up to 200 billion barrels of reserves, which would make it the third largest depository of oil after the Persian Gulf and Siberia.

Despite this untapped wealth, decision makers in the former Soviet Union chose to invest their exploratory and developmental resources elsewhere. Thus, production in what is now the independent nation of Azerbaijan declined from 500,000 barrels per day during World War II to less than 250,000 barrels per day in 1992. All this changed with the breakup of the Soviet Union. In September 1994 a production-sharing agreement that has come to be known as the "deal of the century" was signed between the Republic of Azerbaijan and an 11-company consortium known as the Azerbaijan International Operating Company (AIOC). The participating Financial Reporting System (FRS) companies include Amoco, Exxon, and Unocal (see boxed note on page 3-8). Under the production-sharing agreement, the AIOC was required to drill a minimum of three appraisal wells on its contract area within 30 months of the agreement ratification date of December 1994.

The FRS companies currently hold a 35 percent interest in the AIOC, with Amoco leading the way with 17.01 percent, followed by Unocal and Exxon with interests of 10 percent and 8 percent, respectively. The total U.S. interest is 43.7 percent. The consortium is charged with developing the Azeri, Chirag, and deepwater Gunashli oil fields south of the Ashrafi/Dan Ulduzu area, which have estimated reserves of 4 billion barrels. AIOC expected to begin its own production from those fields late in 1997, with initial production estimated at about 115,000 barrels per day. The agreement stipulates that Azerbaijan is to receive 80 percent of the profits. In a separate agreement signed in December 1996, another group of companies will hold exploration rights in the Ashrafi/Dan Ulduzu area of the Caspian Sea. Again, Amoco and Unocal are major participants, with interests of 30 percent and 25.5 percent, respectively. The contract area lies east of the Apsheron Peninsula and covers 453 square kilometers in water depths ranging from 75 to 200 meters.

The FRS companies are also active in Kazakhstan. Mobil is a member of a consortium exploring for oil and gas in the Kazak sector of the Caspian. Onshore, Mobil and Chevron are participants in the Tengizchevoil joint venture, which operates the Tengiz oil field. Production from this field, one of the largest in the world with an estimated 3 billion to 10 billion barrels of oil, had been declining under Soviet managers.

Under the joint venture, production more than doubled to over 160,000 barrels per day by the end of 1996. While production from a field typically declines over time, the new managers expect that annual production can be increased to almost 750,000 barrels per day by 2010.

Events in Turkmenistan provide further evidence of the important role the FRS companies are playing in developing the oil and gas resources of that region. Recently, the Turkmenistan government decided to auction off oil and gas concessions in its sector of the Caspian Sea. Rather than holding the auction in Ashgabat, the capital, the officials are planning to conduct the auction in Houston, where many of the FRS companies have offices. The major obstacle to developing the oil reserves of the Caspian Basin has been the problem of transporting oil to western markets. Currently, flows of oil from that region have been hampered by Russian interests which control all the export lines from the region. This problem is expected to ease somewhat after the opening of an 870-mile pipeline that will transport the oil from Baku, the capital of Azerbaijan, across Chechnya through Russia to the Black Sea port of Novorossisk. The oil then will be shipped to the west by tankers going through the Turkish Straits into the Mediterranean. A second pipeline route is planned that would avoid Russian territory and control altogether by transporting the oil west to the Turkish port of Ceyhan on the Mediterranean. A decision on this route was expected in the fall of 1998.

The issue of who owns the undersea resources of the Caspian Basin could delay resource development. At issue is whether the Law of the Sea convention applies to the Caspian. If it does, the maritime boundaries of the five states bordering the Caspian could be based on the equidistant division of the sea and undersea resources into national sectors. If the law does not apply, the Caspian Basin and its resources could be developed jointly. Arguing that the Law of the Sea does not apply because the Caspian Sea is landlocked, Russia favors joint development of the sea's resources. This position is supported by Iran. However, Iran's involvement in resource development could pose a major problem for the FRS companies in light of executive orders by the U.S. president which have imposed an embargo on trade with and investment in Iran.

Despite the issue of whether resource development in the Caspian Sea will be governed by the Law of the Sea there is every expectation that the Caspian Basin will be a major oil-producing area in the future. As L. Richard Flury, Amoco's executive vice president for exploration and production, said, "We've identified the Caspian Basin as a high-priority area for growth and spending into the twenty-first century."

Oil demand depends on economic activity; hence, oil consumption projections are dependent on assumptions about economic growth rates. World economic activity began to expand in 1993 after 2 years of essentially flat growth which resulted largely from the economic collapse of the FSU. World economic growth was forecast to continue to accelerate slightly over the period 1995–2000 (from about 2.2 percent annually to an average rate of 2.8 percent annually), leading to rising petroleum consumption. Between 1993 and 1997 world petroleum consumption increased slightly more than 1 percent annually. This growth is expected to increase to slightly more than 2 percent annually in 1998 and 1999 (see Table 3-2).

Much of the forecast worldwide economic growth was concentrated in the Pacific Rim nations. However, the economies of many of those nations are still recovering from the Asian financial crisis that began in October 1997, and could continue to experience an economic slowdown through 1998. Countries such as Hong Kong (PRC), Indonesia, Japan, Malaysia, the Philippines, Singapore, South Korea, Taiwan, and Thailand will probably contribute to a slowing in the region's growth in crude oil demand. Asian nations (excluding Japan) are expected to account for about 29 percent of the total growth in world petroleum consumption between 1997 and 2005, substantially less than the 90 percent share this area was forecast to consume 1 year ago; this provides some indication of the severity of the recent Asian financial crisis.

Latin America is expected to show sizable increases in oil consumption as the economic growth in that region of the last few years is expected to continue. (Between 1995 and 2005, the Central America and South American region are forecast to have an average annual economic growth of approximately 5 percent, according to WEFA Energy. In that period, the European OECD countries are forecast to have average annual economic growth of 0.3 percent and the FSU is forecast to have average annual growth of 2.1 percent.) Alternatively, in the more developed markets of the OECD countries, economic growth and consequent growth in petroleum demand have been more moderate and are forecast to remain so through 2005. The growth in oil consumption in the FSU, eastern Europe, and other developing countries (including Africa) is forecast to be even lower than the growth in oil consumption in the OECD countries taken together (see Table 3-2).

If supply and demand grow at comparable rates, relatively moderate changes in the price of crude oil will result. However, the continued (although slow) recovery of the FSU petroleum industry, marginal (and largely technology-driven) increases in production by non-OPEC producers, eased restrictions on Iraqi crude oil exports, and the apparent lack of adherence to production quotas by OPEC producers have resulted in declining world prices for crude oil. These prices became so low that an extraordinary meeting was held March 30, 1998. OPEC and some key non-OPEC oil producers agreed to reduce production levels 1.5 million b/d in an attempt to reverse the recent downward trend in world oil prices, which reached a 9-year nominal low of $12.80 per barrel on March 17, 1998. (Since December 9, 1996, the United Nations has allowed Iraq to sell a limited amount of oil to pay for food, medicine, and other humanitarian needs. The currently allowed volume is 2.3 million b/d.) However, the anticipated production cuts have appeared increasingly ephemeral since the agreement was reached. On May 29, the Algerian oil minister, Youcef Yousfi, said that OPEC members are discussing further cuts to support oil prices. Yousfi also said that contacts were continuing with non-OPEC oil producers to put an end to the fall in oil prices.

Overseas Investments by U.S. Petroleum Companies

Four of the world's 20 largest petroleum companies in terms of oil production are U.S.-based, 14 are state-owned, and 2 are European-based (both of which have affiliates among the major U.S. oil companies). Opportunities for U.S. multinational petroleum companies to explore, develop, and produce crude oil and natural gas in many areas of the world are increasing rapidly. Since the oil price crash of 1986 the major U.S. petroleum companies have more than doubled their foreign exploration and development spending, and since 1989 the majors' foreign expenditures often have exceeded their domestic expenditures (see Table 3-6). [Some U.S. independent oil and gas companies have significant overseas oil and gas production operations, but the collective value of those operations constitutes a small fraction of the overseas operations of the U.S. majors.] Recent increases in the U.S. majors' exploration and development expenditures have been directed mostly toward the North Sea and southeast Asia (see Table 3-6).

North Sea. OECD Europe, principally the North Sea, is still the largest target of the major U.S. petroleum companies' overseas oil and gas exploration and development spending and accounted for about 32 percent of those expenditures in 1996 (see Table 3-6). Spending by the major U.S. petroleum companies on their upstream North Sea operations should continue to be substantial in the years ahead. The major U.S. companies account for roughly one-third of total North Sea production, with most of the balance produced by European companies.

Asia and the Pacific Rim. The "Other Eastern Hemisphere" region shown in Table 3-6, which essentially consists of Asia and the Pacific Rim, is the second most important target for the major U.S. petroleum companies' exploration and development spending, accounting for about 27 percent of their total foreign expenditures. Exploration and development expenditures in this area increased dramatically in 1996, growing 90 percent. However, much of that increase was due to Mobil's acquisition of the Australian petroleum company Ampolex for $1.3 billion. Additionally, the recent Asian financial crisis may substantially, but perhaps only briefly, diminish future prospects in this area.

Africa. Approximately 15 percent of the U.S. majors' foreign exploration and development spending was directed at Africa in 1996. That spending in Africa more than doubled between 1994 and 1996, increasing $1.4 billion. Although most U.S. upstream petroleum investment in Africa was in Nigeria, Algeria and Angola also were major targets in 1996. Nigeria is an area of comparatively long-time investment by the U.S. majors, and the new investments were employed largely in existing offshore exploration, development, and production. By contrast, Algeria only recently opened its borders to foreign investment in upstream petroleum and has been in need of foreign investment embodying recent technological advances. Angola also recently opened its upstream petroleum to foreign investment. Although the particulars behind increased investment in each of these countries vary, two threads run through those investments: the recent opening of the country to foreign investment and the introduction of investment with advanced technological properties. The U.S. majors also have operations in Egypt, Namibia, and Niger.

Latin America. The "Other Western Hemisphere" region, which principally consists of Latin America, is an area of rapidly growing exploration and development activity for U.S. majors. Although accounting for only 10 percent of the major U.S. petroleum companies' total foreign exploration and development expenditures in 1996, their Latin American exploration and development spending grew more rapidly in 1996 than in any other single region except the Asia and Pacific Rim region.

Recent privatization in Latin America occurred as part of sweeping free market economic reforms. Although the privatization of petroleum assets in Latin America has been sporadic, some countries, such as Argentina, have embarked on far-reaching privatization efforts, while others, such as Mexico (Latin America's largest crude oil producer), have adopted modest reforms. Venezuela, through the state-owned Petroleos de Venezuela, S.A. (PdVSA), is Latin America's second largest crude oil producer. PdVSA has attracted substantial interest and is attempting to attract substantial foreign investment by allowing production-sharing agreements with foreign companies. Thus, foreign companies may take an equity interest in the oil or gas reserves developed rather than simply providing services for fees. However, investment in Venezuela's upstream petroleum industry is not without problems in dealing with government regulations. Colombia and Peru are other Latin American countries that have attracted the interest of the major U.S. oil companies.

Canada. Canada accounted for 9 percent of the U.S. majors' foreign exploration and development expenditures in 1996. That country is the largest combined exporter of crude oil and natural gas to the United States. Currently, most of Canada's crude oil production occurs in the western provinces. However, the Hibernia field, which may be an important area for future oil and gas production, lies offshore of Newfoundland in eastern Canada and may be a part of a substantial oil production area, rivaling the major western Canada deposits. The $6 billion Hibernia field is approximately two-thirds controlled by major U.S. oil companies and has crude oil reserves as large as 1 billion barrels. Hibernia could prove to be the largest North American project since the development of the Prudhoe Bay, Alaska, deposits. Oil production from the Hibernia field began in November 1997, and shipments to refiners began in December 1997.

Socialist and Former Socialist Regions. The former communist countries of eastern Europe and Asia offer enormous opportunities to U.S. petroleum companies through the recent opening of their oil and gas resources to foreign investors. Many foreign investors expect that the move toward a market-driven economy in Russia, Azerbaijan, Kazakhstan, and other countries of the FSU eventually will create new exploration and production opportunities in one of the world's largest petroleum-producing regions outside the Persian Gulf. However, political uncertainties, legal difficulties, and concerns about property rights are large impediments to investment in these countries. Changing tax regimes and political complications regarding pipelines, many of which cross borders between hostile nations, have also limited foreign investment in pipelines. Undeveloped infrastructures hinder the transportation of produced oil and gas to consuming areas, creating disincentives for foreign investment in

related seaports. Thus, although investment by the U.S. major petroleum companies is increasing, it remains low relative to investment in other regions of the world at 3 percent of total foreign exploration and development spending. (Despite these difficulties, Russia determinedly continues to go down the privatization path. In March 1997 an auction of 75 percent of the state oil company Rosneft was announced with a starting price of $2.1 billion. However, the attempted sale was postponed.)

DOMESTIC PETROLEUM INDUSTRY

Since the oil price collapse of 1986, the size of the U.S. petroleum industry has diminished as higher-cost companies have left the industry and higher-cost projects have been abandoned. Thus, the lower-priced oil of the post-1986 period provides a marginally better, but still low, return to companies and their projects today. (For data on U.S.-based major energy producers, see the boxed note: "The Financial Reporting System.") The increased productivity of U.S. exploration and development is reflected in the decline in the cost of adding reserves (finding costs). Finding costs have fallen because of a general reduction in activity combined with more selective drilling (often called prospect high grading). Additionally, the application of advancing technologies to exploration and drilling has made many projects more profitable. Finally, corporate downsizing and reorganization have reduced operating costs through the elimination of redundancies and a refocusing of the uses of corporate resources.

Smaller companies have also been playing a larger role in the development of U.S. oil and gas resources. The share of oil and gas production of nonmajors (independents) increased from 40 percent of total U.S. production in the late 1980s to nearly 50 percent in 1996. Nonmajors accounted for 60 percent of total U.S. production of natural gas from U.S. offshore areas in 1996. These companies tend to drill in smaller fields and have faster depletion rates than do the majors. They also have been able to reduce their finding costs to levels comparable to those of the majors.

THE FINANCIAL REPORTING SYSTEM

The Financial Reporting System (FRS) was established in 1977 under Section 205(h) of the Department of Energy Organization Act (P.L. 91-95). This statute requires the Energy Information Administration to "identify and designate major energy-producing companies" and develop and implement a data reporting program for energy financial and operating information from these companies. The EIA is also required to submit an annual data and analysis report on the FRS information (*Performance Profiles of Major Energy Producers*) to the Congress. Individual company financial reporting is required "on a uniform and standardized basis" for "each line of commerce in the energy industry" in which the company or its affiliates are involved.

Technological Improvements

The introduction of new technologies has reduced finding costs and operating costs at a time when petroleum prices generally have hovered around historic lows after adjusting for inflation. Advanced computers and associated improvements in software have made possible three-dimensional seismic studies, a major breakthrough in exploration and development technology. Three-dimensional seismic images have greater resolution than do two-dimensional images and more thoroughly delineate oil and gas reservoirs that are hidden by complex faulting. Detailed seismic surveys have fostered the use of horizontal drilling, another new technology. Recent technological advances include four-component seismic (also known as multicomponent seismic), which can be applied to geologic structures to indicate whether a structure contains oil, natural gas, or water.

Many petroleum reservoirs are wider than they are deep, and so wells that are drilled horizontally more closely follow the contours of a reservoir and expose the drilling bore to greater amounts of hydrocarbons. Horizontal drilling also allows more than one reservoir to drain with a single well. In the North Sea horizontal wells are doubly effective: They increase the flow from fields that otherwise would be too slow, making them economical, and they reach reservoirs that would be too small to justify the building of a new platform. Another technological advance consists of production platform designs that provide access to offshore fields at previously inaccessible water depths. The Gulf of Mexico and the North Sea, once thought of as having nearly reached their productive limits, have added economic petroleum reserves that surpass previous expectations through the application of technological advances such as three-dimensional seismic images, horizontal drilling, and deep-water platforms.

Domestic Petroleum Production Forecast

Domestic crude oil production peaked in 1970 and has fallen an average of 1.5 percent per year since that time. Low returns on investment in oil and gas production operations account for much of the decline in U.S. exploration and development activity. In recent years the rates of return on such investments have been significantly and consistently lower than those realized by the S&P Industrials' nonenergy companies. Domestic crude oil production is expected to increase only 0.1 percent in 1998 and decline 2 percent in 1999 (see Table 3-1).

An area for domestic crude oil production that has shown some promise in recent years is the Gulf of Mexico. Offshore production, which comes almost exclusively from the Gulf of Mexico, accounted for 21 percent of total U.S. production in 1997, compared with 15 percent in 1989 (see Table 3-4). Also, offshore Gulf of Mexico production is expected to show a sustained increase well into the future (see the boxed note: "Deepwater in the Gulf of Mexico: A New Frontier"). In contrast, the onshore production of the "Lower 48" is projected to decline steadily over the next two decades. Alaska accounted for 20 percent of total U.S. production in 1997 (see Table 3-4). Alaskan production has declined over the last several years from its peak in 1988 of slightly more than 2 million b/d to 1.3 million b/d in 1997. Although the decline is expected to continue, with production falling 7 percent in 1998 and 3 percent in

---

DEEPWATER IN THE GULF OF MEXICO: A NEW FRONTIER

Although the Financial Reporting System companies have explored for oil and gas in the deeper waters of the Gulf of Mexico since the late 1970s, deepwater development generally was considered uneconomical because the costs of a fixed production platform increased exponentially with water depth. Indicative of this, in 1989 less than 3 percent of the oil produced in the Gulf of Mexico came from deepwater projects. Recently, however, significant new discoveries, legislated deepwater royalty relief, and advances in deepwater production systems have transformed the deepwater region of the Gulf into one of the hottest areas for exploration and development.

Helping foster this trend is the DeepStar project, an industry cooperative effort whose goal is to identify economically viable methods of producing oil and gas from the deepwater tracts in the Gulf of Mexico. As a result of this collective effort, as well as the efforts of the individual firms, 17 percent of the total oil production in the Gulf in 1996 was accounted for by projects operating in water depths exceeding 1,000 feet.

The year 1996 also saw the commencement of production at the $1.2 billion Mars project, the largest discovery in the Gulf of Mexico in the last 25 years. Two FRS companies, Shell and BP America, are partners in this project. The project, with a water depth of 2,940 feet, broke the record set by Shell's Auger project in 1994. Because the costs of installing a fixed platform are prohibitive at such a depth, a tension leg platform was used to extract the oil and gas. A tension leg platform is a floating structure that is held in place by tensioned tendons connected to the sea floor. The Mars project also employs another new production technology, the subsea well. This technology extends the areal reach of a project by enabling the operator to place a satellite well on the sea floor and pipe the oil and gas back to the tension leg platform or to other facilities. Production from the first well at the Mars project was a record-breaking 15,000 barrels of oil per day. Overall production from the project exceeds 100,000 barrels of oil per day. The oil is being transported to shore on the new $135 million Mars Pipe Line system. Suggestive of the project's potential, the pipeline has a capacity of 250,000 barrels of oil per day, with expansion planned to 500,000 barrels per day.

Approximately 60 deepwater Gulf projects are in various stages of development. Among those scheduled for start-up in the next few years are Genesis, Gomez, Mensa, Neptune, Popeye, Petronius, Ram-Powell, Troika, and Ursa (see Table 3-7). Reflecting the progress that has been made in controlling the costs of deepwater development in just the short time since the 1994 start-up of Shell's Auger project, the development costs of these projects are expected to average $3.60 per barrel, 36 percent lower than Auger's costs of $5 per barrel.

TABLE 3-7: Selected Deepwater Projects in the Gulf of Mexico

Project	Participating Companies	Water Depth, ft	Start-Up Year	Production System[1]	Estimated Ultimate Recovery, million barrels of oil equivalent	Project Cost, millions of dollars[2]
Genesis	Chevron, Exxon, Fina	2,600	1996	SP	160+	750
Gomez	Union Pacific Resources	3,000	2000	NA	100–140	NA
Mars	Shell, BP America	2,940	1996	TLP	500	1,200
Mensa	Shell	5,300	1997	SS	128	280
Neptune	Oryx, CNG[3]	1,930	1997	SP	50–75	NA
Popeye	Shell, CNG,[3] Mobil, BP America	2,000	1996	SS	67	110
Petronius	Texaco, Marathon	1,754	1999	CT	80–100	NA
Ram-Powell	Shell, Amoco, Exxon	3,214	1997	TLP/SS	250	1,000
Troika	BP America, Marathon, Shell	2,800	1998	SS	200+	NA
Ursa	Shell, BP America, Conoco, Exxon	4,000	1999	TLP	400+	1,450

[1] CT = compliant tower; SS = subsea system; TLP = tension leg platform; SP = spar platform.
[2] These are unofficial estimates. NA = not available.
[3] A non-FRS company.
Source: Press releases and annual reports.

A RENAISSANCE OF ACTIVITY IN ALASKA

Until recently there was very little basis for optimism about the future of oil production in Alaska. Production from Prudhoe Bay was declining approximately 10 percent per year, and potential North Slope projects that could offset the decline were not as profitable as identical projects elsewhere because the ban on exports of North Slope crude depressed the wellhead price of North Slope production. Also, the fiscal climate was anything but hospitable. Some state leases included provisions for a "net profits" tax, or a tax on revenues after capital and operating cost are recovered, as high as 89 percent. Furthermore, Alaska was perceived to be an expensive region in which to develop new reserves, with the development costs of some of the newer proposed fields, such as Northstar, being estimated at an uneconomical $11 per barrel of reserves. This is consistent both with the pattern of wellhead prices since the ban was repealed and with prior projections of the effect of lifting the ban on wellhead values.

This situation has improved significantly over the last 2 years. The repeal of the export ban has increased the wellhead price of Alaskan North Slope crude by approximately $1 per barrel, an amount which has increased the attractiveness of investing in Alaska. Moreover, Alaska has liberalized its fiscal climate by reducing its royalty take on new fields. Finally, operators in Alaska have found ways to reduce the costs of developing new fields. For example, at Prudhoe Bay, ARCO has been able to reduce the cost of drilling a well over 50 percent since the late 1980s. Moreover, through the use of three-dimensional seismic and horizontal drilling technology,

"fishhook" wells now are drilled that curve along with the oil-bearing strata to maximize the amount of the pipe that is in contact with the strata. As a result of these developments, it is now believed that the Northstar field, which was projected to have costs of $11 per barrel of potential reserves in 1991, will now be developed by BP America for less than $3 per barrel.

These developments are having a major impact on resource development in Alaska. ARCO, BP America, and Exxon, the partners in the Prudhoe Bay field, have announced plans to expand the field's enhanced oil recovery project at a cost of $165 million. This project is expected to increase production 20,000 barrels per day. In addition, ARCO has announced plans to develop its Alpine field, which lies 30 miles west of Kuparuk. This field has potential reserves of over 300 million barrels, making it one of largest fields discovered in the United States in the last decade. The costs of developing the field are believed to be less than $2.50 per barrel. To minimize the impact of the field's development on the environment, ARCO will develop the field by using extended-reach drilling technology from just two drill sites. Moreover, the field will operate much like an offshore platform in that there will not even be a road connecting it to the other North Slope infrastructure. ARCO also intends to develop the West Sak field. Phase I of the project calls for 50 wells and will add 50 million barrels of reserves at a cost of $2 per barrel. Phase II of the project is expected to result in the drilling of an additional 500 wells and allow the recovery of 400 million barrels of reserves.

1999, recent changes may improve the future prospects for oil production in Alaska (see the boxed note: "A Renaissance of Activity in Alaska").

Domestic Petroleum Consumption Forecast

In the United States, real economic growth is expected to average about 2.3 percent annually over the period 1997–2005. As

in recent years, crude oil consumption (and energy demand in general) is expected to lag behind overall economic growth. U.S. consumption of crude oil is expected to increase almost 2 percent in 1998 and slightly more than 2 percent in 1999 (see Table 3-2), largely because of increased demand for motor vehicle fuel. Between 1997 and 2005 crude oil consumption is forecast to grow an average of 1.7 percent annually. Meanwhile,

TABLE 3-8: U.S. Trade Patterns in Crude Petroleum and Natural Gas[1] in 1997

(millions of dollars; percent)

Exports			Imports		
Regions[2]	Value[3]	Share, %	Regions[2]	Value[3]	Share, %
NAFTA	452	48.6	NAFTA	19,060	43.9
Latin America	0	0.0	Latin America	7,963	18.3
Western Europe	0	0.0	Western Europe	2,356	5.4
Japan/Chinese Economic Area	238	25.7	Japan/Chinese Economic Area	109	0.3
Other Asia	238	25.7	Other Asia	267	0.6
Rest of world	0	0.0	Rest of world	13,711	31.5
World	929	100.0	World	43,465	100.0
Top Five Countries	Value	Share, %	Top Five Countries	Value	Share, %
Canada	445	48.0	Canada	12,492	28.7
South Korea	238	25.6	Mexico	6,568	15.1
China	119	12.8	Venezuela	5,716	13.2
Japan	71	7.7	Saudi Arabia	4,805	11.1
Taiwan	48	5.2	Nigeria	3,712	8.5

[1] SIC 1311.
[2] For definitions of regional groupings, see "Getting the Most Out of *Outlook '99.*"
[3] Values may not sum to total due to rounding.
Source: U.S. Department of Commerce, Bureau of the Census.

crude oil production is expected to decline less than 1 percent annually over that period. Consequently, imports will account for a growing share of U.S. crude oil consumption. Crude oil imports are expected to grow at an annual average of 3.6 percent through 2005, and prices should remain relatively stable over that period (see Tables 3-1 and 3-3), increasing at an average rate of 1 percent annually. Table 3-8 describes U.S. trade patterns in crude petroleum and natural gas.

An extensive list of citations to this chapter may be found at the Energy Information Administration Web site, http://www. eia.doe.gov/emeu/finance/usi&to/UP_98.html. This chapter was prepared by the Energy Information Administration, the independent statistical and analytical agency of the U.S. Department of Energy, based on EIA's 1998 long-term forecast and its July 1998 short-term forecast. The EIA short-term forecasts are updated monthly and are found at http://www.eia.doe.gov/ emeu/steo/pub. The information in this chapter should not be construed as advocating or reflecting any policy position of the Department of Energy or any other organization.

Neal C. Davis, U.S. Department of Energy, Energy Information Administration, neal.davis@eia.doe.gov, June 1998.

■ **REFERENCES**

"Demand LNG's Torch Passes On," by Andrew Symon, *Financial Times,* April 16, 1998, p. 10.

Energy Information Administration (EIA), *AEO98 National Energy Model System,* AEO98b.d100197a, Table 13.

EIA, *Annual Energy Outlook 1998,* EIA/DOE-0383(98), December 1997.

EIA, *International Energy Annual 1995,* DOE/EIA-0219(95), December 1996.

EIA, *International Energy Annual 1996,* DOE/EIA-0219(96), February 1998.

EIA, *International Energy Outlook 1998,* DOE/EIA-0484(98), April 1998.

EIA, *Natural Gas Monthly,* DOE/EIA-0130(97/08), August 1997.

EIA, *Oil and Gas Developments in the Early 1990's: An Expanded Role for Independent Producers,* DOE/EIA-0600, October 1995.

EIA, *Performance Profiles of Major Energy Producers 1996,* DOE/EIA-02069(96), February 1998.

EIA, *Short-Term Energy Outlook,* DOE/EIA-02029(98/Q2), April 1998.

"Four-Component Seismic Poised for Rapid Growth," by Martin Quinlan, *Petroleum Economist,* Vol. 65, No. 3, March 1998.

"Hibernia Produces First Oil!," Business Wire, November 17, 1997.

"Hibernia—The Launch of the East Coast Petroleum Sector," Discovery Place, April 17, 1998.

"Hibernia's 'First Cargo' Headed to Market," Canada Newswire, December 29, 1997.

"IMF Warns Asia Crisis Could Deepen," by Adam Entous, Reuters Limited, December 20, 1997.

"IMF's Condessus Urges Indonesia to Get Back on Track with Reform," Dow Jones Newswires, The Wall Street Journal Interactive, April 3, 1998.

"Oil Industry Opens to Competition," by George Hawrlywshn, *The Wall Street Journal,* May 28, 1998, p. B13.

"Petroleum Report for Friday," InfoBeat, May 29, 1998.

"Petroleum Report for Wednesday," InfoBeat, April 1, 1998.

"Russia, Kazakstan Agree on Caspian Sea Division," *Energy Alert,* April 14, 1998.

"Russia to End Pumping Excise Tax," *Energy Alert,* March 30, 1998, p. 5.

"State-Owned Companies of OGJ100 Control Big Share of World's Oil," by Robert J. Beck and Marilyn Radler, *Oil and Gas Journal,* Vol. 95, No. 36, September 8, 1997.

"Venezuelan Red Tape Hits Foreign Oil Contractors," by Tom Ashby, Reuters, May 1, 1998.

WEFA Energy, *World Economic Outlook: 20-Year Extension,* Eddystone, Pennsylvania, April 1997.

Worldwide Petroleum Refining and Gasoline Marketing for forecasts of the international and domestic downstream petroleum industry.

■ RELATED CHAPTERS

2: Coal Mining
4: Petroleum Refining

■ GLOSSARY

Lifting costs: Another name for crude oil production costs.

Organization of Petroleum Exporting Countries (OPEC): Members are Algeria, Indonesia, Iran, Iraq, Kuwait, Libya, Nigeria, Qatar, Saudi Arabia, the United Arab Emirates, and Venezuela.

Upstream: In the petroleum industry, this term refers to petroleum exploration, development, and production.

PETROLEUM REFINING
Economic and Trade Trends

U.S. International Trade

($ billions)

Legend: Balance — Exports — Imports

Source: U.S. Department of Commerce: Bureau of the Census; International Trade Administration.

World Export Market Shares

(%)

Legend: United States, Singapore, Venezuela, South Korea

Source: United Nations; U.S. Department of Commerce, International Trade Administration.

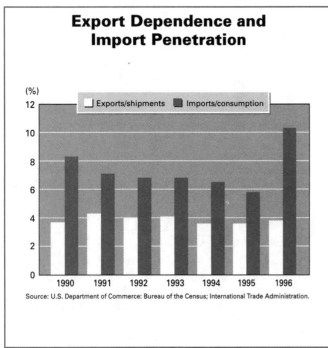

Export Dependence and Import Penetration

(%)

Legend: Exports/shipments, Imports/consumption

Source: U.S. Department of Commerce: Bureau of the Census; International Trade Administration.

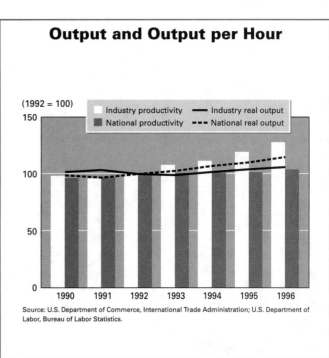

Output and Output per Hour

(1992 = 100)

Legend: Industry productivity — Industry real output, National productivity --- National real output

Source: U.S. Department of Commerce, International Trade Administration; U.S. Department of Labor, Bureau of Labor Statistics.

See "Getting the Most Out of *Outlook '99*" for definitions of terms.

Petroleum Refining

INDUSTRY DEFINITION   The petroleum refining industry (SIC 2911) consists of establishments engaged primarily in producing gasoline, kerosene, distillate fuel oils, residual fuel oils, and lubricants through straight distillation of crude oil, redistillation of unfinished petroleum derivatives, cracking, and other processes. Establishments in this industry also produce aliphatic and aromatic chemicals as by-products.

OVERVIEW

The consumption of refined petroleum products in the United States is expected to increase about 2 percent between 1997 and 1998, 1 percent in 1999, and about 14 percent between 1997 and 2005 (see Table 4-1). [Normal weather conditions and continuing economic expansion of about 2 percent annually are assumed in this forecast.] Refinery output in this country is forecast to increase about 1 percent in 1998, slightly less than 1 percent in 1999, and less than 13 percent between 1997 and 2005. As a result, petroleum product imports by the United States as a share of petroleum product consumption will increase from 6 percent in 1997 to 9 percent in 2005.

Changes in the consumption of petroleum products vary across products. The consumption of motor gasoline is expected to increase 2 percent in 1998 and about the same amount in 1999. Residual fuel oil consumption is anticipated to increase 5 percent in 1998, exhibiting a rebound from the weather-induced low consumption level in 1997, and 2 percent in 1999 (see Table 4-2). [Residual fuel oil consists of the heavier oils that remain after the distillate fuel oils and lighter hydrocarbons are distilled in refinery operations and that conform to ASTM Specifications D396 and 975; common uses for it include electricity generation, commercial and industrial heating, and powering ships.] The consumption of jet fuel and distillate fuel oil also is expected to increase between 1997 and 1999. The national average price of gasoline was expected to decline 12 percent in 1998, since lower crude oil prices and increased worldwide crude oil production were expected to depress prices.

Gross refining margins (refined product revenues minus raw materials expenses and product purchases divided by refined product sales volume) for a composite (weighted) average of petroleum products sold by the major U.S. oil companies fell between 1991 and 1996 (see Table 4-3), as did the margins for motor gasoline. (See the boxed note: "The Financial Reporting System.") Low returns in the first half of the 1990s have lowered expectations for a competitive rate of return, thus eliminating from active consideration many potential investments in refineries. With fewer investment alternatives, relatively less investment has occurred. However, declining product prices and falling margins have increased the pressure to reduce operating costs and spread fixed costs over more output. These incentives have shaped refinery investment in the 1990s.

[Quantities of oil in this chapter are reported in barrels (1 barrel of crude oil is 0.1364 metric ton; of gasoline, 0.1172 metric ton; of distillate fuel oil, 0.1340 metric ton; of residual fuel oil, 0.1502 metric ton).]

THE FINANCIAL REPORTING SYSTEM

The Financial Reporting System (FRS) was established in 1977 under Section 205(h) of the Department of Energy Organization Act (P.L. 91-95). This statute requires the Energy Information Administration to "identify and designate major energy-producing companies" and develop and implement a data reporting program for energy financial and operating information from these companies. The EIA is also required to submit an annual data and analysis report on the FRS information (*Performance Profiles of Major Energy Producers*) to the Congress. Individual company financial reporting is required "on a uniform and standardized basis" for "each line of commerce in the energy industry" in which the company or its affiliates are involved.

TABLE 4-1: U.S. Refinery Output, Trade, and Supply of Petroleum Products, 1987–2005
(millions of barrels per day)

Year	Refinery Output	Net Imports	Stock Changes and Other Adjustments	Products Supplied
1987	14.63	1.39	0.64	16.67
1988	15.02	1.63	0.63	17.28
1989	15.17	1.50	0.65	17.33
1990	15.27	1.38	0.34	16.99
1991	15.26	0.96	0.49	16.71
1992	15.40	0.94	0.69	17.03
1993	15.79	0.93	0.52	17.24
1994	15.79	1.09	0.84	17.72
1995	15.99	0.75	0.98	17.72
1996	16.32	1.10	0.89	18.31
1997	16.76	1.04	0.82	18.62
1998	16.94	0.96	0.96	18.86
1999	17.09	1.12	1.00	19.21
2003	18.30	1.75	0.47	20.52
2005	18.87	1.96	0.32	21.15

Source: U.S. Department of Energy, Energy Information Administration, *Short-Term Energy Outlook* (1987–1999), *Annual Energy Outlook 1998* (2003–2005).

TABLE 4-2: Petroleum Products Supplied to the U.S. Market by Type, 1987–2005
(millions of barrels per day)

Year	Motor Gasoline	Jet Fuel	Distillate Fuel Oil	Residual Fuel Oil	Other Products	Total Products
1987	7.21	1.38	2.98	1.26	3.84	16.67
1988	7.34	1.45	3.12	1.38	3.99	17.28
1989	7.33	1.49	3.16	1.37	3.98	17.33
1990	7.23	1.52	3.02	1.23	3.99	16.99
1991	7.19	1.47	2.92	1.16	3.97	16.71
1992	7.27	1.45	2.98	1.09	4.24	17.03
1993	7.48	1.47	3.04	1.08	4.17	17.24
1994	7.60	1.53	3.16	1.02	4.41	17.72
1995	7.79	1.51	3.21	0.85	4.36	17.72
1996	7.89	1.58	3.37	0.85	4.63	18.31
1997	8.02	1.60	3.44	0.80	4.74	18.62
1998	8.18	1.63	3.49	0.84	4.64	18.86
1999	8.32	1.66	3.60	0.86	4.69	19.21
2003	8.94	2.03	3.78	0.79	4.98	20.52
2005	9.18	2.16	3.88	0.81	5.11	21.15

Source: U.S. Department of Energy, Energy Information Administration, *Short-Term Energy Outlook* (1987–1999), *Annual Energy Outlook 1998* (2003–2005).

TABLE 4-3: Refining and Marketing Margins and Production Costs, 1979–1996
(1996 dollars per barrel)

	1979	1984	1988	1991	1992	1993	1994	1995	1996
Petroleum product gross refining margin	8.384	8.542	8.700	7.982	7.540	7.235	6.243	5.639	6.528
Less petroleum product marketing costs	1.996	2.681	1.996	2.714	2.961	2.325	1.879	1.783	1.858
Less petroleum product energy costs	2.088	2.837	1.355	1.315	1.231	1.252	1.001	0.840	1.071
Less petroleum product other operating costs	2.614	3.012	3.083	3.120	2.934	2.898	2.616	2.516	2.726
Equals petroleum product net refining margin	1.687	0.011	2.267	0.832	0.414	0.759	0.747	0.500	0.873
Motor gasoline wholesaler/reseller margin	NA[1]	2.603	5.726	1.836	4.124	5.701	5.272	5.740	4.403
Motor gasoline retailer margin	NA[1]	4.887	1.625	5.657	3.627	2.440	3.143	2.537	2.648
Refined product sales (thousands of barrels per day)	14,868	12,088	14,114	13,015	13,089	13,178	13,455	13,641	14,024

[1] Not available.
Source: U.S. Department of Energy, Energy Information Administration, Financial Reporting System.

Return on Investment in U.S. Refining and Marketing for Major U.S. Oil Companies, 1977–1996

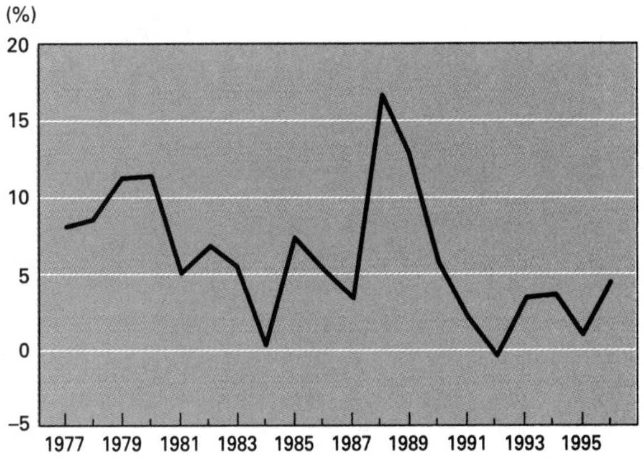

Source: U.S. Department of Energy, Energy Information Administration, Financial Reporting System.

FIGURE 4-1

Domestic Petroleum Refining and Marketing

For the U.S. refining and marketing industry, the 1990s has been characterized by unusually low product margins, low profitability, and selective retrenchment. The costs of complying with environmental laws have grown substantially during this period and thus have affected the profitability of the domestic industry. Profitability (measured by the rate of return on investment) from the refining operations of domestic petroleum companies has varied widely, a trend that began before the 1990s (see Figure 4-1). Although the variability in returns seems to have diminished over the last 5 years, returns have become consistently low. This may be due in part to the capital investment

expenditures needed to comply with environmental legislation. These expenditures appear to have increased the investment base without a resulting increase in net income. Consequently, refiners' ability to recoup their investments has been impaired. The recent low profitability of refining and marketing operations also has been due partially to the narrowing of the spread between petroleum product prices and raw material input costs.

Additionally, persistently low profits have prompted domestic refiners and marketers in recent years to make concerted efforts to realize greater value from their fixed assets and reduce their operating costs. Refining operations have been consolidated, the capacity of existing facilities has been expanded, and several refineries have closed. In particular, 41 refineries were closed between 1990 and 1997, amounting to 20 percent of the number of operable U.S. refineries in 1990 (see Table 4-4).

Joint Ventures

The joint venture is one mechanism that downstream petroleum companies have used to consolidate their operations. These deals may provide these companies with a way to increase the value of their fixed assets and/or reduce their costs by sharing assets and operations with a partner. The largest recent joint venture affecting U.S. refining and marketing was announced late in 1996 but was not completed until early in 1998. That venture merged Texaco, Star Enterprise (a joint venture between Texaco and Aramco, the Saudi Arabian state oil company), and Shell Oil (the U.S. subsidiary of Royal Dutch/Shell). That joint venture resulted in the creation of two companies, Equilon Enterprises L.L.C. and Motiva Enterprises L.L.C., in January and May 1998, respectively. Equilon consists of the companies' western and midwestern U.S. operations as well as their nationwide trading, transportation, and lubricants businesses. (Shell Oil owns 56 percent of Equilon, and Texaco has a 44 percent share.) Motiva consists of the companies' eastern and Gulf Coast U.S. operations [with the exception of Shell's Deer Park, TX, refinery,

TABLE 4-4: U.S. Refineries and Refining Capacities, 1987–1997

Year	Operable Refineries Total	Operable Refineries Operating	Crude Distillation Capacity, thousands of barrels per calendar day Total	Crude Distillation Capacity, thousands of barrels per calendar day Operating	Downstream Charge Capacity, thousands of barrels per stream day Total	Vacuum Distillation	Thermal Cracking	Catalytic Cracking (Fresh and Recycled)	Catalytic Reforming	Catalytic Hydrocracking	Catalytic Hydrotreating
1987	219	195	15,565	14,940	28,656	6,935	1,928	5,716	3,805	1,189	9,083
1988	213	195	15,915	15,018	29,347	7,198	2,080	5,806	3,891	1,202	9,170
1989	204	193	15,655	15,012	29,537	7,225	2,073	5,650	3,911	1,238	9,440
1990	205	194	15,572	15,063	29,823	7,245	2,108	5,755	3,896	1,282	9,537
1991	202	184	15,676	14,959	30,206	7,276	2,158	5,862	3,926	1,308	9,676
1992	192	183	15,696	14,966	30,074	7,172	2,100	5,888	3,907	1,363	9,644
1993	187	175	15,121	14,777	29,560	6,892	2,082	5,784	3,728	1,397	9,677
1994	179	171	15,034	14,704	30,642	6,892	2,107	5,777	3,875	1,376	10,616
1995	175	165	15,434	15,081	31,292	7,248	2,123	5,752	3,867	1,386	10,916
1996	NA[1]	162	15,286	NA	31,353	7,314	2,153	5,599	3,852	1,385	11,050
1997	164	159	15,452	15,168	31,150	7,349	2,050	5,595	3,727	1,388	11,041

[1] Not available.

Source: U.S. Department of Energy, Energy Information Administration.

which is operated as a joint venture between Shell Oil and the state oil company of Mexico, Petroleos Mexicanos (PEMEX)]. The Texaco-Star-Shell alliance is expected to reduce the aggregate operating costs of the companies by $800 million annually. The resulting joint venture will have assets worth approximately $10 billion.

USX-Marathon Group, an affiliate of the USX Corporation, and Ashland Oil, an affiliate of Ashland Corporation, have merged their downstream assets into a joint venture called Marathon Ashland Petroleum L.L.C. USX-Marathon Group is operating the joint venture and is the majority partner, with a controlling interest of 62 percent. The joint venture is anticipated to result in annual savings of $200 million in operating costs.

In addition, substantial mergers have occurred between independent refiners and marketers in the United States, and the resulting companies also appear to be interested in pursuing joint ventures. However, unlike the major U.S. petroleum companies, which are consolidating their refining and marketing operations through joint ventures, the independent refiners and marketers are expanding their operations through mergers (and, at least in one case, joint ventures). For example, in 1997 Ultramar Diamond Shamrock (created by a merger late in 1996) acquired Total Petroleum North America, gaining three refineries, more than 2,100 marketing outlets, and hundreds of miles of pipelines in addition to other associated assets. The acquisition of Total Petroleum is expected to reduce Ultramar Diamond Shamrock's overall costs by $50 million annually. Then, in an apparent attempt at further expansion, Ultramar Diamond Shamrock attempted to create a joint venture with the downstream operations of Petro Canada, the former state oil company of Canada. That venture, which was announced in January 1998, was abandoned in June of that year in the face of a long and potentially losing battle for the approval of the Canadian regulatory authorities.

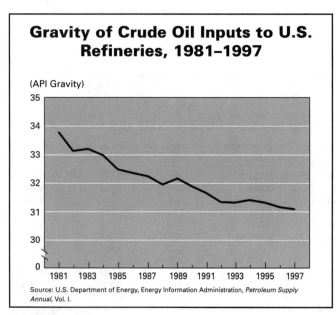

Gravity of Crude Oil Inputs to U.S. Refineries, 1981–1997

(API Gravity)

Source: U.S. Department of Energy, Energy Information Administration, *Petroleum Supply Annual*, Vol. I.

FIGURE 4-2

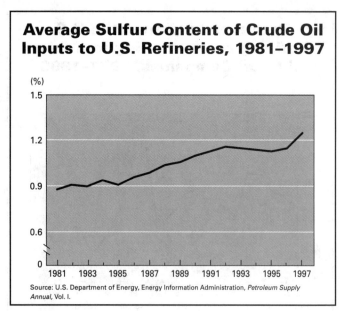

Average Sulfur Content of Crude Oil Inputs to U.S. Refineries, 1981–1997

(%)

Source: U.S. Department of Energy, Energy Information Administration, *Petroleum Supply Annual*, Vol. I.

FIGURE 4-3

Upgrading of Existing Capacity

Investments over the past several years have substantially increased the ability of refineries to utilize crude oils with greater variations in characteristics. Consequently, U.S. refiners now process heavier (i.e., lower gravity; see Figure 4-2) and more sour (i.e., higher sulfur content; see Figure 4-3) crude oil than was the case 15 years ago.

Several producers of comparatively heavy crude oil [including Venezuela's Petroleos de Venezuela, S.A. (PdVSA), Mexico's PEMEX, and, more recently, Norway's Statoil] have allied themselves with U.S. refiners. [PEMEX has a prospective joint venture with Mobil involving the Beaumont, TX, refinery, which has a capacity of 157,500 barrels per day (b/d).] For example, Coastal Corporation recently finalized a joint venture with PdVSA involving its Corpus Christi refinery. That refinery will process heavy crude produced in Venezuela by the joint venture. Phillips Petroleum plans to construct a 58,000-b/d coker unit and related facilities in Venezuela to allow heavy, sour Venezuelan crude to be upgraded, that is, transformed into lighter crude oil. The use of heavier, sour crude oil will allow Phillips to reduce the cost of refining crude oil inputs.

In addition to making a long-term agreement to provide crude oil to the refinery, in some cases crude oil producers have provided a portion of the funding for refinery upgrades needed to enhance the refiner's ability to manufacture light petroleum products such as motor gasoline, jet fuel, and diesel fuel.

Domestic refining capacity has expanded through conventional projects (e.g., adding a catalytic cracking unit) and through debottlenecking investments, which are marginal investments that increase throughput and thus effectively create additional refining capacity from the same physical structure. The additional capacity is termed capacity creep. Moreover, the domestic refining operating capacity of existing refineries has increased substantially over the last decade. Total U.S. distilla-

	1983	1984	1985	1986	1987	1988	1989	1990	1991	1992	1993	1994	1995	1996
Selected independent refiners														
CITGO	31	31	39	39	39	40	42	46	46	46	45	46	46	48
Ultramar Diamond Shamrock[1]														10
Diamond Shamrock[1]	25	24	12	12	9	8	8	8	8	8	8	8	9	
Total Petroleum	22	22	21	19	18	20	22	22	22	20	18	17	18	19
Ultramar/Beacon[1]	3	3	NA	NA	6	2	1	1	1	1	1	1	1	
Tosco[2]	0	9	NA	NA	NA	NA	NA	0	NA	NA	2	4	4	27
Circle K[2]	NA[3]	22	5	NA	12	22	23	22	18	NA	5	27	27	
U.S. majors														
Amoco	35	36	36	30	30	30	31	33	32	30	29	30	30	33
ARCO	24	22	6	6	6	5	5	5	5	5	5	5	5	5
Ashland	7	26	15	16	18	19	18	18	18	13	11	11	11	11
BP/Sohio	20	30	19	29	29	28	26	33	33	28	25	27	27	21
Chevron	39	38	43	33	34	33	33	33	32	31	33	27	27	25
Coastal	NA[3]	NA	NA	NA	22	22	23	28	34	36	36	37	36	36
Conoco	40	40	38	40	39	37	37	37	36	28	28	41	41	41
Exxon	41	38	39	37	37	37	38	40	39	37	37	37	37	41
Fina	20	22	24	24	24	24	23	25	25	11	11	12	12	15
Hess	NA[3]	NA	NA	NA	NA	NA	NA	NA	NA	NA	NA	6	6	6
Kerr-McGee	21	18	20	22	21	21	20	20	13	13	13	13	0	0
Marathon	5	6	6	6	6	8	8	9	9	11	11	11	11	11
Mobil	43	41	40	40	37	36	33	33	34	32	30	27	32	29
Phillips	37	34	34	37	36	33	35	29	29	32	33	33	32	32
Shell Oil	40	38	40	41	41	41	40	41	41	39	40	41	40	41
Sun	27	29	29	29	28	28	28	28	27		20	19	19	19
Texaco	45	46	47	46	44	45	49	49	24	24	24	23	24	25
Unocal	44	42	41	41	41	43	43	41	7	7	7	7	7	7
Average for U.S. Majors	30.5	31.6	29.8	29.8	29.0	28.8	28.8	29.5	25.8	23.6	23.1	22.6	22.1	22.1

[1] Diamond Shamrock and Ultramar merged in 1996, forming Ultramar Diamond Shamrock.
[2] Circle K was acquired by Tosco in 1996.
[3] Not available.
Source: *National Petroleum News.*

tion capacity expanded more than 63,000 b/d between 1988 and 1997 as a result of both conventional investments and debottlenecking investments (see Table 4-4). Those years saw capacity per operating refinery increase 19 percent to 91,400 b/d. However, in that period 43 domestic refineries with capacities totaling more than 1.1 million b/d closed their doors.

Consolidation of Marketing Operations

Gasoline marketing in the United States has undergone dramatic changes over the last 15 years. In their marketing operations the major U.S. oil companies have narrowed their focus to those regions in which they have had the most success (the greatest profitability or the largest market share). The average decline in states of operation per major oil company was from 32 states in 1984 to 22 states in 1996, a drop of 31 percent (see Table 4-5). However, this decline is only part of the consolidation story, as the majors also have substantially fewer branded outlets. Those branded outlets fell from 92,344 in 1984 to 32,325 in 1996, a 65 percent decline. The 4 percent average annual decline in the number of branded outlets of the majors between 1991 and 1996 is even more notable when it is compared with the 2 percent national average annual decline in the number of all U.S. gasoline stations, regardless of ownership, between 1991 and 1996. In other words, by consolidating and refocusing their gasoline

> **EXPANSION BY INDEPENDENT REFINERS**
>
> Recent acquisitions by the independent Tosco have included six refineries from major U.S. oil companies (Exxon-1, BP-2, and Unocal-3) with a total refinery capacity of 747,000 barrels per day and over 1,500 outlets (632 from BP and 1,317 from Unocal) since April 1993. Additionally, Tosco, which had relatively few convenience store operations, acquired the Circle K convenience store chain and its 1,900 gasoline outlets in 1996. Diamond Shamrock, which had 1,324 retail outlets in eight midwestern states, merged with Ultramar, which had 420 outlets in California, late in 1996. Since then the resulting company, Ultramar Diamond Shamrock, has acquired Total Petroleum and has attempted to create a joint venture with Petro Canada in the northeastern United States and Canada. The Total Petroleum acquisition included a total of 560 outlets and three refineries with a distillation capacity of 141,600 b/d.

marketing efforts, the majors have closed gasoline stations at a rate twice as fast as the national average.

In contrast to the majors, independent and foreign-owned refining and marketing companies have expanded their scope of operations through the acquisition of refineries and/or outlets. For example, Citgo, a wholly owned subsidiary of the Venezuelan state oil company PdVSA, expanded its operations from 31 states in 1984, just before its 1986 acquisition by PdVSA, to 48 states in 1996, an increase of 55 percent (see Table 4-5). The Connecticut-based Tosco went from retail operations in no states in 1990 (it had only wholesale operations) to operations in 27 states in 1996. Diamond Shamrock has also increased the scope of its operations. (See the boxed note: "Expansion by Independent Refiners.")

Environmental Issues and Costs

Investment in refining in recent years has been driven largely by the environmental requirements of the Clean Air Act Amendments of 1990 (CAAA90). CAAA90 required a phased reduction in vehicle emissions of regulated pollutants that was met primarily through the use of reformulated gasoline. Phase I of CAAA90 required refiners to produce oxygenated gasoline by November 1, 1992; low-sulfur diesel fuel was required by October 1993; and by January 1, 1995, reformulated gasoline had to be available. Thus, consistently through the first half of the 1990s, domestic refiners were faced with deadlines for new products that required new capital investment. Since reaching a decade peak in 1992 of $5.2 billion, domestic refining capital expenditures by the major U.S. oil companies have fallen an average of 15 percent per year, reaching the decade's low point in 1996 at $2.1 billion. Correspondingly, investment related to pollution abatement also peaked in 1992 and has since declined, according to information from the American Petroleum Institute (see Figure 4-4).

The overall decline in refining investment has roughly paralleled the decline in capital expenditures for pollution abatement. For example, nearly two-thirds of the 1995–1996 decline in refining capital expenditures by the major U.S. oil companies can be attributed to companies with a significant presence in motor gasoline retail markets in California. These companies noted that substantial refinery investment to produce reformu-

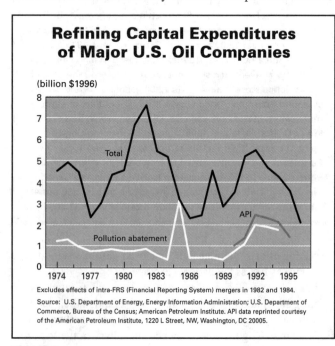

Refining Capital Expenditures of Major U.S. Oil Companies

(billion $1996)

Excludes effects of intra-FRS (Financial Reporting System) mergers in 1982 and 1984.

Source: U.S. Department of Energy, Energy Information Administration; U.S. Department of Commerce, Bureau of the Census; American Petroleum Institute. API data reprinted courtesy of the American Petroleum Institute, 1220 L Street, NW, Washington, DC 20005.

FIGURE 4-4

lated gasoline or low-sulfur diesel that would comply with California's requirements had been completed in 1996.

Overall, environmentally related capital expenditures by the major U.S. oil companies fell approximately 34 percent between 1995 and 1996. From the company annual reports for 1996 the conclusion might be drawn that the major reason for the decline is that Phase I–related (and probably also Phase II–related) CAAA90-motivated investments have been completed. (For example, ARCO in its 1996 annual report noted that in California modifications were completed in 1995 to meet that state's stringent requirements for cleaner gasoline, and Shell Oil Company noted that its reduction in capital spending on oil products in 1996 was due to the completion of a 3-year $1 billion upgrade of its Martinez, CA, refinery in order to produce reformulated motor gasoline, low-sulfur diesel fuel, and jet fuel.) However, compliance with environmental regulations most likely will continue to affect domestic refiners. An interesting recent development related to the environment was the announcement of two partnerships between major U.S. oil companies and U.S. auto manufacturers to develop cleaner and more efficient fuels. The partnerships will focus on development of improved conventional fuels in addition to alternative fuels such as fuel cells and natural gas.

DOMESTIC PETROLEUM PRODUCT FORECASTS

Consumption of domestic petroleum products is forecast to increase about 2 percent in 1998 and another 2 percent in 1999, contributing to an anticipated growth of more than 13 percent between 1997 and 2005 (see Table 4-1). Much of the increase in demand will be for motor gasoline, which is also forecast to increase 2 percent in 1998 and 2 percent in 1999, with an almost 15 percent increase between 1997 and 2005 (see Table 4-2). While overall net imports of petroleum products are forecast to decline almost 8 percent in 1998 because of low crude oil prices and the associated increase in imported crude oil refined domestically, they are expected to increase nearly 17 percent in 1999. The dependency of the United States on foreign petroleum is forecast to increase substantially between 1997 and 2005, with most of the increase occurring after 2000.

The U.S. economy is expected to expand slightly more than 2 percent annually through 2005. Consumption of petroleum products will increase at a slightly slower rate over that period, averaging less than 2 percent annually (see Table 4-1). The share of petroleum product consumption held by motor gasoline is anticipated to hold steady at 43 percent between 1997 and 2005, increasing an average of approximately 2 percent annually. Jet fuel consumption is forecast to increase about 4 percent annually between 1997 and 2005. Consumption of distillate fuel oil is expected to increase less than 2 percent annually on average between 1997 and 2005. Essentially no change in the consumption of residual fuel oil is expected between 1997 and 2005, although consumption was forecast to grow more than 5 percent in 1998.

TABLE 4-6: Petroleum Products Supplied to U.S. End-Use Sectors, 1987–2005

(millions of barrels per day)

Year	Residential and Commercial	Industrial	Transportation	Electric Utilities	Total
1987	1.33	4.25	10.53	0.55	16.67
1988	1.34	4.39	10.87	0.68	17.28
1989	1.32	4.26	11.01	0.74	17.33
1990	1.14	4.32	10.97	0.55	16.99
1991	1.14	4.25	10.80	0.52	16.71
1992	1.12	4.55	10.95	0.42	17.03
1993	1.14	4.45	11.18	0.46	17.24
1994	1.11	4.69	11.49	0.43	17.72
1995	1.13	4.62	11.68	0.29	17.72
1996	1.18	4.85	11.88	0.32	18.23
1997	1.11	4.83	12.23	0.44	18.62
1998	1.10	4.86	12.60	0.30	18.86
1999	1.10	4.30	12.92	0.27	19.21
2003	1.10	5.19	14.06	0.17	20.52
2005	1.09	5.33	14.57	0.16	21.15

Source: U.S. Department of Energy, Energy Information Administration, *Annual Energy Review* (1987–1996), *Annual Energy Outlook 1998* (1997–2005).

The degree to which the different sectors of the domestic economy consume petroleum products continues to change. Petroleum consumption by electric utilities and residential and commercial users was forecast to fall in 1997 and 1998 by 30 percent and 1 percent, respectively. Petroleum consumption by electric utilities is expected to fall by more than 50 percent as natural gas increasingly is the fuel of choice. Meanwhile, residential and commercial consumption is anticipated to fall less than 2 percent (see Table 4-6) over this period as the use of space heating with fuel oil declines.

Conversely, petroleum consumption by the industrial and transportation sectors of the economy is forecast to increase between 1997 and 2005. Among all sectors of the economy, only transportation is expected to increase its consumption of petroleum products over the forecast period, increasing about 3 percent during 1998. The overall importance of petroleum products to the domestic economy (estimated by the share of total domestic energy they constitute) has changed little in the 1990s and is expected to be largely unchanged through 2005.

WORLDWIDE PETROLEUM PRODUCT FORECAST

Worldwide demand for petroleum is anticipated to increase 13 million b/d between 1997 and 2005, an average of more than 2 percent annually. The bulk of the growth is expected to occur in developing countries.

TABLE 4-7: Historical and Forecast World Crude Oil Consumption by Region, 1995–2005

(millions of barrels per day)

	1995	1996	1997	1998	1999	2003	2005
OECD	42.409	43.328	43.869	44.435	45.123	47.201	48.267
United States (states and territories)	17.979	18.565	18.870	19.191	19.653	20.841	21.501
Canada	1.755	1.799	1.822	1.845	1.862	1.960	2.012
Mexico	1.855	1.895	1.941	2.007	2.091	2.301	2.367
Japan	5.711	5.867	5.982	6.100	6.208	6.519	6.670
Australia and New Zealand	0.988	0.935	0.963	0.992	1.020	1.078	1.098
OECD Europe	14.121	14.267	14.291	14.300	14.290	14.502	14.621
Developing countries	18.477	19.149	19.904	20.657	20.929	24.168	26.016
Other Central and South America	3.459	3.544	3.820	4.100	4.381	5.207	5.597
Pacific Rim	4.394	4.548	4.733	4.917	5.095	6.171	6.850
OPEC	5.226	5.394	5.596	5.786	5.498	6.020	6.300
Other developing countries	5.398	5.663	5.755	5.854	5.955	6.770	7.268
Eurasia	9.040	9.047	9.317	9.615	9.928	11.357	12.232
Former Soviet Union	4.617	4.379	4.328	4.309	4.319	4.725	5.067
Eastern Europe	1.092	1.120	1.220	1.316	1.408	1.554	1.601
China	3.331	3.548	3.770	3.990	4.201	5.078	5.564
Total consumption	69.926	71.524	73.090	74.707	75.980	82.726	86.515
Presumed oil prices (1996$/bbl)	17.61	20.52	18.18	18.00	18.57	19.79	20.20

Source: U.S. Department of Energy, Energy Information Administration, *International Energy Outlook 1998.*

TABLE 4-8: U.S. Trade Patterns in Petroleum Refining[1] in 1997

(millions of dollars: percent)

Exports			Imports		
Regions[2]	Value[3]	Share, %	Regions[2]	Value[3]	Share, %
NAFTA	2,448	38.0	NAFTA	3,740	17.1
Latin America	1,623	25.2	Latin America	6,735	30.8
Western Europe	957	14.9	Western Europe	3,354	15.4
Japan/Chinese Economic Area	578	9.0	Japan/Chinese Economic Area	200	0.9
Other Asia	535	8.3	Other Asia	439	2.0
Rest of world	294	4.6	Rest of world	7,370	33.7
World	6,435	100.0	World	21,837	100.0
Top Five Countries	Value	Share, %	Top Five Countries	Value	Share, %
Mexico	1,540	23.9	Venezuela	4,304	19.7
Canada	908	14.1	Saudi Arabia	2,813	12.9
Japan	356	5.5	Canada	2,648	12.1
Netherlands	290	4.5	Nigeria	1,530	7.0
Singapore	183	2.8	United Kingdom	1,143	5.2

[1] SIC 2911.
[2] For definitions of regional groupings, see "Getting the Most Out of *Outlook '99*."
[3] Values may not sum to total because of rounding.
Source: U.S. Department of Commerce, Bureau of the Census.

Currently, prospects for foreign investment by U.S. refining and marketing companies appear to be greatest in Latin America, China, and the Pacific Rim, which are forecast to have the largest growth in petroleum consumption through 2005. Latin America's recent wave of government reforms is anticipated to trigger substantial economic growth (more than 4 percent annually) over the next several years. Consequently, petroleum consumption is forecast to increase 47 percent between 1997 and 2005 (see Table 4-7).

Petroleum consumption in China and the developing countries of the Pacific Rim is projected to grow slightly slower over the forecast period than it is in Latin America (45 percent compared with 47 percent). However, taken together, China and the developing countries of the Pacific Rim are responsible for a substantially greater share of worldwide petroleum consumption (13 percent in 1997 and 14 percent in 2005) than is Latin America (6 percent in 1997 and 6 percent in 2005). Thus, China and the Pacific Rim may actually hold more promise for refining and marketing ventures through 2005. The continued development of China's economy is expected to lead to a 48 percent increase in petroleum consumption between 1997 and 2005. The other developing countries of the Pacific Rim are expected to increase their petroleum consumption 45 percent (see Table 4-7) despite the recent Asian financial crisis.

In the second half of 1998 many environmentally motivated refinery investments were expected in Europe as refiners were forced to meet European Union fuel standards. As many as 15 European refineries were expected to close because the new environmental regulations make closure a more economically feasible option.

Refinery investment has been announced in other countries, including Mexico, Colombia, and India. Mexico plans investments of more than $1 billion by 2001 to modernize its refiner-ies. Colombia plans to invest $655 million by 2002, which will increase its refinery capacity almost 25 percent, to accommodate forecast demand increases. India has announced that it requires $22 billion of refining investment over the next 10 years to accommodate anticipated growth in domestic consumption.

Meanwhile, restructuring and mergers are anticipated in Japan in the face of continuing low earnings from downstream activities. The Middle East (because of diversification into refining) and Asia (because of substantial economic growth) should lead the world in the growth of refining capacity well into the next century.

Thus, worldwide refining presents considerable opportunities and challenges over the next several years as growth in petroleum product consumption, combined with higher environmental standards, leads to continued restructuring and other industrywide adjustments. Table 4-8 describes U.S. trade patterns in the petroleum refining industry.

This document was prepared by the Energy Information Administration (EIA), the independent statistical and analytic agency of the U.S. Department of Energy. The information herein should not be construed as advocating or reflecting any policy position of the U.S. Department of Energy or any other organization. The forecasts for 1998 and 1999 are based on the EIA's *Short-Term Energy Outlook* July 1998 projections. The forecasts for 2005 are based on EIA's *Annual Energy Outlook 1998*. EIA's short-term forecasts are updated monthly and are found at http://www.eia.doe.gov/emeu/steo/pub. An extensive list of citations to this report may be found at the EIA Web site, http://www.eia.doe.gov/emeu/finance/usi&to/down_98.html.

Neal C. Davis, U.S. Department of Energy, Energy Information Administration, neal.davis@eia.doe.gov, July 1998.

■ REFERENCES

American Petroleum Institute, 1220 L Street, NW, Washington, DC 20005. (202)682-8000, http://www.api.org.

"Ashland, Marathon Ink Merger Agreement After FTC Clears Deal," *Octane Week,* Vol. 12, No. 49, December 15, 1997.

"Coastal Corp. Says It Intends To Make Canadian Acquisitions," by Hillary Durgin, *The Houston Chronicle,* May 8, 1998, p. 2.

"Colombia's Ecopetrol Reveals Plan To Raise Refining Capacity 25% Shortly After 2000," by Peter Eisen, *The Oil Daily,* Vol. 48, No. 45, March 9, 1998, p. 5.

Energy Information Administration (EIA), *Annual Energy Review 1997,* DOE/EIA-0384(97), July 1998.

EIA, *Annual Energy Outlook 1998,* EIA/DOE-0383(98), December 1997.

EIA, "Financial Performance: Low Profitability in U.S. Refining and Marketing," November 3, 1997, from *Petroleum 1996: Issues and Trends.*

EIA, *The Impact of Environmental Compliance Costs on U.S. Refining,* November 3, 1997.

EIA, *International Energy Outlook 1998,* DOE/EIA-0484(98), April 1998.

EIA, *Performance Profiles of Major Energy Producers 1996,* DOE/EIA-02069(96), February 1998.

EIA, *Petroleum Supply Annual,* DOE/EIA-0384(97/1), February 1998.

EIA, *Privatization and the Globalization of Energy Markets,* DOE/EIA-0609, October 1996.

EIA, *Short-Term Energy Outlook,* June 1998.

EIA, *Why Do Motor Gasoline Prices Vary Regionally? California Case Study,* June 9, 1998.

EIA, *Worldwide Petroleum and Natural Gas: An Overview and Prospects Through 2005,* June 18, 1998.

"Ford, Mobil To Make Cleaner Fuels," Associated Press, March 5, 1998.

"Fuel Specs to Fall Hard on French Refiners," *Oil and Gas Journal,* May 25, 1998, p. 25.

"Global Refining Addresses Increased Oil Demands, New Challenges," by Tim W. Martin, *Oil & Gas Journal,* March 16, 1998, p. 51.

"India Seeks $22 Billion To Expand Refining Industry," *Octane Week,* Vol. 13, No. 18, May 4, 1998.

"Marketing, Refining Pact Signed; Texaco, Aramco, Shell Teaming Up," by Hillary Durgin, *The Houston Chronicle,* May 28, 1998, p. 1.

National Petroleum News, Adams Business Media, 2101 S. Arlington Heights Road, Suite 150, Arlington Heights, IL 60005. (847) 427-9512, http://www.petroretail.net.npn.

National Petroleum News, Vol. 84, No. 7, mid-June 1992, pp. 35–54.

National Petroleum News, Vol. 89, No. 7, mid-June 1997, pp. 35–52.

"Pemex to Overhaul Three Oil Refineries," by Henry Tricks, *Financial Times,* May 14, 1998.

"Petro-Canada and Ultramar Diamond Shamrock Withdraw Competition Bureau Application," Dow Jones and Company, June 22, 1998.

Petroleum Intelligence Weekly, Vol. 37, No. 24, June 15, 1998, p. 8.

"Phillips, Corpoven Sign Principles of Agreement to Build a New Coker," Business Wire, August 25, 1997.

"Ultramar Diamond Shamrock Completes Acquisition of Total Petroleum," Business Wire, September 25, 1997.

"U.S. Refining Sector Is Said To Show Signs of Real Recovery," by George Stein, *Platts Oilgram News,* Vol. 74, No. 70, April 10, 1996, p. 2.

"Venezuela: US Operations," IAC (SM) Newsletter Database, Arab Press Service Organisation, *APS Review Downstream Trends,* Vol. 49, No. 25, December 22, 1997.

"With Margins Soft, Japan's Refiners May Seek Mergers," by Kanji Ishibashi and Shen Ping, *Platt's Oilgram News,* Vol. 76, No. 85, May 5, 1998, p. 3.

■ RELATED CHAPTERS

2: Coal Mining
3: Crude Petroleum and Natural Gas

■ GLOSSARY

Capacity creep: The increased capacity of refining units resulting from debottlenecking investments.

Catalytic cracking: A refinery process in which larger, heavier, and more complex hydrocarbon molecules are broken down into simpler and lighter molecules. It utilizes a catalytic agent and increases the yield of gasoline from crude oil.

Debottlenecking investments: Upgrades to one or more parts of a refinery that allow fuller use of other parts of the refinery without making any direct changes in them; such relatively inexpensive investments may result in substantial increases in the capacity of the refinery.

Downstream petroleum: Refers to petroleum refining, marketing, and transportation. (However, transportation, chiefly pipelines and marine transport, is not discussed in this chapter.)

ELECTRICITY PRODUCTION AND SALES
Economic and Trade Trends

Electricity Industry Balance of Trade

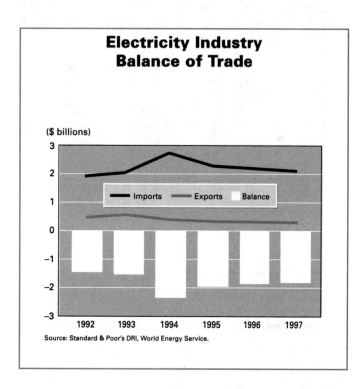

($ billions)

Source: Standard & Poor's DRI, World Energy Service.

Generating Capacity Provided by Nonutilities

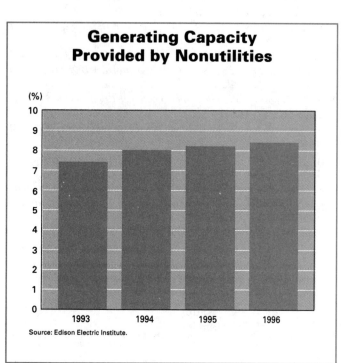

(%)

Source: Edison Electric Institute.

Export Penetration and Import Dependency

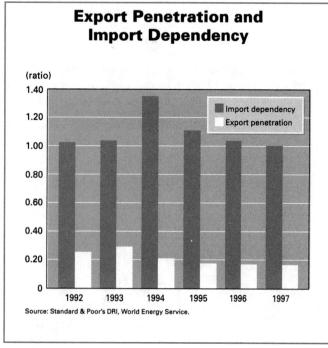

(ratio)

Source: Standard & Poor's DRI, World Energy Service.

Electric Utilities Output per Worker

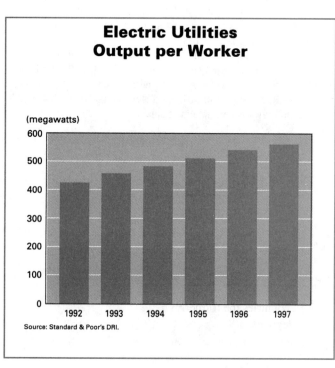

(megawatts)

Source: Standard & Poor's DRI.

Electricity Production and Sales

INDUSTRY DEFINITION The electricity supply industry in the United States is the largest in the world, with approximately one-fourth of global generation capacity and 120 million retail customers. The present industry includes various groups, such as vertically integrated utilities, smaller distribution-only utilities, nonutility power generators, and other players that act as intermediaries between sellers and buyers of energy. However, this traditional pattern is changing rapidly as a result of restructuring, which is creating new corporate structures characterized by varying mixtures of unbundled generation, distribution, and marketing units as well as groups specializing in only one or two functions.

Supplying electricity involves numerous commercial and industrial activities, including purchasing fuel, constructing power stations, generating electricity, building and operating transmission and distribution networks, trading bulk electricity, marketing to retail customers, metering retail sites, and operating customers' billing and accounting systems.

Regulated electricity suppliers fall into two categories: investor-owned utilities and publicly owned utilities. Public power, which serves about 24 percent of all retail users in the United States, is subdivided into municipally owned utilities and rural cooperatives. There are also federally owned power generation utilities and systems which supply the wholesale market and some large retail users. Nonutility power producers fall into several categories, including industrial groups that own on-site generation and cogeneration facilities, small independent power producers and cogenerators that have special "qualifying facility" status, and large-scale independent power producers. Other market participants include power marketers that buy and sell energy, energy brokers that facilitate trades without owning energy, and energy service companies (ESCOs) that sell utility-related services such as conservation programs and energy purchasing services. Transmission capacity tends to be owned by large utilities that sell in an increasingly active market for third-party wheeling.

GLOBAL INDUSTRY TRENDS

In most countries the formerly dominant models of large, vertically integrated utilities and extensive state ownership of the electricity industry are disappearing gradually as a result of deregulation and privatization.

Following the British and Scandinavian practice of the early 1990s, the European Union as a whole is now committed to a gradual restructuring that will start in 1999; some countries, such as Germany, are moving ahead of the others in opening their markets. In eastern Europe, the demise of the communist system has brought a broad restructuring of national power industries that has led to the establishment of separate generation and distribution groups. Elsewhere, countries such as Argentina have adopted a national power pool system.

In the United States the national wholesale market was opened up by the landmark 1992 Energy Policy Act, which gave buyers and sellers open access to the national transmission system. The push for full retail competition has gained in intensity since that time. Most actions to begin establishing retail choice have occurred at the state level so far, with Congress still debating a national restructuring law which would set a target date for action by all the states.

Privatization of state-owned electricity assets has become a worldwide phenomenon. In some cases, such as the United Kingdom in the early 1990s, the main motivation was to break up a national monopoly and shift to a private ownership system. However, in many cases local governments are selling assets to raise cash to balance their budgets or as a means of attracting foreign capital to pay for modernization and expansion of the electricity system. U.S. and western European energy companies have been leading contenders to buy such assets worldwide.

Many governments have invited foreign energy groups to add new capacity in their countries. This can be done either on a build-own-operate basis in which the developer permanently owns the project or on a build-own-transfer basis in which the developer runs the plant for a fixed period to recoup the initial investment and then transfers it to the host government. Developers also may acquire long-term concessions to operate facilities without buying them.

Privatization of the remaining federally owned generation assets in the United States is being debated in the context of deregulation of the generation market, but public power groups, which have priority access to the power generated, oppose any such change.

INDUSTRY RESTRUCTURING ISSUES IN THE UNITED STATES

Restructuring has advanced rapidly at the state level in the last 3 years. A limited number of states with high power costs, led by California, Massachusetts, Rhode Island, Maine, and New York, have already approved deregulation for the period 1998–2000. Many other states are debating the issue and are expected to establish retail choice soon after 2000 without waiting for action at the federal level.

In March 1998 the Clinton administration went on record with a plan which would create a "flexible mandate" for states to deregulate by 2003 but would give them the option to decide against retail choice if their state regulators determine that this would not be in the public interest. However, the chances for passage of a federal bill before the new Congress convenes in 1999 appear to be slim.

Regardless of the outcome at the federal level, the trends among state plans are clear. Distributing and transmitting electricity are being functionally separated from generating electricity. Generation is being deregulated, and a new competitive market is evolving at the retail level.

States are maintaining traditional regulation over electricity distribution and transmission and are using either full divestiture or strict codes of conduct to prevent anticompetitive actions in local retail markets by energy sellers affiliated with distribution companies. On the basis of Federal Energy Regulatory Commission (FERC) guidelines, states and regions are using independent system operators (ISOs) to supervise transmission grids and ensure nondiscriminatory access to those grids by all energy sellers. ISOs have no allegiance or business connection to any market group.

States have generally upheld the principle of stranded cost recovery (having customers pay for above-market costs of unneeded generation), although some, such as New Hampshire and Pennsylvania, have approved less than full recovery and have faced legal challenges. Some states, including California, Massachusetts, Maine, and New York, have required utilities to divest their generation assets to determine stranded cost values. This has led to major asset sell-offs, which began in late 1997. The Clinton administration also supports the recovery of "prudent" and "verifiable" stranded costs and would give FERC the power to step in if states did not approve such recovery.

Industry Participants

There are over 3,100 electric utilities in the United States, including 243 investor-owned utilities (IOUs), 2,000 publicly owned (mainly municipal) utilities, and about 930 cooperative utilities (see Tables 5-1, 5-2, 5-3). Municipal utilities are owned by local towns, while co-ops are owned by their customers. All states regulate IOUs, but only some regulate publicly owned utilities and co-ops. IOUs serve about 76 percent of all retail customers, with municipals and co-ops accounting for the remaining 24 percent.

There are also 10 federally owned generation utilities which provide power to wholesale users on a not-for-profit basis. These include the Tennessee Valley Authority, four regional Power Marketing Administrations, and several agencies, such as the U.S. Army Corps of Engineers, which own large hydroelectric projects.

At the present time IOUs, public utilities, and co-ops own more than 90 percent of the installed nameplate generation capacity in the United States, but this is beginning to change as individual states order utilities to divest their generation assets and as utilities close uneconomical units because of increased competition but do not build new capacity.

Until the mid-1990s most nonutility generation capacity was owned by cogeneration and small power producers that had built projects under the guidelines of the 1978 Public Utilities Regulatory Policy Act (PURPA). Such "qualifying facilities" under PURPA were given special rights to sell power to utilities under protected contracts. However, as competitive wholesale markets developed in the United States in the wake of the 1992 Energy Policy Act, independent power producers (IPPs) began to build new "merchant" power plants designed to sell in whole-

TABLE 5-1: Installed Generating Capacity in the United States by Type of Producer

(as of December 31 in each year; megawatts, nameplate)

	1992	1993	1994	1995	1996
Total electric utility	741,601	744,690	745,954	750,859	754,889
Investor-owned	572,920	575,164	574,834	579,175	581,057
Government and public	168,730	169,526	171,120	171,684	173,832
Total nonutility	55,188	58,134	65,010	66,415	69,328
Cogeneration	40,691	43,144	49,020	50,594	53,293
Small power producers	10,164	10,517	10,529	10,483	10,694
Other	4,332	4,473	5,469	5,338	5,341
Total	796,839	802,845	810,964	817,275	824,217

Source: Edison Electric Institute.

TABLE 5-2: Electricity Generation in the United States by Type of Producer

(million kilowatt-hours)

	1992	1993	1994	1995	1996
Total electric utility	2,797,219	2,882,525	2,910,712	2,994,528	3,073,149
Investor-owned	2,214,475	2,227,185	2,308,684	2,340,481	2,372,985
Government and public	582,744	611,340	602,028	654,047	700,164
Total nonutility	309,726	327,398	372,015	400,506	400,220
Cogeneration	245,190	253,208	292,881	319,939	320,293
Small power producers	46,669	50,067	51,087	51,146	53,665
Other	20,866	24,121	28,047	29,420	26,262
Total	3,106,945	3,209,922	3,382,727	3,395,034	3,473,369

Source: Edison Electric Institute.

sale markets without long-term contracts or special legal protection. Nonregulated affiliates of utilities were also permitted to participate more freely in this market by a provision in the 1992 act allowing "exempt wholesale generator" (EWG) status for their plants.

As utility asset sales have begun, the existing plants that are being auctioned off have entered the same merchant category, frequently with energy sell-back deals with the utilities which had formerly owned those assets (see Table 5-4).

These developments have created a new class of large independent generation owners, including both nonregulated affiliates of existing utilities and traditional IPP groups. Such groups also frequently have large-scale energy marketing operations which started up in the mid-1990s for wholesale markets and are now shifting their focus to emerging retail markets.

TABLE 5-3: Regulated U.S. Electric Utility Industry, 1996

	IOU	Public[1]	Federal	Co-op	Total
Number of utilities	243	2,010	10	932	3,195
Customers (millions)	90.3	16.5	1	12.2	120

[1] Includes municipals, public power districts, state authorities, irrigation districts, and other state organizations.
Source: Edison Electric Institute.

Utility Mergers and Other Company Combinations

The number of mergers between IOUs increased dramatically in the mid-1990s (see Table 5-5) as utilities attempted to form larger groups to enhance their efficiency and prepare for competitive markets. While state and federal authorities have begun to take a harder line against mergers which appear to be anticompetitive, so far most of these deals have been approved. A mid-1997 plan to merge American Electric Power with Central and South West is the biggest such deal proposed so far and will test the limits of such merger activity.

Another major trend has been for IOUs to merge with or acquire gas companies (see Table 5-6). This "combined energy" strategy is aimed at deregulated retail markets in which a single market entity can offer users one-stop shopping for a range of fuels and actually sell British thermal units (Btus) in the most economical package rather than selling specific energy resources. Such mergers have tended to require less antitrust review because of the different market segments of the players, and major 1997 deals between Duke Power and PanEnergy Corp. and between Houston Industries and Noram were closed rapidly. There are several variations of this approach, such as the deal between Southern Company and Vastar to merge their electricity and gas marketing businesses but not the parent companies.

Another key trend which picked up steam in the mid-1990s involves electric utilities diversifying into other service businesses, including energy purchasing and management, energy

TABLE 5-4: Utility Asset Sales in the United States, 1997–1998

Utility	Buyer	Capacity, MW	Price, $ millions	Date Offered	Status
New England Electric	U.S. Generating	4,000	1,600	Mar. 1997	Close likely 8/98
Central Maine Power	FPL Group	1,185	846	June 1997	Pending
Boston Edison	Sithe Energies	2,000	536	July 1997	Sale completed May 1998
Eastern Utilities Associates	Southern Energy	280	75	July 1997	Pending
Eastern Utilities Associates		493		July 1997	No award yet
Commonwealth Electric	Southern Energy	984	462	Sept. 1997	Pending
Maine Public Service	Wisconsin Public Service	92	37.4	Sept. 1997	Pending
PG&E	Duke Energy	2,645	501	Sept. 1997	Sale completed June 1998
SoCal Edison	AES	3,556	781	Sept. 1997	Sale completed June 1998
SoCal Edison	Houston Industries	3,776	280	Sept. 1997	
SoCal Edison	Destec-NRG Energy	1,020	87	Sept. 1997	
SoCal Edison	Thermo Ecoteck	280	9.5	Sept. 1997	
San Diego G&E		2,430		Dec. 1997	Not awarded yet
Fitchburg G&E		50		Jan. 1998	Not awarded yet
Montana Power		1,439		Mar. 1998	Not awarded yet
PG&E		4,712		Mar. 1998	Not awarded yet
GPU New York State E&G	Edison Mission Energy	1,884	1,800	Apr. 1998	Pending
GPU		4,408		Apr. 1998	Not awarded yet
GPU	Peco Energy + British Energy	916	100	Apr. 1998	Pending
New York State E&G	AES	1,424	950	Apr. 1998	Pending
Boston Edison		670		Apr. 1998	Not awarded yet
Niagara Mohawk Power		4,217		Apr. 1998	Not awarded yet
Bangor Hydro Electric		129		May 1998	Not awarded yet
United Illuminating		1,208		May 1998	Not awarded yet
Unicom		5,576		July 1998	Not awarded yet
Western Massachusetts Electric		290		Aug. 1998	Not awarded yet

Source: *Electric Utility Week.*

TABLE 5-5: Recent Mergers of U.S. Investor-Owned Electric Utilities

Company 1	Company 2	New Company	Status
Orange & Rockland Utilities	Consolidated Edison		Pending
Nevada Power	Sierra Pacific Resources		Pending
Wisconsin Public Service	Upper Peninsula Power		Pending
American Electric Power Co.	Central and South West Corp.		Pending
LG&E Energy Corp.	KU Energy Corp.		Pending
Wisconsin Energy Corp.	Edison Sault Electric Co.		Completed June 1998
Ohio Edison Co.	Centerior Energy Corp.	FirstEnergy	Pending
Kansas City P&L Co.	Western Resources Inc.	Western Resources, Westar Energy	Pending
WPL Holdings Inc.	IES Industries Inc.	Interstate Energy	Completed April 1998
Allegheny Power System	DQE Inc.		Pending
Atlantic Energy	Delmarva Power	Conectiv	Completed Mar. 1998
Union Electric Co.	Central Illinois Power Co.	Ameren Corp.	Completed Jan. 1998
Baltimore G&E Co.	Potomac Electric Power Co.	Constellation Energy	Canceled Dec. 1997
Public Service Colorado	Southwestern Public Service	New Century Energies	Completed Aug. 1997
Northern States Power Co.	Wisconsin Energy Corp.	Primergy	Rejected by FERC, May 1997
Washington Water Power	Sierra Pacific Resources	Altus	Canceled June 1996
New England Electric System	Nantucket Electric Co.		Completed Apr. 1996
Midwest Resources	Iowa-Illinois G&E Co.	MidAmerican Energy	Completed July 1995
Cincinnati G&E Co.	PSI Resources	CINergy Corp.	Completed Oct. 1994
Entergy Corp.	Gulf States Utilities Co.		Completed Dec. 1993
Texas Utilities Co.	Southwestern Electric Service Co.		Completed Jan. 1993
Northeast Utilities	Public Service Co. of New Hampshire		Completed June 1992
Unitil Corp.	Fitchburg Gas & Electric Co.		Completed Apr. 1992
Kansas Power & Light Co.	Kansas Gas & Electric Co.	Western Resources	Completed March 1992

Source: *Electric Utility Week.*

conservation, telecommunications, and home security. In these cases utilities are looking for new, nonregulated revenue streams to provide growth once electricity deregulation flattens revenue growth from their core electricity business. A key aim of utilities is to leverage existing retail customer bases, brand names, and distribution networks by providing new products. In some cases the dynamic is reversed, as in a 1997 bid by the gas and electricity marketer Enron to acquire Portland General Electric to provide a base for developing retail products and pursuing West Coast and national energy marketing activities. But this diversification trend showed signs of slowing in mid-1998 as Entergy announced it would sell sev-

TABLE 5-6: Recent Electricity-Gas Mergers and Acquisitions in the United States

Electricity Company	Gas Company	Status	Name
NIPSCO Industries	Bay State Gas	Pending	
Enova Corp.	Pacific Enterprises	Completed July 1998	Sempra Energy
Portland General Electric Co.	Enron	Pending	
Long Island Lighting Co.	Brooklyn Union Gas	Completed May 1998	
Midwest Energy	KN Energy	Completed April 1998	
Western Resources	ONEOK	Completed Dec. 1997	
Houston Industries Inc.	NorAm Energy	Completed Aug. 1997	
PG&E Co.	Valero Energy	Completed July 1997	
Duke Power	PanEnergy Corp.	Completed July 1997	Duke Energy
Puget Sound P&L	Washington Energy	Completed July 1997	Puget Sound Energy
TECO Energy	Lykes Energy Inc.	Completed June 1997	
PacifiCorp	TCP Corp.	Completed Mar. 1997	

Source: *Electric Utility Week.*

eral noncore businesses and LG&E Energy dropped its large power marketing unit.

This expansion of electric utilities into new businesses is occurring at the same time that restructuring at the state level is breaking down the traditional model in which electric utilities are vertically integrated (i.e., the same company generates, transmits, and sells power to retail users and charges a bundled rate covering all costs). While some states are forcing total divestiture of electricity generation to create "distribution only" utilities, others are expected to require only "functional" unbundling, in which utilities will be able to retain all their original upstream and downstream businesses but will have to operate them separately. In some cases utilities are being required to auction their generation assets to determine stranded costs but can bid to buy them back and maintain a separate generation business.

The end result will be a general division between nonregulated energy production and marketing functions on one side and regulated energy distribution and services functions on the other side. However, in many cases large utility corporations will remain active in both areas.

Prices and Demand

Restructuring is bringing more competition to the electricity supply industry, and this should lower prices through the action of normal market forces. This downward price trend will be hastened by the introduction of new baseload gas combined-cycle generation technology, which provides extremely low cost power to replace high-cost output from older fossil fuel and nuclear plants. In the northeast, where existing plants are no longer protected from competition by traditional regulation, over 30 new gas-fired plants with a capacity of 500 megawatts (MW) or more have been proposed since late 1996.

After it became clear that the California deregulation plan (which went into effect in March 1998 after 2 years of debate and allowed all retail users to choose energy suppliers) would provide only minimal up-front rate cuts because of high stranded cost recovery charges, some states proposed plans that would directly mandate rate cuts of 10 percent or more after

stranded cost charges were accounted for to ensure up-front savings for consumers. In Massachusetts rate cuts of 10 to 20 percent have been assured by allowing utilities to provide a low-cost "transition service" based on purchases from groups that have bought their generation assets.

Such cost reductions will tend to take place in states which have retail prices well above the 6.5 cents/kWh (kilowatt-hour) national average and have pushed the hardest for deregulation. Therefore, the first major result of restructuring will be to bring energy prices in such states more in line with those in the rest of the country. A reduction in average rates nationwide should follow, but some states which now have below-average rates are concerned that national restructuring will actually raise their costs as their cheap supplies flow elsewhere.

With generally lower electricity prices nationwide, consumption will continue to rise steadily, but it is unlikely that there will be a price-related surge in the demand for power, in part because of the major drive over the last 15 years to encourage the use of more energy-efficient appliances, lighting, industrial machinery, and building construction materials. This produced a real demand reduction of about 2 percent, or 30,000 MW, nationwide by 1996. Ratepayer-supported energy conservation efforts are being reduced or ended in many states in favor of market-based programs, but a conservation infrastructure probably will remain in place.

Other factors that are expected to limit demand growth include aging of the population, which implies a declining number of persons per household, and the increasing importance in the economy of services and trade jobs relative to traditional manufacturing jobs. Even though commercial demand for power will grow, these industries are not as energy-intensive as manufacturing is.

GLOBAL INDUSTRY TRENDS OF U.S. COMPANIES

Large U.S.-based IPPs and some nonregulated utility affiliates entered overseas energy markets in the early 1990s after opportunities to initiate new independent projects diminished in the domestic market. Their activities included acquiring privatized assets and developing greenfield projects, often through competitive bidding against other energy groups. This trend intensified in the mid-1990s for several reasons. On one side the international marketplace has expanded exponentially as governments have sold existing generation and distribution companies and have begun to depend totally on foreign developers for the large new projects needed to keep up with rapid growth in domestic demand. At the same time U.S. utilities have stepped up overseas expansion as another way to create a new nonregulated revenue stream and leverage their world-class expertise in the electricity business.

In the mid-1990s several large American utilities acquired British regional electric utilities and made major acquisitions in South America and Australia. Southern Company led the pack by being the first into the British market in 1995 and then taking over the Hong Kong–based Consolidated Electric Power of Asia in 1997. Other utility-related developers with extensive overseas activities include Edison Mission Energy, CMS Generation, NRG Energy, Dominion Energy, and Entergy Power.

Among American IPP players, the most successful overseas operator by far is AES, which has amassed a worldwide portfolio of over 20,000 MW of capacity and has been active in up to 50 countries. Other key U.S. IPP players in international markets include Enron and International Generating.

U.S. regulators so far have taken a lenient attitude toward U.S. utility investment in foreign electricity markets despite some concerns that domestic customers could be negatively affected by bad overseas investments. There have been some financial setbacks, such as a 1997 decision by the new British government to impose a windfall profits tax on regional electric companies, which resulted in over $1 billion in write-offs by the U.S. parent companies. Also, the 1998 recession in several Asian counties crimped development plans; and some U.S. groups, including Entenergy and Dominion Resources, have sold off large foreign electric distribution assets. Overall, how-

ever, these foreign investments have been financially successful and show no sign of slacking off.

At the same time several large European-based energy groups have invested in the U.S. IPP market. They include Tractebel of Belgium, which bought the Texas-based CRSS; the French-owned Sithe Energies, which bought Boston Edison's generation assets; and Britain's National Power, which now owns American National Power.

Actual imports and exports of electricity are a minor issue for the U.S. electricity industry. Exports are minimal, and imports have tended to remain in the range of $2 billion per year, or about 1 percent of all sales (see Table 5-7). The main source of imports has been Canadian shipments to the northeast and upper midwest, where there is a logistic and economic advantage. In New England an emerging issue is the competition between low-cost hydroelectric power from new Canadian projects and power from efficient new plants in the region that are fueled by imported Canadian gas.

U.S. INDUSTRY GROWTH PROJECTIONS FOR THE NEXT 1 AND 5 YEARS

Electricity Prices

Retail competition, a proliferation of suppliers, low coal prices, efficient new generation technology, low interest rates, and lower supplier reserve margins have all contributed to the continuation of a fall in electricity prices. While the ability of utilities to win stranded cost payments from retail customers through "transition" charges will prevent a price plunge once restructuring is complete, the collection of such charges will be limited to between 5 and 10 years, after which the full impact of competitive pricing will be felt.

By 2002 the average nationwide price of electricity should be 11 percent lower than the price in 1995, which will mean an average annual decline of roughly 2 percent. Regional price differen-

TABLE 5-7: Electric Utilities Industry (SIC 4911) Trends and Forecasts
(millions of dollars unless otherwise indicated)

	1992	1993	1994	1995	1996	1997[1]	1998[1]	1999[2]	96–97	97–98	98–99	92–96[3]
									Percent Change			
Industry data												
Value of shipments	187,131	197,678	202,330	206,846	211,000	214,628	220,106	223,262	1.7	2.6	1.4	3.0
Value of shipments ($1992)	187,131	196,009	201,255	206,456	208,314	211,439	214,610	217,400	1.5	1.5	1.3	2.7
Employment (thousands)	440	428	417	404	386	378						
Trade data												
Value of imports	1,925	2,056	2,738	2,289	2,179	2,123	2,139	2,148	−2.6	0.8	0.4	3.1
Value of exports	460	561	400	338	321	311	311	311	−3.1	0.0	0.0	−8.6

[1] Estimate.
[2] Forecast.
[3] Compound annual rate.
Source: Standard & Poor's DRI.

tials should narrow as a result of restructuring from a maximum of 150 percent in 1995 to 130 percent in 2002, measured by average prices in each region relative to the average U.S. price.

Generating Capacity

Through the early 1980s virtually all new power plants were built by electric utilities in the context of traditional regulation, which guaranteed a specific rate of return on new rate-base additions as well as secure franchised distribution territories. This began to change in the mid-1980s as federal law required utilities to buy supplies from qualifying facilities under PURPA and state regulators adopted least-cost planning rules which forced utilities to seek competitive bids for new supplies and build capacity themselves only when that was economically justified.

Since the mid-1980s about half the approximately 100,000 MW of new generation capacity in the United States has been built by utilities and half has been built by nonutility generators. For the utilities this has included several large nuclear plants which had been under construction since the 1970s as well as a large number of small oil- and gas-fired units to meet peaking needs without adding to baseload capacity, which remained sufficient to meet normal nonpeak demand.

U.S. nuclear capacity nearly doubled from 55,000 MW in 1980 to 103,000 MW in 1990. However, since that time nuclear plant additions have stopped, with the last one coming in 1995 with the Tennessee Valley Authority's 1,250-MW Watts Bar 1 plant. No new nuclear plants have been ordered in the United States since 1978, and several projects have been canceled. Also, because of competition and increasingly tough safety regulations, the number of nuclear plants which close before their 40-year licenses expire has increased. In recent years Trojan, San Onofre, Maine Yankee, Connecticut Yankee, and Zion have been retired early because of high maintenance and compliance costs.

By 1996 nonutility generators owned 69,300 MW, or 8.4 percent of generation capacity, in the United States and produced 400.2 billion kWh of energy, or 11.5 percent of U.S. output. Cogenerators, which also sell steam to industrial hosts, supplied about 9.2 percent of total energy, selling about half their output to utilities. Small power producers, mainly small hydroelectric units, contributed 1.5 percent of supply, and IPP plants now provide less than 1 percent of total energy.

However, this situation is expected to change for several reasons. Utilities' additions to capacity virtually stopped in the mid-1990s because of the trend toward lower reserve margins and the advent of restructuring, which makes recovery of plant investment costs uncertain. Many states have set a cutoff date for restructuring plans, after which utilities cannot claim stranded cost recovery for new investments. In 1997 Southern Company was considered unconventional in its proposal to build 2,000 MW of new gas-fired capacity in Mississippi and Alabama under normal rate regulation and won state approval only after pledging not to seek stranded cost recovery for those projects.

At the same time, growth in the cogeneration and small power sector has stalled as the rates that providers are offered by utilities for such power had dropped with the overall trend toward lower prices. This has made it almost impossible for new cogeneration plants to get contracts under PURPA rules. This situation may change somewhat, as some states have passed rules requiring competitive energy sellers in deregulated markets to use a fixed percentage of power from renewable and cogeneration sources.

A big shift is expected in the IPP sector as utilities divest their assets and nonregulated energy companies add new gas-fired capacity to serve emerging retail markets. In 1997, for example, FPL Group announced the purchase of 1,185 MW of assets from Central Maine Power and at the same time said that it would build 1,000 MW of new capacity in Maine. U.S. Generating has bought 4,000 MW of New England Electric System assets and is building several new plants in New England. Also, in 1998 about 15,000 MW of utility capacity in California will be sold to several groups, including AES, Houston Industries, and Duke Energy, and will effectively become IPP power. Depending on the extent of divestiture policies in each state, a large amount of current utility-owned generation will change hands and become IPP capacity, while the rest will continue to be owned by the same company but no longer will be vertically integrated with customer load.

The highly favorable economic structure of new gas-fired combined cycle generation has led to a surge in proposals for new projects in several regions. While the main objective is to back out inefficient existing plants, it remains to be seen how many new projects will obtain financing and be built. This situation has put a premium on new projects which use existing sites and back out older capacity to eliminate environmental problems. Other crucial elements are the availability of gas and transmission to move power to markets.

Overall, analysts predict that between asset sales and new capacity additions, the IPP share of U.S. electricity capacity will increase to close to 200,000 MW, or about 25 percent of the national total, by 2002, with about 15 large energy groups holding over half the assets. These groups will be able to offer energy in the range of 2 to 3 cents per kilowatt-hour, forcing down prices in the entire market.

Electricity Consumption

Electricity consumption rose steadily in the mid-1990s at a rate somewhat below 1 percent annually, and electricity use generally has grown faster than has the use of other energy sources. Demand for electricity is expected to grow 1.6 percent per year between 1996 and 2010, driven especially by increases in commercial and industrial demand. Residential growth will remain flat at 1 percent per year (see Table 5-8). Total demand should top 3.5 trillion kWh by the year 2005.

The value of electricity sales in the United States in 1997 was estimated at $211.4 billion. Sales in constant dollars have risen just over 2 percent per year since the early 1990s (see Table 5-8). This growth will continue at a somewhat slower pace through 1999 as declining prices continue to offset growth in demand.

TABLE 5-8: U.S. Electricity Sales
(billions of kilowatt-hours)

	1995	1996	1997	1998	1999	2000	2005	2010	2015	2020	Percent Growth 1996–2010	Percent Growth 2010–2020
Commercial	938	971	984	1,018	1,038	1,057	1,145	1,241	1,319	1,373	1.8	1.0
Industrial	1,008	1,041	1,072	1,091	1,106	1,120	1,249	1,377	1,500	1,612	2.0	1.6
Residential	1,047	1,071	1,062	1,094	1,106	1,122	1,184	1,238	1,311	1,373	1.0	1.0
Other	9	8	8	8	8	9	9	9	9	10	—	—
Total	3,002	3,091	3,126	3,211	3,258	3,308	3,587	3,867	4,139	4,368	1.6	1.2

Source: Standard and Poor's DRI, World Energy Service.

Industrial Use

The industrial sector, with total usage of approximately 1.2 trillion kWh per year, is the largest consumer of electricity in the United States, including both purchases from outside sources and self-generation. This sector purchased just over 1 trillion kWh in 1997 from utilities and other generators, and demand growth is expected to continue in the range of 2 percent per year through 2010, then drop off slightly.

While industrial users have greatly improved their efficiency in the use of power in the last 10 years, this has been closely matched by growth in new applications for electricity in automated production lines, robotics, computers, and heating systems. In this period industrial use of other fossil fuels has declined fairly steadily, driven by high prices, environmental pressures, and the shift of the industrial mix away from so-called smokestack industries. From just 15 percent of final industrial energy consumption in 1980 (excluding raw material uses), electricity now accounts for almost 25 percent of total industrial energy usage.

Industrial users have been able to win major price concessions from utilities in recent years, especially in high-cost states, where they have made a legitimate case that they would be forced to move their operations out of state without lower prices. They have also played a key political role in pushing state governments to consider retail competition.

Commercial Use

Electricity consumption in the commercial sector has traditionally been lower than that in the industrial and residential sectors, accounting for 31.4 percent of total demand in 1997. However, this sector showed strong growth in the early 1990s and is predicted to increase its use of electricity 1.8 percent per year through 2010, catching up to residential use in that year. This strong growth has been pushed by the explosion in personal computing over the last 15 years, along with increased use of photocopiers, printers, fax machines, and communications devices. Indoor shopping centers, amusement complexes, and mass transit systems have increased the demand for electricity in this sector.

Over time, the amount of electricity used per square foot has increased. If that trend continues, it should raise the electricity intensity of the commercial sector to 46 percent by 2002 from 44.5 percent in 1995. In addition to gas absorption chillers and some gas heat pumps in specialized locations, electricity has captured the commercial sectors growth markets. A 1.5 percent annual growth in commercial square footage combined with a rise of 0.25 percent per year in electricity used per square foot will lead to an expected 1.75 percent annual growth increase after 2000.

Commercial users have been less vocal in pushing for retail competition but are expected to make major use of competitive energy sellers and special purchasing and load aggregation techniques once that choice is available. Large institutional users such as school districts, hospitals, and state governments have also made aggressive efforts to tap the competitive market.

Residential Use

Residential use at just over 100 billion kWh accounts for over one-third of U.S. electricity consumption. While residential use rose in the early 1990s, it is expected to stabilize at a steady average annual increase of 1 percent over the next 10 to 20 years. This slow growth will be caused by the modest overall growth in the population and in household formation. Also, gas is expected to share in the growth in residential energy use along with electricity over the survey period. Gas provides competition in traditional areas of cooking, water heating, and clothes drying and increasingly in space heating and cooling as gas heat pumps gain market share.

Home energy savings resulting from more energy-efficient appliances and promotions that encourage the use of such appliances and lighting will be offset by the increased use of appliances and a modest gain in electricity-heated homes, keeping energy use per person constant during this period. With the faster growth of demand for electricity in the commercial and industrial sectors, residential use will gradually fall below 33 percent of total U.S. demand after 2005.

Electricity Trading

Since the passage of the 1992 Energy Policy Act, which encouraged a greater use of regional transmission grids for energy trading, energy sales on the wholesale market have risen dramatically. These sales are carried out by a large group of energy marketers and brokers that are licensed by FERC to deal at market rates.

In 1997, energy marketers handled 1.2 trillion kWh of wholesale energy sales, a remarkable fivefold increase over 1996 and over a growth rate close to zero in 1994. This represented approximately 50 percent of all wholesale electricity sales in 1997, with the other 50 percent made by utility affiliates directly to their own operating companies or to other utilities. Leading national energy marketers by sales volume in 1997 included Enron, Southern Energy Marketing, Electric Clearinghouse, Aquila Power, Duke Energy Trading, and Vitol Gas & Electric. Overall, about 100 separate marketers were registered with FERC and reported some trading activity in 1997.

In 1998 futures trading in electricity began to emerge, with large commodity exchanges in New York and Chicago setting up trading hubs.

CONCLUSIONS

The movement toward restructuring of the U.S. electricity industry appeared to gain irreversible momentum in 1997, and the only questions now are how many states will voluntarily change to a deregulated system and whether federal legislation will force the others to follow suit.

For the electricity supply industry, the introduction of choice will shift the focus of regulation but not eliminate it. Unbundled generation and energy marketing activities will be free from traditional rate regulation but still will come under scrutiny from FERC and state commissions, especially in regard to market power and environmental issues. Most states will have a simple procedure for registering marketers but also will impose a code of conduct to ensure fair competition and protect retail customers from shady sales practices.

Existing utilities generally will retain their transmission assets, but transmission rates and access issues will be supervised by the new ISO groups, usually at the regional level. ISOs also will control system expansion and other reliability-related issues and will manage regional pools for energy, capacity, reserves, and ancillary services.

The distribution operations of present utilities generally will remain intact. These utilities will serve the same franchise areas under regulated distribution rates with an obligation to serve, provide default service, and collect stranded costs charges.

Paul Kemezis, Electric Utility Week, (931) 695-5485, October 1998.

■ REFERENCES

Capacity and Generation of Non Utility Sources of Energy (annual), Edison Electric Institute.
Electric Power Annual (annual), Energy Information Administration, Department of Energy.
Electric Utility Week, McGraw-Hill, New York.
Electrical World (monthly), McGraw-Hill, New York.
Electricity Supply & Demand, Summary of Electric Utility Supply and Demand Projections (annual), North American Electric Reliability Council.
Global Power Report (biweekly), McGraw-Hill, New York.
International Private Power Quarterly, McGraw-Hill, New York.
Power Generation Markets Quarterly, McGraw-Hill, New York.
Statistical Yearbook of the Electric Utility Industry (annual), Edison Electric Institute.

■ RELATED CHAPTERS

2: Coal Mining
4: Petroleum Refining

■ GLOSSARY

British thermal unit (Btu): The standard unit for measuring quantities of heat energy, such as the heat content of fuel. A Btu is the amount of heat energy required to raise the temperature of 1 pound of water 1 degree Fahrenheit.

Cogeneration: Electricity generation in which both electrical energy and excess heat are produced. The heat, usually in the form of steam, is sold as a separate commodity to a host industrial user. Power output from the plant may be sold directly to the host industry, the local electric utility, or both. Cogeneration plants can be owned by the industrial host or by an independent developer.

Combined cycle unit: A type of generation unit, usually gas- or oil-fired, which uses waste heat from an initial combustion turbine cycle to assist a second topping combustion cycle, creating extra efficiencies in fuel use. Gas-fired combined cycle units in the range of 400 to 600 MW currently represent the leading generation technology for new baseload plants in the United States.

Electricity intensity: Energy used per dollar of gross domestic product (GDP) measured in real dollars is referred to as energy intensity; electricity used per dollar of GDP in real dollars is referred to as electricity intensity.

Electricity used per square foot: The average number of kilowatt-hours used per square foot of a building or building sector, such as commercial buildings.

End-use sectors: Residential, commercial, industrial, and transportation markets in which energy is sold at retail.

Final demand: The demand for electricity, natural gas, coal, and oil, excluding the demand for those fuels when used to generate electricity.

Independent power producers (IPPs): Private companies which develop, own, or operate electric power plants and sell power on the wholesale market, frequently under long-term contracts, to utilities and do not have a responsibility to serve a retail load. IPPs also are defined as a class of large nonutility generators that produce electricity only and are not cogeneration plants or small power producers.

Investor-owned utilities (IOUs): Utilities that are financed by the sales of securities and whose business operations are overseen by a board representing their shareholders.

Nameplate capacity: The guaranteed continuous output in megawatts of an electricity generation plant when it is operating under optimal conditions.

Nonutility generators (NUGs): A broad class of privately owned power generators which sell power in wholesale markets. Unlike traditional vertically integrated utilities, they do not sell directly to retail users in franchise territories, although this is changing with the advent of restructuring. Nonutility generators include cogenerators, small power producers, and IPPs.

Qualifying facilities (QFs): Nonutility generation plants which have a special status under the 1978 Public Utilities Regulatory Policy Act and have the right to sell their power to utilities if they can meet a utility's avoided cost. QFs include cogeneration plants and small power units fueled by renewable energy sources.

Restructuring: Action by a state government or the federal government that requires utilities to unbundle their operations into separate generation, transmission, and distribution businesses and gives utility retail customers a free choice of energy suppliers.

Retail choice: The system, under restructuring, in which residential, commercial, and industrial end users obtain the ability to choose their energy suppliers and use the local distribution company's wires to directly access the competitive market.

Self-generation: Production of electricity on site by a retail customer for the customer's use as an alternative to buying from the local utility.

Small power producers (SPPs): Private nonutility power producers whose generating facilities use renewable resources and produce power below a set capacity.

Stranded costs: The value of generation assets owned by utilities which become too costly to operate once restructuring takes place and retail users can access competitive supplies at lower market-based costs. Most state and federal restructuring proposals allow utilities to recover some or all of their stranded costs, usually through a universal "transition" charge on all retail users over a fixed time period.

Unbundling: The process of separating the generation, transmission, and distribution assets of vertically integrated utilities into distinct operating units that can be individual subsidiaries of a parent corporation or can be divested into independent unaffiliated companies. Also refers to the practice of breaking down utility rates into separate energy, transmission, and generation components as a preliminary step toward restructuring.

CONSTRUCTION
Economic and Trade Trends

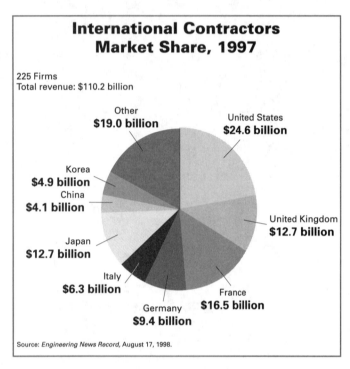

International Contractors Market Share, 1997

225 Firms
Total revenue: $110.2 billion

- Other **$19.0 billion**
- United States **$24.6 billion**
- Korea **$4.9 billion**
- China **$4.1 billion**
- United Kingdom **$12.7 billion**
- Japan $12.7 billion
- Italy **$6.3 billion**
- France **$16.5 billion**
- Germany **$9.4 billion**

Source: *Engineering News Record*, August 17, 1998.

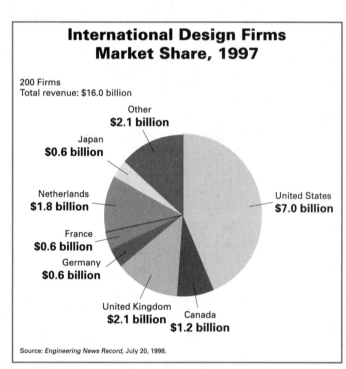

International Design Firms Market Share, 1997

200 Firms
Total revenue: $16.0 billion

- Other **$2.1 billion**
- Japan **$0.6 billion**
- United States **$7.0 billion**
- Netherlands **$1.8 billion**
- France **$0.6 billion**
- Germany **$0.6 billion**
- United Kingdom **$2.1 billion**
- Canada **$1.2 billion**

Source: *Engineering News Record*, July 20, 1998.

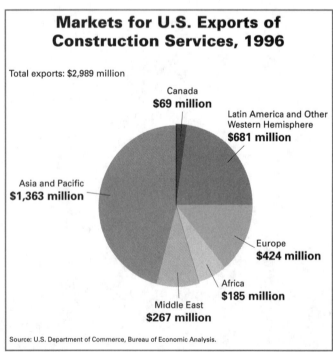

Markets for U.S. Exports of Construction Services, 1996

Total exports: $2,989 million

- Canada **$69 million**
- Latin America and Other Western Hemisphere **$681 million**
- Asia and Pacific **$1,363 million**
- Europe **$424 million**
- Africa **$185 million**
- Middle East **$267 million**

Source: U.S. Department of Commerce, Bureau of Economic Analysis.

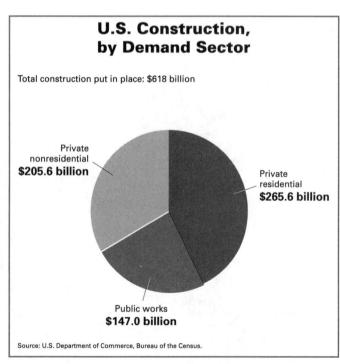

U.S. Construction, by Demand Sector

Total construction put in place: $618 billion

- Private nonresidential **$205.6 billion**
- Private residential **$265.6 billion**
- Public works **$147.0 billion**

Source: U.S. Department of Commerce, Bureau of the Census.

Construction

INDUSTRY DEFINITION This chapter covers construction contracting (SIC 15, 16, 17). Architectural, engineering, and surveying services (SIC 8710) are not included in the domestic analyses, but their international activities are covered in the analysis of the international contracting subsector. The chapter also does not cover real estate (SIC 65), manufactured housing (SIC 245), construction equipment (SIC 3462), and construction equipment leasing (SIC 735).

OVERVIEW

In 1999 the constant-dollar value of new construction put in place will increase 1 percent from the 1998 level. The home building sector will recover as mortgage interest rates decline. Nonresidential construction will increase 2 percent from the 1998 level. Public works construction will increase 4 percent over 1998 as a result of increasing federal and state government investment in infrastructure. U.S. exports of construction services will decline about 5 percent because of weakening Pacific Rim markets, the strengthened dollar, and the booming domestic market.

GLOBAL CONSTRUCTION TRENDS

The United States is one of the leading construction markets in the world, employing 7.1 million and accounting for about 7 percent of gross domestic product (GDP). Nevertheless, about 80 percent of the world's construction activity occurs outside the United States. Enterprising American construction and engineering firms have been successful competitors in the international contracting market, although most of their overseas construction is done by foreign affiliates using local labor rather than cross-border exports of U.S. services (see Table 6-1).

TABLE 6-1: Construction Trends and Projections

	1994	1995	1996	1997	1998[1]	1999[2]
Value of construction put in place ($ billions)[3]	519.9	534.1	568.6	601.0	635	
Value of construction put in place (1992 $ billions)	481.0	474.4	493.2	507.1	520	525
Number of private housing starts (thousands of units)	1,457	1,354	1,477	1,475	1,450	1,410
Shipments of mobile homes (thousands of units)[4]	304	340	363	353	345	340
International construction contracts, U.S. companies ($ millions)[5]		18,900	22,800	24,600		
Exports of construction services ($ millions)[6]	2,474	2,848	2,990	3,100	3,000	2,800
Imports of construction services ($ millions)[6]	280	339	489	600		
Employees (thousands)[7]	4,986	5,158	5,400	5,600		
Self-employed workers (thousands)	1,425	1,455	1,475	1,500	1,550	
Average hourly earnings of construction workers ($)	14.73	15.09	15.46	16.00	16.50	
Construction cost index (1992 = 100)	108.0	112.5	115.0	118.3		
Producer price index for construction materials (1982 = 100)	133.8	138.8	139.6	146.0	149.0	

[1] Proprietors and working partners, not counted as employees.
[2] Estimate.
[3] The data on construction put in place do not include maintenance and repair work.
[4] Manufactured Housing Institute and Bureau of the Census.
[5] *Engineering News-Record;* McGraw-Hill Information Systems Co.
[6] U.S. Department of Commerce, Bureau of Economic Analysis.
[7] Based on establishments surveyed by the Bureau of Labor Statistics. Excludes self-employed workers.
Source: U.S. Department of Commerce: Bureau of the Census, International Trade Administration; U.S. Department of Labor, Bureau of Labor Statistics.

The Asian economic crisis has curtailed construction in the Pacific Rim area, which until recently was the most active construction market in the world. South America and Europe are also large markets for international contractors, and U.S. exporters have a North American Free Trade Agreement (NAFTA) advantage in Canada and Mexico. Although U.S. firms have substantial difficulties entering foreign markets, they have stepped up their efforts in the 1990s. In 1997, American-based design firms received $7 billion in international billings and American general contractors won $25 billion in foreign contracts.

U.S. exports of construction services, measured on a cross-border transactions basis, totaled approximately $3 billion in 1996. The actual value of contracts won by American-owned companies was much larger—about $23 billion. The difference can be explained chiefly by the fact that cross-border transactions exclude most construction done by foreign affiliates, foreign subcontractors, and foreign labor forces. Legal U.S.

imports of construction services amounted to approximately $0.6 billion, giving the United States a large surplus in the balance of trade in construction services. Most U.S. exports of construction services involve management services, engineering know-how, and specialized technology.

U.S. CONSTRUCTION INDUSTRY

In 1998 the inflation-adjusted value of new construction put in place increased 3 percent to set an all-time record (the 1998 current-dollar value of about $635 billion is also a record). This performance occurred in spite of a 1.7 percent decline in the number of housing starts to 1.45 million units. The decline in home building was offset by solid increases in home improvement and nonresidential construction. Public works construction increased 4 percent, led by increases in school and road construction. Private nonresidential construction increased

TABLE 6-2: Value of Construction Put in Place
(billions of 1992 dollars; percent)

Type of Construction	1996	1997[1]	1998[2]	1999[2]	2003[2]	Percent Change[3] 97–98	98–99	98–03
Total construction	493.2	507.1	520.1	525.4	549.8	3	1	1
Residential	212.0	216.1	219.1	216.1	224.7	1	–1	1
Single-family	136.5	136.5	136.5	131.0	136.5	0	–4	0
Multifamily	17.4	19.1	19.7	20.3	18.7	3	3	–1
Home Improvement	58.1	60.5	62.9	64.8	69.5	4	3	2
Private nonresidential	165.8	173.2	178.0	181.8	187.6	3	2	1
Manufacturing facilities	28.0	25.9	25.4	25.9	29.4	–2	2	3
Offices	24.1	27.1	28.5	29.9	28.5	5	5	0
Hotels and motels	10.3	11.0	11.8	11.8	11.8	7	0	0
Other commercial	41.3	41.3	42.5	42.5	38.5	3	0	–2
Religious	4.0	4.9	5.0	5.1	5.5	2	2	2
Educational	5.8	7.0	7.7	8.2	9.4	10	6	4
Hospital and institutional	10.5	11.7	11.8	12.1	13.7	1	2	3
Miscellaneous buildings	6.5	7.7	7.9	8.0	8.7	2	2	2
Telecommunications	10.4	10.1	10.3	10.5	11.9	2	2	3
Railroads	4.0	4.2	4.3	4.4	4.5	3	2	1
Electric utilities	11.2	12.0	12.4	12.9	14.3	3	4	3
Gas utilities	4.3	4.5	4.6	4.6	5.1	2	0	2
Petroleum pipelines	0.9	0.9	0.9	0.9	0.8	0	–3	–2
Farm structures	2.7	2.8	2.9	2.9	3.2	3	2	2
Miscellaneous structures	1.8	2.1	2.1	2.2	2.4	2	2	2
Public works	115.4	117.8	123.0	127.5	137.5	4	4	2
Housing and redevelopment	3.9	4.0	4.1	4.2	4.5	2	4	2
Federal industrial	1.2	0.8	0.8	0.9	1.1	5	7	6
Educational	20.1	20.9	23.0	24.4	26.7	10	6	3
Hospital	4.0	4.3	4.3	4.3	4.7	0	1	2
Other public buildings	20.2	20.7	21.7	22.6	25.2	5	4	3
Highways	33.3	34.9	36.3	37.7	40.1	4	4	2
Military facilities	2.2	2.2	2.2	2.0	1.8	–2	–7	–4
Conservation and development	5.2	4.7	4.8	4.8	5.1	3	0	1
Sewer systems	9.1	8.5	8.5	8.8	8.9	0	3	1
Water supply	5.1	5.2	5.5	5.6	6.3	5	3	3
Miscellaneous public structures	11.1	11.6	11.8	12.1	13.1	2	2	2

[1] Estimate.
[2] Forecast.
[3] Average annual rate of growth.
Source: U.S. Department of Commerce: Bureau of the Census; International Trade Administration.

TABLE 6-3: Construction Expenditures by Type of Structure

(billions of 1992 dollars; percent)

	1996	1997[1]	1998[2]	1999[2]	2003[2]	Percent Change[3] 97–98	Percent Change[3] 98–99	Percent Change[3] 98–03
Total new construction	493.2	507.1	520.1	525.4	549.8	3	1	1
New building construction	333.8	342.9	350.6	351.2	362.8	2	0	1
New housing units	153.9	155.6	156.2	151.3	155.2	0	–3	–0
Private nonresidential	130.5	136.6	140.5	143.4	145.4	3	2	1
Publicly owned	49.4	50.7	53.9	56.5	62.2	6	5	3
Other new structures	101.3	103.7	106.6	109.4	117.5	3	3	2
Private nonresidential	35.3	36.6	37.5	38.4	42.2	2	2	2
Publicly owned	66.0	67.1	69.1	71.0	75.2	3	3	2
Home improvements	58.1	60.5	62.9	64.8	69.5	4	3	2
Home repairs[4]	31.7	32.0	33.0	34.0	38.3	3	3	3

[1] Estimate.
[2] Forecast.
[3] Average annual rate of growth.
[4] Home repairs are not included in construction put in place.
Source: U.S. Department of Commerce: Bureau of the Census; International Trade Administration.

modestly, with commercial buildings and utilities accounting for most of the gain (see Tables 6-2 and 6-3).

Residential remodeling and repair work increased in 1998, reflecting the growing stock of housing and a heavy turnover of used homes. Although the data for maintenance and repair construction are not as complete as those for new construction, the available information indicates that 1998 will be a record year for this type of work. Nonresidential building improvements (commercial remodeling and renovation) probably also have increased since 1997.

The 1992 Census of Construction showed that about 66 percent of the construction industry's work was for new construc-

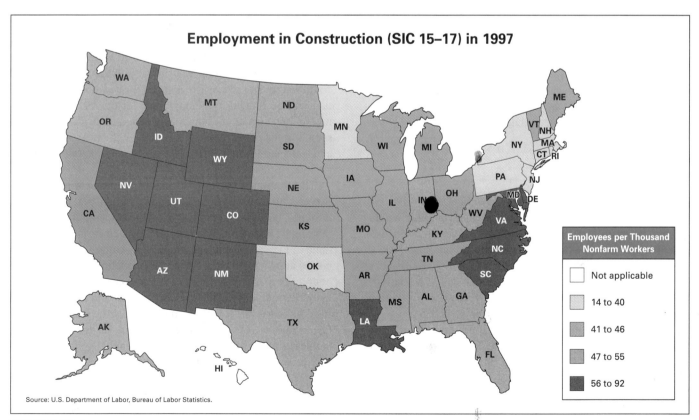

Employment in Construction (SIC 15–17) in 1997

Employees per Thousand Nonfarm Workers

- Not applicable
- 14 to 40
- 41 to 46
- 47 to 55
- 56 to 92

Source: U.S. Department of Labor, Bureau of Labor Statistics.

FIGURE 36-1

tion; 19 percent was for additions, alterations, and reconstruction; 10 percent was for maintenance and repair; and 5 percent was unspecified. In 1998 new construction probably accounted for about 65 percent of the industry's business.

In 1998 the value of new construction put in place was estimated to equal about 7.1 percent of GDP. This share is about the same as that in 1996 but is well below the post–World War II peak of 11.9 percent of GDP attained in 1966. This measure tends to understate the importance of construction in the economy because several types of construction activity that are not included in new construction data have grown rapidly in the past decade. These types include maintenance and repair, some commercial and/or industrial renovation, factory-built structures, and environmental restoration.

Construction costs increased about 2 percent in 1998, as measured by the fixed-weight construction cost deflator of the U.S. Bureau of the Census. This was faster than the average annual rate of increase in the previous 5 years and faster than the rate of increase of the consumer price index. Prices of building materials also rose an average of about 2 percent in 1998. Land prices were fairly stable on average, although there have been double-digit increases in some of the stronger markets. (Land prices are not included in the construction cost index.) Insurance and bonding costs have continued to increase, although the overall availability of insurance has improved. Labor costs have increased because of tight labor markets, with the average hourly earnings of construction workers increasing approximately 4 percent in 1998. Interest costs for real estate and construction loans increased slightly from the 1997 levels.

There were an estimated 5.6 million employees in the construction industry in 1997. This was about 4 percent above the 1996 level and was an all-time record. In addition, about 1.5 million people are self-employed as proprietors and working partners. Construction is one of the higher-paying industries in the United States, as measured by average hourly and weekly earnings (see Table 6-1). State levels of employment in the construction industry are shown in Figure 6-1.

OUTLOOK FOR 1999

The constant-dollar value of new construction in 1999 will increase slightly from the value in 1998. Home building will lag behind nonresidential construction (see Tables 6-2 and 6-3). The most promising markets are commercial buildings, educational buildings, highways, and electric utilities. The weaker construction markets will be military facilities and some types of residential construction. (Detailed prospects for various types of construction are discussed later in this chapter.)

Housing starts will total about 1.40 million units in 1999, about 3 percent below the level in 1998. This drop is entirely attributable to single-family housing starts, which will decrease 5 percent to 1.05 million units. Private nonresidential construction will be about 2 percent higher than it was in 1998, with declines in store construction offset by gains in other categories. Public works construction will increase about 4 percent

in 1998 as a result of increases in federal, state, and local construction expenditures.

Construction activity is likely to be stronger in the west and the south than in the northeast and the midwest, but all four regions will show gains. The recovery in California will continue, especially in home building, but the amount of construction activity will remain below the levels of the late 1980s. The midwest has had less overbuilding than has most of the nation, and has a relatively strong economic outlook. The south has received the greatest share of industrial construction in the last two decades and probably will continue to grow faster than the national average as the economy recovers. Although the northeast has pockets where construction is booming, much of that region will be a slow-growth construction market.

OUTLOOK TO 2003

Between 1999 and 2003 new construction is expected to increase modestly from the current levels. The overall growth rate for construction will be about 2 percent annually, in line with 2 percent growth in GDP. Public works construction is expected to increase faster than is private nonresidential construction. Remodeling and repair construction will increase at about the same rate as GDP.

A key factor supporting construction in the next 5 years will be declining interest rates. This forecast assumes a very small federal deficit and modest inflation, which should lead to lower interest rates and a fairly good macroeconomic climate for construction.

The oversupply of commercial buildings, a drag on new construction, is being eliminated gradually by attrition, remodeling, and a growing economy. Store construction will be affected by the adjustments under way in the retailing industry, which could last several years. The demand for new housing construction will be limited by demographic factors and the declining investment appeal of home ownership. Federal government spending for public works, especially highways, will increase, and state and local governments also will increase their investments in infrastructure.

The continued strength of the U.S. manufacturing sector is expected to result in strong demand for industrial construction through 2003. Electric utility construction and repair also will represent a large growth market. Hospital construction will continue to increase despite strenuous cost-cutting efforts by businesses and health care providers. Remodeling and repair work, both residential and nonresidential, will continue to increase as the U.S. stock of structures becomes older and more extensive. In addition to market factors, the U.S. construction industry will face a number of supply-side challenges in the next 5 years, including foreign competition, the limited supply of workers, and the rising cost of insurance. Most foreign construction contractors that compete in the U.S. market are well financed and have world-class construction expertise. The strong U.S. market has made foreign penetration easier than it was 5 years ago. The supply of young workers, who constitute most of the construction labor force, is fairly tight because of economic and demographic trends. In 1998 there were labor shortages, especially of skilled laborers, in local markets. Some of those shortages were eased by labor migration, but as the economic boom continues, shortages of labor and skills will become more general. The cost of liability insurance has stabilized, but the cost of health insurance and worker's compensation insurance has continued to increase rapidly.

PRIVATE RESIDENTIAL CONSTRUCTION

In 1998 home building expenditures are expected to increase about 1 percent in real terms above the near-record levels of 1997. The huge single-family-home category will drop, while multifamily construction and home improvement will increase.

Housing starts were expected to total 1.45 million units in 1998, a 3 percent decline from the 1.47 million starts in 1997. The single-family market probably will record a 3 percent drop to 1.10 million units, while the multifamily market is expected to see starts increase 3 percent to 0.33 million units (see Table 6-4). This has occurred partly in response to higher vacancy rates and better financial returns from other investments. Although housing starts data do not include mobile homes, they do include panelized and modular units which are built to local or statewide factory-built building codes.

Expenditures for residential repairs and improvements totaled nearly $120 billion in 1997. This amount includes contracted work and purchased materials but excludes the value of do-it-yourself labor. Improvements over the last few years have averaged about 60 percent of all such expenditures, with maintenance and repair accounting for the remainder.

Outlook for 1999

New housing starts are expected to total 1.40 million units in 1999, a slight decline from 1.45 million in 1998. Starts of single-family units should decrease slightly to 1.05 million, while the multiunit segment is forecast to increase about 3 percent to 0.36 million units. Home improvement expenditures are expected to rise about 3 percent.

Interest rates should be slightly higher in 1999, and this will have a modest impact on the single-family sector. Other factors affecting this sector include the continued moderate growth expected in GDP and consumer income, the lure of other investment options, the slowed growth in home owner equity in the 1990s, the heavy debt load of U.S. consumers, and the availability of construction loans to contractors and mortgage funds to home buyers.

Multifamily construction activity will be affected by high vacancy rates and mediocre demographics. However, there will be strong investor interest as a result of easier lending requirements and real estate investment trust (REIT) liquidity. There

TABLE 6-4: Private Housing Starts by Type of House
(thousands of units)

Period	Total Housing Starts	Single-Unit Structures			Multiunit Structures			
		Total One-Unit	Detached Houses	Town Houses[1]	Total Multiunit	Two- to Four- Unit Structures	Town House–Style Apartments[1]	Apartment Units[2]
1980	1,292	852	774	78	440	110	45	285
1981	1,084	705	628	77	379	91	39	249
1982	1,063	663	577	86	400	80	27	293
1983	1,703	1,068	897	171	635	113	44	478
1984	1,750	1,085	875	210	665	121	40	504
1985	1,745	1,075	905	170	670	93	53	524
1986	1,807	1,179	1,013	166	628	84	52	492
1987	1,623	1,146	1,004	142	477	65	35	377
1988	1,488	1,081	968	113	407	59	30	318
1989	1,376	1,003	916	87	373	55	31	287
1990	1,193	895	832	63	298	38	20	240
1991	1,014	840	789	51	174	36	12	126
1992	1,200	1,030	958	72	170	31	14	125
1993	1,288	1,126	95	1,031	162	29	12	120
1994	1,457	1,198	1,091	107	259	35	19	204
1995	1,354	1,076	972	104	278	34	13	231
1996	1,477	1,161	1,054	107	316	45	15	256
1997	1,475	1,134	1,030	104	341	44	17	280
1998[3]	1,450	1,100			350			
1999[4]	1,410	1,050			360			
2003[4]	1,380	1,050			330			

[1] A single-unit town house is separated from adjoining units by a ground-to-roof wall and has separate utilities. Town house–style apartments, though attached, are not separated by a ground-to-roof wall and may share infrastructural facilities.
[2] Apartment buildings are conventional multifamily buildings in which dwelling units may share a common basement, heating plant, stairs, entrance halls, water supply, or sewage disposal system.
[3] Estimate.
[4] Forecast.
Source: U.S. Department of Commerce; Bureau of the Census.

will be increased demand in market areas with high populations and economic growth.

Spending for residential repairs and improvements is expected to increase about 3 percent in 1999. Home repair expenditures probably also will rise about 3 percent. This expected gain will be largely the result of solid sales of new and existing homes over the last few years. (More than half of all improvements occur within 18 months after a new owner moves in or within 12 months before a home is sold.) In addition, the moderately strong economy will allow more home owners to better maintain and improve their homes.

Outlook to 2003

Annual housing starts in the period 1998–2003 probably will average about 1.4 million units, slightly lower than the level in 1998; however, the average size of housing units will increase in line with long-term trends of about 2 percent annually. Home improvement and repair work will continue to increase at about the same rate as GDP.

Demographic factors will restrain the demand for new single-family housing at the end of the 1990s and into the next decade. Because of the "baby bust" that occurred in the United States between 1965 and 1976, declining numbers of young adults are entering the 25- to 45-year-old age group, the prime home buying age. Demographic support for apartment construction is currently soft but will improve steadily over the next 5 years because the group 18 to 25 years old will increase, as will the over-65 population.

Financial factors affecting the demand for housing are less certain. Interest rates are expected to decline slightly over the next 5 years, steadily improving the affordability of home ownership. However, low inflation rates are likely to result in the slower buildup of home owners' equity, which will limit the ability of many people to trade up to newer and larger houses. The slower rise in housing prices is likely to further reduce the investment appeal of home ownership, especially for more expensive homes. Still, record capital gains may lead stock market investors to purchase more luxurious housing. The net effect of these mixed trends will be to support current levels of home building through the beginning of the next century.

Home improvement and repair construction will continue to grow faster than will new home construction. Much of this demand will result from home owners' adding rooms and amenities. In addition, the stock of housing is steadily growing larger and older, providing a growing base demand for home improvement and repair construction.

Single-Family Home Building

Many factors have influenced the single-family housing market in the 1990s, including low interest rates, modest economic growth, and changing demographic patterns. The investment appeal of home ownership has been reduced by the slowdown in the growth of real estate value.

Whereas first-time buyers and trade-up buyers account for most of the demand for new homes, the role of retirement and other specialized housing is also significant. Retirement hous-

ing is becoming a much greater factor in this market, with the units usually being smaller and having specially designed features for seniors. Many of these units are being built outside metropolitan areas.

New housing competes with housing resales and manufactured home sales in the single-family market. Family incomes, consumer confidence, and affordability remain the key considerations that affect decisions to buy or rent. Among the key factors affecting affordability are mortgage interest rates, the availability of funds, and mortgage options.

About 90 percent of new single-family houses are detached. The median sales price of single-family units has continued to rise, with the 1997 level at about $146,000. The size of new single-family homes has been increasing slowly over the years and now averages over 2,100 square feet. New one-family units are characterized by the inclusion of more amenities, which include central air-conditioning, two and a half or more bathrooms, fireplaces, two-car garages, full basements, and three or more bedrooms.

Multiunit Home Building

Multifamily housing starts totaled 350,000 units in 1998—the highest level since 1989—in response to easing restrictions on lenders and increasing interest among investors. This was part of an overall surge in commercial real estate. Increasing vacancy rates and better alternative investment opportunities are expected to slow this market by 2000. Although the level of new multifamily construction rose modestly in 1997, this segment of housing continues to be at historically low levels. The 0.34 million units built in 1997 compare with annual totals in the mid-1980s that were nearly twice as large.

Multiunit housing refers to buildings having two or more dwelling units. These are usually either town house structures or apartment units. Rentals make up about 80 percent of multiunit housing, and most of these units are in structures with five or more dwelling units. In 1998 multiunit housing accounted for 24 percent of all new private housing starts, compared with about 38 percent in 1985.

Among the major factors that influence the level of construction of new multiunit housing are the tax laws, demographics, the financial strength or weakness of the real estate and lending institution sectors, and regulatory requirements such as handicapped accessibility. Another factor supporting greater multiunit construction is the aging of the population. Expected lower property appreciation also may encourage many people to rent rather than buy, as would any changes in tax laws affecting mortgage interest deductions, such as some flat tax proposals. General affordability problems and growing uncertainty among workers also tend to discourage home buying.

Alterations, Repairs, and Additions

This category encompasses spending for upkeep and repairs as well as improvements to existing residential structures. Maintenance and repairs continue to account for the bulk of spending for rental properties, while improvements account for the greater share of spending on owner-occupied units.

Included in this type of work are projects such as painting, appliance replacement parts and repairs, and roof repairs. The improvements category involves additions to structures and major replacements of structures and other property. Examples of improvements include changes in major exterior and interior structures, fences, and replacement furnaces and water heaters. For do-it-yourself work, the costs of materials and parts are included in the data but the labor costs are not.

Expenditures for home improvement and repair have increased fairly steadily in the 1990s. Spending for this type of work tends to be less volatile than is that for new construction, and the growth has been somewhat greater over the long term. This trend is expected to continue into the twenty-first century. The stock of housing will grow larger and older, and sales of existing homes will continue to increase.

PRIVATE NONRESIDENTIAL CONSTRUCTION

The current-dollar value of new private nonresidential construction put in place in 1998 was estimated at $187 billion, of which $149 billion was for buildings and $38 billion was for other structures. In constant 1992 dollars the total was about the same as that in 1996 (see Table 6-2). The largest increases were for manufacturing plants, electric utilities, and telecommunications.

Private nonresidential construction includes all the buildings and other structures owned by American businesses and non-profit organizations except for housing and mining. This includes manufacturing plants, office buildings, stores, hotels, hospitals, nursing homes, farm buildings, electric power plants, gas pipelines, telephone and electric lines, churches, railroads, and private schools (see Table 6-2).

Although demand for each of these categories of construction is influenced by macroeconomic variables such as interest rates and GDP growth, each category also has a unique set of factors that influence demand. For example, store construction is heavily influenced by the trend toward "big box" stores and "demalled" shopping centers rather than traditional malls. Hospital construction is affected by corporate cost cutting and health care legislation. Manufacturing plant demand is influenced by capacity utilization rates and international competitiveness factors.

In addition to the $187 billion in new construction put in place, as much as $120 billion is spent on nonresidential remodeling, repair, and other construction improvements. Spending on the nonresidential category probably is growing faster than is the total. Statistics on this type of construction are very poor.

Outlook for 1999

New private nonresidential construction will remain at the current high levels as the economic expansion continues for the seventh year. The largest construction increases in 1999 are expected to be in manufacturing plants, educational buildings, hospitals and other health institutions, electric utilities, and telecommunications. The outlook is weaker for hotels and other forms of commercial construction.

In 1999 business investment in plant and equipment is expected to increase. Although construction of manufacturing facilities and utility plants is expected to share in this increase, most of the investment will pay for capital equipment rather than buildings and other structures. Investments in equipment tend to be cost-saving measures and are less risky than new industrial plants.

One result of the stock market boom is that REITs are becoming important funding sources for nonresidential construction. These companies will be major sources of funding in 1999 and beyond as they channel large amounts of equity into commercial real estate.

The nonresidential repair and renovation markets probably will continue to grow in 1999 and for the next 5 years. Electric utilities in particular are likely to increase their maintenance and repair expenditures substantially. Investments in nonresidential building improvements will remain at high levels as the owners of commercial buildings strive to keep their buildings attractive in competitive rental markets. A side effect of the turmoil in the retailing industry will be massive remodeling of existing stores.

Outlook to 2003

Total private nonresidential construction is likely to increase moderately over the next 5 years, growing a little more slowly than the average growth in GDP of about 2 percent. Prospects look best for industrial, utility, and hospital construction. The repair and renovation market will grow about as fast as will the new construction market in the next 5 years, and will be less cyclical.

Despite the currently modest oversupply situation in commercial real estate, investor interest in commercial construction will be strong enough to continue the boom through the 1999. The reemergence of REITs will support commercial construction even if interest rates rise. The recovery in this office building cycle has been slower but more sustainable than were several past recoveries.

By 2003 private nonresidential construction will have recovered to its record 1990 levels, but spending on factories, utilities, and hospitals will account for a much larger share of the total and commercial construction will account for a substantially lower proportion. Although the office building market has recovered partly, a dramatic building boom is unlikely early in the twenty-first century because of changes in tax laws, tighter regulatory scrutiny, and greater wariness in the investment community. Currently, existing commercial buildings often can be purchased for less than the cost of construction. The surge in the construction of big box stores appears to have passed its peak and probably will decline over the next several years, although the concept of automobile "megadealers" that sell used cars and multiple brands of new cars may offset this trend partly.

In the twenty-first century the demand for commercial buildings will be affected by technological trends favoring telecommuting, electronic shopping, home offices, teleconferencing, and globalization of information services as well as business management trends toward downsizing, temporary work forces, and inventory reduction.

Manufacturing Facilities

Most manufacturers' expenditures are for equipment rather than structures. Nevertheless, manufacturers are investing heavily in industrial construction to increase capacity, replace old buildings, and adjust to changing conditions. The inflation-adjusted value of industrial construction put in place should increase in 1999, and further gains are expected in 2000 and beyond. The long-term rate of increase may be slower than it was in most previous recoveries because of concern over global competition, but the upswing will last longer.

Changing global trade patterns will continue to have major effects on industrial construction. If the $170 billion trade deficit in manufactured goods were eliminated, the demand for industrial construction could increase $3.5 billion annually. The currently high exchange rate for the dollar and the weakening of important export markets will restrain investment in U.S. manufacturing capacity in 1999, but these restraining factors probably will ease in a few years. The U.S. industries that are expected to gain from increased trade probably will have to invest heavily in new capacity.

The need to modernize the capital stock of U.S. manufacturers will provide strong underlying demand for new construction as well as for repair and renovations. Even though 75 percent of plant and equipment expenditures are for equipment rather than structures, the construction potential is huge.

Although the long-term outlook for industrial construction is uncertain, it is likely to be one of the stronger construction markets during the next 5 years. Because the U.S. economy and U.S. exports are expected to grow during this period, the economic climate should be moderately favorable for industrial construction. Strong common stock prices and fairly low interest rates will make it easier to finance industrial expansion. Negative factors include continued uncertainty about the economy, regulatory burdens, and the heavy debt loads of many companies.

Office Buildings

In 1998 the value of office construction was about 5 percent higher than it was in 1997 but 40 percent below the 1985 record. Further gains are expected in 1999 for both new construction and office renovation.

There is increasing investor interest in office construction because of financial and regulatory factors. Long-term interest rates are much lower than they were at the same stage of the previous building cycle. In addition, lending institutions have gradually eased restrictions on commercial real estate loans. The value of new real estate loans has surged, and commercial construction is at record levels for the 1990s.

Although the office supply and demand situation has improved steadily, the office construction market remains burdened with fairly high vacancy rates, slower growth in white-collar employment, and technology trends that favor the substitution of home offices for office buildings. In many office markets prime office buildings are for sale at prices below the cost of construction. Nevertheless, a sizable amount of office construction will continue because of easier loan conditions and strength in a small number of cities and market niches.

In 1999 white-collar employment will increase very slowly because of tight labor markets, modest economic growth, and corporate cost cutting. During the period 1999–2003 growth in office-type employment will average about 1 percent annually, according to Labor Department forecasts. In addition, the trend toward telecommuting will increase as the improving cost and availability of technology make it more feasible to work at home.

The office renovation business has been strong during the past decade. In some markets expenditures for office renovation are probably higher than are those for new office construction put in place. Much of the growth in this market segment has resulted from overbuilding in the 1980s, which compelled owners to upgrade older buildings to retain tenants. Although expenditures for office remodeling are likely to remain at high levels, the era of rapid growth is largely over because of market maturation.

Hotels and Other Commercial Buildings

Although hotel construction is usually a small category of construction, it boomed in the mid-1990s. The 1998 value of hotel construction was more than double the 1994 value. Many gambling casinos are classified as hotels in the construction statistics, and much of the current boom is attributable to this factor. In addition, travelers' demand for lodging has increased, although after 1998 the level of construction will be in line with the underlying demand for hotel lodging. It is uncertain whether the casino-building boom will last until 2000.

The construction category "other commercial buildings" consists of all commercial buildings except office buildings and hotels and includes warehouses, grain elevators, shopping centers, parking garages, banks, fast-food restaurants, and gasoline stations. In recent years, shopping centers have accounted for about half the value of construction work in this category and warehouses have accounted for about one-fourth.

The value of store construction put in place has remained high despite the financial woes of many established retail chains and weak gains in retail spending. Much of the current strength in store construction involves big box stores and centers, which are nonmall discount stores or large stores which carry a narrow category of products (such as electronics, building supplies, or pet supplies) at discount prices. The boom in big box store construction has waned, but this type of construction will be a major component of commercial construction for the next 5 years. The softness in consumer spending is affecting even the most successful discounters, some of which are suffering from growing pains as well.

Another important segment consists of "neighborhood" shopping centers close to new housing subdivisions. The fairly high level of housing starts expected in 1996 through 1998, along with lower interest rates, was expected to boost neighborhood shopping centers in 1998.

Construction of service stations and auto repair garages will remain at high levels in 1999. The automobile service business has benefited from the increasing complexity of automobiles and the increasing proportion of older cars. Although the number of gasoline stations has declined sharply over the last three decades, most of the remaining stations are investing large amounts in construction to become high-volume sales outlets, convenience shops, fast-food outlets, or specialized service stations. According to economic and demographic forecasts for the next 5 years, there will be further increases in the number of vehicle miles driven and the demand for automobile services and repair.

Private Electric Utilities

This category of construction includes new power plants, transmission lines, and pollution control facilities; the conversion of existing power plants from oil and gas to coal; and the modernization of existing power plants and other buildings. It does not include government-owned facilities and power plants owned by manufacturers.

The electric utility industry is experiencing a moderate construction boom as the demand for electricity approaches capacity in many regions. This trend should continue in 1999 and through 2003. The rate of gain over the long term will be strongly affected by interest rates and the demand for electricity, with new construction growing at about the same rate as GDP and repair construction growing at a faster rate.

Although the industry has experienced high growth in the demand for electricity, competition has increased because of the National Energy Policy Act of 1992 and actions by certain state utility commissions. This has resulted in less construction by the regulated utility companies but more construction for congeneration projects, nonregulated power generators, and municipal supplies. There probably will be a quickening in the pace of new power plant starts, but utilities are unlikely to order large numbers of new plants. Instead, the emphasis will be on energy conservation, the expansion of existing facilities, and heavier use of the existing capacity.

Expenditures for the maintenance and repair of electric utility systems have grown rapidly and are almost as high as spending on new utility construction. Maintenance and repair expenditures will continue to grow rapidly into the next century as the average age of operating power plants increases and as operations become more complex.

Hospital and Institutional Building

This category includes hospitals, outpatient clinics, nursing homes, convalescent homes, orphanages, and similar institutions for prolonged care (buildings that are used primarily as doctors' offices are classified as office buildings.) About 70 percent of the value of this construction is for hospitals and clinics; the remainder is for nursing homes and similar facilities. Seventy percent of hospital and institutional construction expenditures are for additions to and modernization of existing facilities, and only 30 percent are for new facilities. About 75 percent of this construction is used for privately owned facilities, and 25 percent for publicly owned facilities.

Construction of health care facilities has slowed in recent years; in part, this reflects uncertainty about health care financing. In 1999 hospital construction probably will resume its long-term upward trend, and between 1999 and 2003 health care probably will be one of the faster-growing construction markets.

In recent years the health care sector has been affected by many of the down sizing and cost-cutting trends that have influenced the rest of the U.S. economy. A short-term result has been a decline in new hospital construction. This decline is likely to be brief and mild, as was the case in the mid-1980s, during a different round of cost containment. The Maternity and Mental Health Insurance Coverage Act of 1996 will increase hospital demand slightly over the next several years, and this will further reduce the impact of cost-cutting measures.

Aside from health care financing, the most important factor in the longer-term outlook for hospital and institutional construction is the rapid increase in the number of elderly Americans. People over age 65 average about six times as much hospitalization per capita as do persons under 65. Nearly 90 percent of the 1.8 million Americans in nursing homes are 65 or older.

Nursing home construction is likely to increase even faster than is overall health care construction because it is focused on the most rapidly growing segment of the population. Between 1981 and 1991 the United States' nursing home population grew 20 percent, and demographic projections indicate that it may grow even more in the next 10 years.

Additional factors that will support health care construction include the increasing use of new sophisticated medical treatments, the prospect of major increases in federally mandated health insurance coverage, and the need to modernize to attract paying patients and scarce health care personnel. Negative factors in an otherwise bullish outlook include the poor fiscal condition of hospitals with large proportions of charity patients, the declining proportion of workers with employer-paid health insurance, and aggressive cost reduction on the part of major insurance payers. Publicly owned hospitals are less able to cope with these negative factors, and so their construction is expected to lag behind that of privately owned hospitals.

PUBLICLY OWNED CONSTRUCTION

In 1998 the total value of publicly owned construction in current dollars was about $150 billion, of which $42 billion went for highways and bridges and $30 billion for educational buildings. The constant-dollar value of publicly owned construction put in place was about 4 percent higher than the 1997 level. Most categories of public construction increased, except conservation and development, military facilities, and sewerage systems (see Table 6-5).

Public works construction was expected to set an all-time record in 1998, although in per capita terms it was below the level reached in 1968. This category of construction will remain at high levels to prevent deterioration of U.S. infrastructure and

TABLE 6-5: Federal Construction Outlays by Fiscal Years
(millions of dollars; percent)

	1995	1996	1997	1998[1]	1999[2]	Percent Change, 98–99
Military construction	3,654	3,398	3,161	3,108	2,900	–7
Defense family housing	918	1,078	1,012	991	901	–9
Atomic energy defense activities	248	933	537	677	804	19
Highways and bridges	19,216	19,653	20,502	21,751	22,319	3
Mass transportation	3,561	3,698	4,041	3,753	3,660	–2
Railroad transportation	153	282	372	236	500	112
Air transportation	1,844	1,675	1,514	1,609	1,650	3
Water transportation	97	125	111	136	96	–29
Community development block grants	4,333	4,545	4,517	4,989	4,959	–1
Other community and regional development	1,254	1,530	1,507	1,666	1,399	–16
Pollution control and abatement	4,012	3,668	3,646	3,504	3,955	13
Water resources	2,253	2,318	2,078	2,757	2,021	–27
Federal prison system	420	486	307	22	499	
Housing assistance	6,425	6,757	6,849	6,812	6,864	1
General science, space, and technology	573	611	615	492	506	3
Energy	2,961	1,918	1,128	1,051	1,005	–4
Veterans hospitals and other health	1,294	1,404	1,538	1,845	1,715	–7
Postal service	996	1,138	1,261	1,243	1,355	9
Federal buildings funds	1,008	1,478	1,362	1,080	885	–18
International affairs	307	279	315	260	261	0
Other construction programs	801	917	1,373	1,901	1,487	–22
Total federal construction outlays	56,328	57,891	57,746	59,883	59,741	–0

[1] Estimate.
[2] Budget.
Source: Budget of the U.S. government, fiscal years 1995 through 1999.

accommodate population growth and movements and economic development. The condition of infrastructure not only is a quality-of-life issue but also is an important factor in U.S. productivity and international competitiveness. In particular, the vast American highway network increases U.S. industrial productivity by allowing faster and cheaper transportation of products. Other types of infrastructure, such as airports, schools, waterworks, and mass transit, also contribute to the productivity of the U.S. economy.

The Transportation Equity Act for the 21st Century (TEA-21), which was signed into law in June 1998, authorizes a total of $218 billion in federal expenditures for surface transportation between 1998 and 2003. TEA-21 provides for a major increase in construction spending over the 1992–1997 level, depending on future inflation rates. By far the biggest share of this spending will be for construction and maintenance of major highways, although mass transit construction will also receive increased funding.

Federal construction spending programs will increase about 4 percent in 1998 (see Table 6-5) as a result of the high level of obligations incurred during fiscal years 1996 and 1997. (Because of lags in approvals and construction, most of these obligations do not result in construction put in place for a year or more.)

State and local governments also will increase their total construction spending in 1998 as a result of higher federal grants, the booming economy, and the need to curtail the backlog of deferred projects. State and local government spending is especially important for education, highways, water and sewer works, and public safety.

Outlook for 1999

The overall value of publicly owned construction will increase modestly from the 1998 level. Federal spending for public works construction will increase 3 percent faster than inflation, while state and local government spending will increase 5 percent faster in the aggregate. The largest increases are expected in federal industrial facilities, prisons, highways, and water supply systems. Few categories of public works construction are expected to decline other than military facilities and conservation and development.

Although the President's budget of January 1998 did not project growth in federal construction spending in 1999, there probably will be a significant increase in spending because of the recently passed TEA-21 authorization. Large reductions are budgeted for military construction, federal office buildings, and conservation and development, while spending on military waste cleanup, pollution control, and housing and urban development is expected to increase.

Outlook to 2003

Public works construction will increase significantly over the next 5 years, assuming moderate economic growth and gradually declining interest rates. Federal construction spending will pick up substantially because of the balancing of the budget and the reauthorized highway program. The increases in new construction obligations in 1996 and 1997 will be felt mostly in 1999. Over the past two decades construction programs have borne a disproportionate share of the budget cuts needed to control the deficit, and the currently balanced budget will reduce this pressure on infrastructure investment. Since the $59.9 billion in federal construction spending accounts for only 3.6 percent of the total federal budget, substantial increases in public works would have relatively modest effects on overall spending. Furthermore, if the economy performs as predicted, lower interest rates and growing tax revenues will allow state and local funding for public works to remain at high levels.

Government maintenance and repair spending probably will increase at least as fast as will new construction spending because the public works infrastructure is steadily becoming older and larger. While increased maintenance and repair expenditures will provide work for certain types of contractors, this category will consume funds that could have been spent on new construction.

Highway construction is likely to be the largest and most reliable public works market through the rest of the century. However, further increases will be small unless it is decided to draw down the Highway Trust Fund. The federal-aid highways program needed reauthorization in 1997, and there could be support for higher gasoline taxes to pay for needed improvements in roadway infrastructure. Water and sewer construction will remain at high levels but will not increase much. Construction of schools and other public buildings also may increase. Military construction and federal industrial construction probably will decline as measured by new construction put in place, but environmental restoration projects funded by these programs will remain at high levels.

Transportation Infrastructure

New road and bridge construction, which was at a record level in 1997 and 1998, is expected to remain as high in 1999. With the passage of TEA-21 (discussed earlier) high levels of investment in highways and mass transit are assured through 2003. Expenditures for highway maintenance and repair have increased, partly at the expense of new construction.

In 1999 expenditures on highway construction probably will continue to increase to prevent a decline in the condition of the highway infrastructure. The huge Federal-aid Highways Program, which expired in 1998, was renewed at levels that promise to be at least 10 percent higher in inflation-adjusted terms. Any sustained increase in federal funds would require an increase in federal motor fuel taxes, but the large balance in the Highway Trust Fund can accommodate a surge in expenditures. Although total state government spending on road construction has increased only slightly faster than has the rate of inflation, several states have made a commitment to fund massive road building programs.

About 25 percent of the value of highway construction put in place consists of bridges, overpasses, and tunnels; flatwork (primarily roads) accounts for the remaining 75 percent. Bridge work is expected to grow faster than flatwork over the next several years because of the need to replace obsolete or unsafe bridges. According to the Federal Highway Administration's latest estimate, 23 percent of the highway bridges in the United States are structurally deficient and an additional 21 percent are functionally or structurally obsolete.

Highway maintenance and repair expenditures have grown during the past two decades as the road network has become larger and older. In 1997 the current-dollar cost of highway maintenance and repair was about $31 billion, compared with $45 billion in new highway construction put in place. While some of this work is routine maintenance such as mowing grass, much of it involves typical construction activity such as repaving roads and painting bridges. Highway maintenance and repair expenditures may grow more rapidly than does new construction over the next decade (see Table 6-5).

Mass transit construction may decline slightly in 1998 but is expected to increase in 1999 because of increased federal financial support. The outlook for mass transit construction is heavily dependent on the renewal of the Federal-aid Highways Program. Of the $155 billion in ISTEA funds authorized from 1992 through 1997, $35 billion was earmarked for mass transit projects. In addition, a large share of discretionary federal transportation grants was diverted from highways to mass transit because of concern about air pollution and local development policies.

Airport construction has gained dramatically over the last decade in response to large increases in air travel. Federal government spending for airport construction is expected to increase modestly in 1999, while local investments in airports will remain near the current levels. In the longer term overall airport construction spending will not increase much until more domestic airlines improve their financial performance.

Water and Sewer Systems

Water supply construction increased 5 percent in 1998, while sewerage construction was about the same as the level in 1997. Both of these construction categories did well in the mid-1990s, reflecting high levels of building construction as well as work on long-deferred projects. The strong construction market expected in 1999 will help both categories do well.

In the longer term waterworks probably will be one of the more rapidly growing categories of public construction. The aqueduct systems of most older cities are so old that extensive replacement work must be done each year. The current level of construction in the United States is much lower than that needed to replace waterworks every 50 years, which is the recommended practice. Most water utilities are in a good position to raise the needed capital, and so a steady increase in replacement construction is likely through 1999. The Safe Drinking Water Act requires numerous upgrades and replacements of water supply facilities. The Water Resources Act has expanded the role of the federal government in municipal water supply and appears to have facilitated increased federal funding for water supply construction.

After 1999 sewerage construction probably will continue to increase, although at a growth rate lower than that of the overall economy. Federal spending may not keep up with inflation, but the state and local share will increase steadily. A growing market factor is the need to repair, modernize, and replace the sewage treatment plants that were built during the boom of the 1970s. The sustained recovery in building construction also will support sewerage construction.

Solid waste disposal facilities, including those used for resource recovery, constitute a small but rapidly growing construction market. Resource recovery facilities are increasingly common because of improved efficiency, rising land prices, and environmental objections to landfills.

Educational Buildings

New construction expenditures for schools, libraries, and museums were at near-record levels in 1998, and another solid increase is expected in 1999. About 70 percent of this spending was for primary and secondary schools, while colleges and other higher education facilities accounted for an additional 25 percent. More than 80 percent of educational construction expenditures was for publicly owned buildings; the rest went for privately owned buildings.

The school construction boom, which began in the late 1980s, is encountering the budget problems of state and local governments. The underlying demand for school construction is very strong because of the record number of school-age Americans, the need to replace dilapidated schools, and population expansion into underbuilt areas. The net result of these conflicting pressures will be for school construction to remain at high levels with slow growth rates.

Patrick MacAuley, U.S. Department of Commerce, Office of Metals, Materials, and Chemicals, (202) 482-0132, May 1998.

INTERNATIONAL CONSTRUCTION

The international construction market continued to have strong growth in 1996 and most of 1997, and overseas business was buoyant for U.S. design and construction firms (see Table 6-6). Contractors found that financing was the key to securing international jobs, and designers had to provide increasingly higher levels of service. Both found strong growth in new market demand. The markets of the Pacific Rim continued to grow in 1996 and most of 1997, and few firms were prepared for the currency crises that wreaked havoc with projects in Thailand, Indonesia, Malaysia, South Korea, and other countries in that region, beginning in the summer of 1997.

According to *Engineering News-Record (ENR),* U.S. design firms dominated the list of companies reporting the largest billings outside the home country in 1996. Among the top 200 international design firms, 89 companies from the United States billed $5.8 billion in 1996, a 40.2 percent share of the $14.5 billion in total international billings by the group. U.S. firms increased their billings by 23 percent over the $4.7 billion billed in 1995.

U.S. contractors reported $22.8 billion in revenue from projects outside the home country in 1996, 17.8 percent of the $126.8 billion reported by *ENR*'s top 225 international contractors. International work for the top 225 was up 20.7 percent over 1995. A building boom was heating up in many markets, and sales of petroleum and transportation-related projects were on the upswing. In 1996, 75 of the top 400 U.S. general contractors on the *ENR* list earned revenue from international work. Over 21 percent, or $23.8 billion, of the total contracting revenue earned by those contractors came from overseas jobs. Work on the worldwide market accounted for 27 percent of all new contracts reported in 1996 by that group of contractors.

Design firms continued to accelerate their activity on the global scene, and international billings among design firms continued to climb in 1996. Billings from work outside the United States reached $6.2 billion, an 18.2 percent jump from the figure for the previous year. On *ENR*'s top 500 design firms list, 211 firms reported billings outside the United States.

TABLE 6-6: U.S. Trade Patterns in Prefabricated Buildings[1] in 1997
(millions of dollars; percent)

Regions[2]	Exports Value[3]	Share, %	Regions[2]	Imports Value[3]	Share, %
NAFTA	91	26.1	NAFTA	80	76.0
Latin America	60	17.3	Latin America	0	0.1
Western Europe	28	8.0	Western Europe	9	8.6
Japan/Chinese Economic Area	113	32.4	Japan/Chinese Economic Area	0	0.2
Other Asia	27	7.6	Other Asia	14	13.5
Rest of world	30	8.6	Rest of world	2	1.7
World	349	100.0	World	106	100.0
Top Five Countries	**Value**	**Share, %**	**Top Five Countries**	**Value**	**Share, %**
Japan	85	24.5	Canada	80	75.7
Canada	68	19.6	South Korea	13	12.5
China	26	7.4	United Kingdom	5	4.5
Mexico	23	6.5	Belgium	2	1.8
Chile	12	3.4	Australia	1	0.8

[1] SIC 245, 3448.
[2] For definitions of regional groupings, see "Getting the Most Out of *Outlook '99.*"
[3] Values may not sum to total due to rounding.
Source: U.S. Department of Commerce, Bureau of the Census.

Nearly all geographic regions were growth markets for U.S. designers and contractors. Among *ENR*'s top 500 U.S. design firms there was growth in every international region worldwide in 1996. The real eye-opener was the explosion of work in the Americas as firms saw a 56 percent increase in work in Latin America and Canada. Latin America felt little impact from the "tequila effect" of Mexico's financial troubles of 1995, as billings for 159 firms climbed to $576.5 million. In Canada megaprojects such as the massive Hibernia offshore oil facility helped 79 firms bill $419.4 million. The European market grew 28 percent, with 132 firms bringing in $2.4 billion in billings. Work in Asia and Australia continued at a high level, with 179 firms billing $1.7 billion, but this represented only a 2.3 percent increase from the previous year. U.S. design firms billed $610.9 million for Middle Eastern projects, up 5.5 percent; in Africa they billed $334.8 million, a 6.9 percent increase.

U.S. contractors also experienced significant growth worldwide. The bonanza was in Middle Eastern work, where 27 firms brought in revenue of $4.15 billion in 1996, up 83 percent from 1995. Some of this activity was a result of massive infrastructure investments, but an even greater source was the move by many oil-producing countries into downstream petroleum and petrochemical investment, particularly in liquefied natural gas.

The largest market for U.S. contractors continued to be Europe, where 36 contractors earned revenues of $6.6 billion, up 36 percent from 1995. In the Asia and Australia market, 42 contractors saw their work climb just 3.2 percent to $5.53 billion. The only declining market on the list in 1996 was contractors' billings in Latin America, where revenues slid 12.3 percent to $2.84 billion. In Canada revenue increased 8.3 percent to $2.6 billion. In Africa there was a 17.4 percent gain, with 22 contractors bringing in $1.55 billion in revenue.

The *ENR*'s top 500 U.S. design firms again enjoyed significant growth in most regions in 1997. Total design billings for this group reached $7.3 billion from projects based outside the United States. While this billing level was 18.7 percent above the 1996 level, it is not strictly comparable, as *ENR* altered its ranking methodology to include design billings from integrated engineering-procurement-construction contracts and design-build contracts. However, these totals illustrate how important Asia has become to U.S. construction firms as an export market.

Europe continued to be the single largest export market, with over $2.66 billion in design billings. Asia was a close second at nearly $2.46 billion in design work. The Middle East and Latin America showed growth, with each region accounting for $681 million. The Canadian market fell off in 1997 to $378 million from $419 million in 1996, as did the African market to $317 million from $335 million.

Among the market sectors, industrial process and petroleum work continued to dominate U.S. design firms' international billings in 1997. Petroleum work accounted for $2.78 billion in overseas billings for *ENR*'s top 500, while industrial process work accounted for $772 million. The power sector continued to be an import source of export work for U.S. design firms, with $870 million in billings.

General building, including commercial, retail, institutional, and office work, provided *ENR*'s top 500 design firms with $602 million in overseas billings. Basic infrastructure contributed to design firms' export revenues with $757 million in billings for transportation, $367 million for sewer and wastewater work, and $349 million for water supply jobs. Manufacturing design continued to show a surprising lack of strength, with only $205 million in design billings by the top 500. Hazardous-waste work continued to show more promise than revenue in the international market, providing $341 million.

Financing

A major driver of the international construction market and of opportunities for U.S. construction firms in that market has been a surge in private investment in developing countries. In 1997 long-term private capital investment in those countries reached $256 billion, up from $247 billion in 1996, according to the World Bank. This was the seventh straight year of record increases in private investment, and that figure amounted to about six times the level of official capital flows into those countries.

However, the Asian financial crisis, which began in July 1997 in Thailand and spread to Indonesia, Malaysia, and the Philippines while shaking South Korea's previously aggressive economy, deflected those capital flows. Private investment in developing countries in the first 10 months of 1997 were 10 percent above the 1996 level. The fact that total private investment in 1997 exceeded that in 1996 by only 3.6 percent demonstrates the chilling effect of the troubled Asian currencies on the willingness of private investors to put money into developing countries. Bond issues and loan commitments to southeast Asia and Latin America dropped over 50 percent in the fourth quarter of 1997. Thus, only the fact that the impact of Asia's economic troubles did not begin to be experienced until late 1997 permitted the year's investment levels to exceed those of 1996. "This is a year when we saw not just the opportunities but also the risks of private capital flows," said Joseph Stiglitz, the World Bank's chief economist and senior vice president for development economics.

Official aid from international development banks also set a record in 1997, rising to $44 billion from $35 billion in 1996. However, much of this increase was in the form of an international economic rescue package for Thailand rather than being earmarked for specific programs or projects. Official aid should rise to a new record in 1998 with International Monetary Fund (IMF) packages for Indonesia and Korea, but many critics worry that these financial aid packages are drawing much-needed aid from social programs and, in the case of the international construction community, project-specific aid.

The economic troubles in Asia have had another effect on the construction market: Developing countries have found it more difficult to issue bonds, whether project-specific or general obligation. The bonds that have been issued have been at a substantial premium, putting limits on the levels of bonds that developing countries' governments are willing or able to float.

The currency problems in southeast Asia have created new obstacles for U.S. construction firms. Over the past few years those firms have become much more sophisticated in arranging financing to get international projects off the ground. However, investors burned by the Asian meltdown will require greater levels of assurance and guarantees in future project financing agreements.

U.S. firms in the international market also must understand that risks come with international work. Some of the most sophisticated construction firms in the United States lost money in the Asian crisis. Many U.S. firms, despite taking elaborate precautions to hedge currencies, were hurt by local legal restrictions designed to protect those economies from currency speculators.

Regional Markets

Data have not been tallied showing how severely total construction volume in the Pacific Rim region will be affected by the monetary crisis and stock market gyrations of the summer and fall of 1997. Regionally, southeast Asia is expected to taper off in the rate of growth of its total construction activity for 1 to 3 years, but observers expect it to bounce back in a comparatively short time. There is no question, however, that the pressure on those currencies is having an effect on construction.

In Thailand, after a decade of expansion when growth averaged 9 percent a year, construction ground to a halt in the summer of 1997. After years of unrestrained lending for speculative real estate projects, both local and foreign investors started fleeing from Thai stocks and the baht. Then, as the country's foreign exchange reserves plummeted, the Thai government freed the baht from a dollar-linked trading band, sending it into a tailspin that nearly devastated Asian foreign exchange and stock markets. In Thailand the baht fell 40 percent against the dollar, sending the cost of imported materials soaring and bringing work to a standstill on construction sites. The $3.2 billion elevated light rail system, which had been one-fifth completed, for example, was officially scrapped by Thailand's cabinet. It could take years to get the country back on track. The IMF gave Thailand $22 billion to stabilize its financial system. In exchange, the Thai government pledged to deal with the problems of more than 50 troubled finance companies, many of which were overextended in the real estate market.

Malaysia also encountered serious financial problems, resulting in the cancellation of several prominent projects. Malaysia delayed several of its biggest infrastructure projects, including the $5 billion Bakun hydroelectric dam, which would have been one of the largest in the world. In spring 1998 critics were still concerned that the Malaysian government would not hold to its free market reforms, which, like those set up in bailout packages for other countries by the IMF, include letting troubled firms go bankrupt unless they find a buyer.

Indonesia's rupiah was the currency most severely affected by the turmoil in southeast Asia, falling nearly 75 percent against the dollar. Indonesia slashed government spending in September 1997 and postponed 14 major infrastructure projects, including power plants and toll roads, in an effort to keep its economy in balance. The International Labor Organization estimated that 4 million Indonesians lost construction and manufacturing jobs because of the economic crisis.

The Philippines also was hit in the middle of a building boom. Dozens of new residential high-rises were under construction, but many projects were slowed, and U.S. firms pulled staff members out of the country. Even the giant Fort Bonifacio Global City project southeast of Manila began to slow down in the face of currency instability. However, the $1 billion currency stabilization package extended by the IMF is expected to help put the country back on track.

On the positive side, new power plant construction could be a major factor over the coming decades. A report from Hong Kong–based PowerGen forecasts that 6 of the top 10 energy users in the world could be in Asia by 2020, with the region overtaking traditional heavy energy use in Europe.

China has been the powerhouse of development in this region. In Shanghai, in the Pudong foreign trade zone alone, where restrictions have been eased to encourage development, 12 million square meters of space was under construction in 1996, according to the Ministry of Construction. The Jin Mao Tower, for example, was on its way toward completion. It will be an 88-story, 421-meter-tall office and hotel combination owned by the China Shanghai Foreign Trade Company and designed by the Chicago-based architect-engineer Skidmore, Owings and Merrill. A $1.5-billion, 1-square-kilometer General Motors assembly plant was announced for the Xin Jinqiao export processing zone in the fall of 1997.

Early in 1998 officials reported that they were planning to soften the impact of massive privatization with new construction projects worth $750 billion to $1 trillion over the next 3 years. More like $450 billion was actually believed to be in the country's budget over that period, however. The higher figures were considered impossible in a country whose gross domestic product is $900 billion a year. Therefore, one can expect steady growth increases of perhaps 15 percent instead of 10 percent fueled by more home mortgage loans, more readily available credit from banks, and more spending on infrastructure. Projects already approved include a Shenzhen subway, a Nanjing light rail system, and a $2 billion bridge between Hong Kong and Zhuhai as well as irrigation and wastewater treatment projects.

Funding for infrastructure investment is expected to come from local and provincial governments as well as international players. New build-operate-transfer (BOT) financing rules are expected from the planning commission by the end of 1998. Three experimental BOT projects were undertaken and are being evaluated, and more may be allowed to proceed even before a new BOT law is passed by the National People's Congress.

India continues to attract international interest. Bureaucracy is a major hurdle that seems to be improving, but the government has been seen to have an ambivalent attitude toward foreign investment. Early in 1998 political instability led to stock market volatility and economic vulnerability.

Western Europe has not shown any significant growth in total construction since 1991 and was at a low ebb in 1997, especially Germany and France, while Britain and Portugal were exceptions. Germany is still going through a turbulent period. "It's the same all over Europe," experts say, but other countries did not experience the internal boom resulting from German unification. France also has a depressed market. There has been pressure on European governments to curb public spending to ensure that countries satisfy the criteria for the European Monetary Union. Euroconstruct, a federation of industrial and economic forecasting bodies from 15 countries, predicted in June 1997 that western European construction output would rise just 0.4 percent in 1997 after falling 0.7 percent in 1996. French construction activity was expected to fall a further 1.3 percent in 1997 before rebounding 3 percent in 1998 as measures to reverse rising unemployment take effect.

The United Kingdom, where construction has languished for most of the 1990s, could outstrip most of its continental rivals in 1998. U.K. construction activity was predicted to rise at an annual rate of 3 to 4 percent in 1997 and 1998 before slowing to 2.5 to 3 percent in 1999. The Independent Construction Forecasting and Research group in Britain predicted construction activity worth 55.7 billion pounds by 2000, beating the record 55.3 billion pounds set in 1990. However, the industry faces a huge task in converting the increased workload into improved profits. The margins earned by general contractors in the United Kingdom remain very thin, often in the range of 1 to 2 percent. In 1998 the United Kingdom's ministry of defense and environmental department launched initiatives to reduce public sector building costs by 30 percent.

Central and eastern markets are developing quite well, especially in Poland and the Czech Republic. Contractors continue to await action from the perennial emerging market, Russia, but the neighboring republics are active. The Caspian area has been called "pipeline heaven." For hydrocarbon work, Azerbaijan will be the Oman of the region. Nearby Kazakhstan is also active. The region composed of Azerbaijan, Kazakhstan, and Turkmenistan is estimated to have 178 billion barrels of proven and possible oil reserves, which would put it on a par with the richest Persian Gulf states.

The Russians have tried to block energy exports from that region, although their position seemed to weaken in 1997 in the face of pressure from the Clinton administration. For example, in fall 1997 Deputy Prime Minister Boris Nemtsov said that Moscow planned a bond issue to build a $220 million, 176-mile-long pipeline bypassing unstable Chechnya. In 1998 Chinese companies bid for and won two large Kazakhstan oil deals. They will build a $3.5 billion, 2,000-mile-long oil pipeline from Kazakhstan to Xinjiang.

Africa continues to offer construction prospects. An important area is the mining sector, but power demand was stagnant and was focused more on transmission and distribution or service activities. North Africa has high potential, with many privatization opportunities in Tunisia and Morocco. In sub-Saharan and southern Africa the experts see a host of opportunities in mining, power, ports, and infrastructure.

Contractors are optimistic about Latin America, but some will not work in countries where their employees may be at risk. "We are doing procurement on a hydroelectric project in Colombia. The contractor has had five people on the project kidnapped for ransom by rebels so far," one contractor said.

Despite political worries, recent economic weakness, and attacks by guerrilla groups, international investors continue to bring large sums to Colombia's privatization program. Investors spent $3.1 billion to buy power companies, hydroelectric plants, banks, and mines in 1998.

Contractors are doing well in Brazil's oil and gas sector and see opportunities in chemicals. Privatization will provide work for a number of years. Other contractors are looking for privately financed hydroelectric and highway work in Colombia and Peru as well as airport contracts in Chile.

Chile is a standout nation in the region. It has "a good economy and safe environment," the international contractors reported. Its 1996 GDP growth has been estimated at 7 percent, and its unemployment and inflation rates have been estimated to be at historic lows of about 4 percent. Chile is one of the top-rated emerging markets and has great infrastructure development needs—about $11 billion worth by 2000, according to government estimates. It is meeting those needs through a concession program to domestic and foreign private interests. A legal framework for the concessions, which typically last 10 to 30 years, defines the rights and obligations of private sector investors and the states. The government guarantees, for example, minimum revenue equivalent to 70 percent of an investment. Among the projects in the program are the rehabilitation and maintenance of 1,560 kilometers of the Pan American Highway. In 1997 more than $1.5 billion in concessions was scheduled to be awarded.

Contractors remain interested in the Middle East, a tough and very competitive market. Those countries are not spending as freely as they did in the past, but there seems to be greater interest in projects farther downstream from the oil fields, petrochemical work as well as refineries. The oil wealth is being invested in a great deal of infrastructure work, such as wastewater treatment and other improvements. The rapid drop in oil prices in late 1997 and early 1998 may cause a slowdown in growth, exacerbating existing budget deficits in some oil-producing countries. There is not a wild spending spree under way, but there are opportunities as the region sustains its growth.

After a construction slump in 1995, Canada experienced new life in 1996 and 1997. Tar sands development in northern Alberta spurred major development in that province not just in petroleum and petrochemical work but also in commercial and office work in Calgary and Red Deer. The success of the massive Hibernia oil rig off the coast of Newfoundland should add impetus to the Terranova floating oil production facility and later to a similarly planned White Rose facility in the area. There was a general pickup in all sectors of work, including some major transportation projects. U.S. firms have been quite successful there, and new mining work is generating revenue. Some observers say that pulp and paper work is ready to make a comeback.

Long-Term Outlook

The overall outlook for international construction begins and ends with Asia. The Asian market was for years one of the major targets for construction services exports by U.S. construction firms, which earned steadily increasing revenues and had high hopes for the region. However, the financial crisis that swept southeast Asia and Korea, coupled with Japan's economic stagnation, has played havoc with those revenues and hopes. Numerous U.S. construction firms have reported that large and small projects have been canceled or put on hold in the region. Some have reported the downsizing of their offices in the region, and others report that projects that are on the drawing board may not be completed for a year or more, if ever.

Some financially troubled countries in this region show signs of a turnaround. Thailand and Korea stabilized their currencies by early 1998, and the Philippines continues to focus on major development projects, including Clark Field and Manila Bay redevelopment. Other countries continue to struggle.

Some markets in Asia show signs of continued activity. Hong Kong and Singapore are going on with major infrastructure programs, with Singapore moving up the timetable on some transportation projects to spur its economy. China also is planning a major infrastructure program, although some experts question whether the full scope of its $1 trillion plan will be realized. U.S. construction firms continue to look to countries with largely unrealized potential, such as India.

The overall short-term outlook for Asia is negative. In April 1998 the IMF projected a mere 1.8 percent growth in economic output in that year for the newly industrialized economies in Asia after an average of 6.9 percent in the previous 8 years. The IMF is somewhat more optimistic about 1999, forecasting economic growth of 4.5 percent. However, some financial experts worry that the GDP of previously major construction markets such as Thailand, Malaysia, and Indonesia will suffer declines of up to 10 percent in 1998. Some experts see significant declines in GDP in Korea in 1998 and believe that Japan will be hard pressed to maintain its 1997 GDP level. Even India, which has had strong growth over the past few years and which many U.S. construction firms believe can become a huge market, announced in April 1998 that its economy grew at a 5 percent pace in the 1998 fiscal year. This is the lowest level since India enacted free market reforms at the beginning of the 1990s.

U.S. construction firms should expect a drop in revenue in Asia through the end of 1998 amounting to as much as 5 percent. A general recovery in the region should be well under way by 1999, allowing U.S. construction firms to recover most if not all of the lost revenues from the downturn in 1997–1998. By 2000 Asia should once again be a substantial and thriving market. Throughout the financial crisis and into the Asian recovery U.S. construction firms have retained a level of optimism. Many firms maintain that they have the technological sophistication and the ability to bring financing for badly needed infrastructure to increase their market share in the region. While many major U.S. corporations have deferred some of their investments, they maintain that they are committed to long-term expansion in the region and will continue to bring U.S. construction firms along.

Western Europe's construction market should continue to struggle, with only marginal increases, while its nations attempt to cope with unification and the European Monetary Union (EMU). Private sector work will continue, and privatization in areas such as transportation and telecommunications throughout the continent should support the market. However, countries attempting to implement structural reforms and conform their national budgets to the strictures of EMU should put a damper on any increases in publicly funded work. Overall, the European market should remain stable with possible increases of 1 to 2 percent a year through 2000.

The Middle East continues to develop as an overall market rather than one focused on oil-producing states. Depressed oil prices should act as a damper on some construction opportunities in the short term, but the mild winter of 1997–1998 and the economic downturn in Asia bear much of the responsibility for the oil glut. With the return of normal weather patterns and an economic recovery in Asia, oil prices should return to more normal levels. This should spur activity in the region's vast petroleum and petrochemical sector and ease the strain on the national budgets of the oil-producing states, thus allowing for increased infrastructure spending by the end of 1998. In addition, reconstruction of Lebanon and major development plans in many countries in this region should result in overall annual gains in construction activity in the range of 2 to 4 percent in 1998 and 1999 and perhaps higher levels in 2000.

Latin America has suffered for decades from currency problems and inflation. However, the move toward more sound macroeconomic policies by major countries in that region, particularly Argentina and Brazil, have led to a more attractive investment climate which has created a surge in construction activity. Even the collapse of the Mexican peso and, more recently, the Asian financial crisis have had only a limited impact on the region. The Mexican government's willingness to take difficult economic steps to shore up its economy has blunted the "Tequila effect" on the rest of the region and has given Mexico's construction market new opportunities.

Overall growth of Latin American economies averaged better than 5 percent in 1997, the highest rate since 1981, according to the InterAmerican Development Bank, and regional inflation dropped to 10 percent. This has made many of these countries attractive investment destinations. For example, Brazil attracted over $2 billion in foreign direct investment in the first 2 months of 1998. This level of investment has led to a major increase in construction activity throughout the region. For example, construction activity increased 17 percent in the first 2 months of 1998, according to INDEC, Argentina's statistical bureau. However, weather damage to Peru's infrastructure from 1998's El Niño storms is spurring a major road repair program. Overall, the international construction market in Latin America grew at a 5 to 8 percent rate in 1998, and an only slightly lower level is forecast for 1999 and 2000.

Africa has generally been a small and difficult market for U.S. construction firms, and the next few years should not change this pattern. Much of the market in central and southern Africa will remain dependent on international funding agencies despite a general improvement in the economies in this region. A further problem for U.S. construction firms is the level of competition from established firms from former colonial countries such as Britain, the Netherlands, and France and, in the case of former Portuguese colonies, construction firms from Brazil. The emergence of South Africa from apartheid has allowed construction firms from that country to dominate much of the market in southern Africa. Thus, the market for U.S. construction firms in Africa should increase at a low rate.

As a whole, U.S. construction firms would do well to maintain current levels of international work in the short term. More likely, revenue from international work will fall 2 to 3 percent in 1998. However, the resumption of slow growth in Asia and the expected increase in the Middle East and in the petroleum and petrochemical markets in 1999, coupled with a strengthening of U.S. firms' market share, should allow for overall growth in U.S. construction exports to the world market of 3 to 4 percent, and a further increase of 5 percent in 2000.

Jan Tuchman and Gary Tulacz, Engineering News-Record, The McGraw-Hill Companies, August 1998.

■ REFERENCES

Call the Bureau of the Census at (301) 457-1242 for information about ordering Census documents.

America's Infrastructure: Effects of Construction Spending, Associated General Contractors, 1957 E Street, NW, Washington, DC 20006. (202) 393-2040.

Automated Builder (monthly), P.O. Box 120, Carpinteria, CA 93014. (805) 684-7659.

Cahners Building & Construction Market Forecast (monthly), Cahners Publishing Co., 275 Washington Street, Newton, MA 02158-1630. (617) 630-2105.

Census of Construction, 1992, Bureau of the Census, U.S. Department of Commerce, Washington, DC 20233. (301) 457-1242.

Construction Review (quarterly), International Trade Administration, Room H4045, U.S. Department of Commerce, Washington, DC 20230. (202) 482-0132.

Decisions for the 1990s, NAHB Publications, National Association of Homebuilders, 15th & M Street, NW, Washington, DC 20233. (202) 822-0200.

Dodge/Sweet's Construction Outlook, McGraw-Hill Information Systems Company, 1221 Avenue of the Americas, New York, NY 10020.

Engineering News-Record (weekly), The McGraw-Hill Companies, 1221 Avenue of the Americas, New York, NY 10020. (212) 512-4634.

Expenditures for Nonresidential Improvements and Upkeep, 1992, Bureau of the Census, U.S. Department of Commerce, Washington, D.C. 20233. (301) 457-1605.

Housing Starts (Construction Reports, Series C-20), Bureau of the Census, U.S. Department of Commerce, Washington, DC 20233. (301) 457-4666.

Infrastructure: Investing in Our Future, Portland Cement Association, 54 Old Orchard Road, Skokie, IL 60077. (708) 966-6200.

Manufacturing Report (monthly), Manufactured Housing Institute, 2101 Wilson Boulevard, Arlington, VA 22201-3062. (703) 558-0400.

1996 Year-end Report (annual), National Association of Home Builders, Building Systems Councils, 1201 15th Street, NW, Washington, DC 20005. (202) 822-0576.

Quick Facts (annual), Manufactured Housing Institute, 2101 Wilson Boulevard, Arlington, VA 22201-3062. (703) 558-0400.

TEA-21: Moving Americans into the 21st Century (www.fhwa.dot.gov/tea21/), U.S. Department of Transportation, Washington, DC, 20590. (202) 366-4000.

Value of Construction Put in Place (Construction Reports, Series C-30), Bureau of the Census, U.S. Department of Commerce, Washington, DC 20233. (301) 457-1605.

■ RELATED CHAPTERS

7: Wood Products
8: Construction Materials

WOOD PRODUCTS
Economic and Trade Trends

U.S. International Trade

($ billions)

Legend: Balance — Exports — Imports

Source: U.S. Department of Commerce: Bureau of the Census; International Trade Administration.

World Export Market Shares

(%)

Legend: United States, Canada, Indonesia, Malaysia

Source: United Nations; U.S. Department of Commerce, International Trade Administration.

Export Dependence and Import Penetration

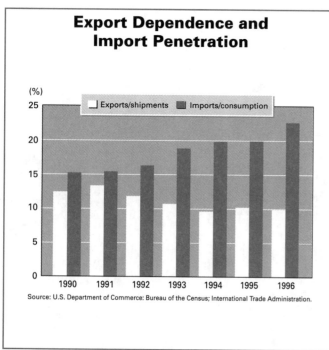

(%)

Legend: Exports/shipments, Imports/consumption

Source: U.S. Department of Commerce: Bureau of the Census; International Trade Administration.

Output and Output per Hour

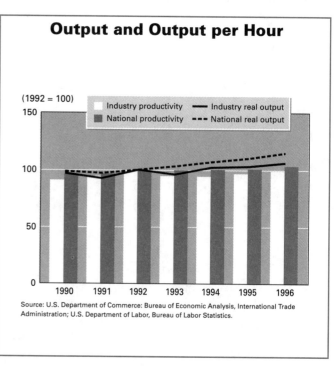

(1992 = 100)

Legend: Industry productivity, National productivity, Industry real output, National real output

Source: U.S. Department of Commerce: Bureau of Economic Analysis, International Trade Administration; U.S. Department of Labor, Bureau of Labor Statistics.

See "Getting the Most Out of *Outlook '99*" for definitions of terms.

Wood Products

INDUSTRY DEFINITION   The U.S. wood products industry consists of 14 manufacturing sectors that process timber and pulpwood into products such as lumber, panel products, and other basic wood materials. This chapter covers the following wood products sectors: general sawmills and planing mills (SIC 2421), hardwood veneer and plywood (SIC 2435), softwood veneer and plywood (SIC 2436), and reconstituted wood products (SIC 2493). Manufactured housing and prefabricated wood buildings are not covered in this chapter.

GLOBAL INDUSTRY TRENDS

The U.S. wood products industry is a world leader in the production of and trade in a multitude of products used for residential and light commercial construction as well as consumer-oriented products. Residential and light commercial construction end uses dominate the market for its products, with more than 81 percent of softwood lumber and 65 percent of structural panels utilized in those activities. Highly skilled labor, access to raw materials, high levels of capital investment, and efficient transportation and logistical systems make the United States the premier producer of wood products in the world.

Trade in wood products has been an important component of the industry, increasing from $13.6 billion in 1992 to $20.8 billion in 1997. However, most of this growth in trade has come in the form of imports, which accounted for nearly half the U.S. trade in wood products in 1992 but now account for 65 percent of that trade. A burgeoning domestic economy with strength in housing starts has increased domestic demand for wood products.

IMPORTANT FACTORS AFFECTING FUTURE U.S. INDUSTRY GROWTH

Growth in residential and light commercial construction and the good health of the repair and remodeling industry are the main factors in the growth of the U.S. wood products industry. However, as the industry becomes increasingly tied to foreign markets, growth in offshore markets is becoming more important.

In 1997, the value of new residential construction put-in-place rose 2 percent while growth in the single-family housing market was flat but remained at a relatively lofty historical level. Whereas the single-family sector has remained strong, growth in private nonresidential construction increased over 4 percent in 1997 as developers that were humbled by the overbuilding and subsequent relatively low occupancy rates of the late 1980s slowly reentered the market

Recently, financial difficulties in Asia, especially in Japan, have taken a toll on the wood products industry as demand in those countries has suffered. Wood products such as softwood lumber, hardwood lumber, and panel products have all suffered pricing setbacks even though the U.S. market for those products is very strong. Compounding this weak pricing is the increase in imports, especially of lumber products. Despite the laws of supply and demand, weakened prices for wood products, especially for softwood lumber, have not caused sawmills to limit their production because producers have tended to increase production to meet financial obligations such as employee compensation. Furthermore, the fragmented nature of the industry has caused a credibility gap in regard to announcements of production cutbacks in the face of weaker pricing.

The resiliency of the industry should be demonstrated again even as the industry is shaken by the developments in Asia. Cutbacks in federally supplied timber once were thought to spell doom for the wood products industry, but the industry responded to that challenge by seeking an increasing supply of timber from privately held lands. While this transition of sourcing has been painful in terms of mill closures and financial uncertainties and is not complete, the industry's resilience and innovation in using previously less desirable tree species have allowed it to remain the premier wood products producer in the world.

U.S. INDUSTRY GROWTH PROJECTIONS FOR THE NEXT 1 AND 5 YEARS

It is forecast that the U.S. gross domestic product will continue to grow, but the level of single-family housing starts is expected to decline 1 percent annually to 1.38 million units in the next 5 years. While this decline in housing starts will affect the wood products industry, the forecast 2 percent annual increase in the repair and remodeling sector should counteract it. As a result, shipments of wood products were expected to increase 1.7 percent in 1998. Prospects for growth in U.S. exports of wood products in the next 5 years are bleak despite improved access to foreign markets resulting from the removal or reduction of tariff and nontariff barriers through the North American Free Trade Agreement (NAFTA) and the Uruguay Round of multilateral trade negotiations under the auspices of the World Trade Organization (WTO). Beset by the financial difficulties in key Asian markets such as Japan, U.S. exports are expected to contract 20 percent in 1998 and 16 percent in 1999. After the financial difficulties ease and Japan emerges from recession, exports of wood products should rebound to the growth rates that existed before the Asian financial distress. Imports of wood products, by contrast, are expected to retain their steady growth as the U.S. market remains the strongest in the world, attracting an increasing variety of suppliers from various countries. Over the period 1998–2003, exports are expected to decline 11 percent annually while imports are expected to increase 3 percent per year. The rate of decline for U.S. exports could be much worse if the Asian economies, especially that of

Japan, remain mired in their malaise throughout the period 1998–2003.

GLOBAL MARKET PROSPECTS

Growth in U.S. exports of wood products is dependent on how the Asian economies, especially that of Japan, handle their difficulties. Exports to Japan, the leading market for U.S. wood products in 1996, only to be replaced by Canada in 1997, declined 24 percent in 1997, and it is expected that exports to Japan in 1998 and 1999 will fall 30 percent. Tough economic conditions in Japan are stunting consumer demand for wood products, especially in housing applications, despite conducive market-opening mechanisms such as the Enhanced Initiative on Deregulation and Competition Policy, which featured, among other things, a housing component. The rise in the Japanese consumption tax from 3 percent to 5 percent in 1996 is thought to be one reason why Japanese demand has fallen, along with the recession that gripped that country starting in late 1997. Canada has overtaken Japan as the largest market for U.S. wood products as the Canadian economy has strengthened. However, industry sources indicate that a good proportion of U.S. exports are destined to be transshipped, mostly to European destinations and to a lesser extent to Asian destinations (see Table 7-1).

The wood products industry is a key sector among the various nascent multilateral market-opening forums, such as the Asia Pacific Economic Corporation (APEC), the Free Trade Area of the Americas, and new applicants seeking to join the WTO. With its housing reform measures, China is an important focus for the wood industry in these negotiations. All these forums call for the removal of tariffs and the harmonization of product standards and codes, two of the key impediments to

TABLE 7-1:   U.S. Trade Patterns in Wood Products[1] in 1997
(millions of dollars; percent)

Exports			Imports		
Regions[2]	Value[3]	Share, %	Regions[2]	Value[3]	Share, %
NAFTA	1,001	27.5	NAFTA	8,128	85.1
Latin America	203	5.6	Latin America	541	5.7
Western Europe	1,230	33.8	Western Europe	243	2.5
Japan/Chinese Economic Area	837	23.0	Japan/Chinese Economic Area	35	0.4
Other Asia	205	5.6	Other Asia	458	4.8
Rest of world	161	4.4	Rest of world	150	1.6
World	3,638	100.0	World	9,554	100.0
Top Five Countries	Value	Share, %	Top Five Countries	Value	Share, %
Canada	800	22.0	Canada	7,991	83.6
Japan	636	17.5	Indonesia	340	3.6
Germany	292	8.0	Brazil	303	3.2
United Kingdom	244	6.7	Mexico	137	1.4
Mexico	202	5.5	Chile	108	1.1

[1] SIC 2421 2435 2436 2493.
[2] For definitions of regional groupings, see "Getting the Most Out of *Outlook '99.*"
[3] Values may not sum to total due to rounding.
Source: U.S. Department of Commerce, Bureau of the Census.

increased growth in U.S. exports of wood products, among their objectives. Work on removing these barriers is farthest along in the APEC arena. Wood products is one of 15 sectors that were selected by the heads of state of the various APEC economies at their November 1997 summit to be slated for "early voluntary sectoral liberalization." The details of this liberalization effort were being discussed throughout 1998. The wood products industry is placing a great deal of emphasis on this effort because of the importance of Asia to their growth potential.

The final stage of tariff removal by Canada on January 1, 1998, under the U.S.-Canada Free Trade Agreement is benefitting U.S. exporters. U.S. wood product exports to Canada increased 21 percent to $800 million in 1997, making Canada the largest export market for U.S. wood products. Similarly, the gradual removal of tariffs as Mexico implements the North American Free Trade Agreement should benefit U.S. exporters. U.S. exports to Mexico continue to rebound from the difficulties that resulted when the Mexican economy contracted at the end of 1994. Wood product exports to Mexico increased 15 percent to $202 million in 1997.

SAWMILLS AND PLANING MILLS

The sawmills and planing mills sector consists of manufacturers that are engaged primarily in sawing rough lumber and timber from logs and bolts or resawing cants and flitches (veneer stock) into softwood and hardwood lumber. This industry also includes establishments engaged in manufacturing softwood furniture and flooring stock, fuel wood, railroad ties, and wood chips from mill residues.

Industry Performance in 1998

Continuation of strong domestic demand for softwood and hardwood lumber was the major reason why product shipments increased 2 percent in 1997 to an estimated $22 billion and shipments were expected to increase 3.5 percent in 1998 (see Table 7-2). The factors driving this increase in demand are the relatively high level of single-family housing starts, the fact that the United States is the largest consumer of lumber products worldwide, and the vigorous residential repair, remodeling, and home improvement sectors.

Sawmills and planing mills are the second largest sector in the forest products industry (as defined by SIC 24 and SIC 26) and the largest sector in the solid wood products industry, with product shipments in 1996 valued at $25.8 billion. Solid sawn softwood and hardwood lumber are the largest components of the sawmills and planing mills sector, with product shipments valued at $19.4 billion in 1996.

Prices for softwood lumber, which were very volatile after completion of the 1996 U.S.–Canada Softwood Lumber Agreement, stabilized, removing some uncertainty among major end users and subsequently subduing the drive to increase the use of substitute products for solid-sawn lumber. Although the market is still adjusting to the curtailment of harvesting from western federal lands and the transition to just-in-time inventory practices, according to industry data, 1997 softwood lumber production surpassed the 1996 level by 2 percent, totaling 14.6 million cubic meters, and was expected to duplicate this level in 1998.

This relatively high level of softwood lumber production is due mainly to stumpage derived from privately owned lands and the decrease in log exports. As supplies from federally

TABLE 7-2: Sawmills and Planing Mills, General (SIC 2421) Trends and Forecasts
(millions of dollars except as noted)

	1992	1993	1994	1995	1996	1997[1]	1998[2]	1999[3]	Percent Change 96–97	97–98	98–99	92–96[4]
Industry data												
Value of shipments[5]	21,061	24,460	26,964	25,776	26,740	28,125	29,100	29,900	5.2	3.5	2.7	6.2
Value of shipments (1992$)	21,061	19,662	21,181	21,716	22,700	23,100	23,550	23,900	1.8	1.9	1.5	1.9
Total employment (thousands)	138.0	142.0	142.0	143.0	138.0	137.0	137.0	135.0	–0.7	–0.0	–1.5	0.0
Production workers (thousands)	118.0	122.0	122.0	122.0	118.0	118.0	117.0	116.5	–0.0	–0.8	–0.4	0.0
Average hourly earnings ($)	9.65	9.83	9.97	10.24	10.51	10.70	10.93	11.15	1.8	2.1	2.0	2.2
Capital expenditures	459	548	694	852	1,000	1,050	1,085	1,105	5.0	3.3	1.8	21.5
Product data												
Value of shipments[5]	20,347	23,641	26,001	24,945	25,849	26,577	27,163	28,259	2.8	2.2	4.0	6.2
Value of shipments (1992$)	20,347	19,004	20,425	21,015	21,943	22,382	23,165	23,802	2.0	3.5	2.8	1.9
Trade data												
Value of imports	3,472	5,022	6,039	5,505	6,813	7,305	7,500	7,750	7.2	2.7	3.3	18.4
Value of exports	2,322	2,450	2,428	2,412	2,393	2,472	1,960	2,015	3.3	–20.7	2.8	0.8

[1] Estimate except imports and exports.
[2] Estimate.
[3] Forecast.
[4] Compound annual rate.
[5] For a definition of industry versus product values, see "Getting the Most Out of *Outlook '99*."
Source: U.S. Department of Commerce: Bureau of the Census; International Trade Administration.

owned lands are expected to be curtailed for the foreseeable future because of various environmental issues, the industry, especially in the western United States, has been forced to derive supplies from private landowners when companies do not own any land themselves. The only alternative is to go out of business. The decrease in softwood log exports has benefited the softwood lumber industry by increasing the available supply, and therefore lower raw material input costs, ultimately leading to an increase in demand-driven production. Softwood log exports have been declining from the 1992 level of 13.8 million cubic meters, falling to 9.4 million cubic meters in 1997. Slackened Japanese demand accounts for most of this decline and is expected to remain weak given the weakness of the Japanese economy and Japan's use of more value-added materials from the United States and other suppliers.

Single-family residential construction remains the main consumer of softwood lumber, and according to industry data, the average unit uses 5.6 cubic meters of framing lumber; this figure, multiplied by the number of single-family housing starts, shows the importance of construction activity to the softwood lumber industry. Although single-family residential construction is the most important consumer of softwood lumber, the residential repair and remodeling market is a close second and is viewed as a growth segment as more homeowners refurbish their existing houses. Buoyed by financial gains from the U.S. stock market and high consumer confidence, homeowners are spending an increasing amount of money for additions and renovations and therefore are consuming more lumber. Expenditures on home improvements increased 4 percent in 1997, reaching a total of $60.5 billion, and this upward trend is expected to continue; this bodes well for the softwood lumber industry.

In 1997 imports accounted for nearly 24 percent of apparent consumption of products from this sector, and this import dependency was expected to increase slightly in 1998. Imports of softwood lumber from Canada are by far the single largest component of this subsector and the entire solid wood products industry.

Other commodities manufactured by this sector are used in a wide range of applications, including residential construction and repairs as well as nonresidential construction, paper and allied products, millwork items, cabinetry and furniture, prefabricated housing units, and sporting goods and toys.

International Competitiveness

The U.S. sawmills and planing mills industry faces formidable competition in international markets, especially in softwood lumber commodities. In spite of this competition, U.S. exports of softwood lumber increased 3.3 percent in 1997 over the 1996 level in terms of value, although they decreased 9 percent in volume. Japan remains the largest U.S. export market for softwood lumber, with a 41 percent share in 1997, down considerably from 54 percent in 1996, reflecting the sluggishness of the Japanese economy, especially in terms of demand for new residential housing. Canada and Spain are the second and third largest markets for U.S. softwood lumber.

Financial difficulties in Asia are having a profound impact on the international competitiveness of the U.S. sawmills and planing mills industry. Since lumber products are priced internationally in U.S. dollars, the depreciation of Asian currencies has had a depressing effect on lumber exports. Furthermore, Asian demand for hardwood and softwood logs, which also are priced in U.S. dollars, has fallen dramatically, allowing domestic sawmillers to process these high-quality logs for domestic consumption. Even with the very strong U.S. housing market, American producers have not been able to pass along price increases because of the weak Asian markets. In fact, the U.S. market is so strong, and lumber prices are so relatively weak, that consumers are reaping large benefits from this position, largely because of the Asian difficulties. Industry sources do not expect any significant price increases or a surge in exports in the next 2 years.

Industry and Trade Projections for the Next 1 and 5 Years

Shipments of sawmills and planing mills products are expected to grow about 3.5 percent in 1998 and about 2.8 percent in 1999 in constant dollars. While the volume of production, according to industry data, is expected to increase around 2 to 4 percent, prices will remain subdued despite the very strong domestic markets.

In 1998 and 1999, U.S. housing markets are expected to retain most of the vitality they showed in 1996 and 1997. Housing starts are expected to decline slightly in 1998 and 1999, but since the average size of a home built in the United States is expected to increase slightly, more lumber products will be consumed in those years. Increasing activity in the repair and remodeling end-use segments will further bolster lumber consumption. Homeowners, flush with receipts from a historically high equities market, have been funneling some of their gains into additions, decks, and furniture items, causing the production of lumber products to increase.

Producers have been caught between strong domestic demand and tepid international demand, especially in Japan and other Asian countries, and have not been able to increase prices readily. However, the hardwood lumber segment has been able to pass along price increases more readily than have its softwood cousins, since international demand has not been affected as much as in the softwood lumber commodity sector. Hardwood lumber, with its vast range of species, is differentiated from the softwood sector because softwood lumber products are used primarily in construction and molding and millwork applications, where species differentiation is not critical. Lighter-colored hardwood lumber such as hard maple has seen a tremendous rise in price and is expected to remain expensive for the next 2 to 3 years. Production of these light-colored hardwoods has been increasing slowly but cannot fully satisfy demand because of increasing logging restrictions on federal lands in the hardwood-producing regions of the country. While not experiencing the same degree of restriction on federal land use that the Pacific northwest is currently facing, the Allegheny National Forest in Pennsylvania, a prime location for hard maple and other highly sought Appalachian hardwoods, has seen logging decrease as a result of various environmental measures. Privately owned land in the eastern United States has been able to increase production to meet the demand, but not totally because of the highly fragmented nature of ownership of the hardwood forest resource.

Internationally, U.S. exports are expected to suffer significant setbacks, declining 21 percent in 1998 mainly because of lackluster demand in Asia. However, 1999 should see a 2.8 percent rebound in exports as the Asians come back into the marketplace and because of resurgent demand from the Europeans, especially for hardwoods, as their economies grow. A major wild card in the future growth of exports in this sector concerns China's housing reform that was launched in the spring of 1998 and that country's acceptance of the use of wood products such as softwood lumber and hardwood lumber in domestic residential construction. China has not been as strongly affected by the Asian financial difficulties as have some of its regional neighbors, but its economy has slowed somewhat and the Chinese government has focused on the residential housing market as a key to increasing growth in its set targets. If China is successful in its housing reform efforts and the use of wooden building materials is accepted by the nascent wood-framed housing market, U.S. exports should respond quite positively and this new, large market should make up for slack demand from China's neighbors.

The recovering European markets will have a positive influence on the growth of this industry, mostly in the hardwood lumber market but also in softwood lumber commodities. However, the United States faces very formidable competition in the European market from Canada and the Scandinavians, especially the Swedes. Sweden, with its European Union member-

ship and proximity to the European market, most likely will be the primary beneficiary of the increased European activity.

Growth in the sawmills and planing mills sector is expected to be moderate over the period 1998–2003. As the Asian economies, especially Japan, sort out their difficulties, this sector will benefit from an increasing supply of logs that once were destined for Asian markets that they will be able to transform into lumber products. The healthy U.S. economy will allow this sector to grow and absorb some of the lumber that previously was manufactured for export. However, this will have a dampening effect on lumber prices, leading to only moderate growth in this sector.

HARDWOOD VENEER AND PLYWOOD

Hardwood veneer and plywood (SIC 2435) producers are engaged primarily in producing commercial hardwood veneer and in manufacturing commercial plywood or prefinished hardwood plywood. This includes nonwood-backed or faced veneer and nonwood-faced plywood from veneer produced in the same establishment or from purchased veneer.

Industry Performance in 1998

The strong domestic housing market and an increase in the consumption of furniture and cabinetry items were the main factors that fueled a 2.5 percent increase in product shipments of hardwood veneer and plywood in 1997. Also contributing to the growth in product shipments were the strong European and Canadian markets, leading to a 14 percent increase in U.S. exports to $419 million in 1997 (see Table 7-3).

TABLE 7-3: Hardwood Veneer and Plywood (SIC 2435) Trends and Forecasts
(millions of dollars except as noted)

	1992	1993	1994	1995	1996	1997[1]	1998[2]	1999[3]	Percent Change 96–97	97–98	98–99	92–96[4]
Industry data												
Value of shipments[5]	2,238	2,537	2,609	2,642	2,623	2,652	2,725	2,805	1.1	2.8	2.9	4.0
Value of shipments (1992$)	2,238	2,371	2,292	2,277	2,236	2,250	2,272	2,298	0.6	1.0	1.1	0.0
Total employment (thousands)	19.9	19.8	21.9	22.0	21.3	21.3	21.1	21.0	0.0	−0.9	−0.5	1.7
Production workers (thousands)	16.9	16.8	18.8	18.8	18.3	18.3	18.2	18.2	0.0	−0.5	0.0	2.0
Average hourly earnings ($)	8.12	8.55	8.21	8.75	8.95	9.00	9.11	9.17	0.6	1.2	0.7	2.5
Capital expenditures	45.1	46.6	52.5	32.2	37.7	38.1	35.0	36.2	1.1	−8.1	3.4	−4.4
Product data												
Value of shipments[5]	2,023	2,305	2,444	2,520	2,556	2,633	2,701	2,771	3.0	2.6	2.6	6.0
Value of shipments (1992$)	2,023	2,154	2,148	2,173	2,179	2,233	2,284	2,339	2.5	2.3	2.4	1.9
Trade data												
Value of imports	729	857	890	924	997	994	1,120	1,250	−0.3	12.7	11.6	8.1
Value of exports	273	292	343	372	369	419	435	462	13.6	3.8	6.2	7.8

[1] Estimate except imports and exports.
[2] Estimate.
[3] Forecast.
[4] Compound annual rate.
[5] For a definition of industry versus product values, see "Getting the Most Out of *Outlook '99*."
Source: U.S. Department of Commerce: Bureau of the Census; International Trade Administration.

According to U.S. Bureau of the Census data, hardwood plywood is the dominant product in this group, with over 38 percent of product shipments in 1996, followed by hardwood veneer at 25 percent. Hardwood plywood products, which include products such as laminated veneer lumber, account for 23 percent of product shipments, and prefinished hardwood plywood paneling accounts for 8 percent. Product shipments of prefinished hardwood plywood paneling continue to decline as consumers are specifying the use of gypsum board because of its ability to be painted or wallpapered. Commodities manufactured by businesses in this sector are used in a wide range of applications, from furniture and case goods to residential repair and remodeling and manufactured housing units.

Producers of hardwood plywood are able to make panels in nearly any dimension that an application demands. A customer can order sizes that go beyond the sizes normally available for the application at hand. However, most hardwood plywood panels come in stock sizes, generally 4 feet wide by 6 to 10 feet long. Industry data show that the production of hardwood plywood has increased 3 percent, the thirteenth consecutive year of growth, to 89.5 million square meters. Continued growth is expected as a result of increased consumption by the furniture industry and other case good manufacturers.

Stock hardwood production accounts for slightly more than half of all the hardwood plywood produced. Eastern producers, given their proximity to the hardwood forest resource, produce 53 percent of hardwood plywood, while western producers account for 46 percent, with the Lake States supplying the remainder. In the not too distant past, western producers were besieged by escalating fiber costs caused by harvesting restrictions and the impact on producer prices of exporting unprocessed logs to Asia. However, because of the financial difficulties facing the Asian region, more logs are available domestically, and the prices paid by producers for logs thus have been reduced.

Hardwood plywood producers use a wide range of species for the face veneers of their product. Red oak remains the most popular with 37 percent of the market, followed by birch (30 percent) and maple (16 percent). Maple continues to increase in popularity as consumers are specifying lighter-colored woods, especially for kitchen cabinetry and other furniture items. The popularity of maple should plateau at 17 or 18 percent of the market because maple is a very difficult species to stain, whereas oak and birch are more readily adaptable to changing consumer preferences in the colors of wood. One of the popular trends in the furniture industry is the Shaker style, which utilizes a lot of maple; this bodes well for the continued popularity of maple.

The use of different cores in the hardwood plywood industry varies from veneer plies (63 percent of the market) to medium-density fiberboard (MDF) cores at 16 percent. The use of MDF and particleboard cores increased steadily after 1991, since these materials allow the panel to be flatter and more dimen-sionally stable. Furthermore, these cores cost less to manufacture than do veneer or lumber cores.

International Competitiveness

U.S. hardwood veneer and plywood exports increased nearly 14 percent in 1997 as demand from the European and Canadian markets increased. Canada, Germany, Spain, and the United Kingdom are the top four markets, representing nearly 60 percent of U.S. exports of these products. U.S. exports were expected to increase in 1998, but not at the same pace that was experienced in 1997, mainly as a result of slack Asian demand. However, it was expected that exports to Europe would pick up, leading exports from this sector to increase 3.8 percent to nearly $435 million in 1998. The United States will continue to face tough competition from southeast Asian, South American, and eastern European producers but is insulated somewhat in that plywood produced from species indigenous to the United States is still highly sought in foreign markets.

U.S. imports of these products were almost unchanged in 1997, totaling nearly $994 million. U.S. importers have numerous choices of species that are available from domestic sources. The importation of tropical species has been stable, with Indonesia being the largest supplier. Aided by weakened southeast Asian currencies, especially in Indonesia, imports are expected to increase nearly 13 percent in 1998 and 12 percent in 1999.

Industry and Trade Projections for the Next 1 and 5 Years

Continued growth in furniture and mobile home construction and a healthy domestic construction market should result in higher product shipments in 1998 and 1999. Those shipments are expected to increase 2.3 percent in 1998 and 2.4 percent in 1999 as domestic demand is sustained and stronger demand comes from Europe and Canada. All categories of products in this sector should participate in the growth, even the recently declining prefinished hardwood paneling plywood used in prefabricated and modular housing units.

Exports of hardwood veneer and plywood products were expected to increase 3.8 percent in 1998, continuing the strong export growth of these products. Europe, Canada, and South America were expected to be the main markets in 1998. Imports are expected to continue to increase, especially hardwood plywood from Indonesia as the rupiah has been pummeled in foreign exchange markets, making luaun plywood very price-competitive in the United States.

Over the period 1998–2003, the hardwood veneer and plywood industry is expected to increase shipments 2 percent annually as the markets for these products improve. Domestic producers are expected to face an increasing amount of competition from Asian countries for the lower end-use markets, especially in inexpensive furniture items that once used hardwood plywood and now are increasingly using vinyl overlaid particleboard and other composite products, thus tempering the growth potential of this sector.

SOFTWOOD VENEER AND PLYWOOD

Softwood veneer and plywood (SIC 2436) manufacturers are engaged primarily in producing commercial softwood veneer and plywood from veneer produced in the same establishment or from purchased veneer. This includes softwood plywood composites and softwood veneer and plywood utilized in hardwood and softwood paneling.

Industry Performance in 1998

The softwood veneer and plywood industry rebounded slightly in 1997, increasing sales as product shipments rose a slim 1 percent (see Table 7-4). Housing starts, repair and remodeling, and general construction products were very healthy in 1997, and the softwood plywood and veneer industry's resilience in shifting production from the Pacific Northwest to the South aided this increase in production. Also contributing to the slight rise in 1997 product shipments were the completion and full operation of the first softwood plywood facility built in the United States in the last 10 years. Along with the increase in product shipments, exports of softwood plywood rebounded in 1997, mostly as a result of strong exports of southern yellow pine softwood plywood. Softwood plywood and veneer exports are facing stiff competition from Canada, Indonesia, and Brazil, especially in the European and Japanese markets. According to Census Bureau data, rough softwood plywood accounted for an estimated 58 percent of this sector's total product shipments, followed by sanded softwood plywood (15 percent) and nonreinforced softwood veneer (13 percent).

The production of softwood plywood has been enhanced by technological and economic breakthroughs in the use of adhe-sives. The employment of phenol-formaldehyde adhesives, which are thermoreactive and set to an infusible solid, allows the use of veneer sheets with a higher moisture content compared with veneer sheets that are glued with protein-based adhesives such as casein. This allows a lower production cost because the manufacturer does not necessarily need to reduce the moisture content of the veneer sheets below the equilibrium moisture content to ensure a good bond. Furthermore, the plywood panel is less likely to warp or shrink because the moisture content of the veneers is near equilibrium with the ambient environment.

One of the greatest challenges to the softwood plywood and veneer industry is competition from oriented strand board (OSB). OSB is a structural panel with alternating layers of compressed wood strands that are glued with exterior-grade adhesives. Since 1992, when OSB was certified to perform as well as softwood plywood, as defined by Performance Standard PS-2, OSB has been rapidly taking market share from softwood plywood. This certification allows OSB to compete directly for the same markets as plywood while offering the consumer a lower cost because OSB is much cheaper to produce. However, there are certain applications that are still dominated by the use of softwood plywood, such as underlayment for floors.

In the United States there are 92 plywood-producing mills and nearly 50 OSB-producing mills. Nearly 75 percent of all grades of softwood plywood are produced in the South. The West, the traditional producer of softwood plywood, especially Douglas fir plywood, is slowly being reduced to production for niche markets because of the changing patterns of raw material procurement that have favored landowners in the south versus the publicly derived stumpage that a large percentage of western mills have relied on.

TABLE 7-4: Softwood Veneer and Plywood (SIC 2436) Trends and Forecasts
(millions of dollars except as noted)

	1992	1993	1994	1995	1996	1997[1]	1998[2]	1999[3]	96–97	97–98	98–99	92–96[4]
										Percent Change		
Industry data												
Value of shipments[5]	5,350	6,035	6,544	6,828	6,033	6,095	6,185	6,200	1.0	1.5	0.2	3.0
Value of shipments (1992$)	5,350	5,172	5,417	5,376	5,264	5,270	5,296	5,335	0.1	0.5	0.7	−0.4
Total employment (thousands)	30.9	30.7	30.3	32.4	31.9	31.8	31.8	31.5	−0.3	0.0	−0.9	0.8
Production workers (thousands)	27.7	27.7	27.2	29.1	28.6	28.5	28.5	28.4	−0.3	0.0	−0.4	0.8
Average hourly earnings ($)	11.08	11.42	11.83	12.14	12.36	12.60	12.87	13.02	1.9	2.1	1.2	2.8
Capital expenditures	95	118	150	184	208	220	236	245	5.8	7.3	3.8	21.8
Product data												
Value of shipments[5]	4,778	5,321	5,700	5,953	5,225	5,272	5,338	5,445	0.9	1.3	2.0	7.3
Value of shipments (1992$)	4,778	4,560	4,719	4,688	4,559	4,593	4,648	4,718	0.8	1.2	1.5	−1.2
Trade data												
Value of imports	59	77	96	99	88	109	112	115	23.3	2.8	2.7	10.6
Value of exports	341	373	327	339	317	392	397	406	23.7	1.3	2.3	−1.8

[1] Estimate except imports and exports.
[2] Estimate.
[3] Forecast.
[4] Compound annual rate.
[5] For a definition of industry versus product values, see "Getting the Most Out of *Outlook '99*."
Source: U.S. Department of Commerce: Bureau of the Census; International Trade Administration.

International Competitiveness

Exports of softwood plywood and veneer rose a healthy 24 percent in 1997 to $392 million, the highest level in 8 years. Exports to the United Kingdom, Canada, and Germany, the top three U.S. export markets for products in this category, experienced healthy gains. The resurgent European markets have increased demand for softwood plywood, especially in the use for concrete-forming applications, as the construction sector throughout Europe has increased its activity. Softwood plywood remains the largest export sector in this category, accounting for nearly 88 percent of exports. However, this percentage has been declining over the last couple of years as international acceptance of OSB and increasing competition from Canada, Brazil, and Indonesia have slowly eroded the export dominance of softwood plywood.

U.S. imports of softwood plywood and veneer increased about 24 percent to $109 million, with over 77 percent originating in Canada. This increase is due mainly to the strong U.S. housing market and repair and remodeling sectors. However, since the United States is the most efficient and least-cost producer, foreign penetration of the U.S. market is very difficult.

Industry and Trade Projections for the Next 1 and 5 Years

Sales of softwood plywood and veneer continued their modest increase in 1997, and this trend should continue in 1998 and 1999. However, these increases are small: 2 percent in 1998 and 1.5 percent in 1999. The U.S. softwood plywood and veneer industry appears to have adjusted to the cutbacks in publicly derived raw materials and the shift in production capacity to the South. Also, the very active construction market in the United States and the invigorated European markets are contributing to the modest growth of this sector. Furthermore, the continuing removal of tariffs and nontariff barriers throughout the world will lead to an increase in export opportunities.

While the European construction markets are slowly awakening, there is cause for concern in Asia, especially Japan, as this region continues to be beset with financial difficulties and recession. Also, the worldwide increase in the production of OSB should sound alarms for softwood plywood and veneer exports. Nonetheless, softwood plywood is still the material of choice for construction-related applications, and this marginal growth should continue as long as domestic demand remains strong. However, it is not expected that substantial growth opportunities will abound for this sector. The domestic market is facing extremely formidable competition from OSB, and so the chance to increase growth substantially resides in foreign markets.

Although the traditional European and Asian markets should remain the main markets, nontraditional markets such as South America and eastern Europe need to be exploited. Softwood plywood has some advantage over OSB in terms of developing these markets because OSB currently is not seen as a performance-based product equivalent to plywood. Also, developments in China and its massive restructuring of its housing market could be a boon to plywood producers.

The South is expected to increase its dominance in production over the West and by 2002 should account for 77 percent of all plywood production. While the timber constraints that western producers have been facing for the last 10 years are starting to abate, the South is a lower-cost producer. However, the West will still have the niche markets for high-end construction applications. Douglas fir and fir plywood products will still be demanded by consumers drawn by the appearance of those products.

RECONSTITUTED WOOD PRODUCTS

The reconstituted wood products (SIC 2493) sector consists of establishments that are engaged primarily in the manufacture of reconstituted wood and panel products. Important products of this industry are hardboard, particleboard, insulation board, medium density fiberboard, waferboard, and oriented strand board. Other major products include wallboard, tile board, insulating siding, and flakeboard.

Industry Performance in 1998

Product shipments of reconstituted wood products increased 3.1 percent in 1997, reaching an estimated nominal value of $5.3 billion. The strong domestic housing market and the increased activity in residential repairs and remodeling projects contributed significantly to this growth. Also, the strong furniture market and similar end-use markets contributed to this growth (see Table 7-5).

The reconstituted wood products sector produces items such as OSB, hardboard, particleboard, MDF, and insulation board. Census Bureau data indicate that OSB constitutes the largest portion of this industry, accounting for 26 percent of total product shipments. Particleboard accounts for 25 percent, followed by hardboard (18 percent) and MDF (10 percent). According to industry data, production of OSB, the main structural item in this group, increased significantly, rising from slightly over 7 million square feet in 1994 to nearly 9.7 million square feet in 1997. OSB uses compressed strands of wood laid in alternating layers with a phenol-formaldehyde adhesive and is structurally equivalent to plywood. OSB has a distinct advantage over plywood in that OSB utilizes tree species that once were deemed to be very undesirable, in particular aspen. OSB production started in the lake states, where aspen is very abundant, grows in pure stands because it is a pioneer species, and is very prolific in propagation from cuttings. Scientists utilized this wood and tweaked the production processes to yield OSB. Since peeler logs are not needed, as they are in the production of plywood products, producers have cheaper raw material costs. Furthermore, producers can use smaller-diameter logs and are not as reliant on raw material derived from publicly owned lands.

The production of OSB has fallen in relation to operating capacity as more mills in the United States and Canada have been built. Consequently, the price received for OSB has fallen, prompting some mills throughout North America to curtail production in the hopes of seeing prices increase. Competition is

TABLE 7-5: Reconstituted Wood Products (SIC 2493) Trends and Forecasts

(millions of dollars except as noted)

	1992	1993	1994	1995	1996	1997[1]	1998[2]	1999[3]	Percent Change 96–97	Percent Change 97–98	Percent Change 98–99	Percent Change 92–96[4]
Industry data												
Value of shipments[5]	3,986	4,669	5,344	5,202	5,141	5,300	5,434	5,560	3.1	2.5	2.3	6.6
Value of shipments (1992$)	3,986	4,180	4,388	4,264	4,470	4,565	4,658	4,755	2.1	2.0	2.1	2.9
Total employment (thousands)	22.8	23.5	24.3	25.0	26.1	26.8	27.0	27.2	2.7	0.7	0.7	3.4
Production workers (thousands)	18.6	19.2	19.7	20.4	21.1	21.9	22.1	22.3	3.8	0.9	0.9	3.2
Average hourly earnings ($)	11.49	11.72	11.85	11.92	12.73	12.98	13.14	13.34	2.0	1.2	1.5	2.6
Capital expenditures	143	171	333	438	573	612	640	645	6.8	4.6	0.8	41.5
Product data												
Value of shipments[5]	3,987	4,658	5,338	5,160	5,111	5,435	5,609	5,906	6.3	3.2	5.3	6.4
Value of shipments (1992$)	3,987	4,170	4,382	4,229	4,444	4,688	4,899	5,095	5.5	4.5	4.0	2.8
Trade data												
Value of imports	402	581	834	963	1,067	1,146	1,270	1,350	7.4	10.8	6.3	27.6
Value of exports	244	256	292	307	308	355	375	398	15.3	5.6	6.1	6.0

[1] Estimate except imports and exports.
[2] Estimate.
[3] Forecast.
[4] Compound annual rate.
[5] For a definition of industry versus product values, see "Getting the Most Out of *Outlook '99*."
Source: U.S. Department of Commerce: Bureau of the Census; International Trade Administration.

expected to intensify, and the export markets are seen as a way to increase the prices received for OSB. Exports of OSB have increased steadily, rising from $238 million in 1992 to over $595 million in 1997, and are expected to continue to increase slightly.

The other products in this category are used mainly in decorative and furniture and case good applications. These products are very fiber-efficient and average around 92 percent recovery rates from a log during the production process. Also, as in OSB production, producers can use smaller-diameter logs, which are less expensive and more available than are the peeler logs used in other types of panel production. A large number of producers also buy waste products such as sawdust from lumber mills and turn them into particleboard, MDF, and hardboard products. Because of its uniformity, flatness, and dimensional stability, particleboard is used primarily for floor underlayment, kitchen counter underlayment, furniture components, and cabinet components. According to industry data, in 1997 particleboard shipments totaled 4.4 billion square feet on a ¾-inch basis, a 2 percent increase over 1996.

Hardboard is used primarily in the construction industry for exterior siding in new residential construction. Unlike particleboard, which uses a relatively high amount of binders, hardboard is produced mainly by compressing wood fibers under extreme heat and pressure to form a panel. Hardboard also is used in industrial applications such as furniture and case goods as well as in the repair and remodeling sector.

MDF is used primarily in furniture and cabinetry applications because of its smoothness, dimensional stability, and paintability and the sharp lines that are left after a decorative cut is made on the panel. MDF uses wood fibers and binders and then is heated and pressed to yield a panel. Consumption of MDF is also increasing in the molding and millwork industries. An increasing amount of newly constructed housing may use MDF wainscoting and other decorative applications. MDF shipments continue to increase, and in 1997 shipments grew to 1.6 billion square feet on a ¾-inch basis. Competition for MDF sales is increasing as capacity rises from both established and new mills.

International Competitiveness

Both value and volume exports of the reconstituted wood products segment increased in 1997 to $355 million. Canada, the United Kingdom, Mexico, and Japan are the largest markets for these products. Exports increased mainly as a result of increasing global acceptance of OSB for use in construction applications. Japan, a rapidly growing market for OSB because of its initiative to reduce housing costs one-third by 2000, may prove to be a troubling market as its domestic economy stagnates. Exports are expected to continue to grow, but at a slower rate than they did in 1997.

In 1997 imports from Canada accounted for over 78 percent of U.S. imports. Those exports are expected to increase at a rate higher than that of export growth as a result of intense competition from Canada and the capacity Canada has added in the last couple of years.

Industry and Trade Projections for the Next 1 and 5 Years

Reconstituted wood products are forecast to increase shipments 4.0 percent in 1998 and 1999 as strong demand from the furniture market will prove to be especially beneficial to particleboard, MDF, and hardboard producers. Furthermore, the increased use of OSB in residential construction and the increase in the number of producing mills should allow this sector to increase shipments.

However, as in other sectors in the wood products industry, growth in this sector will be somewhat restrained by economic conditions in Japan and throughout Asia. OSB has been making significant inroads in the Japanese residential construction market as that country and the United States have worked successfully on addressing the various building code and product standards issues that affect the use of OSB but is now threatened by Japan's recession. As an increasing amount of OSB production is coming on-line in North America, increased export opportunities are paramount for this subsector's longer-term health. Over the period 1998–2003 growth is expected to increase 3.3 percent per year as the furniture markets and residential construction remain healthy.

Chris Twarok, U.S. Department of Commerce, Office of Metals, Materials, and Chemicals, (202) 482-0377, October 1998.

■ REFERENCES

Crow's Weekly Letter, C.C. Crow Publications, Inc., P.O. Box 25749, Portland, OR 97225. (503) 646-8075.

Hardwood Stock Panels Annual Statistical Report for 1995, Hardwood Plywood and Veneer Association, 1825 Michael Faraday Drive, P.O. Box 2789, Reston, VA 22090. (703) 435-2900.

Market Barometer, Composite Panel Association, 1828 Premier Court, Gaithersburg, MD 20879. (301) 670-0604.

1997 Statistical Yearbook of the Western Lumber Industry, Western Wood Products Association, Yeon Building, 522 SW Fifth Avenue, Portland, OR 97204. (503) 224-3930.

Panels: Products, Applications and Production Trends, 2d Edition, Miller-Freeman, Inc., 600 Harrison Street, San Francisco, CA 94107.

Random Lengths, Random Lengths Publications, Inc., P.O. Box 867, Eugene, OR 97440. (503) 686-9925.

Solid Wood Products Statistical Roundup, American Forest and Paper Association, 1111 19th Street, NW, Suite 800, Washington, DC 20036. (202) 463-2700.

Structural Panels, C.C. Crow Publications, Inc., P.O. Box 25749, Portland, OR 97225. (503) 646-8075.

Structural Panels and Engineered Wood Products, APA—The Engineered Wood Association, P.O. Box 11700, Tacoma, WA 98411. (206) 565-6600.

Weekly Hardwood Review, P.O. Box 471307, Charlotte, NC 28247. (704) 543-4408.

■ RELATED CHAPTERS

6: Construction
8: Construction Materials
38: Household Consumer Durables

CONSTRUCTION MATERIALS
Economic and Trade Trends

U.S. International Trade

Source: U.S. Department of Commerce: Bureau of the Census; International Trade Administration.

World Export Market Shares

Source: United Nations; U.S. Department of Commerce, International Trade Administration.

Export Dependence and Import Penetration

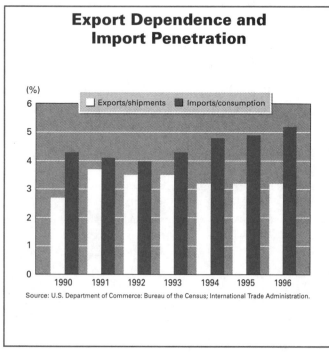

Source: U.S. Department of Commerce: Bureau of the Census; International Trade Administration.

Output and Output per Hour

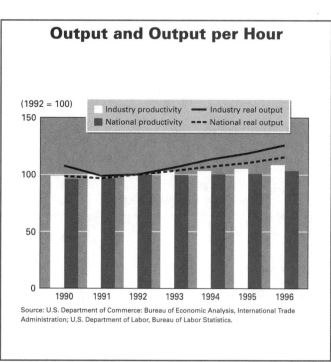

Source: U.S. Department of Commerce: Bureau of Economic Analysis, International Trade Administration; U.S. Department of Labor, Bureau of Labor Statistics.

See "Getting the Most Out of *Outlook '99*" for definitions of terms.

Construction Materials

INDUSTRY DEFINITION The construction materials described in this chapter are produced by industries that make various types of mineral, metal, and plastic building products. The only wood-based products mentioned are manufactured housing and wood prefabricated buildings; other wood products are covered in Chapter 7. The construction materials discussed in detail are fabricated structural metal (SIC 3441), cement (SIC 3241), flat glass (SIC 3211), prefabricated metal buildings (SIC 3448), mobile homes (SIC 2451), prefabricated wood buildings (SIC 2452), gypsum products (SIC 3275), brick and structural clay tile (SIC 3251), ceramic tile (SIC 3253), and plumbing products (SIC 3088, 3261, 3431, 3432).

GLOBAL INDUSTRY TRENDS

Many U.S. construction materials firms of all sizes are active exporters. Some of those firms produce overseas, and others have joint ventures and licensing partners in other countries. Most U.S. producers of construction materials, however, are small companies that are concerned primarily with local or regional domestic markets.

Among the industries covered in this chapter, flat glass, fabricated structural metal, plumbing equipment, and prefabricated metal buildings have the highest levels of exports. Other non-lumber materials with significant levels of exports that are not covered in detail include builders' hardware, plastic pipe and fittings, and mineral wool insulation. The major customers for construction materials are Canada, Mexico, Italy, Taiwan, and Japan. Product categories with high levels of competition from imports include flat glass, ceramic tiles, and cement; the major suppliers have been Canada, Mexico, Italy, and Japan. Information on the export and import roles of the construction materials product categories addressed in this chapter is summarized in Table 8-1.

Internationalization of the construction materials sector continues. Not only are U.S.-based firms moving overseas, but foreign producers have expanded their role in the United States. The latter have purchased U.S. firms of all sizes, built new plants, and licensed their technologies in this country. Foreign participation is particularly high in the U.S. cement, clay brick, and flat glass industries. Among the building product sectors

with high levels of overseas U.S. investment are flat glass, insulation, flooring, and gypsum board.

The popularity of U.S. construction materials in foreign markets is based on both quality and price. U.S. products used in construction often are priced very competitively, but there are many barriers to overseas sales, and those barriers often go well beyond tariff levels. They include restrictive standards, building codes, product certification, and testing procedures. Closed distribution systems in some countries constitute another problem.

DOMESTIC TRENDS

The level of new domestic construction activity is the major factor that determines growth in sales of construction materials. The cyclical nature of construction activity is a short-term factor. The market for specific products depends on the mix of construction, as some products are used mainly in residential buildings, some in commercial buildings, and others in heavy construction or infrastructure work. There are times when some of these elements do well and others do not. The overall strength of the economy and the level of interest rates are key influences. Although it still plays a relatively minor role in construction materials overall, the strength of foreign construction markets and of foreign competition in the United States will become increasingly important. Also meaningful is the market for construction materials used in maintaining, fixing up, and adding to

TABLE 8-1: U.S. Trade Patterns in Construction Materials[1] in 1997
(millions of dollars; percent)

Regions[2]	Exports Value[3]	Exports Share, %	Regions[2]	Imports Value[3]	Imports Share, %
NAFTA	586	42.5	NAFTA	1,297	43.8
Latin America	142	10.3	Latin America	228	7.7
Western Europe	172	12.5	Western Europe	1,005	34.0
Japan/Chinese Economic Area	314	22.8	Japan/Chinese Economic Area	341	11.5
Other Asia	74	5.4	Other Asia	53	1.8
Rest of world	88	6.4	Rest of world	36	1.2
World[2]	1,377	100.0	World	2,960	100.0
Top Five Countries	**Value**	**Share, %**	**Top Five Countries**	**Value**	**Share, %**
Canada	463	33.6	Canada	809	27.3
Japan	231	16.8	Mexico	488	16.5
Mexico	123	8.9	Italy	368	12.4
Luxembourg	60	4.4	Spain	214	7.2
Hong Kong (PRC)	43	3.1	Taiwan	190	6.4

[1] SIC 3088, 3211, 3241, 3251, 3253, 3261, 3275, 3431, 3432, 3441.
[2] For definitions of regional groupings, see "Getting the Most Out of *Outlook '99.*"
[3] Values may not sum to total due to rounding.
Source: U.S. Department of Commerce, Bureau of the Census.

existing structures. Expenditures for residential renovation construction account for about $120 billion in revenues a year.

ENVIRONMENTAL, ENERGY, AND SECURITY ISSUES

Various environmental, energy, and security issues have implications for the design, manufacture, and use of construction materials. The popular products are those which save energy, increase quality and endurance, reduce cost (product and installation), utilize waste materials or substitutes for products that create energy and/or environmental problems, or improve safety and security. These needs are increasing the level of design and product research and development, and expenditures will grow as a result. Better insulation, weather stripping, and design not only will cut heating and cooling costs but will conserve fuel. New technology that allows for better interior air quality, lighting efficiency, and security systems will continue to be a priority. The use of building products that utilize waste materials is growing. Other developments include new building boards, engineered wood products, improved insulation materials, plastic lumber, and concrete with greater utilization of blended cements.

Energy intensity and environmental issues are key factors in the production of several construction materials. Cement is the best example because of important issues involving air pollution, fuel use, and climatic change. Other industries with significant energy and/or environmental involvement are flat glass, fiberglass insulation, and plumbing products. Firms that deal in the many plastic-based construction products face the usual issues that affect petrochemical industries.

PROJECTIONS OF INDUSTRY AND TRADE GROWTH FOR THE NEXT 1 AND 5 YEARS

New U.S. construction in real terms is expected to grow about 3 percent in 1998 after experiencing 2 percent average annual increases from 1991 through 1997 (see Chapter 6: Construction). A similar average annual rise was experienced in the 1980s. The forecast for 1999 calls for a 1 percent rise. Growth of about 1 percent a year is anticipated from 1999 through 2003. A 1 to 2 percent annual increase is forecast for additions, alterations, and repair work on existing structures. These expected trends will support a continuing modest gain in the demand for construction materials in 1999 and over this 5-year period. The market for specific products will depend on the mix of construction activity over these years. For example, some products, such as plumbing equipment, ceramic tile, clay brick, flat glass, prefabricated wood buildings, mobile homes, and gypsum board, are primarily dependent on the residential and nonresidential building markets. Fabricated structural steel and cement are used in all types of construction, particularly public works and nonresidential construction. Prefabricated metal buildings are used in the nonresidential building market.

GLOBAL MARKET PROSPECTS

U.S. exports of construction materials have been increasing over the last several years, but imports have risen at a faster pace. In 1996 U.S. exports of all nonwood construction materials reached $4.94 billion, up 9 percent from 1995. In 1996 imports reached $6.75 billion, a 14 percent increase from 1995. This resulted in a U.S. trade deficit of about $1.8 billion.

For the 13 SIC industries covered in this chapter, current dollar product shipments should total about $51.7 billion in 1998. Exports for those industries should amount to about $2 billion, approximately 4 percent of total shipments. Imports will be higher at $3.3 billion, or about 6 percent of the U.S. consumption of these construction products.

This growth in trade basically reflects the strength of the U.S. and world construction markets. U.S. foreign trade in these products traditionally reflects the strength of the domestic market. When U.S. demand is strong, imports often rise faster than do exports. When the U.S. construction industry is depressed, imports often decline while exports increase.

Over the long term, overall levels of U.S. exports and imports of construction materials are expected to grow annually through 2003. Imports are likely to grow about 8 to 9 percent, while exports should rise 4 to 5 percent annually. The U.S. market will continue to be a large and strong market for foreign suppliers, while rising levels of construction activity worldwide should help U.S. exports. Financial problems in Asia probably will reduce previously expected U.S. sales to that area of the world in 1998 and 1999 while adding to the level of U.S. imports.

FABRICATED STRUCTURAL METAL

The fabricated structural metal industry (SIC 3441) is almost totally demand-dependent on the construction sector, with about 95 percent of its output going into various types of structures. Commercial and industrial buildings account for about 65 percent of this work. Other important markets include various types of public buildings, churches, sports facilities, government buildings, hospitals, infrastructure construction (bridges and tunnels), drilling rigs, and utility facilities. In the residential construction sector most of this material is used in high-rise apartment and condominium buildings.

U.S. shipments of fabricated structural metal in real terms have increased over the last few years (see Table 8-2) as a result of rising levels of nonresidential building construction. In 1996 they rose almost 5 percent in real terms. Increases in the range of 4 to 5 percent occurred in 1997 and 1998. A modest 2 percent rise is forecast for 1999. Expectations through the year 2003 are for average annual increases of 1 to 2 percent.

Fabricated structural steel competes mainly with reinforced concrete construction and factory-produced precast/prestressed, and prefabricated metal building elements. Other masonry, specifically brick, also competes with steel, but it is usually only a facing material and is not used structurally. American Institute of Steel Construction data indicate that steel has about a 50 percent share of the industrial buildings market and a slightly higher share of the market for commercial and office buildings. Masonry (clay brick and concrete) construction accounts for the balance of the nonresidential building market.

Capacity utilization, although rising somewhat, continues to be low. The industry is decreasing production capacity as plants close or downsize.

Research and development (R&D) continues to strengthen fabricated structural steel sales and increase steel product use in the nonresidential construction field and to increase applications in the residential sector. Metal framing systems have been developed and are being used in single-family and low-rise multifamily dwellings, replacing the traditional lumber

TABLE 8-2: Fabricated Structural Metal (SIC 3441) Trends and Forecasts
(millions of dollars except as noted)

	1992	1993	1994	1995	1996	1997[1]	1998[2]	1999[3]	96–97	97–98	98–99	92–96[4]
									Percent Change			
Industry data												
Value of shipments[5]	8,919	9,245	9,857	10,918	11,744	12,542	13,160		6.8	4.9		7.1
Value of shipments (1992$)	8,919	9,144	9,450	10,166	10,551	11,057	11,488	11,740	4.8	3.9	2.2	4.3
Total employment (thousands)	72.0	70.7	71.4	74.3	75.5							1.2
Production workers (thousands)	50.8	50.8	51.6	54.3	55.7							2.3
Average hourly earnings ($)	10.97	11.16	11.24	11.45	11.69							1.6
Capital expenditures	133	130	149	166	172							6.6
Product data												
Value of shipments[5]	8,073	8,455	8,915	9,897	10,751	11,481	12,048		6.8	4.9		7.4
Value of shipments (1992$)	8,073	8,363	8,548	9,215	9,659	10,123	10,518	10,750	4.8	3.9	2.2	4.6
Trade data												
Value of imports	23.4	61.9	79.5	105	134	151	175	185	12.7	15.9	5.7	54.7
Value of exports	60.6	68.5	71.3	81.9	97.8	120	135	140	22.7	12.5	3.7	12.7

[1] Estimate except exports and imports.
[2] Estimate.
[3] Forecast.
[4] Compound annual rate.
[5] For a definition of industry versus product values, see "Getting the Most Out of *Outlook '99*."
Source: U.S. Department of Commerce, Bureau of the Census; forecasts by author.

products. Home builder organizations have been encouraging the use of this technology, as they have encountered higher prices for lumber and wood products and fear future shortages. Specifically, R&D has been funded for metal-deck framing systems that require no interior beams for spans up to 30 feet, metal studding systems, and newer high-yield stress steels.

The United States both exports and imports sizable volumes of fabricated structural metal. U.S. exports have increased considerably in the last several years. In 1997 they totaled $120 million with Canada, Mexico, and the United Kingdom being the major customers. Imports have risen faster in the 1990s, reaching $151 million in 1997. Leading suppliers to the United States include Canada, Germany, Mexico, and Japan.

CEMENT

The output of the cement industry (SIC 3241) is vital to the construction sector. Cement is used in virtually all types of construction activity, but its major market is nonresidential construction; the residential sector accounts for only about 30 percent of demand. The ready-mix concrete industry is the major customer for cement, accounting for about 60 percent of shipments. Concrete product producers (pipe, block, brick, precast, prestressed, and dry mix) purchase another 11 percent. Direct sales to construction contractors account for about 6 percent, and sales to building materials dealers, hardware stores, lumber yards, and home centers represent another 3 percent of demand. The rest is purchased directly by the government, oil well drillers, and miscellaneous users.

Cement demand tends to track levels of overall construction activity, particularly construction in the nonresidential sector (see Chapter 6: Construction). Although domestic shipments will rise, imports will be used to satisfy much of the increase, as domestic production is close to full capacity. Public works construction tends to be especially cement-intensive. With overall construction activity expected to rise slightly in 1999, cement shipments should increase about 1 percent (consumption will be up about 2 percent). Over the period 1999–2003 cement demand should rise about 1 to 2 percent a year on average (see Table 8-3).

Foreign investment in the U.S. cement industry rose rapidly in the 1980s, and about 65 to 70 percent of U.S. capacity is currently foreign-owned. Internationalization of the U.S. and world cement industries is continuing. Large international firms, many with capacity in the United States, have been purchasing firms and plants around the world. Interestingly, firms that produce in the United States account for three-quarters or more of all the imports coming into this country.

The United States is by far a net importer of cement. Imports have become an important part of the U.S. supply; they reached almost 16 million tons in 1996, satisfying 16 percent by volume of U.S. consumption (see Table 8-4). In 1997 import volume rose about 24 percent over 1996, with the imports accounting for 19 percent by volume of U.S. cement consumption. This compares to similar peaks in 1987 and 1988, when U.S. demand was strong and imports were abundant, and contrasts with the 8 to 9 percent levels in 1992 and 1993, when the U.S. construction sector was recovering from a recession. In 1997 most cement imports came from Canada (about 30 percent), with Venezuela, Spain, and Greece being

TABLE 8-3: Hydraulic Cement (SIC 3241) Trends and Forecasts

(millions of dollars except as noted)

| | 1992 | 1993 | 1994 | 1995 | 1996 | 1997[1] | 1998[2] | 1999[3] | Percent Change | | | |
									96–97	97–98	98–99	92–96[4]
Industry data												
Value of shipments[5]	4,051	4,187	4,808	5,342	5,818	5,964	6,205		2.5	4.0		9.5
Value of shipments (1992$)	4,051	3,987	4,278	4,437	4,618	4,710	4,781	4,820	2.0	1.5	0.8	3.3
Total employment (thousands)	17.0	16.6	16.6	16.8	16.9							−0.1
Production workers (thousands)	12.8	12.5	12.4	12.6	12.5							−0.6
Average hourly earnings ($)	15.15	15.48	15.80	16.40	16.75							2.5
Capital expenditures	226	227	280	282	495							21.7
Product data												
Value of shipments[5]	3,929	4,051	4,699	5,172	5,650	5,792	6,025		2.5	4.0		9.5
Value of shipments (1992$)	3,929	3,858	4,180	4,296	4,484	4,574	4,643	4,680	2.0	1.5	0.8	3.4
Trade data												
Value of imports	251	284	444	542	596	753	830	870	26.3	10.2	4.8	24.1
Value of exports	50.3	49.3	46.8	56.0	59.1	60.2	64.5	68.0	1.9	7.1	5.4	4.1

[1] Estimate except exports and imports.
[2] Estimate.
[3] Forecast.
[4] Compound annual rate.
[5] For a definition of industry versus product values, see "Getting the Most Out of *Outlook '99*."
Source: U.S. Department of Commerce, Bureau of the Census; forecasts by author.

TABLE 8-4: Cement Imports in U.S. Consumption
(thousands of short tons)

Year	Domestic Shipments	Exports	Imports	Consumption[1]	Consumption, Percent Change	Imports as a Percent of Consumption
1986	75,441	59	16,128	91,510		17.6
1987	76,402	52	17,536	93,886	2.6	18.7
1988	75,991	101	17,365	93,255	−0.7	18.6
1989	75,447	511	15,741	90,677	−2.8	17.4
1990	76,904	554	13,273	89,623	−1.2	14.8
1991	71,819	698	8,701	79,822	−10.9	10.9
1992	75,770	822	6,797	81,745	2.4	8.3
1993	81,704	689	7,782	88,797	8.6	8.8
1994	83,562	698	12,459	95,323	7.3	13.1
1995	80,295	837	15,265	94,723	−0.6	16.1
1996	84,958	885	15,605	99,678	5.2	15.7
1997	85,987	872	19,396	104,511	4.8	18.6

[1] Shipments plus imports less exports.
Source: U.S. Department of the Interior, U.S. Geological Survey.

the next largest suppliers. Other major suppliers include Turkey, Mexico (which was the largest supplying country before the dumping actions of the early 1990s), Colombia, and Sweden (see Figure 8-1). The United States has little cement available for export. Exports account for about 1 percent of U.S. production, and most go to Canada.

One of the most important issues facing the U.S. cement industry is energy and environmental regulation. In many ways it is difficult to separate the two. The manufacturing process involves a high-temperature, seven-days-a-week, around-the-clock operation that uses coal as the primary fuel. The cement industry has long operated under special U.S. Environmental Protection Agency (EPA) regulations regarding cement dust, including some changes that were proposed in the last few years. This industry also has special emission problems that have become more important because of the coal burning and the chemical process when limestone and other materials are transformed into cement clinker—the material that comes out of the kiln—which is then mixed with gypsum and finely ground into finished cement. This process emits carbon, nitrogen oxide, and sulfur dioxide, which have been named as contributors to climatic change, the thinning ozone layer, and urban smog. The energy intensity in this industry involves the huge volume of coal required to make cement clinker. Energy accounts for 30 to 40 percent of total cement manufacturing costs.

Capital intensity is a related problem. New plants can cost as much as $300 million, and major modernizations and expansions can cost more than $50 million. Most capital expenditures in the late 1980s and early 1990s were for replacement equipment (kilns, crushers, mixers, etc.), to meet environmental requirements, and for energy conservation projects. No new plants were built in that period, largely because of high capital costs, excess capacity in some markets, and the weakened financial status of the producers. Starting in the second half of the 1990s, however, the number of major modernizations has increased, and a few new plants are being built or are in the planning process. Although it is not clear at this time, potentially

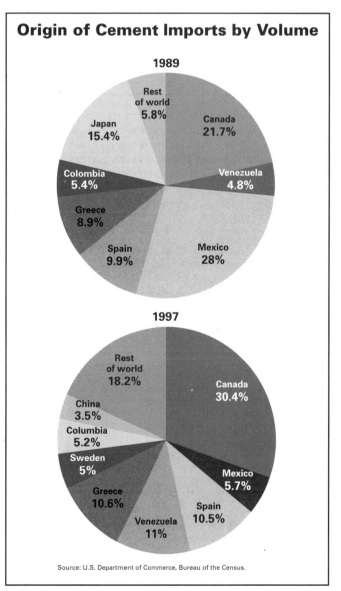

Origin of Cement Imports by Volume

1989

Rest of world 5.8%
Japan 15.4%
Colombia 5.4%
Greece 8.9%
Spain 9.9%
Canada 21.7%
Venezuela 4.8%
Mexico 28%

1997

Rest of world 18.2%
China 3.5%
Columbia 5.2%
Sweden 5%
Greece 10.6%
Venezuela 11%
Spain 10.5%
Mexico 5.7%
Canada 30.4%

Source: U.S. Department of Commerce, Bureau of the Census.

FIGURE 8-1

more stringent environmental regulations for the industry could inhibit domestic capacity expansion and further encourage imports. This will be determined over the next few years as U.S. and international regulations related to climatic change are approved and enforced.

Climatic change issues and proposals could have a significant effect on the industry in the coming years. As a result of the energy crisis of the 1970s, government programs required much of the industry to convert from natural gas and oil to coal. To save energy, the industry accelerated the conversion of kilns from a wet to a dry process and introduced "tightening-up" measures to save energy. In the 1990s there has been pressure to switch back to natural gas because of the environmental climatic change and ozone layer issues involved with coal use. Many cement plants in the United States also burn various waste materials and have worked with some hazardous waste materials, depending on EPA and state regulations. Many in the industry are encouraging a greater use of blended cements, which require less cement in concrete mixes and allow for a greater use of waste material substitutes such as coal ash and slag.

FLAT GLASS

The flat glass industry (SIC 3211) consists of firms that manufacture float glass (i.e., flat glass with a nearly true optical surface made by floating a molten glass sheet on a molten tin bed), and fabricate it into products such as windshields for motor vehicles and architectural glass panes for windows and doors. All six of the U.S. float glass producer companies are vertically integrated and fabricate their float glass into end-use products. They also sell glass to other firms that only fabricate. Some U.S. producers are Japanese- or British-owned. Among the U.S. firms are four of the world's largest producers.

Shipments of flat glass (see Table 8-5) rose 3 percent in real terms in 1997 after an increase of almost 10 percent in 1996. An increase of less than 2 percent is expected for 1998, and the forecast for 1999 calls for a rise in the range of 2 to 3 percent. The longer-term outlook is for about a 2 percent average annual increase through the year 2003. This forecast is based on modest expectations for growth in the construction and automotive sectors.

The production of float glass is both energy- and capital-intensive. A typical new plant costs between $100 million and $120 million. The production of float glass involves a 24-hour-a-day process in which a considerable amount of fuel (natural gas or fuel oil) is consumed.

The float glass producers are export-oriented, while the fabricators, which include small and medium-size companies, are more domestic market–oriented. In the 1990s the U.S. flat glass industry has had a rising level of exports. In 1997 exports totaled $810 million, up from $793 million in 1996 and about $500 million in 1992. This growth was due to aggressive marketing abroad and favorable foreign exchange rates. U.S. imports totaled $492 million in 1997, up from $463 million in 1996 and about $278 million in 1992. Most imports come from Canada, Mexico, and Japan.

Demand for flat glass has been particularly strong in recent years as the construction and motor vehicle sectors have remained healthy after the recession of the early 1990s. The production capacity utilization rate for float glass production

TABLE 8-5: Flat Glass (SIC 3211) Trends and Forecasts
(millions of dollars except as noted)

	1992	1993	1994	1995	1996	1997[1]	1998[2]	1999[3]	Percent Change 96–97	97–98	98–99	92–96[4]
Industry data												
Value of shipments[5]	2,073	2,283	2,600	2,598	2,671	2,746	2,790		2.8	1.6		6.5
Value of shipments (1992$)	2,073	2,234	2,346	2,213	2,417	2,490	2,530	2,595	3.0	1.6	2.6	3.9
Total employment (thousands)	11.8	11.3	11.2	11.2	11.5							–0.6
Production workers (thousands)	9.7	9.2	9.2	9.1	9.3							–1.0
Average hourly earnings ($)	17.45	18.03	19.01	19.73	19.39							2.7
Capital expenditures	148	159	137	170	248							13.8
Product data												
Value of shipments[5]	1,994	2,151	2,474	2,474	2,555	2,625	2,668		2.8	1.6		6.4
Value of shipments (1992$)	1,994	2,105	2,233	2,107	2,312	2,381	2,419	2,480	3.0	1.6	2.5	3.8
Trade data												
Value of imports	278	341	416	399	463	492	520	530	6.3	5.7	1.9	13.6
Value of exports	499	583	620	687	793	810	825	860	2.1	1.9	4.2	12.3

[1] Estimate except exports and imports.
[2] Estimate.
[3] Forecast.
[4] Compound annual rate.
[5] For a definition of industry versus product values, see "Getting the Most Out of *Outlook '99*."
Source: U.S. Department of Commerce, Bureau of the Census; forecasts by author.

grew from about 80 to 85 percent in 1989–1990 to almost 100 percent currently.

Construction applications account for 50 to 55 percent of total flat glass use, and motor vehicles for another 25 percent. Other products, such as furniture, appliances, machines, and other transportation equipment (primarily naval, aircraft, and aerospace equipment), account for the rest. The glass replacement market is also a significant factor in the construction and automotive sectors.

PREFABRICATED BUILDINGS

This section covers three industries that produce prefabricated buildings in permanent plants. The prefabricated metal buildings industry (SIC 3448) is composed of firms that fabricate the components of complete low-rise nonresidential building systems such as office buildings, retail stores, fast-food restaurants, warehouses, recreational facilities, manufacturing facilities, schools, churches, storage buildings, and agricultural buildings. The mobile home industry (SIC 2451) produces units, now also called manufactured homes, that are made to the U.S. Department of Housing and Urban Development National Manufactured Housing Standard. The prefabricated wood building industry (SIC 2452) includes firms that make panelized and modular units. Prefabricated wood units are built to either local building codes or statewide factory-built housing codes. A major advantage of prefabrication in all types of buildings is that these units are built faster and are available much sooner to the buyer. Factory quality and cost controls are also key factors in the success of these industries.

Prefabricated Metal Buildings (SIC 3448)

Prefabricated metal buildings are particularly popular as nonresidential structures of less than 150,000 square feet. These buildings have a 65 percent share of this nonresidential market compared with about 50 percent in 1990 and 35 percent in the early 1970s.

Because the growth of the nonresidential buildings market is expected to continue and as a result of the popularity of this type of building, a growth in product shipments of almost 3 percent is forecast for 1999 (see Table 8–6) and a 2 to 3 percent annual average growth is anticipated through 2003.

Among the reasons for the popularity of these structures are affordability, faster completion and occupation times, and high quality. Faster construction results in a quicker return on investment for the owner. Factory fabrication of components for these structures usually offers better quality control and reduces the weather and seasonality factor.

These structures often are sold through manufacturer representatives who act as builder-dealers. Most of these dealers are independent and provide the staff for engineering and erecting the buildings.

Exports of these structures have been growing significantly. In 1997 they totaled $230 million, down slightly from $233 million in 1996 but up from $143 million in 1992. Although the value of exports is substantial, exports represent only about 5 percent of domestic output. The U.S. industry is considered a leader in the design and production of these units and enjoys a reputation for quality and service. Among the major foreign markets are China, Canada, and Argentina. The size of the construction market in China and that country's need for various

TABLE 8-6: Prefabricated Metal Buildings (SIC 3448) Trends and Forecasts
(millions of dollars except as noted)

| | 1992 | 1993 | 1994 | 1995 | 1996 | 1997[1] | 1998[2] | 1999[3] | Percent Change | | | |
									96–97	97–98	98–99	92–96[4]
Industry data												
Value of shipments[5]	2,789	3,314	3,857	4,352	4,512	4,847	5,102		7.4	5.3		12.8
Value of shipments (1992$)	2,789	3,190	3,532	3,775	3,853	4,026	4,275	4,285	4.5	3.7	2.6	8.4
Total employment (thousands)	20.3	23.2	25.3	27.4	28.7							9.0
Production workers (thousands)	13.1	15.6	17.1	19.3	20.0							11.2
Average hourly earnings ($)	10.03	10.69	10.51	10.82	10.77							1.8
Capital expenditures	28.9	34.3	50.5	67.4	73.0							26.1
Product data												
Value of shipments[5]	2,579	3,048	3,581	3,982	3,998	4,295	4,521		7.4	5.3		11.6
Value of shipments (1992$)	2,579	2,934	3,279	3,454	3,414	3,568	3,700	3,795	4.5	3.7	2.6	7.3
Trade data												
Value of imports	7.7	12.7	20.4	33.9	40.2	62.3	65	75	55.0	10.8	8.7	51.2
Value of exports	143	198	197	201	233	230	250	280	–1.3	8.7	12.0	13.0

[1] Estimate except exports and imports.
[2] Estimate.
[3] Forecast.
[4] Compound annual rate.
[5] For a definition of industry versus product values, see "Getting the Most Out of *Outlook '99.*"
Source: U.S. Department of Commerce, Bureau of the Census; forecasts by author.

types of structures offer the U.S. prefabricated metal building industry excellent export opportunities.

Imports rose to about $62 million in 1997, up from $40 million in 1996 and $8 million in 1992. Import growth has also been rapid as European, Japanese, and Canadian companies have developed their products to compete with U.S. firms in third world markets and even in the United States.

Mobile Homes (SIC 2451)

These units, now called manufactured homes, are produced as single-section or multisection dwelling units. Before 1996 the industry produced more single-section than multisection units. In 1996, 52 percent of the 363,411 total units shipped were double- or triple-wide units (see Table 8-7). A small percentage of these units are used for schoolrooms, bank branches, construction site offices, and other commercial applications.

Shipments of manufactured homes are expected to decline about 2 percent in 1998 and are forecast to increase 1 to 2 percent in 1999 (see Table 8-8). Long-term shipments, however, are expected to grow at about a 2 percent average annual rate through 2003. This is much lower than the rate seen between 1991 and 1995, when unit shipments almost doubled.

The problems facing this industry include the "housing trailer" or "mobile home" image. Although these units have improved, safety and quality concerns still exist. The industry continues to encounter zoning restrictions which in many areas virtually "zone out" the use of mobile homes unless they are placed in a manufactured housing park (community).

Despite these problems, demand has grown. Financing options for buyers of manufactured housing are now closer to those for buyers of conventional housing. Owners who place these units on private property can finance the land with the unit for up to 30 years. Prices per square foot for manufactured housing are about half those for site-built units. Manufactured homes, when put on private lots, now appreciate at a rate simi-

lar to that of conventional units. There is also a sizable market for preowned manufactured homes.

Because these units are shipped in a three-dimensional mode, relatively few are exported. Their weight and volume result in very high transportation costs. Most are exported across the border to Canadian customers. U.S. imports are insignificant.

Prefabricated Wood Buildings (SIC 2452)

Prefabricated wood building shipments in 1997 were down about 2 percent in real terms from those in 1996 (see Table 8-9). Shipments in 1998 should be at about the inflation-adjusted level of 1997. The forecast for 1999 is for about a 1 percent decline. The market for prefabricated wood buildings basically follows the trend in new single-family housing. As the popularity of factory-built housing is expected to continue to grow slowly, growth from 1999 to 2003 is expected to average about 1 percent annually, compared with a 1 percent annual decline forecast for the new single-family housing sector in total.

The annual State of the Industry Shapiro Report published by *Automated Builder* magazine shows that in 1997 the panelized sector had 329 companies with 377 plants. There were 130 companies with 172 manufacturing facilities making modular units. Although they are not necessarily classified under SIC 2452, many firms (about 2,200) produce components for homes (roof trusses, wall and floor units, etc.) and a large group (about 7,000) of "production builders" make their own components in a factory (permanent or temporary) or buy them from component producers. The modular and panelized sectors grew in the 1990s and expect a modest improvement in demand for their products.

Because prefabricated wood buildings are built to local building codes or statewide factory-built codes, they do not encounter serious zoning problems. Also, the difference in appearance between these units and conventional housing has

TABLE 8-7: Manufactured Housing Units
(thousands of units; percent)

Year	Single-Wide Shipments	Multiwide Shipments	Total Shipments	Annual Percent Change in Total Shipments	Single-Family Housing Starts	Annual Percent Change	Total Housing Additions[1]	Manufactured Housing, Percent of Total Additions
1987	139.1	93.5	232.6		1,146.4		1,379.0	16.9
1988	122.4	96.0	218.4	−6.1	1,081.3	−5.7	1,299.7	16.8
1989	103.3	94.9	198.3	−9.2	1,003.3	−7.2	1,201.6	16.5
1990	98.6	89.6	188.2	−5.1	894.8	−10.8	1,083.0	17.4
1991	91.1	79.7	170.7	−9.3	840.4	−6.1	1,011.1	16.9
1992	112.1	98.7	210.8	23.5	1,029.9	22.5	1,240.7	17.0
1993	134.4	119.8	254.3	20.6	1,125.7	9.3	1,380.0	18.4
1994	156.2	147.8	303.9	19.5	1,198.4	6.5	1,502.3	20.2
1995	173.8	165.8	339.6	11.7	1,076.2	−10.2	1,415.8	24.0
1996	173.7	189.7	363.4	7.0	1,160.9	7.9	1,524.3	23.8
1997	148.8	204.6	353.4	−2.8	1,133.1	−2.4	1,486.5	23.8

[1] Manufactured housing shipments are not included in housing starts. This column is the total of the shipments and housing starts.
Sources: Manufactured Housing Institute; U.S. Department of Commerce, Bureau of the Census.

TABLE 8-8: Mobile (or Manufactured) Homes (SIC 2451) Trends and Forecasts

(millions of dollars except as noted)

| | 1992 | 1993 | 1994 | 1995 | 1996 | 1997[1] | 1998[2] | 1999[3] | Percent Change | | | |
									96–97	97–98	98–99	92–96[4]
Industry data												
Value of shipments[5]	4,484	5,786	6,890	8,115	9,019	8,880	8,824		−1.5	−0.6		19.1
Value of shipments (1992$)	4,484	5,537	6,135	6,791	7,338	7,133	6,983	7,075	−2.8	−2.1	1.3	13.1
Total employment (thousands)	36.8	42.4	48.4	54.5	60.4							13.2
Production workers (thousands)	30.6	35.7	40.5	45.8	51.4							13.8
Average hourly earnings ($)	9.52	10.07	10.19	10.43	10.96							3.6
Capital expenditures	50.4	78.4	124	89.3	140							29.1
Product data												
Value of shipments[5]	4,446	5,755	6,844	7,964	8,876	8,740	8,685		−1.5	−0.6		18.9
Value of shipments (1992$)	4,446	5,507	6,095	6,664	7,222	7,020	6,875	6,965	−2.8	−2.1	1.3	12.9
Trade data												
Value of imports	1.1	0.5	1.0	1.1	1.1	1.9	2.0	2.0	72.7	5.3	0.0	0.0
Value of exports	17.4	13.8	13.1	17.7	17.3	21.7	22.5	24.0	25.4	3.7	6.7	−0.1

[1] Estimate except exports and imports.
[2] Estimate.
[3] Forecast.
[4] Compound annual rate.
[5] For a definition of industry versus product values, see "Getting the Most Out of *Outlook '99*."
Source: U.S. Department of Commerce, Bureau of the Census; forecasts by author.

TABLE 8-9: Prefabricated Wood Buildings (SIC 2452) Trends and Forecasts

(millions of dollars except as noted)

| | 1992 | 1993 | 1994 | 1995 | 1996 | 1997[1] | 1998[2] | 1999[3] | Percent Change | | | |
									96–97	97–98	98–99	92–96[4]
Industry data												
Value of shipments[5]	2,161	2,327	2,688	2,745	2,871	2,892	2,947		0.7	1.9		7.4
Value of shipments (1992$)	2,161	2,155	2,337	2,284	2,343	2,296	2,296	2,275	−2.0	0.0	−0.9	2.0
Total employment (thousands)	19.2	19.5	20.7	21.5	21.4							2.7
Production workers (thousands)	13.7	14.1	15.4	16.1	16.1							4.1
Average hourly earnings ($)	9.60	9.32	9.84	9.61	10.07							1.2
Capital expenditures	25.2	39.9	44.3	49.5	41.6							13.4
Product data												
Value of shipments[5]	2,164	2,325	2,749	2,644	2,715	2,735	2,787		0.7	1.9		5.8
Value of shipments (1992$)	2,164	2,153	2,391	2,199	2,216	2,172	2,175	2,150	−2.0	0.1	−1.1	0.6
Trade data												
Value of imports	8.5	9.4	21.4	22.5	41.2	41.7	43.0	44.0	1.2	3.1	2.3	48.4
Value of exports	59.8	45.8	74.3	73.1	93.0	97.0	103.0	115.0	4.3	6.2	11.7	11.7

[1] Estimate except exports and imports.
[2] Estimate.
[3] Forecast.
[4] Compound annual rate.
[5] For a definition of industry versus product values, see "Getting the Most Out of *Outlook '99*."
Source: U.S. Department of Commerce, Bureau of the Census; forecasts by author.

become less apparent. However, a prefabricated unit often is less expensive, and quality control generally is better in a plant than it is at a building site. These units definitely can be put in place faster than can site-built units. Although most of the output of this industry is used for residential purposes, some units, particularly modular ones, are used for schoolrooms, offices, and other commercial applications.

Although the United States exports some prefabricated wood buildings, exports account for a small proportion of production. In 1997 exports totaled about $97 million. Modest long-term export growth of about 2 percent annually can be expected through 2003. The major customers include Canada, Japan, and China. Imports of these units are very low, with most originating from Canada.

GYPSUM PRODUCTS

The main markets for the gypsum products industry (SIC 3275) are new housing, new nonresidential buildings, and alterations, repairs, and additions to existing buildings. Gypsum wallboards (also known as sheetrock and plasterboard) account for more than 90 percent of the output of this industry. Various gypsum plasters and compounds account for the remainder.

On the basis of new residential and nonresidential building construction and renovation work on existing buildings, gypsum product shipments rose about 3.2 percent in real terms in 1997 (see Table 8-10). In 1998 a small decline of less than 1 percent was expected, and for 1999 the forecast is for an additional drop of 1 percent. With favorable prospects for long-term building construction, an average annual growth rate of 2 to 3 percent is expected between 1999 and 2003.

U.S. exports of gypsum products totaled $66 million in 1997, compared with $60 million in 1996 and $71 million in 1992. Imports, however, grew to $125 million in 1997, up from $101 million in 1996 and $13 million in 1992. Canada and several Asian countries are the largest customers for U.S. products, while Canada and Mexico are the major suppliers to the United States.

This is a highly concentrated industry, with the three largest producers accounting for 65 to 70 percent of all wallboard output. These three firms also make several other construction material lines and produce gypsum board and other building products in foreign countries.

Because of the weight and relatively low price of gypsum board, shipments usually go no farther than 200 miles from the plant. Therefore, the larger producers have many plants around the United States. The manufacturing process utilizes mostly gypsum and paper. Most gypsum board production goes directly into the distribution system or directly to major customers; little is warehoused at the plant.

This industry produces several types of boards designed for specific markets and needs. Regular board accounts for about 59 percent of all gypsum board shipments, and the Type X board with its superior fire retardant features has a 28 percent share. The 5/16-inch mobile home board accounts for about 6 percent, and the water- and moisture-resistant board for about 3 percent. The remaining 4 percent of sales include lath, veneer base, sheathing, and predecorated boards.

Gypsum board plays a predominant role in the interior wall and ceiling market, particularly in housing construction. It has the advantages of low price, ease of installation, and excellent fire containment characteristics. Plastering has become very expensive, and wood paneling has specialized uses. Building codes usually require that a type of gypsum board be installed under wood paneling. Various composition boards made of combinations of materials (waste wood and paper, gypsum, and cement) are available. Although they are heavier than ordinary gypsum board, they tend to be easier to cut and install, to be less susceptible to breakage and moisture damage, and to hold nails better. Still, these products do not appear to be likely to affect the demand for gypsum board significantly in the near future.

CLAY BRICK

The brick and structural clay tile industry (SIC 3251) is characterized by local markets. Relatively little clay brick is shipped farther than 200 miles from the plant because of the weight

TABLE 8-10: Gypsum Products (SIC 3275) Trends and Forecasts
(millions of dollars except as noted)

	1992	1993	1994	1995	1996	1997[1]	1998[2]	1999[3]	Percent Change 96–97	97–98	98–99	92–96[4]
Industry data												
Value of shipments[5]	2,100	2,290	2,954	3,476	3,826	4,012	4,036		4.9	0.6		16.2
Value of shipments (1992$)	2,100	2,069	2,161	2,249	2,481	2,560	2,547	2,525	3.2	−0.5	−0.9	4.3
Total employment (thousands)	10.6	10.4	10.8	11.3	13.2							5.6
Production workers (thousands)	8.5	8.3	8.6	9.0	10.4							5.2
Average hourly earnings ($)	12.70	13.06	13.42	14.28	14.09							2.6
Capital expenditures	43.8	39.8	74.6	154	123							29.5
Product data												
Value of shipments[5]	1,948	2,133	2,729	3,221	3,712	3,892	3,915		4.8	0.6		17.5
Value of shipments (1992$)	1,948	1,927	1,996	2,083	2,407	2,484	2,472	2,452	3.2	−0.5	−0.8	5.4
Trade data												
Value of imports	13.2	24.5	50.6	75.2	101	125	140	150	23.8	12.0	7.1	66.3
Value of exports	71.2	55.3	50.5	52.9	60.3	65.8	70.0	74.5	9.1	6.4	5.7	−4.1

[1] Estimate except exports and imports.
[2] Estimate.
[3] Forecast.
[4] Compound annual rate.
[5] For a definition of industry versus product values, see "Getting the Most Out of *Outlook '99*."
Source: U.S. Department of Commerce, Bureau of the Census; forecasts by author.

and relatively low cost. These factors also explain why little clay brick is traded internationally. In the 1980s and early 1990s foreign investment in the U.S. industry resulted in 40 percent of U.S. capacity being foreign-owned, mainly by British firms.

Clay brick shipments tend to track new single-family housing closely. Although there is limited use in commercial and institutional construction, the major use for clay brick is as siding on single-family and low-rise multifamily housing. With continuing strength in the residential sector, demand for clay brick rose about 1 percent in 1997 and should remain at about the same level in 1998. Shipments in 1999 are forecast to decline by about 1 percent (see Table 8-11). Short-term changes in demand for brick usually follow the rise and fall of housing starts closely. Over the longer term, little growth is expected through the year 2003.

Although buyers like brick facing on their homes, the percentage of new single-family units that utilize brick has declined over the long term, although it has remained at about the same level over the last several years. The U.S. Census Bureau's *Current Construction Report: Characteristics of New Housing: 1996* shows that brick had a 21 percent share of all new houses sold, with wood at 23 percent, stucco at 16 percent, vinyl at 33 percent, aluminum at 2 percent, and all others at 6 percent. Although brick is not expensive, bricklaying is costly and time-consuming and requires a relatively rare skill. On the positive side, specially shaped and sized clay architectural bricks and blocks designed for the nonresidential building market have gained in use. Clay pavers also have become popular.

Clay brick has been very popular as a siding material in some parts of the United States, but little is used in other areas. The availability of clays for making brick many years ago had much to do with this situation. Over time a regional tradition of brick use developed. Brick is used most often in Ohio and Pennsylvania, many south Atlantic states (particularly the Carolinas and Virginia), some east south central states, and Texas.

Most U.S. foreign trade in brick involves regular sales across the U.S.–Canadian border between U.S. firms and Canadian customers or between Canadian producers and U.S. customers. Several years ago there were sizable sales of Mexican brick in the United States, but quality and other problems have resulted in a relatively low volume of sales to and from Mexico in the 1990s.

CERAMIC TILE

The consumption of ceramic tile (SIC 3253) has increased over the years. Total sales volume of ceramic tile have risen faster than have industry shipments because of imports. These imports have accounted for 50 to 60 percent of domestic consumption by quantity for many years.

In 1997 ceramic tile shipments increased almost 10 percent in 1992 dollars, while imports by square feet rose 16 percent. Another 3 percent rise in shipments is expected in 1998, and a 3 to 4 percent gain is forecast for 1999 (see Tables 8-12 and 8-13). Imports in these years will continue to rise at a faster pace. Ceramic tile consumption over the period 1999–2003 should rise at a 2 to 3 percent average annual rate, but much of this gain will be accounted for by imported products. As a result, the import-to-consumption ratio will remain over 60 percent.

TABLE 8-11: Brick and Structural Clay Tile (SIC 3251) Trends and Forecasts
(millions of dollars except as noted)

	1992	1993	1994	1995	1996	1997[1]	1998[2]	1999[3]	Percent Change 96–97	97–98	98–99	92–96[4]
Industry data												
Value of shipments[5]	1,110	1,199	1,313	1,283	1,422	1,472	1,495		3.5	1.6		6.4
Value of shipments (1992$)	1,110	1,160	1,234	1,175	1,288	1,303	1,303	1,290	1.2	0.0	–1.0	3.8
Total employment (thousands)	14.1	14.7	14.2	13.9	13.8							–0.5
Production workers (thousands)	11.0	11.2	11.0	11.0	11.1							0.2
Average hourly earnings ($)	9.57	9.80	10.05	10.59	10.68							2.8
Capital expenditures	42.9	56.1	63.5	77.1	133							32.7
Product data												
Value of shipments[5]	1,054	1,125	1,213	1,176	1,293	1,339	1,360		3.6	1.6		5.2
Value of shipments (1992$)	1,054	1,088	1,140	1,077	1,172	1,186	1,186	1,175	1.2	0.0	–0.9	2.7
Trade data												
Value of imports	4.6	3.9	4.3	6.0	5.3	5.8	5.9	5.5	9.4	1.7	–6.8	3.6
Value of exports	11.3	11.8	11.0	11.5	11.9	16.5	17.8	18.5	38.7	7.9	3.9	1.3

[1] Estimate except exports and imports.
[2] Estimate.
[3] Forecast.
[4] Compound annual rate.
[5] For a definition of industry versus product values, see "Getting the Most Out of *Outlook '99*."
Source: U.S. Department of Commerce, Bureau of the Census; forecasts by author.

TABLE 8-12: Ceramic Wall and Floor Tile (SIC 3253) Trends and Forecasts
(millions of dollars except as noted)

	1992	1993	1994	1995	1996	1997[1]	1998[2]	1999[3]	Percent Change 96–97	Percent Change 97–98	Percent Change 98–99	Percent Change 92–96[4]
Industry data												
Value of shipments[5]	731	811	847	938	989	1,097	1,156		10.9	5.4		7.8
Value of shipments (1992$)	731	806	829	902	949	1,041	1,074	1,115	9.7	3.2	3.8	6.7
Total employment (thousands)	8.9	8.7	8.6	9.4	9.2							0.8
Production workers (thousands)	7.3	7.3	7.1	7.8	7.7							1.3
Average hourly earnings ($)	9.50	10.41	9.92	10.35	10.41							2.3
Capital expenditures	48.9	68.0	73.1	61.5	45.6							−1.7
Product data												
Value of shipments[5]	678	739	735	790	839	931	981		11.0	5.4		5.5
Value of shipments (1992$)	678	734	719	760	805	883	911	945	9.7	3.2	3.7	4.4
Trade data												
Value of imports	419	472	519	562	628	716	790	835	14.0	10.3	5.7	10.6
Value of exports	19.3	22.6	23.5	26.1	24.6	28.9	32.0	34.0	17.5	10.7	6.3	6.3

[1] Estimate except exports and imports.
[2] Estimate.
[3] Forecast.
[4] Compound annual rate.
[5] For a definition of industry versus product values, see "Getting the Most Out of *Outlook '99*."
Source: U.S. Department of Commerce, Bureau of the Census; forecasts by author.

Imports will benefit from declining U.S. tariffs resulting from negotiations of the North American Free Trade Agreement (NAFTA) and the Uruguay Round of multilateral trade negotiations. As a result of NAFTA, Mexico will have duty-free access to the U.S. market after several years of staged reductions. Faster staging of tariff reductions has been proposed by Mexican and some U.S. firms but is opposed by many U.S. producers. As a result of the Uruguay Round, tariffs on imports from other countries will be cut in half over a period of 10 years from 20 percent to just under 10 percent *ad valorem*.

Domestic and global competition for U.S.-made ceramic tile comes from many countries. By far the largest supplier to the world and the United States is Italy, but Mexico is increasing its international presence. In 1997 Italy supplied 34 percent of the total U.S. import volume, Mexico 24 percent, Spain 20 percent, and Brazil 6 percent. Other significant suppliers included Turkey, Indonesia, Argentina, France, and Colombia.

Ceramic tile, although expensive to install, has a reputation for strength, endurance, and good looks. It is considered a luxury product. In the 1970s and 1980s tile lost part of its bathroom market to various plastic bathtub wall units, but in the 1990s it made a comeback in bathrooms and expanded its market in other parts of the home, such as kitchens (floors and countertops), foyers, and sunrooms. There have also been rising applications in commercial and institutional buildings as designers and building owners tend to spend more initially on longer-lasting products that are easier to maintain in order to save later ("life cycle costing").

TABLE 8-13: Ceramic Tile Imports in the U.S. Market
(millions of square feet; percent)

Year	U.S. Shipments	Imports	Consumption[1]	Imports-to-Consumption Ratio, %
1986	452	506	958	52.8
1987	479	523	1,002	52.2
1988	471	523	994	52.6
1989	543	712	1,255	56.7
1990	509	572	1,081	52.9
1991	485	472	957	49.3
1992	496	541	1,037	52.2
1993	559	642	1,201	53.5
1994	604	711	1,315	54.1
1995	606	775	1,381	56.1
1996	580	884	1,464	60.4
1997	636	1,028	1,664	61.8

[1] Exports are low, and volume export data are not available.
Source: U.S. Department of Commerce, Bureau of the Census.

PLUMBING EQUIPMENT

The plumbing equipment sector includes industries that produce fixtures made of various materials: plastic (SIC 3088), vitreous (SIC 3261), and metal (SIC 3431). Also covered in this section is the plumbing fixture fittings and trim industry (SIC 3432), which makes faucets, drains, and showerheads. Most larger plumbing equipment producers make products in several, if not all, of these industries. There are, however, hundreds of small companies specializing in products classified under just one or two of these industries.

TABLE 8-14: Plumbing Parts (SIC 3088, 3261, 3431, 3432) Trends and Forecasts

(millions of dollars except as noted)

	1992	1993	1994	1995	1996	1997[1]	1998[2]	1999[3]	Percent Change 96–97	97–98	98–99	92–96[4]
Industry data												
Value of shipments[5]	5,507	6,007	6,539	6,899	7,753	8,462	9,072		9.1	7.2		8.9
Value of shipments (1992$)	5,507	5,886	6,277	6,395	6,979	7,464	7,837	8,185	6.9	5.0	4.4	6.1
Total employment (thousands)	43.1	45.7	47.5	49.0	50.0							3.8
Production workers (thousands)	33.5	35.0	36.3	37.5	38.7							3.7
Average hourly earnings ($)	11.08	11.03	10.78	11.24	10.85							−0.5
Capital expenditures	137	137	167	180	169							5.4
Product data												
Value of shipments[5]	5,224	5,705	6,294	6,647	7,427	8,105	8,685		9.1	7.2		9.2
Value of shipments (1992$)	5,224	5,586	6,037	6,156	6,679	7,147	7,505	7,840	7.0	5.0	4.5	6.3
Trade data												
Value of imports	375	422	524	575	659	717	780	815	8.8	8.8	4.5	15.1
Value of exports	254	260	256	261	245	276	300	320	12.7	8.7	6.7	−0.9

[1] Estimate except exports and imports.
[2] Estimate.
[3] Forecast.
[4] Compound annual rate.
[5] For a definition of industry versus product values, see "Getting the Most Out of *Outlook '99*."
Source: U.S. Department of Commerce, Bureau of the Census; forecasts by author.

Product shipments in these four industries rose about 7 percent in real terms in 1997 compared with 1996 (see Table 8-14). A 5 percent gain is anticipated for 1998, and a 4.5 percent rise is forecast for 1999. Longer-term growth through 2003 is expected to occur at a 3 to 4 percent average annual rate.

The market for plumbing fixtures is dependent mainly on new housing, but commercial and institutional buildings are also important. There are also significant plumbing equipment replacement and addition markets. Adding and renovating bathrooms and modernizing kitchens have become a very big business for contractors, distributors, and product producers. The market situation for fixture fittings, however, is different from that for fixtures. Fittings have a much stronger repair, replacement, and addition market because they are easier and often less costly to replace than are fixtures and tend to wear out faster.

Growth and continuing strength in the new building construction and renovation markets have resulted in favorable trends in the overall plumbing equipment markets. Plastic fixtures and fittings have tended to experience higher growth over the years than have metal and vitreous ones. Plastics have gained in the residential bathtub, shower stall, lavatory sink, and whirlpool markets at the expense of vitreous and metal. The use of vitreous fixtures is primarily in bathrooms (sinks and toilets), while metal fixtures are employed most often in kitchen sinks (stainless and enameled) but also are still used in bathtubs. Vitreous still has much of the toilet market but has lost market share to plastics in the toilet water tank and lavatory sink markets. The plastics category includes fiberglass reinforced plastic (FRP) and other plastics, including cultured marble. FRP products are gel-coated or acrylic. The U.S. Census Bureau's *Current Industrial Reports: Plumbing Fixtures* shows that overall shipments of plastic fixtures (fiberglass and plastics) reached $1.43 billion in 1996, accounting for 46 percent of total plumbing fixture shipments. Vitreous china accounted for $860 million, or 27 percent of the total. Metal fixtures reached $644 million, a 20 percent share. Other materials had the remaining 7 percent share.

Another favorable factor for plumbing equipment markets is the long-term trend toward including more bathrooms in new homes. The U.S. Census Bureau's *Characteristics of New Housing: 1996* shows that the number of new homes with three or more bathrooms has risen to 16 percent of the total. The number with two and a half baths is at 33 percent, with those with two baths at 41 percent and those with one and a half baths or less at just 10 percent.

Water conservation is a major issue in this industry. Water supply devices and toilet flush designs and devices are the key factors. The Energy Policy Act of 1992 set the maximum number of gallons per flush at less than 1.6, less than half the average gallons per flush previously used in most toilets. Some of the new devices and designs have not provided satisfactory flushing. There also have been problems with some supply devices, such as showerheads, which decrease the water pressure and volume to the point of not cleaning properly. Manufacturers have spent much time and money developing products that work satisfactorily for the consumer but still meet government standards.

Foreign trade in plumbing equipment is significant, but the slow growth in exports has been overshadowed by the rapid increase in imports. Imports in 1997 were almost double those in 1992, while exports were up less than 10 percent.

C. B. Pitcher, formerly U.S. Department of Commerce, Forest Products and Building Materials Division, (202) 482-0132, September 1998.

■ REFERENCES

Call the Bureau of the Census at (301) 457-1242 for information about ordering Census documents.

American Institute of Steel Construction, Inc., One East Wacker Drive, Suite 3100, Chicago, IL 60601-2001. (312) 670-2400.

Automated Builder (monthly), 1445 Donlon Street, Suite 16, Ventura, CA 93003. (805) 642-9735.

Brick Institute of America, 11490 Commerce Park Drive, Reston, VA 22091. (703) 620-0010.

Building Systems Councils, National Association of Home Builders, 1201 15th Street, NW, Washington, DC 20005. (202) 822-0576.

Construction Review (quarterly), International Trade Administration, Room H4039, U.S. Department of Commerce, Washington, DC 20230. (202) 482-0132.

Current Construction Reports: Characteristics of New Housing: 1996 (annual), C25/96, U.S. Bureau of the Census.

Current Industrial Reports: Clay Construction Products (quarterly), MQ32D, U.S. Bureau of the Census.

Current Industrial Reports: Plumbing Fixtures (quarterly), MQ34E, U.S. Bureau of the Census.

Glass Digest (monthly), Ashlee Publishing Co., 110 East 42d Street, New York, NY 10017. (212) 682-7681.

Gypsum Association, 810 First Street, NE, Washington, DC 20002. (202) 289-5440.

Manufactured Housing Institute, 2101 Wilson Boulevard, Arlington, VA 22201-3062. (703) 558-0400.

Metal Building Manufacturers Association, 1300 Summer Avenue, Cleveland, OH 44115-2851. (216) 241-7333.

Mineral Industry Surveys: Cement (monthly), Industrial Minerals Section, U.S. Geological Survey, 983 National Center, Reston, VA 20192.

Mineral Industry Surveys: Gypsum (monthly), Industrial Minerals Section, U.S. Geological Survey, 983 National Center, Reston, VA 20192.

National Glass Association, 8200 Greensboro Drive, McLean, VA 22102. (703) 442-4890.

New Steel (monthly), The Chilton Company, Chilton Way, Radnor, PA 19089. (610) 964-4000.

Plumbing Manufacturers Institute, 800 Roosevelt Road, Glen Ellyn, IL 60137. (708) 858-9172.

Portland Cement Association, 5420 Old Orchard Road, Skokie, IL 60077-1083. (847) 966-6200.

Systems Builders Association, 28 Lowry Drive, West Milton, OH 45383. (513) 698-4127.

Tile Council of America, P.O. Box 1787, Clemson, SC 29633. (803) 646-4021.

■ RELATED CHAPTERS

6: Construction
7: Wood Products
18: Production Machinery

TEXTILES
Economic and Trade Trends

U.S. International Trade

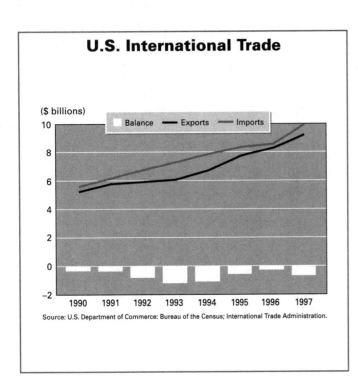

($ billions)

Legend: Balance, Exports, Imports

Source: U.S. Department of Commerce: Bureau of the Census; International Trade Administration.

World Export Market Shares

(%)

Legend: United States, Germany, Hong Kong, South Korea

Source: United Nations; U.S. Department of Commerce, International Trade Administration.

Export Dependence and Import Penetration

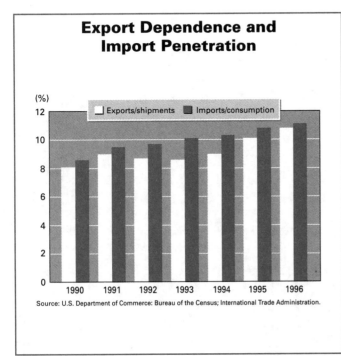

(%)

Legend: Exports/shipments, Imports/consumption

Source: U.S. Department of Commerce: Bureau of the Census; International Trade Administration.

Output and Output per Hour

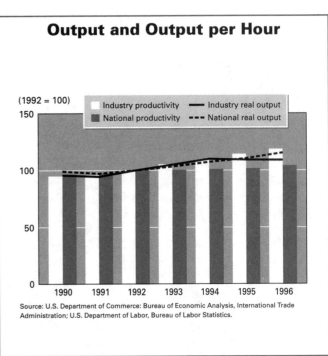

(1992 = 100)

Legend: Industry productivity, Industry real output, National productivity, National real output

Source: U.S. Department of Commerce: Bureau of Economic Analysis, International Trade Administration; U.S. Department of Labor, Bureau of Labor Statistics.

See "Getting the Most Out of *Outlook '99*" for definitions of terms.

Textimes

9

Textiles

INDUSTRY DEFINITION In this chapter portions of the textile mill products sector (SIC 22) are covered: broadwoven fabric mills (SIC 221, 222, 223); weft, lace, and warp knit fabric mills (SIC 2257, 2258); carpets and rugs (SIC 227); and yarn spinning mills (SIC 2281). The chapter also covers the man-made fiber industry (SIC 2823, 2824), which provides primary raw material inputs for textile products. Also included in SIC 22 but not covered in this chapter are narrow fabric and other smallwares mills, cotton, wool, silk, and man-made fiber (SIC 224); women's full-length and knee-length hosiery except socks (SIC 2251); hosiery not elsewhere classified (SIC 2252); knit outerwear mills (SIC 2253); knit underwear and nightwear mills (SIC 2254); knitting mills not elsewhere classified (SIC 2259); dyeing and finishing textiles except wool fabrics and knit goods (SIC 226); yarn texturizing, throwing, twisting, and winding mills (SIC 2282); thread mills (SIC 2284); and miscellaneous textile goods (SIC 229).

FACTORS AFFECTING FUTURE INDUSTRY GROWTH

Global Industry Trends

Global trends in the textile industry are driven by two major factors: automation of production and internationalization of company operations.

Once one of the more low-technology and labor-intensive industrial sectors, the textile industry has seen automation become a reality in an increasing number of its processes. Indeed, the technology now exists to automate almost an entire textile mill, from the opening of fiber bales to the loading of the finished product onto trucks. As production becomes automated, labor accounts for a smaller proportion of the total costs. Of even greater importance are the cost of capital, the availability of personnel with the technical training and skills needed to maintain high-technology equipment, the ready availability of low-cost and high-quality raw materials, and the proximity of and access to markets.

Although the need for constant upgrading of technology in the textile industry may seem obvious to companies in the developed world, such as those in the United States, western Europe, and Japan, no country's industry is immune to pressure to produce higher-quality goods at a lower cost. For example, in

1998 China began a massive restructuring and downsizing of the state-owned segment of its textile industry, which had ceased to be globally competitive.

To a greater extent than most industries, textile companies in the developed countries have expanded in regions close to their home markets. Investment farther afield has been undertaken on a more limited basis, generally to serve local markets. The trend toward regionalization is driven by an increase in production-sharing arrangements for apparel, which continues to be the most important market for man-made fibers and textile mill products. Mexico and the Caribbean have become critical outward processors of U.S. fabric, while textile companies in the European Union look primarily to eastern Europe to serve that function.

The intensification of global competition, coupled with the need for large amounts of capital to fund technological upgrades, is likely to spur further consolidation. The textile marketplace probably will be increasingly dominated by very large companies, with small companies prospering in specialized niche markets. In recent years a number of companies have grown larger through acquisitions and joint ventures, some of which have been cross-border in nature. In pursuing this trend, companies appear to be seeking strategic alliances which will help them become more focused, flexible, and market-driven.

The elimination of quotas in the global trade in textiles and apparel on January 1, 2005, will be a watershed event whose full consequences are difficult to predict. Certainly trade, cross-border investments, and joint ventures will be stimulated, and trade and investment patterns probably will change somewhat. Regional tariff preferences, combined with the possible expansion of such arrangements in various parts of the world, could result in a trend for textile companies to focus their efforts largely on regional markets.

Domestic Trends

The U.S. textile industry has taken significant steps to become more innovative and competitive. Capital investment in the industry has continued at a steady pace, with textile mills spending $2 billion or more a year to modernize and expand their facilities. The textile industry is earmarking from 3 to 4 percent of corporate sales for capital expenditures. U.S. textile mills also have been improving their competitive positions through acquisitions and divestitures, becoming more productive, efficient, and profitable.

Computerization of the industry has been a critical part of the quick response (QR) programs that are being adopted by textile mills to shorten the interval between the placement of retail orders and the delivery of textile goods to stores. The companies that coordinate these programs communicate by using bar codes and electronic data interchange. Companies that have the ability to pinpoint production times and quantities can direct production in accordance with individual orders. The mills, as well as apparel manufacturers and retailers, benefit from the resulting reduction in inventory costs. QR programs also result in more consistent unit growth and a smoother flow of production, significantly improving a textile mill's operating margins. Savings from increased ordering and delivery efficiencies have translated into lower, more consistent prices for consumers.

Another emerging trend in the textile industry is vertical integration into apparel manufacturing—in effect, selling fabric in the form of garments. Rather than simply supplying fabric, some mills are offering a "full package" to their apparel customers by arranging garment production, transportation, and logistics. To date, textile companies have utilized contractors mainly to produce finished garments, and some mills have begun to acquire apparel manufacturing facilities, allowing them to better control production and introduce new technology. For the most part, mills are providing apparel manufacturing services for branded apparel companies and private labels. However, some industry observers speculate that the trend toward vertical integration will culminate in the extensive development by mills of their own apparel brands, as many mills have done successfully in home furnishings.

Employment in the U.S. textile industry has been on a long-term downward trend for nearly three decades, a development related to the effects of international competition, increasing productivity, and consolidation. However, employment levels for workers with higher-skilled and higher-paying jobs have remained relatively constant. Advances in productivity have to some extent allowed U.S. textile manufacturers to maintain output through automation and technological improvements while requiring fewer workers. See Figure 9-1 for employment levels in the textile industry in the various states.

The U.S. textile industry is devoting more resources to complying with environmental requirements which have a direct impact on the industry. Chief among these requirements is the U.S. Environmental Protection Agency's (EPA) proposed Maximum Achievable Control Technology standard, which will go into effect in 2003. That standard, which is designed to reduce hazardous pollutants in the atmosphere, will affect textile printing and dyeing processes. The domestic industry has been working to participate in the drafting of the standard, which the EPA was scheduled to develop by the end of 1998.

The U.S. textile industry and standard-writing organizations are making progress toward developing international standards which would enhance the overseas sales of U.S. textiles. The U.S. industry has asked the International Standards Organization (ISO) Textiles Committee to consider some 50 U.S. textile product standards for adoption at the international level. These standards cover a wide variety of apparel fabrics, home furnishings, and industrial textiles.

PROJECTIONS OF INDUSTRY AND TRADE GROWTH FOR THE NEXT 1 AND 5 YEARS

Strong economic growth in 1997 helped textile mill industry shipments reach a record level that was up 2 percent from the level in 1996. Strength in spending and business investment also stimulated new textile orders, which were up more than 4 percent in 1997. Textile inventories remained under control during 1997 and ended the year 2 percent above the December 1996 level. The Federal Reserve Bank's industrial production index for textile mill products grew 3 percent between 1996 and 1997, and the capacity utilization rate increased from 82.8 percent to 83.4 percent.

According to the Fiber Economics Bureau, mill fiber consumption of cotton, wool, and man-made fibers reached 16.6 billion pounds in 1997, its highest level since 1994. Textile mill profits posted a substantial gain in 1997—5.7 percent over the 1996 level—as bottom-line performance improved, largely as a result of demand for apparel and home furnishing fabrics and a better retail climate.

The U.S. economy began strongly in 1998, with business and consumer confidence very high, and there are indications that 1999 will be another good year for the textile industry. These positive indications include little or no significant upward cost pressure, relatively soft raw material costs, and improved levels of consumer confidence. In a period of low inflation, wholesale textile prices are likely to remain flat. Relatively moderate wage increases should be offset by gains in productivity. The real growth in the value of textile industry shipments should be approximately 2 percent between 1998 and 1999 (see Table 9-1).

An issue that is causing uncertainty is the extent to which the Asian financial crisis will affect imports and prices in the United States. Reductions in import prices resulting from currency

Employment in Textiles (SIC 22) in 1997

Employees per Thousand
Nonfarm Workers

☐ Not applicable

☐ Fewer than 2

☐ 2 to 4

☐ 5 to 9

☐ 10 to 48

Source: U.S. Department of Labor, Bureau of Labor Statistics.

FIGURE 9-1

devaluations in major supplier nations could put pressure on domestic prices and squeeze the profit margins of U.S. producers. However, the impact of these devaluations is being mitigated by several factors. First, Asian producers import large quantities of fiber, yarn, and fabric as inputs for their apparel production; those inputs now cost them more as a result of their devaluations. Second, the credit and foreign exchange crunch in those countries has weakened many Asian producers. Third, with all the significant Asian suppliers subject to comprehensive U.S. textile restraint agreements, import growth on a quantity

TABLE 9-1: Textile Mill Products (SIC 22) Trends and Forecasts
(millions of dollars except as noted)

| | 1992 | 1993 | 1994 | 1995 | 1996 | 1997[1] | 1998[2] | 1999[3] | Percent Change | | | |
									96–97	97–98	98–99	92–96[4]
Industry data												
Value of shipments[5]	70,753	73,955	78,027	79,874	80,242	81,847	83,900	85,750	2.0	2.5	2.2	3.2
Value of shipments (1992$)	70,753	74,276	78,223	77,725	77,246	78,400	79,950	81,200	1.5	2.0	1.6	2.2
Total employment (thousands)	617	610	624	610	577							−1.7
Production workers (thousands)	528	524	534	520	489							−1.9
Average hourly earnings ($)	8.62	8.92	9.29	9.37	9.62							2.8
Product data												
Value of shipments[5]	70,008	73,216	77,249	79,200	79,334	80,950	83,000	84,800	2.0	2.5	2.2	3.2
Value of shipments (1992$)	70,008	73,530	77,459	77,045	76,355	77,500	79,050	80,300	1.5	2.0	1.6	2.2
Trade data												
Value of imports	5,843	6,161	6,534	6,965	7,169	8,369	9,000	9,725	16.7	7.5	8.1	5.2
Value of exports	4,467	4,687	5,151	5,696	6,177	7,081	7,800	8,540	14.6	10.2	9.5	8.4

[1] Estimate except imports and exports.
[2] Estimate.
[3] Forecast.
[4] Compound annual rate.
[5] For a definition of industry versus product values, see "Getting the Most Out of *Outlook '99.*"
Source: U.S. Department of Commerce: Bureau of the Census; International Trade Administration.

basis is limited to the growth rates established in those agreements and the extent to which quotas were not filled in the past.

Exports will play a major role in the future growth of the U.S. textile industry. Between 1992 and 1997, U.S. exports of textile mill products increased at an average annual rate of 10 percent, over three times the rate of growth of the value of industry shipments. The bulk of the increase in these exports was accounted for by the North American Free Trade Agreement (NAFTA) countries Canada and Mexico, but U.S. exports to other markets also should increase as these markets become more open to U.S. textile products. Export growth should be almost 10 percent between 1998 and 1999 (see Table 9-1).

Mill consolidations, increased capital expenditures for new plant and equipment, improved market research and development, and a greater emphasis on QR and other electronic-age technology should play decisive roles in the ability of the U.S. textile industry to compete in both domestic and global markets. Textile mill employment will continue to decline, primarily because of productivity gains. However, these job losses should occur at a slower rate than they did in the last decade. Most textile mill executives and industry analysts believe that the U.S. industry should remain strong and viable in the years ahead as production, shipment, and profit gains continue. Exports should grow 9.8 percent per year from 1999 through 2003, and import growth should average 7.8 percent annually over that period. Real growth in the value of industry shipments is expected to average 2.5 percent from 1999 through 2002.

GLOBAL MARKET PROSPECTS

Canada and Mexico were the top two markets for U.S. textile mill exports in 1997, accounting for about 45 percent of total exports. The growth in exports to the NAFTA market exceeded 19 percent in 1997, outpacing the growth in exports to the rest of the world. Exports to beneficiary countries of the Caribbean Basin Initiative (CBI) accounted for 11 percent of total U.S. textile exports (see Table 9-2). This regional export growth trend shows no sign of abating and suggests that substantial further gains could be achieved from the realization of a Free Trade Area of the Americas Agreement, negotiations for which were launched in April 1998.

Concern about the future prospects for U.S. exports arises from the Asian financial crisis. Lower incomes in the affected countries are reducing the consumption of textiles and apparel, with sales of higher-priced imported products being hit the hardest. The consumption of imported textile products in these countries also is negatively affected by currency devaluations, which increase the price of imports in the local currencies. The price effect of devaluations may have a negative impact on U.S. textile exports to countries which have not experienced major currency devaluations, as U.S. products will become more costly relative to the products of countries that have devalued. However, U.S. exports of textiles to the five countries hit hardest by the crisis—South Korea, Indonesia, Malaysia, the Philippines, and Thailand—accounted for only 3 percent of total U.S. textile exports in 1997. A greater concern is the collateral effect of the crisis on Hong Kong and Japan, which were the fourth and fifth largest U.S. textile export markets in 1997 (see Table 9-2).

As U.S. quotas on textile and apparel imports are phased out, the ability of U.S. textile producers to gain access to foreign markets will be increasingly important. U.S. producers continue to face high tariff and other barriers in major emerging markets such as India and Brazil. In 1997 and 1998, the United States successfully pursued a World Trade Organization (WTO)

TABLE 9-2: U.S. Trade Patterns in Textiles[1] in 1997
(millions of dollars; percent)

Exports			Imports		
Regions[2]	Value[3]	Share, %	Regions[2]	Value[3]	Share, %
NAFTA	3,213	45.4	NAFTA	1,780	21.3
Latin America	1,181	16.7	Latin America	415	5.0
Western Europe	1,144	16.2	Western Europe	2,004	23.9
Japan/Chinese Economic Area	612	8.6	Japan/Chinese Economic Area	1,805	21.6
Other Asia	353	5.0	Other Asia	1,977	23.6
Rest of world	579	8.2	Rest of world	389	4.6
World	7,081	100.0	World	8,369	100.0
Top Five Countries	Value	Share, %	Top Five Countries	Value	Share, %
Canada	1,936	27.3	Canada	1,088	13.0
Mexico	1,277	18.0	Mexico	692	8.3
United Kingdom	330	4.7	South Korea	665	7.9
Hong Kong (PRC)	259	3.7	Italy	625	7.5
Japan	236	3.3	China	611	7.3

[1] SIC 22.
[2] For definitions of regional groupings, see "Getting the Most Out of *Outlook '99*."
[3] Values may not sum to total due to rounding.
Source: U.S. Department of Commerce, Bureau of the Census.

case to remove illegal restrictions on imports of textiles and apparel into Argentina.

INDUSTRY SUBSECTORS

Broadwoven Fabric Mills

The broadwoven fabric mills subsector consists of cotton broadwoven fabric mills (SIC 221), man-made fiber broadwoven fabric mills (SIC 222), and wool broadwoven fabric mills (SIC 223).

The manufacturing of broadwoven fabrics is a mature industry. Since the 1980s major U.S. firms in that industry have achieved growth largely through mergers, acquisitions, and sales in foreign markets. Fabric weavers generally are vertically integrated companies that produce their own yarn. The quantity of broadwoven fabric production rose almost 4 percent between 1996 and 1997 to 16.4 billion square yards.

TABLE 9-3:   Broadwoven Fabric Mills (SIC 221, 222, 223) Trends and Forecasts

(millions of dollars except as noted)

| | 1992 | 1993 | 1994 | 1995 | 1996 | 1997[1] | 1998[2] | 1999[3] | Percent Change | | | |
									96–97	97–98	98–99	92–96[4]
Industry data												
Value of shipments[5]	16,190	16,816	17,638	18,389	18,204	18,505	18,875	19,160	1.7	2.0	1.5	3.0
221 Cotton fabric mills	5,811	5,990	6,172	6,751	6,699	6,875	7,040	7,150	2.6	2.4	1.6	3.6
222 Man-made fabric mills	8,767	9,145	9,605	9,810	9,750	9,850	10,035	10,200	1.0	1.9	1.6	2.7
223 Wool fabric mills	1,612	1,681	1,861	1,829	1,756	1,780	1,800	1,810	1.4	1.1	0.6	2.2
Value of shipments (1992$)	16,190	16,917	17,926	18,174	17,787	17,998	18,290	18,450	1.2	1.6	0.9	2.4
221 Cotton fabric mills	5,811	5,930	6,068	6,375	6,325	6,470	6,600	6,650	2.3	2.0	0.8	2.1
222 Man-made fabric mills	8,767	9,294	9,974	9,959	9,701	9,750	9,900	10,000	0.5	1.5	1.0	2.6
223 Wool fabric mills	1,612	1,693	1,884	1,840	1,761	1,778	1,790	1,800	1.0	0.7	0.6	2.2
Total employment (thousands)	157.0	155.0	152.0	150.0	139.2							−3.0
221 Cotton fabric mills	55.9	55.0	55.0	55.8	51.9							−1.8
222 Man-made fabric mills	87.2	85.8	81.5	80.8	73.9							−4.1
223 Wool fabric mills	13.7	13.8	14.6	13.9	13.4							−0.6
Production workers (thousands)	139.0	137.0	134.0	132.0	121.4							−3.4
221 Cotton fabric mills	50.1	49.9	50.0	50.4	46.7							−1.7
222 Man-made fabric mills	76.7	75.0	71.4	69.7	63.0							−4.8
223 Wool fabric mills	11.8	11.9	12.6	12.1	11.7							−0.2
Average hourly earnings ($)	9.04	9.38	9.86	10.08	10.35							3.4
221 Cotton fabric mills	8.92	9.38	9.82	9.96	10.32							3.7
222 Man-made fabric mills	9.21	9.46	9.91	10.20	10.48							3.3
223 Wool fabric mills	8.46	8.87	9.70	9.92	9.78							3.7
Product data												
Value of shipments[5]	15,596	16,218	17,044	17,819	17,558	17,837	18,193	18,472	1.6	2.0	1.5	3.0
221 Cotton fabric mills	5,708	5,863	6,084	6,640	6,582	6,750	6,910	7,020	2.6	2.4	1.6	3.6
222 Man-made fabric mills	8,500	8,853	9,442	9,716	9,549	9,640	9,820	9,980	1.0	1.9	1.6	3.0
223 Wool fabric mills	1,388	1,502	1,518	1,463	1,427	1,447	1,463	1,472	1.4	1.1	0.6	0.7
Value of shipments (1992$)	15,596	16,315	17,324	17,606	17,148	17,355	17,635	17,794	1.2	1.6	0.9	2.4
221 Cotton fabric mills	5,708	5,805	5,982	6,270	6,215	6,360	6,490	6,540	2.3	2.0	0.8	2.2
222 Man-made fabric mills	8,500	8,997	9,805	9,864	9,502	9,550	9,690	9,790	0.5	1.5	1.0	2.8
223 Wool fabric mills	1,388	1,513	1,537	1,472	1,431	1,445	1,455	1,464	1.0	0.7	0.6	0.8
Trade data												
Value of imports	3,183	3,295	3,310	3,417	3,372	3,758	3,880	4,025	11.4	3.2	3.7	1.5
221 Cotton fabric mills	1,475	1,525	1,482	1,614	1,507	1,689	1,725	1,780	12.1	2.1	3.2	0.5
222 Man-made fabric mills	1,468	1,541	1,586	1,550	1,598	1,777	1,850	1,925	11.2	4.1	4.1	2.1
223 Wool fabric mills	240	230	242	252	267	292	305	320	9.4	4.5	4.9	2.7
Value of exports	1,569	1,680	1,840	2,027	2,206	2,376	2,572	2,795	7.7	8.3	8.7	8.9
221 Cotton fabric mills	579	621	704	813	881	938	1,030	1,125	6.5	9.8	9.2	11.1
222 Man-made fabric mills	891	974	1,049	1,099	1,209	1,303	1,400	1,520	7.8	7.4	8.6	7.9
223 Wool fabric mills	99.3	84.6	87.2	114	116	134	142	150	15.6	5.9	5.6	4.0

[1] Estimate except imports and exports.
[2] Estimate.
[3] Forecast.
[4] Compound annual rate.
[5] For a definition of industry versus product values, see "Getting the Most Out of *Outlook '99.*"
Source: U.S. Department of Commerce: Bureau of the Census; International Trade Administration.

TABLE 9-4: U.S. Trade Patterns in Broadwoven and Knit Fabrics[1] in 1997

(millions of dollars; percent)

Regions[2]	Exports		Regions[2]	Imports	
	Value[3]	Share, %		Value[3]	Share, %
NAFTA	1,361	44.6	NAFTA	818	17.9
Latin America	556	18.2	Latin America	67	1.5
Western Europe	499	16.4	Western Europe	1,009	22.1
Japan/Chinese Economic Area	220	7.2	Japan/Chinese Economic Area	1,167	25.6
Other Asia	137	4.5	Other Asia	1,346	29.5
Rest of world	277	9.1	Rest of world	156	3.4
World	3,050	100.0	World[3]	4,563	100.0
Top Five Countries	**Value**	**Share, %**	**Top Five Countries**	**Value**	**Share, %**
Canada	789	25.9	South Korea	569	12.5
Mexico	572	18.8	Canada	514	11.3
United Kingdom	135	4.4	Italy	443	9.7
Dominican Republic	130	4.3	China	368	8.1
Hong Kong (PRC)	114	3.7	Taiwan	363	8.0

[1] SIC 221, 222, 223, 2257, 2258.
[2] For definitions of regional groupings, see "Getting the Most Out of *Outlook '99*."
[3] Values may not sum to total due to rounding.
Source: U.S. Department of Commerce, Bureau of the Census.

While the production of man-made fiber fabrics rose nearly 2 percent, a strong 8 percent increase in cotton fabrics was the primary driver of the overall production gain. The production of wool broadwoven fabrics increased 15 percent over this period, primarily as a result of increased blending of wool with other fibers.

The broadwoven fabric mills industry had a real growth rate of around 2 percent in the value of industry shipments between 1997 and 1998. U.S. exports of broadwoven fabrics increased over 8 percent between 1997 and 1998 to an estimated $2.6 billion. U.S. exports of broadwoven fabrics to the NAFTA countries increased from 37 percent of total exports in 1993 to 45 percent in 1997. U.S. imports of broadwoven fabrics increased over 3 percent from 1997 to 1998 to an estimated $3.9 billion (see Tables 9-3 and 9-4).

Weft, Lace, and Warp Knit Fabric Mills

The U.S. knit fabric industry sells almost its entire output to apparel firms, largely for the production of high-volume goods such as T-shirts, underwear, sweatshirts, and other fleece apparel. This sector had real growth of 2.5 percent in the value of industry shipments between 1997 and 1998. Imports account for a relatively small but growing share of the U.S. market. Between 1992 and 1998 the share of imports in the domestic market grew from 3.2 percent to an estimated 11.4 percent. U.S. exports of weft, lace, and warp knit fabrics rose 7 percent from 1997 to 1998 to an estimated $725 million (see Table 9-5). This increase primarily reflects larger shipments to the NAFTA countries, which increased from 39 percent of total exports in 1993 to 44 percent in 1997.

The majority of knitters have continued to develop new products, new strategies, and tighter, more streamlined opera-

tions. On the apparel side, business is particularly good for stretch doubleknits in blends of spandex with polyester or nylon, polyester microfibers in piques and jerseys, and stretch ribbed knits. Knitting mills continue to develop and improve performance knit fabrics. These high-tech activewear fabrics, which originally were designed for high-performance sports such as mountain climbing and skiing, are finding new markets in sportswear, which sometimes is called street active or lifestyle apparel.

Carpets and Rugs

Real growth in the value of shipments in the carpet and rug industry has been slow but steady since 1992, with shipments increasing one percent between 1997 and 1998. Exports increased just over 2 percent during that period, accounting for over 7 percent of product shipments in 1998. Imports grew almost 3 percent over the period to an estimated $950 million in 1998 (see Table 9-6). Carpeting is the largest segment of the U.S. floor covering market, which also includes tile and hardwood floors, accounting for over 70 percent of the total market.

The U.S. carpet and rug industry continues to consolidate at all levels from manufacturing through retail. Today about 40 percent of all carpet fiber and filament yarns are produced by carpet manufacturers. The three largest carpet producers in the United States—Shaw Industries, Mohawk, and Beaulieu of America—are also the three largest carpet fiber producers. These three firms account for over 70 percent of the fiber used in carpet manufacturing, which is dominated by nylon and polypropylene fibers.

The carpet industry is seeing increased acquisition activity involving carpet manufacturers and the retail and commercial

TABLE 9-5: Weft, Lace, and Warp Knit Fabric Mills (SIC 2257, 2258) Trends and Forecasts

(millions of dollars except as noted)

	1992	1993	1994	1995	1996	1997[1]	1998[2]	1999[3]	Percent Change			
									96–97	97–98	98–99	92–96[4]
Industry data												
Value of shipments[5]	7,270	7,526	8,110	7,858	7,537	7,700	7,930	8,100	2.2	3.0	2.1	0.9
Value of shipments (1992$)	7,270	7,544	8,182	7,752	7,414	7,540	7,730	7,870	1.7	2.5	1.8	0.5
Total employment (thousands)	63.9	60.6	61.2	57.7	54.8							−3.8
Production workers (thousands)	53.9	50.6	51.5	48.5	46.3							−3.7
Average hourly earnings ($)	8.54	8.90	9.43	9.47	9.58							2.9
Product data												
Value of shipments[5]	7,436	7,478	8,102	7,841	7,580	7,747	7,979	8,147	2.2	3.0	2.1	0.5
Value of shipments (1992$)	7,436	7,492	8,172	7,736	7,459	7,585	7,775	7,915	1.7	2.5	1.8	0.1
Trade data												
Value of imports	233	302	354	356	542	805	930	975	48.5	15.5	4.8	23.5
Value of exports	377	375	400	495	547	675	725	765	23.4	7.4	5.5	9.8

[1] Estimate except imports and exports.
[2] Estimate.
[3] Forecast.
[4] Compound annual rate.
[5] For a definition of industry versus product values, see "Getting the Most Out of *Outlook '99*."
Source: U.S. Department of Commerce: Bureau of the Census; International Trade Administration.

TABLE 9-6: Carpets and Rugs (SIC 227) Trends and Forecasts

(millions of dollars except as noted)

	1992	1993	1994	1995	1996	1997[1]	1998[2]	1999[3]	Percent Change			
									96–97	97–98	98–99	92–96[4]
Industry data												
Value of shipments[5]	9,828	10,234	10,600	10,762	11,184	11,370	11,600	11,810	1.7	2.0	1.8	3.3
Value of shipments (1992$)	9,828	10,286	10,537	10,551	10,722	10,840	10,975	11,150	1.1	1.2	1.6	2.2
Total employment (thousands)	49.4	50.6	55.1	55.5	55.0							2.7
Production workers (thousands)	38.9	39.6	42.9	43.5	43.8							3.0
Average hourly earnings ($)	8.83	9.17	9.54	9.58	9.55							2.0
Product data												
Value of shipments[5]	9,518	9,953	10,141	10,405	10,806	10,990	11,210	11,410	1.7	2.0	1.8	3.2
Value of shipments (1992$)	9,518	10,003	10,081	10,201	10,360	10,475	10,600	10,770	1.1	1.2	1.6	2.1
Trade data												
Value of imports	700	660	736	843	820	925	950	985	12.7	2.7	3.7	4.0
Value of exports	705	698	667	632	702	793	810	825	13.0	2.1	1.9	−0.1

[1] Estimate except imports and exports.
[2] Estimate.
[3] Forecast.
[4] Compound annual rate.
[5] For a definition of industry versus product values, see "Getting the Most Out of *Outlook '99*."
Source: U.S. Department of Commerce: Bureau of the Census; International Trade Administration.

dealer segment and a slowdown of acquisitions involving mills. The U.S. industry is getting more involved in direct retail sales and commercial distribution.

In November 1997 the Carpet and Rug Institute (CRI) launched a $100 million 4-year national carpet advertising and promotion campaign to increase consumer awareness and create opportunities in the domestic marketplace. The CRI also has implemented a Seal of Approval Program to help consumers identify companies that provide services that meet a higher standard with regard to consumer satisfaction.

Yarn Spinning Mills

The U.S. yarn spinning industry is among the largest in the world and is competitive with foreign suppliers to the U.S. market. To a large extent, U.S. cost competitiveness in the production of spun yarn is facilitated by a large domestic supply of raw

TABLE 9-7: Yarn Spinning Mills (SIC 2281) Trends and Forecasts

(millions of dollars except as noted)

	1992	1993	1994	1995	1996	1997[1]	1998[2]	1999[3]	Percent Change 96–97	97–98	98–99	92–96[4]
Industry data												
Value of shipments[5]	7,669	7,618	7,999	8,465	8,543	8,675	8,800	8,890	1.5	1.4	1.0	2.7
Value of shipments (1992$)	7,669	7,960	8,289	8,324	8,526	8,600	8,700	8,750	0.9	1.2	0.6	2.7
Total employment (thousands)	68.7	65.6	66.1	64.5	60.6							–3.1
Production workers (thousands)	62.6	59.7	60.2	58.8	55.1							–3.1
Average hourly earnings ($)	8.48	8.62	8.95	9.13	9.47							2.8
Product data												
Value of shipments[5]	7,756	7,696	8,196	8,619	8,771	8,900	9,025	9,115	1.5	1.4	1.0	3.1
Value of shipments (1992$)	7,756	8,041	8,493	8,475	8,753	8,830	8,940	8,990	0.9	1.2	0.6	3.1
Trade data												
Value of imports	321	337	388	400	420	529	580	630	26.1	9.5	8.6	7.0
Value of exports	169	146	209	299	327	355	410	465	8.6	15.5	13.4	17.9

[1] Estimate except imports and exports.
[2] Estimate.
[3] Forecast.
[4] Compound annual rate.
[5] For a definition of industry versus product values, see "Getting the Most Out of *Outlook '99*."
Source: U.S. Department of Commerce: Bureau of the Census; International Trade Administration.

materials that are available at competitive prices. The United States is a large producer of cotton and man-made staple fibers, which are major raw materials for the spun yarn industry. Man-made staple fiber and cotton are used to produce more than 95 percent of the spun yarn made in the United States.

The primary customer for spun yarn for sale is the knitting mill industry. Knitting mills purchase a high percentage of their yarn because they tend to be small, nonintegrated, style-oriented entities that generally require a great variety of yarns. Weaving mills, in contrast, are primarily large, vertically integrated textile mills that produce their own yarn. U.S. spun yarn producers supply over 90 percent of the spun yarn for sale consumed in the knitting mill industry and sell only a small proportion of their total shipments overseas. However, U.S. exports of spun yarn have increased steadily to an estimated $410 million in 1998, primarily as a result of NAFTA. In 1997 U.S. exports of spun yarn to the NAFTA countries were almost three times the 1993 level and represented more than 50 percent of total spun yarn exports. Imports of spun yarn increased almost 10 percent between 1997 and 1998 to an estimated $580 million (see Table 9-7).

Man-Made Fibers

In the past decade the market for worldwide man-made fiber products has changed markedly, with developing countries taking a larger share as their populations and per capita fiber consumption have grown at faster rates than have those of the developed countries. Historically, the industry has been dominated by the developed countries, but in recent years the developing countries of Asia have become increasingly important.

According to the Fiber Economics Bureau, between 1992 and 1996 the developing countries, led by China, Taiwan, and South Korea, accounted for most of the growth in world man-made fiber production, increasing their aggregate share from 30 percent in 1990 to 50 percent in 1996. In contrast, the production of man-made fibers has remained relatively stagnant in the United States, Canada, western European countries, and Japan. Those countries' aggregate share of world output fell from 40 percent in 1992 to 36 percent in 1996. By the end of 1998 the developing countries of Asia are expected to account for more than half of worldwide man-made fiber capacity.

Since the mid-1980s the U.S. man-made fiber industry has undergone extensive consolidation and reorganization. Domestic fiber producers have taken measures to expand and diversify their operations by purchasing existing plants, enlarging capacity, and creating new capacity in other parts of the world. Today, most fibers are commodity products and the value and trading advantages of branding have almost disappeared. In recent years large fiber producers have sold their operations or left the market. Other companies have reorganized their textile fiber business, focusing on textile market segments with higher margins, larger volumes, and lower business maintenance costs.

The U.S. man-made fiber industry experienced real growth of 1 percent in the value of shipments between 1997 and 1998. Exports grew over 8 percent during that period to almost $2.4 billion, and imports grew 9 percent to $1.7 billion (see Table 9-8). In addition to exporting, many domestic man-made fiber producers have increased their presence in foreign markets by entering into joint venture operations. Domestic fiber producers provide the bulk of the capital needed to construct new plants

TABLE 9-8:   Man-Made Fibers (SIC 2823, 2824) Trends and Forecasts

(millions of dollars except as noted)

	1992	1993	1994	1995	1996	1997[1]	1998[2]	1999[3]	Percent Change 96–97	Percent Change 97–98	Percent Change 98–99	Percent Change 92–96[4]
Industry data												
Value of shipments[5]	12,861	13,293	13,366	14,035	14,179	14,400	14,600	14,825	1.6	1.4	1.5	2.5
Value of shipments (1992$)	12,861	13,289	13,217	13,421	13,425	13,575	13,700	13,845	1.1	0.9	1.1	1.1
Total employment (thousands)	55.4	51.6	46.9	44.7	44.5							−5.3
Production workers (thousands)	41.7	39.8	36.6	35.0	35.1							−4.2
Average hourly earnings ($)	14.22	14.63	14.23	14.87	15.28							1.8
Product data												
Value of shipments[5]	10,924	11,092	11,779	12,529	12,383	12,580	12,750	12,940	1.6	1.4	1.5	3.2
Value of shipments (1992$)	10,924	11,092	11,719	12,023	11,768	11,900	12,010	12,140	1.1	0.9	1.1	1.9
Trade data												
Value of imports	907	1,127	1,302	1,384	1,401	1,558	1,700	1,850	11.2	9.1	8.8	11.5
Value of exports	1,473	1,407	1,594	2,078	2,113	2,168	2,350	2,525	2.6	8.4	7.4	9.4

[1] Estimate except imports and exports.
[2] Estimate.
[3] Forecast.
[4] Compound annual rate.
[5] For a definition of industry versus product values, see "Getting the Most Out of *Outlook '99*."
Source: U.S. Department of Commerce: Bureau of the Census; International Trade Administration.

TABLE 9-9:   U.S. Trade Patterns in Man-Made Fibers[1] in 1997

(millions of dollars; percent)

Exports Regions[2]	Value[3]	Share, %	Imports Regions[2]	Value[3]	Share, %
NAFTA	645	29.7	NAFTA	587	37.7
Latin America	247	11.4	Latin America	17	1.1
Western Europe	599	27.6	Western Europe	437	28.1
Japan/Chinese Economic Area	346	16.0	Japan/Chinese Economic Area	212	13.6
Other Asia	224	10.3	Other Asia	253	16.3
Rest of world	107	4.9	Rest of world	51	3.3
World	2,168	100.0	World	1,557	100.0
Top Five Countries	**Value**	**Share, %**	**Top Five Countries**	**Value**	**Share, %**
Canada	458	21.1	Canada	409	26.2
Mexico	187	8.6	South Korea	185	11.9
United Kingdom	122	5.6	Mexico	178	11.5
Hong Kong (PRC)	117	5.4	Germany	170	10.9
Netherlands	116	5.3	Japan	125	8.0

[1] SIC 2832, 2834.
[2] For definitions of regional groupings, see "Getting the Most Out of *Outlook '99*."
[3] Values may not sum to total due to rounding.
Source: U.S. Department of Commerce, Bureau of the Census.

and/or license their technology. Major trading partners include the NAFTA countries and western Europe, which generally account for more than 55 percent of U.S. exports and almost 66 percent of imports (see Table 9-9).

Maria A. Corey, U.S. Department of Commerce, Office of Textiles and Apparel, (202) 482-4058, maria_corey@ita.doc.gov, September 1998.

■ **REFERENCES**

ATI (America's Textiles International), 2100 Powers Ferry Road, Atlanta, GA 30339. (770) 955-5656, http://www.billian.com/textile.
Broadwoven Fabrics (Gray), Current Industrial Report MQ22T, U.S. Department of Commerce, Bureau of the Census. (301) 457-4620, http://www.census.gov/econ/www/manumenu.html.
Daily News Record, Fairchild Publications, Inc., 7 West 34th Street, New York, NY 10001-8191. (212) 630-4000.

Fiber Organon, Fiber Economics Bureau, Inc., 1150 17th Street, NW, Suite 306, Washington, DC 20036. (202) 467-0916, http://www.fibersource.com.

Industrial Production and Capacity Utilization (G.17), Federal Reserve Statistical Release, Board of Governors of the Federal Reserve System, Washington, DC 20551. (202) 452-3245, http://www.bog.frb.fed.us/releases/G17/about.html.

Quarterly Financial Report for Manufacturing, Mining, and Trade Corporations, U.S. Department of Commerce, Bureau of the Census. (301) 457-3343/3379, http://www.census.gov/mp/www/pub/mfg/msmfg13a.html.

Textile HiLights, American Textile Manufacturers Institute, Inc., 1130 Connecticut Avenue, NW, Suite 1200, Washington, DC 20036. (202) 862-0544, http://www.atmi.org.

Textile Outlook International, Textiles Intelligence Limited, Derwent House, 31 Alma Lane, Wilmslow, Cheshire, SK9 5EY, United Kingdom. Telephone: (44) (0) 1625-536136.

Textile World, Intertec Publishing Corporation, 9800 Metcalf Avenue, Overland Park, KS 66212-2215. (913) 341-1300.

■ RELATED CHAPTERS

■ GLOSSARY

International Standards Organization (ISO): Founded in 1946; represents the standards-setting bodies in 95 countries and governmental organizations. Its purpose is to develop and promote quality standards for the international exchange of goods and services through the development of commonly accepted measures of quality.

Polymer: A high-molecular-weight chainlike structure from which man-made fibers are derived; produced by linking together units called monomers.

Quick response (QR): A strategy that involves the exchange of information among all members of the textile production chain through computer networks. A prime objective is to shorten the response time to changes in consumer taste.

Vertically integrated: Refers to a manufacturing process in which a single firm engages in more than one stage of production, such as a textile mill that produces its own yarn and fabric.

PAPER AND ALLIED PRODUCTS
Economic and Trade Trends

U.S. International Trade

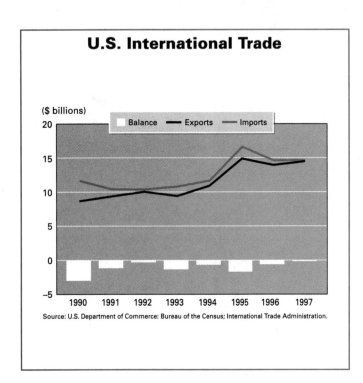

Source: U.S. Department of Commerce: Bureau of the Census; International Trade Administration.

World Export Market Shares

Source: United Nations; U.S. Department of Commerce, International Trade Administration.

Export Dependence and Import Penetration

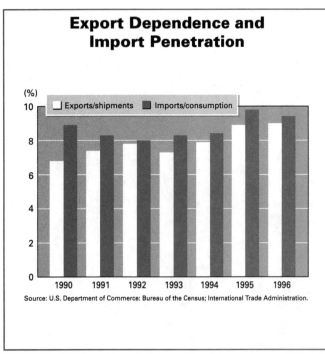

Source: U.S. Department of Commerce: Bureau of the Census; International Trade Administration.

Output and Output per Hour

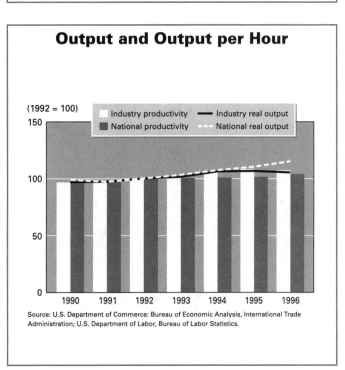

Source: U.S. Department of Commerce: Bureau of Economic Analysis, International Trade Administration; U.S. Department of Labor, Bureau of Labor Statistics.

See "Getting the Most Out of *Outlook '99*" for definitions of terms.

Paper and Allied Products

INDUSTRY DEFINITION The U.S. paper and allied products sector (SIC 26) consists of 17 manufacturing industries which process wood, recovered paper and paperboard, other cellulose fiber sources, and certain plastic and metal films into thousands of end-use products. This sector is divided into three major commodity groupings: (1) SIC 261, 262, and 263, which produce primary products, covering pulp, paper, and paperboard; (2) SIC 265, which consists of five industries producing paperboard containers and box products; and (3) SIC 267, which contains nine nonpackaging converted paper and paperboard products industries, which produce, among other things, pressure-sensitive tapes, labels, and packaging films; plastic and paper bags; envelopes, stationery, and paper office supplies; pressed and molded pulp goods; certain wall coverings; and gift-wrap paper.

GLOBAL INDUSTRY TRENDS

The global paper and allied products industry is one of the most important contributors to the health of the world economy. Although recognized in many circles as a mature sector, this industry is also one of the most dynamic in terms of product development, technological improvements, distribution and handling, processing and converting, and environmental protection. The industry continues to go through a globalization process in which producers are expanding their raw material, product manufacturing, converting, and distribution network to foreign markets that previously were seen as competitors. Leading world producers, especially in the developed, industrialized nations, can no longer simply focus on the domestic market for sales growth; instead, they must expand their customer base to the world marketplace. Competition is rapidly increasing from producers in some less developed countries which have a number of cost advantages over their industrialized counterparts. The growing influence of this globalization process will continue into the next century as free trade becomes more of a reality and market access barriers are removed to create a more open and fair trading marketplace.

The U.S. paper and allied products industry is the world's leading producer and exporter of a variety of consumer-directed commodities, trading many of them with more than 125 countries. A large modern manufacturing base, combined with an adequate transportation and distribution network and a highly skilled labor force, makes the U.S. industry the most competitive and highest-volume supplier in the world. Although the domestic market consumes more than 90 percent of its output, this industry has become a major player in the world paper and allied products market. After 1993 exports as a proportion of total U.S. paper and allied products shipments increased from 7.3 percent in that year to nearly 9 percent in 1998 as exports on a value basis grew from over $9 billion to nearly $15 billion. As much as 65 percent of the industry's growth in shipments over the past decade is directly attributable to increases in foreign shipments of paper and allied products.

As domestic sales have stagnated (up 1.5 to 2 percent) over the past 5 years, the industry has refocused on export sales, placed a greater emphasis on increasing exports by directing more resources toward world markets, and gained a global market share. The globalization of paper and allied products manufacturers has been ongoing for more than a decade. Many U.S. paper and allied products companies are active exporters, but they also are engaged in foreign production, converting, and packaging operations as well as joint ventures and direct foreign capital investment in partnerships and ownerships.

From 1992 through 1998 U.S. paper and allied products exports increased at nearly a 7 percent compound annual growth rate. Most of the increase resulted from shipments to Canada, Mexico, southeast Asia, and certain Latin American and European countries. The commodities exported by the industry are divided into market wood pulp, recovered paper (not included in SIC data), paper and paperboard, and converted paper and paperboard products. In 1998 paper and paperboard on a volume basis represented 41 percent of the industry's exports, followed by recovered paper (28 percent), market wood pulp (22 percent), and converted paper and paperboard products (9 percent). On a value basis, paper and paperboard exports represented 48 percent of the industry's exports, followed by converted paper and paperboard products (25 percent) and wood pulp (21 percent), with the balance coming from exports of recovered paper and paperboard.

FACTORS AFFECTING FUTURE GROWTH OF THE U.S. INDUSTRY

The U.S. paper and allied products sector is recognized worldwide as a high-quality and high-volume low-cost producer that benefits from a number of key operating advantages, including a large domestic consumer market, the world's highest per capita consumption, a modern manufacturing infrastructure, adequate raw materials and energy resources, a highly skilled labor force, and an efficient transportation and distribution network. This industry is among the most modern because of continued large capital expenditures. This spending, which is driven mainly by production improvements (through existing machine upgrades, retrofits, or new installed equipment), environmental concerns, and increased recycling, totaled an estimated $9 billion in 1998.

The industry ranks among the top 10 U.S. manufacturing industries and is in the top 5 for sales of nondurables. Although this sector is the third leading energy consumer (behind chemicals and metals), it has the second highest rate of self-generated energy (behind chemicals), totaling 56 percent in 1996 and 1997. Because nearly all the industry's products are consumer-oriented, product shipments are affected mostly by the overall health of the U.S. economy, although the growth of the world economy is playing a more important role in the industry's outlook than ever before. Gross domestic product (GDP) growth and sector shipment growth typically are tied closely together. In the future, growth in demand in a number of key foreign paper and paperboard markets will play an increasingly important role in the health and expansion of the U.S. paper and allied products industries.

After a poor performance in 1996, the U.S. paper and allied products industry has experienced consecutive years of increased domestic and foreign demand, slowly improving prices, higher capacity utilization rates, and inventory drawdowns. As a result, total shipments of paper and allied products increased 1.5 percent in real terms and 4.1 percent in current-dollar terms in 1998. A general upward movement in prices for a number of primary commodity grades of paper and paperboard and certain converted paper products and packaging materials resulted in the increase in the current value of shipments. Real GDP increased about 3.7 percent in 1998 (first quarter to first quarter), leading to noticeable increases in real disposable income, total U.S. industrial production, and purchases of nondurable goods; all these factors combined to increase domestic paper and paperboard demand and improve the industry's level of shipments.

New paper and paperboard tonnage capacity in 1998 was estimated to grow 1.6 percent above the level in 1997, the smallest increase for the domestic industry since 1993. This helped producers draw down their inventories and set up better industry fundamentals going into 1999. Much of this tonnage is due to come on-line when price and demand levels begin to rise again. By controlling operating rates and allowing inventories to be drawn down for most of 1997, domestic pulp and paper producers were in a better economic and operative position throughout most of 1998, and this bodes well for the industry in 1999. Industry capital expenditures fell 4.8 percent in 1997 to $8.86 billion but increased 1.5 percent in 1998 to $9.0 billion. Since 1992 there has been a leveling off of industry spending after the record levels of the late 1980s. Expenditures for environmental and energy (non-output-related) projects accounted for 13 percent of total capital outlays in 1998.

The earnings of domestic paper and paperboard companies were estimated to improve slowly in 1998 as a result of increasing demand, slightly higher prices, increased operating rates, and the end of a major inventory drawdown cycle. Virtually every major U.S. pulp and paper company saw overall sales, net profits, and average earnings per share improve slightly in 1998 from the same period in 1997. Labor, chemicals, and wood raw materials costs generally were kept in check, but energy prices fell for the industry in 1998 as the mild winter resulted in an excess supply of heating fuel oil and natural gas.

U.S. paper and allied products manufacturers have traditionally been at the forefront of a number of environmental issues. They have a history of successfully addressing many key environmental issues, particularly those relating to air and water quality, recycling, recovery of pre- and postconsumer paper and paperboard, and energy. Protection of the environment not only has become a major capital expenditure but also is near the top of the industry's most challenging and difficult public relations matters. Although the industry's expenditures for the environment increased substantially over the past decade, the public still generally perceives the industry as damaging rather than improving the environment. Significant improvements have been made in environmental protection over the past several years, and producers have worked closely with the U.S. government on a number of key domestic and international environmental policy issues. As the industry looks to the future, it sees the need to continue to improve its environmental performance and increase its collection and utilization of recovered paper and paperboard. Corporate decisions will be based not only on ways to increase production and improve sales but also on ways to improve corporate image, increase recycling, and adapt to increasingly stringent environmental regulations.

The United States is the global leader in the generation, recovery, consumption, and export of recovered paper and paperboard. Once a fiber supplement, this recovered material has become a critical source for papermaking. In 1998 the U.S. paper and paperboard industries consumed more than 33 million metric tons of recovered paper and paperboard, a 3 percent increase from the record level in 1997. U.S. paper and allied products companies not only are the world's leading collectors and consumers of recovered paper, they also are the global leaders in exporting. Data indicate that the United States exported 7 million metric tons to about 80 world markets. These tremendous improvements in pre- and postconsumer paper recovery operations will have to continue for the primary paper and paperboard industry to meet its self-imposed 50 percent recycling goal by 2000.

U.S. INDUSTRY GROWTH PROJECTIONS FOR THE NEXT 1 AND 5 YEARS

With U.S. GDP forecast to continue to expand in 1999, product shipments by the U.S. paper and allied products industries should follow suit with a 2.2 percent increase (see Table 10-1). Over the 1999–2003 forecast period, product shipments should expand 2 percent annually in real terms. The move by this industry to improve its fundamentals over the past several years should allow it to reap positive benefits, especially if demand remains high and the industry is better able to control capacity additions. The U.S. paper and allied products industry should experience improved sales, prices, and earnings over this period, driven by increases in domestic and foreign shipments. As access barriers to foreign markets are reduced as a result of both North American Free Trade Agreement (NAFTA) and World Trade Organization (WTO) Uruguay Round trade agreements, the industry should be in an excellent position to increase exports. This forecast is dependent on the economic performance of key world paper-consuming markets. U.S. exports should increase 3.5 percent in 1999 and 4 percent annually over

the next 5 years. However, imports also should increase as the U.S. economy expands, leading to increased paper and paperboard demand. U.S. imports are forecast to increase 5 percent in 1999 and 4.5 percent annually over the 1999–2003 period. The large U.S. paper-consuming market will continue to be the principal target for many foreign paper producers.

GLOBAL MARKET PROSPECTS

Growth of U.S. exports of paper and allied products will depend on the improved economies of many key foreign markets. Over the past 5 years the industry has been successful in penetrating a number of emerging markets, including Mexico, China, South Korea, and Brazil. In addition, there has been substantial growth in a number of nontraditional, developing markets in Latin America, southeast Asia, and portions of eastern Europe (see Table 10-2). However, it is still too early to determine the long-term impact of the Asian financial crisis, which nearly paralyzed the economies of important paper-consuming markets, including Thailand, Malaysia, the Philippines, South Korea, and Indonesia. The full extent of the impact of Asia's financial difficulties probably will not be felt until late in the forecast period. It is certain that a number of the pulp, paper, and paperboard capacity announcements made by several key Asian producers will be delayed or perhaps canceled as a result of that region's financial problems.

The successful implementation of trade agreements will greatly increase the U.S. paper and allied products industry's ability to compete. The Mexican economy has experienced a number of economic difficulties over the past several years as Mexico has made a transition to a more business-oriented economy. As a result, the benefits of the NAFTA to the U.S. paper

TABLE 10-1: Paper and Allied Products (SIC 26) Trends and Forecasts
(millions of dollars except as noted)

	1992	1993	1994	1995	1996	1997[1]	1998[2]	1999[3]	Percent Change 96–97	97–98	98–99	92–96[4]
Industry data												
Value of shipments[5]	133,201	133,262	143,649	173,716	160,661	167,853	174,739	183,048	4.5	4.1	4.8	4.8
Value of shipments (1992$)	133,201	135,059	141,192	141,915	140,102	143,464	145,616	148,820	2.4	1.5	2.2	1.3
Total employment (thousands)	627	626	622	629	631	633	634	637	0.3	0.2	0.5	0.2
Production workers (thousands)	479	479	480	487	488	489	490	491	0.2	0.2	0.2	0.5
Average hourly earnings ($)	13.81	14.09	14.52	14.73	15.02	15.31	15.56	15.84	1.9	1.6	1.8	2.1
Capital expenditures	7,963	7,370	7,731	8,369	9,302	8,855	8,990	9,100	−4.8	1.5	1.2	4.0
Product data												
Value of shipments[5]	128,941	128,695	138,560	168,137	155,319	162,286	168,944	176,978	4.5	4.1	4.8	4.8
Value of shipments (1992$)	128,941	130,523	136,231	137,048	135,455	138,706	140,787	143,884	2.4	1.5	2.2	1.2
Trade data												
Value of imports	10,356	10,787	11,668	16,624	14,610	14,664	16,130	16,937	0.4	10.0	5.0	9.0
Value of exports	10,042	9,457	11,000	14,943	14,002	14,511	14,801	15,320	3.6	2.0	3.5	8.7

[1] Estimate except imports and exports.
[2] Estimate.
[3] Forecast.
[4] Compound annual rate.
[5] For a definition of industry versus product values, see "Getting the Most Out of *Outlook '99.*"
Source: U.S. Department of Commerce: Bureau of the Census; International Trade Administration.

TABLE 10-2: U.S. Trade Patterns in Paper and Allied Products[1] in 1997

(millions of dollars; percent)

Regions[2]	Exports Value[3]	Exports Share	Regions[2]	Imports Value[3]	Imports Share, %
NAFTA	5,089	35.1	NAFTA	10,841	73.9
Latin America	1,719	11.8	Latin America	435	3.0
Western Europe	2,970	20.5	Western Europe	2,205	15.0
Japan/Chinese Economic Area	2,559	17.6	Japan/Chinese Economic Area	867	5.9
Other Asia	1,339	9.2	Other Asia	216	1.5
Rest of world	836	5.8	Rest of world	99	0.7
World	14,511	100.0	World	14,664	100.0
Top Five Countries	**Value**	**Share, %**	**Top Five Countries**	**Value**	**Share, %**
Canada	3,054	21.0	Canada	10,573	72.1
Mexico	2,035	14.0	Finland	620	4.2
Japan	1,279	8.8	Germany	416	2.8
United Kingdom	597	4.1	Japan	406	2.8
South Korea	546	3.8	Brazil	325	2.2

[1] SIC 26.
[2] For definitions of regional groupings, see "Getting the Most Out of *Outlook '99*."
[3] Values may not sum to total due to rounding.
Source: U.S. Department of Commerce, Bureau of the Census.

industries have not been realized. In the first 2 years of implementation, U.S. paper products manufacturers had significantly higher exports to Mexico, which reached $1.9 billion in 1995. However, the peso devaluation had a negative impact on the industry's ability to compete in the Mexican market in 1996, and U.S. exports to Mexico dropped to less than $1.8 billion. In 1997, the Mexican economy stabilized and the peso strengthened, giving U.S. exporters of paper and allied products an opportunity to increase their exports to Mexico. In 1997 U.S. exports increased a strong 13 percent in value to $2.03 billion. This trend continued in 1998 as exports to Mexico increased an additional 22 percent to $2.48 billion. This has allowed Mexico to become a solid number two export market, surpassing Japan and trailing only Canada as the leading foreign destination for U.S. paper and allied products. Over the next 5 years, NAFTA should confer further benefits on the U.S. paper manufacturers as the Mexican economy strengthens and tariff and nontariff market access barriers are reduced. Beginning January 1, 1994, NAFTA will phase out trade barriers on the majority of primary pulp, paper, and paperboard products over a 5-year period. Corrugated box tariff and nontariff barriers will be eliminated over 7 years, while tariffs on most converted products will be eliminated after a 10-year phaseout.

The ongoing implementation of the Uruguay Round trade agreements initiated in 1995 should have a positive impact on future trade opportunities for the U.S. paper and allied products industries. As a result of the Uruguay Round tariff agreement for paper, foreign tariff barriers in key European and Asian markets will be eliminated by 2005. In the implementing legislation of the GATT agreement (as well as NAFTA), there is specific language that permits the U.S. government to enter into follow-up negotiations which could lead to shortening or perhaps eliminating the tariff reduction period. In addition, efforts are under

way by the Asia Pacific Economic Cooperation (APEC) members to significantly liberalize trade within several product groupings as agreed at the November 1997 Ministerial. Included in the initiative is the paper and allied products sector. Domestic producers have been very proactive in supporting the U.S. efforts toward this end.

PULP MILLS

According to the current Standard Industrial Classification, manufacturers in SIC 2611 produce a variety of chemical and mechanical paper-grade pulps, special alpha and dissolving pulps, and pulp by-products that include turpentine, tall oil, and other cooking liquor–based by-products. The various grades of pulp are made from softwoods, hardwoods, and other fibrous raw material sources, including recovered fiber, rags, flax, and other agricultural fibers (cotton linters, straw, bagasse, and kenaf). Product shipments by this subsector, both for export and domestic, represent 13 to 16 percent of annual U.S. pulp production and do not include pulp utilized in captive paper and paperboard operations and domestic transfer shipments to affiliated and/or nonaffiliated paper and paperboard mills.

Industry Performance in 1998

After a record-breaking 1997 that saw U.S. market pulp suppliers ship an all-time high of more than 10.5 million metric tons, U.S. market pulp shipments declined 3 percent to about 10.23 million metric tons in 1998. The causes included sluggish domestic demand, depressed foreign sales (especially in Asia), continued global overcapacity, and significant increases in the consumption of recovered paper and paperboard in the United States and abroad. Unfortunately, prices for most pulp grades remained under pressure in 1998 because of excess supply, soft global demand, moderately high pulp inventory levels, and abundant supplies of less expensive recovered paper and paperboard; therefore, the current dollar value of shipments fell 2.2 percent. Exports represented slightly less than 55 percent of the volume of all U.S. market pulp shipments in 1998, the lowest market share in this decade. The Asian financial crisis, in combination with increased competition from other foreign pulp suppliers, contributed to the poorest U.S. export performance since 1990.

The U.S. Department of Commerce's Bureau of the Census divides this subsector's shipments into four major commodity groupings: (1) special alpha and dissolving pulps, representing 17 percent of the current-dollar value of product shipments, (2) sulfate (or kraft) paper-grade pulp, accounting for 70 percent, (3) sulfite paper-grade pulp, accounting for 3 percent, and (4) nonwood pulp and pulp by-products, accounting for 9 percent. On a volume basis, sales by the domestic market pulp sector are dominated by chemical paper-grade pulp produced by the kraft or the sulfite cooking process. In 1998 shipments of these commodities constituted about 83 percent (8.5 million metric tons) of the total quantity of U.S. market pulp shipments. The majority of shipments in this category in 1998 consisted of bleached and semibleached kraft pulp, amounting to 96 percent (8.16 million metric tons) of chemical paper-grade market pulp shipments. The remaining 1998 paper-grade chemical pulp sales came from product shipments of sulfite pulps and unbleached kraft pulp. Domestic market pulp capacity is currently dominated by the kraft process rather than mechanical pulping and other chemical processes. Bleached and unbleached kraft pulps have distinct advantages over mechanical and other chemical process–based pulps, including high physical strength and appearance properties, valuable and economically retrievable pulp by-products (including tall oil and turpentine), improved yields, and lower costs for environmental pollution control. In addition, the kraft pulping process is more conducive to the indigenous hardwood and softwood tree species grown in the United States.

Shipments of special alpha and dissolving pulps accounted for 13 percent of the sector total in 1998 on a volume basis. These higher-valued pulps are specialty grades of chemical pulps produced from alpha cellulose, wood, or cotton linters and are tailored for use in the manufacture of man-made fibers (rayon and acetate), certain cellulose-based plastics, textiles, cellophane film, photographic paper, chemicals, and other value-added specialty papers. The alpha and dissolving pulp market has been going through a difficult transition period over the past several years. For instance, the rayon market, which is one of the big end-use markets for alpha and dissolving pulps, is being dislocated from industrialized nations to less developed countries, slowing domestic sales of alpha pulp. Global capacity has fluctuated rapidly in recent years as several mills in the United States, Europe, and Scandinavia have closed or have retrofitted their equipment to make paper-grade chemical pulp, while new mills have been added in Asia and Latin America. According to the United Nations Food and Agriculture Organi-

zation, world dissolving pulp capacity increased from 5.2 million metric tons in 1988 to 5.6 million metric tons in 1997. Nearly three-fourths of this capacity is in the form of market pulp. In the United States, annual production capacity has declined in recent years to 1.2 million metric tons after the closing of several large mills.

Global Commodity

Chemical paper-grade market pulp, which is used primarily in the manufacture of coated and uncoated free sheet printing and writing paper grades, is recognized as a global commodity and a bellwether for the general health of the world paper and paperboard sector. It is produced in about 27 countries, with 1998 global capacity amounting to approximately 38.2 million metric tons. About 62 percent, or 23.7 million metric tons, of world output comes from the Norscan countries (United States, Canada, Sweden, Finland, and Norway). The combined capacities of Canada (the global leader) and the United States represent 47 percent (17.94 million metric tons) of the world total. For more than a decade the Norscan market share of pulp shipments has declined as a result of significant new capacity coming on stream from a number of suppliers in Latin America, Asia, and Africa. Since 1992 the Norscan market share has declined gradually from 68 percent in that year, to 65 percent in 1996, to 62 percent in 1998. Most of the new output is coming from state-of-the-art pulping facilities in Brazil, Chile, and Indonesia. Those countries have a number of operating advantages over their Norscan counterparts, including low-cost, rapid-growing hardwood and softwood tree species, and lower labor, energy, and environmental protection costs. These countries with lower delivered costs are able to undersell Norscan producers in a global market where price has become the principal driving force.

Prices, Inventories, and Operating Rates

Despite competition from a variety of nontraditional producers, Norscan producers, as a result of their large market share of global market pulp output, are the most critical producers in terms of production levels, prices, and inventories. Generally, Norscan producers need to carry no more than 1.5 million metric tons (or the equivalent of a 25-day supply) of inventory for the market to be considered firm. During most of 1997 Norscan inventory levels remained quite high (1.7 to 1.9 million metric tons), and this depressed prices and pushed down operating rates. In 1996 and 1997 heavy discounting from list prices had taken place. As a result, Northern Bleached Softwood Kraft (NBSK), the premium grade of market pulp, was listed at $610 per metric ton at the end of 1997, but the actual transaction price was only about $580 per metric ton. In the first quarter of 1998 inventories declined to 1.5 million metric tons, a situation which should have given producers an opportunity to push their prices closer to list prices. However, the extent of the Asian financial crisis was felt at the same time that inventories declined. The effect of the financial upheaval resulted in lower pulp and paper demand throughout the Asian region, lower market pulp prices, and a slump in market pulp shipments to

Asia, which has been the fastest growing pulp-consuming market for the past decade. As a result, in the first half of 1998 list prices for NBSK declined to $590 per metric ton, with actual transaction prices falling to $540. The full extent of the impact of the so-called Asian flu probably will not be seen until some time in 1999 or 2000, but the impact on 1998 world market pulp prices was significant. Since this was combined with a slowdown in the European paper industry in mid-1998, further price increases for pulp were unlikely in 1998. Operating rates in 1998 declined slightly to 86 percent from the 90 percent level in 1997. This was the lowest level in several years. Market pulp producers typically prefer to run at operating rates of 93 to 96 percent, but this has not happened since 1995.

The practical maximum chemical paper-grade market wood pulp capacity for U.S. mills in 1998 was essentially unchanged from the 1997 level of 8.6 million metric tons. According to industry estimates, capacity increased less than 1 percent, primarily because of a definition-related shift in capacity from captive pulp to market pulp by a domestic manufacturer. Through the year 2000, capacity is forecast to increase less than 0.5 percent annually and will remain in the range of 8.6 to 8.8 million metric tons during that 3-year time frame.

Recovered paper and paperboard consumption by the domestic paper industry continues to increase rapidly, partly as a result of the industry's goal of a 50 percent recycling rate (consumption and export) of paper stock by 2000. The increased consumption of secondary fiber has come at the expense of virgin papermaking fibers. In 1998, U.S. paper and paperboard mills consumed an all-time high of 33.5 million metric tons of paper and paperboard, nearly a 3 percent increase over the record attained in 1997. In 1998 domestic paper mills consumed an estimated 91.8 million metric tons of total papermaking fiber. Of that total, the virgin fiber share was 64 percent and the secondary fiber share was 36 percent. Since 1994 the secondary fiber share of total papermaking fiber consumption has increased steadily from 30 percent to the record share of 36 percent in 1998. Over the next 3 years paper and paperboard consumption is forecast to increase at an average annual rate of 2.1 percent, more than doubling the rate of virgin wood pulp consumption. By 2000 paper consumption will reach nearly 38 percent of the domestic paper industry's total papermaking fiber consumption.

International Competitiveness

The pulp market has a global nature in which large quantities of virgin papermaking fiber are traded principally duty-free from countries with a net surplus of fiber to papermaking countries which by nature are fiber-deficient. Norscan countries are the leading suppliers because of their adequate forest resources, large domestic pulping infrastructures, adequate transportation and distribution facilities, and low-cost pulp-processing facilities. Canada and the United States are the world's leading producers and exporters of market pulp. For most of the 1980s and early 1990s the United States was the global leader in market pulp production, but in 1996 Canada surpassed it. Currently, the United States is the world's largest captive pulp supplier and the

second leading market pulp supplier. Canada's total chemical paper-grade practical maximum capacity is 9.36 million metric tons, compared with the American market pulp capacity of 8.59 million metric tons.

The United States is a large exporter and importer of market pulp and has enjoyed a trade surplus in that sector since 1987. The majority of international trade in this commodity grouping for the United States consists mainly of bleached and semibleached kraft pulp. In 1998 more than 77 percent of U.S. exports and 80 percent of U.S. imports were composed of this particular grade. U.S. exports of market pulp declined for the third consecutive year in 1998, dropping 15 percent in quantity to 5.53 million metric tons and falling 12 percent in value to $2.9 billion. The decline was driven by substantially lower demand in Asia caused by the financial crisis, which affected many leading pulp-purchasing countries, and a global oversupply of pulp. U.S. exporters shipped pulp to 90 countries in 1998, but the leading markets were Japan (15 percent), Italy (11 percent), Germany (10 percent), and Mexico (9 percent). In 1998 U.S. market pulp imports decreased about 3 percent from 5.8 million metric tons to 5.63 million metric tons. Because of falling pulp prices, the value of these imports declined 5 percent, dropping from $2.57 billion to $2.44 billion. The United States imported pulp from 15 countries, but 3 supplying countries (Canada at 82 percent, Brazil at 13 percent, and South Africa at 2 percent) were responsible for 97 percent of the U.S. import total in 1998.

Prospects for 1999

A turnaround in the important Asian pulp-consuming economies combined with an increase in production by domestic paper producers should result in increased demand for U.S. market pulp in 1999 (see Table 10-3). As a result, market pulp shipments (in 1992 dollars) should increase 2 percent. Higher demand by U.S. and Asian producers for printing and writing paper should contribute to this expansion. The industry should have higher shipments, prices, and operating rates in 1999, resulting in a return to profitability for the sector.

The volume of U.S. exports of pulp should increase about 5.5 percent and increase their product share of total pulp shipments to more than 60 percent. For U.S. pulp exporters to improve their sales in 1999, significant improvements will have to be made in the Asian economies which have been adversely affected by the recent financial crisis. The subsector's ability to export to Korea, Thailand, Malaysia, and the Philippines is critical for exports to increase. A rebound of Japan's and China's economies also is important to the subsector's export prospects for 1999. The strengthening of the U.S. dollar throughout the east Asian region has reduced the price competitiveness of U.S. market pulp in that region. A strengthening of the local currencies in that region will aid the ability of U.S. exporters to export to these large paper-producing, fiber-deficient markets.

As the world's leading paper and paperboard manufacturer, the United States will continue to be the target of many countries' pulp output. As a result, U.S. imports of pulp are forecast to increase 2.5 percent on a volume basis and 4 percent on a

TABLE 10-3: Pulp Mills (SIC 2611) Trends and Forecasts

(millions of dollars except as noted)

	1992	1993	1994	1995	1996	1997[1]	1998[2]	1999[3]	96–97	97–98	98–99	92–96[4]
									Percent Change			
Industry data												
Value of shipments[5]	5,466	4,282	4,827	7,513	5,508	5,930	5,798	6,151	7.7	−2.2	6.1	0.2
Value of shipments (1992$)	5,466	4,758	4,992	4,920	4,931	5,104	4,951	5,050	3.5	−3.0	2.0	−2.5
Total employment (thousands)	15.9	14.2	13.3	14.6	15.0	15.1	14.9	15.2	0.7	−1.3	2.0	−1.4
Production workers (thousands)	12.1	10.8	10.2	11.3	11.1	11.1	11.0	11.2	0.0	−0.9	1.8	−2.1
Average hourly earnings ($)	19.15	19.49	20.08	20.40	20.16	20.65	20.80	20.85	2.4	0.7	0.2	1.3
Capital expenditures	772	426	315	564	698	575	488	525	−17.6	−15.1	7.6	−2.5
Product data												
Value of shipments[5]	6,104	4,995	5,952	8,911	6,329	6,814	6,662	7,067	7.7	−2.2	6.1	0.9
Value of shipments (1992$)	6,104	5,550	6,156	5,836	5,666	5,864	5,688	5,802	3.5	−3.0	2.0	−1.8
Trade data												
Value of imports	2,104	1,868	2,285	3,745	2,601	2,572	2,443	2,541	−1.1	−5.0	4.0	5.4
Value of exports	3,236	2,482	2,954	4,698	3,358	3,253	2,863	3,092	−3.1	−12.0	8.0	0.9

[1] Estimate except imports and exports.
[2] Estimate.
[3] Forecast.
[4] Compound annual rate.
[5] For a definition of industry versus product values, see "Getting the Most Out of *Outlook '99.*"
Source: U.S. Department of Commerce: Bureau of the Census; International Trade Administration.

value basis in 1999. U.S. suppliers that ship to the domestic market probably will face increased competition from low-cost, high-volume producers in Indonesia, Brazil, South Africa, and Chile. U.S. producers of pulp will need to monitor their own capacity utilization rates as well as consumer and producer inventory levels around the world and their relationship with the current level of global paper and paperboard production to prevent further significant increases in surplus pulp in the market.

Long-Term Prospects

Over the 1999–2003 forecast period, U.S. market pulp suppliers will experience increased global demand and a corresponding increase in sales as product shipments increase about 1.75 percent annually over those 5 years. Much of the growth in sales will be linked to foreign demand as exports continue to be the major end use for U.S. market pulp shipments. The U.S. dollar must stabilize, especially in the east Asian region, for the United States to remain competitive in world pulp markets. Exports as a proportion of total market pulp shipments are likely to return to the 70 percent level over the 5-year period as U.S. paper and paperboard producers continue to consume even larger quantities of paper and paperboard. Other economic and performance characteristics important to this subsector include domestic and foreign paper and paperboard demand (especially for printing and writing paper), capacity utilization rates, various pulp inventory levels, and market pulp prices. For this industry to remain productive and profitable, utilization rates in the range of 92 to 96 percent should be maintained and producer inventory levels should stay near the 25-day supply level.

U.S. suppliers will continue to experience increased competition from Asian, African, and Latin American suppliers not only in the global pulp market but also in the U.S. market,

which is by far the world's largest pulp-consuming market. Despite these factors, virgin market pulp will continue to be papermakers' fiber of choice because of its high strength and appearance properties, uniformity of quality, cleanliness, and ease of processing. In the U.S. market, virgin pulp will maintain about a 62 to 64 percent share of the fiber consumed in domestic paper and paperboard mills.

According to a recent report, total demand for chemical paper-grade market pulp is forecast to increase about 1.3 million metric tons from 1998 to 2000. However, the survey indicates that supply will increase by only 930,000 metric tons during that period. This differential should allow supply and demand levels to remain close, promoting a price recovery during that period. Although most pulp capacity expansion activity in this decade has come from North American mills, the biggest increases over the next several years will come from Indonesia and Brazil. Indonesia's new capacity additions, which are supposed to involve new mills coming on stream over the next couple of years, may be delayed by the severe economic conditions affecting that country.

PAPER AND PAPERBOARD MILLS

According to the current SIC, paper and paperboard mills (SIC 262 and 263) are engaged primarily in manufacturing a variety of commodity grades of coated and uncoated paper and paperboard from wood pulp and other fiber pulp and also may manufacture converted and packaging paper and paperboard products. Among the commodities manufactured by this subsector are newsprint, coated and uncoated printing and writing papers, tissue, packaging and converting paper, boxboard, bristols, milk carton board, containerboard, pressboard, special food board, wet machine board, and construction paper and paperboard.

Industry Performance in 1998

Product shipments (in 1992 dollars) by the U.S. paper and paperboard mills subsector increased 1 percent in 1998 as a result of global economic gains which led to an increase in domestic and international demand and a subsequent improvement in U.S. sales. In 1998 the industry saw a number of improvements in operating conditions, including an easing of overcapacity, which has plagued the industry for several years, and the end of a long inventory drawdown cycle. There were year-over-year increases in nearly every major commodity in the paperboard subsector and in a select number of paper subsectors, including uncoated printing and writing paper grades, tissue, and several converting and packaging paper grades. The only subsectors that had negative results in 1998 were newsprint, unbleached kraft papers, and coated printing and writing paper grades.

The value of product shipments by U.S. paper and paperboard mills in 1998 increased 6 percent. The weak price structure that had been in place since mid-1995 slowly ended in late 1997 and early 1998 because inventories dropped, capacity additions were minimal, and production rates generally decreased over a 24-month period starting at the end of 1995; this eventually led to higher prices for many paper and paperboard commodities in 1998. Operating rates for the industry, which had shown a steady decline in 1995 and 1996, improved in 1997 and 1998. For the U.S. paperboard subsector, domestic mill operating rates declined from the 1994 high of nearly 97 percent to just under 95 percent in 1995 and to less than 93 percent in 1996. However, as the inventory drawdown process continued and demand remained high in 1997 and 1998, domestic paperboard sector operating rates improved to 95 percent in 1997 and 97 percent in 1998.

The results for the paper segment of the domestic paper and paperboard mills subsector were similar. Operating rates declined from the 1994 level of nearly 95 percent to only 90 percent in 1996. However, in 1997 and 1998 operating rates jumped back to 94 percent. As a result, domestic producers were able to reduce their inventories in late 1995 and 1996, setting the stage for better operating conditions in 1997 and 1998 and enabling many domestic producers to pass along legitimate price increases for the first time in several years.

The principal reason for the industry's poor price performance in the past 3 years was a large buying spree by many domestic and international customers beginning in late 1995 in anticipation of future price increases. Box makers, printers, publishers, and other end users began buying up large quantities of base paper and paperboard grades to obtain raw materials that could ensure effective operations and eliminate the need to buy after the next price hike. In the previous 18 months, price hikes on most commodity grades of paper and paperboard were occurring quarter upon quarter.

Another bright spot for the industry in 1998 was the increase in the quantity of paper and paperboard exports. The globaliza-tion of the world paper and paperboard subsector has been an ongoing process for more than a decade. The United States produces nearly 30 percent of the world's paper and paperboard output. As a result, the domestic industry is well suited to take advantage of growing world paper and paperboard demand. In 1998, because of higher foreign demand and a comparatively low-valued U.S. dollar, U.S. exports of paper and paperboard increased more than 4.5 percent to 10.4 million metric tons, an all-time high for U.S. producers. Despite the financial crisis in Asia, which affected a number of that region's key paper-purchasing markets in 1998, there was increased demand in other portions of Asia and also in Europe and Latin America, which led to the increase in overall U.S. paper and paperboard exports. International trade continues to be the subsector's major source of growth. Over the past 5 years U.S. exports of paper and paperboard have increased nearly 7 percent annually on a tonnage basis.

In 1998 U.S. production of paper and paperboard reached a new record as output rose to 85.6 million metric tons. Paperboard commodities were responsible for 53.5 percent (45.8 million metric tons) of the subsector's output, while paper commodities were responsible for 46.5 percent (39.8 million metric tons). On a current-dollar basis, however, paper commodities have a higher per unit value; therefore, shipments of paper accounted for 63 percent of the paper and paperboard mills total, while paperboard shipments accounted for 37 percent.

Paper Mills

Slowly improving operating rates, slight increases in domestic and international demand, and moderately improved prices characterized the U.S. paper mills subsector in 1998. Although the drawdown of inventories which started in mid-1995 was slower than expected, it contributed to a better overall performance by U.S. producers in 1998. The process of inventory downsizing resulted from producers' efforts to keep operating rates in check, minimize capacity additions, and take advantage of the stronger demand. The strength in the U.S. economy, with real GDP increasing more than 3.5 percent, was the principal cause of the increase in domestic demand. Although exports of paper and paperboard have increased greatly over the past decade, 90 percent of the output from U.S. paper mills is destined for the domestic market. According to the 38th Annual Pulp, Paper, and Paperboard Capacity Survey from the American Forest and Paper Association, from 1997 through 1999 domestic papermaking capacity is forecast to increase only 1.5 percent annually. This should allow supply and demand to continue to be brought more into balance as the industry moves into 1999.

In 1998 production from U.S. paper mills was divided into four principal commodity segments: printing and writing paper, newsprint, tissue, and packaging and converting paper. Printing and writing paper constitutes the single largest commodity group in paper-related production. In 1998 domestic output of this high-value paper products segment was 23.5 million metric tons, which amounted to 59 percent of all paper-related production. Within this commodity grouping, moderate increases in shipments came from the uncoated groundwood paper segment and the uncoated free sheet subsector. Uncoated free sheet, which is used extensively in a variety of printing and publishing applications, was the single largest printing and writing paper commodity in 1998, amounting to 12.2 million metric tons, or 52 percent of all U.S. printing and writing paper production. The second leading commodity grouping in the paper sector in 1998 was newsprint. Production of this newspaper, periodical, and journal raw material in 1998 was just under 6.5 million metric tons, essentially unchanged from the 1997 record level. Newsprint production represented 16 percent of all paper-related output in 1998. The strongest growth in the paper segment of the paper and paperboard mills subsector in 1998 occurred in the tissue segment. Domestic output in 1998 was 5.96 million metric tons, representing 15 percent of U.S. paper output and indicating nearly a 4 percent increase over the 1997 level. The other major paper commodity from U.S. mills in 1998 was bleached and unbleached kraft converting, wrapping, and packaging papers. U.S. production of this material, which is used extensively in the manufacture of bags and grocery sacks, totaled 3.83 million metric tons in 1998, representing 10 percent of all U.S. paper production in that year.

Paperboard Mills

In 1998 U.S. production of paperboard commodities increased nearly 3 percent because of strong domestic and export performances by U.S. containerboard mills. U.S. producers of containerboard (linerboard and corrugating medium) had noticeably higher sales to the export market, domestic corrugated and solid fiber box plants, and nonpackaging containerboard end-use markets. Over the past several years U.S. paperboard mills, especially the containerboard subsector, have had record sales opportunities for many of their products in corrugated box, shipping container, and carton plants in southeast Asia, Europe, and Latin America, leading to a sizable increase in the subsector's exports.

U.S. production of paperboard is divided into two product lines: containerboard and boxboard. Containerboard sales amounted to 32.2 million metric tons (70.5 percent) of all domestic paperboard production in 1998, nearly a 4 percent increase over the 1997 record level. Domestic boxboard production amounted to 13.5 million metric tons (29.5 percent of total paperboard production) in 1998, less than a 1 percent increase over the 1997 level. Softer than expected demand by some folding carton and sanitary food and beverage container end users contributed to only minimal increases in boxboard production in 1998. Although domestic boxboard sales to folding carton plants were soft in 1998, the export market was very strong as foreign shipments by U.S. boxboard producers increased 7 percent to nearly 1.7 million metric tons.

The production of linerboard, which is used by the corrugated box and container subsector and is the largest domestic paperboard commodity, accounted for 58 percent (18.8 million metric tons) of domestic containerboard production in 1998. This was a 4.6 percent increase over the 1997 level and a new record for domestic producers, and it gives an indication of

strong demand by U.S. corrugators and a solid export market. Domestic production of corrugating medium, the other component of a corrugated box, increased 2 percent in 1998 to 8.9 million metric tons. Despite the mostly positive situation for containerboard subsector fundamentals in 1998, announced price increases were held back in the first half that year. Several leading producers indicated that an attempt at price increases of $40 to $50 per ton for both linerboard and corrugating medium might take place in fall 1998. In most of 1998 prices for containerboard remained essentially unchanged.

According to a recent industry capacity survey, domestic paperboard mills will add more than 1.7 million metric tons of capacity by 2000. This reflects an average annual growth rate of 1.2 percent from 1998 through 2000. This is a noticeable drop from the 3 percent average annual increase in capacity over the 1988–1997 period. Nearly 56 percent of the capacity addition will be in the containerboard sector.

International Competitiveness

Strong foreign demand and adequate domestic supplies enabled the U.S. paper and paperboard subsector to increase its exports on both a volume basis (4.5 percent) and a value basis (8 percent) in 1998. Demand was strongest in certain Asian and Latin American markets but also was up in portions of Europe and Africa. In 1998, paper exports represented 31 percent (volume basis) of the total and paperboard represented 69 percent. Paperboard's export market share has increased in recent years from 64 percent in 1994 to the 1998 record share of U.S. exports. In 1998, on the paper side, there were higher exports of tissue (40 percent) and packaging and converting paper (24 percent), while exports of printing and writing paper and newsprint fell 11 percent and 18 percent, respectively. On the paperboard side, there were increases in exports of bleached and unbleached linerboard (8 percent), recycled paperboard (6 percent), semichemical corrugating medium (30 percent), and unbleached kraft paperboard (2.5 percent).

In 1998 the strong U.S. economic performance led to significant increases in paper and paperboard consumption. Other paper-producing countries, including Canada, Sweden, Finland, Indonesia, and Brazil, seized the opportunity to increase their exports to the United States to take advantage of the increase in demand. As a result, there was an 11 percent increase in the volume of U.S. imports of paper and paperboard and an 18 percent increase in the value of U.S. paper and paper imports in 1998. The U.S. market is not protected by significant tariff and nontariff market access barriers; this makes the U.S. market vulnerable to low-cost or surplus paper and paperboard output from a number of foreign competitors.

As a result of the dependence of the U.S. newspaper publishing market on newsprint imports (primarily from Canada), the U.S. paper and paperboard mills sector has traditionally run a trade deficit. In 1998 U.S. imports of newsprint amounted to 6.52 million metric tons, reflecting nearly a 2 percent drop from the 1997 level. However, U.S. imports of nearly every other commodity grade of paper and paperboard surged in 1998. This included significant increases in imports of printing and writing paper (33 percent), packaging and converting paper (10 percent), semichemical corrugating medium (11 percent), kraft paperboard (7 percent), and paperboard (17 percent).

Forecast for 1999

Shipments (in 1992 dollars) from domestic paper and paperboard mills are forecast to increase at least 2.5 percent in 1999 as the U.S. economy continues to expand, resulting in higher domestic demand for a variety of paper and paperboard commodity grades (see Table 10-4). This forecast is contingent not only on an improving U.S. economy but also on better economic conditions in key Asian, Latin American, and European markets and reduced market access barriers in key foreign markets. A stabilized U.S. dollar compared to foreign currencies, especially in Asia and Latin America, will aid U.S. producers in increasing their exports in 1999. Although domestic producers traditionally have directed much of their output to domestic converters and packagers, significant future growth will be centered in vital international markets, especially in Asia and Latin America. Exports to Europe, although still important, will not grow as fast because of competition from Canadian and Scandinavian producers, which already have a strong presence in the European market. Exports of paper and paperboard will increase 3.5 percent on a volume basis and 7 percent on a value basis in 1999.

The outlook for the global paper and paperboard subsector is uncertain. Although demand is forecast to increase about 1.9 percent in 1999, the rate of expansion is well below the 2.3 percent to 2.5 percent levels of the late 1980s and early 1990s. The long-term impact of the Asian financial crisis will not begin to unfold until 1999. Asia is the fastest growing paper-consuming and paper-producing region. Unfortunately for a number of key east Asian paper-producing countries, the financial crisis came

at a time when a number of new operations were being built or were planned. Industry surveys indicate that through announced capacity additions in Asia, 17 million metric tons is scheduled to come on line before the end of 1999. This would represent more than half the world's total increase in paper capacity during that 2-year period. However, the crisis has led to the canceling or at least the delaying of a number of paper machine installations and mill constructions in Asia. It remains to be seen exactly how much output will be canceled or postponed because of the Asian financial crisis.

After successfully passing along numerous price increases in 1994 and through mid-1995, global paper and paperboard producers saw steep price declines from mid-1995 through most of 1996. The cycle of peaks-to-valleys pricing has been one that global paper and paperboard producers have been unable to avoid over the past half century despite their concerted efforts. In 1999 relationships between producers, stockholders, and consumers will experience more friction as producers seek to make up for their disappointing results over the last 24 months. U.S. paper and paperboard producers will have to monitor closely domestic and foreign demand, supply, and inventory levels to prevent further dramatic price swings in 1999. U.S. paper and paperboard mill fundamentals and operating conditions appear to be relatively solid for 1999. As a result, operating rates should increase and prices should improve.

Over the next 2 years the domestic paper and paperboard mills subsector is expected to add 3.2 million metric tons of capacity, with new output being added to both the paper subsector and the paperboard subsectors (paperboard increases will constitute 60 percent of the added capacity). If the global economy improves over the next 24 months, the additional output from U.S. mills will be easily absorbed. If it does not, operating rates in domestic production plants probably will remain in the

TABLE 10-4: Paper and Paperboard Mills (SIC 262, 263) Trends and Forecasts
(millions of dollars except as noted)

| | 1992 | 1993 | 1994 | 1995 | 1996 | 1997[1] | 1998[2] | 1999[3] | Percent Change | | | |
									96–97	97–98	98–99	92–96[4]
Industry data												
Value of shipments[5]	48,926	48,267	53,381	69,638	59,837	64,306	68,186	73,046	7.5	6.0	7.1	5.2
Value of shipments (1992$)	48,926	48,625	52,187	53,571	51,107	52,538	53,063	54,390	2.8	1.0	2.5	1.1
Total employment (thousands)	182	180	177	175	171	172	175	175	0.6	1.7	0.0	−1.5
Production workers (thousands)	140	138	136	135	132	133	135	135	0.8	1.5	0.0	−1.5
Average hourly earnings ($)	17.97	18.22	19.17	19.76	20.34	20.55	20.70	21.00	1.0	0.7	1.4	3.1
Capital expenditures	4,952	4,507	4,960	4,859	5,502	5,320	5,410	5,655	−3.3	1.7	4.5	2.7
Product data												
Value of shipments[5]	47,232	46,513	51,110	67,052	57,971	62,302	66,061	70,768	7.5	6.0	7.1	5.3
Value of shipments (1992$)	47,232	46,866	49,945	51,571	49,514	50,900	51,409	52,694	2.8	1.0	2.5	1.2
Trade data												
Value of imports	6,736	7,224	7,371	10,235	9,154	9,055	10,685	11,219	−1.1	18.0	5.0	8.0
Value of exports	4,263	4,189	4,813	6,437	6,339	6,545	7,069	7,563	3.2	8.0	7.0	10.4

[1] Estimate except imports and exports.
[2] Estimate.
[3] Forecast.
[4] Compound annual rate.
[5] For a definition of industry versus product values, see "Getting the Most Out of *Outlook '99*."
Source: U.S. Department of Commerce: Bureau of the Census; International Trade Administration.

upper 80s to low 90s percentwise to prevent mill and consumer stocks from increasing significantly.

Long-Term Prospects

Over the 1999–2003 period the U.S. paper and paperboard mills subsector should see shipments increase about 1.9 percent annually. As major Asian paper-consuming markets recover and other global economies grow, resulting in increased consumption of paper and paperboard, the U.S. industry should be in the best position to supply much of the increased demand. As further capacity is added, the U.S. industry will expand its overseas activities in Mexico, other Latin American countries, southeast Asia, and eastern Europe. The United States has the world's largest paper and paperboard industry, producing nearly 30 percent of world paper and paperboard output. As market access barriers are reduced over the next 5 years, demand for high-quality, price-competitive U.S. paper and paperboard products will increase. As a result, U.S. exports will grow at least 3.3 percent annually through 2003. As the world's leading paper-consuming market, the United States will continue to be a target for many countries' surplus paper and paperboard output. Low-cost imports from Indonesia, Brazil, Canada, and certain European countries will increase during this period. There are practically no market access barriers which will impede other countries from exporting to the large U.S. market. As a result, imports will increase 3 percent annually in the 1999–2000 period.

Competition on a global scale is expected to increase over this period as world producers seek to maintain their current market share and broaden their customer base. According to the United Nations Food and Agriculture Organization, global paper and paperboard capacity is forecast to grow from 300.5 million metric tons in 1995 to 337.4 million metric tons by 2000. This reflects an annual average increase of 2.3 percent, which is significantly below the 2.9 percent average annual increase that took place from 1990 through 1995. Although the United States will remain the global leader in output, its share of total world production probably will decline over this period when competition from Asian, Latin American, Canadian, and certain European producers increases. The largest growth is expected from Asia as producers in China, South Korea, Japan, and Indonesia seek to satisfy more domestic demand and move into the export arena. By 2003 the U.S. sector's share of global paper and paperboard production will have dropped from the current level of just over 29 percent to 27 percent. However, there will be further technological, product, and distribution innovations on the part of U.S. suppliers, and this will enable domestic producers to remain powerful players in the expanding global paper and paperboard market.

CORRUGATED AND SOLID FIBER BOXES

According to the current SIC, the corrugated and solid fiber box industry (SIC 2653) consists of establishments that are engaged primarily in the manufacture of corrugated and solid fiber boxes and containers and related products from purchased paperboard (produced in SIC 263). The industry's principal commodities are corrugated and solid fiberboard boxes, pads, partitions, display items, pallets, single face products, and corrugated sheets. According to the *Annual Survey of Manufactures* (*ASM*), product shipments for the industry represent more than 60 percent of total U.S. paperboard container and box shipments (SIC 265).

Industry Performance in 1998

The U.S. corrugated and solid fiber boxes industry experienced a third consecutive year of strong growth in 1998 as product shipments (in 1992 dollars) increased 3.2 percent. The 1998 increase is in line with the growth pattern of corrugated product shipments for the past 10 years even when the 4 percent decline in 1995 is taken into account. Domestic corrugators enjoyed record domestic and foreign demand in 1998, which saw the industry ship a record 402.6 billion square feet of finished corrugated boxes, cartons, and shipping containers. Shipments of corrugated products represented just over 99 percent (399 billion square feet) of the 1998 industry total, and shipments of solid fiber boxes made up the remainder.

Strong growth in the U.S. economy in 1998 resulted in increased U.S. manufacturing output (the principal driving force behind corrugated box demand) and higher shipments of industrial and consumer nondurable goods. This translated into record demand for a variety of virgin and recycled corrugated packaging materials and shipping containers. Although the industry struggled in the first half of 1997, it was able to recover in the second half, buoyed by continued growth in the U.S. economy (real GDP increased nearly 4 percent), 7.5 percent growth in U.S. industrial production, and increased domestic and foreign consumption.

In 1998 the U.S. corrugated and solid fiber boxes industry continued to have excellent export opportunities. U.S. exports of a wide variety of corrugated boxes, shipping containers, and related packaging materials have increased each year since 1989. This growth has been remarkable in that the total quantity of exports has increased as well as the actual number of markets. In 1998, the industry experienced another year of record demand despite the Asian financial crisis and the slow growth of many European and Latin American economies. Exports as a percentage of total shipments have grown noticeably over the last eight years, from less than 1 percent in 1989 to nearly 3 percent in 1998. Although the overall percentage remains relatively low, exports have become one of the fastest growing end-use segments for domestic corrugators. The ability of the domestic industry to develop innovative packaging and shipping commodities to meet the increasingly stringent requirements of foreign customers has enabled U.S. corrugators to become the world's leading exporters of finished corrugated products. The U.S. shipment level in 1998 was roughly 30 percent above the foreign sales of European Union (EU) corrugators and almost four times the amount shipped by Japan. The superior quality, price competitiveness, and high strength of U.S.-produced corrugated materials continue to open new export opportunities for U.S. suppliers.

Prices and Inventories

Since the disappointing current-dollar sales value of 1996, the corrugated box industry has experienced back-to-back years of higher current-dollar sales, primarily as a result of the recovery of prices for domestic corrugators. The producer price index (using 1980 as the base year) for SIC 2653 shows a slow, moderate increase since the final quarter of 1996, which has equated to higher current-dollar value sales for the subsector over the past several years. The combination of growing domestic and foreign demand and closely monitored inventories allowed U.S. corrugating converters to implement several small price increases in 1997 and 1998. Box prices were able to catch up to the price hikes made for linerboard and corrugating medium in the final quarter of 1997.

The domestic corrugating industry was able to draw down its containerboard (i.e., linerboard and corrugating medium) inventories to manageable levels (about 2.3 million to 2.5 million tons, which equates to a 4-week supply) and to moderate effectively operating levels for most of 1997 and the early months of 1998. Although U.S. containerboard producers were able to increase their prices slightly in the last half of 1997, they were unable to push through additional price increases in the first half of 1998 as inventory levels at domestic corrugating plants began to creep back up, slowing the pace of containerboard price increases for most of the year. In 1998 U.S. paperboard mills produced nearly 27.6 million metric tons of containerboard for domestic corrugated converting operations, up a strong 4 percent from the 1997 level. To produce combined board, these corrugator plants consumed 27.8 million metric tons of containerboard, reflecting the decrease in year-end inventories from 1997 to 1998. Of the quantity of containerboard consumed, linerboard represented 67 percent of the total and corrugating medium accounted for 33 percent.

International Competitiveness

Spurred by an increase in foreign demand for high-quality, high-strength, competitively priced U.S. corrugated shipping containers and boxes, domestic exports of corrugated paperboard products experienced their ninth consecutive year of growth in quantity and value in 1998 with a 6 percent increase in value and a 4 percent increase in volume. U.S. corrugators exported a record 2.33 million metric tons of finished corrugated boxes, containers, and related products in 1998. Although domestic sales have fluctuated in recent years, foreign sales have continued to be a bright spot for domestic producers. Despite the Asian financial crisis, U.S. corrugators increased their sales noticeably to Japan, Indonesia, China, Taiwan, Singapore, and Hong Kong. U.S. exports of corrugated containers and finished packaging commodities were shipped mainly to Mexico (55 percent) and Canada (21 percent) in 1998. However, there were large increases in exports to Brazil, Honduras, the Dominican Republic, and several other Latin American markets in that year.

Although imports of corrugated containers and other finished corrugated products totaled only $156 million in 1998, they increased for the seventh consecutive year. The growth in the U.S. economy was the principal driver behind the increase in imports in 1998. The only significant suppliers of corrugated containers and related materials to the U.S. market in 1998 were Canada (65 percent) and Mexico (10 percent).

Prospects for 1999

The U.S. corrugated and solid fiber boxes subsector should experience higher domestic and foreign demand in 1999, resulting in a 3.3 percent increase in product shipments (see Table 10-5). The U.S. economy is expected to continue to grow in 1999, resulting in increased industrial activity and higher shipments of nondurable goods. If domestic corrugators are to experience an

TABLE 10-5: Corrugated and Solid Fiber Boxes (SIC 2653) Trends and Forecasts
(millions of dollars except as noted)

	1992	1993	1994	1995	1996	1997[1]	1998[2]	1999[3]	Percent Change 96–97	97–98	98–99	92–96[4]
Industry data												
Value of shipments[5]	19,834	20,623	22,681	27,965	25,914	27,754	30,085	32,591	7.1	8.4	8.3	6.9
Value of shipments (1992$)	19,834	20,895	21,297	20,472	21,051	21,682	22,376	23,114	3.0	3.2	3.3	1.5
Total employment (thousands)	112	114	120	125	127	129	130	132	1.6	0.8	1.5	3.2
Production workers (thousands)	81.4	82.6	89.3	93.5	94.7	95.4	95.6	96.5	0.7	0.2	0.9	3.9
Average hourly earnings ($)	11.37	11.85	11.92	11.77	12.12	12.25	12.65	12.73	1.1	3.3	0.6	1.6
Capital expenditures	465	530	531	788	862	775	795	806	−10.1	2.6	1.4	16.7
Product data												
Value of shipments[5]	19,139	19,876	21,703	26,724	24,816	26,578	28,800	31,250	7.1	8.4	8.5	6.7
Value of shipments (1992$)	19,139	20,138	20,379	19,564	20,159	20,764	21,428	22,135	3.0	3.2	3.3	1.3
Trade data												
Value of imports	62.8	74.7	102	131	139	141	156	166	1.4	10.6	6.4	22.0
Value of exports	392	421	533	698	789	818	867	910	3.7	6.0	5.0	19.1

[1] Estimate except imports and exports.
[2] Estimate.
[3] Forecast.
[4] Compound annual rate.
[5] For a definition of industry versus product values, see "Getting the Most Out of *Outlook '99*."
Source: U.S. Department of Commerce: Bureau of the Census; International Trade Administration.

increase in the current-dollar value of shipments, they will have to do a better of job of monitoring finished product inventories and adjusting their operating rates to reflect current domestic and foreign demand patterns. The availability of raw materials should not be a problem for the industry in 1999. The additional linerboard and corrugating medium output coming on line and the slow recovery of important containerboard export markets in Asia should allow domestic corrugators to secure adequate box-making materials at reasonable prices. However, a significant recent merger in the containerboard subsector could affect the availability, flow, and price of linerboard and corrugating medium. As a result, domestic corrugators, especially independent corrugators, will have to monitor closely their raw material inventories to ensure that high production levels are maintained.

Foreign sales will grow in 1999, with exports increasing on a value basis by 5 percent to $910 million, which will be a record high for U.S. corrugators. Despite a slow recovery in important Asian markets, U.S. corrugated box, carton, and related product converters should find expanded sales opportunities in traditional markets and develop new markets. Growth in the U.S. economy (with real GDP growth averaging 2.2 percent) will result in increased imports of corrugated packaging materials. In 1998 imports are forecast to increase nearly 6.5 percent to a record high of $166 million.

In 1998 shipments of nondurable goods made up 77.7 percent of the total volume of corrugated boxes and related materials shipments, reflecting a slight increase over 1997. This share will decrease slightly in 1999 to 77.5 percent as durable goods grab a slightly larger share of the subsector's shipments. Growth in demand in the food and kindred products (40 percent of corrugated shipments) and paper and allied products (22.7 percent of corrugated shipments) sectors contributed to the increase in the share of nondurable goods in 1998, and that growth will continue in 1999. Durable goods made up just over 22 percent of total corrugated products shipments in 1998 and will increase their percentage of shipments further in 1999. The leading durables end-user segments in 1999 will be miscellaneous manufacturing, which includes toys, amusements, and sporting and athletic goods (4.7 percent of corrugated shipments), and stone, clay, and glass products (4.5 percent of corrugated shipments).

Long-Term Prospects

Product shipments by the U.S. corrugated and solid fiber boxes sector are expected to grow nearly 3 percent annually over the next 5 years. This places the subsector first in projected average annual growth among all domestic paperboard packaging subsectors (SIC 265). The food and kindred products and paper and allied products industries will continue to be the leading end-use markets throughout this period. However, durable goods sectors, as they have done over the past several years, will continue to consume larger quantities of corrugated containers, cartons, and boxes. Competition for domestic and international market share for shipping mediums probably will intensify from flexible plastic films, metal and plastic laminates, and related materials as well as within the paperboard packaging subsectors. For instance, in 1998 some customers in the food

industry, notably the meat and fresh fruit and vegetable sectors, began to replace traditional brown corrugated boxes with returnable, reusable plastic containers. This trend has been under way for some time in parts of Europe.

Despite increased competition, corrugated packaging materials should be able to maintain their dominant role as a shipping medium through more innovative, visually appealing, environmentally friendly, recyclable cost-effective products which will be increasingly directed toward the retail marketplace in the form of consumer-oriented point-of-purchase displays. The continued growth of large "warehouse-style" grocery outlets offering bulk and jumbo-size items will provide new marketing and sales opportunities for domestic corrugators. Although traditional shipping containers (the so-called brown boxes) will continue to dominate sales into the next century, specialty corrugated products, which are largely consumer-directed, will have the fastest rate of growth. The development of new miniflutes (known as E- and F-flutes) has opened up many end-user segments that previously were unavailable for domestic corrugators. These new products are very popular for use as point-of-purchase consumer-oriented displays in both grocery stores and other retail stores and outlets.

U.S. exports of corrugated boxes, containers, and related products are projected to continue to climb through the forecast period 1999–2003, spurred by increasing sales to Latin American countries, the recovery of Asian market economies, and the development of new markets in Europe. Canada and Mexico will remain the dominant foreign markets for U.S. corrugated products not only because of their proximity but also because of a projected acceleration of demand. The removal of market access barriers through the U.S.–Canada Free Trade Agreement and the ongoing reduction of barriers through NAFTA have created a more level playing field for U.S. corrugated products exporters, which have seen their export opportunities improve. Further implementation of NAFTA should help U.S. producers continue to increase their exports.

During the next 5 years the domestic corrugating sector will see expanded product development; an increased recycled content of its corrugated board through improved technologies, paper stock handling, and collection procedures; new uses for preprinted linerboard; increased use of minifluted and microfluted combination board in point-of-purchase displays; increased use of computerization in every aspect of corrugated box design, assembly, and distribution; expanded use of flexographic color printing; and improvements in graphic design. As the world's lowest-cost, highest-volume, most technologically advanced, and highest-quality producer of containerboard and corrugated products, the United States is expected to remain highly competitive in the ever-expanding global marketplace for corrugated shipping containers and similar products over the forecast period.

FOLDING PAPERBOARD BOXES

According to the current SIC, the folding paperboard box (also known as the folding carton) industry (SIC 2657) is made up of establishments that are engaged primarily in the manufacture of folding paperboard boxes from purchased paperboard (manufactured in SIC 263), including folding sanitary food boxes and cartons, except milk cartons. Milk and milk-type paperboard containers and cartons are classified under SIC 2656, sanitary food containers. The principal products manufactured include a variety of folding paperboard boxes, packaging containers, and food packaging components for a number of food and produce (i.e., dry foods, beverages, frozen foods, fast-food restaurant items) and nonfood items (i.e., soaps, detergents, cosmetics, medicinal products, personal health and hygiene products, paper products). The industry is second only to the corrugated and solid fiber box industry in terms of domestic paperboard container and box industry sales. The *ASM* shows that product shipments for this industry represent nearly 30 percent of total U.S. paperboard container and box shipments (SIC 265).

Industry Performance for 1998

The U.S. folding paperboard box industry set all-time records in 1998 in both the quantity and the value of product shipments. The strength of the domestic economy, which led to increased domestic sales, and a stronger than expected export performance enabled the industry to have record sales in nearly all its end-use markets. This was the second consecutive year of significant growth for this sector after a disappointing sales performance in 1996. Based on annualized 5-month 1998 industry data, product shipments in real terms increased 2.5 percent in 1998 after posting a 3.2 percent increase in 1997. On a value basis, prices for folding cartons and related products increased modestly in 1998, resulting in a 3.5 percent increase in the current-dollar value of shipments.

A combination of several factors led to the increase in the volume of folding carton product shipments by domestic box makers in 1998: (1) real GDP growth of 3.7 percent in the U.S. economy, (2) significant improvements in real disposable income [up 3.7 percent], (3) strong growth in total U.S. industrial production [up 5 percent], (4) growth in purchases of nondurable goods [up 1.6 percent], and (5) record U.S. exports of folding cartons and related paperboard boxes materials [up 4 percent on a volume basis].

Sales in the folding carton industry traditionally have been seasonal. The industry typically begins the year on a strong note after a slowdown in sales in December. Sales typically slow moderately from April to July and then turn around from August through November before slowing again in December. In 1998 this traditional pattern held true for most of the year. Shipments started the year strongly, rising moderately above the 1997 record levels in the first quarter of 1998. Sales slowed in the second quarter and into the first portion of the third quarter but picked up noticeably in the latter portion of the third quarter and into the fourth quarter.

Prices and Inventories

In 1998, for the second consecutive year, the average value per ton of folding carton shipments increased noticeably, which indicated a strengthening of finished box prices. According to 5-month 1998 data from the producer price index (PPI) of the Labor Department's Bureau of Labor Statistics, the year-over-year PPI for the U.S. folding carton industry showed a 5 percent increase in the average selling price received by folding paperboard producers. Although a number of domestic box makers experienced some resistance from their customers, the industry was successful in instituting several small price increases in 1998.

Fortunately for the domestic folding carton industry, the cost of its raw materials (predominantly bleached board, recycled board, and kraft paperboard) has changed very little over the past several years, allowing the industry to control a portion of its input costs. According to published price statistics for 1996 through 1998, prices for each of the pertinent raw material grades of folding boxboard changed less than 5 percent during that period. The data also indicate that there has been heavy discounting from the list price during the past 24 months as a result of oversupply and a softer than expected export market. In 1998, production of folding boxboard for domestic packaging uses fell about 1 percent from 7.71 million to 7.64 million metric tons. The production of solid bleached sulfate, the premium virgin fiber grade of folding carton stock, took the biggest fall in 1998 as domestic output declined more than 5 percent to 1.84 million metric tons. In terms of overall folding carton stock consumption in 1998, recycled board grades represented 48 percent of the subsectoral total, followed by solid bleached sulfate grades at 27.5 percent and kraft paperboard grades at 20 percent.

According to industry data, the subsector's inventory of finished goods was kept at fairly even levels through most of 1998, with the exception of the period from April through June, which is traditionally the season of inventory buildup for the fall sales push. In a year-over-year comparison, finished folding carton inventories increased about 3.5 percent from 1997 to 1998. The industry's operating rates remained high for most of 1998, contributing to the slight increase in the subsector's finished goods inventory. However, domestic producers were able to adjust output and operating levels to prevent a large inventory buildup, which would have contributed to lower prices.

Environmental Profile

The U.S. folding paperboard box industry has an excellent environmental performance record, surpassing that of other domestic paper and paperboard segments as well as that of other packaging materials, including plastics, metals, and glass. The industry has a long-established reputation as a leading consumer of paper and paperboard, with many of its products containing more than 75 percent secondary fiber. In many of its applications there is as much as 100 percent secondary fiber content. Unfortunately, this environmental performance is overlooked by many consumers. As a result, a mechanism has been created to promote the environmental efforts and benefits of the folding paperboard box industry. In conjunction with the National Paperbox Association (NPA) and the American Forest and Paper Association (AFPA), the Paperboard Packaging Council created the American Paperboard Packaging Environmental Council (APPEC) to promote the recyclability, renewability, functionality, and durability of paperboard containers. To date, the APPEC has established support and recognition for recovery programs in at least 10 major U.S. cities and has provided product and process informational kits to manufacturers, legislators, and the general public.

Product and Process Innovations

The U.S. folding paperboard box industry has been very aggressive over the past decade in improving its overall productivity and expanding its range of products. This industry has a reputation for providing excellent technical and sales service, innovative packaging ideas, and flexibility in response to customers' requests. As a result, it has become increasingly competitive in an increasingly competitive packaging materials market. The industry has enhanced its printing, pressing, folding, and die-cutting technologies in recent years, establishing itself as a quality supplier of an environmentally preferable form of packaging. Although competition from other packaging alternatives (plastics and corrugated products) has increased in recent years, the industry has experienced slow but steady growth in sales over the past decade.

Domestic producers of folding cartons have expanded their customer bases to include some nontraditional end-user markets. These include cartons and boxes for software and computer-related products; alcoholic beverages, including wines and champagnes; photographic equipment and supplies; and new restaurant and fast-food businesses. Domestic and foreign customers have responded enthusiastically to new lighter-weight, more attractively styled (including multicolored graphics and designs), and more tamper-resistant features. Utilizing this type of protective, visually appealing packaging, folding carton producers have aggressively pursued increased sales opportunities in the high-value pharmaceutical, soap, cosmetics, and toiletries end-user segments as well as the traditional food, bakery, and related products segments. In addition, U.S. folding carton producers have improved their overall operating efficiencies to keep their operating costs down and remain competitive in the large U.S. packaging sector. As the industry's more mature markets have begun to experience fluctuating or stagnating sales, the industry has begun to offer a wider range of modernized, upscale products to spur increased consumption. Efforts to sell to a larger portion of generic and private label marketers in hopes of making inroads into the national brands' market share have led to higher demand for folding cartons in a number of markets.

Industry Structure

According to the 1992 Census of Manufactures report, the domestic folding carton industry consists of 445 companies operating 599 establishments. This reflects a slight decline from the 1987 report. These estimates vary noticeably from those of industry sources. In 1998 *Boxboard Containers* magazine announced the results of an industry survey which indicated that there are approximately 300 companies operating 495 folding carton plants in the United States, essentially unchanged from the 1997 level. Although the industry announced several new

folding carton installations, an equal number of facilities were closed, acquired, merged, or sold. The survey indicates that the reason for the discrepancy between government and industry reports is that many of the facilities contained in the government data are considered very small or captive operations which produce only minimal output for specific packaging applications. These facilities are not included in the overall privately collected industry statistics.

Shipments by the U.S. folding carton industry are broken down into four principal geographic regions: north central, eastern, southern, and Pacific. The north central region continues to be the leading geographic region for folding carton shipments, accounting for just over 37 percent of the industry total. The eastern and southern regions follow at about 28 percent and 27 percent, respectively, while the Pacific region remains at slightly over 7 percent. The southern region continues to be the fastest-growing carton-producing region, while the share of the north central region continues to slip. Over the past 5 years the southern region's share has increased from its 1992 share of 24 percent; the north central share has declined over the same period from 40 percent. Western Europe has a significantly higher number of folding carton plants, estimated at as many as 901, but a significant number of European plants probably are not engaged primarily in manufacturing folding cartons. The average European consumes only about half as many folding cartons as does the American counterpart, who averages 17 kilograms.

Folding Carton End-Use Market Profile

According to a recent industry association report, approximately 62 percent of the volume of folding carton shipments went to food-related applications and 38 percent went to nonfood applications. In the food-related end-use markets for the U.S. folding carton industry in 1998, the leading segments were dry foods and produce (including cereals, crackers, biscuits, cake mixes, and pet food) at 26 percent, beverage cartons and carriers at 15 percent, wet foods (including frozen foods, butter and ice cream, and meats) at 12.5 percent, and bakery and candy items at about 6.5 percent. In the nonfood end-user segments, medicines and cosmetics were first at 7 percent, followed by paper goods at 6.5 percent, hardware supplies at 6 percent, soaps at 4.5 percent, and tobacco products at 4 percent. Over the past decade the areas that have seen the strongest growth have been dry foods and produce, beverage cartons and carriers, and hardware supplies.

The fastest growing end user—the beverage carrier industry—continues to be one of the most competitive and innovative sectors for domestic folding carton producers. As soft drink consumption has increased in recent years, the industry has developed a number of different display units, a variety of carton designs, and creative advertising and packaging products that hold 12 to 24 cans. With many soft drink companies expanding their product lines to include different varieties (regular versus diet, caffeine versus decaffeinated), the folding carton industry has been able to provide products and services that match customers' requirements. The beer industry has been responsive to the "cube" and "twin stack" carton adaptations typically utilized by the soft drink industry. Colorful graphics and eye-catching displays have proved to be effective advertising techniques for domestic beer producers. Competition in the dry foods area (especially snack-related foods and breakfast cereals) has increased tremendously. The snack food and breakfast cereal industries have been very aggressive in their promotional efforts in recent years, and folding carton manufacturers have been able to use innovative advertising campaigns and gimmicks to attract many new customers in these dry food segments. U.S. folding carton producers have created many new products for this competitive subsector, including packages for pretzels, popcorn, chips, cookies, and breakfast cereals. The future prospects for this area look equally positive as these subsectors continue to show flexibility in developing new and different dry food varieties.

International Competitiveness

International trade for the U.S. folding carton industry falls essentially under two separate commodity groupings. The first falls under Harmonized System (HS) code 4819.20.0020, which includes sanitary food and beverage containers of noncorrugated paper and paperboard. The second falls under HS code 4819.20.0040, which includes folding cartons, boxes, and cases of noncorrugated paper and paperboard.

U.S. exports of all folding carton subsector–related commodities in 1998 amounted to 151,250 metric tons and were valued at $292 million. This represents increases of 2 percent and 5 percent, respectively, over the 1997 levels. In 1998 folding cartons represented about two-thirds of the total quantity shipped, while sanitary food and beverage containers made up one-third.

Exports of sanitary food and beverage containers totaled 49,910 metric tons in 1998 and were valued at $105 million. This represents an 11 percent decline in the quantity shipped and a 4 percent increase in value compared with the 1997 data. This was the first decline in U.S. exports of noncorrugated sanitary food and beverage containers in over 7 years. Fortunately, U.S. suppliers were able to make up for the significant drop in the quantity shipped by increasing their prices in certain markets, which resulted in a smaller drop in the value of U.S. exports. On a quantity basis, the leading U.S. sanitary food and beverage container export markets in 1998 were Mexico (29 percent), Canada (28 percent), and Taiwan (17 percent).

In 1998 U.S. exports of finished folding cartons totaled 101,340 metric tons and were valued at $187 million. This reflected a 7.5 percent increase in the volume of exports and a 12 percent increase in the value of exports over 1997. The increase in foreign demand, combined with local folding carton shortages in certain Asian and Latin American markets, enabled the industry to pass along several price increases in 1998, boosting the value of those shipments. Despite the Asian financial crisis in 1998, U.S. suppliers of folding cartons were able to improve their exports to a number of east Asian markets, including China (up 83 percent), Indonesia (up 52 percent), and Singapore. The leading U.S. export markets (on a quantity

basis) for finished folding cartons in 1998 were Canada (40 percent), Mexico (30 percent), and China (11 percent).

The continued expansion of the U.S. economy in 1998 resulted in an increase in demand for a variety of shipping containers, cartons, boxes, and related packaging materials, including folding carton–related products. The increase in domestic demand led to a surge in U.S. imports of both sanitary food and beverage containers and finished folding cartons. In 1998 U.S. imports of these two commodities totaled 160,953 metric tons (up 25 percent) and were valued at $362 million (up 15 percent). In 1998, sanitary food and beverage containers represented 35 percent of the total quantity imported and finished folding cartons represented 65 percent. In recent years the import share of sanitary food and beverage containers has risen substantially as a result of moderate growth in U.S. demand by the domestic soda and beer end-use markets.

In 1998 U.S. imports of sanitary food and beverage containers amounted to 56,333 metric tons and were valued at $86.9 million. This reflects more than a twofold percentage increase in the quantity shipped and a 150 percent increase in the value of imports. Canada is by far the leading supplier to the U.S. market with a 91 percent market share. The only other noteworthy suppliers in 1998 were Denmark (5 percent) and Mexico (2.5 percent).

In 1998 U.S. imports of finished folding cartons totaled 104,620 metric tons and were valued at $275.1 million. The level of imports in 1998 was essentially unchanged from the 1997 level, with the quantity of folding carton imports declining less than 5 percent and the value decreasing less than 1 percent. As is the case with most paper and paperboard products, Canada is by far the principal supplier of folding cartons to the U.S. market. In 1998 Canada supplied 85 percent of the finished folding cartons imported into the United States. Other carton suppliers included China (4.3 percent), Germany (3.6 percent), and Taiwan (2 percent).

Prospects for 1999

Product shipments by the U.S. folding paperboard box industry should increase 1.8 percent in real terms in 1999, buoyed by the continued expansion of the U.S. economy, which should translate into higher consumer spending, increased real disposable income, and more consumer purchases of nondurable food products [i.e., fast food items and dry foods] (see Table 10-6). Economic growth in important export markets, combined with a comparatively high-valued U.S. dollar, will translate into higher overseas demand and a 11 percent increase on a quantity basis in U.S. exports of sanitary food and beverage containers and finished folding cartons. However, U.S. imports of these products should reach all-time records in 1999 as a stronger U.S. economy leads to increased demand for folding cartons and a 13 percent increase on a volume basis in U.S. imports.

If historical paperboard packaging trends continue, the industry should see higher shipments that are due not only to the stronger U.S. economy but also to the growth of the inventories of domestic box consumers. Most of the industry's end-

TABLE 10-6: Folding Paperboard Boxes (SIC 2657) Trends and Forecasts

(millions of dollars except as noted)

	1992	1993	1994	1995	1996	1997[1]	1998[2]	1999[3]	Percent Change 96–97	97–98	98–99	92–96[4]
Industry data												
Value of shipments[5]	7,929	8,009	8,284	8,782	9,026	9,408	9,740	9,965	4.2	3.5	2.3	3.3
Value of shipments (1992$)	7,929	7,993	8,267	8,253	8,396	8,665	8,882	9,042	3.2	2.5	1.8	1.4
Total employment (thousands)	52.6	52.5	53.1	53.0	53.2	53.4	53.3	53.5	0.4	−0.2	0.4	0.3
Production workers (thousands)	41.7	41.5	42.7	42.5	42.8	42.9	42.9	43.0	0.2	0.0	0.2	0.7
Average hourly earnings ($)	12.14	12.63	12.43	12.66	13.00	13.46	13.68	13.76	3.5	1.6	0.6	1.7
Capital expenditures	296	333	282	240	350	315	338	325	−10.0	7.3	−3.8	4.3
Product data												
Value of shipments[5]	7,731	7,754	7,986	8,545	8,814	9,187	9,510	9,729	4.2	3.5	2.3	3.3
Value of shipments (1992$)	7,731	7,738	7,970	8,031	8,199	8,461	8,672	8,828	3.2	2.5	1.8	1.5
Trade data												
Value of imports	144	147	197	275	294	315	362	402	7.1	14.9	11.0	19.5
Value of exports	130	179	192	212	242	278	292	315	14.9	5.0	7.9	16.8

[1] Estimate except imports and exports.
[2] Estimate.
[3] Forecast.
[4] Compound annual rate.
[5] For a definition of industry versus product values, see "Getting the Most Out of *Outlook '99*."
Source: U.S. Department of Commerce: Bureau of the Census; International Trade Administration.

use markets should grow in 1999 as a result of the improved U.S. economy. The strength of the folding paperboard box industry has always been its ability to adapt to an ever-changing domestic packaging subsector and develop new products to maintain its end-user market share. The industry's new technologies and equipment have allowed the development of lighter-weight, more colorful graphics to produce more visually appealing boxes without sacrificing the folding carton's dimensional stability and structural integrity. The industry is expected to continue gradually increasing the use of flexography printing at the expense of the traditional rotogravure process. This should reduce the industry's printing costs and improve production turnaround time. About 25 to 30 percent of the industry uses flexography.

Long-Term Prospects

Product shipments of folding paperboard containers and boxes should increase about 1.6 percent annually over the next 5 years as the domestic economy grows around 2.2 percent per year. Exports and imports of folding carton products should increase about 6 and 7 percent, respectively, on a quantity basis annually throughout this period. Mexico and Canada will remain the principal export markets, but the industry will develop a number of new, nontraditional markets over the next year, primarily in Latin America, east Asia, and eastern Europe.

The north central region of the United States will remain the industry's largest consumer market, but the south, despite a disappointing performance in 1995, will remain the fastest-growing sales region for domestic folding carton producers. The eastern region, with improving economies in portions of New York, New Jersey, and Pennsylvania, should see sales increase as well, but the growth will fluctuate more than it will in the southern region. The Pacific region has experienced a slow decline over the past decade because of natural disaster damage in California and the decline in the Mexican economy and devaluation of the Mexican peso. Nevertheless, sales in the Pacific region should stabilize in the range of 7 to 7.5 percent of total shipments as the California economy improves and gains in Washington and Oregon take place.

Competition in the U.S. packaging subsector is expected to escalate in the future as producers of plastic packaging and other paperboard packaging products (i.e., corrugated and solid fiber boxes) attempt to develop new end-use markets at the expense of the folding paperboard box market share. However, with continuing improvements in process technologies, product development, and operating efficiencies, the folding carton industry is well positioned not only to secure traditional end users but also to expand into new product sectors. The functional durability of the folding carton will find increased uses in products such as compact discs (both software and music), soaps, pharmaceutical and medicinal products, alcoholic and soft drink beverages, and fast and frozen foods. Folding cartons will lose very little market share to other packaging substrates, especially plastic packaging alternatives. The industry's environmental performance should capture sales from companies and organizations that want to utilize products that are environmentally preferable or have a minimal environmental impact. The industry's continuing efforts to promote its environmental efforts will continue to reap benefits.

Gary Stanley, U.S. Department of Commerce, Office of Metals, Materials, and Chemicals, (202) 482-0376, October 1998.

■ REFERENCES

Boxboard Containers, Maclean Hunter Publishing Co., 29 N. Wacker Drive, Chicago, IL 60606. (312) 726-2802.

Fibre Box Association, 2850 Golf Road, Rolling Meadows, IL 60008. (847) 364-9600.

Monthly Statistical Summary, American Forest and Paper Association, 1111 19th Street, NW, Suite 800, Washington, DC 20036. (202) 463-2700.

1994–98 Paper, Paperboard, and Pulp Capacity and Fiber Consumption, American Forest and Paper Association, 1111 19th Street, NW, Suite 800, Washington, DC 20036. (202) 463-2700.

1995 Statistics of Paper, Paperboard, and Wood Pulp, American Forest and Paper Association, 1111 19th Street, NW, Suite 800, Washington, DC 20036. (202) 463-2700.

North American Factbook, Miller Freeman Publications, 600 Harrison Street, San Francisco, CA 94107. (415) 905-2200.

Paper Age, Global Publications, Inc., 51 Mill Street, Hanover, MA 02339. (617) 829-4581.

Paperboard Packaging Council, 888 17th Street, Suite 900, Washington, DC 20006. (202) 289-4100.

Papermaker Magazine, 57 Executive Park, Suite 310, Atlanta, GA 30329. (404) 325-9153.

Pulp and Paper, Miller Freeman Publications, 600 Harrison Street, San Francisco, CA 94107. (415) 905-2200.

Pulp and Paper International, Miller Freeman Publications, 600 Harrison Street, San Francisco, CA 94107. (415) 905-2200.

TAPPI Journal, Technology Park/Atlanta, P.O. Box 105113, Atlanta, GA 30348. (404) 446-1400.

Walden's Fiber and Board Report, Walden-Mott Publications, 225 N. Franklin Turnpike, Ramsey, NJ 07446. (201) 818-8630.

■ RELATED CHAPTERS

18: Production Machinery
25: Printing and Publishing

CHEMICALS AND ALLIED PRODUCTS
Economic and Trade Trends

U.S. International Trade

Source: U.S. Department of Commerce: Bureau of the Census; International Trade Administration.

World Export Market Shares

Source: United Nations; U.S. Department of Commerce, International Trade Administration.

Export Dependence and Import Penetration

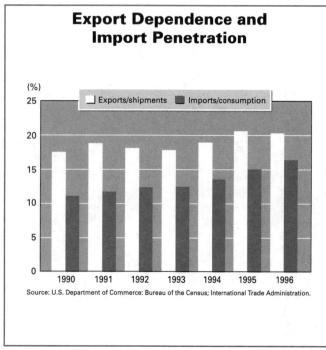

Source: U.S. Department of Commerce: Bureau of the Census; International Trade Administration.

Output and Output per Hour

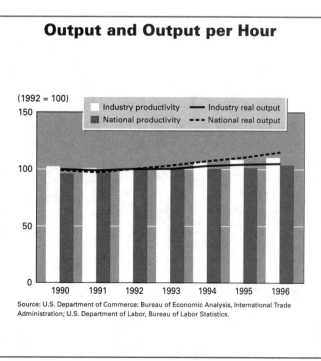

Source: U.S. Department of Commerce: Bureau of Economic Analysis, International Trade Administration; U.S. Department of Labor, Bureau of Labor Statistics.

See "Getting the Most Out of *Outlook '99*" for definitions of terms.

Chemicals and Allied Products

INDUSTRY DEFINITION This chapter covers developments in the following industrial chemicals: industrial inorganics (SIC 281), industrial organics (SIC 286), agricultural chemicals (part of SIC 287), miscellaneous chemical products (SIC 289), and plastic materials and resins (SIC 2821). The specialty chemical subsectors of drugs (SIC 283) and biotechnology are also covered. Cellulosic (SIC 2823) and noncellulosic man-made fibers (SIC 2824) are covered in Chapter 9, "Textiles." The four charts on the opposite page show trends for SIC 28, chemicals and allied products.

INDUSTRIAL INORGANIC CHEMICALS

This subsector covers developments in the industrial inorganic chemicals industry (SIC 281), which includes four main product groups: alkalies and chlorine (SIC 2812); industrial gases such as nitrogen, oxygen, and carbon dioxide (SIC 2813); inorganic pigments such as titanium dioxide and iron oxide (SIC 2816); and miscellaneous inorganics, including acids, aluminum compounds, potassium and sodium compounds, and catalysts, among many others (SIC 2819).

Global Industry Trends

As in the chemical industry overall, globalization has become a key factor in the outlook for industrial inorganic chemicals. The United States now exports almost a third of its inorganic chemical production, notably to Canada, Japan, Mexico, and developing countries in Asia (see Table 11-1). As a result, trends in the global economy are playing a larger role in the U.S. inorganic chemicals sector, a fact that has been emphasized by the recent financial problems in Asia and, earlier, Mexico.

Asia accounted for over a third of total U.S. inorganic chemical exports in 1997. With economic growth in Asia forecast to slow noticeably through 1999, growth in global demand for inorganic chemicals inevitably will decline, which would have a negative effect on U.S. exports while stimulating imports.

Although the Asian economies are expected to rebound by the turn of the century, problems in Japan and indications of slowing in the unpredictable Chinese market could have a further inhibiting impact on U.S. exports.

The effect on U.S. producers is expected to be minor, however, as a result of several factors, particularly continued growth in the North American and Latin American markets. The domestic market remains the most important driver of industry growth, and the U.S. economy has proved quite resilient. In addition, North American Free Trade Agreement (NAFTA) partners Canada and Mexico, along with Latin America, account for around 40 percent of total U.S. inorganic chemical exports, and growth in these regions is expected to be respectable. Although some cancellations and postponements have been announced, most U.S. producers plan to continue to expand into the Asian region and may benefit from reduced construction costs or be able to purchase the assets of struggling local producers at discounted prices.

U.S. Industry Outlook

Key factors affecting the demand for inorganic chemicals include the health of end-use markets, environmental regulations, and trends in foreign trade. Inorganic chemicals are used primarily by the construction, paper, packaging, paints and coatings, and fertilizer industries. Those markets are influenced

TABLE 11-1: Industrial Inorganic Chemicals (SIC 281) Trends and Forecasts
(millions of dollars except as noted)

	1992	1993	1994	1995	1996	1997[1]	1998[2]	1999[3]	2003[3]	96–97	97–98	98–99	92–96[4]
Industry data													
Value of shipments[5]	27,332	26,339	25,018	26,667	27,741	28,950	29,600	30,400	36,250	4.4	2.2	2.7	0.4
Price deflator (1992 = 100)	100.0	100.9	102.7	107.8	110.7	110.9	116.1	117.8	127.6				
Value of shipments (1992$)	27,332	26,092	24,358	24,744	25,052	26,100	25,500	25,800	28,400	4.2	−2.3	1.2	−2.2
Total employment (thousands)	103	93.7	86.5	81.8	80.2								
Production workers (thousands)	54.9	49.7	46.7	45.4	45.2								
Average hourly earnings ($)	16.59	16.93	17.87	19.00	20.74								
Capital expenditures	1,553	1,179	1,304	1,708	2,002								
Product data													
Value of shipments[5]	22,090	21,845	21,286	23,992	24,920	26,020	26,600	27,350	32,600	4.4	2.2	2.8	3.1
Price deflator (1992 = 100)	100.0	100.8	102.7	108.7	111.6	111.0	116.2	117.9	127.8				
Value of shipments (1992$)	22,090	21,670	20,729	22,064	22,333	23,450	22,900	23,200	25,500	5.0	−2.3	1.3	0.3
Trade data													
Value of imports	4,653	4,534	5,247	6,222	6,857	6,899	7,500	8,300	11,500	0.6	8.7	10.7	10.2
Value of exports	5,715	5,399	5,908	7,016	7,165	8,139	8,500	9,100	12,500	13.6	4.4	7.1	5.8

Percent Change spans columns 96–97, 97–98, 98–99, 92–96.

[1] Estimate except imports and exports.
[2] Estimate.
[3] Forecast.
[4] Compound annual rate.
[5] For a definition of industry versus product values, see "Getting the Most Out of *Outlook '99*."
Source: U.S. Department of Commerce: Bureau of the Census; International Trade Administration. Estimates and forecasts by Freedonia Group Incorporated, Cleveland, OH.

by the health of the overall U.S. economy and by consumer spending trends.

After falling over 2 percent in 1998, shipments of industrial inorganic chemicals in constant dollars are forecast to increase just over 1 percent in 1999, limited by sluggish export markets and the lingering effects of economic problems in Asia (see Table 11-1). However, this situation is expected to improve somewhat after the turn of the century, with growth through 2003 projected at about 2 percent annually, boosted by cyclical improvement in U.S. industrial production. The best prospects will continue to be for industrial gases and titanium dioxide. By the turn of the century chlorine demand should improve as environmentally driven losses in the paper industry stabilize and polyvinyl chloride (PVC) becomes the major force driving growth.

There are a great number of inorganic chemical products. The most important are alkalies and chlorine, industrial gases, and inorganic pigments such as titanium dioxide.

Alkalies and Chlorine

The chloralkali industry (SIC 2812) is composed primarily of chlorine, caustic soda, soda ash, sodium bicarbonate, and potassium hydroxide. Chlorine and caustic soda dominate the industry, accounting for more than three-quarters of total demand, while soda ash accounts for more than 20 percent.

Chlorine and caustic soda (sodium hydroxide) are manufactured as coproducts at a set ratio of 1.1 tons of caustic soda to 1 ton of chlorine. Because chlorine is difficult to store, production is geared to meet immediate demand. Thus, the availability of caustic soda is dictated by the level of chlorine production, cre-

ating cyclical problems in matching chlorine and caustic supplies with demand. Chlorine is used in production of both organic and inorganic chemicals, including chlorinated solvents, titanium dioxide, and propylene oxide; as a feedstock in the manufacture of PVC; as a pulp and paper bleach; and as a sanitizer in water treatment. Caustic soda also is used in a range of chemicals as well as in wood pulp delignification. Other uses include soaps and detergents, water treatment, oil drilling, and textiles and fibers.

Demand for chlorine in the United States is expected to increase less than 2 percent in 1999 primarily because of the slowdown in Asian industrial production, which is adversely affecting demand for PVC and its precursors (ethylene dichloride and vinyl chloride monomer). Asia is a leading market for U.S.-produced PVC. The PVC chain is the largest-volume end use for chlorine and has been the primary driver of growth as environmental regulations have sapped the demand for chlorine in pulp bleaching, solvents, pesticides, and chlorofluorocarbons (CFCs). As growth slows, chlorine prices will weaken, leading to contractions in U.S. capacity utilization.

Since caustic soda production is linked to the production of chlorine, the slowdown in chlorine production is expected to cause supply disruptions for caustic soda consumers. With demand for caustic soda having increased about 3 percent in 1998 (primarily because of strong demand in alumina markets), supplies will tighten and prices will continue to rise. Prices for chlorine and those for caustic soda also are linked, with a decline in the price for one commodity necessarily leading to an increase in the price for the other. Over the last several years chlorine has shouldered most of the burden as a result of surprisingly strong demand. Now, however, the cycle is shifting, and caustic soda will bear a larger proportion of the cost.

Soda ash (sodium carbonate) is a naturally occurring mineral whose primary use is in glass production (nearly half of total demand). It also is used as a sodium source in chemical production, as a detergent builder, in pulp and paper, and in environmental and water treatment products. Soda ash production will be affected by the Asian economic slowdown. Exports constitute a vital market for U.S. soda ash producers, accounting for about 35 percent of total domestic production. With exports to Asia accounting for nearly half of all American exports, the downturn in Asian industrial activity will continue to disrupt the U.S. soda ash market, putting pressure on prices and squeezing margins for producers.

The market for soda ash in the United States is mature, with glass (primarily glass containers), chemical production, and pulp and paper being the primary outlets. Competition from plastic packaging and aluminum beverage cans will limit growth in glass markets, while slow advances in paper production will hold back growth increases in that market. Growth will be concentrated in chemical production, where soda ash will benefit from the rising price of caustic soda, opening up opportunities in swing markets which can use either one as a raw material. Demand also will benefit from the shifting balance of power in the chlorine and caustic soda market in another way: Several plants which manufacture caustic soda from soda ash will restart operations to fill the void created by the weakness in chlorine.

Industrial Gases

Volume demand for industrial gases in the United States is forecast to increase about 5 percent a year through 2003. The largest-volume industrial gases are nitrogen and oxygen; other major gases include hydrogen, carbon dioxide, argon, acetylene, and helium. Niche markets exist for krypton, neon, and xenon. Demand for industrial gases will remain heavily reliant on the chemical, oil refining, and primary metals industries. However, the strongest annual gains will occur in the electronics industry and smaller niche markets such as oil recovery and water treatment applications.

The most significant technological development in the industrial gas industry involves the continuing diffusion of noncryogenic air separation technology, particularly membrane systems, pressure swing adsorption (PSA), and vacuum PSA. Although more traditional cryogenic air separation technology will retain the high-volume and high-purity segments of the industrial gas market, noncryogenic methods offer a highly cost-effective alternative for smaller customers of the major atmospheric gases, nitrogen and oxygen. These developments have prompted gas customers to reevaluate their purity requirements and methods of delivery, and most major gas companies now offer customers on-site noncryogenic options in areas where these methods can result in substantial cost savings.

The chemical and primary metal industries are essentially mature, but gas demand for these end uses is outpacing secular expansion in both industries. In chemicals, the use of nitrogen for inerting applications is growing as a result of the rising availability of less costly noncryogenic material, while hydrogen is finding greater use in petroleum refineries because of mandates of the Clean Air Act that necessitate the hydrosulfurization of petroleum products to produce cleaner-burning fuels. Oxygen is by far the largest-volume gas used in the production of primary metals, where it fuels the basic oxygen furnace that converts pig iron into steel as well as blast furnaces and open hearth furnaces. Using oxygen instead of air in furnaces enhances combustion, reduces energy consumption, and reduces emissions, particularly those of nitrous oxides. These advantages are promoting the use of oxygen in combustion processes in many other industries, such as glass manufacturing. Critical to welding operations are a variety of gases, particularly acetylene and oxygen, which serve as a combustible heat source, and carbon dioxide, argon, and helium, which are used as shielding gases to protect the welding surface. Among these gases, argon has the most favorable prospects in shielding applications, where it offers the best cost and performance characteristics.

The electronics industry will remain a leading outlet for high-purity gases, particularly nitrogen, which is used to create an oxygen-free atmosphere that is conducive to the production of sensitive components such as semiconductors and printed circuit boards. The food and beverage processing markets, while mature, are benefiting from efforts to extend the shelf life of perishable foods and rising demand for convenience foods. Nitrogen in particular is benefiting from these trends, since noncryogenic production techniques are making packaging in a low-oxygen atmosphere more cost-effective in many marginal uses (situations in which the potential extension of shelf life does not justify the cost of liquid nitrogen). Oil recovery will remain the market's most rapidly expanding sector; rising demand is attributable to the cost-effectiveness of using gases such as nitrogen and carbon dioxide to improve yields.

Foreign trade in most major industrial gases is negligible as a result of prohibitively high shipping costs. Nevertheless, foreign trade plays a significant role in certain niche gases, particularly helium. With its large natural deposits the United States holds a dominant world position in the supply of helium.

Pigments and Other Inorganic Chemicals

The U.S. market for other inorganic chemicals, including commodity products such as sodium and potassium chemicals, aluminum compounds, and inorganic pigments, is essentially mature and will record relatively slow overall growth. Opportunities exist, however, for certain products, including titanium dioxide and aluminum oxide.

Hundreds of chemical compounds can be formed by utilizing sodium and potassium chemicals because of their high reactivity, which allows them to combine with numerous other chemicals. In general, demand for such chemicals tracks growth in the gross domestic product (GDP), as end-use markets cover the entire scope of industrial manufacturing, including water treatment, pulp and paper, fertilizers, soaps and detergents, foods and beverages, metals, textiles, and leather processing. There are hundreds of producers of these chemicals, primarily companies that have a core focus in commodity chemicals, which exhibit market dynamics different from those of specialty chemicals.

Consumption of aluminum compounds such as aluminum oxide, aluminum hydroxide, and aluminum sulfate will track growth in GDP. Aluminum oxide (alumina) will benefit from growing demand for aluminum metal in the packaging, transportation, construction, and electrical equipment and electronics markets. Aluminum hydroxide is increasing its share of the flame retardant market because of its environmental advantages over competing products, particularly halogenated flame retardants. Demand for aluminum sulfate (alum) will benefit from growing concern over the presence of organic carbons in water supplies. Municipal and industrial water treatment facilities are expected to increase alum use to enhance organic carbon removal via coagulation. Because the United States has almost no commercially significant deposits of bauxite (the ore from which aluminum metal and chemicals are made), basic bauxite demand will continue to be satisfied by foreign sources, primarily Jamaica and Surinam. The United States is largely self-sufficient in downstream aluminum compounds, including alumina, aluminum sulfate, and aluminum hydroxide.

Titanium dioxide, the largest-volume inorganic pigment, is used as the primary white pigment in paper and paperboard, plastics, synthetic rubber, and coatings. Titanium dioxide has an extremely high ability to reflect light, adding brightness to products.

U.S. demand for titanium dioxide is expected to increase about 5 percent in 1998, with the most rapid advances occurring in plastics and coatings. Its use in paper and paperboard will lag behind the overall gains because of slow growth in paper production. Although demand is growing strongly, operating margins are still soft, even after a price increase early in 1998. Already highly concentrated, the global titanium dioxide industry continues to consolidate, with several players announcing deals to sell their operations to better-established competitors. This consolidation is based on chronic weak pricing, a result of substantial overcapacity, which has left producers with eroding margins even in the face of robust growth in demand. The economic disruptions in Asia, which accounts for one-quarter of world demand, will negatively affect world titanium dioxide markets as the production of coatings and plastics slows.

William Baumgartner, Paul Ita, and *Teresa L. Hayes,* Freedonia Group, Incorporated, (440) 646-0809, November 1998.

INDUSTRIAL ORGANIC CHEMICALS

This subsector covers developments in the industrial organic chemicals industry (SIC 286), which includes organic dyes and pigments, aromatics such as benzene and toluene, gum and wood chemicals, pesticides, alcohols, and various cyclic intermediates, such as cumene, cyclohexane, and styrene, along with many other organic chemicals.

Global Industry Trends

The global market for organic chemicals—petrochemicals and dyes and pigments in particular—is increasingly competitive. While this market traditionally was dominated by developed countries such as the United States, Germany, and Japan, in recent years the fastest growth has been registered in the developing regions of Asia, the Middle East, and Latin America. This trend is expected to continue despite the recent financial crisis in Asia.

Although 1997 was a good year for the petrochemical industry, particularly in the United States, cyclical pressures are expected to return, forcing down growth in 1999. This trend will be exacerbated by the aftermath of financial problems in Asia as countries in that region slip into recession. Petrochemicals have been one of the major areas of expansion in the Asian chemical sector but have sustained the greatest damage from the financial crisis. Asian producers, reeling from overcapacity and sluggish domestic demand, are expected to increase export activity and cut prices, risking a price war in petrochemicals, especially if world energy prices remain low.

U.S. Industry Outlook

Key factors affecting the U.S. organic chemical industry include the outlook for key end-use markets and for the overall U.S. economy and competition from foreign producers. As a result of the commodity nature of many of these chemicals, currency fluctuations play an important role in global shipment patterns. Industrial organic chemicals are used primarily in the production of fuels, plastics, fibers, elastomers, fertilizers, and a broad range of other chemical products.

After falling in 1998, shipments of industrial organic chemicals in constant dollars are forecast to increase over 1 percent in 1999 (see Table 11-2). Growth will remain sluggish because of the continuing effects of the downturn in petrochemical production and the reduced export opportunities caused by the recession in key Asian economies. However, steady improvement is expected after 1999, with growth of nearly 3 percent annually through 2003. A cyclical upturn in the petrochemical industry and improvement in the global economy will drive this growth. The United States is expected to remain a net exporter of organic chemicals but will have a significantly smaller surplus than that which it averaged over the last decade; this will result from strong competition from export-oriented producers in Asia and the Middle East.

Organic chemicals encompass a broad range of products, the majority of which are intermediates in the production of other chemicals. However, also included in this subsector are several important finished chemical product classes, such as dyes and organic pigments and pesticides and other nonfertilizer agricultural chemicals.

Dyes and Organic Pigments

Demand for dyes and organic pigments in the United States is projected to rise almost 2 percent annually through 1999, stimulated by ongoing shifts from inorganic to organic pigments

TABLE 11-2: Industrial Organic Chemicals (SIC 286) Trends and Forecasts

(millions of dollars except as noted)

	1992	1993	1994	1995	1996	1997[1]	1998[2]	1999[3]	2003[3]	Percent Change 96–97	97–98	98–99	92–96[4]
Industry data													
Value of shipments[5]	64,397	64,280	70,096	76,729	75,672	77,100	76,500	78,600	97,850	1.9	–0.8	2.7	4.1
Price deflator (1992 = 100)	100.0	104.0	106.7	116.2	118.4	116.4	116.8	118.1	132.5				
Value of shipments (1992$)	64,397	61,826	65,700	66,020	63,902	66,250	65,500	66,550	73,850	3.7	–1.1	1.6	–0.2
Total employment (thousands)	125	123	116	118	126								
Production workers (thousands)	72.3	72.9	68.5	69.7	74.7								
Average hourly earnings ($)	18.55	18.68	19.98	20.31	21.30								
Capital expenditures	4,791	4,061	3,554	4,923	6,269								
Product data													
Value of shipments[5]	59,451	59,912	65,889	73,247	71,478	72,850	72,300	74,300	92,500	1.9	–0.8	2.8	4.7
Price deflator (1992 = 100)	100.0	103.8	106.3	115.8	117.3	116.4	116.8	118.1	132.5				
Value of shipments (1992$)	59,451	57,724	61,955	63,234	60,931	62,600	61,900	62,900	69,800	2.7	–1.1	1.6	0.6
Trade data													
Value of imports	7,334	7,423	8,746	10,672	11,627	13,014	14,500	15,600	21,500	11.9	11.4	7.6	12.2
Value of exports	10,221	10,583	12,534	15,772	14,368	15,664	15,800	16,900	24,100	9.0	0.9	7.0	8.9

[1] Estimate except imports and exports.
[2] Estimate.
[3] Forecast.
[4] Compound annual rate.
[5] For a definition of industry versus product values, see "Getting the Most Out of *Outlook '99*."
Source: U.S. Department of Commerce: Bureau of the Census; International Trade Administration. Estimates and forecasts by Freedonia Group Incorporated, Cleveland, OH.

and increased demand for brighter packaging and printing inks. However, growth will decelerate as a result of waning demand in certain end-use markets (e.g., plastics and paints and coatings) and stringent environmental regulations that have prompted the use of low-volume, cost-effective products. Ongoing competition from low-cost overseas producers will continue to place downward pressure on shipments of colorants, a situation which could be aggravated by the recent Asian financial problems.

In addition to packaging and inks, major markets for dyes and organic pigments include textiles, plastics, paints and coatings, and leather products. Competition from developing countries (particularly India, China, and other Asia/Pacific nations) has been especially prevalent in the textiles sector, the largest end use for colorants, because of the increased production of inexpensive textile fibers and finished goods in those countries. Consequently, U.S. producers have increasingly expanded their operations in the Asia/Pacific region to take advantage of lower labor, environmental compliance, and other operational costs. The move into lower-cost regions also has been prompted by weak U.S. demand for textile goods, particularly apparel products, and the strength of the U.S. dollar relative to other currencies.

Foreign trade has played a significant role in the U.S. organic colorants industry, with the dye sector being more significantly affected than the organic pigments sector. The United States will maintain its position as a net importer of dyes and organic pigments, although exports are expected to increase much more rapidly in the long term than are imports. Western Europe will remain a dominant supplier to the United States,

although less expensive organic colorants (particularly textile dyes) from Asia/Pacific countries are expected to continue to apply downward pressure on most dyestuff prices, squeezing profit margins for U.S. manufacturers. Western Europe, Canada and Mexico, and the Asia/Pacific region will continue to be the most significant markets for U.S. exports of dyes and organic pigments. Canada and Mexico will remain important markets as a result of the impact of NAFTA and the General Agreement on Tariffs and Trade (GATT).

Teresa L. Hayes and *Jae Kennedy,* Freedonia Group, Incorporated, (440) 646-0809, November 1998.

AGRICULTURAL CHEMICALS

Fertilizers

World consumption of fertilizers totaled 134.4 million tons in the 1996–1997 growing season, up 4 percent from the comparable 1995–1996 season, based on data provided by the International Fertilizer Industry Association (IFA). Nitrogen fertilizers accounted for 62 percent of world consumption, phosphate fertilizers for 23 percent, and potash fertilizers for 15 percent.

The fertilizer industry is a relatively mature business in the United States, reflecting stagnant or modest growth in the underlying American farm economy. The overall fertilizer business is highly seasonal, with the most sales occurring prior to the spring and fall plantings. Domestic demand is largely a function of acreage planted, with farmers' planting decisions importantly influenced by grain prices, federal support programs, and weather conditions. Other important factors affecting annual fertilizer sales include carryover inventories from the prior year, production costs, environmental concerns, and soil moisture. A bumper crop in the prior year typically results in lower prices and reduced plantings the following year. However, when favorable weather causes increased grain and bean yields, additional fertilizer application is needed in the following year to compensate for soil nutrient depletion.

Foreign business is important, representing about one-third of U.S. industry shipments. As such, changes in economic conditions abroad and fluctuations in foreign currency exchange rates can also materially affect the fertilizer business. China represents close to 30 percent of U.S. fertilizer exports, other Asia/Pacific markets 33 percent, Latin America 25 percent, and all other markets 12 percent.

Despite the recent downturns in their economies, developing nations in Asia and Latin America represent important growth markets for fertilizers. Strong demographic growth, rising income levels, and efforts to improve diets and general standards of living in those areas should foster greater production of grains and other produce. This, in turn, should result in increased usage of fertilizers to increase production. The total world population is projected to grow from 5.8 billion in 1997 to 6.1 billion in 2000 and 6.9 billion in 2010, with most of the growth occurring in emerging or third world countries.

According to the IFA, developing nations accounted for 59 percent of world fertilizer consumption in 1996–1997, up from 38 percent 10 years ago. World consumption by geographic regions in 1996–1997 broke down as follows: Asia 48 percent, North America 17 percent, western Europe 13 percent, Latin America 7 percent, and other areas 15 percent.

Nitrogen is the most commonly used fertilizer, with anhydrous ammonia being the principal ingredient in most nitrogen fertilizers. Anhydrous ammonia is produced by combining atmospheric nitrogen with methane. Because this compound evaporates from the soil, nitrogen fertilizers must be applied each year, resulting in a relatively stable market for this commodity. Phosphate fertilizers are derived from phosphate rock. Phosphate rock is combined with sulfuric acid to yield phosphatic acid, which is further processed into diammonium phosphate (DAP), the most widely used phosphatic fertilizer. Potash is primarily mined from deposits of potassium salts in Canada, Germany, Russia, the United States, and Israel.

The United States is the largest producer of phosphatic fertilizers, the second largest producer of nitrogen fertilizers, but a relatively small producer of potash. It accounts for about 45 percent of world phosphate fertilizer production, with about a two-thirds share of the total trade in diammonium phosphate. The United States exports about 55 percent of its phosphate fertilizer production, with about 30 percent of that volume going to China. About one-fifth of U.S. nitrogen fertilizer production is exported.

Despite its present lead position, the United States is expected to eventually relinquish its dominant position in phosphate fertilizers to Morocco. With its phosphate deposits estimated at over 50 percent of world rock phosphate reserves,

Morocco is presently the largest phosphate rock exporter, with most of its production going to Europe. China, the former Soviet Union, and India are also large phosphate fertilizer producing countries.

The United States is a net importer of nitrogen and potash fertilizers. Canada, Trinidad, and Tobago are the main sources of U.S. imports of nitrogen fertilizers (4.6 million metric tons in 1996) because of their low-cost supplies of natural gas. The United States imported over 5 million metric tons of potash in 1996, largely from Canada which has huge reserves in Saskatchewan. Such imports accounted for roughly 80 percent of domestic potash consumption. The United States consumes about 40 percent of total world potash production. The Canadian potash industry has been operating at only two-third of capacity in recent years, and therefore has the capacity to fill anticipated growth in world demand well into the next century.

Domestic dollar fertilizer shipments are expected to increase by about 4.4 percent to about $11 billion in 1998, bolstered by increases in planted acreage. Planted acreage for corn rose to 80.8 million acres in the 1998 growing season, as compared with 80.2 million the year before; while soybean acreage climbed to 72.7 million, from 70.9 million in 1997 and 64.2 million in 1996. Farmers opted to plant more soybeans in recent years, given attractive soybean prices and new findings of soil benefits from the annual rotation of soybeans with corn, especially in the midwest. Given the large increases projected for soybean production, soybean prices are likely to decline in 1999, along with planted acreage.

Gains in domestic acreage in 1998 are expected to more than offset reduced export volume to the Chinese market, price weakness in nitrogenous fertilizers, and economic difficulties in southeast Asia. The downturn in China reflected that nation's suspension of urea imports (a nitrogenous fertilizer) in mid-1997 with the opening of its own urea production facilities.

Farmers now have much greater flexibility in the choice of which crops they plant than in the past because of the Federal Agricultural Improvement and Reform Act of 1996. Representing the most significant change in U.S. farm policy since the depression, the new legislation (referred to simply as the Farm Bill) permits farmers to plant crops of their own choice and still maintain eligibility for federal subsidies under farm programs. Decisions with respect to crops chosen for planting are now more reflective of world market conditions, relative crop prices, and other agronomic considerations. This legislation envisions the eventual phaseout of support payments by 2002. In the longer term, grain prices and farm income levels are expected to show greater volatility, with the absence of the stabilizing effects of government price support programs.

Representing the most valuable commercial crop in the United States, corn is also the most important for the fertilizer industry, accounting for about 42 percent of U.S. crop nutrient consumption. Hay and pasture crops account for 15 percent, followed by wheat (14 percent), soybeans (6 percent), cotton (5 percent), and all other (18 percent).

The fertilizer industry has undergone significant consolidation in terms of the number of players in the field. Mergers have reduced the number of phosphate rock producers in Florida to 5, from 11 in 1990; the number of U.S.-based phosphoric acid producers now totals 11, down from 24 in 1980; and North American ammonia producers presently total 25, down from 55 in 1980. Major fertilizer manufacturers include IMC Global, IMC-Arico (a joint venture between IMC Global and Phosphate Resource Partners), Potash Corp. of Saskatchewan, and Agrium and Terra Industries.

Pesticides

Based on data provided by Wood Mackenzie Consultants, a research firm in Edinburgh, Scotland, the global market for pesticides totaled $30.2 billion in 1997, up 2.6 percent from 1996 (excluding currency effects). While continued growth is expected in 1998, the pace is expected to slow somewhat because of unfavorable weather conditions in many parts of the world (due to El Niño) and the economic downturn in southeast Asia.

Pesticides are chemical agents used to destroy or repel plant or animal pests, with herbicides, insecticides, and fungicides representing principal product categories. The United States is the leading global manufacturer of chemical pesticides, with Germany and Japan also important producers.

North America represents the largest geographic market for pesticides, accounting for about 34 percent of 1997 global sales, according to Wood Mackenzie. Other important markets are western Europe (24 percent of 1997 sales), Latin America (13 percent), and Japan (9 percent). Major global pesticide producing corporations include Novartis, Monsanto, Zeneca Corp., Dupont, AgrEvo, Bayer, Rhone-Poulenc, Dow Chemical, BASF, the Cyanamid division of American Homes Products, and FMC Corp.

Total domestic sales of U.S.-made and imported pesticides grew 5.5 percent to $8.8 billion in 1997, according to the American Crop Protection Association (ACPA). Exports of U.S.-made pesticides increased 11 percent, or $2.8 billion. About 83 percent of U.S. pesticide sales in 1997 were shipments to crop markets. Corn represented the largest single market for crop protection products, accounting for 24 percent of domestic pesticide sales in 1997. Other important crop markets included soybeans (19 percent), cotton (10 percent), small grains (6 percent), and vegetables (4 percent). The balance (37 percent) was composed largely of fruits, rice, sorghum, peanuts, and potatoes. Pesticides designed for use in the home, garden, turf, and other noncrop categories totaled $1.5 billion in 1997, representing 17 percent of total domestic pesticide sales.

The pesticide market is also a mature business in the United States, with over 90 percent of corn, soybean, and cotton acreage in major producing states being treated each year with pesticides. Changes in yearly sales is largely a function of starting inventory levels, changes in planted acreage, weather, and farm prices.

Used to control weeds, brush, and other unwanted vegetation, herbicides represent the largest crop protection category, totaling $6 billion or 68 percent of total U.S. pesticide sales in 1997, according to the ACPA. About 88 percent of U.S. herbicide sales were for crop use, of which corn and soybeans accounted for about two-thirds of total volume.

Sales of insecticides or chemicals used to guard growing or stored crops from insect infestation totaled $1.9 billion and accounted for about 21 percent of total U.S. pesticide sales in 1997. Cotton was the major end market for insecticides in 1997 (20 percent of sales), followed by corn (17 percent). Sales of corn insecticides dropped 21 percent in 1997, partially reflecting the introduction of new insect-resistant seeds. Sales of insecticides for cotton rose modestly in 1997, following a sharp drop in 1996 due to the introduction of new insect-resistant plants.

Fungicides accounted for 7 percent of total pesticide sales in 1997. While agricultural uses are the largest end market, fungicides are also used extensively in the lumber, paint, plastics, and pharmaceutical industries.

The emerging field of agricultural biotechnology is likely to impact the pesticide industry more significantly in the coming years. Genetically engineered or transgenic plants have been developed with resistance to insects, herbicides, and plant diseases, thus reducing the need for conventional pesticides. Led by Monsanto, many companies have developed transgenic seeds for corn, cotton, and soybeans. Monsanto's new Roundup Ready herbicide–tolerant soybean seeds were believed to have accounted for about over 20 percent of total U.S. soybean acreage plantings in 1997. This transgenic seed is resistant to Monsanto's Roundup Ready herbicide (the world's largest selling weed killer). Commercial use of transgenic seeds is expected to increase over the coming years.

After several decades of regulatory scrutiny of pesticides because of potential carcinogenic effects related to certain ones, the Food Quality Protection Act (FQPA) passed by Congress in mid-1996 represented a major new layer of regulation on the industry. The legislation contains far-reaching provisions in tolerance standards that pesticides must meet in order to receive marketing approval from the Environmental Protection Agency (EPA). Under the new law, all existing pesticides must be reevaluated against a much stricter set of risk criteria. The EPA is presently reviewing organophosphate and carbamate insecticides, which are widely used pesticides, especially in western states.

Herman Saftlas, Standard & Poor's Corporation, (212) 208-1199, October 1998.

MISCELLANEOUS CHEMICAL PRODUCTS

This subsector covers developments in the miscellaneous chemical products industry (SIC 289), which includes five main product groups: adhesives and sealants (SIC 2891), explosives (SIC 2892), printing ink (SIC 2893), carbon black (SIC 2895), and various miscellaneous chemicals, including fatty acids and gelatin.

U.S. Industry Outlook

Shipments of miscellaneous chemicals in constant dollars are expected to increase almost 2 percent in 1999, with growth accelerating to nearly 3 percent annually through 2003, basically in line with expected changes in U.S. GDP (see Table 11-3). However, the overall growth rate hides rather diverse trends in these products. Included in this category are products ranging from specialty chemicals such as adhesives and sealants and printing inks to commodity chemicals such as carbon black and fatty acids.

Adhesives and Sealants

Demand for adhesives and sealants in the United States is forecast to grow about 3 percent annually through 2003, with market value rising more than 5 percent annually over that period. The average price per pound for formulated adhesives and sealants will increase because of continuing shifts in the product mix that favor highly formulated synthetic adhesives. Although adhesives and sealants are used in nearly all sectors of the economy, final demand will remain strongly linked to two industries: construction and packaging. Corrugated paper boxes are the largest-volume use for adhesives in the packaging industry. Another major market in the packaging industry is pressure-sensitive tapes and labels, particularly for hot melt adhesives based on ethylene vinyl acetate (EVA), acrylic, and styrenic block copolymers. Adhesives and sealants also are used widely in the manufacture of major durables such as motor vehicles, industrial machinery and equipment, and appliances. Most major markets for adhesives and sealants are forecast to have slower growth relative to the solid gains of the period 1992–1997.

As is the case in related industries such as industrial coatings, the general focus of product reformulation activity in the U.S. adhesive and sealant industry is lower solvent content and volatile organic compound emissions. The major beneficiaries of these trends include environmentally compatible systems with higher solids contents, such as water-based and hot melt (100 percent solid) adhesives.

Foreign trade does not play a significant role in the adhesive and sealant industry largely as a result of the fact that shipping costs are prohibitive and most products are based on readily available technology. Nonetheless, U.S. producers hold a leadership position in the global market, particularly for higher-margin products such as structural adhesives and sealants used in more advanced applications. Most trade in adhesives and sealants has traditionally been with Canada, although the enactment of NAFTA has increased trade with Mexico. Exports to Asia have been affected by the financial crisis in that region, which has severely curtailed spending on construction and durables.

The U.S. adhesive and sealant industry continues to undergo restructuring and consolidation. This restructuring is an outgrowth of spiraling costs for regulatory compliance and the trend toward globalization. In particular, European firms, including Imperial Chemical Industries (United Kingdom), Henkel (Germany), and Elf Atochem (France), have invested heavily in the United States in recent years.

Explosives

Demand for explosives, including pyrotechnics and explosive accessories and assemblies, is expected to increase a little over 2 percent annually through 2003. This growth is spurred by the greater use of air bags, many of which use explosive ignitors and propellants. The continued popularity of consumer fireworks also will support these increases. However, growth will

TABLE 11-3: Miscellaneous Chemical Products (SIC 289) Trends and Forecasts
(millions of dollars except as noted)

| | 1992 | 1993 | 1994 | 1995 | 1996 | 1997[1] | 1998[2] | 1999[3] | 2003[3] | Percent Change | | | |
										96–97	97–98	98–99	92–96[4]
Industry data													
Value of shipments[5]	20,512	21,851	22,502	23,830	24,508	26,000	26,550	27,800	34,000	6.1	2.1	4.7	4.6
Price deflator (1992 = 100)	100.0	101.7	105.0	110.0	110.4	112.6	114.7	117.8	130.5				
Value of shipments (1992$)	20,512	21,481	21,426	21,662	22,194	23,100	23,150	23,600	26,050	4.1	0.2	1.9	2.0
Total employment (thousands)	83.7	81.8	79.8	81.6	75.9								
Production workers (thousands)	48.2	47.0	46.7	47.7	45.0								
Average hourly earnings ($)	13.63	13.76	14.27	14.42	14.72								
Capital expenditures	751	790	731	807	1,006								
Product data													
Value of shipments[5]	19,440	20,764	20,950	22,215	22,918	24,300	24,800	25,950	31,700	6.0	2.1	4.6	4.2
Price deflator (1992 = 100)	100.0	101.8	105.0	110.0	110.5	112.7	114.8	117.7	130.5				
Value of shipments (1992$)	19,440	20,406	19,954	20,191	20,734	21,570	21,600	22,040	24,300	4.0	0.1	2.0	1.6
Trade data													
Value of imports	1,429	1,618	1,770	2,186	2,481	2,711	3,200	3,550	6,000	9.3	18.0	10.9	14.8
Value of exports	2,766	3,022	3,216	3,712	4,021	4,541	4,750	5,320	7,850	12.9	4.6	12.0	9.8

[1] Estimate except imports and exports.
[2] Estimate.
[3] Forecast.
[4] Compound annual rate.
[5] For a definition of industry versus product values, see "Getting the Most Out of Outlook '99."
Source: U.S. Department of Commerce: Bureau of the Census; International Trade Administration. Estimates and forecasts by Freedonia Group Incorporated, Cleveland, OH.

trail the rates achieved in the early and middle 1990s because of a decline in mining activity and decelerating construction expenditures. These markets dominate explosives demand, accounting for almost two-thirds of consumption.

The best growth prospects will be found in pyrotechnics as a result of their higher average prices and the extensive use of fireworks in holiday celebrations, stage productions, and amusement park displays. Demand for propellants will exhibit above-average growth because of their use in air bag systems, although a less favorable outlook for ammunition production will moderate these gains. Consumption of blasting agents and other explosives is expected to fare much worse, reflecting slowed construction outlays and maturity in the key mining market. Sluggish mining activity also will limit demand for explosive accessories and assemblies, which is predicted to mirror market averages.

Although the United States is the largest consumer of explosives worldwide, the market is becoming increasingly globalized. The greatest opportunities for producers of explosives exist in the expanding mining and construction industries of southeast Asia, Latin America (e.g., Argentina, Peru, and Bolivia), and Australia. Many U.S. producers are therefore pursuing growth through exports, causing exports to outpace imports by more than two to one through the end of the decade. However, many producers are entering international markets through direct investment in local industries, joint manufacturing ventures, and technological licensing agreements, thus moderating export growth. Imports have similarly been restrained by the construction of manufacturing plants and the use of strategic agreements by foreign-based firms seeking a more direct entry into the U.S. market.

Printing Inks

Demand for printing inks is forecast to rise more than 2 percent annually through 2003, driven by ongoing growth in commercial printing and packaging. Value gains will increase more rapidly, based on continued increases in sales of ink-jet inks and other higher-priced formulations. Although still a factor to some extent, the switch from solvent-based inks to environmentally attractive alternatives (vegetable oil–based products) in applicable markets has for the most part been completed. In addition to commercial printing and packaging, which dominate ink use, inks are utilized in publishing (e.g., for newspapers, periodicals, and books) and miscellaneous applications (e.g., business forms and greeting cards).

Ink-jet printing inks are the most rapidly growing ink type, with demand being driven by greater use of personal and commercial digital printing equipment in the desktop printing industry and the development of new substrates and niche markets. Applications for ink-jet inks include small graphic arts applications (e.g., fliers and banners) and larger commercial printing jobs (e.g., billboards).

Despite ongoing globalization, the United States will remain the largest ink consumer in the world. Continued strong growth is anticipated in both the Asia/Pacific and South America regions because of high demand for packaged and printed goods and thus for printing inks. Nevertheless, most overseas demand will be satisfied by local producers; consequently, trade will not be a significant factor on a worldwide basis. The United States will maintain its position as a net exporter of printing inks, with the trade surplus widening as U.S.-based suppliers expand their multinational presence. While the financial crisis in Asia has affected this industry to some extent, substantial long-term problems are not expected.

Carbon Black

Volume demand for carbon black in the United States is forecast to rise about 2.5 percent annually through 2003, basically tracking overall gains in rubber demand over that period. The rubber industry will continue to account for more than 90 percent of total demand for carbon black. In vulcanized rubber goods, carbon black is used as a reinforcement, since it improves an elastomer's tear, abrasion, and flex resistance. Tires are the primary application in the rubber industry, but carbon black also is used widely in industrial rubber products such as hoses, belts, and mechanical goods. While both of these major markets will see continued gains, demand for carbon black in industrial rubber product applications will be hindered by the strong growth exhibited by thermoplastic elastomers, some types of which do not require carbon black while others require much less carbon black than do the thermoset rubber parts they are replacing.

Although accounting for less than 10 percent of the market, nonrubber applications, called special blacks, are also important, particularly from a value standpoint, since these specialized grades command significantly higher prices than do commodity rubber blacks. In addition to higher margins, a strong position in special blacks offers suppliers greater protection from cyclicity in the rubber and motor vehicle industries. The primary nonrubber use for carbon black is as a pigment in plastics, paints and coatings, and printing inks.

Demand for carbon black in its largest market—tires—is being affected by significant trends. One favorable trend has been the popularity of performance tires, since these types of tires require higher carbon black loadings in the tread compounds relative to all-season radials. Performance tires also have shorter service lives, and so they are replaced more often. In addition, the popularity of sport utility vehicles and full size pickup trucks has increased demand by original equipment manufacturers (OEMs) for larger tires and will benefit the replacement market for years to come. Finally, the production of medium- and heavy-duty trucks has made a solid recovery from cyclical lows in the early 1990s, and this has increased OEM and replacement demand for large truck tires. However, carbon black loadings in tire tread compounds will face downward pressure as a result of efforts to improve wet traction and reduce rolling resistance (and thus improve tire longevity and gas mileage). Carbon black is receiving increased competition from precipitated silica in this regard, although the actual displacement has been minimal. Carbon black suppliers have responded by developing new grades that can reduce rolling resistance while providing a higher level of reinforcement.

Internationally, the Asia/Pacific region will continue to post the strongest gains in carbon black demand, mainly because of the ongoing development of China's tire industry. However, increases will be below prior projections as a result of the financial crisis that swept the Pacific Rim late in 1997. Latin America also offers solid opportunities, particularly in Brazil, while in eastern Europe the strongest prospects are in the Czech Republic, Hungary, and Poland. Demand in western Europe and Japan will recover somewhat from weak showings in the first half of the 1990s, but gains in both regions will remain below those in the robust North American market, mainly because of sluggish demand for major durables such as motor vehicles.

Paul Ita, Jae Kennedy, and *Wendy Jovan,* Freedonia Group, Incorporated, (440) 646-0809, November 1998.

DRUGS AND PHARMACEUTICALS

The drugs and pharmaceuticals sector (SIC 283) consists of four primary components: medicinals and botanicals (SIC 2833), pharmaceutical preparations (SIC 2834), diagnostic substances (SIC 2835), and biological products (SIC 2836). Medicinal and botanical establishments (SIC 2833) are primarily engaged in manufacturing bulk organic and inorganic medicinal chemicals and their derivatives and in processing bulk botanical drugs and herbs. Pharmaceutical preparations (SIC 2834) include establishments primarily engaged in manufacturing, fabricating, and processing medicinal substances into finished pharmaceuticals for human and veterinary use. Ethical brand-name drugs, generic products, and nonprescription or over-the-counter medications constitute the pharmaceutical preparations subsector. The diagnostic substances subsector (SIC 2835) includes companies that make chemical, biological, or radioactive substances for testing blood or other bodily fluids and tissues. These substances may be used for in vitro (test tube) or in vivo (administered in the body) testing. Biologicals establishments (SIC 2836) are primarily engaged in the production of bacterial and virus vaccines, toxoids, and analogous products (such as allergic extracts, serums, plasmas, and other blood derivatives) for human and veterinary use.

Global Industry Trends

Strong and consistent growth in the mid-single digits is expected in the global pharmaceutical market over the next 5 years. It is likely the $300 billion-plus global pharmaceutical market will grow about 6 percent per year through 2000. Growth will be sustained by several factors such as record-setting, long life expectancies, a rising standard of living in developing countries, and a steady stream of new products and line extensions, including the new frontier of quality-of-life pharmacology.

Demographics ensure an expanding global market for pharmaceuticals. Increased life expectancies bring increased health problems. As the world's population ages, the demand for phar-

maceuticals increases. The elderly are the single largest group of users of prescription drugs. The World Health Organization (WHO) reports that the global over-65 population is forecast to rise from 380 million in 1997 to more than 690 million by 2025. As governments around the world consider various ways to tackle the problems of rising health care costs for the elderly, pharmaceuticals emerge as an efficient and cost-effective way to address the problem. Pharmaceuticals provide health care savings by shortening hospital stays, reducing nursing home admissions, lessening doctor visits, and in some cases eliminating the need for surgery.

The rising standard of living in the developing countries offers long-term potential for increased sales of medical products. Health in developing countries is improving as a result of a rising global economy and the new interaction between science, public health, and business. New and improved vaccines and pharmaceuticals are becoming available to more of the world's population. More of the population expects better medical treatment. Pharmaceuticals are the first line of medical therapy worldwide. The global pharmaceutical industry has the ability to develop products to fight infectious diseases wherever they occur. The challenges are of availability, affordability, and effectiveness.

Another major factor fueling the continued growth of the global pharmaceutical industry is the introduction of new products. More than one-third of the global industry's growth in 1997 came from products less than 2 years old. The newest frontier of drug development is quality-of-life pharmacology. The first wave of these products is already in the market. A number of new treatments in the quality-of-life category are under development. These new products help to keep people looking and feeling young into the latter years of life. The new quality-of-life drugs are posing many questions for health care systems. Foremost is the issue of cost. Even though the pharmaceuticals are expensive, skyrocketing sales demonstrate the public is eager for products of this type. Over the next few years, it is expected that pharmaceutical companies will introduce a whole range of new compounds that not only will cure disease but also will slow down the ravages of age.

The pharmaceutical industry has a history of mergers, acquisitions, and buyouts that are not limited by national boundries. Companies pool resources to compete more effectively and to finance the escalating cost of expanded research and development (R&D). Collaborations, alliances, and joint ventures with small drug discovery companies, academia, and research institutions have become popular as a way to access new technologies, breakthroughs, and product leads. Foreign drug manufacturers continue to eye U.S. firms as potential acquisition candidates. The pace of worldwide consolidations in the industry over the past few years shows no sign of abatement. There does, however, appear to be a new factor behind global megamergers. In the early 1990s the mergers were primarily driven by a desire to cut costs. In the late 1990s R&D opportunities appear to be the driving force. R&D is vital to the growth of the global pharmaceutical industry and to new product development.

U.S. Industry Growth Projections for the Next 1 and 5 Years

For the next 1 and 5 years, growth for the U.S. pharmaceutical industry is expected to average in the mid-single digits. Industry shipments are expected to increase to $91.3 billion in 1997, a 5.5 percent increase over those of 1996 (see Table 11-4). The U.S. pharmaceutical industry is likely to continue its upward momentum into the new century fueled primarily by new products and the increased demand for pharmaceuticals. Contrary to expectations, managed care in the United States also is boosting pharmaceutical sales in the brand, generic, and nonprescription markets. In addition, a more conciliatory U.S. regulatory environment for the industry is likely to invigorate growth.

Demand and the introduction of new products have replaced pricing as the primary force behind the U.S. pharmaceutical industry's overall growth. U.S. patients are shifting from older, less costly pharmaceuticals to newer, more expensive ones. In 1997 the U.S. pharmaceutical categories that contained new product recorded the highest growth rates. The U.S. industry appears to be on the edge of a major new cycle, with a number of potential blockbuster products recently introduced or soon to be launched. Examples of new products include more effective cancer drugs, HIV protease inhibitors, oral diabetes therapy, cholesterol reducers, and impotence treatment. U.S. companies are intensifying their efforts on the creation of unique, "breakthrough" therapeutic compounds rather than developing new drugs to compete with existing products, the "me too" drugs of the 80's.

The U.S. pharmaceutical marketplace is being transformed by the rapid growth of managed care. HMOs, preferred provider organizations, and other managed care firms have grown rapidly in recent years. In the 1980s managed care's share of the retail pharmaceutical market was less than 30 percent. By 2000, managed care's share of the retail pharmaceutical market is expected to be 90 percent. Managed care is increasing pharmaceutical sales in the U.S. by widening pharmaceutical usage as a viable alternative to other treatment forms, and this trend should continue over the next 5 years.

In different ways and degrees, each of the three segments of the U.S. pharmaceutical industry—brand-name drugs, generic products, and nonprescription medications—benefit from the growth of managed care. Due in part to the continued trend toward self-care, which is increasingly driven by the managed care industry, the nonprescription retail sales for 1997 reflected a 4 percent increase over 1996 sales. A steady increase in nonprescription sales is expected to continue over the next 5 years. Managed care has contributed to the expansion of the generic market as well. Generic drugs are forecast to supply nearly two-thirds of all prescriptions written by the end of the decade. This is an increase from 42 percent of the market in 1996 and 22 percent in 1985. The generic market is expected to reach $15 billion by 2000, up from an estimated $9 billion in 1996. Growth of the generic market is also aided by the fact that over the next 5 years drugs generating more than $16 billion in 1996 sales are scheduled to lose patent protection. Branded pharmaceutical sales have also been helped by managed care. Managed care providers realize that, many times, newly developed branded pharmaceuticals provide the most effective and cost-efficient means to treat patients. Increasingly, leading-edge branded pharmaceuticals are being used by managed care providers as the preferred form of treatment. To compete with well-established and cheaper generic products and to increase their

TABLE 11-4: Drugs (SIC 283) Trends and Forecasts
(millions of dollars except as noted)

	1992	1993	1994	1995	1996	1997[1]	1998[2]	1999[3]	Percent Change			
									96–97	97–98	98–99	92–96[4]
Industry data												
Value of shipments[5]	67,792	70,985	75,804	80,907	86,532	91,291	95,033	98,645	5.5	4.1	3.8	6.3
Value of shipments (1992$)	67,792	68,179	71,142	73,820	76,824	79,128	81,661	83,702	3.0	3.2	2.5	3.2
Total employment (thousands)	194	200	205	216	213							
Production workers (thousands)	92.7	94.6	102	113	106							
Average hourly earnings ($)	14.78	15.80	16.34	15.99	16.63							
Capital expenditures	3,887	4,047	4,034	4,503	4,301							
Product data												
Value of shipments[5]	60,793	63,970	67,751	71,528	76,293	80,489	83,788	86,973	5.5	4.1	3.8	5.9
Value of shipments (1992$)	60,793	61,428	63,588	65,285	67,754	69,786	72,020	73,820	3.0	3.2	2.5	2.7
Trade data												
Value of imports	5,958	6,094	6,966	8,582	11,160	14,196	18,263	21,003	27.2	28.7	15.0	17.0
Value of exports	6,774	7,222	7,565	7,996	8,889	10,375	12,114	13,325	16.7	16.8	10.0	7.0

[1] Estimate except imports and exports.
[2] Estimate.
[3] Forecast.
[4] Compound annual rate.
[5] For a definition of industry versus product values, see "Getting the Most Out of *Outlook '99*."
Source: U.S. Department of Commerce: Bureau of the Census; International Trade Administration.

share of the managed care market, the branded companies have to ensure a full pipeline of new and innovative pharmaceuticals that offer improved effectiveness or unique solutions. To maintain approximately 10 percent annual growth, branded companies believe that they must bring two or three new products to the market each year.

The U.S. pharmaceutical industry experienced a more industry-friendly regulatory environment during 1997 which aided the growth of the market. In 1997 new legislation was enacted in the United States which streamlines and speeds the Food and Drug Administration's (FDA) approval process for new prescription drugs and medical devices. FDA's user-fee program is extended and the new drug review process is expedited. Under the new law, seriously ill patients are allowed easier access to experimental compounds, and new incentives for the development of pediatric medicines are provided. Drug manufacturers' ability to disseminate information on unapproved uses of new drugs is expanded. The 1997 legislation is expected to aid the industry in its growth over the next 5 years.

International Competitiveness

Highly innovative and technologically advanced, the U.S. pharmaceutical industry has consistently maintained a competitive edge in international markets. The United States leads the world in R&D expenditures (36 percent of the world's pharmaceutical R&D) and new drug discoveries. It also provides an economic, regulatory, and intellectual environment that encourages innovation. As a result, U.S. manufacturers are leading suppliers in the global pharmaceutical market, producing roughly a third of all drugs sold worldwide. In 1997 North America accounted for 35 percent of the worldwide drug market, Europe 27 percent, Japan 17 percent, Latin America 8 percent, Asia/Pacific 5 per-

cent, and all other regions 8 percent. This geographical breakdown is not expected to change much over the next 5 years.

In 1997 the pharmaceutical industry in the United States is expected to export medicines worth almost $10.4 billion. Between 1996 and 1997, exports from the United States increased 16.7 percent from $8.9 billion to $10.4 billion in 1997 (see Table 11-5). U.S. drugmakers generate, on average, close to two-fifths of their sales abroad. Some of the leading pharmaceutical customers for the United States include Canada, the United Kingdom, Germany, the Netherlands, Italy, Belgium, and Japan.

Pharmaceutical imports into the U.S. have grown markedly in recent years. The United States imported about $14.2 billion worth of pharmaceuticals in 1997. This was a 27 percent increase over imports in 1996. Some of the largest pharmaceutical suppliers to the United States are Germany, the United Kingdom, Canada, Japan, Switzerland, Italy, and France. The following factors appear to be contributing to the increase in U.S. imports: the number of companies relocating research and manufacturing operations outside the United States; international mergers and cost concerns that lead to foreign sourcing of raw materials and intermediates for U.S. manufacturing; increase in EU producers' selling advanced pharmaceutical products to the United States; and U.S. efforts to maintain an unrestricted pharmaceutical business environment.

Continued U.S. pharmaceutical international competitiveness is connected to effective worldwide intellectual property (IPR) protection. IPR protection drives medical progress by providing economic incentives for biomedical innovation. Other foreign trade barriers that U.S. pharmaceutical companies encounter include restrictive and expensive registration processes, price controls that discourage market participation,

TABLE 11-5: U.S. Trade Patterns in Drugs[1] in 1997

(millions of dollars; percent)

Regions[2]	Exports Value[3]	Share, %	Regions[2]	Imports Value[3]	Share, %
NAFTA	1,637	15.8	NAFTA	797	5.6
Latin America	688	6.6	Latin America	81	0.6
Western Europe	5,578	53.8	Western Europe	11,058	77.9
Japan/Chinese Economic Area	1,461	14.1	Japan/Chinese Economic Area	1,446	10.2
Other Asia	404	3.9	Other Asia	451	3.2
Rest of world	607	5.9	Rest of world	363	2.6
World	10,375	100.0	World	14,196	100.0
Top Five Countries	**Value**	**Share, %**	**Top Five Countries**	**Value**	**Share, %**
Canada	1,401	13.5	United Kingdom	2,566	18.1
Japan	1,164	11.2	Germany	2,368	16.7
Germany	1,139	11.0	Ireland	1,886	13.3
Netherlands	1,001	9.6	Switzerland	1,284	9.0
United Kingdom	861	8.3	Japan	1,203	8.5

[1] SIC 283.

[2] For definitions of regional groupings, see "Getting the Most Out of *Outlook '99.*"

[3] Values may not sum to total due to rounding.

Source: U.S. Department of Commerce, Bureau of the Census.

and other market interventions that favor purchase of domestic products.

Bill Hurt, U.S. Department of Commerce, Chemicals, Pharmaceuticals, and Biotechnology Division, (202) 482-5125, November 1998.

BIOTECHNOLOGY

Domestic Trends

The relatively young biotechnology industry is rapidly revolutionizing the medical, agricultural, environmental, and other fields through the introduction of breakthrough processes and products. In a span of 20 years, the industry has already successfully commercialized over 40 products. These include a wide variety of therapeutic pharmaceuticals, vaccines, diagnostic products, agricultural products, and environmental products, many generating hundreds of millions of dollars in annual sales.

Total industry product sales are projected to reach about $15.6 billion in 1998. This figure is up from $14.6 billion in 1997 and $10.8 in 1996 (based on data provided by the accounting firm Ernst & Young). The industry generated an additional $4.4 billion of revenues from payments derived from research performed under collaborative agreements with large pharmaceutical companies and others.

While the overall industry is still in a deficit position, its annual losses have been diminishing in recent years because of the successful launch of several new products such as Biogen's Avonex treatment for multiple sclerosis, Centocor's ReoPro blood clot inhibiting agent, and Agouron Pharmaceuticals' Viracept HIV drug. Based on data from Ernst & Young, the industry's net loss shrank to $1.8 billion in the 12 months through June 1997, from $2.2 billion in the comparable preceding period. Some analysts expect the industry to move into a profit position within the next few years.

Although there are nearly 1,300 biotechnology companies presently operating in the United States (of which about 23 percent are publicly held), the industry is fairly concentrated, with the six largest players—Amgen Inc., Biogen Inc., Centocor, Chiron Corp., Genentech Inc., and Genzyme Corp.—expected to account for over one-third of total industry revenues in 1998.

While the large firms are firmly established with multimillion dollar products able to fund ambitious ongoing research and development programs, many of the small firms are typically strapped for cash to finance ongoing research programs. Lacking the assets needed to provide collateral for debt financing, small biotech companies typically rely on equity financing, which may take the form of venture capital from larger private investors or funds raised from the sale of stock in initial public offerings (IPOs) or secondary offerings. As most of these small biotech firms are still in the developmental stage and unprofitable, their common stock valuations are largely determined by investor perceptions as to the future commercial potential of

products in research and development. Thus, clinical developments on those products typically have an important bearing on those perceptions and can result in wide price fluctuations in stock prices.

While the level of funding to biotechnology companies is now significantly higher than it was a few years ago, the pace slowed somewhat in 1998. Based on a survey done by Burrill & Co., the industry raised $8.6 billion in new funds in the first 9 months of 1998, down from $8.9 billion in the first 9 months of 1997. The decline largely reflected reductions in funds derived from public financing due to greater volatility in the stock market, especially in biotechnology stocks. However, funds raised by private biotech firms from partnering arrangements and venture capital exhibited robust expansion in 1998.

Partnering deals tend to be a "win-win" situation for all parties. Eager to gain access to new breakthrough biotech products, leading drug companies and others have found that arranging collaborative agreements with small biotech firms with cutting-edge science is preferable to the substantial expenditures and patent litigation that they would have to endure if they attempted to develop similar biotech products by themselves. The collaborations are especially valuable to drugmakers with limited or no in-house biotechnology capability. From the perspective of the small biotech firms, these arrangements provide them with a "big brother" with deep pockets that is able to fund ongoing research and eventually help in the manufacturing and marketing of approved products.

According to Burrill & Co., upfront payments and equity investments from partnering arrangements totaled $4.7 billion in the first 9 months of 1998, up from $3 billion in the comparable preceding period. All venture capital raised by biotechnology companies aggregated $7.9 billion in 1997, up from $5.2 billion in 1992.

Merger and acquisition activity in the biotechnology industry is also likely to increase in the years ahead, as many of the small firms deplete their cash positions and seek combinations with large, more financially stable firms in order to fund ongoing R&D programs. Acquisition activity may also be fostered by large foreign drug companies eager to gain a foothold in the American biotechnology industry. Hoffman La Roche's purchase of a majority interest in Genentech and Ciba-Geigy's (now Novartis) acquisition of a 49 percent stake in Chiron Corp. are two prominent examples of this trend.

Although biotechnology has been employed for thousands of years in the production of cheese, wine, beer, and other fermented products, the present biotechnology industry did not come on the scene until the discovery two decades ago of recombinant DNA procedures. These techniques, also referred to as gene splicing, involve the transfer of genetic fragments from the cells of one organism to the cells of another in order to manufacture large quantities of desired proteins.

The industry's leading drugs such as Amgen's Epogen red blood cell stimulant and Neupogen white blood cell promoting agent, and Genentech's Activase clot dissolving drug and Humulin Human Insulin are produced through recombinant

DNA methods. Other important areas of development include monoclonal antibodies, which are used extensively in in-vitro diagnostic tests and in many therapeutic products such as Centocor's ReoPro blood clot inhibiting agent, Retavase clot dissolver, and Remicade immune system modulator. Monoclonal antibodies, DNA probes, and other biotechnology techniques are also being used extensively in the production of medical diagnostics, ranging from tests used to screen blood for the AIDS virus to home pregnancy tests.

Biotechnology companies are also benefiting materially from a recently streamlined Food and Drug Administration (FDA), whose new top leadership remains committed to further speeding up and rendering more efficient the agency's new drug review and approval process. In November 1997 the Prescription Drug User Fee Act (PDUFA) was renewed for another 5 years, guaranteeing the FDA close to $600 million in fees to be submitted with new drug applications through 2002. Those funds are to be used to hire additional personnel and make other necessary investments in order to facilitate an efficient and expeditious new drug review and approval system.

Through the PDUFA, the agency has been able to reduce the median review time of new molecular entities from 23 months in 1993 to 12.8 months in 1997. In addition to streamlining and speeding the approval processes for new drugs and medical devices, the reform legislation allows seriously ill patients easier access to experimental compounds; expands the definition of effectiveness to include (besides reduced mortality) such measures as tumor reduction or reduced viral levels in evaluating a drug's efficacy; provides incentives for the development of pediatric medicines; and allows drug manufacturers to disseminate information on off-label (unapproved) uses of new drugs.

Biotechnology companies are continuing to support legislation that would make the 1981 research and development tax credit permanent. This federal credit enables corporate taxpayers to receive a credit of up to 20 percent of qualified research expenditures, in excess of a calculated base amount. The credit has been extended seven times for short periods. Lawmakers had targeted these credits for cutbacks as part of an overall program to reduce the federal budget deficit. The pharmaceutical and biotechnology industries were successful in preventing the cutbacks, and they continue to push for new legislation that would establish permanent R&D tax credits based on a fixed schedule.

Research and Development

Research and development investments that facilitate the discovery of new drugs represent the foundation upon which the biotechnology industry rests. Those investments have increased rapidly in recent years with the advent of new discoveries in genetics, molecular biology, rational drug design, DNA sequencing, and other areas. Total industrywide R&D investments made by the biotechnology industry in 1998 are projected at $10.2 billion, up from $9 billion in 1997 and $7.9 billion in 1996.

Based on data from the 1998 survey of the Pharmaceutical Research & Manufacturers Association (PhRMA), there were approximately 350 biotechnology medicines in development by some 140 pharmaceutical and biotechnology companies. These consisted of 151 for cancer (including 30 for melanoma, 20 for colorectal cancer, and 13 each for breast and prostate cancer); 29 therapeutic agents for HIV, AIDS, and AIDS-related diseases; 36 for other infectious diseases; 28 for heart disease and other cardiovascular-related conditions; 20 for respiratory diseases; 26 for neurological disorders; 19 for autoimmune disorders such as rheumatoid arthritis and lupus; 14 dermatologicals; and 27 for a wide variety of other ailments. In addition, about 77 vaccines were under develoment to prevent HIV infection, AIDS, various cancers, multiple sclerosis, and stroke.

The process of drug discovery has been revolutionized in recent years by new methodologies such as combinatorial chemistry, genomics, rational drug design, high-throughput screening, and signal transduction. Adoption of these methods is fueling industrywide growth by increasing research productivity and innovation, creating a multitude of new drug opportunities. Combinatorial chemistry utilizes state-of-the-art robotics and synthesis methods to automatically synthesize millions of different compounds. These combinations or combinatorial libraries are then screened by researchers in automated, high-volume analyses to provide valuable information in identifying those with the most potential therapeutic benefits. Combinatorial libraries can be screened within a matter of days or weeks, compared with the weeks and months required under the old empirical methods.

Significant advances in understanding genomics (the science of genetics) are expected to accrue from The Human Genome Project, a global initiative whose goal is the mapping and sequencing of the entire human genome by the year 2005. The human genome is the sum of all genetic codes in each person—consisting of some 100,000 genes arranged in 46 chromosomes. Genes contain sequences of DNA, which carry in encoded form all the information necessary for cells to function in specific ways. A greater understanding of the complex combinations and sequences involved in the genetic system is expected to pave the way for the development of new medicines based on gene therapy.

Gene therapy attempts to correct medical conditions by altering or manipulating the patient's genetic system. So far, these procedures have involved the introduction of genes into a patient's body to replace the defective ones or suppress the action of a harmful gene. Although still in its infancy, gene therapy may eventually provide a basis for treating hereditary diseases and cancers by replacing defective genetic material with normal DNA or by delivering therapeutic substances within the body. Cell therapy, meanwhile, involves isolating diseased cells, treating them outside the body, and then returning them to the patient's body.

One of the recent advances in new drug development based on biotechnology is structural rational drug design. This method involves the creation of high-resolution three-dimensional molecular images of proteins to discover their key functional receptor sites. Scientists then construct new compounds designed to bind to those receptors in an effort to correct or cure various medical ailments. High-throughput screening (HTS) is an important tool using computers to perform various tests to identify promising compounds that interact with given protein targets. With HTS, large-scale screening of millions of molecules can be performed in a relatively short time.

While health care will remain the principal market for biotech products, significant strides have also been made through the application of genetic engineering and other biotech processes to other areas, including food processing, agriculture, environmental control, and forensics or crime detection. Advances in veterinary therapeutics involving biotechnology have yielded new medicines to reduce costly disease in livestock, while other applications have involved improvements in animal breeding, milk production in cows, and meat quality in pigs and other food animals.

Herman Saftlas, Standard & Poor's Corporation, (212) 208-1199, October 1998.

PLASTIC MATERIALS AND RESINS

The plastic materials and resins industry (SIC 2821) includes petroleum-derived monomeric and polymeric materials. These products can be divided into two broad subsectors: thermoplastics and thermosets.

Global Industry Trends

The plastics industry has been increasingly globalized, with the base of production for many commodity resins shifting to countries such as Saudi Arabia, China, and South Korea. Producers in highly developed markets such as the United States, western Europe, and Japan have responded to these changes by emphasizing the production of specialty and higher-value-added products and rationalizing their production capacity to improve profitability. This not only capitalizes on the comparative advantages of developed nations in highly advanced production technologies and research but also lessens the effects of market cyclicity.

While producers in developed countries have been increasing exports to fast-growing areas, notably Mexico, South America, and Asia, the economic downturn in Asia will limit export opportunities in that region, at least in the short term. The existing concern over growing Asian exports has been compounded by the recent currency crisis, which is likely to reduce resin prices significantly while prompting Asian companies to increase output to improve cash flow. However, it is likely that western producers will find opportunities to purchase local assets at reasonable prices, giving them a good base for growth when the Asian economies recover.

Research in the plastics industry has been focused on the development of new production processes instead of entirely new plastic materials. For example, the development of metallocene catalyst technology is expected to play a key role in the olefin sector through the end of the century. The production of metallocene-catalyzed thermoplastics has been growing rapidly both in the United States and worldwide, yet it accounts for only a minor proportion of total resin production. As technical

difficulties are resolved and prices fall, this technology is expected to gain greater importance in the global marketplace. Other efforts are aimed at expanding applications for plastics and improving the performance properties of existing resins through alloying and blending.

The global plastics industry is dominated by large multinational chemical companies that are vertically integrated. Although the industry is expanding globally, it has undergone considerable consolidation, especially through the formation of joint venture companies. This trend is likely to continue, especially in struggling Asian countries, where cost-cutting activity is expected to lead to plant rationalization and asset sales. Nevertheless, total plastics production remains fragmented, based on the number of resins produced and the diversity of the markets served. Larger resin sectors, such as polyethylene and polypropylene, tend to be less concentrated than are smaller, specialty-type products. In each of the top four product types— polyethylene, polypropylene, PVC, and polystyrene—fewer than five players have significant global positions.

U.S. Industry Outlook

Factors affecting growth in the U.S. plastics industry include trends in key end-use markets such as packaging, construction, motor vehicles, and consumer durables. These markets in turn are affected by trends in consumer spending, GDP, and population growth. Other issues which influence the industry's outlook include the cost and availability of raw materials, foreign competition, technological advancements, and competition from other materials.

Shipments of plastics are forecast to increase just over 3 percent in 1999, continuing a trend of decelerating growth which began in 1997 (see Table 11-6). Increases will be restrained by limited export opportunities, increasing competition from imports, slowing demand in key markets (both domestic and foreign), and the maturity of the U.S. economic expansion. However, the outlook for plastics is still favorable, and through 2003 shipments are forecast to gain momentum, growing more than 4 percent annually. While import growth will far exceed export growth through 1999, the United States will remain a net exporter of resins because of its feedstock advantages, technological innovation, reduced trade barriers, and focus on more specialized resin grades.

Exports have played an increasingly important role for U.S. plastics producers, accounting for over a quarter of total shipments in 1997. U.S. companies benefit from a strong feedstock position and solid technological capabilities. Export growth should result from economic expansion in large global markets such as western Europe and continuing penetration of developing regions, especially South America and Asia. However, many countries in those areas, notably South Korea and China, are expanding local capacity, which will not only limit further penetration from exports but create competition for U.S. companies in the global arena. In the near term, currency problems are expected to dampen Asian demand, and this will further lower U.S. export potential. As a result, while exports will continue to increase their share of U.S. production, their growth is

TABLE 11-6: Plastic Materials and Resins (SIC 2821) Trends and Forecasts
(millions of dollars except as noted)

	1992	1993	1994	1995	1996	1997[1]	1998[2]	1999[3]	Percent Change 96–97	Percent Change 97–98	Percent Change 98–99	Percent Change 92–96[4]
Industry data												
Value of shipments[5]	31,601	31,546	37,305	43,453	40,097	43,900	45,890	47,710	9.5	4.5	4.0	6.1
Value of shipments (1992$)	31,601	31,172	35,327	35,156	34,567	37,520	38,920	40,160	8.5	3.9	3.2	2.3
Total employment (thousands)	61.2	62.2	68.9	70.0	58.6							
Production workers (thousands)	36.5	36.6	40.4	41.6	36.3							
Average hourly earnings ($)	18.61	18.75	19.39	20.04	20.50							
Capital expenditures	1,712	1,926	2,536	2,324	2,784							
Product data												
Value of shipments[5]	33,299	33,589	38,043	44,017	42,751	45,350	47,340	49,230	6.1	4.4	4.0	6.4
Value of shipments (1992$)	33,299	33,191	36,025	35,612	36,854	38,760	40,155	41,440	5.2	3.6	3.2	2.6
Trade data												
Value of imports	2,062	2,518	3,280	4,084	4,176	4,649	5,140	5,655	11.3	10.6	10.0	19.3
Value of exports	7,007	7,181	8,427	10,337	10,586	11,746	12,860	13,900	11.0	9.5	8.1	10.9

[1] Estimate except imports and exports.
[2] Estimate.
[3] Forecast.
[4] Compound annual rate.
[5] For a definition of industry versus product values, see "Getting the Most Out of *Outlook '99.*"
Source: U.S. Department of Commerce: Bureau of the Census; International Trade Administration. Estimates and forecasts by Freedonia Group Incorporated, Cleveland, OH.

expected to slow through 1999.

Historically, demand for plastics was spurred by the replacement of materials such as glass, paper, and metal, based on plastic's strong performance characteristics, including low cost, light weight, corrosion and moisture resistance, ease of design and fabrication, and parts consolidation capability. These properties allowed plastics to make serious inroads into packaging and industrial markets. However, much of this substitution has already occurred, especially in the packaging and consumer sectors, and further inroads will be more difficult to achieve. Thus, producers are focusing on upgrading resin performance and searching for new applications.

Global Industry Trends

World demand for plastic materials and resins is expected to total almost 160 million metric tons by 2003, with thermoplastics remaining clearly dominant. While the United States, Japan, and western Europe will continue to dominate both production and consumption of plastics, faster growth is expected in the developing regions of Latin America and Asia, especially Brazil, China, and Mexico. While the outlook for growth in Thailand, South Korea, and other fast-growing southeast Asian countries is subdued, by 2003 Asian demand growth should return to its prerecession levels. Of greater concern is the continuing sluggishness of the Japanese market and indications of slowing demand in China.

Thermoplastics

Thermoplastics constitute the largest subsector of the plastics industry and are expected to account for almost 87 percent of total revenues by 1999. Demand is expected to increase almost 4 percent annually through 2003, with better growth anticipated

for certain products, such as engineered plastics. In contrast, prospects for polystyrene and PVC are less favorable despite the recent growth of PVC use in construction applications.

Polyethylene, including both low- and high-density varieties, will remain the most widely used type of thermoplastic. Demand is influenced by a number of variables, including product pricing, process improvements, and the development of more efficient production catalysts. Packaging is by far the largest market for polyethylene in the United States, followed distantly by consumer and construction goods. The commodity nature of polyethylene makes it susceptible to competition from offshore producers with feedstock advantages, primarily Canada and Saudi Arabia at present. Intense global competition and mature markets are driving U.S. producers to focus on the development of higher-performance applications which use sophisticated polymerization technologies.

Although the United States is a net exporter of thermoplastics, domestic producers will face a number of problems in the global arena through 1999, including rising industry capacity, particularly in the Pacific Rim and the Middle East, which is flooding the world market and limiting U.S. export opportunities. This trend is expected to continue, augmented by increasing supplies of low-cost Asian-produced materials. However, the positive trade balance of the United States is expected to continue through 2003, based on the reduction of trade barriers and growing exports of engineering resins and highly specialized grades.

Thermosets

Demand for thermosets in the United States is affected by a number of factors, notably the outlook for end-use markets such as motor vehicles and construction (unlike thermoplastics, packaging is not a key market for thermosets). Consequently, the outlook is for consistent, respectable advances, but at a considerably slower pace relative to the gains experienced during the initial stages of the U.S. economic expansion. Growth in demand reflects the durability, versatility, and lightweight advantages of thermosets over competitive materials.

Phenolics and polyurethane will remain the most widely used types of thermosets, with polyurethane and epoxy resins expected to experience the fastest growth. The United States is a leading global producer of the major types of thermoset resins. However, by 2000 the United States is expected to be a slight net importer of thermosets.

William P. Weizer and *Teresa L. Hayes,* Freedonia Group Incorporated, (440) 646-0809, November 1998.

■ **R E F E R E N C E S**

Industrial Inorganic Chemicals

Chemical Marketing Reporter, Schnell Publishing Company, 80 Broad Street, New York, NY 10004. (212) 248-4177.
Chemical Week, McGraw-Hill Publications, 888 Seventh Avenue, New York, NY 10106. (212)-621-4900.
Industry Studies, 795: *Bromine & Derivatives;* 833: *Chloralkalies,* 841: *Aluminum Compounds,* 855: *Peroxides,* 872: *Industrial Gases,* and 929: *Fluorochemicals,* Freedonia Group Incorporated, 767 Beta Drive, Cleveland, OH 44143. (440) 646-0809. E-mail: info@freedoniagroup.com, www.freedoniagroup.com.

Industrial Organic Chemicals

Chemical Marketing Reporter, Schnell Publishing Co., 80 Broad Street, New York, NY 10004. (212) 248-4177.
Chemical Week, McGraw-Hill Publications, 1221 Avenue of the Americas, New York, NY 10020. (212) 512-2000.
Study 935: *Dyes & Organic Pigments,* Freedonia Group Incorporated, 767 Beta Drive, Cleveland, OH 44143. (440) 646-0809, E-mail: info@freedoniagroup.com, www.freedoniagroup.com.

Miscellaneous Chemical Products

Chemical Marketing Reporter, Schnell Publishing Co., 80 Broad Street, New York, NY 10004. (212) 248-4177.
Chemical Week, McGraw-Hill Publications, 1221 Avenue of the Americas, New York, NY 10020. (212) 512-2000.
Industry Studies (865: *Printing Inks,* 976: *World Carbon Black,* 1004: *Explosives & Pyrotechnics,* 1006: *Fatty Acids*), Freedonia Group Incorporated, 767 Beta Drive, Cleveland, OH 44143. (440) 646-0809, E-mail: info@freedoniagroup.com, www.freedoniagroup.com.

Drugs and Pharmaceuticals

Current Industrial Reports, Manufacturers Shipments, Inventories and Orders (monthly), U.S. Department of Commerce, Bureau of the Census, Washington, DC 20233.
Generic Pharmaceutical Indistry Association, 1620 I Street, NW, Suite 800, Washington, DC 20006.
Nonprescription Drug Manufacturers Association, 1150 Connecticut Avenue, NW, Washington, DC 20036.
Pharmaceutical Research and Manufacturers of America, 1100 Fifteenth Street, NW, Washington, DC 20005.

Plastic Materials and Resins

Facts and Figures of the US Plastics Industry, 1997 edition, Society of Plastics Industry, Inc., 1275 K Street, NW, Washington DC 20005. (202) 371-5200.
Industry Studies, 893: *Reinforced Plastics,* 909: *World Polyethylene,* 926: *World Polyvinyl Chloride,* 928: *Plastics in Construction,* 938: *Engineered Plastics,* 949: *Injection Molded Plastics,* 958: *Polypropylene,* 972: *PET Resins,* 991: *Epoxy Resins,* 995: *Polyethylene,* 1007: *Phenolic Resins,* 1010: *Thermoplastic Compounding,* Freedonia Group Incorporated, 767 Beta Drive, Cleveland, OH 44142. (440) 646-0809, E-mail: info@freedoniagroup.com, www. freedoniagroup.com.

■ **R E L A T E D   C H A P T E R S**

9: Textiles
12: Rubber
20: Environmental Technologies and Services
35: Processed Food and Beverages
45: Medical and Dental Instruments and Supplies

RUBBER
Economic and Trade Trends

U.S. International Trade

($ billions)

Legend: Balance — Exports — Imports

Source: U.S. Department of Commerce: Bureau of the Census; International Trade Administration.

World Export Market Shares

(%)

Legend: United States, Japan, France, Germany

Source: United Nations; U.S. Department of Commerce, International Trade Administration.

Export Dependence and Import Penetration

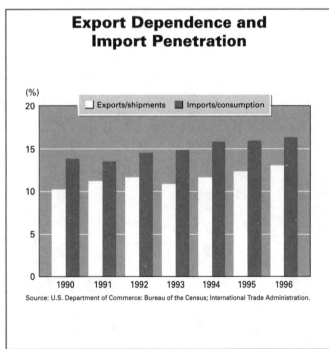

(%)

Legend: Exports/shipments, Imports/consumption

Source: U.S. Department of Commerce: Bureau of the Census; International Trade Administration.

Output and Output per Hour

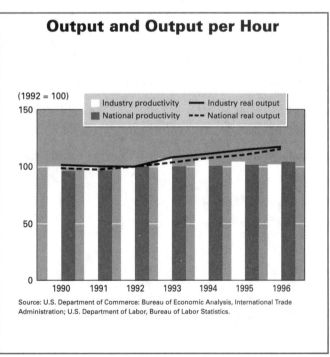

(1992 = 100)

Legend: Industry productivity — Industry real output; National productivity — National real output

Source: U.S. Department of Commerce: Bureau of Economic Analysis, International Trade Administration; U.S. Department of Labor, Bureau of Labor Statistics.

See "Getting the Most Out of *Outlook '99*" for definitions of terms.

Rubber

INDUSTRY DEFINITION The rubber industry covered in this chapter consists of synthetic rubber (SIC 2822), tires and inner tubes (SIC 3011), and fabricated rubber products not elsewhere classified (SIC 3069). In recent years, the U.S. industry has run a trade deficit in this industry (see Table 12-1).

SYNTHETIC RUBBER

SIC 2822 includes establishments primarily engaged in manufacturing synthetic rubber, an elastomer, by polymerization or copolymerization. An elastomer is a rubberlike material that can be further processed by vulcanization, such as polymers and copolymers of butadiene and styrene, as well as butadiene and acrylonitrile, polybutadienes, chloroprene rubbers, and isobutylene-isoprene copolymers. Butadiene copolymers, however, that contain less than 50 percent butadiene are classified under SIC 2821. Natural chlorinated rubbers and so-called cyclized rubbers are considered semi-finished products and are classified under SIC 3069, fabricated rubber products.

Factors Affecting Future Industry Growth

Global Industry Trends. After a strong initial growth phase from the 1960s through the early 1990s, the worldwide synthetic rubber industry settled into a period of maturity. The worldwide average growth of consumption, after reaching all-time highs in the 1960s, entered a period of slow growth at around 4 to 6 percent since then. The 1960s and 1970s saw the

TABLE 12-1: U.S. Trade Patterns in Rubber[1] in 1997
(millions of dollars; percent)

Exports			Imports		
Regions[2]	Value[3]	Share, %	Regions[2]	Value[3]	Share, %
NAFTA	2,487	50.2	NAFTA	1,923	31.6
Latin America	564	11.4	Latin America	260	4.3
Western Europe	966	19.5	Western Europe	956	15.7
Japan/Chinese Economic Area	497	10.0	Japan/Chinese Economic Area	1,538	25.2
Other Asia	192	3.9	Other Asia	1,327	21.8
Rest of world	244	4.9	Rest of world	89	1.5
World	4,950	100.0	World	6,093	100.0
Top Five Countries	Value	Share, %	Top Five Countries	Value	Share, %
Canada	1,662	33.6	Canada	1,653	27.1
Mexico	825	16.7	Japan	1,025	16.8
Japan	384	7.8	Malaysia	618	10.1
Belgium	255	5.2	China	278	4.6
Brazil	158	3.2	Mexico	269	4.4

[1] SIC 2822, 3011, 3069.
[2] For definitions of regional groupings, see "Getting the Most Out of *Outlook '99.*"
[3] Values may not sum to total due to rounding.
Source: U.S. Department of Commerce, Bureau of the Census.

development of more chemically complex polymers, including the so-called thermoplastic elastomers (TPEs). Since the mid-1980s, however, most significant advances in rubber chemistry have involved the development of existing polymers rather than the invention of entirely new materials.

The costs of entry are high, relative to other industrial sectors, leading to high industry concentration worldwide. Twelve firms account for nearly one-half of total world capacity of synthetic rubber. The top four alone—Bayer, Goodyear, Enichem, and Japan Synthetic Rubber—account for nearly one-fourth of total world capacity. The remaining eight firms (Nippon Zeon, Korea Kumho, Exxon, Petroflex, DSM Copolymer, Bridgestone-Firestone, Michelin, DuPont Dow) account for one-fifth. About one-fourth of world capacity, consisting of four specific types of synthetic rubber, goes toward captive production, mostly tires.

The share of world production of synthetic rubber by region has remained fairly steady since the mid-1980s. In 1995 total world production reached an estimated 6,481 thousand metric tons (TMT), an all-time high. North America (Canada and the United States) led the way with nearly 40 percent (2,467 TMT), followed by Asia and Oceania (28 percent, or 1,826 TMT), western Europe (26 percent, or 1,678 TMT), and Latin America (6 percent, or 510 TMT). Two product groups accounted for the bulk of world production in 1995: solid styrene-butadiene rubber (SBR) and butadiene rubber (BR).

The synthetic rubber industry is widely regarded as being very mature. Except for an unusual peak period in 1989–1990, annual worldwide consumption has hovered in the range of 9.0 to 9.5 million metric tons. There has been little change in the overall composition of worldwide consumption by product type and region, with the exception of China, central and eastern Europe, and the former Soviet republics. Geographically, North America remained the world's largest consumer of synthetic rubber (31.5 percent, or 3,002 TMT) in 1995, followed by western Europe (24.2 percent, or 2,311 TMT), Asia and the Pacific (22.7 percent, or 2,174 TMT), Latin America (6 percent, or 576 TMT), and the Middle East and Africa (2 percent, or 165 TMT).

Domestic Trends. In terms of growth, capacity in North America ranked second only to that in Asia and Oceania in the period 1987–1996. Total capacity in North America grew nearly 18 percent in that period, from 2,970 TMT in 1987 to an estimated 3,500 TMT in 1996, second only to Asia and Oceania (27 percent).

In 1996 there were 19 producers of synthetic rubber in the United States that were responsible for an estimated 3,230 TMT. Four categories accounted for nearly 80 percent of total U.S. production in 1996: SBR (31.7 percent), BR (18.6 percent), carboxylated nitrile-butadiene rubber [XSBR] (16.9 percent), and ethylene-propylene copolymer/ethylene-propylene terpolymer [EPM/EPDM] (11.5 percent).

Historically, synthetic rubber (SR) continues to be second only to natural rubber as the elastomer most commonly used in North America. The natural:synthetic ratio was 3:1 over the last decade. U.S. per capita consumption of SR has shown little variability as well, except for a historic low in 1990–1991. This pattern stands in sharp contrast to consumption patterns in the emerging economies, where there has been a greater tendency to use higher percentages of natural rubber in the production process.

In 1996 three end-use sectors accounted for roughly three-quarters of SR shipments: fabricated rubber products (30 percent), tires (27 percent), and miscellaneous plastic products (18 percent). The remainder was used in the paper, floor coverings, and adhesive-sealant and electrical wiring industries.

Compared with other SIC 28 industries, trade dependency is about average. Data for the early 1990s showed a consistent pattern of stable export-to-product shipment ratios of approximately 20 percent. Similarly, imports as a percentage of apparent consumption (imports plus product shipments minus exports) showed even less variability, in the range of 14 percent, in that period.

The United States remains a strong net exporter of synthetic rubber to the world, with exports running at a nearly 2:1 ratio relative to imports. Canada is both the largest supplier and the largest U.S. export market, taking nearly one-fourth of all exports while supplying one-third of all imports. Export patterns showed some reshuffling in 1994–1997 as the slowdown in Asia made itself felt: Exports of SR to Japan, for instance, declined nearly 40 percent in that period. Import shares, by contrast, have been stable except for Brazil, whose share has increased eightfold (see Table 12-2).

As a producer of commodity chemicals, the SR industry has operating costs that are strongly affected by environmental regulation at all levels. Superfund, the Clean Air Act, and more recently issues of liability are likely to dominate industry concerns in the future. Somewhat peripherally, efforts at regulating scrap rubber as "hazardous waste" by treaty have lost momentum.

Projections of Industry and Trade Growth for the Next 1 and 5 Years

In real terms, industry shipments in 1999 will depend largely on conditions prevailing in the three main end-use sectors. Sluggish demand from the tire sector more than likely will be offset by expected growth in the fabricated rubber products and miscellaneous plastic products sectors. Demand for SR probably will quicken later as the tire sector gains strength through the turn of the century, possibly surpassing $5 billion. No significant changes are expected in the composition of overall demand in North America, partly as a result of the maturity of this market (see Table 12-3).

Global Market Prospects

The financial crisis in Asia is expected to depress demand for SR across that region and to affect U.S. exports adversely, particularly exports to Japan, Taiwan, Korea, Hong Kong, Indonesia, and Thailand, as processors scramble for hard currency. In

TABLE 12-2:   U.S. Trade Patterns in Synthetic Rubber[1] in 1997

(millions of dollars; percent)

Exports			Imports		
Regions[2]	Value[3]	Share, %	Regions[2]	Value[3]	Share, %
NAFTA	430	33.0	NAFTA	282	38.8
Latin America	191	14.6	Latin America	38	5.3
Western Europe	440	33.7	Western Europe	242	33.4
Japan/Chinese Economic Area	116	8.9	Japan/Chinese Economic Area	106	14.6
Other Asia	84	6.4	Other Asia	39	5.3
Rest of world	44	3.4	Rest of world	18	2.5
World	1304	100.0	World	725	100.0
Top Five Countries	Value	Share, %	Top Five Countries	Value	Share, %
Canada	316	24.2	Canada	242	33.4
Belgium	178	13.7	Japan	89	12.2
Mexico	114	8.7	France	63	8.6
Brazil	100	7.6	Germany	48	6.6
Japan	63	4.8	Mexico	39	5.4

[1] SIC 2822.
[2] For definitions of regional groupings, see "Getting the Most Out of *Outlook '99*."
[3] Values may not sum to total due to rounding.
Source: U.S. Department of Commerce, Bureau of the Census.

TABLE 12-3:   Synthetic Rubber (SIC 2822) Trends and Forecasts

(millions of dollars except as noted)

	1992	1993	1994	1995	1996	1997[1]	1998[2]	1999[3]	Percent Change 96–97	97–98	98–99	92–96[4]
Industry data												
Value of shipments[5]	4,235	4,739	4,964	5,475	5,291	4,743	4,838	4,964	–10.4	2.0	2.6	5.2
Value of shipments (1992$)	4,235	4,623	4,755	4,543	4,537	4,696	4,790	4,891	3.5	2.0	2.1	2.5
Total employment (thousands)	11.9	12.2	11.9	12.0	12.0							0.7
Production workers (thousands)	7.6	7.7	7.7	8.0	7.9							0.9
Average hourly earnings ($)	18.73	19.27	19.52	20.61	20.68							2.0
Capital expenditures	321	256	266	268	279							7.0
Product data												
Value of shipments[5]	4,318	4,643	4,983	5,430	5,139	4,648	4,693	4,841	–9.6	1.0	3.2	4.5
Value of shipments (1992$)	4,318	4,530	4,773	4,507	4,407	4,602	4,646	4,769	4.4	1.0	2.6	1.9
Trade data												
Value of imports	530	555	624	691	681	725	730	740	6.5	0.7	1.4	16.9
Value of exports	1,010	947	1,081	1,264	1,344	1,304	1,310	1,319	–3.0	0.5	0.7	9.5

[1] Estimate except imports and exports.
[2] Estimate.
[3] Forecast.
[4] Compound annual rate.
[5] For definition of industry versus product values, see "Getting the Most Out of *Outlook '99*."
Source: U.S. Department of Commerce: Bureau of the Census; International Trade Administration.

the longer term, however, the outlook for overall consumption of SR is firm, with consumption expected to hold at around 11 million metric tons by the turn of the century. The highest growth in consumption in the next several years is projected for the states of the former Soviet Union, central and eastern Europe, and China, at about 30 to 40 percent, as a result of continuing liberalization and streamlining of foreign investment regulations in those countries. Consumption rates in Latin America and the rest of Asia probably will keep pace with the overall growth in world consumption rates, reaching 3 to 4 percent annually through the year 2000. Consistent with the realities of a mature market, however, North American and western European producers probably will see little growth in the foreseeable future. Little if any change in consumption patterns by elastomer type is expected worldwide, except for truck and other specialized tire producers.

TIRES AND INNER TUBES

SIC 3011 includes establishments primarily engaged in producing pneumatic casings, inner tubes, and solid and cushion tires for all kinds of vehicles, airplanes, farm equipment, and children's vehicles; tiring and camelback; and tire repair and retreading materials. Establishments primarily engaged in tire retreading and repair, however, are classified under SIC 7534.

Factors Affecting Future Industry Growth

Global Industry Trends. The global tire industry is going through a postconsolidation phase after experiencing a difficult period in the early and middle 1990s. Years of restructuring and consolidation, ensuing plant closings, price wars, cyclical recessions, and, more recently, sharp price hikes for raw materials weeded out the weaker competitors and left the industry with fewer but stronger producers. Among the survivors in 1994 were 19 major manufacturers that accounted for $50.8 billion of the estimated global sales of $57.8 billion. Eleven of those 19 manufacturers were responsible for over $59.2 billion in new tire sales worldwide in 1996, an increase of 6.3 percent over 1995. Three firms—Bridgestone, Groupe Michelin, and Goodyear Tire & Rubber—accounted for nearly two-thirds of total output, or $38.9 billion, in 1996.

Sales and profitability are making a comeback, with many major global players reporting an improved sales and profit climate both in North America and in western Europe. Concern over the prices of raw materials has largely evaporated in the wake of the so-called Asian currency crisis, as the epidemic of currency devaluations has ensured an even greater availability of raw materials and cost savings for the major producers.

More flexible manufacturing has become a necessity for the larger manufacturers, including Michelin, Bridgestone, Goodyear, Continental, Sumitomo, and Pirelli. Cost pressures and an ever-growing proliferation of niche markets are providing an incentive for the development of more adaptable manufacturing processes. These more sophisticated processes allow producers to bring product specifications and quantities into conformance with client needs more economically.

In addition to servicing traditional tire markets (passenger cars and trucks), producers have of necessity turned to product differentiation as their key weapon, especially in the more developed markets. Technological innovation is seen by many producers as a way of attracting attention to a crowded marketplace. Two notable examples are so-called airless tires and low-resistance tires. To date, however, these products do not appear to have gained significant market share.

Domestic Trends. Tire production is highly capital-intensive, as evidenced by extremely high industry concentration (a few firms account for a large share of production), the high cost of manufacturing operations, production technology, and investment in research and development (R&D). Uncertainty over raw materials sourcing, which accounts for a small percentage of total operating costs, is not as critical as it is in other industries, as most major U.S. producers exercise strict control over their own rubber plantations, mostly in southeast Asia. Recent disturbances in southeast Asian currency markets and ensuing drops in dollar-denominated rubber prices have put U.S. producers in an even more advantageous competitive position despite price stabilization agreements (the International Natural Rubber Agreement). U.S. production is now centered in the eastern United States: Oklahoma, North Carolina, and Alabama are home to roughly one-half of all U.S. tire capacity, which was estimated to be 937,200 units in 1996.

In regard to distribution, some realignments in mass merchandising in the United States are becoming evident. Recent trends show shifts in ownership, with national and regional tire dealerships forming buying groups and thus hindering the entry of major manufacturers into the retail end of the business. Independent tire dealerships and chain department stores, however, still keep a firm grip on distribution nationwide. About four-fifths of all domestic passenger car tires were sold through these two channels in 1996.

In terms of trade dependency, this industry is showing signs of becoming increasingly export-dependent, with export-to-product shipment ratios growing nearly 70 percent in the early 1990s. Significantly, imports as a percentage of apparent consumption showed virtually no change (approximately 20 percent through the middle of the 1990s). These tendencies have caused a significant reversal of earlier trends. As a result, import-to-export ratios are running at their lowest point in several years (see Table 12-4).

The United States has been a net importer of tires, although there are signs that trade is becoming more export-oriented. The North American Free Trade Agreement (NAFTA) cosignatories, Canada and Mexico, make up the single largest U.S. export market, taking in 57 percent of all tire exports in 1997. Canada also was the largest supplier of the United States in 1997, accounting for one-third of all tire imports, followed by Japan and Korea. The fastest growing suppliers to the United States in the period 1994–1997 included China and Mexico, possibly at the expense of Brazil and Taiwan.

Scrap tire recycling poses an ongoing challenge to the industry. National trade associations have been active in promoting the benefits of scrap tires, including their high British thermal unit (BTU) content, lower cost, and "greenness." An estimated 236 million scrap tires were consumed in 1996, with the bulk used as so-called tire-derived fuel (TDF). Other outlets for scrap that had high rates of growth were civil engineering and some exports. Industry efforts are now focused on developing demand and finding economically feasible alternatives to dumping. Much remains to be done in this regard, as is evidenced by the ever-increasing national stockpile of scrap tires.

Environmental issues will continue to be a matter of concern to industry, especially Superfund provisions which define scrap tires as hazardous waste, so-called flow control legislation aimed at restricting the use of scrap tires according to their source, and Clean Air Act amendments related to automobile emissions. Earlier successes in negotiating acceptable tire

TABLE 12-4: U.S. Trade Patterns in Tires and Inner Tubes[1] in 1997

(millions of dollars; percent)

Regions[2]	Exports Value[3]	Exports Share, %	Regions[2]	Imports Value[3]	Imports Share, %
NAFTA	1,371	57.2	NAFTA	1,229	36.6
Latin America	290	12.1	Latin America	191	5.7
Western Europe	277	11.6	Western Europe	468	13.9
Japan/Chinese Economic Area	284	11.8	Japan/Chinese Economic Area	1,069	31.8
Other Asia	41	1.7	Other Asia	343	10.2
Rest of world	133	5.5	Rest of world	56	1.7
World	2,394	100.0	World	3,357	100.0
Top Five Countries	**Value**	**Share, %**	**Top Five Countries**	**Value**	**Share, %**
Canada	861	35.9	Canada	1,096	32.6
Mexico	510	21.3	Japan	809	24.1
Japan	259	10.8	South Korea	200	6.0
Germany	83	3.5	Brazil	135	4.0
Venezuela	50	2.1	Mexico	134	4.0

[1] SIC 3011.
[2] For definitions of regional groupings, see "Getting the Most Out of *Outlook '99*."
[3] Values may not sum to total due to rounding.
Source: U.S. Department of Commerce, Bureau of the Census.

TABLE 12-5: Tires and Inner Tubes (SIC 3011) Trends and Forecasts

(millions of dollars except as noted)

	1992	1993	1994	1995	1996	1997[1]	1998[2]	1999[3]	Percent Change 96–97	97–98	98–99	92–96[4]
Industry data												
Value of shipments[5]	11,814	12,601	13,183	14,145	14,209	15,045	15,502	15,814	5.9	3.0	2.0	4.7
Value of shipments (1992$)	11,814	12,614	13,249	14,061	14,604	15,290	15,627	15,767	4.7	2.2	0.9	5.4
Total employment (thousands)	64.6	65.1	65.1	65.9	64.8	65.6	66.1	66.1				0.1
Production workers (thousands)	52.8	53.3	54.0	54.3	54.0	54.6	54.9	54.9				0.6
Average hourly earnings ($)	18.54	18.63	19.00	18.89	19.48							1.2
Capital expenditures	506	490	518	467	579							3.4
Product data												
Value of shipments[5]	11,316	12,241	12,816	13,835	13,753	14,294	14,571	15,024	3.9	1.9	3.1	5.0
Value of shipments (1992$)	11,316	12,253	12,880	13,753	14,134	14,526	14,681	14,979	2.8	1.1	2.0	5.7
Trade data												
Value of imports	2,463	2,680	2,979	3,089	3,020	3,357	3,454	3,413	11.2	2.9	−1.2	5.2
Value of exports	1,395	1,453	1,598	1,856	1,955	2,394	2,451	2,613	22.5	2.4	6.6	8.8

[1] Estimate except imports and exports.
[2] Estimate.
[3] Forecast.
[4] Compound annual rate.
[5] For definition of industry versus product values, see "Getting the Most Out of *Outlook '99*."
Source: U.S. Department of Commerce: Bureau of the Census; International Trade Administration.

labeling and certification standards with Mexico may have provided a useful benchmark for future negotiations.

Projections of Industry and Trade Growth for the Next 1 and 5 Years

The short-term outlook for growth of the original equipment market remains cautious in response to continuing drop-offs in demand from the transportation sector. Steadier demand from the replacement market for major tire subsectors (passenger cars, light trucks, and trucks and buses) may help soften the impact somewhat. In real terms, overall shipments of tires and inner tubes are not expected to grow more than 1 percent in 1999. A reversal in the longer term is expected as shipments pick up speed later, maintaining a growth rate of 2 to 3 percent annually well into the next decade. Export growth is expected to resume in 1999 and gain momentum through 2002. Import growth through 2002, in contrast, probably will continue to lag behind (see Table 12-5).

Global Market Prospects

With the worst of the slump out of the picture, much of the growth in new demand is expected to come from areas outside the already mature markets of North America and Europe.

If current investment trends continue, demand across much of Latin America is expected to balloon as new vehicle production facilities come on line. Over $12 billion in new investment by North American and European interests in the automotive sector, representing nearly half a million new vehicles, is expected to account for much of the new demand in this region.

Observers agree, however, that the Asia/Pacific region still holds the most promise despite the current economic setbacks there. Projected expansion of the automobile population in the long term, partly fueled by growing consumer incomes across Asia, probably will generate substantial markets for both original equipment and replacement tires. The outcome of ongoing talks at the World Trade Organization (WTO) and the Asia-Pacific Economic Conference (APEC) will continue to play a major role in easing the way toward a more transparent trading and investment climate in Asia.

FABRICATED RUBBER PRODUCTS

SIC 3069 includes the output of business entities engaged in the manufacture of miscellaneous rubber items, including but not limited to industrial rubber goods, rubberized fabrics, and vulcanized rubber clothing, as well as miscellaneous rubber specialties not elsewhere classified. Also included in this industry are firms involved in the reclaiming of rubber. Not included, however, are firms engaged in the wholesale distribution of scrap rubber (SIC 5093), establishments engaged in the rebuilding and retreading of tires (SIC 7534), firms that manufacture rubberized clothing from purchased materials (SIC 2385), and producers of gaskets and packing (SIC 3053).

Factors Affecting Future Industry Growth

Global Industry Trends. Exports of miscellaneous rubber products from the rapidly industrializing economies of east Asia and southeast Asia to the developed economies have shown steady and consistent growth throughout this decade. Geographically, producers of natural rubber (NR) have been in a stronger competitive position than have nonproducers, accounting for their sustained higher production and export growth rates. Key producers in this group include Brazil, China, Indonesia, Malaysia, Mexico, the Philippines, Sri Lanka, and Thailand.

Three key factors are responsible for this surge in growth: a wave of rapid industrialization throughout the Asia/Pacific region, disruptions in supply from the central and eastern European region, and the transfer of manufacturing operations, or "plant drift," from the higher-cost developed economies to the more resource-rich and lower-cost regions. The range of products turned out by many of these rubber-producing countries has been limited by price and availability constraints on needed synthetic elastomers and rubber-processing chemicals.

Many of the world's largest producers of natural rubber have been hard hit by the Asian financial crisis. Currency devaluations and the ensuing drop in the export earnings of these nations have made it particularly difficult for many of these producers to finance their day-to-day operations. In this regard the International Natural Rubber Organization (INRO) can initiate price support measures by manipulating stockpiles. To date, however, talks appear to be stalled by differences of opinion between developing country producers (for intervention) and developed country consumers (against intervention).

Domestic Trends. Fabricated rubber products are most often used as intermediates. A high proportion of this production, over 80 percent, is channeled directly to a wide range of industrial users, including the motor vehicle, motor vehicle parts, health care, and auto rental sectors.

There were nearly 1,000 producers of rubber products operating nearly 1,800 plants across the United States in 1992. Historically, production has tended to cluster in the north-central region around Akron, Ohio, and to a lesser extent in parts of the northeast and midwest and in southern California.

Most fabricated rubber products firms fall into two distinct categories: There are a few large, diversified conglomerates and a significant number of niche market players. Top firms in 1996, all with reported sales exceeding $200 million, were Rubbermaid, Standard Products, Carlisle, Textile Rubber & Chemical, Miler Products, Kraco Enterprises, Cooper Tire & Rubber, and Pretty Products.

In comparison with other rubber product (SIC 30) industries, SIC 3069 is one of the less export-dependent sectors, ranking well behind tires (SIC 3011), rubber and plastics footwear (3021), and rubber and plastics hose and belting (SIC 3052). Exports grew faster than shipments during this period as a result of NAFTA and firm demand from Canada and Mexico. In line with industrywide trends in the rubber industry, imports as a percentage of consumption have shown a mild upward tendency, in the range of 14 to 16 percent (see Table 12-6).

In regard to trade, the United States has been a net importer, with imports consistently running at about a 2:1 ratio relative to exports. The main suppliers to the United States in 1996 were Malaysia, Canada, Thailand, China, and Japan. On the export side, the NAFTA trading area (Canada and Mexico) has become the single largest export market for the United States, taking nearly three-fifths of total U.S. exports in 1996.

Projections of Industry and Trade Growth for the Next 1 and 5 Years

As a result of this sector's dependence on the automotive industry, the outlook for 1999 will depend largely on that industry's ability to weather sagging demand (see Table 12-7). In the longer term, however, real output is expected to bounce back in response to recovery in the transportation sectors. Import competition in the U.S. domestic market will remain keen as more competitive, low-cost producers continue to make inroads into this already crowded market. The pace of imports is expected to quicken through 2002.

TABLE 12-6: U.S. Trade Patterns in Fabricated Rubber Products[1] in 1997

(millions of dollars; percent)

Exports			Imports		
Regions[2]	Value[3]	Share, %	Regions[2]	Value[3]	Share, %
NAFTA	687	54.9	NAFTA	411	20.5
Latin America	84	6.7	Latin America	31	1.5
Western Europe	250	20.0	Western Europe	246	12.2
Japan/Chinese Economic Area	98	7.8	Japan/Chinese Economic Area	363	18.1
Other Asia	67	5.3	Other Asia	945	47.0
Rest of world	67	5.4	Rest of world	14	0.7
World	1,252	100.0	World	2,010	100.0
Top Five Countries	Value	Share, %	Top Five Countries	Value	Share, %
Canada	486	38.8	Malaysia	607	30.2
Mexico	201	16.0	Canada	316	15.7
Japan	62	4.9	Thailand	166	8.2
United Kingdom	49	3.9	China	142	7.1
Netherlands	48	3.8	Japan	128	6.4

[1] SIC 3069.
[2] For definitions of regional groupings, see "Getting the Most Out of *Outlook '99*."
[3] Values may not sum to total due to rounding.
Source: U.S. Department of Commerce, Bureau of the Census.

TABLE 12-7: Fabricated Rubber Products not elsewhere classified (SIC 3069) Trends and Forecasts

(millions of dollars except as noted)

	1992	1993	1994	1995	1996	1997[1]	1998[2]	1999[3]	Percent Change			
									96–97	97–98	98–99	92–96[4]
Industry data												
Value of shipments[5]	6,933	7,608	7,748	8,327	8,481	8,118	8,102	8,126	−4.3	−0.2	0.3	5.7
Value of shipments (1992$)	6,933	7,474	7,442	7,632	7,654	7,998	8,014	8,038	4.5	0.2	0.3	1.7
Total employment (thousands)	56.5	58.4	57.9	58.1	58.1							0.2
Production workers (thousands)	42.0	43.4	43.1	43.9	43.5							1.0
Average hourly earnings ($)	10.08	10.33	10.31	10.86	10.93							2.5
Capital expenditures	205	222	215	226	269							−3.4
Product data												
Value of shipments[5]	6,600	7,179	7,384	7,720	7,875	7,631	7,616	7,720	−3.1	−0.2	1.4	4.4
Value of shipments (1992$)	6,600	7,052	7,093	7,076	7,108	7,518	7,533	7,636	5.8	0.2	1.4	0.5
Trade data												
Value of imports	1,045	1,279	1,504	1,758	1,952	2,010	2,108	2,094	3.0	4.9	−0.7	6.5
Value of exports	725	773	916	969	1,044	1,252	1,292	1,349	19.9	3.2	4.4	7.4

[1] Estimate except imports and exports.
[2] Estimate.
[3] Forecast.
[4] Compound annual rate.
[5] For definition of industry versus product values, see "Getting the Most Out of *Outlook '99*."
Source: U.S. Department of Commerce: Bureau of the Census; International Trade Administration.

Global Market Prospects

There is no evidence that southeast Asian producers of fabricated rubber products are attempting to export their way out of their current and largely self-made difficulties. In fact, exports from the major Asian suppliers—Malaysia, China, Thailand, Japan, Taiwan, and Indonesia—show no unusual activity. Given the current instability of rubber prices in dollar terms and the fact that some form of synthetic rubber is used in many fabricated rubber products, the likelihood of input substitution (natural for synthetic) remains high, at least for some product lines. Concern over world prices of NR probably will continue to overshadow other industry issues, such as recycling.

There is still considerable controversy about what role, if any, should be taken by the INRO in initiating market operations with a view to supporting rubber prices. A key issue which divides producers from consumers has been whether existing commodity agreements should be used to correct exchange fluctuations and whether the existing treaty allows for modification of previously agreed-on price-setting mechanisms.

In the longer term, China probably will emerge as a leading world producer as it integrates itself more fully into the world trading system and makes its entry into more and higher value-added sectors. This in turn may intensify competitive pressures against other Asian producers resulting in lower prices and greater availability but, at the same time, more competitive pressure on higher-cost producers in North America and Europe. Reshuffling in Asia will remain a possibility. Ensuing and perhaps unfair terms of competition resulting from this dynamic will have to be scrutinized closely during any future accession talks at the WTO.

Raimundo M. Prat, U.S. Department of Commerce, Chemicals, Pharmaceuticals & Biotechnology Division, (202) 482-0810, October 1998.

■ **REFERENCES**

"Elastomers Overview, January 1995," *Chemical Economics Handbook,* SRI International, Menlo Park, CA 94025. (415) 859-3900.

Institute of Scrap Recycling Industries, 1325 G Street, NW, Suite 1000, Washington, DC 20005. (202) 737-1770.

National Tire Dealer and Retreaders Association, 1250 I Street, NW, Suite 400, Washington, DC 20005. (202) 682-3999.

Rubber and Plastics News, Crain Communications, Inc., 1725 Merriman Road, Suite 300, Akron, OH 44313-5251. (303) 836-9180.

Rubber Products: An Overview of Major Markets and Opportunities for Developing Countries, International Trade Center, UNCTAD/GATT, Geneva, Switzerland, 1995.

Scrap Tire Management Council–Rubber Manufacturers Association, 1400 K Street, NW, Washington, DC 20005. (202) 682-4800.

Tire Business, Crain Communications, Inc., 1725 Merriman Road, Suite 300, Akron, OH 44313-5251. (303) 836-9180.

Web Site: www.rubber.com.

Worldwide Rubber Statistics 1996, International Institute of Synthetic Rubber Producers, 2077 South Gessner Road, Suite 133, Houston, TX. (713) 783-7253.

■ **RELATED CHAPTERS**

36: Motor Vehicles
37: Automotive Parts and Accessories

STEEL MILL PRODUCTS
Economic and Trade Trends

U.S. International Trade

($ billions)

Legend: Balance — Exports — Imports

Source: U.S. Department of Commerce: Bureau of the Census; International Trade Administration.

World Export Market Shares

(%)

Legend: United States ■ Japan □ Germany ■ France

Source: United Nations; U.S. Department of Commerce, International Trade Administration.

Export Dependence and Import Penetration

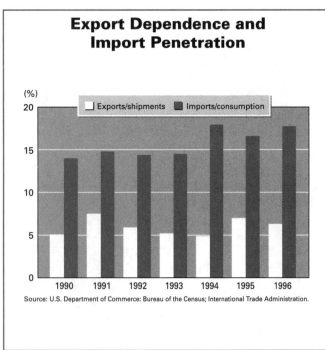

(%)

Legend: Exports/shipments ■ Imports/consumption

Source: U.S. Department of Commerce: Bureau of the Census; International Trade Administration.

Output and Output per Hour

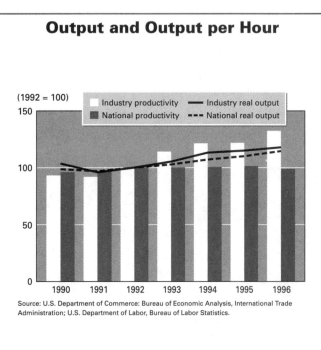

(1992 = 100)

Legend: Industry productivity — Industry real output / National productivity --- National real output

Source: U.S. Department of Commerce: Bureau of Economic Analysis, International Trade Administration; U.S. Department of Labor, Bureau of Labor Statistics.

See "Getting the Most Out of *Outlook '99*" for definitions of terms.

Steel Mill Products

INDUSTRY DEFINITION The U.S. steel industry encompasses the products of steel works, blast furnaces, and rolling mills (SIC 3312); steel wiredrawing and steel nails and spikes (SIC 3315); cold rolled sheet, strip, and bars (SIC 3316); and steel pipes and tubes (SIC 3317). The products in SIC 3312 account for the overwhelming share of this sector.

GLOBAL INDUSTRY TRENDS

Steel demand worldwide was expected to rise 3.5 percent to reach a record 710 million tons in 1998, according to a forecast by the Organization for Economic Cooperation and Development (OECD) Steel Committee. This would represent a smaller increase than the 5.4 percent growth recorded in 1997, reflecting the fallout from the economic crisis in southeast Asia. However, significant improvement was anticipated for Latin America. Demand in North America and Europe was expected to remain firm. Trends in the U.S. steel industry in the period 1992 to 1999 are shown in Table 13-1.

Developments in other parts of the world have an important bearing on the U.S. market because an ever-higher percentage of steel mill products is traded. In 1996, for example, steel exports represented approximately 31 percent of world crude steel production, an increase of 6 percentage points over 10 years.

The financial crisis in southeast Asia is an example of external forces affecting the U.S. market. The rapidly developing economies in that region were large importers of steel in recent years, notably from the Confederation of Independent States (CIS), other Asian countries (e.g., 75 percent of Japan's exports go to this area), and the European Union (EU). However, the area's unfavorable consumption outlook in 1998 was expected to lead to a shift in the balance of trade; its weak currencies and domestic demand will limit imports while encouraging steelmakers to export. U.S. imports from the four major producers in east Asia (Japan, South Korea, China, and Taiwan) had already increased 23 percent in 1997 compared with 1996 as a result of the strong dollar and the developing crisis there, and higher levels of imports continued early in 1998. Still, these currency devaluations constitute a mixed blessing for the region's steelmakers, as many of their imported raw materials are denominated in dollars. This and the resultant

uncertainty complicated financing and delayed the expected increase in exports.

Developments in the CIS also are having a large impact on steel markets worldwide. After the breakup of the Soviet Union, domestic demand for steel virtually collapsed. In Russia, for example, steel consumption dropped from 66 million tons in 1990 to only 17 million tons in 1996. To maintain production and obtain foreign currency, steelmakers sharply boosted exports to foreign markets, many of them new, since traditional markets (the so-called near-abroad) also were depressed. Total exports increased from 3.9 million tons in 1992 to 25.7 million tons in 1996 (the most recent data available). While shipments to the growing markets in the Far East accounted for more than 40 percent of total exports in that year, U.S. imports from Russia were also rising sharply, increasing from virtually nothing in the early 1990s to 3 million tons by 1997, when Russia became the second largest national supplier. The surge in exports, some priced well below market prices and production costs, prompted the filing of antidumping trade cases worldwide, including in the United States, and frequently the imposition of large dumping duties. The collapse of Russia's markets in southeast Asia also raised concern that its huge exports to that region would be diverted elsewhere.

Intense competition and pressure to cut costs are leading to the consolidation of steel companies both nationally and across borders. A recent wave of national consolidations included the merging of the steel units of the German firms Krupp and Thyssen and in the United States the division of Lukens Steel facilities between Bethlehem Steel and the specialty steelmaker Allegheny Teledyne. Some of the less efficient facilities were to be shut and employment was to be reduced as part of these consolidations. Internationally, Arbed of Luxembourg acquired Spain's largest producer, the formerly state-owned Aceralia, adding to existing mills in Luxembourg, France, Belgium, Brazil, and Germany.

TABLE 13-1: Steel Mill Products (SIC 3312, 3315, 3316, 3317) Trends and Forecasts
(millions of dollars except as noted)

	1992	1993	1994	1995	1996	1997[1]	1998[2]	1999[3]	Percent Change 96–97	97–98	98–99	92–96[4]
Industry data												
Value of shipments[5]	57,187	61,301	68,753	73,716	73,238	77,600	79,500	80,900	6.0	2.4	1.8	6.4
Value of shipments (1992$)	57,187	60,338	64,732	65,687	67,422	70,700	72,100	73,200	4.9	2.0	1.5	4.2
Total employment (thousands)	234	225	222	221	217							−1.9
Production workers (thousands)	179	173	172	173	171							−1.1
Capital expenditures	2,568	2,166	3,130	3,283	3,402							7.3
Product data												
Value of shipments[5]	56,132	60,199	67,681	72,347	71,293	75,505	77,354	78,716	5.9	2.4	1.8	6.2
Value of shipments (1992$)	56,132	59,266	63,733	64,472	65,609	68,791	70,153	71,224	4.8	2.0	1.5	4.0
Trade data												
Value of imports	8,508	9,300	13,445	12,908	13,853	14,815	15,600	14,600	6.9	5.3	−6.4	13.0
Value of exports	3,191	2,988	3,205	4,892	4,346	5,117	5,200	5,300	17.7	1.6	1.9	8.0

[1] Estimate except imports and exports.
[2] Estimate.
[3] Forecast.
[4] Compound annual rate.
[5] For definition of industry versus product values, see "Getting the Most Out of *Outlook '99*."
Source: U.S. Department of Commerce: Bureau of the Census; International Trade Administration.

Britain-based Ispat acquired Inland Steel, the sixth largest U.S. producer, to complement its mills in Kazakhstan, Canada, Mexico, Ireland, and Trinidad and Tobago, making Ispat the world's fourth largest steelmaker. The synergy of the various units is expected to improve their competitiveness and boost their capacity.

DOMESTIC TRENDS

Steel demand in the United States has grown rapidly in the 1990s, confounding many experts who early in the decade had foreseen only a limited opportunity for growth. By 1997 apparent consumption of steel mill products (domestic shipments plus imports, including semifinished steel, minus exports) reached 118.6 million tons, an increase of 34 percent since 1990 and 5.6 million tons above the previous peak (see Table 13-2).

Propelling the surge in demand are new products and applications, an increase in the steel intensity of the economy [steel consumption per unit of gross domestic product (GDP)], a narrowing of the deficit in the indirect trade in steel (i.e., the net trade in steel-containing products such as motor vehicles and tractors), and steady GDP growth.

Construction is one market where steel use is rising sharply. Domestic shipments (actual consumption figures are not available) to this sector, the second largest market for steel, increased from 11 million tons in 1990 to 13 million tons in 1997, based on preliminary data from the American Iron and Steel Institute. This increase reflects the growth in construction, especially of low-rise and industrial buildings, as well as the inroads steel has made against other materials, such as wood in framing, because of its relatively stable prices. The price index of galvanized sheet used for light gauge framing rose less than

TABLE 13-2: Tonnage of Steel Mill Products (SIC 3312, 3315, 3316, 3317), 1987–1999
(millions of metric tons except as noted)

	1987	1991	1992	1993	1994	1995	1996	1997	1998[1]	1999[2]	Percent Change 97–98	98–99	Compound Annual Rate of Growth, % 87–97
Raw steel production	80.9	79.7	84.3	88.8	91.3	95.2	94.7	97.4	98.9	100.7	1.5	1.8	1.9
Continuous casting (%)	55.2	75.8	79.3	85.7	89.5	91.1	93.2	94.0	95.5	97.0			
Steel mill product shipments	69.6	71.5	74.6	80.7	86.2	88.5	91.2	95.7	97.5	98.9	1.9	1.4	3.2
Exports	1.0	5.7	3.9	3.6	3.4	6.4	4.5	5.4	5.5	5.6	1.0	2.3	18.5
Imports	18.5	14.2	15.5	17.7	27.3	22.1	26.4	28.3	30.0	27.5	6.0	−8.3	4.3
Apparent domestic consumption	87.0	80.1	86.2	94.8	110.0	104.1	113.0	118.6	122.0	120.8	2.9	−1.0	3.1
Exports/shipments ratio	1.4	8.0	5.2	4.5	4.0	7.3	5.0	5.7	5.6	5.7			
Imports as a percent of apparent consumption	21.3	17.8	18.0	18.7	24.8	21.3	23.4	23.9	22.2	20.8			

[1] Estimate.
[2] Forecast.
Source: American Iron and Steel Institute; U.S. Bureau of the Census. Forecasts by the International Trade Administration.

9 percent between 1988 and 1997, while the index for light wood framing jumped nearly 70 percent.

Steelmakers are also benefiting from consumers' soaring demand for big, steel-intensive light trucks. Owing largely to light trucks' growing share of the market, the total weight of a typical family vehicle rose 48 kg between 1990 and 1997, reversing the trend of falling curb weight that followed the first oil crisis. The steel content in motor vehicles rose 34 kg in that period, and so steel's share of total weight remained relatively stable despite competition from lightweight materials such as aluminum and plastic. The increase occurred largely in the use of high- and medium-strength carbon steels, many only recently developed, and stainless steels, which are being used more widely in exhaust systems. Still, the major boost to steel consumption was the increase of 2.1 million units in motor vehicle production in this period.

To maintain steel's competitiveness for motor vehicles compared with other lighter materials, 35 sheet steel producers from 18 countries (the Ultralight Steel Auto Body Consortium) collaborated to develop a prototype lightweight steel auto body while maintaining performance and affordability. The 4-year, $22 million project, completed early in 1998, resulted in the development of a 238-kg structure, up to 36 percent lighter than comparable vehicles then in use, and the performance in torsion and bending was substantially improved. Yet this structure reportedly costs no more to build than do conventional auto bodies. Some aspects of the technology, which the consortium is offering at no cost to motor vehicle manufacturers, are already being incorporated in some phases of production, although steelmakers did not begin a major campaign to sell its advantages to manufacturers until 1998.

Despite the record demand, steel prices have been relatively steady largely as a result of the huge increase in supply from both domestic and foreign sources. Since 1990 the composite price for steel mill products has increased just 5 percent; since 1995 it has actually slipped 2.6 percent. By the spring of 1998 the prices of some products were under downward pressure as a result of increased competition from low-priced imports and an increase in domestic capacity (see below).

While these relatively flat prices have enhanced the competitiveness of steel against other materials, the industry's profitability has suffered, particularly in the integrated sector. Steelmakers' return on net sales was only a fraction of that for the S&P 500 during much of the 1990s.

With only a limited ability to raise prices, steelmakers have boosted their earnings by cutting costs and improving the product mix. In 1997 this strategy had some success. While prices rose less than 1 percent between 1996 and 1997, the six large integrated mills were able to more than double their operating profits to $1.5 billion.

The higher demand for steel and a revolution in steelmaking and steel rolling technologies have prompted appreciable growth in the steel industry's capacity. After dropping 24 percent between 1981 and 1990, crude steelmaking capacity has increased 7 percent. Electric furnaces accounted for nearly the entire increase (they use scrap as a charge rather than pig iron produced via the integrated process consisting of coke ovens and blast and basic oxygen furnaces). Many of the new electric furnaces have been paired with thin slab casters, a revolutionary technology developed in the late 1980s that has enabled the so-called minimills for the first time to produce flat rolled sheet (flat rolled products account for approximately 60 percent of steel demand in the United States). Capital and operating costs in thin slab/flat rolling mills are low compared with those in traditional steelmaking routes, and improved technologies in the newest mills have improved quality substantially. Since the first of these mills began producing flat products in 1989, capacity has increased to 15 million tons and is expected to rise an additional 2 million tons by the year 2000. Several companies operating these mills are new; their ownership includes Canadian, Brazilian, Japanese, and German interests. This additional capacity is expected to displace some imports and boost exports once world prices improve. The increased competition from these low-cost producers also could lead to the closing of some less efficient integrated facilities.

Another area of technological innovation and/or revolution is in front-end operations (preparing raw materials and steelmaking), where the need for new processes is high. Minimills are being driven to develop alternatives to scrap because of its high cost and the uncertain availability of the high grades required as a charge for the new flat rolled minimills. The integrated mills are under pressure to reduce coke oven emissions, because they are considered carcinogenic, and greenhouse gases. These mills have been shutting their existing coke batteries for environmental reasons and because of obsolescence. As much as one-quarter of existing capacity may ultimately be closed.

To replace its own shuttered coke-making operations, Inland Steel built the first new coke battery in the United States in decades; production began during the spring of 1998. The $350 million project uses a new technology, the so-called heat recovery coke-making process, and includes a cogeneration facility to supply electricity to the mill. Unlike the process in conventional facilities, the by-products are consumed completely in the cogeneration facility so that there is no leakage into the air. In addition, the coke will be produced at a lower cost.

Direct reduced iron (DRI) and to a lesser extent iron carbide and hot briquetted iron (HBI) are some of the ferrous scrap substitutes that are being more widely produced in the United States for or by minimills. A number of other technologies (e.g., Corex, Inmetco, Hismelt) are under development. Each has appeal, depending on the fuel used, the scale of the plant, and the grade of the ore used and the iron produced. In 1998, U.S. capacity to produce DRI will total approximately 3.8 million tons in at least four captive and merchant plants, up from less than 400,000 tons in just one plant 2 years earlier. Numerous additional projects have been announced.

Environmental Issues

As the fourth largest energy-consuming sector, the steel industry is a major source of emissions of greenhouse gases. The Clinton administration agreed at the meeting of the parties to the U.N.

Framework Convention on Climate Change to a binding emissions target of 7 percent below the 1990 level by the period 2008–2012. This has raised concern that such commitments will substantially boost the energy costs and reduce the international competitiveness of U.S. steelmakers, especially against developing countries that have made no commitments and are expanding their steel production.

The steel industry was one of the first sectors to meet with the administration to discuss how it would reduce emissions; the administration had offered to reward firms that pledged to take measures early. The steel industry, as represented by the American Iron and Steel Institute, indicated that it expected at least a 10 percent reduction in greenhouse gas emissions below the 1990 levels by 2010 through voluntary efforts.

Labor Developments

Steelmakers have moved aggressively to reduce costs in order to improve their competitiveness and profitability since they have had a limited opportunity to raise prices. Employment costs have been targeted, as they account for approximately 30 percent of total production costs. As a consequence, the erosion in employment has been relentless. Since 1990 total employment has fallen nearly 15 percent despite a 24 percent increase in industry shipments. The decline in production workers was 14 percent over that period.

One result of these diverging trends has been a sharp rise in productivity. According to the Bureau of Labor Statistics, output per employee hour rose 40 percent between 1990 and 1996 (the most recent available data). This compares favorably with the 23 percent rise for all manufacturing industries during that period.

U.S. INDUSTRY GROWTH PROJECTIONS FOR THE NEXT 1 AND 5 YEARS

Domestic shipments have risen sharply in recent years owing to the robust U.S. demand mentioned above. In 1997 they reached 95.5 million metric tons, an increase of 18.4 million metric tons since 1990 and the highest level since 1974. That growth was expected to continue into 1998, with shipments rising an additional 1.8 million tons. This estimate assumes a boost in deliveries from minimills; higher imports, especially from Asia, will likely limit the rise in shipments below the increase in demand. Exports should remain relatively flat.

With a GDP increase of 2.6 percent forecast in 1999 and continued low inflation, the favorable trend in shipments should persist; shipments are forecast to grow an additional 1.4 percent, or 1.4 million tons, that year (see Table 13-2). The second largest steel-consuming sector, construction (including private nonresidential and public works), which is forecast to rise nearly 3 percent in that year, should provide part of the boost. Highway spending, an important public works component that is a heavy user of steel, is expected to rise 4 percent. The capital goods industries, which have contributed heavily to increased steel demand in recent years, also should stimulate growth owing to continuing high levels of spending on producers' durable equipment. Steel's largest market, motor vehicles, should remain relatively flat, although at a high level.

Through the year 2003 steel shipments should rise at an erratic 1 to 2 percent average rate, assuming continued moderate economic growth.

GLOBAL MARKET PROSPECTS

Exports historically have accounted for a small share of total steel industry shipments. Even though exports increased 20 percent in 1997 from 1996 to a near-record level, they still accounted for just 5.7 percent of shipments (see Table 13-2).

North America, historically the major destination for U.S. steel exports, became even more important in this regard in 1997. Between 1995 and 1997 exports to the region increased 1.4 million tons, reflecting Canada's strong demand and Mexico's ongoing recovery from the peso crisis. As a consequence, North America's share of total U.S. exports jumped from 48 percent to 81 percent over this period. By contrast, shipments to southeast Asia, the second largest market for U.S. steel in 1995, accounted for just 5 percent of the total in 1997 (see Table 13-3). The relatively strong market and the appreciation of the U.S. dollar against the currencies in that area severely reduced export opportunities there.

With export prices currently so far below domestic prices, a substantial boost in exports is unlikely despite the large increase in domestic capacity. The strong domestic demand and near-record imports also may discourage exporting. Still, demand for steel in North America is strong, and prices are relatively firm; thus, this market offers the best opportunity for exports in the near term.

The removal of trade barriers is facilitating trade in steel. Mexico's tariffs on steel mill products from the United States and Canada will be eliminated by 2003; Canada's duties on U.S. steel have already been eliminated. More widespread duty eliminations are occurring in the World Trade Organization (WTO). As a result of the Uruguay Round of trade negotiations, the United States, the EU, Japan, Canada, Norway, Switzerland, Singapore, and Hong Kong agreed to eliminate steel duties by January 1, 2004. Taiwan will begin to eliminate its tariffs once it accedes to the WTO. Together these countries accounted for 53 percent of apparent steel consumption worldwide in 1996.

Negotiations to conclude an agreement to prohibit the use of subsidies and remove all nontariff barriers ended unsuccessfully in 1997. Those talks, which had begun in 1989 to cover all steel products, were at the end limited to specialty steel, with the hope that any agreement might be a model for the rest of the industry. In the end, however, the parties could not agree on which subsidies were permissible. Even without an agreement, government involvement in steel has been substantially reduced as one country after another has come to realize that government intervention does not lead to economic growth. Moreover, budget constraints have pressured governments to reduce subsidies. Privatization has swept the industry, especially in Europe

TABLE 13-3: U.S. Trade Patterns in Steel Mill Products[1] in 1997

(millions of dollars; percent)

Exports			Imports		
Regions[2]	Value[3]	Share, %	Regions[2]	Value[3]	Share, %
NAFTA	3,524	68.9	NAFTA	3,825	25.8
Latin America	498	9.7	Latin America	1,368	9.2
Western Europe	444	8.7	Western Europe	4,426	29.9
Japan/Chinese Economic Area	147	2.9	Japan/Chinese Economic Area	2,362	15.9
Other Asia	222	4.3	Other Asia	889	6.0
Rest of world	283	5.5	Rest of world	1,944	13.1
World	5,117	100.0	World	14,815	100.0
Top Five Countries	Value	Share, %	Top Five Countries	Value	Share, %
Canada	2,509	49.0	Canada	2,596	17.5
Mexico	1,015	19.8	Japan	1,787	12.1
United Kingdom	116	2.3	Mexico	1,229	8.3
Venezuela	106	2.1	Germany	1,175	7.9
Belgium	68	1.3	Brazil	1,013	6.8

[1] SIC 3312, 3315, 3316, 3317.
[2] For definitions of regional groupings, see "Getting the Most Out of *Outlook '99.*"
[3] Values may not sum to total due to rounding.
Source: U.S. Department of Commerce, Bureau of the Census.

and Latin America, where the last remaining state-owned company was sold to private interests late in 1997.

Charles L. Bell, U.S. Department of Commerce, Office of Metals, Materials, and Chemicals, International Trade Administration, (202) 482-0608, October 1998.

■ **REFERENCES**

American Iron and Steel Institute, 1101 17th Street, NW, Washington, DC 20036. (202) 452-7100, www.steel.org.

Steel Manufacturers Association, 1730 Rhode Island Avenue, NW, Washington, DC 20036-3101. (202) 296-1515, Fax: (202) 296-2506, www.steelnet.org.

■ **RELATED CHAPTERS**

1: Metals and Industrial Minerals Mining
2: Coal Mining
6: Construction
8: Construction Materials
36: Motor Vehicles

NONFERROUS METALS
Economic and Trade Trends

U.S. International Trade

($ billions)

Legend: Balance | Exports | Imports

Source: U.S. Department of Commerce: Bureau of the Census; International Trade Administration.

World Export Market Shares

(%)

Legend: United States | Germany | Canada | Chile

Source: United Nations; U.S. Department of Commerce, International Trade Administration.

Export Dependence and Import Penetration

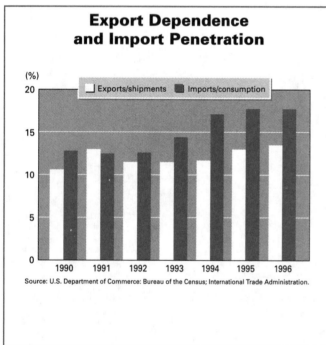

(%)

Legend: Exports/shipments | Imports/consumption

Source: U.S. Department of Commerce: Bureau of the Census; International Trade Administration.

Output and Output per Hour

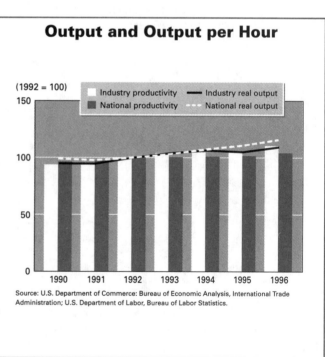

(1992 = 100)

Legend: Industry productivity | Industry real output | National productivity | National real output

Source: U.S. Department of Commerce: Bureau of Economic Analysis, International Trade Administration; U.S. Department of Labor, Bureau of Labor Statistics.

See "Getting the Most Out of *Outlook '99*" for definitions of terms.

Nonferrous Metals

ALUMINUM

The aluminum industry is composed of a primary aluminum sector (SIC 3334), a secondary sector (a portion of SIC 3341), and a semifabricating sector which includes SIC 3353, aluminum sheet, plate, and foil (rolling); SIC 3354, aluminum extruded products; and SIC 3355, aluminum rolling and drawing not elsewhere classified, such as cable, wire, bars, and rods.

Global Industry Trends

The global aluminum industry currently is sorting out the effects on both supply and demand of several major issues which are creating uncertainty in the marketplace. On the demand side, the degree of the impact on global consumption of the economic crisis in Asia has not been determined. A greater influence on demand has been the slow growth in consumption in the Japanese economy and its expected negative growth in 1999. With regard to supply, global consumption has exceeded supply for the past 4 years. However, a considerable amount of primary smelter capacity remains idle and could enter the market fairly quickly. In addition, Russia continues to export large quantities of metal, and the extent of China's status as a net importer causes its effect on the market to remain unclear. Therefore, continued supply deficits are not assured, and in spite of decreasing inventories and a very low ratio of consumption to stock (see Table 14-1), these uncertainties are causing aluminum prices to languish at levels that are considered to be lower than the long-run average cost for the industry.

The economic crisis in Asia should not have a significant impact on the global demand for aluminum (this is not to say that it has not resulted in a decrease in consumption or that it has not had an effect on global markets, particularly in regard to price). In 1996 Asia, excluding Japan, accounted for only 15.7 percent of global primary aluminum consumption; Japan accounted for 14.4 percent. Although these figures seem to indicate that consumption in Japan is roughly equal to that in the rest of Asia, there are huge differences between the two regions in the end-use consumption patterns for aluminum. In its fiscal year ending April 1998 Japan recorded a 2 percent

decline in consumption. Approximately half the aluminum consumed in Japan is accounted for by the automobile sector, which has had large declines in production that are expected to persist (increases in the amount of aluminum per vehicle will not compensate for that decline). Consumption by the building sector is expected to decline as well. The consumption sectors in countries most affected by the economic crisis in the rest of Asia are not as aluminum-intensive as are those in Japan. As a result, the stagnation in the Japanese economy probably will have a greater impact on global aluminum consumption than will the economic crisis in the rest of Asia.

Regarding the global outlook, it appears that in 1997 primary aluminum consumption exceeded supply by about 150,000 tons in spite of an increase in worldwide production of about 4 percent. This was due to continued strong demand in the United States and a resurgence in demand in Europe. Consumption growth in Asia, especially in Japan, was weak. From 1979 to 1996 global primary aluminum consumption increased at a compound annual growth rate of 2.1 percent. This rate has been surpassed substantially in the past few years, and 1998 was not expected to be an exception. In 1998, demand in the United States and Europe was expected to remain strong enough to compensate for a potential decline in consumption in Japan, yielding another increase in global consumption. However, new capacity additions and the fact that close to 1 million annual tons of capacity remains idle globally (a significant portion of which is in the United States) will make a significant supply deficit unlikely.

Industry Structure

The U.S. industry is dominated by three large integrated, multinational U.S. companies—Aluminum Company of America (Alcoa), Reynolds Metals Company, and Kaiser Aluminum and Chemical—as well as one similar Canadian company, Alcan. A fourth, major U.S. company, Alumax, was acquired by Alcoa for $3.8 billion in mid-1998. The primary aluminum segment of the industry is composed of 23 smelters operated by 12 companies located principally in the Pacific northwest, while the semifabricating sector is composed of over 200 companies clustered principally in the midwest. Together these companies have over 60,000 employees and produce over $30 billion in shipments.

TABLE 14-1: Aluminum Industry (SIC 3334, 3341, 3353, 3354, 3355) Trends and Forecasts
(thousands of metric tons)

	1992	1993	1994	1995	1996	1997[1]	1998[1]	1999[2]	Percent Change 96–97	Percent Change 97–98	Percent Change 98–99	Compound Annual Growth Rate, % 92–96
Total shipments	8,083	8,417	9,365	9,565	9,549	10,258	10,575	10,890	7.42	3.00	2.98	4.25
Primary ingot production	4,042	3,695	3,299	3,375	3,577	3,600	3,700	3,800	0.64	2.70	2.70	–3.01
Exports	1,233	1,094	1,195	1,310	1,309	1,378	1,475	1,525	5.27	6.58	3.39	1.51
Ingot	606	404	343	373	421	377	375	375	–10.45	–0.53	0.00	–8.70
Semifabricated products	627	690	852	937	888	1,001	1,100	1,150	12.73	9.00	4.55	9.09
Imports	1,573	2,327	3,136	2,702	2,573	2,974	3,175	3,300	15.58	6.33	3.94	13.09
Ingot	1,163	1,850	2,536	1,976	1,940	2,364	2,525	2,650	21.86	6.38	4.95	13.65
Semifabricated products	410	477	600	726	633	610	650	650	–3.63	6.15	0.00	11.47
Primary metal inventories, end of year	3,244	4,497	3,733	2,581	2,642	2,258						
Week supply	10.9	14.7	11.2	8.2	7.6	6.5						

[1] Estimate: shipments by The Aluminum Association, production by the U.S. Geological Survey.
[2] Forecast.
Source: U.S. Department of Commerce, International Trade Administration (ITA); and The Aluminum Association. Estimates and forecasts by ITA; 1997 shipments by The Aluminum Association

Domestic Trends

Consumption. In 1997 the U.S. aluminum industry set a record for total shipments, approximately 10.26 million metric tons. Shipments in 1998 were expected to increase 3 percent to 10.58 million metric tons. In descending order, the largest end-use sectors were, and probably will remain, the transportation, containers and packaging, and building and construction sectors. Combined, these sectors represented about two-thirds of all shipments. Over half of all shipments were in the form of rolled products such as plate, sheet, and foil. The transportation sector, which supplanted the containers and packaging sector as the largest end-use sector in 1994, continues to expand its share of overall aluminum shipments. The transportation sector now accounts for approximately one-third of the industry's shipments, and just as the aluminum can was the engine for aluminum growth in the 1970s and 1980s, the transportation sector is expected to provide the impetus for demand growth in the future.

Meanwhile, shipments to the container and packaging sector have suffered for a few reasons. First, the industry continues to improve the technology for producing cans to compete with steel and plastic containers. As a result, there are now about 33 cans per pound of aluminum compared with 29 in 1992 and 22 in 1972. Second, the market is saturated; virtually 100 percent of beer and soda cans are made of aluminum, and the possibility for further substitution of glass packaging is minimal. Therefore, increased shipments rely on increases in soda and beer demand, which offset the lightweighting of the can. However, soda consumption is not increasing rapidly, and beer consumption is falling. As a result, in 1997 aluminum can shipments totaled just over 1 billion cans, only a 1.6 percent increase from 1996.

Supply. The domestic supply of aluminum can be divided into three components: primary production, secondary production, and imports. Currently, each of these sectors supplies roughly one-third of the market. This ratio is vastly different from 1992, when domestic production accounted for almost half of supply. This changing ratio has resulted from a decrease in primary production and an increase in secondary aluminum production and imports.

Primary Aluminum. Primary aluminum production was about 3.6 million metric tons in 1997. This represents a capacity utilization rate of about 86 percent, compared with 92 percent globally. This level is well below the 1987 rate of approximately 97 percent but above the nadir in 1994, when the industry was operating at a rate around 79 percent. U.S. production is expected to increase slowly in the next few years as idled capacity is reactivated, depending on global market conditions (the price for aluminum is determined on an international trading exchange). One U.S. producer with considerable idle capacity, Reynolds Metals, intended to have all its idle capacity fully operational by the end of 1998. Another U.S. producer, Alcoa, still maintains approximately 400,000 metric tons of idle capacity, approximately 40 percent of the world's total. Primary aluminum production in 1998 was expected to increase slightly to 3.7 million metric tons.

The production of primary aluminum is an electrolytic process which is energy-intensive. Electricity accounts for approximately one-third of the cost of production, and its cost and availability are the driving force behind decisions on the location of new or expanded smelter capacity. For example, approximately 40 percent of U.S. smelting capacity is located in the Pacific northwest and utilizes hydropower from the Bonneville Power Administration. Currently, new capacity is planned for locations such as Canada (hydropower) and the Middle East (natural gas). There has not been a new smelter constructed in the United States since 1980.

However, changing economics and, in particular, the impending deregulation of the U.S. power industry have renewed interest in the possibility of smelter expansions in the United States. It is believed that once the industry is deregulated, it will be possible for aluminum companies to buy electricity more economically by wheeling power in from areas of the country with excess supply and controlling its cost to the smelter through hedging. As a result, feasibility studies are under way to investigate the possible expansion of smelters in the United States.

Secondary Aluminum. Although its share of total supply has remained constant since 1992 at about one-third, in 1989 secondary aluminum production accounted for only one-quarter of supply. Absolute production of secondary aluminum since 1992, though, has increased over 35 percent. In 1997, for the first time, secondary aluminum production exceeded primary production with 3.76 million metric tons versus 3.60 million metric tons.

A major factor in the increase in secondary production has been the success of the aluminum beverage can and its recyclability. Of the 100 billion aluminum beverage cans produced in 1997, 66.5 percent were recycled. Over half the content of a new aluminum beverage can comes from recycled aluminum. In 1997 a total of 929,000 metric tons of aluminum was recovered from used beverage containers, resulting in a payout to the public of $1.03 billion (about 1.5 cents per can).

Another principal factor in the steadily increasing production of secondary aluminum is the resultant energy savings. Secondary aluminum production saves 95 percent of the energy required to make aluminum from virgin materials.

However, the production of secondary aluminum relies on a loop based on cause and effect. Increased secondary aluminum production is dependent on improved recycling rates and an increasingly larger supply of scrap. The latter probably will occur through the obsolescence of a greater number of products and products containing increasing amounts of aluminum, such as autos. These products, however, initially will require an increase in primary metal production. Therefore, as a consequence of this loop and the fact that primary and secondary aluminum are not perfect substitutes for each other, there is a limit to the potential market share which can be accounted for by secondary aluminum.

Defense National Stockpile. The Defense National Stockpile Center received authority in fiscal year 1997 to dispose of its entire inventory of aluminum, 57,000 metric tons. By the end of the fiscal year in October 1997 the entire quantity had been liquidated.

Environment. Environmental issues pose economic concerns for the primary aluminum industry, but global climate change and measures which may be implemented to reduce greenhouse gas (GHG) emissions loom as the most threatening factors. Approximately half the electricity consumed by the primary aluminum industry is generated by coal-fired power facilities which are heavy emitters of GHGs. Given the sensitivity of the primary sector to electricity costs, it is quite possible that depending on the structure and timing of GHG

reduction measures, a considerable portion of the U.S. industry will become unviable.

Currently, the industry is working with the U.S. Environmental Protection Agency (EPA) to voluntarily reduce some GHGs emitted directly by smelters. The EPA and the aluminum industry have developed a joint program, the Voluntary Aluminum Industrial Partnership (VAIP), designed to improve aluminum production efficiency while improving the environment through the reduction of emissions of perfluorocarbons (PFCs), which are potent greenhouse gases. All but one U.S. producer participates in the program, representing 94 percent of U.S. capacity. The industry has made a commitment to reduce PFC emissions 40 percent from the 1990 levels by 2000. However, these emissions are insignificant in magnitude compared with the problem of indirect emissions from electricity consumption by the industry.

Technology. All segments of the aluminum industry are working to lower costs, improve their environmental performance, and develop new end uses for aluminum. In this regard, in late 1996 the Aluminum Association (U.S.) announced a joint effort with the U.S. Department of Energy to develop technology to reduce the consumption of electricity 30 percent in the production of primary metal, increase the use of continuous casting technology in the semifabricating sector, and enhance joining and forming processes for fabricating finished products.

Because of the importance of electricity to the cost structure of the industry, the industry has continuously sought to reduce the number of kilowatt-hours needed to produce a pound of aluminum. To this end, it has been working to develop modifications of the existing Hall-Heroult electrolytic process for producing aluminum. Two notable techniques under development include a new type of cathode for use in certain prebaked anode cells and a dimensionally stable anode for use in all cells. In addition to improving energy efficiency, this anode would not be consumed during the electrolytic process and would not emit PFCs. However, these developments are many years from commercial application.

U.S. Industry Growth Projections for the Next 1 and 5 Years

Total shipments are expected to increase 3 percent annually from 1999 through 2003, in line with recent annual growth rates. This means that shipments will total 10.89 million metric tons in 1999 and 12.25 million metric tons in 2003. Primary aluminum production should increase slowly as idle capacity is reactivated, climbing to 3.8 million metric tons in 1999 and probably just exceeding 4.0 million metric tons in 2003. It also will be necessary for imports, especially of ingot as a result of domestic capacity constraints, to increase to meet the growing demand.

The transportation sector, autos in particular, should be the driving force behind growth in aluminum demand. Demand in this sector is expected to increase about 5 percent annually through 2003. Although vehicle production will remain fairly constant, the amount of aluminum used per vehicle should increase. The amount of aluminum per light vehicle now averages about 250 lb, compared with 183 lb in 1992. Currently, the majority of aluminum consumed in this sector is in the form of castings, with engines constituting the largest end use, followed by transmissions. Although aluminum may be expected to increase its share of these applications, the real growth potential exists in applying sheet aluminum in areas such as body panels and developing an aluminum space frame.

Demand from another transportation sector, aerospace, should also increase faster than does the industry average. Commercial aircraft deliveries are expected to be very brisk through 2003, peaking in 1998–1999, providing strong demand for plate products. However, the aerospace sector constitutes a very small component of total demand and is not capable of influencing overall growth by itself.

The containers and packaging sector will remain a dominant end-use sector for aluminum through 2003. However, it will grow at a lackluster rate, probably only 1 percent annually. Competition from other materials could dampen even this low growth rate. However, a major factor responsible for the widespread acceptance of aluminum cans has been their recyclability. This has usually proved to be a decisive advantage of aluminum over other materials, but improvements in the recycling rates of these materials will put additional pressure on the aluminum can.

Demand from the building and construction sector should be slightly lower than the overall growth rate for aluminum, particularly as commercial construction begins to slow in the next couple of years. All the other sectors should match the overall growth rate for aluminum in general.

Global Market Prospects

In 1998 the global market for aluminum should be in approximate supply-demand balance. U.S. exports of ingot should remain fairly constant through 2003, since most of what is exported is a result of foreign equity in some U.S. smelters, mostly on the part of the Japanese. Exports of semifabricated products, although growing more slowly than are overall shipments, should not be affected too adversely by the economic crisis in Asia. Canada always has been the largest market for U.S. exports, and this will remain the case.

The United States is the largest market for aluminum; other major markets include Europe and Japan. As an indication of relative size, per capita consumption of aluminum in the United States is 30.6 kg in comparison to 31 kg in Japan, 26.7 kg in Germany, 17.6 kg in France, and 11.1 kg in the United Kingdom. The principal difference in these rates is a result of the end-use consumption patterns in the different markets. The United States and to an increasing degree Japan are large consumers of aluminum beverage cans; this is not the case in Europe. The transportation sector assumes a much larger role proportionally in aluminum demand in Japan and Europe than it does in the United States.

As was mentioned above, the transportation sector already is the source of a considerable amount of aluminum demand. However, consumption in this sector could grow considerably because of efforts to reduce the weight of vehicles for the purpose of conserving energy and reducing GHG emissions. Several programs to develop an all-aluminum vehicle are under way, and Audi has begun to market an all-aluminum vehicle. Currently, such vehicles are in the luxury price range, and efforts to develop an affordable model are ongoing. In the United States a government-industry consortium called the Partnership for a New Generation of Vehicles maintains the goal of a mass-produced vehicle that will carry six people with a fuel efficiency of 80 miles per gallon. This vehicle is expected to weight about 2,000 lb, most of which will be aluminum. Furthermore, certain regions of the United States have mandated that a no-emission vehicle account for a given percentage of new car sales (see the section on lead, below). If this materializes, it could be a boon for aluminum. As an example, the General Motors EV1 electric vehicle has an aluminum unibody frame that weighs only 295 lb.

David A. Cammarota, U.S. Department of Commerce, Office of Metals, Materials, and Chemicals, (202) 482-5157, October 1998.

COPPER

The copper sector includes the primary smelting and refining industry (SIC 3331), which produces refined metal from raw materials, and rolling, drawing, and extruding establishments (SIC 3351), which shape refined copper into semifabricated products such as rods, bars, profiles, plates, sheets, strips, tubes, pipes, and wire. The insulating of copper wire is classified under SIC 3357, nonferrous wire drawing and insulating, and copper and alloy foundries are classified under SIC 3366.

Global Industry Trends

World copper production and consumption continue to set records. Mine output rose in 1997, reaching more than 11.3 million metric tons. This was a 2.8 percent increase over 1996 and represented the third consecutive year of significant growth. Production of refined copper, including that from secondary sources, grew 7 percent to more than 13.5 million metric tons.

Consumption of refined copper worldwide also increased in 1997, reaching over 13.1 million metric tons. This was the third year of consumption growth higher than 4 percent. The older industrialized regions of the world continue to increase their consumption of copper, but ongoing economic development in other parts of the world is resulting in more rapid growth of copper use in those areas.

Encouraged by strong world demand and attractive recent copper price levels, the world copper industry has embarked on significant capacity expansion. Between 1997 and 2001 total mine capacity is expected to grow nearly 30 percent, reaching over 16 million metric tons per year. In that period scheduled increases in refinery capacity will amount to as much as 20 percent, bringing the total to over 18 million metric tons per year. Chile may see its mining capacity grow to as much as 4.5 million metric tons per year, confirming that country's position as the world's top copper miner. Since 1994, when world consumption exceeded production by as much as 450,000 metric tons, output has risen faster than has consumption. In 1997 the world copper market had a surplus of approximately 360,000 metric tons, and inventories held by producers, consumers, merchants, and exchanges rose to an estimated 1 million metric tons by year end. This return to surplus conditions was accompanied by a decline in copper prices, with quotations in New York falling below 80 cents per pound in early 1998 from nearly $1.20 per pound as recently as June 1997. Although it is believed that many newer or more efficient copper production facilities around the world can still operate at such price levels, sustained low copper prices may lead producers to close some operations temporarily or delay some of their planned expansions. Shutdowns have been announced, including some in the United States.

The trend toward privatization of state-owned copper producers is continuing. Bidding and negotiations continue over portions of Zambia Consolidated Copper Mines (ZCCM), which mines and refines over 300,000 metric tons per year. Firms from the United States, Canada, South Africa, and China are among those showing interest in both renovation and expansion projects in Zambia. The negotiations are complicated by questions about responsibility for the various social services previously provided by ZCCM in communities where it operates and the assumption of the debts of the state enterprise. In the Democratic Republic of Congo (the former Zaire), Gecamines, the state copper enterprise, has invited joint venture participation by foreign firms in rejuvenating its operations. The Congo has considerable deposits of copper and other minerals, and as recently as 1988 it produced over 450,000 metric tons of copper annually, the fifth highest output in the world. However, inadequate investment in obsolescent facilities and the political turmoil which ultimately led to a change of government in 1997 resulted in copper production dwindling to an estimate 40,000 metric tons in 1997.

Domestic Trends

Production of refined copper in the United States was more than 2.4 million metric tons in 1997, a 4.3 percent increase over 1996. Of this, 2.06 million metric tons was produced from primary materials, with the remainder refined from scrap. The use of the solvent extraction–electrowinning (SX-EW) technique, in which metal is first leached from ore by a chemical solution and then recovered from the solution by electrolytic means, continued to increase and provided almost 24 percent of the copper refined in the United States. Output from both wire rod mills and brass mills also increased over 1996 levels, growing approximately 10 percent and 3.9 percent, respectively.

The U.S. copper industry is an efficient, competitive producer that is well able to satisfy the bulk of current and future domestic demand. Primary production is dominated by five principal firms, each of which is also involved in other copper-producing regions of the world, particularly Latin America, as well as in other metals and minerals. Two of these operators are foreign-owned: Kennecott is owned by RTZ of the United Kingdom, and the Australia-based BHP has been producing in the United States since it acquired Magma Copper in 1996.

The major producers are continuing to improve their production capabilities. By the end of 1997 Kennecott was reportedly achieving sustained near-capacity output in its Utah facilities. The technical problems which had curtailed production at the smelter there since its 1995 opening apparently were resolved, and in 1997 a flash converting furnace and other equipment were rebuilt. At full capacity this complex will be able to produce over 300,000 metric tons of refined metal per year. In 1997 Cyprus Amax agreed to sell its Mineral Park, AZ, mine and an ore property at Tonopah, NV, to the Australian company Equatorial Mining. Equatorial reportedly is interested in expanding the modest Mineral Park operation and establishing an open pit and SX-EW facility at the Tonopah site. Cyprus suspended mining at Tohono, AZ, although leaching operations are continuing there. Phelps Dodge, the largest U.S. producer, hopes to resume production in 1999 at its Ajo, AZ, mine after installing a new concentrator and other equipment. Annual output of over 60,000 metric tons of copper in concentrate is anticipated. Phelps Dodge also has bought the Continental, NM, mine of Cobre Mining Company. Cobre had planned an expansion program that included a SX-EW plant of 30,000 metric tons per year for this site, where production resumed in 1993 after a 3-year closing.

Consumption of refined copper grew at a vigorous 5.7 percent rate in 1997, reaching 2.77 million metric tons (see Table 14-2). Wire rod mills, which use primary refined metal as the principal feedstock, increased their use 7.6 percent over 1996 to 2.13 million metric tons. This was more than three-quarters of total refined copper consumption. Brass mills, which use remelted scrap as well as refined copper, increased their use of refined metal by only about 1.4 percent in 1997.

Copper continues to face competition from alternative materials. Although aluminum is well established in power cable applications and optical fiber has displaced copper in some communications uses, copper remains the metal of choice for most electrical and electronic purposes (see Table 14-3). The suitability of copper for these uses and the long-term growth in the use of copper-intensive electrical and electronic equipment have assured the continuing importance of copper in these areas. Efforts are under way to improve the competitive position of copper in motor vehicle radiators. In recent years the quest for fuel economy through weight reduction has made aluminum the dominant metal for this use, although copper still competes in certain commercial vehicles and in the replacement market. A new copper-brass radiator design is intended to make better use of copper's superior heat conductivity and reduce or eliminate the traditional weight disadvantage of this metal.

Construction remains the largest single copper-consuming sector of the U.S. economy, with building wiring, plumbing, heating, air-conditioning and refrigeration, lighting, and power utilities absorbing about half of all the copper used.

International Trade

Although the United States has the world's largest refined copper production and is second only to Chile in mine output, it is

TABLE 14-2: Copper Industry (SIC 3331, 3351, 3357, 3366) Trends and Forecasts

(thousands of metric tons; percent)

| | 1992 | 1993 | 1994 | 1995 | 1996 | 1997[1] | 1998[1] | 1999[2] | Percent Change | | | |
									96–97	97–98	98–99	92–96[3]
Refined copper production	2,140	2,253	2,230	2,280	2,340	2,440	2,530	2,610	4.3	3.7	3.2	2.2
Refined copper consumption	2,180	2,364	2,680	2,525	2,620	2,770	2,850	2,910	5.7	2.9	2.1	4.6
By wire rod mills	1,675	1,820	2,060	1,950	1,980	2,130						
By brass mills	458	503	568	533	588	596						
Exports												
Refined copper and alloys	185	239	173	232	184	117						
Wire mill products	44	57	67	48	59	63						
Brass mill products[4]	96	87	103	130	144	142						
Imports												
Refined copper and alloys	301	354	486	442	635	669						
Wire mill products	21	32	43	56	72	73						
Brass mill products[4]	109	125	176	196	189	220						

[1] Estimate by U.S. Department of Commerce, International Trade Administration (ITA).
[2] Forecast by ITA.
[3] Compound annual rate.
[4] Excluding foil.
Source: U.S. Department of the Interior, Geological Survey; U.S. Department of Commerce.

TABLE 14-3: Wire Shipments by Domestic Manufacturers in 1996

	Copper[1], kilotons	Aluminum[2], kilotons	Copper[1], $ millions	Aluminum, $ millions	Optical Fiber, $ millions
Electronic wire and cable	95		2,590		
Communications	225		2,075		1,729
Power wire and cable	113	142	1,411	1,530	
Portable power cable	11		95		
Control and signal wire	18		250		
Building wire and cable	525	27	2,747	786	
Apparatus wire and cordage	98		821		
Magnet wire	317[2]	25	1,163	118	
Other	63		490		1,078
Total	1,464	313[3]	11,643	4,159[3]	2,807

[1] Metal content.
[2] Gross weight.
[3] Includes categories that are withheld to avoid disclosing data for individual companies.
Source: U.S. Department of Commerce, Bureau of the Census.

a major importer. While domestic copper output has risen, the robust growth of consumption has resulted in a doubling of refined (mostly cathode) imports since 1992. Canada supplied nearly three-quarters of those imports in that year and supplies from that country increased to nearly 300,000 metric tons by 1997, but the flow of refined metal from Chile more than tripled to 130,000 metric tons and that from Peru increased tenfold to 100,000 metric tons in that period. In regard to refined copper exports in 1997, Canada and Taiwan each absorbed about 28,000 metric tons, with Japan and Mexico taking 19,000 and 11,700 metric tons, respectively.

Canada and Mexico continue to be the largest markets for U.S. exports of copper semifabricates. Together, these two countries absorbed 84 percent (by weight) of wire exports, 69 percent of rod, bar, and profile products, 60 percent of plate, sheet, and strip items, and 71 percent of tubes and pipes in 1997. Sources

of U.S. imports are more diverse, with Canada providing only 11 percent of rod, bar, and profile imports and the EU and Asia supplying about 36 percent and 19 percent, respectively. The EU and Asia also provide 33 percent and 26 percent of plate, sheet, and strip imports, respectively. Mexico and Canada, however, are again the dominant sources for imports of tube and pipe products, with 41 percent and 23 percent of this flow, respectively, followed by the EU with 19 percent.

U.S. Industry Growth Projections for the Next 1 and 5 Years

Refined copper consumption growth in 1998 was expected to slacken somewhat from its surge in 1997 but to achieve a healthy rate of about 3 percent, increasing to a level of 2.85 million metric tons. The expected 1998 growth in construction put in place, particularly in categories of nonresidential and public construction such as office, hotel, commercial, and educational structures, will contribute to growth in copper demand. In 1999 and beyond, demand growth can be expected to average about 2 percent per year, leading to consumption of more than 3.1 million metric tons in 2003.

Production of refined copper was expected to be about 2.53 million metric tons in 1998, a 3.7 percent increase from 1997. The average rate of growth in refined copper output over the next 5 years will be lower than the rate of increase of consumption, and production may reach 2.8 million metric tons in 2003. The level of output in these years will be influenced by developments in copper prices. If the relatively low prices of early 1998 persist, producers are likely to consider additional closings of some of their less economical facilities and may be discouraged from pressing ahead with capacity enhancements.

Global Market Prospects

Consumption of copper continues to increase throughout the world. In the short run continuing economic strength in the United States and the ongoing recovery in Europe are likely to offset any faltering of copper demand in Asia caused by recent financial problems. The long-established industrialized countries are maintaining or increasing their levels of copper use, but the most impressive growth can be expected to occur in the parts of the world that are undergoing rapid industrialization. Asia and in particular China are developing into strong copper consumers. The Chinese market now accounts for about 10 percent of world copper consumption, more than 1.3 million metric tons, having expanded nearly 50 percent between 1992 and 1997. Its consumption should continue to grow at nearly double-digit rates for the next several years, challenging Japan's place as the largest copper consumer in Asia, and second in the world to the United States. China has considerable copper resources, but they are not always economically attractive for exploitation and supply only a portion of China's needs. China relies on imported materials to satisfy its rapidly growing smelter and refinery capacity and is also an active importer of scrap.

Most of the expected increase in world copper production capacity will occur in the major copper-mining regions, especially Chile and Peru, and in the rapidly industrializing countries, whose consumption is also growing. In the long run these facilities can be expected to supply most of the coming increase in world copper demand. As these foreign economies become more developed, U.S. exporters probably will find more opportunities for shipments of higher-value-added copper-containing products rather than shipments of the metal itself from the United States. The major American copper-producing companies will continue to be involved in many of these foreign expansion projects in addition to their domestic production activities as the world copper market becomes more integrated.

Robert M. Shaw, U.S. Department of Commerce, Office of Metals, Materials, and Chemicals, (202) 482-0606, October 1998.

LEAD

The international lead industry consists of primary producers (SIC 3339) that use either lead ores and concentrates or a mixture of lead ores and concentrates and scrap lead as feedstock, and secondary producers (SIC 3341) that recycle scrap lead primarily in the form of spent lead-acid batteries (LABs). The most important end use for lead is the LAB (SIC 3691), which accounts for 71 percent of global consumption. Lead is an internationally traded commodity whose value is based on the price set daily by the London Metal Exchange (LME). This price may vary in different countries, depending on local market conditions.

Global Industry Trends

The United States is by far the world's largest producer of refined lead metal, accounting for 23.8 percent of total production, followed by China with 10.8 percent, the United Kingdom with 7.5 percent, Germany with 5.5 percent, and Japan with 5.0 percent. In the 1990s the international lead and LAB industries have undergone a process of consolidation, with a number of major producers expanding their operations globally to reduce transportation costs and increase market share in foreign markets. U.S. producers have played an important role in this consolidation by purchasing facilities in South America and western Europe.

The international lead industry faces both increasing opportunities and significant challenges. Since such a large share of the lead consumed worldwide goes into producing LABs used in automotive and various industrial applications, the rapid expansion of the economies and automobile fleets in newly industrializing and developing countries continues to benefit the industry. At the same time, an increasing number of international, regional, and national environmental negotiations and regulations are focusing on lead and some of its end uses. Certain dispersive or readily bioavailable uses, such as lead in gasoline, as a solder in piping for drinking water and food cans, and in house paints, have been or are being phased out in many countries because of environmental and health concerns. Some of these recently proposed regulations focus on nondispersive uses of lead that do not pose unmanageable risks to human health and the environment, using the "precautionary principle" (act on the basis of suspicion of damage rather than proof) and the "substitution principle" (always substitute less hazardous materials for hazardous materials regardless of whether a significant risk exists) as justification.

Domestic Trends

The world's largest producers of lead ores and concentrates are China, accounting for 22.1 percent of total production; Australia, 16.7 percent; the United States, 14.4 percent; Peru, 8.8 percent; and Canada, 6.3 percent. The domestic lead-mining industry includes 16 mines in Alaska, Colorado, Idaho, Missouri, Montana, New York, and Tennessee, with the 9 mines in Alaska and Missouri accounting for approximately 93 percent of domestic production. Primary lead is produced at Doe Run's Herculaneum and Asarco's Glover smelter-refineries in Missouri and at Asarco's East Helena, MT, smelter. In April 1998 Asarco announced its intention to sell its Missouri smelter-refinery and lead mines to Doe Run. If completed, this purchase, along with Doe Run's acquisition of Peru's La Oroya smelter-refinery in October 1997, will make Doe Run the world's largest primary lead producer. Secondary lead is produced at 17 recycling facilities in Alabama, California, Florida, Georgia, Indiana, Louisiana, Minnesota, Missouri, New York, Pennsylvania, Tennessee, and Texas. Since 1995 Exide Corporation, an integrated LAB producer and recycler, has acquired a number of secondary lead refineries in the United States, France, and Spain as well as battery plants in the United States and across Europe, making Exide the world's dominant secondary lead and LAB producer.

Lead is also sold by the Defense National Stockpile Center (DNSC) as a result of legislation passed in 1992 authorizing the disposal of the entire 555,000 metric tons in the stockpile over several years. The law, however, requires the task to be completed without undue disruption of commercial lead markets. At the end of 1997, 362,680 metric tons of lead remained in the DNSC inventory. The fiscal year (FY) 1999 Annual Materials Plan (AMP) authorized the disposal of about 54,000 metric tons of lead between October 1, 1998, and September 30, 1999. Additional authority is being sought by the DNSC to dispose of 54,000 metric tons of lead for the FY 2000 AMP.

The domestic lead market has experienced strong growth since 1993. Domestic lead mine production decreased in 1992 and 1993 as a result of low lead, gold, and silver prices but has since recovered as several mines have expanded or reopened because of improved metal prices. Domestic lead mine production reached 459,000 metric tons in 1997, still below the 497,000 metric tons produced in 1990. Domestic lead metal production rose at an annual rate of 1.5 percent between 1990 and 1997, reaching a record high of 1.43 million metric tons in 1997. This increase occurred despite the closing of Asarco's

Omaha primary refinery and a number of secondary plants, which were more than offset by the opening of a new secondary refinery and an increase in capacity at a number of other secondary refineries. During this period the share of total metal production accounted for by secondary lead increased from 69 percent to 76 percent (see Table 14-4).

The United States accounts for almost 28 percent of global lead consumption and is by far the single largest market worldwide. Domestic lead consumption increased at an average annual rate of 3.8 percent between 1990 and 1997, rising from 1,312,000 to 1,664,000 metric tons. Lead consumption patterns have long been shifting to a market dominated by one major end use, the LAB. Increasing LAB demand has more than made up for all end uses that have declined significantly or been legislated out of existence for environmental and health reasons. The LAB's share of total domestic lead consumption increased from 80 percent in 1990 to an estimated 88 percent in 1997. Nonbattery uses of lead declined at an average annual rate of 2.9 percent between 1990 and 1997. Lead used in ammunition (the largest nonbattery end use) remained fairly constant in that period. Other uses, such as cable covering, caulking, and solder, have declined significantly, while tetraethyl lead additives for gasoline, which once accounted for 20 percent of domestic consumption, have been phased out entirely.

Environment. Thirty-seven states have enacted legislation to encourage the recycling of LABs. These states have adopted laws proposed by the Battery Council International (BCI) which would prohibit the disposal of LABs in municipal solid waste streams and require all levels of the collection chain to accept spent LABs. Four other states ban only the landfilling and incineration of LABs. At the federal level, the Lead-Acid Battery Recycling Act was introduced to promote recycling nationwide. As a result of these bills, which reinforce long-standing industry practices in the collection and recycling of

TABLE 14-4: Lead Industry (SIC 3339, 3341) Trends and Forecasts
(thousands of metric tons; percent)

	1990	1993	1994	1995	1996	1997	1998[1]	1999[2]	Percent Change 96–97	Percent Change 97–98	Percent Change 98–99	Compound Annual Growth Rate, % 90–97
Mine production	497	363	370	394	436	459	460	470	5.3	0.2	2.2	−1.1
Metal production	1,291	1,206	1,249	1,377	1,381	1,431	1,403	1,475	3.6	−2.0	5.1	1.5
Primary	403	335	351	373	326	342	330	345	4.9	−3.5	4.5	−2.2
Secondary	888	871	898	1,004	1,055	1,089	1,073	1,130	3.2	−1.5	5.3	3.2
Percent secondary production	69	72	72	73	76	76	76	77				
Apparent metal consumption	1,312	1,377	1,514	1,613	1,657	1,664	1,767	1,780	0.4	6.2	0.7	3.8
Percent lead-acid battery	80	82	84	85	88	88	88	88				
Imports for consumption	91	196	230	264	268	265	300	287	−1.1	13.2	−4.3	27.3
Percent consumption	6.9	14.2	15.2	16.6	16.2	15.9	17.0	16.1				
Exports	56	51	48	47	44	37	20	20	−15.9	−45.9	0.0	−4.8

[1] Estimate.
[2] Forecast.
Source: U.S. Department of Commerce, International Trade Administration (ITA); U.S. Department of the Interior, Geological Survey; International Lead and Zinc Study Group. Estimates and forecasts by ITA.

batteries, more batteries are being recycled and fewer are being disposed of improperly. The 1995 annual study released by the BCI reported an average annual LAB recycling rate of 94.9 percent between 1990 and 1995. The U.S. Department of Commerce estimates that the recycling rate will remain near this level in the future.

A number of international, regional, and national environmental negotiations and regulations could have an impact on the domestic and global lead markets. The Basel Convention is an international environmental agreement designed to restrict the transboundary movement of hazardous wastes to protect countries (particularly developing ones) that may not have the capability or technology to manage waste properly. Annex VIII of the convention, which contains a list of materials which Annex VII countries (OECD members, the EU, and Liechtenstein) are prohibited to export to non-Annex VII countries after December 31, 1998, includes lead compounds, lead waste and scrap, and scrap LABs. When this ban goes into effect, non-Annex VII countries may find it difficult to obtain feedstock for their secondary lead industries. While some domestic lead waste and scrap is exported to OECD countries, more than half these exports of waste and scrap are currently destined for non-OECD countries. (See page 14-17 for more information on the Basel Convention.)

In February 1998 the Convention on Long-Range Transboundary Air Pollution sponsored by the United Nations Economic Commission for Europe (UNECE; includes all the European countries, Canada, and the United States) concluded a Heavy Metals Protocol which will, among other things, control emissions of lead and restrict the use of leaded gasoline. Strict criteria were included in the protocol to ensure that additional metals or products containing the metals covered under the protocol are added only if they contribute significantly to long-range transboundary air emissions of these metals. This protocol was signed in June 1998. (See page 14-18 for more information on the Heavy Metals Protocol.)

The European Commission and a number of countries have introduced or are considering initiatives that would severely restrict the use of lead in various products. The proposed European initiatives could severely limit the international competitiveness of U.S. producers of lead-containing products, such as the U.S. automotive, electronics, and telecommunications industries. In most cases these initiatives focus on nondispersive uses of lead that do not pose unmanageable risks to human health and the environment. The European Commission's Environmental Directorate (DGXI) has proposed an initiative which would ban the use of lead in electrical and electronic equipment by January 2004. In addition, DGXI has proposed a directive which would require that after January 2003 lead-containing parts, with the exception of lead solder in circuit boards, be removed from scrap motor vehicles before shredding. Since it is not practical to remove many lead-containing parts from end-of-life vehicles before shredding, this proposed regulation would in effect ban most uses of lead in motor vehicles. DGXI has not yet submitted this draft directive to the European Council for approval.

Denmark has proposed banning the importation, sale, and production of most products containing lead compounds and a number of products containing metallic lead. This regulation, which would continue to allow exports of these products, was to go into effect on January 1, 1998, but so far Denmark has not submitted it to the European Commission for approval. Sweden has drafted a proposed chemical policy which would ban the use of lead shot for hunting and sporting purposes and states as a goal that all uses of lead should be banned in the future. If this proposal is adopted, Sweden would have to send any legislation to the European Commission for approval. In Japan, the Ministry of International Trade and Industry (MITI) has asked domestic automobile producers to voluntarily reduce by almost 70 percent the amount of lead used in automobiles by 2005.

U.S. Industry Growth Projections for the Next 1 and 5 Years

Domestic lead consumption is forecast to increase at an average annual rate of 3.5 percent between 1997 and 1999, growing from 1.66 million to 1.78 million metric tons. This growth came despite a sharp drop in the production of automotive replacement batteries in 1998 that was caused by mild temperatures nationwide during the winter of 1997–1998. Warmer-than-normal temperatures in the second half of 1998 resulted in a dramatic increase in replacement automotive battery production in late 1998 as the large number of batteries produced in 1994 reached the end of their service life. Production of industrial batteries increased at an average annual rate of 7 percent in this period. Between 1999 and 2003 domestic lead consumption is expected to rise at an average rate of about 2 percent per year, reaching 1.82 million metric tons in 2003, with the LAB's share of total consumption accounting for about 89 percent.

Lead-Acid Batteries. The LAB is the driving force behind the lead industry both globally and domestically. This sector consists of two main markets: starting, lighting, and ignition (SLI) batteries, which currently account for about 80 percent of the market, and industrial batteries, which account for 20 percent. SLI batteries are used in a number of applications, such as passenger cars and light trucks, heavy commercial vehicles, motorcycles, special tractors, marine craft, aircraft, and military vehicles. Demand for replacement SLI batteries, which currently represent 84 percent of the SLI market, is dependent on the size and age of the motor vehicle fleet, extreme temperature fluctuations, and the service life of the battery. Original equipment (OE) SLI batteries are tied to the level of motor vehicle production and sales.

Between 1990 and 1997 SLI battery production increased at an average annual rate of 3.9 percent, rising from 83.6 million units to 99.6 million units. SLI production is expected to increase to about 104 million units in 1999. Production should rise at an average annual rate of about 2 percent between 1999 and 2003, reflecting both a slight increase in motor vehicle production and a growing automotive fleet. If a large segment of the United States experiences extreme temperature fluctuations during this period, production of replacement SLI batteries could push the rate higher.

The industrial battery market is divided into two sectors: motive power and stationary. Motive power includes batteries for industrial trucks, mining vehicles, and railroad cars and currently accounts for 40 percent of the industrial battery market. Stationary batteries include telecommunications, uninterruptible power supply (UPS), and control and switchgear batteries and account for the remaining 60 percent. This market rose 15 percent in 1997 and registered an average annual growth rate of 11 percent between 1990 and 1997, with the strongest increase involving UPS (13 percent growth) and telecommunications (18 percent growth) batteries.

The industrial battery market is forecast to experience continued strong growth between 1997 and 2003, rising at an average rate of about 12 percent per year, as stationary batteries continue to increase their share of this market to an estimated 68 percent. This growth should be led by telecommunications and UPS batteries, which are tied to the buildup and redefinition of the worldwide telecommunications infrastructure as a result of the advent of new technologies in fiber optics and broadband communications systems and the explosive growth in Internet and networking servers. Industrial batteries are forecast to capture one-quarter of the LAB market by 2003.

Laws passed in California and nine northeastern states mandating the production of electric vehicles (EVs) could also influence lead consumption in this period. California and the Coalition of Northeastern Governors (CONEG) require that by 2003, 10 percent of all vehicles sold in these areas be zero-emission EVs and 15 percent be ultra-low-emission vehicles. Since EVs would be considerably more expensive than conventional motor vehicles and consumers are not required to purchase EVs, overall lead consumption could be slightly lower than has been forecast.

Supply. Domestic production of lead is forecast to rise to 1.475 million metric tons in 1999 and to continue increasing to an estimated 1.52 million metric tons by 2003. While primary production is expected to remain flat in this period, secondary production will continue to rise as a result of capacity expansions at other secondary refineries and the possibility of additional new capacity coming on line. The share of total domestic production accounted for by secondary lead should rise to 77 percent by 2003, reflecting the continued importance of recycling for the lead industry.

Imports of unwrought lead accounted for an estimated 16 percent of consumption in 1997 and are expected to remain at that level through 2002. In 1997 almost all imports came from Canada, Mexico, and Peru. While the United States exported approximately 37,000 metric tons of unwrought lead in 1997, with about 80 percent going to Canada, Malaysia, South Korea, and the United Kingdom, most exports are in the form of LABs or products containing either LABs or other applications of lead.

Global Market Prospects

Between 1993 and 1997 global consumption of lead rose at an annual rate of 2.3 percent, increasing from 5.23 million to 6.04 million metric tons. LABs accounted for 71 percent of consumption, followed by pigments, 12 percent; rolled extrusions, 7 percent; ammunition, 6 percent; and other uses, 4 percent. Global market conditions for lead are forecast to worsen slightly in the near term. Consumption is expected to decline 1 percent to 5.98 million metric tons, while metal production is projected to increase less than 1 percent, rising from 6.07 million to 6.08 million metric tons. As a result, an increased surplus of 119,000 metric tons is expected to overhang the market. The United States will maintain its dominance as the world's largest producer and consumer of lead metal.

Dave Larrabee, U.S. Department of Commerce, Office of Metals, Materials, and Chemicals, (202) 482-0607, October 1998.

TITANIUM

Titanium does not have a specific SIC code. Titanium sponge for metal alloy production is included in the basket industry classification code SIC 3339. The secondary recovery of titanium is covered by SIC 3341, mill product production by SIC 3356, castings by SIC 3369, and forgings by SIC 3463.

Titanium is a lightweight metal noted for its corrosion resistance and high ratio of strength to weight. Less than 10 percent of world titanium consumption is in the form of metal; the bulk is in the form of titanium dioxide, primarily used in pigments for paints, paper, and plastics. There are ample titanium-bearing mineral resources around the world. Through its production of mineral concentrates, Australia provides about half the world's beneficiated titanium raw materials. Titanium-bearing slags from the Republic of South Africa and Canada and concentrates and slags from Norway make up most of the balance. These raw materials are processed primarily by pigment manufacturers and a few integrated titanium metal producers. This section focuses on metallurgical titanium.

Global Industry Trends

The production of titanium sponge, the porous basic titanium metal, is limited to seven companies in five countries: the United States, Japan, Russia, Kazakstan, and China. Sponge consumption for conversion to ingot and slab and the subsequent production of castings and mill products occur principally in the United States, Japan, Russia, the United Kingdom, France, and Germany.

Worldwide demand for titanium continues to grow, largely as the result of increased demand from the aerospace industries in the United States and Europe. The commercial aircraft segment is probably enjoying the most robust demand cycle in its history. Order backlogs by the leading commercial aircraft manufacturers totaled 2,753 planes at the end of 1997, up 16 percent from 1996. As a result, worldwide titanium demand from the commercial aerospace industry has increased to about

21,000 metric tons, representing a 35 percent share of the estimated world titanium demand of 60,000 metric tons in 1997.

A decade ago defense applications, led by aerospace, were the main uses for titanium, but a dramatic decline in defense use after the end of the cold war and the latest cyclical upturn in the commercial aerospace market have resulted in commercial aerospace applications assuming the lead in worldwide titanium consumption. Historically, commercial aerospace applications for titanium centered on jet engine components, but the drive to produce larger and more fuel-efficient aircraft has led commercial aircraft manufacturers to design increasing amounts of titanium into their airframes. The Boeing 777 uses more titanium than does any other commercial aircraft. Approximately 68 metric tons of titanium mill products are shipped to produce one Boeing 777, but only about 14 metric tons is actually included in the finished plane, with the bulk of the balance being recovered as scrap. Depending on the engines employed, roughly 9 percent of the weight of a delivered Boeing 777 consists of titanium, compared with less than 4 percent of the weight of the older and smaller Boeing 737.

Another global trend is the increased presence of titanium products from the former Soviet Union (FSU), especially Russia, on world markets. This is due to substantially reduced demand in the FSU, which has resulted in considerable production capacity available for the export market. There has been a net reduction in world sponge capacity of about 30 percent since the early 1990s, to about 106,000 tons per year in 1997. Owing to rising demand and the lack of sufficient sponge capacity in their home markets, U.S., Japanese, and European titanium producers have entered into long-term supply contracts and other arrangements for obtaining sponge from the two active sponge producers in the FSU. As a result, U.S. imports of sponge from the FSU represented approximately 16 percent of U.S. sponge consumption in 1996 and increased to 27 percent in 1997. The Berenzniki Titanium and Magnesium Works (Avisma) in Russia has a capacity of about 26,000 tons of titanium sponge per year, and the Ust-Kamenogorsk Titanium and Magnesium Works in Kazakhstan has a capacity of about 40,000 tons of sponge per year; together they represent about 60 percent of world titanium sponge capacity. Another titanium sponge plant in the FSU, the Zaporozhye Titanium-Magnesium Plant in Ukraine, closed during the last market downturn in the early 1990s, but work is reportedly under way to modernize and restart that facility.

Domestic Trends

Beginning in 1995, U.S. titanium demand began a dramatic upturn on the back of an upturn in the commercial aerospace market, supplemented by the emergence of and tremendous growth in the golf club market, especially titanium woods. According to data published by the U.S. Geological Survey (USGS) and the U.S. Bureau of the Census, since 1994 U.S. demand, as measured by reported mill product and castings shipments plus imports of these products, has doubled, growing about 26 percent per year to a record 33,812 metric tons in 1997. This was the second consecutive record year for U.S. titanium demand, up 3 percent over 1996 (see Table 14-5).

While demand from the aerospace industry continued to grow in 1997, there are indications from the major producers that demand from the golf club market declined significantly. Much of the decline can be explained by overbuying and inventory buildup by club makers in 1996. The major producers also may be losing some of their direct sales to golf club makers as increased alloy melting and casting services are being provided by other processors. Golf club makers may be purchasing more material from sources other than domestic producers.

Actual titanium shipment levels by end-use areas are not known. This information is estimated from an aggregation of producer perceptions based on sales and producers' knowledge of the likely uses of different titanium mill products and castings. Before 1998 the only survey of U.S. titanium industry shipments was the voluntary quarterly survey conducted by the USGS, which assesses only shipments by product form or mill shape, not end use. Beginning in the first quarter of 1998, however, the International Titanium Association (formerly the Titanium Development Association, Boulder, CO), through the American Bureau of Metal Statistics, began to collect quarterly shipments data by end use from the association's North American members. Successful data collection will go far toward providing greater transparency to the titanium end-use pattern in North America.

In 1997 the three major U.S. titanium producers—Titanium Metals Corporation (Timet), Denver, CO; RMI Titanium Company, Niles, OH; and Oregon Metallurgical Corporation (Oremet), Albany, OR—had their second consecutive year of net profits. In 1997 their combined net profits were up 71 percent to about $174 million. This followed a 5-year period (1991–1995) of weak demand and depressed prices during which none of these producers posted net profits, resulting in reported cumulative losses of about $230 million. In addition to the three major titanium producers, there are four smaller producers of titanium alloy ingot, mainly for internal use in castings production, and about 30 titanium mill product and specialty product fabricators, many of which process other metals as well.

In the current demand upturn titanium producers in the United States, Europe, and Japan are operating at or near their practical capacity for sponge and ingot production. With only two major producers of titanium sponge—Timet and Oremet—U.S. sponge production is withheld to prevent the disclosure of company proprietary information. U.S. titanium sponge imports, however, increased 60 percent to 16,140 metric tons in 1997. The leading U.S. sponge import sources in 1997 were Russia (47 percent), Japan (39 percent), and Kazakstan (7 percent). U.S. ingot production increased 14 percent to a record 58,800 tons, while imports of ingot increased 152 percent to a record 5,189 tons, led by Russia (75 percent), the United Kingdom (17 percent), and China (7 percent).

Since the spring of 1997, acquisitions in the United States have resulted in significant consolidation within the domestic titanium industry. Three titanium companies were reduced to one as Teledyne Industries, with its specialty metals units, including the nonintegrated titanium producers Teledyne Allvac (Monroe,

TABLE 14-5: Titanium Trends and Forecasts

(metric tons except as noted)

	1989	1993	1994	1995	1996	1997	1998[1]	1999[2]	Percent Change 96–97	97–98	98–99	Compound Annual Growth Rate, % 87–97
Sponge metal												
Imports for consumption	903	2,160	6,470	7,560	10,110	16,140	17,800	19,000	59.6	10.3	6.7	33.1
Consumption	24,927	15,100	17,200	21,500	28,400	32,000	34,000	32,000	12.7	6.3	(5.9)	5.9
Imports as percent of consumption	3.6	14.3	37.6	35.2	35.6	50.4	52.4	59.4				
Industry stocks, Dec. 31	2,114	2,910	5,570	5,270	4,390	7,050	7,500	7,000				
Price, Dec. 31 ($/lb)	4.50–5.00	3.50–4.00	3.75–4.25	4.25–4.50	4.25–4.50	4.25–4.50						
Scrap metal												
Imports	5,308	5,520	5,870	11,100	16,400	10,650	13,000	14,000	(35.1)	22.1	7.7	17.0
Consumption	17,956	15,300	15,700	20,600	26,300	26,400	30,000	34,000	0.4	13.6	13.3	4.9
Exports	5,474	3,890	4,120	3,420	3,410	5,500	7,500	7,500	61.3	36.4	0.0	0.8
Stocks, Dec. 31	8,028	8,130	7,930	9,730	15,900	15,200	16,000	18,000				
Ingot												
Production	41,306	27,900	29,500	39,800	51,400	58,800	60,000	63,000	14.4	2.0	5.0	5.7
Imports	168	206	1,463	1,772	2,063	5,189	4,000	4,500	151.5	22.9	12.5	NA[3]
Consumption	31,396	25,700	24,300	30,600	38,300	45,500	48,000	50,000	18.8	5.5	4.2	3.5
Exports	334	275	373	483	269	613	900	900	128.3	46.8	0.0	NA[3]
Stocks, Dec. 31	3,548	2,430	3,270	3,560	4,710	4,350	4,000	3,800				
Mill products and castings												
Net mill product shipments	24,923	16,500	15,600	19,800	25,900	28,200	30,000	31,000	8.9	6.4	3.3	3.4
Net castings shipments	483	469	540	480	680	1,020	1,200	1,500	50.0	17.6	25.0	9.0
Imports (including castings)	1,440	600	802	1,860	6,142	4,592	5,300	6,200	(25.2)	15.4	17.0	17.8
Demand, net shipments + imports	26,846	17,569	16,942	22,140	32,722	33,812	37,700	39,700	3.3	11.5	5.3	4.6
Exports (including castings)	6,559	2,390	3,850	4,580	4,535	5,196	6,200	6,600	14.6	19.3	6.5	11.2

[1] Estimate.
[2] Forecast.
[3] Not available.
Source: U.S. Department of Commerce, International Trade Administration (ITA); U.S. Department of the Interior, Geological Survey. Estimates and forecasts by ITA.

NC) and Teledyne Wah Chang (Albany, OR), was merged with Allegheny Ludlem Steel Corporation, a major specialty steel and superalloy producer, to form Allegheny Teledyne Corporation (Pittsburgh, PA). More recently, Allegheny Teledyne acquired Oremet, an integrated titanium producer. Furthermore, RMI Titanium Company (Niles, OH), a nonintegrated producer, acquired Galt Alloys, Inc. (Canton, OH), a producer and worldwide distributor of ferrotitanium and specialty alloy additives for the production of specialty steels and nonferrous alloys.

In addition to this consolidation, each major producer has embarked on significant capacity expansions, especially cold hearth, to lower production costs. By the end of 1999 U.S. sponge and vacuum arc remelt (VAR) ingot capacity will have increased by 7 percent each to approximately 23,000 and 66,000 metric tons per year, respectively. New installations and expansions of existing plants will result in U.S. cold-hearth capacity increasing 129 percent to about 44,000 metric tons per year by the end of 1999. Cold hearth is an alternative technology that allows cost savings through greater scrap utilization and continuous melting with either electron beams or plasma arcs to mass-melt sponge and scrap, with or without alloying agents, into consumable electrodes in preparation for VAR melting. Cold-hearth technology also is used to produce single-melt industrial-grade ingot and slab.

Timet, an integrated titanium producer of sponge, ingot, and mill products, announced that it was expanding its VAR by about 25 percent to 22,400 metric tons per year, and separately announced that it was expanding electron beam cold-hearth melting at its subsidiary, Titanium Hearth Technologies, Inc. (THT), Morgantown, PA, by about 56 percent to 25,000 metric tons per year. THT is a producer of industrial-grade titanium slab and consumable titanium electrodes for VAR ingot production. These expansions were to be completed by mid-1998. RMI announced its plans to expand Galt to include new scrap preparation facilities and a plasma arc cold-hearth furnace with an initial capacity of 3,200 metric tons per year to produce consumable titanium electrodes. The Galt expansion should be completed by mid-1999. Both Allvac and Oremet announced expansion plans as well. Allvac will double its plasma arc cold-hearth capacity to about 5,000 metric tons per year, and Oremet will expand its sponge production capacity by about 1,500 metric tons to approximately 8,300 metric tons per year and will establish its own electron beam cold-hearth production with an initial melting capacity of about 10,000 metric tons per year. These expansions were to be completed by mid-1998.

Coupled with these capacity expansions, the major U.S. titanium producers have entered into long-term agreements to supply material to the major commercial aircraft manufacturers.

These agreements give the titanium producers a guaranteed minimum level of shipments for a portion of their production and give aircraft manufacturers an assurance of price levels and lead times for a portion of their titanium supplies. It is hoped that these agreements will mitigate the effects of business cycles in the commercial aerospace market. Titanium producers typically do not sell directly to aircraft and jet engine manufacturers but instead sell to companies that fabricate and supply parts and components to aircraft and jet engine manufacturers. There is generally a lag of approximately 18 to 24 months between mill product shipments and a finished aircraft.

Owing to increased domestic and world titanium demand, U.S. activity in titanium production and consumption and trade in titanium products generally increased in 1997, with the exception of scrap imports and imports of mill products and castings, which had significant declines. The chief indicator of the health of the U.S. titanium industry is domestic activity in sponge, scrap, ingot, and mill products and castings.

U.S. sponge consumption increased 12.7 percent in 1997 to 32,000 metric tons, while imports of titanium sponge increased almost 60 percent to 16,140 metric tons valued at about $122 million, up 72 percent from 1996. The import proportion of U.S. sponge consumption increased 42 percent to a 50 percent share. Imports from Russia increased 114 percent to 7,648 metric tons and a 47 percent share of total sponge imports. The average unit value for imported sponge in 1997 was $3.42 per pound, up 8 percent, or 24 cents per pound. On average there is a loss of about 10 percent in converting titanium sponge to ingot.

U.S. titanium scrap imports declined 35 percent to 10,650 metric tons valued at about $49 million, down 40 percent. This decline occurred despite a lower average unit value of $2.09 per pound, down 18 cents per pound. With reported scrap consumption practically unchanged at 26,400 metric tons, year-end scrap stock levels down 4 percent, and exports up 61 percent, the decline in imports probably was caused by ample domestic scrap generation and strong demand for scrap in foreign markets. On average there is a loss of about 30 percent from the conversion of ingot to mill products, but most of this material is recovered as scrap. U.S. titanium scrap export destinations were led by the United Kingdom with a 74 percent share of total scrap exports. Overall, the average scrap export unit value was $1.06 per pound, down 14 cents per pound.

Reported U.S. titanium ingot production increased 14 percent to 58,800 metric tons in 1997, while imports increased 152 percent to 5,189 metric tons valued at about $87 million, up 241 percent from 1996. With a 75 percent share of the total volume, ingot imports were led by Russia, increasing 177 percent to 3,872 metric tons valued at about $70 million, up 338 percent. Imports from the United Kingdom followed with a 17 percent share, increasing 217 percent to 863 metric tons valued at about $12 million, up 220 percent. The average unit value of U.S. imports of ingot was $7.62 per pound, up about $2.00 per pound, or 35 percent. U.S. exports of ingot increased 128 percent to 613 tons valued at about $11 million, up 138 percent, while the average export unit value increased 5 percent, or 35 cents per pound, to $7.96 per pound.

Reported U.S. titanium mill product and castings shipments increased 10 percent in 1997 to a record 29,220 metric tons, 42 percent above the peak of the last titanium market upturn in 1989. In 1997 U.S. imports of titanium mill product and castings declined 25 percent to 4,592 metric tons valued at about $80 million, down 15 percent. With a 74 percent share of the total import volume, Russia was the leading import source for titanium mill products and castings in 1997. However, a 28 percent, or 1,335-metric-ton, decrease in the volume of imports from Russia accounted for most of the 1,550-metric-ton decline in the total volume of titanium mill products and castings imports.

U.S. imports of titanium mill products and castings (wrought titanium) from Russia decreased from $50.6 million in 1995 to $36 million in 1997—a drop of 29 percent. Despite this decrease, Russia continued to be the principal foreign supplier. Meanwhile, U.S. exports of titanium mill products and castings increased to 5,196 metric tons valued at about $269 million—a 15 percent increase in quantity and 33 percent increase in value from 1996. Increased exports to the United Kingdom, France, Germany, China, and Australia led the improved export performance.

The titanium industry was the subject of trade actions during 1998. On July 24, the U.S. International Trade Commission (USITC) found that revocation of the antidumping duties covering imports of titanium sponge from Japan, Kazakstan, Russia, and Ukraine is not likely to lead to continuation or recurrence of material injury to the U.S. industry within a reasonably foreseeable time. As a result of the USITC's negative determinations, the U.S. Department of Commerce will revoke the existing antidumping orders on titanium sponge from Japan, Kazakstan, Russia, and Ukraine.

On June 30, 1998, the United States Trade Representative announced presidential decisions regarding the U.S. generalized system of preferences (GSP) program, two of which affect titanium products. Any change in duty status resulting from these decisions can take effect de facto only upon congressional renewal of the GSP program, which expired on July 1, 1998.

The President's decision restored duty-free treatment for wrought titanium imports from Russia, which account for 22 percent of Russia's titanium shipments to the United States. At the same time, the President announced that the decision to extend duty-free treatment under GSP to unwrought titanium would remain under consideration.

U.S. Industry Growth Projections for the Next 1 and 5 Years

The 1998 and 1999 U.S. and world titanium consumption is not expected to change appreciably from that in 1997. This is the case because about one-half of U.S. and one-third of world titanium consumption are associated with commercial aerospace sales and because no significant downturn in that market is anticipated in the near term despite the Asian financial crisis. Boeing's commercial aerospace unit projects that it will deliver about 300 aircraft to Asia between 1998 and 2000. However, Boeing has conceded that the financial crisis could mean about 60 fewer aircraft deliveries, but delivery cutbacks, if any, will not occur until 1999 and 2000. U.S. and world aerospace demand for titanium therefore is expected to amount to about 17,600 and 22,000 metric tons, respectively, in 1998, increasing slightly in 1999 to 17,900 and 22,400 metric tons, respectively. With worldwide commercial aircraft deliveries projected to peak in 1999 and with a lag between titanium shipments and a finished aircraft of up to 2 years, demand could begin to soften by 2003.

Several aerospace programs continue to drive the defense sector worldwide, and because of the large volume potential, the armor market continues to offer good demand prospects. Worldwide, diminished but stable military aerospace programs are expected to yield fairly flat demand growth at about 5,500 metric tons per year through 2003. Titanium demand from the nonaerospace industrial and consumer sector could approach 21,000 metric tons worldwide in 1999 and grow at a rate of about 2 percent per year to about 22,700 metric tons in 2003. The principal nonaerospace industrial and consumer applications for titanium include chemical processing, pulp and paper equipment, industrial power plants, pollution control equipment, and desalination plants, while emerging applications include end-use areas such as sports equipment, medical implants, automobiles, and energy extraction and processing.

In 1999 U.S. imports of titanium mill products and castings are projected to increase to about 6,200 metric tons, driven by demand from fabricators of jet engine components and airframes. U.S. titanium mill product imports are slated to grow at about 5 percent per year to about 7,500 metric tons in 2003. U.S. titanium mill product exports are projected to increase at a rate of about 3 percent per year from 6,600 metric tons in 1999 to about 7,200 metric tons in 2003.

Graylin W. Presbury, U.S. Department of Commerce, Office of Metals, Materials, and Chemicals, (202) 482-5158, October 1998.

ZINC

The international zinc industry includes primary producers (SIC 3339) that use zinc ores and concentrates as feedstock and secondary producers (SIC 3341) that recycle scrap zinc and crude zinc calcine obtained from steel mill electric arc furnace dust. Secondary zinc has been an increasingly important source of metal in recent years. Zinc is consumed primarily by the galvanizing (SIC 3312), zinc-based die casting alloy (SIC 3369), and brass and bronze (SIC 3364 and 3366) markets. Zinc is an internationally traded commodity whose value is based on the price set daily by the LME. This price may vary in different countries, depending on local market conditions.

Global Industry Trends

The structure of the global zinc industry has changed significantly in the 1990s. In 1990 Japan was the world's largest producer of zinc metal, followed by the Soviet Union, Canada, China, and the United States. By 1997 China had become the dominant producer, accounting for 18.2 percent of the 7.7 million metric tons produced, followed by Canada, 9.1 percent; Japan, 7.8 percent; the United States, 4.9 percent; and Spain,

4.8 percent. China has also become the world's second largest exporter of zinc metal, with exports rising from 17,000 metric tons in 1990 to 544,000 metric tons in 1997. These exports, combined with declining zinc consumption in Europe, Japan, and other countries in the early 1990s, resulted in a record market surplus, with the level of excess supply rising from 25,000 metric tons in 1990 to 619,000 metric tons in 1993. Improved market conditions after 1993 transformed this surplus into a supply deficit in 1995 and 1996 and a slight surplus of 26,000 metric tons in 1997 despite growing Chinese exports.

Domestic Trends

The United States is the world's fifth largest producer of zinc ores and concentrates after Canada, China, Australia, and Peru. The 15 leading domestic zinc mines, which are located in Alaska, Missouri, New York, and Tennessee, account for 95 percent of production, with Alaska accounting for more than 50 percent of total mine production. Primary zinc metal is produced at three refineries: Big River Zinc at Sauget, IL; Savage Zinc at Clarksville, TN; and Zinc Corporation of America (ZCA) at Monaca, PA. Secondary zinc metal is produced from waste and scrap materials at 10 plants. The largest secondary producer, ZCA, obtains a substantial part of its feedstock from crude zinc calcine recovered from steel mill electric arc furnace dust.

Zinc is also sold by the DNSC as a result of legislation passed in 1992 authorizing the disposal of the entire 334,000 metric tons in the stockpile over several years. The law, however, requires that the sale be completed without undue disruption of commercial zinc markets. At the end of 1997, 224,861 metric tons of zinc remained in the DNSC inventory. The FY 1999 AMP authorized the disposal of about 45,000 metric tons of zinc between October 1, 1998, and September 30, 1999. Additional authority is being sought by the DNSC to dispose of 45,000 metric tons for the FY 2000 AMP.

The domestic zinc market has experienced strong growth throughout the 1990s. Zinc mine production declined in 1993 as a result of the temporary closing of the Kennecott Greens Creek mine in Alaska because of low lead, gold, and silver prices and reduced output at other mines, and again in 1996 as a result of the closing of two mines in Tennessee. Despite these closings, zinc mine production increased at an annual rate of 2.3 percent between 1990 and 1997, primarily reflecting increased production at the Cominco Red Dog mine in Alaska. In 1997, domestic zinc mine production reached 632,000 metric tons, compared with 543,000 metric tons in 1990.

Domestic zinc metal production rose from 358,000 metric tons in 1990 to 367,000 metric tons in 1997. In that period the share of total metal production accounted for by secondary zinc increased from 27 percent to approximately 33 percent. This increase occurred despite the 1993 closing of ZCA's Bartlesville, OK, refinery, which was more than offset by an increase in secondary production and the debottlenecking of production at Savage Zinc's Clarksville smelter as well as an increase in capacity at Big River Zinc's Sauget smelter (see Table 14-6).

The United States accounts for almost 17 percent of global zinc consumption and is the single largest market worldwide.

TABLE 14-6: Zinc Industry (SIC 3339, 3341) Trends and Forecasts

(thousands of metric tons; percent)

	1990	1993	1994	1995	1996	1997[1]	1998[1]	1999[2]	Percent Change 96–97	Percent Change 97–98	Percent Change 98–99	Compound Annual Growth Rate, % 90–97
Mine production	543	513	598	644	628	632	730	815	0.6	15.5	11.6	2.3
Metal production	358	382	356	363	366	367	390	400	0.3	6.3	2.6	0.4
Apparent metal consumption	992	1,123	1,182	1,234	1,212	1,256	1,285	1,330	3.6	2.3	3.5	3.8
Imports for consumption	632	724	793	856	827	876	830	890	5.9	−5.3	7.2	5.5
Percent of consumption	63.7	64.5	67.1	69.4	68.2	69.7	64.6	66.9				
Exports	1	1	6	3	2	4	2	1	100.0	−50.0	−50.0	42.9

[1] Estimate.
[2] Forecast.
Source: U.S. Department of Commerce, International Trade Administration (ITA); U.S. Department of the Interior, Geological Survey; International Lead and Zinc Study Group. Estimates and forecasts by ITA.

Domestic zinc consumption increased at an average rate of 3.8 percent per year between 1990 and 1997, rising from 992,000 to 1,256,000 metric tons. In 1997 zinc galvanizing accounted for 55 percent of total consumption, followed by zinc-based die casting alloys at 18 percent and brass and bronze at 13 percent. The remaining 14 percent went to zinc oxides, rolled zinc, and several other uses.

Markets. Zinc is found in a large number of manufactured products, but its role is not always obvious because it tends to lose its identity in a product. Almost all zinc exports are contained in hundreds of products, such as motor vehicles (galvanized steel body, zinc die castings, and tires containing zinc oxide), appliances (zinc die castings), televisions (zinc sulfide), and animal feed (zinc oxide). Rolled zinc is purchased by the U.S. Mint for the production of pennies.

The largest and fastest growing segment of the zinc market is galvanized steel, which includes coated steel sheet and strip, structural shapes, fencing, storage tanks, fasteners, nails, and wire rope. The galvanizing segment is forecast to increase from 697,000 metric tons in 1997 to 750,000 metric tons in 1999 and to rise about 1.3 percent annually between 1999 and 2003, reaching 788,000 metric tons. Galvanized steel is used in the automotive and construction industries to confer corrosion protection. Galvanizing in automotive applications has increased substantially in the past few years as virtually all domestically produced motor vehicles have switched to two-sided galvanized steel. Because of its durability, galvanized steel is targeted for applications such as residential housing and public works, including highways, bridges, and wastewater treatment systems.

As a result of research and extensive marketing, two applications in the construction sector could result in a significant increase in zinc consumption. The International Lead and Zinc Research Organization has worked extensively to promote the use of galvanized rebar. Corrosion of concrete reinforcement bars is a major infrastructure problem that costs billions of dollars in repairs and replacement of reinforced concrete structures. Currently, less than 1 percent of rebar is galvanized, representing 30,000 metric tons of zinc worldwide. If this project is successful, zinc consumption for this use could expand to 150,000 met-

ric tons annually worldwide. Another promising application sponsored jointly by the North American steel and zinc industries is steel framing for residential housing. Steel framing offers not only corrosion protection but a cost saving over lumber, which is used most often in residential framing. An estimated 75,000 steel home frames were produced in 1996, representing 7,000 metric tons of zinc. The American Iron and Steel Institute is attempting to capture one-quarter of the residential frame market by 2000. If it is successful, this could result in a 20,000-metric-ton increase in galvanizing zinc consumption every 3 years.

Zinc-based die casting alloys are used to produce die cast parts such as handles, grilles, brackets, locks, hinges, gauges, pumps, mounts, and housings, which are used extensively in motor vehicles, heavy machinery, business machinery, appliances, household hardware, and scientific and electronic equipment. Domestic consumption in this segment is expected to increase from 221,000 to 232,000 metric tons between 1997 and 1999 and then rise about 1.8 percent per year between 1999 and 2003, reaching 249,000 metric tons.

Brass and bronze products are used as shell casings in ammunition and in tubes, valves, motors, pipes, refrigeration equipment, heat exchangers, communication units, and electronic devices. Consumption in this segment is expected to increase from 165,000 metric tons in 1997 to 175,000 metric tons in 1999. Between 1999 and 2003 brass and bronze consumption is forecast to rise about 1 percent per year to 183,000 metric tons.

Environment. Laws passed in California and nine northeastern states mandating the production of EVs could influence future zinc consumption. California and CONEG require that by 2003, 10 percent of all vehicles sold in these areas be zero-emission EVs and 15 percent be ultra-low-emission vehicles. One technology that could compete in this market is the zinc-air battery. An Israeli company has developed a prototype zinc-air EV battery system that would allow an EV to perform as well as a gasoline-powered vehicle, with a range of 300 miles or more, a top speed of 80 miles per hour, acceleration from zero to 50 miles per hour in 12 seconds, and refueling (mechanical recharging) in only a few minutes at a recharging station.

Annual sales of 100,000 such EVs would translate into 10,000 metric tons of zinc per year for these batteries.

A proposed European Commission directive on batteries and accumulators would ban the use of nickel-cadmium batteries in the EU by 2008. Since cadmium is a by-product of zinc, this proposal would have a severe impact on the price of zinc. The proposed directive is contrary to a joint effort of the OECD and industry to increase the recycling of these batteries.

U.S. Industry Growth Projections

Domestic zinc consumption is estimated to increase at an average annual rate of about 2.9 percent between 1997 and 1999, growing to 1.33 million metric tons, reflecting growth in all zinc markets. Galvanizing is forecast to rise as a result of increases in private nonresidential and public works construction such as highways as well as an expected increase in market share in housing construction as steel frame houses gain wider acceptance. This growth will offset expected stagnation in motor vehicle production. The market for zinc-based alloys should increase slightly, reflecting the decision by several automobile producers to increase their specifications for zinc die castings and an increase in the use of zinc die castings in the building hardware market. Brass and bronze should be positively affected by an increase in end-use markets such as ammunition and plumbing fixtures. Between 1999 and 2003 zinc consumption is forecast to rise 1.3 percent per year, reaching a record level of 1.49 million metric tons.

Domestic production of zinc is forecast to increase to 400,000 metric tons in 1999 as Big River Zinc and Savage Zinc increase capacity. By 2003 production is expected to increase to 410,000 metric tons as a result of an increase in secondary production. The production level could be considerably higher if Savage Zinc increases capacity at its Clarksville refinery by 150,000 metric tons, as planned.

The United States is a net importer of refined zinc, with imports accounting for about 68 percent of consumption. In 1997, 81 percent of the 876,000 metric tons imported came from Brazil, Canada, Mexico, Russia, and Spain. Imports from Brazil, Mexico, and Russia were duty-free, while the Canadian duty was 0.1 percent as a result of the North American Free Trade Agreement (NAFTA). Spanish imports were charged a 1.5 percent duty. Imports are forecast to increase to 890,000 metric tons in 1999 and rise to 940,000 metric tons by 2003. Imports could be considerably lower in the long term, however, if Savage Zinc goes through with its contemplated capacity expansion. Zinc alloy imports in 1997 increased to 267 metric tons from 186 metric tons in 1996, with Canada, Mexico, and the United Kingdom accounting for 94 percent of the total. The tariff for zinc alloy was 19 percent for most countries before 1995 but as a result of the Uruguay Round of the General Agreement on Trade and Tariffs (GATT) will be reduced gradually to 3 percent by January 1999. Imports of zinc alloy from Canada and Mexico are duty-free under the CFTA and NAFTA, respectively. Imports from developing countries are duty-free under the GSP. The U.S. Department of Commerce will monitor zinc alloy imports from WTO countries until 2002 to determine whether imports have an adverse effect on U.S. national security interests.

Given the domestic zinc industry's reliance on imports, only 3,600 metric tons of zinc was exported in 1997, with 94 percent going to Canada. About 12,000 metric tons of zinc alloy was exported, with 97 percent going to Canada.

Global Market Prospects

Between 1993 and 1997 global consumption of zinc rose at an annual rate of 3.5 percent, increasing from 6.61 million metric tons to 7.77 million metric tons. Galvanizing accounted for 47 percent of consumption, followed by brass and bronze, 19 per-

TABLE 14-7: U.S. Trade Patterns in Nonferrous Metals[1] in 1997

(millions of dollars; percent)

Exports			Imports		
Region[2]	Value[3]	Share, %	Region[2]	Value[3]	Share, %
NAFTA	2,551	47.8	NAFTA	3,831	53.2
Latin America	444	8.3	Latin America	906	12.6
Western Europe	792	14.8	Western Europe	1,033	14.3
Japan/Chinese Economic Area	880	16.5	Japan/Chinese Economic Area	977	13.6
Other Asia	472	8.8	Other Asia	178	2.5
Rest of world	202	3.8	Rest of world	277	3.8
World	5,342	100.0	World	7,201	100.0
Top Five Countries	Value	Share, %	Top Five Countries	Value	Share, %
Mexico	1,358	25.4	Canada	2,488	34.6
Canada	1,192	22.3	Mexico	1,343	18.7
Japan	403	7.5	Chile	437	6.1
United Kingdom	300	5.6	China	430	6.0
Hong Kong (PRC)	170	3.2	Japan	347	4.8

[1] SIC 1021, 3331, 3341, 3351, 3357.
[2] For definitions of regional groupings, see "Getting the Most Out of *Outlook '99*."
[3] Values may not sum to total due to rounding.
Source: U.S. Department of Commerce, Bureau of the Census.

cent; zinc-based alloys, 13 percent; chemicals, 9 percent; zinc semimanufactures, 8 percent; and other uses, 4 percent. Global market conditions for zinc are forecast to worsen slightly in the near term. Consumption was expected to remain flat in 1998 at 7.82 million metric tons, while metal production was projected to increase 3.3 percent from 7.77 million metric tons to 8.02 million metric tons. As a result, an increased surplus of 233,000 metric tons is expected to overhang the market. While exports from China were expected to be lower than those in 1997, China will continue to dominate the global zinc market.

For overall trade patterns in the nonferrous metals industries, see Table 14-7.

Dave Larrabee, U.S. Department of Commerce, Office of Metals, Materials, and Chemicals, (202) 482-0607, October 1998.

INTERNATIONAL ENVIRONMENTAL INITIATIVES AND THE METALS INDUSTRY

Basel Convention

The Basel Convention was negotiated under the United Nations Environment Programme (UNEP). Its goals include waste minimization, pollution prevention, national self-sufficiency in waste management, environmentally sound management of waste movement, and accountability for the movement of hazardous and other wastes. The convention prohibits waste exports if they will not be properly managed; waste exports if the proposed recipient state prohibits the importation of the waste or does not consent in writing to the import; and trade in covered wastes.

There are 117 parties to the convention. However, the United States has not ratified the convention, though it has the advice and consent of the Senate. For the United States to become a party, it must adopt the implementing legislation and notify the Basel Secretariat of its ratification.

U.S. ratification of the Basel Convention has been on hold because of a decision adopted by member states at the Third Conference of Parties (COP III) to the convention. This decision, known as the ban amendment, obligates parties listed in Annex VII of the convention (OECD members, the EU, and Liechtenstein) to prohibit immediately the exportation to non-Annex VII countries of all hazardous wastes destined for final disposal and to prohibit such exports for recycling after December 31, 1997. However, the ban amendment did not define hazardous waste and therefore the scope of the ban. This left U.S. industries concerned that they will not be able to trade commoditylike scrap materials to countries that are not in the annex if the United States becomes a party to the convention.

At present, only 8 countries have ratified the ban out of the required 67 parties necessary for the decision to become an amendment to the convention. However, the EU has chosen to implement the ban amendment unilaterally through written requests to nations that import wastes from the EU, and each nation must respond positively to the EU for exports to continue. Such a unilateral implementation could cause a distortion of trade patterns.

To address what is covered by the ban, the Technical Working Group (TWG) of the convention defined two lists of materials: those covered (Annex VIII) and a list of nonhazardous materials not covered (Annex IX). Additionally, there is a short list of materials (the C list) awaiting classification to either Annex VIII or Annex IX. The TWG is establishing a permanent review mechanism for classifying materials to the annexes, with the knowledge that it will be possible to nominate additional materials to the C list.

At COP IV, which was held in Kuching, Malaysia, in February 1998, there were several positive outcomes. Foremost was the adoption of the lists, now annexes to the convention, in a legally binding manner. Furthermore, the annexes include introductory language (chapeau) that allows for individual shipments to be tested and reclassified; for example, an individual shipment of an Annex VIII material that does not exhibit hazardous characteristics per the convention will be reclassified to Annex IX.

COP V will be held in December 1999. The TWG will meet in the interim to work on establishing a review mechanism as well as work toward the hazard classification of items on the C list.

Climate Change

The United Nations Framework Convention on Climate Change (FCCC), signed in Rio de Janeiro in 1992, has been ratified by 166 countries; it entered into force in 1994. The FCCC seeks to address the anthropogenic emissions of greenhouse gases—carbon dioxide (CO_2), methane (CH_4), and nitrous oxide (N_2O)—and of industrial gases—hydrofluorocarbons (HFCs), PFCs, and sulfur hexafluoride (SF_6). These emissions result in part directly from metal-processing facilities and directly and indirectly from consumption of energy. They can be significant for some metals, especially aluminum and steel.

At the COP in Kyoto, Japan, in December 1997, the parties agreed to a protocol for reducing greenhouse gas emissions. The Kyoto Protocol calls for industrialized nations to reduce their average national emissions to 5.2 percent below 1990 levels by 2008–2012. The United States is required to reduce its emissions 7 percent. The protocol includes all the major greenhouse gases and takes into account changes in emissions resulting from forest and land use patterns. COP IV was scheduled to be held in November 1998 in Buenos Aires, Argentina.

Because the competitiveness of the metals industries could be affected adversely by the conditions of the protocol, the administration has begun consultations with industry to determine the best means of achieving reductions in greenhouse gas emissions on a voluntary basis. Technological innovation will assume a major role in the ability of industry to reduce energy consumption and greenhouse gas emissions.

Global Efforts to Reduce and Eliminate Metals Use

Because of risks to human health and the environment, there is growing pressure to reduce the use of many metals. In particular, cadmium, lead, and mercury have been the subject of reduction and elimination efforts, the most prominent of which is the United Nations Economic Commission for Europe Convention on Long-Range Transboundary Air Pollution (LRTAP) Heavy Metals Protocol. However, many other forums have begun to examine these metals, including the OECD, the European Commission, and individual counties.

The United States is a contracting party to the Economic Commission for Europe (ECE)–administered LRTAP Convention of 1979. Under the convention, five protocols have been adopted. The Heavy Metals Protocol is one of four that has been considered in parallel by the contacting parties. Negotiations were concluded in February 1998, and the protocol was signed later that year.

This protocol, which will cover Europe, the United States, and Canada, will control emissions of lead, cadmium, and mercury and restrict the use of a limited number of products containing some of these metals, particularly leaded gasoline and most mercury-containing primary batteries. The targeted emissions are from industrial sources which include primary and secondary ferrous and nonferrous metal foundries, power production plants, and incinerators. To achieve the reductions, the protocol suggests the use of best available techniques, including improvements in production processes and the use of filters, scrubbers, and absorbers.

Several other attempts are under way to reduce or eliminate the use of cadmium, lead, and mercury. In 1995 the OECD, with assistance from Sweden and the Netherlands, began to examine the emissions from and environmental impact of pathways of significant exposure to cadmium and ways to minimize the associated risks. Since then the OECD, in cooperation with industry, has established a successful collection and recycling program for nickel-cadmium batteries.

In spite of the success of the OECD's recycling program, the DGXI has moved to ban nickel-cadmium batteries by January 1, 2008. In addition, DGXI is seeking to ban the use of cadmium, lead, mercury, and hexavalent chromium in electrical and electronic equipment. Furthermore, the EU will require that after January 2003, cadmium, lead (lead-acid batteries and lead solder in circuit boards are exempt), mercury, and hexavalent chromium contained in vehicles be removed from scrap vehicles before shredding.

Individual countries are moving to control metals as well. Sweden is attempting to ban all uses of lead, mercury, and cadmium by 2007. The Netherlands, through the Chemical Substance Act of 1998, seeks to ban all uses of cadmium in pigments and stabilizers and as a surface coating. In Denmark draft legislation has been proposed to ban the importation, sale, and production of numerous lead products, except for export. Finally, Japan has asked its domestic automobile producers to reduce voluntarily by almost 70 percent the amount of lead used in motor vehicles by 2005.

A. J. Campbell, U.S. Department of Commerce, Office of Metals, Materials, and Chemicals, (202) 482-0553, October 1998.

■ REFERENCES

Aluminum

The Aluminum Association, 900 19th Street, NW, Washington, DC 20006. (202) 862-5100.

American Metal Market, Capital Cities, Inc., 825 Seventh Avenue, New York, NY 10019. (202) 887-8550.

Metal Bulletin, Metal Bulletin, Inc., 220 Fifth Avenue, New York, NY 10001. (212) 213-6202.

Platts-Metals Week, McGraw-Hill, Inc., 1221 Avenue of the Americas, New York, NY 10020. (212) 512-6126.

Copper

American Metal Market, Capital Cities, Inc., 825 Seventh Avenue, New York, NY 10019. (212) 887-8550.

Copper Development Association, 260 Madison Avenue, New York, NY 10016. (212) 251-7200.

International Copper Study Group, Rua Almirante Barroso, No. 38, 6th Floor, 1000 Lisbon, Portugal. Telephone: 351-1-352-4039.

U.S. Department of Commerce, Bureau of the Census, Manufacturing and Construction Division, Washington, DC 20233. (301) 457-4736.

U.S. Department of the Interior, Geological Survey, Office of Minerals Information, 989 National Center, Reston, VA 20192. (703) 648-4978.

Lead

American Metal Market, Capital Cities, Inc., 825 Seventh Avenue, New York, NY 10019. (212) 887-8550.

Battery Council International, 401 North Michigan Avenue, Chicago, IL 60611-4267. (312) 644-6610.

International Lead and Zinc Study Group, 2 King Street, London SW1Y 6QP, England. Telephone: 011-44-171-839-8550.

International Lead Zinc Research Organization, 2525 Meridan Parkway, P.O. Box 12036, Research Triangle Park, NC 27709. (919) 361-4647.

Lead Industries Association, 295 Madison Avenue, 19th Floor, New York, NY 10017. (212) 578-4750.

Metal Bulletin, Metal Bulletin, Inc., 220 Fifth Avenue, New York, NY 10001. (212) 213-6202.

Mineral Commodity Surveys, *Lead Industry Monthly,* U.S. Department of the Interior, Geological Survey, Reston, VA 20192. (703) 648-77567.

Platts-Metals Week, McGraw-Hill, Inc., 1221 Avenue of the Americas, New York, NY 10020. (212) 512-6126.

Titanium

American Metal Market, Capital Cities, Inc., 825 Seventh Avenue, New York, NY 10019. (212) 887-8550.

International Titanium Association, 1871 Folsom Street, Suite 200, Boulder, CO 80302. (303) 443-7515.

Metal Bulletin, Metal Bulletin, Inc., 220 Fifth Avenue, New York, NY 10001. (212) 213-6202.

Platts-Metals Week, McGraw-Hill, Inc., 1221 Avenue of the Americas, New York, NY 10020. (212) 512-6126.

Titanium Quarterly, Mineral Industry Surveys, U.S. Department of the Interior, Geological Survey, Reston, VA 20192. (703) 648-7718.

Zinc

American Metal Market, Capital Cities, Inc., 825 Seventh Avenue, New York, NY 10019. (212) 887-8550.

American Zinc Association, Suite 240, 1112 16th Street, NW, Washington, DC 20036.

International Lead and Zinc Study Group, 2 King Street, London SW1Y 6QP, England. Telephone: 011-44-171-839-8550.

International Lead Zinc Research Organization, 2525 Meridan Parkway, P.O. Box 12036, Research Triangle Park, NC 27709. (919) 361-4647

Metal Bulletin, Metal Bulletin, Inc., 220 Fifth Avenue, New York, NY 10001. (212) 213-6202.

Mineral Commodity Surveys, *Zinc Industry Monthly,* U.S. Department of the Interior, Geological Survey, Reston, VA 20192. (703) 648-7767

Platts-Metals Week, McGraw-Hill, Inc., 1221 Avenue of the Americas, New York, NY 10020. (212) 512-6126.

International Environmental Initiatives

Danish Environment Ministry, http://www.mem.dk/mem/ukindex.htm.

European Commission, Environmental Directorate, http://europa.eu.int/en/comm/dg11/dg11home.html.

Japan Environment Corporation, http://www.eic.or.jp/jec/eg/html/engtop.htm.

MITI, http://www.miti.go.jp/index-e.html.

Organization for Economic Cooperation and Development, http://www.oecd.org.

Swedish EnviroNet, http://smn.environ.se/smnproj/miljonat/english/katalog/index.htm.

United Nations Economic Commission for Europe, http://www.unece.org/env/env_eb.htm.

United Nations Environment Programme, http://www.unep.ch.

United Nations Framework Convention on Climate Change, http://www.unfccc.de.

■ RELATED CHAPTERS

6: Construction
21: Aerospace
36: Motor Vehicles

GENERAL COMPONENTS
Economic and Trade Trends

U.S. International Trade

Source: U.S. Department of Commerce: Bureau of the Census; International Trade Administration.

World Export Market Shares

Source: United Nations; U.S. Department of Commerce: International Trade Administration.

Export Dependence and Import Penetration

Source: U.S. Department of Commerce: Bureau of the Census; International Trade Administration.

Output and Output per Hour

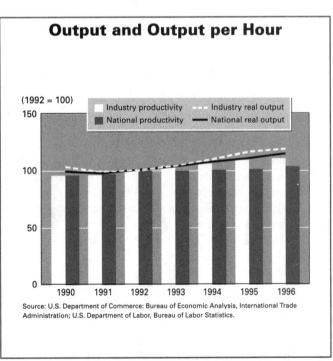

Source: U.S. Department of Commerce: Bureau of Economic Analysis, International Trade Administration; U.S. Department of Labor, Bureau of Labor Statistics.

See "Getting the Most Out of *Outlook '99*" for definitions of terms.

General Components

INDUSTRY DEFINITION The general components sector consists of products used as parts by manufacturers to construct machinery, equipment, buildings, piping systems, and other manufactured goods. This chapter examines screw machine products (SIC 3451), industrial fasteners (SIC 3452), industrial valves (SIC 3491), pipe fittings (SIC 3494), and ball and roller bearings (SIC 3562). Among the general components not discussed here are gaskets, packing, and sealing devices (SIC 3053); fluid power valves and hose fittings (SIC 3492); steel springs (3493); wire springs (3495); speed changers, industrial high-speed drives, and gears (SIC 3566); and mechanical power-transmission equipment not elsewhere classified (SIC 3568).

GLOBAL INDUSTRY TRENDS

General components play a major role in manufacturing world-wide. Most machinery or equipment uses some type of bearings, screw machine products, or industrial fasteners. Valves and pipe fittings are used in most kinds of construction, including industrial plants, power projects, and commercial construction, as well as in pipelines and oil refineries.

General components industries around the world are changing rapidly: Developing countries are establishing their industries, and industrialized countries are using advanced technology to make new and better products. Competition is getting stronger all the time. End users constantly try to cut costs, forcing general components manufacturers to try to cut their costs. General components companies are investing in new technology in the form of improved capital equipment and manufacturing processes. There is also a trend toward consolidation as companies find that the best investment often is to buy other companies or merge rather than build new product lines from scratch. End users such as Chrysler, General Motors, and Ford are using fewer general components suppliers.

Technological advances have facilitated expanded world trade in general components. The general components industries are becoming more globalized. Low-tech commodity-type products are increasing by being made in countries with relatively lower costs of production. The rapid rate of technology transfers has made it possible for developing countries to become major players in international markets for commodity-type products. General components industries that are based in industrialized countries still have a comparative advantage in providing high-quality products and service. Some valve, pipe fitting, and bearing manufacturers in industrialized countries are sourcing components and parts in developing countries.

DOMESTIC TRENDS

The U.S. general components industries have prospered in recent years. A strong domestic manufacturing sector and robust exports combined to produce healthy sales for the valve, pipe fitting, screw machine products, industrial fastener, and bearing industries. For the period 1992–1996 combined product shipments for these industries increased at an average annual rate of 3.0 percent, expressed in constant dollars. The rate of growth was projected to be 4.1 percent in 1997 and 5.3 percent in 1998.

Employment in the four components industries in 1997 in this chapter was approximately 218,000 with production workers accounting for about 164,000 jobs. The industry is faced with a shortage of skilled workers which has been difficult to resolve despite the creation of training programs. The demand for skilled workers continues to grow faster than does the supply. To a limited extent, increased investment in laborsaving machine tools and other production equipment can help alleviate this problem.

A major trend facing the U.S. general components industries is consolidation. Most U.S. general components makers were highly fragmented until fairly recently. With increased domes-

TABLE 15-1: General Components (SIC 3451, 3452, 349A, 3562) Trends and Forecasts
(millions of dollars except as noted)

	1992	1993	1994	1995	1996	1997[1]	1998[2]	1999[3]	Percent Change 96–97	97–98	98–99	92–96[4]
Industry data												
Value of shipments[5]	22,038	23,202	25,014	27,310	28,648	30,255	32,563	34,133	5.6	7.6	4.8	6.8
3451 Screw machine products	3,831	4,170	4,686	5,044	5,278	5,690	6,657	6,976	7.8	17.0	4.8	8.3
3452 Industrial fasteners	5,195	5,373	5,819	6,385	6,519	6,897	7,318	7,706	5.8	6.1	5.3	5.8
349A Valves and pipe fittings[6]	8,723	9,102	9,618	10,600	11,405	11,873	12,526	13,177	4.1	5.5	5.2	6.9
3562 Ball and roller bearings	4,290	4,557	4,891	5,281	5,446	5,795	6,062	6,274	6.4	4.6	3.5	6.1
Value of shipments (1992$)	22,038	22,866	24,174	25,593	26,221	27,257	28,714	29,335	4.0	5.3	2.2	4.4
3451 Screw machine products	3,831	4,137	4,599	4,841	4,993	5,392	6,147	6,301	8.0	14.0	2.5	6.8
3452 Industrial fasteners	5,195	5,320	5,699	6,145	6,209	6,550	6,845	7,050	5.5	4.5	3.0	4.6
349A Valves and pipe fittings	8,723	8,928	9,174	9,731	10,178	10,280	10,486	10,696	1.0	2.0	2.0	3.9
3562 Ball and roller bearings	4,290	4,481	4,702	4,876	4,841	5,035	5,236	5,288	4.0	4.0	1.0	3.1
Total employment (thousands)	194	194	196	207	212	218			2.8			2.2
3451 Screw machine products	46.4	47.1	51.9	54.2	57.1	60.8			6.5			5.3
3452 Industrial fasteners	44.1	43.7	43.4	46.0	46.5	47.4			1.9			1.3
349A Valves and pipe fittings	68.0	69.0	66.8	71.3	71.9	73.1			1.7			1.4
3562 Ball and roller bearings	35.0	33.8	33.4	35.6	36.0	37.1			3.1			0.7
Production workers (thousands)	142	144	147	156	159	164			3.1			2.9
3451 Screw machine products	36.5	38.5	41.9	44.0	46.0	48.9			6.3			6.0
3452 Industrial fasteners	31.9	32.0	31.9	34.1	35.1	36.7			4.6			2.4
349A Valves and pipe fittings	45.6	46.6	45.8	48.9	48.5	49.0			1.0			1.6
3562 Ball and roller bearings	28.2	27.3	27.2	29.2	29.5	29.9			1.4			1.1
Average hourly earnings ($)	12.57	12.70	12.90	13.25	13.52							1.8
3451 Screw machine products	11.29	11.36	11.25	11.55	12.26	12.76			4.1			2.1
3452 Industrial fasteners	12.80	12.74	12.76	13.58	13.36	13.99			4.7			1.1
349A Valves and pipe fittings	12.39	12.76	12.76	13.17	13.55	13.94			2.9			2.3
3562 Ball and roller bearings	14.35	14.48	15.97	15.65	15.72	16.44			4.6			2.3
Capital expenditures	758	778	825	1,194	1,024							7.8
3451 Screw machine products	135	152	226	250	231							14.4
3452 Industrial fasteners	151	163	157	386	190							5.9
349A Valves and pipe fittings	265	257	269	310	331							5.7
3562 Ball and roller bearings	207	206	173	248	273							7.2
Product data												
Value of shipments[5]	20,754	21,930	23,702	25,871	27,030	28,571	30,806	32,375	5.7	7.8	5.1	6.8
3451 Screw machine products	3,660	3,986	4,642	5,324	5,608	6,045	7,073	7,412	7.8	17.0	4.8	11.3
3452 Industrial fasteners	4,854	5,043	5,439	5,916	6,115	6,470	6,845	7,263	5.8	5.8	6.1	5.9
349A Valves and pipe fittings	8,100	8,461	8,828	9,501	10,049	10,461	11,036	11,643	4.1	5.5	5.5	5.5
3562 Ball and roller bearings	4,140	4,440	4,794	5,129	5,258	5,595	5,852	6,057	6.4	4.6	3.5	6.2
Value of shipments (1992$)	20,754	21,616	22,913	24,262	24,772	25,793	27,149	27,740	4.1	5.3	2.2	4.5
3451 Screw machine products	3,660	3,954	4,555	5,109	5,305	5,729	6,531	6,694	8.0	14.0	2.5	9.7
3452 Industrial fasteners	4,854	4,993	5,327	5,694	5,824	6,144	6,420	6,613	5.5	4.5	3.0	4.7
349A Valves and pipe fittings	8,100	8,303	8,422	8,723	8,969	9,059	9,240	9,425	1.0	2.0	2.0	2.6
3562 Ball and roller bearings	4,140	4,366	4,609	4,736	4,674	4,861	4,958	5,008	4.0	2.0	1.0	3.1
Trade data												
Value of imports	4,221	4,630	5,490	6,263	6,458	7,019	7,814	8,675	8.7	11.3	11.0	11.2
3451 Screw machine products												
3452 Industrial fasteners	1,231	1,386	1,666	1,894	1,847	1,907	2,059	2,265	3.2	8.0	10.0	10.7
349A Valves and pipe fittings	2,096	2,240	2,652	2,988	3,221	3,650	4,198	4,744	13.3	15.0	13.0	11.3
3562 Ball and roller bearings	895	1,004	1,171	1,381	1,389	1,462	1,557	1,666	5.3	6.5	7.0	11.6
Value of exports	3,154	3,332	3,849	4,570	5,167	5,568	6,105	6,834	7.8	9.6	11.9	13.1
3451 Screw machine products												
3452 Industrial fasteners	685	710	905	1,061	1,366	1,333	1,466	1,686	-2.4	10.0	15.0	18.8
349A Valves and pipe fittings	1,810	1,964	2,211	2,620	2,890	3,239	3,563	3,991	12.1	10.0	12.0	12.4
3562 Ball and roller bearings	659	658	733	889	912	996	1,076	1,157	9.2	8.0	7.5	8.5

[1] Estimate except imports and exports.
[2] Estimate.
[3] Forecast.
[4] Compound annual rate.
[5] For definition of industry versus product values, see "Getting the Most Out of *Outlook '99*."
[6] Code 349A represents an aggregation of SICs 3491 and 3494.
Source: U.S. Department of Commerce: Bureau of the Census; International Trade Administration.

tic and international competition, U.S. general components companies are finding it harder to survive. This competition has resulted in relatively small profit margins for many companies, which have been forced to cut costs in order to survive. Consolidations allow these firms to do so, by taking advantage of economies of scale.

The future of the U.S. general components industries is dependent on the growth of the U.S. manufacturing base. Despite the large share of product shipments now being exported, the U.S. general components industry is heavily reliant on the U.S. manufacturing industry, as is especially true in the case of bearings, screw machine products, and industrial fasteners. The automotive industry is the most important end user for all three of these industries; expanded domestic motor vehicle production is a key to the future of the general components industries.

With the stiff competition they face from imports, it is important for general components companies to remain competitive. Most U.S. general components manufacturers cannot compete on a price basis in the commodity products sectors of the industries. U.S. companies need to invest in research and product development and incorporate new production techniques into their factory lines. An emphasis on quality and providing good service will be two critical factors in U.S. competitiveness. U.S. companies need to develop and exploit market segments and niches where they enjoy a comparative advantage.

PROJECTIONS OF INDUSTRY AND TRADE GROWTH

The screw machine product, industrial fastener, industrial valve, pipe fitting, and bearing industries are forecast to register a combined growth rate of 2.2 percent in 1999 (see Table 15-1). Major

factors in limiting this growth rate are the leveling off of automobile production and expected slower growth in exports of U.S. machinery and equipment. The increased competitiveness of imports from Asia is also expected to play a role. Strong demand is expected from manufacturers of aircraft, construction machinery, machine tools, farm machinery, and light and heavy trucks.

General component exports are expected to increase about 10 percent in 1998 and 12 percent in 1999. Canada and Mexico will continue to be the most important foreign markets. The European Union will account for a large share of exports outside North America.

Imports of general components are expected to increase about 11 percent in both 1998 and 1999. There could be significant increases in imports from Asian manufacturers based on the depreciation of a number of Asian currencies. Imports from China are expected to gain an increased share of the U.S. import market for general components.

For the 5-year period 1999–2003, shipments for the general components industry are expected to increase at an average annual rate of 2 to 3 percent. Exports and imports are expected to register average annual growth rates between 8 and 12 percent (see Table 15-2).

SCREW MACHINE PRODUCTS AND INDUSTRIAL FASTENERS

A general definition of screw machine products (SIC 3451) is custom-designed products and turned parts made on screw machines as well as other types of turning machinery. As a result of technological advancements in the machine tool industry, many products traditionally made on screw machines can now be made more efficiently on other types of machines. This trend will continue as screw machine prod-

TABLE 15-2: U.S. Trade Patterns in General Components[1] in 1997
(millions of dollars; percent)

	Exports			Imports	
Regions[2]	Value[3]	Share, %	Regions[2]	Value[3]	Share, %
NAFTA	3,153	56.6	NAFTA	1,666	23.7
Latin America	390	7.0	Latin America	67	1.0
Western Europe	867	15.6	Western Europe	1,921	27.4
Japan/Chinese Economic Area	339	6.1	Japan/Chinese Economic Area	2,784	39.7
Other Asia	496	8.9	Other Asia	433	6.2
Rest of world	324	5.8	Rest of world	149	2.1
World	5,568	100.0	World	7,019	100.0
Top Five Countries	Value	Share, %	Top Five Countries	Value	Share, %
Canada	2,261	40.6	Japan	1,398	19.9
Mexico	892	16.0	Taiwan	1,038	14.8
United Kingdom	265	4.8	Canada	850	12.1
South Korea	183	3.3	Mexico	816	11.6
Japan	174	3.1	Germany	582	8.3

[1] SIC 3451, 3452, 3491, 3494, 3562.
[2] For definitions of regional groupings, see "Getting the Most Out of *Outlook '99*."
[3] Values may not sum to total due to rounding.
Source: U.S. Department of Commerce, Bureau of the Census.

uct companies increase the use of computer numerical control (CNC) machines in their production facilities. The industrial fastener industry (SIC 3452) consists of establishments primarily engaged in manufacturing metal bolts, nuts, screws, rivets, washers, formed and threaded wire goods, and special industrial fasteners such as aircraft fasteners.

Global Industry Trends

The standards segment of the industrial fastener industry is global in nature. Countries with relatively low labor costs have an advantage in producing large numbers of standard products at a relatively low cost. For a number of years Taiwan and Japan have been the principal suppliers of standards to the world market. However, as labor costs have increased, those countries have begun to face increased pressure from lower-cost producers such as China. Developing countries seeking to build domestic fastener industries initially are very dependent on exports, as their domestic markets are limited; exports are also a good source of foreign exchange.

The U.S. industrial fastener and screw machine product industries are very competitive in producing custom or specially engineered products. The U.S. competitive advantage lies in providing quality and service. Both industries sell primarily to the North American market.

The specials segment of the industrial fastener industry and the screw machine product industry are localized in nature: Most companies are in proximity to their major customers. The move toward just-in-time delivery gives an advantage to suppliers that are located near major manufacturers. Some industrial fastener companies and, to a limited extent, screw machine product manufacturers follow their major customers overseas, in some cases setting up foreign manufacturing facilities. For example, many Japanese transplants in the United States buy fasteners and screw machine products from their traditional suppliers, some of which have built facilities in the United States. Many U.S. fastener and screw machine product companies have significant exports to Ford, General Motors, and Chrysler operations in Mexico and Canada.

The U.S. screw machine product (SIC 3451) and industrial fastener (3452) industries are concentrated in the large manufacturing states of the midwest—Michigan, Ohio, Illinois, Indiana, and Wisconsin—as well as in New York, Pennsylvania, Connecticut, and California. The screw machine product industry consists of about 1,700 establishments employing 60,800 people, and the industrial fastener industry has 930 establishments with 47,400 workers.

Trends in the U.S. industrial fastener and screw machine product industries are closely related to trends in the major consuming industries. Virtually all machinery and equipment manufacturers use industrial fasteners and screw machine products. The automotive industry is the major consuming industry for both of these industries. Shipments to the automotive industry account for about 30 to 35 percent of U.S. fastener production and a somewhat lower percentage for the screw machine product industry. Other major consuming industries include aerospace, defense, construction machinery, mining equipment, machine tools, medical equipment, and computers. Aircraft fasteners represent a special segment of highly engineered products that are used only by aircraft manufacturers.

The industrial fastener industry has continued its pattern of consolidation with more mergers and acquisitions. As the U.S. fastener industry is composed of a large number of small and medium-size companies, these consolidations improve the competitiveness of these companies by utilizing economies of scale and resources for research and expansion that would not otherwise be available.

The industrial fastener and screw machine product industries are highly competitive. Major customers are asking suppliers to keep a lid on prices. Many large customers, especially in the automotive sectors, are allowing little or no provisions for raising prices. It behooves industrial fastener and screw machine product manufacturers to improve their efficiency and productivity. An important factor in increased productivity and efficiency is the utilization of new technology and production processes. Much of this advanced technology is incorporated in new and improved machine tools and other production machinery.

The automotive industry is the major engine behind the industrial fastener industry and, to a lesser degree, the screw machine product industry. When the automotive industry is booming, so is the industrial fastener industry; when the automotive industry is depressed, the fastener industry also slumps. The U.S. fastener and screw machine product industries have prospered in recent years with expansion of the manufacturing sector and strong demand from the automotive sector in particular. A rebound in the construction industry also has benefited both industries. New residential construction stimulates production in the appliances industry, which is a major consumer of screw machine products. Screw machine product shipments expressed in constant dollars registered a strong increase estimated at 14 percent in 1998 compared with 1997. Strong demand from all major machinery and equipment sectors contributed to that increase. In 1998 the industrial fastener industry registered growth estimated at 4.5 percent in constant dollar terms. Demand from the aircraft industry was particularly strong.

U.S. industrial fastener exports amounted to approximately $1.33 billion in 1997, a 2.4 percent drop from 1996 and the first decline in fastener exports in the 1990s; fastener exports had grown at an average annual rate of 12.2 percent between 1992 and 1996. The decline in 1997 was due to a 40 percent drop in U.S. fastener exports to Mexico that resulted from a slowdown in automotive production in North America. Canada replaced Mexico as the largest export market in 1997 with fastener exports valued at $620 million, a 20 percent increase from 1996. Combined, Canada and Mexico accounted for over 70 percent of U.S. fastener exports in 1997. Fastener exports to a number of countries in Asia and South America registered large increases in 1997. Exports to Malaysia grew from $4.6 million to $23.4 million and exports to the Philippines expanded 10-fold, reaching $21.1 million. U.S. fastener exports to the members of the Association of Southeast Asian Nations (ASEAN) increased 58 percent to $83.4 million in 1997. Fastener exports to the MERCOSUR countries (Argentina, Brazil, Paraguay, and Uruguay) and the ANDEAN countries (Bolivia, Colombia, Ecuador, Peru, and Venezuela) increased 124 percent and 74 percent, respectively, that year.

U.S. imports of industrial fasteners increased 3.2 percent to $1.91 billion in 1997. Taiwan remained the largest supplier to the U.S. import market with a 39 percent share, followed by Japan and Canada with 22 percent and 15 percent, respectively. The fourth and fifth largest suppliers were Germany and China. Imports from China increased 20 percent (see Table 15-3).

Fastener Quality Act

The Fastener Quality Act, Public Law 101-592, is having a major influence on the U.S. industrial fastener industry. This law addresses the issue of mismarked, substandard, and counterfeit fasteners. It mandates certain testing and certification procedures to assure the quality of high-grade fasteners. The purpose of the act is to protect public safety, deter the introduction into commerce of nonconforming fasteners, and provide users with increased assurance that fasteners meet the stated specifications. The act has elements which will enhance traceability, accountability, and responsibility from the manufacturer's plant throughout distribution and finally to the end user. The act places responsibility on the firms that manufacture and sell fasteners to assure that those fasteners have been manufactured in accordance with applicable standards and specifications by having them tested in a laboratory accredited by the National Institute of Standards and Technology (NIST) or an organization approved by NIST. The assurance required is a written certification of conformance which manufacturers, importers, private label distributors, and any person who significantly alters fasteners must keep on file for 5 years. This assur-

ance also must be backed by an original test report in the custody of these individuals, which also must be kept for 5 years.

Coverage applies to any fastener used in a "critical application." Currently, all fasteners which meet the definition in section 3(5) of the act are covered. An estimated 25 to 55 percent of currently available fasteners meet this definition and are therefore subject to these requirements. Revised regulations implementing the act were issued in April 1998. In accordance with the revised regulations and under the provisions of the act itself, the Fastener Quality Act is scheduled to become effective on June 1, 1999.

Projections of Industry and Trade Growth

Growth in screw machine product shipments is expected to moderate to 2.5 percent in 1999 after a strong increase in 1998. Demand from most major machinery and equipment sectors is expected to level off. The expected weakening in machinery and equipment exports to Asia will somewhat dampen the demand for general components such as screw machine products and industrial fasteners. Strong demand from the telecommunications, computer, and aerospace industries is expected to continue in 1999; only modest growth in shipments to the automotive sector is anticipated in that year. An expected healthy residential construction industry should lead to increased demand for screw machine products from appliance manufacturers. Shipments of screw machine products are forecast to grow at an average annual rate of 3 to 4 percent for the period 1999–2003.

Growth in the industrial fastener industry is expected to slow to 3.0 percent in 1999. Continued strong demand for aircraft fasteners is likely to be a major factor in expanded shipments of fasteners. Modest growth in demand is expected from the motor vehicle sector, largely as a result of increased production of light

TABLE 15-3: U.S. Trade Patterns in Bolts, Nuts, Rivets, and Washers[1] in 1997

(millions of dollars; percent)

Exports			Imports		
Regions[2]	Value[3]	Share, %	Regions[2]	Value[3]	Share, %
NAFTA	942	70.7	NAFTA	295	15.5
Latin America	43	3.2	Latin America	5	0.3
Western Europe	166	12.5	Western Europe	276	14.5
Japan/Chinese Economic Area	58	4.3	Japan/Chinese Economic Area	1,233	64.6
Other Asia	95	7.1	Other Asia	86	4.5
Rest of world	29	2.2	Rest of world	11	0.6
World	1,333	100.0	World	1,907	100.0
Top Five Countries	Value	Share, %	Top Five Countries	Value	Share, %
Canada	620	46.5	Taiwan	751	39.4
Mexico	322	24.1	Japan	412	21.6
United Kingdom	85	6.4	Canada	279	14.6
Japan	37	2.8	Germany	90	4.7
Singapore	33	2.4	China	67	3.5

[1] SIC 3452.
[2] For definitions of regional groupings, see "Getting the Most Out of *Outlook '99*."
[3] Values may not sum to total due to rounding.
Source: U.S. Department of Commerce, Bureau of the Census.

and heavy trucks. Increased shipments to the farm machinery, construction machinery, and machine tool sectors are also forecast. For the 5-year period 1999–2003 fastener shipments are expected to grow at an average annual rate of 3 to 4 percent in constant dollars. The trend toward consolidation is expected to continue. In order to grow, U.S. companies will need to invest in product development and emphasize quality and service.

Fastener exports are projected to register strong increases in 1998 and 1999, approaching $1.7 billion in 1999. Most of the increased exports will be destined for Mexico and Canada, but exports to South America are also expected to expand. Demand from Asian markets is projected to be soft. Most exports will be to the automotive sector, with smaller quantities going to the aircraft and heavy equipment sectors.

Fastener imports are also expected to expand at a healthy rate in 1998 and 1999. Strong demand from the automotive sector and the construction industry should see U.S. imports of industrial fasteners grow to $2.27 billion in 1999. The standard fasteners that constitute the majority of fastener imports are very price-sensitive, and the recent devaluations of Asian currencies coupled with weak Asian economies could foster strong increases in U.S. fastener imports as Asian manufacturers look for new export markets. Imports from China are expected to register strong increases.

Global Market Prospects

The global demand for industrial fasteners will continue to grow as most industrialized and developing countries expand their manufacturing bases. The world automotive industry will remain the most important source of demand for industrial fasteners. The industrial fastener industry worldwide is expected to become even more competitive as developing countries expand their fastener industries and acquire the skilled work force and technology needed to produce higher-quality and more sophisticated fasteners. There will be a global trend toward consolidation as individual companies try to improve their competitiveness and expand into new markets.

VALVES AND PIPE FITTINGS

The valve and pipe fitting industry includes industrial valves (SIC 3491) and valves and pipe fittings not elsewhere classified (SIC 3494). It does not include plumbing fixture fittings, which are included in SIC 3432. Industrial valves comprise a wide range of valve types: gates, globes, angles, waterwork valves (IBBW, AWWA, and UL), ball, butterfly, plug, nuclear, automatic, and solenoid-operated. Valves and pipe fittings not elsewhere classified include plumbing and heating valves and metal fittings, flanges, and unions for piping systems.

Global Industry Trends

Demand for industrial valves and pipe fittings is growing with the expansion of the global economy. The world energy sector accounts for a large share of valve and pipe fitting demand. Large industrial and infrastructure projects are also major sources of demand. The world's largest economies—the European Union (EU), Japan, and the United States—have the largest valve and pipe fitting markets. Large oil-producing countries are also major consumers. The fastest growing demand comes from countries with expanding oil and gas sectors and countries with rapidly growing economies. Countries in South America and Asia with rapidly expanding economies are making heavy investments in their infrastructure and manufacturing sectors.

The increased competitiveness within the world valve and pipe fitting industry is leading to increased production in countries with lower production costs. To be competitive, many of the world's largest valve companies are establishing valve and pipe fitting plants in countries with low labor costs. Large valve manufacturers are also increasingly sourcing their valve parts in developing countries. Many castings and other valve parts are being made in developing countries and shipped to industrialized countries where the final production takes place. In addition to lower labor costs, the costs associated with complying with environmental, safety, and health regulations are considerably lower in developing countries. These countries have a comparative advantage in producing commodity or low-tech valves and pipe fittings. The industrialized countries' selling points are quality and service.

The industry is very globalized. The developing countries are present in low-tech commodity-type valves, while the industrialized countries dominate in more high-tech and highly engineered valves. Many large valve companies have plants around the world; this is less prevalent among pipe fitting manufacturers. There has been a trend toward consolidation in recent years. To expand and compete in a global marketplace, many valve and pipe fitting companies are merging or being acquired by other industrial companies. Merged companies can improve efficiency by sharing distribution systems and benefiting from other economies of scale. Standards are playing an increasingly important role in the valve and pipe fitting industries. The EU's efforts to establish standards for valves and pipe fittings is a major concern for U.S. manufacturers. Standards in other countries often become barriers to trade.

Domestic Trends

The U.S. valve and pipe fitting industries consist of about 648 establishments employing about 73,000 workers. Texas has the largest concentration of plants with 73 establishments making products covered in SIC 3491 (industrial valves) and 47 companies making products covered in SIC 3494 (valves and pipe fitting not elsewhere classified). Texas-based companies make a wide variety of valves and pipe fittings for the oil and gas sectors. Other states with concentrations of valve and pipe fitting manufacturers include California, Pennsylvania, Ohio, and Illinois.

The U.S. valve and pipe fitting industries consist of many different segments. Several large companies make a wide range of valve and pipe fitting products, but most companies in the industry can be characterized as small and medium-size manufacturers which focus on certain segments or market niches.

Some segments of the U.S. industry, such as cast iron valves and fittings, have been contracting, while others, such as automated valves, have expanded. To a large extent these market segments are competing with each other. Many companies are seeking to expand their product lines as a means of expanding sales and surviving in the long term. Acquisitions and mergers have been a popular means of expanding product lines. Many smaller valve and pipe fitting companies have limited financial resources as a result of declining profits and have merged or been acquired by larger companies.

The energy sectors are major consumers of valves and pipe fittings. Major energy sector industries that account for a significant share of total valve and pipe fitting consumption are petroleum production, oil and gas transmission, petroleum refining, gas distribution, and power generation and cogeneration, which together account for about 45 percent of total demand. Other major consumers are the chemical, pulp and paper, food processing, commercial construction, and water and sewer industries.

Imports are a major factor in the future of the U.S. industry. Manufacturers of commodity-type valves and pipe fittings are facing stiff competition from the newly industrializing countries and more recently from developing countries such as India and China. A large number of U.S. valve and pipe fitting companies have disappeared. Some sectors of the U.S. pipe fitting industry have only a few U.S. manufacturers left. Among the major factors contributing to these problems is the cost of complying with environmental and safety regulations that many foreign companies do not have to consider. Foundries in particular have a large cost associated with complying with pollution control standards. Many companies went out of business because the cost of complying with these regulations was too high.

In order to survive, U.S. valve and pipe fitting companies need to be diligent in continuously increasing their competitiveness by improving the manufacturing process and expanding product lines to meet the changing needs of their customers; companies that do not do this will find their market shares eroding. World demand for valves and pipe fittings will continue to grow, but the growth in different segments will vary greatly.

Advances in technology are leading to improvements in valve and pipe fitting products. U.S. valve and pipe fitting companies are working closely with customers to engineer products for specific applications. Exports offer U.S. companies excellent opportunities for increased sales as world demand for valves and pipe fittings will continue to grow at a faster rate than will U.S. demand. Exports already account for about 32 percent of U.S. production; the percentage is higher for valves than it is for pipe fittings and higher for large companies than for small manufacturers. Some large U.S. valve companies export more than 50 percent of their production.

Safety and environmental concerns will continue to play an important role in the future of U.S. valve and pipe fitting manufacturers. End users are developing closer working relationships with manufacturers to help resolve specific problems associated with piping systems. With the increased importance of valve reliability, end users are becoming more knowledgeable about valve technology. Greater emphasis is being placed on training and maintenance.

Product shipments of valve and pipe fittings registered a small increase in '92 dollars, estimated at 1 percent, for 1997 and a 2 percent increase in 1998. The growth in pipe fitting shipments was stronger than the growth in industrial valve shipments. Expansion in industrial and commercial construction was a major factor in the rise in value of pipe fitting shipments; domestic demand for industrial valves was very weak. Due to the dearth of big energy and industrial manufacturing projects in the United States, domestic valve demand is largely for replacement valves. Exports continue to be the growth sector for the U.S. valve and pipe fitting industries. Exports increased 12 percent in 1997 and a projected 10 percent in 1998. Strong import growth of 13 percent was registered in 1997, and imports were expected to increase 15 percent in 1998. The depreciation of many Asian currencies improved the price competitiveness of many valves of Asian manufacture.

Projected Trade and Industry Growth

Stronger domestic demand from domestic valve and pipe fitting end-user industries and continued high overseas demand for U.S.-made valves are expected to lead to a 2 percent expansion in valve and pipe fitting shipments in 1999. Healthy demand is expected from the U.S. construction industry in 1998, continuing into 1999. The construction sectors contributing to overall growth in valve and pipe fitting shipments are expected to be manufacturing facilities, office facilities, hospitals, and educational buildings. Demand from increased spending on public works also should benefit the industry, with strong demand from the sewer and water supply sectors. Demand from domestic energy sectors is expected to be weak with the exception of electric utilities.

Export growth of 12 percent was forecast for 1999, with valve and pipe fitting imports also expanding about 13 percent. During the 5-year period 1999–2003 industry shipments of valves and pipe fittings are expected to expand at an average annual rate of 2 to 3 percent, with expanding overseas demand being the major driving force.

The continued growth of this U.S. sector is highly dependent on U.S. valve and pipe fitting companies' maintaining their competitiveness. This will require investing in new technology, improving productivity, and developing new product lines. The strength of U.S. companies lies in customizing products to meet the needs of individual customers.

Global Market Prospects

World demand for valves and pipe fittings is expected to outgrow U.S. demand through the year 2003. Greatly expanded activity in world oil and gas exploration, production, and pipelines will be very important factors in a growing world valve and pipe fitting market. Large investments in infrastructure projects and manufacturing industries in the BEMs (Big Emerging Markets) and other developing countries also will foster large increases in demand for valves and pipe fittings.

U.S. exports of industrial valves and pipe fittings amounted to about $3.2 billion in 1998. Canada was the largest export market with a 37 percent share in 1997, followed by Mexico with 14 percent. The next four largest export markets were South Korea, the United Kingdom, Germany, and Japan, with shares of 3 to 5 percent. The major oil-producing countries, such as Saudi Arabia, Nigeria, Kuwait, and Indonesia, are large importers of U.S. valves and pipe fittings, but their demand fluctuates sharply year to year. The U.S. industry registered a 50 percent increase in exports to Latin American countries other than Mexico in 1997. Three BEMs with very good long-term market potential are India, China, and Brazil.

Imports accounted for approximately 34 percent of valve and pipe fitting consumption in 1997. Mexico was the largest supplier of valves and pipe fitting imports to the United States with a 20.8 percent share, followed by Japan and Canada with 13.4 and 10.8 percent, respectively (see Table 15-4). U.S. imports from several of the largest supplier countries registered significant increases in 1997 compared with 1996. Notable were imports from Mexico, which increased 54 percent to $759 million in 1997. Imports from China and the United Kingdom increased 24 percent and 18 percent, respectively. U.S. valve consumers are also importing increased quantities of valves from a number of other countries with relatively lower labor and production costs, such as Romania, Malaysia, Turkey, and Poland.

BALL AND ROLLER BEARINGS

The ball and roller bearing industry (SIC 3562) consists of establishments primarily engaged in manufacturing ball and roller bearings (including ball or roller bearing pillow block, flange, takeup cartridge, and hangar units) and parts. Major product sectors include miniature and precision instrument bearings, integral shaft and integral spindle ball bearings, thrust ball bearings, tapered roller bearings, and cylindrical, spherical, and needle bearings.

Global Industry Trends

The ball and roller bearing industry is very globalized. The largest bearing producers in the United States are also the largest world producers. Estimates put world ball and roller bearing production at approximately $25 billion. The largest bearing-producing countries are the United States, Japan, and Germany, which still constitute the three major bearing markets despite the rapid growth in demand in other Asian and European countries. The world industry is very price-competitive, particularly in commodity-type bearings. The technology for producing commodity-type bearings is readily available, and developing countries have an advantage in labor costs but a shortage of skilled workers. Developing countries are also plagued by infrastructure problems which create shortages and delays.

The largest bearing companies have plants throughout the world to better serve individual markets. In recent years these companies have been establishing operations in Asia to better serve emerging automotive manufacturing industries and heavy equipment and machinery operations being built in Asian countries. The large European and Japanese bearing companies have established significant production capacity in the United States through acquisitions and new plant construction. To improve competitiveness, the larger companies have modernized their existing plants.

Domestic Trends

The U.S. bearing industry consists of about 183 plants that make a wide variety of ball bearings, roller bearings, mounted

TABLE 15-4: U.S. Trade Patterns in Valves and Pipe Fittings[1] in 1997
(millions of dollars; percent)

Regions[2]	Exports Value[3]	Share, %	Regions[2]	Imports Value[3]	Share, %
NAFTA	1,639	50.6	NAFTA	1,151	31.5
Latin America	270	8.3	Latin America	43	1.2
Western Europe	524	16.2	Western Europe	1,264	34.6
Japan/Chinese Economic Area	230	7.1	Japan/Chinese Economic Area	886	24.3
Other Asia	336	10.4	Other Asia	218	6.0
Rest of world	241	7.4	Rest of world	88	2.4
World	3,239	100.0	World	3,650	100.0
Top Five Countries	**Value**	**Share, %**	**Top Five Countries**	**Value**	**Share, %**
Canada	1,192	36.8	Mexico	759	20.8
Mexico	447	13.8	Japan	487	13.4
South Korea	144	4.4	Canada	393	10.8
United Kingdom	137	4.2	Germany	333	9.1
Germany	105	3.3	Italy	271	7.4

[1] SIC 3491, 3494.
[2] For definitions of regional groupings, see "Getting the Most Out of *Outlook '99*."
[3] Values may not sum to total due to rounding.
Source: U.S. Department of Commerce, Bureau of the Census.

bearings, and bearing parts. There are two large U.S.-based bearing companies, the Timken Company and the Torrington Company, which were traditionally roller bearing manufacturers. Through acquisitions, both companies now own ball bearing operations as well. There are several large foreign-based companies that have large U.S. operations and manufacture a wide range of ball and roller bearing products. The products they do not manufacture in the United States they import from their other plants, primarily in Europe and Asia.

In recent years a number of acquisitions have contributed to a consolidation of the U.S. bearing industry, although there are still a number of small and medium-size producers that make specialty products or have market niches. In recent years bearing companies have refurbished many of their older plants, in addition to improving the capacity of older bearing plants, a number of new plants have been built. Many of the newer plants are being built in the south to take advantage of lower production costs. The states with the largest numbers of bearing plants are Connecticut, New York, Pennsylvania, South Carolina, and Ohio. The bearing industry employs about 37,000 people.

Dumping has been a problem faced by U.S. bearing companies. A number of foreign companies have been found guilty of dumping bearing products on the U.S. market. Dumping margins imposed on the guilty parties have been a contributing factor leading to a number of foreign bearing companies acquiring or building plants in the United States to supply their American customers. In recent years U.S. bearing plants have faced growing pressure from imports from China.

After a decline in 1996, product shipments for the bearing industry in constant dollars rebounded, expanding by an estimated 4 percent in 1997 and 2 percent in 1998. A strong domestic manufacturing sector has led to increased demand for bearings. In that period demand from most industrial machinery and equipment machinery manufacturers was particularly strong; bearing sales for light and heavy trucks also rose significantly. However, weakened demand resulting from lower automobile production levels partially offset strong sales to other end users. Shipments to the defense sector remain depressed. The motor vehicle industry consumes about 30 percent of U.S. bearing production. Other large consumers include the aircraft, railroad, construction machinery, mining equipment, machine tool, and farm machinery industries. The aftermarket plays a very important role in bearing sales, accounting for as much as 30 percent of total production.

Projections of Industry and Trade Growth

Bearing shipments are expected to remain at a high level. The value of U.S. shipments expressed in constant dollars is expected to register a slight increase of 1.0 percent in 1999. Strong demand is expected from manufacturers of aircraft and light and heavy trucks. Shipments to automobile manufacturers are expected to show little growth because of projected lower levels of production. Increased shipments are expected to manufacturers of farm machinery, construction machinery, and machine tools.

Bearing exports are expected to grow a projected 7.5 percent in 1999. Canada and Mexico will remain the largest export markets, but exports to other countries with significant automotive production also could register significant gains. However, the Asian financial crisis could adversely affect exports to Japan, South Korea, and Thailand.

Bearing imports are projected to increase 7 percent in 1999. Expanded production by Japanese and German automotive transplants are expected to contribute to increased import demand. The depreciation of Asian currencies could also lead to expanded imports. Imports from China are likely to continue to make inroads into the U.S. market.

Bearing shipments are expected to expand at an average annual rate of 2 to 3 percent over the next 5 years. Expanding export markets should be a major factor in this growth. The improved competitiveness of the U.S. bearing industry and a rebound in demand from the automotive sector should lead to increased demand from domestic consumers. Demand from most industrial machinery and equipment sectors is also expected to remain strong. The passage of the highway construction bill could result in strong demand from builders of construction machinery. The improved competitiveness of U.S. manufacturing companies should assure a healthy U.S. bearing industry. However, it behooves U.S. bearing companies to remain competitive by investing in research and product development. Achieving this will require even closer working relationships between bearing companies and end users. As machinery, equipment, and motor vehicles become more sophisticated, end users will demand new and improved bearing products.

The rate of growth of bearing exports is expected to exceed the growth in domestic demand during the period 1999–2003. Canada and Mexico will remain the most important markets. Outside the North American Free Trade Agreement (NAFTA) partners, exports to the EU will be the major source of expanded bearing exports in the next 5 years. However, the largest percentage growth will come from smaller markets in South America and Asia. U.S. bearing products must remain competitive in order for U.S. bearing companies to take full advantage of export markets. Dollar exchange rates will play an important role in the success of U.S. companies in expanding export markets. The continued growth of U.S. machinery and equipment exports also will be a major factor in the health of the U.S. bearing industry, as these products utilize large numbers of bearings.

Global Market Prospects

Imports account for about 24 percent of apparent consumption. U.S. bearing imports increased 5.3 percent in 1997 and are projected to increase 6.5 percent in 1998. Japan is still the largest supplier to the U.S. market, with a share of 34 percent, down from 40 percent in 1995. The next largest suppliers to the U.S. market are Canada, Germany, and China with market shares of 12 percent, 11 percent, and 9 percent, respectively. U.S. bearing imports grew at an average annual rate of 10 percent between

TABLE 15-5: U.S. Trade Patterns in Ball and Roller Bearings[1] in 1997
(millions of dollars; percent)

Exports			Imports		
Regions[2]	Value[3]	Share, %	Regions[2]	Value[3]	Share, %
NAFTA	572	57.4	NAFTA	219	15.0
Latin America	78	7.8	Latin America	19	1.3
Western Europe	177	17.8	Western Europe	380	26.0
Japan/Chinese Economic Area	51	5.1	Japan/Chinese Economic Area	665	45.5
Other Asia	65	6.5	Other Asia	128	8.8
Rest of world	53	5.4	Rest of world	50	3.4
World	996	100.0	World	1,462	100.0
Top Five Countries	Value	Share, %	Top Five Countries	Value	Share, %
Canada	449	45.1	Japan	499	34.1
Mexico	123	12.3	Canada	179	12.2
Germany	46	4.6	Germany	160	10.9
United Kingdom	42	4.3	China	134	9.2
Japan	36	3.6	United Kingdom	61	4.2

[1] SIC 3562.
[2] For definitions of regional groupings, see "Getting the Most Out of *Outlook '99.*"
[3] Values may not sum to total due to rounding.
Source: U.S. Department of Commerce, Bureau of the Census.

1992 and 1997. With the recent expansion of production capacity in the United States, more demand can be supplied by U.S. bearing plants. The move to just-in-time delivery by many U.S. manufacturers makes it easier to meet supply schedules with U.S.-made bearings.

U.S. bearing exports increased 9 percent in 1997 and are projected to grow 8 percent in 1998, reaching an estimated $1.08 billion. Canada remains the largest foreign market, accounting for 45 percent of U.S. bearing exports in 1997. Mexico is the second largest export market with a 12 percent share; bearing exports to Mexico registered a 67 percent increase in 1997 compared with 1996, reaching $123 million. Most of the bearings exported to Canada and Mexico are destined for the automotive market. The next largest export markets are Germany, the United Kingdom, Japan, France, and Brazil (see Table 15-5). Most of the largest U.S. manufacturers have plants in Europe from which they can supply European customers with bearings.

In the drive to remain price-competitive, bearing companies are building new plants in countries with lower production costs. Japanese bearing companies have already built a number of plants in other Asian countries. As demand in developing countries grows, bearing industries will develop in those countries. Recently the developing countries and eastern European countries have become important suppliers of low-cost commodity-type bearings.

Industrialized countries' comparative advantage lies in producing high-value bearings of superior quality and in the service these countries provide. In critical applications reliability is often more important than price. The value added by bearing companies is increasing as these companies become more integrated into the manufacturing process. As the world's largest bearing market with relatively easy access, the United States is targeted by countries with bearing production that exceeds domestic demand.

U.S. imports of commodity-type bearings from developing countries are expected to show sustained growth in the next 5 years.

Richard Reise, U.S. Department of Commerce, Office of Energy, Infrastructure, and Machinery, (202) 482-3489, September 1998.

■ REFERENCES

Annual Survey of Manufactures, 1996, M96(AS)-1 and M96(AS)-2, Bureau of the Census, U.S. Department of Commerce, Washington, DC 20233.

Valves and Pipe Fittings
Census of Manufactures, 1992, MC92-I-34F, Bureau of the Census, U.S. Department of Commerce, Washington, DC 20233.
Valve Magazine, Valve Manufacturers Association of America, 1050 17th Street, NW, Suite 280, Washington, DC 20036-5503.

Screw Machine Products and Industrial Fasteners
American Fastener Journal, published by Mike McGuire, 293 Hopewell Drive, Powell, OH 43065-9350. (614) 848-3232.
Census of Manufactures, 1992, MC92-I-34D, Bureau of the Census, U.S. Department of Commerce, Washington, DC 20233.
Fastener Industry News, edited by John Wolz, 2009 NE 16th Avenue, Portland, OR 97212-4430. (503) 335-0183.
Fastener Technology International, Initial Publications, Inc., 3869 Darrow Road, Suite 101, Stow, OH 44334. (330) 686-9544.

Ball and Roller Bearings
Census of Manufactures, 1992, MC92-I-34E, Bureau of the Census, U.S. Department of Commerce, Washington, DC 20233.

■ RELATED CHAPTERS

17: Metal Working Equipment
18: Production Machinery
36: Motor Vehicles
37: Automotive Parts

MICROELECTRONICS
Economic and Trade Trends

U.S. International Trade

($ billions)

Legend: Balance, Exports, Imports

Source: U.S. Department of Commerce: Bureau of the Census; International Trade Administration.

World Export Market Shares

(%)

Legend: United States, Japan, Singapore, South Korea

Source: United Nations; U.S. Department of Commerce, International Trade Administration.

Export Dependence and Import Penetration

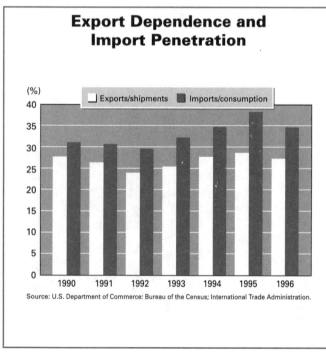

(%)

Legend: Exports/shipments, Imports/consumption

Source: U.S. Department of Commerce: Bureau of the Census; International Trade Administration.

Output and Output per Hour

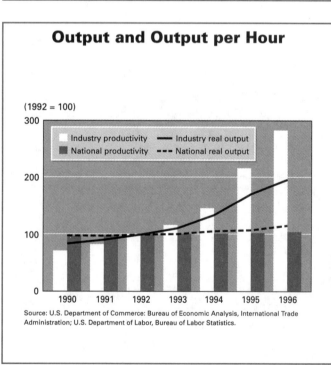

(1992 = 100)

Legend: Industry productivity, Industry real output, National productivity, National real output

Source: U.S. Department of Commerce: Bureau of Economic Analysis, International Trade Administration; U.S. Department of Labor, Bureau of Labor Statistics.

See "Getting the Most Out of *Outlook '99*" for definitions of terms.

Microelectronics

INDUSTRY DEFINITION This chapter covers electronic components and semiconductor manufacturing equipment (SME). The Standard Industrial Classification (SIC) system includes electronic components and accessories under SIC 367. Electronic components comprise electron tubes (SIC 3671); printed circuit boards (SIC 3672); semiconductors and related devices (SIC 3674); electronic capacitors (SIC 3675); electronic resistors (SIC 3676); electronic coils, transformers, and other inductors (SIC 3677); electronic connectors (SIC 3678); and electronic components not elsewhere classified (SIC 3679).

OVERVIEW

Global and Domestic Industry Trends

The microelectronics industry manufactures a vast array of products ranging from relatively simple electrical connectors that cost a few pennies, to thousand-dollar integrated circuits (ICs) that contain millions of transistors on a single chip, to complex machines for semiconductor manufacturing that cost several million dollars per unit. The great majority of these products are sold to manufacturing companies that are part of the global electronics industry.

Worldwide demand for microelectronic products stems from increasing use of computers, telecommunications equipment, instrumentation, medical devices, audio and video equipment, and other electronic products and systems. Demand for semiconductors, one of the most commonly used electronic components, drives the market for SME.

The range of products that contain microelectronics is growing, and the value of the electronic components in many products is increasing as well. The automobile industry illustrates these trends. Twenty years ago the value of electronic components in the average automobile was only 1 percent; today that figure ranges from 8 to 15 percent, depending on the make and model of a car. Highway departments in many states are adopting electronic methods to collect tolls, and so new electronic systems are being created. Analysts believe that the electronics content of an automobile could reach 25 percent in the next decade as electronic navigation systems and intelligent highway systems are implemented.

There is intense pressure for microelectronics manufacturers to be first to market with leading-edge products. By being the first, a supplier often can gain the high profit margins necessary to finance (1) research and development for the next generation of product and (2) the purchase of new equipment to manufacture that generation.

To meet fierce international competition for worldwide sales, U.S. microelectronics suppliers must sell to all major markets, both domestic and foreign. Profit margins on some products, such as dynamic random-access memory (DRAM) chips, are so slim that only through global sales can a supplier generate sufficient profits to remain in business. For other products, such as SME, the markets are so few and specialized that in order to survive, a supplier must pursue sales to all available customers worldwide.

Microelectronics companies compete globally for low-cost labor as well as sales. Many U.S.-based semiconductor manufacturers have moved their test and assembly operations to Asia to take advantage of the low wage rates. However, much of the design and fabrication work for microelectronic products is done in the United States, where a highly educated labor force and top-quality electrical engineers are available. In 1996 the U.S. electronic component industry employed 588,000 workers. Employment has remained relatively stable since 1989 despite growing industry sales, a sign of increased productivity.

The global microelectronics industry is already benefiting from implementation of the Information Technology Agreement (ITA), which will eliminate import duties on information technology products, including electronic components and SME, by

2000. Major information technology markets such as the European Union and South Korea have already cut tariffs as much as 50 percent. Efforts to expand the number of participants and the scope of goods covered by the ITA have been the subject of multilateral negotiations, with results expected in late 1999.

The Asian financial crisis will have a negative but not catastrophic effect on the prospects of U.S. electronic component makers as well as suppliers of electronics manufacturing equipment. Many industry analysts stated that sales of semiconductors, passive electronic components and connectors, and SME to that region would see little if any growth in 1998. The full effect of the Asian crisis on the microelectronics sector will not be known for some time. The primary concern has been that worldwide sales of electronic equipment will slow in 1998 because of lower economic growth in Asia. Some analysts predict that troubled Asian markets will experience lower demand for end-user products and reduced consumer spending and that Asian economies will increase exports to compensate.

In some ways the export factor could be good news for U.S.-based microelectronics manufacturers. Prices for parts and materials traditionally imported from Asia are likely to drop as a result of the weakening of Asian currencies. U.S.-based manufacturers that have plants in Asia may see some bottom-line gains since foreign overhead costs, such as wages and energy bills, are paid in newly devalued local currencies.

However, gains resulting from reduced production costs may erode somewhat as imports challenge U.S.-produced electronic components. Cheaper imports from Asia may particularly hurt U.S. microelectronics companies that compete directly with foreign manufacturers. For example, Micron Technology, an Idaho-based firm that manufactures memory chips in the United States, alleged that South Korean competitors unfairly dumped DRAM chips in the U.S. market in 1997 and 1998.

The U.S. printed circuit board industry has expressed concern over fallout from the Asian financial crisis. Dramatic downward pressure on prices is expected to affect printed circuit boards and related production equipment. U.S. board producers are likely to be most vulnerable in the domestic market, since the U.S. and North American market is the primary outlet for U.S. sales. These developments could present monumental problems for the U.S. industry, which already faces extreme price competition from major producers in Taiwan and China.

One of the most immediate effects of the Asian crisis was a drop in capital investment by Asia-based semiconductor companies which hurt sales by U.S. SME suppliers. Reduced consumer demand in Asia will also slow the growth of the global semiconductor market, causing reduced capital spending by some U.S.-based microelectronics firms as well.

A factor mitigating the effects of the Asian financial crisis on the U.S. electronic components industry is that the economies of China and Taiwan have thus far been relatively unaffected by their neighbors' woes. Both countries should continue to experience strong demand for computer equipment, electronic systems, and communications products, and U.S. sales there are expected to continue to grow over the next several years.

Industry and Trade Projections

In 1997 the U.S. electronic components industry (SIC 367) continued to grow strongly, although at a somewhat slower pace than it did in the boom years of 1994–1995. Electronic component product shipments were estimated at $138.5 billion in 1997, up 9 percent from the 1996 level of $127 billion (see Table 16-1). Shipments were forecast to reach $148.6 billion in 1998. The long-term outlook is favorable, with shipments by the U.S. electronic components industry expected to grow an average of 9 percent annually through 2003.

TABLE 16-1: Electronic Components and Accessories (SIC 367) Trends and Forecasts
(millions of dollars except as noted)

	1992	1993	1994	1995	1996	1997[1]	1998[2]	1999[3]	Percent Change 96–97	97–98	98–99	92–96[4]
Industry data												
Value of shipments[5]	73,642	81,236	97,131	120,129	127,996	136,457	143,747	154,162	6.6	5.3	7.2	14.8
Value of shipments (1992$)	73,642	81,129	97,838	126,734	144,213	158,932	171,703	188,448	10.2	8.0	9.8	18.3
Total employment (thousands)	530	531	551	584	588							2.6
Production workers (thousands)	317	321	340	364	368							3.8
Average hourly earnings ($)	10.83	10.98	11.14	11.41	11.70							2.0
Product data												
Value of shipments[5]	71,372	77,840	92,719	115,202	126,997	138,465	148,603	161,993	9.0	7.3	9.0	15.5
Value of shipments (1992$)	71,372	77,739	93,343	121,272	142,543	160,861	177,942	200,250	12.9	10.6	12.5	18.9
Trade data												
Value of imports	23,116	27,963	36,086	51,505	49,293	51,458	57,921	63,963	4.4	12.6	10.4	20.8
Value of exports	17,381	20,144	26,178	33,440	35,048	42,695	48,291	56,369	21.8	13.1	16.7	19.2

[1] Estimate except imports and exports.
[2] Estimate.
[3] Forecast.
[4] Compound annual rate.
[5] For definition of industry versus product values, see "Getting the Most Out of *Outlook '99*."
Source: U.S. Department of Commerce: Bureau of the Census; International Trade Administration

TABLE 16-2:   U.S. Trade Patterns in Microelectronics[1] in 1997

(millions of dollars; percent)

	Exports			Imports		
Regions[2]	Value[3]	Share, %	Regions[2]	Value[3]	Share, %
NAFTA	11,711	27.4	NAFTA	6,860	13.3
Latin America	1,422	3.3	Latin America	231	0.4
Western Europe	5,475	12.8	Western Europe	4,556	8.9
Japan/Chinese Economic Area	8,568	20.1	Japan/Chinese Economic Area	19,240	37.4
Other Asia	14,799	34.7	Other Asia	20,082	39.0
Rest of world	720	1.7	Rest of world	489	0.9
World	42,695	100.0	World	51,458	100.0
Top Five Countries	Value	Share, %	Top Five Countries	Value	Share, %
Mexico	7,211	16.9	Japan	10,974	21.3
Canada	4,500	10.5	South Korea	6,345	12.3
Malaysia	3,848	9.0	Malaysia	5,691	11.1
Japan	3,690	8.6	Taiwan	4,766	9.3
South Korea	3,213	7.5	Mexico	3,645	7.1

[1] SIC 367.
[2] For definitions of regional groupings, see "Getting the Most Out of *Outlook '99*."
[3] Values may not sum to total due to rounding.
Source: U.S. Department of Commerce, Bureau of the Census.

The U.S. electronic component industry exported roughly 31 percent of its total shipments in 1997. U.S. exports of electronic components totaled $42.7 billion in 1997 and were forecast to reach $48.3 billion by the end of 1998. Exports were expected to grow about 13 percent in 1998 (see Table 16-2). This slowdown in export growth compared to 1997 was due primarily to slower growth of demand in Asian markets hindered by the financial crisis. U.S. exports are forecast to grow 16.7 percent in 1999 as Asian markets recover stability.

U.S. imports of electronic components totaled $51.5 billion in 1997 and were expected to top $57.9 billion in 1998. This 12.6 percent increase was forecast in part because of reduced prices for Asian imports brought on by Asian currency devaluations. The growth of U.S. electronic component imports is forecast to slow to a 10.4 percent rate in 1999. The United States ran a trade deficit in electronic components of $8.8 billion in 1997, and the deficit was forecast to grow to $9.6 billion in 1998.

Robin Roark, U.S. Department of Commerce, Office of Microelectronics, Medical Equipment and Instrumentation, (202) 482-3090, November 1998.

SEMICONDUCTORS AND RELATED DEVICES

Semiconductors are active electronic components that produce and transfer electricity in electronic circuits. Semiconductor devices covered in this section include discrete semiconductors and integrated circuits classified under SIC 3674. Discrete semiconductors perform a single electronic function—acting as a diode or a transistor, for example—and several discrete semiconductors must be connected to form a working circuit.

Integrated circuits (ICs) incorporate thousands or millions of microscopic transistors and other functional components to form complex electronic circuits on the surface of a rigid substrate such as a "chip" of silicon; thus, they are sometimes called computer chips.

Global and Domestic Outlook

The U.S. semiconductor industry is made up of more than 140 firms that design, manufacture, and sell semiconductors. Most semiconductors are purchased by original equipment manufacturers for incorporation into electronic products and systems; a small proportion of ICs are purchased by individual end users, mostly for processor and memory chip upgrades in personal computers or electronic hobby applications.

Leading U.S. semiconductor companies include Intel, Motorola, Texas Instruments, IBM, AMD, National Semiconductor, Micron Technology, and Lucent Technologies, each of which is active in semiconductor design, manufacturing, and marketing. Many small and midsize U.S. semiconductor firms also manufacture chips, and dozens of companies design or market semiconductors that they do not manufacture. According to the U.S. Bureau of the Census, the U.S. semiconductor industry employed 190,000 persons in 1996.

Semiconductors control and amplify electronic signals in most electronic products and systems, including computers and other data processing equipment; consumer electronics; industrial machinery; telecommunications equipment; automobiles, aircraft, and other transportation systems; medical equipment and analytical instruments; and military and defense electronic systems. According to the Integrated Circuit Engineering Corporation (ICE), the computer industry was the largest end user of integrated circuits in 1996, when it accounted for 55 percent of worldwide IC sales. Consumer goods and communications products each accounted for about 15 percent of global demand for ICs in 1996. The communications segment has been one of the fastest growing semiconductor markets in recent years, with the telecommunications business outpacing the personal computer (PC) industry in some countries. The industrial equipment sector accounted for roughly 8 percent of IC sales in 1996, followed by the automotive industry with about 5 percent. The military market, which has shrunk during the 1990s, represented only about 1 percent of IC demand in 1996, according to ICE.

The U.S. semiconductor industry invests heavily in new equipment and facilities (capital expenditures) and research and development (R&D expenditures) to support growth. According to the Semiconductor Industry Association (SIA), the combined investment in capital expenditures and R&D by U.S. companies exceeded 30 percent of sales revenues in the period 1994–1996.

The mean rate of manufacturing capacity utilization of the U.S. semiconductor industry was 82.8 percent in 1996, down slightly from 86 percent in 1995, which was the highest recorded in over 15 years. In response to fast-growing demand for computer equipment in 1994 and 1995, semiconductor companies in the United States and abroad sought to expand their production capacity with major investments in plant and equipment. Much of this capacity became available in 1996 and 1997, just as the overheated market for PCs began to cool. In 1996 computer manufacturers began to sell off the semiconductor inventories they had accumulated during the hot PC market of 1994–1995. This inventory reduction resulted in oversupply and rapidly falling prices for DRAMs and other semiconductors.

Some chip makers reduced their capital expenditures by canceling or delaying new facilities in response to the falling prices in 1996. Other companies, especially in Asia, continued to build and plan new investments in 1997, hoping to gain market share when prices again rose. Unfortunately, average selling prices for semiconductors continued to fall throughout 1997 and into 1998. The continued glut of production capacity, combined with the Asian financial crisis (which dampened demand for semiconductors in the Asian region), is expected to keep semiconductor prices on a downward trend throughout 1998 and perhaps into 1999.

Industry and Trade Projections

Shipments by the U.S. semiconductor industry in 1997 rose an estimated 7.8 percent over 1996, reaching $76.9 billion in current dollars (see Table 16-3). The value of U.S. semiconductor industry shipments was forecast to reach $81.1 billion in 1998, an increase of 5.4 percent. The slower growth of semiconductor industry shipments in 1997 and 1998 compared with 1994 and 1995 was due primarily to continuing excess production capacity worldwide and a resultant decline in the average selling price for all semiconductors, which fell an estimated 15 percent in 1997 and was expected to drop an additional 6 percent in 1998.

The global semiconductor market grew in 1997 to $147 billion, up only 3.5 percent from the 1996 level, according to Dataquest. Worldwide semiconductor revenues are expected to fall by 5.9 percent in 1998 to $138 billion. In 1999 semiconductor sales are forecast to increase 11.8 percent, and revenues should reach $155 billion. The global semiconductor market is forecast to grow at a compound annual rate of roughly 11.5 percent per year through 2003, when the total market value should reach $283 billion.

Analysts expect global revenues for MOS memory chips (especially DRAMs and SRAMs) to experience a compound annual growth rate of nearly 16 percent over the next 5 years. Sales of analog ICs (such as amplifiers, data converters, and

TABLE 16-3: Semiconductors and Related Devices (SIC 3674) Trends and Forecasts
(millions of dollars except as noted)

| | 1992 | 1993 | 1994 | 1995 | 1996 | 1997[1] | 1998[2] | 1999[3] | Percent Change | | | |
									96–97	97–98	98–99	92–96[4]
Industry data												
Value of shipments[5]	32,191	35,152	47,265	65,922	71,413	76,983	81,140	86,414	7.8	5.4	6.5	22.0
Value of shipments (1992$)	32,191	35,222	47,790	71,810	85,833	96,562	105,156	115,882	12.5	8.9	10.2	27.8
Total employment (thousands)	172	163	183	192	190							2.5
Production workers (thousands)	84.8	82.2	92.9	98.1	96.2							3.2
Average hourly earnings ($)	13.55	14.08	14.46	14.89	15.29							3.1
Product data												
Value of shipments[5]	29,391	33,689	44,064	60,330	67,070	72,436	76,420	81,693	8.0	5.5	6.9	22.9
Value of shipments (1992$)	29,391	33,757	44,554	65,719	80,613	91,173	100,108	111,821	13.1	9.8	11.7	28.7
Trade data												
Value of imports	15,275	19,244	25,670	38,618	36,256	36,266	39,841	42,220	0.0	9.9	6.0	24.1
Value of exports	11,465	13,744	17,991	23,189	24,001	28,861	31,401	35,312	20.2	8.8	12.5	20.3

[1] Estimate except imports and exports.
[2] Estimate.
[3] Forecast.
[4] Compound annual rate.
[5] For definition of industry versus product values, see "Getting the Most Out of *Outlook '99*."
Source: U.S. Department of Commerce: Bureau of the Census; International Trade Administration.

voltage regulators) are forecast to achieve a CAGR of about 13 percent. Revenues for both the MOS microcomponent (led by digital signal processors) and MOS digital logic (led by ASICs) categories are expected to have CAGRs of roughly 10 percent during the same period. Worldwide revenues for discrete semiconductors are forecast to grow by nearly 8 percent over the next 5 years.

The fastest growing end-use markets for semiconductors in the long term will be computers (including multimedia PCs, laptops, and hand-held computers), communications equipment (especially wireless mobile equipment and wired network and public switching equipment), and digital consumer electronics products such as video CD players, digital television and set-top boxes, digital cameras and camcorders, digital VCRs, and arcade and home video games.

Global Market Prospects

U.S. semiconductor companies are major players in the global electronics industry, and roughly half of U.S. semiconductor industry revenues are derived from foreign sales. Foreign sales by U.S. semiconductor companies include direct exports from the United States and non-U.S. sales of semiconductors manufactured in U.S.-owned facilities overseas. In 1997 direct exports of semiconductors from the United States were valued at $28.9 billion, up 20.3 percent from 1996. This amount accounts for just under 40 percent of the $72.3 billion in global semiconductor sales recorded by U.S. companies in 1997, according to Dataquest.

The largest markets for U.S. semiconductor exports in 1997 were Malaysia, the Philippines, South Korea, Canada, Mexico, Singapore, Japan, Taiwan, Hong Kong, and Thailand (see Table 16-4). Of these, only Canada and Japan stand out as countries with large domestic electronics markets, followed to a lesser extent by South Korea, Mexico, and Taiwan. The majority of U.S.

semiconductor exports to the other countries listed are unfinished parts that receive further processing (mostly assembly and testing) and are reexported to the United States and third countries. The fastest growing major markets for U.S. semiconductor exports in 1997 were the Netherlands (up 70.4 percent from 1996), South Korea (up 51.3 percent), the Philippines (up 48.6 percent), Thailand (up 39.7 percent), Taiwan (up 27.7 percent), Mexico (up 27.6 percent), China (up 27 percent), France (up 25.1 percent), Hong Kong (up 24.7 percent), and Malaysia (up 18.6 percent).

On a regional basis, analysts forecast semiconductor revenue in North and South America to increase by 13 percent in 1999. The Asia/Pacific region will rank second to the Americas in terms of market size, although it is expected to grow at a slightly higher rate—nearly 15 percent in 1999. The European region is forecast to be the third largest regional market in 1999, growing about 12 percent over the previous year. The Japanese semiconductor market is forecast to grow by only 6 percent in 1999 and will be surpassed in size by the European market.

Dataquest estimated the U.S. semiconductor industry's share of the total world market at 49.2 percent in 1997, up from 45.1 percent in 1996. Among the major competitors, the Japanese share of the global market fell to 32.5 percent in 1997, while European companies' market share grew to 10.1 percent and non-Japanese firms headquartered in the Asia/Pacific region (primarily those in South Korea and Taiwan) held an 8.3 percent share, according to Dataquest estimates.

Access to the Japanese market has been a continuing concern for the U.S. semiconductor industry since the 1980s. With the help of successive U.S.-Japan Semiconductor Arrangements negotiated in 1991 and 1996, the foreign share of the Japanese semiconductor market, as calculated under the agreement, slowly increased, reaching 16.7 percent in 1992, 19.4 percent in 1993, 22.4 percent in 1994, 25.4 percent in 1995, 27.5 percent in 1996, and 33.3 percent in 1997.

TABLE 16-4: U.S. Trade Patterns in Semiconductors and Related Devices[1] in 1997
(millions of dollars; percent)

Exports			Imports		
Regions[2]	Value[3]	Share, %	Regions[2]	Value[3]	Share, %
NAFTA	5,366	18.6	NAFTA	3,145	8.7
Latin America	291	1.0	Latin America	10	0.0
Western Europe	3,198	11.1	Western Europe	2,572	7.1
Japan/Chinese Economic Area	6,375	22.1	Japan/Chinese Economic Area	12,219	33.7
Other Asia	13,393	46.4	Other Asia	18,155	50.1
Rest of world	238	0.8	Rest of world	165	0.5
World	28,861	100.0	World	36,266	100.0
Top Five Countries	Value	Share, %	Top Five Countries	Value	Share, %
Malaysia	3,679	12.7	Japan	7,542	20.8
Philippines	3,036	10.5	South Korea	5,943	16.4
South Korea	2,821	9.8	Malaysia	5,213	14.4
Canada	2,742	9.5	Philippines	3,310	9.1
Mexico	2,624	9.1	Taiwan	3,101	8.6

[1] SIC 3674.
[2] For definitions of regional groupings, see "Getting the Most Out of *Outlook '99*."
[3] Values may not sum to total due to rounding.
Source: U.S. Department of Commerce, Bureau of the Census.

The 1991 accord was succeeded by two bilateral agreements, one for industry and one for government, both signed on August 2, 1996, in Vancouver, Canada. The agreements emphasize cooperation between the industries and reduce the amount of government oversight. The industry agreement created a World Semiconductor Council to address market access issues and promote cooperative industry activities. The council is open to industry associations from major semiconductor-producing countries that have eliminated or made a commitment to eliminate tariffs on semiconductors. The governmental agreement created the Global Governmental Forum, in which major semiconductor-producing countries discuss global issues such as tariffs, taxation, and environmental rules. The governmental agreement also provides for continued consultations between the U.S. and Japanese governments to review progress on cooperative activities between their industry associations and review recommendations made by the World Semiconductor Council.

Robin Roark, U.S. Department of Commerce, Office of Microelectronics, Medical Equipment and Instrumentation, (202) 482-3090, November 1998.

PASSIVE COMPONENTS AND ELECTRON TUBES

Passive components cover a wide range of products. The major categories are capacitors (SIC 3675), resistors (SIC 3676), coils and transformers (SIC 3677), connectors (SIC 3678), and other related devices (SIC 3679), including but not limited to switches, relays, and piezoelectric devices. Electron tubes (SIC 3671) includes but is not limited to television picture tubes (color and black and white); diode, triode, and tetrode tubes; and magnetrons and other microwave tubes.

Global and Domestic Outlook

Globally, U.S. firms continue to capture substantial shares of foreign markets for the passive components and electron tubes industries. Considering the growth of the multimedia era and the sales of the computer, communications, and automotive sectors, the demand for all types of passive components and electron tubes is forecast to increase steadily over 1998–2002. Sales of cathode-ray tubes (CRTs) 27 inches and above are expected to grow strongly to meet consumer demand for "home theater" TV systems. U.S. manufacturers of passive components have established a stellar reputation in the international arena and as a result are in a position to increase their exports worldwide (see Tables 16-5 and 16-6).

In the capacitor sector, Mexico remains the largest export market for the United States, receiving 61 percent of American exports in 1997. Canada was the second largest export market for U.S. capacitors, taking 7 percent of exports. Singapore maintained the third place by importing 6 percent of U.S. capacitor exports. The European Union received 11 percent of U.S. capacitor exports, with Germany and the United Kingdom having the largest shares. Japan remains the primary international competitor for the U.S. capacitor industry. U.S. capacitor exports to Japan totaled only 3 percent, while Japan remained the top exporter to the United States, capturing 39 percent of the import market in 1997.

U.S. manufacturers enjoyed a 20 percent increase in resistor exports in 1997. Mexico remained the top export market, taking 36 percent of U.S. exports. Canada and Japan each took 10 percent, while the United Kingdom and Taiwan received 5 percent each. Japan continues to be the major international competitor for the United States, capturing 38 percent of the U.S. resistor import market in 1997.

TABLE 16-5:   Passive Components (SIC 3675, 3676, 3677, 3678, 3679) Trends and Forecasts
(millions of dollars except as noted)

	1992	1993	1994	1995	1996	1997[1]	1998[2]	1999[3]	Percent Change 96–97	97–98	98–99	92–96[4]
Industry data												
Value of shipments[5]	30,986	35,656	38,302	41,209	42,102	43,449	45,317	48,353	3.2	4.3	6.7	8.0
Value of shipments (1992$)	30,986	35,270	38,119	41,565	43,612	46,054	48,955	52,871	5.6	6.3	8.0	8.9
Total employment (thousands)	260	275	271	290	287							2.5
Production workers (thousands)	165	173	177	190	190							3.6
Average hourly earnings ($)	9.45	9.48	9.53	9.86	10.16							1.8
Capital expenditures	983	1,314	1,248	1,436	1,587							12.7
Product data												
Value of shipments[5]	32,330	33,892	37,540	42,435	46,800	51,480	56,628	62,857	10.0	10.0	11.0	9.7
Value of shipments (1992$)	32,330	33,523	37,350	42,805	48,584	54,900	62,037	70,722	13.0	13.0	14.0	10.7
Trade data												
Value of imports	5,671	6,440	7,730	9,658	9,949	11,997	14,636	18,002	20.6	22.0	23.0	15.1
Value of exports	4,053	4,498	5,578	7,060	7,633	9,568	12,056	15,432	25.4	26.0	28.0	17.1

[1] Estimate except imports and exports.
[2] Estimate.
[3] Forecast.
[4] Compound annual rate.
[5] For definition of industry versus product values, see "Getting the Most Out of *Outlook '99*."
Source: U.S. Department of Commerce: Bureau of the Census; International Trade Administration.

TABLE 16-6:   Electron Tubes (SIC 3671) Trends and Forecasts

(millions of dollars except as noted)

	1992	1993	1994	1995	1996	1997[1]	1998[2]	1999[3]	Percent Change 96–97	Percent Change 97–98	Percent Change 98–99	Percent Change 92–96[4]
Industry data												
Value of shipments[5]	3,145	3,052	3,148	3,500	3,779	4,039	4,225	4,501	6.9	4.6	6.5	4.7
Value of shipments (1992$)	3,145	3,085	3,126	3,434	3,701	3,921	4,082	4,294	5.9	4.1	5.2	4.2
Total employment (thousands)	22.2	20.2	20.4	21.6	23.3							1.2
Production workers (thousands)	16.8	15.3	15.8	16.6	17.9							1.6
Average hourly earnings ($)	13.21	13.73	13.25	13.10	12.95							−0.5
Capital expenditures	61.7	85.5	132	142	181							30.9
Product data												
Value of shipments[5]	3,357	3,330	3,561	3,894	4,178	4,436	4,633	4,883	6.2	4.4	5.4	5.6
Value of shipments (1992$)	3,357	3,367	3,536	3,822	4,092	4,331	4,503	4,719	5.8	4.0	4.8	5.1
Trade data												
Value of imports	928	990	1,218	1,390	1,239	1,123	1,042	1,027	−9.4	−7.2	−1.4	7.5
Value of exports	771	929	1,232	1,541	1,720	2,258	2,586	2,973	31.3	14.5	15.0	22.2

[1] Estimate except imports and exports.
[2] Estimate.
[3] Forecast.
[4] Compound annual rate.
[5] For definition of industry versus product values, see "Getting the Most Out of *Outlook '99*."
Source: U.S. Department of Commerce: Bureau of the Census; International Trade Administration.

With the United States' 35 percent increase in total exports of connectors over 1996, its top foreign markets included Mexico, which took 28 percent of American exports, Canada (17 percent), and the United Kingdom (8 percent). Mexico was also the largest exporter to the United States in 1997, capturing 27 percent of the U.S. connector market. Japan was the second largest source of U.S. imports at 19 percent, while the United States passed only 7 percent of its total exports to the Japanese market in 1997.

Mexico was by far the most important foreign market for U.S. electron tubes in 1997, receiving 60 percent of U.S. exports.

Japan continues to be the major competitor for the U.S. electron tube market, capturing 39 percent of U.S. imports in 1997.

Industry and Trade Projections

The outlook for the passive components and electron tubes industries is very positive, particularly with the expected growth of the information technology era and the continued emergence of new international markets. Shipments of passive components by U.S. industry were expected to total $43.4 billion in 1997, up a modest 3.2 percent from 1996. Passive com-

TABLE 16-7:   U.S. Trade Patterns in Passive Components[1] in 1997

(millions of dollars, percent)

Exports Regions[2]	Value[3]	Share, %	Imports Regions[2]	Value[3]	Share, %
NAFTA	3,744	39.1	NAFTA	2,970	24.8
Latin America	889	9.3	Latin America	199	1.7
Western Europe	1,725	18.0	Western Europe	1,565	13.0
Japan/Chinese Economic Area	1,811	18.9	Japan/Chinese Economic Area	5,449	45.4
Other Asia	972	10.2	Other Asia	1,506	12.5
Rest of world	426	4.5	Rest of world	309	2.6
World	9,568	100.0	World	11,997	100.0
Top Five Countries	**Value**	**Share, %**	**Top Five Countries**	**Value**	**Share, %**
Mexico	2,620	27.4	Japan	2,740	22.8
Canada	1,124	11.7	Mexico	2,399	20.0
Japan	1,061	11.1	China	1,398	11.7
United Kingdom	581	6.1	Taiwan	1,047	8.7
Brazil	470	4.9	Canada	571	4.8

[1] SIC 3675, 3676, 3677, 3678, 3679.
[2] For definitions of regional groupings, see "Getting the Most Out of *Outlook '99*."
[3] Values may not sum to total due to rounding.
Source: U.S. Department of Commerce, Bureau of the Census.

Exports			Imports		
Regions[2]	Value[3]	Share, %	Regions[2]	Value[3]	Share, %
NAFTA	1,404	62.1	NAFTA	316	28.1
Latin America	218	9.7	Latin America	12	1.1
Western Europe	175	7.8	Western Europe	254	22.6
Japan/Chinese Economic Area	226	10.0	Japan/Chinese Economic Area	480	42.8
Other Asia	209	9.3	Other Asia	57	5.1
Rest of world	26	1.2	Rest of world	4	0.3
World	2,258	100.0	World	1,123	100.0
Top Five Countries	Value	Share, %	Top Five Countries	Value	Share, %
Mexico	1,349	59.7	Japan	434	38.6
Brazil	180	8.0	Mexico	297	26.4
Japan	103	4.6	Germany	72	6.4
South Korea	90	4.0	France	67	6.0
Hong Kong (PRC)	86	3.8	Italy	58	5.2

[1] SIC 3671.
[2] For definitions of regional groupings, see "Getting the Most Out of *Outlook '99*."
[3] Values may not sum to total due to rounding.
Source: U.S. Department of Commerce, Bureau of the Census.

ponent shipments were forecast to grow 4.3 percent in 1998 and 6.7 percent in 1999 to reach a value of $48.3 billion.

U.S. industry shipments of electron tubes increased an estimated 6.9 percent in 1997. Shipments were forecast to slow somewhat in 1998, growing 4.6 percent, but should then rebound to reach a value of $4.5 billion in 1999, up 6.5 percent from 1998.

Exports of passive components and electron tubes should continue to grow strongly during the forecast period as new markets abroad develop. Growing markets for U.S. exports include Sweden, Argentina, the Czech Republic, Venezuela, and Ireland. For example, the information technology sector in the Czech Republic is the most rapidly growing market as a result of great demand. U.S. firms have captured 30 to 40 percent of this market, and their share is expected to increase (see Tables 16-7 and 16-8).

Electronics is the largest manufacturing industry in Ireland. There are substantial market opportunities there for U.S. electronic component manufacturers. The most promising sectors are resistors and capacitors. U.S. firms have captured 39 percent of the electronic components market in Ireland. In Sweden the connector industry is the most promising part of the passive components subsector. The United States is the leading supplier of sophisticated components to Sweden, capturing 15 percent of that market.

Marlene Ruffin, U.S. Department of Commerce, Office of Microelectronics, Medical Equipment and Instrumentation, (202) 482-2470, October 1998.

SEMICONDUCTOR MANUFACTURING EQUIPMENT

Semiconductor manufacturing equipment includes that used to fabricate, assemble, and test semiconductors. The SIC system does not currently define SME as a separate industry. The products are classified under such diverse industries as photographic equipment and supplies (SIC 3861); coating, engraving, and allied services (SIC 347); and special industrial equipment (SIC 3559).

Global and Domestic Outlook

SME is one of the fastest growing major industries in the U.S. economy, achieving a compound annual rate of nearly 20 percent since 1992. SME is a highly cyclical industry that is both global and capital-intensive in orientation.

The health of the SME industry is tied closely to trends in the semiconductor industry. Capital spending decisions made by semiconductor producers determine orders to the SME industry. Semiconductor producers buy SME to expand their manufacturing capacity in response to demand for products or to upgrade their production capacity for the manufacturing of more sophisticated products. The semiconductor industry's profitability affects the timing of its capital spending decisions. A collapse in the prices of semiconductor devices generally hurts the profitability of semiconductor manufacturers, which in turn may curtail spending on SME for the next generation of semiconductor devices. Conversely, rising prices encourage the expansion of semiconductor production capacity for both existing and next-generation devices.

The SME industry is highly cyclical, expanding and contracting in tandem with, but more dramatically than, revenue growth in the semiconductor industry. In 1992, at the end of the semiconductor industry recession of 1990–1991, the SME industry contracted 5 percent. During the banner expansion of the semiconductor industry in 1995, the global SME industry grew 65 percent, its best performance in nearly two decades.

In recent years the SME industry has become progressively more global. Today SME firms in the United States, Japan, and

Europe—the major suppliers of SME on the world market—earn on average less than half their revenues from their home markets. In recent years, as semiconductor firms have made more offshore investments and entered into more joint ventures, SME firms have had to follow their customers to new markets. In addition, SME suppliers have started serving an emerging market: foreign semiconductor foundries and contract manufacturing plants.

In the 1990s, as soaring development costs have presented significant barriers to market entry, the SME industry has become increasingly concentrated. Equipment prices have increased an average of 15 percent annually as the technology used to make semiconductors has become more sophisticated. According to some analysts, a steadily decreasing number of companies supply the SME market despite its dramatic growth. The world's 10 largest SME companies supply about 60 percent of the global market, and the top 20 firms supply nearly 80 percent. This trend toward concentration probably will continue as large firms benefit from increasing economies of scale and as mergers and acquisitions within the SME industry become more common.

The long-term prospects for the SME industry are good. As a result of continued growth in both the computer and telecommunications sectors, semiconductor manufacturers will need to add manufacturing capacity to meet growing demand for new generations of the semiconductor devices used by those industries. Many analysts believe that the semiconductor industry will have to construct up to 300 new plants worldwide over the next 5 years to produce the number of semiconductor devices that will be needed by the computer, telecommunications, and other electronic industries. Each of these plants costs in excess of $1 billion, with up to 70 percent of that cost associated with purchases of SME.

Over the next 5 years the SME industry will undergo a major product transition, moving from equipment based on a 200-mm (approximately 8-inch) standard for processing semiconductor wafers to a 300-mm (approximately 12-inch) standard. The transition to the 300-mm standard will increase the productivity of semiconductor manufacturing considerably. However, the up-front costs associated with developing new equipment compliant with the 300-mm standard are substantial: as much as $13 billion. The SME industry is concerned with how to fund these costs and with how quickly semiconductor producers will adopt the new, more expensive generation. Rapid and widespread adoption of 300-mm equipment would invigorate growth, but adoption schedules have been slower than was first expected. The SME industry is concerned that semiconductor producers will hesitate to buy 300-mm SME either because SME vendors have not developed all the equipment needed to implement the standard fully or because semiconductor producers believe that early models of the new generation of equipment are not yet cost-competitive with models of the more established 200-mm generation.

To respond to cyclical market fluctuations while maintaining long-term competitiveness, U.S. SME firms must manage their financial and personnel resources with a high degree of flexibility. In periods of a cyclical downturn, U.S. SME firms often focus on cash flow. Firms on average spend about 15 percent of revenues on R&D. Firms that reduce their absolute level of R&D spending during a downturn can hurt their future competitiveness. During high-growth periods, U.S. firms closely watch their order backlogs to ensure that customers do not defect to rival suppliers that can deliver products more quickly. The availability of qualified engineering and manufacturing personnel became a concern during the boom cycle of the mid-1990s, when the U.S. SME industry increased production so rapidly that firms had trouble filling design and factory positions.

Industry and Trade Projections

The global SME market in 1998 was an estimated $24 billion, a 10 percent decrease compared to 1997. The United States is the largest market for SME, accounting for roughly $8 billion. Japan's market is valued at $5 billion, while Taiwan, the European Union, and South Korea have markets valued between $2 billion and $3 billion each.

In recent years the U.S. SME market growth has closely corresponded to the expansion of the world market, providing evidence of both the developing globalization of the U.S. semiconductor industry and the increased presence in the United States of foreign capital–affiliated semiconductor firms. In 1999 analysts forecast modest growth in the U.S. market of 6 percent to nearly $8.5 billion, while the worldwide market will grow 4 percent to $25 billion. The 5-year outlook is more favorable, with analysts forecasting a compound annual growth rate of 15 percent for the United States and 13 percent worldwide. By 2003, the value of the U.S. SME market will double to $16 billion and the world market will grow to $44 billion.

Historically, the wafer fabrication equipment segment has grown faster than have the assembly and test segments, and this trend probably will continue in the foreseeable future. Wafer fabrication equipment currently accounts for 65 percent of the value of the SME market and probably will account for 70 percent by 2003. Semiconductor producers are demanding greater functionality from wafer fabrication equipment, and this has spurred strong growth in this segment. The test and assembly equipment segments will experience slightly slower rates of growth, and their shares of the total SME market will decline to an estimated 22 percent and 8 percent, respectively, by 2003.

Japan is the United States' chief competitor in SME. Currently, U.S. SME firms hold 48 percent of the world market, while Japanese firms have 44 percent (European firms account for the remaining 8 percent). Analysts expect no major shifts in market shares over the next 5 years.

The United States is a net exporter of SME. In 1997 the United States exported an estimated $6.5 billion of SME, compared with imports of $2.7 billion.

Although U.S. firms currently supply nearly 70 percent of the U.S. SME market, imports are growing rapidly. Analysts expect U.S. imports to grow at a compound annual rate of 20 percent through 2003. This high growth reflects in part the increased manufacturing presence, through greenfield investments and joint ventures, of foreign semiconductor producers in the United States. In these new plants, foreign semiconductor producers frequently transfer manufacturing technology and utilize in U.S.

plants the same foreign-made SME they use in their home markets. The major sources of SME imports into the United States, in order of importance, are Japan, the Netherlands, and Germany. By 2003, foreign firms may supply 40 percent of the U.S. market, most of which will be in the form of imports.

Even though U.S. firms face increased competition at home, the U.S. SME industry now earns the majority of its revenues from exports, and the export outlook is bright. Analysts expect U.S. exports to grow at a compound annual rate of 18 percent through 2003, better than the 13 percent global rate of growth projected during that period. U.S. exporters are strong in several markets that are expected to experience above-average growth.

In 1997 the top five markets for U.S. SME exports, in descending order, were Taiwan, Japan, Korea, Singapore, and France. As these rankings show, Asia is the dominant market for U.S. exporters.

Japan is the largest SME market after the United States. However, the U.S. share of the Japanese SME market is only 20 percent, and Japan's importance to U.S. exporters has been declining in recent years. Although Japan has historically been the largest export market for U.S. firms, its top position has been eclipsed by faster growing markets that are more receptive to U.S. equipment. In 1995 South Korea briefly emerged as the top export market, and in 1997 Taiwan held that position. Analysts expect the Japanese SME market to grow more slowly than the world average. Japanese semiconductor firms have been severely affected by that country's financial crisis and declining profit margins from commodity semiconductors such as DRAMs. Both factors have resulted in cutbacks and delays in Japanese capital investment. Analysts expect Japanese SME market growth to be only half the world average over the next 5 years.

Taiwan is now the top market for U.S. exporters and is the second largest Asian market for SME after Japan. In 1997 Taiwan bought over $1.5 billion of SME from the United States, an amount more than 10 times greater than its purchases just 4 years earlier. Taiwan now has over a dozen semiconductor firms that have ambitious plans to build new semiconductor plants and expand existing ones. Significantly, Taiwan has not been as affected by the Asian financial crisis as have Japan and Korea. Taiwan's chief constraint is the availability of engineering talent. Taiwan is expected to continue to grow faster than the world average over the next 5 years, although its recent explosive growth will be difficult to sustain.

South Korean semiconductor manufacturers built numerous new plants to make DRAMs in the first half of the 1990s, during which time the South Korean SME market experienced explosive growth at a compound annual rate of 50 percent. After peaking in 1996, the South Korean SME market cooled off. South Korean semiconductor producers have had to contend with falling profits from DRAMs, a credit crunch, and a sharply devalued currency. In 1998 the dollar value of South Korean purchases of SME were one-third to one-half lower than those in 1997. South Korean semiconductor producers will of necessity resume purchases of SME to maintain competitiveness, but the South Korean market will not grow as fast as will other Asia/Pacific markets.

Other Asian markets will grow faster than the world average. After Taiwan, Singapore has seen the most solid market growth in the Asia/Pacific region and has surpassed many European nations in market size. Malaysia is a major market for assembly and test equipment, and it still hopes to construct wafer fabrication plants despite its credit difficulties. China is planning to build competitive wafer fabrication capability during the next 5 years, and this may present opportunities for U.S. exporters.

Analysts expect the European Union to experience average growth through 2003. While Germany and France will remain dominant markets, other EU countries, notably the United Kingdom, Italy, the Netherlands, and Ireland, will gain in importance.

Michael Andrews, U.S. Department of Commerce, Office of Microelectronics, Medical Equipment and Instrumentation, (202) 482-2795, October 1998.

PRINTED CIRCUIT BOARDS

Printed circuit boards (PCBs) are at the core of electronic interconnection technology. The interconnection food chain is composed of manufacturers of bare circuit boards, suppliers of PCB manufacturing equipment, and producers of the electronic materials and chemicals used in PCB fabrication. Beyond board manufacturing, there are companies involved in assembling the components on a board and integrating them into final electronic products. When PCBs have other electronic components assembled on them, they are called printed circuit assemblies or "stuffed boards." These interconnected assemblies make up all electronic products. Thus, printed circuit boards and circuit assemblies are at the core of the interconnection sector and the overall electronics industry.

Global and Domestic Industry Trends

The ever-continuing demand for faster, smaller, more functional electronic products drives technological evolution in electronics manufacturing. Product innovations in the PCB industry are driven primarily by developments in the semiconductor industry. As semiconductors change, so must the boards to which they are interconnected so that the final products can run. It has been said that if semiconductors are the brains of electronic devices, PCBs are the nervous system. The stakes are high for PCB companies, since electronic end products are dependent on adequate interconnection solutions; the companies must keep pace with trends in technology.

The PCB industry continues to rise to the technological challenges by providing innovative technical solutions which create continuous improvement in the production processes. For instance, there is a movement under way among many U.S. PCB shops to replace the process that relies on chemically deposited copper baths. The newer alternative process referred to as direct metallization offers performance enhancements and is environmentally more friendly, among other advantages. Advanced production technologies, such as laser drilling and etching of microbore holes in plasma, have yielded considerably smaller hole diameters, blind holes, and buried drill holes or "vias." Through 2000 the trend toward high-density substrates which incorporate microvia technology will be used to achieve smaller holes on PCBs and thus maximize the utilization of space on circuit boards. Efficient use of PCB "real estate" is the key to integrating new functionality and miniaturization into electronic end products.

Overall, U.S. competitiveness in the technology industries for both existing products and emerging technologies will depend partially on consistent advances in global interconnection technologies. Thus, continuous improvement will continue to be the order of the day in the PCB industry as producers scramble to keep up with technical modernization. These imperatives for change in manufacturing require costly capital equipment and R&D investments. For industry participants, remaining competitive is an expensive proposition that requires insightful corporate planning and adept management of resources. Thus, trends toward consolidation or strategic alliances are expected to permeate the PCB industry and the overall interconnection industry in the next 5 years.

Production of PCBs in the United States is performed both by independent PCB firms and by electronic systems companies known as original equipment manufacturers (OEMs). This relationship is described as a merchant dynamic versus a captive dynamic. For example, PCBs produced by OEMs, as in the computer and telecommunications sectors, are for their own consumption (captive production) for use in subsystems within their product lines. Merchant companies produce for the common market, while captive suppliers produce for use and/or consumption in their own product lines. Independent merchant PCB firms focus almost exclusively on PCB manufacturing and are the dominant contributors to PCB production in the U.S. market. In 1997 there were an estimated 650 independent companies producing PCBs in the United States. Approximately 90 percent of printed circuit boards produced in the United States came from independent producers in 1997.

The U.S. printed circuit board industry is composed primarily of relatively small to medium-size electronics companies compared with the OEMs in the electronic systems sector. According to the Institute for Interconnect and Packaging Electronic Circuits (IPC), among the 650 U.S. companies, 500 have annual sales less than $5 million. To put this in perspective, the top 8 independent PCB companies sold over $100 million and supplied 25 percent of the U.S. market in 1996, and the next 20 largest sold between $50 and $100 million, representing 23 percent of the market.

End Markets: PCB Customers.   As was described above, PCB producers sell their products to makers of computer, telecommunication, automotive, consumer electronics, and all other information technology (IT) end markets. In the United States the computer industry has traditionally been the major end market for the PCB supply. Although this is still true, there has been a relative decline in the portion of PCB products that go to computer end markets. PCB sales to the computer and business retail end market declined between 1980 and 1997 from 51 percent to 33 percent. This trend is driven in part by the development of multifunction portable electronic products which have blurred distinctions between end-product definitions. The convergence of PCs, communication devices, televisions, with the Internet is producing many new products. The final products can be identified as hybrids of at least two industries.

Classification disputes aside, strong growth exists in end markets beyond computing, such as telecommunications and automotive electronics. What is certain is that the users' needs have changed because of a more computer-literate and computer-dependent population and a more mobile lifestyle. For instance, by the year 2003, 830 million mobile telephone networks probably will be in use. According to International Data Corporation (IDC), in 1997 the number of users accessing the Internet surpassed 60 million. This represents a jump of 26 million Internet users in 1997, a market that did not really exist 5 years before. Use of the Internet is expected to grow at an astronomical rate, pushing sales of computers, Web TV, and even the "Internet refrigerator" (a product currently under development in Japan) in which the front door holds a display to host topics related to food, such as recipes and nutritional information. As technology continues to saturate modern lifestyles, the interconnection industry will continue to respond with adaptations to meet customer demand.

Global and Domestic Outlook

Employment and Production.   Contributions by the overall interconnection industry to the U.S. economy include the value of PCBs, the components mounted, the service activities involved in the assembly of board products, and overall employment in both PCB manufacturing and assembly operations. U.S. interconnection companies have operations in all 50 states. In 1997 the overall U.S. interconnection industry (PCBs and assembly) employed approximately 225,000 persons and exceeded $20 billion in sales (see Table 16-9).

Employment in PCB manufacturing in 1997 grew 10 percent and was estimated at 97,200. That was a banner year as positive domestic business conditions provided for strong PCB demand. Specifically, PCB growth was driven by strong end-market expansion, ever-increasing electronic content within capital goods, and an overall strong domestic economy with low inflation. Thus, printed circuits followed suit with other U.S. electronic product markets, as PCB shipments continued an aggressive expansion through 1997. Shipments of rigid boards rose almost 13 percent, and orders were reportedly up almost 18 percent; for flex circuits, shipments in 1997 rose 10.2 percent. According to Frost & Sullivan, strong performances in the PCB market contributed an estimated $8.7 billion to the U.S. economy. According to IPC, the estimated total for the PCB U.S. market in 1997 was $8 billion for rigid PCBs and $788 million for flex circuits.

U.S. Export Performance and Prospects.   U.S. exports fared very well in 1997, growing 18 percent to slightly over $2 billion. Strong export performance helped erode the long-standing

TABLE 16-9: Printed Circuit Boards (SIC 3672) Trends and Forecasts
(millions of dollars except as noted)

	1992	1993	1994	1995	1996	1997[1]	1998[2]	1999[3]	Percent Change 96–97	97–98	98–99	92–96[4]
Industry data												
Value of shipments[5]	7,320	7,378	8,416	9,498	10,702	11,986	13,065	14,894	12.0	9.0	14.0	10.0
Value of shipments (1992$)	7,320	7,551	8,803	9,924	11,067	12,395	13,510	15,401	12.0	9.0	14.0	10.9
Total employment (thousands)	76.0	73.6	76.9	81.6	88.3	97.2	104	114.3	10.1	7.0	9.6	3.8
Production workers (thousands)	51.0	50.5	54.0	59.6	63.9	70.3	75	82.5	10.0	6.7	10.0	5.8
Average hourly earnings ($)	10.16	10.58	10.49	10.36	10.75							1.4
Capital expenditures	318	283	381	453	585							16.5
Product data												
Value of shipments[5]	6,293	6,930	7,555	8,543	8,949	10,113	10,922	12,560	13.0	8.0	15.0	9.2
Value of shipments (1992$)	6,293	7,093	7,902	8,926	9,254	10,457	11,294	12,988	13.0	8.0	15.0	10.1
Trade data												
Value of imports	1,243	1,289	1,468	1,840	1,849	2,071 × .16	2,402	2714	12.0	16.0	13.0	10.4
Value of exports	1,092	973	1,377	1,651	1,694	2,007 × 2	2,248 × 18	2,652	18.5	12.0	18.0	11.6

[1] Estimate except imports and exports.
[2] Estimate.
[3] Forecast.
[4] Compound annual rate.
[5] For definition of industry versus product values, see "Getting the Most Out of *Outlook '99*."
Source: U.S. Department of Commerce: Bureau of the Census; International Trade Administration.

trade deficit in PCBs by 50 percent to a level of $64 million. The import-export ratio early in 1998 showed import growth slightly outpacing export growth. In 1997 many new countries moved into the top 20 export markets, including Thailand (ranked ninth), Australia (seventeenth), Belgium (eighteenth), Spain (nineteenth), and the Philippines (twentieth). Some countries demonstrated extremely strong growth rates, including increases of 178 percent for the Philippines, 109 percent for Thailand, 101 percent for Ireland, 87 percent for China, and 57 percent for Singapore.

With 16 percent growth, Mexico surpassed Canada as the largest U.S. export market in 1997 (see Table 16-10). North America remained the largest regional market for U.S. exporters, totaling nearly $1.2 billion, or 60 percent of exports; Mexico accounted for $618 million, and Canada for $580 million. Since these markets are highly integrated with the U.S. economy, strong export opportunities for U.S. PCB suppliers are forecast to continue throughout 1998 and 1999 as the U.S. economy is expected to fuel strong regional performances.

Other large export markets in 1997 were, in descending order after Canada, the United Kingdom, Singapore, Germany, Ireland, Japan, China, Thailand, and Malaysia. U.S. export growth to western Europe paralleled the economic recovery there, with the most remarkable expansion occurring in Ireland. Sales prospects continue to be strong for all PCB products in western European electronic markets; however, U.S. firms may face greater price pressures from Asian board suppliers competing to sell in Europe as a result of Asian economic difficulties,

Although exports to Japan have slowed, possibly as a result of the severe economic downturn in that country since late 1997, other Asian markets, such as those in southeast Asia, including Singapore, Thailand, and Malaysia, continued to be highly receptive to U.S. exports through the end of 1998.

The shakeout from the Asian market upheaval may prove to be particularly challenging to Japan and South Korea, yet market conditions vary greatly. As of early 1998, the Taiwanese, Chinese, and Philippine electronic markets have not plunged the way their east and southeast Asian neighbors have. Taiwan in particular is demonstrating dramatic PCB market growth and seems to have benefited from the Asian economic crisis. However, in contrast to the Philippines and China, Taiwan is not expected to be a growing market for U.S. PCB markets. For instance, the Philippines is an up-and-coming electronics market and is highly receptive to U.S. PCB products.

China's marketplace is flush with foreign investment and new production capacity. U.S. exports to China are expected to continue their strong growth. U.S. exports of PCB products to China increased 87 percent in 1997; thus, that country became one of the top 10 markets for U.S. exports and also moved upward dramatically to become the fourth largest supplier of the U.S. market, behind Taiwan, Canada, and Japan. South China's Guangdong province alone produced electronics goods worth $11 billion in 1997, up almost 35 percent from 1996.

However, subsequent quarterly performances for these markets in 1998 showed medium to severe declines for U.S. exports. As of February 1998 the Asian markets demonstrating a strong downturn were Thailand, Hong Kong, and South Korea. However, Singapore and Malaysia continued to have strong growth, and Japan's market reversed its downward slide as U.S. exports rose there. Since monthly data cannot provide a basis for a solid long-term prediction, most analysts would concur that weak economic conditions in most parts of Asia portend slower export growth overall in Asia and less penetration in some markets through 1999.

TABLE 16-10:   U.S. Trade Patterns in Printed Circuit Boards[1] in 1997

(millions of dollars; percent)

Exports			Imports		
Regions[2]	Value[3]	Share, %	Regions[2]	Value[3]	Share, %
NAFTA	1,198	59.7	NAFTA	430	20.7
Latin America	23	1.1	Latin America	11	0.5
Western Europe	377	18.8	Western Europe	165	8.0
Japan/Chinese Economic Area	156	7.8	Japan/Chinese Economic Area	1,092	52.7
Other Asia	224	11.2	Other Asia	364	17.6
Rest of world	29	1.5	Rest of world	11	0.5
World	2,007	100.0	World	2,071	100.0
Top Five Countries	Value	Share, %	Top Five Countries	Value	Share, %
Mexico	618	30.8	Taiwan	586	28.3
Canada	580	28.9	Canada	388	18.7
United Kingdom	133	6.6	Japan	258	12.5
Singapore	103	5.1	China	150	7.2
Germany	59	2.9	South Korea	134	6.4

[1] SIC 3672.
[2] For definitions of regional groupings, see "Getting the Most Out of *Outlook '99.*"
[3] Values may not sum to total due to rounding.
Source: U.S. Department of Commerce, Bureau of the Census.

U.S. Industry's Place in World Competition. Since 1993 the U.S. PCB industry has staged a successful comeback in global market share versus the Japanese. After being the global leader in the PCB market, the United States slipped behind Japan in 1987. From 1993 through 1998 the United States made great progress in retaining global market leadership in the rigid board market. In 1996 it was estimated that U.S. production, at $7.9 billion, accounted for 26.5 percent of world production; while Japan produced $7.8 billion, which accounted for 26.1 percent of the world market. The region showing the strongest growth in market share was actually the combined "Other Asia" country markets. The rest of Asia accounted for approximately 23 percent of the world market, up from 16 percent. Estimates for 1997 have the near parity continuing for the United States and Japan, while the world PCB market grew to an estimated $32 billion.

In efforts to cut costs, many global PCB makers are expanding their offshore manufacturing in newly developing countries. Many of the boards produced overseas are eventually imported into the United States at prices lower than those of products manufactured domestically. U.S. companies have not embraced offshore manufacturing as much as their international counterparts have. Instead, U.S. firms have tried to employ other strategies to develop process improvements which will yield higher volumes and lower-cost boards.

U.S. PCB manufacturers face major challenges to maintaining their competitiveness in the global PCB market. The U.S. industry must continue to develop cost-competitive PCBs even though manufacturing costs are higher in the United States than they are in many newly industrialized countries. According to the IPC, the cost differential for U.S. producers is attributed mainly to higher labor rates and overall manufacturing costs

related to stricter environmental, labor, and health regulations in the United States. To remain competitive globally, U.S. companies must continue to seek ways to improve the cost-effectiveness of their PCB manufacturing facilities, yet U.S. producers are not alone in facing the challenge to improve cost-competitive manufacturing.

Global PCB Markets. Spurred by growth in the electronic industries, the world market for rigid PCBs was estimated to total $32 billion in 1997. Industry representatives estimate that the global PCB market will grow to between $35 billion and $38 billion by 2000. According to IPC estimates, regional PCB production in 1996 was highest in Asia (including Japan), with slightly over 50 percent of the total dollar value coming from Asia ($14.6 billion). The Americas are second with $8.5 billion (dominated by North America at $8.1 billion); Europe is third with $6.1 billion.

In terms of global market share, the United States and Japan accounted for an estimated 53 percent of the overall global market in 1997. With the turmoil in Asia, the United States should continue to stay ahead, at least through 1998. However, the more recent U.S. lead relative to Japan has been due in part to the impact of the offshore manufacturing strategies of many Japanese producers. The impact of those strategies has been evident over the past 3 years through explosive growth trends in the PCB markets in east and southeast Asia. Market analysts believe that this growth is a result of foreign investment from Japan and to a lesser degree Taiwan.

The larger east Asian PCB producers have increasingly resorted to moving production to areas with lower manufacturing costs, especially in China and southeast Asia. PCB producers in Japan and more recently in Taiwan and South Korea have had to reckon with relative changes in their local manufacturing environments. Although these issues may not be equivalent to those in the United States, these Asian producers are contending with higher labor rates and higher prices for industrial real estate.

The biggest story in global PCB developments appears to be Taiwan's expected rise to the top of the global market. According to China Economic News Service, Taiwan's PCB sales grew 20 percent to $2.2 billion in 1997, of which Taiwan exported approximately 70 percent. Taiwanese firms benefited from the Asian financial crisis as their export prices for multilayer PCBs became more competitive compared with the United States, Japan, and Europe as a result of the devaluation of the New Taiwan dollar (NT$).

Most of the top 10 Taiwanese PCB firms experienced double-digit sales growth, even as high as 46 percent, in 1997. The outlook for Taiwanese PCB companies is strong for 1998 and beyond. Taiwanese PCB powerhouses are forecast to continue aggressive global market expansion. At this rate, in the medium-term future Taiwan's PCB industry probably will pose a challenge to the United States and Japan for leadership in global market share. According to the industry consultant Barry Livingstone, the Taiwanese PCB industry is uniquely capable of gaining global market share amid the economic upheaval in Asia.

For instance, Taiwanese PCB manufacturers do not rely heavily on imported raw materials; 86 percent of that material is available domestically. Therefore, the Taiwanese experienced no significant increase in input costs to PCBs as a result of devaluation of the NT$. In addition, with the exception of a single key piece of processing equipment, all production equipment necessary for PCB manufacturing is made locally. Taiwanese PCB firms are to a great degree insulated from the economic hardships of other Asian economies. Taiwanese PCB output prices probably will continue to benefit from a declining currency without facing higher input or production equipment costs. The sum of these conditions gives Taiwanese PCB manufacturers a competitive advantage over other Asian and even Western PCB manufacturers. Total output in Taiwan was expected to increase 40 percent in 1998, with sales predicted to grow 24 percent to $2.97 billion.

The U.S. PCB market may not be as strongly influenced as are other electronic component or production equipment segments by the ripple effect of the Asian financial crisis. This is due to the fact that the U.S. industry as a whole is not as active in exporting as are other component producers, such as semiconductor or even PCB production equipment or material suppliers. An industry survey conducted early in 1998 by the Institute for Interconnecting and Packaging Electronic Circuits showed very little perceived impact from the Asian financial crisis upon U.S. PCB producers. The U.S. market and the broader North American market are a dominant outlet for most U.S. PCB products. Unfortunately, there is speculation that the U.S. PCB industry is still not in the clear.

It may take longer for the effects of the Asian economic problems to appear because of the partial insulation of many U.S. PCB producers that are not active in exporting to Asia. A possible indication of trouble ahead for U.S. PCB makers was the dip in semiconductor markets early in 1998; PCB market trends usually follow semiconductor market trends with a 3- to 6-month lag time. Thus, uncertainty prevails about U.S. PCB export prospects, especially in regard to the impact on U.S. exports from the largest U.S. PCB firms, which are much more active in exporting.

In addition, there is a clear and present threat to the U.S. PCB industry as a result of stronger challenges from imported board products. As has been the case in the last 5 years, this is especially true of Asian-made products but may increasingly be a factor as pricing pressures in Asian PCB markets spill over into other global markets. In addition, some analysts speculate that affected Asian producers may use the global market to buoy their comeback as economic recoveries progress in their home markets.

Further, U.S. producers may actually feel stronger pricing challenges from board producers that are not thought to have been among the affected Asian economies. For example, Taiwan and China are two economies that thus far have been unscathed by economic turmoil in the rest of Asia. PCB producers from those countries (plus Japan) hold dominant portions of the U.S. imported board market and thus probably will respond in kind to lower pricing just to maintain their growing presence in the U.S. PCB/electronics market, and will increase their production to satisfy strong electronics market demand in the United States.

Industry and Trade Projections

Overall, the U.S. electronics market is expected to maintain its strength through 2000. However, 1998 will be a year of adjustment to the Asian financial crisis. The solid economic conditions in the overall U.S. economy will continue to fuel consumer and business demand in the computer, telecommunications, consumer electronics, and automotive industries. However, the strength of the U.S. market may turn out to be a double-edged sword. Although the expanded market opportunities should mean more business for U.S. electronics firms, there may be stronger competition in the U.S. market. Some foreign firms will be attracted to the U.S. market while other world economies rebuild, and business entities may focus on the U.S. market simply because product demand is high there. Such conditions are likely to make the U.S. market a magnet for PCB imports.

On the one hand, import challenges are likely to increase, but on the other hand, the overall size of the U.S. electronics market is expected to increase in the foreseeable future, and so more prospects exist for PCB sales. Also, the United States will not be the only market consuming more PCB imports. Western European countries are expected to buy more boards as their economies continue relatively strong performances through 2000. On an upbeat note, this may offer continued export opportunities to U.S. exporters as the U.S. PCB industry increasingly is involved in international markets. The only concrete prediction is that market conditions will remain strongly competitive worldwide, especially in regard to price.

Overall confidence exists for solid growth of the global electronics market through 2000, and this bodes well for PCB sales. A small slowdown was expected in the U.S. PCB market in 1998 compared with the torrid growth in 1997, but many analysts expected this to dissipate by early 1999. Competition from Asian board producers will intensify through 2002. Growth in bookings is expected to reach 7 to 8 percent in 1998 and spring back in 1999 to double-digit territory. Certainly these expectations rest on the assumption that the worst is over in Asia, barring any other major global economic surprises. PCB shipment growth estimates are 9 percent in 1998 and 14 percent in 1999 and in 2000. Strong possibilities exist for a near repeat performance of 1997's banner year for PCB shipments, with growth predicted to top 15 percent in 2002. The U.S. PCB market was expected to reach into the neighborhood of $9.3 billion in 1998 and may top $10 billion by the close of 2000. The U.S. market is expected to continue moderate expansion through the coming years, growing at an estimated compound annual growth rate (CAGR) of 8 to 9 percent through 2002.

The traditional end markets will continue to get the bulk of PCB sales; however, prospects are especially strong for expanded sales in newer electronic product markets, such as smart cards and digital cameras. These markets are expected to remain strong, as the United States is among the largest markets for these products. For instance, according to Killen & Associates, the worldwide market for smart cards is expected to grow from $1.2 billion in 1996 to $7.6 billion in 2000, a 59 percent CAGR, with a possible slowdown to 16 percent from 2000 to 2005, reaching $16 billion in 2005. In-Stat expects the dollar value of digital still camera shipments to grow to nearly $6 billion by 2002.

Overall, long-term growth is expected in the PCB-consuming products. Thus, optimism pervades the U.S. interconnection industry's future expectations for growth and expansion into 2002. The outlook for 2000 and beyond is robust, with growth expected as global consumers continue to ground themselves and every aspect of their lifestyles in the information age.

Judee Mussehl-Aziz, U.S. Department of Commerce, Office of Microelectronics, Medical Equipment and Instrumentation, (202) 482-0429, October 1998.

■ REFERENCES

Advanced Packaging, IHS Publishing, 17730 West Peterson Road, P.O. Box 159, Libertyville, IL 60048. (847) 362-8711.

American Electronics Association (AEA), 1225 Eye Street, NW, Suite 950, Washington, DC 20005. (202) 682-9110, Fax: (202) 682-9111, http://www.aeanet.org/.

Circuitree, 700 Gal Drive, Suite 200, Campbell, CA 95008-0901. (408) 364-3949.

Circuits Assembly, Miller Freeman Inc., 2000 Powers Ferry Center, Suite 450, Marietta, GA 30067. (404) 952-1303.

CleanRooms, Penn Well Publishing, Ten Tara Boulevard, 5th Floor, Nashua, NH 03062. (603) 891-0123, Fax: (603) 891-9200, http://www.cleanrooms.com/.

Dataquest, Inc., 251 River Oaks Parkway, San Jose, CA 95134-1913. (408) 468-8000, Fax: (408) 954-1780, http://www.dataquest.com/.

EDN, Cahners Publishing Co., 275 Washington Street, Newton, MA 02158. (617) 964-3030, Fax: (617) 558-4470, http://www.ednmag.com/.

EDN Asia, Cahners Asia Ltd., 19/F, Eight Commercial Tower, 8 Sun Yip Street, Chaiwan, Hong Kong. Phone: 852-2965-1555, Fax: 852-2976-0706.

EDN China, China Electronic News Agency, 23 Shi Jing Shan Road, Beijing 100043, China. Phone: 011-86-10-886-1813, Fax: 011-86-10-886-1805.

Electronic Business Asia, Cahners Asia Ltd., 19/F, Eight Commercial Tower, 8 Sun Yip Street, Chaiwan, Hong Kong. Phone: 852-2965-1555, Fax: 852-2976-0706.

Electronic Business Today, Cahners Publishing Co., 275 Washington Street, Newton, MA 02158. (617) 558-4563, Fax: (617) 558-4470, http://www.ebtmag.com/.

Electronic Buyers' News, CMP Media Inc., 600 Community Drive, Manhasset, NY 11030. (516) 562-5000, Fax: (516) 562-5123, http://techweb.cmp.com/ebn/.

Electronic Design, Penton Publishing Inc., 611 Route 46 West, Hasbrouck Heights, NJ 07604. (201) 393-6060, Fax: (201) 393-0204, http://www.penton.com/ed/.

Electronic Engineering Times, CMP Media Inc., 600 Community Drive, Manhasset, NY 11030. (516) 562-5000, Fax: (516) 562-5325, http://techweb.cmp.com/eet/.

Electronic Industries Alliance (EIA), 2500 Wilson Boulevard, Arlington, VA 22201. (703) 907-7750, Fax: (703) 907-7501, http://www.eia.org/.

Electronic Trend Publications, 1975 Hamilton Avenue, Suite 6, San Jose, CA 95125. (408) 369-7000, Fax: (408) 369-8021, http://www.electronictrendpubs.com/.

Electronic News, Electronic News Publishing Corp., 488 Madison Avenue, New York, NY 10022. (212) 909-5916, Fax: (212) 755-2751, http://www.sumnet.com/enews/.

Electronic Packaging & Production, Cahners Publishing Co., 1350 East Touhy Avenue, Box 5080, Des Plaines, IL 60017. (847) 635-8800, Fax: (847) 390-2770.

Electronic Products, Hearst Business Publishing Inc., 645 Stewart Avenue, Garden City, NY 11530. (516) 227-1300, Fax: (516) 227-1901, http://www.electronicproducts.com/.

Fabless Semiconductor Association (FSA), 13455 Noel Road, Suite 1000, Dallas, TX 75240. (214) 239-5119, Fax: (214) 774-4577, http://www.fsa.org/.

Henderson Ventures, 101 First Street, Suite 144, Los Altos, CA 94022. (415) 961-2900.

HTE Research, Inc., 400 Oyster Point Boulevard, Suite 220, South San Francisco, CA 94080. (415) 871-4377, Fax: (415) 871-0513, http://www.hte-sibs.com/.

Institute for Interconnecting and Packaging Electronic Circuits (IPC), 2215 Sanders Road, Northbrook, IL 60062. (847) 509-9700, Fax: (847) 509-9798, http://www.ipc.org/.

Integrated Circuit Engineering Corp., 15022 North 75th Street, Scottsdale, AZ 85260. (602) 998-9780, Fax: (602) 948-1925, http://www.ice-corp.com/.

Integrated System Design, Verecom Group, Inc., 5150 El Camino Real, Suite D31, Los Altos, CA 94022. (415) 903-0140, Fax: (415) 903-0151, http://www.isdmag.com/.

International Microelectronics and Packaging Society (IMAPS), 1850 Centennial Park Drive, Suite 105, Reston, VA 22091. (703) 758-1060, Fax: (703) 758-1066, http://www.ishm.ee.vt.edu.

N.T. Information LTD., 18 Strawberry Lane, Huntington, NY 11743. (516) 673-8571.

Printed Circuit Directories, P.O. Box 67202, Scotts Valley, CA 95067. (408) 353-4322.

Printed Circuit Fabrication, Miller Freeman Inc., 2000 Powers Ferry Center, Suite 450, Marietta, GA 30067. (404) 952-1303.

Semiconductor Equipment and Materials International (SEMI), 805 East Middlefield Road, Mountain View, CA 94043. (415) 964-5111, http://www.semi.org/.

Semiconductor Industry Association (SIA), 181 Metro Drive, Suite 450, San Jose, CA 95110. (408) 436-6600, Fax: (408) 436-6646, http://www.semichips.org/.

Semiconductor International, Cahners Publishing Co., 1350 East Touhy Avenue, Des Plaines, IL 60018. (847) 390-2296, Fax: (847) 390-2770, http://www.semiconductor-intl.com/.

Solid State Technology, Penn Well Publishing, Ten Tara Boulevard, 5th Floor, Nashua, NH 03062. (603) 891-0123, Fax: (603) 891-0597, http://www.solid-state.com/.

Surface Mount Technology, IHS Publishing Group, 17730 West Peterson Road, P.O. Box 159, Libertyville, IL 60048. (847) 362-8711, Fax: (847) 362-3484.

Technology Forecasts, 1420 Harbor Bay Parkway, Suite 295, Alameda, CA 94502-7083. (510) 747-1900

VLSI Research, Inc., 1754 Technology Drive, Suite 117, San Jose, CA 95110. (408) 453-8844, Fax: (408) 437-0608, http://www.vlsir.com/.

■ **RELATED CHAPTERS**

23: Industrial and Analytical Instruments
27: Computer Equipment
30: Telecommunications Services
31: Telecommunications and Navigation Equipment
36: Motor Vehicles
38: Household Consumer Durables
45: Medical and Dental Instruments and Supplies

■ **GLOSSARY**

Active component: A nonmechanical circuit component that has gain or switches current flow, such as a diode or transistor.

Analog: A continuous value that most closely resembles the real world and can be as precise as the measuring technique allows.

Analog circuit: A collection of components used to generate or process analog signals.

Application specific integrated circuit (ASIC): An integrated circuit designed to meet a specific customer requirement.

Assembly: The final stage of semiconductor manufacturing, where the active device is encased in a plastic, ceramic, or metal package; also referred to as back-end processing.

Capacitor: An electrical component that builds and stores voltage for release on command.

Chip: An integrated circuit or discrete device; also called a die.

Circuit board: The generic name for a wide variety of interconnection techniques, which include rigid, flexible, and rigid-flex boards in single-sided, double-sided, multilayer, and discrete wired configurations.

Clean room: An area specially constructed to control the air flow, temperature, and humidity in such a way that constant filtration keeps contamination below a predetermined level and keeps temperature and humidity within predetermined limits.

Computer-aided design (CAD): A technique of using a computer to aid a person in the design of electrical circuits, integrated circuits, gate arrays, and other complex engineering designs in a reasonable time frame.

Conductor, electrical: A material capable of carrying (conducting) electricity. Silver is the best electrical conductor. Copper, gold, and aluminum are also popular.

Deposition: A heat or physical (sputtering) process by which a thin film of material is deposited over the surface of a wafer.

Die: A single square or rectangular piece of semiconductor material into which a specific electrical circuit has been fabricated; also called a chip or device (integrated circuit or discrete).

Diffusion: A high-temperature process by which selected chemicals (dopants) enter the crystalline structure of semiconductor materials to change the electrical characteristics at desired locations; takes place in a diffusion furnace.

Digital: A method of representing information in an electrical circuit by switching the current on or off. Only two output voltages are possible, usually represented by 0 and 1.

Digital circuit: A circuit that operates like a switch and can perform logical functions; used in computers and similar logic-based equipment.

Digital signal processor (DSP): A primarily digital component used to process either digital or analog signals. An analog signal may first be conditioned and then converted into a digital equivalent by using an analog-to-digital (A/D) converter function. The signal conditioning and A/D functions may be external to or resident in the DSP. A typical DSP application is the compression and decompression of video data.

Diode: A two-terminal device that conducts electricity in only one direction; in the other direction it behaves like an open switch. The term typically is taken to refer to a semiconductor device, although alternative implementations such as vacuum tubes are available.

Discrete device: A semiconductor containing only one active element, such as a transistor or a diode.

Double-sided: Refers to a printed circuit board with tracks on both sides.

Dry etch: Refers to the process that uses radio-frequency energy and gas phase chemicals to remove a specific layer during semiconductor processing.

Dual in-line package (DIP): The most common type of integrated circuit package; circuit leads or pins extend symmetrically outward and downward from the long sides of the rectangular package body.

Dynamic random-access memory (DRAM): A memory device in which each cell is formed from a transistor-capacitor pair. It is called dynamic because the capacitor loses its charge over time and each cell must be periodically recharged if it is to retain its data.

Electrically erasable programmable read-only memory (EEPROM or E2PROM): Similar to read-only memory (ROM), but with the capability of selective erasing and programming through a special electrical stimulus.

Electron: An elementary negatively charged atomic particle.

Electron tube: An enclosed device consisting of at least two electrodes that is capable of varying current from one to the other in response to the characteristics of a signal or under the control of another device. The most basic form of tube, having just two plates, is called a diode.

Erasable programmable read-only memory (EPROM): Similar to read-only memory (ROM), but enables the user to erase stored information. Normally it refers to a memory device whose contents may be erased by exposure to ultraviolet light shining through a window in the ceramic package.

Etch: Refers to the process of removing material (such as oxides or other thin films) by chemical, electrolytic, or plasma (ion bombardment) means.

Fabless: Refers to a semiconductor company that does not have its own wafer manufacturing facility but subcontracts wafer manufacturing.

Fabrication: In semiconductor manufacturing, usually refers to the front-end process of making devices on semiconductor wafers but usually does not include the package assembly (back-end) stages.

Hybrid circuit: A microelectronic device consisting of both film circuits and semiconductor elements.

Insulator: A material that is a poor conductor of electricity; used to separate conductors from one another or to protect personnel from electricity.

Integrated circuit (IC): A semiconductor die containing multiple elements that act together to form the complete device circuit.

Interconnect: A conductive connection between two or more circuit elements; the conductors among elements (transistors, resistors, etc.) on an integrated circuit or between components on a printed circuit board.

Large-scale integration (LSI): Refers to integrated circuits containing 1,000 or more transistors but fewer than 100,000.

Leadframe: A stamped or etched metal frame that provides external electrical connections for a packaged electrical device.

Line width: Usually refers to a dimension on a mask or a feature on an integrated circuit.

Linear circuit: A circuit whose output is an amplified version of its input or a predetermined variation of its input.

Lithography: The transfer of a pattern or image from one medium to another, such as from a mask to a wafer. If light is used to effect the transfer, the term photolithography applies. Microlithography refers to the process as it is applied to images with features in the submicrometer range.

Magnetron: An electron tube used to generate microwave radiation for applications including telephony and radar.

Metal-oxide semiconductor (MOS): A common family of transistors in which the controlling terminal is connected to a plate separated from the semiconductor by an insulating layer. This plate was originally made of metal (now polysilicon is generally used), and the insulator is an oxide.

Microcomputer: A microprocessor complete with stored program memory (ROM), random-access memory (RAM), and input/output (I/O) logic. Microcomputers are capable of performing useful work without additional supporting logic. If all the functions are on the same chip, it is sometimes called a microcontroller.

Micrometer: One-millionth (10^{-6}) of a meter; about 40-millionths of an inch, synonymous with micron, symbolized μm.

Micron: See micrometer.

Microprocessor: The basic arithmetic logic of a computer; also called a microprocessor unit (MPU).

Monolithic device: A device whose circuitry is completely contained on a single die or chip.

Nonvolatile memory: A memory device that maintains the memory state after power is removed.

Package: The protective container of an electronic component, with terminals to provide electrical access to the components inside.

Passive component: An electrical component without "gain," or current-switching capability; commonly used to refer to resistors, capacitors, or inductors.

Printed circuit board (PCB): A substrate on which a predetermined pattern or printed wiring and printed elements have been formed; also called a printed wiring board (PWB).

Programmable read-only memory (PROM): A read-only memory that can be programmed after manufacture by external equipment. Typically PROMs utilize fusible links that may be burned open to produce a logic bit in a specific location.

Random-access memory (RAM): The basic (read/write) storage element in a computer that stores digital information temporarily and can be changed as required.

Read-only memory (ROM): The computer element that permanently stores information that is repeatedly used, such as tables of data and characters of electronic displays. Unlike RAM, it cannot be altered.

Resistor: An electrical component used to modify voltage or current in a circuit by providing resistance.

Semiconductor: A material with the properties of both a conductor and an insulator. Common semiconductors include silicon and germanium.

Silicon (Si): The basic element used in most semiconductor devices, such as diodes, transistors, and integrated circuits.

Small-scale integration (SSI): Refers to integrated circuits containing fewer than 30 transistors.

Submicron: Refers to dimensions smaller than 1 micron.

Substrate: The material on which a microelectronic device is built. Such material may be active, like silicon, or passive, like alumina ceramic.

Transformer: An electrical component used to modify voltage or other characteristics between one circuit and another.

Transistor: An active semiconductor device with three electrodes that may be either an amplifier or a switch.

Ultra large-scale integration (ULSI): Refers to integrated circuits containing 10 million or more transistors.

Very large-scale integration (VLSI): Refers to integrated circuits containing 100,000 or more transistors but fewer than 10 million.

Volatile memory: Refers to memory devices that lose their stored states when power is removed.

Wafer: A thin disk of semiconductor material (usually silicon) on which many separate chips can be fabricated.

METALWORKING EQUIPMENT
Economic and Trade Trends

U.S. International Trade

($ billions)

Legend: Balance — Exports — Imports

Source: U.S. Department of Commerce: Bureau of the Census; International Trade Administration.

World Export Market Shares

(%)

Legend: United States, Germany, Japan, Italy

Source: United Nations; U.S. Department of Commerce, International Trade Administration.

Export Dependence and Import Penetration

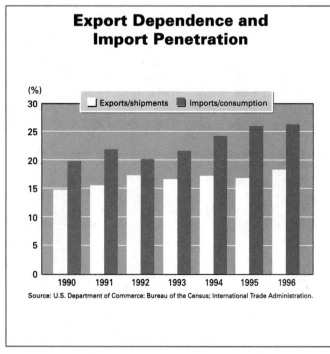

(%)

Legend: Exports/shipments, Imports/consumption

Source: U.S. Department of Commerce: Bureau of the Census; International Trade Administration.

Output and Output per Hour

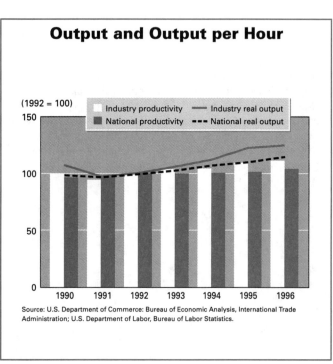

(1992 = 100)

Legend: Industry productivity, Industry real output, National productivity, National real output

Source: U.S. Department of Commerce: Bureau of Economic Analysis, International Trade Administration; U.S. Department of Labor, Bureau of Labor Statistics.

See "Getting the Most Out of *Outlook '99*" for definitions of terms.

Metalworking Equipment

INDUSTRY DEFINITION   Metalworking equipment includes machine tools (SIC 3541, 3542), machine tool accessories (SIC 3545), metal cutting tools (SIC 35415), special dies and tools (SIC 3544), power-driven hand tools (SIC 3546), and welding apparatus (SIC 3548). The United States has a trade deficit in this sector, with the majority of imports originating in Japan, the Chinese Economic Area, and western Europe (see Table 17-1).

MACHINE TOOLS

A machine tool is a power-driven, not hand-held machine used to cut, form, or shape metal. The industry consists of about 16 primary product groups under two codes: SIC 3541, metal cutting machines, and SIC 3542, metal forming machines.

Several sources provided the data used in this section. Table 17-3, Trends and Forecasts, relies on U.S. Census Bureau data for SIC 3541 and 3542, including data on machine tool parts. "Global Industry Trends" and Table 17-2, Machine Tool Pro-

duction in 1997, reflect data from Gardner Publications' *1998 World Machine Tool Output and Consumption Survey*. The Gardner data come from government and trade association sources. The figures for 1997 are estimates based on 6-month data. The Gardner figures reflect complete machines, excluding parts; exceptions are noted.

Global Industry Trends
After several years of growth, worldwide production of machine tools declined in 1997. At $37 billion, global output

TABLE 17-1: U.S. Trade Patterns in Selected Metalworking Machinery[1] in 1997
(millions of dollars; percent)

	Exports			Imports	
Regions[2]	Value[3]	Share, %	Regions[2]	Value[3]	Share, %
NAFTA	2,679	39.2	NAFTA	1,592	15.1
Latin America	572	8.4	Latin America	89	0.8
Western Europe	1,633	23.9	Western Europe	3,427	32.6
Japan/Chinese Economic Area	792	11.6	Japan/Chinese Economic Area	4,885	46.4
Other Asia	746	10.9	Other Asia	233	2.2
Rest of world	419	6.1	Rest of world	296	2.8
World	6,842	100.0	World	10,523	100.0
Top Five Countries	Value	Share, %	Top Five Countries	Value	Share, %
Canada	1,859	27.2	Japan	3,983	37.9
Mexico	820	12.0	Canada	1,369	13.0
United Kingdom	407	5.9	Germany	1,345	12.8
Germany	379	5.5	Taiwan	526	5.0
Japan	336	4.9	Switzerland	424	4.0

[1] SIC 3541, 3542, 3544, 3546, 3548.
[2] For definitions of regional groupings, see "Getting the Most Out of *Outlook '99*."
[3] Values may not sum to total due to rounding.
Source: U.S. Department of Commerce, Bureau of the Census.

was 4.2 percent lower than the output in 1996, according to estimated figures reported in Gardner Publications' 1998 world machine tool survey (see Table 17-2). European producers were affected the most by the 1997 contraction. The 14 countries that form the European Committee for the Cooperation of the Machine Tool Industry (CECIMO) witnessed a 9 percent decline in shipments. Germany was the hardest hit, with a 13 percent drop in dollar-valued shipments.

The U.S. machine tool industry managed to sustain its pattern of growth in 1997. Constant dollar shipments of metal forming and metal cutting machine tools rose 5.3 percent over 1996 as a result of the strength of the domestic economy. U.S. machine tool manufacturers are enjoying the longest industry expansion since the 1960s.

Japan continues to be the largest supplier in the global machine tool industry. In contrast to the lackluster performance of most Asian machine tool producers, Japanese machine tool shipments increased 6.1 percent in 1997 compared with 1996. As the world's top producer, the Japanese industry supplies more than 25 percent of global output, followed by Germany, the United States, Italy, and Switzerland. The Japanese industry rebounded from a stagnant period with a sharp increase in domestic machine tool consumption in 1997. Expectations of continued strong demand from the Japanese automotive industry will ensure the dominance of the Japanese in the future.

European producers collectively play a major role in the global machine tool market, with CECIMO supplying more than 40 percent of total world output. Germany and to a lesser extent Italy are also large consumers of machine tools.

The world's largest machine tool consumer is the United States, which annually consumes approximately one-fifth of world output. The robust domestic economy helped boost U.S. machine tool apparent consumption by 4.5 percent in 1997, according to the Gardner survey. The United States, which typically supplies around 12 percent of world production of machine tools, must import sizable quantities of machine tools to satisfy domestic demand. In 1997 the U.S. machine tool import penetration rate exceeded 50 percent.

Overview of the U.S. Machine Tool Industry

The U.S. machine tool industry is in a period of relative stability, although industry size, employment, and revenues typically fluctuate in response to swings in the business cycle. The number of industry establishments stands at around 600, according to U.S. Census Bureau data. These producers are concentrated in several midwestern and northeastern states; Ohio, Michigan, and Illinois have the greatest concentration of industry establishments.

The industry's customer base continues to follow historical patterns, with the exception of the increasing importance of the job shop sector. The automotive sector remains the industry's largest customer group, followed by the job shop and aerospace sectors. The appliance and off-highway and construction industries are also significant markets. The medical equipment industry is one of the fastest growing customer groups.

The composition of the industry has changed since the beginning of the 1990s as a result of consolidation and foreign investment. A spate of buyouts and acquisitions occurred in the early to middle 1990s, and a number of privately held companies became publicly owned. A wave of investment by the European automotive industry spurred similar investments by continental machine tool producers, which established U.S. production facilities to supply their primary customer group. Japanese investment also picked up in the first half of the decade, driven by the strong yen. The newcomers joined a contingent of Japanese machine tool manufacturers that had established U.S. production facilities in the 1980s in response to U.S. import restrictions that have since been lifted.

A strong commitment to exporting and the sustained expansion of the U.S. economy are key elements in the machine tool industry's newfound stability. Changes in the automotive sector are also important. The automotive industry is far less cyclical

TABLE 17-2: Machine Tool Production in 1997[1]
(millions of dollars, estimated)

Rank and Country	Total	Cutting	Forming
1. Japan	9,746.3	8,259.6	1,486.7
2. Germany	6,566.9	4,465.3	2,101.6
3. United States	4,597.6	3,222.3	1,375.3
4. Italy	3,569.9	2,221.3	1,348.6
5. Switzerland	1,838.4	1,486.1	352.4
6. Taiwan	1,758.1	1,163.9	594.2
7. People's Republic of China	1,700.0	1,140.0	560.0
8. United Kingdom	1,381.6	1,124.6	257.0
9. France	957.3	627.9	329.4
10. Republic of Korea	880.5	781.0	99.4
11. Spain	815.8	587.4	228.4
12. Brazil	p545.0	p441.6	p103.4
13. Canada	p471.2	p278.8	p192.4
14. Czech Republic	261.9	226.9	35.0
15. India	p246.0	p217.8	p28.3
16. Austria	226.0	144.2	81.8
17. Poland	u188.8	u137.9	u50.9
18. Sweden	u180.6	u52.9	u127.7
19. Belgium	u167.8	u8.8	u159.0
20. Russia	167.4	138.3	29.1
21. Finland	159.6	23.6	136.0
22. Netherlands	107.7	17.2	90.4
23. Turkey	u107.5	u33.0	u74.5
24. Denmark	u72.0	u28.5	u43.5
25. Yugoslav Republic	68.0	57.0	11.0
26. Ukraine	u64.2	u52.3	u11.8
27. Romania	57.0	48.7	8.3
28. Croatia	43.5	41.9	1.6
29. Portugal	33.2	4.7	28.4
30. Slovak Republic	pu26.8	pu19.0	pu7.7
31. Mexico	c25.0	c15.0	c10.0
32. Argentina	20.4	13.5	6.9
33. Hungary	u7.0	u4.6	u2.5
34. South Africa	5.3	0.7	4.6
Total	37,064.1	27,086.5	9,977.7
Western Europe	16,338.6	11,019.4	5,319.1
Asia/Pacific Rim	14,331.0	11,562.3	3,052.2
Americas	5,659.2	3,971.2	1,688.0
Eastern Europe	730.1	532.8	185.4
Others	5.3	0.7	4.6

[1] c = circa, rough estimate from fragmentary data; p = includes parts; u = unrevised but converted at current rate.
Source: Gardner Publications, Inc.

than it was in the past. Automakers are undertaking more frequent and less extensive design changes and are becoming globalized, tailoring their products to individual markets. This has led to ongoing investment programs rather than concentrated purchasing cycles. The increasing globalization of the automotive sector is encouraging a similar trend among machine tool suppliers. U.S. machine tool companies are increasing their worldwide presence, often through joint ventures, cooperative agreements, and strategic alliances. The countries that have attracted the largest industry investment to date are Mexico, Brazil, India, and China.

Domestic Trends and Factors Affecting U.S. Industry Growth

Technological Developments. Developments in machine tool technology are leading to increased demand for new, improved products, particularly in the job shop sector. A combination of lower prices and user-friendly personal computer (PC)-based controls has spurred investment in computer numerical control machines. Growing numbers of small shops are investing in new, more sophisticated machine tools that offer increased performance, flexibility, and productivity and are easier to program and operate on the shop floor. The job shop market is being bolstered by expectations that outsourcing trends will continue, with large manufacturers relying more on outside suppliers.

Rapidly changing consumer tastes and shorter product life cycles are driving demand for machine tools with greater flexibility. Manufacturers are making more frequent design changes and increasing small-lot production. As a result, single machines that can perform a range of functions with minimal setups are replacing multiple and less wieldy machines. These new machines have faster turnaround times and can be more readily reconfigured for changing production assignments and more easily integrated into production lines. Traditional transfer line technology—long the mainstay of large-scale production—increasingly is being challenged by these flexible machines. Demand for these new machines also is rising in response to the shifting of more production to job shops through outsourcing. Transfer lines are impractical for small machining shops because of their cost and size.

High-speed machining technology is generating considerable interest in a range of user industries. This technology currently is used most in the aerospace, automotive, and die and mold industries to machine aluminum. Use of the technology is expected to grow steadily as producers across the manufacturing spectrum face mounting pressure to improve accuracy, efficiency, and productivity. High-speed or high-velocity machining combines various advanced technologies, including high feed rates, high rapid traverse rates, high spindle speeds, high acceleration and deceleration rates, and fast tool change times, to achieve high metal removal rates in less time along with better surface finishes. Due to higher spindle speeds and increased feed rates, total machining time has been drastically reduced.

High-speed techniques offer significant benefits to the aerospace sector, making it possible to machine aluminum parts with much thinner walls than can be achieved with traditional techniques and to machine much larger parts. Monolithic parts that are machined from a single block of raw material are generally lighter, stronger, and less expensive than parts assembled out of sheet metal. In the automotive industry high-speed techniques are used widely to machine aluminum components. This trend will continue as automakers, under pressure to reduce vehicle weight, increase their use of aluminum components. This technology is also prevalent in the mold and die industry, where the use of aluminum for prototype tooling is growing. While aluminum is the material most frequently associated with high-speed machining, this technique is being applied to a wider range of materials, such as cast iron and tool steels, as machining shops become more adept at using the technology.

Machine tool builders will have to develop new machining techniques as manufacturers increasingly substitute alternative materials for traditional metal. In addition to the automotive and aerospace sectors' increased use of aluminum and magnesium, polymers such as cast nylon and plastics are being used more by a range of industries. These materials often pose difficulties for conventional machine tools. Traditional machining methods increasingly are being replaced by newer methods, especially for machining exotic materials.

Nontraditional cutting methods that are gaining ground include laser, electrical discharge machining (EDM), and waterjet machining. These technologies currently represent niche markets but have the potential for significant growth. Laser shipments increased over 60 percent in the period 1995–1997 and are the fastest growing segment of the machine tool industry. Laser cutting is replacing work previously done by turret punch presses, plasma cutters, shears, and mills. The advantages of laser machining include the ability to machine burr-free edges and to cut parts directly from a computer-aided-design model, eliminating tooling and secondary finishing costs. Laser technology is particularly useful for prototype work and small production runs because lengthy setups are eliminated and downtime, as well as cutting time, is reduced. The aerospace industry, with its emphasis on increasing quality and accuracy while cutting costs, is a strong market for laser machining technology.

Waterjet technology uses a stream of water and abrasive particles to cut materials. This process, which is effective on a range of materials, offers many benefits. Thermal distortion, a significant problem with many machining techniques, is virtually eliminated. Waterjet machining generates a very concentrated heat that is absorbed by chips so that the properties of the work material are not affected. The process also cuts with very little force, resulting in a better surface finish; as a result, secondary operations such as hand polishing are eliminated in most cases. The use of waterjet machining will grow steadily as the technology becomes less costly and easier to use.

The EDM sector also is expanding. This process, which employs electrical discharge spark erosion to remove metal, is commonly used for die and mold applications. EDM's image of being costly and difficult to use is changing as a range of industries become familiar with its advantages. Because of its ability to produce a mirrorlike surface, EDM is well suited to ultraprecision work such as machining medical products. Traditional machining often necessitates follow-up polishing that can diminish accuracy.

Control technology continues to have a substantial impact on the machine tool industry, playing a key role in improving machining precision, productivity, flexibility, and speed. In the past, controls typically became outdated before machine tools needed replacement. Today software-based open architecture controls can minimize that problem. PC-based controls can be upgraded affordably as technology changes, and software can be reloaded. With the increased use of PC-based controls, more programming can be performed by machine operators on the shop floor. Giving the operator a greater ability to create and modify programs improves efficiency and productivity and often results in a better machined product. PC-based controls will continue to gain market share.

Advances in operator control are bringing an increase in machine tool networking capabilities and the use of multimedia technology. Machine tools now offer remote diagnostics capabilities, allowing for improved operation and maintenance and helping to reduce machine downtime caused by system failures. The use of teleservice and telemaintenance is increasing, leading to improved customer service. These technological advances are improving the design process by facilitating communication between factory floor operators and engineering department designers. Virtual reality technology also is making inroads into the design of equipment and assembly procedures. The technology allows for a thorough evaluation of tooling and setup configurations while avoiding costly machine downtime and the risk of tool damage from unforeseen collisions, which are not uncommon in traditional machining.

Environmental issues and costs remain a concern for U.S. machine tool manufacturers. The industry probably will see increased government regulation of metalworking fluids in the coming years. The Occupational Safety and Health Administration (OSHA) believes that exposure to these fluids and the mists they generate poses a significant risk to workers. OSHA has formed a metalworking fluids Standards Advisory Committee to review the issue and contribute to its rule-making process. In response, the industry is reexamining its use of metalworking fluids. These fluids, or coolants, traditionally have been employed to control thermal distortion and help control chips during the machining process. As it becomes more expensive for the industry to administer fluid management programs to oversee the maintenance, recycling, and disposal of used coolants, interest in innovative materials and machining techniques that reduce or eliminate the need for fluids is growing. Fluidless cutting or "dry machining," is in limited use at present but may become more common as the technology advances. To reduce the need for fluids, tools can be treated with heat-resistant coatings; diamond, cubic boron nitride, and titanium-aluminum-nitride coatings are commonly used. These coatings impart hardness, minimize the effects of high temperatures on a tool, and help prolong tool life. Innovative cutting materials such as coated car-

bide, cermets, and ceramics may be employed. Dry machining methods often require higher metal removal rates and special procedures to remove chips.

Government Efforts. The National Institute of Standards and Technology (NIST) plays an active role in machine tool research and development and provides technical assistance to U.S. machine tool manufacturers through a wide range of programs that involve partnerships with industry, academia, and not-for-profit organizations. NIST's Manufacturing Engineering Laboratory (MEL) serves as a central research laboratory for manufacturing infrastructure technology, measurements, and standards.

The MEL facility's efforts in the area of intelligent machines and systems are accelerating the trend toward a more open systems architecture. The Enhanced Machine Controller program, a collaborative effort that includes machine tool manufacturers, end users, and control component manufacturers, furthers this technology. The goal of this initiative is to reduce the life cycle cost of machine tool controllers, reduce integration costs, and improve performance. The project focuses on controller software, an area in which the United States enjoys a commanding lead.

The National Advanced Manufacturing Testbed (NAMT), which was launched by MEL in 1996, aims to help U.S. industry develop twenty-first-century manufacturing capabilities. This distributed, multiproject testbed allows NIST and a host of research partners to remotely access and share information, demonstrate manufacturing feasibility, and evaluate prototype standards. NAMT provides the means to conduct and distribute manufacturing research in advanced metrology, control, and interoperability technology to create a new information technology–based manufacturing model. The project demonstrates how machines, software, and people can be networked to improve productivity and foster innovation.

Two NAMT projects focus specifically on machine tools. The objective of the Machine Tool Performance Representation Models and Data Repository project is to create a virtual manufacturing environment that simulates the complete manufacturing cycle in order to reduce the time needed for new product introduction. Using standardized data formats, researchers attempt to develop predictive machine tool and inspection system models that allow accurate simulation of performance in specific applications. A standardized approach to structuring and representing detailed performance information is a key element of virtual manufacturing environments. The second project, Characterization, Remote Access and Simulation of Hexapod Machines, represents an effort to measure and extend the capabilities of hexapod machine tools, a new class of parallel-actuated machine tools based on the Stewart platform mechanism. This promising new machine tool technology offers many potential benefits, including increased stiffness, higher speed and acceleration as a result of reduced moving mass, and lower production and installation costs that result from the machine's symmetry and self-contained structure.

The Manufacturing Extension Partnership (MEP) is an NIST initiative to help small and medium-size manufacturers become globally competitive. A partnership of federal, state, and local organizations, MEP provides technical assistance and advice to small manufacturing companies through a nationwide network of more than 70 not-for-profit centers. MEP's in-house engineering experts and outside consultants offer guidance on production techniques and technology applications; technical seminars and training programs are also available.

A government–private sector partnership known as the National Machine Tool Partnership (NMTP) seeks to enhance U.S. nuclear weapons manufacturing capabilities and machine tool industry technology. The initiative, which began in 1993 and is funded by the U.S. Department of Energy, partners various national laboratories, production facilities, and machine tool builders and users on long-term projects that address key government and industry needs. Industry oversight and guidance are provided by the Association for Manufacturing Technology and the National Tooling and Machining Association, which are key industry trade associations. Partnership projects require in-kind matching of activities by industry partners. Current projects include predictive maintenance, intelligent manufacturing cells, and determination of machining center accuracy.

Global Market Prospects

Exports of U.S. metal cutting and metal forming machine tools have risen for 4 consecutive years as a result of aggressive marketing efforts and increasing demand in global markets. U.S. machine tool builders currently export over 40 percent of their annual production. The upward trend in industry exports has helped moderate the cyclical nature of the capital goods sector. Exports climbed to over $2.8 billion in 1997, nearly a 5 percent increase over 1996, and were projected to increase an additional 4 percent in 1998. The top export markets for U.S. machine tools in 1997 were Canada, Mexico, and China. Other strong markets were Brazil, South Korea, and the United Kingdom.

Global demand for machine tools is shifting from the relatively saturated markets in the industrialized world to the fast-growing economies of the newly industrialized countries. While traditional markets such as Europe, Japan, and the United States will remain the largest consumers of machine tools in absolute terms, the emerging markets of Latin America and southeast Asia offer the greatest potential for growth. The trend toward globalization in a range of industries, particularly in the automotive sector, will ensure continued growth in off-shore demand for capital equipment. Manufacturers are establishing more small plants throughout the world to supply markets with local production.

The ongoing upheaval in Asian financial markets has dimmed the outlook for that region. As the crisis has spread throughout the Pacific Rim, slackened demand for capital equipment is affecting machine tool exporting countries, for which Asia was recently a booming market. The region's existing machine tool production capabilities will enable machine tool consumers in that area to substitute locally built equipment for imports. According to Gardner Publications' annual survey,

Asia and the Pacific Rim countries account for nearly 40 percent of world production. The Asian bloc also consumes a large proportion of the world's annual supply of machine tools—over 25 percent—so that a drop in the region's demand will have a strong impact on U.S. and other global machine tool suppliers. U.S. producers can expect significant discounting throughout the region while the malaise lingers. Asian suppliers also are expected to offer increased incentives to purchase their products, further challenging U.S. machine tool exporters.

Global machine tool trade will become increasingly competitive in response to the Asian situation. That region's economic woes will increase the already strong pressure on machine tool prices, which are expected to remain steady or fall somewhat. Falling currencies throughout Asia will boost the region's exports as local markets shrink and excess capacity rises. U.S. production by Japanese machine tool builders probably will be supplemented by increased imports of Japanese-built equipment. Taiwan, another major producer in that region, also will increase its exports to the United States and other parts of the world.

Mexico.   Mexico has been one of the U.S. machine tool industry's most important export markets for many years, surpassed only by Canada. Mexico has recovered from the economic morass that caused panic among many investors several years ago, and U.S. exports have rebounded, approaching precrisis levels. U.S. machine tool manufacturers' exports to Mexico topped $300 million in 1997.

U.S. machine tool exporters have a competitive advantage in Mexico over suppliers from outside the continent as a result of the North American Free Trade Agreement (NAFTA). Under NAFTA, various U.S.-built machine tools have received immediate duty-free status, while the other duties are being phased out. Tariffs for machine tools sourced from nonsignatory countries range from 10 to 20 percent.

Ambitious investment plans for the Mexican automotive, appliance, and heavy equipment industries bode well for the continued strength of U.S. machine tool exports. The automotive sector offers the greatest potential for growth in demand. A number of new plants are being announced by manufacturers, since current capacity is insufficient to meet expected levels of future demand; some projections call for Mexico's annual automotive production to surpass 2 million vehicles around the turn of the century. Similar dynamics are at play in the Mexican automotive parts sector, which is striving to increase domestic production. A large percentage of these parts will be produced with metalworking machinery. U.S. automakers also are increasing the number of parts they are sourcing from Mexico.

The Mexican government is implementing policies to further reform the economy and ensure continued economic growth. These policies include reducing foreign debt and inflation, increasing foreign investment, creating more job opportunities, and creating and strengthening domestic sources of financing. Economic reform will further stimulate the industrial sector. The United States will remain the largest supplier of machine tools to the Mexican market in the near term.

China. Despite Asia's financial problems, China remains a promising market for U.S. machine tool exports. Although China's economic growth rate has slowed, its plans to accelerate domestic manufacturing capability are still on track. That country's ability to stem the slowing of its economy will depend on its success in implementing recently announced reform plans. These plans include revamping the banking system and the state-owned sector. For the time being, China's large cash reserves are insulating its economy from the regional upheaval.

U.S. machine tool builders exported over $98 million of metal cutting and metal forming equipment to China in 1997, making it the industry's third largest export market. Other large suppliers of machine tools to China are Japan, Taiwan, and Germany. China has been one of the U.S. industry's top three export markets since 1993. Despite this ranking, U.S. machine tool exports to China have shown a downward trend in recent years, dropping over 30 percent in 1997 compared with 1996. This decline is explained largely by China's elimination in December 1996 of a tariff exemption on capital equipment imports for government-approved projects. China has reinstituted a tariff exemption that should help strengthen demand for machine tool imports. As of January 1998, capital goods imports of foreign ventures are receiving duty-free treatment.

China's domestic machine tool industry consists of around 400 manufacturers. Although that nation's machinery manufacturing capabilities have developed rapidly and product quality has improved, there is still a large gap between Chinese and U.S.-built machinery. The government of China is undertaking efforts to improve the efficiency of its machine tool industry— a recently announced plan calls for mergers—and improvement of its technological capabilities. U.S. firms can expect demand for their technology and equipment to continue as China pursues its plan to transform its machinery, automotive, and other key sectors into so-called pillar industries in the next 15 years. More direct investment by U.S. machine tool manufacturers is likely as Chinese government policies are expected to favor local coproduction over imports.

The automotive sector in China offers considerable potential for growth. Motor vehicle sales are projected to soar as per capita income rises. Automakers have plans to increase capacity over the next several years, fueling demand for machine tools. However, the performance of this sector has been uneven, and some automakers have experienced losses. At present, automotive investment is outpacing vehicle sales. In response, the Chinese government is seeking to curb the market. Construction of new plants is expected to level off unless sales improve. To fill the gap, China may seek to increase its motor vehicle imports. However, stiff competition from the many nations that also are increasing automotive capacity, particularly elsewhere in Asia as well as Latin America, may thwart this effort. Demand for auto parts is forecast to be strong. China is building up its automotive parts and components industry and is seeking a higher Chinese content level in all vehicles.

Brazil. Brazil and the other countries that form MERCOSUR (the Southern Common Market that includes Argentina, Brazil, Paraguay, and Uruguay) hold significant potential for U.S. machine tool exporters. Efforts are under way to revamp industry in the four countries, lift import restrictions, and lower tariffs and other barriers to trade. All these actions are favorably affecting demand for machine tool imports. The region has a population of over 200 million, and its overall economy is healthy. Its current political stability enhances its potential.

MERCOSUR's automotive, aerospace, and appliance sectors are expanding rapidly, investing in capital equipment to increase capacity and modernize operations. Machine tool consumption in the region currently far exceeds production levels, creating an imbalance that will continue in the near to medium term. The combined industrial activity of the MERCOSUR economies makes it the fourth largest regional market for U.S. machine tools.

Activity is strongest in Brazil, where global automakers are investing in state-of-the-art manufacturing facilities that will supply the entire Latin America region. U.S. machine tool manufacturers exported over $92 million of equipment to Brazil in 1997, the second highest level to date. Although exports were down significantly compared with 1996, the U.S. machine tool industry believes that this trend will be reversed as the Brazilian economic situation continues to strengthen. The turbulence that Brazil's economy experienced in 1996 and 1997 has been attributed to fiscal and monetary difficulties precipitated by Mexico's financial crisis. Opportunities for sales of machine tools were expected to grow throughout 1998 and well into the future in response to continued automotive spending and accelerated development of Brazil's production capacity for consumer goods. AMT, the Association For Manufacturing Technology, the industry's trade group, has established an office at the São Paolo U.S. Commercial Center to better serve the market.

U.S. Industry Growth Projections

Annual U.S. machine tool product shipments have grown for the last 4 years, topping $6.5 billion in 1997 (see Table 17-3). This trend was expected to hold with 1998 shipments on track to exceed $7.1 billion, an increase of 9 percent in current dollars (6.6 percent in constant dollars). Industry exports reflect a similar pattern of growth. U.S. machine tool exports climbed to over $2.8 billion in 1997 and were expected to rise 4 percent in 1998 to more than $3 billion. With continued growth projected for the U.S. economy, U.S. machine tool producers have reason to be optimistic. Machine tool purchases historically are driven by economic prosperity. The industry's upward trend is expected to continue for several more years, in parallel with the domestic economy's projected sustained growth. Product shipments of machine tools, expressed in constant dollars, are forecast to increase 1.5 percent in 1999.

U.S. machine tool manufacturers can expect moderate growth in shipments in the period 1999–2003. Projections call for annual increases of around 3 to 4 percent. The rising demand for capital equipment will be driven by manufacturers' need to improve productivity, increase capacity, and cut labor costs. Price increases will be virtually nonexistent as manufacturers continue to place strong price pressure on machine tool

TABLE 17-3: Machine Tools (SIC 3541, 3542) Trends and Forecasts
(millions of dollars except as noted)

	1992	1993	1994	1995	1996	1997[1]	1998[2]	1999[3]	96–97	97–98	98–99	92–96[4]
									Percent Change			
Industry data												
Value of shipments[5]	5,102	5,231	5,366	6,089	6,357	6,853	7,470	7,769	7.8	9.0	4.0	5.7
Value of shipments (1992$)	5,102	5,152	5,196	5,695	5,771	6,077	6,478	6,575	5.3	6.6	1.5	3.1
Total employment (thousands)	39.9	38.0	37.1	40.4	40.4	40.7			0.7			0.3
Production workers (thousands)	23.3	22.3	22.0	24.5	24.7	25.1			1.6			1.5
Average hourly earnings ($)	15.34	15.72	16.16	16.25	16.74	17.23			2.9			2.2
Capital expenditures	124	95.7	131	190	169							8.0
Product data												
Value of shipments[5]	4,521	4,524	5,098	5,747	6,088	6,563	7,154	7,437	7.8	9.0	4.0	7.7
Value of shipments (1992$)	4,521	4,455	4,934	5,375	5,528	5,821	6,205	6,298	5.3	6.6	1.5	5.2
Trade data												
Value of imports	2,311	2,596	3,389	4,380	4,770	5,329	5,702	6,044	11.7	7.0	6.0	19.9
Value of exports	1,836	1,744	2,179	2,265	2,753	2,886	3,001	3,091	4.8	4.0	3.0	10.7

[1] Estimate except imports and exports.
[2] Estimate.
[3] Forecast.
[4] Compound annual rate.
[5] For a definition of industry versus product values, see "Getting the Most Out of *Outlook '99*."
Source: U.S. Department of Commerce: Bureau of the Census; International Trade Administration.

suppliers. The metal cutting sector is expected to be somewhat stronger than the metal forming sector.

The most active customer markets for U.S. machine tool builders in the near to medium term will be the aerospace, appliance, automotive, construction, farm machinery, and job shop industries. Demand will be particularly robust among job shops. The nation's tool and die businesses are in a retooling mode, investing in a range of new high-technology equipment to improve quality and precision. Job shops are increasing and widening their machining capabilities, particularly in areas such as high-speed cutting and laser, waterjet, and rapid proto-typing technologies. The trend toward outsourcing by a range of producers, most notably the automotive industry, will further increase this sector's demand.

Prospects for export markets are less sure. Key markets that are expected to be soft in the near term include the weakened Pacific Rim region and the European Union, where the introduction of a common European currency in select countries is creating uncertainty. As a result, slower growth in exports is likely, as well as an increase in the U.S. machine tool trade deficit. Machine tool exports are expected to grow around 2 to 3 percent annually in the period 1999–2003. The strongest markets for U.S. machine tool exporters will be Canada, Mexico, Chile, Argentina, and Brazil.

Megan Pilaroscia, U.S. Department of Commerce, Office of Energy, Infrastructure and Machinery, (202) 482-0609, November 1998.

METAL CUTTING TOOLS

Metal cutting tools, (SIC 35451) a subsector of machine tool accessories (SIC 3545), perform the actual cutting on a machine and require frequent replacement and resharpening. They include drills, taps, reamers, and various forms of indexable inserts. An insert is a form of tool with two or more cutting edges that can be repositioned quickly against a cutting surface.

Global Trends

The principal markets for machine tool accessories are in the industrialized countries, which are the primary users of machine tools. Most cutting tools have been supplied by locally or regionally based manufacturers. Each leading international market has developed a discrete set of major suppliers that often are internally based. Consequently, export opportunities for U.S.-based manufacturers of cutting tools have been limited and most U.S. production has gone to domestic or NAFTA markets. Recently, as the domestic industry has consolidated, U.S. manufacturers have begun to establish more international stocking points and acquire foreign manufacturers that can provide the service and parts needed to maintain an effective presence in a foreign market. Additional opportunities for export sales may develop as customers adopt just-in-time inventory practices that require a rapid supply of cutting tools and work holders from local stocking points.

Domestic Trends

The production of machine tool accessories is concentrated in the Great Lakes states, with Michigan the leading producer state, followed by Ohio, Illinois, and Pennsylvania. Rounding out the top 10 producers, mostly outside the Great Lakes region, are South Carolina, California, Massachusetts, Wisconsin, Tennessee, and Connecticut. The industry, which employs a significant portion of its work force in small machine shops, had

55,600 employees in 1996, of whom 39,300 were production workers. This was an 8 percent increase from 1995.

Metal cutting tools constitute the largest product class in this industry, averaging 50 to 55 percent of shipments. Demand for metal cutting tools is closely linked to the performance of the machine tool industry, tracking its overall trends and cycles. Technological development in the cutting tool industry is closely linked to the demands of the machine tool industry and to competitive pressures to increase productivity.

Technological advances include the use of new materials and heat treatments of cutting tools and continued improvements and wider application of cermets (hard ceramic metal composites). The development of polycrystalline cubic boron nitride cutting tools has reduced problems of lifting, peeling, and chipping in the cutting of thermally sprayed aircraft components.

The impact of technology on the value of product shipments has pulled in two opposing directions. High-technology products usually carry higher unit prices and tend to increase the value of product shipments. Conversely, cutting tools have become more efficient and productive and longer-lasting. In addition, the industry has witnessed advances in casting technology and greater use of near net shapes, which reduces the need for metal removal and hence for cutting tools. These trends have combined to slow growth in unit demand and thus shipment value. However, the overall economic performance in the period 1997–1998 was such that product shipments of machine tool accessories rose more sharply than they have at any time since the economic recovery began in 1992.

Mergers and Consolidations

The principal U.S.-based producers of metal cutting tools have engaged in a round of mergers and consolidations in the past 2 years that have reshaped the industry significantly. This activity has taken several different forms, from conventional acquisitions within the industry to the purchase of firms outside the industry (for example, in electric motors) and the purchase of metal cutting tool manufacturers by machine tool producers. The latter type of merger has altered the traditional relationships between producers of machine tools and suppliers of metal cutting tools. Such mergers are driven partly by an increased tendency of cutting tool technology to dictate developments in the machine tool industry rather than the opposite pattern, which has long prevailed.

Projections of Industry and Trade Growth for the Next 1 and 5 Years

Product shipments of machine tool accessories are estimated to have risen by 5.6 percent in 1998 to almost $5.75 billion in constant dollars (see Table 17-4). Substantial growth in shipments is expected for 1999, with product shipments of machine tool accessories expected to rise a further 7.5 percent to almost $6.18 billion. Over the 5-year period 1999–2003 both industry and product shipments should rise at an annual average of 5 percent despite the likelihood that the increases projected in the period 1997–1999 will not be sustained later.

As was noted earlier, international trade remains limited in an industry in which suppliers have traditionally been located close to their customers. Projected increases of 4.3 percent in 1998 and 5.2 percent in 1999 should bring total U.S. imports of machine tool accessories to just over $101 million. U.S. exports of machine tool accessories, after having fallen slightly in 1997, should rebound with an estimated increase of 5.5 percent to over $57 million in 1998 and a further rise of 7.8 percent to $62 million in 1999. Over the 5-year period 1999–2003, U.S.

TABLE 17-4: Machine Tool Accessories (SIC 3545) Trends and Forecasts

(millions of dollars except as noted)

	1992	1993	1994	1995	1996	1997[1]	1998[2]	1999[3]	96–97	97–98	98–99	92–96[4]
									Percent Change			
Industry data												
Value of shipments[5]	3,844	4,003	4,698	5,341	5,893	6,235	6,597	7,105	5.8	5.8	7.7	11.3
Value of shipments (1992$)	3,844	3,940	4,548	5,030	5,416	5,641	5,900	6,284	4.2	4.6	6.5	8.9
Total employment (thousands)	43.3	43.3	46.7	51.1	55.6							6.5
Production workers (thousands)	30.6	30.5	32.7	35.8	39.3							6.5
Average hourly earnings ($)	12.03	12.79	12.48	12.46	13.06							2.1
Capital expenditures	144	164	188	245	283							18.4
Product data												
Value of shipments[5]	3,606	3,798	4,401	4,864	5,146	5,440	5,745	6,176	5.7	5.6	7.5	9.3
Value of shipments (1992$)	3,606	3,739	4,260	4,580	4,730	4,896	5,111	5,438	3.5	4.4	6.4	7.0
Trade data												
Value of imports	59.3	55.1	68.8	85.5	91.6	92.4	96.4	101.4	0.9	4.3	5.2	11.5
Value of exports	41.8	31.6	43.1	50.0	54.8	54.6	57.6	62.1	–0.4	5.5	7.8	7.0

[1] Estimate except imports and exports.
[2] Estimate.
[3] Forecast.
[4] Compound annual rate.
[5] For a definition of industry versus product values, see "Getting the Most Out of *Outlook '99*."
Source: U.S. Department of Commerce: Bureau of the Census; International Trade Administration.

exports of machine tool accessories should show a rise of 5 percent a year in current dollars while imports are expected to increase at an annual rate of approximately 7 percent. International trade, although growing, will continue to be a marginal factor until customers can be assured of just-in-time service from locally based stocking points.

Global Market Prospects

The metal cutting tool industry is largely a domestic industry. Imports currently account for 4 percent of domestic consumption, and only 2 percent of U.S. production is exported. International trade is expected to remain a relatively marginal factor over the 5-year forecast period. Data from 1997 indicate that Japan (26 percent) and Canada (25 percent) account for over half of U.S. machine tool accessory exports. Mexico is third at 9 percent, followed by the United Kingdom at 5 percent and Korea at 4 percent. The next five largest export markets—Germany, France, China, Australia, and Brazil—all received between $1.5 and $2 million of U.S. exports in 1997. The following five largest export markets, in order, were Singapore, Hong Kong, Thailand, Israel, and Indonesia, with U.S. export totals ranging from $880 million to $1.32 billion in 1997. Although Canada has long been the leading export market for U.S. cutting tool manufacturers, a threefold jump in exports to Japan placed that country in the lead in 1997. However, it appears probable that this increase may not be sustained in the period 1998–1999 because of weakness in the Japanese economy. The prominence of Asian countries in the third tier of export markets presages a further slowdown of exports in 1998 and 1999.

Japan supplies just over one-third (34 percent) of U.S. cutting tool imports, followed by China (17 percent), Switzerland (12 percent), Germany (6 percent), and the United Kingdom (5 percent). France, Korea, Canada, Mexico, and India round out the top 10 import sources. The United States did not receive more than $1 million in machine tool accessories imports from any other country in 1997.

Edward D. Abrahams, U.S. Department of Commerce, Office of Energy, Infrastructure, and Machinery, (202) 482-0312, November 1998.

SPECIAL TOOLS, DIES, JIGS, AND FIXTURES

This industry group (SIC 3544) is composed almost entirely of small companies that manufacture special tools, such as dies and molds, and precision machined parts, prototypes, and special machines for other manufacturers. Commonly referred to as tool and die or tooling and machining companies, these firms engage primarily in manufacturing on a job or order basis and also may provide stopgap capacity for other manufacturers. Industry revenues include revenues for the tools, dies, jigs, fixtures, molds, and contract machining industry (SIC 3544) and receipts for machine shop job work (SIC 35995). Machine shop job work is a component of industrial machinery not elsewhere classified.

Global Trends

The tool and die sector is becoming a world market in response to increased globalization in a number of key industries. Manufacturers are moving production closer to local markets, prompting suppliers to follow suit. This trend is most prevalent in the automotive industry, one of the largest sources of demand for custom tooling. Automakers are striving to develop "world vehicles" that with slight adaptations can be sold throughout the global marketplace. This approach reduces investment costs and increases economies of scale. As manufacturers globalize their sourcing, they will look to suppliers that can accommodate their worldwide needs. This trend will expand opportunities for tool and die producers and increase global competition in the industry.

Investment in technology is on the rise throughout the global machining industry. Computer-aided design and manufacturing (CAD/CAM) techniques and high-precision computer-controlled equipment are being used to craft tooling more quickly and less expensively than can be done with manual and time-consuming traditional techniques. The industry is using information systems and communications technology to achieve further improvements. The Internet and manufacturing software packages enable toolmakers and customers to collaborate on product design and engineering across a network, reducing geographic barriers and speeding product development.

Another trend affecting the tooling and machining sector is the increased use of outsourcing by a range of manufacturing industries. Manufacturers that previously maintained in-house machining capability are finding it advantageous to contract parts production to machining shops, creating expanded opportunities for the industry. Contract machining shops also are providing more value-added services to manufacturers, often partnering with a product manufacturer early in the planning and design process. The trend toward outsourcing will continue as manufacturers face pressure to reduce costs and get products to market more quickly.

Domestic Trends

The U.S. tool and die industry (SIC 3544) includes over 7,000 shops; more than 8,000 job shops (SIC 35995) also are in operation around the United States. The combined annual sales of the tool and die and job shop industries exceed $25 billion. The companies that make up the precision tooling and machining industry are generally small and privately owned and operated; most have between 25 and 30 employees.

Tool and die sector shipments have risen steadily over the last 5 years. This pattern of growth continued in 1997, with domestic shipments surging approximately 15 percent over the 1996 level. The robust domestic economy and buoyant conditions in key customer groups, particularly the electronic components, construction, oil field, and mining equipment and aerospace sectors, have fueled demand for special tooling.

Increased outsourcing by the industry's major customer groups is another significant factor in the upward trend in tooling and machining shipments. More manufacturers are contracting the production of parts and components to outside suppliers in an attempt to lower production costs. This trend is particularly prevalent in the automotive and appliance sectors. Outsourcing is expected to increase in the coming years; as a result of this trend, pressure on industry prices, which already is an area of concern, will increase.

The expanded presence of foreign automakers in the United States, especially Japanese and European manufacturers, also is creating opportunities for U.S. contract machining shops. The transplants, which now account for around a quarter of U.S. automotive production, are relying on U.S. tool and die suppliers more than they did in the past. Transplant automakers also tend to outsource more of their parts than do U.S. automakers. However, Japanese contract machining shops still have a presence in the United States; many of these shops were established during previous waves of investment by Japanese automotive transplants.

The U.S. tooling and machining industry is in the middle of a retooling process, increasing its investment in highly sophisticated technology. Machining shops are widening their range of capability, acquiring more high-speed machine tools as well as more nontraditional machine tool technology, such as laser, EDM, and waterjet machines, and rapid prototyping technology. These nontraditional technologies are well suited for just-in-time manufacturing, which often requires the processing of small batches of material. Increased investment in equipment will help the industry counter the growing shortage of workers.

Investment in advanced and easy-to-use programming technology also is on the rise among contract machining shops. Improvements in CAD/CAM software make it easier and faster for shops to design tools and enable machinists to do more programming. The Internet also is having an impact. Greater numbers of U.S. shops are doing business electronically, using the Internet to develop new business opportunities. This trend will increase competition among suppliers, putting further pressure on prices. More shops are receiving customer data electronically, a trend that will lead to shortened delivery times. Virtual manufacturing interfaces enhance the ability of companies and customers to collaborate on the design, testing, and manufacturing of special machines and tooling across continents, potentially boosting industry exports.

The U.S. industry can expect increased competition from overseas suppliers in the future. The Asian financial crisis, which has weakened currencies in that region, may bring an increase in low-priced imports and a decrease in demand for U.S. special tooling exports. Increased competition at home as well as in global markets is leading to a new trend in the contract machining industry—increased industry cooperation—with more tool and die companies forging closer relationships with fellow shops.

Technology. Rapid prototyping technologies enable machining shops to develop physical models quickly. These technologies, which generally use CAD software and different materials or methods of material application or removal to generate a model, shorten prototype development time from a month or more to as little as a week. The latest techniques can reduce development time to an hour or less. One of the best known rapid prototyping technologies is stereolithography, which uses a laser beam to cure light-sensitive polymers into the shape of a part. Newer methods that are even faster and more accurate include laminated object manufacturing, which uses a laser to cut thin layers of paper that are laminated together to form a part; selective laser sintering, which uses a laser beam to bond nylon, metal, or trueform powder into a shape; and solid ground curing, which uses a material that hardens quickly after a brief exposure to ultraviolet light to make models.

Rapid prototyping techniques have been enhanced and are being used to produce durable tooling from steel and other hard metals and cermets faster and cheaper. Traditional production tooling, which typically relies on computer numerical control (CNC) or EDM machining, is very costly and time-consuming. The new rapid tooling technologies help manufacturers respond to shrinking lead times and bring new products to market more quickly. Some of the latest rapid tooling technologies use composite materials as an alternative to metal tooling.

Sandia National Laboratories, a U.S. Department of Energy research and development facility, in conjunction with private sector partners, is working to commercialize a special technology that dramatically reduces the time required to make custom parts and molds. The technology, which is known as Laser Engineered Net Shaping (LENS), extends earlier techniques of rapid prototyping and rapid manufacturing. LENS allows the manufacture of three-dimensional metallic components directly from CAD designs, using computer-controlled lasers to weld air-blown streams of metallic powders into custom parts and molds. This technique can be used to produce shapes that are close enough to the final product to eliminate the need for rough machining. It also makes it possible to create a complex metal part in a matter of hours rather than the weeks typically needed with older methods that require manual carving and sculpting. When perfected, LENS technology will significantly increase manufacturers' ability to vary the shapes and materials of products quickly as market conditions shift.

Skilled Labor Shortage. The National Tooling and Machining Association estimates that demand for skilled machinists exceeds the supply by 20,000. This labor shortage is one of the most critical issues facing U.S. tooling companies and one with serious ramifications: The decreasing pool of highly skilled toolmakers makes the industry particularly vulnerable to overseas competition. Adding to the worry is the aging of the industry's work force: The average age of these machinists is 55 years. The shortage is worsening as demand for industry products and services increases.

The U.S. contract machining industry has stepped in to fill the void created by vanishing federal funding for worker training. National Tooling and Machining Association local chapters have established 21 training centers around the country to teach precision skills, using state-of-the-art equipment. Over half these centers are operated in partnership with local community colleges or vocational schools. Toolmakers, who require expertise in a range of sophisticated technologies, including CNC machine tools and CAD/CAM techniques, typically require at least 4 years of on-the-job training.

The industry also has launched an effort to develop metal-working skills standards and credentialing assessments by creating the National Institute for Metalworking Skills, a consortium of trade associations, labor organizations, the Council of Great Lakes Governors, companies, and educators. Formed in 1995, the group has completed work on a number of standards, with the remainder slated for completion by the end of 1998. The initiative will help give the metalworking industry a high-quality work force and increase its reputation for world-class skills.

Legislative Efforts. Legislative efforts are under way that may affect the U.S. tool and die industry in several key areas. A bill introduced in early 1998, known as the Skilled Workforce Enhancement Act, is intended to alleviate the shortage of skilled workers that plagues many U.S. industries. The bill reflects the growing recognition among industry and legislative leaders that the United States must improve its training in technical skills to ensure that high-paying manufacturing jobs are not transferred to offshore sources of labor. This legislation would give small manufacturers a tax credit for training workers on site.

Tax relief in another area is also a target of industry efforts. The tool and die industry has lobbied for reform in the estate, or death, tax laws for many years. These taxes often imperil small family-owned businesses. Scores of machining shops have been forced to close after an owner's death when surviving family members have been unable to pay the substantial estate taxes that are levied under U.S. law. The 1997 budget agreement's estate tax provisions provide some relief for family-owned small businesses. The battle continues, how-

ever, with the small business community, including the National Tooling and Machining Association, pushing for the repeal of this tax. The contract machining industry also is lobbying for product liability reform; frivolous lawsuits and enormous punitive damage awards are another threat to small machining businesses.

U.S. Industry Growth Projections

The upward trend in industry shipments has been projected to continue through 1998, although at a slower pace than in 1997. Product shipments by U.S. tool and die producers were expected to grow around 3.5 percent in constant-dollar terms in 1998 and 2.3 percent in 1999 (see Table 17-5). Moderate growth is also anticipated in the period 1999–2003, during which time industry shipments should grow around 3 to 4 percent a year. The near-term growth projections are dampened somewhat by uncertain prospects in some export markets. Uncertainty is strongest in Asia, which remains mired in financial turmoil. The strongest customer sectors for the industry in the near term are expected to be the electronic components, aerospace, construction, mining, and oil field equipment industries.

International Competitiveness

Industry exports increased over 20 percent in 1997 compared with 1996 and, at almost $2 billion, are nearly double the 1992 level. The top destinations for U.S. contract machining exports are Canada, Mexico, and the United Kingdom; these markets will remain the primary destinations for U.S. tool and die exports in the foreseeable future. More than 40 percent of U.S. tooling and machining exports went to Canada in 1997. With purchases of U.S.-sourced tooling exceeding $830 million, the Canadian market was more than twice as large as the next largest market, Mexico. The next four largest export markets

TABLE 17-5: Special Tools, Dies, Jigs, and Fixtures (SIC 3544) Trends and Forecasts
(millions of dollars except as noted)

	1992	1993	1994	1995	1996	1997[1]	1998[2]	1999[3]	Percent Change			
									96–97	97–98	98–99	92–96[4]
Industry data												
Value of shipments[5]	9,265	9,951	11,145	12,656	12,949	14,891	15,636	16,261	15.0	5.0	4.0	8.7
Value of shipments (1992$)	9,265	9,708	10,604	11,839	11,902	13,533	14,007	14,329	13.7	3.5	2.3	6.5
Total employment (thousands)	111	118	119	131	133	137			3.0			4.6
Production workers (thousands)	84.9	90.7	91.8	102	104	108			3.8			5.2
Average hourly earnings ($)	14.58	14.70	15.03	15.35	15.64	16.00			2.3			1.8
Capital expenditures	369	532	541	722	699							17.3
Product data												
Value of shipments[5]	10,230	10,990	12,235	13,595	13,834	15,909	16,704	17,372	15.0	5.0	4.0	7.8
Value of shipments (1992$)	10,230	10,722	11,641	12,717	12,715	14,457	14,963	15,307	13.7	3.5	2.3	5.6
Trade data												
Value of imports	1,399	1,880	2,608	2,948	2,656	2,924	3,304	3,634	10.1	13.0	10.0	17.4
Value of exports	1,033	1,239	1,306	1,480	1,616	1,958	2,033	2,094	21.2	3.8	3.0	11.8

[1] Estimate except imports and exports.
[2] Estimate.
[3] Forecast.
[4] Compound annual rate.
[5] For a definition of industry versus product values, see "Getting the Most Out of *Outlook '99*."
Source: U.S. Department of Commerce: Bureau of the Census; International Trade Administration.

for U.S. toolmakers in 1997 were Germany, Japan, the Netherlands, and Hong Kong.

Despite the upward trend in U.S. tool and die exports, exports still account for a paltry share of annual shipments—13 percent. The larger machining firms account for the bulk of industry exports; relatively few of the smaller shops that predominate in the industry try to sell to overseas markets. The pressure to export is growing, however, with increased globalization in the manufacturing sector creating more competition among world suppliers. U.S. suppliers of custom tooling must increase their global market share or risk being marginalized. To maintain current shipment levels, U.S. tooling and machining companies will be forced to pursue overseas markets aggressively and follow their customers.

U.S. imports of tool and die products continue to outpace exports, with the industry registering a trade deficit of nearly $1 billion in 1997. Special tooling imports rose more than 10 percent in response to dynamic conditions in the U.S. manufacturing sector. At over $2.9 billion, U.S. tooling and machining imports in 1997 were more than twice the 1992 level. The largest suppliers of special tooling to the U.S. market in 1997 were Japan, Canada, and Germany, followed by Israel, Sweden, the United Kingdom, and Taiwan.

Growth of U.S. tooling and machining exports was expected to slow in 1998. Dampened by developments in Asia, U.S. exports were projected to grow around 4 percent for the year. Exports are projected to be flat in 1999 and 2000 unless there is substantial improvement in the crisis-stricken economies of the Pacific Rim. Slight growth will be seen in shipments to the industry's traditional leading export markets, Canada and Mexico; South America also will see an increase in imports.

While Asia's ailing economies are cutting back on their purchases of U.S. goods, exports from that region's tool and machining industries threaten to swell. Excess capacity in the region could lead to an upward surge in U.S. tool and die imports from Asia as well as more Asian exports competing for market share in global markets. The plunge in Asian currencies will make Asian products cheaper for U.S. customers and tend to depress product prices and profits in the United States.

Despite Asia's current woes, its machining industry, which consists of many large shops, is particularly strong and poses a growing challenge to U.S. producers. Asian tool and die producers are aggressively pursuing overseas markets; the Asian industry currently controls an estimated 40 percent of the worldwide tooling and machining business. Many of the region's contract machining industries receive generous government assistance, including support for training programs. This assistance has helped countries such as Korea, Taiwan, Thailand, and Singapore establish centers that provide training to machinists and die and mold makers. Asian shops are increasing their ranks of skilled machinists at a time when the U.S. industry is experiencing a shortage of skilled labor.

Megan Pilaroscia, U.S. Department of Commerce, Office of Energy, Infrastructure and Machinery, (202) 482-0609, November 1998.

POWER-DRIVEN HAND TOOLS

The power-driven hand tool industry (SIC 3546) consists of manufacturers of hand-held and portable electric and non-electric power tools. These tools include corded and cordless (battery-powered) electric tools, pneumatic and hydraulic tools, powder-actuated tools, and gasoline-powered and electric chain saws. Stationary woodworking tools are classified under SIC 3524. Hand and edge tools are classified under SIC 3423. Gasoline and electric trimmer/brushcutters, hand-held and backpack blowers, and hedge trimmers are classified under SIC 3524. Handsaws and saw blades are classified under SIC 3425.

Global Trends

The power-driven hand tool subsector has evolved into a global industry, with manufacturers producing tools at locations which yield the greatest efficiencies and largest profit margins yet still provide labor sufficiently skilled to manufacture high-quality tools. The industry's products are sourced from markets with highly skilled labor forces and from newly industrializing countries. Distribution channels, which long were confined to national borders, have internationalized as retail outlets in the United States and Europe have established branches outside their countries of origin. Although the leading brand names have retained their identities, the electric power tool subsector has seen a continuation of the mergers that have altered the locus of capital control among the industry leaders. These mergers and joint ventures have involved both foreign capital purchases of U.S.-based entities and U.S. purchases of foreign, usually European Union, firms (largely to gain easier entry into the European Union). The CE Mark, which is viewed by the industry as a nontariff barrier, has further encouraged the establishment of new U.S.-owned European facilities. In the face of market consolidation, Japan-based suppliers have continued to expand their manufacturing capabilities in the United States.

Domestic Trends

The power-driven hand tool subsector had 16,000 employees in 225 establishments in 1996. Industry employment has stabilized at this level and is expected to remain there for the next several years. The production of nonelectric (hydraulic and pneumatic) power tools is concentrated in New York, Pennsylvania, Ohio, and Illinois. Those states and Wisconsin have significant electric tool production. However, the production of electric power tools has gradually settled in a southern crescent running from Maryland through North Carolina, South Carolina, Georgia, Mississippi, Tennessee, Arkansas, and Texas.

Projected increases in product shipments in the period 1997–1999 will be driven by several factors. These factors include competitive home center outlets that increasingly emphasize tool sales to a broad band of do-it-yourself and contractor customers, step-up purchasing by do-it-yourselfers seeking higher quality and an increased volume of exports, particularly of cordless tools, as well as higher levels of exports to previously underexploited markets.

From the introduction of the power-driven screwdriver in 1987 to the arrival of 18- and 24-volt cordless drills, battery-powered electric tools gained wide acceptability among both do-it-yourselfers and contractors. Battery charging times, which initially were measured in hours, were compressed to minutes. Cordless tools have proved immensely popular on outdoor job sites and in areas, including some foreign markets, where electric power supplies are unreliable. However, U.S. product shipments of cordless power tools, after reaching a record $429 million in 1993, fell and leveled off at just over $350 million between 1994 and 1996. Product shipments of cordless tools are estimated to have risen to approximately $375 million in 1997 and have been projected to reach $405 million in 1998. Manufacturers have sought to increase shipments by exploiting export opportunities in new markets and enlarging the range of products to which cordless technology is applicable.

Shipments of chain saws were reported by industry sources at 2,173,000 units in 1997, an increase of 5.4 percent from the 1996 total of 2,161,000 units. This represented the second consecutive year of substantial increases in unit volume of chain saw shipments. Manufacturers also benefited from a nearly 20 percent increase in unit shipments of hedge trimmers in 1997, although this followed an 8 percent downturn in 1996. In 1998 chain saw shipments were expected to increase 1.5 percent to approximately 2,206,000 units.

On the regulatory front, California regulatory authorities continue to play a major role in shaping the market for chain saw manufacturers. The industry faces a long-pending deadline in its efforts to achieve compliance with the year 2000 Tier II standards for two-cycle engines promulgated by the California Air Resources Board. Additionally, several large municipalities

in that state, including Los Angeles and Santa Barbara, have sought to ban or regulate the use of trimmer/brushcutters and hedge trimmers. In addition to complying with the California standards, the industry must comply with U.S. Environmental Protection Agency Phase I and Phase II exhaust emission standards for two-cycle engines.

Power tool manufacturers continue to be affected by the changing retail environment in which most tools are sold. Sales of electric tools are increasingly funneled through home centers as contractors and professionals have become amenable to purchasing through those outlets and the home centers have adapted to professionals' needs. Home centers selling almost exclusively to the professional trade have appeared in some markets. Greater consolidation among U.S. home center retailers and hardware wholesalers and buying groups has enabled electric power tool manufacturers to sell more tools through fewer retail outlets. Nonelectric power tools continue to be sold largely through industrial distributors.

Projections of Industry and Trade Growth for the Next 1 and 5 Years

As is indicated in Table 17-6, current dollar product shipments of power-driven hand tools are expected to reach record levels of $3.73 billion in 1998 and almost $3.94 billion in 1999. In constant 1992 dollars, product shipments of power-driven hand tools are expected to rise 3.5 percent to $3.38 billion and 4.4 percent to a record level of $3.53 billion in 1999. Over the period 1999–2003 both industry and product shipments are expected to increase at an average annual rate of 4 percent.

International trade in power-driven hand tools should continue to be robust over the period 1997–1999. U.S. imports of power tools should rise an estimated 9.6 percent in 1998 to

TABLE 17-6: Power-Driven Hand Tools (SIC 3546) Trends and Forecasts
(millions of dollars except as noted)

	1992	1993	1994	1995	1996	1997[1]	1998[2]	1999[3]	Percent Change 96–97	Percent Change 97–98	Percent Change 98–99	Percent Change 92–96[4]
Industry data												
Value of shipments[5]	2,873	3,480	3,608	3,791	3,744	3,894	4,081	4,305	4.0	4.8	5.5	6.8
Value of shipments (1992$)	2,873	3,405	3,450	3,566	3,470	3,567	3,695	3,857	2.8	3.6	4.4	4.8
Total employment (thousands)	16.1	17.0	16.1	17.0	16.3							0.3
Production workers (thousands)	10.6	11.7	11.2	11.9	11.3							1.6
Average hourly earnings ($)	11.08	10.98	11.27	12.13	12.17							2.4
Capital expenditures	72.3	112	106	118	118							13.0
Product data												
Value of shipments[5]	2,415	3,074	3,281	3,368	3,426	3,563	3,730	3,935	4.0	4.7	5.5	9.1
Value of shipments (1992$)	2,415	3,008	3,137	3,168	3,175	3,264	3,378	3,527	2.8	3.5	4.4	7.1
Trade data												
Value of imports	766	823	952	1,084	1,209	1,388	1,521	1,647	14.8	9.6	8.3	12.1
Value of exports	568	600	699	738	720	916	1,035	1,189	27.2	13.0	14.9	6.1

[1] Estimate except imports and exports.
[2] Estimate.
[3] Forecast.
[4] Compound annual rate.
[5] For a definition of industry versus product values, see "Getting the Most Out of *Outlook '99*."
Source: U.S. Department of Commerce: Bureau of the Census; International Trade Administration.

$1.52 billion and a further 8.3 percent to nearly $1.65 billion in 1999. Although U.S. exports of power-driven hand tools are expected to expand at a greater rate than are imports over the period 1997–1999, a substantial deficit in the U.S. balance of trade in these tools will continue. Exports are anticipated to rise 13 percent in 1998 to approximately $1.04 billion and a further 15 percent in 1999 to a record level of $1.2 billion. Over the period 1998–2003, imports should increase at an annual average of about 10 percent while exports should rise an annual average of approximately 12.5 percent. The profile of international trade in this industry will continue to rise, but the overall U.S. trade in power-driven hand tools will almost certainly remain in deficit.

Global Trade Prospects

U.S. exports of power-driven hand tools totaled a record $916 million in 1997, representing a 27 percent increase over 1996. Nonelectric tools constituted approximately 60 percent of power tool exports, with electric power tools accounting for approximately 40 percent. Canada, which accounted for $200 million, or 22 percent of U.S. power tool exports, has long been the leading U.S. export market, although its overall export share has declined slowly through the 1990s. Mexico, accounting for $90 million, or just under 10 percent of U.S. power tool exports, emerged in 1997 as the second largest export market. U.S. exports to the Netherlands doubled to $71 million in 1997, or 8 percent of all U.S. power tool exports. Germany (7 percent) and the United Kingdom (7 percent) were the fourth and fifth largest export markets. Belgium showed a nearly $30 million increase to $44 million (5 percent) in 1997, while France, at $43 million (5 percent), was in seventh place. The European Union markets received a substantial volume of exports sent to U.S. subsidiaries, including parts subject to substantive transformation in the manufacturing process. Japan (4 percent), Australia (4 percent), and Brazil (2 percent) rounded out the top 10 U.S. power tool export markets.

U.S. imports of portable power tools totaled an estimated $1.388 billion in 1997, an increase of 14.8 percent over 1996. Japan accounted for 19 percent of U.S. imports in 1997, a total of $262 million. This continued a downtrend in the percentage of imports derived from Japanese sources. A surge in domestic demand apparently encouraged Japanese producers to increase direct importing into the United States of higher-dollar-value power-tool items, reversing the fall in imports. In previous years, direct importing from Japan had fallen as the major Japan-based producers expanded their U.S. operations. Japanese firms have primarily produced drills and other consumer power tools at their U.S. plants.

Although dogged by quality problems, China surged past Mexico into second place as a source of U.S. power tool imports, accounting for $242 million, or 17 percent of U.S. imports. U.S. imports of Mexican power tools totaled $185 million, or 13 percent of all imports, with increased NAFTA-inspired reliance on *maquiladora* (in-bond) production. The remaining top 10 sources of power tool imports into the United

States are Taiwan (11 percent), Germany (11 percent), Sweden (7 percent), the United Kingdom (5 percent), Switzerland (5 percent), Italy (4 percent), and Canada (2 percent.)

Edward D. Abrahams, U.S. Department of Commerce, Office of Energy, Infrastructure, and Machinery, (202) 482-0312, November 1998.

WELDING APPARATUS

The welding apparatus industry consists of manufacturers of welding power sources; arc welding transformers and generators; gas welding equipment; resistance welders; welding robots; welding guns, tips, and torches; soldering equipment; electrodes; and bare and coated welding wire. The industry is formally known as the electric and gas welding and soldering equipment industry (SIC 3548). Manufacturers of shielding gases are classified under SIC 2813.

Global Trends

The United States is the world's largest producer of welding and cutting apparatus, and U.S. welding products maintain a strong competitive position in most of the industrialized countries, which are the leading markets for this apparatus. The United States remains a leading source of welding power sources, electrodes, and resistance welding apparatus. Importers have emerged as the primary sources for robotic welding systems, some types of welding torches, and certain specialty items. Mergers and consolidations of U.S.-based and foreign-owned firms have placed some traditional competitors under common ownership. Although the industry continues to be heavily dependent on its traditional markets in the automotive and shipbuilding industries, it has attempted to develop new markets, such as the aerospace industry.

Domestic Trends

Leading markets for welding equipment include the automotive, automotive repair and aftermarket, nonresidential construction, petroleum, shipbuilding, highway construction and bridge building, and machine and job shop work markets. In 1996 the U.S. welding apparatus subsector employed 19,700 workers, of whom 13,000 were production workers. The production of welding apparatus is widely distributed in the United States, with the greatest concentration in the Great Lakes states. Michigan, with its proximity to the automobile industry, dominates the production of resistance welding equipment. Ohio, Wisconsin, Illinois, and Missouri are among the leading producers of welding power sources and equipment for gas-metal-arc and gas-tungsten-arc welding. New Hampshire has emerged as a major source of plasma cutting equipment.

Mergers and Consolidation

The welding apparatus industry has experienced a spate of mergers over the last 4 years. This trend toward consolidation seems likely to continue and has reshaped the nature of the industry. Major mergers have taken place among the leading producers of welding apparatus and major manufacturers of shielding gases. This merger activity has involved both publicly traded and privately held companies. The overall merger pattern has injected a substantial amount of publicly held capital stock into an industry long characterized by closely held firms even among the U.S. industry leaders.

Standards, Workplace Safety, and the Environment

The safety of the welding work environment has been heavily regulated at the federal level by the U.S. Department of Labor, OSHA, and by related state agencies. These regulations primarily govern workplace safety and have impelled manufacturers to improve the dust and fume extraction capabilities of machinery and the effectiveness of shielding gases. Safety equipment such as gloves and shields has become a major feature of the industry's trade shows. Pulse welding has emerged as an environmentally friendly welding process. The industry has also been active in maintaining and revising welding standards, such as the recently completed revisions of the U.S. standard for welding structural steel. The welding industry is closely involved in efforts to harmonize international welding standards and prevent standards issues from becoming nontariff barriers to the sale of welding apparatus.

Welding Education

The welding apparatus industry has long seen welding education and training as a central tenet of its efforts to attract more workers to the profession and encourage the use of safe processes. The education process runs from the training of apprentice welders to the education of graduate welding engineers. The American Welding Society has embarked on an "Image of Welding" program designed to attract new students to the field. Included in the program is an industry-sponsored video directed at students who are considering a career in welding.

Projections of Industry and Trade Growth for the Next 1 and 5 Years

As is indicated in Table 17-7, product shipments of welding apparatus are expected to grow an estimated 7.4 percent in current dollars and 6.2 percent in constant 1992 dollars in 1998. Product shipments of welding apparatus are expected to reach a record $4.3 billion in 1999, up 8.5 percent in current dollars, while reaching $3.56 billion in constant 1992 dollars, or 7.3 percent above the estimated 1998 level. Over the 5-year period 1999–2003 both industry and product shipments are projected to increase at an average of 5 percent per year in current dollars, with the greatest growth likely to occur in the last years of the twentieth century.

International trade should continue to grow briskly in both directions in the period 1999–2003. Imports of welding apparatus are expected to rise at an annual average rate of 8 percent, while exports should show an increase of approximately 7 percent per year.

Global Market Prospects

The United States remains the world's largest producer of and market for welding apparatus, and a majority of the top manufacturers remain U.S.-based, controlled by U.S. capital. The United States is highly competitive internationally in the production of most types of welding apparatus. However, Japan

TABLE 17-7: Welding Apparatus (SIC 3548) Trends and Forecasts
(millions of dollars except as noted)

	1992	1993	1994	1995	1996	1997[1]	1998[2]	1999[3]	Percent Change 96–97	97–98	98–99	92–96[4]
Industry data												
Value of shipments[5]	2,738	3,101	3,086	3,303	3,496	3,657	3,928	4,261	4.6	7.4	8.5	6.3
Value of shipments (1992$)	2,738	2,984	2,871	2,970	3,067	3,159	3,355	3,600	3.0	6.2	7.3	2.9
Total employment (thousands)	19.6	20.3	18.6	18.9	19.7							0.1
Production workers (thousands)	11.7	13.1	12.0	12.7	13.0							2.7
Average hourly earnings ($)	13.87	14.76	15.28	15.92	16.05							3.7
Capital expenditures	65.3	80.6	73.5	89.3	124							17.4
Product data												
Value of shipments[5]	2,391	2,717	3,043	3,336	3,452	3,607	3,874	4,203	4.5	7.4	8.5	9.6
Value of shipments (1992$)	2,391	2,615	2,830	3,000	3,028	3,122	3,316	3,558	3.1	6.2	7.3	6.1
Trade data												
Value of imports	382	535	530	659	751	882	974	1,118	17.4	10.4	14.8	18.4
Value of exports	624	655	685	770	850	1,081	1,173	1,322	27.2	8.5	12.7	8.0

[1] Estimate except imports and exports.
[2] Estimate.
[3] Forecast.
[4] Compound annual rate.
[5] For a definition of industry versus product values, see "Getting the Most Out of *Outlook '99.*"
Source: U.S. Department of Commerce: Bureau of the Census; International Trade Administration.

has established a clear predominance as a supplier of robotic welding systems to the American market. Germany also is a major supplier of robotic welding systems to U.S. manufacturers. Other producers, such as Italy, which is a major source for the production of inverters and other welding power sources, have established a foothold in the U.S. market.

U.S. welding apparatus exports set a record in 1997, reaching $1.081 billion, marking the industry's first billion-dollar export year. Canada, long the top U.S. export destination for welding apparatus, accounted for $286 million (26 percent) of U.S. exports in 1997, a 41 percent increase over 1996. Mexico easily retained its second ranking as an export destination for U.S. welding apparatus with U.S. exports of $104 million, nearly 10 percent of the industry total and nearly 50 percent above the level in 1996. Rounding out the top 10 U.S. export markets were South Korea (5 percent), Japan (4 percent), the United Kingdom (4 percent), Singapore (3 percent), Brazil (3 percent), Germany (3 percent), India (2 percent), and Australia (2 percent). The Asian financial crisis could slow the growth of U.S. welding apparatus exports. However, as of 1997, other than Japan and China, Malaysia ($15.8 million) was the only Asian country which accounted for over 1 percent of total U.S. welding apparatus exports. Thailand, the Phillippines, and Indonesia accounted for $5 million to $10 million each in U.S. welding apparatus exports in 1997.

The United States imports welding apparatus from fewer countries than it exports to. U.S. imports of welding apparatus nearly doubled between 1992 and 1996 as import penetration rose from 16 percent to 24 percent of estimated product shipments. Import penetration was expected to remain near this level in 1998 and is projected to be slightly above 25 percent in 1999.

U.S. imports of welding apparatus in 1997 showed some divergent trends, with imports from Japan rising 57 percent while imports from Sweden dropped nearly 50 percent and those from Switzerland fell nearly a third. In 1997 Japan accounted for almost 49 percent of U.S. welding apparatus imports, primarily reflecting its domination in imports of high-value robotics welding systems. Japanese imports were more than four times the value of Canadian and German imports, which each accounted for approximately 11 percent of U.S. welding apparatus imports. U.S. imports of Swedish welding apparatus fell sharply in 1997, dropping by nearly half to a 6 percent import share. Rounding out the top 10 U.S. import sources are the United Kingdom (5 percent), Switzerland (4 percent), Italy (4 percent), France (1.5 percent), Austria (1.1 percent), and Taiwan (1 percent.) China accounts for only $4.8 million in U.S. imports and ranks seventeenth on the 1997 import source list. Technical requirements for assembly and the need for a skilled labor force have largely precluded migration of the industry's manufacturing facilities to newly industrializing countries.

Edward D. Abrahams, U.S. Department of Commerce, Office of Energy, Infrastructure, and Machinery, (202) 482-0312, November 1998.

■ REFERENCES

Machine Tools

American Machinist, Penton Publishing, Inc., 1100 Superior Avenue, Cleveland, OH 44114-2543. (216) 696-7000, Fax: (216) 696-0177, http://www.penton.com/am.

Association for Manufacturing Technology, 7901 Westpark Drive, McLean, VA 22102-4269. (703) 893-2900, Fax: (703) 893-1151, http://www.mfgtech.org.

Manufacturing Extension Partnership (MEP), National Institute of Standards and Technology. Telephone: (800) MEP-4MFG, http://www.mep.nist.gov.

Metalworking Insiders' Report, P.O. Box 107, Larchmont, NY 10538-0107. (914) 834-2300, Fax: (914) 834-7035.

Metalworking Machinery, Current Industrial Reports, Series MQ-35W, U.S. Department of Commerce, Bureau of the Census, Industry Division, Washington, DC 20233. (301) 457-4744, http://www.census.gov/econ/www/manumenu.html.

1992 Census of Manufactures, MC92-I-35C, Metalworking Machinery, U.S. Bureau of the Census, Washington, DC 20233.

1998 World Machine Tool Output and Consumption Survey, Gardner Publications, Inc., 6915 Valley Avenue, Cincinnati, OH 45244-3029. Fax: (513) 527-8801, http://www.gardnerweb.com.

Metal Cutting Tools

Assembly, Cahners Business Information, 8773 South Ridgeline Boulevard, Highlands Ranch, CO 80126-2329.

Cutting Tool Engineering, CTE Publications, Inc., 400 Skokie Boulevard, Northbrook, IL 60062-7903.

Job Shop Technology, Edwards Publishing Co., 16 Waterbury Road, Prospect, CT 06712.

Modern Applications News, 2500 Tamiami Trail North, Nokomis, FL 34275-3482.

Tooling and Production, Adams-Huebcore Publishing, Inc., 29100 Aurora Road, Suite 200, Solon, OH 44139.

Special Tools, Dies, Jigs, and Fixtures

Manufacturing Engineering, Society of Manufacturing Engineers, One SME Drive, P.O. Box 930, Dearborn, MI 48121-0930. (313) 271-1500, Fax: (313) 271-2861, http://www.sme.org.

Modern Machine Shop, 6915 Valley Avenue, Cincinnati, OH 45244-3029. (513) 527-8800, Fax: (513) 527-8801, http://www.gardnerweb.com/mms.

National Tooling and Machining Association, 9300 Livingston Road, Fort Washington, MD 20744. (301) 248-6200, Fax: (301) 248-7104, http://www.ntma.org.

Tooling and Manufacturing Association, 1177 S. Dee Road, Park Ridge, IL 60068-4396. (847) 825-1120, Fax: (847) 825-0041, www.tmanet.com.

Tooling and Production, 29100 Aurora Road, Solon, OH 44139. (440) 248-1125, Fax: (440) 248-0187, http://www.toolingandproduction.com.

Power-Driven Hand Tools

Do-It-Yourself Retailing, National Retail Hardware Association, 5822 W. 74th Street, Indianapolis, IN 46278.

National Home Center News, Lebhar-Friedman, Inc., 425 Park Avenue, New York, NY 10022.

1992 Census of Manufactures, MW-92-I-35C, Metalworking Machinery, Bureau of the Census, Washington, DC 20233.

Power Equipment Trade, Hatton-Brown Publishers, 225 Hanrick Street, Montgomery, AL 36104.

Welding Apparatus

Gases and Welding Distributor, Penton Publishing Company, 1100 Superior Avenue, Cleveland, OH 44114-2543.

Practical Welding Today, The Croydon Group, Ltd., 833 Featherstone Drive, Rockford, IL 61107-6302.

Welding Design & Fabrication, Penton Publishing Company, 1100 Superior Avenue, Cleveland, OH 44114-2543.

Welding Journal, American Welding Society, 550 N.W. Le Jeune Road, Miami, FL 33126.

■ **RELATED CHAPTERS**

PRODUCTION MACHINERY
Economic and Trade Trends

U.S. International Trade

($ billions)

Legend: Balance — Exports — Imports

Source: U.S. Department of Commerce: Bureau of the Census; International Trade Administration.

World Export Market Shares

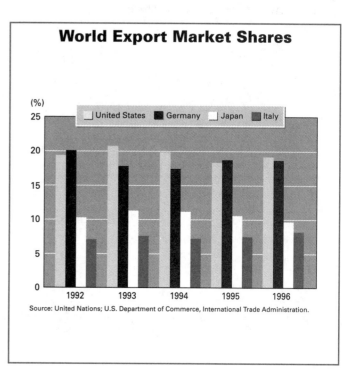

(%)

Legend: United States, Germany, Japan, Italy

Source: United Nations; U.S. Department of Commerce, International Trade Administration.

Export Dependence and Import Penetration

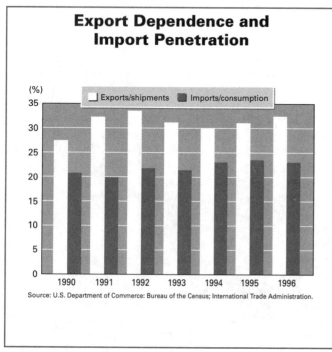

(%)

Legend: Exports/shipments, Imports/consumption

Source: U.S. Department of Commerce: Bureau of the Census; International Trade Administration.

Output and Output per Hour

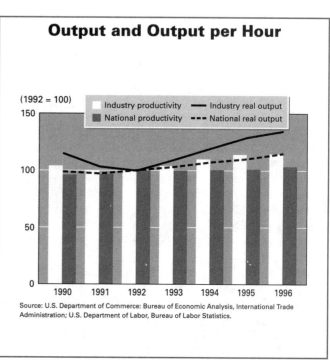

(1992 = 100)

Legend: Industry productivity, National productivity, Industry real output, National real output

Source: U.S. Department of Commerce: Bureau of Economic Analysis, International Trade Administration; U.S. Department of Labor, Bureau of Labor Statistics.

See "Getting the Most Out of *Outlook '99*" for definitions of terms.

18

Production Machinery

INDUSTRY DEFINITION This chapter discusses nine production machinery industries: air conditioning, refrigeration, and heating equipment (SIC 3585); construction machinery (SIC 3531); mining machinery (SIC 3532); oil and gas field machinery (SIC 3533); printing trades machinery (SIC 3555); packaging machinery (SIC 3565); paper industries machinery (SIC 3554); agricultural and farm machinery (SIC 3523); and food products machinery (SIC 3556). Air conditioning, refrigeration, and heating equipment is the largest subsector, followed by construction machinery, then agricultural and farm machinery. These three subsectors account for more than 76 percent of 1996 product shipments of the production machinery discussed in this chapter.

OVERVIEW

The products covered in this chapter are a diverse group, from farm tractors, to printing presses, to air conditioning units, with the common purpose of making the production and distribution processes of manufacturing firms more efficient and profitable. Because many machines manufactured by production machinery firms represent significant capital expenditures for the end users, shipments in the industry tend to follow the business cycle closely, growing rapidly in times of low interest rates and strong profits and decelerating in times of uncertainty and weaker consumer demand.

Evidence of the cyclical nature of the industry can be seen in the experience of the early and middle 1990s. The years 1992–1995 exhibited strong industry growth, with real shipments increasing from nearly $59 billion to over $75 billion, a growth rate of 8.7 percent annually. High levels of consumer confidence and record low interest rates triggered high demand from the end users of production machinery, thus prompting significant levels of capital investment, both in terms of expansion and in terms of upgrading existing equipment. Strong export markets, particularly in Asia and the NAFTA (North American Free Trade Agreement) countries, reinforced the high domestic demand for production machinery. Two exceptions to this strong pattern of growth were the mining machinery subsector, with variable growth throughout the 1992–1995 period, and the oil and gas field machinery subsector, whose shipments declined in inflation-adjusted terms due to overcapacity of oil and gas rigs remaining from the boom of the late 1980s.

However, since 1995 the pace of growth has decelerated. During 1996 and 1997 the constant-dollar value of industry shipments grew more modestly at an average growth rate of 4.4 percent per year. Major factors in the trend toward diminished growth include declining construction rates and more moderate capital spending, despite interest rates which continued at low levels and consumer confidence which remained high. Strongest growth during 1997 was experienced by the construction machinery, oil and gas field machinery, and farm machinery subsectors.

Additional demand for new production machinery will be generated by customers aiming to meet new standards of energy efficiency and conservation. Reduction of paper, water, and ink waste in the printing machinery subsector, elimination of the use of chlorofluorocarbons (CFCs) in air conditioning systems, and compliance with new conservation tillage standards in the farm machinery sector will spur the development of new technologies and will continue to feed orders for equipment adhering to the stricter environmental standards.

The production machinery industry, while cyclical with respect to domestic economic activity, is also dependent on foreign markets for continued strong growth in shipments. Over 34 percent of the shipments in the production machinery sector are destined for foreign markets, with nearly half of the exports bound for countries in the Western Hemisphere (see Table 18-1). The NAFTA countries accounted for nearly 28 percent of exports in 1997, and Latin America accounted for an additional 19 percent. Major export countries include Canada, Mexico, Venezuela, Australia, and the United Kingdom.

TABLE 18-1: U.S. Trade Patterns in Production Machinery[1] in 1997

(millions of dollars; percent)

	Exports			Imports		
Regions[2]		Value[3]	Share, %	Regions[2]	Value[3]	Share, %
NAFTA		7,686	27.5	NAFTA	3,799	22.4
Latin America		5,263	18.8	Latin America	397	2.3
Western Europe		4,996	17.9	Western Europe	8,348	49.3
Japan/Chinese Economic Area		2,045	7.3	Japan/Chinese Economic Area	3,197	18.9
Other Asia		2,857	10.2	Other Asia	747	4.4
Rest of world		5,141	18.4	Rest of world	452	2.7
World		27,988	100.0	World	16,941	100.0
Top Five Countries		Value	Share, %	Top Five Countries	Value	Share, %
Canada		5,867	21.0	Japan	2,920	17.2
Mexico		1,819	6.5	Canada	2,567	15.2
Venezuela		1,262	4.5	Germany	2,476	14.6
Australia		1,185	4.2	United Kingdom	1,677	9.9
United Kingdom		1,141	4.1	Italy	1,425	8.4

[1] SIC 3523, 3531, 3532, 3533, 3554, 3555, 3556, 3565, 3585.
[2] For definitions of regional groupings, see "Getting the Most Out of *Outlook '99*."
[3] Values may not sum to total due to rounding.
Source: U.S. Department of Commerce, Bureau of the Census.

Within the production machinery industry, those subsectors with the largest shipment values also tend to be export leaders (construction machinery, air conditioning, refrigeration, and heating, and farm machinery). The main exception is oil and gas field machinery, which accounted for only 6 percent of the shipments but 21.1 percent of the exports of the sector in 1997. This export intensity is due to the prevalence of oil producers in nations other than the United States and the inclusion of reconditioned goods in the export statistics.

In 1997 shipments from production machinery industries totaled nearly $82 billion. The largest subsectors, in constant-dollar terms, were air conditioning, refrigeration, and heating, accounting for 31.8 percent of shipments, construction machinery with a share of 27.2 percent, and farm machinery with 17.1 percent of industry shipments.

GLOBAL INDUSTRY TRENDS

The production machinery industry is incorporating advances in high technology into its production processes as well as its customer and supplier interface channels. The integration of computer technology into manufacturing processes allows for a more efficient process, as well as one which is more tailored to the needs of the individual customer. For example, digital format systems are being integrated into printing presses to quickly adjust the output to meet the changing needs of a customer. The packaging machinery industry is experiencing a similar revolution with expanded computer use throughout the packaging manufacturing process. In the area of mining machinery, machine-monitoring systems can track individual pieces of equipment throughout the mine site, allowing for a more efficient allocation of resources. As new uses are found for information technology systems, increasing efficiency and cutting costs, the production

machinery sector will continue to experience strong demand from firms looking to upgrade outdated and inefficient equipment.

INDUSTRY AND TRADE FORECASTS

The years 1998 and 1999 will be ones in which the output of these production machinery industries will decline, with constant-dollar industry shipments dropping 1.5 percent and 0.5 percent, respectively. The high levels of capital spending seen in the early 1990s will not continue as uncertainty stemming from the currency crisis in Asia, as well as subsequent volatility on key world equity markets, will lead many firms to postpone further expansion and upgrading of equipment until future profits seem more assured.

The strong export markets which were largely responsible for growth during 1995–1997 are also forecast to experience waning demand during 1998 and 1999. Overall, exports are expected to increase by only 3.9 percent in 1998, followed by growth of 4.5 percent in 1999. These rates are in sharp contrast with the expansion of exports between 1994 and 1997, in which exports grew at an average annual rate of nearly 13 percent, accounting for over 55 percent of the growth in shipments during that period. Lower growth in Asia—indeed, recessions in Japan, South Korea, Thailand, and Malaysia—and the subsequent dampening of economic activity in Asia's major trading partners is the primary factor behind this export slowdown.

CONSTRUCTION MACHINERY

Construction machinery (SIC 3531) consists of earthmoving equipment (bulldozers, shovel loaders, and excavators), off-highway trucks, power cranes, crawlers, draglines, trenchers, compactors, mixers, pavers, graders, and scrapers as well as components, parts, and attachments. This equipment is used for the construction of residential and nonresidential buildings, for new power and manufacturing plants, and for adding to or renovating infrastructures such as sewage and water lines, roads, bridges, and tunnels.

Global Industry Trends

Construction equipment revenues will continue to follow trends in the construction industry. Robust building of new homes, factories, roads, and dams portends strong growth and profits for construction equipment firms. Because of the developed transportation and energy systems in the United States and the trend toward downsizing and consolidation in the industry, companies are focusing on expanding into international markets, particularly in countries intent on developing and expanding their infrastructures. Additionally, these firms are looking to increase sales in the domestic market with specialized machinery for niche projects distributed through the rental market.

Rent-to-rent and rent-to-own options are an increasingly larger part of the construction equipment market as dealer networks not only provide the traditional sales and financing services but also expand their rental fleets, particularly for specialized equipment. For the end user, renting equipment reduces maintenance and warehousing costs and eliminates the problem of equipment obsolescence. The American Rental Association reports that construction and industrial equipment renters saw an increase in profits of 0.3 percent in 1995 along with an increase in net worth of nearly 4 percent. As an example, dealers for the Case Corporation, a leader in the rental trend, will begin to supply telescopic handlers (a piece of equipment used for material-handling applications in the building industry) manufactured by Ingersoll-Rand as part of their rental

and sales fleet. Manufacturers are responding to this trend toward rental distribution by producing more durable equipment as well as a wider range of specialty equipment and equipment of different sizes and specifications.

With limited growth forecast in the United States through 2002, construction equipment firms are increasingly looking to overseas markets to expand their businesses. As a result of increasing emphasis on trade, cost competitiveness, which is tied directly to the strength of the dollar, will be an important factor in the continued growth of construction equipment firms. To avoid the uncertainty of currency fluctuations (for example, the recent experience in east Asia), companies are seeking joint ventures and acquisitions abroad to produce and sell in the same country and to take advantage of the transportation and energy projects being undertaken by developing countries for infrastructure advancement. Firms are increasingly turning to acquisitions and mergers to break into foreign markets, as opposed to the traditional route of licensing agreements. For instance, Volvo acquired the construction equipment division of Samsung Heavy Industries (which produces excavators, trucks, and cranes) and plans to develop a South Korean subsidiary.

Global Market Prospects

While most U.S. exports of construction equipment are shipped to the traditional trading partners such as Canada and western Europe (see Table 18-2), demand for construction equipment is also high in countries undergoing rapid economic growth, such as those in Latin America (Mexico, Chile, Brazil, etc.) and Asia (Singapore, Indonesia, etc.) With product shipment growth in the United States in the low single digits, construction equipment firms are reacting by investigating new markets, with 40 percent of respondents to a recent Construction Industry Manufacturers' Association (CIMA) survey indicating that a signifi-

TABLE 18-2: U.S. Trade Patterns in Construction Machinery[1] in 1997
(millions of dollars; percent)

Exports			Imports		
Regions[2]	Value[3]	Share, %	Regions[2]	Value[3]	Share, %
NAFTA	2,284	34.4	NAFTA	1,247	23.3
Latin America	1,208	18.2	Latin America	141	2.6
Western Europe	1,175	17.7	Western Europe	2,462	45.9
Japan/Chinese Economic Area	324	4.9	Japan/Chinese Economic Area	1,152	21.5
Other Asia	592	8.9	Other Asia	206	3.8
Rest of world	1,065	16.0	Rest of world	156	2.9
World	6,648	100.0	World	5,364	100.0
Top Five Countries	Value	Share, %	Top Five Countries	Value	Share, %
Canada	1,927	29.0	Japan	1,088	20.3
Australia	378	5.7	Canada	884	16.5
Belgium	374	5.6	United Kingdom	718	13.4
Mexico	357	5.4	Germany	496	9.2
Chile	315	4.7	Italy	411	7.7

[1] SIC 3531.
[2] For definitions of regional groupings, see "Getting the Most Out of *Outlook '99*."
[3] Values may not sum to total due to rounding.
Source: U.S. Department of Commerce, Bureau of the Census.

cant proportion of their increased sales in recent years was attributable to rising export demand. In 1997 alone exports rose nearly 15 percent, a double-digit export growth rate not seen since 1994. As in the domestic market, export sales are giving way to rental markets as a distribution tool, particularly for specialized equipment.

This survey further suggested that Central America, the Far East, and eastern Europe will be particularly strong markets in the near term. In fact, 45 percent of the attendees at a recent CIMA conference chose South America for their market focus in 1998 mainly because of that market's rate of infrastructure construction, political stability, and economic growth. Exports in the first quarter of 1998 lend support to the results of this survey, as exports to Mexico, Brazil, Peru, and Venezuela exceeded the 1997 levels.

Although the potential market for construction equipment in the former Soviet Union and the eastern bloc is large by U.S. Department of Commerce estimates, significant obstacles to trade remain. Lack of financing is cited as the biggest impediment to sales, and the willingness of suppliers to agree to flexible payment arrangements is an important element in developing this market. Tariff barriers range from zero to 20 percent ad valorem, and construction equipment is exempt from the value-added tax in Russia. Nonprice barriers, such as equipment certification and obstacles at the local government level, are common.

Industry Projections

Demand for construction machinery is tied directly to trends in residential, nonresidential, and public construction. Construction expenditures increased nearly 3 percent in 1997, adjusted for inflation, with nonresidential building construction increasing more than 4 percent and school construction seeing the

largest increase at over 20 percent. Low interest rates and a "baby boomlet" combined with a robust economy, strong consumer confidence, and high capacity utilization rates were the essential factors in this strong growth. They contributed to increased sales in the construction equipment subsector of over 12 percent, adjusted for inflation. These high rates of growth, however, are not expected to continue as GDP growth moderates, interest rates rise slightly, and retail and manufacturing industries consolidate, thus decreasing their need for additional space. Real growth is expected to slow in 1998 and 1999, with the industry rebounding by the end of 1999 (see Table 18-3). Overall, the compound growth rate from 1996 to 2002 is forecast to be 2.1 percent.

According to CIMA, growth has not been uniform across different types of construction equipment. Bituminous and aggregate equipment (which includes asphalt plants, rollers, asphalt pavers, and crushers) saw gains of only 3.8 percent in 1997, and forecasts indicate nearly a 1 percentage point reduction in growth in 1998. In contrast, the fastest growing area in construction machinery is lifting equipment (cranes, aerial work platforms, and rough-terrain forklifts), with growth of 7.6 percent in 1997 and forecasts that growth would continue to top 7 percent in 1998.

Near-term performance in the construction machinery subsector will be influenced by the new federal transportation spending law known as the Transportation Equity Act for the 21st Century (TEA-21), which was signed into law by President Clinton on June 9, 1998. This highway reauthorization measure provides $216 billion over 6 years for highway and transit upgrades and improvements and represents a compromise between the bills passed by the House and the Senate. The $175 billion in the bill specifically designated for highway repair and

TABLE 18-3: Construction Machinery (SIC 3531) Trends and Forecasts
(millions of dollars except as noted)

	1992	1993	1994	1995	1996	1997[1]	1998[2]	1999[3]	Percent Change 96–97	97–98	98–99	92–96[4]
Industry data												
Value of shipments[5]	13,139	15,444	17,697	19,911	21,627	24,698	24,237	23,162	14.2	-1.9	-4.4	13.3
Value of shipments (1992$)	13,139	15,097	17,049	18,714	19,860	22,323	21,519	20,142	12.4	-3.6	-6.4	10.9
Total employment (thousands)	74.6	74.7	77.9	85.4	88.7							4.4
Production workers (thousands)	47.8	49.1	52.9	58.4	61.1							6.3
Average hourly earnings ($)	15.13	15.33	14.84	14.81	14.93							-0.3
Capital expenditures	395	346	359	443	450							3.3
Product data												
Value of shipments[5]	12,001	14,122	16,123	18,299	20,259	23,053	22,810	21,899	13.8	-1.1	-4.0	14.0
Value of shipments (1992$)	12,001	13,804	15,532	17,198	18,604	20,836	20,232	19,099	12.0	-2.9	-5.6	11.6
Trade data												
Value of imports	2,574	3,403	4,277	4,458	4,433	5,364	5,793	6,320	21.0	8.0	9.1	14.6
Value of exports	4,280	4,361	5,210	5,471	5,792	6,648	6,907	7,177	14.8	3.9	3.9	7.9

[1] Estimate except imports and exports.
[2] Estimate.
[3] Forecast.
[4] Compound annual rate.
[5] For a definition of industry versus product values, see "Getting the Most Out of Outlook '99."
Source: U.S. Department of Commerce: Bureau of the Census; estimates and forecasts by author.

expansion represents a 40 percent increase in spending over current levels.

Christine Siegwarth Meyer, Bentley College, (781) 891-2476, November 1998.

MINING MACHINERY

The mining machinery industry (SIC 3532) includes excavating, crushing, loader, and haulage equipment used in mining as well as pertinent components of and accessories for extraction equipment. Among the industry's key products are excavating machinery, conveyor systems, LHD (load, haul, and dump) machines, underground trucks, ground support equipment, mine seal equipment, and rock crushers. While the basic machinery standards are fundamental to the industry, technological innovation has automated many of the mechanical processes. New applications of robotic and remote control systems, for instance, stand to replace traditional machinery and yield increased productivity and efficiency in the mining industry.

Global Industry Trends

The mining machinery subsector follows the business cycle less closely than do other capital goods subsectors, since demand is derived from the opening of new mines and increased production at old mines, decisions that are based on long-term projections. Long-wall systems and continuous miners are expensive, and the decision to expand a firm's capital base is tied more closely to long-term forecasts of commodity prices than to cyclical patterns in demand.

The mining machinery subsector is integrating mining equipment with high technology by using machine monitoring systems, the Global Positioning System (GPS), and geographic information systems (GIS) to increase efficiency. Machine monitoring systems utilize a communications network to track machine status and movements and thus limit idle time and make more efficient use of a smaller number of machines. Recently, GPS-type systems using Russian and American satellites have been integrated into these machine monitoring systems to better track the movement of machines throughout a mine. GIS (a computer-based mapping and analysis tool) and similar high-precision technologies also are being used to navigate drills, control dozer blades, and track bucket positions on shovels.

Global Market Prospects

Exports from the mining machinery subsector continue to grow, with a 23 percent increase in 1997, and data from the first quarter of 1998 indicated that the upward trend was continuing (see Table 18-4). The North American Free Trade Agreement (NAFTA) countries (Canada and Mexico) account for over a quarter of the exports in this subsector, while many other countries in the western hemisphere (Chile, Colombia, Venezuela, and Peru, for example) also provide major export markets. In total, more than 50 percent of exports in 1997 were destined for Latin American and Canadian customers.

The nations of the former Soviet Union, including Russia and Ukraine, are large potential customers for American mining equipment. The mining industries in those countries are large and need new high-technology equipment. However, U.S. firms are wary of the business risks of trading in a sector that is highly politicized and state-controlled and in which there are limited supplies of hard currency, which is vital to a smooth system of payment. As these countries make the transition to a full market economy, become more aware of U.S. products, and seek high-technology equipment to compensate for the exodus of labor from their mining industries, U.S. exports to these nations are forecast to expand.

TABLE 18-4: U.S. Trade Patterns in Mining Machinery[1] in 1997
(millions of dollars; percent)

Exports			Imports		
Regions[2]	Value[3]	Share, %	Regions[2]	Value[3]	Share, %
NAFTA	391	25.7	NAFTA	116	20.9
Latin America	432	28.4	Latin America	5	1.0
Western Europe	184	12.1	Western Europe	288	52.1
Japan/Chinese Economic Area	69	4.5	Japan/Chinese Economic Area	69	12.4
Other Asia	206	13.5	Other Asia	38	6.8
Rest of world	240	15.8	Rest of world	37	6.7
World	1,523	100.0	World	553	100.0
Top Five Countries	Value	Share, %	Top Five Countries	Value	Share, %
Canada	274	18.0	Canada	82	14.8
Chile	119	7.8	Germany	74	13.5
Mexico	117	7.7	United Kingdom	56	10.2
Indonesia	108	7.1	Italy	51	9.3
Colombia	99	6.5	Japan	51	9.2

[1] SIC 3532.
[2] For definitions of regional groupings, see "Getting the Most Out of *Outlook '99.*"
[3] Values may not sum to total due to rounding.
Source: U.S. Department of Commerce, Bureau of the Census.

Industry Projections

The mining equipment industry was not expected to have strong growth in 1998 despite a robust economy and high capacity utilization rates in the mining industry (90 percent versus 83 percent economywide). Purchases of mining equipment involve large capital expenditures, which do not mirror the business cycle as closely as they do in other industries. Shipments are expected to increase again after 2000, with average annual growth of 1.6 percent from 1998 through 2002, as firms find new equipment profitable again (see Table 18-5).

Underground mining equipment falls into three categories—conventional equipment, continuous miners, and longwall systems—with the latter two used in coal mining. Conventional equipment includes cutters, drills, loaders, shuttle cars, conveyors, and roof bolters. Continuous mining machines eliminate the need for cutting machines, drills, and explosives by removing coal from the face of a seam and loading it directly into cars on conveyors. The advantages of this system are that it increases mine productivity and improves worker safety. Another product known for elevating productivity is the longwall system, which shears coal from the face of a seam in long slices and moves it to the surface on conveyors.

As in many other industries, mining equipment firms are experiencing an increase in the number of acquisitions as the sector consolidates. On March 20, 1998, P&H Mining Equipment, a subsidiary of Harnischfeger Industries, acquired Horsburgh & Scott, a manufacturer of custom-engineered gears, drives, and replacement parts for mining and industrial equipment. In the same month Terek acquired O&K Mining, giving that firm a mining shovel compatible with its trucks and thus vertically integrating the business. As this subsector is increasingly driven by global demand, the ability to achieve acquisitions and mergers which improve the efficiency of the parent company will contribute to the continuing success of the American mining equipment industry.

Christine Siegwarth Meyer, Bentley College, (781) 891-2476, November 1998.

OIL AND GAS FIELD MACHINERY

Oil and gas field equipment (SIC 3533) includes machinery and components used in oil and gas exploration, well servicing and drilling, and the production and processing of oil and gas in the field. Among the specific kinds of equipment produced are geophysical prospecting machinery, drilling rigs and tools, cementing and well-fracturing units, pumping machinery, dehydrators, separators, treaters, and other field processing machines.

Global Industry Trends

The oil and gas field machinery subsector is directly influenced by capital expenditures in the oil and gas extraction industries, which in turn are influenced by volatile supply and demand factors. Firms in the oil and gas field machinery subsector are reacting to recent price improvements in oil and gas with cautious optimism, focusing on mergers and acquisitions to diversify their product lines and new technologies to reduce costs and increase efficiency.

A leading indicator in the oil field machinery subsector is the rig utilization rate (the percentage of U.S. drilling rigs that are currently active). As of May 1, 1998, Offshore Data Services (ODS) reported a worldwide offshore rig fleet utilization rate of 95.6 percent, a figure which has been rising steadily since 1986, when crude oil prices dropped dramatically. High

TABLE 18-5: Mining Machinery (SIC 3532) Trends and Forecasts
(millions of dollars except as noted)

	1992	1993	1994	1995	1996	1997[1]	1998[2]	1999[3]	96–97	97–98	98–99	92–96[4]
									Percent Change			
Industry data												
Value of shipments[5]	1,548	1,881	1,715	2,181	2,397	2,151	1,995	1,983	−10.3	−7.2	−0.6	11.6
Value of shipments (1992$)	1,548	1,844	1,659	2,038	2,193	1,923	1,739	1,678	−12.3	−9.6	−3.5	9.1
Total employment (thousands)	12.6	12.6	12.6	13.8	14							2.1
Production workers (thousands)	7.4	7.7	8.0	8.9	8							3.2
Average hourly earnings ($)	11.92	12.21	13.08	13.30	13.87							3.9
Capital expenditures	33.0	58.9	29.5	29.8	43.8							7.3
Product data												
Value of shipments[5]	1,417	1,745	1,639	2,100	2,202	2,018	1,893	1,887	−8.3	−6.2	−0.3	11.7
Value of shipments (1992$)	1,417	1,711	1,585	1,962	2,014	1,805	1,649	1,597	−10.4	−8.6	−3.2	9.2
Trade data												
Value of imports	268	307	379	466	515	553	604	667	7.4	9.2	10.4	17.7
Value of exports	811	846	987	1,111	1,235	1,523	1,595	1,657	23.3	4.7	3.9	11.1

[1] Estimate except imports and exports.
[2] Estimate.
[3] Forecast.
[4] Compound annual rate.
[5] For a definition of industry versus product values, see "Getting the Most Out of *Outlook '99.*"
Source: U.S. Department of Commerce: Bureau of the Census; estimates and forecasts by author.

rig utilization rates also portend rising day rates (the price paid to drilling contractors for a day's work) and high profits. With the Energy Information Administration forecasting an increase in the market share of petroleum from 38 percent in 1996 to 40 percent in 2020 and a corresponding rise in exploratory and experimental drilling, rig shortages are possible in the Gulf of Mexico and the North Sea by 1999. Despite these improvements in the industry's fortunes, upgrades of existing rigs to incorporate new technologies are expected to be more prevalent than is new construction.

Clouding the picture are projected increases in the worldwide supply of oil resulting from recent discoveries in Algeria and Nigeria as well as an intensive plan by Venezuela to increase capacity. Furthermore, uncertainty about the amount of oil that Iraq will be allowed to sell in international markets further complicates the task of projecting trends in oil prices.

Following economywide trends, firms in the oil and gas machinery industry are expanding the range of services they offer through mergers and acquisitions. For example, the Houston-based IRI International and Norway's Hitec ASA agreed to merge, with the resulting firm, IRI Hitec, focusing on the design, engineering, and manufacturing of advanced technology for offshore and land-based drilling equipment. Additionally, Halliburton Company, which acquired Numar Corporation in September 1997, planned to acquire Dresser by fall 1998, making it the largest provider of oil field services. The purchase of Dresser was cited by Halliburton as a way to better integrate oil field, engineering, and construction services, while Numar was purchased primarily for its patented proprietary well-logging device, the Magnetic Resonance Imaging Logging tool, which is used to evaluate subsurface rock formations in newly drilled oil and gas wells.

Domestic natural gas demand, and thus production, is expected to increase throughout 2002 as a result of the perception on the part of consumers that natural gas is a more environmentally friendly fuel than many of the energy alternatives, thus feeding the downstream demand for gas field equipment. The Energy Information Administration projects that recent discoveries in the Gulf of Mexico will account for a significant portion of the increase in production. New technologies (measurement while drilling, horizontal drilling, slimhole drilling, etc.) and revised operating practices make deep-water wells such as the Mensa project (which holds the deep-water record for production) economically feasible. As these new gas fields are utilized, pipeline capacity and storage facilities will be expanded, particularly on the east coast.

Global Market Prospects

Export markets continue to generate a substantial portion of demand for the oil and gas field equipment subsector. The dominant markets for U.S. oil and gas field machinery include the major oil-producing nations, such as Venezuela, Saudi Arabia, United Arab Emirates, and Nigeria (see Table 18-6). The largest growth in exports in 1997 came from China (with an increase in purchases of 140 percent), and data from the first 3 months of 1998 indicate that this trend will continue despite uncertainties in the Asian economic future.

Export potential is not limited, however, to the traditional oil-producing nations. The markets of the former Soviet Union seem to have especially strong sales prospects as the oil and gas industries in those countries adjust to economic reform. Reform programs in Russia, for example, along with high taxes on energy, led to a 50 percent drop in oil production and a 10 percent drop in natural gas production from 1990 to 1995. However, even with these large cuts in output, Russia remains the third largest producer of oil and the largest producer of natural gas in the world, offering an opportunity for U.S. firms to fulfill

TABLE 18-6: U.S. Trade Patterns in Oil and Gas Field Machinery[1] in 1997
(millions of dollars; percent)

Exports			Imports		
Regions[2]	Value[3]	Share, %	Regions[2]	Value[3]	Share, %
NAFTA	151	2.6	NAFTA	71	34.7
Latin America	1,955	33.1	Latin America	2	1.1
Western Europe	819	13.9	Western Europe	123	60.3
Japan/Chinese Economic Area	330	5.6	Japan/Chinese Economic Area	3	1.6
Other Asia	824	13.9	Other Asia	3	1.5
Rest of world	1,829	31.0	Rest of world	2	0.8
World	5,907	100.0	World	204	100.0
Top Five Countries	Value	Share, %	Top Five Countries	Value	Share, %
Venezuela	877	14.8	Canada	60	29.4
Singapore	403	6.8	United Kingdom	34	16.5
United Kingdom	345	5.8	Netherlands	21	10.5
Saudi Arabia	289	4.9	Austria	20	9.8
China	262	4.4	France	20	9.6

[1] SIC 3533.
[2] For definitions of regional groupings, see "Getting the Most Out of *Outlook '99*."
[3] Values may not sum to total due to rounding.
Source: U.S. Department of Commerce, Bureau of the Census.

TABLE 18-7: Oil and Gas Field Machinery (SIC 3533) Trends and Forecasts
(millions of dollars except as noted)

	1992	1993	1994	1995	1996	1997[1]	1998[2]	1999[3]	Percent Change 96–97	97–98	98–99	92–96[4]
Industry data												
Value of shipments[5]	3,921	3,740	3,758	3,803	4,646	5,147	4,824	4,979	10.8	−6.3	3.2	4.3
Value of shipments (1992$)	3,921	3,762	3,677	3,619	4,290	4,655	4,236	4,244	8.5	−9.0	0.2	2.3
Total employment (thousands)	26.3	24.5	25.5	24.3	26							0.1
Production workers (thousands)	15.4	13.8	14.7	15.0	17							2.5
Average hourly earnings ($)	13.63	14.22	15.57	15.05	16.07							4.2
Capital expenditures	105	79.8	77.7	123	157							10.6
Product data												
Value of shipments[5]	2,981	2,939	2,976	3,023	3,814	4,245	3,992	4,157	11.3	−6.0	4.1	6.4
Value of shipments (1992$)	2,981	2,956	2,912	2,876	3,521	3,838	3,504	3,543	9.0	−8.7	1.1	4.2
Trade data												
Value of imports	36.2	47.1	67.5	93.2	145	204	228	251	40.6	11.8	10.0	41.5
Value of exports	3,986	3,746	3,546	4,168	5,236	5,907	6,510	6,887	12.8	10.2	5.8	7.1

[1] Estimate except imports and exports.
[2] Estimate.
[3] Forecast.
[4] Compound annual rate.
[5] For a definition of industry versus product values, see "Getting the Most Out of *Outlook '99*."
Source: U.S. Department of Commerce: Bureau of the Census; estimates and forecasts by author.

that country's need for advanced technology equipment. The difficulty for firms in filling this demand is due to the lack of hard currency available in Russia. Firms are minimizing the risk from such overseas operations in part by conducting joint ventures, such as the one between Flour Daniel and Brown & Root Energy Services, which will provide engineering, planning, and other support services for the substantial Sakhalin II project in eastern Russia. Other countries in the former Soviet Union also are strong potential markets for U.S. oil and gas field equipment. For example, the Dallas-based Halliburton Company recently agreed to supply drilling services for an exploration and appraisal program in Turkmenistan.

Industry and Trade Projections

The oil and gas machinery subsector experienced a remarkable recovery over the last 2 years. A real growth rate of 23 percent in 1996 was followed by a more modest increase in shipments of 9 percent in 1997, the first 2 years of growth this subsector has seen since 1991 (see Table 18-7). Shipments are expected to decline in the near term as uncertainties regarding energy prices driven by unpredictable supply and demand factors keep new equipment purchases low. Average annual growth is forecast at 1 percent from 1996 through 2002.

Demand for certain types of oil rigs (drill ships and semisubmersible rigs in particular) will continue to be strong, driving the market in the area of rig replacement and leading to an actual expansion of the fleet. This demand is driven in part by the central Gulf of Mexico lease sale in March 1998, in which 539 deep-water (more than 800 meters) leases received bids. Estimates made by Offshore Data Services indicate that at least 29 deep water rigs will be demanded as a result of this sale and of existing leases which have not been drilled.

Christine Siegwarth Meyer, Bentley College, (781) 891-2476, November 1998.

FARM MACHINERY

The farm machinery subsector (SIC 3523) is defined as farm field and farmstead machinery used for the production of crops and agricultural animals. The major product lines of the industry include wheel tractors and parts, planting and fertilizing machinery, tillage equipment (plows, cultivators, harrows), chemical application equipment, harvesting machinery (e.g., combines, cotton pickers, root harvesters), haying and mowing machinery (including balers), farm dairy equipment, poultry house equipment, barnyard machinery, sprayers and irrigation equipment, grain driers and blowers, and commercial turf and grounds care equipment. Machinery parts and components are an important segment of farm machinery production and exports. Because of the rugged construction and long life of many farm machines (e.g., the median age of a farm tractor in the United States is 19 years), replacement parts are significant. Although they are not used in farm agriculture, tractor mowers and some irrigation equipment are used as commercial turf and grounds care equipment and are included under SIC 3523.

Global Industry Trends

As part of the overall agribusiness industry, the farm machinery industry is characterized by ever-increasing globalization. The large manufacturers, such as Deere, Case Corporation, and AGCO, are multinational organizations that have manufacturing joint ventures and assembly operations throughout the world. Many other U.S. companies that may not manufacture overseas have agents and distribution channels in many countries. Conversely, companies such as Kubota Tractor of Japan, Fiat of Italy, and Alfa-Laval of Sweden have set up facilities and distribution networks in the United States and around the globe. Parts and components used as replacements and in original equipment manufacturing account for a large volume of imports and exports of farm machinery. This makes it difficult to determine accurately the local content of machinery produced in the United States and other countries; U.S. farm machinery may contain foreign-manufactured components, and U.S. components are shipped to overseas subsidiaries and other overseas farm machinery producers.

Growth in the size of farms and increased mechanization are prevailing trends in the agricultural industry, particularly in sophisticated mature markets such as the United States, Canada, Europe, and Australia. Most new farm machinery is sold to replace less productive and less powerful older models. The total number of farms and units of farm machinery sold has declined concurrently with the increased acreage of farms and the larger size and capacity of the machinery used to work the land. Major food and cereal producers and independent contractors that provide crop services to farms are the primary purchasers of farm machinery.

Although the trend toward increased mechanization and larger farms or cooperatives has accelerated in some developing and emerging markets, three fundamental types of farming are practiced throughout the world. High-production agriculture characterized by large farms and high-capacity machinery is practiced in the United States, Canada, Australia, Argentina, Saudi Arabia, Mexico, Brazil, former Soviet Union countries such as Ukraine, and African countries such as South Africa. Medium-scale but highly sophisticated farming is practiced in Europe and some parts of Latin America and Asia. Small-scale farming is the norm in most of Asia, Africa, and the Caribbean, and some small-scale and hobby farming is practiced in the United States.

The world farm machinery industry experienced a structural decline in the mid-1980s as a result of plant overcapacity and crop surpluses. In response to those conditions, the industry restructured on a global basis to produce sizes and models of machinery in economically rational locations where the highest volumes of such equipment are used. The export of tractors, harvesting machinery, and other equipment from single rather than multiple manufacturing locations resulted in greater production efficiencies and lower unit costs to customers. The United States and Canada dominate in the production of powerful high-production, high-horsepower equipment; Europe is most prominent in the production of medium-range (40 to 100 horsepower) but highly sophisticated machinery; and Japan is the major supplier of tractors and equipment below 40 horsepower.

The world farm machinery market is increasingly dominated by the Big Four companies, which continue to engage in joint ventures and acquisitions of both domestic and international manufacturers. The estimated market share of the Big Four companies is as follows: Deere & Co., 26 percent; New Holland NV (owned by Fiat of Italy), 17 percent; Case Corporation, 13 percent; and AGCO Corporation, 12 percent. In 1997

Deere established a joint venture with and majority ownership of the Jiamusi Combine Harvester factory of Heilongjiang, China, and purchased 49 percent of Cameco Industries, a major manufacturer of sugarcane harvesting and handling machinery in Louisiana. Deere also agreed to acquire the assets of Maschinefabrik Kemper GmbH, a German manufacturer of forage harvester headers. AGCO Corporation acquired Fendt Tractor of Germany. Case Corporation acquired Agri-Logic, an Indiana software developer of instant yield maps and Gem Sprayers of the United Kingdom in 1997; in 1998 Case broke ground for a new tractor and combine production facility in Sorocaba, Brazil, where it already manufactured construction equipment. New Holland launched its first model in a series of tractors tailored to the Indian market in a new production facility near New Delhi.

Caterpillar, Inc., increased its activity in farm machinery manufacturing with the introduction in 1987 of the rubber-belted Challenger tractor. Today seven different models of that tractor are manufactured. The company formed Cat Ag Products, a wholly owned subsidiary, which Caterpillar announced signaled the company's commitment to become a leader in the farm machinery product industry. In 1997 Caterpillar and CLAAS OHG of Germany, Europe's leading manufacturer of combines and forage harvesters, formed a joint venture to market and manufacture combine harvesters and rubber-belted farm tractors in North America and Europe. The joint company, Caterpillar CLAAS America L.L.C., recently announced its intention to build a manufacturing facility near Omaha, NE, to produce and market the LEXION line of combine harvesters.

Domestic Trends

In 1997 farm machinery shipments in constant dollars rose 7.4 percent over 1996. That large increase was driven by substantial increases in domestic sales of tractors (over 14 percent) and combines (7.2 percent) and a dramatic 21.5 percent (in current dollars) rise in exports. Tractors and heavy harvesting machinery such as combines, cotton pickers, and balers account for almost two-thirds of the dollar value of farm machinery shipments. Generally, increased sales of tractors and harvesters cause sales of short line and other farm machinery to rise; however, sales of other machinery can rise independently of good tractor and harvester sales. Combine sales in the first 5 months of 1998 were 41 percent ahead of sales in 1997, and tractor sales remained ahead of 1997 sales in that period but showed some indications of softening demand. In another sign of possible softening of demand, shortline (specialty) manufacturers reported first quarter 1998 sales that were only 2 percent ahead of 1997 and no increase in orders on hand. Weather problems have delayed plantings in some areas and could account for part of the slowdown (see Table 18-8).

The prevailing trend in American agriculture is toward growth in farm size and increased mechanization. In 1950 there were over 5.4 million farms, whereas today there are just over 2 million. Farms of under 500 acres constitute about 80 percent of all farms but only 20 percent of crop production. About 50,000 of the largest farms produce half the U.S. agricultural output,

TABLE 18-8: U.S. Trade Patterns in Farm Machinery[1] in 1997

(millions of dollars; percent)

Exports			Imports		
Regions[2]	Value[3]	Share, %	Regions[2]	Value[3]	Share, %
NAFTA	1,777	38.5	NAFTA	813	23.9
Latin America	510	11.0	Latin America	21	0.6
Western Europe	995	21.5	Western Europe	1,721	50.6
Japan/Chinese Economic Area	133	2.9	Japan/Chinese Economic Area	691	20.3
Other Asia	154	3.3	Other Asia	40	1.2
Rest of world	1,050	22.7	Rest of world	117	3.4
World	4,620	100.0	World	3,404	100.0
Top Five Countries	Value	Share, %	Top Five Countries	Value	Share, %
Canada	1,371	29.7	Canada	720	21.2
Australia	440	9.5	Japan	650	19.1
Mexico	406	8.8	United Kingdom	500	14.7
France	236	5.1	France	372	10.9
Germany	212	4.6	Italy	356	10.5

[1] SIC 3523.
[2] For definitions of regional groupings, see "Getting the Most Out of *Outlook '99*."
[3] Values may not sum to total due to rounding.
Source: U.S. Department of Commerce, Bureau of the Census.

and today U.S. farmers feed twice as many people as they did in 1950 with approximately the same acreage. The real profits in the farming industry are realized by the large (sometimes corporate) producers, which constitute the largest customer base for farm machinery.

In 1997 U.S. imports of farm machinery rose 13.8 percent from the 1996 level, and imports through April 1998 were up 25.8 percent from the same period in 1997. For more than a decade the top suppliers, accounting for 85 to 90 percent of all U.S. imports for this category, have been: Canada, Japan, the United Kingdom, France, Italy, and Germany. Imports from Mexico grew from just over 1 percent of total imports in 1992 to 2.7 percent of imports for this category in 1997, a fourfold increase in current-dollar amounts for the 5-year period. The emergence of Mexico as a significant supplier of farm machinery to the U.S. is due in large part to the implementation of NAFTA in 1994. More than half of U.S. farm machinery imports are medium- and low-horsepower tractors and parts; many of these imports come from subsidiaries of the Big Four companies and are marketed under their familiar brand names. U.S. farm machinery manufacturers' domestic factories build row crop tractors of 100 horsepower and above; U.S. demand for tractors and attachments in the lower-horsepower ranges are met largely by imports. Fully 82,351 of the 110,568 two-wheel tractors sold in the United States in 1997 were under 100 horsepower, and most were imports.

Because the customer base is static and there is little acreage expansion, most farm machinery sales in the United States consist of replacement machines. Conservation compliance was mandated by the Food Security Act of 1985, which was fully implemented by the end of 1994. These measures to reduce soil erosion by water and wind caused a revolution in tillage practices known as conservation tillage or residue management farming. Newly designed tillage equipment included coulters, disk openers, air drills, row cleaners, and other machines that were the opposite of the traditional moldboard plowing that caused erosion. Conservation tillage also reduced the number of trips through the fields, thus reducing wear on the machinery and extending its life. Precision farming has been another impetus for inventions and includes site-specific and soil-specific crop management with focused fertilizing and site-specific nutrient input systems that can reduce the use of chemicals and fertilizers. Precision farming and environmental requirements will lead to more inventions in the future. There have been no significant breakthroughs in farm machinery in the last several years, but incremental improvements have been made in existing machinery, including increased use of electronics, fewer parts and redesign of equipment for ease of servicing and repair, greater operator comfort and safety, and reduced engine emissions.

The U.S. Environmental Protection Agency (EPA) has determined that emissions of off-road engines, including those used in farm machinery, contribute significantly to air pollution. EPA proposed diesel engine regulations to limit exhaust and smoke emissions from off-road engines and proposed a staggered phase-in period for new engines, with the first set of Tier I requirements to take effect as follows: 175- to 750-horsepower engines in 1996, 100- to 175-horsepower engines in 1997, 50- to 100-horsepower engines in 1998, and engines above 750 horsepower or below 25 horsepower by 2000. Engine modifications for compliance with Tier I requirements have been accomplished with relatively moderate design adjustments; however, EPA Tier II (to be accomplished by 2003) and Tier III (by 2006) requirements are increasingly stringent and may be challenged by the industry as unrealistic.

California has a stricter environmental schedule, and EPA representatives have told the industry that EPA intends to give states and local air quality districts unhindered authority to regulate the place, hours, and circumstances under which off-road equipment can be operated. California is aggressively moving forward with regulations to control emissions from spark-ignition engines. Federal EPA regulations probably will follow. Additional information on the Clean Air Act can be found on the Equipment Manufacturers Institute Web site and numerous EPA Web sites (e.g., http://earth1.epa.gov/oar/caa/contents.html).

According to EPA estimates, 65 percent of nonpoint source water pollution comes from agriculture. The principal pollutants are sediment, animal waste, fertilizers, and pesticides. Odors from animal operations are a growing issue. Under the provisions of the Clean Water Act, efforts are under way among government, agricultural groups, and machinery producers to prevent nonpoint source water pollution. Precision agricultural equipment, which makes possible site-specific nutrient and pesticide inputs, is an example of machinery that reduces pollutants.

Farm policy will increasingly be made outside the agriculture establishment. Congressional committees concerned with the environment and appropriations rather than agriculture will initiate legislation that affects farming. As another example, all highly erodible cropland could come under conservation compliance regulation.

The major manufacturing states for farm machinery are, in rank order, Iowa, Illinois, Wisconsin, Kansas, Nebraska, and Georgia.

Projections of Industry and Trade Growth for the Next 1 and 5 Years

In 1997 shipments of U.S. farm machinery increased an estimated 8.5 percent in current dollars (7.4 percent in constant dollars) over 1996 sales. Unit domestic sales of two-wheel tractors above 100 horsepower rose 12.9 percent, while unit sale of four-wheel-drive tractors grew 33.5 percent. Four-wheel drive

tractors and two-wheel tractors over 100 horsepower are considered the benchmark for production because almost all row crop field tractors manufactured in the United States fall into those size ranges. Domestic combine sales recovered from a slight decline in 1996, rising 7.2 percent. Extremely strong export sales that increased $815.5 million (21.5 percent) over the 1996 level also contributed to strong growth in the industry overall (see Table 18-9).

El Niño of 1997–1998 was one of the strongest recorded since this global weather pattern has been tracked, and it has wreaked climatic havoc around the globe. Mexico has experienced its worst drought in 70 years as well as persistent forest fires, and drought has devastated Russia's grain areas, destroying 10.1 million hectares of that country's grain and affecting 33 million hectares in all, according to preliminary reports from Russia's Ministry of Agriculture and Food. In the United States, Florida has suffered $135 million in crop losses and another $35 million in livestock losses because of the fires. Bad weather has battered cotton crops from Georgia to California, and the 1998–1999 cotton crop could be the smallest in the 1990s. Texas, the biggest cotton producer in the United States, has suffered withering drought and excessive heat since April, and in California, the number two producer, excessive rains from El Niño retarded the development of cotton plants. However, the U.S. Department of Agriculture (USDA) has forecast a record wheat crop, and corn, soybeans, and other crops are progressing well at this point in the growing cycle. Domestic 1998 combine sales were over 40 percent ahead of 1997 sales, tractor sales remain strong, and U.S. farm machinery producers are optimistic about farm income, credit availability, and interest rates as well as replacement demand and farmers' attitudes toward new equipment purchases. Farm machinery exports declined

TABLE 18-9: Farm Machinery and Equipment (SIC 3523) Trends and Forecasts
(millions of dollars except as noted)

	1992	1993	1994	1995	1996	1997[1]	1998[2]	1999[3]	96–97	97–98	98–99	92–96[4]
									Percent Change			
Industry data												
Value of shipments[5]	9,620	11,190	12,759	13,757	14,469	15,699	16,484	17,110	8.5	5.0	3.8	10.7
Value of shipments (1992$)	9,620	10,938	12,163	12,773	13,070	14,037	14,570	14,905	7.4	3.8	2.3	8.0
Total employment (thousands)	61.5	63.5	66.5	65.7	66.6							2.0
Production workers (thousands)	42.6	45.8	47.7	48.3	48.5							3.3
Average hourly earnings ($)	13.18	13.18	13.60	14.37	14.24							2.0
Capital expenditures	196	229	260	290	294							10.7
Product data												
Value of shipments[5]	8,940	10,340	11,911	12,599	13,191	14,312	15,028	15,599	8.5	5.0	3.8	10.2
Value of shipments (1992$)	8,940	10,108	11,355	11,698	11,916	12,798	13,284	13,590	7.4	3.8	2.3	7.4
Trade data												
Value of imports	2,022	2,148	2,917	3,089	2,990	3,404	3,772	3,964	13.8	10.8	5.1	10.3
Value of exports	2,176	2,473	2,647	3,119	3,804	4,620	4,389	4,534	21.4	–5.0	3.3	15.0

[1] Estimate except imports and exports.
[2] Estimate.
[3] Forecast.
[4] Compound annual rate.
[5] For a definition of industry versus product values, see "Getting the Most Out of *Outlook '99*."
Source: U.S. Department of Commerce: Bureau of the Census; International Trade Administration.

somewhat in 1998; however, current-dollar growth for the industry was expected to reach 5 percent, a 3.8 percent increase in constant dollars.

The 1999 outlook for farm machinery sales is unclear. According to the Food and Agriculture Organization of the United Nations (FAO), the worldwide value of all principal agricultural products declined more than 2 percent in 1997, primarily as a result of a decrease in the price of cereals. Declines were expected to continue in 1998 because of weak prices and reduced demand from Asia. Wheat prices are at their lowest levels in the 1990s, and U.S. farmers could forfeit up to 10 million bushels of wheat to the federal government rather than repay their 1997 USDA price support loans. USDA has warned that U.S. farm exports could fall another $4 billion below the $56 billion forecast for 1998. Milk and hog prices are forecast to decrease in 1999. The weather is another complicating factor. The World Meteorological Organization has advised that a La Niña weather pattern is emerging earlier than expected and that it seems more intensive than what has been seen before. The La Niña impact is the opposite of the El Niño pattern and could bring excessive precipitation and colder temperatures. The heavy rains could cause extensive erosion of topsoil in areas that are in a fragile condition after the drought. As a result of these uncertainties and the lagged effect of lower crop prices on farm income, farm machinery sales are estimated to rise a moderate 2.3 percent in constant dollars (3.8 percent in current dollars) in 1999.

Allowing for fluctuations in the weather and crop prices, constant-dollar sales of farm machinery should continue to increase approximately 2 percent per year from 2000 through 2003. Populations continue to grow worldwide, and there is continued demand for dietary improvements in developing countries. Adverse weather conditions could reduce grain stockpiles, thus increasing crop prices. FAO has advised that conventional tilling severely erodes the soil and is supporting reductions in the use of heavy tillage equipment while encouraging greater use of conservation tillage and improved soil management. Conservation tillage is practiced primarily in North America, and the United States is a leader in this technology, which could be exported in the future and further enhance growth in the farm machinery subsector.

Global Market Prospects

Exports account for a significant proportion of U.S. farm machinery shipments, averaging about one-quarter of the total value of shipments. U.S. exports of farm machinery soared 21.5 percent in 1997 compared with 1996, an increase of $815.5 million. Four countries—Turkmenistan, Ukraine, Uzbekistan, and Kazakhstan—accounted for over 30 percent of the increase as 1997 exports to those countries rose 395 percent ($306.3 million) compared with 1996. Those countries placed major orders for equipment in 1996, backed by Export-Import Bank guarantees. Orders of that magnitude may not be repeated soon, and export data through April 1998 show exports to this region down 62.3 percent. Exports to Mexico, the third largest market for U.S. farm equipment, rose 18.2 percent in 1997 but exports will decrease in 1998 as Mexican agriculture was plagued by the

aftermath of the strong El Niño. Asian markets account for about 6 percent of U.S. farm machinery exports, but the continuing economic turmoil in that continent has caused steep declines in exports to those markets. Exports were off about 15 percent in 1997 compared with 1996; exports for the period through April 1998 were down 40 percent from the same period in 1997.

Tariff reductions resulting from the Uruguay Round of multilateral trade negotiations which took effect on January 1, 1995, included the total elimination of tariffs on agricultural equipment in the European Union, Japan, Canada, Australia, and other developed countries and substantial reduction of tariffs in Brazil and other countries. Since that time there has been a dramatic increase in exports to many of those regions; exports to some major European countries have almost doubled, and those to Brazil rose 200 percent in current dollars from 1994 to 1997. Exports of farm machinery to Russia grew 211 percent in 1997 and were up 191 percent through April 1998. It is too early to say that this is a trend; however, Agricultural Committee activities under the U.S.–Russian Joint Commission on Economic and Technological Cooperation are focused on opening the potentially huge Russian market to U.S. manufacturers of farm machinery. Upgrading agriculture and farm mechanization is a major goal of China's ninth Five-Year Plan (1996–2000); however, U.S. exports of farm machinery to China reached a high of $47 million in 1995 and have been dropping steeply since then. China's Ministry of Machinery Industry has still not settled on the agricultural machinery portion of the Five-Year Plan; this factor, rather than Asia's economic crisis, is thought to account for the sharp decrease in exports. Chinese delegations interested in buying farm machinery have increased exploratory trips to the United States. When the agricultural machinery portion of the Five-Year Plan is settled, China could be a substantial market for exports of U.S. farm machinery.

Although farm machinery exports to many markets continue to rise, current-dollar U.S. exports for the category were expected to decline about 5 percent in 1998, partly as a result of agricultural problems faced by countries affected by El Niño, Asia's economic problems, and the 1997 export spike to countries of the former Soviet Union. U.S. imports of farm machinery in 1998 were well ahead of the level in 1997. The United States does not manufacture farm machinery in the lower-horsepower ranges, and many imports reflect U.S. demand for those products. Lawn and garden tractors and large grounds care equipment are included under SIC 3523 and are reflected in the import totals. Current-dollar U.S. imports of farm machinery were estimated to grow 10.8 percent in 1998. The global farming industry is basically sound, and U.S. exports are forecast to increase 3.3 percent in 1999 as farming conditions recover from weather problems in major markets. The lagged effect on U.S. farmer purchases also could affect imports of farm machinery. Current-dollar imports are projected to grow at a slower pace in 1999, increasing about 5.5 percent over 1998.

Mary R. Wiening, U.S. Department of Commerce, Office of Energy, Infrastructure, and Machinery, (202) 482-4708, November 1998.

PACKAGING MACHINERY

The packaging machinery industry (SIC 3565) consists of establishments engaged primarily in manufacturing machinery for uses such as canning, container cleaning, filling, bagging, bottling, sealing and lidding, check weighing, wrapping, case forming, labeling and encoding, palletizing and depalletizing, and related uses. More than 100 specialized types of packaging machines are manufactured and used daily throughout the world.

The purpose of packaging machinery is to take bulk or finished products—in liquid, gaseous, or solid state—and pack them for final shipment to customers, whether industrial, commercial, or retail. The packing process consists of placing a product into containers made of appropriate materials and of uniform sizes that are designed to protect the product against deterioration or damage, and marking and/or labeling them ready for market.

Global Trends

The packaging machinery industry is being increasingly globalized as industrialization and agribusiness spread throughout the world, creating new needs and markets for packaging. With the creation of new products, the dispersion of international packaging technology is facilitating the globalization of the packaging machinery industry. The outlook for growth of the industry is very favorable, although it varies by geographic region and industry segment. The developed markets of Europe, North America, and Japan will progressively update their technologies to maintain their competitiveness, as will the industrializing nations as business conditions permit.

The nations of the European Union, particularly Germany and Italy, followed by Japan and the United States, are the world's leading manufacturers, distributors, and end users of packaging machinery and technology. Packaging machines of various types and degrees of sophistication also are produced in numerous other countries, such as Russia, Hungary, Brazil, Mexico, Taiwan, and India. They often are designed for local or regional use, but increasingly they are exported and may be built in factories that are joint ventures or subsidiaries of large multinational manufacturers. Machinery parts and basic components are available and are purchased from international sources at competitive prices. That there are no international standards for packaging machinery is a concern among U.S. manufacturers, which export roughly one-quarter of their production and are striving to expand their international presence. The U.S. industry supports international cooperation in standards development to prevent standards from becoming trade barriers while assuring that uniformly high-quality safe machinery is delivered to end users worldwide.

Domestic Trends

The United States is the world's largest market for packaging technology, with revenues estimated to exceed $100 billion and employing more than 200,000 professionals. This huge market is still growing, fueled by the highly competitive, industrialized, market-driven U.S. economy. The extensive range of American-made packaging equipment reflects the machinery industry's historical response to the dynamic needs of American manufacturers of packaged goods.

A broad base of standard packaging systems is the foundation of an almost infinite number of system variations customized to meet customers' requirements at low prices. Machinery builders can no longer simply build machines to sell; they must build machines to the customer's orders. This requires that machinery suppliers cultivate partnering relationships with their customers, providing them with technical expertise, engineering services, after-sales support, and developmental planning. In the future some packaging equipment suppliers may become "full-service" suppliers by building equipment, training operators, and employing packaging system managers in customers' plants.

Industrial consumption of packaging machinery is estimated as follows: The processed food and beverage industry uses about 60 percent; pharmaceuticals and drugs, about 20 percent; personal care products, 15 percent; and other industries, about 5 percent. End-user sectors with high growth in demand for new machinery and technology include personal care products, household and industrial chemicals, and food products, followed by beverage and pharmaceutical applications.

The U.S. packaging machinery industry consists of about 650 companies, mainly small and medium-size highly specialized businesses that are mostly privately held (see Table 18-10). The leading machinery manufacturing states are Illinois, Wisconsin, Ohio, and Indiana, which account for about 40 percent of the industry's employment. With the increasing demand for complete packaging lines and systems integration, many of these specialized machinery builders are collaborating on projects by partnering and forming consortia that can undertake very large and diverse projects. There has also been some acquisition activity, both foreign and domestic, as companies attempt to broaden their product lines by acquiring capable companies with complementary machinery lines.

Four major factors drive the demand for new machinery. First are production considerations: the need to expand production and packaging capabilities. This results from the continued growth of the U.S. economy and the rise in industrial production that requires more automated and efficient machinery. In addition to new plant requirements, purchases are made to expand production as additions to or replacements of existing machinery needed to increase productivity and lower manufacturing costs. Second, technological advancements and new features provide a significant incentive for purchases of new machinery. Popular new features include the ability to perform quick changeovers without the need for tools, expanded computer integration, and simpler user-friendly controls. Expanded robotics and fault detection and self-diagnosis systems also are attractive features for efficiency-conscious buyers. The third factor is the adaptation of machinery to new packaging materials such as films and other plastics, which are becoming the materials of choice in a multitude of applications. Coupled with this are requirements for flexibility in handling variations in the

TABLE 18-10: Packaging Machinery (SIC 3565) Trends and Forecasts

(millions of dollars except as noted)

	1992	1993	1994	1995	1996	1997[1]	1998[2]	1999[3]	Percent Change 96–97	Percent Change 97–98	Percent Change 98–99	Percent Change 92–96[4]
Industry data												
Value of shipments[5]	3,150	3,418	3,690	4,185	4,056	4,303	4,565	4,839	6.1	6.1	6.0	6.5
Value of shipments (1992$)	3,150	3,322	3,491	3,864	3,667	3,810	3,959	4,117	3.9	3.9	4.0	3.9
Total employment (thousands)	26.4	24.9	24.8	28.0	27.2							0.7
Production workers (thousands)	15.6	14.2	14.9	16.9	16.3							1.1
Average hourly earnings ($)	13.86	14.29	14.52	14.69	14.68							1.4
Capital expenditures	70.6	90.2	98.6	87.0	111							12.0
Product data												
Value of shipments[5]	2,861	3,098	3,257	3,658	3,435	3,646	3,869	4,103	6.1	6.1	6.0	4.7
Value of shipments (1992$)	2,861	3,011	3,081	3,377	3,105	3,224	3,358	3,492	3.9	4.2	4.0	2.1
Trade data												
Value of imports	699	719	842	932	1,042	1,104	1,148	1,194	5.9	3.9	4.0	10.5
Value of exports	606	672	792	839	841	871	900	945	3.6	3.3	5.0	8.5

[1] Estimate except imports and exports.
[2] Estimate.
[3] Forecast.
[4] Compound annual rate.
[5] For a definition of industry versus product values, see "Getting the Most Out of *Outlook '99.*"
Source: U.S. Department of Commerce: Bureau of the Census; International Trade Administration.

sizes, shapes, and types of new packages. The fourth factor is environmental considerations as packagers try to expand the use of recyclable materials and reduce material use and waste in their operations.

Internet Applications

Packaging professionals foresee that the Internet will continue its transition from a passive to an active reference tool for commerce in packaging technology. A number of machinery builders are utilizing the communication capabilities of the Internet by incorporating modems in their equipment to allow their customers around the world to log on to manufacturers' home sites for "real-time" field adjustments of packaging equipment.

Evolution of Packages

The era of heavy mass-produced stock containers is coming to an end, and a new generation of proprietary lightweight packages is emerging. Rigid containers—bottles, cans, and boxes—are less rigid than they were in recent years. The distinct boundary between rigid and flexible containers is being blurred by ever-lighter containers that use less but stronger material. Environmental and economic drivers that motivate packagers to "contain more with less" also are moving the market away from large dedicated rigid containers. However, the market success of the new generation of packages will rely on the ability of machinery manufacturers to build, install, and service flexible, agile packaging equipment to produce, fill, label, seal, and pack a wide variety of mass-customized packages.

Packaging Education

Globalization is enhancing the need for international packaging education on the training school, continuing education, and university levels. Understanding package design, materials selec-

tion and specification of machinery, labeling, marketing, and the environmental aspects of good packaging are essential to modern manufacturing, distribution, and trade.

Projections of Industry and Trade Growth

The 1996 decline of 5.1 percent in constant 1992 dollars ended a period of growth years that culminated in record high shipments in 1995. In 1996 a decided softening of the market ensued when capital spending by end users rose only 3.5 percent and the vigorous consolidation of the food and beverage industries apparently peaked. The dramatic gains made by the industry in 1995 could not be sustained. Despite the prevalence of soft market conditions in 1996, healthy market fundamentals remained in place, while technological developments by machinery builders continued to be spurred by intensive competition for the slightly smaller market. Exports climbed from 23 percent to 24 percent of shipments. In 1997 shipments resumed an upward trend of about 4 percent as manufacturers, particularly large-volume producers, sought to improve productivity, efficiency, and profitability through the installation of new, more highly automated packaging lines. Renewed market momentum, technological developments demanded by new product packaging, moderate GDP growth, and increased exports carried the packaging machinery forward at about 4 percent growth in 1998. This rate of growth is forecast to continue through 2000 and beyond. As the U.S. market matures, exports are becoming more important to U.S. companies, which find some of their best market opportunities abroad.

Global Market Prospects

The total world market for packaging technology, including machinery, materials, and services, is estimated at around $415

TABLE 18-11:   U.S. Trade Patterns in Packaging Machinery[1] in 1997

(millions of dollars; percent)

Regions[2]	Exports Value[3]	Share, %	Regions[2]	Imports Value[3]	Share, %
NAFTA	234	26.9	NAFTA	168	15.3
Latin America	128	14.7	Latin America	3	0.3
Western Europe	232	26.6	Western Europe	808	73.2
Japan/Chinese Economic Area	94	10.8	Japan/Chinese Economic Area	107	9.7
Other Asia	106	12.2	Other Asia	6	0.5
Rest of world	77	8.8	Rest of world	11	1.0
World	871	100.0	World	1,104	100.0
Top Five Countries	Value	Share, %	Top Five Countries	Value	Share, %
Canada	158	18.1	Germany	348	31.5
Mexico	77	8.8	Italy	234	21.2
United Kingdom	56	6.4	Canada	163	14.8
Japan	51	5.8	Japan	82	7.4
Germany	48	5.5	United Kingdom	64	5.8

[1] SIC 3565.
[2] For definitions of regional groupings, see "Getting the Most Out of *Outlook '99*."
[3] Values may not sum to total due to rounding.
Source: U.S. Department of Commerce, Bureau of the Census.

billion, with nearly one-third of that based in North America. Because of the vast size of the U.S. market, American machinery builders continue to focus most of their development, engineering, and marketing efforts in their home market. However, international sales are an increasingly important factor to U.S. builders as industry exports make up about 24 percent of shipments, in contrast to European and Japanese builders, which traditionally must export to stay in business.

Built robustly to meet the rigorous high-volume, high-speed, and often continuous operating conditions demanded in the domestic American marketplace, and with advanced control systems and software, U.S. packaging machinery continues to enjoy growth in international markets. Increasing numbers of manufacturers report higher growth rates for sales to their international clientele than for their domestic customers. U.S. machinery is exported to more than 150 countries annually. In 1997 Canada and Mexico imported about 27 percent of U.S. exports. Other top 10 markets include the United Kingdom, Japan, Germany, Brazil, Australia, South Korea, France, and the Netherlands. U.S. machinery technology also has a solid customer base in selected markets in western Europe, Latin America, and Asia (see Table 18-11).

With imports in excess of $1 billion, the United States is the world's largest single import market, representing an important customer base to international machinery builders that can meet its high production and technical specifications. The U.S. market is open and accessible, has low tariffs, and offers the greatest variety of machinery applications. The leading suppliers are Germany, Italy, Canada, Japan, and the United Kingdom, which together supplied 81 percent of the machinery imported into the United States in 1997, a year in which imports held a 28 percent share of the market.

As globalization of the world economy expands, so will international requirements for packages and containers of every description to protect and carry the increasing abundance of the world's commerce.

Eugene Shaw, U.S. Department of Commerce, Office of Energy, Infrastructure and Machinery, (202) 482-3494, November 1998.

PAPER INDUSTRIES MACHINERY

The paper industries machinery subsector (SIC 3554) consists of firms that manufacture machinery for the production of pulp and paper. The industry produces equipment for the major papermaking stages: woodyard equipment used to prepare wood for pulping, pulping and fiberline equipment used in the manufacture of pulp, paper machines, and machinery and equipment used in finishing and converting paper into finished goods. The industry includes machinery for off-machine coating but does not include some machinery and equipment commonly used in paper and allied product mills, such as vacuum pumps, fourdrinier wire, and paper machine clothing. Some historical highlights are given in the boxed note: "Two Centuries of Paper Machinery."

Global Trends

Despite intense competition from Finland and Germany, the United States is the largest worldwide manufacturer of paper industries machinery and an effective competitor in international markets. Although paper industries machines are among the largest forms of machinery manufactured for any industry, paper machinery is easily exportable in a completely knocked-down form. Consequently, size has not proved to be a barrier to the movement of paper machinery in international trade.

The paper industries machinery subsector has historically been subject to the cyclical nature of the paper industry. The long lead times for paper machinery make industry activity a lagging economic indicator and can further distort industry performance if the paper industry does not share the favorable economic circumstances prevalent in other sectors.

Asian and Latin American papermakers have substantially increased their capacity to manufacture commodity paper grades, primarily tissue and newsprint. Investments in new or "greenfield" mills in Asia and Latin America have provided new export opportunities for U.S. paper machinery manufacturers in Indonesia, Malaysia, Taiwan, Chile, and Argentina. However, U.S. manufacturers are vulnerable to the recent devaluations of several key Asian currencies and the subsequent regional economic downturn. Both U.S. and foreign paper machinery manufacturers face the prospect of losing projected business if new Asian paper mill projects, often financed by Japanese or Chinese capital, are canceled or delayed.

Domestic Trends

The U.S. paper industry has experienced 6 years of sluggish growth, with increases in product shipments averaging only 1.5 to 2 percent annually. This slow growth has resulted from a combination of falling prices and overcapacity in market pulp and key paper grades such as newsprint and tissue. These factors contributed to a decline in product shipments by the U.S. paper machinery industry in 1997 and 1998 (see Table 18-12). Paper and allied product mills have been reluctant to increase capital spending during the current cycle. Mergers and acquisitions in the paper and allied products industries have eliminated some existing capacity and consequently have reduced demand for both new and rebuilt paper machinery. Long lead times and a large backlog of orders fueled growth in product shipments

TWO CENTURIES OF PAPER MACHINERY

The year 1999 will mark the two-hundredth anniversary of the invention of the paper machine. The first patent for a paper machine was issued in 1799 to Louis Joseph Robert (1761–1828) of France. The London stationers Henry and Sealy Fourdrinier obtained patents in 1806 and 1807 for the fourdrinier machine, but like many other inventors they subsequently derived little financial benefit. John Gamble and Bryan Donkin improved the paper machine, leading to the introduction of machine-made paper in Great Britain in about 1812. John Dickinson patented a cylinder board machine in 1809, and the first U.S. cylinder board machine was installed in Delaware in 1817. The first U.S. fourdrinier machines were installed at Saugerties, NY, in 1827 and North Windham, CT, in 1828. Phelps and Spafford, later Smith and Winchester, of South Windham, CT, began to manufacture paper machinery in 1828. Several leading U.S. paper machinery manufacturers originated in the nineteenth century. A U.S.-made paper machine was displayed at the Chicago World's Fair of 1893. The machine was subsequently installed in a mill and remained in service for nearly 100 years.

In the first half of the twentieth century the pace of technological change in the industry slowed. In the mid-1960s Finnish, German, and other foreign-based suppliers began to penetrate the North American paper machinery market. Technological change quickened with the arrival of twin wire formers, tri-nip presses, improved headboxes, numerical controls, wider-width machines, and other significant, if largely evolutionary, changes in paper machines.

TABLE 18-12: Paper Industries Machinery (SIC 3554) Trends and Forecasts
(millions of dollars except as noted)

	1992	1993	1994	1995	1996	1997[1]	1998[2]	1999[3]	Percent Change 96–97	97–98	98–99	92–96[4]
Industry data												
Value of shipments[5]	2,524	2,529	2,828	3,418	3,419	3,363	3,312	3,324	−1.6	−1.5	0.4	7.9
Value of shipments (1992$)	2,524	2,496	2,751	3,283	3,216	3,140	3,074	3,040	−2.4	−2.1	−1.1	6.2
Total employment (thousands)	18.2	18.1	17.5	19.3	19.5							1.7
Production workers (thousands)	10.2	9.8	9.8	10.9	11.2							2.4
Average hourly earnings ($)	14.76	15.24	16.11	16.55	17.56							4.4
Capital expenditures	65.4	55.9	49.7	90.6	75.3							3.6
Product data												
Value of shipments[5]	2,225	2,253	2,479	2,970	3,039	2,989	2,949	2,959	−1.6	−1.3	0.3	8.1
Value of shipments (1992$)	2,225	2,224	2,411	2,853	2,859	2,794	2,734	2,704	−2.3	−2.1	−1.1	6.5
Trade data												
Value of imports	637	709	907	981	1,182	1,109	1,079	1,115	−6.2	−2.7	3.3	16.7
Value of exports	583	652	653	862	853	990	1,045	1,105	16.1	5.6	5.7	10.0

[1] Estimate except imports and exports.
[2] Estimate.
[3] Forecast.
[4] Compound annual rate.
[5] For a definition of industry versus product values, see "Getting the Most Out of *Outlook '99*."
Source: U.S. Department of Commerce: Bureau of the Census; International Trade Administration.

before 1997. Falling order backlogs and long lead times for the delivery of new machinery now are having the reverse effect of slowing the industry's efforts to recover from the sluggish performance of its primary customer base. The weakness of its domestic paper industry customers has forced the paper machinery industry into a greater reliance on exports to sustain growth in product shipments. Moreover, the ability of exports to sustain that growth is threatened by a possible downturn in exports to Asian markets such as Indonesia and Malaysia, which in recent years have absorbed a rising share of U.S. paper machinery exports.

Additionally, the industry has seen a slowdown in new orders for paper recycling equipment, primarily new deinked paper mills. Several of these mills have been equipped by the manufacturers of recycling machinery with machinery designed to showcase the recycling process. Some of these mills have been forced to suspend operations or take machine downtime. The difficulties have stemmed from price weakness and oversupply of tissue and newsprint grades and from problems in debugging the new recycling machinery. Restarting deinked paper mills has in some instances required further investment by the machinery manufacturers or has led a machinery manufacturer to acquire control of a mill.

The industry continues to undergo extensive restructuring through mergers, acquisitions, and joint ventures. Pulping equipment and primary paper machinery manufacturers have been affected significantly. This activity has increased the industry's concentration and the proportion of product shipments emanating from the leading U.S., Finnish, and German suppliers. Mergers in the paper and allied products industries also have reduced excess pulp and paper machine capacity. Paper industry mergers in some instances have provided new investment capital for greenfield mill projects and paper machine rebuilds. However, these mergers appear to have reduced the total number of paper machines in place at U.S. and Canadian mills and thus have contributed to a drop in the number of new and rebuilt paper machinery projects being announced.

Employment in the paper machinery industry has grown modestly in recent years, reaching 19,500 workers in 1996, of whom 11,200 were production workers. This growth has occurred in spite of mergers and consolidation in the industry. Continued merger activity and the announced plans for future restructuring of certain leading U.S. manufacturers make a fall in overall paper machinery industry employment likely in the period 1998–1999.

The U.S. industry remains concentrated in its traditional centers of production in smaller, mostly northern communities. The industry consists of approximately 298 companies with 333 establishments. Wisconsin, with 40 firms, accounts for nearly 30 percent of industry shipments and maintains its long-held place as the leading state for paper machinery manufacturing. Massachusetts, New York, Ohio, Pennsylvania, Washington, and Illinois follow. The South continues to attract stocking and parts facilities in states such as Alabama, Florida, and Louisiana.

Paper machines installed in domestic mills are aging and offer opportunities for new orders in 1999 and beyond. An industry-conducted survey indicated that in mid-1997 approximately 43 percent of the paper machines operating in domestic mills had been installed before 1986.

Although proposals for greenfield mills in North America are frequently drawn up, the construction of a greenfield mill requires passage through an obstacle course of environmental regulations and planning and zoning permits. This has limited the number of projects completed. Traditionally, rebuilds of machinery in place account for 60 to 70 percent of paper machine orders in North American markets. Rebuilding or replacement of existing machines continues to offer mill operators a less tortuous route toward increasing production capacity or effecting a change of paper grade.

Projections of Industry and Trade Growth

Product shipments of paper industries machinery were expected to drop 1.3 percent in 1998 to approximately $2.95 billion, continuing an apparent decline that began in 1997, when product shipments were estimated to have fallen 1.6 percent from 1996. Product shipments of paper industries machinery are expected to recover only slightly in 1999, rising an estimated 0.3 percent as the industry feels the continued effect of a slowdown in the North American and Asian paper machinery markets.

The balance of trade in paper machinery was expected to reach near parity in 1998 for the first time since it slid into a deep deficit in the early 1990s. U.S. exports of paper industries machinery are projected to reach a record level of $1.105 billion in 1999, an estimated increase of 5.7 percent over 1998. Conversely, imports are predicted to rise 3.3 percent to $1.115 billion in 1999 after 2 years of decline. The long-term sluggishness in the growth of the North American paper market has reduced domestic demand for paper machinery imports. Export growth fueled by the fulfillment of orders with a long lead time and continued growth in exports to Latin American markets should continue through 1999. However, a projected fall in exports to Asian markets such as Indonesia and Malaysia is expected to widen the trade deficit in paper industries machinery again after 1999.

Over the 5-year period 1999–2003, both product and industry shipments are estimated to grow at an annual rate of approximately 2 percent, with most of the growth likely to occur in the later years. Exports are likely to account for an increased percentage of product shipments over that 5-year period. Exports of paper machinery are projected to increase at an average annual rate of 5.5 percent annually between 1999 and 2003. Imports, after falling in the initial stages of that 5-year period, should resume their upward climb as overall demand for paper manufacturing machinery improves. U.S. imports of paper industries machinery should increase at an annual average of about 4 percent between 1999 and 2003. These projected rates of growth should yield a fairly even balance of trade through the period.

Global Market Prospects

Canada, which normally accounts for about one-fourth of all U.S. paper machinery exports, has long been the leading export market for paper industries machinery, with U.S. exports doubling between 1994 and 1997. By eliminating a 9.5 percent

TABLE 18-13: U.S. Trade Patterns in Paper Industries Machinery[1] in 1997
(millions of dollars; percent)

Regions[2]	Exports Value[3]	Share, %	Regions[2]	Imports Value[3]	Share, %
NAFTA	339	34.3	NAFTA	162	14.6
Latin America	114	11.6	Latin America	13	1.2
Western Europe	203	20.5	Western Europe	858	77.3
Japan/Chinese Economic Area	101	10.2	Japan/Chinese Economic Area	62	5.5
Other Asia	153	15.5	Other Asia	4	0.4
Rest of world	78	7.9	Rest of world	11	0.9
World	990	100.0	World	1,109	100.0
Top Five Countries	Value	Share, %	Top Five Countries	Value	Share, %
Canada	267	27.0	Germany	301	27.2
Indonesia	77	7.7	Canada	161	14.5
Mexico	73	7.3	Sweden	118	10.7
United Kingdom	67	6.8	Switzerland	118	10.7
Brazil	54	5.4	Finland	104	9.4

[1] SIC 3554.
[2] For definitions of regional groupings, see "Getting the Most Out of *Outlook '99*."
[3] Values may not sum to total due to rounding.
Source: U.S. Department of Commerce, Bureau of the Census.

Canadian tariff on paper machinery, the U.S.–Canada Free Trade Agreement has encouraged the reorganization of Canadian paper machinery manufacturing facilities and stimulated a sharp rise in U.S. paper machinery exports to Canada. An upward trend seems likely to continue through the period 1998–1999 (see Table 18-13).

Conversely, U.S. exporters of paper machinery are somewhat exposed to fallout from the Asian financial crisis. New commodity-grade mills have been constructed in Latin American and Asian markets, including Indonesia, and are now attempting to manufacture paper grades such as newsprint in exportable quantities. Several new Asian mill projects remained under consideration in 1998. In 1997 U.S. paper machinery exports to Indonesia doubled to $76.7 million, placing that country second among U.S. paper machinery export markets. Singapore ($23.9 million) and Taiwan ($18.6 million) also registered substantial increases in U.S. paper machinery exports in 1997.

Mexico, the United Kingdom, Brazil, Japan, Germany, Korea, China, and Australia rounded out the top 10 markets for U.S. paper industries machinery in 1997. Singapore and Taiwan led the next tier of export markets, followed by the Netherlands, Argentina, and Chile. (see Table 18-13).

The primary suppliers to the U.S. import market in 1997 were Germany, Canada, Sweden, Switzerland, and Finland. The other major import sources include Italy, the United Kingdom, Japan, France, Spain, Brazil, and Taiwan. Imports from Finland, long the third leading import source after Germany and Canada, have fallen in recent years as Finnish suppliers have done more direct manufacturing in the United States. Imports from some sources, especially Canada, Spain, and the United Kingdom, include machinery manufactured in U.S.-owned facilities in those countries.

Ed Abrahams, U.S. Department of Commerce, Office of Energy, Infrastructure and Machinery, (202) 482-0312, November, 1998.

AIR-CONDITIONING, REFRIGERATION, AND HEATING EQUIPMENT

Air-conditioning, refrigeration, and heating equipment (SIC 3585) includes machinery related to heat transfer and cooling systems. Specific products include air conditioners, humidifiers, dehumidifiers, furnaces, compressors and compressor units, heat pumps, and commercial refrigerators.

Global Industry Trends

The air-conditioning, refrigeration, and heating equipment sector is driven in large part by the construction industry, specifically the areas of residential and commercial building. Weather plays a significant role in the sales of this industry, with installations in existing structures highest when temperatures are extreme. For example, unseasonably mild weather in 1997, which according to the Air-Conditioning and Refrigeration Institute (ARI) led to reduced demand for central air conditioners and air-source heat pumps, contributed to a slowdown in growth. Combined unitary equipment shipments (factory-assembled central air-conditioning systems used in both home and commercial settings which enclose all components in one or two units) fell for the first time in 3 years, down 6 percent from a record 5.7 million units in 1996, according to ARI figures. Total industry shipments reversed the growth trend seen in this subsector since 1991, with inflation-adjusted shipments falling 2 percent in 1997. Positive factors in the industry in 1997 and 1998 were low mortgage rates, a robust housing market, and significant income growth.

Global Market Prospects

Despite a weak domestic market in 1997, exports were strong, with Canada being the largest international market (29 percent of all exports) for U.S. air-conditioning, refrigeration, and heat-

TABLE 18-14:   U.S. Trade Patterns in Refrigeration and Heating Equipment[1] in 1997
(millions of dollars; percent)

Exports			Imports		
Regions[2]	Value	Share, %	Regions[2]	Value	Share, %
NAFTA	2,069	39.7	NAFTA	1,018	39.0
Latin America	540	10.4	Latin America	203	7.8
Western Europe	695	13.4	Western Europe	302	11.6
Japan/Chinese Economic Area	658	12.6	Japan/Chinese Economic Area	627	24.0
Other Asia	617	11.8	Other Asia	442	16.9
Rest of world	627	12.0	Rest of world	18	0.7
World	5,206	100.0	World	2,609	100.0
Top Five Countries	Value	Share, %	Top Five Countries	Value	Share, %
Canada	1,518	29.2	Mexico	711	27.3
Mexico	551	10.6	Japan	539	20.6
South Korea	249	4.8	Canada	307	11.8
Saudi Arabia	247	4.7	Brazil	199	7.6
Hong Kong (PRC)	193	3.7	Singapore	134	5.1

[1] SIC 3585.
[2] For definitions of regional groupings, see "Getting the Most Out of *Outlook '99*."
[3] Values may not sum to total due to rounding.
Source: U.S. Department of Commerce, Bureau of the Census.

ing equipment (see Table 18-14). The only potential weakness in export markets comes from Asia, which accounted for 24 percent of total exports in 1997, down from 27 percent in 1996. In the first 3 months of 1998 that figure fell below 20 percent, an indication that the currency crisis and subsequent recession in countries such as South Korea and Thailand may affect imports from the United States for some time. Exports grew in 1997 in spite of the drop in Asian sales, mainly as a result of a strong increase (34 percent) in exports to Latin American countries. This surge accounted for over half the upswing in exports in that year. The impact of the Asian slowdown is expected to be

felt through 2000, with exports expanding at an average annual rate under 5 percent until that time.

Industry and Trade Projections

A further slowdown has been projected for 1998 before the industry's shipments pick up slightly again in 1999 (see Table 18-15). The major factor in this slowdown is an anticipated slackness in new housing starts that have been forecast to fall 1 percent in 1998 and 3 percent in 1999. In the short term, El Niño effects will slow down the shipments of heat pumps, as demonstrated by the 15 percent drop in shipments in the first

TABLE 18-15:   Refrigeration and Heating Equipment (SIC 3585) Trends and Forecasts
(millions of dollars except as noted)

	1992	1993	1994	1995	1996	1997[1]	1998[2]	1999[3]	Percent Change			
									96–97	97–98	98–99	92–96[4]
Industry data												
Value of shipments[5]	19,739	21,530	24,414	26,217	28,094	27,672	27,495	28,550	−1.5	−0.6	3.8	9.2
Value of shipments (1992$)	19,739	21,338	24,029	25,233	26,554	26,129	25,528	26,115	−1.6	−2.3	2.3	7.7
Total employment (thousands)	121	122	131	135	135							2.8
Production workers (thousands)	89.1	90.1	99.1	103	104							3.9
Average hourly earnings ($)	13.26	13.36	13.76	14.16	14.20							1.7
Capital expenditures	557	518	779	672	717							6.5
Product data												
Value of shipments[5]	18,098	19,767	22,441	23,770	25,512	25,206	25,198	26,139	−1.2	0.0	3.7	9.0
Value of shipments (1992$)	18,098	19,591	22,087	22,877	24,114	23,801	23,396	23,911	−1.3	−1.7	2.2	7.4
Trade data												
Value of imports	1,647	1,769	2,155	2,415	2,684	2,609	2,857	2,997	−2.8	9.5	4.9	13.0
Value of exports	3,310	3,582	3,855	4,371	4,679	5,206	5,451	5,712	11.3	4.7	4.8	9.0

[1] Estimate except imports and exports.
[2] Estimate.
[3] Forecast.
[4] Compound annual rate.
[5] For a definition of industry versus product values, see "Getting the Most Out of *Outlook '99*."
Source: U.S. Department of Commerce: Bureau of the Census; estimates and forecasts by DRI/McGraw-Hill.

quarter of 1998 compared with the first quarter of 1997. The good news for air-conditioning manufacturers is the trend toward installing air-conditioning units in new homes. According to U.S. Department of Commerce reports, air-conditioning was installed in only 75 percent of new residences in 1991 and 81 percent of new homes in 1996. This trend is due in part to the population shift toward the South, a region in which 98 percent of new houses have air-conditioning.

The need to replace chillers that use ozone-depleting chlorofluorocarbon (CFC) refrigerants will keep industry shipments above the level required by new residential and commercial construction. Although the production of CFCs was banned in December 1995 under the Montreal Protocol, the ARI estimates that by January 1, 1998, only 30 percent of the original 80,000 units using CFCs had been converted or replaced. One factor influencing the slow conversion to non-CFC products has been the illegal importation of contraband refrigerant into the United States.

Christine Siegwarth Meyer, Bentley College, (781) 891-2476, November 1998.

PRINTING TRADES MACHINERY

Printing trades machinery (SIC 3555) consists of the equipment used in all phases of the printing process, from prepress to bindery. All types of printing presses are included in this category, from conventional offset presses to those incorporating the latest flexographic and digital imaging technologies. This subsector also includes bookbinding machinery and graphic arts accessories used in the prepress stage.

Global Industry Trends
Demand for products produced by the printing trades machinery subsector depends directly on demand for printed products, including advertising, books and magazines, and business applications. Thus, the printing trades machinery subsector is indirectly influenced by changes in demographics, new advertising strategies, and competition from electronic media. To remain profitable, firms in the printing trades machinery industry are focusing on cost reduction, customer service, and improvements in quality, flexibility, and speed derived from new technologies.

The most significant trend in the printing equipment industry is the explosion of digital format systems in all areas of the printing process: prepress, printing, and bindery. Digital prepress allows customers to change and enhance their work quickly and inexpensively during the design approval process. Computer-to-plate technology enables each revolution of the press to print a different image, allowing companies to provide personalized printing for applications such as direct mail and catalogs. A fully digital workflow will integrate all three aspects of the printing process, increasing speed and thus reducing cost. To digitally link all the elements of the printing process, 33 manufacturers formed a study group called the International Cooperation for Integration of Prepress, Press and Postpress. This consortium created a standard format (Print Product Format) containing process control data needed to adopt computer-integrated manufacturing practices. This format not only enhances productivity through shorter production cycles and better quality control but also provides environmental benefits, including a reduction in paper, water, and ink waste.

This industry is using digital technology to establish networked communications systems designed to link suppliers and customers with manufacturers, allowing for rapid, personalized interaction. The Digital Workflow Study conducted by the Association for Suppliers of Printing and Publishing Technologies (NPES) Market Research Committee reported that only 50 percent of printing and publishing sites used computer or digital technology in 1995. NPES expects that number to grow to 70 percent by 2000, with the fastest growth occurring in North American firms. This study also pointed to two factors that may slow the transition to a digital workplace: a slowdown in economywide growth and investment and cultural resistance to new technologies and business methods.

To implement these new digital technologies, firms are turning to mergers, acquisitions, and joint ventures, many of which reach across national borders. Two U.S.-based firms—Eastman Kodak Company and Sun Chemical Corporation—formed a new joint venture company, Kodak Polychrome Graphics, which began operations on January 1, 1998. Shortly thereafter, Kodak Polychrome Graphics announced that it was acquiring Horsell Anitec, a global supplier of graphic arts products. The German firm Heidelberg Druckmaschinen is engaged in a joint venture with Microsoft to develop new color management technology and another joint venture with Kodak whose goal is to create a completely digital printing press by 2000. In another international acquisition, the U.S. arm of BARCO, a Belgian-based company primarily involved with imaging equipment and software systems, bought Gerber Systems, which pioneered advanced computer-to-plate imaging systems. Scitex Corporation, whose digital printing subsidiary is located in Ohio, acquired the Israeli-based Idanit Technologies, an innovator in wide-format digital printing systems. These mergers and acquisitions allow firms to take advantage of complementarities both in products and in distribution systems to increase profitability.

International collaboration in printing equipment manufacturing is not limited to private sector initiatives. The U.S. Commerce Department, together with NPES and several American and Chinese printing and publishing firms, has established the U.S.–China Printing Technologies Training Center in Shanghai. This center will benefit U.S. firms by serving as a demonstration site for companies interested in expanding into the Chinese market. Not only does China have a large potential consumer base for printed products, but also new privatization policies, including expansion of foreign ownership allowances and growth in the types of business that print shops can seek, make the Chinese market potentially lucrative for U.S. firms.

Global Market Prospects
Since 1990 U.S. trade in printing trades machinery has experienced a deficit which is projected to continue, with imports exceeding exports through 2002. By 1999 the excess of imports

TABLE 18-16: U.S. Trade Patterns in Printing Trades Machinery[1] in 1997

(millions of dollars; percent)

Regions[2]	Exports Value[3]	Share, %	Regions[2]	Imports Value[3]	Share, %
NAFTA	251	17.8	NAFTA	152	7.5
Latin America	206	14.7	Latin America	2	0.1
Western Europe	518	36.8	Western Europe	1,344	66.6
Japan/Chinese Economic Area	209	14.8	Japan/Chinese Economic Area	434	21.5
Other Asia	124	8.8	Other Asia	3	0.2
Rest of world	99	7.0	Rest of world	83	4.1
World	1,407	100.0	World	2,019	100.0
Top Five Countries	**Value**	**Share, %**	**Top Five Countries**	**Value**	**Share, %**
Canada	175	12.5	Germany	747	37.0
Germany	144	10.2	Japan	419	20.8
Japan	101	7.2	United Kingdom	169	8.4
Brazil	97	6.9	Canada	144	7.1
United Kingdom	89	6.3	Italy	121	6.0

[1] SIC 3555.
[2] For definitions of regional groupings, see "Getting the Most Out of *Outlook '99*."
[3] Values may not sum to total due to rounding.
Source: U.S. Department of Commerce, Bureau of the Census.

over exports will reach $821 million, up from $612 million in 1997. Germany was the largest single source of imports in 1997, with Japan, Canada, and several other European countries following (see Table 18-16). Exports from the United States flowed to many of those countries, with Canada being the single largest international market for U.S. printing machinery. Exports in the first quarter of 1998 remained roughly at the 1997 levels, indicating a weak 1.9 percent growth rate of exports in 1998. The effect of the Asian financial crisis is being felt in this sector, with exports to South Korea, Hong Kong, Malaysia, Indonesia, Japan, and other Asian economies lower in the first quarter of 1998 than

they were in the same period in 1997. In 1999, as Asia begins a slow climb out of recession, exports are expected to grow 2.9 percent, with growth exceeding 8 percent in the subsequent 3 years.

Industry and Trade Projections

Growth in shipments is forecast to be weaker in 1998 than in 1997, with a drop in real shipments expected in 1999 (see Table 18-17). These forecasts reflect expected general trends in the economy of reduced GDP growth caused in part by the Asian financial crisis and the anticipated weakness in exports. A slowdown in exports reduces demand in the printing trades machin-

TABLE 18-17: Printing Trades Machinery (SIC 3555) Trends and Forecasts

(millions of dollars except as noted)

	1992	1993	1994	1995	1996	1997[1]	1998[2]	1999[3]	Percent Change 96–97	97–98	98–99	92–96[4]
Industry data												
Value of shipments[5]	2,635	2,727	3,079	3,498	3,654	3,902	4,072	4,005	6.8	4.3	−1.6	8.5
Value of shipments (1992$)	2,635	2,668	2,972	3,300	3,371	3,529	3,621	3,527	4.7	2.6	−2.6	6.3
Total employment (thousands)	19.2	18.9	21.4	22	21.8							3.2
Production workers (thousands)	10.7	10.3	11.7	12.1	11							0.7
Average hourly earnings ($)	13.65	14.59	14.48	14.80	15.90							3.9
Capital expenditures	62.7	52.9	74.0	101.0	106							14.0
Product data												
Value of shipments[5]	2,342	2,345	2,814	3,213	3,019	3,224	3,374	3,335	6.8	4.6	−1.1	6.6
Value of shipments (1992$)	2,342	2,294	2,716	3,031	2,785	2,921	3,006	2,946	4.9	2.9	−2.0	4.4
Trade data												
Value of imports	1,217	1,347	1,553	1,988	1,776	2,019	2,187	2,296	13.7	8.3	5.0	9.9
Value of exports	1,054	1,064	1,029	1,215	1,338	1,407	1,434	1,475	5.1	1.9	2.9	6.2

[1] Estimate except imports and exports.
[2] Estimate.
[3] Forecast.
[4] Compound annual rate.
[5] For a definition of industry versus product values, see "Getting the Most Out of *Outlook '99*."
Source: U.S. Department of Commerce: Bureau of the Census; estimates and forecasts by author.

ery industry directly through reduced sales and indirectly through lower profits for the subsector's downstream customers. However, if the industry can capitalize on new technologies and expand into developing markets, growth is expected to average nearly 3 percent from 1999 to 2002. An important factor in the future growth of this subsector could be the National Ambient Air Quality Standards issued by the EPA in July 1997. Firms are in the process of assessing the impact of the change in ozone standards on their production processes.

Christine Siegwarth Meyer, Bentley College, (781) 891-2476, November 1998.

FOOD PRODUCTS MACHINERY

The food products machinery industry (SIC 3556) supplies machinery for all types of operations in the processing of foodstuffs (vegetables, fruits, nuts, meats, poultry, fish, dairy products, grains, cereals, bakery and confectionery products, beverages, and animal foods). Machinery and associated systems for most applications are custom designed and constructed of special materials for highly sanitary operation and ease of thorough cleaning. Depending on their use, these machines must conform to one or more of the sanitary standards established by the U.S. Department of Agriculture, the U.S. Food and Drug Administration, and the International Association of Milk, Food and Environmental Sanitarians. Food products machinery builders regularly provide machinery to the pharmaceutical, drug, cosmetic, and personal-care-products industries.

Global Trends

International demand for processed foods and beverages continues to set the stage for the continued growth of the food products machinery industry. Over the past 25 years the estimated value of world trade in processed foods has increased at an annual rate of more than 10 percent. Fully two-thirds of all international trade in agricultural products involves processed foods and beverages. International economic and lifestyle changes caused by industrialization, urbanization, and rising family affluence coupled with less time for meal preparation will continue to drive the demand for processed food products worldwide.

To meet this escalating demand and capitalize on its opportunities, the processed foods industry is undertaking sweeping reorganizations and changes. Companies are divesting unprofitable lines and undertaking mergers and acquisitions with companies that have complementary lines and objectives. These strategies are leading to an increased concentration of manufacturing and marketing in the hands of fewer and more powerful multinational companies. Globalization of the processed food industry directly affects the strategies and planning of machinery manufacturers and determines the types of machinery and equipment which are most salable and appropriate to the market.

The international market for food products machinery is highly competitive. Most leading manufacturers and distributors, especially of high-technology equipment and systems, are in Germany, Italy, the United States, and Japan. Machines and equipment of various types, operating capacities, and degrees of technology also are produced in other nations, but often for local or regional markets.

Capital investment in food processing ventures is extensive and requires significant support services such as refrigeration equipment, dry and raw materials handling equipment, storage equipment and facilities, waste treatment systems, clean-in-place systems, packaging machinery lines, and laboratories appropriately equipped to perform quality control, hygienic, research and development functions. With some exceptions, most machinery is custom built by the manufacturer in accordance with government product, safety, and health standards and regulations. Standards such as the 3A standards for dairy equipment, U.S. Underwriters Laboratory certification, and ISO-9000 are widely recognized and applied. There is no single set of international standards. The U.S. industry supports international cooperation to prevent machinery standards from becoming trade barriers and to assure that uniformly high-quality, safe equipment is delivered to processors throughout the world.

Domestic Trends

U.S. manufacturers of food products machinery benefit from the huge domestic market. According to the U.S. Department of Agriculture, the processed food industry is the largest manufacturing and distribution sector in the U.S. economy, accounting for more than one-sixth of the nation's industrial activity. In addition, the United States is a major player in the global food industry, manufacturing about one-fourth of the world's processed foods. In 1997 U.S. shipments of processed foods and beverages were estimated at about $471.6 billion. Six of the 10 largest and 21 of the top 50 food processing companies in the world have headquarters in the United States. In addition to providing a large and viable home market for domestic machinery manufacturers and process technologists, the United States is a magnet market for advanced foreign high-technology machinery suppliers and for direct investment in the food industry.

In todays' competitive business environment food processors are on increasingly tight schedules to bring new products to market and must have the ability to make product changes efficiently. This has forced processors to demand more expeditious delivery of plant projects for renovations, expansion of existing facilities, and the design and building of new facilities. Current construction surveys indicate that a record number of food and beverage plant projects are under way or in the planning stages across a full range of product sectors. The leading regions for new development are the South, the Midwest, and the West Coast. The most significant trends in plant design and operation are the increased use of computers in process management technology and the use of more automated equipment. This is also true in sanitation and food safety applications. The factors driving this strong trend are market forces, competition, legislation and regulations, quality standards, and optimization of production performance and plant operations to achieve maximum profitability.

Although some food processors, particularly larger organizations, have historically maintained in-house technical staff to design new production lines and manufacture proprietary machinery and production lines for their own use, those capabilities are disappearing as a result of downsizing measures to reduce costs. The trend is to take advantage of the technology and expertise of dedicated machinery manufacturers and laboratories to fulfill these operational needs.

The majority of machinery builders are small and medium-size businesses which have developed special market niches and technical expertise. However, processors in the United States and abroad are increasingly demanding complete turnkey production systems which almost preclude single machinery sales except through engineering companies or systems integrators. Many niche manufacturers are forming working consortia with manufacturers of complementary machines, enabling them to broaden their effective product base in order to offer turnkey systems.

Implementation of Hazard Analysis and Critical Control Point Plans

The use of hazard analysis and critical control point (HACCP) plans is widespread in U.S. food processing plants of all types. However, in the greatest single change in its 90-year history, the Food Safety Inspection Service of the U.S. Department of Agriculture has augmented existing food safety regulations by mandating that more than 6,200 slaughter and meat and poultry processing plants phase in standard operating procedures and HACCP plans for controlling *Salmonella* and *E. coli* bacteria in poultry and meats. The Food Safety Inspection Service implemented the first stage of the program in January 1998 for more than 300 large plants with 500 or more employees. Small plants with 10 to 500 employees are to implement plans by January 1999, and very small plants must implement plans by January 2000. An HACCP plan is a process control system designed for a specific processing plant to monitor and prevent microbial and other hazards in food production. Such preventive control systems are recognized as the most effective approach to producing safe food. The new regulations create the need and opportunity for machinery builders to manufacture HACCP-friendly machinery that can be easily disassembled and reassembled for thorough cleaning and inspection. A significant proportion of U.S. machinery already meets or can be adapted to meet HACCP requirements.

Technologies for Sanitary Food Treatment

Among equipment developments which are in the forefront of the movement to assure more consistently sanitary and wholesome food products are pasteurization, ozone treatment methods, and electron beam treatment based on nonnuclear laser beam technology. Irradiation is a proven method of food sanitation which can double the shelf life of foods and substantially increase food safety. For more than 20 years irradiation has been an accepted process in many countries. However, there is a resistance to irradiated foods by consumers in many countries, including the United States, where there is a fear of possible radioactivity. Acceptance of irradiation technology may come in the long run, but not without further public debate.

Home Meal Replacements

Home meal replacements (HMRs) are the latest trend and the fastest growing sector of the food industry. HMRs have resulted from the factors of sweeping demographic changes and time. There are many more working families that include teenagers and a proportionately higher number of singles than there were a generation ago. Although eating out has always been an option, in 1996 the value of takeout orders exceeded that of restaurant dining for the first time. Takeout is no longer limited to simple sandwiches and snacks. In response to consumers' demands, supermarkets and food specialty shops across the nation are providing shoppers at all income levels with an increasing variety of foods. By expanding prepared food lines, the grocery industry has been able to capture a share of the lucrative growing fast-food market.

Provision of these foods encompasses three alternatives: in-house preparation, preparation and distribution by central commissaries, and the purchase of packaged HMRs from distant food processors. These alternatives represent opportunities for a wide range of machinery, equipment, and packaging materials suppliers. The technologies that support the processing and delivery of safe refrigerated HMRs require strict sanitary preparations under safe sanitary operating procedures, HACCP plans, and the application of cold-chain management from the acquisition of raw materials, through processing and packaging in a plant or commissary, to transportation and storage of the HMRs at sales outlets. To extend product shelf life, safe food handling techniques are enhanced by processors that employ high-technology packaging methods such as modified gas atmosphere packaging in combination with specially selected packaging materials.

Projections of Industry and Trade Growth

Shipments of food products machinery are projected to outpace U.S. domestic economic growth by about 1 percent, with annual growth in 1992 dollars of about 4 percent through 1999, most of which can be attributed to consolidation and expansion of the food and beverage sectors at home and abroad. The introduction of new food products and technology will have a positive effect on sales of machinery.

Exports are expected to grow about 4 or more percent annually after a small downward adjustment in 1997. The 1997 decline was preceded by several years of annual increases which reached an all time high of $821 million in 1996 (see Table 18-18). The United States is a net exporter of food products machinery. In 1996 exports accounted for 33 percent of product shipments. The opportunities in overseas markets are becoming more evident to U.S. manufacturers as their large home market matures and competition intensifies.

The United States is the world's largest food processor, food innovator, and machinery market; therefore, it is a target market for imports, which in 1996 accounted for 25 percent of the market. The U.S. market is accessible and competitive, and tariffs are low. Foreign manufacturers of a variety of high-quality state-of-the-art machinery and special niche equipment find a receptive audience among U.S. processors.

TABLE 18-18: Food Products Machinery (SIC 3556) Trends and Forecasts
(millions of dollars except as noted)

	1992	1993	1994	1995	1996	1997[1]	1998[2]	1999[3]	96–97	97–98	98–99	92–96[4]
									Percent Change			
Industry data												
Value of shipments[5]	2,417	2,630	2,674	2,819	2,798	3,044	3,248	3,462	8.8	6.7	6.6	3.7
Value of shipments (1992$)	2,417	2,564	2,520	2,579	2,502	2,602	2,706	2,814	4.0	4.0	4.0	0.9
Total employment (thousands)	18.9	18.8	19.8	19.9	21.1							2.8
Production workers (thousands)	11.2	11.3	12.0	12.1	12.1							2.0
Average hourly earnings ($)	13.08	13.23	13.05	13.46	13.66							1.1
Capital expenditures	46.8	48.8	48.5	43.0	67.0							9.4
Product data												
Value of shipments[5]	2,102	2,311	2,266	2,347	2,490	2,709	2,890	3,081	8.8	6.7	6.6	4.3
Value of shipments (1992$)	2,102	2,252	2,136	2,147	2,227	2,316	2,409	2,505	4.0	4.0	4.0	1.5
Trade data												
Value of imports	474	439	481	591	545	575	592	610	5.5	2.9	3.0	3.6
Value of exports	687	696	734	792	821	817	842	875	-0.5	3.0	3.9	4.6

[1] Estimate except imports and exports.
[2] Estimate.
[3] Forecast.
[4] Compound annual rate.
[5] For a definition of industry versus product values, see "Getting the Most Out of *Outlook '99*."
Source: U.S. Department of Commerce: Bureau of the Census; International Trade Administration.

Global Market Prospects

The greatest business opportunities for food products machinery lie in the global markets. The outlook for the continued growth of international markets is generally very good but varies regionally and between countries. In the large and mature markets of western Europe, Japan, and North America and certain large food processing and distributing nations such as Australia, Brazil, and Argentina, the picture continues to be bright as a result of the need for higher output, more efficient machinery, and more automated and flexible processing plants. Cou-

pled with this is international consumer demand for a wider variety of processed foods and beverages ranging from safe and wholesome basic foods in developing nations to convenience foods such as frozen and microwavable easy-to-prepare meals and HMRs in the industrializing and developed nations.

In 1997 the United States exported about $817 million of food products machinery to more than 150 countries. Regional performance was led by North America, followed by Latin America, western Europe, the Japan/Chinese Economic Area, other Asia countries, and other markets. The leading country

TABLE 18-19: U.S. Trade Patterns in Food Products Machinery[1] in 1997
(millions of dollars; percent)

Regions[2]	Exports Value[3]	Share, %	Regions[2]	Imports Value[3]	Share, %
NAFTA	190	23.2	NAFTA	51	8.8
Latin America	169	20.7	Latin America	7	1.1
Western Europe	175	21.5	Western Europe	442	76.8
Japan/Chinese Economic Area	127	15.6	Japan/Chinese Economic Area	53	9.2
Other Asia	80	9.8	Other Asia	6	1.0
Rest of world	76	9.2	Rest of world	17	3.0
World	817	100.0	World	575	100.0
Top Five Countries	**Value**	**Share, %**	**Top Five Countries**	**Value**	**Share, %**
Canada	118	14.4	Germany	102	17.8
Mexico	72	8.8	Italy	97	16.9
United Kingdom	49	6.0	Netherlands	55	9.6
Japan	40	5.0	Canada	45	7.9
Brazil	39	4.8	Japan	42	7.2

[1] SIC 3556.
[2] For definitions of regional groupings, see "Getting the Most Out of *Outlook '99*."
[3] Values may not sum to total due to rounding.
Source: U.S. Department of Commerce, Bureau of the Census.

markets were, in order, Canada, Mexico, the United Kingdom, Japan, and Brazil (see Table 18-19). U.S. machinery is competitive in world markets. Built for heavy-duty continuous operations in hostile environments, U.S. machinery is noted for its technical quality, excellent electronics, robust construction, long service life, serviceability, and good value.

In 1997 the United States imported about $575 million of food products machinery. Regionally, western Europe, Japan and Chinese Economic Area, and the NAFTA nations were the leading suppliers. The leading supplier countries were, in order, Germany, Italy, the Netherlands, Canada, and Japan.

In Asia the current financial problems may dampen the expansion of the food industry in affected markets in the near term. However, the processed food industry is now well grounded, and progress will continue despite any temporary setbacks.

With notable exceptions, the agricultural and food industries of eastern and central Europe, Russia, and the Newly Independent States are greatly in need of modernization in terms of equipment and technology. The food processing industries in many of those countries are using technology that is 10 to 40 years out of date. The need to reduce food waste and improve food quality through better technology is genuine. Even standard western machinery would represent a major improvement. Despite current difficulties in doing business in some of these nations, their markets offer significant opportunities to suppliers that work closely and patiently with potential buyers.

As the world's population grows and industrialization progresses, agribusiness development will continue to spread as a result of the need for increased food production and the reduction of food waste. The increased use of processed and preserved foods is driven by necessity, national government priorities, and foreign direct investment. These factors will combine to increase international trade in food products and food processing machinery and technology.

Eugene Shaw, U.S. Department of Commerce, Office of Energy, Infrastructure and Machinery, (202) 482-3494, November 1998.

■ REFERENCES

American Petroleum Institute, 1220 L Street, NW, Washington, DC 20005. www.api.org.

American Printer, Intertec, 29 N. Wacker Drive, Chicago, IL 60606. www.americanprinter.com/default.htm

American Rental Association, 1900 19th Street, Moline, IL 61265. www.ararental.org/.

BP Statistical Review of World Energy, Britannic House, 1 Finsbury Circus, London EC2M 7BA. www.bp.com/bpstats/.

Construction Industry Manufacturer's Association, 111 E. Wisconsin Avenue, Suite 1000, Milwaukee, WI 53202-4879. www.cimanet. com/.

Federal Reserve Statistical Release G.17, Industrial Production and Capacity Utilization, Board of Governors of the Federal Reserve System, Washington, DC 20551. www.bog.frb.fed.us/releases/g17/default.htm.

House Committee on Transportation and Infrastructure, Washington, DC 20515. www.house.gov/transportation/.

Natural Gas Annual 1996, Energy Information Administration, EI-30, Forrestal Building, Washington, DC 20585. www.eia.doe.gov/fuel-natgas.html.

NPES, the Association for Suppliers of Printing and Publishing Technologies, 1899 Preston White Drive, Reston, VA 22091. (703) 264-7200, Fax: (703) 620-0994, www.npes.org.

Offshore Data Services, P.O. Box 19909, Houston, TX 77224. www. offshore-data.com/

Yatsko, Pamela, "Rethinking China," *Far Eastern Economic Review,* December 18, 1997.

Farm Machinery

Ag Industry Watch, Farm Equipment, Johnson Hill Press, Inc., 1233 Janesville Avenue, Fort Atkinson, WI 53538-0460.

Agricultural Outlook, U.S. Department of Agriculture, Economic Research Service, ERS-NASS, 341 Victory Drive, Herndon, VA 22070. www.econ.ag.gov.

Agricultural Resources and Environmental Indicators, Farm Machinery, U.S. Department of Agriculture, Economic Research Service, ERS-NASS, 341 Victory Drive, Herndon, VA 22070. www.usda. gov/nass.

Agriculture Online, www.agriculture.com.

American Society of Agricultural Engineers, 2950 Niles Road, St. Joseph, MI 49085-9659. http://asae.org.

Current Industrial Reports: Farm Machinery and Lawn and Garden Equipment, MA 35A (96)-1, U.S. Department of Commerce, Bureau of the Census. Washington, DC 20233. www.census.gov.

Flash Reports, Equipment Manufacturers Institute, Suite 1220, 10 S. Riverside Plaza, Chicago, IL 60606. www.emi.org.

Government Information Sharing Project, Oregon State University. http://govinfo.kerr.orst.edu.

1992 Census of Manufacturers: Engines and Turbines and Farm Machinery and Equipment, MC92-1-35A, U.S. Department of Commerce, Bureau of the Census, Washington, DC 20233.

Short Liner, Farm Equipment Manufacturers Association, 1000 Executive Parkway, Suite 100, St. Louis, MO 63141. www.farmequip.org.

10-Digit HS U.S. Trade Date, U.S. Department of Commerce, International Trade Administration. www.ita.doc.gov/industry/otea/trade-detail.

TVA Rural Studies, www.rural.org.

World Agricultural Information Center, web site of the Food and Agricultural Organization of the United Nations, Vialo dello Tarme di Caracalla, 00100, Rome, Italy. www.fao.org.

Food Products Machinery; Packaging Machinery

American Meat Institute, 1700 North Moore Street, Arlington, VA 22209

Exports and Imports of the United States, U.S. Department of Commerce, Bureau of the Census, Washington, DC 20233.

Flexible Packaging Association, 1090 Vermont Avenue, NW, Washington, DC 20005-4960.

Food Engineering. Cahners Business Information, 201 King of Prussia Road, Radnor, PA 19089.

Food Processing, Putnam Publishing Company, 555 W. Pierce Road, Suite 301, Itasca, IL 60143.

Food Processing Machinery & Supplies Association, 200 Daingerfield Road, Alexandria, VA 22314-2800.

Food Production Management, CTI Publications, Inc., 2619 Maryland Avenue, Baltimore, MD 21218-4576.

Globalization of the Processed Foods Market, AER-742, U.S. Department of Agriculture, Economic Research Service, Washington, DC 20005.

Institute of Packaging Professionals, 481 Carlisle Street, Herndon, VA 20170.

International Association of Food Industry Suppliers, 1451 Dolley Madison Boulevard, McLean, VA 22101.

International Dairy Foods Association, 1250 H Street, NW, Suite 900, Washington, DC 20005.

Meat & Poultry, Sosland Companies, 4800 Main Street, Suite 100, Kansas City, MO 64112.

Meat Marketing & Technology, Marketing & Technology Group, Inc., 1415 Dayton, Chicago, IL 60622.

1992 Census of Manufactures: General Industrial Machinery and Equipment, SIC 3565, MC92-I-35E, U.S. Department of Commerce, Bureau of the Census, Washington, DC 20233.

1992 Census of Manufactures: Special Industrial Machinery, except Metalworking Machinery, SIC 3556, MC92-1-35D, U.S. Department of Commerce, Bureau of the Census, Washington, DC 20233.

1996 Annual Survey of Manufactures, M96(AS)-1 and M96(AS)-2, U.S. Department of Commerce, Bureau of the Census, Washington, DC 20233.

Packaging Machinery Manufacturers Institute, 4350 North Fairfax Drive, Suite 600, Arlington, VA 22203.

Panorama of EU Industry '97, vol. 2, Luxembourg Office for Official Publications of the European Community, Agent: Bernan Associates, 4611 Assembly Drive, Lanham, MD 20706.

Quick Frozen Foods International, E.W. Williams Publications Co., Division of Pioneer Association, Suite 305, 2125 Center Avenue, Ft. Lee, NJ 07024.

Refrigerated & Frozen Foods, Stagnito Publishing Company, 935 Shermer Road, Suite 100, Northbrook, IL 60062.

Snack World, Snack Food Association, 1711 King Street, Alexandria, VA 22314.

Paper Industries Machinery

American Forest & Paper Association, *Capacity and Fiber Consumption, 38th Annual Survey, Paper, Paperboard and Pulp,* 1111 19th Street, NW, Suite 800, Washington, DC 20036.

Journal of Pulp and Paper Science, P.O. Box 1144, Lewiston, NY 14092.

1992 Census of Manufactures: Special Industrial Machinery, Except Metalworking Machinery, MC92-1-35D, U.S. Department of Commerce, Bureau of the Census, DC 20233.

1996 Annual Survey of Manufactures, M96(AS)-1 and M96(AS)-2, U.S. Department of Commerce, Bureau of the Census, Washington, DC 20233.

Paper Age, 51 Mill Street, Suite 5, Hanover, MA 02339.

Paper Industry, Two East Office Building, 400 Eastern Boulevard, Suite 4, Suite 204, Montgomery, AL 36117.

PIMA's North American Papermaker, 1699 Wall Street, Suite 212, Mt. Prospect, IL 60056-5782.

Pulp and Paper, Miller Freeman Publishing Company, 600 Harrison Street, San Francisco, CA 94107.

TAPPI Journal, Technical Association of the Pulp and Paper Industry, 15 Technology Parkway S., Norcross, GA 30092.

■ **RELATED CHAPTERS**

ELECTRICAL EQUIPMENT
Economic and Trade Trends

U.S. International Trade

($ billions)

Legend: Balance, Exports, Imports

Source: U.S. Department of Commerce: Bureau of the Census; International Trade Administration.

World Export Market Shares

(%)

Legend: United States, Germany, Japan, France

Source: United Nations; U.S. Department of Commerce, International Trade Administration.

Export Dependence and Import Penetration

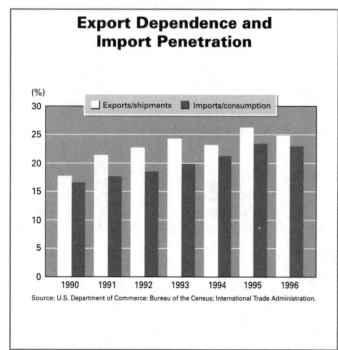

(%)

Legend: Exports/shipments, Imports/consumption

Source: U.S. Department of Commerce: Bureau of the Census; International Trade Administration.

Output and Output per Hour

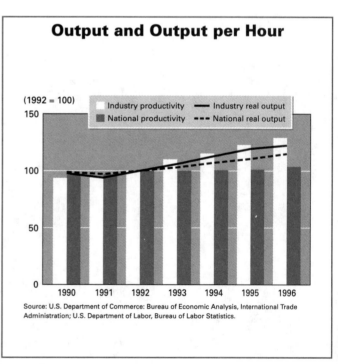

(1992 = 100)

Legend: Industry productivity, Industry real output, National productivity, National real output

Source: U.S. Department of Commerce: Bureau of Economic Analysis, International Trade Administration; U.S. Department of Labor, Bureau of Labor Statistics.

See "Getting the Most Out of *Outlook '99*" for definitions of terms.

19

Electrical Equipment

INDUSTRY DEFINITION Electrical equipment comprises five subsectors: power, distribution, and specialty transformers (SIC 3612); switchgears (SIC 3613); motors and generators (SIC 3621); industrial controls (SIC 3625); and steam, gas, and hydraulic turbines and turbine generator sets (SIC 3511). For statistical purposes, the last subsector is treated separately from the others.

OVERVIEW

The electrical equipment industry supplies products to industrial firms for use in equipment and in end products. Demand for electrical equipment is characterized by sharp cyclical fluctuations, since it is tied to consumers' demand for durable goods such as washers, dryers, and refrigerators as well as to firms' capital spending decisions, which are highly sensitive to movements in interest rates and the perceived path of future demand and thus to expected profits.

Between 1992 and 1996 electrical equipment industry shipments boomed, increasing 5.2 percent in real terms. This growth ended a negative period in 1990 and 1991 during which shipments declined more than 9 percent. The most important factor underlying those boom years was significant investment by firms in terms of both expansion and upgrading of their capital base. Low interest rates, technological improvements, and a healthy export climate stimulated this capital spending. The relays and industrial controls subsector and the motors and generators subsector historically have had the largest shipment val-

TABLE 19-1: U.S. Trade Patterns in Electrical Equipment[1] in 1997
(millions of dollars; percent)

Exports			Imports		
Regions[2]	Value[3]	Share, %	Regions[2]	Value[3]	Share, %
NAFTA	3,646	33.9	NAFTA	3,653	40.8
Latin America	1,084	10.1	Latin America	263	2.9
Western Europe	1,914	17.8	Western Europe	2,078	23.2
Japan/Chinese Economic Area	1,464	13.6	Japan/Chinese Economic Area	2,327	26.0
Other Asia	1,512	14.0	Other Asia	525	5.9
Rest of world	1,150	10.7	Rest of world	105	1.2
World	10,770	100.0	World	8,950	100.0
Top Five Countries	Value	Share, %	Top Five Countries	Value	Share, %
Mexico	2,106	19.6	Mexico	2,545	28.4
Canada	1,539	14.3	Japan	1,536	17.2
Japan	662	6.2	Canada	1,107	12.4
United Kingdom	442	4.1	Germany	644	7.2
South Korea	413	3.8	China	555	6.2

[1] SIC 3511, 361, 3621, 3625.
[2] For definitions of regional groupings, see "Getting the Most Out of *Outlook '99.*"
[3] Values may not sum to total due to rounding.
Source: U.S. Department of Commerce, Bureau of the Census.

ues, and over the period 1992–1996 both subsectors experienced the most vigorous growth, with average annual increases in shipments about 7 percent each.

The pace of growth in electrical equipment shipments ebbed slightly in 1997, with performance varying significantly between subsectors. Turbines and transformers and switchgears, for example, had growth rates which exceeded their 1992–1996 average, while all the other subsectors, including the two largest (industrial controls and motors and generators), experienced a deceleration of growth. The falloff in the growth rate of shipments in most electrical equipment subsectors reflects a tapering off in the demand for industrial equipment as well as durable goods a trend that will intensify through 1999.

Export growth in the electrical equipment sector between 1992 and 1996 surpassed 8 percent per year, with the individual subsectors ranging from a low of 6.3 percent (motors and generators) to a high of 11.3 percent (transformers). Turbine exports in 1997 accounted for 40 percent of all exports in the electrical equipment sector, with strong export demand being generated by developing countries, such as Saudi Arabia, Mexico, India, and China, that are attempting to spur economic development through substantial investment in large generation equipment. Because of this large foreign demand for U.S. turbines as well as other electrical equipment, the American trade surplus in electrical equipment was almost $2 billion in 1997. Imports, however, have been increasing more rapidly than have exports, with shipments of industrial controls from Mexico and Canada as well as several Asian countries (for example, China, Malaysia, Singapore, and South Korea) rising sharply since 1992 as many of these countries are becoming important suppliers in the electrical equipment industry (see Table 19-1).

TURBINES

This subsector comprises the manufacture of steam turbines, hydraulic turbines, gas turbines except aircraft, and complete steam, gas, and hydraulic turbine generator set units. Also included is the manufacture of wind-powered and solar-powered turbine generators and windmills for generating electric power.

Global Market Trends

The bulk of electricity production in the United States comes from steam turbines because of their efficiency and large capacity. However, gas turbines, which are also called combustion turbines, are accounting for the bulk of new manufacturing capacity in the turbine-producing subsector, particularly for peak load times and emergency and reserve power. Of the increase in generating capacity at U.S. electric utilities between 1992 and 1996, the Energy Information Administration estimates that over 60 percent can be attributed to newly installed gas turbines. More than three-quarters of the planned capacity additions at these utilities from 1997 to 2006 are expected to use gas as the primary energy source.

The U.S. Department of Energy (DOE), together with the gas turbine industry, academia, and energy-producing firms, is in the process of developing new gas turbine technology as part of the Advanced Turbine Systems (ATS) program. This program is designed to increase energy efficiency by 15 percent compared with today's turbines while achieving lower emissions, particularly of nitrogen oxide. Consequently, the program anticipates lowering energy costs for domestic consumers while increasing the competitiveness of U.S. turbine producers. Projections indicate that nearly three-quarters of new power generation equipment installed in the United States after 2000 will be related to technologies developed as part of the ATS program. Additionally, high international demand is forecast to provide a market of over $1 trillion for these efficient turbines. One advance is the development of turbines that can operate under high turbine inlet temperatures (2,600°F and above). Although this capability increases the efficiency of a turbine, it also requires new cooling technologies such as the closed-loop concept. Cogeneration—the production of two sources of energy from one burning of fuel—further increases efficiency while keeping emissions at low levels. It is anticipated that gasified coal and gas from biomass (waste from the wood and agricultural industries as well as municipal solid waste) will be utilized as alternative fuel sources. These advances will reduce the risk of a price increase in natural gas to consumers and producers.

Deregulation of the electric power industry will continue to influence turbine manufacturers throughout the forecast period as competition grows after the entry of large-scale energy trading companies as well as independent power producers (IPPs) into the electricity market. The Gas Research Institute projects that by 2015 over 15 percent of energy generation in the United States will come from IPPs, up from only 3 percent in 1996. The increased presence of IPPs will be felt in the turbine market as well. Approximately 20 percent of new equipment demand today comes from IPPs, and this figure is expected to grow to 65 percent early in the next decade. Companies in this new competitive environment will demand more efficient, more reliable, more cost-effective turbines. Although many firms are retrofitting the existing capital stock until the uncertainty in the market dissipates, deregulation eventually could lead to a significant boom in turbine demand, particularly for producers that can satisfy changing customer needs. Gas turbines are especially well poised to fill this market niche because of their flexibility and low cost as well as the relative cleanliness of natural gas as an energy source. Hagler Bailly Consulting reported that as of January 1997 natural gas was the primary energy source for generating capacity controlled by IPPs, accounting for 53 percent of all megawatts produced by these independents. The new competitive environment also will change the capital acquisition decision of both IPPs and conventional utilities. No longer will the need for new capacity alone drive the construction of new plants. Instead, as the Gas Research Institute indicates, a comparison of economic costs and benefits will form the basis for capital investment decisions, hastening the entry of new, energy-efficient gas turbines into the marketplace.

Global Industry Prospects

Exports account for increasingly larger proportions of sales for U.S. turbine producers. Whereas the value of exports accounted for only 40 percent of industry shipments in 1992, that figure rose to 53 percent in 1996 and is forecast to exceed 69 percent by 1999 (see Table 19-2). Exports to the North American Free Trade Agreement (NAFTA) countries and to Asia have been especially strong, with several countries experiencing large average annual increases in shipments from the United States between 1992 and 1997, such as, Mexico (32 percent), India (54 percent), and China (33 percent). Western Europe continues to be an important market for U.S. turbine producers, with over one-fifth of exports headed for that region. The two largest U.S. turbine manufacturers, Westinghouse (being acquired by Siemens) and General Electric, recently announced plans for major turbine sales overseas. Westinghouse reported that over 60 percent of new orders in 1994 came from abroad, for instance, supplying new steam turbine generators to China as well as refurbishing existing foreign power plants. General Electric recently announced the sale of two gas turbines destined for cogeneration power plants in France.

The market for gas turbines in particular is heavily dominated by sales to Asia and western Europe. *Diesel and Gas Turbine Worldwide* reported that between June 1996 and May 1997, 45 percent of all new gas turbine orders originated in Asia and 26 percent in western Europe. This compares with only 10 percent of new orders coming from North America. This expanding reliance on export markets, however, leaves U.S. producers vulnerable to currency fluctuations and recessions abroad.

Imports of turbines come almost exclusively from western Europe and the NAFTA countries. Together, those areas accounted for over 90 percent of the $807 million in turbine imports into the United States in 1997. Canada, the United Kingdom, Germany, and Italy each account for over 10 percent of imports in this industry.

Industry and Trade Projections

The turbine industry continued to display strong growth in 1997, with industry shipments increasing 2.7 percent in real terms. This followed a period of solid growth in 1996 in which the industry rebounded from a slump in shipments of 11 percent in 1995. Uncertainty about the impact of the Asian financial crisis, as well as an expected tempering of economic growth domestically, is expected to dampen production throughout 1999. However, as China, India, and other rapidly developing countries continue to demand increased energy generation capacity and as new high-efficiency gas turbines from the ATS program enter the market, sales are expected to be strong in the first part of the next decade.

Low future prices for natural gas enhance the long-term forecast for gas turbine demand. The Gas Research Institute anticipates that the relatively high gas prices of 1996 and 1997 will not last and that prices will fall by the end of the decade mainly because of increases in supply. Higher levels of gas production both in the Gulf of Mexico and in Canada will offset any increases in demand resulting from a strong economy and the conversion of many applications away from fuel sources with high emissions of greenhouse gases.

Exports rebounded in 1997 after weak worldwide demand in 1996. Exports of U.S. turbines grew over 30 percent in 1997, while firms in the United States increased imports 7 percent in that year. This record level of increase of exports is not expected to continue throughout the forecast period, as slow economic growth in Asia, particularly in Japan, South Korea, Thailand, and Indonesia, will dampen the level of turbine shipments to that region. Total exports to these four countries in the first 5 months of 1998 were down 22 percent compared with the same

TABLE 19-2: Turbines and Turbine Generator Sets (SIC 3511) Trends and Forecasts
(millions of dollars except as noted)

	1992	1993	1994	1995	1996	1997[1]	1998[2]	1999[2]	Percent Change 96–97	Percent Change 97–98	Percent Change 98–99	Percent Change 92–96[3]
Industry data												
Value of shipments[4]	5,843	6,234	6,802	6,144	6,268	6,493	6,630	6,709	3.6	2.1	1.2	1.8
Value of shipments (1992$)	5,843	6,160	6,565	5,846	6,050	6,213	6,319	6,306	2.7	1.7	−0.2	0.9
Total employment (thousands)	27.1	26.7	27.1	24.3	21.8							
Production workers (thousands)	15.0	15.0	15.1	14.8	13.2							
Average hourly earnings ($)	18.38	18.62	19.67	19.03	19.44							
Capital expenditures	312	310	247	162	150							
Product data												
Value of shipments[4]	6,003	6,354	6,546	6,134	6,308	6,516	6,620	6,653	3.3	1.6	0.5	1.2
Value of shipments (1992$)	6,003	6,278	6,318	5,836	6,089	6,235	6,310	6,253	2.4	1.2	−0.9	0.4
Trade data												
Value of imports	638	754	817	802	754	807	889	959	7.0	10.2	7.8	4.2
Value of exports	2,360	2,985	3,040	3,661	3,303	4,306	4,496	4,658	30.4	4.4	3.6	8.8

[1] Estimate.
[2] Forecast.
[3] Compound annual rate.
[4] For a definition of industry versus product values, see "Getting the Most Out of *Outlook '99*."
Source: U.S. Department of Commerce: Bureau of the Census; estimates and forecasts by author.

period in 1997. However, strong shipment levels to several European countries (the United Kingdom, Italy, and Germany) as well as continued demand from China will offset declines in demand from other parts of the world.

TRANSFORMERS

This subsector involves economic activity in the manufacture of power, distribution, industrial, and specialty transformers. Transformers play a crucial role in the transmission of electricity as they increase, decrease, and regulate the voltage of electric current efficiently and safely.

Global Market Trends

Of the roughly 50 million transformers in use in the United States today, approximately 80 percent are owned by electric utilities that serve residential and commercial customers, with the remaining units owned by commercial and industrial facilities. Demand for new transformers arises mainly from demand for additional electricity resulting from new residential or commercial construction or increased electricity use by existing customers. Additionally, some electric utilities are finding that replacing existing transformers with high-efficiency units is becoming cost-effective.

Demand for transformers comes mainly from new construction, since the dependability and long life of transformers do not lead to a vigorous replacement market. Therefore, domestic construction activity is an important factor in sales growth of transformers. As the U.S. construction industry in both the residential and nonresidential sectors has boomed because of low interest rates, high income growth, and robust consumer confidence, the transformer industry has seen impressive growth since 1992, with industry shipments increasing at an average annual rate of over 5 percent. As new construction increasingly places utility lines underground, demand is shifting toward pad-mounted transformers and away from the common pole-top models.

Recent bursts in demand, such as the 7.4 percent growth in shipments (1992$) in 1997, also can be traced to upgrading of the existing transformer stock by electric utilities. Currently, the U.S. Environmental Protection Agency estimates that over 2 percent of all electricity generated in the United States is wasted because of inefficient distribution transformers, which account for 55 percent of all system losses. In an effort to reduce these losses and lower the greenhouse gas emission levels associated with generating this electricity, the agency has instituted the Energy Star Transformer Program, which recognizes utilities that install efficient transformers. Most of the major transformer producers participate in this program, which is expected to improve the competitiveness of electric utilities while boosting demand for high-efficiency transformers which comply with Energy Star requirements. The deregulation of the electricity industry and the ensuing increase in competition are likely to accelerate the move toward this new class of transformers among firms that focus on long-term cost savings rather than short-term reductions in capital expenditures.

Global Industry Prospects

The NAFTA countries (Mexico and Canada) provide the bulk of the international market for United States-made transformers, with 55 percent of exports going to those regions (see Table 19-3). Japan and other Asian countries also import a substantial number of transformers from U.S. producers, which are working to expand their market share in those countries. However, until the countries of southeast Asia overcome their currency crises and the resulting recessions, the future for sales in that region will be uncertain, especially since much of the demand in that region comes from government-sponsored utility projects.

TABLE 19-3: U.S. Trade Patterns in Transformers[1] (Except Electronic) in 1997
(millions of dollars; percent)

Regions[2]	Exports		Regions[2]	Imports	
	Value[3]	Share, %		Value[3]	Share, %
NAFTA	365	55.4	NAFTA	604	62.0
Latin America	59	8.9	Latin America	11	1.1
Western Europe	57	8.7	Western Europe	119	12.2
Japan/Chinese Economic Area	85	12.8	Japan/Chinese Economic Area	201	20.6
Other Asia	63	9.6	Other Asia	37	3.7
Rest of world	30	4.6	Rest of world	2	0.2
World	659	100.0	World	975	100.0
Top Five Countries	**Value**	**Share, %**	**Top Five Countries**	**Value**	**Share, %**
Mexico	265	40.3	Mexico	465	47.7
Canada	100	15.1	Canada	139	14.3
Japan	33	5.1	China	122	12.5
Philippines	27	4.2	Taiwan	44	4.5
Hong Kong (PRC)	27	4.1	South Korea	28	2.9

[1] SIC 3612.
[2] For definitions of regional groupings, see "Getting the Most Out of *Outlook '99*."
[3] Values may not sum to total due to rounding.
Source: U.S. Department of Commerce, Bureau of the Census.

TABLE 19-4: Electrical Equipment (SIC 361, 3621, 3625) Trends and Forecasts
(millions of dollars except as noted)

	1992	1993	1994	1995	1996	1997[1]	1998[2]	1999[3]	Percent Change 96–97	97–98	98–99	92–96[4]
Industry data												
Value of shipments[5]	25,706	27,697	29,787	33,429	34,670	36,472	36,930	37,380	5.2	1.3	1.2	7.8
3612 Transformers	4,118	3,940	4,708	5,213	5,147	5,507	5,507	5,535	7.0	0.0	0.5	5.7
3613 Switchgear & apparatus	5,679	5,849	6,172	6,866	7,184	7,622	7,676	7,691	6.1	0.7	0.2	6.1
3621 Motors and generators	8,168	9,182	9,499	11,163	11,477	11,764	11,705	11,775	2.5	−0.5	0.6	8.9
3625 Relays and controls	7,741	8,727	9,408	10,188	10,862	11,579	12,042	12,379	6.6	4.0	2.8	8.8
Value of shipments (1992$)	25,706	27,329	29,082	31,833	32,536	33,984	33,934	33,895	4.5	−0.1	−0.1	6.1
3612 Transformers	4,118	4,028	4,819	5,192	5,051	5,425	5,403	5,414	7.4	−0.4	0.2	5.2
3613 Switchgear & apparatus	5,679	5,723	5,889	6,363	6,603	6,946	6,898	6,905	5.2	−0.7	0.1	3.8
3621 Motors and generators	8,168	9,064	9,267	10,621	10,787	11,165	10,997	10,887	3.5	−1.5	−1.0	7.2
3625 Relays and controls	7,741	8,514	9,108	9,657	10,095	10,448	10,636	10,690	3.5	1.8	0.5	6.9
Total employment (thousands)	199	199	208	215	215							2.0
3612 Transformers	29.0	27.9	30.7	32.3	32.1							2.6
3613 Switchgear & apparatus	39.1	38.5	39.5	41.6	41.5							1.5
3621 Motors and generators	67.9	69.2	73.7	77.1	75.2							2.6
3625 Relays and controls	62.5	63.1	64.3	64.2	66.2							1.4
Production workers (thousands)	136	138	144	151	150							2.5
3612 Transformers	22.0	21.1	21.7	23.0	22.4							0.5
3613 Switchgear & apparatus	26.0	25.7	27.2	29.0	29.0							2.8
3621 Motors and generators	51.9	53.6	58.0	61.7	59.9							3.6
3625 Relays and controls	36.0	37.2	37.3	37.6	38.6							1.8
Average hourly earnings ($)	11.40	11.79	11.80	12.29	12.71							2.8
3612 Transformers	11.62	12.00	11.91	11.93	12.68							2.2
3613 Switchgear & apparatus	12.25	12.89	13.25	13.29	13.61							2.7
3621 Motors and generators	11.22	11.33	10.85	11.90	12.21							2.1
3625 Relays and controls	10.90	11.58	12.18	12.37	12.82							4.1
Capital expenditures	663	664	862	929	938							9.1
3612 Transformers	85.3	77.8	166	132	144							14.0
3613 Switchgear & apparatus	112	120	146	155	164							10.0
3621 Motors and generators	242	249	290	337	349							9.6
3625 Relays and controls	224	217	260	305	280							5.7
Product data												
Value of shipments[5]	25,435	27,123	29,582	31,885	33,379	34,898	35,233	35,535	4.6	1.0	0.9	7.0
3612 Transformers	4,066	3,906	4,485	4,632	4,746	5,036	5,020	5,015	6.1	−0.3	−0.1	3.9
3613 Switchgear & apparatus	5,469	5,718	5,894	6,526	6,816	7,205	7,233	7,233	5.7	0.4	0.0	5.7
3621 Motors and generators	8,626	9,406	10,255	11,055	11,541	11,714	11,609	11,609	1.5	−0.9	0.0	7.5
3625 Relays and controls	7,274	8,093	8,948	9,671	10,276	10,944	11,371	11,678	6.5	3.9	2.7	9.0
Value of shipments (1992$)	25,435	26,770	28,882	30,348	31,319	32,508	32,354	32,213	3.8	−0.5	−0.4	5.3
3612 Transformers	4,066	3,994	4,591	4,614	4,657	4,950	4,916	4,916	6.3	−0.7	0.0	3.5
3613 Switchgear & apparatus	5,469	5,595	5,624	6,048	6,264	6,565	6,499	6,493	4.8	−1.0	−0.1	3.5
3621 Motors and generators	8,626	9,285	10,005	10,519	10,847	11,118	10,907	10,722	2.5	−1.9	−1.7	5.9
3625 Relays and controls	7,274	7,896	8,662	9,167	9,550	9,875	10,033	10,083	3.4	1.6	0.5	7.0
Trade data												
Value of imports	4,287	4,871	5,899	6,879	7,210	8,143	8,757	9,208	12.9	7.5	5.1	13.9
3612 Transformers	500	608	592	815	828	975	1,057	1,091	17.8	8.4	3.2	13.4
3613 Switchgear & apparatus	306	326	395	413	445	515	557	573	15.7	8.2	2.8	9.8
3621 Motors and generators	2,146	2,365	2,872	3,188	3,233	3,541	3,757	3,982	9.5	6.1	6.0	10.8
3625 Relays and controls	1,334	1,572	2,041	2,463	2,704	3,112	3,386	3,562	15.1	8.8	5.2	19.3
Value of exports	4,031	4,276	4,518	5,289	5,534	6,463	6,751	7,006	16.8	4.5	3.8	8.2
3612 Transformers	338	359	384	469	518	659	691	709	27.2	4.8	2.6	11.3
3613 Switchgear & apparatus	387	405	439	478	550	646	663	669	17.5	2.6	1.0	9.2
3621 Motors and generators	1,969	2,061	2,129	2,540	2,516	2,974	3,099	3,226	18.2	4.2	4.1	6.3
3625 Relays and controls	1,336	1,452	1,567	1,802	1,949	2,185	2,299	2,402	12.1	5.2	4.5	9.9

[1] Estimate except imports and exports.
[2] Estimate.
[3] Forecast.
[4] Compound annual rate.
[5] For a definition of industry versus product values, see "Getting the Most Out of *Outlook '99*."
Source: U.S. Department of Commerce: Bureau of the Census; International Trade Administration; estimates and forecasts by author.

Opportunities for U.S. transformer manufacturers abound in developing countries whose transmission and distribution losses are large (in India, for example, they are estimated at 22 percent) because of the prevalence of old wound-core transformers. The governments in several of those countries want to reduce their losses in electricity distribution and are including the acquisition of modern foil-type distribution transformers as part of the solution. In large potential markets such as China, firms are turning to joint venture projects in an effort to establish a foothold for future sales growth. For instance, Asea Brown Bovieri plans to manufacture transformers in China in a joint partnership arrangement.

Industry and Trade Projections

The outlook for the transformer industry indicates that the rapid expansion of the mid-1990s will not continue, as residential fixed investment as well as the construction of private nonresidential structures will slow in 1998 and beyond. Adjusted for inflation, shipments of transformers are forecast to decrease 0.4 percent in 1998 and then increase 0.2 percent in 1999 (see Table 19-4). Continued low mortgage rates will not by themselves generate a prolonged housing boom, and the sluggish growth of industrial employment will keep commercial construction demand from increasing dramatically; both of these factors portend a weakening in the demand for new transformers. In the longer term, however, deregulation and the ensuing competition should affect the transformer industry positively as IPPs expand operations and existing utility companies look for energy-efficient transformers to lower transmission losses.

The United States currently runs a trade deficit in transformers and will continue to do so over the forecast period. Imports of transformers, particularly from Mexico, Canada, and China, have grown an average of 13.4 percent annually since 1992 and will continue to experience robust growth through the beginning of the next century. Although exports saw impressive growth in 1997 (27.2 percent), this pace will not continue, particularly in light of the uncertainty regarding government projects in economically challenged areas in the Far East. Canada and Mexico will continue to provide a reliable market for U.S. transformer manufacturers.

SWITCHGEARS

Switchgear products include switches, fuses, panel boards, distribution boards, and circuit breakers. They are used primarily in electric generation, transmission, and distribution systems. Switchgears protect electrical systems from problems in voltage, frequency, continuous current, and other operating conditions. They are required for load switching, for short-circuit protection, and in industrial and commercial power systems to protect and control circuit loads.

Global Market Trends

The switchgear market is driven primarily by the demand for electricity, a function of the number of homes and commercial enterprises, as well as by the replacement of outdated equipment by electric utilities. As residential construction grew 8 percent annually from 1992 to 1996 and investment in nonresidential structures rose 6 percent per year in that period, the demand for all electrical equipment, including switchgears, was robust, increasing 3.5 percent annually in real terms.

Global Industry Prospects

In the switchgear industry the value of exports has consistently exceeded the value of imports. The largest export markets for U.S. switchgears in 1997 included Canada (20 percent of exports), Mexico (15 percent), the Dominican Republic (11 percent), and Japan (7 percent) [see Table 19-5]. The single

TABLE 19-5: U.S. Trade Patterns in Switchgears[1] in 1997
(millions of dollars; percent)

Exports			Imports		
Regions[2]	Value[3]	Share, %	Regions[2]	Value[3]	Share, %
NAFTA	228	35.3	NAFTA	213	41.4
Latin America	128	19.9	Latin America	64	12.5
Western Europe	95	14.7	Western Europe	166	32.2
Japan/Chinese Economic Area	99	15.3	Japan/Chinese Economic Area	44	8.6
Other Asia	58	9.0	Other Asia	26	5.0
Rest of world	37	5.7	Rest of world	2	0.3
World	646	100.0	World	515	100.0
Top Five Countries	Value	Share, %	Top Five Countries	Value	Share, %
Canada	131	20.3	Mexico	196	38.1
Mexico	97	15.1	Dominican Republic	49	9.5
Dominican Republic	73	11.3	Ireland	49	9.4
Japan	44	6.8	Germany	41	7.9
Hong Kong (PRC)	31	4.8	Japan	32	6.2

[1] SIC 3613.
[2] For definitions of regional groupings, see "Getting the Most Out of *Outlook '99*."
[3] Values may not sum to total due to rounding.
Source: U.S. Department of Commerce, Bureau of the Census.

largest source of switchgear products imported into the United States is Mexico, with 38 percent of imports originating there. The United States also imports from the Dominican Republic, Ireland, Germany, and Japan, among other countries.

One avenue for U.S. switchgear manufacturers to penetrate overseas markets has been the acquisition of foreign electrical equipment firms and then the sharing of technology and the provision of critical capital investment funds to modernize production facilities. This strategy allows U.S. manufacturers to compete on equal footing with local suppliers, which often are favored in government contracts, and it limits U.S. firms' exposure to currency fluctuations. Two examples of such acquisitions are Asea Brown Boveri's plans to purchase a Polish manufacturer of switchgear and high-voltage equipment and its planned purchase of a Chinese firm specializing in low-voltage circuit breakers.

Industry and Trade Projections

A slowdown in both residential and commercial construction is forecast to affect shipments in the switchgear industry negatively. Much of the demand for switchgears is anticipated to be for electronic switching devices, which are connected to communications systems and are remotely controlled by computer. Such electronic equipment is less labor-intensive and more accurate and reliable than are traditional systems. Overall, output is expected to grow 1.6 percent annually between 1996 and 2002.

Much of the increased demand for switchgear products will come from outside the domestic market as developing countries expand their infrastructure systems and U.S. firms service those markets with a complete line of electrical equipment, including generators, transformers, and switchgears. Exports by the switchgear industry are forecast to grow at an average annual rate of 6 percent in constant dollars between 1996 and 2002.

MOTORS AND GENERATORS

This subsector includes the production of electric motors (other than engine starting motors) and power generators, motor generator sets, railway motors and control equipment, and motors, generators, and control equipment for gasoline, electric, and oil-electric buses and trucks.

Global Market Trends

Demand for motors and generators is related to overall demand for equipment such as consumer and industrial electrical appliances, automobiles, heavy machinery, swimming pools, and agricultural irrigation systems. Motors and generators are purchased primarily by equipment manufacturing firms which incorporate them into end products.

The legislation which has most strongly affected the motors and generators industry is the Federal Energy Act of 1992 (EPACT), which was enacted in October 1997. This legislation imposes efficiency standards on most motors used for industrial purposes and requires that manufacturers label their products with efficiency ratings. The DOE has initiated the Motor Challenge Program, a partnership between industry and government whose aim is to increase the number of energy-efficient motors in key industries in order to increase the overall energy efficiency of industrial-use motors 12 percent and hence reduce carbon emissions. DOE feels that focusing on increasing the efficiency of motors will lead to substantial reductions in emissions because it estimates that nearly 70 percent of all electricity consumed for industrial purposes involves a motor-driven device. These industrial-use motors drive pumps, compressed air systems, and fans as well as being used for material movement and processing and refrigeration. Industry experts estimate that before the enactment of this legislation only 20 percent of motors sold to industry complied with the EPACT

TABLE 19-6: U.S. Trade Patterns in Motors and Generators[1] in 1997
(millions of dollars; percent)

Exports			Imports		
Regions[2]	Value[3]	Share, %	Regions[2]	Value[3]	Share, %
NAFTA	1,274	42.8	NAFTA	1,609	45.4
Latin America	297	10.0	Latin America	77	2.2
Western Europe	431	14.5	Western Europe	673	19.0
Japan/Chinese Economic Area	359	12.1	Japan/Chinese Economic Area	940	26.5
Other Asia	341	11.5	Other Asia	199	5.6
Rest of world	272	9.1	Rest of world	43	1.2
World	2,974	100.0	World	3,541	100.0
Top Five Countries	Value	Share, %	Top Five Countries	Value	Share, %
Mexico	693	23.3	Mexico	1,230	34.7
Canada	581	19.5	Japan	593	16.7
China	114	3.8	Canada	379	10.7
Japan	103	3.5	Germany	242	6.8
United Kingdom	94	3.2	China	239	6.8

[1] SIC 3621.
[2] For definitions of regional groupings, see "Getting the Most Out of *Outlook '99*."
[3] Values may not sum to total due to rounding.
Source: U.S. Department of Commerce, Bureau of the Census.

standards, pointing to a large potential impact of this program on the efficient use of energy.

Aside from motors designed to meet new energy guidelines, technology has been progressing on other fronts in the motor and generator industry. One promising new technology is the switched reluctance motor, which industry analysts predict will become an alternative to conventional electric motors because of its high reliability, high efficiency, variable speed capability, and low cost. The emergence of commercially available switched reluctance motors has been slowed by the lack of training among engineers in this new technology. At this point, switched reluctance technology is being used primarily in automotive and appliance applications.

Another new type of motor, the high-horsepower electric motor using high-temperature superconductors, was developed as part of the Superconductivity Partnership Initiative, a DOE program with American Semiconductor Corporation and Reliance Electric. These motors are smaller, lighter, and more efficient than current models, and their commercialization is expected by the turn of the century.

Global Industry Prospects

The motor and generator industry generates exports to a larger extent than do other electrical equipment subsectors except for turbines. In 1996 over 25 percent of product shipments were bound for foreign markets. The largest export markets for U.S. motors and generators were Mexico (with a 23 percent share), Canada (20 percent), Asia (24 percent), western Europe (15 percent), and Latin America (10 percent). The general pattern of exports has not changed significantly since 1992, with the NAFTA countries purchasing the largest proportion of U.S. motors and generators outside the United States (see Table 19-6).

The United States continues to run a trade deficit in motors and controls, with imports having exceeded exports by $717 million in 1996. Imports in this subsector are primarily from Mexico, Japan, Canada, Germany, and China, with China emerging as the fastest growing exporter of motors and generators to the United States. Shipments of motors and generators from China increased at an annual rate above 23 percent from 1992 to 1997.

Industry and Trade Projections

Because industrial and construction activity is expected to be less vigorous over the forecast period than it has been in the recent past, the outlook for the motors and generators market is for negative growth until 2000. Adjusted for inflation, shipments in this subsector are expected to decline 1.5 percent in 1998 and 1 percent in 1999. The reason for this slowdown is a decline in consumer spending on appliances and motor vehicles, two end products that incorporate many motors and generators. Housing starts are anticipated to decline in 1999, reducing demand for construction machinery and electrical appliances, both driven by motors. After 1999 the motor and generator industry is expected to rebound with a positive growth in shipments, spurred by the demand for the new energy-efficient motors produced as part of the Motor Challenge Program as well as by other emerging technologies.

Exports of motors and generators are expected to be relatively weak in 1998 and 1999 compared with the period 1992 to 1997. The uncertainty generated by significant recessions in Asia will slow capital investment in many regions of the world and thus affect export sales.

INDUSTRIAL CONTROLS

Industrial controls are used primarily for starting, regulating, stopping, and protecting various types of machinery and equipment that incorporate motors and/or other power generating systems. There are two types of industrial controls: advanced industrial controls, which are based on solid-state electronics technology and include programmable logic controllers, computer numerical controls, adjustable speed drives, proximity/positioning sensors, and industrial control software; and conventional (electromechanical) industrial controls, such as starters and contractors, limit switches, and resistors.

Global Market Trends

Industrial controls are used by a myriad of original equipment manufacturers (OEMs) in their products. Industrial controls appear in industrial and production machinery and electrical and electronic equipment, with demand recently shifting to manufacturers of nondurable goods, service industries, utilities, and construction firms. A second important market for industrial controls consists of maintenance/repairs/operating (MRO) firms, which repair and service the original equipment. OEM demand can be cyclical, depending on capital investment and consumer purchases, both of which closely follow the business cycle. MRO demand is more stable because of the large existing capital stock, making the industrial control industry better able to weather downturns in the domestic and international economies.

Within the industrial controls industry, demand is shifting away from conventional controls and toward advanced industrial controls such as computer numerical controls, which allow an end user to program a machine to do basic tasks that previously were done by an operator, such as the movement of parts, changing tool parts, and cooling a machine. Computer numerical controls are found in a variety of industries and applications, including metal removal (drilling, boring, milling, etc.), woodworking, fabrication of metal products, and lettering and engraving. The United States is also strong in the manufacture of programmable logic controllers, computers in whose memory is stored control programs for a series of assembly and manufacturing functions which can produce items such as valves, relays, and motors. The advantage of these systems over their predecessors, the relay logic controllers, lies in their reliability, low cost, and ease of reprogramming.

One source of competition for producers of programmable logic controllers may come from the personal computer market, which offers similar methods for the programming of machines and processes. However, despite the adoption of personal computers for the control of lines by a few high-profile manufacturers, industry experts point out that several features of programmable

TABLE 19-7: U.S. Trade Patterns in Relays and Industrial Controls[1] in 1997

(millions of dollars; percent)

	Exports			Imports	
Regions[2]	Value[3]	Share, %	Regions[2]	Value[3]	Share, %
NAFTA	1,215	55.6	NAFTA	977	31.4
Latin America	95	4.3	Latin America	102	3.3
Western Europe	453	20.7	Western Europe	642	20.6
Japan/Chinese Economic Area	177	8.1	Japan/Chinese Economic Area	1,088	34.9
Other Asia	163	7.4	Other Asia	256	8.2
Rest of world	83	3.8	Rest of world	47	1.5
World	2,185	100.0	World	3,112	100.0
Top Five Countries	Value	Share, %	Top Five Countries	Value	Share, %
Mexico	806	36.9	Japan	840	27.0
Canada	408	18.7	Mexico	607	19.5
United Kingdom	136	6.2	Canada	371	11.9
Germany	96	4.4	Germany	247	7.9
Japan	66	3.0	China	179	5.7

[1] SIC 3625.
[2] For definitions of regional groupings, see "Getting the Most Out of *Outlook '99.*"
[3] Values may not sum to total due to rounding.
Source: U.S. Department of Commerce, Bureau of the Census.

logic controllers—cost, durability at extremes in temperature as well as resistance to dust and other contaminants, and simplicity of coding—will continue to secure their place in the market.

Between 1992 and 1996 real industry shipments of industrial controls grew steadily at an annual rate of nearly 7 percent. After this strong growth, which was fueled largely by strong consumer demand, industrial expansion, and a healthy economy, the subsector grew only modestly in 1997.

Global Industry Prospects

U.S. exports of industrial controls are heavily biased toward the NAFTA region, with 37 percent headed for Mexico and 19 percent for Canada (see Table 19-7). The trade between Mexico and the United States in this subsector has been positively influenced by NAFTA, with exports to Mexico more than doubling in just 4 years. Other important export markets include the United Kingdom, Germany, and Japan.

Since 1993 the United States has run an ever-increasing trade deficit in industrial controls, with strong competition from suppliers in Japan, France, Germany, and the United Kingdom, countries with their high-technology knowledge and traditional strengths in the machinery and electronic industries. The largest increases in imports since 1992 have come from Asian countries, with China leading the way with an average annual growth rate of over 50 percent in shipments to the United States. Malaysia, Singapore, Taiwan, and South Korea are also entering the global industrial controls market, with particular strength in conventional controls.

Industry and Trade Projections

Because of the steady demand from MRO firms, the industrial controls subsector will continue to experience moderate growth even as other subsectors within the electrical equipment indus-

try have declines in shipments in 1998 and 1999. Overall, the inflation-adjusted value of shipments is expected to increase 1.8 percent in 1998 and 0.5 percent in 1999. After 2000 the subsector will see accelerated growth as OEM markets begin to pick up, with growth in shipments between 2 and 4 percent over the remainder of the forecast period.

Exports of industrial controls will continue to be strong, although the average annual growth rates of nearly 10 percent experienced in 1992–1996 will not persist. Rapidly expanding machinery and electrical equipment industries in developing countries, such as those in Latin American and Asia, as well as continued vigorous sales to NAFTA countries will lead to growth rates of 4 to 5 percent per year in 1998 and 1999 despite uncertainties regarding the health of many of the world's economies.

Christine Siegwarth Meyer, Bentley College, (781) 891-2476.

■ REFERENCES

Advanced Turbine System Program, U.S. Department of Energy, Federal Energy Technology Center, 3610 Collins Ferry Road, P.O. Box 880, Morgantown, WV 26507-0880. (304) 285-4603, www.fetc.doe.gov/publications/factsheets/power_sys/ats/atsfacts.pdf.

Diesel and Gas Turbine Worldwide, 13555 Bishop's Court, Brookfield, WI 53005. (414) 784-9177, www.dieselpub.com/ww/ww_toc.htm.

Electric Power Annual, Energy Information Administration, Office of Coal, Nuclear, Electric and Alternate Fuels, U.S. Department of Energy, Washington, DC 20585. www.eia.doe.gov/cneaf/electricity/epa/toc.html.

Electric Power Supply Association, 1401 H Street, NW, Suite 760, Washington, DC 20005. (202) 789-7200, www.epsa.org/.

Gas Research Institute, 8600 West Bryn Mawr Avenue, Chicago, IL 60631-3562. (773) 399-8100, www.gri.org.

ENVIRONMENTAL TECHNOLOGIES AND SERVICES
Economic and Trade Trends

U.S. Environmental Industry Market Segments, 1997

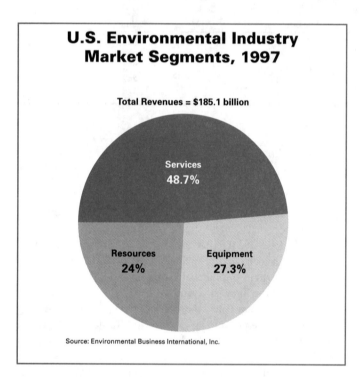

Total Revenues = $185.1 billion

Services 48.7%
Resources 24%
Equipment 27.3%

Source: Environmental Business International, Inc.

U.S. Environmental Export Performance

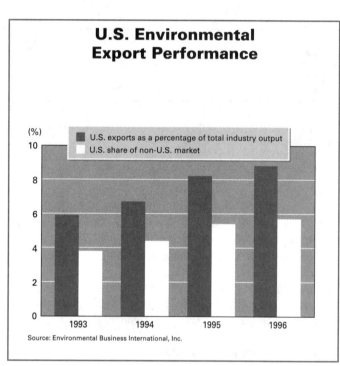

(%)
- U.S. exports as a percentage of total industry output
- U.S. share of non-U.S. market

Source: Environmental Business International, Inc.

U.S. Environmental Trade Balance by Sector, 1996

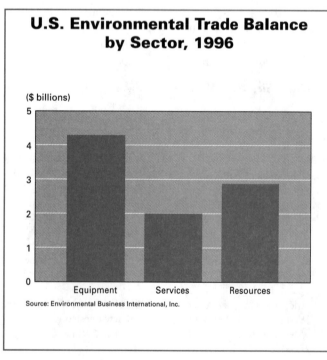

($ billions)

Equipment   Services   Resources

Source: Environmental Business International, Inc.

Environmental Global Market Growth, 1996–2000

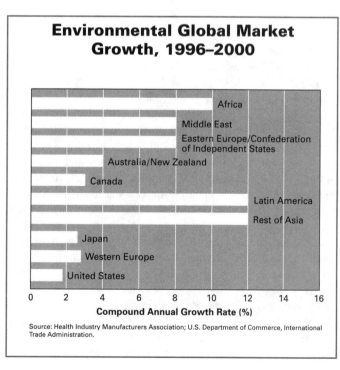

Africa
Middle East
Eastern Europe/Confederation of Independent States
Australia/New Zealand
Canada
Latin America
Rest of Asia
Japan
Western Europe
United States

Compound Annual Growth Rate (%)

Source: Health Industry Manufacturers Association; U.S. Department of Commerce, International Trade Administration.

Environmental Technologies and Services

INDUSTRY DEFINITION Environmental technologies advance sustainable development by reducing risk, enhancing cost-effectiveness, improving process efficiency, and creating products and processes that are environmentally beneficial or benign. The environmental technology industry includes air, water, and soil pollution control; solid and toxic waste management; site remediation; engineering, design, and consulting services; environmental monitoring; recycling; and industrial and clean process technology. This relatively young industry is large and fragmented and has evolved in response to growing concern about the risks and costs of pollution and the enactment of pollution control legislation in the United States and around the world.

OVERVIEW

The U.S. environmental technologies sector consists of more than 115,200 companies and entities that employed 1.3 million workers in 1996. The United States is the largest producer and consumer of environmental goods and services in the world. Environmental Business International (EBI) of San Diego, CA, estimates that the global market for environmental technologies totaled $453 billion in 1996 and projects that it will grow to $530 billion by 2001. EBI estimates that total U.S. industry revenues increased 2.1 percent from $180.8 billion in 1996 to $184.6 billion in 1997 (see Table 20-1; data vary for 1996 in Tables 20-1, 20-2, and 20-6 because of the statistical methods used by the source). Annual growth of 10 to 15 percent in the period 1985–1990 declined to 2 to 5 percent in 1991–1995 and fell to 1 to 2 percent in 1996, the lowest growth rate on record. Projected annual growth for the sector over the next few years is estimated to be in the range of 2 to 2.8 percent. Faced with slower growth, increased competition, and declining profits in the home market, U.S. companies increasingly are turning to export markets to increase their sales. In 1996 exports of U.S. environmental technologies and services generated $16 billion and a trade surplus of $9.3 billion. The global environmental market has been a savior to the industry, with 5 percent growth over the last 2 years and well over 10 percent in much of the

developing world. What was a high-growth industry in the United States is now an industry in transition, as characterized in "Meeting the Challenge: U.S. Industry Faces the 21st Century: The U.S. Environmental Industry," a report by the Office of Technology Policy of the U.S. Department of Commerce. Environmental regulations that fueled market growth in the past now have a diminished influence on demand. Since 1991 substantial compliance with existing regulations has been reached by most major industrial sectors, creating cost pressures on many of the industry's customers. Few new environmental legislative programs have been enacted, and fewer new regulations have been promulgated. With the erosion of regulation-induced demand, buying patterns for environmental products and services are undergoing a fundamental change from a predominant demand for pollution control, waste management, and remediation to an evolving demand for resource productivity and environmental improvements that enhance competitive advantage. As this change gathers momentum, the environmental market is shifting from one dominated by activities making up for the past to one dominated by preparations for the future.

Environmental Technologies and Services

The U.S. environmental market has matured rapidly and has become very dependent on demand by regulation; it now receives little new growth impetus from waning regulation-induced mar-

TABLE 20-1: U.S. Environmental Industry Revenues Trends and Forecasts

(billions of dollars; percent)

Industry Segment	1995	1996	1997	1998	1999	2000	2001	2002	Percent Growth 95–96	Percent Growth 96–97
Equipment										
Water equipment and chemicals	16.5	17.5	18.0	18.7	19.4	20.1	20.8	21.4	6.0	2.7
Instruments and information systems	3.0	3.1	3.2	3.3	3.5	3.6	3.7	3.8	4.2	1.9
Air pollution control equipment	14.8	15.3	15.8	16.3	16.7	17.2	17.6	18.1		
Waste management equipment	11.7	12.0	12.2	12.3	12.4	12.6	12.7	12.8	2.1	1.9
Process and prevention technology	0.8	0.8	0.9	1.0	1.1	1.2	1.3	1.4	2.4	7.1
Services										
Analytical services	1.2	1.2	1.1	1.1	1.1	1.1	1.1	1.1	−2.5	−8.5
Wastewater treatment works	23.4	24.0	24.7	25.6	26.6	27.5	28.5	29.5	2.5	2.8
Solid waste management	32.5	33.9	34.9	35.8	36.7	37.5	38.1	38.6	4.3	2.9
Hazardous waste management	6.2	6.0	5.8	5.6	5.4	5.1	4.9	4.7	−3.5	−3.0
Remediation and industrial services	8.6	8.6	8.6	8.7	8.7	8.7	8.6	8.5	−0.3	−0.2
Consulting and engineering	15.5	15.2	15.0	15.1	15.2	15.2	15.2	15.0	−1.9	−1.4
Resources										
Water utilities	25.3	26.4	27.1	28.0	28.9	29.7	30.5	31.3	4.2	2.8
Resource recovery	16.9	14.3	14.8	15.4	15.9	16.4	16.8	17.2	−14.9	3.2
Environmental energy sources	2.3	2.4	2.6	2.7	2.9	3.1	3.3	3.4	3.5	7.6
Industry total	178.8	180.8	184.6	189.7	194.5	199.0	203.1	206.8	1.1	2.1

Source: Environmental Business International, Inc.

TABLE 20-2: U.S. Environmental Trade Balance by Industry Segment, 1996

(billions of dollars; percent)

Industry Segment	US Industry Revenues	US Market	Exports	Imports	Trade Balance	Exports to Industry Revenues, %
Equipment						
Water equipment and chemicals	17.5	16.0	3.3	1.8	1.5	19
Air pollution control	15.7	15.4	1.6	1.3	0.3	10
Instruments and information	3.1	1.8	1.6	0.3	1.3	51
Waste management equipment	12.0	10.7	1.9	0.6	1.3	16
Process and prevention technology	0.8	0.9	0.0	0.1	−0.1	1
Total	49.1	44.8	8.4	4.1	4.3	17
Services						
Solid waste management	33.9	32.7	1.4	0.2	1.2	4
Hazardous waste management	6.0	5.9	0.2	0.1	0.1	3
Consulting and engineering	15.2	14.2	1.3	0.3	1.0	9
Remediation and industrial services	8.6	8.3	0.3	0.0	0.3	3
Analytic services	1.2	1.2	0.0	0.0	0.0	2
Wastewater treatment works	24.0	24.6	0.2	0.8	−0.6	1
Total	88.9	86.9	3.4	1.4	2.0	3.8
Resources						
Water utilities	26.4	27.0	0.1	0.8	−0.7	1
Resource recovery	14.3	11.6	2.9	0.2	2.7	20
Environmental energy	2.4	1.4	1.1	0.2	0.9	48
Total	43.1	40.0	4.1	1.2	2.9	9.5
Industry total	181.1	171.8	16.0	6.7	9.2	8.8

Source: Environmental Business International, Inc.

ket growth. Many environmental companies face slower industry growth and are cautious about investing in a future with uncertain market demand. Virtually all 14 segments of this large and diverse industry now display the characteristics of a maturing industry: decelerating growth, heightened competition, growing customer sophistication, pricing pressure, consolidation of market share in larger players, reduced profitability, and increased merger and acquisition activity. Without substantial reform in the framework of environmental policy, demand will become even more uncertain, and this will directly affect the competitiveness of the environmental industry.

In general, the U.S. environmental industry is very competitive in most equipment segments but trails in some service segments. However, U.S. companies are notably competitive in service segments such as solid waste management, hazardous waste management, engineering, remediation, analytical services, and information systems. Many of the service segments in which the United States has a comparative advantage (e.g., consulting and engineering, analytical services, and remediation) are not those in strongest demand in the established markets of the developed world or in developing markets. U.S. firms are very competitive in environmental instrumentation and information systems, where they export 51 percent of their output (see Table 20-2). U.S. firms are moving rapidly into the fast-growing pollution prevention sector, but this sector represents only about 1 percent of the industry's current total revenues. U.S. companies have generally been uncompetitive in the design, construction, and management of potable water and wastewater projects overseas. These companies possess competitive technical capabilities but are often noncompetitive in foreign bidding and negotiating deals, largely because of the financial terms. In the water treatment field, this may be explained by the fact that U.S. entities have been run by the public sector and thus are regionally focused. The lack of competitive business practice is contrasted by the experience of leading privatized European companies in the water industry (see the boxed note: "Water and Wastewater Infrastructure Opportunities").

WATER AND WASTEWATER INFRASTRUCTURE OPPORTUNITIES

Multilateral development banks and other international organizations look closely at funding and financing for projects involving environmental technologies. Many environmental technology projects focus on water and wastewater infrastructure. These projects offer American firms attractive opportunities to export environmental technologies and services, particularly in consulting, engineering, and the management of large construction projects.

The Inter-American Development Bank's (IADB) annual lending grew rapidly from $294 million in 1961 to over $6 billion in 1997. In the environmental technology sector, loans valued at $335 million were approved in 1997. Overall, environmental projects make up about 8 percent of IADB's annual business. The approved projects include environmental management of the Mantanza-Riachuelo River Basin in Argentina; a private concession for water and sewerage services in Guayaquil, Ecuador; and restructuring the national water and sewer utility in Panama. The IADB publishes a pipeline of proposed and future projects. IADB's Web site is www.iadb.org.

The Asia Development Bank's (ADB) main operational objective is to ensure the provision of reliable and safe drinking water and sanitation services. Water supply components often are included in integrated urban development projects. The ADB also supports the participation of the private sector in water supply development, management, and maintenance. Overall, environmental projects made up about 7 percent of ADB's 1996–1998 program. Proposed projects include the Melanchi Water Supply in Nepal, valued at $5 million; the Bangkok Metropolitan Region Wastewater Management, valued at $150 million; and the Northeast Region Water Supply and Sanitation project in Thailand, valued at $50 million. Pipeline projects are published monthly and are available by subscription. ADB's Web site is www.asiandevbank.org.

The African Development Fund (ADF), part of the African Development Group, approved loans for the Rural Water Supply Project in Côte d'Ivoire, valued at $20 million; the Nairobi Third Water Supply (supplemental loan), valued at $20 million; and the Rural Water Supply and Sanitation II project in Zimbabwe, valued at $18.5 million. The African Development Bank, another part of the ADF, approved a loan for the Jendouba Irrigated Agriculture Development Project, valued at $26 million. In 1997 one of the group's major achievements that will boost the ADF's project activity was the conclusion of the Seventh General Replenishment of the resources of the ADF. Over the next 2 years ADF envisions providing concessional assistance to 42 African countries that will total about $3.2 billion.

The European Bank for Reconstruction and Development (EBRD) in 1997 expanded its operations into Croatia, Hungary, Poland, the Slovak Republic, and Ukraine, and signed five financing commitments totaling $156 million and a second framework agreement for a municipal services multiproject facility. EBRD projects include the extension and improvement of sewerage and water services in towns along the Adriatic coast and a water and environment investment project in Riga, Latvia. Since the EBRD was established in 1991, the cumulative value of signed operations has been over $9.5 billion. In the municipal and environmental infrastructure sector, EBRD states that the demand for financing is growing rapidly, and estimates indicate that investments in excess of $186 billion are needed to achieve basic levels of services in the EBRD countries.

The World Bank's lending for environment projects in fiscal years 1986–1997 totaled $11.6 billion. In addition, the World Bank shares the responsibility for implementing the Global Environment Facility (GEF) with the United Nations. The World Bank is currently responsible for a GEF work program of about $1 billion, covering four focal areas, including international waters. At the end of fiscal year 1997 World Bank management had approved 69 projects in over 50 countries, totaling GEF commitments of $675 million and leveraging an additional $2.84 billion. For pipeline project information, the World Bank produces *Monthly Operational Summary of Bank and IDA Proposed Projects,* and its Environmental Department produces an annual environmental review each fall. The World Bank's Web site is www.worldbank.org.

In addition to the Internet, the Department of Commerce, Office of Multilateral Development Bank Operations, may be contacted at (202) 482-3399 or (202) 273-0927 for information about multilateral bank programs. U.S. firms with questions about exporting environmental technologies may contact the Department of Commerce, Environmental Technologies Exports, at www.infoserv2.ita.doc.gov/ete or the Department of Commerce Trade Information Center at (800) 872-8723.

Corey D. Wright, U.S. Department of Commerce, Office of Environmental Technologies Exports, (202) 482-0616.

The service sectors are the largest components of the environmental industry. In 1996 the largest service sectors were solid waste management and wastewater treatment works, with estimated revenues of $33.9 billion and $24 billion, respectively. In the equipment sector the dominant revenue producers in 1996 included water equipment and chemicals [$17.5 billion], air pollution control equipment [$15.3 billion], and waste management equipment [$12 billion] (see Table 20-1).

The lack of a precise and comprehensive industry definition represents a significant challenge, and the existing official data on production of and trade in environmental technologies are of limited value. However, ongoing work will address these problems in the near future and produce a more accurate and comprehensive identification of the goods and services which constitute the environmental technologies industry, particularly work being done within the Organization for Economic Cooperation and Development (OECD).

Environmental exports by many states have increased consistently in recent years, with some states already exporting 5 to 10 percent of their environmental technologies and services. California, which has the largest concentration of environmental companies (over 16,000) and more than 160,000 employees, is the largest exporter of environmental technologies at $2.3 billion in 1996. Texas, New York, Pennsylvania, Illinois, and New Jersey were among the top states in terms of both environmental revenues and exports.

U.S. Market Trends

Environmental regulations have been the major driving force in the development of environmental technologies in the United States. Before the 1970s industries developed environmental technologies for their own use. With growing public concern for the environment and the passage of the Clean Water Act and the Clean Air Act, the environmental sector has expanded to meet new challenges. Early technologies, stemming from state and federal policies, focused on end-of-pipe pollution control and remediation issues. In the late 1970s and early 1980s new concerns over waste storage and disposal prompted the industry to develop cleanup and remediation technologies. More recent policy and market shifts toward pollution prevention have stimulated the development of eco-efficient, or green, technologies. Along with these changes, the industry has made major advances in monitoring and assessment techniques to meet industry and government requirements.

Small and medium-size revenue-generating entities are a vital part of the industry. Firms with less than $100 million in annual sales generate a majority of the industry's revenues, and a large majority of these firms generate under $10 million in annual revenues (most earn well under $5 million). Revenue growth that averaged in the double digits until 1991 has slowed or in some sectors become negative. The period of rapid growth, which correlated with the initial rush of new environmental regulations, is now behind most sectors of the industry. A high degree of compliance with existing environmental regulations by its customers, fewer new regulations, and the perception of softened enforcement have reduced the demand for many prod-

ucts and services. According to Standard & Poor's Industry Surveys, industrial companies are basing environmental decisions less on regulations than on economic necessity. The outsourcing of noncore environmental operations, modification of production processes to reduce waste, and mass privatization of publicly owned municipal water supply and sewage treatment utilities are the most noteworthy trends in the industry.

In the remediation and hazardous waste industries demand may be shifting from regulatory-based drivers to economic drivers. In the water supply and treatment sector, privatization of public utilities may become a major trend, creating opportunities for investor-owned water companies. Some industry analysts believe that aside from privatization, Internal Revenue Service (IRS) rule changes may allow municipalities to enter into third-party operations contracts of up to 20 years to fund infrastructure projects. Local laws also may change, allowing U.S. companies to design and bid for utility construction. New markets may develop for investor-owned companies that can build, own, or operate wastewater operations on behalf of industrial companies. The solid waste sector will continue to be negatively affected by declining per capita municipal solid waste (MSW), which will be driven by modest U.S. real annual gross domestic product (GDP) growth of 2.5 percent and moderate population growth.

INDUSTRY OUTLOOK

The environmental industry and environmental policy in the United States are at a critical point. Technology development and investments in environmental improvement by the regulated community have declined along with environmental industry revenues. Great progress has been made in improving environmental quality, but the pace of progress has reached a plateau. Similarly, while the U.S. environmental industry has gradually increased its global market share, future gains will be more difficult in the wake of faltering economies and uncertainty in Asia.

The industry's poor financial returns reveal the diminished circumstances of many of its segments. Median profit margins that routinely exceeded 10 percent in the late 1980s are now in the range of 2 to 3 percent in service segments that are experiencing reduced or negative growth. Stock market performance is another indicator of the industry's problems. Since 1991, the average annual return of the firms listed in the Environmental Business Journal (EBJ) Index of 240 environmental companies has been 6 percent, compared with returns for firms on the NASDAQ (22 percent), Dow Jones (16 percent), and S&P 500 (14 percent) over that period. The environmental industry also has a poor record of attracting capital for venture-stage and public financings. Venture capital placements in environmental technology companies fell steadily from more than $200 million in 1991 to less than $20 million in 1996.

Future growth in environmental industry sectors will continue to reflect the emphasis on pollution avoidance and prevention technologies. In the following discussion of the solid waste, water, and air pollution control sectors, the key forces driving change are indicated. The industry has been a valuable contributor to the U.S. economy not only in terms of the social and economic benefits of a cleaner environment but also in terms of gains in resource productivity and competitive improvement in all industries benefiting from environmental technologies.

David Earle, U.S. Department of Commerce, Office of Environmental Technologies Exports, (202) 482-4503, October 1998.

SOLID WASTE MANAGEMENT

Revenues of solid waste management services and equipment in the United States totaled approximately $47 billion in 1997. This is the largest environmental industry segment and covers collection, transfer, recycling, the conversion of waste to energy, and landfills. It is also the most mature segment, with an estimated moderate annual growth rate of 2.9 percent in 1996–1997. Projected annual growth at the same rate to 2002 will see revenues exceeding $51 billion. Approximately 210 million tons of solid waste was generated in the United States in 1997. Americans produce little solid waste relative to the country's total economic output. The 1996 per capita waste generation was estimated at 4.4 pounds, which is expected to increase to 4.6 pounds in 2010 at an annual average growth rate of 0.6 percent, while GDP is expected to grow at an annual average rate of 2.5 percent in that period. The shift from an industrial to a service-based economy is the primary reason for this trend, according to Standard & Poor's Industry Surveys.

Three types of operations make up the solid waste sector: landfills, where approximately 56 percent of the waste is disposed and 80 percent of the service revenues is generated; recycling (including composting), where 27 percent of the waste is treated and 11 percent of the service revenues is generated; and incineration, where the remaining 17 percent of the waste is treated and 9 percent of the service revenues is generated. In the 1990s the solid waste industry experienced a downturn after it invested about $20 billion in new landfills while environmental regulations at the state and national levels required recycling, composting, incineration programs, and source reduction of municipal solid waste. Curbside recycling and yard trimmings composting programs increased. However, the supply of recyclable materials has exceeded the demand in most cases, and so the market for such materials has not been as lucrative as was hoped. The recycling segment of MSW continues to be driven by government regulations. There has been a trend toward fewer MSW landfills, and overcapacity is likely to affect operators in the near term. The decrease in landfills nationwide from the early 1990s continued into 1997, with the number dropping to 2,514, according to the industry trade publication *BioCycle.* Some states predict capacity rates of landfills from 10 to 20 years and beyond. The number of incinerators has remained stable in the last 10 years.

The solid waste industry consists of 41 percent public companies which account for $14.8 billion in annual revenues, 27 percent private companies which account for $9.7 billion in annual revenues, and 32 percent municipal which account for $11.5 billion in annual revenues. The two largest publicly traded companies are curtailing the acquisition strategies they employed to increase market share and are focusing more on their core municipal solid waste collection and disposal operations, reducing employment, and incorporating share buybacks. Publicly traded companies in the second tier are expanding their operations, primarily through acquisitions. First tier, or major, firms tried diversification into other environmental businesses such as recycling, hazardous waste, and water utilities. Second tier firms, such as USA Waste, Allied Waste, and Republic Industries, are trying to expand by acquiring smaller, independently owned MSW collectors in order to compete. Publicly traded companies acquired assets worth approximately $5 billion from 1995 to mid-1997. Among the 5,500 to 7,000 private companies in the business, some are diversifying or specializing in services such as septic services, scrap metal, and nonwaste services. However, smaller waste handlers find that the investments required by regulations are beyond their reach and are closing or selling out to larger providers with which they cannot compete. In the solid waste sector, market analysts predict continued consolidation and privatization and growth at a moderate rate if the economy remains strong.

The hazardous waste segment generated $5.8 billion in revenues in 1997. The hazardous waste market is composed of combustion (28 percent of revenues), solvent recovery and fuel blending (23 percent), aqueous treatment (15 percent), technical services (10 percent), land disposal (17 percent), and other services (7 percent). Because industry is progressively developing ways to reduce the hazardous waste stream and regulators are blurring the distinctions between hazardous waste and nonhazardous waste, the market for hazardous waste treatment is expected to continue to shrink.

With about 217,000 contaminated sites remaining to be cleaned, the U.S. Environmental Protection Agency (EPA) estimates the market segment of U.S. sites and associated remediation costs at $187 billion in 1996 dollars. This segment includes Resource Conservation Recovery Act (RCRA) corrective actions, underground storage tanks, Superfund sites, and other contaminated sites across the United States. Hazardous waste remediation activities are driven primarily by federal and state regulation and by the availability of public and private funds. The number of sites identified in the last 15 years as possibly requiring remediation exceeds 500,000. These sites include U.S. Department of Defense (DOD) facilities as bases close as a result of downsizing.

Remediation is a high priority for DOD's 8,336 remediation sites (budgeted for $29 billion). The 110,500 U.S. Department of Energy sites remaining to be remediated are estimated to cost $63 billion, the 165,000 sites of underground storage tanks are estimated to cost $21 billion, and over 3,000 corrective RCRA sites are estimated to cost over $39 billion. Reflecting the success of EPA's waste minimization policy, hazardous waste generation and the demand for hazardous waste management services are decreasing. The latest Census Bureau data show that of the total hazardous waste generated and regulated under RCRA, 208 million tons was subsequently managed by treatment, storage, and disposal facilities. Contrary to the fears of a decade ago, not only is there sufficient hazardous waste treatment and disposal capacity but the market may be oversaturated because of increased on-site treatment by generators of hazardous waste, ongoing emphasis on waste minimization, materials substitution for less hazardous components or processes, and uncertainty in the remediation market resulting from possible regulatory changes. In April 1998 the EPA detailed principles for legislation to reform the management of hazardous waste under the RCRA, but Congress has not concluded its work in this matter.

International Markets

U.S. solid waste management companies may find international opportunities in developed nations with regulations covering waste management. In many undeveloped and developing regions waste management is a low regulatory priority. The waste management sector in these regions generally is operated by the public sector or by local companies under government contracts. There is a lot of competition for those contracts, and it is important to have a partner in the country that is familiar with the local and provincial laws regulating waste management. Hazardous materials regulations like those in the United States are rare in other parts of the world, except in some industrialized nations. This sector usually is dominated by a few large contractors.

Anne Novak, U.S. Department of Commerce, Office of Environmental Technologies Exports, (202) 482-8178, October 1998.

WATER AND WASTEWATER

The constant, accessible supply of clean water is often taken for granted in the United States. By contrast, access to safe drinking water is a major problem in many parts of the world, especially developing countries. Ninety-five percent of the world's cities release untreated sewage and wastes into rivers and streams, many of which provide drinking water. Over 5 million children a year die from drinking unsanitary water.

It has been estimated that the annual cost of purifying water, treating wastewater, and filtering and separating process fluids will increase worldwide to $500 billion per year by 2000. However, this is far below the level needed for good health throughout the world. U.S. citizens receive more water per person than the world average, and the quality is substantially above the average. Worldwide, 1.3 billion people have no access to clean water. In Asia, for example, as the population grows from 2.9 billion to a projected 4.2 billion in 2020, water is expected to become an increasingly critical resource. One in three Asians still lacks access to safe drinking water, and one in two has no access to sanitation services.

The major players in the global water and wastewater industry come from the United States, France, England, Germany,

and Japan. U.S. companies, which are more specialized, face stiff competition from foreign companies that are more integrated. This integration can give foreign companies an edge, since they have more experience in owning, operating, and serving privatized facilities in emerging markets whose water and wastewater systems are undergoing privatization. Only 13 percent of the water utilities in the United States are privately managed, and under 1 percent of sewage treatment facilities in this country are privately owned.

U.S. Water and Wastewater Market

The water industry in the United States is driven and regulated by the Clean Water Act of 1972 and the Safe Drinking Water Act, which was reauthorized in 1996. This legislation facilitated the emergence of a strong, high-tech commercial water and wastewater industry in the United States. The U.S. domestic water supply consists primarily of publicly owned facilities, a large majority of which are operating beyond their useful lives and need capital improvements. It has been estimated that over $130 billion is needed to build new facilities and improve the existing ones.

The water and wastewater market can be divided into four subsectors: water supply, wastewater treatment, water equipment and chemicals, and water consulting. The water supply subsector includes government-owned and investor-owned utilities that distribute purified water to consumers. The wastewater treatment subsector consists of government-owned and investor-owned utilities that treat municipal and industrial sewage. The water equipment and chemicals subsector includes companies that make pumps, filters, and chemicals for water purification. The water consulting subsector consists of firms that provide consulting services to water pollution cleanup projects. In terms of spending for water and wastewater treatment, the top U.S. industrial wastewater markets are chemicals, electric utilities, pulp and paper, petroleum refining, food processing, primary metals, and other types of manufacturing. Among these markets, the chemicals sector is the largest at 25 percent.

Major companies in the industry will continue the trend toward consolidation. Small to midsize companies will be limited to acquiring companies that large businesses will not buy. Additional trends in the industry include the following: Engineering and manufacturing costs will continue to decrease as large companies increase their sales of standard products; the number of firms offering build-own-operate systems will increase, which will further erode profit margins; the demand for single-source supply companies will increase; and foreign companies will continue to attempt to increase their market share in the United States.

Household Drinking Water

The drinking water treatment industry is expanding, and industry analysts predict that it will grow 290 percent by 2013. People in the United States spend 10 times as much to assure an adequate clean drinking water supply as does the average world inhabitant. According to the 1997 National Water Quality Survey, one of five Americans is dissatisfied with the quality of his or her household water supply. The survey, which was commissioned by the Water Quality Association, found that a third of the consumers surveyed currently use a home water treatment device. The use of "entry-level" devices such as pour-through pitchers with filters has grown more than has that of any other type of water treatment device on the market. Nearly half of the persons surveyed want additional information about their water, yet 23 percent do not know who to contact to obtain that information.

The Safe Water Drinking Act is the primary statute for the protection of the nation's public drinking water supply. Part of this act includes the creation of a Drinking Water State Revolving Fund (DWSRF) that provides federal funding to states and water suppliers to improve their drinking water infrastructures. (For more information, refer to the EPA Web site: www.epa.gov/watrhome/regs/lgaset/lgtecinf.html.)

Water Utilities

There are more than 58,000 community water systems in the United States servicing about 226 million people, according to EBI, and under 6 percent of these systems provide about 80 percent of the water used by the U.S. population. Based on statistics from the American Water Works Association's Water Industry Database, the water utility business constitutes a $25 billion market in the United States (EBI estimates a slightly larger $27 billion market). Only about 13 percent of this revenue is generated by privately held, investor-owned utilities. Domestic and commercial users obtain 87.1 percent of their water from public water utilities. By contrast, industrial and mining users obtain only 18.7 percent from public water supplies (see Table 20-3).

Water and Wastewater Privatization Trends

One of the most important trends in this industry in recent years has been the contracting of private companies to operate existing facilities or build and operate new facilities. These initiatives have sparked the consolidation of many of the leading companies in this area to enable them to provide a full range of services to their clients and will position them to be more competitive internationally. American Water Works, the largest investor-owned water supply company, has acquired more than 20 water supply operations. U.S. Filter Company, the largest investor-owned water conglomerate, has been aggressively acquiring industrial wastewater treatment companies as well as water equipment and filter makers.

International Markets

While the U.S. market is clearly one of the world's most developed and currently the largest, opportunities also exist for U.S. firms around the world. Estimates put the market for the rest of the world at four to five times the revenue volume of the U.S. market.

Many modern developed countries, such as Japan, have large percentages of the population that are not connected to sewage treatment facilities or do not have access to clean drinking water. Water scarcity is one of the key issues facing China in the next decade. The Chinese government is looking at technologies to help it meet the demand for water of swelling urban and industrial sectors without harming its agricultural sector, which is needed to feed its growing population. Satellite photographs show that lakes and local streams are drying up, challenging the central government and local governments to provide clean

TABLE 20-3: U.S. Water Industry Growth
(millions of dollars; percent)

Business Segments	1996	1997[1]	1998[1]	1999[2]	2000[2]	2001[2]	2002[2]
Full-solution companies	1,380	2,070	3,110	4,670	5,840	6,720	7,730
Water equipment and chemicals							
Separation	2,300	2,390	2,490	2,590	2,690	2,800	2,910
Destruction	1,000	1,050	1,100	1,160	1,220	1,280	1,340
Chemical equipment	360	360	360	360	360	360	360
Delivery equipment	8,200	8,450	8,700	8,960	9,230	9,510	9,800
Biosolids equipment	1,040	1,090	1,140	1,200	1,260	1,320	1,390
Chemicals	3,410	3,440	3,470	3,500	3,540	3,580	3,620
Total	16,310	16,780	17,260	17,770	18,300	18,850	19,420
Services, consulting, and engineering							
Contract operations	1,100	1,320	1,580	1,900	2,280	2,740	3,290
Consulting	1,440	1,500	1,560	1,620	1,680	1,750	1,820
Design engineering	1,630	1,710	1,800	1,890	1,980	2,080	2,180
Maintenance services	1,030	1,090	1,160	1,230	1,300	1,380	1,460
Total	5,200	5,620	6,100	6,640	7,240	7,950	8,750
Instruments	600	670	740	820	910	1,010	1,120
Analytic services	413	420	430	440	450	460	470
Wastewater treatment works	24,020	24,790	25,580	26,400	27,240	28,110	29,010
Water utilities	26,360	27,410	28,510	29,650	30,840	32,070	33,350
Total water industry	74,283	77,760	81,730	86,390	90,820	95,170	99,850
Annual growth, %	3.6	4.7	5.1	5.7	5.1	4.8	4.9

[1] Estimate.
[2] Forecast.
Source: Environmental Business International, Inc.

drinking water. Despite the economic downturn in Asia, several countries plan to invest in water and wastewater treatment facilities, creating opportunities for U.S. equipment and service companies. For example, in South Korea the Ministry of Environment is planning to invest $5.5 billion to build 216 additional wastewater treatment plants throughout that nation by 2005. In Indonesia the market for wastewater pollution equipment reached about $246.3 million in 1996. It has grown at an annual rate of 20 to 25 percent in the past 3 years and is expected to continue to expand no less than 15 to 20 percent over the next 5 years. The rest of the developing countries in Asia will not be far behind in requiring water and wastewater technologies, goods, and services.

Some of the best opportunities for U.S. companies exist in Latin America, especially in the water and wastewater sector. CH2M Hill International, in partnership with a Brazilian engineering firm, was awarded a concession to design, construct, own, and operate a wastewater collection and treatment plant in Brazil. This is the first privatized wastewater treatment project in that country. Brazil has one of the fastest growing economies in the world, with trade investment opportunities worth $1.7 billion in the water and wastewater sector.

According to the United Nations Economic Commission for Europe, over 120 million people in Europe lack access to safe drinking water. Approximately 30 percent of the water in the system is lost from leakage. Albania, Norway, and Romania experience losses of approximately 50 percent, and some cities experience losses as high as 70 to 80 percent.

George Litman, U.S. Department of Commerce, Water and Wastewater Specialist, Office of Environmental Technologies Exports, (202) 482-0560, May 1998.

AIR POLLUTION CONTROL

The air pollution control sector includes products and services that remove air pollutants or convert them to a nonpolluting or less polluting form before release into the atmosphere. The sector includes equipment to control, mitigate, or reduce emissions from both "fixed" (e.g., factories and utilities) and "mobile" (e.g., cars and buses) sources. Customers for air pollution control companies include electric utilities; incinerators and waste-to-energy processors; various manufacturing sectors, such as pulp and paper, mining, metal finishing, and cement; and automobile and vehicle manufacturers that buy catalytic converters and related technologies. The principal categories of air pollutants consist of oxides of sulfur and nitrogen (SO_2 and NO_X) carbon monoxide (CO), volatile organic compounds, hazardous air pollutants, and particulate matter.

The air pollution control industry is driven by government regulations. The first clean air legislation in the United States was enacted in 1955, and the first comprehensive legislation, the Clean Air Act (CAA), was passed in 1963 and amended in 1990. EPA later updated its national air quality standards (NAAQS) for ground-level ozone and small particulate matter, creating a final rule in July 1997.

Air Pollution Control Equipment and Services and Mobile and Stationary Sources

The total U.S. market for air pollution control equipment and related services grew 6 percent from $14.5 billion in 1994 to $15.3 billion in 1996. This growth slowed to just over 3 percent in 1996–1997 registering $15.8 billion in that period. Projections are for the industry to grow just under 3 percent through 2002. Most of this growth will come from equipment sales to control mobile and stationary source pollutants. It is more difficult to estimate revenues tied to services. In general, the services segment, which includes consulting and engineering services, analytical services, and instrumentation, was estimated to generate $3 billion in revenues in 1997 (see Table 20-1).

Mobile source air pollution control technologies and services constitute the largest segment in the air pollution control sector, accounting for $13.4 billion in 1997. This market segment is driven by the health of the automotive industry as well as by government regulations. The mobile air emissions segment includes equipment firms that make catalytic converters and related technologies for vehicles. While this segment is projected to grow only slightly through 1999, in part because of slow growth in the automobile sector, the new EPA standards could generate increased demand for mobile source air pollution control technologies, although implementation and enforcement questions remain. Under new standards, diesel trucks and light-duty vehicles could be affected. Other proposed EPA standards would affect locomotive engines, increasing the demand for air pollution control technologies (see Table 20-4).

Stationary source technologies and services, including equipment, consulting and engineering, instrumentation, and analytical services, accounted for $5.9 billion in revenues in 1997. The Institute for Clear Air Companies (ICAC) estimates the U.S. market for all air pollution control technology for stationary sources to be $3.8 billion.

TABLE 20-4: Air Quality Markets in the United States
(billions of dollars)

	1994	1997[1]	2000[2]
Stationary sources market			
Equipment	3.7	3.5	3.7
Consulting and engineering	1.6	1.3	1.4
Instrumentation	0.6	0.5	0.6
Analytic services	0.1	0.1	0.1
Indoor air pollution	0.5	0.5	0.6
Total	6.5	5.9	6.4
Mobile sources market			
Equipment	10.8	12.3	13.5
Consulting and engineering	0.2	0.2	0.2
Instrumentation	0.2	0.3	0.2
Analytic services	0.4	0.6	0.8
Total	11.6	13.4	14.7
Total air pollution control	18.1	19.3	21.1

[1] Estimate.
[2] Forecast.
Source: Environmental Business International, Inc.

Market Drivers and Trends

Contrary to widely held expectations that the 1990 Clean Air Act Amendments (CAAA) would quickly stimulate strong economic growth, sales of equipment to address stationary source pollution dropped 5 percent and 3 percent in 1995 and 1996, respectively, and grew moderately in 1997 after posting a decade-long average of around 2.6 percent, according to EBI. A contrasting assessment by ICAC, the air pollution control industry's leading trade association, predicts that annual growth will average 7 percent between 1997 and 2000. Many analysts predict that the air pollution control equipment market will decline after that time.

Many factors complicate predictions about growth in this sector predicated on regulatory change. These factors include the ways in which rules are promulgated and enforced and the pace of development of market-based incentive programs such as emissions trading. Certain changes in regulation create economic incentives for industry to lower emissions by using pollution prevention as opposed to pollution control techniques and technologies. A decline in sales of flue gas desulfurization systems between 1992 and 1997 can be attributed to the sulfur dioxide emissions allowance and credit trading program. Industrial control of sulfur dioxide emissions provided 30 percent of total industry revenues in 1992, and that number fell to 21 percent in 1997. Because of the EPA's stricter standards, regulators are now focusing on nitrogen oxides and volatile organic compounds, the precursors of ground-level ozone. The share of the market accounted for by volatile organic compounds has grown to a level of 18 percent from 13 percent in 1992. ICAC notes that there could be a delay in the phase-in of nitrogen oxide regulations but believes that it will not be as cost-effective for power generators to shift to low–nitrogen oxide boilers compared with the earlier shift that occurred for sulfur dioxide. This, of course, depends upon the implementation, domestically and internationally, of nitrogen oxide emissions allowance trading since nitrogen oxide is a greenhouse gas covered under the Kyoto Protocol.

The air pollution control stationary source market historically has been dominated by big-ticket items sold to utilities and major industries and has been a major source of revenue for equipment builders (see Table 20-5). It is expected that there will continue to be a shift by utilities and industries away from pollution control and toward pollution prevention strategies. New and more stringent EPA standards for reducing transported ozone and controlling small particulate matter may require substantial air pollution control investments in the near future. For now, smaller systems, modular equipment and aftermarket parts and services, consulting and process engineering services, and international sales represent the most important emerging opportunities for air pollution control firms. The air consulting market in particular probably will grow as air consulting and pollution prevention engineering replace pollution control strategies. Approximately 95 percent of demand for air pollution control is met by domestic firms, with Germany and Japan being the leading foreign competitors in the U.S. market.

One relatively important unknown is the extent of the effect of the Kyoto Protocol negotiated under the Framework Convention on Climate Change (FCCC) in December 1997. While only a handful of countries have signed, let alone ratified, this treaty, the effects of an agreement to reduce all six greenhouse emissions, including that of nitrogen oxide, could have an important impact on the air pollution control industry. Both carbon dioxide, the most abundantly natural occurring greenhouse gas, and nitrogen oxide, an air pollutant, are produced when fossil fuels are burned. While carbon dioxide is not in itself an air pollutant, any global attempt to reduce its emission will force energy efficiencies on producers and consumers alike. Energy efficiency is a pollution prevention strategy that will decrease the need for air pollution control technologies if it is widely used. The President and the Vice President have said that the earliest date on which the treaty will be submitted to the Senate, which must ratify it if it is to take effect and be implemented in U.S. law, will be 1999.

Pollution Prevention

In its broadest definition, pollution prevention means reducing pollution at its source. Preventing pollution involves changing manufacturing processes and products to reduce waste and pro-

TABLE 20-5: U.S. Air Pollution Control Equipment Market Revenues for Stationary Sources, by Equipment
(millions of dollars)

Equipment Type	1996	1997[1]	1998[1]	1999[2]	2000[2]	2001[2]	2002[2]
Flue gas desulfurization	793.4	663.0	649.7	636.7	624.0	611.5	599.3
Electrostatic precipitators	684.3	698.8	691.8	684.9	691.7	698.6	705.6
Fabric filters and baghouses	601.3	653.1	868.5	884.1	910.7	938.0	966.1
Oxidation systems	520.2	536.6	579.5	625.9	676.0	730.0	788.4
Carbon absorption	125.2	124.9	122.4	119.9	117.5	115.2	112.9
NO$_x$ control systems	296.2	322.3	341.6	362.1	405.5	454.2	508.7
Delivery systems	48.6	28.7	29.6	30.6	31.4	32.3	33.3
Other equipment	39.7	111.3	114.7	118.1	121.6	125.3	129.0
Materials and supplies	81.2	134.0	142.0	150.5	155.1	159.7	164.5
Total equipment market	3,390	3,473	3,540	3,613	3,733	3,865	4,008

[1] Estimate.
[2] Forecast.
Source: Environmental Business International, Inc.

mote the efficient use of energy and materials resources. As modern industrial economies shift from a focus on pollution control and mitigation to a focus on prevention and process and from environmental management to resource management, the environmental industry and ultimately other industrial sectors will change.

While environmental regulation will remain a necessary condition for increased environmental protection, several factors emerging within the economy will increasingly be important drivers of the environmental industry: cost escalation in raw materials and waste disposal, cleanups based on the economic value of land, economic return for waste minimization, and increased profits and better comparative advantage from increased efficiency. These market factors eventually will overtake regulation as the primary means of achieving higher environmental standards, providing new and expanded markets for environmental technologies and giving rise to a shift from cleanup and control to process and prevention. Meeting pollution prevention goals and working toward sustainable development are a question not just of a change in technology but of a change in corporate culture that will lead to enhancing resource efficiency. Prevention technologies could appear in industry segments as diverse as environmental information software, recycling and recovery technology, and materials substitution. Data are available on two fast-growing subsectors that achieve pollution prevention within the environmental industry: process and prevention technologies and environmental energy sources.

Process and Prevention Technology and Environmental Energy Sources

Process and prevention technology refers to equipment and processes designed to achieve waste minimization and resource efficiency rather than end-of-pipe control. Such technology can be used in all environmental technology subsectors: water management (treatment, delivery, recycling), waste management, environmental energy sources, strategic environmental management, risk assessment and cost-benefit analysis, brownfields redevelopment, instruments, and information systems. Specific examples of process and prevention technology include the removal of contaminants from fuel before combustion and the use of "alternative processes" such as biopesticides. While the market for process and prevention technology ($900 million) and environmental energy sources ($2.56 billion) represents only a fraction of all environmental business, data show consistently high growth rates when compared with the other environmental business segments. Growth in process and prevention technology from 1997 to 2000 is anticipated at 10 percent, the highest in all these segments, and there will be 6 percent growth for environmental energy sources (see Table 20-1). These rates could accelerate as a result of the negotiation of targets and timetables at Kyoto under the FCCC and worldwide deregulation of electrical utility production and distribution.

Jane Siegel, U.S. Department of Commerce, Office of Environmental Technologies Exports, (202) 482-0617, October 1998.

INTERNATIONAL MARKET PROSPECTS

Revenues generated outside the United States accounted for 9 percent of the U.S. environmental industry's 1996 total and were responsible for 60 percent of industry growth in 1996. Exports of U.S. environmental goods and services increased from $11.5 billion in 1994 to $16 billion in 1996, making the United States the world's largest supplier in this industry. Despite this growth, the revenues generated by exports represent only 8.8 percent of industrial output. This is in contrast to the performance of Japan, Germany, and other west European nations, in which exports account for 15 to 25 percent of output. The United States imported only $6.7 billion in environmental goods and services in 1996, a $0.5 billion increase from 1995, resulting in a trade surplus of $9.3 billion (see Tables 20-6 and 20-7).

Obstacles to the penetration of foreign markets tend to differ between developed and developing countries. Developed countries may inhibit access through the use of conventional tariff or nontariff barriers (e.g., requiring technology-specific performance or performance-specific equipment). Many local companies may not comply with environmental laws or may choose to pay fines instead of investing in pollution prevention or control

TABLE 20-6: U.S. Environmental Industry Trade
(billions of dollars; percent)

	1994	1995	1996	Percent Change[1] 94–96
U.S. environmental industry revenues[2]	172.1	178.9	181.1	1.2
U.S. environmental market[2]	165.9	170.4	171.8	0.8
U.S. environmental exports[2]	11.5	14.7	16.0	8.8
U.S. environmental imports	5.5	6.2	6.7	8.0
U.S. industry exports to revenues, %	6.7	8.2	8.8	7.5
Trade balance	6.2	8.5	9.3	9.4

[1] Compounded annual rate change.
[2] U.S. industry is revenues generated by U.S. companies worldwide; U.S. market is revenues generated from U.S. customers. Exports include ownership of overseas companies but do not include repatriated profits.
Source: Environmental Business International, Inc.

TABLE 20-7: U.S. Environmental Export Performance
(billions of dollars; percent)

	1993	1994	1995	1996
Global market	413	429	441	453
U.S. market	160	166	170	172
Non-U.S. market	253	263	271	281
Exports, % of total industry output	5.9	6.7	8.2	8.8
U.S. exports	9.6	11.5	14.7	16.0
U.S. share of non-U.S. market, %	3.8	4.4	5.4	5.7

Source: Environmental Business International, Inc.

equipment and services. Developing countries are more reliant on external financing from development assistance or multilateral development banks to pay for their environmental investments. Despite the United States' reputation for high-quality goods and services worldwide, the United States competes with foreign governments' research and technology grants, financial support for private ventures, export subsidies, regional tariff advantages, aggressive business practices, long-standing dependence on international markets because of small domestic markets, and long bilateral commercial histories. Imports into the U.S. market are growing, and foreign competitors have acquired a number of important U.S. environmental firms. This import penetration necessitates continual industry investment to preserve and expand competitiveness.

Global environmental revenues are forecast to grow just over 3 percent annually by 2000. The largest markets will still be the United States, western Europe, and Japan. The most rapid growth is occurring in developing regions: Asia (prior to the Asian financial crisis, and excluding Japan), Latin America, and Africa. However, demand in many of these regions is limited. This lack of demand usually results from the inability to pay (especially now in Asia) rather than an absence of regulations requiring environmental protection. Overseas markets and exports, which in 1996 accounted for 60 percent of total industry growth, will continue to provide U.S. environmental technologies and service firms with excellent opportunities. Between 1995 and 1996, a 16 percent gain was expected in Asia, outside of Japan, which represents the best opportunities for environmental goods and services. Although currently the Asian region's buying power has been dramatically reduced due to the its financial instability, long-term growth prospects still look very promising. Environmental degradation continues, and environmental remedies will continue to be needed. The best markets for U.S. environmental exports are expected to be France, China, Mexico, Indonesia, Spain, the United Kingdom, Chile, Korea, Taiwan, and Italy (see Table 20-8).

Asia

While several countries in Asia have experienced significant economic slowdowns, the outlook for U.S. environmental goods and services in the region is good. In 1997 total U.S. environmental technology imports reached approximately $280 million in Indonesia, $165 million in Korea, $56 million in Malaysia, and $53 million in the Philippines. Today Asia represents about 20 percent of the global environmental market. Environmental degradation, the demand for clean water, and inadequate waste treatment will increase as these countries continue to develop. Meeting these needs will provide tremendous opportunities for U.S. firms in the years ahead.

Despite Korea's economic crisis, regional governments still plan to invest heavily in wastewater treatment plants and other environmental projects. Industry sources believe that these projects have excellent prospects of being funded and completed, and large Korean construction and engineering companies are in fierce competition to win the awards. However, domestic companies' lack of sophisticated technology and experience in the areas of design, engineering, and other technical services may prevent Korea from undertaking some wastewater treatment projects. Local companies are actively seeking joint venture partnerships with foreign firms that have expertise and experience in related advanced technologies or have made an investment in the relevant research and development. In 1998 alone regional governments' investment was estimated to be over $400 million. With particular emphasis on environmental policies by Korea's new administration, industry sources believe that environmental projects have the green light to proceed and offer great potential for a high return on investment.

The Philippines' national environmental protection system is struggling to catch up with that country's booming economic growth of the last few years. With a fairly comprehensive regulatory framework, the environmental market was estimated at $546 million in 1997. The largest sector is water and wastewater treatment, followed by the solid waste management sector.

TABLE 20-8: Estimated Growth in the Global Environmental Market
(billions of dollars; percent)

	1996	1997[1]	1998[1]	1999[2]	2000[2]	2001[2]	Percent Change 96–01[3]
United States	171.8	175.5	179.4	183.4	187.4	191.5	2.2
Canada	11.6	11.9	12.2	12.5	12.8	13.1	2.5
Latin America	8.8	9.8	11.0	12.3	13.8	15.5	12.0
Western Europe	133.6	137.3	141.2	145.1	149.2	153.4	2.8
Eastern Europe/Confederation of Independent States	7.1	7.7	8.3	9.0	9.7	10.5	8.1
Japan	87.1	88.8	90.6	92.4	94.3	96.2	2.0
Rest of Asia	20.0	22.0	24.2	26.6	29.3	32.2	10.0
Australia/New Zealand	6.8	7.1	7.4	7.6	8.0	8.3	4.1
Middle East	4.3	4.7	5.0	5.4	5.9	6.3	7.9
Africa	2.2	2.4	2.6	2.9	3.2	3.5	9.7
Total	453	467	482	497	513	530	3.2

[1] Estimate.
[2] Forecast.
[3] Compounded annual rate change.
Source: Environmental Business International, Inc.

Imports account for 80 to 90 percent of the total market. The United States has an advantageous position in the import market because of its historical ties with the Philippines as well as price competitiveness and the high quality of U.S.-manufactured equipment.

Taiwan remains one of the strongest environmental markets in Asia but is one of the toughest to penetrate. The market for environmental goods and services has remained steady throughout the 1990s as a result of improved enforcement and growing economic pressure that continue to generate high demand. It is estimated that the overall expenditure for environmental technologies was $4.4 billion in 1997. The Taiwan Environmental Protection Administration is planning to increase spending on environmental goods and services from the current level of $4.4 billion to $6 billion by the year 2000. Most of the technologies have been imported from overseas, primarily from Germany, Japan, and the United States. The market share in 1997 was estimated at 27 percent for Japan, 26 percent for Germany, and 20 percent for the United States.

China's acute environmental problems stem from a deteriorating natural resource base, dense population, heavy reliance on soft coal, outmoded technology, underpriced water and energy, and breakneck industrial growth. To combat its environmental challenges, the Chinese government has enacted new environmental legislation, shut down nearly 70,000 small and dirty factories, and decreed that all industrial enterprises comply with pollution discharge standards by 2000. In March 1998 the country's Environmental Protection Agency received ministerial status, raising its standing in the Chinese government. China spent an estimated $7.2 billion on the environment—about 0.8 percent of GDP—in 1997. Since this figure includes the upkeep of environmental institutes and other expenditures, the size of the market accessible to foreign firms is considerably smaller. For the first time, detailed environmental objectives have been written into a Chinese 5-year plan. Fully achieving these goals would require an investment of $54 billion in the period 1996–2000. The central authorities inevitably look to local governments and foreign lenders to provide the majority of investment. Determining which projects will ultimately receive funding and approval is often a daunting task. Local enforcement of environmental laws is spotty, investment in pollution control infrastructure is inadequate, and competition from domestic firms is increasingly strong, further limiting market opportunities for U.S. firms. Most large U.S. environmental firms traditionally have concentrated on World Bank and Asian Development Bank projects. The future may be brighter as affluent coastal cities begin to dramatically increase environmental spending, multinational investors establish new sources of demand, and municipalities experiment with new project-financing models. Products with the best sales prospects include low-cost flue gas desulfurization systems, air and water monitoring instruments, drinking water purification devices, industrial wastewater treatment equipment, and resource recovery technologies.

Thailand has experienced increasingly serious economic difficulties since the government floated the baht in July 1997.

Credit shortages have hindered business dealings in the environmental sector and all other sectors. The current Thai administration, however, has given every indication that it will persist with the adjustment program set forth by the International Monetary Fund (IMF). Despite the country's financial problems, the economy is expected to resume rapid expansion over the longer term. Thailand's GDP more than tripled in the decade leading up to 1996, reaching $184 billion. Government investment in infrastructure projects, which began to expand rapidly at the beginning of the decade, helped propel stable and vigorous growth. The strong dollar currently puts U.S. environmental technologies at a price disadvantage. U.S. firms could improve their competitive position by offering technical training, commissioning of equipment, and after-sales service as part of the sales package. Market opportunities exist for pollution control equipment, water supply and wastewater treatment, and municipal solid waste landfill improvement.

Before being caught in the economic turmoil that spread across Asia, Malaysia had undertaken an ambitious plan to become a fully developed economic powerhouse by 2020. Rapid expansion was planned through conversion from an agricultural and commodities-based economy to a competitive manufacturing economy. In July 1997 Thailand's financial crisis spread to Malaysia, and by December the Malaysian ringgit had depreciated 33 percent against the U.S. dollar. Despite the economic downturn, Malaysian authorities are forging ahead with environmental improvements in the water and wastewater and waste management sectors. Other priority sectors include air pollution control, as a result of the poor air quality caused by fires in both Malaysia and Indonesia, and animal waste technologies.

Singapore's tiny size and population of about 3.4 million are not reflective of the economic status of this Asian powerhouse. As a business-friendly and focused economy, Singapore has become home to several U.S. environmental companies' Asian branch offices. Although hurt by the Asian financial crisis, Singapore has remained a stable base for business and economic growth. Singapore has a major problem with landfill space. The construction of incinerators and solid waste disposal will continue to offer opportunities for U.S. firms. Air pollution caused by the haze from fires in the region and the government's tightening of emissions controls also offer significant trade opportunities.

George Litman, U.S. Department of Commerce, Office of Environmental Technologies Exports, (202) 482-0560, October 1998.

Latin America

Latin America purchased over $8.8 billion in environmental goods and services in 1996, and this market is expected to grow 12 percent annually through 2000. Large investments are urgently needed to meet the region's infrastructure requirements in the water, energy, transportation, and telecommunications sectors. The World Bank estimates that $115 billion in investment is needed in the region's water and wastewater sectors alone to meet its environmental goals by 2000.

Years of uncontrolled industrial growth, urbanization, and overpopulation have created a society that must face serious environmental issues. The principal market drivers that will be responsible for the projected 12 percent industry growth rate in the region are adherence to International Standards Organization (ISO) 14000 standards, especially for multinational corporations; stricter enforcement on the part of governments (a common demand by a rising middle class); and basic unmet needs in water supply and sanitation services.

The Latin American market reflects demand for a broad range of environmental goods and services. These environmental subsectors, from the largest to the smallest, include water utilities, solid waste management, water equipment and chemicals, water treatment works, waste management equipment, air pollution control equipment, consulting and engineering, resource recovery, hazardous waste management, instruments and information systems, analytical services, remediation and industrial services, and environmental waste-to-energy projects. Among all the environmental submarkets, potable water, municipal sanitation services (sewer systems and wastewater treatment plants), and industrial wastewater treatment offer the best opportunities for U.S. environmental technology firms, especially firms that work with U.S. multinational corporations.

In addition to the regionwide need for water pollution control and solid waste management, each Latin American country has its own key industry sectors, such as mining (Peru and Chile), petroleum (Venezuela and Mexico), petrochemicals (Brazil), food and beverage processing (Brazil and Argentina), and paper, that offer significant environmental opportunities for U.S. firms.

A new modality for structuring large, municipal wastewater projects has emerged under the name of the build-operate-transfer or concession mode. While this mode will be a major trend over the next 5 years, traditional multilateral development bank projects will continue to play an important role in the region.

David O'Connell, U.S. Department of Commerce, Office of Environmental Technologies Exports, (202) 482-3509, October 1998.

Central and Eastern Europe

Central and eastern European countries are driven to improve their environments to meet the environmental standards required for full membership in the European Union and to attract investment and tourism. In the most polluted regions improvements are necessary to better the quality and length of life, which are at low levels because of toxic air, water, and soil.

Most of the environmental devastation in this part of the world was caused by decades of industrialization and energy production without regard for the environment. Factories discharged sulfur dioxide from the burning of large quantities of low-quality coal, which polluted the air, water, and soil. Environmental conditions have improved as manufacturing has decreased, but the degradation remains. In addition, former regional Soviet military installations that were vacated in the early 1990s left a legacy of water and soil pollution.

Air pollution control, the protection of water resources, and improvement in the quality of drinking water are the priorities for most central and eastern European governments. The municipalities, the energy and power generation sectors, and the chemical industry are the primary purchasers of environmental technologies. Environmental improvement is funded by state and municipal funds. International funds are available for cofinancing environmental projects. As less developed central and eastern European countries are able to make environmental protection investments a priority and as privatization increases regionwide, the environmental technologies market is expected to grow at an annual rate of 6 to 12 percent.

The primary reason for the purchase of a U.S. environmental product or service is that U.S. products generally provide the best technology available. The United States enjoys a favorable reputation in central and eastern Europe for price and quality competitiveness. However, even in Poland, the largest central and eastern European market at $1.5 billion per year, only 5 percent of the market share is held by U.S. firms. Western European suppliers have the highest market share because of their lower tariffs, geographical proximity, and long commercial histories with these nations.

Anne Novak, U.S. Department of Commerce, Office of Environmental Technologies Exports, (202) 482-8178, October 1998.

Russia and the New Independent States

Seventy years of Soviet industrialization, misuse of water resources, senseless application of chemicals and pesticides, and deteriorating environmental conditions seriously threaten public health and economic productivity throughout Russia and the New Independent States. Industrial bases throughout the region were mostly devoted to military production and are responsible for huge amounts of contamination of water, soil, and air. The post-Soviet manufacturing infrastructure is environmentally hostile, is geared toward unit production, and functions with obsolete technology.

While the need for modern environmental equipment and technologies has been clear for several years, the post-Soviet industrial collapse compelled Russian government agencies and enterprises to assign a low priority to pollution control expenditures. During the stabilization of the Russian economy over the last 2 years prior to the current economic crisis, the Russian environmental technology market made notable progress. The current trend is away from analysis and baseline assessment and toward design and implementation. One indicator—the growth of domestic sales of environmental equipment and services—was increasing at approximately twice the rate of overall Russian firm sales. A recent estimate put the Russian environmental technology market at $4 billion annually (from an unpublished analysis based on the 1997 National Survey of Russian Business by the Tirone Corporation, a U.S. market analysis firm on Russia). Although the actual environmental technology market potential in Russia could be valued in the hundreds of billions, the near-term potential is limited by the rudimentary financing alternatives available and the current lack of economic and political stability. New domestic and international financial institution funding mechanisms were on the horizon that would have removed some of the financial barriers that previously hampered the business of American environmental technology companies. The collapse of the Russian financial markets will undoubtedly delay their introduction.

The market had been improving in response to citizens' demands, the growth of regional bond issues, better enforcement of environmental legislation, pressure from international environmental protection organizations to recognize international standards, pressure from international investors to eliminate environmental risks, and more active involvement on the part of multilateral financing agencies in addressing Russian environmental problems.

Tirone Corporation points out that direct investment is another major driver of the environmental market in Russia. When a direct investor, strategic equity partner, or lender takes a "position" in a Russian firm, a principal component of its evaluation is the risk to that investment. Any item or activity that represents a potential claim on future cash flow is a "risk," and that includes environmental impact. Serious investors consider what will happen to earnings as a result of compliance with environmental regulations by their target investment as opposed to ignoring the regulations. In the past, the costs of violation were far lower than the cost of compliance; yet given the current economic crisis, the costs of violation can be expected to increase as municipal agencies require funds (see below). Also, the present lack of liquidity will cause target firms to eliminate violations as a condition of desperately needed investment. To the degree that direct investment continues in Russian firms, environmental issues (and markets) will benefit. The trend of direct investment remains to be seen.

Other forces will focus attention and resources on the environmental market, according to Tirone Corporation. The current crisis of public debt places emphasis on rapidly increasing revenue in national, regional, and municipal governments. An immediate source of revenue is supplied by environmental fines. As the need for public funding increases, so will enforcement of environmental standards, driving a greater need for environmental equipment and services in the private sector. The scarcity of liquidity will persist, however, and actually increase the leverage and interest of strategic investors, as assets will be very cheap in Russia. If the political and economic climate stabilizes, it is likely that direct investment will resume, with the attendant need to secure investments through the elimination of environmental violations.

Prior to the crisis in Russia, the total market was expected to grow in the next 5 years for certain subsectors. Opportunities for major water treatment, solid and hazardous waste, and greenhouse gas reduction projects in major cities and in the regions offered significant potential. The environmental technology subsectors with the greatest potential for U.S. investment were water supply, wastewater, solid and hazardous waste treatment, and ozone depletion reduction. Rapidly growing industries with significant environmental requirements included oil and gas (upstream and downstream applications, including gas pipelines), transportation, mining (aluminum and ferrous alloys), wood products, and food packaging. At present, those industries with significant foreign currency sales may still hold opportunity.

Almost every large city in Russia cited construction of waste processing facilities as a major municipal project. The trend toward privatizing these municipal operations was accelerating. Public and private sector decision makers sought western financial and technical solutions to solve mounting environmental problems. Major infrastructure projects in larger cities included water supply, sewage treatment, solid waste, methane emission reduction, and radiation remediation projects. In the next 2 or 3 years suppliers of water and wastewater treatment products and services may find their niche in the Russian market. Sales of water treatment equipment were expected to increase over 20 percent. Larger cities also sought treatment and recycling methods to address pollution caused by used tires, batteries, oil waste, and spare auto parts. Russian regions with significant environmental projects include the Urals, northwest and southern Russia, eastern Siberia, and the Russian Far East. The market for air pollution controls should be considered in long-term strategy plans but could balloon significantly if bilateral Kyoto Climate Change terms are ratified. The Bureau of National Affairs' predictions for Russia to meet Kyoto Climate Change obligations estimated that the market for air pollution reduction could reach at least $18 billion by 2005.

While the current economic situation warrants a cautious approach, the ramification of ignoring this vast market are long-term and costly. In the last 2 years very few American environmental technology companies competed for multi-million-dollar infrastructure projects in Moscow and St. Petersburg. American companies face aggressive, well-ingrained competition from European and Japanese companies whose governments provided tied aid, flexible financing options, and donations through the design phase to help them win major environmental projects. However, American environmental technology companies retain a reputation for high quality. When the Russian economy stabilizes, so will the attendant environmental technology industry needs.

Although Ukraine continues to undergo a difficult economic transition, that country is making great advances in privatization. After reviewing international codes regarding the environment, Ukraine pledged to consider the environmental effects when privatizing. New regulations in this area should provide U.S. environmental technology firms with partnership opportunities to purchase Ukrainian industrial enterprises that currently lack environmental safeguards. The best prospects for U.S. companies are municipal water and wastewater treatment, municipal utility development projects, ozone protection, and Chernobyl nuclear power plant closure and remediation projects. As the country retools and reengineers its industries, pollution control systems could become a high priority. In central Asia, key environmental issues include coping with the consequences of the Aral Sea disaster; reducing extensive pollution from largely coal-fueled and heating installations, particularly in Kazakhstan; mitigating environmental degradation of the Caspian Sea caused largely by the rapid development of associated hydrocarbon deposits; and reducing the environmental consequences posed by earlier nuclear tests, nuclear materials processing and storage, and the ongoing destruction of missile silos.

Susan Simon, U.S. Department of Commerce, Office of Environmental Technologies Exports, (202) 482-0713, August 1998, October 1998.

International Environmental Standards

The growing acceptance by companies of international environmental management standards should lead to increased sales of environmental technologies. The International Organization for Standardization (ISO) is currently developing this family of standards which address management systems, including auditing and performance evaluation, and the environmental aspects of products in the areas of life-cycle assessment and labeling. These standards have the potential to exert a significant influence on the design, manufacture, and marketing of products. They are also likely to affect the type of environmental data gathered by businesses and how those data are communicated internally and externally. Although ISO 14000 standards are voluntary, competition could in effect force industrywide conformance, as has been the case with the ISO 9000 series (quality management systems). ISO 14001—the specification for an environmental management system (EMS)—is the only standard in the 14000 series which is applicable to third-party certification. An organization may seek third-party certification of its management system to meet a regulatory requirement or a demand from customers and/or stakeholders for independent verification. Businesses may benefit from implementing ISO 14001 in a facility in any number of ways: by decreasing waste through efficient energy use, pollution prevention, cost-recovery recycling, and decreased liability. EPA recognizes that implementation of an EMS has the potential to improve an organization's environmental compliance with regulatory requirements; however, at this time the agency is not basing any regulatory initiatives on the use of EMSs or certification to ISO 14001.

■ **R E F E R E N C E S**

Air Pollution Control Equipment Market Forecasts, Institute of Clean Air Companies, Inc., Washington, DC, January 1996. (202) 457-0911.

Air Pollution Control Equipment 1995, National Fund for Environmental Protection and Water Management, Warsaw, Poland.

Air Pollution Management Report, McIllvaine Company, Northbrook, IL, 1996. (847) 272-0010.

Asia Environment Review, Asia Environment Trading, 55 Exhibition Road, London SW7 2PG, United Kingdom.

Asia Environmental Business Journal, Environmental Business International, Inc., San Diego, CA.

Asian Development Bank Annual Report 1996, 6 ADB Avenue, Mardaluyong City, 0401 Metro Manila, Philippines.

BioCycle National Survey: "The State of Garbage," *BioCycle,* April 1998, 419 State Avenue, Emmans, PA 18049. (610) 967-4135.

A Bridge to a Sustainable Future, Office of Science and Technology Policy, Old Executive Office Building, Washington, DC 20500.

China: Environmental Technologies Export Market Plan, Trade Promotion Coordinating Committee, Environmental Trade Working Group, March 1996.

Congressional Research Service, by James McCarthy, Environment and Natural Policy Division, Library of Congress, Washington, DC. (202) 707-7225.

Demand for Environmental Technologies in Poland, Hungary, the Czech Republic and Slovakia, Regional Environmental Center, September 1997.

Directions in Development Series: Toward Sustainable Management of Water Resources, 1995, The World Bank, Serageldin, Ismail, 1818 H Street, Washington, DC 20433. (202) 477-1234.

EBI Report 510: The U.S. Water & Wastewater Industry, 1996, Environmental Business International, Inc., P.O. Box 371769, San Diego, CA 92137. (619) 295-5743.

EBI Report 2000: The U.S. Environmental Industry & Global Market, August 1996, Environmental Business International, Inc., P.O. Box 371769, San Diego, CA 92137. (619) 295-5743.

The Environment Industry and Markets in Selected Central and Eastern European Countries, Organization for Economic Co-operation and Development, 1995, Paris, France.

Environmental & Waste Management, Industry Surveys, Standard & Poor's, a division of The McGraw-Hill Companies, New York, NY, April 24, 1997.

Environmental Industry of the United States—Overview by State and Metropolitan Statistical Area, U.S. Department of Commerce, October 1997.

European Bank for Reconstruction and Development Annual Report 1996, EBRD Procurement Opportunities, Subscription Department, 82-84 Peckham Rye, London SE15 4HB, United Kingdom.

Executive Brief, Environmental Industry Associations, May 1998, 4301 Connecticut Avenue, NW, Suite 300, Washington DC 20008. (202) 244-4700.

Global Competitiveness of U.S. Environmental Technology Industries: Air Pollution Prevention and Control, International Trade Commission, Publ. 2974, June 1996. (202) 205-1806.

Global Competitiveness of U.S. Environmental Technology Industries: Municipal and Industrial Water and Wastewater, March 1995, U.S. International Trade Commission, Publ. 2867, Washington, DC 20436.

The Global Environmental Markets and United States Environmental Industry Competitiveness, Environmental Business International, Inc., 1995, San Diego, CA 92137.

The Hazardous Waste Consultant, "Commercial Hazardous Waste Management Facilities: 1998 Survey of North America," March/April 1998, Vol. 16, Issue 2.

India: Environmental Technologies Export Market Plan, Trade Promotion Coordinating Committee, Environmental Trade Working Group, October 1996.

Indonesia: Environmental Technologies Export Market Plan, Trade Promotion Coordinating Committee, Environmental Trade Working Group, August 1996.

Industrial Wastewater, Water Environment Federation, 601 Wythe Street, Alexandria, VA 22314-1994. (703) 684-2400.

Infrastructure Finance, "Turning on the Taps," February/March 1996, Siting World Bank Statistics.

Inter-American Development Bank Annual Report 1997, 1300 New York Avenue, Washington, DC 20577. (202) 623-1000.

International Environment, The Bureau of National Affairs, Inc., Vol. 21, No. 11, May 27, 1998, Washington, DC 20037.

Journal, American Water Works Association, 6666 West Quincy Avenue, Denver, CO 80235. (303) 794-7711.

Motor Vehicle Pollution Controls: The Growing Global Market, by Michael P. Walsh, July 31, 1996. (703) 241-1297.

Report by the Boards of Directors of the African Development Bank and African Development Fund Covering January 1–December 31, 1996, 01 B.P. 1387 Abidjan 01, Côte d'Ivoire.

South Korea: Environmental Technologies Export Market Plan, Trade Promotion Coordinating Committee, Environmental Trade Working Group, November 1994.

Taiwan: Environmental Technologies Export Market Plan, Trade Promotion Coordinating Committee, Environmental Trade Working Group, July 1995.

Technology for a Sustainable Future, Office of Science and Technology Policy, Old Executive Office Building, Washington, DC 20500.

Tirone Corporation, unpublished study with data that resulted from an independent national survey of over 500 Russian businesses in 22 cities conducted by the corporation in 1997. Tirone Corporation, 44 Main Street, Suite 510, Champaign, IL 61820. (217) 359-5433, E-mail: tirocorp@cu-online.com.

US-Asia Environmental Partnership (US-AEP), "Country Assessments," 1996.

The U.S. Environmental Industry, August 1998, "Meeting the Challenge: U.S. Industry Faces the 21st Century," Office of Technology Policy, Technology Administration, U.S. Department of Commerce.

Waste Age 100, by Bethany Barber and John Aquino, September 1997.

Water & Environment International, International Trade Publications Ltd., Redhill, Surrey, RH1 1QS, United Kingdom. Telephone: +44 (0)173-776-8611.

Water & Wastewater International, MacDonald Communications, Inc., 3300 S. Gessner, Suite 119, Houston, TX 77063. (713) 266-0610.

Water Conditioning & Purification Magazine, Water Quality Association, 4151 Naperville Road, Lisle, IL 60532. (708) 505-0160.

Water Environment & Technology, Water Environment Federation, 601 Wythe Street, Alexandria, VA 22314-1994. (703) 684-2400.

WaterWorld, P.O. Box 2847, Tulsa, OK 74101. (918) 835-3161.

World Bank Annual Report 1997, 1818 H Street, NW, Washington, DC 20433. (202) 477-1234.

World Water and Environmental Engineering, Faversham House Group Ltd., South Croydon, Surrey, CR2 8LE, United Kingdom. Telephone: +44 (0)181-651-7100.

■ RELATED CHAPTERS

1: Metals and Industrial Minerals Mining
2: Coal Mining
3: Crude Petroleum and Natural Gas
4: Petroleum Refining
5: Electricity Production and Sales
10: Paper and Allied Products
11: Chemicals and Allied Products
12: Rubber
13: Steel Mill Products
14: Nonferrous Metals
23: Industrial and Analytical Instruments

AEROSPACE
Economic and Trade Trends

U.S. International Trade

($ billions)

Legend: Balance — Exports — Imports

Source: U.S. Department of Commerce: Bureau of the Census; International Trade Administration.

World Export Market Shares

(%)

Legend: United States, France, United Kingdom, Germany

Source: United Nations; U.S. Department of Commerce, International Trade Administration.

Export Dependence and Import Penetration

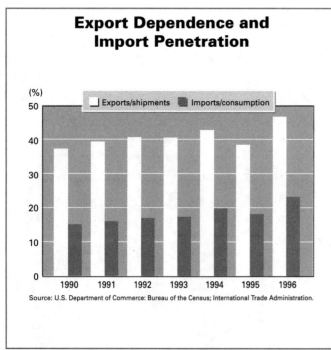

(%)

Legend: Exports/shipments, Imports/consumption

Source: U.S. Department of Commerce: Bureau of the Census; International Trade Administration.

Output and Output per Hour

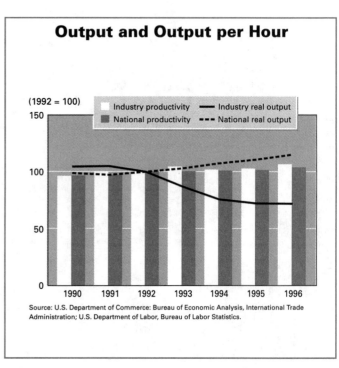

(1992 = 100)

Legend: Industry productivity — Industry real output; National productivity --- National real output

Source: U.S. Department of Commerce: Bureau of Economic Analysis, International Trade Administration; U.S. Department of Labor, Bureau of Labor Statistics.

See "Getting the Most Out of *Outlook '99*" for definitions of terms.

21

Aerospace

INDUSTRY DEFINITION The aerospace industry includes aircraft, aircraft engines and their parts, and aircraft equipment and other parts (SIC 372) and guided missiles and space vehicles, propulsion units and parts, and other parts and auxiliary equipment (SIC 376).

GLOBAL INDUSTRY TRENDS

Growth in the U.S. aerospace industry will be influenced by several factors, including continuing expansion—although at a slower rate—of the global economy, consolidation of manufacturing facilities, lower levels of defense spending by U.S. and foreign governments, increased productivity and technological innovation, products and processes that are more environmentally friendly, foreign competition, investment in research and development, and support by foreign governments for their aerospace industries.

Global Economy

As of October 1998, the International Monetary Fund (IMF) expected the world economy to grow about 2 percent in 1998, taking into account the financial crisis in eastern Asia, especially Indonesia, South Korea, Malaysia, the Philippines, and Thailand. The IMF's *World Economic Outlook* predicted that global growth would recover only moderately in 1999. Eastern Asian nations should see the financial crisis bottom out in the first half of 1999 and be out of recession by the second half of 1999. The Asian financial situation will have at least as much of an effect on the region's aerospace industries as on its airlines.

Japan was expected to show an economic decline of 2.5 percent in 1998 and a 0.5 percent gain in 1999. The IMF report also predicted that South Korea's economy will contract 7 percent in 1998 and a further 1 percent in 1999; as a group, the economies of Indonesia, the Philippines, Malaysia, and Thailand were expected to fall 0.1 percent in 1999 after a contraction of 10.4 percent in 1998—these are the five economies most affected by the Asian financial crisis. The IMF stated that these five nations will benefit from increased trade and investment and financial restructuring.

The crisis could cost the world's airlines $2.5 billion in 1998 operating profits and dampen international passenger demand through 2003, the International Air Transport Association (IATA) warned in September 1998. As a result, IATA revised its 1997–2001 forecast for passenger traffic downward: average international growth to 5.5 percent (from 6.6 percent).

An important consequence of the currency situation in eastern Asia for the aerospace industry is the reduced capacity in funding markets. Japanese banks are among the most important of those institutions with a reduced capacity to lend. At the end of 1995 Japan had 9 of the 10 largest banks in the world and 25 of the top 100. During the period 1988–1997 Japanese banks provided some 25 percent of the new equipment financing raised by the world's airlines. In February 1998 almost no new funding commitments were made by Japanese banks. Although some other banks, especially German ones, have become more active, they have not filled the gap left by the Japanese, especially in Asia. The bad debt which may become apparent in Asia will affect all banks active in that region.

According to the IMF's report, the United States and the European Union will continue to experience solid growth in 1998 and 1999, largely immune to the "Asian flu."

Industry Consolidation

The process of consolidation of the major players in the U.S. aerospace and defense industry is nearly complete. After previous mergers and acquisitions, in August 1997 there were three major players: the Boeing Company, Lockheed Martin Corporation, and Raytheon Company (in descending order). The U.S. Department of Justice (DOJ) looked at the question of vertical integration in the proposed merger of Northrop Grumman and Lockheed Martin. The DOJ had called for the divestiture of certain assets that the government indicated would give the merged company too much market leverage in the defense industry. On

July 16, 1998—rather than meet the DOJ in court less than eight weeks later—Lockheed Martin announced that, in the best interests of the corporation's shareholders and customers, it had terminated the merger agreement with Northrop Grumman.

Consolidation of the aerospace industries in Europe has progressed in fits and starts. In December 1997 the governments of France, Germany, and the United Kingdom agreed that there was an urgent need to restructure Europe's aerospace and defense industries. The heads of the three governments jointly asked industry to come up with a detailed plan and timetable for action by March 31, 1998. The consolidation was expected to be planned around the Airbus Industrie consortium. The report was issued by British Aerospace PLC (BAe); Aerospatiale SA of France; Daimler-Benz Aerospace AG (DASA), a unit of Daimler-Benz AG of Germany; and Construcciones Aeronauticas SA (CASA) of Spain—the four Airbus partners. These companies expressed broad agreement in principle on the objectives, scope, and operational structure of a possible merger of their businesses into a single unified European aerospace and defense company that would encompass aircraft, helicopters, missiles, launchers, and defense systems—a goal considered essential now that U.S. defense contractors have rapidly consolidated into only a few major players. There are deep divisions among the partners on how to proceed toward an integrated European defense company. The lack of a timetable in the 20-page report suggests the difficulty of bringing together companies that historically have maintained fierce independence. The British and German companies are growing frustrated over what they see as continued resistance, or at least ambivalence, by the French government, for which aerospace has traditionally been a matter of national prestige. In July 1998 the French government and Lagardère announced a plan to join the activities of Aerospatiale and Matra Hautes Technologies, to become effective January 1, 1999. Aerospatiale will be privatized with the French government holding a "golden" share.

Although the European partners are making progress toward turning Airbus into a "single corporate entity" (SCE), a process scheduled for completion in 1999, the broader consolidation of Europe's defense industry is proving more complex. The French government has signaled that it seeks sector-by-sector integration, perhaps through joint ventures, rather than a comprehensive approach that would quickly create true rivals to the U.S. giants Boeing, Lockheed Martin, and Raytheon. The British and German governments want to adopt a far more dramatic approach. After the report was issued, the French government said that it was committed to European defense integration and termed the report an important first step in an ambitious process. The various governments and the report itself also recognized the importance of involving other aerospace companies, such as Saab Aircraft AB of Sweden, Dassault Aviation SA of France, and Finmeccanica of Italy, the parent of Alenia SpA.

Environment

Up to 90 percent of the dangerous materials that are generated during the service life of an aircraft come from painting or stripping the fuselage. During the process of painting or stripping it is not possible to accomplish other work on an aircraft. There has been much research on this process with the aim of reducing the environmental damage from use of paints and chemical paint removers. In July 1998 the U.S. Navy put into operation a process which combines pulsed light energy and a steady stream of dry pellets to remove paint. The latest proposal involves the replacement of paint with adhesive films, which can be applied by hand and offer better corrosion protection than does paint.

In other areas of concern, aircraft and engine manufacturers are working to reduce both external and internal noise. Makers of aircraft engines are also studying ways to reduce or eliminate dangerous emissions, including lead from piston aircraft engines and nitrogen oxides, which could contribute to the "greenhouse effect." Industry representatives have pointed to a trade-off in levels of nitrogen oxides and carbon dioxide and have suggested that emissions of both may be reduced through better management of the air transportation system. Reducing air traffic delays, such as the circling of an airport while an airplane is waiting for clearance to land, would promote environmentalist goals.

Defense Spending

With the reduction of military spending over the past few years in the United States and western Europe, the eastern Asian countries became a growing market for the aerospace and defense industries. After the financial crisis began in the summer of 1997, those countries began to delay, reduce, or cancel programs in this industry. The reduction in orders from the United States, western Europe, and eastern Asia is now shifting attention to other regions, such as Latin America.

DOMESTIC TRENDS

The U.S. aerospace industry passed a milestone in 1997 as sales to commercial and foreign customers matched sales to the U.S. government for only the second time since 1908. (The first time was in 1934, when the DC-3 and the Boeing Stratoliner introduced large-scale commercial air travel.) Although sales of civilian products did not quite surpass sales of military products in 1997, they were expected to claim 55 percent of aerospace business in 1998. This historic turning point has resulted from increases in civil sales as well as decreases in military sales. Deliveries of civil aircraft, engines, and parts reached $39.7 billion in 1997, an increase of 50 percent over 1996. Meanwhile, deliveries of military aircraft to foreign customers dropped an estimated 8 percent in 1997, to approximately $30.5 billion. In the first 8 months of 1998, compared with the same period of 1997, U.S. aerospace industry shipments increased 9.9 percent and new orders grew 14.8 percent.

U.S. defense procurement (including new buys, modifications, and parts) in fiscal year (FY) 1997 totaled $13.2 billion for aircraft and $4 billion for missiles and space equipment. The major purchases of military aircraft in that year were the Air Force C-17 Globemaster III transport and E-8C JSTARS surveillance aircraft, the Navy F/A-18E/F fighter, the Navy/Marine AV-

8B Harrier V/STOL fighter and V-22 Osprey tilt-rotor aircraft, and the Army AH-64 Apache and UH-60 Black Hawk helicopters. Procurement in FY 1998 was expected to remain flat, with major purchases similar to those in FY 1997. An increase in military procurement in FY 1999 suggests that the decline in defense spending has hit bottom and that such spending will climb through FY 2003. The U.S. Department of Defense (DOD) expects to reach a target of $60 billion in procurement spending for the first time in FY 2000. Programs that will be emphasized in the FY 1999 budget include production of the F-22 Raptor and boosted production of the Bell-Boeing V-22.

After a decade of decreases in military procurement in which industry sales to the U.S. government dropped from 75 percent to 50 percent of total sales created a wave of mergers among military contractors. Those mergers left only three U.S. prime military contractors—Boeing, Lockheed Martin and Raytheon—representing about two-thirds of all military product sales. Although the military will continue to be a significant customer, there is a new focus on civilian business practices. DOD will use more existing commercial technologies and reform buying practices to reduce red tape.

U.S. INDUSTRY GROWTH PROJECTIONS FOR THE NEXT 1 AND 5 YEARS

The value of total shipments by the U.S. aerospace industry in 1997 was $124 billion, a 23 percent increase over 1996. Shipments are expected to increase in value 21 percent in 1998 over 1997 and about 5 percent in 1999 compared with 1998. U.S. aerospace exports increased 25 percent in 1997 compared with 1996 (see Table 21-1). Aerospace shipments are estimated to increase about three percent per year from 2000 through 2003.

GLOBAL MARKET PROSPECTS

Asia

The financial crisis in eastern Asia should cause only temporary fluctuations in U.S. aerospace production. In early 1997 Indonesia, South Korea, Malaysia, the Philippines, and Thailand were bright spots in an otherwise declining market for military equipment; they were among the countries expected to show the greatest economic growth over the next 20 years. Each sector of the aerospace industry will be affected by the Asian monetary crisis to a different extent. Large commercial aircraft deliveries to the region probably will be delayed rather than canceled. Orders for general aviation airplanes, including regional airliners, and helicopters can be changed more quickly due to shorter production lead times. Defense sales to the region will decline partly because of reduced military budgets, but the greater determinant is the devaluation of the respective countries' currencies and the reduced ability of those nations to make major investments that require foreign exchange. Commercial space launches for countries of eastern Asia also may be delayed. The eastern Asian economic crisis that began in July 1997 did not affect China as severely as it did other Asian countries, but China did experience a significant decline in airline traffic through the first quarter of 1998, reflecting the problems in other Asian countries.

Latin America

The Latin American region is becoming an important market for U.S. aerospace and defense manufacturers as eastern Asian countries delay, reduce, or cancel programs. With the reduction of military spending in the United States and western Europe, U.S. contractors are looking for orders to keep their military production lines going. In a climate of declining defense bud-

TABLE 21-1: Aerospace (SIC 372, 376) Trends and Forecasts

(millions of dollars except as noted)

	1992	1993	1994	1995	1996	1997[1]	1998[2]	1999[3]	Percent Change 96–97	97–98	98–99	92–96[4]
Industry data												
Value of shipments[5]	131,368	116,346	103,316	100,062	101,322	124,309	150,443	157,314	22.7	21.0	4.6	−6.3
Value of shipments (1992$)	131,368	113,815	98,831	94,046	93,798	112,725	136,254	142,635	20.2	20.9	4.7	−8.1
Total employment (thousands)	692.80	611.70	524.50	470.80	457.70							−9.9
Production workers (thousands)	330.10	278.60	240.80	221.10	219.20							−9.8
Average hourly earnings ($)	40.17	39.70	41.09	40.89	42.75							−3.3
Capital expenditures	3,851	2,725	2,363	2,114	2,513							−10.0
Product data												
Value of shipments[5]	198,884	110,312	97,157	95,311	96,223	117,750	141,965	147,053	22.4	20.6	3.6	−5.9
Value of shipments (1992$)	122,800	107,905	92,938	89,576	88,974	106,641	128,368	133,001	19.9	20.4	3.6	−7.7
Trade data												
Value of imports	12,793	11,583	11,513	11,148	13,250	17,054	20,545	21,209	28.7	20.5	3.2	0.9
Value of exports	43,490	37,854	35,920	31,556	38,586	48,175	59,170	61,109	24.9	22.8	3.3	−2.9

[1] Estimate except imports and exports.
[2] Estimate.
[3] Forecast.
[4] Compound annual rate.
[5] For definition of industry versus product values, see "Getting the Most Out of *Outlook '99.*"
Source: U.S. Department of Commerce: Bureau of the Census; International Trade Administration.

TABLE 21-2: U.S. Trade Patterns in Aerospace[1] in 1997

(millions of dollars; percent)

Exports			Imports		
Regions[2]	Value[3]	Share, %	Regions[2]	Value[3]	Share, %
NAFTA	2,820	5.8	NAFTA	3,774	21.7
Latin America	1,890	3.9	Latin America	386	2.2
Western Europe	18,074	37.5	Western Europe	10,357	59.5
Japan/Chinese Economic Area	9,647	20.0	Japan/Chinese Economic Area	1,726	9.9
Other Asia	8,241	17.1	Other Asia	504	2.9
Rest of world	7,564	15.7	Rest of world	654	3.8
World	48,236	100.0	World	17,402	100.0
Top Five Countries	Value	Share, %	Top Five Countries	Value	Share, %
United Kingdom	6,260	13.0	France	3,987	22.9
Japan	4,906	10.2	United Kingdom	3,770	21.7
Saudi Arabia	2,619	5.4	Canada	3,697	21.2
France	2,509	5.2	Japan	1,648	9.5
Canada	2,507	5.2	Germany	1,111	6.4

[1] SIC 372, 376.
[2] For definitions of regional groupings, see "Getting the Most Out of *Outlook '99*."
[3] Values may not sum to total due to rounding.
Source: U.S. Department of Commerce, Bureau of the Census.

gets and reduced international, as well as regional, tensions, Latin American governments must decide whether to continue upgrading their fighter aircraft or buy new ones. The major markets are Argentina, Brazil, Chile, and Mexico, followed by Colombia and Venezuela. The growth in passenger and cargo traffic among the region's airlines should produce further sales in that sector. The degree to which the Asian financial crisis will affect Latin America is unknown, although Japanese banks used to support infrastructure programs in Latin America as well as in Asia (see Table 21-2).

AIRCRAFT AND PARTS

The aircraft and parts industry covers aircraft (SIC 3721), aircraft engines and engine parts (SIC 3724), and aircraft equipment and parts, not elsewhere classified (SIC 3728).

Foreign Manufacturers

Europe. There was further rationalization of the European regional aircraft industry in 1997 with the closure of Fokker (50- and 100-seat aircraft), Saab's decision to cease its production of turboprop airplanes—the 340 (35-seat) and the 2000 (50-passenger)—by the middle of 1998, and BAe's plan to end production of the Jetstream 41 (30-seat). The prospects for Aero International Regional [AI(R)] dimmed at the end of 1997 when the programs for the planned 50- to 80-seat AI(R)JETs were halted. The reason for the common marketing of the products of the partners—ATR (Aerospatiale and Alenia) and British Aerospace—was the realization of a new European regional plane family. When BAe withdrew its support for the 70-seat regional jet, there was no reason for the partners to stay

together. AI(R) was dissolved by mutual consent on June 30, 1998. The British were finally able to break even in their program in 1997 after heavy losses in previous years. The midterm prognosis for the four-engine Avro RJ, which sells for $20 million, is not positive. To make the RJ competitive, BAe had started negotiating with Kazanah Nasional Berhad about part manufacturing in Malaysia to reduce costs. The Asian financial crisis has curtailed that plan.

Europe–United States. Fairchild Aerospace (San Antonio, TX) acquired Dornier Luftfahrt (Oberpfaffenhofen, Germany) from DASA in June 1996. As of September 30, 1998, Fairchild Dornier had received 44 orders for the new Dornier 328JET. The company's German and U.S. designers are thinking of increasing the product range. The new models under consideration are a 40-seat 428JET, a stretched 50-seat 528JET, and a 90-seat 928JET. This development is an outcome of the planned 728JET. Fairchild Dornier predicts a necessary investment for the development and construction of the 728JET at approximately $600 million, which the company does not intend to finance on its own. Seventeen companies are being considered as risk-sharing partners. If the 728 program is successful, Fairchild Dornier will start development of the 528 and the 928JET. The company also is committed to the construction of the 428JET, which is approximately 3 meters longer than the 328JET and is designed to carry 42 to 44 passengers.

Asia. The IMF announced in January 1998 that one of the conditions of its $43 billion rescue of Indonesia was the ending of government subsidies to Industri Pesawat Terbang Nusantara (IPTN), that country's aircraft manufacturing company. The development cost of the N-250 (a 70-seat turboprop regional airliner) was funded in part by a loan from another agency. President Suharto said that IPTN's N-2130 (a 130-seat jet transport) project could go forward, but only if outside money—foreign or Indonesian—took over the financing, a prospect considered unlikely. Dr. B. J. Habibie, then IPTN's chairman, said that there would not be any layoffs at the Bandung plant. Faced with his imminent election as Indonesia's vice president (before replacing Suharto as president), the aviation and space engineer, who was trained in Germany, stepped down officially from his positions at IPTN and various government agencies. The completion of the N-250 development program should require at least another $110 million between January 1998 and 2000. Then, since 70 percent of the aircraft components are imported, IPTN will need a large amount of foreign currency financing to start production.

South Korea's Samsung Aerospace Industries Ltd. is scheduled to provide the U.S.-based Boeing with $30 million worth of plane wing frameworks. Under the contract Samsung Aerospace will provide $13 million worth of wing frameworks for Boeing's 767 series airplanes, beginning in October 1998 and continuing to 2001. The company will sell Boeing an additional $17 million worth of the frameworks from 2002 to 2006. Lockheed Martin also signed a contract with Samsung to develop the advanced KTX-2 combat-trainer aircraft. With a price tag of $2 billion and a high-tech specification, the project indicates why partnership is a required ingredient in aerospace production. Despite South Korea's economic setback, the program remains on track, although some analysts in South Korea believe that it may be delayed.

Taiwan, China, South Korea, and Indonesia have had only moderate success in launching civil aircraft programs. Asian companies do not have the technical know-how or the commercial prowess to compete with aerospace giants for business that is increasingly global. If Asian manufacturers are to grow, they must find a niche market and/or join forces with established manufacturers. Asian companies that have succeeded in building complete aircraft have relied on national defense business in their home markets to develop the industry. While there is a potential for Asian aerospace companies to enlarge their defense business, it is not likely to be fulfilled by major indigenous programs.

Like other regional manufacturers, Taiwan's Aero Industry Development Center (AIDC), a manufacturer that soon will be privatized, has had to reduce its aerospace ambitions. AIDC is set to complete the production of Taiwan's indigenous fighter aircraft (IDF) by 2000. High costs make it unlikely that there will be any more national programs like the IDF in Taiwan. In the future the company hopes to supply parts to larger, more established companies and to enter partnership programs for aircraft such as new regional commercial jetliners.

A new concept in rotorcraft is being developed by the Modus Corporation of Taiwan. The Modus Verticraft uses closely coupled counter-rotating solid disks with rigid bladelets fixed to the end of each one. Control in both vertical and horizontal flight is accomplished by means of gimbal actuation of the entire disk. The program calls for a 30-foot-long aircraft which seats four.

The region's biggest success stories—Japan and Singapore—early embraced the idea of joining forces with larger companies.

Singapore Technologies Aerospace (STA), a state-owned aerospace design, manufacturing, and maintenance concern, could provide a valuable model for other companies in the region. STA is taking advantage of Singapore's status as a major airline hub and has started concentrating on aviation maintenance. STA also has joined with manufacturers such as Europe's Airbus Industrie and Eurocopter, the Franco-German helicopter manufacturer, by producing parts and components and by emphasizing regional maintenance of European-produced aircraft.

Although financially strong enough to compete with the world's biggest players, Japanese manufacturers have chosen to work with them. Japanese firms subcontract and pursue ties with Boeing and Airbus as a key strategy of their business. Mitsubishi, Kawasaki, and Fuji helped design and build about 20 percent of the Boeing 777's airframe structure, making Japan the largest non-U.S. supplier country for the wide-body commercial jet.

Also following the new paradigm, although yet to see results, is Aviation Industries of China (AVIC), which signed an agreement to share the $1.7 billion development of the 95 to 125-seat AE31X airliner. Airbus, Alenia, and Singapore Technologies were to provide technology and AVIC to provide the facilities for final assembly at Xian Aircraft. On September 3, 1998, Airbus Industrie announced that all partners concluded that there was no common basis for further developing the aircraft. Airbus said that it plans to seek another project with the Chinese.

The Americas. The Brazilian plane manufacturer Embraer was privatized in 1994. In 1995 it rolled out the 50-seat regional jet ERJ-145, which competes with Canada's Bombardier/Canadair Regional Jet. The rollout for Embraer's new project, the 37-seat ERJ-135, took place on May 12, 1998. There are few differences between the two planes apart from the fuselage, which is 3.54 meters shorter in the ERJ-135. Deliveries of the new Brazilian regional jet will begin in the first half of 1999. The development of this jet cost $100 million, and Embraer estimates that up to 500 planes will be sold in the next 10 years.

International Markets

Large Civil Transports. Sales of large transport aircraft are expected to result from the retirement and replacement of aircraft to comply with Federal Aviation Administration (FAA) Stage 3 noise regulations, which go into effect at the end of 1999, and from the production of additional aircraft to accommodate growth in air traffic. Because of European Union regulations restricting the use of hushkits, which reduce noise but not pollutants, there will be a higher percentage of new airplanes serving European regions than serving other regions. Manufacturers expect no long-term sales problems in Asia, although delays in deliveries and cancellation of options have occurred causing a decrease in the production rate of long-range, wide-body aircraft. In June 1998 the Boeing Company predicted that during the period 1998–2002, 150 fewer aircraft will be ordered worldwide than was previously expected due to the economic crisis in Asia.

By 2001 the Asia/Pacific region is expected to reestablish its previous growth trend. Latin America, with the possible exception of Brazil, should experience a rebound and have better prospects for new orders. There should be moderate, sustained growth in airline travel within Europe and between Europe and the United States. That growth should lead to the purchase of new aircraft for the additional passengers as well as normal replacement of retired aircraft and aircraft going off lease.

Business Airplanes.   A total of 1,850 business aircraft, worth about $22 billion, are expected to roll off the production lines in Wichita, KS, Savannah, GA, Montreal, and Bordeaux-Mérignac from 1999 through 2003. Following an economic slump in the 1980s and early 1990s, this subsector is now looking toward a profitable future, with its growth having stabilized at a healthy level over the past 3 years. Worldwide, it is estimated that there were a total of 408 deliveries worth $5.1 billion in 1997. In 1998, 420 jets worth $5.4 billion were expected to be delivered. It is possible that this output can be maintained through 1999 and then level off to the high 300s in the following years.

There are three reasons for this positive development: worldwide economic growth in general; the use of improved technologies with efficient ecologically sound economical products; and the stimulation of the market by new market incentives, such as fractional ownership programs, which make it possible to become a partial owner of a business jet at an entry level below $1 million. Fractional ownership programs have generated about 30 percent of the growth. The five dominating manufacturers—Bombardier of Canada; Gulfstream, Cessna, and Raytheon of the United States; and Dassault of France—will benefit the most from the growth in the business jet market. Together those five companies share 90 percent of the market for business aircraft.

In 1998 approximately 17,300 business aircraft were in service worldwide, 8,700 of which were jet aircraft. Almost two-thirds of the world's fleet (approximately 5,800 jets and 5,100 turboprops) fly in North America, which is the largest business aviation market. About 2,000 business aircraft (1,060 jets) are registered in Europe. South America is the third largest market, with a total of 1,620 units. Asia is operating a relatively small fleet of only 768 aircraft. Business aircraft producers have identified China as the main growth market. The development of that market will start at a very low level—China received its first business jet, a Lear 60 delivered to Hainan Airlines, in 1996. The worldwide market potential based on fleet renewal is projected to strengthen at the turn of the century. Used aircraft dealing could account for as much as 85 percent of this business. In 1996, 1,100 aircraft changed owners. Assuming an average service life of 25 to 30 years, a significant need for new business aircraft should occur between 2000 and 2005.

Rotorcraft.   In Latin America the market for helicopters is increasing along with the economic revitalization occurring in that region. Petroleum and natural gas are the key commodities driving this economic boom. About 80 percent of oil industry

helicopter contracts in Latin America are for seismic work (deep probing for geologic conditions conducive to finding oil), and 20 percent are for helirig work (actual drilling projects). Sikorsky delivered S-70/UH-60 Black Hawks to Argentina, Brazil, and Colombia. Between 1993 and 1997 Bell supplied surplus model 205/UH-1 Iroquois to the armed forces of Argentina, Bolivia, Brazil, Chile, Colombia, El Salvador, and Mexico.

In 1997 Argentina's helicopter market was about two-thirds civil and the rest military, the reverse of the situation in 1987. Most privately owned helicopters were bought by executives in the banking, insurance, agricultural, oil, and mineral industries due to the lack of second-party financing. In Brazil, which has Latin America's largest helicopter operator (Lider Taxi Aereo), 71 percent of the helicopter fleet (505 aircraft) in 1997 was civil. The dramatic rise in civil helicopter sales in that country has been driven by traffic congestion and the need for personal security. Light helicopters are being used in electronic news gathering—traffic reporting in particular—and their use is spreading to other segments, such as flight training, police aerial observation, and agricultural spraying.

Colombia has the region's second largest helicopter operator (Helitaxi Ltda.), 90 percent of whose contracts are with that country's petroleum industry. Guatemala has the largest number of helicopters per capita in Latin America; its helicopter fleet is 75 percent civil. The commercial helicopter industry is divided into five basic areas: aerial photography, petroleum and geophysical operations, agricultural spraying, search and rescue, and mineral exploration. Mexico's civil helicopter fleet—68 percent of the total fleet—will continue to grow through 1999 despite troubles on the Mexican stock exchange early in 1998. Mexican operators follow the models of Brazil and Colombia, serving the petroleum and executive transport segments of the helicopter industry.

Only 30 percent of Venezuela's helicopter fleet is civil, with 70 percent operated by the military. There has been a resurgence of activity in the petroleum industry, which, along with mining, is a major source of income for that country. Government agencies have delayed issuing operating permits to the oil companies. Chile's ratio of civil to military helicopters in its fleet is also about 30:70. Environmental work represents a small but growing segment of Latin America's helicopter industry, especially in Venezuela. Major contracts in Venezuela are related to forestry: reforestation, fighting fires, and aerial spraying for pest control. Other areas of work include geologic surveys, transportation of executives, high-altitude topography, high-mountain rescue operations, heliskiing, and adventure tourism.

DOMESTIC SUBSECTOR OUTLOOK

As in the aerospace manufacturing sector, consolidation is occurring in the maintenance, repair, and overhaul (MRO) area of the aircraft and parts subsector, according to a presentation given at the Air Transport Research International Forum

(ATRIF) in March 1998. In 1993 there were 24 aftermarket support companies; in 1998 there were only 13. In a few years there are expected to be four, plus government depots and maintenance operation at the major airlines. Original equipment manufacturers (OEMs) of aircraft and engines (Boeing and General Electric, for example) are acquiring independent centers which service their products. The OEMs would like to smooth out the production boom-and-bust cycle. While major airlines prefer to perform as much maintenance as possible in house, they need to reduce the cost of ownership and operations by outsourcing component MRO and inventory management or by pooling their inventories. The U.S. government continues to expand its outsourcing of noncombatant support in an effort to get the DOD out of the repair and inventory management business. It plans to reduce the number of DOD military support personnel and civilian government workers by shifting them to warfighting aircraft only.

Aircraft

Large Transports. The large civil aircraft subsector includes commercial passenger and cargo aircraft with an operating empty weight greater than 15,000 kilograms: two-, three-, and four-engined jetliners. Passenger aircraft in this category can accommodate at least 70 passengers. New trijet airplanes are being delivered primarily for use as freighters, although Boeing announced in June 1998 that the trijet MD-11 will be discontinued, with the last delivery scheduled for February 2000. The value of shipments of transport aircraft increased 47 percent in 1997 compared with 1996 (see Table 21-3) and a further 38 percent in the first quarter of 1998 compared with the same period of 1997. Exports of large transport aircraft increased 54 percent in 1997 compared with 1996 (see Table 21-4). Imports of that type of aircraft in 1997 increased 30 percent over 1996 (see Table 21-5). Orders for new narrow-

TABLE 21-3: Shipments of Complete U.S. Aircraft, 1971–1999
(millions of current dollars; number of units)

| | Total Aircraft | | Civil Aircraft | | | | | | | | | Military Aircraft | |
| | | | Total | | Large Transports[1] | | General Aviation[2] | | Rotorcraft | | | | |
	Units	Value	Units	Value	Units	Value	Units	Value	Units	Value		Units	Value
1971	11,056	6,607	8,142	2,985	223	2,594	7,466	322	453	69		2,914	3,622
1972	13,100	6,093	10,570	3,290	227	2,660	9,774	558	569	72		2,530	2,803
1973	16,529	7,428	14,708	4,544	294	3,603	13,646	828	768	113		1,821	2,884
1974	16,820	8,242	15,307	5,056	332	3,993	14,166	909	809	154		1,513	3,186
1975	16,988	9,095	15,209	5,078	315	3,779	14,056	1,033	838	266		1,779	4,017
1976	17,812	9,299	16,494	4,628	222	3,078	15,451	1,226	821	324		1,318	4,671
1977	19,041	8,968	17,907	4,388	155	2,649	16,904	1,488	848	251		1,134	4,580
1978	19,952	10,136	18,956	6,417	241	4,308	17,811	1,781	904	328		996	3,719
1979	19,280	15,028	18,443	10,598	376	8,030	17,048	2,165	1,019	403		837	4,430
1980	14,677	18,929	13,630	13,037	387	9,895	11,877	2,486	1,366	656		1,047	5,892
1981	11,978	20,093	10,916	13,223	387	9,706	9,457	2,920	1,072	597		1,062	6,870
1982	6,244	18,446	5,085	8,611	232	6,246	4,266	2,000	587	365		1,159	9,835
1983	4,409	21,769	3,356	9,773	262	8,000	2,691	1,470	403	303		1,053	11,996
1984	3,928	21,787	2,992	7,700	185	5,689	2,431	1,681	376	330		936	14,087
1985	3,610	27,269	2,691	10,385	278	8,448	2,029	1,431	384	506		919	16,884
1986	3,262	29,587	2,155	11,859	330	10,309	1,495	1,262	330	288		1,107	17,728
1987	3,085	28,966	1,875	12,104	357	10,507	1,160	1,320	358	277		1,210	16,862
1988	3,381	30,401	2,076	15,357	423	13,603	1,270	1,420	383	334		1,305	15,044
1989	3,709	31,961	2,448	17,128	398	15,074	1,535	1,803	515	251		1,261	14,833
1990	3,321	38,585	2,268	24,476	521	22,215	1,144	2,007	603	254		1,053	14,109
1991	3,092	44,657	2,181	29,035	589	26,856	1,021	1,968	571	211		911	15,622
1992	2,585	47,397	1,832	30,732	567	28,750	941	1,840	324	142		753	16,665
1993	2,585	41,166	1,630	26,390	408	24,133	964	2,144	258	113		955	14,776
1994	2,309	36,568	1,545	20,666	309	18,124	928	2,357	308	185		764	15,902
1995	2,436	33,658	1,625	18,299	256	15,263	1,077	2,842	292	194		811	15,359
1996[3]	2,232	36,246	1,677	20,883	269	17,564	1,130	3,126	278	193		555	15,363
1997[4]	2,839	46,065	2,289	30,715	374	25,810	1,569	4,674	346	231		550	15,350
1998[5]	3,308	57,345	2,758	42,000	535	37,200	1,890	4,560	333	240		550	15,345
1999[6]	3,485	59,415	2,925	44,015	600	39,000	1,975	4,760	350	255		560	15,400

[1] Includes fixed-wing aircraft over 15,000 kilograms empty weight, including all jet transports plus the turboprop-powered Lockheed L-100.
[2] Excludes off-the-shelf military aircraft.
[3] Revised.
[4] Military estimated.
[5] Estimated.
[6] Forecast.
Source: U.S. Department of Commerce: Bureau of the Census; International Trade Administration (ITA); Department of Defense; General Aviation Manufacturers Association; Aerospace Industries Association; and company reports. Estimates and forecasts by ITA.

TABLE 21-4: U.S. Exports of Aerospace Vehicles and Equipment

(value in millions of current dollars; quantity in number of units or kilograms)

	1992 Quantity	1992 Value	1993 Quantity	1993 Value	1994 Quantity	1994 Value	1995 Quantity	1995 Value	1996[1] Quantity	1996[1] Value	1997 Quantity	1997 Value
Aerospace vehicles and equipment, total		44,960		39,375		37,532		33,320		40,311		50,614
Total aircraft		26,292		21,280		18,810		13,852		18,984		25,560
Civilian aircraft		24,209		19,821		17,718		12,251		15,160		23,164
Under 4,536 kg unladen weight, new	587	298	486	227	436	270	504	296	507	343	492	475
4,536–15,000 kg unladen weight, new	60	295	58	324	66	331	56	306	52	258	83	486
Over 15,000 kg unladen weight, new	384	22,256	278	18,146	222	15,931	137	10,606	172	13,624	252	21,028
Rotorcraft, new	212	112	171	119	159	83	208	170	214	212	259	208
Used or rebuilt	954	1,241	696	996	640	1,097	614	858	547	716	519	959
Nonpowered aircraft		7		9		7		15		8		8
Military aircraft	429	2,084	629	1,458	436	1,093	520	1,601	428	3,824	416	2,397
New	332	1,910	517	1,403	348	826	462	1,539	316	3,549	360	2,297
Used or rebuilt	97	174	112	55	88	266	58	62	112	275	56	99
Aircraft engines and parts		6,714		6,258		6,578		6,192		6,870		8,618
Piston engines and parts[2]		334		296		462		369		344		434
Complete engines, new and used	7,269	101	7,582	114	6,679	143	7,885	147	7,528	144	17,749	229
Engine parts		233		183		319		222		200		205
Reaction/turbine engines and parts[3]		6,380		5,961		6,117		5,823		6,525		8,184
Complete engines, new and used	18,185	2,473	17,028	2,406	4,950	2,484	7,025	1,802	8,638	2,136	11,028	2,275
Engine parts		3,907		3,555		3,633		4,020		4,390		5,909
Propellers, rotors, and parts		289		307		306	2,584,005 kg	334	2,973,786 kg	426	3,360,362 kg	500
Landing gear and parts		362		336		313	3,138,195 kg	386	4,321,328 kg	527	4,996,973 kg	559
Aircraft parts and accessories, not elsewhere classified		8,533		8,570		8,933		9,443		10,662		12,090
Avionics		796		646		673		673		779		871
Flight simulators and parts		206		197		232	1,714,011 kg	122	2,056,499 kg	166	2,044,233 kg	184
Guided missiles and parts		1,431		1,235		1,113		1,508		1,210		1,149
Space vehicles and parts		337		548		574		811		689		1,083

[1] Revised from previously published data. Revisions to trade data based on U.S. Bureau of the Census, Historical Summary 1989–1993 and 1991–1997.

[2] Category changed to include reaction engines, other than turbojets—except missile and rocket—and their parts. Camshafts and crankshafts have been added to both engine categories.

[3] Category revised to include camshafts and crankshafts; and reaction engines, other than turbojets—except missile and rocket—and their parts.

Note: Totals do not correspond to SIC-based trade statistics because of slightly broader coverage. Details may not add to totals due to rounding. Data shown for certain products are not comparable to data before 1989 due to category changes made under the Harmonized System.

Source: U.S. Department of Commerce: Bureau of the Census; International Trade Administration.

body aircraft were expected to slow in 1998 as the U.S. Stage 3 buying surge ended.

General Aviation Aircraft. Manufacturers in the general aviation sector produce fixed-wing aircraft for regional airline service, business transportation, recreation, specialized uses such as ambulance service and agricultural spraying, and pilot training. The General Aviation Manufacturers Association (GAMA) reported that in 1997 its members had the highest industry billings ever, $4.67 billion, up 50 percent from $3.13 billion in 1996; the highest shipments since 1985, 1,569 units, up from 1,130 units in 1996; and single-engine piston sales rose 70.8 percent and jet aircraft sales increased 44.4 percent. Shipments further increased in the first quarter of 1998 by 29 percent over the first quarter of 1997. Exports increased 62 percent in 1997.

Regional airliners include turboprop and turbofan aircraft that seat 10 to 70 passengers or the cargo equivalent. Some turboprop aircraft are being replaced by regional jets (RJs). More often RJs are replacing larger jet aircraft. The regional turboprop airliners produced by U.S. manufacturers—those seating 10 to 19 passengers—should not be affected by the move to jet aircraft.

The effects of the reduced product liability afforded by the 1994 General Aviation Revitalization Act showed up in the reintroduction of Cessna's Skyhawk and Skylane and other single-engine piston-powered airplanes as well as new models. GAMA reported that U.S. shipments of piston-powered aircraft rose 64 percent in 1997 over 1996, while those of single-engine

TABLE 21-5: U.S. Imports of Aerospace Vehicles and Equipment
(value in millions of current dollars; quantity in number of units or kilograms)

	1992		1993		1994		1995		1996¹		1997	
	Quantity	Value	Quantity	Value	Quantity	Value	Quantity	Value	Quantity	Value	Quantity	Value
Aerospace vehicles and equipment, total		13,978		12,616		12,808		12,226		14,391		18,809
Total aircraft		3,863		3,809		3,722		3,655		3,947		4,562
Civilian aircraft		3,807		3,798		3,698		3,589		3,920		4,545
Under 4,536 kg unladen weight, new	119	104	143	39	163	25	213	28	278	30	252	22
4,536–15,000 kg unladen weight, new	125	1,251	130	1,210	152	1,673	157	1,506	209	2,144	206	2,531
Over 15,000 kg unladen weight, new	64	2,007	55	2,078	35	1,137	23	1,050	19	823	23	919
Rotorcraft, new	149	185	156	225	215	317	206	300	183	361	241	462
Powered, used or rebuilt	161	259	246	246	313	545	258	703	275	560	298	609
Nonpowered aircraft		1		1		1		3		3		2
Military aircraft		57		11		25		66		27		18
Powered, new	25	50	36	7	54	16	122	64	47	20	58	3
Powered, used or rebuilt	51	5	33	2	42	6	41	1	9	5	22	11
Nonpowered aircraft		2		2		2		2		2		3
Aircraft engines and parts		5,854		5,357		5,415		4,888		5,839		7,888
Piston engines and parts²		113		95		172		141		191		203
Complete engines, new and used	2,843	41	2,511	28	4,480	84	4,781	54	5,735	70	3,458	47
Engine parts		71		66		88		87		121		156
Reaction/turbine engines and parts³		5,741		5,262		5,243		4,747		5,649		7,685
Complete engines, new and used	2,849	2,650	2,423	2,569	2,298	2,672	2,752	1,774	5,964	1,937	4,247	2,949
Engine parts		3,092		2,694		2,571		2,974		3,712		4,736
Propellers, rotors, and parts		27		22		26	162,446 kg	33	194,634 kg	51	258,265 kg	46
Landing gear and parts		80		57		64	608,960 kg	70	923,106 kg	129	1,225,752 kg	173
Aircraft parts and accessories, not elsewhere classified		3,300		2,639		2,661		2,783		3,601		5,039
Avionics		509		458		472		567		599		699
Flight simulators and parts		206		75		144	322,547 kg	56	391,412 kg	64	550,340 kg	99
Guided missiles and parts		107		108		88		96		128		153
Space vehicles and parts⁴		33		92		216		79		34		151

¹ Revised from previously published data. Revisions to trade data based on U.S. Bureau of the Census, Historical Summary 1989–1993 and 1991–1997.
² Category revised to include camshafts and crankshafts.
³ Category revised to include camshafts and crankshafts; and reaction engines, other than turbojets—except missile and rocket—and their parts.
⁴ Category does not include materials imported by NASA for launching into space.
Note: Totals do not correspond to SIC-based trade statistics because of slightly broader coverage. Detail may not add to totals due to rounding. Data shown for certain products are not comparable to data before 1989 due to category changes made under the Harmonized System.
Source: U.S. Department of Commerce: Bureau of the Census; International Trade Administration.

airplanes alone rose 71 percent. The trend was expected to continue in 1998 and 1999. Student pilot starts were up 8 percent in 1997, reversing a downward trend and providing a good sign for the general aviation industry.

Rotorcraft.   Rotorcraft include helicopters—vertical takeoff and landing vehicles—and tiltrotor or other aircraft that can take off vertically as a helicopter and fly horizontally as an airplane. The shipment and trade figures given below include only helicopters, since tiltrotor aircraft are still under development and have not entered full-scale production.

After reaching a peak of more than $500 million in civil helicopter shipments in 1985, the U.S. industry began a downward trend from which it only recently is emerging. The industry hit a low of $113 million in 1993, and from 1994 to 1997 the shipment value gradually increased to $231 million. The U.S. civil helicopter fleet is expected to reach 5,860 machines by 2002. World production figures for the period 1999–2003 are expected to total $26 billion for both military and civil rotorcraft.

The helicopter industry faces a number of problems, including few properly located public-use heliports, high operating costs, an increasing shortage of realistic actual access to airspace, the release of surplus military helicopters in the civil marketplace, and the use of helicopters owned by public operators, which compete for services provided by private operators. Despite these problems, the industry has some good indicators, such as the outstanding safety record of helicopters, the variety of tasks that only helicopters can do, new models, new corporate mergers and acquisitions, strong sales of new and used helicopters, and new efforts to keep maintenance and operation costs under control.

The year 1997 saw a decline in the number of military surplus turbine helicopters entering the commercial marketplace. From a high of 361 units in 1995, surplused helicopters were forecast to total no more than 250 units in 1997 and no more than 100 units in 1998. Furthermore, many of the helicopters that have been transferred from the military are not in working order. Among the 1,085 military surplus helicopters that were delivered to the commercial market since 1993, about 800 have been assigned to local law enforcement and other public agencies. Of these, about 40 percent are currently unflyable. The public service fleet is a substantial asset which could be upgraded with newer helicopters.

The important civil helicopter markets are largely unchanged. The emergency medical services account for 10 to 20 percent of deliveries. Law enforcement agencies have 5 to 15 percent of the market although they are likely to use military surplus machines, particularly the Bell OH-58. Corporate travel accounts for 25 to 30 percent of the market and general utility roles represent 30 to 35 percent of all civil sales. The offshore oil market for helicopters is quite low at just 10 percent of the world market.

Although no market increases are foreseen in the helicopter industry, the future looks much brighter than it did a decade ago. The current fleet is aging rapidly and will require replacement. Furthermore, the industry has developed more maintenance-friendly, quieter, more fuel-efficient, and more economical helicopters which will encourage experienced customers to move to a new generation of machines.

Other rotorcraft include tiltrotor, tiltwing, advancing blade, X-wing, canard rotor wing, compound helicopter, and verticraft, which combine the vertical takeoff and landing (VTOL) capability with a faster forward speed than that of a traditional heli-copter. One of these is the Bell Boeing V-22 Osprey, a tactical transport and combat assault aircraft that combines the vertical takeoff, hover, and vertical landing qualities of a helicopter with the long range, fuel efficiency, and speed of a turboprop airplane. The V-22 program has been approved for low-rate initial production by the DOD, with aircraft deliveries scheduled to begin in 1999. Bell Helicopter assumed full ownership in March 1998 and is completing the certification basis for the Bell 609 civil tiltrotor with the FAA. The 609 is the first of its kind to be certified by any aviation agency in the world, and it is necessary to come to an early agreement on what will be required of the manufacturers before production of the aircraft begins. The 609 will be the first vertical flight aircraft certified using electronic data submittal, the first "on-line" certification program. Other certification agencies around the world are watching the progress of the 609 so that when the time comes to certify in other countries, those agencies will be ready to handle it. Market acceptance of the aircraft has been greater than expected; in September 1998 Bell had 68 commitments from more than 40 customers. The markets where the 609 will be used vary from corporate shuttle to resource support (offshore oil). Bell is talking to government agencies about using the 609 in place of their existing helicopters and fixed-wing aircraft. Bell also is working on the Eagle Eye Tiltrotor Unmanned Air Vehicle (UAV).

Growth and Trade Projections

The value of aircraft shipments is expected to increase 24 percent in 1998 over 1997 and increase another 4 percent in 1999. Shipments are expected to grow 3 to 4 percent a year through 2003. Exports, representing about 42 percent of 1996 shipments, increased 34 percent in 1997 and are expected to increase 25 percent in 1998 (see Table 21-6).

TABLE 21-6: Aircraft (SIC 3721) Trends and Forecasts
(millions of dollars except as noted)

	1992[1]	1993	1994	1995[1]	1996	1997[2]	1998[3]	1999[4]	Percent Change 96–97	Percent Change 97–98	Percent Change 98–99	Percent Change 92–96[5]
Industry data												
Value of shipments[6]	62,940	55,120	50,970	47,028	47,313	58,668	72,750	75,295	24.0	24.0	3.5	−6.9
Value of shipments (1992$)	62,940	53,775	48,131	42,909	41,870	51,238	63,537	65,760	22.4	24.0	3.5	−9.7
Total employment (thousands)	265	241	218	189	188							−8.2
Production workers (thousands)	122	104	92.9	84.0	84.5							−8.8
Average hourly earnings ($)	20.00	19.90	20.75	22.15	23.12							3.7
Capital expenditures	1,660	1,154	877	568	622							−21.8
Product data												
Value of shipments[6]	56,569	51,006	46,814	44,457	44,584	55,285	68,550	70,950	24.0	24.0	3.5	−5.8
Value of shipments (1992$)	56,569	49,762	44,206	40,563	39,455	48,284	59,869	61,965	22.4	24.0	3.5	−8.6
Trade data												
Value of imports	3,863	3,809	3,722	3,655	3,947	4,668	5,600	5,800	18.3	20.0	3.6	0.5
Value of exports	26,292	21,279	18,810	13,852	18,984	25,509	32,000	33,120	34.4	25.4	3.5	−7.9

[1] Revised.
[2] Estimate except imports and exports.
[3] Estimate.
[4] Forecast.
[5] Compound annual rate.
[6] For definition of industry versus product values, see "Getting the Most Out of *Outlook '99*."
Source: U.S. Department of Commerce: Bureau of the Census; International Trade Administration.

Aircraft Engines and Parts

Due to environmental concerns, cost, and the reduced availability of 100 low-lead (100LL) aviation gasoline (avgas), the FAA's Technical Center is conducting research on an unleaded replacement. That research will lead to the development of a specification, with the American Society of Testing and Materials (ASTM), for an unleaded avgas to replace the currently available 100LL avgas. A number of issues have contributed to the urgency associated with this program. The first issue is the statutory requirements established by the 1990 Clean Air Act Amendments, which called for the elimination of tetraethyl lead from all fuels by January 1, 1996. That legislation also required that all new and remanufactured engines sold in the United States after January 1, 1992, be certified to operate on unleaded fuels. The U.S. Environmental Protection Agency, however, issued an exemption for light aircraft engines, based on efforts to develop a replacement fuel. Additionally, the Montreal Protocol mandated the elimination of methyl bromide compounds, which are products of the combustion of 100LL in general aviation aircraft engines, by 1998. Other considerations that will affect the availability and price of the current avgas include the need to segregate avgas from all other fuels, the cost of maintaining systems that are contaminated with lead, and the political climate, in which it is likely that aircraft will be identified as the principal sources of airborne lead, hydrocarbons, and methyl bromide emissions. (The numbers of general aviation aircraft are small, but each engine is significantly dirtier than a current-technology automotive engine.) Research at the FAA Technical Center is being conducted with industry participation through the Coordinating Research Council to address issues such as engine detonation, material compatibility, volatility (vapor lock), engine performance, storage stability, water reaction, emissions, changes in fuel consumption, and engine durability (engine life and component wear).

While some analysts were looking to unleaded avgas as a solution to environmental problems and cost issues, others were looking to diesel engines to solve those problems for aircraft whose requirement is 500 brake horsepower or less. Turbine aircraft engines run on cheap kerosene, aviation turbine fuel (AvTur), which is available throughout the world. This fuel is not volatile enough to ignite in spark ignition systems. To run on AvTur, a piston engine must burn fuel by compression ignition, that is, the diesel system. There are currently no diesel aeroengines in regular use anywhere in the world. These engines were popular prior to World War II, before turbojet engines replaced large piston engines. In the late 1980s an Italian firm began work on a four-stroke diesel aircraft engine. Since then engine makers in France, Germany, the United Kingdom, Austria, and the United States have developed their own diesel programs. Teledyne Continental is conducting a research and development program with aid from the National Aeronautics and Space Administration's (NASA) General Aviation Propulsion program. Textron Lycoming is also studying the idea.

Growth and Trade Projections for Aircraft Engines and Parts

The value of shipments in the aircraft engine and parts industry is expected to increase 20 percent in 1998 over 1997 and about 3 percent in 1999. Shipments are expected to increase 3 to 4 percent a year through 2003. Exports, representing 40 percent of 1996 shipments, increased 25 percent in 1997 and were expected to increase 20 percent in 1998 (see Table 21-7).

TABLE 21-7: Aircraft Engines and Engine Parts (SIC 3724) Trends and Forecasts
(millions of dollars except as noted)

	1992[1]	1993	1994	1995[1]	1996	1997[2]	1998[3]	1999[4]	Percent Change 96–97	97–98	98–99	92–96[5]
Industry data												
Value of shipments[6]	22,408	18,946	16,584	17,519	18,769	23,085	27,700	28,550	23.0	20.0	3.1	−4.3
Value of shipments (1992$)	22,408	18,538	15,855	16,450	17,315	20,929	25,113	25,884	20.9	20.0	3.1	−6.2
Total employment (thousands)	117	103	84.2	76.3	75.1							−11.1
Production workers (thousands)	66.5	53.6	45.5	41.9	41.4							−11.2
Average hourly earnings ($)	17.25	17.15	18.79	18.17	19.98							3.7
Capital expenditures	598	440	435	475	485							−5.1
Product data												
Value of shipments[6]	20,933	17,995	15,218	15,811	17,017	21,100	25,320	26,080	24.0	20.0	3.0	−5.0
Value of shipments (1992$)	20,933	17,608	14,549	14,846	15,698	19,130	22,956	23,645	21.9	20.0	3.0	−6.9
Trade data												
Value of imports	5,729	5,223	5,243	4,878	5,831	7,685	9,300	9,590	31.8	21.0	3.1	0.4
Value of exports	6,657	6,192	6,517	6,127	6,807	8,536	10,240	10,550	25.4	20.0	3.0	0.6

[1] Revised.
[2] Estimate except imports and exports.
[3] Estimate.
[4] Forecast.
[5] Compound annual rate.
[6] For definition of industry versus product values, see "Getting the Most Out of *Outlook '99*."
Source: U.S. Department of Commerce: Bureau of the Census; International Trade Administration.

(millions of dollars except as noted)

	1992	1993	1994	1995[1]	1996	1997[2]	1998[3]	1999[4]	96–97	97–98	98–99	92–96[5]
Industry data												
Value of shipments[6]	19,511	18,264	17,049	16,848	17,312	21,035	25,240	26,000	21.5	20.0	3.0	−2.9
Value of shipments (1992$)	19,511	17,750	16,206	15,939	16,029	19,210	23,050	23,744	19.8	20.0	3.0	−4.8
Total employment (thousands)	165	139	122	116	113							−8.8
Production workers (thousands)	93.6	78.4	66.1	64.0	64.5							−8.5
Average hourly earnings ($)	16.71	18.37	19.20	19.73	19.98							4.6
Capital expenditures	1,132	713	656	673	916							−4.7
Product data												
Value of shipments[6]	21,940	18,684	17,710	17,701	18,832	22,882	27,460	28,280	21.5	20.0	3.0	−3.7
Value of shipments (1992$)	21,940	18,157	16,835	16,747	17,437	20,897	25,078	25,826	19.8	20.0	3.0	−5.6
Trade data												
Value of imports	3,094	2,443	2,460	2,517	3,344	4,548	5,500	5,670	36.0	20.9	3.1	2.0
Value of exports	9,087	9,126	9,456	10,056	11,481	12,973	15,700	16,150	13.0	21.0	2.9	6.0

The table also has a "Percent Change" heading spanning the last four columns (96–97, 97–98, 98–99, 92–96[5]).

[1] Revised.
[2] Estimate except imports and exports.
[3] Estimate.
[4] Forecast.
[5] Compound annual rate.
[6] For definition of industry versus product values, see "Getting the Most Out of *Outlook '99.*"
Source: U.S. Department of Commerce: Bureau of the Census; International Trade Administration.

Aircraft Parts and Equipment

A major concern of the FAA is the safety of the flying public. To this end, regulations covering helicopters in normal use (Part 27) and in the transport category (Part 29) were revised. The revisions require that helicopters type-certified after 1989 meet stricter seat load standards to improve crash survivability for the passengers and crew. These changes are the result of the experiences of military pilots who suffered back injuries in crashes such that the occupants could not exit the aircraft. The new standards are optional for buyers of earlier helicopters. Energy-absorbing seats are produced in the United States, the United Kingdom, Germany, and Israel.

The U.S. Air Force (USAF) is also interested in seats that enhance the survivability of an aircraft's occupants. In 1997 the Bureau of Export Administration, U.S. Department of Commerce, conducted a national security assessment of the emergency aircraft ejection seat sector at the request of the USAF. The request came in response to congressional language in H.F. 1530, FY 1996 Defense Authorization Bill, Air Force Research Training Development and Evaluation (RTD&E) on aircraft ejection seats, which stated, "The committee is also concerned about the sustainment of the U.S. [ejection seat] industrial base during this period of virtually no aircraft production." Ejection seats were studied because they enhance the national security by preserving the lives and thus the operational experience of war fighters.

Major reductions in U.S. defense procurement of new combat aircraft in the last decade have severely eroded the market for new ejection seats. The smaller market has been accompanied by a sharp drop in employment and in the specialized expertise required to design and produce ejection seats. The United States has one active producer. Based on current projec-tions, the prospects for an expanded market in 1998–2003 are not encouraging. It appears likely that without cooperative industry-government action, the future market for ejection seats will be forfeited to major foreign concerns.

The Bureau of Export Administration's report made the following recommendations: facilitate greater rationalization (elimination of redundancy) and consolidation in the U.S. ejection seat industry with procurement and RTD&E policies and discussions with industry and where appropriate and possible, support U.S. teaming licensing agreements with foreign manufacturers for production sharing and technology exchange on a worldwide basis.

Growth and Trade Projections for Aircraft Parts and Equipment

The value of other aircraft parts and equipment shipments is expected to increase 20 percent in 1998 over 1997 and approximately 3 percent in 1999. Shipments are expected to increase 3 to 4 percent a year through 2003. Exports, representing 60 percent of 1996 shipments, increased 13 percent in 1997 and were expected to increase 21 percent in 1998 (see Table 21-8).

Ronald D. Green, U.S. Department of Commerce, Office of Aerospace, (202) 482-3068, ronald_green@ita.doc.gov, October 1998.

MISSILES AND SPACE LAUNCH VEHICLES

The guided missiles and space vehicle and parts industry covers guided missiles and space vehicles (SIC 3761), guided missile and space vehicle propulsion units and parts (SIC

3764), and guided missile and space vehicle parts and auxiliary equipment, not elsewhere classified (SIC 3769).

Missile Systems

Missiles systems include guided missiles, guided missile propulsion units and parts, and guided missile parts and auxiliary equipment, not elsewhere classified.

Global Outlook

Europe's missile programs have been affected by a stream of budget problems which have jeopardized the success of several programs and have encouraged collaboration and consolidation in the European missile industry. For short-range air-to-air missiles, Germany is developing the IRIS-T with Canada, Greece, Italy, Norway, Sweden, and the Netherlands. The United Kingdom's ASRAAM has nearly finished operational tests and will enter into service in the Royal Air Force in 1998. The United Kingdom also is developing the Beyond Visual Range Air-to-Air Missile (BVRAAM), which is larger and more powerful than the previous standard, the U.S. Aim-9 Sidewinder. Matra BAe is developing the Apache-AP and Storm/Shadow Scalp EG for the air-to-surface market. Russia is developing the Vympel R-74, a follow-on of its R-73 (AA-11 Archer). A smaller but emerging provider is Israel with Rafael's Python-3 and Python-4 missiles. The Python-3 has been exported to Chile, China, Thailand, and South Africa, while the follow-on Python-4 has been designed to be more powerful than the Aim-9 Sidewinder. Outside the short-range sector, in the beyond-visual-range area, the Europeans and Russians effectively do not offer much competition to the United States. Even with the French MICA and the Russian R-77, international orders for the U.S. AIM-120 AMRAAM are foremost.

The French Mistral missile is one of the most successful low-cost, low-altitude air defense missiles. Export sales of the Mistral have been strong while sales of other systems have been weak, mainly because of its adaptability, from being human-portable to vehicle/warship-mounted. The French Aster missiles are being adapted for land and naval use and are currently in initial production. In the antitank and antiship missiles sectors, European programs remain in jeopardy due to budget cuts, causing European governments to look to U.S. missiles as alternatives. The only exception may be the Eryx antitank missile, a lightweight portable system that has been ordered by five countries. In Israel the Arrow2, a theater ballistic missile interceptor, is in the testing stage and successfully destroyed a target missile in March 1997 even though the warhead failed to arm.

Domestic Outlook

Industry consolidation encouraged the merger of Raytheon and Hughes and thus created the world's largest missile manufacturer, currently accounting for more than half the missile market. Raytheon is now the dominant provider of air-to-air missiles and a key provider of air-to-surface and surface-to-air missiles. Other domestic producers include Boeing (incorporating missile-producing units from McDonnell Douglas and Rockwell), Lockheed Martin, and a number of smaller producers. The new Raytheon/Hughes manufactures the U.S. AIM-120 AMRAAM, the follow-on to the AIM-7 and one of the most extensively sold missile systems in the world. The AIM-120's unit price has been cut about 50 percent, with the Pentagon planning to buy these missiles until 2007. The follow-on version probably will not reach production until 2010. The AMRAAM, long considered the standard for medium-range air-to-air missiles, is scheduled for a series of upgrades, including enhanced electronic counter-countermeasures, software refinements, guidance improvements, and an extended rocket motor. Because of the ability to lower costs, the United States is upgrading existing weapons systems rather than looking to new developments such as the British BVRAAM.

Air-to-surface missiles are being improved through the use of the Global Positioning System (GPS) for guidance and navigation. GPS allows a missile to identify its target through the use of satellites and to identify the surface below it by using near-real-time satellite data. Earlier systems used terrain guidance mapping, which did not permit the quick retargeting that GPS allows. Most air-to-surface missiles programs are using upgraded GPS guidance packages. The GPS navigation system may be used alone or in conjunction with inertial guidance systems, depending on the type of missile. In addition to the guidance upgrade, other improvements are being examined for the Joint Direct Attack Munition (JDAM) such as powering up while still on the wing, acquiring the GPS signal after a missile's release from an aircraft, and linking the aircraft's GPS system with the GPS system on the JDAM. In the long run the JDAM also may receive GPS antijam capability, alternative warheads, and extended range capability. The U.S. Navy also plans to increase the JDAM's accuracy from 10 feet to 3 feet through the deployment of a terminal guidance seeker that is scheduled to be used around 2001 or 2002. The Navy has also proposed the Sea Launched Attack Missile (SLAM) for joint service with the Air Force in the Joint Air to Surface Standoff Missile Program (JASSM). The Navy feels that its SLAM-ER (extended range) could meet the needs for both services, while the Air Force believes that proceeding with its version of the JASSM missile would be preferable. In April 1998 Lockheed Martin was selected to produce the USAF JASSM, a contract which is worth up to $2 billion.

Air defense missiles can be divided into low-altitude, infrared systems; sophisticated, high-altitude, radar-guided systems; and midrange, mobile launchers (usually using semi-active radar or command guidance). The low-altitude systems, such as the U.S. Stinger missile, tend to be less expensive and offer varying degrees of sophistication and mobility. This allows them to address a larger market that can select the exact type of weapon needed. The more sophisticated radar-guided missiles have been dominated by the U.S. Patriot. The Patriot is being considered for upgrades, including radar modifications, communications upgrades, and remote launch capability. The United States is developing a number of high-altitude systems, including the Theater High Altitude Defense System (THAAD), the Standard Block 4A, and the PAC-3. The THAAD system has had a series of five test failures which

TABLE 21-9: Guided Missiles and Space Vehicles (SIC 3761) Trends and Forecasts
(millions of dollars except as noted)

	1992	1993	1994	1995[1]	1996	1997[2]	1998[3]	1999[4]	Percent Change			
									96–97	97–98	98–99	92–96[5]
Industry data												
Value of shipments[6]	19,423	15,800	13,954	14,315	13,777	16,945	19,656	21,818	23.0	16.0	11.0	−8.2
Value of shipments (1992$)	19,423	15,628	13,899	14,372	14,262	16,811	19,500	21,645	17.9	16.0	11.0	−7.4
Total employment (thousands)	97.7	86.6	68.5	60.8	55.7							−13.1
Production workers (thousands)	30.1	27.6	23.8	20.0	18.6							−11.3
Average hourly earnings ($)	22.58	20.88	21.30	20.65	21.81							−0.9
Capital expenditures	313	308	297	294	367							4.1
Product data												
Value of shipments[6]	13,972	13,452	10,983	11,756	10,536	12,749	14,406	15,072	21.0	13.0	4.6	−6.8
Value of shipments (1992$)	13,972	13,306	10,939	11,804	10,907	12,648	14,292	14,952	16.0	13.0	4.6	−6.0
Trade data												
Value of imports	4.1	5.2	1.6	2.7	1.1	0.2	0.6	1.0	−81.8	200.0	66.7	−28.0
Value of exports	595	511	376	717	608	462	512	553	−24.0	10.8	8.0	0.4

[1] Revised.
[2] Estimate except imports and exports.
[3] Estimate.
[4] Forecast.
[5] Compound annual rate.
[6] For definition of industry versus product values, see "Getting the Most Out of *Outlook '99*."
Source: U.S. Department of Commerce: Bureau of the Census; International Trade Administration.

have delayed production of 40 operation evaluation system missiles.

Antitank missiles do not constitute a major missile sector, but the Javelin, Hellfire, Longbow, and TOW missiles remain in production in the United States. The Javelin is currently planned to be the first antitank missile to use infrared imaging guidance technology. Little development is planned for the antiship missiles sector, as the U.S. Navy continues to rely on the proven Tomahawk and Harpoon missiles. In addition, the Navy is proposing modifications to the existing Harpoon's guidance systems to enable that missile to attack land-based targets as well. Approximately 3,000 Harpoons have been bought for domestic use, with an equal number being sold internationally. While international sales of ballistic missiles are restricted by the international Missile Technology Control Regime (MTCR), the United States continues to upgrade the Minuteman-3, the primary U.S. intercontinental ballistic missile (ICBM). The maintenance contract for the Minuteman-3 ICBM over the next 15 years was awarded to TRW in January 1998 and is worth up to $3.4 billion.

Growth and Trade Projections

The missile sector will have fewer procurements over the next few years, although the appearance on the market of new, smaller providers such as Israel and South Africa may offer customers more choice. With the expected decline in procurements, consolidation of the industry is expected to continue on a global basis. Efforts through the MTCR to limit the proliferation of nuclear weapons will keep trade in long-range missiles low. The MTCR is strongly enforced by the United States and several European countries in an attempt to keep countries that do not have such capabilities from developing or purchasing them.

Thus, the developing world will continue to have restricted access to cruise missiles. Air defense missiles will remain the largest portion of the global missile market. Exports of the U.S. Aim-120 and exports in the air-to-air sector as a whole will remain strong (see Table 21-9).

LAUNCH VEHICLES

This section covers the space vehicles and parts component, space vehicle propulsion units and parts, and space launch vehicle parts and auxiliary equipment.

Global Subsector Outlook

On a global basis, the international commercial launch services market will thrive over the next 5 years as providers of satellite services rush to get their new satellites into orbit. The current market leader, the European consortium Arianespace, will experience continued success in this period, especially as it continues to use the Ariane 4 rocket and begins to offer commercial launches on the newer and larger Ariane 5 launch vehicle. Arianespace probably will maintain its hold on approximately 40 percent of launches for the commercial satellite market but will face increasing competition from nonmarket economy providers such as Russia, China, and Ukraine. The Ariane 5 launch vehicle was expected to carry its first commercial payload in late 1998, signal the beginning of the phaseout of the Ariane 4 rocket over the next 5 years.

In 1997 Arianespace launched 17 satellites on 11 Ariane 4 launch vehicles and one Ariane 5, up from 10 Ariane 4 launches in 1996. With the appearance of the Ariane 5, commercial launches gradually will be shifted to the new, larger vehicle, which will be able to simultaneously launch one heavy- and one medium-class satellite. Plans also exist for the development of an even larger version of the Ariane 5, which would be capable of carrying two heavy-class payloads to orbit on the same rocket.

The launch vehicles of the former Soviet Union (mostly Russia and Ukraine) are being marketed mainly through international joint ventures with western countries. The Russian Proton launch vehicle is marketed by International Launch Services in conjunction with the American Atlas rocket. The Ukrainian Zenit launch vehicle is marketed by Boeing through the Sea Launch consortium, which will offer launches from a sea-based platform. The Proton had its first commercial launch in 1996 and has a full manifest through 1999, while Sea Launch will begin commercial launches in 1999 with a full schedule. Both companies are developing upgrades of and improvements in these launch vehicles which will allow heavier satellites to be launched with less time between launches.

China is also offering launch services in the international commercial market but has captured only a small market share (3 to 5 percent) because of a string of failures in 1996. China has contract options to launch up to five Loral satellites and five Hughes satellites on its Long March 3B rocket.

Japan is developing a commercial launch vehicle, the H-2A, which is scheduled to have its first commercial launch in 2001. Japan is updating and enlarging the infrastructure at Tanegashima, its launch site, which will be used for a longer proportion of the year, due to a new agreement with Japanese fishermen whose jobs are affected by the launches.

While the majority of launch vehicles mentioned above focus on launches of satellites to geostationary earth orbit (GEO), a number of smaller launch vehicles are targeting the low earth orbit (LEO) market. The Starsem joint venture is a partnership between Russian and French firms to market the Russian Soyuz vehicle for LEO launches. Starsem was scheduled to hold its first launch, for Globalstar, in 1998. India is developing a Polar Satellite Launch Vehicle (PSLV) so that it will have a domestic ability to launch its remote sensing satellites. India has not yet contracted for any international commercial launches. Brazil is also seeking to enter the international commercial market for space launch services with its VLS-1 rocket. It is expanding the capabilities of its launch site, Alcantera, which is attractive to many foreign launch vehicle manufacturers that would like to gain better efficiency from launching at this equatorial site. Brazil has four noncommercial launches scheduled between 1997 and 2001.

Domestic Subsector Outlook

Strong foreign competition in both large and small launch vehicles has pushed U.S. launch services providers to examine international partnerships, new technologies, and new ways of doing business. This type of international partnership led Boeing to acquire Ukrainian Zenit launch vehicles for its Sea Launch project and led Lockheed Martin to market the Russian Proton rocket in coordination with the U.S. Atlas launch vehicle. The Sea Launch project will tow a Ukrainain rocket and a launch pad to the equator and launch from the middle of the Pacific Ocean. In addition to Sea Launch, Boeing maintains its domestic capability through the Delta family of launch vehicles. The newest, largest member of its family, the Delta 3, failed on its maiden launch in August 1998. There are plans to build a still larger vehicle, the Delta 4, for the U.S. Air Force's Evolved Expendable Launch Vehicle program.

TABLE 21-10: Guided Missile and Space Vehicle Propulsion Units and Parts (SIC 3764) Trends and Forecasts
(millions of dollars except as noted)

	1992	1993	1994	1995[1]	1996	1997[2]	1998[3]	1999[4]	96–97	97–98	98–99	92–96[5]
									Percent Change			
Industry data												
Value of shipments[6]	5,121	6,201	3,374	2,954	2,715	3,025	3,406	3,743	11.4	12.6	9.9	−14.7
Value of shipments (1992$)	5,121	6,134	3,360	2,968	2,819	3,001	3,379	3,713	6.4	12.6	9.9	−13.9
Total employment (thousands)	32.0	29.2	22.8	19.6	17.2							−14.4
Production workers (thousands)	13.2	8.9	7.8	6.7	5.5							−19.7
Average hourly earnings ($)	23.81	22.03	22.10	19.60	20.61							−3.5
Capital expenditures	121	85.4	68.9	48.8	77.5							−10.5
Product data												
Value of shipments[6]	5,207	5,862	3,705	2,984	2,803	3,111	3,422	3,696	11.0	10.0	8.0	−14.3
Value of shipments (1992$)	5,207	5,799	3,690	2,999	2,911	3,086	3,395	3,667	6.0	10.0	8.0	−13.5
Trade data												
Value of imports	0.4	0.2	0.0	0.4	14.6	43.1	37.0	39.0	195.2	−14.2	5.4	145.8
Value of exports	12.6	1.1	17.3	40.1	22.3	5.4	5.6	5.9	−75.8	3.7	5.4	15.3

[1] Revised.
[2] Estimate except imports and exports.
[3] Estimate.
[4] Forecast.
[5] Compound annual rate.
[6] For definition of industry versus product values, see "Getting the Most Out of *Outlook '99*."
Source: U.S. Department of Commerce: Bureau of the Census; International Trade Administration.

TABLE 21-11: Guided Missile and Space Vehicle Parts and Auxiliary Equipment, n.e.c. (SIC 3769) Trends and Forecasts
(millions of dollars except as noted)

	1992	1993	1994	1995[1]	1996	1997[2]	1998[3]	1999[4]	Percent Change 96–97	Percent Change 97–98	Percent Change 98–99	Percent Change 92–96[5]
Industry data												
Value of shipments[6]	1,964	2,015	1,386	1,398	1,436	1,551	1,691	1,908	8.0	9.0	12.8	−7.5
Value of shipments (1992$)	1,964	1,991	1,381	1,406	1,504	1,536	1,674	1,889	2.1	9.0	12.8	−6.5
Total employment (thousands)	16.2	12.3	9.1	8.8	8.1							−15.9
Production workers (thousands)	6.8	5.6	4.7	4.6	4.8							−8.3
Average hourly earnings ($)	18.04	19.95	20.29	21.49	20.98							3.8
Capital expenditures	33.8	25.3	29.1	37.0	45.0							7.4
Product data												
Value of shipments[6]	4,179	3,313	2,727	2,602	2,451	2,623	2,807	2,975	7.0	7.0	6.0	−12.5
Value of shipments (1992$)	4,179	3,273	2,719	2,618	2,566	2,597	2,779	2,946	1.2	7.0	6.0	−11.5
Trade data												
Value of imports	103	103	86.2	93.7	112	109	107	109	−2.7	−1.8	1.9	1.9
Value of exports	846	745	744	765	684	690	712	730	0.9	3.2	2.5	−5.0

[1] Revised.
[2] Estimate except imports and exports.
[3] Estimate.
[4] Forecast.
[5] Compound annual rate.
[6] For definition of industry versus product values, see "Getting the Most Out of *Outlook '99.*"
Source: U.S. Department of Commerce: Bureau of the Census; International Trade Administration.

To better serve its launch customers, Lockheed Martin established the International Launch Services (ILS) joint venture to market the Proton, the Atlas, and the smaller Athena launch vehicles. Both the Proton and the Atlas have full launch schedules in 1999–2000, with a backlog of nearly $3 billion in international sales. Lockheed Martin is planning improvements in and upgrades of the Proton and Atlas rockets to make them capable of carrying larger, heavier payloads. For example, Lockheed Martin will use Russian-designed rocket engines on the upgraded Atlas rockets, an idea that was unimaginable during the height of the cold war. The Athena is designed mainly to launch small payloads into LEO, but Lockheed Martin is developing a follow-on Athena (Athena 3) that will be able to launch payloads up to 3,960 pounds to GTO.

Orbital Sciences launches small payloads with its Pegasus and Taurus launch vehicles. Both vehicles offer the unique capability of physically launching from anywhere in the world. The Pegasus is air-launched from the belly of an L-1011 aircraft which takes off from a normal runway, while the Taurus requires only a basic concrete base and a small tower structure for launching.

With the forecast growth in demand for commercial satellites, government agencies as well as entrepreneurial firms are researching new technologies and developing new rockets. NASA is sponsoring the X-33 and X-34 programs to encourage the development of reusable launch vehicle prototypes, which could then be adapted as commercial launch vehicles. Lockheed Martin (X-33) and Orbital Sciences (X-34) plan to finish the prototypes by the end of 2000 and prove that the cost of launch can be reduced and that reusable launch vehicles are a viable option for the commercial sector.

At least four entrepreneurial firms—Kelly Space & Technology, Pioneer Rocketplane, Kistler Aerospace, and Rotary Rocket Company—are using private investments to develop reusable rockets. Each has a unique concept—from towing the rocket behind a Boeing 747 to using helicopter blades for a vertical landing—that separates it from the 20- to 30-year-old technology currently used in rockets. Although it is unclear whether any of these programs will develop into profitable commercial systems, their presence has pushed the development of new technologies while lowering the cost of launch.

Growth and Trade Projections

The commercial space launch industry is expected to experience steady growth through 1998 and 1999, while launches of new satellite systems such as Iridium and Globalstar are in high demand. Once these systems have their basic systems on-orbit, launches will level out for 2 to 3 years, after which replacement and follow-on systems will increase the number of launches again. The high demand for launches will be addressed by the appearance of several new launch services providers. Small launch vehicles will experience steady growth because of the need for remote sensing satellite systems, scientific experiments, and replacement launches for LEO communications systems (see Tables 21-9, 21-10, and 21-11).

Kim Wells, U.S. Department of Commerce, Office of Aerospace, (202) 482-2232, September 1998.

REFERENCES

Aircraft, Engines, and Parts

"Aerospace Daily," 1156 15th Street, NW, Washington, DC 20005. (202) 822-4600.

Aerospace Facts and Figures, 1997–1998, Aerospace Industries Association, 1250 Eye Street, NW, Washington, DC 20005. (202) 371-8400, http://www.aia-aerospace.org.

"Aerospace Industry (Orders, Sales, and Backlog) Current Industrial Report MA37D," Bureau of the Census, U.S. Department of Commerce, Washington, DC 20233. http://www.census.gov/cir/www.ma37d.html.

Air Transport World, 1350 Connecticut Avenue, NW, Washington, DC 20036. (202) 659-8500, http://www.atwonline.com.

Aviation Week & Space Technology, 1221 Avenue of the Americas, New York, NY 10020. (212) 512-2000, http://www.awgnet.com/aviation.

The Boeing Company, P.O. Box 3707, Seattle, WA 98124. http://www.boeing.com.

"Civil Aircraft and Aircraft Engines, Current Industrial Report M37G," Bureau of the Census, U.S. Department of Commerce, Washington, DC 20233. http://www.census.gov/cir/www.m37g.html.

Defense News, 6883 Commercial Drive, Springfield, VA 22159. (703) 658-8400, http://www.defensenews.com.

European Diversification and Defense Market Assessment, A Comprehensive Guide for Entry into Oversears Markets, June 1995. Office of Strategic Industries and Economic Security, Bureau of Export Administration, U.S. Department of Commerce, Washington, DC 20230. http://www.bxa.doc.gov.

FAA Aviation Forecasts, Fiscal Years 1998–2009, Office of Aviation Policy and Plans, Federal Aviation Administration, U.S. Department of Transportation, Washington, DC 20591. http://api.hq.faa.gov.

Flight International, Quadrant House, The Quadrant, Sutton, Surrey, SM2 5AS, United Kingdom. http://www.reedbusiness.com.

Flug Review. http://www.flug-revue.rotor.com.

Future Aviation Activities 10th International Workshop, Transportation Research Board, National Research Council, 2101 Constitution Avenue, NW, Washington, DC 20418. http://www.nas.edu/trb.

General Aviation Statistical Databook, 1998 Edition, General Aviation Manufacturers Association, 1400 K Street, NW, Washington, DC 20005. (202) 393-1500, http://www.generalaviation.org.

"Industrial Production and Capacity Utilization," Board of Governors of the Federal Reserve System, Washington, DC 20551.

Interavia, Swissair Centre, 31 Route de L'Aéroport, P.O. Box 437, CH-1215 Geneva, Switzerland.

International Monetary Fund, Washington, DC 20431. http://www.imf.org.

Market Research Reports, National Trade Data Bank, U.S. and Foreign Commercial Service, International Trade Administration, U.S. Department of Commerce, Washington, DC 20230.

Middle East Diversification and Defense Market Assessment, A Comprehensive Guide for Entry into Oversears Markets, July 1996. Office of Strategic Industries and Economic Security, Bureau of Export Administration, U.S. Department of Commerce, Washington, DC 20230. http://www.bxa.doc.gov.

National Security Assessment of the Emergency Aircraft Ejection Seat Sector, A Report for the U.S. Department of the Air Force, November 1997. Office of Strategic Industries and Economic Security, Bureau of Export Administration, U.S. Department of Commerce, Washington, DC 20230. http://www.bxa.doc.gov.

Office of Aerospace, International Trade Administration, U.S. Department of Commerce. http://www.ita.doc.gov/aerospace.

Pacific Rim Diversification and Defense Market Assessment, A Comprehensive Guide for Entry into Oversears Markets, November 1994. Office of Strategic Industries and Economic Security, Bureau of Export Administration, U.S. Department of Commerce, Washington, DC 20230. http://www.bxa.doc.gov.

"Quarterly Financial Report for Manufacturing, Mining, and Trade Corporations," Bureau of the Census, U.S. Department of Commerce, Washington, DC 20233. http://www.census.gov/agfs/www/qfr.html.

Rotor & Wing, Phillips Business Information, Inc., P.O. Box 61130, 7811 Montose Road, Potomac, MD 20897-5402. (301) 340-2100.

Western Hemisphere Diversification and Defense Market Assessment, A Comprehensive Guide for Entry into Oversears Markets, September 1996. Office of Strategic Industries and Economic Security, Bureau of Export Administration, U.S. Department of Commerce, Washington, DC 20230. http://www.bxa.doc.gov.

"World Military and Civil Aircraft Briefing," Teal Group Corporation, 3900 University Drive, Suite 220, Fairfax, VA 22030. (703) 385-1992.

Missiles and Space Launch Vehicles

"Aerospace Daily," 1156 15th Street, NW, Washington, DC 20005. (202) 822-4600, http://www.awgnews.com.

Aerospace Facts and Figures, 1997–1998, Aerospace Industries Association, 1250 Eye Street, NW, Washington, DC 20005. (202) 371-8400, http://www.aia-aerospace.org.

Aviation Week & Space Technology, 1221 Avenue of the Americas, New York, NY 10020. (212) 512-2000, http://www.awgnet.com/aviation.

Defense News and *Space News,* 6883 Commercial Drive, Springfield, VA 22159. (703) 658-8400, http://www.defensenews.com; http://www.spacenews.com.

International Trade Administration, U.S. Department of Commerce. http://www.ita.doc.gov/aerospace.

Launchspace, Launchspace Publications, Inc., 7929 Westpark Drive, McLean, VA 22102. http://www.launchspace.com.

Low Earth Orbit Commercial Market Projections, Associate Administrator for Commercial Space Transportation, Federal Aviation Administration, Washington, DC 20590. http://ast.faa.gov.

1997 COMSTAC Mission Model Update, Associate Administrator for Commercial Space Transportation, Commercial Space Transportation Advisory Committee, Federal Aviation Administration, Washington, DC 20590. http://ast.faa.gov/comstac.

RELATED CHAPTERS

16: Microelectronics
29: Space Commerce
30: Telecommunications Services
31: Telecommunications and Navigation Equipment
43: Transportation

GLOSSARY

Airframe: Assembled structure of an aircraft, together with the system components that form an integral part of the structure and influence strength, integrity, or shape.

Avionics: Aeronautical electronics, including communications and navigation equipment.

FAA Stage 3 regulations: Requirements that aircraft meet more stringent (lower) noise levels than Stage 2 aircraft as they approach and take off from airports; similar to Chapter 3 of the European Union's regulations.

General aviation aircraft and rotorcraft: Fixed-wing aircraft and rotary-wing aircraft used for regional airline service, business transportation, recreation, specialized uses (such as ambulances and agricultural spraying), and pilot training.

Geostationary earth orbit (GEO): The altitude (22,230 miles) at which a satellite appears to be fixed at a specific spot above the earth.

Global Positioning System (GPS): A system using 24 satellites, all reporting precise time signals, along with location keys; eight satellites are in each of three 63°-incline-plane circular orbits at 11,000 nautical miles altitude; the system is used for navigation and to determine the exact position.

Low earth orbit (LEO): For the purposes of this chapter, any orbit lower than geostationary earth orbit.

Payload: The satellite, instrument package, or equipment carried into space by a launch vehicle.

Rotary-wing aircraft or rotorcraft: An aircraft that delivers lift from a system of rotating airfoils; includes helicopters and the tiltrotor aircraft in the vertical mode.

SHIPBUILDING AND REPAIR
Economic and Trade Trends

U.S. International Trade

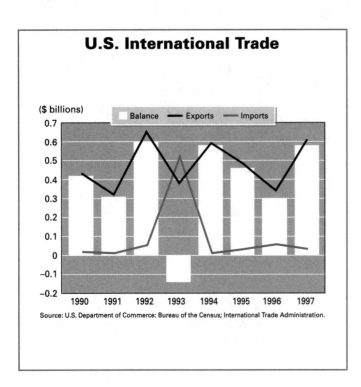

($ billions)

Legend: Balance — Exports — Imports

Source: U.S. Department of Commerce: Bureau of the Census; International Trade Administration.

Commercial Shipbuilding Orderbook

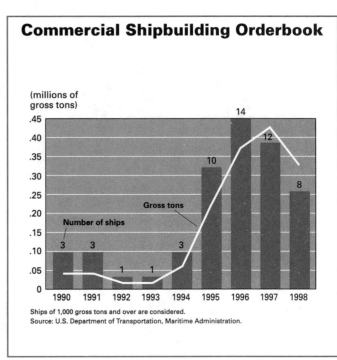

(millions of gross tons)

Gross tons

Number of ships

Ships of 1,000 gross tons and over are considered.
Source: U.S. Department of Transportation, Maritime Administration.

Export Dependence and Import Penetration

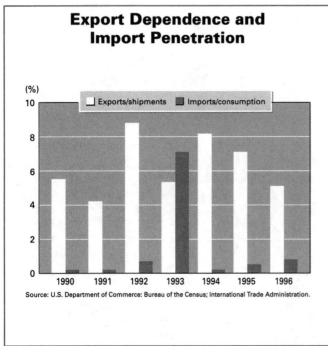

(%)

Legend: Exports/shipments   Imports/consumption

Source: U.S. Department of Commerce: Bureau of the Census; International Trade Administration.

Output and Output per Hour

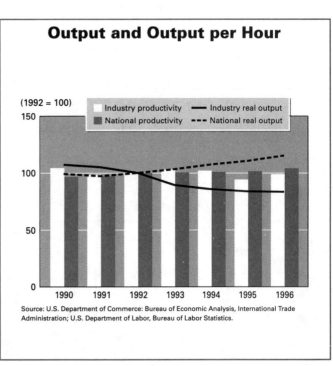

(1992 = 100)

Legend: Industry productivity — Industry real output
National productivity --- National real output

Source: U.S. Department of Commerce: Bureau of Economic Analysis, International Trade Administration; U.S. Department of Labor, Bureau of Labor Statistics.

See "Getting the Most Out of *Outlook '99*" for definitions of terms.

Shipbuilding and Repair

INDUSTRY DEFINITION Shipbuilding and repair (SIC 3731) includes establishments primarily engaged in building and repairing ships, barges, and lighters, whether self-propelled or towed by other craft. This industry also includes the conversion and alteration of ships and the manufacture of off-shore oil- and gas-well drilling and production platforms, whether or not self-propelled. Establishments primarily engaged in fabricating structural assemblies or components for ships and subcontractors engaged in ship painting, joinery, carpentry work, and electrical wiring installation are classified under other industrial codes.

OVERVIEW

The U.S. shipbuilding industry has made progress in reemerging as an active participant in the commercial shipbuilding markets. The stimulus for this development in the industry and the ability of the industry to aggressively enter and compete in these markets was the National Shipbuilding and Conversion Act of 1993 and the expanded Title XI Federal Ship Financing Guarantee Program.

GLOBAL INDUSTRY TRENDS

According to Lloyd's Register *World Shipbuilding Statistics,* the world orderbook for new ships, as measured in gross tons, increased in 1997. As of December 31, 1997, the world orderbook for merchant vessels 100 gross tons (gt) and over consisted of 2,604 vessels totaling 56.6 million gt. This represents a 7.1 percent decline from the 2,802 vessels on order at the close of 1996 but an 18.7 percent increase in gross tonnage from 47.7 million gt in 1996. The average size of merchant ships on order increased a dramatic 27.7 percent from 17,026 gt at the close of 1996 to 21,736 gt at the end of 1997.

At the end of 1997 Japan retained the dominant position in the world merchant shipbuilding market with 35 percent of the gross tonnage of merchant ships on order, followed by South Korea with 33.1 percent and the People's Republic of China with 5.6 percent of the international commercial shipbuilding orderbook (see Figure 22-1).

At the end of 1997 the United States ranked fourteenth among shipbuilding nations with 1 percent of world gross tonnage compared with an orderbook of 1.8 percent of the aggregate in 1996. The U.S. orderbook declined from 854,435 gt to 541,355 gt between the fourth quarter of 1996 and the fourth quarter of 1997, a decrease of 36.6 percent in gross tonnage of ships on order.

U.S. SHIPBUILDING TRENDS

The benchmark used for tracking the U.S. shipbuilding industry is the U.S. Major Shipbuilding Base (MSB), which is defined as privately owned shipyards that are open and have at least one shipbuilding position consisting of an inclined way, a launching platform, or a building basin capable of accommodating a vessel 122 meters in length or larger. With few exceptions, these shipbuilding facilities are also major repair facilities with a drydocking capability. In January 1, 1998, there were 18 major shipbuilding facilities in the United States (see Figure 22-2).

According to the U.S. Department of Labor, aggregate employment in the U.S. shipbuilding and repair industry in December 1997 was 94,300, down 3,400 from the revised December 1996 number of 97,700. MSB shipyards employ about 64 percent of the total work force of the shipbuilding and ship repair industry. The remaining 36 percent worked in the 550 additional establishments (with 10 or more employees) classified under Bureau of Labor Statistics SIC 3731 (ship-

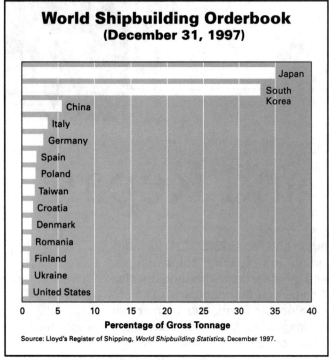

FIGURE 22-1

World Shipbuilding Orderbook
(December 31, 1997)

Japan
South Korea
China
Italy
Germany
Spain
Poland
Taiwan
Croatia
Denmark
Romania
Finland
Ukraine
United States

0   5   10   15   20   25   30   35   40

Percentage of Gross Tonnage

Source: Lloyd's Register of Shipping, *World Shipbuilding Statistics*, December 1997.

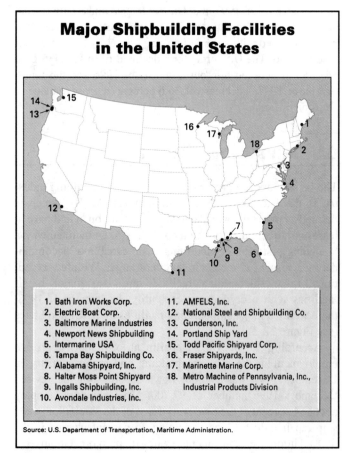

FIGURE 22-2

Major Shipbuilding Facilities in the United States

1. Bath Iron Works Corp.
2. Electric Boat Corp.
3. Baltimore Marine Industries
4. Newport News Shipbuilding
5. Intermarine USA
6. Tampa Bay Shipbuilding Co.
7. Alabama Shipyard, Inc.
8. Halter Moss Point Shipyard
9. Ingalls Shipbuilding, Inc.
10. Avondale Industries, Inc.
11. AMFELS, Inc.
12. National Steel and Shipbuilding Co.
13. Gunderson, Inc.
14. Portland Ship Yard
15. Todd Pacific Shipyard Corp.
16. Fraser Shipyards, Inc.
17. Marinette Marine Corp.
18. Metro Machine of Pennsylvania, Inc., Industrial Products Division

Source: U.S. Department of Transportation, Maritime Administration.

building and repairing). Not included in SIC 3731 are the five government-owned shipyards, which do not engage in new construction but instead overhaul and repair Navy and Coast Guard ships. In October 1997, total employment in the five government shipyards was 22,735.

Industry Revitalization Efforts

Recognizing that U.S. shipyards had to be able to compete in the international commercial shipbuilding market to remain viable, the federal government developed a multifaceted program to improve the industry's competitiveness in the international commercial shipbuilding market. On October 1, 1993, President Clinton submitted to Congress the report *Strengthening America's Shipyards: A Plan for Competing in the International Market*. This report formed the basis for the administration's efforts to help the U.S. shipbuilding industry translate its skills from military requirements to a commercial focus in order to compete and obtain orders from international shipowners, substantially increasing the industry's customer base. The President's five-part plan includes:

■ Ensuring fair international competition

■ Eliminating unnecessary government regulation

■ Assisting international marketing

■ Financing ship sales through Title XI loan guarantees

■ Improving commercial competitiveness through MARITECH

To implement the plan, on November 30, 1993, the President signed into law the National Defense Authorization Act of 1994, which contained the National Shipbuilding and Shipyard Conversion Act of 1993. The latter act expanded the existing Title XI Federal Ship Financing Program by authorizing the Secretary of Transportation to guarantee obligations issued to finance the construction, reconstruction, or reconditioning of eligible export vessels. It also authorized guarantees for shipyard modernization and improvement projects. The Shipyard Act established a National Shipbuilding Initiative (NSI) program to support the industrial base for national security objectives. Its goal is to reestablish the American shipbuilding industry as an internationally competitive industry.

Federal Assistance Programs

For over 40 years the Maritime Administration (MARAD) has provided financial assistance to U.S. shipowners through the Federal Ship Financing Guarantee Program (Title XI) and the Capital Construction Fund (CCF).

The Title XI program was established by the Merchant Marine Act of 1936 as amended and provides for a full faith and credit guarantee by the U.S. government for the purpose of promoting the growth and modernization of the U.S. Merchant Marine and U.S. shipyards. The Title XI program provides for federal government guarantees of private sector financing or refinancing obligations for the construction or reconstruction of U.S.-flag vessels in U.S. shipyards. Vessels eligible for Title XI assistance include, but are not limited to, commercial vessels such as passenger vessels, bulk carriers, cargo vessels, tankers, tugs, towboats, barges, dredges, oceanographic research vessels, and offshore oil vessels.

U.S. operators are permitted to establish a CCF. They can make qualified withdrawals from the fund of tax-deferred dollars to procure new or reconstructed vessels from U.S. shipyards.

In addition, the federal government continues to provide significant direct support to the industry through the procurement of goods and services from a large number of shipyards and related industries to repair government-owned vessels. Principal government contracting agencies include the Naval Sea Systems Command, the Military Sealift Command, the Army Corps of Engineers, the U.S. Coast Guard, the National Oceanic and Atmospheric Administration, the National Science Foundation, and MARAD.

Federal Ship Financing Guarantee Program

Interest in the Federal Ship Financing Guarantee Program (Title XI) has reached levels not seen since the early 1980s as a result of the enactment of the National Shipbuilding and Shipyard Conversion Act of 1993. This act expanded the program to make Title XI financing guarantees available to foreign shipowners and to shipyard modernization projects. This resulted in the approval in fiscal year (FY) 1996 and FY 1997, combined, of more than $1.4 billion in Title XI guarantees. MARAD has been asked to consider a variety of projects, including river and power barges, tugs, double-hulled product tankers, and drilling equipment, including semisubmersible mobile offshore drilling units.

In FY 1997 and the first half of FY 1998 MARAD approved 17 applications for Title XI financing (see Table 22-1). Included

were two export projects and two shipyard modernization projects. The total estimated cost of these projects is $803 million with Title XI guarantees totaling $572 million. The two shipyard modernization projects had a total estimated cost of $91 million with Title XI guarantees totaling $80 million.

In April 1998, MARAD had applications for 19 projects pending, including three shipyard modernization projects, at an estimated cost of $952 million, with Title XI guarantees totaling $803 million. The pending Title XI applications included double-hull product tankers, ferries, various offshore vessels, barges, tug and supply vessels, and passenger ferries.

MARITECH Program

MARITECH is a 5-year federal program that provides matching government funds to encourage the shipbuilding industry to direct and lead in the development and application of advanced technology to improve its competitiveness and preserve its industrial base. The program is industry-led and is jointly funded by government and industry with administration provided through the Defense Advanced Research Projects Agency (DARPA) of the U.S. Department of Defense in collaboration with MARAD.

MARITECH has both near-term and long-term objectives. In the near term it is intended to assist industry in penetrating the international marketplace with competitive ship designs, new marketing strategies, and modern shipbuilding processes and procedures. In the long term the program is meant to encourage advanced ship and shipbuilding technology projects to promote continuous product and process improvement in

TABLE 22-1: Approved Title XI Applications, Fiscal Years 1997–1998[1]

Company	Number and Type of Ships	Loan Guarantee Amount ($ millions)
Ship projects		
COSCO Line (America), Inc.	4 1432 TEU container vessels	137.7
CPD Barge Company	18 jumbo hopper barges	5.4
Trailer Bridge, Inc.	2 triple-stack box carriers	10.5
Riverbarge Excursion Lines, Inc.	2 hotel river barges	15.9
Mersea Ships I, Inc.	2 SWATH 300-passenger commuter vessels	29.9
Trico Marine International, Inc.	1 twin-hull crew boat	9.6
Secunda Atlantic, Inc.	1 73.2-meter anchor-handling tug/supply vessel	17.1
Cashman Equipment Corporation	7 single-skin steel flat barges	6.6
Trailer Bridge, Inc.	3 triple-stack box carriers	16.9
Noble Drilling Corporation[2]	1 semisubmersible mobile offshore drilling unit	96.9
Tugz International L.L.C.	6 twin Z-drive reverse tractor harbor/escort/towing tugs	28.1
Canal Barge Company, Inc.	30 steel open hopper barges 2 79.2-meter deck barges 10 36.6-meter deck barges	11.5
Attransco, Inc.	3 tank vessels	47.4
Western Power Co. (formerly known as Ghana National Petroleum Corp.)[2]	2 power barges	59.9
Shipyard projects		
Massachusetts Heavy Industries, Inc.	(yard reactivation)	55.0
HAM Marine, Inc.	(shipyard modernization)	24.8

[1] As of April 1, 1998.
[2] Export project.
Source: U.S. Department of Transportation, Maritime Administration.

order to maintain and enlarge the U.S. share of the commercial and international market; this will ensure the availability of an experienced industrial base, which is vital to national security in times of crisis.

MARITECH projects awarded during FYs 1994–1997 covered a wide range, from the design of various types of small vessels to large oceangoing ships, shipyard technology, and advanced materials technology. These projects have been awarded to 24 companies and their subcontractors in 40 of the 50 states, the District of Columbia, Puerto Rico, and nine foreign countries.

MARAD MARITECH Program. Since 1994 DARPA and MARAD have jointly selected a total of 65 projects valued at $357 million, among which 40 projects valued at $172 million were assigned to MARAD to administer (see Table 22-2). No funding was provided for new projects in FY 1998. Several existing projects, however, were extended with follow-on work phases.

At present, 27 ongoing MARITECH projects are being administered by MARAD, ranging from innovative design and marketing strategies for high-technology vessels to research in advanced manufacturing technology processes and procedures. Information on MARAD-administered projects is available on the World Wide Web at the National Maritime Resource and Education Center (NMREC) home page (http://nmrec.dot.gov).

Commercial Ship Construction

New Orders. In 1997 the U.S. shipbuilding industry received orders for the construction of six oceangoing commercial ships. Early in 1997 Alabama Shipyards received an order for four 1,432 TEU (twenty-foot equivalent units) containerships for export for COSCO Line (America), Inc.; unfortunately, the order was terminated later in the year. In mid-1997 Avondale Industries received a $332 million order from ARCO Marine, Inc., to build two 82,545-gt [125,000 deadweight tons (dwt)] crude carriers valued at $332 million. The tankers for ARCO are the largest ships ordered from a U.S. shipyard since 1984. Additional orders for these shuttle tankers were expected to be placed by other owners in 1998. In the first quarter of 1998 U.S. shipyards did not receive any new orders for oceangoing commercial ships.

Deliveries. In 1997 and the first quarter of 1998 U.S. shipyards delivered five commercial oceangoing ships. Avondale Industries of New Orleans delivered to American Heavy Lift one 27,854-gt tanker and two 24,474-gt tankers reconstructed as double-hulled product carriers. The reconstruction involved cutting the tanker in two, removing the existing forebody, and constructing and attaching a new 155-meter double-hulled forebody.

Newport News delivered the first of six double-hulled product tankers. The 30,415-gt tanker *American Progress,* which originally was ordered on October 31, 1994, by Fleves Shipping Corporation, was sold to Mobil Oil early in 1997 and delivered to the new owner in September 1997.

Alabama Shipyard delivered the first of two 11,000-gt chemical carriers, which were ordered in late 1995, to Danneborg Rederi AS of Denmark. In addition, Todd Pacific Shipyard Corp. of Seattle delivered one 4,340-gt nonoceangoing passenger-vehicle ferry for the Washington State Ferry System.

Current Orderbook. As of April 1, 1998, the U.S. orderbook for commercial ships consisted of five 30,415-gt tankers at Newport News Shipbuilding, one 11,000-gt chemical tanker at Alabama Shipyard, two 82,545-gt crude carriers at Avondale, and three ferries: two at Todd Pacific Shipyards and one at Halter Moss Point Shipyard. In March 1997 Newport News announced that it would leave the commercial shipbuilding business by the middle of 1999. It announced the cancellation of the construction of three tankers, permitting it to deliver the remaining tankers by mid-1999 and then exit the commercial shipbuilding market.

The tankers at Newport News were being constructed for two different companies: three tankers for Fleves Shipping Corporation of Greece, and two tankers for Hvide Van Ommeron of Miami, FL. The last tanker was originally scheduled for delivery in June 1999. Alabama Shipyard is constructing one chemical tanker for Danneborg Rederi AS of Denmark which is scheduled for delivery in mid-1998.

All the product tankers at Newport News Shipbuilding and the chemical tanker at Alabama Shipyard were made feasible through the assistance of MARAD's Title XI Federal Ship Financing Guarantee Program. The crude carriers under construction at Avondale Industries for ARCO Marine, Inc., a subsidiary of Atlantic Richfield Company, are being financed by

TABLE 22-2: MARITECH Projects by Fiscal Year
(millions of dollars)

Fiscal Year	Number of Projects	Total Value	Government Funded	Industry Matching Funds
1994	19	92.5	43.3	45.2
1995	26	100.9	46.9	53.6
1996	11	83.8	38.5	45.2
1997	9	79.8	36.6	43.1
Total	65	357.0	165.3	187.1
Managed by MARAD	40	172.0	80.0	87.8
Managed by DOD	25	185.0	85.3	99.3

Source: U.S. Department of Transportation, Maritime Administration.

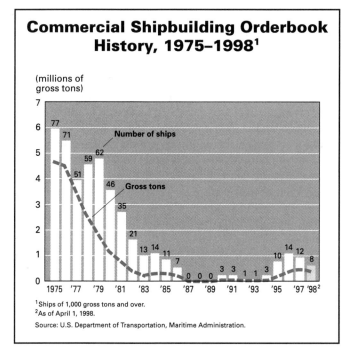

Commercial Shipbuilding Orderbook History, 1975–1998[1]

(millions of gross tons)

FIGURE 22-3

Number of ships

Gross tons

77 71 59 51 62 46 35 21 13 14 11 7 0 0 0 3 3 1 3 10 14 12 8

1975 '77 '79 '81 '83 '85 '87 '89 '91 '93 '95 '97 '98[2]

[1] Ships of 1,000 gross tons and over.
[2] As of April 1, 1998.
Source: U.S. Department of Transportation, Maritime Administration.

the parent company and withdrawals from its MARAD (CCF). The end-of-year orderbook since 1975, updated to April 1, 1998, is shown in Figure 22-3.

In addition, three ferries larger than 1,000 gt are on order or under construction: One 12,904-gt oceangoing ferry is on order at Halter Moss Point Shipyard, and two 4,350-gt nonoceangoing passenger-car ferries are under construction at Todd Pacific Shipyard.

The end-of-year orderbook updated to April 1, 1998, totaled 11 vessels (8 commercial oceangoing ships and 3 ferries) with original contract values of approximately $777.9 million (see Table 22-3). Of the 11 vessels 6 were covered by Title XI with original contract values of $239.3 million, with MARAD providing $209.9 million under the recently expanded Title XI program.

Military Ship Construction

Navy ship construction programs, which had been declining since 1991, have stabilized. A small upward trend is expected, beginning with contracts for the new NSSN submarines, DDG-51 class multiyear procurements, continued procurement of LPD-17 class ships and aircraft carriers, and planned programs such as charter and build. The Navy's ship acquisition budgets are still well below the level reached in the 1980s, when the Navy commenced its largest peacetime combatant ship construction program, with nearly $100 billion appropriated. Although the Navy's ship construction projects have dominated the workload in U.S. shipyards in recent years, they have done so on a much diminished scale.

New Orders. In 1997 and the first quarter of 1998 the Navy ordered 17 new ships, 1,000 light displacement tons (ldt) or larger, from U.S. private shipyards, totaling 217,924 ldt with a total original contract value of $5.7 billion. In that period U.S. private shipyards delivered 12 new Navy vessels and completed three conversions totaling 216,163 ldt with a total original contract value of $4.6 billion.

The Navy's shipbuilding orderbook, as of April 1, 1998, has declined dramatically in the last 10 years as a consequence of the austere new construction budget, dropping from 88 vessels in 1988 to 51 vessels in 1998.

Current Orderbook. On April 1, 1998, the Navy backlog of ships on order or under construction in private shipyards, 1,000 ldt or larger, consisted of 31 combatants and 20 amphibious ships, auxiliary ships, and T-ships, totaling 51 ships (see Table 22-4). Ten Navy vessels are scheduled to be delivered by the end of 1998, eight before the end of 1999, and nine by the end of 2000.

The naval shipbuilding orderbook encompasses a variety of vessels, from the Seawolf submarine to a Coast Guard icebreaker. The Navy's new construction backlog of 51 ships includes 10 different types of ships with the orders dispersed among seven private shipyards on the Atlantic (three), Gulf (three), and Pacific (one) coasts.

Most U.S. shipyards do not have the experience, expertise, or infrastructure required to construct sophisticated naval com-

TABLE 22-3: Commercial Shipbuilding Orderbook[1]

Shipyard	Design Type	Vessel Name	Gross Tons	Award Date	Estimated Delivery Date	Approximate Contract Price, $ millions
Newport News SB	Tanker	*Agathonissos*	30,415	10/31/94	08/15/1998	38.2
Newport News SB	Tanker	*Cape Lookout Shoals*	30,415	07/05/95	04/17/1998	38.2
Halter Moss Point	Ferry	*Kennicott*	12,904	11/06/95	04/17/1998	85.0
Todd Pacific Shipyards	Ferry	*Wenatchee*	4,340	06/20/95	04/28/1998	60.5
Newport News SB	Tanker	*Cape Diamond Shoals*	30,415	07/05/95	05/22/1998	38.2
Newport News SB	Tanker	*Ambrose Channel*	30,415	02/12/96	06/07/1999	49.3
Alabama Shipyard	Chemical carrier	*Aggersborg*	11,000	12/29/95	06/15/1998	26.7
Newport News SB	Tanker	*Brenton Reef*	30,415	02/12/96	12/18/1998	49.3
Todd Pacific Shipyards	Ferry	*Puyallup*	4,340	06/20/95	12/24/1998	60.5
Avondale Industries	Crude carrier	Unnamed	82,545	06/30/97	01/26/2000	166.0
Avondale Industries	Crude carrier	Unnamed	82,545	06/30/97	08/31/2000	166.0
Total	11 vessels		349,749			777.9

[1] Vessels of 1,000 gross tons and over, as of April 1, 1998.
Source: U.S. Department of Transportation, Maritime Administration.

TABLE 22-4: Military Ships under Construction[1]

Symbol	Type	Number
AOE	Fast combat support ship	1
CVN	Aircraft carrier (nuclear-powered)	2
DDG	Guided missile destroyer	27
LHD	Amphibious assault ship (multipurpose)	2
LPD	Amphibious transport ship	1
SSN-21	Attack submarine (nuclear-powered)	2
T-AKR	Military sealift ship	13
WAGB	Icebreaker	1
T-AGOS-23	Ocean surveillance ship	1
T-AGS-60	Ocean survey ship	1
Total		51

[1] Ships of 1,000 ldt or over, as of April 1, 1998.
Source: U.S. Department of Transportation, Maritime Administration.

bat vessels. The Navy's T-ship projects, however, have provided some work for private U.S. shipyards that for the last 15 years have relied heavily on military ship construction. These projects involve the building of civilian-manned Navy auxiliary ships which when completed will be placed under the control of the Military Sealift Command (MSC).

On April 1, 1998, there were 15 T-ships on order or under construction, unchanged from 1997. The orders were distributed among Avondale Industries, Inc., Avondale, LA, for six military sealift ships, and National Steel and Shipbuilding Co. (NASSCO) of San Diego, CA, for seven military sealift ships. Both contracts are scheduled for completion by the end of 2001. Halter Moss Point Shipyard of Moss Point, MS, is constructing one ocean survey ship and one ocean surveillance ship. An additional military sealift ship is planned for procurement in FY 1999.

National Oceanic and Atmospheric Administration

The National Oceanic and Atmospheric Administration (NOAA) is contemplating the detailed design and construction of one or possibly two new classes of fisheries research vessels (FRVs). NOAA anticipates that these vessels will replace the existing fleet of aging FRVs and provide expanded capability by using new technology and improved design. The missions for these new vessels will include stock assessment and life history, physical and biological research, habitat studies, evaluation of fisheries research gear, and atmospheric and sea surface observations and measurement. An extensive suite of state-of-the-art gear and laboratories to support stock assessment and sampling, diving, and oceanography will be required. It is anticipated that the ships will have an overall length of 55 to 65 meters, be able to carry enough supplies to ensure a self-sustained 30- to 40-day voyage, and have accommodations for 38 crew members and scientists. The vessel will comply with all U.S. and international rules and standards applicable to oceanographic research vessels. Currently, NOAA is soliciting for potential sources for design and construction. A major repair and service life extension is also planned for the NOAA ship *Miller Freeman,* which currently conducts fisheries research in the Gulf of Alaska and the Bering Sea.

In early 1997 Halter Moss Point delivered the oceanographic research ship *Ronald H Brown.* One new oceanographic research ship is included in the Navy's FY 1999 budget proposal.

Ship Repair and Conversion Work

The U.S. ship repair industry continues to be very active. Large and small U.S. shipyards have been successful in competing for ship repair and conversion work in the domestic and foreign markets to supplement diminishing repair work on Navy ships. U.S. shipyards have been successful in using location, timeliness of repairs, and competitive prices to gain an edge over many foreign repair yards.

During 1997 U.S. private shipyards performed a large variety of ship repair and conversion work on a large array of vessel types.

The continued high level of activity in the U.S. offshore oil and gas industry has created a need for additional ship repair and conversion services and has increased maintenance capabilities. There has been a great deal of consolidation activity in Gulf Coast shipbuilding and repair and an expansion of shipyard capabilities achieved through an increase in shipyard property and capital equipment, that is, production lines and drydocks. The Gulf Coast shipyards have reported that the demand for repair and construction work, in conjunction with an active building market, has resulted in a continued shortage of skilled labor.

Each year the Navy accomplishes maintenance and modernization work on its ships in both public and private shipyards. In FY 1997 the Navy completed 101 availabilities (overhaul and repair work) with a budgeted value of $1.8 billion. Of these, 37 availabilities were accomplished in the naval shipyards for a budgeted value of $871 million, 48 percent of the budgeted amount, while the private sector completed 64 smaller, less complex availabilities that reflected approximately $959 million, accounting for 52 percent of the budgeted value.

The FY 1998 Navy Maintenance and Modernization projection called for 94 scheduled availabilities with a total budgeted value of $2.0 billion. The naval shipyards are scheduled to accomplish 33 availabilities representing approximately $1.33 billion, or 66 percent of the budgeted value. The private sector's shipyards are scheduled to accomplish 61 smaller, less complex availabilities representing $697 million, or 34 percent of the budgeted value.

Before 1985 Navy repair work was either allocated directly to public yards or awarded to private yards. The bulk of ship repair work is still distributed on an allocation basis.

Naval Base Closings and Realignment

In 1990 Congress established a new set of procedures for military base closings: Title XXIX of Public Law 101-510. These procedures were valid for only 5 years, with closings being proposed for every other year: 1991, 1993, and 1995. As a result of the commission's recommendations, four of the eight naval shipyards in the United States were closed: The Philadelphia Naval Shipyard closed on September 30, 1995, after a 194-year history; the Charleston Naval Shipyard and the Mare Island

Naval Shipyard closed on March 31, 1996; and the Long Beach Naval Shipyard closed on September 30, 1997. The closing of Navy shipyard facilities is having an impact on both public and private shipyards.

Since the completion of the first four rounds of base closings, which included the closing of the four naval shipyards listed above, several commercial ventures have acquired and are redeveloping facilities or have leased facilities at the former naval shipyards. These private ventures may include improvement of the existing facilities for shipbuilding and repair or other commercial ventures and in some cases may provide employment opportunities for skilled and unskilled workers idled as a result of base closings.

In the case of the Charleston Naval Shipyard, two private shipyards—Braswell Services Group, Inc., and Detyens Shipyard, Inc.—have leased facilities at the shipyard from the Charleston Naval Shipyards Redevelopment Association for the repair of ships.

In late 1997 Kvaerner Masa, a Norwegian shipbuilder, acquired the rights to a portion of the southern end of the former Philadelphia Naval Shipyard. Kvaerner is designing a modern compact shipyard to build cargo ships. The new shipyard, which will be named Kvaerner Philadelphia Shipyard, USA, expects to employ about 1,000 multiskilled employees. Kvaerner will receive approximately $480 million in local, state, and federal funding for the design and refurbishment of the shipyard (including two drydocks) and to retrain local employees. Kvaerner has agreed to purchase the first three containerships constructed at the new shipyard, with the first one expected to be delivered in 2001.

National Defense Reserve Fleet

MARAD's National Defense Reserve Fleet (NDRF) is a program which allows the storage and orderly disposal of obsolete or excess government-owned vessels. At the beginning of FY 1998 the NDRF consisted of 217 merchant ships and 90 vessels held for other government agencies, primarily the U.S. Navy, on a reimbursable basis. Many of these ships can be activated to meet U.S. shipping requirements in the event of a national emergency.

A key sealift shipping program that exists as a subset of the NDRF is the Ready Reserve Force (RRF). At the beginning of FY 1998 the RRF was composed of 96 oceangoing cargo ships that are maintained to keep their certificates of inspection current. Vessels in the RRF are owned, managed, and operated by the U.S. Department of Transportation's MARAD under authorization found in the Merchant Ship Sales Act of 1946. In peacetime RRF ships generally are held in various stages of readiness in the United States and are periodically activated in support of Department of Defense (DOD) peacetime exercises. In 1990 the first mass activation of the RRF took place when 79 RRF ships were activated to support Operation Desert Shield/Desert Storm. By the end of the Gulf War the RRF had transported 22 percent of all military supplies, including 45 percent of the ammunition, to the Persian Gulf.

The NDRF is funded by DOD through the National Defense Sealift Fund (NDSF). The budget is typically about $250 million for maintenance and operations. MARAD retains the responsibility for ownership, custody, maintenance, and operational readiness of the fleet. To reduce the existing surge roll-on/roll-off (RO/RO) shortfall, DOD is pursuing expansion upgrades of selected RRF RO/ROs to obtain an additional 5,980 square meters of lift by the year 2002. A DOD directive calls for the retirement of 19 older breakbulk ships from the RRF to the NDRF by FY 2002, as the Navy's newly constructed and/or converted military sealift ships (T-AKRs), which are large medium-speed RO/ROs, become available.

RRF ship maintenance and repair are conducted primarily in commercial U.S. yards with U.S. marine equipment and service suppliers. The RRF uses commercial ship managers that are authorized to do ship maintenance and repair contracting in accordance with commercial practices. MARAD utilizes a combination of surplus government piers and commercial piers to meet its vessel layberthing needs. Operation Desert Shield/Desert Storm indicated a need to berth more RRF ships in a higher state of readiness, some with full-time reduced operating status (ROS) crews aboard. MARAD currently has a total of 65 RRF ships outported. MARAD has received 64 no-notice activations from DOD since the 1990–1991 Gulf War, and all but two ships have met or exceeded the assigned availability time. Through March 31, 1998, operational RRF ships in prepositioning have accumulated over 10,492 operational days while achieving a 99.5 percent full-mission-capable readiness rating. MARAD will continue to rely heavily on the U.S. maritime industrial base for the RRF program, which is now the single largest source of national emergency contingency surge shipping in the world.

Passenger and Cruise Vessels

In 1997 U.S. shipbuilders were not involved in any major construction or conversion projects involving oceangoing passenger ships. However, numerous ship repair companies received a number of work assignments involving the maintenance and repair of major oceangoing passenger ships. In addition, a few U.S. shipyards were still involved in the design, construction, and retrofitting of smaller passenger, cruise, dining, and gaming vessels.

Second-Tier Shipyards

Second-tier shipyards—small and medium-size shipyards that are primarily engaged in supporting inland waterway and coastal operators—constitute an important segment of the U.S. shipbuilding and repair industry. Their activity consists of new construction and repair of smaller vessels such as barges, tugboats and towboats, offshore crew and supply boats, ferries, casino boats, fishing boats, patrol boats, military and nonmilitary craft, and fire and rescue vessels as well as oil rig construction, conversion, and repair.

According to a survey performed by *WorkBoat* magazine, second-tier shipyards received orders for or delivered over 15 percent more vessels during 1997 than they did in 1996, including ferries, casino boats, tugs, and small military craft.

Dry Cargo Barges

The last few years have seen a surge in construction orders for new dry cargo barges as a result of numerous factors: the strong demand for barges created by the rise in commodities shipments, projections of future increases in commodity flows, the age of the barge fleet, the rapid rate of retirement of old dry cargo barges (400-plus annually), and the attractiveness of the capital markets and healthy corporate capital positions. In addition, it was projected that there would be a significant demand for new barge tonnage to replace the large number of barges that were approaching the end of their useful lives. It was estimated that between 800 and 1,000 barges would be delivered in 1998.

As 1997 came to a close, some industry officials began to express concern about the possible existence of excess capacity in the dry cargo market. In spite of fears of near-term overcapacity, MARAD data indicate that the shipyards ended the year with a strong quarter. Over 30 percent of the hopper barges ordered during 1997 were placed in Gulf Coast shipyards in the final quarter of that year. In 1997, according to MARAD data, second-tier shipyards received orders for over 1,000 dry cargo hopper barges.

Tank Barges

According to the U.S. Army Corps of Engineers, there are about 4,000 tank barges in the inland and coastal trades. The inland tanker barge fleet is aging. It has been reported that about 35 percent of these tank barges are over 25 years of age, the typical useful life of a barge. The average age of small tank barges, those with a capacity less than 9,000 bulk barrels (bbl), is about 32 years, while jumbos and semi-integrated unit tow tank barges average around 19 years of age.

Given the double-hull requirements of the Oil Pollution Act of 1990 (OPA-90) and the advanced age of the tank barge vessel fleet, the outlook for offshore tank barge demand remains bright. It is estimated that 66 of the tank barges in the U.S. Jones Act trades will have to be phased out by 2005, along with another 22 tank barges by 2010, because of the double-hull requirements of OPA-90.

MARAD estimates that by the year 2000 about 25 percent of the current domestic tank barge fleet, those ships between 10,000 and 30,000 tons, will be more than 25 years old and that more than 8 percent will be at least 30 years old.

Offshore Supply Vessels

The boom in the Gulf Coast offshore industry has caused a surge in orders for offshore supply vessels (OSVs). As drillers move farther from shore to search in deeper water for oil and gas, larger OSVs with new technology are needed to carry supplies to the rigs, especially large quantities of liquid mud, and to stay around the rigs for prolonged periods in rougher water.

In the closing months of 1997 the OSV market was very active. Contracts to construct a large number of offshore supply vessels were announced, and options were signed for several big OSVs. Edison Chouest Offshore of Galliano, LA, had approximately 30 OSVs under construction. All these supply vessels had extra capabilities because of the greater demand for liquid mud and for the hauling of drilling and production risers into deeper water. These boats were not being built on speculation; there were firm contracts in all cases.

Export Orders

A number of second-tier shipyards have been active in the international market, building a variety of vessels for different clients. Some examples of recent awards and buildings for the export market include an aluminum small waterplane area twin hull (SWATH) vessel for the Hong Kong government; a barge-mounted gas turbine power plant for Puerto Plata, Dominican Republic; and a towboat to work along the Paraguay, Parana, Uruguay, and Alto Parana rivers and waterways.

Capital Investment

In FY 1997 the U.S. shipbuilding and repair industry invested more than $244 million for the expansion and upgrading of facilities. Much of this investment was used to improve the competitiveness and efficiency of shipyards. The capital investments were made to update and convert shipyard facilities to make them more commercially viable. Examples of recent capital investments include new pipe and fabrication shops, dry-dock extensions, automated steel process buildings, expanded design programs, and military applications. Many of these improvements have been made necessary by the increased utilization of U.S. shipyards, particularly those along the Gulf Coast, as a result of the resurgence of the oil exploration and production industry in the Gulf of Mexico.

According to data received by MARAD, it was projected that in FY 1998 U.S. shipyards would make capital investments of about $256 million. The industry's capital investments since 1970 have totaled approximately $6.2 billion, and actual expenditures since 1985 have consistently exceeded those planned, except in 1990.

U.S. INDUSTRY OUTLOOK

According to the current orderbook, three U.S. shipyards have orders for the construction of commercial oceangoing vessels: Alabama Shipyard, Inc., has work through mid-1998 completing the construction of one chemical carrier; Avondale Industries, Inc.–Shipyards Division, has work through the year 2000 with the construction of two tankers for ARCO Marine; and Newport News has work through mid-1999 constructing five tankers. Ferry construction will provide work at Halter Moss Point Shipyard through early 1998 and Todd Pacific Shipyards, Inc., through the last quarter of 1998.

For the foreseeable future, the U.S. shipbuilding and repair industry will continue to have as its principal customer the U.S. Navy, including conversion and repair work, although the level of activity is expected to be lower than that in the previous decade. The FY 1998 Navy budget was $8.1 billion, 48 percent higher than the $5.5 billion appropriated for FY 1997. This increase was the result of the multiyear authorization for 13 DDG-51 destroyers, the lead ship of a new class of submarines, and an aircraft carrier refueling. The Navy's FY 1998 budget is the largest since the $11.4 billion funding level in FY 1990. The Navy's projected ship construction budget for FY 1999 is approximately $6.3 billion. The proposed FY 1999 budget is 22.8 percent lower than the budget for FY 1998. In addition, both public and private shipyards will be affected by the FY 1998 Navy ship repair and modernization budget of $2 billion, which is 10.8 percent larger than the budget for FY 1997.

Major Shipyards

The Navy's long-term fleet expansion program, which began in the 1980s, had a goal of establishing a modern 600-ship fleet. This program was halted as a result of the end of the cold war. Reductions in the Navy ship procurement program, along with the scheduled and early decommissioning of Navy submarines, combatants, and auxiliary vessels, have led to a smaller active U.S. Navy fleet. The Navy's active fleet was reduced by 187 ships between the end of FY 1985 and FY 1997, from 541 to 354 ships. This represents a 34.6 percent decline in the size of the active fleet.

The U.S. Navy's shipbuilding plan for FYs 1998–2003 includes the construction and conversion of 48 new ships costing about $51.7 billion (see Table 22-5). Among the 48 ships, 45 are Shipbuilding and Conversion, Navy (SCN)–funded and 3 are National Defense Sealift Fund (NDSF)–funded. The 45 SCN ships consist of 32 new construction ships, 2 nuclear aircraft carrier refuelings, 7 ship conversions, and 4 service life extensions (SLEPs). The 3 NDSF ships involve the construction of 3 military sealift ships (T-AKRs). The Navy's shipbuilding program represents a 69.4 percent reduction in the quantity of ships being procured, an average of 5.8 ships per year compared with the average of 19 ships annually for Navy programs in the 1980s. SCN funding accounts for $51.5 bil-

lion of the $51.7 billion SCN budget, and NDSF funding accounts for $0.25 billion. New military sealift vessels have been contracted for in each fiscal year since 1993 for a total to date of 13 new vessels. This military sealift construction program is planned to conclude after the procurement of 14 new vessels.

Navy ships require many subcontractors to assist in the construction and installation of a multitude of complex shipboard systems (weapons, radar, etc.). These complex systems dramatically increase the total cost of military ships. The shipyard contract value accounts for only about one-third of the $53.8 billion budget; the remainder goes to items such as government-furnished equipment placed aboard the vessels and government program costs.

It has been projected that foreign demand for naval vessels over the next 20 years will total about 180 destroyers, frigates, and corvettes. Asia is expected to generate the greatest demand, followed by western Europe, the Middle East, eastern Europe, and Latin America. The Asian market may be somewhat softer than expected in the near future as a result of the economic and financial changes that have recently taken place there.

The major full-service shipyards—those which constitute the MSB—in the foreseeable future will continue to depend on Navy shipbuilding and repair work as their primary source of employment. Since mid-1992 these shipyards have experienced a sharp decrease in employment as a consequence of deep reductions in new Navy shipbuilding orders, the decline in complex Navy repair activity, and the absence of significant orders for commercial shipbuilding. The Navy's shipbuilding plan for FYs 1998–2003 will halt the long decline in shipyard employment and will result in a leveling out of the work force through the end of 2006. The shipbuilding industry workload projection (see Figure 22-4) reflects the labor-power requirements for the

TABLE 22-5: Navy Shipbuilding Plan, Fiscal Years 1998–2003

Ship Class	1998	1999	2000	2001	2002	2003	Total
New construction							
CVN					1		1
New Attack Submarine (NSSN)	1	1		1	1		4
DDG 51	3	3	3	4	1	3	17
LPD 17		1	2	2	2	2	9
AOE	—	—	—	—	—	1	1
Subtotal	4	5	5	7	5	6	32
Conversion/major overhaul							
CG (conversion)					1	6	7
CVN (refueling)	1			1			2
T-AE (conversion)					1	1	2
T-AFS (conversion)	—			—	1	1	2
Subtotal	1			1	3	8	13
Total SCN	5	5	5	8	8	14	45
Other funding							
T-AKR (military sealift)	2	1					3
Total	7	6	5	8	8	14	48

Source: U.S. Department of Defense, Department of the Navy; U.S. Department of Transportation, Maritime Administration.

Shipbuilding Industry Workload: Major Shipbuilding Base Summation, 1985–2006[1]

Equivalent production workers (thousands)

Total employment

Firm new construction

Projected Navy construction

Repair and nonship

[1] Number of yards is 18.

Source: Shipyard data from form MA832 when provided; U.S. Department of Transportation, Maritime Administration, Office of Ship Construction.

FIGURE 22-4

commercial shipbuilding orderbook as of December 1997 and the proposed Navy FYs 1998–2003 shipbuilding plan.

Oil Pollution Act of 1990

OPA-90 established the requirement that all tankers entering U.S. ports by the year 2015 have double hulls. OPA-90 was seen as representing a large step in reducing the environmental danger from shipping petroleum and petroleum products as well as an opportunity for the U.S. shipbuilding industry to reenter the commercial market through the construction of double-hulled tankers. The U.S. industry has taken numerous steps to improve its ability to capture a comfortable percentage of the demand for replacement tonnage in the world tanker fleet.

MARAD data indicate that about 1,500 tankers involved in foreign trade—about one-third of the world's petroleum tanker fleet—enter U.S. ports. It is difficult to determine the number of tankers that will be rebuilt, scrapped, or constructed as a result of the enactment of OPA-90, but it is known that a double hull will be required by the year 2015 for all tankers entering a U.S. port.

World Tanker Demand

More than half the tankers in the world's operational fleet by deadweight tonnage were built before 1980. At the end of 1995, according to *Clarkson's Shipping Review and Outlook,* 31 percent of the very large crude carrier (VLCC) tankers in the world fleet were over 20 years old. By September 1996 this percentage had climbed to 37.4 percent, indicating a continuing deterioration in the age of the VLCC fleet. *Clarkson's* reported that the fleet of smaller tankers—"Aframax" tankers, or those in the range of 80,000 to 120,000 dwt—also continued to age. At the end of 1995, 17.3 percent of these tankers were over 20 years

old, and by September 1996 the proportion had climbed to 22 percent.

By the year 2000 about 40 percent of the current world tanker fleet will be more than 25 years old and over 20 percent will be at least 30 years old as a result of the concentration of tankers built between 1972 and 1977. Many of these tankers will have to be replaced with new tonnage in the remainder of the 1990s and early in the next century so that they will be able to enter U.S. ports.

U.S. and foreign shipyards are seeing an influx of orders for double-hulled tankers as a result of the requirements of OPA-90. These orders should be a catalyst for future orders for double-hulled tankers that incorporate design improvements and advanced electronic features. U.S. shipyards continue to make significant capital investments to improve their facilities and increase their productivity in order to participate in the expected opportunities forecast for the next decade, including Jones Act tanker tonnage resulting from OPA-90.

Shipbuilding analysts expect a significant rise in new orders for commercial ships into the next century. This increase results from projections of high growth in the seaborne trade for oil and dry bulk cargoes as well as the continued demand for replacement ships necessitated by the aging of the world fleet. Drewry Shipping Consultants, Ltd., has projected that between 1998 and 2010 total worldwide demand for new tonnage will be approximately 339 million dwt (see Figure 22-5). Drewry forecast that the greatest demand will arise between 1999 and 2000, when more than 76.6 million dwt will be required. To achieve this level, a significant number of orders will have to be made for tankers and dry bulk carriers.

Orders for new tankers are expected to average over 20 million dwt per year in the period 1998–2000, followed by a decline in orders in the first half of the next decade (see Table 22-6). The U.S. shipbuilding industry has already benefited from the increased demand for double-hulled tankers generated

World New Building Demand: Projected Orders

(millions of dwt)

Oil tankers   Bulk carriers   Other

Source: Drewry Shipping Consultants.

FIGURE 22-5

TABLE 22-6: Oil Tanker New Building Demand, 1998–2004

(millions of dwt)

Size, dwt	1998	1999	2000	2001	2002	2003	2004	Total
10,000–45,000	1.8	1.9	2.0	0.5	1.4	1.2	1.4	10.2
45,000–90,000	1.9	3.0	2.8	1.6	2.4	3.1	2.8	17.6
90,000–175,000	3.3	4.8	2.7	0.9	1.4	0.8	0.3	14.2
Larger than 175,000	14.1	12.3	12.4	8.2	5.1	3.7	1.2	57.0
Total	21.1	22.0	19.9	11.2	10.3	8.8	5.7	99.0

Source: Drewry Shipping Consultants.

by OPA-90, receiving orders for 11 new tankers (9 product and 2 chemical tankers) and 4 major tanker reconstructions.

Organization for Economic Cooperation and Development

In December 1994 the world's key shipbuilding nations (the United States, Japan, Korea, the European Union, and Norway) signed an agreement to eliminate shipbuilding subsidies and other trade-distorting practices. The agreement was negotiated under the auspices of the Organization for Economic Cooperation and Development (OECD).

This accord eliminates virtually all direct and indirect subsidies, establishes common rules for government-assisted financing, creates an injurious pricing mechanism to prevent ship dumping, and provides a binding mechanism for dispute settlement. When the agreement takes effect, the Title XI program will be modified to meet its terms, which provide for a maximum repayment period of 12 years and a maximum financing coverage of 80 percent. The current Title XI program allows for a maximum 25-year repayment period and maximum financing coverage of 87.5 percent.

The OECD agreement fulfills a long-sought goal of the United States which President Clinton has pledged to achieve: ensuring fair international competition for U.S. shipyards. The agreement is expected to help restore the competitiveness of American shipbuilding in the world market, since it requires other countries to give up the much more substantial support they have provided to their yards while requiring relatively modest changes in U.S. programs.

Although negotiation of the OECD agreement began as a U.S. initiative, there has been a protracted disagreement within the U.S. shipbuilding industry over its utility. Large military-oriented yards have opposed the agreement, while small and medium-size yards have supported it. The Clinton administration and congressional supporters of the agreement have sought to address critics' concerns through compromise proposals. Various bills to implement the agreement have been considered, but Congress must still act on the legislation. All other parties have ratified the agreement, but it will not go into force unless the United States approves it by passing implementing legislation.

Second-Tier Shipyards

The second-tier shipyards are rich with orders for barges, OSVs, tugs, and other shallow-draft vessels. Several Gulf Coast yards have been expanding their facilities as well as their business lines in an attempt to take full advantage of the thriving Gulf Coast oil and gas markets. In the current environment the industry reportedly is turning away some prospective business opportunities because of the problems caused by the shortage of skilled labor.

The second-tier shipyards have seen a growth opportunity in the rig business and have moved aggressively into that market. The industry observed that the rig fleet was aging and saw a tremendous opportunity in an expected surging demand for rig repairs and conversions. The future portends a healthy construction, repair, and conversion business for this industry.

FACTORS AFFECTING FUTURE U.S. INDUSTRY GROWTH

The availability of long-term Title XI guarantees for eligible vessels constructed or reconstructed in U.S. shipyards and for shipyard modernization projects, together with the extension of the MARITECH program, continues to be a major factor in the revitalization of commercial shipbuilding in U.S. shipyards. The U.S. shipbuilding industry has to make significant strides in building efficient ships at lower prices with on-time deliveries for the Jones Act trade to demonstrate to the international market an ability to produce high-quality commercial vessels. The knowledge and experience gained in the past few years, coupled with a successful domestic building program, should help the U.S. shipbuilding industry secure additional new building tonnage generated by OPA-90, the projected growth in world trade, and the projected demand for replacement tonnage (see Tables 22-7 and 22-8).

The U.S. shipbuilding industry has made significant capital investments to enhance its competitive posture by means of productivity improvements. Through the adoption and development of new technology supported by financing guarantee programs, U.S. shipyards can develop new advanced ship designs, new marketing strategies, and new, more productive shipyard processes which will make them better able to compete in the world market. The federal government, suppliers, shipyard managements, and organized labor continue to work together to achieve increased market penetration through the cost-effective production of high-quality ships and products.

The industry sees opportunities in the years ahead, and a sharp focus on product planning, production, and marketing should afford it a chance to demonstrate achievement first in the

TABLE 22-7: Shipbuilding and Repairing (SIC 3731) Trends and Forecasts
(millions of dollars except as noted)

	1992	1993	1994	1995	1996	1997[1]	1998[2]	1999[3]	Percent Change 96–97	97–98	98–99	92–96[4]
Industry data												
Value of shipments[5]	10,601	9,964	9,865	9,613	9,811	10,302	10,817	11,357	5.0	5.0	5.0	−1.9
Value of shipments (1992$)	10,601	9,436	9,017	8,819	8,807	10,050	10,553	11,080	14.1	5.0	5.0	−4.5
Total employment (thousands)	118	112	102	95.3	92.1	91.5	90.0	90.5	−0.7	−1.6	0.6	−6.0
Production workers (thousands)	87.0	81.9	76.0	70.4	68.4	65.0	62.0	63.0	−5.0	−4.6	1.6	−5.8
Average hourly earnings ($)	13.05	13.45	14.00	14.63	14.39	15.11	15.86	16.26	5.0	5.0	2.5	2.5
Capital expenditures	128	156	166	232	242	244	256	260	0.8	4.9	1.6	17.3
Product data												
Value of shipments[5]	10,381	9,801	9,877	9,590	9,722	9,965	10,214	10,470	2.5	2.5	2.5	−1.6
Value of shipments (1992$)	10,381	9,282	9,028	8,798	8,727	9,722	9,965	10,214	11.4	2.5	2.5	−4.2
Trade data												
Value of imports	50.9	517	12.4	29.4	54.0	30.1			−44.3			1.5
Value of exports	652	379	595	483	346	611			76.6			−14.6

[1] Estimate except imports and exports.
[2] Estimate.
[3] Forecast.
[4] Compound annual rate.
[5] For definition of industry versus product values, see "Getting the Most Out of *Outlook '99*."
Source: U.S. Department of Commerce: Bureau of the Census; estimates and forecasts by author.

TABLE 22-8: U.S. Trade Patterns in Shipbuilding in 1997
(millions of dollars; percent)

Exports Regions[2]	Value[3]	Share, %	Imports Regions[2]	Value[3]	Share, %
NAFTA	8	1.3	NAFTA	8	27.8
Latin America	178	29.2	Latin America	0	0.7
Western Europe	23	3.8	Western Europe	9	28.4
Japan/Chinese Economic Area	33	5.4	Japan/Chinese Economic Area	0	1.5
Other Asia	15	2.5	Other Asia	11	37.0
Rest of world	353	57.9	Rest of world	1	4.7
World	611	100.0	World	30	100.0
Top Five Countries	**Value**	**Share, %**	**Top Five Countries**	**Value**	**Share, %**
Bahrain	140	22.9	Singapore	11	36.6
Trinidad and Tobago	98	16.0	Canada	6	21.4
Nigeria	85	13.9	Norway	4	14.8
Egypt	72	11.8	Mexico	2	6.4
United Arab Emirates	36	5.8	Denmark	1	3.2

[1] SIC 3731.
[2] For definitions of regional groupings, see "Getting the Most Out of *Outlook '99*."
[3] Values may not sum to total due to rounding.
Source: U.S. Department of Commerce, Bureau of the Census.

domestic market and then in the more competitive foreign commercial shipbuilding arena.

Daniel Seidman and Elizabeth Gearhart, Office of Ship Construction, Maritime Administration, U.S. Department of Transportation, (202) 366-5841, September 1998.

■ **REFERENCES**

The Clarkson Shipping Review and Outlook, Autumn 1996, Clarkson Research Studies, 12 Camomile Street, London, England EC3A 7BP. Telephone: 0171-283-8955.

Marine Log, Simmons-Boardman Publishing Corporation, 345 Hudson Street, New York, NY 10014. (212) 620-7263.

Maritime Reporter and Engineering News, Maritime Activity Reports, Inc., 118 East 25th Street, New York, NY 10010. (212) 477-6700.

1997 Report on Survey of U.S. Shipbuilding and Repair Facilities, Maritime Administration, U.S. Department of Transportation, Office of Ship Construction, 400 Seventh Street, SW, Washington, DC 20590. (202) 366-5841.

Shipyard Chronicle (newsletter), Shipbuilders Council of America, 901 North Washington Street, Alexandria, VA 22314. (703) 548-7447.

Workboat Magazine, Journal Publications, 120 Tillson Avenue, Suite 201, P.O. Box 908, Rockland, ME 04841-0908. (207) 594-6222.

The World Shipbuilding Market—Analysis and Forecast of World Shipbuilding Demand, March 1995, Drewry Shipping Consultants, Ltd., 11 Heron Quay, London, England E14 45F. Telephone: 071-538-0191.

World Shipbuilding Statistics, Lloyd's Register of Shipping, 71 Fenchurch Street, London, England EC3M4BS. Telephone: 071-709-9166.

■ RELATED CHAPTERS

INDUSTRIAL AND ANALYTICAL INSTRUMENTS
Economic and Trade Trends

U.S. International Trade

($ billions)

Legend: Balance | Exports | Imports

Source: U.S. Department of Commerce: Bureau of the Census; International Trade Administration.

World Export Market Shares

(%)

Legend: United States | Germany | Japan | United Kingdom

Source: United Nations; U.S. Department of Commerce, International Trade Administration.

Export Dependence and Import Penetration

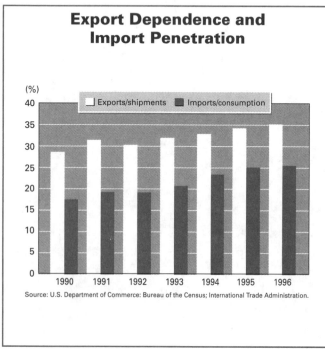

(%)

Legend: Exports/shipments | Imports/consumption

Source: U.S. Department of Commerce: Bureau of the Census; International Trade Administration.

Output and Output per Hour

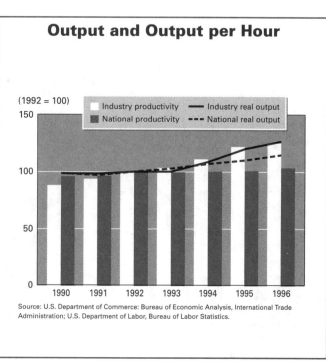

(1992 = 100)

Legend: Industry productivity | Industry real output | National productivity | National real output

Source: U.S. Department of Commerce: Bureau of Economic Analysis, International Trade Administration; U.S. Department of Labor, Bureau of Labor Statistics.

See "Getting the Most Out of *Outlook '99*" for definitions of terms.

Industrial and Analytical Instruments

INDUSTRY DEFINITION The industrial and analytical instruments industry encompasses laboratory instruments (SIC 3821, 3826, 3827), measuring and controlling instruments (SIC 3822, 3823, 3824, 3829), and instruments to measure electricity (SIC 3825). These products are sold in at least 14 different markets, responding to a range of primary economic drivers.

Industrial and analytical instrument (I&AI) product shipments totaled over $48 billion in 1998 and are expected to exceed $51 billion in 1999 (see Table 23-1). By 2003 these shipments are projected to reach $56 billion. Real growth rates in the period 1998–2003 should average about 3 percent annually. In 1998 exports accounted for over 39% of total product shipments and exceeded imports by over $7 billion. The I&AI industry is an important net exporter of U.S. manufactured goods (see Table 23-2).

The worldwide I&AI market in 1998 was $117 billion and is expected to reach $125 billion in 1999 and $150 billion in 2003. The U.S. share of this trade is forecast to decline from 41 percent in 1998 to 37 percent in 2003. As industrial economies mature, their infrastructures become more diversified and instrumentation output begins to expand, reducing the requirements of these economies for imported instruments. Countering this trend, however, is the growing sophistication and software content of instrumentation products, a factor that favors U.S. sourcing.

Within the overall I&AI total, there are five major end-use markets (77 percent of total shipments) and nine other product-specific groupings (23 percent of total shipments). These 14 markets are listed in Table 23-3. The 10 largest U.S.-based manufacturers of I&AI products, based on their worldwide corporate revenues in 1996, are listed in Table 23-4.

Investment expenditures (research and development, capital equipment, and facilities construction) are the principal economic drivers of the I&AI industry. The U.S. I&AI industry is already very globally oriented but will become even more reliant on overseas markets for revenue growth rates that exceed U.S. gross national product (GNP) expansion. The Asian economic crisis will affect these industries. East Asia has been a small market for U.S. I&AI producers in terms of absolute size but has been supplying a major share of overall market growth. The resurgent economies of Europe will offset this decline in demand to some extent.

ELECTRONIC TEST AND MEASUREMENT INSTRUMENTS

The instruments to measure electricity (SIC 3825) industry includes the electronic test and measurement and integrating and electrical measuring instruments markets.

The electronic test and measurement (ET&M) market is the largest I&AI market. In 1998 this sector accounted for 29 percent of total I&AI shipments. In 1999 exports are expected to account for 45 percent of total product shipments. Imports are projected to account for 35 percent of U.S. demand, yielding a trade surplus of over $3 billion. The primary economic driver of this market is the output of electronic products such as semiconductor components, communications equipment, and data processing equipment. As the virtual office becomes commonplace in developed economies, the demand for personal computers, printers, facsimile machines, pagers, cellular telephones, and a host of other electronic products is expected to remain strong through the end of this century.

TABLE 23-1: Industrial and Analytical Instruments (SIC 382) Trends and Forecasts
(millions of dollars except as noted)

	1992	1993	1994	1995	1996	1997[1]	1998[2]	1999[3]	Percent Change 96–97	97–98	98–99	92–96[4]
Industry data												
Value of shipments[5]	34,730	35,409	38,932	43,730	46,741	50,344	54,002	57,482	7.7	7.3	6.4	7.7
3825 Instruments to measure electricity	8,826	8,746	10,124	12,418	13,371	14,284	15,196	16,154	6.8	6.4	6.3	10.9
382A Laboratory instruments[6]	9,823	10,384	11,119	12,254	13,039	13,563	14,512	15,383	4.0	7.0	6.0	7.3
382B Measuring and controlling instruments[6]	16,081	16,279	17,689	19,059	20,331	22,497	24,292	25,945	10.7	8.0	6.8	6.0
Value of shipments (1992$)	34,730	34,708	37,705	41,659	43,955	46,820	49,863	52,351	6.5	6.5	5.0	6.1
3825 Instruments to measure electricity	8,826	8,608	9,800	11,649	12,543	13,284	14,031	14,712	5.9	5.6	4.9	9.2
382A Laboratory instruments	9,823	10,229	10,842	11,761	12,310	12,614	13,400	14,010	2.5	6.2	4.6	5.8
Measuring and controlling instruments	16,081	15,871	17,062	18,250	19,102	20,922	22,432	23,629	9.5	7.2	5.3	4.4
Total employment (thousands)	276	269	266	271	272							-0.4
3825 Instruments to measure electricity	68.5	64.9	63.0	62.3	63.2							-2.0
382A Laboratory instruments	78.2	78.0	76.6	76.8	77.4							-0.3
382B Measuring and controlling instruments	129	126	126	132	132							0.6
Production workers (thousands)	138	134	139	142	141							0.5
3825 Instruments to measure electricity	32.2	30.5	32.0	31.0	33.0							0.6
382A Laboratory instruments	34.3	34.0	35.2	35.1	34.5							0.1
382B Measuring and controlling instruments	71.3	69.4	71.3	75.4	73.7							0.8
Average hourly earnings ($)	13.01	13.32	13.52	13.94	14.28							2.4
3825 Instruments to measure electricity	14.20	14.56	14.84	15.07	15.53							2.3
382A Laboratory instruments	12.74	13.06	13.47	14.14	14.65							3.6
382B Measuring and controlling instruments	12.61	12.91	12.97	13.37	13.54							1.8
Capital expenditures	1,180	1,152	1,156	1,348	1,466							5.6
3825 Instruments to measure electricity	324	402	334	398	469							9.7
382A Laboratory instruments	355	330	325	371	401							3.1
382B Measuring and controlling instruments	501	420	498	579	596							4.4
Product data												
Value of shipments[7]	32,914	33,904	36,214	39,747	42,227	45,310	48,441	51,389	7.3	6.9	6.1	6.4
3825 Instruments to measure electricity	7,985	8,180	9,020	10,882	11,964	12,856	13,866	14,990	7.5	7.9	8.1	10.6
382A Laboratory instruments	9,481	9,654	10,014	11,062	11,451	12,207	12,923	13,554	6.6	5.9	4.9	4.8
382B Measuring and controlling instruments	15,448	16,071	17,181	17,803	18,812	20,247	21,652	22,845	7.6	6.9	5.5	5.0
Value of shipments (1992$)	32,914	33,257	35,092	37,910	39,757	42,139	44,523	46,589	6.0	5.7	4.6	4.8
3825 Instruments to measure electricity	7,985	8,051	8,731	10,208	11,224	11,956	12,744	13,526	6.5	6.6	6.1	8.9
382A Laboratory instruments	9,481	9,516	9,775	10,626	10,815	11,353	11,878	12,237	5.0	4.6	3.0	3.3
382B Measuring and controlling instruments	15,448	15,690	16,585	17,076	17,718	18,830	19,901	20,826	6.3	5.7	4.6	3.5
Trade data												
Value of imports	5,398	6,020	7,424	8,746	9,376	10,407	11,384	12,162	11.0	9.4	6.8	14.8
3825 Instruments to measure electricity	1,200	1,341	1,536	1,966	2,271	2,686	2,981	3,189	18.3	11.0	7.0	17.3
382A Laboratory instruments	1,998	2,069	2,367	2,761	3,095	3,412	3,685	3,927	10.2	8.0	6.6	11.6
382B Measuring and controlling instruments	2,199	2,611	3,521	4,019	4,010	4,309	4,718	5,046	7.5	9.5	7.0	16.2
Value of exports	9,988	10,805	11,926	13,601	14,868	17,426	18,925	20,403	17.2	8.6	7.8	10.5
3825 Instruments to measure electricity	2,957	3,054	3,388	4,166	4,897	5,764	6,221	6,748	17.7	7.9	8.5	13.4
382A Laboratory instruments	3,104	3,263	3,585	4,114	4,565	5,279	5,740	6,139	15.6	8.7	7.0	10.1
382B Measuring and controlling instruments	3,926	4,487	4,953	5,321	5,407	6,383	6,964	7,516	18.1	9.1	7.9	8.3

[1] Estimate except imports and exports.
[2] Estimate.
[3] Forecast.
[4] Compound annual rate.
[5] For a definition of industry versus product values, see "Getting the Most Out of *Outlook '99.*"
[6] The code 382A represents an aggregation of SIC 3821, 3826, and 3827. The code 382B represents an aggregation of SIC 3822, 3823, 3824, and 3829.
[7] Value of products classified in the measuring and controlling devices industry produced by all industries.
Source: U.S. Department of Commerce; Bureau of the Census; International Trade Administration.

TABLE 23-2: U.S. Trade Patterns in Industrial and Analytical Instruments[1] in 1997

(millions of dollars; percent)

Exports			Imports		
Region[2]	Value[3]	Share, %	Region[2]	Value[3]	Share, %
NAFTA	3,956	22.7	NAFTA	2,583	24.8
Latin America	888	5.1	Latin America	84	0.8
Western Europe	4,847	27.8	Western Europe	3,707	35.6
Japan/Chinese Economic Area	3,949	22.7	Japan/Chinese Economic Area	3,258	31.3
Other Asia	2,700	15.5	Other Asia	432	4.2
Rest of world	1,086	6.2	Rest of world	344	3.3
World	17,426	100.0	World	10,407	100.0
Top Five Countries	Value	Share, %	Top Five Countries	Value	Share, %
Canada	2,742	15.7	Japan	2,579	24.8
Japan	2,545	14.6	Mexico	1,559	15.0
Mexico	1,215	7.0	Germany	1,248	12.0
Germany	1,115	6.4	United Kingdom	1,030	9.9
United Kingdom	1,051	6.0	Canada	1,024	9.8

[1] SIC 382.
[2] For definitions of regional groupings, see "Getting the Most Out of *Outlook '99.*"
[3] Values may not sum to total due to rounding.
Source: U.S. Department of Commerce, Bureau of the Census.

TABLE 23-3: I&AI End-Use Market Distribution

	Percent of I&AI Total
End-use market group (SICs)	
Electronic test and measurement (38252)	26.6
Laboratory instrumentation and apparatus (38210, 38260)	20.8
Process control instruments (38230)	17.5
Building and appliance controls (38220)	6.8
Motor vehicle instruments (38244)	5.7
Product-specific group (SICs)	
Optical apparatus and instruments (38274)	4.5
Commercial and meteorological instruments (38295)	3.6
Physical properties testing instruments (38292)	3.5
Integrating fluid meters and counters (38242)	3.4
Integrating and electrical measuring instruments (38251)	2.5
Sighting, tracking, and fire control instruments (38271)	1.6
Nuclear radiation instruments (38294)	1.3
Aircraft engine instruments (38291)	1.2
Surveying and drafting instruments (38295)	1.0
Total	100.0

Source: U.S. Bureau of the Census, MA38B: *Instruments & Selected Products.*

The principal end-use markets for ET&M products consist of manufacturers of semiconductor components, data processing and computer equipment, voice and data communications equipment, consumer electronics (televisions, audio products, and other types) products, medical electronics products, and other industrial and scientific electronic products. ET&M products are also widely used in industrial and government laboratories, by telecommunications service providers, by the military services, and in many other applications. The United States and Japan are the principal producers and markets for ET&M products (see Table 23-5).

The predominant specific products within the ET&M sector are:

- Automatic test equipment
- Semiconductor component test equipment
- Waveform measuring and analyzing equipment
- Microprocessor test equipment
- Microwave generating equipment
- Network analyzers
- Logic test and analysis equipment
- Internal combustion engine test equipment

Suppliers of ET&M products tend to specialize in specific market niches. Hewlett-Packard has the broadest product line in this marketplace and has a worldwide market share of 12 to 15

TABLE 23-4: I&AI Top 10 U.S.-Based Manufacturers

Manufacturer	Primary SIC	Sales[2]	Gross Profit Margin, %	Growth, %[3]	R&D, %[4]
Hewlett-Packard[1]	3825	42,895	43.5	17.5	7.2
Emerson Electric[1]	3823	12,299	40.2	9.8	3.6
Johnson Controls[1]	3822	11,440	NA[5]	NA	NA
Honeywell	3822	7,312	35.6	3.4	4.8
Tektronix	3825	1,940	46.0	8.4	9.7
Elsag Bailey	3823	1,613	36.9	NA	8.0
Perkin-Elmer	3826	1,277	53.1	7.0	10.4
Thermo Instrument Systems	3826	1,209	49.6	29.0	7.0
Teradyne	3825	1,172	45.3	18.1	12.3
KLA-Tencor	3825	1,032	59.3	45.9	13.0

[1] Fiscal year 1997.
[2] Total corporate revenues in 1996.
[3] Compound 5-year revenue growth rate.
[4] R&D as percent of corporate revenues.
[5] NA = not available.
Source: McGraw-Hill/Standard & Poor's; McMahon Technology Associates.

TABLE 23-5:   U.S. Trade Patterns in Instruments to Measure Electricity[1] in 1997

(millions of dollars; percent)

Exports			Imports		
Region[2]	**Value[3]**	**Share, %**	**Region[2]**	**Value[3]**	**Share, %**
NAFTA	688	11.9	NAFTA	426	15.8
Latin America	294	5.1	Latin America	7	0.3
Western Europe	1,395	24.2	Western Europe	1,157	43.1
Japan/Chinese Economic Area	1,698	29.5	Japan/Chinese Economic Area	874	32.6
Other Asia	1,406	24.4	Other Asia	63	2.3
Rest of world	283	4.9	Rest of world	159	5.9
World	5,764	100.0	World	2,686	100.0
Top Five Countries	**Value**	**Share, %**	**Top Five Countries**	**Value**	**Share, %**
Japan	1,029	17.9	Japan	774	28.8
South Korea	495	8.6	Germany	426	15.9
Canada	468	8.1	United Kingdom	415	15.4
Taiwan	415	7.2	Canada	267	9.9
Singapore	362	6.3	Mexico	158	5.9

[1] SIC 3825.
[2] For definitions of regional groupings, see "Getting the Most Out of *Outlook '99*."
[3] Values may not sum to total due to rounding.
Source: U.S. Department of Commerce, Bureau of the Census.

percent. No other supplier has as much as 5 percent of the worldwide market. Important U.S.-based ET&M suppliers include Tektronix, Teradyne, Fluke, Keithley Instruments, and National Instruments. Leading Japanese firms include Anritsu, Advantest, Hitachi, and Yokogawa. Leading European firms include Schlumberger, Philips, and Siemens. In early 1998, General Electric plc (UK) sold Marconi Instruments (Stevenage, United Kingdom), an important ET&M manufacturer, to IFR Systems (Wichita, Kansas) for $107 million. In the same year Danaher Corporation, a Washington, DC–based industrial capital goods manufacturer, acquired Fluke for $625 million.

Some manufacturers of semiconductor components produce their own ET&M gear for specialized applications. These "homemade" devices are not captured in the statistics presented in this chapter. Analog Devices, Inc., a leading producer of real-world signal processing integrated circuits, develops analog component testers internally.

Net exports (exports minus imports) of ET&M products in 1997 accounted for about 45 percent of the overall net exports of I&AI products. ET&M products have the largest net export surplus of any I&AI product sector.

LABORATORY INSTRUMENTS AND APPARATUS

The laboratory instruments (SIC 3821, 3826, 3827) industry includes the laboratory instrumentation and apparatus, optical instruments and apparatus, and sighting, tracking, and fire control instruments markets.

The laboratory instrumentation and apparatus (LI&A) market accounted for over 25 percent of total I&AI product shipments in 1998. In 1999 exports are expected to account for 45 percent of total product shipments. Imports are projected to account for 27 percent of U.S. demand, yielding a trade surplus of over $2 billion. The primary economic driver of this market is research and development (R&D) spending by industry and the federal government. Industrial R&D spending will grow about 5 percent in 1999, and federal government–funded R&D, which has been in a decline since 1991, will grow 3 percent.

LI&A shipments include three primary product groups:

- Laboratory apparatus: 24 percent
- Analytical instruments: 62 percent
- Clinical instruments: 14 percent

Environmental measurements have been a major factor in the growth of this marketplace and should be a source of continuing growth in the future.

Industrial laboratories (R&D, production and quality control, and product testing) account for about 60 percent of this market. Health-care laboratories (hospital, clinical, contract medical testing, and biomedical R&D) represent about 20 percent. All other laboratories (university, government, environmental testing, and nonprofit research) account for the balance (20 percent).

The United States accounts for about 35 percent of the worldwide LI&A market. Europe accounts for about 30 percent, and east Asia for about 20 percent. Japan represents more than half of the east Asian subtotal (see Table 23-6). The largest specific analytical instrument products include:

- Liquid chromatographs
- Gas chromatographs
- Electron microscopes
- Mass spectrometers
- Infrared spectrophotometers

TABLE 23-6: U.S. Trade Patterns in Laboratory Instruments[1] in 1997
(millions of dollars; percent)

Exports			Imports		
Region[2]	Value[3]	Share, %	Region[2]	Value[3]	Share, %
NAFTA	685	13.0	NAFTA	328	9.6
Latin America	236	4.5	Latin America	4	0.1
Western Europe	1,990	37.7	Western Europe	1,391	40.8
Japan/Chinese Economic Area	1,443	27.3	Japan/Chinese Economic Area	1,415	41.5
Other Asia	602	11.4	Other Asia	146	4.3
Rest of world	322	6.1	Rest of world	127	3.7
World	5,279	100.0	World	3,412	100.0
Top Five Countries	**Value**	**Share, %**	**Top Five Countries**	**Value**	**Share, %**
Japan	1,064	20.2	Japan	1,119	32.8
Germany	449	8.5	Germany	520	15.2
Canada	433	8.2	Canada	315	9.2
United Kingdom	401	7.6	United Kingdom	271	7.9
South Korea	257	4.9	China	165	4.8

[1] SIC 3821, 3826, 3827.
[2] For definitions of regional groupings, see "Getting the Most Out of *Outlook '99*."
[3] Values may not sum to total due to rounding.
Source: U.S. Department of Commerce, Bureau of the Census.

- Nuclear magnetic resonance (NMR) spectrometers
- Thermal analysis systems

Biotechnology instrumentation, including DNA/protein sequencers, DNA/protein synthesizers, and polymerase chain reaction (PCR) thermal cyclers, is expected to surpass $0.5 billion in worldwide sales in 1999.

According to a recent survey by *Analytical Instrument Industry Report,* a biweekly newsletter, more than 500 firms worldwide produce LI&A products. The 13 largest firms accounted for over 40 percent of this $21 billion worldwide market in 1997, and the 40 largest for almost 63 percent. The five largest LI&A firms worldwide are Thermo Instrument Systems (United States), Perkin Elmer (United States), Hewlett-Packard (United States), Shimadzu (Japan), and Horiba (Japan), with a combined share of about 25 percent. Horiba acquired Instruments, SA, of France in 1997.

Net exports of LI&A products in 1998 accounted for about 20 percent of the overall net exports of I&AI products.

MEASURING AND CONTROLLING INSTRUMENTS

The measuring and controlling instruments (SIC 3822, 3823, 3824, 3829) industry includes the process control instruments, building and appliance controls, motor vehicle instruments, integrating and fluid meters and counters, commercial and meteorological instruments, physical properties testing instruments, aircraft engine instruments, nuclear radiation instruments, and surveying and drafting instruments markets.

In 1998 this sector accounted for 44 percent of total I&AI shipments. In 1999 exports are expected to account for 33 percent of total product shipments. Imports are projected to

account for 25 percent of U.S. demand, yielding a trade surplus of almost $2.5 billion.

Process Control Instruments

The process control instrument (PCI) market accounted for over 17 percent of total I&AI product shipments in 1998. The primary economic driver of this market is industrial capital spending on plant and equipment, particularly in the nondurable goods and electric and gas utilities sectors. The worldwide PCI market in 1999 is projected to reach over $32 billion. PCIs represent about 70 percent of this overall market. Other products involved in process control that are covered in other chapters include control valves and actuators (SIC 3491), programmable logic controllers (SIC 3625), industrial computers (SIC 3571), and process control software (SIC 7372). In Asia the economic crisis is affecting this market particularly severely. This geographic area is rich in basic industrial development, the principal market for these products.

The primary end-use markets for PCIs are shown in Table 23-7. The chemical process industries account for almost 70 percent of these markets. The United States represents about 33 percent of the worldwide market, with Europe and Japan at about 31 percent and 11 percent, respectively (see Table 23-8).

The predominant specific products within the PCI total include:

- Distributed control systems
- Multifunction process computers
- Process analytical instruments
- Differential pressure transmitters
- Temperature sensors
- Mass flowmeters

TABLE 23-7: End-Use Markets for Process Control Instruments

End-Use Markets	Percent of Total Demand
Chemicals	24
Electric and gas utilities	14
Pulp and paper	10
Petroleum refining	10
Food processing	8
Metals and minerals	7
Water and wastewater treatment	5
Pipelines	5
Oil and gas production	4
Other industries	13

Source: Walton Associates, Menlo Park, CA.

By function, PCI products can be broken down into measurement and display systems (60 percent) and controllers and control systems (40 percent). Industrial process controllers are making significant inroads into process control systems markets, replacing the distributed control systems and programmable logic controllers traditionally used in those applications. Process control software products, including basic operating systems and advanced control packages, are the fastest growing process control product sector. Industrial safety and shutdown systems with fault-tolerant TMR (triple modular redundant) architecture are an important related market. In 1998 ABB acquired August Systems (Crawley, United Kingdom), a leading industrial safety system manufacturer, for $16 million. Siebe Control Systems, Honeywell, and other PCI manufacturers already have units that are active in this specialty.

The top six PCI suppliers worldwide according to *Control Magazine* (December 1997) are ABB (Switzerland), Honeywell (United States), Emerson Electric (United States), Siebe (United Kingdom), Elsag Bailey (the Netherlands), and Yoko-

gawa (Japan), with a combined share of about 45 percent of the worldwide market. Emerson and Honeywell are U.S.-based. ABB, Elsag, and Siebe are based in Europe, but their primary PCI production is sited in the United States. Yokogawa is based in Japan and competes in the U.S. market through a wholly owned subsidiary, Yokogawa Industrial Automation. The top 12 suppliers (worldwide PCI revenues of $0.5 billion or higher) account for about 60 percent of the market. At least 300 firms worldwide produce PCI products, and about half those firms are active in the United States.

In mid-1998, Elsag Bailey's controlling shareholder (Finmeccanica-Italy) announced its intention to divest. The short list of preferred acquirers included Rockwell International, GE, and Emerson Electric.

In the first 4 months of 1998 Siebe acquired three firms for a combined total of almost $1.25 billion. Wonderware and Simulation Sciences are strong software providers for process control applications. Eurotherm plc is an important industrial instrumentation firm with a strong position in temperature controls.

Net exports of PCI products in 1997 accounted for about 17 percent of overall net exports of I&AI products.

Building and Appliance Controls

The building and appliance controls (B&AC) market accounted for about 7 percent of total I&AI product shipments in 1998. The primary economic drivers of this market are construction spending on new buildings, remodeling and refurbishment of existing buildings, and residential appliance production.

Commercial (nonresidential) building controls account for about 50 percent of this market, residential building controls represent 30 percent, and appliance controls account for 20 percent. Pressure to reduce operating expenditures in the huge stock of existing buildings in the developed countries and infrastruc-

TABLE 23-8: U.S. Trade Patterns in Measuring and Controlling Instruments[1] in 1997
(millions of dollars; percent)

Exports			Imports		
Region[2]	Value[3]	Share, %	Region[2]	Value[3]	Share, %
NAFTA	2,583	40.5	NAFTA	1,829	42.4
Latin America	358	5.6	Latin America	73	1.7
Western Europe	1,461	22.9	Western Europe	1,158	26.9
Japan/Chinese Economic Area	808	12.7	Japan/Chinese Economic Area	968	22.5
Other Asia	692	10.8	Other Asia	223	5.2
Rest of world	481	7.5	Rest of world	58	1.3
World	6,383	100.0	World	4,309	100.0
Top Five Countries	Value	Share, %	Top Five Countries	Value	Share, %
Canada	1,840	28.8	Mexico	1,387	32.2
Mexico	743	11.6	Japan	686	15.9
Japan	452	7.1	Canada	442	10.3
United Kingdom	354	5.5	United Kingdom	344	8.0
Germany	352	5.5	Germany	302	7.0

[1] SIC 3822, 3823, 3824, 3829.
[2] For definitions of regional groupings, see "Getting the Most Out of *Outlook '99.*"
[3] Values may not sum to total due to rounding.
Source: U.S. Department of Commerce, Bureau of the Census.

TABLE 23-9: U.S. Nonresidential Building Census, 1995

Principal Building Activity	Buildings, thousands	Floor Space, millions of square feet
Education	327	7,852
Food sales	137	642
Food service	285	1,353
Health care	105	2,333
Lodging	158	3,618
Mercantile and service	1,289	12,728
Office	712	10,486
Public assembly	326	3,948
Public order and safety	87	1,271
Religious worship	269	2,792
Warehouse and storage	580	8,481
Other	67	1,004
Vacant	261	2,384
Total	4,603	58,892

Source: Energy Information Administration, *Commercial Building Characteristics,* DOE-EIA-0246(95).

ture development in the emerging economies are expected to sustain the demand for B&AC products. The U.S. Department of Energy's triennial nonresidential building survey estimated the U.S. population of nonresidential buildings to be 4.6 million, encompassing almost 59 billion square feet of floor space in 1995 (see Table 23-9). Less than 5 percent of these buildings, with under 20 percent of the total floor space, are equipped with computerized energy management and control systems.

According to BCS Partners, the worldwide commercial building controls market in 1997 totaled $7.65 billion. North America accounted for 37 percent of this total, Europe and Japan for 18 percent each, and the rest of the world for 27 percent. B&AC products account for about 20 percent of this market. Other products and services included in the overall total are automatic valves and dampers (SIC 3491), refrigeration and air-conditioning equipment (SIC 3585), and refrigeration and air-conditioning service and repair (SIC 7623), along with a variety of other products and services.

The three leading suppliers of commercial building controls are Johnson Controls, Honeywell, and Siemens (Landis + Staefa), each with a worldwide share of 17 to 19 percent. Siemens' acquisition of the Landis + Staefa building automation business from Electrowatt AG (Switzerland), announced in early 1997, was expected to be completed in late 1998. Siebe and Yamatake together have another 10 percent of the market, giving the top five suppliers about a 65 percent share. Approximately 300 U.S. manufacturers produce B&AC products. Honeywell, Emerson Electric, and Siebe are important suppliers to the residential controls market. Siebe, Eaton, General Electric, and Emerson Electric are important suppliers of appliance controls. Siebe acquired Eaton's $440 million appliance and climate controls business unit in 1997. These products are sold almost exclusively to appliance manufacturers for current production.

In 1998, U.S. imports of B&AC products exceeded exports, reducing the overall net exports of I&AI products by about 4 percent.

Motor Vehicle Instruments

The motor vehicle instruments (MVI) market accounted for about 6 percent of total I&AI product shipments in 1998. The primary economic driver of this market is motor vehicle (automobiles and trucks) production. MVI products are sold almost exclusively for new vehicles, with the ultimate customer being the vehicle manufacturer. Continuing growth in the worldwide demand for motor vehicles is predicted to sustain the growth of MVI shipments. The integration of electronic digital controls in motor vehicles, particularly passenger cars, has significantly expanded the opportunities for the production and sale of automatic regulation devices. The variety of measurements and associated displays is expected to continue to expand, lifting the market for MVI products.

Since most MVI products are dashboard instruments, vehicle manufacturers prefer to purchase a complete subassembly that is ready for installation. The original purchaser of many MVI products is therefore often a large automotive electronics supplier such as Motorola or Siemens. Ametek, Eaton, ITT Industries, Siebe, and TI Group (United Kingdom) are important suppliers of MVI products. Net exports of MVI products in 1998 accounted for about 8 percent of overall net exports of I&AI products.

Other Industrial and Analytical Instruments

Nine other product-specific markets account for almost one-fourth of I&AI shipments. These nine markets accounted for about 14 percent of the overall net exports of I&AI products in 1998.

Optical Instruments and Apparatus. The optical instruments and apparatus market accounts for about 4.5 percent of total I&AI product shipments. It encompasses binoculars, telescopes, optical test equipment, and photographic and other mounted lenses. U.S. and worldwide R&D investments are the principal economic factors that underlie the growth of this market.

Integrating Fluid Meters and Counters. The integrating fluid meters and counters market accounts for about 3.4 percent of total I&AI product shipments. It encompasses turbine and positive-displacement fluid meters for water metering and petroleum product metering. Counting devices are also included in this market. Residential construction is the most important factor that underlies the growth of this market.

Commercial and Meteorological Instruments. The commercial and meteorological instruments market accounts for about 3.6 percent of total I&AI product shipments. These products are quite varied, with the most important types being meteorological instruments for weather forecasting and related uses and geophysical instruments for seismic detection, petroleum exploration, and other uses. Overall GNP growth is probably the most important factor that underlies the growth of this market.

Physical Properties Testing and Inspection Instruments. The physical properties testing instruments market accounts for about 3.5 percent of total I&AI product shipments. Physical properties testing instruments account for about 45 percent of

TABLE 23-10: I&AI Product Shipments, 1997–2003
(millions of dollars; percent)

Industry Sector	1997	1998	1999	2003	Aggregate Growth, 1998–2003, %
Laboratory instruments[1]	12,207	12,923	13,554	15,372	19.0
Measuring and controlling instruments[2]	20,247	21,652	22,845	24,532	13.1
Instruments to measure electricity[3]	12,856	13,866	14,990	15,971	15.2
Total	45,310	48,441	51,389	55,875	15.3

[1] SIC 3821, 3826, 3827.
[2] SIC 3822, 3823, 3824, 3829.
[3] SIC 3825.
Source: McMahon Technology Associates.

these shipments, physical properties inspection equipment for about 40 percent, and kinematic testing equipment for about 15 percent. R&D investment by durable goods manufacturers is the most important factor underlying the growth of this market.

Integrating and Electrical Measuring Instruments. The integrating and electrical measuring instruments market accounts for about 2.5 percent of total I&AI product shipments. Household watt-hour meters and electrical recording instruments are the principal products in this sector. Residential construction is the most important factor that underlies the growth of this market.

Sighting, Tracking, and Fire Control Instruments. The sighting, tracking, and fire control instruments market accounts for about 1.6 percent of total I&AI product shipments. Weapons systems development and deployment are the most important factors that underlie the growth of this market.

Aircraft Engine Instruments. The aircraft engine instruments market accounts for just over 1 percent of total I&AI product shipments. Aircraft engine manufacturers such as GE, United Technologies (Pratt & Whitney), and Rolls-Royce are the principal customers. The products include temperature, pressure, vacuum, fuel and oil flow-rate sensors, and other measuring devices. Aircraft production is the most important factor that underlies the growth of this market.

Nuclear Radiation Instruments. The nuclear radiation instruments market accounts for just over 1 percent of total I&AI product shipments. The U.S. Department of Energy (national laboratories), the U.S. Department of Defense (military services), and nuclear power plant operators are the principal customers. The products include radiation detection instruments, radiation dosage monitoring instruments, pulse analyzers, and nuclear spectrometers. Defense R&D spending is the most important factor that underlies the growth of this market.

Surveying and Drafting Instruments. The surveying and drafting instruments market accounts for just over 1 percent of total I&AI product shipments. Surveying instruments account for about 80 percent of these product shipments. Construction activity is probably the most important factor that underlies the growth of this market.

OUTLOOK THROUGH 2003

Industrial and analytical instrument product shipments are projected to expand at over a 3 percent annual rate through 2003 (see Table 23-10). Total shipments should reach $56 billion in 2003 (current dollars).

Much of the value-added growth in the I&AI industry over the next 5 years is expected to be derived from software and services. Traditionally, this source is not captured in the SIC 38 product categories. The I&AI industry can participate in this growth, but established instrument manufacturing and distribution channels must be reexamined to maximize the value delivered to end-use customers.

Laboratory instruments are projected to expand at a 3.5 percent annual rate through 2003, and analytical instruments should grow at a faster rate. Optical instruments and apparatus and sighting, tracking, and fire-control instruments are expected to record below-average growth. Total shipments of laboratory instruments are projected to grow about 19 percent from 1998 to 2003 in constant dollars.

Measuring and controlling instruments are projected to expand at a 3 percent annual rate through 2003. Process control instruments, motor vehicle instruments, integrating fluid meters and counting devices, and smaller sectors such as aircraft engine instruments are expected to be among the higher-growth segments. Building and appliance controls product shipments are forecast to grow at a slower rate. This industry is strongly affected by the shift to services, with newer technologies replacing established products in some instances (e.g., communications device manufacturers backing out proprietary hardware). Total shipments of measuring and controlling instruments are projected to grow about 13 percent from 1998 to 2003 in constant dollars.

Instruments to measure electricity are projected to expand at over a 3 percent annual rate through 2003. Electronic test and measurement products are expected to expand at a higher rate than are integrating and electrical measuring instruments. Total shipments of instruments to measure electricity are projected to grow about 15 percent from 1998 to 2003 in constant dollars.

Terrence K. McMahon, McMahon Technology Associates, (201) 585-2050, September 1998.

■ REFERENCES

Air Conditioning & Refrigeration Institute, Arlington, VA. (703) 524-8800.

American Electronics Association, Washington, DC. (202) 682-9110.

Analytical Instrument Industry Report, East Grinstead, United Kingdom. Telephone: (011) 44-1342-835935.

Analytical Instruments & Life Science Systems Association, Alexandria, VA. (703) 836-1360.

BCS Partners, Leonia, NJ. (201) 585-2050.

CENTCOM Ltd (ACS Publications), Wayne, PA. (610) 964-8061.

Commercial Building Characteristics, Energy Information Administration, 1995, DOE/EIA-0246(95). (202) 586-1135.

Control Magazine, Putman Publishing Co., Itasca, IL. (630) 467-1300.

Electronic Industries Association, Washington, DC. (202) 457-4900.

Laboratory Products Association, Alexandria, VA. (703) 836-1360.

Measurement, Control & Automation Association, Williamsburg, VA. (757) 877-5100.

National Trade Data Bank, U.S. Department of Commerce. (202) 482-1986.

Opto-Precision Instruments Association, Alexandria, VA. (703) 836-1360.

Selected Instruments and Related Products, Current Industrial Report MA38B(96), 1996, U.S. Bureau of the Census. (301) 763-5434.

Test & Measurement World, Cahners Publishing, Newton, MA. (617) 630-2119.

Walton Associates, Menlo Park, CA. (650) 326-6464.

■ RELATED CHAPTERS

PHOTOGRAPHIC EQUIPMENT AND SUPPLIES
Economic and Trade Trends

U.S. International Trade

Source: U.S. Department of Commerce: Bureau of the Census; International Trade Administration.

World Export Market Shares

Source: United Nations; U.S. Department of Commerce, International Trade Administration.

Export Dependence and Import Penetration

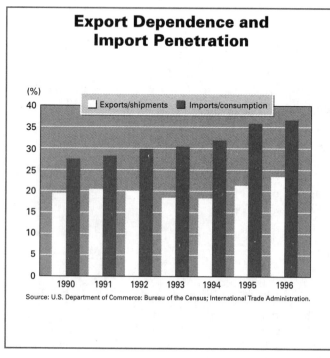

Source: U.S. Department of Commerce: Bureau of the Census; International Trade Administration.

Output and Output per Hour

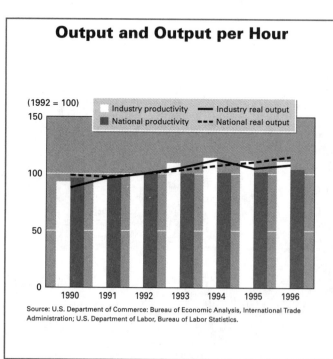

Source: U.S. Department of Commerce: Bureau of Economic Analysis, International Trade Administration; U.S. Department of Labor, Bureau of Labor Statistics.

See "Getting the Most Out of *Outlook '99*" for definitions of terms.

Photographic Equipment and Supplies

INDUSTRY DEFINITION The U.S. photographic equipment and supplies industry (SIC 3861) consists of manufacturers of photographic equipment, accessories, and parts such as still and motion-picture camera and projection apparatus; photofinishing equipment; photocopy and microfilm equipment; and sensitized film, paper, and plates and prepared photographic chemicals. Establishments engaged primarily in developing film and making photographic prints and enlargements for the trade or the general public are classified under SIC 7384, photofinishing laboratories.

FACTORS AFFECTING FUTURE INDUSTRY GROWTH

Global Industry Trends

The blurring of photographic, digital imaging, and computer technologies has placed the photographic equipment and supplies industry in the middle of a period of transition. The move into uncharted waters from traditional silver-based photographic technologies and products, which include photocopying and photofinishing equipment and prepared photographic chemicals as well as cameras and film, makes it impossible to conduct business as usual. The product mix and competition are expanding to include companies from the consumer electronics, computer equipment, and software industries, and this broadening of the imaging industry is bringing challenges and providing opportunities for growth.

Traditional silver-based photography is still the foundation of the industry. The Advanced Photo System (APS), a camera-film format which was introduced in 1996, is gaining momentum and market share, but at a slower rate than manufacturers had predicted. The camera's unique features, including drop-in film loading, the ability to choose between three sizes of photographs when taking pictures, and the ability to link to other capabilities, including image scanning, editing, and transmission by computer, should continue to attract customers. In addition, shipments of photofinishing equipment capable of APS

processing are rising. The expanding infrastructure should ease consumers' concerns about processing cost and the delay in film processing caused by the lack of on-site laboratories. Purchases of single-use cameras (SUCs) continue to grow steadily in most major markets worldwide. New SUC models created for occasions such as weddings and parties, models loaded with black-and-white film, and those designed for children keep the product line in demand. SUCs are also available in the new APS format. Expenditures on research and development have been an important component in maintaining growth in the industry. Often imaginative new products and the refreshing of old products help maintain user interest.

Company restructuring and employment downsizing continue in an effort to lower operating costs and respond to financial losses. In addition, drastic job cuts are intended to strengthen the competitive position of photographic companies as they face new challenges in the expanding market for digital products. Other areas of cost containment include improving manufacturing productivity and reducing inventory levels.

The continued convergence of photographic and imaging technologies is creating new challenges and opportunities for the photographic industry. The expanding marketplace is a driving force for competition in this industry. To improve global competitiveness, companies have formed strategic alliances with domestic and foreign firms. Cooperative efforts typically include joint research and production, technology sharing, and dual product marketing that can result in a stronger market position. Also, these arrangements increase access to new markets and provide economies of scale in production and marketing. In the area of digital photography, for example, Eastman Kodak signed an agreement with Picture Vision, Inc., to create an Internet-based digital photography network that will allow consumers to view, E-mail, store, and use their photos on personal computers. The collaboration between Xerox Corporation and Olivetti Lexikon to extend their products across small office–home office and business markets should enhance both companies' standing. Under the agreement, Xerox will provide Olivetti Lexikon with a range of laser printers and digital copier products, and Olivetti Lexikon will supply Xerox with facsimile, printer, and multi-function products that use ink-jet technology. These products will be marketed under the companies' respective brand names, and each company will add software and image processing capabilities to differentiate its product line.

Global manufacturing is another way for companies to stay competitive. By moving the production of mature products to countries with lower labor rates, companies can hold down costs and gain access to local markets that have nontariff barriers in place. This can be a win-win situation, since the host country gains by obtaining capital, management expertise, and technology. This trend is reflected in U.S. imports of photographic products from countries such as China and Taiwan, which increased at an annual average rate of 74 percent and 15 percent, respectively, between 1993 and 1997.

Opportunities for growth exist in many developing regions, where markets for photographic equipment and supplies are small and penetration is low. Exports of photographic products to the Big Emerging Markets (BEMs) increased 14 percent in 1997, with Mexico and the Chinese Economic Area leading the way. However, the recent Asian economic crisis should cause a slowdown in shipments and sales in an uncertain economic climate. U.S. companies thus may have to reassess their short-term marketing strategies and plans for expansion in the Asian region.

Domestic Trends

Shipments. The industry's wide range of products and applications for end users in the consumer and business markets allows the industry to adjust the product mix to compensate for periods of slow growth. Since the U.S. market is mature and typically experiences slow growth, new technologies and products are necessary to stimulate domestic demand. The production of digital copiers and multifunctional peripherals should make a larger contribution to industry shipments as consumers and businesses demand more functionality from their business equipment and ratios of price to performance improve. In addition, the United States has sustained a healthy economy, with discretionary income recently growing at a 5 percent annual rate. As a result, consumers are more likely to purchase leisure goods and services, such as cameras, film, and photoprocessing services.

Photographic industry shipments increased 3 percent in 1996 to $22.3 billion and maintained a modest growth of 4 percent in both 1997 and 1998 to reach $24.2 billion. Photographic product shipments increased to $20 billion in 1998, of which 24 percent was exported (see Table 24-1). In constant dollars, industry shipments reached $25.7 billion in 1998. Contributing to this growth has been the increased production of the APS and related photofinishing equipment. Other factors include steady demand for single-use cameras and continued expansion of the industry into the arena of digital technologies.

TABLE 24-1: Photographic Equipment and Supplies (SIC 3861) Trends and Forecasts
(millions of dollars except as noted)

	1992	1993	1994	1995	1996	1997[1]	1998[2]	1999[3]	Percent Change 96–97	97–98	98–99	92–96[4]
Industry data												
Value of shipments[5]	22,119	22,368	23,261	21,654	22,297	23,250	24,200	24,700	4.3	4.1	2.1	0.2
Value of shipments (1992$)	22,119	23,276	24,825	23,135	23,796	24,734	25,745	26,200	3.9	4.1	1.8	1.8
Total employment (thousands)	77.3	75.7	63.9	61.1	60.7	60.0	57.9	53.3	-1.2	-3.5	-7.9	-5.9
Production workers (thousands)	39.2	38.0	34.7	35.2	35.7	36.3	36.0	34.2	1.7	-0.8	-5.0	-2.3
Average hourly earnings ($)	14.65	14.64	15.82	16.41	16.72							3.4
Capital expenditures	805	775	753	746	724							-2.6
Product data												
Value of shipments[5]	18,861	19,686	20,227	19,159	19,129	19,500	20,000	20,400	1.9	2.6	2.0	0.4
Value of shipments (1992$)	18,861	20,485	21,586	20,469	20,415	20,745	21,150	21,630	1.6	2.0	2.3	2.0
Trade data												
Value of imports	6,401	7,017	7,702	8,399	8,440	9,083	9,600	10,000	7.6	5.7	4.2	7.2
Value of exports	3,758	3,631	3,702	4,074	4,483	4,687	4,850	5,000	4.6	3.5	3.1	4.5

[1] Estimate except imports and exports.
[2] Estimate.
[3] Forecast.
[4] Compound annual rate.
[5] For definition of industry versus product values, see "Getting the Most Out of *Outlook '99*."
Source: U.S. Department of Commerce: Bureau of the Census; International Trade Administration.

Other contributors to U.S.-based production of photographic products include foreign firms such as Fuji (Japan) with its multiproduct manufacturing facility in South Carolina. The expansion of that factory in 1997 added the production of 35mm film, giving the plant an initial capacity to manufacture 100 million rolls of film annually. The facility also increased its production capacity of color photographic paper 50 percent above the existing levels.

Employment. Employment in the photographic industry continued its downward course, dropping 1 percent in 1997 to about 60,000 workers. Industry restructuring and cost containment efforts have steadily reduced employment since its peak in 1982. By contrast, production workers experienced a slight upturn in employment in 1995 as manufacturers prepared for the introduction of a new camera system and expanded production into digital imaging products. The ratio of production workers to total employees has edged closer to a 60-40 split compared with the historical ratio of 50-50. This change reflects companies' efforts to remove many administrative and management positions and increase productivity. However, this modest increase in production workers may be short-lived, since major photographic manufacturers announced substantial job cuts in 1998. Managers hope that savings from employee reduction will help contain increasing price pressures and allow photographic companies to better position themselves to compete with imaging and consumer electronics firms. Total industry employment was expected to drop nearly 4 percent to 57,900 employees in 1998, of which 36,000 were production workers.

Trade Patterns. The United States continues to rank as the second largest (after Japan) exporter of photographic equipment and supplies, representing 13 percent of the worldwide total. U.S. exports of photographic products rose at a modest rate of 4 percent in 1997 to reach $4.7 billion (see Table 24-2). Europe is the major regional export market for U.S. photographic products, accounting for $1.5 billion, or about one-third of the total. However, the European share declined from 42 percent of the export total in 1992 to 32 percent in 1997, reflecting slow growth in European photographic markets. On an individual country basis, Canada received the largest share of U.S. photographic exports with 16 percent, or $740 million. Rising demand in developing countries, such as the BEMs, plays an increasing role in U.S. photographic exports, going up from 20 percent of the export total in 1992 to 28 percent in 1997 (see Figure 24-1).

By product group, exports of sensitized film and paper accounted for 47 percent of the export total and had the fastest growth rate, up 8 percent to $2.3 billion in 1997. Photocopier and microfilming equipment followed with 19 percent of the export total, or $900 million. In addition to traditional photographic products, exports of still-image video cameras (digital cameras) more than doubled in 1997, rising to $69 million. The primary destinations for digital cameras included Germany with 17 percent of the export total and Canada with 13 percent.

Imports have always been an important contributor to the U.S. photographic market and accounted for 38 percent of U.S. consumption in 1997, rising nearly 8 percent to $9.1 billion. Photocopying and microfilming equipment ($4.0 billion) and still picture equipment ($2.2 billion) together accounted for nearly 70 percent of the U.S. photographic import total. In the related area of digital photography, increased U.S. demand for digital cameras is being met partially by imports, with an inflow of more than 1 million units in 1997. Japan supplied 73 percent of the total units. Taiwan and the Republic of Korea each supplied 11 percent of the total volume. In terms of value, U.S. imports of digital cameras reached nearly $300 million in 1997.

TABLE 24-2: U.S. Trade Patterns in Photographic Equipment and Supplies[1] in 1997
(millions of dollars; percent)

Exports			Imports		
Regions[2]	Value[3]	Share, %	Regions[2]	Value[3]	Share, %
NAFTA	1,221	26.1	NAFTA	619	6.8
Latin America	508	10.8	Latin America	33	0.4
Western Europe	1,544	32.9	Western Europe	1,790	19.7
Japan/Chinese Economic Area	787	16.8	Japan/Chinese Economic Area	6,021	66.3
Other Asia	287	6.1	Other Asia	603	6.6
Rest of world	339	7.2	Rest of world	17	0.2
World	4,687	100.0	World	9,083	100.0
Top Five Countries	Value	Share, %	Top Five Countries	Value	Share, %
Canada	740	15.8	Japan	4,633	51.0
Japan	528	11.3	China	997	11.0
Mexico	482	10.3	Netherlands	438	4.8
United Kingdom	395	8.4	Germany	386	4.2
Netherlands	290	6.2	United Kingdom	331	3.6

[1] SIC 3861.
[2] For definitions of regional groupings, see "Getting the Most Out of *Outlook '99*."
[3] Values may not sum to total due to rounding.
Source: U.S. Department of Commerce, Bureau of the Census.

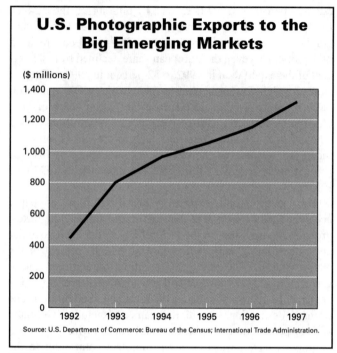

U.S. Photographic Exports to the Big Emerging Markets

($ millions)

Source: U.S. Department of Commerce: Bureau of the Census; International Trade Administration.

FIGURE 24-1

Asia is by far the largest supplier of photographic products to the United States with $6.3 billion, or 72 percent of the import total, in 1997. Some shifts in the country of origin have occurred in recent years as Japan, the largest individual supplier, has moved production offshore to countries with lower labor rates, such as China and Taiwan. As a result, U.S. imports from those Asian countries continue to increase. For example, photographic imports from China rose 39 percent and totaled nearly $1 billion in 1997 versus $83 million in 1992. U.S. photographic imports from China consist primarily of still picture equipment and photocopiers. Similarly, imports from Taiwan showed strong growth, rising 48 percent to $158 million in 1997. In contrast to strong import growth from other Asian countries, U.S. imports from Japan rose only 2 percent to $4.6 billion, or 69 percent of the Asian total, down from 73 percent in 1996.

The U.S. trade deficit in photographic equipment and supplies increased $276 million to $4.2 billion in 1997. The U.S. photographic trade deficit with the Asian region rose 10 percent to $5.3 billion, as deficits with Japan and China increased to $3.9 billion and $971 million, respectively, in 1997.

Other Industry-Specific Information

Photocopiers. Analog plain-paper copiers are the mainstay of the copier industry. These copiers use optical technology to capture and transfer images to paper through an electrophotographic process. This market segment is mature, and products and pricing are similar among suppliers. The common use of original equipment manufacturing (OEM) agreements is one reason for product similarities, since companies agree to source virtually the same product from a variety of manufacturers and distinguish it by adding finishing features, model options, and software under

their own brand names. Analog copiers account for the bulk of photocopier shipments. Profits from this technology fund the research and development of digital technology and products.

Digital Copiers. Business demand for digital copiers will increase as the prices of digital products decline. Digital copiers scan images and transfer them to electronic form. Since the data are digitized, users can edit, copy, print, store, retrieve, and transmit images and documents. According to Dataquest, Inc., the U.S. market for digital copiers more than tripled in 1997 to 100,000 units, up from 33,700 in 1996 (see Figure 24-2). Traditional copier manufacturers will face a challenge from digital technologies and will have to broaden their product lines through the use of OEM agreements. Advances in copier and printer technology are forcing the two industries to compete in the same marketplace. In anticipation of this competition, some copier companies are choosing to market computer printers themselves, such as Sharp with color laser printers and Danka, which announced that it will distribute and service Hewlett-Packard's LaserJet printers. Vendors say that the introduction of digital copiers that can serve as network printers and the increasing use of printers to reproduce documents are part of an industry shift toward multiuse document devices instead of traditional stand-alone printers and copiers. Dataquest predicts that by 2001 the U.S. digital copier market will be close to 600,000 units, or six times its current level.

During the transition period from analog to digital, traditional copier manufacturers may have a competitive edge because of their established channels of distribution and service networks, according to Dataquest. Nearly 90 percent of personal copiers are sold through office superstores, warehouse clubs, and specialty electronic stores. For the other segments, 86 percent of copiers are sold through dealers and branches that

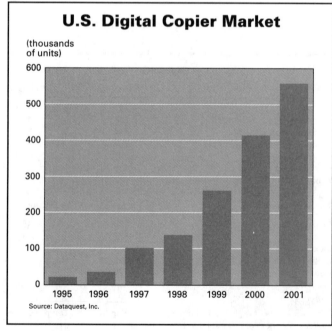

U.S. Digital Copier Market

(thousands of units)

Source: Dataquest, Inc.

FIGURE 24-2

use their service capabilities to their advantage. American vendors primarily use branch distribution, and Japanese vendors primarily use office equipment dealers. However, in an effort to broaden their reach, suppliers have begun to experiment with a variety of distribution channels that include a combination of branch and dealer networks, mergers, joint ventures, and sales agents.

Color Copiers.   Color copiers are significantly more expensive than black-and-white models because color reproduction uses a more complicated technology and requires more consumable supplies. Industry surveys indicate that the cost difference and slower speed are the largest hurdles for most end users in deciding to purchase color copiers. Recent product introductions are aimed at lowering prices and increasing speed to make color products more attractive to businesses. In addition, many newer copiers are network-ready and can serve as auxiliary color output devices.

Toners.   The growing market for color peripherals is spurring demand for color toners-cartridges. CAP Ventures of Norwell, MA, projects that the worldwide market for color toners will grow at an annual rate of about 40 percent and reach $1.8 billion by 2001. The key to this growth will be lower-priced color equipment, which should allow users to compensate for the higher cost of color toners. The average cost of color toners is $100 per pound compared with $25 for monochrome.

Chemicals.   U.S. still-film sales continue to increase despite advances in digital photography. The APS is gaining momentum, and single-use cameras continue to be popular. Both use film and require chemical processing. In industrial markets such as medical x-ray applications, some end users prefer film images to digital images for the archiving of records. Other areas that provide growth opportunities for photographic chemicals are foreign countries with developing photographic markets as they begin to expose and process more color film. However, manufacturers continue to develop ways to reduce the amount of chemicals needed to process film. Processors are also recycling and recovering more chemicals. This trend toward the use of lower quantities may lead to a decrease in overall demand in the future.

INDUSTRY GROWTH PROJECTIONS FOR THE NEXT 1 AND 5 YEARS

Since overall demand for photographic products remains soft, industry shipments are expected to increase at a modest 2 percent to $24.7 billion in 1999. Both the business sector and the consumer sector should contribute to this growth. Lower prices for digital and color copiers, coupled with user demand for more functionality in office equipment, are projected to accelerate the replacement of aging equipment. With an expanded production base, foreign firms producing sensitized materials in the United States will contribute to the overall growth in shipments while strengthening their market position. Consumer confidence and discretionary spending are projected to remain

stable, and this will translate into more purchases of leisure products and recreational travel. The APS is still a relatively new technology, and lower prices for digital cameras should boost sales to amateur photographers.

By 1999 photographic industry employment will fall to about 53,300 workers. This drastic drop in employment will result from the continuation of massive restructuring by U.S. manufacturers to contain costs. Efforts to improve productivity and the use of cooperative agreements will result in a further decline in production workers to about 34,100. Also, streamlining efforts will be necessary as companies begin to compete in digital markets, where profitability may take some time to achieve.

Exports should be sluggish, rising only 3 percent to $5 billion in 1999. Contributing factors include the declining share of photographic product exports to Europe and the lack of comparable increases in developing markets. Exports to Asia will continue to be soft for the third consecutive year because of slowdowns in market growth resulting from the region's economic crisis. Recovery from these economic problems will be an important factor in the rebound of trade and market demand. Interest and investment in China should continue unabated, as manufacturers have not been discouraged by the downturn in economic activity there. China's demographics should lead to strong long-term growth.

Photographic imports will continue to outpace exports and should increase 4 percent to $10 billion in 1999. The photographic trade deficit is expected to increase to an estimated $5 billion.

Assuming favorable industry and market conditions, photographic industry shipments are expected to maintain a modest growth rate and reach $26.7 billion in 2003. As is typical for the industry, periods of expansion and contraction could occur, but overall there should be ongoing improvements in traditional silver halide film technology and growth in the popularity of digital technology. As a result, product shipments should reach $22 billion and should account for a declining share of industry shipments as companies further expand their mix of traditional photographic and digital products. Lower prices and increased demand for digital and color office equipment can be expected to fuel industry expansion. In the digital imaging marketplace, Asian photographic and consumer electronics firms will use lower costs to increase their U.S. market share. Meanwhile, manufacturers will continue to make inroads in both traditional and digital imaging markets in developing countries, particularly in Latin America and Asia. The industry's labor force will stabilize after declining for 20 consecutive years. Production workers should experience a slight upturn in employment, but suppliers will continue to limit growth in hiring by implementing ways to improve manufacturing productivity to keep down costs.

After some weakness in the 1998–1999 period, exports are expected to climb at an annual average rate of about 5 percent to $6.1 billion in 2003. Exports as a percentage of domestic production should decline because the use of global manufacturing will redistribute production bases to areas with a lower labor compensation rate. Asia will continue to be the major supplier of photographic products to the United States. However, Japan's dominance as the major supplier will lessen since most Japanese camera producers have manufacturing operations in other Asian countries (see the box below). U.S. photographic imports should total about $13 billion, resulting in a trade deficit of $6.9 billion in 2003.

Silver halide photographic technology will maintain its dominance in regard to industry revenues. While prices for digital imaging products will continue to fall, traditional photography and digital photography will coexist rather than directly compete, since each has its own advantages and limitations. Photographic suppliers will encounter strong competition from consumer electronics and other products in the information technology industries in regard to consumers' discretionary spending.

THE KODAK 301/WTO CASE

In July 1995, acting on a Section 301 petition filed by Eastman Kodak, the U.S. government initiated a trade complaint and an investigation of Japan's consumer photographic materials sector. After an 11-month investigation, the U.S. government determined that the Japanese market did have unreasonable practices with respect to the sale and distribution of consumer photographic materials, and made three requests through the World Trade Organization (WTO) about a broad range of market access barriers in the consumer photographic materials sector in Japan. Separately, Kodak filed a complaint with the Japan Fair Trade Commission, alleging the existence of anticompetitive practices and a possible violation of Japan's antitrust law in the consumer film and photographic paper market.

The final WTO film panel report, issued on January 30, 1998, did not find Japan in violation of its General Agreement on Tariffs and Trade (GATT) obligations and rejected U.S. claims that Japanese government measures restrict Kodak's ability to sell film in the Japanese market. The United States did not appeal the decision.

The United States noted that pursuing the GATT case led Japan to take some steps that will benefit U.S. and other foreign film manufacturers. These steps include movement toward eliminating the Large Scale Retail Store Law and the relaxation of impediments to foreign firms' ability to promote their products in Japan. Additionally, film was removed from the list of sectors covered by the Business Reform Law, which allows Japan to provide financial support and other assistance to firms facing increased competition.

On February 3, 1998, the Department of Commerce and the United States Trade Representative announced a new market opening initiative aimed at improving access for imported photographic film and paper in the Japanese market. An interagency monitoring committee is reviewing the implementation of formal measures promised by the government of Japan to the WTO panel regarding Japan's efforts to ensure openness of its market to imports of film. It also will review Japan's representations on a regular basis. Its first report was issued in July 1998.

GLOBAL MARKET PROSPECTS

Asia is a major source of and market for photographic products. It is the primary source of U.S. photographic imports and the second largest region for American exports. Industry analysts predict slower growth in the region because of the recent economic crisis. They do not expect a full turnaround for several years and believe that declines in industrial production, widespread layoffs, and rising inflation will affect business practices and trade. Overall, most Asian suppliers of photographic equipment continued to ship products to the U.S. market in 1997. Areas of weakness included imports from Malaysia, which declined 24 percent in 1997 and continued that downward trend in early 1998. Similarly, photographic imports from Indonesia began dropping in December 1997 and had fallen another 60 percent 3 months later.

Industry analysts expect most economies in the Asian region to grow at a much slower rate. With higher unemployment, decreased consumer demand, and currency fluctuations, Asia's ability to absorb exports from the United States could slow down temporarily. A falloff in exports is expected through 2000, but the demographics remain in place for a rebound in demand after that year. Meanwhile, the currency situation could help companies that want to expand their presence in Asia because labor rates and the cost of investing in manufacturing facilities have fallen there.

China has been a primary focus of photographic industry expansion in recent years. Two-way trade with the United States grew 20 percent between 1995 and 1997. China's photographic market is changing at an accelerating pace and, with double-digit annual growth rates, is estimated to be one of the fastest growing in the world. U.S. companies are continuing to invest and expand manufacturing and marketing capabilities there. For example, Kodak announced in 1998 that it will invest more than $1 billion in China over the next several years to upgrade technology, improve manufacturing capacity, and expand distribution and marketing capabilities. Japanese companies are also expanding their presence in China. Fuji reportedly will increase its annual output of cameras fourfold by adding the production of APS cameras. That move, which will increase exports to Japan, the United States, and Europe, also could strengthen Fuji's position in meeting the requirements for marketing rights in China. Canon recently added two Chinese manufacturing and marketing facilities. One plant was established to produce and sell photocopying machines, and the other further expands Canon's Chinese-based camera production.

Many U.S. and foreign companies are eager to pursue the Chinese photographic market even with high tariff rates for cameras [30 percent plus 17 percent of cost, insurance, and freight (CIF) value] and marketing restrictions. China has an enormous, virtually untapped population in regard to photographic products. Less than 15 percent of households in China have cameras, according to industry research. Photofinishing News Inc. projected that 7 million cameras were sold in China in 1996. Official estimates put the market for color film at about 100 million rolls in 1996. Some industry reports suggest higher levels and project sales approaching 200 million rolls in 1997. China's consumer film market is expected to grow 15 percent a year over the next decade, and China may surpass Japan to become the world's second largest consumer film market. Mini-labs continue to proliferate, doubling in a 2-year period to reach about 20,000 in 1997.

PRODUCT SUMMARIES

Traditional Cameras

U.S. camera sales rose slightly in 1996 to 15.1 billion units, and revenue reached $1.4 billion, according to Photo Marketing Association International (PMAI). Sales of 35mm lens shutter cameras slipped 2 percent to 9.8 million but still accounted for approximately 66 percent of the total cameras sold. These compact autofocus cameras had an average selling price under $100 with a standard lens and under $200 for models with zoom and telephoto lenses. Sales of 35mm single-lens reflex (SLR) cameras have remained relatively stable for several years with a unit volume around 800,000 in 1996. Smaller and lighter-weight models and lower-priced autofocus models helped sustain a 5 percent market share. Sales of cartridge cameras dropped 24 percent to 1.6 million units and accounted for 11 percent of the total unit volume but less than 2 percent of total value in 1996. The cartridge camera (110) has been on the market since 1972 and competes with 35mm lens shutter cameras, single-use cameras, and APS format cameras because of its ease of use. Because cartridge cameras are an older technology and newer formats are on the market, sales will continue to fall.

Single-use cameras, also referred to as one-time-use cameras, constitute a segment of the photographic market that continues to grow. These portable, easy to use cameras have helped sustain manufacturers and retailers during periods of slow industry growth, and their popularity continues unabated. Promotional packaging, new APS models, telephoto, and black-and-white versions should boost their popularity even further. Sales increased over 20 percent to an estimated 89 million units in 1997, according to PMAI, and are expected to continue to climb over the next few years.

After a sluggish start, which included supply shortages and limited advertising, the APS ended its first year on the market with U.S. sales of 1.1 million units, according to PMAI. Sales of this totally new camera system captured about 7 percent of the total camera units sold and contributed 11 percent to the total dollar value as a result of the high prices of some early models. While APS photography is silver halide–based, camera, film, and processing costs can be somewhat higher than those for 35mm photography. The original group of five manufacturers has been joined by other producers to provide more than 70 models that range from single-use models to high-end SLR models. APS features include small size, drop-in film loading (24mm), the option to select three different picture formats, index print proof sheets, and film that is magnetically coated to hold digitized data such as exposure parameters. The magnetic encoding on the film is read by APS photofinishing

equipment, and corrections are made automatically to improve color, lighting, and contrast on the prints. In addition, the scannability of APS film should support digital technologies and help boost sales of silver-based photographic equipment and supplies into the next century. PMAI expected sales of APS cameras to increase to about 3 million units, or 20 percent of total camera sales, in 1997.

The APS also made inroads in international photographic markets. According to GfK Marketing Services Europe, APS models captured 6 percent of overall camera sales in Europe in 1996. In Germany, for example, the momentum of APS continued into 1997 as sales almost doubled to 640,000 units, representing a 16 percent share of the German camera market. APS camera sales nearly doubled in Japan, increasing to 1.6 million units in 1997 and accounting for 32 percent of total compact camera sales.

Instant camera and film sales have remained relatively flat over the past several years because of the proliferation of traditional 1-hour photofinishing outlets. Also, low-end digital cameras that allow users to see images immediately have further weakened sales of instant cameras. Key developing markets that provided growth opportunities for instant cameras, such as Russia and China, have experienced significant sales declines over the past 2 years as a result of increased competition from minilabs and traditional photography products. Instant camera sales to the consumer market totaled 1.7 million units in 1996, and instant film remained at 88 million units for the third consecutive year, according to the PMAI. Polaroid, the only U.S. manufacturer of instant-imaging products, announced the development of the first instant single-use camera that will produce prints while the photographer waits but is disposable after the film is exposed. The camera is expected to go on sale in the second half of 1999. Polaroid also provides products to government agencies and professional and industrial markets such as insurance, medical, and real estate, and is attempting to broaden its business base to provide more diversity through the introduction of new digital imaging products.

Digital Cameras

Demand is growing for digital still cameras as new sensors help reduce prices and improve resolution. Charge-coupled devices (CCDs) are currently the most widely used technology for converting light into electrical signals. The recent introduction of megapixel CCDs and complementary metal oxide semiconductor (CMOS) sensors offers the potential for lower power consumption at more moderate costs. As a result of lower consumer prices, some in the range of $250 to $300, digital cameras are gaining greater consumer acceptance. The expansion of the digital camera market has led to more types of cameras with differentiated features, resolution capabilities, and price points. The diverse suppliers include traditional camera manufacturers, producers of consumer electronics products, and computer equipment and software suppliers. There is some variation in market size depending on definitions. Industry reports that placed U.S. digital camera shipments at around 600,000 units in 1996 estimated growth to between 800,000 and 1.2 million units in 1998. On a worldwide basis, International Data Corporation and Future Image, Inc., projected that sales would reach 8.4 million units by 2001, with revenues of $4 billion.

Demand for digital cameras is primarily business-driven, with users in professional and commercial fields such as photojournalism, advertising and publishing, insurance, and real estate. Use among small businesses, especially those which are computer-oriented, is also picking up. Digital images are being used in desktop publishing and are being transmitted over in-house networks and the Internet. Interest in the consumer segment has been boosted by the increase in home computer ownership in the United States. According to industry estimates, 35 to 40 percent of U.S. households own computers. Much of the imaging software that computer owners need to enhance and edit, catalog, and download and save photos as picture files is bundled with the digital camera. However, the consumer segment has a long way to go before digital cameras will be entrenched in the home. A recent Digital Imaging Marketing Association (DIMA) survey revealed that only 0.3 percent of all households actually own a digital still camera, 8.7 percent say they intend to purchase one in 1998, and 13.6 percent plan to purchase one in the near future.

OEM partnerships are common between competitors to develop digital cameras, such as the Sanyo-Olympus high-end model and the 2-million-pixel professional model jointly developed by Kodak and Canon. Another manufacturing strategy was announced by Intel Corporation that could further increase the number of suppliers and bring portable personal computer (PC)–digital cameras to the market more quickly. Intel's design guidelines specify the use of the universal serial bus (USB) to transfer data from digital cameras to personal computers, MMX technology for image processing, and miniature card technology for storage. The Portable PC Camera design guideline is supported by 25 companies, including Hewlett-Packard, Kodak, and Microsoft. This effort should make it easier to use digital still cameras with personal computers, promoting their use as a computer peripheral input device. In November 1997 Intel announced its PC Camera Kit, which has the five key ingredients (sensor, image processing unit, microprocessor, memory, and some form of flash memory) needed to assemble a PC-digital camera. Individual manufacturers will provide other essentials, such as lenses and camera bodies. According to industry reports, Samsung has produced the first PC camera using Intel's design guidelines. Similar OEM agreements have been formed with related software companies for product distribution. For example, Adobe has agreements with most of the major digital camera vendors to bundle its photo-editing software.

Digital imaging should continue to flourish with the combination of falling prices and improving picture resolution. With associated scanner and printer technologies, this segment is quickly becoming one of the most popular and rapidly growing technology markets. Dataquest predicts that worldwide production of digital still cameras will reach 9.2 billion units by 2002 (see Figure 24-3).

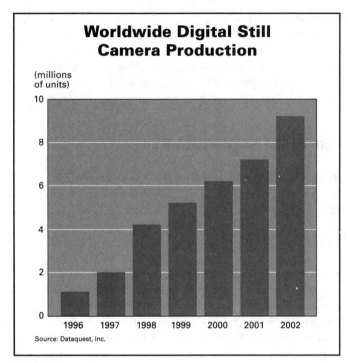

FIGURE 24-3

Digital Cameras in International Markets

Digital cameras have become an essential part of the camera business in Japan, where domestic sales reached an estimated 1 million units in 1997. About 60 models compete in this market, and those with over 1 million pixels are expected to account for one-third of total Japanese sales, according to a survey by Nikkei Market Access of Japan. Casio, a leader in the market, saw its 40 percent share reduced by half during 1997 as other manufacturers introduced competing models. Digital camera sales were forecast to increase 36 percent to 1.5 million units in 1998. Sales are anticipated to exceed 2 million by the year 2000.

Digital camera sales in Europe were estimated at about 100,000 units in 1996, with about one-third sold in the German market, according to Prophoto, a German photographic industry association. In 1997, digital camera sales alone more than doubled over the 1996 level to 80,000 units in Germany, and this could bring Europe's overall total close to 250,000 units.

Film

The APS format has helped renew interest in film photography. Worldwide consumption of conventional roll film increased 7 percent in 1996 to 3 billion units, according to Photofinishing News (see Figure 24-4). Film use in the United States rose 3 percent to 945 million rolls in 1996, up from a 0.3 percent increase the previous year. The U.S. film market is the largest in the world, accounting for one-third of the total. While APS film accounted for less than 1 percent of total U.S. film sales, or about 5 million rolls, in 1996, that share will grow as camera sales rise, according to PMAI. APS film is projected to capture 20 percent of U.S. film sales by the end of the decade. The dominant 35mm film format, accounting for over 80 percent of the total volume, rose 8 percent. In contrast, sales of cartridge and disc film fell 10 percent

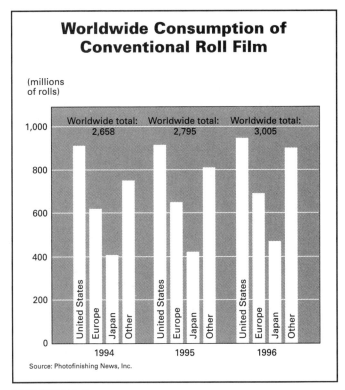

FIGURE 24-4

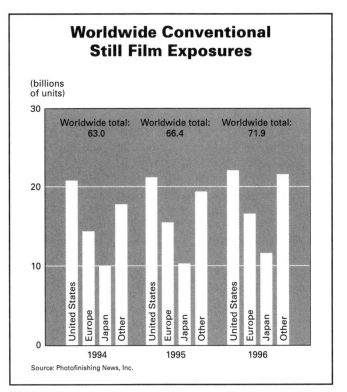

FIGURE 24-5

and 17 percent, respectively. Instant film sales remained flat.

Europe is the world's second largest film market with the consumption of 690 million rolls, or about 23 percent of the worldwide total, in 1996. Germany is the region's largest market, accounting for nearly one-third of sales. In 1997 Germany's film sales increased 3 percent to 182 million rolls. Color negative film represented 83 percent of this total. Japan is the third largest film market with 470 million rolls, or 16 percent of the worldwide total. Virtually all of Japan's film is color, and 35mm film accounted for 85 percent of the total. APS film accounted for 4 percent of the total, including sales of APS single-use cameras. Film consumption in the rest of the world, which accounts for about 30 percent of the total, is growing at double-digit rates as many countries are developing photographic markets.

Worldwide conventional film consumption is projected to reach 3.4 billion units by 2000, according to industry sources. The United States and Japan should maintain their shares of the world market, but the European percentage probably will decline. Film consumption will increase in other regions as companies continue to penetrate those markets.

Exposures

Traditional photographic exposures increased 8 percent to 71.9 billion in 1996 (see Figure 24-5). An additional rise of 1.8 billion in instant film exposures and 600 million digital camera exposures brought the worldwide total to 74.2 billion, according to Photofinishing News. Regional shares are similar to those of film sales. The United States accounted for the largest share of film exposures, followed by Europe and Japan. Both APS and digital exposures should represent an increasing share of overall exposures as consumers accept the new systems and learn the benefits of these evolving technologies.

Photofinishing

The worldwide value of photographic processing services increased 4 percent in 1996 to $32.7 billion, according to Photofinishing News. Amateur photofinishing, which accounts for nearly three-fourths of the market, rose 4 percent to $23.9 billion. The nearly $9 billion professional segment increased at a rate of 5 percent. Europe's combined photofinishing market increased 7 percent to $10 billion, while Japan's declined 5 percent to $6 billion. Photoprocessing in the rest of the world grew 12 percent in 1996 to nearly $5 billion.

In the United States, amateur photofinishing sales rose 2 percent to $5.9 billion in 1996. The volume of film processed rose 3 percent to 647 million rolls, with 97 percent of that total accounted for by color negative film. Discount stores and mass merchandisers have captured the largest share of photoprocessing by volume (33 percent) and are becoming a force among processing outlets. This channel offers consumers the convenience of one-stop shopping and sells nearly 50 percent of all cameras and 60 percent of the film purchased, according to PMAI. Discounters generally have strong promotional pricing programs in place but traditionally have lower sales from enlargements, reprints, and other ancillary processing sales compared with other channels. Drugstores are the second outlet of choice for amateur film processing, with 24 percent, and supermarkets have 16 percent.

In terms of amateur photofinishing by film format, 35mm accounted for the overwhelming share of prints, with close to

94 percent. Cartridge film accounted for 5 percent, while APS and disc film together accounted for 1 percent of the total in 1996, according to PMAI. APS processing should grow significantly after the testing of a flat rate for developing and printing to simplify the pricing structure. Initally consumers were charged processing fees according to whether the APS film was exposed in a 4×6, 4×7, or panoramic format. This new pricing strategy now brings APS in line with 35mm and other film formats that charge the same price for each frame of film processed.

Digital imaging and the blending of this technology with traditional photography should complement and stimulate growth in the processing business. This new technology presents both a challenge and an opportunity to photoprocessors willing to provide support services for images presented in a variety of formats. Among the new services are digital printing, scanning to digitize traditional film, archiving photos on disk, and preparing photos for use on the Internet. To support these services, photofinishers are beginning to purchase new automated equipment that combines the elements of digital technology with traditional chemical-based film processing.

Joyce Watson, U.S. Department of Commerce, Office of Computers and Business Equipment, (202) 482-0574, joyce _watson@ita.doc.gov, May 1998.

■ REFERENCES

CAP Ventures, Inc., 600 Cordwainer Drive, Norwell, MA 02061. (781) 871-9000, http://www.capv.com.

Dataquest, Inc., 251 River Oaks Parkway, San Jose, CA 95134-1913. (408) 468-8000, http://gartner4gartnerweb.com/dq/static/dq.html.

Future Image Inc., 520 S. El Camino Real, Burlingame, CA 94402. (650) 579-0493, http://www.futureimage.com.

International Data Corporation, 5 Speen Street, Framingham, MA. (508) 935-4389, http://www.idcresearch.com.

Manufacturers' Shipments, Inventories and Orders (M3-1), *Current Industrial Reports,* U.S. Bureau of the Census, Washington, DC 20230. (301) 457-4673, http://www.census.gov.

1995–1996 Industry Trends Report and *1996–1997 Industry Trends Report/International,* Photo Marketing Association International, 3000 Picture Place, Jackson, MI 49201. (517) 788-8100, http://www.pmai.org.

1996–1997 Digital Imaging Industry Trends, Digital Imaging Marketing Association, 3000 Picture Place, Jackson, MI 49201. (517) 788-8100, http://www.pmai.org.

1997 International Photo Imaging Industry Report, Photofinishing News, Inc., 10915 Bonita Beach Road, Suite 1091, Bonita Springs, FL 34135. (941) 992-4421, www.photo-news.com.

Photo International, World Press, Inc., 807 Chatore Ichigaya, 11-5, Tomishisa-cho, Shinjuku-ku, Tokyo 162, Japan. Telephone: 81-3-3356-2879.

Photo Trade News, 445 Broad Hollow Road, Suite 21, Melville, NY 11747. (516) 845-2700, www.ptnonline.com.

■ RELATED CHAPTERS

27: Computer Equipment
38: Household Consumer Durables

■ GLOSSARY

Advanced Photo System (**APS**): A 24mm silver-based camera and film system introduced in 1996 that simplifies the picture-taking process and the reprint-ordering process.

Big Emerging Markets (**BEMs**): Argentina, Brazil, China (including Taiwan and Hong Kong), India, Mexico, Poland, South Africa, South Korea, Turkey, and the ASEAN countries (Indonesia, Brunei, Malaysia, Singapore, Thailand, Philippines, and Vietnam).

Minilab: A retail outlet (freestanding or in-house) that processes photographs (usually within an hour), using on-site equipment.

Original equipment manufacturing (**OEM**) **agreement:** An agreement between companies to buy and then sell (under their own brand names) the same basic equipment.

Silver halide photography: A photographic process that uses the interaction of silver compounds coated on a film base and chemicals to make images visible.

Single-use camera (**SUC**): A camera preloaded with film (the film cannot be removed by the photographer) that must be delivered as a unit to a photofinisher for processing.

PRINTING AND PUBLISHING
Economic and Trade Trends

U.S. International Trade

($ billions)

Legend: Balance, Exports, Imports

Source: U.S. Department of Commerce: Bureau of the Census; International Trade Administration.

World Export Market Shares

(%)

Legend: United States, Germany, United Kingdom, France

Source: United Nations; U.S. Department of Commerce, International Trade Administration.

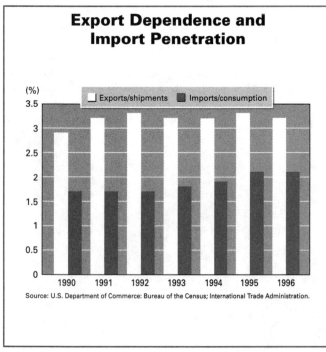

Export Dependence and Import Penetration

(%)

Legend: Exports/shipments, Imports/consumption

Source: U.S. Department of Commerce: Bureau of the Census; International Trade Administration.

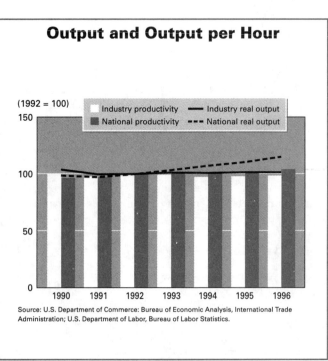

Output and Output per Hour

(1992 = 100)

Legend: Industry productivity, Industry real output, National productivity, National real output

Source: U.S. Department of Commerce: Bureau of Economic Analysis, International Trade Administration; U.S. Department of Labor, Bureau of Labor Statistics.

See "Getting the Most Out of *Outlook '99*" for definitions of terms.

Printing and Publishing

INDUSTRY DEFINITION The U.S. printing and publishing industry consists of the following industry sectors: newspapers (SIC 2711); periodicals (SIC 2721); book publishing (SIC 2731); book printing (SIC 2732); miscellaneous publishing (SIC 2741); commercial printing, lithographic (SIC 2752); commercial printing, gravure (SIC 2754); commercial printing not elsewhere classified (SIC 2759); manifold business forms (SIC 2761); greeting cards (SIC 2771); blankbooks and looseleaf binders (SIC 2782); bookbinding and related work (SIC 2789); typesetting (SIC 2791); and platemaking services (SIC 2796). The typesetting (SIC 2791) and platemaking services (SIC 2796) industries have been combined into one industry, printing trade services (SIC 279).

OVERVIEW

The United States is the world's largest printer, publisher, and importer and exporter of printed products. Its population of 268.8 million has one of the highest per capita expenditures for printed materials among the world's major economies. Virtually every town or county has a newspaper publisher or commercial printer. In 1998 the U.S. printing and publishing industry had an estimated 70,000 establishments, a work force of 1.5 million (see Figure 25-1 for state levels of employment in the industry), and a value of shipments totaling $211 billion (see Table 25-1). With U.S. printed product exports projected to reach $5 billion in 1998, coupled with imports of $3.3 billion, the United States is a dominant force among the world's traders of printed materials.

Global Industry Trends

Although U.S. printers and publishers focus primarily on their domestic markets, the industry is influenced increasingly by global forces. These forces include foreign investment, global sourcing, joint ventures and licensing agreements, and global markets.

Foreign Investment. The large and expanding U.S. market for printed products attracts foreign publishers and printers. Foreign investment in the U.S. publishing industry traditionally came from the United Kingdom, but major investments in the 1990s have been as likely to come from Germany and the Netherlands. Ten of the 20 largest U.S. book publishers are

foreign-owned, and European management of U.S. periodicals companies continues to increase. The U.S. commercial printing industry has attracted significant investments from Canadian and Swiss sources, while Canada is a dominant purchaser of U.S. newspaper properties.

Global Sourcing. Although the U.S. printing and publishing industry meets most of its commodity and equipment needs through domestic suppliers, its vast size accommodates a huge inflow of commodities (paper, ink, plates, chemicals) and equipment (printing presses, binding machines, paper cutters) from foreign sources. Trends in printing technology toward electronic-based (digital) processes and away from film- and chemical-based (analog) processes have created new markets for platemaking equipment from Canada and digital printing presses from Belgium. In the 1990s an increasing proportion of U.S. commodity and equipment needs has been met by suppliers in Germany, Japan, the United Kingdom, Switzerland, Italy, and the Netherlands.

Joint Ventures and Licensing Agreements. Market opportunities abroad have created a surge of U.S. interest in joint ventures and licensing arrangements with foreign partners. Joint venture activity is particularly strong among U.S. commercial printers whose clients are multinational U.S. corporations with global printing requirements. Linkages with foreign printing establishments enable U.S. printers not only to meet their domestic customer's needs but also to identify printing niches in foreign markets that can be served by their U.S. operations.

Employment in Printing and Publishing (SIC 27) in 1997

Employees per Thousand Nonfarm Workers

- Not applicable
- 5 to 9
- 10 to 11
- 12 to 15
- 16 to 21

Source: U.S. Department of Labor, Bureau of Labor Statistics.

FIGURE 25-1

The licensing of property rights between U.S. and foreign publishers has surged in response to the expansion of literary interests across national borders.

Global Markets. U.S. markets for printed products are large and stable but highly competitive. An increasing number of U.S. printers and publishers are finding growth opportunities overseas through exports, direct investment, and joint venture or licensing arrangements. Global needs for printed communications—advertising materials, labels, financial and legal printing—are rising, particularly in Latin America, and U.S. printers are becoming more active in that region. International demand for books, periodicals, and other informational materials has generated a surge of interest from U.S. publishers. Exports and the licensing rights to U.S. books, for example, are growing at rates higher than that of the U.S. book market and thus attract increased attention from U.S. publishers.

Domestic Trends

With U.S. imports of printed products having accounted for just 1.5 percent of U.S. apparent consumption in 1998, it is clear that domestic markets for printed materials are dominated by U.S. printers and publishers. In serving these markets, the U.S. printing and publishing industry is favored by language commonality, customer proximity, communications access, local and national transportation networks, and customers' time requirements. Four principal trends are influencing U.S. markets for printed products: an expanding economy that is accompanied by growth in advertising, more competition from

electronic media, a favorable industry cost structure (although it has been buffeted by changes in technology), and improved demographic factors, especially in relation to education.

Economy and Advertising. Expansion of the U.S. economy in the 1990s has been the single greatest factor in enlarging U.S. demand for printed products. A growing economy creates more business formations (bank, insurance, financial, and legal printing), greater disposable personal income (newspapers, books, periodicals, greeting cards), higher advertising expenditures (direct mail, catalogs, shopping news, printed inserts, telephone directories), and higher tax revenues (educational materials). The U.S. printing industry relies on advertising expenditures for over 70 percent of its revenues, and only economic growth can support larger budgets for advertising. Growth in demand for other printed products—including business forms, ledgers, binders, notebooks, newsletters, and business information services—is tied to the rising needs of U.S. business derived from the expanding economy.

Electronic Media. The competition between print media and electronic media to capture the leisure time activities of U.S. households has not yet had a winner. The amount of time spent reading by the U.S. population has not diminished, but the number of adults age 18 years and older accessing the Internet amounts to 29 million and is growing exponentially. The public's access to information on-line has been a boon to electronic bookstores, but it has cut into markets for checkbooks, newsletters, and business information in printed format. Demand for textbooks and printed educational materials is enhanced when those materials are packaged with videos and CD-ROMs, but U.S. printers find that CD-ROMs are reducing their markets for printed technical manuals and publishers see declining markets for printed directories, encyclopedias, and other reference works.

Technology and Cost Structure. The U.S. economy's steady pattern of growth, coupled with low interest rates, high employment, and stable prices, has benefited the cost structure of the U.S. printing and publishing industry through most of the 1990s. The costs of materials—paper, ink, chemicals, and film—have been held in check, and printers' investments in new equipment have been aided by low interest rates and a favorable tax structure. The industry's technological transition to electronic (digital) processes from film- and chemical-based (analog) processes requires a smaller but more skilled work force whose wages are commensurate with those technological skills. In the short term the installation of the new technology expands printers' plant capacity so significantly that utilization rates are driven down. These short-term costs are justified, however, by immediate gains in plant productivity.

Demographics and Education. Favorable demographic trends have been critical to the growth of the U.S. printing and publishing industry over the last decade. The industry has been supported by a large, well-educated population with rising levels of disposable personal income in the 1990s. Between 1960 and 1998 the U.S. population grew 50 percent to 268.8 million; high school graduates as a percentage of the population age 25 and older doubled to 142.6 million; the number of college graduates as a percentage of the population age 25 or older tripled to 41.7 million; and per capita disposable personal income, adjusted for inflation, increased 131 percent to $20,000. By 1998, 67.8 million students were enrolled at all levels of learning: kindergarten through eighth grade, 38.1 million; high schools, 14.8 million; and colleges and universities, 14.9 million. The combination of these positive demographic factors, along with a strong economy, drove demand for U.S. printed products to record levels in 1998.

Projections of Industry and Trade Growth for the Next 1 and 5 Years

The value of shipments by the U.S. printing and publishing industry is expected to total $219 billion in 1999, a gain of 1 percent over 1998 in constant dollars. This growth is predicated on a rising U.S. economy that generates higher levels of advertising expenditures, especially in newspapers, periodicals, and direct-mail materials. Several cost elements could limit the profits of U.S. printers and publishers in 1999. Higher postal rates are forecast, the first such increases since the mid-1990s. Paper mill capacity is not expected to expand in 1999, leading to potentially higher prices for paper if demand for printed products exceeds expectations. Labor costs are projected to

TABLE 25-1: Printing and Publishing (SIC 27) Trends and Forecasts[1]
(millions of dollars except as noted)

	1992	1993	1994	1995	1996	1997[2]	1998[2]	1999[3]	Percent Change			
									96–97	97–98	98–99	92–96[4]
Value of shipments	166,153	172,633	176,876	188,133	195,435	203,097	211,073	218,907	3.9	3.9	3.7	4.1
2711 Newspapers	33,782	34,651	36,091	37,732	39,171	41,131	42,982	44,701	5.0	4.5	4.0	3.8
2721 Periodicals	22,104	22,653	21,892	23,743	24,930	26,526	27,985	29,384	6.4	5.5	5.0	3.1
2731 Book publishing	16,698	18,616	19,695	20,484	21,363	22,000	23,000	24,000	3.0	4.5	4.3	6.4
2732 Book printing	4,681	4,810	4,745	5,392	5,333	5,385	5,495	5,660	1.0	2.0	3.0	3.3
2741 Miscellaneous publishing	10,908	11,807	11,976	12,025	12,511	13,010	13,620	14,190	4.0	4.7	4.2	3.5
275 Commercial printing	56,229	58,173	60,411	65,101	67,842	70,625	73,240	75,805	4.1	3.7	3.5	4.8
2761 Manifold business forms	7,429	7,491	6,958	7,894	7,724	7,299	7,007	6,797	−5.5	−4.0	−3.0	1.0
2771 Greeting cards	4,190	4,275	4,546	4,689	5,011	5,101	5,274	5,522	1.8	3.4	4.7	4.6
2782 Blankbooks and binders	3,758	3,771	4,276	4,544	4,820	5,135	5,445	5,713	6.5	6.0	4.9	6.4
2789 Bookbinding	1,291	1,258	1,367	1,509	1,608	1,710	1,825	1,935	6.3	6.7	6.0	5.6
279 Printing trade services	5,085	5,129	4,920	5,020	5,123	5,175	5,200	5,200	1.0	0.5	0.0	0.2
Value of shipments (1992$)	166,153	167,352	167,099	168,181	168,517	169,514	171,230	173,000	0.6	1.0	1.0	0.4
2711 Newspapers	33,782	33,222	33,294	32,782	31,718	31,337	31,024	30,559	−1.2	−1.0	−1.5	−1.6
2721 Periodicals	22,104	22,014	20,849	21,903	22,379	22,983	23,305	23,538	2.7	1.4	1.0	0.3
2731 Book publishing	16,698	18,180	18,493	18,257	18,166	18,038	18,218	18,491	−0.7	1.0	1.5	2.1
2732 Book printing	4,681	4,777	4,647	5,043	5,008	5,123	5,149	5,200	2.3	0.5	1.0	1.7
2741 Miscellaneous publishing	10,908	11,320	11,048	10,604	10,504	10,599	10,747	10,876	0.9	1.4	1.2	−0.9
275 Commercial printing	56,229	56,764	58,252	59,454	60,555	61,164	62,509	63,759	1.0	2.2	2.0	1.9
2761 Manifold business forms	7,429	7,027	6,240	5,762	5,494	5,274	5,010	5,164	−4.0	−5.0	3.1	−7.3
2771 Greeting cards	4,190	4,040	4,016	3,960	4,064	4,080	4,104	4,129	0.4	0.6	0.6	−0.8
2782 Blankbooks and binders	3,758	3,668	4,049	4,058	4,152	4,355	4,560	4,665	4.9	4.7	2.3	2.5
2789 Bookbinding	1,291	1,249	1,343	1,431	1,501	1,549	1,594	1,634	3.2	2.9	2.5	3.8
279 Printing trade services	5,085	5,090	4,867	4,928	4,977	5,012	5,010	4,985	0.7	−0.0	−0.5	−0.5

[1] Industry data.
[2] Estimate.
[3] Forecast.
[4] Compound annual rate.
Source: U.S. Department of Commerce: Bureau of the Census; International Trade Administration.

increase at a gradual pace, but wage increases could accelerate if U.S. printers have difficulty obtaining workers with the technical skills needed to operate newly installed digital equipment.

The 5-year period 1999–2003 is expected to be critical for U.S. printers and publishers. The industry's projected value of shipments should rise at an inflation-adjusted compound annual average rate of 1.8 percent, a level slightly below projections for the nation's gross domestic product. For U.S. printers these 5 years represent an investment-laden transition to digital technology to replace analog technology. For U.S. publishers decisions must be made to accommodate the entrance of electronic media into previously print-oriented markets. For both printers and publishers demographic trends should remain favorable, although elementary school enrollments should peak in 2002 and then trend very gradually downward. The capacity of U.S. paper mills should be adequate to meet fluctuations in U.S. print demand, and labor costs should remain at acceptable levels. The international interests of U.S. printers and publishers should become more sharply focused in the period 1999–2003, with increased opportunities for joint ventures and the licensing of rights. Attention could well be drawn to the expanding markets of Latin America, especially if Asian economies remain subdued.

Global Market Prospects

Foreign markets for U.S. printed products show every sign of expanding in the years ahead, building on the solid export base of $5 billion achieved in 1998 (see Table 25-2). Canada should remain the largest purchaser of U.S. printed materials, accounting for approximately 40 to 45 percent of the U.S. export total. Significant shifts in demand are not foreseen for other major buyers of U.S. printed products, with aggregate exports to Australia, Japan, Mexico, and the United Kingdom still expected to represent approximately 25 to 30 percent of total U.S. exports. The leading international opportunities for U.S. printers and

publishers over the next decade appear to be in the southeast Asian and Latin American regions. Southeast Asia was a growth market for U.S. printed products in the 1990s, expanding at a compound annual average rate of 9 percent before the recent financial difficulties. The anticipated economic recovery in that region should again spur U.S. exports. Latin America was an even more attractive market for U.S. printed products in the 1990s, recording growth at a compound annual average rate of 12 percent. Even greater demand for U.S. printed products should be evident in this region in the decade ahead.

Global demand for U.S. printed products is supported by international efforts to strengthen copyright protection, provide market access, and remove trade barriers. The U.S. government has vigorously pursued violators of international copyright and holds a leadership position in promoting copyright enforcement through the World Intellectual Property Organization (WIPO). Removing or reducing foreign tariffs and trade barriers to U.S. printed products is being accomplished through implementation of the tariff reductions negotiated during the Uruguay Round of multilateral trade negotiations. In addition, the United States is participating in sector liberalization negotiations within the Asia Pacific Economic Cooperation (APEC). Completion of the Uruguay Round of trade negotiations in 1994 represented a global step toward opening world markets to U.S. printed products.

William S. Lofquist, U.S. Department of Commerce, Office of Consumer Goods, (202) 482-0379, October 1998.

NEWSPAPERS

Global Industry Trends

Acquisitions and restructuring continued at a brisk pace in the newspaper industry in 1997 and 1998. Earlier forecasts had pre-

TABLE 25-2: U.S. Trade Patterns in Printing and Publishing[1] in 1997
(millions of dollars; percent)

Exports			Imports		
Regions[2]	Value[3]	Share, %	Regions[2]	Value[3]	Share
NAFTA	2,349	50.7	NAFTA	979	31.9
Latin America	245	5.3	Latin America	34	1.1
Western Europe	993	21.4	Western Europe	978	31.8
Japan/Chinese Economic Area	429	9.3	Japan/Chinese Economic Area	791	25.7
Other Asia	243	5.2	Other Asia	210	6.8
Rest of world	373	8.0	Rest of world	81	2.6
World	4,632	100.0	World	3,074	100.0
Top Five Countries	Value	Share, %	Top Five Countries	Value	Share, %
Canada	2,057	44.4	Canada	847	27.6
United Kingdom	486	10.5	United Kingdom	428	13.9
Mexico	293	6.3	China	305	9.9
Japan	280	6.0	Hong Kong (PRC)	282	9.2
Australia	204	4.4	Japan	155	5.0

[1] SIC 2711, 2721, 2731, 2732, 2741, 2752, 2754, 2759, 2771, 2782, 2789, 2791, 2796.
[2] For definitions of regional groupings, see "Getting the Most Out of *Outlook '99.*"
[3] Values may not sum to total due to rounding.
Source: U.S. Department of Commerce, Bureau of the Census.

dicted a leveling off in consolidation activity after a purchasing spree in the period 1994–1996. Especially prevalent in the United States was the buying and swapping of holdings between newspaper companies to achieve a clustering of properties in specific geographic areas that could benefit circulation and advertising. In the United States 162 dailies changed hands in 1997. According to Dirks, Van Essen & Associates, a Santa Fe newspaper brokerage firm, the volume of transactions totaled $6.2 billion, nearly double the prior record of $3.2 billion set in 1995 and three times the 1996 level of nearly $2 billion. On the international front, the Canadian conglomerate Hollinger agreed to sell 167 of its small U.S. dailies, weeklies, and free newspapers to a U.S. buyer, while *The New York Times* signed a distribution agreement with the *The Globe and Mail* of Toronto which should significantly expand the *Times'* Canadian distribution. Overseas, Great Britain's *Financial Times* launched a global strategy to boost its circulation, mainly in the United States, against that of *The Wall Street Journal;* the *Journal* counterattacked with a London edition of *The Wall Street Journal Europe.* France's *Le Monde* and Britain's *The European* formed a partnership to publish *L'Européen,* a French-language edition. An increasingly globalized economy is creating a strong demand for world business and financial news. The most significant expansion for many U.S. and foreign newspapers resulted from their move on-line, and more than 3,600 newspapers worldwide now appear on World Wide Web sites. Foreign media conglomerates such as Hollinger and Thomson of Canada, the News Corp. of Australia, and America's Dow Jones and International Data Group are among the broad-based media conglomerates that continue to pursue global cross-media purchases and investments.

The circulation of daily newspapers continues to drop in most industrialized countries but is rising in many developing countries. According to the 1997 report of the International Federation of Newspaper Publishers, not only did daily newspaper circulation continue to decline in the European Union and the United States in 1996, but the rate of decline increased. Advertising performance in many industrialized countries has fared better than has circulation, with a majority of countries, such as India, continuing to show gains in advertising revenue. Newspaper circulation in developing countries continues to climb along with newspaper advertising revenues. Developing countries, especially those in Latin America, have seen significant gains in both circulation and advertising. Among the developing countries Poland, Mexico, Brazil, India, and China saw their overall advertising revenues grow in the range of 10 to 30 percent in 1997. For some developing countries, particularly those in Asia that have been hard hit by the recent financial crisis, advertising gains have been more moderate than they were in the past.

Important Factors Affecting the Future Growth of U.S. Industry

The U.S. newspaper industry initiates, designs, publishes, and prints newspapers. The industry's major product segments are daily, weekly, and Sunday newspapers. Publishers of daily and Sunday newspapers have their own production facilities, but publishers of weekly newspapers may contract out their printing requirements to commercial printers. Shopping news circulars are free-circulation information and advertising products by miscellaneous publishers.

The majority of U.S. newspapers serve local markets, although large newspaper groups own many community newspapers. According to *Editor and Publisher,* the number of U.S. dailies continued to drop, falling from 1,533 in 1995 to 1,520 in 1996. Based on a summary of Audit Bureau of Circulation data, Morton Research's *Newspaper Newsletter* reported that in 1996, 126 media chains owned 1,165 U.S. dailies, about 77 percent of the total. Only 77 U.S. newspapers with a circulation of 30,000 or more were independently owned in 1997. Among the chains, swapping and bartering for papers to achieve better geographic proximity for their individual newspaper groups became a frequent occurrence. A growing number of newspapers sold their broadcast operations to focus more closely on their newspaper core. Among the major publicly owned U.S. newspaper companies with most of their holdings in newspapers are Pulitzer Publishing, Knight Ridder, Central Newspapers, and McClatchy Newspapers.

Newspaper receipts in constant dollars were projected to decline slightly in 1998, since slower growth was anticipated in the overall economy and in total U.S. advertising expenditures. Industry receipts were expected to total about $43 billion in 1998 (see Table 25-3). Both newspaper advertising and circulation receipts were expected to post smaller gains in 1998 than they did in 1997. Advertising accounts for the major portion of the newspaper industry's revenues, with most advertising coming from the local community. In general, real growth in this industry has been declining in recent years, although profits and earnings have remained high for large newspaper chains. Morton Research's *Newspaper Newsletter* reported that among the 15 largest newspaper chains it tracks, the average after-tax profit margin (weighted) in 1997 was 11.4 percent. Earnings and profit growth were expected to slow in 1998.

Despite the fact that the financial performance of newspapers over the last several years has been strong, many challenges are facing the industry. Among the issues are a declining share of U.S. advertising expenditures going to newspapers; falling circulation, especially at newsstands; unstable newsprint prices; postal reforms; competition from a growing number of information providers; and cross-ownership of newspapers and broadcast media in the same market.

Advertising. According to the Newspaper Association of America (NAA), in 1997 advertising expenditures in daily newspapers rose at a considerably faster rate than did the gross domestic product (GDP) and outpaced total U.S. advertising growth. Although newspaper advertising revenues have been projected to rise at a slower rate in 1998 as the economy cools off slightly, they should continue to grow at a faster rate than total advertising and GDP. The NAA expected newspaper advertising receipts to increase about 6.7 percent in 1998. Newspapers' share of total U.S. media advertising probably will hold at about 22 percent

TABLE 25-3: Newspapers (SIC 2711) Trends and Forecasts

(millions of dollars except as noted)

	1992	1993	1994	1995	1996	1997[1]	1998[2]	1999[3]	96–97	97–98	98–99	92–96[4]
									Percent Change			
Industry data												
Value of shipments[5]	33,782	34,651	36,091	37,732	39,171	41,131	42,982	44,701	5.0	4.5	4.0	3.8
Value of shipments (1992$)	33,782	33,222	33,294	32,782	31,718	31,337	31,024	30,559	−1.2	−1.0	−1.5	−1.6
Total employment (thousands)	414	410	412	415	403							−0.7
Production workers (thousands)	134	132	134	135	136							0.4
Average hourly earnings ($)	12.94	12.90	13.39	13.58	13.61							1.3
Capital expenditures	1,665	1,262	1,329	1,229	1,277							−6.4
Product data												
Value of shipments[5]	31,933	32,853	34,040	35,577	37,225	39,086	40,844	42,478	5.0	4.5	4.0	3.9
Value of shipments (1992$)	31,933	31,499	31,402	30,909	30,142	30,082	29,781	29,334	−0.2	−1.0	−1.5	−1.4
Trade data												
Value of imports	53.4	50.3	9.2	8.7	8.7	9.1	8.5	9.5	4.6	−6.6	11.8	−36.5
Value of exports	30.1	27.3	34.9	30.8	28.3	33.9	31.0	33.0	19.8	−8.6	6.5	−1.5

[1] Estimate except imports and exports.
[2] Estimate.
[3] Forecast.
[4] Compound annual rate.
[5] For definition of industry versus product values, see "Getting the Most Out of *Outlook '99.*"
Source: U.S. Department of Commerce: Bureau of the Census; International Trade Administration.

after declining from 25.1 percent of the total in 1990 to 21.9 percent in 1996. NAA reported that the growth of classified advertising would remain strong in 1998, up about 8 percent after a 10.2 percent gain in 1997. According to NAA estimates, retail advertising, which accounts for about half of total newspaper advertising, was expected to grow about 5.2 percent in 1998 after climbing 5.8 percent in 1997. Buoyed by a strong economy, national newspaper advertising staged strong performances in the last 2 years, rising 12 percent in 1997 and about 8 percent in 1998. This remains newspapers' smallest advertising sector, accounting for about 13 percent of total advertising expenditures in newspapers. Closings of and consolidations in retail chains over the last decade have had a substantial impact on the amount of advertising that goes into newspapers. Furthermore, both classified and retail newspaper advertising are increasingly threatened by old and new competitors with products that are eroding these advertising bases. Business shifts from higher-priced run-of-press newspaper advertising to newspaper preprints also have contributed to the slower growth in newspaper revenues. The trend toward specialty publications and on-line postings for automotive, real estate, and employment advertising has made newspapers take stock of their capabilities for providing classified advertising services.

Circulation. According to an NAA analysis of Audit Bureau of Circulation data, while overall newspaper circulation declined slightly in 1997, in every circulation category of newspapers, large and small, the losses incurred were smaller than those in 1996. The weekday circulation of U.S. dailies dropped 1.1 percent, declining from 58,193,391 in 1995 to 56,989,800 in 1996; morning circulation, which totaled 44,789,322 in 1996, was up 1.1 percent from the 1995 level; and evening circulation,

which stood at 12,200,486 in 1996, was down 12.2 percent from 1995. The continuing decline in the number of evening papers and the gain in the number of morning papers partly account for these trends; 15 of the 19 dailies that ceased publication in 1997 were evening papers. Competition from other media for readers' leisure time and difficulties in delivering evening papers also have contributed to the erosion in circulation. Sunday circulation, totaling 60,797,814 in 1996, fell 1.2 percent from the 1995 level. The newspaper industry's 25 largest companies had about a 1 percent gain in circulation in 1997, while the number of newspapers these companies owned dropped from 643 to 598. Newspapers are paying greater attention to boosting circulation but are not pursuing circulation price increases as aggressively as they did in the last several years. Although many companies expected to increase their circulation in 1998, the gains were projected to be small. A major factor affecting circulation in 1997 was the trend among newspaper companies to cluster their newspaper properties to increase circulation and advertising reach in a geographic region. Companies have achieved clustering by selling off properties in some geographic areas and buying properties in regions in which they already have sizable holdings. This gives them a stronger circulation and advertising presence in those areas. According to Dirks, Van Essen & Associates, from 1990 to 1997 newspapers that belonged to a cluster avoided the nationwide trend toward declining circulation.

Newsprint Costs. Since newsprint costs consume about 15 to 20 percent of a newspaper's operating budget, volatile newsprint prices can be a major problem for newspaper publishers, as occurred in 1995. As newspaper publishers built up their newsprint inventories in the first half of 1997, this strong demand allowed newsprint producers to boost their prices after having delayed an increase earlier in the year. Newsprint analysts anticipated more price increases in 1998. Publishers have turned to European and Asian countries for some of their newsprint in recent years as the U.S. supply has dwindled and risen in price. Publishers would like to count on an average price for newsprint, but since 1994 the longest period in which an average price has stayed in place has been 6 months. Publishers and newsprint suppliers are concerned that newspapers could cease to be an inexpensive source of information and a cheap advertising medium if newsprint costs become too high.

Postal Reform. The U.S. newspaper industry is concerned about pending postal reform legislation in Congress that would reduce the authority of the Postal Rate Commission and give more autonomy to the U.S. Postal Service (USPS) in setting rates. The bill also would allow the USPS to provide volume discounts for large mailers. Newspaper publishers believe that the proposal makes it easier for the USPS to compete with the private sector, including newspapers. They also are convinced that with greater flexibility the USPS would tend to favor high-volume mailers, including direct-mail marketers, one of the newspapers' chief competitors. Because of the devastating impact this legislation could have on smaller-volume users, including newspapers, the NAA has actively pursued changes in the legislation that would be more favorable to the industry.

Growing Competition. Over the years newspapers have had to compete for advertising dollars and audience with direct mail, the broadcast media, the Yellow Pages, community-based shopper publications, and other specialty advertising publications. More recently the industry has focused on its on-line competitors, which hope to gain some of newspapers' advertising and circulation revenues by offering a broad range of information services. According to the NAA, over 500 U.S. dailies now have Web sites; more than 60 percent of those papers have circulations under 60,000. Many publishers have done little to develop a competitive advantage over other on-line service providers that are trying to enter local advertising markets, which have mostly been the domain of newspapers.

Cross-Ownership Rules. Among newspapers that want to acquire broadcast properties, the Federal Communications Commission (FCC) regulations that limit cross-ownership of newspaper and broadcast media in the same market are considered outdated and are being challenged. Newspapers believe that with the diverse range of media that now exist in many markets, those rules are unfair to newspapers. The FCC was scheduled to review those rules in 1998; also, a bill that would lift the cross-ownership ban is pending in Congress.

U.S. Industry Growth Projections for the Next 1 and 5 Years

Newspaper industry receipts in constant dollars probably will decline about 1 percent or less in 1998 and over the next 5 years. The industry's continuing well-being will depend on a healthy economy, steady consumer confidence, strong advertising expenditures, and the diligence of newspapers in adapting to changing technologies. Employment growth and gains in retail, automotive, and real estate sales would raise retail and classified newspaper advertising receipts. Higher interest rates could weaken consumer confidence and hurt newspaper advertising, which is heavily dependent on the retail, automotive, and real estate sectors of the economy. Newspaper advertising receipts, which account for about three-fourths of total newspaper receipts, are likely to grow in the range of 5 to 7 percent over the next 5 years. More siphoning off of newspapers' advertisers and audience by competitors such as direct-mail marketers, television, and on-line service providers could further erode the advertising base. As baby boomers age over the next 5 years, newspaper receipts should benefit, since daily readership of newspapers rises with age.

Global Market Prospects

While most U.S. newspapers serve local markets and several, including *The Wall Street Journal, U.S.A. Today,* and *The New York Times,* have a national audience, only a few U.S. newspapers have an international presence (see Table 25-4). Both *The Wall Street Journal* and *U.S.A. Today* also are published internationally, along with the *International Herald Tribune (IHT),* a joint venture of the *Washington Post, The New York Times,* and Whitney Communications. The *IHT* is sent by facsimile transmission to 14 sites around the world, where it is printed and then distributed to more than 180 countries. A Russian-language edition of *The New York Times* called *The New York Times in Review* is jointly published by the *Times* and *Moscow News.* The *Miami Herald,* a regional paper, also prints by satellite transmission in several Latin American countries. Many foreign papers have national audiences in their own countries; national papers are prevalent in such countries as Japan, the United Kingdom, and Germany. A few foreign papers, such as the *Financial Times* in the United Kingdom, are also expanding to serve an international audience.

A major factor in taking newspapers rapidly into the global market is their presence on the World Wide Web and their ability to offer products that attract both customers and advertisers to their Web sites. According to a Newslinks Associates survey, more than 3,600 newspapers now have Web sites; about 500 of these are U.S. newspapers. More than 1,700 of these papers started publishing on the Web in 1997. The number of papers on the Web could easily double over the next few years. The NAA reported that less than a third of newspapers expected to make a profit from their Web sites in 1997. Newspapers have led all other media in the development of electronic on-line services. Because the audience for newspapers is increasingly turning to the Internet, newspapers must provide their services on-line as well. According to a survey conducted by Maritz Marketing Research Inc. of St. Louis, computer penetration in households with incomes over $75,000 has reached 75 percent and 42 percent of all U.S. households own personal computers. Among home computer users, 65 percent have Internet access. A Neilsen Media Research survey reported in 1998 that the number of people who had made purchases on the Internet increased 50 percent

TABLE 25-4: U.S. Trade Patterns in Newspapers[1] in 1997

(millions of dollars; percent)

Regions[2]	Exports Value[3]	Exports Share, %	Regions[2]	Imports Value[3]	Imports Share, %
NAFTA	25	73.3	NAFTA	3	38.3
Latin America	0	0.8	Latin America	0	0.0
Western Europe	7	20.0	Western Europe	4	46.6
Japan/Chinese Economic Area	1	2.7	Japan/Chinese Economic Area	1	5.8
Other Asia	0	1.4	Other Asia	1	7.9
Rest of world	1	1.9	Rest of world	0	1.3
World	34	100.0	World	9	100.0
Top Five Countries	**Value**	**Share, %**	**Top Five Countries**	**Value**	**Share, %**
Canada	20	59.0	United Kingdom	3	37.3
United Kingdom	6	18.1	Canada	3	34.8
Mexico	5	14.3	India	1	7.8
China	1	2.2	Japan	1	5.8
Thailand	0	1.0	Spain	1	5.8

[1] SIC 2711.
[2] For definitions of regional groupings, see "Getting the Most Out of *Outlook '99.*"
[3] Values may not sum to total due to rounding.
Source: U.S. Department of Commerce, Bureau of the Census.

to nearly 10 million, and as many as one-quarter of those surveyed stated that they went on-line daily.

Thus, the key issue facing newspaper publishers worldwide over the next few years is how to best approach electronic publishing. Newspaper publishers are aware that they stand to lose a major portion of their classified advertising revenues if they do not actively pursue on-line opportunities. The stakes are getting higher for some newspapers, since they realize that they must enter the market quickly to capture some of the $2 billion in on-line classified advertising sales that are forecast for 2001. While many U.S. newspapers already have established a presence on the Web which includes classified advertising listings, so have many nonnewspaper companies. To counter on-line employment classifieds, several large newspapers joined forces a few years ago to establish an on-line employment-listing service called Careerpath.com. This network now has over 70 prominent U.S. newspapers on its site and has become the major career and job management network on the Internet. Still, nonnewspaper providers are challenging newspapers' on-line classified advertising position by offering a broad spectrum of classified advertising. These nonnewspaper competitors are selling classified advertising listings on-line, mainly employment but also real estate and automotive, and providing local, regional, and national news and information services traditionally provided by newspapers. Recently, Classified 2000, the leading on-line provider of classified advertising content and distribution on the Internet, began providing users of the Switchboard Internet Directory with quick, easy access to its listing of classified advertisements. Switchboard is considered the leading White Pages and Yellow Pages directory provider on the Web, with more than 40 million hits a month from consumers seeking a broad range of information. According to *PR Newswire,* this agreement further strengthens the growing Classified 2000 Network, which distributes an extensive database of classified advertising listings in multiple categories to leading Web publishing partners, including the major search sites Excite, Lycos, Infoseek, WebCrawler, and HotBot; top Internet service providers such as AT&T and WorldNet Concentric Network Corp.; and popular destinations sites, including GeoCities, Hotmail, and Tripod. In addition to generating its own advertising content, the Classified 2000 Network aggregates advertising content in categories such as automotive, employment, and real estate from its leading Web partner sites and distributes that content throughout its network.

Newspapers are in a strong position to provide news and information for other on-line service providers' sites. The challenge for some papers will lie in deciding whether it is more advantageous to be on-line providers or to supply other service providers with content. Because of the high quality of newspapers' information content, their Web sites attract high-quality audiences. These are consumers whom advertisers want to reach, especially advertisers in the local communities that newspapers serve. Some newspapers are capitalizing on their ability to provide both print and on-line advertising in addition to high-quality editorial content, which makes them a more attractive buy for advertisers than are their nonnewspaper competitors. However, local and metropolitan newspapers are facing competition at the local level from America Online's Digital Cities, CitySearch, Knight Ridder's Real Cities, and Sidewalk, as well as television station sites. Nonnewspaper on-line service providers also are offering information that traditionally has been found in newspapers, such as local sports and entertainment information. In a venture with the Tribune Company in Chicago, America Online launched Digital City, an on-line service that now covers at least six large metropolitan areas and provides information on local entertainment, restaurants, and the like. A looming threat to newspapers on the Web could be Microsoft, which plans to offer news and other service information, both nationally and locally, in certain metropolitan areas. Microsoft wants to form ties with local newspapers and other publications to gather local information. *Presstime* magazine reported that when Microsoft officials cut back on staff for its on-line Sidewalk city guides early in 1998, the newspaper industry took some comfort in the fact that editorial integrity and long-standing community relations had helped the industry win a victory in its battle against other electronic service providers. However, newspaper on-line service providers such as Knight Ridder, which has 34 sites on-line under a Real Cities umbrella, are aware of the threat Microsoft still poses with its plan to expand into the top 50 U.S. markets by the end of 1998. Since many newspaper on-line local community efforts are less than a year old, it is too early to know whether they can ward off potential competitors. As the strategies of their nonnewspaper rivals shift, newspaper publishers will have to reevaluate their own on-line development strategies. Already a number of metropolitan newspapers have realized that their own resources are not sufficient to build adequate community content and traffic on their Web sites. Newspapers such as the *Boston Globe* have launched sites in partnership with other community media sources to create "city.com" Internet addresses. Some newspapers have done this in connection with America Online's Digital City network to cut down on their Web responsibilities. The Tribune Company of Chicago has actively pursued a dual approach to its online presence by developing separate newspaper and community sites. Whether they follow the "newspaper.com" approach or the "city.com" approach, publishers are frequently offering value-added services on Web sites for entertainment guides, Yellow Page business directories, and classified products. In the future their ability to measure their audiences and target their services to narrower segments of those audiences should help them maintain preeminence among local news and information on-line service providers and capture advertising and paid subscribers for their Web sites.

Over the next several years newspaper publishers will face operational challenges to their core product, printed newspapers. In particular, they will need to maintain their leadership in producing high-quality editorial content in order to utilize that content to generate new revenue streams. Newspapers will have to strengthen their links to both readers and advertisers by providing both of those customer bases with more of what they want and making it more easily available to them. Many papers are realizing that the needs and wants of their customers are rapidly changing and that if they do not provide for those needs, other information service providers will. Newspapers will have to upgrade their database capabilities continually to better store and more quickly retrieve and disseminate information in various formats, both print and electronic. They will need to focus more of their circulation efforts on single-copy sales and subscription renewals rather than on obtaining new home delivery customers. Publishers will have to include more targeting of women, younger readers, and minority groups in their marketing plans. They will have to fine-tune their distribution systems

continually to deliver advertisers' messages to more targeted segments of their readers. Some technological improvements high on newspapers' agendas are digital advertisement delivery from advertisers and advertising agencies in standardized formats, prepress systems that can produce a complete page negative, and computer-to-plate systems which image digital-page information directly on a printing plate. Greater use of color and more attention to consistent quality control of color will help newspapers compete more effectively against other media for advertisers and audiences.

If publishers develop effective strategies for attracting readers and advertisers and make good use of emerging technologies in the next few years, they will position themselves to succeed in the next decade. Since newspapers are better able to deliver larger audiences in their local markets than is any other source and because of the huge consumer information databases newspapers possess, they have a unique opportunity to be a dynamic force in the delivery of both print and electronic information.

Rose Marie Zummo Bratland, U.S. Department of Commerce, Office of Consumer Goods, (202) 482-0380.

PERIODICALS

Global Industry Trends

In most areas of the world the economic outlook for periodicals continues to be promising, but in some areas economic activity in 1998 was unstable and advertising expenditures in magazines declined or grew at a slow rate. The United States remains the largest magazine market in the world, and Germany, France, the United Kingdom, and Japan are very big markets. Although many magazine markets in the Asia/Pacific region experienced sharp growth in the early and middle 1990s, the economic uncertainty in that region more recently has affected the level of advertising spending in magazines. Magazines in South America continue to show rapid growth, with both foreign and domestic publishers expanding the number of publications and with advertising in magazines showing significant gains. More recently, magazine advertising expenditures in mature markets such as the United States, Europe, and Japan have been rising 10 percent or less a year, while those in developing markets such as China, Brazil, and eastern Europe have been growing 20 percent or more a year.

U.S. and European publishers have expanded their titles to other foreign markets and have created spin-off titles and other products to attract more advertising and readers. With the increasing demand for name-brand U.S. and European products in Asia, South America, and other foreign markets, large companies expanding into those markets look to magazines to promote their brand-building profiles. Companies want to advertise in magazines abroad that reflect the images they have in their home markets.

Magazine circulation in more mature markets is slowing, with some countries continuing to show substantial losses in newsstand sales, while circulation in developing world markets is rising. Consumer and business magazines have shown strong gains in South America, Asia, and Europe. Worldwide, publishers continue to express concern about paper supply and costs, but rising postal costs have become an even more important issue, especially for small-circulation publications. Publishers are paying close attention to new media, particularly on-line ventures, which potentially threaten but also could enhance publishers' products and operations. More publishers are assessing their opportunities to provide services electronically through various arrangements with other foreign and domestic media and advertisers.

As large magazine publishers have found their home markets saturated, many have begun to focus on international markets. Their global publishing arrangements have become very extensive and complex over the last few years. Some of these large publishers are now giant multinational media companies with magazine publishing ventures on several continents. Among the most active internationally are media giants such as Time-Warner, Reader's Digest, Hearst, Conde Nast, and International Data Group (United States); Reed Elsevier and EMAP (United Kingdom); Bertelsmann and Burda (Germany); Hachette (France); VNU (Netherlands); Ringier (Switzerland); Rizzoli (Italy); and Nikkei Business Publications (Japan). These multinationals have shown great interest in establishing a presence in Latin America and Asia, where economic growth, advertising spending, and magazine circulation have been increasing at faster rates than they have in other regions. These areas have become very attractive magazine publishing markets because of their expanding consumer economies, better educated populations, advancing technology bases, and greater market access. Some large European publishers have increased their presence in the U.S. market by buying magazine publishing properties or forming joint ventures with U.S. partners. Many magazine publishers that operate abroad have realized the importance of finding local partners for their ventures to bridge the cultural gap and obtain an understanding of the local market.

Globally, merger and acquisition activity remained strong for the periodicals industry in 1997 and early 1998. The big news in the global magazine market was the merger of the United Kingdom's multinational Reed Elsevier with the Dutch giant Wolters Kluwer in an alliance valued at $7.8 billion that includes holdings on three continents. According to the *Financial Times* (United Kingdom), this merger created the world's largest supplier of professional and scientific information. In its first acquisitions outside Europe, Britain's EMAP Group bought the Australian publishing firms Mason Stewart Publishing and Bounty Services, which had been publishing some of EMAP's titles under license. *Folio Magazine* reported that in the U.S. magazine publishing sector, foreign buyers and U.S. financial investors accounted for the 10 biggest buyouts in 1997 (see Table 25-5). Among these buyouts were Reed Elsevier's purchases of Chilton Business Group, consisting of 39 trade publications, from Walt Disney Co. for $447 million and 40 legal titles from the Thomson Corporation of Canada. Reed merged Chilton and its Cahners Publishing Group into Reed Elsevier Business Information to form nearly a $1 billion venture with 131 business titles. Veronis, Suhler & Associates, a U.S. investment banker that focuses on media, acquired T/SF Communications Corp., a publisher of trade magazines and information services, for $145 million. In another Disney sale, Euromoney Publications P.L.C., a United Kingdom publisher, purchased *Institutional Investor* for $142 million. The German magazine publisher Axel Springer Verlag bought the *Medical Tribune* group (United States), including its main publication, *Medical Tribune.* Early in 1998 Primedia, formerly KIII, acquired Cowles Enthusiast Media and Cowles Business Media from McClatchy Newspapers for $200 million. Cowles Business Media is the publisher of *Folio Magazine,* the leading industry trade publication. In the medical publishing sector Wolters Kluwer of Amsterdam purchased Waverly Inc., a U.S. medical publishing firm, for $375 million.

Worldwide, in 1997 and 1998 joint ventures and licensing agreements continued at a brisk pace as publishers joined with partners that could strengthen their position or increase their profits in their home markets or in targeted foreign markets. U.S. and European publishers have been the most active in pursing foreign ventures. Hearst's entry into Thailand and the Philip-

TABLE 25-5:   Ten Largest U.S. Magazine Transactions in 1997

Purchaser	Property	Seller	Price, $ million
Reed Elsevier	Chilton Business Group	Walt Disney Co.	447
Veronis, Suhler & Associates Communications Partners Limited Fund II	T/SF Communications	T/SF Communications, Inc.	145
Euromoney Publications PLC	*Institutional Investor*	Walt Disney Co.	142
Miller Freeman	Telecom Library	Telecom Library, Inc.	130
Cygnus Publishing	PTN	Stanley Sills and the investment banker Golder, Thoma, Cressey, Rauner	97
Wasserstein Perella's U.S. Equity Partners, LP	American Lawyer Media	Time Inc.	63
Rural Press USA Inc.	Farm Progress Group	Walt Disney Co.	57
Primedia	Cardinal Business Media	Brentwood Associates	45
Miller Publishing Group LLC	*Spin Magazine*	Spin Magazine, Inc.	40
Miller Publishing Group LLC	Six sports titles (including *Tennis* and *Snow Country*)	New York Times Company	35

Source: *Folio Magazine,* January 1, 1998.

pines continued the expansion of *Cosmopolitan,* which now has 36 foreign editions. In a joint venture with Recruit Company (Tokyo), *Entrepreneur* magazine (United States) launched a Japanese-language version. *Entrepreneur* has subscribers in 65 countries and newsstands sales in 33 countries. Rodale Press continued its international launches of *Men's Health* with start-ups in Russia, South Africa, and Australia. By the end of 1998 Rodale could have as many as 10 international editions of *Men's Health.* The *Newsletter of International Publishing* reported that Rodale had earlier converted from a licensing agreement to a joint venture with Editorial Televisa, a Latin American publisher in Mexico, to help reshape *Men's Health*'s global brand name and editorial mission. It has become very important to U.S. publishers for the basic image and concepts of a home-based title to be conveyed in a foreign edition of a magazine while having the edition reflect the lifestyle of the country in which it appears. Maintaining a magazine's image abroad permits publishers to attract global advertisers that are interested in reaching similar audiences in a number of countries. Other ventures included the launch in Russia of France's *Marie Claire,* the result of a joint venture between Marie Claire Group, Hearst Magazines, and Independent Media (Moscow). This was followed by a launch of *Marie Claire* in South Africa under a licensing arrangement with Africa's Perskor (Republican Press). *Marie Claire* now has more than 25 international editions. According to the *Newsletter of International Publishing,* the Manager Media Group (Thailand), an active magazine publisher in Asia, entered a joint publishing venture with the Dutch publisher VNU to publish *Asian Advertising & Marketing.* This was VNU's first venture in the Asian publishing market. Editorial Televisa of Mexico joined with *National Geographic* to launch a Spanish-language edition for the Latin American market. That Mexican publisher also entered

a partnership with Hachette-Filipacchi (France) to launch *Quo* in Spain. *National Geographic* recently started Italian- and Hebrew-language editions of its magazine with foreign partners.

Important Factors Affecting the Future Growth of U.S. Industry

The U.S. periodicals industry initiates, designs, and publishes periodicals. The industry's major product segments are farm, religious, specialized business and professional, and general and consumer periodicals, including comics. Publishers of periodicals contract out their printing requirements to commercial printers.

After an outstanding year of growth in 1997, publishers remained cautious about 1998. U.S. periodicals' receipts were expected to grow about 1.4 percent in that year, a smaller gain in constant dollars than occurred over the past few years, reflecting the slower growth rates expected in the overall economy and in total U.S. advertising spending. Industry receipts were expected to total about $28 billion in 1998 (see Table 25-6). U.S. consumer and business publications were expected to show slower growth in advertising receipts and advertising page totals than they did in 1997, although business publications' advertising revenues were expected to increase at a faster rate than were those of consumer magazines. Circulation volume for consumer magazines could be up slightly or flat compared with the 1997 level, and circulation revenues were expected to rise at a slower rate than they did in 1997.

According to Samir Husni's *Guide to New Consumer Magazines,* the number of consumer magazine start-ups in 1997 totaled 852, down from 933 in 1996. This was the first drop in new launches since 1991. Husni reported that the average cover price of new magazines continued to rise, reaching $4.75 in 1997. Popular growth categories in 1997 included fitness,

TABLE 25-6: Periodicals (SIC 2721) Trends and Forecasts

(millions of dollars except as noted)

| | 1992 | 1993 | 1994 | 1995 | 1996 | 1997[1] | 1998[2] | 1999[3] | Percent Change | | | |
									96–97	97–98	98–99	92–96[4]
Industry data												
Value of shipments[5]	22,104	22,653	21,892	23,743	24,930	26,526	27,985	29,384	6.4	5.5	5.0	3.1
Value of shipments (1992$)	22,104	22,014	20,849	21,903	22,379	22,983	23,305	23,538	2.7	1.4	1.0	0.3
Total employment (thousands)	115	117	117	122	121							1.3
Production workers (thousands)	20.2	19.7	18.2	17.8	16.4							−5.1
Average hourly earnings ($)	13.40	12.51	12.78	13.58	14.85							2.6
Capital expenditures	235	290	308	332	311							7.3
Product data												
Value of shipments[5]	20,942	21,692	21,642	22,951	24,352	25,911	27,336	28,734	6.4	5.5	5.1	3.8
Value of shipments (1992$)	20,942	21,080	20,611	21,173	21,860	22,450	22,764	22,992	2.7	1.4	1.0	1.1
Trade data												
Value of imports	134	194	209	222	217	204	190	194	−6.0	−6.9	2.1	12.8
Value of exports	731	737	788	825	819	864	907	948	5.5	5.0	4.5	2.9

[1] Estimate except imports and exports.
[2] Estimate.
[3] Forecast.
[4] Compound annual rate.
[5] For definition of industry versus product values, see "Getting the Most Out of *Outlook '99.*"
Source: U.S. Department of Commerce: Bureau of the Census; International Trade Administration.

music, and science fiction, while among the declining launches were epicurean, gardening, and travel. Among the start-ups were titles targeted at special audiences, including children and their parents (*Kids Wall Street News, KidStyle, MaMaMedia*), generation X (*Wine X, Jane*), sports enthusiasts (*Sports for Women, Sports Illustrated Women/Sport, Eye on the Tiger*), and holistic health followers (*Alternative Medicine Digest, New Herbal Remedies*). New titles in 1998 included more targeted publications of already popular magazines: *Teen People, Golf Digest Woman,* and *Travel & Leisure Family.*

According to the *1998 National Directory of Magazines,* the number of U.S. consumer and business magazines published in 1997 was 18,047, up from 17,195 in 1996. Standard Rate & Data Service Consumer & Farm Magazines listed a total of 2,746 consumer and farm magazines in 1997, up from 2,716 in 1996.

Magazine advertising cutbacks, rising paper costs, new postal regulations, falling newsstand sales, and consolidation among distributors remain major concerns for publishers. For some publishers 1998 was a year for making difficult decisions concerning advertising rates, circulation prices, Internet involvement, and marketing strategies which could have long-range implications for their businesses.

Advertising.   A slow downward movement in magazines' share of total U.S. advertising has occurred over the 1990s, but in 1997 magazines accounted for 7.6 percent of the total, up slightly from their 1996 share of 7.5 percent. *Advertising Age* reported that in 1997 consumer advertising expenditures rose 9 percent from the 1996 level. Advertising spending in business publications was up 7.9 percent. According to *Advertising Age,* both of these media had growth rates that surpassed the 7 percent rise in total U.S. advertising in 1997, although both lagged behind total advertising growth in 1996. According to the Publishers Information Bureau, consumer magazine advertising revenues were up 13.1 percent in 1997, the highest growth rate in magazine advertising revenue in 13 years. Consumer magazine advertising pages rose 5.2 percent, the second highest growth rate in 13 years. A healthy economy, a robust business climate, and high consumer confidence gave advertising a boost. For consumer magazines, all the top 10 advertising categories showed gains in 1997, with automotive, retail, and drugs and remedies showing increases of more than 20 percent from their 1996 levels. Automotive, toiletries and cosmetics, and direct-response companies were the top three advertisers in terms of spending. Advertising revenues were especially strong in magazines focusing on computers and the Internet.

Magazine advertising expenditures were expected to moderate in 1998 because of slower or flat growth in advertising spending by automakers, food manufacturers, and pharmaceutical companies. Cuts in magazine advertising spending by U.S. automakers and the impact of the Asian economic crisis also had their effects. Magazine advertising rates were up 5 to 6 percent in 1998 in anticipation of increases in paper and postal prices. It may still surpass growth in the overall economy, since total U.S. advertising growth is likely to exceed growth in the U.S. economy, as it did in 1997.

Circulation.   Newsstand circulation for consumer magazines has dropped steadily since the late 1970s as subscriptions have continued to climb. In 1997, newsstand circulation accounted for 18 percent of total magazine circulation, down from 24 percent a decade earlier. Higher single-copy prices, fewer magazine outlets, and the proliferation of new magazines sold mainly by subscription hurt newsstand sales over the last decade. Larger general-interest magazines, especially news magazines, have been especially hard hit at the newsstand in the 1990s. More recently, a slight gain in newsstand sales has occurred which may be attributable in part to an increasing number of outlets for magazines, particularly in large bookstores and retail outlets such as Barnes & Noble and Walmart. The Audit Bureau of Circulation reported a 0.2 percent increase in 1996 and a 1.2 percent rise in 1997 in the number of magazines sold on newsstands; the number of subscriptions rose 0.2 percent in 1996 and 0.7 percent in 1997.

In recent years publishers have been reluctant to raise newsstand or subscription prices, anticipating that their circulation would sustain sizable losses. At the same time publishers have been sending more magazine copies to newsstands but selling a smaller percentage. Many magazine publishers that are using direct-mail promotions to obtain new magazine subscribers are losing money on those promotions because of low response rates. The price of a single-copy magazine has on average increased 4.3 percent a year in the last 3 years, while the price of a magazine subscription has risen on average 0.3 percent a year.

In its *1996 Annual Survey of Manufactures* the U.S. Bureau of the Census reported that the growth of magazine circulation receipts has slowed over the last few years while magazine advertising receipts have increased. Circulation revenues represented 48.9 percent of total magazine receipts in 1996, compared with 51.6 percent in 1992, according to the Census Bureau.

Paper Costs.   Cyclical paper prices remain an ongoing concern for magazine publishers. Since the sharp paper price increases of 1994 and 1995, when the price of some paper grades rose more than 50 percent, publishers have kept a close eye on their paper inventories. They have not hoarded paper as they did during the 1994–1995 crisis, an action which further drove up prices. Strong growth in advertising pages and many new magazine titles have spurred paper demand, but rises in paper prices were moderate in 1997 and 1998.

Distribution Changes.   In the aftermath of the magazine wholesaler consolidations which swept through the industry in 1995 and 1996, newsstand distribution problems persist for publishers. With more and more magazines vying for a position on already crowded newsstands and higher magazine returns to publishers, *Folio Magazine* reports that a few distributors who cover retail chains have begun charging for titles that are not posting high sales. Some industry officials are expressing concern that this new practice could drastically alter the magazine circulation process. Wholesalers claim that they are handling many titles that are not profitable for them. According to *Folio Magazine,* part of the problem has resulted from chain retailers establishing more control over their magazine operations, a process which has left less money in the hands of distributors. The distributors have responded by charging publishers for services which were previously free. Smaller, niche-title magazines are more likely to be hurt by this new policy.

Postal Costs. Most magazine publishers were pleased with the new postal rate increases for magazines, although the 4.6 percent increase was higher than the 3.9 percent the USPS had requested from the Postal Rate Commission. For nonprofit magazines the 8 percent rate increase imposed was considered steep. Some nonprofit magazines may resort to alternative delivery systems. In recent years publishers have claimed that postal costs have represented an increasing share of their costs. Postal officials reported that the increase in rates for periodicals was related to some degree to the difficulty in automatically processing magazines. Rising postal processing costs for periodicals have been a long-standing point of contention between the magazine industry and USPS.

Competition from Other Media. Magazine publishers not only are confronting increasing competition from other publishers launching similar or more narrowly focused publications but also are facing challenges from on-line information and service providers that could siphon off advertising and readers from their existing publications. More and more magazine publishers are making the decision to have a Web presence for fear that a competitor may establish an on-line presence first. Business magazines are especially aware that the threat from other on-line business information providers could upstage their own valuable content. Already many business magazine publishers have joined on-line information service providers in establishing Web sites or have created their own sites. A growing number of cable television channels also are targeting audiences that tend to be readers of special-interest magazines and are competing for these readers' attention and for advertisers that want to reach those audiences.

U.S. Growth Projection for the Next 1 and 5 Years

Having fared well in attracting advertising to their magazines in the last few years, publishers will work hard over the next 5 years to maintain their share of total media advertising. Magazine industry receipts should increase at an average annual rate of about 1.5 to 2 percent in constant dollars if the GDP and U.S. advertising grow at a moderate rate. This growth will depend on expanding corporate profits, strong consumer confidence, rising consumer spending, and the magazine industry's establishment of a strong foothold in new media. Many magazines should prosper in the next 5 years as advertisers continue to emphasize brand building for their products and services in magazines. Magazine publishers also will benefit from extending the reach of their titles by creating spin-off print, broadcast, and on-line media products. Continued growth of special-interest magazine titles on-line will attract advertisers that want to reach more targeted audiences. Aging baby boomers and their children should provide more demand for narrowly focused titles in a number of consumer magazine sectors,

including health, leisure, and finance. According to Veronis, Suhler & Associates' annual report on the media, growth trends will favor media that provide consumers with a high degree of control through interactivity, such as on-line publication, or a greater choice of products. The high-quality editorial content and products of magazine publishers offer many options in providing consumers with what they want through a diverse range of media.

Global Market Prospects

The demand abroad for U.S. magazines has been growing at a moderate rate over the last several years. With the strengthening of developing economies, especially in Asia and South America, U.S. magazine exports are expected to grow about 5 percent annually over the next several years. U.S. periodical exports were up about 5 percent in 1998, earning an estimated $907 million. From 1992 through 1998, these exports increased at a 3.7 percent compound annual rate. The leading export markets for U.S. magazines in 1997 were Canada, accounting for more than 73 percent of the total; the United Kingdom, more than 8 percent; and the Netherlands, about 3 percent (see Table 25-7).

In 1997 the WTO issued its final ruling ordering Canada to end discriminatory policies that have protected that nation's domestic magazine industry. The ruling gives foreign publications, mainly U.S. magazines, greater market access to the Canadian magazine market and makes possible the start-up of Canadian editions of U.S. magazines. Over the past 30 years Canada had imposed a number of restrictions that limit the entry of U.S. publications containing Canadian advertising and prohibit foreign magazines from producing Canadian editions with local advertising. The Canadian government will remain very sensitive to U.S. magazine dominance in this market since it claims that the WTO ruling has disastrous implications for Canadian culture.

Instead of exporting U.S. editions of their magazines abroad to areas with large populations and growing economies, more U.S. publishers are licensing their publications to foreign publishers or launching foreign-language editions of their magazines, mainly through joint ventures. Large global-brand advertisers and local advertisers in those markets are providing advertising content to support these ventures. Over the next 5 years a growing number of multinational media conglomerates will increase their media holdings by purchasing other print and electronic media properties internationally to strengthen their position in the global market. This trend is expected to continue at a brisk pace. Among the largest and most active U.S. multinational publishers are Hearst Magazines and International Data Group. Hearst Magazines has more than 93 international editions distributed in over 100 countries, including *Country Living, Good Housekeeping, Esquire,* and *Cosmopolitan.* International Data Group publishes more than 285 computer magazines and newspapers and 500 book titles in 75 countries.

With increasing trade, investment, and trade agreements worldwide has come growth in the number of both business and consumer magazine titles. Rapid economic growth in countries such as China, Brazil, and Chile and a strong recov-

TABLE 25-7: U.S. Trade Patterns in Periodicals[1] in 1997
(millions of dollars; percent)

Exports			Imports		
Regions[2]	Value[3]	Share, %	Regions[2]	Value[3]	Share, %
NAFTA	646	74.8	NAFTA	130	64.0
Latin America	24	2.8	Latin America	2	1.1
Western Europe	146	16.9	Western Europe	57	27.8
Japan/Chinese Economic Area	13	1.5	Japan/Chinese Economic Area	11	5.5
Other Asia	12	1.4	Other Asia	1	0.7
Rest of world	22	2.5	Rest of world	2	0.9
World	864	100.0	World	204	100.0
Top Five Countries	Value	Share, %	Top Five Countries	Value	Share, %
Canada	633	73.2	Canada	118	57.9
United Kingdom	71	8.2	United Kingdom	38	18.4
Netherlands	25	2.8	Mexico	12	6.1
France	21	2.4	Japan	7	3.6
Mexico	14	1.6	Spain	5	2.6

[1] SIC 2721.
[2] For definitions of regional groupings, see "Getting the Most Out of *Outlook '99*."
[3] Values may not sum to total due to rounding.
Source: U.S. Department of Commerce, Bureau of the Census.

ery in other Latin American and Asian economies will increase the demand for consumer and business magazines in those markets. Rapidly expanding advertising markets in Asia and Latin America will support growth in the magazine sectors of those economies, making those regions very attractive publishing targets for foreign publishers. *Magazine World* reports that magazines' share of total media advertising ranges from 2 to 12 percent in Asia and from 3 to 10 percent in Latin America. With over half the world's population, the Asia/Pacific region will be the prime focus of many magazine publishers over the next few years despite the recent economic downturn in that region. *Folio Magazine* reports that a growing demand for brand-name consumer products exists in Asia, especially China, Taiwan, and South Korea. For these countries the greatest magazine growth will be in special-interest and special-audience magazines, which will be supported by expanding economies that will feature increased spending on leisure time activities and products. Over the next few years more U.S. publishers will publish an increasing number of Spanish-language versions of their publications to take advantage of Latin America's growing need for consumer and business information. In Brazil the number of magazine titles has climbed sharply, but more titles will be launched in this market that are targeted to smaller population sectors.

With an increasing array of media choices available to U.S. advertisers and a growing number of leisure time options open to consumers, U.S. publishers will need to be more responsive to the needs of both groups. Magazines that do the best job of identifying their readers and their readers' interests will have an advantage over other magazines and media competitors in attracting advertisers. Increasingly, publishers will have to demonstrate to advertisers the importance of magazines to their overall marketing plans.

With the growth rate for subscribers to on-line services expected to triple over the next 5 years, magazine publishers will have to weigh their strategies for on-line participation carefully. Some publishers, especially those of trade magazines, that have actively pursued on-line opportunities are doing well, but many publishers of consumer and trade magazines are likely to find it very difficult to attract on-line advertising and subscription revenues over the next few years. A few trade magazine giants, such as International Data Group and Reed Elsevier, have already established large on-line resources both on their own and in conjunction with other on-line providers. *PR Newswire* reports that in early 1998 International Data Group's Web network encompassed 210 local Web publications in 52 countries worldwide, making it the largest global on-line network serving the information technology sector. Consumer special-interest magazines are likely to fare better on the Web than are general consumer-interest publications since they appeal to a more targeted audience and to advertisers trying to reach that audience. While the costs of starting on-line magazines are generally lower than those for print publications, publishers know that they will need to attract both advertisers and subscribers to make their magazines viable on the Web. On-line sources such as Electronic Newsstand are assisting many magazine publishers with subscription and advertising sales.

Although the health of most print magazines over the next 5 years will not be endangered by on-line publications and services, magazine publishers are aware that they stand to lose both subscribers and advertisers to on-line publications and services. Factors affecting the success of magazines on the Web will include consumers' desire to obtain more immediate access to information, the development of more user-friendly on-line media sites, the ability of magazines to satisfy consumers' and advertisers' desires in a range of formats, and the ability of the magazine industry to devise a measurement standard that permits auditors to measure traffic and interests at magazine publishing sites.

The greatest strength of magazine publishers over the next 5 years will continue to be their ability to provide high-quality content for print and electronic publications and on-line services. With much of magazine content already in digital form, this content is very adaptable to on-line applications. Electronic distribution of information transcends global boundaries and permits the rapid and timely distribution of editorial content in various formats. Magazine publishers will have to determine how their editorial content can best be adapted to the new technologies of the digital information age. More magazine publishers will seek new revenue streams by using their editorial content for television programming and by licensing a magazine's name to other producers. *Folio Magazine* reports that Hearst magazine imprints are found on more than 3,000 products, including calendars, apparel, and paints. An increasing number of magazine publishers will need to give serious attention to developing print and electronic products and services that can be marketed globally as well as nationally.

Rose Marie Zummo Bratland, U.S. Department of Commerce, Office of Consumer Goods, (202) 482-0380, October 1998.

BOOK PUBLISHING

Global Industry Trends
The United States is the world's largest publisher, exporter, and importer of books. Industry shipments were expected to total $23 billion in 1998, with exports projected to exceed $2 billion

and imports estimated at about $1.4 billion (see Table 25-8). The U.S. population of 268.8 million provides a huge market for books, but American publishers also serve an expanding international clientele. Global demand for U.S. books is determined largely by language skills, educational attainment, income levels, and currency exchange rates. This demand is supported by expanded international copyright protection, improved global distribution systems, and greater awareness of product availability.

Book publishing in the United States is changing from an essentially domestic activity to one with global implications. Publishers view potential markets for authors' manuscripts from both a foreign and a domestic perspective. The marketing strategies of U.S. publishers cater increasingly to international audiences whose preferences tend toward American arts and sciences. An explosion of Internet activity has enlarged the sphere of international contacts for U.S. publishers, further expanding global markets for U.S. books. Major trends influencing the global perspective of the U.S. book publishing industry are the internationalization of the world book industry, advances in book distribution, strengthened international copyright protection, and growth in the use of the English language.

Publishing Globally. The commercial interests of the world's largest publishing enterprises have rarely been confined to their domestic borders, but in the 1990s the pace of global expansion accelerated. Major publishers in Europe, Asia, and the Americas continually cross global borders to expand market share, achieve economies of scale, and enhance profitability. The ebbs and flows of publishers' international interests are tied inevitably to economic opportunities. In the early 1990s market access to the previously controlled

TABLE 25-8: Book Publishing (SIC 2731) Trends and Forecasts
(millions of dollars except as noted)

	1992	1993	1994	1995	1996	1997[1]	1998[2]	1999[3]	Percent Change 96–97	97–98	98–99	92–96[4]
Industry data												
Value of shipments[5]	16,698	18,616	19,695	20,484	21,363	22,000	23,000	24,000	3.0	4.5	4.3	6.4
Value of shipments (1992$)	16,698	18,180	18,493	18,257	18,166	18,038	18,218	18,491	−0.7	1.0	1.5	2.1
Total employment (thousands)	79.0	83.2	83.5	83.5	85.4							2.0
Production workers (thousands)	18.2	18.2	18.2	18.5	18.5							0.4
Average hourly earnings ($)	12.51	12.90	13.56	13.61	13.27							1.5
Capital expenditures	327	282	283	345	365							2.8
Product data												
Value of shipments[5]	14,761	16,596	17,229	18,409	19,114	19,650	20,475	21,295	2.8	4.2	4.0	6.7
Value of shipments (1992$)	14,761	16,207	16,177	16,407	16,254	16,247	16,393	16,606	−0.0	0.9	1.3	2.4
Trade data												
Value of imports	953	966	1,023	1,184	1,240	1,298	1,365	1,440	4.7	5.2	5.5	6.8
Value of exports	1,637	1,664	1,703	1,779	1,776	1,897	2,040	2,175	6.8	7.5	6.6	2.1

[1] Estimate except imports and exports.
[2] Estimate.
[3] Forecast.
[4] Compound annual rate.
[5] For definition of industry versus product values, see "Getting the Most Out of *Outlook '99.*"
Source: U.S. Department of Commerce: Bureau of the Census; International Trade Administration.

economies of eastern Europe and the New Independent States of the former Soviet Union created a brief surge in publishers' investments. In the mid-1990s publishers' attention was focused on the high-growth, knowledge-based economies of countries in southeast Asia. In the late 1990s Asia's financial instability redirected international publishers' efforts toward expansion into the United States, an economy whose large and open markets are the envy of the world. Publishers' attention after the millennium may well be directed toward the economies of Latin America.

Book Distribution.   Printing on paper is one of the world's oldest's technologies, but new ways of finding global markets and achieving international distribution of printed products result from the use of the newest technology: the Internet. Growth in global access to the Internet by foreign audiences has been a boon to the world's book buyers and distributors and a bane to book retailers, whose storefronts are bypassed electronically. The ease of locating books on the Internet and making payment by credit card spurs book exports and challenges the efficiencies of international book distributors. Increased movements of books by airlines rather than shipping companies reflects market requirements for faster deliveries. Some book publishers must deal with the fact that the negotiated rights purchased by publishers to obtain exclusive geographic sales territories for certain books are devalued to the degree that Internet purchases are made outside the control of those publishers. However, for most book publishers the Internet is a powerful sales tool with a truly global reach.

International Copyright.   The international protection of publishers' properties through strong copyright regimes has been a dominant trend in the last decade. Perhaps the most significant outcome of the recent set of multilateral trade negotiations—the Uruguay Round of the General Agreement on Tariffs and Trade (GATT)—was the acceptance of the copyright provisions in the agreement Trade-Related Aspects of Intellectual Property Rights (TRIPS). Further enhancement of the TRIPS provisions is being addressed through another international body, WIPO, whose interests are to extend copyright duration and expand protection to all forms of electronic media. The most appealing aspect to publishers is the growth of coordinated efforts among governments to enforce copyright protection. Enforcement efforts are shifting away from the successes achieved in southeast Asia and focusing on the growth of copyright piracy in countries in the Middle East.

English Language.   English has not yet achieved full adoption as the world's language, but this radical concept of English primacy has an expanding cadre of supporters. Electronic communication—the Internet—has further enhanced its acceptance and value. English has become at least the world's second language and is firmly first in the sciences. Publishers of technical and scientific books can develop notable international markets for their products only if their works are published in or translated into English. Internationally, it is estimated that the number of persons with an occupation classified as professional is approximately 50 million to 60 million, a group whose commonality rests on having English as either the first or second language. The benefits derived by U.S. publishers from the global popularity of the English language are incalculable but are implied by the growth of U.S. exports of textbooks and technical, scientific, and professional books.

Domestic Trends

The economic success of the 2,700 establishments that constitute the U.S. book publishing industry rests on the growth of a literate U.S. population whose propensity to read books is supported by rising levels of income, occupation, and educational attainment. The industry's total value of shipments in 1998—$23 billion—was spread among three principal product categories: educational materials, primarily textbooks; trade books, or adult and juvenile works of fiction and nonfiction generally sold through retail outlets; and all other books, including religious books, reference books, technical, scientific, and professional books, book club and mail order publications, university press books, music books, and pamphlets.

Book publishing in the United States is an industry with a large number of small establishments (under 20 employees) whose total output in the 1990s failed to keep pace with the rise in GDP. Publishers are being affected by several major trends: an expansion of merger and acquisition activity, substantial changes in retail trade, favorable U.S. demographics, and gains in school and library funding.

Mergers and Acquisitions.   The huge U.S. book market is attracting more foreign, primarily European, publishers. The attractiveness of this market is aided by its openness and relative ease of entry, the political and economic stability of the United States, and the market's significant growth potential. Entry to this market is accomplished increasingly through mergers or acquisitions. Publishing firms based in Canada and the United Kingdom have traditionally been the most active in this endeavor, but the 1990s has witnessed a pronounced increase of interest from Germany, Australia, France, Switzerland, and the Netherlands. U.S. scholarly publishing tends to draw keen attention from German and Dutch publishers, while British and Canadian publishers focus on the trade book sector. The gradual but progressive entry of foreign firms into the cultural and commercial business of U.S. book publishing received significant publicity when it was revealed that 10 of the 20 largest U.S. publishing companies in 1998 were foreign-owned.

Retail Trade.   A virtual revolution has occurred in the channels through which American books are sold. While the 1980s was characterized by the expansion of chain bookstores into shopping malls, the retail book trade of the 1990s is increasingly being dominated by book superstores: retail establishments with 50,000 to 100,000 titles spread over 30,000 square feet or more of floor space. Competition from these superstores, coupled with the growth of retail book sales through warehouse clubs, general mass merchandise stores, and the Internet, has reduced significantly the number of independent bookstores. The rise of book superstores has had a twofold effect on book publishers. The huge space dimensions of these stores generate an increase in the number of titles available for display, but the stores' tight sales turnover requirements hasten the return of unsold books for store credit. The net effect has been to expand the number of U.S. book titles published but reduce the quantities of books printed.

Demographics. Book publishers have benefited from a favorable set of U.S. demographic factors that extend back to 1960. The U.S. population grew to 268.8 million in 1998 from 179.3 million in 1960. This represents an additional 89.5 million persons, or an increase of 50 percent. The educational attainment of the U.S. population has taken enormous strides. By 1998 the proportion of the U.S. population with a high school degree stood at 82 percent, double the 41 percent level in 1960. Even more impressive is growth in the number of college graduates. In 1998, 24 percent of the U.S. population achieved status as having attended 4 or more years of college, three times as many individuals as in 1960. The U.S. population is both increasing and becoming more educated, and its financial well-being has improved. In terms of dollars adjusted for inflation, the per capita disposable personal income of the population rose to approximately $20,000 in 1998 from $8,660 in 1960, a compound annual rate of growth of 3 percent.

Education and Libraries. With over 40 percent of the U.S. book industry's products being sold to schools, colleges, and libraries, publishers are extremely sensitive to changes in those critical markets. In 1998, enrollment at U.S. schools and colleges totaled 67.8 million, representing 25 percent of the U.S. population. Enrollment trends were relatively stable over the period 1988–1998: up 17 percent in elementary schools (to 38.1 million in 1998 from 32.5 million in 1988), 15 percent in high schools (to 14.8 million in 1998 from 12.9 million in 1988), and 16 percent in colleges and universities (to 14.9 million in 1998 from 13.1 million in 1988). In the aggregate, U.S. enrollments increased 16 percent (9.3 million students) between 1988 and 1998, but until 1997 state and local government funds for instructional materials generally failed to keep pace with this growth. Expansion of the U.S. economy since the mid-1990s has generated more tax dollars for educational purposes, but school board initiatives to get more computers in classrooms have diverted some textbook-earmarked funds to the electronic media. The nation's 37,000 libraries, also funded through tax revenues, faced expenditure scenarios similar to those of U.S. schools in the period 1988–1998. Library budgets emphasized the funding of computers and networks, with the goal of becoming Internet-connected, and allocated increased expenditures for reference materials in CD-ROM rather than in print.

Projections of Industry and Trade Growth for the Next 1 and 5 Years

The opening of more retail superstores, gains in U.S. disposable personal income, and more tax revenues available for U.S. schools and libraries should raise shipments of the U.S. book publishing industry to $24 billion in 1999, an increase of about 2 percent over 1998 in constant dollars. Enrollments at U.S. schools and colleges should increase by 763,000 students, generating more demand for textbooks and instructional materials. State adoption schedules for the purchase of school textbooks in 1999 show a stable buying pattern compared with those in previous years. The budgets of U.S. schools and libraries should benefit in 1999 from continued growth of tax revenues resulting from an expanding economy. An increase of 2.3 million in the population, coupled with gains in disposable personal income, should support growth in U.S. markets for adult and juvenile trade books. Exports of U.S. books in 1999 are expected to reach $2.2 billion, up 7 percent from 1998 in nominal dollars. Expectations of improved sales to Canada and countries in the European Union should counter the negative effects of a strong U.S. dollar and continued weakness in book demand from Asian countries.

Shipments of the U.S. book publishing industry over the next 5 years should grow at a compound annual average inflation-adjusted rate of 2 percent. Demand for U.S. books will be aided by a gain of 11.5 million in population and the enrollment of an additional 2.4 million students in U.S. schools and colleges. A strong, stable, inflation-tamed, job-producing U.S. economy is expected to generate tax revenues and disposable personal income that will support a steady demand for books through 2003. Overseas demand for U.S. books is largely a function of market economies and currency exchange rates, conditions that could change noticeably in the next 5 years. Asian countries should improve their financial situations markedly, and the strength of the U.S. dollar could abate, creating greater demand for U.S. exports, including books.

The 5-year demand scenarios for individual categories of U.S. books has a varied pattern. Book categories exceeding the projected annual growth rate of 2 percent include religious books, college textbooks, technical, scientific, and professional books, and elementary and high school textbooks. The search for a life with spiritual meaning consistently raises the level of U.S. religious book purchases above the all-industry average. Improved sales of college textbooks should result from higher enrollments and more materials and course packs tailored by instructors for individual classrooms. Growth in occupational specialties at the technical, scientific, and professional levels, combined with more funds for libraries and institutions, should improve markets for technical, scientific, and professional books. Gains in elementary and high school enrollments and greater funding of educational materials to support those enrollments are expected to raise demand for elementary and high school textbooks.

Book categories that are projected to experience growth rates below the 5-year all-industry annual average of 2 percent include adult and juvenile trade books, mass market paperbound books, and reference books. The expanding number of book superstores has encouraged the publication of more adult trade U.S. titles but has not demonstrated an ability to raise overall market demand for those books. In addition, demand for U.S. adult trade books lowered by a reduction in the number of independent bookstores may not be totally compensated for by the rise of superstores. Juvenile book demand is not helped by projected U.S. demographics. The number of persons age 13 years or younger is forecast to increase by only 230,000 over the next 5 years. Mass market paperbound books suffer from competition from heavily discounted best-selling hardcover books, thus restricting their markets. Increased competition from the electronic media is expected to further limit markets for U.S. reference books in the years ahead.

Global Market Prospects

With U.S. apparent consumption of books in 1999 forecast at $20.6 billion, the focus of the U.S. book publishing industry is clearly on serving the reading needs of the domestic market. Projected exports of books in 1999 should reach about $2.2 billion, representing approximately 11 percent of U.S. apparent consumption. To an increasing degree, data on U.S. book exports understate the growing international interests of U.S. publishers. Export shipments valued under $2,500 are not reported in the book classification, yet world growth of the Internet has created a surge of international access to global products, especially U.S. books. In addition, foreign revenues received by U.S. publishers from the sale of rights and translations, which are estimated to range annually from $200 million to $400 million, are not reported in the export data.

International sales of U.S. books are concentrated primarily in five countries: three where English is the predominant language—Canada, the United Kingdom, and Australia—and two where it is not—Japan and Mexico (see Table 25-9). These five economies accounted for over 73 percent of U.S. book exports in 1997, a ratio that has shown little variance over the last decade. An additional 25 countries, each purchasing at least $5 million in U.S. books annually, accounted for another 22 percent of the export total. A breakout of U.S. book exports by geographic area identifies the leading regions as Asia excepting Australia and Japan (11 percent), Europe excepting the United Kingdom (10 percent), Latin America excepting Mexico (4 percent), and Africa (2 percent). All four regions offer potentially attractive markets for U.S. books, assuming an awareness of changes in economic conditions and fluctuations in currency valuations.

Global demand for U.S. books essentially is accounted for by three sectors: textbooks, technical, scientific, and professional books, and adult trade books. Exports of U.S. textbooks represent 20 percent of the export total, with foreign demand for these books strongest at the college and university level. Foreign markets for U.S. technical, scientific, and professional books account for 30 percent of U.S. book exports. Global demand for such books emanates from foreign libraries and institutions, but these products also meet the informational needs of individuals in the professions. Although the top-selling U.S. adult trade books eventually appear abroad in translation, many more trade books, including non-best-sellers, are exported in English. International demand for U.S. adult trade books published in English is so significant that this book category represents 45 percent of the U.S. book export total. The remaining 5 percent is represented by foreign sales of U.S. reference and religious books.

Global market prospects for U.S. book publishers are uniformly favorable, especially considering the long-run potential for improved economies in eastern Europe and Asia. However, U.S. publishers' access to the world's economies will continue to be inhibited unless trade barriers are removed and international copyright protection is enforced and enhanced. Improved market access to the world's publications was improved in the Uruguay Round of GATT and is being addressed in the APEC forum. Enforcement of international copyright continues to be a major concern among the world's publishers, and the U.S. government has taken the lead in this important issue. WIPO has

TABLE 25-9: U.S. Trade Patterns in Book Publishing[1] in 1997

(millions of dollars; percent)

Regions[2]	Exports Value[3]	Share, %	Regions[2]	Imports Value[3]	Share, %
NAFTA	882	46.5	NAFTA	208	16.1
Latin America	83	4.4	Latin America	17	1.3
Western Europe	417	22.0	Western Europe	557	43.0
Japan/Chinese Economic Area	179	9.5	Japan/Chinese Economic Area	355	27.3
Other Asia	118	6.2	Other Asia	123	9.5
Rest of world	217	11.5	Rest of world	38	2.9
World	1,897	100.0	World	1,298	100.0
Top Five Countries	Value	Share, %	Top Five Countries	Value	Share, %
Canada	824	43.4	United Kingdom	283	21.8
United Kingdom	254	13.4	Hong Kong (PRC)	203	15.7
Australia	138	7.3	Canada	189	14.6
Japan	120	6.3	Singapore	92	7.1
Mexico	58	3.1	Italy	86	6.6

[1] SIC 2731.
[2] For definitions of regional groupings, see "Getting the Most Out of *Outlook '99*."
[3] Values may not sum to total due to rounding.
Source: U.S. Department of Commerce, Bureau of the Census.

proposed extending copyright protection to include both print and electronic media, a potentially contentious issue pitting authors and publishers against educators and librarians. Successful resolution of this issue is critical since the world's publishing industries seek to advance knowledge, information, and entertainment through print and electronic formats.

William S. Lofquist, U.S. Department of Commerce, Office of Consumer Goods, (202) 482-0379, October 1998.

COMMERCIAL PRINTING

Commercial printing is one of the nation's oldest and largest manufacturing activities. The industry's 40,000 establishments and 437,000 employees are dispersed geographically among virtually all states, regions, and localities. The products of U.S. commercial printers, which were estimated at $73 billion in 1998, serve the diverse economic, cultural, and informational needs of an expanding citizenry (see Table 25-10). The bulk of U.S. printing production—labels, decals, cards, coupons, forms, periodicals, catalogs, maps, stamps, and financial, legal, and advertising materials—is geared to domestic markets, but an active international component serves foreign markets. Exports estimated at almost $1.3 billion in 1997 place U.S. commercial printing second only to that of Germany in meeting the printed product needs of a global society. (see Table 25-11)

Global Industry Trends

Demand for printing among the world's developed economies is met largely through indigenous industries. The experience of the United States is typical: U.S. imports of printed matter account for less than 2 percent of apparent consumption, and U.S. exports represent less than 2 percent of the value of shipments. Nonetheless, a rise in global perspective in the U.S. printing industry is evidenced by the trends discussed below.

Foreign Investment. Serving the international printing needs of U.S. multinational companies has encouraged the largest U.S. printers to establish foreign subsidiaries or form partnerships with printing firms abroad. Much of this activity was focused on Europe in the 1980s and Asia in the 1990s, but Latin America is now the region of choice. Relatively robust printing markets in Argentina, Brazil, Chile, and Mexico invite U.S. investment, a trend that is expected to continue in the foreseeable future. In turn, foreign investment in the large U.S. printing market tends to ebb and flow. Several Asian and European printers have established a presence in the United States or been active in acquiring U.S. printing firms, but the largest and most consistent U.S.-focused merger and acquisition actions have been generated by Canada's major printing firms

International Standards. To an ever-increasing degree, U.S. printers seeking international markets, especially in Europe, are denied entry unless their manufacturing operations comply with international standards. In particular, Standard 9000 of the International Standards Organization (ISO) establishes benchmarks for consistency of quality control in manufacturing, while ISO 14000 addresses the management of factors relating to the environment. The costs of complying with these standards are not inconsequential, but a lack of certification would render U.S. printers ineligible to compete in potentially attractive foreign markets.

TABLE 25-10: Commercial Printing (SIC 275) Trends and Forecasts

(millions of dollars except as noted)

	1992	1993	1994	1995	1996	1997[1]	1998[2]	1999[3]	Percent Change 96–97	Percent Change 97–98	Percent Change 98–99	Percent Change 92–96[4]
Industry data												
Value of shipments[5]	56,229	58,173	60,411	65,101	67,842	70,625	73,240	75,805	4.1	3.7	3.5	4.8
Value of shipments (1992$)	56,229	56,764	58,252	59,454	60,555	61,164	62,509	63,759	1.0	2.2	2.0	1.9
Total employment (thousands)	567	572	577	598	604							1.6
Production workers (thousands)	408	415	417	433	437							1.7
Average hourly earnings ($)	11.50	11.69	11.75	11.86	12.31							1.7
Capital expenditures	2,144	2,238	2,708	2,680	2,959							8.4
Product data												
Value of shipments[5]	54,902	56,960	58,902	63,819	66,624	69,490	72,130	74,725	4.3	3.8	3.6	5.0
Value of shipments (1992$)	54,902	55,577	56,791	58,277	59,466	62,108	63,536	64,870	4.4	2.3	2.1	2.0
Trade data												
Value of imports	442	505	584	756	748	825	925	1,045	10.3	12.1	13.0	14.1
Value of exports	1,056	1,201	1,061	1,197	1,195	1,248	1,310	1,362	4.4	5.0	4.0	3.1

[1] Estimate except imports and exports.
[2] Estimate.
[3] Forecast.
[4] Compound annual rate.
[5] For definition of industry versus product values, see "Getting the Most Out of *Outlook '99*."
Source: U.S. Department of Commerce: Bureau of the Census; International Trade Administration.

TABLE 25-11: U.S. Trade Patterns in Commercial Printing[1] in 1997
(millions of dollars; percent)

Exports			Imports		
Regions[2]	Value[3]	Share, %	Regions[2]	Value[3]	Share, %
NAFTA	497	39.9	NAFTA	435	52.8
Latin America	96	7.7	Latin America	3	0.4
Western Europe	305	24.4	Western Europe	246	29.8
Japan/Chinese Economic Area	164	13.1	Japan/Chinese Economic Area	93	11.2
Other Asia	86	6.9	Other Asia	20	2.4
Rest of world	100	8.0	Rest of world	29	3.5
World	1,248	100.0	World	825	100.0
Top Five Countries	Value	Share, %	Top Five Countries	Value	Share, %
Canada	347	27.8	Canada	410	49.7
Mexico	150	12.0	Germany	59	7.1
Japan	102	8.2	United Kingdom	55	6.6
United Kingdom	99	7.9	Japan	37	4.4
Germany	52	4.2	France	36	4.3

[1] SIC 275.
[2] For definitions of regional groupings, see "Getting the Most Out of *Outlook '99*."
[3] Values may not sum to total due to rounding.
Source: U.S. Department of Commerce, Bureau of the Census.

Global Sourcing. Although the focus of U.S. printers is servicing domestic markets, both the materials and the equipment used to reach those markets are being determined globally. The principal material consumed—paper—is frequently sourced from Canada or the Scandinavian countries. Even if paper is purchased domestically, its prices are subject to demand forces that are determined internationally. Film, printing plates, inks, and chemicals are increasingly sourced from supplier firms in the Netherlands, Japan, the United Kingdom, and Mexico. Expanding U.S. markets for imports of printing machinery and equipment from Germany, Italy, the United Kingdom, and Japan illustrate a growing dependency on international sources for the basic means of print production.

Domestic Trends

Most products of the U.S. commercial printing industry target the diverse needs of domestic consumers and businesses. The industry's economic fortunes track fluctuations in the nation's GDP and are closely tied to the level of U.S. advertising expenditures. Changes in U.S. demographics are soon reflected by changes in the markets for printed products. Expansion of the school-age population generates more comics, textbooks, juvenile books, and youth-oriented periodicals. Growth in household formation promotes the interests of direct mail, newspaper insert, and catalog producers. New business formation creates markets for trade advertising, forms, directories, and financial and legal printing. An increase in the number of senior citizens increases the demand for newspapers and books.

Commercial printing is a mature industry that is undergoing a significant transition. Forces affecting U.S. commercial printing include changes in technology, shifts in the industry's structural dynamics, changes in demand for print advertising, and imposition of new electronic media on traditional print markets.

Technological Change. Traditional printing operations were long centered on analog technology, a process dependent on photographic film, light-sensitive printing plates, solvent-based inks, and an array of chemicals and developers. By 2000 a decadelong shift into digital technology will be the dominant process in the plants of many medium-size and large U.S. printers. The changes wrought by this shift in technology are dramatic. Gone are thousands of typesetting firms, rendered obsolete by digital type produced on desktop computers. Gone are hundreds of platemaking and color separation shops, whose film-based skills have become worthless as digital processors produce color-corrected films or the digital text and images are applied directly to printing plates. The impact of digital technology was first concentrated on the printing operations—typesetting and platemaking—required before the running of the press. More recent applications of digital technology to the press itself are yielding cost-effective, full-color short production runs of text and image variable printed products that were cost-prohibitive before the advent of digital imaging.

Structural Dynamics. Owing in part to changes resulting from digital technology, the U.S. commercial printing industry is undergoing structural changes designed to achieve economies of scale while retaining a marketing focus that is sensitive to local and regional printing opportunities. A wave of merger and acquisition activities supported by a growing U.S. economy and a buoyant stock market is consolidating ownership among medium-size and large printers. The intent is the geographic dispersion of affiliated plants among all U.S. regions and principal localities, producing a cohesive marketing structure that is attentive to the printing needs of U.S. businesses. This structure also generates economies of scale in the purchase of machinery, equipment, and consumable supplies. Plant affiliation also is aided by growth in the application of digital technology, which yields a higher output per worker without a significant increase in payroll costs.

Advertising Expenditures. While commercial printing's value of shipments closely parallels fluctuations in GDP, the industry is largely dependent on U.S. expenditures on print advertising. Since 1980 U.S. advertising through various print media has held steady at approximately 60 percent of total advertising expenditures. Although print advertising's trends in the 1990s show overall growth in nominal dollars, gains in advertising expenditures among print media vary significantly. This is of substantial importance to U.S. printers, since the unique printing, binding, and delivery requirements of each print medium necessitate a large capital investment. Marginal growth in the advertising revenues of newspapers, periodicals, and Yellow Pages directories lessens the attractiveness of these markets to U.S. printers, while the higher advertising growth rates achieved by direct mail, catalogs, inserts, and coupons offer greater returns on the printing industry's investments. Greater use of digital printing equipment enables U.S. printers to respond more rapidly to changes in print demand.

Competition from Electronic Media. Although total demand for U.S. printed products continues to expand, the electronic media provide strong competition. Examples include electronic banking, which lowers demand for checkbooks; CD-ROMs, which reduce the need for technical manuals, encyclopedias, and directories; Web sites on the Internet, which provide electronic access to digital catalogs, annual reports, and other company information, obviating the need for certain materials in printed format; and E-mail, including electronic commerce, which lessens the demand for newsletters and printed business information and forms. The Internet is used on a regular basis at work or at home by over 29 million U.S. residents age 18 or over, a sector currently representing 15 percent of the U.S. adult population. A doubling of this Internet-accessed sector over the next decade is virtually assured, guaranteeing further inroads in demand for selected U.S. printed products.

Projections of Industry and Trade Growth for the Next 1 and 5 Years

Growth in the U.S. economy, more new business formation, and increasing demand for print advertising are expected to raise the shipments of the U.S. commercial printing industry to $76 billion in 1999, an increase in constant dollars of 2 percent over 1998. Markets for catalogs and direct-mail materials are expected to exceed this rate of growth, driven by continued strong U.S. business demand for these products. Printed products expected to match this 2 percent growth rate in 1999 include decals, labels, newspaper and periodical printing, and legal and financial printing, with U.S. demand for these products supported largely by gains in GDP. Inroads made by the electronic media, especially the Internet and CD-ROMs, should reduce U.S. markets for printed directories, newsletters, business-to-business information, annual reports, and technical manuals. Profits of U.S. printers are forecast to edge downward

in 1999 as a result of constraints on paper supply and larger investments in capital equipment.

A series of favorable factors should support the growth of U.S. printed product output over the next 5 years. The U.S. population is projected to reach 280.4 million by 2003, an increase of 8.1 million persons. This population growth should be accompanied by higher levels of educational attainment and gains in personal income. A rising U.S. economy, coupled with growth in aggregate demand for print advertising, should support an annual growth rate averaging 2 percent, adjusted for inflation, in the value of shipments of the U.S. commercial printing industry through 2003. Competition from the electronic media is expected to reduce U.S. markets for some printed products, but commercial printing's aggregate demand is projected to stay relatively aligned with growth in the nation's economy. The costs of the printing industry's principal material input—paper—are expected to increase over the period 1999–2003, adversely affecting printers' profit margins.

Global Market Prospects

The ability of the U.S. commercial printing industry to expand its interests globally depends largely on the industry's success in addressing a critical set of domestic issues: industry consolidation, the absorption of new technology, and the industry's response to competition from electronic media. Since commercial printing is a mature industry with long-established markets, U.S. printers recognize that future growth hinges on creating new products that satisfy predominantly domestic customers.

Consisting of approximately 40,000 plants, 85 percent of which have fewer than 20 employees, the U.S. printing industry is ripe for consolidation. This condition is abetted by intense competition for large-market, high-volume products, including labels, decals, catalogs, directories, periodicals, coupons, and inserts, that require large capital investments. Acquisitions among the printing industry's larger firms are pressuring the smaller firms, creating price competition that should lead to a long-term reduction in the number of printing establishments. Other factors pointing toward consolidation among printing plants are the significant costs associated with investments in digital technology (deemed essential to enhance plant productivity) and a reduction in some markets for printed products as a result of increased competition from the Internet, CD-ROMs, E-mail, and other electronic media.

Economic, demographic, and technological changes influence markets for printed products. A strong, stable U.S. economy generates high levels of advertising expenditures and creates new business formation. Commercial printers whose markets focus on advertising and new businesses should experience real growth rates in excess of the 2 percent industry average projected through 2003. Printed products tied to advertising include direct mail, signs, coupons, circulars, fliers, shopping news, posters, inserts, point-of-purchase items, and display cards. Growth in the number of U.S. business establishments promotes more bank, insurance, financial, and legal printing; business forms; and trade advertising.

Projected changes in U.S. demographics will have a varied effect on printers' markets. An aging population should enlarge U.S. markets for newspaper printing, but shrinkage in the teenage component could hinder the growth of magazine printing. Higher levels of educational attainment enlarge U.S. markets for books and informational materials, but scarcity of leisure time could lead to greater use of computer-related electronic media to the possible detriment of print media. The changes wrought by advances in computer technology have a negative impact on markets for a variety of printed products. Printers of newsletters, business forms, directories, technical manuals, maps, and check-books have experienced decreased demand for their products as a result of competition from the electronic media. Growth of Web site use by U.S. households could reduce the demand for printed coupons as those items become accessible electronically. In contrast, markets for printed catalogs may experience short-term increases as familiarity with Web sites grows.

International markets for U.S. printed products recorded an uneven pattern of growth in the 1990s, with projected exports in 1999 reaching $1.4 billion. The proximity of Canada and Mexico to the United States encourages a strong trade relationship, and those two countries account for 40 percent of U.S. printers' exports. Foreign demand for U.S. printed products is strongly influenced by global economic conditions, especially currency exchange rates. Advertising printing—including catalogs, posters, and tourist literature—is traditionally the largest U.S. export category, followed by security printing: certificates, legal documents, and financial materials. Other U.S. printed products that attract global attention include labels, decals, playing cards, and pictorial matter.

Global prospects for increasing exports by the U.S. commercial printing industry should improve significantly in the years ahead. Most of these products have their access to foreign markets challenged by tariffs and other trade barriers. As noted earlier, the removal of barriers to international trade, a priority activity of the U.S. government, is being accomplished through implementation of the Uruguay Round tariff cuts and the APEC negotiations. The opening of foreign markets to U.S. printed products should enlarge the global vision of U.S. printers. The development of an international trade strategy would complement the printing industry's traditionally domestic focus.

William S. Lofquist, U.S. Department of Commerce, Office of Consumer Goods, (202) 482-0379, October 1998.

BOOK PRINTING

As a result of the unique printing, binding, and finishing requirements associated with book printing, establishments in this industry are distinctly separate from general commercial printers. The U.S. book printing industry consists of approximately 550 firms that serve the printing and binding needs of 2,700 domestic book publishers. Book printers tend to be large, with just 54 plants employing about two-thirds of the industry's work force. The industry displays some geographic concentration, with the majority of plants located in the mid-Atlantic and midwestern states. Access to major truck and rail facilities is a critical determinant of plant location. Printers' plants tend to be specialized, with equipment geared to a distinct product: textbooks, hardcover or paperbound trade books, or religious, reference, and scholarly books.

Changes in the U.S. book printing industry's value of shipments are linked to the manufacturing requirements of the customers: U.S. book publishers. Demand for U.S. books has increased at stable but marginal rates in recent years, and this is reflected in the sales trends experienced by book printers. The book printing industry's value of shipments in 1999 is projected

TABLE 25-12: Book Printing (SIC 2732) Trends and Forecasts
(millions of dollars except as noted)

	1992	1993	1994	1995	1996	1997[1]	1998[1]	1999[2]	Percent Change			
									96–97	97–98	98–99	92–96[3]
Industry data												
Value of shipments[4]	4,681	4,810	4,745	5,392	5,333	5,385	5,495	5,660	1.0	2.0	3.0	3.3
Value of shipments (1992$)	4,681	4,777	4,647	5,043	5,008	5,123	5,149	5,200	2.3	0.5	1.0	1.7
Total employment (thousands)	50.5	49.8	46.5	49.0	50.3							-0.1
Production workers (thousands)	38.7	38.3	36.1	38.0	38.5							-0.1
Average hourly earnings ($)	12.13	11.77	12.08	12.58	13.63							3.0
Capital expenditures	195	174	283	323	253							6.7
Product data												
Value of shipments[4]	4,730	4,938	4,994	5,358	5,323	5,370	5,465	5,615	0.9	1.8	2.7	3.0
Value of shipments (1992$)	4,730	4,904	4,891	5,013	4,998	5,110	5,130	5,175	2.2	0.4	0.9	1.4

[1] Estimate.
[2] Forecast.
[3] Compound annual rate.
[4] For definition of industry versus product values, see "Getting the Most Out of *Outlook '99*."
Source: U.S. Department of Commerce: Bureau of the Census; International Trade Administration.

to be almost $5.7 billion, an increase in constant dollars of 1 percent over 1998 (see Table 25-12). Book printers have noted a surge in the number of new U.S. book titles and/or editions published annually—to a range of 55,000 to 65,000 in the late 1990s from 40,000 to 50,000 in the early 1990s. However, they also have experienced a decline in the number of copies printed per title—to under 5,000 copies per title in the 1990s from 5,000 to 10,000 in previous years. This reflects U.S. publishers' decision to maintain low book inventories and U.S. printers' ability to return to press quickly when demand for a particular title exceeds supply. Expansion in U.S. book markets over the next 5 years should raise shipments of the U.S. book printing industry to gains averaging 1.5 percent annually, adjusted for inflation, through 2003.

The U.S. book printing industry faces both short-term and long-term challenges in the years ahead. Printing competition from nations in southeast Asia is expected to intensify, especially in light of the export-favorable currency situation resulting from the financial crises in several of those countries. This competition should not be onerous, however, since in addition to predictions that the currency situation may be short-lived, rapid technological changes in global printing are expected to reduce significantly the cost advantages of printing in low-wage economies. A longer-term challenge is the contraction of some U.S. book printing markets resulting from growth in the electronic media. The printed output of encyclopedias, directories, and other reference works is being reduced as a result of demand for these products in CD-ROM or other electronic formats. However, the U.S. book printing industry takes comfort from the knowledge that although some books may be electronically challenged, publishers and readers remain essentially print-dependent.

William S. Lofquist, U.S. Department of Commerce, Office of Consumer Goods, (202) 482-0379, October 1998.

MISCELLANEOUS PUBLISHING

The U.S. miscellaneous publishing industry is an amalgam of essentially informational products, the most significant of which are telephone books, directories, catalogs, shopping news, newsletters, loose-leaf business service publications, calendars, souvenir cards, and maps. This diversity is indicative of the variety of markets these companies serve and the multiple factors influencing demand. Factors common to all these firms include changes in GDP and levels of personal income, but for most products the dominant influence is U.S. expenditures for advertising. Businesses engaged in miscellaneous publishing tend to be small, with just 17 percent of the industry's 3,500 firms having more than 20 employees. The industry's focus is almost exclusively on domestic markets, with less than 1 percent of its products destined for international sale.

Expansion of the U.S. economy in 1999 is expected to help raise the value of shipments of the miscellaneous publishing industry 1.2 percent, adjusted for inflation, over the level in 1998 (see Table 25-13). Higher levels of advertising expenditures aid publishers of catalogs, shopping news, calendars, and telephone directories. Continued growth in U.S. business formation, an active stock market, and more occupational specialties should support greater sales of newsletters, directories, and business service publications. Rising levels of disposable personal income should help publishers of yearbooks, souvenir cards, travel guides, sheet music, maps, and atlases. With neither exports nor imports representing as much as 2 percent of U.S. apparent consumption, foreign trade considerations should not be a significant factor in the marketing strategies of the industry in 1999. Stable markets for most of the industry's products through 2003 should result in a compound average annual rate of growth of 1 percent in U.S. miscellaneous publishers' value of shipments.

TABLE 25-13: Miscellaneous Publishing (SIC 2741) Trends and Forecasts
(millions of dollars except as noted)

	1992	1993	1994	1995	1996	1997[1]	1998[2]	1999[3]	96–97	97–98	98–99	92–96[4]
									Percent Change			
Industry data												
Value of shipments[5]	10,908	11,807	11,976	12,025	12,511	13,010	13,620	14,190	4.0	4.7	4.2	3.5
Value of shipments (1992$)	10,908	11,320	11,048	10,604	10,504	10,599	10,747	10,876	0.9	1.4	1.2	−0.9
Total employment (thousands)	65.1	66.6	65.6	67.3	68.8							1.4
Production workers (thousands)	23.5	22.8	24.2	25.4	25.4							2.0
Average hourly earnings ($)	10.91	10.41	10.40	11.56	13.04							4.6
Capital expenditures	189	139	173	159	144							−6.6
Product data												
Value of shipments[5]	11,493	12,400	12,893	12,722	12,898	13,360	13,920	14,450	3.6	4.2	3.8	2.9
Value of shipments (1992$)	11,493	11,888	11,894	11,219	10,829	10,905	11,036	11,146	0.7	1.2	1.0	−1.5
Trade data												
Value of imports	97.1	103	118	148	148	165	185	210	11.5	12.1	13.5	11.1
Value of exports	66.2	86.9	102	99.2	124	103	120	135	−16.9	16.5	12.5	17.0

[1] Estimate except imports and exports.
[2] Estimate.
[3] Forecast.
[4] Compound annual rate.
[5] For definition of industry versus product values, see "Getting the Most Out of *Outlook '99*."
Source: U.S. Department of Commerce: Bureau of the Census; International Trade Administration.

Technological change is expected to have a marked impact on the industry in the years ahead. The issuance of these products in electronic rather than printed format is expected to increase, with consequences that are still obscure. Publications not dependent on advertising, such as newsletters, directories, and business service publications, may retain and expand their circulation bases through their availability on the Internet or CD-ROM. Publishers of catalogs may find the use of electronic formats revenue-enhancing, with Web sites on the Internet creating greater demand for a publisher's products or services and encouraging viewers to send for the printed catalog. However, some publications, specifically telephone directories, may encounter a reduction in market demand as advertisers trim their expenditures on the printed product to accommodate greater exposure on the Internet. The full impact of electronic media on print media has not run its course. The coming decade should see products of the U.S. miscellaneous publishing industry experiencing marketplace conflicts of consequence.

William S. Lofquist, U.S. Department of Commerce, Office of Consumer Goods, (202) 482-0379, October 1998.

GREETING CARDS

U.S. greeting card companies are undergoing a transition in terms of their product lines, product formats, and retail distribution because of changing lifestyle and demographic trends in the population. Many companies are producing new card lines that are more relevant to consumers' situations and relationships. They are targeting specific ethnic, religious, and lifestyle markets. Large and small publishers are introducing many alternative card lines that are nonoccasion, everyday cards expressing consumers' thoughts and feelings that relate to their lifestyles and experiences. While Christmas and Valentine's Day cards still represent the major product sectors for greeting card publishers, everyday cards are the fastest growing area of the market. Aging baby boomers and growing ethnic populations in the United States are contributing to this growth. Cards and related product lines which celebrate cultural and racial diversity and values are being targeted especially to African-Americans, Hispanic-Americans, Asian-Americans, and Jews. While small greeting card publishers initially created many of the ethnic and more targeted specialty card lines, the major card companies have developed their own specialty lines that compete in these niche markets.

Three companies dominate the U.S. greeting card industry, dividing about 85 percent of the total receipts in this competitive market; about 1,000 small and medium-size firms share the remaining 15 percent. Industry receipts should increase on average no more than 1 percent yearly in constant dollars over the next 5 years, reflecting a slow but fairly steady growth pattern. Total industry shipments should exceed $5.5 billion in 1999 (see Table 25-14). Demographic factors probably will have more of an impact on greeting card sales over the next few years than will the performance of the overall economy. The fact that middle-aged women account for over 90 percent of the greeting card market has limited card sales, but with the large number of women baby boomers moving into this age group, card sales should rise. Greeting card publishers will create even greater variety in their product lines for the ethnic populations in the United States, since these segments will continue to grow at faster rates than will other segments. To increase sales, greeting card publishers will create more new and diverse card lines that address many nontraditional events in consumers' lives. Supermarkets and drugstores will continue to bolster sales of

TABLE 25-14: Greeting Cards (SIC 2771) Trends and Forecasts

(millions of dollars except as noted)

	1992	1993	1994	1995	1996	1997[1]	1998[2]	1999[3]	Percent Change			
									96–97	97–98	98–99	92–96[4]
Industry data												
Value of shipments[5]	4,190	4,275	4,546	4,689	5,011	5,101	5,274	5,522	1.8	3.4	4.7	4.6
Value of shipments (1992$)	4,190	4,040	4,016	3,960	4,064	4,080	4,104	4,129	0.4	0.6	0.6	−0.8
Total employment (thousands)	22.8	22.2	22.7	22.1	21.4							−1.6
Production workers (thousands)	11.7	12.2	12.4	12.4	11.9							0.4
Average hourly earnings ($)	10.78	11.51	11.72	12.35	12.65							4.1
Capital expenditures	85.7	53.8	71.6	67.0	66.4							−6.2
Product data												
Value of shipments[5]	3,075	3,349	3,564	3,617	3,751	3,819	3,949	4,134	1.8	3.4	4.7	5.1
Value of shipments (1992$)	3,075	3,165	3,148	3,055	3,042	3,054	3,072	3,090	0.4	0.6	0.6	−0.3
Trade data												
Value of imports	47.2	49.8	91.3	97.8	108	121	133	146	12.0	9.9	9.8	23.0
Value of exports	51.3	50.1	61.7	123	130	153	176	202	17.7	15.0	14.8	26.2

[1] Estimate except imports and exports.
[2] Estimate.
[3] Forecast.
[4] Compound annual rate.
[5] For definition of industry versus product values, see "Getting the Most Out of *Outlook '99.*"
Source: U.S. Department of Commerce: Bureau of the Census; International Trade Administration.

greeting cards by expanding their product lines as consumers pursue convenience in their shopping. In regard to publishers' costs, recent postal rate hikes could have an impact on the number of greeting cards sent, especially during the holidays. While paper prices remain a constant concern, they are expected to rise only moderately compared with the sharp increases of several years ago.

On the international front the major companies are marketing their cards and a wide range of related paper products through subsidiaries, foreign partners, and foreign distributors. U.S. greeting card exports totaled $153 million in 1997, an increase of about 18 percent from the 1996 level. Since 1992 card exports have tripled as more card companies have sought international customers. Much of the gain has come in the Canadian market, which is generally the first foreign market that greeting card publishers pursue. Other major markets include the United Kingdom, Australia, Mexico, Japan, Hong Kong, and Singapore. In addition to selling printed greeting cards around the world, major card publishers are marketing electronic greeting cards and other gift products on-line. Some greeting card Web sites are offering free electronic greeting cards to attract customers on-line. Over the next few years publishers will enlarge their Web ventures as more customers go on-line. As they continue expanding globally, large U.S. mass market retailers will support international distribution and growth of U.S. greeting cards as they have done in the U.S. market. Over the next few years, greeting card publishers will move toward creating a social expressions group which will have cards as the core product but also will include gift wrap, party goods, candles, and small gift items.

Rose Marie Zummo Bratland, U.S. Department of Commerce, Office of Consumer Goods, (202) 482-0380, October 1998.

BLANKBOOKS AND LOOSELEAF BINDERS

The U.S. blankbook and looseleaf binder industry meets the information and storage access requirements of U.S. businesses, students, and consumers through the manufacture of products that include blankbooks (such as albums, diaries, notebooks, and appointment books) and binders in looseleaf and ringed formats. Data on U.S. production of checkbooks, which account for approximately 40 percent of the industry's value of shipments, move statistically to SIC 275, commercial printing, in the 1997 Census of Manufactures.

Blankbook and binder making is undergoing a significant change. The industry's plants are growing larger, a shift in geographic concentration is taking place, and more product lines are being manufactured overseas. The industry's 550 firms have shown only marginal growth in the number of establishments, but the size of these firms is increasing: Two-thirds of all plants have over 20 employees, up from 57 percent of plants two decades ago. Geographic concentration of the industry's plants is shifting gradually to the west and south, decreasing the industry's presence in the mid-Atlantic and midwestern regions. Foreign manufacturing of diaries and address books, often under U.S. license or joint venture agreements, accounts for two-thirds of the U.S. market for these items.

Shipments by the U.S. blankbook and looseleaf binder industry in 1999 should total over $5.7 billion, a gain, adjusted for inflation, of 2.3 percent over 1998 (see Table 25-15). The industry's growth is supported by expansion of the U.S. economy, higher levels of educational enrollments, the formation of more businesses, and an increasing need to manage and control data and information generated by computers. Gains in U.S. acceptance of electronic banking are reducing the demand for printed checkbooks, a market that peaked at $2 billion in the

TABLE 25-15: Blankbooks and Looseleaf Binders (SIC 2782) Trends and Forecasts
(millions of dollars except as noted)

	1992	1993	1994	1995	1996	1997[1]	1998[2]	1999[3]	Percent Change			
									96–97	97–98	98–99	92–96[4]
Industry data												
Value of shipments[5]	3,758	3,771	4,276	4,544	4,820	5,135	5,445	5,713	6.5	6.0	4.9	6.4
Value of shipments (1992$)	3,758	3,668	4,049	4,058	4,152	4,355	4,560	4,665	4.9	4.7	2.3	2.5
Total employment (thousands)	38.7	37.5	39.6	38.5	35.8							−1.9
Production workers (thousands)	28.9	27.0	28.3	27.0	25.4							−3.2
Average hourly earnings ($)	10.24	10.28	10.61	10.74	11.08							2.0
Capital expenditures	101	86.8	99.8	114	93.3							−2.0
Product data												
Value of shipments[5]	3,396	3,487	3,927	3,972	4,096	4,240	4,375	4,495	3.5	3.2	2.7	4.8
Value of shipments (1992$)	3,396	3,392	3,719	3,547	3,528	3,595	3,620	3,627	1.9	0.7	0.2	1.0
Trade data												
Value of imports	221	233	254	310	305	337	380	420	10.5	12.8	10.5	8.4
Value of exports	34.0	33.8	27.9	36.5	44.0	54.2	60.0	65.0	23.2	10.7	8.3	6.7

[1] Estimate except imports and exports.
[2] Estimate.
[3] Forecast.
[4] Compound annual rate.
[5] For definition of industry versus product values, see "Getting the Most Out of *Outlook '99.*"
Source: U.S. Department of Commerce: Bureau of the Census; International Trade Administration.

mid-1990s and now faces a long-term decline. Another electronic competitor—organizers—is capturing the U.S. market for appointment books. Demand for U.S. blankbooks and binders through 2003 is forecast to increase the industry's value of shipments at a compound annual average rate of 2 percent.

Blankbook and binder making is a mature industry characterized by unsophisticated technology and a relatively unskilled work force. To the degree that customization is required, the products are increasingly sourced from low-wage economies. Competition from imports and the electronic media is challenging the domestic manufacture of several product lines—especially checkbooks, diaries, and address books—and growth in this industry is not assured. The expansion of U.S. investment in blankbook and looseleaf binding operations overseas, particularly in the Far East, addresses U.S. industry's concern regarding competition from abroad. However, the gradual shift to the management and control of information electronically rather than in a printed format poses a challenge to the U.S. blankbook and looseleaf binder industry that could require new recourses and resources.

William S. Lofquist, U.S. Department of Commerce, Office of Consumer Goods, (202) 482-0379, October 1998.

BOOKBINDING

The binding of books has a long manufacturing history, and the 1,100 plants that constitute the U.S. bookbinding industry rely on old world craft skills coupled with modern technology. The output of U.S. binderies consists of bound and rebound hardcover books; the binding of newspapers, periodicals, pamphlets, and brochures; and the preparation of sample books, swatches, and cards—bound packages containing items such as carpets, upholsteries, draperies, and souvenir cards. Bookbinding plants tend to be large: Over 60 percent of the industry's work force is employed by 154 establishments. Although bookbinding plants are found throughout the United States, one-third of all binderies are located in California, Illinois, and New York. The 1990s has witnessed a shift in the industry's customers away from the reduced binding needs of U.S. book printers and libraries and toward the increased binding requirements of the nation's commercial printers.

The value of shipments of the U.S. bookbinding industry is forecast to total over $1.9 billion in 1999, a rise of 2.5 percent, adjusted for inflation, over 1998 (see Table 25-16). A growing U.S. economy should stimulate more demand for printed materials, especially bound advertising and informational materials from U.S. commercial printers. The library binding market should expand, with more tax revenues expected to be channeled into the nation's libraries. The binding of books for U.S. book printers should remain soft, in line with the modest gains projected for the U.S. book publishing industry. Bookbinding's export markets are relatively negligible, consisting of bound newspapers and periodicals destined primarily for Canada, the United Kingdom, and Japan. The industry's value of shipments through 2003 is projected to achieve a compound annual average rate of growth of 3 percent.

The U.S. bookbinding industry appears to have made a remarkable transition. In an old-line industry in need of new markets, U.S. binderies changed their base of customers without changing their base of operations. With book printers integrating their binding and finishing operations and libraries reducing their binding requirements, a growing core of U.S. commercial printers found its bindery needs increasing exponentially. This has resulted from changes in digital technology that have

TABLE 25-16: Bookbinding and Related Work (SIC 2789) Trends and Forecasts
(millions of dollars except as noted)

	1992	1993	1994	1995	1996	1997[1]	1998[2]	1999[3]	96–97	97–98	98–99	92–96[4]
									\multicolumn{4}{c}{Percent Change}			
Industry data												
Value of shipments[5]	1,291	1,258	1,367	1,509	1,608	1,710	1,825	1,935	6.3	6.7	6.0	5.6
Value of shipments (1992$)	1,291	1,249	1,343	1,431	1,501	1,549	1,594	1,634	3.2	2.9	2.5	3.8
Total employment (thousands)	26.9	25.6	27.6	28.7	28.8							1.7
Production workers (thousands)	22.1	21.5	23.3	24.0	24.5							2.6
Average hourly earnings ($)	8.70	8.54	8.99	9.28	9.49							2.2
Capital expenditures	41.1	24.9	45.8	35.0	37.0							-2.6
Product data												
Value of shipments[5]	1,312	1,276	1,376	1,455	1,525	1,585	1,655	1,705	3.9	4.4	3.0	3.8
Value of shipments (1992$)	1,312	1,267	1,352	1,379	1,424	1,434	1,456	1,449	0.7	1.5	-0.5	2.1
Trade data												
Value of imports	2.9	2.1	2.2	2.6	4.1	2.9	3.5	4.0	-29.3	20.7	14.3	9.0
Value of exports	16.7	19.3	18.7	16.8	17.7	16.6	17.5	18.0	-6.2	5.4	2.9	1.5

[1] Estimate except imports and exports.
[2] Estimate.
[3] Forecast.
[4] Compound annual rate.
[5] For definition of industry versus product values, see "Getting the Most Out of *Outlook '99*."
Source: U.S. Department of Commerce: Bureau of the Census; International Trade Administration.

enabled printers to provide their customers with a variety of full-color printed products in cost-effective production runs of as few as 50 copies. The binding and finishing of these products frequently become the responsibility of U.S. bookbinders, whose growth-oriented future is becoming less tied to books and more dependent on the fortunes of commercial printers.

William S. Lofquist, U.S. Department of Commerce, Office of Consumer Goods, (202) 482-0379, October 1998.

PRINTING TRADE SERVICES

Changes in technology are adversely affecting establishments in the U.S. printing trade services. The industry's former role of supplying typeset materials to advertisers and publishers, and color film separations and imaged printing plates to commercial printers, is eroding severely as the U.S. printing industry moves to electronic-based (digital) processes and away from film- and chemical-based (analog) processes. The number of printing trade service firms is expected to decline from its mid-1990s base of approximately 4,000 as the markets for typesetting, platemaking, and film separation services shrink. Advertisers and publishers have found that the ease, control, and cost-effectiveness of preparing print-ready materials in house mitigate the need for outside typesetting services. Commercial printers' investments in productivity-enhancing digital equipment either move film preparation into the printing plant or obviate film and chemical requirements entirely, reducing if not eliminating the requirement for color film separations and imaged printing plates.

The value of shipments by the U.S. printing trade services industry is expected to total $5.2 billion in 1999, a decline of 0.5 percent from 1998 in constant dollars (see Table 25-17). Growth of the U.S. economy in 1999 is expected to support higher levels of investment by the U.S. printing industry in digital technology, further reducing demand for printing trade services. The prices of these services should remain essentially flat in 1999, a reaction both to declining markets and to intense competition among printing trade service firms to retain as much of their customer base as possible. Over the period 1998–2003 the value of shipments of the U.S. printing trade services industry is forecast to decline at a compound annual average rate of 3 percent. The nation's 40,000 commercial printing establishments, along with their formidable base of U.S. advertisers and publishers, are absorbing the new digital technology, a process that is expected to take a decade or more.

With traditional markets in decline, printing trade services firms are seeking new niches in their relationships with printers, publishers, and advertisers. Using their knowledge of digital imaging and creative design skills, service firms are transforming themselves into image managers. These firms are capable of creating, manipulating, inventorying, and storing their clients' digital image materials so that they can be accessed as required. Some printing trade service establishments are moving into short-run digital printing and supplying customers with color digital proofs. Since the vast majority of the nation's 40,000 commercial printers are still analog-oriented, the replacement of film-based printing with digital equipment will be a gradual process. The U.S. printing trade services industry will have an indeterminate period of accommodation to the new technology, but the digital era is almost here.

William S. Lofquist, U.S. Department of Commerce, Office of Consumer Goods, (202) 482-0379, October 1998.

TABLE 25-17:   Printing Trade Services (SIC 279) Trends and Forecasts
(millions of dollars except as noted)

									Percent Change			
	1992	1993	1994	1995	1996	1997[1]	1998[2]	1999[3]	96–97	97–98	98–99	92–96[4]
Industry data												
Value of shipments[5]	5,085	5,129	4,920	5,020	5,123	5,175	5,200	5,200	1.0	0.5	0.0	0.2
Value of shipments (1992$)	5,085	5,090	4,867	4,928	4,977	5,012	5,010	4,985	0.7	–0.0	–0.5	–0.5
Total employment (thousands)	65.0	63.7	57.5	57.7	54.9							–4.1
Production workers (thousands)	46.2	45.3	40.9	41.7	39.3							–4.0
Average hourly earnings ($)	14.06	14.33	14.88	15.27	16.05							3.4
Capital expenditures	230	179	224	193	210							–2.2
Product data												
Value of shipments[5]	5,393	5,435	5,253	5,323	5,400	5,445	5,460	5,450	0.8	0.3	–0.2	0.0
Value of shipments (1992$)	5,393	5,392	5,194	5,223	5,245	5,255	5,230	5,175	0.2	–0.5	–1.1	–0.7
Trade data												
Value of imports	58.3	67.5	79.3	90.1	106	113	125	135	6.6	10.6	8.0	16.1
Value of exports	169	148	165	238	258	262	265		1.6	1.1		11.2

[1] Estimate except imports and exports.
[2] Estimate.
[3] Forecast.
[4] Compound annual rate.
[5] For definition of industry versus product values, see "Getting the Most Out of *Outlook '99.*"
Source: U.S. Department of Commerce: Bureau of the Census; International Trade Administration.

■ REFERENCES

Call the Bureau of the Census at (301) 763-4100 for information about ordering Census documents.

Advertising Age, Crain Communication Inc., 740 Rush Street, Chicago, IL 60611. (312) 649-5200.

American Bookseller, American Booksellers Association, Inc., 828 South Broadway, Tarrytown, NY 10591. (914) 591-2665.

American Printer, an Intertec publication, 29 N. Wacker Drive, Chicago, IL 60606. (312) 726-2802.

Book Industry Trends, Book Industry Study Group, Inc., 160 Fifth Avenue, New York, NY 10010. (212) 929-1393.

Book Publishing Report, SIMBA Information Inc., P.O. Box 4234, Stamford, CT 06907. (203) 358-9900.

Business Publication Rates and Data, Standard Rate & Data Service, 3004 Glenview Road, Wilmette, IL 60091. (708) 256-6067.

Commercial Printing and Manifold Business Forms, 1992 Census of Manufactures, MC92-I-27B. Bureau of the Census, U.S. Department of Commerce, Washington, DC 20233. (301) 457-4768.

Communications Industry Forecast, Veronis, Suhler & Associates, Inc., 350 Park Avenue, New York, NY 10022. (212) 935-4990.

Consumer Magazine and Agri-Media Rates and Data, Standard Rate & Data Service, 3004 Glenview Road, Wilmette, IL 60091. (708) 256-6067.

Editor & Publisher, Editor & Publisher Company, 11 West 19th Street, New York, NY 10011. (212) 675-4380.

Employment and Earnings, Bureau of Labor Statistics, U.S. Department of Labor, Washington, DC 20212. (202) 606-6555.

Folio: The Magazine for Magazine Management, Cowles Business Media, 6 River Bend, P.O. Box 4949, Stamford, CT 06907-0949. (203) 358-9900.

The Gale Directory of Publications, Gale Research, Book Tower Building, Detroit, MI 48226. (313) 961-2242.

Graphic Arts Monthly, Cahners Publishing Co., 249 West 17th Street, New York, NY 10011. (212) 463-6828.

Graphic Communications World, Green Sheet Communications, Inc., P.O. Box 727, Hartsdale, NY 10530. (914) 472-3051.

Greeting Card Association Newsletter and Publications, Greeting Card Association, 1350 New York Avenue, NW, Suite 615, Washington DC 20005. (202) 393-1778.

Greeting Cards; Bookbinding; Printing Trade Services, 1992 Census of Manufactures, MC92-I-27C. Bureau of the Census, U.S. Department of Commerce, Washington, DC 20233. (301) 457-4768.

High Volume Printing, Innes Publishing Co., P.O. Box 368, 425 Huehl Road, Building 11, Northbrook, IL 60062. (312) 563-5940.

Industrial Production and Capacity Utilization, Industrial Output Section, Mail Stop #82, Division of Research and Statistics, Board of Governors of the Federal Reserve System, Washington, DC 20551. (202) 452-2570.

Industry Statistics, Association of American Publishers, Inc., 71 Fifth Avenue, New York, NY 10003. (212) 255-0200.

Magazine World, International Federation of the Periodical Press, Queens House, 55/57 Lincoln's Inn Fields, London WC2A 3LJ, UK. Telephone: 44 171 379-3822.

Newsletter of International Publishing, Magazine Publishers of America, 919 Third Avenue, New York, NY 10022. (212) 872-3700.

Newspaper Newsletter, Morton Research, P.O. Box 40, Spencerville, MD 20868. (301) 879-9806.

Newspapers, Periodicals, Books and Miscellaneous Publishing, 1992 Census of Manufactures, MC92-I-27A and B. Bureau of the Census, U.S. Department of Commerce, Washington, DC 20233.

PR Newswire, New York Headquarters, 810 Seventh Avenue, 32nd Floor, New York, NY 10019. 800 8776-8090, http://www.prnewswire.com.

Presstime, Newspaper Association of America, 1921 Gallows Road, Suite 600, Vienna, VA 22182. (703) 902-1600.

Print Business Register, PTN Graphic Arts Network, 20 E. Jackson Boulevard, Chicago, IL 60604. (312) 922-5402.

Printing Business Report, National Association of Printers and Lithographers, 780 Palisade Avenue, Teaneck, NJ 07666. (201) 342-0700.

Printing Impressions, North American Publishing Co., 401 N. Broad Street, Philadelphia, PA 19108. (215) 238-5300.

Printing News, PTN Publishing Co., 445 Broad Hollow Road, Melville, NY 11747. (516) 845-2700.

Producer Price Indexes, Bureau of Labor Statistics, U.S. Department of Labor, Washington, DC 20212. (202) 606-7716.

Publisher's Auxiliary, National Newspaper Association, 1627 K Street, NW, Washington, DC 20006. (202) 466-7200.

Publishers Weekly, a Cahners/R.R. Bowker Publication, 249 West 17th Street, New York, NY 10011. (212) 463-6758.

Publishing Trends, Market Partners International, Inc., 232 Madison Avenue, #1400, New York, NY 10016. (212) 447-0855.

Ratio Studies, Printing Industries of America, Inc., 100 Daingerfield Road, Alexandria, VA 22314. (703) 519-8100.

Statistics for Industry Groups and Industries, 1996 Annual Survey of Manufactures, M96 (AS)-1. Bureau of the Census, U.S. Department of Commerce, Washington, DC 20233.

Subtext, Open Book Publishing, Inc., P.O. Box 2228, 90 Holmes Avenue, Darien, CT 06820. (203) 316-8008.

Sumir Husni's Guide to New Magazines, Department of Journalism, University of Mississippi, P.O. Box 2906, University, MS 38677.

Technology Forecast, Graphic Arts Technical Foundation, 200 Deer Run Road, Sewickly, PA 15143-2600. (412) 741-6860.

U.S. & World Printing Industry—1997 & 2002, Clayton/Curtis/Cottrell, 1722 Madison Court, Louisville, CO 80027. (303) 665-2005.

Value of Product Shipments, 1996 Annual Survey of Manufactures, M96 (AS)-2. Bureau of the Census, U.S. Department of Commerce, Washington, DC 20233.

What's New(s) in Graphic Communications, Michael H. Bruno, 228 Orchard Lane, Glen Ellyn, IL 60137. (630) 469-9984.

Worldwide Graphics, Reebius Research Labs, Inc., 3952 N. Southport, #143, Chicago, IL 60613-2699. (773) 935-2135.

■ RELATED CHAPTERS

10: Paper and Allied Products
18: Production Machinery
24: Photographic Equipment and Supplies
49: Business and Professional Services

INFORMATION SERVICES
Economic and Trade Trends

Revenue Growth of Information Services

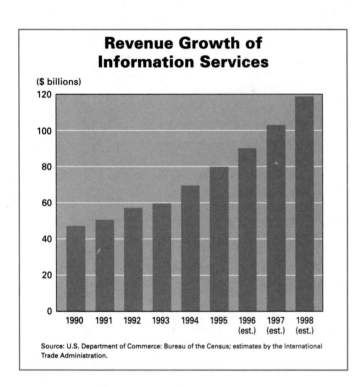

($ billions)

Source: U.S. Department of Commerce: Bureau of the Census; estimates by the International Trade Administration.

Revenues of Top Information Services Suppliers in 1996

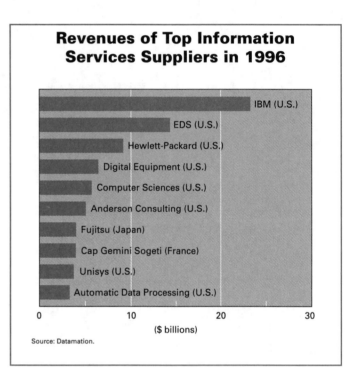

($ billions)

Source: Datamation.

Sales of Computer and Data Processing Services by U.S. MOFAs

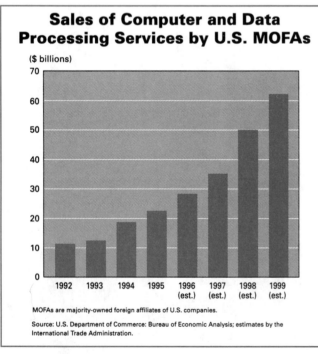

($ billions)

MOFAs are majority-owned foreign affiliates of U.S. companies.

Source: U.S. Department of Commerce: Bureau of Economic Analysis; estimates by the International Trade Administration.

U.S. International Trade in Information Services

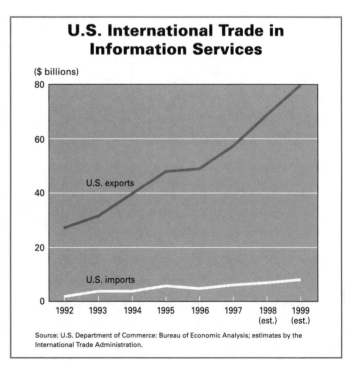

($ billions)

Source: U.S. Department of Commerce: Bureau of Economic Analysis; estimates by the International Trade Administration.

Information Services

INDUSTRY DEFINITION It is difficult to draw firm boundaries in defining information services, but information services can be said to consist primarily of professional computer services, data processing and network services, and electronic information services. According to U.S. Department of Commerce statistics, professional computer services constitutes the largest information services subsector (70 percent of total value added), data processing and network services is second (25 percent), and electronic information services is third (5 percent) [see Table 26-1]. These rankings are inexact, however, because the U.S. SIC codes do not always fit these and other areas of information services. For the purposes of this chapter, professional computer services are partially covered by SIC 7371, 7373, 7377, 7378, and 7379; data processing and network services are partially covered by SIC 7374 and 7376; and electronic information services fall under SIC 7375. Other information services include outsourcing, electronic commerce, and Internet-related services. While they do not easily fit into preexisting statistical categories, these services represent some of the fastest growing areas of value-added information services, and providers and users have begun to define and measure these activities as distinct areas and revenue sources.

OVERVIEW

The United States is the world leader in the production and consumption of information technology and services. In every area of information technology—computer hardware, software, data communication equipment, and information services—the United States is both the largest market and the largest supplier internationally. In the 1990s information technology altered the way businesses and consumers interact. Domestic and worldwide use of computer hardware and software products and communications equipment and services is becoming a single market. Information services and information technology products have become fundamental to the overall growth and development of the U.S. economy and many other economies around the world. Virtually every sector—manufacturing, transportation, energy and utilities, retail and wholesale trade, finance, and government—employs information technology and information services in its operations. As a result, information services represent one of the fastest growing sections of the U.S. economy (see Table 26-1).

The growth of information services is tied to the information technology product base—from microprocessors, to computers, to communications equipment, to multimedia—which makes up the infrastructure of many information services. For instance, advances in microprocessors, modems, and data storage have permitted data and graphics to be transferred and received at much faster speeds, allowing multimedia, content, and information service providers to expand their businesses. A similar process occurs after each technical breakthrough, generating new demands and capabilities. Advances in technology are one of the main factors contributing to the growth of and continued demand for professional computer services. Broadly speaking, information services constitute an increasingly large and important component of the information technology hierarchy. Another major impetus to the growth of information services has been the Telecommunications Act of 1996, which has ushered in greater competition, lower access charges, and a wider variety of services.

TABLE 26-1: Information Services Share of the Economy

(value added in millions of dollars; percent)

	1990	1991	1992	1993	1994	1995	1996[1]	1997[1]	1998[1]
Gross domestic product (GDP)	5,743,800	5,916,700	6,244,400	6,558,100	6,947,000	7,265,400	7,636,000	8,079,900	8,344,900
Year-to-year GDP change, %		3.01	5.54	5.02	5.93	4.58	5.10	5.82	4.71
SIC 7371 Computer programming services	14,902	16,341	18,137	19,548	22,673	26,178	29,712	33,723	38,647
SIC 7373 Computer-integrated systems design	9,424	10,033	11,505	12,465	13,829	15,025	16,497	18,114	19,889
SIC 7374 Computer processing and data preparation	10,256	10,833	12,226	13,009	15,332	17,924	20,433	23,294	26,951
SIC 7375 Information retrieval services	2,435	2,534	2,803	1,963	3,188	3,768	4,262	4,820	6,107
SIC 7376 Computer facilities management	1,369	1,514	1,860	1,811	1,932	2,135	2,338	2,560	2,793
SIC 7377 Computer rental and leasing	1,587	1,438	1,488	1,352	1,324	1,329	1,348	1,369	1,389
SIC 7378 Computer maintenance and repair	4,273	4,244	4,859	4,615	4,740	5,023	5,224	5,433	5,661
SIC 7379 Computer-related services not elsewhere classified	3,006	3,424	4,291	5,147	6,685	8,549	10,686	13,358	16,964
Total information services	47,255	50,365	57,170	59,913	69,706	79,933	90,504	102,673	118,405
Year-to-year information services change, %		6.60	13.50	4.80	16.30	14.70	13.20	13.40	15.30
Share of GDP, %	0.82	0.85	0.92	0.91	1.00	1.10	1.20	1.30	1.40

[1] International Trade Administration estimate except for GDP.

Source: U.S. Department of Commerce: Bureau of the Census; Bureau of Economic Analysis; International Trade Administration.

TABLE 26-2: Information Services Employment Trends and Projections

(thousands of units except as noted)

	1985	1990	1991	1992	1993	1994	1995	1996	2006[1]	Difference 85–96	Average Annual Growth 85–96, %	Difference 96–06	Average Annual Growth 96–06, %
Total private employment	80,992	91,098	89,847	89,956	91,872	95,036	97,885	100,076	115,168	19,084	1.9	15,092	1.4
Year-to-year change, %			–1.4	0.1	2.1	3.4	3.0	2.2					
SIC 7371 Computer programming services	79	150	156	168	188	209	245	271	708	192	11.9	436	10.0
SIC 7373 Computer integrated systems design	60	97	98	102	109	116	129	142	244	82	8.2	102	5.6
SIC 7374 Computer processing and data preparation	192	196	198	204	207	209	223	231	268	39	1.7	37	1.5
SIC 7375 Information retrieval services	39	47	45	45	46	48	56	68	98	29	5.2	29	3.7
SIC 7376 Computer facilities management / SIC 7377 Computer rental and leasing / SIC 7379 Computer related services not elsewhere classified	91	126	131	141	154	172	205	242	643	151	9.3	401	10.3
SIC 7378 Computer maintenance and repair	25	39	42	42	41	44	48	52	69	27	7.0	16	2.8
Total information services	486	659	672	704	748	801	909	1,009	2,032	523	6.9	1,023	7.3
Share of total employment, %	0.6	0.72	0.75	0.78	0.81	0.84	0.93	1.00	1.76				

[1] Estimates by U.S. Department of Commerce, Economics and Statistics Administration, based on BLS projections.

Source: U.S. Department of Labor, Bureau of Labor Statistics.

Information services often supply the "value-added" or specific knowledge that allows firms to utilize information technology hardware to meet their needs in the areas of operations, marketing, electronic communications, databases, and information. In combination, information services and information technology products enable businesses to streamline their operations and become more productive and efficient. They also are instrumental in helping U.S. businesses remain competitive both at home and abroad.

EMPLOYMENT AND WAGES

In the information technology work force, providers of information services have experienced rapid growth of employment (see Table 26-2). From 1985 to 1996 employment in the information services industries more than doubled from under one-half million workers to over 1 million workers, with the fastest growth occurring in the computer programming services industries. By 2006, the Bureau of Labor Statistics projects that the demand for these workers will double again to 2 million.

In addition to the information technology industries, information technology workers are needed across the economy to install, operate, program, repair, maintain, design, and develop equipment and services. In 1996, 4.2 million people worked in information technology–related occupations. About one-third of those workers (1.4 million) were employed by information technology industries, and 2.8 million worked in non–information technology industries. For example, in 1996 there were 1.4 million computer scientists, systems analysts, computer engineers, and computer programmers. The services sector employed 47.7 percent of those workers, primarily in business services, health services, education, and engineering services.

The Bureau of Labor Statistics predicts that 5.6 million workers will be needed to fill information technology–related jobs by 2006. The demand for higher-skilled information technology workers is expected to grow dramatically, while the demand for lower-skilled workers is expected to decline. The Internet is also driving the demand for workers with these skills. Workers are needed to design Web pages, create graphics, code documents in Hypertext Markup Language (HTML), and program in Internet languages such as Java and C++.

In 1996 the average annual wage paid to workers in the information services industries was almost $51,000, compared with just over $28,000 for all private employees (see Table 26-3). Among the information technology industries, workers in the information services industries earned the highest annual wages. This group also had the fastest increase in annual wages, which grew annually since 1985 (see Table 26-4).

Web masters, who are responsible for the design, development, operation, and maintenance of Web sites, earn starting salaries between $35,000 and $50,000; highly experienced Web masters earn $100,000 or more. Web developers, who are responsible for the actual creation of Web sites, are reported to

TABLE 26-3: Annual Wages per Information Services Worker
(dollars; percent)

	1985	1990	1991	1992	1993	1994	1995	1996	Difference 85–96	Average Annual Growth 85–96 %
Average all private industries	18,843	23,209	23,952	25,375	25,746	26,248	27,164	28,352	9,509	3.8
SIC 7371 Computer programming services	29,311	41,857	43,053	46,222	47,552	50,057	52,731	57,818	28,507	6.4
SIC 7373 Computer integrated systems design	31,569	43,795	44,640	48,556	49,689	52,749	54,711	59,810	28,241	6.0
SIC 7374 Computer processing and data preparation	23,228	30,452	30,772	34,374	36,131	36,625	39,749	43,098	19,870	5.8
SIC 7375 Information retrieval services	25,121	32,704	35,044	36,704	38,895	38,583	42,197	46,501	21,380	5.8
SIC 7376 Computer facilities management SIC 7377 Computer rental and leasing SIC 7379 Computer-related services, not elsewhere classified	30,345	41,185	43,242	45,970	46,830	48,924	51,827	57,150	26,805	5.9
SIC 7378 Computer maintenance and repair	26,929	34,296	34,071	36,589	37,488	37,236	37,819	40,072	13,143	3.7

Source: U.S. Department of Commerce, Economics and Statistics Administration, based on Bureau of Labor Statistics data.

TABLE 26-4: Information Services Wage Growth
(millions of dollars; percent)

	1985	1990	1991	1992	1993	1994	1995	1996	Difference 85–96
All private industries	1,526,164	2,114,282	2,152,022	2,282,598	2,365,301	2,494,459	2,658,927	2,837,335	1,311,171
SIC 7371 Computer programming services	2,316	6,312	6,755	7,793	8,954	10,507	12,935	15,721	13,405
SIC 7373 Computer integrated systems design	1,894	4,270	4,406	4,977	5,441	6,140	7,107	8,517	6,623
SIC 7374 Computer processing and data preparation	4,460	5,990	6,099	7,026	7,490	7,673	8,868	9,968	5,509
SIC 7375 Information retrieval services	980	1,560	1,584	1,659	1,797	1,852	2,401	3,181	2,201
SIC 7376 Computer facilities management SIC 7377 Computer rental and leasing SIC 7379 Computer-related services, not elsewhere classified	2,761	5,214	5,669	6,491	7,254	8,459	10,640	13,853	11,092
SIC 7378 Computer maintenance and repair	673	1,365	1,448	1,566	1,567	1,657	1,838	2,108	1,435
Total information services	13,084	24,711	25,961	29,512	32,503	36,288	43,789	53,348	40,264
Share of all private industries, %	0.9	1.2	1.2	1.3	1.4	1.5	1.6	1.9	3.1

Source: U.S. Department of Labor, Bureau of Labor Statistics.

earn a median salary of $55,000. On the lower end of the skill level in Internet jobs, customer service representatives who work for Internet service providers earn from $14,000 to $17,000 per year but may earn up to $35,000, depending on their experience.

GLOBAL INDUSTRY TRENDS

The United States is the world's largest producer and consumer of information technology products and services. *Datamation* magazine's 1996 survey of information technology companies worldwide indicates that 8 of the top 10 companies are U.S. companies (see Table 26-5). Within each specific product or service sector, the U.S. proportion of leading companies is equally high. Additionally, most of the innovative and fastest growing information services companies are in the United States. Because of the world dominance of U.S. companies, global trends and issues in the international information services sector tend to be the same as those which affect the domestic industry.

One of the most significant trends in information services is convergence within the information technology industry. Companies in diverse areas—computer hardware, software, information services, data communications, telecommunications—are rapidly forming alliances with each other through joint ventures, mergers, and acquisitions. These alliances allow companies to integrate information technology products with information services so that they can offer a greater selection of products and services. A key objective of these alliances is to remain viable in an increasingly competitive national and international marketplace.

In the past alliances were common between hardware and software companies and hardware and communications equipment companies. Today they are springing up between firms in much more diverse areas: hardware and software, data communications, Internet applications and World Wide Web develop-

ment, graphic development, networking, and information publishing. Not only are large, well-known companies forming alliances among themselves, they also are forming them with smaller, more obscure companies. Locally, small companies are forming alliances to keep a firm grip on their markets. These alliances are designed to ensure the participating firms' competitiveness in the marketplace by offering business and residential consumers a broader range of higher-quality products and services.

International megaalliances in the various information technology information services, and telecommunications areas are also being formed at a rapid pace. This development is in part a result of the ubiquity and rapid growth of the Internet in addition to the need to gain access to global markets.

Another trend affecting the information services sector is the blurring of traditional industry categories in information technology and communications. In the past distinctions among hardware manufacturers, software developers, communication equipment producers, service providers, and telecommunications companies were relatively clear. In recent years, however, information technology companies have been diversifying their operations to enter the more lucrative information services sector. Today companies are branching out into a wide variety of activities through alliances with or acquisitions of other companies and diversification of their own internally developed service mixes.

In a related trend, firms that traditionally specialized in information technology products are developing new services and generating a higher proportion of their revenues from them. This has occurred as prices for information technology components have fallen in a fiercely competitive environment. According to Standard and Poor's, the computer giant IBM Corp. earned about $18.4 billion—about 24 percent of its revenues—in the 12 months that ended September 30, 1997, from computer-related services. Digital Equipment Corp. derives about 42 percent of its revenues from computer services, an amount totaling $6.2 billion in that period. The database market leader Oracle Corp. has expanded its consulting business: In the 12 months that ended August 30, 1997, computer services accounted for $3 billion (51 percent) of that company's revenues. Its closest competitor, Sybase Inc., derives about 46 percent of its revenues from consulting, education, and other computer services associated with the sale of its core software products.

A further indication of the extent this diversification is the continued merger of telecommunications companies with information services companies. MCI, AT&T, and Sprint are offering new value-added information services related to the Internet. Providers of Internet access have begun to offer other information services. Telecommunications companies and Internet access providers have aligned themselves with information services companies while striving to create and develop their own content services, electronic information services, and other value-added information services internationally.

An additional trend in the global information services sector is the record levels at which foreign businesses have been purchasing computers, software, and data communication equip-

TABLE 26-5: Top 10 Global Service and Support Suppliers, 1996[1]

(millions of dollars)

Company	Country	Revenues, $
IBM	U.S.	22,785
Electronic Data Systems	U.S.	14,441
Hewlett-Packard	U.S.	9,462
Digital Equipment	U.S.	5,988
Computer Sciences	U.S.	5,400
Anderson Consulting	U.S.	4,877
Fujitsu	Japan	4,160
Cap Gemini Sogeti	France	4,104
Unisys	U.S.	3,949
Automatic Data Processing	U.S.	3,567

[1] Service and support includes outsourcing, facilities management, systems integration, IT counseling, contract programming, and disaster recovery.
Source: Datamation.

ment. This buying rush has been stimulated in part by reduced tariffs on information technology products in many countries. This expansion of the information technology infrastructure internationally benefits U.S. information services companies by providing greater opportunities for U.S. exports.

Another important trend in the industry is the growing proportion of spending on information services relative to spending in the information technology market overall, both at the national level and at the international level. Expenditures on software and information services have increased continuously compared with those on hardware, particularly in countries whose information technology and telecommunications infrastructures are relatively strong and developed. On average, one-fifth of information technology expenditures go to support services such as facilities management, systems integration, consulting, custom programming, and disaster recovery. That share of spending is now the single largest segment of IT spending.

This increase in spending is due partly to advances in technology and the growing complexity of information technology, communication, and telecommunications systems. In addition, maintaining, supporting, and integrating information technology, information services, and telecommunications in a multivendor environment generate a greater demand for certain kinds of information services, such as consulting. Another factor in this increased spending is the trend toward client-server architectures and away from traditional mainframe architectures. These factors are providing great opportunities for professional computer services such as systems integration, computer and information technology consulting, maintenance, and disaster recovery.

FACTORS AFFECTING FUTURE GROWTH

International Agreements

The information services sector is affected by government policies and actions regarding market access, security and encryption, intellectual property protection, copyright, privacy protection, and telecommunications services. A number of national and international efforts are under way to harmonize disparate approaches to these issues. Also, governments are working on several of these issues in various international policy forums. A number of countries reached agreements concerning trade in computer services during the Uruguay Round; those agreements were set out in the General Agreement on Trade in Services (GATS) in 1993.

Discussions are under way among governments and private sector groups in various forums on electronic commerce and the business-to-business and business-to-consumer interfaces the Internet has facilitated. The advances made possible by the Internet are increasing access to information services around the world. In December 1996 the World Intellectual Property Organization (WIPO) in Geneva concluded two treaties on international copyright protection which updated international public law regarding copyright and performance rights in the digital era. The Model Law on Electronic Commerce, which

was completed by the United Nations Commission on International Trade Law (UNCITRAL) in 1996, provides for the acceptability of electronic signatures for legal and commercial purposes. The enabling provisions of the Model Law provide a good basis for a legal framework that recognizes, validates, and enforces electronic commercial transactions.

Efforts to develop guidelines for international cryptography policy were concluded by the Organization for Economic Development and Cooperation (OECD) in spring 1997. OECD member countries are examining a wide range of policy issues, including privacy protection and illegal or harmful content. In November 1997 in Turku, Finland, OECD members brought together the private sector, international organizations, and governments to identify barriers and uncertainties that restrict the growth of electronic commerce. The OECD organized a ministerial-level conference, "A Borderless World—Realizing the Potential of Global Electronic Commerce," that was scheduled to take place in Ottawa in October 1998. This conference was designed to build on previous conferences and provide a forum for OECD member countries to meet with private sector and public interest groups to develop a common action plan to promote economic growth on a global basis.

In December 1997 a Transatlantic Business Dialogue (TABD) was held in Rome, Italy. Almost one-fifth of the Rome Communiqué recommendations addressed the new information society, and the TABD's electronic commerce group has an ever-increasing prominence in the field. Discussions on the export of encryption and decryption software are taking place in the United States. Also, a number of international agreements on issues that affect information services have been concluded between the U.S. Trade Representative and this country's trading partners. These agreements will greatly benefit the U.S. industry.

Also important is the Information Technology Agreement (ITA), which was concluded in December 1996 in Singapore. The ITA eliminates the overwhelming majority of participating countries' tariffs by 2000 on a number of information technology products critical to the continued development of the global information infrastructure. All tariffs will be eliminated by 2005. The successful conclusion of the ITA will boost sales of U.S. information technology products in key markets, especially Europe and the Asia/Pacific region, enhancing the development and growth of the global information technology infrastructure and providing consumers around the world with better access to information services. Negotiations to eliminate tariffs on additional products were underway in 1998.

Large and small companies are increasingly networked and are creating new efficiencies through increased access to pools of information, an enhanced capacity for collaborative work efforts, the speed with which data and information can be transmitted, and the emerging technologies that support innovation and dynamism. These new "wired" business models are transcending traditional geographic borders, unleashing creative forces and linking them in previously unimagined business relationships.

The growth of intranets, extranets, and other networks is linked to the emergence of the Internet as a global communications medium. The Internet is making possible new means of business-consumer interaction and creating vast new opportunities for enterprises of all sizes, from multinational companies to one-person entrepreneurial ventures, particularly companies managing information services, which can be distributed more efficiently and expeditiously than ever over the Internet. All these developments are leading to an increased worldwide demand for information services of every variety as the breakneck pace of technological innovation continues, fueled by a growing global appetite for business, financial, and market information as well as expanded business-consumer applications such as marketing and transactional and distribution interfaces.

Telecommunications Negotiations

To conduct business, electronic information companies and data processing and network service providers need access to reliable, low-cost telecommunications infrastructures. In many countries the public telecommunication infrastructure is government-owned and government-controlled, with high usage prices. In other cases access to the telecommunications network over leased lines is controlled by government monopolies. Both situations can hinder the growth of information services in international markets.

The Group on Basic Telecommunications (GBT), previously known as the Negotiating Group on Basic Telecommunications (NGBT), under the auspices of the World Trade Organization (WTO), concluded an agreement on February 15, 1997. Sixty-nine nations, including the United States and most of its major trading partners, took the historic step of concluding the WTO Basic Telecommunications Agreement and making a commitment to open their markets to basic telecommunications services. The WTO Basic Telecom Agreement is intended to replace the traditional regulatory regime of monopoly telephone service providers with procompetitive and deregulatory policies. The 69 nations earn more than 90 percent of worldwide revenues from telecommunications services.

Before the conclusion of the WTO Basic Telecom Agreement, the United States and many foreign nations had looked for ways to encourage governments to open their telecommunications markets. By removing obstacles to entry into telecommunications service markets, including its own, the United States could deliver tangible benefits to U.S. consumers, U.S. companies, and the world at large. The WTO Basic Telecom Agreement helps achieve this goal by furthering the principles of open markets, private investment, and competition as well as the adoption of procompetitive regulatory principles. The agreement allows U.S. companies to enter other nations' basic voice telephony markets within their national borders and removes barriers to foreign investment in telecommunications services. These provisions will greatly benefit business information services firms, consumer on-line services, and their customers.

1996 Telecommunications Act

The U.S. Telecommunications Act of 1996 creates opportunities for and challenges to U.S. information service providers over the long term. The act allows for competition among long-distance carriers, local exchange carriers, and utility and cable companies in key communications and information areas under certain conditions. Even before the effective date of the WTO Basic Telecommunications Agreement, significant procompetitive changes in global telecommunications markets have been evident. Since the U.S. Telecommunications Act of 1996, there has been a significant change in the structure of international telecommunications markets. Throughout the world, markets are opening, more traffic is being exchanged outside the traditional settlements process, and new technologies are having a profound impact on traffic patterns. In January 1996 only 17 percent of the world's top 20 telecommunications markets were open to U.S. companies. Pursuant to the WTO Basic Telecommunications Agreement, 92 percent of major markets are covered by commitments to remove restrictions on competition and foreign entry. Competitive forces will soon result in higher-quality, lower-price, more innovative service offerings. Carriers are adopting nontraditional, more cost-efficient means of routing traffic, such as routing switched traffic over private lines and switched hubbing. Some experts predict that by 2005 the resale market will be worth 10 times what it was worth in 1996. As competition increases among communications companies, they will need to distinguish themselves from their competitors by enhancing their value-added information services, including the provision of access to news, media, entertainment, business, and educational information and databases. Finally, the 1996 act opens domestic markets to expanded foreign competition, adding to the competitive forces already prevalent in this area.

Year 2000 Problem

As the turn of the century approaches, one of the greatest challenges from a technology perspective is the year 2000 (Y2K) problem. Many of the computers and a certain proportion of the software in use today will not work correctly in the twenty-first century because many of these systems calculate dates by using a two-digit year. Once the year 2000 arrives, the systems will not know how to read the date or may misinterpret it as 1900.

Size and Scope of the Problem. For the past 30 years the information technology industry has adhered to a de facto standard of representing a year as two digits. This standard evolved primarily because of the high cost of storage space in the fledgling years of the computer era and has remained in place because of the common assumption that software will be replaced routinely in 10 years or less. With the approach of the year 2000, this seemingly innocuous standard threatens to wreak havoc on businesses, governments, and private citizens throughout the world that depend on computers to support their operations, serve and protect their citizens, and conduct their daily lives. The impact could well mean the economic failure of businesses and the inability to achieve critical missions of government organizations.

If it is not fixed, this problem will affect numeric validations, date comparisons, arithmetic operations, and chronological sorts. The result will be system failures, corrupt databases, and faulty reports and screen displays. The Gartner Group estimates that without correction, 90 percent of all applications will fail and/or create erroneous results by 1999. The problem is not limited to mainframes and legacy applications and/or databases; it extends across the board to distributed systems, personal computers (PCs), and user interfaces. It is not specific to certain programming languages and will affect operating systems, transaction monitors, database management systems, and other types of software. This anomaly of modern technology is in effect the most devastating "virus" ever experienced and has an enormous potential economic impact.

Many Y2K problems will begin to appear before that year. Systems that perform date projections (forecasts, long-term expirations, multiyear financial transactions, etc.) will misinterpret time-dependent data before January 2000. Some systems will stop completely, but many will simply spread erroneous data across the enterprise. Faulty date calculations could result in the misappropriation of money, the rejection of valid transactions, and the loss of legitimate revenue. To avoid this, organizations must ensure that all their systems are Y2K-compliant by calendar year 1999 at the latest.

International Issues. While organizations and governments are increasingly aware of the Y2K issue, in the opinion of the world information technology industry, they are not treating it with the required urgency. Estimates of the global cost to fix this problem are very high. One of the most commonly accepted estimates comes from the information technology industry analyst organization the Gartner Group, which prices the global fix between $300 billion and $600 billion (the higher figure is approximately equal to global expenditures on telecommunications in 1997).

Since the problem is simple to state, many people assume that it will be easy to fix, but this is not the case. We live in an automated information technology world with interlinked and interdependent systems on a global scale, and the continued operation of such systems is threatened by this problem. Major industrialized nations with the longest history of computer-related automation are at the greatest risk. For example, about 80 percent of suppliers to United Kingdom manufacturers are not Y2K-compliant. According to the Gartner Group, over the next 3 years 80 percent of manufacturers that do not develop a supplier millennium compliance program will have lower profit margins because of increased inventory levels and expediting costs.

It is clearly in the best interests of countries to coordinate their actions and assign and reallocate resources to avert the potential problems. It is not necessary to introduce new legislation to deal with this problem, but governments need to give this matter the highest priority.

U.S. Government Status. Of the almost 8,600 mission-critical systems governmentwide, 27 percent were Y2K-compliant in November 1997. Among the U.S. Department of Commerce's 470 mission-critical systems, 63 percent were Y2K-compliant in February 1998. All department systems have been reviewed, and work is under way to repair or replace all noncompliant systems by March 31, 1999.

Impact on Services Companies. Despite the serious threats it poses to companies worldwide, the Y2K problem is a bonanza for computer software and services firms that can help with related consulting, code maintenance services, and software fixes. According to International Data Corporation (IDC), 56 percent of the total spending to address this issue, including software and repair services, will be done internally, leaving 44 percent of the pie for computer services firms.

Professional computer services firms that are assisting new clients with the Y2K problem are trying to develop those relationships into longer-term contracts. In that regard, longer-term opportunities could have even more potential than do short-term ones.

International Trade

Information services and computer services are traded primarily through foreign affiliates of U.S. companies in foreign markets, which are referred to as majority U.S.-owned foreign affiliates (MOFAs). U.S. sales of computer services by MOFAs reached $22.7 billion in 1995, growing at a compound rate of 34 percent since 1993 (see Table 26-6). Europe is the United States' largest market, followed by the Asia/Pacific region. Sales in Europe by MOFAs in 1995 posted a 26 percent increase over the 1994 levels; sales in the Asia/Pacific region and Latin America also had very strong growth in 1995.

The United States also has a sizable export trade surplus in information services. Although imports of information services rose at a compound rate of 24 percent a year between 1992 and 1996, the U.S. trade surplus continued to increase (see Table 26-7). In 1996 U.S. information services generated a $4.3 bil-

TABLE 26-6: Sales of Computer and Data Processing Services by Majority U.S.-Owned Foreign Affiliates (MOFAs)
(millions of dollars; percent)

	1992	1993	1994	1995	1996[1]	1997[1]	1998[1]	1999[1]	2003[1]
Total sales	11,664	12,675	18,777	22,662	28,282	35,296	49,976	62,370	162,764
Percent change		8.7	48.1	20.6	24.8	24.8	41.6	24.8	27.1

[1] Estimate.
Source: U.S. Department of Commerce: Bureau of Economic Analysis; International Trade Administration.

TABLE 26-7: Information Services Balance of Trade

(millions of dollars; percent)

	1992	1993	1994	1995	1996	1997[1]	1998[1]	1999[2]	2003[2]
U.S. exports	2,543	3,002	3,822	4,660	4,771	5,582	6,698	7,937	
Percent change		18.0	27.3	21.9	2.4	17.0	20.0	18.5	17.7
U.S. imports	213	414	385	594	508	631	701	825	
Percent change		94.4	−7.0	54.3	−14.5	24.2	11.1	17.7	21.3
Balance of trade	2,330	2,588	3,437	4,066	4,263	4,951	5,997	7,112	
Percent change		11.1	32.8	18.3	4.8	16.1	21.1	18.6	

[1] Estimate.
[2] Forecast.
Source: U.S. Department of Commerce: Bureau of Economic Analysis; International Trade Administration.

lion surplus, the largest to date, according to the U.S. Department of Commerce. Exports of information services totaled nearly $5 billion in 1996, 2 percent higher than the 1995 level. In each of the preceding 4 years, double-digit increases in information services exports were the norm, growing at a compound rate of 17 percent a year between 1992 and 1996.

Europe is the largest market for information services exports as well as for sales by affiliates of U.S. companies. In 1996 it accounted for approximately 47 percent of total U.S. cross-border exports. Exports to the Asia/Pacific region are also on the rise, representing close to 31 percent of the total. Japan was the single largest export market, followed closely by the United Kingdom, Canada, and Germany.

International trade opportunities in information services will continue to increase rapidly through the end of the decade and well into the twenty-first century. The information technology and telecommunications infrastructures needed to support many information services are still relatively underdeveloped in much of the world. Many governments are embarking on ambitious programs to extend or modernize this infrastructure in recognition of the benefits of the diffusion of information technology and telecommunication products and services. The benefits for business are a primary reason for this effort; information services enable firms in these nations to enhance their operations and work processes and reach customers around the globe. Services to rural areas are another strong selling point, especially in the areas of medicine, education, news, and other business and social services. Thus, the outlook for the expansion of U.S. information services internationally is very positive.

The developed world will remain a significant market as well. Strong demand for information services in Europe will continue into the twenty-first century. A number of European countries already have a strong and well-developed information technology and telecommunications market that is ideally suited for U.S. information services providers. Other European countries are developing and modernizing their infrastructures.

As Europe liberalizes its telecommunications infrastructure, opens it to competition, and continues to decrease tariffs on information technology products, the demand for information services will increase among European businesses. Advantages for U.S. firms in the European market include Europe's relative

proximity to the United States and the long history of trade between the United States and that continent.

Future demand for information services also will be strong in the Asia/Pacific and Latin American regions. Asia is the fastest growing region for sales by U.S. affiliates. The Latin American market for information services is growing faster than is that in the Asia/Pacific region, although its absolute market size is still small. As countries in these regions build their telecommunications and information technology infrastructures, demand for value-added information services will continue to grow rapidly.

In this discussion of international information services activity, it should be noted that the trade statistics issued by the U.S. Department of Commerce do not cover certain areas of the information services industry. They do not include export revenues generated by professional computer services, one of the industry's strongest areas.

PROFESSIONAL COMPUTER SERVICES

The professional computer service subsector includes systems integration, custom computer programming, consulting, training, disaster recovery, and facilities management and maintenance. This subsector constitutes the largest portion of the U.S. information services market: 70 percent in 1995. It is a fast-growing subsector, having expanded 14 percent annually between 1993 and 1995 (see Table 26-8).

Domestic Trends

In the coming years the professional computer subsector overall will experience strong growth, except in certain areas, such as custom programming. Growth in this area may level off as a result of the wide selection of sophisticated off-the-shelf hardware and software. Other factors, such as greater hardware compatibility, the efficiencies offered by next-generation languages, and growing standardization of data types, are contributing to this trend.

Numerous factors will stimulate growth in this subsector as a whole, however. Foremost among them are businesses' continued preference for client-server architectures, the increasing complexity of new information technology products, and the

TABLE 26-8: Professional Computer Services (SIC 7371, 7373, 7377, 7378, 7379) Trends and Forecasts

(millions of dollars; percent)

	1990	1991	1992	1993	1994	1995	1996[1]	1997[1]	1998[1]	1999[2]	2003[2]
Value added	33,194	35,483	40,280	43,129	49,253	56,105	63,469	71,998	82,552	94,983	160,423
Percent change		6.9	13.5	7.1	14.2	13.9	13.1	13.4	14.7	15.1	14.0

[1] Estimate.
[2] Forecast.
Source: U.S. Department of Commerce: Bureau of the Census, Bureau of Economic Analysis; International Trade Administration.

need to integrate them successfully into business operations. Additional factors contributing to growth are the multiplicity of information technology vendors, the convergence of information technology and communications technology products, and the need to integrate these products efficiently and effectively into business operations.

Perhaps the most important factor in the growth of professional computer services is the Internet. Businesses are attempting to take advantage of the Internet's potential while maintaining security and control over critical business data and information. This has generated great demand for systems integration and computer consulting to resolve these sometimes divergent goals. Since the Internet is fast, flexible, and in constant flux, tools and applications designed to interface with it are changing constantly. Businesses are seeking new Internet tools to exploit this vast potential. "Middleware" and other World Wide Web interface tools provide a link between the vast expanse of the Internet and databases. Computer professionals capable of building efficient, secure, and transparent bridges between the two will have enormous opportunities in the coming years.

Businesses are also seeking systems integration and computer consulting services to provide solutions to the challenge of maintaining and upgrading information and communication technology amid the rapid development of more advanced products and despite the constraints of leaner budgets for information systems. Businesses are increasingly confronted with the choice between investing in completely new systems and investing in bridging systems to new networks. Businesses have become more selective in their purchases, emphasizing long-term corporate goals in their choice of information systems. Such challenges have elevated the importance of systems integrators and computer consultants and have contributed to continued strong demand for their services. In the government systems integration market, declining federal and state budgets generally have had a negative impact. Although federal information systems remain antiquated, the need to maintain them creates a niche for computer professionals who can understand them.

Internationally, the market for professional computer services is quite strong. Many large U.S. systems integrators and computer consulting firms continue to win multi-million-dollar contracts with foreign companies and governments. Since U.S. computer professionals generally have more experience then do their international counterparts in integrating the Internet and Internet-related applications with existing systems, they have a competitive edge in overseas markets.

Growth of the Internet and Intranets

In July 1997, the administration issued its Framework for Global Electronic Commerce, which identified nine key areas that must be addressed to realize the Internet's potential as a commercial medium and encouraged private sector leaders to develop effective self-regulatory regimes. The President also directed the Secretary of Commerce to work with the private sector, the states, and foreign governments to support the development of a legal framework that would recognize, facilitate, and enforce electronic transactions worldwide.

When President Clinton released the Framework, he made clear that the administration expects the Internet, a collection of thousands of computer networks, to transform the world and the way business is conducted. Originally, the Internet was an inexpensive and helpful communication device for academics and defense industry engineers. In the mid-1980s it began to be used for broader purposes after the invention of the World Wide Web. The development in the early 1980s of graphic viewers to interface with the Web was the breakthrough that enabled a large portion of the computer-using population to embrace the Internet. As Internet growth continued into the mid-1990s, the Web and on-line transactions remained in their infancy. However, just 3 years later the ability to buy and sell electronically has matured, and a fundamental transformation is occurring in the American and global marketplace.

Internet use is now oriented more toward business needs: advertising, marketing, communication, and to an extent sales. While the Internet is still used for functions such as file access and transfer, the corporate world's use of the Internet as a business tool has outpaced those earlier uses. Internet technology is having a profound effect on global trade in software and entertainment products, information services, and technical, financial, professional, and other services in which the United States is the world leader. It also is changing retail and direct marketing. Perhaps most important, the Internet will make it easier for companies to operate on a global basis, giving even small and medium-size companies access to a worldwide network of customers. The explosive growth of the Internet and other computer networks over the past several years has revolutionized communications in this country and heralds the development of an electronic marketplace.

The Internet can be considered the great equalizer. Because of its virtual transparency, small and large businesses, organizations, and individuals appear more or less the same and can be viewed equally easily by anyone anywhere in the world. Further, providers of similar products or services generally are viewed, accessed, and filed in much the same way by the different search engines and browsers. Given its relatively low cost compared with traditional advertising modes, the Internet can level the playing field for some businesses—at least initially—and allow them to compete effectively.

According to Access Media International, the number of small businesses—companies with fewer than 100 employees—that have Web sites has grown dramatically and will continue to expand through 2000. In 1997, 900,000 small firms had Web sites. In 1998, the number was expected to grow to 2 million firms, and in 2000, 2.7 million small businesses will have Web sites.

With approximately 62 million people in the United States having access, the Internet is an increasingly popular medium for advertising goods and services and conducting commercial transactions. It has been estimated that businesses spent $906.5 million for advertising on the Internet in 1997. Advertisements on the World Wide Web often have pages which may contain text, pictures, video, sound, interactive graphics, or a combination of all these features. Commerce on the Internet could total tens of billions of dollars by the turn of the century, and the U.S. government has been actively involved in the development of telecommunications and information policies that will facilitate the rapid expansion of the electronic marketplace for the benefit of all Americans. Estimates of on-line sales vary dramatically. One survey estimates that in the fourth quarter of 1997, 37.2 million users shopped on-line and 10.5 million users purchased on-line.

The Internet is a medium which has expanded, developed, and been successful largely because it has not been subject to government intervention. In such a rapidly changing environment, industry will need to develop solutions to the challenges facing the Internet. The imposition of rigid solutions, often designed to apply to all participants in the same way, will hamper the growth and expansion of the Internet and stymie economic growth in the newly emerging electronic information economy. The approaches adopted should be flexible and versatile and have the ability to adapt to the changing environment of the Internet.

The U.S. Department of Commerce has released a discussion draft, *A Proposal to Improve Technical Management of Internet Names and Addresses,* that recommends privatizing domain name system management functions in a new, not-for-profit corporation and proposes a framework for introducing competition into the domain name registration system.

A unifying effort among the states is under way to revise the Uniform Commercial Code (UCC) to accommodate electronic commerce. Other efforts are seeking to modify contract laws on matters related to electronic commerce that are not covered by the UCC. The National Conference of Commissioners on Uniform State Laws (NCCUSL) has convened a drafting committee for a Uniform Electronic Transaction Act.

Because of the success of the Internet as a mainstream business and communications tool, businesses are developing internal networks based on Internet protocols that are called intranets. Intranets give businesses a new way to organize and structure their internal operations. Intranets provide a more efficient means to collect, manage, and disseminate a firm's internal information among different divisions and subsidiaries. They also provide an integrated conduit or gateway for doing business externally on the Internet. Unlike the current, open state of the Internet, intranets are relatively secure environments that are suitable for businesses. For this reason the growth of the intranet market is expected to greatly exceed that of the Internet market.

Next-Generation Internet

In October 1996 the Clinton administration announced its support for the Next-Generation Internet (NGI) initiative, aimed at providing funding to academic, government, and industry research communities to advance research on experimental network applications, services, and infrastructure. The Clinton administration's fiscal year 1999 budget allocates $850 million for research and development for the Large-Scale Networking and High-End Computing and Computation research and development program. Of this proposed funding, $110 million will go to the NGI initiative.

The NGI will allow the development of high-performance test networks among research centers to provide system-scale testing of advanced services and technologies and support the testing of advanced applications. Two NGI goals are to develop a broadly based network that will connect research institutions across the country at end-to-end performance speeds 100 times that of the current Internet and to develop an ultra-high-speed network among a select group of institutions that will function at speeds 1,000 times that of the current Internet.

The NGI initiative also will work in conjunction with networking projects such as Internet2, a collaborative effort by more than 100 U.S. research universities to create and sustain a leading-edge network for developing network engineering and management tools and broadband applications for advanced research and education.

As in the development of the early networking technologies that foreshadowed the Internet, the next generation of networking technologies probably will stem from the study of precompetitive technologies by the academic, government, and industrial research communities. This research will provide a foundation for a faster, more reliable, and more secure public Internet in the future.

DATA PROCESSING AND NETWORK SERVICES

Network service companies provide a broad range of value-added network services, including electronic data interchange services, electronic mail delivery, file transfer, and electronic funds transfer. Network service firms also provide access to databases and electronic bulletin boards. These firms are increasingly providing more sophisticated forms of electronic commerce, including services which facilitate sales and customized research over the Internet. The data processing subsec-

TABLE 26-9:   Data Processing and Network Services (SIC 7374, 7376) Trends and Forecasts
(millions of dollars; percent)

	1990	1991	1992	1993	1994	1995	1996[1]	1997[1]	1998[1]	1999[2]	2003[2]
Value added	11,625	12,348	14,086	14,820	17,264	20,059	22,771	25,854	29,745	34,230	59,247
Percent change		6.2	14.1	5.2	16.5	16.2	13.5	13.5	15.0	15.1	14.7

[1] Estimate.
[2] Forecast.
Source: U.S. Department of Commerce: Bureau of the Census; Bureau of Economic Analysis; International Trade Administration.

tor is composed principally of companies that provide services such as data entry, credit card authorization and billing, and payroll processing. This subsector's value added to the U.S. economy totaled $20 billion in 1995, an increase of 16 percent from 1994; this duplicated the increase from 1993 to 1994 (see Table 26-9). It is the second largest information services subsector, accounting for approximately 25 percent of total U.S. revenues in the industry.

The dominant factor in the future growth of network services is the acceptance of the Internet as a business tool. In addition, the growth of the Internet as a means of electronic communication in residential markets will have a positive effect on certain network service companies. The growth of traditional network services will continue to accelerate as a result of new applications and tools designed for the Internet and intranets. The Internet also is likely to spur the development of new forms of network services.

The international outlook for network services is in part a function of the level of the network, data communication, and telecommunication infrastructure in a country. Simply put, spending on networking equipment internationally is soaring, generating a concomitant demand for network services. Governments and businesses around the world are purchasing networking and data communications equipment at record levels. Spending on networking equipment is increasing at double-digit and triple-digit rates in much of the Asia/Pacific region. Some of these high growth rates reflect the low installed base of networking equipment in some countries. However, countries with relatively well developed information and telecommunications technology infrastructures, such as Japan, Australia, Singapore, and Hong Kong, also increased their purchases of networking equipment at double-digit rates in 1996. Newly developing countries, including Vietnam, India, and China, also bought networking equipment at record levels.

Spending on network products and services has been boosted by the Internet and by the desire on the part of businesses and governments to develop their information technology and telecommunications infrastructures. A major beneficiary of growing spending on network products will continue to be U.S. network service providers.

The outlook is also very good for data processing, management, and preparation services. Traditional data processing services still have strong growth opportunities. These services include payroll processing, billing, and health care claims processing. They are commonly referred to as back-office functions because they are routine, high-volume, easily automated functions. Many service providers in this area are small companies that target local businesses as their clients. Since these services are affected by the strength of the local and national economies, the demand for traditional data processing services should remain strong, in keeping with U.S. economic growth.

Internationally, opportunities for U.S. data processing companies will remain good. The demand for automated routine functions is increasing with the growth of the global information technology infrastructure and as individual businesses around the world build their own information technology bases. U.S. companies that can provide these services on a large scale stand to benefit greatly from the developing international information technology infrastructure.

A rapidly growing area that is closely related to data processing is outsourcing. A growing number of small and large businesses are entering this market, which resembles data processing but encompasses more critical business functions, including less-automated market-driven, consumer-oriented functions. Outsourcing companies include a few very large key providers as well as a number of new smaller players that cater to niche markets. The Internet will have a profound impact on outsourcing. Web operations and Web page management, along with some Internet security service operations, represent new sources of business for outsourcing firms.

ELECTRONIC INFORMATION SERVICES

Electronic information services include companies that provide proprietary databases and information on-line, on CD-ROM, or on media such as magnetic tape, floppy disc, and audiotext. Examples include financial and economic information for business users, marketing information on specific industries and products, information specific to a geographic area, and news and media information. In addition, certain highly specialized companies provide abstracts of the latest research in specialized medical and scientific fields or technical databases containing patent information, legal abstracts, and the like.

Another important part of electronic information services consists of consumer on-line services. These services give their subscribers access to a wide array of information and data packaged for ease of use. The services may include bulletin boards, chat rooms, live conferencing, software, and home shopping. The information topics offered include entertainment, education, and personal finance as well as electronic versions of magazines and newspapers and information on local events. Consumer on-line services also have begun to offer access to the Internet, the World Wide Web, and global E-mail.

The value added to the U.S. economy by electronic information services totaled nearly $4 billion in 1995, making this the smallest segment of the information services sector (see Table 26-10). This subsector grew 18 percent between 1994 and 1995.

The leading users of electronic information services are the financial and business sectors, which make use of proprietary databases that contain large amounts of timely and accurate information. To meet the needs of the market, most electronic information databases are time-sensitive, and some even require up-to-the-minute updating. Since there is a continuing need for the most recent and accurate information, demand for electronic information services will remain high.

In areas where time sensitivity is not as important, CD-ROM data distribution is a low-cost alternative for accessing large amounts of data. Additionally, CD-ROMs are an important educational tool. The United States leads the CD-ROM market in terms of the production of titles and in having the largest base of installed CD-ROM readers. Europe is the next largest market for CD-ROM use and production. The largest proportion of CD-ROM readers are found in households, indicating the importance of the residential market for this medium.

Consumer on-line services have grown tremendously over the past few years as a result of a number of factors, especially the decline in the cost of powerful PCs with installed high-speed modems that enable users to access graphic interfaces over telephone lines. This has led to an explosion of on-line services in the residential market. Various sources estimate that approximately 40 percent of U.S. households own a PC, and the number of home PCs with an installed modem is increasing. Estimates, though sketchy, indicate that consumer on-line services had on the order of 9 million to 11 million subscribers in 1995, a 70 to 100 percent increase over 1994. In 1997 the number of American subscribers was estimated at 62 million. Growth of this magnitude probably will continue through 2000. Additionally, while some of the largest on-line services are getting bigger, often at the expense of their competitors, smaller regional on-line service providers and those catering to specific interests or niche markets are surviving.

Consumer on-line services are beginning to pursue overseas markets aggressively. The growth of sales of home PCs over-

seas is continuing at record levels. Europe is the second largest market for electronic information services and consumer on-line services. That continent had between 1 million and 1.5 million subscribers to on-line services in 1995, and the number increased greatly in 1996. Currently, the major European markets for on-line services are the United Kingdom, Germany, and France, in part because of their large populations and in part because of the relatively prevalent Integrated Services Digital Network (ISDN) wiring throughout those areas. However, other areas in Europe, particularly some of the Nordic countries, have a telecommunications and technology infrastructure that is well suited for on-line service providers. Additionally, some of the Nordic countries have lower telecommunication costs and greater computer penetration per capita than do their larger neighbors. Asia is still far behind the United States and Europe in terms of on-line services and Internet users. Many estimates of the size of the market refer to the number of Internet users in Asia, not necessarily to the on-line service market.

A number of challenges will affect the growth of electronic information services and on-line services around the world. Many of these challenges are technical issues, others are of a legal or regulatory nature, and still others are sociopolitical. Issues such as censorship, privacy concerns, intellectual property protection, and language requirements may have to be addressed at both national and international levels because of the ubiquity of the Internet. In addition, high local dial-up costs, time-metered phone charges, and inadequate telecommunications infrastructures pose challenges to the growth of these services internationally.

On-line services have been following the general information services trend and aligning themselves with foreign companies to gain access to overseas markets. Expansion into Europe by on-line service providers has been accomplished in a variety of ways, such as establishing joint ventures with local partners, including joint ventures with media, telecommunications, and Internet access providers. Establishing overseas subsidiaries is another method of expanding into overseas markets.

The most significant challenge to the growth of on-line services is the entrance of telecommunications firms, entertainment companies, and Internet access providers into the residential on-line service market. As competition increases, prices for service and access to unique and useful content will be the main areas of competition, possibly cutting into already narrow profit margins. Stiff competition has already forced the

TABLE 26-10: Information Retrieval Services (SIC 7375) Trends and Forecasts
(millions of dollars; percent)

	1990	1991	1992	1993	1994	1995	1996[1]	1997[1]	1998[1]	1999[2]	2003[2]
Value added	2,435	2,534	2,803	1,963	3,188	3,768	4,262	4,820	6,107	7,738	15,833
Percent change		4.1	10.6	−30.0	62.4	18.2	13.1	13.1	26.7	26.7	19.6

[1] Estimate.
[2] Forecast.
Source: U.S. Department of Commerce: Bureau of the Census; Bureau of Economic Analysis; International Trade Administration.

three largest consumer on-line services to switch to flat-rate pricing to maintain their subscriber bases.

The Internet represents a major source of competition for electronic information and consumer on-line services. More and more businesses, educational institutions, governments, and other groups are developing Web pages to provide information about themselves, their regulations, statistics, advertisements about their products and services, and a wealth of other information and data. Some electronic news and media companies are developing their own Web pages for the dissemination and delivery of information directly to the end user rather than using an on-line service provider. At a certain level, therefore, providers of electronic information services may face competition from the "original" source. Consumer on-line services may be able to retain significant markets, however, by continuing to repackage and make Internet data and information more user-friendly.

North American Industry Classification System

The Office of Management and Budget established a new classification system, in conjunction with Canada and Mexico, for use in the United States called the North American Industry Classification System—United States 1997 (NAICS). The NAICS replaces the Standard Industrial Classification System (SIC), which has been used in the United States since the 1940s. Table 26-11 shows the conversion from the SIC to the NAICS. Information services industries included in business services under the SIC will be included under the retail trade; information; real estate and rental and leasing; professional, scientific, and technical services; and other services (except public administration) sectors under the NAICS. Beginning with data for calendar year 1997, U.S. government agencies will begin to release data according to the NAICS rather than the SIC. When the Bureau of the Census releases data from the 1997 Economic Census in 1999, the data will be tabulated according to the NAICS-defined industries with cross-reference tables included to indicate the relationship to the old SIC industries.

The new information sector combines communications, publishing, motion picture and sound recording, and on-line services in recognition of the advent of the new information age. Twenty new industries mark this sector, including software

TABLE 26-11: Information Services: SIC and NAICS

	SIC	NAICS
Computer programming services	7371	541513
Computer integrated systems design	7373	541512
Computer processing, data preparation	7374	51421
Information retrieval services	7375	514191
Computer services management	7376	541513
Computer rental and leasing	7377	53242
Computer maintenance and repair	7378	44312, 811212
Computer-related services not elsewhere classified	7379	541512, 541519

Source: Office of Management and Budget.

publishing, satellite telecommunications, paging, and cellular and other wireless telecommunications.

Electronic Commerce

Many industry observers see electronic commerce as one of the most important techniques affecting future business practices, yet there is no consensus on exactly what electronic commerce is. Generally, the term *electronic commerce* refers to commercial transactions, involving both organizations and individuals, that are based on the processing and transmission of digitized data, including text, sound, and visual images, and are carried out over open networks such as the Internet or closed networks that have a gateway into an open network.

Although much media attention has focused on on-line merchants selling books, wine, and computers, the vast majority of products marketed electronically from businesses to consumers are intangibles such as travel and ticketing services, software, entertainment (on-line games, music, and gambling), banking, insurance and brokerage services, information services, legal services, real estate services, and health care, educational, and government services.

A variety of electronic commerce applications, services, and development tools have existed for many years, albeit in closed, well-defined networks. Electronic data interchange (EDI) software and services are a cornerstone for businesses and government alike. EDI consists of protocols for computer-to-computer transactions for billing, purchasing, invoicing, and other business functions. Electronic mail and electronic funds transfers also can be considered forms of electronic commerce. Most of these services and applications take place over private networks which make use of private and leased public telecommunications lines and are designed to be secure.

Because electronic commerce provides a fundamentally new way of conducting commercial transactions, it will have far-reaching economic and social implications. Current ways of doing business will be modified profoundly: Anyone with a computer and Internet access can become a merchant and reach consumers all over the world, and any consumer can acquire products and services offered anywhere in the world. New and far closer relationships will be forged between businesses and consumers, many of the traditional intermediaries will be replaced, and new products and markets will be developed.

The cost of doing business on new electronic networks is significantly lower than the cost of traditional methods. This advantage, along with the ability to offer high-value, content-rich products and services, has led to exponential growth in the number of firms entering electronic commerce and related businesses. This is most evident in the United States but is becoming evident in other countries as well. Electronic commerce over the Internet was estimated at more than $8 billion in 1997 for trade between businesses (excluding transfers of funds and purchases of financial securities). Business-to-business transactions, which far exceed on-line transactions between businesses and consumers, are expected to grow to $326.4 billion in 2002. Commercial transactions over the Internet are also expanding at a rate too rapid to gauge. By bringing buyers and sellers closer together, electronic commerce will facilitate trade growth.

According to Access Media International, the number of small businesses that are conducting electronic commerce transactions has grown dramatically and will continue to expand through 2000. In 1997, 400,000 small firms conducted electronic commerce transactions. In 1998, the number was expected to grow to 600,000 firms, and in 2000, 1.3 million small businesses will trade electronically. These electronic transactions captured sales totaling $3.5 billion in 1997. Sales in 1998 should increase to $7.5 billion, and in 2000 they should reach $25 billion.

The primary issue affecting Internet commerce is security. Some current concerns over security are justified, while others are more of a function of perceptions and norms of acceptability. Until some of the more salient issues surrounding the security of networks and the Internet are resolved, businesses and individuals may be hesitant to place sensitive financial and personal information on the Internet. Network security issues are being addressed at the national and international levels to arrive at uniform guidelines for businesses and consumers.

Concern over Internet security has spawned new niche industries. A number of hardware and software firms are developing specific technologies and techniques to provide varying degrees of security over private networks and the Internet. On the hardware side, a variety of equipment is being developed to establish firewalls that guard against intrusions into sensitive business data and information systems. New software and services are being designed to ensure secure payment over the Internet. Additionally, a number of information service companies are emerging as electronic commerce facilitators, offering services that enable individuals and businesses to exploit different aspects of the vast Internet market. Some offer a variety of Internet payment mechanisms and act as clearinghouses (payment and billing centers) for Internet commerce. Others certify the integrity of Internet sites and vendors, essentially offering a seal of approval for Internet sites.

These are just a few of the emerging products and services that promise to spur a phenomenal surge of electronic commerce over the Internet. Growth projections vary widely. Analysts predict that businesses will trade as much as $300 billion over the Internet in the next 3 to 5 years; others think the figure could be much higher. These transactions would generate between $3 billion and $30 billion in revenues for electronic commerce service facilitators. While many issues remain, the only question is when, not if, electronic commerce will be widely and easily available.

Claudia Cox Wolfe, U.S. Department of Commerce, Office of Service Industries, (202) 482-5086, October 1998.

■ **R E F E R E N C E S**

Bank Technology News, Faulkner & Grey, 11 Penn Plaza, 22nd Floor, New York, N.Y. 10001-2006. (800) 535-8403.

Census of Service Industries, Bureau of the Census, U.S. Department of Commerce, Washington DC 20230. (301) 457-2689.

Computers: Commercial Services, Standard & Poor's Corp., 25 Broadway, New York, New York 10004.

Computers: Consumer Services & the Internet, Standard & Poor's Corp., 25 Broadway, New York, New York 10004.

Computerworld, International Data Group, Inc., 500 Old Connecticut Path, P.O. Box 9171, Framingham, MA 01701-9171. (508) 879-0700.

Current Business Report: Services Annual Survey, Bureau of the Census, U.S. Department of Commerce, Washington, DC 20230. (301) 457-2787.

Database, Online Inc., 462 Danbury Road, Wilton, CT 06897-2126. (203) 761-1466.

Data Communications, McGraw-Hill Inc., P.O. Box 477, Hightstown, NJ 08520-9360.

Datamation, Cahners Publishing Co., 275 Washington Street, Newton, MA 02158. (617) 558-4281.

EDI World, EDI World Inc., 2021 Coolidge Street, Hollywood, FL 33020-2400. (954) 925-5900.

Electronic Messaging Association, 1655 North Fort Myer Drive, Arlington, VA 22209.

The Emerging Digital Economy, U.S. Department of Commerce, Washington, DC 20230. (202) 482-8369.

Employment and Earnings, Bureau of Labor Statistics, U.S. Department of Labor, Washington, DC 20210. (202) 606-6373.

Federal Communications Commission, *Rules and Policies on Foreign Participation in the U.S. Telecommunications Market,* FCC97-398, Washington, DC 20554.

Federal Computer Week, FCW Government Technology Group, 3110 Fairview Park Drive, Falls Church, VA 22042-4599. (703) 876-5100.

Forrester Research Inc., 1033 Massachusetts Avenue, Cambridge MA 02138. (617) 497-7090.

Gartner Group, Inc., Gartner Park, 56 Top Gallant Road, P.O. Box 10212, Stamford, CT 06904.

Imaging (magazine), Telecom Library Inc, 12 West 21 Street, New York, NY 10010. (212) 691-8215.

Information Industry Bulletin, Digital Information Group, P.O. Box 110235, Stamford, CT 06911-0235. (203) 840-0045.

Information Technology Association of America, 1616 N. Fort Myer Drive, Arlington, VA 22209-3106. (703) 522-5055.

Information Technology Outlook, Organization for Economic Cooperation and Development, Paris, France.

Information Today, Information Today, Inc., 143 Old Marlton Pike, Medford, NJ 08055. (609) 654-6266.

Information Week, 600 Community Drive, Manhasset, NY 11030. (800) 292-3642.

Input, Inc., 1280 Villa Street, Mountain View, CA 94041. (415) 961-3300.

Interactive and Services Report, BRP Publications Inc., 1333 H Street, NW, Washington, DC 20005. (202) 842-3022.

Interactive Services Association, 8403 Colesville Road, Suite 865, Silver Spring, MD 20910. (301) 495-4959.

International Data Corporation, 5 Speen Street, Framingham, MA 01701. (508) 872-8200.

Internet World, Mecklermedia Corporation, 20 Ketchum Street, Westport, CT 06880. www.iw.com.

Online, Online Inc., 462 Danbury Road, Wilton, CT 06897-2126. (203) 761-1466.

Survey of Current Business, October 1997, Economics and Statistics Administration, U.S. Department of Commerce, Washington, DC 20230. (202) 606-9900.

U.S. International Trade Commission, *Industry, Trade and Technology Review,* 500 E Street, SW, Washington DC 20436.

Washington Technology, TechNews, Inc., 8500 Leesburg Pike, Suite 7500, Vienna, VA 22182-2412. (703) 848-2800.

The Yankee Group, 31 St. James Avenue, Boston, MA 02116-4114.

■ R E L A T E D C H A P T E R S

24: Photographic Equipment and Supplies
25: Printing and Publishing
27: Computer Equipment
28: Computer Software and Networking
30: Telecommunications Services

COMPUTER EQUIPMENT
Economic and Trade Trends

U.S. International Trade

($ billions)

Balance ▪ Exports ▪ Imports

Source: U.S. Department of Commerce: Bureau of the Census; International Trade Administration.

World Export Market Shares

(%)

United States ▪ Japan ▪ Singapore ▪ Taiwan

Source: United Nations; U.S. Department of Commerce, International Trade Administration.

Export Dependence and Import Penetration

(%)

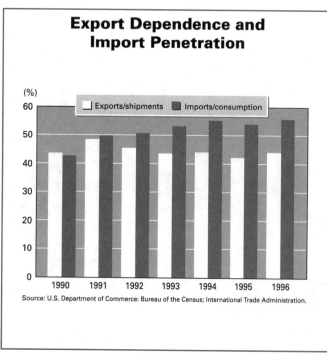

Exports/shipments ▪ Imports/consumption

Source: U.S. Department of Commerce: Bureau of the Census; International Trade Administration.

Output and Output per Hour

(1992 = 100)

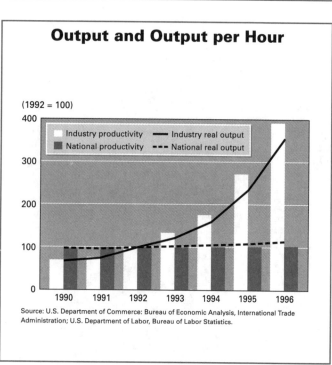

Industry productivity ▪ Industry real output
National productivity ▪ National real output

Source: U.S. Department of Commerce: Bureau of Economic Analysis, International Trade Administration; U.S. Department of Labor, Bureau of Labor Statistics.

See "Getting the Most Out of *Outlook '99*" for definitions of terms.

Computer Equipment

INDUSTRY DEFINITION Computer equipment includes computer hardware and peripherals (SIC 3571, 3572, 3575, 3577).

FACTORS AFFECTING FUTURE INDUSTRY GROWTH

Global Industry Trends

The U.S. computer equipment industry is global in both its operations and its outlook. U.S. companies invested $22 billion overseas in 1996, continuing to establish research, manufacturing, and sales operations throughout the world to serve local and regional markets more effectively and to benefit from foreign technical talent. They also outsourced many of their key components, subsystems, and peripherals worldwide. For example, more than 60 percent of the hardware value of a typical U.S. personal computer (PC) system is made up of floppy and hard disk drives, video cards, multimedia kits, monitors, motherboards, mouse devices, power supplies, and random-access memory (RAM) imported from Asia. Some sourcing of complete PCs systems and other computer equipment is done through arrangements with contract electronics manufacturers (CEMs). In their efforts to reduce costs, several leading U.S. suppliers, such as Dell, Hewlett-Packard, and IBM, reportedly have shifted more of their production over the past few years to U.S. and foreign CEMs that have plants in Asia and Latin America as well as in the United States.

Foreign computer suppliers followed the trend set by their U.S. counterparts by becoming more global in the 1990s. The Japanese in particular invested heavily in China and various countries of the Association of Southeast Asian Nations (ASEAN) to gain access to lower labor rates and cheaper components. Some Asian firms also began manufacturing in Mexico to take advantage of the zero tariff rates offered under the North American Free Trade Agreement (NAFTA). These competitors are making serious efforts to challenge the leadership of U.S. companies in a broad range of computer equipment.

In 1996 cumulative foreign direct investment in the U.S.-based computer industry increased for the third consecutive year after hitting a low in 1993. This spending on U.S. operations and equity positions in U.S. computer firms rose 6 percent to $2.8 billion in 1996, the latest year for which data are available. However, this figure represents little more than a tenth of what U.S. computer equipment companies invested overseas. Japanese firms remained the largest foreign investors, accounting for 74 percent of this total, followed by European companies with 20 percent.

U.S. affiliates of foreign companies have recently had a greater impact on the U.S.-based computer equipment industry and the overall American economy than they had a few years ago. Their gross product dropped to $1.1 billion in 1996, down from the 1995 level of $1.9 billion, while their investment in new plant and equipment decreased by 29 percent to $372 million. Their sales decreased 20 percent to $14.5 billion, with a net loss of $1.3 billion, adding to these affiliates' long-term trend of losses. Their labor force also decreased 9 percent to 38,600 workers, still representing almost 17 percent of total employment in the U.S.-based computer industry. They also continue to be a factor in the ever-widening U.S. trade deficit in computer equipment. They imported 3.2 times what they exported, creating a trade deficit of $4.3 billion in 1996. The fact that they exported less than 10 percent of their sales shows that these affiliates focus on serving U.S. computer demand.

Continuing growth in worldwide Internet use and increasing interest in electronic commerce have helped fuel the global demand for computer equipment. Net Wizards, a market research firm, estimated that the number of Internet host computers grew from 1.3 million at the beginning of 1993 to 29.7 million in 1998. This number is expected to more than triple to 100 million host systems by 2000. Most of these computers are using the Internet for commercial and educational purposes.

The use of electronic commerce to buy and sell products and services should expand rapidly over the next several years. Consumer and business purchases on the Internet around the world will grow from $7.6 billion in 1997 to $331.1 billion in 2002, according to International Data Corporation (IDC). At least a third of these sales in the United States have involved PC hardware, reflecting the growing importance of electronic commerce as a marketing vehicle for U.S. computer equipment companies. For example, Dell Computer sold less than $1 million a day in 1996 but was able to boost its on-line sales to $3 million daily by December 1997, taking in roughly $1 billion for the year. Dell expects to conduct half its business over the Internet in the near future.

Global computer demand has continued to shift to low-cost desktop and portable systems. The world computer systems market totaled $222 billion in 1997, of which PCs alone had a 71 percent share, according to Dataquest. This trend should continue in the future, with the advent of PCs that cost under $1,000 stimulating greater sales to consumers for home use. However, continued growth in corporate intranets and local area networks should also increase the demand for servers.

The global computer market became more concentrated in the 1990s. Although small and medium-size suppliers have prospered in some computer equipment niche markets, a handful of U.S. and foreign manufacturers dominate the markets for computer systems. The control exercised by the top five vendors ranges from 60 percent for midrange computers to 90 percent or more for hand-held PCs and mainframes, according to estimates from Dataquest. In the peripherals area these vendors have an 84 percent share of sales of hard disk drives worldwide.

Competition in desktop and notebook computers was so severe in 1997 that suppliers cut prices almost on a monthly basis to gain market share, reduce inventories, and stimulate sales of older models. In addition to benefiting from lower costs for key components such as microprocessors, dynamic random-access (DRAM) memories, and flat panel displays, the leading U.S. computer companies obtained cost savings from their build-to-order and distribution channel efficiency programs and transferred those savings to users through cheaper prices for PC systems.

In the second half of 1997 fully configured corporate desktop models with Pentium II microprocessors were available for prices below $2,000. Further cuts drove their price down to around $1,200 by early 1998. Some home-use PCs without monitors sold for as low as $600 at many mass merchandisers in the United States. Notebook prices were reduced up to 25 percent during that period, bringing some systems down to $2,500 and a few low-end models to $1,000.

Prices for a wide range of peripherals also fell to record lows. Production overcapacity in hard disk drives swelled inventories and, along with increased foreign competition in the U.S. market, significantly lowered prices for disk arrays and stand-alone drives. The price per megabyte plummeted in a decade from $11.50 in 1987 to only 10 cents in 1997, according to Disk Trend, a market research firm in San Jose, California. An oversupply of notebook screens and an aggressive South Korean pricing strategy pushed liquid crystal display (LCD) manufacturers into the desktop monitor market earlier than had been expected. Prices for 14-inch active-matrix LCDs dropped as much as 50 percent, decreasing from $1,500 in mid-1997 to below $800 early in 1998.

The much-discussed Asian economic crisis should have a positive effect on computer equipment pricing in the United States. U.S. suppliers with manufacturing operations in that region should have even lower labor, plant operations, and component costs from the devaluation of local currencies and are likely to pass those savings on in their exports to consumers in the United States. Similarly, U.S.-based computer equipment companies that source from Asia will benefit from a substantial decline in their cost of goods sold as they purchase cheaper logic and memory chips, boards, other parts, and peripherals from Japan, South Korea, Taiwan, and the ASEAN members. This scenario should result in greater price competition in the U.S. computer systems market between U.S. and Asian firms.

The full impact of this crisis on computer exports from the United States is still difficult to determine, since growth rates in exports to this region have oscillated throughout the 1990s. From the perspective of U.S. computer exports to the world, shipments to Asia have accounted for only a third of the total export value, and any weakness in demand there may be offset to some extent by sales to Canada and major trading partners in Europe and Latin America. What happens to the economy of Japan, the largest single-country computer market outside the United States, and that of China, the fastest growing economy in the region, will probably be the key to how severe a blow is dealt to the industry over the long term. In the short term U.S. computer exports to this region may decline 3 percent in 1998.

For U.S. computer imports, the Asian crisis may be a double-edged sword. Asia has traditionally been the source of roughly 80 percent of U.S. computer import value. Currency devaluation will make these imports cheaper and may boost U.S. demand for them substantially if the domestic computer market remains strong. However, another possibility is that the crisis will restrain imports from this region and thus negatively affect total imports in the near future. In this scenario, substantial shortages of key computer parts and peripherals will occur if the economic malaise in certain countries worsens and the financial problems of several major Asian suppliers force them to go out of business. The likelihood of this will remain slim as long as International Monetary Fund (IMF) financial aid succeeds in improving economic and financial conditions in that region.

Domestic Trends

The trend toward industry consolidation continues among U.S. computer manufacturers, particularly the more established players. The number of mergers and acquisitions in the U.S. computer equipment industry increased 34 percent from 290 in 1995 to 389 in 1997, according to Broadview Associates. The value of those transactions more than doubled to $48.8 billion in 1997. Examples of major transactions during the past few years include Seagate's $2.9 billion purchase of Conner Peripherals, Silicon Graphics' acquisition of Cray Research, and Compaq Computer's $3 billion takeover of Tandem and $9 billion purchase of Digital Equipment Corp.

Computer systems should remain the mainstay of the U.S.-based computer equipment industry in the future. They have generally accounted for more than 50 percent of total product shipment value since 1992, and their production has expanded faster than that of peripherals and parts (see Figure 27-1). Most

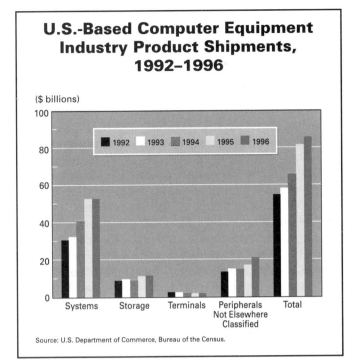

U.S.-Based Computer Equipment Industry Product Shipments, 1992–1996

($ billions)

Legend: 1992, 1993, 1994, 1995, 1996

Categories: Systems, Storage, Terminals, Peripherals Not Elsewhere Classified, Total

Source: U.S. Department of Commerce, Bureau of the Census.

FIGURE 27-1

of this output has been for domestic consumption rather than for export markets. Shipments of disk storage devices have grown slowly, battered by severe price competition and lower than expected demand. Terminal production has declined abruptly and appears to be dying out, since Asian suppliers now dominate the global market. However, shipments of peripherals not elsewhere classified, which consist primarily of printers and parts, increased at a healthy 12 percent annual rate through 1996.

The industry continues to export more than 40 percent of what it manufactures, three-quarters of which consists of peripherals and parts. Its computer export shipments increased nearly 11 percent each year since 1992, reaching over $41 billion in 1997. On a regional basis, the major customers for its exports are the European Union and NAFTA, but Latin America and Other Asia show the fastest growing demand. Canada and Japan remain the top countries of destination (see Table 27-1 and Figure 27-2). Export prices for U.S. computers and peripherals were slightly lower than those of imports of similar products from 1995 through 1997. However, the prices of computer parts exports versus imports were sharply higher during most of this period. This trend probably reflects the steep decline in prices for certain major electronic components sourced mainly from Asia, such as semiconductor memory and flat panel displays.

Imports of computer equipment and parts more than doubled from $31 billion in 1992 to $68 billion in 1997. Asia remained the principal regional source of these imports. However, with the advent of NAFTA, Mexico emerged as the fourth largest and the fastest growing supplier of parts among the top five. Japan is still the leading country of origin (see Table 27-1). Imports significantly outpaced exports during this period and steadily gained a dominant share of the U.S. computer market. Some of this import value represents trade between U.S. subsidiary operations overseas and their parents at home. For example, U.S. imports from Singapore, the second largest supplier, largely consist of hard disk drives produced by U.S. companies that have established plants there to serve the world market. As a result of these mounting imports, the U.S. computer trade deficit soared from $6 billion to $27 billion in just 5 years.

TABLE 27-1: U.S. Trade Patterns in Computer Equipment[1] in 1997
(millions of dollars; percent)

Exports			Imports		
Regions[2]	Value[3]	Share, %	Regions[2]	Value[3]	Share, %
NAFTA	7,701	18.6	NAFTA	7,862	11.5
Latin America	4,192	10.1	Latin America	45	0.1
Western Europe	15,186	36.7	Western Europe	5,518	8.1
Japan/Chinese Economic Area	7,328	17.7	Japan/Chinese Economic Area	28,501	41.6
Other Asia	4,530	10.9	Other Asia	25,765	37.7
Rest of world	2,443	5.9	Rest of world	741	1.1
World	41,380	100.0	World	68,433	100.0
Top Five Countries	Value	Share, %	Top Five Countries	Value	Share, %
Canada	5,343	12.9	Japan	14,659	21.4
Japan	4,896	11.8	Singapore	12,959	18.9
United Kingdom	4,134	10.0	Taiwan	9,600	14.0
Netherlands	3,263	7.9	Mexico	4,436	6.5
Germany	2,656	6.4	Malaysia	4,193	6.1

[1] SIC 3571, 3572, 3575, 3577.
[2] For definitions of regional groupings, see "Getting the Most Out of *Outlook '99*."
[3] Values may not sum to total due to rounding.
Source: U.S. Department of Commerce, Bureau of the Census.

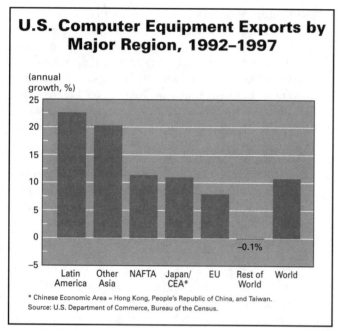

U.S. Computer Equipment Exports by Major Region, 1992–1997

(annual growth, %)

* Chinese Economic Area = Hong Kong, People's Republic of China, and Taiwan.
Source: U.S. Department of Commerce, Bureau of the Census.

FIGURE 27-2

Manufacturing. The U.S. computer equipment industry is experiencing a dramatic shift in the way it manufactures, manages inventory, and distributes products. Responding to the success of Dell Computer's efforts, other major vendors, such as Compaq, IBM, and Hewlett-Packard, have begun implementing build-to-order (BTO) programs for individual buyers and configure-to-order (CTO) programs for their distribution channel partners, covering desktops and some notebook products. Instead of manufacturing to meet a forecast demand and building up costly inventories as they had in the past, companies that use these distribution models have been able to match supply more closely with actual demand and to control more precisely their inventories of parts and finished machines. These programs are providing significant benefits to both manufacturers and customers. Manufacturers have lower inventory costs and deliver their products more quickly. Dell, for example, has its parts shipped on a just-in-time basis and reportedly can build a custom PC 4 hours after it obtains an order over the telephone or the Internet. These firms receive a continuous flow of important information from their customers on their needs and on product quality and performance which they can use to work with parts suppliers to redesign and improve their systems. Customers have a greater range of choices and purchase exactly what they want in terms of performance and functionality. They also receive some of the manufacturers' savings in inventory costs through cheaper prices.

After declining steadily through 1994 partly as a result of restructuring and layoffs, total and production worker employment in the U.S.-based computer industry has been on an upswing over the last few years. Many of the leading U.S. computer systems and peripheral manufacturers, such as Compaq, Dell, Hewlett-Packard, IBM, Quantum, and Seagate, signifi-

cantly expanded their employment rosters in 1996 and 1997. Numerous small to medium-size firms entering the market to supply high demand growth products have been another major source of increased employment. An estimated 20,000 new employees were added to the industry's labor force in the United States from 1995 to 1997, more than half of whom were production workers. This resurgence resulted in part from the strength of the overall U.S. economy.

This upward growth trend in employment may moderate in the future. According to the Bureau of Labor Statistics (BLS), the U.S. computer manufacturing industry will have the fastest projected rate of growth in real output of any U.S. industry, achieving 14.9 percent annual increases through 2006. The BLS predicts that the downside of this growth in output is that competitive pressures and the necessity to keep up with market demand will force the industry to produce more with a smaller number of workers. Other factors which may adversely affect U.S.-based employment include a shift among U.S.-based computer firms from equipment manufacturing toward software development and services, ongoing consolidation within the industry, and increasing use of electronic commerce to market products, which will reduce the need for additional sales staff.

Research and Development. R&D will continue to be an important factor in maintaining the technological leadership of the U.S. computer industry and determining the capabilities and applications of computer equipment in the years to come. According to the January–February 1998 issue of *Research Technology Management,* U.S. computer firms were expected to increase their spending on R&D nearly 7 percent in 1998 and devote 6.3 percent of their sales to this activity, the highest ratio in any major U.S. manufacturing industry. IBM in particular has moved to the top of the list of companies that develop advanced technologies, receiving 1,867 U.S. patents in 1996 with an investment of nearly $4 billion. Along with other major U.S. computer firms, IBM has begun to focus on extracting greater value from its research dollars, sometimes through collaborative efforts.

In the area of high-performance computing research, the U.S. Department of Energy (DOE) has a $940 million Accelerated Strategic Computing Initiative (ASCI) to build supercomputers that will operate at 100 trillion floating point operations per second (teraflops) by 2004 and can be used to test the safety and reliability of the nation's nuclear stockpile through simulation rather than physical testing. Cray Research and IBM were slated to deliver systems with a performance of 3 teraflops to DOE laboratories in 1998.

The U.S. government has initiated broadly based, $1 billion a year Federal Computing, Information, and Communications (CIC) programs to advance the state of the art in supercomputer hardware, software, and networking technologies and to use information technology to improve biomedical research, education, emergency response times, manufacturing, national security, public health, and science and engineering. The three largest R&D efforts within the CIC are High End Computing and Computation (HECC), Large Scale Networking (LSN), and Human Centered Systems (HuCS). Among the goals of HECC is the eventual development of computer systems with performances approaching a million billion floating point operations per second (petaflops), a thousand times more powerful than the largest massively parallel computer today. This program also is investigating advanced concepts in quantum, biological, and optical computing.

The Next Generation Internet (NGI) initiative is an important part of the LSN and will work on creating high-performance networks with data transfer rates 1,000 times faster than that which is currently available over the Internet. It is closely associated with the $500 million Internet2 program, an independent cooperative effort involving 122 U.S. universities and firms in the computer and communications industries that will create broadband applications, engineering technologies, and network management tools for academic research and education. It is hoped that both programs will provide the basis for revolutionary applications such as remote medicine, more sophisticated weather forecasting, and distance learning.

The HuCS program in fiscal year 1998 will continue to focus on ensuring that advanced computing systems and communications networks are readily accessible to and usable by federal agencies and the general public. Its efforts will include developing knowledge repositories and information agents that sort, analyze, and present massive amounts of multimedia and multisource information; systems that permit multimodal human-systems interactions such as speech, touch, and gesture recognition and synthesis; and virtual reality environments and their use in scientific research, health care, manufacturing, and training.

PROJECTIONS OF INDUSTRY AND TRADE GROWTH FOR THE NEXT 1 AND 5 YEARS

The U.S. computer equipment industry's product shipments in current dollars should rebound in 1999, rising 10 percent to an estimated $112 billion (see Figure 27-3 and Table 27-2). Unit shipments of computer systems will increase at a rapid pace, but severe price competition in PCs and hard disk drives will dampen overall growth in computer equipment value slightly. U.S. business and government purchases of computers will slow temporarily as those users divert some of their spending from information technology products to handle the year 2000 problem. On the positive side, product shipments will gain from a recovery in exports and greater worldwide demand for servers, workstations, and PCs costing under $1,000 in the home user sector from first-time buyers and others replacing and adding systems.

U.S. computer equipment trade should be vibrant (see Figure 27-3). Exports are expected to increase 9 percent to $48 billion in 1999, benefiting from continued strong demand in Europe and Latin America and a gradual economic recovery in Asia. Imports again will grow faster than will exports and should reach $92 billion as a result of U.S. companies' continued dependence on Asia for the sourcing of peripherals and parts and the efforts of foreign firms to expand their presence in the U.S. computer systems market. As a result of this surge in imports, the U.S. computer equipment trade deficit should continue to worsen, rising to an estimated $44 billion.

The principal driving force behind computer demand over the next 5 years will continue to be the development of the Global Information Infrastructure (GII) through the expansion of the Internet and corporate local area networks (LANs) and

TABLE 27-2: Computers and Peripherals (SIC 3571, 3572, 3575, 3577) Trends and Forecasts

(millions of dollars except as noted)

	1992	1993	1994	1995	1996	1997[1]	1998[2]	1999[3]	Percent Change 96–97	97–98	98–99	92–96[4]
Industry data												
Value of shipments[5]	61,969	64,374	73,345	86,078	97,592	106,000	115,000	125,000	8.6	8.5	8.7	12.0
Total employment (thousands)	221	211	201	210	221	230	240	250	4.1	4.3	4.0	0.0
Production workers (thousands)	74.2	73.9	75.8	78.9	83.4	92	96	100	10.3	4.3	4.0	3.0
Average hourly earnings ($)	12.26	12.77	13.67	13.49	14.84							4.9
Capital expenditures	2,137	2,045	1,907	1,902	2,684							5.9
Product data												
Value of shipments[5]	54,722	57,928	65,635	81,356	85,441	94,000	101,500	112,000	10.0	8.0	10.3	11.8
Product shipments (1992$)	54,722	67,686	87,679	130,046	192,492	286,833						36.9
Trade data												
Value of imports	30,710	36,978	45,124	55,185	60,245	68,433	79,300	92,000	13.6	15.9	16.0	18.3
Value of exports	24,879	25,276	28,956	34,294	37,621	41,380	44,100	48,000	10.0	6.6	8.8	10.9

[1] Estimate except exports and imports.
[2] Estimate.
[3] Forecast.
[4] Compound annual rate.
[5] For definition of industry versus product values, see "Getting the Most Out of *Outlook '99.*"
Source: U.S. Department of Commerce: Bureau of the Census; International Trade Administration.

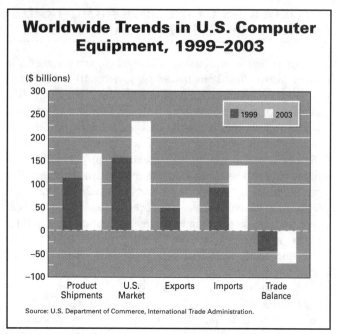

Worldwide Trends in U.S. Computer Equipment, 1999–2003

($ billions)

Source: U.S. Department of Commerce, International Trade Administration.

FIGURE 27-3

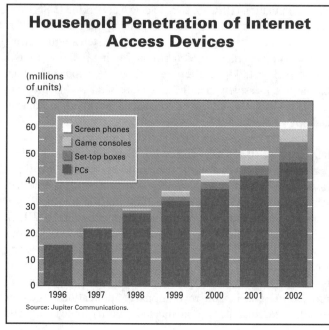

Household Penetration of Internet Access Devices

(millions of units)

Screen phones
Game consoles
Set-top boxes
PCs

Source: Jupiter Communications.

FIGURE 27-4

intranets. This development will be stimulated by a growing awareness in governments and the private sector in the big emerging markets (BEMs) and other developing nations that computers are critical to economic development and international competitiveness. Corporate markets for desktop PCs in the United States and Europe will become saturated, essentially replacement markets, but those markets still will have a significant need for servers to manage networks. Larger enterprises in the BEMs and small to medium-size enterprises overseas will emerge as important customers for U.S. computer equipment suppliers. Business use of palmtop and mobile computers will increase, especially in service occupations.

PC manufacturers will face a growing challenge from products produced by other information technology industries such as information appliances, set-top boxes, Web TVs, and personal communication devices, especially in the area of Internet access. In 1996 there were only 15.2 million household Internet access devices, virtually all of them PCs (see Figure 27-4). By 2002 PCs will account for only 75 percent of the estimated 62.3 million Internet access devices. The impact on computer equipment shipments is unclear, since some information appliances may be considered computers.

Computers may become ubiquitous in the future as personal-use applications grow. In "smart" cars they not only will be used to control engine functions as they do today but will handle navigation, climate control, and security systems as well as providing hands-free communications, Internet access, and driver information. They will allow people in remote areas to discuss their health problems with and receive diagnosis and treatment for certain illnesses from distantly located doctors and hospitals. The use of computers in the home will continue to broaden and will include formal education, entertainment, environmental and appliance control, security, electronic banking, and videoconfer-

encing with family members, friends, and vendors. Computers also will act as intelligent agents to provide people with personal counseling, scheduling, and instruction services. Home users in the United States and other developed nations will need more than one PC to handle this wider range of applications. Many of them are likely to develop their own networks to tie together these systems. Because of their continued strength in many of these areas, U.S. companies should be well suited to serve this demand. In this scenario, product shipments of the U.S.-based computer industry should increase 10 percent each year in current dollars to $165 billion by 2003 (see Figure 27-3).

Trade. In the area of trade, exports of U.S. computer equipment will remain strong and will continue to bolster the industry's product shipments. These exports should grow at a solid 10 percent rate, reaching $70 billion in 2003. The U.S.-based computer industry will continue to make major export sales to Canada and Europe but will depend more on Asia and Latin America for future growth. Demand in Asia and Latin America is expected to increase at a much faster rate as long as there is long-term economic and financial stability. U.S. exporters also should find greater opportunities for sales in other markets, such as eastern Europe, Russia, and the Middle East.

Imports are expected to expand at a 11 percent average annual rate to an estimated $140 billion in 2003. They should maintain nearly a 60 percent share of the U.S. computer equipment market as foreign suppliers use aggressive pricing to compete for corporate accounts and home users and U.S. firms continue to source from overseas suppliers. Although most of this import value will continue to come from Asia, Mexico may play a larger role because of NAFTA. Foreign suppliers are also likely to establish new facilities or expand their existing U.S. production facilities to help meet U.S. demand. These suppliers, mainly Asian, will continue to rely on parts and peripherals from their parent companies, contributing to the ever-widening computer equipment trade deficit. The overall computer trade deficit should increase to around $70 billion, which will equal the value of U.S. computer equipment exports in 2003.

GLOBAL MARKET PROSPECTS

Sources of Future Demand

Opportunities for U.S. computer equipment exporters will be very promising well into the next century if major barriers to information technology product and services trade continue to fall. The worldwide computer equipment market is expected to grow 9.2 percent annually from 1997 to reach an estimated $442.5 billion by 2001, according to IDC. Although commercial users still will represent the majority of this market, the home user sector will expand rapidly with the continued introduction of low-cost desktop and portable PC systems and growing consumer interest in the Internet. Spending on multi-user systems will increase at an average annual rate just slightly ahead of PC growth projections through 2001. However, the value of this market still will be less than half that projected for PCs by the end of this period.

Asia and western Europe will remain the largest regional computer equipment markets outside North America during this period, according to IDC. Although considerably lower in value, emerging markets in Africa and the Middle East, eastern Europe, and Latin America will grow at much faster average annual rates of 19, 14, and 17 percent, respectively. Severe price competition among U.S. and foreign suppliers should make low-end systems more affordable and increase purchases of PCs in markets where penetration rates are currently much lower than they are in the United States and where disposable incomes are rising. Japan will continue to be the largest single market for systems overseas despite the dampening effect of its economic woes on computer demand over the past several years. While not approaching the total value of the Japanese market, some countries are poised for phenomenal growth in the future. China is a prime example: Its computer systems market is expected to nearly triple to $15 billion by 2001. Other countries with high growth potential include Brazil, India, Mexico, Russia, South Korea, and Turkey.

Competition from Asian computer equipment manufacturers should continue to intensify. Japanese firms will pose the biggest challenge and will try to use their substantial financial resources to price their products aggressively and wrest market share from U.S. suppliers. Several Chinese, South Korean, and Taiwanese companies are also likely to emerge as major competitors in low-end PCs. U.S. leadership in the markets for high-performance systems, workstations, desktop PCs, and key peripherals such as hard disk drives and nonimpact printers will depend largely on the industry's retaining its strength in research, design, software development, marketing, and customer service and support.

Effects of International Agreements and Issues

The Information Technology Agreement (ITA), which was implemented on July 1, 1997, will have a positive impact on U.S. computer exports and the industry's international competitiveness. Under the terms of the agreement, most of the 43 participating countries will eliminate tariffs on covered products by 2000. As of May 20, 1998, signatories to the ITA included Australia, Canada, Chinese Taipei, the Czech Republic, Costa Rica, El Salvador, Estonia, the European Union (15 nations), Hong Kong, Iceland, India, Indonesia, Israel, Japan, Liechtenstein, Macao, Malaysia, New Zealand, Norway, the Philippines, Poland, Romania, Singapore, the Slovak Republic, South Korea, Switzerland, Thailand, Turkey, and the United States. A few developing countries have been granted extensions on a limited number of products, but in no case will tariffs be permitted after 2005. Tariff elimination generally will take place in four equal steps on July 1, 1997; January 1, 1998; January 1, 1999; and January 1, 2000.

The ITA covers over 93 percent of world trade in information technology products. Global trade in products covered by the ITA is expected to exceed $1 trillion by the turn of the century. Products covered by the ITA include semiconductors and other electronic components, most semiconductor manufacturing equipment, analytical instruments, computer software, digital photocopiers, most telecommunications equipment, printed circuit boards, and process controls. In addition to the existing 43 signatories, several countries are actively considering participating in the ITA, including Armenia, Egypt, Guatemala, Latvia, Lithuania, Panama, and the People's Republic of China.

Negotiations, initially slated to conclude by June 30, 1998, continued in order to expand product coverage and accelerate tariff reductions for the ITA; this process is generally known as ITA-II. The United States has indicated strong interest in addressing nontariff measures. Failure to reach agreement on additional product coverage by June 30 led to continuation of the negotiations during July 16–17, which also resulted in participants being unable to reach consensus on an agreed list of product additions. Since no party wanted to close out the negotiation or have a result which could not be accepted by consensus, countries agreed to consult bilaterally and plurilaterally until late September with a view toward reconvening at a date later in 1998.

Tim Miles, Daniel Valverde, Richard Dickerson, and Bryan Larson, U.S. Department of Commerce, Computer Systems Division, Office of Computers and Business Equipment, (202) 482-0571, October 1998.

PERSONAL COMPUTERS

The personal computer product sector includes a growing variety of devices, among them desktop and deskside computers, network servers, portable computers (including notebooks, hand-held pen-based tablets, and transportables), network terminals, and even wearable PCs. Personal computers usually are differentiated from more powerful workstations, which generally are used in financial modeling, graphics design, and engineering and scientific applications. Workstations have fast reduced instruction-set computing (RISC) microprocessors, more graphics capabilities, and better display resolution and usually run on a UNIX operating system rather than Windows, OS/2, or the Macintosh OS. However, a new category of PC workstations is emerging as PC-based processors, operating systems, hard drives, and other components become more powerful. Prices for PCs range from below $100 for used computers to more than $10,000 for the most powerful, fully configured systems. Personal computers fall under SIC 3571, electronic computers.

Market Size and Growth

U.S. PC market growth accelerated in 1997 after a period of slower growth in 1996. Shipments, including PC servers, desktops, and portables, totaled 30 million units, up 21 percent from 1996, according to Dataquest (see Figure 27-5). Sales revenues, which were affected by declining prices, rose 17 percent to $70 billion after growing 26 percent in 1996. These figures cover computers manufactured in the United States by domestic and foreign firms, plus imports. PCs with fifth- and sixth-generation Pentium-type processors represented almost 95 percent of the market, while new PCs based on older 80486 and 68xxx chips were almost nonexistent. RISC-based PCs using PowerPC, MIPS, and Alpha processors accounted for the remainder of the market. In 1997 the U.S. installed base of personal computers exceeded 110 million units.

The PC market will continue to experience favorable growth rates through 1998, but while unit sales rise, market competi-

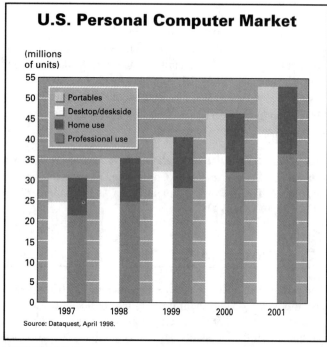

U.S. Personal Computer Market

(millions of units)

Legend: Portables, Desktop/deskside, Home use, Professional use

Source: Dataquest, April 1998.

FIGURE 27-5

tion and the move to PCs costing under $1,000 will continue to put pressure on revenues and profits. Unit shipments should grow around 15 percent with revenues increasing 10 percent, according to IDC. Prices for mainstream Pentium computers will continue to fall throughout 1998 as Intel further reduces the prices of Pentium II chips. Because of market saturation, PC firms must concentrate on the replacement market, which is characterized by more sophisticated buyers who want new and useful technology. Interest from first-time buyers also will increase, stimulated by declining prices and the availability of less expensive scaled-down machines.

Market growth in the range of 14 to 17 percent should continue into the next century, with annual shipments exceeding 60 million units by the year 2002. By that time computer use in the United States will be substantially more pervasive, especially in households and educational institutions, and will affect more human activities. Consumer sales will define the market as telecommuting, electronic commerce, digital home "infotainment" systems, and Internet access attain high levels of market penetration. There will be more types of computers, from single-use to multipurpose devices; networks will be all-encompassing (including in the home); and the use of portable and wireless technologies will be widespread. Many of the distinct and competing technologies that exist today for communications, entertainment, education, and commerce will be obsolete or will converge into single systems. New computer designs will take advantage of this convergence to exploit new technologies.

Market Trends

One factor that sets computers apart from most other products is their constantly improving ratio of price to performance. System performance continues to improve, while prices for similarly configured computers decline, although purchasers continue to spend in the range of $1,500 to $2,000 for a complete PC system with fresh technology. Storage capacity in standard desktop systems has moved to multigigabyte ranges, CD-ROM (read-only memory) drive access times have increased significantly, digital video disk (DVD) and recordable CD-ROM drives are now available, microprocessor speeds continue to increase, typical internal memory allocation is expanding beyond 32 megabytes, 17-inch and larger cathode-ray tube (CRT) monitors are becoming standard, flat panel displays for notebook computers have swelled to 14 inches, and LCD panels are now available for desktop computers. Communication bandwidth and speeds have also risen with the advent of 56K modems, integrated services digital network (ISDN) lines, cable modems, and higher-capacity networks.

Intense price competition and declining prices continue to define the PC landscape. Average prices for all PCs should drop 10 percent in 1998, over twice the decline in 1997, while notebook computers as a group could approach a 15 percent reduction. However, discounts on some PCs will range as high as 25 to 35 percent. Pushed by strong competitors, foreign production in the United States, and an increasingly price-sensitive market at home and abroad, U.S. vendors continue to cut operating and distribution costs and introduce less expensive models. In 1997 there were continuing steep declines in prices for microprocessors, flat panel displays, disk drives, and memory chips because of excess inventories and softening demand. Prices for 16-megabit DRAM dropped as much as 30 percent in 1997. Because of narrow profit margins, future price cuts for computers will depend more on reduced production, distribution, and component costs. Manufacturers will place more emphasis on these factors to balance the demands of a competitive marketplace with the need for an adequate return on investment.

Rapid technological advances continue to shorten product life cycles, putting more pressure on companies' bottom lines and making product delivery and inventory control more critical exercises for PC producers. The estimated product life of a personal computer has decreased from 5 years in 1981 to less than 6 months today, with R&D and market introduction phases shrinking accordingly. PC product cycles are mainly a function of the introduction of new microprocessors. Since 1978 Intel has moved to a new generation of chips (P1 through P6) every 42 months on average and has introduced a growing variety of versions with progressively faster speeds and improved features within each generation. In 1997 over 20 Intel Pentium and Pentium Pro processors with different megahertz (MHz) ratings were sold in PCs. AMD and Cyrix marketed 10 Pentium-equivalent chips, while Motorola and IBM offered more than 30 PowerPC microprocessors. In early 1998 Intel unveiled its 440BX Accelerated Graphics Port (AGP) chipset with 350- and 400-MHz Pentium IIs. These new processors are designed for a 100-MHz external bus which will allow speedier communications among components on the motherboard and provide more realistic three-dimensional images, videoconferencing capabilities, and better-quality movies. Intel also debuted Celeron, which is a stripped-down Pentium II chip, for the sub-$1,000 PC market.

Market saturation is another critical issue faced by PC vendors. Lucrative sectors such as medium-size to large businesses, government agencies, and upper-income consumers now constitute replacement markets, and this has forced suppliers to focus on more cost-conscious customers. While replacement markets respond mostly to technical innovation, success in the new areas depends more heavily on marketing skills and meeting the needs and whims of individual customers. As PCs proliferate and become more like consumer electronics commodities, suppliers must adopt new marketing strategies to promote brand awareness and differentiate their products from the competition. Since the birth of the PC two decades ago marketing campaigns have focused on technology features, performance, and, more recently, price reductions, but tactics increasingly emphasize ease of use, functionality, esthetics, product support, and the bundling of popular software. Specific examples include adding scanners and telephones to computers, designing in modularity and upgrade features, incorporating "plug-and-play" standards, producing ergonomically improved equipment, customizing user interfaces, and offering new cabinet designs.

Another indication of commoditization in the industry is companies' use of multiple distribution channels to reach new customers. The foray of PC vendors into mass-marketing channels and national television advertising that began in the 1990s has become an industry fixture. Now PCs are sold through the same marketing channels as are consumer electronic items. In 1997 these channels included dealers (27 percent of sales), direct-response telemarketers (18 percent), PC specialty stores and superstores (17 percent), value-added resellers [VARs] (14 percent), direct-sales forces (8 percent), consumer electronics stores (8 percent), and other retail outlets (8 percent), according to Dataquest. With the exception of significant growth in sales over the Internet, there should be minimal shifts in market share among the various market channels. The outlets with the highest projected growth through 2000 are direct-response and large computer and office product stores. Large retailers will focus on providing more product support and services to their customers, while major computer vendors will try to emulate the success of direct-response sellers, such as Dell Computer, which have perfected the BTO manufacturing and marketing model. Suppliers that sell through dealers and distributors are moving more custom configuration and assembly out to the distribution channel to better meet customer demand.

As the market expands, the user base continues to fragment into more distinct segments. Businesses in 1997 purchased about 57 percent of all the PCs sold. In 1998 prospects for this sector remained good as companies continued to upgrade to faster computers to accommodate improved operating environments such as Windows 98 and Windows NT 5.0 and more robust 32-bit software applications. Companies also continue to downsize from mainframe and midrange-based systems to PC-based client-server networks and intranets and to extend PC use into blue-collar service areas with pen-based and other special application devices. The corporate sector will lead the market in the foreseeable future as more companies strive to improve productivity and global competitiveness.

Subsectors. Major vendors are beginning to target small businesses, which constitute the least penetrated, fastest growing business sector. Dataquest estimated that sales to this sector would grow over 31 percent in 1998, with the fastest increase occurring in firms with 10 to 49 employees. Market drivers include strong U.S. employment and economic growth, the improved availability of PCs in consumer outlets at attractive prices, and new efforts by major vendors to address the specific needs of these companies, most of which have limited resources and technical know-how. Sales to the more than 9 million firms with fewer than 100 employees, which represent more than 60 percent of all business employees, constitute the largest share of shipments to the U.S. business sector. This share could exceed 40 percent by the year 2000.

In the home sector over 40 percent of the approximately 100 million U.S. households owned PCs in 1997, while one-fourth of PC households had more than one computer. Given the size of this potential market, vendors must base computer designs on consumer preferences and needs in addition to performance enhancement. After years of slow growth, sales to the nation's households jumped dramatically in 1994 and 1995 as major vendors focused on consumer marketing, which previously had taken a backseat to corporate sales. Growth in that period averaged 30 percent per year. Aggressive pricing, initiated by Compaq, and mass merchant marketing, pioneered by Packard Bell, set the stage for jump starting this sector. However, this rapid growth has slowed, and home purchases in 1997 were estimated at 9.2 million units, representing a 19 percent increase over 1996.

In addition to lower prices, improved consumer software, educational needs, and the popularity of on-line information services and the World Wide Web, this sector is driven by growth in the work-at-home phenomenon. IDC reports that there were 34.7 million U.S. households with home offices in 1997, including home-based businesses (full-time and part-time), after-hours workers, and telecommuters, up 16 percent over 1996. Two-thirds of those households owned computers. Corporate trends (downsizing and outsourcing), lifestyle choices (spending more time at home), and technological advances (the Internet, remote computer access, better voice and data communications, affordable multifunction peripherals) have combined to drive this market. It is estimated that the number of work-at-home households will grow around 10 percent annually into the next decade.

Sales of PCs to all educational institutions in the United States in 1997 exceeded 1.8 million units, about 6 percent of total shipments for that year, according to Dataquest. In the 107,700 public and private kindergarten-to-twelfth-grade schools, about 7 million PCs have been installed, but most are located in computer laboratories and libraries and have not significantly penetrated the classroom for instructional purposes. Additional funding, more curriculum-based software, lower prices, and greater technological awareness among teachers and administrators will lead to higher growth in this sector. Sales also will be driven by the growing number of students with PCs at home, more on-line connectivity, and the government's push to wire schools for Internet access. The proliferation of computers capable of multimedia presentations, given that most new PCs come multimedia-ready, will render the installed base increasingly useful for teaching purposes. IDC has estimated that U.S. spending on instructional technology (hardware, software, training, services, on-line access, and networks) will grow from $4.16 billion in the 1996–1997 school year to $9.88 billion in 2001–2002. Expenditures for on-line services and networks will grow the fastest, with LAN penetration reaching 80 percent during this period. Hardware sales represented about half of total spending in 1996–1997. With almost 68 million students in 15,000 school districts throughout the United States, this market sector will invite heightened vendor interest as technology increasingly pervades the classroom. By comparison, there are about 70 million corporate "seats" in the United States.

National, state, and local governments represent a small but growing market segment, accounting for about 7 percent of all PCs shipped in the United States in 1997, according to Dataquest. Shipments exceeded 2.2 million units and were valued at over $5.8 billion in that year. Changes in the federal government's procurement process and the elimination of maximum order limits in 1996 have spurred a significant increase in microcomputer purchases off the General Services Administration's (GSA) Schedule 70 B/C. Because buying off the GSA Schedule and by credit card in the open market offers more choices and is quicker with less paperwork, there has been a marked shift away from large indefinite-delivery, indefinite-quantity (IDIQ) contracts, which offer fixed configurations and prices. There is also a trend toward agencies leasing PCs and outsourcing their procurement and management. IDC estimated that over 670,000 PCs valued at over $2 billion would be shipped to the federal government during fiscal year 1998. There is currently an installed base of around 2.7 million PCs in the federal government, over 90 percent of which are connected to LANs. Future demand for information technology at all levels of government will be stimulated by a greater emphasis on enhancing employee productivity through the ongoing modernization of government programs.

Future Outlook

In addition to declining prices, three areas of technology drive the PC market today: multimedia, mobile computing, and computer networking. These technologies extend the functionality of PCs, adapting them to serve new consumer uses and an expanding array of operations in the business world.

The concept of multimedia evolved during the 1990s from a group of technologies that enabled PCs to process graphics, sound, and video files along with text into a more encompassing concept that covers interactive television, videoconferencing, voice recognition, electronic games, virtual reality, and the World Wide Web. Today most PCs come standard with some multimedia capability, defined as the ability to process a combination of more than two media (e.g., text, animation, and sound), some of which are time-sequenced. Fully equipped multimedia PCs include video and sound boards, speakers, CD or DVD drives, and sufficient memory, storage, and processing power to handle this capability.

Estimates of the size of the multimedia hardware and software market vary, depending on the scope of its definition. Dataquest put the 1997 market at $124 billion, growing to over $260 billion by 2001, and divided the market into four categories: (1) computer-based hardware (PCs, add-in boards, CD-ROM drives, videoconferencing systems, etc.), which makes up over 80 percent of the total, (2) computer-based software (multimedia authoring tools, voice recognition software, video servers, etc.), (3) television-based hardware (set-top boxes, digital broadcast system [DBS] receivers, video game players, etc.), and (4) television-based software (video game cartridges and CD-ROMs). Average revenue growth over the next several years has been estimated at 16 percent for computer-based multimedia products and 25 percent for television-based multimedia products.

The integrated and interactive capabilities of multimedia bring PCs a step closer to realizing their enormous potential in education, training, entertainment, and information services. However, multimedia is still an evolving set of technologies and products, and serious issues remain to be solved. The delivery of increasing amounts of video and graphics information over communications lines requires significantly more bandwidth capacity than exists today in many networks. There are also continuing vendor disputes over technical standards for file formats, user interfaces, data compression schemes, and communications protocols. All this activity is advancing before a backdrop of uncertainty concerning the types of new information products and services that will emerge and the magnitude of user demand for those services. It is likely that with affordable pricing, consumers will purchase improved opportunities for person-to-person communications (cellular, paging, E-mail, satellite communications, etc.), but demand is less certain for more engaging electronic entertainment and more abundant and interactive sources of information. For example, the number of cellular telephone subscribers has grown 44 percent a year since 1989 and now almost equals the number of cable television subscribers. However, experiments with interactive television and video-on-demand services in selected communities have not been overly successful because of steep development costs, high fees, and lack of consumer acceptance. Nevertheless, the introduction of digital television and programming at the end of 1998 was expected to provide new opportunities for home-based interactive media and another test bed for consumer demand. However, the initial high costs of digital television sets will delay their widespread use.

CD-ROM drives, based on optical technology and having a storage capacity of 700 megabytes, are a key component of a multimedia computer. These devices were introduced in the early 1990s, first as parts of upgrade kits and then as standard components on most PCs. The market is now entering a transition phase from CD-ROM to DVD-ROM. Although DVD drives are about double the price of CD drives, they have better audio-video quality and can store from 4.7 gigabytes on single-sided, single-layer models to 17 gigabytes on double-sided, dual-layer models. That is enough capacity for full-length Hollywood movies and complex three-dimensional computer games. Delayed by controversies, recently resolved, over content copyright protection and DVD format protocols, the market reached 754,000 units sold in 1997 and should grow to over 123 million by 2001, according to IDC. In 1999, DVD sales should take off and surpass CD sales worldwide as prices drop and content is developed. Like CD-ROMs, DVD drives will initially be sold mostly as add-on kits.

The popularity of mobile computing and complementary wireless voice communication devices, like that of cellular phones, reflects America's changing work patterns and lifestyles. Consumers want to compute while traveling and communicate with anyone from anywhere, while businesses are adapting mobile devices for such tasks as inventory control, equipment maintenance, delivery services, and remote sales. At the heart of mobile computing is a growing array of portable devices, including notebook computers, hand-held PCs, pen-based tablets, and personal information devices. Technological advances in size reduction, power consumption, function integration, usability, and wireless transmission continue to expand market frontiers. The portable computer market, representing

about 20 percent of total PC sales in the United States, has always grown faster than have desktop sales. If technology and infrastructure development continue to advance, its share could rise to 30 percent by 2000.

Portable computers are projected to have an average annual worldwide growth of 17 percent through 2002, outpacing the 15 percent estimate for desktops in terms of unit shipments. Notebook computers make up the bulk of this category, while sub-notebooks continue to cater to a more highly mobile market niche and search for more market acceptance. Notebooks with faster processors (such as the Pentium II), larger displays (up to 14 inches), more magnetic storage and memory, built-in DVD and CD-ROM drives, expanded docking station options, and network capabilities are increasing interest in this form factor as a primary or complementary computing device. Growth is moderating in developed markets as replacement sales outpace sales to new users. Weakness in the Japanese economy has reduced demand in a market where portables account for about 40 percent of total PC sales. However, as prices have dropped below $2,000 for mainstream models, new opportunities have arisen in the telecommuting, education, and small office–home office (SOHO) markets in the United States and overseas. When price points drop closer to desktop levels, the consumer market for portables should begin to take off.

With improving technologies, hand-held computers are making a significant comeback since the days when the ill-fated Newton PDA (personal digital assistant) was introduced by Apple Computer. These devices are entering a new generation of product development which is characterized by a growing proliferation of form factors with varying sizes, weights, processors, input technologies (keyboard, stylus, and voice), and operating systems. Despite these hardware differences, hand-helds share similar functions: personal information management (calendars, address lists, memos), mobile data collection, and remote data, E-mail, and Internet access. As these devices become more functional and user-friendly while maintaining their sub-$500 prices and portability, they will begin to replace notebook computers for certain purposes. Handwriting recognition and voice input are two technologies that are key to making hand-held computers ubiquitous personal companions for both professional and private use.

Networking and the Internet. Networking is having an increasingly profound effect on the PC industry, from LANs and wide area networks (WANs) to the Internet and intranets. Most of the business PCs in the United States are now connected via a LAN, and 85 percent of all organizations with more than 100 employees have a LAN installed. In 1997, $41 billion was spent worldwide on network interface cards, switches, routers, hubs, modems, and other data communications equipment, up 20 percent from 1996, according to IDC. Networking and client-server technologies have enabled the PC to play a greater role in mission-critical business functions, expanding its value to companies and reducing the status of legacy mainframe and midrange systems. LAN functions are graduating from traditional print sharing, file transfer, and E-mail uses to transaction processing, management support, and Internet access applications. To alleviate bandwidth limitations brought on by increasing LAN traffic and file complexity, organizations are adopting new switching technologies and installing higher-speed communications backbones. Users are also seeking to link LANs to wider areas to accommodate regional offices and provide remote access to home workers.

The burgeoning growth in dedicated network server sales has paralleled the spread of networks. The U.S. PC/NT server market, which represents about 35 percent of worldwide shipments, exceeded 658,000 units in 1997 and grew 55 percent over 1996, according to IDC. Three-quarters of these units were multiprocessor-capable systems. While a number of converted desktop PCs are currently used as servers, they are steadily being replaced by increasingly more powerful multiprocessor machines that are designed solely to operate networks. The demand for these servers has been pushed by growing organizational needs for E-mail, groupware, and file/print-sharing capabilities. The increasing performance and economies of PC-based architectures, the growing robustness of network software, and the popularity of Windows NT are also factors in stimulating demand. Dataquest estimated 1997 worldwide PC server shipments at 1.7 million units, which were divided by type: file/print servers (74 percent), database servers (10 percent), E-mail servers (6 percent), compute servers (3 percent), media servers (2 percent), and other servers (5 percent).

As PC technology further penetrates corporate data centers and mission-critical functions, server sales will continue to expand substantially in every region of the world. In the United States, PC servers should exceed 25 percent growth over the next several years but should show slightly lower growth globally because of the expected slowdown in sales in Japan and other Asian markets. PC vendors are also positioning their high-end computers to compete with traditional UNIX and RISC processor-based workstations in the graphics and computer-aided design/computer-aided manufacturing (CAD/CAM) markets. Pressured by competition from low-end suppliers and the need for higher profit margins, major PC vendors will continue to expand the performance capabilities of their machines. In the PC server area there is growing consolidation among vendors; in 1997 the top four vendors had over 65 percent of the market.

Like multimedia in the early 1990s, the Internet is creating a revolution in the way PCs are used in organizations and households. In 1997 the number of Internet users worldwide was estimated at 100 million by Computer Industry Almanac Inc., and there were over 29 million host computers on the Internet. After traditional business applications, the Internet could historically be the biggest driver of PC sales, especially in the home, as the World Wide Web takes on more electronic commerce and consumer applications. Since the Internet is a global phenomenon, demand for PCs and network servers will be stimulated in all regions. Although the United States accounts for about two-thirds of host computers and over half of all Internet users, other countries are creating sites and users at a fast pace, led by Japan and western Europe, and so the U.S. share will diminish accordingly. In fact, the United States ranks

fourth in Internet users per capita, lagging behind the Scandinavian countries. Organization-specific intranets are also gaining in popularity. It has been estimated that over 90 percent of Fortune 1000 companies have either established or plan to establish intranets. These are closed or tightly controlled networks within the Internet that are used for E-mail, information dissemination, and other business functions.

To meet the call for computers that cost less to purchase and manage in a network setting, a new "paradigm" was introduced in 1996: the thin client or network computer. These devices harken back to the days of terminals connected to mainframe computers. They are simplified, "closed box" computers with minimal local memory and storage capability that are designed to access applications and data from servers. There are currently two varieties: (1) Network computers, promoted by Oracle, Sun Microsystems, and IBM, are intended to work on most server platforms and allow some local processing via a Java Virtual Machine, and (2) Windows-based terminals, supported by Microsoft and Intel and slated for volume shipments in 1998, run mainly Windows applications, utilize the Windows CE operating system, and are totally server-centric with no local processing. These computers should appeal more to enterprises with large amounts of legacy data on traditional mainframe systems.

The market for network computers is still undeveloped and uncertain and is characterized by more marketing hype than actual product. Only 300,000 units were sold in 1997, representing a lackluster 13 percent growth over 1996, which was well below expectations. However, the market could take off if corporations see increased economic and operational benefits in a more centrally controlled client-server environment with reduced system life-cycle costs and if vendors devote more resources to this segment. Although thin clients will cost less than do more fully configured PCs, the cost differentials will not be as great as the savings that come from more cost-efficient network management. Other factors that will affect market growth include the development of more Java applications and systems software for terminal servers. IDC forecasts that the U.S. market will exceed 4 million units and $2 billion by 2002.

The PC industry is profoundly affected by the analog-to-digital conversions that are occurring in many information technology product areas. This development has precipitated both convergence and contention among formally distinct industry sectors—computers, telecommunications, consumer electronics, entertainment, publishing, and television—providing both opportunities and challenges for PC manufacturers. The multimedia revolution that put movies on computers and the progress made in expanding bandwidth for data communications brought PCs to the attention of entertainment and information content providers. However, these developments also placed PCs increasingly in competition with consumer electronics product and service providers.

The continuing digitization of electronic technology, along with increases in the capacity, efficiency, and flexibility of the communications infrastructure, allows a digital computer to incorporate more user functions in a single box, broadening its base of applications and users. Unlike current consumer electronic products that are primarily single-use devices, a microprocessor-based PC can incorporate a number of previously distinct functions. Over the last several years PC manufacturers have launched hybrid PC-TV systems. These devices use new user interface software that mimics television controls, along with add-in cards and services that process satellite and over-the-air broadcast signals. The industry's goal is to broaden the entertainment value of PCs to attract television viewers to the PC platform. In December 1996 the U.S. Federal Communications Commission issued standards for digital television after a long dispute among television makers, broadcasters, and PC companies over specifications for the new technology. Digital televisions with high-definition pictures and clearer audio were scheduled to be available in stores late in 1998.

Digital convergence also gives consumer electronics and television companies an opportunity to encroach into the PC arena by providing interactive products. The Web TV set-top boxes introduced in late 1996 by Philips Electronics and Sony are examples. These devices allow users to navigate the Internet on their home televisions over regular telephone lines. Other initiatives include proposals by cable television companies to offer Internet access via cable modems.

Global Market Overview

To sustain profits and revenue growth, most technology companies today must look for sales overseas. Trade barriers are falling, global commercial and communications systems are improving, and foreign computer markets are becoming more sophisticated. U.S. exports of computer systems and parts have risen almost 9 percent annually since 1989, and this does not take into account the considerable amount of overseas production by U.S. computer manufacturers. Reacting to a saturated U.S. market and increasing foreign competition, U.S. suppliers continue to look abroad for sales and expanded market share, with some companies selling as much product overseas as they do domestically. Foreign vendors also seek to become global players, as is reflected in the efforts of major Asian suppliers to enlarge their presence in the lucrative U.S. market. Since PC applications and market trends are similar around the world and since the technology is relatively standard, global marketing is easier to implement, and this has intensified competition. To be successful in this environment, vendors must establish export marketing strategies, increase overseas investment, and adapt products to foreign markets.

According to Dataquest, factory revenue for PCs sold worldwide exceeded $162 billion in 1997, an 8 percent increase in current dollars over 1996. Unit shipments grew 16 percent to more than 80 million, feeding a worldwide installed base of over 270 million machines. The largest national markets were the United States (38 percent of global shipments) and Japan (10 percent), followed by the major western European countries. Regionally, North America represented 41 percent of the world market, western Europe 23 percent, Asia Pacific 22 percent, Latin America 4 percent, and the rest of the world (eastern Europe, Africa, and the Middle East) 10 percent (see Figure 27-6). Dramatic sales growth will occur in many countries as

their economies mature, incomes rise, and industrial and government infrastructures are modernized. Consequently, the U.S. market share of worldwide demand should decline gradually.

Western Europe. Western Europe is composed of the 15 members of the European Union (EU) plus Norway and Switzerland. Most of these countries have relatively developed computer markets that more or less follow trends in the United States, but at a slower pace. After 11 percent growth in 1996, the western European PC market accelerated to a 17 percent growth pace in 1997, surpassing 18 million units valued at over $39 billion. Unit shipments in 1998 have been estimated to grow 16 percent, according to Dataquest. In 1997, the four largest markets in Europe were Germany (23 percent), the United Kingdom (21 percent), France (14 percent), and Italy (8 percent). The leading PC suppliers in ranked order were Compaq Computer, IBM, Hewlett-Packard, Dell Computer, and Siemens Nixdorf.

Market drivers in Europe are very similar to those in the United States. Advancing market maturation relegates lucrative but relatively saturated corporate and high-income buying sectors to the replacement market, while intense price competition reduces profit margins. This trend compels vendors to focus on less saturated market sectors. In addition, the relatively higher costs of doing business in Europe, along with high value-added taxes, can add significantly to PC prices. On the plus side, sub-$1,000 PCs are generating consumer sales, and European corporations are continuing to upgrade to faster machines and new operating systems. In 1997, PCs with Pentium-type chips dominated sales with more than 96 percent of the market. Corporations are also installing networks and adopting client-server solutions at a fast pace. PC server sales grew 37 percent in 1997, representing almost 3 percent of the total PC market.

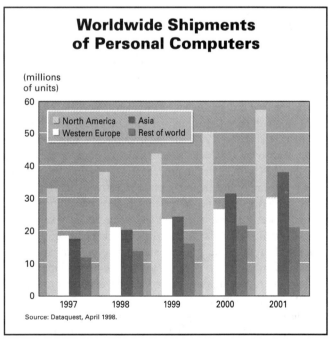

FIGURE 27-6

The market is stimulated by the growing popularity of the Internet and the availability of high-performance notebook computers at lower prices. Portables constituted 14 percent of the PC market in 1997 with a growth rate close to 17 percent, according to Dataquest. Sales to households and small businesses will continue to provide good opportunities in this region over the next several years, although purchases are beginning to taper off in the more highly penetrated German and British markets. Consumer sales represented about one-quarter of the market in 1997 and were expected to grow 14 percent in 1998.

Many computer and software producers locate manufacturing and sales facilities in the EU to take advantage of the opportunities a large, increasingly homogenized market offers. These companies are also in a good position to deal with EU efforts to establish and harmonize national commercial standards and regulations. With developed economies and sophisticated markets, an installed base of more than 60 million PCs in 1998 (about 60 percent of the U.S. total), and a population larger than that of the United States, western Europe is the largest customer for U.S. computer products. In 1997, 37 percent of all U.S. computer equipment exports went to the EU. Expansion of this market is linked to the development of broader distribution channels, better pricing, and further progress in the home and small business sectors.

Eastern Europe. There are 27 countries in eastern Europe, including the former Soviet states, but most are small and have newly established governments. Dataquest estimated that over 3 million PCs were shipped to the region in 1997, resulting in a 17 percent growth rate over 1996. U.S. exports of all computer equipment to eastern Europe totaled almost $300 million in 1996 (about 2 percent of exports to the EU). However, much of this market also is supplied by U.S. operations in western Europe. The region's largest PC markets are Russia (44 percent), Poland (18 percent), the Czech Republic (8 percent), and Hungary (4 percent).

Unlike the markets in the EU, which are dominated by U.S. multinationals, the major markets in eastern Europe are supplied largely by local companies that assemble PCs with less expensive Asian components. In Russia (Vist), Poland (Optimus), and Hungary (Albacomp), local companies had the leading market share in 1997, although Compaq Computer had a slight lead over the local assembler AutoCont in the Czech Republic. PCs from local producers are cheaper than name brands, an important factor in price-sensitive countries where computer prices can be 20 percent higher than those in the United States because of import and value-added taxes. However, the multinationals are intensifying price competition, and this should reduce the future market share of local suppliers. One problem in eastern Europe, as in most emerging markets, is the lack of product support and service that results from a shortage of skilled technicians.

Internet use is relatively low in eastern Europe but is poised for massive growth as outdated telecommunication infrastruc-

tures are modernized throughout the region. Usage is hampered by long delays in obtaining telecommunications hookups and a relative lack of localized content. Despite these obstacles, some countries have made significant strides in connecting their populations. Thousands of commercial and government offices in the region maintain home pages and increasingly have access to the Web on a daily basis. According to Network Wizards, there were over 355,000 Internet hosts in the region at the end of 1997. Russia (26 percent), Poland (22 percent), the Czech Republic (15 percent), and Hungary (13 percent) accounted for most of these hosts.

Japan. In the mid-1990s Japan was the world's fastest growing major PC market with a phenomenal 70 percent growth rate in 1995 and a 35 percent rate in 1996 that was spurred by steep price competition, the widespread use of Japanese-language versions of DOS and Windows, the adoption of the de facto Wintel standard by Japanese computer manufacturers, and a nascent home market. However, continuing economic problems, the completion of the first round of corporate buying, and a stagnant home user sector have overwhelmed the Japanese computer market. As a result, sales in 1997 grew only 8 percent, significantly less than was expected. Despite an initial sales flurry triggered by the consumption tax hike in April 1997, shipments for that year amounted to only 8.3 million units, according to Dataquest.

The computer market should pick up, with growth exceeding 10 percent over the next several years, as the Japanese economy recovers and first-time buyers from the mid-1990s purchase replacement machines. Factors in 1998 that were expected to stimulate the market include the introduction of Windows 98, price declines for Pentium II–type computers, and the availability of sub-$1,000 PCs. Japan is still behind the United States in terms of PC utilization, and this has resulted in a lower demand for corporate network and client-server systems, multimedia applications, home computers, Internet hookups, and high-performance notebook computers. Portable PCs, which are popular in Japan because of space limitations, currently represent about 40 percent of the market, compared with 20 percent in the United States. While desktop shipments declined in 1997, sales of mobile computers rose almost 40 percent. LCD desktop computers (deskbound PCs with flat panel displays) are another form factor that is popular in that country. Dataquest has estimated that sales could triple those of desktop PCs with conventional CRT monitors in 2000, when 13- and 14-inch LCD panels are priced equivalently to CRT displays.

Over the next several years demand for home PCs should recover as more Japanese consumers become interested in the Internet and other on-line services, whose sales are now hampered by high telephone charges and a lack of compelling local content. PC penetration of households is estimated at less than 20 percent, compared with over 40 percent in the United States. According to a Nikkei Market Access survey, there were an estimated 8.6 million on-line users in 1997, accounting for almost 7 percent of the population. This represents an explosive jump over the 3.5 million users reported in 1996. Hoping to spur demand, the Japanese government is promoting the development of a National Information Infrastructure that includes the installation of fiber-optic networks that will connect homes, businesses, and government offices by 2010.

Overt trade barriers to computer imports, such as tariffs and quotas, no longer exist in Japan, but cultural and commercial factors still make this market difficult to enter. Unlike most markets, Japan is dominated by formidable domestic computer manufacturers that control over two-thirds of the domestic market and benefit from extensive dealer networks. To be competitive, foreign vendors must deal with exclusive product distribution systems and redesign their computers and software to accommodate the Japanese language. Despite these obstacles, U.S. firms have made inroads into the Japanese market by selling competitively priced world-class technology that is based on international standards.

Other Asia/Pacific Countries. Fueled by pent-up demand, rising living standards, and growing economies in need of information technologies, the Asia Pacific region has some of the most dynamic economies in the world along with over half the world's population. This region, minus Japan, consumed almost 10 million PCs in 1997, or about 12 percent of global sales. Despite an economic crisis which is resulting in negative or reduced gross domestic product (GDP) growth in most of the Asian markets over the next several years, growth in PC sales is expected to exceed 20 percent through 2002, led by the Chinese Economic Area and India. Vendors in the most developed of these markets (Australia, Hong Kong, New Zealand, Singapore, Taiwan, and South Korea), where electronic goods manufacturing already takes place, are beginning to focus on the small business and consumer sectors to increase sales.

Among the region's developing markets, China is the largest, followed by India, Thailand, Indonesia, Malaysia, the Philippines, and Vietnam. Market potential is significant in these countries. China, which will soon have the largest Asian computer market after Japan, has experienced 50 to 60 percent annual growth rates since 1994 as large and midsize public and private organizations have computerized for the first time. There has also been noteworthy demand for sales of computers to families. In 1997, almost 3 million PCs were sold in China. Even though these levels are expected to slow to the range of 20 to 30 percent, this market remains vibrant. India, another potentially large market, could move into a high-growth phase toward the end of the century if it can speed up economic development while maintaining political stability. After growth rates of more than 40 percent between 1994 and 1996, Indian sales growth dipped below 20 percent in 1997, when about 450,000 PCs were sold, totaling over $850 million in revenues. The policies of many of these governments stimulate demand in the business sector by promoting information technologies as a means of achieving global competitiveness.

The Asia/Pacific region is both an important outlet for U.S. products and a major source of imports. U.S. exports of all computer equipment to this region, minus Japan, equaled $7.5 billion in 1997, or 18 percent of worldwide exports. Since their national incomes are lower than those in more mature markets, these countries often demand reduced levels of technology at lower prices. There can also be difficult obstacles to selling in developing countries. Problems include high import taxes, arbitrary customs enforcement, smuggling and gray market activities, arcane government regulations, investment restrictions, software piracy with inadequate international property rights enforcement, and skilled labor shortages. Despite these impediments, the Asia/Pacific region is a key area, representing one-quarter of the world's information technology market.

Latin America. Latin America represents almost 4 percent of the global PC market but has significant potential with some of the fastest growing and least penetrated markets in the world. U.S. computer equipment exports to the region have grown 23 percent annually since 1990 and increased 25 percent from 1996 to 1997 to $6.5 billion. The area is becoming more democratic and open market-oriented, but the specter of political and economic instability, together with high interest rates, government controls on spending, and inefficient marketing channels, continues to hamper commercial relations. Trade barriers are falling, and free-trade agreements, such as NAFTA and MERCOSUR, are spreading. Privatization and government deregulation have provided more market access to foreign computer vendors, but government policies in Brazil, the largest market, discourage imports in favor of local manufacturing through tax and investment incentives. Major U.S. PC manufacturers have established plants in Brazil to take advantage of those policies.

Total regional PC shipments reached nearly 3.7 million units in 1997, growing 27 percent over 1996, according to IDC. The highest growth rates were in Mexico (34 percent) and Venezuela (43 percent). Brazil represented over 36 percent of the market, followed by Mexico with 22 percent and Argentina with 8 percent. Slightly lower growth has been forecast for the $5.6 billion regional PC market in 1998. The Latin American market generally lags behind U.S. market trends but moves in the same direction. There is increasing interest in intranets and Internet access, groupware and workflow technologies, mobile computing, and networks. In 1997, the region's consumer market represented 19 percent of total sales, 15 percent of retail sales, and 8 percent of notebook sales, compared with 30 percent, 33 percent, and 20 percent, respectively, in the United States. With liberalizing trade policies and maturing markets, Latin America holds good prospects for U.S. exporters that focus on pricing, financing, product support, and distribution channel strategy.

R. Clay Woods, U.S. Department of Commerce, Computer Systems Division, Office of Computers and Business Equipment, (202) 482-0571, October 1998.

■ REFERENCES

Market Research Firms

DataPro International, 600 Delran Parkway, Delran, NJ 08075. (800) 328-2776.

Dataquest, Inc., 1290 Ridder Park Drive, San Jose, CA 95131. (408) 437-8000, www.dataquest.com.

International Data Corporation, 5 Speen Street, Framingham, MA 01701. (800) 343-4952, www.idcresearch.com.

Articles

"Bad Times for PC Makers," by Lisa DiCarlo, *PC Week,* April 6, 1998, Ziff-Davis Inc., 10 Presidents Landing, Medford, MA 02155. (781) 393-3690, www.pcweek.com.

"The Best CPU for Your Next PC," by Michael Slater, *PC Magazine,* September 23, 1997, PO Box 54093, Boulder, CO 80322. (212) 503-5255, www.pcmag.com.

"Cheap PCs," by Peter Burrows, *Business Week,* March 1998, New York, NY 10020. (800) 635-1200, www.businessweek.com.

Computer Industry Almanac, by Karen Petska-Juliussen, Glenbrook, NV. (800) 377-6810, www.c-i-a.com.

"Computer Manufacturing: Change and Competition," *Monthly Labor Review,* August 1996, Bureau of Labor Statistics, U.S. Department of Labor, Washington, DC 20212. (202) 606-5900.

"Computer Networking in Switzerland," February 1998, U.S. Department of Commerce, *National Trade Data Bank.* (202) 482-1986, www.stat-usa.gov.

"Computing's Outer Limits," by Chris O'Malley, *Popular Science,* March 1998, Times Mirror Magazines, 2 Park Avenue, New York, NY 10016. (800) 289-9399, www.popsci.com.

"DTV Gear Boom?" by Peter Brown, *Electronic News,* April 6, 1998, 2105 Landings Drive, Mountain View, CA 94043. (415) 691-1690, www.electronicnews.com.

"Foreign Direct Investment in the United States: Detail for Historical-Cost Position and Related Capital and Income Flows, 1996" and "U.S. Direct Investment Abroad: Detail for Historical-Cost Position and Related Capital and Income Flows, 1999," *Survey of Current Business,* September 1997, Bureau of Economic Analysis, U.S. Department of Commerce, Washington, DC 20230.

"Foreign Direct Investment in the United States," *Survey of Current Business,* June 1997, Bureau of Economic Analysis, U.S. Department of Commerce, Washington, DC 20230.

"400 MHz Pentium IIs: The Great Leap Forward," by Laurianne McLaughlin, *PC World,* June 1998, PO Box 55029, Boulder, CO 80322. (800) 234-3498, www.pcworld.com.

"Fujitsu to Build to Demand," by John G. Spooner, *PC Week,* March 23, 1998, Ziff-Davis Inc., 10 Presidents Landing, Medford, MA 02155. (781) 393-3690, www.pcweek.com.

"High-End PCs," by Jim Cope, *PC Today,* November 1997, Lincoln, NB 68521. (800) 544-1426, www.pctoday.com.

"Industrial Research Institute's R&D Trends Forecast for 1998," *Research-Technology Management,* January–February 1998, Industrial Research Institute, 1550 M Street, NW, Washington, DC 20005. (202) 776-0759, www.irinc.org.

"Industry Output and Employment Projections to 2006," *Monthly Labor Review,* November 1997, Bureau of Labor Statistics, U.S. Department of Labor, Washington, DC 20212. (202) 606-5900.

"Innovation and Global Competitiveness," by Charles F. Larson, *Sigma Xi Forum on Trends in Industrial Innovation: Industry Perspectives and Policy Implications,* November 20, 1997, Arlington, VA.

"Intel Initiative Addresses Build-to-Order Movement," by Ismini Scouras and Diane Trommer, *Electronic Buyers' News,* April 27, 1998, CMP Publishing, 600 Community Drive, Manhasset, NY 11030. (516) 562-5899, www.ebnonline.com.

"Margin Pressures Jar OEMs," by Jennifer L. Baljko, *Electronic Buyers' News,* May 4, 1998, CMP Publishing, 600 Community Drive, Manhasset, NY 11030. (516) 562-5899, www.ebnonline.com.

"The Networked PC Family," by Susan Gregory Thomas, *U.S. News & World Report,* December 1, 1997, 2400 N Street, NW, Washington, DC 20037-1196. (202) 955-2000.

"Open Market & Schedules Win PC Buyers' Business," by Joshua Dean, *Federal Computer Week,* March 23, 1998, PO Box 3023, Northbrook, IL 60065. (847) 291-5214, www.fcw.com.

"Personal Computers U.S. Forecast" and "Personal Computers Worldwide Forecast," *Dataquest,* April 1998, San Jose, CA 95131. (408) 468-8000, www.dataquest.com.

"The Power of Virtual Integration: An Interview with Dell Computer's Michael Dell," by Joan Magretta, *Harvard Business Review,* March–April 1998, Harvard Business School, 60 Harvard Way, Boston, MA 02163. www.hsbp.harvard.edu.

"Price Drops Create Buyer's Market for PCs," *PC Week,* April 13, 1998, Ziff-Davis Inc., 10 Presidents Landing, Medford, MA 02155. (781) 393-3690, www.pcweek.com.

"Prices Nosedive for LCDs," by David Lieberman, *Electronic Engineering Times,* May 4, 1998, CMP Media, Inc., 600 Community Drive, Manhasset, NY 11030. (516) 562-7405, www.techweb.cmp.com/eet.

"Smart Autos Roll towards Smart Roads," by George Leopold and Terry Costlow, *Electronic Engineering Times,* April 27, 1998, CMP Media, Inc., 600 Community Drive, Manhasset, NY 11030. (516) 562-7405, www.techweb.cmp.com/eet.

"Special DELL-ivery," by Joseph E. Maglitta, *Electronic Business,* December 1997, Cahners Publishing, 275 Washington Street, Newton, MA 02158. (617) 964-3030, www.ebt@cahners.com.

"Taking Computers to Task," by W. Wayt Gibbs, *Scientific American,* July 1997, 415 Madison Avenue, New York, NY 10017-1111. www.sacust@sciam.com.

"Thin-Client Market Picks Up Steam," by Dan Briody, *Infoworld,* April 27, 1998, 155 Bovet Road, Suite 800, San Mateo, CA 94402. (415) 572-7341, www.infoworld.com.

"3-D Video Cards," by Larry Stevens, *Government Computer News,* March 9, 1998, Silver Spring, MD. (301) 650-2111, www.gcn.com.

"Unclogging the PC Bottlenecks," by Tom R. Halfhill, *BYTE,* September 1997, PO Box 552, Highstown, NJ 08520. (800) 232-2983, www.byte.com.

Books and Reports

Computing, Information, and Communications: Technologies for the 21st Century, Committee on Computing, Information, and Communications (CIC), National Science and Technology Council, 4201 Wilson Boulevard, Arlington, VA 22230. (703) 306-1234.

High Performance Computing in the U.S.—The Next Five Years, by Horst D. Simon, Lawrence Berkeley National Laboratory, Berkeley, CA.

IDC Worldwide Black Book, December 1997, International Data Corporation, Framingham, MA, 01701. (508) 872-8200, www.idcresearch.com.

The National Technology Roadmap for Semiconductors, 1997 ed., Semiconductor Industry Association, 181 Metro Drive, Suite 450, San Jose, CA 95110. (408) 436-6600, www.semichips.org.

1996 Annual Survey of Manufacturers and *Current Industrial Report,* Bureau of the Census, U.S. Department of Commerce, Washington, DC 20230. (301) 457-4673, www.census.gov.

Trade Associations

American Electronics Association, 1225 Eye Street, NW, Suite 950, Washington, DC 20005. (202) 682-9110.

Information Technology Industry Council, 1250 Eye Street, NW, Suite 200, Washington, DC 20005. (202) 626-5736.

Interactive Multimedia Association, 48 Maryland Avenue, Suite 202, Annapolis, MD 21401-8011. (410) 626-1380.

Internet Society, 12020 Sunrise Valley Drive, Suite 270, Reston, VA 22091-3429. (703) 648-9888.

■ RELATED CHAPTERS

COMPUTER SOFTWARE AND NETWORKING
Economic and Trade Trends

Average Annual Employment in U.S. Packaged Software Industry

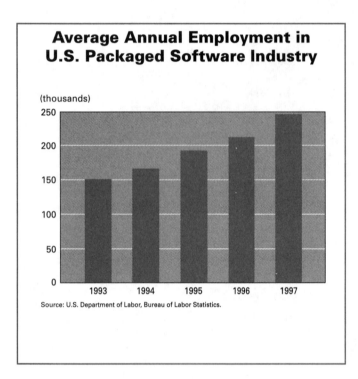

(thousands)

Source: U.S. Department of Labor, Bureau of Labor Statistics.

Software Market Growth, 1999–2003

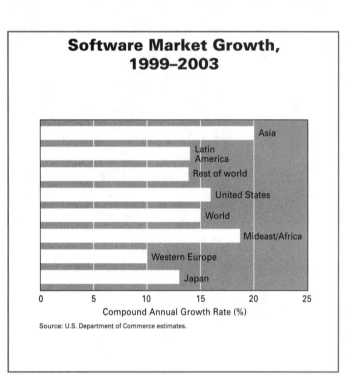

Compound Annual Growth Rate (%)

Source: U.S. Department of Commerce estimates.

World's Top 10 Software Suppliers, 1997

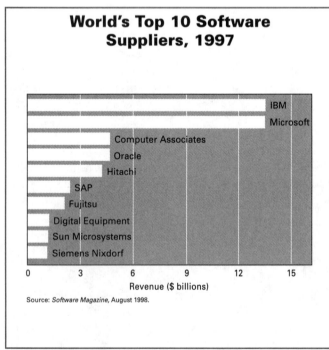

Revenue ($ billions)

Source: *Software Magazine*, August 1998.

Shares of Worldwide Packaged Software Market, 1997

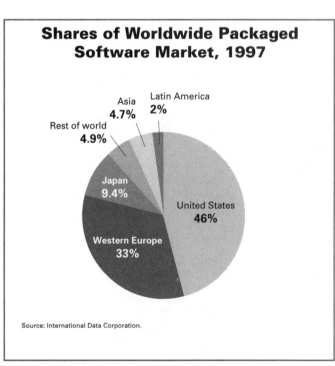

Latin America 2%
Asia 4.7%
Rest of world 4.9%
Japan 9.4%
Western Europe 33%
United States 46%

Source: International Data Corporation.

Computer Software and Networking

INDUSTRY DEFINITION The U.S. computer software and networking industry consists of the following industry sectors: computer programming services (SIC 7371), prepackaged software (SIC 7372), computer integrated systems design (SIC 7373), and computer peripheral equipment (SIC 3577).

GLOBAL INDUSTRY TRENDS

A pioneer in communications, business transactions, and worldwide information access, the U.S. computer software industry continues to make the transition into the twenty-first century. This industry has remained one of the most dynamic and promising sectors of the American economy. It has thrived through competition, innovation, and responsiveness to markets worldwide. Growth rates for the packaged software industry have consistently remained vigorous throughout the 1990s, with average annual growth rates of 12 percent or higher.

Although the United States and western Europe currently account for 80 percent of the world packaged software market, there is real growth potential for companies in countries outside the more highly saturated software markets, where a considerable increase in demand for packaged software will take place. While the U.S. and western European markets will continue to be of vital importance to U.S. software producers and resellers, many Asian, Latin American, and Middle Eastern markets will grow more rapidly. Asian information technology (IT) markets are still widely underpenetrated, and significant room for growth will exist after the currency crisis is resolved. The Chinese and Vietnamese packaged software markets are expected to be among the fastest growing, while the Middle East/Africa region and eastern Europe should continue to grow in importance. Companies that want to expand their sales and market presence will increasingly look toward these growing markets as engines for their growth.

The personal computer (PC) has continued to be the most widely used platform, with Microsoft Corporation's Windows 95 and Windows NT being the most popular operating systems. Business applications software sold in "suites," or packages of different applications, continued to have a dominant presence in the packaged software market. Hundreds of complex multipurpose computer software programs are now available for less than $100. The relatively low cost of buying software and computers has been accompanied by a continuing stream of technological innovations. Software applications that harness the power of computers have become increasingly important to consumers. Businesses must computerize to stay ahead of the competition. The Internet has been a fundamental factor in the development of a host of innovative software products. Many software companies are integrating Web features into their products, making it easier for consumers to access and manipulate the Web from within applications and to export documents to the Web.

The Year 2000 Problem

The software industry will be highly affected by the year 2000 (Y2K) problem. With a new century fast approaching, the coming century date change is of great concern to many computer users. This problem has resulted from the fact that software programs traditionally use a two-digit format for date generation: DD/MM/YY (dayday/monthmonth/yearyear) or MM/DD/YY (monthmonth/dayday/yearyear). This format was developed to save computer storage space, which at the time was expensive and was in limited supply. The difficulty now is that rather than reading 01/01/00 as January 1, 2000, older software programs will read that date as January 1, 1900. Therefore, it is necessary to change all year fields to a four-digit format (DD/MM/YYYY).

It has been estimated that between 200 million and 250 million lines of code will have to be reviewed in affected computer systems and individual programs. A further complication is that many of these systems and programs, particularly those written in the 1970s or earlier, were not consistently programmed. An application of this type must be studied one line of code at a time to identify the proper way in which to correct it.

The date change problem could affect computer hardware, software, and networks as well as devices containing central processing unit (CPU) chips in matters ranging from building access and security systems to telephone switchboards and robotics. Any company that fails to solve the date change problem may find that the year 2000 begins with employees locked out; payroll, sales, purchasing, and stock systems inoperative; and production machinery at a standstill. Between 1997 and January 1, 2000, new releases of compliant auditing software from systems manufacturers and packaged software companies will arrive on the market. However, since buying new hardware and software is costly, software vendors also are offering programs and on-line advisory services as well as providing information to consumers to protect them from buying noncompliant software and hardware. For users looking to address the problem on their own, seminars and workshops are available, along with various software tool kits that will audit the date-stamped code for the century date change.

FACTORS AFFECTING FUTURE U.S. INDUSTRY GROWTH

Employment in the U.S. software industry continues to flourish in a technology-driven market, with the creation of many new opportunities for software developers and programmers. Demand for graduates with the latest training is very high. The Bureau of Labor statistics (BLS) reports that total software industry employment is growing 9 percent annually, with salaries that are among the highest in the U.S. economy. The market for systems and applications programmers is expected to grow faster than the average for all employment growth through the year 2006. These high wages indicate the importance of "human" capital to the software industry and the growing scarcity of highly skilled workers. The BLS estimates that total employment in the U.S. packaged software industry increased 16 percent in 1997 to 245,800 employees, and that jobs generated by this industry will account for nearly 3 percent of all U.S. employment by 2005.

Offshore Outsourcing
Offshore outsourcing as a way to produce customized software less expensively has become a factor in the globalization of the software industry. Some industry observers feared that U.S. programming jobs would be lost to lower-salaried offshore workers. However, some observers contend that the United States is experiencing a significant shortage of qualified computer programmers. Companies see offshore programming and overseas recruitment as an answer to this problem. Many off-

shore programmers are now combining year 2000 compliance work with other software initiatives. Programming services are being provided by many companies in such countries as India, Ireland, and Israel, which have a large pool of English-speaking highly skilled workers.

U.S. companies now hold a two-thirds share of the global software market, yet only one-third of the world's estimated 6 million programmers live in the United States. In the United States there is a growing recognition that collaborative partnerships among educators, government, and industry leaders must be strengthened to solve this problem.

Research and Development
The expansion in U.S. industry's investment in research and development (R&D) appears to have continued into 1998, as forecast by Schonfeld & Associates, Inc.'s, annual R&D Ratios and Budgets. It was expected that a strong U.S. economy would further boost R&D in many industries throughout that year. The packaged software industry was projected to continue its surge in R&D spending, reaching $13.5 billion in 1998, an increase of 18 percent over 1997.

Software Company Rankings
According to *Software Magazine*'s Software 500 listing, which annually ranks 500 companies as the world's foremost software providers, software revenue from licensing fees, maintenance, and support reached $82.4 billion in 1997, an increase of nearly 17 percent over 1996. Among the Software 500 top 10 companies (of which 6 are hardware vendors), 7 are American, 2 are Japanese, and 1 is German. By individual company, the top 10 included IBM, Microsoft, Computer Associates, Oracle, Hitachi, SAP, Fujitsu, Digital Equipment, Sun Microsystems, and Siemens Nixdorf, which collectively accounted for $46.3 billion or 56 percent of the total Software 500 revenues. Revenues of the 7 American companies totaled $37.9 billion and accounted for 46 percent of worldwide revenues for the Software 500 companies and 82 percent of the top 10 company revenues. Four of the top 10 companies reported double-digit revenue increases. Microsoft led the way, expanding its revenues with a 39 percent increase, followed by SAP (35 percent), Oracle (25 percent), and Computer Associates (13 percent). Hardware vendor Sun Microsystems, within the top 10, reported an increase of 21 percent.

The average Software 500 provider allocated 19 percent of corporate revenue back into research and development. A popular growth strategy for many of the software companies continues to be the merger and acquisition route. Of the 1997 Software 500 companies, 137 (27 percent) acquired a company or product line during the year or merged with another company. Among the Software 500, 27 more companies plan to go public in 1998. The biggest trend in 1997 noted by *Software Magazine* was that electronic commerce finally became a reality. Another trend, due largely to the existence of the Internet/intranet/extranet, was the idea of obtaining software solutions without buying the software, thereby enabling software to be provided as a service.

Intellectual Property Rights

In 1997 substantial progress was made in improving intellectual property protection, even in countries whose practices were a major concern in the past. Progress occurred throughout the world, encouraged by the U.S. government's continued commitment to the enforcement of protection for intellectual property. Implementation of the World Trade Organization's (WTO) Agreement on Trade Related Aspects of Intellectual Property Rights (TRIPS) was instrumental in improving this situation. The TRIPS agreement provides a base level of protection to software as a literary work for 50 years and exclusive rental rights for the owners of computer programs. Whereas developed countries were required to implement the agreement by January 1, 1996, countries in transition to a market economy have been given until January 1, 2000, and the least developed countries until January 1, 2006.

The annual Special 301 review examines in detail the adequacy and effectiveness of intellectual property protection in more than 70 countries. Foreign countries that deny adequate and effective protection of intellectual property rights (IPR) or do not provide fair and equitable market access to U.S. individuals who rely on intellectual property protection are designated by the U.S. Trade Representative (USTR) as "priority foreign countries" or placed on the "priority watch" or "watch" list. On January 16, 1998, Paraguay was identified as a "priority foreign country," the most serious designation, which initiated an ongoing Special 301 investigation.

On May 1, 1998, the USTR announced the results of the eleventh annual Special 301 review of intellectual property protection and intellectual property rights–related market access practices of U.S. trading partners. As a result of that review, a WTO dispute settlement action was initiated against Greece and the European Union.

During the 1998 Special 301 review, 15 trading partners were placed on the priority watch list and 32 trading partners were placed on the "watch list." (See the boxed note: "1998 Special 301 Review List.") The priority watch and watch lists identify countries that have serious deficiencies in intellectual property protection but do not meet all the statutory criteria for designation as priority foreign countries. Five of these trading partners—Bulgaria, Hong Kong, Colombia, Jordan, and Vietnam—were also designated to have "out-of-cycle" reviews during the year. In addition, China's IPR practices are subject to monitoring under Section 306 of U.S. trade law, which authorizes imposition of trade sanctions if commitments of a bilateral trade agreement are not met. Continued progress occurred in China regarding enforcement of intellectual property protection resulting from the 1995 and 1996 Bilateral IPR Agreements between the United States and China, as well as extensive follow-up work with Chinese officials. However, concerns remain regarding some IPR-related practices, including end-user piracy of business software.

Although noticeable improvements have been made in intellectual property protection, there remains a need to combat continuing worldwide losses caused by software piracy. According to the Business Software Alliance (BSA), unauthorized elec-

1998 SPECIAL 301 REVIEW LIST	
Priority Foreign Country	
Paraguay	

Priority Watch List	
Argentina	**Indonesia**
Bulgaria	**Israel**
Dominican Republic	**Italy**
Ecuador	**Kuwait**
Egypt	**Macao**
European Union	**Russia**
Greece	**Turkey**
India	

Watch List	
Australia	**Oman**
Bahrain	**Pakistan**
Canada	**Peru**
Chile	**Philippines**
Colombia	**Poland**
Costa Rica	**Qatar**
Czech Republic	**Saudi Arabia**
Denmark	**Singapore**
Guatemala	**South Africa**
Honduras	**South Korea**
Hong Kong	**Sweden**
Ireland	**Thailand**
Jamaica	**Ukraine**
Japan	**United Arab Emirates**
Jordan	**Venezuela**

tronic distribution of copyrighted works over the Internet is growing and represents a substantial threat to the software industry. Common types of software piracy on the Internet include exchanges of software via E-mail, news groups, Internet chat rooms, mail order, file transfer protocol (FTP), serial numbers, and even the World Wide Web, which allows pirates to offer point-and-click, one-stop shopping to even novice users. BSA reports that, worldwide, more than 40 percent of all software in use has been copied illegally. In 1997 piracy cost the software industry $11.2 billion in lost revenues. In the United States alone, BSA states that software piracy cost 130,000 jobs in 1996, and by 2005 it is expected to cost an additional 300,000 jobs. The BSA points out that software piracy translates into fewer jobs, less innovation, and higher costs to consumers.

PACKAGED SOFTWARE

U.S. Industry Growth Projections for the Next 1 and 5 Years

The U.S. packaged software market retained its place as the world's largest and most energetic in 1997, valued at $54 billion. According to the International Data Corporation (IDC) packaged software is the IT market segment with the highest growth potential. Business spending on IT equipment continues to represent nearly 50 percent of the total business equipment investment.

The worldwide packaged software market, defined by the IDC as application solutions software, application tools, and system infrastructure software, was expected to reach $130.6 billion in 1998. This total should grow to $149.7 billion in 1999, and based on IDC data through 2001, is forecast by the U.S. Department of Commerce to rise to $257.3 billion in 2003, with annual increases of over 14 percent.

On an individual segment basis, the worldwide packaged software market for application solutions, including consumer applications, cross-industry applications, and vertical industry applications, was forecast by IDC to increase to $66 billion in 1998. In 1999 this total is expected to rise to $76.6 billion, with a 16 percent annual increase. If this trend continues, this category will reach $137.6 billion in 2003 (IDC data through 2001). The worldwide market total for application tools, which consist of information access tools and programmer development tools, is projected to increase by nearly 14 percent to reach $33.9 billion in 1998 and up 12 percent to $38.1 billion in 1999. By 2003 (based on IDC data through 2001) this segment is expected to grow to $62.2 billion. The last segment included in the definition of packaged software—systems infrastructure software, which incorporates system management software, middleware, serverware, and system-level software—was expected to rise to $30.6 billion in 1998, an annual increase of 12 percent. This segment is projected to reach $34.9 billion by 1999 and $58.3 billion by 2003 (IDC data).

The U.S. packaged software market total was estimated to increase to $62.1 billion in 1998, up 15 percent from 1997. According to IDC estimates, the U.S. market for application solutions software was expected to rise to $32.2 billion in 1998, with an annual increase of 18 percent. This segment is forecast to increase to $37.5 billion in 1999 and $69 billion by 2003 (IDC data through 2001). The application tools segment in the U.S. market was expected to grow to $15.9 billion in 1998, up 11 percent over 1997, and $17.5 billion in 1999, with an annual increase of 10 percent. Based on IDC data the U.S. Department of Commerce projects this segment will increase to $28.0 billion in 2003. In 1998 the U.S. market total for system infrastructure software was expected to rise to $13.9 billion, up 14 percent over the 1997 figure. IDC projected this segment total should increase to $16.2 billion by 1999. The U.S. Department of Commerce forecast this segment to grow 16 percent annually to reach $29.8 billion by 2003.

Global Industry Trends

In 1997 international packaged software markets totaled $60.0 billion and accounted for a 53 percent share of the worldwide market total. International markets in 1998 are expected to reach $68.5 billion. By 1999 this total is expected to grow to $78.3 billion and it should continue to increase to reach $128.1 billion in 2003 (IDC data through 2001), representing half the worldwide packaged software market total. The top 10 countries in the international marketplace reached $46.7 billion in sales in 1997, accounting for 77 percent of the international packaged software market total. The western European region was the largest international market, totaling $35.6 billion in 1997. Six of the top 10 country markets were located in the western European region, representing a 61 percent share of the international market total. Japan was the second largest single-country international market with revenues totaling $12 billion and a 17 percent share of the international markets. The remaining Asian region followed at $4 billion, and a 9 percent share of the 1997 international market total. Annual growth in the regional packaged software markets is projected to range from 9 to 19 percent between 1999 and 2003 (IDC data).

Western Europe

Based on IDC the western European markets were estimated to reach $39.7 billion in 1998 and increase 12 percent to $44.6 billion in 1999. By 2003 the U.S. Department of Commerce projected this total should rise to $65.7 billion in 2003, with an average annual growth rate of 10 percent. The five largest country markets in this region in 1998 were estimated to be Germany ($8.2 billion), the United Kingdom ($9 billion), France ($5.6 billion), Italy ($3.1 billion), and the Netherlands ($2.3 billion). These markets were expected to reach $28.2 billion by 1998, and account for more than 70 percent of the western European market total.

Application solutions is forecast to be the largest segment in the western European region and was projected to rise to $19.4 billion in 1998, up 11.6 percent over 1997. This segment is estimated to increase to $21.9 billion in 1999, and is forecast by the U.S. Department of Commerce, based on IDC data through 2001, to grow to $32.8 billion by 2003. The application tools segment was expected to reach $10.2 billion in 1998 and $11.4 billion by 1999, and in 2003 (IDC data) should total $17.0 billion. Systems infrastructure software was estimated to increase to $10.0 billion in 1998 and $11.3 billion in 1999, and based on IDC data through 2001, this segment total is projected by the U.S. Department of Commerce to rise to $16.4 billion in 2003.

Japan

The Japanese software market was estimated by IDC to increase by 14 percent to $11.7 billion in 1998. In 1999 this market should total $13.2 billion, and is forecast by the U.S. Department of Commerce to increase over 12 percent annually to reach $21.2 billion by 2003. Japan has consistently remained the second largest single-country market throughout the 1990s. The largest segment of this market—application solutions— was estimated to increase to $6.2 billion in 1998 with an annual growth rate of 14 percent. This segment total was projected to rise to $7.9 billion in 1999 and based on IDC Data through 2001, the U.S. Department of Commerce forecast the Japanese application solutions market to reach $12.0 billion in 2003. The application segment tools in this region was expected to rise to $2.5 billion in 1998 and $2.9 billion in 1999, and is estimated by the U.S. Department of Commerce to reach $4.8 billion by 2003. The system infrastructure segment is expected to grow to $2.8 billion in 1998 and $3.1 billion in 1999, with an annual increase of 8 percent. By 2003 (IDC data) this market segment should reach $4.7 billion.

Asia

According to the IDC, the packaged software market in Asia, excluding Japan, has had fast-paced growth, experiencing annual growth rates up to 50 percent. This market has been identified as the software industry's fastest growing region. The Asian packaged software market was expected to increase 14 percent, growing from $5.7 billion in 1997 to $6.5 billion in 1998. If this trend continues, the market should total $8.0 billion in 1999 with an annual increase of 23 percent. Based on IDC data through 2001, the U.S. Department of Commerce forecast this market would reach $17.2 billion in 2003. In this region, excluding Japan, the top three markets—Australia, Korea, and China—were estimated to total $3.2 billion in 1998, with individual market shares of $2.0 billion, $723 million, and $535 million, respectively.

Application solutions has been estimated to be the largest segment in this region and was expected to increase 15 percent to reach $3.1 billion in 1998 and $4 billion in 1999 with an annual increase of 29 percent. By 2003 based on IDC data through 2001, the U.S. Department of Commerce projected this total should rise to $10 billion. The application tools segment was forecast to increase 11 percent over 1997 and reach $2.1 billion in 1998, and in 1999, grow to $2.6 billion. Based on IDC data through 2001, this segment is estimated to total $4.8 billion by 2003. In 1998 the systems infrastructure software segment was expected to reach $1.3 billion, with an average annual increase of 23 percent. This figure should grow to $1.6 billion by 1999, and is projected to rise to $2.2 billion in 2003, increasing by 10 percent annually.

Latin America

According to IDC, the Latin American packaged software market is expected to continue to experience healthy growth with the spread of computer technology in many countries. The Latin American region has remained the software industry's second fastest growing market. The country markets in this region and their estimated market shares for 1998 include Brazil ($1.7 billion), Mexico ($541 million), Argentina ($502 million), Chile ($142 million), Venezuela ($125 million), and Colombia ($113 million). These markets total $3.1 billion, up 24 percent over 1997. These markets are estimated to increase to $4.4 billion in 1999 and, based on IDC data through 2001, the U.S. Department of Commerce forecast this figure will rise to $8.1 billion by 2003.

The application solutions market segment is expected to be the highest-yielding segment in this region, reaching $1.4 billion in 1998, up 27 percent over 1997. This segment should increase to $1.9 billion in 1999 and is estimated to reach $4.9 billion in 2003 (IDC data through 2001). The application tools market has been projected to total $1.3 billion by the end of 1998 and grow to $1.6 billion in 1999, an annual increase of 23 percent. The U.S. Department of Commerce estimates this segment total will reach $3.1 billion by 2003. The last segment—system infrastructure—was forecast to average annual increases of 15 percent to rise to $833 million in 1998, and to $956 million in 1999. The Latin American system infrastructure market total should rise to $1.6 billion in 2003 (IDC data through 2001).

Outlook

Based on IDC data, the U.S. Department of Commerce estimates that the worldwide packaged software market will maintain continued steady growth. From 1998 to 2003 (IDC data through 2001) the market world total should reach $258.1 billion, averaging annual increases of 14 percent. IDC estimated market shares in 1999 should include United States (48 percent), western Europe (30 percent), Japan (9 percent), Asia (6 percent), and Latin America (2 percent), with the two remaining regions (the Middle East/Africa and eastern Europe) and the rest of the world accounting for 5 percent. Based on IDC data through 2001, the U.S. Department of Commerce estimated application solutions market will be the largest segment in 2003, growing to $137.6 billion, followed by application tools ($62.2 billion) and systems infrastructure ($58.3 billion). The fastest growing markets in 1999 are expected to be in Asia: China (49 percent), Vietnam (50 percent), India (40 percent), Taiwan (25 percent), and Korea (36 percent).

Patricia Johnson, Office of Computers and Business Equipment, International Trade Administration, (202) 482-2053, June 1998.

CAD/CAM/CAE

The computer-aided design, computer-aided manufacturing, and computer-aided engineering (CAD/CAM/CAE) sector has four major segments: mechanical computer-aided design and engineering (MCAD/MCAE); electronic design automation (EDA); architectural, construction, and engineering (AEC); and geographic information systems (GIS)/mapping.

MCAD and MCAE include tools used to design, analyze, document, and manufacture single-function parts, components, and assemblies. EDA encompasses tools that automate the design process for a variety of electronic products. This sector has three components: CAE, integrated circuit (IC) layout, and printed circuit board (PCB)/multichip module (MCM)/hybrid.

AEC refers to software tools used by architects, contractors, and plant and civil engineers to aid in the design and management of buildings and industrial plants. AEC represents architectural, civil engineering, facilities design and management, and process plant design. GIS/mapping software enables users to capture, edit, display, and analyze various geographic data.

Factors Affecting Future U.S. Industry Growth

The CAD, CAM, and CAE industry is projected to grow steadily over the next 5 years, as some mechanical CAD companies have formed alliances to remain competitive in the development of new products. Architects and engineers demand power and performance from their computer systems. Windows NT is in competition with UNIX to become the standard operating system for CAD designers and engineers. The advantages cited for Windows NT include improved price and performance and interoperability among applications.

For CAD applications, users have seen the price of software decline, allowing them to purchase software tools to help improve their competitive position and shorten design cycles. As the year 2000 approaches, two-dimensional drawings will be replaced by three-dimensional CAD. Three-dimensional CAD tools will improve the relationship between architectural designers and their clients, for example, by allowing a client to virtually walk through the interior of a new building.

Both systems administration and interoperability are fast-evolving issues because of the Web and the Internet. The use of intranets and the Internet will have a positive affect on CAD applications. Using the Internet as an extension to a CAD system through the use of browsers and browser plug-ins allows an entire project team and its clients to view and manipulate models and drawings in various Web formats early in the design process.

Additionally, the use of electronic commerce has increased the revenues of some CAD/CAM companies, further promoting growth in the market. The potential of the Internet to provide virtual links is beginning to make a difference in the distribution channels for CAD/CAM software. For example, CAD/CAM value-added resellers (VARs) are consolidating. Many resellers are investigating new methods for providing better service to their customers to address the changes in the marketplace.

Numerical control (NC) software drives the CAM segment of the CAD/CAM market. This software enables manufacturers to quickly program, set up, and run the machine tools used in various cutting and fabricating operations. The NC market remains robust as new users buy NC software and veterans upgrade their technology. Among the factors fueling growth are increased worldwide competition, shorter product cycles, and more companies investing in more sophisticated machine tools. The acceptance of concurrent engineering and flexible manufacturing practices is also promoting greater use of NC software, as is the growth of Windows NT–based NC software and the less expensive computers on which they run.

Mechanical CAD

According to Dataquest, Inc., a market research firm in San Jose, CA, as leaders in the mechanical CAD/CAM/CAE market continue to consolidate, the larger companies are beginning to offer more capabilities and the smaller companies are becoming more specialized. With companies forming alliances, mechanical CAD software vendors such as EDS Unigraphics and Intergraph and Dassault and SolidWorks have formed partnerships to address issues that affect the mechanical CAD market.

Newly introduced PC-based solutions in the MCAD market may soon make it possible for users to do high-end workstation-level solid modeling on their desktops. New midrange solutions are leading to significant growth in the MCAD market and putting solid technology on every engineer's desktop. The many new desktop mechanical design systems include SolidWork's SolidWorks 95, a solid modeling system for Windows 95 and Windows NT; Intergraph's Solid Edge, a mechanical assembly and parts modeling package; and Autodesk's release Mechanical Desktop, a suite of existing applications that combines integrated surface modeling with solid modeling. Rand Technolo-

gies is the largest independent VAR for mechanical engineering development tools, CAD/CAM/CAE, and services.

Many engineers and their companies are no longer willing to pay high prices for CAD software because of the availability of less costly midrange systems. Suppliers of midrange solid modelers such as SolidWorks, Microcadam's Helix, and Intergraph's Solid Edge offer increasing functionality in their systems. Some users are finding that they can get an impressive amount of design work done with these packages.

To attract architects and engineers, Microsoft has added to Windows NT the capabilities needed to run CAD software efficiently. For example, Windows NT includes support for multiple-microprocessor workstations. This program also supports a variety of three-dimensional graphics accelerators, an advantage for architects who work with large designs. Software vendors see architectural firms moving toward Windows NT, while Macintosh use is declining rapidly. Architectural customers continue to move from DOS and Windows 3.11 to Windows 95 and Windows NT. Making the move to Windows NT has been relatively painless for most architects because many of them have home computers that run some version of Windows, making the learning curve for Windows NT short. The transition for architectural firms is also smooth because their architects for the most part readily accept the change and because the transition usually lowers a firm's overhead costs. Because hardware performance is changing rapidly, many architectural firms now lease their hardware.

Electronic Design Automation

The EDA industry has blossomed over the last 20 years, becoming a multi-billion-dollar industry with double-digit annual growth worldwide. This growth is attributed to the need to speed development projects with advanced EDA technology. This market is expected to have steady growth over the next 5 years. The EDA vendors community has expanded to include several hundred companies that market a wide variety of automated design solutions. The user base has grown to hundreds of thousands of users, and virtually every major electronic and hardware company in the world has purchased an automated design package. Accordingly, most developers of systems have grown dependent on automated design tools to increase their productivity and decrease the time to market.

Hoping to take advantage of advances in semiconductor processing to develop more capable devices, IC designers are finding that the currently available tools for design and testing are impeding their efforts. Design engineering productivity is falling behind the capabilities of silicon processing. Advanced semiconductor processes are developing more quickly than are the EDA tools needed to design, verify, and test chips with tens of millions of transistors. Engineers need effective tools to design more complex chips. Designers are also under pressure to bring products to market more quickly. As a result, chip-based design reuse may be inevitable. Designs will be supplied as components in software, just as chips, resistors, and capacitors are components to be soldered onto printed circuit boards. One proposed solution to the problem is to reuse basic building-block circuits such as CPU, memory, and input/output (I/O) cores. However, stitching together circuits designed at different times by different companies is not a simple task.

In 1998 top EDA vendors were optimistic about solving problems in deep submicron (DSM) design. Some companies are preparing to team up to solve the issues laid out over the past year or to bring out solutions alone. EDA vendors will have to provide the next-generation tools for DSM design, or the semiconductor companies will develop their own tools, becoming the driving force behind tool development. The task of design has changed so much that EDA customers and vendors have no choice but to restructure their relationships. Many of the new EDA tools and technologies are too complex to be handed off to customers. The inability to achieve expected design productivity improvements has caused many top managers to become skeptical of claims from tool vendors. Every 4 to 6 years designers have to change their methodology completely, along with the tools and technology around it, as a direct result of increasing chip complexity.

EDA companies provide fundamental development technology to the worldwide electronics market. A growing number of EDA vendors are expanding their design service activities in an effort to boost revenue growth and facilitate the use of leading-edge tools in complex design projects. The EDA Consortium is an international association of companies engaged in the development, manufacture, and sale of design tools to the electronic engineering community. The consortium represents over 50 companies which together account for a large majority of international EDA revenues.

Industry organizations such as the Virtual Socket Interface Alliance (VSIA) aim to speed the acceptance of intellectual property supplied by various vendors, but the task of standardizing the interface between cores remains complex.

Architectural, Engineering, and Construction

The AEC CAD software market is expected to grow steadily in the next 5 years as users move to three-dimensional (3-D) CAD technology. The need to provide 3-D models of buildings has always posed design problems. Basically, one had to be an architect to access these designs, and they have been costly and time-consuming to produce. With powerful 3-D CAD software, designers can walk their clients around a proposed building in a short period, and physical models can be made to exact scale. Clients then can offer input very early in the design process, avoiding costly and frustrating change orders during construction and misunderstandings about the design. The benefits of 3-D CAD are so significant for both designers and clients that their use has more than doubled in a two-dimensional year. Moving from 2-D CAD to 3-D CAD design requires a bit of effort. While the hardware and software investments are considerable, the largest obstacle for design firms is usually training time.

Geographic Information Systems Mapping

The GIS software market is expected to grow steadily in the next 5 years. Several factors have contributed to growth in the use of GIS in government and industry. With the drop in prices of computers and the ability of more powerful PCs to process large graphics files, GIS vendors have responded by making more products for Windows NT. The use of GIS by the federal government continues to promote growth in this segment. Commercial satellites and the influence of the Global Positioning System (GPS) will further increase the availability of high-resolution, high-precision imagery.

GIS technology, which traditionally was driven by the buying power of the federal government, has developed into a booming commercial market and is changing the way agencies buy GIS and creating more federal users. Users also have less need to go to the expense of collecting or creating their own data, because many commercial companies now sell geospatial data. GIS users will be able to view a map consisting of databases across the nation, and that ability offers tremendous potential for being able to share data.

Another important new development is the ability to work with spatial data in a relational database environment. Both Oracle Corp. and Informix Software Inc. now offer products that make it possible to manage standard and geospatial data types within the same databases. The nature of GIS is changing as it moves away from the notion of large software systems and toward geospatial capabilities that people can integrate on their own or with other types of applications, such as spreadsheets and word processors. This is placing GIS-type technology into the hands of more users for many different applications.

In the last 10 to 15 years the government used GIS technology primarily to create spatial databases that employed GIS tools. Now agencies are focusing on how they can use GIS tools to disseminate and manage those data. Agencies have become more aware of the benefits of sharing data across an enterprise or among different departments and levels of government. The U.S. Department of Housing and Urban Development (HUD), for example, provides GIS software to its local grantees to help them make better-informed decisions regarding community development and the allocation of federal funds. The U.S. Environmental Protection Agency (EPA) is one of many agencies taking advantage of the Internet by combining its Envirofacts relational database (containing data about EPA-regulated facilities) with a GIS database. Providing this information through the Internet has saved EPA staff the research time needed to fulfill each request for information.

Federal GIS applications cover a broad spectrum. For example, the Library of Congress is assembling a GIS application for users interested in studying environmental or other changes, giving them access to digitized historical maps. The Federal Emergency Management Agency (FEMA) uses GIS technology to help guide disaster recovery efforts. The Justice Department is using GIS to track crime patterns. The Department of Defense (DOD) is the most extensive federal GIS user. DOD has applied this technology to tasks as diverse as managing base-level activities, tracking unexploded mines, and negotiating diplomatic settlements.

The use of GIS for diplomacy spotlights a growing user group: high-level decision makers. GIS technology is moving into the resource management and decision-making realm. Users do not need to know the details of the technology to employ spatial data to make quick decisions. The cost of GIS technology has decreased, allowing the market to expand. The investment required from a hardware and software point of view is dropping. The real issue relates to whether the data are available and affordable. Data represent the highest cost in any GIS system. Sources of data are increasing, but it is still difficult to develop a nationwide database at the level of resolution required to support many decision makers.

The growth in each of these applications stems largely from the continued need to keep ahead of the technology curve. The use of GIS by the federal government continues to promote growth in this segment. More efficient data storage media, such as CD-ROM, are available, and the growing use of the Internet has made it an effective distribution method. New Internet tools are expected which will allow users to access data directly over the Internet without downloading an entire database. Users will spend less on collecting or creating their own data because many commercial companies now sell geospatial data.

U.S. Market Leaders

The top CAD/CAM/CAE companies are IBM, Parametric Technology, Autodesk, Cadence, Intergraph, Environmental Systems Research Institute (ESRI), Mentor Graphics, and EDS Unigraphics. The top three CAD software leaders are Autodesk, Intergraph, and Bentley Systems, Inc. Parametric Technology Corp. is a leading supplier of CAD/CAM/CAE software tools used to automate the mechanical development of a product from conceptual design through production. Autodesk is the world's leading supplier of PC design software and PC multimedia tools and the leader in the architecture, engineering, and construction design software markets. ESRI and Intergraph Corp. are leaders in GIS/mapping.

U.S. Industry Growth Projections for the Next 1 and 5 Years

In 1997, the U.S. CAD/CAM/CAE software market was estimated to grow 12 percent, with revenues reaching $2.6 billion. The growth in revenues for GIS/mapping and EDA is expected to exceed growth forecasts for mechanical CAD/CAE and AEC applications (see Table 28-1).

In 1998, the U.S. CAD/CAM/CAE software market increased 13 percent over 1997, with revenues of over $2.9 billion (see Table 28-1). Of this amount, mechanical CAD/CAE continued to dominate the market with revenues of almost $1.2 billion (40 percent), followed by EDA with revenues of $887 million (30 percent), GIS/mapping with revenues of $509 million (17 percent), and AEC with revenues of $374 million (13 percent). The fastest growing segments continued to be EDA and GIS, at 16 percent and 14 percent, respectively.

In 1999 the U.S. CAD/CAM/CAE software market should increase 14 percent over 1998, reaching an estimated $3.3 billion. In the 5-year (1999–2003) growth projections, the U.S. CAD/CAM/CAE software market should increase to almost $6.2 billion at a compound annual growth rate (CAGR) of 16 percent (see Table 28-1). The EDA and GIS/mapping segments will continue to be the fastest growing markets in the period 1999–2003.

Global Market Prospects

In 1997 the worldwide CAD/CAM/CAE software market reached an estimated $7.8 billion in revenues, growing 12 percent over 1996. North America is estimated to be the largest region with revenues of over $2.8 billion (36 percent), followed by Europe with revenues of almost $2.4 million (30 percent), Japan with $1.9 billion (24 percent), the Asia/Pacific region with $534 million (7 percent), and the rest of world with $140 million (2 percent) (see Table 28-2). The world market leaders were IBM, Parametric Technology, Autodesk, Cadence, Synopsys, Intergraph, Dassault, ESRI, Mentor Graphics, and EDS Unigraphics.

In 1998 the worldwide CAD/CAM/CAE software markets were projected to increase 10 percent over 1997, with revenues of almost $8.6 billion (see Table 28-2). Of this amount, North America was the largest region, representing 37 percent of the total. Europe followed with revenues of $2.6 billion (30 percent), and Japan was next with $2 billion (24 percent). The Asia/Pacific region stood at $566 million (7 percent), and the rest of the world represented $154 million (2 percent). Europe and the rest of the world should join North America as the fastest growing markets, rising at rates of 13 and 10 percent, respectively. In 1999 the worldwide CAD/CAE/CAM software market is expected to increase 11 percent, reaching an estimated $9.5 billion. For the 5-year period 1999–2003, the world-

---

TABLE 28-1: U.S. CAD/CAM/CAE Software Market by Application

(millions of dollars; percent)

	1997[1]	1998[2]	1999[2]	2000[2]	2001[2]	2002[2]	2003[2]	1999–2003[3]
Mechanical	1,041	1,166	1,316	1,503	1,735	2,028	2,401	16
EDA	765	887	1,035	1,211	1,426	1,694	2,030	18
AEC	345	374	411	458	510	573	643	12
GIS/mapping	447	509	585	677	795	929	1,091	17
All applications	2,598	2,936	3,347	3,849	4,465	5,224	6,164	16

[1] Estimate.
[2] Forecast.
[3] Compound annual growth rate.
Source: *Dataquest;* U.S. Department of Commerce, International Trade Administration (ITA). Estimates and forecast by ITA.

TABLE 28-2: Worldwide CAD/CAM/CAE Software Markets by Region
(millions of dollars; percent)

	1997[1]	1998[1]	1999[2]	2000[2]	2001[2]	2002[2]	2003[2]	1999–2003[3]
North America	2,824	3,191	3,619	4,133	4,761	5,513	6,445	16
Europe	2,363	2,602	2,870	3,194	3,574	4,053	4,604	13
Japan	1,893	2,044	2,216	2,418	2,638	2,891	3,192	10
Asia/Pacific region	534	566	602	646	693	750	812	8
Rest of world	140	154	170	189	210	236	267	12
All regions	7,754	8,557	9,476	10,579	11,876	13,443	15,319	13

[1] Estimate.
[2] Forecast.
[3] Compound annual growth rate.
Source: *Dataquest;* U.S. Department of Commerce, International Trade Administration (ITA). Estimates and forecasts by ITA.

TABLE 28-3: Worldwide CAD/CAM/CAE Software Market by Application
(millions of dollars; percent)

	1997[1]	1998[1]	1999[2]	2000[2]	2001[2]	2002[2]	2003[2]	1999–2003[3]
Mechanical	3,579	3,930	4,327	4,816	5,369	6,041	6,850	10
EDA	2,207	2,483	2,808	3,190	3,656	4,222	4,890	12
AEC	944	1,009	1,080	1,164	1,264	1,379	1,510	7
GIS/mapping	1,024	1,136	1,262	1,409	1,587	1,801	2,069	10
All applications	7,754	8,557	9,476	10,579	11,876	13,443	15,319	10

[1] Estimate.
[2] Forecast.
[3] Compound annual growth rate.
Source: *Dataquest;* U.S. Department of Commerce, International Trade Administration (ITA). Estimates and forecasts by ITA.

wide CAD/CAM/CAE software market is expected to grow at a steady CAGR of 13 percent, reaching $15.3 billion by 2003.

In 1997 mechanical CAD/CAE represented the largest share of the market, with 46 percent, followed by EDA with 28 percent, GIS/mapping with 13 percent, and AEC with 12 percent. In the period 1999–2003, mechanical CAD/CAE should continue to represent the largest market share, followed by EDA. The fastest growing segments are expected to be EDA and GIS/mapping (see Table 28-3).

Asia/Pacific Region

In 1998 the Asia/Pacific market for CAD software reached $566 million. This is estimated to be the slowest growing region, at a rate of 6 percent, and slow growth is expected to continue in 1999 and over the next 5 years. The Asian economic crisis will limit opportunities for CAD/CAM vendors. Recessions are expected in South Korea, Indonesia, and Thailand, and no significant growth is likely in Japan. Prospects for the future growth of mechanical CAD sales will be limited in Hong Kong, Singapore, and Taiwan.

Europe

The European market is growing as industries restructure their IT investments. The European CAD/CAM/CAE software market is projected to grow at a CAGR of 13 percent between 1999 and 2003. Germany, the United Kingdom, and France are expected to be the markets with the highest growth. A factor fueling CAD/CAM/CAE software growth in the mechanical CAE segment is the move by software vendors into the design engineering market to provide software for high-performance mechanical design and drafting. Other factors driving CAD software growth include a growing momentum in Europe for the Microsoft Windows CE operating system.

Export Market Size

In 1998 the total worldwide CAD/CAM/CAE market for software, hardware, and services was estimated to increase 11 percent from the level in 1997, with revenues reaching an estimated $26 billion. CAD/CAM/CAE software accounted for 34 percent of the market with revenues of $8.8 billion, hardware 48 percent with revenues of over $12 billion, and services 19 percent with revenues of almost $5 billion (see Table 28-4).

The total worldwide CAD/CAM/CAE market is expected to continue to experience double-digit growth in all segments. In 1999 this market is expected to increase 12 percent from 1998, with revenues reaching $29 billion. For the 5-year period (1999–2003) the market is forecast to grow at a 13 percent CAGR, reaching $48 billion. Of this amount, hardware is forecast to represent the largest share, with 44 percent, followed by software with 36 percent and services with 21 percent (see Table 28-4). The top market leaders are forecast to be Parametric Technology, Autodesk, IBM, and Intergraph.

TABLE 28-4: Worldwide CAD/CAM/CAE Markets

	1997[1]	1998[1]	1999[2]	2000[2]	2001[2]	2002[2]	2003[2]	1999–2003[3]
Software	7,754	8,762	9,901	11,287	12,867	14,798	17,017	14
Hardware	11,239	12,363	13,599	15,095	16,756	18,766	21,018	11
Services	4,261	4,858	5,538	6,368	7,323	8,495	9,854	15
All applications	23,471	25,982	29,038	32,751	36,946	42,059	47,890	13

[1] Estimate.
[2] Forecast.
[3] Compound annual growth rate.
Source: *Dataquest;* U.S. Department of Commerce, International Trade Administration (ITA). Estimates and forecasts by ITA.

U.S. and Foreign Competition

U.S. vendors supply more than two-thirds of the worldwide CAD/CAM/CAE software market, followed by vendors from Japan and others in the Asia/Pacific region with 20 percent. European suppliers account for 10 percent, and suppliers from the rest of the world account for 2 percent. Foreign competitors include Dassault, Fujitsu, Racal-Redac, Siemens Nixdorf, Nihon Unisys, and Hitachi. The leading foreign competitors in Asia are Japan's Fujitsu and NEC. In Europe the French firm Dassault and the German firm Siemens Nixdorf are the leaders. Foreign suppliers continue to have limited success in penetrating the U.S. market. U.S. market leaders continue to dominate the market, although there have been some business alliances with foreign companies (e.g., Digital and Dassault).

Prospects for 1999

In 1999 the total worldwide CAD/CAM/CAE market is forecast to increase 12 percent over 1998, with revenues reaching an estimated $29 billion. Of this amount, CAD/CAM/CAE software will account for 34 percent of the market with revenues of $10 billion. North America will continue to lead with the largest market share at 37 percent.

Vera A. Swann, Office of Computers and Business Equipment, International Trade Administration, (202) 482-0396, June 1998.

COMPUTER NETWORKING

Global Industry Trends

The computer networking and data communications industry rose from obscurity several years ago to become one of the fastest growing and most technologically dynamic industries in the IT sector. U.S. networking companies have grown in size and public recognition. Cisco Systems, the current leader among networking hardware companies, saw its operating revenues increase from $183 million in 1991 to $4.1 billion in 1996, a CAGR of over 86 percent, according to Standard & Poor's. On the 1997 Forbes 500 list of largest companies, Cisco ranked forty-second by market value.

The computer networking industry is relatively young even by IT standards. It began with the rise of client/server computing in the 1980s; this is a method of computing in which infor-

mation and applications reside on a central computer (the server) that can be accessed by terminal computers such as PCs and workstations (clients). In a few short years computer networking companies have grown to rival the size and profitability of the most dominant players in the U.S. IT sector.

The client/server model of computing is most prevalent in the United States, but other advanced economies are beginning to catch up to American levels of deployment. Although this has tended to be primarily a developed country phenomenon, there is great interest worldwide in computer networking technologies. The primary drivers of this interest are increased efficiency and productivity gains for the work force and lower IT expenditures. Instead of colleagues having to save programs and work products to a disk and physically hand them to a coworker on a "sneaker" network, files and programs can be shared remotely. The gains in efficiency can be tremendous, depending on the application and the size of the teams and work groups.

Computer networks are proliferating throughout the world. For instance, *Dataquest* reports that in October 1997 approximately three-quarters of medium-size to large enterprises in western Europe had 90 percent of their PCs connected to a local area network (LAN). At the end of 1997 in Japan, by contrast, just over 60 percent of PCs were connected to a LAN. The rates are growing, however, and *Dataquest* predicts that Japan's PC-LAN connection ratio will top 80 percent by 2001.

The developing world lags in both its adoption of PCs and its connection ratios. However, interest in networking technology is high in all regions, and the highest growth rates in both areas are found in developing countries that are eager to adopt the latest technology. While the developing countries do not rival the more advanced economies in absolute terms, their growth rates are higher because of their relatively low starting point.

Developed economies are both the largest source of demand for networking products and the home of the largest competitors of U.S. networking companies. Large multinationals such as Fujitsu, Hitachi, and Siemens, along with a variety of other foreign firms, are active in the networking equipment and software field, especially in servers, but U.S. firms are the unrivaled leaders. Cisco Systems, Bay Networks, 3Com, Cabletron, Ascend, and a host of others form the front lines of global competition in networking and data communications technology. These companies also are beginning to compete with large telecommunications equipment makers such as Lucent and Nortel of Canada. In fact, in 1998 Canada's Nortel purchased Bay Networks in an effort to exploit opportunities in the fast-growing data communications field. In LAN technologies especially, U.S. firms compete primarily among themselves for global business opportunities. The largest U.S. networking firms also have a vast global presence in all the world's major and developing markets.

Domestic Trends

Very few trends in the networking industry are truly domestic, but a number of technologies and issues that affect demand for networking and data communications products have a domestic aspect, primarily because most of the companies at the forefront are American.

Technologies. One of the most important factors driving this industry is the pace of technological change. That pace is so rapid at times that networking companies must adapt quickly or face marginalization. For every new, better technology that is developed, several technologies will die a painful death. Betting on a technology's prospects has made or broken several smaller firms in this industry.

Only a couple of years ago asynchronous transfer mode (ATM) was thought of as the technology of the future. Most LANs at that time were Ethernet or Token Ring, but the ability of ATM to carry any type of data (such as text files, voice conversations, and videoconferencing images) at high speed was thought to be a sure winner by many pundits as an increasing number of multimedia applications were developed and widely deployed. It was thought that high-bandwidth (the amount of data or information that can be sent) applications such as videoconferencing would clog Ethernet LANs and leave little room for more mundane functions such as E-mail. However, the backers of Ethernet technologies increased the bandwidth functionality by a factor of 10, and now Gigabit Ethernet (increasing the bandwidth capability by a factor of 100) has marginalized the threat of ATM. Ethernet survived as a result of its ability to increase speed as well as the fact that it was considerably cheaper to add a few pieces of equipment to upgrade networks to high speed, or "Fast" Ethernet, than to replace a LAN completely to make the switch to ATM technology. As a result of these changes, Ethernet, ATM, and Token Ring, among others, continue to exist in various parts of the network, although Ethernet continues to dominate the LAN environment. However, IDC predicts that by 2005 or 2010 ATM will be the primary technology for LAN environments because it can carry data, voice, and video signals. Other industry pundits, however, predict its demise because it is not very efficient, with a high overhead relative to the amount of payload it can carry. As with so many technologies in this sector, only time will tell who is correct.

Another recent technology shift involves the rise of switching technologies. LAN traffic originates on one computer and is sent to another, as in E-mail. Traditional LANs used a router (a device that examines the destination address of a message and determines the appropriate or most efficient route) to direct files and messages. Routers once were called the kings of the LAN environment because they were sophisticated, intelligent pieces

of equipment—as well as expensive. A router will stop a message for a just a few nanoseconds, read an E-mail's destination address, compare that address with a list of all the addresses on the LAN, and send the message on the most efficient path to its destination.

The current buzz in the networking field concerns the "switched LAN." Traditional "shared media" LANs incorporated routers in the backbone to direct messages on the LAN and client computers attached to the LAN through a series of hubs, or devices where various cables intersect. Hubs are typically "dumb" devices that simply pass along information and messages from the PC to the LAN.

In a switched LAN a series of switches will perform some of both tasks. A switch will connect the cables that fan out to the client computers and direct messages to the section of the LAN where the destination computer is located. Unlike routers, switches do not have software tables that list all the possible destination computers, but switches can direct messages in a simplified manner. Switches are both speedier and less costly than routers.

Many analysts believe that this is part of a larger process that will decrease the cost of networking and simplify the management of the networking environment. Switches cost less than routers, and with switching, companies can replace hubs with even less sophisticated "unmanaged hubs" that require no staff time or expertise to administer. As a result, the network equipment is cheaper and the cost of administering the LAN can be reduced.

A third technology issue concerns the so-called network computer (NC). Several U.S. companies have touted the NC as the wave of the future. An NC is essentially a "dumb terminal," a device that includes only the minimum components needed to access information and computing power from a central server. Unlike a PC, which includes a CPU, a hard drive, and disk drives, an NC would eliminate most of these components and connect directly to a server for functionality.

An NC would reduce equipment costs and ease network administration. For instance, network managers could upgrade software on the network server only, avoiding the need to replace programs on each PC individually. However, NCs require a functioning network to operate. If the network crashes, all the NCs connected to it will be unusable.

The debate over the future of the NC is contentious and far from resolved. In practice, NCs are likely to be adopted in companies and industries in which ease of administration, cost factors, and software issues are important. *Dataquest* reports that the industries most interested in deploying NC terminals running Java software are banking and transport/agriculture. The industries expressing the most reluctance to shift to an NC model are the legal profession and retail.

Factors Affecting Demand for Networking. Numerous factors are increasing the demand for networks and networking products and services.

The Internet has dramatically increased both business and consumer interest in networking. As the Internet and the World Wide Web (WWW) grow in terms of the number of Web sites connected, the amount and quality of content, and functionality, the number of users that wish to access the Internet also increases. However, the Internet has had a more profound impact on networking than merely increasing user interest. One factor is the widespread (and spreading) use of Internet Protocol (IP), which governs the transmission of information moving over the Internet.

Internet technologies have expanded beyond the WWW to find a home on a smaller scale within companies and organizations. For instance, internal Internets (intranets) have been deployed in vast numbers and in a variety of companies around the world. Intranets are confined mini-Internets that are accessible only to a select group of employees or individuals of the company's choosing. An intranet may provide frequently used documents that employees can download, provide newsletters and other information without the need to send out paper memos, and allow employees to access a library CD-ROM system or other stored electronic information, all using Internet technologies.

Another example of Internet technology deployment is the extranet. An extranet essentially involves the connecting of two or more intranets. Extranets have been deployed primarily between a company and its suppliers. As a result of this linkage, a company can post an offer for suppliers to bid on a procurement project on the extranet, the suppliers can bid electronically, and the company can evaluate the numbers and grant the project to a bidder in a much more compressed time frame than can be accomplished with traditional methods. In this scenario the company in question can avoid having to advertise a bid, send out paper copies of the bid documents, and rely on the postal service to deliver the documents. Several companies expect to save thousands or millions of dollars by using Internet technologies such as intranets and extranets. In fact, the U.S. military has been providing for electronic bidding on tenders for some time, and the U.S. government is augmenting its Web-based tender system to enable electronic bidding for all tenders, regardless of size.

As telecommuting becomes more prevalent and an increasing number of professionals find it necessary to connect to a corporate LAN when they are out of the office, remote access needs are driving the demand for networking products and services. In fact, remote access servers represent one of the fastest growing networking product segments. Remote access also requires a host of additional services and products. For instance, the ability to tap into a corporate LAN from outside a discrete building or location raises significant security concerns. A variety of technologies and software have been developed to protect networks from unauthorized access, including firewalls, encryption, and password protection. The markets for security products are growing dramatically. According to *Dataquest,* the market for firewalls increased to over $250 million in 1997, an 80 percent increase in revenue over 1996.

Remote access also requires a method of contacting the LAN server, and a variety of methods for doing this are currently in place or in development. The most common appara-

tus used by both businesses and individuals for connecting over public networks to the Internet or a LAN is a traditional analog (telephone) line and modem. According to *Dataquest,* 54 percent of the businesses surveyed used an analog line for dial-up access to a LAN. Nearly 30 percent used Integrated Services Digital Network (ISDN), 7 percent used a private leased line connection, and 10 percent used another form of connection technology. New technologies are being developed. One of the more promising is Digital Subscriber Line (DSL), which allows broadband transmission of data over standard copper phone lines. DSL, in a variety of versions and forms, is being developed to provide high-speed access without an extraordinary investment in new telecommunications infrastructure.

In addition, network demand has increased merely as a result of the increase in the number of PCs connected to LANs. These numbers have increased substantially for homes, schools, and businesses.

Finally, network demand has increased as a result of the proliferation of high-bandwidth applications. Videoconferencing, images, and voice all require more than the usual amount of bandwidth to be sent over LANs, and network managers are struggling to catch up. As the need to send more messages and/or images of greater complexity increases, so does the need for greater bandwidth in the LAN. High-bandwidth technologies such as ATM and Gigabit Ethernet should help alleviate these concerns.

Issues and Challenges

Technological Change. The computer networking and data communications industry has undergone a dramatic change in terms of technology in recent years. Some of the most promising new technologies of only a couple of years ago have died painful deaths. For instance, several years ago fiber optic cabling to the computer desktop was seen by many analysts as a logical progression as computer applications grew larger and ate up all the available bandwidth on traditional cables. However, the high cost of fiber cables and the ability to add capacity to traditional cables combined to head off the switch to fiber.

Industry Consolidation. Several networking companies have grown to become behemoths of the computer industry by acquiring numerous smaller software and hardware firms to shore up their product lines or add functionality to their existing products. Cisco Systems has been particularly active in this regard. According to its web site, Cisco acquired 4 companies in the first 5 months of 1998 and 10 since the beginning of 1997. 3Com Corporation acquired U.S. Robotics, among others, and Lucent Technologies bought out three small networking companies since December 1997, according to the *Financial Times.* The networking industry is rapidly becoming an industry with a few giant firms and many niche players around the core group.

Voice and Data Integration. All the major vendors for computer networking equipment are implementing or considering the marriage of voice and data networks. As was mentioned above, the larger telecommunications equipment manufacturers are also moving into data markets. For example, Nortel of Canada purchased Bay Networks in 1998. The reason is clear: While data traffic increases exponentially, voice traffic on the public network is increasing at a slow and steady pace. Several market research firms predict that the share of data traffic will be as high as 90 percent of public network traffic. UUNet, the largest U.S. Internet service provider (ISP), predicted at Networld+Interop in May 1998 that the share of data will equal 99 percent of all traffic.

The rationale for the convergence of voice and data in a local network is that significant cost savings may be realized when these two previously distinct networks are merged under one management system. *Dataquest* reports that 40 percent of the organizations questioned are considering integrating their voice and data networks in the next 5 years. In response, large vendors have developed pieces of equipment that act as both data communications devices and private branch exchanges (PBXs) for voice. The integration of voice and data will have a significant impact on producers in both markets. Considerable attention should be paid to this issue as these technologies converge further.

Security. As was mentioned above, network security has become a more important issue with the rise of remote access and the Internet. Several networking vendors have acquired security companies or developed their own security measures to implement in their products. For instance, Cisco acquired WheelGroup Corporation in February 1998. WheelGroup produces intrusion detection and security scanning software products which can identify and react to unauthorized access and hackers.

Complexity. As networks grow in size and number of users, complexity necessarily increases. According to IDC, network managers are looking primarily for simplicity from networking vendors. Managers need easy installation solutions; want to maximize the use of their current resources, including staff time and energy; and hope to make network management as invisible as possible, that is, render network management easy if not nonexistent.

Data Communications Equipment Markets

The United States is by far the largest market for data communications equipment. IDC reports that the U.S. market for data communications equipment (routers, switches, etc.) was worth almost $19 billion in 1997. The next largest market is Japan at $3.7 billion in 1997, and that market is expected to be just over $5 billion in 2001. However, the U.S. share of the worldwide market is expected to decrease over the next few years. In 1997 the U.S. proportion was over 46 percent of the worldwide market, and that share, despite a substantial increase in absolute terms, will be just over 43 percent in 2001. This indicates that

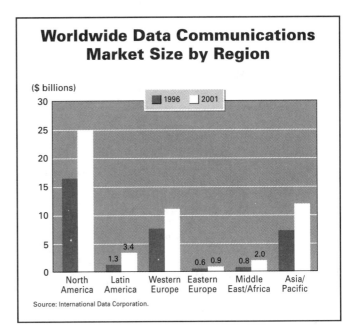

FIGURE 28-1

the fastest growing markets for U.S. networking and data communications products will be outside the United States.

As is shown in Figure 28-1, North American data communications equipment markets were worth over $16.5 billion in 1996 and are expected by IDC to be worth over $25 billion in 2001, for a CAGR of 8.6 percent. Latin America is expected to be the fastest-growing market in the world. That market was worth less than $1.3 billion in 1996, and IDC predicts that it will grow to over $3.4 billion in 2001, for a CAGR of 21.8 percent. Western Europe's market was valued at $7.6 billion in 1996 and is expected by IDC to grow to over $11.1 billion by 2001, for a CAGR of 7.8 percent. Eastern European markets were worth just over half a billion U.S. dollars in 1996 and are expected to reach nearly $900 million by 2001, for a CAGR of 10.9 percent. The Middle East and Africa are two additional high-growth regions for data communications equipment. In 1996, those markets together were valued at less than $800 million, but they are expected to be worth almost $2 billion by 2001, for a CAGR of 20.5 percent. The Asia/Pacific region is one of variety and fluctuation. The Asian currency crisis of 1997 has made predictions difficult, especially if the crisis spreads to additional countries. In addition, predictions for that region are complicated by the fact that some countries have very stable markets, such as Australia, and others show negative growth. IDC reports that the Asia/Pacific market was worth almost $7.3 billion in 1996 and will grow to almost $12 billion in 2001, for a CAGR of 10.5 percent. Regional proportions of worldwide data communications equipment markets are shown in Figure 28-2.

NICs. Network interface cards (NICs) are the devices that actually connect a computer to a LAN or another network. NICs generally are considered commodity products, and thus

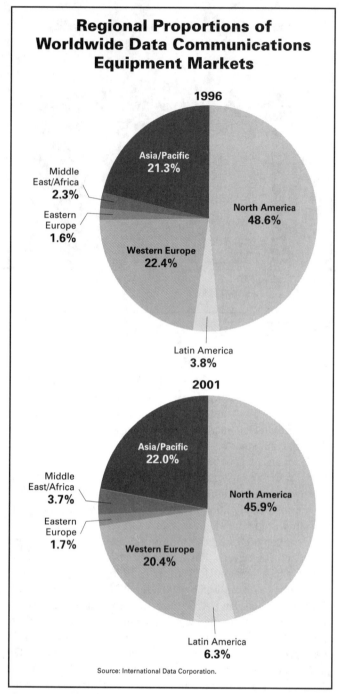

Regional Proportions of Worldwide Data Communications Equipment Markets

1996

- Asia/Pacific **21.3%**
- Middle East/Africa **2.3%**
- Eastern Europe **1.6%**
- Western Europe **22.4%**
- North America **48.6%**
- Latin America **3.8%**

2001

- Asia/Pacific **22.0%**
- Middle East/Africa **3.7%**
- Eastern Europe **1.7%**
- Western Europe **20.4%**
- North America **45.9%**
- Latin America **6.3%**

Source: International Data Corporation.

FIGURE 28-2

However, the fastest growing NIC market was that for high-speed NICs. The market for 10/100Mbps Fast Ethernet NICs increased to around 4.5 million units in 1996, and total shipments of all high-speed NICs grew to 5 million cards from only 1 million in 1995. This constituted a 400 percent increase in just 1 year, and high-speed NICs in 1996 represented 14 percent of the total NIC market, up from 4 percent in 1995.

The "server-NIC" is a relatively new market segment that is growing rapidly. A server-NIC is essentially a device that connects a server to the network the way a traditional NIC does for a PC or other end-user device. IDC predicts that the server-NIC market will continue to grow, and it represents a solid long-term opportunity for manufacturers to escape the commodity nature of the NIC market, at least until competition in this market segment increases.

For both NICs and server-NICs, the fastest growing markets will continue to be outside the United States and western Europe.

According to IDC, the forecast for server-NICs is strongly positive. NIC shipments are expected to grow from 3,419 units in 1996 to 6,657 units in 2001, for a CAGR of 14.3 percent. The server-NIC installed base will increase from 8,576 units in 1996 to 23,305 in 2001, a CAGR of 22.1 percent.

Routers. Routers are the heart of a computer network. They direct the flow of information and messages and determine the best route for information to flow.

The worldwide router market will continue to experience strong growth, according to IDC. Although pundits have predicted the extinction of the router for some time as a result of changes in technology, the router has retained its prominence in most networks. Its usefulness in the center of complex networks and the rise of the Internet are the primary reasons for its resiliency.

Worldwide router shipments totaled just over 1 million in 1996 and are expected to almost triple by 2001, for a CAGR of 24 percent. The worldwide installed base will more than triple over that period to reach over 9 million routers, a CAGR of 32 percent.

The regional variations in router shipments and the installed base of routers show that the U.S. market is expected to be the slowest growing. Router shipments in the United States are expected to increase from over 466,000 in 1996 to 1.2 million in 2001, for a CAGR of 21 percent. The U.S. installed base will increase at a CAGR of 29 percent. Western Europe is expected by IDC to be the fastest growing market in terms of shipments and installed base growth. Router shipments in Europe will increase from just under 300,000 in 1996 to 954,000 in 2001, a CAGR of 27 percent. The installed base will increase at a CAGR of 35 percent. The Asia/Pacific region, as reported by IDC, will increase its shipments from over 188,000 in 1996 to 558,075 in 2001, for a CAGR of 24 percent and an installed base CAGR of 32 percent. For the rest of the world (ROW), shipments in 1996 were just over 81,000 routers and are expected to climb to almost 245,000 units in 2001, a shipment CAGR of 25 percent and an installed base CAGR of 33 percent (see Figure 28-3).

the market is competitively priced. Different NICs are needed for different network speeds and platforms. For instance, there is a 10Mbps (megabits per second) Ethernet NIC, a 100Mbps Ethernet NIC, and NICs for ATM networks of various speeds. IDC predicts that the market for NICs will continue its trend toward higher-speed technologies and new geographic markets.

According to the IDC, the worldwide NIC market grew to about $4 billion in end-user expenditures in 1996, while unit shipments increased strongly to over 37 million worldwide. The market for 10Mbps Ethernet NICs was already large and increased 19 percent to reach around 28 million units in 1996.

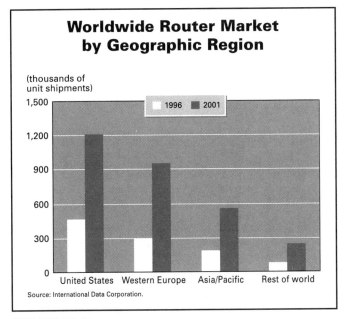

FIGURE 28-3

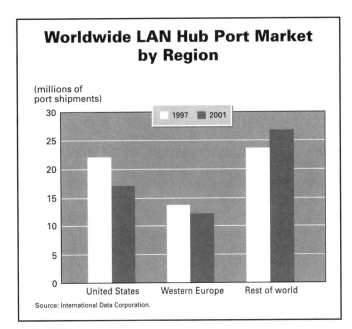

FIGURE 28-4

Hubs. Hub shipments are measured in "ports," or the physical access points to a computer or another device. Hubs have multiple ports, depending on their size and sophistication.

Hubs have the distinction of being the only computer networking product market that is expected to decline in volume. Multiple explanations have been discussed above, such as the increasing use of switches to perform hub functions and the desire of network managers to reduce complexity. The worldwide volume of hub shipments in 1997 was just 25.1 million ports, whereas the number of port shipments in only the second half of 1996 was 25.6 million. According to IDC, the only subsegment that showed growth was unmanaged hubs, which had 5 percent growth in 1997 over the level in the second half of 1996.

Worldwide LAN hub port shipments totaled 59.33 million in 1997, and IDC predicts that they will total only 55.83 million in 2001. The regional breakdown is considerably more interesting (Figure 28-4). Hub port shipments in the United States totaled 20 million in 1995, and they are expected to decrease to just under 17 million in 2001, for a CAGR of −6 percent. The western European market also is expected to decrease, but by a lesser amount, for a CAGR of −3 percent. Hub port shipments outside those two regions did show signs of continued growth, however, offsetting decreases in growth in those markets. IDC predicts that port shipments will increase to 26.7 million units in 2001, for a CAGR of 7 percent. The installed bases in the three regions will all increase by 2001, however. For the United States the CAGR is 8 percent, for western Europe the figure is 10 percent, and for the ROW it is 23 percent. Particularly for hubs, the significant markets in the foreseeable future will be outside the most mature networking markets.

Switches. As was stated above, the market for switches is expected to grow rapidly in the coming years. As the number of networks grows and as vendors continue to add functionality to switches, demand will increase dramatically. Once again, however, the United States is expected to be the slowest growing market.

Worldwide switch port shipments are expected to increase from just over 2 million in 1995 to over 57 million in 2001. Port shipments for the various regions in 2001 are as follows: 26.4 million to the United States for a CAGR of 42 percent, 17.2 million to western Europe for a CAGR of 55 percent, and 13.7 million to the ROW for a CAGR of 57 percent (see Figure 28-5).

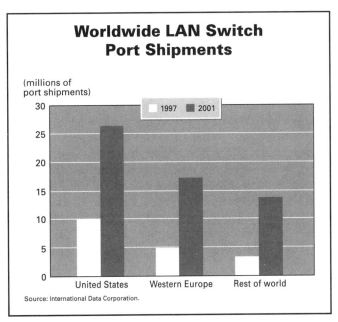

FIGURE 28-5

LAN Servers. Servers are a varied group and come with several different functions and in various positions on the price-performance spectrum. Most market research firms group servers into high-end, midrange, and low-end categories, and servers can perform different functions. For instance, there are print servers, E-mail servers, and data warehousing servers.

IDC predicts that the U.S. market for all types of servers will increase from $19.2 billion in 1996 to over $31.7 billion in 2001, which represents 34.2 percent of the total worldwide market for servers. The next largest market for servers is Japan, which will increase from $12.6 billion in 1996 to $17.6 billion in 2001, reaching a 19 percent world share. The next four largest markets are European Union (EU) countries, which have market sizes ranging from 6.5 percent for Germany to 2.0 percent for Italy. The total worldwide market for servers will increase from $56.6 billion in 1996 to $92.8 billion in 2001.

The fastest growing subsegment in the server category is remote access servers (RASs). Although this market, according to IDC, has not lived up to pundits[1] expectations, the outlook for RASs is bright. RASs are in high demand as a result of the rise of the Internet and new opportunities in international markets. The total worldwide markets for RASs is expected to increase from 174,600 units in 1995 to 690,000 units in 2001. Growth rates are expected to decrease slowly over this period.

Modems. There are two primary categories of modems: analog and cable. Analog modems have been around for years, and the public always anticipates the latest high-speed technology to increase their speed. The latest variety is the 56K modem. Although 56K speeds have been around for a while, a common standard was established only in 1998. Until then the two primary producers, U.S. Robotics (3Com) and Rockwell, had conflicting products that could not work together. However, in December 1997 the two companies agreed on a compromise standard, which was adopted in February 1998 by the International Telecommunications Union (ITU), the international standard-setting body. Since this decision was made, all producers have agreed to adhere to the standard. As a result, analog modem unit sales are expected to increase substantially, driven primarily by the growth of the Internet.

Regional analog modem shipments (see Figure 28-6) indicate that by far the fastest growing markets lie outside the United States and western Europe. Unit shipments for the United States in 1996 were almost 16.9 million and are predicted by IDC to be 32.2 million in 2001, for a CAGR of 13.8 percent. Western European markets are expected to be the smallest in terms of size and growth, increasing from 5.4 million in 1996 to 9.8 million in 2001, for a CAGR of 12.6 percent. The ROW is where significant growth lies for this market. ROW unit shipments are expected to increase from 6.8 million in 1996 to 28 million in 2001, a CAGR of 32.7 percent.

Cable modems are a relatively new product whose demand has been strong in areas that offer Internet service over cable wiring. Since the technology was developed to enable television

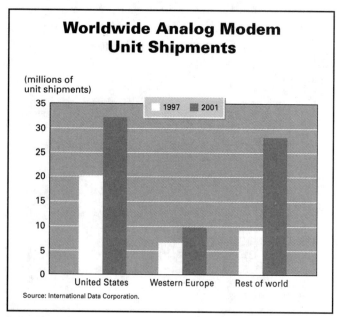

FIGURE 28-6

cables to carry signals in both directions, cable companies have investigated the possibility of becoming ISPs. Several cable companies have deployed upgraded systems that can provide Internet access, but these test markets cover only a few select cities in the United States. Cable is an attractive option, since download speeds are significantly higher than they are with analog lines.

The worldwide number of homes with cable modems is expected to grow substantially over the next few years, according to IDC. For instance, as is shown in Figure 28-7, in the United States (whose market is expected to grow the most slowly) the number of cable modems was 100,000 in 1997, but that is expected to increase to almost 2.3 million in 2002, a CAGR of

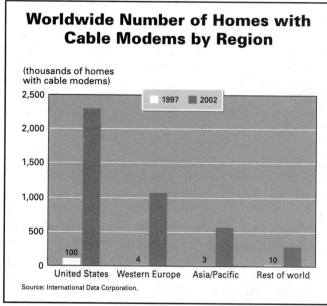

FIGURE 28-7

86.9 percent. Western Europe is expected to have the fastest growing market, increasing from only 4,000 units in 1997 to over 1 million in 2002, a CAGR of 205 percent. Asian markets will increase from 3,000 in 1997 to 556,000 in 2002 and the ROW markets will increase from 10,000 in 1997 to 274,000 in 2002, for CAGRs of 184.2 percent and 93.9 percent, respectively.

Cable modem markets will be aided both by interest in high-speed Internet access and by the increase in the number of homes with televisions and cable subscriptions. Again, and not surprisingly, markets outside the United States are the fastest growing and show the most potential. According to IDC, the limiting factor for cable modems is a lack of availability of this service, not a lack of consumer demand. End users generally have been very pleased with the service, and many parts of the country and the world are eagerly awaiting full-scale deployment of cable access.

Network Operating Systems

The biggest story in this segment of the networking industry is Microsoft's Windows NT. NT is an operating system (OS) for computer networks. Microsoft deployed Windows NT several years ago, and since then it has taken the media by storm. Its acceptance as an OS has grown quickly, and it is constantly referred to as the OS that will challenge the more established players in this market. The 5-year CAGR for Windows NT will reach 100 percent in 2000, according to *Dataquest.*

NT has grown substantially over the past few years, but it has not displaced all the other OSs for network computing. The perceived dominance of Windows NT has resulted largely from the marketing abilities of Microsoft Corporation. When networking professionals were asked by IDC why they were implementing Windows NT, many of them stated that they considered NT the de facto standard.

Many business organizations use more than one OS. For instance, Windows NT is currently installed in about 62 percent of organizations, as reported by IDC. Novell's NetWare is installed in 53 percent of organizations, UNIX (in all its varieties) in 45 percent, and IBM's OS/2 in 12 percent. Although NT has a significant share of the market, it is certainly not cannibalizing all the other OSs. Even more interesting is the number of organizations that stated which OSs they were adding and which OSs would replace legacy systems. Fifty-nine percent of the organizations surveyed planned to add Windows NT, and 39 percent said that NT would be their replacement system. However, 23 percent of these organizations planned to add NetWare and 29 percent said that they would replace their current systems with NetWare. For UNIX the numbers were 26 percent and 14 percent, respectively.

In the same IDC survey, decision makers who stated that they would not adopt NT were asked why. The reasons were varied, but some of them included their past investment in NetWare, their reluctance to be dependent on a single vendor, and a lack of staff expertise with NT.

Different OSs have strengths and weaknesses for various organizations and applications. Windows NT has come to virtually dominate low-end systems with relatively few users. UNIX, by comparison, is the dominant environment for large-scale databases and other high-performance functions, such as transaction processing. UNIX also supports a very large number of users compared with NT systems. NT and NetWare systems are used primarily for file and print applications, E-mail, and Internet access, whereas the primary functions of UNIX systems include database management, file and print, and custom applications.

As can be seen from this analysis, certain OS vendors may be more vulnerable than others to the onslaught of Windows NT. While the media play up the importance of NT in the network and NT continues to gain market share, it is clear that for the foreseeable future at least, several OSs will coexist even within the same organization. Each has its niche and place in the networking environment.

Steven Harris, Office of Computers and Business Equipment, International Trade Administration, (202) 482-0568, June 1998.

THE INTERNET AND ON-LINE TECHNOLOGIES

Global Industry Trends

The Internet is one of the few "industries" that is truly global in character. Although most Internet traffic still passes through the United States, no single country controls the Internet, nor can one.

Examples abound of the interest of governments or industries in restricting Internet sales or activities. In May 1998 the *Financial Times* reported on an effort by the music industry in the United Kingdom to restrict sales of music over the Internet. The British Phonographic Industry is concerned because U.S. Internet Web sites sell CDs and singles at significantly lower prices than those charged at retail stores in the United Kingdom. Preventing such sales is nearly impossible because of the global and unrestricted nature of the Internet, however.

The Internet is a vast global communications medium. With its roots in the U.S. military and research communities, it has grown substantially to involve primarily commercial interests and users. As can be seen in Table 28-5, interest in the Internet and its use have grown faster than have all other methods of communication in this century.

In 1997 the Internet became substantially more global in appearance. More foreign companies, governments, and users have gone on-line, increasing the international flavor of the Inter-

TABLE 28-5: Time to Reach 50 Million U.S. Users

Method of Communication	Years	Time Period
Telephone	25	1920–1945
Radio	38	1922–1960
Television	13	1951–1964
Cable	10	1976–1986
Internet	5	1993–1998

Source: Andersen Consulting.

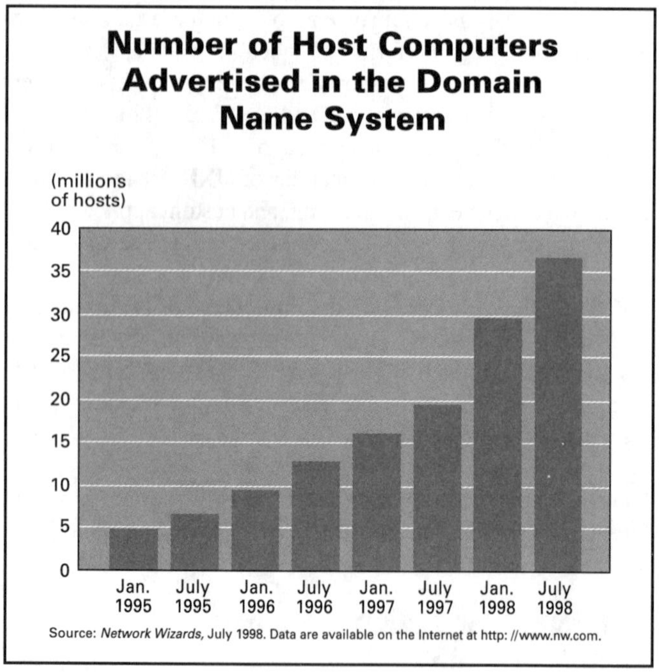

Number of Host Computers Advertised in the Domain Name System

(millions of hosts)

Source: *Network Wizards*, July 1998. Data are available on the Internet at http://www.nw.com.

FIGURE 28-8

net. The number of users outside the United States has shown an incredible increase in the past few years, especially in 1997.

Hard data and numbers on the size of the Internet, the number of users, and the amount of business conducted over it are both difficult to come by and suspect. Various organizations and market research firms have such data, but the definitions of a "connection" and a "business transaction" vary with the source. For instance, some firms report "electronic commerce" numbers that involve only sales done over the Internet, while other firms report all transactions completed as a result of on-line information, both sales done on the Internet and sales completed because a person found information about a product on the Internet but bought the product at a store or dealership. For this reason, users of data should examine the composition of the data closely for consistency. The numbers reported in this section come from a variety of sources and generally follow relatively conservative methods of data collection.

According to *Network Wizards*, the number of computers connected to the Internet worldwide in July 1998 was 36,739,000. It reports that the number of Internet hosts grew over 50 percent between June and the end of 1997 and 84 percent throughout 1997 (see Figure 28-8). According to IDC, the number of devices accessing the WWW is expected to have a CAGR of 67 percent between 1995 and 2001.

The growth of the Internet continues to accelerate. Much of this growth is the result of the increase in interest and users in developing countries primarily in Latin America and Asia. According to *Network Wizards*, Taiwan had the biggest increase in the number of hosts, going from 40,000 in June 1997 to 180,000 in January 1998. Other large increases were reported in New Zealand, which doubled its number of hosts to 169,264; Korea's hosts grew 84 percent and Brazil's grew 52 percent in that period.

Increasing Internet Globalization

The Internet is expected to become even more global over the next few years for a variety of reasons. PC penetration in the rest of the world is expected to increase significantly. In addition, telecommunications deregulation in many countries is expected to decrease prices and thus allow more people to afford Internet access. Also, deployment of broadband and other high-capacity networks will allow an increased number of users. Finally, the United States is expected to experience relative Internet saturation compared with the rest of the world. The biggest markets for electronic commerce, PCs, and Internet services will be in developing countries that are expected to experience huge growth rates in Internet use. As a result of the factors mentioned above, *eMarketer* projected that non-U.S. net users would begin to outnumber U.S. users by the end of 1998.

Despite the increase in non-U.S. users, the Internet is essentially an English-language medium. Several governments have expressed concern as a result, notably the government of China. That government is currently developing a "China Wide Web" to provide Chinese-language content for its population.

Most of the devices used to access the Web are PCs and NCs. The installed base of PCs and NCs is often used as a indicator for how big the Internet is or could get. According to IDC, the percentage of world PCs and NCs accessing the WWW continues to increase. Only 7 percent of these computers were connected to the Web in 1995, but that number is expected to grow to 29 percent in 1998 and 55 percent in 2001.

Trends

Non-PC Access Devices. Although IDC reports that only 14 percent of net users access the Web from non-PC devices (television set-top boxes, hand-held computers, etc.), it predicts that the number of those devices will grow considerably in the next few years. Whereas there were 1.05 million non-PC access

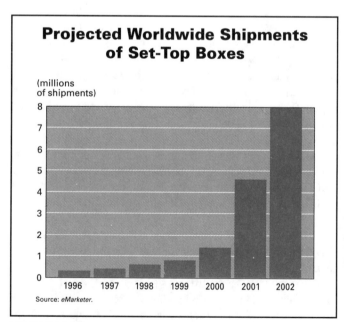

Projected Worldwide Shipments of Set-Top Boxes

(millions of shipments)

Source: *eMarketer*.

FIGURE 28-9

devices in 1997, that number is expected to increase to 26.5 million in 2001. The *eMarketer* estimates of shipments of set-top boxes are shown in Figure 28-9.

Business on the Web. The Internet has grown from its use as a specialty tool for professors and scientists to a mass phenomenon involving consumers and businesses. As recently as 1996 the Internet was used primarily for educational and entertainment purposes. Increasingly, the Internet is used as a tool for businesses to connect with consumers and suppliers. For example, in April 1998 Chevron Corporation announced the deployment of a Web-based purchasing system. The oil and chemicals giant expects to move $2.7 billion worth of purchases to the Internet from 200 suppliers. After testing, the company expects to extend its on-line purchasing system to all of its $9.9 billion procurements because such a system is considerably more time- and cost-effective than the traditional bidding process.

Chevron is just one company that is utilizing the Internet to cut costs and procurement times to improve efficiency and reduce expenditures. Chevron's system is an example of an extranet—the linking of companies and their suppliers via the WWW. Extranets, as was mentioned earlier in this chapter, are an extension of an intranet, or an internal Internet. Intranets are accessible only by employees and those granted explicit access. However, intranets and extranets are created using Internet protocols and are based on Internet technology. These forms of "mini-Internets" are transforming the way companies disseminate information to employees, suppliers, and customers.

The growth of intranets and extranets and the use of the Internet as a business tool are still occurring primarily in the developed countries, especially the United States. In much of Latin America, the Middle East, and Africa, the Internet is still used primarily for entertainment and education. In Latin America in particular, the Internet is largely used for chat, reflecting the fact that the majority of on-line users are between the ages of 19 and 31 years. These regions are following the same path as the United States and slowly increasing Internet use for business purposes. Developing countries represent large potential markets for Internet business tools in the years to come.

Businesses are continually finding new ways for the Internet to increase or improve business contacts. For instance, Web site help desks are becoming more common. As the WWW becomes an increasingly significant source of information about companies, more users are accessing Web sites to ask questions or get help. For instance, at Networld+Interop in May 1998, a Cisco Systems spokesperson announced that 70 percent of customer assistance was done over the Internet. This can result in very practical benefits for companies, since Web site help is considerably less expensive than call centers.

ISPs, Telecommunications Competition, and Consolidation. In 1997 the major U.S. telecommunications companies substantially increased their presence in the ISP market. The U.S. market for Internet service thus followed a different path from that taken by much of the rest of the world. In most countries the first ISP is almost always the national telecommunications

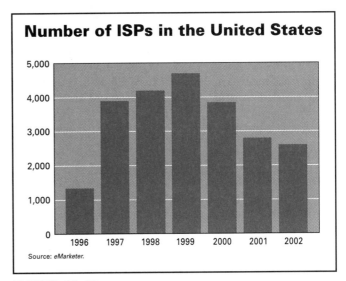

FIGURE 28-10

monopoly. This situation often occurs as a result of government fiat or the fact that the dominant provider is the only provider of telecom services.

The ISP market has undergone considerable consolidation over the past couple of years in the United States. According to *eMarketer*, there were 1,340 ISPs in 1996, and that number was expected to first increase and then shrink to 2,600 in 2002 (see Figure 28-10). Obviously, most of these ISPs are small firms with a relatively small customer base, but a few ISPs are large, national providers. America on Line (AOL) captured 55 percent of the on-line market after its acquisition of Compuserv in late 1997. Another high-profile merger occurred in early 1998 when Sprint, a U.S. long-distance telecommunications provider, acquired Earthlink. Despite the significant rise in the number of subscriptions to ISPs generally, the number of subscriptions claimed by the largest ISPs is decreasing. A report by *The Interactive Services* found that major ISP subscriptions declined 4.9 percent. The report found that one of the reasons for this decrease was the rise in subscriptions to new Internet services provided by the Regional Bell Operating Companies, such as U.S. West and GTE.

Internet Telephony. In 1997, "voice-over-IP" (Internet Protocol) became the cry of industry analysts. Simply put, voice-over-IP (VoIP) allows telephone conversations to take place over the Internet. Perhaps as a method of countering this threat to their core business, many telecommunications companies have aggressively entered the ISP market.

Internet phone calls essentially allow customers to dial their local ISP access number and complete a call over the Internet at a substantially reduced cost. Cost saving is the primary reason for interest in Internet telephony currently. Problems with this method of communication are beginning to ease as latency (time delay) decreases and quality increases.

According to IDC, price arbitrage as the primary driver of Internet telephony will end in 2 years and will be replaced by value-added services. In addition, the use of Internet telephony is expected to skyrocket. In 1997 only 0.2 percent of the 857 billion minutes of long-distance and international calling was done using Internet telephony. IDC predicts that that will increase to 11 percent by 2002 and that the revenue generated by IP voice minutes in 2002 will be $25 billion. Although the growth of Internet telephony is projected to be huge, standard voice telephony is not expected to disappear.

Barriers to Growth

Infrastructure Issues. The lack of adequate telecommunications infrastructure in much of the world is a significant barrier to future Internet development. National monopolies and governments have struggled for years to build telecommunications infrastructures capable of handling high-volume data traffic. Many governments (typically the majority, if not the only, shareholder in telecommunications monopolies) have found the only practical answer to be privatization of the national monopoly carrier. With the costs of infrastructure deployment so high and the nearly universal constraints on government budgets so intense, privatization is seen as the best, if not the only, option.

Existing telecommunications systems have limited capacity to carry voice and data traffic. U.S. infrastructure needs for Internet use continue to increase at a dramatic rate, and ISPs are constantly increasing capacity. The pressure on foreign ISPs is often more intense. As demand in developing countries increases even faster than it does in the United States and considering that the telecommunications infrastructure in most countries is less extensive and technologically advanced, the problem of gaining Internet connectivity abroad is becoming increasingly acute.

Although deregulation of telecommunications markets internationally is taking place, it is occurring at a painfully slow pace in many cases. This situation represents another significant barrier to Internet growth. Since telecommunications services are considered a social good in many countries, agreement on the method of privatization and even the decision to privatize can be difficult and very political. Not only must a country's government develop and implement a plan for deregulation, some countries require a change in their constitutions. Governments, parliaments, and national courts are often all involved in the process. As a result, the process of privatization and deregulation is progressing at a slow pace in many parts of the world. Growth in Internet usage is one casualty.

Privacy. Privacy concerns are another barrier to growth of the Internet. Over the years studies designed to document Internet users' fears and concerns have shown that privacy issues continue to rise on the priority lists of many people. The collection and use of personal information by Web sites, the fear that credit card numbers and other personal data may be intercepted, and the perceived threat from hackers have combined to produce varying levels of concern among the Internet population.

Various industry groups and governments have begun to address these concerns. In the United States, computer and service sector industry groups are raising awareness among businesses that collect information and consumers who supply it. Also, the Federal Trade Commission's (FTC) Bureau of Consumer Protection has studied the prevalence of Web site privacy statements and the fraudulent use of such statements.

The EU has developed by far the most extensive regulations on privacy. The EU data directive requires that personal information about European citizens be kept private and secure. The directive applies extraterritorially to any jurisdiction to which information about EU citizens is sent. Other countries are to be "certified" as adequately safeguarding personal information or not. If a country is not certified, the transmission of personal data about European citizens to that country is not allowed.

The EU directive has caused much concern in other countries because of its extraterritorial nature. The directive was expected to take effect in 1999.

Content. Government regulation or even prohibition of Internet content is the most subjective and potentially most threatening barrier to Internet growth. While most countries agree that using the Internet to transmit child pornography and other "obscene" materials should be banned, substantial disagreement exists regarding less extreme issues. Some countries object to the widespread transmission of political information that they consider subversive or a threat to social peace, and others object to any form of pornography whatsoever. The Communications Decency Act in the United States was an example of an attempt by a national government to impose standards on Internet content. Key portions of the act were struck down by the U.S. Supreme Court in 1997. In Germany the head of CompuServe Deutschland was found guilty of aiding the dissemination of pornography on the Internet. The guilty verdict came despite a plea by both the defense and the prosecution to find him innocent and a German law passed in 1997 that explicitly states that on-line service providers cannot be held responsible for the information to which they provide access. The judge in the case has come under heavy criticism both within and outside of Germany.

As a global phenomenon that is not subject to any one country's laws, the Internet makes regulation of this kind difficult, if not impossible. The only way in which a government can truly control Internet information is to have a server located within its territory, but other methods have been attempted by various governments. It is not clear how effective such methods will be. What is clear is that no efficient and effective method has been devised by any government. The Internet imposes new constraints on government action.

Internet Commerce

On-Line Sales. As was mentioned above, it is difficult to determine the value and volume of on-line sales because of the sketchiness of the data and the definitions used by various research firms in this constantly evolving and fluid market. According to IDC, business-to-business commerce over the Web amounted to $8 billion in 1997 and will grow to $333 billion by 2002. According to ActivMedia, Web commerce accounted for $21.8 billion in 1997 and will increase to $1.2 trillion in 2001.

The value of on-line consumer revenue from Web commerce (business-to-consumer transactions) was estimated by Forrester Research to be $1.1 billion in 1997 and to increase to $6.5 billion by 2000.

Percentages of On-Line Users Making Purchases. The firm @plan estimates that 24 percent of active U.S. Internet users make purchases on-line. That company also estimates that 27 percent of Latin American Internet users make on-line purchases.

IDC stated that electronic commerce revenue in the year ending December 1997 would total $8.5 billion in the United States, rising to $155 billion in 2001, for a CAGR of 107 percent. Western Europe's revenue for 1997 totaled $1.1 billion and is expected to reach almost $26 billion in 2001, for a CAGR of 120 percent. Similar numbers for the Asia/Pacific region (excluding Japan) are about $234 million in 1997 and $12.5 billion in 2001, for a CAGR of 170 percent. E-commerce revenue in Japan is expected to increase from $486.5 million in 1997 to $18.1 billion in 2001, for a CAGR of 147 percent. In the ROW this will increase from $255.2 million in 1997 to $11.4 billion in 2001, for a CAGR of 159 percent. As is clear from these numbers, staggering growth is expected in all parts of the world, but the best prospects are outside the United States, where the process is more advanced (see Figure 28-11).

Business Models and Products. For obvious reasons, computer equipment and software are some of the most popular

goods sold on the Internet. Dell Computer has been a pioneer in this market. Dell makes $3 million a day of sales on its Web site. Cisco Systems reports that it has made $10 million in sales on its site.

IDC's 1997 WWW Survey polled Internet purchasers on the products they bought. The most common answers were software and books—39.6 percent purchased software, and 22.1 percent purchased books. According to @plan, the top five on-line purchase categories were books, computer hardware, airline tickets, general software, and music recordings. Given the relatively immature nature of on-line purchasing, it is not surprising that purchases to date have been limited primarily to small-ticket commodity items. As consumer confidence increases and the technology develops, the amount and variety of electronic purchases should increase substantially.

One industry undergoing substantial change as a result of the Internet is the travel industry. Companies and services such as Travelocity, Expedia, and Yahoo! Travel enable customers to find the cheapest fares for airline travel, hotel rooms, and rental cars. Consumers can customize their user profiles on many such sites to allow services such as notification when airline fares change. Many hotels, car rental agencies, and other travel services offer discounts for on-line purchases, since Web purchases reduce overhead by selling directly to the consumer and avoiding travel agents.

Global Market Trends

Growth in the On-Line User Population. While statistics are difficult to obtain and verify, a number of firms have published numbers on the growth of the Internet population. All of them, however, include a warning about the reliability of such numbers.

According to IDC, the WWW population is expected to grow from 82 million in 1997 to 329 million in 2002. According to CommerceNet, the world total is currently 99.54 million users. The regional breakdown is United States and Canada, 58 million; Africa, 1 million; Europe, 23 million; the Asia/Pacific region, 15 million; the Middle East, 0.54 million; and South America, 2 million.

Today more than 150 countries have direct access to the Internet, although roughly two-thirds of all users are from the United States and Canada and about two-thirds of all Internet hosts are located in the United States. However, the Internet is expected to become more global in the coming years as PC penetration increases substantially in other parts of the world, deregulation of global telecommunications markets accelerates, and relative saturation takes place in the United States.

Given the substantial lead of the United States in Internet development and the growing global interest in this technology, it makes sense that the fastest growing markets for U.S. business are in the international arena as other parts of the world catch up to U.S. levels of PC penetration and Internet use. Given their already substantial lead and the dominance of the English language on the Internet, U.S. firms are clearly in an excellent position to compete on an international scale.

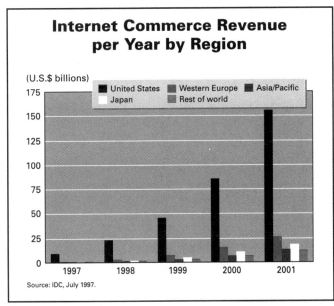

Internet Commerce Revenue per Year by Region

(U.S.$ billions)

Legend: United States, Western Europe, Asia/Pacific, Japan, Rest of world

Source: IDC, July 1997.

FIGURE 28-11

Steven Harris, Office of Computers and Business Equipment, International Trade Administration, (202) 482-0568, June 1998.

■ REFERENCES

ActivMedia, http://www.activmedia.com.

@plan, http://www.nytimes.com/library/tech/98/03/cyber/articles/03survey.html, and the main site at http://www.webplan.net.

Business Software Alliance, 1150 18th Street, NW, Washington, DC. (202) 872-5500, http://www.bsa.org.

Business Wire, http://www.businesswire.com.

Cahners Publishing, 1350 East Touhy Avenue, Des Plaines, IL 60018. http://www.cahners.com.

CommerceNet & Nielson Media Research, http://www.commerce.net.

Computer-aided Engineering, 270 Madison Avenue, New York, NY 10016. http://www.penton.com/cae.

Computerworld, 375 Cochitutate Road, Framingham, MA 01701-9171. http://www.computerworld.com.

Dataquest, Inc., 1290 Ridder Park Drive, San Jose, CA 95131. http://www.dataquest.com.

Electronic Engineering Times, 600 Community Drive, Manhasset, NY 11030. http://pubs.cmpnet.com/eet.

Electronic News, 475 Park Avenue South, 2nd Floor, New York, NY 10016. http://www.electronicnews.com.

eMarketer, http://www.emarketer.com.

Financial Times, The Financial Times Limited, 14 East 60th Street, New York, NY 10022. http://www.ft.com.

Forrester Research, http://www.forrester.com.

Government Computer News, Cahners Publishing Co., 8601 Georgia Avenue, Suite 300, Silver Spring, MD 20910. http://www.cahners.com.

Government Executive, "GIS Puts Information on the Map," October 1997. http://www.governmentexecutive.com.

Infoworld, InfoWorld Publishing Co., and IDG Co., 155 Bovet Road, Suite 800, San Mateo, CA 94402. http://www.infoworld.com.

The Interactive Services, http://www.cyberatlas.com.

International Data Corporation, 5 Speen Street, Framingham, MA 01701. (508) 872-8200, http://idcresearch.com

Network Wizards, http://www.nw.com. *Network Wizards* information is also found at www.cyberatlas.com.

Software Magazine, 257 Turnpike Road, Suite 100, Southboro, MA 01772. (508) 366-2031, http://www.softwaremag.com.

U.S. Department of Labor, Bureau of Labor Statistics, 2 Massachusetts Avenue, NE, Washington, DC 20212. http://stats.bls.gov/blshome.html.

U.S. Trade Representative, 600 17th Street, NW, Washington, DC 20006. http://www.ustr.gov.

The Yankee Group. http://www.emarketer.com.

SPACE COMMERCE
Economic and Trade Trends

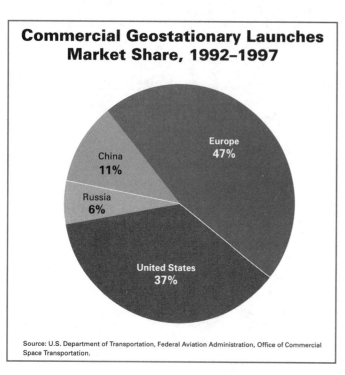

Commercial Geostationary Launches Market Share, 1992–1997

Europe 47%
China 11%
Russia 6%
United States 37%

Source: U.S. Department of Transportation, Federal Aviation Administration, Office of Commercial Space Transportation.

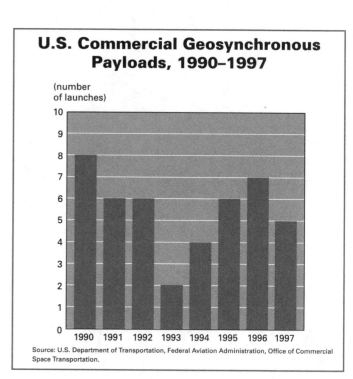

U.S. Commercial Geosynchronous Payloads, 1990–1997

(number of launches)

Source: U.S. Department of Transportation, Federal Aviation Administration, Office of Commercial Space Transportation.

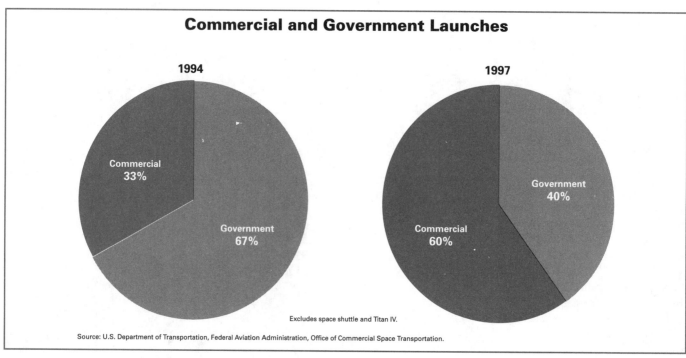

Commercial and Government Launches

1994
Commercial 33%
Government 67%

1997
Government 40%
Commercial 60%

Excludes space shuttle and Titan IV.

Source: U.S. Department of Transportation, Federal Aviation Administration, Office of Commercial Space Transportation.

Space Commerce

INDUSTRY DEFINITION Space commerce consists of a number of major areas, four of which are covered in this chapter: commercial space launch vehicles and launch services, satellite remote sensing services, space insurance, and noncommercial activities that relate to future commercial prospects. Included in the fourth category are emerging applications such as microgravity research and manufacturing, solar power activities, waste removal, space infrastructure, and less developed sectors such as space tourism.

GLOBAL INDUSTRY TRENDS

The leading competitors in the commercial space market are generally countries that have had a strong historical interest in space: the United States, France and other European nations, Russia and Ukraine, China, and more recently Japan and Canada. These countries have developed the ability to launch satellites, and in most cases manufacture both telecommunications and remote sensing satellites. Established providers are being challenged by a new wave of entrepreneurial firms that are trying to provide commercial space products and services at a lower cost. Many companies are developing reusable launch vehicles rather than continuing to rely on expendable, or one-shot, rockets. Efforts are also being made around the world to improve the performance of commercial space systems while reducing their cost and their manufacturing time.

Most large commercial space companies have become more vertically structured in the last few years and now manufacture satellites, launch vehicles, and ground control equipment and even provide telecommunications services. Firms are forming international joint venture partnerships to improve the performance of commercial space systems, reduce costs, and pursue global markets. Internationalization of the industry has been a steady trend which will continue in the near future, especially since the cost of developing space assets (such as the International Space Station and new launch systems) will remain high. However, this internationalization process blurs distinctions between national assets, raising legal questions about issues such as liability for damages that national governments must address.

DOMESTIC TRENDS

While most basic rocket technology is approximately 20 to 30 years old, several American entrepreneurial firms are designing unique reusable launch vehicles to address the growing demand for commercial satellite launches. Additional discoveries about the usefulness of microgravity for scientific research and the development of pharmaceuticals, semiconductors, and new materials are driving the demand for the commercialization of space assets. Growing applications for remotely sensed images are pushing software manufacturers to design new and better programs that can quickly provide customers with easily understood images.

A growing trend in the commercial launch industry is the "block" purchase of a number of launch services at one time by satellite manufacturers. In the recent past an end customer purchased the satellite and the launch services separately. To gain guaranteed access to launch slots, satellite manufacturers have altered this demand pattern by purchasing a number of launches at once and then selling a customer a satellite and a launch as a package. While this has helped lower costs for some customers, customers that do not purchase a satellite "on orbit" are having difficulty finding launches for their satellites. In effect, the satellite manufacturers have become the new brokers of commercial launch services around the world.

INDUSTRY GROWTH PROJECTIONS FOR THE NEXT 1 AND 5 YEARS

The commercial space market will continue its steady growth over the next 5 years, driven by increased demand for all com-

TABLE 29-1: Commercial Launches to Geostationary Transfer Orbit

	1993	1994	1995	1996	1997
United States	4	4	6	8	7
Rest of world	6	10	11	13	17
Total	10	14	17	21	24

mercial space subsectors. The 14 percent increase in global commercial satellite launches to geostationary transfer orbit (GTO) in 1997 was expected to be duplicated in 1998 (see Table 29-1). In the context of this global launch growth, U.S. launch service providers have seen a corresponding growth in revenues (see Table 29-2). Growth in the number of commercial launches will remain steady through 2001, when the rate of growth will level off. With the arrival of several new commercial remote sensing satellite systems, revenues from sales of imagery data will increase rapidly and will take market share from the aerial photography industry. The space insurance market will increase in capacity and revenues as more underwriters enter the market, more satellites are launched relative to previous years, and the decreasing cost of premiums (as a result of factors such as better launch reliability and a larger market base) causes buyers to demand greater insurance coverage.

Prices for launch services, remote sensing imagery, and space insurance are expected to remain level, if not decrease, as a result of the entry of new competitors in these markets and technological improvements. The cost of remote sensing imagery should be driven down by the availability of data from foreign systems.

U.S. and foreign commercial launch providers are increasing their production rates to meet the demand of satellite manufacturers for launches. The production time for a satellite has decreased to under 18 months on average, and manufacturers of launch vehicles are being pushed to reduce their production times accordingly. Currently, it takes approximately 18 to 24 months to build a rocket, which is a reduction from previous production times. Satellite manufacturers are also investing in new launch services programs to increase the available supply of launch vehicles and promote competition among existing providers. Boeing's Delta 3, the Sea Launch joint venture, Japan's H-2A, and several entrepreneurial reusable launch vehicles have been financially supported by the satellite manufacturers Hughes and Loral, which have a strong interest in increasing launch capacity. Several U.S. companies are investing in domestic upgrades as well as forming international partnerships to develop new launch vehicles and provide competitive arrangements for commercial remote sensing data.

Export of U.S. launch services will increase as additional foreign customers demand launches of their telecommunications systems. The sale of remote sensing systems and data from those systems also may increase U.S. exports. However, the increased purchase of foreign remote sensing data will increase the level of imports.

Employment in the launch services sector will remain steady or increase as new systems begin to provide commercial launches. Entrepreneurial ventures also will increase employment in this sector. Employment in remote sensing will be centered on the value-added computer software and data processing industries, but a slight increase will occur as turnkey remote sensing systems are sold internationally. Employment related to programs such as the Space Shuttle will decrease as the ongoing programs become more efficient and cost-effective. In the near term, employment in microgravity experiments and space research will be concentrated largely in the public and academic sectors.

GLOBAL MARKET PROSPECTS

Future export markets for U.S. commercial space products are likely to be found mainly in Asia, although the expected growth

TABLE 29-2: U.S. Commercial Space Revenues
(millions of dollars)

	1990	1991	1992	1993	1994	1995[1]	1996[2]	1997[2]	1998	1999	Percent Change 94–95	95–96	96–97	97–98	98–99	90–99
Total	3,385	4,370	4,860	5,295	6,640											
Commercial satellites delivered	1,000	1,300	1,300	1,100	1,400											
Satellite services	800	1,200	1,500	1,850	2,330											
Fixed	735	1,115	1,275	1,600	1,980											
Mobile	65	85	225	250	350											
Satellite ground equipment	860	1,300	1,400	1,600	1,970											
Mobile equipment	145	280	350	420	480											
Commercial launches	570	380	450	465	580	483	553	750	870	992	(17)	14	36	16	14	74
Remote sensing data and services	155	190	210	250	300	340	480	590	661	713	13	41	23	12	8	460
Commercial research and development infrastructure	0	0	0	30	60	55	65	68	73	80	(8)	18	5	7	10	

[1] Revised from previously published data.
[2] Forecast.
Source: U.S. Department of Commerce: Bureau of the Census; International Trade Administration.

will be limited by the recent Asian financial crisis. Latin America will continue to demand new space-based telecommunications services and remote sensing imagery for applications such as forestry maintenance, agriculture, and drug enforcement.

Most competition for U.S. firms comes from Europe and Russia. Both are established providers of reliable launch vehicles and offer launch services at competitive prices. Europe, Canada, Russia, India, Israel, and Brazil, among others, provide remote sensing data. Countries such as China and Japan may gain some market share, but not in the next few years. Japan's H-2A rocket will offer commercial launches no earlier than 2000, and China is still recovering from a series of launch failures which have left satellite manufacturers wary of using Chinese rockets.

Future demand for commercial space products will be driven by the demand for the various applications of those products. Heavy demand for telecommunications and remote sensing satellite systems will drive the demand for commercial space launches. Emerging applications and the creation of computer software will stimulate continued demand for remote sensing data. Emerging applications include weather forecasting, drug enforcement, agriculture improvements, urban planning, fishing, and zoning.

LAUNCH VEHICLES

Launch vehicles are included in SIC 376, guided missiles and space vehicles and parts. This section covers the space vehicles and parts component (SIC 3761), space vehicle propulsion units and parts (SIC 3764), and space launch vehicle parts and auxiliary equipment. It should be noted that guided missile parts, propulsion units, and auxiliary equipment also are included in these SIC codes and are addressed in Chapter 21, Aerospace.

Global Outlook

The European consortium Arianespace is the current market leader in international commercial launch services. Arianespace is owned by 49 European aerospace and financial groups, with the French space agency Centre National d'Etudes Spatiales (CNES) owning 55.54 percent. In 1997, Arianespace launched 11 Ariane 4 launch vehicles (which carried 17 satellites) and 1 Ariane 5 rocket. In 1996, Arianespace generated sales of 6285 million francs (FF) [$1.257 billion], based on 10 Ariane 4 launches, which was down from 11 launches worth FF7022 million [$1.4054 billion] in 1995. However, several of these launches were performed for noncommercial government projects. In January 1998 the Ariane 4 had a backlog of 43 spacecraft waiting to be launched.

The largest Ariane 4 rocket, the Ariane 44-L, is capable of launching 9,965 pounds (lb) to GTO or 21,100 lb to low earth orbit (LEO) and can carry more than one satellite at a time. To address the growing size of satellites, Arianespace developed the larger Ariane 5 rocket, which can carry one large-class satellite weighing up to 15,000 lb to GTO or one large-class and one medium-class satellite (weighing a total of up to 13,160 lb) at

the same time to GTO. The Ariane 5 also is capable of lifting payloads of up to 39,600 lb to LEO. The Ariane 5's first launch attempt, in 1996, failed. The second Ariane 5 launch took place in October 1997, and even though the payload was left short of the targeted orbit, Arianespace views the launch as a successful proof of the system's technology. The next Ariane 5 flight, scheduled for the second half of 1998, was expected to carry the Ariane 5's first commercial payload, even though it was technically still a validation flight.

Arianespace is planning to convert its commercial business from the Ariane 4 to the Ariane 5 but has extended the transition period to reduce the risk to commercial customers. Arianespace has ordered an additional 20 Ariane 4 rockets, which will continue the Ariane 4's use until 2002. At that time, Arianespace hopes to have 12 to 14 Ariane 5 launches per year, up from a projected 8 to 10 launches per year during the period 2000–2002. However, because GEO telecommunications satellites have grown beyond expectations, the Ariane 5 can no longer carry two heavy-class satellites simultaneously during a launch, as was originally planned. As a result, Arianespace plans to increase the Ariane 5's capability to 15,400 lb by the year 2000, 19,800 to 22,000 lb by 2003, and 24,200 to 28,400 lb by the period 2005–2007. In addition, Arianespace would like to develop the ability to launch a LEO satellite and a GEO satellite on the same vehicle by developing the ability to restart one of its engines after the LEO satellite has separated from the vehicle.

China has been offering commercial space launches since the late 1980s but has suffered technical difficulties which have hampered the program. China's most powerful rocket, the Long March 3B, can carry payloads of 29,900 lb to LEO or 9,900 lb to GTO. The LM-3B has 50 percent greater capability than China's previous vehicle, the LM-2E. China uses three sites for its launches, depending on the type of launch. Since the string of failures in 1996, China has lost several customers that were dubious about the reliability of Chinese rockets. However, early in 1997 Loral announced that it had contracted with China for options to launch up to five payloads to GTO. Hughes has re-signed a contract for five launch options through 2001. In the LEO sector, China has conducted launches for Iridium and is attempting to win future contracts for more LEO communications systems.

One of the market's upcoming commercial competitors is Japan's H-2A launch vehicle, which will be capable of carrying 8,000 lb to GTO in its standard variant and 12,000 lb to GTO on an H-2A with liquid rocket boosters attached. These two versions of the H-2A will be capable of carrying 20,000 lb and 28,000 lb to LEO, respectively. Japan's National Space Development Agency (NASDA) is constructing a second launch pad and a large rocket assembly building at the Tanegashima launch complex for commercial launches that are planned to begin in 2001. To improve the performance and reduce the cost of the H-2A rocket, NASDA selected Thiokol's Castor IVA-XL solid rocket motors. This contract is worth an estimated $50 million to Thiokol. In 1997 Japan negotiated a new agreement with Japanese fishermen that will allow that country to launch as many as five H-2 rockets per year.

In addition to an International Launch Services (ILS) joint venture (see below), Russia is positioning itself to compete better in the international launch services market. President Yeltsin recently ordered the Ministry of Defense to transfer responsibility for all the Baikonur launch complex's operations to the civilian Russian Space Agency within 2 years. The edict also made the Russian Space Agency responsible for strategic missile development, another responsibility historically held by the Ministry of Defense. In addition, the Russian Space Agency's budget was increased to 3,805 billion rubles (about $670 million at 1997 exchange rates) in 1997, up from 2,094.4 billion rubles in 1996. Russia's budget figures for civil space activities remained flat for 1998 at 3.683 billion rubles (about $605 million), but the federal space program has been reclassified into the top-priority budget category. Russia is increasing its emphasis on the commercial market vis-à-vis the Russian government market in order to obtain hard currency, and in 1997 provided 582.2 billion rubles ($102.5 million) for improvements at the Baikonur Cosmodrome launch site to be implemented in 1998. For the first time in history, commercial launches on Russian rockets will be more numerous than those launches provided for the government.

In the small launch vehicle sector, an international partnership involving Arianespace, the French satellite manufacturer Aerospatiale, the Russian Space Agency, and the Russian firms Progress and TsSKB will provide launches to LEO or middle earth orbit (MEO) on a two- or three-stage Russian Soyuz rocket. The Starsem venture had three launches in support of the Globalstar LEO communications system scheduled for 1998, and performed extensive ground facility upgrades at the Baikonur Cosmodrome launch site to enhance its services. A new international partnership, Kosmotras, is also offering converted SS-18 ICBMs for commercial launches of small payloads (up to 7,040 lb) to LEO.

While not a provider of international commercial launches, India in 1997 successfully launched its Polar Satellite Launch Vehicle (PSLV), which carried an Indian remote sensing satellite (weighing approximately 2,000 lb) for the first time. The PSLV can carry up to 6,400 lb to LEO, and launches from a site on the southeast coast of India. Before that launch India had contracted for Russian launches for its remote sensing satellites. The Indian Space Research Organization lost contact with its $148 million satellite after the successful PSLV launch, leaving the satellite useless. The follow-on INSAT-2E satellite was scheduled to replace it in 1998.

Another up-and-coming launch provider is Brazil. Brazil's space agency, INPE, is ready to enter the commercial market and is attracting interest from companies in several countries, including France, the United States, Germany, and Canada. INPE's 1997 budget is four times larger than it was in 1993. Brazil's first launch of its VLS-1 launch vehicle from the domestic launch site Alcantera ended in failure. Many foreign companies are interested in gaining access to this launch site because of its favorable position near the earth's equator. Brazil has four noncommercial launches scheduled between 1997 and 2001 and plans to continue the development and upgrading of Alcantera's infrastructure for international use.

In summary, the planned launch vehicle improvements in France, Russia, Ukraine, and China will attract customers through a combination of proposed lower prices and technology updates. Japan's further entry into the commercial launch market may be stalled by the Asian financial crisis, and India's hopes to enter the commercial market will likely be stifled by sanctions imposed on India for its nuclear weapons activities. Overall, the U.S. industry will face strong global competition from foreign providers.

International Trade Agreements

During the period 1993–96, the United States signed trade agreements with Russia, China, and Ukraine so that U.S. satellites could have increased access to space. The agreements allowed those countries to enter the international commercial space launch services market, which previously had been restricted for national security reasons. With the growing satellite market and increasing demand for space launch services, the U.S. government developed these agreements to provide for a gradual entry of these nonmarket economies into the commercial market, increasing supply and competition while avoiding undue market disruption. The agreements allow each of those countries to provide up to 20 launches to GEO through the years 2000 (Russia) and 2001 (China and Ukraine). In addition, the agreements contain pricing provisions which state that those foreign providers must price on a par (within 15 percent) with western commercial providers. While these agreements are scheduled to remain in place for another 2 to 3 years, the booming commercial launch industry and the changing international partnerships have driven the U.S. industry to request that the quantitative restrictions be removed from the agreements. The U.S. government is considering several options related to that request and hopes that any action taken will further encourage free and fair trade in the commercial launch industry.

Export Licensing Agreements

Because of the historically military nature of the space industry and the continuing ability to use space assets for both commercial and military purposes, the obtaining of export licenses for commercial space products remains a burdensome task. Launch vehicles and their components remain Category 1 items in the international Missile Technology Control Regime and therefore generally cannot be traded internationally. Remote sensing satellites, which are performing commercially at levels formerly reserved for the intelligence community, are licensed by the State Department but are being considered for inclusion on the Commerce Control List (CCL), a list of items which require an export license from the U.S. Commerce Department, usually a much less arduous process. If these satellites are indeed transferred to the Commerce Department's jurisdiction, exporting of some remote sensing satellites will be easier, allowing improved competitiveness for the U.S. satellite industry.

Domestic Outlook

As a result of strong foreign competition, U.S. launch service providers have sought innovative partnerships to improve competitiveness and obtain technology. At the same time, the U.S. industry is experiencing a consolidation which has brought together domestic resources with those of other countries. The domestic commercial space launch industry is now positioned to regain market share from Arianespace while cooperating with countries such as Russia and Ukraine to provide better launch services for global satellite manufacturers.

U.S. launch providers have sought new international partnerships to improve competitiveness, and the rewards from this innovation are starting to be realized. Through the merger of Boeing and McDonnell Douglas, the "new" Boeing now launches the American-built Delta 2 rocket as well as the Ukrainian-Russian Sea Launch vehicle. The Delta 2 can carry payloads of up to 11,220 lb to LEO and up to 4,060 lb to GTO. In January 1997 a Delta 2 rocket carrying a U.S. government GPS satellite exploded near the launch pad in Cape Canaveral, Florida, and this delayed further Delta launches until May 1997. The failure was due to a split in the case of one of the Delta's nine solid rocket motors. There have been several successful launches since Delta's return to flight status, including launches for the Iridium and Globalstar LEO communications systems.

To address the growing size of payloads, Boeing is developing a Delta 3 launch vehicle, and subsequently an even larger Delta 4. The Delta 3's first launch in August 1998 ended in failure. The Delta 4 is discussed below in relation to the Evolved Expendable Launch Vehicle (EELV) project.

Through its international partnership with Ukraine's Yuzhnoye, Russia's Khrunichev, and Norway's Kvaerner, Boeing's Sea Launch venture is preparing for its first launch, scheduled for early 1999. Sea Launch had sold 18 launch slots as of May 1998, even though a launch from an ocean platform has never been attempted. Hughes Space and Communications, which has contracted for 13 of the 18 launches, believes that launching from the sea at the equator will allow it to provide customers with a longer satellite lifetime because of the advantage gained by launching from a low latitude. Sea Launch's command ship and the launch platform have completed their "sea tests," and all the launch control equipment has been installed in the command ship. In addition, the facility in Long Beach, California, where the satellite will be mated with the launch vehicle, has been completed.

Lockheed Martin Corporation (LMC), the other major U.S. provider of launch services for heavy payloads, entered an international partnership, ILS, in 1994. ILS launches the American-built Atlas and Athena launch vehicles from Cape Canaveral, Florida, and Vandenburg Air Force Base in California, and it also launches the Russian Proton rocket from the Baikonur Cosmodrome in Kazakhstan. As of May 1998, ILS had 49 confirmed sales of launch services and a backlog worth nearly $3 billion of international sales. ILS is preparing for a period of accelerated launch activity over the next few years and plans to hold an average of 1.6 launches per month through the end of 1999. Of the 49 launches sold, 20 are scheduled for the Proton, while Atlas has 29, including 6 military payloads.

The Atlas 2AS is capable of carrying 18,959 lb to LEO and 8,150 lb to GTO. Currently ILS's major American vehicle, that rocket is going to be upgraded to the Atlas 3A, with the first launch scheduled for the first quarter of 1999. The Atlas 3A will be capable of carrying 19,010 lb to LEO and 8,940 lb to GTO, with the higher capability largely being achieved through the use of Russian-designed RD-180 engines. The first Atlas 3A was in final assembly in April 1998. The follow-on Atlas 3B will be capable of lifting 9,920 lb to GTO and will launch in mid-2000. Overall, the Atlas should be able to launch 12 rockets per year from Cape Canaveral and another 4 for LEO satellites from Vandenburg.

The current Proton rocket can carry 44,220 lb to LEO and 11,220 lb to GTO and is able to do 8 to 12 launches for either LEO or GTO per year. Proton held three successful commercial launches in 1997 through the ILS joint venture and had at least nine scheduled for 1998. Proton has launched three sets of satellites for the Iridium LEO communications system. Proton suffered a failure in December 1997, when the rocket's fourth-stage booster failed to place the *Asiasat 3* satellite into proper orbit. This was the fifth time since 1987 that the upper stage failed, and it left all Proton flights temporarily on hold through April 1998, when a launch was held for Iridium. ILS released plans in April 1997 for a Proton upgrade, the Proton-M, which would have the capacity to lift 12,125 lb to GTO or 48,400 lb to LEO. The Proton-M will have an upgraded upper stage, avionics system, and engines. The first flight of the Proton-M was scheduled for late 1998.

The U.S. government has encouraged the private sector to upgrade its vehicles through the EELV program in addition to the industry's private investments in new vehicle development. The EELV program is intended to provide more affordable and reliable access to space, which should help the U.S. commercial industry be more competitive internationally. The EELV will evolve from existing medium- and heavy-lift launch vehicles and will consolidate manufacturing, infrastructure, support systems, and operations with a goal of up to a 25 to 50 percent savings over current launch costs. While the U.S. Air Force planned to select one provider to create a family of vehicles that would meet U.S. government launch needs, the air force determined in 1996 that it would be better to select two contractors: Boeing for its Delta family, and LMC for its Atlas family. Several government agencies have strongly recommended that all weight classes of satellites be addressed through this competition so that the U.S. government can maintain an independent ability to launch from the United States.

Boeing's EELV entrant is the Delta 4 rocket, and LMC's is the Atlas 3B. LMC is planning to use Russian-designed RD-180 engines on its EELV entrant. This is possible because of Pratt & Whitney/UTC's joint venture with Russia's NPO-Energomash, RD Amross LLC. Engines built in Russia will be used on the commercial Atlas vehicles, while the same RD-180 engines built in the United States will be used for U.S. government EELV launches.

In addition to these larger launch vehicles, several U.S. firms provide launches on smaller rockets. Orbital Sciences Corporation has been successful with its Pegasus and Taurus launch vehicles and had eight launches planned for 1998. Orbital's Pegasus-XL rocket can carry up to 1,015 lb to LEO and has had 20 launches since its inaugural launch in 1990, including an experimental launch for the Teledesic LEO communications system in February 1998. The Pegasus launch vehicle is unique in that it is carried to a high altitude on the belly of an L-1011 aircraft and then released and launched from the air. This type of launch gives Orbital the theoretical ability to launch from any runway. In April 1997 Orbital launched a Spanish satellite from the Canary Islands, the first time Orbital launched outside the United States and the first time a U.S. satellite launch was controlled from western Europe. Orbital's larger, ground-launched rocket, the Taurus, can carry 3,000 lb to LEO or 900 lb to GTO. The Taurus has had two successful flights (in 1994 and 1998) and has three scheduled for 1999. The Taurus is unique because it can be transported easily to any site for a launch.

LMC also has a family of small launch vehicles, the Athenas. An Athena-1 (capable of launching 1,760 lb to LEO) lifted NASA's Lewis spacecraft into orbit in August 1997. In January 1998 a larger Athena-2 (capable of launching 4,180 lb to LEO) launched the National Aeronautics and Space Administration's (NASA) Lunar Prospector. The Athena is an all-solid-propellant commercial launch vehicle that was originally developed under NASA's small spacecraft technology initiative. To increase the Athena family's range, LMC also is assessing an Athena 3, which would be capable of launching 11,440 lb to LEO or 3,960 lb to GTO. The Athena overcame a major setback when its inaugural launch flew off course and had to be destroyed. Athena now has six more launches scheduled: three in 1998 and three in 1999.

With the growth of commercial satellite demand, a number of entrepreneurial ventures have announced plans to manufacture commercial launch vehicles, including a number of private proposals for reusable launch vehicles (RLVs). In addition, NASA is cofunding the development of two experimental RLVs, the X-33 and the X-34.

The X-33 technology demonstrator is being built by LMC, with a first suborbital flight scheduled for July 1999. A key technology to be tested on the X-33 vehicle is the aerospike engine, a hydrogen-cooled engine that will fire its thrusters in a line along 4 feet of copper alloy. While the engine has not been fully developed, the prototype has been tested and LMC hoped to test the full engine in the fall of 1998. The X-33 will launch vertically, like a rocket, and land horizontally, like an aircraft. Originally, the X-33 was to have its first flight in March 1999, but typical technical development delays have forced NASA and Lockheed Martin to accept a July date. LMC hopes to build a full-scale follow-on to the suborbital demonstrator, the VentureStar, which would provide commercial launches by using the X-33 design.

The X-34 is an experimental vehicle that is being developed by Orbital Sciences Corporation and is smaller than the X-33. The X-34 prototype is designed to carry small payloads comparable to those carried on Orbital's Taurus launch vehicle, but at a much lower cost. NASA and Orbital would like to reduce the turnaround times on the follow-on RLV to 24 hours. The first test flight of the X-34 was scheduled for June 1999. As a follow-on, NASA is studying whether to use Russian NK-39 engines on a second X-34 prototype to further improve the vehicle's performance.

The private company that is possibly the farthest along in terms of development is Kistler Aerospace with its K-1 rocket. The K-1 is planned to be the first fully commercial RLV designed to carry payloads up to 5,700 lb into a 500-mile-high orbit. The K-1 will use Russian NK-33 rocket engines on its first and second stages. Once those stages separate, the first stage will fly back to the launch site on its own and use parachutes and air bags to land. Kistler hopes to have the first stages ready for another use with only 2 weeks between launches. The second stage will continue its ascent to deliver the payload and then return to the launch site to be used again. Kistler hopes to test-fly the launch vehicle in 1998 but is still deciding whether to launch from a Nevada test site or from Woomera range in Australia; launching from Australia creates export license problems.

Another entrepreneurial venture still in development is Kelly Space & Technology's Eclipse tow-launch technique. A Boeing 747 would tow the Eclipse RLV from a runway to a launch altitude of approximately 45,000 feet. At that point the engine would ignite, the tow line would release, and the launch vehicle would be free to inject the satellite into orbit and then return safely to earth. In fall 1996 Kelly signed its first customer, Motorola, to an $89 million contract for the option to launch up to 20 commercial satellites for Motorola's Iridium LEO satellite communications system.

Pioneer Rocketplane Corporation is developing the Pathfinder RLV as an entry into NASA's Bantam System Technology Project. The Pathfinder will take off and land like an airplane and will use a combination of jet and rocket engines to place satellites into orbit. The Pathfinder's rocket engines will be fueled in flight by an L-1011 aircraft, a technology which separates the Pathfinder from other RLVs.

Another inventive proposal is Rotary Rocket Company's Roton RLV, which will use a single-stage rocket with an aerospike engine to launch satellites, will then return to earth, and will deploy helicopter blades to land. Additionally, Space Access LLC is proposing an "aerospacecraft" which would use an air-breathing ejector ramjet propulsion system while flying through the atmosphere and rocket engines in space. Space Access claims to have adequate financing for the venture and is developing partnerships with other companies; its goal is to greatly reduce turnaround times between missions, increase annual launch rates, and lower the current high cost of launchings.

Growth and Trade Projections

The commercial space launch industry will experience continued high growth (at approximately 15 percent) through 1998 and 1999, as the demand for launching of new satellite communications systems is strong. Through 2003, demand for commercial launches will remain strong but growth will begin to level off. Continued demand, with matched supply from launch services providers, will remain high because of the need for the maintenance of LEO commercial satellite communications systems, the replacement of GEO telecommunications satellites, and the arrival of several new launch providers to the market. Small launch vehicles will also see an increase in demand during this period, partially because of the need to maintain LEO communications systems that require launches of one or two small satellites at a time and remote sensing systems.

REMOTE SENSING SATELLITES

Remote sensing satellites collect images of the earth by using various methods, including electro-optical sensors and radar. Electro-optical sensors may collect images by using one light frequency (panchromatic) or several frequencies (multispectral) or may collect images contiguously over a broad range of frequencies (hyperspectral). Radar satellites bounce radar signals off the earth's surface and record the energy returned. Radar imagery can be used to "see" through clouds and collect images in the day or at night. The sharpness and detail of photographs can be related to a satellite sensor's resolution, which usually is measured in meters.

Global Outlook

Over the last several years a number of commercial firms have contracted with foreign government agencies that operate remote sensing satellites to sell data from those satellites in the international marketplace. Simultaneously, a number of U.S. firms have begun to develop commercial private systems which would distribute their own data to the commercial market. This has initiated a fierce competition between satellite operators-owners and data distributors which should drive down the price of imagery.

The SPOT satellite Earth Observation System was designed by CNES of France and developed with the participation of Sweden and Belgium. As the current global leader in remotely sensed images, SpotImage had revenues of approximately $37 million in 1997, a 5 percent increase over 1996; SpotImage projected its revenues for 1998 at over $40 million. The *Spot 4* satellite, which was launched in March 1998, provides 10-meter resolution for panchromatic images and 20-meter resolution for multispectral images. *Spot 4* also carries an infrared imager and a payload called Vegetation which will be used to monitor trends in vegetation, such as soil moisture, vegetation cover, and leaf moisture content. In addition, the Vegetation payload will be used to improve cartography, wetlands studies, and geological studies. As a follow-on, the *Spot 5* satellite is being developed for launch in 2001 and will provide improved resolution, with 5-meter resolution panchromatic images and 10-meter multispectral images.

The European Space Agency (ESA) operates the *ERS-1* satellite, which provides synthetic aperture radar (SAR) imagery with a resolution of 30 meters. ERS imagery is sold in the United States by Space Imaging. ESA is also developing the *Envisat* satellite, which will offer 30-meter SAR imagery in 1999.

Canada operates the *Radarsat* satellite, which provides 8-meter resolution radar images. *Radarsat* is equipped with a single-frequency C-band SAR. The SAR is a powerful microwave instrument that can transmit and receive signals to "see" through clouds, haze, smoke, and darkness and obtain high-quality images of the earth in all types of weather 24 hours a day. Plans are under way to develop a follow-on satellite, *Radarsat-2,* which will improve imagery resolution to 3 meters. The launch for *Radarsat-2* is projected for 2001.

Russia joined the commercial remote sensing market by launching the *Spin-2* photo reconnaissance satellite in early 1998; this satellite will take pictures at 2-meter resolution for commercial customers. The satellite's path will allow it to image a majority of North America and will keep the images in its database, which will be sold by a joint venture of the Russian firm Sovinformsputnik Interbranch Association and three U.S. firms: Aerial Images, Lambda Tech International, and Central Trading Systems. This venture will develop detailed maps for farmers, agriculturalists, rescue services, and many other users. Russia also sells raw remote sensing data from Russian government satellites and historical archives on the Internet.

Brazil signed an agreement with China to coproduce a family of remote sensing satellites called the Chinese-Brazil Earth Resources Satellites (CBERS). Brazil will provide one-third of the money and technology needed for the program, the first satellite of which is to be launched on a Chinese Long March rocket in 1998; the second satellite is scheduled for launch in 1999. The CBERS program will provide high-resolution imagery through a widefield camera and will collect data in the visible and infrared bands. As a result of its large size and the vast unpopulated areas, Brazil has used remote sensing data for studies of the environment (especially forest and jungle monitoring), weather prediction, drug enforcement, and urban planning.

India is a leading nation in commercial remote sensing imagery. To date, India has launched eight satellites in the India Remote Sensing (IRS) satellite series. These satellites have allowed India to hold a significant portion of the global commercial imagery market. The *IRS-1C* satellite, which was launched in 1995, provides the highest spatial resolution of these satellites, producing 5.8-meter panchromatic images. Additional satellites are under development, including *Cartosat-1,* which will provide 1-meter resolution imagery starting in 1999.

The Australian Resource Information and Environment Satellite (*Aries-1*) is being developed by a consortium that includes Australia's Commonwealth Scientific and Industrial Research Organization (CSIRO), the Australian Centre for Remote Sensing (ACRES), and Auspace Limited (a subsidiary of Matra Marconi). This satellite will provide hyperspectral images with 30-meter resolution and panchromatic images with 10-meter resolution. The hyperspectral sensor will gather data from 32 contiguous bands in the visible and near infrared spectrums, and 32 contiguous bands in the shortwave infrared spectrum. The hyperspectral imagery will be used for mineral detection by the mining industry. Satellite launch is expected in 2000.

Israel is developing the EROS series of high-resolution satellites. These satellites will produce panchromatic images with a resolution of 1 meter. Launch is expected in 1999.

The *Korean Multi-Purpose Satellite* (*KOMPSAT*), which is scheduled for launch in 1999, will be built, tested, and operated by teams of personnel from TRW and the Korea Aerospace Research Institute (KARI). *KOMPSAT* will house instruments to map Korea and monitor earth resources. The satellite will provide 10-meter resolution panchromatic images and 20-meter multispectral images.

Alenia Aerospazio of Italy is developing plans for the Skymed/COSMO constellation of earth observation satellites, which will consist of seven satellites: four radar and three optical. The radar satellites will have X-band SAR instruments capable of 3-meter imagery. The optical satellites will include a high-resolution (2.5-meter) panchromatic camera, a coarse-resolution multispectral imager, and a medium-resolution infrared camera. The launch of the first satellite is planned for 2001.

Foreign providers of remote sensing imagery will offer strong competition to U.S. industry through a large assortment of services. U.S. industry will need to develop applications for value-added products, provide lower-cost services, and provide timely images to remain competitive.

Domestic Outlook

Until the launch and operation of the proposed 1-meter resolution commercial remote sensing satellites, the *Landsat* satellite system will remain the primary source of remote sensing data in the United States. In 1984, *Landsat* was commercialized through the Land Remote Sensing Commercialization Act, which allowed the Earth Observation Satellite Company (EOSAT) to operate the satellites and market the raw data.

Under the U.S. policy allowing high-resolution satellites to market data commercially, the U.S. industry is leading the world in the development of these high-resolution remote sensing satellites. Three U.S. companies are developing high-resolution (less than 1-meter) satellites which should be in operation by the end of the decade. These satellites will compete directly with aerial photography for the high-resolution imagery market. Satellites offering pictures of the earth which have the same clarity as aerial photographs will subsequently compete in terms of price and the timeliness of the images.

While no other commercial providers have developed 1-meter resolution systems, the market demand that evolves will determine how many systems with that level of detail are needed in the marketplace and whether the data can be made available at a reasonable cost. Many experts argue that only moderate resolution (10 to 20 meters) is necessary for most purposes and that a wider field of view (usually available on lower-resolution systems) is acceptable for many applications. However, SpotImage is concerned that Earthwatch's 5-meter imagery (obtained through joint ventures with India's IRS spacecraft and data from the U.S. *Landsat* system and Canada's *Radarsat*) may take market share from the *Spot 1, 2,* and *4* satellites' 10-meter images.

Earthwatch launched the first U.S. commercial high-resolution satellite, *Earlybird-1,* in December 1997. *Earlybird* was designed to provide 3-meter resolution imagery, but the satellite failed on-orbit soon after its launch. The second-generation Earthwatch satellite, *Quickbird,* will provide 1-meter panchromatic images and 3.3-meter multispectral images. *Quickbird* is scheduled for launch in 1999.

Space Imaging EOSAT was scheduled to launch its first satellite, *Ikonos-1,* in the summer of 1998. If successful, *Ikonos-1* will be the first commercial satellite to provide 1-meter imagery; this imagery will be useful for applications such as mapping, agriculture, environmental monitoring, disaster management, and city planning. A second *Ikonos* satellite is under construction and was expected to be available for launch late in 1998. Both satellites will provide 1-meter panchromatic images and 4-meter multispectral images.

OrbImage currently operates two low-resolution remote sensing satellites. *OrbView-1* provides information on lightning and severe weather patterns and measures atmospheric temperatures, humidity, and pressure. *OrbView-2* is the first spacecraft to provide daily color images of the earth's changing surface conditions on a global scale. It can be used to identify phytoplankton in the oceans and monitor the health of forests and farm crops. OrbImage will launch its first high-resolution satellite, *OrbView-3,* in 1999. This satellite will be capable of collecting 1-meter panchromatic and 4-meter multispectral imagery data. A fourth OrbImage satellite, *OrbView-4,* is planned for 2002. *OrbView-4* will have the same imagery characteristics as *OrbView-3* but will add an additional 280-channel hyperspectral imaging instrument with 8-meter resolution. Data from the hyperspectral sensor will be used for mineral exploration, agriculture management, environmental monitoring, and security purposes.

Resource 21 is planning a constellation of satellites to serve the agricultural imagery market. By flying four satellites, Resource 21 will be able to shorten revisit times and decrease the time between cloud-free images. The satellites will provide 10-meter resolution imagery in the panchromatic, multispectral, and near-infrared spectrums. The system is projected to start launching in 2000.

The Geophysical and Environmental Research Corporation (GER) plans a constellation of six remote sensing satellites. The GER Earth Resource Observation Satellites (GEROS) will provide 10-meter panchromatic and multispectral images.

Growth and Trade Projections

Growth in the remote sensing industry can be divided into two sectors: the space-based sector, which includes the manufacture and sale of satellites, ground stations, and hardware; and the value-added sector, which converts raw data for specific uses. Both sectors will experience strong growth, with the value-added sector's growth being stronger. Growth in the hardware area will derive from the sale of satellite systems internationally and the sale of ground stations for receiving and interpreting data. Growth in the value-added sector will come from end-user demand driven by the ability to adapt the data to specific purposes in a timely, low-cost manner.

Revenues for raw data and value-added images in the remote sensing industry should reach over $1 billion by the year 2000, with approximately 90 percent of the revenues coming from the value-added sector. This nearly will double the 1996 revenue of approximately $600 million. On the basis of these data, the remote sensing industry will experience solid growth during the next 1-year and 5-year periods. With higher-resolution images and the ability of computer software companies to convert the satellite data into useful end products, the remote sensing industry will begin to cut into the aerial photography market. Therefore, competition will occur not only among satellite remote sensing providers but also between the satellite industry and the aerial photography industry. The amount of competition will be determined by the public's demand for images in the resolution range provided by the aerial photography market and the development of new applications for remote sensing data. It also will depend on the speed and cost at which satellite data can be converted to support such applications. New applications include forestry, urban planning, telecommunications system planning, search and rescue operations, fleet management, product tracking, zoning, and fishing, among many others.

The remote sensing industry will earn commercial profits from the development of several purely commercial systems and the presence of worldwide data distributors that use many countries' satellites to compile image libraries for future use. In addition, the demand for different types of images, such as radar and hyperspectral imagery, will increase the demand for remotely sensed images of the earth. With the number of remote sensing satellites scheduled to increase in 1998 and 1999, the price of imagery should be driven down by stiff competition.

SPACE INSURANCE

Space insurance is a growing subsector of the insurance industry which provides coverage for all aspects of commercial space. Included are a satellite's preparation, assembly, and transportation; its mating with the launch vehicle; the launch and delivery of the satellite into the proper orbit; and the testing and operation of the satellite for a specified period. Satellites often are insured against delays in the launch schedule, during which time a company could lose revenue.

Global Outlook
The space insurance market is growing in conjunction with the booming demand for commercial satellites and launches. With the commercial launch market at its largest size ever, many new insurance providers and underwriters have been attracted to it. Many proven launch vehicles are based on technologies which are 20 to 30 years old, so that the technology is well understood and predictable, reducing the risk to insurers. At the same time, the well-established providers have worked hard to make improvements in production, launch operations, and technology, and thus in the reliability of their launch vehicles. Because of this greater reliability and the common 2-year period from contract to launch, insurance providers are able to realize returns on these investments in a relatively short time.

The space insurance market has become a profit-making sector within the last 5 years. Previously, the lower reliability of launch vehicles and a lesser understanding of the relevant technologies caused problems for many launch and satellite operations. The market grew to approximately $1.6 billion for overall space insurance in 1997 and is projected to continue experiencing substantial growth over the next 4 or 5 years as satellite launches increase. At the same time, the amount of liability the insurance market is able to handle is increasing with the appearance of additional underwriters.

As the growth in this market has increased, premiums have decreased, with launch premiums remaining higher than operational premiums because of the higher risk involved during a launch. With lower premiums, satellite manufacturers' and operators' demand for various types of insurance also has increased. Operators have extended their time of coverage for satellites on orbit and are investigating the need to insure them against solar weather problems. Additionally, with more launches occurring from new foreign sites, such as Kazakhstan (for Russian and Ukrainian launches) and China, customers are seeking political risk insurance against unforeseen political problems which could delay or prohibit a launch.

Underwriters assign varying rates to launch vehicles on the basis of their reliability record. With the emergence of many new commercial providers, insurers will maintain conservative positions until these vehicles demonstrate a steady, reliable track record. This philosophy applies to some extent to new satellite designs as well.

Domestic Outlook
Within the last 2 years the insurance market has adjusted to a favorable change in the commercial satellite industry: the development of LEO satellite communications systems, which often launch several satellites at a time on one launch vehicle and maintain spares on orbit in the case of satellite failure. While the risk at the time of launch is higher, the presence of the spares allows a satellite operator to replace quickly any satellite which fails, thus reducing the amount of potential revenues lost and the risk to insurers.

Growth and Trade Projections
The space insurance market will continue to see steady growth over the next 1 and 5 years as a result of the expanding commercial satellite and launch market. As new vehicles prove their reliability, the space insurance market will continue to expand, premiums will continue to be reduced, and volume and capacity will increase.

OTHER NONCOMMERCIAL SPACE PROJECTS

This section deals with projects that are on the verge of becoming commercial but remain in the government realm and have not begun to be exploited. It includes the commercialization of human space flight, the commercialization of the

International Space Station, and projects such as microgravity experiments, manufacturing in space, space-based solar power, and space tourism.

Global Outlook

The drive to commercialize space has gained momentum as government space budgets have been cut, pushing this market toward the commercial sector. Driving this commercialization are government agencies, such as NASA, which is trying to shed its operational functions and focus its limited resources on core research and development missions such as space exploration. NASA is working with commercial space firms to explore ways in which LEO space projects can be financed with private funds so that it can focus on the exploration of Mars and other planets. Both the public sector and the private sector recognize that the development of commercial space will rely on public-private partnerships, and hope that those relationships will spread the risk of these projects enough that more projects will materialize. To support continued commercialization, the House of Representatives passed legislation in 1997 which would promote expanded business opportunities for the commercial space industry.

Historically, the commercialization of space was restricted both by high risk and by the high cost of developing and launching space assets. For investments in commercial space to be worthwhile, end markets have to be developed further, which will drive demand for these products. The government has tended to fund all space science activities, but new companies are beginning to establish entrepreneurial ventures to capitalize on the resources of space.

In support of commercial space development, NASA's fiscal year (FY) 1998 commercial technology program budget was $146 million, and FY 1999 will feature a budget of $130.4 million. Innovative small business research programs will get $101.5 million in FY 1998 and $100 million in FY 1999. The Spacelab will receive $11.9 million in 1998 but is scheduled to receive no funds in 1999. Space products development funds will increase from $12.9 million in FY 1998 to $14.4 million in FY 1999. Commercial technology programs will be reduced from $25.2 million in FY 1998 to $23.2 million in FY 1999.

Domestic Outlook

Human Space Flight Privatization. NASA has turned over the day-to-day management and operation of the U.S. Space Shuttle to a Boeing–Lockheed Martin joint venture, United Space Alliance (USA). USA was formed in the fall of 1995 and began operations in 1996. Since that time cost reductions have occurred, while the safety record of the Space Shuttle has improved. As of May 1998, USA had flown 11 shuttle missions, and it has a full schedule for the rest of that year and through 2000. USA is interested in expanding the use of the Space Shuttle to include commercial payload launches between the missions used to build the Space Station. This would increase the flight rate and thus lower the cost per flight. However, law and policy in place since the 1986 *Challenger* accident prohibit the use of the Space Shuttle to launch commercial payloads. Not only would this pose an unnecessary risk to human life, but it would also place a government-funded system in direct competition with the commercial launch industry. It also is not clear that the Space Shuttle could ever be made into a commercially attractive launch system. Nevertheless, the question of Space Shuttle commercialization is likely to be reopened in the next 2 years as NASA faces tighter budgets.

As a follow-on to the commercialization of the Space Shuttle, NASA may consider the commercialization of the International Space Station (ISS), possibly as early as 10 years after its construction, so that NASA will have more resources to focus on traveling to Mars. NASA believes that commercial activities could account for approximately one-third of the ISS's space for scientific experiments in its first 10 years of operation. The ISS is currently projected to cost approximately $21 billion, but many aerospace experts believe that the cost could go up, perhaps by another $3 billion, and many also assume that further delays will increase the price. Launch of the first module is scheduled for late 1998, and construction is scheduled to be finished around 2003. The ISS is being developed mainly by the United States, Russia, Japan, and Europe, with 180 companies working on the space laboratory. Efforts are under way to commercialize ISS functions such as communications and to develop a strategy for turning the entire facility over to private industry at the end of its 10-year government occupancy.

The 1996 National Space Policy Act directed U.S. government agencies to increase their reliance on the commercial industry for the purchase of products and services. Congress has encouraged the reduction of costs for access to space and believes that this will allow the commercial development of space infrastructure. The U.S. military is examining ways to best use commercial space assets for its operations in times of peace and times of crisis. However, the military is also faced with the need to protect sensitive commercial space assets at times of crisis. The presence of commercial satellites creates a vulnerability as well as a dependency for the military.

Emerging Markets. The commercial use of space is growing, mainly as a result of the continued development of new applications. The satellite telecommunications sector is today the largest profit-making space-related industry (see Chapters 30 and 31). Even though the use of satellites for telecommunications has become standard, several other sectors of this industry have just begun to enter the commercial market, while others are poised to enter the next few years. Remote sensing satellites, as was discussed above, are beginning to take market share from the aerial photography industry because of the increased number of high-resolution satellites on orbit and the use of computer software to translate satellite data into a useful tool for numerous applications. The Global Positioning System (GPS) has seen explosive growth resulting from the increasing numbers of applications for navigation, location, and timing needs (see Chapter 31).

In addition to remote sensing and GPS, emerging markets such as asset tracking, data processing, logistics, fleet management, and remote management and control will increase their dependence on space assets. One such application is the use of a microgravity atmosphere for the development of tissues, proteins, crystals, and semiconductors in space. Manufacturing such materials in a microgravity environment produces much larger and purer specimens than can be produced on the ground. NASA has performed several experiments on the Space Shuttle and the Russian *Mir* Space Station. NASA and several pharmaceutical firms are increasingly interested in the use of microgravity to speed biomedical research toward cures for diseases such as AIDS and cancer.

A number of new U.S. companies have developed proposals for commercial space ventures. For example, Applied Space Resources is developing a "Lunar Retriever" which will retrieve and return to earth lunar samples that can be sold to researchers and the general public. Applied Space Resources plans to use off-the-shelf technology and hopes that ice will be discovered on the moon through these experiments. In addition, Cry-X, Inc., is developing a commercial protein crystal unit for use on the ISS and would charge pharmaceutical companies for creating proteins and crystals in a microgravity atmosphere. Cry-X was spun off from the Center for Macromolecular Crystallography, but it is unclear whether this type of function will be profitable in the near future.

While not all microgravity experiments are performed on the Space Shuttle or the ISS, approximately 20 companies perform experiments related to physical properties in the absence of gravity. Companies interested in the manufacture of thin semiconductor films and crystal development believe that profits are still a few years away. Limited short-term access to the microgravity atmosphere is available through parabolic aircraft flights, and long-term access is available through the European "Eureka" platform and SpaceHab, a commercial company which offers the ability to perform experiments on the Space Shuttle or *Mir* Space Station. The future ISS and reusable launch vehicles will greatly increase this segment's ability to perform microgravity experiments.

There are a number of other applications which have not been tapped. Many scientists believe that satellites could be used as space power stations to generate electricity even though technical problems and cost have limited their development so far. A number of groups have proposed that outer space be used as a dumping ground for radioactive waste, but safety during launch and environmental concerns have stopped this proposal for the near term. Further in the future, many groups, such as the Space Transportation Association, believe that space tourism will become a valid market sector, allowing the general public to take trips into space. In fact, space tourism already exists in the form of parabolic aircraft flights.

Growth and Trade Projections

Space commercialization, research and manufacturing in space, and other, more established sectors such as GPS and remote sensing will continue to experience growth, but several of these sectors will not enter the commercial realm for at least a few years. Scientific research in space for the most part will remain in the domain of governments in the near term. With the development of the ISS, the commercial use of space for scientific (especially pharmaceutical) research will move this market toward profitability.

Kim Wells, U.S. Department of Commerce, Office of Aerospace, (202) 482-2232, kim_wells@ita.doc.gov, September 1998.

■ **REFERENCES**

Aeronautics & Space Report of the President, Fiscal Year 1997 Activities, National Aeronautics and Space Administration, Washington, DC 20546.

Aerospace Daily, 1156 15th Street, NW, Washington, DC 20005.

Aerospace Facts and Figures, 1997–1998, Aerospace Industries Association, 1250 Eye Street, NW, Washington, DC 20005.

Aviation Week & Space Technology, The McGraw-Hill Companies, 1221 Avenue of the Americas, New York, NY 10020.

International Reference Guide to Space Launch Systems, 2d ed. Steven J. Isakowitz, American Institute of Aeronautics and Astronautics, 370 L'Enfant Promenade, SW, Washington, DC 20024-2518.

Launchspace, Launchspace Publications, Inc., 7929 Westpark Drive, McLean, VA 22102.

Low Earth Orbit Commercial Market Projections, Federal Aviation Administration, Associate Administrator for Commercial Space Transportation, Washington, DC 20590.

1997 COMSTAC Mission Model Update, Commercial Space Transportation Advisory Committee, Federal Aviation Administration, Associate Administrator for Commercial Space Transportation, Washington, DC 20590.

Office of Air and Space Commercialization home page, U.S. Department of Commerce, Washington, DC 20230.

Space News and *Defense News,* The Times Journal Company, 6883 Commercial Drive, Springfield, VA 22159.

Via Satellite, Phillips Publishing Inc., 7811 Montrose Road, Potomac, MD 20854.

Sources of Further Information

Aerospace Industries Association, 1250 Eye Street, NW, Washington, DC 20005.

Arianespace home page, www.arianespace.com.

Boeing home page, www.boeing.com.

Federal Aviation Administration, Office of Commercial Space Transportation. 800 Independence Avenue, SW, Washington, DC 20591.

Globalstar home page, www.globalstar.com.

Hughes Electronics home page, www.Hughes.com.

Iridium home page, www.iridium.com.

Lockheed Martin home page, www.lmco.com.

Orbital Sciences home page, www.orbital.com.

Thiokol home page, www.thiokol.com.

TRW, Inc., home page, www.TRW.com.

United Technologies home page, www.utc.com.

■ **RELATED CHAPTERS**

Big LEO system: A system of satellites working together in low earth orbit that will provide all the services of the Little LEO systems as well as mobile voice and fax capabilities.

Block launch agreement: A strategy used by satellite manufacturers of purchasing numerous launches from a supplier at one time to reserve access to space and receive a price discount based on the number of launches procured.

Evolved Expendable Launch Vehicle (EELV): A U.S. Air Force program that will incorporate existing launch vehicles into the development of a more capable and less expensive rocket.

Geostationary earth orbit (GEO): The altitude (22,230 miles) at which a satellite appears to be fixed above a specific spot over the earth.

Low earth orbit (LEO): For the purposes of this chapter, any orbit lower than geostationary earth orbit.

Payload: The satellite, instrument package, or equipment carried into space by a launch vehicle.

Remote sensing: The process of imaging the earth from space.

TELECOMMUNICATIONS SERVICES
Economic and Trade Trends

Top U.S. Traffic Routes, 1996

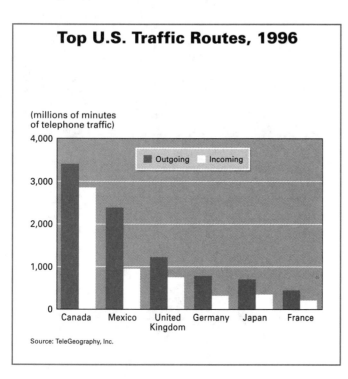

(millions of minutes of telephone traffic)

Source: TeleGeography, Inc.

Distribution of Main Telephone Lines, 1996

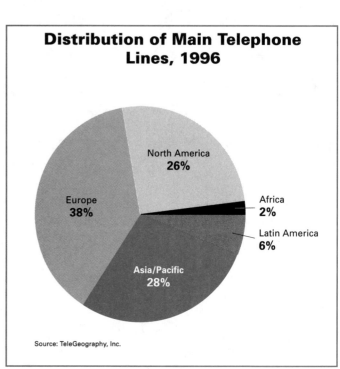

North America 26%

Africa 2%

Latin America 6%

Europe 38%

Asia/Pacific 28%

Source: TeleGeography, Inc.

Top Telecommunications Markets, 1996

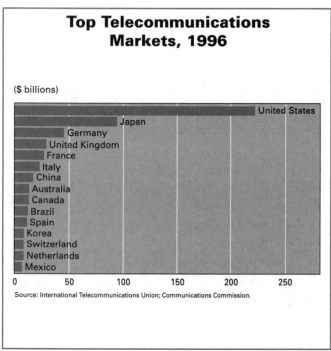

($ billions)

United States
Japan
Germany
United Kingdom
France
Italy
China
Australia
Canada
Brazil
Spain
Korea
Switzerland
Netherlands
Mexico

Source: International Telecommunications Union; Communications Commission.

U.S. International Trade

($ billions)

Imports

Exports

Balance

Exports are for trade between nonaffiliated companies.

Source: U.S. Department of Commerce, Bureau of Economic Analysis.

Telecommunications Services

INDUSTRY DEFINITION The telecommunications services industry (SIC 4812, 4813, 4822) is broadly divided into providers serving the communications markets for basic voice and data services. These services include local exchange, cellular telephony and paging, long-distance (toll), and international services, whether provided by wire (coaxial or fiber cable) or wireless (terrestrial radio systems or satellite) technologies. This chapter focuses on telecommunications firms, both regulated and unregulated, offering basic services that transmit information of the user's choosing without change in the form or content of the information as it is sent and received. Enhanced services, including value-added and on-line information services, are discussed in Chapter 26.

OVERVIEW

Traditional telephone services include local, long-distance, and international voice telephony and data transmission services. The "wireline" services industry (SIC 4813 and 4822) uses terrestrial cable and fiber-optic technology to provide voice and data communications. Some wireline services are now provided through the use of wireless technologies or a combination of wireline and wireless facilities. Radiotelephone communications (SIC 4812), including cellular, paging, and personal communication services, are discussed in the wireless communications services section of this chapter. The satellite services sector includes fixed and mobile services (voice, data, and video) provided through communications satellites.

The Telecommunications Act of 1996 removed the last domestic barriers to competition. However, competition in local markets has not yet expanded beyond some large urban business markets, and the former Bell companies have not yet secured authorization to offer long-distance services within their own service areas. The recent opening of many international markets to competition, which was formalized by the World Trade Organization's (WTO) Agreement on Basic Telecommunications

Services, represents a milestone in the industry. Major American and foreign firms already are competing in large segments of the $825 billion worldwide market for telecommunications services estimated for 1999.

GLOBAL INDUSTRY TRENDS

Historically, telecommunications companies in virtually all countries were state-owned enterprises (generically known as PTTs for the postal, telegraph, and telephone services they offered). PTTs had exclusive rights to provide telephone services both domestically and internationally. Privatizing some or all of the monopoly carrier has become a first step many countries are taking as they get government out of the telephone business and allow greater private sector participation. Governments do this for several reasons: to raise capital to invest in telecommunications infrastructure; bring "market discipline" to an often inefficient, poorly managed bureaucratic enterprise so that it can develop into a competitive business operation; and help set the stage for competition by separating the government regulator from the provider of telecommunications services. In the United States, however, the government never owned or controlled any telephone company, and so it had no interest in perpetuating the AT&T monopoly. British Telecom was the first PTT to go private, with a 51 percent public offering that raised $5.2 billion in 1984. Since then, governments in Denmark, Ghana, Mexico, Pakistan, and Singapore have sold stakes in their telecommunications operators, while France, El Salvador, Kenya, Poland, and Zambia are taking steps in that direction.

Mergers and business alliances continue to take place within the U.S. and foreign telecommunications markets. These strategic alliances are ways for companies to enter new markets and strengthen their competitive position in the markets they already serve. U.S. companies with long experience in the telecommunications sector are potentially desirable partners for foreign firms eager to gain access to the American market. As competition increases within and beyond the United States, companies are looking for new business partners that can provide capital, customers, and/or marketing and technological expertise, and are developing new services.

Continued market liberalization, accompanied by growing competition, is a third global trend. Some governments have introduced competition by allowing private sector participation in building and operating networks for cellular communications and paging services. Since PTTs never provided these services, they do not view the new carriers as a competitive threat. A more significant step in market liberalization is to open all sectors of telephony to competition without limiting the number of firms that may be authorized to provide telephone service or restricting the degree of foreign participation (investment) in the market. Under legislation passed by the European Union (EU), 10 of its member states fully opened their markets to competition on January 1, 1998. The WTO Telecommunications Agreement, which was implemented in February 1998, saw more than 20 countries fully liberalize their telecommunications markets on a multilateral basis, and many other countries are moving toward full or partial liberalization on a phased-in basis.

FACTORS AFFECTING FUTURE U.S. INDUSTRY GROWTH

New laws, together with judicial and regulatory decisions, have played a critical role in introducing and promoting competition in telecommunications services in the United States. After a 20-year effort, Congress passed the Telecommunications Act of 1996, which promised far-reaching changes in the telecommunications industry. However, there is widespread dissatisfaction because local competition has not developed to any significant degree. Future legal decisions and modifications of regulatory policy could have a large impact on the pace of competition in local telephony.

The fundamental role telecommunications now plays in the operations of all businesses and its importance in promoting economic growth and increasing trade assure its future growth.

The United States is the world's largest telecommunications services market, accounting for about 30 percent of world market revenues. Hence, gaining access to the U.S. market is a key strategic objective of many foreign firms.

U.S. companies are world leaders in the development and marketing of telecommunications services and, unlike most foreign operators, already have gained considerable experience functioning in a competitive marketplace. U.S. firms have demonstrated expertise in utilizing new technologies to lower the costs and improve the quality of their services. Many new features and applications in telecommunications are based on sophisticated software programs, such as billing systems that provide valuable information to the customer and the carrier alike.

Growth in the U.S. telecommunications industry also will be fueled by expanding opportunities in foreign markets. U.S. companies, often in partnership with a firm in the host country, already have won nearly 200 bids to build and operate cellular networks abroad. As more countries adopt policies that allow the construction of new networks to provide basic telephony, U.S. firms will be in an excellent position to compete in the bidding process. Expanding opportunities abroad for U.S. service firms will also stimulate the U.S. market for network equipment, since many of the countries where new telecommunications networks will be built do not manufacture the advanced equipment that will be needed.

U.S. firms also participate in foreign markets by investing in privatized national operators and/or new private sector firms. In Mexico, for example, SBC Communications is part of a consortium that has invested in Telmex, while MCI WorldCom is a 45 percent coowner of the competitive Mexican long-distance carrier Avantel, in which it has invested nearly $1 billion. U.S. firms also have invested in the former PTT carriers in Belgium, Ireland, and Italy. More typical in Europe are investments in consortia, one of whose partners owns a telecommunications network that competes against the former PTT. AT&T is an investor in Arcor, a German private network operator formed by an alliance of Mannesmann, Unisource, and DBKom, which owned the telecommunications facilities of the German railway system. BellSouth plans to join another German alliance, O.TEL.O, which also competes with Deutsche Telekom in Europe's largest telecommunications market. Among the major foreign telecommunications services markets, only China remains closed to any type of foreign investment in or operation of its networks.

Although the United States registers a large net deficit in international telecommunications services, this is more a reflection of the inadequacies of foreign market conditions (service monopolies, high prices, less extensive and lower-quality networks) and artificially high accounting rates than of the competitiveness of the U.S. industry. Net settlement payments ("imports"), which exceeded $5 billion in 1997, should decline somewhat, however, as the Federal Communications Commission (FCC) and the forces of competition reduce accounting rates closer to the costs of service.

U.S. INDUSTRY GROWTH PROJECTIONS FOR THE NEXT 1 AND 5 YEARS

It is a challenging exercise to forecast U.S. local, long-distance, and international telephone revenues. Increased competition certainly will affect future prices, traffic volume, and revenue growth, but the timing and extent of that competition are uncertain in several submarkets. At the local level, important questions, such as whether and when cable television operators as well as long-distance providers such as AT&T will enter the local telephone business, remain to be answered. AT&T reportedly thinks that it could capture about one-third of local service revenues within 3 years in the areas where it decides to compete.

In the long-distance sector key questions include how soon the Bell companies enter that market, especially the markets within their own service territories. It is anticipated that by early 1999, one Bell company will be permitted to offer long-distance services throughout at least one state in its region. Will there be price wars as new entrants offer very low rates in an effort to "buy" market share? How much of an effect will voice over the Internet have on revenues, particularly those of the smaller resellers? How many European and other foreign firms will establish U.S. operating companies to provide domestic long-distance and international services, and how effective will they be as competitors?

How soon will the local Bell companies be able to provide in-region international services? How fast will international accounting rates fall? As settlement payments are reduced to comply with current FCC-mandated benchmark rates, how much of those savings will be passed on to customers in the form of lower international rates? What will be the effect on international service revenues after U.S. firms gain access to the markets of the EU member states and other countries in 1998? What effect will new low-cost technologies, such as Internet telephony, have on overall revenues? All these variables will affect prices, traffic volumes, and revenues.

At this point it appears that the demand for all telecommunications services will remain strong and revenues will increase, although at different rates, in the three primary basic services market segments. Revenues derived from all local services should increase about 4 percent a year in 1999 and the following 4 years to reach about $200 billion in 2003. Growth in long-distance minutes should maintain an annual rate of about 5 percent, with revenue growth at close to the same figure. The market should maintain 5 percent annual growth, and so total toll revenues could reach $170 billion in 2003. International outbound U.S. minutes of traffic will grow at an annual rate of 15 to 20 percent from 1998 to 2003, while inbound minutes should increase from 10 to 15 percent annually over that period. Billed revenues should increase about 6 percent annually through 2003, at which time U.S. billed revenues for international telephony could reach $32 billion.

Total U.S. revenues for basic voice and data services are expected to increase about 8 percent in 1999 to reach nearly $270 billion (see Table 30-1). Annual revenue growth is expected to continue at that level, bringing telecommunications service revenues to nearly $375 billion in 2003.

The number of jobs in the telecommunications services industry grew very slightly from 1992 to 1996 but increased 7 percent in 1997. The number of jobs in the wireless sector nearly doubled from 1992 to 1996, although this sector still accounts for less than 20 percent of all industry jobs. The forecasts for continued substantial growth rates in wireless subscribers and revenues and the anticipated entry by new foreign competitors into the open U.S. telecommunications market suggest that overall the telecommunications services industry will continue to create new jobs.

GLOBAL MARKET PROSPECTS

Prospects are good for an overall 8 percent annual growth rate in global telecommunications services revenues through 2000 (see Table 30-2). Continued expansion of foreign networks (leading to improvements in service quality and increases in the number of subscribers on the network) and lower prices arising from competition and/or the use of newer, cost-effective technologies will fuel demand.

There are two significant aspects of future global demand for U.S. telecommunications service providers. The first is the

TABLE 30-1: Telecommunications Services (SIC 4812, 4813, 4822) Trends and Forecasts

(millions of dollars except as noted)

| | 1992 | 1993 | 1994 | 1995 | 1996 | 1997 | 1998[1] | 1999[1] | Percent Change | | | | |
									94–95	95–96	96–97	97–98	92–98[2]
Operating revenue	153,409	165,342	174,890	190,076	211,782	231,168	249,661	269,634	8.7	11.4	9.2	8.00	8.46
Revenue (constant 1992$)	153,409	160,995	165,820	175,817	197,135	215,823			6.0	12.1	9.5	8.0	8.5
Total employment (thousands)	893.3	886.0	901.0	908.2	919.8	984.2			0.8	1.3	7.0		
Production workers (thousands)[3]	670.4	668.4	668.7	678.8	703.2	736.7			1.5	3.6	9.8		
Average hourly earnings ($)[3]	15.09	15.61	15.92	16.22	16.63	17.51			1.9	2.5	5.3		

[1] Forecast.
[2] Compound annual rate
[3] Production or nonsupervisory workers only.
Source: U.S. Department of Commerce: International Trade Administration (ITA), Bureau of Census; U.S. Department of Labor, Bureau of Labor Statistics; Federal Communications Commission. Estimates and forecasts by ITA.

TABLE 30-2: International Traffic, Revenue, and Subscriber Growth[1]

	Historical Trend			Forecast	
	1987	1996	87–96[2]	2000	96–00[2]
Indicator					
Calls (billions)	4.3	20.2	18.8	38	17.1
Estimated call length (minutes)	4.5	3.5	–2.8	3	–3.8
Minutes (billions)	19.1	70.0	15.5	114.1	13.0
Per main line subscriber	42.4	94.0	9.2	123.4	7.0
Per main line plus mobile	42.2	79.3	7.3	88.8	2.9
Revenue (billion $)	23.9	61.3	11.0	82.2	7.6
Assumptions					
Price per minute of telecommunications traffic (MiTT) ($)	1.25	0.88	–3.8	0.72	–4.9
Main lines (millions)	451	745	5.7	925	5.6
Mobile subscribers (millions)	2.5	138	56.1	360	27.1

[1] 1986–1995 based on reported data. 1995–2000 based on International Telecommunications Union forecasts.
[2] Compound annual rate.
Source: Adapted from TeleGeography, Inc.

demand for "traded" services: U.S.-originated and -terminated international voice traffic. Outbound call volume should continue to increase 15 to 20 percent annually. Large manufacturing and service companies in the United States are and will remain heavy users of telecommunications services. Strong U.S. industries such as financial services, travel and tourism, software development, and some manufacturing sectors maintain close overseas business connections with subsidiaries, customers, and suppliers and depend heavily on private telecommunications networks and services to carry out their operations. In addition, the presence of large immigrant populations in the United States and the prospect of lower international calling rates will encourage residential use of international voice services. The value of U.S. telecommunications services "exports" (traffic received from foreign destinations) should remain slightly under $3 billion a year or decline slightly as accounting rates are lowered, thus reducing the settlement rate per minute.

The second aspect of global market prospects involves the new business opportunities that will emerge for U.S. firms as the large telecommunications service markets in Europe, the Far East, and Latin America begin to open to U.S. service suppliers. In pursuing commercial opportunities of these sorts, U.S. telecommunications firms may establish a commercial presence in a foreign country directly or through joint venture arrangements. Although the future revenues and exports those ventures generate can become a source of profit to the company, the revenues earned will not show up in U.S. market figures.

There are tremendous unmet demands throughout the global telecommunications services marketplace. Many nations have ambitious plans to invest huge sums in their infrastructures and make those services more widely available to their citizens. Under China's ninth Five Year Plan the communications and information industry has been designated as a strategic area for development. The objective is to establish a national information infrastructure based on the broadband integrated service

digital technologies by 2010. By 2000 China aims for an annual capital investment of $12 billion, with a network that reaches every village. India's government hopes to see $41 billion invested in that country's telecommunications sector over the next 15 years. Annual expenditures by the member states of the EU should approach $50 billion in 1999, with estimates for the telecommunications and multimedia markets together representing a $100 billion opportunity in 2001.

In the global marketplace developing countries, where typically less than 10 percent and often under 5 percent of the population has ready access to a telephone, have made it a priority to promote "universal service." In the United States, Japan, and western Europe, where 85 to 95 percent of households have telephone service, the emphasis is on upgrading existing networks (popularly referred to as information superhighways or national information infrastructures) to accommodate advanced "multimedia" (combining voice, data, and video applications) and other information technology services.

TELEPHONE SERVICES

Development and Competition

As the United States approaches the twenty-first century, it is appropriate to look back briefly to gain perspective on the remarkable development of the telephone industry over the last century. In 1900 the United States had about 1.36 million phones in service, or a teledensity of 1.8, a penetration rate similar to that of India and Pakistan today. Only 8.5 percent of U.S. households had telephone service. Bell System company revenues totaled $46.4 million. The network of the Bell System consisted of 1.96 million miles of wire connected to 2,775 central offices and maintained by 37,000 employees at the dawn of the century. The value of the Bell companies' communications plant was $181 million. Statistics for the independent companies are not available, but those companies may have increased these totals by about one-half. The U.S. telephone network carried an average of 7.9 million calls in 1900, and industry revenues were under $75 million.

A hundred years later the United States may have 190 million access lines and more than 400 million telephones, with an average of 1.85 billion calls a day. The country's teledensity should approach 70, with 96 percent of all households having telephone service. In 1999 total industry communications facilities worth $400 billion could generate annual revenues of nearly $280 billion. The telecommunications network of the United States is likely to have 28,000 switches, including remote and competitive local exchange carrier switches. The backbone transmission portion of this network is expected to have about 1.6 billion miles of copper wire, over 25 million miles of fiber strands, and as much as 90,000 miles of terrestrial microwave radio systems. Although new technology and computerization eliminated or reduced many types of telephone company positions in the postwar period, there probably will be 15 times as many jobs in the telecommunications services industry in 1999 than there were in 1900. A call between New

York and Chicago that cost $5.45 a hundred years ago can be made for 25 cents or less today.

Many people do not realize that during the industry's early years the provision of telephone services in the United States operated as a competitive enterprise. The original patents the Bell System held gave it a complete monopoly in the telephone field from 1879 to 1894, and its cautious business policy restricted the development of telephone service. As a result of the widespread unsatisfied demand for telephone service, a large number of independent companies entered the field after 1894. The Bell System and the independents contested with each other to acquire new territory. By 1900 there were more than 200 phone companies in Indiana alone. Of course the absence of a mandated interconnection requirement among the various systems, particularly between the local telephone companies, and the fact that AT&T operated the only truly national network ultimately made multiple competing systems within the same territory impractical. Another factor that doomed the independents was their inability to raise the capital needed to continue an aggressive expansion that would include the construction of intercity networks. One method the Bell System employed to eliminate competition was to use its financial backers and their influence to prevent the financing of large independent units. These and other alleged Bell System violations of the antitrust laws led to the Kingsbury Commitment in late 1913. In this agreement with the U.S. attorney general, the Bell System agreed, among other things, not to acquire control over any competing company. However, the Bell System could and did continue to acquire noncompeting telephone companies, so that by 1936 its monopoly of the desirable telephone exchange territory in the United States was virtually complete. With its interconnected long-distance network and its manufacturing arm, Western Electric, the primary equipment manufacturer in the country, AT&T dominated the industry for the next 50 years.

However, some notable results were achieved during this period of free competition that lasted until 1913. Between 1900 and 1905 the Bell companies and the independents together added nearly 2.5 million new phone lines, a development that was stimulated by the lowering of charges for renting a telephone instrument. Under the impetus of competition, the number of Bell phones increased an average of more than 21 percent per year between 1895 and 1906. The independents installed as many lines in their first 5 years of operation as the Bell companies had during their 20 years of monopoly. New telephone manufacturing companies were established to meet the need for transmission and switching equipment, and this led to improvements in technology and equipment. While the Bell System concentrated on serving the big cities, the independents built out into many rural areas; by 1907 almost half the independent companies' lines served farmers and small towns. Competition brought a reduction in the rates Bell System companies had charged. Operating revenue per station for a Bell phone declined from $88 in 1895 to $43 in 1907. Bell companies reacted to the competition by working to connect their many exchanges through a system of long lines into a nationwide system.

In the following decades, although hundreds of independent telephone companies continued to provide local exchange services on a monopoly basis in their own franchised areas, there was no competition in telephone services. This did not change until the early 1970s, when MCI and several other "specialized common carriers" began offering limited private line services to business users in competition with AT&T. Competition emerged in the public switched services market after MCI's introduction of Execunet service in 1976, and MCI became the world's first competitive international voice carrier when it reached an operating agreement with Canada to provide international telephony to that country in 1981. When the U.S. Department of Justice's antitrust suit against AT&T was settled and the Bell System was broken up on January 1, 1984, the United States went back to a policy of encouraging the telephone industry, now the telecommunications industry, to operate on the basis of competition instead of monopoly. The final step in the "policy return" to 1900 was achieved by the Telecommunications Act of 1996, which opened local telephony to competition. In 1999, as in 1900, robust competition reigns in the U.S. telecommunications marketplace. Unlike 1900, there are well-established regulatory policies, interconnection rules, and antitrust laws in place to help ensure a competitive marketplace and good telephone service.

Telecommunications Service Providers

Although well over 90 percent of wireline service revenues are controlled by a few large companies (the five former regional Bell companies, GTE, and the three largest long-distance companies), the introduction of new services based on new or improved technologies provides ample scope for niche market players in telecommunications services. There are nearly 1,400 local telephone service companies in the United States. About 150 firms offer long-distance services over network facilities of which they own at least a part. Another 400 companies provide toll services by reselling the long-distance services of the large carriers that have built their own nationwide networks (e.g., AT&T, MCI WorldCom, and Sprint). More than 100 competitive access providers have built fiber networks in urban business districts that connect with the networks of long-distance carriers.

Approximately 50 firms own a part (e.g., a switch) of the facilities they use to provide international telecommunications services, and at least another 3,000 offer international services on a resale basis. Other companies that report toll revenues include operator service providers and pay telephone operators. On the wireless side, about 850 firms provide cellular, paging, and other mobile services. Although the precise number of firms providing telecommunications services in the United States is unknown since many are unregulated, small, privately held enterprises, the total is not less than 3,800.

As was noted above, approximately 350 firms provide some form of international voice and data services, including resellers and call-back companies. However, the three biggest players still account for nearly 80 percent of international revenues. Each of these three companies has established business relationships with leading foreign telecommunications companies. The benefits of those alliances include securing instant access to large foreign markets already served by the partners, the ability to provide domestic customers with a greater range of seamless global services carried over the partners' network, strengthening of the competitive position of a carrier in its home market against its traditional rivals, and allowing the carrier to expand into domestic markets by obtaining funds to invest in building new network facilities and developing new services.

Mergers and Business Alliances

Mergers continued to occur at all levels of the telecommunications industry in 1997 and 1998, and that trend is expected to continue in the absence of sharp antitrust or regulatory opposition in 1999 and beyond. Some analysts believe that before these activities end, the structure of the telecommunications industry in the United States will be fundamentally altered. They predict that at the end of this period only three of the original seven former Bell regional companies will remain, each allied or merged with one of the three big U.S. long-distance carriers (AT&T, MCI WorldCom, and Sprint), which in turn will have investments in or exclusive business relationships with three large international (European or Asian) firms. Industry leaders claim that in a few years there may be only a handful of truly global telecommunications carriers and that recent mergers are only a reflection of the financial and marketing alliances necessary for a company to be a global competitor.

The big unanswered question is whether the creation of such national and ultimately global behemoths will increase competitive choices for consumers or whether a telecommunications oligarchy will be created. Such an oligarchy among the international record carriers, such as Western Union International in the 1970s, resulted in "Tweedledum" and "Tweedledee" firms that essentially offered the same services at similar prices and service quality and did little to prepare for the day when telegraph and telex services no longer would be the staple of international communications.

Clearly, a case can be made that "market forces" are partly responsible for this wave of mergers, but others argue that misguided or vague legislation, combined with regulatory micromanagement, is part of the explanation. It was widely believed that the Telecommunications Act of 1996 would lead to vigorous competition in the last segment of the telecommunications market dominated by monopolies: local telephone services. The theory was that allowing cable television companies to offer local telephony and allowing long-distance carriers to serve local markets, while letting the former Bell companies into the domestic long-distance and international markets, would spur innovation and competition that would benefit consumers.

Criticism is heard on Capitol Hill and among many telecommunications firms and consumer organizations because competition in the "local loop" has not developed, at least not to a degree that offers benefits to most consumers. Some argue that the act has to be "fixed" by resolving a number of issues that are being litigated and are slowing the progress of competition. Others allege that the act tried to advance contradictory objectives: promoting universal service by maintaining billions of dollars of industry subsidies for local telephone service while encouraging competition in the same market, where the costs of service have been skewed in favor of rural and residential users. In areas where prices have been subsidized historically, competition can result in an increase, not a decrease, in prices as they rise toward the true costs.

Similarly, the old Bell companies are still precluded from offering in-region long-distance and international services. Some observers believe that consolidation among local exchange carriers has become a key strategic goal because these companies have not been granted authority to expand into long distance or because they (and other large telecommunications firms) see little to gain from a fierce struggle to compete in new markets, a struggle that could result in higher costs, loss of market share, and lower profits.

Local telecommunications companies have a different explanation for their desire to grow through mergers. Merging is the best way for them to gain a presence internationally and strengthen their position in the U.S. market. Merging increases the financial and marketing resources at their disposal and makes it possible for them to invest the large sums needed to compete in local markets outside their own service territories. With a greater geographic coverage in the United States and telecommunications alliances abroad, they are better able to offer more customers end-to-end connectivity and seamless services among global locations. Do mergers essentially eliminate the possibility of future competition among rival firms or enhance the prospect of such competition, although among a reduced number of firms?

Whatever one's views on these complicated issues, the headlines of the past 12 months involve some of the best-known U.S. companies. SBC Communications (formerly known as Southwestern Bell), which had bought the former regional Bell Pacific Telesis, in 1996 for $16 billion, concluded its merger with Connecticut's Southern New England Telecommunications in October 1998. SBC offered to buy Ameritech for $62 billion in May 1998. If this deal is approved by the U.S. Department of Justice and the FCC, SBC will directly serve 57 million local telephone lines, about one-third of those in states that account for 70 percent of the U.S. population and half the nation's business lines. There is controversy over whether SBC faces competition in its current local market and whether it has moved to implement provisions of the Telecommunications Act of 1996 regarding opening up its networks to competitors. SBC says that 3 to 5 percent of its local business has gone to new competitors, mostly competitive local exchange carriers, so that there is real competition in its market. Critics argue that the vast majority of SBC customers do not have a choice of local carriers and cite a Texas Public Utility Commission ruling in May 1998 that SBC has not opened its local exchange network adequately. In July 1998, Bell Atlantic and GTE, the largest of the non-Bell telephone companies, announced plans to merge, forming a company with revenues exceeding $53 billion and serving more than 63 million access lines in 38 states. The merged company would be the largest local exchange carrier and cellular service provider in the United States as well as the world's largest publisher of telephone directories. As a new firm, both companies could become a stronger provider of data and advanced Internet services and expand their reach internationally, already having a presence in more than 30 countries.

The long-distance market, where prices of 8 to 15 cents a minute apply to domestic and many foreign locations, may not be as attractive to the local exchange carriers now, but they need to be able to offer those services to their local customers in the future as part of a "one-stop shopping" package. Although no former Bell company has met the Telecommunications Act's conditions for entry into long distance, it is widely expected that Bell Atlantic will be the first to receive such authorization and will enter the New York long-distance market. Recently, Ameritech and US West formed relationships with a growing long-distance carrier (Qwest) to offer residential and small business customers combined local and long-distance services. Carriers believe that combining ("bundling") services in this way provides them with an appealing product to market to customers: a single bill and a single contact for customer service. Also, bundled services can be packaged in ways that provide special discounts or value-added features to distinguish them from standard telephone services. Many telecommunications companies would like to achieve one-stop shopping by which they could offer their customers a variety of voice, data, and Internet-related services, providing for a customer's total communications needs. These marketing alliances have been challenged by several long-distance companies on the grounds that they allow these Bell firms to provide in-region long-distance services before receiving approval from the FCC, as is required under the 1996 act. The legal proceedings regarding this and other provisions stemming from the implementation of the act (e.g., the FCC's order on interconnection) promise to keep the courts busy and the industry in a state of uncertainty for the rest of 1998, if not beyond.

In the interexchange (long-distance) arena MCI had been the target of firms both larger and smaller than itself. In late 1996 British Telecom, which already had about a 20 percent investment in MCI, put forward an offer of $23 billion to buy all of MCI, and the FCC gave its approval. However, two other suitors emerged with bids that British Telecom decided not to match. GTE, already a provider of local telephony in many regions of the United States and an investor in several international carriers, believed that MCI would give it a strong presence in the long-distance and international services market and offered $28 billion. Seemingly out of nowhere came WorldCom, a company that had aggressively been building a fiber network in America and local fiber networks in European cities. It made a bid of $37 billion for MCI, an offer based on the exchange of WorldCom's high-growth stock. MCI chose the WorldCom bid. A concern of some firms (shared by the EU Directorate of Competition, which also had to approve the deal since WorldCom has licenses in EU member states) was that a merged WorldCom/MCI could control up to 60 percent of Internet backbone traffic. While disputing that figure, MCI decided to sell its Internet backbone facilities to Britain's Cable & Wire-

less but kept its consumer Internet access business, a market that WorldCom does not serve. WorldCom has maintained its stake in the data market as its subsidiary, UUNet, continues to expand its Internet facilities. The merger was completed on September 14, 1998, and MCI WorldCom was in business as a company with $30 billion in annual revenues and established operations in 65 countries.

A cross-national merger announced in June 1998 joins the fifth largest American long-distance carrier, Excel Communications, with Canada's Teleglobe in a $3.5 billion arrangement in which each party acquires new capabilities. Teleglobe brings a global network infrastructure linked by cable and satellite facilities to 240 countries and territories to the table, with licenses in 18 countries and a large customer base of Internet service providers. Traditionally, it was largely a wholesale carrier. Excel is a reseller that brings marketing and retail experience in a U.S. customer base and offers dial-around long-distance services, calling cards, and paging services.

Another kind of arrangement between carrier networks that may become more common is demonstrated by the long-term contact between GEInformation Services (GEIS) and MCI WorldCom. The two firms will integrate their global networks, with MCI WorldCom being responsible for managing GEIS's global electronic commerce and EDI networks as well as its own network while GEIS provides value-added network engineering and management for its customers. The arrangement gives WorldCom a guaranteed source of traffic, while GEIS will be able to work mostly with one telecommunications carrier rather than the many carriers from which it currently leases dedicated lines around the world. MCI WorldCom's objective of deploying technology that will support future Internet protocol traffic requirements appeals to GEIS and other firms that offer Internet-based electronic commerce applications.

While AT&T maintains marketing relations with its loose consortia of foreign carriers known as World Partners, it took a step in July 1998 to strengthen its role in international telecommunications by agreeing with British Telecom to form a $10 billion global venture. This firm, which will incorporate BT's existing Concert at its start, will combine the transborder assets, operations, and international traffic of both companies and develop a managed IP-based global network to support such applications as global call centers and electronic commerce. The new carrier will start with an annual international traffic base of about 25 billion minutes, more than one-quarter of the world's total.

On the domestic front, AT&T announced two mergers to speed its entry into the business local services market and to provide a broad set of consumer communications services. AT&T completed its $11 billion merger with Teleport Communications Group (TCG) in July 1998. TCG was the largest of the competitive local services companies, with a network in 65 markets around the country. AT&T now uses TCG's network infrastructure where available to get access to business customers instead of paying established local telephone companies for use of their networks. AT&T also announced plans in June to merge with Tele-Communications, Inc. (TCI) in a deal valued at approximately $48 billion. Once the merger is approved (and regulatory approvals may not be granted before mid-1999), AT&T will combine its current consumer long-distance, wireless, and Internet services units with TCI's cable, telecommunications, and high-speed Internet businesses to create a new subsidiary. The aim of that firm is to upgrade its existing cable infrastructure for use in providing digital telephony, video, and services to consumers.

Several factors account for this trend toward creating larger companies in the telecommunications market. Traditional *telecommunications* companies (providing basic voice and data services) are seeking to become *communications* companies (offering integrated voice, enhanced data, video, and multimedia services) and are looking for partners that increase the ability of the combined firms to compete in the global marketplace. Telecommunications firms may look for partners that can help them maintain market share in already competitive markets and achieve revenue growth by entering newly opened markets. These companies are likely to seek out partners that offer different types of services in adjacent markets or have developed expertise in new technologies. Voice, data, and video communications markets are merging, and different technologies (Internet, digital wireless, broadband networks, and low-orbiting satellite systems) have been developed to transmit digital signals. A company that wants to provide its customers with one-stop shopping for all their communications needs (domestic and international voice, cellular, paging, cable television, Internet, on-line and information services, etc.) is unlikely to have the necessary resources and expertise in-house and will need to buy or form a joint venture with niche market companies.

Internet Telephony

As in many other areas of communications, the Internet is having an impact on the market for basic telecommunications ser-

vices. Internet telephony began in 1995, but it required both parties to have an Internet connection, be on line at the same time, and talk through the sound system of personal computers. Now, however, calls can be made to any telephone from an ordinary phone in cities where the service is available. Users may encounter uneven voice quality and sound delays, but the savings can be dramatic. Although home users, relying on personal computer software, pioneered the use of Internet telephony, a growing percentage of calls now travel over the Internet Protocol (IP) telephony services of established carriers or over corporate intranets (see Figure 30-1).

In 1998 several companies began offering rates as low as 5 cents a minute in selected cities for domestic U.S. calls using the Internet to carry the traffic and 10 cents a minute or less for some international destinations. Average U.S. consumer telephone rates (based on carrier calling plans) are currently about 12 cents a minute for domestic long-distance calls and 60 cents a minute for international calls. Internet telephony, like competitive long-distance services before the advent of equal access dialing (1 plus the 10-digit phone number), currently requires a user to enter a 12-digit local or 800 number and account number and then dial the number desired. The local number is connected to a "gateway," a computer that converts voices to digital signals and then sends those signals over the Internet backbone (a packet-switched network) to another gateway, where the signals are converted back to voice and sent over the (circuit-switched) network of the local telephone carrier.

The future of Internet telephony will be greatly affected by whether regulators define it as a form of ordinary voice telephone service or, by virtue of its use of the Internet Protocol, a distinct information service. If Internet-related telephony becomes subject to access charges and universal service obligations, the prices charged to consumers will have to be

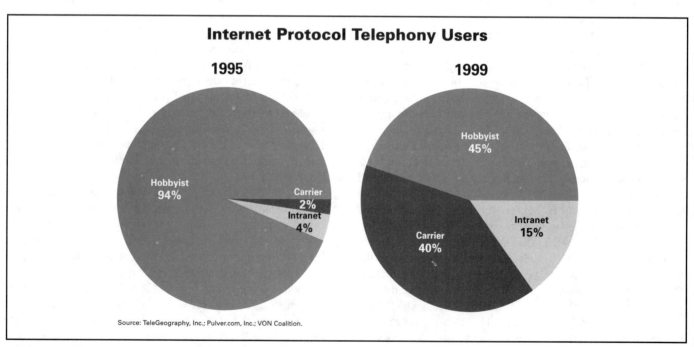

FIGURE 30-1

increased substantially, making the service less attractive and perhaps undermining the growing utilization of the Internet by telecommunications firms. Favoring a policy of allowing Internet-based services to continue developing in an unregulated environment, a section of the 1996 act reads, "It is the policy of the U.S. . . . to preserve the vibrant and competitive free market that presently exists for the Internet and other interactive computer services."

At the moment packet-switched voice is exempt from both interstate access charges and international settlements. However, changes in regulatory policy in this country or abroad could profoundly affect the growth and market appeal of telephony over the Internet. In April 1998 the FCC sent a report to Congress in which it reaffirmed its policy that Internet access (provided by Internet service, providers or ISPs) is an information service and should not be subject to the regulations that govern voice telephony. However, the FCC noted that some forms of phone-to-phone Internet Protocol telephony have the characteristics of telecommunications services.

Packetized voice traffic can flow over private networks too, and private corporate intranets represent a significant potential market. International fax traffic currently may account for as much as 40 percent of the total international telecommunications services market. Faxing over the Internet may become a major application because of the cost savings that can be realized. One consulting group envisions that one-third of long-distance telephone calls will be carried on packet networks by 2005. Although the rapid growth of the Internet in the United States is impressive, projections for Internet-transmitted services must be treated with caution. Some market studies have estimated that from a $10 million to $20 million revenue base in 1996, spending on Internet telephony may reach $240 million in 1998 and nearly $2 billion by 2001.

The potential for Internet telephony has caught the attention of the largest telecommunications firms that currently send huge amounts of voice traffic over the public switched telephone network. AT&T has helped finance ITXC Corporation, which is developing technology to provide settlement and billing services for calls routed across gateways from one carrier to another. AT&T reportedly is testing a prepaid Internet long-distance service that will charge 7.5 to 9 cents a minute. AT&T also offers Internet-based telephone service in Japan. Deutsche Telekom took a nearly $50 million stake in Vocaltec Communications, an Israel-based maker of gateways, in 1997. In the next few years it is not expected that Internet telephony will have much of an impact on the established long-distance services. Internet telephony revenues will remain modest in absolute terms, and the growth of all types of Internet services should help stimulate, not reduce, continued growth in toll volumes.

U.S. Industry Growth Projections for the Next 1 and 5 Years

There are about 190 million telephone access lines in the United States. A 4 percent annual growth rate can be anticipated as a result of continued growth of the number of households with access and demand for second or third lines in existing homes. These lines will be used to support home-based businesses and heavy use of on-line and Internet services and to give family members individual personal communications links in addition to pagers and cellular and portable phones.

Wireline telecommunications services will generate about 84 percent of telecommunications services revenue in 1999, while the wireless share could increase to 20 percent of total revenues in 2003. Local exchange service revenues should increase at an annual rate of 4 percent to reach $59 billion in 1999 and about $69 billion in 2003. New entrants (cable television companies and long-distance firms) will incur expenses in building their own facilities to offer services and are unlikely to offer local telephony at a significant discount. Access charges that totaled about $36 billion in 1996 may increase slightly to $39 billion in 1999. Beyond that, the annual amounts depend on policy changes the FCC could initiate to modify the fundamental nature of the access charge regime.

Growth in long-distance use should stay at a 5 percent annual rate, but prices may decline somewhat, particularly when the Bell companies enter the market. Total toll service revenues (switched and private line) are projected to increase 7 percent in 1999 to about $115 billion. Entry by the Bell local exchange carriers into the interexchange toll market should reduce the 80 percent market share now held by the three largest carriers: AT&T, MCI WorldCom, and Sprint. In future years toll revenue growth should increase at an 8 percent annual rate, bringing toll revenues to $157 billion by 2003.

U.S. international-billed revenues for telecommunications services amounted to $15 billion in 1996. International minutes of use are expected to increase 15 to 20 percent annually over the next 5 years, with billed revenues going up about 9 percent per year. Demand should remain strong in this period, with price reductions resulting from increased competition from the former regional Bell companies and new foreign competitors. Sharp reductions in accounting rates, if they occur, will bring lower rates for callers and stimulate increased call volumes. High volumes of fax traffic that are recorded by networks as international voice calls also are likely to continue. On some U.S.–Asian routes, where time and language differences are obstacles to voice communications, 40 to 50 percent of international calls may be fax transmissions.

Telecommunications Liberalization in Foreign Markets

The largest international carriers, with one exception, are based in open or soon to be open telecommunications markets (see Table 30-3). The entry into force of the WTO Basic Telecommunications Services Agreement on February 5, 1998, provided formal recognition of the increasing degree of telecommunications service liberalization in the world's major markets. The agreement codifies existing policies in some countries and challenges other nations to ensure that their new regulatory structures operate effectively to promote real marketplace competition. The words *privatization, liberalization, competition,* and *deregulation* sometimes are used interchangeably to refer to this general trend, but it is useful to make distinctions among them. Privatiza-

TABLE 30-3: Top 20 International Carriers

Rank	Company	Country	Outgoing Traffic, millions of MiTTs[1] 1997
1	AT&T	United States	10,290
2	MCI	United States	5,907
3	Deutsche Telekom	Germany	5,333
4	BT	United Kingdom	3,735
5	France Télécom	France	3,545
6	Sprint	United States	2,759
7	Telecom Italia	Italy	2,352
8	Swisscom	Switzerland	2,164
9	C&W Communications	United Kingdom	2,065
10	Stentor	Canada	1,778
11	Hong Kong Telecom	Hong Kong (PRC)	1,718
12	China Telecom	China	1,632
13	KPN	Netherlands	1,535
14	WorldCom	United States	1,400
15	Belgacom	Belgium	1,340
16	Telefónica	Spain	1,355
17	Singapore Telecom	Singapore	1,161
18	KDD	Japan	1,105
19	Teleglobe	Canada	1,112
20	Telmex	Mexico	1,009

[1] MiTT (minutes of telecommunications traffic) data are for public voice circuits only, rounded to the nearest million MiTT.
Source: Adapted from TeleGeography, Inc.

tion may refer to the sale of state-owned telecommunications operators to private investors or to allowing private sector firms to participate in a market formerly reserved for government-owned companies. Privatization may be a first step toward liberalization and competition, but in other cases the government-owned PTT may not be privatized until years after other firms enter the market. Most experts agree that continued state ownership of dominant carriers makes it harder for a country to deal successfully with operational and policy decisions to promote fair competition. The WTO agreement did not address the question of privatization directly, and some countries maintained investment limitations in their government-owned carriers.

Liberalization refers to improved or unrestricted market access to provide telecommunications services. It also has a more theoretical reference, suggesting the absence of legal and nontariff barriers in this market. The term *competition,* by contrast, refers to marketplace realities. If the market has been liberalized (old laws and regulations have been changed) but no new players have appeared to offer services, there still is no competition. However, some competition may exist even though the market has not been liberalized, as is the case in China.

The word *deregulation* often is used interchangeably with *competition,* but in fact, introducing competition into a formerly monopolistic industry may call for new regulations, at least during a transitional period. Once the market has become truly competitive, there is less need for regulations and the industry may be deregulated. Because of the current structure of many national telecommunications regimes and the dominant roles of large firms in the industry, deregulation may not be advisable for some time.

Liberalization has not proceeded at the same pace in all countries or within all sectors or submarkets of telecommunications. Often the equipment market was liberalized first, followed by value-added or enhanced services and finally basic (voice) services. In the United States liberalization in voice telephony proceeded over a number of years, driven by the development of new technologies and equipment and backed by critical regulatory policies and court decisions along the way. Now basic voice telephony is regarded as a service that can (although many countries choose not to do so) be liberalized all at once whatever its geographic reach or technology base.

The EU issued two directives in 1990 that led to the liberalization of telecommunications services, but progress in Europe has been uneven. For example, the German regulator has issued more than 80 operator licenses, while Italy's new regulatory authority has just begun doing so. Five EU member states (Denmark, Finland, Netherlands, Sweden, and the United Kingdom) had liberalized voice telephony by 1997 and are farther along in establishing a competitive market. Five more countries (Austria, Belgium, France, Germany, and Italy) liberalized their markets on January 1, 1998, and are making progress in dealing with some key issues (regulating the former monopoly carrier, establishing nondiscriminatory policies) that must be settled before competition can flourish. An emerging interconnection issue involves the proposals introduced or under consideration by several European regulators to require new entrants to meet a minimum switch requirement to qualify for the lowest interconnection rates. The practical result of such a policy could make it difficult for smaller carriers, especially resellers, to enter the market and compete with former monopolists.

In five countries (Greece, Ireland, Luxembourg, Portugal, and Spain) full liberalization will be achieved only between December 1998 and January 1, 2003. These countries were allowed to do this under EU procedures, but whether they will benefit by postponing liberalization is debatable. It may be significant for other countries that have delayed market liberalization that Ireland has announced that it will move the date for liberalizing voice telephone up a year to December 1, 1998. Even in advance of the formal date of liberalization, Irish consumers are beginning to reap the benefits of prospective competition as Telecom Eireann has announced wide-ranging tariff reductions. Reports are that Ireland realized that its closed market was putting it at a competitive disadvantage vis-à-vis its regional neighbors when a multinational firm decided not to locate a major communications operation there because of the lack of competitive alternatives.

Many of the important Latin American countries have made a commitment to phase in full liberalization of their markets by 2000 under the WTO agreement. Chile began the process of privatizing and liberalizing its telecommunications sector in the mid-1970s and today is the most liberal market in its region. Brazil has moved ahead with reform of its telecommunications sector. In 1995 that country passed a constitutional amendment to allow private participation in telecom, and in 1997 it passed a new General Telecommunications Law that created an independent regulatory authority. The government of Brazil recently completed the auction of nine Band-B cellular licenses, and sold the A-band cellular operations and an 18.2 percent stake in the Telebras telephone system. This initial sale of Telebras assets brought in $19 billion.

Asia has some of the world's most and least liberalized telecommunications markets, but a number of countries there may liberalize faster than their cautious WTO commitments would suggest. Australia, Japan, and New Zealand already are fully liberalized; South Korea, although it maintains foreign investment limitations, provides full market access for all basic services. Hong Kong recently liberalized its international services market beyond its WTO commitments, although it has not yet decided whether to offer full access or limit the number of suppliers to its domestic services market. China continues to keep its market closed to foreign telecommunications service providers, but many of its trading partners are insisting that it make some commitments to permit market access and foreign investment as part of its package for accession to the WTO. Taiwan has indicated that as part of its offer to join the WTO, it is prepared to allow majority foreign ownership in its telecommunications companies, significantly reduce the interconnection fees its monopoly carrier charges cellular phone providers, and phase in other measures to liberalize voice telephony in 2001.

Asian countries that have taken some steps to liberalize what are potentially high-growth telecommunications markets include India, Indonesia, Thailand, and the Philippines. These countries, however, are competing with more liberalized nations to attract foreign investment and technology. They may find that their failure to make a commitment under the WTO agreement to a more ambitious program of opening up their telecommunications services (combined with the financial or political uncertainties some of them now confront) will make it difficult for them to meet planned targets for expanding their telecommunications infrastructures. Thailand and Indonesia have multiple service providers in operation but limit foreign investment and have not indicated that they want to make a fast transition to a fully open and competitive market.

India is expected to open its domestic long-distance market to competition in 1999, and its newly elected government has indicated a need to speed the development of competition and private sector participation in the market. However, its government-owned carrier, the Department of Telecommunications, still controls most of the market for wireline telephony and continues to play a major role in setting telecommunications policy. Additionally, the Department of Telecommunications has gone to court to challenge decisions the new regulatory authority takes that are not favorable to its interests. At present it is unclear to what extent the U.S. sanctions invoked by President Clinton after India tested five nuclear bombs in May 1998 will result in diminished U.S. exports to and investment in India's telecommunications sector.

Full liberalization is still several years off in eastern European countries such as the Czech Republic, Poland, Hungary, and Romania, but they all have taken the initial steps and are committed to wide-scale liberalization within a few years. Hungary, for example, driven in part by its government's desire to make that country a regional communications hub, has encouraged extensive privatization in the telecommunications sector. The national carrier, Matav, is 67 percent owned by Magyarcom, a consortium of Deutsche Telecom and Ameritech, and provides local telephony in many districts. The other districts are served by 13 local operating companies typically owned by Hungarian and foreign partners.

Hungary also has set up a regulatory body separate from the operator and has made a commitment to liberalize international long-distance and domestic services in 2003. Meanwhile, paging and data transmission are open to competition, and VSAT services are provided by more than 15 companies. There is no legal restriction against building alternative infrastructure, although currently PSTN services can be provided only by concessionaire companies. Hungary has granted two mobile operators Global System for Mobile Communications (GSM) licenses and one NMT 450 license and expects to announce a tender for an undetermined number of GSM 1800 licenses by the end of 1998.

There are signs of new liberalization in the Middle East and Africa as well. Israel continues to increase the degree of privatization and competition in its market. Its government gradually has been selling off its share of Bezeq, the major Israeli carrier, and should hold less than 50 percent when a new international strategic partner is brought in before the end of 1998. Two long-distance and international service operators are consortia that include American and European firms. The licenses for the three cellular telephone networks are also consortia made up of Israeli and foreign companies. Private networks, cellular, paging, satellite voice and data, and international fax services already have been liberalized, and the government has announced plans to open the domestic telephone market to competition in 1999.

Nine national operators have been privatized in sub-Saharan Africa since 1990. Several African countries, including Botswana, Ivory Coast, Ghana, Mozambique, Namibia, South Africa, Tanzania, Uganda, and Zambia, recently established independent telecommunications regulators, a critical step toward effective market competition. In addition, a competitive environment with multiple providers for nonbasic services has been created. For example, in Ivory Coast, South Africa, and Ghana consumers may choose from a variety of firms that offer cellular, paging, value-added, and data services.

Implementation of the WTO Agreement on Basic Telecommunications Services

Sixty-nine countries that account for more than 90 percent of the world's telecommunications revenues reached a telecommunications services agreement on February 15, 1997, under the auspices of the WTO in Geneva. Since then four more countries have taken steps to join the agreement, while a few countries have adopted policies that go beyond the degree of liberalization under the WTO. The agreement entered into force on February 5, 1998.

Four countries have failed to ratify the agreement but are expected to do so shortly. A country that does not ratify becomes a "free rider"; that is, it has no obligations under the agreement but enjoys all the benefits (market access and national treatment commitments) provided by the WTO members that have ratified.

The agreement has three components: market access, national treatment, and procompetitive regulatory principles. With regard to market access, U.S. companies are given varying degrees of market access to other markets, based on individual country commitments, for local, long-distance, and international services. Services can be provided through any network technology either on a facilities basis or through resale of existing network capacity. As a result of the national treatment obligation, U.S. companies can acquire, establish, or hold a significant stake in telecommunications companies around the world, with the exact percentage of ownership dependent on individual countries' commitments. Sixty-four countries adopted procompetitive regulatory principles based on the landmark U.S. Telecommunications Act of 1996. This agreement is fully enforceable under WTO dispute settlement procedures.

Implementation of the agreement is under way, and it is apparent that some countries face greater challenges in conforming their institutions and policies to their commitments than do others. In 1997 the FCC proposed and adopted new rules to implement U.S. commitments under the agreement. Under the new rules the FCC granted more than 200 applications to provide international service during the first 3 months in which the agreement was in force. Among these were 26 applications from foreign telecommunications carriers to enter the U.S. market.

The EU Commission has released a series of reports on the implementation of telecommunications liberalization within the EU. The commission found that nine member states had not completely or adequately implemented the directives that provided for an open EU market in the 10 member states affected as of January 1, 1998. In May the EU Commission announced the initiation of infringement procedures against five member states for failing to meet EU licensing requirements. Ongoing EU reviews should continue to provide incentives for member states to live up to their commitments to liberalize their markets as called for under EU directives and the WTO Telecom Agreement. It appears that Italy is one EU state that is seriously behind schedule in meeting market liberalization requirements, for example, in establishing a licensing regime.

During the first few months of implementation U.S. telecommunications firms generally had few complaints about the progress countries were making in carrying out their obligations under the agreement. Of course concerns often do not arise until a specific application or request is made by a firm at the time it prepares to enter a market. Thus, the number of complaints may increase as the number of companies seeking to provide services in a greater number of markets increases. In Europe's largest telecommunications market, Germany, the progress of liberalization is of particular interest to U.S. firms. The new German regulatory authority has been active in monitoring actions by the dominant market player that could have a deleterious effect on competition.

During the annual "Section 1377" congressionally mandated review of telecommunications trade agreements entered into by the United States, the U.S. industry filed complaints against Canada and Mexico regarding implementation of their WTO obligations. Since then, the Canadian Radio-Television and Telecommunications Commission has eliminated Canada's international bypass restriction, thus addressing the U.S. industry's complaint.

The issues with Mexico are still under discussion. They involve a 58 percent surcharge on inbound international calls, Mexico's failure to allow international simple resale, and the absence of cost-oriented interconnection rates for connecting domestic and international long-distance traffic to the local network in Mexico. Talks on these issues have been held between the United States and Mexico but have not been concluded satisfactorily.

Daniel Edwards, U.S. Department of Commerce, Office of Telecommunications, (202) 482-4331, October 1998.

WIRELESS COMMUNICATIONS SERVICES

Wireless service providers—cellular, personal communications services (PCS), and paging operators—constitute a thriving industry sector in the United States that has enormous growth potential well into the next century. Catalyzed by a progressive regulatory environment that has encouraged a wave of new market entrants, coupled with increasing price competition and unfulfilled demand, cellular services in the United States grew markedly in 1997. Demand was driven by greater marketing and advertising efforts, rapidly expanding networks, and technological advances. These trends are spreading throughout the world. While voice telephony has been the predominant application and is expected to remain so, new services applications such as advanced messaging, data and video transmission, location technology, and remote monitoring are in the early stages of what most analysts predict will be a period of explosive growth around the turn of the century.

Commercial networks for mobile voice communications services in the United States generally are divided into two categories: cellular and PCS. These systems are distinguished mainly by the frequency used: Cellular in the United States utilizes the 800 MHz band, while PCS utilizes the 1,900 MHz band. In addition, PCS systems are entirely digital, while most cellular networks in the United States are still analog. Many cellular operators are converting their networks to digital and positioning themselves to be all but indistinguishable from PCS operators.

Cellular systems currently represent the largest segment of wireless communications services in the United States. In 1997 there were more than 1,500 cellular systems operating in 750 U.S. markets. Many new PCS operating licenses in six different blocks of spectrum have been issued in the United States since 1994. Competition between PCS carriers and existing cellular carriers has been intensifying as PCS service providers seek sufficient market share to cover development costs and established cellular carriers fight to maintain their market share. Despite the current predominance of cellular subscribers in the U.S. wireless market, PCS is growing rapidly. PCS operators reportedly gained 20 percent of all mobile wireless additions in 1997, for a total of about 2.5 million in the United States at the end of that year, a figure that was expected to more than double in 1998. Few analysts predict that PCS will eclipse cellular in the United States in the near term; however, the gap between the two systems is expected to close gradually over the next 5 years.

Industry Growth

The number of new cellular subscribers in the United States increased dramatically from 1992 to 1996, and 1997 saw a continuation of that growth. For the second year in a row the number of new subscribers exceeded 10 million, with a record 11.5 million net new subscribers in 1997, for a total of over 55.3 million at the end of that year. The number of new subscribers in the United States is expected to again top 10 million and approach a total of 70 million by the end of 1998, with analysts predicting more than 80 million subscribers by the turn of the century. One analytical firm believes that 82 percent of U.S. adults from households with an income higher than $35,000 per year (approximately 90 million people) will be subscribers by 2002. While projections differ, the number of cellular and PCS subscribers in the United States from 1997 to 2002 is expected to have a compound average growth rate (CAGR) of 12 percent. Most of this growth is expected to occur in the next 4 years, with an easement in demand after 2001.

The cellular and PCS industries continued to attract more nonbusiness than business users in 1997, largely as a result of a decline in the cost of handsets and bundled service packages. The average customer's bill dropped about 10 percent to $42.78 at the end of 1997 from $47.70 at the beginning of the year. The FCC reported that overall revenues for cellular and PCS services reached $30 billion in 1997, up about 27 percent from $23.6 billion in revenue for 1996 and nearly $2 billion more than most analysts had projected. Industry revenues are expected to continue to increase over the next few years as higher-capacity digital networks are implemented and new services become available. According to the Cellular Telecommunications Industry Association, industry investment grew to $46 billion in 1997, up over 41 percent from 1996 (see Table 30-4).

Although cellular services still dominate the wireless sector in the United States, there is already at least one PCS system operating in areas serving over 70 percent of the United States. PCS was poised for tremendous growth in 1998 as competition intensified and additional systems began operating. While PCS was introduced commercially only in the last few years, the total number of subscribers at the end of 1997 was 2.5 million in the United States. Dataquest estimates that average annual revenue per subscriber for PCS was about $576 in 1997, with total revenue for 1997 at $1.03 billion, over 3 percent of the combined total for cellular and PCS. By 2001, however, there are expected to be about 40 million U.S. PCS subscribers and total revenue for the year of $15.9 billion, according to Dataquest. Other predictions vary: Decision Resources forecasts that PCS will account for only 21.8 percent (19.5 million) of U.S. mobile voice subscribers, while cellular will account for the remaining 78.2 percent (70 million) by the end of 2001, but estimates total revenues will reach $31.4 billion. On average, however, it is projected that PCS subscribers will account for 40 to 45 percent of subscribers and about half of total service revenues by 2002.

Market Trends

The dust has begun to settle from the frenetic year 1997, with its scramble for new licenses, agonizing over technology choices, and burgeoning subscriber rolls. Significant and sudden changes, however, are a hallmark of the wireless industry, and wireless operators will still have to deal with these and newer challenges arising from stiffer competition and the demand for advanced services in 1998 and 1999. As the price of many wireless devices continues to decline, wireless subscribers soon will demand access to the same types of broadband services, including video and intelligent networks, that they have on their wired phones.

A study entitled "A Strategic Vision of the Wireless Industry" published by the Institute for Communication Research and Education aptly summarizes current trends in the U.S. wireless market. The study states that the plethora of new players that are entering the wireless service provision marketplace

TABLE 30-4: U.S. Wireless Industry Data, December 1990 to December 1997, Reflecting Domestic U.S. Cellular, ESMR, and PCS Providers

Year	Estimated Total Subscribers	Annualized Total Service Revenues, $ thousands	Annualized Roamer Revenues, $ thousands	Direct Service Provider Employees	Cumulative Capital Investment, $ thousands	Average Local Monthly Bill, $	Average Local Call Length, min
1990	5,283,055	4,548,820	456,010	21,382	6,281,596	80.90	2.20
1991	7,557,148	5,708,522	703,681	26,327	8,671,544	72.74	2.38
1992	11,032,753	7,822,726	973,871	34,348	11,262,070	68.68	2.58
1993	16,009,461	10,892,175	1,361,613	39,775	13,956,366	61.48	2.41
1994	24,134,421	14,229,922	1,830,782	53,902	18,938,678	56.21	2.24
1995	33,785,661	19,081,239	2,542,570	68,165	24,080,467	51.00	2.15
1996	44,042,992	23,634,971	2,780,936	84,161	32,573,522	47.70	2.32
1997	55,312,293	27,485,633	2,974,205	109,387	46,057,911	42.78	2.31

Source: Cellular Telecommunications Industry Association.

will create a sea change in competitive intensity in the industry. The authors assert that as a result, buyers will have a broader selection and therefore greater purchasing power. Analysts generally agree that a window of opportunity will open for companies that are moving away from network coverage issues to focus on providing effective hardware and software solutions or services that will allow more efficient customer acquisition, better provisioning of services, more flexible billing, and effective churn and fraud management.

Revenue growth and subscriber gains in 1997 resulted from a number of factors, including increased competition and resulting declines in the cost of service, the introduction of digital technology, wider area coverage at lower rates, the increasing availability of advanced services, and significant reductions in handset prices. In many cases handset costs were kept artificially low through bundling with service packages, an approach many customers seemed to prefer. The fundamental reason for the growth of wireless services, however, remains the fact that consumers enjoy being unfettered by the limitations of wireline networks. These trends were expected to continue in 1998 as competition from new market entrants (notably PCS) increases.

A number of studies indicate that the price of wireless services is relatively inelastic and that any elevation in price must have commensurate service features associated with it that subscribers value, such as call screening and call routing, short message services (SMS), and in the future the advent of personal numbering and modem, fax, and computer functionality. In a 1997 study cost was cited by 37 percent of those surveyed as the most important factor in selecting a wireless service, while 27 percent cited call quality and 10 percent cited concern about dropped or disconnected calls. Although the cost of services is expected to decline gradually, current monthly service fees for cellular and PCS continue to prevent some subscribers from entering the market. According to Allied Business Intelligence, premiums of less than 20 percent per call (over wireline costs) for local usage are needed for greater acceptance by the next population of users. In other words, a significant price reduction may be required to sustain the surge in usage seen to date and to penetrate the next socioeconomic layer of customers.

As was noted above, incumbent cellular service providers face competition from both PCS operators with designs on their customers and new cellular operators (e.g., in unserved areas) that, as a result of telecommunications reform legislation passed in 1996, have greater latitude to cross borders and explore one another's markets. The last few years have seen industry giants such as Sprint, AT&T Wireless, and Primeco Personal Communications aggressively roll out their PCS networks. Although many PCS licensees are carrying heavy debt loads, declining prices eventually will lead many consumers to consider PCS as their primary wireless carrier. Increasing competition is affecting the decisions made by incumbent cellular service providers in a variety of ways, including decisions about structuring prices and deciding which alliances will be the most beneficial. Many cellular carriers are accelerating the buildout and digitalization of their systems to provide enhanced coverage, increase the subscriber base, improve voice quality,

and gain a marketing edge. Although costly, for many cellular operators digital network upgrades are no longer an option but a competitive necessity.

Most of the market share for cellular services remains in the hands of large, established U.S. telecommunications service providers such as AT&T Wireless and the Regional Bell Operating Companies. Many analysts predict that four or five national service providers of cellular and PCS will remain preeminent over the next 5 years. Dataquest noted the following criteria for successful operators: financial viability, marketing acumen, wireless expertise (a well-crafted business plan), an adequate subscriber base, and the ability to construct and optimize the network and the human resources needed to sustain it.

The auctioning of new licenses over the last few years increased competition and helped bring about the current boom in wireless services; however, some expected participants have fallen by the wayside. The Office of Management and Budget has estimated that defaults on auctioned FCC licenses will surpass $6 billion in 1998. However, FCC officials expect actual losses from defaults on license payments to be lower because revenue from reauctioned licenses was not taken into account by the Office of Management and Budget. In 1999 defaults are expected to total $119 million.

The following material offers a brief description of some of other significant issues and trends in 1997 and 1998.

Calling Party Pays. Local wireline services are offered at a flat rate for unlimited calls, whereas mobile services charge by the minute. To date in the United States, calling charges for wireless have been billed mainly to the recipient of a call: the wireless subscriber. In Europe and other parts of the world the reverse is true: It is the calling party that pays for calls to mobile phones. Proponents of this type of approach believe that it helps expand the market and that the current U.S. approach actually stifles the market. Many cellular subscribers give out their phone numbers discreetly to limit the number of incoming calls. PCS carriers have used this to their advantage by offering the first minute free on all incoming calls. The FCC has been reexamining the impact of the calling party pays (CPP) practice to determine whether wider availability of CPP in the United States would stimulate competition with wireline services provided by local exchange carriers (LECs).

Number Portability. Number portability—the ability to retain a phone number when a customer switches carriers—is a prominent goal of the wireless industry. It also is a requirement of the Telecommunications Act of 1996. Number portability is seen as essential by wireless carriers, especially if they are to compete head to head with wireline carriers for local exchange customers.

Prepaid Services. Prepaid wireless services, in which services are purchased in advance of their use, are being mass-marketed successfully by most service providers. Encouraging customers to prepay cuts down on fraud and bad debt and relieves operators of the need to conduct expensive credit checks. The service is enormously popular abroad, where prepaid customers constitute an estimated 30 to 40 percent of all new applicants for wireless service. In 1997 Omnipoint and PrimeCo reported that more than 50 percent of their subscribers used prepaid services.

Digitalization. Although analog systems remain predominant in the United States, many analog systems are reaching capacity. Conversion to digital technologies holds the promise of greater spectral efficiencies as well as a range of new applications that provide better value for users. Digital features such as SMS often translate into increased air time use and therefore more revenue for carriers. About half of worldwide wireless subscribers currently use digital technology, although the proportion in the United States is closer to one-quarter. The number of digital subscribers in the United States is expected to overtake the number of analog subscribers around 2002.

Fraud Prevention. The war against fraud remains a notable phenomenon in cellular services, with some analysts estimating the cost of wireless fraud to operators to be $1.5 million per day. Increased penalties and advanced technology are two ways wireless companies are combatting fraud, which costs the wireless industry over a half billion dollars a year. The U.S. House of Representatives passed a bill to penalize persons convicted of cellular telephone cloning. Corsair Communications, among others, is marketing a radio frequency fingerprinting system to provide fraud protection to cellular carriers, and in 1997 Electronic Data Systems introduced a system designed to reduce cellular carriers' exposure to cloning fraud and decrease its costs by providing near-real-time authentication. As a result of these and other measures, fraud is reportedly on the decline in the United States.

Industry Consolidation. Consolidation is occurring rapidly in the cellular services industry as major players ally. A recent notable example was the merger of MediaOne Group's (formerly U S West Media Group) U.S. cellular and PCS interests into AirTouch Communications in April 1998, creating the second largest wireless provider in the United States. AirTouch reported the total value of the transaction at $5.9 billion.

Move toward Multimedia. Although voice services will continue to drive the cellular and PCS market, network operators are moving steadily toward multimedia services, incorporating video and data. In the future enhanced services (e.g., Internet access and E-mail) will become the norm. Key enabling technologies such as silicon integrated circuits, software, and photonics are creating increasingly sophisticated equipment. The eventual goal of service providers is to deliver ubiquitous, affordable wireless services to small lightweight handsets that can handle voice, data, and video.

Wireless data services are expected to continue to have low growth for a few more years because of relatively slow transmission speed and high cost. However, data transmission is expected to constitute an ever-increasing portion of the future wireless services market (see Figure 30-2). Over the last 2 to 3 years the wireless data market entered a sustained growth cycle driven by increasing market penetration of portable computers and personal organizers, the introduction of additional new products incorporating radio frequency modems, broader user familiarity with networking, and the development of mobile data protocols. Today wireless applications enable users to query databases and access E-mail through cellular modems and phones. Some industry observers predict that within the next 6 years data transmission will account for over 70 percent of wireless traffic. Others predict that as subscribers begin to access the Internet by using wireless devices, air time demands will force the extinction of analog systems except in areas with modest traffic.

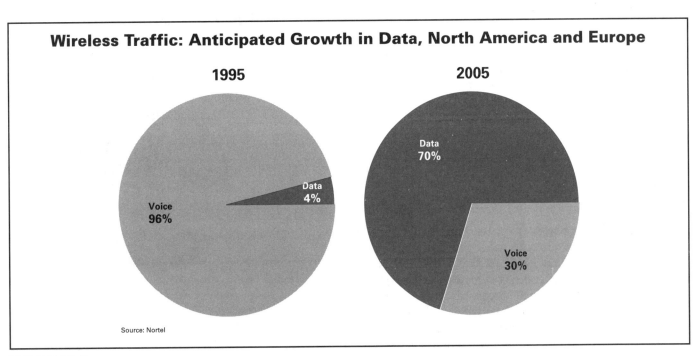

Wireless Traffic: Anticipated Growth in Data, North America and Europe

1995

Voice 96%

Data 4%

2005

Data 70%

Voice 30%

Source: Nortel

FIGURE 30-2

Another hallmark of wireless data is the continued success of Cellular Digital Packet Data (CDPD), which breaks data into packets and "mails" them over the cellular airwaves. It is considered economical for short messages such as E-mail, transmits both voice and data over the same cellular equipment, and supports a broad base of applications. Long-distance carriers and Bell regional holding companies are pursuing alliances and expanding their CDPD service capabilities so that mobile users can have seamless service when sending faxes or receiving E-mail messages.

Standards

For a number of years the European wireless standard, the Global System for Mobile Communications (GSM), benefited greatly from being the only commercially available and widely supported digital standard globally, and it has been selected by over 150 carriers in more than 100 countries throughout the world. Other operators have chosen between Digital AMPS (D-AMPS)/Time Division Multiple Access (TDMA), Code Division Multiple Access (CDMA), and the PCS 1900 variant of GSM in the United States.

Most digital systems today use a form of TDMA technology (e.g., European GSM, Japanese PHS/PDC, and North American IS-136). TDMA advocates emphasize that the standard was devised largely for the smooth conversion of AMPS to digital and cite its seamless interworking with AMPS-based systems. They also note that TDMA is a proven technology and that enhanced services can be introduced (based on IS-136), including a message waiting indicator, caller ID, voice privacy, authentication, data communications, and SMS.

CDMA advocates claim that CDMA has superior spectral efficiency, the ability to reduce deployment costs by simplifying network configuration and lowering required base station density, and better voice quality and longer handset battery life. Customers' response to CDMA service—factors such as superior voice quality and fewer dropped calls—and the features it offers are among the elements that service operators will use to guide future network deployment. Allied Business Intelligence anticipates that CDMA will account for 125 million subscribers in 2002 and possibly approach 300 million subscribers, depending on the number of carriers that turn to CDMA.

The truth of various claims can be borne out only in a commercial environment, as capacity and quality levels cannot be tested seriously before the number of subscribers on a network approaches the hundreds of thousands. For the foreseeable future multiple digital standards will continue to coexist.

Global Market Prospects

The growth of wireless services globally continues to increase rapidly as wireless becomes nearly ubiquitous. Cellular coverage is almost universal in developed countries, and in developing countries it is increasingly becoming a substitute for wireline networks as the cost of installing wireless networks declines. In the 1990s the benefits of cellular telephony—mobility, usability, and, more recently, affordability—have made cellular attractive to consumers in developed countries

and an urgent requirement in many developing countries. Most telecommunications opportunities in non-U.S. markets involve significant wireless capabilities as developers have come to recognize that wireless networks are often less expensive to construct and operate than traditional landline networks and can be brought to market in one-third the time. The auctioning of licenses has become increasingly prevalent as digital technologies have given foreign governments and regulators an opportunity to create competition in line with prevailing political trends toward a more open environment in telecommunications services. This in turn provides a better deal for users and attracts potential investors to the country.

At year end 1997 there were about 200 million cellular subscribers worldwide, an increase of close to 70 million from 1996. By the end of the first quarter of 1998 that figure had reached 225 million. North America accounted for nearly 30 percent of the total number of subscribers, followed by western Europe with 27 percent. Western Europe was the fastest growing region in 1997 and, if this trend continued, was expected to surpass North America in 1998. The number of subscribers in the Asia/Pacific region continued to grow, although at a slower pace than it did in 1996. Although starting from much smaller bases, Latin America and central Europe also experienced strong growth in 1997 (see Figure 30-3). Predictions for cellular and PCS subscribers globally now call for the number of cellular subscribers to exceed 500 million by 2000 (see Figure 30-4). This projection represents a CAGR of 27 percent between 1998 and 2003. Dataquest pegged the global value of cellular services in 1997 at $128 billion and projects that it will reach $276 billion by 2001. PCS subscribership is projected to grow to 151.3 million worldwide by 2000. The degree to which wireless

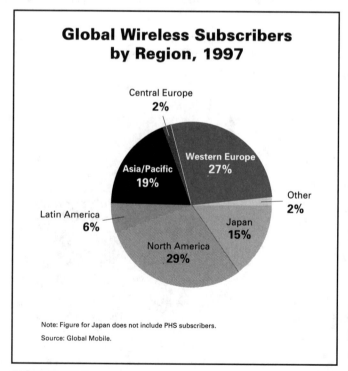

Global Wireless Subscribers by Region, 1997

Central Europe 2%

Western Europe 27%

Asia/Pacific 19%

Other 2%

Latin America 6%

Japan 15%

North America 29%

Note: Figure for Japan does not include PHS subscribers.
Source: Global Mobile.

FIGURE 30-3

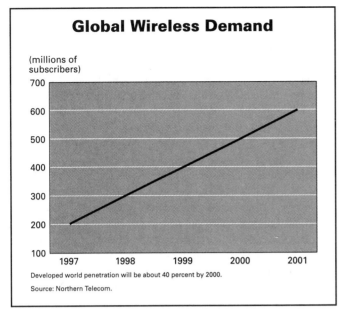

Global Wireless Demand

(millions of subscribers)

Developed world penetration will be about 40 percent by 2000.

Source: Northern Telecom.

FIGURE 30-4

has developed in different regions of the world depends largely on factors such as economic development, income distribution, cost of entry, affordability, free market orientation, and the effectiveness of distribution systems.

The year 1998 ushered in new advances in hemispheric roaming. BellSouth International's roaming and clearinghouse operation, International Wireless Services, for example, began offering hemispheric roaming to telecommunications carriers in the Americas, connecting wireless carriers in South America and Central America to one another and to carriers in North America. France Telecom and Deutsche Telekom offered wireless roaming between Europe and North America. These companies intend to open the service to all GSM operators. In the near future it is expected that handsets will allow users to access services by using up to three different frequencies. For example, a GSM phone affording access to GSM900/1800/1900 is expected on the market in 1999.

Asia/Pacific. Emerging markets in the Pacific Rim have low teledensities and abundant populations, making them key future markets for companies vested in wireless services. Dataquest has estimated 1997 cellular service revenues for the Asia/Pacific region at $53 billion and projects that they will exceed $100 billion by 2001. It is difficult to assess the Asian marketplace without looking at countries individually. Cellular and PCS licensing procedures, for example, have varied from no public tendering (China), to quasi-public tendering (Thailand), to public tendering (Taiwan, Hong Kong), to spectrum auctions (Australia). The ownership characteristics of operating entities also differ throughout the region, from complete state ownership to total foreign control and varying degrees in between. The most spectacular growth in the region in 1997 occurred in Japan, where cellular subscriber totals rose 133 percent to 38 million, reflecting falling handset and service prices.

Europe. According to analysts, the cellular service market in western Europe will grow from $31 billion in 1997 to nearly $52 billion in 2001, an average annual growth rate of 13.8 percent. The number of cellular subscribers in western Europe is expected to exceed 133 million by 2002. Liberalization, falling prices, and greater competition between operators will be the main drivers of growth.

Current penetration rates among the countries of western Europe range from about 9 percent in Greece to over 40 percent in Finland, with an overall average of over 10 percent. Italy, the largest services market in Europe in 1997, had over 11 million subscribers. France, Germany, Portugal, and Belgium all had subscriber growth rates that exceeded 100 percent in 1997. The number of wireless customers in the United Kingdom increased notably in the first quarter of 1998, and operators in Britain are thriving. At the end of March 1998 the British market counted 9 million customers, up from 8.5 million at the end of December 1997, representing a growth rate of about 6 percent.

Finland's market is notable for what it portends. In Finland wireless is growing so rapidly that in the first half of 1997 cellular revenues surpassed domestic wireline revenues. Finland may be establishing a trend that will be followed by many other countries in Europe, with huge implications for future trends in infrastructure investment.

Dataquest estimated the eastern and central European wireless service market at about $2.7 billion for 1997 and projects that it will grow to $15.9 billion by 2001. Eastern and central Europe had about 3.1 million subscribers in 1997, with penetration rates ranging from about 0.1 percent in Belarus to about 7 percent in Hungary and an average penetration rate of less than 1 percent.

Latin America. Cellular and PCS markets in Latin America will swell from around 10 million subscribers in 1997 to about 45 million in 2002, according to The Strategis Group. Dataquest estimated that the Latin American wireless services market reached $6.5 billion in 1997. Revenues are projected to reach $18 billion to $20 billion annually in that region, and service revenues will ultimately reach $30 billion by 2002. The Strategis Group predicts that 60 percent of the subscriber base will use TDMA IS-136, while most of the remainder will use CDMA.

Much of Latin America's market is concentrated in four countries: Brazil, Mexico, Argentina, and Colombia. Brazil is clearly the largest Latin American market, with more than 3 million subscribers at the end of 1997. The number of users in Brazil is expected to grow to approximately 6 million by the end of the decade. After protracted delays, Brazil tendered a series of 10 Band-B licenses in 1997 valued at $7.75 billion. The cellular telephone market in Mexico grew 70 percent in 1997. The government of Mexico took bids for seven radio frequency bands in three sets of auctions in 1997 and 1998. The number of subscribers in Mexico is expected to increase 42 percent by 2000 to reach almost 2.4 million. Colombia ranked third in Latin America with 1.7 million subscribers in 1997, followed by Argentina with around 1.2 million users and Venezuela with about 1 million subscribers.

Africa and the Middle East. Most countries in Africa and the Middle East had multiple operators in 1997, and digitalization continues to take hold. While the region has mostly analog—AMPS, TACS, and NMT—networks, digital networks are growing in number. South Africa clearly dominates the market; Africa had over 2 million users at the end of 1997, about 1.8 million of whom were in South Africa. The second largest market is Egypt, which, with its growing middle class and commitment to privatization, saw significant activity in 1997 and 1998. After a number of false starts, Egypt has seen the addition of two new GSM operators since November 1997.

Growth in wireless services in the Middle East has been relatively slow and has been limited to certain segments of society. Total service revenues for the Middle East exceeded $1.2 billion in 1997. As South Africa dominates Africa, Israel dominates the Middle East in wireless subscribership, with almost two-thirds of the region's 3 million subscribers. Dataquest projects that this region will have over 10 million subscribers by 2001, when over 90 percent of subscribers will be on digital networks (mostly GSM). Israel will spend an estimated $1 billion to set up its third mobile phone network, which was awarded in 1997.

Although next- or third-generation (3G) wireless systems are not expected to be deployed until 2002 at the earliest, a tremendous amount of international standards activity is already taking place (see Chapter 31). These systems will deliver broadband services with high-speed data capabilities as well as new mobile multimedia services such as full-motion video. Thus far, these activities have been driven by manufacturers, based on the assumption that the trend on the wireline side toward increased data traffic eventually will permeate the wireless sector as well. Several trials were scheduled to commence in 1998 in Europe, Japan, and the United States, in part to assess demand. In a study commissioned by the Personal Communications Industry Association and conducted by The Strategis Group in May 1998, executives of leading wireless companies were polled about demand estimates for third-generation terrestrial wireless services in 2010. The respondents estimated 58 percent penetration for toll-quality voice services, followed by messaging at 40 percent, switched data at 19 percent, and multimedia services at 3 to 13 percent. To the extent that the number at 3G standards can be minimized, economies of scale will drive the cost of service down more quickly. The EU is drawing up plans to issue 3G licenses as early as 2000.

Paging

In the United States the number of paging subscribers increased over 15 percent from 43.1 million in 1996 to an estimated 49.8 million in 1997. The number of subscribers using pagers for personal rather than business reasons grew as a proportion of the total paging market from 23 percent in 1993 to 46 percent in 1997. This trend was particularly evident among new paging subscribers; almost 70 percent of new customers are personal paging users. The increase in personal users is quickly changing the demographics of the paging market. Half of these sub-

scribers are under the age of 30, in contrast to the less than 20 percent of business subscribers who are under the age of 30.

While traditional numeric paging continues to constitute the bulk of the U.S. market, alphanumeric paging has experienced strong growth, rising from just 7 percent of the market in 1994 to 16 percent in early 1998. Growth in the U.S. paging industry also is being spurred by increased demand for advanced messaging services, in particular two-way paging. Also known as narrowband PCS (N-PCS), two-way paging allows messages to be transmitted in two directions. The various applications include voice messaging, two-way text transmission, and "acknowledgment" or "guaranteed" messaging (return confirmation that a message has been received error-free). Guaranteed messaging was introduced in 1997 and by the end of that year accounted for 40 percent of the N-PCS market, with voice messaging representing another 20 percent and two-way text messaging accounting for 40 percent.

To stay competitive with other wireless technologies, the paging industry will increasingly move away from traditional numeric paging. Alphanumeric paging is forecast to account for 24 percent of the total paging market by 2001. In 2001 voice messaging is projected to increase to 50 percent of the N-PCS market, while two-way text and guaranteed messaging will decline to 19 percent and 31 percent, respectively.

Global Market Prospects for Paging

Globally, the number of paging subscribers was 143 million in 1996 and is expected to increase to more than 220 million by 2001. The fastest growing regions are western Europe, Latin America, and Asia, in descending order.

Paging penetration in western Europe is relatively low in comparison to North America and Asia, although western Europe is now the fastest growing region in the world. According to The Strategis Group, western European subscribers are forecast to grow from 8.9 million at the end of 1997 to 17.8 million by 2003. In particular, countries such as France, Germany, the Netherlands, Russia, Spain, and the United Kingdom are expected to lead subscriber growth in the region. Western Europe's fast growth is attributed to the introduction of CPP, which eliminates all connection charges, rental charges, and tariffs for a pager owner after purchase; the growth in advanced messaging as operators adopt high-speed protocols such as ERMES and FLEX; and better marketing and distribution by service providers.

In contrast, the Asia/Pacific region has much higher rates of penetration, although its growth rate has lagged behind that in western Europe. The Strategis Group reported that there were 87 million paging subscribers in that region in 1997, and the number is expected to climb to 168 million by 2003. The region's leaders in paging growth will be China, South Korea, Taiwan, India, and Thailand, while countries such as Japan, Malaysia, and Australia will see declining subscriber growth. China in particular will drive the region's growth. From an estimated base of 50 million subscribers in 1997, China is forecast to have 121 million subscribers by 2003. Asia's high subscriber growth has been driven by the expansion of current networks, the introduction of high-speed FLEX networks throughout the region, and declining service prices.

Latin America, like Asia and Europe, is a high-growth region for paging. Latin America's low wireline teledensity is driving strong growth in the wireless sector as subscribers substitute wireless technologies for insufficient telephone networks. In Brazil, for example, paging has had dramatic growth since its introduction in mid-1991. In 1996 there were 800,000 paging subscribers in Brazil; that number is expected to grow to more than 5 million by 2000.

Richard Paddock, Linda Gossack Astor, and Cecily A. Cohen, U.S. Department of Commerce, Office of Telecommunications, (202) 482-4466, June 1998.

SATELLITE COMMUNICATIONS SERVICES

Satellite communications services include one- and/or two-way delivery of voice, video, and data via satellite to discrete geographic locations. Satellites are used to deliver international telephone calls as well as broadcasting and enhanced data services. Fixed satellite services (FSS) refer to broadcasting, data transmission, and telephony using fixed earth stations, while mobile satellite services (MSS) utilize mobile receivers such as cellular-size phones which are able to receive and transmit satellite signals. FSS traditionally represented the majority of satellite service revenues, but new MSS are expected to generate a significant proportion of future earnings.

Revenues for U.S.-based satellite services used in this section include revenues derived from satellite-delivered video and data services, which are not represented in the overall telecommunications services revenue figures given in the Overview section of this chapter. Revenues for satellite services include more than the revenues derived from basic voice and video telecommunications services.

Global Industry Trends

Revenues from global satellite services, both fixed and mobile, amounted to $19.2 billion in 1997, according to a Satellite Industry Association/Futron Corporation survey report. The United States accounted for $6.6 billion, or 34 percent, of this total. Although there is continued growth in the market for fixed services [especially direct broadcast satellite (DBS) services], rapid growth is widely expected in the market for the new mobile satellite services which will be offered in the next 1 to 4 years. Satellite Industry Association/Futron breaks down satellite service revenues into two primary categories: (1) transponder leasing and (2) subscription and retail services, which refer to the revenues generated through DBS, mobile satellite telephone, mobile satellite data, VSAT, and value-added remote sensing services (see Figure 30-5).

The International Telecommunications Satellite Organization (INTELSAT), an international treaty organization that was founded in 1964, was the first organization to provide global satellite coverage. It continues to be the communications

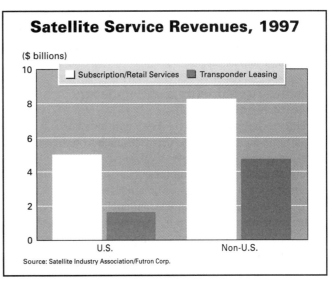

Satellite Service Revenues, 1997

Source: Satellite Industry Association/Futron Corp.

FIGURE 30-5

provider with the broadest reach and the most comprehensive range of services, providing telecommunications services to more than 200 countries. In April 1998 INTELSAT's 142 member nations agreed to partially privatize and form a new company, New Skies Satellites, N.V. While INTELSAT concentrates on FSS, the International Mobile Satellite Organization (INMARSAT) provides MSS worldwide. Established in 1979, INMARSAT has 82 member countries and provides global mobile satellite communications for air, sea, and land applications. INTELSAT and INMARSAT activities in the United States are carried out through COMSAT Corporation. COMSAT in fact is the largest owner and user of both entities. COMSAT's revenues from continuing operations in 1997 were $526.6 million. In September 1998, Lockheed Martin agreed to buy Comsat Corp. for $2.7 billion. Although the deal may not be finalized for some time due to necessary governmental approvals, it will certainly change the face of the U.S. satellite market.

Although INTELSAT only recently completed its partial privatization, there are calls for the complete privatization of both INTELSAT and INMARSAT. INMARSAT members recently agreed on a restructuring and privatization plan. The trend toward privatization of international treaty organizations has resulted from requests for improved services, more advanced technology, and lower prices.

In May 1997 PanAmSat, the world's first private international satellite services provider, merged with Hughes to become the new PanAmSat Corporation. In many areas of the world the number of private satellite operators has begun to increase significantly. The result has been heightened competition, lower prices, and better technology.

Another factor which will influence the future of the global satellite service industry is the increasing use of digital compression technology. Digital compression, or the ability to include multiple digital feeds in the space formerly occupied by a single analog channel, allows more efficient use of satellite technology and lower transponder costs. Although many users are hesitant to switch from analog to digital because of the short-term costs associated with the transition and a lack of familiarity with the new technology, long-term price advantages are expected to persuade the majority of businesses to make the switch as early as 2001.

Satellite Agreements and Regulatory Developments

Several regulatory actions in 1997 will affect the ability of satellite service providers to derive revenue from international operations. In February 1997 the United States and 49 other countries made binding commitments to open satellite markets to competition immediately or on a phased-in basis under the WTO Agreement on Basic Telecommunications Services. To ensure implementation of the agreement, the FCC issued orders in November 1997 that effectively liberalized market access for foreign telecommunications providers in the United States and provided for enhanced competition in the U.S. satellite services market. The objective of these regulations is to ensure that foreign and U.S. carriers will have new opportunities to compete in previously inaccessible markets.

In addition to the WTO agreement affecting satellite services, the United States has negotiated several bilateral agreements pertaining to the provision of satellite services. In October 1997 the United States and Mexico signed a bilateral agreement on FSS which will allow U.S. and Mexican satellites to provide these types of services in both countries. A separate agreement on the provision of direct-to-home (DTH) satellite services was signed in November 1996. The United States and Argentina signed a similar agreement in June 1998 which will allow U.S. and Argentinian companies to provide FSS (including DTH) in both countries. These agreements should ensure that U.S. operators will be poised to take advantage of opportunities to serve Latin America, which is a very promising market for DBS services.

Fixed Satellite Services

FSS provides point-to-point or point-to-multipoint communications between fixed locations. Applications include telephony, video broadcast, data transmission, and teleconferencing. Users of these services were previously limited to INTELSAT and several regional and national systems, many of which were owned by governments or quasi-governmental agencies.

According to *Via Satellite,* the number of geostationary orbit (GEO) satellite operators increased from about 25 operators in the 1980s to about 50 operators in 1996; it is estimated that there will be up to 60 operators by 2000. [The geostationary orbit is the orbit 22,237 miles above the earth at which a satellite appears to move at the same rotational speed as the surface of the earth, therefore appearing to stay "fixed" over a specific place. Only three GEO satellites are necessary to cover the entire earth. Low earth orbit (LEO) satellites orbit the earth at a distance between 500 and 1,000 miles, while medium earth orbit (MEO) satellites orbit the earth at a distance between 4,000 and 7,000 miles.] U.S. domestic FSS operations include (but are not limited to) AT&T Alsacom, Columbia Communications Corporation, COMSAT, GE American Communications

(GE Americom), Loral Skynet, and PanAmSat. Satellite manufacturers have increasingly become involved in the service side of the business, integrating vertically so that they manufacture the satellites and also offer services to consumers. Although the number of operators is expected to continue to increase, industry consolidation, increased competition from new mobile systems, and the phase-out of older systems will limit the increase in the number of new operators in the next 10 years.

One of the new satellite service operators that was expected to emerge in 1998 was Lockheed Martin Intersputnik (LMI). In June 1997 Lockheed Martin announced a joint satellite venture with the Russian-based Intersputnik consortium. LMI will provide a full range of satellite products and services and is expected to become one of the largest commercial communications satellite operators in the world. LMI plans to launch its first satellite, the LMI-1, by the end of 1998. The 1990s have seen an increase in the number of satellite manufacturers seeking valuable orbital slots and service providers looking for the most advanced satellite technology. Another example of this trend is a U.S.–Mexican joint venture announced in October 1997. Loral (United States) and Telefonica Autrey (Mexico) won a 75 percent interest in SatMex, which owns orbital slots above North America. These slots will allow the new company to provide television and data services throughout the Western Hemisphere.

Direct Broadcast Satellite Services

DBS services are formally defined by the FCC as radiocommunication services in which signals transmitted or retransmitted by space stations are intended for direct reception by the general public (both individual reception and community reception). The FCC does not have a formal definition for direct-to-home satellite–fixed satellite services (DTH-FSS), but it does note that there are differences between DBS and DTH-FSS in terms of frequencies, allocation of orbital positions, and interference coordination. Generally speaking, many use the terms *DBS* and *DTH* interchangeably. DBS, one of the fastest growing fixed satellite services, involves the delivery of audio and video signals directly to a household via a receiver dish placed outside the home. DBS subscribers receive anywhere from 150 to 200 channels by paying approximately $200 for equipment and about $30 to $35 in monthly programming fees (this varies depending on the service provider and the programming package selected). U.S. DBS service providers include DIRECTV, Primestar, United States Satellite Broadcasting (USSB), and DISH (Echostar). Another U.S. provider, Alphastar, went out of business in August 1997. In August 1998 there were 9.6 DBS subscribers in the United States, according to the Satellite Broadcasting and Communications Association (see Figure 30-6).

DIRECTV, a business unit of Hughes Electronics, is the largest single player in the market with the greatest number of subscribers to its Digital Satellite System and the broadest distribution system in the country. DIRECTV recorded 1997 revenues of $1.2 billion, representing 23.6 percent of Hughes Electronics' total revenues. Primestar, which has the second

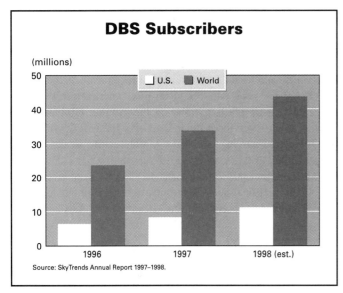

DBS Subscribers

(millions)

U.S. — World

Source: SkyTrends Annual Report 1997–1998.

FIGURE 30-6

place position in the U.S. market, is a consortium of leading cable television companies that originally envisioned providing satellite-delivered television to noncabled areas. Primestar is in the middle of a significant reorganization which will ensure that the company is far removed from the cable companies with which DBS competes so heavily. Echostar's DISH network ranks third but has been growing steadily and hopes to draw new customers by offering local stations via satellite, a service that is not available from the other firms. Echostar had revenues of $477 million in 1997. USSB is a provider of subscription television programming and is the primary movie source for DSS subscribers. It markets programming through a partnership with DIRECTV and earned revenues of $348 million in 1997.

Although it has been claimed that the Digital Satellite System has been the fastest-selling consumer product in history—selling more quickly than the VCR—the DBS industry faces many challenges from the established cable industry, which has 67 million subscribers in the United States, as opposed to 9.6 million DBS subscribers. Future competition from digital cable, regulations pertaining to the carriage of local channels, increases in copyright fees for DBS companies, and infighting among U.S. DBS companies are just a few of the hurdles the industry must overcome in order to thrive. However, analysts predict that there will be 15.7 million subscribers in the United States by 2002 and nearly 18 million by 2007.

The global DBS market has been very strong, and most analysts predict continued growth despite competition from cable and a number of governmental regulations banning the service because of concerns about foreign programming content. In 1997 there were approximately 33.5 million subscribers worldwide generating programming revenues of approximately $11.6 billion, up from 23.4 million and $8 billion in 1996, according to the Futron Corporation. Western Europe leads the world in terms of the number of subscribers, followed by the United States, the Asia/Pacific region, eastern Europe, Africa and the Middle East, and Latin America.

The Asia/Pacific region is thought to be one of the regions with the greatest future growth potential. Paul Budde Communication of Australia predicts that there will be up to 67 million subscribers to DBS services in Asia by 2005. In Japan, DirecTV Japan (Hughes) acquired 167,400 subscribers from its December 1997 market debut through August 1998. SkyPerfecTV (a recent merger of PerfecTV Corporation and Japan Sky Broadcasting), which began service in October 1996, captured 834,000 subscribers by August 1998 and expects to garner more than 2 million by the end of 1999 according to *Sky Report*. China, however, has banned the use of satellite television dishes by consumers, although hotels and other organizations are allowed to obtain DBS services. India has temporarily banned DBS services while legislators consider a bill that will provide for a formal licensing process. The financial crisis in Asia may also have a temporary negative impact on DBS growth over the next few years.

Observers note that the temporary downturn in the Asia/Pacific region may lead to renewed interest in Latin America. The Strategis Group predicts that cable and satellite subscribers in Latin America will increase from 13 million in 1997 to 57 million in 2007, with revenues growing from $4.2 billion to $26.9 billion. Hughes' Galaxy Latin America/PanAmSat and Sky Latin America (backed by TCI International and News Corp.) compete fiercely for subscribers in the region. The Strategis Group notes that the top five markets for cable and satellite include Brazil, Mexico, Argentina, Colombia, and the Caribbean. Further privatization, regulatory liberalization, and continued economic growth send positive messages about the growth of DBS services in that region.

DBS services have been tremendously successful in Europe, although the transition to digital services and burgeoning competition in the region are mitigating factors. Providers in the region include U.K. British Sky Broadcasting, France's Canal Satellite, Germany's DF1, and the Société Europeenne des Satellites, which operates the Astra satellite system. DBS services in Africa and the Middle East hold potential for growth but are somewhat limited as a result of economic conditions and government concerns about foreign content.

North America has seen substantial DBS growth in the United States but less than expected results in Canada. There are currently two Canadian companies providing DBS service in Canada: StarChoice and Expressvu. According to the Canadian Association of Broadcasters, StarChoice and Expressvu should attract 180,000 Canadian subscribers by September 1998. This number is relatively low compared to the size of the "gray" market of Canadian customers receiving U.S. programming not approved for distribution in Canada. In 1997 it was estimated that between 300,000 and 800,000 Canadians received illegal DBS service from the United States. With the enhancement of service offerings by StarChoice and Expressvu, and the launch of Canada's first DBS satellite, many expect that the size of the gray market will begin to decrease. Several U.S. companies have expressed an interest in offering legitimate DBS services in Canada, but their efforts have been hindered by strict Canadian content and license requirements.

Mobile Satellite Services

Mobile satellite services refer to the transmission of voice and data by satellite to mobile receivers such as pagers and cellular-size phones. Existing providers of mobile satellite services in the United States include Qualcomm's OmniTRACs, American Mobile Satellite Corporation (AMSC), and INMARSAT. There were 300,000 subscribers to these data communications and positioning services with revenues of approximately $1.2 billion in 1997, according to Leslie Taylor Associates. A majority of these subscribers (75 percent) are using data-only messaging services.

In January 1997 INMARSAT introduced the world's first truly portable global satellite phone service (mini-M), which utilizes a laptop-sized mobile satellite phone that supports voice, fax, and data communications. These phones cost approximately $3,000, with calling charges of about $2.40 to $3.30 per minute. It is estimated that there are over 20,000 users worldwide of this service. COMSAT markets the INMARSAT mini-M phone service in the United States under the name Planet 1. At this time Planet 1 is subject to FCC authorization in the United States, meaning that one may use the service to place calls to the United States but not to place calls from the United States.

Several companies were planning to offer new mobile satellite services that will allow any type of communications transmission—voice, paging, fax, or data—anywhere on earth beginning in 1998. Subscribers will use lightweight digital dual-mode (cellular and satellite-compatible) handsets or pagers to communicate with other subscribers at any location. Iridium, Globalstar, ICO Global Communications, MHCI/Ellipso, and Constellation are the five primary players in this market (see Table 30-5). [These systems are also referred to as LEOs, or low earth orbit constellations of satellites. Big LEO generally refers to LEO satellite systems used for voice and paging, while Little LEO generally refers to LEO systems used for nonvoice (E-mail, paging, and messaging) services.] Odyssey, an additional service that was to be offered by TRW and Teleglobe of Canada, announced in December 1997 that it was withdrawing its proposed service and investing in the ICO system. Many analysts predict that Odyssey's decision to join ICO in December 1997 represents the beginning of a trend toward consolidation in this segment of the industry. These systems are not expected to compete directly with existing cellular or PCS but instead to fill the geographic gaps in cellular and other wireless services, such as expansive rural areas with poor telephone coverage. All these systems target slightly different market niches or will take different approaches to interacting with terrestrial telephone service providers.

Although there is some concern about the demand needed to support all these services, it is important to note that the systems differ both in structure and in target markets. Iridium is a constellation of 66 satellites that will use cellular and satellite-compatible phones to allow customers to receive and place calls anywhere in the world beginning in November 1998. Iridium has said that its primary target market will be the international businessperson who can pay to have connectivity anywhere in the world at any time. Iridium also will offer paging services,

which it expects will contribute significantly to its revenues. Leslie Taylor Associates predicts that Iridium will sign up 225,000 subscribers in 1999, yielding $486 million in total revenues. By 2003 Leslie Taylor predicts 2 million Iridium subscribers with over $4.3 billion in total revenues.

Globalstar's 48-satellite "bent-pipe" network relies to a larger extent on earth stations on the ground. Globalstar has partnered with service providers all over the world, which will set the final charges. Globalstar's architecture is expected to allow for lower costs, with the handset selling for $750 and per minute charges to the retailer of 35 to 55 cents. Globalstar is targeting international businesses but also is heralding its ability to provide rural telephony solutions. Leslie Taylor Associates predicts 500,000 subscribers for Globalstar by 1999, with revenues of $465 million. By 2003 Globalstar is expected to have 4 million subscribers and $4 billion in revenue.

ICO is a London-based private subsidiary of INMARSAT that will offer service in 2000 using 12 MEO satellites. Ellipso has a patented satellite orbit which will allow the satellite to serve the most populated areas during daylight hours, and rotate to less populated areas during the evening hours when traffic is not as heavy. In May 1998 Boeing took an equity stake in the MHCI/Ellipso system. Constellation will focus on providing coverage in equatorial countries, such as Brazil and Indonesia, that have remote villages and low-density populations spread over vast geographic regions. In May 1998, Orbital Sciences invested in the Constellation system and ended its relationship with MHCI/Ellipso.

Although it appears that there is a need for these types of services, especially in developing regions of the world, the main determinant will be cost and whether customers are willing to pay higher prices for satellite-delivered telephone services. Leslie Taylor Associates predicts a market of 7 million to 12 million subscribers for all mobile satellite services by 2003, with revenues of $8 billion to $20 billion by that year. As only one of these services is being offered at the time of this publication, it is difficult to predict how large this market will be. These complex satellite systems must overcome many hurdles, both technological and regulatory, to ensure that customers are able to use the services effectively. With this satellite-delivered service, there are potential launch problems, in-orbit satellite difficulties, a need to obtain the necessary interconnection and regulatory approvals from governments all over the world, and the need to ensure that customers have easy access to the handsets and services.

These Big LEOs will face competition from several regional systems that will provide MSS in the next 3 years. There are several primary regional systems, including (1) Asian Cellular Systems, which was slated to serve Indonesia and Asia in 1998, (2) Satphone International, which will serve the Middle East and North Africa in 1999, (3) ASC/Agrani, which was scheduled to serve India and Asia in 1998, (4) Euro-African Satellite Telecommunications, which will serve Africa, the Middle East, and parts of Europe in 2000, and (5) Thuraya, which will serve the Middle East, central Asia, India, and eastern Europe in 2000. Most of these systems utilize satellites in geostationary orbit, meaning that there may be significant delays in voice transmission.

TABLE 30-5: Mobile Satellite Systems for Telephony

Name of System and Applications	Major Investors	Number of Satellites in Orbit	Estimated Cost of Project and Cost of Service	Operational in
Iridium Hand-held dual-mode phones, paging, low-speed data transmission	Motorola, Raytheon, Lockheed Martin, Sprint, Khrunichev State Research (12 smaller investors)	66 LEOs	$6 billion Handset: $2,000–$3,000 Charges: $3–$5/minute (retail)	November 1998 (Iridium had launched 66 satellites as of July 1998)
Globalstar Hand-held dual-mode phones, fixed ordinary phones, paging, low-speed data transmission	Loral Space & Communications, Qualcomm Inc., AirTouch Communications, and others	48 LEOs	$2.6 billion Handset: $750 Charges: 35–55 cents/minute (wholesale) Access fee: Service providers will set fees	Fall 1998 (partial), 1999 (full) (Globalstar had launched 8 of 48 satellites as of July 1998)
ICO Global Communications[1] Hand-held dual-mode mobile phones; phones for cars, ships, aircraft; fixed phones in developing areas	ICO is a London-based private offshoot of INMARSAT;[2] 47 investors including COMSAT, TRW, and Hughes	12 MEOs	$4.5 billion Handset: $1,000 Charges: $1.00–$3.50/minute (retail)	2000 (ICO was expected to launch its first satellites by the end of 1998)
MHCI/Ellipso Hand-held phones for mobile and fixed uses; will use smaller satellites in highly inclined and equatorial orbits to provide low-cost service	Mobile Holdings Communications Inc. (Boeing, Spectrum Astro, Lockheed Martin, Israel Aircraft Industries, Vula Communications, and Harris Corp.)	17 LEOs	$1.1 billion Handset: $1,000 Charges: 50 cents/minute Access fee: $35/month	2000
Constellation Hand-held phones for mobile and fixed uses; focus on providing telecom coverage in equatorial countries, such as Indonesia and Brazil, with remote villages and low-density populations spread over vast geographic areas	Constellations Communications (Orbital Sciences, Bell Atlantic, Raytheon E-Systems, Space Vest, Matra Marconi)	12 LEOs	$1.2 billion Handset: $750–$1,000 Charges: 60–90 cents/minute Access fee: $20–$40/month	2001

[1] Odyssey announced on December 20 that it had relinquished its license and invested in ICO
[2] INMARSAT is the International Maritime Satellite Organization. It operates a network of satellites for international transmissions for all types of international mobile services, including maritime, aeronautical, and land mobile.
Source: Compiled by U.S. Department of Commerce, Office of Telecommunications, from company materials, July 1998.

Little LEO services, which primarily offer store-and-forward communications such as E-mail, two-way paging, and messaging, are expected to be offered beginning in 1999. These services are different from the Big LEO systems in that they provide data-only services (no voice) and use less bandwidth. This means that both the satellites and the user equipment are less expensive, reducing the cost of service to the consumer. ORB-COMM (Orbital Sciences Corporation and Teleglobe of Canada), LEO One USA (dbx Corporation), FAISat (Final Analysis), and E-Sat (GEMS) will compete to provide these services worldwide. ORBCOMM has launched all 28 satellites for its system. Subscriber costs are anticipated to be 25 cents per message, with terminals costing anywhere from $100 to $400.

LEO One USA is expected to be the second player to market, with service commencing in 2001. Leslie Taylor Associates predicts that the market for Little LEO data services could grow from 200,000 users in 1997 to more than 20 million by 2004.

Broadband LEOs

Several LEO satellite systems have been proposed to offer high-speed two-way data communications such as Internet, corporate intranet, videoconferencing, and other services. Teledesic (backed by Bill Gates, Craig McCaw, Motorola, Matra Marconi, and Boeing), Alcatel's Skybridge, and Loral's Cyberstar are some of the major players in this market. Teledesic's $9 billion "Internet in the Sky" project will use 288 LEO satellites to provide these data services beginning in 2003. Other broadband (also known as Ka-band) systems include GE's GE Star, Lockheed Martin's Astrolink, and Hughes Spaceway. More than 13 systems have been licensed by the FCC to provide satellite-delivered data services. Most of these systems plan to launch service in 2002, with the exception of Loral's Cyberstar, which was scheduled to lease transponders to offer service in 1998, with full service expected in 2001.

With the large number of companies proposing broadband satellite services, it is certain that consolidation, lack of financing, and demand factors will limit the number of systems that are implemented. The trend toward consolidation was exemplified by the May 1998 announcement that Teledesic would join forces with Motorola's Celestri project. In June 1997, Motorola had proposed its own $12.9 billion, 64-satellite system, called Celestri, to offer high-speed data services in 2002. Celestri and Teledesic were characterized as fierce competitors that would have to fight one another for both financing and customers. For many reasons, Motorola decided to abandon its own project and become the primary contractor for the Teledesic project. Many analysts believe that that move significantly strengthens Teledesic's position by bringing in Motorola's experience in mass-producing LEO satellites (it has already built approximately 70 LEO satellites for the Iridium system) and ensuring that the project will be able to attract the necessary financing.

These systems must first overcome certain technical and marketing challenges, including producing a large number of technologically sophisticated satellites at very low cost, finding a way to launch a large number of satellites by the planned service dates, surmounting domestic and international regulatory hurdles, and dealing with a problem known as "rain fade," or ensuring the transmittal of high-frequency signals through the rain. In addition, these broadband services face competition from fiber-optic cable, which has proved to be an effective and economical way of transmitting large amounts of data from point to point. Satellites offer a more suitable solution when there is a need to deliver data to multiple locations.

One project which may compete with the proposed broadband satellite systems is Sky Station International. Sky Station would provide Internet connectivity and other interactive communications services via high-powered balloons 13 miles above the earth. The technology behind Sky Station is rooted in former President Reagan's Strategic Defense Initiative. Although the technology behind the project is as yet unproven, Sky Station certainly requires much less investment than some of the broadband systems which have been proposed. The Sky Station system is expected to cost about $800 million, while most of the other satellite projects require investments between $4 billion and $13 billion.

The Pioneer Consulting Group estimates that more than $76 billion will be invested in broadband satellite systems by 2010. This figure includes expenditures for the space and ground segments, including the construction cost of the satellites and the respective launch, launch vehicle services, launch insurance, and ground equipment costs. As none of these ser-

vices has been implemented it is difficult to estimate future revenues, but undoubtedly it will take some time to recoup this sizable investment.

Digital Audio Radio Services

Several companies plan to offer satellite-delivered radio direct to consumers. These systems will allow the delivery of 50 to 100 channels of digital radio to vast geographic areas. In the United States, CD Radio (backed by Loral Space and Communications of the United States and Arianespace of France) and XM Satellite Radio Inc. (backed by American Mobile Satellite Corporation and WorldSpace) are the key players. CD Radio will offer a subscription-based satellite radio system to deliver 100 channels of news and music to vehicles across the United States. Subscribers should be able to insert a radio card into a car's radio cassette or compact disc slot and place a battery-powered satellite dish the size of a silver dollar on the car's rear window. The cost of both the radio card and the satellite dish is expected to be about $200 to $250, with monthly subscription fees of about $10. CD Radio expects to launch its first satellite in August 1999 and its second in October, with service beginning by the end of the year.

XM Satellite Radio Inc. will offer a similar service in 2000, charging about $400 for an AM/FM/satellite radio with monthly fees of $5 to $10. The two companies will compete to attract consumers who purchase 12 million new cars and trucks annually, the 5 million people who install upgraded car stereo systems each year, and the 174 million vehicles already equipped with radios and CD players. The two companies will also compete with Lucent Digital Radio, which plans to develop technology that will enable radio stations to receive AM/FM radio broadcasts with near-compact-disc sound. The critical determinant in the success of the satellite-delivered radio services is whether consumers will pay fees in order to receive radio programming anywhere in the United States.

Estimates for DARS subscriber growth in the United States varies greatly, with analysts from Merrill Lynch predicting 1 million users and the Yankee Group estimating 6 million users by 2000. Merrill Lynch predicts 15.6 million users by 2004, while Yankee estimates 32.8 million. The number of subscribers will most likely fall midway between those two estimates—perhaps 2.5 million subscribers by 2000 and 24 million by 2004.

WorldSpace (Alcatel Espace of France, Matra Marconi of the United Kingdom, and others) plans to launch three satellites that will offer portable digital direct audio broadcasting to Africa (AfriStar), the Middle East, Asia (AsiaStar), Latin America, and the Caribbean (AmeriStar). Over 100 radio stations providing news, music, sports, talk, and drama will be delivered via portable or hand-held radios to consumers in their homes, offices, cars, parks, shops, restaurants, etc. AfriStar was launched in October 1998, with launches of AsiaStar and AmeriStar planned in mid-to-late 1999. A WorldSpace receiver is expected to initially cost about $200 to $250. WorldSpace's satellite radio service will be free to listeners. WorldSpace plans to derive revenues from advertising, royalty fees, receiver sales, and the leasing of satellite capacity to programmers. Many analysts question the ability of consumers in these developing regions to pay up to $250 for a radio, but the idea of delivering news, information, and educational programming to people in these vast geographic areas certainly has potential. WorldSpace also says it will subsidize the purchase of radios to certain areas through the WorldSpace Foundation.

Global Positioning System

The Global Positioning System (GPS) is a constellation of 24 radio transmitting satellites operated by the U.S. Department of Defense and used for both military and nonmilitary applications to determine the precise position of a radio receiver on the ground. By determining the time it takes a radio signal to arrive from each satellite's known position in space to a GPS receiver on the ground, the receiver calculates its own position with a high degree of accuracy. The signals derived from these satellites are used to produce precise timing, location, and velocity information.

Commercial applications of the U.S. government's GPS are expected to expand significantly over the next 5 years. Approximately 301 companies provided some form of GPS-related goods or services in 1997. GPS equipment and services are used for aviation, communications, environmental protection, forestry and agriculture, ground transportation, health care, law enforcement and safety, maritime applications, mining and construction, recreation, infrastructure development, and public safety. In 1995 the number of users in the United States alone surpassed 500,000. This is expected to increase to more than 2.5 million users by the year 2000. A September 1998 study by the Department of Commerce estimates that worldwide sales of GPS products will reach $8 billion by 2000 and could exceed $16 billion by 2003.

Remote Sensing

Since the advent of satellite remote sensing, the uses of imagery from space have evolved from more traditional applications such as meteorology, hydrology, cartography, and reconnaissance to more consumer-oriented applications such as agriculture, forestry, environmental monitoring, mining, transportation, utilities, disaster management, civil planning, tax mapping, zoning, and oil and gas.

The commercial remote sensing market consists of companies which sell imagery and value-added enhancements using remote sensing satellites. Currently, LandSat 5 and OrbView 1 and 2 are the U.S.-based satellites used for commercial remote sensing imagery applications. In addition, over 30 remote sensing satellites for commercial operations have been proposed for launch in the next 5 years. Companies from France, Russia, Canada, and India provide for significant competition for U.S. remote sensing companies. It is estimated that worldwide revenues from the commercial sale of remote sensing imagery was $550 million in 1997. Many analysts note remote sensing may become one of the most significant commercial applications in the space industry, second only to telecommunications. Rev-

enues are expected to grow dramatically over the next 5 years as additional commercial remote sensing satellites come online. (For additional discussion of remote sensing, see Chapter 29: Space Commerce.)

U.S. Industry Growth Projections for the Next 1 and 5 Years

The satellite services market is expected to experience rapid growth in the next 1 to 5 years, driven by growth in the mobile telephone and broadband data markets. Revenues from FSS will continue to grow, largely as a result of increasing demand for DBS services. Iridium will garner a great deal of attention when it launches service in November 1998, and many analysts will judge the future of the MSS industry by its success or failure. Globalstar will follow soon afterward with a different architecture and less expensive service. Little LEO data-only services most likely will see rapid growth as they are significantly cheaper than the Big LEO services and offer popular two-way paging, messaging, and E-mail options.

It will be some time before broadband high-speed data and Internet services are offered, and revenues will depend on many factors, including convenience and price. Digital audio radio services are expected to have reasonable growth as consumers take advantage of the opportunity to receive 50 to 100 channels of digital radio anywhere in the country. Revenues from commercial GPS and commercial remote sensing services also should increase as more services become available to consumers. The Pioneer Consulting Group estimates that the global satellite communications services market will exceed $131 billion by 2007, with fixed data representing 18 percent of the market and DBS/DTH and mobile voice and data representing 35 and 40 percent each. These estimates are quite optimistic; untested technology, unknown demand, consolidation, regulatory issues, and other factors may limit some of the explosive growth rates that have been predicted. Although these growth rates may be somewhat overstated, it is clear that the satellite services industry will have healthy growth rates over the next 5 years.

Krysten B. Jenci, U.S. Department of Commerce, Office of Telecommunications, (202) 482-2952, November 1998.

■ R E F E R E N C E S

APEC Telecom Working Group, www.apec-wg.com/.

Cellular Telecommunications Industry Association, www.wow-com. com/.

Communications Week International, P.O. Box 550, Bromley BR2 9TA, U.K. Telephone: (44) 181 956 3017, Web site: www.commweek.com.

Competition in International Satellite Communications, October 1996, U.S. General Accounting Office, GAO/RCED-97-1, GAO Reports & Publications. (202) 512-6000.

Competitive Impact of Restructuring the International Satellite Organizations, July 8, 1996, U.S. General Accounting Office, GAO/RCED-96-204, GAO Reports & Publications. (202) 512-6000.

CTIA Semi-Annual Data Survey, Cellular Telecommunications Industry Association, 1250 Connecticut Avenue, NW, Suite 200, Washington, DC 20036. (202) 785-0081, Fax: (202) 785-0721.

European Messaging/Paging Markets: 1998, Inside Paging, The State of the U.S. Paging Industry: 1997, The Strategis Group, 1130 Connecticut Avenue, NW, Suite 325, Washington, DC 20036-3915. (202) 530-7500, Fax: (202) 530-7550.

FAA Office of Commercial Space Transportation, www.dot.gov/faa/cst/.

Global Mobile, Baskerville Communications Corp., 15165 Ventura Boulevard, Suite 310, Sherman Oaks, CA 91403. (818) 461-9660, Fax: (818) 461-9661.

Global Wireless, Crain Communications Inc., 777 E. Speer Boulevard, Denver, CO 80203-4214. (303) 733-2500, Fax: (303) 733-9941, www.globalwirelessnews.com.

A Guide to Telecommunications Markets in Latin America and the Caribbean, S/N PB96-145073, June 1996, National Technical Information Service.

Industry Analysis Reports from the FCC's Common Carrier Division, www.fcc.gov/ccb/stats.

INTELSAT, www.intelsat.int/.

International Cellular, Kagan World Media, Ltd., 126 Clock Tower Place, Carmel, CA 93923-8734. (408) 624-1536, Fax: (408) 625-3225.

International Telecommunication Union, www.itu.ch/.

Long Distance Market Shares, Federal Communications Commission, 1919 M Street, NW, Room 533, Washington, DC 20254. (202) 418-0940.

Lynx Global Telecom Database, Lynx Technologies, 710 Route 46 East, Fairfield, NJ 07004. (201) 256-7200.

Market Demand Forecast for Terrestrial Third Generation (IMT-2000) Services, Personal Communications Industry Association, 500 Montgomery Street, Suite 700, Alexandria, VA 22314-1561. (703) 739-0300, Fax: (703) 836-1608, www.pcia.com.

Mobile Communications International, MCI Subscriptions, Central House, 27 Park Street, Croydon CRO 1YD, England, Telephone: 011-44-081-686-5654 or 011-44-071-383-5757, Fax: 011-44-071-383-3181.

Mobile Phone News, PCS Week, Wireless Business & Finance, Phillips Business Information, Inc., 1201 Seven Locks Road, Potomac, MD 20854. (301) 340-1520, Fax: (301) 424-2058, www.phillips.com.

Newaves in Personal Communications, Imagination Publications, 820 W. Jackson Boulevard, Suite 450, Chicago, IL 60607. (312) 627-1020.

1997 PCIA Wireless Market Portfolio, Compiled by Personal Communications Industry Association, 500 Montgomery Street, Suite 700, Alexandria, VA 22314-1561. (703) 739-0300, Fax: (703) 836-1608.

Office of Telecommunications of the International Trade Administration, U.S. Department of Commerce, www.infoserv2.ita.doc.gov/ot/home.nsf.

Personal Communications Industry Association, www.pcia.com/.

Personal Communications North America (PERS-NA-MT-9701), December 15, 1997, Dataquest Inc., 251 River Oaks Parkway, San Jose, CA 95134-1913. (408) 954-1780, Fax: (408) 954-1780.

Phone Facts 1997, United States Telephone Association, 1401 H Street, NW, Suite 600, Washington, DC 20005-2164. (202) 326-7300.

RCR Radio Communications Report, RCR Publications Inc., 777 East Speer Boulevard, Denver, CO 80203. 1-800-678-9595, www. rcrnews.com.

Reference Book of Rates, Price Indices, and Household Expenditures for Telephone Service, Federal Communications Commission, 1919 M Street, NW, Room 533, Washington, DC 20036. (202) 418-0940.

Satellite International, Baskerville Communications Corp., 15165 Ventura Boulevard, Suite 310, Sherman Oaks, CA 91403. (310) 978-6073, www.baskerville.co.uk.

Satellite Markets, April 1998, Media Business Corp., Futron Corporation, Satellite Industry Association, 807 Arapahoe Street, Golden, CO 80401. (303) 271-9960, www.skyreport.com.

SkyTrends Annual Report 1997–1998, Media Business Corp., 807 Arapahoe Street, Golden, CO 80401. (303) 271-9960, www. skyreport.com.

Space News, Army Times Publishing Co., 6883 Commercial Drive, Springfield, VA 22159. (703) 750-8696, www.spacenews.com.

State of the Space Industry—1997 Outlook, SpaceVest, 11911 Freedom Drive, Suite 500, Reston, VA 20190. (703) 904-9800, www. spacevest.com.

Statistics of Communications Common Carriers, Federal Communications Commission, 1997/98, 1919 M Street, NW, Room 533, Washington, DC 20036. (202) 418-0940.

Telecommunications Industry Association, www.industry.net/tia.

Telecommunications Industry Revenue: TRS Fund Worksheet Data, Federal Communications Commission, 1919 M Street, NW, Room 539, Washington, DC 20254. (202) 418-0940.

Telecommunications Reports, Business Research Publications, Inc., 1333 H Street, NW, 11th Floor-West, Washington, DC 20005. (202) 842-3006.

TeleGeography 1997/98, TeleGeography, Inc., Suite 1000, 1150 Connecticut Avenue, NW, Washington, DC 20036. (202) 467-0017.

Telephony, Telephony Publishing Corp., P.O. Box 12976, Overland Park, KS 66282-2976.

Trends in the International Telecommunications Industry, Federal Communications Commission, 1919 M Street, NW, Room 539, Washington, DC 20254. (202) 467-0017.

U.S. Long Distance Markets; Local Exchange Carrier Markets: 1995 Edition, Northern Business Information, DataPro Information Services Group, 1221 Avenue of the Americas, New York, NY 10020-1095. (212) 512-2900.

The U.S. Stake in Competitive Global Telecommunications Services, Strategic Policy Research, 7500 Old Georgetown Road, Suite 810, Bethesda, MD 20814. (301) 718-0111.

Via Satellite, 1997 Global Satellite Survey, Phillips Business Information Inc., 1201 Seven Locks Road, Suite 300, Potomac, MD 20854. (301) 340-7788, www.phillips.com/ViaOnline.

WirelessNow (daily wireless update), www.commnow.com.

Wireless Systems Outlook: 1998, The Evolving Landscape, Allied Business Intelligence, Inc., P.O. Box 452, 202 Townsend Square, Oyster Bay, NY 11771. (516) 624-3113, Fax: (516) 624-3115.

Wireless Week, Chilton Publications, 600 South Cherry Street, Suite 400, Denver, CO 80222. (303) 393-7449, Fax: (303) 399-2034.

World Telecommunications Development Report 1997/98, International Telecommunication Union, Geneva, Switzerland, available from Telegeography, Inc., Suite 1000, 1150 Connecticut Avenue, NW, Washington, DC 20036. (202) 467-0017.

■ RELATED CHAPTERS

26: Information Services
27: Computer Equipment
28: Computer Software and Networking
29: Space Commerce
31: Telecommunications and Navigation Equipment

TELECOMMUNICATIONS AND NAVIGATION EQUIPMENT
Economic and Trade Trends

U.S. International Trade

Source: U.S. Department of Commerce: Bureau of the Census; International Trade Administration.

World Export Market Shares

Source: United Nations; U.S. Department of Commerce, International Trade Administration.

Export Dependence and Import Penetration

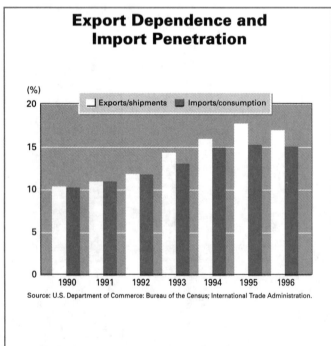

Source: U.S. Department of Commerce: Bureau of the Census; International Trade Administration.

Output and Output per Hour

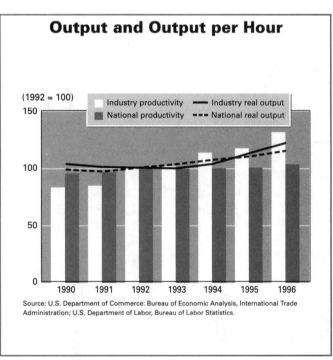

Source: U.S. Department of Commerce: Bureau of Economic Analysis, International Trade Administration; U.S. Department of Labor, Bureau of Labor Statistics.

See "Getting the Most Out of *Outlook '99*" for definitions of terms.

Telecommunications and Navigation Equipment

INDUSTRY DEFINITION This chapter covers network equipment, which includes switching and transmission equipment; customer premises equipment that can be attached to a telephone network, such as telephones, answering machines, and fax machines; fiber optics, including optical fiber and fiber-optic cable; wireless communications equipment, including cellular, paging, and personal communications systems; and satellite communications systems, including communications satellites and related ground equipment. Search and navigation equipment, which covers radar and sonar systems, and surveillance equipment also are included. The chapter omits radio and television broadcasting equipment [closed-circuit and cable television transmission equipment and studio (audio and video) equipment] and terrestrial microwave communications equipment.

GLOBAL INDUSTRY TRENDS

The global market for telecommunications equipment is widely thought to have surpassed $200 billion in 1997 and is expected to expand at an average annual rate of 14 percent until it reaches nearly $300 billion in 2000. The overall global telecommunications equipment market is expected to remain robust, but growth will continue to be strongest in the wireless sector. Research in 1998 by the DMG Technology Group indicates that the global wireless infrastructure equipment market should grow from 12 percent of spending on overall telecommunications equipment in 1997 to 21 percent by 2001.

No single country accounts for more than 20 percent of the world telecommunications equipment market, and no single region accounts for more than a third. As privatization and market liberalization occur in 1998–1999, Europe is expected to surpass North America as the largest regional market. In addition to new service entrants constructing networks, existing European operators are beginning to upgrade and enhance their networks to prepare for competition. Asia, regarded as one of the most attractive and fastest growing markets, has been plagued by a financial crisis which has dampened demand in

some countries, although in others, including China, the markets remain strong. Although the Latin American market is considerably smaller, it is growing at a very fast pace.

This robust growth on all continents is being driven primarily by three factors: large unmet demand for dial tone in emerging markets and for second lines for Internet and electronic mail in developed markets, continued expansion of wireless networks, and liberalization and deregulation of telecommunications services as a result of the World Trade Organization (WTO) Agreement on Basic Telecommunications Services.

Although four leading suppliers are European-based, the world telecommunications market is highly global. In this capital-intensive business requiring large outlays for research and development, a handful of suppliers command the majority of the world market, and most have a significant manufacturing presence on every continent. Trade accounts for a substantial portion of U.S. production and consumption, with 23 percent of U.S. product shipments exported and imports accounting for 20 percent of apparent consumption in 1997. In the telephone and telegraph apparatus market, 23 percent of U.S. product shipments were exported in 1997 and imports accounted for 25 percent of apparent consumption. In the radio and television broadcasting and communications equipment market, 23 percent of U.S. product shipments were exported and imports accounted for 15 percent of apparent consumption in 1997.

DOMESTIC TRENDS

Shipments by the U.S. telecommunications equipment industry were expected to increase about 11 percent in 1998, reaching $79.2 billion, up from $71.6 billion in 1997. Industry shipments of telephone and telegraph apparatus (SIC 3661), which constitute about 47 percent of the total, were predicted to reach $35.1 billion in 1998, up 5 percent from $33.6 billion in 1997. Industry shipments of radio and television broadcast-

ing and communications equipment (SIC 3663), which represent 53 percent of the total, were estimated to rise about 16 percent to $44.1 billion in 1998, up from $38 billion in 1997 (see Table 31-1).

Employment in the telecommunications equipment industry rose 3 percent to about 240,000 in 1997, reflecting continued growth in the industry. Pressure to reduce costs and improve productivity in a highly competitive market environment, coupled with mergers and consolidation among manufacturers, was expected to contribute to slower growth in employment in 1998. Smaller companies are increasingly finding it advantageous to join forces with larger partners to gain access to additional research and development (R&D) funds, expanded product lines, and economies of scale.

TABLE 31-1: Telecommunications Equipment (SIC 3661, 3663) Estimates and Forecasts

(millions of dollars except as noted)

	1992	1993	1994	1995	1996	1997[1]	1998[2]	1999[3]	Percent Change 96–97	97–98	98–99	92–96[4]
Industry data												
Value of shipments[5]	40,031	42,190	49,371	54,915	63,807	71,585	79,233	85,396	12.2	10.7	7.8	12.4
3661 Telephone apparatus	20,510	21,540	23,243	26,183	31,727	33,586	35,097	36,361	5.9	4.5	3.6	11.5
3663 Radio/TV communications equipment	19,521	20,650	26,128	28,733	32,080	37,999	44,136	49,035	18.5	16.2	11.1	13.2
Value of shipments (1992$)	40,031	41,736	48,498	54,166	62,619	69,105	75,860	81,128	10.4	9.8	6.9	11.8
3661 Telephone apparatus	20,510	21,411	23,081	26,052	31,412	33,218	34,590	35,731	5.7	4.1	3.3	11.2
3663 Radio/TV communications equipment	19,521	20,325	25,416	28,114	31,206	35,887	41,270	45,397	15.0	15.0	10.0	12.4
Total employment (thousands)	216	208	220	216	234	239.6			2.6			2.0
3661 Telephone apparatus	91.1	84.9	86.5	89.3	93.6	94.6			1.1			0.7
3663 Radio/TV communications equipment	125	123	133	127	140	145			3.6			2.9
Production workers (thousands)	103	94.5	100	103	107	106.3			-0.9			1.0
3661 Telephone apparatus	44.8	38.5	41.3	40.8	38.1	37.3			-2.1			-4.0
3663 Radio/TV communications equipment	58.6	56.0	59.0	61.7	68.9	69			0.1			4.1
Average hourly earnings ($)	14.28	14.35	14.25	15.69	16.33	17.08			4.6			3.4
3661 Telephone apparatus	14.90	15.34	15.35	16.65	16.57	16.95			2.3			2.7
3663 Radio/TV communications equipment	13.82	13.66	13.51	15.08	16.18	17.20			6.3			4.0
Capital expenditures	1,317	1,445	1,518	1,899	2,088							12.2
3661 Telephone apparatus	615	595	662	742	731							4.4
3663 Radio/TV communications equipment	702	851	856	1,157	1,357							17.9
Product data												
Value of shipments[5]	36,106	38,151	45,495	52,481	60,706	68,102	75,303	81,079	12.2	10.6	7.7	13.9
3661 Telephone apparatus	18,328	19,589	21,661	24,816	30,516	32,341	33,767	34,932	6.0	4.4	3.5	13.6
3663 Radio/TV communications equipment	17,778	18,562	23,834	27,665	30,190	35,761	41,536	46,147	18.5	16.1	11.1	14.2
Value of shipments (1992$)	36,106	37,742	44,695	51,762	59,582	65,739	72,116	77,080	10.3	9.7	6.9	13.3
3661 Telephone apparatus	18,328	19,472	21,510	24,692	30,214	31,966	33,277	34,357	5.8	4.1	3.2	13.3
3663 Radio/TV communications equipment	17,778	18,269	23,185	27,069	29,368	33,773	38,839	42,723	15.0	15.0	10.0	13.4
Trade data												
Value of imports	7,307	8,066	10,218	10,883	11,895	12,981	13,745	14,752	9.1	5.9	7.3	13.0
3661 Telephone apparatus	5,172	5,633	6,647	6,813	7,431	8,219	8,650	9,300	10.6	5.2	7.5	9.5
3663 Radio/TV communications equipment	2,135	2,433	3,572	4,071	4,464	4,762	5,095	5,452	6.7	7.0	7.0	20.2
Value of exports	6,199	7,884	9,904	12,341	12,773	15,674	18,595	21,806	22.7	18.6	17.3	19.8
3661 Telephone apparatus	3,278	4,010	4,799	5,783	6,576	7,326	7,950	8,500	11.4	8.5	6.9	19.0
3663 Radio/TV communications equipment	2,922	3,874	5,106	6,558	6,197	8,349	10,645	13,306	34.7	27.5	25.0	20.7

[1] Estimate except imports and exports.
[2] Estimate.
[3] Forecast.
[4] Compound annual rate.
[5] For definition of industry versus product values, see "Getting the Most Out of Outlook '99."
Source: U.S. Department of Commerce: Bureau of the Census; International Trade Administration.

Regulatory Developments

Legal maneuvering continues to delay implementation of the local competition authorized by the U.S. Telecommunications Act, signed into law in February 1996. As a result, the anticipated benefits of the act for manufacturers have not been realized. The ongoing trend toward deregulation, liberalization, and the licensing of competitive networks was given further impetus by the passage and implementation of the WTO Agreement on Basic Telecommunications Services. Largely as a result of this agreement, this trend is widely expected to continue in the foreseeable future, ensuring a steady market for equipment suppliers.

PROJECTIONS OF INDUSTRY AND TRADE GROWTH FOR THE NEXT 1 AND 5 YEARS

Shipments by the telecommunications equipment industry are projected to increase about 7 percent in 1999. Product areas leading this growth include wireless communications equipment and network equipment, including that for wireless networks. Shipments of telephone and telegraph apparatus (SIC 3661) should increase about 3 percent in 1999, while shipments of radio and television broadcasting and communications equipment (SIC 3663) are expected to rise about 10 percent in that year. Although the outlook for telecommunications equipment shipments through 2003 will continue to be positive, the rate of growth should decline to an average of 5 percent per year as new wired and wireless networks are more fully built out.

New market entrants and the emergence of enhanced services will continue to drive demand for equipment in the United States and abroad. New technologies will generate growth in many sectors of the telecommunications equipment industry. For example, the trend toward the deployment of fiber-optic cable in the local loop will spark growth in both fiber-optic equipment and new network equipment such as optical switching and transmission equipment. The continuing migration to digital networks in the wireless sector and the advent of global mobile satellite systems over the next few years will continue to fuel demand for radio base stations, earth stations, and antennas as well as new wireless end-user equipment. In the longer term, as the increasing demand for data applications and on-line services extends from wired to wireless networks and as demand for interoperability and mobility continues to grow, networks will evolve into high-capacity, high-speed, software-driven networks which integrate fixed and mobile services.

GLOBAL MARKET PROSPECTS

U.S. Trade Performance

The United States registered a record high surplus in telecommunications equipment trade in 1997, the fifth consecutive year in which U.S. telecommunications suppliers enjoyed a surplus (see Figure 31-1). In 1997 the sectoral trade surplus surged to nearly $5.1 billion from $2.4 billion in 1996. This expanding

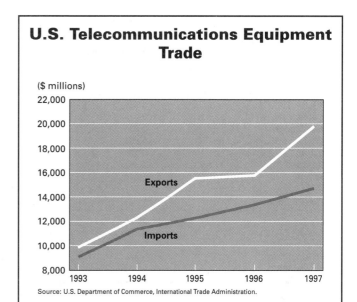

U.S. Telecommunications Equipment Trade

($ millions)

Source: U.S. Department of Commerce, International Trade Administration.

FIGURE 31-1

surplus resulted from strong export growth, which resumed double-digit numbers after leveling off in 1996. Exports, which have doubled since 1993, increased 26 percent (up $4 billion) to $19.8 billion in 1997. Although imports increased 10 percent to $14.7 billion (up $1.3 billion), the rate of import growth has stayed about the same since 1995.

While the data in Tables 31-1 and 31-2 indicate a trade surplus of $2.7 billion, it is important to note that the SIC trade concordances for SIC 3661 and SIC 3663 do not correspond precisely to typical definitions of telecommunications equipment. Several products are classified under SIC 3663 because they use radio frequencies, such as citizens' band (CB) radios, low-power radio transceivers (walkie-talkies), and infant nursery monitors. In addition, fiber-optic cable and coaxial cable, which are used in telecommunications systems around the globe, technically are classified under other SIC codes. Parts for radio-based products also are not included in the official concordance, since some of them can be used for multiple end products. (This discussion of U.S. trade performance and the global market is based on a more conventional definition of the telecommunications sector which corresponds closely to the SIC codes but does not include the items specified above.)

Canada remained the largest export market, with U.S. telecommunications exports to that country rising 19 percent to nearly $2.7 billion, accounting for 14 percent of total exports. Telecommunications exports to Japan, the second largest U.S. export market with 10 percent of the total, rose 9 percent in 1997, reaching a record high of nearly $2.1 billion. After 2 years of relatively flat growth, exports to Mexico surged almost 50 percent to more than $1.4 billion in 1997, accounting for 7 percent of total exports. Exports to the European Union (EU), which declined in 1996, increased 18 percent to reach $3.2 billion in 1997. As a share of the total, exports to the EU accounted for 16 percent of U.S. telecommunications exports in 1997.

TABLE 31-2: U.S. Trade Patterns in Telecommunications Equipment[1] in 1997

(millions of dollars; percent)

Exports			Imports		
Regions[2]	Value[3]	Share, %	Regions[2]	Value[3]	Share, %
NAFTA	3,450	22.0	NAFTA	4,429	34.1
Latin America	2,773	17.7	Latin America	123	0.9
Western Europe	2,884	18.4	Western Europe	925	7.1
Japan/Chinese Economic Area	2,881	18.4	Japan/Chinese Economic Area	4,459	34.4
Other Asia	2,135	13.6	Other Asia	2,488	19.2
Rest of world	1,552	9.9	Rest of world	556	4.3
World	15,674	100.0	World	12,981	100.0
Top Five Countries	Value	Share, %	Top Five Countries	Value	Share, %
Canada	2,244	14.3	Canada	2,601	20.0
Mexico	1,206	7.7	Japan	1,954	15.1
Japan	1,187	7.6	Mexico	1,828	14.1
United Kingdom	884	5.6	China	1,460	11.2
Hong Kong (PRC)	878	5.6	Taiwan	955	7.4

[1] SIC 3661, 3663.
[2] For definitions of regional groupings, see "Getting the Most Out of *Outlook '99*."
[3] Values may not sum to total due to rounding.
Source: U.S. Department of Commerce, Bureau of the Census.

Regionally, Asia represented the largest market for U.S. telecommunications exports, with a total of $6.7 billion in 1997, although U.S. export performance varied throughout the region. Telecommunications exports to Latin America as a whole rose a healthy 60 percent to reach almost $5 billion in 1997.

Asia continues to play a dominant role on the import side, accounting for $7.7 billion of imports in 1997, or 52 percent of the total. Reversing a decadelong trend of Japanese dominance of the U.S. import market, for the second year in a row Canada outranked Japan as the largest source of U.S. telecommunications imports. New suppliers in the Far East continue to play a significant role in the U.S. market. China and Malaysia were the fourth and sixth largest sources of U.S. telecommunications imports, respectively, in 1997, surpassing three of the "Four Dragons" (South Korea, Hong Kong, Singapore, and Taiwan). After 3 years of increases, imports from Mexico, the third largest supplier, fell 5 percent to nearly $2.1 billion in 1997. After leveling off in 1996, telecommunications imports from the EU rose 24 percent to $1.25 billion in 1997, accounting for 8 percent of the total.

The largest export categories in 1997 were radio transceivers and parts for radio equipment, followed by cellular phones, parts for telephonic apparatus, and switching equipment. On the import side, the leading categories in 1997 were parts for telephonic apparatus, cordless phones, television transmitters, parts for radio equipment, and radio transceivers.

In keeping with history, the United States once again registered a sizable deficit of $2.28 billion in relatively low-end, commodity-type customer premises equipment, much of which is no longer manufactured domestically. This was offset by trade surpluses in the areas of network and transmission equipment at $3.8 billion and "other" telecommunications equipment (wireless communications equipment, radio and television broadcasting equipment, and basket categories of telephone

equipment which cannot be allocated to either of the other two categories) at $3.55 billion. Parts continue to represent a substantial percentage of U.S. telecommunications equipment trade. In 1997 parts exports of $5.8 billion accounted for 29 percent of the total. Parts for radio equipment accounted for about half of U.S. exports of telecommunications parts. By comparison, parts imports of nearly $3.8 billion represented nearly 26 percent of total imports in 1997.

Trade Agreements

Multilateral negotiations to liberalize telecommunications services markets conducted under the auspices of the WTO were concluded successfully in February 1997 with the Agreement on Basic Telecommunications Services. The first multilateral telecommunications trade agreement ever reached, it went into force in February 1998. The agreement's three principal achievements were improved market access for telecommunications services, the allowance of foreign investment in telecommunications services and facilities, and the adoption of procompetitive regulatory principles to ensure that improved market access is fully realizable. With over 70 countries making a commitment to some degree of liberalization of their telecommunications regimes, the agreement should serve as a stimulus for equipment purchases for many years to come.

The Information Technology Agreement (ITA) was implemented on July 1, 1997. Under its terms, most of the 43 participating countries will eliminate tariffs on covered products by 2000. A few developing countries have been granted extensions for a limited number of products, but in no case beyond 2005. Tariff elimination generally will take place in four equal steps on July 1, 1997; January 1, 1998; January 1, 1999; and January 1, 2000.

The 43 ITA signatories account for over 93 percent of world trade in information technology products. Global trade in products covered by the ITA is expected to exceed $1 trillion by the turn of the century. Those products include semiconductors and other electronic components, most semiconductor manufacturing equipment, analytical instruments, computer software, digital photocopiers, most telecommunications equipment, printed circuit boards, and process controls.

As of May 20, 1998, the signatories to the ITA included Australia, Canada, Chinese Taipei, the Czech Republic, Costa Rica, El Salvador, Estonia, the European Union (15 countries), Hong Kong, Iceland, India, Indonesia, Israel, Japan, South Korea, Liechtenstein, Macau, Malaysia, New Zealand, Norway, the Philippines, Poland, Romania, Singapore, the Slovak Republic, Switzerland, Thailand, Turkey, and the United States. In addition, several other countries are actively considering participation, including Armenia, Egypt, Guatemala, Latvia, Lithuania, Panama, and the People's Republic of China.

Negotiations are under way to expand and more clearly define the product coverage of the ITA and address related non-tariff measures. This process generally is known as ITA-II. Unfortunately, the participants were unable to complete the ITA-II negotiations by June 30, 1998. They seek to conclude the negotiations during the fall of 1998 and implement any agreement that is reached as soon as possible thereafter.

A mutual recognition agreement with the EU was ratified on October 30, 1998, and enters into force on December 1, 1998. It is intended to reduce the time and cost involved in having U.S. equipment tested and approved for the European market. Three of the six annexes to the mutual recognition agreement apply to equipment for connection to public telecommunications networks (the annexes on telecommunications terminal equipment, electromagnetic compatibility, and safety of electrical equipment). The first two annexes are subject to a transition period of 2 years, during which they provide for mutual recognition of product testing to each country's requirements. After the completion of the transition period, they provide for mutual recognition of product approvals to each country's requirements. These two annexes will allow U.S. suppliers of telecommunications terminal equipment to have the equipment tested and approved in the United States (instead of in Europe) to the requirements of the EU and its member states.

A mutual recognition agreement for telecommunications equipment was endorsed at the Asia Pacific Economic Cooperation (APEC) Telecommunications Ministerial Meeting in Singapore in June 1997. It should facilitate trade in telecommunications equipment between APEC member economies by reducing the time and cost involved in testing and certifying equipment. This mutual recognition agreement provides a process that will allow APEC members to test and/or certify equipment to other members' standards. It was endorsed by the APEC ministers in June 1998, and member economies are beginning to negotiate (usually on a bilateral basis) the terms for mutual recognition of test data or certification. This process is expected to take 1 or 2 years to achieve any agreements as a result of required changes in national laws and regulations.

GLOBAL MARKET PROSPECTS

The priority being given to infrastructure development in most nations means that enormous sums are being invested in telecommunications networks. Contributing factors include worldwide demand for basic dial tone in emerging markets and for additional lines for Internet and E-mail applications in developed markets, the continued robust demand for wireless services, and public policies that promote deregulation and competition. The International Telecommunication Union (ITU), based on a historically constant growth trend, estimates that the number of main telephones will increase from 800 million in 1997 to nearly 1 billion by 2000. The number of wireless subscribers is expected to more than double from 200 million at the end of 1997 to 500 million by 2000. The following sections address regional market prospects.

Europe and the Newly Independent States

As a result of regional standardization and regulatory liberalization, the value of the market for telecommunications equipment (including radio communications and public broadcast equipment) in the original 12 members of the EU was unchanged from 1988 to 1995 at a level of about $32 billion. This resulted from large price decreases associated with increased competition in the supply of telecommunications equipment. Since 1996 the EU telecommunications equipment market has resumed its historical growth rate of 5 to 10 percent per year, spurred by privatization of public network operators, liberalization of regulations governing mobile and data communications and related infrastructure, and expansion of existing networks in eastern Germany, Ireland, Portugal, Spain, and Greece. This growth rate is accelerating to a level estimated at 13 percent per year as a result of the liberalization of regulations governing basic telecommunications and cable television services and related infrastructure in 1998 and the convergence of the telecommunications, multimedia, and information technology sectors. Consequently, the value of expenditures on telecommunications and multimedia equipment in western Europe is expected to increase from $60 billion in 1997 to $100 billion in 2001.

The best opportunities for U.S. suppliers to penetrate this market in western Europe are offered by the expenditures of new entrants to the telecommunications services market. Ten EU member states have authorized competition in basic telecommunications services and have licensed one or more new providers of voice telephony and public telecommunications infrastructure. In addition, every country in western Europe has one or more private cellular communications operators and has already licensed or is preparing to license one or more personal communications services network operators using the European (GSM 1800) standard.

Eighty-two companies are licensed to offer basic telephone services in Germany, which is the third largest telecommunications market in the world. Led by the EU, western Europe has recognized that open competition in telecommunications equipment and services will assure economic growth through investment in the European Information Society. Both EU directives and the WTO Agreement on Basic Telecommunications Services commit the EU to full competition, and the EU Green Paper on Convergence proposes minimizing regulatory burdens for the telecommunications, multimedia, and information technology sectors.

As the countries of central and eastern Europe look to the next century, virtually all have recognized that efficient, reliable, and cost-effective telecommunications will be essential for economic growth and development. Regional authorities clearly recognize the shortcomings of existing networks and are working diligently to expand and improve their communications systems. Since 1990 increased investment has occurred in almost every segment of telecommunications: satellites, mobile telephony, paging, fiber optics, switching, transmission systems, and other network equipment. Many countries have laid out ambitious modernization plans, moved toward adopting international norms for regulation and competition, revised their legal climates to reflect a transparent regulatory environment, begun privatization, and introduced competition in some sectors. Accordingly, heavy investment in telecommunications will continue for the foreseeable future, and there is great potential for U.S. companies interested in selling equipment or providing services in that region.

The Newly Independent States (NIS) are also struggling to remove obstacles to economic growth and development, including aging communications systems. Governments in that region face insufficient capacity, low telephone penetration rates, highly variable call completion rates, and antiquated equipment. This, combined with vast distances, high demand for basic telecommunications infrastructure, and the lack of modern network services, makes the NIS a potentially lucrative market for U.S. telecommunications companies. Governments in that region have made great strides toward expanding and modernizing their networks and services, and a number of U.S. companies already are working there. However, telecommunications companies interested in doing business in the NIS will have to contend with a number of difficulties, including unclear regulatory and legal structures, inconsistent enforcement of laws, standards issues, equipment certification and approval procedures, and confusing and multilayered authorities and licensing procedures. Despite these challenges, the NIS represents a large and growing market for U.S. telecommunications companies.

Estimates of the size of the services and equipment markets for central and eastern Europe and the NIS vary widely. In general, service revenues are expected to exceed $90 billion by 2003, up from approximately $65 billion in 1997. Equipment sales are expected to exceed $25 billion in 2003, up from approximately $15 billion in 1997. A few forecasters have suggested that the value of the markets of central and eastern Europe and the NIS will approach $200 billion by 2005, but those estimates appear to be overly optimistic. Even if the more conservative estimates exceed the actual revenues, it is clear that there is a great need for telecommunications development in these regions and that many opportunities exist for U.S. companies.

Asia

The Asia/Pacific region is currently the largest single market for telecommunications products and services in the world. While the overall Asia/Pacific market is expected to experience strong growth in the forseeable future, it is important to recognize that this region is a collection of many markets with very diverse characteristics. These markets run the gamut from very small to very large and from some of the least developed to some of the most developed in the world. While the economies of some countries have been crippled by the Asian financial crisis, other economies remain strong.

Asia is in the middle of a broad trend toward market liberalization and competition, generating a variety of opportunities for equipment vendors and service providers. For example, Singapore issued new licenses in 1998 for a second local exchange carrier and additional cellular operations. Malaysia is implementing its Multimedia Super Corridor project, offering a range of opportunities for providers of advanced information technology. In Hong Kong, government regulators "bought out" the long-term monopoly of Hong Kong Telecom in international service and licensed additional competitors. South Korea, the Philippines, Taiwan, and Indonesia have licensed new carriers in the past few years and continue to build out their network infrastructures.

The rapid growth of the Asia/Pacific region has made it the largest regional market for U.S. telecommunications equipment exports, accounting for 32 percent of U.S. exports in 1997. Japan is the United States' largest export market in Asia, accounting for $2.1 billion in exports in 1997, while Hong Kong was second at $1.1 billion (some exports to Hong Kong probably are destined for China). South Korea received $892 million in U.S. exports in 1997, and China was the fourth largest export market at $765 million. Indonesia, Singapore, Taiwan, Australia, the Philippines, Thailand, and Malaysia each accounted for more than $100 million in U.S. telecommunications equipment exports in that year.

While the financial crisis has significantly slowed growth rates in some Asian countries, others, especially China, continue to grow at a rapid rate. According to the ITU, investment in the markets of the Asia/Pacific region could exceed $300 billion over the next 5 years. China reports that it plans to invest $12 billion per year in its telecommunications infrastructure through 2000 and to increase spending beyond the turn of the century. Wireless communications, such as cellular, has been one of the fastest growing segments of the telecommunications market in the Asia/Pacific region.

Latin America

In 1997 Latin America represented nearly 18 percent of the world market for U.S. telecommunications products, with U.S. exports to that region rising at an explosive rate of 60 percent to nearly $5 billion from just over $3 billion in 1996. The wireless segment experienced the strongest growth, as the number of cellular subscribers in Latin America soared from just 1.3 million in 1994 to more than 9 million by the end of 1997.

The boom in U.S. telecommunications equipment exports in Latin America is driven by strong economies that have recovered from the "tequila effect," the economic downturn that resulted from Mexico's recession, experienced in 1995. The explosion in demand for telecommunications equipment also has been spurred by a firm commitment by that region's governments to continue reforming the telecommunications sector.

Countries that privatized their state-owned telecommunications operators in the early 1990s are pushing ahead with liberalization. Chile, the region's most liberalized market, launched personal communications services in March 1998. Argentina is issuing new personal communications services licenses and has made a commitment to end the duopoly in basic telecommunications services by 2002. Colombia also is offering such concessions and has begun to introduce competition into its long-distance market. Mexico, which introduced long-distance competition in January 1997, has moved ahead with the licensing of personal communications services and wireless local loop (WLL). Brazil forged ahead with its ambitious plan to privatize telecommunications services by first licensing nine new Band-B cellular concessions and accelerating the scheduled sale of the state-owned Telebras system to private investors to July 1998. The region's smaller countries, such as the Central American states, which missed the first wave of privatization and liberalization, are focusing on privatizing their state-owned telephone companies and introducing modern liberalizing telecommunications legislation. This trend toward more open markets has been fortified by the commitments 17 Latin American countries made under the WTO Agreement on Basic Telecommunications Services.

There are an estimated 40 million main telephone lines in Latin America and a teledensity rate of approximately 9 percent. By 2000 it is estimated that the number of main lines will surpass 65 million and that teledensity will reach 13 lines per 100 inhabitants. The Latin American equipment market will continue to experience tremendous growth as unmet demand remains at high levels. Latin America was expected to spend $10 billion on telecommunications equipment in 1997, and this investment is expected to increase to $15 billion in 2001.

Africa

According to U.S. government trade data, U.S. exports of telecommunications equipment to sub-Saharan Africa totaled $148 million in 1997, a $27 million increase from 1996. Approximately 43 percent, or $64 million, of those exports were shipped to South Africa. The ITU recently reported that there are an estimated 12 million phones in sub-Saharan Africa (less than in the city of Tokyo alone), 5 million of which are in South Africa. Approximately 700 million people live in Africa, and the ITU reported that the teledensity rate there was only 1.85 lines per 100 inhabitants in 1996. While 12 percent of the world's population lives in Africa, they have access to only 2 percent of the world's telephone lines.

Clearly, there is a large potential market for telecommunications equipment in Africa, making it one of the last "great frontiers" for substantial growth. The ITU predicted that Africa will construct $20 billion worth of infrastructure by 2003, with 20 million mainline users and 3 million cellular subscribers by 2000. Deregulation, privatization, improving economic situations, and investment incentives are stimulating U.S. interest in the largely untapped African telecommunications market. According to the World Bank, nine national operators have been privatized in sub-Saharan Africa since 1990: Cape Verde, Cote d'Ivoire, Eritrea, Ghana, Guinea, Guinea-Bissau, Senegal, South Africa, and Sudan. Upcoming partial privatizations in Cameroon, Kenya, Madagascar, Mauritius, Mozambique, Nigeria, Tanzania, Togo, Uganda, and Zambia bode well for future export opportunities for U.S. and other foreign companies. Although European and Asian companies have won many of the already completed privatization projects, SBC International's (formerly Southwestern Bell Corp.) stake in South Africa's operator and increasing U.S. interest in the region may shift the balance in the future. In addition, many African nations, including Ghana and Tanzania, have opened their cellular and value-added services markets to foreign operators. The Regional African Satellite Communications Organization (RASCOM) has been funding a project to put the continent's first satellite in space. Several U.S. companies have been vying for the contract, and a decision is expected by the end of 1998. RASCOM expects the satellite to be launched by 2000 or early 2001.

South Africa is the largest telecommunications equipment market in sub-Saharan Africa and is a key market entry point for the entire sub-Saharan region. In May 1997 SBC International finalized an agreement to become a strategic equity partner in Telkom South Africa, the formerly 100 percent state-owned telecommunications company. The $1.26 billion deal was the first major privatization in South Africa and represents the largest direct investment in that country to date. Thintana Communications (the consortium of SBC International and Telekom Malaysia that won a 30 percent stake in Telkom S.A.) will install 2.7 million new lines by the end of 2002.

The advent of global mobile personal communications by satellite (GMPCS) services late in 1998 with the launch of the Iridium system may spur exports of mobile handsets and ground station equipment to Africa. As additional providers, such as Globalstar, ICO, Ellipso, and ECCO, commence service over the next several years, the costs associated with these systems may decrease and usage in sub-Saharan Africa may increase rapidly.

Of the 48 countries in sub-Saharan Africa, Senegal, Ghana, Cote d'Ivoire, Mauritius, and South Africa are signatories to the WTO Agreement on Basic Telecommunications Services. Although this is a low percentage, the general lack of participation may be due to limited familiarity with the WTO process and the desire of nonparticipants to study how the initial signatories are faring now that the accord is in place. If the experiences of those five countries prove rewarding, many more countries in sub-Saharan Africa may sign on to the agreement in the future.

The remainder of this chapter provides analyses of specific high-profile segments of the telecommunications and navigation equipment industries.

Linda Gossack Astor, U.S. Department of Commerce, Office of Telecommunications, (202) 482-4466, November 1998.

Network equipment consists of the transmission and switching equipment purchased by public and private network operators. Switches complete connections between callers and route information from one network user to another. Transmission systems include the multiplexing equipment, repeaters, and line conditioning equipment used to transmit information. Network equipment is classified under SIC 3661.

Global Industry Trends

The worldwide market for wireline network equipment is projected to reach $54 billion in 1999, up 0.7 percent from $53.6 billion in 1998. The increase will occur in the transmission equipment sector, which will grow from $18.7 billion to $19.7 billion [this figure does not include fiber-optic transmission systems (FOTS), satellite transmission systems, and microwave systems, which were included in 1997]. According to Northern Business Information (Dataquest), revenues from switching equipment will decrease slightly from approximately $34.9 billion in 1998 to $34.3 billion in 1999 after peaking at $36.2 billion in 1996. Worldwide demand for network equipment is expected to grow to $57.6 billion in 2003. Growth will continue to occur in the transmission sector, with the market reaching $24.5 billion, while the value of the worldwide switched market will continue to decline gradually to $33.2 billion.

World demand for network equipment is being driven by a variety of market forces. In less developed regions network expansion and investment can be attributed to the vast infrastructural needs of new market-based economies; a desire to modernize aging and technologically obsolete communications infrastructures; the need to provide telephony to a larger number of residents, especially in rural areas; and the need to provide greater overall reliability and better service in both telephony and data transmission.

In more developed regions new equipment is being deployed to provide advanced new services. Technological advances in network equipment allow network operators not only to offer the new services that customers demand but also to realize cost savings from improvements in network operating efficiencies. Worldwide, liberalization and competition in the telecommunications services sector attract new entrants that need to build new networks, while existing operators are forced to upgrade their networks to remain competitive. The Agreement on Basic Telecommunications under the WTO will reinforce this trend over the next 7 years as the signatories, accounting for over 90 percent of world telecommunications services market, introduce competition into their markets.

Software is increasingly important in the public switching market as manufacturers continue to produce switches that can be upgraded with software rather than with the installation of new equipment. Northern Business Information (Dataquest) predicts that in some developed markets software revenues may be as high as 50 percent of total revenues by 2001. In addition, for most switch-producing companies software upgrades to installed switches will be the largest source of revenues over the next decade, and reliability and maintenance of software will be essential in gaining revenue and market share.

Factors Affecting U.S. Industry Growth

The future of the network equipment industry in the United States will be determined to a large extent by changes in the U.S. telecommunications services industry resulting from the Telecommunications Act of 1996. This complex piece of legislation promises to fundamentally restructure the telecommunications, computer, and cable television industries by removing many barriers to market entry and cross-ownership.

For example, local service companies and long-distance service providers can compete in each other's markets, although competition has not yet developed because of regulatory requirements and the large investments needed to build alternative wireless infrastructures. Cable television companies are permitted to offer local telephone service in their franchise areas, but few have taken steps to do so.

While it is too early to determine the ultimate effects of the new law, it seems clear that new infrastructure needs will promote increased demand for network equipment. U.S. equipment companies are considered to be in the best position to take advantage of these new opportunities.

Other factors driving the demand for network equipment in the United States include the growing trend toward working from home (telecommuting) on a full-time or part-time basis and consumer demand for connections to the Internet and other information services. As a result, more people are finding it necessary to bring additional phone lines into their homes.

These demand drivers will be partially offset by the maturation of the U.S. market. In 1999 Dataquest forecasts that central office switches in the United States will be 91 percent digitized. In 1996 digital switches served 81 percent of local lines, a figure which is expected to rise to 95 percent by 2001 and will continue to move upward through 2003. Vendors in the United States and other mature markets will earn much of their revenue, as was mentioned above in regard to the global switching market, by upgrading features on the installed base of switches rather than by selling new equipment. Although local line shipments are predicted to decrease slightly, revenue should rise from approximately $6.8 billion in 1999 to $7.5 billion in 2003.

Internationally, the continuing worldwide trend toward privatization, liberalization, and competition in telecommunications services markets, bolstered by the Agreement on Basic Telecommunications under the WTO, not only will sustain the demand for equipment but also will help erode market access barriers and allow U.S. equipment suppliers to compete for business in formerly closed markets.

While worldwide demand for network equipment will remain strong, U.S. suppliers will continue to face strong competition from long-established suppliers in Europe and Japan as well as from newer manufacturers in countries such as South Korea and Taiwan. Industry experts generally agree that there is surplus capacity in certain sectors, such as central office switching equipment, and predict that some sort of consolidation is inevitable.

U.S. Industry Growth Projections for the Next 1 and 5 Years

U.S. shipments of network equipment are expected to reach $12.9 billion in 1999 and increase to approximately $14.2 billion in 2003, with an average annual growth rate of 2.5 percent (these figures do not include fiber-optic transmission systems, satellite transmission systems, and microwave systems, which were included in the figures for 1997).

Global Market Prospects

The world market for network equipment is expected to remain strong in the foreseeable future as developing countries continue to build out their telecommunications infrastructures and developed countries invest in new technologies.

Nevertheless, the high growth rates seen in worldwide demand for network equipment in past years are expected to come down and level off over the next 5 years, although this will vary regionally, depending on the level of economic development. Strong growth is expected to continue in the developing world, where infrastructure is weak and telephone penetration rates are still very low. However, this growth will be offset by stagnation and decline in mature markets, where the demand will primarily involve product replacement and new product offerings.

The strongest growth is expected to occur in central and eastern Europe, which Northern Business Information (Dataquest) predicts will have a compound annual growth rate in digital local lines of 24.4 percent between 1996 and 2001. This region is followed by Latin America with 19.5 percent and Africa and the Middle East with 19.1 percent. The Asia/Pacific region is predicted to have a compound annual growth rate (CAGR) of only 1.6 percent, reflecting a slowing of demand in mature markets which growth in developing markets will not offset. The CAGRs for the mature markets of North America and western Europe will decline 1.5 and 2 percent, respectively. It is likely that these trends will continue at least through 2003.

Even with a low growth rate in switching, Asia remains an important market. In fact, it will continue to be the world's largest market for switching equipment. Northern Business Information figures show that in 1999 Asia will have an installed main line base of 276,294,000, or 31.3 percent of world's main lines in service. China is the largest market both in Asia and in the world, with an installed base of main lines in service of 117 million predicted for 1999. Asia has surpassed North America and western Europe in the size of its installed base of main lines, which are predicted to total 212,995,000 and 218,535,000, respectively.

In 1999 North America and Asia will remain the largest markets for transmission equipment in the world, with each accounting for about 30 percent of demand. Western Europe is the third largest market, accounting for about 17 percent of demand. These markets are followed by central Europe, Latin America, and Africa–Middle East, with shares of world demand of 10 percent, 9 percent, and 3 percent, respectively.

In 2003 Asia will surpass North America, reaching 35 percent of world demand, and North America will have a 32 per-

cent share. Markets in other regions will decline or grow only slightly.

Competition in the network equipment market continues to intensify worldwide, with large telecommunications equipment vendors such as Lucent, Alcatel, Siemens, NEC, NorTel, and Fujitsu emphasizing their ability to provide total network solutions, while firms serving niche markets, such as DSC, Hughes, and Scientific Atlanta, offer expertise in specialized equipment subsectors.

Intense competition has led to significant downward pricing pressures. Price declines have resulted in declining margins for manufacturers; the resulting pressures have contributed to the trend toward mergers and consolidation.

Jason Leuck, U.S. Department of Commerce, Office of Telecommunications, (202) 482-4202, May 1998.

CUSTOMER PREMISES EQUIPMENT

Customer premises equipment, or terminal equipment, consists of a wide range of privately owned telecommunications equipment which attaches to the public network. Such shipments are classified under SIC 3661. The largest product sectors of customer premises equipment are modems, private branch exchanges, voice processing equipment, video communications equipment, telephones, key systems, and facsimile machines.

Global Industry Trends

The customer premises equipment industry is composed of a wide variety of products that range from simple telephone handsets costing a few dollars to complex private branch exchange (PBX) systems that can cost millions. Most are mature markets characterized by intense competition and declining unit prices. The majority of low-end products (e.g., telephone sets and answering machines) are commodity products that are manufactured in countries with low labor (production) costs. In the United States most of these products are imported, primarily from manufacturing facilities in Asia. There are also an increasing number of higher-technology products for broadband applications such as high-speed data and video. Domestic manufacturing tends to be concentrated on the more technically sophisticated products, such as videoconferencing and voice processing equipment, which have high value-added content and in which U.S. manufacturers are technological leaders.

Market Trends

Manufacturers of high-end customer premises equipment are increasingly influenced by trends in the computer industry. The convergence of telephony and computers is especially noticeable in the customer premises equipment industry, where vendors of everything from PBXs to voice processing equipment are attempting to facilitate the integration of voice, data, and video communications for users at the desktop.

In the PBX and key telephone system (KTS) markets, manufacturers have shifted their attention to developing advanced features which will provide additional value to their customers. PBXs and KTSs have changed from being stand-alone equipment to being part of a company's communications network. PBX/KTS manufacturers have moved from proprietary to open systems to meet the needs of customers that want to integrate their premise switching equipment with the rest of the enterprise network. Computer telephony integration (CTI) and call centers have brought increased complexity to the task of integrating the different components of the enterprise network. PBX vendors consequently have become much more software-focused. In fact, most PBX and KTS manufacturers have formed alliances with computer software and hardware companies for applications development.

As in the PBX/KTS industry, voice processing equipment manufacturers are becoming more software-intensive in their product development as they move to open, personal computer (PC)-based architectures. Manufacturers are also focusing increasingly on developing enhanced applications for the business and home markets, such as voice-activated dialing.

Wireless capabilities are another promising feature offered by some PBX and KTS vendors. In-building wireless applications have considerable potential because they give corporate users mobility without losing contact within the office setting. The success of wireless phones in the consumer market is helping to popularize this feature in the office, as users have come to expect added mobility in the office as well. Some wireless PBXs promise interoperability with personal communications services or cellular phones, allowing consumers to use the same handset in the office that they use on the road.

Increased interest in on-line technologies and sales of PCs bundled with modems have spurred dramatic growth in the modem market while blurring the distinction between telecommunications and computer equipment.

The U.S. market for consumers' customer premises equipment is quite mature. The Consumer Electronics Manufacturers Association reports that in 1997, 66 percent of U.S. households had cordless phones, 65 percent had answering machines, 34 percent had cellular phones, 19 percent had modems, 18 percent had caller ID equipment, and 9 percent had facsimile machines. Most of this equipment is imported.

U.S. Industry Growth Projections for the Next 1 and 5 Years

The value of domestic shipments of customer premises equipment is estimated to increase to $6.5 billion in 1999. Growth in U.S. shipments will occur primarily in the high-end and technically sophisticated product segments. The value of overall shipments is forecast to grow annually at around 8.5 percent, reaching an estimated $9 billion by 2003. The performance of individual product sectors will vary.

PBX shipments are expected to experience solid growth through the forecast period. Growth will come primarily from manufacturers that provide value-added features such as computer telephony integration and wireless applications. U.S.

shipments of PBX equipment will grow about 5 percent yearly through 2003, and the KTS market will grow at about the same pace. While overall shipments of voice processing equipment should remain strong, voice processing shipments will experience slower growth because of a slowdown in sales to the largely saturated high-scale systems market.

According to Dataquest, overall shipments of modems grew only 14 percent (in terms of quantity) in 1997, compared with a growth rate of 66 percent in 1996. This decline is primarily attributable to a strong falloff in shipments of low-speed modems. Shipments of high-speed modems are expected to continue to increase 10 to 20 percent per year over the next few years, driven primarily by the demands of new PC users and upgrades by existing users. While shipments of conventional modems should continue to grow through 2003, ISDN (integrated services digital network) terminals, xDSI (digital subscriber loop), and cable modems will account for a significant portion of the overall market as the demand for broadband applications increases.

Videoconferencing equipment also should experience increased growth as improvements in compression technologies are made, standards issues are resolved, and broadband transmission facilities become more available. According to Datapro, year-on-year growth of videoconferencing systems may reach 40 percent by the end of 1999.

Global Markets

The global market for customer premises equipment is characterized by intense competition, and in many markets U.S. companies face stiff competition from European and Asian manufacturers. Although the United States runs a consistent deficit in its customer premises equipment trade balance ($2.3 billion in 1997), primarily because of imports of commodity-type products (telephones, answering machines, and fax machines), there are significant opportunities in the international market for U.S. exports, especially in products that incorporate advanced technologies.

During the forecast period the developing economies of the Latin America and the Asia/Pacific region should offer the most promising growth markets for the customer premises equipment industry, as growth in the mature markets of North America and western Europe is expected to slow. Most analysts predict that the top growth markets for PBXs and KTSs will be in the Pacific Rim economies, eastern Europe, and Latin America. The market for voice processing products outside North America is expected to grow at a healthy rate as foreign companies recognize the cost and productivity benefits of such products. U.S. manufacturers stand to gain from this trend, as U.S.-based multinationals have been some of the first global companies to implement worldwide voice processing systems. For the sake of compatibility, these companies tend to favor manufacturers with a large U.S. presence. In the short term the most promising international markets for modems will be in Europe and Japan, where there is the highest penetration of PCs outside the United States. The developing markets of Asia and Latin America should present additional opportunities as the penetration of PCs increases there. In the short term the worldwide market for videoconferencing equipment is expected to experience the strongest growth outside North America, in Europe and the Pacific Rim.

John R. Henry, U.S. Department of Commerce, Office of Telecommunications, (202) 482-1193, November 1998.

FIBER OPTICS

Fiber-optic equipment consists of optical fiber and fiber-optic cable, fiber-optic transmission systems, connectors, and test equipment (SIC 3231, 3357, 3663, 3674, 3678, 3825). A typical fiber-optic system carries voice, data, and video by means of light pulses through a glass fiber. Transmit/receive terminals convert electrical signals to optical signals for transmission at speeds from 6.3 megabits per second to 10 gigabits per second.

Fiber-optic equipment comprises optical fiber and fiber-optic cable, transmission systems, connectors, and test equipment. Telecommunications remains the predominant application, accounting for over 80 percent of the total market. Other industry sectors, such as those involved in medicine, manufacturing, and transportation, are increasingly attractive markets for manufacturers and suppliers of optical fiber and cable. This section focuses on the telecommunications markets for fiber-optic systems and equipment.

Throughout most of the 1990s strong export growth and rapid domestic deployment of fiber-optic cable in long-distance, local loop, and cable television (CATV) networks as well as private networks have contributed greatly to the growth of the U.S. fiber-optic industry. Although this industry is expected to have continued growth through the rest of the decade, overall growth rates will begin to slow, primarily as a result of saturation in long-haul telephony markets in most developed countries. However, growth in short-haul, trunk/feeder/distribution markets in developed countries, coupled with continued growth of backbone applications in developing countries, will continue to fuel the market for fiber-optic equipment. In the United States the Telecommunications Act of 1996 is expected to benefit the fiber-optic industry by encouraging greater competition in the local loop. This in turn will accelerate the deployment of broadband technologies as voice, data, and video service providers transmit more broadband-based services to their subscribers to remain competitive.

Domestic and Global Trends

At the end of 1997 the worldwide installed base of optical fiber was approximately 166 million fiber kilometers, according to Kessler Marketing Intelligence. A vast majority of the total deployed optical fiber is single-mode as opposed to multimode fiber. Multimode fiber is used primarily in local area networks (LANs) and other computer networks that do not operate over long distances. Although multimode fiber has the advantage of using less costly connector components and optical power sources such as light-emitting diodes (LEDs), it is more prone to signal delay and distortion than is single-mode fiber. There-

fore, single-mode has become the fiber of choice for most telecommunications applications and today accounts for more than 90 percent of the total market volume of cable installed worldwide and about 75 percent of the market value of all cable installed.

The United States remains the largest single-country market for optical fiber and cable, representing over 40 percent of the worldwide installed base with 56 million fiber kilometers at the end of 1997. Kessler Marketing Intelligence estimated that an additional 12.1 million fiber kilometers was deployed in the United States in 1997, an increase of 18 percent from 1996. Multimode fiber accounted for approximately 9 percent of this amount. In 1997 the largest deployers of fiber by user group were the local exchange carriers (LECs) and CATV providers with 29 percent each, followed by the interexchange carriers (IXCs) with 15 percent and competitive access providers (CAPs) with 8 percent. Other entities that deploy single-mode fiber include major utilities, railroads, and some private network operators.

It is anticipated, however, that the rate of growth in the U.S. market for optical fiber will begin to slow and drop into the single digits in 1999 and early into the next decade. U.S. deployment was expected to grow 12 percent to 13.6 million fiber kilometers in 1998 and will grow only 5 percent to 14.3 million fiber kilometers in 1999. By 2003 fiber deployment is forecast to reach 17.4 million fiber kilometers, reflecting an annual growth rate of about 5 percent. This decreasing growth rate will be attributable to slackening demand for optical fiber in most of the major market segments. Demand is already beginning to wane in the interexchange carrier segment, where several smaller long-distance providers, such as IXC Communications Inc., Qwest, and Worldcom, are in the last stages of their network expansion programs. The largest interexchange carriers (AT&T, MCI, and Sprint) have extensive fiber-optic networks that were constructed in the 1980s and early 1990s, and therefore are no longer major deployers of optical fiber.

CATV providers, particularly multiple systems operators such as Media One, Time Warner, and TCI, became one of the largest customer groups for optical fiber in the late 1990s. Throughout the 1990s CATV providers have been aggressively deploying fiber in their networks and restructuring their network architectures to provide fiber optic–based broadband services to their subscribers. It is also anticipated that CATV providers will begin to offer local telephone and data communications services in direct competition with local exchange carriers and Internet service providers. Although demand for fiber will continue to grow in the short term, it is anticipated that many of these CATV providers will be nearing the end of their fiber deployment programs as they enter the next decade and that overall demand in this segment will fall off.

The competitive access providers have been aggressively expanding their urban fiber systems as their customer bases have grown rapidly over the last 5 years. Although they started out as long-distance access providers primarily to high-volume business customers (bypassing an incumbent local exchange carrier's network), most competitive access providers are now positioning themselves to offer their own local switched services to their customers and are essentially becoming competitive local exchange carriers (CLECs). Several of the latter are negotiating with utilities, city governments, and other entities that possess rights-of-way that will enable them to target residential customers in addition to business customers. According to Federal Communications Commission (FCC) data, fiber deployment by the competitive access providers and the competitive local exchange providers grew 74 percent annually during the period 1991–1996, a rate faster than that of any other category of fiber end user. Although both of these providers are expected to continue expanding their fiber systems over the next few years, demand for fiber is expected to level off by the end of 1999.

Although demand for fiber in the local exchange carrier market segment has experienced slower growth over the past 5 years relative to the other market segments, it is expected to resume modest annual growth rates into the next decade, particularly as the Regional Bell Operating Companies (RBOCs) continue to apply their fiber-in-the-loop or similar hybrid fiber-coax architecture deployment strategy to their networks. Fiber applications within the local exchange carrier segment range from trunk and feeder network applications to business and residential distribution network applications. Interoffice trunk networks are nearly saturated with fiber, while the residential distribution networks contain relatively little fiber. Over the past few years many RBOCs have concentrated on increasing their fiber deployment in the feeder and business distribution portions of their networks but have installed relatively little fiber in the residential distribution portions. At present most RBOCs are concentrating on fiber-to-the-curb installations in only the most lucrative residential markets but do not foresee wide-scale fiber-to-the-home installations for at least another 10 to 15 years. However, burgeoning consumer demand for more broadband services, such as multimedia and high-speed data communications, together with the decreasing cost of optical components, could ultimately speed deployment plans for fiber-to-the-home.

Generally, in heavily populated urban areas the first-time cost of deploying a fiber-based network is actually lower than that of deploying a copper-based network (the cost drops further when depreciation costs, maintenance costs, and the durability of fiber over copper in the network are considered). Although the cost of upgrading a copper network with fiber is dropping, fiber-in-the-loop deployment is still somewhat costly relative to copper the closer it is installed to the home. Many network operators believe that there is not yet sufficient consumer demand for the types of broadband services that fiber would carry to the home to justify the cost of deploying an all-fiber network. Therefore, many local exchange carriers are turning to lower-cost "interim" solutions such as asymmetric digital subscriber line and high-bit-rate digital subscriber line technologies. Digital subscriber lines basically allow a carrier to use its existing copper plant to offer high-speed services such as Internet access and can achieve an increase in data speeds of 50 to 200 times that of regular phone lines.

According to Northern Business Information (NBI), the U.S. market for fiber-optic transmission systems, which consist of the transmit-receive terminals that convert electrical signals to optical signals and back again for transmission over optical fiber, was expected to reach $3.7 billion in 1998. As a whole, the U.S. market for fiber-optic transmission systems is expected to experience nominal growth of around 5 percent a year through 2003, with some product areas experiencing higher growth, particularly equipment based on the synchronous optical network (SONET) standard. In addition, the equipment market for wave division multiplexing (WDM) and the derivative technology dense wave division multiplexing (DWDM) will continue to enjoy strong growth. As carriers have deployed bandwidth-hungry asynchronous transfer mode switches and transmission equipment based on the synchronous optical network standard some of them have experienced congestion in their fiber-optic networks. As a result, an increasing number of carriers are utilizing dense wave division multiplexing technology to increase network capacity without installing additional fiber. Essentially, this technology combines a number of optical channels in a single fiber according to different wavelengths. First-generation systems developed in the early 1990s had up to 8 channels; however, 16- and 32-channel systems have been introduced and 100-channel systems are being developed. Because of the current cost of components such as pump lasers and optical amplifiers, dense wave division multiplexing is generally a more economical method for operators of long-haul fiber networks compared with short-haul networks. However, as the cost of these components comes down, the market for short-haul local network applications of dense wave division multiplexing should expand. In April 1998 Bell Atlantic was the first RBOC to announce that it had installed such equipment, in this case supplied by Ciena Corporation. Reflecting this growth potential, it has been predicted that the market for dense wave division multiplexing in North America alone will grow from only $95 million in 1996 to $1 billion by 2003.

The fiber-optic industry has also been experiencing a move toward greater integration in recent years. An example is the successful implementation of various technical standards that have evolved over the past decade in the telecommunications and fiber-optic industries. Although standards have been slow to develop in the fiber-optic industry, mostly because of the constantly changing and evolving nature of the business, standards such as SONET—and its international equivalent, synchronous digital hierarchy (SDH)—for telecommunications networks and fiber distributed data interface for LANs have gained universal acceptance among deployers of fiber-optic systems and equipment. These standards have created a more uniform environment which allows competing manufacturers to create compatible products for deployment in telecommunications networks, contributing to market growth. Going into the twenty-first century, the advent of the all-optical network, which will utilize only optical components as opposed to the current mix of electronic and photonic components, is prompting standards bodies to examine the transparency level to which such a network will have to conform and the interoperability criteria that vendors will have to meet. Currently, manufacturers are developing all the new optical components necessary for an all-optical network, such as optical add-drop multiplexers, optical cross-connects, optical switches, and nonzero dispersion shifted optical fiber. In fact, the development of WDM/DWDM technology has represented the first step toward such a network.

Corning and Lucent Technologies remain the largest U.S. manufacturers of optical fiber. Corning is also the largest producer of optical fiber worldwide, and its joint venture with Siemens of Germany, Siecor, is the largest manufacturer of fiber-optic cable in the world. Other major producers of optical fiber and fiber optic cable include Alcatel (France), Alcoa-Fujikura, Ltd. (United States/Japan), Berk-Tek (United States), BICC Cables (United Kingdom), CommScope (United States), Optical Fiber Corporation (United States), Pirelli (Italy), Spectran Corp (United States), and Sumitomo (Japan). The leading U.S. producers of fiber-optic transmission equipment include ADC, AMP, Ciena Corporation, DSC, and Lucent Technologies. Major foreign manufacturers include Alcatel, Fujitsu (Japan), NEC (Japan), NorTel (Canada), Pirelli, and Siemens (Germany).

Global Market Trends

Currently the world market for fiber-optic equipment is estimated at approximately $8 billion. According to a recent study by Frost & Sullivan, the market is expected to exceed $15 billion by 2003. Approximately 36 million fiber kilometers was deployed worldwide in 1997, an increase of 21 percent over 1996. It was expected that annual worldwide deployment would grow 14 percent to 41 million kilometers by the end of 1998. It is forecast that worldwide deployment will increase 15 percent in 1999 and reach 84 million kilometers annually by 2003. Over the last few years worldwide production of optical fiber has been at its limit, resulting in a shortage and rising prices. As new manufacturing facilities came on-line in 1998, this capacity shortage began to ease, and there may be a capacity surplus in the period 1998–1999 which should result in gradually declining prices. However, unless sufficient capacity is added over the next 5 years, industry analysts predict that another fiber shortage could arise early in the next century.

U.S. trade in fiber-optic cable continued to show a surplus in 1997 (see Figure 31-2). Total imports increased 26 percent from the 1996 level, and total exports also increased 24 percent during that period. In 1997, U.S. imports of fiber-optic cable totaled $38 million and those of optical fiber totaled $238 million. While U.S. exports of fiber-optic cable grew only 4 percent to $348 million in 1997, exports of optical fiber surged 48 percent to $459 million. Accurate data for U.S. trade in active fiber-optic components (transmission systems, connectors, and test equipment) are not available.

According to Kessler Marketing Intelligence, the Asia/Pacific region led all regions with 40 percent of worldwide fiber demand in 1997, followed by North America at 36 percent, western Europe at 13 percent, and eastern Europe at 4 percent. All other countries, which Kessler categorizes as emerging markets, accounted for 7 percent. The fastest growing regional mar-

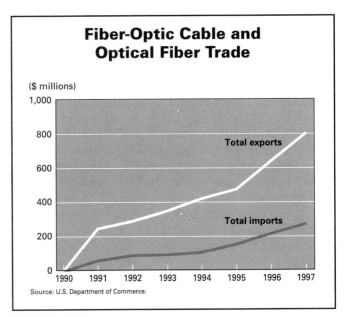

Fiber-Optic Cable and Optical Fiber Trade

FIGURE 31-2

kets in 1997 were the emerging markets (Latin America, Africa, and the Middle East) and eastern Europe, which increased their annual installation in 1997 by 53 percent and 36 percent respectively, over 1996. The five largest individual deployers of optical fiber worldwide were NTT of Japan, MPT/China Telecom, Time Warner, Bell South, and Media One.

North America accounted for the majority of worldwide demand for fiber-optic transmission systems in 1997 with a 45 percent share, according to NBI. This was followed by the Asia/Pacific region with 23 percent, western Europe with 16 percent, Latin America with 7 percent, eastern Europe with 6 percent, and the remaining countries with 3 percent. The fastest growing regional markets in 1997 were eastern Europe at 19 percent and North America at 12 percent compared with 1996.

World market growth for fiber-optic equipment continues to be fueled by increased deployment of fiber-in-the-loop architectures in most industrialized nations and the deployment of fiber in backbone networks by emerging market economies in the Asia/Pacific region, eastern Europe, and Latin America. Many of these newly industrializing countries are modernizing their telecommunications networks, which in some cases predate World War II. As these antiquated networks are modernized, telephone operators are increasingly utilizing SONET/SDH fiber ring topologies and digital overlay networks to improve network performance and reliability. In the industrialized nations fiber deployment is moving from long-haul networks into the interoffice trunk, feeder, and distribution portions of local networks. In both developed and developing countries, competition is being introduced into the telecommunications sector, prompting incumbent telephone operators to upgrade their networks to compete with new market entrants such as utilities and CATV providers. In addition, most of these new entrants already have their own fiber-based networks that they are expanding and upgrading to offer voice and data communications services to the public.

Submarine Systems

Several new submarine fiber-optic cables came on line or were announced in 1997. The much-anticipated Fiberoptic Link Around the Globe (FLAG) commenced service in November 1997. FLAG is a privately financed venture with five principal investors: Bell Atlantic Corporation (through its merger/acquisition of NYNEX), the Dallah Al Baraka Group, Telecom Holdings, Marubeni Corporation, and the Asian Infrastructure Fund. FLAG is a high-capacity, SDH undersea fiber-optic cable linking Japan to the United Kingdom via the Indian Ocean, with landing points in 11 other countries. At 28,000 kilometers and an estimated cost of $1.5 billion, FLAG is the longest undersea cable in the world. The cable consists of two optical fiber pairs operating at 5 gigabits per second (Gbps). One pair provides local transmission, carrying traffic between the landing point countries, and the other pair functions as an express lane, quickly transmitting traffic along several of the busiest routes.

In spring 1997 the last major supply contracts were announced for the Southeast Asia–Middle East–Western Europe (SEA-ME-WE 3) submarine cable, which upon completion will be the world's longest submarine fiber-optic cable at 38,000 kilometers. Fujitsu and Alcatel Submarine Networks have been awarded the largest supply contracts for the $1.3 billion project, which will be built in three phases. Other major suppliers include Kokusai Denshin Denwa (KDD) of Japan, Tyco Submarine Systems Incorporated of the United States, and Pirelli. The system will use 10-Gbps wave division multiplexing technology and SONET/SDH transmission. Upon completion at the end of 1998, SEA-ME-WE 3 will serve a combined population of 3 billion people from 39 landing points stretching from Germany to Singapore.

The recently completed $1.24 billion TPC-5 transpacific undersea cable spans more than 24,000 kilometers between the United States and Japan. Built by AT&T and KDD, TPC-5 is a closed-loop network as opposed to a point-to-point cable and is "self-healing," meaning that if there is a network disruption, traffic can be shifted to spare fibers on the network and thus be restored almost instantaneously. TPC-5 is double the length of TPC-4 (still in service) and is capable of transmission speeds of 5 Gbps over one fiber pair, which is equivalent to 320,000 simultaneous telephone calls.

Two transatlantic cables, Gemini and Atlantic Crossing-1 (AC-1), are nearing completion and will bring much-needed capacity at a time when most existing transatlantic cables are near their capacity limits partly because of surging Internet-related traffic. The 12,600-kilometer Gemini cable, which is owned by Cable & Wireless and Worldcom, was expected to be fully operational by the fourth quarter of 1998 and will consist of three SDH closed loops connecting the United States and the United Kingdom. Gemini will provide transmission speeds of 30 Gbps (15 Gbps per fiber pair) and will feature wave division multiplexing technology. AC-1 promises to boost the level of transatlantic cable capacity by 50 percent upon completion in early 1999 and will directly connect the United States, the United Kingdom, Germany, and the Netherlands. The 14,000-

kilometer undersea cable will have four fiber pairs capable of 10-Gbps transmission (40 Gbps total) and will use wave division multiplexing and erbium doped fiber amplifier (EDFA) technologies. AC-1 is unique in that it will be built, owned, and operated by a single contractor, Tyco Submarine Systems International, which will sell services to carriers. Tyco entered the submarine cable business when it purchased AT&T Submarine Systems Inc. (SSI) for $850 million in 1997.

Several new cable projects were announced in 1997, including Columbus III (transatlantic), the Atlantic Express Cable System, the Pan-American Crossing (PAC-1), Pacific Crossing (PC-1), and the U.S.–China cable. Perhaps the most ambitious submarine fiber-optic cable project announced to date is Project Oxygen, which proposes to connect over 265 landing points in 171 countries via a 320,000-kilometer integrated network of 32 cable loops (mostly undersea). Project Oxygen promises transmission speeds of up to 320 Gbps on any one link and plans to deliver services such as full-motion videoconferencing and real-time international cable television as well as telemedicine and distance learning multimedia applications. Commissioned by CTR Group Ltd. (New Jersey), Project Oxygen will cost $14 billion when it is fully completed in 2003, 10 percent of which will be provided by 30 international telecommunications carriers that have tentatively made a commitment to the project. Carriers will purchase capacity on the network, with ownership proportional to investment. The price of capacity will be based on the revenues of the respective carriers.

Outlook for the Next 1 and 5 Years

Over the period 1993–1998, U.S. shipments of fiber-optic equipment grew from $3.1 billion to almost $5.7 billion (see Table 31-3), reflecting a compound annual growth rate of about 13 percent. With the continuing deployment of fiber-optic equipment in both developing and industrialized countries, it is estimated that total shipments will grow 11 percent to over $6.3 billion in 1999. Optical fiber, fiber-optic cable, and fiber-optic connectors are expected to experience the highest annual growth rates (about 12 percent). Shipments of optical sensors and emitters and light-emitting diodes, which are used primarily in multimode fiber systems), should grow 10 percent each. Shipments of fiber-optic transmission systems and equipment will grow 9 percent, with SONET/SDH-based equipment continuing to experience healthy growth and asynchronous/PDH-based equipment continuing to decline. Shipments of fiber-optic test equipment such as optical time-domain reflectometers and signal-to-noise meters should experience growth of about 8 percent. As with fiber-optic systems and equipment, fiber-optic test equipment designed for SONET/SDH applications will experience the strongest growth.

Over the 1999–2003 period it is estimated that total shipments of fiber-optic equipment will increase at a slower rate of about 9 percent annually, exceeding $8.9 billion in 2003. This relatively lower rate of growth will be due largely to decreased fiber deployment in the U.S. market. Demand for fiber-optic equipment in Canada and Mexico also will peak by the end of the decade, after which time annual growth is expected to be

TABLE 31-3: U.S. Shipments of Fiber-Optic Cable and Equipment

(thousands of U.S. dollars; percent)

SIC	Product	1996	1997[1]	1998[1]	1999[2]	2003[2]	Compound Annual Rate of Growth, % 93–98	98–03
3231892	Optical fiber (data and nondata)	1,032,537	1,187,418	1,365,530	1,529,394	2,199,200	16	10
33579	Optical fiber cable	1,774,476	2,040,647	2,346,745	2,628,354	3,779,456	15	10
36631	Fiber-optic systems and equipment[3]	733,059	806,365	878,938	958,042	1,232,756	4	7
3674914	LEDs[4]	441,851	481,618	524,963	577,460	845,459	9	10
3674924	Optical sensors and emitters	149,879	164,867	181,354	199,489	292,072	16	10
3678553	Fiber-optic connectors	194,244	223,381	256,888	287,714	413,720	33	10
3825285	Fiber-optic test equipment (OTDR)	104,527	111,844	120,791	130,455	169,416	5	7
Percent change, all products							13	9
Total products		4,430,573	5,016,139	5,675,208	6,310,907	8,932,078		

[1] Estimated.
[2] Forecast.
[3] No shipment data for SONET-based equipment for 1991–1996.
[4] Estimated shipments for 1993–1996.
Source: U.S. Department of Commerce.

nominal or flat. However, demand for fiber-optic equipment in emerging markets, particularly for long-haul, backbone telephony applications, should continue to experience strong growth, which will help mitigate decreasing growth in the North American market.

Global Market Prospects

While the U.S., western European, and Japanese markets still constitute the bulk of the world market for fiber-optic equipment, emerging markets in Asia, eastern Europe, and Latin America are experiencing the most rapid growth. Some industry analysts predict that these emerging markets will collectively surpass the industrialized countries in terms of market size sometime in the next century. In the coming years there will be ample sales opportunities in both developing and developed countries for fiber-optic equipment manufacturers. Although long-haul applications still constitute the largest market segment, fiber-in-the-loop applications are expected to gain a larger share of the total market for fiber going into the next century.

In western Europe, recent market liberalization in many EU countries has cleared the way for new market entrants to build new fiber-based networks or expand existing networks to compete with the former monopoly carriers. Incumbent carriers such as Belgacom, Deutsche Telekom, France Telecom, and Telefónica are responding by upgrading and expanding their existing networks to compete with these new market entrants. At present the bulk of demand will be for backbone applications as the long-distance markets are the first to experience this new competition. The western European market for fiber-optic equipment will benefit and should grow about 20 percent annually in the next few years, reaching $4 billion by 2000. Germany is still the largest European market, followed by the United Kingdom, Italy, and France. Together, those four countries account for over 70 percent of the western European market for fiber-optic equipment.

Eastern Europe/NIS has been one of the fastest growing markets for fiber-optic equipment as many countries in that region pursue ambitious network upgrading and expansion programs to rehabilitate woefully archaic and inadequate telecommunications networks inherited after the dissolution of the Soviet Union. The Russian fiber-optic equipment market, the largest in the region, will benefit over the next 5 years from the $40 billion Project 50×50, which will involve the installation of 50 digital switches connected by 50,000 kilometers of fiber-optic cable and microwave radio systems in large metropolitan areas. Several other countries, such as Bulgaria, Hungary, and Poland, are constructing entirely new fiber-based "digital overlay networks" and are beginning to deploy fiber in the local loop. Interregional cable projects such as the Trans European Line (TEL) also will contribute to demand for fiber-optic equipment. Although fiber-optic equipment markets in eastern Europe/NIS should continue to experience strong growth over the next 5 years, the region as a whole will account for less than 10 percent of the world market during in that period.

The countries in the Asia/Pacific region collectively constitute one of the fastest growing and largest markets for fiber-optic equipment. Even with the Asian financial crisis, which is expected to slow the overall growth rate slightly, sales of fiber-optic equipment in that region will reach almost $8 billion by 2003. In terms of installed fiber, the region will surpass in volume the entire 1996 worldwide market by 2003. Japan is currently the largest fiber market in the region and accounted for more than half the installed fiber there in 1997. As part of its national information infrastructure (J-NII) project, Japan has made a commitment to introduce a fiber-optic network to every home by the year 2010. Other industrialized countries in the Asia/Pacific region, such as Australia and the Republic of Korea, are also actively pursuing some variation of a nationwide fiber plan. China has become the second largest market in the region and is expected to overtake Japan as the largest market for transmission equipment by 2001, according to NBI. As part of its ambitious telecommunications development and expansion plans, China recently installed 12 new fiber-optic trunk routes extending over 51,000 route kilometers. Demand for fiber in China is expected to grow 23 percent a year and reach 4.5 million kilometers by 2001. Finally, the developing countries in the region, such as Malaysia, Thailand, and Indonesia, are upgrading their long-distance terrestrial networks with fiber, although it remains to be seen whether the Asian financial crisis will cause serious delays in any of their deployment programs. Telekom Malaysia has plans to upgrade its high-capacity trunk network to SONET/SDH and is investing in the new infrastructure needed for the Multimedia Super Corridor project, which will be a high-tech hub with a world-class voice and data communications network. Both projects will involve significant purchases of fiber-optic equipment. Throughout the region, increasing demand for international services has led to significant growth in the undersea cable market, with several major undersea projects now under construction.

The fiber-optic equipment market in Latin America is expected to experience strong growth through the remainder of the 1990s and into the next decade as privatization and liberalization in several countries in that region spur network upgrading and expansion programs. As a whole, the Latin American fiber-optic equipment market should grow to $2 billion by 2003. Brazil and Mexico are the largest markets in the region and accounted for more than half the fiber deployed there in 1996. In Brazil the government is moving forward simultaneously on two fronts: network upgrading and/or expansion and privatization (followed by market liberalization). Brazil's ambitious Recovery and Expansion Program for Telecommunications and Postal Systems (PASTE) will involve investments in local and long-distance networks of $75 billion in the period 1995–2003 and will add 26 million additional fixed lines by 2003. A priority of PASTE is the installation of fiber-optic systems for interurban, intrastate, and national connections to meet the burgeoning demand for telecommunications services in Brazil's main cities. Once competition is allowed for basic telecommunications services early in the next decade, this will further drive demand for fiber-optic equipment. In Mexico competition in the long-distance market is spurring increased deployment of fiber, which totaled 680,000 fiber kilometers in 1996. The planned fiber deployment of the six new long-distance carriers amounts to about 9,700 route kilometers per year until 2001, representing an annual investment of $1 billion. Elsewhere in the region several undersea cables have been deployed or announced that will serve the international telecommunications needs of many Latin American nations. In particular, the newly constructed Columbus II, Americas-1, and UNISUR undersea cables will be used to facilitate telecommunications transmissions between Latin American countries as well between Latin America and other regions.

Future Growth

In the industrialized countries the fiber-optic industry will continue to focus on local and regional networks as fiber moves closer to the home. In the United States and many other coun-

tries regulatory barriers used to stifle competition have been removed, and this should prompt incumbents and new market entrants to increase the deployment of the fiber-optic infrastructure needed to offer broadband services such as full-motion interactive video, high-speed data communications, distance learning, and telemedicine. Developing countries will account for most of the future growth of fiber in the long-haul market segment and eventually will account for an increasing share of the local loop and CATV market segments. Once fiber-to-the-home proves to be economically feasible in more than a few countries, demand for optical fiber will expand tremendously over the next two decades. Given this future promise and today's favorable economic and regulatory climate, there will continue to be ample opportunities for the U.S. fiber-optic equipment industry to expand sales domestically and abroad over the long term.

G. Stuart Sandall, U.S. Department of Commerce, Office of Telecommunications, (202) 482-2006, May 1998.

WIRELESS COMMUNICATIONS EQUIPMENT

Wireless communications equipment consists of complete radio-based communications systems, including mobile switching, transmission, and subscriber equipment, for the provision of cellular, paging, and personal communications services. Switches complete connections between mobile users or between mobile users and the public switched telephone network. Transmission equipment includes radio transmitters, receivers, and transceivers as well as other base station equipment such as antennas and amplifiers. Subscriber equipment includes mobile and portable handsets. Wireless communications equipment is classified under SIC 3663.

Global Industry Trends

While the overall global telecommunications equipment market is expected to remain robust, industry analysts believe that the focus of growth will be on companies that are vested in the wireless sector. Research in 1998 by DMG estimates that the global wireless infrastructure equipment market will grow from 12 percent of overall telecommunications equipment spending in 1997 to 21 percent by 2001. DMG also estimates that wireless spending worldwide increased about 36 percent to $30 billion in 1997 from $22 billion in 1996 and will grow an additional 33 percent in 1998, tempered somewhat by a slower growth outlook in southeast Asia (see Table 31-4).

The wireless communications sector continued to have extraordinary growth levels in 1998, fueled by a continual stream of wireless license offerings around the globe, coupled with the accelerated movement from analog to digital technology. This licensing of competitive systems, which has been driving the wireless equipment market both in the United States and globally for many years, is expected to proceed, with the number of licenses possibly tripling by the turn of the century.

TABLE 31-4: Wireless Telecommunications Equipment Market Outlook

(millions of dollars; percent)

Year[1]	Global Telecom Equipment	Total Global Spending	Total Spending, Percent Change	Global Wireless Infrastructure Spending	Wireless as Percent of Equipment Spending	Wireless Spending, Percent Change
1995	152	754	16	17	11	NA
1996	200	850	13	22	11	NA
1997	250	950	12	30	12	36
1998	300	1,050	11	40	13	33
1999	325	1,150	10	52	16	30
2000	350	1,275	11	68	19	31
2001	400	1,405	10	85	21	25
Five-year compound annual rate of growth, %	15	11		31		

[1] Estimated for 1996–2001.

Source: International Telecommunication Union; DMG Technology Group.

Infrastructure vendors also benefit from the effect of new licenses on incumbent players, which are motivated to upgrade and/or expand their networks to improve quality, coverage, and capacity. The installed base of wireless infrastructure is estimated to be about $200 billion. Global wireless infrastructure sales were estimated at about $40 billion in 1998, up from $30 billion in 1997. On the subscriber end of the market, new competitors are driving down the cost of service, stimulating subscriber growth and handset sales.

The pace of growth is expected to accelerate over the next 5 years as the industry continues to build on the expanding platform of worldwide privatization and deregulation and technological advances (see Figure 31-3). Wireless network coverage is now nationwide in most developed countries, and in developing countries it is growing rapidly, acting in many cases as a substitute for wireline networks as the cost of installing wireless networks declines. The worldwide movement toward increased competition even in developing nations and the conversion of systems from analog to digital are viewed as the two principal catalysts in the global wireless equipment market. Competition in the global wireless subscriber and infrastructure equipment markets is fierce, and suppliers are scrambling to adapt to a rapidly changing environment and position themselves for the future.

U.S. Market Trends

Since late 1994 the issuance of about 2,400 wireless operating licenses in six different blocks of spectrum in the United States has been a significant market driver for wireless equipment, especially in conjunction with the accelerated conversion of many networks from analog to digital technology. Digitalization has been driven by the need for greater capacity, competition from existing carriers and new entrants, greater spectral efficiency, and new service applications. The auctioning of spectrum and the migration to digital have made this a period of significant demand for wireless subscriber and infrastructure equipment in the United States.

Cellular systems—wireless networks that operate in the frequency range of 800 MHz—continue to represent the largest installed base of wireless communications networks in the United States. According to Allied Business Intelligence (ABI), in 1997 there were more than 1,500 cellular systems in operation in 750 U.S. markets. The Cellular Telecommunications Industry Association (CTIA) reported that over 11 million new cellular subscribers were added in the United States in 1997 (a new 12-month record) for a total of over 55 million subscribers at the end of that year, a penetration rate of nearly 22 percent of the U.S. population. This 25 percent increase marked the second year in which the U.S. wireless sector added more than 10 million new subscribers. The number of cellular subscribers in the United States was expected to approach 70 million by the end of 1998. U.S. subscribers to personal communications services (PCS) were estimated at 2.5 million at the end of 1997 and 3 million by mid-1998.

Despite the current predominance of cellular systems in the United States, most of the new licenses issued over the last few

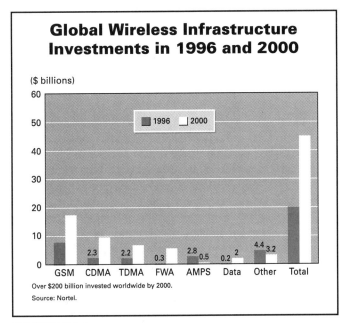

Global Wireless Infrastructure Investments in 1996 and 2000

($ billions)

Legend: 1996, 2000

GSM, CDMA (2.3), TDMA (2.2), FWA (0.3), AMPS (2.8, 0.5), Data (0.2, 2), Other (4.4, 3.2), Total

Over $200 billion invested worldwide by 2000.

Source: Nortel.

FIGURE 31-3

years were awarded for PCS networks operating in the range of 1850 to 1990 MHz. Manufacturers of terminal and infrastructure equipment subsequently reaped the benefits as PCS licensees set out to match cellular operators' coverage and build out new networks in major markets even more rapidly than did their cellular predecessors. Although cellular network equipment continues to account for the majority of the U.S. market, network equipment revenues for PCS are expected to grow to nearly half those of cellular equipment by the end of 1999.

Although there was some concern that PCS would capture a large portion of the prospective cellular market, the U.S. experience to date suggests that advances in digital and microcellular technologies, as well as competition from PCS, have stimulated purchases of new equipment by cellular carriers and consumers.

The United States is expected to remain the world's largest market for cellular/PCS equipment in 1998. CTIA reports that cumulative capital investment by such U.S. PCS operators totaled more than $46 billion in 1997, an increase of 72 percent over the $26.7 billion reported in 1996.

Infrastructure Equipment

The United States has been experiencing a peak period of wireless infrastructure development, and the marked increase in the sale of infrastructure equipment—switching systems, base stations, and operation support and maintenance systems—is expected to continue into early 1999. Growth after that time will depend on a number of variables, such as subscriber growth and antenna siting issues, some of which are difficult to predict.

In 1997 new license holders relied on infrastructure vendors for turnkey network services to meet their aggressive build-out schedules. The speed at which vendors are able to ship equipment was paramount, and suppliers of total systems had a competitive advantage over point-product suppliers. In addition, given the large number of systems to be financed, access to capital has become tight and many licensees are seeking vendor financing as a condition of sale. Many of the large PCS contracts awarded in the United States have been multivendor in nature.

The wireless infrastructure market continues to be dominated by a handful of global companies, among which U.S. manufacturers figure prominently. Ericsson (Sweden–United States), Motorola, Nokia (Finland–United States), Lucent, NorTel (Canada–United States), and Alcatel (France) are the major competitors. Many smaller vendors, however, view the growing PCS market as a major opportunity to strengthen their position.

The United States has the largest number of cell sites in the world. According to ABI, there were 38,700 cellular/PCS base stations in the U.S. market in 1997, representing about 31 percent of the world total of 126,000, an increase from 24,800 in 1996. This number was expected to increase to 57,300 in 1998 and surpass 120,500 by 2001. This would represent a CAGR of 28 percent. Much of this increase will arise from the fact that PCS systems generally require a larger number of antennas to cover the same geographic area covered by cellular networks because of the shorter range of signals at higher frequencies.

Although the pace of growth may subside as initial system construction is completed, DMG's survey of PCS carriers indicates that carriers in the United States have not scaled back their planned expenditures as a result of delays in antenna siting. By 2002 the U.S. share of the world's installed cell sites is expected to decrease to under 24 percent.

Sophisticated new antennas known as smart antennas represent a significant development in the infrastructure market. Smart antennas provide cellular operators with an economical method for expanding network service before, during, and after digital migration, as they allow new networks to be built with fewer base stations. Carriers also are expected to use this technology to expand their coverage into areas where it has not been cost-effective to operate. In addition, dramatic improvements in the quality of service will provide additional market stimulation. Other recent milestones include advances in repeater technologies (repeaters enable operators to expand coverage or enhance the capacity of a network), which have been shown to lower infrastructure costs as much as 45 percent.

The market for in-building wireless equipment for offices and other work environments remains largely untapped, and many vendors and carriers see wireless PBX (private branch exchange) offerings as a future growth opportunity in the next phase of PCS evolution. Wireless PBXs can employ unlicensed frequencies with system-specific handsets providing service to office, campus, and warehouse environments or, alternatively, provide in-building wireless capability as part of a wide-area service, essentially automatic roaming from a cordless phone to a cellular network when out of a specified range.

Subscriber Equipment

According to ABI, the total number of analog and digital cellular and PCS handsets shipped in the United States exceeded 12.5 million in 1997, representing an overall decrease of about 23 percent from the 1996 figure of 16.3 million, for a total estimated shipment value of $3.7 billion. Replacement handsets represented 4.8 million units, or about 38 percent of the total shipped. ABI projected that handset sales would level off to between 10 million and 12 million units in 1998, with an estimated value of $3.4 billion, and then begin to climb again in 1999. The number of handsets projected to be sold in 2001 in the United States ranges from 22 million to 27 million units.

Data on cellular handset exports became available for the first time in 1997 and revealed a trade surplus. The value of cellular handsets exported from the United States in 1997 was $1.8 billion, and the value of handsets imported into the United States was $1 billion. Hong Kong, considered the gateway to China, was the largest export market, with $348 million in 1997, followed by Israel with about $127 million. Regionally, U.S. suppliers exported about $835 million in handsets to the Asia and about $455 million to Latin America in 1997. On the import side, South Korea was the leading supplier of handsets to the U.S. market, with a value of $281 million.

ABI reported the average real price, compared with the often subsidized purchase price, of an analog handset in 1997 was about $150, a number that is is expected to decline further, although less precipitously than it did in previous years. The average real price of a digital handset, based on an assessment of 16 of the most widely bought models, was $338 in 1998. If high-end models such as the Nokia 9000 Communicator are factored in, the average real price of a digital handset was about $465 in 1998. These prices are expected to decline to between $220 and $250 by 2001, making them more attractive to a broader range of consumers.

One study noted that in 1997 more than 60 percent of all U.S. households had never used a cellular or PCS phone and three-fourths of that group had never considered buying one. Nonetheless, the image of wireless—the sense of elitism once evoked by the sight of a wireless handset user in a business attire—is fading rapidly because of increased public awareness and acceptance brought about by factors such as markedly decreasing costs, increased advertising, and an array of new features. Despite the decrease in sales in 1997, wireless handsets remain one of the fastest growing consumer electronics products.

For handset manufacturers unit sales will continue to exceed the number of new service customers by up to one-third because of the replacement handset market. While predicting handset sales worldwide—or in any individual market—has often proved difficult, one rule of thumb is that subscribers tend to replace their phones on average every 3 years. Analysts note that this cycle is likely to shorten as the transition to digital wireless continues and as handsets become more feature-rich and affordable.

Although price continues to drive the low-end market, other factors, including operating features, design, size, and weight, are still significant considerations in a medium- to high-end buyer's decision process (see Figure 31-4). Palm-sized handsets weighing as little as 68 to 100 grams were very popular in 1997

and 1998. Brand loyalty also was a major factor in buying decisions. One analytical group reported that about 73 percent of mobile professionals who intended to purchase a cellular phone within the next 6 months planned to stay with the brand they already owned. Among those using a Motorola, Nokia, or Ericsson phone, 86 percent planned to stay with the current brand. Other factors in buying decisions included battery life, which has increased significantly with lithium ion batteries, moving into the range of 5-day standby/5-hour talk times. Suppliers of cellular accessories, including batteries, chargers, carrying cases, hands-free kits, and data transmission accessories, continue to thrive as these items become increasingly important purchases.

Leading handset manufacturers in the U.S. market include Motorola, Ericsson, Nokia, Qualcomm/Sony, and NEC. According to some estimates, Motorola remained the number one supplier in the U.S. market for wireless phones in 1998, but its share has fallen about 30 percent in the past 3 years to just above one-third of the industry's sales. Although Motorola reportedly would continue to dominate overall handset sales in the U.S. market in 1998, Ericsson was expected to lead in sales of digital handsets, with Qualcomm a close second. [Ericsson is not expected to produce a code division multiple access (CDMA) handset in the near term, and much depends on the future development of CDMA in the U.S. market.] Finally, while 1998 will see a certain amount of consolidation in the existing handset market, it will also be the year when new suppliers enter the market.

Despite relatively healthy sales of analog handsets, 1997 saw a dwindling number of analog handset suppliers as carriers moved toward digitalization. Digital services are now available to 76 percent of the U.S. population (72 percent of the American populace have at least one PCS competitor). Some manufacturers, however, remain committed to the analog market in the United States through the sale of dual-mode (analog/digital) handsets, including Motorola, NEC, and Toshiba. Factory prices have gone below $100 for some analog handsets, and a significant portion of the customer base does not require the more sophisticated features offered in digital handsets. A market for analog handsets probably will continue to exist into the next century.

Clearly, however, as digital handset prices approach those of analog (some digital handsets reached the range of $150 to $200 in 1998), suppliers must position themselves for a digital future. Handset manufacturers are already feeling pressure from consumers and operators to further decrease prices, and margins are expected to continue to drop, thanks in part to the entrance of new vendors such as Philips, Siemens, and Samsung into the U.S. market. The migration to digital has caused the wireless handset industry to increase in-house research and development and distributors to carry only leading brands under the assumption that consumers are looking for recognizable brand names.

Wireless handset production in the United States is complicated by the challenge presented by multiple frequencies (800 and 1,900 MHz) and technologies [advanced mobile phone ser-

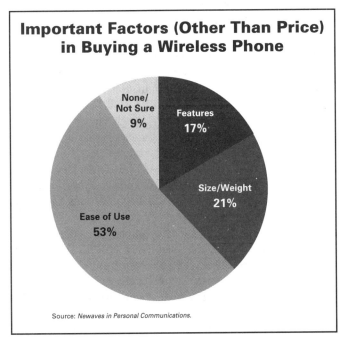

Important Factors (Other Than Price) in Buying a Wireless Phone

None/Not Sure 9%
Features 17%
Size/Weight 21%
Ease of Use 53%

Source: *Newaves in Personal Communications.*

FIGURE 31-4

vice (AMPS), code division multiple access (CDMA), time division multiple access (TDMA), and global system for mobile communications (GSM)]. Most successful handset manufacturers offer a broad product portfolio. Sales of handsets based on TDMA (IS-136) technology increased in 1997 and 1998 as a result of its adoption by the largest U.S. cellular operator, AT&T Wireless, as well as improvements in voice quality. While CDMA handset sales also have been growing steadily, the sale of TDMA handsets is expected to continue to outpace that of CDMA in the near term because of TDMA's 2-year head start in the market. Also, although additional CDMA manufacturers are preparing to enter the market, only a few companies were producing CDMA handsets in early 1998, and some cellular carriers were reportedly waiting for additional CDMA suppliers to enter the market before making a commitment to the technology. Sales of GSM handsets for PCS are also proliferating in the United States, with over 2 million subscribers in mid-1998.

Some chipset vendors have introduced software-driven programmable components that enable users to define and apply multiple standards in a single handset. Using parts that allow costs to be amortized across more than one system will help suppliers achieve economies of scale through a reduction in manufacturer inventory and shared design costs.

In 1997 cellular and PCS handset suppliers continued to use operators as distributors, although retail distribution also has been increasingly common. Subsidies for analog handsets of up to 100 percent offered for signing on to services continued to drive the cellular handset market. (In surveys, many consumers have stated that they prefer to defer the cost of a handset by buying a handset bundled with a service package.) The sale of digital cellular handsets is expected to accelerate because of the application of larger subsidies by service operators acting as distributors.

Smart Devices

New enabling technologies, including advanced silicon integrated circuits, software, and photonics, are creating increasingly sophisticated wireless terminal units, and the wireless equipment industry is entering what some analysts have dubbed the era of smart devices. Today's relatively tiny cellular/PCS phones, for example, have processing power comparable to that of the ordinary desktop PCs of less than a decade ago. In the future, the cellular terminal will become a portable platform for an array of new and advanced services for business and personal communications, information management, and even entertainment. Voice communications eventually will incorporate mobile multimedia—video and data—and enhanced services will proliferate as the industry moves into the next century. Smart products will further alter the way consumers view wireless communications and will markedly change the way wireless companies conduct business as new technologies provide new avenues for revenue generation.

Smart phones—the combination of a cellular phone and a personal data assistant to offer remote access to E-mail, fax, and short messaging services as well as voice capabilities—

emerged on the market as early as 1996. Their numbers grew modestly in 1997 and 1998; industry observer Herschel Shosteck estimated that wireless phones purchased for computer and fax use remained below 2 percent of the market in 1997. Smart phones are not expected to preempt the majority of devices on the market that serve primarily voice functions; instead, users are expected to continue to "mix and match" in the near term. Nevertheless, there is a significant market ready to support smart phones, and a growing number of suppliers are poised to go to market. AT&T Wireless, for example, is already marketing a Mitsubishi smart phone that uses cellular digital packet data (CDPD), a technology that allows data files to be broken into a number of packets and sent along channels of existing wireless voice networks. Cost remains an issue, however, and until smart phone prices break the $500 price point, they are not expected to grow at a pace comparable to that of today's basic voice handsets.

U.S. leaders in software platforms such as Microsoft and Sun are clearly interested in wireless smart products, and companies such as Unwired Planet and Geoworks are developing content for smart devices. Companies such as Wink Communications and Tacit Software are working on graphical interfaces and icons for portable devices to more easily and quickly exploit the capabilities of wireless operating systems and their applications. The development of higher-resolution screens on phones is expected in the near future, with color already available from some vendors. In addition, there have been technological advances in handset antennas, with some models having the antenna built into the case of the handset rather than using an external antenna.

Standards

Digitalization is a significant market driver in the wireless equipment market, and a battle between North American digital standards persists. CDMA, TDMA, and GSM 1900 are the three digital technologies vying for dominance, with competing claims regarding cost, capacity, voice quality, and enhanced service. While competing standards make various claims in regard to superiority, the evolution of wireless in the marketplace will make the ultimate determination.

All three standards probably will continue to coexist in the sizable U.S. marketplace and have enough supporters to create virtually nationwide coverage "footprints." Each standard has a supporting organization—the Universal Wireless Communications Consortium (UWCC) for TDMA, the CDMA Development Group (CDG), and the North American GSM Alliance—designed to promote the interests of their constituents. Many analysts see the issue of interoperability as largely a business question rather than a technology question. For example, AT&T Wireless offers a dual-band, dual-mode AMPS/TDMA phone that defaults to AMPS in areas where there is no TDMA coverage at 800 MHz or 1900 MHz. In 1997 and 1998 Qualcomm successfully demonstrated CDMA/GSM interoperability in a European trial.

In the future, as digital systems become more ubiquitous and new product generations become more software-driven and protocol-independent, standards may become less problematic and divisive. For example, mobile phones eventually may have the ability to automatically download the appropriate software supporting various air interface standards. Although dual-band, dual-mode phones have been on the market for some time, several manufacturers plan to introduce a triband "World Phone" within a year; Ericsson, for example, plans to market a GSM 900/1800/1900 handset in the near future. In addition, the industry is moving toward more open interfaces. With advances in digital signal processing technology, base stations are already moving toward software-configurable digital radios that enable system operators to easily customize their networks to support multiple communications standards based on specific market needs and business plans. Software radios have the principal advantage of replacing many hardware-based dedicated radios, thus minimizing space, power, and equipment as well as maintenance costs. Superconducting technologies are giving wireless carriers an increased ability to receive weaker signals more clearly, potentially reducing the number of base stations needed in a given area.

Paging

Leading a global trend, the U.S. paging industry is migrating from the Post Office Code Standardization Advisory Group (POCSAG) protocol, which has long been the industry standard, to Motorola's FLEX protocol. The capacity limits of the existing POCSAG systems and competition from other wireless services (such as cellular, PCS, and enhanced specialized mobile radio) have led U.S. paging operators to turn to high-speed protocols, such as FLEX, which allow for greater network capacity and two-way messaging. Nearly 20 major U.S. paging operators had adopted the FLEX protocol by May 1998. The two major FLEX system vendors are Motorola and Glenayre. There are no U.S. shipment data available for paging infrastructure and end-user equipment.

Projections of Industry and Trade Growth for the Next 1 and 5 Years

The U.S. wireless network equipment market is expected to surpass $14 billion in 1999. Some analysts are predicting that expenditures on wireless infrastructure equipment in the United States may begin to peak in 1999 and 2000, with one analytical group anticipating that capital spending in the United States will lag behind the overall global average. Other analysts note, however, that while the initial build-out for PCS was winding down in 1998, cellular carriers were accelerating their migration to digital technology to compete with PCS operators. Still others point out that over the next decade the number of licenses around the globe may triple, providing overseas sales opportunities that will keep the industry on a strong growth path.

Other market drivers include the growing need on the part of many businesses and consumers for additional phone lines as users begin to rely on a wireless phone as a supplementary voice channel or, more notably, for Internet access. Although Internet and data communications are driving spending on

telecommunications and computer equipment, voice communication continues to drive spending on wireless infrastructure and subscriber equipment. Over the longer term this shift toward data usage is expected to permeate the wireless sector as well.

DMG Technology Group has predicted that U.S. subscriber sales will pick up in 1998 as footprints grow, subscriber tariffs decline, and data strategies are clarified. While handset sales are expected to experience healthy growth, overall revenues are expected to level off and then decline as the average cost of handsets falls.

Global Market Prospects

Governments throughout the world are strongly committed to developing wireless networks. The reasons range from poor wireline infrastructures in developing countries to increasing consumer appeal in developed countries. Accordingly, major market drivers for wireless equipment in 1997 and 1998 were government actions—deregulation, liberalization, and privatization—driven, in turn, by lucrative revenues from the sale of the spectrum and the understanding that improving communications infrastructures will help attract needed foreign investment. As in the U.S. market, the conversion to digital technology is propelling sales of wireless equipment globally. Factors that will affect the market include the potential tripling of new licenses around the world over the next decade, higher overall use of wireless networks, the growth of wireless use for data transmission over the long term, and increasingly feature-rich services that require infrastructure upgrades.

Roughly half of all new telephones installed in the world in 1997 were wireless. The number of new subscribers worldwide increased by an estimated 63.2 million in 1997, bringing the total to 200 million. This represents a world penetration rate of 3.9 percent at the end of 1997, compared with 2.7 percent at the end of 1996. The vast majority of these subscribers are cellular users. PCS has continued to experience remarkable growth levels, with the number of global subscribers increasing 87 percent from 7.5 million at the end of 1996 to about 14 million at the end of 1997. By March 1998, this figure had surpassed 20 million and there were PCS systems in commercial operation or planned in 42 countries worldwide. Dataquest believes that the number of wireless subscribers will reach 265 million by the end of 1998. Many groups, including the ITU, expect subscribers to more than double by 2001, when as many as 500 million of the 1.4 billion telephones in the world are expected to be wireless. The European Commission estimates a world market of 2.5 billion users by 2015.

Total world expenditures for wireless infrastructure equipment are expected to reach $40 billion in 1998, an increase of 33 percent from the estimated $30 billion spent in 1997. This would represent 13 percent of overall worldwide expenditures for telecommunications equipment in 1998. Estimates vary widely on the projected size of the future market. DMG Technology Group has predicted that worldwide spending for infrastructure equipment should continue to increase in the range of 30 to 33 percent in 1998 and 1999 (see Table 31-4), reaching

$68 billion in 2000. Although other observers are more conservative, the worldwide wireless infrastructure market is expected to double between 1997 and 2000. (see Figure 31-5). This growth could be affected by an accelerated movement to next-generation wireless technology (discussed below). The peak for infrastructure spending in the United States and the rest of the world is at least several years away because of recently issued and anticipated licenses and improvements to existing networks that are needed to remain competitive and add capacity. For some U.S. suppliers, at least half the opportunities for sales of telecommunications equipment sales are overseas.

New network operators will continue to place a premium on the speed of network rollout as the time allowed to construct an operational network is being compressed by stringent license requirements and the perceived advantages of quick time to market. Consequently, the ability to deliver base stations on short lead times constitutes a definite advantage for infrastructure suppliers. The main criterion for winning new contracts (and renewing existing ones) in most cases is the ability to deliver base station equipment on a tight schedule in accordance with subscriber growth.

Of the more than 200 million wireless handsets in service worldwide at the end of 1997, analog units still predominated, with about 50 percent of subscribers using analog technology (mainly AMPS) and the remainder using digital or dual-mode phones. The share of analog is expected to decline markedly, however, to about 20 percent worldwide by 2002. GSM handsets are expected to be in the majority by then, with about 60 percent of the world share. Cahners In-Stat Group estimates that the value of the world handset market reached $33 billion in 1997 and project that it will increase slightly in 1998. Other analysts project that the market for subscriber handsets could grow as much as 17 to 20 percent annually. As in the United States, replacement handsets are expected to fuel the world market and may represent as much as 50 percent of new phone sales in 2000.

Some studies point out that cellular phone sales in certain developed regions, such as North America and Europe, may already be starting to plateau, noting that remaining demographic segments with low penetration levels (e.g., older and low-income consumers) may be poor sales prospects. As prices decline and profit margins narrow, sales revenues may decline in the near term. This trend may be mitigated if digital handsets prove to be more expensive than has been projected.

The wireless industry is having a significant impact on peripheral (component) industries. About 55 percent of the cost of a handset is accounted for by the electronics. The world market for integrated circuits used in wireless communications devices, for example, is expected to more than double by 2003, according to a 1998 report, growing from $5.3 billion to $13.7 billion.

A myriad of forces—economic, socioeconomic, political, technological, geographic, and regulatory—are influencing the global wireless equipment market, and although their impact often differs from region to region and country to country, there are certain commonalities. Virtually everywhere, for example, political and economic pressures dictate the creation of consortia in the bidding for new licenses, and political considerations often influence the selection of operators. Technologically, the migration to digital is also a major force in the aggregate world market.

Certain regional and country markets, however, have distinguishing characteristics. The European wireless marketplace has been characterized by a high level of cooperation between governments and operators in developing and implementing GSM technologies. North America, notably the United States, has chosen a more market-driven approach, and multiple standards are in use. Far from monolithic, the Asia/Pacific market must be examined on a country-by-country basis; while China's market has been burgeoning and seems to be relatively unscathed by the recent Asian financial crisis, currency woes have caused southeast Asian nations such as Thailand to reevaluate their planned rate of network development. Africa and the Middle East must also be disaggregated for analysis, as some of those countries have remarkably successful wireless markets (South Africa and Israel). Virtually all of Latin America is charging ahead with wireless network development, with some countries (Brazil and Mexico) proceeding far more rapidly than are others (Ecuador and Paraguay).

Asia/Pacific. Most analysts view the Asia/Pacific region as the regional wireless equipment market with the greatest potential for the future. Subscriber levels in that region grew from 45 million at the end of 1996 to 75 million at the end of 1997, representing about 38 percent of the world's subscriber base. The Strategis Group estimates there will be about 220 million subscribers in the region by 2002, for a regional penetration rate of about 6.5 percent, with significant variances by country. Japan and China are expected to remain the largest markets in the region, with China rapidly overtaking Japan's lead in the subscriber base. These two countries, along with South Korea and Australia, accounted for 82 percent of the Asia/Pacific sub-

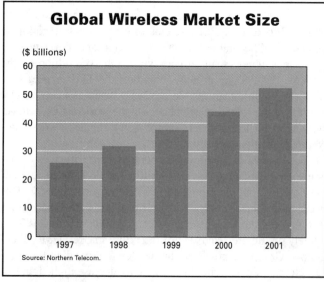

Global Wireless Market Size

($ billions)

Source: Northern Telecom.

FIGURE 31-5

scriber base at the end of 1997. All the countries in that region with the exception of a handful of smaller nations have at least three licensed wireless operators.

According to the Strategis Group, the number of handsets sold in the Asia/Pacific region is expected to increase from 34.8 million in 1997 to 54.2 million in 2001. Handset sales revenues (reflecting a notable decline in price per unit) for the entire region are expected to grow from about $18 billion in 1997 to $19.7 billion in 2001, with analog handsets garnering only about $316 million of the total in 2001.

Uncertainties in regard to continued growth include the economic impact of the Asian monetary crisis, since Asia is such an important market for wireless manufacturers. All major infrastructure manufacturers have significant exposure in Asia and are battling for position throughout that region. All countries involved in the current financial crisis have found it necessary to impose much stricter fiscal and monetary policies, and the crisis has altered suppliers' expectations and understanding of the market. Some forecasters have lowered their forecasts for certain countries in southeast Asia (Thailand and Malaysia), and a number of analysts predict that Japan's wireless market will cool somewhat until an economic recovery takes hold. Korea has sharply scaled back its development plans for the near term. By contrast, growth in China's wireless equipment market is expected to remain strong (Ericsson predicts that sales of mobile phones in China will go as high as 14 million units in 1998). Overall, despite a possible slowing of international investment, Asian countries are still committed to building out their infrastructures.

The Asia/Pacific region has adopted virtually every global wireless standard as well as a few that are unique to the region. The Pacific Digital Cellular (PDC) standard is limited to Japan and has the largest installed base in that region, with over 32 million subscribers in April 1998. Another digital wireless market segment in Japan is the Personal Handyphone Service (PHS). PHS has certain limitations; for example, the system does not lend itself to vehicular use or conventional roaming. The estimated 7 million PHS subscribers has been declining since mid-1997. This system has found acceptance in some Asian countries and has been approved for consideration in China.

GSM is the standard most widely used in the region at present, and Dataquest predicts that the Asia/Pacific GSM infrastructure equipment market will explode around 1999, exceeding all other regional markets by 2001. CDMA and TDMA are in use in a significant number of countries in that region. Telecom New Zealand, for example, is in the process of completely migrating its AMPS subscribers to TDMA. While CDMA was introduced in Hong Kong in 1995, its true foothold in Asia/Pacific is now South Korea, which, along with Singapore, selected CDMA as its national standard for PCS. South Korea has the largest CDMA subscriber base of any country in the world. Economic woes in South Korea in 1998 might have slowed the advance of CDMA networks there but also helped make Samsung more competitive in the world market.

Europe. Western Europe is expected to be a major battleground for wireless infrastructure manufacturers in the period 1998–1999. Every country except Switzerland had at least two wireless operators in 1997, and in the next few years each country in the region is expected to license from one to five new operators, all of which will have immediate infrastructure equipment needs. The handset market also expanded greatly in 1997; western Europe added about 20 million new subscribers, for a total of about 56 million subscribers, compared with 9 million new subscribers in 1996. A number of analysts predict that overall wireless penetration in western Europe will exceed 27 percent by 2001, with some projecting over 40 percent by 2006.

In addition to common technologies (GSM 900/1800) and favorable demographics [high per capita gross domestic product], analysts cite liberalization in the wireline sector as a major factor in the development of wireless in Europe, as this liberalization is expected to provide opportunities for both revenue growth and cost savings for wireless companies. Many existing network operators in Europe had a good revenue year in 1997 as the combined market capitalization of six of the largest European wireless operators nearly doubled. Relatively stable capital expenditures are projected for the next 2 years as competitive networks are built out. New services entrants, a decline in equipment prices resulting from increased competition, and the increased availability of dual-band (GSM 900 and GSM 1800) handsets will help propel the market.

The total GSM wireless infrastructure equipment market in Europe was estimated at over $10 billion in 1997. That market was expected to remain at about $10 billion in 1998 and to decline to about $8.6 billion in 2001, for a compound annual growth rate of −4.8 percent from 1997 through 2000. Ericsson, Nokia, NorTel, and Motorola remain the dominant base station suppliers in the western European market, with Ericsson and Siemens continuing to dominate the switching market. Other prospective entrants will have an uphill struggle to gain market share.

The sale of handsets in Europe was robust in 1997, and all those handsets were digital, as might be expected given the European Community's mandate to use GSM 900 and GSM 1800. Despite strong growth in wireless subscribers, however, the European market is among the regions cited in a number of studies which forecast a leveling off or potential decline in the value of handset sales. Total annual sales of cellular phones in Europe totaled 27 million in 1997, and while the number is expected to rise to 30 million by 2002, the average price of a handset in Europe is expected to decline about $100 per unit. Total revenue for handset sales in Europe therefore is expected to decline at a rate of 4.5 percent per year from about $9.3 billion in 1997 to $7.4 billion in 2002. Suppliers reportedly are planning to focus more attention on the GSM handset market in Asia, especially China; however, China has begun to manufacture its own GSM equipment.

Some U.S. manufacturers supply GSM equipment to carriers around the world. Compatibility has been established between Motorola's GSM base station and switches produced by Ericsson, Alcatel, Nokia, and Siemens. Motorola produces GSM equipment in Europe and has had considerable success with its lightweight, inexpensive GSM handsets. In May 1998 Motorola announced a $500 million GSM contract in Turkey, the largest GSM contract ever awarded.

Central and eastern Europe—especially Russia, with its estimated $200 million infrastructure market for 1998—remains a potentially huge market for wireless equipment if market access barriers such as complicated licensing procedures and burdensome testing and certification requirements can be resolved. At least one new license was awarded in virtually every country in that region in 1997, and there were close to 100 commercially operating systems there at the end of 1997. Improving economic conditions in countries such as Hungary, Slovenia, and Poland are creating environments for strong, sustainable growth of wireless equipment sales. Nokia, Ericsson, Siemens, and Motorola are the dominant equipment suppliers to that region. The total GSM infrastructure market in this region was estimated to exceed $1.2 billion in 1997 and is projected to reach $4.6 billion by 2001.

Canada and Latin America. In Canada new PCS licenses and the expansion and enhancement of existing networks in an effort to keep up with burgeoning demand have combined to expand opportunities in the wireless market. About 30 percent (3.2 million) of Canadian households reportedly own at least one wireless phone, and according to one study, another 1.3 million households are considering purchasing a wireless phone in the next year. Canada's wireless equipment market has been dominated by NorTel and Ericsson. Some analysts think that other suppliers, notably Lucent and Motorola, will make inroads into the market, assuming that CDMA continues to take hold.

The cellular telephone market in Mexico grew 70 percent in 1997, and the number of cellular subscribers in that country is expected to increase about 42 percent by 2000. The total cellular and PCS infrastructure market is expected to reach nearly $473 million in 2001. Motorola holds a strong equity position in four of the six independent cellular systems in Mexico and provides all the network equipment for those operations. Ericsson, through Telmex, plays a major role in the cellular and paging markets, and its equipment dominates Mexico's leading nationwide cellular system, Telcel. Qualcomm is building a nationwide PCS system based on CDMA technology.

Mexico's new regulatory authority has aggressively moved to auction parts of the spectrum, introduce competition in new sectors, and license new technologies. The auctioning of personal communications service licenses in nine regions of Mexico was completed in May 1998. Analysts estimate that total investment in Mexico's wireless communications sector (including cellular, fixed wireless, personal communications service, paging, and trunking) will be $400 million in 1997, $647 million in 1998, and $1.1 billion in 1999.

Telecommunications privatization and liberalization programs are spurring wireless growth in Central America and South America. Other market drivers include the low cost of development relative to wireline and the introduction of calling party pays and prepaid services. The Latin American cellular market is forecast to grow at a 45 percent CAGR up to 2000, with wireless lines approaching parity with wired lines. According to various assessments, cellular and PCS markets in Latin America will grow from around 10 million subscribers in 1997 to as many as 55 million in 2002. The Strategis Group projects that 60 percent of the subscriber base in Latin America will use GSM or TDMA IS-136 and that most of the remainder will use CDMA IS-95. Dataquest predicts that the total GSM infrastructure market in Latin America will rise from $122 million in 1997 to about $3.3 billion in 2001. The digital-AMPS IS-136 (TDMA D-AMPS) infrastructure market in Latin America is projected to grow to $14.7 billion in 2001. While CDMA has established a foothold in Latin America (Chile, Mexico, and Brazil), statistics on market size are not available.

Pent-up demand for basic telecommunications services made certain markets in Latin America particularly attractive for future investment and export opportunities. A number of telecommunications sectors in the region grew dramatically as a result of constitutional reforms allowing private sector participation. Brazil's state-owned telecom company, Telebras, for example, moved to privatize 27 cellular telephone spin-offs, representing the largest privatization in Latin American history, and issued 9 new Band-B licenses in 1997. These 27 entities were consolidated into 8 beginning in summer 1998 and auctioned off to private investors. Infrastructure equipment contracts in Brazil in 1997 were sizable; Ericsson, for example, signed a contract valued at $360 million with Tess in Brazil to supply a D-AMPS IS-136 (TDMA) network for the state of São Paulo. Global Telecom's DDI reports that its consortium will invest $1.5 billion in its Band-B licenses. In the cellular market alone the government expects 3.3 million new lines to be contracted for installation in 1997, 3.1 million in 1998, and 2.9 million in 1999.

Overall, the cellular market in Brazil was expected to boom in 1998, with even stronger growth predicted for 1999. DMG Technology Group predicts that Brazilian equipment opportunities may reach $3 billion to $5 billion over the next 3 years. In 2001 growth in this market should level off and eventually drop slightly as both Band-A and Band-B cellular carriers will have completed most of their infrastructure development and expansion to meet consumer demand. In 1997 NEC estimated its share of the $2 billion Brazilian cellular market at 36 percent, followed by Ericsson, NorTel, Lucent, and Motorola. Wireless infrastructure needs also are drawing suppliers to manufacture in-country; Motorola, for example, is producing analog as well as CDMA base stations at its newly constructed manufacturing facility in Brazil.

Other Latin American infrastructure and terminal equipment markets are growing rapidly. In Venezuela the number of cellular telephone subscribers nearly doubled in 1997, fueled by lower prices from the operators Telcel and Movilnet. Investments in the cellular sector to date have amounted to $558 million, but to maintain market share and cover the estimated demand in 2000, cellular operators will have to invest an additional $900 million. Chile became one of the first Latin American countries to launch PCS in March 1998, and other Latin countries are poised to follow its lead. Argentina and Colombia also planned to auction licenses for PCS networks in 1998.

Africa and the Middle East.   Africa was estimated to have about 2.26 million cellular users in mid-1998. With more than 1.8 million of those users, South Africa clearly dominates the African market. The second largest market is Egypt, which, with its growing middle class and commitment to privatization, had significant activity in 1997 and 1998. After a number of false starts, Egypt saw the addition of two new GSM operators. While other country markets, notably Morocco, Mauritius, and Ghana, are experiencing modest levels of market and investment growth, most other African nations are struggling with development plans.

Africa has a number of the characteristics of a regional wireless marketplace with good potential. Certainly the need for basic telephony exists, as many wireline networks are inadequate. In Lagos, for instance, only 10 percent of the population has access to a phone and copper fixed line networks are pilfered routinely. Cellular telephones are extremely popular in Africa; in fact, cellular service has become so popular in some countries that sometimes difficulties develop because of network congestion. There is a movement toward liberalization in countries such as Tanzania and Cote d'Ivoire, and increasing private sector participation in some countries. Prepaid packages have been extremely effective in driving the markets in certain African countries. South Africa's success offers a blueprint for the rest of the continent. Finally, African nations realize the need for communications capabilities to improve their economies.

Companies pursuing wireless opportunities in Africa have had to face their share of disappointments. In many countries there remains an unstable or confusing regulatory climate. Many Africans still view telephony in general and wireless telephony in particular as a luxury which the majority of the population cannot afford. With the exception of South Africa, handsets usually are not subsidized as they are elsewhere, and the cost of a basic handset can run as high as $1,000 or more in many countries. Economic stagnation, political unrest, and corrupt bureaucracies also have hampered progress. Getting equipment through customs can be difficult, and power sources are not always reliable; as a result, some networks have generators at each base station.

Most countries have multiple operators, and digitalization is taking hold. While Africa has many analog—AMPS, total access communications systems (TACS), and Nordic Mobile Telephone (NMT)—networks, digital networks are growing in number. GSM has become the dominant mobile technology, with a presence in 26 African countries. Siemens, Alcatel, and Ericsson are the dominant GSM equipment suppliers, often bringing attractive financing packages to the regional market. Motorola has sold both GSM and CDMA equipment in Africa. Zambia has a CDMA network, and Qualcomm has CDMA contracts in Congo and Nigeria. In addition, NorTel has supplied TDMA equipment to Africa.

The Middle East, which added more than 1 million subscribers in 1997, has had selected successes in wireless, and planned equipment expenditures are growing in scope. Israel dominates wireless subscribership in the Middle East, with 57 percent of the region's estimated 3 million subscribers in 1997. Israel was expected to spend an estimated $1 billion to set up its third mobile phone network in 1998. The New Territories of Palestine are also planning to establish a wireless network. A second GSM license has been issued in Jordan, and the Jordanian Mobile Telephone Services provider (Fastlink) is expanding its GSM network to extend coverage from the capital city of Amman to Aqaba.

Paging

In the paging industry, POCSAG has long been the global industry standard. However, as POCSAG systems are reaching capacity limits and other wireless services (such as cellular, PCS, and enhanced specialized mobile radio) are presenting stiff competition, the international paging industry is turning to high-speed protocols to allow for greater network capacity and two-way messaging services. An international battle is being waged between Motorola's FLEX high-speed messaging protocol and the European Radio Messaging Service (ERMES). FLEX, already the de facto global industry standard and industry leader in two-way messaging, was approved for use as an international standard by the Radiocommunications Sector of the International Telecommunication Union in 1997. This endorsement will further increase the acceptance and deployment of FLEX as an international protocol.

ERMES was developed as Europe's high-speed paging protocol, much as GSM was developed as that continent's digital cellular standard, and was recommended by the European Commission as a pan-European standard to be adopted by all EU nations. Unlike GSM, however, ERMES has not been as successful in its own region or outside. In 1990 the EC issued a recommendation that ERMES-based systems be deployed beginning in 1992 with the goal of covering 50 percent of western Europe's population by 1995 and 80 percent by 1997. At that time analysts estimated that the number of ERMES subscribers would reach 3 million by 1998. However, Europe's first ERMES-based system in France was not launched until 1994. As of mid-1997 there were only six ERMES systems in operation covering 10 percent of western Europe and a total of only 1 million ERMES subscribers worldwide. Nearly 95 percent of ERMES subscribers are in France and Saudi Arabia. Much of the failure of ERMES to develop as a robustly competitive high-speed paging standard can be traced to the competitive situation into which it was introduced. While GSM faced little competition from U.S. manufacturers, which had not united behind a common digital standard, ERMES faced Motorola's FLEX high-speed protocol, which was already becoming the de facto standard in Europe and other regions. Additionally, ERMES networks were slower to deploy than originally was anticipated, and some ERMES systems, such as Germany's operators, encountered interference problems. The ITU's approval of FLEX for use as an international standard has put ERMES at a further competitive disadvantage. There are currently six countries in Europe with commercially available

ERMES-based systems and four countries with FLEX-based networks in operation; by 2003 it is estimated that 50 percent of western European subscribers will use high-speed paging systems. With the ITU stamp of approval, it is possible that some current POCSAG operators that need to upgrade their systems to a high-speed paging protocol will opt for the more commercially successful FLEX standard.

As a result of the trend toward high-speed paging in general and the FLEX standard in particular, the Strategis Group estimates that paging equipment sales in western Europe will see POCSAG's market share decline from 61 percent in 1998 to 15 percent in 2003, while the market share of FLEX will rise from 15 percent to 45 percent and that of ERMES will increase from 25 percent of the total market to 40 percent. In western Europe the leading markets for paging growth are expected to be France, the United Kingdom, Spain, Germany, and the Netherlands.

In Asia and Latin America FLEX has long been a de facto international standard. In the Asia/Pacific region nearly every major country had at least one FLEX-based system in operation in 1997. The Strategis Group estimates that the number of FLEX users will rise from 8 million in 1997, or 10 percent of the total market, to 47 million subscribers, or 28 percent of the region's total subscriber base, by 2002. There are no commercially available ERMES systems in Asia. As a result of this trend, FLEX pager sales are projected to double from 20 percent of total pager sales in 1998 to 40 percent in 2002. FLEX is expected to show its most significant gains in some of the region's fastest growing markets for paging: China, Taiwan, South Korea, and India.

FLEX has long been the de facto standard in Latin America as well, which traditionally aligns its telecommunications standards with North American rather than European protocols. FLEX-based systems are currently in operation in Argentina, Bolivia, Brazil, Chile, Colombia, Costa Rica, the Dominican Republic, Mexico, Peru, Uruguay, and Venezuela. Pagemart Wireless Inc., which provides messaging services to over 2.5 million subscribers through an extensive alliance of paging carriers in the United States, Canada, Mexico, Central America, and the Caribbean, recently announced plans to launch a FLEX-based system. There are no ERMES systems in operation in Latin America.

There are approximately 1.5 million paging subscribers in the Middle East. ERMES was introduced in that region and has established a strong presence in countries such as Saudi Arabia, which has expanded its ERMES network to have the capacity for 1 million subscribers covering 44 cities, making it the largest ERMES network in the world. Many Middle Eastern companies (including Iran's Telecommunications Co.; Jordan's United Saudi Communications; Kuwait's Mobile Communications Company; Saudi Arabia's Ministry of Post, Telegraph and Telecommunications; Turkey's Turk Telecom; and the United Arab Emirates' Etisalat) have signed onto the ERMES Memorandum of Understanding Association. However, FLEX has been adopted by Qatar, Jordan's Radio Paging, Palestine, a second operator in Turkey, and Israel's Beeper Paging. The adoption of FLEX as an international standard by the ITU probably will lead other regional operators to consider adopting FLEX instead of ERMES.

Although Africa's telecommunications infrastructure lags behind that in the rest of the world, the ITU's approval of the FLEX standard is expected to drive the installation of FLEX systems there, particularly in the region's paging hub, South Africa. In South Africa only one national system operates on the FLEX protocol; all other paging systems operate on the POCSAG protocol. South Africa's paging industry has seen its share of wireless subscribers decline as newly introduced cellular services provide direct competition and POCSAG systems reach their capacity limits. Two-way paging could potentially revive the paging market in South Africa.

Wireless Local Loop

Despite a relatively slow evolution to date, wireless local loop (WLL), or fixed wireless access (FWA), telephony is an auspicious market which is expected to expand dramatically. By the end of 1997 more than 60 countries, primarily in the developing world, had implemented WLL systems or trials, for a combined total of about 2 million subscriber lines contracted. The WLL market was expected to approach an estimated $3 billion in 1997.

U.S. firms with varying degrees of experience in the cellular market—Motorola, NorTel, Hughes Network Systems, and Qualcomm—play a commanding role in the WLL market segment and have won the vast majority of WLL system contracts. Most of these systems are based on existing cellular and PCS standards and have limited data capabilities. A number of vendors, such as InterDigital, which offer systems based on proprietary protocols have been successful internationally. In March 1998 InterDigital formed the Broadband CDMA Alliance with Siemens, Samsung, and Alcatel to market its Truelink WLL solution, which claims to offer features such as high-speed data transmission and Internet access. Lucent Technologies, a relatively late entrant into the FWA market, has a broad portfolio of WLL products but appears to be focusing on its proprietary AirLoop system. Other new WLL technologies are on the horizon, including synchronous code division multiple access (SCDMA) and convolutional ambiguity multiple access (CAMA). SCDMA technology, developed under China's Ninth Five-Year Plan (1996–2000), will wirelessly connect switches with users and will go into production soon. CAMA, developed in the United States, promises far lower investment costs per subscriber compared with the systems currently being marketed.

The slow pace of WLL growth to date can be attributed to a variety of factors. First, most of the systems being marketed are derivatives of established cellular and/or PCS standards. Although little in the way of additional R&D is required, the R&D costs for the development of the associated mobile technologies have kept the investment cost per subscriber line comparable to that of wired networks. Second, there are no common standards or frequency allocations for WLL, and many competing solutions, a source of potential confusion among customers. In addition, wireless vendors often sell to different customers—

landline telephone companies rather than new wireless licensees. However, WLL solutions offer many advantages, such as quick installation, the ability to match investment with demand, and ease of maintenance.

As costs have continued to decline, the pace of orders for and deployment of WLL systems is clearly beginning to accelerate. For example, India recently announced plans to build WLL systems in 11 cities. In Bombay, India's most populous city, the licensee is installing a $200 million WLL system. In May 1998 Mexico completed an auction of eight WLL licenses. Qualcomm, through its partnership in a winning consortium, will build a nationwide CDMA WLL network in Mexico.

Data on international telecommunications clearly show a lack of access to basic service throughout the developing world. Although global teledensity, as reported by the ITU, reached an estimated 13.7 percent in 1997, that average conceals the immense disparity in teledensity levels, which range from less than 1 percent to as high as 99 percent. ITU calculations show that 62 percent of all main telephone lines at the beginning of 1997 were installed in just 23 developed countries, even though this group (the United States, Canada, the European Union, Japan, Australia, New Zealand, Switzerland, Norway, and Iceland) accounts for less than 15 percent of the world's population. Over 950 million households in the world, or 65 percent of the total, do not have telephones. Outside the high-income countries, only 16 percent of households have telephones. Although admittedly an inaccurate indicator of the true level of unmet demand, the number of people officially registered as waiting for a telephone line amounted to 42 million in 1996, pointing to a tremendous pent-up demand for basic telephony.

Given the demonstrated need for telephone infrastructure as well as cost sensitivity in the developing world, it is widely assumed that wireless technologies will be the predominant means of meeting this demand in the future. As WLL equipment will be increasingly cost-competitive with wired equipment over the next several years, it will be a likely choice for improving universal service. The pace of WLL growth is expected to accelerate considerably to over $15 billion in revenues by 2002, driven by rapidly declining subscriber line costs. ABI estimates that this level of WLL deployment will generate $36 billion in infrastructure expenditures by 2002, when subscribers could number 60 million (see Figure 31-6). Between 2002 and 2006 WLL growth should be even more dramatic, surpassing 200 million users.

In developed countries, landline providers have extensive networks, high data rates, high voice quality, and low, flat-rate pricing models. These are characteristics that wireless cannot match at present. As a result, it is difficult to make a convincing business case for constructing a WLL or fixed system that will compete with the landline provider. Nonetheless, there are already a few examples of WLL systems being installed in developed countries, such as Ionica in the United Kingdom and 21st Century Telecom, a PCS licensee, in the United States. As technological developments drive improvements in wireless voice quality and data rates toward levels comparable with those of wireline and competition makes volume levels of cus-

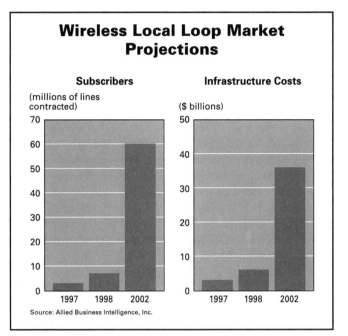

FIGURE 31-6

tomer usage more affordable, a shift toward increased implementation of WLL in developed countries should begin.

Third Generation
Efforts to develop a third-generation (3G) standard that will lead the wireless community into the new millennium intensified in 1997 and 1998 (analog cellular is considered the first generation, and digital cellular/PCS the second generation). Although these systems are not expected to be deployed until 2002 at the earliest, with the possible exception of Japan, the stakes for equipment vendors are potentially enormous. All the major wireless vendors are jockeying for position, forcing a contentious debate over next-generation standards long before second-generation cellular and PCS technologies hit their stride and before demand for the new services is apparent.

The 1992 World Radio Conference identified 1,885 to 2,025 MHz and 2,110 to 2,200 MHz as intended for use on a worldwide basis by administrations that wanted to implement Future Public Land Mobile Telecommunications Services. The ITU now refers to these third-generation systems as International Mobile Telecommunications 2000 (IMT-2000) because they will be introduced early in the next decade. IMT-2000 is envisaged as having a single, universal air interface that will enable global roaming, high-speed data capability, and new mobile multimedia services such as full-motion video. In addition, the minimum performance capabilities for data transmission established by the ITU were 144 kbps at vehicular speeds, 384 kbps at pedestrian speeds, and 2 Mbps in fixed applications—data transmission rates that are many times higher than those available with the current generation of mobile telephone systems. In April 1997 the ITU issued a request for technical proposals, which had to be submitted by June 1998. The ITU has chosen December 1999 as the time frame for completing the development of its IMT-2000 recommendation.

In mid-1997 the European Telecommunications Standards Institute (ETSI) solicited a debate on next-generation wireless technology for the European market in which it explicitly cited an urgent need to preserve the competitiveness of the European telecommunications industry. Five of the world's seven leading wireless equipment vendors are European. After considering five proposed standards, in January 1998 ETSI announced a consensus declaration between the final two candidate technologies—wideband CDMA (W-CDMA) and TDMA/CDMA (TD-CDMA)—for Universal Mobile Telecommunications Service (UMTS), the European name for IMT-2000. The compromise reached between the two groups of manufacturers (nine companies in total) was to adopt W-CDMA for the paired bands identified in 1992 and adopt TD-CDMA for the unpaired bands. In conjunction with ETSI's decision, the name was changed to UMTS Terrestrial Radio Access (UTRA). Japan's standards body also endorsed ETSI's decision. This Japanese support increases the likelihood of UTRA at least becoming a de facto international standard, reminiscent of the path of GSM. In February 1998 the European Commission issued a proposal for the coordinated introduction of 3G among its member countries, directing the member states to license the IMT-2000 band exclusively for UTRA and thus mandating its preferred air interface.

Soon after the ETSI announcement, Lucent, Motorola, Nor-Tel, and Qualcomm joined with the CDG to begin to develop 3G specifications that would enable current CDMA operators to evolve their networks to the next generation, which is not possible with W-CDMA. These efforts resulted in a wideband version of the U.S. CDMA standard, which is called CDMA2000. Although the terminology is similar to that for the ETSI standard, the two standards have significant differences. The goal of CDMA2000 is to give existing CDMA operators the ability to leverage their considerable investment in second-generation digital networks with a clear migration path to 3G. The UWCC also developed a 3G version of its TDMA standard. The United States submitted four proposals to the ITU.

Given the pace and immense amount of investment by wireless operators in second-generation wireless infrastructure, estimated at $200 million at the end of 1997, and the expected introduction of global satellite systems by the end of 1998, an argument can be made for at least partial backward compatibility with second-generation systems. Moreover, there are no solid indications of significant levels of demand for broadband applications and global interoperability, particularly in the near term. Some technology leaders are calling for the development of a converged standard which would incorporate the best features of each technology, allowing backward compatibility with existing systems and breathing room for 3G demand to develop.

Even before the deadline for proposals, efforts to harmonize several of the leading proposals were under way. An ETSI work group dealing with modulation issues released a joint paper in May 1998 that could put everyone on the same higher data rate path and utilize much of the same physical equipment infrastructure hardware. The ITU has already endorsed a "family of systems" concept on the network side, under which both the European "GSM map" and the U.S. IS-41 internetworking standards will be interoperable, narrowing the debate to the air interface. Technical discussions involving regional standards bodies from Europe, the United States, Japan, and South Korea suggest that convergence is possible in a way that will allow the 3G air interface to provide evolution paths from both systems. However, ETSI has refused to modify its decision on the W-CDMA air interface.

If industry efforts to unify the proposals prove unsuccessful, multiple 3G standards are likely to emerge. Although the maximum benefits of economies of scale for manufacturers and operators will not be realized, sizable markets are still anticipated and seamless roaming is still feasible. Interoperability is increasingly becoming a fact of life, as evidenced by the successful implementation of AMPS-PCS 1900 handoff in North America and GSM-CDMA trials in the United Kingdom. In July 1998 Japanese carriers are expected to inaugurate second-generation CDMA systems which will have the capability of automatically roaming on the Japanese digital cellular (PDC) network.

A key issue which also needs to be resolved concerns intellectual property rights, since all proposed standards submitted to the ITU must be "open" standards in terms of such rights. ETSI is in the process of gathering information about intellectual property rights for its W-CDMA proposal, although U.S. firms are expected to be in a very strong position as inventors of CDMA technology. The intellectual property rights issue has become highly politicized, since CDMA technology has been all but barred from the European market to date.

Japan may well be the first country to commercially deploy a 3G network, which is planned for the end of 2000 or 2001. Motorola and Lucent will be conducting 3G trials in Japan based on CDMA2000 technology. Separately, NTT has awarded a $60 million development contract to Ericsson, Nokia, and Lucent for W-CDMA. For the first time in the wireless sector Japan has made a clear decision to utilize global standards.

In Europe, where the market is expected to reach at least $100 billion by 2005, telecommunications ministers of the European Union tentatively approved a draft plan in May 1998 that would give carriers in the 15-country alliance until January 2000 to come up with interconnection treaties and licensing rules for UMTS. The United Kingdom and the Netherlands are already making plans to issue UMTS licenses, with the United Kingdom planning to auction these licenses in 1999, while the Netherlands anticipates a 2-year time frame. In Germany, Ericsson and two German GSM network operators are conducting a W-CDMA research and evaluation project that will last for about a year. The project will generate practical experience regarding the use of 3G technology, which can be integrated into ongoing standardization activities. To the extent that the EU is accelerating not only the debate but implementation plans, European vendors could have an advantage in this process.

An important issue for the United States, with global repercussions, is that the U.S. spectrum allocation for PCS occupies a portion of the band that was identified for IMT-2000 back in 1992. With the increased focus on 3G, manufacturers of PCS infrastructure are already finding that some governments are reluctant to authorize such services based on the U.S. band plan because it may jeopardize their choices in the future in regard to IMT-2000. Although U.S. operators are free to deploy 3G services in their existing spectrum allocation and some may decide to roll out the services as an overlay in areas where they expect sufficient demand, the lack of dedicated 3G spectrum, compounded by the reversal of the base transmit/mobile receive bands with IMT-2000, in practical terms may increase the likelihood of multiple 3G standards.

The decision on a 3G air interface standard will have enormous implications for both suppliers and operators because it will determine how much of the existing wireless networks can continue to be utilized. It is unclear whether the ITU's consensus-building process will be successful in resolving the outstanding differences among proponents of the technologies under consideration. The financial stakes in these 3G standards decisions are very high. Each technology has different economic beneficiaries, and all the factions are well capitalized, are politically powerful, and have vested interests stemming from their existing installed bases. Vendors are already forming strategic alliances, often based on the core competencies of each firm, and devoting substantial R&D dollars to 3G. Some are hedging their competitive positions by participating in multiple working groups. Phone chips for W-CDMA are being developed and tested, and manufacturers are beginning to evolve terminal equipment for data applications such as wireless E-mail and Internet. Development efforts on all fronts are likely to intensify over the next several years.

Once a standard is adopted for the air interface, it could take 1½ to 2 years before the equipment is commercialized (mid-2001 or 2002). Thus, at this juncture the precise impact of 3G on equipment demand is difficult to predict. Although it is clear that the majority of the world's wireless operators will have to replace a substantial portion of their infrastructure, it is less clear how quickly they will move to do so.

Linda Gossack Astor, Richard H. Paddock, and Cecily A. Cohen, U.S. Department of Commerce, Office of Telecommunications, (202) 482-4466, November 1998.

SATELLITE COMMUNICATIONS SYSTEMS

The satellite telecommunications equipment sector consists of satellites and associated ground equipment used for voice, data, and video transmission. The ground segment includes telemetry, tracking, and control as well as receivers ranging in size from 30-meter earth stations to hand-held receivers. It does not include space and ground segment equipment associated with remote sensing meteorology, nor does it include boosters and launch facilities. The sector may include some SIC-coded equipment, but it is not SIC-coded as an entity.

Satellite communications systems may be divided into two categories: the space segment and the ground segment. The space segment includes the satellite itself and the satellite subsystems which are placed in orbit around the earth. The satellite consists of several major components, including transponders or channels, a power system (battery modules and solar panels), an antenna system, a command and control system, and satellite housing. The ground segment includes equipment used to receive and/or transmit signals to the satellites in orbit and consists of everything from large earth stations used for tracking, telemetry, and control of the satellite to dishes as small as 18 to 24 inches which are used by consumers to receive direct broadcast satellite services. Telemetry, tracking, and control systems are used to monitor the operations of satellites. Telemetry involves reporting the status of satellite systems, such as voltage, current, temperature, and transponder configuration. Tracking equipment is used to enable controllers to locate a satellite's exact position and track the direction of the antennas. Control equipment entails sending commands to a satellite to operate systems, configure transponders and antennas, and perform orbital maneuvers such as adjusting the position of the satellite in orbit.

Global Industry Trends

Via Satellite reported that there were 192 commercial communications satellites in geostationary earth orbit (GEO) in May 1998 and 67 more GEO satellites on order. (The geostationary orbit is the orbit 22,237 miles above the earth at which a satellite appears to move at the same rotational speed as the surface of the earth, therefore appearing to stay "fixed" over a specific place. Since the launch of the first satellite in 1957, satellites have traditionally been placed in this orbit to provide the most efficient global service.) The number of GEO contracts signed annually has been declining since a peak of 36 in 1995 (there were 25 contracts in 1996 and 21 in 1997). Advances in technology and new applications for satellites ensure that the market for GEO satellites will remain stable in the near term and that overall growth in the satellite manufacturing industry will continue to expand. Satellites have traditionally been used to provide voice and telecommunications services, but applications such as direct broadcast satellite (DBS) services, mobile telephone services, Internet access, and data broadcasting will expand their use significantly.

According to a market survey completed by Euroconsult in March 1998, satellite operators worldwide will order approximately 300 GEO satellites over the next 10 years (approximately 30 orders per year). These satellites will be worth an estimated $30 billion to $38 billion. Euroconsult notes that nearly 500 non-GEO satellites were under contract as of February 1998, but it is unclear how many of those satellites will be launched. Over the past few years a wide variety of systems have been proposed to offer many similar satellite-based services. Because of regulatory hurdles, increased competition, and financing needs, many of these systems may not be implemented.

The strongest competition to U.S. manufacturers for GEO commercial communications satellite contracts comes from

European manufacturers such as Aerospatiale (France), Matra Marconi (France–United Kingdom), Alcatel (France), and Alenia Aerospazio (Italy). The primary customers for these companies include the European Telecommunications Satellite Organization (Eutelsat), Société Europeenne des Satellites (SES), and the European Space Agency (ESA). A new privately owned European satellite company was expected to be created in 1998. Tentatively called Société Commune des Satellites (SCS), it would include all of Alcatel's satellite activities as well as the satellite manufacturing arm of Aerospatiale. This would leave Matra Marconi, SCS, and Alenia Aerospazio as the main satellite manufacturers in Europe. U.S. companies have been in direct competition with these companies in numerous tenders in Europe and the Middle East.

Additional countries, such as Japan, Russia, Canada, India, China, and Israel, are active in the manufacture of communications satellites for domestic use; they also export parts, components, and subassemblies to U.S. satellite manufacturers. Japan continues to pose a serious competitive challenge to U.S. manufacturers of advanced components and parts. In Japan, Mitsubishi Electric Corp., NEC, and Toshiba produce internationally competitive satellite components but have not yet served as primary contractors for complete satellites. The government of Japan has funded a satellite called the *Unmanned Space Experiment Recovery System* (*USERS*), which will give Mitsubishi significant experience in integrating satellite components. The satellite is scheduled to be launched early in 2001. Many analysts believe that these Japanese companies will have the ability to manufacture GEO commercial communications satellites within 5 years.

Russia has a significant domestic satellite manufacturing capacity. It has built many satellites for domestic use but has not been successful in selling its satellites to overseas customers. Nauchno-Proivzvodstvenoe Obiedinenie Prikladnoi Mekhaniki (NPOPM) is the leading designer of Russian satellites, and RSC Energiya and JSC Gascom are also involved in satellite manufacturing.

Although contracts from international organizations such as the International Telecommunications Satellite Organization (INTELSAT) and the International Mobile Satellite Organization (INMARSAT) and U.S. and foreign government entities continued to represent a significant market for the satellite industry in 1997, contracts from privately owned customers are on the rise. This increase in private contracts may be attributed to some extent to the trend toward privatization of telecommunications institutions in many areas of the world. Even INTELSAT recently finalized a plan to spin off six of its satellites into a new private entity tentatively dubbed New Skies. INMARSAT is moving forward with plans to privatize by January 1, 1999.

According to *Via Satellite,* among the 192 commercial communications satellites in GEO orbit, 44 serve the Asia/Pacific region, 40 serve Europe, 10 serve Latin America, and 8 serve the Middle East and north Africa. Two satellites are expected to serve Africa in the near future: An American Mobile Satellite Corporation (AMSC) satellite will provide mobile telephone service, and WorldSpace's Afristar satellite will provide digital

audio broadcasting services beginning in April. The Regional African Satellite Communications Organization (RASCOM) recently issued a tender for a satellite to provide rural telephony, television, and radio services to Africa. The financial crisis in Asia has had an impact on the satellite market there, with two programs being placed on hold. Many analysts view the impact as temporary, stating that the demand for rural telephony and telecommunications services is so great that satellites will certainly play a role in that region. Space Systems/Loral (SS/L) was forced to downsize by an estimated 300 employees in January 1998 because of uncertainty about future orders from customers in Asia. The temporary downturn in the Asia/Pacific region has generated renewed interest in Latin America. Developments such as the rapid growth of direct-to-home (DTH) services in that region and a joint venture between Loral Skynet and SatMex ensure that Latin America will present significant opportunities in the long term.

With advances in satellite technology, the number of manufacturers of small satellites has increased. These satellites orbit the earth at much lower altitudes [500 to 1,000 miles for low earth orbit (LEO) and 4,000 to 7,000 miles for medium earth orbit (MEO) as opposed to 22,237 miles for geostationary orbit]. As these satellites have become much more powerful and are in orbit much closer to the earth, the reception device does not need to be as powerful and is therefore much more compact. Instead of the larger earth stations that are necessary to receive signals directly from a GEO satellite, hand-held cellularlike phones can easily receive signals from a LEO or MEO satellite. U.S. manufacturers of these small satellites include Boeing, Motorola, Orbital Sciences, Spectrum Astro, and TRW. As companies rush to offer services using LEO and MEO satellites, the market for these small satellites will continue to grow substantially. For example, the Teledesic system, which promises to offer broadband services such as Internet, two-way videoconferencing, and telemedicine services in 2002, plans to build 288 satellites over the next 5 years to operate its service.

A clear trend of truly global ventures has emerged in the market for small satellites for use in the LEO and MEO systems. As providers have attempted to find the best technology, the lowest prices, and guaranteed access to markets all over the world, U.S. and foreign companies have formed numerous partnerships. Globalstar, for example, has established strategic partnerships with DACOM/Hyundai (South Korea), France Telecom/Alcatel, Daimler-Benz (Germany), and Alenia Spazio (Italy). Major components of the Globalstar satellites will be built at Loral's facilities in northern California, but the final assembly and testing of the satellites will be done in Italy by Alenia Spazio. As an increasing number of international ventures are created, it becomes more difficult to identify precisely the U.S. contribution to many of these ventures. However, the United States is still considered the world leader in the advanced technologies that are critical to the success of these projects.

U.S. government export controls continue to have an impact on the ability of U.S. companies to enter into joint venture projects overseas. As many countries seek to develop their own satellite manufacturing capacities, export controls and technology transfer issues have a significant impact on the ability of U.S. companies to enter into joint ventures with government and private entities in countries such as Russia and China.

Satellite manufacturing and sales have been strong in the 1990s. Although many observers predicted that satellite companies would lose out to fiber-optic competitors in the late 1980s and early 1990s, satellites have been resilient as a result of the inherently global "instant" infrastructure they provide. In fact, more GEO satellites have been launched in the 1990s than were launched in the preceding three decades combined.

Domestic Trends

The United States leads the world in satellite manufacturing. Hughes Space and Communications, Lockheed Martin Telecommunications, and Space Systems/Loral are the top manufacturers of traditional commercial communications satellites built for operation in geostationary orbit. (Aerospatiale, Alcatel, Alenia Spazio and Daimler-Benz sold their shares of Loral in February 1997, rendering Loral a majority U.S.-owned company). While Hughes, Lockheed Martin, and SS/L remain the key U.S. players in the manufacture of large communications satellites, Boeing, Motorola, Orbital Sciences, Spectrum Astro, and TRW are gaining increased recognition for the manufacture of small satellites to be used for a variety of emerging satellite services. An SIA/Futron Corporation report estimates that in 1996 the United States held approximately 59 percent of the global satellite manufacturing market. This share increased to 61.5 percent ($8.3 billion out of $13.5 billion, including payments to subcontractors) by the end of 1997 (see Figure 31-7). The report notes that satellite manufacturing supported approximately 57,340 jobs in the United States.

U.S. suppliers dominate the world satellite manufacturing industry in regard to large GEO satellites and are also very competitive in the manufacture of the small satellites that will be

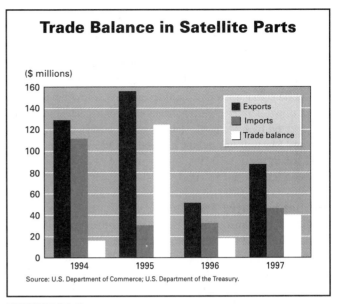

Trade Balance in Satellite Parts

($ millions)

Source: U.S. Department of Commerce; U.S. Department of the Treasury.

FIGURE 31-8

used in LEO and MEO systems. Because of customs tracking procedures, U.S. government statistics for exports of communications satellites (HS 8802.60.3000) are representative only of the countries where satellites are launched. Since only a few countries have commercial communications satellite launch facilities, the statistics are not useful in tracking the number of satellites that are sold to entities in foreign countries.

Via Satellite's "1997 Global Satellite Survey" reported that Hughes has built more than one-third of the GEO satellites in orbit and has contracted to build more than a quarter of those under construction. Lockheed Martin and SS/L are strong competitors and will continue to challenge Hughes' leadership in this area. The manufacturing of GEO satellites is highly capital-intensive, and the nature of the process does not encourage new competitors. Lockheed Martin, Hughes, and SS/Loral have upgraded their satellite manufacturing facilities over the last few years to implement more efficient modular manufacturing practices. This involves reducing complexity by lowering the number of parts and part types, simplifying design and testing procedures, moving toward assembly-line production processes, using common buses, and tailoring user payloads. The implementation of these procedures has resulted in lower costs as well as a reduction in the length of time it takes to manufacture a large GEO satellite from more than 30 months to 18 to 24 months.

U.S. manufacturers also contribute technology to many of the commercial communications satellites made today. U.S. government trade statistics indicate a positive trade balance for U.S.-made parts for communications satellites (HS 8803.90.3000) from 1994 to 1997 (see Figure 31-8). U.S. exports of satellite parts totaled $88 million in 1997, up from $52 million in 1996. Nonetheless, U.S. exports have fallen dramatically from a peak of $156 million in 1995. This drop in U.S. exports of satellite parts may be attributed to several factors, including an increase in the technological capabilities of manufacturers in other countries.

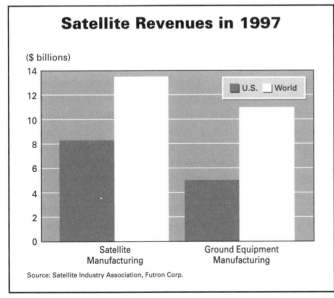

Satellite Revenues in 1997

($ billions)

Source: Satellite Industry Association, Futron Corp.

FIGURE 31-7

The satellite ground equipment industry includes manufacturers of large fixed earth stations, complex telemetry, tracking, and control equipment, very small aperture terminals (VSATs), direct broadcast satellite dishes, and mobile satellite receivers. An earth station is a piece of equipment that can send or receive a satellite signal and consists of an antenna, a low-noise amplifier, a down-converter, and receiver electronics. The high end is represented by large earth stations which cost between $1 million and $10 million, and the low end by DBS receivers that are sold for as little as $199. In the middle, VSATs are priced between $3,000 and $15,000.

Global Industry Trends

Euroconsult estimated that 21.4 million earth stations were sold worldwide in 1996, accounting for over $18 billion in total annual sales. Euroconsult predicts that 108.7 million earth stations will be sold in 2006, with sales of $46 billion (see Table 31-5). Growth in this market may be attributed to several factors: technological improvements that have led to smaller, less expensive, and more sophisticated equipment; global deregulation; and new satellite applications which have translated into higher demand for equipment to utilize satellite technology. Ten years ago satellites were used primarily for telecommunications and television delivery services. New services such as DBS, expanded VSAT applications for business, mobile telephone systems, and satellite radio will help boost the ground equipment market to new heights. Several industry analysts note that the ground segment for supporting space systems is one of the single largest markets in the space industry and is typically the most underestimated. Frost & Sullivan predicts that VSAT, DBS, and mobile terminals will drive the future growth of the ground equipment industry.

Large Earth Stations. Large earth stations used for "fixed" (the receiver is not mobile) telecommunications services are still in demand in developing countries. Developed regions such as North America and Europe tend to utilize the extensive terrestrial wireline infrastructure and do not rely as heavily on satellites for telephone service. The Asia/Pacific and Latin American regions, however, utilize satellites to provide quick and efficient service to both densely populated urban areas and hard-to-reach rural areas. Some analysts predict that satellite-delivered telephone services will decrease in use as the terrestrial infrastructure develops in these areas. Although many regions of the world are still in dire need of telecommunications

services (including India, China, and Africa), satellites do not always provide the lowest-cost solution. Euroconsult predicts that 759,635 fixed telecommunications earth stations, or 62 percent of the world total, will be sold in regions other than North America and Europe by 2006. Some of the largest gateway manufacturers include NEC, Globecomm Systems, IDB Systems Corporation, Alcatel Telspace, Comsat RSI, and Scientific Atlanta. Consolidation has been taking place in the industry: California Microwave recently sold its Satellite Transmission Systems unit to L3 Communications, and TIW was recently sold to Vertex. The advent of mobile satellite services has spurred the market for large earth stations, since companies such as Iridium and Globalstar need large earth stations to send signals from their satellites to terrestrial networks. Scientific Atlanta constructed 57 global gateways for Iridium, and Qualcomm is the prime contractor for the construction of 60 gateways for Globalstar.

VSATs. A VSAT is a small earth station, usually a satellite dish between 1.2 and 2.4 meters in diameter, that is used to provide narrow-cast transmission of video, voice, and data to a satellite. VSATs are commonly used for business applications. Growth in the VSAT segment may be attributed to several factors, including the development of new VSAT applications such as credit authorization, electronic payment systems, transmission of sales and pricing information between retail outlets and headquarters sites, travel- and financial-related services, hotel and motel management, automatic tellers, and real-time inventory control. The world's largest VSAT equipment manufacturers include Hughes Network Systems, Scientific Atlanta, NEC, Fujitsu, Bosch Telecom, and Gilat Satellite Networks. According to Northern Business Information, the VSAT equipment market was valued at $1.2 billion in 1996. Industry sources estimate that 325,000 terminals have been ordered since 1985, with the average terminal price falling to less than $3,000. The fastest growing world market for VSATs was the Asia/Pacific region, where the VSAT market grew 14.8 percent in 1996, according to that report. The Global VSAT Forum was established to combat regulatory and license constraints that are inhibiting the growth of VSAT services worldwide. The forum is based in London and currently has 40 members.

DBS and TVRO. Small satellite antennas that receive digital direct broadcast signals have experienced significant growth since their introduction in 1994. As of August 1998, there were 9.6 million subscribers, of which 2 million are C-band, in the United States, according to the Satellite Broadcast and Communications Association. A group of analysts from Morgan Stanley Dean Witter recently projected that there will be about 15.7 million DBS customers in the United States by 2002 and almost 18 million by 2007. There were 33.5 million DBS subscribers worldwide in 1997, and this number was expected to increase to 43 million in 1998. DBS services include the transmission of signals to both large C-band dishes and 18- to 24-inch dishes. Although these DBS services face stiff competition from the cable industry (and in the future from digital cable), many analysts predict that this segment of the industry, and thus

TABLE 31-5: World Satellite Communications Ground Equipment Market

	1986	1996	2006
Annual sales (units)[1]	510,000	21.4 million	108.7 million
Annual sales ($)[1]	2.48 billion	18.13 billion	46.28 billion
Average price ($)	4,860	850	425

[1] On average.
Source: Euroconsult, May 1997.

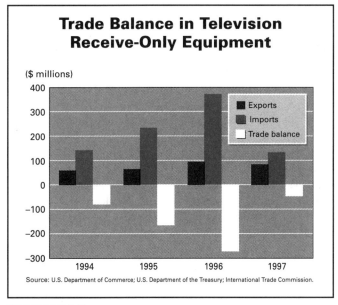

Trade Balance in Television Receive-Only Equipment

($ millions)

Legend:
- Exports
- Imports
- Trade balance

Years: 1994, 1995, 1996, 1997

Source: U.S. Department of Commerce; U.S. Department of the Treasury; International Trade Commission.

FIGURE 31-9

the equipment necessary to utilize these services, will continue to grow. Government statistics show that the United States had a negative trade balance in television receive-only (TVRO) equipment from 1994 to 1997, although the trade balance improved from –$275 million in 1996 to –$48 million in 1997. This negative trade balance can be attributed in large part to the competitive strength of Asian manufacturers of these products (see Figure 31-9).

Two primary components are necessary for direct-to-home satellite television: the 18- to 24-inch dish which is placed outside the home and the set-top box (integrated receiver-decoder) which sits on top of the television set. The manufacturing of these components is highly competitive, and service providers frequently subsidize the equipment to gain subscribers and earn monthly service fees. Prices for this type of equipment have been driven down by competition in the service market, and service providers have forced equipment prices below actual costs. There is, however, high potential for growth in the satellite television industry, which will ensure a large market for this equipment.

Mobile Satellite Receivers. Recently, economically priced commercial mobile satellite services have been offered to consumers, with charges of about $2.40 to $3.30 per minute. This has stimulated sales of INMARSAT's mini-M laptop-sized mobile satellite phones. Sales of these telephones, which cost approximately $3,000, reached 21,600 in March 1998. Manufacturers of mini-M phones include KVH (United States), NEC (Japan), NERA (Norway), and Thrane (Denmark). INMARSAT soon will face competition from companies such as Iridium and Globalstar, which plan to offer mobile telephone service with hand-held phones at similar costs.

Sales of mobile handsets should increase and prices should decline as companies such as Iridium, Globalstar, and ICO roll out service over the next 2 to 4 years. These services will allow customers to use hand-held cellularlike phones to make and receive telephone calls anywhere on earth. Iridium launched its service in November 1998, with Globalstar following in 1999. The entry of providers of high-speed data, videoconferencing, and Internet services such as Teledesic in 2001 will further fuel the satellite receiver market. Frost & Sullivan predicts that spending on mobile satellite earth stations, including hand-held phones and computer receivers, will grow to $6.4 billion in 2001, with sales of over 3 million mobile stations.

In May 1998 the FCC proposed the adoption of interim type-approval rules for global mobile personal communications by satellite (GMPCS) terminals. The FCC took this step in an effort to implement the GMPCS Memorandum of Understanding adopted in March 1998, originated by an informal group of the International Telecommunication Union (ITU).

Mobile services for paging, messaging, tracking, and data (offered by the "Little LEOs") are expected to be provided by a number of companies, such as E-Sat, FAISat, LEO One USA, and ORBCOMM. ORBCOMM is expected to offer two-way data and messaging services beginning in 1999, with terminals costing approximately $400 each. Sales of pagers and other equipment needed for the rollout of these services will increase over the next several years.

GPS. Sales of receivers using the U.S. Global Positioning System constellation of radio-emitting satellites for location, tracking, and timing services are expected to continue to grow rapidly over the next 5 years. Companies involved in the GPS equipment market include Honeywell, Magellan, Motorola, Rockwell, Trimble Navigation, and the NOMOS Corporation. Car navigation systems such as OnStar, PathMaster, and Guidestar cost from $1,000 to $2,500 and constitute one of the fastest growing segments of the GPS market. Currently, these systems are installed in some models of high-end luxury cars. It is projected that as receivers come down in price, automotive GPS will proliferate. Dataquest estimates that the worldwide market for GPS in the automotive industry will increase from 2 million units in 1997 to more than 11 million in 2001, resulting in an increase in market value from $364 million to $1.6 billion. A September 1998 study by the U.S. Department of Commerce estimates that worldwide sales of GPS products will reach $8 billion by 2000 and could exceed $16 billion by 2003.

DARS and DABS. Digital audio radio satellite (DARS) services from companies such as CDRadio and XM Satellite Radio Inc. (formerly AMRC) are expected to increase the demand for satellite receiver radios in the United States over the next few years. WorldSpace plans to offer digital audio broadcasting services (DABS) primarily to developing markets around the world. The system will include satellites serving Africa, the Caribbean, Central America and South America, and northern, southeastern, and western Asia. The current cost of a WorldSpace radio is about $300. WorldSpace has signed contracts with several Japanese companies for the manufacture of this equipment.

While growth in the satellite ground equipment market is solid at this time, competition is intensifying among the manufacturers of this equipment. This competition is driving manufacturers to lower prices while improving features and performance, to differentiate and continually redevelop products, and to tolerate low profit margins.

Domestic Trends

There are no official production or revenue statistics for U.S.-made satellite ground equipment, and industry estimates vary. According to an April 1998 SIA/Futron Corp. survey, the United States manufactures approximately 45 percent ($5 billion of $11 billion) of the world's satellite ground equipment. It is expected that the U.S. share will stay at the same level or decrease slightly. The ground equipment industry supports about 19,404 jobs in the United States, according to that survey. U.S. companies are strong in the market for large earth stations and VSAT equipment, while companies in Asia and Europe excel in the manufacture of the small DBS and new mobile terminals.

In the early 1990s U.S. manufacturers had a large share of the world market for most satellite ground segments, but that share has decreased as competition from Japan and Europe has become more intense. As the industry has grown, so has the number of competitors. Manufacturers face significant price competition, demands for more advanced technology, and the need for continued financial investment. U.S. companies such as Comsat RSI and Scientific Atlanta face fierce competition from NEC and Alcatel.

With regard to large earth stations, U.S. companies have benefited from the launch of new mobile satellite systems such as Iridium and Globalstar, although competition from Japanese and European manufacturers is growing for other large projects. While the VSAT market is expected to grow overall, the U.S. share of that market may slip as companies such as NEC, Fujitsu, and Gilat Satellite Networks make inroads into world markets. Although many analysts predict that DBS subscribers will increase significantly in the next 5 years, manufacturers from Asia have garnered a large portion of this market. The United States continues to import more TVRO equipment than it exports, although the imbalance decreased from 1996 to 1997. The market for mobile handsets and pagers will see significant growth in the next few years as new services for voice, paging, and messaging are introduced. The United States should retain a fair share of this market. Many U.S. companies excel in the production of the higher-technology GPS receivers used for location, tracking, and timing services, although companies from Japan are also strong in this area. The market for satellite receiver radios should increase, although much of that business may go to European and Japanese companies.

While the space segment will continue to receive most of the attention, the earth station market is critical to the success of the overall industry. Without equipment to effectively receive signals from satellites, no satellite system can be commercially viable.

Outlook for the Next 1 and 5 Years

The U.S. commercial satellite communications systems industry (both the space segment and the ground segment) generated estimated revenues of $13.3 billion in 1997, according to the SIAI Futron Corp.'s 1998 survey. The U.S. share represents about 54 percent of world revenue and most likely will increase in 1998 and 1999, based on the strength of the U.S. satellite manufacturing segment. The U.S. satellite component market should also maintain a positive trade balance, although the size of the surplus may slip as component manufacturers in other countries introduce technological advances. The ground segment will remain the same or grow slightly, although competition in this segment is fierce.

It important to consider several factors in forecasting growth in the commercial satellite industry sector over the next 5 years: continued competition from both wireline and other wireless technologies, more advanced satellites with longer lifetimes that will not have to be replaced as often, large up-front investment requirements, the significant risks inherent in launching highly sophisticated equipment into space, and the domestic and international regulatory hurdles operators face in trying to offer global service. As the number of commercial satellites in orbit increases, the allocation of valuable orbital slots and parts of the radio-frequency spectrum becomes more challenging. The International Telecommunication Union, which is part of the United Nations, provides an international forum for the coordination of slots and spectrum. It has been increasingly difficult to ensure that adequate frequency is available for the large number of satellite services that companies are promising to provide.

The United States will certainly dominate the market for large GEO satellites in 1999, although the consolidation of several companies in Europe may make for increased competition in the long term. Orders for GEO satellites will remain at an average of about 30 per year, while contracts for new and next-generation LEO satellites will increase significantly, depending on the number of systems that are implemented. In regard to the overall commercial satellite manufacturing industry over the next 5 years, an increase in the manufacture of small satellites most likely will balance any potential downturns in the growth of the GEO satellite manufacturing market.

Ground equipment sales will continue to be driven by strong growth in VSATs and DBS in the developed regions, while demand for large earth stations for telecommunications services will continue to grow in the developing areas of the world. The areas of high growth will likely continue to be VSAT, DBS, and mobile terminals, including GPS. While the space segment will continue to receive most of the attention, the earth station market is critical to the success of the overall industry.

Global Market Prospects

Continued international demand, coupled with new applications such as mobile telephony, DBS, satellite radio, satellite messaging, and data services, will sustain U.S. satellite equipment industry revenues through the early part of the next century. Many analysts predict some consolidation as the industry grows, but the United States should continue to have a strong presence in the space and ground segments.

The U.S. government is in the process of trying to include satellites and satellite parts in the product coverage list as part of the Information Technology Agreement II (ITA II) negotiations. The inclusion of these products in ITA II would ensure lower tariffs over time and thus facilitate trade.

The U.S. satellite manufacturing industry will continue to dominate the GEO satellite market, and companies such as Boeing, Motorola, Orbital Sciences, Spectrum Astro, and TRW will still represent the United States successfully in the manufacture of small, non-GEO satellites. The ground equipment industry will continue to see strong growth as these new applications are rolled out. Although the U.S. industry will face more pronounced competition from overseas competitors, U.S. companies should be able to maintain their lead in the space segment and remain competitive in certain segments of the ground equipment market, such as large earth stations, VSAT systems, and GPS receivers.

The future of the industry will rely to some extent on three factors: deregulation, which will allow companies to offer service globally; rising demand for telephony and data services; and continued technological developments. Many experts believe that the ability of companies to overcome regulatory hurdles, coordinate spectrum and slot allocations with the ITU, and obtain licenses from foreign governments will be key to the future success of the industry.

Krysten B. Jenci, U.S. Department of Commerce, Office of Telecommunications, (202) 482-2952, November 1998.

SEARCH AND NAVIGATION EQUIPMENT

Search and navigation equipment (SIC 3812) consists of search, detection, navigation, guidance, aeronautical, and nautical systems, instruments, and equipment. It includes radar and sonar systems, light reconnaissance and surveillance equipment, and electronic warfare equipment.

Domestic and Global Industry Trends

U.S. shipments of search, detection, navigation, guidance, aeronautical, and nautical systems instruments and equipment (SIC 3812) continued their downward trend in 1998. Shipments totaled approximately $27 billion in constant dollars, representing a 4 percent decrease from 1997. After a high of $35 billion in 1992, shipments have been decreasing at an average annual rate of 3 percent (see Table 31-6). Search and detection, ground navigation, and guidance systems and equipment account for approximately 92 percent of the shipments. Aeronautical, nautical, and navigation equipment accounts for the remaining 8 percent.

Demand for search and navigation equipment comes from both military and civilian sources. Radar, navigation equipment, and guidance systems are used by the military for installation in military aircraft and ships, and for smart weapons. The end of the cold war has spurred a drop in defense spending. The President's fiscal year (FY) 1999 defense budget will reflect more of the same, with the request for $257.3 billion being about 40 percent below the level in FY 1985 in real terms. Many U.S. companies that once relied on the military for contracts have left the defense business. Raytheon, having previously acquired E-Systems and Texas Instrument's defense electronics division, recently acquired Hughes' Defense Operations Division. In addition, Litton acquired Delco's Navigation and Guidance Systems, Boeing acquired McDonnell Douglas, and Trimble Navigation acquired Terra Corporation. AlliedSignal Inc. is seeking to sell its communications systems division. These are a few examples of the mergers and consolidations that are still taking place in this industry as firms strive to remain competitive. The total number of U.S. companies that produce search, detection, navigation, guidance, aeronautical, and nautical systems has been dropping since 1995.

TABLE 31-6: Search and Navigation Equipment (SIC 3812) Trends and Forecasts
(millions of dollars except as noted)

	1992	1993	1994	1995	1996	1997[1]	1998[2]	1999[3]	Percent Change 96–97	97–98	98–99	92–96[4]
Industry data												
Value of shipments[5]	35,039	33,546	30,110	32,000	30,371	29,360	28,479	27,625	-3.3	-3.0	-3.0	-3.5
Value of shipments (1992$)	35,039	32,856	29,204	30,506	28,925	27,829	26,741	25,698	-3.8	-3.9	-3.9	-4.7
Total employment (thousands)	253	225	199	200	186	179	172		-3.8	-3.9		-7.4
Production workers (thousands)	103	88.5	80.3	71.6	67.8	61.2	55.1		-9.7	-10.0		-9.9
Average hourly earnings ($)	17.28	18.79	18.84	19.95	20.31							4.1
Capital expenditures	849	706	688	730	1,223							9.6
Product data												
Value of shipments[5]	34,171	31,203	29,160	27,755	26,653	25,587	24,563	23,580	-4.0	-4.0	-4.0	-6.0
Value of shipments (1992$)	34,171	30,561	28,283	26,458	25,383	24,253	23,064	21,935	-4.5	-4.9	-4.9	-7.2
Trade data												
Value of imports	965	862	863	994	1,044	1,273	1,349	1,430	21.9	6.0	6.0	2.0
Value of exports	2,133	2,105	2,031	1,978	2,046	2,515	2,590	2,668	22.9	3.0	3.0	-1.0

[1] Estimate except imports and exports.
[2] Estimate.
[3] Forecast.
[4] Compound annual rate.
[5] For definition of industry versus product values, see "Getting the Most Out of *Outlook '99*."
Source: U.S. Department of Commerce: Bureau of the Census; International Trade Administration.

Declining total employment in the search and navigation industry (SIC 3812) reflects the displacement of workers as a result of consolidation. From a high of 253,000 in 1992, total employment decreased to 179,000 in 1997. There also has been a decline in the number of production workers, from 67,800 in 1996 to 55,100 in 1997. Over the last 5 years the number of production workers has dropped at an annual average rate of 10 percent.

Commercial applications of radar, search, and detection equipment are causing many companies to shift their resources to civilian markets. Satellite navigation via the GPS is spurring opportunities for manufacturers of search and navigation equipment. The U.S. Department of Defense and the U.S. Department of Transportation signed a memorandum of agreement in 1993 to establish policies and procedures for the civil use of GPS. The application of radio navigation systems such as GPS in areas such as surveying, weather research, and positioning is being recognized and developed.

The Department of Defense, which has the responsibility for implementing radio navigation systems, has decided to phase out most of the navigational aids currently in use. The two departmental agencies that are responsible for radio navigation systems are the U.S. Coast Guard and the Federal Aviation Administration (FAA). The Coast Guard provides U.S. aids to navigation for maritime navigation, and the FAA has the responsibility for safe aircraft navigation. Under the Federal Radio Navigation Plan, a joint document by the Departments of Defense and Transportation, GPS will become the primary radio navigation system. GPS is a satellite-based navigation system that represents the most dramatic change in navigation in decades. The technology can be applied to aviation, marine, and vehicle navigation. As satellite navigation systems take over, the need for present-day ground-based systems will diminish, with most being phased out completely by 2010. A satellite-based navigation system will be the future technology for aviation internationally. The International Civil Aviation Organization (ICAO) has endorsed the use of a global navigation satellite system to serve as the most important element of an international system for communications, navigation, and surveillance and air traffic management.

Global Market Prospects

Exports of search and detection equipment totaled approximately $2.5 billion in 1997, an increase of 23 percent over 1996. Increased foreign demand for search and navigation equipment has helped keep this industry growing. As a result of their ability to provide technologically advanced equipment, U.S. suppliers maintained an overwhelming trade surplus in this industry.

Canada remained the largest export market for U.S.-manufactured search and detection equipment, accounting for 15 percent of total exports (see Table 31-7). The other major purchasers were Japan (12 percent), the United Kingdom (8 percent), France (6 percent), and Taiwan (6 percent), which accounted for approximately 48 percent of all exports.

Radar apparatus and parts were the major products exported, and accounted for 18 percent of all exports. Exports of radar apparatus totaled approximately $457 million in 1997, representing a 105 percent increase from $223 million in 1996. Parts for radar apparatus, which had historically been the top item exported by this industry, followed with approximately $376 million in 1997. Substantial purchases of radar apparatus by Kuwait and Saudi Arabia propelled those countries to the eighth and ninth positions, respectively, as major new purchasers of U.S. search and navigation equipment in 1997. These two countries accounted for 44 percent of all purchases of radar apparatus.

Imports totaled $1.3 billion in 1997, up 22 percent from $1 billion in 1996. Canada and the United Kingdom supplied

TABLE 31-7: U.S. Trade Patterns in Search and Navigation Equipment[1] in 1997
(millions of dollars; percent)

	Exports			Imports		
Regions[2]	Value[3]	Share, %	Regions[2]	Value[3]	Share, %	
NAFTA	498	19.8	NAFTA	430	33.8	
Latin America	72	2.9	Latin America	1	0.1	
Western Europe	725	28.8	Western Europe	402	31.5	
Japan/Chinese Economic Area	496	19.7	Japan/Chinese Economic Area	250	19.6	
Other Asia	297	11.8	Other Asia	117	9.2	
Rest of world	427	17.0	Rest of world	74	5.8	
World	2,515	100.0	World	1,273	100.0	
Top Five Countries	Value	Share, %	Top Five Countries	Value	Share, %	
Canada	382	15.2	Canada	302	23.7	
Japan	306	12.2	United Kingdom	177	13.9	
United Kingdom	203	8.1	Japan	129	10.1	
France	158	6.3	Mexico	128	10.1	
Taiwan	150	6.0	France	109	8.5	

[1] SIC 3812.
[2] For definitions of regional groupings, see "Getting the Most Out of *Outlook '99*."
[3] Values may not sum to total due to rounding.
Source: U.S. Department of Commerce, Bureau of the Census.

almost 38 percent of all imports for this industry. Accounting for 27 percent of all imports, radio remote control apparatus ($197 million) and radio navigational aid apparatus, reception only ($149 million), were the major imported products. Imports have been growing at an annual average rate of 6 percent over the last 5 years.

Air traffic control (ATC) has provided U.S. manufacturers with many opportunities both overseas and domestically. Russia, the NIS, and China have aging ATC systems or no radar coverage at all. ATC equipment includes terminal control centers, microwave landing systems, voice switching systems, secondary surveillance radars, remote control equipment, radio navigation devices, antennas, and compasses. The Federal Aviation Authority of Russia plans to contract for a three-phase program to modernize the Moscow ATC Center. Raytheon is already installing radar systems in China and recently signed a contract for turnkey radar systems in Shanghai and Prudom. Lockheed Martin won a contract to provide ATC systems at Hongqiao and the Prudom airports. Many countries in Africa and the Middle East as well as Latin American countries such as Chile, Peru, and Brazil are seeking to upgrade their ATC systems.

U.S. Industry Growth Projections for the Next 1 and 5 Years

Shipments of search and navigation equipment will fall an estimated 4 percent in 1999, with further declines anticipated over the next 5 years. Defense opportunities overall will be limited in this period as the proposed defense budgets for FYs 1999 through 2003 call for Department of Defense spending to merely keep up with inflation. Defense procurement for FY 1999 is expected to be funded at $49 billion, with a target of $62 billion in 2003. However, under the Department's comprehensive Quadrennial Defense Review implementation process, recommendations were made regarding security threats and opportunities facing the United States in the post–cold war era. Out of the Quadrennial Defense Review process came several initiatives to modernize and upgrade aging systems. Under the framework of Joint Vision 2010, the Department of Defense will allocate increased funds to the procurement budget to implement these specific initiatives. These modernization efforts will create continuing opportunities for U.S. suppliers of search and navigation equipment to the military through 2003, with an emphasis on command, control, communications, computers, intelligence, surveillance, and reconnaissance capabilities (surveillance includes navigation aids such as GPS). Illustrative programs that will benefit U.S. manufacturers of search and navigation equipment include the procurement of the DDG-51 Destroyer, the New Attack Submarine, the tenth and final Nimitz-class carrier, F/A-18E/F aircraft, approximately 120 C-17 aircraft, the first production F-22s (with a gradual buildup to 36 per year by 2004), and precision munitions such as SLAM-ER land attack missiles, Tomahawk missiles, and Longbow Hellfire missiles. Major avionics upgrades are also projected for all KC-135 tankers. State-of-the-art inertial navigation systems, gyroscopes, and magnetic compasses are among the standard types of search and navigation equipment needed.

Procurement of radar, search, detection, and navigation equipment under NATO's Security Investment Program have continued to be a source of sales opportunities for U.S. manufacturers. Many of the member countries of NATO have been procuring equipment to meet NATO's operational needs heading into the twenty-first century. Among the NATO projects in 1998 were procurements by the Royal Norwegian Air Materiel Command to replace existing antenna array modules and radar signal processors, procurement by the NATO C3 Agency for multiband transportable satellite ground terminals, the Hellenic Air Force's procurement of a ground-to-ground/ground-to-air communication system for the air defense system, and the supply and installation of a perimeter intrusion detection system by NATO headquarters. The pending expansion of NATO to include the Czech Republic, Poland, and Hungary will offer additional sales opportunities for U.S. manufacturers as those countries modernize their air defense systems.

Long-Term Prospects

Prospects for the search and navigation industry beyond 2003 are good. The impetus for future growth will be increased Department of Defense spending and the introduction of new products in the civilian sector. The U.S. search and navigation industry will continue to be the world's technological leader in producing advanced products.

Procurement spending in the U.S. defense budget is projected to reach approximately $62 billion by FY 2003. A large portion of that spending will go to modernize navigation aids. U.S. suppliers of search and navigation equipment to the Department of Defense should expect greater sales opportunities.

Commercial applications of GPS technology offer the best prospect for growth in this industry. GPS technology applied to various civilian uses provides unlimited potential in marine and aviation navigation and in vehicle location and tracking. The integration of GPS receivers with digital maps is allowing automobile and truck drivers to determine their locations. Hertz has already installed GPS receivers on many of its fleet rentals. Consumer products for bikers, hunters, and boaters are expected to use GPS devices. Traffic congestion and the need for safety in automobiles and aircraft have fostered the creation of new applications for GPS equipment, making GPS the technology of choice to meet these demands in the twenty-first century.

Intelligent transportation systems (ITS) constitute one such emerging market. Examples of ITS already in use include vehicle location systems for emergency service, route navigation for private automobiles, and tracking and scheduling of commercial vehicles. Radio navigation equipment will be instrumental in the development of this sector, which is not well defined. The Department of Transportation supports the ITS market through research and development programs. Collision avoidance and automated highway operation are technologies that are still in the research stage. There will be competition from foreign manufacturers in the ITS market as Japan and Germany make advances in research and development and in actual applications.

The commitment of the FAA to move from an extensive ground-based navigation system to one which will rely primarily on satellite navigation will have a worldwide impact on search and navigation suppliers. Many of the current ground-based stations that provide navigational services will be phased out. Manufacturers of the equipment used to support these systems have already stopped production. The Omega system, which provided global radio navigation coverage in the past, has been terminated. Loran-C, which provides coverage for maritime navigation in the United States, is scheduled to be terminated on December 31, 2000. Even with the commitment to GPS, much of the current ground-based equipment employs old technology and will need to be modernized.

Alexis Kemper, U.S. Department of Commerce, Office of Telecommunications, (202) 482-1512, May 1998.

■ REFERENCES

APEC Telecom Working Group: www.apec-wg.com/.

Bureau of the Census, U.S. Department of Commerce: www.census.gov/ftp/pub/industry/ma36p96.txt.

Cellular Telecommunications Industry Association: www.wow-com.com/.

Communications Week International, CMP Publications, Inc., 600 Community Drive, Manhasset, NY 11030. (516) 562-5000, www.commweek.com.

Datapro, The McGraw-Hill Building, 37th Floor, 1221 Avenue of the Americas, New York, NY 10020-1095. (212) 512-2900, http://www.datapro.com/datapro1.html.

Dataquest, 251 River Oaks Parkway, San Jose, CA 95134-1913. (408) 954-1780, Fax: (408) 954-1780, http://www.dataquest.com/.

FAA Office of Commercial Space Transportation: www.dot.gov/faa/cst/.

Federal Communications Commission: www.fcc.gov.

Frost & Sullivan: www.frost.com.

Global Telephony; Telephony; Telephony Publishing Corporation, 55 East Jackson, Chicago, IL 60604. (312) 922-2435

Guide to Telecommunications Markets in Latin America and the Caribbean, June 1996, NTIS S/N PB96-145073. (703) 487-4650.

INTELSAT: www.intelsat.int/.

International Cable Protection Committee: http://elaine.teleport.com/~ptc/iscw/iscw.shtml.

International Telecommunication Union: www.itu.ch/.

1998 Multimedia Telecommunications Market Review & Forecast, Multimedia Telecommunications Association & Telecommunications Industry Association, Arlington VA.

Office of Telecommunications of the International Trade Administration, U.S. Department of Commerce: www.infoserv2.ita.doc.gov/ot/home.nsf.

Personal Communications Industry Association: www.pcia.com/.

Strategis Group: www.strategisgroup.com.

Telecom Insider: www.clnewsnet.com/telecom.html.

Telecom Market Report: China, India & Pacific Rim; Telecom Market Report: Latin America & the Caribbean; Wireless Local Loop: Prospects for Profits; International Technology Consultants, 4340 East-West Highway, Suite 1020, Bethesda, MD 20814-4411. (301) 907-0060, Fax: (301) 907-6555, www.intl-tech.com.

Telecommunications Industry Association: www.industry.net/tia.

Telecommunications Reports, Business Research Publications, Inc., 1333 H Street, NW, 11th Floor-West, Washington, DC 20005. (202) 842-3006.

Trends in the International Telecommunications Industry, Federal Communications Commission, 1919 M Street, NW, Room 539, Washington, DC 20254. (202) 467-0017.

Wireless Cable Association: http://www.wirelesscabl.com.

WirelessNow (daily wireless update): www.commnow.com.

World Telecommunications Development Report 1997-98, International Telecommunication Union, Geneva, Switzerland, available from Telegeography, Inc., Suite 1000, 1150 Connecticut Avenue, NW, Washington, DC 20036. (202) 467-0017.

Network Equipment

America's Network, Advanstar Communications, 201 Sandpointe Avenue, Suite 600, Santa Ana, CA 92707-8700. (714) 513-8400, Fax: (714) 513-8634, www.americasnetwork.com.

Central Office-North America, Dataquest.

World Public Switching Markets: 1997 Edition and Database, Northern Business Information (Dataquest).

World Transmission Equipment Markets: 1997 Edition and Database, Northern Business Information (Dataquest).

Customer Premises Equipment

1995 North American Modem Market; Modems North American Market Share and Forecast, August 1996, Dataquest.

Voice Networking Systems Strategic Analysis, July 1996; *World PBX and KTS Markets, Telefacts,* December 1996; Datapro Information Services Group.

World PBX and KTS Markets: 1995 Edition; *U.S. PBX, KTS, and Related Markets:* 1995 Edition; *U.S. Voice Processing Equipment Market:* 1994 Edition; Northern Business Information.

Fiber Optics

Fiber Deployment Update, End of Year 1996, Jonathan Kraushaar, Industry Analysis Division, Common Carrier Bureau, Federal Communications Commission, July 1997.

Fiber Optics News, Phillips Business Information.

KMI Newport Conference Proceedings on Fiberoptics Markets, October 1997, KMI Corporation, America's Cup Avenue, at 31 Bridge Street, Newport, RI. (401) 849-6771.

Laser Focus World, PennWell Publishing Company, 10 Tara Boulevard, Fifth Floor, Nashua, NH 03062. (918) 831-9424.

Lightwave, PennWell Publishing Company, 10 Tara Boulevard, Fifth Floor, Nashua, NH 03062. (918) 832-9349.

Photonics Spectra, A Laurin Publication, P.O. Box 4949, Pittsfield, MA 01202-4949. (413) 499-0514.

World Transmission Equipment Markets: 1997 Edition, and *Database,* Northern Business Information (Dataquest).

Wireless Communications Equipment

Cellular Infrastructure Worldwide, 1992-2001 Market Trends (PERS-WW-MT-9703), December 31, 1997, Dataquest.

CTIA Semi-Annual Data Survey, Cellular Telecommunications Industry Association, 1250 Connecticut Avenue, NW, Suite 200, Washington, DC 20036. 202-785-0081, Fax: 202-785-0721.

Global Mobile, Baskerville Communications Corp., 15165 Ventura Boulevard, Suite 310, Sherman Oaks, CA 91403. (818) 461-9660, Fax: (818) 461-9661.

International Cellular, Kagan World Media, Ltd., 126 Clock Tower Place, Carmel, CA 93923-8734. (408) 624-1536, Fax: (408) 625-3225.

Mobile Communications International, MCI Subscriptions, Central House, 27 Park Street, Croydon CRO 1YD, England. Telephone: 011-44-081-686-5654 or 011-44-071-383-5757, Fax: 011-44-071-383-3181.

Mobile Phone News; PCS Week; Wireless Business & Finance; Phillips Business Information, Inc., 1201 Seven Locks Road, Potomac, MD 20854. (301) 340-1520, Fax: (301) 424-2058, www.phillips.com.

Newaves in Personal Communications, Imagination Publications, 820 W. Jackson Boulevard, Suite 450, Chicago, IL 60607. (312) 627-1020

1997 PCIA Wireless Market Portfolio, compiled by Personal Communications Industry Association, 500 Montgomery Street, Suite 700, Alexandria, VA 22314-1561. (703) 739-0300, Fax (703) 836-1608.

Personal Communications North America (PERS-NA-MT-9701), December 15, 1997, Dataquest.

RCR Radio Communications Report, RCR Publications Inc., 777 East Speer Boulevard, Denver, CO 80203. 1-800-678-9595.

WirelessNOW (on-line service), CommunicationsNOW, Inc., The Strategis Group, 1130 Connecticut Avenue, NW, Suite 325, Washington, DC 20036-3915. (202) 530-7500, Fax: (202) 530-7550.

Wireless Systems Outlook: 1998, The Evolving Landscape, Allied Business Intelligence, Inc., P.O. Box 452, 202 Townsend Square, Oyster Bay, NY 11771. (516) 624-3113, Fax: (516) 624-3115.

Wireless Telecom Equipment, Deutsche Morgan Grenfell Technology Group, 31 West 52nd Street, New York, NY 10019. (212) 469-5000, Fax: (212) 469-5381.

Wireless Week, Chilton Publications, 600 South Cherry Street, Suite 400, Denver, CO 80222. (303) 393-7449, Fax: (303) 399-2034.

Paging

Asia-Pacific Paging Markets: 1998; European Messaging/Paging Markets: 1998; The State of the U.S. Paging Industry: 1997; The Strategis Group, 1130 Connecticut Avenue, NW, Suite 325, Washington, DC 20036-3915. (202) 530-7500, Fax: (202) 530-7550.

"Europe Sees Shifting Allegiances in Market," *Global Wireless,* January-February 1998.

"Small Wonders Change the Picture," *Wireless Week: Paging Product Supplement,* January 26, 1998.

Satellites

Satellite Communications Ground Stations Market Survey—Worldwide Prospects, 1997-2006, Euroconsult, 71,79 boulevard Richard Lenoir 75011, Paris, France. Telephone: 33-1-49-23-75-30, www.euroconsult-ec.com.

"Satellite International," Baskerville Communications Corp., 15165 Ventura Boulevard, Suite 310, Sherman Oaks, CA 91403. (310) 978-6073, www.baskerville.co.uk.

"Satellite Markets," Media Business Corp., Futron Corporation, Satellite Industry Association, 807 Arapahoe Street, Golden, CO 80401. (303) 271-9960, www.skyreport.com.

SkyTrends Annual Report, 1997-1998, Media Business Corp., 807 Arapahoe Street, Golden, CO 80401. (303) 271-9960, www.skyreport.com.

Space News, Army Times Publishing Co., 6883 Commercial Drive, Springfield, VA 22159. (703)750-8696, www.spacenews.com/.

State of the Space Industry—1997 Outlook, SpaceVest, 11911 Freedom Drive, Suite 500, Reston, VA 20190. (703) 904-9800, www.spacevest.com.

Via Satellite 1997 Global Satellite Survey, Phillips Business Information Inc., 1201 Seven Locks Road, Suite 300, Potomac, MD 20854. (301) 340-7788, www.phillips.com/ViaOnline.

World Satellite Ground Segment Equipment Markets, Frost & Sullivan, 2525 Charleston Road, Mountain View, CA 94043. (415) 961-9000, www.frost.com.

World Transmission Equipment Markets, 1997 Edition, Northern Business Information/Dataquest, 251 River Oaks Parkway, San Jose, CA 95134. (408) 468-8000, gartner11.gartnerweb.com/dq/.

Search and Navigation Equipment

Avionics News, Aircraft Industries Association, 13700 E. 42nd Terrace, Suite 102, Independence, MO 64055. (816) 373-6565.

Federal Radio Navigation Plan, U.S. Department of Transportation (OST/P), and U.S. Department of Defense (USD/A&T), Washington, DC 20301.

ICAO Journal, Magazine of the International Civil Aviation Organization, Suite 1205, University Street, Montreal, Quebec, Canada, H3C5H7. (416) 259-9631, Fax: (416) 259-9634.

Journal of Electronic Defense, Horizon House Publications, Inc., for the Association of Old Crows, The AOC Building, 1000 N. Payne Street, Alexandria, VA 22314-1696.

Market Reports ATC, 4001 N. 19th Street, Suite 904, Arlington, VA 22203. (703) 524-1630.

Signal, Armed Forces Communications and Electronics Association, 4400 Fair Lakes Court, Fairfax, VA 22033-3899. (703) 631-6100.

State of the Space Industry, 1997 Outlook, KPMG Peat Marwick, 2001 M Street, NW, Washington, DC 20036. (202) 467-3083, Fax: (202) 239-5437.

■ R E L A T E D   C H A P T E R S

27: Computer Equipment
28: Computer Software and Networking
29: Space Commerce
30: Telecommunications Services

ENTERTAINMENT AND ELECTRONIC MEDIA
Economic and Trade Trends

Non-Cable Shares of Subscription Television Revenues

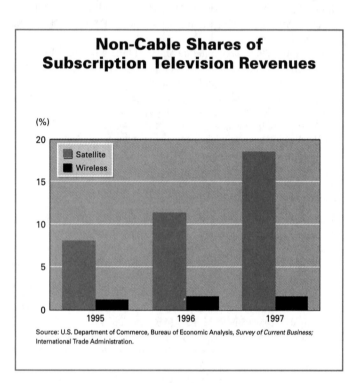

Source: U.S. Department of Commerce, Bureau of Economic Analysis, *Survey of Current Business;*
International Trade Administration.

Entertainment Employment Trends

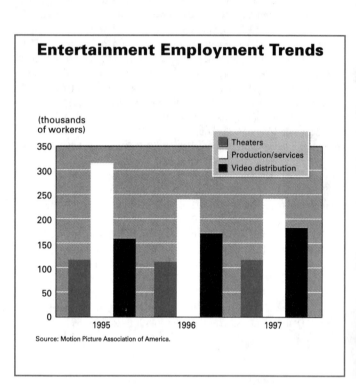

Source: Motion Picture Association of America.

Consumer Expenditures on Entertainment

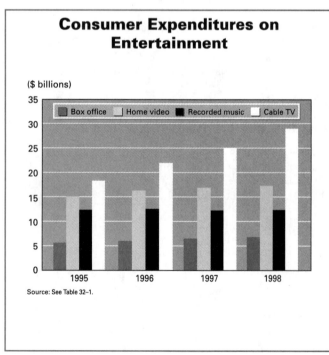

Source: See Table 32–1.

U.S. International Trade

Includes cross-border sales and sales through subsidiaries.
Source: U.S. Department of Commerce: Bureau of Economic Analysis; International Trade Administration.

Entertainment and Electronic Media

INDUSTRY DEFINITION Entertainment covers recorded music and filmed entertainment, which includes movies and series television programming, whether shown on movie screens, broadcast on network or cable television, or viewed on videocassettes. The industries are motion picture and videotape production (SIC 7812), motion picture and videotape distribution (SIC 7822), motion picture theaters (SIC 783), phonograph records and prerecorded audiotapes and disks (SIC 3652), record and prerecorded tape stores, retail (SIC 5735), videotape rental (SIC 7841), radio broadcasting stations (SIC 4832), television broadcasting stations (SIC 4833), and cable and other pay-television services (SIC 4841).

OVERVIEW

Global Industry Trends

The U.S. entertainment industry is the world leader in terms of size and revenues, and international markets are crucial to its continued success: In 1997 those markets accounted for about 40 percent of the revenues of the major U.S. film companies, up from 34 percent in 1988. New technology continues to offer opportunities and challenges to the entertainment industry. At the same time that growth in the videocassette and cable television markets has slowed, the Internet is offering new possibilities as a delivery system for entertainment programming. New technologies will no doubt continue to contribute to the worldwide success and even dominance of the U.S. entertainment industry. However, those technologies bring new problems, such as video piracy and the need for protection of copyright both in the recorded music now available on the Internet and in the filmed entertainment soon to be available there.

Audiovisual services are covered by the General Agreement on Trade in Services (GATS), one of the agreements under the World Trade Organization (WTO). The United States is one of 13 countries which made commitments regarding audiovisual services during the Uruguay Round. These commitments can cover one or more subsectors, including principally motion picture and videotape production and distribution services, motion picture projection services, radio and television services, and sound recording. The GATS is the first multilateral, legally enforceable agreement covering trade and investment in services; it includes basic trade-liberalizing rules such as most-favored-nation treatment, national treatment, market access, transparency, and the free flow of payments and transfers. The small number of country commitments in audiovisual trade and the generally modest steps toward liberalization mean that to date the GATS has played only a minor role in liberalizing this sector. Furthermore, some major trading partners, such as the European Union, did not make a commitment involving audiovisual services. Continuing efforts to expand coverage of audiovisual services are made in talks with countries that wish to join the WTO, and will be part of the new round of GATS services negotiations slated to begin no later than 2000.

Important Factors Affecting Future Growth of the U.S. Industry

Worldwide demand for U.S. entertainment is vigorous and is likely to grow in the long run. Sales of U.S. entertainment both domestically and abroad will depend in part on how new technologies are used for the delivery of entertainment and the barriers that U.S. entertainment is likely to encounter in foreign markets, in addition to general economic conditions. New technologies include the Internet; satellite delivery systems for programming, especially the Direct Broadcast Satellite (DBS); and telephone company entry into markets for programming and music. These technologies are expected to play an increasingly large role in the delivery of filmed entertainment and recorded music. Some industry observers, including the Motion Picture Association of America (MPAA), believe that within a decade the Internet will play a major role in delivering filmed entertainment and recorded music to homes. The rapid growth of DBS appears likely to continue through 2003.

The Internet offers promise as a new method for distributing entertainment products, but unresolved problems may delay its full utilization. For example, use of the Internet will depend on meeting the requirements of entertainment companies for intellectual property protection (IPR) of programming and recorded music and nondiscriminatory access to the network for all users. In addition, trade barriers relating to entertainment, coupled with the lack of IPR protection, can impede the growth of U.S. sales abroad. Trade barriers also include quotas on importing and exhibiting foreign films, import monopolies, and film censorship. Despite these problems, the outlook for U.S. entertainment abroad is strong, with steady growth a likely prospect.

U.S. Industry Growth Projections for the Next 5 Years

Consumer expenditures in the United States on movies, home video, cable television, and recorded music will continue to grow through 2003. Entertainment spending by consumers totaled about $56.5 billion in 1996 and reached an estimated $60.3 billion in 1997. The amount is expected to climb to more than $65.1 billion in 1998, $69.2 billion in 1999, and $90 billion in 2003, in current dollars. Between 1997 and 1999 the industry overall should grow 14.8 percent; from 1999 to 2003 growth is estimated at 30 percent. The growth of individual subsectors of the entertainment industry should vary. However, these growth projections for industry revenues may not correlate with the prospects for profitability. In fact, according to the *Wall Street Journal* and *Variety,* the future profitability of the large entertainment companies will be affected significantly by heavy corporate debt and the cost of integrating the diverse operations that have merged or been acquired.

Global Market Prospects

The Bureau of Economic Analysis (BEA) of the U.S. Department of Commerce collects official data on U.S. trade in film. These data include recordings of film and television as well as home video. Since 1987, total sales of filmed entertainment to foreign buyers increased from $3.73 billion to more than $14 billion in 1996, with some ups and downs along the way. For at least the next 5 years, similar growth probably will continue, with neither sharp increases nor large declines.

According to the BEA, U.S. revenues from exports of film and television tape rentals were roughly $4.8 billion in 1995 and $5 billion in 1996. The figure is expected to rise to $7.6 billion by 1999 and $10 billion by 2003. Foreign affiliates of the major U.S. film companies play a crucial role in distributing American films abroad. BEA data show that in 1996 foreign affiliates of U.S. companies sold $9.5 billion worth of rights to motion pictures, including television, tape, and film. These sales are expected to rise to $12.6 billion in 1999 and $16.6 billion in 2003. BEA data include revenues from home video but do not identify them separately (see Table 32-1).

MOTION PICTURES

This subsector includes motion picture and videotape production (SIC 7812), motion picture and videocassette tape distribution (SIC 7822), and motion picture theaters (SIC 783).

The wave of acquisitions which led to the formation of giant entertainment companies such as Disney, Viacom, and Time Warner appeared to wane in 1997. In commenting on these acquisitions, many observers saw a need for these companies to reduce costs, including the costs of film production and distribution. However, it is doubtful that film companies have made much progress in reducing costs. According to the MPAA, the average cost to its members of producing a motion picture rose from $39.8 million in 1996 to $53.4 million in 1997, an increase of 34 percent, the highest year-to-year increase since 1980 (the earliest data available). Furthermore, the number of new releases by MPAA member companies declined from 215 in 1996 to 197 in 1997. This small year-to-year decline is probably of minor significance, and the number of new MPAA releases appears likely to remain in the range indicated above. Releases by all U.S. companies, though, rose from 420 in 1996 to 458 in 1997, an increase of 9 percent. Thus, independent (smaller) film companies, which rely less on well-known and highly paid stars, may be affected less by these trends, although they face problems in competing with the major studios' marketing muscle.

The cost of distributing films, which often is handled by film production companies or their subsidiaries, has risen over the last several years, especially the costs of printing (making prints of films) and advertising. According to the MPAA, the combined average cost per film to its member companies for advertising and printing was $22.3 million in 1997, up 12.2 percent from $19.8 million in 1996. These costs have increased every year since 1986.

Theatrical exhibition of films remains the principal method for introducing new movies to the public. For the last 2 years box office receipts have shown sizable growth, while the growth in admissions has been moderate. Specifically, box office receipts increased 8.5 percent in 1997 to $6.4 billion and are expected to reach $7.0 billion in 1999 and $8.2 billion in 2003. Admissions increased from 1.37 billion in 1996 to 1.39 billion in 1997, a growth rate of 1.5 percent. Since 1992 admissions have increased in every year except 1995. However, the earnings of film companies from theatrical exhibition probably will continue to decline as a percentage of total revenues, which consist of box office, videocassette, and television revenues (see Table 32-2).

TABLE 32-1: Trends and Forecasts for Motion Picture Theaters, Video Rental Stores, Phonograph Records and Prerecorded Audiotapes and Disks, Cable/Pay-Television, and Recorded Music (SICs 783, 5735, 4841, 3652)

(billions of dollars; percent)

	1994	1995	1996	1997	1998	1999	2003	Percent Change 96–97	97–98	98–99
Box office receipts[1]	5.4	5.5	5.9	6.4	6.7	7.0	8.2	8.5	4.7	4.5
Home video[2]	14.2	15.0	16.2	16.8	17.2	17.6	19.2	3.6	2.3	2.3
Cable television[3]	NA	18.2	21.9	24.9	28.9	32.1	48.6	13.7	16.1	11.1
Recorded music[4]	12.1	12.3	12.5	12.2	12.3	12.5	14.0	–2.4	1	1.6
Employment										
Theaters	109.9	115.8	112.1	116.2						
Production/services	237.4	314.4	240.4	241.7						
Distribution/video	158.8	160.1	172.1	183.8						

[1] Data are from the Motion Picture Association of America and cover 1994–1997; 1998 and later years are estimated by the International Trade Administration (ITA).
[2] Data are from the Video Software Dealers Association and cover 1994–1996; estimates for later years are by the ITA.
[3] Revenues are per Table 32-3.
[4] Data are from the Recording Industry Association of America and cover 1994–1997; estimates for later years are by the ITA.

The steady increase in the number of U.S. movie screens is a sign that the exhibition industry has been profitable for both film companies and exhibitors. According to the MPAA, the total number of screens was 31,640 in 1997, up 6.6 percent from 1996. The number of screens has increased slightly every year since 1990; similar small increases are likely over the next few years. As a result of growth in multiplex theaters, the number of screens is five to six times the number of sites. Generally, owners of film rights and exhibitors divide box office receipts roughly in half, with the owners' share referred to as film rentals.

International

U.S. movies continue to dominate the international trade in motion pictures, including film rentals (a percentage of box office receipts), videocassette rentals and sales, and sales of television rights. In many developed country markets the theatrical exhibition of films has declined for several years, while other methods of exhibition, such as videocassettes and cable,

have grown. In many of these countries U.S. films have also acquired a share of box office receipts equal to or higher than that of domestic films, a situation which encourages protectionism. Recently, however, some foreign markets have been showing increases in film production, box office receipts, and admissions. For example, *Variety* reported that local films accounted for about 50 percent of box office in the United Kingdom in the second half of 1997; in Italy, local films accounted for about one-third of box office, a high point in recent years; and in Germany, 5 of the 10 top films were European-made.

Official data from the BEA for film rentals from theatrical exhibition are unavailable. Thus, the only information on revenues from foreign film rentals comes from the American Film Marketing Association (AFMA), whose 130 members are independent film companies that account for roughly 20 percent of foreign film revenues. The AFMA reported that its members earned $565 million from foreign film rentals in 1997, or about

TABLE 32-2: Trends and Forecasts for International Receipts and Payments (Trade) for Film and Tape Rentals; and Sales by Foreign Subsidiaries of Motion Pictures, Including Television, Tape, and Film

(billions of dollars; percent)

	1994	1995	1996	1997	1998	1999	2003	Percent Change 96–97	97–98	98–99
Cross-border sales[1]										
U.S. receipts	4.4	4.8	5.0	6.2	6.9	7.6	10.0	22.8	11.74	10.1
U.S. payments	0.23	0.23	0.25	0.25	0.25	0.26	0.30	0.0	1.2	4.0
Sales by foreign subsidiaries[2]										
U.S. receipts	6.6	7.5	9.6	10.6	11.6	12.6	16.6	10.9	9.4	8.6
U.S. payments[3]	7.7	8.5	9.0[4]	9.5	9.9	10.2	11.4	5.6	4.2	3.0

[1] Data are available through 1997; all other figures are estimates by the International Trade Administration (ITA).
[2] Data are available through 1996; all other figures are estimates by the ITA.
[3] Payments include sales in the United States by film companies which are subsidiaries of foreign companies.
[4] Estimated by the U.S. Department of Commerce, International Trade Administration.
Source: U.S. Department of Commerce, Bureau of Economic Analysis, *Survey of Current Business,* October 1998. Estimates and forecasts by the U.S. Department of Commerce, International Trade Administration.

31 percent of their total foreign revenues of $1.8 billion (see Table 32-2).

MUSIC

This subsector includes manufacturers of phonograph records and prerecorded audiotapes and disks (SIC 3652).

Sales of prerecorded music in all formats—CDs, cassettes, vinyl records, singles, and music videos—were $12.2 billion in 1997, according to the Recording Industry Association of America (RIAA). This figure represents a decrease of 2.4 percent over sales of $12.5 billion in 1996. This decrease in manufacturers' dollar value—manufacturers' recommended list price for recordings—was the first year-to-year decline since 1980. In addition, unit sales of 1.1 billion in 1997 showed a decline of 6.5 percent from 1996. The higher cost of CDs compared with other formats and the continued growth in sales of the CD format account for the smaller decline in dollar value compared with unit sales (see Table 32-2).

Sales of recorded music have barely progressed since 1994, when revenues surpassed $12 billion for the first time. Furthermore, neither a technological phenomenon such as the introduction of digital video discs (DVDs) nor demographics over the next few years seems likely to push recorded music sales into high year-to-year percentage growth.

The industry, though, finds promise in several aspects of the results from 1997. For example, although retail sales, referred to as total retail value by the RIAA, remained relatively flat between 1996 and 1997, increasing from $10.76 billion to $10.79 billion, sales of CDs by retailers increased 2.3 percent from $8.4 billion to $8.6 billion. The RIAA also noted that sales were strong in the fourth quarter of 1997 and that several albums had very strong sales—all signs of a healthy industry.

Also noteworthy is the likely growth in music sales over the Internet. Record companies as well as retailers and other distributors have Web sites where the public can order and pay for CDs and other recorded music. Some sites permit a customer to select music and create a customized CD or receive music in a digital format to record on a computer disk. Industry observers estimate that music sales over the Web could reach 7.5 percent of total sales by 2002. Unfortunately, the sale of music over the Internet has increased the risk of piracy, and the RIAA has taken legal action against three operators of Internet sites to put an end to copyright infringement. The RIAA views the potential harm to copyright owners from infringement on the Internet as "exponentially greater" than that from traditional piracy. The result of all these trends is that total sales of recorded music should reach about $12.5 billion in 1999 and $14 billion in 2003.

In 1997, CDs accounted for approximately $9.9 billion, or 81 percent of all recorded music sales, a figure that has increased steadily over the last 10 years. CDs should continue to dominate recorded music for a number of years despite the planned introduction of DVDs.

Young consumers have long been crucial to the success of the recording industry. In 1997 consumers age 15 through 24 years accounted for 30.6 percent of all recorded music sales. However, as reported by the RIAA, most of the sales growth in 1997 occurred among the youngest and oldest age groups; those 10 to 14 years old and those over 45.

International

U.S. music has long been very successful internationally. Over the last decade foreign markets have accounted for an increasing share of total sales by U.S. record companies. Some Asian countries, notably China, have the potential to become vast new markets for U.S. music if intellectual property protection improves to the point where companies can protect their recordings. *Variety* has reported growth in the market share of local groups in a number of foreign markets. *Variety* also suggests that local groups may benefit from two phenomena: Current styles that are popular in the United States have not done well abroad, and local groups have attracted increased consumer attention in their own countries.

Determining U.S. sales of music overseas is difficult, in part because, according to the RIAA and the International Federation of the Phonographic Industry (IFPA), most major record companies use licensing agreements with foreign manufacturers to serve foreign markets. With this type of agreement, very little, if any, merchandise will cross a border, as opposed to recorded music shipped in merchandise trade.

The U.S. government reports trade in recorded music under "records, tapes, and other recorded media for sound or other similarly recorded phenomena." Despite more detailed product descriptions introduced in 1996 that permit better identification of exports of recorded music, uncertainty remains in regard to the volume of U.S. exports of recorded music. According to U.S. government data, total exports of recorded music were about $757 million in 1997, a decline of 16 percent from 1996. The 1997 data also indicate a U.S. trade surplus of about $447 million, down from $561 million in 1996.

However, these numbers give an incomplete picture of U.S. trade in recorded music, primarily because they do not include U.S. receipts from licensing agreements with foreign record companies. U.S. licensing receipts from recorded music are certain to be large, because many U.S. record companies sell to foreign markets by entering into license agreements with local companies, which then produce recorded music to meet the demand of the local market. Most industry observers believe that the percentage of total foreign recorded music revenues from licensing agreements is high, although the exact figure is unknown.

The International Federation of the Phonographic Industry (IFPI), an international trade association based in London, estimated that in 1996 total recorded music sales worldwide reached $39.8 billion, an increase of $400 million over 1995. Despite this small increase, the growth over several years remains impressive: Sales were 50.6 percent higher in 1996 than the 1991 total of $26.4 billion.

Based on U.S. domestic sales of about $12 billion, total sales of music worldwide of $40 billion, and the assumption that U.S. music accounts for about 50 percent of all sales worldwide, foreign sales of U.S. music amount to approximately $8 billion. Despite the recent success of local groups abroad, the U.S. recorded music industry is likely to continue experiencing growth in foreign markets.

VIDEOCASSETTES

This subsector includes videocassette rental (SIC 7841) and recorded and prerecorded tape stores (SIC 5735). Establishments that sell videotapes are more diverse than those that rent tapes and therefore fall under the SIC of the establishment's primary business, such as department stores, variety stores, grocery stores, etc.

The retail videocassette industry includes both rental and sale of videocassette tapes, and the revenues of the U.S. retail videocassette market include rental and retail sales figures. Industry observers have concluded that the video rental market has matured, so that double-digit growth is unlikely in the future. According to the Video Software Dealers Association (VSDA), total 1996 revenues from sales and rentals of videocassettes reached $16.2 billion. According to International Trade Administration (ITA) estimates that are based on industry data, total 1997 revenues were about $16.8 billion. The ITA also estimates that 1998 and 1999 revenues will be $17.2 billion and $17.6 billion, respectively, before reaching $19.2 billion in 2003 (see Table 32-2).

Video specialty stores earn about 78 percent of their revenues from rentals of videocassettes and most of the rest from videocassette sales (called the sell-through market). Video retailers have to maintain a high percentage of their revenues from rentals because the profit margin is higher for rentals than for sales. Sales generally account for about 10 percent of the revenue of a specialty video retailer.

Industry sources believe that the number of specialty video stores in the United States is between 25,000 and 30,000. According to the VSDA, the video market is still dominated by small retailers with five or fewer stores despite growing concentration among video retailers, the 50 largest of which account for almost half of video rental revenue. Sales and rentals of video games, snack foods, blank tapes, etc., account for the rest.

The VSDA has described two problems facing the video retail industry. The first is competition from small dish (DBS) satellite systems as a method to deliver movies directly to homes. Sales of DBS systems rose substantially in 1996 and 1997, but from a base so small that this barely threatens the video industry. Nonetheless, DBS remains a potential competitive threat to video rental, according to market research suggesting that DBS households curtail movie viewing generally, including the renting of videos.

The second problem is the time period (called the window) between the video release and the pay-per-view release of a film.

This window has often been 30 to 45 days, but as pay-per-view has grown on cable television and DBS, video retailers have concluded that this period is too short and undermines their rental revenues. They accordingly have pressed for a longer window of up to 120 days.

Despite these problems, the industry has significant strengths. For example, home video receipts are more than twice as large as box office receipts. At 82 percent of television households, VCR penetration is higher than cable penetration and assures a prominent place for video in consumer expenditures on filmed entertainment.

Film companies are the primary suppliers of programming on videocassettes to video retailers. As a result of U.S. copyright law, they derive their revenue from the sale, but not the rental, of videocassettes. In 1996 total supplier revenue was about $6.6 billion from both the higher-priced videocassettes intended for rental and the cassettes intended for the sell-through market. At present film companies derive over half their total movie revenue from sales to video rental stores and to the home market.

International

The popularity of U.S. films in foreign markets appears to ensure the success of U.S. videos there. Revenues from U.S. films sold abroad in video format are likely to continue to be a strong contributor to industry revenues as long as videocassettes remain popular. The MPAA estimates that the foreign revenues of all U.S. film companies from videocassettes were $4.4 billion in 1995, or 43 percent of the total foreign revenues of $10.2 billion earned by U.S. film companies. In addition, the AFMA, which publishes foreign revenues for the association's 130 independent film company members, reports that in 1997 AFMA members earned foreign revenues of $476 million from the exhibition of films in the videocassette format, or 26 percent of their total foreign revenues. This is a significant source of income, though it is nowhere near the percentage earned by the major film companies.

John Siegmund, U.S. Department of Commerce, Office of Service Industries, (202) 482-4781, November 1998.

CABLE TELECOMMUNICATIONS

This subsector (SIC 48) includes cable system operators that transmit programming over their systems to cable subscribers.

Cable television is a delivery system that provides from 30 to several hundred channels of video programming to subscribers through a coaxial cable or optical fiber network connected to the subscriber's television set. For a monthly fee, subscribers receive basic cable service and have the option of subscribing to additional channels of video programming, audio, or other services for extra monthly fees.

Unlike broadcast television stations, cable system operators derive most of their revenues from monthly subscriber fees. In addition to recurring subscriber programming revenues, cablers get revenues from installation charges, sales of pay-per-view movies and events, set-top converter rentals, remote control sales and rentals, advertising, and carriage fees from home shopping channels and others, including advertorial or infomercial presenters.

Total revenues for U.S. cable system operators, including subscription fees, advertising, and other fees and charges, is expected to advance nearly 12 percent in 1999, following an 11 percent rise estimated for 1998. The average annual rate of growth through 2003 is projected at over 13.7 percent. Those attractive gains reflect several positive factors, including growth in subscribers, price inflation, growth in demand for higher-priced programming packages, and strong advertising.

Cable is a relatively mature industry, but it continues to enjoy moderate growth in number of subscribers, largely due to gains in household formation but also due to increased penetration. In spite of inroads made by direct broadcast satellite (DBS) services, the number of U.S. cable subscribers should grow by nearly 3 percent in 1999, followed by increases in the narrow range of 2.5 to 3.3 percent in each year through 2003. Subscriber growth averaged just under 3 percent in the 3 years through 1998.

In addition to sustained subscriber growth, cable is benefiting from rising rates charged for service. Passed in 1992, the Cable Television Consumer Protection and Competition Act reimposed rate regulation on the industry and forced some operators to lower rates for basic-service packages such as equipment rental and installation. Then the Telecommunications Act of 1996 put in place a regulatory framework around which cablers have been allowed to raise rates for various ser-

vices, depending on a number of factors. Because of the politically sensitive nature of cable charges, few cablers have taken full advantage of the increases allowed by the Federal Communications Commission (FCC). Nevertheless, rate hikes have been generous in comparison to inflation, rising an estimated 6.5 percent on average in each of the 3 years through 1998. (Such rates actually declined 2.3 percent in 1994, reflecting the impact of the 1992 act.) Average price hikes of 7 to 8 percent through 2003 are expected in spite of the phasing out of regulatory guidelines and ceilings.

Although cablers are spending heavily to upgrade their systems and program offerings, escalating programming costs are also a major driver behind the rising rates to subscribers. Not only are cablers adding channels each year, but cable program suppliers are hiking fees in large increments. Many of the programming cost increases are justified by the higher spending to acquire sports, news, original and first-run movies, and other programming. Cable's enhanced program offerings draw subscribers to the more expensive programming packages.

Cablers' advertising revenues continue to grow rapidly, outpacing the growth rate of both television and radio. U.S. cable advertising revenues are expected to advance roughly 13 percent on average each year through 2003 (see Table 32-3) and nearly 20 percent in 1999. (Roughly one-third of advertising revenues on cable accrues directly to cable system operators from such sources as infomercials and advertisements sold on some syndicated programs; roughly two-thirds of the advertising goes in the coffers of cable networks such as American Movie Classics and Nickelodeon for advertisements sold on their programs.) Special marketing and promotions related to the millennium will boost advertising in 1999 and 2000.

TABLE 32-3: Cable Television and Satellite TV Trends and Forecasts
(billions of dollars except as noted)

	1995	1996	1997	1998	1999	2000	2001	2002	2003
Cable									
Subscribers (millions)	61.5	63.1	65	67	69	70.7	72.8	75.1	77.6
Basic subscription revenues	15.2	17	18.4	20.3	22	23.7	26	28.7	31.9
Advertising revenues	5.1	6.4	7.5	8.6	10.3	11.3	12.8	14.5	16
Other revenues	9.1	9.9	11.1	12.3	13.7	16.8	19.4	22.5	27.5
Total cable revenues	29.4	33.3	37.0	41.2	46.0	51.8	58.2	65.7	75.4
Direct broadcast satellite									
Subscribers (millions)	2.3	4.4	6.2	8.2	10.2	12.2	14.6	16.8	18.6
Revenues	1.5	3.3	4.8	6.8	8.2	9.7	11.2	12.1	14.3
Wireless (MMDS)									
Subscribers (millions)	0.8	1.2	1	1	0.9	0.9	0.9	0.9	0.9
Revenues	0.4	0.6	0.5	0.5	0.5	0.5	0.5	0.6	0.6
Satellite master antenna (SMATV)									
Subscribers (millions)	0.9	0.8	1	1.1	1.1	1.1	1.2	1.2	1.3
Revenues	0.4	0.3	0.5	0.6	0.6	0.7	0.8	0.9	1
Satellite dish (C-band/Ku band)									
Subscribers (millions)	1.8	1.7	1.6	1.4	1.2	1.2	1.1	1	1
Revenues	0.7	0.7	0.7	0.7	0.8	0.8	0.8	0.8	0.8
Total Revenues for all segments	32.4	38.2	43.5	49.8	56.1	63.5	71.5	80.1	92.1

Source: Standard & Poor's; A.C. Nielsen; Cablevision; Broadcasting & Cable; Multichannel News Online; DBS Dish.com! Forecasts by Standard & Poor's.

Enhanced programming is attracting growing audiences, and the increase in viewers in turn is boosting cable's appeal to advertisers. The rapid growth in number of cable channels is also a factor.

William A. Donald, Standard & Poor's, (212) 208-8153, November 1998.

SATELLITE AND WIRELESS TECHNOLOGY

This subsector (SIC 48) includes direct broadcast satellite (DBS) services, wireless (MMDS) services, satellite master antenna (SMATV) services, and C-band/Ku-band satellite dish (DISH) services.

Satellite and wireless technology, or direct-to-home (DTH) satellite broadcasting systems, foregoes terrestrial wires and instead beams satellite programming directly to subscribers' satellite receiving dishes (dish antennas). DTH providers include DBS, MMDS, SMATV, and DISH technologies.

With the introduction of the 18-inch receiving dish, combined with substantially lower prices and stepped-up marketing, growth in DBS skyrocketed beginning in 1995, and double-digit growth continues without letup. From $1,000 or more in 1995, dish prices and installation costs have plunged. DBS operators keep new subscribers pouring in by frequently offering deeply discounted installation and equipment packages, typically starting at $49 for professional installation (discounted from the standard installation charge of $199) and $149–199 for the basic equipment, which includes the 18-inch dish. Pricing is not the whole story. Operators of DBS have taken advantage of their superior channel capacity over that of cable, touting their ability to offer subscribers 150 or more channels of entertainment.

DBS operators should enjoy nearly 18 percent average annual growth in number of subscribers in the 5 years through 2003. Industry revenues should rise 16 percent on average. The industry is losing money on the discounts offered on new-customer installation and equipment deals, but savvy packaging and pricing of programming fare and supplemental services fairly guarantee that revenues will continue to advance with new customer growth. From subscriber totals estimated at 8.2 million and revenues of $6.8 billion in 1998, DBS subscribers could climb to 18.6 million by 2003 with industry revenues at $14.3 billion.

Although DBS continues to grow rapidly, its inroads into cable's market share have been relatively minor. The proof is that cable subscriptions continue to grow at a 2 to 3 percent rate each year in spite of the phenomenal success of DBS marketing and awareness efforts. DBS systems provide sharper, clearer pictures than cable, and they also provide more programming choices. Both factors will become less advantageous as time passes. In 1998 cable began to make a significant start in upgrading to digital system delivery, which provides exceptional picture quality and superior channel capacity. DBS has several shortcomings relative to cable, including cost. Although much cheaper in 1998 than in 1995, the cost of the DBS dish, installation, and maintenance is borne by the subscriber. With cable, such costs are included in the monthly programming service fee. In most markets, DBS subscribers cannot receive locally originated over-the-air broadcast signals. The DBS subscriber must put up a rabbit ear antenna or subscribe to cable to receive the local channels. That explains why roughly one-fourth of DBS subscribers also subscribe to cable. DBS reception is limited to one television set per household without a special hookup for a second set. More than two television sets require additional DBS dishes. Furthermore, without another special hookup, all sets in a DBS household must be tuned to the same program. Cable systems do not have those limitations. Finally, DBS reception can be lost or badly disturbed in severe weather conditions.

The outlook for other DTH technologies is not nearly as positive as DBS or cable. Wireless, or MMDS (based on microwave broadcasts to rooftop or backyard antennas), has been at a disadvantage to cable for a number of years, hurt by its weaker signal quality, limited number of channels, and poor marketing. Therefore, the number of wireless subscribers has remained relatively stable, at about 1 million for several years. Rapid advancements in digital compression technology have virtually eliminated the disadvantages of channel capacity and signal quality. But the telcos, which were expected to be the industry's savior, seem to have given up on the medium as a way to compete with cable and at the same time sidestep the expense that extensive overbuilding of terrestrial cable plant would entail. For now at least, MMDS appears to be stuck in limbo, in need of deep financing to reinvent itself, in need of creative marketing and alliances, and in need of time to accomplish those things. Although the picture could change, it is more realistic to assume that over the next 5 years, through 2003, subscribers will average less than 1 million, and industry revenues will languish in the $500 million to $600 million range.

The C-band (backyard satellite dish) market has matured and is expected to continue to gradually shrink through 2003. Backyard satelllite dish subscribers grew by nearly 30 percent on average each year from 1990 through 1995, but the advent of the cheaper and smaller DBS dish halted the market for backyard dishes. C-band subscribers are primarily rural dwellers who are not served by cable systems. The C-band receiving dish is 7 feet in diameter and costs about $2,700. DBS dishes, in contrast, can be installed on a window ledge, thanks to their 18-inch diameter, and are substantially cheaper to own, install, and maintain.

William A. Donald, Standard & Poor's, (212) 208-8153, November 1998.

RADIO AND TELEVISION BROADCASTING

Radio broadcasting refers to the transmission of sound. Television signals—technically another form of radio—involve the transmission of both visual and aural content. With federal deregulation, the number of U.S. radio stations has expanded from roughly 10,500 in 1985 to over 12,275 in 1998. In the United States, commercial television broadcasting is conducted on 68 channels. The U.S. television market is the largest in the world, served by roughly 1,575 full-power television stations.

Radio and television stations derive the bulk of their revenues from advertising. In each market, stations use program formats and on-air talent to attract specific demographic audiences. The station's program ratings (audience size measures), the time of day the advertising runs, and the demographic qualities—mainly age and sex—of each program's typical listener or viewer determine the advertising rates that station owners charge and the attractiveness of that station or program to advertisers.

Factors Affecting U.S. Industry Growth

The radio and television industries include thousands of individual companies, but most of them are small mom-and-pop operations. However, broadcasting is an industry where size does matter. Within each segment, the biggest players claim a disproportionately large share of the business.

The Big Three television networks—ABC, CBS, and NBC—generally rake in more than 40 percent of the broadcast television industry's annual advertising revenue, and as much as 47 percent or more during Winter or Summer Olympics years. Although the Big Three will continue to see their future audience share whittled away by cable and other media outlets, they will still dominate television viewership and advertising for the foreseeable future. The top 25 owners of television stations together control 36 percent of the more than 1,200 commercial television stations in the United States as of April 1998. The top 25 owners controlled 33 percent in 1997 and 25 percent in 1996.

The 15 largest radio broadcasters, which own about 11 percent of all U.S. stations, accounted for about 42 percent of radio industry advertising revenues in 1997. In 1996 the top 15 radio broadcasters owned 6 percent of the stations and accounted for 34 percent of advertising revenues.

Audience size and demographic range are sought so that broadcasters can woo large national advertisers. At the same time, broadcasters are narrowing their focus, usually on a station-by-station or program-by-program basis, to attract narrowly defined audiences with distinct consumer profiles that appeal to certain advertisers. The challenge of reaching these niche groups is magnified by their growing elusiveness. Expanded choices for consumers and media users essentially splinter audiences, making them hard to target.

In general, the Big Three networks' (their combined affiliates number roughly 650 television stations) share of the prime-time television audience has declined over the past few decades. Their share has been whittled away in recent years by the growing popularity and availability of cable television (see Table 32-3); by the success of the 11-year-old Fox network; and since January 1995, by the growth of two new networks, United Paramount Network (UPN) and Warner Brothers Television Network (WB).

The dollar amount of broadcast television advertising continues to grow each year. However, broadcast television's share of the whole pie, compared with cable's, is shrinking, from 88.7 percent in 1990, to 80.8 percent in 1997, to a projected 68.6 percent in 2000 and 67.1 percent in 2003. Nevertheless, broadcast television is healthy and will remain so for years, bolstered by its ability to reach mass audiences. Supply and demand comes into play as the number of advertisers expands year after year. Yet the availability of advertising time slots on broadcast television remains relatively static. Although the broadcast television networks continue to lose share of viewers, the absolute dollars going into network television advertising continue to rise, largely reflecting pricing increases. Viewers are flocking to cable television, and there are plenty of cable stations with available time slots. Thus, cable advertising gains are more a function of volume gains rather than price increases.

Radio, formerly a poor laggard behind television in terms of advertising growth, has been in a healthy uptrend since 1993. Radio's resurgence was jump-started by a number of successful, industrywide marketing and training programs. Extensive research was spearheaded by the industry's trade group, Radio Advertising Bureau, beginning in the early 1990s. The effort increased advertising agency and advertiser awareness of radio's many pluses as an attractive medium. With greater visibility and improved marketing programs, the radio industry was primed to take advantage of eased station ownership rules in 1992 and further relaxation of station ownership limits in 1996. National limits on the number of radio stations that an entity can own have been removed. Depending on the number of radio stations operating in a market, a radio broadcaster can own as many as eight stations in that market but no more than five of one kind (AM or FM). The ensuing consolidation has allowed for the centralization of back-office functions such as sales, billing, and marketing. Cost savings are being successfully redeployed into product and sales efforts. The concentration of ownership across local markets and regions appeals to advertisers and advertising agencies that can now blanket a market with only one ad buy rather than negotiating on a station-by-station basis. This one-stop-shopping concept boosts the attractiveness of radio as an advertising medium, no matter whether the advertiser is a local merchant, a regional advertiser, or a national marketer.

Station trading has slowed from the heady pace of the early 1990s but should remain strong for the next 2 to 4 years. The positive impact on advertising growth should last well into the 2000s.

U.S. Industry Growth Projections for the Next 1 and 5 Years

The outlook for radio and broadcast television advertising is good both on a relative basis (compared with growth in total U.S. advertising) and on an absolute dollar basis. In addition to the factors already cited, advertising demand will be bolstered over the next 5 years by a fairly healthy U.S. economy, albeit one that is likely to be growing at a slower pace. Viewed as a whole, the radio and broadcast television industries should hold

TABLE 32-4: Radio and Television Advertising Revenues Trends and Forecasts
(millions of dollars)

	1995	1996	1997	1998	1999	2000	2001	2002	2003
Broadcast television	27,910	31,270	32,460	34,790	37,200	41,428	43,600	46,230	50,190
Radio	11,470	12,410	13,490	15,050	17,000	18,955	20,660	22,519	24,600
Total	39,380	43,680	45,950	49,840	54,200	60,383	64,260	68,749	74,790

Source: Television Bureau of Advertising; Radio Advertising Bureau. Forecasts by Standard & Poor's.

onto their share of the total U.S. advertising market over the next 5 years. Broadcast television garnered nearly 20 percent of the total U.S. advertising pie in 1997, while radio accounted for over 7 percent of total advertising spending in all media. By 2002, broadcast television should still be in the 20 percent range, while radio's share should be nearing 8 percent.

Combined advertising spending in broadcast television and radio is expected to rise to $54.20 billion in 1999, up 8.7 percent from the $49.84 billion estimated for 1998 (see Table 32-4). Combined gains should average 8.5 percent in each of the 5 years through 2003.

Radio will continue to exhibit the strongest growth of the two media, advancing 13 percent in 1999, nearly 12 percent in 2000, and averaging 10.4 percent in each year through 2003. Radio's momentum is being sustained by the factors just enumerated, including ownership deregulation, and aggressive and creative marketing innovations, augmented by rising rates charged per advertisement.

Broadcast television advertising growth should average 7.6 percent through 2003, with the heaviest growth coming in the year 2000, boosted by the Summer Olympics and election spending, including the presidential race. Both 1999 and 2000 will receive an additional boost from advertising and marketing related to the millennium. Although much of this will be entertainment related, all marketers are expected to take advantage of this once-in-a-lifetime occurrence. All advertising media will benefit from the year 2000 phenomenon.

William A. Donald, Standard & Poor's, (212) 208-8153, November 1998.

■ REFERENCES

Call the U.S. Bureau of the Census at (301) 457-2820 for information on ordering Census documents.

Advertising Age, Crain Communications, 220 E. 42nd Street, New York, NY 10017. (800) 992-9970, http://www.adage.com. Biweekly magazine with news of advertisers and ad agencies.

Alexander & Associates, 38 East 29th Street, 10th Floor, New York, NY 10016. (212) 684-0291.

American Demographics, Cowles Business Media, 108 N. Cayuga Street, Ithaca, NY 14850. (800) 828-1133, http://www.demographics.com. Monthly magazine with consumer market news.

American Film Marketing Association, Suite 600, 10850 Wilshire Boulevard, 9th Floor, Los Angeles, CA 90024. (310) 446-1000, www.afma.com.

Annual Survey of Communication Services: 1995, U.S. Department of Commerce, Bureau of the Census, Washington, DC 20230. (301) 457-2766. *Report BC/95,* a *Current Business Report,* covers telephone communications services, broadcasting services, and cable and other pay television Services, www.census.gov/prod/www/abs/msbus24a.html.

Billboard, Billboard Publications, Inc., 1515 Broadway, New York, NY 10036. (202) 764-7300, www.billboardonline.com.

Boxoffice, RLD Communications, Inc., 1800 North Highland Avenue, Hollywood, CA 90028. (213) 465-1186.

Broadcasting and Cable, Broadcasting Publications, Inc., 1735 DeSales Street, NW, Washington, DC 20036. (202) 659-2340.

Broadcasting & Cable, Cahners Publishing Co., 245 W. 17th Street, New York, NY 10011. (212) 645-0067, http://www.broadcasting-cable.com. Weekly magazine with news of the television, radio, and cable industries.

Cable Television Advertising Bureau (CAB), 757 Third Avenue, New York, NY 10017. (212) 751-7770. National association of cable system operators and programmers providing advertising and marketing assistance to members and advertisers. Also provides statistics and promotes cable advertising.

CableVision, Chilton Publications, 245 W. 17th Street, New York, NY 10011. (212) 887-8400, http://www.cvmag.com. Biweekly magazine with broad coverage of developments in cable television.

Cambridge Associates, Inc., 157 Breezy Hill Road, Stamford, CT 06903. (203) 322-6600.

Census of Service Industries, U.S. Department of Commerce, Bureau of the Census, Washington, DC 20233. (301) 457-2668, www.census.gov/epcd/www/sc92html.html.

DBS Digest, 140 W. 29th Street, #363, Pueblo, Colorado 81008. (719) 545-1210.

Federal Communications Commission (FCC), 1919 M Street, NW, Washington, DC 20554. (202) 632-7260, http://www.FCC.gov. Independent government agency whose mission is to encourage competition in all communications markets and to protect the public interest. At the direction of Congress, the FCC develops and implements policy concerning interstate and international communications by radio, television, wire, satellite, and cable.

Motion Picture Association of America, Inc., 1600 Eye Street, NW, Washington, DC 20006. (202) 293-1966, www.mpaa.org.

Movie & Home Entertainment, October 2, 1997, Standard and Poor's, 25 Broadway, New York, NY 10004.

Multichannel News Online, Cahners Business Information, http://www.multichannel.com/.

National Association of Broadcasters (NAB), 1771 N Street NW, Washington, DC 20036. (202) 429-5366, http://www.nab.org. National association of television and radio broadcasters providing legislative, legal, research, technical, marketing, and operational services and information.

National Association of Theater Owners, 4605 Lankershim Boulevard, Suite 340, North Hollywood, CA 91602. (818) 506-1778.

National Cable Television Association (NCTA), 1724 Massachusetts Avenue, NW, Washington, DC 20036. (202) 775-3550. National association of cable system operators and programmers providing legislative, legal, research, technical, marketing, and operational services and information, www.cable-online.com/ncta.htm.

Paul Kagan Associates, Inc., 126 Clock Tower Place, Carmel, CA 93923. (408) 624-1536.

Radio Advertising Bureau (RAB), 261 Madison Avenue, New York, NY 10016. (212) 681-7200. National association of radio broadcasters providing advertising and marketing statistics; also seeks to promote a favorable advertising climate and helps stations in their marketing efforts.

Radio Business Report, 6208-B Old Franconia Road, Alexandria, VA 22310. (703) 719-9500. Weekly newsletter about the radio industry.

Radio Business Source Guide, Radio Business Report, 6208-B Old Franconia Road, Alexandria, VA 22310. (703) 719-9500. Annual radio industry source guide and directory with industry statistics.

Recording Industry Association of America, Suite 300, 1330 Connecticut Avenue, NW, Washington, DC 20036. (202) 775-0101, www.riaa.com.

Television Bureau of Advertising (TVB), 850 Third Avenue, New York, NY 10022. (212) 486-1111. National association of television broadcasters providing advertising statistics. The group seeks to promote a favorable advertising climate in the television industry.

TVB News, Television Bureau of Advertising, 850 Third Avenue, New York, NY 10022. (212) 486-1111. Quarterly newsletter with statistics related to television advertising.

U.S. International Sales and Purchases of Services, Survey of Current Business, October 1997, U.S. Department of Commerce, Bureau of Economic Analysis, Washington, DC 20230. (202) 606-9573, www.bea.doc.gov.

Variety, Variety, Inc., 154 West 46th Street, New York, NY 10036. (212) 779-1100, www.variety.com.

Veronis, Suhler & Associates, 350 Park Avenue, New York, NY 10022. (212) 935-4990.

Video Software Dealers Association, 16530 Ventura Boulevard, Encino, CA 91436. (818) 385-1500, www.vsda.com.

■ RELATED CHAPTERS

25: Printing and Publishing
28: Computer Software and Networking
38: Household Consumer Durables

APPAREL AND FABRICATED TEXTILE PRODUCTS
Economic and Trade Trends

U.S. International Trade

Source: U.S. Department of Commerce: Bureau of the Census; International Trade Administration.

World Export Market Shares

Source: United Nations; U.S. Department of Commerce, International Trade Administration.

Export Dependence and Import Penetration

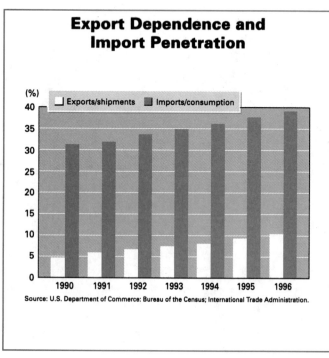

Source: U.S. Department of Commerce: Bureau of the Census; International Trade Administration.

Output and Output per Hour

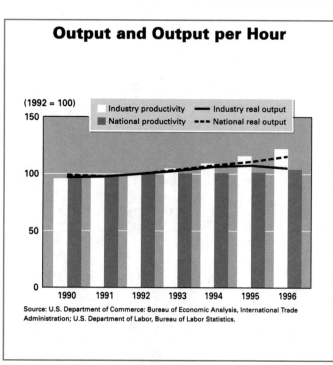

Source: U.S. Department of Commerce: Bureau of Economic Analysis, International Trade Administration; U.S. Department of Labor, Bureau of Labor Statistics.

See "Getting the Most Out of *Outlook '99*" for definitions of terms.

Apparel and Fabricated Textile Products

INDUSTRY DEFINITION SIC 23 covers 31 four-digit industries. These industries fall into the following nine groupings, as defined by the third digit: men's and boys' suits, coats, and overcoats (231); men's and boys' furnishings, work clothing, and allied garments (232); women's, misses', and juniors' outerwear (233); women's, misses', children's, and infants' undergarments (234); hats, caps, and millinery (235); girls', children's, and infants' outerwear (236); fur goods (237); miscellaneous apparel and accessories (238); and miscellaneous fabricated textile products (239). The fabricated textile products industry consists of eight four-digit industry groups: curtains and draperies (2391), home furnishings (2392), textile bags (2393), canvas and related products (2394), pleating and stitching (2395), automotive and apparel trimmings (2396), schiffli machine embroideries (2397), and fabricated textile products not elsewhere classified (2399). Products in the last group include items such as banners and flags, sleeping bags, nondisposable diapers, fishing nets, parachutes, and seat belts.

OVERVIEW

The apparel and fabricated textile products industry is a mature, slow-growing industry that plays an important role in the U.S. economy. Intense competition characterizes this industry and drives its ever-changing structure and operations. The most successful companies have recently undergone restructuring, become more involved in retailing, and increased overseas sourcing. Larger companies continue to gain an advantage over many smaller firms, and branded goods have become more important in the marketplace.

The apparel and fabricated textile products industry consists primarily of firms that produce and coordinate the production of wearing apparel, both cut and sewn and knit to shape, for all population groups. Apparel accounted for 70 percent of total industry shipments in 1997, while fabricated textile products, which include home furnishings, canvas products, and automotive trimmings, accounted for 30 percent.

Employment levels by state in this industry are shown in Figure 33-1.

FACTORS AFFECTING FUTURE INDUSTRY GROWTH

Intense competition for consumers' dollars, changing work habits, demographic changes, an evolving retail structure, new technology, and increasing levels of imports produced with low-cost labor have led to major structural changes in the apparel and fabricated textile products industry.

The U.S. economy has grown at a slow, steady pace in the 1990s. Key positive factors for the apparel and fabricated textile products industry have been low unemployment in the overall economy, rising incomes, a record-setting stock market, low inflation, and low interest rates, which keep consumer confidence high and maintain high levels of spending at

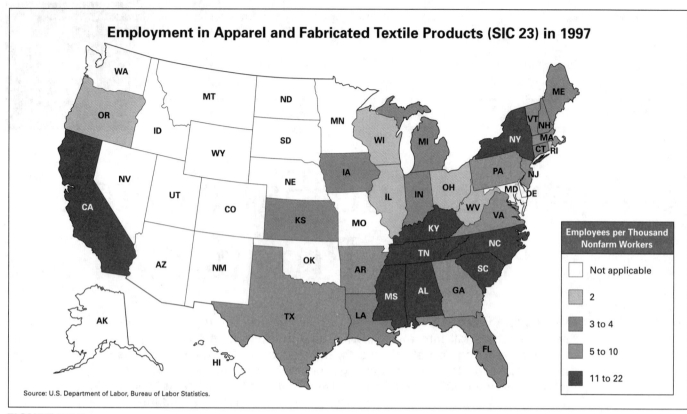

Employment in Apparel and Fabricated Textile Products (SIC 23) in 1997

Employees per Thousand Nonfarm Workers

- Not applicable
- 2
- 3 to 4
- 5 to 10
- 11 to 22

Source: U.S. Department of Labor, Bureau of Labor Statistics.

FIGURE 33-1

retail. Forecasts call for continued solid, sustainable growth.

However, U.S. expenditures for apparel have grown more slowly than have expenditures for all goods and services. Between 1992 and 1997 total personal consumption expenditures grew at an average annual rate of 5.4 percent compared with 4.2 percent growth for spending on clothing. This represents a significant slowdown from the rate of growth of apparel expenditures in the 1980s. The markets for apparel and home furnishings are mature and relatively saturated. Changes in consumer buying habits, with an emphasis on value, have led to more shopping at discounters, warehouses, and off-price stores.

Changing demographic trends have played a significant role in the slowdown in the growth of expenditures for apparel. The segment of the population age 45 years and over accounts for 34 percent of the total population, a number that is expected to grow to 38 percent by 2005. The aging of the U.S. population has many ramifications for the apparel and fabricated textile products industry. Baby boomers are moving away from their free-spending days of the last two decades and focusing on other priorities. An older population tends to spend a greater proportion of its income on mortgages, college expenses, and retirement savings.

Changing demographic trends also are providing a boost for some segments of the apparel industry. The children of baby boomers (the "echo boom") are rapidly becoming consumers. For the next 10 years the teenage segment of the population is expected to grow much faster than is the overall population. Today's teenagers have greater amounts of spending money than ever before, spend more than they earn, and will account for a growing proportion of apparel spending, particularly on products targeted for this market. Teens also readily adapt to Internet marketing promotions, creating opportunity for technology-oriented companies. The growth in the 65-and-older segment of the population also bodes well for apparel manufacturers because this segment is more fit and active and has more disposable income than ever before and requires clothing suitable for an active lifestyle.

Consumers have less time to shop because of their busy work schedules and prefer to spend more of their leisure time at home with family and friends. This trend is known as "cocooning." It benefits manufacturers of home furnishings as consumers attempt to make their homes comfortable and attractive but has a negative impact on apparel manufacturers. Cocooning makes buying new clothes less important for many people. Lack of time to shop also leads to an increasing share of clothing and home furnishing purchases being made through direct mail and the Internet.

The growing number of employers that accept more casual dress has caused major changes in the apparel industry. The one-day-a-week casual dress code, which began with high-tech firms, has been widely implemented by major corporations and has spawned a new market called "Friday wear," which has been very successful.

Consumers' search for value and the availability of low-cost imports have had enormous implications for the apparel and fabricated textile products industry. Price and quality have become the key factors in apparel purchases, and this has led to price pressures in the industry. Wholesale apparel prices increased 3 percent over the period 1993 to 1997, while consumer apparel prices declined 2 percent. Consumers' demand for quality and value increasingly has been met by imports from low-wage countries and a shift of production offshore.

GLOBAL INDUSTRY TRENDS

Many factors influence demand for U.S. apparel and fabricated textile products, but none is as significant as the impact of global competition. Global apparel trade has become much less concentrated, with more countries participating every year.

The World Trade Organization Agreement on Textiles and Clothing (ATC) provides for the phaseout of existing import quotas over a 10-year period beginning on January 1, 1995. Although most quotas are still in effect, the eventual phaseout and the current annual growth in existing quotas have allowed U.S. imports of apparel and fabricated textile products to continue to grow.

The largest suppliers of imported apparel and fabricated textile products to the U.S. market in 1997 in terms of value were China, Mexico, Hong Kong, Taiwan, and the Dominican Republic (see Table 33-1). Among these five countries, the growth of imports from the Asian countries has been slower than that from Mexico. These five countries account for nearly half of U.S. imports of all apparel and fabricated textile products. Imports from the traditional Big Four suppliers (China, Taiwan, Hong Kong, and Korea) have been losing some of their share of the U.S. market since the beginning of the 1990s. The countries that have gained a larger share of the market are Mexico and the Caribbean nations that

receive production-sharing trade preferences. Arrivals of Harmonized Tariff Schedule of the United States (HTSUS) 9802 (formerly 807) goods now account for 26 percent of all apparel imports, up from 9 percent in 1990. HTSUS 9802 permits apparel components to be shipped to low-wage countries for assembly and then returned to the United States, with duty paid only on the value added. Apparel assembled in Mexico from fabric formed and cut in the United States reenters the United States duty-free. In 1997 apparel imports grew 16.5 percent, more than double the 7 percent average annual growth rate between 1992 and 1996, with growth in most segments of the industry increasing sharply.

A significant uncertainty in the global apparel market is the impact of the Asian financial crisis. The five countries most affected by that crisis—Indonesia, Korea, Thailand, the Philippines, and Malaysia—are important apparel producers. The currency devaluations in those countries tend to make their products cheaper in the global marketplace and exert downward pressure on the pricing of the products of competitor countries. However, the price effect of the devaluations is mitigated by certain factors, including the fact that the Asian producers import large quantities of fiber, yarn, fabric, and other inputs to apparel production; those inputs cost them more as a result of the devaluations. Another factor is that the credit and foreign exchange crunch in those countries has had a negative impact on the operations of their domestic producers.

DOMESTIC TRENDS

The U.S. apparel and fabricated textile products industry is large and highly fragmented. Almost all manufacturers in the industry are dealing with increased pressure to improve the design of their products while keeping prices low and meeting growing demands made by retailers.

TABLE 33-1: U.S. Trade Patterns in Apparel and Fabricated Textile Products[1] in 1997
(millions of dollars; percent)

Exports			Imports		
Regions[2]	Value[3]	Share, %	Regions[2]	Value[3]	Share, %
NAFTA	3,294	36.9	NAFTA	7,708	15.4
Latin America	3,842	43.0	Latin America	8,271	16.5
Western Europe	626	7.0	Western Europe	3,402	6.8
Japan/Chinese Economic Area	786	8.8	Japan/Chinese Economic Area	14,378	28.6
Other Asia	141	1.6	Other Asia	14,034	28.0
Rest of world	242	2.7	Rest of world	2,396	4.8
World	8,930	100.0	World	50,190	100.0
Top Five Countries	Value	Share, %	Top Five Countries	Value	Share, %
Mexico	2,349	26.3	China	7,964	15.9
Dominican Republic	1,088	12.2	Mexico	6,275	12.5
Canada	945	10.6	Hong Kong (PRC)	4,027	8.0
Honduras	800	9.0	Taiwan	2,291	4.6
Japan	691	7.7	Dominican Republic	2,251	4.5

[1] SIC 23.
[2] For definitions of regional groupings, see "Getting the Most Out of *Outlook '99*."
[3] Values may not sum to total due to rounding.
Source: U.S. Department of Commerce: Bureau of the Census.

TABLE 33-2: Apparel and Fabricated Textile Products (SIC 23) Trends and Forecasts

(millions of dollars except as noted)

	1992	1993	1994	1995	1996	1997[1]	1998[2]	1999[3]	Percent Change 96–97	97–98	98–99	92–96[4]
Industry data												
Value of shipments[5]	71,658	74,010	76,979	78,103	77,628	79,025	80,053	80,933	1.8	1.3	1.1	2.0
Value of shipments (1992$)	71,658	73,339	76,063	76,601	74,976	75,645	75,766	75,992	0.9	0.2	0.3	1.1
Total employment (thousands)	985	980	954	947	865							-3.2
Production workers (thousands)	824	825	799	792	726							-3.1
Average hourly earnings ($)	7.12	7.34	7.44	7.56	7.67							1.9
Product data												
Value of shipments[5]	68,844	70,986	73,258	73,780	73,319	74,639	75,609	76,441	1.8	1.3	1.1	1.6
Value of shipments (1992$)	68,844	70,345	72,382	72,370	70,843	71,446	71,560	71,773	0.9	0.2	0.3	0.7
Trade data												
Value of imports	32,644	35,475	38,561	41,208	43,075	50,190	56,808	64,704	16.5	13.2	13.9	7.2
Value of exports	4,659	5,433	6,009	6,979	7,836	8,930	9,450	10,301	14.0	5.8	9.0	13.9

[1] Estimate except imports and exports.
[2] Estimate.
[3] Forecast.
[4] Compound annual rate.
[5] For a definition of industry versus product values, see "Getting the Most Out of *Outlook '99*."
Source: U.S. Department of Commerce: Bureau of the Census; International Trade Administration.

U.S. industry shipments of apparel and fabricated textile products continued to have a modest expansion in 1997, but employment remained on a downtrend (see Table 33-2). Despite improvements in technology and increases in productivity, the manufacturing processes in this industry are still labor-intensive. Wages and profit margins in this sector are low relative to those in other manufacturing industries. In 1996 the hourly earnings of production workers averaged $7.67, having risen at a compound annual growth rate of 2 percent since 1992. Employees making men's neckwear and tailored clothing had the highest hourly wages, while workers making men's underwear and women's blouses earned the least. The Clothing Manufacturers Association and the largest apparel labor union, UNITE, recently reached an agreement on a new contract covering 25,000 tailored clothing workers which calls for pay hikes of $0.65 per hour over 3 years. The earnings of apparel and fabricated textile product workers were about 38 percent below the average for all U.S. manufacturing employees and about 33 percent below those of workers in nondurable goods industries in 1996.

Total employment in the apparel and fabricated textile products industry was approximately 865,000 workers in 1996, representing an average 3 percent annual decline since 1992. Employment has been declining almost steadily since 1973, and this is reflected in all industry segments except fabricated textile products. Production workers constituted 84 percent of the work force in 1996, compared with 69 percent for all U.S. manufacturing. Women, blacks, and Hispanic workers constitute a larger share of the work force in this industry than they do in total U.S. manufacturing employment. A few large apparel companies announced significant layoffs in 1997, in some cases because of a shift in production offshore or a decline in demand for their products.

The continuing decline in employment has resulted from a variety of factors. Imports from low-wage countries have been a key factor, and their share of the U.S. apparel market has increased significantly. The North American Free Trade Agreement (NAFTA) and the Caribbean Basin Initiative (CBI) encourage production sharing within the western hemisphere, with many of the more skilled and higher-paying jobs remaining in the United States. Advances in productivity have allowed manufacturers to maintain their production levels with fewer workers.

Manufacturers have had their profits consistently squeezed since the prices of raw materials rose in the mid-1990s, when cotton was in short supply. Although these input prices have eased, competition from cheap imports, the reluctance of consumers to pay higher prices, and growing pressure from retailers have forced U.S. manufacturers to restrain price increases. The Asian financial crisis is expected to provide additional downward pressure on prices.

Retail sales of apparel and accessory stores were sluggish in 1995 but picked up in 1996–1997 and in mid-1998 were running about 6 percent higher than the level in 1997. Consumers continue to shift retail purchases from department stores to discounters and off-price stores and also to catalog shopping and the emerging area of Internet shopping, which may not be reflected in retail sales statistics.

STRUCTURAL CHANGES

Several trends particular to the apparel and fabricated textile products industry will have a profound impact on U.S. companies in coming years. The trend toward casual dress at work, coupled with the escalating number of people working at home full time or part time, has increased the demand for casual clothing, including slacks, sport shirts, and sweaters. This has come to be known as "corporate casual" or "Friday wear." This trend toward wearing casual clothing is expected to continue. Recently, a partial recovery has occurred in the noncasual segment. In the future there may be more blending between casual and other styles. Following the trend toward casual wear, ease of care is becoming more important, with wrinkle-free fabrics growing in popularity. Manufacturers that offer fashionable, comfortable, value-priced casual clothes should have growing sales.

The increasing importance of brand apparel, particularly among the affluent teenage segment of the population, bodes well for brand marketing companies and their licensees. Consumers rely on brand merchandise to provide quality and consistency. In addition to the traditional brands established by apparel companies, proprietary retail brands backed by aggressive marketing and competitive pricing are becoming more familiar and are more in demand among consumers.

Structural changes in the industry include manufacturers becoming retailers and retailers becoming contractors to increase efficiency in production and eliminate middlemen. Many companies that participate in these arrangements are also interested in creating brands. On the manufacturing side, both textile mills and apparel firms have become involved in assembling apparel and retailing. The advantage of the closer integration of manufacturing and retailing lies in control over the entire process, including quality and scheduling, and the ability to react quickly to changes in demand. Some textile firms are experimenting with one-stop shopping for retailers or apparel firms that are moving from manufacturing to concentrate on marketing. These textile companies make and cut the fabric, have it assembled by contractors, and then take care of packaging and delivery, creating ready-to-retail garments.

Mass merchandisers, specialty retailers, and upscale retailers are participating in the trend toward private labels. The biggest advantage for retailers is that they quickly can judge what consumers are buying and then quickly make more of those products. Some retailers have turned to selling exclusively private label merchandise and maintain large design departments. Private label retailers can control the quality and schedule the manufacturing of the products they sell as well as control the pricing. Traditional apparel manufacturers are evolving into marketing firms that promote traditional brands, manufacture private label goods, or, more recently, form partnerships with textile suppliers to provide finished products.

Retail consolidation has had a significant impact on apparel manufacturers, shifting industry dominance from large apparel manufacturers to larger and more powerful retailers. About two-thirds of apparel is now sold through just 12 major retail groups. With fewer strong retail outlets, manufacturers are being forced to deal with retailers' pressure to keep prices down and increasing demand for ready-to-retail goods. Most retailers have narrowed both the assortment of goods they carry and the number of vendors they use in order to reduce costs. This increases competition among domestic manufacturers and foreign suppliers.

LABOR STANDARDS

Many apparel manufacturers and retailers have taken action to make sure they do not operate sweatshops or employ child labor domestically or offshore. Consumers have become more aware of and concerned about the source of goods available to them. In 1997 President Clinton announced the establishment of an Apparel Industry Partnership which is attempting to end sweatshop conditions around the world and guarantee American consumers that the clothes and shoes they buy are not made by exploited workers. In the partnership leaders from the apparel and footwear industries, labor, nongovernmental organizations, and consumer groups have agreed to a code of conduct and independent monitoring systems that will assure that

TABLE 33-3: U.S. Trade Patterns in Apparel[1] in 1997
(millions of dollars; percent)

Exports			Imports		
Regions[2]	Value[3]	Share, %	Regions[2]	Value[3]	Share, %
NAFTA	2,625	33.7	NAFTA	6,392	13.9
Latin America	3,709	47.6	Latin America	8,156	17.7
Western Europe	516	6.6	Western Europe	2,955	6.4
Japan/Chinese Economic Area	697	8.9	Japan/Chinese Economic Area	13,059	28.4
Other Asia	90	1.2	Other Asia	13,169	28.6
Rest of world	159	2.0	Rest of world	2,274	4.9
World	7,797	100.0	World	46,005	100.0
Top Five Countries	Value	Share, %	Top Five Countries	Value	Share, %
Mexico	2,093	26.8	China	6,956	15.1
Dominican Republic	1,072	13.7	Mexico	5,137	11.2
Honduras	793	10.2	Hong Kong (PRC)	4,006	8.7
Japan	624	8.0	Dominican Republic	2,231	4.8
Canada	532	6.8	Taiwan	2,035	4.4

[1] SIC 231, 232, 233, 234, 235, 236, 237, 238.
[2] For definitions of regional groupings, see "Getting the Most Out of *Outlook '99*."
[3] Values may not sum to total due to rounding.
Source: U.S. Department of Commerce: Bureau of the Census.

the clothing and shoes available in the marketplace are made under decent and humane working conditions. The strong workplace code of conduct, which companies voluntarily adopt and require their contractors to adopt, includes the prohibition of child labor, worker abuse and harassment, and discrimination; recognition of workers' rights to freedom of association and collective bargaining; a minimum or prevailing industry wage; a cap on mandatory overtime to 12 hours a week; and a safe and healthy working environment. The partnership also has agreed to recruit others in the industry and develop an independent association to assure compliance and inform consumers about the code and the companies that comply with it.

Eighteen manufacturers and other groups are members of the partnership. These companies and certain other manufacturers and retailers have signed the "No Sweat" pledge to help eradicate sweatshops in America and try to ensure that their shelves are stocked only with "No Sweat" garments.

PROJECTIONS OF INDUSTRY AND TRADE GROWTH

A tough retail environment, rapid changes in communications, shifts in global production, and demanding consumers have forced changes in the apparel and fabricated textile products industry. Retailers' demands for lower prices have forced many manufacturers to choose between shifting some or all production to other countries and closing up shop. Many companies are trying to balance their production mix to take advantage of low-cost foreign labor but maintain enough domestic workers to take advantage of the much quicker domestic delivery schedules.

Information technology will be the key to helping companies cope with these new demands. Rapid data exchange is essential to two methodologies which give domestic companies an advantage over offshore producers: quick response (QR), which is used for seasonal merchandise, and vendor-managed inventory (VMI), which is used for basic products such as jeans and underwear. In using the QR strategy, a vendor ships a portion of the retailer's goods before the selling season and then adjusts the remainder of the product mix on the basis of point-of-sale (POS) data provided by the retailer. Under VMI, the stock of basic garments is managed by using POS data to replenish styles and sizes which have been sold. These methodologies help retailers keep inventories low but also help prevent lost sales because of out-of-stock situations. Manufacturers which can respond quickly to retail needs will increasingly have the advantage over faraway sources.

Government agencies are helping the industry develop and apply new technologies. The American Textile Partnership (AMTEX), a joint venture of the industry and the U.S. Department of Energy, is working to link textile mills, apparel manufacturers, wholesalers, and retailers in an electronic network that allows all industry segments to respond more quickly and efficiently to changing consumer spending patterns. The National Textile Center (NTC), a research consortium of six universities, and the Textile/Clothing Technology Corp. (TC^2), both of which receive funds through the U.S. Department of Commerce, are working with the industry to develop technology to automate product design, production, and distribution.

Successful companies are looking for niche markets and new ways to sell products to consumers. Custom-fit apparel was pioneered several years ago and, while still constituting a small portion of the market, continues to increase its share. Producing garments for individual shoppers is featured for jeans, swimsuits, and upper-end suits. In school systems, a growing trend

TABLE 33-4: U.S. Trade Patterns in Fabricated Textile Products[1] in 1997
(millions of dollars; percent)

Exports			Imports		
Regions[2]	Value[3]	Share, %	Regions[2]	Value[3]	Share, %
NAFTA	668	60.2	NAFTA	1,317	31.5
Latin America	126	11.4	Latin America	115	2.7
Western Europe	105	9.5	Western Europe	448	10.7
Japan/Chinese Economic Area	87	7.8	Japan/Chinese Economic Area	1,319	31.5
Other Asia	49	4.4	Other Asia	865	20.7
Rest of world	75	6.8	Rest of world	122	2.9
World	1,110	100.0	World	4,186	100.0
Top Five Countries	Value	Share, %	Top Five Countries	Value	Share, %
Canada	413	37.2	Mexico	1,138	27.2
Mexico	256	23.0	China	1,008	24.1
Japan	66	5.9	India	265	6.3
United Kingdom	31	2.8	Pakistan	258	6.2
Australia	19	1.7	Taiwan	256	6.1

[1] SIC 239.
[2] For definitions of regional groupings, see "Getting the Most Out of *Outlook '99*."
[3] Values may not sum to total due to rounding.
Source: U.S. Department of Commerce: Bureau of the Census.

TABLE 33-5: Selected Men's and Boys' Apparel (SIC 231, 2321, 2323, 2325, 2326) Trends and Forecasts

(millions of dollars except as noted)

	1992	1993	1994	1995	1996	1997[1]	1998[2]	1999[3]	Percent Change 96–97	97–98	98–99	92–96[4]
Industry data												
Value of shipments[5]	16,991	16,819	17,088	17,426	17,208	17,507	17,692	17,888	1.7	1.1	1.1	0.3
231 Men's/boys' suits/coats	2,430	2,463	2,362	2,078	1,968	1,988	2,023	2,038	1.0	1.8	0.7	−5.1
2321 Men's/boys' shirts	5,921	5,012	5,082	5,186	4,939	5,045	5,078	5,131	2.1	0.6	1.0	−4.4
2323 Men's/boys' neckwear	618	619	705	792	652	664	670	674	1.8	1.0	0.5	1.3
2325 Men's/boys' trousers	6,519	7,055	7,226	7,506	7,658	7,785	7,873	7,968	1.7	1.1	1.2	4.1
2326 Men's/boys' work clothing	1,503	1,670	1,714	1,863	1,991	2,025	2,047	2,077	1.7	1.1	1.5	7.3
Value of shipments (1992$)	16,991	16,538	16,669	16,837	16,437	16,698	16,796	16,678	1.6	0.6	−0.7	−0.8
231 Men's/boys' suits/coats	2,430	2,471	2,338	2,044	1,915	1,909	1,897	1,911	−0.3	−0.6	0.7	−5.8
2321 Men's/boys' shirts	5,921	4,938	5,017	5,104	4,880	5,021	5,157	5,134	2.9	2.7	−0.4	−4.7
2323 Men's/boys' neckwear	618	611	695	772	628	632	651	646	0.7	2.9	−0.8	0.4
2325 Men's/boys' trousers	6,519	6,889	6,975	7,169	7,190	7,293	7,252	7,167	1.4	−0.6	−1.2	2.5
2326 Men's/boys' work clothing	1,503	1,629	1,644	1,748	1,823	1,843	1,839	1,820	1.1	−0.2	−1.0	4.9
Total employment (thousands)	245	229	225	216	185							−6.8
231 Men's/boys' suits/coats	44.0	41.2	34.0	31.1	27.1							−11.4
2321 Men's/boys' shirts	84.4	72.7	73.8	71.0	59.1							−8.5
2323 Men's/boys' neckwear	7.5	6.3	6.2	5.6	4.7							−11.0
2325 Men's/boys' trousers	78.9	78.5	82.2	79.4	70.9							−2.6
2326 Men's/boys' work clothing	30.4	30.0	28.5	28.6	23.4							−6.3
Production workers (thousands)	214	199	197	190	163							−6.6
231 Men's/boys' suits/coats	37.4	34.7	28.7	26.3	22.2							−12.2
2321 Men's/boys' shirts	74.2	64.1	67.0	64.4	53.1							−8.0
2323 Men's/boys' neckwear	5.8	4.8	4.6	4.0	3.5							−11.9
2325 Men's/boys' trousers	69.8	68.4	71.9	70.4	64.3							−2.0
2326 Men's/boys' work clothing	26.4	26.5	24.4	24.8	19.6							−7.2
Average hourly earnings ($)	6.94	7.21	7.18	7.45	7.67							2.5
231 Men's/boys' suits/coats	7.96	8.32	8.35	8.13	8.40							1.4
2321 Men's/boys' shirts	6.85	6.90	6.96	7.20	7.38							1.9
2323 Men's/boys' neckwear	7.39	8.43	9.21	9.82	10.16							8.3
2325 Men's/boys' trousers	6.81	7.15	7.03	7.40	7.69							3.1
2326 Men's/boys' work clothing	6.06	6.47	6.49	7.19	7.17							4.3
Product data												
Value of shipments[5]	15,810	15,405	16,129	16,096	15,441	15,708	15,875	16,051	1.7	1.1	1.1	−0.6
231 Men's/boys' suits/coats	2,387	2,257	2,417	2,020	1,913	1,933	1,967	1,981	1.0	1.8	0.7	−5.4
2321 Men's/boys' shirts	5,318	4,632	4,709	4,792	4,303	4,395	4,424	4,470	2.1	0.6	1.0	−5.2
2323 Men's/boys' neckwear	544	529	594	618	574	584	590	593	1.8	1.0	0.5	1.4
2325 Men's/boys' trousers	6,065	6,338	6,636	6,771	6,757	6,869	6,947	7,031	1.7	1.1	1.2	2.7
2326 Men's/boys' work clothing	1,495	1,650	1,773	1,895	1,894	1,926	1,947	1,975	1.7	1.1	1.5	6.1
Value of shipments (1992$)	15,810	15,147	15,733	15,550	14,744	14,975	15,059	14,955	1.6	0.6	−0.7	−1.7
231 Men's/boys' suits/coats	2,387	2,263	2,393	1,986	1,861	1,856	1,844	1,858	−0.3	−0.6	0.7	−6.0
2321 Men's/boys' shirts	5,318	4,563	4,649	4,717	4,252	4,374	4,493	4,473	2.9	2.7	−0.4	−5.4
2323 Men's/boys' neckwear	544	521	586	602	553	557	573	569	0.7	2.9	−0.8	0.4
2325 Men's/boys' trousers	6,065	6,190	6,405	6,467	6,344	6,435	6,399	6,324	1.4	−0.6	−1.2	1.1
2326 Men's/boys' work clothing	1,495	1,609	1,700	1,777	1,734	1,753	1,750	1,731	1.1	−0.2	−1.0	3.8
Trade data												
Value of imports	7,624	8,281	9,178	10,873	11,426	13,282	15,454	17,930	16.2	16.4	16.0	10.6
231 Men's/boys' suits/coats	789	824	954	1,042	1,134	1,317	1,430	1,559	16.1	8.6	9.0	9.5
2321 Men's/boys' shirts	4,028	4,519	4,917	5,875	6,006	6,810	8,298	9,957	13.4	21.9	20.0	10.5
2323 Men's/boys' neckwear	151	158	156	167	174	184	185	191	5.6	0.7	3.0	3.6
2325 Men's/boys' trousers	2,657	2,780	3,151	3,789	4,113	4,972	5,541	6,223	20.9	11.5	12.3	11.5
2326 Men's/boys' work clothing	0	0	0	0	0	0	0	0				
Value of exports	1,478	1,795	2,036	2,158	2,374	2,661	2,300	2,336	12.1	−13.6	1.6	12.6
231 Men's/boys' suits/coats	197	237	292	269	264	251	223	226	−4.9	−11.1	1.3	7.6
2321 Men's/boys' shirts	457	595	721	842	919	1,091	982	992	18.8	−10.0	1.0	19.1
2323 Men's/boys' neckwear	15.5	21.1	17.9	18.4	21.1	20.6	22.5	23.7	−2.4	9.3	5.1	8.0
2325 Men's/boys' trousers	809	942	1,005	1,029	1,170	1,298	1,071	1,094	11.0	−17.5	2.1	9.7
2326 Men's/boys' work clothing	0	0	0	0	0	0	0	0				

[1] Estimate except imports and exports.
[2] Estimate.
[3] Forecast.
[4] Compound annual rate.
[5] For a definition of industry versus product values, see "Getting the Most Out of *Outlook '99*."
Source: U.S. Department of Commerce: Bureau of the Census; International Trade Administration.

toward requiring student uniforms is providing an opportunity for companies that can meet the demand. Other companies are creating markets for new products by using high-tech materials such as Gore-tex and other moisture-management fabrics, wrinkle-resistant comfortable fabrics, and Polartec and other fabrics designed for warmth.

In addition, retailers and manufacturers are exploring new ways to sell their products. Catalog shopping is becoming more popular as consumers reduce the amount of time they spend in stores. Some traditional store-based retailers recently introduced catalogs. The Internet, which is rapidly becoming available to American households, especially those with children and teenagers, is being used by retailers and manufacturers to dispense product information and offer merchandise for sale. Some sites offer exclusive on-line discounts to lure customers. Some start-up apparel companies have found that opening a Web site is the easiest way to break into the market. Internet commerce is expected to become more significant as the Internet usage and content expands and security is improved. Manufacturers have found that both catalog and Internet retail methods encourage international sales.

GLOBAL MARKET PROSPECTS

While the U.S. sewn products industry historically has not been export-oriented, U.S. manufacturers have turned their attention to overseas markets in recent years rather than depend solely on the relatively slow-growing domestic market. Exports of apparel and fabricated textile products accounted for 12 percent of product shipments in 1997, up from 7 percent in 1992. In the period 1992–1997, exports achieved a compound annual gain of 14 percent (see Table 33-2).

Exports of apparel rose 16 percent from 1996 to 1997, reaching $7.8 billion. Apparel export data include components exported for assembly in other countries and returned to the United States as imports under HTSUS 9802. Exports to the NAFTA member Mexico and to the CBI beneficiary countries, which are the main partners in these production-sharing arrangements, have advanced sharply in recent years and accounted for about 70 percent of total apparel exports in 1997.

Canada, Japan, and the European Union (EU) are the major destinations for finished U.S. apparel exports (rather than cut parts). These markets are exhibiting contrasting trends. The ongoing integration of the North American economy driven by NAFTA, coupled with a robust Canadian economy, has resulted in strong growth in apparel exports to Canada, a trend which appears to be continuing (see Table 33-3).

Japan, which has been suffering from a weak economy and currency, sharply curtailed its imports of U.S. apparel in 1997 and the first half of 1998. The relatively high-cost lifestyle and fashion-forward merchandise the United States exports to Japan is vulnerable to weak discretionary consumer spending. The Asian financial crisis also has had a negative impact on U.S. exports to the markets most affected by it, such as Korea and the Philippines, although these historically are small markets for U.S. apparel.

The EU market for U.S. apparel has been relatively flat with a downward bias. Men's and boys' trousers and knit shirts are the largest exports to Canada, Japan, and the EU. Although the volume is relatively small, exports of U.S. clothing to South America, eastern Europe, and China also have been growing because in those areas demand for upscale goods, status symbols, and western looks is increasing.

U.S. manufacturers have taken advantage of their reputation for high-quality, long-term export strategies, and U.S.

TABLE 33-6: Men's and Boys' Underwear and Nightwear (SIC 2322) Trends and Forecasts
(millions of dollars except as noted)

									Percent Change			
	1992	1993	1994	1995	1996	1997[1]	1998[2]	1999[3]	96–97	97–98	98–99	92–96[4]
Industry data												
Value of shipments[5]	820	581	664	592	590	595	602	608	0.9	1.1	1.0	−7.9
Value of shipments (1992$)	820	578	660	586	578	576	573	576	−0.3	−0.6	0.5	−8.4
Total employment (thousands)	14.2	11.3	10.5	7.8	6.9							−16.5
Production workers (thousands)	13.1	10.5	10.1	7.5	6.5							−16.1
Average hourly earnings ($)	6.67	6.48	7.03	7.10	6.46							−0.8
Product data												
Value of shipments[5]	808	689	743	674	578	583	590	596	0.9	1.1	1.0	−8.0
Value of shipments (1992$)	808	685	738	667	567	565	561	564	−0.4	−0.6	0.5	−8.5
Trade data												
Value of imports	396	528	652	963	1,229	1,661	2,045	2,556	35.2	23.1	25.0	32.7
Value of exports	218	314	331	431	531	624	549	532	17.6	−12.1	−3.0	24.9

[1] Estimate except imports and exports.
[2] Estimate.
[3] Forecast.
[4] Compound annual rate.
[5] For a definition of industry versus product values, see "Getting the Most Out of Outlook '99."
Source: U.S. Department of Commerce: Bureau of the Census; International Trade Administration.

government–sponsored foreign trade fairs and export seminars to increase the level of their shipments abroad. Occasionally modifications in design and fit are necessary to sell in foreign markets, but many times customers are seeking the American look and ease of care and wearing. In addition to export sales through traditional distribution channels, apparel exporters are selling directly to foreign consumers through catalogs and the Internet.

Exports of fabricated textile products continued to increase in 1997, reaching $1.1 billion. The NAFTA partners Canada and Mexico accounted for about 60 percent of the market for these products and are among the fastest growing markets. In 1997 exports of fabricated textile products were up to the EU and were stable to the Far East (see Table 33-4).

The U.S. Department of Commerce's Office of Textiles and Apparel (OTEXA) provides firms with assistance in selling to foreign countries, including a new exporting database with information on country markets and listings of overseas buyers and U.S. exporters. OTEXA also facilitates participation in trade fairs in many parts of the world.

TABLE 33-7: Selected Women's Outerwear (SIC 2331, 2335, 2337) Trends and Forecasts
(millions of dollars except as noted)

	1992	1993	1994	1995	1996	1997[1]	1998[2]	1999[3]	Percent Change 96–97	97–98	98–99	92–96[4]
Industry data												
Value of shipments[5]	13,733	14,123	14,598	14,413	13,851	14,117	14,415	14,611	1.9	2.1	1.4	0.2
2331 Women's/misses blouses	3,970	4,012	4,147	3,797	3,649	3,700	3,792	3,826	1.4	2.5	0.9	−2.1
2335 Women's/misses dresses	5,366	5,602	6,396	6,928	6,606	6,730	6,876	6,982	1.9	2.2	1.5	5.3
2337 Women's suits and coats	4,397	4,509	4,055	3,688	3,596	3,687	3,747	3,802	2.5	1.6	1.5	−4.9
Value of shipments (1992$)	13,733	14,063	14,644	14,604	14,248	14,567	14,582	14,725	2.2	0.1	1.0	0.9
2331 Women's/misses blouses	3,970	3,976	4,053	3,686	3,563	3,651	3,694	3,694	2.5	1.2	−0.0	−2.7
2335 Women's/misses dresses	5,366	5,597	6,507	7,128	6,896	6,992	6,936	7,036	1.4	−0.8	1.5	6.5
2337 Women's suits and coats	4,397	4,491	4,084	3,790	3,789	3,924	3,952	3,995	3.6	0.7	1.1	−3.7
Total employment (thousands)	188	190	182	186	169							−2.5
2331 Women's/misses blouses	56.1	52.9	51.8	47.8	42.9							−6.5
2335 Women's/misses dresses	83.2	87.1	87.5	99.3	93.3							2.9
2337 Women's suits and coats	48.3	49.6	43.1	38.8	33.0							−9.1
Production workers (thousands)	156	159	151	156	143							−2.2
2331 Women's/misses blouses	47.1	44.7	42.2	39.3	35.6							−6.8
2335 Women's/misses dresses	71.0	74.5	74.8	85.1	80.5							3.2
2337 Women's suits and coats	37.8	40.0	34.1	31.1	26.8							−8.2
Average hourly earnings ($)	6.88	7.02	7.09	6.99	6.92							0.1
2331 Women's/misses blouses	6.44	6.96	6.61	6.55	6.35							−0.4
2335 Women's/misses dresses	6.82	6.71	7.10	6.93	6.87							0.2
2337 Women's suits and coats	7.56	7.64	7.68	7.75	7.95							1.3
Product data												
Value of shipments[5]	13,581	14,275	14,400	14,083	13,734	13,997	14,293	14,486	1.9	2.1	1.3	0.3
2331 Women's/misses blouses	4,195	4,580	4,425	4,012	3,752	3,804	3,899	3,934	1.4	2.5	0.9	−2.8
2335 Women's/misses dresses	5,278	5,431	6,042	6,397	6,336	6,455	6,595	6,697	1.9	2.2	1.5	4.7
2337 Women's suits and coats	4,108	4,264	3,933	3,674	3,646	3,738	3,799	3,855	2.5	1.6	1.5	−2.9
Value of shipments (1992$)	13,581	14,211	14,433	14,253	14,119	14,439	14,458	14,597	2.3	0.1	1.0	1.0
2331 Women's/misses blouses	4,195	4,539	4,325	3,896	3,664	3,754	3,798	3,798	2.5	1.2	−0.0	−3.3
2335 Women's/misses dresses	5,278	5,426	6,146	6,582	6,614	6,706	6,652	6,749	1.4	−0.8	1.5	5.8
2337 Women's suits and coats	4,108	4,247	3,961	3,775	3,842	3,978	4,007	4,050	3.6	0.7	1.1	−1.7
Trade data												
Value of imports	7,073	7,718	7,960	8,430	8,943	9,768	11,290	12,781	9.2	15.6	13.2	6.0
2331 Women's/misses blouses	3,501	3,864	3,948	3,906	3,980	4,658	5,742	6,890	17.0	23.3	20.0	3.3
2335 Women's/misses dresses	1,054	1,130	1,339	1,688	1,870	1,930	2,063	2,168	3.2	6.9	5.1	15.4
2337 Women's suits and coats	2,518	2,724	2,673	2,836	3,093	3,180	3,486	3,723	2.8	9.6	6.8	5.3
Value of exports	519	590	591	713	725	820	839	871	13.1	2.3	3.7	8.7
2331 Women's/misses blouses	171	213	243	342	339	376	349	351	10.8	−7.2	0.6	18.7
2335 Women's/misses dresses	98.3	105	103	112	115	148	147	149	28.7	−0.7	1.4	4.0
2337 Women's suits and coats	250	272	245	259	272	297	343	371	9.2	15.7	8.0	2.1

[1] Estimate except imports and exports.
[2] Estimate.
[3] Forecast.
[4] Compound annual rate.
[5] For a definition of industry versus product values, see "Getting the Most Out of *Outlook '99*."
Source: U.S. Department of Commerce: Bureau of the Census; International Trade Administration.

INDUSTRY SUBSECTORS

Many of the industry trends discussed so far in this chapter cut across all segments of the sewn products industry. The following sections provide information on the three major sectors of that industry. According to BEA National Income Accounts, personal consumption expenditure data show that in 1997 women's and girls' apparel accounted for 56 percent of consumer apparel expenditures, men's and boys' 36 percent, and infants' 8 percent.

Men's and Boys' Apparel

The value of men's and boys' outerwear shipments was fairly constant from 1992 to 1996 and is expected to remain so (see Table 33-5). The falloff in the production of suits, coats, and shirts was balanced by increases in trousers and work clothing.

Designers have made it easier for men to buy casual wear by providing all the items needed to complete a wardrobe category. Golf wear, particularly knit and woven sport shirts, showed a marked increase. The production of men's and boys' shorts, sweatshirts, and jeans showed significant increases. Dress shirt purchases were mainly for replenishment. Underwear shipments declined in value as a result of a shift of production offshore and intense price competition (see Table 33-6). Shipments of men's and boys' sweaters were stable. In terms of sales, brand name apparel recorded an above-average performance, but in general consumers looked for value.

Employment in men's and boys' outerwear and underwear continued to decline. Hourly earnings in men's and boys' apparel grew at a faster rate than did the industry average. Sharply expanding exports in both outerwear and underwear accounted for a large proportion of the growth in shipments.

TABLE 33-8: Women's and Children's Undergarments (SIC 234) Trends and Forecasts
(millions of dollars except as noted)

	1992	1993	1994	1995	1996	1997[1]	1998[2]	1999[3]	96–97	97–98	98–99	92–96[4]
									Percent Change			
Industry data												
Value of shipments[5]	3,943	3,943	4,245	4,577	4,244	4,301	4,377	4,412	1.4	1.7	0.8	1.9
2341 Women's/child underwear	2,368	2,155	2,438	2,494	2,330	2,356	2,403	2,420	1.1	2.0	0.7	−0.4
2342 Bras and allied garments	1,575	1,789	1,807	2,083	1,914	1,946	1,974	1,992	1.6	1.5	0.9	5.0
Value of shipments (1992$)	3,943	3,884	4,129	4,418	4,071	4,096	4,139	4,109	0.6	1.1	−0.7	0.8
2341 Women's/child underwear	2,368	2,135	2,390	2,431	2,264	2,280	2,320	2,315	0.7	1.8	−0.2	−1.1
2342 Bras and allied garments	1,575	1,748	1,739	1,988	1,807	1,816	1,819	1,794	0.5	0.1	−1.4	3.5
Total employment (thousands)	53.7	52.1	47.1	45.9	38.1							−8.2
2341 Women's/child underwear	41.6	38.0	33.5	30.2	25.5							−11.5
2342 Bras and allied garments	12.1	14.1	13.6	15.7	12.6							1.0
Production workers (thousands)	45.4	43.7	39.4	38.0	32.0							−8.4
2341 Women's/child underwear	35.8	33.0	29.0	26.3	22.6							−10.9
2342 Bras and allied garments	9.6	10.7	10.4	11.7	9.4							−0.5
Average hourly earnings ($)	6.74	6.89	6.70	7.01	7.31							2.1
2341 Women's/child underwear	6.46	6.54	6.51	6.96	7.21							2.8
2342 Bras and allied garments	7.80	7.93	7.22	7.09	7.53							−0.9
Product data												
Value of shipments[5]	3,821	3,587	3,917	4,180	3,922	3,975	4,043	4,077	1.4	1.7	0.8	0.7
2341 Women's/child underwear	2,237	1,928	2,128	2,135	1,980	2,002	2,042	2,056	1.1	2.0	0.7	−3.0
2342 Bras and allied garments	1,584	1,659	1,789	2,045	1,941	1,973	2,002	2,020	1.6	1.5	0.9	5.2
Value of shipments (1992$)	3,821	3,532	3,808	4,032	3,758	3,779	3,816	3,786	0.6	1.0	−0.8	−0.4
2341 Women's/child underwear	2,237	1,911	2,086	2,081	1,924	1,937	1,972	1,967	0.7	1.8	−0.2	−3.7
2342 Bras and allied garments	1,584	1,621	1,722	1,951	1,833	1,842	1,844	1,819	0.5	0.1	−1.4	3.7
Trade data												
Value of imports	1,519	1,787	2,067	2,443	2,492	2,884	3,400	3,947	15.7	17.9	16.1	13.2
2341 Women's/child underwear	985	1,168	1,342	1,540	1,646	1,938	2,325	2,743	17.7	19.9	18.0	13.7
2342 Bras and allied garments	534	619	725	902	845	946	1,075	1,204	12.0	13.6	12.0	12.2
Value of exports	407	466	521	654	650	816	841	958	25.5	3.1	14.0	12.4
2341 Women's/child underwear	155	186	222	267	273	347	265	238	27.2	−23.7	−10.0	15.2
2342 Bras and allied garments	252	280	299	387	376	468	576	720	24.5	22.9	25.0	10.5

[1] Estimate except imports and exports.
[2] Estimate.
[3] Forecast.
[4] Compound annual rate.
[5] For a definition of industry versus product values, see "Getting the Most Out of *Outlook '99*."
Source: U.S. Department of Commerce: Bureau of the Census; International Trade Administration.

TABLE 33-9: Girls' and Children's Outerwear (SIC 236) Trends and Forecasts

(millions of dollars except as noted)

	1992	1993	1994	1995	1996	1997[1]	1998[2]	1999[3]	Percent Change 96–97	97–98	98–99	92–96[4]
Industry data												
Value of shipments[5]	3,145	3,221	3,926	3,605	3,874	3,935	3,995	4,038	1.6	1.5	1.1	5.4
2361 Child's dresses/blouses	1,619	1,567	1,716	1,631	1,636	1,663	1,687	1,706	1.6	1.5	1.1	0.3
2369 Children's outerwear nec.	1,525	1,655	2,210	1,973	2,238	2,272	2,308	2,332	1.5	1.6	1.0	10.1
Value of shipments (1992$)	3,143	3,203	3,932	3,594	3,832	3,917	4,003	4,018	2.2	2.2	0.4	5.1
2361 Child's dresses/blouses	1,619	1,570	1,728	1,572	1,567	1,603	1,672	1,693	2.3	4.3	1.3	−0.8
2369 Children's outerwear nec.	1,525	1,633	2,203	2,022	2,265	2,314	2,332	2,325	2.2	0.8	−0.3	10.4
Total employment (thousands)	53.3	49.2	48.0	42.7	33.5							−11.0
2361 Child's dresses/blouses	23.9	23.1	19.5	17.3	11.6							−16.5
2369 Children's outerwear nec.	29.4	26.1	28.5	25.4	21.9							−7.1
Production workers (thousands)	43.6	39.8	38.4	34.1	27.4							−11.0
2361 Child's dresses/blouses	19.1	18.6	15.2	13.1	8.8							−17.6
2369 Children's outerwear nec.	24.5	21.2	23.2	21.0	18.6							−6.7
Average hourly earnings ($)	6.36	6.63	6.78	6.54	7.01							2.5
2361 Child's dresses/blouses	6.49	6.24	6.53	6.33	7.36							3.2
2369 Children's outerwear nec.	6.26	6.97	6.96	6.65	6.87							2.4
Product data												
Value of shipments[5]	3,503	3,452	3,636	3,565	3,585	3,642	3,697	3,737	1.6	1.5	1.1	0.6
2361 Child's dresses/blouses	1,719	1,626	1,680	1,616	1,590	1,616	1,640	1,658	1.6	1.5	1.1	−1.9
2369 Children's outerwear nec.	1,784	1,826	1,957	1,949	1,995	2,026	2,057	2,079	1.5	1.6	1.0	2.8
Value of shipments (1992$)	3,503	3,432	3,642	3,554	3,542	3,621	3,703	3,718	2.2	2.3	0.4	0.3
2361 Child's dresses/blouses	1,719	1,629	1,692	1,557	1,523	1,558	1,625	1,646	2.3	4.3	1.3	−3.0
2369 Children's outerwear nec.	1,784	1,803	1,951	1,997	2,019	2,063	2,078	2,072	2.2	0.8	−0.3	3.1
Trade data												
Value of imports												
236 Girls' and children's outerwear	8,016	8,196	8,926	8,890	9,191	11,258	13,150	15,148	22.5	16.8	15.2	3.5
Value of exports												
236 Girls' and children's outerwear	625	703	920	1,273	1,723	1,977	2,372	2,586	14.7	20.0	9.0	28.9

[1] Estimate except imports and exports.
[2] Estimate.
[3] Forecast.
[4] Compound annual rate.
[5] For a definition of industry versus product values, see "Getting the Most Out of *Outlook '99*."
Source: U.S. Department of Commerce: Bureau of the Census; International Trade Administration.

Women's, Girls', and Children's Apparel

Women's outerwear shipments increased faster than the industry average in 1997 (see Table 33-7). In line with the trend toward casual dressing, women's active wear, jeans, and sweaters have been the brightest spots in this segment of the apparel industry. Employment in the women's outerwear sector continued to decline sharply, and earnings increases were below average, largely because of the impact of imports on the women's apparel industry. Women's and children's underwear shipments also increased in 1997 (see Table 33-8).

Sales of girls' wear have shown considerable strength in recent years. As with boys' wear, demographic trends have had a major impact on this segment of the market. Imports of children's outerwear grew sharply in 1997 (see Table 33-9). Employment in girls' and children's wear manufacturers continued to decline sharply, while average hourly earnings increased modestly.

Fabricated Textile Products

The fabricated textile products sector has perhaps the brightest outlook in the sewn products industry (see Table 33-10). It is also the subsector of the industry in which U.S. firms continue to dominate and is less affected by increasing imports. Textile mills, which formerly sold the majority of their print cloth production to apparel producers, have seen that market affected by imports and have increased their emphasis on supplying home furnishings and industrial markets.

The trend toward spending leisure time at home, coupled with record housing starts and home sales, has propelled demand for home furnishings such as draperies and bedding. Strength in the home remodeling business is expected to continue. Manufacturers have increased their offerings of coordinated decorating packages and new products which are designed for comfort.

Shipments of home furnishings and miscellaneous textile products have grown much faster than have shipments from

TABLE 33-10: Miscellaneous Fabricated Textile Products (SIC 239) Trends and Forecasts
(millions of dollars except as noted)

	1992	1993	1994	1995	1996	1997[1]	1998[2]	1999[3]	Percent Change 96–97	Percent Change 97–98	Percent Change 98–99	Percent Change 92–96[4]
Industry data												
Value of shipments[5]	19,118	20,264	21,738	22,488	22,934	23,588	24,051	24,356	2.9	2.0	1.3	4.7
239A Home furnishings[6]	6,886	7,154	7,411	7,616	7,517	7,698	7,860	7,966	2.4	2.1	1.4	2.2
239B Miscellaneous textile products[6]	12,232	13,110	14,327	14,872	15,418	15,890	16,191	16,390	3.1	1.9	1.2	6.0
Value of shipments (1992$)	19,118	20,034	21,318	21,740	21,236	21,463	21,261	21,290	1.1	–0.9	0.1	2.7
239A Home furnishings	6,886	7,022	7,217	7,305	7,002	7,109	7,115	7,079	1.5	0.1	–0.5	0.4
239B Miscellaneous textile products	12,232	13,012	14,101	14,436	14,234	14,354	14,145	14,212	0.8	–1.5	0.5	3.9
Total employment (thousands)	211	212	222	228	224							1.5
239A Home furnishings	73.7	72.1	71.3	74.4	68.6							–1.8
239B Miscellaneous textile products	137	140	151	154	155							3.1
Production workers (thousands)	168	171	179	182	179							1.6
239A Home furnishings	61.0	59.5	59.0	60.0	55.8							–2.2
239B Miscellaneous textile products	107	112	120	122	123							3.5
Average hourly earnings ($)	8.34	8.61	8.78	8.90	9.02							2.0
239A Home furnishings	7.24	7.79	7.90	7.98	8.20							3.2
239B Miscellaneous textile products	8.98	9.06	9.21	9.33	9.39							1.1
Product data												
Value of shipments[5]	18,220	19,555	20,738	21,240	21,866	22,490	22,930	21,644	2.9	2.0	–5.6	4.7
239A Home furnishings	6,540	6,980	7,230	7,096	7,071	7,241	7,393	7,425	2.4	2.1	0.4	2.0
239B Miscellaneous textile products	11,681	12,575	13,508	14,143	14,795	15,248	15,537	14,219	3.1	1.9	–8.5	6.1
Value of shipments (1992$)	18,220	19,331	20,339	20,534	20,243	20,461	20,267	18,927	1.1	–0.9	–6.6	2.7
239A Home furnishings	6,540	6,851	7,043	6,808	6,587	6,687	6,693	6,598	1.5	0.1	–1.4	0.2
239B Miscellaneous textile products	11,681	12,480	13,296	13,726	13,657	13,774	13,574	12,329	0.9	–1.5	–9.2	4.0
Trade data												
Value of imports	2,698	3,116	3,428	3,556	3,614	4,186	4,925	5,873	15.8	17.7	19.2	7.6
239A Home furnishings	1,178	1,334	1,553	1,736	1,734	2,078	2,806	3,647	19.8	35.0	30.0	10.1
239B Miscellaneous textile products	1,520	1,782	1,875	1,820	1,880	2,108	2,120	2,226	12.1	0.6	5.0	5.5
Value of exports	862	971	944	939	1,018	1,110	1,195	1,262	9.0	7.7	5.5	4.2
239A Home furnishings	338	349	362	350	371	439	473	497	18.3	7.6	5.1	2.4
239B Miscellaneous textile products	523	623	582	590	647	671	723	765	3.7	7.7	5.8	5.5

[1] Estimate except imports and exports.
[2] Estimate.
[3] Forecast.
[4] Compound annual rate.
[5] For a definition of industry versus product values, see "Getting the Most Out of *Outlook '99.*"
[6] 239A includes SIC 2391 and 2392; 239B represents all other components of SIC 239.
Source: U.S. Department of Commerce: Bureau of the Census; International Trade Administration.

other industry sectors. Employment has been increasing in the miscellaneous textile products sector while trending downward in the home furnishings sector. Hourly earnings grew at the same rate as did the industry average.

Joanne Tucker, U.S. Department of Commerce, Office of Textiles and Apparel, (202) 482-4058, June 1998.

■ **REFERENCES**

Apparel Industry Magazine, Shore Communications, 180 Allen Road, Suite 300-N, Atlanta, GA 30328. (404) 252-8831.

Apparel Manufacturing Strategies, American Apparel Manufacturers Association, 2500 Wilson Boulevard, Arlington, VA 22201. (703) 524-1864.

Bobbin, Bobbin International, Inc., 1110 Shop Road, P.O. Box 1986, Columbia, SC 29202. (803) 771-7500.

Current Industrial Reports, SIC 23, U.S. Department of Commerce, Bureau of the Census, Industry Division, Washington, DC 20233. (301) 457-4100, http://www.census.gov.

Daily News Record, Fairchild Publications, 7 West 34th Street, New York, NY 10001. (212) 630-4000.

Focus: Economic Profile of the Apparel Industry, American Apparel Manufacturers Association, 2500 Wilson Boulevard, Arlington, VA 22201. (703) 524-1864.

Home Textiles Today, 245 West 17th Street, New York, NY 10011. (212) 337-6900, http://www.hometextilestoday.com.

Monthly Labor Review, U.S. Department of Labor, Bureau of Labor Statistics, Washington, DC 20211. (202) 606-5900.

OTEXA's "Export Advantage," U.S. Department of Commerce, International Trade Administration, Office of Textiles and Apparel, Washington, DC 20230. (202) 482-3400, http://otexa.ita.doc.gov.

Seidman News Bulletin, 51 Pine Mountain Road, West Redding, CT 06896. (203) 544-8249.

Women's Wear Daily, Fairchild Publications, 7 West 34th Street, New York, NY 10001. (212) 630-4000.

■ R E L A T E D   C H A P T E R S

FOOTWEAR, LEATHER, AND LEATHER PRODUCTS
Economic and Trade Trends

U.S. International Trade

($ billions)

Legend: Balance, Exports, Imports

Source: U.S. Department of Commerce: Bureau of the Census; International Trade Administration.

World Export Market Shares

(%)

Legend: United States, Hong Kong, Italy, China

Source: United Nations; U.S. Department of Commerce, International Trade Administration.

Export Dependence and Import Penetration

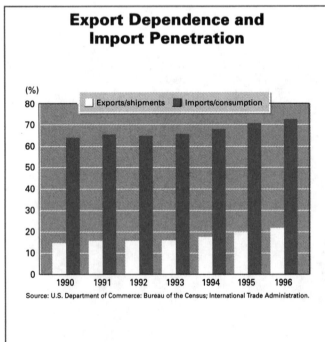

(%)

Legend: Exports/shipments, Imports/consumption

Source: U.S. Department of Commerce: Bureau of the Census; International Trade Administration.

Output and Output per Hour

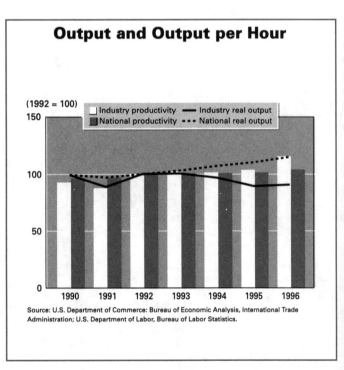

(1992 = 100)

Legend: Industry productivity, Industry real output, National productivity, National real output

Source: U.S. Department of Commerce: Bureau of Economic Analysis, International Trade Administration; U.S. Department of Labor, Bureau of Labor Statistics.

See "Getting the Most Out of *Outlook '99*" for definitions of terms.

Footwear, Leather, and Leather Products

INDUSTRY DEFINITION The footwear, leather, and leather products group consists of seven industries: nonrubber footwear (SIC 314), leather tanning and finishing (SIC 3111), leather gloves and mittens (SIC 3151), luggage (SIC 3161), handbags (SIC 3171), small personal leather goods (SIC 3172), and leather wearing apparel (SIC 2386).

OVERVIEW

Industry shipments of nonrubber footwear, leather, and leather products declined about 2 percent in 1997 to an estimated $8.62 billion. In constant dollars the value of shipments declined about 4 percent in 1997 as strong competition from imports and reduced domestic demand limited production in all industry segments except leather tanning. Tables 34-1 and 34-2 show the distribution and change in industry shipments in current dollars and constant dollars.

GLOBAL INDUSTRY TRENDS

U.S. imports of nonrubber footwear, leather, and leather products increased 10 percent to $18 billion in 1997. China was the largest supplier by far, accounting for 50 percent (see Table 34-3). All these industries, with the exception of leather tanning and finishing, are extremely labor-intensive. In comparison with U.S. producers, manufacturers in China and developing countries have a substantial cost advantage as a result of their lower labor compensation rates.

In 1997 U.S. exports of nonrubber footwear, leather, and leather products totaled about $1.93 billion, up 12 percent over 1996. Thus, in 1997 imports of these products exceeded exports by about $16.1 billion, an increase in the trade deficit of 10 percent from 1996. Nonrubber footwear accounted for $11.2 billion of that deficit. By value, imports were 75 percent of apparent consumption (product shipments plus imports minus exports) for the nonrubber footwear, leather, and leather products group in 1997. The leather apparel industry had the highest percentage of imports to apparent consumption at 89 percent, followed by 86 percent for handbags, 82 percent for nonrubber footwear, 80 percent for luggage, 74 percent for gloves, and 59 percent for personal leather goods. Leather tanning had the lowest at 38 percent.

LEATHER TANNING AND FINISHING

The leather tanning and finishing industry (SIC 3111) consists of establishments engaged primarily in tanning, currying,

TABLE 34-1: Distribution of Industry Shipments of Footwear, Leather, and Leather Products in 1997
(millions of dollars; percent)

SIC and Industry	Shipments[1]	Percent of Total
3111 Leather tanning and finishing	3,353	38.9
314 Nonrubber footwear	3,352	38.9
3161 Luggage	1,105	12.8
3172 Small personal leather goods	266	3.1
2386 Leather wearing apparel	204	2.4
3171 Handbags	203	2.3
3151 Leather gloves and mittens	137	1.6
Total	8,620	100.0

[1] Estimate.
Source: U.S. Department of Commerce, International Trade Administration.

TABLE 34-2: Industry Shipments of Footwear, Leather, and Leather Products, 1998–1999
(millions of 1992 dollars)

SIC and Industry	1998[1]	1999[2]	97–98	98–99
3111 Leather tanning and finishing	2,970	2,881	0.7	–3.0
3142 House slippers	93	96	–19.8	–3.2
3143 Men's footwear except athletic	1,963	2,022	–4.5	–3.0
3144 Women's footwear except athletic	359	363	–19.1	–1.1
3149 Footwear except rubber not elsewhere classified	405	413	–6.7	2.0
3151 Leather gloves and mittens	96	93	–17.9	–3.1
3161 Luggage	1,011	1,044	–5.9	3.3
3171 Handbags	180	160	–13.9	–11.1
3172 Small personal leather goods	231	209	–9.4	–9.5
2386 Leather wearing apparel	213	211	0.0	–0.9
Total	7,521	7,492	–4.4	–0.4

[1] Estimate.
[2] Forecast.
Source: U.S. Department of Commerce, International Trade Administration.

and finishing hides and skins into leather. It also includes leather converters, which buy hides and skins and then have them processed into leather on a contract basis, and finishers, which color and finish crust leather under contract for others, including leather importers.

Global Trends

The most recent data published by the Food and Agriculture Organization of the United Nations show that in 1995 the United States ranked fourth in world bovine (cattle, calf, and buffalo) population with 103.3 million head, behind India (274.1 million), Brazil (154.1 million), and China (123.5 million). The world bovine population totaled 1,448 million head; the sheep and lamb population, 1,070 million head; and

the goat and kid population, 628 million head. Data on the pig and hog populations were not included in the Food and Agriculture Organization report. Goatskin production is concentrated in developing countries, particularly those in Africa and Asia. China was the largest producer of sheepskins and goatskins. The U.S. livestock population consists primarily of cattle.

Developing countries have more than 70 percent of the world bovine herd but produce only half the world's hides by quantity. The United States produced 36 million hides, making it third in the number of hides produced but first by a wide margin in the weight of hides produced, primarily because extensive U.S. feedlot operations permit cattle to be grown to an average in excess of 1,000 pounds before being slaughtered. Total world production of hides was estimated at 287.5 million in 1995 and increased at a compound annual rate of only 0.4 percent from 1986 to 1995.

The United States and the European Union have the highest takeoff, or recovery, rates (37 percent) for hides among all countries. By contrast, recovery rates in the developing countries average only 15 percent. However, some countries, such as China, have improved their rates considerably since 1992, and if major producers such as Brazil, China, and India increase their rates to levels comparable to those of the United States and the European Union, the available world supply of hide will increase substantially.

Because hides and skins are by-products of the much larger meat and wool industries, leather tanners constitute the only market for these raw materials and the entire takeoff is utilized by the tanning industry and converted into leather. The quality and yield of the raw material produced in a country depend largely on animal husbandry, feeding, slaughtering, preservation, and transportation practices. The quantity of raw material

TABLE 34-3: U.S. Trade Patterns Footwear, Leather, and Leather Products[1] in 1997
(millions of dollars; percent)

	Exports			Imports	
Region[2]	Value[3]	Share, %	Region[2]	Value[3]	Share, %
NAFTA	613	31.7	NAFTA	978	5.4
Latin America	189	9.8	Latin America	1,722	9.6
Western Europe	282	14.6	Western Europe	3,031	16.8
Japan/Chinese Economic Area	550	28.5	Japan/Chinese Economic Area	9,471	52.5
Other Asia	219	11.3	Other Asia	2,633	14.6
Rest of world	78	4.1	Rest of world	192	1.1
World	1,932	100.0	World	18,026	100.0
Top Five Countries	**Value**	**Share, %**	**Top Five Countries**	**Value**	**Share, %**
Mexico	358	18.6	China	8,971	49.8
Japan	324	16.8	Italy	1,715	9.5
Canada	255	13.2	Brazil	1,197	6.6
Hong Kong (PRC)	157	8.1	Indonesia	894	5.0
South Korea	115	5.9	Mexico	823	4.6

[1] SIC 2386, 3111, 314, 3151, 3161, 317.
[2] For definitions of regional groupings, see "Getting the Most Out of *Outlook '99*."
[3] Values may not sum to total due to rounding.
Source: U.S. Department of Commerce, Bureau of the Census.

depends in most cases on the animal population, which in turn is affected by the demand for meat or wool.

Domestic Trends

The current-dollar value of leather tanning and finishing industry shipments declined about 3 percent in 1998 to $3.25 billion from $3.35 billion in 1997. This decline resulted from a drop of about 4 percent in leather prices, although the quantity of leather shipped increased slightly. In 1998 current-dollar product shipments declined about 3 percent to $3.3 billion. The quantity of leather shipped by U.S. tanners increased less than 1 percent to 19.73 million cattlehide units from 19.59 million units in 1997. Included in these totals are leather produced from the hides and skins of cattle, calves, goats, sheep, lambs, cabretta, horses, other animals, birds (e.g., ostriches), and reptiles. Shipments of cattlehide leather accounted for about 19.1 million units, or 97 percent of the total (see Table 34-4).

The shoe industry uses approximately 35 percent of all domestic leather shipments. In 1997 about 61 percent of all nonrubber footwear was produced with leather uppers, up from 57 percent in 1995. This increase probably was due to a 6 percent decline in leather prices in 1996 compared with 1995. Leather usage for soles is now limited mostly to high-priced men's and women's footwear of welt or cement construction with uppers of calfskin, hand-sewn moccasins, and more expensive styles of western boots. Synthetic substitutes are favored over leather because new equipment and technology reduce labor costs in shoe bottoming operations. The fastest growing and potentially largest markets for leather in the United States are those for automotive and furniture upholstery. In 1992 upholstery leather represented 26 percent by value of all finished and unfinished leather shipments, and industry estimates indicate that this share has grown since that time to over 35 percent. Leather is used to upholster about 20 percent of all the furniture manufactured in the United States and is now an option in most medium-priced cars and sport-utility vehicles and trucks. Leather is standard in higher-priced foreign and domestic models. The production of wet-blue (partially processed, chrome-tanned) cattlehide leather also increased in 1997 as one U.S. meat packer and several independent tanners increased their production.

In 1997 the quantity of cattlehides derived from the total commercial slaughter declined about 1 percent from 1996 to 36.3 million hides. Cattle slaughter reached a record high of 43 million in 1976 and has been in a long-term decline ever since, dropping to a recent low of 32.7 million head in 1991.

Cattlehides are a by-product of the meatpacking industry, and the supply depends solely on the demand for meat, not on the demand for leather. A long-term decline in demand for beef discouraged the rebuilding of cattle herds, even though feed grains have been favorably priced until recently, for most of the 1980s and 1990s.

The cattle population dropped to 101.2 million head in January 1997 from 103.5 million head in 1996. The record high of 131.8 million head was reached in January 1995. The population is expected to fall back to 97.5 million head in 1999 as herd liquidation continues as a result of the higher feed costs that have been in place since 1996. In mid-1998 dry pasture conditions in the southwest caused growers to move cattle to feedlots earlier than usual. Although slaughter was expected to drop to about 35.7 million head in 1998, a large decline of over 2 million head to 33.5 million head is forecast for 1999. Because the spring calf crop in 1998 was down for the third consecutive year

TABLE 34-4: Leather Tanning and Finishing (SIC 3111) Trends and Forecasts
(millions of dollars except as noted)

| | 1992 | 1993 | 1994 | 1995 | 1996 | 1997[1] | 1998[2] | 1999[3] | Percent Change | | | |
									96–97	97–98	98–99	92–96[4]
Industry data												
Value of shipments[5]	2,905	3,198	3,041	3,119	3,134	3,353	3,249	3,152	7.0	−3.1	−3.0	1.9
Value of shipments (1992$)	2,905	3,096	2,808	2,717	2,821	2,949	2,970	2,881	4.5	0.7	−3.0	−0.7
Total employment (thousands)	16.6	16.9	15.9	15.3	14.8	14.7	14.6	14.2	−0.7	−0.7	−2.7	−2.8
Production workers (thousands)	13.3	13.8	13.4	12.5	12.4	12.3	12.4	12.0	−0.8	0.8	−3.2	−1.7
Average hourly earnings ($)	10.56	10.65	10.62	10.54	10.98							1.0
Capital expenditures	48.5	52.2	45.5	57.6	51.9							1.7
Product data												
Value of shipments[5]	2,952	3,218	3,064	3,138	3,184	3,407	3,301	3,201	7.0	−3.1	−3.0	1.9
Value of shipments (1992$)	2,952	3,115	2,829	2,733	2,866	2,996	3,017	2,926	4.5	0.7	−3.0	−0.7
Trade data												
Value of imports	631	736	960	1,089	1,139	1,376	1,690	1,850	20.8	22.8	9.5	15.9
Value of exports	705	764	812	870	951	1,146	1,410	1,510	20.5	23.0	7.1	7.8

[1] Estimate except imports and exports.
[2] Estimate.
[3] Forecast.
[4] Compound annual rate.
[5] For a definition of industry versus product values, see "Getting the Most Out of *Outlook '99*."
Source: U.S. Department of Commerce: Bureau of the Census; International Trade Administration.

and is not expected to increase until 1999 and because cow slaughter remains at high levels, growth in the cattle population is unlikely to begin until 2000, and growth in slaughter no earlier than 2001. Even so, such growth will require an extended period of low, stable feed grain prices and favorable pasture and forage conditions.

In 1997 the price of cattle hides increased about 5 percent from 1996. The U.S. Bureau of Labor Statistics wholesale price index for cattlehides rose to 196.1 (1982 = 100) from 186.5 in 1996. The Bureau of Labor Statistics producer price index for leather rose 2.6 percent in 1997. The hide price index was down 28 percent in January–May 1998 compared with the same period in 1997 and was expected to remain at lower levels for the balance of the year. The producer price index for leather was down 4 percent in January–May 1998 but was expected to drop further to reflect the larger decline in hide prices.

Raw cattlehide exports fell about 6 percent in 1997 to 19.2 million hides. This quantity represented 53 percent of the total commercial slaughter in 1997, down from 56 percent in 1996. This ratio exceeded 70 percent as recently as 1988, when foreign demand for U.S. hides pushed up prices to historically high levels.

Trends in Technology

The environmental regulations affecting the leather tanning and finishing industry are administered by the U.S. Environmental Protection Agency (EPA). The EPA has established standards to control the pretreatment of wastes that tanners discharge indirectly into publicly owned waste treatment facilities and directly into waterways. Standards for indirect discharges do not require treatment to reduce the biological oxygen demand of the effluent, but they do require control of sulfides, chromium, and acidity. Most indirectly discharging tanners meet these federal standards, although local restrictions and more stringent standards in certain states have forced some of them to cease production or confine it to the processing of wet-blue or crust leathers, which create less pollution.

Tanneries that discharge wastes directly to waterways and all new plants are required by the EPA to control conventional pollutants, such as solids and biological oxygen demand, in addition to sulfides, chromium, and acidity. Furthermore, these tanners must operate with EPA-approved permits. Control of these wastes currently requires both primary and secondary (biological) treatment, although in the future the EPA may tighten or broaden standards to include pollutants such as ammonia, biocides, chlorides, and surfactants. These waste products may require tertiary treatment but probably can be controlled through less costly process modification.

The EPA has continued to exclude from hazardous waste regulation waste scrap leather, wet-blue trimmings and shavings, and tannery sludges that contain chromium because studies have not proved that nontoxic trivalent chromium in these products is oxidized in landfill disposal to the toxic hexavalent form. Therefore, the majority of chromium-containing solid wastes are not classified as hazardous and do not require treatment before land disposal. Tanning systems that recycle chromium are used extensively throughout the industry to reduce concentrations of chromium in the final effluent. In addition, the industry has developed and is adopting new tanning systems that will use other, nontoxic metal salts to replace some or all of the chromium currently used. Vegetable, synthetic, and other organic tanning materials can substitute for some of this chromium. The industry also has successfully reduced emissions of volatile organic compounds by adopting solvent-free or aqueous finishing or coating technologies.

The recycling of materials, the introduction of new processes that reduce the quantities of chemicals used, and the installation of new equipment have reduced the industry's adverse impact on the environment. Moreover, these new processes have lowered labor, material, and energy costs, helping U.S. leather maintain a price-competitive edge in world markets.

Trade

In 1997 U.S. leather imports increased 21 percent to $1.376 billion. This increase was due primarily to an increase in domestic demand for upholstery leather. The United States imported leather from 88 countries in 1997. Mexico was the largest supplier with a 31 percent share of total U.S. leather imports, followed by Argentina with 19 percent, Italy with 15 percent, the United Kingdom with 5 percent, and Brazil with 4 percent (see Table 34-5).

Cattlehide, calfskin, buffalo, and equine leathers accounted for about 90 percent of all U.S. leather imports in 1997. Mexico again was the major supplier, providing the largest share of imported automotive upholstery leather cut parts for assembly in the United States. Sheepskin leathers accounted for 3 percent of total leather imports, and goatskin and kidskin leathers accounted for 1 percent. Miscellaneous types of leathers from other animals, birds, and reptiles made up the balance.

In 1997 U.S. leather imports from designated beneficiary developing countries (BDCs)—those receiving U.S. tariff concessions under the Generalized System of Preferences section of the Trade Act of 1974—accounted for 10 percent of U.S. leather imports in that period, down substantially from 34 percent in 1996. Most BDCs are recovering and converting more of their own raw material to leather and finished leather products with higher added value for export to developed countries.

In 1997 leather exports increased 21 percent to $1.146 billion, mainly in response to increased demand from footwear and leather products manufacturers in the Far East and for automotive upholstery leather in Mexico. In 1997 the United States exported leather to 85 countries. Mexico received the largest share with 27 percent of total U.S. leather exports, followed by Japan with 13 percent, Canada with 12 percent, Hong Kong (PRC) with 12 percent, and South Korea with 8 percent.

In 1997 about 45 percent of U.S. leather exports consisted of whole hides or cut parts for upholstery leather, which were shipped primarily to Mexico, Canada, and Japan for assembly into auto seats. Wet-blue leathers, including both grains and splits, accounted for 20 percent of total leather exports. International trade in wet-blue leathers continues to grow because

TABLE 34-5: U.S. Trade Patterns Leather Tanning and Finishing[1] in 1997
(millions of dollars; percent)

Exports			Imports		
Region[2]	Value[3]	Share, %	Region[2]	Value[3]	Share, %
NAFTA	452	39.4	NAFTA	466	33.9
Latin America	73	6.3	Latin America	389	28.2
Western Europe	94	8.2	Western Europe	413	30.1
Japan/Chinese Economic Area	344	30.0	Japan/Chinese Economic Area	17	1.2
Other Asia	169	14.8	Other Asia	44	3.2
Rest of world	14	1.2	Rest of world	47	3.4
World	1,146	100.0	World	1,376	100.0
Top Five Countries	Value	Share, %	Top Five Countries	Value	Share, %
Mexico	314	27.4	Mexico	429	31.2
Japan	148	12.9	Argentina	256	18.6
Canada	138	12.0	Italy	203	14.8
Hong Kong (PRC)	137	12.0	United Kingdom	74	5.3
South Korea	86	7.5	Brazil	60	4.3

[1] SIC 3111.
[2] For definitions of regional groupings, see "Getting the Most Out of *Outlook '99*."
[3] Values may not sum to total due to rounding.
Source: U.S. Department of Commerce, Bureau of the Census.

of lower shipping costs, quality advantages, and the environmental benefits of these products compared with raw cattlehides. The largest meat packer in the United States is estimated to produce more than 4 million wet-blue hides annually, and one large independent tanner produces over 3 million of those hides annually. Much of the production of these two companies is exported. Also in 1997, U.S. exports of all types of bovine upper leathers for shoes had a 16 percent share of U.S. leather exports.

The share of U.S. leather exported to the BDCs and China, including Hong Kong, in 1997 was 56 percent, unchanged from 1996 but up considerably from the 20 percent share exported to those countries in 1991. The increasing demand for leather from those countries reflects the steady movement to low-wage countries of labor-intensive footwear and leather products production.

Trade Actions

Australia. In August 1996 a coalition of U.S. upholstery tanners filed a Section 301 (Trade Act of 1974) petition with the United States Trade Representative alleging that Australia significantly subsidized its leather tanning industry through programs that denied the United States its rights under the General Agreements on Tariffs and Trade (GATT). Subsequent negotiations and consultations between the United States and the government of Australia did not lead to a resolution of the complaint. Consequently, in January 1998 the United States requested a WTO dispute settlement panel to rule on the legality of the subsidies and order their removal. The WTO dispute settlement process is underway.

Argentina. In August 1997, when the U.S. Department of Commerce removed a countervailing duty order of 15 percent on leather imports from Argentina because of the absence of an injury determination for the domestic industry, leather imports from Argentina soared. By mid-1998 the United States was importing substantial quantities of cut leather automotive upholstery leather parts from Argentina.

U.S. Industry Growth Projections for the Next 1 and 5 Years

Leather shipments were expected to increase about 1 percent to 19.7 million equivalent cattlehides in 1998, although the value of industry shipments may drop because of lower hide and leather prices. In 1999 leather shipments are expected to fall about 3 percent to 19.1 million equivalent cattlehides, reflecting an anticipated decline in total commercial slaughter of about 6 percent.

The longer-term outlook for the leather tanning and finishing industry has become unsettled. The U.S. hide supply will be tight until at least 2001, and so U.S. tanners and packers may find it difficult to convert a larger proportion of that supply to wet-blue and finished leather. Wet-blue leather's share of total U.S. production should continue to increase, although new joint production ventures overseas involving U.S. tanners and other tanners may have an adverse effect on domestic finished leather production by reducing the supply of wet-blue leather available for further domestic processing and pushing up hide prices. New waste treatment technology and equipment, often embodied in new wet-blue plants, should help tanners control waste discharges. Some of these newer plants may add capacity and equipment to further process wet-blue hides into crust or finished leathers. U.S. government negotiations and trade actions could give U.S. tanners greater access to international raw material and leather markets, improving opportunities to expand exports and achieve at least some growth over the longer term.

The nonrubber footwear industry (SIC 314) produces all types of footwear, including house slippers (SIC 3142), men's footwear except athletic (SIC 3143), women's footwear except athletic (SIC 3144), and footwear except rubber not elsewhere classified (SIC 3149). Nonrubber footwear does not include rubber-fabric and rubber-protective footwear, both of which are classified under SIC 3021.

Domestic production of nonrubber footwear declined about 14 percent in 1998 to an estimated 99.4 million pairs. In 1998 the value of industry shipments declined about 6.4 percent to an estimated $3.14 billion. By industry sector, unit shipments of house slippers declined 21 percent in 1998 to 27.5 million pairs, shipments of men's footwear except athletic declined 5 percent to 32.6 million pairs, shipments of women's footwear except athletic dropped 19 percent to 26.8 million pairs, and shipments of footwear except rubber nec declined 6.5 percent to 12.5 million pairs.

Global Trends

Because the footwear manufacturing process is so highly labor-intensive, requiring a large number of cutting, sewing, and stitching operations, manufacturing activities have been transferred to countries that can provide cheap labor. Wholesalers, distributors, and retailers of branded, unbranded, and private label footwear continually seek contract manufacturers in the countries with the lowest labor costs. Because production machinery and equipment for producing most types of footwear do not require a large investment, manufacturing operations can be moved readily from one country to another with little difficulty.

For these reasons, Asia has become the largest shoe manufacturing area. According to the industry publication *World Footwear Markets,* that area produced 68.3 percent of all footwear, rubber and nonrubber, manufactured in the world in 1996. That publication also estimated world footwear production in 1996 at 10.525 billion pairs, up 5.4 percent from 1995. In Asia production has moved away from the two largest supplying countries of the early 1980s—Taiwan and Korea—to China, the lowest-cost producer, and Indonesia, Thailand, India, and Vietnam. In 1996 China's footwear production of 4.5 billion pairs represented almost 43 percent of world production. India produced 700 million pairs, or 6.7 percent; Indonesia, 635 million pairs, or 6 percent; Brazil, 586 million pairs, or 5.6 percent; Italy, 483 million pairs, or 4.6 percent; and Thailand, 320 million pairs, or 3 percent. Turkey ranked seventh with 264 million pairs, or 2.5 percent. The United States ranked eighth, producing 220 million pairs of all types of footwear, or 2.1 percent of world production. Turkey and Mexico entered the list of the top 10 producers in 1996.

In 1996 the United States was by far the largest importer, receiving 1.376 billion pairs, or 25.2 percent of total world imports of 5.471 billion pairs. Japan (7.1 percent), Germany (6.4 percent), the United Kingdom (4.5 percent), and France (4.4 percent) were the next largest importers. Western Europe's footwear imports represented 26.9 percent of the world total. China ex-

ported directly, or indirectly as reexports through Hong Kong, about 4.032 billion pairs in 1996, representing almost 74 percent of the world total of exports. China's share far exceeded that of the second largest exporter, Italy, which had 430 million pairs, or 7.8 percent of the world total. Indonesia (4.4 percent), Thailand (3.3 percent), and Brazil (2.6 percent) had the next largest shares. Spain, India, Vietnam, and Portugal, in that order, followed.

World Footwear Markets estimated total world footwear consumption (defined as production plus imports minus exports) at 9.541 billion pairs in 1996. China's consumption was the largest at 1.868 billion pairs; the United States ranked second at 1.561 billion pairs. U.S. per capita consumption was the largest of any of the major countries at 5.9 pairs. By contrast, China's population of 1.209 billion people consumed 1.5 pairs per capita in 1996.

That publication noted that leather shoes accounted for 39 percent, or 4.150 billion pairs, of total world footwear production. This quantity utilized about 6.75 billion square feet of leather from the hides and skins of 135 million equivalent cattlehides.

Domestic Trends

Nonrubber footwear shipments declined about 14 percent in 1998 to approximately 99 million pairs. Shipment declines of about 20 percent each were largest for slippers and women's footwear. Over the long term nonrubber footwear shipments have fallen from 642 million pairs in 1968 to the current level, a compound annual rate of decline of about 6 percent. Production stabilized only during the 4-year period of the Orderly Marketing Agreements with South Korea and Taiwan from 1977 to 1981 and again from 1986 to 1988.

Apparent consumption of nonrubber footwear increased in 1998 to 1.327 billion pairs from 1.282 billion pairs in 1997. This resulted primarily from an increase of about 5 percent in imports. In 1998 per capita consumption of nonrubber footwear was about 4.9 pairs, up slightly from the level in 1997 but considerably below the levels in most of the 1980s, when the demand for athletic-type footwear consistently kept consumption above 5 pairs per capita.

Personal consumption expenditure (PCE) on all types of footwear reached an annual rate of $41.2 billion in the first quarter of 1998, up almost 5 percent from 1997. PCE in constant dollars also increased 5 percent in that period as the price deflator for footwear at the retail level was unchanged. PCE increased only 1.5 percent during the entire 6-year period 1992–1998. PCE on footwear in 1998 was about $153 per capita. In 1998 the consumer price index for footwear dropped about 1.5 percent as the stronger U.S. dollar brought down the price of imports, particularly from countries in the Far East.

The *Census of Manufacturers* for 1992 listed 318 companies operating 391 establishments in the nonrubber footwear industry. In 1968 more than 1,000 plants were operating. Published reports indicate there were 7 net closings in 1993, 11 in 1994, 10 in 1995, 10 in 1996, and 3 in 1997. In 1998 total employment and production employment dropped about 13 percent each to 29,600 and 24,900, respectively.

Trends in Technology

To maintain competitiveness, shoe manufacturers must respond to trends in fashion within days or even hours rather than weeks. The industry uses computers to shorten production time, control inventory, reduce costs, improve quality, and respond rapidly to customers' orders. Computer-aided design and computer-aided manufacturing shoemaking systems help manufacturers improve competitiveness through better quality, greatly expanded design capability, timely delivery, and lower inventory and production costs. Three-dimensional computer-aided design systems are used for developing styles, visualizing three-dimensional unit sole designs, and producing lasts and selecting materials.

The latest developments in automatic stitching use some of the most advanced techniques in vision and computer technologies to improve quality and vastly reduce labor costs. In lasting operations, cameras can sense the position of a shoe's topline in the last and compare it with a preprogrammed optimum position so that the pull is adjusted automatically to place the topline in the proper position. Many operations have been combined so that two-machine lasting can speed the process.

Machines that are programmable with computers are now available for virtually every operation in the shoe manufacturing process, including cutting, sewing, folding, lasting, making, and bottoming. Much of this new technology has been developed and used in Europe and, depending on the availability of capital, can be transferred readily to Far Eastern producers. However, the labor-saving benefits of this technology are not as great for producers with low unit labor costs. The net effect of such technology would be to reduce the cost, increase the quality, and shorten the response time for U.S. production relative to Far Eastern production, although the Far East will continue to have a substantial competitive advantage for almost all types of footwear.

Trade

Nonrubber footwear imports increased about 9 percent in 1997 to 1.195 billion pairs from 1.093 billion pairs in 1996. The customs value increased about 10 percent to an estimated $11.54 billion (see Table 34-6). The unit value of imports was $9.66, unchanged from 1996 but still about 52 percent below an estimated $20.18 per pair for domestic production. In 1997 the unit value of nonrubber footwear imports from China was $7.38, the lowest of all major foreign suppliers.

In 1997 the five largest suppliers by quantity of nonrubber footwear to the United States were China with 70 percent of the total, Brazil with 7.5 percent, Indonesia with 5.7 percent, Italy with 4.4 percent, and Spain with 2 percent. Those five countries accounted for almost 90 percent of all U.S. nonrubber footwear imports in that year. The United States imported footwear from 112 countries in 1997, but only 3 other countries—Taiwan, Mexico, and Thailand—accounted for more than a 1 percent share of those imports.

In 1997 imports of nonrubber footwear from China increased about 12 percent and reached a record high of 836 million pairs valued at an estimated $6.2 billion. Taiwan and South Korea, the two largest suppliers until the mid-1980s, are no longer major producers or exporters. These countries are now supplying China's rapidly expanding footwear manufacturing operations with a large amount of technological and financial support.

In 1997 China was the leading supplier in all 19 major gender and material subcategories of nonrubber footwear imports. Italy ranked second in men's leather footwear, Brazil was second in women's leather footwear, and Indonesia was second in both juvenile and athletic leather footwear.

U.S. leather footwear imports accounted for about 53 percent of total nonrubber footwear imports in 1997, considerably below leather's share of about 60 percent for domestically pro-

TABLE 34-6: U.S. Trade Patterns Footwear Except Rubber[1] in 1997
(millions of dollars; percent)

Exports			Imports		
Region[2]	Value[3]	Share, %	Region[2]	Value[3]	Share, %
NAFTA	68	18.1	NAFTA	308	2.7
Latin America	65	17.1	Latin America	1,231	10.7
Western Europe	83	22.0	Western Europe	2,078	18.0
Japan/Chinese Economic Area	102	27.0	Japan/Chinese Economic Area	6,369	55.2
Other Asia	15	4.0	Other Asia	1,436	12.4
Rest of world	45	11.8	Rest of world	122	1.1
World	378	100.0	World	11,544	100.0
Top Five Countries	Value	Share, %	Top Five Countries	Value	Share, %
Japan	88	23.3	China	6,158	53.3
Canada	52	13.8	Italy	1,172	10.2
Netherlands	25	6.6	Brazil	1,135	9.8
Mexico	16	4.3	Indonesia	761	6.6
United Kingdom	13	3.4	Spain	412	3.6

[1] SIC 314.
[2] For definitions of regional groupings, see "Getting the Most Out of Outlook '99."
[3] Values may not sum to total due to rounding.
Source: U.S. Department of Commerce, Bureau of the Census.

duced nonrubber footwear. In 1997 the average unit price for imported nonrubber footwear with leather uppers was about $13.82, up less than 2 percent from 1996 but still far below that for domestic production.

U.S. manufacturers export large quantities of cut footwear parts and components to countries such as Mexico and the Dominican Republic, where they are reexported to the United States as finished or partly finished footwear. Under the U.S. Tariff Schedule (Heading No. 9802), duties are assessed only on the value-added content. Moreover, U.S. duties on partially finished but unlasted nonrubber footwear are less than 4 percent, compared with 8 percent or more for completed footwear. Consequently, final manufacturing operations that require less labor, such as lasting, bottoming, finishing, and packing, often are performed in the United States. In 1997 imports of such unlasted footwear with leather uppers exceeded 26 million pairs, valued at $373 million. About 17 percent by quantity of U.S. production was exported. The stronger U.S. dollar and expanding global inventories limited export growth.

In 1997 Japan was the largest export market, receiving 15 percent by quantity of total U.S. nonrubber footwear exports, followed by Canada with 11 percent, Mexico with 5.5 percent, and the United Kingdom with 5 percent. The average unit price for nonrubber footwear exports in 1997 was $17.41 per pair, up 6.4 percent from 1996. Leather footwear's share of nonrubber footwear exports was 61 percent.

Certain types of U.S. footwear are price-competitive in the Japanese market, particularly leather athletic footwear, which is exempt from Japan's restrictive global tariff rate quotas on leather nonathletic footwear. These quotas, combined with the import-licensing procedures required to administer them, discourage U.S. manufacturers from engaging distributors and expanding exports in Japan. Industry sources estimate that Japan's market for leather footwear exceeds 200 million pairs, that country's global tariff rate quotas restrict leather footwear imports to about 10 million pairs, or 5 percent of the market for those types.

Trade Actions
The government of Argentina increased tariffs on certain textiles, apparel, and footwear imports in 1995 to levels substantially above its WTO-bound rate of 35 percent. Subsequently, the WTO found the duty increases on textiles to be illegal, but the Argentinian government was able to avoid such a determination on footwear by reimposing the duties under WTO-legal safeguard rules. This action appeared to stymie the efforts of several major U.S. footwear exporters to increase exports to Argentina.

House Slippers
Shipments of house slippers (SIC 3142) declined about 4.5 percent in 1997 to an estimated 34.8 million pairs. Their product value dropped to an estimated $112 million. Slippers accounted for 30 percent of the quantity but only 4 percent of the value of total nonrubber footwear product shipments in 1997, primarily because most slippers are produced from lower-cost vinyls and textiles rather than from more expensive leather. In 1997 the ratio of imports to apparent consumption for slippers was an

estimated 60 percent by quantity, the lowest among the four sectors (see Table 34-7).

Men's Footwear Except Athletic
Shipments of men's footwear, which includes dress, casual, and work shoes and boots, totaled an estimated 34.3 million pairs in 1997, down 7 percent from 1996. Their value declined about 5 percent from that in 1996. Leather is the most widely used upper material for men's footwear. By quantity, the ratio of imports to domestic supply for men's footwear was about 84 percent in 1997. Work footwear production accounted for about 34 percent of total men's production. Western-style boots captured about 13 percent.

Women's Footwear Except Athletic
Shipments of women's footwear declined about 15 percent in 1997 to an estimated 33.1 million pairs valued at about $628 million. Women's footwear accounted for about 29 percent by quantity and 22 percent by value of all nonrubber footwear product shipments in 1997. By quantity, the ratio of imports to domestic supply for this sector was 94 percent, the highest among the four sectors.

Footwear Except Rubber Not Elsewhere Classified
Shipments of youths' and boys', children's, infants' and babies', and athletic and other miscellaneous types of footwear declined 11 percent in 1997 to 13.4 million pairs. Their value dropped 10 percent to $320 million. Shipments of footwear in this group accounted for 11 percent by both quantity and value of all product shipments of nonrubber footwear in 1997.

About 97 percent of the domestic supply of nonrubber footwear in this sector is imported. Ninety-nine percent of athletic footwear is imported. In 1997 consumption of athletic footwear declined for the fifth consecutive year as worldwide inventories reached record levels. In 1997 athletic footwear's share of the total footwear market dropped to 540 million pairs, or 33 percent of combined nonrubber and rubber footwear consumption, totaling about 1.64 billion pairs.

U.S. Industry Growth Projections for the Next 1 and 5 Years
Shipments of nonrubber footwear were expected to decline about 14 percent in 1998 to 105 million pairs. The decline was expected in all four sectors: men's footwear, −5 percent; footwear nec, −6.5 percent; women's footwear, −19 percent; and slippers, −21 percent. Imports by quantity were expected to increase 5 percent to an estimated 1.25 billion pairs. The ratio of imports to apparent consumption was projected to reach 93 percent in 1998 as apparent consumption and per capita consumption showed modest increases.

In 1999 nonrubber footwear shipments are expected to increase more than 2 percent. Shipments by quantity of men's footwear and slippers are expected to increase about 3 percent each. Shipments of footwear nec and women's footwear will rise 2 percent and 1 percent, respectively (see Table 34-7).

TABLE 34-7: Footwear Except Rubber (SIC 314) Trends and Forecasts

(millions of dollars except as noted)

	1992	1993	1994	1995	1996	1997[1]	1998[2]	1999[3]	Percent Change 96–97	97–98	98–99	92–96[4]
Industry data												
Value of shipments[5]	3,898	3,974	3,923	3,688	3,605	3,352	3,139	3,270	−7.0	−6.4	4.2	−1.9
3142 House slippers	285	302	204	113	128	123	101	106	−3.9	−17.9	5.0	−18.1
3143 Men's footwear	2,210	2,351	2,461	2,420	2,413	2,295	2,226	2,327	−4.9	−3.0	4.5	2.2
3144 Women's footwear	1,095	1,010	950	758	555	474	384	394	−14.6	−19.0	2.6	−15.6
3149 Footwear nec	309	310	309	397	509	460	428	443	−9.6	−7.0	3.5	13.3
Value of shipments (1992$)	3,898	3,907	3,816	3,477	3,345	3,050	2,820	2,894	−8.8	−7.5	2.6	−3.8
3142 House slippers	285	310	205	109	122	116	93	96	−4.9	−19.8	3.2	−19.1
3143 Men's footwear	2,210	2,305	2,382	2,257	2,218	2,056	1,963	2,022	−7.3	−4.5	3.0	0.1
3144 Women's footwear	1,095	987	927	730	522	444	359	363	−14.9	−19.1	1.1	−16.9
3149 Footwear nec	309	305	302	381	483	434	405	413	−10.1	−6.7	2.0	11.8
Total employment (thousands)	48.8	48.5	46.8	44.4	36.7	33.9	29.6	30.4	−7.6	−12.7	2.7	−6.9
Production workers (thousands)	41.4	41.3	40.3	37.7	31.1	28.6	24.9	25.5	−8.0	−12.9	2.4	−6.9
Average hourly earnings ($)	7.33	7.43	7.44	7.85	8.32							3.2
Capital expenditures	51.2	40.3	58.8	34.1	34.5							−9.4
3142 House slippers	2.1	2.5	4.8	1.5	1.2							−13.1
3143 Men's footwear	32.8	26.1	43.3	23.6	25.8							−5.8
3144 Women's footwear	10.5	6.8	7.6	4.3	2.4							−30.9
3149 Footwear nec	5.8	4.9	3.1	4.7	5.1							−3.2
Product data												
Value of shipments[5]	3,608	3,707	3,739	3,402	3,128	2,890	2,674	2,783	−7.6	−7.5	4.1	−3.5
3142 House slippers	259	256	208	122	116	112	92	97	−3.4	−17.9	5.4	−18.2
3143 Men's footwear	1,807	1,970	2,040	1,926	1,924	1,830	1,775	1,857	−4.9	−3.0	4.6	1.6
3144 Women's footwear	1,229	1,188	1,190	959	735	628	509	523	−14.6	−18.9	2.8	−12.1
3149 Footwear nec	314	293	301	394	354	320	298	306	−9.6	−6.9	2.7	3.0
Value of shipments (1992$)	3,608	3,643	3,639	3,217	2,906	2,636	2,407	2,468	−9.3	−8.7	2.5	−5.3
3142 House slippers	259	263	209	118	110	105	85	88	−4.5	−19.0	3.5	−19.3
3143 Men's footwear	1,807	1,931	1,975	1,797	1,768	1,640	1,566	1,613	−7.2	−4.5	3.0	−0.5
3144 Women's footwear	1,229	1,160	1,161	924	692	589	477	482	−14.9	−19.0	1.0	−13.4
3149 Footwear nec	314	289	294	378	336	302	279	285	−10.1	−7.6	2.2	1.7
Trade data												
Value of imports	8,616	9,290	9,698	9,984	10,478	11,544	12,410	13,030	10.2	7.5	5.0	5.0
Value of exports	343	332	382	370	385	378	367	370	−1.8	−2.9	0.8	2.9

[1] Estimate except imports and exports.
[2] Estimate.
[3] Forecast.
[4] Compound annual rate.
[5] For a definition of industry versus product values, see "Getting the Most Out of *Outlook '99.*"
Source: U.S. Department of Commerce: Bureau of the Census; International Trade Administration.

Long-Term Prospects

The production of footwear has become truly a global business. The U.S. market is completely dominated by imports, and large domestic manufacturers, importers, wholesalers, and retailers continue to move product sourcing to countries with abundant low-cost labor, particularly those in the Far East, such as China, Indonesia, India, and Vietnam. Per capita consumption of footwear will remain steady, although consumption will continue to shift away from athletic types to casual footwear as demographic factors push the average age of the population higher. This shift in demand will result in the production of fewer pairs of higher-quality, more comfortable footwear that wear longer than most of the current styles.

The industry has demonstrated an ability to respond quickly and effectively to changes in the market. However, large producers in the Far East, particularly in China, have adopted some of the new technology and probably will become even more price-competitive than they are today. A stronger U.S. dollar could give them an even larger price advantage over U.S. producers. Consequently, lower-cost foreign production combined with stable per capita consumption should continue to provide stiff competition for domestic producers and limit their opportunities to increase their share of the U.S. footwear market.

LUGGAGE AND PERSONAL LEATHER GOODS

The luggage and personal leather goods industries produce a wide variety of consumer goods, including leather gloves and mittens (SIC 3151), luggage (SIC 3161), women's handbags and purses (SIC 3171), personal leather goods (SIC 3172), and leather and sheepskin-lined clothing (SIC 2386).

The total value of industry shipments for all five of these industries declined about 5.7 percent in current dollars in 1998 to an estimated $1.81 billion. The value of product shipments fell about 6 percent to approximately $1.6 billion. When measured in constant (1992) dollars, both industry and product shipments declined about 7.3 percent from 1997. In 1997, total employment in these industries dropped 4.7 percent to 16,300 and production employment declined about 7.6 percent to 12,100.

Global Trends

The luggage and leather goods industries continue to encounter significant competition from imports, especially from China and developing countries, since labor costs represent a large proportion of total production costs. In 1997 the value of imports of luggage and personal leather goods increased about 7 percent to $5.1 million. The value of exports for the group increased about 6 percent in 1997 to $408 million, mostly because of an 8 percent gain in luggage exports.

Leather Gloves and Mittens

The U.S. leather glove industry includes manufacturers of both dress and work gloves, with work gloves accounting for more than 90 percent of production. These products are made from leather or from combinations of leather and cotton, wool, or synthetic fibers.

The value of shipments of these products declined about 6 percent in 1997 to $118 million. In constant dollars the decline was also about 6 percent. Total employment declined about 4 percent to 2,200, and production employment fell almost 5 percent to 1,900. In 1997 apparent consumption of gloves and mittens increased about 2.5 percent to $420 million from $410 million in 1996.

Imports rose about 5 percent to $309 million and represented almost 74 percent of consumption. China had a 74 percent share of imports; India was the next largest supplier with 5 percent. In 1997 exports of leather gloves and mittens declined 34 percent from 1996 to $6.6 million. Canada was the largest customer for these exports, but Mexico, Hong Kong (PRC), and China received significant quantities of cut parts which were assembled in those countries and reentered the United States under Section 9802 (formerly Section 807) of the Harmonized Tariff Schedule of the United States. This section subjects such items to U.S. duties only on the value-added content. U.S. duties on gloves from Mexico will be reduced to zero in 1999 under the North American Free Trade Agreement.

Luggage

The luggage industry produces a wide variety of products, including suitcases, briefcases, attaché cases, hand luggage, tote bags, backpacks, occupational cases, and musical instrument cases. The materials used include leather, plastics, textiles, metals, and various combinations. Leather use is highest in attaché cases and briefcases. Construction methods include sewing, molding, and laminating. An ever-growing proportion of luggage is made of fabric and incorporates wheels, which allow a traveler to pack more clothes with very little increase in weight compared with earlier styles of luggage.

In 1997 the value of shipments of these products dropped about 1 percent to $823 million. Measured in constant dollars, product shipments fell about 2.5 percent. Total employment declined 2 percent to 5,700, and production employment dropped 3 percent to 4,200. Apparent consumption of luggage increased about 9 percent in 1997 to $2.89 billion, primarily because of a large increase in imports of about 13 percent to $2.31 billion, or 80 percent of apparent consumption. The principal sources of luggage imports were China with 45 percent of the total, followed by Thailand with 9 percent, the Philippines with 8 percent, and Taiwan with 7.5 percent. In 1997 the United States imported luggage from 102 countries. U.S. luggage exports increased 8 percent in 1997 to $250 million. The largest export markets were Japan and Canada.

Handbags

The U.S. handbag industry produces women's handbags and purses made of leather and other materials except precious metal. About 64 percent of handbag shipments in 1992 were made wholly or partially of leather. In 1997 the value of handbag product shipments declined about 29 percent to $214 million from $301 million in 1996. Product shipments in constant dollars declined about 28 percent. Apparent consumption of handbags declined about 7 percent to $1.22 billion from $1.31 billion in 1996. Imports of handbags totaled $1.05 billion, unchanged from 1996, and represented 86 percent of apparent consumption. Most manufacturers, distributors, and retailers of well-established and higher-priced brands are now sourcing a large proportion of their handbag requirements from overseas manufacturers. In 1997 China was the largest supplier of handbags to the U.S. market with a 63 percent share of total U.S. imports; Italy had a 19 percent share. In 1997 exports of handbags were up 1 percent from 1996 and totaled $46.5 million. Japan, Mexico, and Canada were the leading export markets, although a substantial proportion of U.S. handbag exports to Mexico consisted of cut handbag parts that were assembled there and reexported to the United States.

Personal Leather Goods (Flat Goods)

Manufacturers in this industry sector produce small articles carried on the person or in a handbag, such as billfolds, wallets, key cases, French purses, credit card cases, and cases for eyeglasses and cigarettes. These products often are referred to as flat goods. They are made mostly of leather or leather combined with textiles or plastics.

In 1997 product shipments of flat goods declined about 9 percent to $348 million from $384 million in 1996. Product shipments in constant dollars dropped about 12 percent from 1996. In 1997, total employment declined 12 percent to 4,500 and production employment declined a similar percentage to 3,200.

Apparent consumption of flat goods fell over 6 percent to $771 million from $825 million in 1996. Imports declined 3 percent in 1997 to $457 million and accounted for 59 percent of apparent consumption, up from 57 percent in 1996 and the low-

TABLE 34-8: Luggage and Personal Leather Goods (SIC 2386, 315, 316, 317) Trends and Forecasts
(millions of dollars except as noted)

	1992	1993	1994	1995	1996	1997[1]	1998[2]	1999[3]	96–97	97–98	98–99	92–96[4]
									\(Percent Change\)			
Industry data												
Value of shipments[5]	2,207	2,106	2,070	1,891	2,030	1,915	1,806	1,798	−5.7	−5.7	−0.4	−2.1
2386 Leather and sheepskin-lined clothing	209	224	237	206	190	204	206	201	7.4	1.0	−2.4	−2.4
3151 Leather gloves and mittens	140	169	145	114	145	137	114	115	−5.5	−16.8	0.9	0.9
3161 Luggage	968	930	991	946	1,115	1,105	1,061	1,099	−0.9	−4.0	3.6	3.6
3171 Women's handbags and purses	463	387	304	305	286	203	175	155	−29.0	−13.8	−11.4	−11.3
3172 Personal goods not elsewhere classified	428	395	393	321	294	266	250	228	−9.5	−6.0	−8.8	−9.0
Value of shipments (1992$)	2,207	2,090	2,064	1,888	2,007	1,868	1,731	1,717	−6.9	−7.3	−0.8	−2.3
2386 Leather and sheepskin-lined clothing	209	225	247	218	201	213	213	211	6.0	0.0	−0.9	−1.0
3151 Leather gloves and mittens	140	168	137	103	125	117	96	93	−6.4	−17.9	−3.1	−2.8
3161 Luggage	968	922	979	942	1,102	1,074	1,011	1,044	−2.5	−5.9	3.3	3.3
3171 Women's handbags and purses	463	385	313	307	291	209	180	160	−28.2	−13.9	−11.1	−11.0
3172 Personal goods not elsewhere classified	428	389	388	317	289	255	231	209	−11.8	−9.4	−9.5	−9.4
Total employment (thousands)	26.4	24.3	22.1	18.5	18.1	17.1	16.3	15.8	−5.5	−4.7	−3.1	−9.0
Production workers (thousands)	21.1	19.0	17.7	14.8	14.4	13.1	12.1	11.7	−9.0	−7.6	−3.3	−9.1
Average hourly earnings ($)	7.43	7.41	7.55	7.85	8.13							2.3
Capital expenditures	27.9	28.2	26.8	30.9	36.7							7.1
2386 Leather and sheepskin-lined clothing	1.3	1.6	0.1	0.6	0.2							−37.4
3151 Leather gloves and mittens	0.5	0.3	12.2	18.4	12.3							122.7
3161 Luggage	15.9	16.4	9.5	6.1	17.8							2.9
3171 Women's handbags and purses	3.4	4.2	3.1	3.7	3.6							1.4
3172 Personal goods not elsewhere classified	6.8	5.7	1.9	2.1	2.8							−19.9
Product data												
Value of shipments[5]	2,109	2,013	2,050	1,818	1,822	1,700	1,598	1,550	−6.7	−6.0	−3.0	−3.6
2386 Leather and sheepskin-lined clothing	199	216	222	194	183	197	199	195	7.7	1.0	−2.0	−2.1
3151 Leather gloves and mittens	114	115	115	93.5	125	118	98	100	−5.6	−16.9	2.0	2.3
3161 Luggage	864	814	880	778	830	823	790	782	−0.8	−4.0	−1.0	−1.0
3171 Women's handbags and purses	411	366	328	315	301	214	184	170	−28.9	−14.0	−7.6	−7.5
3172 Personal goods not elsewhere classified	522	503	505	438	384	348	327	303	−9.4	−6.0	−7.3	−7.4
Value of shipments (1992$)	2,109	1,997	2,045	1,816	1,804	1,661	1,539	1,488	−7.9	−7.3	−3.3	−3.8
2386 Leather and sheepskin-lined clothing	199	217	231	205	193	206	206	204	6.7	0.0	−1.0	−0.8
3151 Leather gloves and mittens	114	114	109	85.1	108	101	82	81	−6.5	−18.8	−1.2	−1.3
3161 Luggage	864	807	869	775	820	800	753	743	−2.4	−5.9	−1.3	−1.3
3171 Women's handbags and purses	411	364	338	318	305	220	189	175	−27.9	−14.1	−7.4	−7.2
3172 Personal goods not elsewhere classified	522	495	498	433	378	334	309	285	−11.6	−7.5	−7.8	−7.8
Trade data												
Value of imports	3,884	4,069	4,562	4,675	4,774	5,106	5,465	5,872	7.0	7.0	7.4	5.3
2386 Leather and sheepskin-lined clothing	1,231	1,222	1,241	994	912	977	933	891	7.1	−4.5	−4.5	−7.2
3151 Leather gloves and mittens	171	214	261	291	295	309	348	392	4.7	12.6	12.6	14.6
3161 Luggage	1,273	1,403	1,700	1,965	2,042	2,312	2,606	2,937	13.2	12.7	12.7	12.5
3171 Women's handbags and purses	890	910	959	972	1,055	1,051	1,087	1,124	−0.4	3.4	3.4	4.3
3172 Personal goods not elsewhere classified	319	321	401	454	470	457	491	528	−2.8	7.4	7.5	10.2
Value of exports	270	283	311	355	384	408	448	492	6.3	9.8	9.8	9.2
2386 Leather and sheepskin-lined clothing	65.5	69.5	64.9	88.7	67.6	71.0	72.1	73.3	5.0	1.5	1.7	0.8
3151 Leather gloves and mittens	12.2	14.0	13.8	13.4	10.0	6.6	6.9	7.3	−34.0	4.5	5.8	−4.8
3161 Luggage	135	138	166	176	231	250	283	320	8.2	13.2	13.1	14.4
3171 Women's handbags and purses	35.1	41.3	42.4	49.6	46.0	46.5	49.2	52.1	1.1	5.8	5.9	7.0
3172 Personal goods not elsewhere classified	22.8	20.0	23.9	27.2	29.3	33.7	36.4	39.3	15.0	8.0	8.0	6.5

[1] Estimate except imports and exports.
[2] Estimate.
[3] Forecast.
[4] Compound annual rate.
[5] For a definition of industry versus product values, see "Getting the Most Out of *Outlook '99*."
Source: U.S. Department of Commerce: Bureau of the Census; International Trade Administration.

est percentages for all the industries in the luggage and leather goods group. The largest suppliers were China with a 53 percent share of total imports and Italy with 14 percent. In 1997 U.S. exports of personal leather goods were up 15 percent to about $34 million and went primarily to Canada and Japan.

Leather and Sheepskin-Lined Clothing

Manufacturers of leather wearing apparel produce leather coats, jackets, and other garments for men, women, and children. Shipments include leather pants, vests, dresses, skirts, suits, caps, and other clothing. Demand for these products is highly seasonal, with most retail sales concentrated in the fall and winter, and is directly related to trends in fashion. Therefore, consumer spending on leather wearing apparel is largely discretionary, and consumption patterns can vary widely from year to year because of fluctuations in the price of leather, weather conditions, and styles.

In 1997 product shipments of leather wearing apparel increased about 8 percent to $197 million from $183 million in 1996. Measured in constant dollars, product shipments increased 7 percent. Total employment was unchanged from 1996 at 1,800, but production employment increased 6 percent to 1,600. In 1997 apparent consumption of leather wearing apparel increased 7 percent to $1.1 billion.

In 1997 imports of leather apparel were up about 7 percent to $977 million. Import penetration in 1997 was 89 percent, the highest for the entire luggage and leather products group. China was by far the largest supplier in 1997, with 66 percent of total U.S. leather apparel imports. India and Pakistan followed with about 7 percent each. U.S. exports of leather wearing apparel in 1997 were up about 5 percent over 1996 to $71 million, and Japan was the largest export market.

U.S. Industry Growth Projections for the Next 1 and 5 Years

Although consumption of luggage and leather products was expected to increase about 3.5 percent in 1998 to an estimated $6.62 billion, imports were expected to rise about 7 percent and reach 83 percent of consumption. As a result, product shipments in constant dollars were expected to drop about 7 percent. The rate of decline varied among categories; luggage, −6 percent; personal leather goods, −7 percent; handbags, −14 percent; and leather gloves and mittens, −19 percent. Leather wearing apparel will remain unchanged (see Table 34-8).

In 1999 product shipments in constant dollars for the group are expected to drop about 3 percent. Luggage, gloves and mittens, and leather wearing apparel will decline about 1 percent each. Handbags will drop 7 percent, and personal leather goods will fall almost 8 percent (see Table 34-8).

Over the next 5 years the constant-dollar value of luggage and leather product shipments is expected to decrease at a compound annual rate of almost 5 percent. Four sectors are expected to decline: luggage by 2 percent, leather gloves by 5 percent, personal leather goods by 8 percent, and handbags by 11 percent. Leather wearing apparel will increase less than 1 percent.

Global Market Products

Among the five subsectors in the luggage and leather goods group, only luggage appears to have an opportunity to increase exports significantly. From 1992 through 1997 luggage exports increased at a compound annual rate of 13 percent, reflecting the fact that this industry has some large manufacturers that can produce and sell worldwide. European countries, Japan, and certain South American countries are expected to become growing markets for U.S. luggage exports. The fact that the other four industries face such intense import competition in the U.S. market indicates that they must confront the same competition in other world markets and will be unable to increase exports significantly.

James E. Byron, U.S. Department of Commerce, Office of Consumer Goods, (202) 482-4034, October 1998.

■ REFERENCES

American Shoemaking (monthly), *World Footwear* (monthly), and *American Shoemaking Directory,* 1998, Shoe Trades Publishing Co., Inc., 61 Massachusetts Avenue, Arlington, MA 02174.

Footwear: Current Industrial Report (quarterly, with annual summary), MQ31A, U.S. Department of Commerce, Bureau of the Census, Industry Division, Washington DC 20233.

Footwear Manual and World Footwear Markets (SATRA), Footwear Industries of America, Inc., 1420 K Street, NW, Washington, DC 20005.

Footwear News (weekly), Fairchild Publications, 7 West 34th Street, New York, NY 10001.

Journal of the American Leather Chemists Association, Leather Industries of American Research Laboratory, Campus Station, Cincinnati, OH 45221.

Leather Gloves, Luggage, and Miscellaneous Leather Goods, SIC 3151, 3161, 3171, 3172; 1992 Census of Manufactures, U.S. Department of Commerce, Bureau of the Census, Washington, DC 20233.

Leather International Journal of the Industry (monthly), and *International Leather Guide,* 1998, Miller Freeman Publishers Ltd., Sovereign Way, Tonbridge, Kent TN91RW, England.

Membership Bulletin Leather Industry Statistics, 1997 Edition, Leather Industries of America, Inc., 1000 Thomas Jefferson Street, NW, Suite 515, Washington, DC 20007.

Miscellaneous Apparel and Accessories, SIC 2371, 2385, 2386, 2387, 2389; 1992 Census of Manufactures, U.S. Department of Commerce, Bureau of the Census, Washington, DC 20233.

Nonrubber Footwear Quarterly Statistical Reports, U.S. International Trade Commission, Washington, DC 20436.

Travelware, Business Journals, Inc., 50 Day Street, Norwalk, CT 06854.

World Footwear Markets, Shoe and Allied Trade Research Association (SATRA), Kettering Northants NN169JH, England.

World Statistical Compendium for Raw Hides and Skins, Leather and Leather Footwear, 1976–1995, Seventh Edition, Food and Agriculture Organization of the United Nations, United Nations Publications.

■ RELATED CHAPTERS

33: Apparel and Fabricated Textile Products

PROCESSED FOOD AND BEVERAGES
Economic and Trade Trends

U.S. International Trade

($ billions)

Legend: Balance, Exports, Imports

Source: U.S. Department of Commerce: Bureau of the Census; International Trade Administration.

World Export Market Shares

(%)

Legend: United States, France, Netherlands, Germany

Source: United Nations; U.S. Department of Commerce, International Trade Administration.

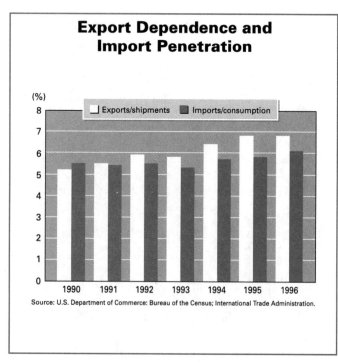

Export Dependence and Import Penetration

(%)

Legend: Exports/shipments, Imports/consumption

Source: U.S. Department of Commerce: Bureau of the Census; International Trade Administration.

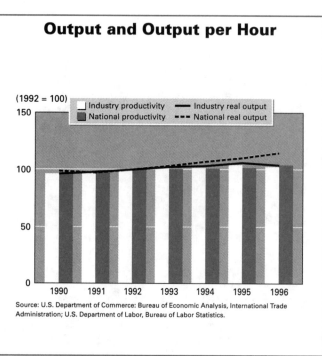

Output and Output per Hour

(1992 = 100)

Legend: Industry productivity, National productivity, Industry real output, National real output

Source: U.S. Department of Commerce: Bureau of Economic Analysis, International Trade Administration; U.S. Department of Labor, Bureau of Labor Statistics.

See "Getting the Most Out of *Outlook '99*" for definitions of terms.

Processed Food and Beverages

INDUSTRY DEFINITION This industry includes establishments that manufacture or process foods and beverages for human consumption and related products such as manufactured ice, chewing gum, vegetable and animal fats and oils, and prepared feeds for animals and fowl. Subsectors in this chapter include red meats and poultry (SIC 2011, 2013, and 2015), snack food (SIC 2068 and 2096), and alcoholic beverages such as beer (SIC 2082), wines and brandy (SIC 2084), and distilled spirits (SIC 2085).

OVERVIEW

Globalization of the processed food and beverage markets is occurring as most developed countries face mature domestic processed food markets. The food and beverage industries of those countries depend on future growth resulting from exporting or making foreign direct investment. The industries may find niche markets in developed economies or export a wide range of products to countries that do not have a fully developed processed food and beverage industry to supply growing middle-income and upper-income populations.

The U.S. processed food and beverage industry is a major participant in the global economy. The United States accounts for approximately one-fourth of the industrialized world's production of processed foods and beverages. Seven of the largest 10 and 22 of the largest 50 food processing firms in the world have their headquarters in the United States.

The processed food and beverage industry sector (SIC 20) is the United States' largest manufacturing sector, accounting for approximately one-sixth of industrial activity. State employment levels in this industry are shown in Figure 35-1. In 1998 the value of food and beverage industry shipments was expected to reach an estimated $480.5 billion (see Table 35-1). In constant dollars, shipments were expected to rise 1.6 percent.

U.S. total processed food and beverage exports were flat in 1998 as a result of the Asian economic crisis. Nevertheless, the

U.S. processed food and beverage industry continues to have a trade surplus. The surplus has been shrinking in recent years due not only to the recent economic crisis in Asia but also to the strengthening of the U.S. dollar. In 1998 the trade balance was only $600 million, compared with a high of $4.9 billion in 1995. Although total U.S. processed food and beverage exports were flat in 1998, U.S. exports of high-value-added consumer-packaged foods grew about 1 percent, while U.S. exports of low-value-added processed food items fell almost 1.5 percent. U.S. processed food and beverage exports are forecast to reach $32.1 billion, or 6.8 percent of domestic production, by 1999 (see Table 35-2).

In 1999 the U.S. food and beverage industry will grow 2 percent in constant dollars. Although exports or other international arrangements will continue to play an important role in the future growth and financial health of the processed food industry, meeting ever-changing consumer needs at home remains important. For example, salad bar sales and packaged salad sales are increasing, along with sales of vegetarian-based cuisine. While supermarket sales have been stagnant in constant dollars, restaurant sales are increasing. In response, supermarket chains are pushing home meal replacements (HMRs). These HMRs, or "meal solutions," are ready-to-finish dinners that require minimal final effort before serving at home.

On the structural side, consolidation continues in the processed food and beverage industry. Less efficient plants are

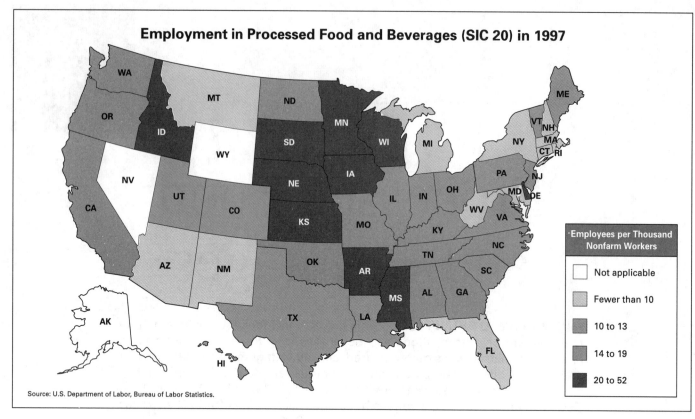

Employment in Processed Food and Beverages (SIC 20) in 1997

Employees per Thousand Nonfarm Workers

- Not applicable
- Fewer than 10
- 10 to 13
- 14 to 19
- 20 to 52

Source: U.S. Department of Labor, Bureau of Labor Statistics.

FIGURE 35-1

closing or merging with more efficient ones. In 1997 mergers and acquisitions in this industry rose more than 30 percent. Of particular interest is the number of Mexican companies that are aggressively seeking alliances with North American companies to gain distribution channels. In the next 5 years constant-dollar shipments of the U.S. processed food and beverage industry are expected to grow between 1.5 and 2.5 percent annually as these markets are increasingly globalized.

RED MEAT AND POULTRY

Red meat production includes establishments primarily engaged in slaughtering, for their own account or on a contract basis for the trade, cattle, hogs, sheep, lamb, and calves for meat to be sold or to be used on the same premises in canning, cooking, curing, and freezing and in making sausage, lard, and other products (SIC 2011) and establishments primarily engaged in manufacturing sausages, cured meats, smoked meats, canned meats, frozen meats, and other prepared meats and meat specialties from purchased carcasses and other materials (SIC 2013). Poultry production includes establishments primarily engaged in slaughtering, dressing, packing, freezing, and canning poultry, rabbits, and other small game or in manufacturing products from such meats for their own account or on a contract basis for the trade. This industry also includes the drying, freezing, and breaking of eggs (SIC 2015).

Global Industry Trends

According to the U.S. Department of Agriculture (USDA), global production by the major producing and trading countries of red meat (beef and pork) and poultry increased approximately 3 percent annually in the last 10 years; these countries include the United States, the nations of the European Union, Canada, Mexico, Japan, China, Brazil, Argentina, and Australia. Worldwide increases in production have been led by increased poultry production and, to a lesser extent, increased pork production. Since 1988 poultry meat production has expanded more than 5 percent annually, offsetting almost no growth in beef production in that period. Global poultry meat production surpassed beef production in 1995, and the gap has continued to widen as beef production has remained stagnant. Pork is the most widely produced meat, with China accounting for over half the world total.

The meat output of China has determined trends in global red meat and poultry production over the last decade. That nation's total meat production has jumped 10 percent annually since 1988. When China's production is excluded, global production of red meat and poultry has risen only about 0.5 percent per year: Beef and pork production have actually declined, and only poultry meat has shown an increase—nearly 4 percent—each year.

Poultry meat is a cheaper source of protein than is beef, and the growth of consumption has been strong in China, Russia, and Mexico in recent years. Even in a developed market such as

TABLE 35-1: Food and Kindred Products (SIC 20) Trends and Forecasts
(millions of dollars except as noted)

	1992	1993	1994	1995	1996	1997[1]	1998[2]	1999[3]	96–97	97–98	98–99	92–96[4]
									| Percent Change			
Industry data												
Value of shipments[5]	406,963	422,220	430,963	446,869	461,324	477,791	480,513	499,879	3.6	0.6	4.0	3.2
Value of shipments (1992$)	406,963	415,112	419,160	431,001	422,973	435,200	442,100	450,900	2.9	1.6	2.0	1.0
Total employment (thousands)	1,503	1,520	1,511	1,520	1,517	1,517	1,533		0.0	1.1		0.2
Production workers (thousands)	1,100	1,118	1,112	1,120	1,113	1,115	1,128		0.2	1.2		0.3
Average hourly earnings ($)	10.41	10.58	10.74	10.96	11.17	11.46	11.77		2.6	2.7		1.8
Capital expenditures	9,898	9,389	10,093	11,812	11,717							4.3
Product data												
Value of shipments[5]	382,889	397,633	405,490	421,507	435,009	450,784	453,340	471,609	3.6	0.6	4.0	3.2
Value of shipments (1992$)	382,889	391,090	394,447	406,291	398,717	410,600	417,100	425,400	3.0	1.6	2.0	1.0
Trade data												
Value of imports	20,883	20,890	22,842	23,956	26,498	29,052	30,300	31,900	9.6	4.3	5.3	6.1
Value of exports	22,642	23,138	25,801	28,868	29,667	30,893	30,900	32,106	4.1	2.3	3.9	7.0

[1] Estimate except imports and exports.
[2] Estimate.
[3] Forecast.
[4] Compound annual rate.
[5] For a definition of industry versus product values, see "Getting the Most Out of *Outlook '99*."
Source: U.S. Department of Commerce: Bureau of the Census; International Trade Administration.

TABLE 35-2: U.S. Trade Patterns in Food and Kindred Products[1] in 1997
(millions of dollars; percent)

Exports			Imports		
Regions[2]	Value[3]	Share, %	Regions[2]	Value[3]	Share, %
NAFTA	7,297	23.6	NAFTA	8,090	27.8
Latin America	2,672	8.6	Latin America	4,500	15.5
Western Europe	5,304	17.2	Western Europe	7,773	26.8
Japan/Chinese Economic Area	9,098	29.5	Japan/Chinese Economic Area	1,539	5.3
Other Asia	2,886	9.3	Other Asia	4,454	15.3
Rest of world	3,636	11.8	Rest of world	2,697	9.3
World	30,893	100.0	World	29,052	100.0
Top Five Countries	Value	Share, %	Top Five Countries	Value	Share, %
Japan	6,367	20.6	Canada	6,024	20.7
Canada	4,907	15.9	Mexico	2,066	7.1
Mexico	2,390	7.7	Thailand	1,648	5.7
South Korea	1,530	5.0	France	1,535	5.3
Hong Kong (PRC)	1,272	4.1	Italy	1,369	4.7

[1] SIC 20.
[2] For definitions of regional groupings, see "Getting the Most Out of *Outlook '99*."
[3] Values may not sum to total due to rounding.
Source: U.S. Department of Commerce, Bureau of the Census.

the United States, consumers are buying more poultry. Lower prices compared with red meats, the convenience of processed poultry products, and the promotion of poultry products in the fast-food industry have contributed to this trend.

According to the USDA, because of strong and growing demand for poultry meat, global exports advanced at a double-digit pace in the 1990s. Pork exports have increased an estimated 3 percent annually, while beef exports have declined. The United States supplies over half of global poultry imports.

Although global production and consumption of red meat (beef, veal, and pork) and poultry meat grew an estimated 3 percent to nearly 188 million tons in 1998, exports from the leading meat exporting countries, except those in the European Union, declined. The red meat and poultry sectors of these countries were confronted with the lingering effects of food safety concerns and the Asian financial situation.

In 1996 the presence of bovine spongiform encephalopathy in the European Union contributed to a slowdown in the growth of global meat consumption and trade. The lingering effects of concerns about food safety began to dissipate in 1997, and the outlook for beef consumption and trade began to improve in the latter part of that year. However, in the last quarter of 1997 Asian beef imports began to slow as reports of *Escherichia coli* and *Listeria* contamination in Asian markets raised concerns about the safety of beef. In 1998 beef consumption in Asia was expected to fall as consumers returned to eating more pork.

The avian influenza outbreak in Hong Kong and the subsequent slaughter of the poultry flock there added more uncertainty in one of the largest poultry trade markets. An outbreak of foot-and-mouth disease in Taiwan in 1997 shut that country, one of the largest pork exporters, out of the global export market. Classical swine fever has disrupted the pork markets in the European Union.

Partly because of the Asian financial crisis, the competition in global markets is probably as great as ever. The bulk of global meat trade is concentrated in a few major markets, and as the growth of consumption slows or shrinks in key markets, competition will intensify. The devaluations of the currencies of Thailand and South Korea substantially improved their competitive position in the export market for poultry and pork. The strengthening of the U.S. dollar against the Australian dollar helped increase the Australian share of the Asian beef market.

World production and demand for seafood will affect the growth of red meat and poultry consumption. According to the USDA, global demand for seafood will grow more than 60 percent over the next 35 years. Today 16 percent of the fish consumed is produced by aquaculture, which may soon account for nearly half the world's fish population. Whereas there are natural limits on fish from the sea, there are fewer limits on fish grown like crops. Several species of fish are raised commercially, but currently catfish farms lead in aquaculture.

Factors Affecting Future U.S. Industry Growth

The red meat industry, the largest sector in the processed food and beverage industry, experienced a 3.4 percent increase in constant-dollar product shipments in 1998 (see Table 35-3).

The health of the U.S. red meat industry is heavily dependent on mother nature and the demand for red meats at home and abroad. According to the USDA, total red meat production rose an estimated 3 percent in 1998. While pork production increased almost 10 percent, beef production in 1998 was down 100 million pounds from 1997 (a drop of 0.04 percent). Beef production should begin to decline sharply in 1999, reflecting cattle inventory declines since 1996. Excluding near-record beef production from 1994 through 1998 (ranging from 24.3 billion to 25.4 billion pounds annually), production in 1999 will be the highest since 1978. Declining cattle inventories will continue to reduce feedlot placements over the next couple of years. Lower feeder cattle supplies, combined with increased heifer retention for herd rebuilding, reduced beef production in the fall of 1998, and that trend will continue through 2000.

In recent years, a larger proportion of Prime and Choice beef has been sold in the hotel-restaurant and export markets, while other cuts have been destined for the domestic retail market. The trend of offering lower-quality meat on the retail market with great variability in eating quality will make it more difficult to recapture the consumer acceptance that accrued under the old Choice grades and thus to raise retail prices for beef. Both white meat chicken and pork loin are increasingly able to compete against beef, and both provide a desirable consistency and size of cut acceptable to consumers, particularly at lower relative prices.

Constant-dollar product shipments of the poultry and poultry products industry were expected to grow 3 percent in 1998 (see Table 35-4).

TABLE 35-3: Red Meat (SIC 2011, 2013) Trends and Forecasts
(millions of dollars except as noted)

	1992	1993	1994	1995	1996	1997[1]	1998[2]	1999[3]	96–97	97–98	98–99	92–96[4]
									Percent Change			
Industry data												
Value of shipments[5]	70,107	73,941	70,701	72,025	71,943	75,216	74,668	75,511	4.5	−0.7	1.2	0.6
Value of shipments (1992$)	70,107	71,389	71,609	74,312	71,003	71,140	73,564	74,300	0.2	3.4	1.0	0.3
Total employment (thousands)	207	209	204	214	218	219	223		0.5	1.8		1.3
Production workers (thousands)	171	173	169	178	180	180	184		0.0	2.2		1.3
Average hourly earnings ($)	8.99	9.06	9.43	9.81	9.64	9.86	10.06		2.3	2.0		1.8
Capital expenditures	719	703	699	862	1,135							12.1
Product data												
Value of shipments[5]	64,351	68,216	64,839	65,878	65,839	67,625	67,132	69,154	2.7	−0.7	3.0	0.6
Value of shipments (1992$)	64,351	65,856	65,679	67,977	64,988	65,118	67,332	68,000	0.2	3.4	1.0	0.2
Trade data												
Value of imports	2,926	3,070	2,984	2,662	2,638	2,989	3,140	3,300	13.3	5.1	5.1	−2.6
Value of exports	4,807	4,698	5,273	6,303	6,226	6,233	5,900	6,070	0.1	−5.3	2.9	6.7

[1] Estimate except imports and exports.
[2] Estimate.
[3] Forecast.
[4] Compound annual rate.
[5] For a definition of industry versus product values, see "Getting the Most Out of *Outlook '99*."
Source: U.S. Department of Commerce: Bureau of the Census; International Trade Administration.

TABLE 35-4: Poultry Slaughtering and Processing (SIC 2015) Trends and Forecasts
(millions of dollars except as noted)

	1992	1993	1994	1995	1996	1997[1]	1998[2]	1999[3]	Percent Change 96–97	97–98	98–99	92–96[4]
Industry data												
Value of shipments[5]	23,965	25,501	27,415	28,929	30,160	30,478	30,500	31,044	1.1	0.1	1.8	5.9
Value of shipments (1992$)	23,965	24,783	25,937	27,525	27,122	27,936	28,770	29,710	3.0	3.0	3.3	3.1
Total employment (thousands)	194	205	216	214	215	216	219		0.5	1.4		2.6
Production workers (thousands)	173	184	193	192	190	190	192		0.0	1.1		2.4
Average hourly earnings ($)	7.39	7.40	7.49	8.09	8.27	8.49	8.76		2.7	3.2		2.9
Capital expenditures	469	555	594	726	697							10.4
Product data												
Value of shipments[5]	23,592	24,983	27,027	28,708	29,981	30,297	30,319	31,844	1.1	0.1	5.0	6.2
Value of shipments (1992$)	23,592	24,279	25,570	27,315	26,961	27,770	28,600	29,450	3.0	3.0	3.0	3.4
Trade data												
Value of imports	25.8	29.9	25.3	30.5	44.7	45.6	50.0	52.5	2.0	9.6	5.0	14.7
Value of exports	990	1,157	1,633	2,097	2,585	2,509	2,470	2,425	–2.9	2.0	–1.8	27.1

[1] Estimate except imports and exports.
[2] Estimate.
[3] Forecast.
[4] Compound annual rate.
[5] For a definition of industry versus product values, see "Getting the Most Out of *Outlook '99*."
Source: U.S. Department of Commerce: Bureau of the Census; International Trade Administration.

The growth of the U.S. poultry industry is affected by what happens not only domestically but also internationally. World poultry production has increased dramatically compared with the production of beef and pork. Although U.S. poultry exports will level off as other countries direct more resources to poultry products, a less expensive form of meat protein compared with beef or pork, total U.S. poultry production will continue to increase. Although the increased supply of poultry, particularly broilers, in the domestic market will lower producers' prices, lower feed costs in 1998 were expected to offset those lower prices, improving net returns to broiler producers. Finally, instead of relying solely on U.S. poultry exports for international opportunities, many major U.S. poultry producers are developing joint ventures around the world (with Russia and China, for example) and will continue to do so in the future.

U.S. Industry Growth Projections for the Next 1 and 5 Years

Constant-dollar product shipments of red meat are forecast to rise a nominal 1 percent in 1999. While beef production is expected to decline in 1999 (but still be at record levels), pork production is expected to increase about 2 percent. In the recent past the financial health and growth of the industry depended partially on exports. The financial crisis in Asia probably will remain a drag on beef trade through 1999, but the situation could ease in the latter part of 1999 if financial reforms stimulate consumer confidence. While stagnating demand is expected to limit U.S. sales to Korea, continued strong growth in exports to Mexico and an expected modest increase in exports to Japan could boost U.S. red meat exports 3 percent in 1999.

According to the USDA, although pork supplies are expected to rise, hog prices will be about the same as they were in 1998 because of the sharp reduction in beef supplies. With abundant pork supplies and reduced amounts of beef available, retailers probably will feature pork over beef. Pork exports are expected to increase 3 percent in 1999 as Mexico and Russia purchase attractively priced lower-value products. Despite the appreciation of the dollar against the yen, shipments to Japan are not expected to decline. Japan is the largest U.S. market for higher-valued pork products.

In 1999 constant-dollar product shipments of poultry and poultry products are forecast to rise approximately 3 percent. Chicken production is expected to increase 4 percent in 1999. Chicken producers are expected to remain cautious in making production decisions, as there will continue to be very large domestic meat supplies and uncertainty in the export market. Turkey production is expected to decline almost 2 percent in 1999 after 3 years of negative returns for turkey producers. According to the USDA, modest export demand and competition from large pork supplies in the domestic market are expected to prevent price rises. Some turkey production facilities will convert to chicken production.

According to industry sources, poultry exports will drop almost 2 percent in 1999 as a result of uncertain prospects for a recovery in the economy of Russia, the largest export market for U.S. poultry. Also, slower growth is expected in shipments to Mexico, South Africa, and many Asian markets (chiefly Japan). U.S. exports to Hong Kong are forecast to rebound somewhat in 1999 (but be below 1997 levels) after a 32 percent drop in 1998. U.S. poultry exports will face strong competition from U.S. pork exports and foreign poultry producers. U.S. pork exports compete as a prime ingredient in processed products and sausages.

U.S. per capita consumption of poultry has increased steadily from 88 pounds in 1995, to an estimated 93 pounds in

1998, to a forecast 95 pounds in 1999. Per capita beef consumption was flat at 67 to 68 pounds between 1995 and 1998 and is forecast to drop to 63 pounds per capita in 1999. Per capita consumption of pork, after declining from 52 pounds in 1995 to 49 pounds in 1997, rebounded to 53 pounds in 1998 and is forecast to reach 54 pounds in 1999.

Over the next 5 years the red meat industry should experience a compound annual growth rate of 1 to 1.5 percent. The industry will face sluggish domestic demand and less than optimum export markets, especially in Asia. Domestic red meat supplies will be tight until after 2000. After the economic crisis in Asia ends, the export markets will again play a greater role in the profitability of the U.S. red meat industry.

Although per capita poultry consumption will increase over the next 5 years, it will not grow as fast as it has during the last decade. This, coupled with a slowdown in U.S. poultry exports, will result in a compound annual growth rate of 2 to 3 percent over the next 5 years.

Global Market Prospects

There was a substantial increase in U.S. imports of red meat products in 1998, when U.S. red meat imports reached an estimated $3.1 billion, an increase of 5 percent over 1997. U.S. exports experienced a 5.3 percent decline to just under an estimated $5.9 billion because of the Asian crisis, which reduced the United States' exports to our major Asian markets for red meat products. For trade patterns in red meat (beef, pork, hides, and skins) see Table 35-5.

In 1997 the top five export markets for beef accounted for almost 95 percent of total exports. Japan was the United States' largest export market for beef, accounting for 55 percent, followed by Mexico, Canada, and South Korea with about 12 percent each and Taiwan with 2 percent. U.S. beef exports to

Mexico have rebounded since the 1995 peso crises and increased from $88 million in 1995, to $315 million in 1997, to an estimated $500 million dollars in 1998.

The top five U.S. export markets for hides and skins accounted for about 80 percent of the total in 1997. South Korea was the largest export market, accounting for about 38 percent, followed by Taiwan with 14 percent, Japan and Mexico with 10 percent each, and China with 7 percent. While U.S. exports of hides and skins to Asia declined dramatically in 1998 (20 to 60 percent depending on the particular Asian country), exports to Mexico increased an estimated 66 percent in 1998. U.S. exports to Mexico increased from $63 million in 1995, to over $150 million in 1997, to an estimated $250 million in 1998.

The top five U.S. export markets for pork accounted for almost 90 percent of the total. As with beef, Japan is by far the largest market with 56 percent, followed by Canada with 13 percent, Russia with 11 percent, Mexico with 6 percent, and Hong Kong with 3 percent. In 1997 approximately 40 percent of U.S. red meat products exports consisted of beef and beef products, followed by hides and skins with 24 percent, pork and pork products (including sausages) with 20 percent, and offals and similar products with 10 percent.

Although U.S. poultry imports rose more than an estimated 9 percent in 1998, these imports represent less than 0.2 percent of domestic supply. U.S. exports of poultry were expected to decline 1.6 percent in 1998, as U.S. poultry exports to the number one market, Russia, declined an estimated 16 percent. U.S. exports to Mexico were expected to remain flat. Each of these two countries has expanded its domestic poultry production. Even with the decline, U.S. poultry exports still represent about 8 percent of domestic production. On the bright side, U.S. exports to Canada have increased steadily from $176 million in 1995, to $216 million in 1997, to an estimated $240 million in

TABLE 35-5: U.S. Trade Patterns in Red Meat[1] in 1997
(millions of dollars; percent)

Exports			Imports		
Regions[2]	Value[3]	Share, %	Regions[2]	Value[3]	Share, %
NAFTA	1,341	21.5	NAFTA	1,313	43.9
Latin America	152	2.4	Latin America	357	11.9
Western Europe	295	4.7	Western Europe	337	11.3
Japan/Chinese Economic Area	3,140	50.4	Japan/Chinese Economic Area	46	1.6
Other Asia	987	15.8	Other Asia	31	1.0
Rest of world	318	5.1	Rest of world	905	30.3
World	6,233	100.0	World	2,989	100.0
Top Five Countries	Value	Share, %	Top Five Countries	Value	Share, %
Japan	2,562	41.1	Canada	1,279	42.8
South Korea	901	14.5	Australia	455	15.2
Mexico	738	11.8	New Zealand	413	13.8
Canada	603	9.7	Denmark	195	6.5
Taiwan	273	4.4	Argentina	129	4.3

[1] SIC 2011, 2013.
[2] For definitions of regional groupings, see "Getting the Most Out of *Outlook '99*."
[3] Values may not sum to total due to rounding.
Source: U.S. Department of Commerce, Bureau of the Census.

TABLE 35-6: U.S. Trade Patterns in Poultry[1] in 1997
(millions of dollars; percent)

Exports			Imports		
Regions[2]	Value[3]	Share, %	Regions[2]	Value[3]	Share, %
NAFTA	451	18.0	NAFTA	23	51.3
Latin America	163	6.5	Latin America	0	0.0
Western Europe	60	2.4	Western Europe	1	2.6
Japan/Chinese Economic Area	671	26.7	Japan/Chinese Economic Area	6	13.8
Other Asia	71	2.8	Other Asia	3	5.7
Rest of world	1,094	43.6	Rest of world	12	26.6
World	2,509	100.0	World	46	100.0
Top Five Countries	Value	Share, %	Top Five Countries	Value	Share, %
Russia	791	31.5	Canada	23	51.0
Hong Kong (PRC)	433	17.3	New Zealand	10	23.0
Mexico	235	9.4	Taiwan	4	8.3
Canada	216	8.6	China	2	3.5
Japan	178	7.1	Israel	2	3.4

[1] SIC 2015.
[2] For definitions of regional groupings, see "Getting the Most Out of *Outlook '99*."
[3] Values may not sum to total due to rounding.
Source: U.S. Department of Commerce, Bureau of the Census.

1998. Exports to Latvia, Poland, and Haiti also expanded between 1995 and 1997 and into 1998. For trade patterns in 1997, see Table 35-6.

Japanese Meat and Poultry Market. Japan's sluggish economy is likely to temper any increase in meat consumption. The United States is expected to face increased competition in supplying the Japanese market. According to Japanese trade statistics, South Korea nearly tripled its pork exports to that country in 1997. The sharp devaluation of the South Korean won has substantially improved the competitive position of South Korean pork in the Japanese market. Japanese beef consumption and imports are not expected to increase and will not reach the high levels of 1996, before food safety concerns associated with an *E. coli* incident arose. In any case, U.S. beef exporters will continue to face strong competition from the Australians. Japanese consumption of poultry meat will experience marginal increases in 1999. Both China and Thailand have increased exports to Japan, especially those of boneless chicken leg meat. Thailand has made inroads into the Japanese market not only because of its devalued currency but also by providing more processed chicken to the growing convenience-conscious Japanese customer market. This growing market provides an opportunity for U.S. suppliers.

South Korean Meat Market. South Korea's beef consumption rose steadily until 1998, when the Asian economic crisis began. In 1998 Korean consumers bought less meat and chose cheaper cuts. As a result, beef consumption dropped in 1998. South Korea is one of the world's leading beef importers. Although it agreed to import 187,000 tons of beef in 1998 as a result of its World Trade Organization commitments, South Korea imported only 25,000 tons as of August 31, 1998, 60 percent below the level in 1997. In response to the South Korean credit squeeze, the United States provided nearly $147 million

in GSM-102 credit guarantees (a USDA export credit program) to facilitate beef shipments to South Korea.

Russian Meat Market. Russia continues to be one of the world's leading importers of meat. In 1998 Russia imported an estimated 2.5 million tons, of which poultry accounted for 1.3 million tons, followed by 750,000 tons of beef and 450,000 tons of pork. Russia has boosted its meat protein consumption with imports of poultry meat. While beef and pork consumption continues to decline, imports of poultry meat have allowed Russian consumption of meat to decline at a much slower rate than its meat production. U.S. suppliers dominate the Russian poultry meat import market by providing ample supplies of low-cost leg quarters. U.S. businesses' major competitors in the Russian market are from the European Union. These EU competitors have aggressively targeted the Russian market and will continue to do so.

Mexican Meat and Poultry Market. Mexico continues to be a critical expanding market for meat producers. Based on estimates of a partial year, Mexico's meat consumption grew faster than did its production in 1998, resulting in an estimated 15 percent increase in meat imports. Beef consumption grew 4 percent in 1997, reflecting strong growth in incomes as the economy continued to expand at a healthy pace. Domestic beef production in Mexico is not sufficient to meet consumer demand. In 1997 Mexican beef imports surged 83 percent to 150,000 tons, and they were expected to increase another 30 percent in 1998. U.S. producers supply the vast majority of beef imports to Mexico.

Mexico's pork consumption also has increased. A 5 percent increase in pork consumption to 960,000 tons was seen in 1997 as pork supplies increased and the economy continued to strengthen. An increase of 2 percent was expected in 1998.

Pork imports increased 28 percent to 41,000 tons in 1997, much of which was imported from the United States by Mexican sausage producers. The U.S. average share of the Mexican pork market has been 97 percent, and almost no change is expected over the next couple of years. Mexican imports have been projected to increase to 47,000 tons in 1998, encouraged by lower U.S. pork prices.

Mexican poultry meat production will continue to expand at a much higher rate than will beef and pork production through 1999; economic recovery since the peso devaluation and falling grain prices are boosting poultry production. The pace is only slightly ahead of consumption gains, and imports have been projected to increase in 1998 and are forecast to increase in 1999.

Canadian Meat Production and Market. Canada expanded meat production in 1998, led by gains in pork and poultry meat production. The cattle industry's liquidation in the period 1996–1997 boosted beef production, and cattle inventories are expected to stabilize at the 1997 level. Canada's beef imports are estimated not to have increased in 1998, and the U.S. share has also declined in favor of Australia. Expansion and aggressive marketing by western Canadian packers are competing with U.S. exports into eastern Canadian markets.

The United States has historically been the largest market for Canadian pork, but record U.S. pork supplies and lower pork prices were likely to keep more Canadian pork at home in 1998. With the help of new processing facilities, Canada's exports increased in 1998. They are expected to increase again in 1999, competing in third markets with U.S. pork products.

SALTED SNACKS AND SNACK FOODS

The salted snack industry consists of establishments primarily engaged in manufacturing potato chips, corn chips, and similar snacks (SIC 2096) and establishments primarily engaged in manufacturing salted, roasted, dried, cooked, and canned nuts or processing grains or seeds in a similar manner for snack purposes (SIC 2068). Salted snacks are part of snack foods, a broader category that also includes consumer-ready packaged cookies and crackers, snack nuts, popcorn (microwavable or unpopped), meat snacks, and other types of foods that are ready to eat in casual, between-meals settings. Although most of this section focuses on salted snacks (the only part of snack foods for which industry-level census data are available), data and information on other snack foods are presented in the discussions of the prospects for markets in individual countries.

Global Industry Trends

Between 1992 and 1996 the worldwide salted snacks market grew 21 percent, and it is expected to reach almost $50 billion in 1999. The United States is the largest market, accounting for approximately 30 to 33 percent of the total, followed by Japan with 16 to 18 percent and the United Kingdom with 7 to 8 percent.

The strong growth in the market is a result of the spread of western eating habits to emerging markets in eastern Europe, Latin America, and Asia as lifestyles in those regions become

busier and the tradition of family meal times becomes impractical. This increase in the amount of time spent at work and in leisure pursuits has led to an increase in snacking that is being tempered by the presence of more health-conscious consumers. As a result, manufacturers around the world are attempting to counter the unhealthy image of their products and profit from this healthy-eating trend. Therefore, they are inventing low-fat but tasty products, as was done in the United States in the last decade.

Factors Affecting Future U.S. Industry Growth

Constant-dollar shipments of salted snacks increased an estimated 3 percent in 1997 and were expected to increase 2.3 percent in 1998 (see Table 35-7). Although there has been a lack of growth in salted snacks sales through traditional supermarkets, gains have taken place in mass merchandising stores. The craze for "good-for-you" healthy-type snack foods has subsided but could resurge if the fat-free olestra ingredient that is being used in some salted snacks catches hold.

U.S. demographics continue to affect the growth of this industry. Three major population sectors have had a balancing effect. According to the latest U.S. Bureau of Labor *Consumer Expenditures Survey* and the U.S. Bureau of the Census's population estimates, the age group 35 to 44 years that consumes annually more than the national average ($102.19 compared with $80.50) grew 17 percent between 1990 and 1997 and accounts for 16 percent of the population. This growth is offset by the age groups 25 to 34 and 55 to 64 years, which consume 10 percent less than the national average, account for almost a quarter of the population, and have grown approximately 15 percent since 1990.

Although Frito-Lay continues to dominate the manufacturing of salted snacks in the United States, regional manufacturers have prospered by finding niche markets that take into account changes in consumer preferences. The sustained growth of the industry also will be dependent on the ability to tap overseas markets influenced by western eating habits.

U.S. Industry Growth Projections for the Next 1 and 5 Years

Since U.S. demographics and consumption patterns in 1998 remained similar to those mentioned above, constant-dollar shipments of salted snacks are likely to increase an estimated 2.1 percent in 1999. Although U.S. exports to Asia will not fully recover in 1999, U.S. salted snack exports to the rest of the world will be strong. Exports are expected to increase 5 percent in 1999.

Demographic projections do not indicate substantial growth in the salted snack sector. Although the age category 35 to 54 years, which consumes about 25 percent more than the national average and will grow in number, is slightly above the national average, the age category 55 to 64 years, which consumes about 10 percent less than the national average, will grow almost five times the national average. These factors, coupled with expectations of growing exports, suggest that the salted snack sector will grow between 2 and 4 percent annually over the next 5 years.

TABLE 35-7: Snack Foods (SIC 2068, 2096) Trends and Forecasts
(millions of dollars except as noted)

	1992	1993	1994	1995	1996	1997[1]	1998[2]	1999[3]	96–97	97–98	98–99	92–96[4]
									Percent Change			
Industry data												
Value of shipments[5]	10,146	10,779	11,266	11,997	12,523	13,220	13,438		5.6	1.6		5.4
2068 Snack nuts and seeds	2,837	3,044	3,098	3,248	3,390	3,555	3,558		4.9	0.1		4.6
2096 Potato chips and snacks	7,309	7,735	8,167	8,749	9,133	9,665	9,880		5.8	2.2		5.7
Value of shipments (1992$)	10,146	10,479	10,712	11,182	11,445	11,785	12,056	12,310	3.0	2.3	2.1	3.1
2068 Snack nuts and seeds	2,837	2,955	2,934	2,905	2,973	3,104	3,200	3,280	4.4	3.1	2.5	1.2
2096 Potato chips and snacks	7,309	7,524	7,778	8,277	8,472	8,681	8,856	9,030	2.5	2.0	2.0	3.8
Total employment (thousands)	45.3	45.1	44.1	45.4	45.4	45.6	45.9	46.9	0.4	0.7	2.2	0.1
2068 Snack nuts and seeds	10.5	10.0	9.8	10.5	9.4	9.5	9.7	10.0	1.1	2.1	3.1	−2.7
2096 Potato chips and snacks	34.8	35.1	34.3	34.9	36.0	36.1	36.2	36.9	0.3	0.3	1.9	0.9
Production workers (thousands)	32.1	32.0	31.1	33.0	32.6	32.7	33.0	33.7	0.3	0.9	2.1	0.4
2068 Snack nuts and seeds	8.1	7.7	7.9	8.4	7.1	7.2	7.4	7.6	1.4	2.8	2.7	−3.2
2096 Potato chips and snacks	24.0	24.3	23.2	24.6	25.5	25.5	25.6	26.1	0.0	0.4	2.0	1.5
Average hourly earnings ($)	9.94	10.17	10.55	11.55	12.42	12.64	13.03		1.8	3.1		5.7
2068 Snack nuts and seeds	8.79	9.07	9.35	9.27	10.06	10.50	10.86		4.4	3.4		3.4
2096 Potato chips and snacks	10.35	10.56	11.00	12.44	13.16	13.24	13.59		0.6	2.6		6.2
Capital expenditures	304	321	349	400	611							19.1
2068 Snack nuts and seeds	44.9	70.5	75.5	72.1	195							44.4
2096 Potato chips and snacks	259	250	273	328	415							12.5
Product data												
Value of shipments[5]	10,199	10,739	11,016	11,466	11,718	12,324	12,541		5.2	1.8		3.5
2068 Snack nuts and seeds	2,671	2,820	2,854	2,860	2,514	2,636	2,638		4.9	0.1		−1.5
2096 Potato chips and snacks	7,527	7,919	8,163	8,607	9,204	9,688	9,903		5.3	2.2		5.2
Value of shipments (1992$)	10,199	10,441	10,476	10,700	10,743	11,051	11,300	11,535	2.9	2.3	2.1	1.3
2068 Snack nuts and seeds	2,671	2,738	2,702	2,558	2,205	2,302	2,375	2,435	4.4	3.2	2.5	−4.7
2096 Potato chips and snacks	7,527	7,703	7,774	8,142	8,538	8,749	8,925	9,100	2.5	2.0	2.0	3.2
Trade data												
Value of imports	410	428	438	427	454	502	455	480	10.6	−9.4	5.5	2.6
2068 Snack nuts and seeds	388	405	413	402	427	470	420		10.1	−10.6		2.4
2096 Potato chips and snacks	22.9	22.9	25.2	24.4	27.8	31.3	35.0		12.6	11.8		5.0
Value of exports	912	1,027	1,205	1,210	1,450	1,258	1,390	1,460	−13.2	10.5	5.0	12.3
2068 Snack nuts and seeds	775	851	953	984	1,228	1,033	1,100		−15.9	6.5		12.2
2096 Potato chips and snacks	137	176	252	226	222	225	290		1.4	28.9		12.8

[1] Estimate except imports and exports.
[2] Estimate.
[3] Forecast.
[4] Compound annual rate.
[5] For a definition of industry versus product values, see "Getting the Most Out of *Outlook '99*."
Source: U.S. Department of Commerce: Bureau of the Census; International Trade Administration.

Global Market Prospects for Snack Foods

A broader definition of snack foods, for which trade data are available, includes not only salted snacks (potato chips and similar snacks and snack nuts) but also consumer-ready packaged cookies and crackers, popcorn (microwavable or unpopped), and meat snacks. U.S. exports of these snack foods declined 2.8 percent in 1997 to $792 million (see Table 35-8). Most of this decline can be attributed to a drop in U.S. exports of snack nuts, which fell 15 percent to $190.9 million. Excluding snack nuts, which are highly dependent on weather and climate changes, U.S. exports of snack foods have done well over the past 5 to 8 years. Excluding snack nuts, U.S. snack food exports rose almost 2 percent in 1998 and almost 45 percent since 1992 (see Table 35-9; Figure 35-2).

The North American Free Trade Agreement (NAFTA) countries, Canada and Mexico, continue to be the United States' leading markets for snack food exports. In 1997 they accounted for over one-third of U.S. exports. Western Europe, the next largest market, accounted for almost one-fifth of U.S. exports. Other major market regions included Japan and the Chinese Economic Area with 18.5 percent, other Asian countries (including Australia and New Zealand) with 12.5 percent, and Latin America with 9.6 percent (see Table 35-10).

In 1997 cookies and crackers were the top export snack food category. Exports of these products have increased each year, reaching $208.6 million in 1997 and posting a 37 percent increase since 1992. The second-largest export snack category is salted nuts at $190.8 million (followed by potato chips at $161.7

TABLE 35-8: U.S. Exports of Snack Food Products[1]
in 1997

(millions of dollars)

Regions[2]	Value[3]	Share, %
NAFTA	275.6	34.8
Latin America	76.4	9.6
Western Europe	152.2	19.2
Japan/Chinese Economic Area	146.8	18.5
Other Asia	98.7	12.5
Rest of world	42.3	5.3
World	792.0	100.0

Top Five Countries	Value	Share, %
Canada	227.0	28.7
Japan	81.4	10.3
Mexico	51.5	6.5
Hong Kong (PRC)	42.6	5.4
United Kingdom	33.1	4.2

[1] SIC 2068, 2096.
[2] For definitions of regional groupings, see "Getting the Most Out of *Outlook '99*."
[3] Values may not sum to total due to rounding.
Source: U.S. Department of Commerce, Bureau of the Census.

million), which has increased 71 percent since 1992. Microwavable and unpopped popcorn exports, the fourth largest export category, have shown steady growth since 1992, increasing from $84.8 million to $100.5 million.

The following discussions of country markets are taken from a variety of sources, which typically focus on different types of snack food products, depending on industry practices and consumer preferences in the individual countries.

U.S. Exports of Snack Food in 1997

Corn chips and pretzels 7.97%
Meat snacks 8.47%
Potato chips 20.43%
Popcorn 12.69%
Cookies and crackers 26.34%
Snack nuts 24.10%

Source: U.S. Department of Commerce, International Trade Administration, based on official Bureau of the Census trade data.

FIGURE 35-2

French Snack Food Market. The demand for snack food is increasing in France, since, according to the recently published French report "Aliments Demain" (Food of Tomorrow), the French are tending to reduce their meal time and size, but are increasing food consumption between meals. Almost 75 percent of the French say they consume food three to five times a day. Although the French consume meals principally at home and in restaurants, up to 15 percent eat lunch at their workstations even if there is a company cafeteria, resulting in a high demand for snack food and drinks at the workplace. Increasing the number of vending machines would help meet this growing demand. The French seem to prefer sweet to salted products. Cookies, nuts (pistachios, pecans, walnuts, and hazelnuts), dried fruits (raisins and prunes), candies, ice cream, and soft drinks have market potential. Many Paris Metro stations were recently equipped with vending machines, and they have been a booming success.

There is also a demand for prepared meals and snacks consumed at lunchtime at the workplace. Both sweet and salted products are wanted, such as tortilla chips, salsa, guacamole, chili, popcorn, and dried meat, as well as the products previously mentioned foods.

United Arab Emirates Salted Snacks Market. According to United Arab Emirates (UAE) trade data, imports of U.S. salted snacks reached a record $4.5 million in 1996, up 36 percent from the record set in 1995. According to trade contacts, salted snack consumption will increase 15 percent annually over the next 5 years. Industry estimates indicate that the UAE salted snacks market is about 10,000 metric tons, or about $30 million, and per capita consumption is about 2 kilograms. The peak consumption of salted snacks occurs between September and June, when school is in session and the tourist season is in full swing. Consumption declines significantly in the summer months, when many residents leave the country to escape the heat and tourism falls.

Although local production of salted snacks has doubled over the past 5 years, demand for imported high-quality salted snack products remains strong. U.S. salted snacks are well known for their high quality. In addition, U.S. exporters offer the widest variety of snacks packed in canisters and bags and are the only suppliers of large bags (300 to 420 grams), which are popular with families and institutional buyers. European salted snacks, especially those from Germany, provide limited competition for U.S. products. Salted snacks from Asia, which generally are lower in quality, compete primarily against locally produced snacks.

According to trade contacts, Oman is the principal foreign supplier of salted snacks to the UAE market, commanding about a 50 percent share of total imports. Saudi Arabia and the United States follow with 25 percent and 15 percent, respectively. The remaining 10 percent of imports is supplied by other countries, including the United Kingdom, Germany, India, Japan, the Philippines, South Korea, and Malaysia.

Imported products from neighboring countries and from Asia compete in price and quality with local production. European and U.S. salted snacks, which are higher in quality and price, dominate the upper range of the salted snack market and

TABLE 35-9: U.S. Exports of Snack Food Products by Product Category
(millions of dollars)

Product Category	1989	1992	1995	1996	1997	Percent of 1997 Total
Salted snacks						
Potato chips	20.7	94.6	168.4	163.0	161.8	20.4
Corn chips and pretzels	14.9	42.2	57.7	65.8	63.1	8.0
Snack nuts	137.7	300.6	140.2	224.4	190.9	24.1
Subtotal	173.3	437.4	366.2	453.2	415.8	52.5
Other snacks						
Cookies and crackers	64.9	152.6	184.8	189.8	208.6	26.3
Meat snacks	15.8	41.1	71.8	73.0	67.1	8.5
Popcorn	49.5	84.9	87.1	98.6	100.5	12.7
Subtotal	130.2	278.7	343.7	361.4	376.2	47.5
Total	303.5	716.0	710.0	814.6	792.0	100.0

Source: Compiled from Official Statistics of the U.S. Department of Commerce.

TABLE 35-10: U.S. Exports of Snack Food Products by Region and Product Category in 1997
(millions of dollars)

Regions	Potato Chips	Corn Chips and Pretzels	Snack Nuts	Cookies and Crackers	Meat Snacks	Popcorn	Total
NAFTA	55.0	17.2	20.9	111.8	40.1	30.6	275.6
Latin America	18.5	10.5	6.3	30.5	1.4	9.2	76.4
Western Europe	14.1	6.3	76.6	26.1	1.4	27.7	152.2
Japan/Chinese Economic Area	43.8	6.9	60.6	17.4	6.0	12.1	146.8
Other Asia	30.1	5.7	26.3	14.4	4.1	18.1	98.7
Rest of world	0.3	16.5	0.2	8.4	14.1	2.8	42.3
World	161.8	63.1	190.9	208.6	67.1	100.5	792.0

Source: Compiled from Official Statistics of the U.S. Department of Commerce.

therefore do not compete directly with local production. In addition, most U.S. salted snacks are sold in 300- to 420-gram bags and canisters of various weights, while locally produced snacks are sold in 10- to 50-gram bags.

Singaporean Snack Market. The snack market is substantial in Singapore. Snacks are popular sales items at supermarkets, gasoline stations, and thousands of small provision shops and minimarts throughout Singapore. Over the past 5 years the market for chips and extruded snacks (such as Cheetos) has been expanding 5 to 10 percent annually on a volume basis. Small retailers reported slower sales expansion than did the larger supermarket chains.

Estimates of annual growth in the market for western dried fruit in the last 5 years have been approximately 5 percent. However, some importers of traditional western fruit have reported that this market is stagnant. Sales of cereal bars have been growing 3 percent per year. The growth in sales of dried fruit and cereal bars is attributed to the increasing affluence of consumers and their growing health consciousness.

The snack market in Singapore is very dynamic. For example, at least two new U.S. brands have entered the marketplace very strongly and several other American items have disappeared in recent years. Supermarket buyers report that con-

sumers are not brand-loyal and are relatively price-insensitive in this category. Strong advertising and promotion and brand positioning are extremely important.

Forecasts for future snack market expansion, including cereal bars and dried fruit, are slightly higher than recent growth figures. It has been estimated that over the next 5 years sales of chips, extruded snacks, and dried fruit will grow 6 to 10 percent. Annual increases in the volume of cereal bars sold is predicted to grow 5 percent annually over the next 5 years.

The United States is expected to maintain its lead as a major supplier of chips and extruded snacks, dried fruit, and cereal bars as a result of the high quality and technological superiority of its products. However, increasing competition is anticipated, especially in chips and extruded snacks, since a number of large snack manufacturers, including Frito Lay and Keebler, are now located in the Far East and are beginning to produce innovative snacks for local tastes. The implementation of the Association of Southeast Asian Nations (ASEAN) Free Trade Agreement will give these manufacturers greater access to southeast Asian markets as a whole.

There is a market for healthier-type snacks as consumers in Singapore are becoming more health-conscious. Singaporeans are paying more attention to the labels on products and the content of food items. Also, as the southeast Asian region continues to grow, there will be expanding opportunities for exports of snack items. In general, the market will remain dynamic. Snacks that are innovative in terms of flavors, ingredients, shapes, and sizes will have the best sales prospects, particularly if they are backed by strong advertising and promotion programs.

Venezuelan Salted Snacks and Snack Nut Market. Annual consumption of dry, salty snacks in Venezuela amounts to approximately 15,000 metric tons, or 0.7 kilogram per capita. The principal types of dried snacks consumed by Venezuelans are pellet (a fried corn kernel type of product) and extruded products, corn and potato chips, popcorn, and processed nuts. Pellet and extruded snacks and chips constitute about 65 percent of snack consumption, while popcorn and processed nuts have roughly 22 percent and 13 percent shares of the market, respectively. Two local multinational corporations—Savoy and Frito Lay—dominate the markets for pellet and extruded snacks, chips, and cocktail peanuts. A small volume of processed snacks is imported, mainly under the Planters and Pringles brands. Peanuts also are imported in bulk for repackaging. Annual consumption of popcorn amounts to about 4,000 metric tons, or 0.2 kilogram per capita.

Venezuela does not produce varieties of corn for popping. Most popcorn is imported in bulk and repackaged locally. Per capita consumption of other processed snack nuts, such as cashews, pistachios, and mixes, is marginal because they are unaffordable for most consumers. Although the United States holds a substantial share of imports in most segments of the market, total import volumes are small compared with domestic production. Locally produced snacks have a competitive edge over imports because domestic manufacturers have extensive sales and distribution networks and employ sophisticated promotional strategies. Although some U.S. products are at a price disadvantage (often because of tariff preferences extended to other Latin American countries), U.S. snack manufacturers and exporters could easily increase their sales of several product lines if brand representations or marketing agreements were established with local food companies and retailers that already have established sales and distribution systems.

ALCOHOLIC BEVERAGES

The alcoholic beverage industry consists of establishments primarily engaged in manufacturing malt beverages (SIC 2082) and wines, brandy, and brandy spirits (SIC 2084) and establishments primarily engaged in manufacturing alcoholic liquors by distillation and manufacturing cordials and alcoholic cocktails through blending processes or by mixing liquors and other ingredients (SIC 2085).

Global Industry Trends

The alcoholic beverage industry has three sectors: malt beverages, wines and brandy, and distilled spirits. For the most part, producers have kept to themselves and only a handful have ventured into producing alcoholic beverages outside their respective sectors. As per capita consumption of alcoholic beverages levels off in many major developed countries, industries there must find niche markets for their products overseas to continue to grow. For a number of years malt beverage and distilled spirit companies have been relying not only on exporting to increase sales but also on establishing licensing agreements and joint ventures. This will continue through 2000.

Beer. According to Canadean Ltd., a major international alcoholic beverage research firm, multinational brewers are pouring billions of dollars into the high-risk, high-reward Central and South American beer market. Pan-regional groups are emerging out of various alliances with domestic partners. These alliances also compete against local brewers with international ambitions, a sizable volume base, and financial muscle. Totaling just under 200 million hectoliters in Central and South America, volumes are growing around 4 percent annually, compared with a global beer market that is growing at 1 to 2 percent per year and static to declining markets in Europe and North America. According to industry sources, in 1980 the European and North American beer market accounted for 75 percent of world production and South America and Asia each had about 8 percent. By 2000 Europe and North America will account for only 50 percent, while Asia will account for 30 percent and South America 13 percent.

Worldwide mergers, acquisitions, joint ventures, and other financial arrangements are on the rise, making the beer industry more global. For example, in spring 1998 Pete's Brewing Company, the second largest U.S. microbrewer, merged with PBC Holding, an affiliate of the Gambrinus Company of Texas. Gambrinus is the exclusive importer of Corona (Mexican) in the eastern United States and Moosehead (Canadian) in the entire United States. Gambrinus also owns a smaller microbrewery in Texas. Anheuser-Busch bought a 27 percent stake in San-Miguel in the Philippines. Al-Ahram Beverages, an Egyptian company, will be brewing a nonalcoholic Guinness beer for the Middle East and north Africa.

Wine. Internationally, the wine industry relied on exports to increase sales in the past. According to *Impact International,* the wine market is evolving into a global, marketing-oriented industry. Soaring demand created by positive health messages, strong economies, and earlier supply shortages in Australia, California, and elsewhere initially pushed winemakers to seek new supply deals in foreign markets. With trends more akin to those in the distilled spirits industry, the global wine market is now alive with international joint ventures, global consolidation, and increased branding. Marketing strategies have fueled a shift in market philosophy from old world (regional) wines such as those from western Europe to new world (branded varietal) wines such as those from the United States, Australia, Chile, Argentina, and South Africa. Although new world wines still have a relatively small global export share, 12.5 percent, there has been growth since 1990, when these wines accounted for only 5 percent of world exports.

Distilled Spirits. According to Canadean Ltd., the world's distilled spirits market was approximately 2,420 million cases in 1996, down 3 percent from 1995. While sales of brown spirits, such as whiskies and brandy, remained solid, the dominant white spirits (such as vodka and rum) suffered a major setback. Vodka, the hardest hit of all international spirits, fell 20 percent by volume in 1996 after 4 years of relative stability. Russia, the world's leading vodka market, accounted for much of this decline. The weakness of its economy and the availability of low-priced, low-quality spirit helped bring about a 50 percent decline in domestic demand. Sales of the number two international spirit, whiskey, ended slightly up in 1996 compared with 1995. The less traditional beverages were among the most successful in 1996. Just 4 years after their introduction, alcoholic carbonates ("alcopops") reached a peak in excess of 13 million cases. There were also further advances in the global market for

TABLE 35-11: Alcoholic Beverages (SIC 2082, 2084, 2085) Trends and Forecasts

(millions of dollars except as noted)

	1992	1993	1994	1995	1996	1997[1]	1998[2]	1999[3]	Percent Change 96–97	97–98	98–99	92–96[4]
Industry data												
Value of shipments[5]	25,035	24,739	24,983	25,652	27,441	28,308	28,552	29,459	3.2	0.9	3.2	2.3
2082 Malt beverages	17,340	16,656	16,795	17,151	18,220	18,259	18,250	18,803	0.2	0.0	3.0	1.2
2084 Wines and brandy	4,301	4,514	4,301	4,798	5,548	6,265	6,454	6,665	12.9	3.0	3.3	6.6
2085 Distilled liquor	3,394	3,569	3,888	3,703	3,673	3,784	3,848	3,991	3.0	1.7	3.7	2.0
Value of shipments (1992$)	25,035	24,802	25,333	25,251	26,160	26,499	26,870	27,273	1.3	1.4	1.5	1.1
2082 Malt beverages	17,340	16,859	17,332	17,100	17,655	17,700	17,870	18,050	0.3	1.0	1.0	0.5
2084 Wines and brandy	4,301	4,465	4,267	4,723	5,175	5,434	5,600	5,766	5.0	3.1	3.0	4.7
2085 Distilled liquor	3,394	3,478	3,734	3,429	3,330	3,365	3,400	3,457	1.1	1.0	1.7	−0.5
Total employment (thousands)	55.6	56.4	53.8	55.6	57.6	56.0	55.6		−2.8	−0.7		0.9
2082 Malt beverages	34.5	35.3	33.5	32.6	34.0	32.3	31.7		−5.0	−1.9		−0.4
2084 Wines and brandy	14.0	14.1	13.7	16.3	17.0	17.0	17.4		0.0	2.4		5.0
2085 Distilled liquor	7.1	7.0	6.6	6.7	6.6	6.7	6.53		1.5	−3.0		−1.8
Production workers (thousands)	36.7	37.0	34.9	35.9	36.8	35.4	34.5		−3.8	−2.5		0.1
2082 Malt beverages	25.1	25.3	23.6	23.6	24.6	23.1	22.1		−6.1	−4.3		−0.5
2084 Wines and brandy	6.5	6.6	6.6	7.5	7.5	7.5	7.7		0.0	2.7		3.6
2085 Distilled liquor	5.1	5.1	4.7	4.8	4.7	4.8	4.7		2.1	−2.1		−2.0
Average hourly earnings ($)	19.83	19.81	20.15	20.37	20.22	21.00	21.89		3.9	4.2		0.5
2082 Malt beverages	22.89	22.71	23.01	23.92	23.39	24.35	25.10		4.1	3.1		0.5
2084 Wines and brandy	12.68	12.80	13.53	13.05	13.56	13.77	13.96		1.5	1.4		1.7
2085 Distilled liquor	15.05	15.49	15.43	15.38	16.07	16.32	16.55		1.6	1.4		1.7
Capital expenditures	736	668	754	1,138	1,200							13.0
2082 Malt beverages	565	479	564	861	877							11.6
2084 Wines and brandy	115	146	151	209	269							23.7
2085 Distilled liquor	56.3	42.1	39.7	67.3	54.0							−1.0
Product data												
Value of shipments[5]	24,607	24,324	24,370	25,155	26,794	27,677	27,909	28,942	3.3	0.8	3.7	2.2
2082 Malt beverages	17,302	16,629	16,714	17,108	18,196	18,283	18,274	18,828	0.5	−0.0	3.0	1.3
2084 Wines and brandy	4,050	4,355	4,196	4,675	5,411	6,110	6,295	6,650	12.9	3.0	5.6	7.5
2085 Distilled liquor	3,255	3,340	3,460	3,372	3,188	3,284	3,340	3,464	3.0	1.7	3.7	−0.5
Value of shipments (1992$)	24,607	24,394	24,735	24,780	25,568	25,894	26,254	26,647	1.3	1.4	1.5	1.0
2082 Malt beverages	17,302	16,831	17,249	17,057	17,631	17,674	17,844	18,024	0.2	1.0	1.0	0.5
2084 Wines and brandy	4,050	4,308	4,163	4,601	5,047	5,300	5,460	5,623	5.0	3.0	3.0	5.7
2085 Distilled liquor	3,255	3,255	3,324	3,122	2,890	2,920	2,950	3,000	1.0	1.0	1.7	−2.9
Trade data												
Value of imports	3,527	3,387	3,668	3,980	4,619	5,198	6,005	6,530	12.5	15.5	8.7	7.0
2082 Malt beverages	881	961	1,072	1,192	1,341	1,514	1,750	1,870	12.9	15.6	6.9	11.1
2084 Wines and brandy	1,347	1,152	1,268	1,402	1,724	2,031	2,500	2,800	17.8	23.1	12.0	6.4
2085 Distilled liquor	1,299	1,274	1,328	1,386	1,554	1,653	1,755	1,860	6.4	6.2	6.0	4.6
Value of exports	742	766	973	1,242	1,342	1,409	1,410	1,510	5.0	−5.4	7.1	16.0
2082 Malt beverages	221	234	391	526	453	418	355	370	−7.7	−15.1	4.5	19.7
2084 Wines and brandy	182	184	201	246	330	423	570	620	28.2	34.8	9.8	16.0
2085 Distilled liquor	339	349	380	470	559	568	505	520	1.6	−11.1	5.6	13.3

[1] Estimate except imports and exports.
[2] Estimate.
[3] Forecast.
[4] Compound annual rate.
[5] For a definition of industry versus product values, see "Getting the Most Out of *Outlook '99*."
Source: U.S. Department of Commerce: Bureau of the Census; International Trade Administration.

premixed drinks, with flavored and lower-alcohol spirits receiving growing consumer support.

Factors Affecting Future U.S. Industry Growth

Between 1989 and 1996 total U.S. production of malt beverages, wines, and distilled spirits declined a modest 0.6 percent for malt beverages to 5,786.4 million gallons and 12 percent for distilled spirits to 326.5 million gallons. Although wine production increased 2.4 percent to 483.7 million gallons in 1996, it still is almost 7 percent below the 1989 level. However, exports have been increasing. Between 1992 and 1996 wine exports increased more than 130 percent, reaching 8 percent of total production, up from 4 percent in 1992.

The reduction in the production of alcoholic beverages stems from two possible causes: Either consumers have embraced moderation in their consumption patterns as a result of public service announcements about the dangers of excessive drinking as well as studies linking moderate drinking with good health, or the number of consumers who regularly consume alcoholic beverages is shrinking. According to Jon P. Nelson, a Pennsylvania State University economist, an aging population may be responsible for the decline in alcohol consumption. According to the Census Bureau, the estimated number of individuals between 21 and 40 years old declined from 81.8 million in 1995 to 78.9 million in 1998.

Consumers have shifted to higher-priced alcoholic beverages, choosing (1) microbrews and other premium-priced beers over massed-produced beers, (2) varietal wines over lower-priced semigenerics such as Burgundy and Chablis, and (3) single-malt whiskies or single-barrel, small-batch bourbons and other high-end whiskies over the more common blended whiskies. Also, while total consumption of vodka fell from 36 million cases in 1993 to slightly less than 35 million

cases in 1997, the consumption of premium vodka increased from about 4.4 million cases in 1993 to 6.3 million cases in 1997.

U.S. Industry Growth Projections for the Next 1 and 5 Years

Although domestic consumption of alcoholic beverages will remain relatively stable, constant-dollar industry shipments will increase 1.5 percent in 1999 and 1.2 to 2 percent over the next 5 years (see Table 35-11). U.S. consumers will continue to demand higher-priced alcoholic beverages, and exports are expected to rebound, increasing over 7 percent in 1999. As the Asian crisis plays itself out and other markets continue to open up, U.S. alcoholic beverage exports are expected to increase 3 to 8 percent annually in the next 5 years.

Global Market Prospects

In 1998 U.S. total exports of alcoholic beverages are not expected to increase. Although the Asian financial crisis has taken a toll on U.S. exports of both beer and distilled spirits, which declined an estimated 15 percent and 11 percent respectively, U.S. wine exports increased 35 percent as the worldwide demand for varietal wines has increased. The current situation aside, exports have been an important factor in the overall financial health of the alcoholic beverage industry. Since 1992 U.S. exports of alcoholic beverages have doubled and now account for 5.1 percent of U.S. production compared with 3 percent in 1992.

Table 35-12 shows trade patterns in 1997 for the malt beverage industry. In this industry three-quarters of the exports in 1997 consisted of beer, followed by brewing dregs and waste (21 percent), which other countries import as a feed input. In 1997 the top five country markets for U.S. beer included Japan

TABLE 35-12:   U.S. Trade Patterns in the Malt Beverage Industry[1] in 1997
(millions of dollars; percent)

Exports			Imports		
Regions[2]	Value[3]	Share, %	Regions[2]	Value[3]	Share, %
NAFTA	60	14.5	NAFTA	610	40.3
Latin America	55	13.2	Latin America	31	2.0
Western Europe	122	29.2	Western Europe	825	54.5
Japan/Chinese Economic Area	145	34.8	Japan/Chinese Economic Area	23	1.5
Other Asia	8	2.0	Other Asia	7	0.5
Rest of world	26	6.3	Rest of world	18	1.2
World	418	100.0	World	1,514	100.0
Top Five Countries	Value	Share, %	Top Five Countries	Value	Share, %
Japan	80	19.1	Netherlands	530	35.0
Canada	40	9.7	Mexico	417	27.6
Taiwan	35	8.5	Canada	193	12.8
United Kingdom	35	8.3	Germany	127	8.4
Hong Kong (PRC)	29	6.9	United Kingdom	91	6.0

[1] SIC 2082.
[2] For definitions of regional groupings, see "Getting the Most Out of *Outlook '99.*"
[3] Values may not sum to total due to rounding.
Source: U.S. Department of Commerce, Bureau of the Census.

(25 percent), Canada (11 percent), Taiwan (11 percent), Hong Kong [PRC] (9), and Paraguay (8 percent).

Wine industry exports include grape wine, sparkling wines, and brandy (see Table 35-13). In 1997 grape wine accounted for more than 85 percent of wine industry exports. The top five countries accounted for almost two-thirds of U.S. grape wine exports. The United Kingdom was the largest export market for grape wine with 28 percent, followed by Canada with 19 percent, Japan with 8 percent, Germany with 6.5 percent, and Switzerland with 5 percent.

In 1997 approximately 62 percent of U.S. distilled spirit exports consisted of branded items, such as whiskey (51 percent), rum (6 percent), liqueurs and cordials (3 percent),

vodka (2 percent), and gin (0.3 percent). Japan is the largest market for U.S. whiskey, accounting for about 20 percent, followed by Germany with 19 percent, Australia with 14 percent, the United Kingdom with 11 percent, and Spain and France with 4 percent each. With an improved Japanese economy, U.S. whiskey exports to that country increased an estimated 50 percent. Japan's adherence to the World Trade Organization ruling that imported distilled spirits are to be taxed similarly to domestic *shochu* also helped U.S. exports. U.S. distilled spirit exports to Japan should continue to grow. Before this agreement, imports were faced with higher excise taxes. Trade patterns for distilled spirits in 1997 are shown in Table 35-14.

TABLE 35-13:   U.S. Trade Patterns in Wines and Brandy[1] in 1997
(millions of dollars; percent)

Regions[2]	Exports Value[3]	Share, %	Regions[2]	Imports Value[3]	Share, %
NAFTA	82	19.3	NAFTA	12	0.6
Latin America	22	5.1	Latin America	151	7.4
Western Europe	224	52.9	Western Europe	1,714	84.4
Japan/Chinese Economic Area	78	18.4	Japan/Chinese Economic Area	10	0.5
Other Asia	14	3.3	Other Asia	1	0.0
Rest of world	4	1.1	Rest of world	143	7.0
World	423	100.0	World	2,031	100.0
Top Five Countries	Value	Share, %	Top Five Countries	Value	Share, %
United Kingdom	107	25.4	France	1,053	51.8
Canada	78	18.5	Italy	456	22.5
Japan	43	10.2	Chile	126	6.2
Germany	25	5.9	Australia	123	6.1
Taiwan	21	4.9	Spain	94	4.6

[1] SIC 2084.
[2] For definitions of regional groupings, see "Getting the Most Out of *Outlook '99*."
[3] Values may not sum to total due to rounding.
Source: U.S. Department of Commerce, Bureau of the Census.

TABLE 35-14:   U.S. Trade Patterns in Distilled Spirits[1] in 1997
(millions of dollars; percent)

Regions[2]	Exports Value[3]	Share, %	Regions[2]	Imports Value[3]	Share, %
NAFTA	59	10.5	NAFTA	489	29.6
Latin America	23	4.1	Latin America	22	1.3
Western Europe	204	35.9	Western Europe	1,069	64.6
Japan/Chinese Economic Area	104	18.4	Japan/Chinese Economic Area	2	0.1
Other Asia	15	2.7	Other Asia	2	0.1
Rest of world	162	28.5	Rest of world	69	4.2
World	568	100.0	World	1,653	100.0
Top Five Countries	Value	Share, %	Top Five Countries	Value	Share, %
Japan	95	16.7	United Kingdom	529	32.0
Georgia	60	10.6	Canada	344	20.8
Germany	59	10.3	Sweden	147	8.9
Canada	43	7.6	Mexico	145	8.8
Australia	43	7.6	Ireland	135	8.1

[1] SIC 2085.
[2] For definitions of regional groupings, see "Getting the Most Out of *Outlook '99*."
[3] Values may not sum to total due to rounding.
Source: U.S. Department of Commerce, Bureau of the Census.

Eastern Europe Highlight. According to the *Euromonitor,* retail sales of alcoholic beverages in eastern Europe are expected to increase 8 to 15 percent in volume in the next 5 years. The beer sector will be more dynamic not only because of the privatization and modernization that have taken place or are under way but also because of the abolition of import duty on beer among the European Free Trade Association (EFTA) countries. This will put beer exporters in EFTA on the same level with domestic manufacturers, opening new opportunities for beer exporters. Although there is also the potential for joint ventures or other financial arrangements with wineries in Hungary, Bulgaria, and Romania, which are in need of investment and redevelopment, this is not the case for distilled spirits. National protectionism has prevented full privatization and development of the spirits industry in the vodka-producing countries Poland, Ukraine, and the Russian Federation.

Donald A. Hodgen, U.S. Department of Commerce, Office of Consumer Goods, (202) 482-3346, November 1998.

■ REFERENCES

Call the Bureau of the Census at (301) 457-4100 for information about ordering Census documents.

Agra Europe, Agra Europe (London) Ltd., 25 Frant Road, Tunbridge Wells, TN2 5JT, England. Telephone: 011-0-1892-533813, Fax: 011-0-1892-544895/524593.

Agricultural Outlook, Economic Research Service, U.S. Department of Agriculture, 1800 M Street, NW, Washington, DC 20036. 800 (999)-6779 or 202 (694)-5050.

Alcoholic Beverage Executives' Newsletter, Alcoholic Beverage Executives' Newsletter Inc., P.O. Box 3188, Omaha, NE 68103. (402) 397-5514, Fax: (402) 397-3843.

Aliments Demain (Food of Tomorrow), University of Toulouse Le-Mrail, Toulouse, France (funded by the French Ministry of Agriculture and Fisheries in conjunction with the French Ministry of Education, Research and Technology). Telephone: 011-33-561-656132 or 011-33-562-25800.

American Meat Institute, P.S. Box 3556, Washington, DC 20007. (703) 841-2400, Fax: (703) 527-0938.

Beverage Aisle, Strategic Business Communications, 226 West 26th Street, 10th Floor, New York, NY 10001. (212) 822-5930, Fax: (212) 822-5931.

Brauwelt, Fachverlag Hans Carl GmbH & Co. KG, P.O.B. 99 01 53, D-90268 Nurnberg, Germany. Telephone: 011-49-911-952850, Fax: 011-49-911-9528548.

Brewing and Beverage Industry—International, Verlag W. Sachon GMBH+CO, D-87714 Mindelheim, Germany. Telephone: 011-49-08261-966-0, Fax: 011-49-08261-999-132.

Consumer and Producer Price Indexes, Bureau of Labor Statistics, U.S. Department of Labor, Washington, DC 20211. (202) 606-6950 and (202) 606-7700.

Consumer Expenditure Survey, Bureau of Labor Statistics, U.S. Department of Labor, Washington, DC 20211. (202) 606-6900.

Drinks International, Wilmington Publishing Ltd., 5-8 Underwood Street, London, United Kingdom N1 7JQ. Telephone: 011-44-181-841-3970, Fax: 011-44-181-845-7696.

Empirical Economics, "Economic and Demographic Factors in U.S. Alcohol Demand: A Growth-Accounting Analysis," by Jon P. Nelson, December 1997.

Euromonitor, 60-61 Britton Street, London EC1M 5NA, England. Telephone: 011-44-171-251-8024, Fax: 011-44-171-608-3149.

Food & Drink Weekly, Sparks Publishing, 6708 Whittier Avenue, McLean, VA 22101. (703) 734-8787, Fax: (703) 893-1065.

Food Engineering, Cahners Business Information, 201 King of Prussia Road, Radnor, PA 19089. (610) 964-4000, Fax: (610) 964-2915.

Food Engineering International, Chilton Company, Chilton Way, Radnor, PA 19089. (610) 964-4000, Fax: (610) 964-4273.

Food Institute Report, American Institute of Food Distribution, 28-12 Broadway, Fairlawn, NJ 07410. (201) 791-5570, Fax: (201) 791-5222.

Food Marketing Institute, 800 Connecticut Avenue, NW, Washington, DC 20006-2701. (202) 452-8444, Fax: (202) 429-8272.

Impact International, M Shanken Corporation, 387 S. Park Avenue, New York, NY 10016. (800) 848-7113, Fax: (212) 630-0731.

International Wine Industry Report, Wine Institute and JBC International, 1620 I Street, NW, Suite 615, Washington, DC 20006. (202) 463-8493, Fax: (202) 463-8497.

Liquor Handbook, Adams/Jobson Publishing Inc., 1180 Avenue of the Americas, New York, NY 10036. (800) 827-4700, Fax: (847) 427-2006.

Livestock and Poultry: World Markets and Trade, Foreign Agricultural Service, U.S. Department of Agriculture, AG Box 1044, South Agriculture Building, Washington, DC 20250. (202) 720-8252.

Meat: Marketing & Technology, Marketing and Technology Group, 1415 N. Dayton, Chicago, IL 60622. (312) 266-3111, Fax: (312) 266-3363.

Milling and Baking News, Sosland Publishing Company, 4800 Main Street, Suite 100, Kansas City, MO 68112. (816) 756-1000, Fax: (816) 756-0494.

Monthly Statistical Release, Beer, Wine and Distilled Spirits, Marketing Compliance Division, Department of the Treasury, Bureau of Alcohol, Tobacco and Firearms, Washington, DC 20226. (202) 927-8130.

National Broiler Council, 1155 15th Street, NW, Suite 614, Washington, DC 20005. (202) 296-2622, Fax: (202) 293-4005.

1992 Census of Manufacturers, Meat Products, Dairy Products, Canned, Frozen and Preserved Fruits, Vegetables, and Specialty Foods, Grain Mill Products, Bakery Products, Sugar and Confectionery Products, Fats and Oils, Beverages, and Miscellaneous Food Preparations, Bureau of the Census, U.S. Department of Commerce, Washington, DC 20233.

1996 Statistical Information for the U.S. Distilled Spirits Industry, Distilled Spirits Council of the United States, Inc., 1250 Eye Street, NW, Suite 900, Washington, DC 20005. (202) 628-3544.

1997 Brewers Almanac, Beer Institute, 122 C Street, NW, Suite 750, Washington, DC 20001. (202) 737-2377, Fax: (202) 737-7004.

Population Projections of the United States by Age, Sex, Race and Hispanic Origin: 1995 to 2050, Ser. P-25, No. 1130, Bureau of the Census, U.S. Department of Commerce, Washington, DC 20233.

Poultry: Marketing & Technology, Marketing and Technology Group, 1415 N. Dayton, Chicago, IL 60622. (312) 266-3111, Fax: (312) 266-3363.

Prepared Foods, Cahners Publishing Company, 1350 E. Touhy Avenue, Des Plaines, IL 60018-3358. (847) 635-8800, Fax: (847) 390-2445.

Render, National Renderers Association and Sierra Publishing, 2820 Birch Avenue, Camino, CA 95709. (530) 644-8428, Fax: (530) 644-8429.

Snack Food & Wholesale Bakery, Stagnito Publishing, 1935 Sherner Road, Suite 100, Northbrook, IL 60062. (847) 205-5660, Fax: (847) 205-5688.

State of the Snack Food Industry Report and Snack World, Snack Food Association, 1711 King Street, Suite One, Alexandria, VA 22314. (703) 836-4500, Fax: (703) 836-8262.

Statistics for Industry Groups and Industries, 1996 Annual Survey of Manufacturers, M96(AS)-1, Bureau of the Census, U.S. Department of Commerce, Washington, DC 20233.

Supermarket News, Fairchild Publications, P.O. Box 10600, Riverton, NJ 08076. (609) 786-0963, Fax: (609) 786-4415.

Thomas Food Industry Register, 5 Penn Plaza, New York, NY 10001. (212) 290-7262, Fax: (212) 290-7373.

Value of Product Shipments, 1996 Annual Survey of Manufacturers, M96(AS)-2, Bureau of the Census, U.S. Department of Commerce, Washington, DC 20233.

The Wine Institute, 914 Post Street, San Francisco, CA 90505, (415) 512-0151, Fax: (914) 442-0742.

MOTOR VEHICLES
Economic and Trade Trends

U.S. International Trade

($ billions)

Legend: Balance, Exports, Imports

Source: U.S. Department of Commerce: Bureau of the Census; International Trade Administration.

World Export Market Shares

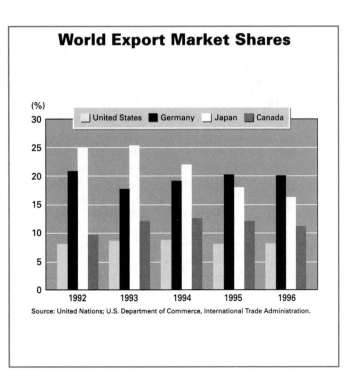

(%)

Legend: United States, Germany, Japan, Canada

Source: United Nations; U.S. Department of Commerce, International Trade Administration.

Export Dependence and Import Penetration

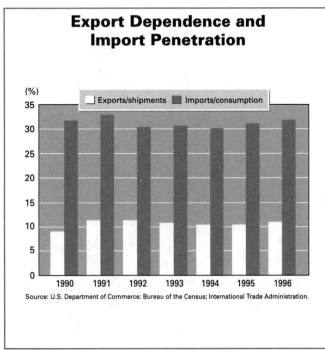

(%)

Legend: Exports/shipments, Imports/consumption

Source: U.S. Department of Commerce: Bureau of the Census; International Trade Administration.

Output and Output per Hour

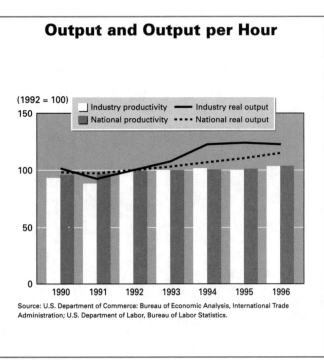

(1992 = 100)

Legend: Industry productivity, Industry real output, National productivity, National real output

Source: U.S. Department of Commerce: Bureau of Economic Analysis, International Trade Administration; U.S. Department of Labor, Bureau of Labor Statistics.

See "Getting the Most Out of *Outlook '99*" for definitions of terms.

Motor Vehicles

INDUSTRY DEFINITION   The motor vehicle industry includes new on-road, volume-produced completed vehicles that carry cargo or passengers (SIC 3711, 3713). The automotive parts and accessories industry is covered in Chapter 37.

OVERVIEW

The United States is a major player in the world automobile industry. Both globally and in the United States, this industry is cutting the number of stand-alone companies and unique platforms, engines, and parts in an effort to reduce investment costs and improve economies of scale. As a result, the major automakers are combining their research and development efforts to create platforms and parts that can be used throughout the world.

Another trend is related to timeliness as well as cost control: Manufacturers are using supercomputers and paperless design tools to reduce the time from concept to production. Reduced development time means that key decisions affecting product marketability are made at a stage in the development process that is closer in time to the product launch. It also means that engineers and designers can evaluate several iterations of a given part or even an entire vehicle as computer simulations instead of using the costly and time-consuming method of building and testing physical prototypes. Although this new technology requires significant investments, the payoff should be fairly immediate.

GLOBAL INDUSTRY TRENDS

Many of the barriers that have separated the world's automotive markets are slowly falling away. As a result, the light-vehicle market (cars plus light trucks) worldwide has become much more integrated with production. Similarly, vehicle trends in the world's mature markets (the United States, western Europe, and Japan) are appearing in the developing markets as well. Conversely, new production techniques used in developing markets will find their way into the production of vehicles in mature markets.

The changing face of the world market means that automakers can move production to less costly locations. The U.S. automakers (General Motors, Ford, and the former Chrysler) have been increasing production in Mexico, for example. Honda and BMW, however, are moving production to the United States to avoid relatively high domestic labor costs. Another global trend is that production has moved closer to a vehicle's primary market, in part to minimize the effect of currency fluctuations. In keeping with that trend, Mercedes-Benz is building its M-Class sport utility vehicle exclusively in Alabama, making that state the worldwide location for M-Class production. Suppliers to the industry have followed the manufacturers and with the original equipment manufacturers have made the new sites centers for automobile production.

World Commonality

The changes taking place in today's world industry are in ways reminiscent of Henry Ford's idea of mass-producing vehicles in the interest of achieving economies of scale. The industry is expanding the concept of economies of scale from the country level to the world level by reducing the number of unique platforms (a vehicle's underpinnings) and components (e.g., engines and transmissions). The idea is to design a single platform or component that can be used on several vehicles worldwide. An example is the new Ford Focus, which is built and sold in Europe but also will be built in North America and sold as the replacement for the Ford Escort.

This global approach has a number of advantages. First, product development costs are reduced (one design in place of many). Second, development costs can be spread over a larger number of vehicles, reducing the development cost per vehicle and thus allowing lower prices and increased profit margins. Third, commonality of parts allows a manufacturer to concentrate production in areas where costs are lowest. Fourth, the use of common parts reduces development time and costs for a new product because not all the components for the new vehicle must be created from scratch.

Several examples of this approach can be seen in an engine made by General Motors (GM). In mid-1996 GM awarded a contract for its L850 world engine to its engine plant in Tonawanda, New York. Although the engine was to be built in upstate New York, GM engineers in Michigan and Germany designed it in consultation with Lotus Engineering in the United Kingdom. Ultimately, the New York plant and one in Europe will source the L850 engine. The output from these two plants will supply GM cars worldwide. Total L850 production is expected to reach 800,000 units per year eventually. The first vehicle in the United States likely to have this engine is a new model from Saturn that is code-named Innovate but is likely to be called Saturn LS when introduced.

This world perspective brings both opportunities and risks for the U.S. auto industry. For the Tonawanda plant, the opportunities are huge, as it will be able to supply engines for vehicles produced throughout the world. Moreover, if the United States enters a recession, U.S. L850 output can remain strong as long as the auto industry in other parts of the world stays healthy. This means that U.S. plants will be competing with factories throughout the world. In addition, many factories in more recently industrialized nations will have more modern equipment, a lower-wage-rate labor force, and reduced production-related costs (i.e., lower costs in the absence of environmental regulations). However, U.S. plants should remain attractive in the near future because of a well-trained work force, an advanced infrastructure, a stable political climate, and an established supplier base.

Industry Consolidation

As automakers move toward producing a reduced number of parts, the industry is moving toward a reduced number of manufacturers and component suppliers. That does not imply an impending wave of business shutdowns but instead a consolidation of smaller companies into larger ones. For example, Ford now effectively controls Mazda and owns the British makes Jaguar and Aston Martin outright. GM owns half of the Swedish automaker Saab and is expected to obtain full ownership by the end of the decade. GM also has interests in Isuzu and Suzuki, and Nissan owns part of Subaru. If the proposed acquisition of Rolls Royce by Volkswagen is completed, one more major automobile manufacturer will be eliminated. Chances are that today's small automakers worldwide will need the support of a "big brother" to survive the establishment of a world market.

This trend toward consolidation, however, is not new. Foreign and U.S. auto manufacturers have been following a path of consolidation for some time. Chrysler Corporation, for instance, has combined with Daimler-Benz. Chrysler itself grew out of Maxwell and Dodge Brothers and previously purchased AMC/Jeep. AMC was in turn the sum of a number of companies from Kaiser Jeep (formerly Willys-Overland), Nash, and Hudson. For a time Chrysler even owned the Italian

supercar maker Lamborghini as well as shares of Mitsubishi and DeTomaso.

Although consolidation on the manufacturing side has been going on for a long time, such activity on the supplier front has recently begun to heat up at levels never before seen. One of the reasons for consolidation of suppliers is an attempt to increase economies of scale. Another is that suppliers are moving from being component suppliers to being module and systems suppliers. For example, rather than supplying only the seats for a given model, a system supplier may supply the entire interior.

For suppliers as well as automakers, consolidation has both advantages and disadvantages. On the positive side, consolidation lets manufacturers deal with only one large company, rather than many small ones, to buy an entire interior. That should allow automakers to negotiate a lower total price from suppliers, which have much more at stake because the deals as well as the profits are now larger. Conversely, consolidation ultimately means larger but fewer companies, a situation that typically results in less competition and thus potentially higher prices, all of which could result in monopoly or oligopoly situations. In an effort to prevent these and other possible anticompetitive situations, automakers have doled out contracts to strategically position suppliers so that they can still compete against one another and keep quality high and prices low. Although some automakers have expressed concern about that potential situation, others have been selling off their component divisions. Reduced vertical integration allows vehicle makers to buy parts from the best suppliers. The spun-off parts companies are assumed to operate more efficiently and become more competitive (and thus yield lower unit costs) as independent entities. GM's Delphi, for example, was expected to be spun off before the end of 1998.

Suppliers are not only consolidating but also going global. As auto manufacturers have spread out across the globe, their respective suppliers have moved with them. The United States, for example, has seen a growth of Japanese suppliers as those companies have followed their auto manufacturers across the Pacific to the United States. Japanese suppliers have formed joint ventures with existing American firms and have gained not only the business of the transplanted Japanese companies but also business with the American manufacturers. Another advantage to going global is access to developing markets or at least to markets where a company did not have a significant presence. For example, an axle manufacturer in the United States may merge with one in Europe or Japan or a U.S. company may form a joint venture with a foreign counterpart, giving it an inroad into developing markets, many of which cannot be penetrated without partnering with an existing local company.

DOMESTIC TRENDS

The settling pattern of U.S. automakers is best described as an iterative process. That is, originally suppliers settled around the manufacturers they were supplying. However, as a network of suppliers builds in an area, more manufacturers tend to gravi-

Light-Vehicle Output by State in 1997

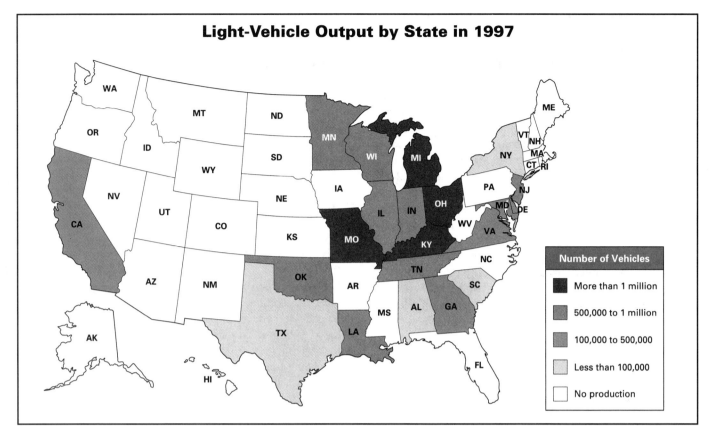

Number of Vehicles

- More than 1 million
- 500,000 to 1 million
- 100,000 to 500,000
- Less than 100,000
- No production

FIGURE 36-1

tate toward and settle near the existing network of suppliers. In this way, the shipping costs and delivery times are minimized. Plants also tend to be built near major freeways and railways to facilitate the shipping of components and finished vehicles.

Plants are thus clustered in specific areas of the country, partly explaining why North American light-vehicle production has long been centered in the midwest. Top manufacturing states, which include Michigan, Ohio, Missouri, and Kentucky, each produce in excess of 1 million vehicles a year. Michigan outproduces the rest of the country by far, with a total annual output averaging just over 3 million units between 1990 and 1997. The Detroit area is home to 19 light-vehicle assembly plants, all of which are owned by Ford, GM, or Chrysler. Total output for 1997 came in at 3.0 million units and probably will increase to 3.1 million units by 2000. Mazda is the sole foreign-based producer in the state, building vehicles through a venture with Ford at a facility in Flat Rock, Michigan. With Michigan as the hub, Ohio, Missouri, and Kentucky made up the top four producer states in 1997 (see Figure 36-1).

The "More Than a Million" Producer States

Ohio's light-vehicle production averages around 2 million units per year. That state is the current home of eight vehicle-manufacturing facilities. Unlike Michigan, however, which is controlled by the Big Three, about 33 percent (650,000 units) of Ohio's annual production comes from Honda, which produces its popular Accord and Civic models out of two plants.

Honda has done a lot to increase total output for the state: Production at its East Liberty plant has more than doubled since 1990, and demand-driven increases at its Marysville plant have added another 50,000 vehicles to the state's annual total. Despite Honda's attempts to make its North American plants the sole production source for Accords and Civics sold in the United States, excess demand for those models has occasionally forced the company to turn to its plants in Japan to help supply the U.S. market.

Production output in Ohio may decrease slightly by the year 2000, but the state should be able to retain its number two standing. The reason for the possible decrease in output is that Ford has permanently shut its Lorain car-production facility as part of its effort to maximize its light-vehicle capacity utilization (straight-time capacity for the company stood at 90 percent in 1996). The shutdown also is intended to establish common platforms among several vehicles. The closing of the Lorain facility means an annual loss of roughly 100,000 vehicles for the state.

Missouri and Kentucky are the other two states that produce more than 1 million vehicles per year. While all light-vehicle production in Missouri is done by the Big Three, output in Kentucky is split about 60-40 percent between the Big Three (Ford, GM, and Chrysler) and the transplants (Toyota). Kentucky has experienced the strongest overall growth among the "more than a million" states: Its output rose by 400,000 units between 1990 and 1996. That growth can be attributed to the addition of a

Ford light-truck plant in that state and the expansion of Toyota's Georgetown production facility. Continued strong production is forecast for Kentucky, as it is the home of many popular vehicles, such as the Ford F-Series, the Ford Explorer, and the Toyota Camry. Continued strong demand is forecast for these vehicles. That, combined with the addition of the Avalon sedan and the Sienna minivan to the Georgetown facility, should ensure production in excess of 1 million units through 2000.

Missouri also experienced strong production growth between 1990 and 1997. Output in the state rose by more than 200,000 units (23 percent) during that period and reached nearly 1.2 million units in 1996. Missouri's success is due largely to strong demand for light trucks. Indeed, light-truck production was responsible for 85 percent of the state's total output in 1997. Because production in Missouri is expected to remain heavily weighted toward light trucks [as a result of continued strong demand for pickups, minivans, and sport utility vehicles (SUVs)] and because of the near-term replacement of the state's production of cars with light trucks, Missouri's light-vehicle production is forecast to remain at its current level through 2000.

Joint Ventures

Historically, the Big Three and foreign-based manufacturers formed joint ventures and alliances as a way for the foreign-based producers to gain access to the North American marketplace and as a way for the Big Three producers to fill gaps in their vehicle lineups. Although several transplant manufacturers simply set up shop in North America, others, such as Toyota, decided to test the waters first. The resulting alliance, the New United Motors Manufacturing, Inc. (NUMMI)—the first of its kind in North America—is located in Fremont, California. That plant was set up originally by GM to build Chevy Novas and today produces the Toyota Corolla and Tacoma as well as the Chevrolet Prizm.

The alliance of Ford and Mazda is an interesting one because the lines between the two companies have started to fade. In fact, as Mazda has continued to struggle with falling market share, its dependence on Ford has been increasing. The new Mercury Cougar is being built at the Flat Rock (Ford-Mazda) production facility, based on Ford's CDW27 platform. Currently, the Mazda B-Series pickup is the only vehicle based on a Ford platform, but forward product plans indicate that future versions of the Protege will be based on Ford platforms, with more to follow in the future.

The long-standing on-again, off-again relationship between Chrysler and Mitsubishi is now expected to continue. Talk of severing the ties between the two automakers began to surface when Mitsubishi was struggling to find enough production space to build its Galants. In place of Chrysler, Volvo was a likely candidate to take up some of the remaining space in Normal, Illinois, after Chrysler pulled up roots. However, reports now indicate that Chrysler will continue to contract with Mitsubishi to produce its Sebring and Avenger alongside the Galant and Eclipse in Illinois. Despite the Daimler-Chrysler merger, no significant change in this production agreement is expected before 2005, since the Avenger and the Sebring are based on Mitsubishi components.

Product Cycles and Design

Years ago car body styles seemed to change almost yearly, with the addition of at least some new sheet metal. In the 1960s body styles began to last longer, with minor trim changes being the only indication of a new model year. Some models today have cycles as long as 8 or even 10 years. These longer product cycles are most often associated with the Big Three, as the Asian nameplates generally seem to have cycles of 4 to 5 years.

Freshness of product was one of the key factors that cost American companies market share. When most Asian nameplate production took place overseas, the loss of share resulted in increased vehicle imports and cuts in U.S. car production. In recent years, with more import nameplate (transplant) production in North America, the negative effect of longer cycles on U.S. and North American companies has been mitigated somewhat. In addition, the increased popularity of light trucks has helped the production picture because the Big Three dominate the U.S. light-truck market. Thus, the light-truck trend should mean an increase in U.S. and North American production, all else being equal. Interestingly, trucks tend to have longer product cycles than do cars because consumers do not seem to demand freshly styled trucks as often as they do cars; this also works to the Big Three's advantage.

Impact of Technology

The advent of supercomputers has allowed automobile designers to create engines, interiors, and even entire vehicles in record time. Many automakers have expressed interest in shortening the time to market to 24 months or less. The time includes designing, testing, and producing a vehicle once corporate decision makers give the final approval. That allows the production of state-of-the-art designs and prevents situations in which designs are dated by the time they reach production.

The use of computer-aided design ultimately should lead to more uniform product cycles because key design questions can be answered in days rather than months. Similarly, a part can be modeled and prototyped in an hour instead of days. These technological innovations no doubt save time and also reduce development costs. In addition, the design and production aspects of the U.S., North American, and world industries may become so integrated that once a part design is complete, computer-driven production equipment can instantly configure the tooling needed to make the part, so that actual part production can begin almost immediately after completion of the design.

Regulatory and Environmental Issues

Air-Quality Standards. Ozone depletion, global warming, and concern about air quality continue to spur the development of low-emission and alternatively fueled vehicles. California, which has become the main force behind tough zero-emission vehicle mandates, has eased its standards; but the California Air Resources Board (CARB) is still requiring that 10 percent of automakers' fleets sold in that state be zero-emission vehicles by 2003. While CARB has agreed to relax its mandate that automakers begin selling zero-emission vehicles in 1998, New York State continues to hold to that requirement. Automakers selling vehicles in California must begin selling low-emission vehicles in 2001, 3 years ahead of the U.S. Environmental Protection Agency's (EPA) required date. In exchange for the 3-year reprieve on zero-emission vehicles, automakers will be rolling out electric vehicles in the near future. In addition to electric vehicles, automakers are increasingly considering alternative power plants and fuels, such as hybrid electrics and fuel cells.

At a recent summit in Kyoto, Japan, most of the industrialized nations agreed to lower carbon dioxide emissions. This would have an effect on the American automakers, which would be forced to lower the emissions of their vehicles, but the treaty has not been approved in the United States. For another international effort to control emissions of motor vehicles, see the boxed note: "A Worldwide Effort to Improve the Environment."

Passenger Safety. Airbags have recently taken center stage as a result of several fatalities from the force of a bag's deployment. Warning labels inform that children and adults shorter than 5 feet, 4 inches, are at risk from driver and front passenger seat airbags. The National Highway Traffic Safety Administration (NHTSA) also has mandated warning labels for vehicles equipped with passenger-side airbags. Currently, NHTSA allows airbags to be shut off for people who have a valid letter from a physician detailing medical reasons for the shutoff. The NHTSA regulations allow for a shutoff in cases where there is a small-statured person (under 5 feet tall), and in a two-seat vehicle NHTSA allows a shutoff for children. Also, cutoff switches are currently available in most pickup trucks. All newly installed airbags have slower propulsion. The industry has begun to offer airbags that can sense the size of the occupant and automatically adjust deployment accordingly. New technology employing weight, heat, and sonic detection of passengers is on the horizon.

Employment

As long as the economy can avoid a recession and light-vehicle demand remains near 15 million units, employment in the industry should hold steady through 1998 and begin to improve early in the next decade. The employment outlook is bolstered by increased domestic production driven by the surging light-truck market and the substitution of domestic production for imports. On the downside, however, are the ongoing attempts by both the original equipment manufacturers (OEMs) and the parts suppliers to control vehicle costs. The cost savings will be driven in large part by productivity gains, which will typically mean less labor input into the production process. Cost savings should also result from continued consolidation in the supply community, which inevitably means fewer jobs as the merged companies streamline their sales, administrative, procurement, and production arrangements.

The labor agreements signed by the Big Three and the United Auto Workers (UAW) point to declining employment among the major automakers. These agreements allow a 5 percent cut in the number of union jobs over the contract period at Ford and Chrysler and up to a 14 percent cut at GM. The number of jobs lost at the Big Three could go higher if an economic downturn has a negative impact on light-vehicle demand. Many of the job cuts are expected to reflect the continued move toward component outsourcing and could be offset by increased employment among parts makers. The parts makers, however, often are not unionized and therefore pay less than do the Big Three.

MEDIUM- AND HEAVY-DUTY TRUCKS AND BUS BODIES

Medium- and heavy-duty vehicles are used primarily for commercial purposes, including the transport of raw or finished goods as well as passengers. Medium-duty vehicles tend to be used for short- and medium-distance hauling and transportation, with the weight capacity generally proportional to the average distance traveled.

Domestic Trends

Seven major companies supplied medium- and heavy-duty trucks to the U.S. market in 1997, although nearly 65 percent of sales came from three major manufacturers: Ford, Freightliner, and Navistar. In 1997 Ford lost market share while the six other competitors took up its loss.

In 1997 Ford abandoned the class 6–8 truck market. Shortly after introducing its new HN80 truck series, including the Louisville and Aeromax models, Ford sold the entire division to Daimler-Benz, the parent company of Freightliner. Daimler-Benz's new truck division was renamed Sterling Truck Corporation, with sales beginning in the 1999 model year. While Freightliner continues to lead the sales of class 8 trucks, Sterling will help gain ground in the class 6 and 7 markets for Daimler-Benz.

TABLE 36-1: U.S. Medium- and Heavy-Duty Truck Sales by Manufacturer

	1997		2003	
	Units	Share, %	Units	Share, %
Ford	77,228	21	74,711	21
Freightliner	70,368	19	69,510	20
GM	34,102	9	31,358	9
Mack	23,667	6	21,659	6
Navistar	96,353	26	86,619	25
PACCAR	40,347	11	36,490	10
Volvo/GM	17,622	5	17,190	5
Others	16,452	4	11,713	3
Total	376,139	100	349,250	100

Source: Standard & Poor's DRI.

The other truck manufacturers are not standing still. PAC-CAR, the owner of Peterbilt and Kenworth, purchased the Dutch truck manufacturer DAF in 1997 and the English manufacturer Leyland in 1998. Mack became part of the Renault organization a number of years ago. Volvo Heavy purchased GM's shares of Volvo/GM in 1996. Navistar had a great year in 1997 and has expanded operations in the United States through a contract with Marmon and in Mexico and South America (see Table 36-1).

U.S. medium- and heavy-duty truck sales grew considerably during the period 1992–1995. Growth slowed in 1995, but domestic sales exceeded 388,000 units, their highest level to date. In 1996, sales totaled roughly 359,000 units, a decline from the previous year's peak but in line with the 1994 level. The slowing economy and the exhaustion of pent-up replacement demand contributed to this sales weakness. However, the absence of a strong cyclical recovery, combined with a slow period for replacement demand after the boom years of 1993 and 1994, suggests that this weakness will extend into 1998. U.S. medium- and heavy-duty sales should recover to the range of 325,000 to 350,000 units by 2002 if the current trend in gross domestic product (GDP) growth remains steady and a normal replacement-demand cycle occurs.

Global Trends

World medium- and heavy-duty truck production grew rapidly in 1994 and 1995, averaging 17 percent annual growth (see Table 36-2). Unit production climbed from less than 950,000

in 1993 to nearly 1.3 million in 1995 as coinciding replacement cycles in Europe and the United States combined with strong underlying economic growth across the world. In 1996 world output declined 9 percent to 1.18 million units as a result of economic weakness in the major developed economies of North America, western Europe, and Japan. World truck output was forecast to continue declining through 1998 but should begin to rise in 1999, assuming normal replacement cycles. The U.S. share of world medium- and heavy-duty truck output is projected to decline through 2002, falling to nearly 26 percent from 30 percent in 1995. Although part of this decline is due to slower economic growth in the United States compared with that in developing regions, the expected shift of production to faster-growing markets in Latin America and Asia is also a factor.

Importers include Mitsubishi FUSO, Hino, Isuzu, Nissan Diesel, and the upstart Hyundai (sold under the Bering brand), along with captive imports (vehicles manufactured domestically by companies based in foreign countries) sold by GM and Mack. Isuzu is the largest medium-duty importer, accounting for roughly 45 percent of the 11,800 import units sold through November 1996. Mitsubishi FUSO ranked second among the importers, with a 20 percent share, while Nissan Diesel and Mack rounded out the top four with shares of 12 percent and 11 percent, respectively.

U.S. export sales of medium- and heavy-duty trucks have traditionally been rather low, averaging 10 percent of U.S. factory sales. The weakness in the Canadian economy in 1996 mostly explains the falloff in sales, as more than 60 percent of U.S. truck exports go to Canada. Moreover, the bulk of U.S. exports (60 to 65 percent) consists of class 8 trucks, which are particularly vulnerable to economic cycles. U.S. truck export sales (in units) are not expected to grow significantly over the next several years but should grow in the range of 3 to 5 percent annually, as demand growth remains slow in the major developed markets and as U.S. producers continue to shift production to faster-growing regions of the world.

The largest amount of output generated by U.S.-based companies outside the United States is in Canada. In 1996, roughly 87 percent of total Canadian medium- and heavy-duty truck production (29,000 units) came from the factories of U.S. producers. However, the U.S. share of Canadian production has fallen steadily over the last few years as Ford, Mack, and Ken-

TABLE 36-2: World Medium- and Heavy-Duty Truck Production
(thousands of units)

	1995	1996	1997	1998	1999	2000	2001	2002	2003
United States	386	318	362	400	344	309	309	320	335
Western Europe	344	303	332	344	341	334	331	335	344
Japan	288	267	267	233	276	276	287	295	275
Other	640	601	601	563	595	706	789	828	865
World	1,658	1,489	1,562	1,540	1,556	1,624	1,716	1,778	1,820
Annual percent change	1.9	−10.2	4.9	−1.4	1.0	4.4	5.6	3.6	2.4

Source: Standard & Poor's DRI.

worth have reduced or eliminated medium- and heavy-duty truck operations to the north. In contrast, the share of Mexican medium- and heavy-duty truck production generated by U.S.-based firms has grown significantly, increasing from less than 30 percent in 1993 to more than 45 percent in 1996. In 1995 Ford and General Motors joined Chrysler and Kenworth in the Mexican market. Although production volumes have been down since Mexico entered a recession in 1994, output is expected to climb to roughly 30,000 units in 2002, of which 12,000 to 15,000 units will come from U.S. plants.

LIGHT TRUCKS

When a nation first has sufficient per capita income to make vehicle ownership feasible on a large scale, the first vehicles purchased usually are trucks, such as compact pickups. Businesses typically make such purchases because they need trucks to get goods to market. As the market matures, personal-use vehicles, beginning with small cars, begin to take a share of the market, causing light-truck sales to dwindle. The U.S. market has shown an uncharacteristic rebound in light-truck sales, however.

Domestic Trends

Over the past 10 years, the U.S. automobile industry has witnessed a dramatic change in truck offerings and a resulting jump in the demand for and market share of light trucks. The U.S. market provides a sound illustration of the evolution of the light truck from a primarily business and commercial product to a consumer-oriented product.

Despite the maturity of the U.S. market, the light-truck share in the United States is on the way up and is approaching parity with car share. However, today's U.S. truck purchases are different from those of an emerging market in that they are not primarily business-related. The models are larger and more luxurious, designed for personal transportation. Part of the U.S. demand for trucks can be attributed to more open space as well as lower gasoline prices in the United States compared with western Europe and Japan, where the light-truck share remains low.

Because of corporate average fuel economy (CAFE) restrictions, automakers cannot sell enough economical small cars to balance their sales of the large fuel-hungry cars that the American public desires. This has been a major contributing factor to the rise in the popularity of light trucks for personal use. Automakers can produce more V8-powered trucks because of lower CAFE requirements on the vehicles. With profit margins of $5,000 to $15,000 per truck, automakers have been encouraged to abandon car projects in favor of trucks and truck-based vehicles.

Global Trends

Although overseas markets are relatively small, light trucks are starting to increase in popularity as personal-use vehicles in western Europe and Japan. Minivans are gaining ground in Europe, as most of the major manufacturers have begun to offer models. Likewise, Japanese purchases of compact sport utilities and some smaller minivanlike offerings are on the rise.

North American light-vehicle production capacity is also growing. A majority of the gains in plant space have resulted from expansion by the transplant manufacturers. However, domestic manufacturers in North America are working to reconfigure their current production allocation to make better use of their plants' floor space. For these domestic manufacturers, changes over the next several years should mostly involve the conversion of plant output from cars to trucks in response to market demand. Total North American straight-time production capacity for 1997 was 17.3 million units. Planned additions and expansions, the majority of which were targeted for the United States and Canada, were expected to bring that total to 17.8 million units. In 1997 the United States accounted for nearly 76 percent of the total North American output. Of that total, Canada and Mexico contributed 16 percent and 8 percent, respectively. Despite the planned expansions in the United States, expansion of Canadian light-vehicle output should be somewhat stronger, and by 2000 Canada is expected to gain a 1 percent share of North American output at the expense of the United States.

Globally, total capacity and production will be affected by the Asian economic crisis. South Korea, which was the most overcapacitized country, was heavily affected by this crisis, and expansion plans probably will be put on hold, perhaps reducing some of the worldwide underutilization problems. Although the crisis has not affected U.S. sales or production, it is likely to affect emerging economies that have significantly higher income elasticity for car demand and from which most of the world's net new growth in demand was expected to come.

Long-Term Prospects

U.S. light-vehicle sales growth should reflect the maturing age of the U.S. driving population. Unlike previous periods, there is no untapped portion of the population that is about to enter the market. For example, when women entered the work force en masse, a part of the population with low demand for light vehicles began purchasing them. Similarly, when the baby boomers were old enough to afford new vehicles, sales surged. Over the forecast period, most of the growth in the population will be in the 40- to 60-year-old age bracket. As these buyers are already in the buying pool, growth in this age bracket will not affect the total number of new vehicles sold, though it is likely to affect the types of vehicles purchased.

In general, trucks worldwide probably will offer more car-like amenities, such as heated seats, power windows, and traction control. These added features should broaden the range of consumers who choose a light truck over a car. In addition, partly in the interest of reducing unique platforms (and costs) and partly to further soften ride characteristics, many of the latest small truck models are actually based on cars (e.g., many minivans). As many cars are beginning to follow truck styling cues, the world market (with mature markets leading the way) most likely will offer hybrid models that have the styling and visibility of light trucks and the comfort and features traditionally offered by cars.

NEAR-LUXURY VEHICLES

The traditional luxury car market in the United States has certainly found competition from the increasingly luxury truck market as well as from a portion of the near-luxury market. Near-luxury vehicles usually are priced above traditional family sedans but below most standard luxury models. They also tend to be a bit smaller than standard luxury models and in some cases smaller than traditional family sedans. Near-luxury models, however, offer many of the accoutrements formerly found exclusively in the top-end luxury models, including CD players, traction control, and heated mirrors and seats. Thus, consumers are finding it more difficult to identify what they are getting for their money in choosing a luxury car rather than a near-luxury model.

Together, the European and Asian luxury nameplates have dominated this market, with 90 percent of near-luxury entries coming from outside North America. Solely on the basis of growth numbers, it might seem wise for the Big Three to become more involved in this segment. Indeed, Cadillac has introduced its Catera, and Lincoln is expected to offer a near-luxury LS model in 1999. Although the Lincoln model most likely will be made in the United States, the Cadillac entry is based on a vehicle made in Germany by GM of Europe (GM, however, has been evaluating whether to build a version of its Catera stateside).

Although growth in this segment has been impressive, the best segments overall are both large and growing, which is not the case in the near-luxury segment. In 1997, even after several years of strong growth, near-luxury vehicles accounted for only about 4.5 percent of the U.S. market, or slightly more than 368,000 sales. Moreover, these sales were split among 12 different models, meaning that sales per model were below 31,000. In comparison, the full-size SUV market (also a fast grower) has sales that average nearly 52,000. The sales situation for near-luxury vehicles is less important for the Asian and European nameplates because U.S. sales constitute only a small part of their sales worldwide. Conversely, as the Big Three move into this segment, they may find higher unit costs because they will not have a European and/or Asian sales base over which to spread development costs if they develop models especially for the U.S. market.

An approach to reducing unit development costs that has been used successfully by Asian automakers is to create near-luxury models based on dressed up standard models. For example, the Lexus ES300 is heavily based on the Toyota Camry and the Infiniti I30 is heavily based on the Nissan Maxima. Similarly, the Catera is a revised version of the Omega model currently sold in Europe.

In addition, recent price cuts (not just rebates) in the traditional luxury segments could herald a price drop for many near-luxury vehicles. This would certainly cut into profit margins.

Thus, the risks are slowing growth, a fairly small market share, low average sales, and the potential for reduced profits.

In terms of U.S. and North American production, the potential is far greater. Most near-luxury models sold in the United States are imported. As most mainstream models sold in the United States by the Asian brands are now made in North America, there is a move to bring the production of some near-luxury models to these shores. Honda has already moved the production of the Acura CL coupe and TL sedan to Ohio. Toyota is likely to bring the production of a Lexus coupe or sedan to Canada. Nissan will be bringing the production of the Maxima to the United States in the near future and thus could move the production of the Infiniti I30 to the United States as well.

GLOBAL MARKET PROSPECTS

The motor vehicle industry in the United States is a large, mature market, and most of the cars and light trucks produced here are geared toward the unique U.S. market. For example, many vehicles are large, have powerful engines, and are well equipped compared with products in the rest of the world. This is the case even in comparison with other mature markets, such as those in Japan and western Europe, both of which demand much smaller models than those sold in the United States, in part because of the high price of fuel overseas.

Canada is the market that is most accepting of U.S.-made vehicles. Because of lower incomes, higher taxes and vehicle prices, and a weak Canadian dollar, the best-selling models in Canada tend to be smaller and less expensive than the U.S. best-sellers. As the Mexican market continues to expand, automakers will increase the number of models tailored for that market. Chrysler is forecast to introduce a model below the Neon in both price and size around the 2000 model year, and the forthcoming Fiesta will boost Ford's sales. However, the Canadian light-vehicle market in total is expected to reach only 1.5 million by 2002, with the Mexican market hitting between 700,000 and 800,000 units. In other words, the two export markets with the greatest potential for U.S.-made products have limited growth potential and are far smaller than the U.S. market. As in the United States, sales peaks in the coming forecast years are unlikely to exceed past high-water marks.

Japanese automakers with plants in the United States have begun exporting vehicles from the United States to Japan. Honda, for example, is exporting Accords made in Ohio to Japan and Europe, and Toyota is exporting Camry coupes and wagons to Japan. European automakers are following suit: Mercedes sport utilities and BMW roadsters will be shipped worldwide from their U.S. sources. Although the volumes of these vehicles will be fairly minimal compared with those of some of the high-volume products made in the United States, their unit value will be higher.

Unfortunately for the U.S. industry, most of the growth in the world's markets will be in the developing auto markets, such as those in China, India, Latin America, and eastern

Europe. Thus, the typical product made in the United States has a very limited sales potential in these growing markets because it is overequipped and prohibitively expensive. Even without local production requirements, the low vehicle prices needed to be successful in the evolving markets are incompatible with the production costs (labor, energy, regulatory compliance, etc.) associated with U.S. manufacturing efforts.

Additionally, many of the countries with the biggest poten-tial gains in light-vehicle sales are requiring that the vehicles sold there be made there in the interest of establishing a local production base and jobs. Specific groups of countries in which "semilocal" production is encouraged are creating trade agree-ments to leverage their common interests. Brazil, for example, has local production content requirements, but it has an agree-ment allowing Mexican production to count as local; produc-tion in Brazil also can be considered local for Mexican domestic requirements. Thus, even if American manufacturers can establish a presence in the evolving markets, the vehicles they sell there most likely will have to be made there.

For U.S. government efforts at increasing exports of motor vehicles, see the boxed note: "International Trade Negotiations."

Import Penetration

A key factor affecting U.S. production is import penetration. GM, Ford, and Chrysler have faced a seemingly never-ending battle for market share with the import nameplates (e.g., Toyota, Honda, and Nissan). The trough of the 1991 recession saw the Big Three's market share bottom out as consumers tended to buy less expensive vehicles that seemed to be a sound value. At that time those criteria pointed toward an Asian nameplate vehicle.

Since then, however, the gap between domestic production and domestic sales has narrowed because many of the import

nameplates have moved production to North America. Although the major U.S. automakers have essentially held mar-ket share flat, the share of U.S. sales imported from outside North America declined from a high of about 26 percent in 1986 to just over 11 percent in 1997. As the import nameplates have been stronger in cars than in light trucks, the import share of car sales has traditionally been higher in the car sector than in the light-truck sector. This trend is expected to continue (see Figure 36-2).

The 1997 increase in import share was due largely to the U.S. consumers' love of SUVs, whose popularity has resulted in higher prices for SUVs than for many car models. In response, import nameplates are attempting to tap into this demand by offering smaller, less expensive SUVs, such as Honda's CR-V, Toyota's RAV4, and Subaru's Forester, all of which will be at least initially sourced from Japan. Over time, however, the production of most of these vehicles will come to the United States. In addition, the Big Three are expected to introduce a number of smaller models in an attempt to capture part of this lower-end SUV market. When these vehicles are made mostly in North America, the domestically produced light-truck share will increase.

On the car side, new versions of a number of sporty and lux-ury models went on sale in 1998. Sporty and luxury models tend to have very strong sales in the first full year, followed by a fairly rapid tapering off. The coinciding introductions of a number of models result in a short-term increase in the import light-vehicle share. In addition, Honda's Civic has been so pop-ular that Honda has been forced to resume some imports. Honda planned on ending all imports of Civics except for the low-volume Del Sol model, beginning with its 1996 models, as it had done with the Accord; however, despite increased North American Civic production, strong U.S. demand for the entire 1996 Civic line forced Honda to import models from Japan to supplement production at its Ohio and Canadian plants. That

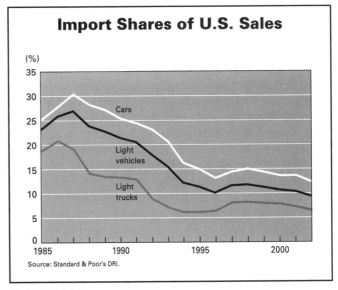

FIGURE 36-2

situation is expected to be short-lived. More recently, the European nameplates have been managing somewhat of a recovery in the United States by dramatically cutting production costs and repricing vehicles (changes for which the Japanese have become famous). However, with the exception of Volkswagen, the high-volume European manufacturers Peugeot, Renault, and Fiat have left the U.S. market.

At the same time, the South Korean "second wave" is under way. The first wave consisted solely of Hyundai. Second-wave imports now consist of Kia, Daewoo to join later, and tentatively Ssangyong. Most of these vehicles are based on designs for the South Korean home market. Even though these vehicles are smaller than most in the American market, they have been performing well. This performance is expected to continue.

Despite this ongoing and increasing competition, the Big Three have maintained market share because of the popularity of light trucks, producing the majority of vehicles in the largest and hottest segments (such as SUVs, minivans, and full-size pickups). With trucks expected to remain popular in the face of relatively stable gas prices and increasingly carlike attributes, the Big Three should be able to at least maintain their share.

When a segment remains strong for an extended period, new entrants are likely to appear. Toyota in particular has been aggressively pursuing the hot U.S. light-truck markets. Toyota's current T100 model is larger than any Asian compact pickup before it and was to be offered with a V8 engine and made in the United States by 1998. U.S. production of a new minivan began in 1997; it will be more on a par with the minivans offered by the Big Three than is Toyota's current model. Similarly, the U.S.-made version of the T100 (renamed the T150) could make an excellent foundation for a large, V8-equipped SUV model (a segment exclusively held by the Big Three). Honda also will bring minivan production from Japan to North America and is likely to produce a replacement for today's imported CR-V in the United States or Canada.

Effects of NAFTA

Four years after its implementation, the North American Free Trade Agreement (NAFTA) has been boosting automotive trade across borders. NAFTA has enabled vehicle producers to rationalize their production in the United States, Canada, and Mexico (the three member countries), improving their productivity and profitability. Additional volume for the United States is being sourced from Mexico, and U.S. vehicle shipments to Mexico have grown substantially. In 1994, the year the agreement was implemented, exports of all road motor vehicles to Mexico jumped from $167 million to $656 million, according to data assembled by the Office of Automotive Affairs. In 1995 a severe slump in the Mexican economy resulted in a drop in U.S. vehicle exports to $383 million; that figure was still twice the 1993 level.

In 1996 shipments to Mexico totaled nearly $1.3 billion, an increase of more than 225 percent for the year. The year 1997 also saw a large increase in shipments to Mexico, with a value totaling almost $2 billion, an increase of almost 58 percent from the previous year. In 1993 vehicle imports from Mexico totaled $3.7 billion on a volume of 339,000 units. Imports of 414,000 vehicles from Mexico in 1994 generated a trade value of $4.8 billion. Shipments in 1996 of 771,000 vehicles from Mexico to the United States represented a gain of 31 percent over the previous year and produced a 45 percent increase in the customs value to a total of $11.3 billion. Imports from Mexico grew again in 1997, reaching a total value of about $12.1 billion, a 7 percent increase from 1996.

The devaluation of the peso in Mexico and its subsequent negative effects on the economy acted to decrease exports from the United States to Mexico in 1995, while healthy demand in the United States enabled Mexican-based producers to increase their share of exports over that period. U.S. exports of new cars and new trucks to Mexico rose sharply from 5,686 in 1993 to 39,388 in 1994. The economic crisis cut exports to Mexico in half in 1995, but they were still considerably higher than the level in the pre-NAFTA period. The Mexican economy has been recovering slowly. As a result, new vehicle imports from the United States more than doubled between 1995 and 1996, reaching 82,698 units. The growth from 1996 to 1997 was not as good. At a 60 percent increase, total units shipped reached 131,700. These data include only new trucks and cars. A broader definition that includes all exported road motor vehicles for the transport of goods or people, which the U.S. government uses for trade policy purposes, would result in unit exports to Mexico totaling 16,530 in 1993, 46,660 in 1994, 28,141 in 1995, 90,664 in 1996, and 140,652 in 1997.

Canada accounts for the majority of U.S. exports and imports. Most of the bilateral trade is generated from intracompany shipments by GM, Ford, and Chrysler. Total exports to Canada gained 6.3 percent in 1996, reaching $12.2 billion (720,000 units), and imports from Canada rose 1 percent, totaling $33.7 billion (2.1 million units). The year 1997 brought an increase in exports to Canada, with levels rising above $14.4 billion (877,000 units). Imports from Canada in 1997 increased 6.4 percent to $35.8 billion. Thus, Canada represented more than 56 percent of the total value of U.S. exports in 1997 and more than 40 percent of total U.S. general imports.

According to 1996 data from the American Automobile Manufacturers Association (AAMA), direct factory export shipments of cars and light trucks to Canada by all manufacturers in the United States totaled 594,000 units, while Canadian factories shipped 1.7 million vehicles to the United States. AAMA data also show that factory export sales of cars and light trucks to other countries by the U.S. plants of the Big Three and the Japanese affiliates totaled 424,000 units. Before NAFTA was in place, Canada and the United States had very open bilateral trade, with little or no tariffs. As a result of this open trade, the implementation of NAFTA did not have as dramatic an effect as it did on trade with Mexico.

Japan's Impact on the U.S. Industry

In 1997 the value of U.S. exports to Japan declined, dropping by more than 14 percent for the year to $1.6 billion. The decline accelerated through the first six months of 1998, when the value dropped nearly 43 percent as a result of the economic crisis in Asia. According to data provided by the Japan Automobile Importers Association and the Japan Automobile Dealers Association, sales in Japan of North American–built products manufactured by the Big Three dropped 20 percent in 1997, falling to a total of 62,459 units. Japanese sales of vehicles produced in North America by Honda, Mitsubishi, and Toyota dropped 48 percent, falling to 36,206 units. For details on an underlying agreement with Japan, see the boxed note: "U.S.-Japan Automotive Agreement."

Most Japanese manufacturers are following a strategy of producing high-volume, lower-cost vehicles in local markets while reserving most low-volume, high-value units for production in Japan. Consequently, U.S. vehicle imports from Japan have been declining steadily, falling from a peak of 3.6 million units in 1986 to 1.2 million units in 1996. In 1997, however, imports from Japan grew 15 percent to 1.4 million units worth $23.6 billion, a gain of 15 percent.

U.S. retail sales of light trucks imported from Japan grew 33 percent in 1997, reaching a total of 526,000 units, whereas sales of cars imported from Japan recovered slightly to gain 9 percent and rise to 726,000 units. Toyota experienced such strong demand for its 4-Runner, RAV4, and LX450 SUV models (all of which are assembled only in Japan) that its total 1997 sales of light-truck imports increased 10 percent to 246,000 vehicles. Imported truck sales were expected to grow even more vigorously in 1998, when Toyota was slated to introduce its new Lexus RX300 SUV to the U.S. market. In the first half of 1998, total imports from Japan increased 5.6 percent in units (721,000) worth $12.4 billion, a 9.8 percent gain.

The popularity of Hondas and Toyotas could continue to generate a net increase in their imports. Because both companies appear to remain committed to transferring capacity here, their import growth is probably a short-term phenomenon.

U.S.-JAPAN AUTOMOTIVE AGREEMENT

The U.S.-Japan Agreement on Autos and Auto Parts was signed in 1995. The 5-year agreement was made in the hope of opening up the Japanese market to U.S. exports. Since then, the Big Three have been working to increase sales in the Japanese market and improve their distribution network in the region. Although some progress has been made in both areas by U.S. domestic auto manufacturers, growth has been slow. The industry and government continue to make progress toward improving the trade relationship with Japan.

Much like the United States, Japan has a mature motor vehicle market that is an unlikely prospect for long-term high growth; it is, however, a large market, and improved access is of great interest to U.S. vehicle and parts producers. In February 1997 Japan rejected a petition by the United States that would have deregulated some of its parts market and allowed the United States to become more competitive in that arena.

The speed at which they move to establish additional U.S. capacity, however, probably will be greatly influenced by the yen-dollar exchange rate trend, which currently favors imports from Japan.

Nissan, the third major Japanese player in the U.S. market, has much less flexibility in its sourcing decisions than does either Toyota or Honda. Nissan will continue to rely heavily on truck imports to supplement the one pickup model it produces in Tennessee until an SUV is added to the production mix. A recent downturn has forced Nissan to adjust its product mix, and it will add two new SUVs, one built in the United States and one imported, to the lineup over the next few years.

U.S. INDUSTRY PROJECTIONS FOR THE NEXT 1 AND 5 YEARS

Although the U.S. market is expected to grow little over the forecast period, domestic production has increased faster than have sales over the past decade. The reason for this is that the import share of U.S. sales has fallen dramatically as major Japanese and German manufacturers have moved vehicle production to North America. Also related to import penetration is the increasing popularity of light trucks, which have far lower import penetration than do passenger cars.

Over time, the Big Three may have greater production increases in Canada and Mexico than they do in the United States. Offsetting this effect will be continued efforts by the import nameplates to make inroads into U.S. markets. By the end of 1997 Toyota, Honda, Nissan, Mazda, Mitsubishi, Subaru, Isuzu, BMW, and Mercedes were producing vehicles in the United States. The import nameplates are also expected to continue to increase production efforts elsewhere in North America—in particular, Honda and Toyota in Canada and Nissan and Volkswagen in Mexico (see Table 36-3).

From 1990 to 2002 the United States may lose some of its light-vehicle production predominance in NAFTA, as its share of total North American light-vehicle output is expected to fall from 77 percent to 72 percent. On a percentage point basis, Mexico will gain the most from the loss by the United States. It is important to note that despite a loss in the U.S. North American share, U.S. production is expected to remain at approximately 12 million units.

Comparisons of capacity with production indicate that North American factory utilization hit 91 percent in 1997. This represents a slight imbalance between plant space and actual output, but it offers manufacturers room to breathe in years with stronger demand. While some automakers are struggling to make use of their plant floor space, others are finding themselves in need of extra space just to keep up with demand. For example, Nissan is working hard to rearrange and add production in North America to take advantage of its greatly underutilized Mexican plants. Honda, in contrast, is expanding its North American production capabilities. As these adjustments are made over the next few years, North American automakers should see capacity utilization surpass 90 percent.

TABLE 36-3: U.S. Trade Patterns in Motor Vehicles–1997[1]
(millions of dollars; percent)

Exports			Imports		
Regions[2]	Value[3]	Share, %	Regions[2]	Value[3]	Share, %
NAFTA	16,092	65.6	NAFTA	48,026	51.7
Latin America	1,489	6.1	Latin America	12	0.0
Western Europe	2,650	10.8	Western Europe	14,709	15.8
Japan/Chinese Economic Area	2,171	8.9	Japan/Chinese Economic Area	27,909	30.1
Other Asia	234	1.0	Other Asia	1,901	2.0
Rest of world	1,889	7.7	Rest of world	313	0.3
World	24,525	100.0	World	92,869	100.0
Top Five Countries	Value	Share, %	Top Five Countries	Value	Share, %
Canada	14,141	57.7	Canada	35,770	38.5
Mexico	1,950	8.0	Japan	27,906	30.0
Japan	1,563	6.4	Mexico	12,256	13.2
Germany	1,091	4.4	Germany	9,762	10.5
Belgium	696	2.8	South Korea	1,900	2.0

[1] SIC 3711, 3713.
[2] For definitions of regional groupings, see "Getting the Most Out of *Outlook '99*."
[3] Values may not sum to total due to rounding.
Source: U.S. Department of Commerce, Bureau of the Census.

TABLE 36-4: Motor Vehicles and Car, Truck, and Bus Bodies (SIC 3711, 3713) Trends and Forecasts
(millions of dollars except as noted)

	1992	1993	1994	1995	1996	1997[1]	1998[2]	1999[3]	Percent Change 96–97	97–98	98–99	92–96[4]
Industry data												
Value of shipments[5]	156,309	173,702	204,373	209,035	209,184	209,272	216,702	218,848	0.0	3.6	1.0	7.6
Value of shipments (1992$)	156,309	167,951	190,691	192,975	190,849	187,314	195,799	195,919	−1.9	4.5	0.1	5.1
Total employment (thousands)	263	259	271	278	263							0.0
Production workers (thousands)	219	217	230	239	225							0.7
Average hourly earnings ($)	20.64	21.28	22.03	22.93	23.04							2.8
Capital expenditures	3,059	4,113	4,419	4,681	4,503							10.1
Product data												
Value of shipments[5]	151,629	168,682	201,307	205,644	205,930	217,694	220,141	227,665	5.7	1.1	3.4	8.0
Value of shipments ($1992)	151,629	163,091	187,816	189,946	187,892	194,900	199,901	205,196	3.7	2.6	2.6	5.5
Trade data												
Imports	59,805	67,803	78,806	84,042	86,992	92,369	94,032	98,550	6.2	1.8	4.8	9.8
Exports	17,539	18,399	22,123	21,522	22,904	24,525	27,854	28,034	7.1	13.6	0.6	6.9

[1] Estimate except imports and exports.
[2] Estimate.
[3] Forecast.
[4] Compound annual rate.
[5] For a definition of industry versus product values, see "Getting the Most Out of *Outlook '99*."
Source: U.S. Department of Commerce: Bureau of the Census; International Trade Administration. Estimates and forecasts by Standard & Poor's DRI.

In 1997, the United States produced 22 percent of world vehicle output. Combined, the NAFTA countries accounted for 29 percent of total output. The U.S. share of worldwide production is forecast to rise through 2003 to 27 percent of total output. Although U.S. output will expand at a modest rate (4.6 percent) over this period, other regions, such as eastern Europe and Latin America, are expected to grow at a much faster rate. One reason for this is that U.S. light-vehicle demand is expected to be relatively flat for the next several years. At the same time, other regions that are experiencing expansion in light-vehicle sales are not likely to buy North American–produced vehicles, the majority of which are too large and expensive to meet the needs of emerging markets. Consequently, expansion in U.S. and North American production will be due largely to domestic production replacing imports. Although exports are expected to rise, they will not figure as dramatically in the growth of North American output.

In the long term the markets with the greatest potential for growth include India, China, Latin America, and eastern Europe. Unfortunately, average income levels in those countries are far below those in the mature markets and cannot bear the cost of U.S.-made products. Also, in the short term these developing areas will have to deal with the effects of the economic conditions in Asia and may experience short-lived dips in production. Moreover, the size and relative fuel inefficiency of U.S.-made vehicles would make most of them incompatible with market conditions in those countries. Finally, many of those countries have trade barriers in the form of tariffs or domestic content requirements. For U.S. car companies to be competitive in many large untapped markets, they need to manufacture there, which further limits the likelihood that cars and light trucks made in the United States will be sold in quantity in the evolving markets.

Altogether, U.S. industry shipments were expected to grow 3 percent in 1998, reaching almost $228 billion in that year and $285 billion by 2002 (a further 25 percent gain) [see Table 36-4]. Gains are expected to come from a variety of sources, including increased exports to the recovering Mexican market and to a reviving Canadian market, increased import penetration of North American–made products in Asia and Europe, continued gains in the light-truck share of the U.S. market, and increased output from transplant manufacturers.

The movement by the import nameplates over the past decade has allowed both U.S. and North American production to increase faster than have U.S. sales. In fact, in 1994 North American production outpaced U.S. sales for the first time in recent memory. From 1994 to 2002, however, the U.S. picture is not likely to be as bright as that for North America overall. Like U.S. sales, U.S. production levels are expected to change little from today's levels. In contrast, light-vehicle production in North America overall is expected to continue to grow. The strongest growth is expected in Mexico as a result of the use of that country as a base for export production to other Latin American countries as well as to Europe and the recovery of the Mexican economy, which will boost sales and production for the local market.

Phil Gott, (781) 860-6964; *Suzanne Murtha,* (781) 860-6805; *Sam Fiorani,* (781) 860-6655—Standard & Poor's DRI Global Automotive Group, October 1998.

■ **REFERENCES**

American Automobile Manufacturers Association (for pre-1985 U.S. vehicle production data) in *Ward's Automotive Yearbook,* 1996, Ward's Communications, Southfield, MI.
American Association of Automobile Manufacturers
American Trucking Association
Commercial Carrier Journal
Standard & Poor's DRI Global Automotive Group
Transport Topics
Ward's Automotive Reports

■ **RELATED CHAPTERS**

13: Steel Mill Products
16: Microelectronics
37: Automotive Parts

AUTOMOTIVE PARTS
Economic and Trade Trends

U.S. International Trade

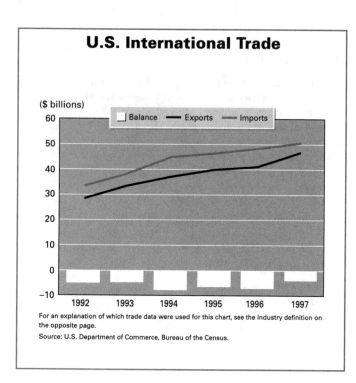

($ billions)

Legend: Balance, Exports, Imports

For an explanation of which trade data were used for this chart, see the industry definition on the opposite page.

Source: U.S. Department of Commerce, Bureau of the Census.

World Export Market Shares

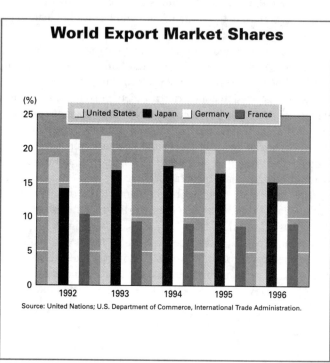

(%)

Legend: United States, Japan, Germany, France

Source: United Nations; U.S. Department of Commerce, International Trade Administration.

Export Dependence and Import Penetration

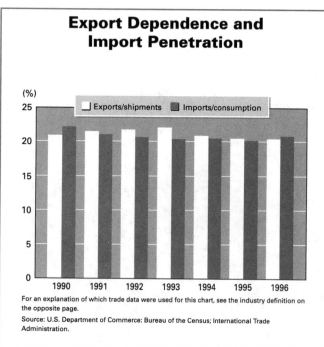

(%)

Legend: Exports/shipments, Imports/consumption

For an explanation of which trade data were used for this chart, see the industry definition on the opposite page.

Source: U.S. Department of Commerce: Bureau of the Census; International Trade Administration.

Output and Output per Hour

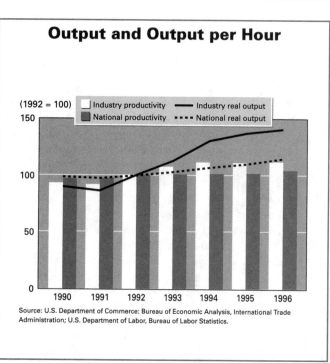

(1992 = 100)

Legend: Industry productivity, Industry real output, National productivity, National real output

Source: U.S. Department of Commerce: Bureau of Economic Analysis, International Trade Administration; U.S. Department of Labor, Bureau of Labor Statistics.

See "Getting the Most Out of *Outlook '99*" for definitions of terms.

Automotive Parts

INDUSTRY DEFINITION The U.S. automotive parts industry includes manufacturers of automotive stampings; carburetors, pistons, piston rings, and valves; vehicular lighting equipment; storage batteries; engine electrical equipment; and other motor vehicle parts (SIC 3465, 3592, 3647, 3691, 3694, and 3714, respectively).

(Note on trade data: Two different sets of trade data are used in this chapter: a narrow set that is based solely on the six automotive parts SIC codes and a broad one that includes those SIC codes as well as other automotive products classified under other SIC codes, such as automotive tires and tubes and glass. The trade data in the chart titled "Export Dependence and Import Penetration" on the facing page and in Table 37-2 are based on the narrow set. The broad data are used in the chart titled "U.S. International Trade" on the facing page, in Table 37-4, and in the text. The U.S. government uses the broad definition for trade policy purposes. Another important difference is the fact that the narrow set is based on imports for consumption and the broad set is based on general imports. Imports for consumption include products coming out of U.S. Foreign Trade Zones, some of which have undergone a transformation; general imports measure all imports into the country in the condition in which they arrived. For example, under imports for consumption, products are imported into Foreign Trade Zones as automotive parts but come out as a car, leading to an undercount of parts imports. General imports include all parts imports.)

OVERVIEW

The automotive parts industry supplies two markets: the original equipment market for parts used directly in the manufacture of vehicles and the replacement (repair) parts market, or aftermarket. The U.S. industry consists of approximately 5,000 firms, including about 500 Japanese, European, and Canadian manufacturers. The industry is dominated by 100 large manufacturers that supply both the original equipment market and the aftermarket and account for the vast majority of sales. The industry and trade data cited in this chapter are not collected or reported in a way that allows a distinction to be made between the original equipment market and the aftermarket.

FACTORS AFFECTING FUTURE INDUSTRY GROWTH

Global Industry Trends

The world's major motor vehicle manufacturers continue to restructure their manufacturing operations in the important markets of North America, Europe, Asia, and Latin America, with each one striving to create its own "world vehicle." Leading automotive parts manufacturers have responded to this form of globalization by revamping their operations to manufacture products and supply their customers in markets worldwide. This trend has resulted in a sharper focus by parts manufacturers on core competencies in an attempt to become "systems integrators and the assumption of more research and development responsibilities that once were the province of motor vehicle manufacturers. These major trends have changed the face of the global automotive parts industry, which has been undergoing strategic mergers and making crucial acquisitions in order to pool their resources and gain a competitive advantage as global suppliers. Manufacturers that were unable to adapt to these trends have disappeared from the market. According to industry studies, the number of tier one suppliers worldwide was halved from 3,000 to 1,500 between 1990 and 1996, while the value of mergers and acquisitions soared annually, nearing a record $19 billion in 1997, up almost 27 percent from $15 billion in 1996.

As motor vehicle manufacturers have begun to supply overseas markets with vehicles produced in those markets, the tier one suppliers have followed their customers into those markets by establishing new production facilities or entering into joint ventures with local manufacturers. Between 1993 and 1997 global sales by the world's top 10 automotive parts manufacturers jumped nearly 47 percent to $114 billion, with much of that growth coming from sales in foreign markets. (See Table 37-1.) For example, the world's number one supplier, Delphi Automotive Systems, has attempted to augment its overseas sales by $8 billion to $9 billion, and in 1996 it announced new operations and joint ventures in Asia, particularly in the Association of Southeast Asian Nations (ASEAN) region. These investment decisions were made in tandem with the plans of its parent company, General Motors Corp. (GM), to invest $750 million in Asia by 2000. GM scaled back its planned investment in Thailand to $500 million in late 1997 as a result of that country's economic downturn and the economic crisis in other Asian countries. However, between 10 and 20 other GM suppliers have made a commitment to follow the automaker into that region.

Another example involves the number 3 global supplier, Robert Bosch of Germany. Bosch has been attempting to add another $5 billion in North American and Asian sales. To achieve that goal, the German supplier acquired AlliedSignal Automotive's braking group for $1.5 billion in 1996, one of the largest purchases in the industry in that year. Bosch currently gets more than half its business from outside Germany, with close to 20 percent coming from North America. Japan's Nippondenso Co. Ltd., which once relied largely on Toyota Motor Corp. for its business, is seeking to diversify and expand its international presence. The Japanese industry giant Unisia Jecs Corp. plans to invest $20 million to $25 million in a new U.S. plant to supply U.S.-based Japanese vehicle manufacturers and its major customer, Nissan, in Mexico. Globalization, however, is not limited to the largest automotive parts firms: Smaller suppliers are also looking for partners in foreign markets to expand and maintain their current customer base.

In the past decade motor vehicle manufacturers have begun requiring their tier one parts manufacturers to become systems integrators—suppliers of modular or preassembled units that can be installed in a vehicle as a single system, such as an entire fuel supply system. In Brazil, Volkswagen (VW), Daimler-Benz, GM, and Ford are experimenting with new vehicle

TABLE 37-1: Sales of Top 10 Global Automotive Parts Suppliers
(millions of dollars)

Rank	Company	1997 Sales
1	Delphi Automotive Systems	26,600
2	Visteon Automotive Systems	17,000
3	Robert Bosch Corp.	16,500
4	Nippondenso Co. Ltd.	13,104
5	Aisin World Corp.	7,790
6	Lear Corp.	7,343
7	Johnson Controls Inc.	7,280
8	TRW Inc.	7,032
9	Dana Corp.	6,217
10	Magna International Inc.	5,500
	Total	114,366

assembly facilities that locate some suppliers within a vehicle assembly plant. In late 1996 VW pioneered this practice with the production of a commercial truck: Eight of VW's tier one suppliers provide modular components and essentially assemble the vehicle. GM's new Brazilian plant, the Blue Macaw, will manufacture a low-cost version of the Opel Corsa by using a similar assembly process. Ford has announced plans to build a plant, Project Amazon, that will build a small sedan and a hybrid sport-utility vehicle by using comparable production processes. Dana Corp. announced in late 1996 that it will supply Chrysler's Brazilian operations with a complete chassis (the frame, driveshaft, axles, brakes, and suspension components) for the Dodge Dakota. This practice will become more prevalent as motor vehicle manufacturers begin a worldwide consolidation of platforms that will be common to several vehicle models. Some industry sources expect 1 million unit platforms to be built by the decade's end.

While these new production processes enable vehicle manufacturers to save time and money in product development, they have forced multinational automotive parts manufacturers to revamp their operations to focus on core competencies. In preparation for the production of global vehicles, leading tier one suppliers are shedding diverse divisions or snapping up firms with complementary product lines. For example, megasuppliers in the seating and interiors sector emerged when the U.S. seat maker Johnson Controls Inc. acquired the French seat supplier Roth Freres SA and the interior trim specialist Prince Automotive Group and the Canadian giant Magna International purchased the seat manufacturer Douglas & Lomason Co. The braking system giant Lucas-Varity plc was established by the $4.8 billion merger between the U.S.-based Varity Corp. and Lucas Automotive of the United Kingdom. The world's largest supplier of safety systems was formed when the merger between Sweden's Autoliv AB and Morton International Inc.'s Automotive Safety Products operations led to the establishment of Autoliv Inc. Even the competing number one and number four suppliers—GM's Delphi and Ford's Visteon—are considering a partnership in Asia.

Today the supplier's role does not end at parts production but has expanded into areas once controlled solely by motor vehicle manufacturers. In addition to producing parts for vehicle manufacturers, tier one suppliers have increasingly been required to take on engineering, managerial, and financial responsibilities. Vehicle manufacturers are increasingly relying on their suppliers for design, research and development expertise and new product ideas, and this trend has resulted in significantly shorter product development cycles for supplier-engineered parts. As vehicle manufacturers have culled the pool of suppliers with which they deal directly, the surviving tier one megasuppliers have had to form their own strategic partnerships with lower-tier suppliers, managing the sourcing of parts from tier two and tier three suppliers. Finally, tier one suppliers now are required to finance these engineering and managerial duties while complying with vehicle manufacturers' requirements for lower-priced parts.

As the evolution of the automotive parts industry into a community of world suppliers continues into the twenty-first century, the ability of tier one suppliers to adapt to these major trends will determine their fate. The decimated ranks of tier one suppliers should shrink further, with only 375 of the current 1,500 expected to exist by the decade's end; 450 (most of which have less than $100 million in annual sales) will go out of business, 375 will be acquired, and 300 will leave the business. The survivors will be divided into three categories: very large, diversified multinational tier one parts manufacturers with major financial resources; smaller, specialty tier one firms with partners in strategic global markets; and lower tier suppliers.

Domestic Trends

In this decade the U.S. automotive parts industry has restructured itself in an effort to maintain its competitive position relative to its main rival, Japan. The ability to maintain its standing as a worldwide leader as it enters the twenty-first century will depend not only on its ability to comply with the specific requirements of its current customers—an increased foreign presence, finely honed core competencies, and the assumption of traditional functions normally handled by vehicle manufacturers—but also on its ability to deal successfully with larger domestic and international factors.

Competitive Pricing. A chief domestic factor affecting the growth of the U.S. parts industry has been U.S. motor vehicle manufacturers' continued demand for improved quality and lower costs. This issue continues to be a long-term concern for U.S. suppliers. In the mid-1980s the Big Three motor vehicle manufacturers, faced with competition in their own market from state-of-the-art Japanese vehicle manufacturers, were forced to revamp their operations to remain competitive and demanded lower-priced, higher-quality parts from their suppliers. As a result, supplying high-quality, continuously improved parts with falling price tags has become an industry norm. Since 1993, productivity has increased slightly more than 2 percent annually and product quality has improved measurably. Despite the parts industry's past successes, the Big Three will continue to demand significant cost cuts from their suppliers, with Ford seeking cost cuts averaging 5 percent annually through 1999 and Chrysler asking its tier one suppliers to propose money-saving ideas equal to 5 percent of their sales to that company. Although the bigger and more efficient suppliers with low unit costs, such as TRW and Dana, have been able to increase their profit margins despite lower prices, many smaller suppliers have encountered diminishing returns as each additional improvement is becoming more costly and technologically more difficult to achieve, resulting in lower growth in profits.

Consolidation. The consolidations and strategic partnerships that improved the competitive stance of many U.S. suppliers during the industry's restructuring promise to play a key role in the future growth of the industry. As a result of restructuring, each of the Big Three motor vehicle manufacturers has reduced its pool of tier one suppliers, preferring to source entire systems from a single supplier. To meet these demands, suppliers have consolidated their operations, becoming systems integrators by forming strategic partnerships with other firms or by shedding unwanted product lines.

The independent supplier community continues to undergo a spate of mergers, acquisitions, and bankruptcies: Between 1993 and 1996 the industry giant Dana completed 24 purchases or joint ventures. In July 1998 Dana announced its acquisition of Echlin, creating a company with $13 billion in annual sales and establishing one of the world's largest independent companies supplying components to both automotive original equipment manufacturers and the aftermarket. Even the Big Three's in-house parts operations underwent upheaval: GM's and Ford's in-house suppliers emerged as the industry giants Delphi and Visteon, while Chrysler divested noncore business divisions of Acustar and reorganized its procurement and supply operations to work more efficiently with its vehicle development teams.

The parts divisions spun off by the Big Three will sharpen competition in the already-cutthroat supplier community. Although Visteon will have to compete with independent suppliers for Ford contracts, the company hopes to raise component sales to non-Ford customers from 5 percent of total sales to 10 percent. The plants that Delphi has earmarked for sale will create a $1 billion independent parts supplier.

Consolidation in the supplier industry could force vehicle manufacturers to rely on a single source for a part. This could create monopolistic conditions, with reduced competition leading to higher prices. The risks of a production system based on a single source for a critical component were underscored in early 1997 when a fire razed an Aishin Seiki plant in Japan that supplied nearly 100 percent of a small brake part for Toyota. The fire forced the automaker to suspend operations at its 18 vehicle assembly plants in Japan for 4 days and resulted in an estimated 100,000-unit decrease in production.

Technology. Future growth for U.S. automotive parts firms will continue to be technology-driven as a result of increasingly stringent safety, fuel efficiency, and environmental regulations as well as increasing demand for enhanced passenger comfort systems. The Clean Air Act of 1990 has been the major catalyst for this change, prompting U.S. suppliers to develop new technologies to produce lightweight body materials and weight-saving mechanical components. In recent years U.S. suppliers have developed composite materials—a mix of plastics with glass and carbon fibers or other substrates—to substitute for metal in vehicles, while new heat-resistant technologies have enabled the automotive industry to use more plastic in engine blocks, significantly lowering an engine's weight. In-car electronics, which have risen to 15 percent of total content from nominal levels in the 1950s, are expected to rise to 20 percent by 2010. Electronic systems will continue to control more functions in vehicles, which thus will require more computer-based technology. As a result, computer software and hardware companies will be more involved in vehicle production, becoming major suppliers to the industry.

The development of new technology is also a key factor in the Clinton administration's Partnership for a New Generation of Vehicles (PNGV). The long-term goal of the PNGV is to develop technologies for a new generation of affordable midsize passenger cars that will travel 80 miles per gallon. Currently, more than 300 U.S. suppliers are involved in this historic industry-government partnership, which includes the development of new power plant, drivetrain, and chassis technologies. With safety, noise-absorption, exhaust-cleaning, and passenger ergonomic systems adding about 440 pounds of indispensable weight to a vehicle, continued improvement of the technology in these areas will become an even more critical factor in vehicle weight reduction as traditional options dwindle. Steelmakers have been developing the ultralight steel auto body, or body-in-white, which weighs about 25 percent less than traditional bodies and costs less to make than bodies made from traditional materials and composites. They hope that this development will allow them to become more involved in the PNGV program.

Outsourcing.   Another major factor for the U.S. automotive parts industry is outsourcing. Since the mid-1980s the Big Three have continued their efforts to cut costs and pare down their in-house parts operations. The June 1998 strike at GM parts facilities is illustrative of issues underlying cost-cutting efforts. GM is seeking higher productivity and claims that union work rules inhibit efficiency; the United Auto Workers (UAW) is protesting that speeding up production to increase productivity is dangerous to workers. Workers are also protesting the outsourcing of work formerly done by the plant and claim that GM has not kept its promise to invest $300 million in the plant. Disagreements about outsourcing between the motor vehicle manufacturers and the UAW also were highlighted by a 17-day strike in March 1996 at GM's Delphi brake plants in Dayton, OH. Although GM retained the right to outsource an antilock brake system instead of sourcing it from Delphi, as a result of 1996 contract negotiations with the UAW, the Big Three have effectively restricted the amount of business they can conduct with independent suppliers (those not owned by an automaker). According to the 3-year contract, the Big Three must maintain 95 percent of their work force, an agreement which will restrict their ability to outsource. If similar contract provisions remain in effect, the proportion of outsourced parts should remain relatively flat through 1999.

Foreign Competition.   Foreign competition in the U.S. market will continue to challenge American automotive parts producers as they attempt to comply with the worldwide sourcing strategies of vehicle manufacturers. Foreign, mainly Japanese, competition in the U.S. market was a major catalyst for the industry's restructuring, and U.S. suppliers have increasingly been challenged by imports and U.S.-based foreign-affiliated automotive parts manufacturers. Since 1989 U.S. imports of automotive parts have grown an average of 6 percent annually, resulting in import penetration levels between 20 and 21 percent. Parts imports from Japan, which have increased to supply the growing number of U.S.-produced Japanese vehicles, have accounted for the vast majority of the U.S. deficit in automotive parts trade since the mid-1980s. Although imports from Japan continue to account for most of the deficit in parts trade, as a result of the 1995 U.S.–Japan Framework Agreement, imports from that country over the period have fallen 24 percent and exports have risen 36 percent, resulting in a 27 percent decrease in the parts deficit with Japan.

The share of U.S. production by foreign-affiliated, U.S.-based parts producers continues to increase. While the vast majority of this investment is Japanese, European firms have increased their investments as they have followed BMW and Mercedes-Benz to the U.S. market. Developments in the Japanese and European industries may also drive their interest in the U.S. market. Leading Japanese suppliers, facing demands for drastic price cuts from Japanese vehicle manufacturers intent on cutting production costs, are breaking away from their *keiretsu* relations with vehicle companies and turning to foreign vehicle manufacturers, including the U.S. Big Three, for business. High manufacturing and labor costs have forced many German automotive parts manufacturers to invest in plants outside Germany, with much of that investment going to the United States. The German Automobile Association predicts that more than half the German supplier industry will invest in facilities outside Germany by 2000.

Finally, intense foreign competition will pose challenges to U.S. automotive parts manufacturers that are seeking to capitalize on growth opportunities in key emerging markets. The Japanese automotive industry is firmly entrenched in the Asian markets, while the European industry is eyeing key eastern European countries. The U.S. industry can expect to see the Japanese and Europeans work hard to win more of the Mexican market, while recent Japanese and European plans for investment in the Brazilian automotive industry should heat up competition in Latin America.

PROJECTIONS OF INDUSTRY TRADE GROWTH FOR THE NEXT 1 AND 5 YEARS

The U.S. automotive parts industry has historically played a vital but little noted role in the U.S. economy. In 1997, industry shipments accounted for slightly over 4 percent of total U.S.

TABLE 37-2: Automotive Parts Industry (SIC 3465, 3592, 3647, 3691, 3694, 3714) Trends and Forecasts
(millions of dollars except as noted)

| | 1989 | 1992 | 1993 | 1994 | 1995 | 1996 | 1997[1] | 1998[2] | 1999[3] | Percent Change | | | Compound Annual Growth Rate |
										96–97	97–98	98–99	89–96
Industry data													
Value of shipments[4]	99,945	105,841	119,678	138,982	147,773	152,134	157,154	161,869	166,078	3.30	3.00	2.60	9.5
Value of shipments (1992$)	102,600	105,841	119,264	137,842	145,124	148,775	151,840	154,455	156,677	2.06	1.72	1.44	8.9
Total employment (thousands)	650	609	633	679	706	691							3.2
Production workers (thousands)	521	482	506	548	566	558							3.7
Average hourly earnings ($)	15.00	15.84	16.22	16.57	17.05	17.05							1.9
Capital expenditures	4,404	4,585	5,308	6,010	7,824	7,572							13.4
Product data													
Value of shipments[4]	94,379	104,109	118,293	134,462	143,859	148,201	152,647	157,074	161,001	3.00	2.90	2.50	9.2
Value of shipments (1992$)	96,802	104,109	117,882	133,371	141,294	144,954	147,201	150,310	153,042	1.55	2.11	1.82	8.6
Trade data													
Exports	14,266	22,437	26,064	27,927	29,323	30,285	35,150	38,489	40,183	16.06	9.50	4.40	10.0
Imports	20,365	21,055	23,461	27,267	28,800	30,837	33,093	34,913	35,961	7.32	5.50	3.00	7.8

[1] International Trade Administration (ITA) estimate except for trade data.
[2] Estimate.
[3] ITA forecast.
[4] For a definition of industry versus product values, see "Getting the Most Out of *Outlook '99*."
Source: U.S. Department of Commerce: Bureau of the Census; International Trade Administration.

manufacturing shipments and the 691,000 jobs provided by the industry accounted for almost 4 percent of total manufacturing employment. Among the top 50 global automotive parts suppliers, 19 are headquartered in the United States. These 19 U.S. companies accounted for 47 percent of the top 50 companies' worldwide sales in 1997. In addition, this industry is one of the largest U.S. export industries, accounting for 6.8 percent of total U.S. merchandise exports.

In 1997 industry shipments totaled a record $157 billion, a 3 percent increase over 1996 (see Table 37-2). North American sales by the top 50 U.S. automotive parts suppliers totaled $118 billion, up 11 percent from 1996. This upward trend is expected to continue through 1999, with industry shipments rising to $166 billion. By 2003 industry shipments should approach $189 billion. Modest growth in U.S. vehicle production, which is predicted to remain at around 12 million units annually, and a 2 to 3 percent annual growth rate in sales of aftermarket parts should sustain the domestic supplier industry over the next few years (see Tables 37-2 and 37-3).

During the industry's restructuring in the late 1980s and early 1990s, foreign trade became an important issue for the U.S. automotive parts suppliers (see Table 37-4). Not only was the influx of imports a catalyst in the industry's restructuring, but exports helped sustain the industry, jumping from 27 percent of total output in 1992 to 31 percent in 1997. Even with this growth in exports, the United States has posted a deficit in automotive parts trade since the early 1980s.

In 1997 U.S. exports of automotive parts totaled $47 billion, an increase of 13.9 percent from 1996. The majority of those exports were shipped to traditional U.S. automotive markets, with almost 73 percent going to North American Free Trade Agreement (NAFTA) partners Canada and Mexico and 9 per-

TABLE 37-3: North American Original Equipment Sales of Top 50 Suppliers in 1997
(millions of dollars)

Rank	Company	Sales
1	Delphi Automotive Systems	19,950
2	Visteon Automotive Systems	13,932
3	Dana Corp.	4,974
4	Johnson Controls Inc.	4,950
5	Lear Corp.	4,672
6	Delco Electronics Corp.	4,350
7	Magna International Inc.	3,740
8	TRW Inc.	3,516
9	Robert Bosch Corp.	3,300
10	Chrysler Component Operations	3,000
11	Eaton Corp.	2,913
12	Nippondenso Co. Ltd.	2,700
13	ITT Automotive	2,600
14	Goodyear Tire & Rubber Co.	2,200
15	Budd Co.	2,178
16	American Axle & Manufacturing Inc.	2,150
17	UT Automotive Inc.	2,020
18	Yazaki Corp.	1,980
19	LucasVarity Inc.	1,788
20	Motorola Inc.	1,680
21–50	Other	29,189

Source: Extracted from *CRA/Automotive News,* March 30, 1998, copyright Crain Communications, Inc., and company Web pages. All rights reserved.

cent going to the European Union. U.S. penetration of key Asian and Latin American markets has increased significantly in recent years: Between 1993 and 1997 U.S. parts exports to Japan grew 105 percent, shipments to ASEAN countries grew 85 percent, and exports to Brazil climbed nearly 175 percent. With respect to Latin America and Brazil, these growth trends have continued in 1998 and should continue in 1999, with total

TABLE 37-4: U.S. Trade Patterns in Automotive Parts and Accessories

(millions of dollars)

Regions	Exports[1] 1996	1997	Share of Total, %	Regions	Imports[2] 1996	1997	Share of Total, %
World	41,119	46,643	100.00	World	48,421	50,720	100.00
Asia and the Pacific				**Asia and the Pacific**			
Total ASEAN[3]	602	623	1.34	Total ASEAN[3]	1,267	1,251	2.47
Total Chinese Economic Area	522	882	1.89	Total Chinese Economic Area	1,556	1,691	3.33
Select Other Asia and the Pacific				Select Other Asia and the Pacific			
Australia	740	652	1.40	Australia	103	149	0.29
India	63	44	0.09	India	110	134	0.26
Japan	2,049	2,312	4.96	Japan	13,417	11,830	23.32
Korea	942	661	1.42	Korea	606	657	1.30
Europe				**Europe**			
Total European Union[4]	4,145	4,121	8.84	Total European Union[4]	5,483	5,877	11.59
Select Eastern Europe				Select Other Europe			
Hungary	39	54	0.12	Hungary	81	111	0.22
Poland	10	12	0.02	Poland	15	14	0.03
Russia	44	66	0.14	Russia	7	6	0.01
Western Hemisphere				**Western Hemisphere**			
Total Andean Community[5]	617	970	2.08	Total Andean Community[5]	150	168	0.33
Total MERCOSUR[6]	670	945	2.03	Total MERCOSUR[6]	979	1,277	2.52
Total Central America[7]	151	173	0.37	Total Central America[7]	19	25	0.05
Total NAFTA	29,307	33,969	72.83	Total NAFTA	24,284	27,139	53.51
All others	1,217	1,158	2.48	All Others	338	374	0.74
Top Five Countries				**Top Five Countries**			
Canada	22,228	24,387	52.28	Canada	12,639	13,825	27.26
Mexico	7,078	9,582	20.54	Mexico	11,645	13,314	26.25
Japan	2,049	2,312	4.96	Japan	13,417	11,830	23.32
Germany	898	1,006	2.16	Germany	2,544	2,616	5.16
Austria	899	757	1.62	Brazil	944	1,233	2.43

[1] Total exports, f.a.s.
[2] General imports, customs value.
[3] The ASEAN region includes Brunei, Indonesia, Malaysia, Philippines, Singapore, Thailand, and Vietnam.
[4] The European Union includes Belgium, Denmark, France, Germany, Greece, Ireland, Italy, Luxembourg, the Netherlands, Portugal, Spain, and the United Kingdom. As of 1995, Austria, Finland, and Sweden are included in the total.
[5] The Andean Community includes Bolivia, Colombia, Ecuador, Peru, and Venezuela.
[6] The MERCOSUR countries are Argentina, Brazil, Paraguay, and Uruguay.
[7] Central America includes Costa Rica, El Salvador, Guatemala, Honduras, and Panama.

exports of U.S. automotive parts exports expected to reach $51 billion and $53 billion, respectively. By 2003 exports should near $62 billion as original equipment parts demand increases. Much of this growth will be due to accelerating European light-vehicle production and sustained growth in vehicle output in rapidly developing countries such as Mexico, China, and Brazil. Demand for aftermarket parts should rise because of the increasing popularity of light vehicles in the rapidly growing markets of Asia and Latin America.

U.S. imports of automotive parts totaled $50.7 billion in 1997, up 4.8 percent from 1996. Again, the NAFTA countries were the source of the majority (53 percent) of these imports, with Mexico experiencing an 81 percent increase in exports to the United States since 1993. Shipments from Japan accounted for 23 percent of U.S. automotive parts imports. Other foreign suppliers have had increased penetration of the U.S. market since 1993, with imports from South America and ASEAN countries up 70 percent and 42 percent, respectively. U.S.

imports of automotive parts should continue to grow slowly, reaching an estimated $54 billion in 1998 and $55 billion in 1999. By 2003 imports are expected to reach $63 billion. With U.S. vehicle production expected to be flat at 12 million units, parts growth will be buoyed mostly by increased aftermarket demand (see Table 37-4).

GLOBAL MARKET PROSPECTS

The world's largest traditional markets, the United States and western Europe, have become mature, offering little opportunity for growth. Therefore, U.S. automotive parts suppliers are looking in other parts of the world for export and investment opportunities, especially in key Latin American and Asian countries. Vehicle sales in South America are predicted by DRI to grow 37 percent by 2003, with annual sales reaching 4 million units, up from just under 3 million in 1997. Production in 1997 totaled 2.8

million units; it is expected to decline slightly in 1998 and reach 2.9 million units in 1999 and 4 million in 2003. Forecasts for sales of vehicles in southeast Asia and Korea remain positive in the long term, with 85 percent growth expected by 2008. The Thai market is expected to recover to its 1996 levels between 2002 and 2004. Although short-term growth has been severely affected, most analysts agree that Asia will continue to be one of the world's fastest growing markets over the next decade.

U.S. suppliers' export efforts have been supplemented by recent trade agreements and other U.S. government initiatives. NAFTA, the Uruguay Round of the General Agreement on Tariffs and Trade, and the U.S.–Japan Automotive Framework Agreement were negotiated in the early and middle 1990s to facilitate trade and investment with and access to these major and emerging markets. New initiatives, including the Global Automotive Standards Agreement under the auspices of the Transatlantic Business Dialogue and the Asia-Pacific Economic Cooperation (APEC) Early Voluntary Sector Liberalization discussions in the automotive sector, may offer further opportunities for increased trade and investment.

Mexico

Brazil and Mexico and other Latin American markets hold the greatest potential for U.S. automotive parts manufacturers. Mexico has been one of the U.S. automotive industry's most significant foreign markets since the early 1980s. In their efforts to rationalize North American production, U.S. motor vehicle manufacturers and suppliers have regarded the Mexican market as part of their North American operations. Along with the Big Three, most leading U.S. automotive parts suppliers manufacture in Mexico, which has consistently been the second most important U.S. export market (behind Canada). Implementation of NAFTA in January 1994 further enhanced the importance of Mexico, providing U.S. suppliers with increased access to the growing Mexican market and an opportunity to structure their overall North American manufacturing operations to achieve economies of scale and maximize quality and international cost competitiveness.

Mexico is clearly on its way to a full recovery from the December 1994 devaluation of the peso and the subsequent economic crisis that severely affected its automotive industry. The industry's performance in 1997 was assisted by the increased availability of "cheaper" credit, interest-free factory financing, lower down payments, and extended payment terms, making vehicles more affordable. Mexican motor vehicle output increased 50 percent in 1997 over the 1996 level, and as a result U.S. parts exports rose 35 percent. The market performance in 1997 bodes well for future growth. Exports in 1997 exceeded 1994 levels by 25 percent and should continue to grow as the Mexican economy improves. With vehicle sales expected to reach pre-1995 levels in 1998, U.S. parts firms operating in Mexico should be able to attain predevaluation sales levels. On January 1, 1998, the 5-year staging for duty elimination on light trucks and many automotive parts was completed. Exports of U.S. automotive parts should continue to

grow, aided by the phasing out and elimination of all Mexican automotive parts tariffs by 2003. In the coming years U.S. producers of replacement parts should benefit from supplying the Mexican market for the increasing number of U.S.-made models now being sold in Mexico.

Mexico also promises to be a springboard for supplying other Latin American countries. The Mexican government has negotiated preferential trade agreements with Costa Rica, Colombia, Venezuela, and Chile and is negotiating similar agreements with other countries, including Ecuador and Peru and the MERCOSUR nations. Negotiations with the European Union may result in an agreement by 2000. As Mexico's preferential trade arrangements are fully implemented, cost advantages for producers in Mexico exporting to these countries will range from 10 to 35 percent in terms of duties saved.

Brazil

In recent years Brazil has emerged as one of the world's fastest growing automotive markets. Since 1990 vehicle production has more than doubled to reach 2.1 million units in 1997, making Brazil the world's number eight automobile producer. However, the Brazilian fiscal plan of November 1997 has slowed economic growth and vehicle production was expected to drop 10 percent to 1.86 million units in 1998. Despite this slowdown, by 2000 that country should be able to reach the number four global ranking, with new automotive investment expected to surpass $16 billion and motor vehicle sales conservatively estimated to top 2.5 million units. Car sales alone are expected to increase 45 percent to 2.6 million units by 2003. U.S. automotive parts exports to Brazil jumped 175 percent between 1993 and 1997 as a result of growth in the market in that period. U.S. investment in the Brazilian supplier industry also has increased. Ford, for example, brought 20 of its U.S. suppliers—including Budd Co., ITT Industries, Inc., and Johnson Controls—to Brazil to supply its Fiesta. TI Group Inc., a subsidiary of Bundy Corp., which built a plant in Brazil to supply Fiat's Palio "world car," hopes to land similar contracts with Fiat as Palio production spreads to Argentina and other Latin American countries.

U.S. parts exports to Brazil should continue their rapid increase as the Brazilian automotive boom continues into the twenty-first century. Recent investments by Honda, Chrysler, and Navistar should provide additional opportunities for U.S. parts exports, although exports will be limited by regional content requirements in the short term and by MERCOSUR rules of origin in the long term. U.S. firms that manufacture in Brazil will be aided in the short term by tariff reductions under the Brazilian government's automotive regime and motor vehicle manufacturers' plans to supply Brazil's MERCOSUR partners Argentina, Paraguay, and Uruguay. Future U.S. supplier investment is likely as rapid growth has put pressure on indigenous parts manufacturers to modernize their products and plants, and vehicle manufacturers in Brazil are pressing local suppliers to team up with foreign firms to improve their cost, quality, and just-in-time delivery competitiveness.

Under the recent Memorandum of Understanding Concerning Trade in the Automotive Sector between the U.S. government and the Brazilian government, parts manufacturers have until December 31, 1998, to apply for benefits under the current regime, while vehicle assembly companies had until June 30, 1998. Benefits for parts manufacturers include lower tariffs and "export" credits for imports or purchases of new capital equipment. On January 1, 2000, a common MERCOSUR automotive policy will go into effect. This policy has not been developed fully but will include the removal of most trade barriers among the four member countries and implementation of a common external tariff. Parts suppliers that have invested in Brazil or other MERCOSUR countries will be well positioned to take advantage of these markets.

Asia

The Asian markets that have the most favorable long-term potential are those of China and the nine-member ASEAN. Although the Asian economic crisis has severely affected short-term prospects for the region's automotive markets, the ASEAN region remains the most promising for U.S. automotive parts firms over the next decade. In the early 1990s the Big Three vehicle manufactures began assembling in that region, as did several leading U.S. suppliers, including Dana Corp., UT Automotive Inc., Lear Corp., and Delphi. Since 1993 exports of U.S. automotive parts to the ASEAN members have nearly doubled. U.S. automotive parts investment in and exports to the region are expected to expand as companies try to take advantage of the potential of the ASEAN members to become the hub of Asian automotive manufacturing.

That potential was based on forecasts that Thai and Indonesian vehicle production capacity would reach 1 million and 600,000 units, respectively, by 2000. Those forecasts have now been pushed out to between 2002 and 2004 for Thailand and even later for Indonesia. Thailand, the world's second largest pickup market (after the United States), is currently the most mature and largest ASEAN automotive market, followed by Indonesia, Malaysia, the Philippines, Vietnam, Singapore, and Brunei. Although the market forces affecting the economic recovery of the region remain uncertain, the region will continue to be the Asian base for manufacturers that plan to export components and finished vehicles in significant volume to the rest of Asia and other markets. Long-term opportunities, however, will not be easily realized. The ASEAN markets are proving difficult to penetrate because of Japan's virtual monopoly in the automotive sector, prohibitively high tariffs, stringent investment restrictions, and low annual per capita income. Foreign market penetration is especially difficult in two ASEAN countries—Indonesia and Malaysia—which have automotive programs that discriminate against foreign vehicles and parts. Although Indonesia's national car program has been abolished as a result of the International Monetary Fund (IMF) bailout package, the U.S. government is continuing to pursue World Trade Organization (WTO) action against other remaining automotive trade barriers contained in the 1993 automotive program. If these efforts are successful, U.S. automotive produc-

ers' interest in Indonesia may be revitalized. However, much depends on Indonesia's adherence to its agreements with the IMF and the time it takes that country's economy to recover. The APEC Early Voluntary Sector Liberalization discussions in the automotive sector (which include most of the ASEAN members), if successful, will lead to further liberalization in access to these markets.

Despite the recent financial crisis in Asia, the long-term outlook for U.S. automotive products in China remains strong. The Chinese market combines the world's highest rate of economic growth with one of the lowest vehicle-density rates, roughly 9 vehicles per 1,000 people. Analysts state that China has the potential to become one of the largest vehicle markets by 2010, with sales reaching 5 million new vehicles per year. In 1997, while vehicle production reached an estimated 1.47 million units, sales declined 1.54 percent, leading manufacturers to slash prices. Although U.S. exports of automotive parts have been limited by 20 to 30 percent tariff rates and restrictive local content requirements, U.S. exports to China increased 139 percent in 1997, growing from $130 million to $311 million. Increased opportunities will result from continued discussions to admit China to the WTO and to supply Shanghai GM, a joint venture between General Motors and Shanghai Automotive Industry Corporation, which is expected to generate an estimated $1 billion in U.S. exports over the next 5 years.

Trade Agreements

The 1994 passage of the Uruguay Round of GATT greatly improved the export and foreign investment prospects of the U.S. supplier industry in most of the world's major and emerging automotive markets. The Uruguay Round agreement, which established the WTO, included a 58 percent reduction in the automotive parts tariffs in major markets and put a ceiling on tariffs in many developing countries. In agreeing to these provisions, major automotive markets made a commitment to keep import duties on their automotive parts below certain ("bound") rates. The Uruguay Round provisions on trade-related investment measures (TRIMs) and dispute settlement procedures should help eliminate nontariff trade barriers that have long plagued U.S. automotive parts firms in foreign markets. This agreement requires the elimination of performance requirements such as local content and foreign exchange balancing requirements. The dispute settlement procedures improve the enforcement of these WTO agreements and ensure that governments will take action—either removing a barrier or negotiating compensation—when foreign barriers to U.S. exports are found to be illegal.

In 1996 the U.S. government examined the legality of the automotive regimes of several foreign countries under the WTO. The United States held several rounds of consultations with Brazil (in which the European Union and Japan also participated) on its automotive regime and with Indonesia on its national car program, completing the preliminary steps needed to request the formation of WTO Dispute Settlement Panels in both cases. As a result of bilateral consultations between the United States and Brazil, the WTO case was dropped, and early in 1998 the two countries entered into a memorandum of understanding concerning the Brazilian regime. On January 15, 1998, as part of its agreement to receive $43 billion in financing from the IMF, Indonesia agreed to end support for its WTO-violating national car program. However, the U.S. government is continuing to pursue WTO action against Indonesia's 1993 automotive program (which predates the national car program by 3 years) and is seeking to redress the nearly $1 billion in benefits which have already been granted under that program. The U.S. government is currently analyzing India's automotive regime for TRIMs violations and will continue to pursue any violations that impede the conduct of U.S. automotive business interests. In addition, the expected accessions to the WTO of key emerging countries, such as China and several eastern European countries, should continue to help U.S. manufacturers gain a stronger foothold in those markets.

The U.S.–Japan Automotive Framework Agreement has improved opportunities for U.S. automotive parts suppliers with the Japanese industry both in Japan and in the United States. Since the 1995 signing of the agreement, significant progress has been made in improving opportunities for U.S. original equipment parts suppliers in Japan and Japanese transplants in the United States as well as in eliminating regulations that restricted access to the parts aftermarket in Japan. U.S. parts companies that had been unsuccessful in penetrating the Japanese market reported significant new contracts and sales opportunities during the first 2 years of the agreement. The Japanese Ministry of Transport has completed deregulatory actions that should provide new opportunities for U.S. firms in Japan's lucrative aftermarket. However, the current economic crisis in Japan has significantly decreased the opportunities for U.S. parts suppliers.

As the automotive industry has become more global, differing safety and environmental standards have become a major impediment to automotive trade. What began under the auspices of the Transatlantic Business Dialogue, which was initiated in late 1995, has evolved into a proposal for a Global Automotive Standards Agreement. Under the Transatlantic Business Dialogue, U.S. and European industries and governments began discussions on international automotive regulatory harmonization. These discussions included the intergovernmental regulatory process necessary to achieve such harmonization and the coordination of vehicle safety and environmental research. In March 1998 the United States, the European Union, and Japan approved the text of an Agreement on Global Technical Regulations to supplement the revised 1958 United Nations/Economic Commission for Europe Working Party on the Construction of Vehicles (known as Working Party 29) to provide for the development of global technical regulations for motor vehicles and motor vehicle equipment (automotive parts). The text of the agreement is still subject to a final round of comments from interested governments. The establishment of harmonized or functionally equivalent standards should increase the U.S. industry's export potential to European and other markets as well as reduce the costs of regulatory compliance for the industry, give consumers more choices and lower prices, uphold and improve safety and environmental standards, and improve the competitiveness of producers.

OUTLOOK FOR U.S. AFTERMARKET SUPPLIERS

The U.S. automotive parts aftermarket consists of some 2,000 firms that manufacture exclusively for the replacement parts market and numerous original equipment parts manufacturers that also supply the aftermarket. Depending on how the industry is defined, the size of the market in 1997 was estimated to range from $151 billion to $249 billion. According to the Automotive Parts & Accessories Association (APAA), 1996 retail sales of replacement parts and accessories reached $143 billion, up 6 percent from 1995. Major segments of the aftermarket include the service repair market, the tire aftermarket, and the do-it-yourself market.

Traditionally, growth in U.S. aftermarket sales has been directly related to the size and age of the vehicle fleet as well as the number of miles driven. In 1996 the 198 million passenger vehicles on U.S. roads had an average age of 8.5 years and had been driven a total of 2.5 trillion miles, up from 157 million vehicles, 7.8 years, and 1.8 trillion miles in 1985. Despite these increases, growth of U.S. aftermarket sales continues to hover around the 3 percent average annual level. The primary reason for this relatively low level of growth has been the dramatic improvement in quality and durability of original equipment parts, with vehicle manufacturers' specifications for a part's life rising from 50,000 miles to 100,000 miles in certain product lines. These improvements will hold average annual U.S. sales growth at around 2 percent into the twenty-first century. Weather is also a factor that can influence the aftermarket. Some producers are blaming lower sales of replacement parts in 1997 and early 1998 on the warmer weather caused by El Niño. Sales of parts that suffer the greatest stress during extreme cold, such as batteries, brakes, and brake pads, are reportedly down.

Consolidation and competition will remain major issues for U.S. aftermarket suppliers over the long term. In recent years, U.S. aftermarket manufacturers, like original equipment suppliers, have been undergoing a dramatic restructuring. The APAA estimates the value of mergers and acquisitions among aftermarket manufacturers between 1995 and 1997 to have totaled almost $18 billion (for SIC 3714 only), with the number of such deals continuing to increase. Similar consolidations are expected to continue into the next decade as firms regroup to reduce costs and debt and enhance their competitive positions at home and abroad. Competition in the aftermarket has increased dramatically in the 1990s. Original equipment suppliers, squeezed by automakers' restructuring plans, are vying for a greater share of the replacement parts market. Also, many U.S. aftermarket parts manufacturers have found it difficult to supply the increasing number of Japanese imports in the U.S. fleet, since replacement parts for Japanese imports historically have been manufactured by Japanese original equipment suppliers.

However, the 1995 signing of the U.S.–Japan Automotive Framework Agreement has aided U.S. aftermarket manufacturers in their efforts to supply parts for Japanese vehicles in the United States, in Japan, and in other markets where Japanese vehicles are sold. The agreement encourages Japanese automakers to purchase more U.S. parts for use in their U.S.-based operations, some of which will be used to supply the aftermarket for transplant and imported Japanese vehicles, and makes it easier for Japanese consumers to modify their vehicles with independent aftermarket parts and accessories. As of August 1996, the Japanese Ministry of Transport (MOT) had released eight parts—shock absorbers, struts, trailer hitches, power steering systems, torque rods, stabilizers, torsion bar springs, and clutches for motorcycles—from the requirement to use government-approved mechanics and garages to remove or replace certain critical, or safety-related, parts. MOT also has liberalized its regulations regarding the number of government-qualified mechanics for approved garages and the requirements for government-approved garages. This includes the creation of specialized certified garages that need only facilities appropriate for the repair of any one or more of the seven, rather than all seven, critical parts systems. These changes should increase the opportunities for U.S. suppliers to break into the $60 billion Japanese aftermarket as they allow smaller, independent garages and automotive parts stores that tend to use a larger percentage of imported parts to perform work they formerly could not; the changes also create an incentive for more garages to carry competitive foreign parts. As the U.S. and Japanese governments continue to monitor progress under the agreement, MOT is expected to further deregulate its aftermarket. For example, MOT held public hearings in May 1998 to solicit views from U.S. and Japanese automotive parts associations and other interested parties in which MOT proposed a parts type designation system that would be the same as the one currently used in Europe. This new set of regulations would make it easier for U.S. companies, especially those producing parts in Europe, to import their parts into Japan.

One of the best growth markets for U.S. aftermarket parts manufacturers is Mexico as a result of NAFTA. Between 1997 and 2003 the Mexican aftermarket is expected to more than double to $11.4 billion as the Mexican fleet of 13 million vehicles grows and ages. U.S. parts currently account for about 23 percent of the replacement parts market, as the Mexican fleet contains a high level of U.S.-origin parts. As the Mexican automotive industry recovers from the peso devaluation and subsequent market collapse and Mexican duties on automotive parts are phased out under NAFTA, U.S. exports of replacement parts are expected to exceed pre-1995 growth levels. In addition, increasing use of Mexico as an automotive export platform to other Latin American markets should help pave the way for increased sales of U.S. parts in these markets.

Robin L. Gaines, U.S. Department of Commerce, Automotive Parts and Suppliers Division, (202) 482-1418, June 1998.

■ REFERENCES

Automotive News, Crain Communications Inc., 965 E. Jefferson, Detroit, MI 48207-3185, (800) 678-9595.

The Autoparts Report, International Trade Services, P.O. Box 5950, Bethesda, MD 20824-5950. (301) 857-8454.

Impact of the North American Free Trade Agreement on U.S. Automotive Exports to Mexico: Fourth Annual Report to Congress, U.S. Department of Commerce, International Trade Administration. (202) 482-1418, http://www.ita.doc.gov/auto.

Motor and Equipment Manufacturers Association, P.O. Box 13966, Research Triangle Park, NC 27709-3966. (919) 549-4800.

Motor Vehicle Facts and Figures, 1997 (annual), American Automobile Manufacturers Association, Suite 900, 1401 H Street, NW, Washington, DC 20005. (202) 326-5500.

1998 APAA Aftermarket Factbook, Automotive Parts and Accessories Association, 4600 East-West Highway, Third Floor, Bethesda, MD 20814. (301) 654-6664

Report to President William Jefferson Clinton of the Interagency Enforcement Team Regarding the U.S.-Japan Agreement on Autos and Auto Parts, April 12, 1996 (four subsequent reports have been written), U.S. Department of Commerce, International Trade Administration. (202) 482-0554, http://www.ita.doc.gov/auto.

The Shape and Size of the USA Motor Vehicle Aftermarket: A Profile, 1998 Edition, Automotive Service Industry Association, 25 Northwest Point Boulevard, Suite 425, Elk Grove Village, IL 60007-1035. (847) 228-1310

U.S. Department of Commerce, Office of Automotive Affairs, http://www.ita.doc.gov/auto.

U.S.-Japan Automotive Agreement and Supporting Documents, August 23, 1995, U.S. Department of Commerce, International Trade Administration. (202) 482-0554, http://www.ita.doc.gov/auto.

Ward's Automotive Reports (weekly), *Ward's Automotive International* (bimonthly), and *Ward's Automotive Yearbook,* Ward's Communications, Suite 2750, 3000 Town Center, Southfield, MI 48075. (313) 962-4433.

World Motor Vehicle Data 1996 (annual), American Automobile Manufacturers Association, Suite 900, 1401 H Street, NW, Washington, DC 20005. (202) 326-5500.

■ RELATED CHAPTERS

12: Rubber
13: Steel Mill Products
14: Nonferrous Metals
36: Motor Vehicles
43: Transportation

HOUSEHOLD CONSUMER DURABLES
Economic and Trade Trends

U.S. International Trade

Source: U.S. Department of Commerce: Bureau of the Census; International Trade Administration.

World Export Market Shares

Source: United Nations; U.S. Department of Commerce, International Trade Administration.

Export Dependence and Import Penetration

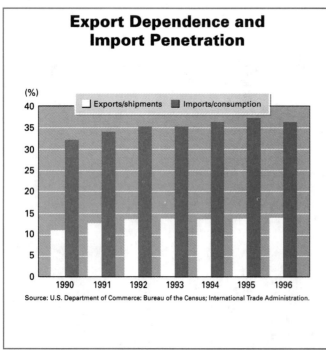

Source: U.S. Department of Commerce: Bureau of the Census; International Trade Administration.

Output and Output per Hour

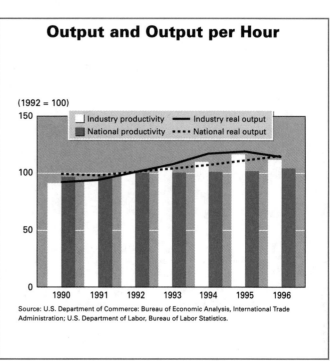

Source: U.S. Department of Commerce: Bureau of Economic Analysis, International Trade Administration; U.S. Department of Labor, Bureau of Labor Statistics.

See "Getting the Most Out of *Outlook '99*" for definitions of terms.

Household Consumer Durables

INDUSTRY DEFINITION The household consumer durables sector includes household furniture (SIC 251), household appliances (SIC 363), household audio and video equipment (SIC 3651), and lawn and garden equipment (SIC 3524).

OVERVIEW

The four household durable goods industries in this chapter are cyclical industries. All are highly affected by such factors as housing activity, employment, consumer disposable income, and consumer confidence levels. Since these household products are often large purchases, consumer interest rates and credit availability are also important.

The year 1998 was another good one for these industries as the economic expansion that began in 1991 continued. Economic indicators were generally quite favorable with several reaching record highs or at least cyclical highs. Especially strong were the stock market, housing sales, employment, and consumer confidence levels. Housing starts were quite strong, although not as high as in the boom years of the 1970s and 1980s. Housing starts and home sales were aided by low mortgage interest rates. These low rates resulted in substantial amounts of mortgage refinancing, which increased available consumer spending for other goods and services.

The major dark cloud on the horizon is the economic crisis in Asia which began in 1997 when Thailand devalued its currency. Several other Asian countries were sucked into the economic turmoil as their currencies and securities markets plummeted in value. Unfortunately, it does not appear that Japan will be of much help in pulling the other Asian countries out of their economic crisis since Japan's own economy has been stagnant in recent years. Even if the economic crisis does not spread directly into other regions, it will ultimately have an adverse effect on several countries, including the United States, because of international trade. Because of the changes in cur-

rency values in foreign exchange markets and falling demand in Asia, some sharp changes in imports and exports have already resulted. Several U.S. companies reported substantial declines in sales to Asian customers in 1998 as U.S. exports to Asia were adversely affected by the crisis. At the same time, U.S. imports from Asia have increased sharply in several industries. These trade trends are not expected to be reversed soon since the recent currency adjustments are likely to prove to be long-term in nature, having resulted from fundamental banking and financial market problems and the increasing competitive pressure of steadily rising Chinese exports.

HOUSEHOLD FURNITURE

The household furniture industry (SIC 251) comprises manufacturers of wood furniture (SIC 2511), upholstered wood furniture (SIC 2512), metal furniture (SIC 2514), mattresses, foundations, and convertible beds (2515), wood television, radio, and sewing machine cabinets (SIC 2517), and miscellaneous household furniture (SIC 2519).

Factors Affecting Future Industry Growth

U.S. furniture manufacturers' shipments totaled an estimated $28.5 billion in 1998 as a strong economy translated into an estimated increase in real (inflation-adjusted) shipments of 4 percent over 1997 shipments. A number of factors contributed to the rosy scenario for furniture shipments. (See the boxed note: "Factors Affecting Furniture Demand.") With mortgage rates nearing their lowest levels of the decade and home prices still at moderate levels, houses were more affordable than they had been at any time since the mid-1970s: according to the Harvard University Joint Center for Housing Studies, the after-tax cost of a mortgage was taking about 22 percent of income in 1997, down from a peak of 34 percent in the early 1980s. The rate of the common 30-year fixed-rate mortgage has remained below 8 percent since early 1997, and was between 7.0 percent and 7.3 percent for the first half of 1998, according to HSH Associates, a Butler, NJ, research firm.

A combination of low mortgage rates and moderately increasing home prices, together with demographic factors, led to a record level of home ownership—65.9 percent of American households, according to first-quarter data from the U.S. Census Bureau. The National Association of Realtors (NAR) projected 4.53 million existing-home sales for 1998, which represented a 7.5 percent increase over the record of 4.22 million sales posted in 1997. According to NAR president R. Layne Morrill, this heavy activity is fueled in part by increasing numbers of nontraditional households entering the market—such as immigrants, singles, and older people trading down—reflecting a shift that will continue in years to come. The year 1998 would mark the seventh in a row that existing home sales have exceeded the 3.5 million level. According to NAR consulting economist John A. Tuccillo, this is the level at which such sales provide a significant stimulus to other sectors of the economy, such as furniture, appliances, and other home furnishings. New homes were also sold at a record pace as of May 1998, at a seasonally adjusted annual rate of 890,000 units. That was the ninth straight month that sales exceeded the 800,000-unit annual rate, a record streak. Combined sales of new and existing homes were projected to reach a record level of nearly 5.4 million in 1998 (see Figure 38-1).

Like the housing market, the economy in general was very strong in the first part of 1998. Spurred by low unemployment, which reached 4.3 percent—its lowest level in 28 years—the Conference Board's Consumer Confidence Index reached a 29-year high of 137.6 (1985 = 100) in June (see Figure 38-2). Real disposable income growth was also strong in the first quarter of 1998 (see Figure 38-3). That, combined with the wealth effect of strong growth in stock prices the last 4 years, has left con-

sumers flush with income to spend and feeling wealthier, thus enabling purchases of large-ticket items such as furniture. Furthermore, the historically high ratio of consumer credit to personal income has been falling over the last 2 years, giving consumers more breathing room to take on more credit for purchases such as furniture (see Figure 38-4).

The major negative consideration for the furniture industry is the possible effects of the Asian financial crisis. As a result, the dollar achieved an 8-year high against the yen in 1998, surpassing 140, and is expected to remain strong against many currencies. This tends to make U.S. imports less expensive and exports more expensive. Furthermore, the weakness in many

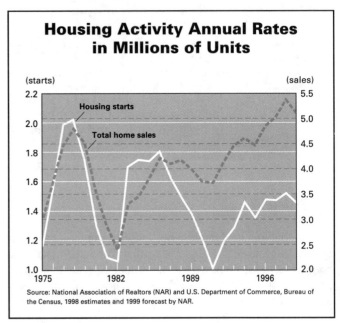

Housing Activity Annual Rates in Millions of Units

(starts) / (sales)

Housing starts

Total home sales

Source: National Association of Realtors (NAR) and U.S. Department of Commerce, Bureau of the Census, 1998 estimates and 1999 forecast by NAR.

FIGURE 38-1

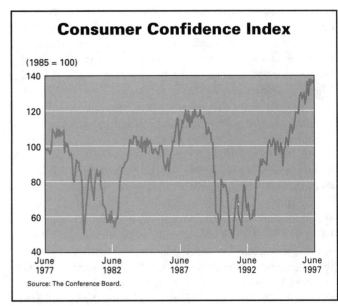

Consumer Confidence Index

(1985 = 100)

Source: The Conference Board.

FIGURE 38-2

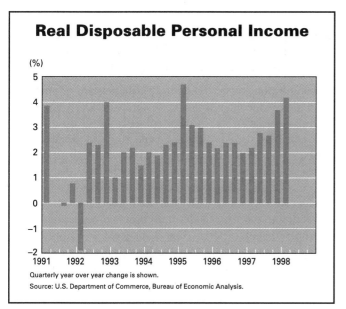

Real Disposable Personal Income

(%)

Quarterly year over year change is shown.

Source: U.S. Department of Commerce, Bureau of Economic Analysis.

FIGURE 38-3

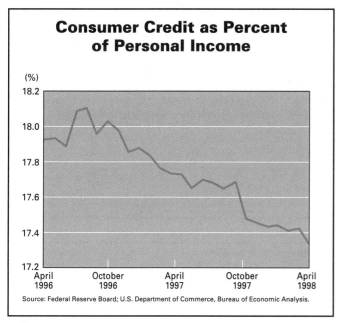

Consumer Credit as Percent of Personal Income

(%)

Source: Federal Reserve Board; U.S. Department of Commerce, Bureau of Economic Analysis.

FIGURE 38-4

Asian economies means demand is off, and since the U.S. economy is relatively strong, many of the Asian exporters will look to the U.S. market to make up for lost sales in their region. U.S. exports were still expected to be up by about 10 percent in 1998, largely on the strength of sales to Canada and Mexico, the largest and the third largest foreign destinations for U.S. furniture, respectively. Imports were also expected to be up substantially in 1998 because of strong domestic demand and low prices for imports because of the strong U.S. dollar.

Ironically, the initial impact of the Asian crisis has boosted domestic furniture demand by lowering interest rates and thus spurring housing activity. According to the American Furniture

Manufacturers Association (AFMA), total furniture shipments for the first 4 months of 1998 were up 15 percent and orders were up 17 percent. For upholstery products alone, shipments were up 17 percent and orders had jumped 25 percent from the same period in 1997. The effects of the Asian slowdown are expected to be felt on final demand in the second half of 1998 and into 1999. Early indications were that furniture orders in May had already begun to slow.

Global Industry Trends

International trade has been increasingly important to the furniture industry. U.S. imports, especially from China, have shown dramatic growth and account for an increasing share of U.S. consumption of furniture (see Figure 38-5). Imports now account for about 1 of every 5 dollars of apparent consumption, up from about 1 in 7 dollars in 1992. Part of the import growth is accounted for by U.S. manufacturers, which often import parts or import certain pieces to augment their product lines. Exports are less of a factor, accounting for about 1 out of every 16 dollars in U.S. manufacturers' shipments. Still, exports have contributed positively to U.S. producers' sales growth, increasing at a compound annual rate of 11 percent from 1990 to 1997.

The reduction of trade barriers, especially tariffs, under various trade programs and agreements have lowered or eliminated U.S. tariffs to most countries and lowered or eliminated tariffs on U.S. furniture products in many foreign markets. These programs and agreements include the Generalized System of Preferences, U.S.-Canada Free Trade Agreement, North American Free Trade Agreement (NAFTA), and Uruguay Round Market Access Agreements under the General Agreement on Tariffs and Trade (GATT; now called the World Trade Organization, or WTO). Under the U.S. Generalized System of Preferences, developing countries have had duty-free access to the U.S. mar-

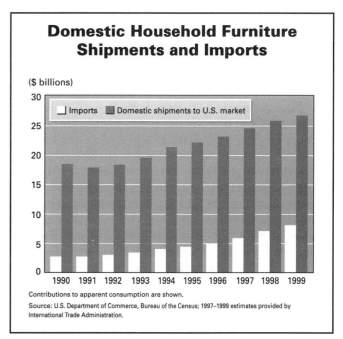

Domestic Household Furniture Shipments and Imports

($ billions)

Imports   Domestic shipments to U.S. market

Contributions to apparent consumption are shown.

Source: U.S. Department of Commerce, Bureau of the Census; 1997–1999 estimates provided by International Trade Administration.

FIGURE 38-5

ket on furniture products since 1976. Tariff reductions under the U.S.-Canada Free Trade Agreement removed tariffs on household furniture as of January 1, 1993. Beginning in 1994, Mexican tariffs on certain furniture products were eliminated and on others were lowered in stages of 5 years or 10 years. As a result, in 1998 Mexican tariffs on most furniture trade were either already zero or reduced to 8 or 6 percent ad valorem from their original rates of 20 and 15 percent, respectively. By 2003, Mexican tariffs on all U.S. furniture products will be completely eliminated. Under the Uruguay Round of multilateral trade negotiations, the United States, Canada, the European Union, Hong Kong, Japan, Korea, Norway, Singapore, and Switzerland agreed to eliminate their furniture tariffs to Most Favored Nation countries over a 5-year period beginning in 1995.

In addition to these completed negotiations, the U.S. government is negotiating to reduce or eliminate furniture tariffs with a number of countries that want to join the WTO. Significant furniture markets among these include China, Taiwan, Saudi Arabia, and countries of eastern Europe and the former Soviet Union. Furniture is also included in negotiations for nine initial sectors slated for early voluntary sectoral liberalization among Asian Pacific Economic Cooperation (APEC) members. APEC countries with good prospects for furniture exports whose tariffs are not already scheduled for elimination include Australia, Chile, China, Indonesia, Malaysia, the Philippines, Taiwan, and Thailand. In the Western Hemisphere, the U.S. government and 33 other democratically elected governments have agreed to liberalize trade in the Americas under the Free Trade Area of the Americas by 2005. Together, these agreements and negotiations offer the promise of virtually worldwide free trade for the furniture industry in the twenty-first century. With the advent of tariff-free trade, issues of implementation, compliance, and enforcement come to the fore and nontariff issues, such as standards, labeling, and certification, will become more important. Labor and environmental issues are expected to play increasingly prominent roles.

Domestic Trends

Distribution. The consolidation of the retail residential furniture industry has made access to distribution channels an important competitive advantage for manufacturers. Some major companies are integrating forward into retailing both through company-owned stores and through partnerships with independently owned dealers and chains. A pioneer in this trend is Ethan Allen, which sells its products in free-standing stores, 20 percent of which are company-owned. An example of partnering is the February 1998 announcement of a strategic alliance between the number one manufacturer, Furniture Brands International, and Havertys, a major regional retailer, that eventually will result in half of Havertys' floor space being devoted to furniture from Thomasville, Broyhill, and Lane, the three companies owned by Furniture Brands International. These are further steps in the trend toward establishing brand awareness at the retail level through dedicated space that was begun in the 1980s with the gallery concept.

While consolidation is occurring in the traditional retail channels, new distribution channels such as electronic retailers, wholesale clubs, catalog retailers, and television home shopping are opening up and becoming important.

Consolidation. The trends in distribution are driving consolidation in the manufacturing sector, particularly among the largest manufacturers. In order to serve the diverse distribution channels such as furniture centers, independent dealers, national and local chain stores, department stores, specialty stores, and decorator showrooms, supported by dedicated sales forces covering each channel, companies need to have a broad product line. Companies benefit from economies of scale in marketing to the trade under one corporate banner and to the consumer under different brands targeted to different consumers. According to the trade publication *Furniture/Today,* the top 25 manufacturers' market share grew from 40 percent in 1990 to 46 percent in 1997 (see Table 38-1).

In November 1996, Chromcraft Revington acquired Cochrane, a producer of case goods and upholstered furniture. In 1997 the high-end upholstery producer Sherrill acquired Hickory White. Showing a hint of internationalism, the ready-to-assemble (RTA) specialist Bush Furniture acquired a 51 percent interest in the German furniture producer Rohr Gruppe. Bush continued its external growth with the purchase in 1998 of RTA producer Fournier. Also in 1998, La-Z-Boy acquired Sam Moore, a producer of upscale upholstered occasional chairs and Centurion Furniture, PLC, an English producer of upholstered furniture that supplies to outlets in the United Kingdom and Europe.

TABLE 38-1: Top 10 U.S. Furniture Manufacturers Based on 1997 Sales

(millions of dollars; excludes nonfurniture sales)

Manufacturers and Companies Owned	1997 Shipments
Furniture Brands International	1,808.3
Broyhill, Lane, Thomasville	
LifeStyle Furnishings International, Ltd.	1,693.6
Beacon Hill Showrooms, BenchCraft, Berkline, Drexel Heritage, Henredon, La Barge, Lexington, LifeStyle Contract Furnishings, Maitland-Smith, Robert Allen/Ametex, Sunbury, Universal	
La-Z-Boy, Inc.	1,074.0
Centurion, England/Corsair, Hammary, Kincaid, La-Z-Boy Canada; acquired Sam Moore Furniture in 1998	
Klaussner	668.0
Klaussner of California, Klaussner International, Stylecraft, Paoli, Realistic; acquired DJI in 1998	
Ashley Furniture Industries, Inc.	530.0
Ashley, Millennium	
LADD Furniture, Inc.	525.5
American Drew, American of Martinsville, Barclay, Clayton Marcus, Lea Inds., Pennsylvania House, Pilliod	
Ethan Allen Interiors, Inc.	511.9
Ethan Allen, Knob Creek	
Sauder	475.0
Bassett Furniture Industries, Inc.	446.9
Bassett, E.B. Malone	
O'Sullivan Industries	320.4

Source: *Furniture/Today,* May 11, 1998.

Despite these trends toward consolidation, particularly at the top, the furniture industry still consists of mostly small manufacturing facilities. According to the Census Bureau's 1995 County Business Patterns, less than 2 percent of furniture manufacturing plants had more than 500 employees and two-thirds had less than 20 employees. The most recent census data on concentration in the industry (1992) indicated that for most furniture categories the eight largest manufacturers account for between 31 and 36 percent of total industry shipments. This compares to 98 percent for household refrigerator and freezer producers and 91 percent for the motor vehicle industry. By factoring in the import penetration for the furniture industry, concentration is even less.

Regulation. Two major regulatory issues could have an impact on the U.S. furniture industry. The Consumer Product Safety Commission is investigating whether it should require upholstery fabrics to be treated with fire-retardant chemicals. The furniture and decorative fabrics industries are opposed to such a requirement because of the unknown toxicity effects of such chemicals, the effect on the aesthetic or tactile qualities and pricing of treated furniture, and the significant costs that would be imposed especially on the mostly small manufacturers even if the other concerns could be overcome. Through the Upholstered Furniture Action Council (UFAC), the furniture and fabric industries already have a voluntary program of fire safety standards, and they argue such a voluntary approach has worked well in the past and should continue. Currently, only the United Kingdom and Ireland require such treatment for residential upholstered furniture. The European Union Commission rejected harmonizing on the U.K. standards for all Europe because of concerns about the possible long-term health and economic effects. Instead, many safety authorities endorsed the voluntary standards patterned after the UFAC program in the United States.

The second major issue has to do with Environmental Protection Agency (EPA) regulations to enforce the 1990 Amendments to the Clean Air Act. The EPA has proposed regulations for the combustion of wood, a significant by-product of the furniture manufacturing process. In addition, it is requiring reductions in airborne pollutants that are a by-product of the coating and finishing operations for virtually all wood and metal furniture products beginning in 1998 and continuing into the first decade of the next century. The industry will need to develop a water-based coating or some other compliant coating to meet the new standards. Such changes require additional administrative and research and development (R&D) costs, which may be burdensome, especially for the many small furniture producers.

Projections of Industry and Trade Growth for Next 1 and 5 Years

U.S. furniture shipments are expected to slow to a 2 percent growth rate in 1999 in constant dollars. U.S. imports will continue to increase significantly, though they are expected to slow to 15 percent, down from the 20 percent estimated growth in 1998. U.S. exports are also expected to slow, to 5 percent from an estimated 10 percent growth in 1998 (see Table 38-2).

Several factors point to a slowdown in the recent strong growth of furniture industry shipments. Foremost is the Asian financial crisis, which was expected to slow the growth of the U.S. economy from its strong first-half showing and into 1999. This is partly due to a slowdown in exports and continued growth in imports because of weaker foreign economies and the stronger dollar. In addition, the housing sector is expected to cool off from its torrid pace of the last 2 years as demand by those who took advantage of low interest rates becomes satisfied and interest rates rise again. Finally, the U.S. economy will

TABLE 38-2: Household Furniture (SIC 251) Trends and Forecasts
(millions of dollars except as noted)

	1992	1993	1994	1995	1996	1997[1]	1998[2]	1999[3]	Percent Change 96–97	97–98	98–99	92–96[4]
Industry data												
Value of shipments[5]	20,507	21,906	23,603	24,458	25,426	27,033	28,508	29,514	6.3	5.5	3.5	5.5
Value of shipments (1992$)	20,507	21,373	22,363	22,563	23,010	24,161	25,127	25,629	5.0	4.0	2.0	2.9
Total employment (thousands)	253	255	267	271	273	273.8			0.3			1.9
Production workers (thousands)	213	217	229	231	232	234.3			1.0			2.2
Average hourly earnings ($)	8.36	8.77	8.83	8.89	9.21	9.56			3.8			2.5
Capital expenditures	346	393	436	528	481							8.6
Product data												
Value of shipments[5]	19,517	20,825	22,690	23,530	24,571	26,164	27,591	28,565	6.5	5.5	3.5	5.9
Value of shipments (1992$)	19,517	20,328	21,508	21,739	22,270	23,384	24,319	24,805	5.0	4.0	2.0	3.4
Trade data												
Value of imports	2,995	3,397	3,965	4,448	4,988	5,882	7,058	8,117	17.9	20.0	15.0	13.6
Value of exports	1,113	1,183	1,307	1,320	1,326	1,530	1,683	1,767	15.4	10.0	5.0	4.5

[1] Estimate except imports and exports.
[2] Estimate.
[3] Forecast.
[4] Compound annual rate.
[5] For definition of industry versus product values, see "Getting the Most Out of *Outlook '99*."
Source: U.S. Department of Commerce: Bureau of the Census; International Trade Administration.

be in its ninth year of expansion (assuming continuation through the fourth quarter of 1999), tying with the period 1961–1969 for the longest continuous postwar expansion. Beginning in 2000, the economy will be in unchartered territory, raising the chances of a downturn that year. Furthermore, some analysts have increased their estimates of a recession in 2000 based on problems associated with converting software systems to accommodate four digits for that year.

Over the long term, demographics play an important role in demand for household durable goods such as furniture. The postwar baby boom, comprising individuals born in the years 1946–1964, has had an impact on economic growth in every stage of these people's lives. In addition, the baby boom echo, essentially the children of the baby boomers, born between 1979 and 1995, will also have a significant effect on economic activity. The baby boomers fueled the growth of the housing market in the 1970s and the growth in size of homes during the 1980s, and are driving the growth of vacation homes and luxury goods in the 1990s. The leading edge of the baby boom, those in the 45–54 age group, are in their peak earning years and generally have the highest levels of discretionary income. This age group is expected to grow rapidly over the next 5- and 10-year periods (see Figure 38-6), fueling growth in higher-priced furniture. A 1998 *Washington Post* article reported that the luxury mattress market—defined as mattress and box spring sets selling for more than $1,500—is the fastest growing segment of the mattress business. It noted that consumers are paying as much as $6,000 for an ultrapremium set with hand-tied English coils, German foam, plush French tufting, and gold thread embroidery.

Those in the 35–45 age group are the largest segment of the population and also the age group that tends to spend the most on furniture (see Figure 38-7). This age group will peak in the year 2000 and decline slightly during the subsequent 5 years, but will still maintain its place as the largest 10-year cohort.

Figure 38-6 shows the 5–14 age group increasing between 1995 and 2000 and the 15–24 age group increasing between 2000 and 2005 relative to the total population as the baby boom echo children grow up. This is adding to spending by the baby boomers on categories such as youth furniture, ready-to-assemble furniture, and entertainment centers. With the baby boomers aging (note the growth in the 55–64 age group in Figure 38-6) and increased life expectancy, demand for health-care-type furniture is expected to grow.

Figure 38-6 also shows the decline of the 25–34 age group, the so-called Generation X. This is a prime age group for marriages, starting families, and entry or relocation in the job market. The lower number of people in this generation has led to slower household formations and slower growth in the labor force. While total households increased 7.4 percent between 1990 and 1996, households headed by those in the 25–34 age group declined by the same percentage. The Bureau of Labor Statistics projects growth in the labor force from 1996 to 2006 to be 11 percent. This change is compared with the 14 percent growth rate over the 1986–1996 period. The labor force 25 to 34 years of age is expected to decline by almost 3 million, or 9 percent, during the same period. Such changes are largely responsible for the increasingly tight labor markets in the late 1990s. Although strong expenditures by baby boomers are currently masking the effects of Generation X on furniture expenditures, these demographics are likely to have a negative impact beyond 2005 as baby boomers' influence wanes.

Global Market Prospects

The reduction of trade barriers through international agreements has opened up many foreign markets for U.S. furniture. The democratization and privatization of countries in the former Soviet Union, eastern Europe, and Latin America have created new opportunities in those markets. Furthermore, many

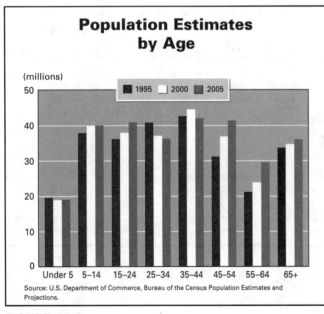

FIGURE 38-6

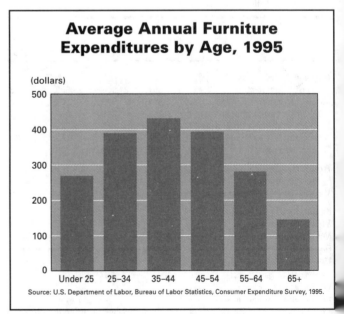

FIGURE 38-7

developing economies are maturing, creating a growing consumer class with purchasing power and a taste for American culture, styles, and products. Traditionally, the rapidly growing Asian economies have been a source of export growth for the furniture industry. However, the Asian financial crisis has curtailed exports to most of the Asian markets except China. U.S. exports to Asia grew at a compound annual rate of 25 percent between 1992 and 1996, then slowed to a 1 percent growth rate in 1997, and dropped 22 percent during the first quarter of 1998. Despite high trade barriers, exports of furniture to China grew at a 45 percent compound annual rate between 1992 and 1997 and more than tripled in the first quarter of 1998 compared to the same period in 1997 (see Table 38-3).

Some of the most rapid growth has been to the markets in South America. For example, exports to Brazil, the largest South American market for U.S. furniture, grew at a compound annual rate of 87 percent from 1992 to 1996. In the spring of 1997 Brazil imposed restrictive import financing measures that negatively affected shipments of furniture, among other products. In 1997 export growth to Brazil slowed to 21 percent, and for the first quarter of 1998 such exports declined 20 percent. Other significant South American markets include Venezuela, Chile, Columbia, Argentina, and Peru.

Exports to Central America are also significant, accounting for 7 percent of U.S. exports. While not as rapid as growth to South America, export growth to Central America has been relatively steady, growing at a 12 percent compound annual rate between 1992 and 1997 and increasing 5 percent in the first quarter of 1998.

By far the largest markets for U.S. furniture exports are the NAFTA partners, Canada and Mexico (see Table 38-8). Together, they account for nearly half of U.S. exports. Canada accounted for 41 percent in 1997, and the strength of its econ-

omy, particularly consumer spending, has boosted U.S. exports of furniture to Canada, which were up 18 percent in 1997 and 20 percent in the first quarter of 1998. The Canadian economy showed some signs of slowing in mid-1998, and that slowdown was expected to continue into 1999, indicating that exports to Canada are likely to cool from their pace. U.S. exports to Mexico dropped dramatically in 1995, down 57 percent, as a result of the recession following the peso crisis. As the Mexican economy recovered, U.S. exports picked up, growing 15 and 20 percent in 1996 and 1997, respectively. For the first quarter of 1998, exports to Mexico jumped 78 percent, and Mexico was expected to overtake slumping Japan as the number two export market in 1998.

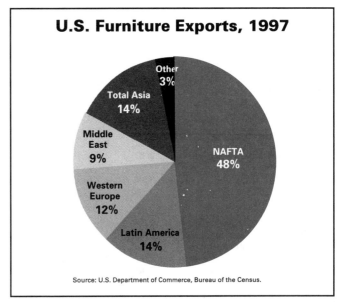

U.S. Furniture Exports, 1997

Source: U.S. Department of Commerce, Bureau of the Census.

FIGURE 38-8

TABLE 38-3: U.S. Trade Patterns in Household Furniture[1] in 1997

(millions of dollars; percent)

Exports			Imports		
Regions[2]	Value[3]	Share, %	Regions[2]	Value[3]	Share, %
NAFTA	739	48.3	NAFTA	1,623	27.6
Latin America	209	13.7	Latin America	167	2.8
Western Europe	184	12.0	Western Europe	1,114	18.9
Japan/Chinese Economic Area	150	9.8	Japan/Chinese Economic Area	1,824	31.0
Other Asia	66	4.3	Other Asia	1,038	17.7
Rest of world	182	11.9	Rest of world	115	2.0
World	1,530	100.0	World	5,882	100.0
Top Five Countries	Value	Share, %	Top Five Countries	Value	Share, %
Canada	632	41.3	China	1,104	18.8
Japan	114	7.4	Canada	1,075	18.3
Mexico	106	6.9	Taiwan	669	11.4
Saudi Arabia	64	4.2	Italy	656	11.2
United Kingdom	55	3.6	Mexico	548	9.3

[1] SIC 251.
[2] For definitions of regional groupings, see "Getting the Most Out of *Outlook '99*."
[3] Values may not sum to total due to rounding.
Source: U.S. Department of Commerce, Bureau of the Census.

Western Europe and the Middle East are the other major export regions for U.S. furniture. U.S. exports to western Europe, led by the United Kingdom, increased 16 percent in 1997 and 18 percent in the first quarter of 1998. The strong British economy was expected to slow in 1998 and 1999, slowing the growth in exports to Europe. U.S. exports to the Middle East accounted for 9 percent of total furniture exports and were up a robust 17 percent in 1997, largely on the strength of strong sales to the largest market, Saudi Arabia. An expected slowdown in 1998 had exports relatively flat for the first quarter of 1998. If the Saudi Arabian economy picks up in 1999 as projected, U.S. exports should follow.

Kevin M. Ellis, U.S. Department of Commerce, Office of Consumer Goods, (202) 482-1176, July 1998.

HOUSEHOLD APPLIANCES

Household appliances (SIC 363) include household cooking equipment (SIC 3631; household electric and nonelectric cooking equipment such as stoves, ranges, and ovens, including microwave and convection ovens); household refrigerators and home and farm freezers (SIC 3632); household laundry equipment (SIC 3633; laundry equipment such as washing machines, dryers, and ironers, for household

TABLE 38-4: Household Appliances (SIC 363) Trends and Forecasts

(millions of dollars except as noted)

	1992	1993	1994	1995	1996	1997[1]	1998[2]	1999[3]	Percent Change 96–97	97–98	98–99	92–96[4]
Industry data												
Value of shipments[5]	18,633	20,435	22,829	21,776	22,157	22,108	22,086	22,288	−0.2	−0.1	0.9	4.4
3631 Household cooking equipment	2,950	3,010	3,849	3,918	3,565	3,631	3,649	3,684	1.9	0.5	1.0	4.8
3632 Household refrigerators	4,232	4,463	5,149	5,200	5,605	5,414	5,385	5,465	−3.4	−0.5	1.5	7.3
3633 Household laundry equipment	3,329	3,871	4,612	4,133	4,233	4,269	4,290	4,351	0.9	0.5	1.4	6.2
3634 Electric housewares and fans	2,897	3,106	3,053	3,298	3,032	2,898	2,760	2,707	−4.4	−4.8	−1.9	1.1
3635 Household vacuums	1,905	2,096	1,933	2,045	2,425	2,316	2,277	2,300	−4.5	−1.7	1.0	6.2
3639 Home appliances nec	3,320	3,889	4,233	3,183	3,297	3,580	3,725	3,781	8.6	4.1	1.5	−0.2
Value of shipments (1992$)	18,633	20,179	22,512	21,498	21,717	22,000	22,437	22,640	1.3	2.0	0.9	3.9
3631 Household cooking equipment	2,950	2,911	3,755	3,856	3,481	3,580	3,690	3,725	2.8	3.1	0.9	4.2
3632 Household refrigerators	4,232	4,436	5,068	5,154	5,538	5,530	5,730	5,815	−0.1	3.6	1.5	7.0
3633 Household laundry equipment	3,329	3,887	4,668	4,191	4,258	4,430	4,585	4,650	4.0	3.5	1.4	6.3
3634 Electric housewares and fans	2,897	3,087	3,065	3,328	3,066	3,000	2,875	2,820	−2.2	−4.2	−1.9	1.4
3635 Household vacuums	1,905	2,037	1,843	1,941	2,303	2,235	2,257	2,280	−3.0	1.0	1.0	4.9
3639 Home appliances nec	3,320	3,820	4,114	3,028	3,070	3,225	3,300	3,350	5.0	2.3	1.5	−1.9
Total employment (thousands)	103	105	111	110	108	104			−3.7			1.2
Production workers (thousands)	83.2	85.0	90.6	87.7	87.0	82.2			−5.5			1.1
Average hourly earnings ($)	11.34	11.72	11.74	12.23	12.81	13.02			1.6			3.1
Capital expenditures	556	481	517	630	721							6.7
Product data												
Value of shipments[5]	16,789	18,027	19,841	20,095	20,581	20,532	20,492	20,676	−0.2	−0.2	0.9	5.2
3631 Household cooking equipment	3,007	3,162	3,821	3,904	3,766	3,834	3,832	3,872	1.8	−0.1	1.0	5.8
3632 Household refrigerators	4,048	4,309	4,995	5,121	5,356	5,174	5,141	5,216	−3.4	−0.6	1.5	7.3
3633 Household laundry equipment	2,995	3,299	3,671	3,541	3,699	3,729	3,747	3,803	0.8	0.5	1.5	5.4
3634 Electric housewares and fans	2,653	2,710	2,651	2,875	2,501	2,391	2,280	2,232	−4.4	−4.6	−2.1	−1.5
3635 Household vacuums	1,809	2,015	1,788	1,907	2,341	2,233	2,194	2,204	−4.6	−1.7	0.5	6.7
3639 Home appliances nec	2,279	2,531	2,916	2,748	2,919	3,171	3,298	3,349	8.6	4.0	1.5	6.4
Value of shipments (1992$)	16,789	17,792	19,559	19,834	20,160	20,420	20,820	21,005	1.3	2.0	0.9	4.7
3631 Household cooking equipment	3,007	3,058	3,727	3,842	3,677	3,780	3,875	3,915	2.8	2.5	1.0	5.2
3632 Household refrigerators	4,048	4,283	4,916	5,075	5,292	5,285	5,470	5,550	−0.1	3.5	1.5	6.9
3633 Household laundry equipment	2,995	3,312	3,715	3,592	3,721	3,870	4,005	4,065	4.0	3.5	1.5	5.6
3634 Electric housewares and fans	2,653	2,694	2,662	2,902	2,529	2,475	2,375	2,325	−2.1	−4.0	−2.1	−1.2
3635 Household vacuums	1,809	1,958	1,705	1,809	2,223	2,155	2,175	2,185	−3.1	0.9	0.5	5.3
3639 Home appliances nec	2,279	2,486	2,834	2,614	2,717	2,855	2,920	2,965	5.1	2.3	1.5	4.5
Trade data												
Value of imports	4,322	4,535	4,915	5,131	5,444	5,764	7,138		5.9	23.8		5.9
Value of exports	2,307	2,482	2,568	2,621	2,791	2,958	3,150		6.0	6.5		4.9

[1] Estimate except imports and exports.
[2] Estimate.
[3] Forecast.
[4] Compound annual rate.
[5] For definition of industry versus product values, see "Getting the Most Out of *Outlook '99.*"
Source: U.S. Department of Commerce: Bureau of the Census; International Trade Administration.

use, including coin-operated); electric housewares and fans (SIC 3634; electric housewares for heating, cooking, and other purposes, and electric household fans, except attic fans); household vacuum cleaners (SIC 3635); household appliances not elsewhere classified (SIC 3639; household appliances such as water heaters, dishwashers, food waste disposal units, and household sewing machines).

Factors Affecting Future Industry Growth

In 1998, product shipments of household appliances were estimated to be $20.5 billion, a constant dollar increase of 2.0 percent from 1997. The increase in shipments reflected the continued strong economy of the past few years. Favorable factors included a high rate of housing starts, very low unemployment levels, and increased consumer confidence. Housing starts remained at high levels, declining slightly from 1.47 million in 1997 to an estimated 1.45 million in 1998. The housing industry benefited from low mortgage rates during 1998. During the first half of the year, mortgage rates were generally below 7.5 percent. Also favorable was the unemployment rate which dropped to 4.3 percent early in the year, a 28-year low. Consumer confidence, as measured by the Conference Board, soared to a 30-year high in February 1998 when it reached 138.3 (1985 = 100). This was near the historical high of 142.3 set in October 1968. The consumer confidence index remained near the February peak into the summer months.

Global Industry Trends

The appliance industry is rapidly globalizing. In the developed countries, appliance markets are generally saturated and increasingly price competitive. This has resulted in a number of acquisitions and mergers as companies try to increase in size to obtain a greater market share and a competitive advantage through increased economies of scale. There has also been increased international trade in appliances as many countries have lowered their tariffs in recent years. While small appliances may be shipped economically long distances, trade in the major appliances tends to be more regional although high-end major appliances often can also be profitably shipped longer distances.

In addition to increased foreign trade, there has been a substantial increase in investments by appliance companies in foreign countries through acquisitions and joint ventures. The investing companies are seeking low-cost sources of appliances and/or a share in rapidly growing markets. Much of this investment has taken place in the former communist countries as well as in rapidly industrializing countries in Asia and Latin America.

In the U.S. appliance market in 1998, pressure on prices was keen and persistent. Much of the pressure resulted from sharply increased imports led by soaring imports from the two largest foreign suppliers, China and Mexico. In addition, imports from several other Asian countries, such as South Korea and Japan, were also up sharply because of the weakness of their currencies in foreign exchange markets stemming from the Asian economic crisis. Pressure on prices from increased imports was a major factor in causing U.S. appliance producer prices to decline during the year (see Tables 38-4 and 38-5).

Severe competition has induced several companies to restructure, often resulting in major layoffs and plant closings. For example, Black & Decker, a leading small appliance producer, exited the household appliance industry, selling its household products division to Windmere-Durable Holdings, Inc., in early 1998. Sunbeam Corporation, which had had substantial layoffs to reduce costs, purchased Mr. Coffee, Coleman, and First Alert brands during the year and then proceeded to squeeze costs from those operations.

Restructuring was not restricted just to the small appliance producers. In mid-1997, Raytheon began exiting from the industry when it sold its Amana home appliance business to Goodman

TABLE 38-5: U.S. Trade Patterns in Household Appliances[1] in 1997
(millions of dollars; percent)

	Exports			Imports	
Regions[2]	Value[3]	Share, %	Regions[2]	Value[3]	Share, %
NAFTA	1,356	45.9	NAFTA	1,674	29.0
Latin America	524	17.7	Latin America	84	1.5
Western Europe	416	14.1	Western Europe	870	15.1
Japan/Chinese Economic Area	171	5.8	Japan/Chinese Economic Area	2,328	40.4
Other Asia	177	6.0	Other Asia	784	13.6
Rest of world	312	10.6	Rest of world	23	0.4
World	2,958	100.0	World	5,764	100.0
Top Five Countries	Value	Share, %	Top Five Countries	Value	Share, %
Canada	974	32.9	China	1,709	29.7
Mexico	383	12.9	Mexico	1,191	20.7
Venezuela	96	3.2	Canada	483	8.4
United Kingdom	92	3.1	Taiwan	429	7.4
South Korea	88	3.0	South Korea	421	7.3

[1] SIC 363.
[2] For definitions of regional groupings, see "Getting the Most Out of *Outlook '99*."
[3] Values may not sum to total due to rounding.
Source: U.S. Department of Commerce, Bureau of the Census.

Holding Company. This was followed in early 1998 by the sale of its Speed Queen laundry equipment business to Bain Capital Inc. Meanwhile, A.B. Electrolux of Sweden was closing its Frigidaire headquarters in Dublin, Ohio, after that division was combined with the lawn products divisions. The combined headquarters is in Augusta, Georgia. This was part of a long-term global restructuring by Electrolux to eliminate 12,000 jobs. Whirlpool, going through a restructuring to cut 7,900 positions worldwide, terminated two of its four joint ventures in China. However, Whirlpool was moving forward in Brazil as it completed the purchase of a majority voting interest in Brasmotor S.A., a holding company that controls Multibras S.A., the largest appliance company in Latin America. Whirlpool has had an interest in these two Brazilian companies for several years.

Energy Efficiency Standards

The National Appliance Energy Conservation Act of 1987 mandates the Department of Energy (DOE) to set national energy efficiency standards for several categories of major household appliances, including refrigerators and freezers, water heaters, dishwashers, clothes washers and dryers, and kitchen ranges and ovens. Over the past decade, the DOE has raised the standards for these appliances, taking into consideration life-cycle costs (initial cost plus operating cost).

On April 28, 1997, the DOE published final energy efficiency standards for refrigerators and freezers. The standard becomes effective in July 2001, 14 months later than the legal minimum of 3 years from the date of publication to allow more time for the development of HCFC-141b substitutes. HCFC-141b is used by many companies as a foam insulation blowing agent in the manufacture of refrigerators. The Environmental Protection Agency is banning the manufacture and importation of HCFC-141b, effective January 1, 2003, since it is a stratospheric ozone-depleting chemical. The revised energy efficiency standards will result in the production of refrigerators and freezers using approximately 23 to 30 percent less electricity than those manufactured in 1997. Manufacturers are expected to meet the new standards through several incremental improvements that together produce significant energy savings. Improvements could include the use of better insulation, more efficient motors and compressors, and sensors to control defrost times. In developing the final standards, the DOE relied substantially on a joint recommendation negotiated by refrigerator manufacturers and their trade association, energy efficiency advocates, electric utilities, and state energy offices, which was submitted to the DOE in 1994.

In mid-1998, the DOE was in the final stages of developing revised energy efficiency standards for kitchen ranges, cooktops, ovens, and microwave ovens. It was expected to publish final energy efficiency standards for these appliances by the end of 1998. The standards may ban the use of pilot lights in all gas ranges. It has been estimated that in the average household the amount of gas used by pilot lights is approximately equal to the amount used for cooking.

Also in the pipeline are revised energy efficiency standards for clothes washers and hot water heaters. Final rules for both of these appliance categories are expected to be published by the end of 1999. New standards for clothes washers may result in horizontal-axis washing machines becoming much more common than vertical-axis washers in the market. An estimated 90 percent of the energy used by clothes washers is for heating the water. Therefore the best way to improve efficiency is to reduce the amount of water, particularly hot water, that is needed to wash the clothes. Horizontal-axis machines use approximately one-third the energy and water used by vertical-axis machines. Horizontals also spin-dry clothes drier because of faster spin speeds, saving on drying energy. Manufacturers of hot water heaters will likely meet the expected new standards for that appliance category through the use of improved heat traps, flue baffles, flue dampers, insulation, heat exchangers, and possibly electronic ignition. While appliances meeting the new standards are expected to cost more than the older designs, they will have lower life-cycle costs because of reduced operating expenses.

U.S. Industry Growth Projections for the Next 1 and 5 Years

With the U.S. economic expansion in its 8th year in 1998, it is showing signs of age. Although the economy has managed to avoid most of the dangers resulting from the crises in Mexico and Asia in recent years, there have been some effects on the appliance industry. U.S. imports of appliances from many of the affected countries have increased sharply while exports to those countries have fallen rapidly. Exports to those countries are expected to rebound as their economies get back on track, but imports to the United States may not be reversed so easily, especially for those countries where production costs are substantially lower than those in the United States.

Domestically, housing starts are expected to decline slightly in 1999, down 3 percent to 1.40 million starts, still a relatively high level. Mortgage interest rates are expected to increase to about 7.7 percent for 1999 from an estimated average 7.4 percent in 1998. While the unemployment rate and consumer confidence level will be hard pressed to remain at their current near-record levels, they likely will still be quite favorable for the economy. Assuming continued growth in the U.S. economy, constant-dollar product shipments of appliances are expected to increase 1 percent in 1999.

During the next 5 years, product shipments of appliances are expected to increase at an estimated annual compound rate of 1.5 percent in constant dollars. Continued high levels of employment are expected to result in higher rates of household formations than might otherwise have been the case. The total number of households is expected to increase at a rate of about 1 percent per year over the 5-year period. In addition, the trend toward two-income families will continue, although at a slower rate than in the past decade. This will result in the need for labor-saving appliances by more families with the disposable income to purchase them. Such families are also more inclined to purchase high-end appliances.

Global Market Prospects

In 1997, appliance imports and exports increased approximately 6 percent from 1996. Appliance imports increased to $5.8 billion and appliance exports to $3.0 billion. The leading foreign appliance suppliers to the United States were, in descending order, China, Mexico, Canada, Taiwan, and South Korea. Together, these countries accounted for 66 percent of total imports. The three leaders have substantially increased their share of imports in recent years. Mexico and Canada are benefiting from the continued realignment of their appliance industries with that of the United States because of NAFTA and the U.S.-Canada Free Trade Agreement, respectively, as well as to their proximity to the United States, while China is quite competitive with other countries because of its low labor rates.

The leading export markets for U.S. appliance producers in 1997 were Canada, Mexico, the United Kingdom, Japan, and South Korea. These countries accounted for about 53 percent of total U.S. exports.

In 1998, exports were expected to increase at approximately 6.5 percent, as in 1997. However, imports were expected to increase at a much faster rate, over 23 percent; a major cause was the strength of the U.S. dollar on foreign exchange markets. Most of this strength was in comparison to certain Asian currencies following the economic crises in several countries that began when Thailand devalued its currency in 1997. While several Asian countries whose currencies were substantially affected by the crisis were expected to record sharp increases in appliance shipments to the United States during the year, so were China and Mexico. Although the currencies of China and Mexico were relatively strong during the year, both countries were expected to record 1998 appliance shipments to the United States increasing at a much higher rate then they had in recent years.

John M. Harris, U.S. Department of Commerce, Office of Consumer Goods, (202) 482-1178, October 1998.

LAWN AND GARDEN EQUIPMENT

Global Industry Trends

Lawn and garden equipment is used in similar ways regardless of the country. Factors influencing choice of products are more due to lawn size, grass variety, and environmental requirements than to cultural practices. In the United Kingdom, many consumers prefer the common grass variety to be cut short and pressed down. For that market, manufacturers produce mowers with a roller instead of back wheels. In much of the rest of Europe, grass is cut longer. Bagging is common, mulching virtually unknown.

Electric lawnmowers have become more sophisticated and powerful. But consumers still find cords inconvenient, and even the best battery models can cut only about one-third of an acre before needing a recharge. This limitation is less important in Europe, where lawns are usually smaller than in the United States and Canada. Higher gas prices in Europe also make electric mowers more popular there than in North America.

For maximum coverage there are the riding mowers, particularly the powerful and expensive garden tractors. They are popular in the United States, and U.S. exports are strongest to France, Germany, Canada, Australia, and the United Kingdom. While some mowers exported to Europe, especially riders, are essentially similar to the American versions, U.S. manufacturers also produce models just for export. These export-only models include walk-behinds two-thirds the width of U.S. mowers, riders with rear bagging instead of side discharge, and small riders powered by diesel rather than by gas as in America.

The U.S. industry is competitive in the world marketplace. Despite low tariffs, U.S. imports in 1997 accounted for only about 4 percent of apparent consumption. The value of U.S. exports was three times the imports, and accounted for 12 percent of U.S. producers' shipments (see Table 38-6).

TABLE 38-6: Lawn and Garden Equipment (SIC 3524) Trends and Forecasts
(millions of dollars except as noted)

	1992	1993	1994	1995	1996	1997[1]	1998[2]	1999[3]	Percent Change 96–97	97–98	98–99	92–96[4]
Industry data												
Value of shipments[5]	5,164	5,828	6,836	6,971	6,823	7,369	7,590	7,742	8.0	3.0	2.0	7.2
Value of shipments (1992$)	5,164	5,788	6,682	6,723	6,480	6,934	7,072	7,143	7.0	2.0	1.0	5.8
Total employment (thousands)	24.9	25.7	28.0	27.7	27.0	28.6						2.0
Production workers (thousands)	19.9	20.5	22.4	22.3	21.5	22.9						2.0
Average hourly earnings ($)	10.73	10.88	10.56	10.26	11.05	11.34						0.7
Capital expenditures	125	92.1	129	126	120							–1.0
Product data												
Value of shipments[5]	4,344	4,884	5,730	6,061	5,908	6,381	6,572	6,704	8.0	3.0	2.0	8.0
Value of shipments (1992$)	4,344	4,850	5,601	5,845	5,611	6,004	6,124	6,185	7.0	2.0	1.0	6.6
Trade data												
Value of imports	134	162	175	172	225	264	251	266	17.3	–5.0	5.9	13.8
Value of exports	612	686	740	765	721	788	750	795	9.3	–4.8	4.2	4.2

[1] Estimate except imports and exports.
[2] Estimate.
[3] Forecast.
[4] Compound annual rate.
[5] For definition of industry versus product values, see "Getting the Most Out of *Outlook '99.*"
Source: U.S. Department of Commerce: Bureau of the Census; International Trade Administration

Domestic Trends

Continuing changes to product design, along with economic and demographic factors, appear to be influencing the growth of the high-end market: self-propelled walk-behinds and front-engine riding equipment. While production of the lower-quality rear-engine riding mowers has experienced a decade-long decline, front-engine models, including lawn tractors and garden tractors, have more than made up for it. The main difference between lawn tractors and garden tractors is the latter's ability to tow attachments such as utility carts, snow blowers, and tillers. Lawn and garden tractor sales have benefited from manufacturers' efforts to make them more familiar to potential users, that is, more like a car. Consumers encounter fewer difficulties when a rider mower has automatic transmission, power steering, and even cruise control, as many models now do.

The value of new construction put in place for single family houses in the mid-1990s matched or exceeded the high levels in the mid-1980s. This strength in construction along with economic growth coincided with shifts in the market toward self-propelled walk-behind and riding mowers. Some consumers are even buying commercial-grade lawn mowers, a trend that mirrors the growth of private residential use of commercial-grade cookware, kitchen appliances, and building materials, especially in home improvement projects. The ratio of home improvement projects to total residential construction generally increased from the late 1970s through 1997 (the most recent Census data available), and this trend is expected to continue. Remodeling can involve room additions, extensions, or decks that decrease the size of the lawn. Both average and median plot sizes of new one-family houses sold have been declining throughout the recent housing boom, even while house sizes have increased. Thus, the growing sales of riding units may be less a function of bigger lawns than of higher discretionary income and a desire to save time.

Some people may have less leisure time because, according to the Bureau of Labor Statistics, the percentage employed in nonagricultural jobs working an average of 49 or more hours a week rose from 13 percent in 1976 to 18.5 percent by 1993. (This percentage appears to have grown from 1994–1997 as well, but because of a redesign of the survey, data from 1994 on are not comparable to earlier years.) Among the groups that have highest percentages of people working these long hours are managers and professionals. Because they are likely to earn high salaries, they are most able to afford more expensive, time-saving equipment such as self-propelled walk-behind or riding mowers. Though more difficult to quantify, there may also be style and status factors. Dealers report that sales of riding mowers are often spurred by neighbors' purchases of such equipment. The growth of sales in riding mowers also parallels increased sales of sport utility vehicles, four-wheel-drive light trucks that have recently been adapted to consumer use.

In addition to time constraints and affluence, demographics influence this industry. The first baby boomers are now in their early 50s, and the 45- to 64-year-old segment of the population is predicted to increase each year from 1999 through 2005. Thus there will be more people who are likely to have condi-

tions that impair their pushing a 40- to 85-pound machine over the lawn. Not all will buy more expensive equipment, however. Some will leave the market for consumer lawnmowers entirely, opting for professional lawn care. According to a Gallup poll, 24.4 million households planned to purchase such services in 1998, an increase of 9 percent from 1997. Nearly half of all professional lawn and landscape services in 1997 were hired by households led by people aged 50 and older. About the same percentage of households hiring professional lawn care had incomes of at least $100,000.

Electric mowers have made gains in power and convenience. While earlier versions were basic, now some models can even mulch. This feature went from an option in gas mowers in the early 1990s to a standard feature on many models by the later years of the decade, because of environmental concerns and restrictions on yard waste at some landfills. The biggest change in electric mowers has been improvements in battery models, some of which can now cut one-third of an acre before needing a recharge. While these products are easy to turn on and require almost no maintenance, they are still impractical for large lots and can cost up to twice as much as gas mowers with comparable features. That price difference is not the same in all countries, however. In the United Kingdom, electric models are generally less expensive than those with internal combustion engines. Until range is increased and price is reduced, the electric mower share of the U.S. market may not grow significantly higher than the 5 to 7 percent estimated by one manufacturer. The lawn and garden industry may benefit from the increased interest in battery technology caused by emission regulations for cars. And the lawn and garden industry does see potential for electric mowers. A major supplier to many lawnmower companies states that almost all manufacturers that do not already make electric models are considering adding them to their product lines.

The simplest and usually least expensive lawnmower of all, a push reel mower, continues to enjoy a resurgence because of its simplicity, quiet operation, and according to many users, superior cut. Another attraction for some users is the exercise, but that generally limits these models to small lots. Powered reels have disappeared from the consumer market since they are less adaptable than rotary blades to safety standards.

From the mid-1980s through the early 1990s, the growth of mass merchants like Wal-Mart and "big box" home improvement stores like Home Depot and Builders Square contributed to a bifurcation in the market for lawn and garden equipment. While specialty dealers offered high-end products, the mass merchants offered lawnmowers at prices as low as $99. These models, however, were generally of inferior quality. Many manufacturers produced different lines, with less expensive ones sold mostly by the mass market stores and better ones sold exclusively by dealers. In the mid to late 1990s, there has been increased competition by both manufacturers and retailers for the middle ground, trying to pull customers away from the competition by offering workmanship better than that found in the least expensive models, but at prices lower than the high end. In 1996, John Deere, probably the best-known brand in the industry, introduced a new line, "Sabre by John Deere," an attempt to gain the middle market. Now there are numerous good-quality walk-behinds priced below $200, capable of bagging, dispersing, or mulching. Dealers are usually the only retailers that provide service for the product, though some are now contracting with mass market stores for after-sales service.

Probably the biggest influence on lawn and garden equipment design in recent years has been environmental regulations. In January 1998, the U.S. Environmental Protection Agency (EPA) proposed Phase 2 standards for nonroad small spark ignition engines that power lawnmowers and other equipment. These engines currently produce approximately one-tenth of U.S. emissions of hydrocarbons from "mobile sources" (i.e., vehicles and equipment). These regulations, which will be phased in between 2001 and 2005, are intended to reduce emissions by both hand-held and non-hand-held equipment of certain pollutants by 30 percent beyond the Phase 1 standards, in effect since the 1997 model year. Unlike the Phase 1 standards, the Phase 2 standards require engines to meet air quality standards not just when new but for a set number of operating hours that vary by category of equipment. EPA efforts to minimize the burden of complying with these proposed regulations include phase-in schedules; a certification averaging, banking, and trading program for non-hand-held equipment; and other special provisions. The regulations are unlikely to change the engines used for walk-behinds significantly, but manufacturers will be likely to switch from side-valve to overhead-valve engines for their riding mowers. Phase 2 for hand-held equipment, like string trimmers, will require cleaner two-stroke engines. An industry official estimates that original owners keep walk-behinds an average of 5 years and riding equipment 7 years. Since equipment is sometimes transferred to other users, any changes in technology take at least several years to dominate the product mix.

The more stringent standards promulgated by the California Air Resources Board (CARB) could affect the entire country because manufacturers typically find it more expedient to make all their products compliant with California rules than to make different versions of engines. The CARB Tier 1 standard took effect in 1995. Tier 2 is scheduled to take effect in 2002 for horizontal-shaft engines (frequently used in tillers) and in 2006 for vertical-shaft engines (generally used in lawn mowers). Early data had underestimated the engine deterioration that caused higher emissions, so, like the EPA's Phase 2, the CARB's Tier 2 for non-hand-held equipment will require manufacturers to demonstrate that their products are "emissions durable" (i.e., emissions-controlled for a set number of operating hours). Furthermore, larger manufacturers must provide additional emissions reductions through the early introduction of clean engines or other measures. Like the EPA, the CARB would allow some products to exceed emissions standards as long as other models had sufficiently low emissions so that the class, on average, met the requirements. Unlike the EPA's Phase 2, the CARB's stricter Tier 2 will likely result in the increased use of overhead-valve engines for walk-behind as well as for riding mowers.

For hand-held equipment, the CARB's Tier 2 requirements will go into effect in 2000. Those will result in the decreased use of basic two-stroke engines and the increased use of improved two-stroke engines and of micro four-stroke engines. Hand-held equipment is included in the CARB averaging program, which would allow the continued production of some high-emitting products as long as other models had emissions sufficiently low that the manufacturer met the requirements on average.

Manufacturers have been able to meet these standards in part because, while there are many brands of lawn mowers, the engines themselves are made by relatively few companies. This concentration allows more money to be devoted to research and development than would be the case if the industry were composed of numerous small manufacturers.

From 1987 to 1996 (the latest year for which Census data are available), employment in this industry tracked the economy in general. The lowest employment for production workers (18,300) was in 1990, and the lowest for all employees (24,400) was in 1991. In 1994, employment peaked for production workers (22,400) and for total employees (28,000). By 1996, employment had declined both for production workers (21,500) and for total employees (27,000).

Projections of Industry and Trade Growth for the Next 1 and 5 Years

The lawn and garden industry generally tracks economic growth with one substantial exception: the weather. Most consumers purchase lawn equipment in the spring. A spring that is either unusually hot and dry or cold and wet is a deterrent to retail sales not just for March-May but for the entire season. There can also be a spill-over effect as retailers, faced with excess inventory, reduce purchases the following year. Even more difficult to predict are snow thrower sales which can be flat for months but then jump on the report of a major snowfall or immediately after a blizzard.

This is a mature industry, and while some products have become easier to use, most recent product change has been in levels of emissions. Therefore, consumers generally replace this equipment because it has worn out, not because new products are faster (like computers) or more fashionable (like cars, clothes, or home decor). Domestic shipments of this equipment are apt to fluctuate with the economy and the weather, growing 1 percent in 1999 in constant dollars, and averaging 4 percent growth over the next 5 years. Inflation in this industry is expected to remain approximately 1 percent. Probably the most significant effect on growth in this industry over the next 5 years is the aging of the baby boomers, which should spur interest in higher-end products like self-propelled walk-behinds and riding mowers. In an increasingly service-oriented economy, however, baby boomers may be more likely to hire lawn care services than to upgrade their equipment. So far, there is no evidence that those who came of age during the environmental movement are disproportionately willing to pay a premium for electric mowers.

Global Market Prospects

The United States is a net exporter of the lawn and garden equipment covered in this chapter (see Table 38-7). The percentage of U.S. domestic production that is exported rose from

TABLE 38-7: U.S. Trade Patterns in Lawn and Garden Equipment[1] in 1997
(millions of dollars; percent)

	Exports			Imports		
Regions[2]	Value[3]	Share, %	Regions[2]	Value[3]	Share, %
NAFTA	197	24.9	NAFTA	145	55.0
Latin America	42	5.3	Latin America	0	0.1
Western Europe	419	53.2	Western Europe	32	12.0
Japan/Chinese Economic Area	25	3.2	Japan/Chinese Economic Area	82	30.9
Other Asia	16	2.0	Other Asia	5	1.9
Rest of world	89	11.4	Rest of world	1	0.2
World	788	100.0	World	264	100.0
Top Five Countries	Value	Share, %	Top Five Countries	Value	Share, %
Canada	187	23.8	Canada	92	34.9
France	110	13.9	Japan	66	24.9
Germany	99	12.6	Mexico	53	20.0
United Kingdom	57	7.2	Sweden	13	4.8
Australia	52	6.6	China	8	2.9

[1] SIC 3524.
[2] For definitions of regional groupings, see "Getting the Most Out of *Outlook '99*."
[3] Values may not sum to total due to rounding.
Source: U.S. Department of Commerce, Bureau of the Census.

11.4 percent in 1990 to a peak of 14.1 percent in 1992 before slipping to 12.3 percent in 1997. This decline may be due in part to increased production of riding mowers, which are even more likely than the rest of the product mix to be sold in the United States than abroad. By far the biggest market for U.S. exports is Canada ($187.7 million in 1997). France and Germany ($110.1 and $99.1 million, respectively), Australia ($52.0 million), some other European Union (EU) members, and Japan ($17.1 million) constitute the rest of the top 10 export destinations. There are relatively few artificial barriers to trade in this industry. The EU had been considering stringent noise standards, which also would have affected European-made products. The EU now appears to be rethinking these proposed regulations in light of evidence that the technology is not advanced enough for products to meet them.

In 1997, U.S. imports were approximately one-third the value of its exports. Imports are low, having captured only about 4 percent of the U.S. market. Over one-third of U.S. imports came from Canada, whose steady growth dislodged Japan from the number one spot. Mexico, Sweden, and China constituted the rest of the top five import sources which together accounted for 88 percent of all U.S. imports of these products. The value of Chinese imports grew each year from 1992 ($71,000) to 1997 ($7.7 million). Mexico's imports were $7.3 million in 1992, stagnated at one-third that level from 1993 to 1995, but resumed their climb, reaching $53.1 million in 1997. Import figures for the first eight months of 1998 show the value of Mexico's imports to exceed Japan's, and China's imports to be close to Sweden's.

Despite an economic slowdown in Canada and serious systemic problems in Japan, exports of lawn and garden equipment have grown or remained stable from the early 1990s through the first four months of 1998. If the Japanese economy worsens, that will have a negative effect on U.S. exports, but the effect will be limited. Although Japan was the ninth-largest U.S. export market for these product in 1997, U.S. exports to Canada were 11 times higher. None of the countries immediately affected by the Asian economic crisis have been major export markets for these products. Unless the crisis spreads, U.S. exports should average 6 percent annual growth, close to the level they have enjoyed for the past several years. Imports are also likely to maintain their average annual growth of 6 percent, particularly if Canada and China continue their significant gains.

Jonathan Freilich, U.S. Department of Commerce, Office of Consumer Goods, (202) 482-5783, November 1998.

HOUSEHOLD AUDIO AND VIDEO EQUIPMENT

Although overall factory sales of consumer electronics products rose by 5.7 percent in 1996 and 5.5 percent in 1997, the keystone product categories of audio and video equipment experienced a significant sales decline in the same period. Factory sales of home and portable audio products dropped 7.2 percent in 1996 and 1 percent in 1997, while video products, including televisions, videocassette recorders (VCRs), and home satellite systems experienced a decline of 1 percent in 1996 and 7.4 percent in 1997 (see Table 38-8).

There are numerous reasons why sales in these product categories have been falling. In particular, home information products such as personal computers have been a more immediate focus of the spending of consumers' disposable income. Further, household penetration levels for these products are already substantial. The first wave of the mainstream home theater boom drove the industry's success throughout the mid-1990s, with 1995 being the peak sales year. Consumers expect audio

TABLE 38-8: Total Factory Sales of Consumer Video and Audio Products[1]

(millions of dollars)

	1994	1995	1996	1997	1998[2]	1999[3]	Percent Change			
							96–97	97–98	98–99	94–99[4]
Video products										
Direct-view color TV	7,225	6,798	6,492	6,026	6,298	6,229	−7.2	4.5	−1.1	−2.9
Projection TV	1,117	1,417	1,426	1,361	1,629	1,625	−4.6	19.7	−0.2	7.8
Monochrome TV	38	34	29	27	22	20	−6.9	−18.5	−9.1	−12.0
LCD color TV	42	44	39	38	37	37	−2.6	−2.6	0.0	−2.5
LCD monochrome	32	31	32	30	25	23	−6.3	−16.7	−8.0	−6.4
TV/VCR combinations	710	723	697	684	782	784	−1.9	14.3	0.3	2.0
Videocassette players	64	59	43	39	20	14	−9.3	−48.7	−30.0	−26.2
VCR decks	2,869	2,767	2,815	2,618	2,273	2,171	−7.0	−13.2	−4.5	−5.4
Camcorders	1,985	2,130	2,084	1,894	1,919	1,925	−9.1	1.3	0.3	−0.6
Laserdisc players	122	108	66	25	11	4	−62.1	−56.0	−63.6	−49.5
Direct to home satellite systems	900	1,265	1,493	1,254	1,084	1,092	−16.0	−13.6	0.7	3.9
Digital versatile disc players (DVD)				171	323	535		88.9	65.6	
TV/PC combinations				174	317	397		82.2	25.2	
Set-top Internet access devices				80	145	196		81.3	35.2	
Total	15,104	15,376	15,216	14,419	14,884	15,052	−5.2	3.2	1.1	−0.1
Home and portable audio products										
Rack audio systems	595	515	380	271	189	167	−28.7	−30.3	−11.6	−22.4
Compact audio systems	1,108	1,162	1,157	1,419	1,606	1,673	22.6	13.2	4.2	8.6
Separate audio components	1,686	1,911	1,808	1,609	1,555	1,500	−11.0	−3.4	−3.5	−2.3
Home theater-in-a-box			164	282	218	226	72.0	−22.7	3.7	
Portable equipment	2,495	2,506	2,149	2,033	2,259	2,083	−5.4	11.1	−7.8	−3.5
Home radios	306	284	291	300	330	335	3.1	10.0	1.5	1.8
Total	6,190	6,378	5,949	5,914	6,158	5,984	−0.6	4.1	−2.8	−0.7

[1] Factory sales reflect total industry sales (domestic sales and imports to the United States).
[2] Estimate.
[3] Forecast.
[4] Compound annual rate.
Source: Consumer Electronics Manufacturers Association.

and video products to have a longer technological life cycle than personal computers, which are designed for frequent upgrades. Most important, several new audio and video technologies, recently introduced or soon to debut, have resulted in significant consumer confusion regarding potential new purchases of audio and video products.

Some of these new technologies are the result of efforts by the consumer electronics industry to bring audio and video equipment together in the digital realm and eventually to meld them with the capabilities of the personal computer as part of a new "convergence" medium. The goal is to create hardware that can play back passive or interactive entertainment that has been delivered digitally from fixed media such as audio and video discs or from broad- or narrow-band networks such as home satellites and dial-up Internet connections. This trend is exemplified by two key products from the video industry. The digital videodisc (DVD), introduced in the spring of 1997, is intended to be an entertainment carrier that can play movies, music, and games through a home entertainment system or a personal computer. Soon to be introduced, digital television (DTV) formats, which will incorporate the high-definition television (HDTV) format as a subset, are envisioned as video media that just as easily can be delivered to a personal computer (PC) as to a traditional television.

Because home audio and video equipment represents a sizable investment of discretionary income and because there is considerable consumer confusion regarding the viability of today's products in the light of emerging technologies, sales in the audio and video categories have been flat. But the new technologies that are keeping older products on dealers' shelves are expected eventually to spur substantial consumer interest, particularly through the new entertainment possibilities that are inherent in these technologies. As part of this natural technological market cycle, prices are expected to continue to drop on existing products, resulting in even lower profit margins in industries where margins are already thin.

Digital Television

The next-generation video system that has been known for more than a decade as high-definition television is now known by the more general but accurate name of digital television. In DTV, video and computer data travel in a digital bitstream, much like computer data. This bitstream can be modified and optimized for content purposes and intended display and/or playback environments.

Justifiable confusion surrounded the expected autumn 1998 introduction of DTV has affected consumers, hardware manufacturers, and the broadcast community. In fact, there are 18 officially approved digital video formats that can legitimately be called DTV. The differences between these formats are mainly expressed in terms of picture resolution, picture shape (aspect ratio), and scanning technique. The present National

Television Standards Committee (NTSC) video system that has been in use throughout the United States since the late 1940s delivers 525 lines of picture information in an alternating series of odd and even lines, called interlaced scanning. The computer industry uses a different technique for video displays called progressive scanning, whereby the lines of information are represented in sequenced order.

Because of the desirability of making digital video signals playable on either a computer or TV monitor, a compromise had to be reached between interlaced and progressive scan, so a plethora of legitimate DTV formats was accepted by the Advanced Systems Television Committee (ATSC). These formats ranged from extremely high-resolution pictures with 1,080 interlaced lines or 720 progressively scanned lines, to lower-resolution pictures that are not high-definition yet are still digital. While HDTV is an iteration of DTV, and indeed is the highest-quality iteration, there are numerous versions of digital television that are not considered high definition. These formats, called standard-definition television (SDTV), feature digital video and data delivered as smaller, more economical bitstreams.

This confusion has affected the manufacture, marketing, and sales of an entire range of video products, from professional broadcast gear to home consumer television sets. Not all digital television sets sold to consumers will be able to play all 18 approved DTV signals. Furthermore, the major broadcast networks have split camps on their chosen DTV technologies, and there are still questions as to whether the major cable carriers have the ability or motivation to carry the highest-quality HDTV signals. Since most Americans receive their television programming via cable, this potential bottleneck has serious implications for the immediate future of DTV and for television sales overall.

The confusion over DTV and the question whether it will be possible for consumers to upgrade their present analog television sets to DTV have caused a slump in new television sales despite rock-bottom retail prices. With so much uncertainty over how much the first digital TVs will cost (estimates range from $2,000 to $5,000 more than a comparable analog television) and how much the analog-to-digital TV converter boxes will cost (estimates range from $300 to $1,700), consumers have voted with their pocketbooks and stayed with their present equipment. The introduction of HDTV broadcasts in October 1998 may present early-adopter consumers with a compelling reason to buy into the new technology. However, manufacturers were circumspect over the prospects for DTV sales in the format's first year and pointed to color television as an equally compelling technology that took a decade to become mainstream. The Consumer Electronics Manufacturers Association estimates that DTV will be in 30 percent of U.S. households by 2006, with the first 10 million sets being sold between 1998 and 2003 and the second 10 million in 2004 and 2005.

Home Theater

Home theater, which can be loosely defined as the combination of a big-screen TV (27 inches or larger) with surround-sound audio equipment, has become a mainstream product category.

The vast majority of mass-manufactured audio gear is now designed or equipped for surround and/or home theater play. Sales of high-quality video source components meant for home theater, such as home satellite systems and videodisc players, have also been on the upswing. The concept has become commonplace enough for manufacturers to market home theater upgrade packages for as little as $400 and complete entry-level home theater packages, including TV, for less than $1,000 at retail.

As a result of these attractive prices and bargains on higher-end systems, the volume of sales of home theater products remained high in 1997 at $8.1 billion, only a slight drop from $8.3 billion in 1996. This relative market consistency was surprising, considering that sales of key category products were markedly down. Sales of direct broadcast satellite (DBS) systems were down almost 51 percent in 1997 compared with 1996. One reason for this dip is escalating market penetration, which now includes 11 percent of American homes. Another reason is consumer disappointment in that DBS systems sold in 1997 were unable to receive local broadcasts or deliver Dolby Digital surround sound, a multichannel digital audio technology that represents the current state of the art in home theater sound. Both shortcomings have been rectified. Hardware manufacturers such as Thomson (RCA) are beginning to build VHF antennas into the small DBS dishes for local reception, and broadcasters such as DirecTV planned to transmit programming with Dolby Digital beginning in summer 1998.

Consumer confusion over technologies like Dolby Digital has been a factor in sluggish home theater sales. Dolby Digital is a fully digital audio medium that requires specific equipment to receive and decode its signals. These decoders, which are typically built into audio-video receivers, are an advance over the earlier analog Dolby ProLogic surround-sound format which had driven home theater sales until the recent slump. Not only is new hardware necessary for Dolby Digital play, but the early equipment was difficult to use and confusing to most nonenthusiast consumers. Hardware with Dolby Digital capability also costs more. While mainstream audio-video receivers with analog surround sound sell for as low as $250 for an entry-level unit, entry-level receivers with Dolby Digital capability start at $500.

While surveys consistently reveal that home theater is well understood and generally desired by consumers, it is clear to many consumers, particularly the early-adopter demographic that drives sales trends, that substantial changes in this category are imminent. This has resulted in a spiral of price slashing on older technologies, damaging profitability throughout the category despite strong volume shipments.

Analog Television Market

Television sales epitomize the current malaise of the audio and video industries. Sales of traditional direct-view sets were down more than 7 percent in 1997 versus 1996, with the larger projection TVs experiencing a 5 percent drop over the same period. This decline occurred despite the fact that the technology stands at the highest quality level of its analog iteration before it begins to be supplanted by digital TV in 1998. The technological refinement of analog TVs, coupled with inexpensive mass manufacturing throughout Asia and Mexico, has made television sets an outstanding consumer value. In the last 5 years the average unit price to dealers of a direct-view color television set dropped more than 11 percent, from $318 to $283. Unfortunately, the low prices of these products, which are often highly discounted in a cutthroat retail landscape, have made high-volume shipments necessary in order to make profits. A 98 percent household penetration level does not bode well for a product category dependent on volume.

The newest television sets, called plasma display panels (PDPs), feature a flat-profile screen of 42 inches or more. Rather than use a traditional cathode-ray tube or liquid-crystal-display picture tube, these TVs use a gas-plasma technology that can be manufactured to an extremely low-profile form factor. These sets, introduced to the consumer market by Philips and Pioneer, fill a long-standing consumer wish for a large-screen TV that can be "hung on the wall." Because of price tags of over $10,000, the excitement over this technological advancement has not resulted in significant product sales. Worse, it has dampened enthusiasm for big-screen upgrades using more traditional technologies.

The intended industry savior is DTV, which is scheduled to be broadcast in selected markets in late 1998. The first digital television sets were announced for fall delivery from Thomson, Zenith, and Panasonic; it is likely that Sharp and Philips will have this product as well. The advantages of these TVs, particularly in the ability to present HDTV pictures, are already surprisingly well known to consumers, according to a recent Verity Group survey. Much of this consumer awareness is tied to the media attention given to the confusion about the DTV and HDTV formats. As of mid-1998, broadcasters were evenly split in their plans for digital television. CBS and NBC have committed to 1,080-interlaced HDTV pictures, while ABC and Fox have committed to 720-progressive pictures. All the networks except CBS have announced additional plans for lower-resolution SDTV programming.

None of these formats will play in their optimal resolutions on today's television sets, which is a major reason for the sales slump in the television category. While manufacturers have promised converter boxes that will allow analog television sets to play HDTV signals (though only in analog quality), the demand for these boxes is likely to be low: At first there will be little HDTV programming for consumers to watch, and later the prices on DTV sets will likely experience a natural market drop within the first 2 years of the product's introduction.

VCR and Videodisc Market

The VCR remains an important item in American households, with penetration at 90 percent. As a result, VCRs have become an inexpensive commodity that have suffered the same retail fate as television sales. While unit shipments of VCRs were up more than 6 percent in 1997 over 1996 and more than 12 percent over 1995, dollar sales were down more than 7 percent from 1996 and more than 5 percent from 1995. Consumers are buying VCRs at a healthy pace, mostly as replacement units.

However, there are slim profits because the average dealer price for a VCR in 1997 was down to $157, a 15 percent drop from 1996 and a 30 percent drop from 1995.

VCR sales were also marred by the introduction of a new home entertainment technology called DVD. This optical disc is similar to the CD or CD-ROM but has many times more data capacity, enough to store full-length movies and interactive games with video footage. The DVD is the first true convergence carrier in that it theoretically can play in either a home entertainment or PC environment. The first DVD hardware in the marketplace came in the form of home theater components that interfaced with a TV and surround-sound components. The first software titles were Hollywood movies meant for display in this environment, though also playable on a PC.

The consumer electronics industry was pleased with the market reaction to DVD. According to CEMA, DVD in its first year performed twice as well as VCRs during their first two years 1975-1977, and more than 12 times as well as CD players in their debut year, 1983. Some 437,000 DVD players were sold to dealers in the format's first year. By April 1998, several hundred DVD titles had been released, with most of the major entertainment studios having committed, at least in principle, to support the new format. The introduction of DVD in April 1997 came amid much fractious politicking between consumer electronics and PC manufacturers, the entertainment industry, and the software industry, with the bulk of the contention over consumer ownership of perfect digital copies of copyrighted entertainment. These squabbles were eventually resolved by the development of effective data encryption methods. But the idea of a super encrypted disc soon led to a new conception of DVD, called Divx, which undermines the format's original conception as a universal digital carrier and now threatens the market viability of the DVD format.

The Divx disc is named for its parent company, Digital Video Express, LP, which is a partnership between the electronics retail chain Circuit City and a Los Angeles–based entertainment law firm. The main hardware partner for Divx is Matsushita (Panasonic), which is also a proponent of open DVD, the name given the original format to differentiate it from Divx DVD. Divx, which was scheduled to launch in summer 1998, is a radical rethinking of the role of prerecorded media in the digital age. Divx is essentially a pay-per-view disc. Divx discs, which look like DVD discs, will not play in an open DVD player. They are given a special digital encryption that can be decrypted only by a Divx-equipped hardware deck or drive. Whereas open DVD discs sell for $20 to $30, Divx discs are intended to sell for $4 to $5. When the customer inserts the disc into a Divx home player, the machine dials up a server at the Divx central station, which then sends a signal back over the phone line to "unlock" the disc for a 48-hour play period. At the end of this period, the disc is encrypted again. Customers can then order additional plays at any time for an additional fee; some software studios have announced that a flat-rate permanent-play buyout will be possible for the consumer. The advantage to the consumer is that these discs, unlike rentals, need never be returned to the store.

Retail and consumer confusion caused by the scheduled Divx launch has had a significant impact on the tenuous market position of the new DVD format. Early adopters who had invested in DVD were shocked to find that their investment might already be obsolete in view of announcements of Divx support from major entertainment studios like Disney, Paramount, Universal, and Dreamworks. Furthermore, competing retail chains expressed reservations about supporting hardware marketed by a leading retail competitor, and the hardware makers that had pushed the launch of open DVD—particularly Toshiba and Sony—were faced with a format war with a major manufacturing competitor. It remains to be seen whether Divx can establish a market toehold beyond its two first test markets, Richmond, Virginia, and San Francisco.

In the meantime, DVD and Divx have spelled market death for the former optical disc format meant for home theater, the laserdisc. Sales of laserdisc players were down more than 68 percent in 1997 over 1996, and down almost 80 percent from 1995. Given that laserdisc never achieved market penetration of more than 2 percent of U.S. households, even after 18 years of product availability, it is safe to say that laserdisc has no market future. Unless DVD can iron out its problems, it may experience the same fate. There is already consumer confusion regarding open and pay-per-view DVD, and most consumers are unaware that today's DVD technology may not be sufficient to carry HDTV signals when entertainment in that format becomes available. Furthermore, the upcoming recordable DVD technology is already fractured between competing formats, including a write-once technology called DVD-R (recordable) and a rewritable format called DVD-RAM (random access memory).

Convergence Products

In 1997, consumer electronics and PC manufacturers began marketing convergence appliances that would serve as a dual-purpose entertainment and information center. The consumer electronics manufacturers saw this confluence of traditional passive and interactive media as an addendum to the television environment, and began to market set-top boxes that could turn the TV into a medium through which consumers could access the Internet. PC manufacturers developed the same idea in a line of products that were for all intents and purposes a multimedia-equipped computer with TV reception and input connections for VCRs and DVD players.

Although it is too early to make predictions over which iteration of this convergence idea will prevail, especially once DTV arrives, early sales figures show substantial consumer apathy toward the convergence idea. Dealer sales of set-top Internet boxes for connection to TVs totaled 400,000 units. The major proponents were Sony and Philips, which marketed set-top boxes featuring Microsoft's WebTV software client. RCA had hoped to compete with Sony and Philips through the NC Network Computer, another set-top box made in collaboration with software maker Oracle. However, the NC product was abandoned by Oracle in April 1998, and units were purchased back from consumers through an RCA consumer refund. The software "front end" used for the NC set-top boxes was then purchased by America Online, which intends to use the software's television orientation and compliance as part of the company's own convergence initiatives.

The PC makers that have been selling "TVPCs" have approached the convergence medium with caution. Compaq and Gateway2000 have been the leaders, with other companies offering inexpensive TV tuner upgrade cards which would theoretically turn any multimedia-capable PC into a convergence machine. So far the TVPCs that consumers have reacted to have been high-end, expensive machines. Some 60,000 of these machines were sold in the United States in 1997, the first year in which the technology was seriously marketed. However, the average dealer price for a system was $2,900, more than double the average price of a typical multimedia-equipped PC. Clearly, the rapid downward spiral of PC pricing will have an impact on future TVPC sales. These price drops, along with the TV compliance in the new Windows 98 operating system meant for mainstream PC use, may spur increased consumer interest in the category.

Home Audio Market

Despite high household penetration and lagging dollar sales, home and portable audio remains a strong category for the consumer electronics industry. Overall sales were down only 1 percent despite larger percentage drops in most of the major product lines. The introduction of high-quality minisystems, which blend the audio performance of separate components with the compactness of a small rack system, was the category's biggest success story. Sales of these systems were up over 22 percent in 1997 over the previous year. Another strong showing came from inexpensive home theater upgrade packages called "home theater-in-a-box." These systems, which consist of a complement of surround speakers and an outboard decoder to play back analog (not Dolby Digital) surround information, typically retail for $500 or less, with dealer costs averaging $288 per system. Sales of these units were up 57 percent in 1997 versus 1996, the first year that these systems came to market.

The strong sales in the aforementioned categories mitigated dipping sales and profitability in the other home audio categories. Factory sales of separate audio components, including those meant for home theater, were down almost 12 percent in 1997 from 1996. Rack audio systems suffered an even worse year with a 38 percent drop in factory shipments over the same time period. Figures for CD players, which are a commodity to the audio industry as the VCR is to the video industry, are emblematic of the current climate in the audio market. Despite increased dealer sales, which were up almost 12 percent in 1997 over 1996, actual dollar sales for the same period rose less than 2 percent. This is because the cost of CD players continues to drop; the average $130 dealer cost of a player was 9 percent lower in 1997 than 1996, and almost 15 percent lower than the cost in 1995.

The lull in audio sales is also due to consumer anxiety over emerging audio media. Dolby Digital technology is not yet widespread and faces a format challenge in the new DVD arena from a largely incompatible technology called Digital Theater Sound (DTS). Furthermore, plans are under way to utilize DVD as a next-generation carrier of super audio music discs. These discs, which have been announced by Sony, Philips, Meridian, Toshiba, and others, will utilize the increased storage capability of DVD discs to offer a much-higher-resolution audio experience than can be attained with today's CDs. This audio experience will likely be multichannel (surround sound) as opposed to the two-channel stereo sound standard on today's CDs. Specifications and techniques are still being fought over by the competing technology camps, but it is clear that this new superdisc will not be usable in existing CD players. The new format is expected to be introduced into the U.S. market by 2001.

International Competition

The consumer electronics industry has long been dominated by Japan, with secondary roles assumed by Korea, the Netherlands, and France. However, economic instability throughout Asia, soft worldwide demand for home entertainment products, and increasing competition from American high-technology firms have caused a shift in the landscape. U.S. firms produced $13 billion in audio and video electronics in 1997, with 60 percent ($7.8 billion) of this figure consumed in the domestic market. Of the 40 percent going to export, the top international markets for U.S. sales were Canada, Mexico, Japan, Brazil, and Hong Kong.

Most consumer electronics products worldwide are manufactured in Japan or Japanese offshore plants in Malaysia, Thailand, and Singapore. The recent financial instability throughout the region was felt throughout the electronics industry, but the industry was resilient. For example, the Electronics Industry Association of Japan (EIAJ) predicted that Japanese production of consumer electronic equipment would drop 2.7 percent in 1998, a modest decline in consideration of worldwide trends. Singapore expected an increase of 2.5 to 4.5 percent in electronics exports to the United States in 1998. Korea also has responded well to its recent reforms, pulling back from a globalization strategy to an export-driven strategy reminiscent of the country's boom years of the 1970s and 1980s, with electronics leading the way. The Electronics Industry Association of Korea (EIAK) estimated the country's electronics exports would reach $46.6 billion in 1998, up 10.4 percent from 1997. An extremely weak won, down 57 percent in value against the U.S. dollar in March 1998 compared with 1997, is a big reason for the increase in exports.

Consumer electronics products sold by the United States are manufactured and assembled both domestically and abroad. Of all the product categories, U.S. manufacturing accounts for the most sales in the home information and mobile products. In 1997, 54 percent of home information products sold by the United States were produced domestically, which points to a healthy PC industry. Some 66 percent of U.S. sales of mobile electronics, including pagers, cellular phones, auto sound, and aftermarket vehicle security systems, were produced domestically. Only a minority of home entertainment products accounting for U.S. sales were attributable to U.S. production. Some 43 percent of video equipment sold was produced in the U.S., and 20 percent of audio equipment. This latter figure is almost completely attributable to an American specialty hi-fi industry that has enjoyed significant success in overseas markets, including China and Russia.

U.S. Industry Growth Projections for the Next 1 and 5 Years

The audio and video industries experienced a disappointing year in 1997. With the exception of DVD, both categories were hampered by a lack of compelling new technologies, and the established technologies such as home theater experienced slower sales growth than the industry had become accustomed to over the previous several years. The boom in home information products was a factor here. In direct terms, consumers are spending more of their electronics budgets on computers than audio-video gear. In indirect terms, the computer industry's business model of frequent consumer upgrades through accelerated technological evolution and drastic price reductions has hurt the audio and video industries. A consumer base familiar with these cycles is increasingly aware that digital technologies can now change in a matter of months rather than years. Because consumers know that next year's hardware will be more powerful and less expensive than last year's, they have shown a greater propensity to wait for significant new products before investing.

These significant products are ready to come to market. DTV is especially important because the digital data that it can receive point to the possibility of new interactive media—in essence, a new entertainment category. The arrival of DTV occurs at a fortuitous time in the television product life cycle. The average consumer turnaround for a television is 8 years. With the majority of large-screen TVs in U.S. households having been sold since 1995, the all-important early adopter and enthusiast will be ready to buy a new television within the first 3 years of DTV broadcasts. Industry estimates point to 18 million households identified as such consumers, which means that an optimistic projection could put DTV in as many as one of every five households within 10 years. The industry confidently predicts a 30 percent penetration for DTV by 2006, the cutoff point by which the FCC has mandated full DTV delivery.

Unfortunately for the audio and video industries, the first DTV sets will be expensive and rare so that the technology is expected to have little impact on audio and video sales in 1998. The video product segment was expected to show a modest sales increase from $14.5 billion in 1997 to $14.7 billion in 1998. The audio segment was expected to show a slight drop in factory sales from $5.9 billion in 1997 to $5.7 billion in 1998. These declines stand in contrast to overall industry projections, which see a 5 percent increase in overall sales from $72 billion in 1997 to $75.6 billion in 1998. The consumer electronics industry projects that it will grow 31 percent between 1996 and 2000 to overall sales of $86 billion (see Tables 38-8 and 38-9).

The market success of the industry's new products will depend in large part upon the cooperation and participation of content providers across a wide spectrum of media. In the age

TABLE 38-9: U.S. Trade Patterns in Consumer Electronics[1] in 1997
(millions of dollars; percent)

Exports			Imports		
Regions[2]	Value[3]	Share, %	Regions[2]	Value[3]	Share, %
NAFTA	1,958	47.1	NAFTA	5,550	28.4
Latin America	730	17.5	Latin America	283	1.4
Western Europe	619	14.9	Western Europe	382	2.0
Japan/Chinese Economic Area	470	11.3	Japan/Chinese Economic Area	8,177	41.8
Other Asia	245	5.9	Other Asia	5,155	26.3
Rest of world	136	3.3	Rest of world	23	0.1
World	4,158	100.0	World	19,570	100.0
Top Five Countries	Value	Share, %	Top Five Countries	Value	Share, %
Mexico	1,037	24.9	Mexico	5,436	27.8
Canada	922	22.2	Japan	4,266	21.8
Japan	238	5.7	China	3,385	17.3
Brazil	178	4.3	Malaysia	2,478	12.7
Germany	141	3.4	Thailand	863	4.4

[1] SIC 3651.
[2] For definitions of regional groupings, see "Getting the Most Out of *Outlook '99*."
[3] Values may not sum to total due to rounding.
Source: U.S. Department of Commerce, Bureau of the Census.

of DTV, intellectual property such as movies, music, games, and publications will be cross-purposed by the content holders to take advantage of new delivery systems and media outlets, including interactive television and the World Wide Web. Computer functionality will be grafted onto television sets and vice versa; but unless the copyright holders supply the content for these advanced media, consumers will have little incentive to invest in new hardware.

Ample software availability will be the key to driving these new technologies, but content creators have thus far been reluctant to commit to full support until the hardware penetration has reached an acceptable level. This scenario may be complicated by an increasing trend toward incompatibility among hardware playback systems. There are format wars brewing in several key categories: DTV, DVD, recordable DVD, and the superfidelity audio disc. The first of these technologies to market, the DVD player, is already stricken with incompatibilities between open system and pay-per-play media. The recordable iteration of DVD has split into two camps; not all discs recorded through one technology will play back on another. Unlike the PC industry, the consumer electronics industry has been built on adhered-to standards like NTSC, VHS, and CD. The fragmented platforms of the PC environment are a foreign concept to mainstream consumer electronics customers, who balk at a purchase that might be outdated and insufficient in a year or two. To achieve balance and maintain growth, the PC and computer electronics industries will need to learn marketing and manufacturing techniques from each other, particularly since products of both industries converge more with each technological season.

Ron Goldberg, New York, NY, (212) 732-7206, rgold@interport.net.

■ **REFERENCES**

Furniture

To order Bureau of the Census documents, call (301) 457-4100. A growing number of Census Bureau documents and services, including shipment and demographic data, are available via the Internet. The home page is http://www.census.gov/.

AKTRIN Furniture Information Center, 164 S. Main Street, P.O. Box 898, High Point, NC 27261. (336) 841-8535, Fax: (336) 841-5435. Or, 151 Randall Street, Oakville, Ontario, Canada, L6J 1P5. (905) 845-3474, Fax: (905) 845-7459, http://www.aktrin.com/.

American Furniture Manufacturers Association (AFMA), P.O. Box HP-7, High Point, NC 27261. (336) 884-5000, Fax: (336) 884-5303, http://www.afmahp.org/.

Bed Times, International Sleep Products Association, 333 Commerce Street, Alexandria, VA 22314. (703) 683-8371, Fax: (703) 683-4503, http://www.sleepproducts.org/.

Civilian Labor Force by Sex, Age, Race, and Hispanic Origin, 1986, 1996, and Projected 2006. Bureau of Labor Statistics, U.S. Department of Labor, Washington, DC 20212. (202) 606-5711, http://stats.bls.gov/emphome.htm.

Consumer Expenditure Survey, 1995. Bureau of Labor Statistics, U.S. Department of Labor, Washington, DC 20212. (202) 606-6900, http://stats.bls.gov/csxhome.htm.

Employment and Earnings, Bureau of Labor Statistics, U.S. Department of Labor, Washington, DC 20212. (202)606–7705. http://stats.bls.gov/ceshome.htm.

The Furnishings Digest, Mann, Armistead, & Epperson, Ltd., 121 Shockoe Slip, Richmond, VA 23219. (804) 644-1200, Fax: (804) 644-1226.

Furniture Insights, BDO Seidman, LLP, 101 South Main Street, Suite 802, High Point, NC 27261. (336) 883-0181, Fax: (336) 841-8764, http://www.bdo.com/publications.html.

The Furniture Quarterly, Wheat, First Securities, Inc., P.O. Box 1357, Richmond, VA 23211. (804) 782-3297, Fax: (804) 782-3636, http://www.wheatfirst.com/newresearch/rafurn.html.

Furniture/Today, Cahners Business Newspapers, P.O. Box 2754, High Point, NC 27261-2754. (336) 605-0121, Fax: (336) 605-1143, http://www.furnituretoday.com/.

National Association of Home Builders (NAHB), 1201 15th Street, Washington, DC 20005. (800) 368-5242 or (202) 822-0555, Fax: (202) 822-0377, http://www.nahb.com/.

National Association of Realtors (NAR), 700 11th Street, NW, Washington, DC 20001. (202) 383-1225, Fax: (202) 383-7563, http://nar.realtor.com/databank/home.htm.

1992 Census of Manufactures, Bureau of the Census, U.S. Department of Commerce, Washington, DC 20233. http://www.census.gov/prod/www/abs/msmfg02a.html.

1996 Annual Survey of Manufactures, Bureau of the Census, U.S. Department of Commerce, Washington, DC 20233. http://www.census.gov/prod/www/abs/m96as1.html.

Personal Consumption Expenditures, Bureau of Economic Analysis, U.S. Department of Commerce, Washington, DC 20230. (202) 606-9375.

Population Estimates and Projections, Bureau of the Census, U.S. Department of Commerce, Washington, DC 20233. (301) 457-2422, http://www.census.gov/population/www/.

Producer Price Indexes, Bureau of Labor Statistics, U.S. Department of Labor, Washington, DC 20212. (202) 606-7705, http://stats.bls.gov/ppihome.htm.

Random Lengths, Weekly Report on North American Forest Products Markets, P.O. Box 867, Eugene, OR 97440-0867. (541) 686-9925, Fax: (541) 686-9629, http://www.randomlengths.com/.

Survey of Current Business, Bureau of Economic Analysis, U.S. Department of Commerce, Washington, DC 20230. (202) 606-9900, http://www.bea.doc.gov/bea/pubs.htm.

TWICE (This Week in Consumer Electronics), 245 West 17th Street, New York, NY 10011. (212) 337-6980, http://www.twice.com/.

U.S. Consumer Product Safety Commission, Office of Information and Public Affairs, Washington, DC 20207. (301) 504-0400, http://www.cpsc.gov/.

Weekly Hardwood Review, P.O. Box 471307, Charlotte, NC 28247-1307. (800) 638-7206, Fax: (800) 444-2237, http://www.hardwoodreview.com/.

Household Appliances

Appliance, Dana Chase Publications, Inc., 1110 Jorie Boulevard, Oak Brook, IL 60522. (708) 990-3484, E-mail: scot@appliance.com, http://www.appliance.com.

Appliance Manufacturer, Business News Publishing Co., 5900 Harper Road, Suite 105, Solon, OH 44139. (216) 349-3060, http://www.bnp.com/am.

Dealerscope Consumer Electronics Marketplace, North American Publishing Co., 401 North Broad Street, Philadelphia, PA 19108. (215) 238-5300, http://www.dealerscope.com.

Electric Housewares and Fans, Current Industrial Reports, MA-36E, Bureau of the Census, U.S. Department of Commerce, Washington, DC 20233. (301) 457-1604.

HFN, Home Furnishings Network, Fairchild Publications, 7 West 34th Street, New York, NY 10001. (212) 630-4000, http://www.hfn-mag.com.

Household Appliances, 1992 Census of Manufactures, MC92-1-36B, Bureau of the Census, U.S. Department of Commerce, Washington, DC 20233.

Major Household Appliances, Current Industrial Reports, MA-36F, Bureau of the Census, U.S. Department of Commerce, Washington, DC 20233. (301) 457-1604.

1996 Annual Survey of Manufactures, Bureau of the Census, U.S. Department of Commerce, Washington, DC 20233.

Lawn and Garden Equipment

California Air Resources Board, Mobile Sources Lab, 9420 Telstar Avenue, El Monte, CA 91731. (626) 575-6676, Fax: (626) 575-6686, http://www.arb.ca.gov/.

Consumer Reports, Consumer's Union, 101 Truman Avenue, Yonkers, NY 10703. (914) 378-2000, Fax: (914) 378-2900, http://www.consumerreport.org.

Engines and Turbines and Farm Machinery and Equipment, 1992 Census of Manufactures, SIC 3524, MC92-I-35A. Bureau of the Census, U.S. Department of Commerce, Washington, DC 20233. (301) 457-4100, http://www.census.gov/.

Farm Machinery and Lawn and Garden Equipment (the product series described in this publication is similar, but not identical to the series described in the other two Census publications listed), 1996 Current Industrial Report, Ser. MA35A(96)-1. Bureau of the Census, U.S. Department of Commerce, Washington, DC 20233. (301) 457-4100, http://www.census.gov/.

National Centers for Environmental Prediction, National Oceanic and Atmospheric Administration, U.S. Department of Commerce, Camp Springs, MD 20746. (301) 763-8000, http://www.noaa.gov/.

Outdoor Power Equipment Institute, 341 South Patrick Street, Alexandria, VA 22314. (703) 549-7600, Fax: (703) 549-7604, http://www.opei.mow.org.

Personal Consumption Expenditures, Bureau of Economic Analysis, U.S. Department of Commerce, Washington, DC 20230. (202) 606-9735, http://www.bea.doc.gov/.

Producer Price Indexes; Employment and Earnings, Bureau of Labor Statistics, U.S. Department of Labor, Washington, DC 20212. (202) 606-7705, http://www.bls.gov/.

U.S. Consumer Product Safety Commission, Office of Information and Public Affairs, Washington, DC 20207. (301) 504-0400, http://www.cpsc.gov/.

U.S. Environmental Protection Agency, National Vehicle and Fuel Emission Laboratory, Ann Arbor, MI 48105. (734) 214-4849, Fax: (734) 214-4050, http://www.epa.gov/omswww/.

Value of Product Shipments, 1996 Annual Survey of Manufactures, Bureau of the Census, U.S. Department of Commerce, Washington, DC 20233. (301) 457-4100, http://www.census.gov/.

Yard & Garden, Johnson Hill Press, Inc., P.O. Box 803, Fort Atkinson, WI 53538-0803. (920) 563-6388, Fax: (920) 564-1699.

Household Audio and Video Equipment

Consumer Electronics Manufacturers Association, 2500 Wilson Boulevard, Arlington, VA 22201. (703) 907-7764.

■ RELATED CHAPTERS

6: Construction
7: Wood Products
42: Retailing

RECREATIONAL EQUIPMENT
Economic and Trade Trends

U.S. International Trade

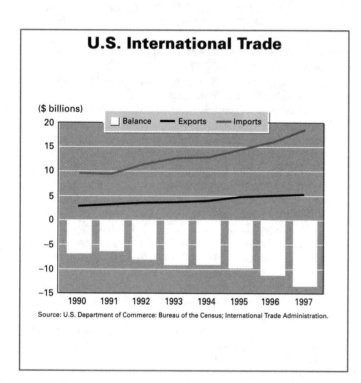

($ billions)

Balance — Exports — Imports

Source: U.S. Department of Commerce: Bureau of the Census; International Trade Administration.

World Export Market Shares

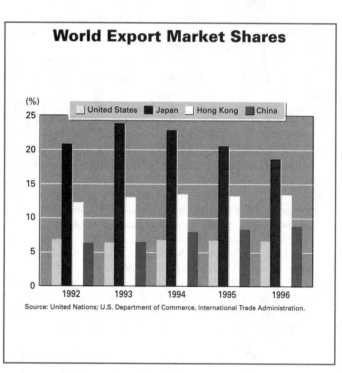

(%)

United States ■ Japan □ Hong Kong ■ China

Source: United Nations; U.S. Department of Commerce, International Trade Administration.

Export Dependence and Import Penetration

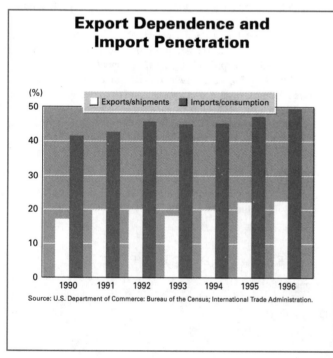

(%)

Exports/shipments ■ Imports/consumption

Source: U.S. Department of Commerce: Bureau of the Census; International Trade Administration.

Output and Output per Hour

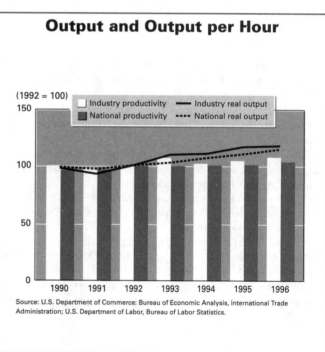

(1992 = 100)

Industry productivity — Industry real output
■ National productivity ---- National real output

Source: U.S. Department of Commerce: Bureau of Economic Analysis, International Trade Administration; U.S. Department of Labor, Bureau of Labor Statistics.

See "Getting the Most Out of *Outlook '99*" for definitions of terms.

Recreational Equipment

INDUSTRY DEFINITION   This chapter includes analyses of SIC 3949, sporting and athletic equipment; SIC 3942 and 3944, dolls, toys, and games; SIC 37511, bicycles and parts; SIC 37512, motorcycles and parts; and SIC 3732, boat building and repairing. Among the products not included in this chapter are camping equipment, sports apparel and footwear, coin-operated games, large ships and vessels, and recreational motor homes and camping trailers. More specific industry definitions appear with certain individual industry descriptions.

GLOBAL INDUSTRY TRENDS

International trade is an important aspect of the recreational equipment industry. Many companies import low-end branded products, use parts made overseas, or face stiff competition from importers. Labor is an important input in the production of many recreational products, particularly entry-level products. The less developed countries have wage rates significantly lower than those in the United States. Many firms import products with U.S. brand names; this practice is prevalent in the dolls, toys, games, sporting goods, and bicycle industries. The motorcycle industry relies on imported parts from both developed and developing countries. Many of those parts no longer are manufactured in the United States. As a result of these trends in completed products and parts, the ratio of imports to apparent consumption in the recreational equipment industry is high, reaching 52 percent in 1997. The single exception to this trend is the U.S. boat industry, in which that ratio was only 15 percent in 1997.

Exports are also important in this industry, driven by increasing demand for "made-in-the-USA" products. U.S. products such as titanium golf clubs, Harley-Davidson motorcycles, inboard-outdrive boats, and mountain bikes are in high demand overseas. In addition, industries that typically are not thought to be export-oriented have had export successes recently. For example, toys, particularly educational software, have been in demand overseas; U.S. exports of toys increased 8 percent in 1997. Export growth in the various recreational equipment industries ranged from 2 to 16 percent in 1997. The U.S. industry manufactures primarily high-quality recreational equipment products and is viewed by overseas consumers as a leader in product development. As a result, U.S. name brands are recognized and sought throughout the world. Innovations such as mountain bikes, in-line roller skates, and snowboards were developed in this country by small entrepreneurs and companies which now are large, profitable firms. Servicing the world's largest market for recreational equipment in the United States, large American firms are aware of consumer tastes and preferences in recreational products. Many U.S. firms recognize their advantages in overseas markets. Export sales are an important factor in U.S. manufacturers' business plans. The ratio of exports to domestic shipments was 23 percent for the entire recreational equipment sector in 1997.

IMPORTANT FACTORS AFFECTING THE FUTURE GROWTH OF U.S. INDUSTRY

Current-dollar product shipments for recreational equipment totaled $22 billion in 1997, growing 1 percent over 1996 in real terms. These shipments were expected to reach $22.4 billion in 1998, up only 0.4 percent in real terms. Growth in domestic shipments can be traced to strong export growth. U.S. exports of recreational equipment totaled $5 billion, increasing 5 percent in 1997, and were expected to reach $5.3 billion, up 6 percent, in 1998. However, the shifting of production from U.S. sourcing to overseas sourcing, particularly for the toys, dolls, games, and bicycle industries, weakened domestic manufacturers' growth. Constant-dollar product shipments for these two industries declined 5 percent, while imports, not adjusted for

TABLE 39-1:   Recreational Equipment (SIC 3732, 3751, 3942, 3944, 3949) Trends and Forecasts
(millions of dollars except as noted)

	1992	1993	1994	1995	1996	1997[1]	1998[2]	1999[3]	Percent Change			
									96–97	97–98	98–99	92–96[4]
Industry data												
Value of shipments[5]	18,904	20,969	21,459	23,065	23,665	24,490	25,104	25,841	3.5	2.5	2.9	5.8
Value of shipments (1992$)	18,904	20,755	20,943	22,034	22,196	22,302	22,490	22,699	0.5	0.8	0.9	4.1
Total employment (thousands)	155	165	167	170	171							2.5
Production workers (thousands)	116	123	127	130	130							2.9
Average hourly earnings ($)	9.12	9.44	9.61	10.12	10.29							3.1
Capital expenditures	449	493	524	567	636							9.1
Product data												
Value of shipments[5]	17,461	19,385	19,891	21,023	21,411	21,979	22,438	23,010	2.7	2.1	2.5	5.2
Value of shipments (1992$)	17,461	19,181	19,410	20,080	20,078	20,002	20,081	20,189	−0.4	0.4	0.5	3.6
Trade data												
Value of imports	11,423	12,582	12,901	14,370	16,007	18,491	21,519	23,667	15.5	16.4	10.0	8.8
Value of exports	3,394	3,471	3,844	4,595	4,737	4,988	5,309	5,559	5.3	6.4	4.7	8.7

[1] Estimate except imports and exports.
[2] Estimate.
[3] Forecast.
[4] Compound annual rate.
[5] For definition of industry versus product values, see "Getting the Most Out of *Outlook '99*."
Source: U.S. Department of Commerce: Bureau of the Census; International Trade Administration.

inflation, increased 19 percent. Imports increased in every recreational sector except boat building from 1996 to 1998. U.S. imports of recreational equipment totaled $18.5 billion, increasing 16 percent in 1997. Imports were expected to grow an additional 16 percent to total $21.5 billion in 1998. These increases are closely related to the Asian financial crises, as most Asian currencies fell against the dollar, making the prices of imported products from Asia significantly lower. Demand in the U.S. market also grew, partly in response to cheaper imported products. As real gross domestic product (GDP) and disposable income increased 3.8 and 2.9 percent, respectively, in 1997, apparent consumption climbed 7 percent in real terms to total $35.5 billion. In 1998, GDP was expected to grow 2.2 to 2.8 percent while apparent consumption in the recreational equipment sector was expected to total $38.6 billion, increasing 8 percent in real terms. Consumer confidence, as measured by the Conference Board, remained high at over 120 throughout most of 1997 and the first half of 1998 (see Table 39-1).

U.S. INDUSTRY GROWTH PROJECTIONS FOR THE NEXT 1 AND 5 YEARS

Current-dollar product shipments are forecast to reach $23 billion in 1999, up 0.5 percent from 1998 in constant dollars. Constant-dollar product shipments for the sports equipment, boat, and motorcycle industries are forecast to increase, while product shipments in the bicycle and dolls, toys, and games industries are expected to be down, reflecting the trend of imports displacing domestic production. However, apparent consumption will grow to a forecast $41.1 billion, up 5 percent in real terms. Imports are the primary benefactors of the increased

demand as U.S. imports of recreational equipment are forecast to increase 10 percent to total $23.7 billion. The ratio of imports to apparent consumption will grow to 58 percent in 1999, up from 49 percent as recently as 1996. U.S. exports of recreational equipment will continue to increase, growing 5 percent in 1999 as the weighted sum of top 20 overall export markets is forecast to grow 3.6 percent. The ratio of exports to shipments will reach 24 percent in 1999. Highlighting the growth of exports are the 10 percent and 7 percent projected increases in U.S. exports of toys and motorcycles, respectively.

Constant-dollar product shipments are forecast to increase 1.5 percent annually over the next 5 years. Trade will continue to be one of the important factors affecting shipments. The ratio of exports to shipments for recreational equipment is likely to reach 26 percent as U.S. exports are projected to grow 6 percent annually. Meanwhile, imports will continue to increase at a 4 percent annual rate. The ratio of imports to apparent consumption probably will remain between 56 and 59 percent, depending on fluctuations in exchange rates.

Demographic trends will be a key factor for these industries. The baby boom generation has helped these industries over the last three decades. The parents of baby boomers bought their children toys and bicycles in the 1960s, and the boomers themselves bought sports equipment and motorcycles in the 1970s and boats and campers in the 1980s. In the early 1990s they upgraded to high-quality recreational products of all kinds. Over the next 5 years this generation will be entering the age group 45 to 64 years. The older segment of the group, the age group 55 to 64 years, will be the fastest growing age cohort over the next 5 years. Getting these soon to be senior citizens to continue to participate in recreational activities will be a growing concern as this period progresses. However, early indications are that the baby boomers will continue to enjoy recreational activities, especially less strenuous ones such as exercising with equipment, golfing, and motorcycle touring.

GLOBAL MARKET PROSPECTS

Overseas markets for recreational equipment are growing faster than is the domestic market as leisure time is increasing faster in most foreign countries, particularly in the newly industrialized nations and the Big Emerging Markets. Western Europe currently is the largest market for U.S. recreational equipment, accounting for 28 percent of American exports in 1997. The next largest market consists of the North American Free Trade Agreement (NAFTA) countries, Canada and Mexico; U.S. exports of recreational equipment to this region accounted for almost 27 percent of total recreational equipment exports. The Japan/Chinese Economic Area accounted for almost 23 percent of exports. In 1997, U.S. exports of recreational equipment to western Europe grew 4 percent and exports to the NAFTA countries rose 23 percent. However, because of the Asian financial crisis, U.S. exports of recreational equipment to the Japan/China Economic Area fell 8 percent (see Table 39-2).

The largest single market for U.S. recreational equipment exports was Canada, with exports totaling $929 million in 1997. U.S. exports of sports equipment and dolls, toys, and games reached $625 million, accounting for 67 percent of recreational equipment exports to Canada. U.S. exports to Japan, the next largest export market, totaled an estimated $786 million. Exports of sports equipment to Japan totaled $515 million, accounting for 65 percent of U.S. recreational equipment exports, as Japanese consumers have increased leisure time and a passion for many sports activities, especially golf. Mexico was the third largest market, reaching an estimated $395 mil-

lion and increasing 49 percent in 1997. As the Mexican economy began its turnaround in 1996, opportunities for manufacturers of leisure equipment increased, particularly for sports equipment, pleasure boats, and dolls, toys, and games manufacturers, which have benefited from the growth of the tourism industry in Mexico. The United Kingdom and Germany were the fourth and fifth largest markets for U.S. exports of recreational equipment, totaling an estimated $369 million and $270 million, respectively, in 1997.

Trade in the recreational equipment sector is clearly dominated by imports, as U.S. imports of recreational equipment surpassed exports by an estimated $13.5 billion. Only the golf industry had a favorable balance of trade in 1997.

China was the largest foreign supplier of recreational products, as U.S. imports from that country totaled an estimated $9 billion, or about 49 percent of total U.S. recreational equipment imports, up 28 percent from 1996. China is the world's largest exporter of several recreational products, including dolls, toys, and bicycles. U.S. imports from Japan, the second largest foreign supplier, totaled an estimated $3.6 billion in 1997. Imports of motorcycles and parts accounted for a significant share—23 percent—of total U.S. imports of recreational products from Japan. U.S. imports from Taiwan, the third largest foreign supplier, totaled an estimated $1.3 billion. Taiwan has become a major supplier of medium-price and medium-quality recreational products, especially bicycles and sports equipment. The fourth largest foreign supplier in 1997 was Canada, from which U.S. imports of recreational equipment totaled an estimated $0.9 billion. Canada is a major supplier of pleasure boats to the United States; imports of pleasure boats accounted for 48 percent of total recreational imports from Canada in 1997.

It is likely that imports will continue to increase over the next 5 years, although at a slower rate. With disposable income growing and with many consumers reaching an age at which

TABLE 39-2: U.S. Trade Patterns in Recreational Equipment[1] in 1997
(millions of dollars; percent)

	Exports			Imports	
Regions[2]	Value[3]	Share, %	Regions[2]	Value[3]	Share, %
NAFTA	1,324	26.5	NAFTA	1,758	9.5
Latin America	467	9.4	Latin America	63	0.3
Western Europe	1,395	28.0	Western Europe	1,224	6.6
Japan/Chinese Economic Area	1,128	22.6	Japan/Chinese Economic Area	14,185	76.8
Other Asia	293	5.9	Other Asia	1,165	6.3
Rest of world	381	7.6	Rest of world	98	0.5
World	4,988	100.0	World	18,493	100.0
Top Five Countries	Value	Share, %	Top Five Countries	Value	Share, %
Canada	929	18.6	China	8,984	48.6
Japan	786	15.8	Japan	3,584	19.4
Mexico	395	7.9	Taiwan	1,336	7.2
United Kingdom	369	7.4	Canada	935	5.1
Germany	270	5.4	Mexico	823	4.5

[1] SIC 3732, 3751, 3942, 3944, 3949.
[2] For definitions of regional groupings, see "Getting the Most Out of *Outlook '99*."
[3] Values may not sum to total due to rounding.
Source: U.S. Department of Commerce, Bureau of the Census.

they have a higher level of discretionary income, consumers may be more apt to purchase higher-quality domestic products. However, discretionary income also could be used to ease personal debt and increase savings as the baby boom generation approaches retirement age.

SPORTING AND ATHLETIC EQUIPMENT

The sporting and athletic equipment industry (SIC 3949) consists of firms that produce equipment for golf, fishing, tennis, physical fitness, gymnastics, archery, bowling, billiards, winter sports, and team sports. This industry does not include camping equipment, athletic apparel and footwear, hunting equipment, or most leisure-related vehicles, such as boats, bicycles, motorcycles, and snowmobiles.

Global Industry Trends

The U.S. sporting goods market performed well in the 1990s as real apparent consumption grew 4 percent annually from 1989 to 1998. The baby boom generation has continued to drive up sales as it has pursued healthy living. This generation continues to dominate trends in the industry. For the past 30 years the effect has been positive on sports equipment sales as the baby boomers have shown a strong desire to participate in sports and stay fit. In the 1970s baby boomers were in their teens and twenties, and strenuous activities such as running, football, and tennis had all-time-high participation totals. In the 1980s that generation mellowed a bit as its members swelled the ranks of the thirty somethings, pushing activities such as weight training, baseball, and softball to peak participation rates. In the 1990s, with baby boomers reaching middle age, fitness activities became one of the most popular forms of sports recreation. Exercise walking was the most popular sports activity in 1997, with 76 million participants, followed by swimming (60 million), exercising with equipment (48 million), and bicycle riding (45 million).

A changing retail environment is affecting sales of sports equipment. A major problem for the industry is an oversaturation of retail space. Today there are more places and more choices for consumers. This has created a survival-of-the-fittest mentality in the sports retail business. It appears that the large super sporting-goods stores have been winning most of the battles. Chains such as the Sports Authority and Gant Sports Systems are putting added pressure on many small store chains. Many retailers have opted to go to a larger store; some have created a "shoppertainment" format with in-store features such as basketball courts, golf driving ranges, and exercise facilities. The large-store chains have continued to increase the number of outlets. These chains not only are affecting their competitors but also wield substantial power over manufacturers in regard to price and product offerings. Many manufacturers find themselves in a partnership with retailers in order to lower costs to consumers and maximize profits for both retailer and manufacturer. These partnerships typically deal with inventory controls, with manufacturers taking more of the risk in exchange for more shelf space.

Important Factors Affecting the Future Growth of U.S. Industry

Factors affecting the growth of U.S. sports equipment consumption and U.S. manufacturers' shipments include the Asian financial crisis, stable prices, and steady growth of disposable income. As was indicated above, demographics also plays a key role in industry growth. Constant-dollar product shipments of sporting and athletic goods were expected to grow about 2 percent in 1998 after an estimated 0.5 percent growth in 1997. Apparent consumption in real terms was up an estimated 3 percent in 1997 and 4 percent in 1998.

U.S. imports grew about 2 percent in 1997 and were expected to increase about 11 percent in 1998. In 1997 U.S. exports increased 2 percent to reach $2.4 billion. U.S. exports in 1998 were expected to increase 1 percent. The Asian financial crisis has driven up imports, while export opportunities have been curtailed as U.S. products have become less price-competitive versus Asian products. However, U.S. export sales have been buoyed by continued growth in the major European markets and continued demand by overseas consumers for sports products that are "made in the USA."

Low inflation in the sporting goods industry also has helped fuel the demand for sports equipment. The industry's producer price index rose only 1.7 percent in 1997 over 1996. Annual inflation has not topped 3 percent since 1990, and there was a 2.2 percent annual inflation rate from 1989 to 1998. In that period the overall consumer price index had only 3 years with inflation under 3 percent and grew at an annual inflation rate of 3.1 percent. Manufacturers have become much more efficient, cutting their largest input, labor, 3 percent from 1994 to 1996 while increasing real production as measured by real product shipments 7 percent over that period. The retailer pressures that were mentioned earlier and pressures for low-cost imports have been factors in the low inflation rates in the sports industry.

The growth of apparent consumption of sporting and athletic goods has been aided by higher personal income. Real disposable personal income (DPI) increased 3 percent annually from 1989 to 1997. In that period real personal consumption expenditures for sporting goods increased 6 percent annually. Real DPI grew 4 percent in the first quarter of 1998 from the same period in 1997. As a result, consumers had more income to spend on sports activities. However, the Asian financial crisis may dampen the growth of personal income in the second half of 1998 as increased imports cut into the sales of domestic manufacturers. Any loss of market share by U.S. firms probably will mean fewer wage increases and lower growth in personal income.

Golf Equipment

In 1997 current-dollar domestic shipments of golf equipment totaled an estimated $2.5 billion, up 5 percent in constant dollars from 1996. Imports of golf equipment jumped 23 percent to reach $784 million, while exports grew only 5 percent to about $804 million. However, the U.S. golf industry still had a favorable balance of trade as exports of its products surpassed imports by $20 million in 1997. Several manufacturers have decided to take advantage of lower Mexican labor costs and lower tariffs as a result of NAFTA by starting assembly operations just across the border. Imports of golf equipment from Mexico increased 22 percent in 1997. Apparent consumption totaled an estimated $2.4 billion, up 11 percent in real terms. The demographics of the United States have played a large role in the growth of consumption. The baby boom generation has high levels of disposable income at a time when its available leisure time is high. Although participation in golf has not increased greatly, sales have soared. Golf is an equipment-intensive activity whose participants are eager to have the proper tools to maximize their talent. Golfers desire the latest items, such as clubs (titanium), balls, shoes (spikeless), gloves, and even apparel that will make them play or look better. Now this generation has the income needed to purchase the best equipment. As a result, there are many new manufacturers with new products that they hope will become the next big trend, such as titanium clubs. With the new entrants also comes the need to increase marketing so that one's company stands out. Industry experts believe that spending on infomercials and other media advertisements has never been higher.

Fishing Tackle and Equipment

In 1997 apparent consumption of fishing equipment was estimated at $951 million, up almost 1 percent in real terms from 1996. This reflected a 3 percent decline in U.S. imports of fishing equipment, which totaled $349 million. The decline in imports can be attributed to a major oversupply of products in 1995, when imports increased 26 percent. Imports, mostly from South Korea, Japan, and China, accounted for about 41 percent of apparent consumption. Current-dollar domestic product shipments totaled an estimated $750 million in 1997, up 2 percent in constant dollars. However, U.S. exports of fishing equipment fell 5 percent, declining to $148 million in 1997. Many industry experts predict that sales of fishing equipment will grow significantly as the baby boomers get older, since fishing is a sport with high participation rates among people over age 50 years. However, continued development of waterfront real estate has made it difficult to find appropriate locations to go fishing. Therefore, U.S. consumption of fishing equipment is likely to grow moderately at an estimated 2 to 3 percent from 1998 to 2003.

Exercise and Gymnastic Equipment

The exercise and fitness sector, the second largest sector of the sporting goods industry, has grown the fastest among major industry segments in the 1990s. Real apparent consumption rose at an estimated compound annual rate of 5 percent from 1990 to 1997. Imports declined 15 percent from 1996, totaling $638 million in 1997, while exports increased 9 percent to reach $355 million. Current-dollar shipments reached an estimated $1.6 billion in 1997, an increase of 6 percent in constant dollars. A slight decline in popularity and an oversupply of devices for working the abdominal muscles probably were the main reasons for the decline in imports. These abdominal

machines were low-tech devices that typically were imported from countries with low-wage manufacturing capacity. However, overseas consumers were interested in more sophisticated products, such as cross-country ski machines, treadmills, and stair climbers, that typically are manufactured in the United States, and this led to an increase in exports.

Playground Equipment and Other Sporting and Athletic Goods

This category includes all other sporting goods products, including skis, water sports apparatus, swing sets, and team sports equipment. Major segments that have experienced growing participation rates include snowboarding, soccer, softball, and in-line skating. Snowboarding participation nearly doubled from 1988 to 1997 to total 2.5 million participants, according to a National Sporting Goods Association (NSGA) survey. The inclusion of snowboarding in the 1998 Nagano Olympics was expected to fuel the growth of this market segment. However, much of snowboarding's popularity has come at the expense of alpine skiing, which from 1988 to 1997 lost 3.5 million participants.

In the 1970s soccer was forecast to be a major spectator sport and participatory activity. However, that sport is just beginning to meet those lofty claims. Participation in soccer increased 40 percent between 1987 and 1997, reaching 13.7 million participants. The U.S. men's and women's teams' participation in the World Cup is expected to attract more participants over the next few years. Based on participation statistics from the NSGA, soccer is the number one team sports activity among individuals less than 10 years old. However, the sport has lost young participants and spectators to basketball, football, and baseball as these participants have grown older. However, several factors may change that trend. The percentage of the U.S. population that is of Asian and Hispanic descent is expected to grow significantly. Hispanic and Asian individuals are projected to constitute 17 percent of the population by 2005, compared with 12 percent in 1990. Soccer is very popular in these cultures, and it is unlikely that these individuals will give up the sport. In addition, the development of a first-rate professional league (Major League Soccer) may entice young people to stay involved in the sport.

U.S. Industry Growth Projections for the Next 1 and 5 Years

Growing more slowly than personal income and GDP, constant-dollar product shipments for the sports equipment industry will increase only an estimated 1 percent in 1999. A potential decline or leveling off of consumer confidence and historically high levels of consumer debt will be the main factors limiting growth. The economy is expected to continue to experience modest annual growth. Restraining growth may be a continuation of the trend among consumers toward lowering debt, which is still at record levels, 17.4 percent of personal income in the first quarter of 1998. As the year continues, consumers may use less credit and pay off more of their debts. Apparent consumption should total $11.9 billion in 1999, growing 3 percent in real terms. Imports will be the beneficiary of the increase in consumption as imports rise over 7 percent in 1999, reaching $4.2 billion. Exports will continue to rise, but at a moderate rate of 2 percent, to reach $2.5 billion. Economic growth in the major industrialized countries will be counteracted by weak Asian markets as U.S. manufacturers continue to search for export opportunities. (See Tables 39-3 and 39-4.)

Constant-dollar product shipments for sports equipment are expected to grow 2.5 percent annually over the next 5 years. The long-term outlook for the U.S. sporting goods industry will be affected by two major factors: demographic trends and the growth of the domestic and world economies. More aging baby boomers are likely to participate less in many sports activities. The effects on shipments, however, will not be that significant because the baby boomers who continue to participate probably will be engaged in equipment-intensive activities such as golf and working out. The real challenge will be to entice the next generation, sometimes called the X generation, to participate in and spend on sports activities. These individuals have shown some interest in sports activities but have not sustained a high level of participation. Individuals in this generation typically are entertained by many activities besides sports, such as computers, the Internet, and media entertainment (television and motion pictures). One recreational sports activity which has maintained a strong level of participation among individuals in the X generation is in-line skating. The number of in-line skating participants increased 33 percent annually from 1990 to 1997. Recently, participation rates have increased only modestly, but the increases have been sustained, which indicates that the sport probably is not a fad. Recognizing this trend, mainstream manufacturers such as Nike, Fila, and K2 have begun producing in-line skates.

One aspect of the X generation that has been extremely positive has been the participation of women in sports activities, which is at an all-time high. Some of the activities in which women have strong participation rates are all fitness activities and sports such as softball, in-line skating, and soccer. The success of women's team sports at the 1996 Olympics may be a key reason for this increased participation. U.S. women's Olympic teams in softball, basketball, and soccer all won gold metals in the 1996 Atlanta games. Sparked by increasing women's participation, fast-pitch softball was the fastest growing team sport in 1997, according to a study prepared for the Sporting Goods Manufacturers Association. Also spurring growth may be a federal law called Title IX, which requires federally funded universities to offer equal opportunities to participate in athletics to both men and women. Title IX has meant more scholarships for women and more money for women's sports programs.

Another positive demographic factor for the industry is the "echo baby boomers," the offspring of the baby boomers. Although not as large a group as their parents, this age cohort appears to have many of the same propensities toward sustained sports participation. The echo boomers will be entering the age group 10 to 19 years old over the next 5 years. The members of this group appear to have significant purchasing power, perhaps because their parents are at their maximum income levels. Many sports equipment manufacturers are already directing advertising toward this group. Popular sports activities among individuals 10 to 19 years old include snowboarding, in-line skating, and mountain biking.

The U.S. economy is experiencing one of its longest periods of sustained growth since World War II. Many forecasters expect the economy to continue to experience modest growth.

TABLE 39-3: Sporting and Athletic Goods n.e.c. (SIC 3949) Trends and Forecasts
(millions of dollars except as noted)

	1992	1993	1994	1995	1996	1997[1]	1998[2]	1999[3]	Percent Change 96–97	97–98	98–99	92–96[4]
Industry data												
Value of shipments[5]	7,581	8,459	8,943	9,543	9,882	10,680	11,200	11,610	8.1	4.9	3.7	6.9
Value of shipments (1992$)	7,581	8,401	8,734	9,149	9,340	9,691	10,045	10,211	3.8	3.7	1.7	5.4
Total employment (thousands)	62.0	64.4	68.2	67.7	66.1							1.6
Production workers (thousands)	44.2	46.8	49.7	48.8	47.6							1.9
Average hourly earnings ($)	8.52	8.74	8.67	9.26	9.51							2.8
Capital expenditures	178	218	192	222	254							9.3
Product data												
Value of shipments[5]	6,994	7,865	8,285	8,802	9,203	9,630	9,890	10,175	4.6	2.7	2.9	7.1
Value of shipments (1992$)	6,994	7,810	8,091	8,440	8,698	8,739	8,870	8,949	0.5	1.5	0.9	5.6
Trade data												
Value of imports	2,518	2,543	3,129	3,392	3,472	3,531	3,900	4,200	1.7	10.5	7.7	8.4
Value of exports	1,289	1,490	1,758	2,171	2,313	2,366	2,400	2,450	2.3	1.4	2.1	15.7

[1] Estimate except imports and exports.
[2] Estimate.
[3] Forecast.
[4] Compound annual rate.
[5] For definition of industry versus product values, see "Getting the Most Out of *Outlook '99*."
Source: U.S. Department of Commerce: Bureau of the Census; International Trade Administration.

TABLE 39-4: Major Sports Industry Segments Trends and Forecasts

(millions of dollars except as noted)

	1992	1993	1994	1995	1996	1997[1]	Percent Change 91–92	92–93	93–94	94–95	95–96	96–97
Fishing equipment (SIC 39492)												
Product data												
Value of shipments[2]	493	629	657	685	724	750	3.8	27.5	4.5	4.2	5.7	3.6
Value of shipments (1992$)	493	621	632	649	668	681	0.9	26.0	1.7	2.6	3.0	1.9
Trade data												
Value of imports	321	289	309	388	358	349	28.8	−10.0	7.0	25.6	−7.7	−2.5
Imports to apparent consumption (%)	43.4	34.7	35.7	41.0	38.6	36.7	13.5	−20.2	3.1	14.7	−5.7	−5.0
Value of exports	76	85	102	126	155	148	2.9	12.2	20.0	24.3	22.6	−4.5
Exports to shipments (%)	15.3	13.5	15.5	18.5	21.4	19.7	−0.9	−12.0	14.8	19.3	16.0	−7.8
Market data												
Apparent consumption	738	833	864	946	927	951	13.5	12.8	3.8	9.5	−2.0	2.6
Real apparent consumption	738	823	831	896	855	863	10.3	11.4	1.0	7.8	−4.6	0.9
Golf equipment (SIC 39492)												
Product data												
Value of shipments[2]	1,782	1,926	1,976	2,098	2,286	2,450	18.6	8.1	2.6	6.2	9.0	7.2
Value of shipments (1992$)	1,782	1,903	1,900	1,987	2,109	2,223	15.3	6.8	−0.2	4.6	6.1	5.4
Trade data												
Value of imports	461	492	541	579	639	784	25.8	6.6	10.1	7.0	10.3	22.7
Imports to apparent consumption (%)	25.4	25.5	27.4	29.1	29.6	32.3	−0.4	0.5	7.3	6.4	1.5	9.0
Value of exports	428	491	542	690	766	804	−1.1	14.9	10.3	27.3	11.1	5.0
Exports to shipments (%)	24.0	25.5	27.4	32.9	33.5	32.8	−16.6	6.3	7.5	19.9	1.9	−2.0
Market data												
Apparent consumption	1,816	1,927	1,976	1,988	2,159	2,430	26.3	6.1	2.5	0.6	8.6	12.5
Real apparent consumption	1,816	1,904	1,900	1,883	1,992	2,205	22.8	4.9	−0.2	−0.9	5.8	10.7
Exercise and gymnastic equipment (SIC 39494)												
Product data												
Value of shipments[2]	1,376	1,407	1,370	1,452	1,510	1,625	−3.4	2.3	−2.6	6.0	4.0	7.6
Value of shipments (1992$)	1,376	1,390	1,317	1,375	1,393	1,475	−6.1	1.0	−5.3	4.4	1.3	5.9
Trade data												
Value of imports	382	384	513	517	751	638	24.2	0.5	33.5	0.9	45.1	−15.0
Imports to apparent consumption (%)	24.3	24.0	31.4	30.8	38.8	33.4	26.8	−1.0	30.8	−1.9	25.9	−13.8
Value of exports	183	191	249	290	325	355	47.6	4.4	30.7	16.3	12.2	9.1
Exports to shipments (%)	13.3	13.6	18.2	20.0	21.5	21.8	52.8	2.1	34.2	9.7	7.9	1.4
Market data												
Apparent consumption	1,575	1,600	1,633	1,679	1,936	1,908	−2.0	1.6	2.1	2.8	15.2	−1.4
Real apparent consumption	1,575	1,581	1,571	1,590	1,786	1,731	−4.8	0.4	−0.7	1.3	12.3	−3.0

[1] Estimate except imports and exports.
[2] Value of products classified in the sporting and athletic goods, n.e.c., industry produced by all industries.
Source: U.S. Department of Commerce: Bureau of the Census.

If this occurs, it is likely that apparent consumption and product shipments will grow moderately. However, if personal income declines or consumer debt increases, this may dry up disposable income and sales of discretionary purchases such as sports equipment. Currently, the consumer confidence index is relatively high (134.3 in May 1998), as measured by the Conference Board. Consumers' attitudes toward and expectations about the economy can be volatile, however. With stock market fluctuations and the Asian financial crisis, it is possible that consumers will limit further growth of the economy by consuming less. Consumption accounts for over two-thirds of GDP.

If the major industrialized economies mirror the modest U.S. GDP growth, as is expected, U.S. exports of sports equipment will continue to support the growth of domestic manufacturers. Many industrialized countries are experiencing a boom in sports participation, similar to what happened in the United States in the 1970s and 1980s. However, consumers in these markets are not as committed to leisure spending and typically cut back on purchases of sports equipment at the first sign of economic hardship. GDP in major sports equipment markets such as Canada, the United Kingdom, and Germany is expected to grow an estimated 3.6 percent in 1999. U.S. brand names are well respected for quality and service in those countries. Opportunities for U.S. exports of sports equipment also will be opening up in the Big Emerging Markets, particularly in Latin America (see Table 39-5).

Global Market Prospects

The U.S. sports equipment industry is focused on global competitiveness, especially in terms of the manufacturing process. The production process of sports equipment is diverse in that varying amounts of labor and capital are needed to manufacture

TABLE 39-5: U.S. Trade Patterns in Sporting and Athletic Goods, nec[1] in 1997
(millions of dollars; percent)

Exports			Imports		
Regions[2]	Value[3]	Share, %	Regions[2]	Value[3]	Share, %
NAFTA	580	24.5	NAFTA	611	17.3
Latin America	103	4.4	Latin America	36	1.0
Western Europe	557	23.6	Western Europe	398	11.3
Japan/Chinese Economic Area	759	32.1	Japan/Chinese Economic Area	1,906	54.0
Other Asia	211	8.9	Other Asia	556	15.7
Rest of world	156	6.6	Rest of world	25	0.7
World	2,366	100.0	World	3,531	100.0
Top Five Countries	Value	Share, %	Top Five Countries	Value	Share, %
Japan	515	21.8	China	1,166	33.0
Canada	360	15.2	Taiwan	580	16.4
Mexico	220	9.3	Canada	310	8.8
United Kingdom	202	8.5	Mexico	301	8.5
China	105	4.4	South Korea	156	4.4

[1] SIC 3949.
[2] For definitions of regional groupings, see "Getting the Most Out of *Outlook '99*."
[3] Values may not sum to total due to rounding.
Source: U.S. Department of Commerce, Bureau of the Census.

different types of sports products. Sports balls are a good example of the varying cost of production inputs. Inflatable and stitched balls such as basketballs and baseballs require a high degree of labor intensity, while solid and noninflatable hollow balls such as golf balls and tennis balls rely on more capital or machinery. As a result, the U.S. industry manufactures and competitively exports many capital-intensive products, such as golf and exercise equipment, in the United States. Labor-intensive products such as baseball and fishing equipment tend to be manufactured overseas through licensing contracts or joint ventures, since labor costs are generally lower in many less developed countries, and are imported into the United States. U.S. manufacturers rely on imported products to complete product lines; the ratio of imports to apparent consumption was 33 percent in 1997.

In 1997 China was the largest foreign supplier and sold almost $1.2 billion of sporting goods to the United States, an increase of 19 percent over 1996. U.S. imports from Taiwan were down 23 percent in 1997, yet Taiwan remained the second largest foreign supplier at $580 million. China and Taiwan combined accounted for over 49 percent of U.S. imports, down only slightly from 50 percent in 1996. Many sporting goods firms are changing their source for imports from Taiwan to China to take advantage of lower labor costs. U.S. sports equipment imports from Canada, the third largest foreign supplier, totaled $310 million, up 17 percent from 1996 and accounting for 9 percent of total imports. U.S. sports equipment imports from Mexico, the fourth largest foreign supplier, were slightly lower at $301 million but also accounted for almost 9 percent of total imports. Imports from Mexico were up more than 40 percent for the second straight year as many tariffs on sports equipment were reduced to zero as a result of NAFTA. Some U.S. companies which had produced in Asia may have switched production

to Mexico to be closer to the U.S. market and take advantage of lower import duties and lower relative wages.

Many products that have a capital-intensive production process and are made in the United States are price-competitive worldwide. The ratio of exports to shipments for the U.S. sports equipment industry was 25 percent in 1997. U.S. exports totaled $2.4 billion in that year.

U.S. exports to Japan accounted for the largest share of total U.S. sports equipment exports at almost 22 percent, totaling an estimated $515 million, down 5 percent from 1996. The financial crisis has weakened the Japanese market for most U.S. exports except for exercise equipment. U.S. exports of exercise equipment to Japan increased 4 percent in 1997. Japanese consumers have continued to try to stay fit, and they usually buy the best equipment. U.S. manufacturers have been the primary beneficiaries because they produce some of the highest-quality exercise equipment in the world.

Canada was the second largest foreign market for U.S. sports equipment exports, increasing its purchases 14 percent to $360 million in 1997. Canada is the largest foreign market for exercise equipment, as U.S. exports of exercise equipment totaled $108 million, up 28 percent from 1996. Mexico became the third largest market, increasing its purchases 42 percent to $220 million. U.S. manufacturers have benefited from lower Mexican tariffs on sports equipment as a result of NAFTA and a recovery of the Mexican economy, which had been depressed in 1995. The United Kingdom was the fourth largest market for U.S. sports equipment exports as exports to that country climbed 14 percent to $202 million. U.S. exports of sporting goods to China, the fifth largest market, fell 13 percent in 1997. Bowling equipment accounts for nearly 90 percent of U.S. sports equipment exports to China. However, because of the Asian financial crisis and the completion of several bowling centers in Asia, sales opportunities have been restrained. In addition, China continues to have high tariffs and an inadequate distribution system for most consumer products. However, if market restraints are removed in China, U.S. sports equipment manufacturers will benefit significantly by selling to one of the world's largest consumer markets.

DOLLS, TOYS, GAMES, AND CHILDREN'S VEHICLES

Global Industry Trends

The toy industry is dominated by large U.S. corporations that make products mostly in developing countries and sell them throughout the world. The two largest U.S. toy companies, Mattel and Hasbro, are also the world's largest, with 1997 sales of approximately $4.8 billion and $3.2 billion, respectively. Although some other toy companies are privately held and do not report earnings, industry sources suggest that none approach Mattel's or Hasbro's sales figures. The one possible exception is the Japanese firm, Nintendo, which had $3.4 billion in sales in 1997. However, since it makes only video games, which are not classified as toys or games in terms of U.S. domestic production, Nintendo is not directly comparable to Mattel and Hasbro, both of which make a wide variety of products.

The toy industry is becoming increasingly consolidated. In early 1998 Hasbro purchased Tiger Electronics, a maker of cyberpets, the hot product in 1997, as well as the rights to Atari's video games, which are now old enough to inspire nostalgia and licensing. Mattel purchased Tyco, formerly the third largest toy manufacturer, in 1997, adding Tyco's Matchbox line of toy cars to the its own Hot Wheels. In 1998 Mattel, the sales of whose mainstay, Barbie, continue to increase but at a lower rate, purchased Pleasant Co., the maker of the American Girl dolls. Mattel's strengths continue to be in girls' and preschoolers' toys, not boys' toys. Among those remaining independent of the Big Two are Little Tykes, a division of Rubbermaid, and Ty, the maker of Beanie Babies.

Domestic Trends

Distinguishing global from domestic trends in this industry is difficult since children's play patterns do not appear to vary dramatically among cultures. Construction toys, for instance, are popular in many countries. Among the best known companies that make construction toys are Lego, a Danish company with factories in the United States and other nations. Lego's MindStorms CD-ROMs will allow children to design robots on a computer and then build them with Lego sets. This mingling of traditional toys with modern electronics has become increasingly common, as is exemplified by Fashion Designer Barbie, which allows girls, who generally are less involved than boys in electronic gadgetry, to design and then make outfits for Barbie dolls on a computer. Hasbro is making interactive versions of the board games baby boomers played as children.

The lines separating computers, video games, the Internet, and toys have become blurred. Consumers can now surf the Web on a television, play sophisticated games on a computer, design games for a video game console (Sony's Net Yaroze), and, melding technology with emotional connection, program stuffed animals (Actimates' Barney). Little Tykes and IBM have collaborated on the $2,400 Young Explorer computer designed for 3- to 7-year-olds, which comes encased in a purple and yellow plastic desk. At this price, the target markets are institutional settings such as day care centers, kindergartens, and cruise ships, not individual consumers. Rather than being supplanted by computers, video game machines remain popular. Perhaps this is the case because many people still regard computers as user-unfriendly, or perhaps video games are an anticipation of a predicted development: cheaper, easier-to-use computers with fewer functions. Sega, which currently offers only a 32-bit model, planned to introduce the 128-bit Dreamcast in Japan in 1998 and North America in 1999, leapfrogging over Nintendo 64, which was introduced in 1996. Neither Sony nor Nintendo has announced its intentions, but a 256-bit video game machine no longer seems as improbable, as did a 64-bit machine when Atari 8-bit games were new.

On the other end of the spectrum in terms of sophistication (and usually price) are perennial favorites such as yo-yoes, puzzles, and small stuffed animals, including the phenomenally popular Beanie Babies. These items had been sold exclusively through small retailers before McDonald's started Happy Meal tie-ins with the even smaller Teenie Beanie Babies. In 1997 McDonald's began a 10-year marketing agreement with the Walt Disney Co., an arrangement that will promote both companies' products.

Cross-marketing, a practice as internationally popular as are American movies, does not always yield enormous profits, however. Although products based on the live action *101 Dalmatians* and the rereleased *Star Wars* trilogy did well, those associated with *The Hunchback of Notre Dame, Men in Black,* and *Starship Troopers* disappointed their licensees. So far sales of *Godzilla* have been lower than anticipated, though, as a summer movie, it may be profitable during the increasingly important Halloween season. Banking on earlier success, Hasbro, Galoob, and, in its first license ever, Lego all will have products related to the upcoming three *Star Wars* "prequels."

From 1987 to 1996, the latest year for which census data are available, employment generally tracked the economy, with 1991 having the lowest employment figures for production workers (22,900) and for all employees (32,400). Production worker employment peaked in 1995 at 30,000, while total employment peaked in 1993 at 39,000. Employment declined in 1996 to 28,500 production workers and 36,800 overall. In 1997, after its acquisition of Tyco, Mattel laid off 2,700 employees, about 10 percent of its work force. In late 1997 Hasbro announced 2,500 job cuts worldwide, about 20 percent of its work force, including 700 in Texas. Despite the growing domination of made-in-Asia products, domestic employment in this industry is not plummeting. However, neither high earnings by Mattel and Hasbro nor their continuing acquisitions necessarily will spur domestic production of small mass-market toys.

Low production costs abroad make it difficult for U.S.-made toys to compete with the least expensive imports. Therefore,

U.S. production is increasingly geared toward an upscale market. U.S.-made dolls are a prime example of this trend; they are usually expensive collector items. In contrast, mass-market dolls such as Barbie and "male action figures" generally are not "born in the USA." While some other American-made toys are also high-end, the United States produces many less expensive construction sets, puzzles, electric trains, ride-on vehicles, and games. Many large plastic products, such as those from Little Tykes, are still made in the United States because their production is less labor-intensive and their potential shipping costs from overseas are more significant. Making products closer to their intended customers allows manufacturers to respond more quickly to changes in demand. When Tickle Me Elmo became an unexpected hit late in 1996, Tyco was unable to increase its imports in time for Christmas.

Toy retailing is changing. Toys "R" Us, Wal-Mart, K-Mart, and Target continue to lead the pack, but the share of Toys "R" Us fell from 25 percent in 1994 to 20.3 percent in 1997. Wal-Mart's market share grew from 9.5 percent to 15.6 percent in that period. Warehouse clubs are selling more toys, although they devote shelf space to those products mostly during the Christmas season. (In 1997, a federal judge ruled that Toys "R" Us had pressured manufacturers not to sell popular toys to such warehouses except in more expensive combination packs.) Internet shopping has increased, prompting Toys "R" Us to start using that medium for sales in 1998. In that year the Internet company eToys acquired Toys.com. Catalog shopping for toys is also up. American Girl dolls, which feature historical re-creation costumes and accompanying novels and CD-ROMs, are available only through catalogs.

Rather than attempting to compete with big box and discount stores on price, smaller toy stores offer more convenience, better service, and preselection of products. Although their price points can be higher, they offer some products that are not sold at mass merchandisers, including the phenomenally popular and reasonably priced Beanie Babies. There also has been growth in chains specializing in educational toys. Zany Brainy, Noodle Kidoodle, Imaginarium, Learning Express, and the Store of Knowledge are more likely than are international retail chains such as Toys "R" Us to feature products from smaller manufacturers.

The trends underlying changes in distribution and product use include decreased free time among parents and children, increased money spent in the service sector, the growth of the Internet, and improved computer games. With increased household income and more parents working full time, the prospect of negotiating traffic, traversing a vast parking lot, and then roaming aisle after aisle of a big box store such as Toys "R" Us may not seem worth the savings, particularly if parents already have planned to make a trip to Wal-Mart for other household needs. Small retailers have complained that even McDonald's can eliminate some casual visits to the toy store with its Beanie Baby and Disney products.

Parents are not the only family members who are pressed for time. With more children lacking a parent at home full time, children spend more time in institutional settings such as after-school day care or in organized activities such as soccer prac-

tice, which appears to have attracted more young girls to organized athletics than have other team sports. When they finally get home, even first-graders may have homework. Particularly after they start school, children simply have less time to play. With the time that remains, even young schoolchildren are spending less time on traditional toys and more on computer games and the Internet. Toys "R" Us has lost much of that market to computer stores.

Projections of Industry and Trade Growth for the Next 1 and 5 Years

Growth in demand for toys in the United States is strongly correlated with growth in the population of children. Demographic trends over the next 5 years will lead to a slight decline in demand for toys. Children under 5 years old represent an especially important segment to the industry because older children's interests are increasingly diverted from toys, especially traditional toys such as dolls, cars, blocks, and stuffed animals. The number of children in the United States under 5 years old is predicted to edge down about 0.5 percent from 19.04 million in 1999 to 18.96 million in 2001 and then remain nearly constant through 2003. This age bracket also will decline in terms of its share of the total U.S. population from 7.6 percent in the early 1990s, to 6.7 percent by 2003. A similar decline will occur among 5- to 9-year-olds, still a significant group for this industry. This group will fall from 20.06 million in 1999 to 19.46 million in 2003, with its share of the total population decreasing from 7.4 percent to 6.9 percent. A partial mitigation of these trends may be seen in anecdotal reports that on average, children are likely to receive more toys per capita now than their counterparts did in previous decades. Some of the reasons for this trend may be found in statistical data indicating that average family and household sizes are continuing to fall. Children whose parents do not live in the same household may receive more toys. The aging of the population means that children are more likely to have living grandparents and possibly step-grandparents, providing more potential toy givers per child. However, these factors will not completely negate the changes in demand caused by the decline in the population of children.

From 1992 to 1997 imports grew at an average annual rate of 11 percent as the manufacturing of mass-market toys shifted to countries with lower production costs. During that period U.S. exports grew at an average annual rate of 6 percent. Apparent consumption is derived by adding domestic production to imports and then subtracting exports. Imports represented 69 percent of apparent consumption in the early 1990s, dipped to 64 percent in 1995, and then climbed to 75 percent in 1996 (see Table 39-6). Over the next 5 years, this statistic may climb to the mid-80s or even the low 90s, depending on the product mix sold and when the balance of U.S. versus overseas production of mass-market toys stabilizes. Already companies have moved production abroad for many goods that are significantly cheaper to produce offshore, and so the ratio of imports to apparent consumption may not reach the high levels that were noted above. Present trends do not always continue. Imports rose dramatically from 1994 to 1997, with a peak annual per-

TABLE 39-6: Dolls, Toys, and Games (SIC 3942, 3944) Trends and Forecasts

(millions of dollars except as noted)

	1992	1993	1994	1995	1996	1997[1]	1998[2]	1999[3]	Percent Change 96–97	97–98	98–99	92–96[4]
Industry data												
Value of shipments[5]	4,542	4,968	4,550	5,092	4,867	4,779	4,665	4,716	−1.8	−2.4	1.1	1.7
Value of shipments (1992$)	4,542	4,954	4,510	4,967	4,708	4,580	4,423	4,426	−2.7	−3.4	0.1	0.9
Total employment (thousands)	35.5	39.0	35.3	38.7	36.8							0.9
Production workers (thousands)	26.8	28.8	27.5	30.0	28.5							1.5
Average hourly earnings ($)	8.43	9.03	9.31	9.58	9.59							3.3
Capital expenditures	146	142	140	138	142							−0.7
Product data												
Value of shipments[5]	3,983	4,248	4,170	4,495	4,154	4,079	3,981	4,025	−1.8	−2.4	1.1	1.1
Value of shipments (1992$)	3,983	4,235	4,132	4,384	4,019	3,909	3,774	3,777	−2.7	−3.5	0.1	0.2
Trade data												
Value of imports	7,111	7,897	7,445	8,041	9,523	12,063	14,468	16,017	26.7	19.9	10.7	7.6
Value of exports	719	743	867	915	898	973	1,167	1,292	8.4	19.9	10.7	5.7

[1] Estimate except imports and exports.
[2] Estimate.
[3] Forecast.
[4] Compound annual rate.
[5] For definition of industry versus product values, see "Getting the Most Out of *Outlook '99*."
Source: U.S. Department of Commerce: Bureau of the Census; International Trade Administration.

centage increase of 27 percent in 1997. First quarter 1998 imports were up from the same period in 1997, although the percentage increase was less striking, perhaps indicating slower growth in the future. Unless the Asian crisis worsens, U.S. exports should be able to maintain 6 percent annual growth, helped by the Mexican recovery and the gradual removal of a Brazilian tariff on toy imports.

Domestic production of the merchandise that is classified in the category of dolls, toys, games, and children's vehicles is likely to fluctuate, averaging a 1 percent compound annual growth rate over the next several years. Largely as a result of low production costs abroad and a high U.S. dollar, inflation in this industry is expected to remain at a low 1 percent. Domestic production is particularly difficult to predict since the toy market is dominated by imports. Continuing acquisitions and layoffs by Mattel and Hasbro will tend to reduce U.S. employment in this industry. As the production of less expensive mass-market toys continues to move abroad, there will be increased product stratification between those imports and U.S.-made higher-end products. This niche helped the ratio of exports to total U.S. factory shipments reach 22 percent in 1996. Educational software, computer games, and electronic toys represent potential growth areas. However, as a result of the way U.S. production is classified, while the Junior Explorer computer is considered a toy, the disks, tapes, and cartridges that contain computer or video games are not classified as games but instead as software or services. Thus, the latter products are not reflected in the factory shipment figures discussed in this chapter.

Global Market Prospects

With fewer than 3.3 percent of the world's children under 9 years old living in the United States, U.S. manufacturers have to look overseas (see Table 39-7). With an aging population in traditional export markets such as Canada and western Europe, U.S. manufacturers have had to broaden their scope to include markets in Asia, South America, and the Middle East. Unfortunately, exporting to some of those countries and the sale of products made by U.S. companies there have proved difficult.

Continuing economic troubles in Asia, including a major U.S. export destination, Japan, have inhibited U.S. export penetration in that region. This financial crisis also could hurt the economies of non-Asian countries, further depressing U.S. exports. The United States and China continue to work to eliminate China's tariffs on toys, which are applied even to products manufactured in China by foreign companies, and its nontariff barriers, such as intellectual property rights violations and confusing license requirements. India's growing consumer class finally may be able to buy imported consumer goods if that country's quantitative restrictions are eliminated in 1999, a possibility but not a certainty. Sales to Brazil should grow as its "safeguard" measure, which has increased tariffs, is phased out over the next few years. Argentina rejected a petition by its domestic industry for a similar measure in 1997 but was considering a revised petition in 1998. The European Union is contemplating banning phthalates, chemical compounds used to plasticize polyvinyl chlorides, in toys intended to be placed in children's mouths, such as teething rings.

Toy tariffs levied by Canada, Japan, and Korea are being reduced through the General Agreement on Tariffs and Trade (GATT) Uruguay Round negotiations and will be eliminated no later than January 1, 2004. In addition, the United States voluntarily removed its import tariffs in 1995, and Hong Kong does not impose tariffs on these products. Under the U.S.–Canada Free Trade Agreement, all U.S.–Canadian trade became duty-

TABLE 39-7: Population of Newborns to 9-Year-Olds

(thousands)

	1998		2010		1998–2010	
	0–9 Years Old Group	0–9 as Percent of Population	0–9 Years Old Group	0–9 as Percent of Population	Change in 0–9 Years Population	Percent Change in 0–9 Years Old Group
NAFTA						
Canada and Mexico	27,895	21.59	27,735	18.11	−160	−0.57
Canada	4,027	13.13	3,749	10.94	−278	−6.90
Mexico	23,868	24.22	23,986	20.19	118	0.49
United States	39,141	14.48	39,501	13.25	360	0.92
Western Europe						
France	7,272	12.37	5,956	9.98	−1,316	−18.10
Germany	8,267	10.07	6,311	7.79	−1,956	−23.66
United Kingdom	7,321	12.68	6,410	11.05	−911	−12.44
South America						
Argentina	6,764	18.65	7,442	17.73	678	10.02
Brazil	33,780	19.89	32,102	16.81	−1,678	−4.97
Chile	2,743	18.69	2,283	13.94	−460	−16.77
Africa						
South Africa	10,169	23.74	9,687	20.39	−482	−4.74
Asia						
China	208,607	16.87	169,886	12.73	−38,721	−18.56
Hong Kong (PRC)	796	11.87	864	11.17	68	8.54
India	230,857	23.46	233,724	19.77	2,867	1.24
Japan	12,136	9.64	12,808	10.07	672	5.54
Singapore	501	14.36	414	10.63	−87	−17.37
South Korea	6,892	14.85	6,866	13.40	−26	−0.38
Taiwan	3,176	14.50	3,202	13.21	26	0.82
Thailand	9,631	16.04	9,290	14.06	−341	−3.54
Vietnam	11,460	15.03	15,186	17.14	−61,050	−80.08
Middle East						
Egypt	23,811	36.05	16,832	20.85	−6,979	−29.31
Israel	1,075	19.05	1,165	17.40	90	8.37
Jordan	1,368	30.85	1,542	25.27	174	12.72
Kuwait	409	21.38	485	17.45	76	18.58
Saudi Arabia	6,476	31.16	9,469	30.35	2,993	46.22
United Arab Emirates	452	19.63	536	18.79	84	18.58

Source: U.S. Department of Commerce, Bureau of the Census, International Data Program.

free as of January 1, 1998. Mexico is gradually removing duties under the NAFTA. Representatives of the economies of the Asia Pacific Economic Cooperation group, including the countries mentioned above and 13 others, are discussing removing tariffs on toys.

The U.S. Standard Industrial Classification System groups products differently than does the Harmonized System, the classification system used worldwide for international trade. Thus, some products that may be thought of as toys may not be classified as such by one or both of these systems. For example, for international trade purposes, educational computer games and personal computers for preschoolers are classified not as toys but as "electronic flash cards" and computers, respectively. For U.S. factory production, no computer games, whether or not they are educational, are classified as toys but personal computers for preschoolers are. As distinctions among categories blur, both domestic production data and international trade data become less clear.

According to the definitions used, toy imports rose almost 27 percent from 1996 to 1997. Imports from China, many pro-duced by U.S. companies, constituted 62 percent of all U.S. toy imports in 1997, only a slightly higher proportion than in 1996. The second largest import source was Japan, with a 21 percent share of toy imports, up sharply from 14 percent in 1996. The share of the third largest supplier, Mexico, was essentially unchanged at 4 percent, slightly more than those of Taiwan and Hong Kong, the next biggest import sources, combined. Among the top 10 import source countries, only China and Mexico have grown steadily in import values since 1992. First quarter 1998 figures showed China with a 67 percent share of imports, Japan with 15 percent, and Mexico with 6 percent. China's domination of this market seems likely to increase. (See Table 39-8.)

U.S. toy exports are also growing, but not as fast as are imports. Therefore, toy exports fell from one-tenth the value of imports in 1992 to one-twelfth in 1997. However, since the United States has a sophisticated electronics industry, some of whose products might be thought of as toys but not be classified as such, U.S. toy export figures may be understated. As is the case for many industries, our NAFTA partners are the most important

TABLE 39-8:   U.S. Trade Patterns in Dolls, Toys, and Games[1] in 1997
(millions of dollars; percent)

Exports			Imports		
Regions[2]	Value[3]	Share, %	Regions[2]	Value[3]	Share,. %
NAFTA	393	40.4	NAFTA	653	5.4
Latin America	191	19.7	Latin America	10	0.1
Western Europe	158	16.2	Western Europe	390	3.2
Japan/Chinese Economic Area	127	13.1	Japan/Chinese Economic Area	10,442	86.6
Other Asia	43	4.4	Other Asia	549	4.5
Rest of world	61	6.3	Rest of world	19	0.2
World	973	100.0	World	12,063	100.0
Top Five Countries	Value	Share, %	Top Five Countries	Value	Share, %
Canada	265	27.3	China	7,491	62.1
Mexico	128	13.2	Japan	2,474	20.5
Japan	82	8.4	Mexico	489	4.1
United Kingdom	69	7.1	Taiwan	249	2.1
Brazil	39	4.0	Hong Kong	229	1.9

[1] SIC 3942, 3944.
[2] For definitions of regional groupings, see "Getting the Most Out of *Outlook '99.*"
[3] Values may not sum to total due to rounding.
Source: U.S. Department of Commerce, Bureau of the Census.

export destinations. NAFTA immediately lowered many of Canada's and Mexico's tariffs, giving U.S. exporters greater access to those economies. Before NAFTA, Mexican imports had entered the United States duty-free under the Generalized System of Preferences. On January 1, 1995, the United States eliminated its tariffs on toys for all its trading partners. Therefore, NAFTA was all gain and no loss for U.S. toy manufacturers. NAFTA also protected U.S. exports from being assessed Mexico's higher tariff rates when that nation's economy suffered a crisis in 1996. Sales to Canada represented 27 percent of U.S. toy exports in 1997, with Mexico coming in second at 13 percent. Japan (8 percent), the United Kingdom (7 percent), and Brazil (4 percent) completed the top five.

BICYCLES AND PARTS

Global Industry Trends

The major trend in the bicycle and parts industry has been the shift of production of mass-merchandiser bicycles to China. Over the last 30 years the U.S. bicycle industry has been losing market share to Asian manufacturers. The production of bicycles is a fairly labor-intensive process. Therefore, much bicycle production in the last 30 years has been moved to low-wage countries with a labor force that has the skills required for bicycle production. In the early 1970s Japan's low labor rates and developing skilled labor pool became attractive to bicycle producers looking to cut costs. Japan became a major supplier of bicycles, taking some market share away from the U.S. industry. The ratio of imports to apparent consumption for bicycles and parts was 30 percent in 1973. However, toward the end of the decade the six major U.S. manufacturers were able to improve their product offerings, mainly by selling lightweight bikes, and regain market share, driving that

ratio down to 14 percent by 1978. In the 1980s Taiwan became the major foreign supplier of bicycles, accounting for 86 percent of U.S. imports in 1986. The ratio of imports to apparent consumption climbed to 59 percent that year. This increase in imports had an effect on the makeup of the domestic industry. Four major manufacturers remained, three of which primarily serviced the mass-merchandiser markets through stores such as Toys "R" Us, Sears, and K-Mart. The independent dealer market was very much in disarray, with bicycle shops going out of business, merging, and changing manufacturer-sourcing arrangements.

The lone bright spot for the dealer market industry was the development of the mountain bike. Small U.S. entrepreneurs started this trend by adapting beach cruisers with fat tires, high handlebars, and strong frames with 10 to 18 gears that normally were found on racing bikes for use on the rough mountainous terrain of the western United States. New innovations continued to be developed as more mainstream consumers were attracted to those bikes. Although the U.S. bicycle industry initially benefited from this trend, importers eventually were able to produce the same types of bikes more cheaply.

From 1987 to 1994 U.S. manufacturers were able to cut their costs by improving production efficiencies and moving toward more capital-intensive production techniques, maintaining and actually gaining market share. The ratio of imports to apparent consumption was as low as 47 percent in 1993.

China has long been a major producer of bicycles, but until recently Chinese bicycles were so poor in quality that they could not be exported. However, in the early 1990s Taiwanese and American capitalists started to invest in bicycle production facilities in China. Armed with new capital and production techniques, Chinese manufacturers improved the quality of their bicycles dramatically. U.S. imports from China increased at a compound annual rate of 44 percent from 1989 to 1997.

Chinese imports have been particularly damaging to the U.S. industry. Many of those imports were marketed for the low-end mass merchandisers, competing directly with the bikes made by U.S. producers. The retail price for mass-merchandiser bikes from China typically has been 15 percent lower than that of comparable U.S. models, making it virtually impossible to compete against them on price, the most important factor at this level. The three major U.S. manufacturers of bicycles now all have sourcing arrangements with overseas suppliers in Mexico or China. The ratio of imports to apparent consumption was nearly 61 percent in 1997 and probably will go higher. Huffy recently announced that it was closing a plant in Ohio which employed nearly 1,000 employees. The company claimed that it will still source 60 percent from its other U.S. production facilities. The Brunswick Corporation, which recently acquired Roadmaster and Mongoose, producers of name-brand bicycles, has closed at least one plant and cut employment at others. How the industry will respond to this crisis is not known. One scenario has the U.S. industry becoming more of a high-end manufacturer, supplementing its low-end products with imports from China and Taiwan, as at least two U.S. mountain bike companies currently do.

Bicycling in general remains a popular recreational activity and mode of transportation both domestically and internationally. It is the fourth largest participatory sport in the United States. However, in 1997 an NSGA study reported only 45 million active participants in bicycling, down 15 percent from 1996. In-line skating probably has taken away some of the growth potential of the industry. The same study reported that in-line skating participation increased 4 percent in 1997. Children and young adults traditionally have thought of cycling as an enjoyable activity and a mode of transportation. In previous generations, going to see a friend and traveling to the local store usually were done on a bicycle. With skates, there is another viable option; children can still get to where they need to go on skates. In addition, skates have a portability bonus. Although it is unlikely that skating will ever get as big as bicycling, it has taken a piece of the youth transportation pie.

Important Factors Affecting the Future Growth of U.S. Industry

With U.S. manufacturers closing several plants and with not particularly strong demand for biking products, U.S. shipments are expected to be weak in 1999. Constant-dollar product shipments of bicycles and parts decreased an estimated 3 percent in 1997 and 13 percent in 1998 (see Table 39-9). Current-dollar product shipments totaled an estimated $825 million in 1998. However, export growth of about 16 percent in 1997 and 9 percent in 1998 kept U.S. shipments from declining further. Strong overseas markets and a demand for U.S.-made high-priced mountain bikes were the key reasons for the continued increase in exports. Imports rose almost 12 percent in 1997 and were expected to increase an estimated 17 percent in 1998. U.S. companies are expected to import more to offset decreases in domestic manufacturing.

Current-dollar shipments of apparent consumption totaled $1.6 billion in 1998, growing an estimated 3 percent in 1997 and 1 percent in 1998 in real terms. Although mountain bike sales are not as strong as they were in years past, consumers continue to purchase new bicycles. Personal consumption expenditures increased 8 percent and 3.1 percent in 1997 and the first 5 months of 1998, respectively. The strong economy and lower prices of bicycles compared with 1996 are the primary reasons for the growth of apparent consumption. The U.S. economy remained strong the last 2 years as real disposable personal income grew 3 percent in the first 4 months of 1998 after increasing 2.9 percent in 1997. In addition, the growth in the number of low-priced bicycles from China has meant a decline in the average price of bicycles. In general, current prices of bicycles are equal to 1989 prices. These low prices have enticed consumers to purchase bikes, particularly for children. Imports of children's bicycles increased 42 percent in 1997 and 57 percent in the first quarter of 1998.

Greater competition has led to improved quality of bicycles. Manufacturers producing for mass merchandisers have been able to increase the quality of bicycle components such as gear shifters and brakes without increasing prices significantly. In

TABLE 39-9: Bicycles and Parts (SIC 37511) Trends and Forecasts
(millions of dollars except as noted)

	1992	1993	1994	1995	1996	1997[1]	1998[2]	1999[3]	Annual Growth 96–97	97–98	98–99	92–96[4]
Product data												
Value of shipments	1,023	1,083	1,103	1,048	996	940	825	775	−5.6	−12.2	−6.1	−0.7
Value of shipments (1992$)	1,023	1,092	1,112	1,039	981	949	829	767	−3.2	−12.7	−7.5	−1.0
Trade data												
Imports	734	841	825	968	878	979	1,150	1,270	11.6	17.4	10.4	−4.6
Exports	175	197	200	257	268	310	337	350	15.7	8.7	3.9	−11.2

[1] Estimate except imports and exports.
[2] Estimate.
[3] Forecast.
[4] Compound annual rate.
Source: U.S. Department of Commerce: Bureau of the Census; International Trade Administration.

addition, most domestic manufacturers have made extensive changes to improve production efficiency. This has led to increased consumer satisfaction and bicycles that last longer, lengthening the replacement cycle and resulting in fewer replacement sales in any given year.

U.S. Industry Growth Projections for the Next 1 and 5 Years

Imports of bicycles probably will increase an estimated 10 percent in 1999, primarily at the expense of U.S. manufacturers. Constant-dollar product shipments of bicycles and parts are forecast to fall about 8 percent in 1999. Exports, however, will continue to increase, but at a lower rate of an estimated 4 percent in 1999, reaching $350 million. Stronger GDP growth in some of the major foreign markets for U.S. bicycles will spur this increase. Meanwhile, U.S. apparent consumption adjusted for inflation is forecast to increase an estimated 2 percent. With growth of real disposable income expected to be 2 percent, the domestic bicycle market should be able to sustain limited growth.

Five-year growth in the market is likely to be weak at only 1 percent annually. However, real domestic product shipments probably will decline at an estimated 1 percent compound annual rate. Demographics will play a key role in this modest growth. According to data from the U.S. Bureau of the Census, the increase in the number of children in the age group 5 to 14 years is expected to be lower than the increase in population of the nation from 1998 to 2003. Historically, U.S. shipments have tended to be correlated with growth in this age group.

In addition, baby boomers entering the age group 55 to 64 years, which should be the fastest growing age group over this period, may affect sales in two major ways. First, many members of this age cohort may limit their participation in all sports activities, including biking. In the 1996 NSGA sport participation survey, participation in all activities was 21 percent lower and that in biking was 40 percent lower in the age group 55 to 65 years compared with the age group 45 to 54 years. However, bicycling is somewhat unusual in that it can be participated in on many different levels, from casual and light workouts to racing and serious aerobic exercise. This could mean more sales opportunities for hybrid bikes that combine lightweight features with more comfortable features. The baby boom generation is getting older but still has a high degree of purchasing power and may want to stay involved with the sport in a more casual way.

Global Market Prospects

In 1997 U.S. imports of bicycles and parts totaled $979 million, increasing about 12 percent from 1996. Imports accounted for 61 percent of apparent consumption. Taiwan, China, and Japan are the three largest foreign suppliers of bicycles and parts, accounting for a combined 87 percent of U.S. imports. Taiwan remains the largest supplier of bicycles and parts to the United States, supplying $419 million, or almost 43 percent of total U.S. imports, in 1997; U.S. imports from Taiwan declined about 8 percent that year. The impact of Chinese bicycle manufacturers was documented earlier in this chapter; China was our second largest foreign supplier of bicycles, supplying $323 million, or 33 percent of total U.S. imports, in 1997, 52 percent more than in 1996. Imports from Japan fell 2 percent, totaling $112 million, or about 11 percent of total U.S. bicycle imports (see Table 39-10).

Taiwan is the world's largest exporter of bicycles in terms of value but is second in terms of units. Labor is a significant

TABLE 39-10: U.S. Trade Patterns in Bicycles and Parts[1] in 1997
(millions of dollars; percent)

Exports				Imports			
Regions[2]	Value[3]	Share, %	Percent Change 96–97	Regions[2]	Value[3]	Share, %	Percent Change 96–97
NAFTA	60	19.4	29.5	NAFTA	30	3.1	150.0
Latin America	30	9.7	79.5	Latin America	1	0.1	0.0
Western Europe	132	42.6	12.3	Western Europe	49	5.0	0.0
Japan/Chinese Economic Area	66	21.3	2.8	Japan/Chinese Economic Area	860	87.9	10.3
Other Asia	5	1.6	-0.5	Other Asia	38	3.9	8.6
Rest of world	17	5.5	-4.2	Rest of world	1	0.1	0.0
World	310	100.0	15.9	World	979	100.0	11.5
Top Five Countries	Value	Share, %	Percent Change 96–97	Top Five Countries	Value	Share, %	Percent Change 96–97
Netherlands	39	12.6	8.1	Taiwan	419	42.8	-7.5
Taiwan	38	12.3	13.8	China	323	33.0	52.0
Canada	34	11.0	13.3	Japan	112	11.4	-1.7
Germany	29	9.4	-4.5	Italy	24	2.5	-9.4
Mexico	26	8.4	60.2	Mexico	24	2.5	241.9

[1] SIC 37511.
[2] For definitions of regional groupings, see "Getting the Most Out of *Outlook '99*."
[3] Values may not sum to total due to rounding.
Source: U.S. Department of Commerce, Bureau of the Census.

input in the cost of producing a bicycle. Thus, as Taiwan's wage rates have risen, the price competitiveness of its products in the mass-merchandiser market has declined. However, the quality of the products of Taiwanese manufacturers has improved greatly as they supply many of the world's high-quality bicycles through bicycle dealer distribution. Wage rates in China have remained much lower, making that country's products far more competitive. China has long been the world's largest producer of bicycles through its servicing of its domestic population of more than 1 billion. However, with the improved quality of its bikes, China has become a major exporter. China may have become the largest exporter earlier, but its manufacturers face high safeguard or antidumping duties in several major markets, including the European Union, Canada, Mexico, and South Korea.

U.S. exports of bicycles and parts increased from $13 million in 1987, accounting for only 2 percent of domestic shipments, to $310 million in 1997, or about 33 percent of domestic production. In 1997 U.S. exports of bicycles and parts increased 16 percent. The increased popularity of mountain bikes in foreign markets has been the primary reason for the tremendous growth of exports. U.S.-made and -branded mountain bikes and parts have a favorable image in many industrialized nations. The inclusion of mountain biking in the 1996 Summer Olympics brought further attention to the sport and increased its international popularity.

The Netherlands was the largest market for U.S. exports of bicycles and parts in 1997 with $39 million, representing an increase of 8 percent. Only slightly behind the Netherlands in terms of the amount of U.S. exports was Taiwan. Exports to that country jumped 14 percent in 1997, totaling $38 million. Virtually all (97 percent) U.S. exports to Taiwan consist of bicycle parts. The Asian financial crisis has not had a great effect on Taiwan, and sales opportunities for U.S. parts manufacturers remain strong and have not been affected by a strong U.S. dollar vis-à-vis Asian currencies. U.S. bicycles and parts exports to Canada, the third largest market for U.S. bicycles, totaled $34 million, up 13 percent. Germany was the fourth market for U.S. exports of bicycles and parts in 1997 with exports totaling $29 million, declining 5 percent. U.S. bicycles and parts exports to Mexico, the fifth largest market for U.S. bicycles, totaled $26 million, growing 60 percent.

It is expected that countries in Europe and North America will experience healthy growth in 1999 and beyond which should continue to boost U.S. exports of high-quality mountain bikes. Bicycling is more ingrained and accepted as a part of life in many countries in Europe and Asia. The Netherlands, Vietnam, and of course China have the highest percentage rates of bicycle usage. Vietnam and China are just beginning to open up, spurring U.S. opportunities to sell bicycles and parts. These countries are negotiating to join the World Trade Organization (WTO), and this probably will ease market barriers such as high tariffs and an inefficient distribution system. Competition is likely to be fierce, but there is also a great demand for the "made in the USA" label, particularly on mountain bikes.

MOTORCYCLES AND PARTS

Global Industry Trends

The motorcycle industry may refer to the 1990s as the decade of the luxury or big bike as motorcycles with engines larger than 800 cc have had dramatic increases in sales. Baby boomers, who rode small recreational motorcycles in the middle to late 1960s and then off-road motorcycles in the early 1970s, are buying the bikes of their dreams in the 1990s. The unit share of the market accounted for by heavyweight motorcycles increased from 18 percent in 1987 to 46 percent in 1996. As baby boomers matured and as their average age and income increased, they traded up for newer, bigger, more comfortable, and more expensive motorcycles. Large touring, racing, and custom-styled motorcycles became the most popular motorcycles among members of the baby boom generation.

The U.S. motorcycle industry has benefited from this trend, since all three domestic manufacturers produce primarily large-engine motorcycles. The two Japanese-owned manufacturing facilities in the United States produce nearly all their companies' heavyweight motorcycles for the U.S. market. However, the biggest beneficiary has been the sole major American-owned manufacturer, Harley-Davidson, which has rebounded to become the dominant supplier of heavyweight motorcycles to the U.S. market.

Harley-Davidson's products have a unique style that has attracted many motorcycle owners in the baby boom generation. In 1997 Harley-Davidson motorcycles accounted for 67 percent of the heavyweight market. What makes Harley-Davidson unique? According to the company, image, history, quality, and attention to the customer make its products unique. The Harley motorcycle is most often associated with free-spirited individuals. Whether they were renegades or just individuals seeking solitude, baby boomers were attracted by motorcycling when they were young. In fact, motorcycle registrations peaked at 5.7 million in 1980, when most young adult baby boomers were seeking their own, sometimes rebellious, identities. However, Harley products appear to be the ultimate expression of one's free spirit and uniqueness, as has been portrayed on television and in movies such as the 1969 *Easy Rider*.

Harley-Davidson claims it is the oldest motorcycle company in the world, having started production in 1903. In 1998 Harley celebrated its ninety-fifth anniversary in Milwaukee, where its headquarters are located. Milwaukee police estimated that over 100,000 bikers and Harley aficionados attended the celebration. Riders from all over the country and the world came to those events. The Harley product has one of the highest levels of satisfaction among its owners. Harley-Davidson motorcycles have not changed much over the last 95 years. The company still uses a "V-twin" engine and its frames and suspension arrangements are modifications from developments in the 1940s, 1950s, and 1960s.

However, the company's product offerings are quality machines that use many advances in technology and production. In the early 1980s the company almost went out of business because it was not producing a high-quality product and consumer loyalty, then its greatest strength, was waning. The management team decided to buy the company and change it into a manufacturer of high-quality motorcycles. The move worked; as quality improved, so did consumer loyalty and, more important, sales.

Consumer loyalty is stronger than ever today, as can be seen in the 100,000 Harley riders who traveled to the company's ninety-fifth anniversary reunion, but that loyalty is not one-sided. Harley has established Harley Owners Groups with local chapters of riders and supporters. The company uses these rider groups and other venues to canvas the riders on what they enjoy and dislike about riding a Harley motorcycle. Engineers and stylists work together to design a product that matches the consumer's needs. The company has gone to great lengths to improve styling and keep aspects of the bike that people like while producing a technologically first-rate piece of equipment. The Harley's heavy use of chrome and distinctive noise have made the company a huge success. In some cases, certain typical engine parts demand unusually high-precision crafting; others must be crafted more loosely to maintain traditional styling. It is a fine line that the company must continue to walk, given changing environmental and performance standards. However, its customers still demand high performance, and so Harley-Davidson will continue its efforts.

The consumer's choice of larger motorcycles has helped increase the industry's dollar value of shipments. However, motorcycle registration figures show that registrations were virtually the same in 1996 as they were in 1990: In 1990 there were 4.088 million motorcycles registered in the United States, compared with 4.008 million in 1996. Traditionally, motorcycling has attracted younger consumers who enjoy the thrill and excitement of riding; generally these consumers have less disposable income and therefore tend to purchase small motorcycles, which are less expensive. However, sales of smaller motorcycles have declined over the last several years. Three factors probably are hurting sales of smaller motorcycles: the popularity of all-terrain vehicles (ATVs), the greater availability of financing to younger riders who want a larger motorcycle, and the fact that proportionately there are fewer young people

to buy small motorcycles. ATVs are four-wheel off-road vehicles which are very similar to motorcycles and are popular with teenagers and new enthusiasts. These vehicles may now serve as an introduction to the sport. In addition, younger motorcyclists and other first-time buyers can acquire a more desirable larger motorcycle through loans and other credit terms as more motorcycle dealers offer their own financing packages. The last major factor affecting sales of small motorcycles is the lack of potential new riders. The number of individuals in the 15–29 age group declined from 23 percent of the population in 1990 to 21 percent in 1998.

Important Factors Affecting the Future Growth of U.S. Industry

Current-dollar product shipments of motorcycles and parts totaled an estimated $1.7 billion and $1.8 billion in 1997 and 1998, respectively (see Table 39-11). Constant-dollar product shipments increased 5 percent in both 1997 and 1998. Sales of heavyweight motorcycles accounted for an estimated 45 percent of the domestic market by units in 1997 versus 35 percent in 1993. Moderate to slow growth in the other motorcycle segments, such as off-road and entry-level motorcycles, has negated some of the positive performance of the heavyweight markets. Imports of motorcycles and parts totaled an estimated $1.1 billion, decreasing 3 percent in 1997, and were expected to reach an estimated $1.3 billion in 1998, increasing 15 percent. The Asian financial crisis is giving Japanese manufacturers favorable exchange rates, enabling them to lower prices. Meanwhile, exports of motorcycles and parts increased 5 percent in 1997 and were estimated to increase another 4 percent in 1998. The demand for U.S.-manufactured motorcycles overseas continued as U.S. exports grew 18 percent annually from 1987 to 1997. In 1997 and 1998 apparent consumption totaled $2.1 billion and $2.4 billion, increasing 0.2 percent and 10 percent in real terms, respectively.

A major restraint on foreign and domestic sales has been the lack of supply of Harley-Davidson motorcycles. While that company has increased production significantly over the last several years, it has not been able to keep up with demand.

TABLE 39-11: Motorcycles and Parts (SIC 37512) Trends and Forecasts
(millions of dollars except as noted)

	1992	1993	1994	1995	1996	1997[1]	1998[2]	1999[3]	96–97	97–98	98–99	92–96[4]
									Annual Growth			
Product data												
Value of shipments	968	1,277	1,228	1,387	1,585	1,702	1,820	1,935	7.4	6.9	6.3	13.1
Value of shipments (1992$)	968	1,225	1,143	1,218	1,371	1,438	1,507	1,554	4.8	4.8	3.2	9.1
Trade data												
Imports	803	877	937	1,162	1,137	1,104	1,266	1,355	–2.9	14.7	7.0	9.1
Exports	497	506	511	593	638	666	690	735	4.5	3.5	6.5	6.4

[1] Estimate except imports and exports.
[2] Estimate.
[3] Forecast.
[4] Compound annual rate.
Source: U.S. Department of Commerce: Bureau of the Census; International Trade Administration.

Dealers typically have waiting lists, and buyers must wait a year or more to purchase a Harley. Overseas, the expected wait is longer and there are high prices on the used-Harley market. However, the company has opened a new facility and improved production capacity at its older facilities and will increase production substantially by 2003, its centennial anniversary.

U.S. Industry Growth Projections for the Next 1 and 5 Years

Constant-dollar product shipments of motorcycles and parts are forecast to increase 3 percent in 1999. Apparent consumption will continue to grow in real terms by an estimated 4 percent. Real apparent consumption has grown at an annual rate of 8 percent since 1989. Slower growth in personal disposable income probably will slow the growth of personal consumption expenditures on motorcycles. Exports will continue to increase, growing an estimated 7 percent in 1999. This increase is largely due to an increasing supply of Harley-Davidson motorcycles and a forecast improvement in the Asian financial situation in the latter half of 1999. In addition, U.S. exports of motorcycles should benefit from continued economic growth in the major markets for motorcycles. GDP in the top 20 markets for U.S. total exports are expected to grow 3.6 percent on average in 1999. Imports are expected to rise 7 percent, again largely based on advantageous exchange rates for Japanese suppliers.

Real domestic product shipments are expected to grow at an annual rate of 4 percent between 1998 and 2003, benefiting from growth of the export sector and the domestic market in addition to an increasing supply of touring and custom-style motorcycles. Domestic and foreign demand for large motorcycles should remain strong, particularly in the early years of this time period.

Demographics played a key role in past growth and will continue over this time period. Motorcyclists of the baby boom generation are primarily in the 45–54 age group. This is a time when individuals have the highest level of discretionary income. According to the 1995 Consumer Expenditure Survey prepared by the U.S. Bureau of Labor Statistics, consumers in the 45–54 and 54–65 age groups had the highest level of expenditures on motorcycles. The 55–64 age group will be the fastest growing and the 45–54 age group the second fastest growing age groups, increasing 4 percent and 3 percent annually, respectively, from 1998 to 2003.

The surprise for the industry has been the addition of a new manufacturer of motorcycles, Polaris, the first new mass production manufacturer in the United States since 1960. Polaris entered the heavyweight market with a bang with its new Victory V92C cycle, which has the biggest V-twin engine in a cruiser-style bike. So far the bike has been well received. *Cycle World,* a major U.S. consumer motorcycle magazine, chose the Victory V92C as Best Cruiser of the Year. The addition of a new motorcycle manufacturer may spark the interest of consumers in motorcycling or improve production efficiencies typically associated with increased competition.

Global Market Prospects

In 1997 U.S. imports of motorcycles reached $1.1 billion as imports accounted for 52 percent of apparent consumption. Japan was the largest foreign supplier of motorcycles, accounting for 76 percent of total U.S. imports, or $849 million. Imports from the four major manufacturers of motorcycles in Japan—Honda, Kawasaki, Suzuki, and Yamaha—accounted for an estimated 40 percent of U.S. consumption. Germany and Italy were the other major suppliers of motorcycles to the United States, supplying $58 million and $51 million, respectively; each accounted for roughly 5 percent of U.S. imports of motorcycles in 1997. Most of those imports came from BMW in Germany and Ducati in Italy (see Table 39-12).

TABLE 39-12: U.S. Trade Patterns in Motorcycles, Bicycles, and Parts[1] in 1997

(millions of dollars; percent)

Exports			Imports		
Regions[2]	Value[3]	Share, %	Regions[2]	Value[3]	Share, %
NAFTA	160	16.4	NAFTA	48	2.3
Latin America	76	7.8	Latin America	4	0.2
Western Europe	448	45.9	Western Europe	219	10.5
Japan/Chinese Economic Area	177	18.1	Japan/Chinese Economic Area	1,750	84.0
Other Asia	18	1.8	Other Asia	46	2.2
Rest of world	97	9.9	Rest of world	16	0.8
World	976	100.0	World	2,083	100.0
Top Five Countries	Value	Share, %	Top Five Countries	Value	Share, %
Japan	130	13.3	Japan	961	46.1
Canada	128	13.1	Taiwan	458	22.0
Germany	112	11.4	China	326	15.6
Netherlands	88	9.0	Italy	75	3.6
United Kingdom	63	6.5	Germany	61	2.9

[1] SIC 3751.
[2] For definitions of regional groupings, see "Getting the Most Out of *Outlook '99*."
[3] Values may not sum to total due to rounding.
Source: U.S. Department of Commerce, Bureau of the Census.

U.S. exports have become a more important factor in domestic production. The ratio of exports to shipments was 39 percent in 1997. Harley-Davidson continues to have difficulty meeting foreign demand, providing most foreign markets with an allocated percentage of the available supply. As was stated earlier, demand exceeded supply in many foreign markets. As a result, many entrepreneurs have stepped in and begun exporting used or new Harleys, inflating the ratio of exports to shipments to some degree.

The European Union (EU) is the largest foreign market for U.S. motorcycle exports, totaling an estimated $287 million in 1997, or 43 percent of U.S. exports. However, the European markets are primarily performance markets in which manufacturers such as BMW, Honda, Kawasaki, and Ducatti dominate the overall market. In addition, the market share of U.S. companies would be greater if not for the stringent noise emission standards in the EU. The EU has the strictest noise emission standards in the world, and larger-engine motorcycles, particularly cruisers such as Harley-Davidson motorcycles, tend to make more noise. Currently, most American-made products must be altered to meet European noise standards. Some models cannot be imported into the EU at all.

U.S. motorcycle manufacturers exported $106 million to Japan, which became the largest individual country export market for U.S. motorcycles in 1997. Those exports grew 18 percent in 1997 and 22 percent from 1994 to 1997. U.S. exports to Japan have benefited from new regulations which make it easier for consumers to obtain an operator's license for large motorcycles (engines over 400 cc). These changes came about after several years of efforts by Harley-Davidson and the U.S. government to persuade Japanese officials to change rigorous and cumbersome test procedures for the potential operators of large motorcycles. Export sales to the Japanese market are still hampered by the prohibition of tandem riding on expressways and a low speed limit on expressways. Many potential Japanese owners of heavyweight motorcycles may pass up the opportunity to buy a Harley-Davidson because riding with a passenger is prohibited on Japanese expressways and other roads are slow and potentially dangerous.

Canada was the second largest market for U.S. exports of motorcycles and parts as exports increased 9 percent in 1997 to total $94 million. U.S. exports of motorcycles and parts to Germany and the Netherlands, the third and fourth largest markets in 1997, totaled $83 million and $50 million, down 19 and 15 percent, respectively.

Increasing motorcycle sales to the Big Emerging Markets will be an important factor in the future of the industry. Argentina, Brazil, and Mexico are the largest Big Emerging Markets for U.S. exports, totaling $14 million, $13 million, and $7 million, respectively, in 1997. However, many emerging markets in Asia have restrictive practices which hamper U.S. exports. In addition, the Asian financial crisis has hurt efforts to find potential economically viable distributors and dealers in many Asian countries. However, as domestic production increases, U.S. manufacturers hope for expanded international opportunities worldwide.

BOAT BUILDING AND REPAIRING

The boat building and repairing industry (SIC 3732) consists of manufacturers that produce primarily pleasure boats, including motorboats, sailboats, rowboats, and canoes. The industry does not include ship building and repairing, inflatable boats, or marine engines. Although this industry also includes small commercial and military craft, the discussion here will center on trends in leisure craft.

Global Industry Trends

The U.S. pleasure boat market is the largest in the world. U.S. consumption of pleasure boats and marine accessories accounts for an estimated 60 percent of the worldwide market for those products. Typically, U.S. manufacturers hope for a strong U.S. market to bolster sales and profits. A strong U.S. market also helps exports to a degree, as economies of scale play an important role in the production of boats. If U.S. manufacturers are able to produce a large number of boats for the U.S. market, prices will decline for domestic buyers and international buyers, making U.S. firms more price-competitive overseas.

However, since 1995 there has been relatively weak growth, and real industry shipments were slightly lower in 1998 than they were in 1994. The boat industry usually grows when the economy grows and declines when the economy stalls. In addition, the industry has typically outperformed the overall economy, sometimes after a 1-year lag. Conversely, it declines at a greater rate and a year or 2 before recessionary or slowdown periods in the overall economy. In 1989 the boating industry went into a recession, with real industry shipments falling 10 percent, followed by decreases of 15 percent, and 28 percent in the next 2 years. The overall U.S. economy began slowing in 1990 and 1991; real GDP grew only 1.2 percent in 1990 and declined 0.9 percent 1991. As the economy rebounded in 1992 with real GDP up 2.7 percent, so too did real industry shipments, which rose a robust 23 percent. However, while real GDP has grown 2 percent or better annually since 1995, the boating industry has been virtually unchanged.

Seeking to understand the reasons for this lackluster performance, the industry commissioned a study of the reasons why previous owners are not upgrading and why potential newcomers are not buying a boat. The study, called "Boating Market Evaluation & Opportunities Study," was issued by the industry's trade association, the National Marine Manufacturers Association. Key highlights of the study were that affordability, the lack of sufficient leisure time, and confusion about products were causing consumers to refrain from purchasing a boat. The affordability of a boat involves two factors: a person's personal wealth or disposable income, which will be discussed later, and the rising prices of boats as a result of rising production costs. Although the industry cannot control disposable income, it can try to control costs, which it has not done well the last several years. The producer price index increased 3 percent annually from 1994 to 1997. During that period most recreational equipment industries saw wholesale prices increase less than 2 percent annually, making those products more affordable than boating. The industry must lower costs by improving efficiency or lower input costs such as labor. One way to do this could be continued consolidation of production, distribution, and retail outlets to improve economies of scale.

Although the second factor cited in the study, leisure time, is also largely out of the industry's control, the industry feels that it can address the situation in a limited way by educating potential buyers about the joys of boating, particularly versus other leisure activities, both indoor and outdoor. The industry hopes to launch a marketing campaign in conjunction with the National Marine Manufacturers Association to promote boating as an enjoyable and affordable family activity.

The final finding of the study was product confusion among boat buyers. Buying a boat is a major purchase for most families, probably the second or third largest lifetime expenditure after a house and a car. Thus, confusion on the part of the buyer that cannot be adequately addressed tends to delay or discourage a boat purchase. Some points of confusion concern the comparison of the product with its competition and finding the boat that meets a buyer's needs. The industry hopes it can address these concerns by creating closer ties between manufacturers and dealers and establishing better marketing practices, such as demos, test drives, and better advertising.

In addition, the boat industry continues to worry about the increased costs associated with new legislation regulating and taxing the industry. The U.S. Environmental Protection Agency and the industry began implementing stricter emissions standards that would be phased in gradually over 8 years. These stricter emissions standards require a large capital investment by marine engine companies such as Brunswick and OMC. Although new technologies for two-stroke outboard marine engines will be required, the U.S. industry believes that it can meet these standards over the phase-in period. Currently, these restrictions apply only to outboard engines, but they soon will apply to the engines of personal watercraft as well. Personal watercraft are one- to three-person boats that are propelled by a jet-pump and have handlebars and seats most closely resembling those of motorcycles. Outboard motorboats and personal watercraft are two of the most popular types of pleasure boats, especially among first-time buyers and fishing boat owners.

Similar outboard engine emissions standards are being proposed in the EU. The engine industry has been negotiating with the Europeans for a phase-in period similar to that of the U.S. Environmental Protection Agency. If emissions regulations have no phase-in period, they will cause a severe disruption in the supply of outboards to the EU, all of which are imported, mostly from the United States. Other regulations being considered, including operator licensing, marine wildlife protection laws, and various user fees and taxes, may have a significant impact on the industry.

Important Factors Affecting the Future Growth of U.S. Industry

Consumer debt has played a major role in the growth of product shipments over the last 5 years. From 1990 to about 1994 the ratio of consumer credit to personal income fell from around 17 percent to about 15 percent. Lagging 1 year behind that decline, real domestic product shipments were able to rebound from one of the industry's most severe recessions. From 1991 to 1995 real product shipments increased 3 percent annually. As the ratio of consumer credit to personal income increased from around 15 percent in 1994 to nearly 18 percent in 1996, real product shipments of boats declined an estimated 1 percent annually in 1997. (See Table 39-13.)

Apparent consumption (shipments plus imports minus exports) totaled an estimated $5.7 billion in 1998, virtually un-

TABLE 39-13: Boat Building and Repairing (SIC 3732) Trends and Forecasts

(millions of dollars except as noted)

	1992	1993	1994	1995	1996	1997[1]	1998[2]	1999[3]	Percent Change 96–97	Percent Change 97–98	Percent Change 98–99	Percent Change 92–96[4]
Industry data												
Value of shipments[5]	4,648	4,975	5,334	5,597	5,823	5,850	6,045	6,235	0.5	3.3	3.1	5.8
Value of shipments (1992$)	4,648	4,887	5,154	5,255	5,284	5,105	5,123	5,153	–3.4	0.4	0.6	3.3
Total employment (thousands)	44.5	47.0	47.6	47.9	49.2							2.5
Production workers (thousands)	34.6	36.8	38.4	38.9	40.1							3.8
Average hourly earnings ($)	9.58	9.57	9.70	10.49	10.57							2.5
Capital expenditures	63.6	83.2	98.9	89.0	109							14.4
Product data												
Value of shipments[5]	4,331	4,632	4,887	5,072	5,214	5,350	5,635	5,800	2.6	5.3	2.9	4.7
Value of shipments (1992$)	4,331	4,550	4,722	4,763	4,732	4,668	4,775	4,793	–1.4	2.3	0.4	2.2
Trade data												
Value of imports	257	425	564	807	997	814	735	825	–18.4	–9.7	12.2	40.3
Value of exports	714	534	507	658	621	673	715	732	8.4	6.2	2.4	–3.4

[1] Estimate except imports and exports.
[2] Estimate.
[3] Forecast.
[4] Compound annual rate.
[5] For a definition of industry versus product values, see "Getting the Most Out of *Outlook '99*."
Source: U.S. Department of Commerce: Bureau of the Census; International Trade Administration.

changed from 1997 in real terms. However, real apparent consumption was down an estimated 5 percent in 1997. This decline reflected falling imports in 1997. U.S. imports of boats declined 18 percent in 1997 and an estimated 10 percent in 1998. The fall in imports probably was due to weakening demand for personal watercraft, as the leading manufacturer of personal watercraft is Canadian. Sales of personal watercraft increased rapidly from 1991 to 1995 but have suffered a decline since 1995. According to annual retail estimates of the National Marine Manufacturers Association, sales of personal watercraft peaked at 200,000 units in 1995 and dropped to 176,000 units in 1997. Meanwhile, U.S. exports of boats increased 8 percent in 1997 and an estimated 6 percent in 1998. The Canadian market and several European markets have continued to have strong overall growth, which has boosted U.S. exports of boats. However, the Asian financial crisis has greatly diminished sales opportunities for U.S. boat manufacturers. U.S. exports to Japan, Singapore, Hong Kong, and Malaysia were down 23 percent, 48 percent, 66 percent, and 97 percent, respectively, in the first quarter of 1998 compared with the first quarter of 1997.

Demand for marine products has been inconsistent since 1995. Some segments of the market have grown in one year only to decline the next. Boats powered by water pumps, personal watercraft, and jet boats have grown one year and then declined the next, as has the demand for inboard boats and outboard boats. Multihulled boats, typically with outboard engines, have been experiencing strong growth. These vessels have advantages in offshore pleasure boating, providing more stability in ocean waves. However, this trend toward yachts has not had much of an effect on production; domestic shipments to the U.S. market were up only 3 percent.

U.S. Industry Growth Projections for the Next 1 and 5 Years

U.S. industry shipments of boats are forecast to reach $6.2 billion but will be virtually unchanged in real terms in 1999. U.S. exports will continue to grow, but at a slower rate of about 2 percent. Although the Canadian and European markets are expected to grow, the Asian financial crisis will continue to hamper U.S. sales opportunities, making American products more expensive. For example, the value of the dollar relative to the Japanese yen was at an 8-year high in 1998. U.S. apparent consumption is expected to reach $5.9 billion in 1999, increasing 1 percent in real terms, largely from imports. While the overall economy as measured by GDP is expected to grow around 2 percent in 1999, consumers will need to continue reducing their debt burden before seeking additional credit to purchase a boat. The ratio of consumer credit to personal income declined from 18 percent to 17 percent in the second half of 1997 and the first half of 1998. If that ratio goes much lower, perhaps to 15 percent, U.S. domestic shipments and imports may jump much higher than expected. Also important concerning the forecast will be consumer expectations. Consumer expectations as measured by the Conference Board may have reached their peak in April and may decline slightly in the second half of 1998 and the first half of 1999.

Five-year growth in the market probably will mirror the overall economy's trend line growth as real domestic shipments will increase approximately 2 percent annually. Imports are likely to grow 8 percent annually, while exports will increase 5 percent. Changing demographics and continued foreign demand will be the key factors. The industry benefited from favorable demographic trends in the 1980s, mainly the movement of the baby boomers into their thirties. In the first half of this decade these individuals were part of the 35–54 age group, in which they reached their maximum earning potential, and continued to purchase boats. From 1998 through 2003, the 55–64 age group will be the fastest growing age cohort. This age group, according to the 1996 Consumer Expenditures Survey of the U.S. Bureau of Labor Statistics, has the second highest expenditure level for boats with or without a motor, behind the 45–54 age group.

Global Market Prospects

Exports are becoming increasingly important as foreign markets discover pleasure boating and build the needed infrastructure. The ratio of exports to shipments for boat building and repairing was an estimated 13 percent in 1997. The U.S. boat building industry is the world's largest supplier of recreational craft. Supplying the sizable U.S. market gives American manufacturers many advantages in overseas markets, including economies of scale and product innovation insights. Many consumers in overseas markets look for the "made in the USA" label because they believe that U.S. manufacturers provide the highest-quality products. U.S. manufacturers are competitive overseas and do produce high-quality products. Overseas markets are typically volatile from year to year, since managing the proper amount of supply can be tricky, particularly for many small dealers and suppliers. However, over the last several years U.S. exports of boats have experienced healthy growth.

The one exception was provided by the Asian markets, which fell dramatically in 1998. Asian markets had been growing significantly, and U.S. exports to that region increased 7 percent annually from 1993 to 1997. Many new marinas and pleasure boating facilities have been built over the last 5 years. However, with the current financial crisis, sales have shrunk drastically. Many U.S. manufacturers are hoping that once exchange rates improve and U.S. boats become more affordable, exports again will grow rapidly.

The largest market for U.S. exports was Canada. Exports of pleasure boats to that country increased 26 percent, totaling $177 million in 1997 (see Table 39-14). This increase was a big factor in the overall increase of U.S. exports of boats, as the increase of exports to Canada accounted for 69 percent of the increase in total U.S. boat exports. Japan was the second largest foreign market for U.S. pleasure boats. However, exports fell 3 percent, totaling $59 million in 1997. Early fallout from the financial crisis has been the most common reason given for the small decrease. U.S. exports to the Netherlands, the third largest foreign market for U.S. boats, decreased 22 percent to $41 million. Germany was the fourth largest market, and exports to that country fell 29 percent to $36 million. These

TABLE 39-14: U.S. Trade Patterns in Boat Building and Repairing[1] in 1997

(millions of dollars; percent)

Exports			Imports		
Regions[2]	Value[3]	Share, %	Regions[2]	Value[3]	Share, %
NAFTA	191	28.4	NAFTA	446	54.8
Latin America	97	14.5	Latin America	13	1.6
Western Europe	232	34.4	Western Europe	217	26.6
Japan/Chinese Economic Area	65	9.7	Japan/Chinese Economic Area	87	10.7
Other Asia	21	3.1	Other Asia	14	1.7
Rest of world	67	9.9	Rest of world	38	4.6
World	673	100.0	World	814	100.0
Top Five Countries	Value	Share, %	Top Five Countries	Value	Share, %
Canada	177	26.3	Canada	446	54.8
Japan	59	8.7	Italy	73	8.9
Netherlands	41	6.2	United Kingdom	68	8.4
Germany	36	5.4	Taiwan	49	6.0
United Kingdom	35	5.2	Netherlands	32	3.9

[1] SIC 3732.
[2] For definitions of regional groupings, see "Getting the Most Out of *Outlook '99*."
[3] Values may not sum to total due to rounding.
Source: U.S. Department of Commerce, Bureau of the Census.

markets are still suffering from the oversupply of U.S. products in 1995, when U.S. exports of boats nearly doubled from 1994, reaching $66 million in the Netherlands and $57 million in Germany. The fifth and sixth largest markets for U.S. pleasure boat exports were the United Kingdom and Australia, respectively. U.S. exports to the United Kingdom rose 54 percent, totaling $35 million. U.S. exports to Australia grew 61 percent, totaling $27 million in 1997. Two notable growing markets for U.S. exports of boats in 1997 were Italy and the Bahamas. U.S. exports to those markets grew 103 percent and 199 percent and totaled $22 million and $16 million, respectively. The Bahamas is a major market for the largest yachts, but year-to-year sales often fluctuate, since a half dozen yachts can make a big difference in terms of the value of U.S. exports to that country.

U.S. imports of pleasure boats in 1997 fell for the first time in 5 years, decreasing 18 percent from 1996. The largest foreign supplier of pleasure boats to the United States was Canada. U.S. imports from Canada totaled $446 million in 1997, decreasing 28 percent. Italy was the second-largest foreign supplier of pleasure boats to the United States. U.S. imports from Italy totaled an estimated $73 million, growing 45 percent in 1997. The United Kingdom became the third largest foreign supplier of pleasure boats to the United States in 1997, with imports totaling $68 million, up 73 percent. Boat manufacturers in the United Kingdom have been more aggressive in the U.S. market. By becoming competitive in the U.S. market, overseas manufacturers probably will be competitive in all world markets. U.S. pleasure boat imports from Taiwan were up 9 percent, totaling $49 million. Taiwan's industry could become a major source of production over the next 5 to 10 years. Taiwan has a growing supply of skilled labor, the type needed for the production of boats, and low wage rates relative to U.S. workers' wages. However, the lack of a strong domestic market and the

lack of locally made parts probably will likely slow any movement of production from the United States to Taiwan.

John A. Vanderwolf, (202) 482-0348, and ***Jonathan Freilich,*** (202) 482-5783, U.S. Department of Commerce, Office of Consumer Goods, October 1998.

■ REFERENCES

Call the Bureau of the Census at (301) 457-4100 for information about ordering Census documents.

Bicycle Business Journal, 1904 Wenneca Street, Fort Worth, TX 76102. (817) 870-0341.

Bicycling Magazine, 33 E. Minor Street, Emmaus, PA 18049. (215) 967-5171.

Boat and Motor Dealer, 3949 Oakton, Skokie, IL 60076. (312) 982-1810.

Boating, Diamandis Communications, Inc., 1633 Broadway, New York, NY 10019. (800) 525-0643.

Boating Industry, 850 Third Avenue, New York, NY 10022. (212) 715-2600.

Boating 1997, National Marine Manufacturers Association, 200 East Randolph Drive, Suite 5100, Chicago, IL 60601. (312) 946-6200.

Boating Market Evaluation & Opportunities Study, National Marine Manufacturers Association, 200 East Randolph Drive, Suite 5100, Chicago, IL 60601. (312) 946-6200.

Dealernews, Edgell Communications, Inc., P.O. Box 19531, Irvine, CA 92714. (800) 346-0085.

Dolls—The Collector's Magazine, Collectors Communications Corp., 170 Fifth Avenue, New York, NY 10010. (212) 989-8700, Fax: (212) 645-8976.

Electronic Industries Alliance, 2500 Wilson Boulevard, Arlington, VA 22201. (703) 907-7751, Fax: (703) 907-7769, http://www.eia.org/.

International Data Base, International Programs, Bureau of the Census, U.S. Department of Commerce, Washington, DC 20233. http://www.census.gov/ipc/www/idbsum.html.

Marine Business Journal, 1766 Bay Road, Miami Beach, FL 33139. (305) 538-0700.

Motorcycle Product News, P.O. Box 2338, 6633 Odessa Avenue, Van Nuys, CA 91406. (818) 997-0644.

Musical Instruments and Parts; Toys and Sporting Goods, 1992 Census of Manufactures, MC92-1-39B, Bureau of the Census, U.S. Department of Commerce, Washington, DC 20233. (301) 457-4100.

1992 Census of Retail Trade, SIC 5551, Boat Dealers, Retail, Series RC92-A-52 (quinquennial). SIC 5571, Motorcycle Dealers, Retail, Series RC92-A-52 (quinquennial). SIC 5941, Sporting Goods Stores and Bicycle Shops, Retail, Series RC92-A-52 (quinquennial). Bureau of the Census, U.S. Department of Commerce, Washington, DC 20233. (301) 763-7304.

The 1997 Motorcycle Statistical Annual, Motorcycle Industry Council, 2 Jenner Street, Suite 150, Irvine, CA 92718. (714) 727-4211.

Personal Consumption Expenditures, Wheeled Goods. Bureau of Economic Analysis, U.S. Department of Commerce, Washington, DC 20233. (202) 606-5302, http://www.bea.doc.gov.

Playthings, Cahners Business Information, 51 Madison Avenue, New York, NY 10010. (212) 689-4411, Fax: (212) 683-7929.

Producer Price Indexes, Employment and Earnings, Bureau of Labor Statistics, U.S. Department of Labor, Washington, DC 20212. (202) 606-7705, http://www.bls.gov.

Ship and Boat Building, Railroad and Miscellaneous Transportation Equipment, SIC 3732, 1992 Census of Manufactures, Series MC92-I-37C (quinquennial). Bureau of the Census, U.S. Department of Commerce, Washington, DC 20233. (301) 763-7304.

Soundings Trade-Only, Pratt Street, Essex, CT 06426. (203) 767-3200.

Sport Style, Fairchild Publications, 7 East 12th Street, New York, NY 10003. (212) 741-5971.

Sporting Goods Business, Gralla Publications, 1515 Broadway, New York, NY 10036. (212) 869-1300.

Sporting Goods Dealer, Sporting News Publishing Co., 1212 N. Lindbergh Boulevard, St. Louis, MO 63132. (314) 997-7111.

The Sporting Goods Market in 1997, National Sporting Goods Association, Mt. Prospect, IL 60056. (847) 439-4000.

Sports Participation in 1997, National Sporting Goods Association, Mt. Prospect, IL 60056. (847) 439-4000.

Sports Trend, Shore Communications Inc., Suite 300, N Building, 180 Allen Road NE, Atlanta, GA 30328. (404) 252-8831.

Survey of Current Business, Bureau of Economic Analysis, U.S. Department of Commerce, Washington, DC 20230. (202) 606-9900, http://www.bea.doc.gov.

Toy Book, Adventure Publishing Group, Inc., 1501 Broadway, Suite 500, New York, NY 10036. (212) 575-4510, Fax: (212) 575-4521.

Toy Manufacturers of America, 1115 Broadway, New York, NY 10010. (212) 675-1141, Fax: (212) 633-1429, http://www.tma-toy.com.

U.S. Consumer Product Safety Commission, Office of Information and Public Affairs, Washington, DC 20207. (301) 504-0400, http://www.cpsc.gov.

OTHER CONSUMER DURABLES
Economic and Trade Trends

U.S. International Trade

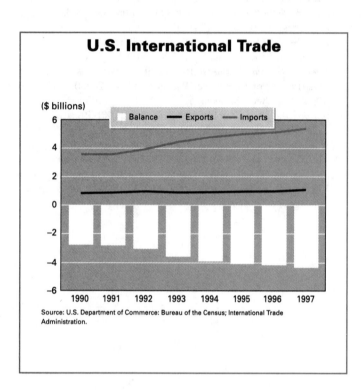

($ billions)

Legend: Balance, Exports, Imports

Source: U.S. Department of Commerce: Bureau of the Census; International Trade Administration.

World Export Market Shares

(%)

Legend: United States, Italy, United Kingdom, Switzerland

Source: United Nations; U.S. Department of Commerce, International Trade Administration.

Export Dependence and Import Penetration

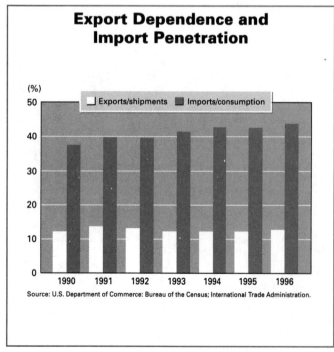

(%)

Legend: Exports/shipments, Imports/consumption

Source: U.S. Department of Commerce: Bureau of the Census; International Trade Administration.

Output and Output per Hour

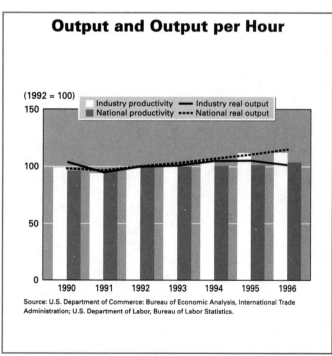

(1992 = 100)

Legend: Industry productivity, Industry real output, National productivity, National real output

Source: U.S. Department of Commerce: Bureau of Economic Analysis, International Trade Administration; U.S. Department of Labor, Bureau of Labor Statistics.

See "Getting the Most Out of *Outlook '99*" for definitions of terms.

Other Consumer Durables

JEWELRY

Precious metal jewelry (SIC 3911) includes jewelry and other articles worn on or carried about the person, made of precious metals (including base metals clad or rolled with precious metals), with or without stones. Costume jewelry and costume novelties (SIC 3961) includes costume jewelry, costume novelties, and ornaments made of all materials except precious metal, precious or semiprecious stones, and rolled goldplate and gold-filled materials.

Global Industry Trends

The U.S. domestic jewelry industry, which consists of precious metal jewelry manufacturers and costume jewelry manufacturers, remains under heavy pressure from imports. This situation explains why the industry has benefited only slightly from increased consumer spending fueled by recent record levels of employment, stock market indexes, and consumer confidence. In 1998 the constant dollar values of shipments of both precious metal jewelry and costume jewelry increased 1 percent.

In the domestic market in 1998, white gold, platinum, silver, pearls, and diamond solitaires had great popularity. Although basic sales of pearls and diamonds were strong, increasing numbers of consumers, buoyed by high profits on Wall Street, opted for purchases of high-end designer pieces.

In 1998 Europe and the United States remained the strongest markets for jewelry. Asia, beset with economic difficulties since mid-1997, when Thailand devalued its currency and set off a chain reaction of competitive devaluations in other Asian countries, has seen jewelry sales plummet in many countries, along with consumer confidence. Before mid-1997, Asia had been emerging as a major market for jewelry. Sales have dropped not only in countries with large devaluations, such as Thailand, Korea, Indonesia, and Malaysia, but also to a lesser extent in neighboring countries, such as Japan and Taiwan, whose cur-

rencies have held up much better. The result has been increased competition for consumers' cash not only in Asia but also in markets such as Europe and North America. While less jewelry is being exported to Asia from Europe and North America, more jewelry is going in the opposite direction. Many Asian jewelry producers, facing the worst economic crisis since World War II, are looking to foreign markets for survival. To increase their exports rapidly, many are willing to cut their prices.

Thailand is a major source and cutting center of gems, including rubies and sapphires. Price cuts between 20 and 40 percent from 1997 prices were reported in 1998 as many Thai dealers were forced to reduce their inventories. With decreased demand, sales of most categories of gems, including diamonds, slowed sharply for many dealers operating in Thailand. In fact, De Beers reported a 16 percent drop in diamond sales in the second half of 1997 as a result of the Asian economic crisis. Much of this decline was due to a substantial downturn in demand in Japan, the second largest market for diamonds. To strengthen diamond prices, De Beers drastically cut the amount of rough diamonds it distributes through its sights or offerings to its distributors in early 1998.

Increased Asian competition in finished jewelry has been slower to develop in foreign markets than has been the case for gems because of differences in jewelry styles. Asian manufacturers that wish to sell successfully in western markets for the first time needed to design and manufacture jewelry for a specific market, since styles can differ widely between markets in Asia, Europe, North America, and Latin America. This preparation work, along with proper marketing, takes time and effort to do correctly. Therefore, much of the increased Asian competition caused by the economic crisis will build up gradually. However, once these manufacturers have made the effort to profitably enter a foreign market, they will be reluctant to exit after the crisis is over. Therefore, increased competition in the global jewelry industry for some time to come is a likely legacy of the Asian economic crisis.

Also affecting jewelry prices in 1998 was the drop in gold prices. In recent years gold generally has fluctuated in the range of $350 to $400 per ounce. However, from a 1996 high of $416 per ounce, gold fell throughout 1997, hitting a low of $278 per ounce in January 1998. Rebounding from that point, gold prices hovered around $300 in the first half of 1998. It is unclear whether this downward shift is a long- or short-term trend. The economic crisis in Asia is assumed to account for part of this price change through a drop in demand. In addition, low inflation rates in many countries have obviated the need for hedges against inflation such as gold for many individuals. Also affecting the demand and supply for gold was the decision by the central banks of some countries, such as Australia, to reduce their gold reserves in 1997.

Many jewelry retailers passed the savings resulting from lower gold material costs on to their customers. Lower prices were especially evident in products, such as gold chain, in which labor compensation and other costs are minimal. These lower prices in turn often spurred increased consumer demand for gold jewelry.

U.S. Industry Growth Projections for the Next 1 and 5 Years

Continuing economic improvement is expected to boost domestic consumer spending for jewelry in 1999. However, increasing jewelry imports are expected to capture most of this additional consumer spending. The value of shipments of precious metal jewelry in constant dollars is expected to remain unchanged from 1998, while costume jewelry shipment, in constant dollars are expected to increase 1 percent (see Tables 40-1 and 40-2).

As the domestic economy enters its eighth year of expansion, the likelihood for continued improvement gets less and less certain. While the domestic economy has weathered economic crises in Latin America and Asia in recent years, eventually the good times will end. Since jewelry is a very cyclical industry, when the economy turns down and consumer discretionary spending slows, this industry will feel the adverse conditions more than most others will. In addition, the threat from foreign producers is not expected to subside soon. On the contrary, the likelihood is for more global competition in the industry as tariff rates fall. In the next 5 years shipments of precious metal jewelry are expected to remain unchanged in constant dollars. Costume jewelry shipments in constant dollars are expected to increase 1 percent, compounded annually.

Global Market Prospects

U.S. imports of precious metal jewelry rose 5 percent in 1997 to $4 billion. The leading suppliers of precious metal jewelry were Italy, Thailand, Hong Kong, India, and Israel (see Table 40-3). Italy was by far the largest supplier, accounting for over 30 percent of total imports. While this was an impressive performance, Italy has nonetheless lost a substantial portion of its share of imports since 1983, when it accounted for 55 percent of imports. Among the countries that have increased substantially in importance in recent years as suppliers of precious metal jewelry are India, Mexico, Canada, and Turkey. India has evolved into an important diamond-cutting center and jewelry manufacturer, while the Mexican and Canadian jewelry industries are developing close relationships with the U.S. market under the auspices of the North American Free Trade Agreement (NAFTA) and the U.S.–Canada Free Trade Agreement.

TABLE 40-1: Jewelry, Precious Metal (SIC 3911) Trends and Forecasts
(millions of dollars except as noted)

	1992	1993	1994	1995	1996	1997[1]	1998[2]	1999[3]	Percent Change 96–97	Percent Change 97–98	Percent Change 98–99	Percent Change 92–96[4]
Industry data												
Value of shipments[5]	4,190	4,278	4,459	4,444	4,443	4,483	4,500	4,545	0.9	0.4	1.0	1.5
Value of shipments (1992$)	4,190	4,215	4,350	4,297	4,243	4,285	4,313	4,313	1.0	0.7	0.0	0.3
Total employment (thousands)	32.5	34.0	31.1	30.1	29.4	28.6			-2.7			-2.5
Production workers (thousands)	22.5	23.6	20.1	20.3	20.1	19.5			-3.0			-2.8
Average hourly earnings ($)	9.41	9.53	9.78	9.61	10.06	10.33			2.7			1.7
Capital expenditures	36.8	45.3	49.2	58.0	91.4							25.5
Product data												
Value of shipments[5]	3,739	4,006	4,063	4,034	4,016	4,054	4,070	4,111	0.9	0.4	1.0	1.8
Value of shipments (1992$)	3,739	3,947	3,964	3,902	3,836	3,875	3,901	3,901	1.0	0.7	0.0	0.6
Trade data												
Value of imports	2,711	3,142	3,438	3,573	3,766	3,959	4,400	4,650	5.1	11.1	5.7	8.6
Value of exports	476	388	366	375	392	471	375	400	20.2	-20.4	6.7	-4.7

[1] Estimate except imports and exports.
[2] Estimate.
[3] Forecast.
[4] Compound annual rate.
[5] For definition of industry versus product values, see "Getting the Most Out of *Outlook '99*."
Source: U.S. Department of Commerce: Bureau of the Census; International Trade Administration.

TABLE 40-2: Costume Jewelry (SIC 3961) Trends and Forecasts

(millions of dollars except as noted)

	1992	1993	1994	1995	1996	1997[1]	1998[2]	1999[3]	Percent Change 96–97	97–98	98–99	92–96[4]
Industry data												
Value of shipments[5]	1,444	1,429	1,627	1,660	1,525	1,562	1,573	1,605	2.4	0.7	2.0	1.4
Value of shipments (1992$)	1,444	1,417	1,603	1,624	1,472	1,475	1,490	1,505	0.2	1.0	1.0	0.5
Total employment (thousands)	17.4	17.1	18.8	16.1	16.2	15.8			−2.5			−1.8
Production workers (thousands)	12.5	12.0	14.3	12.4	12.5	12.2			−2.4			0.0
Average hourly earnings ($)	7.25	7.50	8.06	7.77	8.41	8.82			4.9			3.8
Capital expenditures	12.8	9.7	13.6	11.8	10.1							−5.8
Product data												
Value of shipments[5]	1,532	1,556	1,679	1,770	1,666	1,705	1,715	1,748	2.3	0.6	1.9	2.1
Value of shipments (1992$)	1,532	1,542	1,654	1,732	1,608	1,610	1,625	1,640	0.1	0.9	0.9	1.2
Trade data												
Value of imports	550	561	586	513	484	486	520	545	0.4	7.0	4.8	−3.1
Value of exports	121	135	149	150	151	166	170	175	9.9	2.4	2.9	5.7

[1] Estimate except imports and exports.
[2] Estimate.
[3] Forecast.
[4] Compound annual rate.
[5] For definition of industry versus product values, see "Getting the Most Out of *Outlook '99*."
Source: U.S. Department of Commerce: Bureau of the Census; International Trade Administration.

TABLE 40-3: U.S. Trade Patterns in Jewelry[1] in 1997

(millions of dollars; percent)

Exports			**Imports**		
Regions[2]	Value[3]	Share, %	Regions[2]	Value[3]	Share, %
NAFTA	129	20.2	NAFTA	294	6.6
Latin America	89	14.0	Latin America	402	9.1
Western Europe	272	42.7	Western Europe	1,716	38.6
Japan/Chinese Economic Area	96	15.1	Japan/Chinese Economic Area	699	15.7
Other Asia	28	4.4	Other Asia	978	22.0
Rest of world	23	3.7	Rest of world	355	8.0
World	637	100.0	World	4,445	100.0
Top Five Countries	Value	Share, %	Top Five Countries	Value	Share, %
Switzerland	130	20.4	Italy	1,338	30.1
Canada	100	15.6	Thailand	392	8.8
Japan	64	10.0	Hong Kong (PRC)	391	8.8
Italy	46	7.1	India	384	8.6
United Kingdom	31	4.9	Israel	246	5.5

[1] SIC 3911, 3961.
[2] For definitions of regional groupings, see "Getting the Most Out of *Outlook '99*."
[3] Values may not sum to total due to rounding.
Source: U.S. Department of Commerce, Bureau of the Census.

In 1997 imports of costume jewelry were virtually unchanged from the level in 1996 at $486 million. The leading suppliers of costume jewelry were China, Korea, Austria, and Taiwan. China, which accounted for 31 percent of total costume jewelry imports in 1997, is steadily increasing its share of imports as a result of its labor cost advantage. Meanwhile, imports from Mexico more than doubled between 1995 and 1997. Mexico was the seventh largest supplier in 1997 and was expected to be fifth or sixth in 1998.

Exports of precious metal jewelry increased 20 percent in 1997 to $471 million, while exports of costume jewelry increased 10 percent to $166 million. The leading export markets for precious metal jewelry were Switzerland, Canada, Japan, and Italy, while the leading export markets for costume jewelry were Canada, Japan, Mexico, and the United Kingdom. Exports to Mexico more than doubled in both categories over 1997–1998, reflecting that country's continued recovery from its recession, which began at the end of 1994. Increased exports of parts used in the manufacture of jewelry in Mexico were also a factor. Further encouraging exports to Mexico have been the reductions in Mexican tariffs on U.S. goods that are being implemented under NAFTA.

Over the past 15 years foreign trade has become more important for this industry as tariff barriers have dropped. Between 1983 and 1997, imports of precious metal jewelry increased from 26 percent of domestic consumption (production plus imports and exports) to 52 percent. Imported costume jewelry increased from 19 percent of domestic consumption to 24 percent in that period. Today, after recent minor reductions in jewelry tariffs under the Uruguay Round of General Agreement on Tariffs and Trade (GATT) negotiations, the average U.S. tariff for precious metal jewelry is about 6 percent and that for costume jewelry is about 11 percent. In addition, imports of both categories of jewelry from beneficiary developing countries are eligible for duty-free treatment under the Generalized System of Preferences (GSP). The U.S.–Canada Free Trade Agreement has eliminated tariffs on imports of each country's jewelry. Under NAFTA, Mexico has eliminated tariffs on costume jewelry from the United States. Its tariffs on precious metal jewelry imported from the United States are being eliminated over a 10-year period that began in 1994. Its tariff on such jewelry was 10 percent in 1998. The United States has eliminated tariffs on both categories of jewelry from Mexico.

Further tariff reductions are likely. Gems and jewelry constitute one of nine industry sectors for which members of the Asia-Pacific Economic Cooperation (APEC) forum are seeking to reduce tariff and nontariff barriers. Negotiations within APEC continued throughout 1998. The 18 members of APEC include the United States, Canada, Australia, New Zealand, China, Taiwan, Korea, Japan, Thailand, Malaysia, Indonesia, and the Philippines. Since tariffs in several of these countries are substantial, tariff reduction could offer substantially improved export opportunities for the U.S. industry. For example, China and Thailand have duties of 60 percent for jewelry, while several other APEC countries, such as Malaysia, the Philippines, Indonesia, and New Zealand, have duties ranging between 10 and 25 percent. While the United States does have duties slightly above 10 percent for several jewelry categories, imported jewelry from several APEC countries is currently eligible for duty-free treatment under GSP.

Also during 1998, negotiations formally began to form a Free Trade Area of the Americas. The decision to agree to a free-trade area by 2005 had been made by all the leaders in the Americas other than Cuba at the Miami summit in 1994. Leaders from the Western Hemisphere nations launched negotiations at the Santiago summit in April 1998. Negotiating groups began meeting in September 1998.

MUSICAL INSTRUMENTS

Musical instruments (SIC 3931) includes pianos with or without player attachments, organs, other musical instruments, and parts and accessories for musical instruments.

Global Industry Trends

Product shipments of musical instruments in 1998 were estimated to account for $1.28 billion in revenues. In constant dollars this represented an increase of 2 percent over 1997. Consumer spending in 1998 was aided by high consumer confidence, low unemployment, and a strong stock market. Consumer confidence, as measured by the Conference Board, reached 137.4 in February 1998, its highest level since it rose to 137.9 in June 1969. Also reflecting a strong economy was the unemployment rate, which fell to 4.3 percent in April 1998, the lowest since 4.2 percent was recorded in February 1970. Other good economic news during the year included the soaring stock market, which surged past the 9,300-point level, as measured by the Dow Jones Industrial Average, in July.

There are two major categories of musical instruments: acoustic and electronic or electric. Acoustic instruments include pianos, pipe and reed organs, stringed instruments, woodwinds, brass winds, percussion instruments, harmonicas, and accordions. Electronic or electric instruments include electric organs, electric and digital pianos, electronic keyboards, synthesizers, and electric guitars.

After several years of declining sales, unit production of acoustic pianos turned upward in 1997. Also doing rather well in recent years has been the production of school instruments, including stringed, woodwind, and brass instruments, as the number of students enrolled in kindergarten through high school reached the historically high level of 53 million in 1998. This sector has benefited as more schools have been able to budget additional funds for music education without incurring taxpayer wrath, as a result of the strong economy of the 1990s.

By contrast, sales have continued to be soft for musical instruments such as portable keyboards and home organs. Sales of both of these instruments have declined substantially over the past decade as they have lost popularity with consumers. Portable keyboards suffer from a perception by many consumers that they are of low quality, while home organs are considered old-fashioned by many young consumers. Other electronic music products with newer features hold more interest for most consumers than does either of these products.

U.S. Industry Growth Projections for the Next 1 and 5 Years

The projection for 1999 is for a 2 percent increase in music instrument product shipments in constant dollars (see Table 40-4). This assumes that the economy will continue expanding at a moderate rate in spite of the advanced age of the current economic expansion.

Similarly, the long-term outlook for the musical instrument industry is favorable. Over the next 5 years shipments of musical instruments are expected to increase at a compound rate of

TABLE 40-4: Musical Instruments (SIC 3931) Trends and Forecasts
(millions of dollars except as noted)

	1992	1993	1994	1995	1996	1997[1]	1998[2]	1999[3]	Percent Change 96–97	97–98	98–99	92–96[4]
Industry data												
Value of shipments[5]	982	1,037	1,062	1,144	1,173	1,222	1,280	1,330	4.2	4.7	3.9	4.5
Value of shipments (1992$)	982	990	976	998	986	1,000	1,020	1,035	1.4	2.0	1.5	0.1
Total employment (thousands)	12.2	12.5	12.3	12.8	12.9	13.2			2.3			1.4
Production workers (thousands)	9.4	9.7	9.8	10.4	10.3	10.5			1.9			2.3
Average hourly earnings ($)	9.87	10.14	9.63	10.61	10.59	10.70			1.0			1.8
Capital expenditures	13.8	17.1	11.4	23.7	15.3							2.6
Product data												
Value of shipments[5]	902	965	977	1,167	1,182	1,229	1,282	1,333	4.0	4.3	4.0	7.0
Value of shipments (1992$)	902	922	898	1,018	993	1,005	1,025	1,040	1.2	2.0	1.5	2.4
Trade data												
Value of imports	666	711	751	880	855	905	1,000	1,070	5.8	10.5	7.0	6.4
Value of exports	327	340	370	397	412	409	415	425	–0.7	1.5	2.4	5.9

[1] Estimate except imports and exports.
[2] Estimate.
[3] Forecast.
[4] Compound annual rate.
[5] For definition of industry versus product values, see "Getting the Most Out of *Outlook '99*."
Source: U.S. Department of Commerce: Bureau of the Census; International Trade Administration.

2 percent in constant dollars. Favoring the industry during this period will be a relatively large cohort of students passing through their school years, with many having the opportunity to learn to play a musical instrument. During their teenage years and into their twenties, these students will be major purchasers of musical instruments.

Another demographic cohort that will benefit the industry is the baby boom generation. This generation, with its older members now in their early fifties, will soon be looking toward retirement. Many, having put aside musical instruments many years ago in order to work and raise families, will have enough leisure time to take them up again. There will be much interest among this group in examining the advances that have taken place in musical instruments over the past few decades and in purchasing many of these new and improved products.

Global Market Prospects

The currency turmoil in southeast Asia in 1997 and 1998 had a moderate effect on U.S. imports and exports of musical instruments. Surges of imported goods from Asian manufacturers did not develop as some in the industry had feared despite the fact that a large percentage of imported musical instruments comes from Asia. However, of the four principal Asian suppliers, only Korea suffered a major decline in the value of its currency. The currencies of the others—Japan, Taiwan, and China—suffered only relatively minor losses in value.

U.S. imports of musical instruments accounted for $905 million in 1997, an increase of 6 percent from 1996. Imports rose an estimated 10 percent in 1998. The four leading suppliers to the United States—Japan, Korea, Taiwan, and China—together accounted for about two-thirds of total U.S. imports (see Table

40-5). China continues to increase its share of total imports, although at a slower rate than obtained a few years ago. In 1997 imports from China increased 23 percent from the 1996 level. While this is impressive, it pales in comparison with the increases recorded in 1994 and 1995. Imports from China doubled in each of those years, albeit from a much lower base. Steady growth in imports from China is expected to continue because of its labor cost advantage.

U.S. musical instrument exports were not affected drastically by the Asian currency crisis, since the developed countries are the leading import markets for these products. Total product demand in those countries generally was not affected, since their currencies remained relatively strong. However, U.S. exporters may lose some market share in these traditional export markets as a result of increased imports from Asian countries. Any such market impact is expected to be minor, since most U.S. exporters compete primarily by selling a quality product rather than competing primarily in terms of price.

Among the southeast Asian countries that experienced sharp declines in the value of their currencies in 1997, only South Korea had been a major market for U.S. musical instrument exports in the recent past. While U.S. exports to that country were off only 2.5 percent in 1997, they declined substantially in 1998. Although several other southeast Asian countries affected by falling currency values also recorded major declines in imports of U.S. musical instruments in 1998, they had not been major markets for U.S. exports in the past.

In 1997 U.S. exports of musical instruments totaled $409 million, somewhat less than half the value of imports. This was a decrease of 1 percent from 1996. Exports increased slightly in 1998, rising an estimated 1.5 percent. The leading export mar-

TABLE 40-5: U.S. Trade Patterns in Musical Instruments[1] in 1997
(millions of dollars; percent)

Regions[2]	Exports Value[3]	Exports Share, %	Regions[2]	Imports Value[3]	Imports Share, %
NAFTA	56	13.8	NAFTA	70	7.8
Latin America	42	10.2	Latin America	2	0.2
Western Europe	139	33.9	Western Europe	137	15.1
Japan/Chinese Economic Area	118	28.8	Japan/Chinese Economic Area	469	51.8
Other Asia	29	7.0	Other Asia	206	22.8
Rest of world	26	6.4	Rest of world	21	2.3
World	409	100.0	World	905	100.0
Top Five Countries	**Value**	**Share, %**	**Top Five Countries**	**Value**	**Share, %**
Japan	99	24.3	Japan	295	32.6
Canada	39	9.5	South Korea	136	15.0
United Kingdom	34	8.3	Taiwan	96	10.6
Germany	32	7.8	China	77	8.5
Mexico	18	4.3	Germany	50	5.5

[1] SIC 3931.
[2] For definitions of regional groupings, see "Getting the Most Out of *Outlook '99*."
[3] Values may not sum to total due to rounding.
Source: U.S. Department of Commerce, Bureau of the Census.

kets were Japan, Canada, the United Kingdom, and Germany, which accounted for 50 percent of U.S. exports in 1997.

Musical instruments in all product categories are imported. However, the categories in which imports are especially strong include pianos, guitars, and electric instruments. Similarly, the United States exports instruments from all product categories, with the emphasis being on parts, high-quality guitars, and electric instruments. Musical instrument parts, which are exported to all countries that produce high-quality instruments, account for approximately one-third of total exports.

John M. Harris, U.S. Department of Commerce, Office of Consumer Goods, (202) 482-1178, September 1998.

◼ REFERENCES

Call the Bureau of the Census at (301) 763-4100 for information about ordering Census documents.
1996 Annual Survey of Manufactures, Bureau of the Census, U.S. Department of Commerce, Washington, DC 20233.

Jewelry

American Jewelry Manufacturer, Manufacturing Jewelers and Silversmiths of America, Inc., 1 State Street, Providence, RI 02908-5035. (401) 274-3840, ajm.magazine@internetMCI.com.
Jeweler's Circular-Keystone, Chilton Company, Chilton Way, Radnor, PA 19089. (215) 964-4000, jck.polygon.net.

Jewelry, Silverware, and Plated Ware, 1992 Census of Manufactures, MC87-I-39A, Bureau of the Census, U.S. Department of Commerce, Washington, DC 20233.
Modern Jewelers, Vance Publishing Corporation, 400 Knightsbridge Parkway, Lincolnshire, IL 60060. (913) 451-2200.
National Jeweler, Gralla Publications, 1515 Broadway, New York, NY 10036. (212) 869-1300, national-jeweler.com.
Office Supplies, Costume Jewelry and Notions, 1992 Census of Manufactures, MC87-I-39C, Bureau of the Census, U.S. Department of Commerce, Washington, DC 20233.

Musical Instruments

Musical Instruments and Parts, 1992 Census of Manufactures, MC87-1-39B, Bureau of the Census, U.S. Department of Commerce, Washington, DC 20233.
Music, Inc. Maher Publications, Inc., 180 West Park Avenue, Elmhurst, IL 60126. (630) 941-2030, E-mail: musicincupbeat@worldnet.att.net.
The Music Trades, Music Trades Corporation, 80 West Street, PO Box 432, Englewood, NJ 07631. (201) 871-1965, E-mail: MUSIC@MUSICTRADES.com.
Music USA 1998, National Association of Music Merchants, 5140 Avenida Encinas, Carlsbad, CA 92008-4391. (619) 438-8001, http://www.namm.com/namm, E-mail: namm@namm.com.

◼ RELATED CHAPTERS

16: Microelectronics
42: Retailing

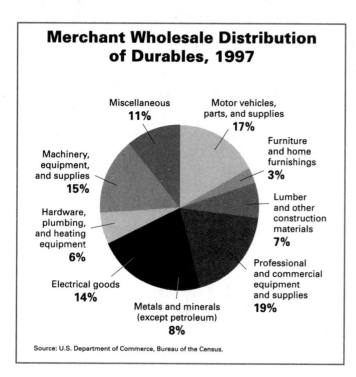

Merchant Wholesale Distribution of Durables, 1997

- Miscellaneous **11%**
- Motor vehicles, parts, and supplies **17%**
- Furniture and home furnishings **3%**
- Machinery, equipment, and supplies **15%**
- Lumber and other construction materials **7%**
- Hardware, plumbing, and heating equipment **6%**
- Electrical goods **14%**
- Professional and commercial equipment and supplies **19%**
- Metals and minerals (except petroleum) **8%**

Source: U.S. Department of Commerce, Bureau of the Census.

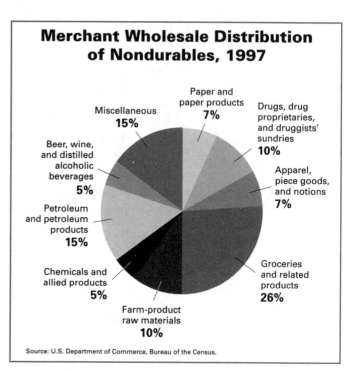

Merchant Wholesale Distribution of Nondurables, 1997

- Paper and paper products **7%**
- Miscellaneous **15%**
- Drugs, drug proprietaries, and druggists' sundries **10%**
- Beer, wine, and distilled alcoholic beverages **5%**
- Apparel, piece goods, and notions **7%**
- Petroleum and petroleum products **15%**
- Chemicals and allied products **5%**
- Groceries and related products **26%**
- Farm-product raw materials **10%**

Source: U.S. Department of Commerce, Bureau of the Census.

Sales Size of Merchant Wholesaler-Distributors, 1992

Legend:
- Percent of total firms
- Percent of total sales

Categories: Less than $1 million; $1 million to $9.9 million; $10 million to $24.9 million; $25 million or more

Source: U.S. Department of Commerce, Bureau of the Census.

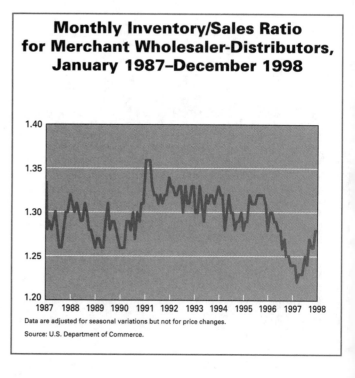

Monthly Inventory/Sales Ratio for Merchant Wholesaler-Distributors, January 1987–December 1998

Data are adjusted for seasonal variations but not for price changes.

Source: U.S. Department of Commerce.

41

Wholesaling

INDUSTRY DEFINITION The wholesale distribution industry includes establishments (places of business) that sell products to retailers, merchants, contractors, and/or industrial, institutional, and commercial users but do not sell in significant amounts to the ultimate consumers (end users). The industry includes companies that distribute durable goods (SIC 50) and those that distribute nondurable goods (SIC 51). Durable goods are principally items that can be used repeatedly because they are not consumed as they are used (or are consumed very slowly); examples include furniture (SIC 5021), office equipment (SIC 5044), plumbing and heating equipment and supplies (SIC 5074), and industrial supplies (SIC 5085). Nondurable goods are principally items that are consumed as they are used, such as printing and writing paper (SIC 5111), groceries (SIC 5141), chemicals and allied products (SIC 5169), and books, periodicals, and newspapers (SIC 5192).

OVERVIEW

Three types of operations can perform the functions of wholesale distribution: merchant wholesaler-distributors, manufacturers' sales branches and offices, and agents, brokers, and commission agents. Merchant wholesaler-distributors are independently owned and operated firms that buy and sell products of which they have taken ownership. Generally, wholesaler-distributors operate one or more warehouses in which they receive and inventory goods for later reshipping. Manufacturers' sales branches and offices are captive wholesaling operations that are owned and operated by domestic (U.S.) manufacturers. Agents, brokers, and commission agents buy or sell products for commissions or fees but do not take ownership of those products.

Merchant wholesaler-distributors are the largest and most important of these three groups. According to the most recent census data (1992), merchant wholesaler-distributors accounted for 57 percent of wholesale sales volume compared with 32 percent for manufacturers' sales branches and offices and 11 percent for agents, brokers, and commission agents. Although the share accounted for by merchant wholesaler-distributors declined slightly from the 1987 census data, overall that share has been increasing steadily from a low of 48 percent in 1958. There were 341,376 merchant wholesaler-distributors operating

414,836 establishments in 1992, but only 301,167 of those firms were operating throughout the census year. Wholesale distribution sales in 1997 totaled approximately $4.3 trillion, of which $2.5 trillion was booked by merchant wholesaler-distributors. The wholesale distribution industry is represented by the National Association of Wholesaler-Distributors (NAW), a federation of 112 national wholesale distribution line of trade associations and 45 state, local, and regional associations. NAW represents more than 40,000 individual companies.

Wholesale distribution has constituted a remarkably stable proportion of U.S. national income over the past 70 years. According to the Distribution Research Program at the University of Oklahoma, the proportion of national income attributable to wholesale distribution increased from 5.1 percent in 1929 to 5.6 percent in 1994. Furthermore, the wholesaling industry has consistently accounted for about 1 in every 20 jobs in the United States throughout this century. (Employment levels by state in the wholesaling industry are shown in Figure 41-1.)

The economic value added of merchant wholesaler-distributors derives from their performance of multiple functions for both manufacturers and customers. At the most basic level, customers want to purchase small quantities of many different products, while manufacturers produce large quantities of a few products. Merchant wholesaler-distributors simplify product, payment, and information flows between the princi-

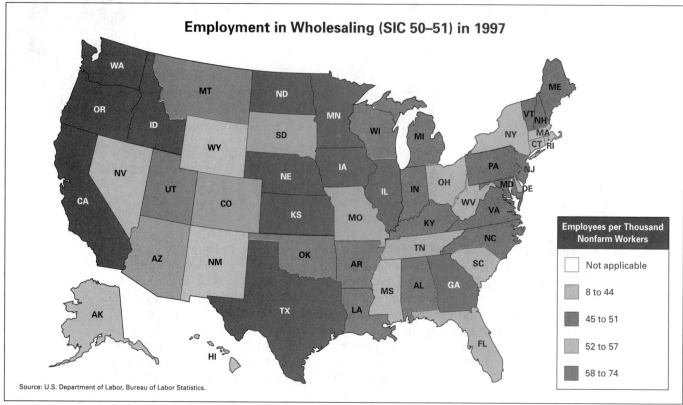

Employment in Wholesaling (SIC 50–51) in 1997

Employees per Thousand Nonfarm Workers

Not applicable

8 to 44

45 to 51

52 to 57

58 to 74

Source: U.S. Department of Labor, Bureau of Labor Statistics.

FIGURE 41-1

pals to a given transaction—a customer and a supplier—by bridging the gap between the assortments of goods and services available from individual producers and the assortments demanded by industrial, retail, institutional, and commercial customers. Among the functions performed for manufacturers are sales contact, order processing, customer support, and market information. The functions performed for customers include product availability, credit and finance, customer service, sales advice, and technical support. One reason why merchant wholesaler-distributors have increased their share of total wholesale sales is that they can perform those functions more effectively and efficiently than can either manufacturers or customers.

The majority of wholesaler-distributors are very small companies that operate in a single location; 92 percent of wholesaler-distributors had annual sales less than $10 million in 1992. These companies accounted for 25 percent of total merchant wholesaler-distributor sales. In contrast, the largest wholesaler-distributors, defined as companies with sales over $250 million, represented 0.2 percent of these firms but made 37 percent of total sales (see Table 41-1).

The size difference between the smallest and largest firms has been growing. In 1982 wholesaler-distributors with annual sales less than $10 million accounted for a slightly higher proportion of total wholesale distribution firms (94 percent) but made a much greater percentage of the sales (31 percent). Another

TABLE 41-1:   Size Distribution by Sales of Merchant Wholesaler-Distributors, 1992[1]

Sales of Firms	Number of Firms	Number of Establishments	Total Sales, $ millions	Average Number of Establishments per Firm	Average Sales per Firm, $ thousands	Average Sales per Establishment, $ thousands
Less than $1 million	153,657	155,072	61,638	1.0	401	397
$1 million to $9.9 million	123,689	143,252	389,727	1.2	3,151	2,721
$10 million to $24.9 million	15,256	27,797	232,223	1.8	15,222	8,354
$25 million to $49.9 million	4,819	13,001	165,502	2.7	34,344	12,730
$50 million to $99.9 million	2,145	9,331	146,209	4.4	68,163	15,669
$100 million to 249.9 million	984	8,134	147,147	8.3	149,540	18,090
$250 million or more	617	17,619	679,117	28.6	1,100,676	38,545
Total	301,167	374,206	1,821,564	1.2	6,048	4,868

[1] Includes firms that operated during the entire year only.
Source: U.S. Department of Commerce, Bureau of the Census.

important disparity between large and small firms relates to their geographic scope of operation. Wholesaler-distributors with sales less than $10 million operate in one or two locations, while the largest merchant wholesaler-distributors operate at an average of 29 locations (see Table 41-1). The disparity in establishment size is even greater. The largest merchant wholesaler-distributors run establishments that average $38.5 million in sales, roughly 10 times the figure for the establishments run by firms with sales below $10 million.

Despite these trends, traditional measures of industry concentration are low relative to those of most manufacturing sectors. The average four-firm concentration ratio among merchant wholesaler-distributors was 17 percent at the four-digit SIC level in 1992. The four-firm concentration ratio is the percentage of total industry sales contributed by the largest four companies. To some extent, this low level of concentration reflects the fact that competition among wholesaler-distributors traditionally occurs in geographically distinct markets. A wholesaler-distributor can dominate one region of the country yet account for a very small proportion of national sales. Thus, the apparent fragmentation of merchant wholesale distribution may not reflect the true nature of concentration in a single region.

GLOBAL INDUSTRY TRENDS

In 1992, 7.8 percent of merchant wholesaler-distributor sales were for export, a sharp increase from 6.1 percent in 1987. This represents a dollar increase in export sales of $53.9 billion. The following industries had the highest proportion of merchant wholesaler-distributor sales for export in 1992: grain and field beans (SIC 5153), 41 percent; coal and other minerals and ores (SIC 5052), 37 percent; farm-product raw materials (SIC 5159), 35 percent; and transportation equipment and supplies excluding motor vehicles (SIC 5088), 31 percent. Collectively, these four industries represented 6.5 percent of all merchant wholesaler-distributor sales.

The importance of merchant wholesaler-distributors in international trade will grow substantially over the next 5 years. Domestic merchant wholesaler-distributors are expanding internationally in two ways. First, they are acquiring foreign wholesaler-distributors at a record rate. According to *Mergers & Acquisitions Journal*'s annual compilation of publicly announced transactions, there were 81 acquisitions of foreign firms by domestic wholesaler-distributors in 1996. In fact, wholesale distribution now accounts for approximately 1 in 10 of all cross-border acquisition transactions that involve at least one U.S. company. In contrast, there were only nine cross-border acquisitions by domestic wholesaler-distributors in 1981. For example, Arrow Electronics, a $7.8 billion wholesaler-distributor of electronic components that has expanded internationally through acquisition, now derives 29 percent of its annual sales from European subsidiaries and 7 percent from subsidiaries in Asia. Second, merchant wholesaler-distributors are expanding internationally by acquiring U.S.-based export firms. For instance, Hughes Supply, a $1.8 billion wholesaler-

distributor of building materials, recently purchased Merex Corp., a $15 million trading company that does business in South America.

Wholesaler-distributors are expanding internationally to meet the needs of both customers and suppliers. Global manufacturers and customers are demanding that their distribution partners have a presence in all major markets. The reduced cost of cross-border shipping and falling trade barriers are also encouraging expansion. For the same reasons, foreign wholesaler-distributors are making inroads into the domestic market. There were 61 acquisitions of U.S.-based wholesaler-distributors by foreign companies in 1996, mirroring the overseas expansion of U.S. companies.

DOMESTIC TRENDS

Industry Consolidation

Consolidation, defined as a decline in the number of companies in a single line of trade, has been sweeping through the wholesale distribution industry. Consolidation is closely related to increased sales concentration. In many lines of trade a few wholesaler-distributors have grown much larger than their competitors, leading to greater concentration in the sales that go through the wholesale distribution portion of the channel.

A report published by the Distribution Research & Education Foundation (DREF) of NAW, *Consolidation in Wholesale Distribution: Understanding Industry Change,* found evidence of significant consolidation in 42 of the 54 lines of trade studied. In 14 of those 42 industries, the number of wholesaler-distributors declined by more than 40 percent. (However, census data have not documented a pronounced decline in the number of merchant wholesaler-distributors. This apparent discrepancy is due to aggregation biases in the SIC code relative to conventional industry definitions and a tendency for industry participants to underestimate the number of very small merchant wholesaler-distributors.)

Consolidation among wholesale customers has been an important cause of consolidation. Customer consolidation occurs through the emergence of a few dominant customers, the exit of the small companies that form the traditional distribution customer base, and the banding together of customer organizations into cooperative purchasing groups. These changes have led to industry consolidation for two reasons. First, the emerging needs of larger customers create incentives for geographic expansion among wholesaler-distributors. Second, customer consolidation limits the business prospects for wholesaler-distributors that cannot provide the geographic reach or level of service required by customers.

Customer consolidation allows a wholesaler-distributor to grow geographically and exploit the benefits of operating in multiple regions. Large national manufacturers, multiunit retailers, and national purchasing groups often welcome the combination of broad geographic coverage and wide brand availability. It can be more efficient to deal with merchant wholesaler-distributors that are able to provide access to multiple manufacturers across multiple geographic regions. Similarly, industrial purchasers that operate multiple regional manufacturing facilities but use local or regional wholesaler-distributors in each area present a profitable opportunity for a national wholesaler-distributor.

For example, changes in customers' buying practices were the primary driver of rapid and intense consolidation among wholesalers of periodicals and magazines. Retailers put their contracts up for competitive bids, encouraging wholesalers to cross previously exclusive geographic boundaries. The contract-winning companies rapidly acquired former competitors in an effort to cover larger territories and service larger accounts. Smaller, regional wholesalers that did not or could not react were forced to sell out or dissolve. John Harrington of Harrington Associates, a company that specializes in publishing distribution services, estimates that the number of wholesalers dropped from nearly 182 companies in 1990 to 56 in 1997. The top five wholesalers now control an estimated 60 percent of the national market.

To take advantage of external consolidation forces, some wholesaler-distributors have adopted a growth-by-acquisition strategy, sequentially folding competitors into their operations through friendly takeovers. Many of the largest merchant wholesaler-distributors have been formed through sequential acquisitions. According to *Mergers & Acquisitions Journal*'s annual survey, wholesale distribution is now the second most active industry in the United States in terms of merger and acquisition activity.

In response to this trend toward consolidation, smaller merchant wholesaler-distributors are banding together in alliances. Members can bid for national or multiregional contracts and thus offer the same geographic reach provided by a larger, multiestablishment company. These groups can also take advantage of volume purchasing opportunities from suppliers. At the same time, the alliance members retain operational autonomy, enabling them to maintain high levels of service for their local customers. According to *Modern Distribution Management,* two of the largest alliances are Affiliated Distributors, which has 281 members and aggregate sales of $13 billion, and iPower Distribution Group, which has 220 members and aggregate sales of $10 billion.

Despite pressure for consolidation, the aggregate number of merchant wholesaler-distributors is not likely to decline sharply. However, the disparity between large and small firms documented in Table 41-1 will continue to prevail. In many lines of business there will be a top tier of very large, national wholesaler-distributors that coexist with much smaller, local firms. Although the long-term viability of the alliances described above is not certain, the continued success of these groups will provide a way for smaller companies to survive as independent entities.

Impact of Outside Financial Investment

Strong interest in consolidation investments on the part of the financial community is bringing enormous amounts of financial capital into the wholesale distribution industry. For example,

Consolidation Capital Corporation raised over $500 million in November 1997 to "become the leading consolidator of distribution companies and service providers in one or more fragmented industries," according to the prospectus. Private equity firms also are financing industry consolidation in wholesale distribution. For example, Golder Thoma Cressey Rauner, a prominent Chicago firm that partners with executives to consolidate service industries, recently formed American Sanitary to consolidate the distribution of janitorial and sanitary supplies.

The roll-up phenomenon is another indication of the financial community's recent interest in wholesale distribution. In a roll-up, a group of 5 to 10 merchant wholesaler-distributors in the same line of trade simultaneously merge to create a new holding company. At the same time, the holding company goes public and lists its shares on the stock market. Prominent actions in this area include Industrial Distribution Group (nine industrial wholesaler-distributors with combined sales of $251 million), USA Floral (nine floral products wholesaler-distributors with combined sales of $175 million), and Pentacon (five fastener wholesaler-distributors with combined sales of $152 million). These companies raised over $60 million each in the public capital markets between September 1997 and March 1998.

Integrated Supply

An important trend in industrial distribution channels has been the growth of integrated supply agreements for maintenance, repair, and operating products (MROP). These products include production consumables, spare parts, maintenance supplies, and many other frequently used low-value items. Under these agreements, a buying customer agrees to give a single wholesaler-distributor or a group of wholesaler-distributors all of its business for MROP. In exchange, the distributor agrees to provide a high level of service for an entire group of products at agreed on, contractually negotiated prices. Integrated supply is seen as a way to eliminate waste and redundancy from the distribution channel.

Larger end-user customers have been driving the integrated supply phenomenon. According to a 1992 survey by *Purchasing* magazine, industrial customers spent 17 percent of MROP purchasing dollars but generated 36 percent of all purchase orders for those products. In other words, these customers face enormous organizational costs in purchasing the lowest-cost, most frequently used items. Integrated supply represents an attempt by customers to minimize their total acquisition costs by reducing the supplier base, shrinking internal purchasing staffs, and applying supply chain management technologies such as electronic commerce (including electronic data interchange and on-line ordering) to reduce inventory. This process also allows customers to leverage their buying power by bundling their purchases. Integrated supply agreements can also involve the complete outsourcing of the procurement function to the merchant wholesale distribution channel.

Ideally, integrated supply agreements eliminate redundancies in the supply chain while lowering costs through more efficient purchasing by customers. To meet the integrated supply needs of customers, wholesaler-distributors have developed a number of innovative strategies. Some companies are positioning themselves to manage the entire supply chain for their customers by acquiring wholesaler-distributors from other lines of trade and aggregating the products from multiple industries. Strategic marketing alliances of large wholesaler-distributors from multiple lines of trade are also being formed. In 1997, VWR Scientific Products, one of the largest wholesaler-distributors of laboratory supplies, entered into an alliance with W. W. Grainger, a nationwide wholesaler-distributor of MROP. This alliance allows customers to place consolidated orders with Grainger for VWR products and vice versa. Another alternative is provided by Pure Integrators—companies that focus their entire business on integrated supply contracting without a branch-based distribution system. Two such companies are Bruckner Supply and Industrial Systems Associates.

Alternative Channels

During the past 15 years one of the biggest threats to merchant wholesaler-distributors has been the rise of "power retailers" that purchase directly from manufacturers. The 1995 DREF report *Competing for Customers: How Wholesaler-Distributors Can Meet the Competitive Challenge* describes two different types of power retailers: (1) general merchandise power retailers that sell a broad variety of product lines, either discount department stores such as Wal-Mart and Kmart or membership warehouse clubs such as Price/Costco and Sam's Club, and (2) category-dominant power retailers that concentrate on one or more closely related merchandise lines [examples include Toys R Us (toys), Petco (pet supplies), Staples (office supplies), and Home Depot (home improvement supplies)]. Since direct purchases by retailers are not included in the Census of Wholesale Trade, the aggregate sales impact of power retailers is hard to determine.

A key source of competitive advantage for these companies is the ability to buy in large quantities in select product categories, which gives them a very prominent position in the channel. This large purchase volume has caused many power retailers to adopt a "buy direct" approach. Retailers such as Wal-Mart have squeezed costs out of the channel by creating in-house distribution systems in which wholesaler-distributors play a small role. Manufacturers have been forced to respond to the demands of dominant buyers, often at the expense of wholesaler-distributors. In addition, power retailers have triggered industry consolidation among the small and medium-sized retailers that were traditional wholesale distribution customers.

Electronic Commerce

Electronic commerce—the process of buying and selling by using the Internet—is the most important wild card for the future of merchant wholesaler-distributors. The Gartner Group, an information technology advisory company, has outlined two possible scenarios for the way in which the Internet will negatively affect merchant wholesaler-distributors. In the first scenario, manufacturers post their products on the Internet by using a bulletin board system, letting customers search and

source globally by using on-line search engines. In the second scenario, manufacturers can use the Internet to gain direct access to customers, taking on important functions currently performed by merchant wholesaler-distributors.

Bruce Merrifield, an expert in the way in which electronic commerce affects wholesale distribution, has noted that electronic commerce offers the capacity to "empower final customers to let them buy anywhere, anytime, their way, for less, now, and fast." When real-time total information availability is provided to the end user on the Internet, the traditional value of merchant wholesaler-distributors declines sharply. Products that can be shipped by small-package carriers can be globally sourced and delivered overnight to almost any place in the world. For these products, large public warehouses or third-party shipping organizations can perform the logistics roles, eliminating the need for thousands of specialized wholesaler-distributors.

Large industrial buyers have begun to experiment with dynamically priced open sourcing over the Internet. For example, FreeMarkets Online, a Pittsburgh-based start-up company, has brokered $103 million in goods through Internet-based auctions for clients such as Caterpillar, United Technologies, and General Motors. Polymerland, Inc., a subsidiary of GE Corp., lets engineers search its on-line database of polymers to find the resin that has the exact qualities of heat and shrink resistance needed in a new laptop or toaster. Similar consumer-oriented services use Internet buying agent utilities to compare prices among competing on-line retailers. Companies such as NECX, an on-line computer retailer, lets customers compare the prices of identical items on competitors' sites without forcing them to leave the NECX site.

Electronic commerce thus poses the threat that technology could replace some functions of independent wholesale distribution intermediaries. Three common technologies have been identified by Bob Segal, a consultant with Frank Lynn & Associates: (1) Telemarketing permits manufacturers to communicate cost-effectively with end-user customers, (2) relational databases allow manufacturers to give end users a level of customization previously available only from a local reseller, and (3) advanced inventory management systems, just-in-time manufacturing, and express delivery services such as Federal Express and UPS diminish the importance of maintaining high levels of local inventory. So far, wholesaler-distributors have not been replaced by electronic commerce solutions because it is extremely complex to replace all of the valuable functions performed by wholesale distribution intermediaries.

U.S. INDUSTRY GROWTH PROJECTIONS FOR THE NEXT 1 AND 5 YEARS

In 1997, the sales of merchant wholesaler-distributors exceeded $2.5 trillion, a 4.3 percent increase over 1996 (see Table 41-2). Sales growth for merchant wholesaler-distributors has been very strong in recent years, exceeding overall U.S. economic growth. The compound annual growth rate (CAGR) for durable goods wholesale distribution from 1993 to 1997 was 7.2 percent and the CAGR for nondurable wholesale distribution during that period was 6.4 percent (see Table 41-3). These strong aggregate growth rates indicate clearly that merchant wholesaler-distributors have been an attractive channel for manufacturers and customers during the current economic expansion. Actual growth for both 1996 and 1997 exceeded the forecasts made in *U.S. Industry & Trade Outlook '98.*

It is very difficult to interpret growth rates for the subsectors of wholesale distribution. Total sales growth for wholesale distribution can be broken down into four underlying components: (1) changes in the volume of product handled, (2) changes in the price of products, (3) changes in revenues from value-added services, and (4) changes in the proportion of channel volume going through merchant wholesaler-distributors. These four elements cannot be analyzed in a meaningful and consistent manner across lines of trade.

Sales by merchant wholesaler-distributors are forecast to exceed the growth rate of the overall U.S. economy. Growth is predicted to be strong through 1998, with a slight weakening by the end of the decade. By the year 2000 sales by merchant wholesaler-distributors should approach $3 trillion (see Table 41-3). According to the U.S. Department of Commerce, gross profit margins have been remarkably steady for merchant wholesaler-distributors at approximately 21 percent of sales in each of the last 10 years. Gross margins as a percentage of sales are expected to remain at approximately the same level during the next 3 years.

Many of the domestic trends discussed earlier in this chapter support favorable prospects for wholesale distribution. The

TABLE 41-2: Merchant Wholesaler-Distributor Sales by Category
(billions of dollars)

	SIC	1987	1988	1989	1990	1991	1992	1993	1994	1995	1996	1997
Durable goods												
Motor vehicles and parts and supplies	501	156	167	167	174	167	171	179	197	203	211	218
Furniture and home furnishings	502	27	30	32	34	32	33	35	37	41	44	43
Lumber and other construction materials	503	58	61	63	64	58	64	71	78	77	86	88
Professional and commercial equipment and supplies	504	85	94	110	114	124	140	159	166	195	231	256
Metals and minerals (except petroleum)	505	68	79	80	78	76	77	80	92	101	98	106
Electrical goods	506	94	102	113	116	113	115	132	150	170	174	178
Hardware, plumbing, and heating equipment	507	41	45	49	53	50	53	56	64	68	71	76
Machinery, equipment, and supplies	508	118	138	149	157	146	149	161	170	183	187	193
Miscellaneous durable goods	509	84	86	89	91	93	107	114	128	143	144	147
Total		731	802	852	881	860	909	987	1,082	1,179	1,246	1,304
Nondurable goods												
Paper and paper products	511	41	47	51	52	52	55	59	68	82	83	89
Drugs, drug proprietaries, and druggists' sundries	512	34	40	45	52	60	67	72	83	95	103	119
Apparel, piece goods, and notions	513	47	53	61	65	64	68	70	73	71	76	87
Groceries and related products	514	223	236	259	273	277	279	285	289	305	315	329
Farm-product raw materials	515	102	124	120	108	105	106	96	95	114	130	118
Chemicals and allied products	516	26	34	33	36	37	39	39	42	48	53	56
Petroleum and petroleum products	517	125	122	136	149	140	143	139	143	151	178	182
Beer, wine, and distilled alcoholic beverages	518	42	43	45	49	52	50	51	53	54	56	58
Miscellaneous nondurable goods	519	105	113	123	131	133	133	140	148	168	181	183
Total		745	812	874	913	920	941	953	993	1,087	1,175	1,221
Grand total		1,476	1,614	1,725	1,794	1,780	1,850	1,940	2,076	2,266	2,421	2,526

Source: U.S. Department of Commerce, Bureau of the Census.

TABLE 41-3: Merchant Wholesale Distribution (SIC 50, 51) Trends and Forecasts
(billions of dollars; percent)

	1993	1994	1995	1996	1997	1998[1]	1999[2]	2000[2]	97–98	98–99	99–00	93–97[3]
									|	Percent Change		|
Durable goods sales	987	1,082	1,179	1,246	1,304	1,384	1,445	1,520	6.1	4.4	5.2	7.2
Nondurable goods sales	953	993	1,087	1,175	1,221	1,285	1,331	1,384	5.2	3.6	4.0	6.4
Total	1,940	2,076	2,266	2,421	2,526	2,669	2,776	2,904	5.7	4.0	4.6	6.8

[1] Estimate.
[2] Forecast.
[3] Compound annual growth rate.
Source: U.S. Department of Commerce, Bureau of the Census; estimates and forecasts by the author.

amount and quality of outside financing signal the fundamental strength of the wholesale distribution industry. The continued interest of the public capital markets in wholesale distribution should lead to further consolidation; this consolidation will create larger, well-funded merchant wholesaler-distributors that are better able to serve manufacturers and customers.

Continued consolidation of the purchasing function by industrial customers will fuel a need for integrated supply contracts. Frank Lynn & Associates, an international consulting firm that specializes in channels issues, estimates that the integrated supply market will exceed $10 billion by the year 2000. During the next 5 years wholesaler-distributors' strategies to service integrated supply contracts will lead to a blurring of traditional industry definitions. A few very large, multicategory wholesaler-distributors will emerge to serve the needs of larger customers. The integrated supply trend will also increase the proportion of wholesale sales that are made through wholesaler-distributors because manufacturers will not be able to fully serve the multicategory needs of industrial customers.

Although power retailers pose an ongoing competitive threat to merchant wholesaler-distributors, there are few consumer products for which the power retailer concept has not already been attempted. Therefore, the impact of alternative retail channels is likely to diminish over the next 5 years. Furthermore, merchant wholesaler-distributors have found ways to provide valuable services to large retail customers, limiting the direct-buying activities of power retailers. For example, Central Garden and Pet, a fast-growing merchant wholesaler-distributor with over $600 million in annual sales, has built an efficient national distribution network. By combining a national scale with a broad menu of value-added services, Central Garden & Pet has reversed a direct-buying trend and become the preferred supply source for retail chains such as Wal-Mart.

It is still too early to forecast the ultimate impact of electronic commerce on merchant wholesaler-distributors. Merchant wholesaler-distributors in many lines of trade are innovating to retain a place in the distribution channel. The Gartner Group has suggested that wholesaler-distributors can thrive by using the Internet to communicate more frequently with suppliers and customers, strengthening their bonds with other members in the channel. Some wholesaler-distributors have already begun to use Internet information-sharing capabilities to share forecasts, order information, inventory levels, and shipment status with their trading partners. For example, Marshall Industries was one of the first wholesaler-distributors to put its entire product catalogue on the Internet. Like many wholesaler-distributors, Marshall offers its customers the ability to access the status of their orders electronically by linking to its internal databases.

The inventory-sales ratio measures the monthly turnover of inventories at current sales rates. From 1991 through 1995 the ratio averaged 1.31, indicating that merchant wholesaler-distributors held inventory that would be used up in roughly 6 weeks if inventories were not replenished. The ratio began trending downward in late 1995, reaching a low of 1.22 in February 1997. However, the ratio increased in 1997, ending the year at 1.28. Despite this recent rise, the inventory-sales ratio for merchant wholesaler-distributors is expected to decline to 1.20 by mid-1999, driven by increased supply chain efficiencies on the part of larger wholesaler-distributors and the use of electronic commerce by all the participants in the supply chain. Note that these figures represent a mix of durable and nondurable goods. The inventory-sales ratio for nondurable was close to 1.00 at the end of 1997, while the ratio for durable goods was 1.50.

GLOBAL MARKET PROSPECTS

The wholesale distribution industry is globalizing, creating a top tier of merchant wholesaler-distributors that compete in multiple countries. Export activity is expected to continue to expand, and the nondomestic operations of merchant wholesaler-distributors should grow in importance. By 2002 more than 10 percent of merchant wholesaler-distributor sales will be for export. Large, sophisticated, and well-funded wholesaler-distributors will continue to engage in international expansion.

International growth opportunities are particularly substantial in countries with unsophisticated distribution infrastructures. For instance, Russia has seen the formation of large domestic merchant wholesaler-distributors such as Uniland, which was founded in 1991 and now has sales of $1 billion, and Soyuzontrakt, which has annual sales of $300 million. These companies have had difficulty raising capital to expand and modernize their operations. Furthermore, distribution is still in its formative stages in Russia and other emerging markets. During the next 10 years domestic merchant wholesaler-distributors will leverage their superior operating procedures, access to capital, and information technology systems to become market leaders in those countries.

Adam J. Fein, Pembroke Consulting, (215) 238-1505, September 1998.

■ REFERENCES

Baden, Jeff, "Integrated Supply Distributors: Their Strengths and Challenges," *Modern Distribution Management,* July 10, 1998.

"Comparison Shopping: Unable to Beat 'em, Web Sites Join 'em," *New York Times,* March 27, 1998.

"Distribution in Russia: Palletable," *The Economist,* February 14, 1998.

Enslow, B., A. Mesher, and C. Smith, *SCM and the Internet: Beyond Disintermediation and Product Commodization,* The Gartner Group, 1997, Stamford, CT. (203) 964-0096.

Fein, A. J., *Consolidation in Wholesale Distribution: Understanding Industry Change,* 1997, Distribution Research and Education Foundation, Washington, DC. (202) 872-0885.

Fein, A. J., "A Primer on IPO Roll-ups," *Modern Distribution Management,* April 10, 1998. Available at http://www.pembroke-consulting.com.

Fein, A. J., "The Triggers of Consolidation in Drug Wholesaling," *HealthCare Distributor,* November 1997. Available at http://www.pembroke-consulting.com.

Hartman, C., "Sales Force," *Fast Company,* 1997. Available at http://www.fastcompany.com.

Lusch, R. F., and D. Zizzo, *Competing for Customers: How Wholesaler-Distributors Can Meet the Power Retailer Challenge,* 1995, Distribution Research and Education Foundation, Washington, DC. (202) 872-0885.

Lusch, R. L., and D. Zizzo, *Foundations of Wholesaling: A Strategic and Financial Chart Book,* 1996, Distribution Research and Education Foundation, Washington, DC. (202) 872-0885.

Merrifield, B., "Understanding Channel Chaos," *Modern Distribution Management,* 1997. Available at http://www.merrifield.com.

Morgan, Jim, "Is Integrated Supply the Way of the Future?" *Purchasing,* May 1, 1997.

Purchasing magazine, *How Industry Buys MRO,* 1992, Cahners Publishing, Newton, MA. (617) 964-3030, ext. 4348.

Rosenbloom, B., *Marketing Functions and the Wholesaler-Distributor: Achieving Excellence in Distribution,* 1987, Distribution Research and Education Foundation, Washington, DC. (202) 872-0885.

Segal, B., "Electronic Commerce = Disintermediation?", 1997. Available at http://www.franklynn.com.

Stern, L. W., and A. El-Ansary, *Marketing Channels,* 4th ed., 1992, Prentice-Hall, Englewood Cliffs, NJ.

Vurva, R., "The Allied Invasion," *Progressive MRO Distributor,* January/February 1998.

■ **RELATED CHAPTERS**

6: Construction
7: Wood Products
38: Household Consumer Durables
42: Retailing

RETAILING
Economic and Trade Trends

Retail Trade versus GDP

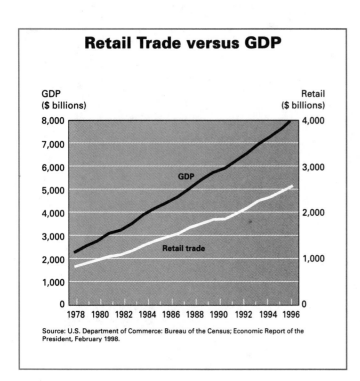

GDP
($ billions)

Retail
($ billions)

GDP

Retail trade

Source: U.S. Department of Commerce: Bureau of the Census; Economic Report of the President, February 1998.

Retail Trade and Consumer Sentiment

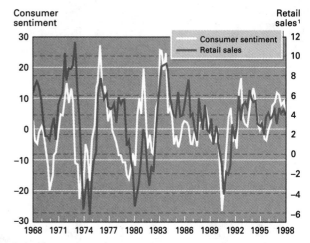

Consumer
sentiment

Retail
sales[1]

Consumer sentiment
Retail sales

[1] Annual percent change (1992$).

Source: Surveys of Consumers, University of Michigan; U.S. Department of Commerce, Bureau of the Census.

Retail Trade, 1997

Building materials
and garden supplies
6%

Miscellaneous stores
14%

Eating
drinking places **9%**

Apparel and
accessory stores **5%**

Gasoline
service stations **6%**

Food stores
17%

Automotive
dealers
24%

Furniture and
home furnishings **6%**

General merchandise stores
13%

Miscellaneous stores include stores with SIC 59 (sporting goods, book, jewelry, drug and proprietary, liquor, nonstore retailers, fuel dealers, and miscellaneous shopping goods stores).

Source: U.S. Department of Commerce, Bureau of the Census.

Retail Trade Employment as a Percent of Total U.S. Employment

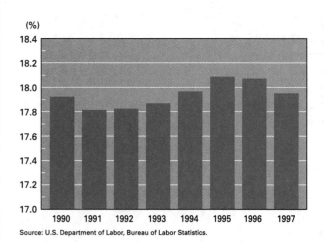

(%)

Source: U.S. Department of Labor, Bureau of Labor Statistics.

Retailing

INDUSTRY DEFINITION   Retailers sell two major subgroups of products: durable goods, which are expected to last at least 3 years, and nondurable goods. Most durable goods are sold by retailers of building materials and garden supplies (SIC 52), automobiles (SIC 55), and home furnishings and furniture (SIC 57). Most nondurable goods are sold in general merchandise stores (SIC 53), food stores (SIC 54), drugstores (SIC 591), apparel and accessory stores (SIC 56), and eating and drinking places (SIC 58). Miscellaneous retail stores (SIC 59) can sell both durable goods and nondurable goods.

DOMESTIC RETAIL TRADE PROSPECTS

Growth of sales in the retail trade sector is expected to be moderate between 1998 and 2003, increasing approximately 4 percent annually in nominal terms (see Table 42-1), which is slightly less than the 5.8 percent average annual growth rate between 1992 and 1996. It is expected that sales will increase 4.5 percent in 1998 and slow to a 3.8 percent increase in 1999 primarily as a result of the effects of the Asian financial crisis and a projected decline in real consumer spending. In the long term, retail sales tend to parallel the gross domestic product (GDP), and it is expected that as GDP changes, so will the retail sector.

A key indicator of how the economy is performing and where it is going is the Index of Consumer Sentiment (ICS) produced by the University of Michigan. The ICS measures how well consumers feel the economy is doing, and it is a fairly good predictor of GDP. The ICS currently stands at 108.7, slightly down from the all-time record of 110.4 posted in February 1998. These high numbers indicate that consumers are extremely confident in the economy and feel that good economic conditions will continue to prevail in the near future. Indeed, the United States is experiencing nearly record low levels of unemployment, low inflation, and low interest rates with no signs of major swings in the near future.

Despite the strength of the economy, a factor that could negatively affect the retail industry is high consumer levels of debt. Although these levels are decreasing, debt service payments as a percentage of disposable incomes are close to record levels. For example, revolving consumer credit increased 21 percent in 1995, 12.7 percent in 1996, and 4.7 percent in 1997, so the level

of this type of debt is increasing, although at a decreasing pace. At the same time, 17 percent of household income is being devoted to paying off debts, including mortgage payments.

Another factor influencing the forecast for a relative slowdown in retail sales over the next 5 years is an expected decline in real consumer spending. According to DRI, a data research company, real consumer spending is expected to increase 2.5 percent between 1998 and 2002, compared with 2.9 percent between 1992 and 1997. In percentage terms, over the next 5 years consumer spending is expected to increase, but at a pace 14 percent lower than that of the preceding 5 years.

Retail sales typically are classified as either sales of durable goods, such as automobiles, hardware items, furniture, household appliances, books, sporting goods, and jewelry, or sales of nondurable goods, such as food, apparel and accessories, and restaurant meals. Durable goods accounted for 40 percent of retail sales in 1996, and nondurable goods 60 percent. Sales of durable goods are expected to increase 7 percent between 1998 and 2003, which is slightly lower than the 9 percent average annual growth rate between 1992 and 1996. A primary reason for the expected decline in the growth of sales of durable goods is the projected decline in real consumer spending over this period. Real consumer spending on durable goods grew an average of 5.7 percent between 1992 and 1997, and this is expected to decline to 4.2 percent between 1998 and 2002. Real consumer spending on nondurables is expected to remain relatively stable over the next 5 years, and it is projected to increase 3.5 percent between 1998 and 2003.

Underlying these trends are the continual revamping and retrenching of retail stores. The retail industry is one of the most competitive industries in the United States, which means that

TABLE 42-1: Retail Trade (SIC 52-59) Trends and Forecasts
(millions of dollars unless otherwise noted)

	1992	1993	1994	1995	1996	1997[1]	1998[1]	1999[2]	96–97	97–98	98–99	92–96[3]
									\<Percent Change\>			
Total retail sales	1,951,589	2,072,788	2,227,325	2,324,038	2,445,296	2,587,279	2,703,706	2,803,743	5.8	4.5	3.7	5.8
Total, durable goods	703,604	776,126	873,408	925,017	993,336	1,083,074	1,148,059	1,205,462	9.0	6.0	5.0	9.0
Building materials and garden supplies	100,838	109,444	122,342	125,831	134,485	144,588	151,094	157,591	7.5	4.5	4.3	7.5
Automotive dealers	406,935	456,332	518,492	551,330	592,919	651,673	690,774	733,601	9.9	6.0	6.2	9.9
Furniture and home furnishings	96,947	105,399	118,649	127,270	133,486	144,645	152,456	159,622	8.4	5.4	4.7	8.3
Total, nondurable goods	1,247,985	1,296,662	1,353,917	1,399,021	1,451,960	1,507,974	1,538,134	1,576,587	3.9	2.0	2.5	3.9
General merchandise stores	246,420	264,613	283,203	299,169	312,792	332,028	345,309	355,669	6.1	4.0	3.0	6.1
Food stores	377,099	384,978	398,845	409,617	423,318	435,739	444,454	453,343	2.9	2.0	2.0	2.9
Gasoline service stations	136,950	138,172	141,671	146,080	154,967	159,856	164,652	168,768	3.2	3.0	2.5	3.1
Apparel and accessory stores	104,212	107,176	109,862	110,429	113,608	116,092	118,414	120,782	2.2	2.0	2.0	2.2
Eating and drinking places	200,164	213,461	223,485	232,060	236,526	246,638	256,503	264,198	4.3	4.0	3.0	4.3
GAF, total[4]	519,230	552,967	593,788	622,940	654,236	693,184	720,912	746,144	6.0	4.0	3.5	5.9
Employment (thousands)	19,356	19,773	20,507	21,187	21,625	22,490	23,210	23,906	4.0	3.2	3.0	2.8
Percent of total nonfarm employment	17.8	17.9	18.0	18.1	18.1							

[1] Estimate.
[2] Forecast.
[3] Compound annual rate.
[4] GAF represents stores which specialize in department store types of merchandise (general merchandise, apparel, furniture, miscellaneous shopping goods).
Source: U.S. Department of Commerce, Bureau of the Census; Department of Labor, Bureau of Labor Statistics, January 1998.

retailers will continue competing with each other along all their margins. For instance, some retailers will pursue the strategy of providing better customer service, while others will try to make the shopping experience more pleasant by investing in entertainment; some retailers will invest heavily in new technologies to try to reduce their costs and pass the savings on to consumers, while others may expand the merchandise mix or develop a store-specific brand; some may consolidate or merge with other retailers to provide better service. Retailers may focus on such strategies, but in any case it is expected that they will continue to invest in their stores to ensure that customers return. In short, retailers will compete with each other along any margin that increases the value customers receive from shopping at a particular store.

To remain competitive and maintain market share, retailers are implementing measures to make customers loyal to their store. Retailers are offering frequent shopper programs, in-store cards which offer rewards for shopping at a store more often, and more specialized service. Some retailers are investing in complex databases that will better enable them to identify customers with whom they can build a long-term relationship. By compiling detailed consumer preferences and tracking consumer purchasing patterns, these databases allow retailers to market their merchandise more effectively.

It was expected that many retailers would begin issuing in-store cards in 1998. For example, Petco Animal Supplies issues store cards that have a picture of the customer's animal. Petco hopes that the cards will encourage customers to keep returning to its stores because of the personal nature of the cards and the benefits customers receive from using the cards, such as in-store discounts and repeat purchase discounts. Petco will bene-

fit from these cards by using them to develop a data warehouse on its customers and gaining a better understanding of consumer buying patterns. Rite-Aid has announced a similar program in which it will substitute store cards for gift certificates. Rite-Aid plans to distribute approximately 250,000 store cards in the second half of 1998.

A chief advantage of a store card is that it better enables a retailer to maintain a data warehouse on its customers. Data warehousing helps retailers understand customer needs so that they are better equipped to satisfy consumer demand. Before the development of the concept of data warehousing, retailers maintained records on their customers by using separate databases, which made it difficult for them to assess consumer spending patterns. With better understanding of consumer spending patterns, retailers can promote certain products to a particular class of consumers (e.g., teenagers may prefer purple nail polish), stock inventory more efficiently, and determine which products may be big sales items in the future.

To remain competitive, retailers must continue to explore new ways to provide convenience and value to consumers. They must change their stores to adapt to changing consumer preferences. For instance, a recent trend is for consumers to make fewer trips to the shopping mall. According to a recent study by Management Horizons, the number of trips to the mall has decreased 50 percent since the early 1990s. That study also revealed that the number of stores consumers visit once they are at a mall is down two-thirds. In other words, consumers are precision shopping by visiting shopping malls to make specific purchases rather than browsing or window-shopping. This implies that successful retailers will continue to revamp their stores to make it easier for consumers to find the products they are looking for.

In addition to being one of the most competitive industries in the U.S. economy, retailing is one of the most important in terms of generating employment and trade. According to the National Retail Federation, retail trade represented nearly 27 percent of GDP and employed approximately 18 percent of the nation's work force in 1997 (see Figure 42-1). Contrary to popular opinion, retailers are primarily small businesses: Approximately 88 percent of all retailers employ fewer than 20 people, 95 percent operate only one store, and nearly 90 percent earn less than $2 million in annual sales. In addition, the retail sector is expected to be a primary source of employment growth in the period 1998–2005, generating approximately 3 million new jobs, according to the U.S. Department of Labor. Clearly, the retail industry is vitally important to the U.S. economy.

Retailing and Electronic Commerce

An exciting new technology that is having a profound impact on the retailing industry is the Internet. More and more retailers are setting up Web sites and using the Internet as a way to increase the services they offer to consumers. Today, even though Internet retail represents only a small fraction of total retail sales, Internet consumers have a wide variety of shopping alternatives and products from which to choose. They can access sites that specialize in books, computer goods, groceries, music, magazines, hosiery, sporting goods, candles, flowers, and a range of other products.

With sales topping $850 million in 1997, personal computer (PC) hardware and software is the largest specialty retailing area on the Internet. Consumers can shop for desktop computers, notebooks, software, and accessories direct from the manufacturer, through a reseller, from well-known retailers with large store networks, and from new retailers with a presence limited to the Internet. Egghead.com, a $361 million computer reseller, began offering hardware and software products on its Web site in February 1996; 9 months later consumers could directly download selected software products to their PCs. In January 1998 Egghead announced that it would close its network of retail stores and stake its future on Internet commerce.

Books and music are other large categories of Internet commerce. Amazon.com ended 1997 with sales of $148 million. Barnes and Noble reported that its Web-based business, launched in mid-May 1997, generated about $14 million in its first 9 months of business. The company expects its 1998 Internet sales to exceed $100 million.

N2K and CDNow, two of the largest music sites, posted $6.5 million and $9.5 million in net revenues, respectively, in the first 9 months of 1997. N2K's full-year 1996 revenues were just under $1.7 million; CDNow's were $6.3 million.

Gifts and flowers are other important Internet retail categories. 1-800-FLOWERS had on-line sales of $40 million in 1997, accounting for 10 percent of its total revenues. Garden Escape, a Web site selling plants, gardening supplies, tools, and equipment, reports that its sales have been growing 30 to 40 percent every month since its fall 1995 launch.

Hallmark, the world's leading creator and marketer of greeting cards and personal expression products, launched its

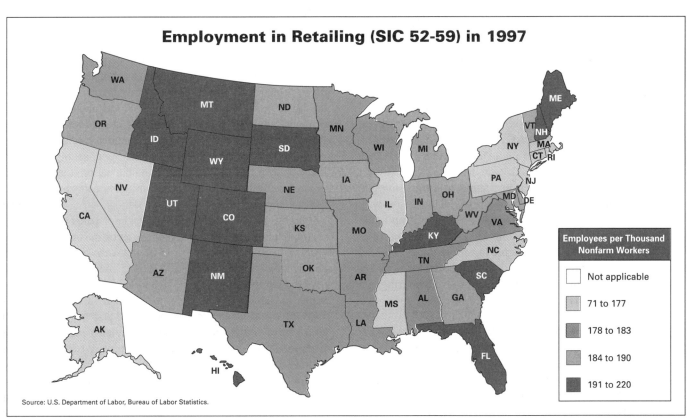

FIGURE 42-1

site in December 1997, offering more than 1,100 cards and 100 multimedia and animated greeting cards, gifts, and other services.

Superretailers such as Wal-Mart and the direct marketer Cendant Corporation (formerly CUC International) offer consumers one-stop shopping under one roof. Both companies' Web sites offer a vast selection of products across different categories. As in stores, shopping at Walmart.com is free of charge, and consumers can make single or bulk purchases. Shoppers at Cendant's netMarket pay a $69 annual membership fee to make purchases from over 1 million products.

Even buying a car, which is more of an investment than a typical retail purchase, can be done through auto marketplaces, on-line classified sites, and manufacturers' sites. Consumers use these sites to access vehicle inventory, schedule sales appointments, order new and used cars, and apply for financing. According to the National Automobile Dealers Association (NADA), approximately 50 percent of new-car dealerships have a Web site, 40 percent of the remainder plan to launch one within 6 months, and dealers with Web sites sell five cars a month on average over the Internet—double the number in 1997.

According to a fall 1997 survey conducted by CommerceNet and Nielsen, 10 million people in the United States and Canada have used the Internet to make a purchase. This represents almost a doubling from their survey conducted 6 months earlier, which found 5.6 million purchasers using the Internet in North America. Analysts estimate Internet retail sales at between $1.3 billion and $4 billion for 1997, a small fraction of the $2.5 trillion consumer retail market. By the year 2000, U.S. on-line consumer retail could account for $7 billion to $37 billion. If mail order sales are used as an indication of the potential for Internet retailing, the figure could reach $115 billion in 5 to 8 years. Some analysts believe that the Internet has three advantages over mail order: It offers consumers a more complete assortment, better and more complete information, and, over the long term, better prices.

Selling over the Internet offers retailers cost advantages, gives them greater market access, and has the potential to permit retailers to do one-to-one marketing. Virtual stores have lower operating costs compared with their physical counterparts. They typically limit their operations to advertising and marketing, site content, establishment of relationships with manufacturers or distributors, accounting functions, and customer service. Rent and depreciation, store personnel, utilities, and other expenses of a physical store infrastructure are avoided almost entirely. Internet-only stores may not even take possession of goods, leaving fulfillment activities—warehousing and distribution functions—to third parties. More than one-fourth of Web sellers currently outsource these functions.

Many retailers use the Internet as a means of advertising their goods and services as well as selling their product. However, most on-line retailers have not made a profit from on-line sales. This trend will likely reverse in the near future as new technologies evolve to provide safer and faster access to the Internet. As consumers become more comfortable making on-line financial transactions, it is likely that on-line sales will increase.

Although this is not yet widely practiced, the Internet offers the opportunity to profitably market directly to narrow bands of customers and even to market to customers one by one. Software programs detect when an individual customer enters a Web site, greeting the customer by name. Querying one or more databases reveals that the customer has recently purchased a pair of blue jeans and an extra-large sweater or books on travel in Italy. On the Internet, the store may prompt the customer to purchase another sweater in a similar style or a complementary shirt; it may notify the customer when new travel books about Italy have been published or suggest books on Renaissance art. Researchers are working to develop software agents that learn the behaviors and preferences of individuals. As these technologies become more sophisticated, Internet businesses are likely to employ them in one-to-one marketing.

It is expected that the retail sale of tangible goods on the Internet probably will grow more slowly than will business-to-business Internet commerce and commerce in goods and services that can be delivered digitally. How quickly Internet retailing evolves will depend on consumers' trust of the medium, the sophistication and efficiency of distribution, and the speed at which the Internet becomes a mass market.

The most frequent complaint from on-line shoppers is that finding and buying things on the Internet is slow and complex. Some of this is due to delays in accessing information because of slow modems, and some of it is due to poorly organized sites that make finding things difficult. As bandwidth to the home increases, these delays should be minimized. Search and categorization tools that are currently being developed should make navigating the Internet easier and more intuitive.

The growth of the Internet also will depend on how quickly retailers and manufacturers establish a presence on the Web. Most of them have a Web presence, but it tends to be limited to information about a company and store locations. Only 12 percent of retailers and 9 percent of manufacturers currently sell on the Internet. Few have the experience or infrastructure to deliver orders directly to end customers. In addition, selling on-line is likely to have a negative impact on their existing store sales and, in the case of manufacturers, on their relationships with wholesalers and retailers.

Perhaps one of the biggest advantages of going on-line is the widespread accessibility virtual stores offer. For instance, a retailer that manages a Web site is accessible around the globe at a relatively low cost. Very few retailers now sell merchandise over the Internet internationally, but the potential exists. A consumer in Canada or China can just as easily access a retailer's Web site as can a consumer in the United States. In the long run consumers around the globe will be able to make purchases from retailers in the United States. For many retailers, setting up a Web site today and servicing the domestic market will better equip them for selling internationally on the Internet once the logistics are worked out and the use of the Internet becomes more widespread.

INTERNATIONAL RETAILING

Because the domestic retail market is highly competitive and maintains an excessive number of stores, American retailers in search of higher profits increasingly are looking to opportunities overseas. As emerging economies continue to experience growth and open their borders to foreign investment, expanding internationally is becoming a reality for many retailers. In addition, trade agreements such as the North American Free Trade Agreement (NAFTA), Asia Pacific Economic Cooperation (APEC), and General Agreement on Trade in Services (GATS) are reducing trade barriers and tariffs, and this should open up some markets to American retailers over the next few years.

According to Ernest and Young's survey of global retailing, 42 of the top 100 retailers in the world in 1997 were American, up from the 1996 total of 38. Despite this prominence, American retailers have been relatively slow to expand overseas. A recent study showed that only 12 percent of 250 U.S. retailers surveyed had international operations. Many analysts expect this number to increase over the next few years, since many countries are experiencing impressive real growth and rising disposable incomes. In 1996, Hong Kong, Poland, Mexico, Singapore, Chile, India, and China experienced a growth rate above 5 percent in real GDP. In addition, consumer purchasing power is increasing around the world. The middle class in Korea and Taiwan (defined as the middle 60 percent of the population) is earning relatively more than does the middle class in the United States. Furthermore, American retailers have a distinct advantage over their foreign counterparts: Many American retailers employ the latest technologies and management techniques in their stores, and American culture is recognized around the world because of Hollywood movies, CNN, and MTV.

Many analysts attribute the recent growth in international retailing to push and pull factors which are occurring simultaneously. The push factors that are inducing retailers to explore overseas operations include saturation of the home market or overcompetition, limited growth in consumer spending, a declining or aging population, high operating costs, and pressure from shareholders to maintain profit growth. Among the forces that are pulling retailers overseas are the underdevelopment of some markets or weak competition, strong economic growth or rising standards of living, high population growth or a high concentration of young adults, a relaxed regulatory framework, favorable operating costs (labor, rents, taxation), the geographical spread of trading risks, the opportunity to innovate under new market conditions, and the potential to find alternative sourcing for their merchandise. These push and pull influences are expected to draw many American retailers overseas in the next few years.

American retailers are beginning to expand aggressively internationally. For example, Toys "R" Us is planning to open 35 international stores in 1998, as opposed to only 15 domestic stores. Starbucks Coffee plans to open 200 stores in Taiwan. Wal-Mart announced that it plans to open 50 to 60 retail units overseas in 1998. In 1997, of Wal-Mart's $105 billion in sales, approximately $5 billion came from international operations. This trend of expanding aggressively overseas is expected to continue over the next few years. It has been predicted that by the end of 1999, of the top 100 global retailers, 90 will have international operations, as opposed to the current total of 30.

In terms of retail expansion, the best long-term investment location continues to be countries in the Asian region. For retailers with a long-term outlook, China continues to be a promising market because of its large population base and rising disposable incomes. In addition, some large foreign retailers, such as Wal-Mart, Carrefour (a French retailer), and Makro/Metro (a German retailer), have opened up stores in China and have the potential to create growth in this market because of their management expertise, sophisticated distribution techniques, and advanced technologies. China's retail sales are increasing steadily. In the first half of 1996 retail sales of consumer goods reached RMB1,441 billion ($173 billion), a 13 percent increase in real terms from 1995. However, before China's 1.2 billion population, its middle-class consumers, and the benefits of trade liberalization become a reality for foreign retailers, the Chinese government must remove many restrictions on foreign retailers. The government of China heavily regulates this market, for example, by requiring a different joint venture partner for each retail outlet and restricting retailers to opening no more than two stores in a city, which makes it extremely costly for American retailers to achieve economies of scale. In addition, retail legislation differs from province to province as well as at the national level, requiring retailers to keep abreast of changes in retail legislation. These restrictions are very burdensome and make this market only a long-term prospect for retailers.

Other countries in the Asian region that offer sales potential include Japan, South Korea, and the Philippines, all of which are implementing measures to open up investment to foreign retailers. Korea's income per capita rose steadily from $1,640 in 1980 to $10,550 in 1996, an increase of approximately 540 percent. Japan offers potential because its consumers have high disposable incomes and the local retail market has room for improvement. With some restrictive retail laws being abolished in Japan, opportunities for American retailers, some of the most technologically advanced retailers in the world, should abound in the next few years. The Philippine government is considering legislation to open its retail sector to foreign firms. Retailers have entered this market, however, through franchising and have been relatively successful. According to the National Trade Data Bank, U.S. franchisers enjoy a 94 percent success rate in the Philippines. Given the recent economic turnaround and the increased per capita income, the Philippine retail industry should expand 5.5 percent through the year 2000.

Other regions that offer great potential to U.S. retailers are eastern Europe and South America. In eastern Europe, the population is extremely large with over 300 million people (in comparison, western Europe has about 350 million people), the work force is well trained and highly educated, and governments are becoming more politically stable; also, since people lived under communism for so long, many consumers have a pent-up demand for consumer goods. In addition, many of the economies in that region are projected to grow steadily in the foreseeable future. For example, Slovakia is expected to grow around 7 percent over the next few years, Poland and the Czech Republic between 5 and 6 percent, and Hungary about 3 to 4 percent. Although eastern Europe offers potential for investment, it has largely been western European retailers who have taken advantage of this emerging opportunity. As these countries become more politically stable and experience greater economic growth, it is expected that American retailers will seek out sales opportunities more vigorously.

The retail industry in South American countries is relatively undeveloped and has room for expansion, as evidenced by the fact that no South American retailer generated enough sales to qualify for Ernest and Young's list of the top 100 global retailers. In addition, many South American countries, such as Brazil, Chile, and Argentina, are becoming more politically and economically stable. Brazil has implemented a tight monetary policy and reined in inflation to 10 percent in 1996, compared with a 1,000 percent increase in consumer prices in 1994. In addition, the economy of Brazil, with a population of 164 million, is expected to grow steadily over the next few years. Chile is a relatively free market economy and has posted impressive growth rates in the 1990s. Over the period 1991–1996, Chile's GDP grew an average of more than 6.5 percent annually, with inflation near a 40-year low. Argentina offers potential to American retailers because its retail market has room for development and because disposable income is expected to rise over the next few years as the Argentine economy grows about 5 percent annually.

Although there seem to be many opportunities for U.S. retailers to invest internationally, a number of barriers must be overcome. The first is adapting to new cultures. A format that has worked well in the United States may not work well in an overseas market. Differences in tastes, spending patterns, and even religious customs can have a substantial effect on a retail establishment. Government regulatory policies—for example, tax and tariff structures and restrictions on trading hours, store size, and foreign ownership—can impose significant costs. Furthermore, key resources such as land and labor may be scarce, and a vast array of established local supplier relationships may be difficult to breach.

With these factors in mind, retailers considering operations abroad must carefully study demographic, economic, and cultural trends; must be flexible in choosing retail formats; and must be willing to enter into partnerships with local operators. Retailers also must be prepared to commit capital resources to sustain what may be losing operations for several years before consumers accept them. To be sure, overseas expansion is risky and requires a long-term outlook, particularly in countries with a great potential for growth in the next century. The prospective profits in those markets is so large, however, that many retailers cannot afford to miss these opportunities.

HOME FURNISHING RETAILERS

Retailers in the home furnishing subsector cater primarily to the do-it-yourself home improvement market. This market posted impressive returns in 1997. According to the National Home Center News, the top 500 home improvement retailers earned $79.3 billion, up 10.5 percent from 1996. Most of these gains came from the two largest home improvement retailers, Home Depot and Lowes, which account for nearly 21 percent of this market. The impressive sales gains in this subsector are being driven primarily by a strong housing market, low interest rates, and a robust economy. Between 1993 and 1996 the number of homeowners increased 5.5 percent, pushing the proportion of homeowners to 65.1 percent, just below the all-time high recorded in the 1980s. Interest rates are relatively low, and many consumers are buying new homes or borrowing money to make home improvements. With no signs of swings in inflation or interest rates, it is expected that this market will increase steadily over the next 5 years.

In their efforts to provide better convenience and value to consumers, home improvement chains will continue to invest in their stores to differentiate themselves from their competitors. For example, it is likely that in the foreseeable future these chains will offer services such as in-store food, repairs, training and education centers to teach consumers a particular skill, and child care facilities. Home improvement retailers probably will hire plumbers, electricians, architects, interior designers, landscape designers, and other professionals specializing in home improvement so that they will be better equipped to solve consumers' problems. These retailers also may hire more female employees as many chains are targeting female consumers. Some chains are venturing onto the Internet to provide better customer service. Ace Hardware and Home Depot have launched Web sites where consumers can read how to make a home repair, find the nearest store location, and browse through monthly specials.

DRUGSTORES

The drugstore industry grew 6.9 percent in 1996, reaching $121.4 billion in revenues, and is expected to maintain this growth rate over the next 5 years. The drugstore industry is benefiting from an aging population that requires more prescription drugs, the leading sales category in a drugstore.

The dominant trend in the drugstore industry is the number of mergers that have occurred since 1996. Some of the major drugstores, such as Revco D.S., Thrifty PayLess Inc., Thrift Drugs Inc., Rite-Aid, and CVS, as well as some small chains and independent operators have been involved in mergers. The drugstore industry is very competitive, and room for domestic expansion is limited. Since this market is relatively overstored, one strategy used by drugstores to increase their market share is to merge with other firms that already have a number of stores in prime locations. Merging with other drugstores provides a number of advantages: It allows drugstores to achieve economies of scale in marketing, advertising, distribution, and overhead expenses; a merged drugstore will have greater bargaining power with its suppliers; and a merged drugstore will have better access to financial markets for acquiring capital. This trend is likely to continue over the next 5 years as drugstores attempt to increase their customer base.

Since this industry is so competitive and is facing competition from supermarkets and discount stores, drugstores will continue to invest in new ways to differentiate themselves from their competitors by offering more services or merchandise, training pharmacists and staff to solve customer problems, increasing store hours, and offering drive-in facilities. Phar-Mor is offering shoe repair, key making, postal services, party services, copy and faxing capabilities, and a notary public to provide more services to its consumers. Eckerd is hiring trained cosmeticians in the majority of its stores to assist customers in their purchases. It is likely that the drugstore industry will continue to see such innovations over the next 5 years.

FOOD STORES

Sales at food stores, which include grocery stores, meat and fish markets, and retail bakeries, increased 3.3 percent in 1996, slightly above the previous 5-year annual average growth rate of 2.9 percent. Sales at food stores are expected to increase around 3 percent over the next 5 years. This is a very mature market without much room for growth. For example, in 1996 there were 29,900 supermarkets, an increase of only 2 percent over 1995. Since the market is so competitive, it is expected that supermarkets will restructure their general operations to try to increase their margins over the next 5 years.

Supermarkets are restructuring through mergers and consolidation. In 1996, Whole Foods Markets, Inc., a natural food grocery chain, merged with Fresh Fields Markets, Inc., and increased its store base by about 40 percent. Also, Safeway Inc., the third largest grocery chain, merged with the tenth largest grocery chain, Vons Co., to make it the nation's second largest grocery company with a total of 1,375 stores generating more than $22 billion in sales. It is likely that this trend will continue over the next 5 years as acquiring stores in a mature market helps firms gain market share and reduce costs by taking advantage of economies of scale.

It is expected that supermarkets will compete by focusing on programs that will make customers loyal to their stores or by restructuring their operations to reduce costs. For example, Safeway Inc., recently introduced a Safeway savings card with which customers can receive additional savings at the register. Furthermore, many grocery stores are offering home meal replacement programs to cater to customers who shop for convenience. Stores with such programs offer gourmet and prepared foods, salad bars, and ready-to-heat meals with side dishes. Another way supermarkets can generate customer loyalty is by offering private label brands. These brands are gener-

ally good business for grocery stores, because the price is usually cheaper but the margin is typically two to three times as high as it is on national brands. If customers enjoy a private label brand, it is likely that they will continue shopping at that store because it is the only place to purchase that product.

Supermarkets will also compete by investing in new technologies that could save a store money in the long run. For instance, some supermarkets are experimenting with a new self-checkout system in which consumers scan the products they have selected and then pay with a credit card or debit card, all without the assistance of a store clerk, reducing the store's labor costs.

EATING AND DRINKING PLACES

Sales at eating and drinking places increased 2 percent in 1996, considerably below the 4 percent average annual increase from 1992 to 1996. The primary reason for this slowdown is that the industry overexpanded in the early 1990s, creating a surplus of restaurants. From 1990 to 1993, the number of eating and drinking establishments increased 10 percent while the population expanded just over 1 percent annually. This means that the pie is not getting any bigger and that restaurants are competing with each other for the same consumer dollar, putting pressure on margins and profitability. It is expected that sales at eating and drinking establishments will increase in the range of 3 to 4 percent over the next few years as the industry adjusts to the overexpansion of the early 1990s.

In addition to the overstored environment, there is a shortage of labor which puts upward pressure on costs. Since restaurant labor is relatively scarce, restaurant owners have to offer better incentives to attract employees. The reason for the shortage of labor is that the primary source for restaurant employees is the 16- to 24-year-old cohort, which is relatively small because of the sharp decline in births during the 1960s and 1970s. Since the labor pool has shrunk, the quality of skilled restaurant employees has dwindled. To combat this problem, restaurant owners are investing in programs to train their employees in the skills required for good customer service. A recent survey showed that 75 percent of respondents offered a training program in 1996, as opposed to only 66 percent in 1992.

Another method restaurant owners are using to combat the high costs of a shrinking labor pool is to employ new technologies by looking to other areas of the business to keep costs low. A good example is the automation of labor scheduling. In 1996, 50 percent of restaurant owners scheduled employees' work electronically, as opposed to only 25 percent in 1990. Also, databases can help employers schedule laborers more efficiently and thus save on the total labor bill. A database can help an employer determine seasonal swings in demand, labor productivity, and the effects of labor incentive programs.

As is the case with most mature industries, the restaurant industry is expected to experience a number of consolidations and mergers over the next few years. This will allow restaurants to expand their market share while taking advantage of economies of scale.

To combat the overstored environment, restaurants are seeking opportunities in overseas markets. Many fast-food and casual restaurants are aggressively exploring international markets. For instance, Wendy's is looking at Canada, Europe, Latin America, and the Pacific region for its international expansion plans, while Lone Star Steakhouse and Saloon has opened 20 restaurants in Australia. As the middle class in many foreign countries becomes larger and trade barriers are brought down, it is expected that this trend of overseas expansion will continue well into the future and will be profitable for many restaurants.

GENERAL MERCHANDISE STORES

Sales at general merchandise stores, which include department stores, discount stores, and variety stores, increased 4.5 percent in 1996. Sales at general merchandise stores are expected to increase in the range of 6 to 7 percent over the next few years as consumers are becoming more value-conscious and the stigma of shopping at discount stores is declining. Consumers seeking value and convenience are increasingly making apparel purchases at discount stores, whereas a decade ago they were reluctant to do so. In addition, department and discount stores are offering private label brands. For example, Wal-Mart's Kathie Lee private label brand was expected to generate sales of more than $250 million in 1997, while sales of private label brands at Sears were expected to generate $4 billion in sales.

General merchandise stores are also focusing on ways to operate more efficiently and reduce unnecessary costs through mergers and consolidations to take advantage of economies of scale. For example, Dillard's, the fifth largest department store chain, has agreed to purchase Mercantile Stores, an independent department store chain, adding 103 stores to its base of 272 stores. Since acquiring new stores is a way to gain market share quickly in a mature industry, it is likely that mergers and consolidations will continue over the next 5 years.

It is also expected that there will be a number of liquidations among smaller, regional department store chains in the near future. Currently, there is approximately 20 square feet of shopping space for every man, woman, and child in the United States, which is an all-time high. A number of department stores, such as Woodward & Lothrop, Abraham & Straus, and John Wanamaker, closed their doors recently. It is expected that a number of stores will consolidate or liquidate in the years ahead as retail square footage contracts to a level more on a par with the level of consumer demand.

A number of department and discount stores are seeking overseas opportunities. Wal-Mart is the leader in this category, with current operations in Puerto Rico, Mexico, Canada, Argentina, Brazil, China, Indonesia, and most recently Germany; JCPenney has operations in Mexico, Chile, and Puerto Rico; and K Mart has operations in Puerto Rico, Guam, and the Virgin Islands. This trend is likely to continue since opportunities are limited in the United States.

APPAREL AND ACCESSORY STORES

Total sales of apparel and accessory stores reached $113.6 billion in 1996, an increase of 2.9 percent from 1995. Sales at these stores have been relatively slow over the last few years, since general merchandise stores and discounters are beginning to compete with specialty apparel stores and are taking away some of their market share. Another factor contributing to the slow growth in apparel stores is a change in consumer preferences: Consumers are spending less time shopping and have placed a lower priority on purchasing apparel items. According to a recent study, consumer visits to the shopping mall decreased from 3.3 visits a month in 1995 to 3.0 in 1996. In addition, consumers placed investments, dining out, and vacations ahead of making apparel purchases in their financial priorities for 1997. It is expected that sales at apparel and accessory stores will remain in the range of 2 to 3 percent over the next 5 years.

Intense competition in the apparel sector has resulted in a significant restructuring of the industry in recent years. One contributing factor has been the rise of mass marketing stores and discount retailers with low overhead costs and low prices. These retailers have captured a significant share of the sales of traditional apparel retailers such as department and specialty stores. In addition, discount stores and general merchandise stores are offering store-specific brands such as JCPenney's Original Arizona Jean Co. and Wal-Mart's Kathie Lee line, which are generating impressive sales gains.

Many experts point to changes in consumers' attitudes as a driving force behind the restructuring in the apparel industry. Not only have consumers become more cautious in their buying habits, but they are increasingly demanding high-quality goods at low prices. Retailers have often been forced to sell merchandise permanently at "sale" prices, with promotions occurring throughout the year. This has put downward pressure on apparel stores' profit margins.

Since the apparel industry is a mature market, many specialty apparel stores are seeking opportunities in overseas markets. For example, the Gap has stores in Canada, the United Kingdom, France, Germany, and Japan; Eddie Bauer has stores in Canada, Japan, Germany, and the United Kingdom; Land's End has operations in the United Kingdom, France, Germany, Japan, and the Netherlands; and Brooks Brothers plans to open 20 stores in southeast Asia over the next 2 years. It is expected that apparel stores will continue to expand overseas aggressively as the opportunities for domestic expansion are limited. The best markets for apparel stores to expand into in the short term include western Europe, Canada, and Japan, and in the long run the southeast Asian countries.

Aaron Schavey, U.S. Department of Commerce, Office of Service Industries, (202) 482-4117, October 1998.

■ REFERENCES

"Brooks Brothers Opens First Stores in Hong Kong," *Business Wire,* New York, March, 6, 1998.

Chain Store Age, Lebhar-Friedman Publication, 425 Park Avenue, New York, NY 10022. (212) 756-5252.

Combined Annual and Revised Monthly Retail Trade, 1996, Bureau of the Census, Economics and Statistics Administration, U.S. Department of Commerce, Washington, DC 20230. (301) 457-2688.

Discount Merchandiser, Macfadden Publishing, Inc., 233 Park Avenue South, New York, NY 10003. (212) 979-4860.

Discount Store News, Lebhar-Friedman Publication, 425 Park Avenue, New York, NY 10022. (212) 756-5220.

The Emerging Digital Economy, Appendix 5, Retail of Tangible Goods: Analysis and Case Studies, U.S. Department of Commerce, Washington, DC, April 1998.

"Restaurants," *Standard & Poor's Industry Surveys,* October 30, 1997, 25 Broadway, New York, NY 10004. (212) 208-8768.

"Retailers Rush to Capture New Markets," by D. Ross and M. Finney, *Financial Times,* London, February 13, 1998.

"Retailing: General," *Standard & Poor's Industry Surveys,* July 24, 1997, 25 Broadway, New York, NY 10004. (212) 208-8768.

"Retailing in South Korea: Bargain Hunters," *Economist,* April 26, 1997.

"Retailing: Specialty," *Standard & Poor's Industry Surveys,* January 22, 1998, 25 Broadway, New York, NY 10004. (212) 208-8768.

Stores, National Retail Federation, Inc., 325 7th Street NW, Washington, DC 20004. (202) 783-7971.

"Supermarkets & Drugstores," *Standard & Poor's Industry Surveys,* September 18, 1997, 25 Broadway, New York, NY 10004. (212) 208-8768.

Surveys of Consumers, University of Michigan, Index of Consumer Sentiment, 1998.

World Factbook, Central Intelligence Agency, 1998.

■ RELATED CHAPTERS

TRANSPORTATION
Economic and Trade Trends

U.S. International Trade

($ billions)

Balance — Exports — Imports

Exports comprise passenger fares, freight transportation, and port services.

Source: U.S. Department of Commerce, Bureau of Economic Analysis.

Growth in World Waterborne Trade by Service Type, 1993–1997

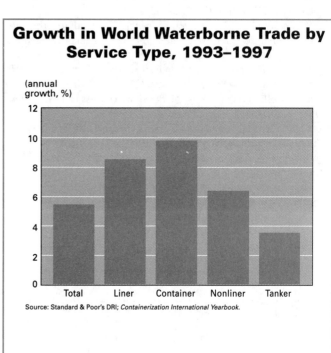

(annual growth, %)

Source: Standard & Poor's DRI; *Containerization International Yearbook*.

Domestic Shipments by Mode and Volume, 1996 and 2006

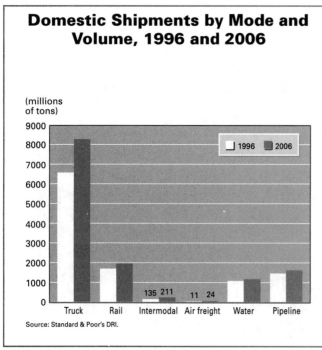

(millions of tons)

1996   2006

Source: Standard & Poor's DRI.

Intercity Freight Ton-Miles by Mode, 1996

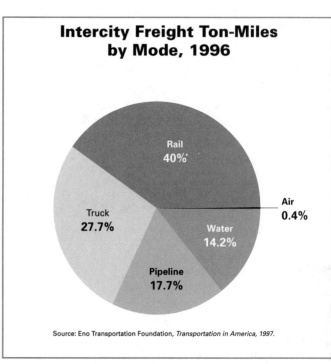

Source: Eno Transportation Foundation, *Transportation in America, 1997*.

Transportation

AIRLINES

Airlines (SIC 4512, 4513, 4522) provide regularly scheduled and nonscheduled air transportation of passengers, cargo, and mail. Integrated air express operators constitute a sector of this industry whose operations are limited to the delivery of letters, parcels, and packages.

Air Transport Services

The airline business, a global industry that generates $150 billion in annual revenues, specializes in the movement of people and goods by air. Growth rates for passengers and cargo have been outpacing world economic growth for more than 35 years. Since the mid-1990s the airline business has reflected the dynamism of the world economy (see Table 43-1). Low-cost, low-fare airlines are increasing the level of competition. Travel in long-haul markets is growing rapidly as aircraft with an improved range are entering the world fleet. While airline service between traditional international gateways continues to grow, more cities are receiving nonstop airline service. Boeing predicts that over the next 20 years nonstop flights between pairs of cities will double.

The deregulation of airlines, which began in the United States in 1978, has played a major role in creating a structural change in this industry. Competition has displaced government regulation as the driving force in many marketplaces. Once wholly dominated by government-owned national flag carriers, international aviation now has a larger proportion of profit-seeking privatized carriers. To extend their reach, airlines have formed regional and international alliances with other carriers, combining route networks and sharing revenues from joint enterprises.

Twenty years into the deregulation era, U.S. airlines appear to have adjusted finally to the demands of the competitive environment. Profits have been at record levels in recent years. Following in the footsteps of the United States, the European Community is experiencing increased competition arising from regulatory liberalization, the removal of trade barriers, and the entry of low-cost carriers. Market opportunities and service choices have increased, and free trade agreements referred to as "open skies" are proliferating between nations.

The financial and economic problems of the Asia/Pacific region have engendered uncertainty. The outlook for the region as a whole remains positive, but projections of growth rates have been reduced from the optimistic forecasts of the recent past. The International Air Transport Association (IATA), the industrial group for world airlines, suggests that the economic downturn will have a stronger impact on carriers based in Asia than it will on those based elsewhere. The IATA has revised its passenger and freight forecast for the period 1996–2001 to reflect this downturn. The IATA's director general, Pierre J. Jeanniot, expects the Asian crisis to trim $2 billion in profitability from airlines operating in the Asia/Pacific region through 2001.

TABLE 43-1: Traffic, Capacity, and Load Factor For U.S. Commercial Carriers
(billions of dollars; percent)

	1992	1993	1994	1995	1996[1]	1997[2]	1998[2]	1999[3]	2000[3]
Revenue passenger miles	475	483	510	537	570	599	620	638	657
Available seat miles	745	768	776	804	828	853	883	914	946
Load factor (percent)	63	62	65	66	68	70	70	69	69

[1] FAA estimate.
[2] Author estimate.
[3] Forecast.
Source: Federal Aviation Administration (FAA); forecasts by the author.

U.S. Industry Trends

In 1997 U.S. airlines broke the all-time record for earnings, producing operating profits of $7.9 billion. This record year, the fourth consecutive year of earnings growth, represented a 32 percent increase over the 1996 record of $6 billion (see Figure 43-1). A strong U.S. economy has fueled traffic demand. Ticket prices, especially for business travelers who pay full fares, have been rising steadily. However, more than 96 percent of airline tickets are sold at a discount, reflecting the powerful role of marketing in the promotion and sale of air transportation. The revenue passenger mile yield—the average ticket price for each mile traveled—continues to decline under the trend toward discounting.

Commercial aircraft have been unusually crowded with passengers, in large part as a result of the airlines' reluctance to add capacity, which is defined as the number of seats offered. In 1997, the average passenger load factor (the percentage of the aircraft occupied) was 70 percent, the highest since the World War II era. The load factor was 7 percent higher than the figure in 1993. Edmund S. Greenslet, president of ESG Aviation Services of Ponte Vedra Beach, FL, points out that the major airlines have recorded a 20 percent gain in traffic over 4 years while capacity has increased only 8 percent. He regards this phenomenon as the impetus for the huge increase in operating earnings, which improved from a $1.3 billion net loss in 1993 to a $4.6 billion net profit in 1997.

Airlines also have benefited from cost containment. Between 1993 and 1997 the operating cost per available seat mile for the 10 major airlines increased only from 9.17 cents to 9.40 cents, not including a rate of inflation of 3 percent per year. In 1997 the airlines achieved a major turnaround in constraining the cost of travel agents' commissions. Traditionally one of the highest expenses after fuel and labor, the cost of commissions was flat in 1997 after years of escalation. Providing further evidence of containment, the cost of travel agents' commissions as a share of total airline costs has declined. In 1993 these commissions represented 10.9 percent of total costs; in the third quarter of 1997 that proportion dropped to 8.1 percent. The share of tickets marketed through travel agents declined in 1997, and this was reflected in a slight fall in the cost per passenger.

The widespread practice known as yield management has contributed to the airlines' profit-making ability. When they use computer-based programs for yield management, the airlines can control the numbers of passengers who pay full fares and those who buy discounted tickets, thus managing the mix of passengers and earning the maximum revenue from each flight. As tickets have been relatively affordable and traffic demand has been strong during a period of tight seat capacity, profit making has been less of a challenge for U.S. carriers than has been customary.

The forecast for 1998 accords with the positive trend in recent years. Although traffic growth was slow in the first 2 months, system traffic (which includes domestic and international traffic) was expected to rise 3 to 3.5 percent for the year. The slow-growth scenario for January, with an increase of only 1 percent, is regarded as a residual effect of the off-and-on imposition by Congress of the 10 percent airline ticket tax. In January 1997, when the ticket tax was not in place, traffic jumped 10.7 percent over January 1996. The ticket tax was reimposed for most of 1997, and so monthly comparisons are expected to be normal for most of 1998.

The key to the positive earnings forecast is lower fuel costs, which were apparent in the first quarter of 1998. A 1-cent difference in the price of a gallon of fuel has a $170 million impact on U.S. airlines. For an extended period in that quarter, airlines bought fuel for 14 cents per gallon less than the average price in 1997. David Swierenga, chief economist with the Air Transport Association of America in Washington, DC, said that reduced fuel costs will allow the airlines to improve their management of ticket pricing. If there is softening in the economy, the carriers will be better able to lower their prices to stimulate lagging traffic.

In the years ahead air carriers face potential problems and uncertainties: The volatility of fuel prices is always an issue, Asia's financial ills could have a ripple effect on other regions, and the traffic and revenue impact of the Asian crisis could be deeper than anticipated. Another area of concern in the United States is rising labor costs. Some concessionary labor contracts of the period 1993–1994 have expired and have been replaced by amended contracts that provide increased wages. The average compensation and benefit package for airline employees now exceeds $60,000 a year. To offset higher costs, management is relying on gains in productivity.

U.S. airlines face a dilemma in regard to the system of fares. The airlines rigidly control the passenger mix by imposing restrictions on the use of discount tickets. Some examples are the requirement for the purchase of tickets in advance of a trip and the requirement for a passenger to remain at a destination over the weekend, which is known as the "Saturday night stay." Business fliers who cannot or will not meet these requirements

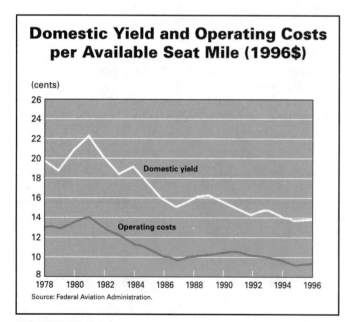

Domestic Yield and Operating Costs per Available Seat Mile (1996$)

(cents)

Domestic yield

Operating costs

1978 1980 1982 1984 1986 1988 1990 1992 1994 1996

Source: Federal Aviation Administration.

FIGURE 43-1

are charged the full fare. Unlike many discounted tickets, a full-fare ticket is completely refundable and has no restrictions. In 1997, 94.6 percent of travelers on U.S. airlines received some form of discount and 5.4 percent paid the full fare. However, many companies that have felt the sting of high fares are complaining and in some cases are criticizing the lack of competition at certain hub airports.

Although pricing and competition have been matters of concern in Congress since the dawn of deregulation, Congress has tread lightly in this area. However, dozens of bills containing remedies to pricing and competition problems were filed in Congress in late 1997 and early 1998. Meanwhile, the Department of Transportation (DOT) and the Department of Justice (DOJ) have investigated the impact on competition of airline alliances. These departments also have reviewed allegations of predatory pricing and other anticompetitive actions brought by new entrants against major carriers. In the first quarter of 1998 the DOT prepared guidelines that defined predation, signaling a more aggressive government position toward competition issues than obtained in past years.

The fare system created by U.S. airlines, which is unwieldy and many-tiered, is a candidate for change. Fare revisions numbering in the hundreds of thousands occur daily in a computer-driven electronic marketplace operated by the Airline Tariff Publishing Company, an airlines-owned unit based at Washington's Dulles International Airport. In the past the airlines were unable to agree on a means to simplify this complex system. The last attempt to inject order was made by American Airlines in 1992. That plan—Value Pricing—would have established a four-tier fare structure. Its principal effect would have been a reduction in the fares paid by business fliers, while leisure fares would have increased slightly. However, the carriers were unable to agree on the plan, and the effort collapsed into a series of fare wars. Part of the problem in that period was industry overcapacity (too many seats offered to meet demand), a condition that usually results in intense fare competition.

In more recent years airline capacity has been tightly controlled. Traffic and earnings trends have been favorable for the members of the Air Transport Association of America, which carry 95 percent of all passengers and cargo in the United States. There are 22 U.S. members of that association and 5 non-U.S. associate members. In 1997 those airlines flew 574.7 billion revenue passenger miles (RPMs) in domestic and international services (an RPM equals one passenger carried 1 mile). This was a 4.7 percent increase over the record numbers in 1996. Capacity increased 3.2 percent to 811.8 billion available seat miles (an ASM equals one seat carried 1 mile). The record load factor of 70.8 percent reflected an increase of 2.8 percent over the 1996 figure.

Growth rates for cargo in the United States have surpassed those for passenger traffic. Total cargo revenue ton miles (RTMs) flown in 1997, including freight and mail, increased 10.1 percent over the figure for 1996. In 6 of the 12 months of 1997 the increase in cargo traffic was in double digits.

Air cargo in the United States is increasingly moved by integrated-express carriers, defined as carriers which control both the ground segment and the air segment. The integrated carriers, UPS and FedEx being the largest, specialize in door-to-door shipments as opposed to airport-to-airport services. MergeGlobal, Inc., a consultancy based in London and Washington, estimates that integrated companies hauled 64 percent of total U.S. domestic air freight, an estimated 6.39 million metric tons, in 1996. The remainder was carried by airlines as belly cargo. By 2002 the percentage of freight carried by integrated carriers is forecast to rise to 75 percent.

Factors Affecting U.S. Industry Growth

After 1997, an excellent year for earnings ($7.9 billion operating, $4.3 billion net), U.S. airlines can expect continued growth at a moderating pace. The industry produced profits in each quarter in 1997 and weathered a 7.5 percent increase in fuel prices, though that increase reflected steadily moderating prices throughout the year. Management efforts at controlling costs have had a positive impact. Real unit costs, excluding fuel and oil expenses, declined for 6 of the 10 major carriers. In 1997 system average real operating cost per available seat mile, excluding fuel and oil, was 8.23 cents, a 1.8 percent decline from 1996.

The positive trends that were expected in 1998 were:

■ Lower fuel prices, which will increase carriers' flexibility in operating whether the economy grows or softens

■ Continued emphasis on cost reduction

■ An industry policy of limiting supply through constraints on the growth of seat capacity

The negative trends that were forecast for 1998 were:

■ The impact of Asian financial and structural problems

■ Rising labor costs

■ Moderating growth as the business cycle matures

■ Continued downward pressures on yields

U.S. Major Carriers

The 10 U.S. major carriers, defined as airlines that produce revenues of $1 billion or more a year, have undergone a radical transformation in the 1990s. In the beginning of the decade multiple factors—including an economic recession and international tensions related to the Persian Gulf War—critically wounded an unprepared industry, leading to bankruptcies and widespread restructuring. With the cooperation of labor, the major airlines adopted a variety of survival tactics (cutting costs, rolling back new aircraft deliveries, and negotiating concessionary labor contracts) that have aided their strong recovery in a growing economy. By 1995 the recovery was complete as the majors produced operating income for the year of $4.8 billion. Profits have improved since then and should continue to grow, though at a moderating rate.

One reason for this success has been the airlines' tight grip on capacity growth. In spite of increasing demand, airlines have maintained capacity below the level of traffic growth. As a consequence, the average load factor has been climbing steadily, reaching an all-time high of 70.8 percent for Air Transport Association carriers in 1997. The coordination of supply with demand has been economically beneficial for those carriers. In 1998 capacity was forecast to increase 3.5 percent, in line with traffic growth.

Other factors have contributed to the reining in of capacity. Boeing's inability to obtain parts has slowed the schedule of new aircraft deliveries. While 1997 was the peak of the order cycle for new aircraft, only 46 new aircraft were delivered to U.S. carriers that year, a fleet increase of a scant 0.9 percent. However, the U.S. commercial fleet is forecast to grow from 4,953 aircraft in 1997 to 7,400 in 2009. Another factor that holds down capacity is the guidelines for meeting the standards of U.S. antinoise legislation. Aircraft that meet only Stage 2 standards (older-model DC-9s, Boeing 737s, and Boeing 727s) will be parked or are being replaced, reengined, or hush-kitted. At the end of 1997 the fleet included more than 1,300 Stage 2 aircraft, approximately one-quarter of the total fleet.

In another competitive development, in 1998 US Airways launched a low-cost, low-fare carrier, MetroJet, as an adjunct to its normal scheduled flight operations. The tactic followed the successful start-up of low-fare carriers by United Airlines (Shuttle by United) and Delta Air Lines (Delta Express) in recent years. Continental Lite, an experiment undertaken by Continental Airlines in 1993 after its emergence from bankruptcy, failed in the east coast marketplace; it disappeared during a restructuring that restyled Continental and directed it on the path toward profitability. These low-fare adjunct carriers, organized under special labor agreements, are designed to compete with low-fare services offered by Southwest Airlines and other new-entrant carriers. The development of affiliated low-fare carriers has been the most significant structural change in U.S. majors since the 1980s, when the majors began establishing links with commuter and regional carriers.

National, Regional, and Commuter Airlines

Competition in this sector of commercial aviation has increased considerably and will continue to accelerate. The entry of turbofan-powered pure jet aircraft into a field dominated by turboprop-powered aircraft is altering the commercial aviation landscape. New 50-seat jet aircraft that rival large transports in comfort and speed have created opportunities for regional and commuter airlines to serve markets up to 1,000 miles or more from airport hubs. The success of the twin-jets—the Canadair RJ and the Embraer EMB-145—is likely to result in route rationalizations by the major carriers and their allied regional and commuter carriers. Commuter jets will displace large transport aircraft on routes of 500 miles or more.

Because of the high level of passenger acceptance of regional jets, their deployment is expected to accelerate. The manufacturers Embraer and Fairchild Dornier have selected designs for jet transports in the 30- to 40-seat range. Canadair and Aero International Regional have designs for jet-powered transports that will carry up to 70 passengers.

Despite structural changes in regional and commuter networks, the airlines will not abandon their primary role of feeding traffic to major carriers at airport hubs. Commuter aircraft have provided that service since the early days of airline deregulation, after the major airlines departed from many short-haul markets and later established traffic agreements with the smaller operators. In the 1980s the major carriers solidified their positions by investing in or acquiring regional and commuter airlines, leading to consolidation in that sector. Between 1981 and 1997 the number of commuter and regional carriers declined from 250 to less than 100. In 1997 the top 50 commuter airlines carried 98.7 percent of the total number of passengers. Trends toward consolidation and further integration with the major airlines are expected to continue.

Traffic growth in the regional and commuter sector will outpace the growth of major airlines. The U.S. Federal Aviation Administration (FAA) forecast a 10.2 percent increase in 1998 to 15.5 billion RPMs. A 7.5 percent increase has been projected for 1999.

Corporate Strategies

Strict cost controls and a pattern of carefully restrained growth have become routine components of U.S. airlines' operating plans. The robust health of the industry is attributable in part to these strategies and the restructuring of individual carriers in the aftermath of the economic downturn of the early 1990s. The concessionary labor contracts of the early to middle 1990s reduced costs and played an important role in restoring the airlines to financial health.

In their quest to reduce costs, airlines have broken the strong grip that travel agents had on them as third-party distributors of airline tickets. Travel agents are still the chief distributors, but direct ticket sales by airlines to passengers through the Internet have injected a new element of competition in ticket distribution. For the first time under deregulation the cost of travel agents' commissions has declined in tandem with the commission rates paid by carriers. Airlines will continue to exploit Internet sales and other alternatives to third-party distribution. In compensation for the loss of revenues, some travel agents have begun to charge fees to serve their clients' travel needs.

In the future airlines will keep capacity fairly closely in line with expected traffic growth, a cautious strategy that has won accolades on Wall Street. This restraint protects carriers from an oversupply in the marketplace and diminishes the threat of fare wars. For these reasons, Wall Street regards the carriers as better prepared for an economic downturn than they were in the early 1990s. The decisions by carriers' managements to disdain a market-grabbing strategy also reflect the new-style, post-deregulation, business-oriented airline executives who have come to work at the airlines after gaining experience in other industries.

The break in fuel prices in 1998 may delay an earnings decline, but a decline appears to be an inevitable consequence of the industry's operating dynamics in the coming years. The airlines are expecting parallel rates of growth for traffic and capacity, while costs rise and pressures on yield remain constant. In these circumstances the airlines can substantially improve earnings only by raising their prices. Reductions in costs will ease the challenge. An overhaul of the fare system that will redistribute the burden from business travelers to leisure and other travelers also could help, but a concerted effort by the airlines in this area is unlikely. The carriers could produce additional earnings by squeezing more passengers into airplanes, causing the load factor to go even higher into the 70 percent range, but there is little room for growth of that kind.

U.S. airlines will continue to pursue alliances and partnerships. By aligning networks, the airlines have crafted a substitute for the mergers and acquisitions seen in other industries. Alliances have had a positive influence on traffic for the carriers concerned. Studies of traffic flows by the DOT over a 4-year period show 35 percent traffic growth through European hub airports where alliances and open skies agreements are in effect. This compares with 27 percent growth at hubs where the carriers only jointly sell tickets and share computer reservations system codes. In gateways with no code sharing the traffic increase was 3 percent.

Furthermore, alliances are lucrative. KLM Royal Dutch Airlines and Northwest Airlines started joint operations in April 1991 with a flight connecting Minneapolis–St. Paul with Amsterdam. After the United States and the Netherlands penned the first open skies agreement in December 1992, the United States granted antitrust immunity to the alliance. Since that time the airlines have discussed and established prices. Under this arrangement, alliance flights have grown to 160 a week in the transatlantic sector alone. KLM has said that the partnership contributes about $150 million a year to its profits.

Alliances also offer side benefits. Centralization of purchasing has resulted in a reduction in costs. DSS World Sourcing AG was founded in June 1995 to serve the carriers in the Global Excellence Alliance, which then comprised Delta Air Lines, Singapore Airlines, and Swissair. DSS has concentrated on purchasing cabin service items and food catering services. Other alliance affiliates are working to standardize commonly used items such as fuel, avionics, and in-flight entertainment.

The U.S. government has spearheaded the drive toward open skies bilateral civil aviation agreements, which have increased competition. Since the first open skies agreement—in 1992 with the Netherlands—the United States has approved free trade bilateral agreements with 31 nations and a liberal trans-border pact with Canada. However, the European Commission has said that the bilateral agreements with eight European countries are in violation of European Union law, alleging that they have distorted competition. The commission has charged that airlines not associated with the agreements have been discriminated against. A lengthy court dispute is expected. In both Europe and the United States airline alliances are coming under increasing scrutiny by the authorities. Some form of restriction can be expected.

U.S. Industry Growth Projections for the Next 1 and 5 Years

Slowing of the U.S. economy will affect traffic growth rates in the period 1998–2002. For 1998, the Air Transport Association forecast system traffic growth of 3 percent or more, down from the 4.7 percent increase recorded in 1997. The FAA was more optimistic, projecting a 4.5 percent increase in RPMs in 1998, but that agency recognized a lower growth pattern related to the economic slowdown in later years of the FAA forecast.

U.S. carriers are expected to offer increasing amounts of capacity as the composition of the commercial fleet changes under the influence of noise regulations and new aircraft. Capacity growth probably will outpace traffic growth in these years. Then the average load factor will decline from its record peaks.

The FAA predicts relatively large declines in real yield (with inflation factored in), with an average 2.2 percent decline annually through the turn of the century. This prediction is based on the assumption that air carriers will reduce their fares to attract passengers during the economic slowdown. The yield decline will occur as a consequence of increased competition, largely from low-fare carriers. The shoehorning of additional landing slots for new-entrant carriers into slot-controlled airports such as Chicago's O'Hare International, New York's LaGuardia, and Washington's Ronald Reagan National Airport will kindle competition in the networks serving those large marketplaces. In overseas markets, open skies agreements and alliances should enhance competition, leading to lower yields.

International traffic will outpace domestic traffic in the 5-year outlook period. U.S. airlines have been increasing their international operations steadily. In 1980 the international proportion of U.S. scheduled airlines traffic was 21.1 percent. This share increased to 26.5 percent in 1997 and will continue climbing to more than 30 percent in 2009.

In 1997, international traffic among U.S. airlines increased 4.7 percent but growth varied over the three largest regions. Traffic to Latin American markets increased 9.2 percent; to Atlantic markets, 5 percent; and to Pacific markets, 2.4 percent. The small growth in the Pacific market reflected Asian economic turbulence in 1997 evidenced by the devaluation of currencies, huge stock market declines, bankruptcies, and problematic loans. The impact on airline traffic was immediate in the region and extended to the principal U.S. carriers—Northwest Airlines and United Airlines—which operate in the Pacific Rim. Both carriers have adjusted their schedules to minimize the damage and seek opportunities in some Asian markets that have been less affected.

The regional and commuter segment has the most positive outlook in the U.S. airline industry. The FAA forecasts that 1998 enplanements will grow 7.8 percent to 66.7 million passengers. Reflecting the steady increase in stage lengths flown by regional and commuter carriers, the growth of RPMs will be higher, up 10.2 percent. The FAA forecast excludes aircraft with 60 seats or more, and thus the numbers differ from those reported by the Regional Airline Association of Washington, DC. That association estimates that enplanements reached 66 million in 1997 and are likely to grow to 96 million by 2000.

Echoing the effects of the economy's slowdown, the U.S. domestic cargo market is expected to grow at a slower rate than it achieved over the 1993–1997 period. In a 1998 forecast MergeGlobal predicted 5.7 percent annual growth for cargo from 1997 through 2002. Boeing has forecast 5.5 percent annual cargo growth in the U.S. market through 2015.

Global Industry Trends

As world aviation has expanded and matured, the rate of growth of passenger traffic has moderated from the double-digit levels of the 1960s to an average annual growth rate of 3.4 percent in the period 1990–1995. The spiral of growth was reversed only once in modern times, in 1991, during the Persian Gulf War, when passenger and cargo traffic declined about 1 percent from the 1990 level. Passenger and cargo traffic rebounded throughout the 1990s, after the airlines restructured, rolled back aircraft orders, and rewrote labor contracts.

Concern about aviation safety and security has dominated the 1990s and is likely to continue. The International Civil Aviation Organization (ICAO), with the support of its nation members, is expanding the Safety Oversight Program it launched in 1995. Under that program, teams of specialists have been reviewing licensing and airworthiness programs at the invitation of the nation members. In March 1998 the ICAO Council approved a plan to expand the inspections to all 185 member nations. The inspection program would extend from airworthiness, licensing, and aircraft operations to all safety-related ICAO annexes, including those covering security, air traffic services, airports, support systems, and facilities. A key deficiency found by inspection teams has been a lack of qualified personnel to carry out safety oversight of airlines and other aviation enterprises. Training programs are expected to expand to meet this need.

In recent years the growth of the airline business has reflected the dynamism of the global economy. In the future growth will depend, as it has in the past, on the health of the world's economies, trade, and cost considerations. Over the longer term air transport is being nurtured by the expansion of free trade. The chief obstacles to growth are airport congestion—most serious in the developed countries—environmental issues, and other uncertainties. One of those issues is the exemption of airlines from the payment of national fuel taxes. Most international carriers are exempted from national taxes under the system of bilateral aviation agreements that govern air services between nations. Environmentalists criticized that exemption at the 1997 world conference on the environment held in Kyoto, Japan.

The outlook for air transport is dominated by the economic turbulence in the Asia/Pacific region, the fastest growing of the six world regions. The world industry group IATA suggested an impact on airline profits in 1998 of more than $2 billion and has revised its forecast for 1996–2001. In regard to passenger service, the average annual growth rate was reduced from 7.7 percent to 4.4 percent. For cargo service, that rate was reduced from 9 percent to 6.5 percent. The revisions were made after consultation with the chief executive officers of 46 airlines that serve the Asia/Pacific region.

The forecast community has been divided over the impact of the economic and financial turmoil in the Asia/Pacific region. One view has held that the impact will be as severe as that of the 1991 downturn, which affected all regions of the world. Other views are more optimistic, yet all agree that there will be a dampening effect on traffic over an extended period of recovery. The chief effects of the downturn should be confined to the Asia/Pacific region. Traffic was expected to be hardest hit in 1998, with the recovery being slow and steady. Factors other than financial and economic issues are at work in a short-term assessment of the Asia/Pacific region, including the impact of air pollution over a wide area of southeast Asia, which reduced tourism in 1997, and a widely publicized health problem in Hong Kong. The reversion of Hong Kong from British rule to Chinese sovereignty has provided further uncertainty for the region.

The 1995–2005 forecast for air transport issued by the ICAO, the United Nations affiliate that establishes world aviation standards, did not take into account the Asia/Pacific economic problems. It was based on a prediction that world economic growth would increase at an average annual rate of 2.5 percent in real terms. Scheduled airline traffic for the world was forecast to rise at an average annual rate of 5.5 percent. The international portion was expected to have the majority of that growth at 7 percent per year, while domestic travel was expected to grow 3.5 percent per year.

Taking into account the impact of the Asia/Pacific downturn, world economic growth will decline from the forecast rate, but the principal effect on aviation will be to lower growth in world airline traffic to 5 percent a year. The decline from previous optimistic forecast levels will be steepest in the Asia/Pacific region. Downward pressure on airline yields should be strong in the world's six regions through 2000, followed by a period of stable yields through 2005 as the Asia/Pacific region recovers.

Forecasts for Scheduled Services through 2005 by Region

Asia/Pacific.   Extreme devaluation of currencies in this region has placed imported items out of financial reach while exports are increasing. The traffic impact will be felt primarily in services within the region. Average annual traffic growth between 1985 and 1995 was 9 percent. The rate of growth was forecast to be 8.5 percent a year by ICAO, but in view of the downturn, it can be expected to moderate to 5 percent per year through 2005. The decline from the forecast represents a loss of 300 billion passenger kilometers through 2005 that will not be recovered. The impact will be reflected by a decline in the number of new aircraft deliveries to the region, perhaps as many as several hundred transports, through 2013.

Latin America and the Caribbean.   This region has benefited from economic growth, air carrier privatization, and new competition. The average annual growth rate between 1985 and 1995 was 4.7 percent. Passenger traffic will grow 5 percent or more a year through 2005.

Europe.   The European airline industry is being transformed under the influence of new competition and new carriers. The average annual growth rate between 1985 and 1995 was 2.5 percent, which reflected the traffic decline in Russia after the fall of the Soviet Union. Passenger traffic will grow 4.5 percent a year through 2005.

Middle East. This region has shared in world economic growth and will continue to do so. The average annual growth rate between 1985 and 1995 was 4.6 percent. Passenger traffic will grow 5.5 percent a year through 2005.

Africa. Spurred by South Africa, the continent's growth rate is rising. Privatization and interairline alliances will expand opportunities. The average annual rate between 1985 and 1995 was 3.3 percent. Passenger traffic will grow 4 percent a year through 2005.

North America. This mature market will grow 4 percent a year through 2005, a decline from the average annual rate between 1985 and 1995 of 4.7 percent. Because of the large stake in international services held by U.S. and Canadian airlines, international scheduled services will grow 8 percent a year through 2005.

James Ott, Aviation Week, The McGraw-Hill Companies, (606) 341-8484, November 1998.

RAILROADS

Railroads (SIC 4011) are establishments engaged primarily in intercity (line-haul) railroad passenger and freight operations.

In 1997 the railroad freight industry generated an estimated $35 billion in revenue. Nine major railroad systems accounted for roughly 90 percent of that figure. In that year Amtrak, the quasi-governmental passenger railroad corporation serving 45 states and Washington, DC, had estimated revenues of $1.7 billion.

Freight Service

In 1997 the railroad industry increased its carloadings of freight for the sixth consecutive year (see Table 43-2).

Structure. In 1997 there were nine Class I freight railroad systems—systems with an annual operating revenue of approximately $255 million or more—in the United States. Those systems employed 178,000 people, down from nearly 236,000 in 1987. In 1996 there were 32 regional railroads (line-haul railroads operating at least 350 miles of road and/or earning revenue between $40 million and the Class I threshold) which employed about 10,500 workers, down from 10,900 in 1987.

Approximately 500 local railroads (line-haul railroads smaller than regional railroads) employed 13,000 people, compared with 15,800 in 1987. Between 1987 and 1996, 237 regional and local railroads were created while the number of Class I systems dropped from 16 to 9, primarily because of mergers.

Mergers were common in the industry in the early 1980s and seemed to become prevalent again in the mid-1990s. For example, the Union Pacific Railroad (UP) acquired the Chicago and North Western in 1995 and the Southern Pacific in 1996, and the Burlington Northern merged with the Atchison, Topeka and Santa Fe in 1995. In June 1998 the Surface Transportation Board (STB), formerly the Interstate Commerce Commission (ICC), voted to approve the application by Norfolk Southern and CSX to acquire the lines of Conrail. The transaction involved Norfolk Southern acquiring 58 percent and CSX 42 percent of Conrail's lines and joint operation areas in northern New Jersey, Philadelphia, and Detroit. During the proceeding, the STB, following input from the DOT's Federal Railroad Administration (FRA), required the parties to submit Safety Implementation Plans indicating how the acquisition would be completed to assure safe operations. In view of the magnitude of the transaction, the STB, for the first time in a railroad consolidation proceeding, required the preparation of an environmental impact statement. The final statement included recommendations by the STB's Section of Environmental Analysis for appropriate environmental mitigation.

In April 1998 the Canadian National Railway, the Illinois Central, and the Kansas City Southern Railway announced a 15-year agreement that will coordinate sales and marketing, operations, use of equipment, and application of information systems. Traffic in areas where any two of the railroads provide the only direct rail service will not be included. This agreement will provide customers of all three railroads with new competitive options in key north-south continental freight markets.

The STB is expected to vote in spring 1999 on the Canadian National Railway's proposed acquisition of the Illinois Central Corporation. This proposed transaction would allow the Canadian National, which serves from Vancouver to Halifax, Canada, to serve the rapidly growing north-south trade corridor, including service between Detroit, Chicago, St. Louis, Memphis, Jackson, New Orleans, and Mobile. Under a separate agreement, subject to STB approval of this proposed acquisition, Canadian National and Kansas City Southern plan to grant rights over

TABLE 43-2: Railroads (SIC 4011) Trends and Forecasts

	1992	1993	1994	1995	1996	1997	1998[1]	1999[2]	Percent Change			
									96–97	97–98	98–99	92–96[3]
Carloads (thousands)	21,206	21,683	23,179	23,726	24,159	25,016	25,500	25,900	3.5	1.9	1.6	3.3
Tons (millions)	1,399	1,397	1,470	1,550	1,611	1,585	1,610	1,630	−1.6	1.6	1.2	3.6
Ton-miles (billions)	1,067	1,109	1,201	1,306	1,356	1,349	1,370	1,390	−0.5	1.6	1.5	6.2

[1] Estimate.
[2] Forecast.
[3] Compound annual growth rate.
Source: *Railroad Facts, 1997,* and *Analysis of Class I Railroads 1997,* Association of American Railroads; estimates and forecasts by the author.

each other's tracks in Mississippi, Louisiana, and Alabama. Both parties will invest in automotive, intermodal and transload facilities in Memphis, Dallas, Kansas City, and Chicago.

Other STB Activities. Starting in mid-1997, the STB came under increasing pressure from Congress and shippers concerning congestion in the west. These problems were associated with the Union Pacific's difficulties in integrating the Southern Pacific at the same time that rail volumes and intermodal volumes were increasing. Serious bottlenecks developed, particularly for the Gulf Coast region's chemical industry and for containers arriving in Los Angeles from the Far East for the holiday season. In addition, grain, coal, and lumber shippers were among the industries complaining of major service difficulties. In October and December 1997 the STB held hearings on service problems faced by western railroad shippers. After the first hearing the STB issued an emergency order concluding that a transportation emergency existed in the west and granting trackage rights to the Texas-Mexican Railroad to relieve congestion in the Houston area and provide the area's shippers with alternative routing. The STB ruled in summer 1998 that the congestion had dissipated and that emergency service in Houston was no longer warranted.

Through the winter and spring of 1998 shippers continued to complain about inadequate service in the west. In spring 1998 the STB requested that interested parties express their views on several issues, including (1) whether additional opportunities should be considered to allow railroads to access the lines of other railroads, such as requiring railroads to open their lines to another railroad if shippers demonstrate that there has been a substantial and measurable deterioration of service, and (2) how to improve the definition of railroad revenue adequacy, that is, earning more than their cost of capital. (Railroad revenue adequacy is determined by the STB. It is a measure of whether a railroad is earning a rate of return equivalent to the cost of capital as calculated by the STB. A rate of return less than the cost of capital generally indicates that a railroad will not be able to replace capital assets over the long run, and it effectively lessens scrutiny over rail rates.) In addition, the STB opened a proceeding on reducing the burden on shippers in rate reasonableness complaint cases by limiting the use of discovery by defendant railroads to obtain information on competition from other potential supplying locations or from other commodities.

Commodities. In 1997 the major rail-carried commodities, in terms of total carloads, included intermodal traffic [trailers and containers on flatcars] (29 percent), coal (27 percent), chemical products (7 percent), and farm products and motor vehicles and equipment (6 percent each). The fastest growing segment of rail traffic has been intermodal traffic, in which the number of trailers and containers increased substantially from 5.8 million in 1988 to 8.7 million in 1997.

Rates. Since 1980, the year the Staggers Rail Act partially deregulated rail rates and services, the railroads have invested over $240 billion in track and equipment. Freight rates adjusted for inflation declined 2 percent a year between 1993 and 1997

and 1 to 2 percent a year since the passage of the Staggers Act, compared with an increase of nearly 3 percent per year in the 5 years before 1980. Between 1993 and 1997, the Class I freight railroads averaged an 8 percent return on their net investment, up from a 2 percent average in the 1970s.

The Staggers Act reduced the authority of the ICC in areas where competition served to limit rail rates. In 1995 the ICC estimated that only 16 percent of the revenue earned by freight railroads came from traffic subject to maximum-rate regulation.

Three factors are tending to reduce regulation of rates: competition, which is keeping rates at levels below the threshold for STB authority; STB/ICC exemptions; and shipments moving under contract. In the early 1980s all traffic moving in boxcars or in trailers or containers on flatcars was exempted, but rates are still regulated for specific commodities, including grain, coal, ores, certain food products, certain pulp and paper products, and certain oversized heavy machinery.

By legalizing railroad-shipper contracts, the Staggers Act has had a significant impact on the industry's ability to market its services. Today roughly 70 percent of all freight shipped by rail moves under contract. (For more background on the Staggers Rail Act, see the *1990 Industrial Outlook,* Chapter 42.) For more information on the ICC Termination Act of 1995, see the *U.S. Industry & Trade Outlook '98,* Chapter 43, page 43-16.)

Productivity. Between 1987 and 1996 freight railroads made major strides in improving productivity. In that 10-year period the railroads nearly doubled the output per employee from 3.8 to 7.5 million revenue ton-miles as traffic increased and crew size was reduced.

The railroads also have increased the traffic density of their operations from 6.4 to 10.7 million revenue ton-miles per mile of road operated. Two factors are at work here. First, traffic has increased; second, Class I railroads have been selling light-density lines to smaller railroads. A by-product of that trend is better service on those lines.

Freight railroads also are making more efficient use of fuel. Between 1987 and 1996 ton-miles per gallon of fuel consumed rose from 309 to 379. To make their operations more fuel-efficient, the railroads have been rebuilding equipment and buying more locomotives that conserve fuel, using innovative equipment (for example, aluminum freight cars and double-stack cars), and reducing locomotive idling time.

Future Growth. The railroads' major commodities—coal, chemicals, intermodal traffic, and farm products—account for roughly two-thirds of railroad traffic measured in carloads, tons, and ton-miles. Each of these measures is forecast to increase from 1998 through 2003 for coal, chemicals, and intermodal traffic, with farm products forecast to be relatively flat.

Coal traffic is expected to continue to grow modestly as the demand for coal increases, especially for electricity generation. The emissions standards under the 1990 amendments to the Clean Air Act will continue to spur the use of low-sulfur coal mined in the west, in part at the expense of coal mined in the midwest. Western coal is expected to increase its penetration of more distant eastern utility markets.

Chemical traffic should continue to grow moderately as the demand by plastics producers, such as makers of plastic packaging, will continue to increase the demand for the resins used in making plastics and the raw materials used in making resins. The demand for whitening agents by textile mills and paper mills also is expected to grow. Some of the growth in chemical traffic will reflect an increase in U.S. imports of chemicals as more production shifts to plants outside the United States.

Intermodal traffic is projected to grow at a slower pace than it did in the 1980s and early 1990s because the current economic and financial problems in the Far East and the strong U.S. dollar are expected to hamper U.S. exports to the Far East to an extent that will not be balanced by the expected increase in imports from the Far East. Rail traffic crossing the Canadian and Mexican borders in both directions is expected to continue to increase.

With the trend toward longer hauls—particularly as coal production shifts westward and as mergers reduce the need for interchanges between railroads—ton-miles should increase more rapidly than will carloads and tons originated. At the same time, intermodal traffic should compete more effectively in closer markets, offsetting increases in haul length somewhat. Imports through the east coast will increase, in part at the expense of imports through the west coast, as suppliers from southern parts of the Pacific Rim choose to ship via the Suez Canal instead of the transpacific route.

Passenger Service

Amtrak. The National Railroad Passenger Corporation (Amtrak) started its twenty-sixth year of operation in May 1997. Amtrak operates more than 200 intercity trains a day over a 22,200-mile route system, serving more than 500 communities in 45 states and the District of Columbia. In fiscal year (FY) 1997 (October 1, 1996, to September 30, 1997) Amtrak carried 68.6 million passengers (20.2 million on its intercity trains and 48.4 million metropolitan commuters), generating a total of 5.17 billion passenger miles (up about 2 percent from 5.05 billion in FY 1996).

Amtrak continues to face serious financial and operational challenges, although it has shown some improvement in recent years. Several years ago inadequate capital investment, stagnant traffic and passenger revenue levels, outdated equipment in need of modernization, and declining federal subsidies worsened Amtrak's performance. The company incurred an operating shortfall of $834 million in FY 1994, the worst in its history.

In FY 1995, under new management, the corporation implemented a reorganization that divided Amtrak into several strategic business units and set in motion a strategic business plan that called for revenue enhancement initiatives, programs to reduce overhead expenses and improve productivity, and major changes in service. The plan also was designed to recapitalize Amtrak's assets and make the company more efficient, increase ridership, and make the passenger business more profitable. Since that time Amtrak has demonstrated modest improvement in its bottom line, and by the end of FY 1997 it was able to

reduce its operating loss to $762 million, a reduction of about 9 percent from FY 1994.

Despite the recent improvement, Amtrak still spends almost $2 for every dollar it earns in revenues from its intercity passenger service. In fact, only 1 of its 40 intercity routes, the Metroliner service between Washington, DC, and New York City, was profitable in FY 1997. Controlling expenses and increasing operating efficiencies on one hand and increasing revenues on the other, particularly in its intercity passenger operation, remain difficult obstacles.

Contributing to the corporation's financial problems are lower federal subsidies. Since FY 1995 Congress has been reducing Amtrak's operating subsidies, and it plans to eliminate them altogether (except for excess railroad retirement payments) by 2002. In FY 1997, for example, the corporation received a federal subsidy of $668 million and an additional $175 million to continue electrifying the line between New Haven and Boston as part of the Northeast Corridor Improvement Project. In constant dollars, Amtrak's FY 1997 subsidy was almost 60 percent lower than its FY 1981 appropriation.

In response to its financial problems, Amtrak has undertaken an aggressive capital improvement program, primarily to replace outdated equipment and thus improve service. Over the past several years Amtrak had ordered and taken delivery of close to 200 bilevel Superliners, designed to replace the aging Heritage equipment, and 50 Viewliners, scheduled for service in the midwest and the east coast. The Viewliner equipment represents the first single-level sleeping cars manufactured in the United States in 40 years.

More recently Amtrak placed orders with General Electric and General Motors for close to 150 locomotives to replace its aging F-40 locomotives, and most of them have been delivered. Furthermore, an international consortium led by Bombardier, Inc., of Canada and GEC Alsthom of France is under contract to design and build 20 high-speed all-electric train sets. This contract is a vital component of Amtrak's plan to introduce high-speed passenger service along the Washington–Boston Northeast Corridor in late 1999 and 2000. Assembly of component parts has begun, and preproduction locomotives and coaches are scheduled to be ready for testing by early 1999. The new trains will be equipped with tilt technology (designed to improve ride quality through curves), reach speeds of 150 miles per hour (mph), and offer the latest communications technology to the traveling public. The $750 million contract includes 15 additional high-powered locomotives and three train set maintenance facilities.

Several recent developments in its performance have improved Amtrak's long-term outlook. First, Amtrak's ridership has shown healthy gains, increasing 2.7 percent in FY 1997 over FY 1996, while ridership in the first half of FY 1998 grew 6.4 percent over the prior year's level. Strong ridership growth in both the west and the Northeast Corridor was made possible by improved marketing and a relatively mild winter, despite some weather-related service disruptions in the west. Second, Amtrak's service quality improved. Amtrak's customer service index, which measures the level of customer satisfaction, improved from 81 in FY 1995 to 83 in FY 1997. After the first 6 months of FY 1998 that index was at 85. Similar gains were evident in Amtrak's on-time performance measures. That index improved from 70.9 percent on time in FY 1996 to 74.4 percent in FY 1997, and 6 months into FY 1998 the index was at 80.5 percent, 3.7 percent higher than in FY 1997.

Finally, the recent passage of two Amtrak-related statutes is likely to have an important effect on Amtrak's future. The Taxpayers Relief Act and the Amtrak Reform and Accountability Act (ARAA) provide Amtrak with sufficient capital and reform to improve the company's chances for survival and stay on the path toward operating self-sufficiency by 2002. The Taxpayers Relief Act provides $2.2 billion for capital investment through two direct payments to Amtrak from the U.S. Treasury, while ARAA authorizes future appropriations and allows Amtrak to operate more like a private business. ARAA also replaces Amtrak's existing board of directors with a new seven-member reform board and grants its unions increased flexibility to negotiate on key issues and improve productivity.

High-Speed Passenger Service

Congestion at airports and on highways costs millions of hours in delays. Although alleviating that congestion is increasingly expensive, the need for cost-effective and efficient movement of growing numbers of people is greater than ever.

In August 1996 the FRA released its Commercial Feasibility Study, a major study of high-speed ground transportation (HSGT) and its potential in the United States. The report concluded that public-private partnerships could implement HSGT systems and that those systems could be self-sustaining after the initial capital investment is made.

In its projections of HSGT system requirements and performance, the report described three basic technology options:

- Accelerail is an upgraded rail passenger service that travels over existing rights-of-way and makes use of state-of-the art tilting trains with top speeds of 90 to 150 mph and many other technological advances.

- The new high-speed rail (HSR) is a 200-mph equivalent of systems such as the French high-speed service (TGV) and the Japanese bullet trains (Shinkansen).

- Maglev, or magnetic levitation, is an entirely new technology that allows vehicles to glide at up to 300 mph over specially designed and constructed guideways.

For illustration, the report focused on the potential for HSGT systems in eight heavily populated high-speed corridors: California, the Pacific Northwest, the Texas Triangle, the Chicago Hub network, New York State's Empire Corridor (New York City–Albany–Buffalo), the Northeast Corridor (Washington, DC, to Boston), Florida, and the Southeast Corridor (Washington, DC, Virginia, and North Carolina). In each of the corridors at least one of the technologies exhibited the potential to spark interest in a private-public partnership. Conversely, each technology showed potential in at least one corridor. According to the study, detailed analyses at the state level will be needed to

---

HIGH-SPEED GROUND TRANSPORTATION

The Federal Railroad Administration study of high-speed ground transportation (HSGT) examined the potential of high-speed passenger service in eight corridors. The states in each of those corridors have shown tangible support for HSGT initiatives. In fact, most have received federal funds to invest in HSGT infrastructure or conduct planning. Following are a few of the major initiatives:

Florida. Early in 1996 Florida announced its selection of the Florida Overland Express (FOX) consortium to develop a high-speed rail (HSR) system using French TGV technology. In its multi-billion-dollar proposal, which relies on public and private funding, FOX included a dedicated right-of-way for high-speed passenger trains along the 320-mile line that connects Miami, Orlando, and Tampa. The Florida Department of Transportation has pledged $70 million a year to the project and is working with the consortium on environmental impact and corridor alignment studies while it develops a funding plan.

California. In a report and action plan issued late in 1996 the California Intercity High Speed Rail Commission found that based on expected growth in travel demand and using a new HSR or maglev system, a high-speed line linking the state's largest areas—Los Angeles and the San Francisco Bay Area with extensions to San Diego and Sacramento—could be feasible from an environmental, engineering, and technical viewpoint and could generate annual operating surpluses. The only major obstacle is the substantial capital needed for construction. To address financial issues and develop plans for the implementation of an HSGT line, the state legislature established a High Speed Rail Authority. The authority will inform the public about the plan while preparing for a referendum in 2000.

Pacific Northwest. Washington will take delivery of two trains custom-built by TALGO (a transportation equipment manufacturer in Spain) starting in November 1998, and Amtrak will also add two similar TALGO trains beginning late in 1998.

Other State-Sponsored HSGT Activities. Other states are in the process of studying or implementing Accelerail systems. These plans involve adapting existing (mainly freight) railroads to improve passenger service. Several involve the adoption of new technologies, among them onboard computers and databases.

---

confirm whether the development of any particular HSGT system there can or should be realized (see the boxed note: "High-Speed Ground Transportation").

Safety and Technology

Safety and Regulatory Initiatives. In 1995 FRA implemented the Safety Assurance and Compliance Program (SACP), a new approach to safety inspection and encouragement of compliance. This innovative approach is applied simultaneously as FRA continues site-specific inspections and penalties. SACP involves a safety partnership with representatives from the federal and state governments, labor and the rail industry, and the public to identify and correct problems on individual railroads through cooperative actions. By focusing on the root causes, FRA's regional safety inspectors and headquarters personnel help address potential safety concerns before they become safety problems by developing comprehensive, cooperatively created solutions. The SACP effort comprises a series of joint meetings over many months on an individual railroad's safety issues. The process may include FRA's gathering specific safety information from railroad employees by setting up listening posts at the railroad. Safety Action Plans are developed by the railroad and collaboratively monitored by FRA and the railroad until all the safety problems are resolved. FRA is moving toward more collaborative rulemaking, bringing the railroads, labor, suppliers, passenger advocates, state agencies, and others into the process. On April 1, 1996, the agency convened the Railroad Safety Advisory Committee (RSAC), which will make rules by consensus. Among its first tasks, RSAC appointed work groups to revise track safety standards, power brake regulations, and rules related to railroad communications. The group working on track safety standards reported the first consensus product to the full committee in October 1996. FRA also has finalized regulations for roadway worker safety, the product of its first formal rule-making negotiations.

Regulations resulting from this collaborative process are more likely to be reflective of all the affected interests and more readily implemented. Because the final rule is based on consent, acceptance and understanding are widespread and compliance has been at high levels from the start.

Among the safety issues FRA has addressed through regulation are power brake regulations, requiring two-way end-of-train devices by July 1, 1997, enabling locomotive engineers to apply an emergency brake from both ends of the train, and revision of the regulations governing accident and incident reporting, effective January 1, 1997. Additionally, final rules on track safety standards, Tourist and Historic Railroads operation, and revision of federal standards for radio communications are being reviewed.

RSAC also is considering the revision of certain rules, including Qualification and Certification of Locomotive Engineer Regulations, safety standards for track motor vehicles and self-propelled roadway equipment, locomotive crashworthiness and working conditions, event recorder requirements, and the safety implications of processor-based signal and train control technologies, including communications-based operating systems.

1997 UP Safety Compliance Report.
FRA undertook a comprehensive review of safety on the Union Pacific Railroad after safety deficiencies were discovered during safety audits prompted by several major collisions which resulted in the deaths of seven UP employees. The Safety Assurance and Compliance Program (SACP) was established in 1997 in cooperation with the UP and its labor organizations to address operational problems on the UP which compromised safety, including insufficient staffing for train and engine crews, varying attitudes toward safety on the merged UP and Southern Pacific railroads, and unsafe practices attributable to lack of training and work overload. An FRA report issued in February 1998 found that UP was making progress in remedying these safety deficiencies.

Safety Audit on CSX Transportation. FRA also conducted a comprehensive audit in 1997 on CSX Railroad, based on FRA's SACP model. The audit identified several deficiencies, including hazardous materials operations and crew management inadequacies, along with the need to more effectively manage signal and train control operations. CSX Transportation, its labor organizations, and FRA subsequently initiated actions to implement new rules on hazardous material cars, improve crew management, and create a team to improve the process of locomotive inspection and repair.

Conrail Acquisition. FRA made recommendations, which were adopted by the STB, concerning the acquisition of Conrail by CSX and Norfolk Southern, identifying specific safety concerns which had not been addressed by the applicants and requiring both CSX and Norfolk Southern to prepare Safety Implementation Plans to fully resolve safety issues and assure a safe integration of the Conrail properties into the acquiring railroads' systems. FRA worked with STB to secure detailed commitments of the resources and steps necessary to implement the Safety Implementation Plans properly.

Technology Initiatives. Among the technologies being developed by the rail industry and the FRA are new train control systems for positive train separation. These systems utilize Global Positioning System technology and onboard computers to keep trains apart, thus preventing collisions and increasing throughput capacity. The new control systems should increase safety and allow trains to operate at higher speeds; at the same time, they are expected to cost only half of what conventional track circuit-based control systems cost. A Positive Train Control demonstration for freight and passenger revenue service on a 123-mile segment of a Union Pacific railroad line between Springfield, IL, and Chicago will take place over a 4-year period through a cooperative effort involving the Illinois Department of Transportation, the Association of American Railroads, and the FRA. An onboard computer will automatically monitor a train's speed, assuring that locomotive engineers do not exceed permitted speeds, do not pass red signals, and do not operate the train beyond track limits approved by the UP's Control Center in Omaha. The demonstration will determine the validity of the proposed technology and assess the potential safety and productivity gains it offers.

The FRA is also working with Amtrak, New York State, and others to develop nonelectric high-speed locomotives. In one effort, an Amtrak turbine-powered train set was retrofitted with new engines and the cars were refurbished. In a battery of tests, the train set achieved its goal of 125 mph cruise speed with improved acceleration. The train now operates daily at up to 110 mph on the Empire Corridor between Albany and New York City. In another effort, the FRA has signed an agreement with Bombardier, Inc., to develop a new turbine-powered nonelectric locomotive which may use an energy storage system under development by FRA which could increase acceleration.

Another initiative being developed specifically to improve rail operations is the interline-settlement system, a project supported by all the Class I railroads and 30 short lines. That industry effort to produce electronic, timely, error-free bills for moving goods over multiple carriers should streamline the billing process and the division of interline shipping revenue.

In an effort to develop high-speed passenger rail service and reduce highway-rail grade crossing incidents, FRA has granted funds to North Carolina to improve safety along its designated high-speed rail corridor. The initiative includes the installation of innovative highway-rail crossing devices, the consolidation of crossings, the use of long arm gates and articulated gate arms, video enforcement, video monitoring and data collection, studies of driver behavior and an analysis of the demographics of violators, and innovative warning devices and the use of improved signs at private crossings.

To curb the problem of trespassing and vandalism on railroad property and to work toward the goal of zero fatalities, accidents, and injuries, FRA has developed and offered to state and local governments model legislation which addresses both urban and rural trespassing and vandalism issues and recommends penalty provisions.

Privatization of the Mexican National Railways. The Ferrocarriles Nacionales de Mexico, the nationally owned Mexican National Railways, has offered to investors the opportunity to operate concessions on three major Ferrocarriles rail lines and 30 short lines. Concessions for 50 years for the use of mainline track with a 50-year renewal option and up to 49 percent foreign investment were offered, and the rail system was segmented into four major regions: the Northeast, the Pacific North, the Southeast, and the Valley of Mexico Terminal.

The licensing process for the Northeast region was concluded on December 5, 1996, with the successful bid of Transportacion Ferroviaria Mexicana, coowned by Kansas City Southern Industries, the parent of Kansas City Southern Railway and Texas Mexican Railway, and the Mexican ship operator Transportacion Maritima Mexicana. The Northeast Railway began operation on June 23, 1997, linking the busiest United States–Mexico rail interchange at Laredo, TX, as well as Brownsville, TX, with the Mexican ports of Lazaro Cardenas, Veracruz, and Tampico/Altamira and the cities of Monterrey and Mexico City.

Grupo Ferroviario Mexicano (Ferromex), of which Union Pacific Railroad is a minority partner, was the successful bidder on June 19, 1996, for the Pacific North region, starting operations on February 20, 1998. The line links the ports of Calexico, CA; Nogales, AZ; and El Paso and Eagle Pass, TX, with Mexico City, Guadalajara, Tampico, Monterrey, and Manzanillo.

Additionally, the Burlington Northern Santa Fe Railway now has a direct interchange with the Pacific-North Railroad at Eagle Pass, TX. Similarly, as was mentioned in the section on railroad industry structure, Canadian National, Illinois Central, and the Kansas City Southern Railway have formed a 15-year marketing alliance that will give shippers a coordinated rail network linking points in Canada with major U.S. midwestern and southern markets as well as access to Mexico's largest rail system, Ferromex. It is expected that private investment in Mexico's railway system will boost rail utilization and encourage the modernization of existing routes, the creation of new rail connections, and the expansion of markets for shippers between the United States and Mexico.

Exporting U.S. Technology and Know-How. The pace of commercialization, privatization, and/or concessioning of government-owned and -operated railways around the world continues. All the continents are making these changes to some degree. The most common model used is the so-called Swedish Model, by which the government retains ownership (and maintenance) of the infrastructure, while operations are spun off and commercialized or privatized outright. Anyone interested in participating in the rail export market should research the various privatization models as well as potential limitations in multicountry markets such as the European Union.

Concessioning has clearly emerged as the most promising avenue for debt-ridden railways to regain profitability. When concessioning is coupled with the all-important political will to allow a railway to operate in a free market enterprise environment, financial stabilization and even profitability most often result. To date, the greatest success story remains the privatization-concessioning of the Argentinian railway system, a story that has prompted countries as far away as Africa's Côte d'Ivoire to venture into this arena by restructuring and concessioning SITARAIL.

The U.S. privately owned and operated rail system remains the model for other countries to emulate. Its highly efficient and effective rail-related products and services have clearly proved to have materially and positively affected the profit margin of railroads, and this has not gone unnoticed by foreign governments. For instance, in 1997 the FRA was visited by over 60 foreign delegations in search of briefings on and discussions about the success of the U.S. rail industry.

Commercialization, privatization, and concessioning—and therefore export opportunities—in the 1998–1999 time frame appear likely in sub-Saharan Africa, southeastern and central Europe, central Asia, and China. Furthermore, a number of large projects and/or initiatives are in various planning stages, including the Trans-Asia Rail Project (Malaysia, Thailand, Cambodia, Vietnam, and points north), rail-related alliances in the Caspian Sea region (all the "-stan" and Black Sea countries), southeastern Europe (Bulgaria, Romania, Macedonia, Albania, and Hungary) and Turkey, and continued rapid expansion of the rail system in China to overcome the fact that only 65 to 70 percent of demand in that country currently is being met.

Rolling stock, signaling and train control, safety, management systems, management expertise, and financing all provide opportunities for the U.S. rail-related manufacturers, suppliers, and service providers to contribute to the process.

NAFTA. The United States, Mexico, and Canada have a history of cooperation and interchange of rail traffic. The North American Free Trade Agreement (NAFTA) formalized that rail partnership; it also promotes operating efficiencies and safety. NAFTA established a Land Transport Standards Subcommittee to address the development of more compatible standards related to rail, truck, and bus operations and the transportation of hazardous materials between NAFTA partners.

In June 1995 the subcommittee issued a report stating that no major impediments to cross-border rail transportation are posed by the NAFTA countries' existing safety regulations but that greater compatibility among those standards could increase efficiencies. Timetables and a mechanism for making safety regulations compatible have been developed to address any future changes in cross-border operations and their impact on safety. Work will continue through the formal process on facilitating transborder rail service and through ongoing cooperation on improving operating procedures and infrastructure.

In 1997 U.S. railroads carried $59 billion worth of goods between the United States and Canada (including $7 billion of transshipments, that is, traffic moving through Canada to or from a third country), up from $44 billion in 1994. U.S. railroads carried $18 billion worth of goods between the United States and Mexico in 1997 (including $29 million of transshipments through Mexico), up from $12 billion in 1994. Excluding transshipments, motor vehicles and motor vehicle parts hauled by railroads in 1997 accounted for nearly 70 percent of the rail-delivered U.S. value of traffic with Mexico and more than 50 percent of rail-delivered traffic with Canada. For example, a number of automobile assembly plants have opened on the Mexican side of the border in the past several years. U.S. companies ship motor vehicle parts to those plants for assembly, and the assembled vehicles are shipped back to the United States. Other major shipments include over $4 billion worth of imports (excluding transshipments) of wood and of paper and allied products from Canada.

Joel Palley, U.S. Department of Transportation, Federal Railroad Administration (202) 493-6409, October 1998.

TRUCKING

Trucking companies (motor carriers) provide ground-based transportation of raw materials, including dry bulk and liquid commodities and finished and semifinished manufactured products. Cargo is transported by dry van, hopper, or tank trailer. Local carriers (SIC 4212) are those which handle shipments exceeding 100 pounds within a single municipality, contiguous municipalities, or a municipality and its suburbs. Long-distance truckers (SIC 4213) provide highway transport of commercial and household items. Package, parcel, and courier services (SIC 4215) handle items weighing less than 100 pounds and may move locally or over long distances.

Domestic Trends

The trucking industry, which accounts for an estimated 79 percent of the total U.S. commercial freight market, or about $347 billion in 1997, has grown rapidly over the last 50 years at the expense of railroads, inland waterway operators, and pipelines. Motor carriers have been able to garner the major share of the

freight market because, unlike those other transportation modes, there are no physical limits on their route structure. Ten of the top trucking companies are listed in Table 43-4.

Until the development of the interstate highway system after World War II, nearly all trucking was local in nature. After the construction of permanent all-season roads, motor carriers, which according to the Eno Foundation for Transportation handled only 5.4 percent of all interstate traffic in 1944 (based on ton-miles), were able to expand their share to 22 percent by 1960 and 29 percent in 1997. The trucking industry's share of commercial freight revenue is far higher than its share based on weight, since this industry specializes in higher-valued manufactured goods rather than the low-value bulk commodities moved by rail, barge, and pipeline.

Although motor carriers have had above-average growth for several decades, their share of the freight market has been stagnant since 1993. Standard & Poor's DRI anticipates that trucking will lose market share between 1996 and 2006 as trucking revenue, which is projected to increase 29 percent over this period, will lag the 121 percent increase expected for air freight and the 55 percent aggregate gain projected for rail intermodal. It has been projected that as costs fall for air freight and manufacturers strive to establish shorter order fulfillment cycles, they will increasingly turn away from trucks for the transport of high-value items. Also, rail intermodal, which already has a significant price advantage over motor carriage for long-haul shipments, will gain ground as it improves its service performance, expands double-stack container routes for domestic freight, and creates new long-haul, single-system intermodal corridors through mergers (see Table 43-3).

Shrinkage of Private Trucking's Share. Some $200 billion worth, or 45 percent of all commercial freight, was moved by privately operated truck fleets in 1997. About $115 billion of that

TABLE 43-3: Transportation Market, 1997
(billions of dollars)

Mode	Revenue
Private, interstate	115
Private, local	85
Truckload, interstate	65
Truckload, local	40
Less-than-truckload, national	8
Less-than-truckload, regional	10
Package/express (ground)	24
Total trucking	347
Railroad	36
Pipeline (oil and gas)	26
Air freight, integrated (domestic)	20
Air freight, forwarder (domestic)	5
Water (Great Lakes and rivers)	7
Total transportation	441
Warehousing	65
Logistics administration	30
Total distribution and transportation	546

Source: Standard and Poor's DRI; Cass Information Systems.

TABLE 43-4: Leading Trucking Companies, 1997
(billions of dollars)

Company	Revenue
United Parcel Service[1]	15.73
Roadway Express	2.58
Yellow Freight System	2.51
Schneider National	2.51
Consolidated Freightways	2.19
RPS Inc.	1.58
J.B. Hunt Transport	1.36
Con-Way Transportation	1.35
Ryder Integrated Logistics	1.30
ABF Freight System	1.14

[1] Revenue from U.S. surface transportation only.
Source: *Transport Topics*, August 10, 1998.

figure involved interstate moves, with local hauling accounting for the balance. Private carriers are defined as shippers whose primary business is not transportation but which operate truck fleets to haul their own raw materials or finished goods. Standard & Poor's DRI estimates that private freight transportation revenues will shrink to a 42 percent share of the freight market by 2006 as they grow a lackluster 13 percent during the period 1996–2006.

Before deregulation in 1980, many private fleets were established to provide a lower-cost alternative to commercial motor carriers. With premium truckload carriage now at a discount compared with private fleet costs, manufacturers and distributors increasingly are choosing to outsource their transportation activities. Nevertheless, a significant portion of the trucking market remains private, as many operators believe they can gain a competitive edge by offering a more responsive and reliable delivery service. Private fleets also create goodwill and serve as mobile billboards. A private operation is high-cost and complex; therefore most private carriers limit their activities to shipments moving under 250 miles and ship with for-hire carriers during their seasonal peaks.

Growth of Third-Party Logistics. Logistics is defined as the process of planning, implementing, and controlling the efficient and effective flow and storage of goods, services, and related information from the point of origin to the point of consumption (the supply chain). Third-party logistics administration, which has been estimated by Cass Information Systems at $30 billion, is expected to grow at a double-digit pace over the next 5 to 10 years, and that rate of growth would make it the fastest growing segment of the transportation and distribution industry. Until the early 1990s most manufacturing companies took responsibility for the transportation, warehousing, and coordination of the flow of materials. Leaders in logistics management such as Ryder System gradually convinced corporations that their systems were inefficient and that they should outsource those activities.

Many trucking companies entered the logistics field during the early and middle 1990s, such as Schneider National, Caliber Systems (part of FDX Corporation), and Menlo Logistics (part of CNF Transportation). Truckers were drawn to the field because there were higher margins than those earned in traditional trucking. There can be conflicts of interest when a logis-

tics administrator also operates a transportation mode, since the administrator's obligation is to route freight on the carrier that offers the best value. A shakeout in the logistics field is under way as some truckers have found that they cannot offer, except at great cost, the complex information systems required to maintain this service.

Advancement of Rail Intermodal Service. A major trend in the motor carriage industry is the growth of rail intermodal service (the movement of containers or trailers on rail flatcars). Standard & Poor's DRI has estimated that rail intermodal revenues, which reached $5.6 billion in 1996, will grow 55 percent to $8.7 billion by 2006. Some of this growth reflects the expansion of international trade, while a large part reflects a diversion of domestic traffic from truckload carriers. Rail intermodal will benefit from the shortage of long-haul drivers and a cost advantage over highway transport for long hauls.

Rail intermodal service was ignored by most shippers in the 1970s and early 1980s because of its lack of reliability. Deregulation in 1980, accompanied by a wave of mergers in the rail industry, created more efficient long-haul intermodal routes. The opening up of double-stack service (containers piled two high on a flatcar) further increased the cost advantage of intermodal over highway transport. Accordingly, the growth of intermodal increased from a 2.8 percent annual compound rate in the 1970s to a 6.2 percent annual rate in the 1980s.

The trucking industry contributed to these gains by forming alliances with railroads to feed them long-haul traffic that was increasingly difficult to handle because of a shortage of drivers. Truckers such as J.B. Hunt Transport decided to join the rails as partners because they recognized that lower-cost railroads eventually would dominate the long-haul market.

Less-than-truckload (LTL) carriers also have turned to rail intermodal to handle long-haul moves as a way to cut costs. In their 1994 contract with the Teamsters, LTL carriers won the right to increase their intermodal use from 10 percent to 28 percent of total vehicle miles. Intermodal service has helped these carriers boost their margins by reducing overall costs by 5 to 10 percent (see Table 43-5).

Intermodal, which is projected by Standard & Poor's DRI to grow at a 4.9 percent annual pace between 1997 and 2003, will

TABLE 43-5: Operating Ratios for Leading Less-Than-Truckload Carriers

Year	Ratio	Year	Ratio
1980	96.4	1989	96.2
1981	96.8	1990	95.0
1982	98.4	1991	97.1
1983	95.5	1992	96.6
1984	95.7	1993	96.5
1985	95.2	1994	97.2
1986	94.0	1995	99.1
1987	96.7	1996	99.0
1988	94.6	1997	95.5

Source: Standard & Poor's.

get a boost from the division of Conrail between CSX Transportation and Norfolk Southern. Those two railroads plan to create new long-haul, single-system north-south routes that will divert freight from the heavily used I-95 highway. The growth scenario for intermodal service could fall flat if Congress lifts its ban on long combination vehicles.

Popularity of JIT. In the LTL segment carriers are being influenced by a manufacturing practice imported from Japan that is known as *kanban.* In the United States it is called "just-in-time" (JIT) and is employed to reduce costs by holding inventories to a bare minimum. JIT provides savings, as warehouse space is reduced and less capital is tied up in inventory. As stocks are depleted, fresh deliveries are made. Illustrating the popularity of JIT is the dramatic drop in manufacturers' ratio of inventory to sales over the last few years. Although JIT is popular among large manufacturers of high-value products, there is much room for growth, as it has been estimated that only 30 percent of companies currently use it.

Growing employment of the JIT inventory management system has been accompanied by changes in the transportation field. JIT promotes more frequent shipment of materials and components in smaller lots. To assure a continuous flow, JIT practitioners limit supply sources to a few firms within a day's haul or a 300- to 500-mile radius. The chief beneficiaries of JIT have been high-grade regional LTL carriers and to a lesser extent air cargo carriers. Because of the high risks associated with JIT, shippers demand that their carriers meet exacting reliability expectations and possess state-of-the art shipment tracing and communication systems.

While national LTL carriers also can provide short-haul service, the majority of JIT-inspired business has gone to the purely regional LTL lines. To capture a piece of the faster-growing short-haul market spurred by JIT, national carriers have had to restructure their terminal networks radically to shorten transit times and cut costs. The old "hub-and-spoke" terminal arrangements operated by national LTL carriers, which is very efficient for maximizing truck utilization, produce extremely slow service, particularly on shorter routes. Replacing the hub-and-spoke system is direct loading with strict cutoff times. Freight is gathered at one terminal, loaded into a larger truck, and promptly sent out, whether the truck is fully or partially loaded, to a destination terminal. With direct loading, handling is reduced, transit times are cut, and the potential for damage is limited.

Shortage of Drivers. In the truckload sector a chronic shortage of drivers is pushing up costs and forcing operating changes. Many industry observers consider the current driver shortage the major challenge that will face truckload carriers in the next decade. Contributing to the paucity of available drivers are economic growth and demographic and regulatory changes. In March 1998 the U.S. economic expansion reached its seventh year, making it one of the longest on record as well as generating record amounts of freight and creating jobs in industries more attractive than trucking. Demographically, fewer people were born in the current generation than were born during the baby boom years. Consequently, truckers have had to broaden their recruitment efforts to nontraditional segments of the labor pool, such as women and immigrants. Reduced government support for driver training schools, the tightening of licensing procedures, and drug and alcohol screening have exacerbated the shortage.

To close the gap between the demand for truckload service and the supply of drivers, motor carriers are lifting pay scales significantly. J.B. Hunt Transport raised drivers' pay 33 percent in 1997 and now pays out more than $50,000 annually to each of several thousand long-haul drivers. Hunt, along with other carriers that have raised pay, believes that the extra pay will be offset by reduced spending for training, recruitment claims, insurance, and fuel as these firms attract more experienced and skilled operators. A novel solution to the driver shortage is for big, well-capitalized companies to buy up smaller carriers to get their drivers.

Besides higher payments per mile, truckload drivers are attracted by lushly appointed tractors, increased motel allowances, higher layover pay, higher loading and unloading pay, 401(k) retirement plans, profit-sharing schemes, medical and dental coverage, and incentive bonuses that are based on safety, fuel consumption, and on-time performance. Higher monetary compensation alone cannot resolve this issue. Carriers have begun to recognize that drivers need to return home more frequently and at predictable intervals. To accomplish this, the carriers are turning to sophisticated computer software that matches drivers with loads moving in the direction of their homes. This practice results in more empty mileage but lower driver turnover. To get drivers home sooner, truckers are abandoning long-haul freight or are using rail piggyback for the line-haul portion of a move.

Regulatory Issues

The dismantling of the ICC at the end of 1995 eliminated most economic regulation of the motor carrier industry. Truckers still must file certain financial reports, obtain operating certificates, and file proof of insurance coverage with the ICC's successor, the Surface Transportation Board, while the U.S. Transportation Department oversees certain safety-related issues. The ICC Termination Act ended the legal distinction between contract carriage and common carriage for truckers, allowing carriers to craft any type of contract they want. Carriers now can legally offer released rates (discounted rates) in exchange for a cap on their liability for lost or damaged cargo.

One vestige of regulation is the rate bureau system of setting rates collectively. The ICC Termination Act stipulated that all rate bureau agreements expire by December 31, 1998, unless they are renewed by the Surface Transportation Board. The seven remaining rate bureaus, where motor carriers can meet to set rates collectively, currently are immune from antitrust laws. The rate bureau system is likely to be scrapped as few, if any, shippers pay the inflated class rates published by the bureaus.

The Trucking Industry Regulatory Reform Act (TIRRA), which was enacted in 1994, relieved carriers of the costly and time-consuming process of filing tariffs with the ICC each time a discounted rate is offered. Previously, TIRRA carriers filed over 1 million tariffs each year, many in coded language or so narrowly defined as to preclude their application to any firm except the one shipper intended. TIRRA ended this system, enabling motor carriers to compete more effectively through more timely rate adjustments. An outgrowth of the Trucking Industry Regulatory Reform Act has been an effort by carriers to simplify their rate structures to make them more user-friendly.

Initially, carriers disseminated their rates by mailing out free diskettes that required only the specification of a shipment's origin and destination ZIP codes and a freight description to determine the appropriate rate. Since the advent of the Internet, rating software can be downloaded through a carrier's Web site. By keying in a few bits of information, shippers can get their freight priced; truckers benefit by avoiding the cost of mailing out thousands of new rate diskettes each time their rates are adjusted. Other carriers are using the Internet as a marketing tool to provide information about the array of services they offer. Beginning in 1997, motor carriers began to make their Web sites more interactive, allowing shippers to trace their freight, schedule pickups, review claim status, and generate shipping documents.

The trucking industry, while largely free of regulations relating to entry and rates, is still subject to governmental rules covering safety and environmental issues which influence operating costs and capital spending plans. Local, state, and federal governments also influence trucking profits through the imposition of fuel excise taxes.

Freeze on Long Combination Vehicles. A policy issue which will influence trucking productivity is vehicle size. Truckers want to use the largest practicable trailers or operate with triple trailer combinations that employ smaller "pup" (28-foot) trailers. The Intermodal Surface Transportation Efficiency Act (ISTEA) of 1991 froze size and weight limits on trucks. The freeze was extended in 1998, when ISTEA came up for reauthorization.

Currently, only 16 states, mostly in the west, allow the operation of triple trailers. Another 18 states, also mainly western, permit the use of "turnpike doubles," which use 48-foot tandem trailers. Standard double trailer combinations using pup trailers are legal in all 50 states. The use of long combination vehicles (LCVs) is attractive for motor carriers because it greatly reduces line-haul costs. Although motorists worry that LCVs will result in more highway fatalities, truckers counter that LCVs promote highway safety since their greater use will result in the presence of fewer (although longer) trucks on the road.

Although no change in policy on LCVs is anticipated in the near term, ultimately these vehicles may be allowed to use the highways, in which case traffic may shift from rail back to highway. Arthur D. Little, Inc., a Cambridge, MA, consulting firm, found in a 1995 survey that 14 percent of intermodal users would switch to trucks if trucking rates were cut just 10 percent.

Changes in Hours of Service. With drivers in short supply, truckers want to make sure that revisions in hours of service regulations are designed to enhance, not detract from, produc-

tivity. Since late 1996 the Federal Highway Administration (FHWA) has been working to revise these regulations, which have not changed since the 1930s. Implementation of the new rules is anticipated by mid-1999.

Driver fatigue is the top cause of accidents involving heavy trucks. Despite the considerable public concern about trucks, statistics show a general decline in fatalities since 1982. Nevertheless, the trucking industry thinks highway safety can be improved by setting hours of service regulations that offer greater flexibility and let drivers worker longer hours when they are alert and fewer hours when they are tired.

Under the current rules workers can drive 10 hours, followed by an 8-hour break, and can log no more than 70 hours over an 8-day period. Truckers want this changed to 14 hours on and 10 hours off with 100 hours over an 8-day period. Truckers say that the present system, although it allows fewer driving hours, leads to greater fatigue since drivers' hours are constantly shifting. Under the proposed system of 14 hours on and 10 hours off, a driver would repeat the shift at the same time each day, conforming to the body's natural clock.

The current hours of service regulations, coupled with demand for JIT freight delivery, compels drivers to violate the law. The Insurance Institute for Highway Safety, which claims that 73 percent of long-distance drivers violate hours of service regulations, wants to force compliance by directing trucking companies to install onboard computers (black boxes) that monitor vehicle performance. While better-capitalized carriers already have these devices, their installation could place a burden on marginal lines. If the FHWA's new hours of service regulations in 1999 conform to the industry's proposals, they could greatly alleviate the current shortage of long-haul drivers.

Environmental Regulations

The U.S. government's policies concerning air quality are shaping the trucking industry's cost structure and capital investment patterns. Federal fuel taxes, which add 24.4 cents, or 18 percent, to a gallon of diesel fuel, have prompted truckers to buy new fuel-efficient vehicles. The tightening of clean air standards in recent years also has added to the cost of fuel, which absorbs about 15 percent of truckers' revenues, or some $52 billion.

In 1997 the U.S. Environmental Protection Agency (EPA) issued its final emissions standards for heavy-duty diesel trucks. The new rules require a 50 percent reduction in emissions by 2004. Nitrogen oxide emissions are to be cut from 5 grams to 4 grams in 1998 and 2.9 grams by 2004. Nonmethane hydrocarbons (soot) are to be limited to 0.5 gram. Most existing diesel engines already meet the EPA's soot standard, but more costly engines will have to be installed in new trucks to meet the nitrogen oxide limits.

Truckers also face costly environmental regulations governing the use of petroleum product tanks and the discharge of pollutants into storm water runoff. By the end of 1998 all underground fuel tanks installed before 1988 will have to be upgraded to include corrosion, spill, and overfill protection. The cost of upgrading average tanks, only half of which had gone through this procedure by the end of 1997, has been estimated at $100,000 and up. The EPA's rules regarding storm water require any facility that engages in the washing or maintenance of motor vehicles to obtain a permit and collect water samples to determine whether pollutants are getting into the storm water system. Truckers estimate that compliance will cost at least $5,000 per facility (if no pollution is found).

International Trends

U.S. motor carriers compete aggressively with Canadian carriers for cross-border traffic. Some 1,000 Canadian truckers can provide service to all 48 mainland states, and $360 billion worth of trade was conducted between Canada and the United States in 1997. Penetration by Canadian carriers into the United States and by American truckers into Canada was facilitated by the implementation of NAFTA, which was adopted on January 1, 1994. Effective January 1, 1998, all remaining tariffs on U.S. and Canadian products were mutually eliminated, providing an additional boost to U.S.–Canadian trade. The majority of this increased trade may not be moved by truck. In 1998, CN agreed to acquire the U.S. railroad IC for $2.4 billion. This transaction, which could be completed in 1999, will create the first North American transcontinental railroad. The merger will establish seamless long-haul north-south routes that will capture cross-border highway traffic through the use of less expensive intermodal service.

When fully implemented with Mexico, NAFTA will have a more pronounced impact on U.S.–Mexican truck competition than on U.S.–Canadian competition because there is a wider cost disparity between Mexican and U.S. motor carriers. In 1996, $130 million of trade was conducted between the United States and Mexico, of which 80 to 85 percent was moved by truck.

Mexican carriers legally have access to the 20-mile commercial zone on either side of the border. In December 1995 Mexican carriers were scheduled to gain full access to deliver cross-border freight throughout California, New Mexico, Texas, and Arizona. Similarly, U.S. carriers were scheduled to gain access to the six Mexican border states. With the support of the Teamsters Union, and citing safety concerns over poorly maintained Mexican trucks, the DOT was reluctant to comply with the NAFTA timetable. Mexico retaliated by effectively barring U.S. truckers from its markets by banning 53-foot trailers. As of fall 1998, restrictions on Mexican truckers had not been lifted. In the meantime, freight is streaming across the border by railroad. In 1997 KCS invested $520 million to buy a stake in Mexico's Northeast Line, while UP spent $400 million to gain control of the Pacific North Railway. As costs are lower on these lines and track infrastructure has improved, an increasing portion of the trade between Mexico and the United States is likely to move by rail.

Outlook

The near-term outlook for motor carriers is positive, as is the economic backdrop. Standard & Poor's has estimated that industrial output will grow 3.3 percent in 1998 and 1.5 percent in 1999. Through 2003 the economy is anticipated to grow between 2.5

and 3.0 percent annually. Additionally, both the truckload and the LTL segments of the for-hire industry have adjusted to deregulation. Consolidation in the LTL segment has helped stabilize freight rates. Having reined in capacity for several years, LTL carriers now have the upper hand in pricing matters. LTL rates increased 5.8 percent in 1997 and are expected to go up 2.9 percent in 1998 and 2 percent in 1999.

Despite the improvement in rates, LTL carriers continue to manage their costs aggressively and pursue only freight that contributes to the bottom line. The bloody battle for market share is now a dark chapter in the history of the trucking industry. Standard & Poor's has estimated that profits for leading LTL carriers will climb 2 percent in 1998 on top of a 384 percent gain in 1997; in 1999 profits could increase another 8 percent. This improvement, off an extremely depressed base, is deceptive. Profits remain at less than half the levels posted in 1978, before deregulation. The industry's operating ratio of 95.5 percent in 1997 and an estimated 95.6 percent in 1998 is inferior to the 94.0 percent ratio that was common before deregulation. Aggregate industry revenues for the LTL sector, which have been estimated at $20 billion in 1998 and $21 billion in 1999, should reach $23 billion by 2003.

Truckload carriers, while currently benefiting from strong profit and volume trends, face the challenge of raising wages to attract and retain drivers and sustaining higher capital costs to invest in the new equipment needed to retain drivers. Lower fuel costs in 1998 and rate hikes of 1 to 2 percent were projected to help truckload carriers increase their profits in 1998 by 25 to 30 percent. In 1999 profits could rise just 5 percent as the overbuilding of trucks and a rebound in intermodal traffic cut rates and limit volume growth. The for-hire truckload sector is projected to have revenues of $68 billion in 1998, $70 billion in 1999, and $80 billion in 2003.

Stephen R. Klein, The McGraw-Hill Companies, (212) 208-8148, November 1998.

WATER TRANSPORTATION

The U.S. water transportation industry (SIC 44) consists of companies that carry freight or passengers on the open seas or inland waterways and companies that offer lighterage and towing services, operate canals and terminals, charter vessels, and handle cargo. The major segments of the industry are deep-sea foreign transportation of freight (SIC 441), deep-sea domestic transportation of freight (SIC 442), Great Lakes and St. Lawrence Seaway transportation of freight (SIC 443), inland waterways transportation of freight (SIC 444), passenger transportation (SIC 448), and port and cargo-handling services (SIC 449).

Global Industry Trends

Three types of vessels operate in the deep-sea trade: liners, which offer scheduled service; nonliners, which carry dry cargo on demand; and tankers, which carry liquid cargo on demand. In the period 1993–1997 world liner trade increased 8.5 percent

TABLE 43-6: Water Transportation (SIC 44) Trends and Forecasts

	1993	1994	1995	1996	1997[1]	1998[2]	2002[3]	Percent Change 97–98	Percent Change 93–97	Percent Change 98–02[3]
Industry data										
Employment (thousands)	168	172	174	173	177	179	187	1.0	1.3	1.0
Real GDP ($ billion 1992)	10.4	10.9	11.0	10.7	11.2	11.4	12.4	2.0	1.9	2.0
Waterborne trade data (million metric tons)										
World trade (imports)	3,586	3,810	4,122	4,273	4,423	4,469	5,069	1.0	5.4	3.2
Liner	346	393	433	447	479	494	618	3.1	8.5	5.8
Nonliner	1,600	1,736	1,915	1,977	2,053	2,087	2,455	1.6	6.4	4.1
Tanker	1,640	1,681	1,774	1,849	1,891	1,888	1,996	–0.1	3.6	1.4
Container (million TEUs)	51	56	64	69	74	80	109	8.1	9.8	8.0
U.S. foreign trade	894	939	982	1,019	1,051	1,088	1,239	3.5	4.1	3.3
Imports	539	599	571	627	667	701	820	5.1	5.5	4.0
Liner	55	57	59	58	65	73	95	12.3	4.3	6.8
Container (million TEUs)	6.0	6.6	6.8	6.9	7.8	8.3	10.9	6.4	6.7	7.0
Nonliner	106	134	134	143	153	168	206	9.8	9.6	5.2
Tanker	378	408	378	426	449	460	519	2.4	4.4	3.1
Exports	355	340	411	392	384	386	419	0.5	2.0	2.1
Liner	60	66	77	67	69	70	82	1.4	3.5	4.0
Container (million TEUs)	5.0	5.7	6.4	6.5	7.0	7.4	9.4	5.7	8.7	6.0
Nonliner	229	228	286	279	269	271	287	0.7	4.1	1.4
Tanker	66	46	48	47	46	46	50	0.0	–8.6	2.1
North American cruise passengers (millions)	4.5	4.4	4.3	4.7	5.0	5.4	7.2	8.0	2.7	7.5
U.S. domestic trade	969	997	991	998	1,010	1,016	1,066	0.6	1.0	1.2
Domestic ocean	251	257	248	249	244	243	238	–0.5	–0.7	–0.5
Inland waterways	618	636	638	645	655	668	723	2.0	1.5	2.0
Great Lakes	100	104	105	104	111	105	105	–5.4	2.6	0.0
Passengers (million)	143	145	148	146	146	149	161	2.0	0.5	2.0
Fleet data (million metric DWT unless otherwise specified)										
World oceangoing fleet	678	687	697	719	744	755	805	1.5	2.3	1.6
Container	35	39	43	48	55	59	81	7.2	12.0	8.0
Bulk	250	251	261	271	281	284	295	1.0	3.0	1.0
Tanker	298	298	294	300	308	311	324	1.0	0.8	1.0
Other	95	99	99	100	100	101	105	1.0	1.3	1.0
North American cruise Capacity (million passengers)	5.3	5.2	5.3	5.7	5.8	6.5	8.8	12.1	2.3	7.9
Domestic Fleet										
Dry cargo ships	0.7	0.7	0.6	0.8	0.8	0.8	0.8	–0.5	3.3	–0.5
Tankers	9.4	9.1	8.1	8.6	8.2	7.7	5.6	–6.1	–3.3	–7.6
Dry cargo barges	35.1	35.0	36.2	38.7	39.9	40.3	42.1	1.0	3.3	1.1
Coastal	4.3	4.3	4.3	4.4	4.5	4.6	5.0	2.0	1.1	2.0
Great Lakes	0.4	0.3	0.3	0.4	0.4	0.4	0.4	0.0	0.0	0.0
Inland	30.5	30.4	31.7	34.0	35.0	35.3	36.7	1.0	3.5	1.0
Tank barges	9.7	10.0	10.2	10.3	10.5	10.6	11.2	1.5	2.0	1.5
Coastal	3.4	3.5	3.4	3.4	3.5	3.5	3.8	2.0	1.0	2.0
Great Lakes	0.0	0.0	0.1	0.1	0.1	0.1	0.1	0.0	0.0	0.0
Inland	6.3	6.5	6.7	6.8	6.9	7.0	7.2	1.0	2.3	1.0
Tugs and towboats (number)	5,224	5,179	5,127	5,103	5,077	5,052	4,951	–0.5	–0.5	–0.5
Coastal	1,745	1,753	1,714	1,700	1,691	1,682	1,649	–0.5	–0.8	–0.5
Great Lakes	188	190	198	208	207	206	202	–0.5	2.4	–0.5
Inland	3,291	3,236	3,215	3,195	3,179	3,163	3,100	–0.5	–0.9	–0.5
Passenger/ferries (thousands of passengers)	297	311	325	331	349	356	385	2.0	4.1	2.0

[1] Estimate.
[2] Forecast.
[3] Compound annual rate.
Source: Industry data: U.S. Bureau of Economic Analysis; World Trade: DRI/McGraw-Hill and Mercer Management Consulting, Inc., World Sea Trade Service; Cruise: *Cruise Industry News;* Domestic: U.S. Army Corps of Engineers.

per year, nonliner (bulk) trade increased 6.4 percent per year, and tanker trade increased 3.6 percent per year. Container trade, a major segment of liner trade, increased 9.8 percent per year from 1993 to 1997.

Steady growth in world waterborne trade contributed to increased earnings for merchant vessels in the mid-1990s (see Figure 43-2). However, despite continued trade growth, earnings for liners and bulk vessels have fallen in recent years. These declines can be attributed to a surge in fleet capacities (see Table 43-6).

Several factors are driving new construction in the world merchant fleet, including the age of the existing fleet. New vessels are being built to replace old ones and, in the case of tankers, to comply with double-hull regulations imposed by the United States and the International Maritime Organization (IMO). Product tankers are also being built to accommodate the expansion of refinery capacity in the Middle East and southeast Asia. New construction in the liner segment of the fleet is being driven by the deployment of large [4,000-plus 20-foot equivalent units (TEUs)], fast (20 or more knots) containerships in the mainstream liner trades (United States–Europe, United States–Far East, and Europe–Far East), and containerization of intraregional trade.

Factors Affecting Future U.S. Industry Growth
U.S. waterborne trade (both foreign and domestic) drives the growth of the U.S. water transportation industry. From 1993 to 1997, U.S. foreign waterborne trade grew 4.1 percent per year and domestic waterborne trade increased only 1 percent. The recovery of U.S. grain exports from the 1993–1994 floods had a substantial impact on the industry, increasing both nonliner exports and long-haul domestic barge shipments on the inland waterways.

The Jones Act (Section 27 of the Merchant Marine Act of 1920) precludes foreign-owned and foreign-flagged vessels from participating in U.S. domestic trade. Thus, U.S.-based companies receive all payments for domestic water transportation, including payments for port and cargo-handling services. However, both foreign and U.S. companies receive transportation payments from international trade.

In 1997 U.S. importers paid over $11.4 billion in freight payments to foreign carriers, representing a balance of payments outflow (see Table 43-7). In that year foreign carriers paid about $7.7 billion for U.S. port and cargo-handling services, representing a balance of payments inflow. U.S. carriers received over $4.5 billion in freight payments from foreign importers but paid over $2.2 billion for foreign port and cargo-handling services. That is, net receipts of the U.S. port industry largely offset the negative balance in the freight account. With receipts from and payments for passenger fares and charter hires, the U.S. water transportation industry had a $1.9 billion deficit in its balance of payments in 1997.

U.S. Industry Growth Projections for the Next 5 Years
The contribution to the nation's real gross domestic product (GDP) from water transportation is expected to increase about 2 percent per year from 1998 to 2002. This is significantly less than the projected growth in international waterborne trade but more than the projected growth in domestic trade. The primary drag on the industry will be the decline in Alaska North Slope production of crude oil, which will reduce domestic ocean crude oil movements.

Employment in water transportation is expected to increase about 1 percent per year from 1998 to 2002. In water transportation, employment growth historically has not kept pace with real GDP growth—a sign that productivity is going up—and this relationship is expected to continue.

Global Industry Prospects
The growth of world deep-sea trade, which is projected at 3.2 percent per year over the next 5 years, will generally exceed fleet growth (1.6 percent per year) in that period, improving earnings for water carriers.

The rate at which tankers and bulk carriers are scrapped (broken up) is expected to accelerate as vessels built during the boom in the years 1974–1978 reach 25-plus years in service (see Figure 43-3). The age of the fleet is only one factor in the replacement of tankers. Also at work here are U.S. and IMO safety and environmental regulations. The Oil Pollution Act of 1990 (OPA-90) mandates that single-hull tankers that serve U.S. ports be phased out in stages (based on age and size) beginning in 1995. IMO regulations for tankers that serve foreign ports require that new tankers delivered after July 6, 1996, have double hulls and that 25-year-old single-hull tankers be retrofitted with double hulls beginning in 1995. As of the end of 1997, Clarkson's Tanker Register (a comprehensive registry of seagoing tankers) reported that only 22 percent of the world's tankers were equipped with double hulls, up from 12 percent at the beginning of 1995.

In terms of safety, the IMO Safety of Life at Sea (SOLAS) convention requires that all ships of at least 500 gross registered

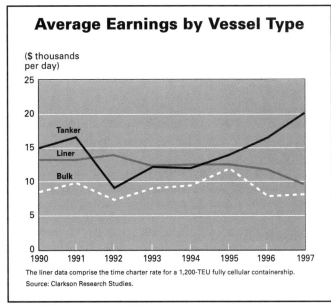

Average Earnings by Vessel Type

($ thousands per day)

Tanker
Liner
Bulk

1990 1991 1992 1993 1994 1995 1996 1997

The liner data comprise the time charter rate for a 1,200-TEU fully cellular containership.
Source: Clarkson Research Studies.

FIGURE 43-2

TABLE 43-7: U.S. Balance of Payments in Water Transportation
($ millions)

	1992	1993	1994	1995	1996	1997
Receipts						
Passenger fares	176	237	287	285	329	329
Export freight	3,980	3,951	4,447	5,213	4,647	4,545
Port expenditures	7,192	7,477	7,899	8,299	7,788	7,751
Charter hire	156	104	56	68	57	81
Total	11,504	11,769	12,689	13,865	12,821	12,706
Payments						
Passenger fares	301	341	353	353	453	453
Import freight	9,269	10,030	10,967	11,132	10,930	11,433
Port expenditures	2,029	2,010	2,326	2,553	2,230	2,202
Charter hire	563	529	513	486	432	491
Total	12,162	12,910	14,159	14,524	14,045	14,579
Balance	−658	−1,141	−1,470	−659	−1,224	−1,873

Source: U.S. Department of Commerce, Bureau of Economic Analysis.

tons meet International Safety Management (ISM)-mandated standards. Passenger ships, tankers, bulk carriers, and high-speed cargo ships had to be ISM-certified by July 1, 1998. Other cargo ships must be ISM-certified by July 1, 2002. Vessels that do not have ISM certification will be denied access to U.S. ports. So far, ISM certification has not restricted the shipping capacity available for deep-sea trade.

For passenger vessels, the Safety of Life at Sea convention requires significant changes in shipboard infrastructure. By 1997 ships were required to have low-level lighting, smoke detection, and alarm, and sprinkler systems. By 2000 ships must have steel frames in stairways, ventilation ducts equipped with fire dampers, and fire-extinguishing systems for certain machinery. For many shipowners the steel-frame stairway requirement in 2000 represents a significant expense and is likely to accelerate the removal of older vessels from service.

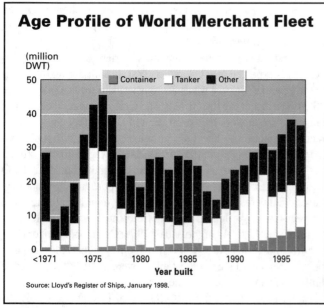

Age Profile of World Merchant Fleet

(million DWT)

Legend: Container, Tanker, Other

Year built

Source: Lloyd's Register of Ships, January 1998.

FIGURE 43-3

Reflecting the fact that expansion of global refinery capacity has been concentrated in crude oil producing areas (the Middle East and Asia), it is expected that growth of the product tanker fleet will be faster than that of the crude oil tanker fleet and that the average size of product tankers will grow in response to long-haul shipping requirements.

The containership fleet is expected to grow at a significantly higher rate than are other vessel types as larger containerships are introduced into mainstream east-west trade and containerships continue to replace traditional breakbulk ships in the world liner trades. The containerization of fleets will occur most rapidly in intraregional trades.

Freight Transportation

Four of the major segments of the U.S. water transportation industry carry freight: deep-sea foreign transportation, deep-sea domestic transportation, inland waterways transportation, and Great Lakes and St. Lawrence Seaway transportation.

Deep-Sea Foreign Transportation. This segment of the water transportation industry carries imports and exports on the deep seas between the United States and foreign ports. Servicing this segment are liners, nonliners, and tankers. Between 1993 and 1997 U.S. liner trade increased 3.9 percent per year, U.S. nonliner trade increased 5.9 percent, and U.S. tanker trade increased 2.8 percent. U.S. container trade increased 7.7 percent in that period, reflecting the continuing containerization of U.S. liner trades.

Liner vessels, largely containerships with some breakbulk and roll-on/roll-off ships, operate between advertised ports of loading and discharge on a regular basis. In 1997 liner service accounted for 13 percent of U.S. waterborne trade on a metric ton basis but 66 percent on a value basis.

Containerships generally move faster and spend much less time in port than do traditional breakbulk ships. Liners carry a variety of manufactured and semimanufactured products. With containerization, different commodities are handled in the same way, facilitating cargo transfers. As a result, highly specialized line-haul/feeder services, connecting carrier services, vessel-sharing agreements, and intermodal services have been developed, increasing carrier productivity in the liner trades.

As of the end of 1997 approximately 39 percent of the containership capacity [in deadweight tons (DWT)] deployed in U.S. liner trade was deployed in round-the-world (RTW)/tricontinental services, up from 31 percent 4 years earlier. Containership capacity deployed in RTW/tricontinental services increased 89 percent. The average age of the containership fleet deployed in these trades is 7 years, compared with 10 years for vessels in other services.

The growth in RTW/tricontinental services reflects the fact that major shippers prefer shipping lines that operate on a worldwide scale. Shipping lines want to be able to offer a global service package with operations on all the major routes (transatlantic, transpacific, and Europe–Far East) supplemented by operations or operating agreements covering north-south trades.

In contrast to liner vessels, nonliner dry cargo vessels do not operate on fixed schedules or itineraries; instead, they are hired for specific jobs. In 1997, of the 422 million metric tons of nonliner cargoes (imports and exports), 21 percent were grains, 19 percent were coal and coke, and 13 percent were ores and scrap. These trades are affected by general economic conditions as well as external shocks, such as midwestern floods (grains in 1993–1994), United Mine Workers' strikes (coal in 1994), and the expansion of trade with China (grains in 1995).

Tankers carry liquid cargoes in bulk: crude oil, petroleum products, liquid chemicals, liquefied gases, vegetable oils, water, and wine. In 1997 crude oil accounted for 69 percent of all U.S. tanker cargoes and petroleum products accounted for 24 percent. In 1995 there was a decline of 7 percent in tanker imports primarily as a result of an increase in world petroleum prices and a drawdown in domestic stocks. New EPA rules, however, have reduced the cost of producing Clean Air Act–compliant gasoline at Caribbean refineries and have contributed to a recovery in U.S. tanker imports.

The U.S. liner trade is expected to grow at a rate significantly higher than the rates for the nonliner and tanker trades. In the period 1998–2002 U.S. liner trade (imports and exports) is expected to grow 5.5 percent per year, compared with 2.9 percent for nonliner trade and 3.5 percent for tanker trade. This is attributable to the fact that reductions in trade barriers, privatization, and technological advances in transportation, distribution, and communications have a more immediate positive impact on demand for manufactured products, which are shipped in liner service, than on demand for primary commodities.

Overall, U.S. foreign deep-sea trade is expected to grow 3.3 percent per year in the period 1998–2002, down from 4.3 percent in the period 1993–1997. The 1993–1997 growth rates reflect recoveries in tanker imports and nonliner (bulk) exports from the temporary disruptions of the mid-1990s.

Deep-Sea Domestic Transportation. This segment of the market includes carriers that transport freight on the deep seas between U.S. ports, including noncontiguous U.S. territories.

Of the 244 million metric tons moved in the domestic ocean trade in 1997, petroleum products accounted for 44 percent, crude petroleum for 29 percent, chemicals for 6 percent, and coal for 6 percent. Traditional liner cargoes move primarily in the noncontiguous trades (U.S. mainland to Alaska, Hawaii, Puerto Rico, and Guam) on both self-propelled and barge vessels.

Total cargo moving in the domestic deep-sea trade has been declining steadily in the 1990s, reflecting the decline in Alaska North Slope crude oil shipments (see Figure 43-4). Domestic deep-sea trade declined about 0.7 percent per year from 1993 to 1997. In that period, crude oil shipments declined 6 percent per year while other shipments increased 2 percent per year. Furthermore, the decline in long-haul crude oil shipments contributed to a 23 percent decline in average haul (miles) in the deep-sea domestic trade from 1993 to 1997.

In the period 1998–2000 total domestic deep-sea shipments are expected to decline about 0.5 percent per year. Most of that decline will be in shipments of crude oil, which are expected to fall about 5 percent per year. Shipments of other commodities are expected to increase about 1 percent per year. For other commodities, the expected growth rate is below the 1993–1997 growth rate, primarily because of an expected recovery in petroleum product imports.

Starting in 1995, the Clean Air Act amendments of 1990 required that reformulated (oxygenated) gasoline be used year-round in high–carbon monoxide areas, principally on the Atlantic and Pacific coasts. According to the U.S. Department of Energy, methyl tertiary butyl ether (MTBE) production capacity is concentrated at U.S. Gulf refineries. MTBE-gasoline blends cannot be shipped through pipelines from U.S. Gulf refineries to the U.S. west coast. Consequently, long-haul (5,000 to 6,500 nautical miles) product tanker shipments of reformulated gasoline from the U.S. Gulf to the U.S. west coast doubled from 1995 to 1997.

While the U.S. Gulf–west coast petroleum product trade represents a significant source of demand for product tanker ser-

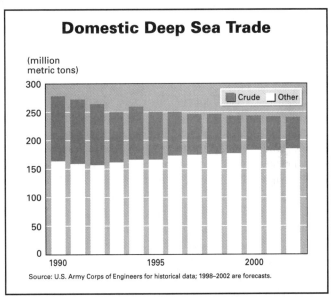

Domestic Deep Sea Trade

(million metric tons)

Source: U.S. Army Corps of Engineers for historical data; 1998–2002 are forecasts.

FIGURE 43-4

vices, it accounts for only 1 percent of domestic ocean shipments in terms of metric tons and therefore will have little impact on the forecast discussed above.

In 1997, the fleets serving U.S. domestic deep-sea trade included 39 dry cargo vessels (0.8 million DWT), 122 tankers (8.2 million DWT), 3,393 dry cargo barges (4.8 million DWT), and 669 tank barges (3.4 million DWT). The capacity of the dry cargo vessel fleet is expected to remain at the 1997 level through 2002, reflecting limited growth in U.S. noncontiguous trade.

While some limited construction of crude oil tankers and product tankers is under way for domestic trade, the capacity of the tanker fleet, particularly crude oil carriers (most with a dead-weight capacity of 70,000-plus metric tons), is expected to decline about 7 percent per year from 1998 to 2002. At the end of 1997 approximately 72 percent of the crude oil fleet was at least 20 years old. A significant part of this fleet probably will be scrapped or removed from service in 1998–1999 as the domestic crude oil trade continues to decline and these ships approach their next special survey and/or OPA-90 phase-out dates.

The capacities of the dry cargo and tank barge fleets are expected to increase about 2 percent per year from 1998 to 2002. The projected growth in tank barge capacity reflects increasing demand for barges for intracoastal and short-haul intercoastal shipments of petroleum products. The projected growth of the dry cargo barge fleet reflects an increase in demand for container-trailer barges for short-haul noncontiguous trade (e.g., Florida–Puerto Rico) and for penetration of the overland (truck and rail) container markets.

Inland Waterways. In 1997, 655 million metric tons moved on the inland waterways, including the intracoastal waterways on the Atlantic and Gulf coasts. Most of it (96 percent) moved by barge. The primary commodities were coal (27 percent), petroleum (27 percent), crude materials (20 percent), and farm products (12 percent) [see Table 43-8].

However, in terms of demand for transport services, farm products accounted for 28 percent of the ton-miles on the inland waterways in 1997. The average haul for inland shipments of farm products was 988 miles, compared with 332 miles for all other inland shipments. The temporary surge in shipments of farm products (grain exports) in 1995 had a significant positive impact on the demand for inland dry cargo barge services and on freight rates (see Figure 43-5).

The projected growth rate for inland waterways trades (2 percent per year) is higher than actual performance in the period 1993–1997 (1.5 percent), largely as a result of a projected increase in domestic consumption of eastern coal. In the 1990s many utilities complied with the emissions requirements of the Clean Air Act of 1990 by substituting low-sulfur western coal carried primarily by rail for high-sulfur eastern coal carried primarily by barge. To satisfy the act's more stringent year 2000 emissions requirements, utilities will be forced to install emissions-reducing equipment. As this equipment is put into use, demand for eastern coal and related barge services will increase, as is already evident in the 6 percent increase that occurred in domestic coal trade from 1995 to 1997.

TABLE 43-8: Major Commodities Shipped on the Inland Waterways in 1997[1]

	Billions of Metric Ton-Miles	Millions of Metric Tons	Average Miles
Coal and coke	66.1	175.8	376
Petroleum	33.7	177.9	189
Chemicals	27.6	56.8	486
Crude materials	45.2	128.9	351
Primary manufactures	18.6	23.6	789
Food and farm products	75.7	76.6	988
Manufactured products	1.0	10.7	94
Waste and scrap	0.3	5.0	60
Total, excluding food and farm products	192.6	578.7	332
Total	268.3	655.3	410

[1] Includes intraport shipments.
Source: U.S. Army Corps of Engineers.

In 1997 the inland barge fleet consisted of 25,997 dry cargo barges (35 million DWT) and 3,384 tank barges (6.9 million DWT). Total inland barge capacity increased 6.2 percent from 1995 to 1996, the largest annual increase in capacity since 1980–1981. The 1996 increase was largely a function of the 1995 surge in barge freight rates that limited dry cargo barge scrapping and led to a sharp increase in orders of new dry cargo barges for delivery in 1996 and 1997 (see Figure 43-6). In contrast, underlying a good part of the 1980–1981 increase were new deliveries spurred by investment tax credits.

Inland tank barge capacity is expected to grow about 1 percent per year from 1995 to 2002, reflecting modest growth in U.S. consumption of petroleum products.

Dry cargo barge capacity on the inland waterways is expected to increase about 1 percent per year from 1996 to 2002. Capacity growth will be limited by the following factors:

- Scrapping, since approximately 41 percent of the inland barge fleet will be at least 25 years old by 2002.

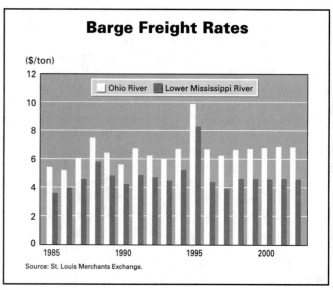

Barge Freight Rates

Source: St. Louis Merchants Exchange.

FIGURE 43-5

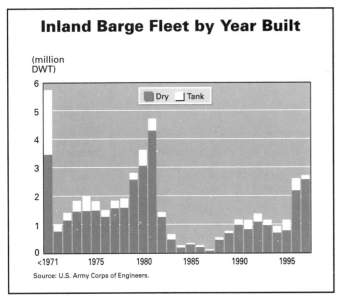

Inland Barge Fleet by Year Built

(million DWT)

Source: U.S. Army Corps of Engineers.

FIGURE 43-6

- Low freight rates in 1996–1997, which tend to increase scrappings and limit the industry's financial resources for new barge construction.

- Weather-related factors, which contribute to unexpected year-to-year fluctuations in traffic and barge freight rates.

Great Lakes. Ships in this segment of the water transportation industry move freight on the Great Lakes and the St Lawrence Seaway, either between U.S. ports or between U.S. ports and Canadian ports.

In 1997, 111 million metric tons of cargo moved on the Great Lakes. The major commodities were iron ore (49 percent), limestone (24 percent), and coal (18 percent). Iron ore and limestone are used in steel production, and coal fuels electric plants. Ninety-one percent of the trade is moved in dry bulk ships.

Shipments (imports plus exports) between U.S. and Canadian ports on the Great Lakes amounted to 34.5 million metric tons in 1997, and projected growth rates are included with those for other U.S. foreign trade. The major commodities were iron ore and scrap (27 percent), coal (24 percent), and sand, stone, and gravel (15 percent).

At the end of 1997 the U.S. Great Lakes fleet consisted of 129 dry cargo vessels (1.9 million DWT), 5 tankers (0.02 million DWT), 258 dry cargo barges (0.4 million DWT), and 41 tank barges (0.1 million DWT). From 1996 to 1997 Great Lakes traffic increased 6.7 percent to 111 million metric tons. In the mid-1990s the trade has been in the range of 104 to 105 million metric tons. The 1996–1997 increase was due largely to abnormally mild weather which facilitated shipping on the Lakes in the early spring of 1997. Thus, the demand for Great Lakes shipping capacity has remained fairly constant in the mid-1990s, and this pattern is expected to continue in the period 1998–2002. Great Lakes fleet capacity is therefore expected to remain at about its 1997 level through 2002.

Tugs and Towboats. The tug and towboat fleet consists of coastal tugs and inland towboats (pushboats). Coastal tugs are used in ship assisting, tanker escorting, barge towing, and salvage. Some recently built coastal tugs have oil spill skimming equipment, contributing to their usefulness in the U.S. tanker and tank barge trades. In contrast, inland towboats are used primarily for pushing barges.

The overall tug and towboat fleet in terms of the number of vessels declined steadily in the mid-1990s. This decline can be attributed to the fact that new tugs and towboats are replacing an aging fleet of smaller (less than 3,000 horsepower), less efficient vessels. This trend of improved productivity is expected to continue over the next 5 years.

Water Transportation of Passengers: Cruise Ships and Ferries

Cruise ships are floating resorts which tend to offer round trips of 3 days or more. Ferries tend to convey passengers on daily one-way trips between two or more points.

Cruise Ships. After a 2-year decline in passengers in the mid-1990s, North American cruise passenger growth increased at an average rate of 7.8 percent per year from 1995 to 1997 (the long-term average rate of growth for the period 1980–1997 was 7.6 percent per year).

The recovery in passenger growth is due primarily to two factors. The first is the introduction of new ships. The market traditionally has been driven by such new ships, which attract new and repeat passengers. New ships offer new technologies and a rich mix of cabins and amenities. Thirty-three of the 122 cruise ships serving U.S. ports in 1998 were introduced as new-builds after 1995. An additional 26 newbuilds will be introduced from 1998 to 2002.

The second factor is consolidation. The industry has consolidated through acquisitions and mergers. For instance, in 1998 the top four North American cruise lines controlled 82 percent of North American cruise capacity, up from 61 percent in 1995. In fact, these companies control an even larger share of the mar-

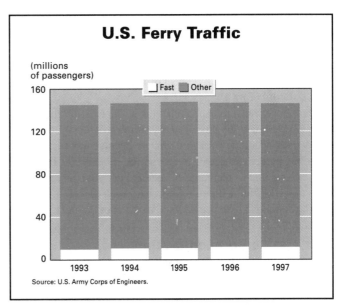

U.S. Ferry Traffic

(millions of passengers)

Source: U.S. Army Corps of Engineers.

FIGURE 43-7

TABLE 43-9: Top 20 U.S. Ports for Waterborne Commerce of the United States
(million metric tons)

Port	1994			1995			1996		
	Domestic	Foreign	Total	Domestic	Foreign	Total	Domestic	Foreign	Total
South Louisiana	89.2	78.5	167.7	97.1	88.5	185.5	96.2	76.0	172.2
Houston	57.6	72.8	130.4	57.8	64.9	122.7	55.4	79.0	134.4
New York	69.8	44.6	114.4	64.7	43.6	108.2	68.1	51.3	119.4
New Orleans	34.2	32.3	66.5	34.5	35.4	69.9	33.4	42.5	75.9
Baton Rouge	40.5	37.7	78.2	41.2	34.7	75.8	41.0	32.5	73.5
Corpus Christi	22.2	48.6	70.9	23.5	40.5	64.0	21.6	51.3	73.0
Valdez	77.2	0.0	77.2	73.3	0.1	73.5	68.0	1.9	69.9
Plaquemine	39.9	18.9	58.8	44.0	22.1	66.1	41.9	18.8	60.7
Long Beach	21.4	29.9	51.3	17.9	30.4	48.3	20.3	32.7	53.0
Texas City	18.0	22.3	40.3	17.4	28.3	45.7	19.1	32.0	51.2
Pittsburgh	44.5	0.0	44.5	44.3	0.0	44.3	46.2	0	46.2
Mobile	22.2	18.6	40.8	22.8	23.5	46.3	23.0	23.1	46.2
Tampa	28.6	18.5	47.1	28.8	18.2	47.1	29.4	15.2	44.7
Norfolk Harbor	9.3	32.2	41.5	9.3	33.9	43.3	9.4	35.3	44.7
Lake Charles	18.7	25.1	43.8	17.9	24.3	42.3	17.9	26.6	44.5
Los Angeles	16.0	23.2	39.1	17.3	24.9	42.2	16.2	25.2	41.5
Baltimore	13.8	23.9	37.6	11.9	28.7	40.6	12.7	26.9	39.5
Philadelphia	13.0	24.0	36.9	11.6	25.3	36.8	11.8	26.2	38.0
Duluth-Superior	29.4	8.5	37.9	31.7	9.2	40.8	27.5	10.1	37.6
Port Arthur	5.6	35.7	41.4	6.2	39.0	45.2	6.0	27.9	33.7
Total, top 20	671.1	595.3	1,266.3	673.2	615.5	1,288.6	665.2	634.6	1,299.8
Total, all ports	1,918.8	1,012.2	2,931.0	1,907.8	1,040.9	2,948.7	1,916.4	1,073.2	2,989.6
Top 25, percent of total	35.0	58.8	43.2	35.3	59.1	43.7	34.7	59.1	43.5

Source: U.S. Army Corps of Engineers, *Waterborne Commerce of the United States.*

ket because their vessels are newer and tend to sail fuller than do those of smaller lines. Consolidation has provided the top companies with more financial strength and marketing muscle to promote their ships and control costs, contributing to the stability of the industry in the late 1990s.

Ferries. At the end of 1997 there were 1,204 ferry vessels serving U.S. waterways; 176 of these were fast ferries, capable of speeds of at least 25 knots. In terms of passenger capacity, 34 percent of the overall fleet was built before 1975, and a substantial number of these vessels will be replaced over the next 5 years. In contrast, only 8 percent of fast ferry passenger capacity was built before 1975.

Fast ferries have replaced other ferries on existing routes and have enabled new longer-haul ferry routes to open up. In 1997, fast ferries accounted for 7.4 percent of total ferry traffic, up from 5.8 percent in 1993. In the period 1993–1997 fast ferry traffic (passengers) increased 6.8 percent per year. In that period other ferry traffic declined 0.1 percent per year (see Figure 43-7). These trends are expected to continue over the next 5 years.

Port and Cargo-Handling Services

This segment of the water transportation industry handles foreign and domestic marine cargo from the time cargo (for or from a vessel) arrives at a dock, pier, terminal, staging area, or

TABLE 43-10: Top 20 U.S. Container Ports
(thousand TEUs)

Port	1993	1994	1995	1996	1997
Long Beach	1,543	1,939	2,137	2,357	2,673
Los Angeles	1,627	1,786	1,849	1,873	2,085
New York	1,306	1,404	1,537	1,533	1,738
Charleston	579	655	758	801	955
Seattle	781	967	993	939	953
Oakland	772	879	919	803	843
Norfolk	519	570	647	681	770
Miami	469	497	497	505	624
Houston	392	419	489	538	609
Tacoma	547	510	545	506	551
Savannah	406	418	445	456	529
Port Everglades	230	281	403	422	453
Baltimore	291	310	305	276	260
New Orleans	188	197	206	204	231
Portland	179	233	239	210	210
Jacksonville	142	151	184	185	198
San Juan	82	113	134	154	143
Gulfport	90	97	108	106	121
West Palm Beach	89	91	90	101	112
Wilmington, DE	99	83	83	106	103
Total, top 20 ports	10,331	11,600	12,568	12,756	14,161
Total, all ports	10,971	12,238	13,173	13,328	14,794
Top 20 ports, percent of total	94.2	94.8	95.4	95.7	95.7

Source: *Journal of Commerce*, PIERS.

in-transit area until the cargo is loaded or unloaded. This segment also involves the operation and maintenance of piers, docks, and associated buildings and facilities.

In 1997 a total of 350 U.S. ports handled foreign and/or domestic waterborne trade. By tonnage, the 20 leading coastal and inland ports handled 43 percent of waterborne trade that year. The leading ports accounted for 59 percent of U.S. foreign trade but only 35 percent of U.S. domestic trade (see Table 43-9).

International container trade through U.S. ports is highly concentrated. The 20 leading container ports accounted for just under 96 percent of container traffic, measured in 20-foot equivalent units moving in U.S. foreign trade in 1997. The top 10 ports accounted for almost 80 percent of the total TEUs (see Table 43-10).

Three of the top five container ports in the United States are on the west coast. Two of them—Los Angeles and Long Beach—had the largest absolute growth in container traffic between 1993 and 1997 (measured in TEUs), but Houston, Jacksonville, Charleston, Port Everglades, and San Juan showed the largest rates of growth over that period, reflecting high growth in U.S.–Latin American container trade.

Russell Byington, U.S. Department of Transportation, Maritime Administration, (202) 366-2278, August 1998.

■ REFERENCES

Airlines

The Airline Monitor, January–February 1998, ESG Aviation Services, P.O. Box 1781, Ponte Vedra Beach, FL 32004.

Aviation Daily, 1200 G Street, NW, Washington, DC 20005.

Aviation Week & Space Technology, 1200 G Street, NW, Washington, DC 20005.

Boeing: Current Market Outlook, Boeing Company, P.O. Box 3707, Seattle, WA 98055.

FAA Aviation Forecasts, Fiscal Years 1998–2009, U.S. Department of Transportation, Federal Aviation Administration, Office of Aviation Policy and Plans, Washington, DC 20591.

The Impact of Recent Events on the Asia Pacific Aviation Market and Prospects for Future Growth to 2001, International Air Transport Association, Aviation Information and Research Department, London, March 1998.

1996/1997 World Air Cargo Forecast, Boeing Commercial Airplane Group Marketing, P.O. Box 33707, MS 75-14, Seattle, WA 98124-2207.

1997 World Air Freight Industry Analysis and Forecast, MergeGlobal, Inc., 3 Balston Plaza, 1100 North Glebe Road, Suite 720, Arlington, VA 22201.

Outlook for Air Transport to the Year 2005, Circular 270, International Civil Aviation Organization, 999 University Street, Montreal, Quebec, Canada H3C 5H7.

Airlines Interviews

Brian Clancy, Principal, MergeGlobal, Inc., Arlington, VA.

Thomas Clark, Vice President, Aerospace Group, Makino, Mason, OH.

Walter Coleman, President, Regional Airline Association, Washington, DC.

Edmund S. Greenslet, President, ESG Aviation Services, Ponte Vedra Beach, FL.

Pierre J. Jeanniot, Director-General, International Air Transport Association, Montreal and Geneva.

David Swierenga, Chief Economist, Air Transport Association of America, Washington, DC.

Vernon F. Thomas, Manager, Market Analysis and Management Information, GE Aircraft Engines, Cincinnati, OH.

U.K. Wickrama, Forecast Branch, International Civil Aviation Organization, Montreal.

Railroads

Accident/Incident Bulletin (annual), Office of Safety, Federal Railroad Administration, U.S. Department of Transportation, 400 Seventh Street, SW, Washington, DC 20590. (202) 493-6211.

Amtrak Annual Report, National Railroad Passenger Corporation (Amtrak), 400 North Capitol Street, Washington, DC 20001. (202) 906-3939.

Analysis of Class I Railroads (annual), Policy, Legislation and Economics Department, Association of American Railroads, 50 F Street, NW, Washington, DC 20001. (202) 639-2211.

Directory of Transportation Data Sources (annual), Bureau of Transportation Statistics, U.S. Department of Transportation, 400 Seventh Street, SW, Washington, DC 20590. (202) 366-DATA.

Employment and Earnings (monthly), Bureau of Labor Statistics, U.S. Department of Labor, Washington, DC 20212. (202) 606-6555 or (202) 606-6373.

Enhancing Rail Safety Now and into the 21st Century: The Federal Railroad Administration's Safety Programs and Initiatives, A Report to Congress, October 1996, Office of Safety, Federal Railroad Administration, U.S. Department of Transportation, 400 Seventh Street, SW, Washington, DC 20590. (202) 493-6211.

Freight Commodity Statistics (annual), Policy, Legislation and Economics Department, Association of American Railroads, 50 F Street, NW, Washington, DC 20001. (202) 639-2211.

High-Speed Ground Transportation for America, August 1996, Federal Railroad Administration, U.S. Department of Transportation, 400 Seventh Street, SW, Washington, DC 20590. (202) 493-6379.

Highway-Rail Crossing Accident/Incident and Inventory Bulletin (annual), Office of Safety, Federal Railroad Administration, U.S. Department of Transportation, 400 Seventh Street, SW, Washington, DC 20590. (202) 493-6211.

Intercity Freight and Passenger Rail: State and Local Project Reference Guide, September 1996, Office of Policy and Program Development, Federal Railroad Administration, U.S. Department of Transportation, 400 Seventh Street, SW, Washington, DC 20590. (202) 493-6410.

Intermodal Freight Transportation, vol. 1: *Overview of Impediments, Data Sources for Intermodal Transportation Planning, and Annotated Bibliography* (DOT-T-96-04), and vol. 2: *Fact Sheet and Federal Aid Eligibility* (DOT-T-96-05), December 1995, Federal Highway Administration, U.S. Department of Transportation, 400 Seventh Street, SW, Washington, DC 20590. (202) 366-9236.

National Transportation Statistics (annual), Bureau of Transportation Statistics, U.S. Department of Transportation, 400 Seventh Street, SW, Washington, DC 20590. (202) 366-DATA.

1993 Commodity Flow Survey: State Summaries, September 1996, Bureau of Transportation Statistics, U.S. Department of Transportation, 400 Seventh Street, SW, Washington, DC 20590. (202) 366-DATA.

1993 Commodity Flow Survey: United States, October 1996, U.S. Department of Commerce, Economics and Statistics Administration, Bureau of the Census, Commodity Flow Survey Branch, Services Division, Washington, DC 20233. (301) 457-2788 or (301) 457-2114.

North American Transportation Quarterly (formerly *Transportation Monitor;* monthly), Standard & Poor's DRI, 24 Hartwell Avenue, Lexington, MA 02173. (800) 933-3374.

PPI [Producer Price Index] Detailed Report (monthly), Bureau of Labor Statistics, U.S. Department of Labor, Washington, DC 20212. (202) 606-7705.

Privatization of Intercity Rail Passenger Service in the United States, March 1998, Federal Railroad Administration, U.S. Department of Transportation, 400 Seventh Street, SW, Washington, DC 20590. (202) 493-6379.

Profiles of U.S. Railroads (annual), Policy, Legislation and Economics Department, Association of American Railroads, 50 F Street, NW, Washington, DC 20001. (202) 639-2211.

Rail Rates Continue Multi-Year Decline, February 1998, Office of Economics, Environmental Analysis and Administration, Surface Transportation Board, 1925 K Street, NW, Washington, DC 20423. (202) 565-1596.

Railroad Facts (annual), Policy, Legislation and Economics Department, Association of American Railroads, 50 F Street, NW, Washington, DC 20001. (202) 639-2211.

Railroad Ten-Year Trends (annual), Policy, Legislation and Economics Department, Association of American Railroads, 50 F Street, NW, Washington, DC 20001. (202) 639-2211.

Railway Age (monthly), Editorial and Executive Offices, 345 Hudson Street, New York, NY 10014. (212) 620-7233. Circulation: (800) 895-4389.

Safety Assurance and Compliance Program Report for CSX Transportation, Inc., Federal Railroad Administration, U.S. Department of Transportation, 400 Seventh Street, SW, Washington, DC 20590. (202) 493-6244.

Safety Assurance and Compliance Program Report for Union Pacific Railroad, Federal Railroad Administration, U.S. Department of Transportation, 400 Seventh Street, SW, Washington, DC 20590. (202) 493-6244.

Short-Term Energy Outlook Quarterly Projections, Energy Information Administration, U.S. Department of Energy, Washington, DC 20585. (202) 586-8800.

Sources of Financial Improvement in the U.S. Rail Industry, 1966–1995, by Carl D. Martland, Massachusetts Institute of Technology, *Transportation Research Forum Proceedings, 39th Annual Meeting, 1997,* vol. 1, pp. 58–86.

Traffic World (weekly), 741 National Press Building, Washington, DC 20045. (202) 383-6140. Circulation: (800) 245-8723.

Transportation Expressions 1996, Bureau of Transportation Statistics, U.S. Department of Transportation, 400 Seventh Street, SW, Washington, DC 20590. (202) 366-DATA.

Transportation in America (annual), Eno Transportation Foundation, Inc., One Farragut Square South, Washington, DC 20006. (202) 879-4700.

Transportation Review: Rail Traffic Focus (annual) (now North American Commodity Flow Outlook), Standard & Poor's DRI, 24 Hartwell Avenue, Lexington, MA 02173. (800) 933-3374.

Transportation Statistics Annual Report (annual), Bureau of Transportation Statistics, U.S. Department of Transportation, 400 Seventh Street, SW, Washington, DC 20590. (202) 366-DATA.

The Ultimate ICCTA [Interstate Commerce Commission Termination Act] Outline, by Mark J. Andrews and Richard H. Streeter, *The Transportation Lawyer,* vol. 5, no. 1, July 1996, pp. 38–52.

Selected World Wide Web Sites

Association of American Railroads: http://www.aar.org for the web sites of the Class I railroads and AAR speeches, press releases, data, catalog of publications and services.

Bureau of Transportation Statistics, U.S. Department of Transportation: http://www.bts.gov for national transportation library; geographic information systems; BTS programs, products and services; and searchable databases.

Federal Railroad Administration, U.S. Department of Transportation: http://www.fra.dot.gov for news releases, public education campaigns and programs, safety data; http://www.fra.dot.gov/hsgt/ for information on high-speed rail passenger transportation.

U.S. Department of Transportation: http://www.dot.gov for news and press releases, DOT web search, browse DOT modal administrations, what's new, transportation and government Internet sites.

Additional Department of Transportation Sources

The Bureau of Transportation Services provides the Statistical Information Line at (800) 853-1351; Fax-On-Demand at (800) 671-8012; and technical assistance for customers experiencing difficulties in accessing or using BTS electronic products at (800) 366-6664.

Trucking

American Trucking Trends, American Trucking Associations, 2200 Mill Road, Alexandria, VA 22314. (703) 838-1799.

Commercial Carrier Journal, Chilton Co., 201 King of Prussia Road, Radnor, PA 19089. (610) 964-4513.

Distribution, Chilton Co., 1 Chilton Way, Radnor, PA 19089. (610) 964-4386.

Financial & Operating Statistics, 1995 Motor Carrier Annual Report, American Trucking Associations, 2200 Mill Road, Alexandria, VA 22314. (703) 838-1793.

Journal of Commerce, 2 World Trade Center, 27th Floor, New York, NY 10048. (212) 837-7000.

Logistics Management, Cahners Publishing Co., 275 Washington Street, Newton, MA 02158. (617) 558-4473, www.logisticsmgmt.com.

Standard & Poor's Industry Survey: Commercial Transportation, 1998 ed., 25 Broadway, New York, NY 10004. (212) 208-8148.

Traffic World, Journal of Commerce Inc., 1230 National Press Building, Washington, DC 20045. (202) 783-1101, www.trafficworld.com.

Transportation & Distribution, Penton Publishing Inc., 1100 Superior Avenue, Cleveland, OH 44114-2543. (216) 696-7000.

Transport Topics, American Trucking Associations, 2200 Mill Road, Alexandria, VA 22314. (703) 838-1781.

Water Transportation

Annual Energy Outlook, 1997, Energy Information Administration, Washington, DC, January 1998.

Bond, Mary, ed., "Cruise and Passenger Ferries Report," *Seatrade Review,* E.T. Heron, Ltd., London, October 1995.

Box, William, "Tomorrow's Ships Today," *Seatrade Review,* Seatrade Organization, Colchester, U.K., February 1995.

Fearnley, Astrup, ed., *Fearnleys Review, 1997,* Fearnresearch, Oslo, Norway, January 1998.

Global Container Markets, Prospects and Profitability in a High Growth Era, Drewry Shipping Consultants, London, July 1996.

Holland, D.J., *Future IMO Legislation, To Enter Into Force Between 1993 and 2010,* U.K. Lloyd's Register, London, 1993.

Kalosh, Anne, "Cruise Shipping, The Big Fish Keep Growing," *Seatrade Review,* Seatrade Organization, Colchester, U.K., March 1996.

Lambert, Jack, ed., *Barge Fleet Profile of Inland River Barges,* Phalanx Publishing, St. Paul, MN, 1997.

MARPOL 73/78, 1992 Amendments to Annex I, International Maritime Organization, London, 1992.

101st Congress, Public Law 101-380, Oil Pollution Act of 1990, August 18, 1990.

Logsdon, Charles, et. al., *Revenue Sources Book, Fall 1995,* State of Alaska, Department of Revenue, Juneau, November 1997.

Longley, Claire, ed. "Medium-Size Boxship Market Cooling Off," *Lloyd's Shipping Economist,* Lloyd's of London Press, June 1996.

Mathiesen, Oivend, ed., *Cruise Industry News, Annual 1997,* Cruise Industry News, New York, 1997.

Mentz and Decker, "Charter Report," *Containerization International,* Containerization International, London, February 1998.

Nicoll, Stuart, ed., "Tanker Regulatory Costs, Pressures and Challenges," *Lloyd's Shipping Economist,* Lloyd's of London Press, December 1994.

Oil Daily Company, "U.S. Loses WTO Appeal on Gasoline, Has 30 Days to Consider Course of Action," *The Oil Daily,* Oil Daily Company, New York, April 30, 1996.

"Oxygenate Distribution," *Petroleum Supply Monthly,* Energy Information Administration, Washington, DC, December 1994.

Petroleum Supply Annual 1997. Energy Information Administration, Washington, DC, June 1997.

Product Tankers, Drewry Shipping Consultants, London, August 1997.

Seatrade Cruise Shipping Convention, Transcript, Miller/Freeman, Princeton, NJ, March 1998.

Shipbuilding Industry Outlook, Product Tankers, IMA Associates, Washington, DC, September 1995.

The Shipbuilding Market, Analysis and Forecast of World Shipbuilding Demand, 1995–2010, Drewry Shipping Consultants, London, March 1995.

Shipping Review and Outlook, Clarkson Research Studies, London, Spring 1998.

Short Sea Container Markets, Drewry Shipping Consultants, London, September 1997.

Transportation Review 1996, DRI/McGraw-Hill, Lexington, MA, November 1996.

Waterborne Commerce Statistics Center, *Transportation Lines of the United States,* U.S. Army Corps of Engineers, New Orleans, 1996.

Waterborne Commerce Statistics Center, *Waterborne Commerce of the United States,* Part 5, U.S. Army Corps of Engineers, New Orleans, 1996.

World Sea Trade Service Review, First Quarter 1997, DRI/McGraw-Hill, Lexington, MA, and Mercer Management, November 1997.

■ GLOSSARY

Trucking

Backhaul: A return trip for a carrier, often involving empty vehicles on certain routes (see Deadhead).

Common carrier: A motor carrier, railroad, or other transportation company that offers its services to any business or individual.

Contract carriers: Regulated motor carriers, generally with a limited number of shipper clients to which they guarantee trucks and drivers when needed.

Deadhead: The process of returning on a backhaul without a load.

Double-stack: Refers to the transportation of containers piled two high on a rail flatcar; a form of piggybacking.

For-hire carrier: A trucking firm that transports goods for monetary compensation; may be a common carrier or a contract carrier.

Headhaul: A carrier's primary trip, bringing a shipment to its destination.

Hub-and-spoke system: A freight distribution system employed by railroads, motor carriers, and airlines to maximize equipment efficiency; shipments are fed into a few consolidation centers from several satellite terminals.

Intermodal: Refers to consumer goods and light industrial products that are transported by railroad in a trailer or container that originates from and terminates with a motor carrier or an ocean shipping line.

Just-in-time (JIT) system: A production management system under which inventories are kept to bare minimum levels through greater coordination between materials purchases, transportation, and production schedules; known as *kanban* in Japan, where it originated.

Less-than-truckload (LTL) freight: Refers to shipments weighing 10,000 pounds or less; involves more intermediate handling than does truckload freight.

Logistics: The management of a company's total distribution, transportation, and warehousing needs.

Line-haul: The longest leg of a shipment; the movement of freight between terminals.

Owner-operators: Independent truckers that operate their own vehicles to transport exempt goods or regulated freight under a lease agreement with a common carrier or shipper.

Piggybacking: The transporting of truck trailers or marine containers on flatbed railroad cars.

Private carrier: A shipper that transports its goods in truck fleets that it owns or leases.

Regular-route service: Transportation of goods by a for-hire motor carrier over standard routes, generally on a fixed schedule.

Tariffs: Schedules of rates charged for hauling freight specific distances or between specific points; still published by railroads, tariffs are no longer required in the motor carrier industry.

Truckload (TL): A shipment exceeding 10,000 pounds; a motor carrier may haul more than one TL in a single vehicle.

HEALTH AND MEDICAL SERVICES
Economic and Trade Trends

Health Care Expenditures as a Percentage of GDP for Selected Countries, 1995

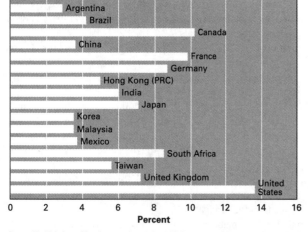

Source: Health Industry Manufacturers Association; U.S. Department of Commerce, International Trade Administration.

U.S. Health Care Expenditures as a Percentage of GDP

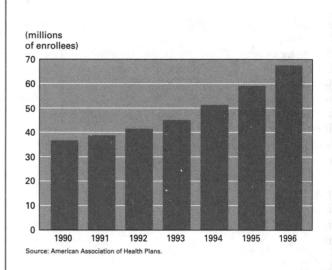

Source: U.S. Department of Health and Human Services, Healthcare Financing Administration.

Proportion of Medicare Beneficiaries in Managed Care, 1992–1997

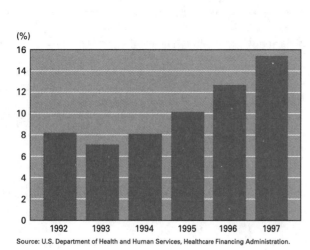

Source: U.S. Department of Health and Human Services, Healthcare Financing Administration.

Growth in HMO Enrollment, 1990–1996

Source: American Association of Health Plans.

Health and Medical Services

INDUSTRY DEFINITION The health care industry (SIC 80) consists of public, private, and nonprofit institutions. These institutions include hospitals, offices and clinics of medical doctors, nursing homes, and home health care facilities; other specialized health care facilities; and managed care organizations consisting of prepaid plans such as health maintenance organizations (HMOs), preferred providers organizations (PPOs), and independent practice associations (IPAs). The health care industry includes thousands of independent medical practices and partnerships as well as public and nonprofit institutions and major private corporations, such as the Columbia/HCA, Tenet, and Kaiser Permanente companies, which have assets of billions of dollars and are major employers in the U.S. economy.

GLOBAL INDUSTRY TRENDS

Health care reform, a prominent issue in the United States in the 1990s, is an increasingly significant objective in most regions of the world. Modifications of countries' social security systems are reshaping delivery systems as governments enhance private competition and thus encourage the availability of new medical services. Hand in hand with this greater private sector activity are the imperatives of efficiency and cost containment. Increasingly sophisticated medical technologies and pressures on central government budgets compel providers to deliver treatment in a more affordable manner, yet the wide variation in countries' levels of spending on health care and differences in the forms and quality of medical services ensure variability in countries' response to these changes.

Rising per capita incomes and a substantial growth in the middle class have spurred appreciably greater demand and access to quality services in Latin America. The movement of multinational corporations into that region also has contributed to this result.

The pioneering of multiple forms of managed care in the United States frequently has led to the incorporation of components of this approach abroad. Emulation is not always total, of course, because many countries do not permit the broad range of private sector medical activity that occurs in the United States. Nevertheless, the payment of physicians on a capitated basis (a flat payment to cover treatment for a fixed period of time or a fixed number of patients) and consortia among health care providers for the purpose of exacting discounts from suppliers of medical equipment and pharmaceuticals are becoming prevalent internationally. Since 1980 the high expense of inpatient hospital care has induced practically all west European countries to cut the total number of hospital beds substantially and explore more cost-effective alternatives. In the wake of severe economic downturns in east Asian economies, the movement to rationalize health care systems in order to reduce expenditures should gain even greater momentum.

The tendency toward more vigorous competition in the delivery of health care services is not without challenge or political opposition in most countries. The common valuation of health care as a universal right with significant public welfare and ethical dimensions ensures that the sector will remain a highly regulated one, and for-profit activity thus carries a burden of proof.

International influences affect the U.S. health care service market. Although the breadth of the U.S. middle class and a high per capita gross domestic product (GDP) inevitably affect the demand for health care, the comparatively high proportion of this country's expenditures devoted to medical care and the greater discretion for private sector health care activities and reimbursement practices are of fundamental importance in spurring foreign interest. The relative openness of U.S. foreign investment and profit repatriation regulations in the health care sector act as an additional stimulus, since the operation of medical facilities requires a long-term presence in the United States and thus calculability in regard to investment matters. Foreign providers operating in the United States can count on legal protection against expropriation of medical equipment, although medical specialists must comply with certification and registration requirements.

DOMESTIC TRENDS

The costs of health care in the United States grew about 4.6 percent in 1997, reaching an estimated $1.1 trillion, or about $3,900 per capita. Total health care expenditures amounted to 13.4 percent of U.S. GDP.

The dominance of managed care in the health care delivery system slowed the cost of health care to an annual growth rate of 4.4 percent in 1996, an unprecedented rate for the past three decades since the Medicare and Medicaid programs were introduced. The rapid displacement of traditional fee-for-service indemnity plans by managed care has created a degree of price stability in the health care system. From 1993 to 1996 the rate of growth for health care expenditures fluctuated from 4.4 percent to 8.6 percent compared with 11.0 percent to 12.9 percent from 1970 to 1990. Moreover, health care expenditures maintained the same share of GDP of 13.6 percent from 1993 to 1996 and stood at 13.4 percent in 1997. This is due partly to the healthy state of the economy and the reduced rate of growth of health care spending. The percentage rate, however, is still the highest among the industrialized economies of the world. Since 1989 the public share of total health care costs has been increasing rapidly, from 40.5 percent in that year to 46.7 percent in 1996.

In recent years, many employers have expanded the range of health plans they offer their employees to include managed care plans that have much lower average employer premiums than do traditional indemnity plans and that tend to control utilization through gatekeepers. The best known managed care plans are HMOs and PPOs, which offer a wide range of preventive services. HMOs continue to offer comprehensive benefits. All HMOs cover primary care visits with no limit on the number of appointments, and their copayments are as low as $5 to $10 for primary care visits and prescription drugs. Managed care plans tend to restrict patient choice, use primary care physicians as gatekeepers for specialized services, and negotiate fees directly with health care providers. Managed care offers enrollees lower premium costs, better benefits, reasonable copayments, and lower deductibles.

Before the arrival of managed care, health care professionals focused mainly on providing care to patients, but now they have to focus on costs and management issues as well. Physicians are forming their own provider groups. Health care insurers are involved in health plans. Hospitals are diversifying as well as merging and acquiring other health institutions. Through mergers and acquisitions Columbia/HCA, a health care corporation, became the largest and most prestigious hospital corporation in America, although it is now ranked number 10. Fierce competition in the industry has resulted in slim or no profit margins for some hospitals, home health agencies, and managed care plans, including HMOs. However, other providers have done well in the market.

Historically, a period of high profits in the industry usually is accompanied by low premium rates. Premium rates usually follow a cycle. The industry is now preparing for higher rates of increase in premiums. As rates decreased through managed care, enrollment increased. A recent industry survey estimated that 85 percent of employed Americans are enrolled in some form of managed care. The traditional fee-for-service plans which accounted for 23 percent of all employees covered in 1996 dropped to 15 percent in 1997. PPOs have a market share of 30 percent; HMOs, 30 percent; and point-of-service (POS), 20 percent.

Managed care companies are providing information that will help consumers better manage their health care needs. Health plans have launched Internet programs that allow consumers to access medical research, support groups, and professional advice as well as exchange E-mail with providers.

Biomedical research has provided medicines to improve patient care. At the same time, this research has brought economic gains to pharmaceutical drug companies, investors, and physicians.

In the Balanced Budget Act (BBA) of 1996, Congress reformed the Medicare program to make it operate more cost-effectively, saving $115 billion through 2002. The administration proposed in its 1999 budget to provide health care coverage to some uninsured workers and children. About 41 million individuals have no health coverage in the U.S. system. Currently, there is debate about the changes needed in managed care, particularly in the areas of assessing quality, accountability, access, and cost. One pivotal issue involves achieving a balance between patients' rights and reasonable profit for providers of health care services.

DOMESTIC PROJECTIONS

Outlays for U.S. health care (SIC 80) are estimated at $1.2 trillion in 1999, a 5.6 percent increase over 1998 (see Table 44-1). In the next 5 years health care expenditures are expected to undergo an average annual increase of 6.5 percent. Since 1993 health care spending as a percentage of GDP has remained relatively stable at 13.6 percent, except in 1997, when it fell to 13.4 percent. During the next 5 years health care spending as a percentage of GDP will range from 13.4 to 14.5. This can be explained by the fact that GDP will rise faster than or fall a little below the rate of growth of health care spending. Managed care has effectively reduced health care costs, and with some adjustments it will continue to contain costs well into the next century. Uncertainties exist for Medicare payments. The BBA of 1997 seeks to strengthen the traditional Medicare program by making major revisions to fee-for-service payment policies, ensuring the ongoing availability of the program to Medicare beneficiaries. These legislative changes are expected to prolong the life of the Medicare Part A Trust by a decade. Over the next few years new prospective systems developed for Medicare payment will affect the operations of skilled nursing facilities, hospital outpatient services, home health agencies, long-term care hospitals, and rehabilitation facilities. The BBA will also revise many payment policies to improve volume controls for physicians' services and reduce payments to teaching hospitals for the indirect costs of medical education. The BBA will mandate new preventive services for Medicare beneficiaries. These new developments will have spillover effects on all areas of the industry, affecting prices and the quality of services.

Managed care will dominate the industry with a market share of about 90 percent by 2002. HMOs will modify their operational practices to accommodate patients' complaints as well as to increase the number of enrollees. Managed care premiums will increase about 6 to 8 percent per year during the period 1999–2001 and thus help enhance profits for health care providers. Managed care will contract with specialists to better control high-cost disease treatments.

Mergers and acquisitions will continue to occur among health care organizations, but at a much slower rate than that which obtained in the early 1990s. Small and inefficient HMOs and PPOs will be bought by larger ones.

In the next few years the number of home health care entities may shrink as a result of limited sources of funding; however, the number of nursing home patients will increase. Some of the proposals by the President in the 1998 State of the Union Address will be implemented within the next 5 years. They include (1) allowing those who are approaching the age of 65 years to buy into Medicare, (2) extending Medicaid to cover more children and legal immigrants, (3) providing more funding for biomedical research, (4) enacting rules to protect consumers in managed care plans, and (5) expanding health coverage to some of the 41 million uninsured persons.

Competition within managed care markets is narrowing price differences among plans; therefore, in the future consumers will switch plans on the basis of quality of care rather than price differences in premiums.

In 1999 U.S. exports of medical services, a category that is dominated by the treatment of foreigners in U.S. facilities, will grow approximately 4.4 percent. This represents a slight decrease from the estimated 4.8 percent rise in 1998, partly as a result of a sharp dip in economic growth in Asian countries. However, the 1999–2003 period will experience a U.S. revenue expansion of 5.5 to 6.5 percent. The export level will depend largely on the

TABLE 44-1: Health and Medical Services Trends and Forecasts
(billions of dollars; percent)

	1992	1993	1994	1995	1996[1]	1997[2]	1998[2]	1999[3]	Percent Change						
									92–93	93–94	94–95	95–96	96–97	97–98	98–99
National health expenditure	836.6	895.1	945.7	991.4	1,035.1	1,082.7	1,136.8	1,200.5	7.0	5.6	4.8	4.4	4.6	5.0	5.6
Health services and supplies	809.1	866.1	915.2	960.7	1,003.6	1,050.2	1,102.7	1,163.3	7.0	5.7	5.0	4.5	4.6	5.0	5.6
Personal health care	740.7	787.0	828.5	869.0	907.2	947.1	992.6	1,044.2	6.2	5.3	4.9	4.4	4.4	4.8	5.2
Hospital care	305.3	323.0	335.7	346.7	358.5	370.0	384.4	403.3	5.8	3.9	3.3	3.4	3.2	3.9	4.9
Physicians' services	175.9	183.6	190.4	196.4	202.1	209.2	215.1	222.6	4.4	3.7	3.1	2.9	3.5	3.3	3.5
Dental services	37.0	39.1	41.7	44.7	47.6	51.3	55.1	58.8	5.6	6.6	7.3	6.4	7.8	6.8	6.8
Other professional services	42.1	46.3	50.3	54.3	58.0	61.9	66.2	71.0	9.9	8.8	7.9	6.8	6.8	7.0	7.2
Home health care	19.6	22.9	25.6	28.4	30.2	31.9	33.1	34.4	16.5	12.2	10.9	6.2	5.5	5.0	4.0
Drugs and other medical nondurables	71.2	75.6	79.5	84.9	91.4	98.3	108.2	116.4	6.2	5.2	6.8	7.7	7.5	10.0	7.9
Vision products and other medical durables	11.9	12.3	12.5	13.1	13.3	13.5	13.9	14.3	3.4	1.5	4.9	1.4	1.5	2.9	3.0
Nursing home care	62.3	66.3	70.9	75.2	78.5	81.3	84.4	87.8	6.5	6.8	6.2	4.3	3.6	4.5	4.0
Other personal health care	15.4	18.0	21.9	25.3	27.6	29.9	32.2	35.6	16.9	21.8	15.4	9.4	8.3	9.8	10.5
Program administration and net cost of private health insurance	45.0	53.8	58.2	60.1	60.9	62.1	64.8	69.3	19.6	8.2	3.3	1.2	2.0	4.3	6.9
Government public health activities	23.4	25.3	28.5	31.5	35.5	40.8	45.3	50.8	8.2	12.5	10.7	12.5	14.9	13.0	12.2
Research and construction	27.5	29.0	30.5	30.7	31.5	32.5	34.1	37.2	5.3	5.1	0.8	2.6	3.2	4.0	2.8
Research[4]	14.2	14.5	15.9	16.7	17.0	17.4	18.6	19.9	2.2	9.6	5.0	1.9	2.4	6.9	7.2
Construction	13.4	14.5	14.6	14.0	14.5	15.1	15.5	17.3	8.7	0.5	–3.8	3.4	3.8	3.3	2.5

[1] Preliminary.
[2] Estimate.
[3] Forecast.
[4] Research and development expenditures of drug companies and other providers and suppliers of medical equipment are excluded from research expenditures but are included in the expenditure class in which a product falls.
Source: U.S. Department of Health and Human Services, Health Care Financing Administration, Office of the Actuary; U.S. Department of Commerce, International Trade Administration (ITA); estimates and forecasts by ITA.

TABLE 44-2: U.S. International Trade in Medical Services, 1992–1997

(millions of dollars)

	1992	1993	1994	1995	1996	1997
Medical Services						
Exports	708	750	794	841	872	925[1]
Imports			Not available			
Sales to Foreigners by U.S. Nonbank Affiliates						
	367	381	476	469	490[1]	515[1]
Sales to Americans by Foreign Nonbank Affiliates						
	Not available	1,514	1,630	1,786	1,775[1]	1,760[1]

[1] Estimated value.

success of U.S. providers in "bundling" domestic treatment of foreigners with long-term health insurance coverage, an arrangement that is attractive for individuals such as Latin Americans, who spend many months of the year in the United States.

U.S. medical service firms also secure business by extending their services to foreigners through their nonbank affiliates abroad. Examples include a U.S.-owned acute care hospital operating in Germany and a U.S.-owned dental clinic providing service in Russia. Such U.S. sales totaled approximately $469 million in 1995, the most recent year for which figures are available, while the corresponding amount for sales by nonbank U.S. affiliates of foreign medical providers was $1.8 billion (see Table 44-2). U.S. affiliates should see an increase in their sales of about 2.6 percent in 1999 as well as an average annual expansion of about 2.9 percent between 1999 and 2003. U.S. affiliates of foreign companies will experience some stabilization of sales, with a 2.2 percent rise in 1999 and average annual growth of about 1.8 percent between 1999 and 2003.

GLOBAL MARKET PROSPECTS

Private spending for health care services is increasing in a majority of countries. As the middle class grows and populations contain more old people, governments face intensified demands for better treatment and greater pressure on budgets. Such conditions have contributed to the popularity of U.S.-style managed care schemes even when foreign medical practitioners are reluctant to accept the lower fees and more constrained personal autonomy such systems entail. Some large U.S. managed care companies are actively exploring opportunities in Latin America and Asia. Cigna Healthcare, for example, reported revenues of $200 million from its managed care operations abroad in 1997 and predicts that its revenues will increase at an annual rate of about 20 percent in the future.

A look at international health care systems from region to region reveals differences in attitudes and approaches to questions such as foreign investment, the scale of for-profit activity, and the autonomy of the medical profession. Because of its geo-graphic proximity to and the presence of its large expatriate communities in the United States, Latin America remains the most promising region for U.S. health care providers. Moreover, its physicians and medical decision makers are among those most receptive to incorporating the cost containment methods associated with managed care and are continuing with privatization efforts. Interest in Asia, although still significant, was tempered in 1998 by that region's financial and economic disturbances, leading to a more cautious approach in reshaping the traditional structure of health care treatment in Asian medical communities. Western Europe, a strong prospective market because of its affluence and large middle classes, has not spawned health care service opportunities commensurate with its potential, as restrictions on for-profit medical activity and a high degree of state regulation of delivery systems somewhat impede entrepreneurial ventures.

While opportunities for telemedicine continue to be identified, barriers to this type of treatment can pose challenges for U.S. medical service firms. An important consideration is reimbursement for telemedicine services, because whether such treatment will be covered under a country's health insurance plans is often unclear. Host governments may impose ceilings on what a U.S. health care service firm can charge for services. However, determined companies have overcome these difficulties through patient negotiations.

In Latin America a larger segment of the population is gaining access to health care services, a development that is providing new openings for U.S. firms. Both the broadening of the middle class and an upward trend in incomes are fueling opportunities, in addition to the fact that the movement of multinational corporations to the region continues. These companies are looking for reliable alternatives in extending cost-effective health care coverage to both expatriate and indigenous employees. Part of the strategy entails forging relationships with managed care providers and private clinics in Latin American countries. Equally significant are governments' social security reforms, which have resulted in the establishment of private competition and a demand for new forms of treatment that can be provided efficiently. Latin American health care systems are incorporating components of U.S. managed care programs, including payment of physicians according to the principle of capitation (a flat fee per patient or per period of time), salaried medical specialists working under staff plans, and preventive care.

Mexico has moved to the forefront in vigorous U.S. medical service involvement, most notably in hospital operation and construction, managed care, primary care clinics, and health insurance. That country supports a sprawling, frequently outdated medical system in which approximately 6 percent of the population purchase private medical insurance. However, approximately half a million higher-income Mexicans often choose to get treatment across the border in cities such as San Diego and Houston. While Mexican law requires that workers approve their transfer from the public social security system to a private insurance scheme, various U.S. companies have begun to offer private plans, including one aimed at bank employees

Some U.S. insurers are refraining from major involvement, awaiting the creation of more transparent regulations in this area. Mexican authorities have planned the construction of 100 clinics throughout their country by 2000.

In the hospital sector plans are well under way for the construction of a $100 million Mexico City facility by a private Mexican hospital owner. This project may include the establishment of an HMO that will provide primary care treatment. In line with a continuing need for new hospitals, a Dallas hospital corporation has finished building a hospital in Hermosillo, Mexico, and is working on similar future projects. Hospital renovation is also fueling private sector interest. Patients for these hospitals invariably are drawn from the middle and upper classes. However, it is not simply the "high end" of the patient population that is attracting foreign interest. Small clinics that offer primary care have been established under a U.S.–Mexican joint venture in Leon, Cancun, and Toluca.

Legislation which became effective in 1993 introduced private competition into Colombia's health care system. The law permitted the establishment of "health promotion companies" for the provision of a bundle of health care services termed the "obligatory health plan." Despite recent political instability, that country is becoming the focus of foreign health care providers. An estimated 4.6 percent of Colombian GDP goes for health care expenditures, in contrast to around 2.1 percent before 1993. The number of individuals with access to health care has expanded to approximately half the population. Hospital construction, renovation, and management are providing significant business opportunities.

The tightening of fiscal policies in Brazil has put immense pressure on the financing of the health care sector and has complicated the task of providing high-quality services. Foreign managed care providers and health insurance companies are nevertheless targeting this large country, whose private health insurance sector expanded an estimated 41.5 percent in 1996. Although Brazil devotes only 3.9 percent of its GDP to health care, around 40 million inhabitants are covered under private health care policies. The Brazilian government provides a guarantee of universal health care coverage to citizens and pays about 72 percent of health care costs. U.S. insurers such as Aetna, Cigna, and Liberty have entered into joint ventures in the medical insurance field. HMOs were responsible for roughly 35 percent of the private health care market in 1996, a share which is expected to rise because of the government's attempts, through modified legislation, to draw foreign investors in order to rein in medical costs. Profits of HMOs increased to $3.7 billion in 1996, a 24 percent rise over 1995.

The Brazilian Ministry of Health is considering proposals that would permit private firms to operate some specialized public hospitals. Under this scheme, which has incurred the opposition of labor unions, these hospitals would be converted into nonprofit organizations that would contract out services.

Private health insurance grew at a staggering rate after its inauguration in Chile in the early 1980s. With the current cooling off in this pace, the health care system is experiencing an increased emphasis on managed care, outpatient treatment in community centers, and investment outside the country. Health care expenditures as a share of GDP have risen to just under 5 percent. The 25 percent of the Chilean population covered under private plans, representing 3.8 million individuals, can access care that is markedly superior to that provided by the public medical service. The need to contain health care costs, particularly in the hospital sector, which absorbs 70 percent of medical expenditures, has spurred vertical integration in the industry. For example, spending per bed in one of Chile's better private hospitals is currently estimated to be approximately $150,000 per year. As a result, outpatient care has expanded dramatically, garnering around 60 percent of all private health care spending. Private clinics are losing patients to public hospitals that offer private beds outside Santiago. U.S. providers may find opportunities by teaming up with the health care facilities that have emerged in shopping malls in Chile.

Argentina's government has initiated attempts at reform of health care, taking aim at inefficiency and escalating costs. This program is expected to create opportunities in managed care, integration of delivery systems, and the training of health care managers and primary care specialists. Spending $640 per person annually, the country tops the list of Latin American countries in medical expenditures per capita. The 2.5 million Argentines who can afford to purchase private health insurance are covered under approximately 200 plans. The quality of coverage varies, and costs are substantial because of the encouragement of overuse as well as an absence of regulation.

In general, the recent downturn in a number of Asian economies has increased the importance of providing affordable health services so that U.S. firms can maintain their competitive position. In spite of financial upheavals in a number of countries, the World Bank estimates that total Asian expenditures on health care will rise to $1.5 trillion by 2025. Export-minded firms continue to seek opportunities, especially in areas such as hospital and clinic management, operation, and construction. In one recent instance, a U.S. company formed a joint venture in Indonesia to provide treatment in eight hospitals and train medical specialists.

Asia's Pacific Rim is emerging as a pivotal region for the establishment of telemedicine ventures. U.S. providers of telemedicine are already active in the region. Noteworthy are a project in Indonesia and another with the government of Malaysia to construct an information highway linking that country's hospitals. Given the potential for telemedicine in this part of the world, Indonesia and Malaysia, along with Taiwan, Singapore, and Korea, are vying to serve as the region's "downlink" that would receive and diagnose the electronic images emanating from remote areas.

The dramatic rise in income levels in China during the period 1994–1998, particularly in eastern urban areas, has led health care firms to pay increasing attention to this market. Several foreign joint ventures have emerged in the hospital and dental service sectors. Approximately 80 percent of China's population is uninsured for medical treatment, and care is provided largely on a "cash and carry" basis. Medical providers from Australia and Hong Kong, for example, are establishing a presence, particularly in southern China. However, opportunities in the hospital sector are somewhat limited by the fact that participating foreign doctors may work only in an educational context, and hospital joint ventures typically are permitted in a temporary time frame and must pass a needs test. Chinese citizens traveling to the United States for medical reasons are obligated to obtain visas from the authorities.

In spite of these challenges, Chinese medical authorities are receptive to incorporating Western-style management expertise into their facilities. Some Chinese hospitals are attempting to set up consortia with foreign health service firms, especially those which include a training or educational component. In the coming years China will also need to modernize and renovate its existing hospitals and clinics as expectations rise with increasing affluence. While the overall opening of the country's health insurance market will be a gradual process, the inauguration of a unified health care program in Chinese cities slated for the next 3 to 5 years has spurred interest because of the requirement for mandatory contributions by employers and employees. Several hospital joint ventures with foreigners have been established in Beijing and Shanghai.

Because of increasing family incomes, consumer expenditures on medical care in Taiwan are rising. Spending in the health care sector has expanded at an annual average rate of 13 percent since 1991, reaching more than $21.3 billion in 1996. Taiwan's passage of a universal health insurance program in 1995 launched a social welfare initiative for the elderly which should be of interest to firms specializing in such care.

Australia is attracting the attention of foreign health care companies as a result of its decision makers' desire for assistance in the management and development of new public hospitals. Expenditures for private hospitals are increasing at a rate of 8.3 percent a year; the country has 334 private hospitals out of a total of about 1,150 hospitals. In Victoria providers of acute, specialist, aged, and mental health services have found opportunities in hospital care. Hospital management services also may be provided on a private basis, with some other type of private patient coverage under consideration. Australians are permitted to purchase private health insurance for coverage of private hospital charges as well as to have private status in public hospitals. Other potentially profitable activities include hospital upgrades and outsourcing.

In Japan most health care services that have proved viable as exports are not permitted on a for-profit basis. Rather than operating hospitals and clinics, U.S. firms would do better by concentrating on the provision of consulting expertise to not-for-profit Japanese medical organizations, a modest market but one which is expected to expand in the coming years. Services for medical laboratories are another area that can be tapped. Health care firms are also looking at treatment of the elderly, who are expected to make up 25 percent of Japan's population by 2025. The 1997 entitlement program for nursing services for the elderly, which will take effect in 2000, applies to home health care as well as institutional care.

The sharp depreciation of the won, the certainty of negative GDP growth in the near future, and the austerity measures negotiated during South Korea's agreement with the International Monetary Fund have combined to lower the expectations of foreign health care providers significantly. The ensuing cost containment pressures, however, have shifted domestic providers' focus from purchases of medical equipment, which have declined recently, to the methods by which health care services are provided. This development should create opportunities for U.S. firms with experience in managed care as well as health care financing and strategic management.

Public and private spending on health care in Canada reached an estimated $55.4 billion in 1996, with an additional $1 billion for purchasing health care services in the United States. Privately insured services and uninsured out-of-pocket payments accounted for approximately $10.1 billion of the total. In the face of severe cost pressures in the medical arena, about 30 percent of the domestic spending took place in the private sector. Budgetary tightening has encouraged a gradual shift to greater private sector health care activity. U.S. health care firms that specialize in medical consulting, rehabilitation clinics, and facilities management should have particularly favorable prospects.

Health service providers continue to look for investment opportunities in Eastern Europe, especially Hungary, the Czech Republic, and Poland. Under the influence of Western European health care systems, Hungary has erected a primarily publicly financed structure of delivery with an expanding sphere of private services. Seven percent of the country's GDP is devoted to health care expenditures. The trend toward private services has been most evident in dentistry and pharmaceuticals, with a larger proportion of the costs being shouldered by households. Health authorities are devising new schemes that encourage private physicians to contract independently with medical financing agencies. The scale of privatization is less marked in diagnostic and ambulatory services and is barely perceptible in hospital services, as the public sector remains responsible for reimbursement and cost practices. Spurred by Hungarian reform efforts, the number of hospital beds declined 20 percent in 1996 and 1997 and should further contract in the future.

In the Czech Republic, long considered one of the most promising east European markets, health care authorities have been attempting to move treatment away from the earlier state-controlled system and into a more flexible and economically rational system. This transformation is expected to entail greater direct payments by patients as well as a continued reduction in the number of hospital beds. Currently, the country devotes about 10 percent of GDP to expenditures on health care. The hospital sector has been plagued by excessive debt, and significant opportunities are emerging for U.S. medical consultant and financial and management expertise. While only a small number of the roughly 200 hospitals have been privatized, foreigners are permitted to take part in their privatization. Training of medical staff in the operation of hospital equipment represents another sphere for U.S. private sector involvement.

The Middle East and south Asia should provide some possibilities for export-minded firms. The high income per capita in some Persian Gulf states has prompted interest, notably in regard to hospital construction and operation projects. In India the presence of a middle class of more than 200 million has drawn a half dozen U.S. companies that provide a range of services in the hospital sector. Managed care ventures represent a marketable service, as do emergency and evacuation services for trauma, cardiac, and critical care. Indian decision makers are also looking for foreign partners in the fields of health care consultancy and hospital construction.

MANAGED CARE

Managed care, a health care system of prepaid plans that provide comprehensive coverage to members, has become the growth leader in the health care market. The system has brought some stability in containing health care costs. In the United States employees' health care coverage rose only 0.2 percent from 1996 to 1997.

The system controls the use of health care services to provide cost-effectiveness. For example, managed care plans seek providers with lower-cost practice patterns and offer them a defined patient base in exchange for a favorable payment rate. Managed care may limit the number of providers or create financial incentives to choose a particular set of providers. These plans can use discount fee-for-service rates to control costs such as per case, per day payments to hospitals, or per person payments to physicians to shift some of the financial risk of treating patients to providers.

Managed care organizations are very complex, and their characteristics vary. For instance, some are long established and have millions of enrollees, while others are small companies with relatively few members. Some provide indemnity coverage and collaborate with insurance companies. The well-known ones, such as HMOs, PPOs, and POSs, are sometimes owned by integrated delivery systems that operate clinics and hospitals. Many managed care organizations operate for profit, while others are nonprofit.

Managed care plans cover more than 85 percent of all U.S. employees. In January 1997 there were 651 HMOs in the United States with over 67.5 million enrollees. The percentage of enrollees in PPOs has overtaken that in HMOs. In 1996 PPOs had 97.8 million members. The largest HMO enrollment is in California, with over 14 million members. Table 44-3 provides information on the development of U.S. HMOs in respect to

enrollment pattern, market expansion, and rate of growth in the top five states in each category.

An industry survey reported that families with children enrolled in managed care realized savings of $375 to $500 in 1996, and families without children saved $324 to $440. In Massachusetts, average savings per family were even higher at $775 to $1,055. Because of the lower premiums paid under managed care plans, the number of uninsured persons was reduced 3.1 percent to 5 million.

The shift of membership from less expensive plans seems to work in the managed care system, but this trend may be tapering off. The profit margins of managed care plans, especially HMOs, were lean in 1997 because of competitive pricing. To increase profits and pay dividends to shareholders in 1998 and 1999, premium increases in the range of 6 to 8 percent are expected. In 1996 the average monthly premium under HMOs was $395.42 for a family and $146.41 for a single person. Managed care premiums are lower than charges in fee-for-service plans. This is a major reason for the dominance of managed care in the industry.

GOVERNMENT PROGRAMS

The U.S. Department of Health and Human Services (HHS) is the federal government's lead agency for health programs. The HHS Strategic Plan states the agency's mission is to enhance the health and wellbeing of Americans by providing for effective health and human services and fostering strong, sustained advances in the services underlying medicine, public health, and social services.

The plan includes six goals: (1) reducing the major threats to the health and productivity of all Americans, (2) improving the economic and social wellbeing of individuals, families, and communities in the United States, (3) improving access to health services and ensuring the integrity of the nation's health entitlement and safety net programs, (4) improving the quality of health care and human services, (5) improving public health systems, and (6) strengthening the nation's health sciences research enterprise and enhancing its productivity.

Besides providing billions of dollars for Medicare and Medicaid programs and medical research through the National Institutes of Health, federal tax laws help finance health insurance and care. Employers' contributions for health insurance premi-

TABLE 44-3:   Some Characteristics of HMOs in the Top Five States

Largest HMO Enrollment (1997), millions		Highest Market Share (1997), %		Largest New Enrollment (1996–1997)		Highest Annual Rate of Growth (1996–1997), %	
California	14.0	Oregon	47	New York	1,237,017	Mississippi	103
New York	6.5	Massachusetts	45	California	971,420	Kansas	76
Florida	4.2	California	44	Florida	676,592	Kentucky	68
Pennsylvania	4.0	Utah	40	Kentucky	432,084	Maine	66
Texas	2.9	Delaware	39	Minnesota	335,388	Arkansas	61

Source: American Association of Health Plans.

ums are excluded from employees' taxable income. It is estimated that total health-related tax expenditures, including other provisions, will reach $86 billion in 1999 and total $491 billion in the period 1999–2003.

Medicare

Medicare is a federal program that reimburses hospitals, physicians, and other medical providers for serving patients 65 years and older, certain disabled people, and most persons with end-stage renal disease. About 38 million elderly and disabled people are enrolled in the program. There are two basic programs under Medicare: Hospital Insurance (HI), which pays for inpatient hospital care, and Supplementary Medical Insurance (SMI), which pays for physicians' services, outpatient hospital services, and other services.

The Medicare program is subject to statutory and regulatory changes; administrative rulings, interpretations, and determinations; and government restrictions. All these changes may materially increase or decrease the federal budget and payments to hospitals, physicians, and other medical providers. For instance, the BBA of 1997 will slow the rate of growth of Medicare spending between 1997 and 2002 as well as control the quantity and quality of care provided.

Assuming that Congress makes no changes in current law, the Congressional Budget Office projects that Medicare spending will increase from $187 billion in 1997, to $246 billion in 2002, to $393 billion by 2008 (see Table 44-4). Annual growth in spending will increase from 5.6 percent between 1997 and 2002 to 8.1 percent between 2002 and 2008. Most Medicare beneficiaries pay a premium of $42.50 per month which helps reduce the federal government's allocation.

Medicare accounted for about 11 percent of total federal spending in 1995. Thus, it was a target as the federal government attempted to reach a balanced budget. The BBA of 1997 is expected to reduce Medicare spending by $115 billion relative to the baseline projection from 1998 through 2002.

Medicaid

Medicaid is a program jointly funded by the federal government and state governments. It is administered by the individual states operating within federal guidelines and provides medical care to low-income people, including children, pregnant women, and the elderly, blind, and disabled. The guidelines give states discretion to establish income and resource criteria for program eligibility; determine the amount, duration, and scope of covered services; and determine provider reimbursement methodologies and the administration of their own programs. This federal-state health care program served approximately 33 million low-income Americans in 1997 at a cost of about $167.5 billion. The federal share of the total amount spent was $95.6 billion (57 percent), and the states' share was $72 billion (43 percent). Under current law Medicaid is expected to grow at an average annual rate of 7.2 percent from 1998 to 2003.

From 1990 to 1992 Medicaid spending rose from $75.3 billion to $106 billion, a 41 percent increase. In 1996 the increase in Medicaid spending dropped to 5.3 percent, the lowest rate in the program's history. The decrease is attributable to (1) low rates of medical price inflation that dampened growth in spending per recipient, (2) prosperity in the economy that reduced the number of people eligible for Medicaid, (3) the full effect of tightened disproportionate share of hospital payments (DSH) and provider-based taxes, and (4) voluntary donations (T&D) to increase state funds for providing care and increase enrollment in capitated managed care programs.

Balanced Budget Act of 1997 and Its Implication for Medicare Programs

The Medicare Payment Advisory Commission Report to Congress on Medicare Payment Policy indicated that the BBA of 1997 incorporated several changes that will affect almost every sphere of the Medicare program. These changes will result in significant savings, provide more choices to beneficiaries in the

TABLE 44-4:   Medicare Mandatory Outlays by Selected Fiscal Year
(billions of dollars; percent)

	1990	1997	2002	2008	Average Annual Growth Rate, %		
					90–97	97–02	02–08
Gross mandatory outlays					9.9	5.9	8.3
Benefits	107	207	276	447			
Mandatory administration and grants[1]	>0.50	1	2	1			
Total	107	208	277	448			
Premiums[2]	−12	−20	−31	−55	8.4	8.8	10.0
Mandatory outlays net of premiums	96	187	246	393	10.1	5.6	8.1
Discretionary outlays for administration	2	3	3	4	1.7	4.7	4.8
All Medicare outlays net of premiums	98	190	249	398	9.9	5.6	8.1

[1] Mandatory outlays for administration of support peer review organizations and of controlling activities such as fraud and abuse.
[2] Includes collections of civil penalties and criminal fines beginning in 1997.
Source: Congressional Budget Office.

selection of health plan options, and strengthen the traditional Medicare program.

The BBA is expected to reduce Medicare spending by $115 billion over the next 5 years. Since Medicare consumed about 11 percent of the total federal budget in 1995 and was growing annually by approximately 8 to 9 percent, Congress was willing to reduce its rate of growth to about 6 percent until the year 2002.

The most profound change in the new legislation is the creation of the Medicare + Choice program. The BBA broadens the health plan choices for Medicare beneficiaries to reflect changes that are under way in the private insurance marketplace and in the Medicare program itself. These changes include risk-contracting programs, PPOs, provider-sponsored organizations, private fee-for-service plans, and demonstration medical savings account plans. Enrollment in Medicare risk-contracting plans grew from 3.8 percent in 1995 to 14 percent in 1997.

To ensure choice, the BBA strengthened the traditional Medicare fee-for-service program by designing and implementing prospective payment systems for providers of ambulatory and postacute care. In addition, the BBA will change many payment policies, such as improving volume controls for physicians' services, and reduce payments to teaching hospitals for the indirect costs of medical education. Other changes include direct payment to nurse practitioners and clinical nurse specialists and various fraud and abuse provisions. The BBA also mandates new preventive services for Medicare beneficiaries. This act not only extends the range of health plan options but also will facilitate choice by expanding the availability of consumer information to explain benefits, costs, and grievance and appeal process in the Medicare + Choice program. The BBA further encourages health plans to participate by improving the capitation payment policy.

Fraud and Abuse

Fraud and abuse have been a major contributing factor in rising health care costs. It has been estimated that fraud accounts for as much as 10 percent of total annual health care expenditures. To reduce fraudulent practices in government health care programs, the President's budget for 1999 contains several proposals to improve compliance with the Medicare program. Among the proposals are assessing a fee on providers to cover administrative costs such as auditing and settling their medical claims and imposing new civil monetary penalties on physicians who falsely certify a beneficiary's need for mental health and hospice benefits and providers who participate in kickback schemes. Medicare fines or overpayment would be given priority in bankrupcy cases. In recent years many health care providers have been penalized for fraudulent medical practices.

HEALTH BENEFIT COSTS IN PRIVATE INDUSTRY

Health care benefits are a major component of U.S. compensation packages to workers. Wages and benefits constitute a significant cost factor in the production of medical services.

Therefore, increased or decreased compensation costs could result in rising or decreasing health care prices and eventually increased or decreased employer health care costs. After 1986 annual percentage increases in compensation costs (wages and salaries and benefits) for workers employed in health services establishments fluctuated widely, ranging from a high of 7.1 percent at the start of 1990 to a low of 1.8 percent in December 1996. Table 44-5 provides a breakdown of the cost per hour worked for compensation among private health care industry workers in March 1996.

Many factors affect health care compensation, such as (1) increases in real wages, (2) increased consumer demand for health care services, and (3) workers' productivity. Other factors include industry's desire for increased profits, the introduction of new technologies, changing competition in the market, and the supply of skilled workers.

The latest data available show a significant drop in health benefit costs in private industry. In March 1997 benefit costs in private industry averaged 99 cents per hour worked, or 5.5 percent of total compensation. In that period, in the goods-producing industries, health benefit costs were $1.49 (6.8 percent), compared with 83 cents (4.9 percent) for service-producing industries. In average dollar amount and proportion of compensation, employers' costs for health benefits were highest in blue-collar occupations ($1.19 per hour worked and 6.9 percent of total compensation). Service occupations had the lowest costs (0.40 cent per hour worked and 4.5 percent compensation). White-collar occupations averaged $1.07 (5.0 percent). Union workers carried higher employer costs for health benefits, averaging $2.01 (8.5 per cent), than did nonunion workers, whose average was 85 cents. Geographically, the cost of health benefits ranged from 86 cents in the South to $1.17 in the Northeast. The size of health care establishments also played an important role in determining the average amount of health care compensation. For instance, establishments with fewer than 100 employees averaged 72 cents, or 4.7 percent; those with 100 to 499 employees averaged 98 cents, or 5.8 percent; and those with 500 or more employees averaged $1.57, or 6.3 percent.

TABLE 44-5: Private Industry Compensation Component Cost per Hour Worked
(current dollars; percent)

Compensation Component	Cost per Hour Worked	Percent of Compensation
Total compensation	17.10	100.0
Wages and services	12.58	71.9
Total benefits	4.91	28.4
Legally required	1.59	9.3
Health insurance	1.14	6.5
Paid leave	1.12	6.4
Retirement savings	0.55	3.1
Supplemental pay	0.49	2.8
Other benefits	0.03	0.2

Source: Bureau of Labor Statistics.

The Health Insurance Portability and Accountability Act of 1996 gurantees people losing group health care coverage through retirement or other termination of employment continued access to coverage in the market regardless of their health status. In testimony before Congress, Director of Health Financing and System Issues William J. Scanton indicated that consumers attempting to exercise this right have been hindered by carrier practices and pricing or by their own misunderstanding of the law. However, many have had difficulties obtaining individual market coverage with guaranteed access rights or have been charged significantly higher premiums for such coverage, as some carriers charge premiums as much as 600 percent higher than the standard rates. Many consumers do not realize that the guarantee of access applies only to those losing group coverage who meet other eligibility requirements. For example, an individual must apply within 63 days of losing group coverage or lose the right to coverage.

Insurers believe that the act poses an excessive administrative burden, has had unanticipated consequences, and has the potential for consumer abuse. State insurance regulators have encountered difficulties in attempting to implement and enforce the act's provisions when they have found federal guidance lacking in clarity or detail. Even federal regulators face an unexpectedly large regulatory role under the act.

DOMESTIC SUBSECTORS

The health care services delivery system in the United States has changed with the advent of managed care. Hospital and physician services are the largest components of the health care system, but their share of total spending is diminishing. These services, which amounted to 57.6 percent of total national health care spending in 1990, declined to 54.1 percent in 1996. The drop of 3.5 percentage points in spending was allocated to long-term care, prescription drugs, other professional services, and alternative delivery of services.

With respect to revenues, hospitals did not perform as well as home health agencies did because the government reimbursed home health agencies for services rendered to Medicare patients on a full-cost recovery basis, whereas with hospital inpatient services for Medicare patients the government paid those hospitals for the established diagnosis-related groupings (DRGs). The DRG payments are lower than the full-cost recovery payments. When the BBA amends this discrepancy, the profit margins of home health care agencies will be reduced.

The major developments in the subsectors include the effect that managed care operation has had on them. The number of inpatient days and stays in the hospital has declined as a result of payment incentives in managed care and Medicare. Between 1990 and 1996, inpatient days declined 15 percent and length of stay declined 1.1 days.

While inpatient hospital days and stays have gone down, the revenues derived from outpatient services rose an average of 11.8 percent annually from 1990 to 1996. During that time hospitals were operating with stable profit margins. Hospitals increased their revenues by engaging in the business of post-acute home health care and providing nursing home services. Hospital expenditures rose from an estimate $358.5 billion in 1996 to $370.0 billion in 1997, a 3.2 percent increase. In this competitive environment hospitals will have to be more creative to attract patients.

Outlays for nursing home care amounted to $84.4 billion in 1998. Annual spending growth for home health care decreased from a high of 23.4 percent in 1992 to 9.5 percent in 1996. Growth in the number of visits per person served fell from 33 percent in 1990 to 3 percent in 1996. This was due partly to the detection of fraud and abuse in the industry. There is a moratorium on licensing and certification of new Medicare-participating home health agencies.

Expenditures for physicians' services rose to an estimated $208.2 billion in 1998, a 3 percent increase over 1997. Spending on physicians has grown at a low rate since 1990 because of the expanding role of managed care contracts and changes in physicians' practices. For instance, managed care contracts to physicians grew from 61 percent to 88 percent between 1990 and 1996, resulting in managed care revenues rising from 28 to 44 percent of total revenues. By 1996, 31 percent of physicians in practices with 25 or more physicians did direct contracting with employers. The trend of having a solo practice has changed for physicians, many of whom are now employees of managed care organizations. The proportion of physicians who were employees rose from 32 percent to 42 percent during the period 1990–1996.

HOME HEALTH CARE

Home-delivered health and medical services have become an integral part of the U.S. health care system. The high cost of hospital and nursing home care has emphasized the need for alternative, less expensive ways of delivering care to the elderly sick and disabled who do not require continuous skilled nursing care. One of the major ways of containing health care costs is by providing care in a patient's home.

Home care consists of home health agencies, home care aide organizations, and hospices. The National Association for Home Care identified 20,215 home care institutions in the United States in 1996 (see Table 44-6). This included 10,027 Medicare-certified home health agencies, 2,154 Medicare-certified hospices, and 8,034 other organizations such as home health agencies, home care aides, and hospices that do not participate in Medicare. Home health care agencies have provided services to over 7 million individuals with an acute illness, a long-term medical condition, a permanent disability, or a terminal illness. An estimated 3.9 million Medicare enrollees received home health services in 1997. Annual expenditures for home care rose from $19.6 billion in 1992 to an estimated $31.6 billion in 1997. The

TABLE 44-6: Growth of Medicare-Certified Home Health Care Agencies, 1992–1996

Year	Total	Home Health Care Agencies	Hospices	Other
1992	12,497	6,004	1,039	5,454
1993	12,959	6,497	1,223	6,239
1994	15,027	7,521	1,459	6,047
1995	18,874	9,120	1,857	7,897
1996	20,215	10,027	2,154	8,034

Source: National Association for Home Care.

TABLE 44-7: Comparison of Hospital, Skilled Nursing Facility, and Home Health Medicare Charges, 1994–1996
(current dollars)

	1994	1995	1996
Hospital charges per day	1,754	1,910	1,965
Skilled nursing facility charges per day	356	402	414
Home health charges per visit	83	84	86

Source: National Association for Home Care.

average cost per home care visit increased from $47 in 1987 to $77 in 1997.

The momentum in the growth of home health care is reflected in its cost-effectiveness compared with care from service providers in institutions such as hospitals and skilled nursing homes. Table 44-7 provides some examples of the charges paid by patients in these institutions per day and per visit. Several studies have also compared inpatient care to home care costs for a specified group of patients. Huge savings were realized for services provided under home care (see Table 44-8). Home care not only reduces health care costs but also generates employment. Employment in home care rose from 344,000 in 1991 to 666,000 in 1996.

New Medicare payment levels for home care may result in greater Medicare savings and budget surplus but lower revenues for home care companies. Interim rules enacted by Congress in 1997 cap reimbursement at agencies' actual costs, per visit cost limits, or per beneficiary cost limits, whichever is lowest.

GLOBAL SUBSECTORS

The emergence of new viable subsectors in the health care service sphere has resulted from innovations in the organization and financing of medical delivery as well as advances in technology. Because of this complexity, countries which seek foreign partners in health care are increasingly looking to so-called turnkey agreements in which a provider not only provides the needed management and consulting services but also provides the equipment, supplies, and construction supplements for the arrangement. Training of both medical specialists and the personnel who operate medical devices frequently is added to this "package."

Treatment of foreigners who travel to a provider's home facilities, often on a "cash and carry" basis, has long been a mainstay of health care service export revenues. However, the ownership, operation, or management of foreign health care facilities, especially with accompanying health insurance coverage, is becoming a more prominent activity each year. Moreover, since few health care systems have been able to escape the escalating costs that helped fuel the expansion of managed care in the United States, hybrids of this form of treatment and related modifications to traditional indemnity insurance have followed in its wake, producing opportunities for export-minded companies.

Because of the aging of the population in a number of industrialized countries, such as Germany and Japan, home health care is emerging as another promising export subsector. This form of care, like telemedicine, is being encouraged by the considerable expense of maintaining hospitals and clinics. Emergency and ambulatory services, dental care, and hospital design and construction are also proving to be among the more dynamic services sought by those developing health systems.

Although the desire to relieve the patient burden on hospitals is evident globally, in most countries the development of alternative means of care has not taken place with the same rapidity as it has in the United States. This condition, combined with the fact that medical professions in nations such as Japan constitute political forces that can resist new forms of competition in health care, ensures that the management and operation of hospitals will continue to be a critical subsector in most countries.

Internationally, telemedicine treatment represents one of the most promising services that has emerged in the health care service sector in recent years. Telemedicine represents a means for

TABLE 44-8: Cost of Inpatient Care Compared to Home Care, Selected Conditions
(current dollars)

Conditions	Per-Patient Per-Month Hospital Costs	Per-Patient Per-Month Home Care Costs	Per-Patient Per-Month Dollar Savings
Low birth weight	26,190	330	25,860
Ventilator-dependent adults	21,570	7,050	14,520
Oxygen-dependent children	12,090	5,250	6,840
Chemotherapy for children with cancer	69,870	55,950	13,920
Congestive heart failure among the elderly	1,758	1,605	153
Intravenous antibiotic therapy for cellulitis, osteomyelitis, others	12,510	4,650	7,860

Source: National Association for Home Care.

providing health care and communicating health care information over vast distances through the use of telecommunication technology. This method can include the transmission of basic patient data through computer networks as well as the transmission of x-ray, ultrasound, and magnetic resonance images. Consultations with medical specialists and patient interviews constitute another application of this form of treatment.

The objective of telemedicine is to upgrade the quality and minimize the cost of medical care by easing the communication of critical information between health care specialists. One of its chief benefits is the elimination of the necessity for a physician and a patient to be in the same geographic region. U.S. hospitals, managed care firms, physician groups, and other providers have recognized the commercial benefits that can be realized by offering such services, especially in developing countries, where they are well suited to providing a cost-effective alternative to the maintenance of expensive medical facilities. Moreover, by linking up with medical specialists in a developing country, a U.S. telemedicine provider can avoid many of the regulatory barriers it would encounter with an "on the ground" operation.

U.S. medical service firms have acted to reap the domestic benefits of this technologically advanced form of health care delivery. In particular, mergers among managed care plans have introduced challenges in the integration of computer data and communications because of widely dispersed and often disparate computer systems in the newly merged facilities. Telemedicine linkups have proved effective in coordinating such patient information and systems in addition to their cost-containment dimension. U.S. health care firms are increasingly seeking telemedicine opportunities abroad. Some instances include a telemedicine venture in two Indian cities and similar projects in developing countries such as South Africa. Another firm which specializes in long-distance satellite medical education has teamed with a U.S. satellite service provider to offer worldwide delivery of medical education and information. Companies are also seeking these opportunities in Russia, notably the Russian Far East, and a U.S. consulting firm has concluded a telemedicine arrangement with Jordan.

Some U.S. providers are taking a close look at "distance medical education" and informational programs. This application of telemedicine is intended to respond to the U.S. reduction in funding for the training of foreign physicians here by using sophisticated telecommunication and technology satellites to train physicians, especially in primary care and low-technology care, in developing countries. Fields such as teleradiology, dermatology, retinal visual imaging, and cardiac care are viewed as some of the most promising subspecialties of telemedicine.

U.S. management of foreign health care facilities, the only subsector for which import-export figures are available, should rise 5.2 percent in 1999 and approximately 7 to 7.5 percent between 1999 and 2003. Projection of future growth in this medical subspecialty is a highly problematical exercise because of providers' dependence on governmental budget allocations and often unsolicited requests for partnerships. The growth of these U.S. services, which remained stable at about $18 million in 1996, will continue to be spurred by intense demand for American management and health care financing know-how. Foreign management of U.S. facilities will fare less well in these 5 years, posting a rise between 3 and 4 percent in the face of stiff domestic competition. Foreign revenues in 1999, it is anticipated, will expand 3.3 percent, down from their 25 percent expansion in 1996.

Simon Francis, (202) 482-2697, and **Ernest Plock,** (202) 482-4783, U.S. Department of Commerce, Office of Service Industries, October 1998.

■ REFERENCES

Basic Statistics About Home Care 1997, National Association for Home Care, 228 Seventh Street, SE, Washington, DC 20003.

The Budget of the United States Government, Fiscal Year 1999, U.S. Government Printing Office, Washington, DC 20402.

Compensation and Working Conditions, Vol. 2, No. 4., U.S. Department of Labor, Bureau of Labor Statistics, Washington, DC 20212.

The Economic and Budget Outlook: Fiscal Years 1999–2008; A Report to the Senate and House Committees on the Budget, January 1998, U.S. Government Printing Office, Washington, DC 20402.

Health Affairs, Project Hope, 7500 Old Georgetown Road, Suite 600, Bethesda, MD 20814.

Health Care Financing Review, Health Care Financing Administration, Office of Research and Demonstration, U.S. Department of Health and Human Services, Baltimore, MD 21244.

Health Systems Review, FAHS Review Inc., 1405 N. Pierce Street, Suite 308, Little Rock, AR 72207.

HMO and PPO Industry Profile, 1995–1996 Edition, American Association of Health Plans, 1129 20th Street, NW, Suite 600, Washington, DC 20036.

Hospitals and Health Networks, American Hospital Publishing, Inc., 737 North Michigan Avenue, Chicago, IL 60611.

The Lagniappe Letter, Latin American Information Services, Inc., 159 West 53rd Street, 28th Floor, New York, NY 10019.

Managed Care Facts, American Associations of Health Plans, 1129 20th Street, NW, Washington, DC 20036.

National Trade Data Bank, U.S. Department of Commerce, Economics and Statistics Administration, Washington, DC 20230.

1996 HIMA Emerging Market Report, Health Industry Manufacturers Association of America, 1200 G Street, NW, Washington, DC 20230.

Report to the Congress Medicare Payment Policy, Medicare Payment Advisory Commission, 1730 K Street, NW, Suite 800, Washington, DC 20006.

Survey of Current Business, U.S. Department of Commerce, Bureau of Economic Analysis, Washington, DC 20230.

■ RELATED CHAPTERS

11: Chemicals and Allied Products
45: Medical and Dental Instruments and Supplies

■ GLOSSARY

Copayment: Any required cost sharing that involves a fixed dollar amount paid by the member each time a health care service is rendered.

Fee-for-service: The requirement that payment for health care services be made as those services are delivered.

Health maintenance organization (HMO): A health plan that offers comprehensive health care from an established panel of providers to an enrolled population on a prepaid basis.

Home health care: A method of providing services to disabled people in their homes rather than in medical facilities.

Indemnity plan: A health-care insurance program in which an insured person is reimbursed for covered expenses. The insured person may choose any provider and is subject to cost sharing, usually in the form of a deductible and coinsurance.

Managed care: A system of prepaid plans providing comprehensive coverage to voluntarily enrolled members. Managed health care typically covers professional fees, hospital services, diagnostic services, emergency health care services, limited mental services, medical treatment for drug or alcohol abuse, home health services, and preventive health care.

Medicaid: A federally supported and state-administered assistance program that provides medical care for certain low-income individuals and families.

Medicare: A U.S. government program that pays hospitals, physicians, and other medical providers for serving patients age 65 years and older, certain disabled people, and most persons with end-stage renal disease (ESRD).

Out-of-pocket payments: Payments that are not covered by insurance plans; instead, they are paid by the recipient of the medical services.

Point-of-service (POS): A health plan in which a member is enrolled in an HMO but may self-refer to providers outside the established network, typically with deductibles or other cost-sharing requirements. Also known as an open-ended HMO product.

Preferred provider organization (PPO): A health plan in which a member may self-refer to any provider but the plan offers the member the option of more comprehensive benefits and/or fewer cost-sharing requirements if the member uses the plan's designated network providers.

MEDICAL AND DENTAL INSTRUMENTS AND SUPPLIES
Economic and Trade Trends

U.S. International Trade

($ billions)

Legend: Balance, Exports, Imports

Source: U.S. Department of Commerce: Bureau of the Census; International Trade Administration.

World Export Market Shares

(%)

Legend: United States, Germany, Japan, Netherlands

Source: United Nations; U.S. Department of Commerce, International Trade Administration.

Export Dependence and Import Penetration

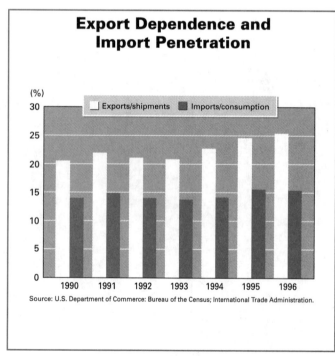

(%)

Legend: Exports/shipments, Imports/consumption

Source: U.S. Department of Commerce: Bureau of the Census; International Trade Administration.

Output and Output per Hour

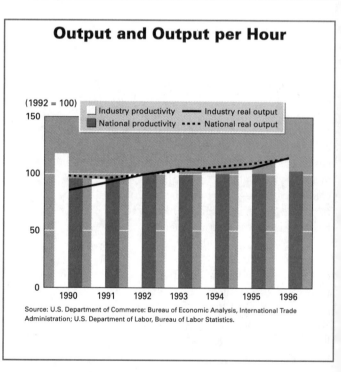

(1992 = 100)

Legend: Industry productivity, Industry real output, National productivity, National real output

Source: U.S. Department of Commerce: Bureau of Economic Analysis, International Trade Administration; U.S. Department of Labor, Bureau of Labor Statistics.

See "Getting the Most Out of *Outlook '99*" for definitions of terms.

Medical and Dental Instruments and Supplies

GLOBAL INDUSTRY TRENDS

The United States is the recognized global leader in the production of medical equipment and supplies. According to statistics provided by the Health Industry Manufacturers Association (HIMA), U.S. firms commanded about 44 percent of the $124 billion worldwide market for medical devices in 1997. The rest of the market consisted of medical products produced in Europe (27 percent), Japan (14 percent), and other areas (17 percent).

Based on HIMA data, worldwide sales in 1997 were divided by product category as follows: surgical and medical instruments, 28 percent; orthopedic devices and surgical supplies, 28 percent; diagnostic reagents, 19 percent; electromedical equipment, 14 percent; x-ray equipment, 7 percent; and dental equipment, 4 percent. Hospitals accounted for approximately two-fifths of worldwide industry sales, with the balance derived from physicians and dentists, nursing homes, clinics, home health care operators, and others.

The conventional hospital supply market is a mature business, consisting largely of commodity-type products marketed by a relatively small number of large manufacturers. This business, which includes such items as intravenous products, anesthesia items, surgical apparel, and a wide range of other conventional diagnostic and therapeutic products, is characterized by low margins, high volume, and long-term contracts with hospital management chains and other large customers.

A second, more profitable sector of the industry comprises innovative high-technology products, such as implantable cardiac defibrillators and sophisticated diagnostic imaging systems, that are designed for highly specific markets. These products typically target smaller patient populations, but are significantly more profitable than commodity items. But with these profits comes a significant risk—product obsolescence. Companies specializing in the high-tech sector typically see new products (those introduced within the preceding 2 years) accounting for more than 30 percent of sales.

The global medical device industry is expected to continue to grow at above-average rates in the years ahead. Relatively unaffected by economic cycles that impact other industries, demand for medical products should continue to increase in the years ahead, bolstered by aging populations in developed and developing countries who are disproportionately larger users of medical products and new breakthrough medical devices emerging from ambitious research and development efforts. In addition, many developing countries are modernizing their health care delivery systems, which will increase the demand for more advanced medical technologies.

Based on a study done by the World Health Organization (WHO), the global over-65 population is forecast to rise from 390 million in 1997 to over 800 million by 2025. Although more people than ever will be living longer,that does not mean they will be free from health problems. According to WHO, cancer, heart disease, and other chronic diseases, which presently cause some 24 million deaths per year, are expected to increase in the years ahead. This increase is due to a large extent to unhealthy lifestyles led by many people which include smoking, obesity, poor diet and lack of exercise.

WHO projected a doubling in cancer cases in most countries over the next 25 years, along with a 33 percent increase in lung cancers in women and a 40 percent rise in prostate cancer in men in Europe by 2005. The increasing elderly population increases the demand for cardiovascular products such as pacemakers, defibrillators, and angioplasty catheters used mostly on elderly patients. Orthopedic knee and hip implants and related products are also used primarily by the elderly, as are diagnostic imaging products such as magnetic resonance imaging (MRI) and computerized tomography (CT) machines.

New products are the engine of continuity and growth in the medical device industry. Fueled by aggressive R&D spending and increasing investment in new medical technologies, a plethora of sophisticated new medical instruments has come on the market in recent decades. These devices have helped to extend life expectancy and to improve the quality of life for millions of Americans and others around the world. Medical product manufacturers have enjoyed a relatively high rate of commercial success from their R&D efforts. Their success has, in turn, motivated them to invest increasingly large sums in new medical technology. For example, coronary artery bypass surgery and balloon angioplasty, unheard of 30 years ago, are routine procedures today. Meanwhile, new defibrillators are treating previously untreatable cardiac arrythymias.

Diagnostic procedures have been revolutionized, with state-of-the-art magnetic resonance imaging (MRI) and positron emission tomography (PET) devices now offering enhanced diagnostic capabilities for a wide range of conditions. And surgical practices have been drastically revised, reducing trauma to the patient. For example, noninvasive or minimally invasive lithotripsy and laparoscopic methods are being used to perform complex gastrointestinal operations.

The primary impetus behind new medical product development has been the desire to increase benefits to patients. In recent years, because of managed care's influence, cost-cutting has become another strong motive. In the years ahead, there should be strong demand for equipment that can reduce labor expense (which typically absorbs more than half of a hospital's budget), improve labor productivity, reduce patient hospital stays, or facilitate patient care in less expensive settings.

Examples of efficiency-fostering technological advances include the use of lasers to perform eye surgery in a physician's office rather than more expensive acute-care facilities; fiber-optics to diagnose knee and joint injuries; premixed drug solutions; continuous ambulatory peritoneal dialysis (CAPD) for patients with kidney failure, instead of more costly inpatient hemodialysis; enteral nutritional feeding systems, which use a tube to provide nutrition to a patient directly; and cardiac angioplasty and similar devices used to clear clogged arteries, instead of more costly bypass surgery.

U.S. INDUSTRY TRENDS

The U.S. medical and dental instruments and supplies manufacturers saw shipments rise 12.8 percent in 1997 in constant dollars, for a current-dollar value of $54.9 billion. The impact of the Asian financial crisis and medical health care cost containment programs limited growth of U.S. production to 3.73 percent in 1998 in constant dollars. HIMA estimated tht domestic production reached $58.1 billion that year. Boosted by strong demographic trends in the elderly, ongoing economic prosperity in the United States, new products emerging from ambitious R&D efforts, overseas expansion, and a more industry-friendly FDA, the outlook for 1999 is good with constant-dollar growth estimates of 5 percent (see Table 45-1).

The United States remains a major supplier to the world market for medical equipment with exports reaching $12.7 billion in 1998, while imports were limited to only $7 billion. The U.S. medical device manufacturers enjoyed a trade surplus of $5.7 billion. The U.S. industry continually seeks methods to maintain its international competitiveness. The industry regularly spends 8 percent of its sales on research and development. It has worked closely with the government to open foreign markets to U.S.-made devices and has supported global efforts to harmonize the regulatory system.

TABLE 45-1: Medical Instruments and Supplies (SIC 384) Trends and Forecasts
(millions of dollars except as noted)

	1992	1993	1994	1995	1996	1997[1]	1998[1]	1999[2]	96–97	97–98	98–99	92–96[3]
									Percent Change			
Industry data												
Value of shipments[4]	39,535	42,237	42,309	43,413	47,406	54,900	58,100		15.8	5.8		4.6
Value of shipments (1992 $)	39,535	41,386	41,057	41,960	45,629	51,470	53,390	56,060	12.8	3.7	5.0	3.6
Total employment (thousands)	264	271	264	265	268							0.4
Production workers (thousands)	154	157	152	154	157							0.5
Average hourly earnings ($)	11.22	11.48	11.68	12.00	12.23							2.2
Capital expenditures	1,560	1,627	1,433	1,477	1,648							1.4
Product data												
Value of shipments[4]	36,001	38,733	38,715	39,963	44,130	51,100	54,080		15.8	5.8		5.2
Value of shipments (1992 $)	36,001	37,949	37,568	38,657	42,549	48,000	49,790	52,280	12.8	3.7	5.0	4.3
Trade data												
Value of imports	4,584	4,869	4,913	5,534	5,935	6,470	7,010		9.0	8.4		6.7
Value of exports	7,574	8,041	8,734	9,802	11,161	11,940	12,750		7.0	6.8		10.2

[1] Estimate.
[2] Forecast.
[3] Compound annual rate.
[4] For a definition of industry versus product values, see "Getting the Most Out of *Outlook '99*."
Source: U.S. Department of Commerce: Bureau of the Census; International Trade Association. Estimates and forecasts based on Health Industry Manufacturers Association data.

Based on projections made by the U.S. Census Department, the over 65 segment of the U.S. population is expected to increase 34 percent from 1997 through 2015, compared with a 16 percent rise in the total U.S. population over the same period. The faster pace in the elderly reflects the baby boomer generation turning 65. The "graying of America" is especially bullish for cardiovascular products, such as pacemakers, defibrillators, and angioplasty catheters, which are used mostly on elderly patients. Orthopedic knee and hip implants and related products are also used primarily by the elderly, as are such diagnostic imaging products as magnetic resonance imaging (MRI) and computed tomography (CT).

American manufacturers of medical equipment have by now by in large adapted to the increasing influence of managed care providers in the health care marketplace. In the past, nealry all device sales were generated by company salespeople who traveled the country to apprise hospitals and surgeons of their product's merits. But major purchasing decisions are now being made by managers of health maintenance organizations (HMOs), preferred provider organizations (PPOs), large hospital consortiums, government agencies, and other large managed care buyers who wield substantial leverage in terms of product selection.

More than 60 percent of all medical device purchases in the United States are believed to be made by managed care buyers, with the proportion projected to rise to over 80 percent within the next five years. Managed care providers use their collective purchasing clout to secure discounts on bulk purchases of pharmaceuticals and medical products, as well as on physician and hospital services.

Managed care providers also typically insist on using lower-cost products whenever possible. They often employ therapeutic substitution, in which a less expensive therapy is used instead of a more expensive one. This policy has fostered greater use of low-cost pharmaceutical treatments instead of surgical procedures that use medical devices. Even when medical device procedures are sanctioned, many managed care plans limit reimbursement to a set number of approved devices.

Trends favoring the use of capitated plans and gatekeepers have generally hurt medical device sales in recent years, especially for big-ticket items such as MRI machines. Unlike conventional "fee-for-service" plans—under which hospitals and physicians are paid separately for each service provided—"capitated plans" pay hospitals a prenegotiated fixed amount each month based on the number of members enrolled in the plan. Providers in capitated contracts, whose annual top-line revenues are fixed by the number of subscribers in the customer base, can operate profitably only when their costs are below that ceiling. They are thus motivated to hold down costs and unnecessary inpatient services that could result in operating losses.

Another method that managed care operators use to hold down costs is employing "gatekeepers"—often doctors or administrative workers—to screen incoming patients to determine if hospitalization is required or whether the needed services can be done at less-expensive outpatient settings.

The ongoing movement of Medicare recipients into HMOs and other managed care plans is another trend that the medical device industry must contend with. While cost conscious managed care providers tend to limit the use of expensive procedures, the increasing number of Medicare beneficiaries in their ranks is not entirely a negative for the medical device industry.

This is because seniors enrolled in managed care plans are usually covered for most inpatient and outpatient services, while outpatient reimbursement under conventional Medicare plans is more limited. In addition, managed care efforts to hold down hospital budgets have not prevented new medical devices from achieving notable commercial success, especially for products aimed at reducing hospital stays and overall treatment costs. Federal and state health agencies are intensifying efforts to move Medicare and Medicaid recipients into HMOs and similar managed care systems because of the cost savings. Based on HCFA data, Medicare beneficiaries in managed care plans account for about 12 percent of all 38 million Medicare beneficiaries, compared with managed care's over 60 percent penetration of the general population. Based on estimates made by the Congressional Budget Office (CBO), the proportion of Medicare recipients enrolled in managed care plans will reach 27 percent by 2002.

So far, managed care has had more success in Medicaid than in Medicare, due largely to the federal government's incentives that encourage Medicaid beneficiaries to join managed care plans. About 13 million Medicaid beneficiaries, representing 35 percent of the total, are presently enrolled in managed care plans, up from 7.6 million at the end of 1992.

Faced with managed care's transformation of principal markets, an increasing number of medical device companies are seeking to enhance their competitive positions by pooling their resources via mergers and acquisition. Consolidation activity in the medical device industry is expected to continue worldwide, although probably not at the heady pace seen in pharmaceutical mergers in recent years.

After a lull of several years, merger and acquisition activity in the medical device industry picked up in 1998, with a number of high-profile mergers taking place in several different industry sectors. Key factors underlying the urge to merge include the effects of heightened competition throughout the industry, price discounting, constrained Medicare reimbursement, and the growing influence of cost-conscious managed care in the health care marketplace. The value of medical device mergers could exceed $20 billion in 1998, more than double from the estimated 1997 level.

Mergers and acquisitions are often viewed as more efficient means of growth than internal product development, which involves substantial expenditures in research and development and production and marketing, as well as battles with established products. Acquisitions, by contrast, can often be accomplished for common stock without requiring cash outlays. Significant gains in the stock prices of many leading medical products firms have fueled a significant increase in stock-for-stock or pooling-of-interests mergers in recent years. The need to create critical mass is another reason behind many mergers.

In today's marketplace, which is oriented toward managed care, size is key to success. Large hospital management chains would rather deal with one or two suppliers that can deliver their entire product needs than with numerous individual device manufacturers. Large companies are also in a better position to offer more significant price discounts and product servicing.

Another by-product of managed care is that price inflation in medical devices has been significantly curtailed. Prices for many medical and surgical products, in contrast to many other health care sectors, have actually declined in recent years. Weak pricing conditions in the medical device industry has reflected competitive pressures brought on by a more cost-conscious hospital market. This, in turn, mirrors managed care's widening influence, consolidation in the hospital industry, and less-generous Medicare reimbursement in recent years. Price weakness was especially noted in conventional surgical instruments, diagnostic apparatus, cardiac defibrillators, and cardiac pacemakers.

Demand for medical devices used in physicians' offices and ambulatory clinics has increased significantly in recent years with an increasing number of operations now being done in less-expensive outpatient settings. According to the American Hospital Association, well over half of all surgeries performed in community hospitals are now done on an outpatient basis, compared with about 20 percent 10 years ago. Within the next three or four years, nearly 75 percent of all surgical procedures are expected to be performed on an outpatient basis.

New technology has helped fuel this trend. With the aid of new medical products, surgeons now perform one-day procedures on an outpatient basis that once required expensive inpatient surgery, extensive hospital stays, and weeks of recuperation. A growing number of mobile care units now provide easier access to cardiac catheterization, magnetic resonance imaging (MRI), mammography, laparoscopy, computerized tomography (CT), and ultrasound. Technologies that offer therapeutic advantages along with cost efficiencies have been the most prominent success stories in medical technology in recent years. Some examples of these products would be minimally invasive laparoscopic surgical devices that shorten hospital stays, and balloon angioplasty, which often eliminates the need for more costly cardiac bypass procedures.

Some of the newer procedures finding widespread acceptance include radial keratotomy and photorefractive keratectomy, which use excimer lasers to cure nearsightedness and other vision problems; endometrial ablation, which removes the inner lining of the uterus to help patients suffering from exceptionally heavy or prolonged menstrual bleeding; and TMR skin resurfacing, which uses a special laser to remove wrinkles, acne scars, and other blemishes and facial imperfections.

The 1997 FDA Modernization Reform Act is proving to be a major boon to manufacturers of medical devices. Most of the bill's medical device provisions are aimed at alleviating FDA delays and the excessively long new product approval conditions that have beleaguered medical device companies in recent years. Implementation of the overall reform program entails the drafting of some 42 regulations, more than 20 guidance notices, and 45 other reports from 1998 through 2001. Key features of

this legislation with respect to medical device manufacturer include the following: exempting low-risk devices from filing requirements; eliminating other unnecessary or redundant regulations in order to free up valuable FDA resources for the review of higher-risk and potentially much more lucrative medical devices; expanding a program allowing independent outside experts to review Class II (intermediate risk) devices; and lessening restrictions on distributing reliable information about unapproved, or "off-label," uses of approved medical devices. The 1997 FDA reform legislation also makes several important changes that improve the ability of the United States to implement the medical device Mutual Recognition Agreement with the EU, discussed in detail later in this chapter.

Another recent piece of legislation affecting the U.S. medical products industry has been The Biomaterials Access Assurance Act, which was signed into law by President Clinton in August 1998. Under the new law, suppliers of raw materials used in medical devices and implants are exempted from liability lawsuits involving finished medical devices, provided they met device manufacturers' requirements. However, the new law does not protect suppliers if a court found evidence of negligence on the part of the supplier. This legislation addressed the problem of potential worsening shortages of various raw materials used in the manufacture of implantable medical devices such as pacemakers, heart valves, artificial hip and knee replacement and similar items. This condition was fostered by the previous law which allowed suppliers to be sued for defective finished products even though the supplier had no part in the design, manufacture, or sale of the finished product. The risk of huge legal costs combined with the relatively small markets for many of these biomaterials have caused most manufacturers to shun this business in recent years.

The most visible example of biomaterials shortages has been in silicone following a decision by Dow Corning and Shell not to sell silicone, Teflon, and related materials to medical device markets in the wake of the substantial lawsuits levied against Dow Corning because of alleged injuries suffered from silicone breast implants. Large class action suits and jury verdicts against Dow Corning forced that company into Chapter 11 bankruptcy.

Representing a major breakthrough in what has been one of the longest, most contested, and thorniest litigation issues in recent years, Dow Corning Corp. and attorneys for some 170,000 women alleging injuries from silicone breast implants agreed in July 1998 to a tentative settlement. The proposed settlement is part of an overall plan that would allow the company, which is a joint venture between Dow Chemical and Corning Inc., to emerge from bankruptcy. Dow Corning has been operating under Chapter 11 bankruptcy since 1995, after seeking protection from more than 19,000 breast implant suits.

Along with government agencies, banks, insurance companies, and others that rely on massive chronologically-arranged computer files, manufacturers of medical and laboratory products may experience difficulties beginning January 1, 2000. This is because their internal computer hardware and software systems are mostly encoded with two-digit year fields. As a result, computers will be unable to distinguish between the years 1900 and 2000, 1901 and 2001, and so forth. This is commonly called the Y2K problem. Although Y2K problems can usually be solved by rewriting programming software, finding the source of the problem can be extremely difficult. The search and repair process can involve sifting through billions of lines of computer code.

Responding to the problem, the federal government's Health and Human Services Department has requested that all manufacturers of medical devices and biomedical equipment review their products for Year 2000 compliance. A special alliance called the National Patient Safety Partnership (NPSP)—made up of the Veterans Administration, the American Hospital Association, and five other well-known health organizations—has also asked medical device makers to identify potential Y2K compliance issues and present this data to the public before the end of January 1999.

While most medical devices do not need correct date information in order to function, certain kinds of equipment—defibrillators, dialysis machines, EKG readers, drug-infusion pumps, and radiation equipment, to name a few—may require it. For example, incorrect dates could entail risk if those dates are incorporated into diagnostic or therapeutic systems evaluating a patient's condition over a period of time.

Generating close to two-fifths of their sales abroad, leading U.S. medical device manufacturers are significantly impacted by overseas demand, foreign business and regulatory conditions, as well as fluctuations in the dollar compared with other currencies. In recent years, export growth has benefited from the development of sophisticated diagnostic equipment and an increasing emphasis by foreign governments on providing their citizens with quality health care. Buoyed by robust demand from key markets abroad, exports of medical equipment increased about 10 percent to $12.2 billion in 1997, based

on estimates made by the U.S. Commerce Department. Imports rose 6.7 percent to $6.6 billion, resulting in a net trade surplus of $5.6 billion (see Table 45-2).

These favorable trends are expected to continue in the years ahead. Record trade surpluses with Europe and Asia (excluding Japan) occurred in 1997, but trade comparisons with Canada and Japan were negative. Despite ongoing economic woes in Asia, key markets such as Taiwan, India, and Hong Kong are expected to show continued trade growth in 1998. U.S. firms continue to build manufacturing and marketing infrastructures abroad to better serve local markets and to improve manufacturing efficiency. Relocation of production and R&D facilities overseas offers many advantages in terms of lowering production costs and being able to ship and deliver products on a more timely basis. Easier product development is another important incentive spurring foreign expansion. New product approval times in Europe are usually faster than in the United States, which is restrained by tougher FDA approval requirements.

Although emerging markets accounted for about 14 percent of the world medical technology market in 1997, they are expected to grow significantly by 2005. The U.S. medical device market is expected to expand by about 6 percent a year over the next few years, comparable to the pace projected for the whole world. Growth may slow to 5 percent in Europe, partially reflecting greater conservatism in government health care spending. Meanwhile, the annual growth rate for 1997–1999 for Asia and Latin America is expected to be higher than the growth rate in Europe or in the United States.

The 1999 debut of the euro, Europe's new currency, has favorable implications for the medical device industry. Besides helping to equalize prices for medical products throughout the European Union (EU), the common currency should also help standardize business practices and enhance marketing strategies throughout the EU.

TABLE 45-2: Trade Patterns in Medical Instruments and Supplies[1]
(millions of dollars; percent)

Exports			Imports		
Regions[2]	Value[3]	Share, %	Regions[2]	Value[3]	Share, %
NAFTA	1,534	12.6	NAFTA	1,176	18.0
Latin America	932	7.6	Latin America	376	5.7
Western Europe	5,559	45.5	Western Europe	2,762	42.2
Japan/Chinese Economic Area	2,530	20.7	Japan/Chinese Economic Area	1,580	24.1
Other Asia	675	5.5	Other Asia	414	6.3
Rest of world	989	8.1	Rest of world	244	3.7
World	12,219	100.0	World	6,552	100.0
Top Five Countries	Value	Share, %	Top Five Countries	Value	Share, %
Japan	2,037	16.7	Japan	1,114	17.0
Germany	1,171	9.6	Germany	1,082	16.5
Netherlands	1,082	8.9	Mexico	923	14.1
Canada	1,076	8.8	China	338	5.2
France	802	6.6	United Kingdom	306	4.7

[1] SIC 384.

[2] For definitions of regional groupings, see "Getting the Most Out of *Outlook '99*."

[3] Values may not sum to total due to rounding.

Source: U.S. Department of Commerce, Bureau of the Census.

The euro will also foster the consolidation trend that has been in place in the healthcare industry. The use of one currency will allow U.S. companies a better understanding of the relative profitability among prospective acquisition candidates in Europe. The common currency should also encourage greater unity among European nations in attempts to standardize regulatory approval processes and reimbursement procedures for medical products.

In June 1998 the EU's Medical Devices Directive (MDD) went into effect on a mandatory basis. These rules require products to comply with specified standards of design, performance, and safety. Devices conforming to these requirements are eligible to apply for the CE mark, which is the stamp of approval that allows the device to be marketed in each of the 15 nations of the European Union.

Similar to FDA guidelines, the MDD provides for medical products to be classified under one of four different categories based on their relative level of risk: Class I, for low-risk items; Class IIa and IIb, medium-risk; and Class III, high-risk. MDD also provides for conformity assessment procedures, which include independent expert assessment of the product.

The United States and the EU have recently entered into a Mutual Recognition Agreement (MRA) with respect to medical devices (medical devices is one of several MRAs). The medical device MRA allows for mutual product approval and inspection of medical device manufacturing facilities in the United States and EU. For product approval, for an agreed-upon list of medium risk (Class II) medical devices, European-based notified bodies will review European medical devices to be exported to the United States based upon FDA standards. Similarly, U.S.-based Conformity Assessment Bodies (CABs) will review U.S. products for export to the EU based upon the EU's Medical Device Directive (MDD).

For plant inspections, U.S. manufacturing facilities will be inspected by U.S.-based CABs based upon the EU's Quality System Requirements (QSRs). Similarly, EU manufacturing facilities will be inspected by EU CABs based upon U.S. QSRs. While product approvals are limited to specific devices indentified in the medical device annex of the MRA, plant inspections apply to all U.S. and EU manufacturing facilities. The MRA, which goes into force December 1, 1998, is a 3-year agreement which is viewed as a confidence-building period with the goal of expanding the number of medical devices covered both during the 3-year confidence-building period and after.

It is the goal of the MRA to establish a model MRA between the EU and the United States in which each party will normally endorse the reports of listed CABs for certain medical device product approvals and plant inspections, simplifying and improving two-way trade. It is also hoped that the success of the U.S.-EU MRA will be an important step toward global harmonization under the Global Harmonization Task Force. For this reason, the United States does not support or seek multiple MRAs, but only *one* with the EU. Multiple MRAs between developed countries would result in 200 MRAs, a system which would be far more difficult than harmonization under one global system agreed to by all developed

countries. USG and U.S. medical device industry associations hope the U.S./EU harmonization process will lead to global harmonization among developed countries under the Global Harmonization Task Force (GHTF). The GHTF is composed of developed economies (United States, Canada, the EU, Australia, and New Zealand) with certain Asian countries as observers. The goal of the GHTF is to establish uniform medical device regulations among these developed countries, which will likely be adopted by other countries to form new global medical device regulatory standards.

The U.S. medical device industry exported over $1 billion to emerging markets in Asia in 1998 according to HIMA. The leading U.S. export markets in that region in 1998 are summarized in Table 45-3.

Along with other U.S. export industries, medical device manufacturers have been hurt by widespread currency devaluations and sagging economies in Asia. Nonetheless, U.S. exports of medical products to that region should increase in 1998.

Furthermore, the area still offers promising long-term growth opportunities. Based on rising standards of living and greater governmental emphasis on improving overall health levels, the market for medical products in Asia is expected to grow rapidly in the years ahead. The region accounted for about 9 percent of worldwide medical technology sales in 1997.

Now, more than ever, future exports of medical devices around the world will be driven by each country's reimbursement issuance systems and regulatory requirements. The U.S. Department of Commerce and U.S. medical device industry associations work closely together in many markets to encourage development of reimbursement systems which recognize advantages of advanced medical technologies, as well as transparent and unrestricted regulatory procedures.

Meanwhile, the industry is taking several steps to weather the present economic crisis in Asia. Acting on behalf of U.S. medical companies, the Health Industry Manufacturers Association has persuaded several Asian countries to raise device reimbursement rates to compensate for currency losses. Fearing a possible supply shortage of critical medical devices, regulatory agencies in Korea granted a 30 percent increase in reimbursement rates for many medical products, while Thailand offered an 18 percent hike. Presently, devalued Asian currencies also offer U.S. firms more attractive investment opportunities in Asia. In that

TABLE 45-3: U.S. Exports to Asia (Excluding Japan) in 1998

Country	$ millions	Percent Change from 1997
India	89.9	13
Hong Kong (PRC)	239.8	8
Taiwan	196.0	5
China	131.4	No change
Singapore	152.9	−7
Malaysia	35.7	−46
Philippines	16.8	−46
South Korea	143.3	−54
Thailand	27.6	−63
Asia total	1,017.8	−20

region, expenses involved in constructing manufacturing facilities, as well as the cost of labor to operate the plants, are typically significantly below those of industrialized nations.

When assessing the effects of the Asian financial crisis on the medical device market, it is most useful to group countries according to the strength of their currencies, rather than to analyze the market as a whole. Those countries that have been most affected by the financial crisis imported only 2 percent of all U.S. medical device exports in 1996, when demand in those countries was at its highest. Countries that have not suffered radical currency devaluation, namely Singapore, India, China, Hong Kong (PRC), and Taiwan, are still increasing their demand for U.S. medical devices. U.S. medical device exports to these countries totaled approximately 6 percent of all U.S. medical device exports in 1997, and trade statistics indicate that the percentage will increase in 1998.

The statistics reflect a distinct pattern. In those countries that devalued—Thailand, the Philippines, Malaysia, South Korea, and Indonesia—U.S. medical device exports decreased by an average of 44 percent between the second quarter of 1997 and the second quarter of 1998. However, for the same period, those countries that did not undergo severe currency devaluations—Singapore, India, China, Hong Kong, and Taiwan—averaged an increase of U.S. medical device exports of 105 percent.

This growth pattern should encourage U.S. device manufacturers, considering the intensified competition from Japan. The yen has considerably weakened against the dollar, making Japanese medical devices more attractive to cost-conscious purchasers. Asian countries that have not devalued their currencies may have increased purchases of Japanese devices, but this has not slowed the rate of demand for U.S. devices.

Herman Saftlas, Standard & Poor's Corporation, (212) 208-1199, October 1998; and *U.S. Department of Commerce,* Office of Microelectronics, Medical Equipment and Instrumentation, (202) 482-2587, November 1998.

INSURANCE
Economic and Trade Trends

Asset Distribution for Life Insurance

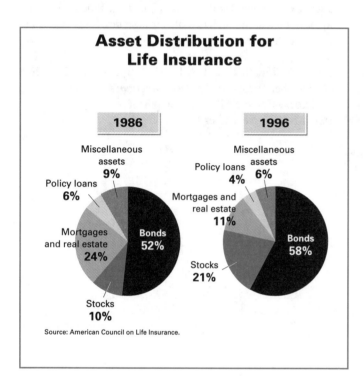

1986

Miscellaneous assets 9%

Policy loans 6%

Mortgages and real estate 24%

Bonds 52%

Stocks 10%

1996

Miscellaneous assets 6%

Policy loans 4%

Mortgages and real estate 11%

Bonds 58%

Stocks 21%

Source: American Council on Life Insurance.

Asset Distribution for Property/Casualty Insurance

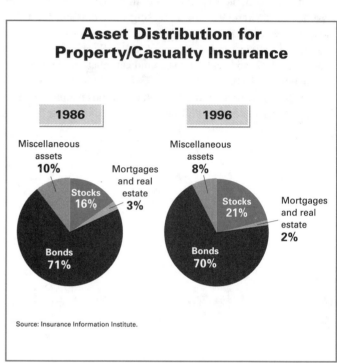

1986

Miscellaneous assets 10%

Mortgages and real estate 3%

Stocks 16%

Bonds 71%

1996

Miscellaneous assets 8%

Mortgages and real estate 2%

Stocks 21%

Bonds 70%

Source: Insurance Information Institute.

Growth Trends in Global Insurance Industry

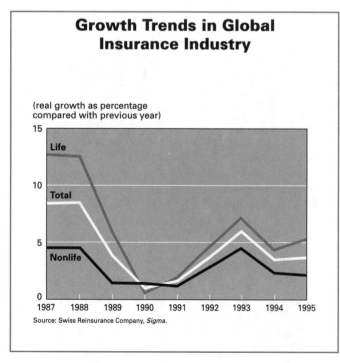

(real growth as percentage compared with previous year)

Life

Total

Nonlife

1987 1988 1989 1990 1991 1992 1993 1994 1995

Source: Swiss Reinsurance Company, *Sigma*.

Regional Growth Rates for the Insurance Industry

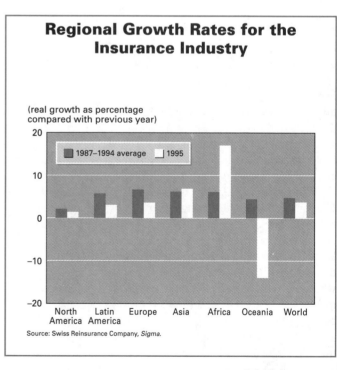

(real growth as percentage compared with previous year)

■ 1987–1994 average   □ 1995

North America   Latin America   Europe   Asia   Africa   Oceania   World

Source: Swiss Reinsurance Company, *Sigma*.

Insurance

INDUSTRY DEFINITION Insurance provides financial protection for individuals, commercial businesses, and others against illness, death, loss of property, or losses by a third party for which the insured is liable. Insurance companies are classified mainly under life insurance (SIC 631), accident and health (SIC 632), and property/casualty (i.e., fire, marine, and casualty insurance, SIC 633).

OVERVIEW

Insurance in the United States can be divided into two broad categories: life and health insurance and property and casualty (P/C) insurance. Approximately 7,900 domestic insurance companies are based in the United States. Together, the life insurance and P/C insurance markets provided 2.2 million jobs and had assets of $3.1 trillion at the end of 1996.

The insurance market is a vital component of the U.S. economy, providing individuals and businesses with financial security and generating large amounts of capital for investment. Insurance companies account for a significant proportion of financial assets in the U.S. economy, and life insurers hold about a fifth of American pension funds and mutual funds.

Individuals and families rely on life, retirement income, health, automobile, and homeowner insurance to provide protection against financial loss. Businesses count on insurance to protect factories against fire losses, provide worker's compensation when there is a workplace injury, pay for product liability losses, and provide health and retirement benefits to workers and their families.

With more than $549.5 billion in premiums in 1996, the U.S. insurance market is the second largest in the world, behind that of Japan. The U.S. market is arguably the most competitive in the world. Many analysts consider the U.S. market to be essentially saturated, and future growth in premiums, therefore, will be limited. The U.S. insurance industry as a whole is financially healthy, although the threat of environmental liabilities and catastrophic losses could affect the well-being of the P/C industry.

Increased competition in the U.S. market, the dominant trend in the industry, will come from banks and other financial institutions, alternative risk mechanisms such as captives and increased self-insurance, and foreign providers as the market becomes increasingly global. These competitive pressures will continue to force insurance providers to reduce costs through new information technology, product specialization, and consolidation. Reducing the costs of distribution, particularly agency systems, should remain especially important in an increasingly competitive environment.

Growth of the U.S. insurance industry will come primarily from markets outside the United States. American companies continue to invest overseas, where markets are growing faster and are more profitable. Growing economies in Asia and Latin America are becoming priority markets for many U.S. insurance providers. Global trends toward open markets and deregulation are providing U.S. insurers with opportunities for growth that cannot be found in the mature U.S. market. Recent trade agreements directly affecting insurance have strengthened these trends. Foreign insurers from Europe and other regions are entering the U.S. market, mainly through acquisitions, to compete with U.S. insurers on a global basis.

Life Insurance

At the end of 1996 the U.S. life insurance industry consisted of nearly 1,700 companies engaged in underwriting life insurance and annuities, a decline of 1.2 percent from 1995. Life insurance companies also underwrite accident and health insurance and manage pension and trust funds. These companies are classified mostly under life insurance (SIC 631) and accident and health insurance (SIC 632). Most life insurance firms are stock companies (owned by shareholders), while a large proportion of the rest are mutual companies (owned by policyholders).

TABLE 46-1:   Premium Receipts of U.S. Life Insurance Companies
(millions of dollars)

	1992	1993	1994	1995	1996
Life insurance premiums					
Ordinary	65,788	74,872	75,592	78,069	82,430
Group	15,977	17,407	18,297	18,560	19,968
Industrial	481	459	462	410	390
Credit[1]	1,622	1,710	1,921	1,886	1,826
Total	83,868	94,448	96,272	98,925	104,614
Annuity considerations					
Individual	61,348	76,987	80,832	77,370	84,067
Group	71,297	79,458	73,017	82,565	92,228
Total	132,645	156,445	153,849	159,935	176,295
Health insurance premiums					
Individual	16,718	18,641	20,442	22,809	20,746
Group	47,319	48,405	53,822	55,708	50,814
Credit[1]	1,508	1,612	1,957	1,835	1,642
Total	65,545	68,658	76,221	80,352	73,202
Total premium receipts	282,058	319,551	326,342	339,212	354,111

[1] Credit insurance is limited to insurance on loans of 10 years or less.
Source: American Council of Life Insurance.

Life insurance companies receive funds from two main sources: premiums paid by policyholders and earnings on investments. Overall, premium growth for life insurance companies has barely kept ahead of growth in the economy, increasing just under 6 percent annually from 1992 to 1996 to total just over $354 billion (see Table 46-1). Life companies receive premium income from three major product areas: life insurance, annuities, and health insurance. The growth of annuity income and the relative decline of premiums from life policies constitute an industry trend. In 1996, life insurance policies accounted for 29.5 percent of premium income at almost $105 billion while annuities accounted for nearly half at $176.3 billion. This is in stark contrast to the situation in the 1970s, when life insurance premiums accounted for nearly half of all income and annuities accounted for only 21.1 percent. Income from health insurance fell slightly in 1996 to 20.7 percent of total premium income, or $73.2 billion, from 22.7 percent 10 years earlier. The growth in annuities can be attributed largely to increases in group annuities related to tax-favored 401(k) pension plans. This shift from traditional life insurance products to annuity and retirement products—from managing mortality risks to managing investment risks—has brought life insurers into direct competition with banks, securities firms, and mutual funds. The slowing of growth in health care costs and the move to managed care have constrained the growth of premiums for health insurance.

The assets of life insurance companies have increased steadily over the last few years to total over $2.3 trillion in 1996, an increase of 8.4 percent from 1995, compared with a growth rate of 10.4 percent from 1994. Life insurance ranks third among institutional sources of funds, providing 10.8 percent of all the funds that go into financial markets. The assets of

life insurers are placed into four major investment areas: bonds (government and corporate), stocks, mortgage and real estate holdings, and policy loans. The mix of assets in life insurers' portfolios changed significantly from 1986 to 1996. Holdings of mortgages and real estate declined by more than half to 11.1 percent in 1996, while stock holdings more than doubled to 20.6 of total assets. Bond holdings also increased, going from 51.9 percent of total assets in 1986 to 58 percent in 1996. While bond holdings continue to represent a majority of assets for life insurers, a situation prompted in part by concerns about solvency in the early 1990s and the adoption of risk-based capital standards by state regulators, changes in investment yields have contributed to the growth of stock assets. Life insurers have shifted much of the reliance on mortgages of the 1980s to other sources.

Many larger life insurers have been affected by questionable market conduct practices, such as deceptively selling life insurance as retirement annuity products and making overly optimistic predictions about investment performance that do not come true. This has hurt many companies and the industry as a whole at a time when the products of life insurers are competing more directly with those of other financial institutions.

Employment by life and health insurers totaled 909,000 in 1996, a decrease of 2.5 percent from 932,000 in 1995 (see Table 46-2). Employment by companies selling mainly life insurance fell to 521,600 in 1996 from 575,100 in 1995 after experiencing fast growth in 1993 and 1994. Employment by insurers that sell primarily health insurance increased to 322,100 in 1996 from 306,100 in 1995. These increases are mainly attributable to growth in the operation of health maintenance organizations and other managed care entities by insurance companies.

TABLE 46-2: Employment in Insurance
(annual averages)

Year	Property/Casualty	Life and Health	Agents, Brokers, and Service Personnel	All Industry
1987	588,000	828,000	612,000	2,027,000
1988	599,000	836,000	640,000	2,075,000
1989	609,000	830,000	652,000	2,090,000
1990	620,000	843,000	663,000	2,126,000
1991	620,000	875,000	666,000	2,161,000
1992	618,000	878,000	657,000	2,152,000
1993	617,000	912,000	668,000	2,197,000
1994	616,000	936,000	684,000	2,236,000
1995	597,000	932,000	696,000	2,225,000
1996	601,000	909,000	707,000	2,127,000

Source: U.S. Department of Labor, Bureau of Labor Statistics.

Property/Casualty Insurance

The P/C insurance industry provides financial protection for individuals, commercial businesses, and others against losses of property or losses by third parties for which the insured are liable. P/C insurance companies are classified under fire, marine, and casualty insurance (SIC 633). There are more than 2,600 P/C companies in the United States. Most are organized as stock companies, with some organized as mutual companies.

P/C products include individual and commercial automobile, homeowner, commercial property (e.g., fire, multiple peril), general liability, medical malpractice, and marine insurance. P/C insurers also write accident and health insurance policies.

Premiums in the P/C industry increased 3.4 percent from 1995 to 1996, reaching a total of $268.4 billion (see Table 46-3). Personal insurance led this growth: Automobile insurance increased 5.2 percent, and homeowner insurance increased 6 percent. The largest increase in net premiums written by P/C firms was in the area of financial guaranty, which grew 27.2 percent from 1995 to 1996 but accounted for only $2.7 billion in total premiums in that year. Underwriting profitability for

personal lines has stabilized recently as a result of better control of health care costs and more selective underwriting of catastrophic risks.

At 2 percent per year, growth in commercial insurance premiums was lower than the rate of inflation in the period 1995–1996. This resulted from excess capacity and competition suppressing premium rates and the use of alternative risk-financing mechanisms by corporate insureds, particularly for worker's compensation. Most of the growth in premiums was in property lines, in which the prospect of catastrophe losses kept rates somewhat firm. This was reflected in reinsurance markets as well. Underwriting profitability has been strained by unprecedented catastrophic losses and increased reserving for environmental liabilities.

Employment by P/C insurers increased in 1996 to 601,000 over the 1995 figure of 597,000, a growth rate less than 1 percent (see Table 46-2). Expenses for P/C insurers remained a problem. Only a strong investment performance kept P/C insurers profitable in those years. The industry also strengthened its balance sheet by increasing its reserves and enhancing its capital in response to new risk-based capital requirements. Assets increased to $802.3 billion (6.1 percent growth) as the industry maintained its high reliance on bonds. The policyholder surplus improved to $255.5 billion (13.6 percent growth) in 1996.

TABLE 46-3: Property/Casualty Premiums by Line of Business
(billions of dollars)

	1990	1996	Percent Change
Personal lines			
Private automobile	78.4	107.7	37.3
Homeowner multiple peril	18.6	25.4	36.6
Total	97.0	133.1	37.2
Commercial lines			
Commercial automobile	17.0	17.6	3.5
Liability (nonauto)	22.1	24.4	10.4
Worker's compensation	31.0	25.1	−19.0
Others	50.8	68.2	34.2
Total	120.9	135.3	11.9
Total	217.9	268.4	23.2

Source: A.M. Best; Insurance Information Institute.

GLOBAL MARKET PERFORMANCE

World premium volume was $2.143 trillion in 1995, exceeding $2 trillion for the first time. The 1994 premium figures were $1.986 trillion. The growth rate in the global insurance market was 3.7 percent in 1995, compared with 3.5 percent in 1994. The United States had the second largest insurance market in the world in 1995 with 29.11 percent of worldwide premiums, slightly lower than its 30.2 percent share in 1994. Japan remained the largest insurance market in 1995 with $637.3 billion, or 29.73 percent of world premiums, a decrease of 1 percent from 1994. This included $510.4 billion of premiums in the life insurance market, reflecting the propensity of the Jap-

TABLE 46-4: World's Leading Insurance Countries in 1995
(written premiums in millions of dollars)

Rank	Country	Nonlife Premiums[1]	Life Premiums	Total Premiums	Percent of Total World Premiums
1	Japan[2]	126,808	510,448	637,256	29.73
2	United States[3]	359,466[4]	264,509	623,975	29.11
3	Germany	92,752	62,299	155,051	7.23
4	France	48,392	83,245	131,637	6.14
5	United Kingdom	55,230	72,674	127,904	5.97
6	South Korea[2]	13,251	46,738	59,989	2.80
7	Italy	24,306	14,260	38,566	1.80
8	Canada	20,821	16,348	37,169	1.73
9	The Netherlands	16,514	18,760	35,274	1.65
10	Switzerland	11,357	20,374	31,731	1.48

[1] Includes accident and health insurance.
[2] April 1, 1995 to March 31, 1996.
[3] Net premiums written.
[4] Includes health insurance premiums written by commercial insurers.
Source: Swiss Reinsurance Company, *Sigma,* No. 4/97.

anese to save through insurance products. Germany, France, and the United Kingdom were the next largest markets after the United States (see Table 46-4). Growth rates varied considerably from region to region. Insurance volume grew fastest in Africa in 1995 (16.9 percent), followed by Asia (6.7 percent), Europe (3.4 percent), Latin America (2.9 percent), and North America (1.4 percent). Oceania was the only region to record a decline in insurance volume, at −14 percent. The significant rates of change in Africa and Oceania were due primarily to the volatile single premium life insurance business in each region's respective dominant markets, South Africa and Australia.

U.S. insurers have expanded their presence in foreign markets in recent years, although foreign activities still constitute a relatively small proportion of their overall business. Table 46-5 shows that U.S.-owned insurers in foreign countries had sales (premium income plus investment income plus other income) of $54.5 billion in 1995, up 16 percent from $47 billion in 1994. Canada, Europe, and Japan continue to be key markets for U.S. insurers. Most foreign sales have been nonlife operations, but U.S. life insurers also have become more active overseas. Additionally, according to U.S. Commerce Department statistics, foreign markets were more than twice as profitable as the U.S. market for U.S. insurers in that period.

Foreign-owned insurers in the United States had sales of $88.1 billion in 1995, up from $54.4 billion in 1989 and $78.3 in 1994, mainly as a result of acquisitions. They captured more than 16 percent of the U.S. premium market in 1995, up 6 percent from 1994. Most foreign-owned insurers in this country are from Europe or Canada.

Cross-border trade in insurance constitutes a small but important part of the U.S. insurance market. U.S.-based insurers received more than $5.8 billion in premiums from overseas (exports) in 1995. Premiums of $13.7 billion, of which $12 billion consisted of reinsurance, went to foreign-based insurers (imports) to cover risks in the United States. Among the premi-

TABLE 46-5: Operations of Foreign Insurance Affiliates of U.S. Companies[1]
(billions of dollars except as noted)

	1990	1995[2]	Percent Change
All insurance			
Number of affiliates	627	701	11.8
Total assets	111.6	206.6	85.1
Sales[3]	34.8	54.5	56.6
Employment (thousands)	98.5	96.1	−2.4
Life insurance			
Number of affiliates	109	139	27.5
Total assets	41.5	71.7	72.8
Sales[3]	11.9	19.6	64.7
Employment (thousands)	25.7	32.9	28.0
Other insurance[4]			
Number of affiliates	514	562	9.3
Total assets	70.1	134.9	92.4
Sales[3]	22.9	34.9	52.4
Employment (thousands)	72.8	65.2	−10.4

[1] Affiliates include entities with at least 10 percent ownership by a nonbank U.S. parent.
[2] Preliminary estimates.
[3] Sales equal premium and investment income plus other income.
[4] Includes nonlife insurers, agencies, brokerage firms, and other insurance-related companies.
Source: U.S. Department of Commerce, Bureau of Economic Analysis.

ums sent abroad, most went to Europe or offshore centers such as Bermuda. Reinsurance premiums sent abroad represent about one-third of the reinsurance market in the United States and provide much of the capacity for large property and liability risks. The performance of the U.S. reinsurance market in 1996 was similar to that of previous years, with sluggish premium gains. Premiums reached $18.9 billion in 1996, up 4.5 percent from 1995. However, most companies were able to increase their premiums, mainly through acquisitions.

FACTORS AFFECTING FUTURE U.S. INDUSTRY GROWTH

Financial Market Integration

With the freeing up of interest rates and reforms in capital markets, the regulatory lines separating banking, securities, and insurance that have existed in the United States since the 1930s are being eroded by the realities of the marketplace and the actions of regulators, courts, and legislatures. Life insurers have shifted their focus from traditional life insurance products to annuities and other investment-type products. Banks have changed their emphasis by attempting to deliver a broader array of financial products to their customers, including investment products such as annuities and asset management services. Life insurers and banks therefore are competing head to head with securities firms, including mutual funds, to manage personal and institutional savings and investments. Furthermore, banks are seeking additional fee income through the sale of insurance company products. An expansion of this sales outlet will continue to put pressure on the high-cost agency systems most insurers now have in place.

This trend has been supported by recent U.S. Supreme Court decisions holding that annuities are investment products, not insurance products, and that national banks in towns with a population of 5,000 or less can sell insurance. The comptroller of the currency, who regulates national banks, has been actively approving the right of banks to engage in insurance activities. The 105th Congress, in the Financial Services Competition Act of 1997 (H.R.10), addressed issues of functional regulation and affiliations among financial institutions as it considered financial modernization legislation. This adds up to more competition for insurance companies now and in the future.

Alternative Risk Mechanisms

Alternative risk mechanisms include captives, risk retention groups, self-insurance, and other mechanisms employed by commercial insureds to avoid the high costs and availability problems of the commercial insurance market or to capture profits from these risk-bearing activities. Self-insurance is commonly used for worker's compensation, whereas risk retention groups and captives are used for liability coverages such as product and medical malpractice liability. It has been estimated that these mechanisms now account for more than one-third of commercial insurance overages, and they have contributed to the slow growth of premiums in the last few years. In addition, these mechanisms tend to underwrite the more predictable risks, leaving the more volatile risks in the portfolios of P/C insurers. This naturally brings into question the adequacy of insurance company reserves for these unpredictable liabilities.

Globalization

As in the economy in general, insurance and financial markets are becoming increasingly global. Advances in information gathering and communications have made it possible for even the smallest investor to purchase financial instruments from almost anywhere abroad. The rise in personal income and savings in many areas of the world, combined with the need to protect this wealth, provides significant opportunities for life insurers. This environment makes it possible for life insurance companies to seek premiums and place investments globally.

The growth of multinational companies and international trade and investment has prompted the growth of international nonlife insurance companies and insurance brokers that service the local and global needs of companies for protection from all types of risk. Therefore, insurers from Europe, Asia, and the United States have expanded internationally. In addition to providing insurance products, insurance companies create jobs, provide for capital formation, transfer services and technologies such as claims adjusting, risk management, actuarial and investment services, and information technologies in these markets.

Because of globalization, most countries are moving toward establishing more liberal insurance markets. The pressure of the global economy, the lack of local insurance capacity, and the demand for trade liberalization have pushed many countries to accelerate insurance market reforms, privatize government-owned insurers, and invite foreign participation. Private insurance markets have proved to be a very effective means for dealing with some of the larger economic and social issues all governments face, including providing pension and retirement income, financing and delivering health care, and encouraging sound worker safety and environmental practices.

With multilateral and bilateral trade actions such as the General Agreement on Trade in Services (GATS) and the financial services agreement reached in December 1997, barriers to insurance which limit foreign participation and opportunities in domestic markets are falling. As they adjust to globalization, insurance supervisors are beginning to cooperate to set common standards, guard against problem companies, and prevent fraud and abuse.

However, some barriers are still in place. Certain markets, such as India and China, either are completely closed to foreign competition or maintain a high degree of government control over the licensing process which denies equal opportunity to foreign insurers. Malaysia and China, as well as other Asian countries, limit foreign ownership. Local companies often receive preferential treatment, such as exclusive government procurement and tax benefits. Brokers are not recognized in many countries, and the lack of transparency of government regulations in many markets remains a major barrier.

Consolidation

Over the last few years the new global competitive environment and the search for cost efficiencies have spurred mergers and acquisitions in the insurance industry. This merger and acquisition boom is expected to continue. In 1996, merger and acquisition activity in the insurance sector totaled a record $40.8 billion, up 51.7 percent from of $26.9 in 1995 and a staggering 226.4 percent from $12.5 billion in 1994. Approximately 40 percent of the mergers and acquisitions activity in 1996 occurred in the health and managed care areas.

Although this trend has increased concentration, both the life and health industry and the P/C industry remain highly competitive. Much of the merger and acquisition activity involves foreign entities acquiring U.S. insurance companies. This trend began to accelerate in 1988 with the purchase of Farmers Group, an insurance company in California, by Batus Inc. of the United Kingdom. Other foreign investments include Axa Groupe's (France) majority investment in the Equitable Life Assurance Society of New York and the 1991 purchase by Allianz (Germany) of the Fireman's Fund of California. In 1995 Zurich Insurance Group of Switzerland purchased Kemper Corporation of Illinois.

However, whereas merger and acquisition activity used to revolve around the acquisition of "vulnerable" companies, it is now focused much more on strategic alliances as companies stress building market share through acquisition rather than international growth. In 1996, Aetna of Connecticut sold its domestic P/C operations to the Travelers Group and acquired U.S. Healthcare, Berkshire Hathaway acquired the balance of GEICO, and the CNA Financial Group acquired Continental Insurance. In 1998 St. Paul agreed to acquire USF&G. Citibank and Travelers shocked the financial community by announcing their $70 billion merger. It is expected that the proposed creation of Citigroup will transform financial services in the United States by unifying disparate industries and accelerating the globalization of markets. Strategic alliances between banks and insurers may continue to be formed, especially if Congress passes the Financial Services Competition Act to ease restrictions on bank ownership of insurance companies. However, the spate of large-firm mergers is likely to force smaller, independent insurance companies to seek creative solutions to stay competitive.

Consolidation has affected reinsurance markets on a global basis as insurers seek stronger reinsurers at better prices. The highlights of this activity have been General Reinsurance's acquisition of National Reinsurance (United States) and Cologne Reinsurance (Germany) to become the second largest reinsurer in the world. Competition in commercial P/C lines has affected even large insurance brokers, with the Aon Group picking up Bain Hogg (United Kingdom) and Alexander and Alexander (United States) and Marsh and McLennan acquiring Johnson & Higgins. Similar trends toward insurance consolidation are occurring in Europe, spurred by European Union aspirations for a single market, and in other foreign markets as well. Market conditions strongly suggest that consolidation trends in insurance are likely to continue in the foreseeable future.

Technology

Advances in information and communications technology are rapidly changing the nature of the insurance and financial markets. The insurance industry has invested heavily in information technology equipment, and there is evidence that this investment has resulted in lower operating costs. Competition in the industry, especially among personal lines, suggests that these cost savings are passed on to customers in the form of lower prices and better service. State insurance regulators are exploring ways to use information technology to reduce regulatory costs and burdens on the industry, such as the Insurance Regu-

latory Information Network, in which standard information o agents and brokers will be kept to allow more efficient mult state licensing.

Information technology should continue to have a profoun long-term effect on the structure and operation of the industry Technology will allow niche players to compete locally an financial conglomerates to compete globally and vice versa Much of this consolidation is driven by a desire to captur information cost efficiencies. Technology will allow the deve opment of new products and new businesses as insurance an financial risks are unbundled. Certainly, advances in informa tion technology are setting the stage for the integration of finar cial services.

U.S. INDUSTRY GROWTH PROJECTIONS

In general, the insurance industry should grow at the same rat as the economy but probably will be restricted by the sam forces that have determined its performance over the last fev years. The maturity of the U.S. market and the high degree c competition in the industry will keep prices down, profit mai gins thin, and consolidation the norm. The market should favc insurance consumers. Insurers will attempt to offer new finar cial services and enter foreign markets to meet their revenu and profit goals. Although the balance sheet of the industr should remain strong, a sharp upswing in catastrophic losses c turmoil in economic and financial markets could disrupt it future performance.

Net written premiums for P/C insurers are expected to grov 3.1 percent in 1999 to reach $296 billion. Premium receipts fc life insurers should increase to $395 billion in 1999, up 4 pe cent from 1998. These trends are expected to continue at leas through 2003, when P/C premiums will total about $324 billio and life and health insurance premiums will increase to abou $443 billion (see Table 46-6).

Income growth, wealth accumulation, population and wor force changes, and home ownership will determine the deman for the products of life insurers over the long term. The aging c the baby boom generation is creating demand for products t provide retirement income and health care financing. The cor cern with health care costs, however, should maintain the tren toward managed care insurance.

Competition in insurance markets should increase. Wit favorable government policies, banks will be authorized to se favorable government insurance and securities and insurers wi be able to enter the banking and securities markets. In an event, banks, mutual funds, and other financial institutions wi offer investment and savings products that will compet directly with insurance and annuity products. Banks also shoul increase their sales of automobile and homeowner insurance Foreign insurers should continue to expand into the largel unrestricted U.S. market, and U.S. insurers probably wi expand abroad to capture faster growing and more profitabl foreign markets. Large commercial insureds can be expected t continue, and may expand, their use of alternative risk mecha

TABLE 46-6: Insurance Trends and Forecasts

(millions of dollars except as noted)

	1989	1993	1994	1995	1996	1997[1]	1998[1]	1999[2]	2003[2]	Percent Change			
										96–97	97–98	98–99	89–96[3]
Life and health													
Premium receipts	244	320	326	339	353	366	380	395	443	3.5	4.0	4.0	5.4
Life insurance in force[3]	8,694	11,105	11,674	12,577	13,395	14,198	15,050	15,393	18,331	6.0	6.0	6.0	8.7
Assets	1,300	1,839	1,942	2,144	2,336	2,523	2,738	2,984	3,864	8.0	8.5	8.0	8.0
Employment (thousands)[4]	1,430	1,477	1,521	1,538	1,578	1,594	1,620	1,645	1,751	1.0	1.6	1.6	1.4
Property/casualty													
Net written premiums	208	242	251	260	269	278	287	296	324	3.3	3.2	3.1	3.7
Assets	527	672	705	765	829	877	929	989	1,194	5.8	6.0	6.5	6.7
Policyholders' surplus[5]	134	182	193	230	249	265	281	299	356	6.2	6.0	6.0	9.3
Employment (thousands)[4]	548	544	540	533	536	535	536	538	545	-0.2	0.2	0.4	-0.3

[1] Estimate.
[2] Forecast.
[3] Compound annual rate.
[4] Employees on payroll only.
[5] Represents capital base of industry.
Source: American Council of Life Insurance; A. M. Best; U.S. Department of Labor, Bureau of Labor Statistics. Estimates and Forecasts by U.S. Department of Commerce, International Trade Administration.

nisms such as self-insurance and captives at the expense of commercial insurers.

Insurers will be seeking new information and communications technology to increase efficiency in underwriting, distributing, investment, claims, and administrative activities. There will be pressure on the distribution system to reduce costs. Insurers probably will be forced to look for more cost-efficient alternatives for distribution, such as direct mail, other financial institutions, and financial advisors and consultants. Agents may have to accept less compensation or increase their production. Many agents may affiliate with banks.

Consolidation in the industry should proceed as larger, better capitalized companies take a bigger share of the market from less efficient insurers, but smaller niche players should be strong in selected markets, especially in reinsurance. Reinsurers also will compete with capital market products as insurers look for ways to better use their capital in underwriting larger and more volatile risks such as catastrophic and environmental liabilities.

GLOBAL INDUSTRY TRENDS

Regulatory, market, and trade developments around the world continue to create opportunities for U.S. insurance companies.

Europe

The European Commission is directing its members to liberalize their markets for insurance. This already has resulted in strong growth and significant consolidation in the life and non-life sectors. Opportunities in the European Union should be enhanced by the development of private health insurance markets and the privatization of pension systems as governments look to private markets to deal with those costs. Additionally,

the advent of a single European currency will improve market access conditions for foreign insurers.

In some regards, European Union countries have a market that is more liberal than that in the United States. Insurers established in the European Union are able to structure and price their products freely throughout the union with only one license. There also is a long experience in Europe of bank and insurance affiliations, including the sale and underwriting of insurance products and ownership affiliations.

The economies of central and eastern Europe are developing quickly, especially in Poland, Hungary, and the Czech Republic, as these countries look to join the European Union. Poland has taken significant steps in the development of its insurance and pension markets, and other European countries are following suit. While many insurance markets in this region are small and remain underdeveloped, their long-range prospects are positive as they move forward on insurance-related reforms. Russia, with one of the largest market potentials in the region, continues to struggle with the establishment of basic market and regulatory institutions.

Latin America

The economies of Latin America, although small, are growing quickly. Many Latin American countries are liberalizing their insurance markets by privatizing government-owned insurers, allowing foreign investment, and deregulating their markets to be more competitive. Chile privatized its pension system in 1980 with individually controlled pension accounts, and U.S. insurers are major providers of pension services in Chile. The success of the Chilean system has sparked similar changes in Argentina, Colombia, Peru, Brazil, and Mexico. Other insurance reforms have led to opportunities in private life and health insurance, commercial insurance, and worker's compensation. Insurance technology firms are finding new markets with Latin

American insurance firms that are trying to become more competitive. Latin America so far has managed to avoid the financial problems currently besetting Asia, and economic reforms in countries such as Brazil, Argentina, Chile, and Mexico are being accelerated as a result of the Asian financial crisis. Privatization of Brazil's state reinsurance monopoly, slated for the end of 1999, will have a significant impact on the development of that market.

Asia

Large opportunities are available in the economies of Asia. While the Asian financial crisis has discouraged the use of this region as a destination for foreign investment, most foreign insurers in the market have taken a long-term view and continue to see opportunities down the line. Taiwan and South Korea have attracted many U.S. insurers in recent years. Korea's accession to the Organization for Economic Cooperation and Development has spurred additional reforms that, combined with that country's rebound from its economic woes, will provide more opportunities in the future. China looms as a priority market for U.S. insurers if it enacts market access reform consistent with that negotiated in December 1997 under the World Trade Organization (WTO) financial services agreement. China is being pressed to open its insurance market in conjunction with its WTO accession commitments. Japan is slowly progressing with regulatory reform in financial services and insurance that should create more commercial opportunities for U.S. insurers and brokers over the next few years. This trend is being enhanced by the U.S.-Japan Framework Agreement on Insurance, which Japan agreed to bind to its WTO commitments on financial services, and has resulted in Japan making specific progress on reforms affecting foreign insurance providers. India's parliament is scheduled to consider legislation in December 1998 to open its insurance market to domestic competition with minority foreign participation in joint ventures.

The financial crisis in Asia has negatively affected the short-term premium receipts of many companies operating in that region. However, U.S. insurers take a long-term view of the Asian market. Therefore, the majority of insurers in Asia are likely to weather the financial storm and keep their operations open because the region still has vast potential in regard to business opportunities and premium growth. One short-term result of the crisis may be a renewed focus on other markets, such as Latin America and eastern Europe. However, the long-term prospects in Asia remain strong.

Multilateral Trade Agreements

Long-term opportunities for U.S. insurers in foreign markets will depend in part on the effectiveness of the rules and principles negotiated by the United States in the WTO's GATS. GATS establishes a multilateral framework of principles and rules for trade in services. Among other things, GATS promotes transparency in laws and regulations and treats service providers from all countries on an equal basis (the most-favored-nation principle). Perhaps most important, this agreement sets up a strong, binding dispute settlement system to enforce adherence to its commitments. A country found to be in violation of GATS could face WTO-sanctioned retaliatory actions such as punitive tariffs and license denials by injured parties to compensate for the economic harm done to the trade of an injured party.

Another major component of GATS is its annex covering financial services, which was completed in December 1997. The financial services pact covers 95 percent of the global financial services market as measured by revenue. Commitments by WTO members encompass $2.2 trillion in worldwide insurance premiums. Under the agreement, 52 countries will permit 100 percent foreign ownership of subsidiaries or branches in insurance, with 61 percent (accounting for over 93 percent of world insurance premiums) permitting majority control. A significant achievement was Japan's agreement to extend to all signatory countries certain concessions it made to the United States in the U.S.-Japan insurance agreement. One disappointment was Malaysia, which refused to grandfather (i.e., to exempt current situations from new law) existing levels of foreign ownership, as was done by all the other WTO members. Another shortcoming was seen in India, which made commitments in banking and securities but did not make an offer regarding its insurance sector. (It is not clear if India will alter its WTO commitment to reflect any proposed changes in its domestic insurance law.) South Korea initially made unsatisfactory service commitments when it refused to extend to all the other signatories the liberalizing provisions it accepted when it joined the Organization for Economic Cooperation and Development. However, after the agreement was signed on December 13, 1997, South Korea agreed to extend its OECD commitments to its WTO package. The U.S. government is continuing to negotiate improved market access commitments with all the WTO partners before the pact's implementation in March 1999.

Although GATS covers cross-border trade and purchases of services, it also covers the ability of insurance providers to establish subsidiaries, branches, and joint ventures in foreign countries. Unlike most prior trade agreements, GATS covers the trade and investment activities of service providers. GATS promotes the idea that service providers have the right to enter foreign markets and enjoy the same competitive opportunities as local providers. It improves the predictability and transparency of the trading system for an insurance company making international business decisions. The next round of WTO talks, which are expected to be comprehensive and to address all sectors, including financial services, is planned for 2002.

Tim Fisher, U.S. Department of Commerce, Office of Finance, (202) 482-0346, November 1998.

■ REFERENCES

A. M. Best Company, Ambest Road, Oldwick, NJ 08858. (908) 439-2200.

American Council of Life Insurance, 1001 Pennsylvania Avenue, NW, Washington, DC 20004.

Insurance Information Institute, 110 William Street, New York, NY 10038. (800) 331-9146.

Swiss Reinsurance Company, 50/60 Mythenquai, P.O. Box 8022, Zurich, Switzerland. Telephone: 0041-1-285-21-21.

■ **RELATED CHAPTERS**

44: Health and Medical Services

47: Financial Services

48: Securities, Mutual Funds, and Commodity Futures Trading

FINANCIAL SERVICES
Economic and Trade Trends

U.S. International Trade

($ billions)

Legend: □ Balance — Exports — Imports

Trade is between nonaffiliated companies.

Source: U.S. Department of Commerce, Bureau of Economic Analysis.

Number of Banking Companies with 25 Percent of Domestic Deposits

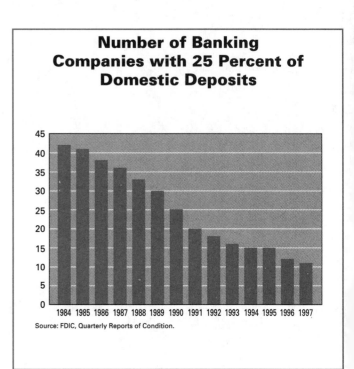

Source: FDIC, Quarterly Reports of Condition.

Noninterest Income as Percent of Bank Net Operating Revenue

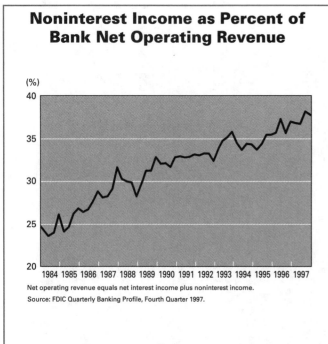

(%)

Net operating revenue equals net interest income plus noninterest income.

Source: FDIC Quarterly Banking Profile, Fourth Quarter 1997.

Output and Output per Hour

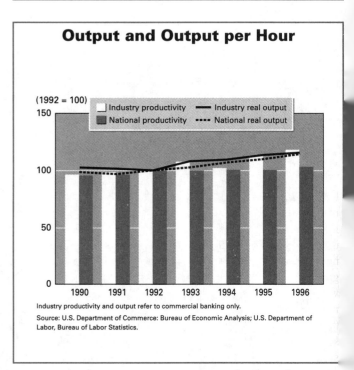

(1992 = 100)

Legend: □ Industry productivity — Industry real output ■ National productivity ---- National real output

Industry productivity and output refer to commercial banking only.

Source: U.S. Department of Commerce: Bureau of Economic Analysis; U.S. Department of Labor, Bureau of Labor Statistics.

See "Getting the Most Out of *Outlook '99*" for definitions of terms.

Financial Services

INDUSTRY DEFINITION Financial services comprise commercial banks (SIC 602), which accept deposits and conduct other related banking functions; savings institutions (SIC 6035, 6036); equipment leasing (SIC 735, 6159), including financial leasing (SIC 6159) and miscellaneous equipment rental and leasing (SIC 735); and property/casualty insurance (SIC 633), life insurance and annuities (SIC 631), and health coverage (SIC 6321).

OVERVIEW

The financial services sector in the United States is in the midst of significant changes. Merger and acquisition activity has produced both a consolidation in the number of financial service providers and a concentration of a growing share of industry assets in a smaller number of companies. The traditional lines separating banking from other financial services activities have been increasingly blurred as banks and thrifts offer new financial products and as more nonfinancial firms enter into the banking business through ownership of limited-service bank charters and unitary thrifts. These developments are occurring at a time of unprecedented prosperity for depository institutions. Favorable operating conditions—a growing economy, combined with low and stable interest rates—have helped lift bank and thrift profits to record levels and have positioned these industries to be able to take advantage of opportunities for expansion.

COMMERCIAL BANKING

Recent years have witnessed an evolution in the structure and nature of commercial banking. The removal of long-standing legal barriers to geographic expansion has unleashed an unprecedented wave of merger activity that has reduced the number of commercial banks by more than one-third and greatly increased the concentration of financial resources within the industry. At the same time, banks have been steadily moving away from reliance on traditional lending and deposit-taking toward a greater emphasis on transactions services as a source of profits. Although deregulation has proceeded more slowly in expanding the range of financial products that banks

are permitted to offer, it has further supported the trend toward fee-based activities.

U.S. commercial banks registered a sixth consecutive year of record profits in 1997. Industry earnings totaled $59.2 billion, an increase of 13.1 percent over 1996. Commercial banks' return on assets (ROA) reached 1.23 percent in 1997, the highest annual level reported in the 64 years since the introduction of federal deposit insurance (see Figure 47-1). More than 95 percent of all commercial banks were profitable in 1997, and almost 69 percent reported ROAs of 1 percent or higher for the year. The improvement in industry earnings was largely attributable to higher net interest income, increased income from trust activities, and growth in other fees.

A favorable environment of economic growth and low, stable interest rates helped sustain loan demand in 1997. The growth in loans and other interest-earning investments in turn supported an increase of 7.2 percent in net interest income, even as net interest margins (the difference between the average yields on banks' interest-earning assets and the average cost of funding these assets) declined for the fifth year in a row. Noninterest income continued to increase in relative importance, growing 11.7 percent in 1997 and providing 37.5 percent of the industry's net operating revenue. As recently as 1992, noninterest income accounted for less than one-third of net operating revenue. Banks' trust income increased 17.8 percent, and other fee income was 14 percent higher than in 1996. Commercial banks' foreign operations accounted for 10.3 percent of industry profits in 1997, the lowest proportion since the industry posted a net loss on its foreign operations in 1989. The improvement in commercial bank earnings was limited by rising loan-loss expenses and higher noninterest expenses. Provisions for loan losses increased 21.5 percent in 1997, reflecting rising charge-offs on credit card loans. Noninterest expenses rose 5.8 percent.

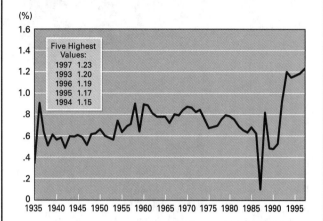

Annual Return on Assets (ROA) of Commercial Banks, 1934–1997

(%)

Five Highest
Values:
1997 1.23
1993 1.20
1996 1.19
1995 1.17
1994 1.15

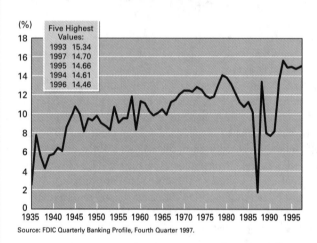

Annual Return on Equity (ROE), 1934–1997

(%)

Five Highest
Values:
1993 15.34
1997 14.70
1995 14.66
1994 14.61
1996 14.46

Source: FDIC Quarterly Banking Profile, Fourth Quarter 1997.

FIGURE 47-1

Commercial bank asset growth reached a 17-year high in 1997, although loan growth slowed for a second consecutive year. Total assets increased 9.5 percent, the largest percentage since 1980. Net loans and leases increased 5.7 percent, led by growth in leases (up 28.3 percent), real estate construction and development loans (up 15.5 percent), home equity loans (up 15 percent), and commercial and industrial loans (up 12.2 percent). Asset growth was also concentrated in short-term credit extended in the form of federal funds sold and securities purchased under resale agreements, which increased 59.7 percent; in trading account assets, which were up 23.1 percent; and mortgage-backed securities, which grew 14.4 percent. Loans to non-U.S. borrowers increased only 1.2 percent during the year, but assets in foreign offices of U.S. banks increased 11.3 percent. At the end of 1997, total assets of commercial banks surpassed $5 trillion for the first time.

Commercial bank deposits also registered strong growth in 1997. Total deposits increased 7 percent, the highest annual

growth rate since 1986. Domestic office time deposits increased 9 percent, savings deposits grew 8.4 percent, and demand deposits declined 2 percent. Deposits booked in foreign offices increased 11.1 percent. Despite the strong growth, deposits continue to provide a shrinking share of funding for commercial banks. At the end of 1997, deposits constituted 74.4 percent of all commercial bank liabilities. Growth in nondeposit liabilities was strongest in federal funds purchased and securities sold under repurchase agreements, which increased 31.1 percent, and trading account liabilities, which grew 37 percent. Equity capital rose 11.6 percent in 1997.

Asset quality remained favorable in 1997, although loan losses continue to rebound from cyclical lows. Net loan charge-offs increased 18 percent, with credit card loans accounting for most of the increase. Of the $18.3 billion in loans charged off by commercial banks in 1997, 64 percent were credit card loans. While the net charge-off rate on credit card loans has risen to a historically high level, credit card lending has remained very profitable because of the high interest rates charged on credit card loans and the strong fee income generated by credit card loan portfolios. The average ROA for specialized commercial bank credit card lenders was 2.08 percent in 1997.

Noncurrent loans (loans 90 days or more past due on scheduled payments plus loans in nonaccrual status) declined to 0.96 percent of total loans at the end of 1997. This is the lowest level in the 16 years that banks have reported noncurrent loan data. As banks' noncurrent loans have declined, the industry's "coverage ratio" has risen to a record $1.92 in reserves for every $1.00 of noncurrent loans. However, the industry's ratio of reserves to total loans has been declining since early 1992, and is now at its lowest level since the first quarter of 1987.

The process of consolidation that has reduced the number of commercial banks by more than one-third since 1984 continued in 1997. The number of insured commercial banks reporting financial results declined by 385 in 1997, to 9,143 institutions at

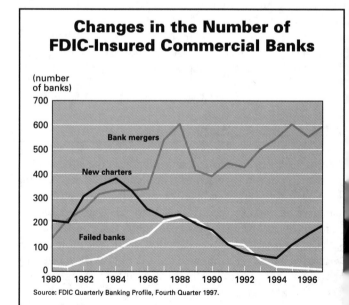

Changes in the Number of FDIC-Insured Commercial Banks

(number of banks)

Bank mergers

New charters

Failed banks

Source: FDIC Quarterly Banking Profile, Fourth Quarter 1997.

FIGURE 47-2

year end (see Figure 47-2). The pace of bank mergers remained high, as 599 institutions were absorbed during the year, but the rate of consolidation was slowed by an increase in the number of new commercial bank charters. The 188 new banks chartered in 1997 represented the largest number since 1989, when 193 new banks were chartered.

On June 1, the Riegle-Neal Interstate Banking and Branching Efficiency Act removed most federal restrictions on interstate branching. The elimination of these restrictions meant that banking companies with multiple subsidiary banks in different states could consolidate affiliated institutions into one bank with branches outside its home state. This change provided an immediate boost to merger activity, as many multistate banking companies restructured themselves. On June 1, insured commercial banks had 5,414 interstate branches. By year end, the number of interstate branches had risen to 11,630. Of the 599 banks absorbed by mergers in 1997, 189 were absorbed by out-of-state banks. The number of intrastate mergers declined to 410 in 1997, from 503 in 1996.

Industry consolidation has increased the concentration of financial resources in the banking industry. Ten years ago, the 36 largest banking companies held 25 percent of all the domestic office deposits in commercial banks and savings institutions. At the end of 1997, the same share of domestic deposits was controlled by only 11 companies. While the Riegle-Neal Act limits deposit concentrations in any one banking organization to 30 percent of a state's deposits and 10 percent of the nation's deposits, these limits leave considerable room for further consolidation of the industry. Also, these concentration limits apply only to interstate mergers and branching transactions and do not affect intrastate transactions.

Outlook

The recent flattening of the yield curve will continue to put downward pressure on banks' net interest margins. Declining loan demand will also increase the difficulty of sustaining lending profitability, as increased competition for a shrinking pool of loans erodes lending spreads and underwriting standards. The boom in home mortgage refinancings will provide some temporary relief for consumer debt burdens, and may give a boost to

Credit Risk Diversification at Commercial Banks: Consumer Loans versus Loans to Commercial Borrowers

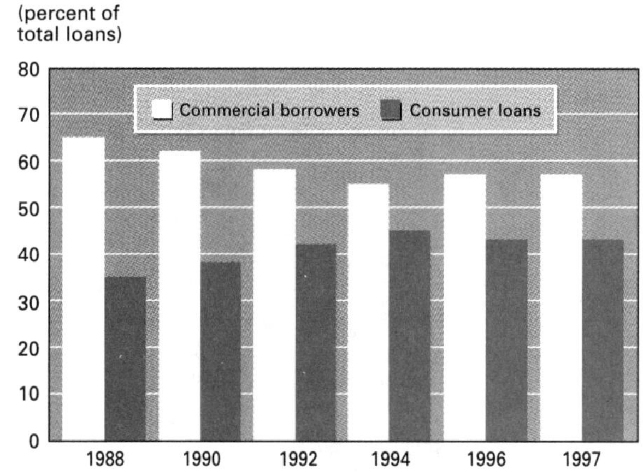

Source: FDIC Quarterly Banking Profile, Fourth Quarter 1997.

FIGURE 47-3

lending and credit quality in the short run. Overhead expenses will be increased by higher technology costs associated with the Year 2000 problem. The Year 2000 problem may also accelerate the pace of mergers in 1998 if potential acquirers are concerned that the 2000 trigger date will be too close in 1999 for new acquisitions. Some increases in troubled loans related to the Asian financial crisis will occur at a few large banks, but these problems are unlikely to have a significant impact on industry earnings. The challenge of maintaining current levels of bank profitability will reinforce the emphasis on expansion of fee-based activities and efficiency improvements at commercial banks.

Table 47-1 gives trends and forecasts in the commercial banking industry, provided by Standard & Poor's DRI.

Ross Waldrop, Federal Deposit Insurance Corporation, Division of Research and Statistics, (202) 898-3951, May 1998.

TABLE 47-1: Commercial Banking Trends and Forecasts

(billions of dollars except as noted)

	1990	1991	1992	1993	1994	1995	1996	1997	1998	1999	Percent Change 96–97	97–98	98–99	92–96[1]
Consumer debt, excluding mortgages	789	777	780	839	960	1094	1180	1233	1279	1330	4.5	3.7	4.0	10.9
Commercial and industrial loans at all commercial banks	640	622	597	586	640	714	777	847	907	964	9.0	7.1	6.3	6.8
Real estate loans at commercial banks	819	873	893	915	965	1053	1107	1190	1276	1368	7.5	7.2	7.2	5.5
Deposits at commercial banks	2298	2428	2489	2514	2527	2605	2754	2993	3321	3505	8.6	11	5.6	2.6
Commercial bank prime rate (%)	10.0	8.5	6.3	6.0	7.1	8.8	8.3	8.4	8.4	7.7				
Conventional 30-year mortgage rate—all lenders (%)	10.1	9.3	8.4	7.3	8.4	8.0	7.8	7.6	6.9	6.0				
11th District cost of funds at insured S&L's— San Francisco (%)	8.2	7.1	5.1	4.1	3.9	5.1	4.9	4.9	4.9	4.5				

[1] Compound annual rate.
Source: Standard & Poor's DRI.

Global Market Trends

The year 1997 was an excellent year for banks. *The Banker*'s "Top 1,000" banks in the world showed a record 25.8 percent growth in profits to reach a stunning $216.2 billion total and provide a welcome 14.5 percent average return on capital. Figure 47-4 illustrates the worldwide geographical breakdown of the Top 1,000. Of the Top 1,000 banks, ranked according to their Tier One Capital strength, 148 are headquartered in the United States. Nineteen U.S. banks are ranked in the Top 100.

The commercial banking industry is consolidating worldwide. Banks in the United States and abroad continue to find

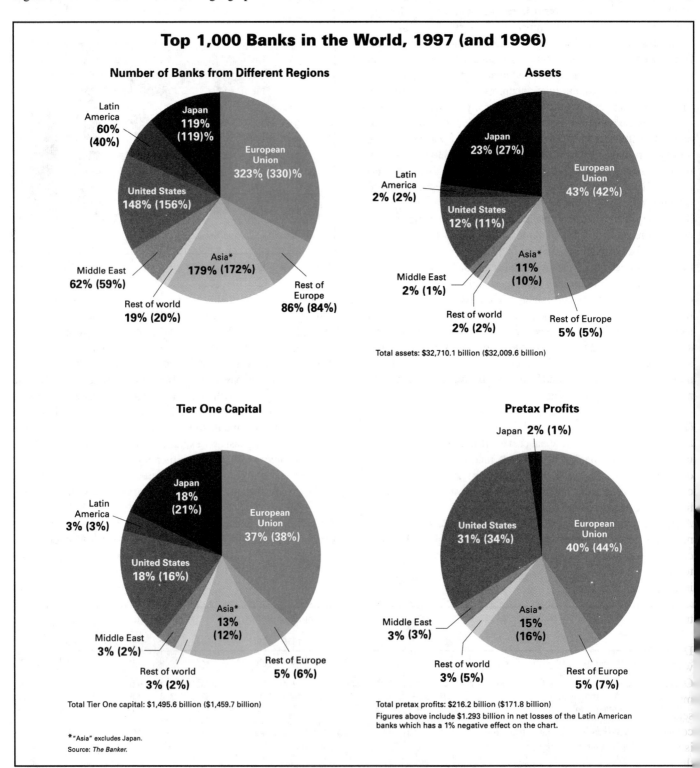

Top 1,000 Banks in the World, 1997 (and 1996)

Number of Banks from Different Regions

- Latin America 60% (40%)
- Japan 119% (119)%
- European Union 323% (330)%
- United States 148% (156%)
- Middle East 62% (59%)
- Rest of world 19% (20%)
- Asia* 179% (172%)
- Rest of Europe 86% (84%)

Assets

- Japan 23% (27%)
- Latin America 2% (2%)
- European Union 43% (42%)
- United States 12% (11%)
- Middle East 2% (1%)
- Asia* 11% (10%)
- Rest of world 2% (2%)
- Rest of Europe 5% (5%)

Total assets: $32,710.1 billion ($32,009.6 billion)

Tier One Capital

- Japan 18% (21%)
- Latin America 3% (3%)
- European Union 37% (38%)
- United States 18% (16%)
- Middle East 3% (2%)
- Rest of world 3% (2%)
- Asia* 13% (12%)
- Rest of Europe 5% (6%)

Total Tier One capital: $1,495.6 billion ($1,459.7 billion)

Pretax Profits

- Japan 2% (1%)
- United States 31% (34%)
- European Union 40% (44%)
- Middle East 3% (3%)
- Asia* 15% (16%)
- Rest of world 3% (5%)
- Rest of Europe 5% (7%)

Total pretax profits: $216.2 billion ($171.8 billion)
Figures above include $1.293 billion in net losses of the Latin American banks which has a 1% negative effect on the chart.

*"Asia" excludes Japan.
Source: *The Banker.*

FIGURE 47-4

partners for their persistent quest to shed overcapacity and achieve efficiencies. Even in markets such as Switzerland, Canada, the United Kingdom, France, and the Netherlands, where banking is already concentrated among a handful of institutions, consolidation is continuing as competition intensifies and financial markets integrate. Though consolidation is not new to the financial services sector, it is moving in new directions as banks acquire investment banks and asset management firms to build expertise in specialized domains. Also, in an attempt to serve as "one stop shops" for consumer and corporate financial needs, banks are taking a greater interest in insurance companies and insurance products to take advantage of cross-selling opportunities.

What is the benefit of a larger-scale financial service organization? It is better able to spread its marketing, administrative, and systems costs and to redeploy capital by securitizing assets off the balance sheet. Also, a large organization is in a better position to diversify across business lines, geographies, and income sources to enhance stability. As information becomes the most prized asset, information management systems will enable bankers to work with customers anywhere anytime.

What does the future hold for this trend toward consolidation? Most definitely, more mergers are in the works. The big question is whether mergers will be done between banks headquartered in different countries. Most observers predict that, in the short run, U.S. and foreign banks will be buying equity stakes in each other as a likely prelude to mergers. Such cross-shareholdings could be gradual steps toward creating globe-spanning institutions. Even short of an outright merger, members of such alliances could combine to offer a consistent range of international banking services.

Cross-border mergers are an increasing possibility, especially between U.S. banks and globally minded British, Dutch, and Swiss institutions which already have a large presence in the United States. However, such mergers likely would not occur until there is further consolidation in the European financial industry. Also, such speculation could become academic if there is a serious downturn in the international economy. Another impediment to achieving a cross-border merger is the necessity to pay cash because of complications in cross-border exchanges of stock and the likelihood of Europeans hesitating to accept stock of a regional U.S. bank which does not have an international reputation.

Deregulation, technology, and globalization are driving this trend.

Deregulation. On a global basis, substantial deregulation was achieved on December 12, 1997, when 102 World Trade Organization (WTO) members reached a multilateral agreement which established a set of rules with respect to financial services. These rules created the right to establish and operate competitively, provided the same access to domestic markets as is accorded to domestic companies and required treatment on the same basis as domestic companies, removed restrictions on cross-border services, and granted majority ownership by for-

eign entities. This agreement levels the playing field in global financial markets and provides new opportunities for financial service firms to operate globally. The agreement does not go into effect until enabling legislation is enacted in each signatory country. In the United States, for example, the Senate has until January 29, 1999, to ratify the agreement. Though generally well received by the U.S. banking community as a pact that will facilitate U.S. bank entry to foreign markets, according to major U.S. bank players it needs to be modified to ease lending limits and restrictions on transferring information across national borders to allow banks to efficiently do business overseas.

Deregulation occurred in national markets as well. In the United States, deregulation recently occurred in the form of regulatory/legislative changes and court decisions in regard to banks' ability to expand across state lines, their broadened securities underwriting activities, and their ability to sell insurance. The U.S. Congress is still grappling with the issue of whether and in what form financial service industries will be modernized. Such actions are partially responsible for the record dollar volumes of mergers of financial service firms in the U.S. and will continue to influence future merger activity.

Also, in the United States the Federal Reserve Board proposed a substantial revision of Regulation K which would significantly expand the powers of U.S. banks overseas. These regulations, if finalized, would drop some limits on underwriting and dealing in equities and debt securities, permit more venture capital investments, and expedite branch applications. The whole purpose is to increase the competitiveness of U.S. banks overseas.

In Japan, reforms dubbed the "Big Bang" are aimed at rebuilding the banking industry and changing the way the world's second largest economy does business. Measures scheduled to take effect by 2001 include reforms which will open financial markets to greater foreign competition, bringing new services and the abolition of barriers between the work of banks, brokerages, and insurers. (See the section on Japan.)

In Europe the prospect of a single currency has already helped to create a huge leap in mergers and acquisitions within the European financial sector. In 1997 the total value of deals was $104.4 billion, compared with $48.6 billion in 1996 and $46.9 billion in 1995. (See the section on Europe.)

In Latin America the increased presence of U.S. banks and other foreign financial institutions and the adoption of financial-sector liberalization measures should help create more competitive conditions, facilitate the development of more efficient market-oriented and privately owned Latin banking institutions, and provide greater opportunities to U.S. and other foreign financial institutions. (See the section on Latin American markets.)

Technology. Today customers demand everything that can be done in a branch, and banks must respond in kind. Banks' huge investments in technology have necessitated consolidation in order to spread costs over an organization which generates more revenue than a single bank could produce. Also, technology has made it possible for banks to manage their operations worldwide and to provide certain products which depend on such sophistication, e.g., electronic bill presentment, a precursor to a marketplace for truly integrated on-line financial services.

Globalization. Globalization, the third driver for consolidation, springs as much from the need for modernizing emerging economies as from the explosive expansion of the middle classes of these economies. The banking industry is well poised to facilitate global trade due to its keen understanding of how to manage risk abroad. Financial institutions follow their clients. As more of their clients do business with overseas customers, it is only natural that their banks will support their business.

U.S. Banks' Foreign Market Trends and Opportunities

U.S. bank loan growth in international markets outpaced domestic activity in the 12 months that ended June 30, 1997, according to the *American Banker*. Non-U.S. commercial and industrial loans (C&I) on the books surged 17 percent to $124 billion, compared with a 13 percent jump in loans to U.S. borrowers to $578 billion. The data exclude loans to foreign governments, banks, and consumers. Last year a survey conducted by a Wall Street investment bank showed that international cross-border exposure at U.S. banks jumped 26 percent for the period 1996–1997 to nearly $102 billion. However, foreign C&I loans still account for less than 18 percent of a total $702 billion in such loans at U.S. banks. Confirming the trend toward increased international activities at U.S. banks, an accompanying survey by the *American Banker* found that outstanding standby letters of credit issued abroad rose nearly 15 percent to $46 billion, or roughly 20 percent of all standby letters of credit issued by U.S. banks. In contrast, the amount of U.S.-based standby letters of credit rose 11.5 percent to $165.8 billion.

Typically, banks' foreign opportunities are viewed solely from a geographic perspective. However, when viewed from a product panorama, regional, if not global, possibilities become more realistic. As multinational companies increasingly view Latin America in terms of regional trading blocs, global banks are stepping in with European-style services designed to meet the needs of financing regional operations. Eyeing growth in intraregional trade in the Americas, a few U.S. banks have started offering a new cash-management service known as national cash pooling. The tool allows companies to optimize their liquidity in their regional operations by using the excess cash in one country to offset the borrowing needs of another country. In essence, multinationals can pool their cash and better manage their needs providing that they maintain an overall credit surplus. For example, if a company had a $10 million surplus in Argentina and was establishing a new operation in Peru that set it back $8 million, it would not need to look for local financing in Peru and could handle such needs out of its pooled resources. This product is geared toward the trend of multinationals establishing hub centers for cash management.

Another product which knows no national boundaries is money management. A recent study said pension fund assets, a prime target of money managers, in non-U.S. markets are expected to grow 70 percent to $7 trillion by 2001, whereas growth in the United States is expected to be only 48 percent. A leading U.S. money manager expects its worldwide assets under management will climb to $500 billion from $292 billion over 3 years, with the non-U.S. portion rising to $250 billion from $60 billion. Much of the overseas growth should be propelled by the privatization of state pension programs. U.S. institutions have been doing pension fund management for more than 20 years, are bigger than their competitors, have better access to U.S. capital markets than foreign competitors, and are better at it, according to a leading U.S. asset manager. The high-growth economies of Latin America and Japan, where wealth is plentiful despite its recent economic slowdown, are seen as offering the greatest growth potential.

Looking at opportunities from a geographic perspective, most U.S. banks are being selective about the territories they want to penetrate. Although recently the direction has been away from mature western economies and into some of the emerging markets that over the long term have better growth and profit prospects, very attractive opportunities have surfaced in mature markets due in large part to structural changes brought about by deregulation of these markets.

Mature Economies

Japan. Japan is on the brink of the "Big Bang," a financial overhaul aimed at rebuilding a faltering banking system and changing the way the world's second-largest economy does business. When Japan announced these deregulatory measures, it promised that the Tokyo market would become a level playing field offering equal access to foreign and domestic financial institutions. These reforms, combined with a growing demand for western-style pension fund management and deepening problems facing local banks, are helping to open up markets that had historically discouraged expansion.

Among measures included in the "Big Bang" which should unclog the arteries of the banking system and make better use of the $9.23 trillion that Japanese people have in low-interest savings accounts (annual interest as low as 0.1 percent) include:

- Further liberalization of sales of mutual funds and securities and brokers' commissions and the abolition of the securities transactions tax
- Tougher guidelines to keep banks from amassing too much debt
- Greater disclosure of corporate information which will allow investors to better judge whether a stock is a good buy
- Abolition of barriers between the work of banks, brokerages, and insurers

Best prospects for U.S. banks include a range of specialized activities, including institutional and retail asset management, securities custody and processing, capital markets, and loan securitization.

Japan's aging population is putting enormous pressure on pension funds to produce higher yields. By 2020 one-third of the population will be over 60. Though Japan has one of the highest savings rates in the world, yields on these accounts were historically low. In search of better returns, the Japanese are now looking to foreign banks which have cut their teeth in much more highly competitive markets than Japan and are well prepared to produce results for Japanese savers by investing the funds overseas. According to recent reports, two U.S. banks have been given the opportunity to manage portions of Nempuku, Japan's largest pension fund, with $185 billion of assets under management. Still, foreign banks' share of Japanese pension fund management has climbed slowly, from less than 3 percent in 1989 to between 7 percent and 8 percent in 1997. However, recent trends could open the door to business with other funds, especially corporate pension funds. U.S. banking companies stand to gain not only in asset management but also in the related securities custody and processing businesses.

Europe. Considered the biggest political event of the European continent in 25 years, a single currency system was adopted by the European Union (EU). Except for the United Kingdom, Denmark, and Sweden, which have decided not to join for political reasons and have adopted an opt-out, opt-in clause, and Greece, which did not qualify to join based on economic and exchange-rate criteria, the remaining 11 EU members will form the Euro bloc. On January 1, 1999, these 11 currencies will merge into the new euro and become the book-entry transactions of capital markets, government agencies, and wholesale corporate payments. Government and corporate bonds, listed futures, and options will all be quoted, priced, and settled in euro.

During the 3-year changeover phase, use of the euro will be encouraged alongside national currencies. On January 1, 2002, euro bank notes and coins will be introduced to the public and all the technical processes should be complete. Six months later, individual European currencies will retire, leaving the euro as the only valid currency. Monetary policy will be set by a European Central Bank, which is now being set up in Frankfurt.

The introduction of a single European currency will create the world's largest monetary bloc, serving a population of 370 million people, 15 countries, and a combined gross domestic product of $84 trillion. That compares with the U.S.-dollar bloc's 260 million people in a market with a gross domestic product of $71 trillion.

Introduction of the single currency is expected to trigger major changes in banking and cut into European banks' profitability, increasing pressure there to consolidate. A well regarded consulting group recently predicted that within 8 years no more than five truly global banks will control about 66 percent of the cross-border payments market in Europe. Three of the candidates angling to be hubs in the new payment environment, which will be radically changed by the introduction of a single European currency, are U.S.-based. The reasons for U.S. banks' competitive advantage is simple—they are the only institutions that have put pan-European banking systems in place over the last decade. U.S. banks have operated with inte-grated technology platforms and are in a good position to compete, especially since they play to technology and scale. As a result, these banks should grab a major portion of the market for cash management, funds transfer, and securities trading in the near future. It is estimated that to build such an integrated platform on a pan-European scale could take 5 or 6 years. Monetary union could offer some long-term benefits as well. The larger single market will create opportunities, particularly in the area of investment banking and the cross-border sale of deposits, mutual funds, and other savings products.

Introduction of a single European currency may also prompt some big European banks to expand into the U.S. and emerging markets to increase revenues and profits. Such expansion would be needed to substitute for the revenue loss due to the elimination of much of the corresponding banking and clearing businesses, as well as foreign exchange trading, which many European banks rely on for profits. The forces of a single market will make many banks uncompetitive or unprofitable. However, different regulations, tax, and accounting systems of EU members will continue to influence the pace of consolidation and banks' need to adjust.

Canada. Though Canada has not yet fully deregulated, most observers are expecting changes in the near term which will allow more foreign competition. Canada intends to adopt a law permitting foreign branch banking. Such a law would give force to their WTO financial services offer and also help them meet their commitment to the North American Free Trade Agreement (NAFTA) under Article 1403. It is worth noting that foreign branch banking would not mean full service retail banking. Many of the foreign banks, which now operate in Canada as wholesale subsidiaries of the parent banks in their home countries, will switch to wholesale branches. Any retail services would have to be offered through subsidiaries. Most foreign banks, and certainly the U.S. banks, do not see a big market in Canada for full service retail banking. The real opportunities lie in the corporate banking sector and in "near banking," which includes almost everything from mutual funds, small business loans, and mortgages to credit cards and other limited financial services which do not require the taking of deposits. Already, hoping to cash in on Canada's closeness and similarity to home, U.S. financial service companies are turning to Canada as the next frontier for growth. It is a natural extension of U.S. business to market to people with strong common interests.

The big news coming out of Canada might not yet have been written. Knowledgeable observers believe that Canada's and the United States' financial systems may be fusing together and that cross-border mergers may be on the horizon. The two Canadian megamergers announced in 1998 (Royal Bank/Bank of Montreal and CIBC/Toronto-Dominion) look like preliminaries to things bigger and multinational. The already close cultural affinity is carrying over to market and corporate structures. Assuming the circumvention or removal of remaining legal limitations on foreign ownership of Canadian banks, a principle supported by the Canadian bankers, the largest U.S. banks are likely to want to broaden their horizons.

Emerging Economies

The hottest emerging markets for banks are in eastern Europe and Latin America. These markets have inefficiencies and growth, and that creates opportunities, especially for trading and risk management.

Key Eastern European Markets. Bankers are eyeing countries, including Russia, Poland, Hungary, and the Czech Republic, which are growing faster and generating wider spreads than mature markets such as the United States and western Europe. The rush into eastern Europe is grounded in the belief that these markets will develop even faster than the markets of Latin America. Experts point out that a legacy of pre-World War free-market infrastructures and educated work forces are some of the reasons why eastern Europe's financial markets will approach western standards. These markets are in the initial steps of development, but the pace of change is faster in eastern Europe than elsewhere.

The extent to which U.S. banks are increasing their involvement in that part of the world is clearly reflected in cross-border lending statistics. According to the Federal Reserve Board, cross-border lending by U.S. banks to eastern Europe rose 126 percent to $6.6 billion in 1996, including a fivefold rise in lending to Russia to more than $3 billion.

Banks plan to expand corporate banking by underwriting capital market issues, including high-yield securities, local currency financing, risk management, trading, and financial advisory activities in the region. Other banks will emphasize trade, project finance in areas such as oil and gas, as well as private equity investments in middle market companies, while still others will function as loan syndicators or participants.

It may seem odd that U.S. banks waited more than 5 years after the collapse of communism to move in with such verve. However, a number of occurrences have encouraged them to commit significant resources to the region: the improving credit ratings of several countries, rapid increases in demand for funding and flow of capital, and a rise in interest in trading in eastern European currencies and securities.

One reason why this region has fared so well is its close trade links to western Europe. With the EU well on track for solid growth this year, central Europe's current account will be cushioned against the pressures coming from Asia. However, two potential negatives loom on the horizon: future increases in the cost of international capital would depress growth, and increased competition from Asian exporters benefiting from a drop in their currencies' value may undercut eastern European exporters.

Another factor encouraging greater U.S. bank interest is a growing appetite among bankers and investors for riskier but higher-yielding assets. Banks are looking for new frontiers and eastern Europe is moving away from being a hinterland and becoming part of western capital markets. Most countries in the region are moving in the right direction politically and economically. Even if the risks are still there, they are diminishing. The key is not where these countries are today but what measures they are taking for tomorrow.

Even if yields decline, banks see ample room to continue expanding by moving deeper into local markets and into other specialties, such as real estate and securitization.

Key Latin American Markets. The financial sectors of key Latin American countries, particularly Argentina, Brazil, Chile, and Mexico, can provide substantial opportunities for foreign investment in national banking systems. These financial sectors typically provide a wide variety of services through their banking institutions. An increased presence of U.S. banks and other financial institutions in these Latin American banking markets should help create more competitive conditions in those markets and should facilitate the development of more efficient market-oriented and privately owned Latin American banking institutions. Moreover, the adoption of financial-sector liberalization measures in major Latin American markets should also provide greater opportunities to U.S. banks and other financial institutions.

Today Latin America's middle-class, a prime target of banks, is only emerging. Only the top 10 percent or so of the typical Latin American nation's population has household income comparable to the median household income in developed countries. Ever so slowly, consumers are shifting holdings out of physical assets, such as cars and homes, and putting cash from under the mattress into deposit accounts. As this phenomenon runs its course, growth in bank deposits of 30 percent to 50 percent per year will falter.

What does this mean for banks? Basically, foreign banks expanding into Latin America may need to take an approach that differs from conventional commercial banking. As reported in the *American Banker,* the real opportunities lie in:

- "developing consumer finance (at high rates!), possibly through separate subsidiaries, that will help meet the enormous pent-up demand for automobiles and homes
- "expanding pension fund management and creating pension fund investment opportunities by originating and securitizing consumer banking assets such as mortgage-backed securities
- "reducing the costs of branch networks and shifting away from a 'generalist' distribution to 'specialist' distribution that will serve the mass-market banking needs of low-income economies, most likely through consumer finance companies or minimum-service branches
- "building commission-related sales forces in specialized areas such as credit cards, mortgages, mutual funds, and consumer finance in order to boost productivity
- "rationalizing operations along cross-border regional rather than national lines. This would create economies of scale that could, for example, yield significant reductions in the cost of credit card operations. Call centers also can be set up on a cross-border rather than national basis, while treasury and capital markets operations can also be centralized, further reducing costs."

So far, the strategy pursued by big U.S. banks that have been in the region for a long time has been to focus on corporate activ ities. However, with the prospect of an emerging middle class, even U.S. regional banks, which are excessively domestically focused, will be enticed to look across international borders to the beckoning Latin American market.

Argentina. Argentina has liberalized various banking sector limitations and restrictions. In 1994 the Argentine Central Bank eliminated legal constraints on the establishment, acquisition, and branching of foreign banks. During that year the Central Bank removed the legal distinction between domestic and foreign banks.

A substantial number of U.S.-based banks have been active in the local market, and two U.S. banks—Bank of Boston and Citibank—are among the largest foreign retail banks in Argentina. Moreover, most Argentine banks maintain correspondent arrangements with U.S. banks. According to a recent report, foreign-controlled banks hold about 35 percent of total Argentine bank deposits. In addition, three of Argentina's top 10 commercial banks were sold to European financial institutions in 1997.

New foreign banks should help create a more competitive and stronger banking sector with new bank products and an upgraded technological infrastructure. Argentina already has a large financial sector that provides a wide variety of services through the banking system. However, Moody's Investors Service reported in early 1998 that the Argentine banking system is relatively weak despite improvements in bank regulation and supervision. Bank asset quality is considered poor and profitability is weak by Latin American standards.

The financial system is supervised by the Central Bank of the Argentine Republic. Argentina's financial system includes both publicly owned and privately owned banks that operate as commercial, investment, or mortgage banks. Various banks have not been allowed to own industrial, commercial, or agricultural firms without a Central Bank general authorization for the entire system.

Brazil. Brazilian policy basically welcomes foreign investment, and despite certain restrictions numerous U.S. banks have a presence in Brazil and are well represented in Brazilian markets. Foreign commercial access to Brazil's banking sector has been based on a case-by-case authorization and a presidential decree. However, the Brazilian central bank has sent out signals of its willingness to let foreign groups play an important role in the banking system.

Some barriers to foreign participation in Brazil's long protected financial sector have already come down. For example, some foreign banks in Brazil have boosted minority stakes they previously held. In recent years foreign banks have also been able to expand into new areas by converting into multiple banks. Moreover, Brazilian authorities have recently given permission to a number of foreign banks to actually acquire Brazilian banks or to enter the Brazilian market.

Brazil has a large and sophisticated financial sector that provides a wide range of services, including commercial banking and investment banking. The nation's Central Bank, among other duties, regulates banks and other financial institutions.

Brazil's banking sector comprises both private-sector and government banks. All-service multiple banks—which have dominated the market—provide commercial banking, brokerage, and investment services. Brazilian commercial banks and subsidiaries of international banks are active in trade finance.

Chile. Chile's banking sector has been rated as the most solid in Latin America. The banking system provides numerous asset and liability products available in international financial centers. Moreover, foreign trade financing and money exchange operations are particularly active and efficient by Latin American standards.

A key feature of the government of Chile's development strategy is a welcoming attitude toward foreign investors. In the banking sector U.S. banks with operations in Chile include Republic National Bank of New York, Citibank, Bank of Boston, Chase Manhattan, American Express, and Bank of America. U.S. banks have concentrated mainly on corporate lending to medium and small-size businesses. In Chile, private banks handle most corporate business.

Chilean authorities, however, have considered Chile an overbanked nation and for years have not allowed new banks to enter the market, except by purchasing existing banks. This restriction has been applied to both domestic and foreign firms. Moreover, restrictions have been imposed on the domestic and foreign banks' ability to enter several promising areas of business, including securities brokerage, pension fund management, factoring, and leasing.

The Chilean banking system is regulated by the Superintendent of Banks and Financial Institutions, an agency under the Finance Minister. The Central Bank, which has autonomy from the government in conducting monetary and exchange rate policy and regulating international capital movements, also regulates bank operations. There is another state-owned bank (aside from the Central Bank): the Banco del Estado, Chile's largest bank, which accounts for a substantial percent of loans and deposits.

Mexico. In recent years Mexican authorities have implemented significant market-oriented reforms in the financial system. Mexico's large, liberalized financial sector provides a variety of services through the banking system and other financial institutions. The Mexican government has used NAFTA's financial services chapter as a means to open up the local financial sector to foreign investment.

The implementation of NAFTA in January 1994 marked the start of a process that, over time, should level the playing field for U.S. investors in the Mexican banking industry. Through wholly owned subsidiaries, U.S. investors have been allowed to engage in the full range of activities permitted to their Mexican counterparts, with relatively minor exceptions. Moreover, under NAFTA, various U.S.- or Canadian-based financial institution subsidiaries of foreign banks may also establish bank subsidiaries in Mexico.

Thus, Mexico's banking sector has been opened to foreign competition. Foreign institutions, barred from acquiring majority stakes in Mexican banks prior to 1995, claim total shareholdings exceeding one-quarter of the financial sector.

Moreover, Mexico has indicated it has plans to remove remaining restrictions on foreign ownership of Mexican banks.

The Secretariat of Finance, the National Banking and Securities Commission, and the Bank of Mexico (the Central Bank) are the principal regulators of the banking system.

John R. Shuman, U.S. Department of Commerce, Office of Finance, (202) 482-3050, with input on Latin American markets from Tino Perera, (202) 482-5822, May 1998.

SAVINGS INSTITUTIONS

At the end of 1997, mergers, acquisitions, charter conversions, and failures had reduced the number of U.S. savings institutions to 1,779 from a peak of 4,842 in 1966 (see Figure 47-5). Despite continued shrinkage in the number of institutions, thrift industry assets have remained relatively unchanged over the past 5 years. As of December 31, 1997, savings institutions held $1 trillion in assets. The most important cause of recent declines in the number of thrifts has been acquisitions by commercial banks. Tax law changes in August 1996 significantly reduced the cost to commercial banks of acquiring thrifts. In 1997 commercial banks acquired 77 savings institutions—a record for unassisted acquisitions of thrifts by commercial banks in a single year. In each of the 4 previous years, commercial banks had purchased more than 60 thrifts. A smaller reduction in the number of thrifts resulted from mergers within the thrift industry. In 1997 there were 50 thrift mergers, and in each of the 4 preceding years the number was approximately the same.

Charter conversions, too, have reduced the number of savings institutions. From 1990 to 1997, 135 thrifts converted their charters to commercial bank charters. Only eight conversions occurred in the 1980s. Recent conversions were facilitated by Public Law 104-188, enacted in August 1996. Until 1996, if savings institutions switched to a bank charter, they had to recapture any bad debt reserve taken on their tax returns. The 1996 law, besides eliminating the tax consequences resulting from conversions of savings institutions to bank charters, also eliminated the tax consequences from the acquisition of savings institutions by commercial banks. Before 1996, probably most of the thrifts converting had had small bad-debt reserves for tax purposes.

In the other direction, recent legislative changes have made it less difficult for commercial banks to convert to thrift charters. The Economic Growth and Regulatory Paper Reduction Act (Public Law 104-208), passed in September 1996, eased restrictions on lending activities so that more commercial banks could qualify for a thrift charter if they wished. Specifically, this legislation relaxed the qualified thrift lender test (QTL) by removing limits on the amount of credit card loans and student loans that thrifts may hold. The limitation on commercial loans was eased as well: savings institutions may now invest up to 20 percent of their assets in commercial loans, although any commercial lending beyond 10 percent of assets must be to small businesses. Between the enactment of PL 104-208 in 1996 and April 15, 1998, 14 commercial banks had converted to savings institution charters.

Profitability

The thrift industry broke several profitability records in 1997. Full-year net income, at $8.8 billion, was the highest ever reported by the industry. The industry's ROA for 1997, at 0.93 percent, was the highest since 1946 (see Figure 47-6). Full-year earnings were $1.8 billion higher than in 1996. Noninterest expense was $4.7 billion lower in 1997 than in 1996, largely because of the special assessment paid in the third quarter of 1996 by institutions insured through the Savings Association Insurance Fund (SAIF). Thanks to the capitalization of their insurance fund, thrifts with SAIF-insured deposits paid lower deposit premiums in 1997, resulting in pretax savings of approximately $800 million. Taxes were $1.8 billion higher in 1997 because the special assessment's deductibility had kept tax expenses unusually low in 1996.

The previous record earnings year for the thrift industry was 1995, when thrifts reported $7.6 billion in earnings for an ROA

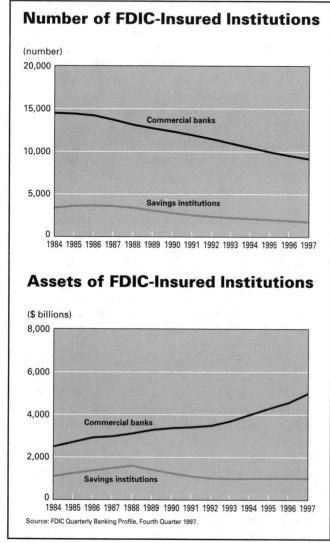

FIGURE 47-5

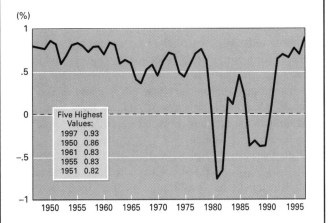

Annual Return on Assets (ROA) of Savings Institutions, 1947–1997

(%)

Five Highest Values:	
1997	0.93
1950	0.86
1961	0.83
1955	0.83
1951	0.82

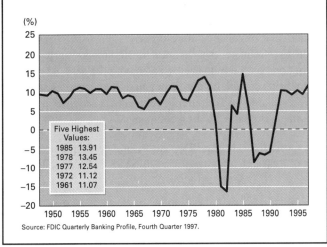

Annual Return on Equity (ROE), 1947–1997

(%)

Five Highest Values:	
1985	13.91
1978	13.45
1977	12.54
1972	11.12
1961	11.07

Source: FDIC Quarterly Banking Profile, Fourth Quarter 1997.

FIGURE 47-6

of 0.77 percent. Earnings in 1997 surpassed 1995 results by $1.2 billion, with much of the difference in earnings accounted for by gains on the sales of securities. In 1997 these gains contributed $1.3 billion to pretax earnings compared with $463 million in 1995.

Net Interest Margins and Yields on Assets

The industry's core profitability improved in 1996 and 1997, when net interest margins were considerably wider than in 1995. Net interest income was 3.23 percent of earning assets in 1997 and 3.22 percent in 1996 compared with 3.09 percent in 1995. In 1997 the yield on earning assets was 9 basis points higher than in 1995, and the cost of funding earning assets was 5 basis points lower. Funding costs have declined with the general decline in interest rates.

The improvement in margins has coincided with two major portfolio shifts from 1995 through 1997. First, thrifts have raised their asset yields by replacing securities with loans; yields on loans tend to exceed yields on securities (see Figure 47-7). In 1996 and 1997 thrifts increased their loans by more than $43 billion and decreased their holdings of securities—mainly U.S. Treasury and mortgage-backed securities—by almost $40 billion. Second, thrifts' funding costs have declined. During the same two-year period their deposits decreased by $38 billion, while nondeposit borrowings increased by $34 billion. Much of the increase in nondeposit borrowings was in the form of Federal Home Loan Bank (FHLB) advances.

Asset Quality

Noncurrent loans continued to decline even as total loans increased. Noncurrent loans totaled $9.2 billion at the end of 1995; by the end of 1996 they had fallen slightly to $8.8 billion, and during 1997 they fell to $7.7 billion. At the end of 1995 noncurrent loans were 1.4 percent of total loans, and at the end of 1997 they had fallen to 1.1 percent.

As asset quality improved, loan losses declined dramatically. Loan losses were 27 percent ($584 million) lower in 1997 than in 1995. Thrifts charged off 0.25 percent of their loans in 1997, down from 0.34 percent in 1995. The lower loan losses allowed thrifts to build up reserves in 1997. At the end of 1997 thrifts held 91 cents in loan-loss reserves for every dollar of noncurrent loans—a record level.

Industry Capitalization

Equity capital reached 8.71 percent of total assets at the end of 1997. This was the highest capital ratio for the industry since 1943. The return on equity (ROE) reached 10.90 percent for all of 1997. This was the highest annual ROE reported by thrifts since 1985, when ROE reached 13.91 percent. That year capital

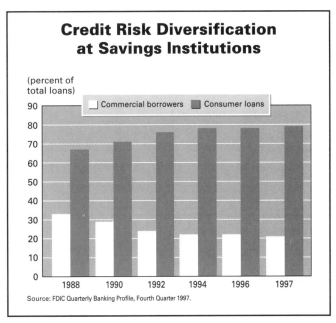

Credit Risk Diversification at Savings Institutions

(percent of total loans)

□ Commercial borrowers ■ Consumer loans

Source: FDIC Quarterly Banking Profile, Fourth Quarter 1997.

FIGURE 47-7

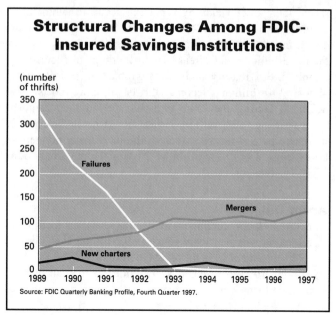

Structural Changes Among FDIC-Insured Savings Institutions

(number of thrifts)

Failures

Mergers

New charters

Source: FDIC Quarterly Banking Profile, Fourth Quarter 1997.

FIGURE 47-8

was just 3.52 percent of industry assets, and the record ROE was attained with earnings of just $5.5 billion.

Healthy capital ratios were widespread throughout the industry as most savings institutions met or exceeded the highest regulatory capital standards. At the end of 1997, 1,744 savings institutions (representing 98 percent of the industry) were considered well capitalized. Another 32 institutions were considered adequately capitalized, and just 3 thrifts were classified as undercapitalized.

Since the Resolution Trust Corporation stopped taking failed institutions at midyear 1995, only one institution has failed (see Figure 47-8). [Union Federal Bank, FSB, Los Angeles, CA, was closed by the Office of Thrift Supervision on August 9, 1996. At closure, the Federal Deposit Insurance Corporation estimated the cost of this transaction to the SAIF to be approximately $10.3 million.] No thrifts failed in 1997, the first calendar year since 1959 with no thrift failures. Thus, costs for resolving failing institutions have not had a significant effect on the SAIF. At the end of 1997 the industry had had no thrift failures for 16 consecutive months.

Outlook

The thrift industry is currently well capitalized and its profitability is at record levels. Asset quality is good, and the trend is favorable. In the near term—and so long as the economy remains strong—the industry's health is likely to continue to improve. Continued progress would be threatened by any weakening in the economy or by adverse changes in the current interest-rate environment.

With the rise in capital held by thrift institutions, many thrifts now have the resources to increase their market share through acquisitions. Washington Mutual, Inc., Seattle, WA, recently announced an acquisition plan that would rank it among the 10 largest banking and thrift companies. Consolidation within both the thrift and banking industries is expected to continue in the near term. An increasing trend in new thrift charter applications could have a slight moderating influence on the pace of thrift industry consolidation.

The future attractiveness of the thrift charter depends on legislative and regulatory developments. Proposals have been made to eliminate the separate thrift charter or to impose restrictions on the industry by narrowing the activities permitted to thrifts or their holding companies. Other proposals would leave a separate thrift charter but expand the activities permitted to commercial bank holding companies.

Tim Critchfield, Federal Deposit Insurance Corporation, Division of Research and Statistics, (202) 898-8557, May 1998.

■ RELATED CHAPTERS

SECURITIES, MUTUAL FUNDS, AND COMMODITY FUTURES TRADING
Economic and Trade Trends

Fiscal Year 1997 Futures Volume by Commodity Type

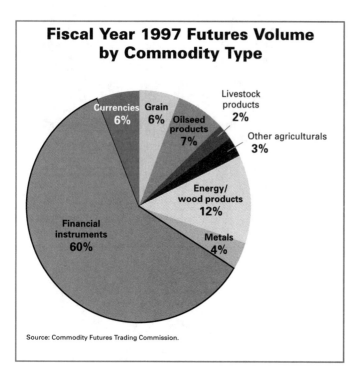

Source: Commodity Futures Trading Commission.

Family Financial Assets

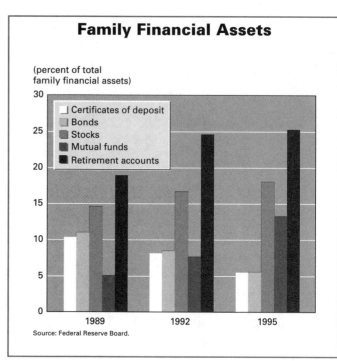

Source: Federal Reserve Board.

Stock and Commodity Prices, 1993–1997

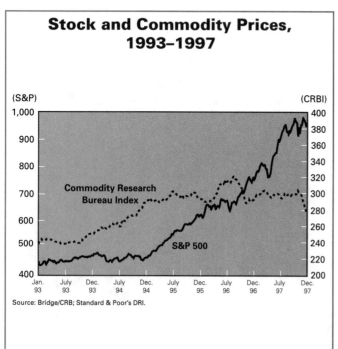

Source: Bridge/CRB; Standard & Poor's DRI.

Average Annual Employment in the Securities Industry

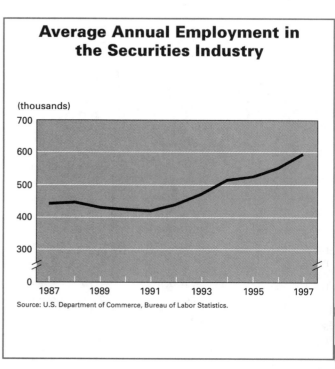

Source: U.S. Department of Commerce, Bureau of Labor Statistics.

Securities, Mutual Funds, and Commodity Futures Trading

INDUSTRY DEFINITION This chapter describes the industries defined in SIC 62 (security and commodity brokers, dealers, exchanges, and services) and SIC 672 (investment offices). The companies involved trade and underwrite stocks, bonds, options, futures, and other financial instruments and provide investment services, including mutual fund management.

OVERVIEW

The increasing globalization of the securities industry was illustrated in the world financial upheaval that resulted in a 7 percent decline in the U.S. market on over 1 billion shares traded on October 28, 1997. Markets all over the world set records for trading volume and volatility. Just as developments overseas affected U.S. markets, trauma in U.S. markets—such as the announcement of possible earnings disappointment for the semiconductor manufacturer Intel on March 6, 1998—drove down prices in foreign markets. Yet another volume record of 1.2 billion shares was set on September 1, 1998, in the midst of

a 20 percent market "correction," and signs pointed to continuing turbulence ahead. As will be described in the three sections below, this industry is exceptionally vibrant and is a major engine of growth in the U.S. economy. Although historically very cyclical, domestic employment in this industry has been growing steadily, and earnings are far above the U.S. average (see Table 48-1). The securities industry is also a major consumer of technology, including high-performance computers that keep orders flowing on major exchanges and in brokerage firms, software that both drives and accommodates demand for trading, and Internet technology.

SECURITIES

The securities industry includes SIC 6211 (securities brokers, dealers, and flotation companies), SIC 6231 (securities and commodity exchanges), and SIC 628 (services allied with the exchange of securities and commodities), which includes both investment advice and services such as clearing and account custodial functions. As can be seen in the SIC names, the national accounts do not distinguish clearly between securities and commodities. It is also difficult to make a clear distinction between the securities industry and the mutual fund industry.

TABLE 48-1: Annual Payroll: Securities and Commodities Brokers (SIC 62)

	1993	1994	1995
Number of employees	449,826	506,981	522,895
Payroll ($ thousands)	39,506,781	39,848,735	45,542,660
Average annual earnings ($)	87,827	78,600	87,097
U.S. average annual earnings ($)	24,934	25,723	26,575

Source: U.S. Department of Commerce, Bureau of the Census, *County Business Patterns*.

Global Industry Trends

Continuing recent trends, 1997 was a year of superlatives in both U.S. and world markets. Trading volumes set new records, and there were record or near-record levels of initial public offerings, mergers, and acquisitions. U.S. markets completed a third consecutive year of returns that exceeded 20 percent. Many of these trends were positive for both investors and the securities industry, but calamities here and abroad illustrated the risks involved in this business. As currency woes spread from Thailand to the rest of Asia, stock markets plummeted, wiping out a decade of growth almost overnight. What had been another 20 percent year-to-date gain in U.S. markets during 1998 evaporated in August in part due to Russia's collapse. Even so, world securities markets continue to become more attractive and influential in raising capital as a result of several forces.

Privatization. Governments all over the world are divesting themselves of businesses they run directly or introducing competition in long-standing state-sanctioned monopolies. This is true in both former planned economies, such as Russia and China, and major industrialized countries. Thus, the four biggest initial public offerings of 1997 were the Australian telecommunications company Telstra, France Telecom, China Telecom, and Electricidade of Portugal. Combined, these offerings accounted for over $22 billion, of which $2 billion was raised in the United States. Richard Grasso, chairman of the New York Stock Exchange, estimated that up to 18,000 companies will be privatized in China alone in the next decade, and many of them could qualify for listing on U.S. exchanges.

Securitization. Whereas real estate has traditionally been held privately by families or partnerships, the real estate investment trust (REIT) industry has blossomed into a sector that commands over $140 billion in U.S. market capitalization. The liquidity that comes with being a publicly traded company facilitates the acquisition of, and reduces the risk of holding, real estate for individual investors and pension funds. Securitization of less liquid assets such as real estate has created an enormous potential for worldwide industry growth.

Consolidation and Restructuring. As domestic and global competition leads to consolidation of companies or the shedding of a particular company's less strategic operations, the issuing of various forms of securities often plays a major role in consummating these deals. Worldwide merger activity in 1997 amounted to $1.6 trillion, representing an increase of almost 50 percent over 1996, and continued liberalization of international financial services suggests that this trend will continue.

International Investing. The increasing sophistication of investors worldwide is leading to more and more international investing. In the United States, trading of international issues increased from $268 billion in 1991 to over $1 trillion in 1996. Similar flows from foreign investors into U.S. stocks will continue to increase trading volume and improve liquidity.

Competition in the securities industry exists at many different levels. First and most important, international exchanges compete for capital and listings, and exchanges such as the New York Stock Exchange, the London Stock Exchange, and the Paris Bourse work hard at being the exchange of choice within segments they serve (see Table 48-2). As a result of competitive pressures, 1998 saw the most significant restructuring of U.S. markets in decades with the merger of the Nasdaq, American, and Philadelphia exchanges. Initial steps were also taken in Europe between the London Stock Exchange and the Deutsche Boerse which could ultimately lead to a Pan-European market.

There are, however, physical limitations on any exchange's capacity (space, telecommunications, computers) as well as issues of market response. For example, experience with U.S.-listed American Depositary Receipts (ADRs) shows that investors' interest in foreign companies is not always sustained after the initial offering. Another limitation that is especially related to competitiveness is that non-U.S. companies that want to be listed on U.S. exchanges are required to comply with U.S. Generally Accepted Accounting Procedures (GAAP). This can be an expensive undertaking because of the initial investment required and the recurring cost of maintaining duplicate sets of books. Although this is unlikely in the very near term, work by the International Organization of Securities Commissions (IOSCO) and the International Accounting Standards Committee (IASC) may pave the way for simpler requirements for international listing. (See the boxed note: "U.S. Securities Trading: Structure and Competition.")

TABLE 48-2: Selected International Stock Markets at End of 1996

Market	Listed Companies		Domestic Market Capitalization		Annual Turnover (millions of ECUs)	
	Domestic	Foreign	Millions of ECUs	Percent of GDP	Domestic	Foreign
United States (New York Stock Exchange)	2,617	290	5,395,889	90.2	3,014,383	190,392
Tokyo	1,766	67	2,374,733	64.9	738,711	1,214
London	557	833	1,368,000	153.6	335,644	580,777
United States (Nasdaq)	5,138	418	1,192,290	19.9	2,505,177	98,767
Germany	681	1,290	531,553	28.3	621,454	18,778
Paris	686	187	472,426	38.5	220,608	4,828
Amsterdam	217	216	302,452	96.1	149,587	653
Milan	244	4	206,997	21.8	82,532	18
Madrid	357	4	194,681	42.3	63,869	18

Source: International Monetary Fund, *European Monetary Union and International Capital Markets: Structural Implications and Risks,* May 1997.

U.S. SECURITIES TRADING: STRUCTURE AND COMPETITION

The largest U.S. stock exchange by trading volume is no longer an exchange. Since 1994, more shares have been traded on Nasdaq than on the New York Stock Exchange (which still commands a far higher market capitalization). Nasdaq, the National Association of Securities Dealers Automated Quotation System, is actually a virtual marketplace where dealers bid competitively for trades by using electronic screens. Typically, five or more securities dealers commit to make a market in a particular Nasdaq stock, such as Microsoft, and traders ultimately choose the best prices from competing bids through their brokers.

While heavily into various forms of electronic trading, the New York Stock Exchange (NYSE) and the American Stock Exchange (Amex) rely on floor traders who buy and sell shares at trading posts on the floor of the exchange, using an auction or "open outcry" system. Only members of the exchange are allowed to trade, and they must own one of a fixed number of "seats" to have trading privileges. An NYSE seat changed hands at $1.8 million dollars in February 1998. Ultimately, specialists in each stock are responsible for guaranteeing a market if there are no willing buyers or sellers, though trading in individual stocks sometimes may be halted as a result of imbalances. Regional exchanges (Boston, Philadelphia, Chicago, Cincinnati, Pacific) are also part of the national exchange system. In addition to trading purely local issues, they account for about 15 percent of the volume in national issues.

Exchanges also compete for listings with each other and with Nasdaq by emphasizing certain industry segments or products. Interestingly, the security traded most heavily on the Amex in 1997 was not a stock but a derivative product called Standard & Poor's Depositary Receipts (SPDRs, or "Spiders"). In 1998 a similar derivative of the Dow Jones Industrial Average known as "Diamonds" had its first full year of trading. Debates persist within the industry and in academia about whether an auction or dealer market provides the best prices for investors. Nasdaq claims that it is the wave of the future, while exchange proponents assert that floor traders provide better service and maintain more orderly markets. Ultimately, as evidenced by the 1998 merger of the Nasdaq, Amex, and Philadelphia exchanges, the pure auction and pure dealer markets will converge as a result of both domestic factors and global competition. Other consolidations within the industry may also occur.

Just as exchanges compete to raise capital, companies in the securities industry compete for trading commissions, underwriting shares, assets to place under management, and all other aspects of this business. Table 48-3 shows some of the major global competitors for underwriting, and similar lists of names would appear across other business segments. The biggest companies are truly global in nature, with all having assumed this status through acquisitions. Merrill Lynch, the largest U.S.

company, derived roughly one-quarter of its 1996 revenues outside the United States, and foreign revenue growth in 1995 and 1996 exceeded that of U.S. markets. These figures indicate what is possible for companies that execute well, and the potential is not close to being realized. In Japan, for example, pension fund liberalization could expose $125 billion of assets to international competition. As was noted in the November 20, 1997, *Wall Street Journal,* whereas Merrill once centered an ad campaign on being bullish on America, it is now bullish on the world. The same is certainly true for its U.S. and foreign competitors.

Domestic Trends

The U.S. securities industry continued to ride the tails of a historic bull market from 1990 through mid-1998. To put a billion-share day of the New York Stock Exchange (NYSE) in perspective, this volume would have amounted to roughly 20 percent of total annual trading volume just 20 years earlier. This trend has resulted from ever-increasing money flow and technology. In regard to money, individual investors continue to prefer financial assets to hard assets such as real estate in their portfolios, and within their stock of financial assets they continue to move into securities either directly or indirectly through mutual funds and 401(k) plans (see Table 48-4). Analysts at *The New York Times* estimate that total stock ownership by families has reached 43 percent of financial assets—a 50-year high. Although this trend could be reversed in the future, investors have shrugged off several market setbacks and have even, according to some observers, shown more discipline during times of stress than have institutional investors, which are prone to shift strategies on the basis of short-term indicators.

Technology acts as both an enabler and a driver of securities trading. On October 19, 1987, when the market dropped over 20 percent, the NYSE choked on a volume of 600 million shares, and it took several days before the situation returned to normal. By contrast, investment in technology since that time expanded capacity to a theoretical 2.3 billion to 2.7 billion shares, and thus the billion-share day in October 1997 was relatively more manageable. In terms of capacity demand, technology is making it possible for traders to profit, or at least try to profit, from various mathematics-based trading schemes involving individual trades of hundreds of millions of shares. According to an article in the December 1, 1997, *Business Week,* modeling of tick-by-tick movements in search of new trading strategies is one of the fastest growing areas of academic research. Demand for the execution of large volumes of securities on short notice has led to the widespread use of "blind bids," in which traders commit to prices on huge baskets of stocks without knowing which individual stocks will be part of the trade.

The most visible technology-related trend is the growth of Internet trading. Although electronic trading was introduced as early as 1985 by Charles Schwab, using an MS-DOS-based software package with a dial-up modem, a few tenuous steps into Internet trading for several years were soon followed by a stampede. Some of the new Internet trading firms do not even

TABLE 48-3: Top 10 Underwriters in 1997

U.S. Securities			Non-U.S. Securities		
Underwriter	Amount, $ billions	Share, %	Underwriter	Amount, $ billions	Share, %
Merrill Lynch	208.1	16.1	Merrill Lynch	37.1	7.5
Salomon Smith Barney	167.0	12.9	Goldman, Sachs	31.9	6.4
Morgan Stanley Dean Witter	139.5	10.8	SBC Warburg DR	29.0	5.8
Goldman, Sachs	137.3	10.6	Deutsche Morgan Grenfell (UK)	28.6	5.8
Lehman Brothers	121.0	9.4	Credit Suisse First Boston (Switzerland)	27.1	5.5
JP Morgan	104.0	8.0	JP Morgan	23.5	4.7
Credit Suisse First Boston (Switzerland)	67.7	5.2	Morgan Stanley Dean Witter	23.0	4.6
Bear, Stearns	57.5	4.4	ABN AMRO HC (Netherlands)	22.0	4.4
Donaldson, Lufkin, & Jenrette	46.0	3.6	Lehman Brothers	18.0	3.6
Chase Manhattan	33.1	2.6	Paribas (France)	17.8	3.6
Top 10[1]	1,081.3	83.6	Top 10[1]	258.1	52.0
Industry total	1,293.0	100.0	Industry total	496.2	100.0

[1] Totals may not add exactly because of rounding.
Source: Securities Data Co.

have brokers. Many firms use Internet trading as only one of their channels, while some full-service brokerage firms allow clients to view their accounts on the Internet but employ brokers to execute trades. According to Forrester Research, Internet trading will rise from 3 million brokerage accounts totaling $120 billion in 1997 to 15 million accounts handling $688 billion by 2002. Internet trading has been accompanied by an explosion of Web sites providing quotes, research, and other investor information. Many of these sites are maintained by brokerage and mutual fund firms, while many others are maintained by companies in the business of offering free content to sell advertising (e.g., Yahoo!) or offering research and other services on a subscription basis (e.g., S&P Personal Wealth). Many of these services and providers are outside SIC 62 but clearly depend on activity in this industry as a source of growth.

TABLE 48-4: Family Financial Asset Distribution
(percent)

Financial Asset	1989	1992	1995
Transaction accounts	19.7	17.7	13.5
Certificates of deposit	10.4	8.2	5.5
Savings bonds	1.6	1.2	1.4
Bonds	11.0	8.5	5.5
Stocks	14.6	16.6	18.0
Mutual funds (excluding money market funds)	5.0	7.7	13.2
Retirement accounts	18.8	24.4	25.1
Cash value of life insurance	6.2	6.3	7.9
Other managed assets	6.6	5.5	5.7
Other	6.0	3.9	4.2
Total[1]	100.0	100.0	100.0
Financial assets as a percentage of total assets	27.9	30.5	34.1

[1] Numbers may not add exactly because of rounding.
Source: Federal Reserve Bulletin, *Family Finances in the U.S.: Recent Evidence from the Survey of Consumer Finances,* January 1997.

Industry Projections for the Next 1 and 5 Years

Table 48-5 shows historical data reported by securities firms to the Securities and Exchange Commission. Before discussing the outlook for this industry, some definitions will be helpful.

- Commissions are fees that customers pay to execute trades on an exchange.

- With Nasdaq and other over-the-counter trades, customers pay an amount related to the difference between bid and asked prices for a security (the "spread"). Much of the brokerage revenue is reflected in the category "Trading and investment gains."

- Underwriting profits are fees and other gains or losses incurred in connection with a public securities offering. The performance of an offering is an important factor, because the underwriter is obliged to sell and to an extent maintain a market for securities it has issued on behalf of a sponsoring company. Although new issues, such as Yahoo!, which soar on opening usually garner the media coverage, many new issues fall flat when demand is lower than the underwriters hoped for, and losses can be substantial.

- Margin interest is revenue realized when customers borrow funds from their brokers to buy securities. If a customer is confident that the market will rise, the use of borrowed money is a way to increase return, though at higher risk.

- Mutual fund sales reflect commissions (or loads) on mutual funds. Therefore, while they are part of the securities industry's revenue base, they do not represent activity in the larger mutual fund industry.

- The category "Other," which accounts for fully half of reported revenues, reflects the diversity in this industry and the difficulty of fitting different types of revenue into fixed categories. However, this is the most consistent set of data available.

TABLE 48-5: Securities Industry (SIC 62) Trends and Forecasts
(millions of dollars; percent)

| | 1992 | 1993 | 1994 | 1995 | 1996 | 1997[1] | 1998[2] | 1999[3] | Percent Change | | | |
									96–97	97–98	98–99	92–96[4]
Commissions	16,249	19,905	19,847	23,215	27,865	32,689	37,592	40,600	17.3	15.0	8.0	14.4
Trading and investment gains	21,838	25,427	20,219	28,963	30,768	36,055	39,661	43,627	17.2	10.0	10.0	8.9
Underwriting profits	8,300	11,249	6,844	8,865	12,613	14,641	15,812	16,761	16.1	8.0	6.0	11.0
Margin interest	2,690	3,235	4,668	6,470	7,386	10,615	13,269	15,259	43.7	25.0	15.0	28.7
Mutual fund sales	5,950	8,115	6,887	7,434	10,081	12,418	14,902	17,882	23.2	20.0	20.0	14.1
Other	35,557	40,913	54,293	68,468	83,697	101,241	116,427	133,891	21.0	15.0	15.0	23.9
Total	90,584	108,844	112,758	143,415	172,410	207,659	237,663	268,020	20.4	14.4	12.8	17.5

[1] Preliminary.
[2] Estimate.
[3] Forecast.
[4] Compound annual rate.
Source: U.S. Securities and Exchange Commission; estimates and forecast by Standard & Poor's DRI.

Although the outlook for the securities industry in general remains very positive, it is unlikely that revenue growth will maintain the pace that has been set in the last few years. There are some secular trends, notably the shifting of assets into equities, that will take a long time to unwind, and continued growth in the mutual fund industry powered by savings for retirement will have a positive effect on securities trading. However, there are several factors on the horizon that point toward lower growth.

First, commission rates are continuing to fall, especially with the growth of Internet trading. Trades are now available to individual investors for as little as $7.95, and commission revenues as a percentage of the underlying value of the securities being traded continue to trend downward, totaling roughly 0.6 percent in 1995 compared with 0.75 percent in 1991 and 1992. A study by Greenwich Associates determined that average institutional trade commissions declined from 6.4 cents per share in 1992 to an estimated 5.6 cents in 1997. Increased trading volume has more than compensated for falling prices, but at some point the competition could cause revenues to stagnate, particularly if poor or even average stock market performance (compared to the atypical 20-plus percent annual returns in recent years) resulted in slower volume growth. Spreads on Nasdaq and over-the-counter markets can be expected to narrow as trading efficiency continues to improve, and though the securities industry would like to postpone the day of reckoning, the markets eventually will move to decimal trading, which also will narrow spreads.

On the underwriting front, there are signs that the best times in terms of initial public offerings may be past, at least for a while. Underwriting is a cyclical business. Volume in 1997 was off slightly from a record 1996, and anecdotal evidence suggests that profits are being squeezed as a result of competition. According to Securities Data, underwriting continued to be active in the first quarter of 1998, but many of the larger deals were bond issues, which have much lower profitability. Strength returned in the second quarter, although investor response to many initial public offerings (IPOs), especially out-

side the high-flying Internet sector, was cool. The Securities and Exchange Commission (SEC) has also proposed streamlined disclosure requirements, which could cut down on the fees generated and make it easier for companies to offer shares directly to the public. Competition will strengthen from abroad as a result of the European Monetary Union (EMU). The remaining categories of margin interest and mutual fund commissions are likely to remain strong, since investors do not appear to be motivated to reduce their debt level, mutual fund sales remain strong, and load funds appear to be coming back into vogue (see "Mutual Funds," below).

On the basis of the definitions and rationale outlined above, growth in this industry is forecast to tail off in commissions and underwriting but remain strong in the remaining categories. This will result in an aggregate growth rate of nearly 15 percent estimated in 1998, falling to under 13 percent in 1999. Assuming continued major market corrections between the present time and the year 2003, average annual growth through the 5-year period will be approximately 10 percent.

MUTUAL FUNDS

The mutual fund industry (SIC 672) creates and manages pools of securities, such as stocks, bonds, and money market instruments, on behalf of investors. Open-end mutual funds (SIC 6722), which issue and redeem shares on demand, account for the great majority of the economic activity in this industry, and all the tabular data presented in this section pertain to open-end funds. Closed-end funds and unit trusts (SIC 6726) maintain a fixed number of shares, and investors who wish to buy or sell after an initial public offering to do so in the securities markets.

Global Industry Trends

According to the Investment Company Institute, worldwide assets in mutual funds grew from $2.9 trillion in 1991 to $7.2 trillion in 1997. It is hazardous to compare data across countries

TABLE 48-6: Selected Global Activity in the Mutual Fund Industry
(assets in millions of U.S. dollars)

	1992	1993	1994	1995	1996	1997
Australia						
Number of funds	404	366	698	752	1,117	571
Assets	19,280	24,556	44,036	36,505	47,761	50,627
Belgium						
Number of funds	126	161	211	277	340	472
Assets	8,954	15,149	18,877	25,553	29,247	35,748
Canada						
Number of funds	549	633	813	916	954	1,023
Assets	52,921	86,567	90,349	107,812	154,529	197,984
France						
Number of funds	4,538	4,577	4,826	4,878	5,379	5,836
Assets	447,338	483,327	496,743	519,376	534,145	499,881
Japan						
Number of funds	5,701	6,086	6,306	6,408	5,879	5,203
Assets	346,924	454,608	435,603	469,980	420,103	311,335
Sweden						
Number of funds	435	467	314	298	316	344
Assets	18,108	24,356	20,208	27,388	34,981	45,452
United Kingdom						
Number of funds	1,373	1,420	1,452	1,490	1,532	1,550
Assets	91,153	131,455	133,092	154,452	201,304	235,683
Total non-U.S.						
Number of funds	18,183	19,889	22,001	29,050	29,017	27,813
Assets	1,625,543	2,086,147	2,315,054	2,573,814	2,813,786	2,669,383
Total U.S.						
Number of funds	3,850	4,558	5,357	5,761	6,293	6,778
Assets	1,646,259	2,075,366	2,161,495	2,820,355	3,539,205	4,489,681
Total world						
Number of funds	22,033	24,447	27,538	34,811	35,310	34,591
Assets	3,271,802	4,161,513	4,476,549	5,394,169	6,352,991	7,159,064

Source: Investment Company Institute.

because of differences in definitions, regulatory structures, and reporting requirements, but Table 48-6 gives a general idea of international activity. As can be seen in the table, the mutual fund industry is very much a global industry, but compared with securities or commodities trading, the competitive forces are quite restrained. This point is illustrated by the growing U.S. interest in international investing. Whereas a U.S. investor might buy a closed-end regional (e.g., Asia) or country (e.g., Korea) fund on the NYSE or buy any of the dozens of U.S.-based international open-end funds, it is unlikely that the investor would shop for alternative funds in France. In fact, direct ownership of a foreign account would create currency translation problems and increase tax reporting requirements in return for a minimal advantage, if any.

Although global competition is somewhat muted, fund companies are actively pursuing international business. There are at least two business models that fund companies use. The first is to open up shop in-country and sell funds directly to the local population. Examples include Scudder Kemper and Fidelity in Canada, Fidelity in Japan, and Vanguard in Europe. This model requires the company to meet foreign regulatory requirements and market itself to a population for which Fidelity, for example, is not a household name. Second, management companies are finding success by signing on to manage assets for existing funds in other countries. This allows them to capture fee income

from asset management without having to establish brand awareness. The growth potential for U.S. mutual fund companies is particularly significant in Asia, where personal savings rates are high (especially in Japan), awareness of fund investing is relatively low, and investors seem receptive to "foreign" funds.

Domestic Trends

As is shown in Table 48-7, at the end of 1997 mutual fund assets accounted for $4.5 trillion, up 27 percent from 1996. This increase was in part a manifestation of increases in underlying stock prices (and thus higher net asset values of mutual fund shares), but net sales (see Table 48-8) were up 28 percent to $874 billion. Funds not only are an increasingly popular way for investors to hold securities but also are playing a growing role in retirement accounts. Whereas mutual funds accounted for 25 percent of individual retirement accounts (IRAs) in 1991, their share exceeded 37 percent in 1996.

The U.S. mutual fund industry is extremely competitive. Fund empires such as Fidelity and Vanguard have captured huge amounts of assets. If, hypothetically, the average management fee is 0.5 percent of assets, this industry is generating revenues of almost $20 billion, excluding sales charges. In addition to offering regular funds directly to investors, fund managers market their products and services to the insurance industry in the form of variable annuities. Through these annuity products,

TABLE 48-7: Mutual Fund Industry (SIC 672) Trends and Forecasts

(billions of dollars; percent)

	1992	1993	1994	1995	1996	1997	1998[1]	1999[2]	Percent Change			
									96–97	97–98	98–99	92–96[3]
Equity funds												
Net new cash flow	79	130	119	128	222	231						
Assets	523	749	866	1,269	1,751	2,399	2,759	3,311	37.0	15.0	20.0	35.3
Bond and income funds												
Net new cash flow	94	114	−43	−5	13	45						
Assets	577	761	684	798	887	1,032	1,238	1,423	16.3	20.0	15.0	11.3
Money market funds												
Net new cash flow	−16	−14	9	89	89	102						
Assets	546	565	611	753	902	1,059	1,271	1,461	17.4	20.0	15.0	13.4
Total												
Net new cash flow	157	230	85	212	324	378						
Assets	1,646	2,075	2,161	2,820	3,540	4,490	5,268	6,196	26.8	17.3	17.6	21.1

[1] Estimate.
[2] Forecast.
[3] Compound annual rate.
Source: Investment Company Institute; estimates and forecast by Standard & Poor's DRI.

clients have the opportunity to achieve tax-deferred savings while they are young and gain protection against outliving their retirement nest eggs by establishing a monthly income stream for life. Variable-annuity purchasers can direct their investments toward different fund types and take advantage of higher rates of return (although with higher risk) than are available with fixed annuities. Variable annuities have been one of the life insurance industry's best-selling products.

As is indicated by the growing number of fund offerings, new and existing companies are constantly creating new products to capture market share. While nothing beats performance as a selling point, the fund business is extremely marketing-intensive, starting from the creation of the funds themselves. Stein Roe & Farnham achieved great success several years ago with its Young Investors fund, which concentrates on companies of interest to children (such as Disney and McDonald's) and provides educational materials and fun features in its quarterly reports. This fund has combined an innovative and appealing approach with excellent performance. Funds are also created to invest in socially responsible companies (tobacco and pesticide firms are not likely to be found in such a portfolio) or exploit a particular investment theme that appeals to people. One of the most popular unit investment trusts buys the "Dogs of the Dow," exploiting research suggesting that, of the 30 stocks in the Dow Jones Industrial Average, the 10 with the highest dividend payout ratios at the end of the year tend to outperform the market in the following year. Whether or not past performance guarantees future results (and a warning to the contrary is required by the SEC on any fund prospectus), this concept sells.

Success in this industry can create its own complications as funds become bigger. Some studies suggest that as a fund grows large, it gets harder and harder for it to outperform the market because at some point it accumulates a portfolio that looks like

TABLE 48-8: Mutual Fund Sales

(millions of dollars; percent)

Fund Objective	1996 Sales	1997 Sales	1997 Share, %	96–97 Percent Change
Aggressive growth	95,309	109,012	12.5	14.4
Growth	127,832	163,908	18.7	28.2
Growth and income	130,213	179,454	20.5	37.8
Precious metals	3,290	2,352	0.3	−28.5
International	61,869	86,649	9.9	40.1
Global equity	28,812	37,175	4.3	29.0
Income equity	24,029	30,578	3.5	27.3
Flexible portfolio	12,201	14,594	1.7	19.6
Balanced	23,514	29,820	3.4	26.8
Income—mixed	25,819	25,285	2.9	−2.1
Income—bond	38,130	55,914	6.4	46.6
U.S. government income	18,131	19,380	2.2	6.9
Ginnie Mae	7,755	9,529	1.1	22.9
Global bond	10,044	12,008	1.4	19.6
Corporate bond	10,373	11,447	1.3	10.4
High-yield bond	26,279	37,678	4.3	43.4
National municipal bond, long-term	22,439	27,187	3.1	21.2
State municipal bond, long-term	18,776	22,294	2.5	18.7
Total	684,813	874,263	100.0	27.7

Source: Investment Company Institute.

the market. As a practical consideration, funds have certain limitations on owning more than 10 percent of any company, and this can limit a fund manager's choices. Even 1 percent of a $60 billion fund may be larger than 10 percent of the value of some of the most promising small American companies. For this reason, funds such as Fidelity Magellan (on September 30, 1997), Contrafund, and Growth & Income (both on April 3, 1998) chose to stop accepting new accounts. Of course, fund families that close a particular fund generally start up new versions at the same time, hoping to duplicate the success of their parents.

At the retail level, the landscape has been shifting rapidly as discount brokerages have established a major presence. While companies such as PaineWebber and Dean Witter have long sold in-house funds and other load funds on commission, no-load companies such as Janus and Invesco have traditionally depended on their own marketing and 800 numbers to sell directly to the public. Several years ago Charles Schwab initiated its OneSource program, allowing its customers to buy funds of many different families through Schwab while maintaining shares in a Schwab account. This facilitates transactions and eliminates the need for the customer to receive and keep track of separate statements. In exchange for this service, the fund group pays an account maintenance fee for each customer who uses the service. Many discount brokers now provide this service, and Fidelity, which also operates a discount brokerage service, even opened its doors to funds of competing families. Fund companies must make trade-offs between the fees they have to pay under these programs and the potential to sell additional shares. Turnaround being fair play, some fund companies are getting into the brokerage business.

FUND MANAGEMENT: DO INVESTORS GET WHAT THEY PAY FOR?

Peter Lynch put Fidelity Magellan on the map by establishing a long-term performance record that no other fund manager has come close to matching. He did this by building a world-class research team and spending much of his time jetting around the world and visiting companies to personally assess their businesses. George Sauter of Vanguard has made his Index 500 Portfolio the second largest U.S. mutual fund. With no research budget and no travel budget, he has outperformed at least three-quarters of all the other mutual funds for the past 5 years simply by mirroring the composition of the Standard & Poor's 500 stock index in his portfolio.

Several theories have been advanced to explain the underperformance of active managers. Proponents of the efficient market hypothesis expect that on average even professional investors cannot beat the market because they all have access to the same information. Another theory suggests that as indexing gains popularity, outperformance of index funds becomes a self-fulfilling prophecy since a disproportionate amount of money flowing into the S&P 500 basket causes the underlying prices to appreciate. It is undeniable that index funds have a clear cost advantage over actively managed funds (expenses of about 0.2 percent of assets compared with 1.0 percent), and all other things being equal, investors can therefore expect an additional return of 0.8 percent per year. Another attractive aspect is that since these funds do little trading, they typically declare only minimal capital gains dividends on which investors have to pay income tax. This tax efficiency effectively increases returns to investors, who can defer tax payments to future years.

Although somewhat counterintuitive in an environment o better information and more financial education, funds tha charge loads seem to be making a comeback. A January 28 1998, article in *The Wall Street Journal* summarized recen activity, including the commitment of Young Investors to allo cate over $500 million for sales through brokers and the cre ation of additional load funds or the conversion of no-loac funds in families such as Scudder, Pilgrim Baxter & Associates and Montgomery Asset Management. This trend is attributable to the large sums that people are dealing with through retire ment plan rollovers, causing them to seek professional advice and to the hypothesis that activity in the do-it-yourself compo nent of the investing public is peaking.

A looming issue for this industry is compensation for func managers. Regardless of whether managers add value, the fac that managers such as Peter Lynch of Fidelity in its heyday anc Tom Marsico, recently of Janus Capital, attract billions o dollars makes them exceptionally valuable to mutual fund com panies. Their star status is enhanced by the investment media— print, broadcasting, and Internet—which follow their every move and clamor for interviews. As managers' compensation increases costs rise and managers are more prone to jump ship for bette offers. This leaves investors in a quandary about whether to stick with the fund or follow the manager. (See the boxed note: "Fund Management: Do Investors Get What They Pay For?")

Industry Projections for the Next 1 and 5 Years

Although it is strongly affected by the stock and bond markets the mutual fund industry is insulated from some of the cyclicity of securities trading. Mutual funds are becoming an investmen vehicle of choice for retirement plans, and 401(k) dollars in par ticular provide a steady source of new cash. Millions o investors in IRAs or taxable accounts also invest monthly through direct deposit and other automated deposit mecha nisms, and despite short-term fluctuations and reallocation: from month to month, investors are clearly committed to funds for the long haul. Table 48-7 provides historical data on net new cash flow (sales excluding reinvested dividends minus redemp tions) and historical and forecast data on assets. Although asse values are subject to wide fluctuations because of movements ir underlying prices, income in this industry is largely based or the assets managed. Therefore, though somewhat fragile, asse values best represent activity in the fund industry.

In the three categories of funds shown in Table 48-7, net cash flows associated with bond and income and money marke funds vary directly with interest rate movements. Bond funds attract money when interest rates decline because bond prices and thus the net asset values of bond funds, rise. As interes rates rise, though, investors stand to lose money in bonds anc tend to move into money market funds, where they can realize the benefits from increasing rates. Both bond and money mar ket funds also act as safe havens for assets when equities turr down. Assuming a fairly stable interest rate environment ahead bond and money market funds should grow by 15 percent ir 1999. The estimated asset growth in bond and equity funds ir 1998 reflects favorable conditions in fixed income markets dur ing this period coupled with a correction in equities. The 1999 forecast assumes a less ebullient but still rewarding market environment. Asset growth is predicted to be 15 percent annually for the entire industry through the year 2003.

COMMODITY FUTURES

Commodity futures trading is covered largely under SIC 6221, commodity contracts brokers and dealers. Firms in this industry trade contracts on behalf of others as members of national commodity exchanges or trade for their own accounts. The exchanges themselves are combined with securities exchanges in SIC 6231. Services allied with the exchange of securities or commodities (SIC 628) includes investment advice, data support, and custody and transfer services.

Global Industry Trends

According to the Futures Industry Association, world trading on futures and options increased 9 percent to 1,930,225,775 contracts in 1997. The breakdown of trading by futures and options on U.S. and international exchanges is shown in Table 48-9. This performance was notable in an environment in which the U.S. share of the world market had been declining, at least on the basis of these measures. Some background, however, is required to understand what the numbers may mean.

Futures originally evolved from forward contracts, in which farmers and other commodity producers entered into agreements with the owners of grain elevators or with other consumers or intermediaries to deliver specified quantities of commodities to a particular location on a certain date in exchange for a specified price. This allowed the producers to protect themselves from falling prices and allowed consumers to be protected from rising prices that were influenced by demand and uncontrollable factors such as weather. Whereas a forward contract was typically an individual arrangement between two parties, futures contracts developed around recognized commodity exchanges in major trading centers. They differed from forward contracts in that their specifications (date, place, quantity, grade, etc.) were standard and in that while they could be settled by the physical exchange of a product, they did not have to be.

TABLE 48-9: World Futures and Options Volume
(millions of contracts; percent)

	1996	1997	Percent Change
Futures			
U.S. volume	397	444	11.8
Non-U.S. volume	703	757	7.7
Total	1,101	1,200	9.0
Options			
U.S. volume	396	462	16.7
Non-U.S. volume	272	269	−1.1
Total	668	730	9.3

Source: Futures Industry Association.

TABLE 48-10: Top 10 International Contracts
(millions of contracts; percent)

Contract	Exchange	Country	1996	1997	Percent Change
U.S. T-bonds	CBOT	United States	84.7	99.8	17.8
3-Month Eurodollar	CME	United States	88.9	99.8	12.3
German Bund	LIFFE	United Kingdom	39.8	45.0	13.1
3-Month Euromark	LIFFE	United Kingdom	36.2	43.3	19.6
U.S. dollar	BM&F	Brazil	45.1	40.4	−10.4
Interest rate	BM&F	Brazil	49.5	36.5	−26.3
S&P 100 Index Options[1]	CBOE	United States	54.9	36.6	−33.3
Notional bond	MATIF	France	35.3	33.8	−4.2
DAX options	DTB	Germany	26.0	31.5	21.2
Bund	DTB	Germany	16.5	31.3	89.7

[1] The S&P index option listed is a stock option on the Chicago Board Options Exchange, not an option on a future.
Source: Futures Industry Association.

Options on futures became major trading vehicles in the mid-1980s. Although futures buyers do not necessarily have to deliver or accept 10,000 pork bellies, they are exposed to significant financial risk because futures are so highly leveraged. That is, traders commit only a small fraction of the contract value in cash but are liable for the value of the entire contract. Options give traders a way to participate in futures ownership while limiting their potential loss to the amount they invest. Futures contracts originally involved commodities such as grain, precious metals, and silver, but financial instruments have long since dominated commodity trading (see Table 48-10). The resulting difficulty in tracking this industry derives from the question of what is a commodity and what is not.

As world financial markets have become increasingly sophisticated, the type and volume of so-called derivatives have exploded. Although these instruments share characteristics of leverage and risk with commodities, they are not defined as commodities and are not counted in commodity trading statistics but do amount to a sizable and growing economic activity. A March 20, 1998, article in the *Financial Times* cited an estimate of the notional amount outstanding (the underlying value of the contracts) of approximately $28 trillion. Separately, the International Monetary Fund estimated the 1996 worldwide exchange-traded notional value of derivative contracts (futures and options on interest rates, currencies, and stock market indexes) at $9.9 trillion, while the value of the non-exchange-traded (over-the-counter) market for interest rate and currency swaps was $21.1 trillion. While these numbers are not directly comparable, they are indicative of significant activity that is bypassing the exchanges.

As a result of this trend, international regulators have been reassessing their role. Losses suffered by firms such as the United Kingdom–based Barings and the U.S.-based Niederhoffer Investments suggest that more oversight is needed. In a March 1998 speech to the Futures Industry Association, Brooksley Born, chairperson of the Commodity Futures Trading Commission, cited a General Accounting Office (GAO) study that had cataloged over $11 billion in derivatives-related losses between 1987 and 1997 to make a case for better regulation. However, trade associations and traders believe that there is already too much regulation, and they are forcing regulators to streamline the procedures that are already in effect.

Setting aside the role of the over-the-counter market, it is hard to glean much meaning from what on the surface appears to be comparable statistics. This is the case because a contract that hedges the value of 50,000 pounds of cattle is worth five times as much as a contract specifying 10,000 pounds, and ultimately it is the notional principal amount outstanding that is the better measure. Unfortunately, there are no recent data across international exchanges. Also, as described in a 1994 GAO report, much of the growth in commodities trading in other countries has occurred in products that are traded locally. The failure of a U.S. commodity exchange to capture trading volume in a Brazilian commodity cannot be taken as a sign of lack of competitiveness.

In any case, there is fierce competition among exchanges to establish new products and attract trading. This is forcing alliances both overseas and within the United States to cut costs and improve service. In September 1997 the three largest European exchanges—Germany's Deutsche Borse, the French Matif, and the Swiss Schweizer Borse—agreed to standardize their contracts and develop a common trading system called EUREX. In March 1998 the Chicago Board of Trade (CBOT) and the Chicago Mercantile Exchange agreed to consolidate their clearing functions and the New York Cotton Exchange and the Coffee, Sugar, and Cocoa Exchange agreed to merge into the New York Board of Trade. CBOT and EUREX also entered into an alliance which allowed members to trade on each other's floors. As with securities, there is a spirited debate between open outcry advocates and electronic trading proponents, but the stakes in international commodity trading are probably higher because commodities with high global demand, such as bond futures, can be traded anywhere in any time zone.

Domestic Trends

Table 48-11 shows the volume of futures trading on U.S. exchanges. Since the time period (fiscal year versus calendar year) is different from that in Table 48-10, the data do not

match, but the similar growth trends are evident. Like stock trading, aggregate volumes and volumes associated with individual contracts vary widely with both macroeconomic and microeconomic factors. The most significant macro driver in 1997 was the Asian financial upheaval, which started as a currency crisis (translating immediately into high volatility and volume in currency-related futures) and then spread to other commodities, such as copper. Otherwise, 1997 was generally a down year for commodities other than the U.S. dollar, and prices measured by the Commodity Research Bureau index hit record lows in 1998. On the plus side, silver prices climbed sharply on news that Warren Buffett was accumulating positions in that metal. This sharp price rise was accompanied by heavy trading volume, which is good for the industry, and windfalls or stunning losses for individual traders, depending on which side of the trade they were on.

In addition to volatility, the commodities market thrives on new products. The importance of new product development becomes more clear when one compares the stock market, where dozens of new issues join the thousands of listings every week, with the commodity markets, where contracts number in the hundreds and new contract types are introduced more sporadically. Typically, a contract will trade on only one exchange and the exchange that establishes the market first will keep it assuming that there is sufficient interest in the contract to maintain volume and liquidity. Otherwise, the exchange stands to lose a significant investment in contract design, following the regulatory process, and marketing.

The two most popular new commodity products in 1997 were both stock index futures. On September 9, 1997, the Chicago Mercantile Exchange introduced the "E-mini" contract based on the Standard & Poor's (S&P) 500 stock index, which compared with the existing S&P 500 contract, required a margin (or down payment) of only $2,100 that was based on the index price then in effect—one-tenth of the existing S&P 500 future. Also traded electronically and over the Internet, this contract was intended to appeal to retail investors. Subsequently, the rival CBOT started trading a contract based on the rival Dow Jones Industrial Average (DJIA) on October 6. This product was unveiled at the same time that the first-ever stock

TABLE 48-11: U.S. Commodities Futures Trading
(millions of contracts; percent)

Exchange	Fiscal Year		Percent Change
	1996	1997	
Chicago Board of Trade (CBOT)	169.379	179.293	5.9
Kansas City Board of Trade (KCBT)	2.137	2.119	−0.8
Minneapolis Grain Exchange (MGE)	1.001	1.075	7.4
MidAmerica Commodity Exchange (MCE)	3.250	3.321	2.2
Chicago Mercantile Exchange (CME) and International Monetary Market (IMM)	141.141	147.875	4.8
New York Mercantile Exchange (NYMEX) and Commodity Exchange, Inc. (COMEX)	63.391	68.213	7.6
New York Cotton Exchange & Associates (NYCE) and New York Futures Exchange (NYFE)	4.854	5.805	19.6
Coffee, Sugar, and Cocoa Exchange (CSCE)	8.983	9.603	6.9
Philadelphia Board of Trade	0.047	0.036	−23.4
Total	394.182	417.342	5.9

Source: Commodity Futures Trading Commission.

TABLE 48-12: Commodity Trading Industry (SIC 6221, 6231, 628) Trends and Forecasts by Fiscal Years
(millions of contracts; percent)

| | 1992 | 1993 | 1994 | 1995 | 1996 | 1997 | 1998[1] | 1999[2] | Percent Change | | | |
									96–97	97–98	98–99	92–96[3]
Futures contracts	289.5	325.5	411.1	409.4	394.2	417.3	438.2	462.3	5.9	5.0	5.5	8.0
Options on futures	69.6	76.9	99.2	95.4	100.3	105.1	112.5	121.5	4.8	7.0	8.0	9.6

[1] Estimate.
[2] Forecast.
[3] Compound annual rate.
Source: Commodity Futures Trading Commission; estimates and forecast by Standard & Poor's DRI.

index based on the DJIA began trading on the Chicago Board Options Exchange. Both products were accompanied by a blitz of marketing and educational activities and have been doing very well in the marketplace.

Industry Projections for the Next 1 and 5 Years

Among the three subsectors covered in this chapter, commodities trading is the most difficult to forecast (see Table 48-12). In a sense, the relationship of volume to volatility leaves analysts with the need to predict the unpredictable. The greatest positive factor for the industry is the growth in derivatives. As all financial and product markets continue their trend toward globalization, investors need to find new ways to hedge risk, and derivatives creators are responding to that need with ever-increasing sophistication. At issue for an industry defined in the context of recognized commodities exchanges is how much of this activity will be on- or off-exchange. One of the more interesting areas for nonfinancial futures is electricity, because deregulation of electric utilities creates volatility and risk which needs to be hedged.

The major risk for the U.S. commodities industry lies in competition from Europe and the EMU. European exchanges are becoming more integrated, and that integration is occurring as a single currency is about to supplant several national currencies. The eventual disappearance of those currencies, assuming that the EMU succeeds, will reduce the need for hedging risk and eliminate the economic basis for several important contracts and options. As a result, world exchanges in the near term will be competing for shares of a smaller pie. To hang on to market share, the U.S. exchanges are likely to continue forming partnerships and cross-trading agreements with their major European counterparts.

In the absence of specific shocks, the outlook for commodities trading is for continued slow growth. The estimated growth in futures and options volume for fiscal year 1998 is 5 and 7 percent, respectively, with a slight uptick in 1999 as a result of EMU-related activity in advance of and during the transition to a unified currency.

Harvey R. Greenberg, Standard & Poor's DRI, (781) 860-6527, September 1998.

■ REFERENCES

Barron's, 200 Liberty Street, New York, NY 10281.
Business Week, 1221 Avenue of the Americas, New York, NY 10020.
Commodity Futures Trading Commission, *Annual Reports,* available at http://www.cftc.gov.
Commodity Futures Trading Commission, *A Study of the Global Competitiveness of U.S. Futures Markets,* April 1994, 1155 21st Street, NW, Washington, DC 20581. (202) 418-5000.
Federal Reserve Bulletin, *Family Finances in the U.S.: Recent Evidence from the Survey of Consumer Finances,* January 1997, Washington, DC 20551.
Futures Industry Association, 2001 Pennsylvania Avenue, NW, #600, Washington, DC 20006-1823. (202) 466-5460, http://www.fiafii.org.
Greenwich Associates, 8 Greenwich Office Park, Greenwich, CT 06831-5195. (203) 629-1200.
International Monetary Fund, *European Monetary Union and International Capital Markets: Structural Implications and Risks* (Working Paper 97/62), May 1997, 700 19th Street, NW, Washington, DC 20431-0002. (202) 623-7000, http://www.imf.org.
International Monetary Fund, *International Capital Markets: Developments, Prospects, and Key Policy Issues,* November 1997.
Investment Company Institute, *Mutual Fund Fact Book* (annual editions), 1401 H Street, NW, #1200, Washington, DC 20005-2110. (202) 326-5800, http://www.ici.org.
U.S. Securities and Exchange Commission, 450 Fifth Street NW, Washington, DC 20549. (202) 942-8088.
The Wall Street Journal, 200 Liberty Street, New York, NY 10281.

■ RELATED CHAPTERS

46: Insurance
47: Financial Services

■ GLOSSARY

Broker: A person or firm acting as an intermediary between the buyers and sellers of securities.
Commodity future: A contract tied to a particular commodity's price movement, which is determined on the floor of a commodity exhange.
Derivatives: A contract whose value is based on the price of an underlying financial asset, index, or other investment.

Exchanges: Locations where securities or futures trading takes place, such as the New York Stock Exhange.

Mutual fund: A pool of money raised from individual shareholders and managed by an investment company that invests in stocks, bonds, options, futures, and money market and other securities.

Option: A contract that gives the holder the right, but not the obligation, to buy or sell a certain security at a predetermined price, typically until an agreed upon date.

Primary market: The market for new securities, where proceeds from securities sales are retained by the issuer of the securities.

Secondary market: The market where securities are bought and sold subsequent to original issuance, with proceeds retained by selling dealers and investors.

Security: A financial instrument that represents ownership interest in a corporation, creditor relationship with a company or government or some other underlying right.

PROFESSIONAL BUSINESS SERVICES
Economic and Trade Trends

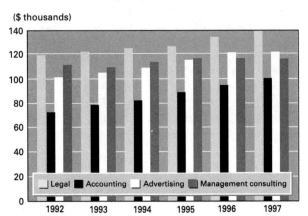

Business Service Receipts Per Employee

($ thousands)

Legend: Legal, Accounting, Advertising, Management consulting

Source: U.S. Department of Commerce: International Trade Administration, Bureau of the Census; U.S. Department of Labor: Bureau of Labor Statistics.

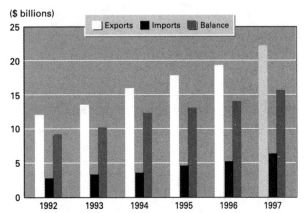

Business, Professional, and Technical Services, 1992–1997

($ billions)

Legend: Exports, Imports, Balance

Transactions between affiliated parties are excluded.

Source: U.S. Department of Commerce: International Trade Administration, Bureau of the Census; U.S. Department of Labor: Bureau of Labor Statistics.

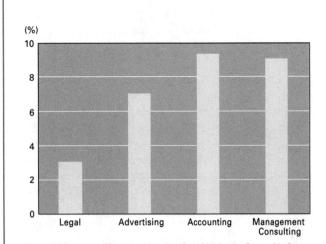

Revenue Growth by Sector, 1992–1996

(%)

Legal, Advertising, Accounting, Management Consulting

Source: U.S. Department of Commerce: International Trade Administration, Bureau of the Census; U.S. Department of Labor: Bureau of Labor Statistics.

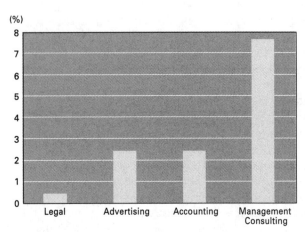

Employment Growth by Sector, 1992–1996

(%)

Legal, Advertising, Accounting, Management Consulting

Source: U.S. Department of Commerce: International Trade Administration, Bureau of the Census; U.S. Department of Labor: Bureau of Labor Statistics.

Professional Business Services

INDUSTRY DEFINITION The professional business services industry includes accounting, auditing, and bookkeeping services (SIC 8721); advertising services (SIC 731); legal services (SIC 81); and management consulting and public relations services (SIC 874).

OVERVIEW

Professional business service companies are functioning on a global scale because of improved communications technology and faster information exchange. More of these firms are expanding internationally to capture new markets and/or capitalize on lower operating costs. Exports of private services grew $16 billion, or about 7 percent, in 1997. The largest dollar increase was attributed to growth in U.S. receipts of "other private services," a category which includes business, professional, technical, and financial services. Technological advances, mergers and acquisitions, and rapid globalization should continue to affect all four of these professions. The objective for many of these firms is not to transform an inefficient professional firm into an efficient one but to make an already efficient professional business service organization more efficient.

Global Trends

The market for professional business services continues to grow more rapidly overseas than in the United States. The leading U.S. firms are multinational and are leaders in innovation and technology worldwide. Client demand is driving firms' growth internationally as more businesses expand globally.

Although U.S. professional business service providers are considered leaders in the industry and U.S. regulations for these sectors are used as models worldwide, there are considerable impediments to doing business internationally. U.S. government efforts are concentrated on these market access barriers in multilateral and bilateral governmental discussions.

Globalization and harmonization are leading to changes in international standards. The momentum for change in international accounting standards in particular has intensified as more and more companies view business as global. Several key factors support international harmonization. The technological ability to transmit information and a business environment that is globally oriented are especially significant factors. This combination has energized companies' willingness to think beyond domestic boundaries. To this end, there is broad agreement that international generally accepted accounting principles (GAAP) are needed urgently. The lack of international accounting standards has an inhibiting effect on global capital flows, causing investors to limit their investments in companies with unfamiliar or opaque accounting methods. However, a number of international bodies, including the European Union (EU), the United Nations (UN), the Organization for Economic Cooperation and Development (OECD), the International Federation of Accountants (IFAC), and the International Accounting Standards Committee (IASC), are involved in international accounting and would have to be included in the harmonization. National authorities also would have to be included.

Technological innovations and improvements in information technology are having a significant effect on professional business service firms. More firms are using sites on the World Wide Web for marketing and advertising or to establish an identity in their industries. The Internet also is being used to provide a higher level of service while keeping costs down. Consultants have real-time information access to technology providers through the Internet and a "self-service" consulting model that allows clients to access a firm's knowledge and templates to do their work. According to a Price Waterhouse/World Economic Forum Survey, Asian and European firms will be influenced more by electronic commerce than will North American firms.

The demand for professional services should continue to come from the major trading partners of the United States. Canada, Europe, and Japan have been the largest purchasers of these services, and this trend should continue for several more years. Latin America is developing new opportunities for professional business firms. Although the Asian financial crisis has hurt a number of industry sectors, some professional business firms are finding increasing opportunities in Asian countries.

Assessments of international sales of professional business services must include sales by nonbank majority-owned foreign affiliates (MOFAs) of U.S. firms. International sales must include both cross-border transactions (exports) and MOFA transactions to fully reflect the international business activity that occurs. For instance, exports of advertising services accounted for cross-border transactions worth approximately $597 million in 1996. However, sales of services by MOFAs for similar activities recorded approximately $4.9 billion in that year (latest available data).

Domestic Trends

The professional business services sector is experiencing large-scale mergers and separations. The Big Six (Arthur Andersen, Ernst & Young, Deloitte & Touche, KPMG Peat Marwick, Coopers & Lybrand, and Price Waterhouse) are about to become the Big Five after the merger of Coopers & Lybrand and Price Waterhouse. Mergers are being assembled to provide clients with more services and firms with higher revenues and greater efficiency. Whereas services were traditionally supplied by a distinct industry sector firm, such as a law firm, the same services may now be supplied by a multidisciplinary service provider through a management consulting firm. However, not all the major partnerships are successful. A major separation involves the megamanagement consulting firm Andersen Consulting, which is filing for separation from the giant accounting firm Arthur Andersen.

Because of computer glitches caused by date formatting, the year 2000 (Y2K) may create hardships for some professional service companies and opportunities for many others. The Y2K issue stems from the fact that many computerized systems, including both financial and operational software applications, identify the year in a date field by the last two digits (for example, 98 represents the year 1998). In this type of system 2000 is simply recorded as 00. Problems may arise when the system uses this date to perform a check or calculation. Minor errors and/or major systems malfunctions may not become apparent until January 1, 2000. Technology consultants estimate that the total global expenditures for the Y2K problem will range from $300 billion to $600 billion through 1999. However, the Y2K issue does not by itself give rise to any modification of an auditor's report on financial statements unless there is or may be a material effect on the financial statements being audited.

Growth in U.S. management consulting and public relation services is expected to continue to increase internationally 14 to 15 percent through 2002. Demand for legal services is estimated to increase about 6 to 7 percent in that period. Advertising services could have a growth rate of approximately 5 to 6 percent into the next century. It is estimated that the demand for accounting, auditing, and bookkeeping services will increase 4 to 5 percent through 2002.

ACCOUNTING, AUDITING, AND BOOKKEEPING

The top 100 accounting, auditing, and bookkeeping companies in the United States include 91 regional accounting practices plus the Nine Nationals. The Nine Nationals define the domestic practice of accountancy (see Table 49-1). Among the Nine Nationals, the Big Six currently dominate this industry subsector globally and produce the majority of revenues.

Auditors are facing a decreasing demand for their traditional services, such as auditing and accounting services, and a greater demand for value-added consulting services. The price of the average audit has declined to about 2 cents per $10,000 of corporate revenue from 3.3 cents in 1985, and this trend shows no sign of abating. To be competitive, certified public accountants (CPAs) are shifting their focus toward helping clients understand all areas of business performance rather than financial matters alone. The accountant is becoming more of a coach than a scorekeeper. The future success of a CPA will be based on the ability to become market-driven rather than being dependent on regulations to stay in business.

Domestic Activity and Performance

A major development in the accounting sector in 1998 involved Andersen Consulting filing for separation from the accounting giant Arthur Andersen because of "breaches of contract and irreconcilable differences." Since Andersen Worldwide created Andersen Consulting in 1989, that firm has grown to become

TABLE 49-1: Gross Revenues Worldwide of the Top Nine National Accounting Firms in 1997
(millions of dollars; percent)

	Revenues	Percent Change 96–97
Andersen Worldwide[1]	11,300	19.0
Ernst & Young	9,100	17.4
Deloitte & Touche	7,400	13.8
KPMG Peat Marwick	8,219	11.1
Coopers & Lybrand	7,500	10.7
Price Waterhouse	5,630	12.2
Grant Thornton	1,403	9.2
McGladrey & Pullen	1,060	12.2
BDO Seidman	1,450	9.0
National firms	53,062	13.9

[1] Arthur Andersen and Andersen Consulting are business units of Andersen Worldwide.
Source: *Public Accounting Report,* 1998, Strafford Publications, Inc., Atlanta GA. (800) 926-7926.

the largest management consultancy, and this activity has become more important than the accounting unit. The proposed breakup of Arthur Andersen and Andersen Consulting is contentious, with both entities intending to keep the Andersen name after the breakup. The separation is being reviewed in private by an independent arbitrator at the International Chamber of Commerce in Paris.

A ruling by the U.S. Supreme Court in 1998 may affect the relationship between accounting firms, management consulting firms, and state regulatory boards in the United States. That ruling allows employees of American Express Tax and Business Services to use their CPA credentials and grants this firm the right to advertise that it employs CPAs. Although the ruling went against the Florida State Board of Accountancy, the board still may assert jurisdiction over these professionals in regard to technical standards.

A controversial ruling announced in 1998 that will affect accounting practices concerns the use of derivatives. The Financial Accountant Standards Board (FASB) is issuing a standard which will require public companies to report their use of derivatives at fair values as of January 1, 2000. The FASB's movement toward fair-value accounting and away from traditional cost accounting is based on the American tendency to support standards with conceptual underpinnings. However, there is not total agreement on applying this methodology. Some financial officers believe that the fair-value accounting method introduces artificial volatility, while supporters of this methodology believe that values are not misstated when the numbers are smoothed out. Some governmental authorities, such as the Securities Exchange Commission, are active proponents of the proposed changes, while the Treasury opposes them. In its current form the FASB proposal does not have full support internationally. Until this situation is resolved, there may be volatility in the equity accounts of those following the standards and some hesitancy by other companies which may decide not to use derivatives for crucial management decisions to avoid the accounting implications.

Accounting Today's top 100 accounting firms reached more than $25 billion in overall revenues in the United States in 1997, a record-setting 21 percent increase over 1996. According to the *Public Accounting Report,* the Nine Nationals posted an unprecedented U.S. net revenue increase of 20 percent to $21.8 billion in 1997, which dwarfed those firms' 14.7 percent growth

rate in 1996. The Big Six are leading the surge, having added more than 20,000 new professionals in 1998. In general, business services are replacing consulting services. In 1998 auditing and accounting services were expected to grow 11 percent, while tax services were expected to increase 19 percent. The fastest growing firms are the strongest niche businesses, as local firms with strong specialties can become national powerhouses.

In 1997 all Big Six practices experienced double-digit growth ranging from 16 to 24 percent. While the proposed merger between Ernst & Young and KPMG Peat Marwick is officially off, the merger of Coopers & Lybrand and Price Waterhouse is still going forward. If it succeeds, the partnership will represent the largest public accounting firm globally in terms of both revenue and number of employees. Worldwide revenues for the Nine National accounting firms increased to more than $53 billion in 1997. Revenues for the accounting services sector should continue to grow approximately 10 percent per year for the next few years (see Table 49-2).

International Activity

Increasing globalization of the economy is affecting the worldwide accounting profession in many ways and increasing the need for that profession to respond through the international accountancy bodies. Accountancy bodies such as IFAC and IASC are considering issues regarding ethical guidance in the disclosure of confidential information, the practice of "lowballing," employing the services of nonaccountants, and the use of the code of national accountancy bodies. Another international professional body, the Institute of Social and Ethical Accountability (ISEA), was recently established in the area of nonfinancial disclosure and works toward the development of international standards for social and ethical disclosure and the auditing of those disclosures. Social accounts focus on social rather than financial matters. Currently, there are no accounting standards for social accounting and no common format for producing these accounts. Social accounts may affect the data and how the data are collected and analyzed. There are clear and distinct differences between the type of information that is audited for financial accounts and the type audited for social accounts. Social accounts are more difficult to audit, since they have many qualitative and quantitative values. The issue of possible future social accounting audit standards is clearly important for the accountancy profession as a whole.

TABLE 49-2:   U.S. Accounting, Auditing, and Bookkeeping Services (SIC 8721) Trends and Forecasts
(millions of dollars except as noted)

	1992	1993	1994	1995	1996	1997[1]	1998[2]	1999[2]	Percent Change			
									96–97	97–98	98–99	92–96[3]
Revenues	37,191	39,807	42,633	48,769	54,484	60,000	65,750	72,000	10.1	9.6	9.5	10.0
Employment (thousands)	513	508	519	550	575	600	626	655	4.3	4.3	4.6	2.9

Estimate.
Forecast.
Compound annual growth rate.
Source: U.S. Department of Commerce: International Trade Administration (ITA), Bureau of the Census; U.S. Department of Labor: Bureau of Labor Statistics. Estimates and forecasts by ITA.

A single body of principles for recording financial transactions and reporting global entities has not been created. As cross-border transactions increase, so does the need for international compatibility in financial reporting. One possibility is to establish an internationally recognized set of accounting standards and procedures. Another is the creation of country-specific GAAP to be applied in the financial reports of companies listed on the world's major stock exchanges.

A key country-specific set of standards is the U.S. GAAP. Many analysts believe that the U.S. process allows for pooling of interests and immediate write-offs of spending on in-process research. Some authorities believe that the U.S. GAAP gives U.S. firms a competitive advantage by avoiding or limiting the reduction in earnings per share. However, some analysts note weaknesses in the U.S. GAAP and argue that the costs for small businesses of complying with GAAP are out of proportion to the size of those businesses. Although GAAP are accepted by many countries, including some in the Asia/Pacific region, continental European countries are more comfortable using international accounting standards (IAS) than using the U.S. GAAP. U.S. decision makers, however, are reluctant to accept international standards in total because the disclosure requirements in the United States are considered the most rigorous in the world and the system is perceived to have fairness, integrity, and carefully monitored regulation.

Selecting appropriate country-specific standards and international standards is especially important in regard to the quality of the financial reporting and growth of the emerging capital markets (ECMs). However, pursuing accounting harmonization is not a risk-free policy option for ECMs because a problem may occur if an ECM selects an inappropriate standard; however, the greater risk is for the ECM not to have a sound basis of accounting.

There are many opportunities for U.S. accounting firms to expand their services around the world. This expansion is occurring at a more rapid pace overseas than it is in the United States (see Table 49-3). Mergers and acquisitions still play an important role in expansion. For example, the major CPA firm Deloitte & Touche merged with the European law firm Thomas & Associates in 1998. Not all mergers are accepted with openness. In particular, the prospect of merging with Price Waterhouse caused Coopers & Lybrand to join Arthur Andersen in Chile. Regulatory changes in various markets are creating additional opportunities for expansion. Because of these changes in several Latin American markets, accounting firms are able to develop their cases in advance and significantly reduce their exposure risk and also find it easier to attract local lawyers to work in their legal departments. Several proposed regulations in China may allow foreign accountancy firms to offer a full range of services in that country. The leading foreign markets for accounting, auditing, and bookkeeping services are with the major U.S. trading partners: the EU, Canada, and Japan. This sector also has some growth opportunities in Latin America.

ADVERTISING

The United States continues to have the largest advertising industry in the world, an industry which is responsible for almost 50 percent of all advertising expenditures globally. This industry consists of advertisers, the media, and advertising agencies. Advertisers include large manufacturers of brand-name consumer products. Media services include broadcast television, cable television, magazines, newspapers, and radio. Advertising agencies create advertising campaigns and place advertisements in the media. In 1997, 6 of the top 10 advertising agencies in the world in terms of gross income were in the United States (see Table 49-4). Traditional advertising is growing at single-digit rates, while direct advertising promotions are growing at double-digit rates. The new emphasis on regional marketing and media, rapid globalization, and increased use of the Internet is changing the way people are advertising.

Many changes and new opportunities will be created for advertisers in the next few years. Mergers and acquisitions created by the deregulation of the $100 billion telecommunications industry are causing industrywide shifts in marketing and advertising strategies as spending on advertising is increasing and telephone companies are changing from passive monopolies to

TABLE 49-3: International Revenues of U.S. Accounting, Auditing, and Bookkeeping Firms
(millions of dollars except as noted)

	Sales of Services by MOFAs[1]		U.S. Balance of Trade		
	Sales	Percent Change	Exports	Imports	Balance
1992	3,978		164	104	60
1993	5,661	29.7	164	103	61
1994	5,702	0.7	142	130	12
1995	6,015	5.2	178	141	37
1996	6,500	7.4	200	152	48
1997[2]	7,200	9.7	225	165	60
1998[3]	8,000	10.0	255	180	75
2002[3]	13,000	9.6	350	235	115

[1] MOFA = majority-owned foreign affiliate.
[2] Estimate.
[3] Forecast.
Source: U.S. Department of Commerce: Bureau of Economic Analysis.

TABLE 49-4: Gross Income Worldwide of the Top 10 Advertising Organizations in 1997

(millions of dollars; percent)

	Income	Percent Change 97–98
Omnicom Group (New York)	4,154	10.8
WPP Group (London)	3,647	6.3
Interpublic Group of Companies (New York)	3,385	11.4
Dentsu (Tokyo)	1,988	3.0
Young & Rubicam (New York)	1,498	10.4
True North Communications (Chicago)	1,212	21.6
Grey Advertising (New York)	1,143	11.2
Havas Advertising (Paris)	1,033	6.0
Leo Burnett (Chicago)	878	1.4
Hakuhodo (Tokyo)	848	−5.5
Total	19,786	7.6

Source: *Advertising Age,* 1998.

assertive competitors. Banks created by megamergers are spending more on advertising to build brand recognition as they move into new regions and offer new products and services. Besides spewing out cash and phone cards, automated teller machines (ATMs) have video screens that are being transformed into advertising billboards for in-store coupons. Whereas stadiums have been major venues for facilities sponsorships, malls represent the hot new long-term marketing partnerships. The new millennium should bring commercial benefits as long as marketers avoid fueling public cynicism with easy promotions and public relations stunts. A beer company will soon announce that it is the official beer sponsor for the Old Royal Observatory's year 2000 program at Greenwich, England, which is promoted as the "home of world time." A candy company has declared itself the official candy of the new millennium. The New Year's Eve ball-lowering event in Times Square in New York City is offering sponsorships. The event is estimated to attract more than 1 billion viewers worldwide in the year 2000. Nobody controls the "official rights" to the year 2000. There are no fees to pay, no licensing hurdles, and no discussions on the placement of the official logo. Pitches for other millennium-associated products are being created.

Mergers and acquisitions are causing conflict between advertising agencies and their clients. Creative assignments for various brands could be in jeopardy as agencies change business profiles. One result may be more turf battles within companies as media buying may become unbundled. Other tensions may arise between advertising agencies and their clients because of the use of consultants. According to the American Association of Advertising Agencies (Four As), 70 percent of all new-business reviews in 1996 involving the top 10 advertising agencies included a consultant. Guidelines have been developed by the Four As for the ways in which agencies manage new business with consultants. However, the guidelines drew criticism from the consultants for being too narrow and not taking their input into consideration.

Advertisers are experiencing pressure because the brands they represent are facing increasing competition from both traditional challenges such as fickle consumers and crowded store shelves and new business factors such as global attractiveness. Brands that lack global potential or reside below the top tier are being removed from the portfolios of product marketers. Advertisements will continue to be judged on the basis of the profit they generate, not just the traffic they pull.

Domestic Trends and Performance

U.S. advertising expenditures were strong throughout 1997. Industry analysts predicted that U.S. advertising in 1998 would top $200 billion, a gain of 6 percent over 1997 (see Table 49-5). According to *Advertising Age,* General Motors was the number one spender on measured advertising, with $2.2 billion in 1997, and Procter & Gamble (P&G) was the second largest spender, buying $1.7 billion worth of advertisements for television, magazines, radio, billboards, and other media. Those two companies were followed by Philip Morris, Chrysler, and Ford Motor Co.

A consolidation strategy was implemented by P&G, the purpose of which was to buy time in a new show-specific method, based on individual viewing patterns, instead of buying by day parts. Other marketers also reviewed and consolidated their media buying. These changes reflected the importance of buying expertise, media planning, and the fact that media could be unbundled from creative activities without detrimental results.

One of the major record-breaking advertising activities in 1998 occurred in the series finale of NBC's "Seinfeld," which received the highest advertising rates in history, about $1.7 million for a 30-second commercial. In comparison, ads in Super Bowl XXXII, which was broadcast on NBC, sold for a record

TABLE 49-5: U.S. Advertising Services (SIC 731) Trends and Forecasts

(millions of dollars except as noted)

	1992	1993	1994	1995	1996	1997[1]	1998[1]	1999[2]	Percent Change 96–97	Percent Change 97–98	Percent Change 98–99	Percent Change 92–96[3]
Revenues	22,672	23,416	24,212	27,068	30,652	32,500	34,550	37,000	6.0	6.3	7.1	7.8
Employment (thousands)	225.8	223.7	222.5	235.7	252.9	268	284	302	6.0	6.0	6.3	2.9

Estimate.
Forecast.
Compound annual growth rate.
Source: U.S. Department of Commerce: International Trade Administration (ITA), Bureau of the Census; U.S. Department of Labor: Bureau of Labor Statistics. Estimates and forecasts by ITA.

$1.3 million per 30 seconds. Only one of the top-rated, regularly scheduled cable network programs, ESPN regular season NFL football, has broken the six-figure mark, while most cable 30-second spots are in the four-figure, or even three-figure, range.

Another development in the advertising sector will involve digital broadcasting, which was scheduled to be available in major markets in 1998. Currently, approximately 20 digital satellite platforms serve about 9 million subscribers worldwide. Digital television will allow more efficient audience research. The hundreds of channels will offer more opportunities for niche programming.

Revenues for the cable industry from direct-response advertising have climbed about 17 percent over 1996 to more than $300 million. The infomercial industry estimates that between $450 million and $550 million is spent in media for these long-form ads. About 60 percent of this amount goes to cable. It is much more cost-effective to use cable than to use national networks for the amount of times an infomercial is aired during a monthly period.

Advertising on cable television, in particular spot cable, was up 24 percent for the first 6 months of 1997, partly as a result of advances in digital insertion technology. Progress in this technology has allowed advertisers to purchase more television advertising locally. Currently, cable industry executives are looking for improved rating measurements, greater market consolidation, and more use of electronic data interchange (EDI). The employment of EDI to conduct transactions reduces paperwork for sales orders and simplifies the process of buying and selling cable television advertising for agencies and their clients. Agencies are mindful of the current consumer trend toward more cable television viewing and less network viewing.

Micromarketing on cable programs is providing more efficient media spending in terms of getting the right message to the right audience. This one-to-one relationship marketing allows the testing of advertising and new products. National advertisers have shied away from local cable because it is expensive on a cost-per-thousand basis and difficult to buy. Normally, to purchase advertising on local cable, marketers must deal with numerous invoices, bookkeeping strains, and more than one system in a market.

Through innovations in fiber-optic technology, cable companies are introducing sophisticated products such as voice and data telephone service and high-speed modem service. The upgraded technology is driving new advertising initiatives directed from the local rather than the corporate level. Currently, these services are concentrated in several metropolitan areas, but in time they will be extended to larger regions. Interactive advertising will be the main feature of the next-generation digital set-top boxes for cable television. This medium has the potential to revolutionize merchandising and advertising.

Magazine advertising, like television advertising, has experienced record highs. Magazines ended 1997 with a record high of over 231,000 advertising pages, up 5.2 percent from 1996. Advertising revenue was up 13.1 percent to $12.8 billion, the highest growth rate since 1984. Drugs and remedies topped all categories in revenue growth, up almost 30 percent to $617.3

million, while automotive grew about 20 percent to $1.3 billion. Analysts were cautiously optimistic about 1998.

National advertising in newspapers totaled $5.3 billion in 1997, an increase of 14.1 percent over 1996. Retail advertising grew to $19.3 billion, a 5 percent increase, and classified advertising grew to $16.8 billion, an increase of 11.3 percent. One reason for the increase is the practice of newspaper advertising departments moving from a traditional order-taking approach to a more aggressive relationship-building approach with advertising customers. Also, from an advertiser's perspective, newspapers offer customers the ability to target deliveries, including zone editions. Analysts expected newspaper advertising growth to continue throughout 1998.

National and retail preprinted newspaper insert advertising increased 11 percent in 1997, the highest gain since 1991. Advertisers spent about $12.6 billion on national and retail preprints in 1997, up from $11.3 billion in 1996. With a strong economy, consumers are making purchases throughout the year rather than waiting for holiday season sales. However, there is movement toward eliminating couponing via free standing newspaper inserts (FSI coupons).

Newspaper departments are learning to harness the Internet rather than view it as a challenge. Jupiter Communications estimates that total on-line classified advertising revenue will grow from $123 million in 1997 to $830 million in 2000 and $1.9 billion by the end of 2002, or 10 percent of the classified market. Classified advertisements are emerging on a nationwide basis rather than just by geographic region. The most popular categories are automobile, employment, and real estate.

In 1997 advertising companies recorded their highest level of expenditures for Internet advertising, totaling close to $1 billion. Factors contributing to this growth included the increase in on-line advertising, the growth in cross-promotion of Web sites in other media, the emergence of cyberbrands, and improvements in Web content and entertainment. Consumer-related advertising was the top category, constituting more than 30 percent of overall Internet advertising spending. However, there is not a consensus that Web advertising is driving sales, even though the technology exists to monitor the results. Banner advertising on the Web has been found to be responsible for 9 percent of ad awareness. Click-throughs to an advertiser's Web site have contributed to only 4 percent of ad awareness. The question for marketers is whether to invest advertising dollars for ad banners on popular content sites or for advertiser-created Web sites or to piggyback on big content providers which are delivering large audiences even when these sites are not directly linked to their marketing objectives.

The Internet is increasing revenues and cutting costs since marketers can now evaluate an advertising campaign in real time instead of having to wait months for mail-in results or phone tallies. The Internet's interactive capabilities such as in-line ads, interstitials, and pop-up windows are providing innovative ways to build brand awareness and leverage site content. Requested E-mails, not "pushed information" to a list of involuntary users (i.e., "Spam"), are also proving successful in reaching a targeted audience and provide an instant and easy way for consumers to respond. Companies that are using E-mail include Shopping.com and DirecTV. Another new development in electronic advertising is the use of eye candy, which allows users to indulge in a mini-interactive treat, such as playing a video game, in the advertisement rather than being linked to a Web site. The Internet allows direct marketers to pay only when a user clicks on their advertisements, fills out a lead form, or actually makes a purchase.

New technology is transforming on-line advertising to personalized ads. For example, if a person is looking for a new camera, an on-line service can locate deals and promotions and send them to the buyer in high-resolution graphic imagery. Virtual imagery ads will allow an image to move up, down, and all around. Ads are also beginning to make appearances on intranets as the Internet is changing from an information utility to a marketing vehicle. Advertisers are integrating promotions into business functions such as providing competitive and promotional information. Sponsorship of content for market research and business news will become more widespread. Currently, the intranet market is estimated at $1.2 billion.

The World Wide Web has become a valuable tool for advertisers to obtain information regarding on-line products and services and feedback from customers and to test new on-line advertising campaigns. On-line surveys produce results more quickly than do conventional research methods such as telephone surveys and "mall interceptions" (stopping consumers in malls to ask questions). Whereas the average mall interception of 1,000 respondents may cost about $30,000, the digital marketing service for an on-line survey may cost $20,000. Marketers have the ability not only to reach the consumers in a specific targeted audience but also to learn more about them and target them more efficiently in the future.

The effectiveness of advertising on the Web is still far from proven. There is disagreement on how effective the Internet is for branding products and services. For many, the Internet is known for its ability to build sales and loyalty, not to build awareness. Most likely, marketers of low-priced goods such as groceries and household products will shift more spending to on-line advertising, while marketers of high-priced goods such as computers and travel services will shift more money to Web site development. Some analysts believe that the Internet is an effective vehicle to brand, suggesting that Web advertising is perceived as more credible than television or print advertising.

A problem with and risk to increasing Web advertising expenditures is the lack of adherence to privacy. Although guidelines are being developed for privacy by the Direct Marketing Association and the Children's Advertising Review Unit of the Council of Better Business Bureaus, not all Web users are adhering to privacy guidelines. A possible method for securing the privacy and integrity of a Web site is the development of a WebTrust seal. This is a service in which an accounting company audits customers' home pages to verify their ability to handle secure electronic commerce. If a site meets predefined standards for proper business procedures, privacy, transaction integrity, and security, it qualifies for a WebTrust Seal. The seal eventually may become equivalent to the Good Housekeeping Seal of Approval and foster consumer confidence in buying goods and services on-line. The stakes are high, as on-line sales are expected to grow to $2 billion by 2000.

Although revenues are up in many categories, advertisers are facing some national and regional restrictions as a result of tobacco legislation. The ultimate consequences of the global tobacco settlement may not be fully realized for some time, but unprecedented marketing concessions are imminent. The proposed tobacco legislation would regulate how tobacco products can be advertised. Under the proposal, advertisers would not be allowed to use animal images on tobacco products or to use billboards, vending machines, point-of-sale displays, sports sponsorship, or Internet advertising. Companies would halt giveaways and event sponsorships under brand names, limit magazine advertising to publications with 85 percent adult readership, and discontinue outdoor advertising. The proposed law may require tobacco industry agreement for the restrictions on advertising and marketing, as the companies may exchange First Amendment rights for legal protection. One of the tobacco manufacturers noted that it would begin aggressively advertising cigarettes and fighting for their legitimacy in court.

New York has approved the toughest local ordinance to restrict tobacco advertising. As in other cities, outdoor signs within 1,000 feet of schools or playgrounds are barred, but the ordinance also bans outdoor advertisements near amusement arcades and day care facilities and internal signage that is visible to clients when they first enter a store. Merchandising giveaways are also prohibited. Advertiser groups believe that the ordinance is unconstitutional and effectively bans all tobacco advertising and marketing in New York outside taxis. The advertising groups plan to sue the city over the proposed ban because it is too broad and violates the First Amendment. This is the first direct challenge of such regulations in the United States.

Advertisers also may be influenced by the Federal Trade Commission's new "green" guidelines for environmental ad claims which use terms such as *degradable, ozone-friendly,* and *recyclable.* Direct advertisers are required to display qualifiers and disclaimers prominently, avoid overstatements and generalizations, and articulate clear and specific comparative claims. Some states are proposing mandating their own green guidelines.

International Activity

Client demand is driving agency expansion as more clients are going global. Clients are assigning more accounts on a global rather than regional basis as advertisers continue to align their businesses with fewer agencies worldwide. The top 23 international agency networks are handling more than 500 clients in five or more countries. International advertising spending by the top 50 global marketers increased 3.1 percent to $49.3 billion in 1996 because of a strong economy and the growing penetration of multinational brands worldwide. Telecommunication deregulation around the world is helping new marketers promote their products and services.

The figures for 1997 outpaced even the more optimistic assessments made in late 1996. Expenditures among the top seven marketer categories were up 7.3 percent in the first 8 months of 1997 compared with the same period in 1996. The computer and resorts and tours segments were up 16 percent and 13 percent, respectively. Worldwide advertising expenditures are expected to rise 6.8 percent in 1998 to $298.8 billion and 6.35 percent in 1999 to $317.8 billion. In Europe, advertising expenditures in 1998 were expected to grow only 1.8 percent over 1997. Different languages and cultures are complicating multimarket campaigns using European Web advertising. Advertising spending in Asia is down because of financial problems such as the currency crisis and the collapse of banks in Japan. The expenditures in the Asia/Pacific region will continue to be adversely affected by this currency crisis, since Japan accounts for 57 percent of media spending in that region. The days of annual growth rates of more than 20 percent for advertising agencies in Asia are over, at least for now. Analysts believe that the significant drop in 1997 should be reversed in 6 months to 2 years. However, overall spending in Asia was expected to increase only about 4 percent on an inflation-adjusted basis in 1998. The decline in Asia is prompting marketers to pitch more products with price-value campaigns rather than status brands. The agencies in Thailand, where the currency crisis began, are perhaps most affected. Commissions in Thailand have been slashed from the previously standard 17.65 percent to as low as 3 percent. However, the advertising industry in Hong Kong and China is buoyant because of a strong currency and a booming economy.

China seems to be insulated from many of the currency problems in Asia. According to China's State Administration for Industry and Commerce, there are 25,443 official advertising agencies in China, employing more than 500,000 people, and spending was $2.28 billion in 1997. Shanghai is emerging as a media capital and should become the advertising center in China, as New York is in the United States. There are more than 2,700 advertising agencies in Shanghai, varying from international firms to solo shops. Internet advertising performance in China remains uncertain. Currently, no accurate data exist on the number of hits each site is receiving. China Internet estimates that 2 million Chinese businesses will soon be wired to the China Wide Web, a domestic version of the World Wide Web.

A major development affecting international advertising is Omnicom's acquisition of GGT Group, London, for approximately $235 million in cash, making it the largest advertising company in the world. Other acquisitions and reorganizations are expected. The leading holding companies will continue to acquire other holding companies as well as individual advertising agencies and marketing specialists. Some industry experts predict that there will be only a small number of advertising organizations in the world within the next few years.

Latin America is offering some new advertising opportunities, but the financial tightening experienced in Asia is spreading to that region. The Brazilian government is setting an example by pledging to reduce its advertising budget $450 million, or 20 percent, even though a presidential election was scheduled in 1998. Advertisements for automobiles, durable goods, and financial services were expected to experience the largest declines in Brazil in 1998. For Latin American business, Miami continues to be the top location from which to operate agencies in the United States. However, Buenos Aires is emerging as a good regional headquarters.

Projections

Estimated spending for advertisements in the United States was expected to reach $186 billion in 1998, up 6.2 percent over 1997. U.S. ad spending has increased every year since 1980, except for 1991, when there was a recession. Although the economy appears strong, advertisers are delaying buys until the last minute and are being very cautious.

Worldwide forecasts for advertising spending in 1998 call for a figure of $317 billion, a 6.4 percent increase over 1997. However, some of the biggest challenges faced by advertisers are budget reduction, profitability, and finding good personnel. Media and marketers worldwide are being affected by the Asian economic slowdown as some Asian advertisers try to renegotiate dollar-denominated rates to reflect the severe declines in the baht, rupia, ringgit, and won. Ad schedules for Asia are covering shorter periods, and media owners are divided on how to address the concerns of Asian advertisers. Some are considering rate protection on future buys, and

TABLE 49-6: International Revenues of U.S. Advertising Organizations
(millions of dollars, except as noted)

| | Sales of Services by MOFAs[1] | | U.S. Balance of Trade | | |
	Sales	Percent Change	Exports	Imports	Balance
1992	4,199		315	450	(135)
1993	3,544	−18.4	338	646	(308)
1994	3,700	4.2	487	728	(241)
1995	3,850	3.9	558	718	(160)
1996	4,917	21.7	597	971	(374)
1997[2]	5,200	5.4	610	990	(380)
1998[3]	5,600	7.1	650	1,100	(450)
2002[3]	7,650	6.7	700	1,175	(475)

[1] MOFA = majority-owned foreign affiliate.
[2] Estimate.
[3] Forecast.
Source: U.S. Department of Commerce: Bureau of Economic Analysis.

others are considering renegotiating bills for ads that have already run. Luxury goods, infrastructure services, and tourism are most vulnerable to the ailing economies in Asia. Purchasing power is dropping as Asian governments are tightening their finances to comply with International Monetary Fund rules.

Unlike many U.S. service industries which usually generate a trade surplus, imports of advertising services typically have exceeded exports. This trend should continue for the next couple of years (see Table 49-6). The trade deficit for advertising services was $374 million in 1996 and was estimated to be $380 million in 1997. Table 49-6 also reflects sales of the MOFAs of U.S. companies in foreign markets, such as sales in the United Kingdom by a U.S.-owned advertising agency there. These sales to foreign affiliates are much larger than the exports reported in the table. In 1995 MOFAs of U.S. advertising agencies in Europe had receipts of $3.5 billion. Europe is the largest foreign market for the affiliates of U.S. agencies, followed by Canada, Japan, and Australia.

LEGAL SERVICES

The top U.S. law practices define the legal services sector (see Table 49-7). The shape of the legal profession will continue to be influenced by technology, mergers and acquisitions, and global issues. In particular, technology is changing the way companies and people interact with each other and with the law. Questions of what belongs to whom on the Internet and the security of monetary exchanges over the Internet are becoming prevalent issues for the legal profession. As a result of mergers and acquisitions both within the legal profession sector and between the companies law firms represent and responses to global issues, law firms are becoming much more oriented toward full service and less specifically focused on litigation and tax advice services.

TABLE 49-7: Gross Revenues Worldwide of the Top 10 U.S. Law Firms in 1996
(millions of dollars; percent)

	Revenues	Percent Change 95–96
Skadden, Arps, Slate, Meagher & Flom	710	11.8
Baker & McKenzie	646	9.4
Jones, Day, Reavis & Pogue	450	12.5
Latham & Watkins	363	21.0
Davis Polk & Wardwell	346	22.7
Sullivan & Cromwell	346	11.6
Mayer, Brown & Platt	325	10.1
Shearman & Sterling	324	13.6
Weil, Gotshal & Manges	322	5.2
Morgan, Lewis & Bockius	321	7.7
Total	4,153	12.2

Source: The American Lawyer, July–August 1997.

Many firms generated some of their highest revenues of the decade in 1997, but for some law firms it is not important only to generate revenue. These firms are contributing to society through pro bono work, including donating legal work and offering services such as professional role model programs for inner-city youth. Attorneys in the top 100 firms in the United States put in more than 1.6 million pro bono hours in 1997, 8.1 percent more hours than they logged for similar work in 1995.

Many American law firms have significant competitive advantages in providing legal services outside the United States. The U.S. system of law is extremely effective, and several of its elements, including antitrust and antibribery, are being utilized in other countries. However, there are still many obstacles for legal professionals attempting to enter other markets. Some of these market access issues are being examined in bilateral and multilateral discussions.

Domestic Trends and Performance

Some U.S. law firms are not pleased with the "legal consulting" that is available at large accounting firms. Law firms maintain that accounting firms have no right to provide these legal services, while the accounting firms stand by open competition and consumer choice. The Big Six have long argued that many large commercial law firms are poorly managed, and they believe that if they can bring a more professional management image to their stand-alone law firms, they should be able to attract significant amounts of business from the legal sector. The displeasure of law firms has resulted in one major accounting and management consulting firm being charged in a state supreme court for the unauthorized practice of law.

Technological advances and innovations have rapidly improved the work environment for attorneys. About 10 years ago the desktop computer system replaced typewriters, but today documents and calendar schedules are shared through networks. The practicing legal professional is receiving a vast amount of communications and information over the Internet. Law firm Web sites are more than a "shingle" on the Internet; they increasingly are being used to relay messages to clients and to attract new clients.

Despite this unrelenting progress, there will always be glitches in the ever-changing world of modern technology, although this should not deter the search for opportunities. Specifically, there are legal ramifications of the Y2K computer problem which include contracts, cost recovery, insurance, regulatory compliance, and remediation. Litigation costs are estimated to range between $400 billion and $800 billion. After repair costs are added to litigation figures, total costs for Y2K could exceed $1 trillion. Litigation issues could include whether company officials have met the applicable due diligence legal standards when taking action to solve their organizations' Y2K problems. The federal and state tax law treatment of these costs will in most cases have a large impact on a company's after-tax income. Many lawyers forecast a boom in "alternative dispute resolution" with regard to Y2K problems; arbitrators, rather than judges and juries, could be used to reconcile differences.

According to *American Lawyer*, the top 100 firms experienced double-digit growth in revenue and profits in 1996, making it one of the most successful years ever for many firms. In total, the "Am Law" 100 firms brought in $18 billion in 1996, netting almost $800 million more than they did in 1995, an 11 percent increase. Average fees for partners increased 10.3 percent to $492,000, and average revenue per lawyer, one of the best indicators of a firm's overall health, was $448,000, an increase of 6 percent. Some of the highest levels of growth occurred in firms involved in product liability litigation and/or securities litigation and companies in Silicon Valley. Even after adjusting for inflation for all the key measures, such as revenue, average partner profits and revenue per lawyer increased. Much of this success has been due to the firms being better managed and more efficiently run. Overall revenues for legal services are expected to grow approximately 6 percent per year in the next couple of years (see Table 49-8).

International Activity

As corporate transactions are increasingly international, the largest firms with the most experience and depth have a competitive advantage. Mergers and acquisitions allow legal firms to reinforce services in some areas and overcome lack of services in other areas. To bolster some of the services in one of the United Kingdom's leading law firms, Wilde Sapte will merge with Arthur Andersen's United Kingdom law firms, Garretts and Dundas & Wilson. The new firm is expected to be called Wilde Sapte Andersen in the short term. It will have 750 lawyers and a turnover of $167 million, making it the sixth largest legal firm in the United Kingdom. In general, the top 20 or so firms are doing the most premium work and making the most money.

Asia's financial turmoil is creating opportunities and generating revenue for lawyers with debt-restructuring expertise. Specialist lawyers expect to involve themselves in the mergers, acquisitions, and privatization that will follow the economic problems, which may continue in some markets for the next few years. Lawyers who can offer litigation and counseling services regarding intellectual property issues will continue to find opportunities in this region. The level of expansion of the legal profession should continue to rise globally in the foreseeable future (see Table 49-9).

MANAGEMENT CONSULTING AND PUBLIC RELATIONS

Innovation and change are driving the growth of consulting firms. The differences between large accounting practices and management consulting and public relations are becoming less noticeable (see Table 49-10). The consulting units of the Nine Nationals dominated the management consulting and public relations sector globally and produced the majority of its revenue.

TABLE 49-8: U.S. Legal Services (SIC 81) Trends and Forecasts

(millions of dollars except as noted)

	1992	1993	1994	1995	1996	1997[1]	1998[1]	1999[2]	Percent Change 96–97	97–98	98–99	92–96[3]
Revenues	108,443	112,145	114,603	116,000	124,565	131,000	139,000	148,000	5.2	6.1	6.5	3.5
Employment (thousands)	913.5	924	924	923	932	945	960	990	1.4	1.6	3.1	0.5

[1] Estimate.
[2] Forecast.
[3] Compound annual growth rate.
Source: U.S. Department of Commerce: International Trade Administration (ITA), Bureau of the Census; U.S. Department of Labor: Bureau of Labor Statistics. Estimates and forecasts by ITA.

TABLE 49-9: International Revenues of U.S. Legal Services

(millions of dollars; percent)

	Sales of Services by MOFAs[1]		U.S. Balance of Trade		
	Sales	Percent Change	Exports	Imports	Balance
1992	264		1,358	311	1,047
1993	127	−107.8	1,442	321	1,121
1994	222	42.7	1,617	383	1,234
1995	240	7.5	1,664	468	1,196
1996	260	7.6	1,910	516	1,394
1997[2]	285	8.7	2,200	600	1,600
1998[2]	310	8.0	2,400	800	1,600
2002[3]	450	7.7	2,700	1,000	1,700

[1] MOFA = majority-owned foreign affiliate.
[2] Estimate.
[3] Forecast.
Source: U.S. Department of Commerce: Bureau of Economic Analysis.

TABLE 49-10: Gross Revenues Worldwide of the Top 10 Management Consulting Firms in 1997
(millions of dollars; percent)

	Revenues	Percent Change 96–97
Andersen Consulting	5,726	21
CSC	3,000	20
Ernst & Young	2,680	29
Coopers & Lybrand Consulting	2,400	25
Deloitte & Touche	2,300	30
McKinsey & Company	2,200	10
KPMG Peat Marwick	2,011	26
Cap Gemini	1,648	20
Price Waterhouse	1,400	24
Mercer Consulting Group	1,338	15
Total	24,703	

Source: Kennedy Information (800-531-0007), *Consultants News,* June 1998.

Management consulting grew significantly in 1997 as pretax profit margins for all consulting firms averaged 27 percent. Consulting firms with fewer than 10 employees are reporting profit margins above 30 percent, while issues such as deregulation, privatization, and market complexities are creating consulting opportunities.

Forecasters predict that more than 250,000 new consultants will be hired over the next 3 years. As a result of this rapid growth and natural attrition, training and retaining staff are becoming a key consideration at many consulting firms which are having difficulty finding skilled workers. Training and education will ensure that these firms continue to groom future partners and provide their clients with the same level of services. Companies are also finding new ways to define and combine jobs, share information and the governing power of the firm, involve employees in work decisions, and improve compensation packages.

Between 1992 and 1996 major strategy-type firms grew faster than did other types of consulting operations in the United States. According to Kennedy Research Group, compound annual growth for strategy consulting segments was about 18 percent, while information technology–oriented segments increased 16 percent, operations management 14 percent, and human resources 10 percent. Consulting growth should remain constant in the near future because of the strong global economy, deregulation, and technological innovations (see Table 49-11).

Domestic Trends and Performance

Management consulting and public relations firms are rapidly expanding and generating large revenues by focusing on the business process. This sector has continued to expand more rapidly than has any other professional business services sector since the early 1990s. These growth trends should continue as management consulting generally does not experience economic downturns as do other professions because companies still value direction and advice from good management consultants.

A major development in this industry in 1998 was the proposed $11 billion to $12 billion megamerger between Price Waterhouse and Coopers & Lybrand. This merger will result in the world's second largest consulting firm and largest accounting firm. The U.S. Justice Department has approved the merger since it is expected to be below the 40 percent threshold. European regulators have indicated that they will also approve the combination. A second merger in this industry was considered between KPMG Peat Marwick and Ernst & Young. However, the proposed $18 billion merger was dropped because of issues such as high costs, disruption of client service, and protracted regulatory processes in Australia, Canada, Europe, Japan, Switzerland, and the United States.

Reliance on technological advances and the need of companies to improve their quality of services will continue to shape the ways in which management consultants serve their clients. Based on a survey sponsored by Deloitte & Touche LLP, executives expect that by 2005 they will rely on the Internet as their primary source of business news, pushing aside traditional news media. Currently, only 7 percent of senior executives cite the Internet as the technology with the greatest positive impact on their business, but this number triples to 21 percent when the same question is asked about 2005. Many executives expect the Internet to be an important news source for them in 2005, while only half expect to get their news from daily newspapers. Companies are also still opting for ISO 9001 certification, the most comprehensive of the 9000 standards of the International Standards Organization. This standard verifies that a company's quality procedures meet rigorous international standards for design, development, manufacturing, production, testing, installation, and services.

TABLE 49-11: Management Consulting and Public Relations Services (SIC 874) Trends and Forecasts
(millions of dollars; percent)

	1992	1993	1994	1995	1996	1997[1]	1998[2]	1999[2]	Percent Change 96–97	97–98	98–99	92–96[3]
Revenues	72,490	75,026	81,439	94,787	104,975	116,000	130,000	147,000	10.5	12.1	13.1	9.7
Employment (thousands)	655.1	688.4	718.7	817	905	1,000	1,100	1,245	10.5	10.0	13.2	8.4

[1] Estimate.
[2] Forecast.
[3] Compound annual growth rate.
Source: U.S. Department of Commerce: International Trade Administration (ITA), Bureau of the Census; U.S. Department of Labor: Bureau of Labor Statistics. Estimates and forecasts by ITA.

TABLE 49-12: International Revenues of Management Consulting and Public Relations Services
(millions of dollars; percent)

| | Sales of Services by MOFAs[1] | | | U.S. Balance of Trade | | |
	Sales	Percent Change		Exports	Imports	Balance
1992	3,978			728	243	485
1993	5,661	29.7		826	287	539
1994	6,177	8.3		1,134	321	813
1995	6,800	9.1		1,456	475	981
1996	7,500	9.3		1,473	543	930
1997[2]	8,300	9.6		1,550	590	960
1998[2]	9,200	9.7		1,700	620	1,080
2002[3]	14,000	8.5		2,400	650	1,750

[1] MOFA = majority-owned foreign affiliate.
[2] Estimate.
[3] Forecast.
Source: U.S. Department of Commerce: Bureau of Economic Analysis.

International Activity and Trends

Companies are expanding more rapidly internationally than they are in the United States (see Table 49-12). Kennedy Research Group estimates that management consulting total revenues worldwide were $62 billion in 1996 and are growing between 10 and 30 percent annually, depending on the country. The biggest U.S. firms are multinational and are leaders in innovation and technology. Many U.S. firms have maintained business relationships with their clients as the clients have expanded internationally.

Management consultants which position themselves as experts in "competitiveness" are likely to do very well in the next couple of years. Even though consulting projects priced in some of the Asian currencies may contribute only half as many dollars to the U.S. firms, growth prospects for management consultants in Japan are likely to average 14 percent over the next 5 years despite the recession. China appears to be lifting some restrictions on the professional services sector, and this may offer new opportunities for management consulting firms. Cross-border trade data in management consulting services indicate that European countries accounted for over 40 percent of these U.S. service exports in 1996. Among the European countries, the United Kingdom was the largest single export market for U.S. management consulting services, accounting for 10 percent of cross-border sales. That country was also the largest supplier of management services to the U.S. market, accounting for 24 percent of U.S. imports in 1996.

Bruce Harsh, U.S. Department of Commerce, Office of Service Industries, (202) 482-4582, October 1998.

■ REFERENCES

Advertising Age, Crain Communications, Inc., 740 Rush Street, Chicago, IL 60611. (312) 649-5200.

AMCF, World Association of Management Consulting Firms, 521 Fifth Avenue, 35th Floor, New York, NY 10175. (212) 697-9693.

American Association of Advertising Agencies, 666 Third Avenue, New York, NY 10017. (212) 682-2500.

American Bar Association, 750 North Lake Shore Drive, Chicago, IL 60611. (312) 998-5000.

American Institute of Certified Public Accountants, 1211 Avenue of the Americas, New York, NY 10036. (212) 644-6469.

The American Lawyer, July/August, 1997, American Lawyer Media, L.P., 600 Third Avenue, New York, NY 10016. (212) 973-2800.

Census of Service Industries, 1992, Bureau of the Census, U.S. Department of Commerce, Washington, DC 20230. (301) 763-1725.

Consultants News, Kennedy Publications, Fitzwilliam, NH 03447. (603) 585-6544.

Current Business Report: Services Annual Survey, Bureau of the Census, U.S. Department of Commerce, Washington, DC 20230. (301) 763-1752.

Direct, 11 River Bend Drive South, P.O. Box 4949, Stamford, CT 06907. (203) 358-9900.

Direct Marketing Association, 1120 Avenue of the Americas, New York, NY 10036. (212) 768-7277.

DM News, 100 Avenue of the Americas, New York, NY 10013. (212) 925-7300.

Employment and Earnings, Bureau of Labor Statistics, U.S. Department of Labor, Washington, DC 20210. (202) 523-1221.

Insider's Report by Robert Coen Presentation on Advertising Expenditures, McCann-Erickson, 750 Third Avenue, New York, NY 10017. (212) 697-6000.

Public Accounting Report, Strafford Publications, Inc., 590 Dutch Valley Road, NE, Postal Drawer 13729, Atlanta, GA 30324. (404) 881-1141.

Public Relations Society of America, 845 Third Avenue, New York, NY 10022. (212) 995-2230.

Survey of Current Business, October, 1997, Economics and Statistics Administration, U.S. Department of Commerce, Washington, DC 20230. (202) 482-3727.

Target, 401 N. Broad Street, Philadelphia, PA 19108. (215) 238-5300

Why Newspapers?, Newspaper Association of America, 11600 Sunrise Valley Drive, Reston, VA 22091. (703) 648-1000.

■ RELATED CHAPTERS

25: Printing and Publishing
26: Information Services
28: Computer Software and Networking

EDUCATION AND TRAINING SERVICES
Economic and Trade Trends

U.S. International Trade

($ billions)

Legend: Balance — Exports — Imports

Exports refer to education only.

Source: U.S. Department of Commerce: Bureau of Economic Analysis.

Origin of Foreign Students in U.S. Colleges, 1996

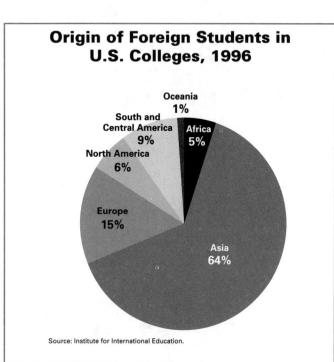

Oceania 1%
South and Central America 9%
North America 6%
Africa 5%
Europe 15%
Asia 64%

Source: Institute for International Education.

Expenditures per Student in Grades K–12, 1970–1996

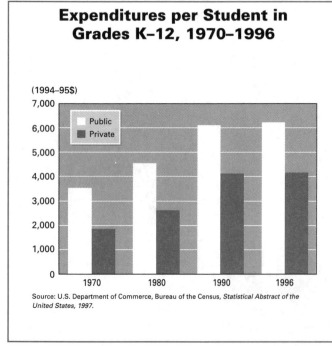

(1994–95$)

Legend: Public, Private

Source: U.S. Department of Commerce, Bureau of the Census, *Statistical Abstract of the United States, 1997.*

U.S. Educational Attainment of Individuals 25 Years or Older

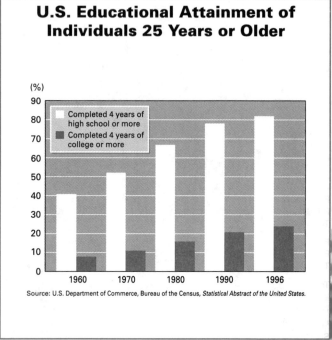

(%)

Legend: Completed 4 years of high school or more; Completed 4 years of college or more

Source: U.S. Department of Commerce, Bureau of the Census, *Statistical Abstract of the United States.*

Education and Training

50

INDUSTRY DEFINITION The education and training industry comprises all public and private institutions engaged in educational activities, including public and private schools for kindergarten through twelfth grade (SIC 821), 2-year community colleges, public and private colleges and universities, vocational schools, and other certificate-granting institutes (SIC 822). Private providers of training and education, particularly formal training programs in public entities and private corporations, whether employer-provided or contracted out (SIC 833), are discussed as well.

OVERVIEW

At 7.4 percent of the gross domestic product (GDP), the $514.7 billion spent for all public and private educational institutions in 1996–1997 and the additional $55.5 billion spent on workplace training accounted for a larger percentage of the economy than did any other sector except health and medical services. In 1996, the education sector in the United States employed over 7 million people. In that same year, more than 66 million children and adults, over 25 percent of the total population, were in school for part of the year (see the boxed note: "U.S. Education Sector Statistics"). Even with the economy expected to slow in 1999–2000, education-related services will maintain their position relative to overall GDP through the first decade of the next century.

Between 1997 and 2000, enrollment at all levels will increase from 1 to 2 percent annually. The rise in the number of students will be most noticeable in the postsecondary grades. Growth will be fueled by an increase in the school-age population after a birthrate spike which peaked in 1990, according to the U.S. Census Bureau, which says elementary enrollments will grow through 2007. Total enrollment for higher education is projected to increase from 14.3 million students in 1995 to about 16 million at all postsecondary institutions by 2000, according to the National Center for Education Statistics (NCES) (see Table 50-1).

Total elementary and secondary school (kindergarten through twelfth grade) expenditures for the school year 1996–1997 are estimated by the NCES to have been $339.7 billion; expendi-

TABLE 50-1: School Enrollment
(millions of students)

	1992	1993	1994	1995	1996[1]	1997[2]	1998[2]	1999[2]	2000[2]	Percentage Change			Annual Average	
										96–97	97–98	98–99	92–96	96–00
Public elementary and secondary	42.82	43.46	44.11	44.66	45.89	46.53	46.99	47.37	47.66	1.4	1.0	0.8	1.7	1.0
Private elementary and secondary	5.38	5.47	5.60	5.70	5.80	5.88	5.93	5.98	6.01	1.4	1.0	0.7	1.9	0.9
Total K–12	48.20	48.94	49.70	50.36	51.68	52.40	52.92	53.34	53.67	1.4	1.0	0.8	1.8	0.9
Public, postsecondary	11.38	11.19	11.13	11.09	11.25	11.41	11.63	11.89	12.09	1.3	1.9	2.2	–0.3	1.8
Private, postsecondary	3.10	3.12	3.15	3.17	3.15	3.19	3.26	3.34	3.41	1.5	2.1	2.5	0.3	2.0
Total postsecondary	14.49	14.30	14.28	14.26	14.40	14.60	14.89	15.23	15.50	1.4	2.0	2.3	–0.2	1.9
Total	62.69	63.24	63.98	64.62	66.08	67.00	67.81	68.57	69.17	1.4	1.2	1.1	1.3	1.1

[1] Estimate.
[2] Forecast.
Source: U.S. Dept. of Commerce, Bureau of the Census, *Statistical Abstract of the United States, 1997.*

tures for colleges and other higher education institutions were about $224.5 billion for that period. The cohort of school-age children now working its way through the system will drive education expenditures at all levels through the next decade. Expenditures for public elementary and secondary schools are forecast to increase at about 5 percent a year (in constant 1994–1995 dollars) from the 1993–1994 levels through the school year 2006–2007, provided the annual inflation remains between 2.8 percent and 4.1 percent, fertility rates average 2.1 births per woman through 2007, net immigration stays at about 820,000 per year, and mortality rates continue to drop. The net increase for this period will be about 32 percent. This figure may seem high, but between 1981–1982 and 1994 expenditures on elementary and secondary education increased 47 percent from $161.6 billion to $238.2 billion, using constant 1994–1995 dollars and the consumer price index. Expenditures will continue to rise not only because more pupils are enrolling but because of efforts to lengthen the school day, to increase school choice through charter schools and vouchers, and to finance programs to implement Standards 2000 (a Department of Education initiative to improve academic curriculum and performance standards for kindergarten through twelfth grade). Total domestic expendi-

tures on education are up from 1993–1994, when public and private education expenditures in the United States accounted for 4.2 percent of GDP for the primary and secondary levels, 2.5 percent for higher education, and 6.8 percent for all levels combined. Current-fund expenditures for public and private higher education institutions are projected to increase at roughly the same annual 5 percent rate (in constant 1994–1995 dollars), or 38 percent, between 1993 and 2007 (see Tables 50-2 and 50-3).

Higher Education Trends

Between 1984 and 1994 college tuitions rose, partly to offset decreased government funding for higher education. During this period government appropriations per full-time equivalent (FTE) student at universities fell both in constant dollars and as a share of all revenues at public institutions. For example, at public universities, government appropriations declined from $8,327 to $7,393, and from 53 percent to 42 percent as a share of all revenue.

College tuitions have risen steadily since 1981–1982 due largely to three factors: economic growth as a whole (including the expansion of public institutions and state and local governments), the inflation rate, and enrollments. The greatest increases in higher education expenditures occurred between 1981 and 1987, when current fund expenditures rose 27 percent. The economy grew steadily at that time, and per-capita disposable income rose 13 percent. There was a 51 percent increase in educational and general expenditures in public colleges from 1981 to 1994 and a 78 percent increase in private colleges. Today, the economy is cooling slightly after a 6-year expansion; tuitions are leveling off somewhat, and more federal student loans are available for 2- and 4-year postsecondary schools under a variety of tuition tax credit and community service work programs. Many colleges offer parents attractive financial breaks on tuition, provided they pay for the entire academic program up front, rather than using loans or year by year.

The number of community colleges continues to increase. In 1970, there were only about 900 of these 2-year schools. Now they number over 1,600 and enrollment exceeds 5.4 million. Community colleges now teach more than 38 percent of all students in postsecondary institutions.

TABLE 50-2: Cost of Education
(billions of 1994–95 constant dollars)

	1992	1993	1994[1]	1995[1]	1996[1]	1997[2]	1998[2]	1999[2]	2000[2]	Percentage Change			Annual Average	
										96–97	97–98	98–99	92–96	96–00
Public education	381.0	388.7	397.0	406.1	414.4	424.0	432.0	437.7	443.4	2.3	1.9	1.3	2.1	1.7
Elementary and secondary	262.3	266.9	272.9	279.4	285.4	292.2	296.8	299.6	302.3	2.4	1.6	0.9	2.1	1.4
Postsecondary	118.7	121.8	124.2	126.7	129.0	131.7	135.2	138.1	141.0	2.1	2.6	2.1	2.1	2.3
Private education	91.4	93.6	95.8	98.4	100.3	103.1	105.8	108.0	110.2	2.8	2.7	2.1	2.3	2.4
Elementary and secondary	22.0	22.7	22.8	23.5	24.1	24.7	25.1	25.4	25.6	2.6	1.7	1.0	2.3	1.6
Postsecondary	69.4	70.9	72.9	74.9	76.2	78.3	80.7	82.6	84.6	2.8	3.0	2.4	2.3	2.7
Total public and private	472.4	482.3	492.8	504.5	514.7	527.0	537.9	545.7	553.6	2.4	2.1	1.5	2.2	1.8

[1] Estimate.
[2] Forecast.
Source: U.S. Department of Commerce, Bureau of the Census, *Statistical Abstract of the United States, 1997*.

TABLE 50-3: Per-Student Cost

(1994–1995 constant dollars)

	1992	1993	1994[1]	1995[1]	1996[1]	1997[2]	1998[2]	1999[2]	2000[2]	Percentage Change 96–97	97–98	98–99	Annual Average 92–96	96–00
Public elementary and secondary	6,126	6,141	6,187	6,256	6,220	6,281	6,317	6,325	6,344	1.0	0.6	0.1	0.4	0.5
Private elementary and secondary	4,090	4,147	4,081	4,123	4,158	4,206	4,235	4,247	4,265	1.2	0.7	0.3	0.4	0.6
Public, postsecondary	10,422	10,882	11,152	11,422	11,459	11,550	11,628	11,617	11,663	0.8	0.7	−0.1	2.4	0.4
Private, postsecondary	22,382	22,768	23,184	23,632	24,227	24,552	24,764	24,725	24,839	1.3	0.9	−0.2	2.0	0.6
Total public and private	12,072	12,206	12,324	12,494	12,473	12,598	12,681	12,697	12,746	1.0	0.7	0.1	0.8	0.5

[1] Estimate.
[2] Forecast.
Source: U.S. Dept. of Commerce, Bureau of the Census, *Statistical Abstract of the United States, 1997.*

Graduate school enrollment, after remaining steady through the late 1970s and early 1980s, rose about 26 percent between 1985 and 1995 and is expected to grow well into the next century. Foreign students continue to account for more than 25 percent of the doctorates awarded annually in the United States. According to the 1997 *U.S. Statistical Abstract,* out of 43,149 doctorates awarded in 1994, 11,538, or 26.7 percent of the total, went to noncitizens. This figure represents a 109 percent increase from 1981, when 12.8 percent of all doctorates went to foreign nationals. The high representation of foreign students is particularly striking in graduate engineering, computer, and medical programs. In 1996, there were 454,000 foreign students in all postsecondary schools, compared with 218,700 in 1976. Asians account for the vast majority of nonresident aliens in American postsecondary schools, with 290,000 students or 64 percent. Europeans follow with 15 percent, with Latin America, North America (Canada), and Africa trailing (see the second chart at the beginning of this chapter). The "Asian economic flu" decreased the number of foreign applicants to graduate and professional degree programs in the United States in 1997–1998. This trend is likely to continue for the near term.

Educational Attainment

Americans are better educated than ever before, but the U.S. literacy rate is still well below that of other industrialized nations such as Japan, Germany, and Sweden. According to *The Digest of Education Statistics 1997,* more than 82 percent of those 25 and older in the U.S. had finished high school in 1996, while 24 percent had completed 4 or more years of college. This completion rate represents a healthy increase since 1980, when 69 percent finished high school and only 17 percent had graduated from a 4-year college. Professional degrees were also up in 1996, with about 5 percent of people age 25 or older holding a master's degree. In the same year, just over 1 percent held a professional degree in medicine or law; 1 percent earned doctorates. (See the boxed note: "How Much Is Your Degree Worth?")

At the high school level, however, standardized scores on the Scholastic Assessment Test (SAT; formerly the Scholastic Aptitude Test) continue to stagnate, failing to reach levels set in the mid-1960s, although there have been modest improvements in mathematics in recent years. Average SAT math scores for college-bound seniors rose from 466 in 1980 to 482 in 1995.

In 1996, the National Assessment of Educational Progress (NAEP) found that 97 percent of all 17-year-olds in public high schools performed at or above selected mathematical proficiency levels when asked to do basic numerical operations and problem solving. But when NAEP measured these same students' proficiency at problems using moderately complex procedures and reasoning, only 59 percent were proficient. Multistep problems involving algebra posed an even bigger challenge, with only 7 percent reaching the NAEP's target proficiency levels. Students at private schools did considerably better at solving moderately

HOW MUCH IS YOUR DEGREE WORTH?

The correlation between level of education and potential future earning power has never been more relevant. In an increasingly high-tech, skills-based economy, it is no longer possible to support a family with a high school education alone.

In 1994, a 4-year college degree was worth 52 percent more in wages than was a high school diploma. In manufacturing, workers with less than a high school education made less in constant dollars in 1995 than they did in 1959, while college graduates in manufacturing earned nearly one-third more (about $60,000). Across all jobs, males 25 years and older with only a high school diploma earned an average of $24,000 a year in 1995, according to the U.S. Census Bureau; women in the same age and education bracket fared far worse, netting only about $13,000.

In stark contrast, male and female college graduates age 18 and older in 1996 made about $46,000 and $26,800, respectively (see Figure 50-1). To track the relationship between education and potential earning power, the Census Bureau's education branch has created an entry called "How Much Is Your Degree Worth?" which is quickly becoming one of the hottest spots on its Web site. To visit, go to: www.census.gov. and click on E for "education." The latest population and educational attainment figures are also found there.

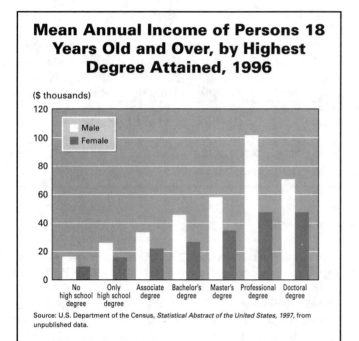

Mean Annual Income of Persons 18 Years Old and Over, by Highest Degree Attained, 1996

($ thousands)

Source: U.S. Department of the Census, *Statistical Abstract of the United States, 1997,* from unpublished data.

FIGURE 50-1

complex problems (72 percent reached the target), but only marginally better at the most advanced level, with 10 percent mastering multistep algebra problems. Similarly discouraging performances were measured in geography and history. In all cases, students' scores climbed as the level of their parents' education rose. Never before has the level of educational attainment translated so directly into future earning power.

Concern about the inability of U.S. workers to adjust to a rapidly changing marketplace has increased pressure on secondary schools to deliver better-prepared students to universities. In response to these and other concerns, Congress passed President Clinton's education initiative, Standards 2000, which calls for states to implement uniform national academic performance goals and testing. Yet at a time when poor scores on reading, math, science, and critical thinking tests have parents clamoring for more rigorous instruction and smaller class sizes, many school districts are reporting record teacher shortages.

EDUCATIONAL INNOVATIONS AT SCHOOL AND AT WORK

The computer-based information revolution will continue to transform the classroom well into the new millennium. Fueling the spending on computer technology in education is President Clinton's pledge to provide all eighth graders with access to the Internet by 2000. The number of public elementary and secondary schools with Internet access already increased from 35 percent in 1994 to 65 percent in 1996, according to Market Data Retrieval (MDR), a private marketing company. A majority of middle schools and junior high schools (78 percent) reported having Internet access. In 2000, over 90 percent of senior high schools plan to be wired; a significant number of all schools already have satellite dishes, cable, local area networks (LANs), CD-ROM, modems, and other hallmarks of the computer and information age (see Table 50-4).

Classroom Technology Explosion

An increase in the school-age population coupled with the computer and technology revolution has forced school districts to enlarge the size of educational facilities they build. Multimedia facilities, computer centers, and/or expanded research libraries with access to the Internet and computers dedicated to interactive research are now commonplace. Increasingly, schools also house day-care centers, and run afterschool math, science, and language enrichment programs. (See Chapter 6: Construction for a discussion of school construction.)

The ratio of computers to pupils has risen significantly since computers first appeared in the classroom in the early 1980s. In the 1985–1986 school year, there were 45.3 pupils for each computer in all schools. By 1996–1997, the national average had dropped to 7.4 students per computer, with some states such as Wyoming doing even better at 4.1 students per machine. Louisiana had the least favorable ratio at 10.7 pupils per computer, according to MDR. Senior high schools do slightly better than do elementary schools at providing classroom access to technology (see Table 50-5).

TABLE 50-4: Public Schools with Access to the Internet, 1994–1996

	Percent of Schools with Internet Access			Percent of Instructional Rooms with Internet Access		
	1994	1995	1996	1994	1995	1996
Total schools	35	50	65	3	8	14
Elementary	30	46	61	3	8	13
Secondary	49	65	77	4	8	16

Source: U.S. National Center for Education Statistics, "Advanced Telecommunications in U.S. Public Elementary and Secondary Schools, Fall 1996," NCES 97-944, from U.S. Department of Commerce, Bureau of the Census, *Statistical Abstract of the United States, 1997.*

TABLE 50-5: Students per Computer in Elementary and Secondary Schools, 1985 and 1997

Students per Computer	1984–1985	1996–1997
U.S. total	62.7	7.4
Public schools, total	63.5	7.3
Elementary	79.3	8
Middle/junior high	61.2	7.4
Senior high	51.5	6.4
Catholic schools, total	73.5	9.4
Elementary	85.1	9.9
Secondary	57.8	8.5
Other private schools, total	40.5	8.3
Elementary	42.7	9.1
Secondary	40.1	5.2

Source: Market Data Retrieval, Shelton, CT, unpublished data (copyright), from U.S. Department of Commerce, Bureau of the Census, *Statistical Abstract of the United States, 1997.*

Over a 5-year period, the number of computers for instructional use grew 186 percent, from 2.2 million in 1991 to 6.3 million in 1996–1997, according to MDR. Since 1995–1996, schools have added 1.2 million classroom-use machines. Nationally, about 81 percent of schools reported having at least one multimedia computer capable of running the latest software and CD-ROMs and (usually) accessing the Internet.

According to MDR, 89 percent of middle schools have LANs in addition to traditional gymnasiums, bleachers, and art and music rooms. Some elementary schools are still being built without telephone hookups for computer modems in the classroom, but MDR reports that many are installing fiber optics or cable as alternative ways of delivering technology to the learning environment. Currently, middle schools seem better equipped technologically than many high schools.

At the university level, MDR predicted that total spending for computer hardware and software would reach $2.8 billion for the 1997–1998 school year. Spending on software alone will climb to $746 million, over half of it pegged for instructional and academic use. Administrative departments are upgrading and linking computer systems at most institutions of higher learning, with larger colleges (10,001 to 25,000 students) spending the most on software and hardware. Libraries are at the cutting edge with online services, giving many students in remote dormitory rooms access to card catalogues, books, and databases for research purposes. University professors routinely accelerate and deepen classroom sessions through interactive discussions of written and oral work by students between formal class meetings.

Over the next decade, the ratio of computers to students will continue to improve, especially in affluent and heavily white school districts. Retraining teachers so they can keep pace with their students and make maximum use of computers remains a challenge. Some analysts say that as many as 25 percent of elementary and secondary teachers are computer illiterate. Teacher training consistently lags behind the acquisition of technology in most secondary and elementary schools. Most school districts do not spend enough money or time training teachers, nor do they encourage staff to upgrade their technological skills by subsidizing course work or offering tuition rebates or regular training workshops.

Business-and-School Partnerships

In 1998, the National Science Foundation's (NSF) advanced technology education program launched some 200 partnerships between potential employers and community colleges in an effort to tailor curricula to fit the hundreds of thousands of high-technology jobs expected to be created nationally in the next 5 years. According to the Bureau of Labor Statistics' (BLS) Office of Employment Statistics, jobs for systems analysts, computer engineers, and computer scientists will increase 108 percent over the 1996 level of 933,000 jobs to reach 1.9 million jobs in 2006. This compares with a 14 percent rise in the number of jobs across all occupations. The NSF fears many of these jobs will go unfilled or go to better-educated noncitizens unless the skills taught are radically overhauled. The challenge will be

to create a knowledge mix that is both broad and deep, combining critical thinking and problem solving skills with precision repair, manufacturing, and quality control. Rather than train workers for a single computer or machine or for an isolated plant's work style, the NSF wants educators to give students skills that can travel from job to job.

On-the-Job Training

According to the American Society for Training and Development (ASTD) and the BLS, U.S. organizations spent an estimated $55.3 billion on formal and informal work place training in 1995. Over the years, the BLS's *Survey of Employer-Provided Training* became the most reliable source on the extent of workplace training because of its size, scope, and precision, but after 1995 the study was not repeated. Instead, in 1997 the ASTD partnered with several private organizations and the U.S. Department of Labor to conduct its own survey of training practices at 540 leading-edge and smaller employers, each of which had at least 50 workers.

Another survey of businesses employing 100 or more workers published in the widely quoted October 1997 *Training* magazine estimated that U.S. companies budgeted $58.6 billion for formal training in 1997 and predicted that figure would grow if modest economic growth continued. *Training*'s survey looked at U.S. businesses with 100 or more employees, based on Dun & Bradstreet figures indicating that there were 136,605 such companies as of the summer of 1997 (see Figure 50-2).

The $55.3 billion to $58.6 billion spent on formal training may seem high, but it pales by comparison to that being spent by some competitor G-7 countries. Many of the United States' international rivals have formalized vocational education systems, highly developed school-to-work or apprenticeship programs, and a history of partnerships between industry and universities. With obvious weaknesses and a different philosophical approach to worker training, the U.S. education and job training system nevertheless has produced workers who are

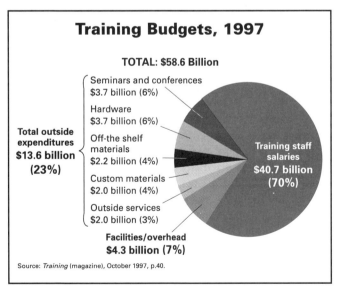

Training Budgets, 1997

TOTAL: $58.6 Billion

Seminars and conferences
$3.7 billion (6%)

Hardware
$3.7 billion (6%)

Off-the shelf materials
$2.2 billion (4%)

Custom materials
$2.0 billion (4%)

Outside services
$2.0 billion (3%)

Facilities/overhead
$4.3 billion (7%)

Total outside expenditures
$13.6 billion
(23%)

Training staff salaries
$40.7 billion
(70%)

Source: *Training* (magazine), October 1997, p.40.

FIGURE 50-2

more employable, productive, and flexible on balance than are those in many other countries.

Business In-House Training

The most successful companies say that ongoing retooling of employee skills builds stability, loyalty, and flexibility into the workplace. Most successful companies guarantee employees a certain number of training hours per year. Motorola, for example, offers workers approximately 40 hours of skills upgrading every 12 months.

Most formal training courses (81 percent) take place in a classroom with a live instructor, according to *Training* magazine, which estimated that 56.6 million workers received some formal training from employers in 1997. Among the 1,559 companies surveyed by *Training,* 94 percent said that they provided some instruction in computer skills. Among all the courses on computer technology, 76 percent are taught by live teachers rather than CD-ROM, video, or other written or visual learning aids used alone.

Money spent on informal training is harder to calculate but is believed to account for significantly more than the amount spent on formal training. Informal training includes new-employee orientation, production-line techniques, new equipment, tools, and safety procedures.

According to the BLS, 70 percent of employees polled at 1,000 businesses had received training of some sort during the 12 months before the latest (1997) survey. Men, white people, and prime-age workers were more likely to receive training than were women, minority members, and people younger than 25 and older than 55. College graduates were three to four times more likely to receive training than were workers with less than a high school education, another clear indication that education is pegged to future earnings. Those who receive regular workplace training earned up to 16 percent more than their similarly educated nontrained peers, according to the ASTD and BLS surveys.

Worries about long-term job security persist in the midst of continuing restructuring. However, once employed and in the job market, U.S. workers do far better than their global counterparts in weathering dramatic changes in the workplace as the economy continues to shift from manufacturing to information systems and service-based jobs. With the lowest jobless rate in 30 years and a modestly positive economic forecast, U.S. workers have a good chance to avoid the layoffs and erosion in earnings that workers in many other G-7 countries are experiencing.

Business Outsourcing of Training

Leading-edge companies in the United States are devoting significant resources to hiring outside consultants to upgrade workers' computer, technical, interpersonal, managerial, and team-task skills. At the same time, larger companies are increasing their internal human resource department budgets, although these departments may lose funding if the economy slows significantly. A training gap continues to exist between what the most successful companies in the United States are doing to keep their workers globally competitive and what the industry norm is.

The 1997 ASTD Human Performance Practices Survey (HPPS) indicated that the typical U.S. private-sector organization with 50 or more employees spent about $504 per employee on training in 1996. "Benchmark" and leading-edge companies, defined as being "among the best places to work in America," told HPPS they spent between $1,245 and $1,659 per worker in 1996. Estimates of training costs to private industry vary widely because of differing methodologies, difficulty in collecting useful data, and problems defining what falls under the rubric of training, but it is generally accepted that in 1996 slightly over $1 of every $15 that employers spent on education went toward formal or informal training.

According to the HPPS, tuition reimbursement represents the smallest portion of the training budget at 13.9 percent. The largest proportion, 39.6 percent, goes to pay salaries for outside trainers. The most frequently offered training courses include basic skills, sales, executive development, product knowledge, professional skills, customer services, quality, competition and business practices, teams, occupational safety, job-specific technical skills, computer literacy, and management and supervisory skills. Job-specific technical skills account for the most training time at 15 percent, while management and supervisory seminars account for 12 percent of all training; basic skills (remedial math, language, and reading) finishes last at 2 percent, according to HPPS.

INTERNATIONAL EDUCATION COMPARISONS

In 1996, the United States had the highest percentage of college graduates (90 million people) in the developed world as well as the largest number of functionally illiterate citizens. The United States spent comparatively more on all levels of education combined than did most of its global competitors. Unfortunately, soaring per-pupil expenditures do not automatically translate into stellar academic performance.

In the Third International Mathematics and Science Study (TIMSS), 1997, American high school seniors trailed behind pupils in 20 countries in mathematics and behind 15 countries in science. American students averaged 461 on the General Mathematics Knowledge Assessment compared with those from the Netherlands (560), Sweden (552), France (523), Canada (519), Germany (495), Italy (476), and the Russian Federation (471). In the science portion, American high school seniors did better, averaging 480, but this score was well below the international average and among the lowest of the 21 countries that participated (see Table 50-6). The 1997 TIMSS is well regarded by educators and is considered a fair comparison of achievement because it was jointly prepared and reviewed by participants to ensure that the areas covered accurately reflected curricula that are considered important in all countries. The test was monitored to make sure countries did not exclude more than 10 percent of their students from testing for any reason. Of

TABLE 50-6: International Comparison of Scores on Mathematics and Science General Achievement Tests

	Mathematics Average Score		Science Average Score
Netherlands	560	Sweden	559
Sweden	552	Netherlands	558
France	523	Canada	532
Canada	519	**International average**	**500**
International average	**500**	Germany	497
Germany	495	France	487
Italy	476	Russian Federation	481
Russian Federation	471	United States	480
United States	461	Italy	475
South Africa	356	South Africa	349

Source: Mullis et al. "Mathematics and Science Achievement in the Final Year of Secondary School," Boston College, Chestnut Hill, MA, 1998.

course, educators in the United States rightly point out that the student population here is among the most diverse in the world and poses real instructional challenges. Canada, for example, recruits highly skilled immigrants to fill specific labor needs, while the United States has a much less targeted immigration policy. This affects literacy levels across the entire school-to-work population. Other nations also have adhered to more stringent national education standards. The United States now has Standards 2000, a package of performance goals, implementation of which is currently bogged down at the state level.

In general, the greater the wealth of a nation, the bigger its education budget. In 1993, Sweden, the United States, and Switzerland ranked at the upper end of per-pupil expenditures for primary education. By 1997, the G-7 countries France and Canada spent a larger percentage of GDP on primary and secondary education, but only Canada spent a larger percentage of GDP on higher education and on all levels of education together than did the United States. The ratio of U.S. expenditures on education to GDP and percentage of per-capita GDP is also fairly high, although not as high as some of the United States global competitors.

High teacher attrition and dropout rates in the United States continues to be a major factor in retaining quality educators in a tight labor market. While the United States pays starting teachers a salary competitive with that of other similarly educated professionals, salary maximums and overall job status lag well behind those afforded teachers in other industrial, G-7, and Pacific Rim countries. Between 1990 and 1996, average teacher salaries in public elementary and secondary schools increased 24 percent from $20,292 to $25,167. Even with that increase, when salaries were adjusted for inflation, the average beginning teacher was making almost the same in 1996 as in 1972. Average teacher salaries are relatively low compared with salaries in other fields college graduates can go into. Teacher salaries in 1995 averaged $38,456 compared with $45,773 as an average annual salary of people over 25 with a bachelor's degree, using 1996 constant dollars.

CHALLENGES FOR THE NEW MILLENNIUM

The main task in the first decades of the next century will be to increase opportunities in poorer, high-minority school districts. By 2015, some 19 states will have school enrollments that are at least 30 percent nonwhite. Studies show that schools with high percentages of nonwhite students tend to be less well funded and to lag in the acquisition of cutting-edge instructional materials, computers, and educational technologies. Perhaps student opportunities can be enlarged through Title I and the new Technology Literacy Challenge Fund, among other programs. Without a major, decades-long commitment, well-documented disparities in skill acquisition and income will persist between poorly endowed schools and those in more affluent areas. Without such an effort the high school graduates now entering community colleges and vocational schools in record numbers will continue to arrive without the minimal computer and problem solving skills needed to survive in tomorrow's work force. In the coming century an inadequate education will act as a greater social and economic destabilizing agent than at any previous time.

Joan McQueeney Mitric, Washington, DC, (301) 933-3042, jmitric1@aol.com, November 1998.

■ REFERENCES

Call the U.S. Bureau of the Census at (301) 457-4701 for information about ordering Census documents or call the Census Education Branch at (301) 457-2464. Visit www.census.gov for the latest population interim data.

Beyond the School Doors: The Literacy Needs of Job Seekers Served by the U.S. Department of Labor, September 1992, Educational Testing Service, ISBN 0-88685-136-X.

"Community Colleges: A Vision Deferred," by Anthony P. Carnevale, Donna M. Desrochers, and Stephen J. Rose, 1997. To get a copy, contact A. Carnevale at The Manufacturing Institute, Suite 600, 1331 Pennsylvania Avenue, NW, Washington, DC 20004-1790.

The Condition of Education 1997. National Center for Education Statistics (NCES 97-388), U.S. Department of Education, National Library of Education, 555 New Jersey Avenue, NW, Washington, DC. (800) 424-1616 or (202) 219-5992. See numerous databases at www.ed.gov.

"Declining Job Security," by Robert G. Valletta, November 1997, Economic Research Department, Federal Reserve Bank of San Francisco.

The Digest of Education Statistics 1997, National Center for Education Statistics (NCES 98-015). See address above.

Education and Training for America's Future, by Anthony P. Carnevale, 1998 Growth Papers for the Manufacturing Institute, Suite 600, 1331 Pennsylvania Avenue, NW, Washington, DC 20004-1790.

Education at a Glance: OECD Indicators 1997, Centre for Educational Research and Innovation, Organization for Economic Co-operation and Development. Or contact the U.S. office at 2001 L Street, Washington, DC 20036-4922, (202) 785-6323. For the economic assumptions underlying this document and other data, visit www.oecd.org/els/stats/els_stat.htm.

Education Market News Data Points, various 1997 reports by Market Data Retrieval and the Dun & Bradstreet Corporation, including "Technology Explosion: Key Trends in Public Schools" (July 1997),

"School Construction in the U.S." (March 1998), and "MDR Unveils Initial Higher Education Technology Survey Findings" (December 1997).

Educational: Mailing Lists & Customized Services 1995–1996. Market Data Retrieval, 1 Forest Parkway, Shelton, CT 06484-9913. (203) 926-4800 or 1-800-333-8802, www.schooldata.com.

"Employer Training: The High Road, the Low Road and the Muddy Middle Path," by Anthony P. Carnevale and Donna M. Desrochers, Educational Testing Service. Prepared for the Conference on Restoring Broadly Shared Prosperity at the University of Texas-Austin and sponsored by the Economic Policy Institute and the Lyndon B. Johnson School of Public Affairs, May 1997.

"The Great Outsourcing Stampede That Never Happened," by Jack Gordon, *Training* (magazine), February 1998. E-mail: jgordon@trainingmag.com.

Involving Employers in Training: Literature Review, (97-K), U.S. Department of Labor, Employment and Training Administration, 1997. To obtain a copy, call (202) 219-7664.

"Learning Ecologies," by David Stamps, *Training* (magazine), January 1998, E-mail: dstamps@trainingmag.com.

Literacy, Economy and Society, results of the first International Adult Literacy Survey, Organization for Economic Co-operation and Development, 1995. See address above.

The National Education Goals Report Summary 1997. National Goals Panel, 1255 22nd Street, NW, Suite 502, Washington, DC 20037. (202) 724-0015, E-mail: NEGP@goalline.org, www.negp.gov.

The 1998 ASTD State of the Industry Report, by Laurie J. Bassie (lbassi@astd.org) and Mark E. Van Buren (mvanburen@astd.org), January 1998. Results of the American Society for Training and Development Human Performance Practices Survey on employer-provided formal training done with the U.S. Department of Labor and Employment and Training Administration, (202) 219-6871. Call ASTD at (703) 683-8100.

Occupational Outlook Quarterly Winter 1997–98, U.S. Department of Labor, Bureau of Labor Statistics, 800 North Capitol Street, Washington, DC 20211. (202) 606-5902, stats.bls.gov.

One-Stop Career Centers and Learning Lab for state-by-state information on vocational education and retraining grants, Job-Training Partnership Act, adult and veterans education opportunities, www.ttrc.doleta.gov/sites.htm.

Projections of Education Statistics to 2007, National Center for Education Statistics (NCES 97-382). See address above.

Statistical Abstract of the United States 1997, U.S. Department of Commerce, Bureau of the Census, Washington, DC.

Training (magazine), October 1997, "Industry Report," annual report on employer-provided training in the United States, Lakewood Publications, 50 S. Ninth Street, Minneapolis, MN. (800) 328-4329 or (612) 333-0471, E-mail: www.lakewoodpub.com.

Washington Post, "Classrooms and Class" and "Science," www.washingtonpost.com.

What Work Requires of Schools: A SCANS Report for America 2000, U.S. Department of Labor, June 1991. The followup is being done at the Institute for Policy Studies at Johns Hopkins University by Dr. Arnold Packer, (410) 516-7160.

■ **RELATED CHAPTERS**

6: Construction
27: Computer Equipment
28: Computer Software and Networking

Index

F

G

M

T

Permissions

A.M. Best Company
Ambest Road
Oldwick, NJ 08858
(908) 439-2200

Advertising Age
Crain Communications, Inc.
740 Rush Street
Chicago, IL 60611
(312) 649-5200

Aerospace Industries Association
1250 Eye Street, NW, Suite 1200
Washington, DC 20005-3924
(202) 371-8502

Allied Business Intelligence, Inc.
P.O. Box 452
202 Townsend Square
Oyster Bay, NY 11771
(516) 624-3113

Aluminum Association
900 19th Street, NW
Washington, DC 20006
(202) 862-5116

American Association of Health Plans
1129 20th Street, NW, Suite 600
Washington, DC 20036
(202) 778-3289

American Council of Life Insurance
1001 Pennsylvania Avenue, NW
Washington, DC 20004

American Iron and Steel Institute
01 17th Street, NW
shington, DC
2) 452-7100

erican Lawyer Media, LP
Third Avenue
York, NY 10016
972-3399

American Petroleum Institute
1220 L Street, NW
Washington, DC 20005
(202) 682-8000
http://www.api.org

Andersen Consulting
1 Market Plaza
Spear Tower, Suite 3700
San Francisco, CA 94105
(415) 537-5000

Association of American Railroads
50 F Street, NW
Washington, DC 20001
(202) 639-2211

Automotive News
Crain Communications, Inc.
965 E. Jefferson
Detroit, MI 48207-3185
(800) 678-9595

Bridge/CRB
3 World Financial Center
New York, NY 10281
(800) 927-2734

Cellular Telecommunications Industry
    Association
1250 Connecticut Ave, NW, Suite 200
Washington, DC 20036
(202) 785-0081

Clarkson Research Studies
12 Camomile Street
London EC31 7BP, England
44 (0) 171 334 3134

The Conference Board
845 Third Avenue
New York, NY 10022
(212) 339-0233

Consumer Electronics Manufacturers
    Association
2500 Wilson Boulevard
Arlington, VA 22201
(703) 907-7764

Cruise Industry News
Nissen-Lie Communications, Inc.
441 Lexington Avenue, Suite 1209
New York, NY 10017
(212) 986-1025

Datamation
PlugIn Datamation
10 Post Office Square, Suite 600 South
Boston, MA 02109

Dataquest
251 River Oaks Parkway
San Jose, CA 95134-1913
(408) 437-8000

Deutsche Morgan Grenfell Technology
    Group
31 West 52nd Street
New York, NY 10019
(212) 469-5381

Drewry Shipping Consultants
Drewry House
213 Marsh Wall
London E14 J4JF, England

Edison Electric Institute
701 Pennsylvania Avenue
Washington, DC 20004-2696
(202) 508-5000

eMarketer
821 Broadway
New York, NY 10003

Eno Transportation Foundation
One Farragut Square South
Washington, DC 20006
(202) 879-4700

Environmental Business International,
Inc.
P.O. Box 371769
San Diego, CA 92137
(619) 295-7685

Folio Magazine
Cowles Business Media
11 Riverbend Drive South, Box 4272
Stamford, CT 06907
(203) 358-4119

Furniture Today
P.O. Box 2754
High Point, NC 27261
(336) 605-0121

Futron Corporation
807 Arapahoe Street
Golden, CO 80401
(303) 271-9960

Futures Industry Association
2001 Pennsylvania Avenue, NW
Washington, DC 20006
(202) 466-5460

Gardner Publications, Inc.
6915 Valley Avenue
Cincinnati, OH 45244-3029

General Aviation Manufacturers
    Association
1400 K Street, NW, Suite 801
Washington, DC 20005
(202) 393-1500

Global Mobile
Baskerville Communications Corporation
15165 Ventura Boulevard, Suite 310
Sherman Oaks, CA 91403
(818) 461-9660

Global Wireless
777 E. Speer Boulevard
Denver, CO 80203
(303) 733-2500

Health Industry Manufacturers
    Association
1200 G Street, NW
Washington, DC
(202) 434-7210

Imagination Publications
820 W. Jackson Boulevard, Suite 450
Chicago, IL 60607
(312) 627-1020

Insurance Information Institute
110 William Street
New York, NY 10038
(800) 331-9146

International Data Corporation
5 Speen Street
Framingham, MA 01701
(508) 872-8200

International Monetary Fund
700 19th Street, NW
Washington, DC 20431
(202) 623-7000

International Telecommunications Union
Sales and Maketing Service
Place des Nations
CH-1211 Geneva 20, Switzerland
41 22 730 61 41
http://www.itu.int/publications

Investment Company Institute
1401 H Street, NW, Suite 200
Washington, DC 20005
(202) 326-5800

Journal of Commerce
PIERS, Port Import Export Reporting
    Service
Two World Trade Center, Suite 2750
New York, NY 10048
(212) 837-7051

Kennedy Publications, Inc.
Kennedy Place, Route 12 South
Fitzwilliam, NH 03447
(800) 531-0007

KMI Corporation
America's Cup Avenue at 31 Bridge Street
Newport, RI
(401) 849-6771

Lloyd's Register of Shipping
100 Leadenhall Street
London EC3A 3BP, England
011-44-171-709-9166

Motion Picture Association of America
1600 I Street, NW
Washington, DC 20006

National Association for Home Care
228 Seventh Street, SE
Washington, DC 20003
(202) 547-7424

National Association of Realtors
700 11th Street, NW
Washington, DC 20001
(202) 383-1000

National Mining Association
1130 17th Street, NW
Washington, DC 20036
(202) 463-2625

National Petroleum News
Adams Business Media
2101 S. Arlington Heights Road,
    Suite 150
Arlington Heights, IL 60005
(847) 427-9512
http://www.petroretail.net/npn

Network Wizards
P.O. Box 343
Menlo Park, CA 94026
(650) 326-2060
http://www.nw.com

Northern Telecom (Nortel)
4001 E. Chapel Hill-Nelson Highway
Research Triangle Park, NC 27709
1-800-4 NORTEL
(919) 992-5000

Photo Marketing Association
    International
3000 Picture Place
Jackson, MI 49201
(517) 788-8100

Photofinishing News
10915 Bonita Beach Road,
    Suite 1091
Bonita Springs, FL 34135
(941) 992-4421

Public Accounting Report
Strafford Publications, Inc.
590 Dutch Valley Road, NE
Postal Drawer 13729
Atlanta, GA 30324

St. Louis Merchants Exchange
230 S. Bemiston, Suite 1450
St. Louis, MO 63105
(314) 725-5222

Satellite Industry Association
225 Reinekers Lane, #600
Alexandria, VA 22314
(703) 549-8697

SATRA Technology Centre
SATRA House
Rockingham Road
Kettering, Northamptonshire
NN16 9JH
England
44 1536 410000

Securities Data Company
Two Gateway Center
Newark, NJ 07102

SIGMA, Swiss Reinsurance
50/60 Mythenquai
P.O. Box 8022
Zurich, Switzerland

Software Magazine
257 Turnpike Road, Suite 100
Southboro, MA 01772
(508) 366-2031

The Strategis Group
1130 Connecticut Avenue, NW
Washington, DC 20036
(202) 530-7500

TeleGeography, Inc.
Suite 1000
1150 Connecticut Avenue, NW
Washington, DC 20036
(202) 467-0017

Tirone Corporation
44 Main Street
Lincoln Building, Suite 510
Champaign, IL 61820
(217) 359-8276

Transport Topics
American Trucking Associations
2200 Mill Road
Alexandria, VA
(703) 838-1778

University of Michigan
Survey Research Center
P.O. Box 1248
Ann Arbor, MI 48106
(313) 763-5224

Video Software Dealers Association
16530 Ventura Boulevard, Suite 400
Encino, CA 91436

Walton Associates
208 Encinal Avenue
Menlo Park, CA 94025
(650) 326-6464

Wireless Week
600 S. Cherry Street
Denver, CO 80246
(303) 393-7449